A Preview of *The United States*

"After many years of teaching, I've finally found a

A Comprehensive, Up-To-Date Survey of Our Nation's History . . .

- **Extensive coverage** of the major people, events, and ideas that have shaped our nation
- **In-depth treatment** of pivotal events including the writing of the Constitution, the Civil War, the Civil Rights Movement, and the Vietnam War
- Told in a **rich, story-like narrative** appropriate for high school students
- Three **repeating themes** connect the flow of historical events
  - ★ Balancing Unity and Diversity
  - ★ Shaping Democracy
  - ★ The Search for Opportunity

With Differences That Help You Get Students Involved . . .

- A **modern design,** based on recent research, visually motivates students.
  - inviting ★ clear ★ discussion-provoking photos
- **Multicultural information** infused into every chapter enables all students to trace their own heritages while learning about the heritages of others.
  - balanced ★ sensitive ★ eye-opening
- More than 280 **primary sources** integrated throughout the text personalize history.
  - ★ famous and ordinary voices
  - ★ culturally diverse selections
- More than 160 **maps, charts, graphs, diagrams,** and **time lines** clarify and enrich the narrative.
- **Extensive coverage of the late 20th century** creates interest in the history students are living.
  - ★ U.S. in the post-Cold-War world
  - ★ Clinton administration

"We cannot dedicate—we cannot consecrate—we cannot hallow this ground. The brave men, living and dead, who struggled here have consecrated it far above our poor powers to add or detract. The world will little note nor long remember what we say here, but it can never forget what they did here. . . . It is rather for us to be here dedicated to the great task remaining before us—that from these honored dead we take increased devotion to the cause for which they gave the last full measure of devotion—that we here highly resolve that these dead shall not have died in vain—that this nation, under God, shall have a new birth of freedom—and that government of the people, by the people, for the people shall not perish from the earth."

—from Abraham Lincoln's Gettysburg Address, given at the dedication of the Gettysburg National Cemetery, November 19, 1863

The Battle of Gettysburg was fought at great human cost: 23,000 Union and 28,000 Confederate casualties.

Vicksburg. While Lee's and Meade's forces battled at Gettysburg, Grant was finally subduing Vicksburg. Since mid-1862 he had been trying to capture the city, which was perched on cliffs above the Mississsippi and partly surrounded by marshland. All attacks from the north had failed.

In March 1863 Grant tried a bold new plan. From Memphis he led 20,000 troops across the Mississippi and down its west bank to a point below Vicksburg. Union gunboats, which had slipped past Vicksburg's deadly cannons, ferried the troops to the east bank of the river. Grant's army drove eastward, defeating Confederate forces, then turned back west to attack Vicksburg.

After two attempts to storm the city had failed, Grant besieged, or encircled, it while Union gunboats bombarded it. For over six weeks Vicksburg held out. Civilians hid in caves for safety and ate dogs, cats, and mules for food. "We are utterly cut off from the world, surrounded by a circle of fire," one girl wrote in her diary. Finally, on July 4, 1863, the day after the battle at Gettysburg, the city surrendered.

Five days later, Port Hudson, the last Confederate stronghold on the Mississippi, gave up after a six-week siege. The Union now controlled the entire river, and the Confederacy was cut in two. Delighted, Lincoln declared, "Grant is my man and I am his for the rest of the war."

Although the … more years, the U… Vicksburg turned …

Chattanooga. … 1863 occurred at Ch… the Tennessee River… under General Wi… Chattanooga. Confe… Braxton Bragg evacu… Georgia. Rosecrans re…

The two armies c… Chickamauga, an Indi… death." The Union fo… nooga. The Confederate…

A month later, Lincol… all Union forces in the W… ing the starving Union… Grant assembled a migh… vember swept down on the… ing the city. After a two-day… crumbled. With victory a… forces secured control of … prepared to move into Georg…

The Treaty of Vers…

Many of Wilson's Fourteen … Europeans' aims. The fina… marks of both Wilson's id… mands. It included an ag… Nations, but it also redrew… severely punished Germa…

- A unique, end-of-year **epilogue, The History of the Future,** enables you to help students
  - ★ review 20th century history
  - ★ consider how the past has shaped the present
  - ★ look into their future

Addison-Wesley

The United States and Its People

Teacher's Edition

Authors

David C. King

Norman McRae

Jaye Zola

Project Team Acknowledgments

Editorial	Susan Hartzell, Jan Alderson, John Burner, Jeannie Crumly Cole, Bobbi Watkinson, Diane Whitworth
Design	Debbie Costello, Barbara Robinson, Kevin Berry, Christy Butterfield, Dana Chan-Hawkins, Emily Hamilton
Product Management	Sharryl H. Davis
Market Research	Shirley Black
Photo Edit	Karen Koppel, Lindsay Kefauver, Inge Kjemtrup, Margee Robinson
Production	Jenny Blackburn, Steve Rogers, Don Shelonko, Therese DeRogatis, Meredith Ittner, Cathleen Veraldi, Ellen Williams
Production Editorial	Nina Pohl
Manufacturing	Sarah Teutschel, Eva Wilson
Marketing Services	Greg Gardner
Permissions	Marty Granahan

ISBN 0-201-81129-4

2 3 4 5 6 7 8 9 10 - VH - 98 97 96

ADDISON-WESLEY PUBLISHING COMPANY

Menlo Park, California • Reading, Massachusetts • New York
Don Mills, Ontario • Wokingham, England • Amsterdam • Bonn
Sydney • Singapore • Tokyo • Madrid • San Juan • Paris • Seoul
Milan • Mexico City • Taipei

and Its People

textbook that excites both the teacher and the student."

Theresa Carmody, Southington High School, Southington, Connecticut

Supported by a Teacher's Edition That Helps You Build Student Interest Each Day. . .

- a wealth of flexible teaching ideas to meet your daily objectives and schedule
- worthwhile, practical active learning strategies
- suggestions for meeting varying student abilities
- provisions for both traditional and alternative assessment

Enriched by a Resource Package that Enables You to Create Memorable Learning Experiences for Every Student . . .

Read to Remember
Chapter Summaries
Reinforcement and Reteaching Activities
Enrichment Activities
Tests and Quizzes
Geography Activities
Readings in Literature and Primary Sources
Active Learning
Twentieth Century Issues

Plus . . .

Transparencies with Activities
Testing Software and Test File for Macintosh and IBM

Organization of the Student Text

The United States and Its People is a comprehensive, well-balanced program that helps students link the past to their life today and to their future. The text integrates content, concepts, and skills to help students gain a broad understanding of United States history. Below is an overview of how the text's organization will engage students in their study of the United States and its people.

Unit Organization

Each of the ten units in the text begins with **History Through Literature**, excerpts from diverse literary works *of* and *about* the period, which provide thoughtful insights into our past. In the **Unit Survey** closing each unit, **Making Connections** questions help students link concepts presented in the unit; **Projects and Activities** provide individual and group learning opportunities. Some questions and activities are based on the time line, **Milestones**, which places political, economic, social, and technological events in perspective. **Assessment: Demonstrating What You Know** challenges students to display their competency in an active individual or collaborative performance task.

Chapter Organization

Each of the thirty-two chapters opens with a colorful collage of illustrations representing the time period covered in the chapter. An opening primary source, **American Voices**, conveys the thoughts and experiences of an ordinary person or a noted figure, giving students an up-close glimpse of the time. An illustrated **Time Line** on the next two pages offers a visual preview of key events.

Chapters are divided into sections. Each section title is followed by a reading objective, the **Focus Question**, which guides students to the key concept of the section. Each section closes with **Section Review** questions that check whether students have achieved the reading objective. Section Reviews also reinforce new vocabulary and call for higher-level thinking with questions labeled *Application*, *Analysis*, *Synthesis*, and *Evaluation*. The *Data Search* questions ask students to analyze specific data from maps, charts, or graphs in the text. *Linking Past and Present* questions require students to relate the past to the present day. Each chapter closes with a mini-essay, **Connections to Themes**, which connects chapter content to one of the three themes in American history. These themes, introduced in Chapter 1 and woven throughout the text, are *balancing unity and diversity, shaping democracy*, and *the search for opportunity*.

At the end of each chapter, a **Chapter Survey** provides vocabulary activities that emphasize word relationships and derivations, questions that test comprehension and higher-level thinking, questions to help students review chronology and geographic location, and activities that ask students to relate past to present and to assess the impact of history on their own lives. Students also have opportunities to apply social studies and thinking skills to information in the chapter, and to consider controversial issues and then take a stand in a writing assignment.

Special Features

Special features stimulate student interest and help students develop skills. **History Through Literature** provides ten extensive excerpts from our diverse literary heritage. **American Voices** and hundreds of other primary sources, set off by colored quotation marks throughout the text, bring history alive by reflecting personal responses to events and conditions. Biography features entitled **The American Spirit** provide inspiring examples of individuals who have played a part in our nation's history.

Each unit includes an **Exploring Issues** feature that focuses on a critical issue of continuing importance. Ten **Point of View** features present a variety of viewpoints on a given topic and ask students to think critically about them.

Geography: A Key to Our Past focuses on five fundamental concepts, or themes, in geography: location, place, relationships within places, movement, and regions. Each of the ten geography features uses a specific historical example to demonstrate an aspect of one of these geographic concepts. To further help students link history and geography, **Geography Skills** questions based on the five geographic concepts accompany maps.

Five pictorial essays called **Young in America** give students a glimpse of what it was like to be young at different stages in our nation's history. **The Creative Spirit** pictorial essays focus on creative contributions to our nation's culture by diverse individuals and groups. These six displays of art, crafts, inventions, lifestyles, and pastimes highlight the multicultural nature of our nation. Detailed and carefully labeled **Learning From Art** illustrations enable students to "step into history," giving them a sense that "you are there." **Spotlight** boxes present the lighter side of history, including anecdotes, little-known events, word origins, sports, and glimpses of social life.

Reference Center

A Reference Center at the back of the book includes an **Atlas** of maps of the United States and the world, information about **The Presidents and Vice-Presidents**, and **Facts about the States**. The Reference Center also contains **The Declaration of Independence**, an annotated **Constitution of the United States**, a **Glossary**, and an **Index**.

Organization of the Teacher's Wraparound Edition

The Teacher's Wraparound Edition of *The United States and Its People* provides creative instructional strategies for teaching students of all abilities and learning styles.

Chapter Interleaf Pages

Four teacher planning pages at the beginning of each chapter help you in building your lessons. They provide a **Planning Guide** with pacing information, an **Overview** of the chapter, **Activity Objectives**, five teaching strategies, a **Bibliography** for teachers and students, and a list of **Audio-Visual Materials and Computer Software**.

Planning Guide

The Planning Guide organizes all the information and resources a teacher needs to teach the chapter. Each Planning Guide lists, section-by-section, the special features in the Student Edition, the activities in the Teaching Strategy references, and all of the support material in the *Teacher's Resource Package*.

Teaching Strategy

The Teaching Strategy for each chapter includes five types of activities. Each activity is identified as an individual, cooperative, or class project, and is given a suggested time frame.

- **Introducing the Chapter** stimulates student interest.
- **Teaching the Main Idea** suggests two activities that focus on major themes and concepts of the chapter.
- The **Reinforcement Activity** reviews information and concepts to ensure retention.
- **Evaluating Progress** assesses students' understanding of chapter material.
- The **Enrichment Activity** extends and enriches chapter content and provides students with opportunities for creativity.

Bibliography and Audio-Visual Materials

The Wraparound Teacher's Edition also provides a bibliography for both teacher and students, which includes recommended reference books, literature, and a list of audio-visual materials and computer software related to each chapter.

Wraparound Margin Pages

Teaching notes in the top and side margins around each student page provide the teacher with background information, ideas for discussions and activities, on-page answers to all questions, and videodisc bar codes.

Top Margin Notes

Background notes in the top margins provide the teacher with additional information and insights. Topics include multicultural perspectives, linking past and present, social history, citizenship, and connections with art and music, religion, literature, economics, science and technology, geography, politics, and global events.

Side Margin Notes

Teaching notes in the side margins provide a flexible section-by-section instructional plan including **Section Objectives**, **Introducing the Section**, **Developing the Section**, and **Section Review**. The side columns also provide a wealth of teacher support to enhance chapter study: ideas for discussions and activities to help students understand the rich multicultural heritage of the United States, suggestions for meeting Limited English Proficiency needs, small group and cooperative learning activities, questions that require higher-level thinking, topics for investigating local history, opportunities to interpret and analyze primary sources, motivators for writing about history, and links to other curriculum areas. Special boxes call attention to **Critical Thinking** and **Active Learning** suggestions.

This special symbol identifies items with multicultural connections.

On-page **Answers** are provided for all Section Reviews, Chapter Surveys, Unit Surveys, and special features and Geography Skills questions.

In the Unit Surveys, teaching notes for **Demonstrating What You Know** offer suggestions for introducing the task and for follow-up activities. The notes also propose a means for developing a scoring system, or rubric, for each performance task.

Videodisc bar codes correlate the text to the GTV's *A Geographic Perspective on American History*, a set of videodiscs and Macintosh software produced by the National Geographic Society and Lucas Film Learning Systems. They enable the teacher to access a variety of still images and film segments, primary sources, and animated maps and graphics on the videodiscs to enhance presentations and bring history alive.

General Bibliography for the Teacher

Annals of America. 18 Vols. Chicago: Encyclopaedia Britannica, 1968.

Banks, Ann, ed. *First Person America*. New York: Alfred A. Knopf, 1980.

Bennett, Lerone. *Before the Mayflower: A History of Black America*. Chicago: Johnson Publishing Company, 1987.

Blanche, Jerry. *Native American Reader: Speeches, Poems, and Stories of the American Indian*. Juneau, Alaska: Denali Press, 1990.

Catton, Bruce, and William B. Catton. *The Bold and Magnificent Dream: America's Founding Years, 1492–1815*. New York: Doubleday, 1978.

Clarke, Leon E., ed. *The African Past and the Coming of the Europeans*. New York: Praeger, 1971.

Cockcroft, James D. *Outlaws in the Promised Land*. New York: Grove Press, 1986.

Cole, Michael and others. *Atlas of Ancient America*. New York: Facts on File, 1986.

Degler, Carl N. *Out of Our Past: the Forces That Shaped Modern America*, 3rd ed. New York: Harper Collins, 1983.

Foner, Jack D. *Blacks and the Military in American History: A New Perspective*. New York: Praeger, 1974.

Foner, Philip S. *Women and the American Labor Movement*. New York: The Free Press, 1979.

Gutman, Herbert G. *The Black Family in Slavery and Freedom, 1750–1925*. New York: Pantheon Books, 1976.

Hawke, David F. *Everyday Life in Early America*. New York: Harper & Row, 1988.

————. *Nuts and Bolts of the Past*. New York: Harper & Row, 1988.

Hosokawa, Bill. *Nisei: The Quiet Americans*. New York: William Morrow and Company, 1969.

Hoxie, Frederick E., ed. *Indians in American History*. Arlington Heights, 1988.

Ingraham, Gloria D. *Album of American Women: Their Changing Roles*. New York: Watts, 1987.

Jaynes, Gerald David and Robin M. Williams, Jr., eds. *A Common Destiny: Blacks and American Society*. Washington D.C.: National Academy Press, 1989.

Litwack, Leon F. *Been in the Storm so Long: The Aftermath of Slavery*. New York: Alfred A. Knopf, 1979.

McCunn, Ruthanne L. *An Illustrated History of the Chinese in America*. San Francisco: Design Enterprises, 1979.

McWilliams, Carey. *North From Mexico*. New York: Greenwood Press, 1968.

Meing, D.W. *The Shaping of America: A Geographical Perspective on 500 Years of History, Atlantic America, 1492–1800*. New Haven: Yale University Press, 1986.

Meier, Matt S. and Feliciano Rivera, eds. *Readings on La Raza*. New York: Hill and Wang, 1974.

Melendy, Brett H. *Asians in America: Filipinos, Koreans, and East Indians*. Boston: G.K. Hall, 1977.

Meltzer, Milton. *In Their Own Words: A History of the American Negro*. New York: Thomas Crowell Company, 1967.

Moquin, Wayne and Charles Van Doren, eds. *A Documentary History of the Mexican Americans*. New York: Bantam, 1978.

Morris, Richard B., ed. *Encyclopedia of American History*. New York: HarperCollins, 1982.

Nabokov, Peter, ed. *Native American Testimony: An Anthology of Indian and White Relations, First Encounter to Dispossession*. New York: Crowell, 1978.

Oswalt, Wendell H. *This Land Was Theirs: A Study of North American Indians*. Mountain View, CA: Mayfield Publishing, 1987.

Ploski, Harry A. and James Williams. *The Negro Almanac, A Reference Work on the African American*, 5th edition. New York: Gale Research Inc., 1989.

Prucha, Francis P. *The Great Father*. Lincoln: University of Nebraska Press, 1984.

Santoli, AL. *New Americans: An Oral History*. New York: Viking, 1988.

Sterling, Dorothy, ed. *We Are Your Sisters: Black Women in the Nineteenth Century*. New York: W.W. Norton, 1984.

Stetson, Erlene, ed. *Black Sister: Poetry by Black American Women, 1746–1980*. Bloomington: Indiana University Press, 1981.

Tindall, George B. *America: A Narrative History*. New York: W.W. Norton, 1984.

Takaki, Ronald. *Strangers from a Distant Shore: A History of Asian Americans*. Boston: Little, Brown, 1989.

Ver Steeg, Clarence L. *The Formative Years*. New York: Hill and Wang, 1964.

Waldman, Carl. *Atlas of the North American Indian*. New York: Facts on File, 1985.

Weatherford, Jack. *Indian Givers*. New York: Crown, 1988.

Weyr, Thomas. *Hispanic U.S.A.* New York: Harper & Row, 1988.

Women in the World: An International Atlas. New York: Simon and Schuster, 1986.

Zinn, Howard. *A People's History of the United States*. New York: Harper & Row, 1980.

Audio Visual and Computer Software Sources

Audio-Visual Sources

ABC Video (ABC)
Division of Capital Cities
825 7th Avenue
New York, NY 10019

AIMS Media (AIMS)
9710 DeSoto Avenue
Chatsworth, CA 91311

Ambrose Video Publishing
Distributor of Time-Life Video
1290 Avenue and the Americas,
Suite 2245
New York, NY 10104

BFA (see Phoenix/BFA)

Braverman Productions (BRVMN)
Div. of Images Communication
Arts Corp.
366 N. Broadway
Jericho, NY 11753

Columbia Broadcasting Company (CBS)
2211 Michigan Blvd.
Santa Monica, CA 90404

Center for Humanities
Mount Kisco, NY 10549

Churchill Media
662 N. Robertson Blvd.
Los Angeles, CA 90069

Coronet/MTI (CORT)
108 Wilmot Road
Deerfield, IL 60015-5196

Walt Disney Educational Media
See Coronet/MTI

Encyclopaedia Britannica Educational Corporation (EBEC)
310 South Michigan Avenue
Chicago, IL 60604-9839

Educational Audio-Visual, Inc. (EAV)
29 Marble Avenue
Pleasantville, NY 10570

Educational Enrichment Materials of the *New York Times*
357 Adams Street
Bedford Hills, NY 10507

Films Incorporated (FI)
5547 Ravenswood Avenue
Chicago, IL 60640

Guidance Associates
Communications Park, Box 3000
Mount Kisco, NY 10549-9989

Journal Films, Inc.
930 Pitner Avenue
Evanston, IL 60202

Karol Video
22 Riverview Drive
Wayne, NJ 07470

Learning Corporation of America (LCA)
Distributed by Coronet/MTI
108 Wilmot Road
Deerfield, IL 60015

Mastervision
969 Park Avenue
New York, NY 10028

McGraw-Hill Films (MCGH)
110 15th Street
Del Mar, CA 92014

Meridian
9903 Santa Monica Blvd. #256
Beverly Hills, CA 90212

Multi-Media Productions
P.O. Box 5097
Stanford, CA 94305

National Geographic Society Educational Services
Dept. 91
Washington, D.C. 20036
(GTV distributor)

National Women's History Project
7738 Bell Road
Windsor, CA 95492-8518

New York Times (see Educational Enrichment Materials)

National Broadcasting Company (NBC)
30 Rockefeller Plaza
New York, NY 10112

Optical Data Corporation
30 Technology Drive
Warren, NJ 07059
(GTV distributor)

Phoenix/BFA
468 Park Avenue South
New York, NY 10003

PBS Video
Public Broadcasting Service
1320 Braddock Place
Alexandria, VA 22314-1698

Pyramid Films & Video
P.O. Box 1048
Santa Monica, CA 90406

Random House
Educational Enrichment Materials
Dept. 9280
400 Hahn Road
Westminster, MD 21157

Right on Programs
755 NY Av. Suite 210
Huntington, NY 11743

Scholastic, Inc.
P.O. Box 7502
2931 E. McCarthy Street
Jefferson City, MO 65102

Society For Visual Education (SVE)
Department VS
1345 Diversey Parkway
Chicago, IL 60614-1299

Time-Life Video
Time-Life Building
New York, NY 10020

United Learning, Inc.
6633 Howard Street
Niles, IL 60648-9875

Video Yesteryear
Box C
Sandy Hook, CT 06482

Westport Media, Inc.
155 Post Road East
Westport, CT 06880-3475

Zenger Video
10200 Jefferson Boulevard, Room VC
P.O. Box 802
Culver City, CA 90232-0802

Software Sources

Aquarius Software
P.O. Box 128
Indian Rocks Beach, FL 34635

Britannica Software (see EBEC)

Educational Activities, Inc. (EAI)
P.O. Box 392
Freeport, NY 11520

Educational Publishing Concepts
P.O. Box 715
St. Charles, IL 60174

Focus Media (FM)
839 Stewart Avenue
Garden City, NY 10016

Hartley Software
c/o Michaels Associates
5171 Greensburg Rd.
Murrysville, PA 15668

Heizer Software
1941 Oak Park Blvd. Suite 30
Pleasant Hill, CA 94523

Intellectual Software
798 North Ave
Bridgeport, CT 06606

MECC
3490 Lexington Avenue N.
St. Paul, MN 55112

Micro Learn/Word Associates
P.O. Box 162
Amboy, MN

Mindscape, Inc.
3444 Dundge Rd.
Northbrook, IL 60062

Queue Educational Software
338 Commerce Dr.
Fairfield, CT 04630

Sliwa Enterprises, Inc. (SEI)
P.O. Box 978
Yorktown, VA 23692

Social Studies School Services
10200 Jefferson Blvd.
P.O. Box 802
Culver City, CA 90232

Tom Snyder Productions
90 Sherman St.
Cambridge, MA 02140

Scope and Sequence

		CHAPTER 1	CHAPTER 2	CHAPTER 3
Knowledge and Understanding	**History**	Diversity in colonial America	Arrival of first people in North America; interaction of Native Americans and Europeans; European desire for trade with Asia; effects of European exploration and conquest on world history	Reasons for European immigration to and colonization of North America; creation of colonial society; conquest of Native-American lands; enslavement of Africans; French and Indian War
	Ethics & Religion	Treatment of Native Americans and Africans by white colonists; religious diversity; existence of sexism and racism today	Religious ideas shared by Native-American cultures; conflicting beliefs of Native Americans and Europeans; Spanish missions	North America as religious haven; Puritans in New England; Catholic roots in Maryland; Quakers in Pennsylvania; racism in colonies; African religious beliefs; Quaker and Mennonite opposition to slavery
	Culture	Colonial culture: European, Native-American, and African roots; cultural diversity today	Similarities and differences among Native-American cultures; early Middle American civilizations; early farming cultures; Native-American religious beliefs and attitude toward nature	Development of a unique colonial society based on European culture; African-American culture; Native-American culture
	Geography	Resources of colonial America; effective use of natural resources	Ice Age; ancient migration from Asia to North America; adaptation to the environment; diffusion of plants and animals; beginning of corn culture; location of Native-American cultural areas	Natural resources and colonial economies; young people at work
	Economics	The United States as a land of economic opportunity; changing economic opportunities—from agriculture to industry	Traditional economic patterns of Native Americans; economic motives for European exploration—the lure of the Indies	Effects of mercantilism on English colonies in N. America; diverse economies in the colonies; development of triangular trade; effects of Navigation Acts on colonies; dependence on slavery in South
	Sociology & Politics	Government's changing role	Diverse Native-American political structures; Spanish/English rivalry	Establishment of limited self-government; House of Burgesses in Virginia; Mayflower Compact; bicameral legislature in Massachusetts; elected assemblies in all colonies
Themes in United States History	**Balancing Unity and Diversity**	Status of Native Americans and African Americans in the colonies; views of religious diversity; intolerance of newcomers; flow of new immigrants	Native-American diversity; European rejection of Native-American structures; influence of Spanish missions and the encomienda system on Native-American ways of life	Diversity of interests and purposes among colonies; conflicting attitudes of Native American and Europeans toward land; African-American culture; clashes between Native Americans and white settlers
	Shaping Democracy	Individual rights vs. common good; balance between state and national power; voting rights; voter indifference; barriers to equality	Iroquois League; Strong Native-American community values; democratic values held in many Native-American societies	Limited self-government in Virginia; House of Burgesses, Mayflower Compact; Mass. bicameral legislature; influence of Magna Carta and Eng. Bill of Rights; freedom of the press; assemblies
	Search for Opportunity	U.S. as a land of plenty; limits in the land of plenty; changing economic opportunities	European discovery and exploration led to opportunity for Europeans, but enslavement for Africans and disaster for Native Americans	Promise of religious toleration, lure of a better life, and search for profits as motives for many migrants to North America
Skills	**Critical Thinking**	Analyzing; applying information; evaluating; recognizing point of view; synthesizing	Analyzing; synthesizing; applying information; evaluating	Analyzing; synthesizing; evaluating; applying information; interpreting political cartoons
	Social Studies Skills	Analyzing bar and line graphs; drawing a bar graph	Understanding geography concepts: movement; relationships within places; using time lines and maps	Comparing maps; understanding geography concepts: movement, location, place
	Writing Skills	Writing a letter expressing an opinion	Writing a letter expressing an opinion; writing a report on the effect of the development of printing on the spread of knowledge after the mid-1400s (Unit 1 Survey)	Writing a letter to a newspaper publisher expressing an opinion
	Active Learning	Making posters that illustrate contributions of a particular culture to life in the community	Researching and reporting on origin of common foods (Unit 1 Survey)	Learning about your ancestors; researching and coming to conclusions about changes in occupations; compiling a class list of laws to help in setting up a new colony (Unit 1 Survey)

	CHAPTER 4	CHAPTER 5	CHAPTER 6	CHAPTER 7
	Causes of American Revolution; Proclamation of 1763; Stamp Act, Townshend Acts; Tea Act; Intolerable Acts; colonial militias; British moves against Lexington; Concord; Rev. War; terms of peace	Creating state governments; ratification of the Articles of Confederation; Northwest Ordinance	Creation and ratification of the United States Constitution; 20th century case studies on constitutional issues	Defining powers of federal government; development of political parties; stabilizing the economy; foreign policy of neutrality; XYZ Affair; Alien and Sedition Acts; Kentucky and Virginia Resolutions
	Revolution undertaken partly to establish natural rights	Bill of rights in state constitutions; religious pluralism	Constitution generally protected individual rights and dignity; Constitution ignored rights and dignity of certain groups; Three-Fifths Compromise	Native Americans forced to cede lands through Treaty of Greenville; speculators and inside information; suppression of free speech
	"Give Me Liberty or Give Me Death" speech (Unit 2—History Through Literature); other persuasive revolutionary literature; role of women in war; African-American participation in the Revolution	Diversity of American culture; establishing an American identity; suppression of African cultures; separation of Native-American, European-American cultures	Cultural traditions of Western world provided roots of Constitution	Values that led to political parties; education in the new American nation
	Effect of location in outcome of the Revolution; Treaty of Paris and establishment of American boundaries	The Northwest Survey System: location; control of development of western lands	Geographic regionalism and creation of Constitution	Boundary disputes settled by Pinckney and Jay treaties; geographic regionalism and political parties
	Effects of British taxation	Impact of Revolution: unfavorable balance of trade with Britain, state debts, worthless American currency, inflation, deflation	Constitution guarded economic interests of delegates and those they represented	National and state debts and Hamilton's policies; national bank; protective tariff proposal; excise tax and the Whiskey Rebellion; trade embargo against Britain
	Organization of local, colonial resistance to British policies; committees of correspondence; First and Second Continental Congresses	Civil unrest and conflict; efforts to limit central government's power	Separation of powers among three branches of gov't; bicameral legislature; representation in Congress; The Great Compromise; indirect election of Pres. and Vice-Pres. through electoral college; federalism	Organization of executive and judicial branches; continuing divisions between Federalists and Anti-Federalists; rise of political parties; farmers and aristocrats; education
	Division of some Americans over revolution; diversity of motives among revolutionaries; diversity of goals of revolutionary colonies	Tensions among diverse states; suppression of African-American culture; policy of assimilation of Native-American cultures; challenges to the narrowly defined national identity	Three-Fifths Compromise; compromise over slave trade	Political parties; origin of the Alien Act; free speech; education
	Declaration of Independence; Revolution fought to establish government based on natural rights; Revolutionary War	Writing of state constitutions; democracy extended slowly: no voice for women, African Americans, Native Americans; expansion of voting rights	Historical origins of constitutional concepts; flexibility of Constitution through checks and balances, amendment process, judicial review; 20th century case studies on constitutional issues; Bill of Rights	Political parties; conflicting views of American democracy; states' rights doctrine; political dissent
		Shays' Rebellion		Political participation; speculation and financiers; farmers protest excise tax; thriving trade; new global markets
	Analyzing; synthesizing; applying information; evaluating	Evaluating; analyzing	Analyzing; evaluating; synthesizing; identifying point of view	Analyzing; evaluating; interpreting political cartoons
	Understanding geography concepts: movement, location; using maps; analyzing line graphs	Using maps; understanding geography concepts: place, location; analyzing maps and graphs	Analyzing diagrams; understanding geography concepts: location; interpreting flow charts	Understanding geography concepts: location
	Writing an essay expressing an opinion	Writing a speech expressing an opinion	Writing an essay regarding the legacy of the framers	
	Writing slogans; gathering information about local Revolutionary War sites	Finding information on state constitutions	Researching census data; reporting on current constitutional issues (Unit 2 Survey)	Role-playing; small group discussion of tolerance of U.S. toward diversity of opinion in times of threats from abroad; researching "third parties"; reenacting election of 1800 (Unit 2 Survey)

Scope and Sequence

		CHAPTER 8	CHAPTER 9	CHAPTER 10
Knowledge and Understanding	History	Jefferson and Republicanism; conflict with Barbary States; exploration and settlement of the West; Louisiana Purchase; causes and effects of War of 1812; Monroe Doctrine	Jacksonian democracy; social reform; abolitionism	Settlement of the Far West; Texan independence; manifest destiny; war with Mexico
	Ethics & Religion	Native-American efforts to keep lands threatened by eastern settlers; controversy over slavery; Missouri Compromise	Spoils system; presidential power; forced migration of Native Americans; revivals/camp meetings; utopias; religion's role in reform; temperance; women's rights; antislavery movement	Religious reasons for westward movement; effects of western movement on Native Americans; religion as source of tension in Texas
	Culture	Contributions of Tecumseh; Native-American identity	Popular campaign art; women's fashions; utopian communities; women and African-American writers	Growth of Hispanic-American culture from contact between Native Americans and Spanish
	Geography	Westward expansion beyond Mississippi; Louisiana Purchase; Lewis and Clark expedition; Lowell: relationships within places; growth of industry in North; "cotton kingdom" in South; Adams-Onís Treaty	Forced movement of Indian tribes; westward expansion; underground railroad routes	Trails to the Far West; Treaty of Guadalupe Hidalgo; Gadsen Purchase; California gold rush
	Economics	Causes and effects of Embargo Act; causes and effects of Industrial Revolution; invention of cotton gin; use of interchangeable parts; invention of steam engine; American System; Panic of 1819	Tariff; Panic of 1837; depression	California gold boom
	Sociology & Politics	Social changes caused by industrialization; growth of sectionalism; one-party politics; end of Republican era	Nullification controversy; states' rights debate; changes in political parties; sectionalism; religious revivals; social reform movements; abolition	Manifest destiny; Mormon theocracy
Themes in United States History	Balancing Unity and Diversity	War brought national unity; controversy over slavery increases sectionalism; westward expansion and Republican policy toward Native Americans	Sectional disagreement over tariff policy and slavery; nullification controversy	Unity threatened by westward expansion; diversity extended by westward expansion
	Shaping Democracy	Republican principles; federal power strengthened through *Marbury* v. *Madison*; *Fletcher* v. *Peck*, *McCulloch* v. *Maryland*; controversy over strict vs. loose construction of Constitution	Expansion of participation; Cherokee Constitution of 1828; lack of rights for Native Americans; states' rights debate; women's rights; antislavery movement; presidential power; social action	Texas constitution of 1836; Oregon constitution and bill of rights of 1843; California constitutional convention of 1849
	Search for Opportunity	Industrial opportunities for women; impacts of technological change	Westward expansion of European Americans into Native-American lands; opportunity for women	Westward movement spawned by desire for: trade, furs, farm land, religious freedom, gold
Skills	Critical Thinking	Analyzing; evaluating; synthesizing; applying information; recognizing point of view; identifying arguments	Analyzing; evaluating; interpreting political cartoons	Analyzing; evaluating; synthesizing; recognizing point of view
	Social Studies Skills	Understanding geography concepts: place, movement, relationships within places; using time lines; analyzing maps	Understanding geography concepts: movement; analyzing graphs; using time lines	Understanding geography concepts: relationships within places, movement, location; using a road map; analyzing maps
	Writing Skills		Writing notes for a class debate	Writing a letter for or against annexing Texas in 1844 (Unit 3 Survey)
	Active Learning	Researching origins and platform of modern Republican party; finding example of Supreme Court's use of judicial review; arguing a character's position; making a time line; (Unit 3 Survey)	Researching recent protective tariffs; researching current reform movements; creating a diagram showing changes in political parties, 1828–1840 (Unit 3 Survey)	

	CHAPTER 11	CHAPTER 12	CHAPTER 13	CHAPTER 14
	Political, economic, social causes of Civil War	Preparations for Civil War; strengths and weaknesses of North and South; military actions; effects of war	Effects of Civil War; effects of Reconstruction; undoing of Reconstruction	Contact and conflict between settlers and Plains Indians; transcontinental railroad; settlement of the Great Plains
	Racism and discrimination; passage of slave codes; violence vs. nonviolence in opposition to slavery; Protestant nativism; exploitation and labor organization	Racism and discrimination; Grant's total war strategy	Racism following Reconstruction; poll tax and Jim Crow laws; *Plessy v. Ferguson*; lynch mobs	Reservation system; broken treaties; Indian resistance; Native-American Ghost Dance; the Dawes Act; frontier justice
	African-American music, arts and crafts; *Uncle Tom's Cabin* (Unit 4—History Through Literature); societies of North and South; literature and antislavery	Wartime roles of women and African Americans	Fisk University Jubilee singers; founding of Tuskegee Institute and other black colleges	Alteration of traditional Indian cultures through contact with European-American culture; Hispanic origins of cowboy traditions; *Cimarron* (Unit 5—History Through Literature)
	Improved transportation system links East and West; immigration from northern Europe; regional differences between North and South	Union and Confederate strategies; battle sites; Gettysburg: relative location	War destruction of Southern farm land, crops, livestock	Mineral, timber, soil resources; alteration of environment of West by newcomers; establishment of railroad network; Leadville, Colorado: place
	Free labor in North; slave labor in South; industry in North; predominance of agriculture in South; immigration; rise and fall of union membership	Strengths and weaknesses of North and South; Union/Confederate finances; economic effects of war	Increased taxes to pay for new programs; tenant farming and sharecropping system	Homestead Act; ranching, mining, agriculture; impact of railroad on trade and settlement
	Popular sovereignty; compromises fail; formation of modern Republican party; sectionalism; labor movement; nativist politics; activism in German and Irish communities	Lincoln and Davis presidencies; debate over presidential power; political effects of war weariness in North	Establishment of Reconstruction governments in South; power struggle between President Johnson and Congress over Reconstruction; impeachment and acquittal of Johnson; inauguration of President Hayes	Development of distinct agricultural society in West
	Irish and German immigrants; nativism; slave revolts; secession; industrial, urban North; agrarian, slaveholding South	Dissent on both sides during war; role of African Americans in war effort and emancipation	Reestablishment of national unity; the issue of segregation	Treaties between Native Americans and U.S. government; Grant's "peace policy"; diverse origins of the homesteaders
	National sovereignty vs. popular sovereignty; Missouri Compromise ruled unconstitutional; immigrant activism and nativist response; free African Americans	Suspension of right of *habeas corpus*; Emancipation Proclamation	13th, 14th, 15th Amendments; Civil Rights Act; suffrage for black men; election of blacks to Cong., state and local gov'ts; extension of some political and social rights to women and African Americans	Woman suffrage in the West; Standing Bear's case—Indians declared persons under the law; "cow custom"
	Immigration from northern Europe; growth of trade and industry; early labor movement	Effects of black service in Civil War; impact of war on northern agriculture and industry	Freedmen seek opportunity; Freedmen's Bureau established	Homesteading; railroading, ranching, mining, land speculation
	Analyzing, applying information; evaluating; synthesizing; recognizing point of view	Analyzing; synthesizing; applying information; evaluating; analyzing cause and effect	Analyzing; recognizing point of view; evaluating; synthesizing	Analyzing; evaluating; synthesizing; applying information; detecting bias
	Understanding geography concepts: region; analyzing maps and statistical tables	Understanding geography concepts: location, movement; using time lines	Understanding geography concepts: location; using statistical tables; using time lines, maps, and graphs	Understanding geography concepts: location, place; using time lines
		Writing notes for a speech	Writing out life story of 60-year-old southerner in 1900 (Unit 5 Survey)	Writing a letter expressing an opinion
	Role play members of the new Republican party as they discuss its goals (Unit 4 Survey)	Researching conscription after the Civil War; researching opposition to the draft in the 1960s; presenting a speech about modern-day protection of battlefield sites	Using newspapers to find current examples of power struggles between the President and Congress	Researching railroad service today

Scope and Sequence

		CHAPTER 15	CHAPTER 16	CHAPTER 17
Knowledge and Understanding	**History**	Technological change; industrialization; growth of big business; immigration; urbanization; political and social reform efforts	Gilded Age; effects of economic and technological change on industrial workers and farmers; support of and opposition to organized labor	Progressive movement
	Ethics & Religion	Diverse religious views of immigrants; corrupt political machines; social Darwinism; business practices and the pursuit of wealth	Corruption; unhealthy and unsafe working conditions; child labor	Temperance movement; child protective laws
	Culture	Inventions and scientific discoveries; advertising; industrialists' support of the arts; depiction of new industrial, urban era by writers and photographers	Influence of industrialization on values	John Dewey and progressive education; sports, toys, and games
	Geography	Migration of farmers to cities; urban environments; immigration; ties of industry, raw materials, and markets	Spread of populism; regionalism and the election of 1896	Conservation and preservation of natural resources
	Economics	Consumerism; industrialization; new forms of business organization; free enterprise system; entrepreneurship; poverty and urban problems	Effects of factory system; labor movement; cause and effect of Haymarket Affair; labor strikes; Depression of 1893; "free" silver issue	Workers' compensation laws; antitrust legislation; federal arbitration of labor disputes; increased federal regulation of big business; Federal Reserve Act
	Sociology & Politics	Debate over role of government in economy; Social Darwinism; immigration debate in Congress; power of political machines; poverty and social action; urbanization	Political corruption; civil service reform; Farmers' Alliances; Populist party; election of 1896	Woman suffrage; Roosevelt's square deal; Progressive party; extension of progressivism by Presidents Taft and Wilson
Themes in United States History	**Balancing Unity and Diversity**	Hostility toward immigrants; immigration restrictions; urbanization and the immigrant population in cities	Racism and sexism in labor movement	Founding of NAACP
	Shaping Democracy	Debate over federal regulation; congressional debate over immigration; political machines extend democracy in cities; poverty and social action	Effect of uncontrolled growth of economy on workers; Populist ideas for getting people more directly involved in politics	Woman suffrage movement; 16th and 17th Amendments; commission and city manager systems; direct primary; initiative, referendum, and recall; secret ballot
	Search for Opportunity	New inventions and industries; growing consumerism; entrepreneurship; immigrants in search of political and religious freedom and economic opportunity	Impact of technological change on workers; Populist call for government role in the economy	W.E.B. Du Bois's and Booker T. Washington's differing views on opportunity for African Americans; collective bargaining
Skills	**Critical Thinking**	Analyzing; evaluating; applying information; synthesizing; identifying an argument	Applying information; analyzing; evaluating; recognizing point of view; synthesizing	Analyzing; synthesizing; evaluating; interpreting political cartoons
	Social Studies Skills	Using time lines; using a bar graph	Understanding geography concepts: region; analyzing line graphs	Analyzing graphs; using time lines
	Writing Skills		Writing an editorial expressing an opinion	Writing a letter expressing an opinion
	Active Learning	Investigating current government regulation of business; investigating current urban problems; researching immigration; making a poster of urban growth from 1850 to early 1900s (Unit 4 Survey)	Researching unions in the community; compiling "Ten Commandments of Big Business" from varying points of view (Unit 4 Survey); making an annotated map of the world (Unit 4 Survey)	Comparing today's high school curriculum to typical curriculum in 1900; investigating state reforms during progressive era

	CHAPTER 18	CHAPTER 19	CHAPTER 20	CHAPTER 21
	Imperialism; enforcement of Monroe Doctrine; causes and effects of Spanish-American War; foreign policy in Asia and Latin America	Causes, course, and effects of World War I	Causes and effects of postwar unrest in the U.S.; causes and effects of business boom; changing values	Causes of 1920s business boom; causes and results of the 1929 stock market crash; Hoover's approach to ending the Great Depression
	Imperialist and anti-imperialist racist beliefs; moral diplomacy	Use of propaganda; suppression of free speech; racial discrimination in military; war and profits; pacifism; Armenian genocide; use of force in promoting values; chemical warfare	Increased nativism and racism; anti-black violence; revival of Ku Klux Klan; Scopes trial; fundamentalism	Religion as Smith campaign issue in 1928; dishonesty in business; charitable aid to depression victims
	Yellow journalism; Spread of Anglo-American values and beliefs	Music and literature from WWI (Unit 6—History Through Literature); propaganda and patriotism	Impact of automobile, electricity, synthetics industry, movies, radio, automobile; popularity of blues music and jazz; "the lost generation"; prohibition; Harlem Renaissance	Dorothea Lange and Margaret Bourke-White, photographers of the depression
	U.S. expansion in Asia; Panama Canal: relationships within places	WWI battlefronts; trench warfare; division of Europe and the Near East after WWI; migration from South to North	Spread of Ku Klux Klan; Mexican and African-American migration to the North; immigration quotas to the U.S.	Election maps of 1928 and 1932
	Expansionists motivated by economic gain; dollar diplomacy	Trade blockades; effects of war on business and labor; government regulation of industry; raising money for war effort	Effect of Mexican labor on U.S. economy; government support for business; business boom; hard times for coal and textile industries and farmers; increase of women in work force	Advertising; credit buying; end of 1920s boom; speculation; underlying weaknesses of 1920s economy; relation between the crash and the depression; depression; business cycle; gov't. response; RFC
	Jones Act; Open Door policy; Big-stick diplomacy; Roosevelt Corollary	Public opinion and the war; propaganda; preparedness; the draft; expansion of role of federal government; woman suffrage; League of Nations debate	Anti-union feelings; political corruption; growth and decline of Ku Klux Klan's political power; "Red scare"; prohibition	Effects of the depression on people of various racial and cultural backgrounds; Bonus Army
	Anti-American feelings in Asia and Latin America	National origins and diversity of opinion about war; racial discrimination in armed forces; moral values and opposition to war; discrimination against German Americans	Racial violence; discrimination toward Asians in U.S.; restricting immigration; unionization efforts by African-American, Mexican, and Japanese workers; "black power" and Marcus Garvey	
	Debate over right of U.S. to exercise its power abroad	Limiting freedom of speech during wartime; Wilson's Fourteen Points; American role and methods in promoting democracy abroad; discrimination; woman suffrage	Civil rights campaigns of the NAACP	Government responsibility in form of indirect aid
	Expansionism for a "fair share" in foreign trade; the Open Door policy; U.S. intervention in Latin America	War mobilization creates opportunities for women and African Americans	Women in the labor force; Mexican and African-American migrations north; formation of the National Urban League	Playing the stock market; dream of opportunities struck down by stock market crash; overproduction by factory owners and farmers
	Analyzing; applying information; evaluating; synthesizing; detecting bias	Analyzing; evaluating; synthesizing; recognizing point of view; interpreting political cartoons; identifying unstated assumptions	Evaluating; analyzing; synthesizing; applying information	Evaluating; synthesizing; recognizing point of view; applying information
	Understanding geography concepts: location, region, relationships within places, movement; using maps	Understanding geography concepts: movement, location, place; using time lines; interpreting graphics; making maps (Unit 6 Survey)	Using time lines; analyzing bar graphs	Using graphs; understanding geography concepts; analyzing statistical tables
	Writing a letter to the editor; writing a speech	Writing a speech	Writing a paragraph expressing an opinion; writing a memoir of the 1920s (Unit 7 Survey)	Writing a memoir of the Great Depression (Unit 7 Survey)
	Debating principles determining foreign policy, role-playing (Unit 6 Survey)	Discussing impact of television in reporting today; researching forms of gov't. before and after WWI, debating moral values and foreign policy, making maps of Europe (Unit 6 Survey)	Researching the air traffic controllers' strike of 1981; making a poster of clothing styles of the 1920s, making a chart of changes brought about by the automobile (Unit 7 Survey)	

Scope and Sequence

		CHAPTER 22	CHAPTER 23	CHAPTER 24
Knowledge and Understanding	**History**	First Hundred Days of the New Deal; Second New Deal	Attempts at ensuring peace; involvement in Latin America; causes and effects of totalitarianism in Europe; Japanese expansion; American response to war; build-up of U.S. defenses	Mobilization for war; major events of World War II
	Ethics & Religion	Father Charles E. Coughlin, critic of New Deal	Kellogg-Briand Pact; U.S. business practices and military involvement in Latin America; fascism; Naziism, anti-Semitism; expansionism; *Kristallnacht*; appeasement vs. direct action	Racist attitudes limit opportunities for African Americans in armed services; internment of Japanese Americans; the Holocaust; debate over use of the atomic bomb
	Culture	*The Grapes of Wrath* (Unit 7—History Through Literature); FDR's fireside chats; WPA writers' and artists' projects; books, music, movies as relief	Will Rogers in radio, movies, and newspapers	*Farewell to Manzanar* (Unit 8—History Through Literature) contributions of young people to the war effort
	Geography	The Dust Bowl: region; migration from Great Plains to the Far West; the TVA; the CCC and national parks	Japan: place; Japan's physical characteristics as a cause of aggression; attempts to "quarantine" aggression; aggression in Europe and Asia	Movement within U.S. to pursue jobs or serve in military; "Second Great Migration" by African Americans; Allied and Axis troop movements; American "island-hopping" strategy
	Economics	Bank crisis; economic relief and reform measures; government and the TVA; union strikes; economic slump of 1937; deficit spending	American investments in Latin America; U.S. as creditor nation; attempts to stimulate world trade; effects of reparations and tariffs; Dawes Plan; economic causes for Japanese expansion; Lend-Lease Act	Conversion of industry to wartime production; booming farm economy; end of Great Depression; government controls of wages and prices; rationing; WLB victory gardens
	Sociology & Politics	The "Black Cabinet"; conservative opposition to the New Deal; radical opposition; Social Security Act; new Democratic coalition; FDR and the Supreme Court	Causes of totalitarianism; American isolationism; Good Neighbor Policy; appeasement; end of isolationism; public opinion and the war	Supreme Court upholds internment policy; stresses of wartime on families
Themes in United States History	**Balancing Unity and Diversity**	Effect of New Deal programs on African Americans and Native Americans; Indian Reorganization Act	Extreme racism and persecution; American role in preserving peace in midst of racial and religious hatred	Women in work force; segregation in armed forces; racial violence against Mexican and African Americans; Executive Order 8802; Japanese-American internment
	Shaping Democracy	FDR and his advisors	American isolationism; U.S. at war; Atlantic Charter; American democracy in the world	African-American and Mexican-American campaigns against discrimination and segregation; investigation of internment
	Search for Opportunity	Expansion of role of government to aid economy and American people	Business interests in Latin America; financial leadership as a creditor after WWI; tariffs and trade agreements	Native-American and Mexican farm workers; Women and African Americans in industry; black migration from South to pursue jobs
Skills	**Critical Thinking**	Synthesizing; applying information; analyzing; evaluating; determining the strength of an argument	Analyzing; evaluating; synthesizing; recognizing point of view; recognizing propaganda	Analyzing; evaluating; synthesizing; applying information
	Social Studies Skills	Understanding geography concepts: region; using time lines; analyzing bar graphs	Understanding geography concepts: place, movement; using maps and time lines; making time lines of German, Russian, and Japanese expansion	Using time lines; interpreting graphics
	Writing Skills	Writing a memoir of the Great Depression (Unit 7 Survey)		
	Active Learning	Researching current job programs for youth; researching New Deal programs still in effect; interviewing; reviewing classic films of the 1920s and 1930s (Unit 7 Survey)	Researching and reporting on a gov't. today with policy of discrimination; making an annotated time line of events leading up to WWII, debating possibility of stopping Hitler's aggression (Unit 8 Survey)	Researching biological effects of radiation; making an annotated time line of major events of WWII, debating U.S. intervention in WWII, interviewing people who lived through WWII (Unit 8 Survey)

	CHAPTER 25	CHAPTER 26	CHAPTER 27	CHAPTER 28
	Causes of the Cold War and arms race; containment and "massive retaliation" policies; Korean War; U.S. policy in Indochina, the Middle East, and Latin America	Post-WWI era in U.S.; changed expectations of women and of ethnic groups facing discrimination; fear of Communist subversion; features of American life in the 1950s	Domestic policies of Kennedy, Johnson; Cold War tensions	African-American civil rights movement of the 1950s and 1960s
	Nuremberg trials; Dulles's view of Cold War as forces of good against evil of communism	McCarthyism; threat of nuclear war	Religion as Kennedy campaign issue; Supreme Court decision on school prayer; efforts toward disarmament; values of counterculture; new religious sects and revival of traditional faiths	Legal and de facto segregation; nonviolent resistance to segregation and discrimination
	Nasser and Arab nationalism	Social conformity	Peace Corps and volunteerism; culture and the arts in the White House; youth culture of the 1960s: music, art, fashion, religion; literature of environmental and social concern; counterculture	Role of TV and newspapers in bringing acts of racism before American public
	Redivision of Europe after WWII; Berlin airlift; Korean War battleground; NORAD map; identifying Cold War trouble spots	Growth of suburbs: relationships within places; decline in population of cities	Environmentalism; Water Quality Act of 1965; creation of EPA; reapportionment; location of Communist Cuba influenced superpower decisions	African-American migration from South to cities throughout U.S.
	Marshall Plan	Post-war abundance; increased consumerism; poverty amid prosperity; impact of automation	Alliance for Progress; increased deficit spending; War on Poverty; Economic Opportunity Act; consumer movements	Boycotts and sit-ins; cycle of racism and poverty; relationship between white racism and riots
	United Nations; Truman Doctrine; NATO; Eisenhower Doctrine	McCarthyism; social impact of the baby boom	Kennedy's New Frontier; LBJ's Great Society; policy of flexible response	Development of mass movement based on direct action; role of federal government; "black power"; separatism
	Views of Eleanor Roosevelt on interracial relations	Fear of communism; lack of diversity in suburbs	End of immigration quotas based on national origin; struggle for civil rights	Massive resistance to *Brown* v. *Board of Education*; effects of African-American migrations to northern cities
	Issue of relation of containment policy to democratic principles; MacArthur controversy and principle of presidential control of military; issue of CIA covert operations	Impact of McCarran Act and HUAC; "separate but equal" facilities ruled unconstitutional; Civil Rights Act of 1957; NAACP black voter registration drives	Opposition to communism; efforts to promote democracy abroad; democracy not reality for many; rights of the accused; Civil Rights Act of 1964; Voting Rights Act of 1965; youth protests	*Brown* v. *Board of Education*; Civil Rights Acts of 1957, 1960, 1964; civil rights movement; Freedom Summer; Voting Rights Act of 1965
	Langston Hughes: "Let America Be America Again" (Unit 9—History Through Literature) conflict over Palestine as Jewish refugees arrive from Europe	Expanding economic and educational opportunities for some members of ethnic groups, while others found poverty and continuing discrimination; labor strikes; impact of Fair Deal policies and automation	Job Corps; VISTA; Head Start	African-American struggle for equal rights; March on Washington for Jobs and Freedom; effect of changing U.S. economy on black migrants
	Analyzing; evaluating; synthesizing	Synthesizing; analyzing; evaluating; detecting bias	Applying information; evaluating; analyzing; synthesizing; interpreting political cartoons	Analyzing; synthesizing; evaluating
	Understanding geography concepts: region, movement, location; using maps and time lines; analyzing bar graphs	Understanding geography concepts: relationships within places; using time lines	Understanding geography concepts: location; using time lines	Understanding geography concepts; analyzing bar graphs
	Writing a speech expressing an opinion	Writing an editorial expressing an opinion; writing an article for a news magazine (Unit 9 Survey)	Writing a letter expressing an opinion	
	Interviewing people about the effect of *Sputnik* I	Making an illustrated time line of major developments in space exploration, 1950s-1960s, interviewing people who remember key events of the Fifties (Unit 9 Survey)	Researching gun control; making an illustrated time line of space exploration; interviewing (Unit 9 Survey)	Interviewing people to learn their opinions about the civil rights movement; role-playing a conversation with a famous person about the civil rights movement (Unit 9 Survey)

Scope and Sequence

		CHAPTER 29	CHAPTER 30	CHAPTER 31	CHAPTER 32
Knowledge and Understanding	History	Causes and effects of Vietnam War	Movements for social justice for women, Hispanics, Native Americans; presidencies of Nixon, Ford, Carter	Reagan era of conservatism; Reagan's foreign policy; George Bush presidency; challenges facing Bill Clinton's presidency	Impact of increasing diversity on all Americans; movement toward a more representative democracy; changing economic opportunities in the 1990s; foreign policy issues
	Ethics & Religion	Racism toward Vietnamese; racial tensions between American soldiers; attitudes toward civilian casualties; conscientious objectors; treatment of Amerasian children	Abortion debate; Carter's human rights policy	The religious right; nuclear freeze movement; use of force to promote democracy abroad; Iran-contra scandal; apartheid in South Africa	Continuing quest for dignity of individual; the problem of hate crimes; responsibility toward environment
	Culture	Cultural misunderstandings between Americans and the Vietnamese	Mexican-American art and literature	Public health issues, including drugs and AIDS; issue of health-care system reform	Increase in cultural pride; multicultural contributions to the arts
	Geography	Impact of terrain and climate on warfare; environmental impact of napalm and Agent Orange	Redistricting; Native-American land and mineral deposit claims; environmental concerns	Relaxed environmental regulations; 1991 Gulf War environmental damage	Shifting population: movement; toxic waste, air pollution, acid rain, global warming; renewable/nonrenewable resources
	Economics	Economic problems in Vietnam under Communist regime	Law guaranteeing equal pay to women; César Chávez and United Farm Workers; grain-export deal with Soviet Union; stagflation; deregulation; opening of trade with China	Reaganomics; recession/recovery; increased deregulation; deficit spending; "new federalism"; growth of poverty, homelessness; supply-side economics; savings and loan crisis	Increasing gap between rich and poor; urban poverty; increasing number of women and people of diverse ethnic groups in work force; global interdependence; trade deficit
	Sociology & Politics	Gulf of Tonkin Resolution; Johnson's withdrawal from election of 1968; War Powers Act of 1973; debate between "hawks" and "doves"; difficulties facing veterans in adjusting to civilian life	NOW; Hispanic political organizations; American Indian Movement (AIM); détente with Soviet Union; Yom Kippur War and energy crisis; Watergate scandal; Iran hostage crisis	Conservatism; Moral Majority; "new federalism;" intervention in Latin America; Iran-contra affair; *glasnost* and *perestroika* in Soviet Union; unification of Germany; break up of Soviet Union	Increase in number of women, Hispanics, and African Americans as elected state and local officials; small, but steady progress in national government
Themes in United States History	Balancing Unity and Diversity	Racial tensions within armed forces; anti-war movement	Women, Hispanics, Native Americans move for equality; upswing of ethnic pride; bilingual education; affirmative action and backlash	Debate over conservative policies; the democratic "rainbow coalition"	Increasingly diverse American population; individual and institutional racism; hate crimes
	Shaping Democracy	Issue of relation of containment policy to democratic principles; abuse of presidential power during war; impact of media on public opinion; issue of presidential war-making power	ERA defeat; abuse of presidential power	Conservative appointments to Supreme Court; opposition to communism in Latin America; defrosting the Cold War; promoting democracy abroad	Voter apathy; efforts by women, African Americans, and Hispanic Americans to gain political power; party images; government gridlock
	Search for Opportunity	War refugees in the United States	Women's movement; Chicano movement; Native-American legal defense of treaty rights; affirmative action	Yuppies; "credit card prosperity"; the "rainbow coalition"; the fight against joblessness and homelessness	Global competition; technological change; trend toward temporary and part time jobs; efforts to reduce poverty
Skills	Critical Thinking	Analyzing; evaluating; recognizing point of view; determining the strength of an argument	Applying information; analyzing; evaluating; synthesizing; identifying point of view; recognizing stereotypes	Synthesizing; evaluating; analyzing; applying information	Evaluating; analyzing; synthesizing; interpreting diagrams
	Social Studies Skills	Understanding geography concepts: location; analyzing graphs	Analyzing graphs; using time lines	Understanding geography concepts: place, location; using graphs and time lines; interpreting diagrams	Understanding geography concepts: movement; using maps; analyzing graphs
	Writing Skills	Writing an editorial expressing an opinion	Writing a paper expressing an opinion		Writing a memorandum expressing an opinion
	Active Learning	Interviewing people who were adults during the Vietnam War (Unit 9 Survey)	Planning a museum display about a political, social, cultural, or technological event of the 1970s (Unit 10 Survey)	Researching the gap between rich and poor; making an energy survey of the community (Unit 10 Survey)	Making a bulletin board display illustrating continuity and change in community, 1970–1990 (Unit 10 Survey)

“A people without history is like wind on the buffalo grass.”

—Lakota/Dakota proverb

ADDISON-WESLEY PUBLISHING COMPANY
Menlo Park, California • Reading, Massachusetts • New York
Don Mills, Ontario • Wokingham, England • Amsterdam • Bonn
Sydney • Singapore • Tokyo • Madrid • San Juan • Paris • Seoul
Milan • Mexico City • Taipei

Addison-Wesley

The United States and Its People

Authors

David C. King

Norman McRae

Jaye Zola

Authors

David C. King, M.A., is the author of several textbooks, as well as short stories and biographies on American history themes. He has taught high school American history and English and has served as a history consultant for the Corporation for Public Broadcasting, National Assessment of Educational Progress, National Council for the Social Studies, and school districts throughout the nation.

Norman McRae, who holds a PhD in history from the University of Michigan, is former director of Social Studies for the Detroit Public Schools. He has conducted many workshops and taught African-American history at two universities. He has also published books, articles, and curriculum materials on the black presence in the United States.

Jaye Zola, a social studies teacher in Boulder, Colorado, has developed an interdisciplinary course on American culture, literature, and history. She has written curriculum and teaching activities on political and social issues, nuclear war, and religion in American history. At her high school she is helping to create an interactive curriculum.

Consultants and Reviewers

Ron Banaszak, associate professor, College of Education, University of Alabama, Tuscaloosa

Carlos Cortes, professor of Latin American history, University of California, Riverside

Carl Degler, Margaret Byrne Professor of American History, Stanford University, Stanford, California

Lloyd Elm, principal, Native American Magnet School, Buffalo, New York

Gloria Ladson-Billings, professor, Department of Curriculum and Instruction, University of Wisconsin, Madison

Mabel McKinney-Browning, staff director of the American Bar Association's Committee on Youth Education for Citizenship

Gary Mukai, coordinator, the Japan Project, Stanford Program on International and Cross-Cultural Education

Brenda Rudman Padial, teacher, Phillips Exeter Academy, Exeter, New Hampshire

Frances J. Powell, supervising director, History/Social Studies, District of Columbia Public Schools

Jack Rakove, professor of history, Stanford University, Stanford, California

Karen Sawislak, assistant professor of history, Stanford University, Stanford, California

Donald Schwartz, credential coordinator for social sciences, California State University at Long Beach; former coordinator of social studies for White Plains, NY, public schools

Patricia Sullivan, assistant director of the Center for the Study of Civil Rights, Carter B. Woodson Institute for Afro-American and African Studies, University of Virginia

Acknowledgments of permission to reprint copyrighted materials appear on pages 973–974.

ISBN 0-201-81128-6

2 3 4 5 6 7 8 9 10 - VH - 98 97 96 95 94

Contents

20th Anniversary
JOBS, PEACE AND FREEDOM
WE SHARE THE DREAM
AMERICAN POSTAL WORKERS UNION, AFL-CIO

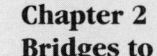

v

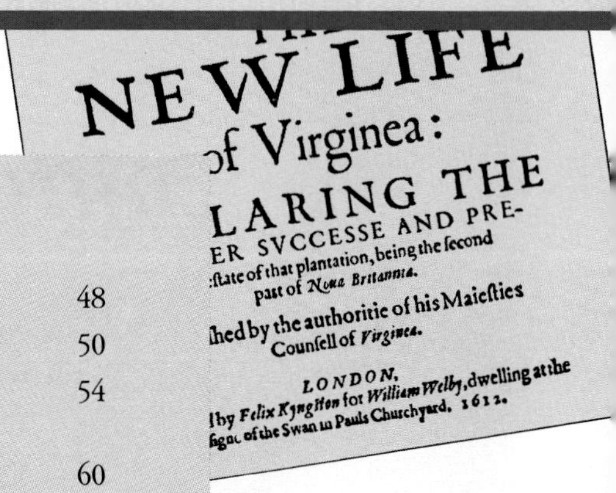

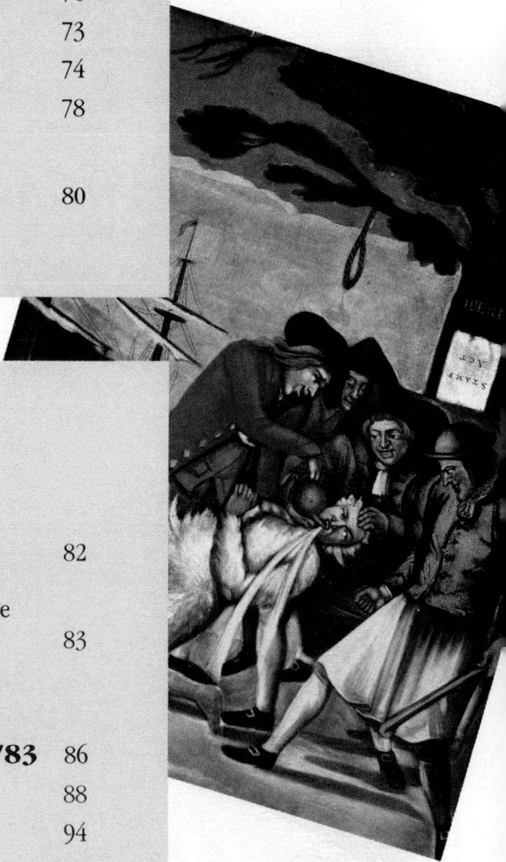

Unit 2 1763–1801

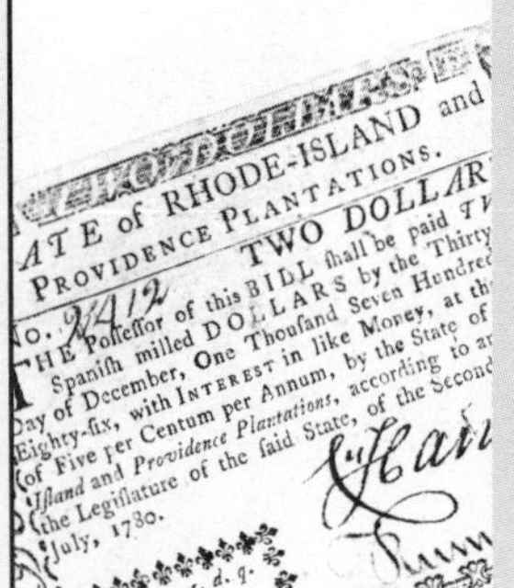

vi

vii

Unit 3 1801–1850

Building a Nation

Unit 4 1850–1905

A House Divided

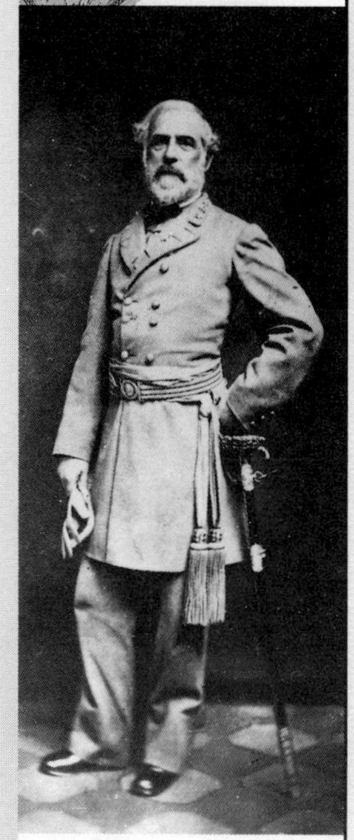

Unit 5 1850–1910

New Horizons 352

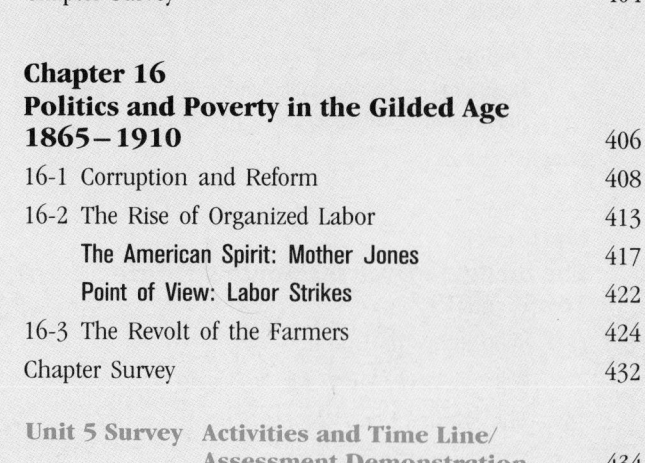

Unit 6 1890–1920

Questions of Power

Unit 7 1919–1939

Prosperity and Depression 522

DON'T YOU KNOW WHEN YOU'VE HAD ENOUGH?

SOMEBODY HAD TO SAVE HIM FROM H—
—Gale in the Los Ang

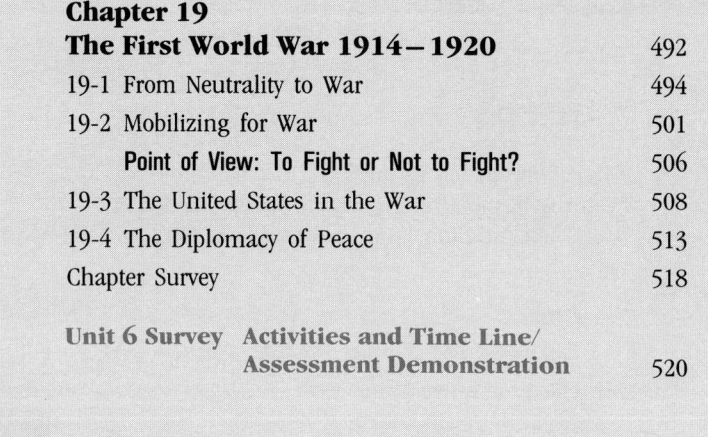

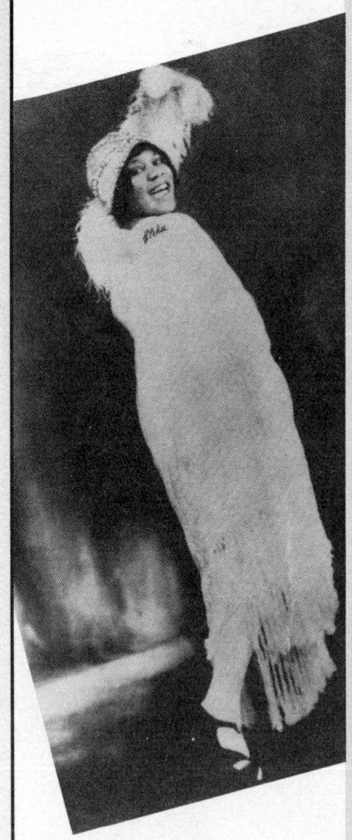

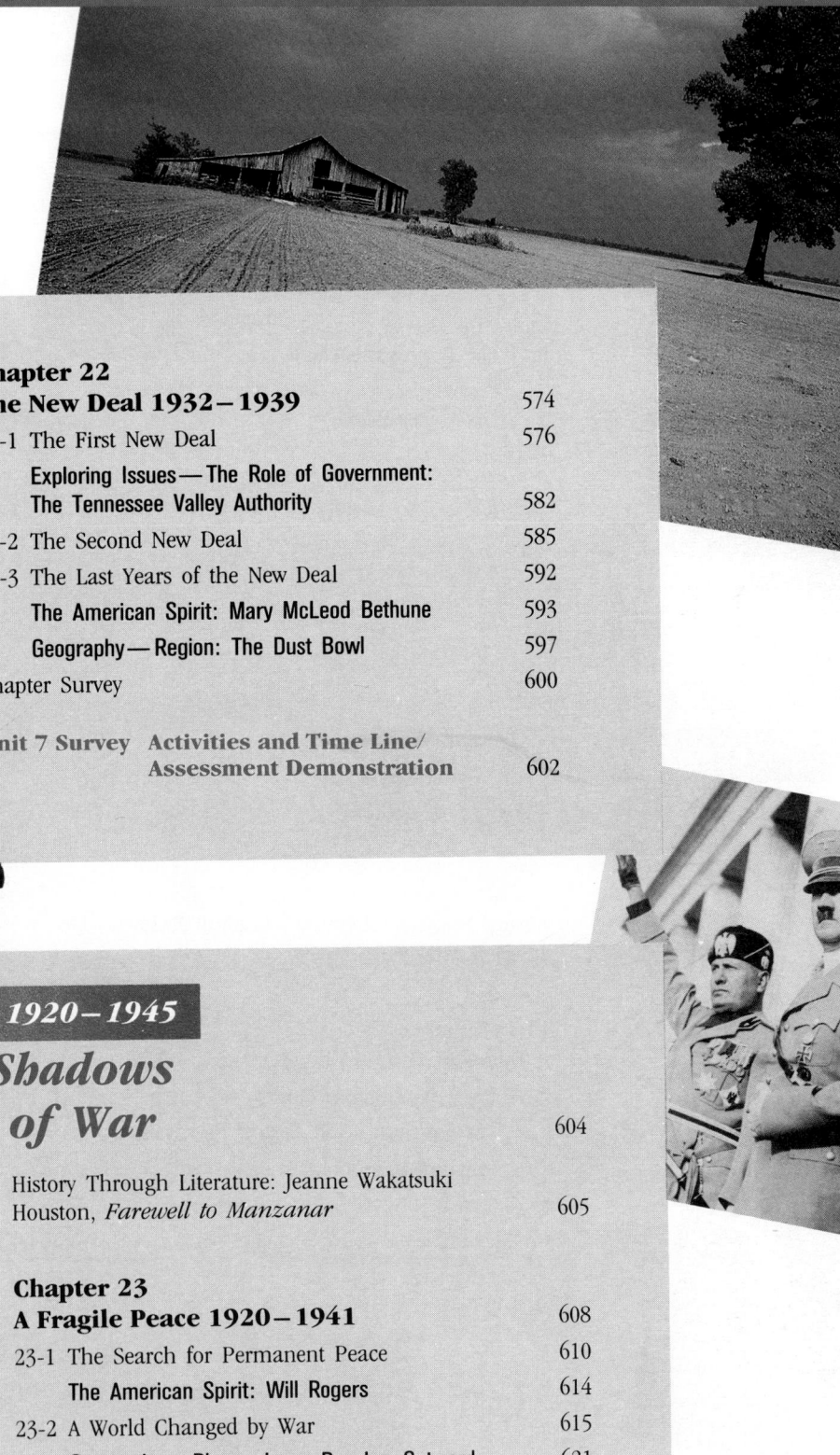

xiii

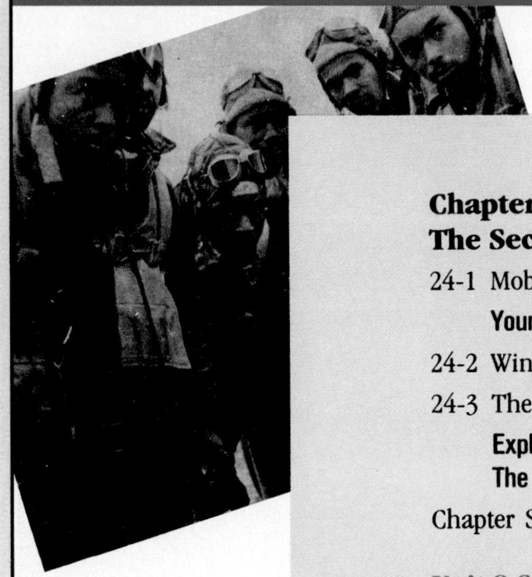

Unit 9 1945–1975

From Confidence to Self-Doubt

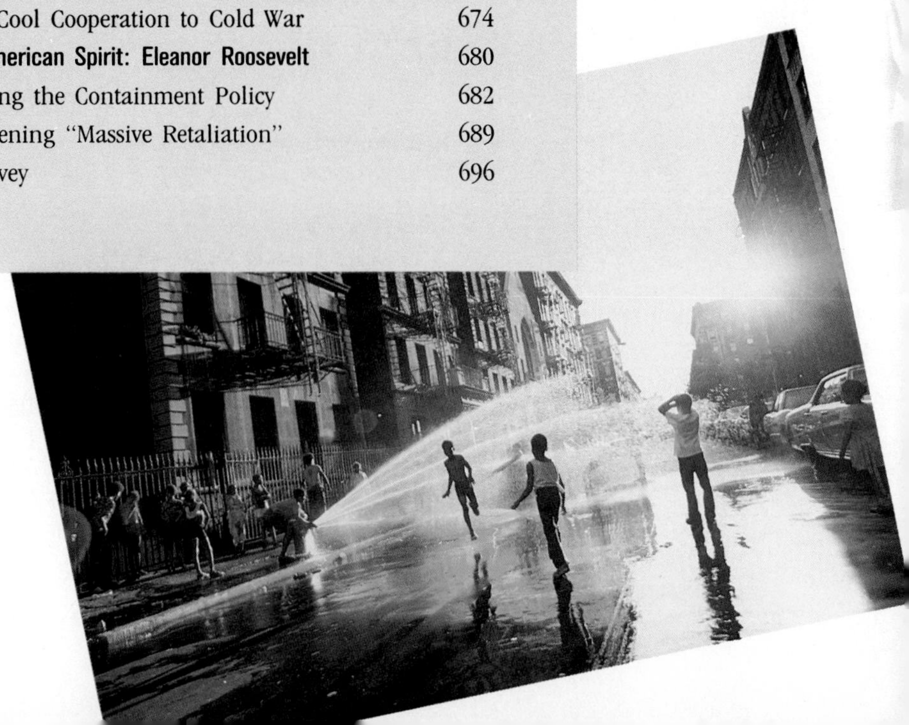

xiv

xv

Unit 10 1969–Present

xvi

Reference Center 898

Special Features

History Through Literature

xvii

American Voices: Selected Primary Sources

Among the hundreds of primary sources throughout the text, the following appear at the beginning of each chapter:

Point of View

Geography

Young in America

The Creative Spirit

Reduced student page in the Teacher's Edition

The American Spirit

Exploring Issues

Learning From Art

Skills

Applying Thinking Skills

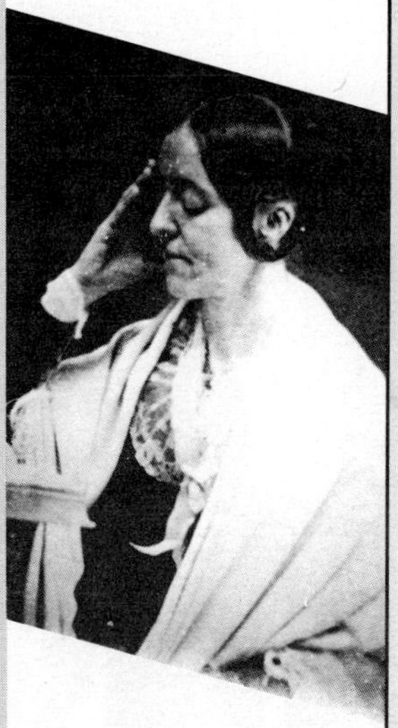

Applying Social Studies Skills

Writing About Issues

Maps

xxiii

Reduced student page in the Teacher's Edition

Charts, Graphs, Diagrams

XXV

Introducing the Book

To Our Readers

Your journey through American history will be a process of discovery— of exploring the hopes, ideas, and fears that have driven Americans from the past up to the present. We have tried to bring these to life by looking at events through the eyes of those who experienced them. You will meet many people from the past— some famous, others little known— and share the thoughts they recorded in letters, diaries, newspapers, and other writings. You will see how they pictured themselves in paintings, drawings, cartoons, posters, and photographs, all of which are tools historians use to interpret the past.

To help you keep the "big picture" in mind on your journey, we have focused on three central themes that have shaped this nation's history and will continue to affect its future. These themes are explained in Chapter 1, and the "Connections to Themes" discussions at the end of each chapter help you trace their development throughout the text.

The first theme is balancing unity and diversity. The United States has always been a land of many peoples and cultures. Diversity has led to strength and tension, as Americans have faced the challenge of building one nation.

The second theme is shaping democracy. Our nation was founded on the democratic ideals of liberty and justice for all, but making those ideals a living reality is a challenge that still faces us today. The third theme is the search for opportunity. This land has been blessed with abundance, and each generation has faced the question of how to use these natural resources to create economic opportunities for all Americans.

On the next five pages you will learn how the book also helps you see the "big picture" through thinking critically, comparing different points of view, and exploring geography. For, in the words of novelist Robert Penn Warren, without a broad understanding of American history, "you have no context for your life. You don't know where you are; you don't know where you're going." Our goal is to help you link the past to your life today and to your future.

David C. King

Norman McRae

Gaye Zola

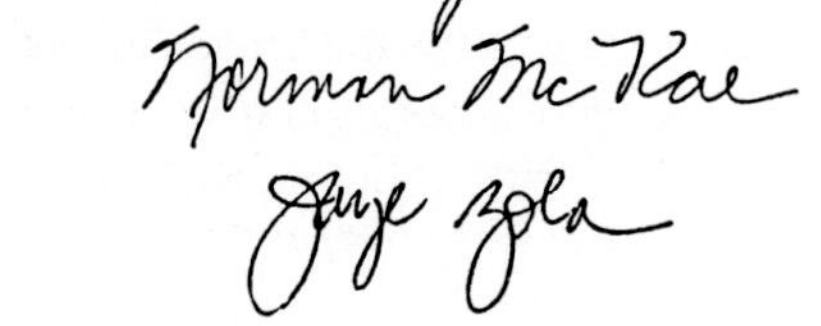

Applying Thinking Skills

In section reviews and chapter surveys, you will see the following labels next to questions: *Identification, Comprehension, Application, Analysis, Synthesis,* and *Evaluation.* They refer to the different types of thinking required.

Identification/Comprehension. To identify means to tell who or what a person or thing is. In this book, identification questions ask you to define new terms.

To comprehend means to grasp the meaning of something. You may be asked to describe, list, or explain what you have read. Each section review has at least one such question, and "Reviewing the Chapter" questions in chapter surveys focus on comprehension.

Example: Describe two issues of concern to women in the 1970s.

Application. To apply means to take something learned in one situation and use it in another. Application questions ask you to link ideas or facts to related topics.

Example: Explain how the challenge of balancing unity and diversity was evident in the late 1800s, using examples from your reading.

Analysis. To analyze means to break something down into its parts to study the relationships. You will often be asked to compare and to identify causes and effects.

Example: Compare treatment of African Americans and Native Americans in the 1960s.

Synthesis. To synthesize means to put together information to create something new. Often you will make predictions or imagine how people in the past might have viewed events.

Example: Describe the battle of the Alamo from the point of view of a Mexican soldier.

Evaluation. To evaluate means to judge the worth, value, or accuracy of something. You are asked to form your own opinion.

Example: How effective do you think nonviolent protests were during the civil rights movement?

Thinking Critically

As you can see, exploring history means more than remembering and understanding what was said, written, or done in the past. It involves thinking about relationships between statements and events, as well as forming opinions about the past and its links to the present. In short, the answers are not all "in the book." You will have many opportunities to think critically about history.

Critical thinking is making informed, thoughtful judgments about the meaning, accuracy, and worth of what you see, hear, or read. Questions calling for synthesis and evaluation, and for application and analysis to some degree, all involve critical thinking. In addition, "Applying Thinking Skills" activities in chapter surveys provide practice in a variety of critical-thinking skills.

The cartoon above, from "Applying Thinking Skills" in Chapter 27, refers to three leaders' conflicting views of an event. Critical thinking involves making your own judgments— thinking for yourself rather than simply accepting what others say is true. By thinking critically, you get "into" the history rather than just getting the history into you.

xxvii

Recognizing Point of View

" A Congressman is a green toad on a green tree, a brown toad on a brown tree. He reflects his constituents. "

This comment by Carrie Chapman Catt, a leader in the movement to gain voting rights for women, reflects her view of national lawmakers in the early 1900s. However, some Congressmen may have disagreed with Catt's view, seeing themselves as leaders not easily swayed by pressure from voters. Exploring American history involves recognizing that people and events can be seen from different points of view.

"Point of view" can mean "opinion," but a more general meaning refers to all factors that affect opinions. In this definition, a **point of view** is the position from which a person observes or considers something.

Many factors may be involved in forming a point of view, including age, sex, personality, family, race, culture, economic condition, job, religion, values, and goals. Experiences also play a role. Catt's view of Congressmen, for example, was colored by her frustrated efforts to gain their support for women's rights.

A point of view can lead someone to focus on certain aspects of a person, issue, or event and to ignore or pay less attention to other aspects. One person's interpretation of the "facts" may differ from another's. Consider, for instance, how an enslaved person and a slaveholder in the early 1800s might differ in their descriptions of working conditions. Or think about how a general and a Vietnam War protestor in the 1960s might disagree over that war's impact. The examples are endless.

In each chapter you will come across many primary sources telling how people saw and reacted to events and conditions. You will also find ten "Point of View" features that explore in more depth viewpoints on a variety of topics. Shown here are pictures from one feature, reflecting different views of factory working conditions in the 1800s.

Recognizing point of view is an important critical-thinking skill that helps you determine the accuracy, reliability, and fairness of accounts and images. By trying to look at people and events from different points of view, you will gain a better understanding of the "big picture" of American history. Perhaps your own views may change as a result.

Linking Geography and History

"Studying history without geography is like watching a movie with your eyes closed. You can follow the plot, but you can't see where the story takes place or how the setting affects what's happening."

As this comment by a history student suggests, the study of history and geography are closely linked. Geography provides the stage on which the historical drama unfolds. And sometimes geography is a key player in that drama, a cause of the action as well as its setting.

Geographers have identified five concepts, or themes, that are fundamental to our learning to think geographically, to ask questions about places and their relationships to people and events. As you will read in the following paragraphs, each concept suggests different questions about the where, why, and how of human events— questions you will encounter throughout this book.

Concept 1: Location

The first geographic concept—**location**— deals with two basic questions: Where? and Why there?

Location can be described in both absolute and relative terms. The **absolute location** of a place or thing identifies precisely where it is on the earth. A common way to indicate absolute location is to give a postal address. Geographers are more scientific, using a system of latitude and longitude to pinpoint the absolute location of a town or lake, for example.

Relative location refers to where a place is in terms of other places. When you say a place is "next door to," "not far from," or "ten miles east of" some other known place, you are describing its relative location.

Knowing something about the relative location of a city, an industry, or a battle is often essential to an understanding of "why there?" As this map of Gettysburg suggests, a great Civil War battle was fought near this Pennsylvania town, not on the whim of a general, but because of the town's location relative to a network of roads. Planning to invade the North, Confederate troops marched along one of these roads toward Pennsylvania's capital, Harrisburg. Union troops moved along another of the roads, hoping to stop the invasion. They met at Gettysburg, a fateful confrontation.

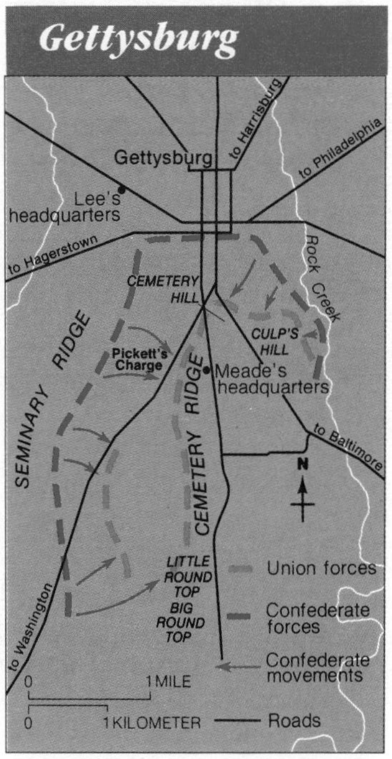

xxix

Concept 2: Place

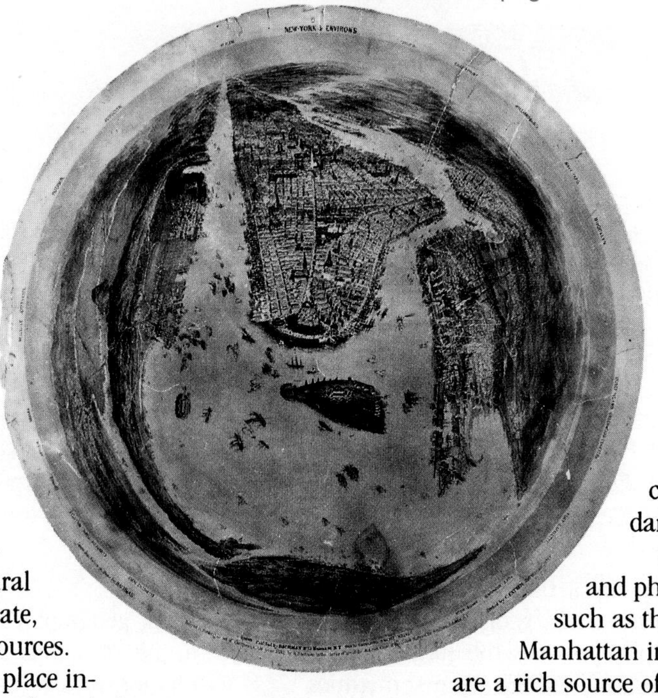

The second geographic concept—**place**— centers on the question: What features give a particular location its unique identity?

Any place on earth can be described in terms of its distinctive physical and human characteristics. *Physical characteristics* include a variety of natural features such as landforms, climate, vegetation, soil, and mineral resources. The *human characteristics* of a place include such factors as the number of people living there and their language and culture. Human characteristics also include changes people have made in the natural landscape, including such features as farms, roads, cities, and dams.

Old drawings and photographs, such as this view of Manhattan in the 1850s, are a rich source of information about unique features of a place. These images reveal how a place looked and help us to see how its characteristics have changed over time.

Concept 3: Relationships Within Places

The third concept—**relationships within places**— focuses on the relationship between people and the environments in which they live. This concept addresses the question of how humans both adapt to and modify their environments to meet their changing needs.

How people relate to a place is influenced by many factors. One factor is the nature of the place— its physical features, climate, and resources. Another is the nature of the people— their way of life, economy, and level of technology. As these factors change over time, relationships within places change as well.

This photo of the Levittown suburb shows how relationship to a place can change. Until the end of World War II, people valued this part of Long Island for its fertile soil. It was a sleepy potato-growing area. Then builder William Levitt bought up some of the potato fields and planted a new "crop"— low-cost homes. In a matter of months, Levitt's potato patch became an instant suburb, a place where many could own a home in the country.

Concept 4: Movement

The concept of **movement** focuses on this question: How do people, things, and ideas move from place to place?

Many kinds of movement interest historians and geographers, from the flow of people and goods through migration and trade to the spread of information and ideas through electronic communication networks. The concept of movement also encompasses the spread of music, words, dances, games, and other forms of popular culture around the world.

The Phillips Collection, Washington, D.C.

This painting of a crowded railway station by Jacob Lawrence was inspired by a massive population movement—the great migration of African Americans out of the rural South during and after World War I. That historic movement of more than a million African Americans to northern cities changed the racial landscape of the United States forever.

Concept 5: Regions

Rather than try to study the whole earth all at once, geographers often divide it into **regions.** A region is any area that people define by one or more unifying characteristics. When defining a region, geographers begin with this question: What feature or interplay of features unites this area while setting it apart from other areas?

There are countless ways of defining regions. A region may be defined in terms of its cultural heritage (Latin America), its main crop (the Cotton Belt), a unifying physical feature (the Great Plains), or a dominant industry (Silicon Valley). A region may be as small as a no-smoking area or as large as a hemisphere. Definitions of regions change as this map shows. Early maps identified part of the plains as a region called the "Great American Desert." After farmers covered the plains with wheat fields, the plains region became known as "America's Breadbasket." Then, in the 1930s, the plains were hit by drought, and winds carried the dry soil away. Once again a part of the plains was redefined, this time as a region called the "Dust Bowl."

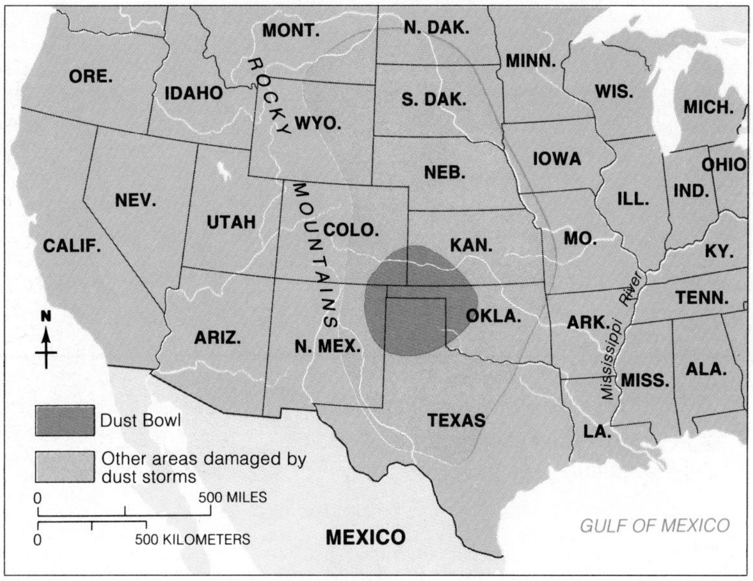

Unit 1

Objectives

- Discuss the three major ongoing themes in American history.
- Describe the diverse cultures that were developed by the first Americans.
- Explain how opportunities for Europeans in the Americas meant disaster for Africans and Native Americans.
- Discuss motives for people from different nations coming to America.

Introducing
THE UNIT

For thousands of years the original inhabitants of the Americas developed their civilizations unaware of the existence of Europe, Asia, and Africa. Europe's explorations of North and South America and the consequences for people on both sides of the Atlantic Ocean are the subjects of Unit 1.

B · A · C · K · G · R · O · U · N · D

Unit Opener Background Photo

The Painted Desert in north-central Arizona received its name from early Spanish explorers, who called it *El Desierto Pintado.* The desert is a wasteland of buttes, mesas, pinnacles, and valleys formed by wind and rain cutting into volcanic ash. Heat, light, and dust often change the pastel colors of the desert from blue, amethyst, and yellow to russet, lilac, and red.

Connections: Geography

The Laguna Pueblo Reservation is located on the Colorado Plateau in New Mexico. Flat-topped mesas, steep-walled canyons, and desert are typical land forms of the region. Precipitation may average less than four inches of rainfall a year.

About 5,000 people live in seven villages on the reservation. Cattle ranching and jobs in Albuquerque provide work

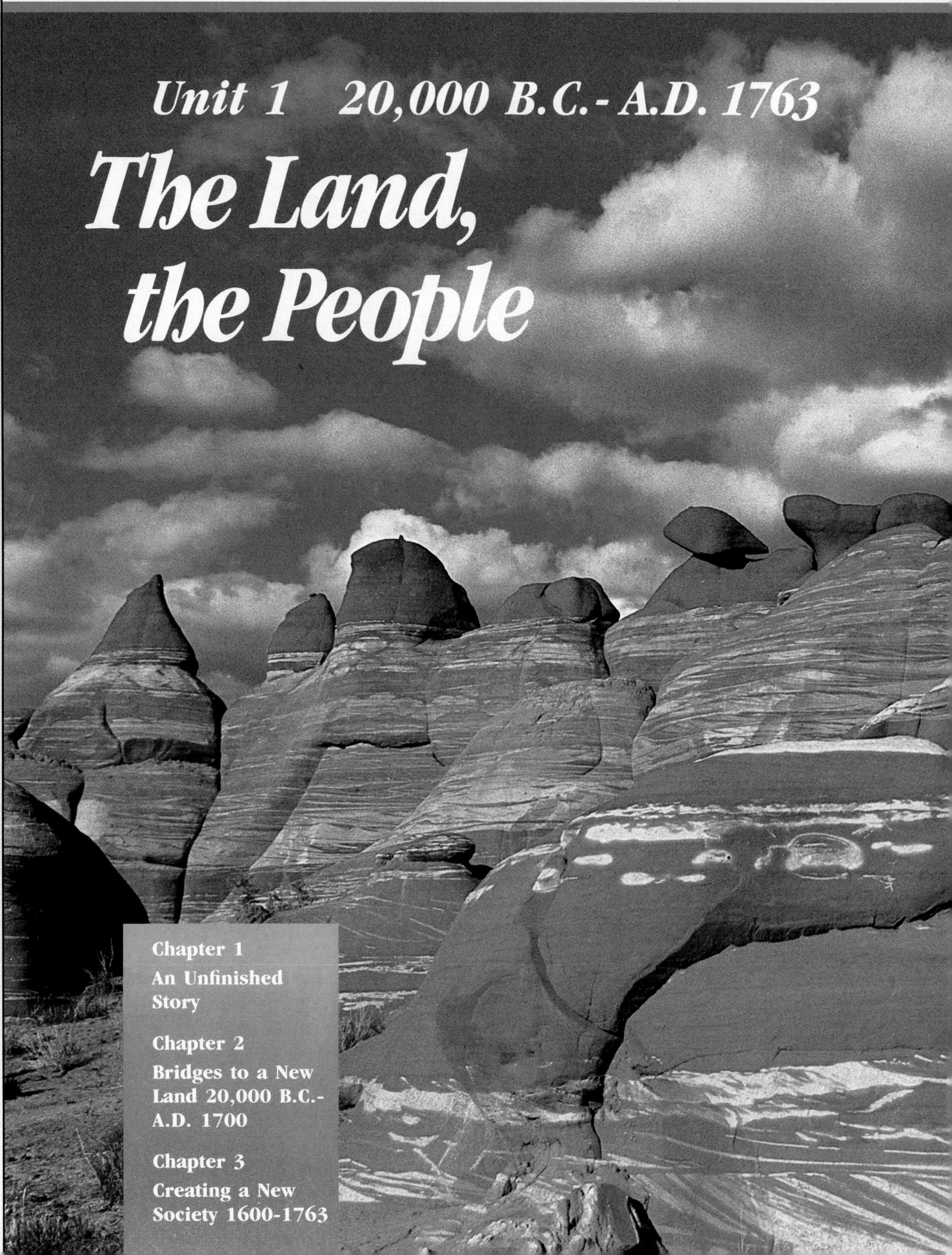

Unit 1 20,000 B.C.-A.D. 1763

The Land, the People

for most families.

Laguna Pueblo, located approximately 45 miles west of Albuquerque, dates from 1699. It is still inhabited by a mixed population of Tano, Keres, Shoshoni, and Zuni Indians.

Connections: Literature

For thousands of years, the Pueblo people have passed on their culture through the art of storytelling. Leslie Marmon Silko's published novels include *Ceremony* and *Storyteller*. Part Pueblo Indian herself, and raised on the Laguna Reservation, Silko comments, "Storytelling has always been a part of my life."

Guided Reading

Discussion. As students read this selection from *Ceremony*, have them look for evidence of a clash of cultures. Which characters cling to their traditional Native-American heritage? Which characters question their heritage, and why?

GTV Side 1

Chap. 1, Frame 01025

The Lay of the Land (Movie)

Search:

Play:

History Through Literature

Leslie Silko, who lives on the Laguna Pueblo Reservation in New Mexico, describes herself as of mixed ancestry—Laguna Pueblo, Mexican, and European. Silko's novels and poetry reflect her rich heritage. In the novel *Ceremony* (1977), Tayo, a Native American, searches for his identity and the meaning of tradition in a culture undergoing transition. In the process, he is reconnected to his land and his Indian heritage.

from

Ceremony

by Leslie Marmon Silko

"I'm thinking about those cattle, Tayo. See, things work out funny sometimes. Cattle prices are way down now because of the dry spell. Everybody is afraid to buy. But see, this gives us the chance. Otherwise, we probably never would get into the cattle business."

The sun was shining in the back window of the truck, and Tayo had the window rolled down and his arm hanging out, feeling the air rush past. He felt proud when Josiah talked about cattle business. He was ready to work hard with his uncle. They had already discussed it. He was graduating in a month, and then he would work with Josiah and Robert. They would breed these cattle, special cattle, not the weak, soft Herefords that grew thin and died from eating thistle and burned-off cactus during the drought. The cattle Ulibarri sold them were exactly what they had been thinking about. These cattle were descendants of generations of desert cattle, born in dry sand and scrubby mesquite, where they hunted water the way desert antelope did.

"Cattle are like any living thing. If you separate them from the land for too long, keep them in barns and corrals, they lose something. Their stomachs get to where they can only eat rolled oats and dry alfalfa. When you turn them loose again, they go running all over. They are scared because the land is unfamiliar, and they are lost. They don't stop being scared either, even when they look quiet and they quit running. Scared animals die off easily." They were driving down the gravel road, going east from Magdalena to catch the highway near Socorro. Tayo was used to him talking like that, going over his ideas and plans out loud, and then asking Tayo what he thought.

"See, I'm not going to make the mistake other guys made, buying those Hereford, white-face cattle. If it's going to be a drought these next few years, then we need some special breed of cattle." He had a stack of books on the floor beside his bed, with his reading glasses sitting on top. Every night, for a few minutes after he got in bed, he'd read about cattle breeding in the books the extension agent had loaned to him. Scientific cattle breeding was very

Connections: Art

The Hopi are one of the largest Native-American groups in North America. They are skilled artisans, especially famous for their beautiful baskets and pottery.

Hopi baskets are woven of wild grasses, and reflect the sun-drenched landscape of the Southwest. Baskets serve as cradles, food carriers, and religious offerings.

Most Hopi pottery is made by the coil method, in which slender ropes of clay are laid on top of one another in spiral fashion. The surface is then scraped smooth and dried. The zigzags on the Pueblo wedding jar below might represent lightning, forerunner of rain to ease the drought that may have driven early Pueblo farmers from their homes.

complicated, he said, and he used to wait until Rocky and Tayo were doing their homework on the kitchen table, and then he would come in from the back room, with his glasses on, carrying a book.

"Read this," he would tell Rocky, "and see if you think it's saying the same thing I think it says." When Rocky finished it, Josiah pushed the book in front of Tayo and pointed at the passage. Then he'd say, "Well?" And the boys would tell him what they got out of it. "That's what I thought too," Josiah would say, "but it seemed like such a stupid idea I wasn't sure if I was understanding it right." The problem was the books were written by white people who did not think about drought or winter blizzards or dry thistles, which the cattle had to live with. When Tayo saw Ulibarri's cattle, he thought of the diagram of the ideal beef cow which had been in the back of one of the books, and these cattle were everything that the ideal cow was not. They were tall and had long thin legs like deer; their heads were long and angular, with heavy bone across the eyes supporting wide sharp horns which curved out over the shoulders. Their eyes were big and wild.

"I guess we will have to get along without these books," he said. "We'll have to do things our own way. Maybe we'll even write our own book, *Cattle Raising on Indian Land,* or how to raise cattle that don't eat grass or drink water."

Tayo and Robert laughed with him, but Rocky was quiet. He looked up from his books.

"Those books are written by scientists. They know everything there is to know about beef cattle. That's the trouble with the way people around here have always done things—they never knew what they were doing." He went back to reading his book. He did not hesitate to speak like that, to his father and his uncle, because the subject was books and scientific knowledge—those things that Rocky had learned to believe in.

Tayo was suddenly sad because what Rocky said was true. What did they know about raising cattle? They weren't scientists. Auntie had been listening but she did not seem to notice Rocky's disrespect. She valued Rocky's growing understanding of the outside world, of the books, of everything of importance and power. He was becoming what she had always wanted: someone who could not only make sense of the outside world but become part of it. She did not like the cattle business and she was pleased to have a scientific reason for the way she felt. This cattle deal was bound to be no good, because Ulibarri was a cousin to that woman. She was almost certain it was that woman who had been talking to Josiah, telling him things which were not true, things which did not agree with the scientific books that the BIA [Bureau of Indian Affairs] extension man had loaned them. But it was his

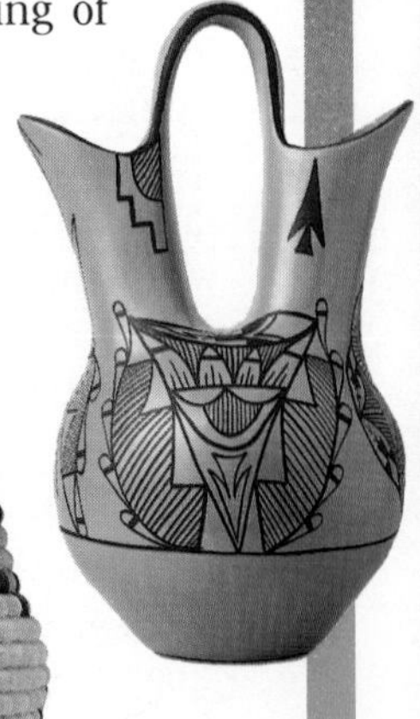

Background photo: the Painted Desert of northern Arizona. Pueblo wedding jar and Hopi basket (right); Hopi kachina (above).

Connections: Religion

The Hopi hold religious ceremonies in which the men mask themselves as kachinas—supernatural beings, spirits of their ancestors. At festival times, the spirits borrow men's bodies and come down from their sacred mountain-top homes and enter the villages to bring rain, health, and bountiful harvests. There are about 335 different kachinas, each with its own distinct personality and mask.

The Hopi carve wooden figures called kachina "dolls," which represent these spirits. Such painted "dolls" are often given to children, not to play with, but to help them learn to recognize the real kachinas at performances.

money, and if that's what he wanted to do with twenty years of money he saved up, then let him make a fool of himself.

"I think it was some kind of trick," she told Rocky and Tayo one evening, when old Grandma was snoring in her chair. Auntie glanced over at her to be sure she was asleep before she said it. "That dirty Mexican woman did it so Ulibarri could get rid of those worthless cattle. They gypped him. They made an old fool out of him."

Rocky did not hear her; he was reading a sports magazine. But Tayo had heard; he always listened to her, and now his stomach felt tense; he was afraid maybe she was right, because he already knew she was right about some things.

"One thing after another all the time." She looked at Tayo, and he turned away and stared at old Grandma. Her mouth hung open a little when she slept, and occasionally he could hear a snoring sound.

"Well," she said with a big sigh, "it will give them something else to laugh about."

Rocky didn't say anything; but when he turned the page he looked up at her as though he were tired of the sound of her voice. Tayo knew that what village people thought didn't matter to Rocky any more. He was already planning where he would go after high school; he was already talking about the places he would live, and the reservation wasn't one of them.

Auntie got out her black church shoes and wiped them carefully with a clean damp cloth; she examined them closely by the lamp on the table to make sure that any dust or spots of dirt left from last Sunday had been removed. She had gone to church alone, for as long as Tayo could remember; although she told him that she prayed they would be baptized, she never asked any of them, not even Rocky, to go with her. Later on, Tayo wondered if she could show the people that she was a devout Christian and not immoral or pagan like the rest of the family. When it came to saving her own soul, she wanted to be careful that there were no mistakes.

Old Grandma woke up. She asked Auntie what she was doing. She asked Tayo and then Rocky. Auntie had to speak to Rocky because he didn't hear old Grandma the first time when she asked him what he was doing. Then old Grandma straightened up in her chair.

"Church," she said, wiping her eyes with a Kleenex from her apron pocket. "Ah Thelma, do you have to go there again?"

Taking a Closer Look

1. *Compare Josiah's views on raising cattle to Rocky's. How do they show a clash of cultures?*

2. *What do Tayo and Rocky want to do after they graduate from high school?*

3. *In what ways does this passage illustrate Tayo's search for identity? How is his search reflected in his relationship to Josiah? to Rocky? to Auntie?*

Taking a Closer Look

ANSWERS

1. Josiah believed a special breed of cattle was needed for the drought-stricken Southwest. He thought that books on how to raise cattle did not deal with the reality of droughts, blizzards, and other problems encountered in the desert. Rocky, on the other hand, agreed with what the scientific books had to say about raising cattle. Rocky believed in what the outside world had to offer. He felt the old ways of doing things were wrong. Josiah saw value in his Indian heritage.

2. Tayo wants to stay on the reservation and work with Josiah and Robert. Rocky wants to leave the reservation and live elsewhere.

3. Tayo feels happy about his Native-American heritage as he plans his future working with his uncle and Robert. He has doubts, however, when he realizes that Rocky and his aunt may be right in their way of thinking.

Chapter 1

An Unfinished Story

Planning Guide

	Student Text	TWE Lesson Plans	Support Materials
SECTION 1	**Section 1–1** (1 Day) **Theme: Balancing Unity and Diversity,** pp 6–8 Review/Evaluation Section Review, p 8	**Introducing the Chapter:** Close to Home—Group Activity, one class period, p 3B	★ **Read to Remember,** Section 1 ● **Section Activities,** Section 1 Δ **Enrichment Activities,** Section 1 Δ **Readings** ● **Tests and Quizzes,** Section 1 Quiz
SECTION 2	**Section 1–2** (1–2 Days) **Theme: Shaping Democracy,** pp 9–11 Review/Evaluation Section Review, p 11	**Teaching the Main Ideas:** A Poll of Citizen Views—Cooperative Activity, 30 minutes introduction, homework, and one class period, p 3B	★ **Read to Remember,** Section 2 ● **Section Activities,** Section 2 Δ **Enrichment Activities,** Section 2 Δ **Readings** ● **Tests and Quizzes,** Section 2 Quiz
SECTION 3	**Section 1–3** (1–3 Days) **Theme: The Search for Opportunity,** pp 12–15 Point of View: The Official English Debate, pp 16–17 Review/Evaluation Section Review, p 15 Chapter 1 Survey, pp 18–19 Skills, pp 18–19 Thinking Critically Applying Social Studies Skills: Analyzing Line Graphs Writing About Issues	**Teaching the Main Ideas:** Clippings on Continuing Challenges—Cooperative Activity, homework, 30 minutes, p 3C **Reinforcement Activity:** If Elected I Will . . . —Cooperative Activity, one class period, p 3C **Evaluating Progress:** Stamp It—Individual Activity, one class period, p 3C **Enrichment Activity:** Understanding Diversity Through Poetry—Individual Activity, homework, 30 minutes, p 3C	★ **Read to Remember,** Section 3 ● **Section Activities,** Section 3 ● **Geography Activities,** Section 3 Δ **Readings** ● **Tests and Quizzes,** Section 3 Quiz, Chapter 1 Test (Forms A and B) **Additional Resources** Δ **Twentieth Century Issues: Links to the Past** ● **Active Learning** Δ **Transparencies and Activity Book** ● **Testing Software** ★ **Chapter Summaries** **Key:** ★ For Extra Support ● For All Students Δ For Enrichment

Overview

Woven throughout the text of *The United States and Its People* are three themes. The first theme focuses on the challenge of balancing unity and diversity in forging a single nation from many cultures and races. The second theme examines our nation's continuing effort to shape a democratic government based on the will of the people and guided by the ideals of liberty, equality, and justice. The third theme deals with the challenge of fulfilling the promise of economic opportunity for all Americans. Students are alerted to the recurrence of these themes throughout our nation's history and to the continuing challenge they pose for Americans today.

Activity Objectives

After completing the activities, students should be able to

- recognize different viewpoints on the balance between contributing to the common good and protecting individual freedoms.
- identify recent examples of the challenge of balancing unity and diversity, shaping democracy, and searching for opportunity.
- create a visual image representing at least one of the three themes.
- propose steps that might be taken toward meeting the challenges represented by the three themes.
- express in poetic form feelings about American diversity.

Introducing the Chapter

Close to Home

This group activity requires one class period.

This activity is designed to introduce students to the themes in a way that allows them to discover for themselves how basic and "close to home" the themes are.

Begin the activity by dividing the class into groups of three or four. Assign each group a theme so that each theme is represented by about the same number of groups. Use the following phrases, or something similar, to suggest the themes: "American Diversity," "American Democracy," and "The American Dream." Have one member of each group write its phrase in the center of a large piece of poster paper. Direct group members to "free associate," adding words that the phrase brings to mind so that a "cluster" of related words and phrases radiates out from the center, connected by lines.

As the cluster expands, students can build upon new words and phrases to create sub-clusters. For instance, the phrase "American Diversity" might prompt a student to draw a short line out from the center and write the word "Hispanics." Others might then draw lines radiating out from "Hispanics" and add phrases like "Mexican Americans" and "Cuban Americans" to create a sub-cluster. Group members can continue adding to sub-clusters as well as creating new ones. The activity should be as spontaneous as possible.

Although the activity primarily illustrates the themes through clusters of words, a variation could allow students to add symbols or other images. For instance, the word *diversity* might prompt an illustration of a rainbow or drawings of various ethnic foods and clothing.

Allow the groups approximately 20 minutes to create their clusters of words and images. Then write the three central phrases on the chalkboard, leaving a large space under each. For each phrase, ask members of appropriate groups to give examples of words, phrases, and images that it suggested to them. List these on the board. To provide closure, above each central phrase write the theme it suggests. Then ask students what issues they anticipate encountering as they explore each of these themes.

Teaching the Main Ideas

Section 1-2: A Poll of Citizen Views

This cooperative activity requires 30 minutes for introduction and preparation, out-of-class time to gather data, and a full class period to compile and discuss the data.

In this activity students conduct an opinion poll of local citizens on the balance between protecting individual freedoms and contributing to the common good. The activity heightens students' awareness of diverse views regarding the nature of democracy. Before class prepare and duplicate a questionnaire with the following "yes or no" questions. To the right of the questions make three columns labeled *Teen*, *20s–30s*, and *40+*.

- Are you willing to give up your right to free speech during a time of war?
- Are you willing to ride mass transit to help reduce pollution?
- Are you willing to pay higher garbage-collection fees to support an expanded city recycling program?
- Are you willing to pay more taxes to provide health insurance for people who cannot afford it?

On the chalkboard write the following:

- common good = the well-being of society as a whole
- individual freedoms = the freedoms of individual members of society to do as they wish without unnecessary interference from the government

Ask students to describe laws or governmental actions designed to promote the common good. (Some examples are regulations prohibiting smoking in public places, the use of roadblocks to catch criminals, and affirmative action laws.) Discuss what limits are placed on individual freedoms by such laws and actions. Explain that Americans of all ages hold conflicting views on what is the common good and on how far individual rights extend.

Tell students that, to assess various opinions on these issues, they will conduct a poll of local residents. Distribute the questionnaires and read each question, asking how it relates to balancing individual freedoms and the common good. You may wish to have the class add more questions. If there are too many suggestions, have them vote on which three or four to add.

After finalizing the questionnaire, assign each student the task of interviewing three people who represent three different age groups: teenagers, people in their 20s or 30s, and people over 40. If you are concerned about students fabricating responses, you might require them to identify respondents by name, age, and address. Set a date for completing the interviews.
On the day the assignment is due, draw a grid on the chalkboard with "yes" and "no" columns for each question by age group. Column spaces should be large enough to include tally marks reflecting all responses to the questions. When all the data has been posted, discuss the responses. Conclude by asking students to generalize from the data. Do respondents seem to place more value on promoting the common good or on protecting individual rights? Do attitudes seem to differ by age group? If so, how might students explain the differences?

Teaching the Main Ideas

Section 1-3: Clippings on Continuing Challenges

This cooperative activity is assigned as homework, requiring 15 minutes to introduce and 30 minutes to discuss the data.

This activity involves collecting newspaper and magazine articles that provide present-day examples of the three themes introduced in the chapter. It will be most effective if students work on it throughout their study of the chapter, completing it after reading Section 1-3.

Write the three themes on the chalkboard and call on students to describe their importance today. Assign students to find six recent newspaper or magazine articles, two exemplifying each theme. They are to cut out or copy the articles and bring them to class by a designated date. On the due date, have them post their articles by theme on a bulletin board or on large pieces of poster paper.

Discuss the articles by having students tell how the events they describe relate to the themes. Challenge students to continue to add to their article display in the coming months.

Reinforcement Activity

Section 1-3: If Elected I Will . . .

This cooperative activity requires one class period, or it can be assigned as homework.

This activity requires students to develop a platform statement for a fictitious political candidate. The platform is to spell out the candidate's proposals for meeting the challenge of the three themes introduced in Chapter 1.

Ask students to review the chapter by sections and write down specific current issues that are discussed in relation to the themes. After their review, have them choose partners with whom to work on the platform. Each pair should specify the office for which their candidate will run and create a profile of him or her. Then they are to write for their candidate a platform that describes specific proposals for dealing with current issues related to the three themes.

Have the pairs present their platforms to the class. Discuss the different proposals that the platforms outline for meeting the challenges of diversity, democracy, and opportunity.

Evaluating Progress

Section 1-3: Stamp It

This individual activity requires most of a class period, or it can be assigned as homework.

This activity challenges students to design a postage stamp that illustrates one or all of the chapter's three themes. To stimulate creativity, you may wish to bring a variety of postage stamps for examination.

Begin by asking students to describe their favorite postage stamps. Emphasize that the Postal Service creates different stamps to commemorate special events, honor outstanding Americans, and promote certain themes. Allow students time to look at the stamps you brought to class. Point out the use of colors, symbols, illustrations, and words. Stress the need for a concise image to represent an idea.

Explain that the assignment is to design a postage stamp to reflect one or all three themes introduced in the chapter. Direct students to design their stamps in an oversize format but to use the rectangular shape of stamps.

Ask students to present their completed stamps to their classmates. Have the class select the stamps that best illustrate the chapter themes, show the most creativity, and make the most lasting impression. Discuss why certain stamps were considered most effective in representing the themes.

Enrichment Activity

Section 1-1: Understanding Diversity Through Poetry

This individual activity is best assigned as an out-of-class project.

This activity has students reflect on the role of diversity in the United States by writing a cinquain (sin-KAYN) poem. Begin the activity by writing on the chalkboard the following question: *What does it mean to be an American?* Review information in Section 1-1 that relates to the question. Explain to students that the concept of diversity creates both intellectual and emotional responses in most people. To express their feelings about diversity, students are to write a cinquain poem addressing the broad theme of diversity. Specific topics they might consider include conflict, cultural exchange, unity, discrimination, and the history of American diversity.

For students unfamiliar with the format of cinquain poetry, explain that it is a five-line poem with a structure based on a syllable count.

Line	Syllables	Content
1	two	topic
2	four	describes topic
3	six	expresses action
4	eight	expresses feeling
5	two	refers to the topic

The following is an example of a cinquain relating to discrimination:

Unjust
Nothing for me
Confront, marching, protest
Anger explodes, restlessness boils
Unfair

Post students' completed poems and allow time for them to read their classmates' work. Discuss the different dimensions of diversity expressed in the poems. Conclude by emphasizing that acknowledging diversity can help foster unity.

Bibliography and Audiovisual Material

Teacher Bibliography

Dinnerstein, Leonard, Roger L. Nichols, and David M. Reimers. *Natives and Strangers: Ethnic Groups and the Building of America.* New York: Oxford University Press, 1990.

Friedel, Frank, ed. *Harvard Guide to American History.* Cambridge: Harvard University Press, 1974.

Handlin, Oscar. *The Americans: A New History of the People of the United States.* New York: Atlantic Monthly Press, 1963.

Makers of America. 10 vols. Chicago: Encyclopaedia Britannica, 1971.

Morison, Samuel Eliot. *The Oxford History of the American People.* New York: Oxford University Press, 1965.

Terkel, Studs. *The Great Divide: Second Thoughts on the American Dream.* New York: Pantheon Books, 1988.

Student Bibliography

Acuna, Robert. *Occupied America: A History of Chicanos.* New York: HarperCollins, 1987.

Freedman, Rusell. *Immigrant Kids.* New York: Dutton, 1980.

Filmstrips

Accent on Ethnic America. Multi-Media Productions.

How Nations are Governed. Filmstrip House/United Learning.

Refugees, Immigrants, Illegal Aliens: Impact on America. SVE.

Films, Videocassettes, and Videodiscs

Bilingual Americans. 55 min. Karol Video. Videocassette.

The Girl Who Spelled Freedom. 90 min. Disney.

Journey to Freedom: The Immigrant Experience. 13 min. AIMS Media. Videodisc.

Computer Software

The American People. Apple, Commodore. Focus Media.

Democracy. Apple, Commodore. Right on Programs.

Chapter 1

Objectives

- Explain how the United States has remained united amid increasing diversity.
- Discuss the issues faced by Americans in shaping a democratic government.
- Discuss whether the promise of economic opportunity is a reality for all Americans.

Introducing THE CHAPTER

For suggestions on introducing Chapter 1, refer to pages 3B in the Teacher's Edition.

Developing THE CHAPTER

For activities and teaching strategies to help you reinforce and enrich chapter content, see pages 3B–3D in the Teacher's Edition.

Chapter Opener Illustrations

Americans live in many different kinds of places. The poster below might have attracted immigrants to California where they would find opportunities to own their own farms or businesses. Note the virtues extolled: land for millions, ideal weather, and so on.

Political parties play a key role in government and provide opportunities for citizens to take part in the political process. The most important role is selecting candidates for public office. Parties hold national conventions, complete with people waving signs and banners and wearing hats and buttons, to select presidential nominees.

Members of the American Indian Movement (AIM) are active in protests to secure the rights and benefits that they believe they deserve. AIM members participated in the Trail of Broken Treaties, a 1972 march on Washington, D.C., to

Reduced student page in the Teacher's Edition

Chapter 1

An Unfinished Story

4

demand the rights and property guaranteed Indians by treaties.

Americans belong to many religious groups. In fact, more than a thousand different religious groups can be found in the United States today. The youth group members pictured here are cooking food for a fund raiser in Austin, Texas.

Suffragists display banners at Washington Mews in Greenwich Village, New York in 1912. In 1919 the Nineteenth Amendment was proposed; it states that no American citizen can be denied voting rights "on account of sex." The amendment was ratified in 1920.

César Chávez is committed to a "totally nonviolent struggle for justice." Since 1965 he has led strikes to gain higher wages and better working conditions for farm workers.

American Voices

Tens of thousands of years ago, a small band of Ice Age hunters gazed upon a new land. These wanderers from Asia may have been the first people to discover America. But they would not be the last. As Thomas Wolfe wrote in his novel *You Can't Go Home Again,* each of us discovers America anew in our own time.

"I think the true discovery of America is before us. I think the true fulfillment of our spirit, of our people, of our mighty and immortal land, is yet to come. I think the true discovery of our own democracy is still before us. . . . I say that our America is Here and Now, and beckons on before us, and that this glorious assurance is not only our living hope, but our dream to be accomplished."

As you make your journey through America's past, you will find that each generation of Americans has faced challenges that have become ongoing themes in the nation's history. Three major themes are:

- The challenge of balancing unity and diversity in a nation of many races, religions, and cultures
- The shaping of democracy into a working system of government
- The search for opportunity for all Americans

The history of the United States is largely the story of how each generation has tried to meet these challenges. That history is far from finished: your generation will be writing the next chapter.

Poster celebrating California's fertile farm land; political convention; Native-American protest near White House; church-group fundraiser in Texas; suffragist march, 1912; United Farm Workers leader César Chávez.

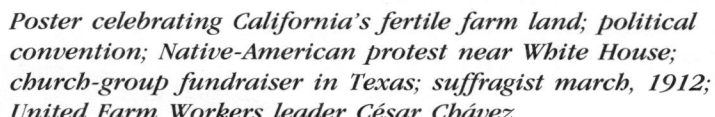

Analyzing Primary Sources

American Voices

Thomas Wolfe (1900–1938) was noted for his autobiographical novels. His first, *Look Homeward Angel,* was published in 1929. *You Can't Go Home Again* was published in 1940, after his death.

Refer students to the selection from *You Can't Go Home Again.* **Ask:** Do you agree with Wolfe's assessment of America? Why or why not? Do you think Wolfe would agree with the title of Chapter 1? Why or why not? **(Wolfe believes the fulfillment of Americans' ideals lies in the future.)**

Section 1-1

Objectives

- ***Answer the Focus Question.***
- *Compare diversity in colonial America with diversity in the United States today.*
- *Contrast the differing views of what unites Americans as a nation.*

Introducing THE SECTION

Begin by asking students to define the word *diversity* and give examples. Then read to students the following statement by writer Ralph Ellison: *"The diversity of American life is often painful, frequently burdensome, and always a source of conflict, but in it lies our faith and our hope."*

Have students discuss the proposition: Our nation's diversity is one of its greatest assets. Ask them to identify arguments for and against the proposition. Ask students why the challenge of balancing unity and diversity is not always easy.

Reduced student page in the Teacher's Edition

1-1 *Theme: Balancing Unity and Diversity*

Focus: How can this nation remain united amid increasing diversity?

From time beyond memory, the land that is now the United States has attracted a great diversity, or variety, of peoples. As the writer Herman Melville noted over a century ago, "America has been settled by people of all nations. All nations may claim her for their own. . . . We are not a nation so much as a world."

Representing many cultures and races, Americans have faced the challenge of forging a single nation. Each generation has wrestled with such questions as:

- How does diversity strengthen or weaken the nation?
- How much unity can this nation achieve without crushing diversity?
- How diverse can this nation be and remain united?

The Origins of American Diversity

Typically, a nation is a group of people who share not only a homeland but also a common culture and language. The land we call America, however, was never home to people of just one culture or language. The Native Americans who settled its forests, grasslands, and deserts thousands of years ago lived in hundreds of separate cultural groups, each with its own language, beliefs, and way of life.

Since the European discovery of a "new world" in the Americas 500 years ago, millions of Europeans, Africans, Asians, and Latin Americans have come to America. Historian John Hope Franklin, an African American, writes of this movement:

> *"From virtually every corner of the globe they came—some enthusiastically and some quite reluctantly. Britain and every part of Europe provided prospective Americans by the millions. Africa and Asia gave up great throngs. Other areas of the New World saw inhabitants desert their own lands to seek their fortunes in the colossus to the North."*

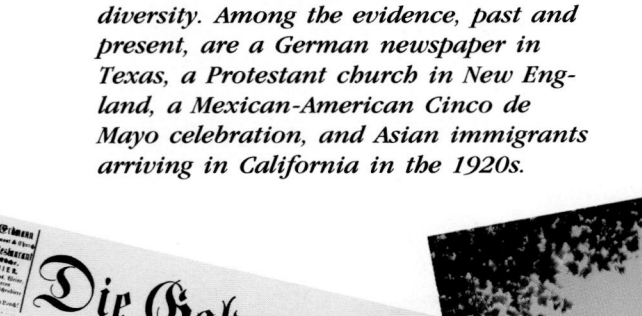

Languages, religions, cultures, and races have all contributed to the nation's rich diversity. Among the evidence, past and present, are a German newspaper in Texas, a Protestant church in New England, a Mexican-American Cinco de Mayo celebration, and Asian immigrants arriving in California in the 1920s.

Connections: Literature

Ralph Ellison was born in Oklahoma in 1914 and moved to New York City in the late 1930s. He is best known for his classic novel, *Invisible Man*, about the black experience in America. Ellison has received many awards for his literary achievements, including the Medal of Freedom in 1969 and the national Medal of Arts in the 1980s.

This gathering of peoples has made the United States unique among nations. As Franklin says, "No other country in the world can point to such a variety of cultural, racial, religious, and national backgrounds in its population."

Diversity in Colonial America

The theme of balancing unity and diversity appears early in American history. The colonies founded along the Atlantic shore of North America attracted settlers who came from many countries in Europe, spoke different languages, and belonged to many religious groups. Two other groups added to colonial diversity: Native Americans who had lived for centuries in the eastern forests, and Africans kidnapped from West Africa and brought to the colonies in chains.

Because they differed so much from Europeans in appearance and culture, neither the Native Americans nor the Africans were accepted into colonial society. Furthermore, many Europeans did not even think of them as human, much less as equals. Native Americans were driven out of the colonies in a series of brutal wars, and most Africans were treated as property and forced to labor for white colonists as slaves.

The first generation of English colonists dealt with diversity in different ways. Some, such as the Puritan leaders of Massachusetts Bay Colony, crushed it. During the 1600s Quakers and others who disagreed with Puritan religious beliefs were fined, flogged, and expelled from the colony. Some were even hanged. Roger Williams, founder of the nearby Rhode Island Colony, took a very different view of religious diversity. Williams, who had been expelled from Massachusetts, welcomed settlers of all faiths. Quakers, Baptists, Catholics, Jews, and others flocked to Rhode Island. An amazed visitor wrote that never had there been "such a variety of religions on so small a spot of ground." Rhode Island was an early sign that a diverse society might thrive in America.

American Voices

"The diversity of American life is often painful, frequently burdensome, and always a source of conflict, but in it lies our faith and our hope."

—Ralph Ellison

How Much Unity?—How Much Diversity?

Since the founding of the United States, the diversity of its people has prompted disagreements over what unites the nation. A basic question has been repeatedly asked: What does it mean to be an American?

Throughout the nation's history, many Americans have been intolerant of diversity. They have readily accepted immigrants similar to themselves but eyed with suspicion and fear those who were "different." This fear was particularly noticeable in the mid 1800s, when more than 2 million Irish Catholics entered the United States. A mayor of Boston during the 1830s thought that the Irish were so different that they would remain forever "distinct and hostile" to American ways. Similar attitudes toward newcomers have continued to the

Developing THE SECTION

Multicultural Perspectives

Discussion. From our perspective, the Europeans who first settled in America do not seem particularly diverse—most were fair-skinned Protestants with similar values. From the colonists' point of view, however, the variety of nations, languages, and religious denominations made for a highly diverse population.

Ask: How does a person's community shape his or her view of what constitutes a diverse society? **(Degree of diversity is relative to one's experiences.)** What is your understanding of a diverse community? Has this changed over time?

Thinking Critically

Evaluation. Have students identify arguments for and against the proposition: The United States' doors should be open to all who want to enter. Group students into teams to debate the issue.

Active Learning

Role Play. Have students work in pairs, one playing the role of an American citizen, the other a recent immigrant. Have the "citizen" explain an expression or custom that the "immigrant" knows nothing about. Examples include the expression "letting the cat out of the bag," a baseball game, the custom of trick-or-treating. Have each pair share their experiences and reactions with the class.

Limited English Proficiency

Activity. Have students form small groups in which each member finds a newspaper article about a culture different from his or her own. Each student should read the article carefully and ask questions of the teacher, librarian, or parents until he or she understands it.

Then have students explain their articles to members of their group so that they understand it, too. They can discuss how the issues in the articles may affect their lives.

Section Review

ANSWERS

1. From colonial beginnings, America has been populated by diverse groups: first, Native American tribes, followed by Europeans with different cultures and religions, enslaved Africans, and later Asians and Latin Americans.
2. Predominant Anglo-Saxon culture, heritage; belief in individual liberty and justice.

Multicultural Perspectives

Anthropologist Margaret Mead communicated to Westerners the wisdom of the distant cultures in Samoa, New Guinea, and Bali. Her research led her to believe that Americans should embrace rather than fear diversity. She stated:

"If we are to achieve a richer culture, rich in contrasting values, we must recognize the whole gamut of human potentialities, and so weave a less arbitrary social fabric . . . one in which each diverse human gift finds a fitting place."

Reduced student page in the Teacher's Edition

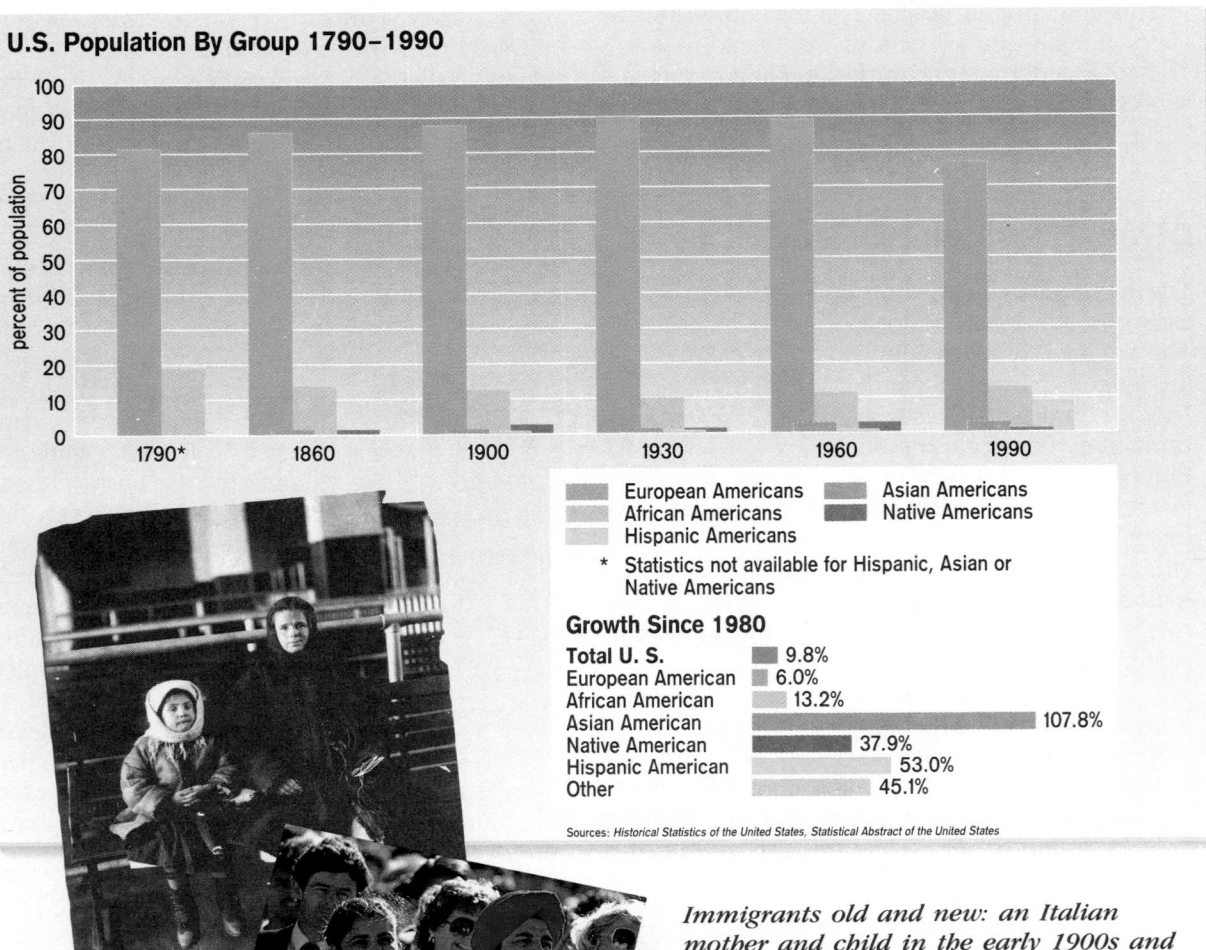

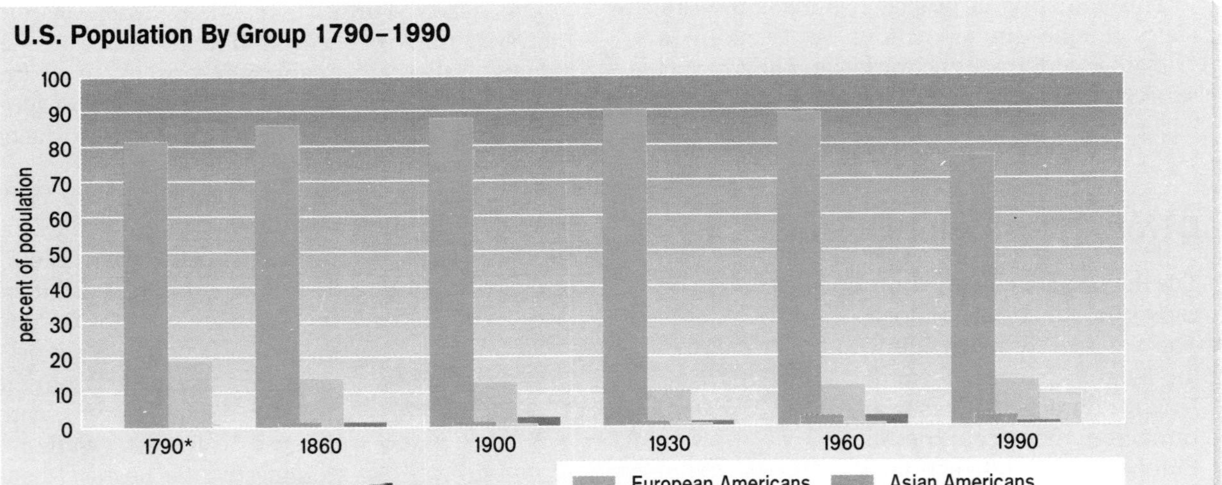

Immigrants old and new: an Italian mother and child in the early 1900s and two new citizens from India.

present day, often spurring calls for stricter immigration limits.

On the other hand, many Americans have argued that cultural diversity is not a problem. In the United States, they believe, people of all cultures are united by a common commitment to American ideals of individual liberty and equal justice. In this view, the country has room for people of all races, religions, and cultures and, in fact, is enriched by the energy, skills, foods, music, arts, religions, and ideas of people from all parts of the world.

Recent immigrants from Asia, Latin America, and the Middle East are making the United States more diverse than ever. In California, for example, students of European descent make up less than half of the public school enrollment, and one of every four students does not speak English at home. This great variety of newcomers brings the nation face to face again with the challenge of creating unity amid increasing diversity.

Section Review

1. Analysis. Why can it be said that the United States has always been diverse?

2. Analysis. Contrast the differing views of what unites Americans as a nation.

Multicultural Perspectives

In 1937 William Hastie became the first African-American federal judge in the United States. He served in the federal District Court in the Virgin Islands and later in a Circuit Court of Appeals. From 1940 to 1942 Hastie was the civilian aide to the Secretary of War. He resigned in anger, though, after the military showed little interest in changing its policy of racial segregation. Hastie was also the first black governor of the Virgin Islands.

Section 1-2

Objectives

- ***Answer the Focus Question.***
- *Explain why the history of American democracy is an unfinished story.*
- *Give examples of the tension between individual liberty and the common good.*

Introducing THE SECTION

Use the following quotation by a Swedish immigrant in the 1850s as the basis for a discussion of equality in the United States:

> *"This is a free country and nobody has a great deal of authority over another. . . . There is no pride and nobody needs to hold his hat in his hand for anyone else. This is not Sweden, where the higher classes and employers have the law on their side so that they can treat subordinates as though they were not human beings."*

Ask: What does the quotation reveal about the immigrant's probable experience in Sweden? **(probably required to defer to wealthier and more powerful people)** Is the immigrant's view of the United States as a nation of political and social equality accurate? **(Native Americans, African Americans, Asians, women were not treated equally in the 1850s.)** For what group of immigrants was this statement true? **(white upper class males)**

1-2 Theme: Shaping Democracy

Focus: How can a democratic government be shaped to meet the ideals on which this nation was founded?

The United States is unique among nations, not only for its diversity but also as the world's oldest democracy. For more than two centuries, Americans have worked to shape a government based on the will of the people and guided by the ideals of liberty, equality, and justice. They have learned that democracy is not something fixed or permanent. Judge William H. Hastie once wrote:

> *"Democracy is a process, not a static condition. It is becoming, rather than being. It can easily be lost, but never be fully won. Its essence is eternal struggle."*

As each generation of Americans has faced changing conditions, it has taken up the challenge of shaping democracy. In the process, each generation has struggled with questions such as:

- What is the meaning of equality?
- What is the common good, and how should it be balanced against the rights of individuals?
- Who should have the right to vote and run for office?
- How should power be divided between the national and state governments?

Widening "We the People"

In shaping a democracy, Americans have faced the issue of who should be allowed to participate in government. The first words in the Constitution are "We the People of the United States." Yet when the Constitution was adopted in 1788, only white adult males could vote in most of the states.

Like other groups, African Americans have struggled long for equal rights, as reflected in a 1912 march in New York City and a 1983 rally honoring the 1963 civil rights march in Washington, D.C.

Multicultural Perspectives

Through provisions like the Dawes Act, the blanket grants of citizenship to certain Native-American groups, and the provisions made for citizenship for Native-American veterans of World War I, perhaps two thirds of the Native-American population in the United States had achieved citizenship by the 1920s. The Snyder Act of 1924 granted citizenship to all Native Americans.

Developing

THE SECTION

Citizenship

Discussion. The most significant factor in predicting voter behavior is level of education: the higher the level of an individual's education, the more likely the person is to vote. The second most significant factor is age, with the voting rate highest among people in their mid-forties to mid-sixties.

Ask: Why do you think many people don't exercise their right to vote? **(no choices, one vote won't matter, inconvenient)** What suggestions can you make to turn nonvoters into voters? Interested students might research and report on voter participation in other countries.

Active Learning

Decision Making. Divide students into groups of four to determine how the powers of government should be divided between federal and state government for the following tasks: declaring war, determining the drinking age and driving age, passing draft laws, regulating immigration, deciding school curriculum.

A short statement should be prepared by each group giving reasons for its decisions. A spokesperson from each group can report to the class the group's decisions and rationale.

Reduced student page in the Teacher's Edition

Recent marchers for the Equal Rights Amendment follow in the footsteps of Susan B. Anthony and other leaders of the women's rights movements of the 1800s and early 1900s.

American history has been marked by a series of struggles to widen the meaning of "We the People" to include all ethnic groups and women. Not until after the Civil War did the Fifteenth Amendment declare that suffrage—the right to vote—could not be denied on account of race. Women did not gain voting rights nationwide until 1920. Carrie Chapman Catt, a leader of the woman suffrage movement, declared, "To get the word *male,* in effect, out of the Constitution cost the women of the country fifty-two years of pauseless campaign."

Today our democratic system faces a new challenge. The right to vote—for which so many struggled so long—is ignored by about half of today's adult Americans. Why do so many Americans choose not to vote? Can a democracy survive such widespread voter indifference?

Dividing the Power

For most of human history, the power to govern has been held by those strong, wise, or wealthy enough to command obedience. American government, though, is in theory based on consent of all the people. Turning theory into practice has involved facing not only the question of who votes but also how power is shared between state and national government.

Drawing lines between state and national power has always been difficult. It ignited debate at the Constitutional Convention in 1787, flared into the Civil War in 1861, and arises today over such issues as the death penalty and environmental protection. How far should the national government go in making policies for all Americans? Are state governments better able to meet the needs of their citizens? Shaping our democracy continues to involve seeking a balance between state and national power.

Toward Equality

"We hold these truths to be self-evident, that all men are created equal, that they are endowed by their Creator with certain unalienable Rights, that among these are Life, Liberty, and the pursuit of Happiness."

These eloquent words in the Declaration of Independence express the most basic American ideals. Throughout our nation's history, however, Americans have debated the meaning of equality. When Thomas Jefferson penned those words in 1776, equal rights were granted only to white males. Indeed, almost a century would go by before slavery was abolished in the United States.

The ending of slavery, of course, did not settle the issue of equal rights. The question of what is fair and equal treatment under the law has arisen again and again. After more than two centuries, Americans still face the challenge of further narrowing the gap between the ideal and reality.

Of course, moving toward the ideal of equal rights requires more than passing laws. It involves

Multicultural Perspectives

Martin Luther King, Jr., a Baptist minister, believed that nonviolent protest, such as sit-ins and boycotts, was the best way to gain equality. His philosophy was widely adopted in the civil rights movement of the 1950s and 1960s. Students will read more about King and the struggle for equality in Chapter 28.

Backyard History

Research and Report. Have students find out about situations in their school and community in which the exercise of individual rights was deemed a threat to the common good. Examples include: screening the school newspaper; city laws regulating curfew, skateboarding.

Students should report the situation, identify the individual right(s) involved, explain how the right was perceived as a threat to the common good, and tell whether they believe the situation was resolved fairly.

changing the attitudes and behavior of individual people, as well as correcting long-established patterns of institutional sexism and racism, such as company hiring practices that intentionally or unintentionally discriminate against women or members of particular ethnic groups.

"The laws are all in place to make true equality possible," notes one writer. "But racism and sexism still exist in the hearts and minds of too many people." The words of civil rights leader Reverend Dr. Martin Luther King, Jr., continue to echo today. "Now is the time," he declared, "to make real the promises of democracy."

Individual Rights vs. the Common Good

A community passes a law limiting how loudly car stereos can be played. Police set up roadblocks to check for drunk drivers on New Year's Eve. A county forbids smoking in public areas. In these cases, and thousands like them every year, the liberty of individuals to act as they choose is balanced against the common good—the needs of all the members of the community.

The word *freedom* is frequently associated with our country. However, under our Constitution the government must balance the rights of individuals against the rights of society. This continuing challenge raises questions: How far do the rights of individuals extend? What exactly is "the common good"? Debates over these issues have long been part of the price of living in our democracy.

Most Americans believe that our system of government can strike a fair balance between the rights of individuals and the needs of society. Expressing this confidence, historian Barbara Tuchman has said that if "it is still possible to reconcile democracy with social order and individual liberty . . . it will be here [in the United States]."

Section Review

1. Analysis. Why can the history of American democracy be described as an unfinished story?

2. Application. Give two examples of the tension between individual liberty and the common good.

In the name of "the common good," the rights of Japanese Americans were violated during World War II. Despite this sign displayed the day after Pearl Harbor, the store owner and his family were sent to an internment camp.

Thinking Critically

Analysis. Using the index at the back of the book, have students research and analyze how each of the following have helped expand equal rights to all Americans: Amendments 13, 14, 15, 19, 23, 24, 26; Civil Rights Act 1964; Voting Rights Act 1965; *Brown* v. *Board of Education.*

Section Review

ANSWERS

1. Each generation of Americans attempts to shape democracy to its vision of equality for all.
2. Examples may relate to equal rights, student rights, and the right to free speech.

Section 1-3

Objectives

- ***Answer the Focus Question.***
- *Discuss how discrimination has affected some people's search for opportunity.*
- *Explain the role of government in creating economic opportunity.*

Introducing THE SECTION

Remind students that every society has a system for producing and distributing goods and services to fulfill people's wants. Ask what this system is called—an economy. The American economy is considered a market—or free enterprise—system. Business owners are free to compete with each other to produce and distribute goods and services.

Have students name countries that have economic systems different from the United States. **(for example, a command economy, where the central government has charge of major resources and makes most economic decisions)** Then compare the rules of these economies with our economic freedoms and limitations.

Reduced student page in the Teacher's Edition

1-3 Theme: The Search for Opportunity

Focus: Can the promise of economic opportunity be made a reality for all Americans?

The first Spanish explorers who wandered through what is now the American Southwest in the early 1500s were spurred on by tales of cities of gold. In the 1600s English settlers along the Atlantic shore found a land of unbelievable abundance—with strawberries four times the size of those in Europe and cornstalks "as high as a man can reach, and higher." To the rest of the world, notes historian David M. Potter, America has always seemed to be a land of plenty:

> *"Explorers have marveled at wealth previously undiscovered. Travelers have contrasted the riches of America with the scarcity of the lands from which they came. Millions of inhabitants of the Old World have responded as immigrants to the lure of the land of plenty, the land of promise."*

For many Americans during the early 1800s, economic opportunity meant the chance to farm their own land.

B · A · C · K · G · R · O · U · N · D

Connections: Science and Technology
Although Native Americans used crude oil for fuel and medicine, few other people found value in oil until the 1840s, when Canadian geologist Abraham Gesner discovered kerosene, which could be distilled from coal or oil.

The steel plow was invented in 1837 by John Deere, a blacksmith in Illinois. He knew that local farmers were not satisfied with wood and iron plows because the heavy prairie sod stuck to the plow and clogged the furrows. The sod fell easily away from Deere's steel plow, making clear furrows.

The effort to make the United States a land of opportunity for every American is another main theme in our nation's history. In this effort, Americans have searched for answers to these questions:

- How can the nation's natural resources be used most effectively?
- How can opportunity be preserved as the economy changes?
- Why have some Americans been excluded from the dream of opportunity?
- What role should the government play in creating economic opportunity?

Limits in the Land of Plenty

Like the first colonists, later generations of Americans were amazed by the richness of the land. They discovered that, besides fertile soil, the United States was blessed with other natural resources such as timber, coal, iron, copper, gold, silver, petroleum, and uranium.

Resources, however, are valuable only when people know how to use them. Petroleum seeping out of the ground seemed a nuisance until someone discovered how to make a useful fuel out of it. As another example, the first westward-moving pioneers viewed the area as worthless grasslands, unlike Native Americans living on the Great Plains. Only after the invention of a steel plow that could cut through the thick prairie sod did farmers turn those vast plains into the nation's breadbasket. By searching out and using natural resources in new ways, Americans have created new opportunites—and an overall standard of living that has been among the highest in the world.

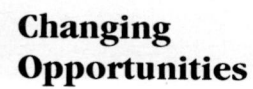

This World War I poster stresses the importance of American industry.

Throughout much of the nation's history, natural resources have seemed limitless. The country was so vast that people were sure they could always find more land to farm, more forests to log, or more minerals to strip from the soil. Only in the late twentieth century did it become clear that there are some limits to the nation's natural resources. Today Americans face the challenge of using familiar resources more wisely—and discovering new ones—in order to maintain a society of abundance for the benefit of all.

Changing Opportunities

"There is room for everybody in America," wrote Hector St. John de Crèvecoeur in the 1780s. No matter what a person's talents or interests were, Crèvecoeur believed, this country offered economic opportunity to anyone:

> *"Is he a laborer, sober and industrious? He need not go many miles . . . before he will be hired, well fed at the table of his employer, and paid four or five times more than he can get in Europe. Does he want uncultivated lands? Thousands of acres present themselves, which he may purchase cheap. . . . I do not mean that every-one who comes will grow rich in a little time. No, but . . . instead of starving, he will be fed. Instead of being idle, he will have employment. And these are riches enough for such men as come over here."*

Developing THE SECTION

Writing about History

Report. How can the nation's natural resources be used more effectively? Have students select a resource, perhaps one important in the local economy, and write a report suggesting ways to use it more effectively. Students can consult an environmental organization or government agency for additional information.

Backyard History

Editorial. Have students write editorials about a situation in their community that involves a conflict between protection of the environment and industrial or economic growth.

Analyzing Primary Sources

Essay. French soldier Michel Guillaume Jean de Crèvecoeur settled in the American colonies in 1759, and by 1765 had become a naturalized citizen. Writing under the pen name of J. Hector St. John, Crèvecoeur portrayed rural life in the colonies in a series of essays, *Letters From an American Farmer.* Refer students to the words of Crèvecoeur on this page.

Ask: What personal characteristics did Crèvecoeur believe were needed for economic success in America? **(serious attitude, willingness to work)** What economic opportunities existed in America but were not available in Europe? **(guarantee of work, high wages, ample food, cheap, plentiful land)** Do these opportunities still exist? Explain.

Connections: Geography

Analyzing Maps. Discuss changes in economic opportunity. Refer students to the maps on text pages 906–907. **Ask:** How has agriculture changed since 1890? **(Farm production more diverse in 1990 than in 1890s.)** How has manufacturing changed since 1890? **(Manufacturing now includes airplane and motor vehicle production, petroleum refining, production of synthetics and electronic equipment.)**

Connections: Literature

Analyzing Poetry. Read the poem *Harlem*, by Langston Hughes:

What happens to a dream
deferred?

Does it dry up like a raisin in the sun?
Or fester like a sore—
And then run?
Does it stink like rotten
meat?
Or crust and sugar
over— like a syrupy
sweet?

Maybe it just sags
like a heavy load.

Or does it explode?

Ask: To what dream does Hughes refer? **(the American Dream)** Whose dream has been deferred? **(people of Harlem)** Have students explain each simile. What are the consequences to people whose dream is deferred? **(loss of hope, frustration, sickness, violence)** Compare dreams that individuals can fulfill for themselves with those that require cooperative social conditions.

Multicultural Perspectives

Hispanic Americans are the fastest growing group in the United States. In 1960 Hispanics had numbered about 3 million; by 1990 they numbered about 22 million. Such growth translates to voting power and political clout, especially in states with key electoral votes. Since the eighties, presidential candidates have courted the Mexican-American vote in California and the Southwest, the Puerto-Rican vote in New York, and the Cuban-American vote in Florida.

The computer revolution that began in the 1970s created new types of high-technology businesses. Increasingly, job opportunities have meant "office work" rather than farm or factory labor.

In Crèvecoeur's day, the United States was a small agricultural nation, with 90 percent of its population living and working on farms. Until the late 1800s the economic promise of America for new settlers lay in its seemingly endless supply of land— regardless of whether Native Americans wanted to sell the land or not. The dream of owning farm land brought millions of immigrants here.

Over time opportunities changed. As the best land was taken from Native Americans and settled, and as industries grew, opportunity still beckoned for many— but with factory jobs rather than land. Only 3 percent of Americans now make their living by farming.

Moving into a new century, the nation stands as an industrial giant with economic interests spanning the globe. Today new technologies and global economic forces are once more reshaping the nation's economy. "We are looking for people who can think," says one employer. "There simply aren't many jobs for people who can lift things." Through all these changes, though, America remains for many a beacon of opportunity.

Reduced student page in the Teacher's Edition

Discrimination and the American Dream

Although America remains a land of promise, the search for opportunity has brought many Americans face to face with discrimination, especially discrimination based on race and sex. Barriers to equal opportunity have taken many forms. Early in our history, most colleges would not admit women. In the 1800s job-hunting immigrants from Ireland met signs saying "No Irish Need Apply." Early in this century, Asian immigrants in California were denied the right to buy farm land.

Pointing to effects of racism on people of color, John Hope Franklin writes:

> *"Their struggle for full equality has been an ongoing one, and they would have much to tell each other both about their limited successes and numerous failures. They are, in general, clustered at the lower end of the occupational and economic scale, victims of discrimination in employment and in compensation [pay] for work done."*

In the years ahead, will the American dream of abundance and opportunity be expanded to include all groups? Or will it remain for some, in the words of African-American poet Langston Hughes, "a dream deferred"?

Government's Changing Role

For over two hundred years, Americans have debated about the role of government in creating a society of abundance. Some argue that government should be actively involved in the economy. Others believe individuals should be left alone to pursue the American dream on their own. The fact remains, though, that the government has always had an impact on economic opportunity— or lack of opportunity— in the lives of various groups of Americans.

In the early 1800s, for instance, the government enforced laws to seize Native American lands and give them to settlers at almost no cost. Later, both

Expectations for government's role in the economy have changed. Not until the early 1900s was there a widespread demand for laws limiting child labor. The 1980s saw the first major efforts to pass laws helping the homeless.

the national and state governments helped build roads, canals, and railroads linking farms to markets. In the late 1800s, as the economy shifted to industry, government helped to protect businesses from foreign competition.

During the Great Depression of the 1930s, when one worker out of four was jobless, the national government created millions of jobs and supported workers in their struggle to earn decent wages. More recently, it has begun to deal with job discrimination against women and other people who have been discriminated against. As our economy changes, government's role will probably continue to be a source of debate.

What History Tells Us

As you study the American past, you will encounter again and again the three themes discussed in this chapter: the balancing of unity and diversity, the shaping of American democracy, and the search for opportunity. You will find that history tells us where this nation has succeeded in living up to its ideals, and where it has failed. From past successes we can find the hope and courage to face the future with confidence. From failures we can learn not to accept things as they are, but to work for and welcome change.

Section Review

1. Analysis. In what ways has economic opportunity changed in America, and how has the role of government changed in response?

2. Evaluation. Do you think the phrase "America: Land of Opportunity" is misleading? Explain why or why not.

Active Learning

Interviewing. Have students review the theme discussed in this section—the search for opportunity. Ask students to interview senior citizens about how the search for opportunity has affected their lives. Students can ask: What has the search for opportunity meant for you? When have you been pleased in your search? Disappointed? How has the search for opportunity affected other people you know?

Section Review

ANSWERS

1. The basis of economic opportunities has changed from land and natural resources to factories to skilled service jobs. The government has developed and encouraged economic opportunities through land policies, infrastructure development, and laws. Presently, the government is concerned with providing greater opportunities for women and minority groups.

2. Answers may include that some opportunities have greatly diminished, certain groups have been denied a full measure of these opportunities. Or, opportunities have always been available to certain people, the government has sought to provide such opportunities.

Global Connections

Activity. In his argument against the amendment, David Fried cites problems that official bilingualism has brought to Canada and Belgium. Have students research those effects and discuss whether they think similar problems would arise in the United States if the government adopted an official language. The discussion could be expanded to look at multilingualism in other nations.

Multicultural Perspectives

The amendment was proposed by S. I. Hayakawa, who was born of Japanese parents and raised in Canada. After becoming a United States citizen in 1954, he became a university professor and later served one term as senator from California. He was dedicated to the twin goals of making English the official language of the United States and of promoting opportunities for all people living in this country to learn English. As an immigrant, Hayakawa believed that "*English is the key that unlocks the door of opportunity in the United States.*" He also argued that "*the movement to make English our official language acknowledges our ethnic diversity. But if our society's strength rests in its diversity, its unity is derived from and preserved by our common language. To say otherwise is to deny reality.*"

Reduced student page in the Teacher's Edition

POINT OF VIEW

The Official English Debate

In 1981 a constitutional amendment was proposed to declare English the official language of the United States. It would make English the only language used for government business. The proposal sparked debate over the role of English in American society. By 1990 eighteen states had declared English their official language, but three states had passed laws supporting the use of more than one language in government. The following editorials present two views in this ongoing debate.

A Common Language

"Spanish is the language in which I conduct most of my personal, social, and professional business. Furthermore, my entire career has been devoted to the promotion of Hispanic culture through teaching, writing, and directing a Spanish-language theater group. There is nothing in the Constitution to prevent me from operating in a language other than English, and if English becomes the official language of the United States, this will not change.

. . . in order to participate fully in the social, economic, and political life of this country, English is essential. . . . Congress debates in English. The President addresses the nation in English. The large newspapers and news magazines use English. Without English, a person is dependent upon secondary sources—politicians and media that may or may not interpret the facts accurately. It is fair and logical that people who wish to exercise the rights of citizenship be required to do so in English.

. . . In states such as California and Florida it is possible to go through school and graduate without learning English. Yet, without English, youngsters will find it nearly impossible to go on to college or to obtain any but menial jobs. . . . Making English the official language of the United States would send a clear message that in order to reap the benefits of U.S. residency, it is essential to know English. But the point of officializing English is to strengthen our common bond, not to obliterate our individual identities. . . . Ethnic diversity is one of the greatest strengths of the United States. English should be our official language, but it should not be our only language."

—Barbara Mujica, in the *Dallas News,* July 24, 1989

In San Francisco ballots are in English, Spanish, and Chinese.

Saying No to 'English Only'

"On the day after the [Official-English] amendment is passed, state and local governments will still face the same problems. But the decisions on every detail of policy will be taken out of their hands and confided to federal judges appointed for life. The statement 'English shall be the official language' provides no intelligible basis for decision. Therefore the judges may do just as they please. At best, they may decide that the amendment merely expresses a pious wish. (If so, it doesn't belong in the Constitution.) At worst, they will be making decisions that are none of their business—for example, that the Constitution forbids the hiring of social workers who speak the language of their clients, lest they be deprived of their incentive to learn English. . . .

The United States is a republic in which national identity is defined by democratic and universal principles, and not by ethnic or linguistic identity. A naturalized citizen is a person who has voluntarily joined our community by subscribing to those principles, whatever his color, culture, or language. People around the world flock here, not only for economic opportunity, but for a chance to leave behind the stifling exclusiveness of their communities and ethnic groups. They are happy to exchange ethnic loyalties for loyalty to a political community that welcomes them. And they are happy to learn English, the language of that community and the key to success. . . .

Proponents of the amendment apparently believe the amendment will cause foreigners to redouble their efforts to learn English. This is one possible reaction. More likely, though, is increased cultural and linguistic separation. In fact, once we admit the principle of an official language, American Hispanics as they increase in numbers may eventually demand a new amendment establishing official bilingualism in recognition of the demographic facts. Then we will have brought down upon our heads the troubles of Canada and Belgium, and we will deserve them.

We can best avoid this fate by following the first rule of constitutional jurisprudence: 'If it ain't broke, don't fix it.'"

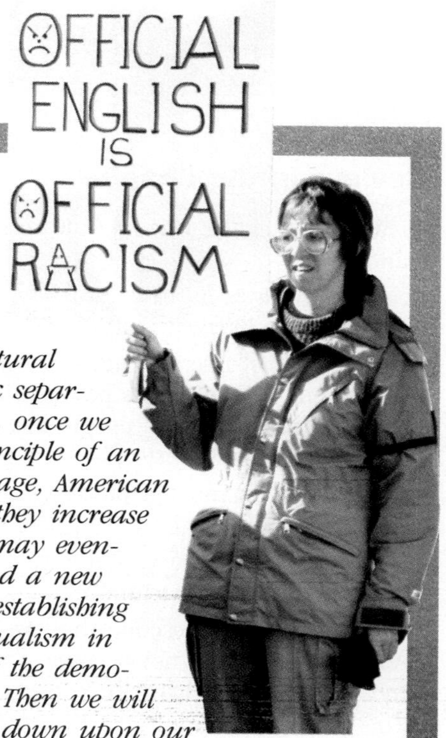

—David J. Fried, in the *Christian Science Monitor,* May 10, 1989

1. Why does Barbara Mujica think that English should be this nation's official language?

2. Why does David Fried oppose making English the official language of the United States?

3. On what points do these two writers agree?

4. Imagine that you are a representative or senator about to vote on an official English amendment. What additional information or viewpoints would you like to have before deciding how to vote?

Point of View

ANSWERS

1. Mujica argues that making English the official language would send a message that to enjoy the benefits of this country and to fulfill the responsibilities of citizenship, it is essential to know English. She also argues that a single official language will strengthen our common bond and promote communication among diverse groups.
2. Fried believes such an amendment would be either a "pious wish," and therefore meaningless, or an invitation to judicial meddling in government affairs. He also suggests that making one language official could open the door to official bilingualism which could create worse problems.
3. They agree that knowing English is key to success in this country and that ethnic diversity does not necessarily weaken national unity.
4. Answers will vary. Some may want more information on the effects of such an amendment. Others may want more data on English acquisition among immigrants in the absence of such an amendment. Still others may want to hear the views of immigrant groups on this issue.

Chapter Survey
ANSWERS

Reviewing the Chapter

1. Great mixing of racial, ethnic, religious groups; oldest ongoing constitutional democracy.
2. Colonists in colonial America came from many European countries, spoke different languages, and belonged to different religious groups. Colonial America was also home to Native Americans and enslaved Africans. The United States today, is home to immigrants from Europe, Asia, Latin America, and the Middle East. Diverse religious practices and customs still exist.
3. A government can get its power from the strongest or wealthiest people in society, from religious leaders, or from consent of the governed. In the United States, government authority is based on consent of the governed. Who gets a say in government has expanded from adult white males with property to include all adults not in prison.
4. Democracy is a process of participation, debate, and compromise.
5. The common ways of making a living have changed from farming to factory work to service industries.
6. The American dream is that everyone has the chance to earn a good living and live a comfortable life. Racism, sexism, lack of education have been obstacles to achieving the American dream.

Reduced student page in the Teacher's Edition

Chapter Survey

Reviewing the Chapter

1. What makes the United States unique among nations?

2. Compare diversity in colonial America with diversity in the United States today.

3. Contrast the differing views on where a government should get its power. What are some ways government by the people has changed during the nation's history?

4. Why is democracy "a process, not a static condition"?

5. How has economic opportunity changed in America since colonial times?

6. How would you describe the "American dream"? Why has it not become a reality for all Americans? Give at least three reasons.

Thinking Critically

1. Analysis. American writer Ralph Ellison has said, "The diversity of American life is often painful, frequently burdensome, and always a source of conflict, but in it lies our faith and our hope." What are the faith and hope of which he speaks?

2. Evaluation. American writer Mark Twain once said, "There is not a single human characteristic which can be safely labeled as 'American.'" Do you agree or disagree? Give reasons to support your answer.

3. Evaluation. Mikhail Baryshnikov, a famous dancer from the Soviet Union, became an American citizen. When he was asked how "American" he considered himself to be, he responded, "How American am I? Well, I'm not a Yankee fan, and don't like Coca-Cola. But I love television, fast cars, and corn on the cob. That's pretty American." What is your reaction to Baryshnikov's statement? Explain.

4. Synthesis. What would a society be like in which the rights of individuals were of the greatest importance? What would a society be like in which the common good was always considered more important than the rights of individuals?

5. Evaluation. Do you think there should be limits on the number of immigrants coming to the United States each year? Why or why not?

6. Synthesis. For each of the three main themes, state in your own words what ideal it represents. As you study different periods in American history, what general signs will you be looking for to check how well our nation has lived up to each ideal? For example, one sign of the ideal of democracy not being lived up to was the denial of voting rights to women.

History and You

Refer to the bar graph on page 8 for the estimated percentages of the American population in 1990 that were European American, African American, Hispanic American, Asian American, and Native American. Then create a similar bar graph showing the percentages of each of these general groups in your class. How does the graph for your class today compare with the graph for the nation as a whole in 1990?

Applying Social Studies Skills

Analyzing Line Graphs

Study the line graph on the next page and then answer the following questions.

1. Which ten-year period between 1820 and 1990 saw the greatest number of European immigrants to America? Compare the general trend in European immigration before that period with the trend after that period.

2. Compare the general trend in European immigration to America after 1960 with the trends in Asian, North American, and South American immigration.

3. Describe at least two ways in which this line graph helps to explain the changes in percentages on the bar graph on page 8.

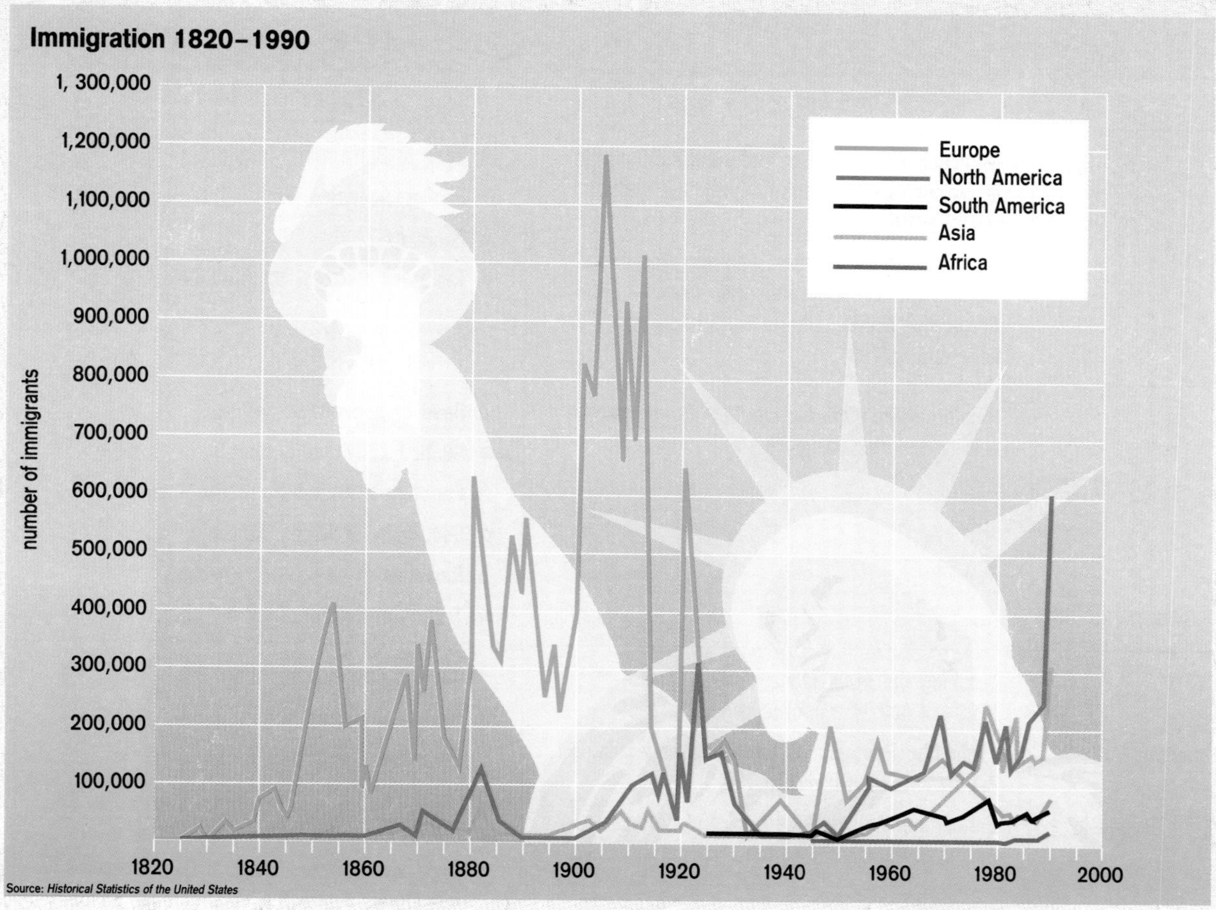

Writing About Issues

The Issue: *Should Congress make English the official language of the United States?*

Recently legislation was introduced in Congress to make English the official language of the United States. While such legislation would allow the private use of any language, it would make English the only language used in government documents such as voting ballots and in public agencies such as courts.

Proponents of such legislation argue that immigrants must be encouraged to learn English so that they can participate fully in this nation's economic and political life. Efforts to provide ballots and public services in other languages foster a divided society, they say. Nations that have supported bilingualism, such as Canada and India, are now deeply divided into language-group factions.

Opponents argue that the proposal is at best unnecessary and at worst racist. Making English the only language of government would deny Americans who do not speak English the right to vote and access to government services. Immigrants have every incentive to learn English without such legislation.

Read more about this issue on pages 16 and 17. Then write to your Representative in Congress expressing your view on the issue. Address your letter to:

The Honorable (name of Representative)
House of Representatives
Washington, D.C. 20515

Thinking Critically

1. Faith in people's ability to learn to tolerate each other's differences; hope that they will do so.
2. Agree: Since America is a mixture of peoples from all over the world, there are no uniquely American characteristics. Disagree: perhaps uniqueness lies in the extent of its diversity.
3. Answers will vary.
4. Individual rights most important: no social fabric, no caring for others, no protection for rights of the dispossessed. Common good most important: individual rights ignored, individual human life is less valued.
5. Reasons for limit: too many people place a strain on natural resources, immigrants threaten "American way of life." Reasons against limit: U.S. has long stood for open immigration, diversity is America's strength, exclusion is undemocratic.
6. Answers will vary.

History and You

Answers will vary.

Applying Social Studies Skills

1. 1900 to 1910; before, European immigration was increasing, after, decreasing.
2. While European immigration decreases the others increase.
3. Immigration from Asia, North America, and South America has increased, European immigration has decreased.

Chapter 2

Bridges to a New Land

Planning Guide

	Student Text	TWE Lesson Plans	Support Materials
SECTION 1	**Section 2–1** (1–2 Days) **The First Americans,** pp 22–29 Review/Evaluation Section Review, p 29	**Introducing the Chapter:** Assessing the Demands of Exploration—Cooperative Activity, one class period, p 19B **Teaching the Main Ideas:** Demonstrating the Diversity of Early Native-American Nations—Cooperative Activity, introduction 30 minutes, homework, p 19B	★ **Read to Remember,** Section 1 ● **Section Activities,** Section 1 Δ **Readings** ● **Tests and Quizzes,** Section 1 Quiz
SECTION 2	**Section 2–2** (1 Day) **The Explorers,** pp 30–35 The Creative Spirit: Native Americans, pp 36–37 Review/Evaluation Section Review, p 35	**Reinforcement Activity:** Who Am I?—Cooperative Activity, one class period, p 19C	★ **Read to Remember,** Section 2 ● **Section Activities,** Section 2 Δ **Enrichment Activities,** Section 2 ● **Geography Activities,** Section 2 Δ **Readings** ● **Tests and Quizzes,** Section 2 Quiz
SECTION 3	**Section 2–3** (1–3 Days) **The Conquerors,** pp 38–45 Geography—Movement: The First American Revolution, p 44 Connections to Themes: The Search for Opportunity, p 45 Review/Evaluation Section Review, p 45 Chapter 2 Survey, pp 46–47 Skills, pp 46–47 Using New Vocabulary Thinking Critically Using a Time Line Applying Social Studies Skills: Analyzing Maps Writing About Issues	**Teaching the Main Ideas:** Unsung Heroes—Individual Activity, two class periods, p 19C **Evaluating Progress:** Where and When—Individual Activity, one class period, p 19C **Enrichment Activity:** The Legacy of Columbus—Individual Activity, one or two class periods, p 19C	★ **Read to Remember,** Section 3 ● **Section Activities,** Section 3 Δ **Enrichment Activities,** Section 3 Δ **Readings** ● **Tests and Quizzes,** Section 3 Quiz, Chapter 2 Test (Forms A and B) **Additional Resources** Δ **GTV Videodiscs** ● **Active Learning** Δ **Transparencies and Activity Book** ● **Testing Software** ★ **Chapter Summaries** **Key:** ★ **For Extra Support** ● **For All Students** Δ **For Enrichment**

Overview

The story of the United States begins with the history of the Western Hemisphere and its native people. According to widely-held theory, human beings crossed into the North American continent from Asia and then moved southward. The diverse environments that the many small migrating bands of people encountered as they spread out across the Americas led them to develop different ways of life.

Some evidence suggests that Europeans, Africans, and Asians might have made contact with the Americas before 1492. However, it was Columbus's voyage in that year that set off a series of European expeditions to the continents that became known as the "New World." Driven by the lure of a shorter passage to the riches of the Indies, Europeans of several nationalities explored the Americas. News of these explorations sparked the determination of other Europeans to find riches in these lands.

Spaniards made the first conquests in the Americas, planting settlements and imposing their ways on the native peoples. Their quest for religious dominance, wealth, and power (God, gold, and glory) resulted in oppression and death for many Native Americans, as well as for many Africans brought as slaves. The Spanish conquest, however, also brought about the birth of a new way of life, as European, African, and Native-American ideas and customs influenced each other.

Spain's dominance in the Americas was soon challenged by European rivals.

Activity Objectives

After completing the activities, students should be able to

- describe how the different environments of the Western Hemisphere led groups of Native Americans to develop diverse ways of life.
- explain European motivations for exploration and conquest.
- recognize that explorations and conquests were conducted by Europeans of several nationalities.
- identify important persons and recount the sequence of events in the early period of European conquest and settlement.
- discuss different interpretations of the legacy of European exploration and conquest of the Americas.

Introducing the Chapter

Assessing the Demands of Exploration

This cooperative activity requires a full class period.

To appreciate more fully the migrations of the early Native Americans and the explorations of later Europeans, students need to consider the personal characteristics required of such adventurers. By participating in the activity, students will begin to realize that certain characteristics such as the willingness to face danger and uncertainty are common to explorers of all time periods.

Introduce the activity by explaining that many people consider astronauts to be modern-day explorers. Then divide the class into groups of three and ask each group to brainstorm to create a list of possible dangers faced by space flight crews, especially those on early missions. Next, have them list desirable personal characteristics of people who make these flights.

When their lists are complete, ask groups to share their work with the rest of the class. As the groups report, compile a class list of the dangers and personal characteristics. Ask the class to review the list of dangers and assess whether they are similar to those faced by the explorers of the Americas. Delete from the list those dangers which would not be comparable. Conduct the same review and revision of the personal characteristics list.

Save the edited class lists. Have students reevaluate the accuracy of their lists after they have finished the chapter.

Teaching the Main Ideas

Section 2-1: Demonstrating the Diversity Of Early Native-American Nations

This cooperative activity requires half a class period and students will need a week or more to complete the projects on their own time.

This activity will help deepen students' understanding and appreciation of the significant diversity that existed among pre-Columbian Native-American peoples.

Divide the class into groups of three. Explain that each group is to assemble a diorama that illustrates the way of life of one of the early Native-American nations discussed in Section 2-1. Encourage students to create representations of homes and household goods, tools and weapons, foods, and clothing, and to make backdrops that illustrate the environment in which the group lived. Each display should be accompanied by captions explaining how the material goods reflect the environment. Suggest that students consult reference books for additional information.

Arrange a showing of the dioramas and have each group explain its project. Conclude the activity by summarizing on the chalkboard characteristics common to the several cultures represented and characteristics unique to particular cultures. Have students relate these characteristics to the relationship between humans and their environment.

Teaching the Main Ideas

Section 2-3: Unsung Heroes

This individual activity requires two class periods, or it may be assigned as homework, with students finishing and sharing their projects in class the next day.

This activity emphasizes the point that although the leaders of expeditions are the ones remembered in history, each was accompanied by a crew he depended on for labor or a military force he depended on for protection. Expeditions often included others, too, such as religious figures, government representatives, and artists who made a visual record of the journey.

Introduce the activity by discussing with students the importance of the "unsung heroes" who accompanied expedition leaders on their travels. Then ask each student to imagine that he or she is a recruiter whose job is to recruit volunteers for an expedition to search for the "Indies" or explore the Americas. Direct students to choose an explorer or a conqueror mentioned in Chapter 2 and begin his or her recruiting task by outlining the purpose of that explorer's mission, the route the explorer expects to follow, and the benefits those who join the expedition can expect to enjoy.

Explain that one way to attract recruits is to create a recruiting poster. Have each student design a poster encouraging people to join the explorer's expedition. Discuss briefly with students various advertising techniques such as catchy slogans, use of color, and illustrations. The poster should be persuasive but provide prospective recruits with adequate information about reasons for the journey and the duties and economic opportunities to be expected.

Display the completed posters. Have students discuss the techniques they used and evaluate each others' posters for both accuracy of claims and persuasiveness.

Reinforcement Activity

Section 2-2: Who Am I?

This class activity may take an entire period, or it may be carried out for a few minutes at the beginning of several class periods.

Section 2-2 discusses a number of explorers, all of whom were major forces in this historical period. To help students remember the names of these explorers, their countries of origin, and the importance of their explorations, the class will engage in a game of "I'm Thinking of Someone or Something."

The rules of the game require that each student think of a person (explorer), a place (a location explored), or a notable achievement. Students write their "thought" on slips of paper. When it is a student's turn, he or she begins by saying, "I am thinking of a person (place or achievement)." The other students then try to determine what the student is thinking by asking a series of questions that can be answered with a "yes" or "no." Questions continue until the class is ready to make a guess. To encourage students to focus questions rather than venturing random guesses, limit the number of guesses in each round to two or three. On the chalkboard tally the number of questions asked of each student. The winner is the student who stumps the class by being asked the most questions.

Evaluating Progress

Section 2-3: Where and When?

This individual activity requires one class period or can be assigned as homework.

Chapter 2 covers the vast area that is the Western Hemisphere and a long time period. This activity can be used to make sure that students have developed an accurate awareness of where and when the events described in the chapter took place.

Ask students to review the chapter and from it select ten individuals, groups, places, and events they would like to have seen with their own eyes. Distribute atlases or maps of the Western Hemisphere and have the students locate sites where they might find their ten selections. Direct students to create hand-drawn maps on which to show the locations.

Have students use their maps to write itineraries describing the route they would follow to see the ten people, groups, places, and events they have identified. Explain that their "journeys" will take them through both space and time, and therefore the itineraries should include the approximate date of each visit. A student might write, for example, "I would like to go to the easternmost tip of South America where Cabral landed while trying to follow Vasco da Gama's route to India in 1500. I would like to fish for salmon with the Tlingits in the Pacific Northwest sometime before the Europeans arrived."

Criteria for evaluation should include explicitness in describing the people, locations, or events selected; accuracy in locating the sites on the maps; and correctness in identifying the appropriate time periods.

Enrichment Activity

Section 2–3: The Legacy of Columbus

This group activity requires one and a half to two class periods.

Section 2–3 describes some of the outcomes of encounters between the native peoples of the Americas and European explorers and conquerors. Much of the Europeans' treatment of Native Americans is judged today to have been unethical and inhumane. This activity is designed to help students consider the legacy of this collision of cultures.

Organize the class into groups of four or five students. Students will consider the impact of the European conquest of the Americas and express their conclusions by suggesting an appropriate observance of Columbus Day. Explain that while most people agree that the voyage of Christopher Columbus in 1492 forever changed life in the Americas, Europe, and Africa, they do not agree about whether this momentous event should be celebrated, mourned, or marked in some other way. Have the groups consider the following views:

- Columbus and the European explorers who followed him brought civilization to the nearly empty continents of North and South America. Their discoveries, in turn, led to a rapid development of western knowledge, in such areas as science, geography, agriculture, and government, which they then spread around the globe.

- The first voyage of Columbus was the beginning of a European invasion of the Americas that brought misery and death to Native Americans, damaged their environment, and destroyed their cultures. At the same time, the Europeans enslaved millions of Africans in order to loot the riches of the Americas.
- As a result of Columbus's voyage, new and vibrant cultures arose in the Americas, where European, African, and Native-American ideas merged. At the same time, Native-American products and knowledge were carried to Europe, greatly benefiting Europeans.

Other views lie somewhere between these three.

Each group will write a statement expressing its stand on the meaning of Columbus's voyage. The statement should be supported with evidence from the text, personal knowledge, observation, and research. The group will also make recommendations for a community Columbus Day observance consistent with the stand it has taken.

Have one member of each group read the group's recommendations and the reasoning behind them. After a discussion of the merits of each position, ask the class to vote on which Columbus Day proposal they would recommend to local officials.

Bibliography and Audiovisual Material

Teacher Bibliography

John, Elizabeth A.H. *Storms Brewed in Other Men's Worlds: The Confrontation of Indians, Spanish, and French in the Southwest, 1540–1795.* Lincoln: University of Nebraska Press, 1975.

Josephy, Alvin M., Jr. *The Indian Heritage of America.* New York: Alfred A. Knopf, 1968.

Marrin, Albert. *Aztecs and Spaniards: Cortes and the Conquest of Mexico.* New York: Atheneum, 1986.

Morrison, Samuel Eliot, ed. and translator. *Journals and other Documents on the Life and Voyages of Christopher Columbus.* New York: Heritage, 1963.

Oswalt, Wendell H. *This Land Was Theirs. A Study of North American Indians.* Mountain View, Ca.: Mayfield Publishing, 1987.

Student Bibliography

Bakeless, John. *America as Seen by its First Explorers.* New York: Dover Publications, 1961.

Bolton, Herbert Eugene, ed. *Spanish Exploration of the Southwest: 1542–1706.* New York: Barnes & Noble, 1991.

Horgan, Paul. *Conquistadors in North American History.* Texas Western, 1982.

Josephy, Jr., Alvin. *The Indian Heritage of America.* Boston: Houghton Mifflin Co., 1991.

O'Dell, Scott. *The King's Fifth.* Boston: Houghton Mifflin, 1966.

Snell, Tee Loftin. *The Wild Shores: America's Beginnings.* Washington, DC: National Geographic Society, 1974.

Weatherford, Jack. *Native Roots.* New York: Crown Publishers, 1991.

Wilford, John N. *The Mysterious History of Columbus.* New York: Alfred A Knopf, 1991.

Films, Videocassettes, and Videodiscs

Age of Discovery: English, French, and Dutch Exploration. Coronet/MTI. Film.

Discovery and Exploration. Westport Media. Videocassette.

The First Americans. NBC. Videocassette.

Indian Cultures from 2000 B.C. to 1500 A.D. Journal Films. Film.

Life in the Woodlands Before the White Man Came. AIMS Media. Videodisc.

The Spanish Explorers. EB. Film.

Computer Software

The Explorer Series: Discover the World. 3 Apple Diskettes. Hartley.

Into the Unknown: Voyages 1 and 2. Apple/Commodore. Focus Media.

Other Cultures. Apple/IBM. Intellectual Software.

Chapter 2

Objectives

- Explain why so many diverse cultures developed in America.
- Cite the factors that led to European exploration of the Americas.
- Describe the effects of European conquests on Native Americans.

Introducing THE CHAPTER

For suggestions on introducing Chapter 2, refer to page 19B in the Teacher's Edition.

Developing THE CHAPTER

For activities and teaching strategies to help you reinforce and enrich chapter content, see pages 19B–19D in the Teacher's Edition.

B · A · C · K · G · R · O · U · N · D

Chapter Opener Illustrations

The map shows French explorer Jacques Cartier and his party on Cartier's third trip to Canada in 1541–1542. The people they met, shown hunting, were the Iroquoians. On this map, north is at the bottom. If the map is turned upside down, a rough outline of the eastern coast of the United States can be recognized. The large earthen-colored island at the left is Newfoundland. The large river is the St. Lawrence.

Although the Greeks are credited with the first astrolabe—an instrument which measures the angle of the sun or stars above the horizon, from which the observer's latitude can be determined—the Arabs perfected it, and European mariners used it in their explorations.

Reduced student page in the Teacher's Edition

Chapter 2 20,000 B.C.-A.D. 1700

Bridges to a New Land

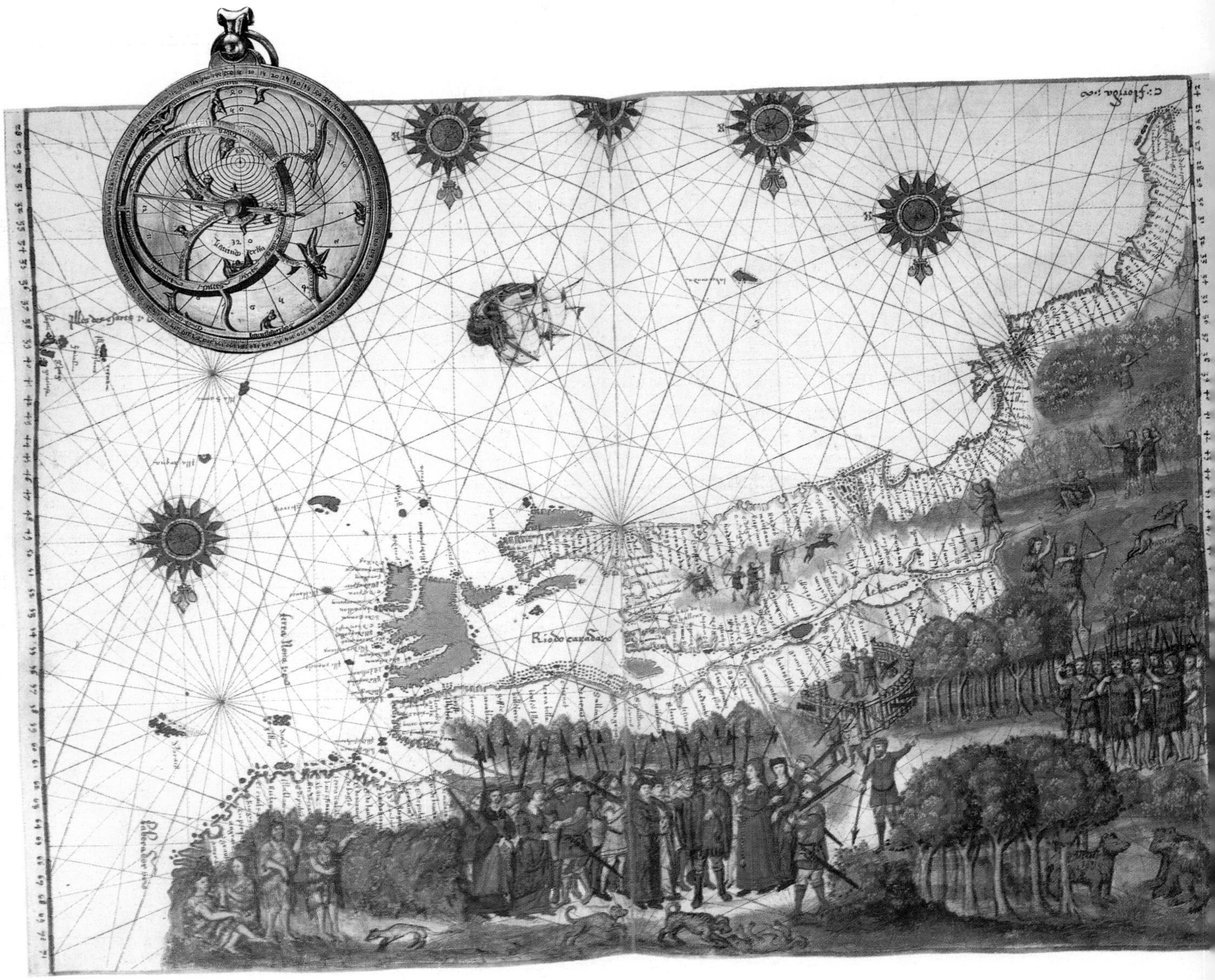

The desire for Asian products led many European nations to search for sea routes to Asia. When Vasco da Gama returned to Portugal from a 24,000-mile trip to India, he brought back goods valued at sixty times the cost of his expedition.

Explorers such as Balboa and Magellan came into contact with the diverse civilizations of native inhabitants of the Americas. Europeans and Americans introduced new ideas and ways of life to each other. The drawing by White shows a bird eating corn, a food native to America. The turquoise snake typifies the sophisticated art created by the Aztecs of Middle America.

American Voices

One of the oldest settlements in the United States, the Hopi village of Oraibi is nestled on a mesa that rises high above the deserts of northern Arizona. Even older than this village is the Hopis' account of how they came to live in their present home.

According to the Hopis, Creator made Nephew to carry out his plan, and Nephew created Spider Woman as a helper. She made human beings in different colors, speaking different languages. At first people lived in caverns. Three times, however, because of people's fighting, greed, and selfishness, Nephew destroyed their underground world. At last Spider Woman directed them to a fourth world. The *Book of the Hopi* continues:

" . . . Alone they set out, traveling east and a little north, paddling hard day and night for many days as if they were paddling uphill. At last they saw land. It rose high above the waters, stretching from north to south as far as they could see. A great land, a mighty land, their inner wisdom told them. 'The Fourth World' they cried to each other. . . .

[Nephew appeared and said,] 'The name of this Fourth World is . . . World Complete. You will find out why. It is not all beautiful and easy like the previous ones. It has height and depth, heat and cold, beauty and barrenness; it has everything for you to choose from. What you choose will determine if this time you can carry out the plan of Creation on it or whether it must in time be destroyed. . . . Now you will separate and go different ways to claim all the earth for the Creator. "

Some historians tell a similar story about a long, difficult journey to an unknown land. They tell of people who scattered across this land, met the challenges of new environments, and were changed by their experiences.

Astrolabe; detail from Cartier Map, 1547; Vasco da Gama; 17th-century copy of John White's North American towhee; Aztec mosaic chest ornament.

Analyzing Primary Sources

American Voices

In the *Book of the Hopi,* thirty-two Hopi elders in northern Arizona tell about the history, mythology, and rituals of the Hopis of the American Southwest. Before this book was written in 1963, Hopi history and traditions had been handed down orally.

Research for the book took nearly three years, with the words of the Hopis recorded on tape and then translated into English. The elders regarded the compilation of this book as a sacred task. It gave to their descendants a written history of their people and an account of their religious beliefs.

1. How does the Hopi description of the land give an idea of the physical characteristics of the American Southwest? **(mountains and valleys, high and low temperatures, beauty and barrenness)**

2. How does the story account for the existence of diverse cultures in the world? **(People separated and went different ways.)**

3. Why are stories important in providing people with a sense of identity? Which stories today provide us with our sense of identity?

Section 2-1

Objectives

- ***Answer the Focus Question.***
- *Describe and compare theories of how humans first came to the Americas.*
- *List characteristics of various Native American cultures.*
- *Cite similarities in religious beliefs and attitudes toward nature among different Indian tribes.*

Introducing THE SECTION

According to widely-held scientific theory, human beings originated in Africa, spread gradually to Europe and Asia, and finally to Australia and North and South America. Ask students which is closest to North America—Africa, Europe, or Asia. Have students use a globe or the map on text pages 890–891 to describe the location of North America relative to Asia. Ask what present-day nation on the Asian continent lies closest to the United States. **(Russia)**

Have students examine the inset map of Alaska on text page 888 to estimate the distance between Asia and North America across the Bering Strait. **(56 miles.)** Most archaeologists think that people entered North America from Asia in small groups over a long period of time. Ask students how people likely reached North America. **(Scholars think that people reached North America in small boats as well as by means of the land bridge described in the text.)**

B · A · C · K · G · R · O · U · N · D

Time Line Illustrations

1. Mammoth skeleton: Early people crossed into North America, hunting migrating herds of animals, such as the now-extinct woolly mammoth. Some mammoths measured more than 14 feet high with tusks 14 feet long.

2. Mimbres pottery: The Mimbres were a branch of the Mogollon culture of the American Southwest. Most Mimbres bowls were intended as burial offerings and were "killed" by punching holes in their bases.

3. Ninth-century Viking ship unearthed at Gokstad, Norway: This warship measured nearly eighty feet long with holes for sixteen pairs of oars and a large steering paddle near the stern. It carried a crew of thirty-five. In 1893 an exact replica sailed from Norway to Newfoundland, demonstrating

Reduced student page in the Teacher's Edition

CHAPTER TIME LINE

20,000 B.C.-A.D. 1700

6000 B.C. Eskimos settle in North America

300 B.C. Farming cultures emerge in Southwest

20,000 B.C. — **A.D. 1100**

20,000 B.C. Hunters cross into North America

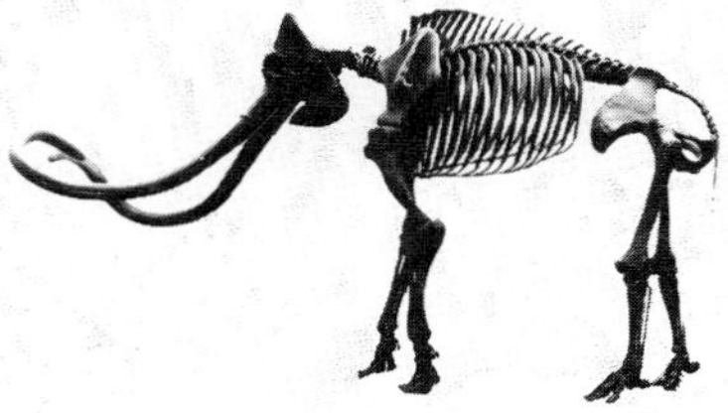

1200 B.C. Olmec civilization arises

A.D. 1000 Vikings reach North America

2-1 The First Americans

Focus: Why did the first Americans develop many diverse cultures?

When Europeans of the sixteenth century first learned of North and South America, they talked about "discovering a new world." But these lands were not new to the people already living there. Thousands of years before, Native Americans, or "Indians," had already "discovered" the Americas—two huge continents on which roamed mammoths and mastodons, antelopes, and armadillos.

Early People in the Americas

Many archaeologists theorize that human beings first began arriving in North America from Asia about 20,000 years ago, when the sparsely inhabited earth was in the grip of an Ice Age. Gigantic sheets of ice called glaciers spread southward from the North Pole, gouging and scraping their way across much of North America and Eurasia.

Because much of the earth's water was frozen in glaciers, the level of the seas dropped. Thus, vast shelves of land, once under water, were laid bare, creating natural bridges from land mass to land mass. One such bridge joined Siberia to Alaska across the Bering Strait. Animals crossed this land bridge from Asia into North America in search of food. Small bands of Ice Age hunters, who depended on the animals for food, clothing, and shelter, tracked them into this new world.

About 10,000 years ago, the Ice Age came to an end. The ice sheets melted as the climate warmed.

the ship's seaworthiness. In 1991 another replica sailed to Iceland with modern navigational equipment.

4. *Santa Maria*: This 1493 engraving of a ship much like Columbus's ship, the *Santa Maria*, was included in the official report of his explorations.

5. Elizabeth I: The English victory over the Spanish Armada can be seen in the two pictures behind Elizabeth. Heaven-sent winds fill the sails of the English ships, left, while at the same time dashing the Armada on the rocks off the coast of Scotland, right.

6. Spanish cavalryman: The mounted soldier is equipped with broadsword, lance, musket, pistols, shield, and *cuera*, or coat of arrowproof leather.

1492 Columbus crosses Atlantic

1418 Prince Henry establishes school of navigation

1521 Cortés conquers Mexico

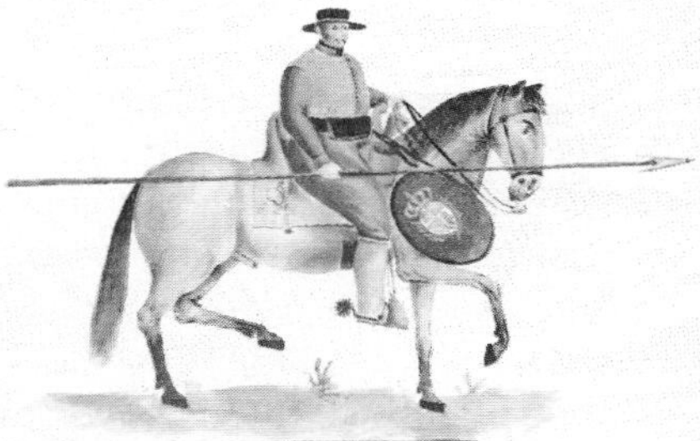

1610 Spanish establish Santa Fe, New Mexico

1300 1500 1700

1588 English defeat Spanish Armada

The seas rose, and the Americas were once again separated from Asia. But this time, according to the land-bridge theory, the Americas were peopled. Gradually, people spread throughout the two continents, with some people reaching the tip of South America by about 6000 B.C.

When the climate changed, the giant beasts died out. People adapted to the new circumstances, relying on fishing, hunting smaller game, and gathering wild plants and seeds to survive. These early people also began to fashion tools from wood, stone, bone, antler, and copper. They wove cloth and baskets from different plant materials, made boats, and tamed the wild dog.

The Beginning of Corn Culture

No one knows exactly where agriculture in the Americas was invented, or by what people. However, sometime around 7000 B.C. gatherers of wild plants and seeds discovered the secret of raising their own crops. The oldest evidence of farming comes from Mexico, where ancient seeds of domesticated gourd, chili pepper, and squash and cobs of domesticated corn lay in caves until they were discovered in the twentieth century.

Corn became North America's most important food crop, proving more dependable than game or wild plants. Gradually, agriculture led to a new way of life. Hunting and gathering required that people follow the migrations of animals or the ripening of wild plants, but with agriculture, people settled down to tend crops. Middle America—present-day Mexico and Central America—became dotted with villages and towns. Some communities grew into cities, and eventually large civilizations arose.

The Olmec culture was the first great civilization to arise in Middle America. From about 1200 B.C. Olmec towns flourished on Mexico's eastern coast, where corn can be grown year-round. The Olmecs were ruled by an elite class of priests devoted to the worship of gods and ancestors. Government officials took care of daily affairs while merchants and artisans carried out a bustling trade.

The Olmecs were skilled artisans. They built stone altars and erected monuments made of great mounds of earth. They also produced beautiful terra cotta, stone, and jade figurines depicting gods

Developing

THE SECTION

Thinking Critically

Analyzing Cause and Effect. Ask students:
1. What changes over time occurred in the size of the groups people lived in? (Gradually the groups became larger, communities grew into cities, large civilizations arose.) What caused this change? (agriculture)
2. What advantages did agriculture have over hunting and foraging? (People no longer had to move to get food; more dependable supply.)
3. How else did agriculture change the way people lived? (People began to perform specialized tasks because everyone did not have to spend time obtaining food. There were trades-people, artisans, and scientists, for example.)

GTV Side 1
Chap. 2, Frame 07200
Bering Land Bridge (Animated Map)
Search and Play:

GTV Side 1
Chap. 2, Frame 06459
Linking Life and Land (Movie)
Search:

Play:

Linking Past and Present

Discussion. In this passage an Aztec woman describes the education of young men. Read it to students and have them compare the Aztec school day with their own class schedules.

“And when they had breakfasted, they began teaching them how to live, how to obey, and how to honor people . . . at midday . . . when they had eaten, right away they began teaching them again . . . how to do battle, or how to hunt. . . . Others were taught song composition and oratory . . . also the science of the heavens. . . . And indeed some they took to the fields . . . to teach them how to sow seeds . . . and to cultivate and work the land. They taught them all it was needful to know by way of service, knowledge, wisdom, and prudent living.”

Limited English Proficiency

Cooperative Activity. Ask students to identify the major groups of early people discussed in this section—hunters, foragers, farmers, Mayas, Toltecs, Aztecs, Incas. Write their names on the chalkboard.

Then divide the class into small committees, assigning each a group of early people. Have each committee reread the text and write down the important facts about the group.

When finished, have a spokesperson from each group read its list and record key words under the appropriate headings.

B · A · C · K · G · R · O · U · N · D

Multicultural Perspectives

No one knows what the Olmecs called themselves. However, since they were the first people to tap rubber trees for sap, they have been called the Olmecs, meaning “rubber people.”

Connections: Science and Technology

The first corn, developed from wild grains, had ears about the size of strawberries. After 3500 B.C., farmers began to breed corn with larger ears. By the time European explorers arrived in about A.D. 1500, Native-American farmers were growing all the main types of corn we know today.

Reduced student page in the Teacher's Edition

and supernatural creatures, including a jaguar god, creator of all beings. For their monuments, drainage systems, and grinding tools, the Olmecs dragged stone over long distances. At one Olmec site stand eight colossal heads carved of a black stone called basalt, which had been dragged almost 50 miles from the coastal mountains to its inland site.

Olmec civilization disappeared about 400 B.C. However, later civilizations built on the ideas of the Olmecs—their social organization, religion, agriculture, art, and architecture.

The Empires of Middle America

Other civilizations based on the cultivation of corn, squash, and beans followed the Olmecs in Middle America. Between A.D. 300 and A.D. 900, Mayan civilization blossomed in the jungles of the Yucatan Peninsula, Guatemala, and Honduras. Most Mayas lived in farming villages near cities, which were the centers of trade and religion. In the cities, scientists and priests developed a written language and studied astronomy, creating an accurate calendar.

Meanwhile, another people, the Toltecs, established an empire to the north in central Mexico. By A.D. 1000 they had conquered the Mayas, and for nearly two hundred years they ruled much of what is today central and southern Mexico. Then civil war broke out and their empire toppled.

About A.D. 1200 the Aztecs created an empire that came to include much of Mexico. They built their capital, Tenochtitlán (teh-NOCH-tee-TLAHN), in the drained marshes of a large lake that used to exist at the site of present-day Mexico City. Tenochtitlán's 300,000 people were fed by the crops that grew on terraced hillsides around the lake or on man-made islands called *chinampas* (chee-NAHM-pahs).

Far to the south of Mexico, another magnificent empire extended some 3,000 miles along the Andes, a chain of mountains in South America. In the 1400s the Inca people conquered many other peoples that lived in these mountains, and their empire came

A great ceremonial pyramid was built by the Toltecs about A.D. 1000 at Chichén Itzá in Yucatan, Mexico. (above) The Aztec rain god Tlaloc holds a cornstalk.

Linking Past and Present

Pueblo Bonito was the largest "apartment building" in North America until a larger one was built in New York City in 1882. The Pueblo covered almost two-and-a-half acres.

Connections: Science and Technology

Scientists have helped historians fix accurate dates for the building and occupation of Pueblo Bonito. They use *dendrochronology*, the science of dating wood. Rings on trunks of trees tell how old the tree is. The width between the rings also provides information: the narrower the space, the drier the year. Historians have used this data to determine the age of timber used to build houses at Pueblo Bonito. They think the Pueblo was built around the year 1300.

to include over 6 million people. Building on the achievements of peoples they had conquered, they terraced mountainsides for farmland and created irrigation systems. They also constructed beautiful cities high in the mountains, linking them by roads and bridges.

Farming North of Mexico

Beginning around 300 B.C., three farming cultures arose in what is today the Southwest United States: Mogollan, Hohokam, and Anasazi. The people settled into permanent villages and towns to grow corn, beans, squash, cotton, and tobacco.

The Mogollans or "mountain people" tended crops along streams high in the mountains of southern Arizona and New Mexico. They settled in villages of pit houses that were partially sunk into the ground and covered with roofs of twigs, reed, and mud. This type of house was well suited to the climate of the Southwest, remaining cool in the hot summer months. The Mogollans also made a distinctive painted black and white pottery.

To the west, in the arid deserts of Arizona, the Hohokams also developed agriculture, pit houses, and pottery. Because of the barrenness of their surroundings, the Hohokams devised an intricate irrigation system of dams and canals.

The Hohokams carried on an extensive trade with Middle America. They used mirrors made in Middle America, kept tropical birds as pets, and imported rubber balls to play a game that had begun in Middle America. So successful were the Hohokam farmers and traders that one of their villages—Snaketown, near modern-day Phoenix—was occupied for 1,500 years.

Northeast of the Hohokams, where present-day Utah, Colorado, Arizona, and New Mexico meet, were the Anasazis, a name meaning "enemy ancient ones" in the Navajo language. At first, like their neighbors, the Anasazis lived in pit houses. Gradually the pit houses gave way to above-ground structures of stone. Eventually the structures became many-storied apartment houses, with the different levels connected by ladders. One Anasazi structure still standing is Pueblo Bonito, in Chaco Canyon, New Mexico. It has five stories with eight hundred rooms.

Spotlight on Native Americans Today

In 1900 the Indian population of the United States reached a low of about 250,000. Then it began to rise. Here are seven facts about the Native American population of the United States today.

- Total Native American population: Nearly 1.75 million
- Number of reservations: 300 federal, 21 state
- Largest reservation: Navajo
- Fraction of Indian population living in urban areas: One-third to one-half
- Urban area with the greatest Native American population: Los Angeles
- States with the greatest Indian populations: California, Oklahoma, Arizona, and New Mexico
- Most commonly spoken languages: Navajo, Iroquois, Inuit, Papago-Pima, Apache, and Sioux

The villages abandoned. Between 500 and 900 years ago, these early civilizations vanished, perhaps because of crop failure, drought, or war. The Mogollans and Hohokams scattered into smaller groups, becoming the ancestors of the Zunis, the Pimas, and the Papagos. The Anasazis also abandoned their great villages and built the new, smaller villages of the modern-day Pueblo (PWEB-lo) Indians.

Pueblo, the Spanish word for "town," is the name Spanish explorers gave to the Indians who lived in villages near the upper Rio Grande. Religion was the heart of village life. At the center of each village was the **kiva** (KEE-vuh), an underground room used by the men of the community for religious ceremonies.

The Pueblo men farmed much as their ancestors had done. Women cooked and made pottery and baskets. Neighboring Pueblo villages traded with one another as well as with the Apaches and Navajos, who migrated to the area from Canada about A.D. 1400.

Writing About History

Linking Past and Present. By studying fragments of history—skeletons, fossils, tools, etc.—people have tried to read the past.

Ask: What artifacts of our culture might people find 1,000 years from now? What would the artifacts reveal about the way we live?

Have students imagine that they are archaeologists in the year 3000 and write an account of twentieth-century American life based on examination of the following artifacts: pocket calculator, lawn mower, saw, shovel, carving knife, clock, hair dryer, and telephone.

Analyzing Primary Sources

Papago Rain Song. Below is a rain song of the Papago, a southwestern tribe. Read it to students and have them note the word pictures that appeal to the senses.

"Close to the west the great ocean is singing.
The waves are rolling toward me, covered with many clouds.
Even here I can catch the sound.
The earth is shaking beneath me and I hear the deep rumbling."

Ask: What word pictures appeal to the eye? **(waves rolling; clouds)** ear? **(ocean singing, earth rumbling)** sense of touch? **(earth shaking)** How does this song illustrate the Papago's closeness to nature? **(Every line in the song addresses nature and the earth.)**

Thinking Critically

Analysis. The complex culture of the Mississippian Mound Builders may have been influenced by Middle American neighbors. **Ask:** What cultural characteristics are shared by Mississippian Mound Builders and Middle Americans, such as the Mayas and Aztecs? (intensive agriculture, large cities, large monuments) How might these peoples have come in contact? (through trade)

Connections: Science and Technology

Discussion. Woodland peoples practiced land management with *slash and burn farming.* In preparing fields, they would kill the trees by stripping bark from their trunks. Then they would burn the underbrush.

Discuss the advantages and disadvantages of this method. The ashes from the fires added nutrients to the soil. Berries and grass were likely to grow on the burned ground. These plants attracted animals such as deer and bear to the area.

Today slash and burn farming is used on a much larger scale. Where the Native Americans burned small plots, today's large scale farming burns up thousands of square miles.

Ask: Where is slash and burn farming used today? How has it affected the environment? **(parts of Latin America, Asia, and Africa; it has led to deforestation and erosion)**

Social History

In many tribes of the Five Nations and in numerous other North American Indian groups, women held important social positions. They often supervised the farming, controlled the distribution of food, and owned property. European women of the time had lower status than men and fewer rights and were generally treated as inferiors.

Reduced student page in the Teacher's Edition

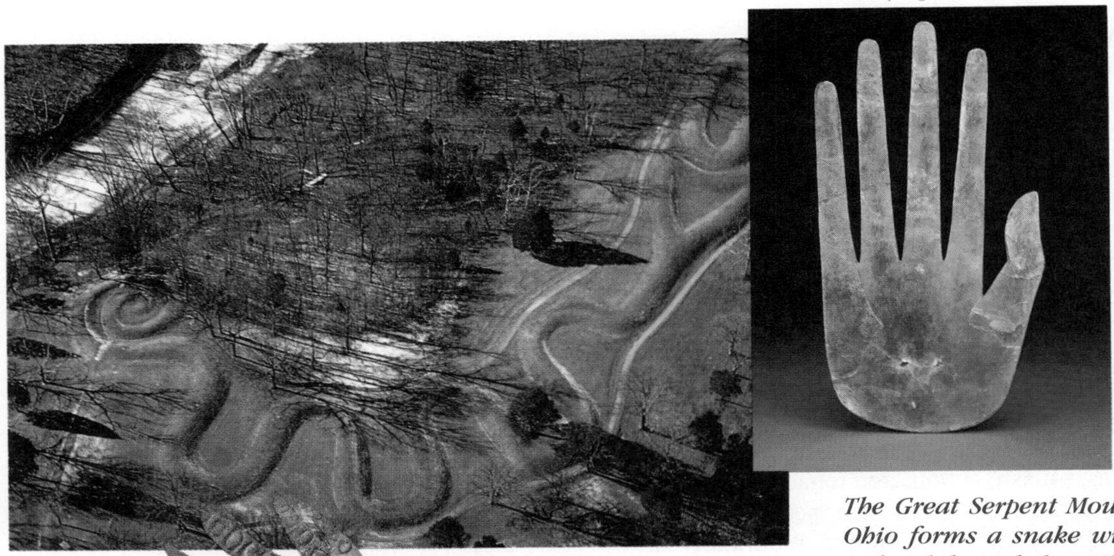

The Great Serpent Mound in Ohio forms a snake with its tail tightly coiled, at the left, and its mouth agape around a large oval ring. Burial goods from other mounds include a copper falcon, an engraved shell throat-piece, and a sheet-mica hand.

The Mound Builders

Native Americans also settled down to farm in the fertile Mississippi and Ohio valleys. About 700 B.C. the Adena culture arose in the Ohio River Valley, where the people cultivated sunflowers, squash, pumpkins, gourds, and tobacco. Their villages clustered near huge earthen mounds—the burial sites of important persons. The Adenas also built earthworks in the shapes of symbols and animals, like the 1,330-foot Great Serpent Mound in Ohio.

Hopewell culture gradually replaced the Adena after about 300 B.C. The Hopewells also built towns around burial mounds. Their mounds were rich in grave goods—items buried with the dead. Many grave goods came from afar: obsidian from the Black Hills, copper from Michigan, shells from the Gulf of Mexico, mica from the Appalachians, and alligator skulls from Florida.

Later people in the Mississippi Valley built sizeable towns around large mounds crowned with temples. A Mississippian town at Cahokia, in present-day Illinois, extended for six miles and had a population of at least 10,000 people. One of its 85 mounds covered 16 acres and was 100 feet high. The Mississippians must have traded widely, for they grew varieties of corn and beans imported from Mexico. Artisans made objects of clay, shells, mica, marble, and copper brought from great distances.

Like the early cultures of the Southwest, the Mound Builders also eventually vanished. Other tribes followed them into the valleys and wooded areas of the Southeast—the Cherokees, Creeks, Seminoles, Choctaws, and Chickasaws. These five tribes may have descended from the Mound Builders, for they had similar forms of government and farming techniques.

Woodland Farmers

Extensive agriculture like that of the Mississippi and Ohio river valleys was not possible in the dense forests to the east. Instead, people there practiced a different kind of farming. Burning trees and underbrush to create farmland, the woodland tribes

Connections: Science

The Algonquian culture is an example of Native Americans co-existing with nature. From plants and trees they derived shelter (frames for homes), clothing, storage (baskets and wood containers), fuel (firewood), transportation (dugout canoes), furniture (cradleboards), and medicines (bitterroot: chewed for sore throat; fuchsia: leaves applied to sores; gum plant: fluid used for stomach ache, poison ivy rash, toothache; watercress: leaves or juice used to treat pimples and gallstones; goldenrod: leaves boiled to clean wounds and wash sores).

raised hardier strains of corn and beans. They hunted, fished, and gathered wild plants to add to their food supply and traded with each other along canoe routes and forest trails.

Algonquian and Iroquoian tribes lived in the area extending from the Atlantic Coast to the Great Lakes and from southeastern Canada to as far south as present-day Virginia. Algonquians such as the Narragansetts, Algonkin, Massachusets, and Delawares, and Iroquoians such as the Mohawks, Eries, Iroquois, and Hurons were among the first Indians met by European explorers and settlers.

Many eastern tribes lived in villages protected by log stockades, but the longhouses of the Iroquois and Algonkin were among the most elaborate. Each sturdy, wood-framed structure housed several families. Whole villages were moved every twenty years or so as old fields became infertile.

The Five Nations. For many years Iroquoian and Algonquian tribes warred with each other. Five of the Iroquoian tribes—the Mohawks, Oneidas, Onondagas, Cayugas, and Senecas—fought both the Algonquian tribes and one another.

Around 1570 a Huron known as Peacemaker was joined by his Mohawk follower, Hiawatha, in urging an end to the wars among the Iroquoians. The five Iroquoian tribes united to form a **confederation,** or alliance of independent groups, that became known as the League of the Iroquois, or the Five Nations. The women of each tribe named the sachems (say-CHUMS), or chiefs, who made up the ruling council that met each summer to make laws and settle disputes.

Buffalo Hunters

To the west of the great woodlands, between the Mississippi River and the Rocky Mountains, lie the Great Plains—the heartland of North America. On the eastern plains the grasses were tall, and streams were lined with trees. To the west the land rose, the climate became drier, the grass grew shorter, and trees were rare. The western plains were too dry for farming. Instead, the Native Americans who lived there depended on the buffalo. Following the great herds meant a nomadic way of life for tribes such as the Kiowas and Comanches.

Buffalo hunting was done on foot, for horses were then unknown in the Americas. The hunters stampeded buffalo over a cliff, then moved in with their spears or bows and arrows. The women and children did the butchering. The meat was eaten, the hides were used for robes and cone-shaped shelters called *tepees*, and the bones were made into scrapers and knives.

Some peoples of the eastern plains, such as the Mandans, Hidatses, and Arikaras, settled along the Missouri and other rivers. The people of these village communities grew corn and beans and traded with their neighbors for buffalo meat.

The Wealth of the West

In the Pacific Northwest, warm currents swirled along the coast, creating a mild, moist climate. Here, caribou, deer, and bear roamed forests rich with roots and berries. Rivers swarmed with salmon. The abundant food supply enabled the people of the region to live in large, permanent settlements even though they were not farmers. In this rich land, the Tlingits, Kwakiutls, Chinooks, Coos, and other tribes developed complex cultures.

These plains hunters, painted by George Catlin, draped themselves in wolf skins to stalk buffalo.

Linking Past and Present

Discussion. The Huron leader, Peacemaker, had a vision in which he saw all Native Americans united, with peace throughout the world.

"I . . . and the Confederated Chiefs now uproot the tallest pine tree, and into the cavity thereby made we cast all weapons of war. Into the depths of the earth, deep down into the underearth currents of water flowing to unknown regions, we cast all weapons of strife. We bury them from sight and plant again the tree. Thus shall the great Peace be established."

Discuss Peacemaker's words. Have students name present-day movements that echo Peacemaker's vision—disarmament, pacifism, anti-nuclear protests, for example. Do students think any of these movements will produce lasting changes?

Global Connections

Discussion. In the 1500s the Spanish brought horses to North America. Some escaped to the plains. At first, the Plains people called the wild horses "mystery dogs." They quickly learned how to tame them and used them for hunting and carrying supplies.

Horses became signs of wealth and position. People who had to travel on foot were considered inferior to those who had horses to ride.

Ask: Do people today feel the same about any of their possessions?

Limited English Proficiency

Cooperative Activity. Have students work in small groups to find information about one of the regions discussed in the section. Each group should record information about the climate, plant and animal life, geographical features, etc., that distinguish the region. Have a spokesperson for each group report the group's findings to the class.

Ask: What changes in daily life might students have to make if they moved to one of these regions? Lead them to consider how environment influenced the ways of life developed by early American peoples.

Writing About History

Poetry. Read the following Yokut poem to students:

My words are tied in one with the great mountains,
With the great rocks, with the great trees,
In one with my body and my heart.
Do you all help me with supernatural power,
And you, day, and you, night!
All of you see me one with this world.

Ask students to cite references to nature in the poem. How do they know the writer valued the relationship between nature and people?

Have students write poems describing the beauty of the land where they live, their feelings about nature, or ways that people can better appreciate nature.

Multicultural Perspectives

The word *totem* is from central Algonquian for "family" or "clan." Totem poles were carved for many reasons. Some blended myth and history to depict the history of the family that owned it. Others were erected to commemorate the dead. Some told of important historical events. A totem might even serve to ridicule or shame a scoundrel.

Reduced student page in the Teacher's Edition

These people were skilled carpenters who built large wood-planked houses using tools of stone and sharp-edged seashells. Elaborately carved door posts called *totems* displayed the symbols of the family—the animal spirits of their clan. They also built large dugout canoes to reach trading partners and to follow schools of halibut and cod.

The Native Americans who lived in this land often held winter festivals called **potlatches**—ceremonies during which they celebrated abundance by giving away their wealth as gifts. The festivity included a feast that sometimes went on for days. At the feast, the hosts showered their guests with blankets, furs, canoes, and sometimes even slaves captured from enemy tribes. A family's rank and prestige were judged by how much wealth it could give away.

California and the Great Basin. To the south, in California, with its warm summers and mild winters, food was nearly as abundant as in the Pacific Northwest. Oak trees grew nearly everywhere, and their acorns were a main source of food for the Hupas, Pomos, Chumashes, and other semi-nomadic groups. Their diet of acorns, pounded into flour for bread and mush, was supplemented by small game, fish, and berries.

In the Great Basin country to the east of California, survival was more difficult. The land was too dry for farming and game animals. The people of the Great Basin—the Paiutes, Shoshones, and Utes—roamed in small bands, gathering wild plants and catching small animals.

The Frozen North

In the subarctic region of the far north, a vast forested land of chilly summers and bitterly cold winters, the weather was too harsh for farming. But the forest was teeming with game—caribou, moose, bear, and smaller animals.

Most of the people in this region, such as the Crees, Chipewyans, and Kaskas, were nomadic, traveling in small groups to hunt, fish, and gather wild plants. These subarctic peoples used the bones, sinews, and hides of animals to fashion sleds, toboggans, and snowshoes. They glided along the rivers and lakes in canoes of birch bark.

Southeast: Devil mask, Cherokee.

Arctic: Bubbles mask, Eskimo.

Each Native-American group had a unique tradition, but cultures within a region were similar, influenced by the land and its resources.

North of the dense forests—at the northernmost edge of the continent—is the Arctic, a land of vast frozen plains called tundra. Here lived the Eskimos, or Inuits, and Aleuts, who may have been the last Native Americans to cross the Bering Strait into North America, arriving about 6000 B.C.

The Eskimos and Aleuts had no organized governments. Instead, they lived by rules of conduct, and the most important rule was that everyone cooperate in order to survive.

Most Arctic people spent part of the year near the sea or inland lakes, hunting seals with harpoons and fishing with spears and hooks made of bone. The people lived in igloos—dome-shaped houses made of tundra or blocks of snow. In summer they often followed caribou across the tundra.

Native American Culture

Although the different groups of Native Americans developed distinct clothing, tools, foods, shelter, customs, and languages, there were—and con-

Active Learning

Cooperative Activity. Divide students into five groups. Tell one group of students to imagine they are members of the mound builders culture; one group, woodland farmers; one group, buffalo hunters; one group, tribes of the Northwest; and one group, people of the Arctic. Suggest that each group choose a recorder.

Have students make a list of the skills they would need to survive as members of the culture. Then each group should write an account of a typical day. The recorder may read the list and the account to the class.

The Art Institute of Chicago

Southwest: Kachina figure.

Native American Culture Areas

Northwest: Sun mask, Bella Coola.

Northeast: Corn husk mask, Seneca.

tinue to be—similarities among the different tribes. Most share a belief in a creator. Some call this creator "Giver of Breath." Others call it "Great Spirit" or "Grandfather." All these terms refer to a spiritual being who is the giver of life.

Religion is a part of daily life. A woman who makes and decorates a pot with symbols of water is reminded that the water she carries in the pot is a gift of the Great Spirit. In this way, her religion, art, and daily life become entwined.

Another similarity is in attitudes toward the relationship between humans and nature. Native Americans tend to see themselves as part of the community of plants, animals, and other natural objects. They believe that each person shares the task of maintaining the balance in nature. To this day, the Lakota People of the Great Plains express this belief by ending their prayers with a phrase that means "we are all related."

Native American traditions have been passed from generation to generation orally—through songs and stories based on a tribe's myths and legends. These songs and stories have taught Indian children how to live. Today many of the legends are still being told and the songs are still being sung, passing on knowledge gained in the past.

Section Review

1. Identification. Define *pueblo, kiva, confederation,* and *potlatch.*

2. Comprehension. Explain how the ancestors of the American Indians came to North America.

3. Analysis. In what ways did the different environments of North America lead to diverse ways of life?

4. Synthesis. At one archaeological site, bits of pottery, the foundation of a large stone building, and traces of an irrigation canal have been found. How do you know that the people who lived here were not nomads?

5. Comprehension. Explain two religious ideas shared by many different Native Americans.

Section Review

ANSWERS

1. Definitions for the following terms are on text pages indicated in parentheses: *pueblo* (25), *kiva* (25), *confederation* (27), *potlatch* (28).
2. Came from Asia across a land bridge.
3. Farming cultures developed in fertile valleys and along rivers; hunters and gatherers lived where extensive agriculture was not possible because of climate or geography; more complex cultures developed where abundant food supply allowed permanent settlements.
4. They were not nomads because evidence of agriculture, pottery making, and permanent shelter.
5. Answers may include that Native Americans shared belief in a creator and in humans' relation to nature; religion was part of daily life.

Section 2-2

Objectives

- ***Answer the Focus Question.***
- *Cite evidence that indicates Asians, Africans, or Europeans may have reached the Americas before Columbus.*
- *Identify major European explorers and their achievements.*
- *Explain the significance of the Treaty of Tordesillas.*

Introducing THE SECTION

In the early 1500s Portuguese and Spanish explorers came into contact with the inhabitants of the Americas. Have students speculate about what ideas and ways of life Europeans and Native Americans might have introduced to each other.

B · A · C · K · G · R · O · U · N · D

Connections: Literature
Starting in 1271, seventeen-year-old Marco Polo, with his father and uncle, journeyed by ship and then by camel from Venice to China. They reached the court of Kubla Khan in 1274. Returning to Europe at the age of forty-one, Polo wrote about the Chinese use of coal for heat, and their paper money, public carriages, and street drains—all ideas new to Europeans at that time.

Polo's original manuscript of *Description of the World* has not survived. However, about 120 hand-copied versions, with many variations, have been found in Italian, French, and other languages.

2-2 *The Explorers*

Focus: What events led to European contact with the Americas?

In ancient times, Roman and Egyptian rulers wore silks imported from China. People in China and Southeast Asia practiced religions that had come to them from India. Mediterranean mariners traded with peoples on the Atlantic coast of Africa. Then the world's great empires declined, and the links between Europe, Asia, and Africa grew weaker.

In fact, from the fifth to the fourteenth centuries, the peoples of Europe, Asia, and Africa knew little about each other— let alone about people living in the Americas. And Native Americans knew little or nothing about the rest of the earth's people. Then, in 1492, Christopher Columbus sailed to the Americas. His voyages were the beginning of European explorations and conquests that changed the history of the world forever.

Contacts with the Americas Before 1492

Other people may have reached the Americas before Christopher Columbus. Evidence uncovered by archaeologists raises interesting questions about them but does not always provide firm answers. For example, evidence shows that about 2500 B.C. people living along the coast of Ecuador suddenly began to make a fine pottery unlike any they had made before. No one around them shaped clay in this way. At the time, pottery of the same type was made at only one other place— southern Japan. Had Japanese ships sailed as far as Ecuador?

The appearance of colossal stone heads in a sacred Olmec city around 600 B.C. also raises questions. The facial features of these heads look much like the features of sub-Saharan Africans. Did a Libyan or Ethiopian ship carrying an African crew land on the eastern shores of Mexico centuries ago, leaving behind an echo of Africa?

People who study America before Columbus are sharply divided on these questions. At the present time, however, the strongest case can be made for the Vikings— daring, seafaring Scandinavians.

For centuries, the Vikings told a tale of Leif Ericson and his voyage to a mysterious land somewhere across the stormy Atlantic. About A.D. 1000, he and his sea-weary sailors reached a land where "they found wild wheat . . . and grape vines." They named the land Vinland, "land of grapes."

Several years later, Viking colonists tried to settle in Vinland. But people whom the Vikings called "Skraelings" soon drove them away. Eventually the land was forgotten except in the sagas told on long winter evenings.

Then in 1963 evidence of Viking homes dating from the year 1000 was uncovered in Newfoundland. The discovery shows that the Vinland saga was probably based on fact.

If voyagers did come to the Americas from Europe, Africa, or Asia in the centuries before Columbus's "discovery," they did not stay long and their effect on Native American cultures is unknown. Not until Europeans reached the Americas in the fifteenth century did outsiders significantly change Native American ways of life.

Had the Olmecs who shaped the stone head (near left) seen features like those on the sculpture from Benin, in Africa?

Connections: Geography

Upon his return home, Bartholomew Días wanted to call the southern tip of Africa the Cape of Storms. However, the Portuguese king, certain that a sea route to the Indies could now be found, named it the Cape of Good Hope.

Connections: Technology

Exploration of the Americas was made possible by several advances in technology. The magnetic compass, first used by the Chinese, was widely used in navigation by the 1100s. The sternpost rudder, a flat piece of wood attached to the rear of the ship made steering easier. A third innovation, the triangular sail, could be turned easily, making it possible to sail both with and into the wind.

In Description of the World, *Marco Polo wrote of his amazing travels in China from 1274 to 1292. The book awakened European interest in the splendors of Asia.*

The Lure of the "Indies"

The European explorers of the 1400s found the Americas unexpectedly. They were searching for routes to the "Indies," as they called the Asian lands of China, India, and the East Indies islands.

Europeans knew little about the Indies. For centuries, Arab rulers had controlled the routes to Asia. They brought the gold, pepper, ginger, cloves, perfumes, and silks of the Indies by ship and camel caravan to Mediterranean ports. Soon, European merchants began to look for ways to trade directly with the Indies. Since overland routes were closed to them, they began to wonder if they could reach the Indies by sea.

The Portuguese Explorations

By the late 1400s, four unified nations had emerged in western Europe— Spain, Portugal, France, and England. The rulers of these nations realized that by expanding trade with Africa and the Indies, they could increase their national wealth and power. Thus, they were eager to support voyages of exploration and to set up trading outposts.

The first European ruler to encourage exploration was Prince Henry of Portugal. In 1418 he founded a school of navigation, gathering together many of Europe's best sea captains, map makers, and shipbuilders. Year after year Prince Henry's ships pushed cautiously southward along the west coast of Africa. The ships returned to Lisbon laden with ivory, gold, and enslaved Africans.

Prince Henry died in 1460, but the Portuguese pressed on along the seemingly endless African coastline. Finally, in 1488 Bartholomeu Dias (DEE-ahs) rounded the southern tip of Africa and sailed into the unfamiliar Indian Ocean. Fearing the unknown, Dias's crew forced him to return home.

In 1497 another Portuguese captain, Vasco da Gama, followed Dias's route and then ventured across the Indian Ocean to India. Da Gama returned to Portugal more than two years later with only 44 of his original crew of 170. However, the hold of his ship was filled with spices and jewels. Keeping the route a secret, the Portuguese built trading posts from India to the Spice Islands.

The Voyages of Columbus

Despite the veil of secrecy cloaking the Portuguese voyages, other Europeans knew of their search for an eastern route to the Indies. Meanwhile, an Italian navigator, Christopher Columbus, thought

Developing

THE SECTION

Active Learning

Cooperative Activity. Tell students that European traders began arriving in Africa in the mid-1400s. Some African rulers allowed the Europeans to influence the trade and even governments of their kingdoms. Others chose to control European trade.

Divide students into small groups to research an African state that existed at about the time that Europeans began to trade with Africans. Such states include Bornu, Songhai, Kongo, Luba, Lunda, Rwanda, Buganda, Benin, Oyo, Zimbabwe, Mwenemutapa, and the Hausa city-states.

Have each group prepare a written report and a display about the state, its natural resources, people, art, literature, and response to European traders.

GTV Side 1

Chap. 4, Frame 11056

Columbus' Voyage, 1492 (Animated Map)

Search and Play:

Writing About History

Diary Entry. Ask students to imagine themselves as Columbus or a member of his crew. Have them write a diary entry for one day during the first voyage. The entry might deal with Columbus calming his crew's fears or with the day when land was first sighted.

Multicultural Perspectives

Discussion. Refer students to Columbus's description of his landing on San Salvador. Discuss his interpretation of the Taino's reaction to the explorer's arrival. **(He thought the Tainos were happy to see Columbus and his party and that they thanked God.)** Ask students to speculate about what the Tainos might really have been thinking.

Thinking Critically

Synthesis. Columbus kept two journals of his journey. One showed his best guess about the distance he and his crew had traveled. The second, the one he showed his crew, gave a much shorter distance. What might have been his motives?

B · A · C · K · G · R · O · U · N · D

Using the Visuals

No portraits were ever made of Columbus in his lifetime. Fifty years after his death, when the significance of his voyages became apparent, likenesses of the Admiral were created by the hundreds. Of course, by then, no one could be certain what Columbus looked like.

His son Ferdinand reported that his father "was a well-made man, of a height above the medium, with a long face, and cheekbones somewhat prominent; neither too fat nor too lean. He had an aquiline [hooked] nose, light-colored eyes, and a ruddy complexion."

Many scholars believe the portrait shown on this page most closely corresponds to written accounts.

that he could reach the Indies by sailing westward around the earth.

Columbus sought backing from Spain in 1485. Because she was eager to expand Spanish power, Queen Isabella listened to Columbus. But the Spanish were engaged in a war to drive out the North Africans who ruled southern Spain. Not until this war ended in 1492 did Isabella agree to Columbus's proposal.

The Spanish king and queen gave Columbus supplies and three caravels—the *Niña, Pinta*, and *Santa María*. On August 3, 1492, Columbus set out from Spain into the Atlantic, the "sea of pitchy darkness." Columbus kept two records of the voyage. His own secret record showed the actual distances traveled. The other showed shorter distances so the crew would not be alarmed at how far they had come. Even so, some of the crew began to demand that the expedition turn back.

Finally, on October 12, a lookout yelled, "Land! Land!" The land sighted was a small island in the Bahamas, probably the one known today as Samana Cay. Columbus named it San Salvador, Spanish for "Blessed Savior."

Here, for the first time, the European explorers met inhabitants of the Americas. They were the Tainos, a farming people of the Caribbean islands. Believing he was in the Indies, Columbus called the Tainos "Indians." Columbus wrote:

> *"[We] went along the island on a north-northeast course in order to see the other part, which was the eastern part, and also in order to see the settlements. And I saw then two or three, and the people who all came to the beach calling us and giving thanks to God."*

Columbus and his men sailed further into the Caribbean, sighting Cuba, which they thought was Japan, and another island they called Hispaniola, "Little Spain." Columbus returned to Spain as a hero. The Spanish court buzzed with excitement. Soon a hopeful king and queen sent Columbus back with a grand fleet of seventeen ships and orders to establish a colony and find China.

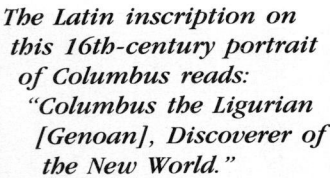

The Latin inscription on this 16th-century portrait of Columbus reads: "Columbus the Ligurian [Genoan], Discoverer of the New World."

Columbus planted a colony on Hispaniola but discovered neither spices nor China. On a third voyage, some colonists seized his ships and returned to Spain to complain of his rule of the colony. Ferdinand and Isabella had Columbus brought home in chains, but he pleaded for a last chance. The king and queen finally agreed.

In 1502 Columbus set out again. This time he combed the coast of Central America, searching in vain for a passage to the Indian Ocean. He spent his last years in Spain, disappointed yet stubbornly claiming that he had reached the Indies.

The Treaty of Tordesillas

To fifteenth-century Europeans it seemed perfectly natural for Spain to claim lands inhabited by other people. They believed that the Pope, being Jesus Christ's representative, "has power not only over Christians, but also over infidels. For all, the faithful and infidels alike, are the sheep of Christ." Therefore, they reasoned, the Pope had the power to assign to Christian kings and queens any lands not already ruled by Christians.

Because they planned to spread Christianity as they explored, Spain and Portugal turned to the Pope for help in dividing any newly discovered lands. In 1494 the two countries signed the Treaty of Tordesillas (TOR-deh-SEE-yahs). Under this treaty, an imaginary line was drawn through the Atlantic from north to south. The Pope gave Spain the right to all lands west of the line, while all lands to the east were to belong to Portugal.

In 1500, sailing under the Portuguese flag, Pedro Alvares Cabral set out to follow Vasco da Gama's route to India. Blown off course, Cabral landed on the part of South America that bulges out into the Atlantic to within only about 2,600 miles of Africa.

Connections: Language

Many English terms related to commerce are derived from the languages of the western Asian and northern African merchants who dominated trade routes to India and China during Europe's Middle Ages. From Persian we get *bazaar*, *caravan*, and *check*; from Arabic, *tariff*, *magazine* (meaning "storehouse"), *admiral*, and *algebra*; and from Sanskrit by way of Arabic, *cipher* and *zero*.

Thinking Critically

Evaluation. Have students agree or disagree with this statement and support their opinions with evidence: The times were right for Europeans to find the Americas. If Columbus had not, someone else would have. (Students should consider European interest in direct trade with Asia and European rivalry for power and wealth.)

Global Connections

Debate. Have students debate the right of European nations to claim any part of the Americas as their own. One side should support the Europeans' notion that they had the right; the other side should oppose this notion.

That land was east of the Pope's imaginary line and thus in Portugal's area. Now Portugal, too, had a claim in the Americas—Brazil.

The Americas, Lands Unknown

In the report Cabral sent back to Portugal he suggested planting a settlement in Brazil, if for no other reason "than to have a stopping place for the voyage to Calicut," in India. A sea route to Asia was still the prize that lured the Portuguese and the Spanish, not the lands that they had found.

John Cabot also dreamed of getting to Asia—particularly Japan, where, according to a friend, "he believes that all the spices of the world have their origin, as well as the jewels." Cabot turned to Henry VII of England, who, with some merchants, agreed to sponsor the expedition.

In 1497 Cabot landed at either Newfoundland or Labrador. On a second voyage, he explored the coastline as far south as New England. There, in the manner of Europeans of the time, "he hoisted the royal standard and took possession for the king." Like Columbus, Cabot believed that he had reached Asia. However, his voyage established an English claim to lands north of Spain's discoveries.

News of the Atlantic voyages spread rapidly. Europeans speculated about the lands the seafarers had reached, and maps of the day show their confusion. Land masses are sketchily drawn and labeled *Terra Incognito*, or "lands unknown." Amerigo Vespucci (ves-POO-chee), an Italian who had sailed along the South American coast aboard a Spanish ship, put a name to these lands. "These parts we may rightly call a New World," Vespucci wrote in a widely published letter. When a German geographer drew a map of this new world, he gave it the Latin version of Vespucci's name—Americus. The name took hold, and Europeans began to call their new world "America."

American Voices

"They found a trail that went inland, they saw a site where a fire had been made, . . . and they saw a stick half a yard long pierced at both ends, carved and painted . . ., and by such signs they believe the land to be inhabited."

—John Day to Columbus, 1497, on the voyage of Cabot

A Sea Route to Asia

In 1510 the Spanish built a colony in Panama, the narrow isthmus that joins Central and South America. For the colony's sake, Governor Vasco Núñez de Balboa (bal-BO-ah) sought the favor of Comaco, a local chieftain, by helping him against his enemies. When Comaco gave the Spaniards a pile of gold in return, his son scattered the gold in disgust, saying:

"If your hunger of gold be so insatiable that only for the desire [for gold] . . . you disquiet so many nations, . . . I will show you a region flowing with gold, where you may satisfy your ravening appetites."

Comaco's son then told of ships that sailed a great sea to the west.

Balboa organized an expedition of Spaniards and Indians. For weeks, they struggled through steaming, snake-infested jungles, hacking a path across Panama. Finally, from the summit of a mountain, they looked down on "the other sea." A few days later Balboa—clad in full armor—planted the Spanish flag on the shore. He named the ocean the South Sea and claimed it and all of the lands bordering it for Spain.

Around the world. Balboa's discovery proved to the Europeans that they had not yet reached the Indies. Ferdinand Magellan (muh-JEHL-uhn) was convinced, however, that this South Sea would lead them there. Unable to gain support in his native Portugal, Magellan, like Columbus, turned to Portugal's rival, Spain, to sponsor his voyage.

With five old ships and more than two hundred sailors, Magellan set sail from Spain in September of 1519. The small fleet moved slowly down the coast of Brazil, seeking a passage to the South Sea.

Thinking Critically

Evaluation. Ask students to agree or disagree with this statement: Until about 1500 the Atlantic Ocean had been a barrier, an end. Then it became a bridge, a starting place. Have them use evidence from the map and the text to support their opinions.

Geography Skills

ANSWERS

Asia, Africa, North and South America.

Writing About History

Letter. In the 1400s Europeans thought that there were four continents, possibly connected—Europe, Africa, Asia, and a huge land mass somewhere in the Southern Hemisphere called *Terra Australis Incognita*, or "Unknown Southern lands."

They also thought that the earth contained more land than water, that Asia and Africa were connected and surrounded the Indian Ocean, and that the earth was about 18,000 miles in circumference.

For each 10-year period from 1480 to 1520, have students write letters from a voyager to a mapmaker telling how to correct the world map. **(Notes may include descriptions and dates of various explorations such as 1488: Dias; 1492: Columbus; 1497: Cabot.)**

Connections: Science and Technology

Prevailing winds, winds caused by the circulation of air around the earth, were a factor in navigating the Atlantic Ocean. They almost always blow from the same direction and travel long distances.

Columbus traveled from northeast to southwest. In his path, north of the equator, prevailing winds blow from the northeast to the southwest. These "northeast trade winds" literally blew Columbus's ships from Spain to the Caribbean Islands.

Getting back to Europe was more difficult. In time, navigators found "prevailing westerlies" farther north along the Atlantic coast of North America. They blew from a westerly direction, carrying ships from North America to Europe.

Reduced student page in the Teacher's Edition

European Voyages of Exploration 1487-1522

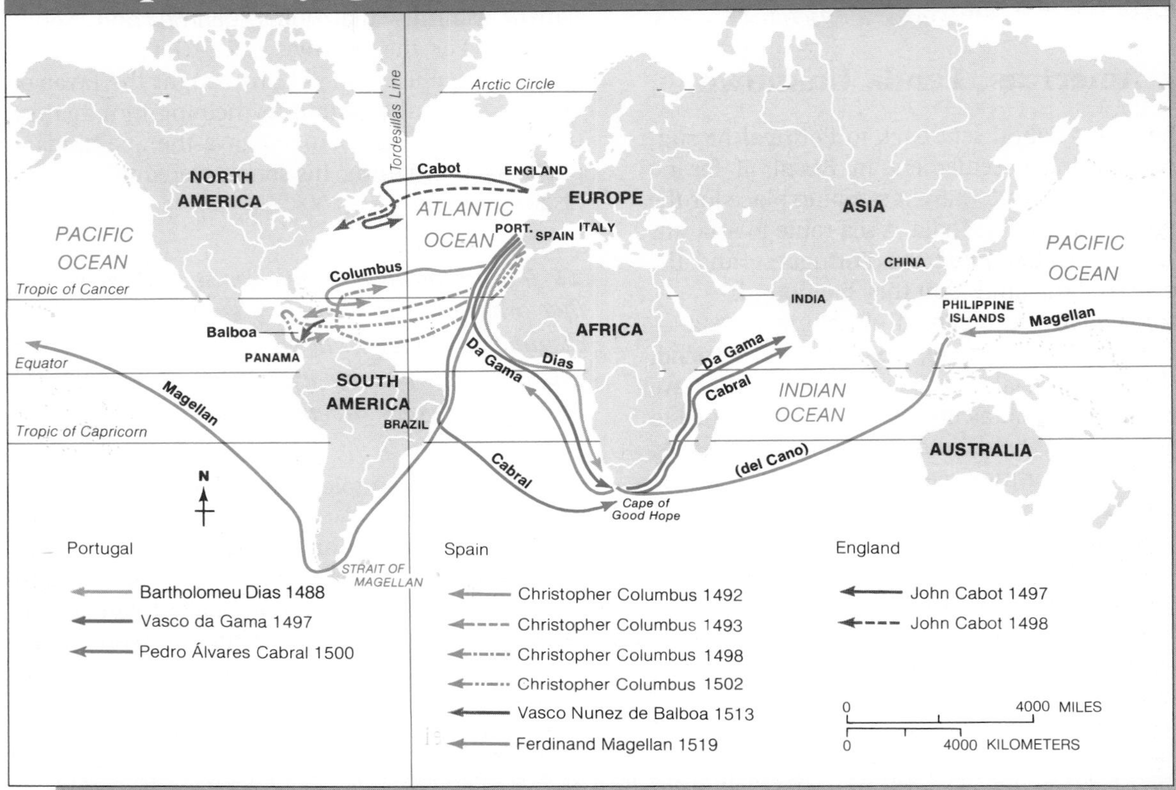

Geography Skills—Movement: The European voyages of exploration led to a gradual spread of European influence. Judging from the routes of early explorers, which continents were most likely to be affected?

Along the way one ship was wrecked, another was taken over by mutineers, and Magellan discovered that he was running out of food.

Yet, in October 1520, Magellan finally found the route he was seeking. Fighting fierce winds, for six desperate weeks Magellan and his crew threaded a course through the rocky 334-mile passage that now bears the name Strait of Magellan. At last, they emerged into Balboa's sea. It was so peaceful that Magellan renamed it the Pacific. The crews set a course for China, and in the vastness of the ocean, one torrid day melted into the next. One of the crew described their hardships:

> *"The biscuit we were eating no longer deserved the name of bread; it was nothing but dust and worm. The water . . . was putrid and offensive. We were even so far reduced to eat pieces of leather, sawdust, and even mice that sold for half a ducat [a coin] apiece."*

It was more than three months before they found an island with fresh water and fruit. Then they pushed on to the Philippines, where they were caught in a local war. After sailing nearly around the world, Magellan died in the clash. "They killed

Global Connections
Samuel de Champlain traveled with a Spanish convoy to the West Indies, Mexico, and Panama between 1599 and 1601. He was one of the first to propose that a canal be built across Panama.

our mirror, our light, our comfort, and our true guide," one of his crew said.

The remaining sailors escaped in two ships. One was captured by the Portuguese. The other, under Juan Sebastián del Cano, finally reached the Indies, took on a load of spices, then followed da Gama's route around Africa to Europe. In September 1522, three years after leaving Spain, the ship *Victoria* returned. The eighteen sailors on board were the first Europeans to circle the earth.

The voyage ended any doubts that America was indeed a new world to the Europeans. And it showed that the earth was far larger than Columbus had believed.

The Search for a Northwest Passage

Magellan had found a way to Asia by sailing west from Europe. But the difficulty of Magellan's voyage led other explorers to look northward for a better route to Asia.

In 1524 France, joining the European search for the wealth of the Indies, sent Giovanni da Verrazano (VER-eh-TSAH-nō), an Italian sea captain, to seek a Northwest Passage. Verrazano searched from the Carolinas to Newfoundland. He found no promising water routes, but he did claim land for France.

Ten years later, French explorer Jacques Cartier (KAR-TYAY) continued the search for a Northwest Passage. Despite ice floes and heavy fog, he negotiated the Gulf of St. Lawrence, and on his second trip he followed the St. Lawrence River far inland. "As far as the eye can reach, one sees that river large, wide, and swift," he wrote, hoping it would lead to China.

Cartier and his crew returned to France with ten Native Americans they had kidnapped. The Indians' stories, furs, and bits of copper raised French interest in trade with North America.

The riches of North America. Many European explorers followed Cartier, still seeking the passage they believed existed. They were often defeated by the fog and ice of harsh Arctic winters, but their voyages added to the map makers' knowledge of North America. Furthermore, they began to discover the riches of the continent—the furs, fish, fruits, forests, harbors, and streams.

In 1609 English explorer Henry Hudson, sailing for the Dutch East India Company, explored New York harbor and a broad river flowing into it. In his ship, the *Half Moon*, he sailed up the river until it narrowed abruptly. Once more, hope for the Northwest Passage was dashed. However, he claimed the lands bordering the river for the Dutch. The crew of the *Half Moon* found the Indians willing to trade furs for metal goods, and soon a Dutch company had set up a thriving trade.

Samuel de Champlain (sham-PLAYN) established French trade in North America. Energetic and endlessly curious, he made eleven trips between 1603 and his death in Canada in 1635. In 1608 he founded Quebec as a fur-trading post.

While some explorers sought wealth or a Northwest Passage, others had different ideas for the Western Hemisphere. "We might inhabit some part of those countries," said English explorer Sir Humphrey Gilbert, "and settle there such needy people of our country which now trouble the commonwealth." Indeed, Portugal, England, France, and the Netherlands were all considering establishing colonies in the Americas. All three, though, lagged far behind their powerful neighbor, Spain.

Section Review

1. Comprehension. What evidence is there that Asians, Africans, or other Europeans may have reached the Americas before Columbus?

2. Analysis. Explain the importance of the voyages led by each of the following explorers: Da Gama, Cabot, Magellan, Cartier.

3. Comprehension. Why did Europeans claim lands already occupied by Native Americans?

4. Synthesis. Agree or disagree with this statement: During the 1500s, the reasons Europeans had for exploring the Americas changed. Support your answer with examples.

Linking Past and Present. Many place names in the United States have Spanish or French origins. List ten Spanish or French place names and tell the location of each. What conclusions can you draw from the locations of the places on your list?

Linking Past and Present

Activity. A bridge in New York City that connects Brooklyn and Staten Island, is named after Verrazano. Have students use an atlas or a geographical dictionary to discover what other places are named after explorers. Examples: Champlain **(a lake between Vermont and New York)**; Hudson **(a river in New York; a bay in Canada)**

Section Review

ANSWERS

1. Archaeological evidence, such as pottery similar to Japan's in Ecuador about 2500 B.C.; African-looking stone heads in an Olmec city around 600 B.C.; Viking homes dating to 100 B.C. in Newfoundland.
2. Da Gama: first European to reach India wholly by sea; Cabot: established first English claim in "New World"; Magellan: his crew were first Europeans to circle the earth; Cartier: stirred French interest in establishing trade in North America.
3. Europeans believed the Pope had power to assign rulers over lands not ruled by Christians.
4. During the 1500s Europeans were still seeking a sea route to Asia; for example, Verrazano, Cartier, Hudson sought a northwest passage.
Linking Past and Present: Answers will vary. Students may conclude these places were first established by French or Spanish explorers.

Connections: Economics

Using the Visuals. Refer students to the illustration of the Secotan village on this page. This drawing by John White shows cornfields in various stages of growth. Have students identify how the economy of the settlement is represented. **(Hunters shown at upper left; corn, squash, and pumpkin raised as crops.)**

Global Connections

Before European contact, Native Americans of the Northeast, Subarctic, Northwest Coast, and Great Plains used specially prepared porcupine quills as well as shells and feathers to decorate clothing, bags, arrow quivers, pipes, and other articles.

Starting about 1675, eastern Indians began decorating with European glass beads that they had received in trade. The beadwork technique gradually spread to other parts of the continent where quillwork had developed.

Thomas Gilcrease Institute, Tulsa, Oklahoma

Secotan villagers reaped bountiful harvests from their fields of corn, beans, peas, and pumpkins.

National Museum of the American Indian/SI

This Cherokee basket, woven of river cane, was used for storage.

The color of porcupine quills on this southeastern Ojibwa pouch is from indigo.

Porcupine quills, softened in water and dyed, decorate Sioux moccasins.

Multicultural Perspectives

North American Indians played two basic kinds of games: those of chance and gambling—dice, guessing games, and hand games—and those requiring skill and dexterity—archery, spear throwing, racing, juggling, chunkey (played with a ring and pole), shinney (played with a ball and stick).

Native-American children also had a variety of toys—dolls were common, as well as boats, sleds, bows and arrows, balls, blocks, tops, stilts, and string for cat's cradles.

Connections: Science and Technology

Using the Visuals. Have students cite ways that the objects and illustrations on these two pages are evidence that Native Americans adapted to their environments. **(Native Americans utilized natural materials for clothing and other practical objects, transportation, and entertainment.)**

GTV Side 1

Chap. 4, Frame 10927

Land of Opportunity (Movie)

Search:

Play:

THE CREATIVE *Spirit*

Native Americans

Native Americans can be thought of as the first pioneers of the Americas. When Europeans reached North America, Native Americans shared with them the results of thousands of years of experience on the continent.

In order to survive, the colonists turned to the crops that Indians had grown for centuries, often using Indian methods of planting and cultivation. Most important was Indian corn, which appeared on the table in some form at practically every meal. Europeans also fed corn to their horses, mules, oxen, hogs, and poultry.

In addition, colonists benefited from Native-American medicines, smoked Indian clay pipes, and used Indian pottery, baskets, and mats in their homes. They also adopted elements of Indian dress, traveled in Indian canoes, and lived at times in Indian-style housing.

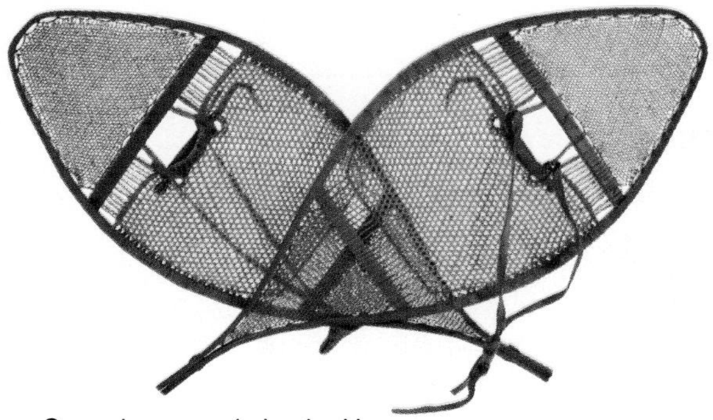

Snowshoes, made by the Hurons, made winter travel easier.

Each lacrosse player used two webbed sticks to gain control of the ball.

Lacrosse developed from an Indian game in which players tried to fling a ball into the opposing team's goal. Hundreds of warriors took part.

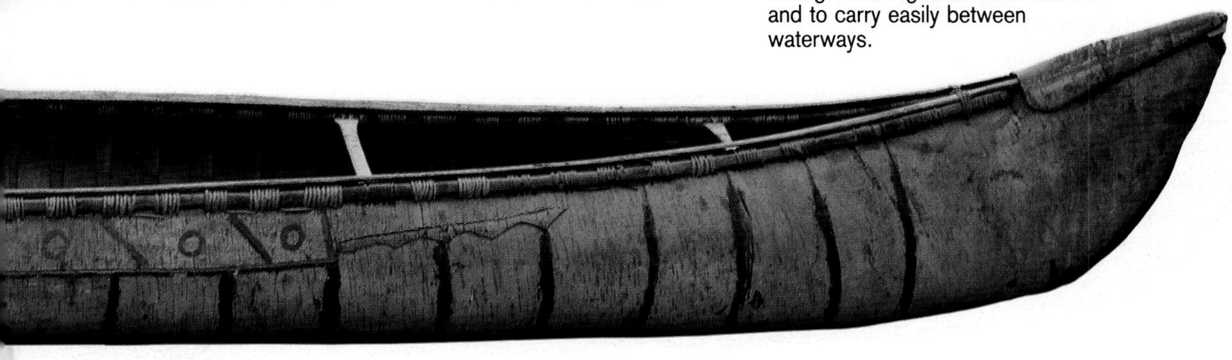

A Penobscot bark canoe was light enough to navigate shallow streams and to carry easily between waterways.

Section 2-3

Objectives

- ***Answer the Focus Question.***
- *Cite Spain's goals in the Americas.*
- *Discuss how Spanish settlement affected Native Americans.*
- *Explain why the English established American colonies.*

Introducing

THE SECTION

Tell students that Hernando Cortés was one of the first Spanish conquerors in the Americas. Cortés told a Mexican noble that he had come to the Americas because *"the Spaniards are troubled with a disease of the heart for which gold is the specific remedy."*

As students read this section, have them find evidence that either supports or refutes Cortés's statement.

Multicultural Perspectives

Cortés acquired the services of a valuable interpreter—Malinche—the daughter of an Aztec chief. Sold into slavery to the Mayans after her father's death, she was presented as a peace offering to Cortés. Malinche, whom the Spanish named Dona Marina when she became a Christian, knew many languages, and served Cortés as an interpreter, guide, and diplomatic representative.

The Mexican attitude toward Malinche is mixed. On the one hand, she is seen as a traitor to her people for helping foreign invaders conquer the Aztec empire. Another view is that Malinche was a heroine for urging Cortés to treat her people leniently. Whatever Malinche's true role, Cortés rewarded her with a large estate north of Mexico City.

Reduced student page in the Teacher's Edition

2-3 The Conquerors

Focus: How did Spanish conquerors bring their way of life to the Americas?

Spain planted its first lasting settlement in the Americas in 1493. In that year, Spanish settlers arrived on the island they called Hispaniola, where they established sugar plantations. Soon they began to bring enslaved Africans to work the plantations. From Hispaniola, the Spaniards conquered and settled Cuba and Puerto Rico.

These colonies were just the first Spanish footholds in the Americas. Other Spanish colonies were to follow, and for the next hundred years Spanish explorers, settlers, and priests were to be the dominant European presence in the Americas.

For God, Gold, and Glory

Spanish conquest of the North American mainland began in 1519. One day a runner brought news to Moctezuma II, ruler of the Aztecs. Pale, bearded strangers were marching from the east toward Tenochtitlán, heart of the Aztec empire. According to Aztec legend, the white-skinned god Quetzalcoatl was to come from that direction to claim the Aztec empire for his own. Moctezuma sent messengers bearing gifts—game birds, fruit, and chocolate—and a plea to Quetzalcoatl to stay away. The strangers, however, kept coming.

The people Moctezuma's messenger had seen were not gods but an army of five hundred Spanish soldiers. Their leader, Hernando Cortés, was one of the first of the ***conquistadores*** (kohn-KEES-tah-dor-ehs), the Spanish adventurers who conquered large parts of the Americas in the 1500s.

By the time Cortés landed with his army on the coast of Mexico, he had already heard about Moctezuma and his wealthy empire. Cortés's duty seemed clear to him: to bring the Christian faith to the Native Americans; to acquire wealth, especially gold, for the Spanish treasury; and to add to Spain's power and prestige by claiming new lands. God, gold, and glory, then, were his goals. Cortés ordered his own fleet burned. There would be no turning back.

Cortés and his army struggled through 500 miles of jungles and mountains. At every settlement along the way, Cortés destroyed images of gods and replaced them with Christian altars. The Indians whose gods Cortés smashed were not Aztec, and many of them were ready to rebel against their powerful Aztec neighbors. Sometimes through persuasion and sometimes through battle, Cortés made allies of one group of dissatisfied Indians after another. Said Cortés, "I was very pleased to see discord between the various parties. It strengthened my design."

By the time Cortés and his party reached Tenochtitlán, they had been joined by thousands of the Aztecs' enemies. The Spaniards were dazzled by Tenochtitlán. It was, wrote Cortés, "the most beautiful city in the world." Moctezuma greeted the Spaniards and presented Cortés with gifts of gold.

Although the Aztecs treated the Spaniards as guests, they were suspicious of these newcomers. The Spanish sensed this hostility. They also saw that they would be outnumbered in any fighting. So to protect themselves, they took Moctezuma hostage. Then they persuaded him to swear allegiance to the Spanish king and to send his own treasure to Spain. It took three days to carry all of Moctezuma's gold from his treasury and count it.

The Aztecs rose up in revolt and on July 1, 1520, drove the Spaniards from the city. In the fighting, Moctezuma was killed and half the Spaniards were cut down. Cortés retreated to the coast, where he reorganized his army of Spaniards and Indians. Then he set off for a final attack on Tenochtitlán.

For more than three months, a fierce battle raged. When the Spanish-led army finally took the city in August 1521, the mighty Aztec empire died. An Aztec poet wrote in anguish: "We have pounded

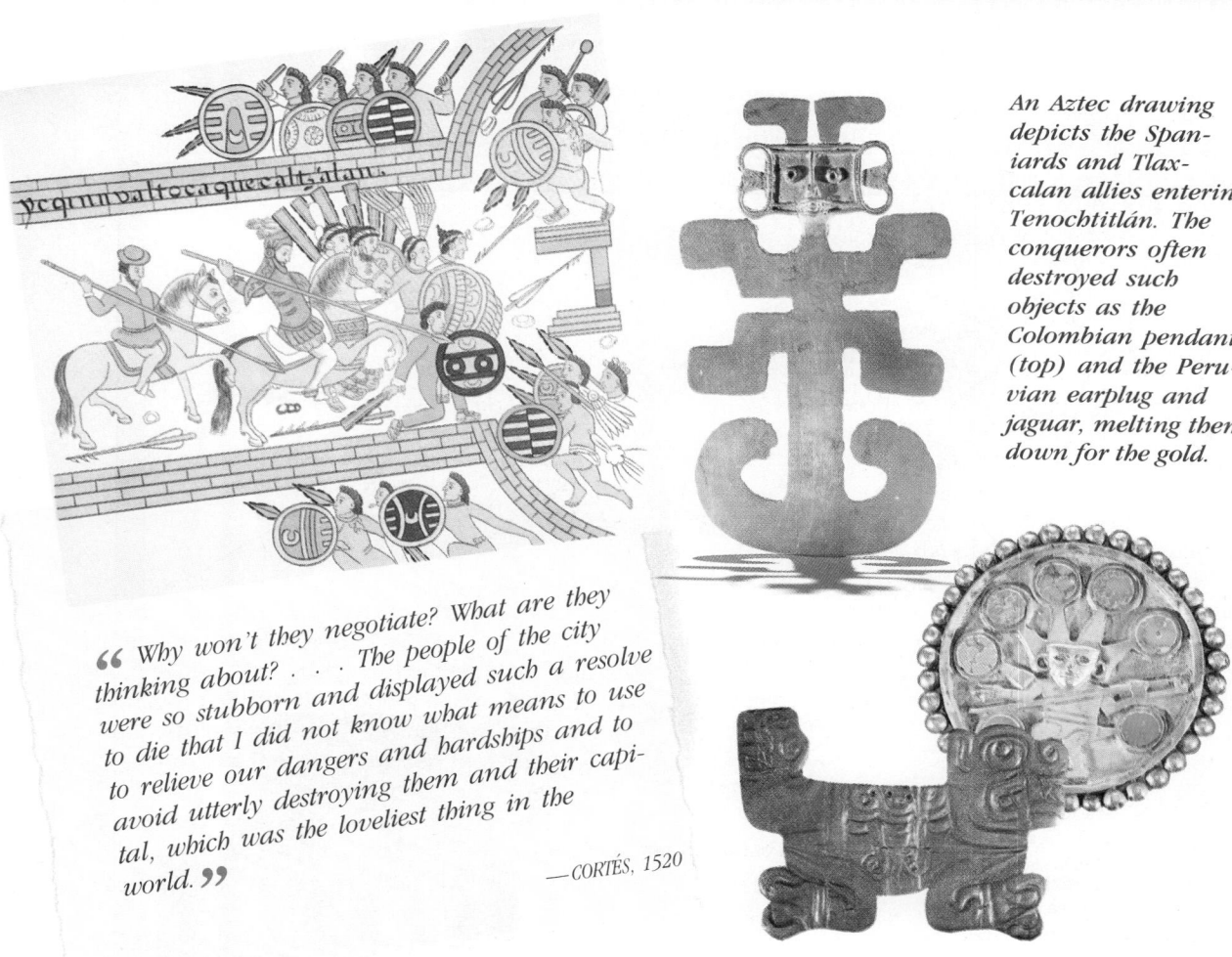

An Aztec drawing depicts the Spaniards and Tlaxcalan allies entering Tenochtitlán. The conquerors often destroyed such objects as the Colombian pendant (top) and the Peruvian earplug and jaguar, melting them down for the gold.

“Why won't they negotiate? What are they thinking about? . . . The people of the city were so stubborn and displayed such a resolve to die that I did not know what means to use to relieve our dangers and hardships and to avoid utterly destroying them and their capital, which was the loveliest thing in the world.”

—CORTÉS, 1520

our hands in despair against the adobe walls, for our inheritance, our city, is lost and dead."

Cortés ordered the beautiful city destroyed. A Spanish capital was built at Mexico City, not far from the ruins of Tenochtitlán. Ships loaded with Aztec treasure sailed back to Spain from its new empire in Middle America—New Spain.

The conquest of Peru. Just ten years later, another conquistador, Francisco Pizarro (pih-ZAHR-ro), set out to add to the gold and glory of Spain. The Spanish Crown gave Pizarro permission to conquer a rich Indian empire rumored to lie south of Panama. In 1531 Pizarro and his soldiers landed on the Pacific coast of South America. As they trekked inland to scale the lofty Andes, they learned that the Inca Empire in Peru possessed the riches they sought. They also heard that the Inca were in the midst of a civil war.

Taking advantage of the political unrest, Pizarro's troops captured the Inca ruler, Atahualpa (AHT-ah-WAHL-pah), in 1532. Pizarro demanded a ransom for Atahualpa's freedom. The Incas handed over great stores of treasure, but the Spaniards executed their ruler anyway. Then the Spaniards took over towns, set up military outposts, and enslaved Incas to work the gold and silver mines. Still more treasure ships sailed for Spain.

North from New Spain

Meanwhile, dreaming of gold and other treasures, conquistadores also pushed north into what is now the United States. Juan Ponce de León (POHN-seh deh le-OHN) claimed and explored Puerto Rico for Spain in 1508. Drawn by legends of a "Fountain of Youth," in 1513 and again in 1521 he explored

Developing

THE SECTION

Thinking Critically

Analysis. Why were the conquistadores, though vastly outnumbered, so successful in defeating the Aztecs and the Incas? (gunpowder, military experience, greed for gold, disease, Indian fears, Aztecs' thinking Cortés was a god, Pizarro aided by civil war in Peru)

Geography Skills

ANSWERS

1. To teach Christianity, acquire wealth, and add to Spain's power and prestige (God, gold, and glory).

2. The map shows the planting of missions, the journeys to Quivera to find gold, and the exploration of new territories with the establishment of presidios.

Thinking Critically

Synthesis. Ask students what character qualities the leader of a voyage of exploration in the 1500s and 1600s would probably possess. Have them explain why they chose particular qualities. (aggressive, patriotic, egotistical, greedy, adventurous, courageous, self-righteous, driven by religious zeal)

Connections: Geography

In 1906 Mesa Verde National Park was established in southwestern Colorado. The name Mesa Verde, Spanish for "green table," is an appropriate one because the region is covered with forests of juniper and piñon pines. The park preserves one of the largest archaeological sites in the country and features Pueblo Indian cliff dwellings built in the 1100s. The largest cliff house contains more than 200 rooms and probably housed about 400 people.

Reduced student page in the Teacher's Edition

Spanish Exploration and Settlement 1513-1720

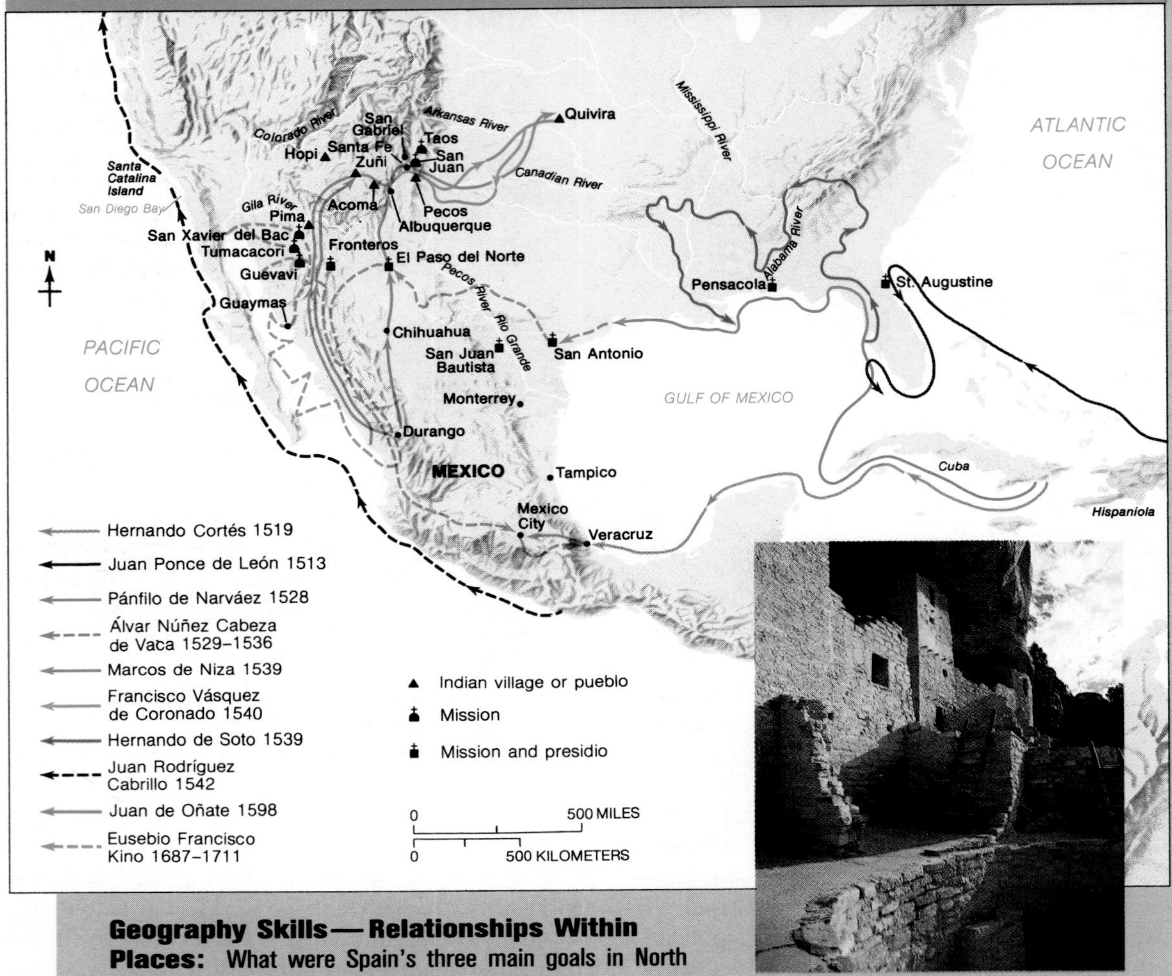

Mesa Verde, Colorado.

Geography Skills—Relationships Within Places: What were Spain's three main goals in North America? How are they reflected by the activities represented on the map?

and claimed for Spain a peninsula that he named Florida, meaning "filled with flowers."

The next conquistador to explore Florida, in 1528, was Pánfilo de Narváez (nahr-VAH-ays). Finding no gold, Narváez and his crew returned to the coast and set sail for New Spain, but they were shipwrecked off the coast of Texas.

Four survivors of the wreck were the treasurer, Alvar Núñez Cabeza de Vaca (kah-BEH-sah day VAH-kah); two other Spaniards, Castillo and Dorantes; and Estevanico (es-teh-vah-NEE-ko), Dorantes's African servant. These four were enslaved for years by the local Indians, but eventually they escaped.

After six years of wandering through what is today Texas, New Mexico, and Arizona, the four finally reached Mexico City in 1536. There, Spaniards listened with fascination as Cabeza de

Multicultural Perspectives

Many people associate Thanksgiving with the feast held by Pilgrims and Native Americans near Plymouth, Massachusetts, in 1621. Much less well known is the commemoration of the four-month journey of Don Juan de Oñate and several hundred Mexican and Spanish colonists from Santa Barbara, Mexico, through the Sonora Desert to what is now El Paso, Texas. When they reached the Rio Grande in April 1598, Oñate called for a Feast of Thanksgiving with Native Americans from the Pico and Mango tribes.

Vaca told tales of well built cities to the north, and Estevanico told of the Seven Cities of Cibola, said to be built of gold.

Such stories prompted Spanish authorities to launch new expeditions. In 1539, leaving his wife, Doña Ysabel, to rule Cuba, the governor of Cuba, Hernando de Soto, set sail for Florida.

Any report of gold drew De Soto onward. For the next three years he and his party pushed on across the South from the Atlantic Coast to present-day Texas and Oklahoma. On their trek they came upon the continent's mightiest river, the Mississippi. This stream was so wide, reported one of the explorers, that "a man standing on the shore could not be told whether he were a man or something else, from the other side."

Meanwhile, the Spanish authorities in New Spain chose Marcos de Niza (NEE-sah), a priest, to lead an expedition into New Mexico and Arizona in 1539. Niza was to search for the Seven Cities. Estevanico would act as guide.

Posing as a medicine man in a plumed headdress, Estevanico was sent ahead to pave the way among the Pueblo Indians. He sent a message to Niza that he had learned of cities with houses four stories high, decorated with turquoise. Niza followed Estevanico's trail until he got word that his guide had been killed. Climbing a hill, he saw in the distance cities of gold-colored stone—the pueblos of the Zunis. Then he quickly turned back toward New Spain.

The search for the golden cities was not over, however. A dashing officer named Francisco Vásquez de Coronado (KOR-oh-NAH-do) was chosen to lead a grand Spanish expedition to find them. Between 1540 and 1542 the company wandered through the southwestern desert and north into the Great Plains as far as Kansas. They found villages, "monstrous beasts" called buffalo, and "much very fine pasture land, with good grass." However, a discouraged Coronado reported, "There is not any gold . . . in all that country."

Meanwhile, the Spanish were laying claim to the westernmost parts of the continent. In 1542 Juan Rodríguez Cabrillo (kah-BREE-yo) sailed up the western coast, seeking riches. For years, Spaniards had read of "an island named California," said to abound with gold, pearls, and precious stones. Cabrillo did not find such wealth, but he did claim for Spain San Diego Bay, Santa Catalina Island, and other points along the California coast. More than two hundred years would pass, however, before Spaniards settled California.

Spanish North America

For two hundred years, on the basis of the explorers' claims, Spain worked to establish colonies at the northernmost fringes of its empire. These settlements were to leave a lasting Spanish influence in the Southeast and Southwest of what would one day be the United States.

The first permanent Spanish settlement in the north was a fort at St. Augustine, Florida, in 1565. The Spaniards were spurred by the fear that rival France was planning a base nearby for pirates raiding Spanish treasure ships. Soon Spanish missionaries and settlers also came to St. Augustine.

In 1598 and 1599 Juan de Oñate (oh-NYAH-teh) led a band of followers into the arid lands along the Rio Grande, establishing the first Spanish settlements in northern New Spain. In 1610 Pedro de Peralta founded a new colony, calling it Santa Fe, meaning "Holy Faith." Santa Fe became the capital of Spain's northern territories.

From Santa Fe and the settlements along the Rio Grande, Spanish missionaries spread out to nearby villages, forcing Christianity upon often unwilling Native Americans. Some of the settlers and soldiers compelled Native Americans to work on ranches and in mines. Many Indians resented the religion and labors that were forced on them.

As the Pueblo Indians' bitterness grew, a Tewa Indian named Popé (pō-PAY) urged his people to revolt. In August 1680 Popé and his followers struck. They killed more than four hundred Spaniards, burned their churches, and drove the survivors out of New Mexico. The Spaniards were not to be kept out for long, and in 1692 a strong Spanish force reconquered New Mexico.

Meanwhile, a priest named Eusebio Francisco Kino (KEE-noh) was exploring what is today southern Arizona. From 1687 until his death in 1711, he set up a chain of towns and missions. In 1700 he laid the foundations of San Xavier del Bac Mission, which still stands on the land of the Papago tribe, just south of modern Tucson.

Active Learning

Cooperative Activity. Have Students meet in small groups to prepare reports about Spanish settlement in North America. Each group should choose one area: Florida, Arizona, or New Mexico and then research significant people, events, and places.

Groups that choose Florida might report on Lucas Vázquez de Ayallón, Tristán de Luna y Arellano, Pedro Menéndez de Avilés, or the first stone fort—Castillo de San Marcos—built in St. Augustine.

Reports about the settlement of New Mexico and Arizona might include Pedro de Peralta, Juan de Oñate, Eusebio Kino, Diego de Vargas, Antonio de Espejo, or the oldest government building in the United States—the Palace of the Governors in Santa Fe.

GTV Side 1

Chap. 4, Frame 13871

Spanish Claims in the Americas, Early 1600s (Animated Map)

Search and Play:

Thinking Critically

Analysis. Spanish soldiers, priests, and settlers greatly affected the ways of life of Native Americans with which they came in contact.
Ask: What role did the Church play in Spanish America? (to convert all Native Americans to Christianity and to teach European ways) How did this affect native peoples? (Though Indians gained an education, they lost their independence.) How did Spanish settlers disrupt Indian life? (brought diseases; established the encomienda system in which Indians were often treated as slaves)

Connections: Health

Europeans introduced diseases new to the Americas, such as smallpox, measles, typhus, and the common cold, against which Native Americans had no immunity. Estimates of the native population in 1492 range from 8 to 100 million. By 1650, epidemics had caused a 50 to 90 percent decline.

Connections: Geography

Laguna Pueblo is located approximately 45 miles west of Albuquerque, New Mexico. It is still inhabited today by a mixed population of Tano, Keres, Shoshoni and Zuñi Indians.

Reduced student page in the Teacher's Edition

Soldiers, Priests, and Settlers

Throughout the sixteenth and seventeenth centuries, Spanish soldiers, priests, and settlers streamed into Spain's American colonies. To guard Spain's claims, soldiers built military garrisons called **presidios.** Presidio soldiers not only fought Native Americans, they also escorted shipments of gold and silver, delivered mail, and served as police.

Spanish missionaries accompanied the soldiers. Dedicated Catholic priests believed that they were serving God and saving souls by converting the Indians to Christianity. To teach their religion, and also European ways, the priests established self-sufficient little communities called **missions.** There, the priests taught the Indians about European livestock and crops. They introduced horses, cattle, wheat, cucumbers, artichokes, and a variety of fruits. In mission workshops, Indians made objects useful for a European way of life, such as hoes, plows, and candlestick holders.

Missionaries disagreed about the best way to save souls. Some priests said the native peoples should convert to Christianity of their own free will. Other priests thought the Indians should be forced to accept Christianity, sometimes punishing, even executing, those who refused.

The* encomienda *system. Spanish settlers were often more interested in the Indians' strength than in their souls. The Crown had forbidden slavery, but a system called ***encomienda*** (en-ko-mee-EN-dah) developed to meet Spanish needs. Under this system, a group of Indians was entrusted to a Spanish settler, usually a conquistador or other privileged colonist. The settler was allowed to use the Indians as laborers but was expected to care for them and teach them Christian ways. In practice, though, settlers often treated the Indians as if they were slaves.

Some priests, such as Bartolomé de Las Casas and Antonio de Montesinos (mohn-teh-SEE-nohs)

Learning From Art Spanish Mission at Laguna Pueblo

Mission San Jose de Laguna was built using Pueblo techniques—stones mortared with adobe.
Pueblo Indians had long made use of ladders to go from one level to the next in multi-storied dwellings.
The roof was a Pueblo construction of pine-log beams, with cross poles covered by brush and plaster.
Pueblo blanket weaving was traditionally done by men.
Pueblo women baked bread once a week in clay beehive ovens.
A missionary usually carried a few metal tools from Spain.
Pueblo pottery was decorated with natural pigments and fired for strength.

Multicultural Perspectives

When Francis Drake vowed to "singe the king of Spain's beard," he had no idea his vow would lead him to rely on a colony of some 3,000 African Americans living in Panama. These were some of the many Africans who had escaped slavery on Spanish plantations in the Caribbean. They became known as the *Cimaroons*, or *maroons*, from the Spanish *cimarrón*, meaning "wild and unruly." Historians estimate that in 1570, besides the 3,000 in Panama, there were about 7,000 Cimaroons in Hispaniola and thousands more in Cuba, Jamaica, Brazil, and Surinam. Drake and the Panamanian Cimaroons became allies in 1571, and together they raided Spanish towns and ships, especially in the southwestern Caribbean.

Active Learning

Cooperative Activity. Bartolomé de Las Casas and Antonio de Montesinos might be considered early advocates for human rights. Ask students if they agree. Why or why not?

Tell students that many countries today have accepted an agreement called the Universal Declaration of Human Rights, which cites political rights, such as the right to vote; economic rights, such as freedom from hunger; and social rights, such as the right to marry.

Have students work in small groups to develop a list of basic human rights that everyone should have. They can present their ideas to the class for discussion. Then the class can draft its own Declaration of Human Rights.

bitterly protested the settlers' treatment of Indians. As early as 1511, Montesinos told his congregation in Hispaniola:

"You are in mortal sin . . . for the cruelty and tyranny you use in dealing with these innocent people. . . . Tell me by what right or justice do you keep these Indians in such cruel and horrible servitude? . . . Are these not men?"

In response, Spain's government made attempts to correct the abuses. But Spain was too far away to enforce policies protecting the Indians.

British Challenge to Spanish Supremacy

In the sixteenth century, Spain's King Philip II ruled over the world's greatest empire. Spain controlled the Netherlands and parts of Italy. In 1580 Spain conquered the kingdom of Portugal, which it held for sixty years. As Europeans said: "When Spain moves, the world trembles." Nevertheless, Europe was changing, and soon other nations would challenge Spain's supremacy.

The Roman Catholic Church had long controlled the religious life and much of the political life of Western Europe. However, in 1517 Martin Luther, a German priest, protested what he felt were false doctrines and corrupt practices within the Church. Other voices, like John Calvin's in Switzerland, joined Luther's, starting a movement known as the Protestant Reformation.

The Reformation split the Church in two: Roman Catholicism on the one hand and a number of Protestant denominations, including Lutheranism and Calvinism, on the other. The Reformation also broke the Catholic Church's political hold in several nations, such as the Netherlands, which became Protestant.

In 1534 King Henry VIII of England cut his country's church loose from Rome's control and declared himself "pope, king, and emperor" of England. The English church moved toward a form of Protestantism known as Anglicanism.

Henry's daughter, Elizabeth I, ruled England from 1558 to 1603. She became the champion of Protestant nations against the great defender of Catholicism, Spain. She helped Protestants in the Netherlands throw off Spanish rule. Religious conflict alone would have been enough to cause trouble between Spain and England. But there were other sources of friction, too.

At first, Queen Elizabeth avoided challenging Philip II for a share of the Western Hemisphere's wealth. However, in the 1560s English interest in overseas colonies and trade was beginning to stir.

One English sailor, John Hawkins, found that he could buy enslaved people in Africa and sell them in the Caribbean for gold, silver, and pearls. Spain, however, banned foreign ships from Caribbean ports. Spaniards captured Hawkins's ships and imprisoned their crews.

Vowing to "singe the king of Spain's beard," Francis Drake, another English sailor, plundered Spanish ships and towns in the Americas. Drake and other "sea dogs" were often joined by groups of Africans who had escaped from the Spaniards and settled throughout the Caribbean.

In 1578, with Elizabeth's unofficial backing, Drake sailed his ship, the *Golden Hind*, through the Strait of Magellan and up the west coast of South America, raiding Spanish towns and ships along the way. He continued as far north as San Francisco, claiming the surrounding land for England. Then, rather than face Spanish warships on the return voyage, he crossed the Pacific. Laden

Laguna Pueblo and Taos Pueblo, New Mexico (shown here), are among those that are still home to Native Americans.

Limited English Proficiency

Making Maps. Distribute to students an outline map of the world. Have them work in pairs to do research to find out where various plants and animals—such as horses, pigs, dogs, rice, and citrus fruits—originated.

Then have them use symbols and arrows to show the diffusion of these plants and animals throughout the world. For example, the peanut originated in America and then spread to Africa.

Geography: A Key to Our Past

ANSWERS

1. Diffusion means "spread out in different directions."
2. Sugar cane probably originated in the South Pacific, spreading to India and then China.
3. Led to a more stable food supply, resulting in a population boom in northern Europe. Gradually power shifted from Mediterranean countries to the north.

Connections: Language

The culture of the Spaniards and the Portuguese took root in the Americas. Because the Spanish and Portuguese languages derived from Latin, the Americas from Mexico southward became known as Latin America.

Geography

A KEY TO OUR PAST

The First American Revolution: Movement

Imagine Italian foods without zucchini or thick tomato sauces and Chinese foods without cashews or fiery chili peppers, Hungarian goulash without paprika and Irish stew without potatoes. Yet until the Age of Exploration, tomatoes, squash, chili peppers, sweet red peppers, potatoes, and countless other foods were unknown outside of the Americas.

The great movement of people across the globe between 1500 and 1800 led to a revolutionary diffusion, or spread, of domesticated plants and animals. The European ships that headed boldly westward carried horses, pigs, dogs, rice, wheat, and citrus fruits. These and other plants and animals originating in the Middle East, Southeast Asia, or Africa were new to the Americas. When those same ships returned to Europe or to Africa, they were loaded with produce grown by American Indians, including corn, many kinds of beans, pineapples, and an astounding new food the Aztecs called *xocoatl* or *chocoatl*— chocolate.

Columbus was the first European to taste a bitter, peppery drink made with chocolate. He was not impressed. When Cortés was served a frothy brew of chocolate, honey, vanilla, and spices, however, he called chocolate "the divine drink that builds up resistance and fights fatigue."

In 1528 Cortés took back to Spain cacao tree pods and utensils for grinding dried pods into chocolate. There, he offered King Charles V "the divine drink." Charles thought the drink could be improved by adding sugar, which Europeans had already obtained from Africa. After that, cacao pods were regularly processed for wealthy Spaniards by monks in Spanish monasteries.

The Spaniards tried to keep their discovery a secret. Gradually, however, the secret leaked out. By the 1700s, chocolate was a fashionable beverage in the capitals of Europe. Today, chocolate is popular throughout most of the world. The largest producers include nations in Africa as well as in Central and South America.

The diffusion of American foods like chocolate not only led to enticing new dishes, but it also led to a more stable food supply. Northern Europe had suffered severe famine whenever cold, wet weather killed off grain crops. Nutritious varieties of potato from the Andes, however, could withstand the weather. Replacing grains, the potato became a reliable food source for northern Europe. The resulting population boom contributed to a gradual shift in power from the Mediterranean to northern Europe.

The voyages of the European explorers began a revolution in the world's food supply— a revolution that continues today. Three fifths of all crops in cultivation originated in the Americas.

Corn goddess pot, Peru.

1. Define *diffusion*.
2. Sugar cane was growing in the South Pacific by 6,000 B.C., in India by 325 B.C., and in China by 100 B.C. What conclusions about movement might a geographer draw from this evidence?
3. How did the diffusion of foods affect the political balance in Europe?

with Spanish treasure, the *Golden Hind* sailed up England's River Thames in 1580, the second ship in history to sail around the world.

Drake's success and booty—including tons of silver and gold—enraged King Philip. He demanded that Drake and his crew be punished. Instead, Queen Elizabeth made Drake a knight.

The Spanish Armada

For Philip of Spain, the English challenge had gone far enough. In 1588 he launched an invasion force to crush England and return it to Catholicism. Heavily armed, the 130 ships carried more than 19,000 soldiers and 8,000 sailors. "Invincible Armada," the Spanish called their fleet, because they thought it could not be defeated.

The Armada sailed into the English Channel, and the two sides blasted away at each other for a week. Then the English filled eight ships with gunpowder, set them ablaze, and sent them into the Spanish fleet. To escape the flames, the Armada fled to open waters. As the Armada scattered, English guns crippled the fleet. A storm wrecked more of the Spanish ships, and only half the Armada limped home to Spain.

The defeat of the Armada weakened Spain. As Spain's power declined, England, France, and the Netherlands saw their chance. By the 1600s, all three were challenging Spain—and each other—for claims in North America.

Section Review

1. Identification. Define *conquistadores, presidios, missions*, and *encomienda*.

2. Comprehension. What were Spain's goals in the Americas? Describe one way Spain carried out each of these goals.

3. Analysis. Why do you think Queen Elizabeth allowed the "sea dogs" to plunder Spanish ships and towns in the Americas?

Data Search. Study the maps on pages 34 and 40. List the present-day states that the Spanish had explored or settled by 1720. How much of the United States was once part of Spain's empire?

Connections to Themes

The Search for Opportunity

European discovery and exploration led to sweeping population changes in North and South America, Europe, and Africa. Europeans from many nations poured into the Americas seeking opportunity—wealth, land, a chance to practice their religion—in what they called "a New World."

However, golden opportunities for Europeans meant misery for many Africans. As early as 1503, the Spanish brought Africans to the Americas as forced labor for plantations and mines. Some did come freely as members of ships' crews and exploring parties. Pedro Niño, navigator of Columbus's ship *Niña*, might have been an African. Some soldiers in the armies of Cortés and Balboa were African. However, millions of Africans were wrenched from their homes and shipped to the Americas as slaves.

Slavery had existed in African societies for centuries. In many places, criminals and prisoners of war were enslaved by law. However, when European traders began to pay well for slaves, illegal ways of obtaining them, such as slave-raiding and kidnapping, increased.

Opportunities for Europeans in the Americas also meant disaster for the original inhabitants. Native Americans were pushed off their lands and slaughtered in battle. Many more were felled by diseases the invaders brought.

By the 1700s Europeans and Africans of many different languages, faiths, and customs were permanently settled in the Americas. And European culture, touched by the ideas and skills of Africans and Indians, had taken firm root.

Section Review

ANSWERS

1. See definitions for the following terms on text pages indicated in parentheses: *conquistadores* (38), *presidios* (42), *missions* (42), *encomienda* (42).

2. Spain's goals were God, gold, and glory. Conquistadores like Cortés and Pizarro added to gold and glory by conquering the Aztec and the Inca. Spanish missionaries forced religion on unwilling Native Americans in New Spain.

3. Elizabeth probably wished to increase England's wealth and power while decreasing the power of England's rival, Spain.

Data Search. Florida, California, New Mexico, Arizona, South Carolina, Georgia, Alabama, Louisiana, Mississippi, Texas, Oklahoma, Kansas; about one third.

Chapter Survey

ANSWERS

Using New Vocabulary

1. *Potlatch* and *kiva* both relate to Native-American ceremonies. A *potlatch* is a winter festival celebrating abundance. A *kiva* is used for religious ceremonies.
2. The Spanish established *presidios* and *missions* in America. *Presidios* were military garrisons; *missions* were self-sufficient communities established by priests.

Reviewing the Chapter

1. Allowed people to remain in one place; communities, cities, and civilizations arose.
2. Olmec, Mayan, Inca. Olmecs were skilled artisans and monument builders. Mayans developed a written language, studied astronomy, created accurate calendar. Incas created beautiful cities, built roads, bridges, and irrigation systems.
3. Iroquois warred among themselves; formed a confederation.
4. Belief in a creator, belief that nature and people are closely related.
5. To increase wealth and power.
6. Balboa: discovery of Pacific showed that the Americas were not the Indies; Magellan: proved Americas were new continents; Cartier: aroused Europeans' interest in furs and minerals; Hudson: sailed up Hudson River from New York Harbor searching for Northwest Passage; found Indians willing to trade furs for metal goods.
7. Spain: Mexico, Central America, most of South America, Florida, west coast of North America; England: land north of Spain's claims in eastern North America; France: North American coast from Carolinas to Newfoundland; Netherlands: land around New York harbor and the Hudson River; Portugal: Brazil.
8. Abuse of Indians under encomienda system disputed. Spain's government made weak attempt to correct abuses, but too far away to enforce its policies.
9. To crush power of England. Spain's power declined and other nations sought claims in North America.

Thinking Critically

1. Answers may include: fertile valleys of Mississippi and Ohio rivers enabled growth of mound-building communities and sizeable towns; nomadic buffalo-hunting tribes of Great Plains, which were too dry for farming; abundant food supplies of Pacific Northwest permitted permanent settlements; nomadic hunter/fishers of the far north, where weather too harsh for farming.

Reduced student page in the Teacher's Edition

Chapter Survey

Using New Vocabulary

The vocabulary terms in each pair listed below are related to each other. For each pair, explain what the two terms have in common. Also explain how they are different.

Example: *Conquistadores* and *encomienda* are related in that a *conquistador* might receive an *encomienda,* a grant of Indian labor, for his service to the king. A *conquistador* was a person, however, while *encomienda* was a system or practice.

1. potlatch, kiva
2. presidios, missions

Reviewing the Chapter

1. How did the coming of agriculture change life in the Americas?
2. Name three early civilizations of Middle America and give two accomplishments of each.
3. What problem did the Iroquoian tribes of the eastern woodlands face? How did they resolve this problem?
4. What beliefs did many Native-American cultures share?
5. Explain two reasons why European rulers backed voyages of exploration.
6. How did the explorations of Balboa, Magellan, Cartier, and Hudson expand European knowledge of the Americas?
7. By the early 1600s, which European nations had claims in the Western Hemisphere? Where were each nation's claims?
8. What disagreement took place among Spaniards over treatment of Native Americans? What was the outcome of this dispute?
9. Why did Spain build an Armada? How did the outcome of its battle with the English affect international relations in the Americas?

Thinking Critically

1. Application. The resources of their environments caused Native Americans to develop different cultures. Illustrate this concept with three examples from the chapter.
2. Evaluation. What standards would you use for judging the Spanish conquest of the Americas from the Spanish point of view? From the Native American point of view? Evaluate Spanish activity from both perspectives.
3. Synthesis. What might relations between Spain and England have been like if the Protestant Reformation had not occurred? Give evidence to support your answer.

Using a Time Line

Match each item on the list below with the correct date. Write your answers in chronological order and explain the importance of each event.

(A) Columbus's first voyage
(B) Hohokam in Southwest
(C) Cortés's conquest
(D) Spanish Armada
(E) Inca Empire
(F) First American agriculture
(G) Aztec Empire
(H) Coronado's explorations
(I) Prince Henry's school
(J) Magellan's voyage

7000 B.C. — 300 B.C. — A.D. 1200 — 1400 — 1418 — 1492 — 1519 — 1521 — 1540 — 1588

2. Answers may include from Spanish point of view: belief they were a superior civilization; Native Americans were inferior, uncivilized, non-Christians; Native American point of view: Spanish were cruel, savage barbarians, blind to achievements of Indian civilizations and had come openly to destroy.
3. Answers may include: England and Spain were natural enemies, both being seafaring nations coveting riches of the Americas. Students might cite England's distrust of Spain as great power, the aggressive sea dogs, Queen Elizabeth's approval of their feats.

History and You

Spanish exploration and colonization changed the face of the Americas profoundly in the fifteenth and sixteenth centuries. Today, the influence of Spain is still causing changes. In the last decade, immigration from Spanish-speaking countries into the United States has greatly increased. What issues and opportunities does this immigration raise in American society?

Applying Social Studies Skills

Using Maps

The Spanish led the way in the discovery, exploration, and colonization of the Western Hemisphere. Use the maps on pages 34, 40, and 900–901 to answer the questions below about the Spanish empire in North America and its legacy.

1. Which Spanish explorer was the first to visit an area that is now part of the United States? When and where did he explore?

2. Which Spanish explorer was probably the first to cross the Mississippi? the Rio Grande?

3. Why does the route of Cabeza de Vaca pick up where Narváez's route ends? Estimate the distance that Cabeza de Vaca traveled.

4. Which Spanish explorers traveled farthest North?

5. By 1720 what areas of North America had been explored by the Spanish?

6. Where in the present United States were early Spanish settlements concentrated?

7. List present-day states that occupy areas the Spanish had explored or settled by 1720.

8. Thousands of places in the United States bear Spanish names. Describe the location of each of the following places, then, consulting a dictionary if necessary, give the meaning of its name in English: Rio Grande, Brazos River, Sierra Nevada, Puerto Rico, California, Colorado, Florida, Toledo, El Paso, San Antonio, Albuquerque, Las Vegas, Mesa, Santa Fe, San Francisco, Los Angeles, and Sacramento.

Writing About Issues

The Issue: *Should the gray wolf be reintroduced into Yellowstone National Park?*

For thousands of years, the haunting call of the gray wolf was part of the American landscape. Native Americans respected this fierce hunter and did nothing to upset the natural balance between predator and prey. Today, however, the gray wolf is listed as an endangered species in every state except Alaska and Minnesota.

In 1991 the National Park Service began work on a plan to reintroduce the gray wolf into Wyoming's Yellowstone National Park. While wolves were once plentiful in this 2.2 million acre park, they were eliminated from this region 60 years ago. If gray wolves are reintroduced into Yellowstone, they will be the first major predator ever returned to a United States national park.

Support for reintroducing wolves to Yellowstone has come mainly from wildlife managers and environmentalists. They see the wolf as an essential part of Yellowstone's ecosystem, or natural community. "Many of us feel it's a moral imperative [necessity] and a biological imperative," says David S. Wilcove, senior ecologist for the Wilderness Society.

Strong opposition to plans for reintroducing wolves has come from livestock and hunting interests. These groups view the wolf as a threat both to domestic cattle and sheep and to wild game prized by hunters. As Carolyn L. Paseneaux of the Wyoming Woolgrowers' Association says, "Our livelihood is at stake." Montana Congressman Ron Maranee states bluntly, "Montana needs wolves like we need another drought."

Should the howl of the gray wolf once again be heard in Yellowstone? Or is the wolf too great a threat to livestock and wildlife? State your opinion and your reasons in a letter to the National Park Service. Address your letter to:

Associate Director of Natural Resources
Department of Interior
National Park Service
P.O. Box 37127
Washington, D.C. 20012-7127

Using a Time Line

(F) 8000 B.C.: allowed permanent communities.
(B) 300 B.C.: relatively advanced society based on farming.
(G) A.D. 1200: advanced empire crushed by Spanish.
(E) 1400: advanced Middle American empire.
(I) 1418: school that encouraged exploration.
(A) 1492: led to discovery of continents unknown to Europeans.
(J) 1519: first Europeans to circle the earth.
(C) 1521: encouraged Spain to step up exploration of the Americas.
(H) 1540: exploration of southwestern desert and Great Plains.
(D) 1588: destruction of Armada signalled end of Spain's world dominance.

History and You

Answers may include the following issues and opportunities: whether there will be enough jobs for immigrants, whether they should be encouraged to assimilate or keep traditional cultures; whether Spanish or English should be primary language; opportunity for Americans to learn new cultural ways.

Applying Social Studies Skills

1. Juan Ponce de Leon; 1513, Florida.
2. Hernando de Soto; Alvar Nunez Cabeza de Vaca.
3. Narvaez was shipwrecked; survivors of his crew, including Cabeza de Vaca, continued westward; 2,250 miles.
4. Coronado, Juan de Onate.
5. Southeast, southwest.
6. Southwest.
7. Florida, Alabama, Georgia, Texas, New Mexico, Arizona, California.
8. Refer students to a regular dictionary or a Spanish language dictionary.

Chapter 3

Creating a New Society

Planning Guide

	Student Text	TWE Lesson Plans	Support Materials
SECTION 1	**Section 3–1** (1 Day) **English Beginnings in America**, pp 50–54 Review/Evaluation Section Review, p 54	**Introducing the Chapter:** Appreciating Diversity in the Classroom—Cooperative Activity, half a class period, p 47B **Teaching the Main Ideas:** Pursuing Money and Power—Cooperative Activity, one class period, p 47B	★ **Read to Remember**, Section 1 ● **Section Activities**, Section 1 Δ **Enrichment Activities**, Section 1 ● **Tests**, Section 1 Quiz
SECTION 2	**Section 3–2** (1–2 Days) **Settling Colonies**, pp 54–61 Exploring Issues—Freedom of the Press: The Trial of John Peter Zenger, pp 60–61 Review/Evaluation Section Review, p 61	**Reinforcement Activity:** Foundations of Democracy—Individual Activity, one class period, p 47C	★ **Read to Remember**, Section 2 ● **Section Activities**, Section 2 Δ **Readings**, Anne Bradstreet ● **Tests**, Section 2 Quiz
SECTION 3	**Section 3–3** (2 Days) **Shaping New Patterns of Life**, pp 62–73 The American Spirit: Olaudah Equiano, p 70 Young in America: At Work, p 73 Review/Evaluation, Section Review, p 72	● **Teaching the Main Ideas:** Regional Diversity—Cooperative Activity, 3–4 days student preparation, p 47B Δ **Enrichment Activity:** Echoes of Africa—Individual Creative Writing Activity, two class periods, p 47C	★ **Read to Remember**, Section 3 ● **Section Activities**, Section 3 ● **Geography Activities**, Section 3 Δ **Enrichment Activities**, Section 3 Δ **Readings**, Jonathan Edwards, Olaudah Equiano ● **Tests**, Section 3 Quiz
SECTION 4	**Section 3–4** (1 Day) **The Struggle for North America**, pp 74–77 Connections to Themes: Shaping Democracy, p 77 Review/Evaluation, Section Review, p 77 Chapter 3 Survey, pp 78–79 Unit 1 Survey, pp 80–81 Skills, pp 78–79 Thinking Critically Applying Thinking Skills: Interpreting Political Cartoons Writing About Issues	● **Evaluating Progress:** The French Point of View—Individual Creative Writing Activity, two class periods, p 47C	★ **Read to Remember**, Section 4 ● **Section Activities**, Section 4 Δ **Readings:** Benjamin Franklin ● **Tests**, Section 4 Quiz, Chapter 3 Test (Forms A and B), Unit 1 Test (Forms A and B) **Additional Resources** Δ **Twentieth Century Issues: Links to the Past** ● **Active Learning** Δ **GTV Videodiscs** Δ **Transparencies and Activity Book** ● **Testing Software** ★ **Chapter Summaries** **Key:** ★ **For Extra Support** ● **For All Students** Δ **For Enrichment**

Overview

Prompted by the desire for wealth and power, the English government encouraged colonization of the east coast of North America. Between 1607 and 1732, English joint-stock companies, royal favorites, and English settlers, acting on mercantilist, nationalist, or religious visions, established thirteen colonies.

With help from Native Americans, the colonies survived. Colonists found sources of income and gained a limited degree of self-government in the form of representative legislatures modeled after the Parliament of England. Population grew rapidly as thousands of English and Europeans, fleeing economic problems, religious conflict, and war, settled in the colonies in the hope of a fresh start.

The colonies were characterized by regional economic interests and religious, ethnic, and racial diversity. Despite traditional distrust between ethnic and religious groups, cooperation and religious toleration began to develop. However, colonists' views of Native Americans and Africans, based on differences in appearances and ways of life, hardened into racist attitudes. Such attitudes condoned destruction of Indians and enslavement of Africans.

In 1754 war broke out between England and France over political dominance in Europe and colonial expansion in North America and other parts of the world. England's victory ended France's role as a colonial power in North America and expanded the English empire.

Activity Objectives

After completing these activities, students should be able to

- explain why the English established colonies in North America.
- describe the diverse economic interests in the English colonies.
- identify political developments that were important to the growth of democracy in the English colonies.
- explain the significance of the English victory in the French and Indian War.
- recognize that enslaved Africans came from unique cultures with rich literary traditions.

Introducing the Chapter

Appreciating Diversity in the Classroom

This cooperative activity requires half a class period.

A major objective in Chapter 3 is student understanding of the similarities and differences among people in England's North American colonies. It will help students to appreciate colonial diversity if they first understand the diversity in their own classroom. This activity will give students the opportunity to learn how their classmates are similar and different.

Divide the class into groups of four. Direct each group to brainstorm to find fifteen characteristics that all members have in common. Have one student record the group's responses. Encourage students to go beyond obvious similarities, such as race or sex, and consider unusual ones, such as family membership, behavior, beliefs, and experiences.

Then have each student name four ways in which he or she is different from the others in the group. Again, encourage students to go beyond consideration of appearance and age and select examples that show special abilities and different family traditions and backgrounds.

Conclude the activity by having the class discuss the following questions:

- Which were more difficult to find—similarities or differences? Why? (Answers will vary depending on the diversity of the class. A class that has difficulty finding differences may not be very diverse.)
- What were the most common similarities and differences mentioned?
- How may similarities strengthen the bonds among group members? How may similarities among group members be harmful?
- How may diversity strengthen the bonds among group members? How may diversity be harmful?
- What did you learn about your class in doing this activity? How do you think your experience might relate to the people in England's North American colonies?

Teaching the Main Ideas

Section 3-1: Pursuing Money and Power

This cooperative activity requires a class period.

In Section 3-1 students learn that England's colonies in North America were an essential part of its mercantilist system. The following activity will enable students to expand their understanding of mercantilism.

Begin the activity by reminding students that the first English joint-stock companies colonizing North America expected to find gold, silver, and other valuable metals. They also expected colonies to supply products that England could not produce, such as naval stores and furs. England could then sell such products or at least not have to buy them. Thus the companies needed to make informed decisions about establishing and running the colonies to ensure financial success.

Organize students into groups of five. Have each group imagine that it manages a joint-stock company that is preparing to establish a colony in North America. Ask each group to spend 30 minutes writing a plan for colonization, addressing the following issues:

- Where will the colony be located?
- What supplies will be needed to establish the colony?
- How can the company ensure profits for investors?
- How many people will be sent?
- What kind of skills will the colonists need?
- What will the colonists get in return for their work?
- Will indentured servants or slaves be sent to the colony?
- What laws will govern the colony?

When assignments are complete, have a representative from each group present its colonization plan to the class. Acting as company investors, the class should determine whether each plan represents a good investment. Conclude the acitivity by taking a class vote to determine which plan is the most likely to succeed in establishing a profitable colony. Have students give reasons to support their decisions.

Teaching the Main Ideas

Section 3-3: Regional Diversity

This cooperative activity requires class time for students to plan projects, two or three days to make or collect items for display, and class time to assemble projects.

To understand conflicting colonial interests, students need to understand the different economic interests of the Southern, Middle, and New England colonies. In the following activity students create displays to illustrate regional diversity in the colonies.

Ask students to recall differences in the geographical features and economic activities of the three colonial regions described in Section 3-3. Then divide the class into groups of four and have each group complete a three-part project, as follows:

- First, they are to write a description of the geography of the Southern, Middle, and New England colonies. They may use encyclopedias and other available sources for resarch on this and other parts of the project.
- Second, they are to list the major products and economic activities (agriculture, trade, manufacturing) in the major colonial regions.
- Third, they are to prepare illustrative displays of the major colonial regions, using pictures, drawings, and/or actual objects.

Direct groups to display their completed projects. Have the class comment on the most original and informative features. Conclude by comparing colonial interests by region and speculating about future sources of conflict based on such differences.

Reinforcement Activity

Section 3-2: Foundations of Democracy

This individual activity requires one class period.

In this activity students will organize information in a chart to reinforce their understanding of events in England and its North American colonies that laid the foundations for democratic government in the United States.

Begin the activity by asking students what individual rights the colonists believed they had and why. Discuss the importance of precedents established by royal decree, the English Parliament, and colonial governments.

Remind students that Section 3-2 lists eight examples of documents that influenced the rights of colonists. Direct students to review the section and organize this information by creating a chart with the following headings: *Document, Date,* and *Significance.* Students should include the following documents: Magna Carta (1215); Mayflower Compact (1620); Massachusetts law creating a representative legislature (1630s); Rhode Island charter (1644); Fundamental Orders of Connecticut (1639); Maryland Toleration Act (1649); Pennsylvania Frame of Government (1680s); English Bill of Rights (1689).

When students have completed their charts, review their work. Discuss the charts by asking: How did these documents extend political and religious rights of the times? In what ways would many of these documents be considered unjust by standards today?

Evaluating Progress

Section 3-4: The French Point of View

This individual activity requires one class period, or it may be assigned as homework and shared in class the following day.

In Section 3-4 students learn about the French and Indian War. Use this creative writing activity to evaluate students' understanding of the events and issues surrounding the war.

Have students review Section 3-4 from the point of view of a French citizen in 1763. Encourage them to jot down events that are significant from the French perspective. Then direct them to write a one-page letter to a friend describing events and issues before, during, and after the French and Indian War.

Criteria for evaluating students' work should include at least five accurate references to specific events or beliefs of the French.

Enrichment Activity

Section 3-3: Echoes of Africa

This individual activity requires a full class period, but students can complete it as homework. Set aside a full class period the following day for students to present their work.

In Section 3-3 students learn that enslaved Africans created an African-American culture of their own by blending old and new ways of life. The following activity will enable students to appreciate praise poems, a part of the literary heritage of Africans.

Remind students that although enslaved Africans brought few material possessions to North America, they carried in their hearts and minds the forms of music, speeches, and stories of their homeland. One such art form is the praise poem, found throughout Sub-Saharan Africa, but especially common among the southern Bantu people.

Among the Sotho, a Bantu people of South Africa, the creation of praise poems is part of the special coming-of-age ceremonies that mark the transition from adolescence to young adulthood. As part of the ritual, youths compose poems in praise of themselves, then recite them to the assembled village. Praise poems are usually solemn tributes, but they can also be satirical or humorous. The poems may be used to introduce oneself to others, show kinship with a family or other group, reveal what one would like to be, or express determination to achieve certain goals.

Read to students the following Bantu praise poem. Help them identify the subject and the characteristics of the poem. (The poet is comparing himself to animals. Characteristics include a repeated phrase and metaphors—the young lion, the fine elephant. Interjections, alliteration, and assonance are also common in praise poems.)

"I am the young lion!
The wild animal with pad-feet and black back!
Whose father has given up hope from the beginning
and whose mother has wept for a long time.
I am the fine elephant of the Mathubapulu, the finest
elephant in the Matsaakgang."

Now have students create their own praise poems of five lines or more. Give the following guidelines.

- First line: an introduction or salute. Begin with a phrase like "Praise to," "Here's to," or "I am."
- Next two or three lines: refer to yourself by different descriptive names and phrases. Compare or identify yourself with something without using the words *like* or *as.* Some examples: nicknames like Wolf, Moonlight; phrases like "a storm thundering across the plain." Animals and natural occurrences are most commonly used, but you may use others.
- Next-to-last line: refer to some action or deed.
- Last line: begin the same way as the first line. Repeat the idea of the first line, but vary the words.

Conclude the activity by asking students why the creation of self-praising poems might be a vital part of coming-of-age ceremonies. (formal presentation of oneself and one's interests and goals as an adult) Explain that African literary traditions were, for the most part, oral, or spoken, rather than written. Have students speculate about why European colonists might have failed to recognize the value of such traditions. (belief that the written word is superior to the spoken one, differences in African and European culture)

Bibliography and Audiovisual Material

Teacher Bibliography

Boorstin, Daniel J. *The Americans: The Colonial Experience.* New York: Random House, 1985.

Demos, John P. *Family Life in Plymouth Colony.* New York: Oxford University Press, 1970.

Demos, John P. *Entertaining Satan: Witchcraft and the Culture of Early New England.* Oxford University Press, 1982.

Hawke, David Freeman. *Everyday Life in Early America.* New York: Harper & Row, 1988.

Morris, Richard B. *The Indian Wars.* Minneapolis: Lerner Publications, 1985.

Nabokov, Peter. *Native American Testimony.* New York: Crowell, 1978.

Williams, Selma R. *Demeter's Daughters: The Women Who Founded America 1587–1787.* New York: Atheneum, 1976.

Literature for Students

Cooper, James Fenimore. *The Last of the Mohicans.* New York: Macmillan, 1986.

Franklin, Benjamin. *Autobiography.* New York: Random, 1990.

Hawthorne, Nathaniel, *The Scarlet Letter.* New York: Penguin, 1983.

Miller, Arthur. *The Crucible.* New York: Viking, 1953.

Films and Videocassettes

Anne Hutchinson: 50 minutes. Zenger Productions Company, Inc. Videocassette.

Colonial America: 60 minutes. SVE/Society for Visual Education. Videocassette.

The French and Indian War: 7 Years War in America. 16 minutes. EBEC. Movie.

Witches of Salem: The Horror and the Hope. 30 minutes. Learning Corporation of America. Videocassette.

Filmstrips

Colonial Sports and Amusements. 1 filmstrip. Colonial Williamsburg Foundation.

Notable Women of the United States: The Beginnings. 1 filmstrip. National Geographic.

The Jamestown Settlement. 1 filmstrip. Multi-Media.

The Puritan Legacy. 2 filmstrips. Guidance Associates.

Computer Software

Colonial Merchant. EAC/Educational Activities, Inc. 2 Apple diskettes.

The Time Tunnel: American History Series. (1760–1970) 2 Apple diskettes. Focus Media.

Chapter 3

Objectives

- Explain why Europeans established colonies in North America.
- Identify the factors that brought Europeans to settle in the colonies.
- Describe the effects of racial and cultural diversity in colonial society.
- Explain how Britain expanded its American empire.

Introducing THE CHAPTER

For suggestions on introducing Chapter 3, refer to page 47B in the Teacher's Edition.

Developing THE CHAPTER

For activities and teaching strategies to help you reinforce and enrich chapter content, see pages 47B–47D in the Teacher's Edition.

B · A · C · K · G · R · O · U · N · D

Chapter Opener Illustrations

The Benin mask, made in the 1500s, is evidence of the advanced African culture that enslaved Africans were forced to leave behind when brought to North America.

The journey by ship was dangerous. The map, drawn by John White in 1585 and engraved in Germany by Theodore de Bry, shows shipwrecks of earlier expeditions along the Outer Banks. There were so many shipwrecks along the Virginia coast that it later became known as "the graveyard of the Atlantic."

Persuasive pamphlets like "The New Life," printed in 1612, attracted settlers to the English colonies of North America, or "New Britain." The land was often described in enthusiastic terms as more abundant and beautiful than any yet known.

Mrs. Elizabeth Freake, wife of a successful Boston mer-

Reduced student page in the Teacher's Edition

Chapter 3 1600-1763

Creating a New Society

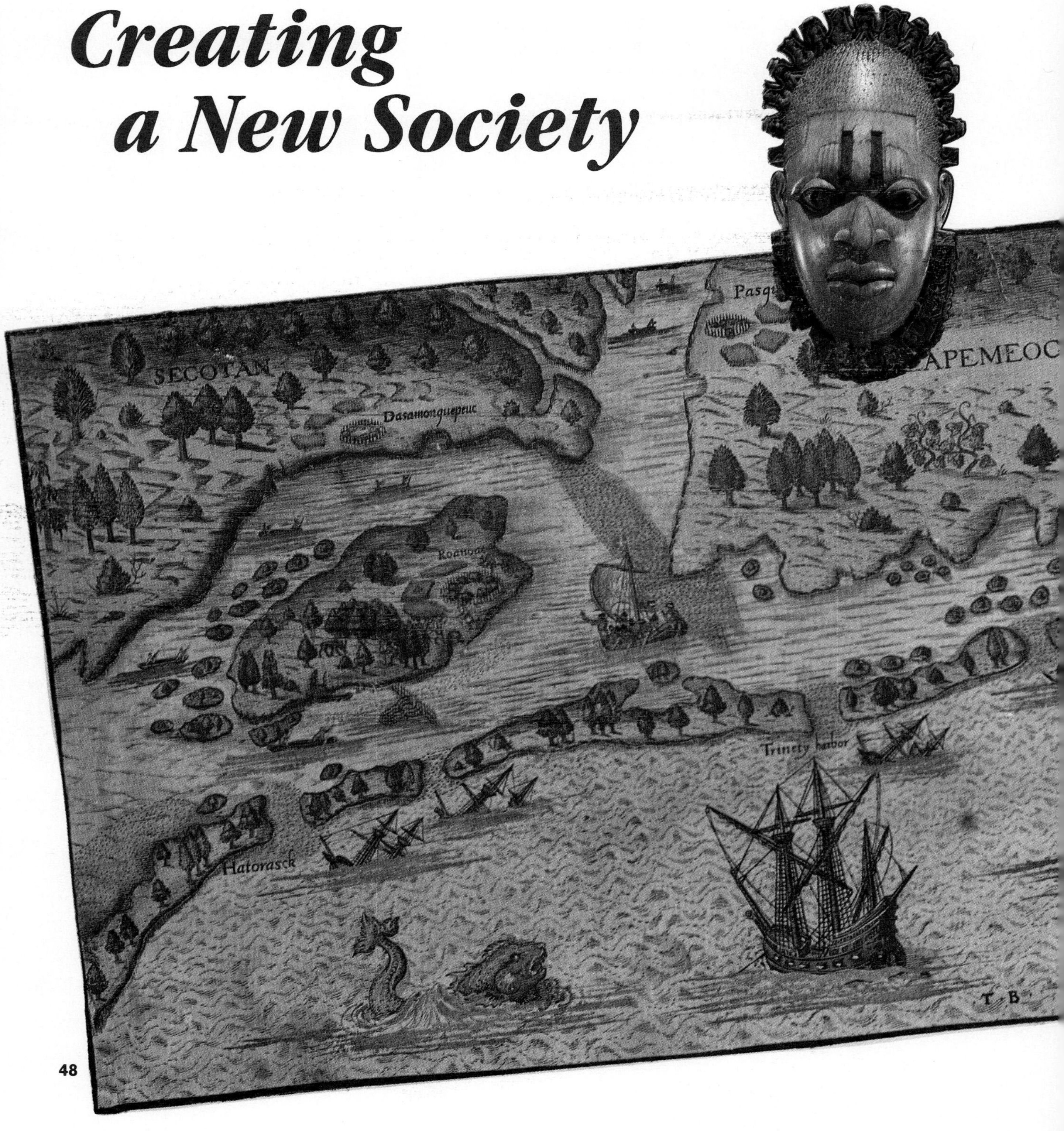

chant-attorney, sat for this portrait in 1671. The lace collar and Baby Mary, Elizabeth's eighth child, were added in 1674.

John White's 1585 drawing of a Florida Timimucuan Indian was probably drawn from a lost original by Frenchman Jacques LeMoyne since there is no record of White ever having been in Florida. Both White and LeMoyne were employed by Sir Walter Raleigh and each endeavored to portray a true picture of Native-American life before white settler's ways changed it.

American Voices

In 1623 Lady Margaret Wyatt wrote a letter to her sister in England. Wyatt had voyaged from England to North America and found the Atlantic crossing miserable. Her only defense against illness and crowding was her lively sense of humor:

" Dear Sister, eare this you should have heard from me, had not th' extremitie of sickness till now hindered me. For our Shippe was so pestered with people and goods that we were so full of infection that after a while we saw little but throwing folks over board: It pleased God to send me my helth till I came to shoare. . . . Few else are left alive that came in that Shipp: for here have dyed the Husband, wife, children & servants. . . . There never came Shipp so full to Virginia as ours. Our Capt[ain] seemed to be troubled at it, and . . . to make the people amends died himself. . . .

"This was our fortune at the Sea, and the land little better, . . and [unless] our Freinds help us it will go hard with us next Wynter. "

Four major European nations competed to establish colonies on North America's eastern seaboard: Spain, the Netherlands, France, and—after a late start—England. The rush to colonize set off a vast movement of people. From 1500 to the present, this movement has involved more than 50 million immigrants from six continents. The story of the United States is based on the mingling and clashing of diverse groups of people, both new and native to North America.

Benin ivory mask, West Africa, 1500s; map of arrival of English in Virginia; travel pamphlet, 1612; Elizabeth Freake and Baby Mary of Boston; drawing of Timucuan man, 1500s.

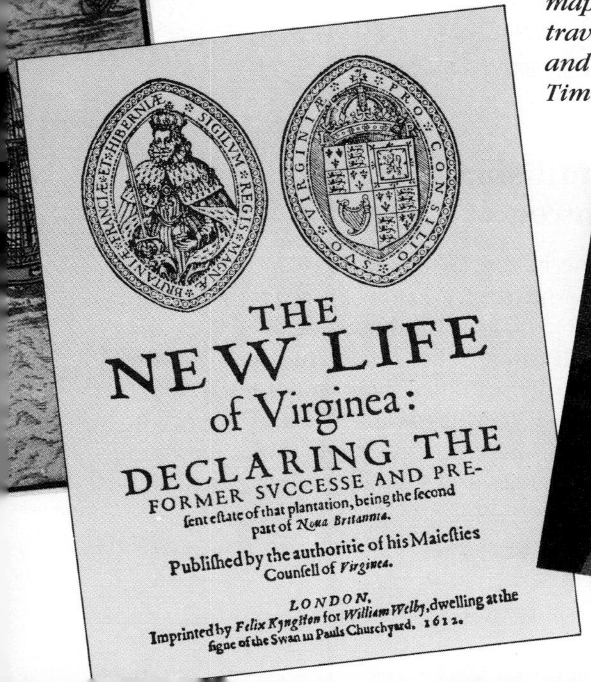

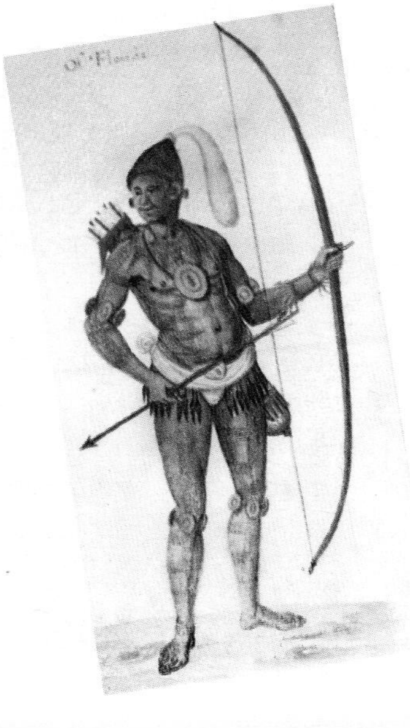

Analyzing Primary Sources

American Voices

Lady Margaret Wyatt's letter, written in 1623, takes students into the mind of a woman who experienced the rigors of crossing the Atlantic Ocean and settling in North America.

1. What perils does Wyatt describe on sea and land? **(disease, overcrowding)**
2. Why do you think people would subject themselves to such perils? **(Forces such as poverty, political or religious persecution, and war, might convince people to leave their homes.)**
3. What impression do you get of Wyatt's ability to cope with hardship? **(Her letter indicates a sense of humor.)**

As students read the chapter, encourage them to look for the reasons that European settlers endured such grim voyages and hardships upon arrival.

GTV Side 1

Chap. 6, Frame 17656

Hoping for the Best in America (Movie)

Search:

Play:

Section 3-1

Objectives

- ***Answer the Focus Question.***
- *Explain how the poor of England could afford to come to the colonies.*
- *Describe how representative government gained a foothold in Virginia.*

Introducing THE SECTION

Read to students from a pamphlet published by the London Company in 1609:

“There are valleys and plains streaming with sweet springs . . . hills and mountains . . . of hidden treasure, never yet searched. . . . The soil is strong and sends out naturally fruitful vines . . . mulberry trees and silkworms, many skins and rich furs, many sweet woods, and costly dyes; plenty of sturgeon, timber for shipping . . . there is a world of means to set many thousands to work.”

Ask: How might such a pamphlet affect people who were dissatisfied at home? Does the pamphlet exaggerate?

Time Line Illustrations

1. Chief Powhatan's deerskin cape is decorated with shells.
2. 150 years after the first Africans were sold in Jamestown, slave ships were still arriving in colonial ports, as this 1769 hand bill indicates.
3. A gravestone rubbing shows a New England preacher.
4. Colonial figures appear on a Pennsylvania Dutch pie plate.
5. James Oglethorpe, an Englishman, founded the colony of Georgia.
6. The powder horn is a souvenir of the French and Indian War. The engraved map shows regions of heavy conflict in central New York.

Reduced student page in the Teacher's Edition

CHAPTER TIME LINE

1600 - 1763

1607 Jamestown Colony founded

1619 First Africans arrive in Jamestown

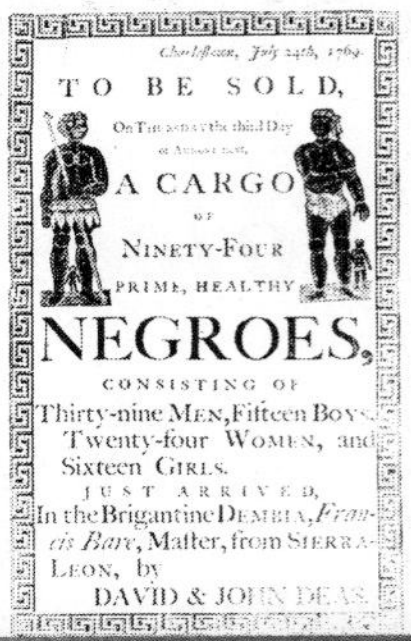
Charlestown, July 24th, 1769.
TO BE SOLD,
On THURSDAY the third Day of AUGUST next,
A CARGO
OF
NINETY-FOUR
PRIME, HEALTHY
NEGROES,
CONSISTING OF
Thirty-nine MEN, Fifteen BOYS,
Twenty-four WOMEN, and
Sixteen GIRLS.
JUST ARRIVED,
In the Brigantine DEMBIA, *Francis Bare*, Master, from SIERRA-LEON, by
DAVID & JOHN DEAS.

1663 Carolinas founded

1664 England seized New Netherland

1600 | 1630 | 1660

1600 Powhatan Confederacy

1620 Mayflower Compact

1630 Puritan migration

3-1 English Beginnings in America

Focus: Why did Europeans establish colonies in North America?

Gold in the Americas! The Spanish had shown that fortunes could be made from the precious metals of the Western Hemisphere. This lesson was not lost on the French, the Dutch, and the English, who had their own hopes of getting a foothold in the Americas. Whatever other motives they may have had, the dream of riches was a vivid one they all shared. In an English play written in 1605, a sea captain describes the America of his dreams:

“I tell thee, gold is more plentiful there than copper is with us. Why, man, all their dripping pans are pure gold, and all the chains . . . are massive gold; all the prisoners they take are fettered in gold; and for rubies and diamonds, they gather 'hem by the sea-shore, to hang on their children's coats and stick in their children's caps.”

Mercantilism: Money and Power

Gold shone in the dreams of sea captains. It also formed the heart of a European economic system pioneered by the Spanish that came to be known as **mercantilism.** Under mercantilism, governments carefully regulated their economies in an effort to fill their treasuries with gold and silver. With such wealth, governments could build powerful armies and navies and strengthen their rule.

Connections: Geography

In 1585 the first English settlers in North America, dispatched by Sir Walter Raleigh, landed on Roanoke Island, just off present-day North Carolina. They returned to England, however, after only a year.

In 1587 a group of men, women, and children landed on Roanoke. A visitor there in 1590 found the colony deserted. There were no signs of a struggle and no evidence of what had happened to the colonists. The only clue left by this "lost colony" was the word CROATOAN carved on a doorpost.

1688 Mennonite protest against slavery

1732 Oglethorpe founds Georgia

1735 Trial of John Peter Zenger

1690 | 1720 | 1750

1682 Penn founds Pennsylvania

1722 Tuscaroras join League of the Iroquois

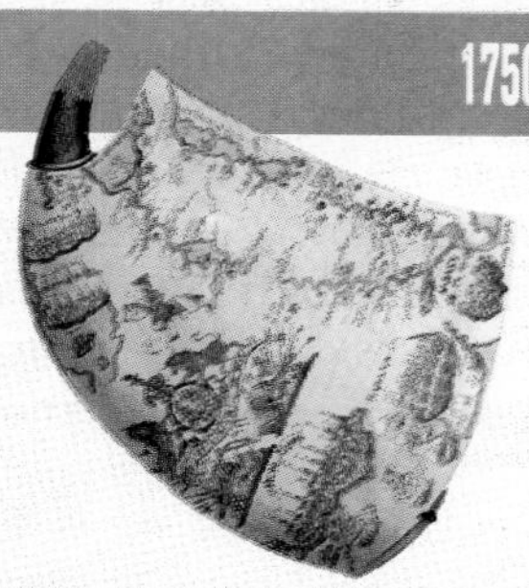

1754 French and Indian War

But the supply of gold and silver was limited. Thus, mercantilist nations needed to improve their **balance of trade,** the difference between the value of goods exported, or sold abroad, and the value of goods imported, or bought from other nations. If they could export more goods than they imported, they would have a favorable balance of trade. More gold and silver would flow into their treasuries than would flow out.

The idea of a "colony" was new. But colonies quickly became the centerpiece of the mercantilist system. European merchants saw that colonies could supply raw materials for workers in the parent country to make into manufactured goods. Colonies could also provide a ready market for those goods. And if a nation were as lucky as Spain had been, colonies themselves might be a source of gold and silver.

Financing Colonies

Establishing a colony was expensive and risky. Therefore, the English Crown encouraged merchants to form **joint-stock companies,** a business organization in which money was raised by selling shares, or stock, in the company to investors. Such companies were in many ways like modern corporations. With many people investing, a joint-stock company could obtain the large amounts of money needed for ships and supplies. The profits were divided among the investors according to the number of shares each held.

In December 1606 a joint-stock company called the London Company sent three ships carrying 144 men and boys across the Atlantic to Virginia. A ballad composed for the venture reflected their hopes:

> "*And cheerfully at sea,*
> *Success you still entice,*
> *To get the pearl and gold,*
> *And ours to hold,*
> *VIRGINIA,*
> *Earth's only Paradise.*"

Establishing Jamestown

"Earth's only Paradise," in reality, was a rude shock. For the site of their settlement the colonists chose a swampy area near a river they named the

Developing

THE SECTION

Connections: Economics

Discussion. Discuss with students the theory of mercantilism and why it led Spain and other nations to colonize North America.

1. What is the main goal of a mercantilist nation? **(to sell more goods than it buys)**
2. What term is used to describe this situation? **(favorable balance of trade)**
3. Why did mercantilist nations try to achieve this goal? **(With greater wealth, they could build strong military forces to increase their power.)**
4. How did Spain, France, and England achieve this goal? **(by establishing colonies as sources of gold and raw materials, and as markets for products)**

Active Learning

Paired Activity. Divide students into pairs. One should be a colonist; the other a mercantilist from the colonizing nation. Have each pair debate advantages and disadvantages of the mercantilist system.

BACKGROUND

Multicultural Perspectives

Powhatan's real name was Wa-hun-sen-a-cawh, but the colonists called him King Powhatan after the town where he lived. The confederation that he ruled was made up of some 200 villages and 32 tribes, with a total population of about 10,000 people.

Connections: Geography

In 1614 John Smith set off to hunt whales in the North Atlantic. Before returning to England, Smith mapped the east coast as far south as Cape Cod. He gave such English place names as Plymouth, Dartmouth, and Cambridge to sites along the way. Smith was the first to give the name "New England" to the territory previously known as Northern Virginia.

Analyzing Primary Sources

Pocahantas's Concerns. At first, Native Americans under Chief Powhatan helped the Jamestown colonists. Later, the Indians had second thoughts. Pocahantas, Powhatan's daughter, stated:

> *"Some doubt I have of your coming hither, that makes me not so kindly seek to relieve you as I would [like]. For many do inform me your coming is not for trade, but to invade my people and possess my country."*

1. What is Pocahantas's concern? **(Colonists will take over Indian lands.)**
2. Remind students that in 1618 the London Company granted colonists the right to own land. How might this have affected future relations between colonists and Native Americans? **(Hurt relations by confirming Indians' suspicions that European wanted to take over their lands.)**

Note that Section 3 will provide more information about how different views of land ownership caused conflict between Native Americans and white settlers.

Thinking Critically

Evaluation. Have students consider the advantages and disadvantages of the indenture system. **Ask:** Who took the greater risk in signing up an indentured servant—the person signing the indenture or the master?

Reduced student page in the Teacher's Edition

James, after their king. The site could be defended easily, but it swarmed with mosquitoes that carried malaria, a deadly disease. In addition, the drinking water was impure.

Most of the settlers were "gentlemen," unused to work, who brought starch for their ruffs and silver buckles for their shoes. They had no idea how to live in the wilderness. They had come to search for gold, and there was "no talke, no hope, nor work, but dig gold, wash gold, refine gold, load gold." Their "gold" turned out to be iron pyrite, a common mineral called "fool's gold."

Thirty-nine colonists had died crossing the Atlantic. During the first seven months, seventy-three more died of hunger and disease. That the rest survived was due to the efforts of Captain John Smith, a soldier, explorer, and self-proclaimed leader. Smith approached a confederation of tribes under the rule of the powerful Chief Powhatan. "It pleased God (in our extremity) to move the Indians to bring us corn, ere it was half ripe, to refresh us," Smith wrote, "when we rather expected they would destroy us."

Without Powhatan's help, the settlement probably would not have survived. The Indians not only brought food but taught the settlers how to grow new crops such as corn and yams and to use nets to fish.

Chances for survival improved in 1608. Two ships arrived with fresh supplies and more colonists. During the winter of 1608–1609, Smith forced order on Jamestown. Quoting from the Bible, Smith declared, "You must obey this for a law: He that will not work neither shall he eat." Soon the gentlemen were planting corn.

The colony suffered a major setback in the fall of 1609 when Smith was burned in a gunpowder explosion and returned to England. Discipline declined and relations with the tribes soured. Still more colonists had arrived, but without the necessary provisions. The winter of 1609–1610 became known as the "starving time." Only sixty of the more than eight hundred colonists survived, eating rats and anything else they could catch. Rumors circulated in England that some of the settlers had resorted to cannibalism.

Many colonists almost gave up. If Jamestown failed to make profits for the London Company, they reasoned, then surely it was doomed. But in 1610 another group of settlers arrived, and the colony struggled on. As one colonist wrote in *Newes from Virginia:*

> *"Let England knowe our willingnesse,*
> *For that our worke is good;*
> *Wee hope to plant a[n English] nation,*
> *Where none before hath stood."*

Changes in Jamestown

Very slowly, Jamestown edged toward prosperity. Around 1612 a colonist named John Rolfe planted some West Indies tobacco seeds in the fertile soil of Virginia. He also developed a method to cure the tobacco in a smokehouse rather than in the open air—as the Native Americans did—so that the product could be shipped long distances.

The sweet Jamestown tobacco was an instant success in England, despite King James's disapproval. Tobacco smoking, he said, was "loathesome to the eye, hateful to the nose, harmful to the brain, dangerous to the lungs." At last the colonists had a valuable product to export. They began to plant tobacco everywhere, even in the streets.

Because tobacco crops quickly exhausted the soil, the planters began taking over Native American lands for new fields. As the settlement inched up the James and other nearby rivers, the Powhatan Confederacy became alarmed. John Rolfe improved relations when he married Pocahontas, daughter of Chief Powhatan.

Land ownership and new arrivals. The London Company saw that it might yet make a profit from the Virginia tobacco trade. To attract more settlers, the company made several important changes. First, in 1618 colonists were given the right to own land. Now colonists who paid their own way to Virginia were granted fifty acres of land. They could receive another fifty acres for each new settler they brought to Virginia.

Settlers who were unable to pay their own way to the colony came as **indentured servants.** That is, they signed an indenture— a contract— agreeing to work four to seven years for the colonist who paid their passage.

Multicultural Perspectives

The first African-American child born in the English colonies, William Tucker, was born in 1621. Tucker's parents were among the first twenty Africans brought to Virginia in 1619.

Writing About History

Diary Entries. Have students imagine that they are colonists in Jamestown and write diary entries for the following times: winter of 1608–1609, fall of 1609, winter of 1609–1610, 1612, and 1619. Diary entries should give first-person accounts of problems colonists faced and their actions and attitudes.

Thinking Critically

Analysis. At first, grants of land were issued by the King of England. In part because of lack of knowledge of American geography, sometimes grants overlapped. Grants usually consisted of both the territory and the power to govern it.

Ask: How did the king get the land in the first place? (Explorers claimed land in the name of the king.) Who might dispute such a claim? Why? (Native Americans, foreign powers)

John Smith credited Pocahontas with saving Jamestown from famine. Native Americans also introduced the English to "drinking smoke." Virginia tobacco, which became the rage in England, provided Jamestown with a source of income.

The company also encouraged women to come to Virginia. It hoped that settlers who married and started families would make Virginia their permanent home. Company agents combed the English countryside telling poor farm families that their daughters could escape a life of poverty by going to Virginia. Many women signed marriage contracts that they could break on arrival if the men did not meet with their approval. In 1619 the first shipload of women arrived in the colony.

In that same year a Dutch ship brought twenty Africans to Virginia. Historians disagree about how many of these Africans were treated as indentured servants and later freed and how many were considered slaves, the permanent property of a master who bought them. The introduction of slavery opened a dismal chapter in the English settlement of America.

Steps to self-government. Another important chapter opened in 1619 when the London Company changed the way that Virginia was governed. Previously, a company-chosen governor and council of advisors had run the colony's affairs. Now the company decided that the colonists should "have a hand in the governing of themselves."

To achieve this limited degree of self-government, the settlement was divided into eleven districts. Adult males in each district were allowed to elect two representatives, called burgesses, to an assembly called the House of Burgesses. The assembly, together with the governor's council, became the colony's **legislature,** or group of people chosen to make laws. The Virginia House of Burgesses first met in the summer of 1619.

The House of Burgesses was the first representative assembly in colonial America. However, the burgesses were not representatives of the people as "the people" is meant today. By law, members were white male landowners. And they were more

GTV Side 1

Chap. 8, Frame 23002

Gottfried Mittelberger: Indentured Servants (American Journal)

Search:

Limited English Proficiency

Making Diagrams. Help students prepare diagrams showing the limited form of self-government in Virginia in 1619. The diagrams should show the relationship between the governor, the governor's council of advisors, and the burgesses from the eleven districts.

Backyard History

Research. Have students find out how and when the land in their community was first settled. Help them formulate questions to guide their research. For example, What Native-American peoples inhabited the land? In what order did various ethnic groups who now live in the community arrive?

Section Review

ANSWERS

1. Definitions for the following terms are on text pages indicated in parentheses: *mercantilism* (50), *balance of trade* (51), *joint-stock companies* (51), *indentured servants* (52), *legislature* (53), *veto* (54).
2. To improve its balance of trade, Britain established colonies that provided raw materials and markets for manufactured goods.
3. By signing indentures or marriage contracts.
4. White male landowners; it represented their interests.

Citizenship

In the English colonies, only white adult males who owned property could vote. African-American men did not gain the right to vote in national elections until ratification of the Fifteenth Amendment in 1870. Women gained suffrage with ratification of the Nineteenth Amendment in 1920. In 1924 the Indian Citizenship Act granted citizenship to Native Americans who had not yet acquired citizenship through treaty agreements and special congressional action. Citizenship did not automatically entitle Indians to vote. Some states, e.g. Arizona did not allow them to vote. The Twenty-sixth Amendment, ratified in 1971, gave the vote to eighteen-year-olds.

Reduced student page in the Teacher's Edition

concerned with efficiently managing the fortunes of the colony than with creating a new manner of governing.

Virginia Becomes a Royal Colony

The change in government failed to solve Virginia's problems. For the next few years the colony struggled, losing hundreds of settlers to disease, accidents, and departures back to England. More than one third of the population was killed in clashes with the Powhatan Confederacy, which was resisting the English takeover of Indian lands. Between 1619 and 1624, about 6,000 settlers came to Virginia, but the actual increase in Jamestown's population was only about 200.

As a result of warfare, much of Jamestown lay in ruins. The London Company had little hope of making a profit for investors or even paying its debts. Convinced that the colony was being mismanaged, King James sued the London Company. The king won the case in 1624, and the court took away the company's charter.

Now Virginia became a royal colony, with the governor and council of advisors appointed by the king. The authority for an assembly had disappeared with the company's charter, but the House of Burgesses continued to meet and pass laws, which either the governor or the king could **veto,** or reject.

Despite the London Company's failure, the Virginia Colony was relatively secure. The colonists had found a valuable crop—tobacco—that grew well in Virginia's climate. And with the House of Burgesses, they had taken a historic first step toward self-government.

Section Review

1. **Identification.** Define *mercantilism, balance of trade, joint-stock companies, indentured servants, legislature,* and *veto.*
2. **Comprehension.** How did mercantilism promote the colonization of North America?
3. **Analysis.** How could the poor in England afford to come to Virginia?
4. **Synthesis.** Which Jamestown dwellers do you suppose welcomed the creation of the House of Burgesses? Why?

3-2 Settling Colonies

Focus: What factors brought Europeans to settle in the English colonies?

Desire for profit led a few merchants and people of property to invest in the joint-stock companies that were attempting to plant colonies on the eastern coast of North America. But what motivated the thousands of ordinary people who pulled up stakes and risked their futures in an unknown land? What drew or forced them to take up life thousands of miles from their former homes? What were they giving up? And what were they hoping to find?

People in Motion: Reasons for Migration

Answers to the question of why settlers came to the colonies can be found partly in conditions in England in the 1600s. There, economic problems and religious conflict drove waves of the poor and the persecuted to America when the opportunity arose.

The roots of the economic conditions lay in basic changes in land ownership. Beginning in the

Global Connections

Land was a magnet that drew settlers to North America. In Europe the oldest child in a family, often the oldest son, inherited the family estate, a practice called *primogeniture.* This system kept large landholdings from being divided among the children into many small estates. Peasants as well as nobles practiced primogeniture. Many landless younger offspring sought land and opportunity in North America. Primogeniture in England ended in 1925, except for the royal family.

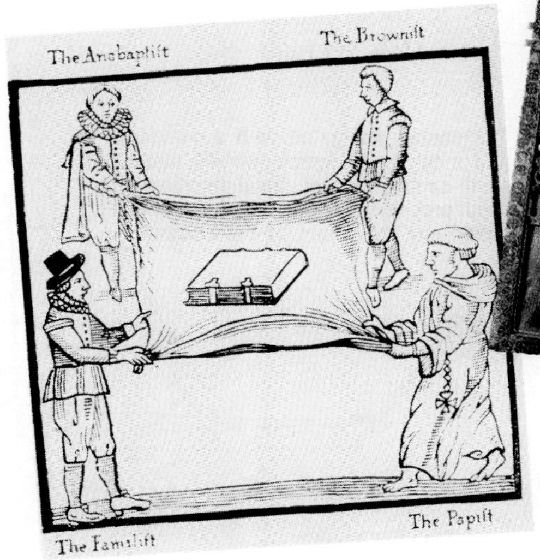

English Christians opposed to the Church of England (left) and Protestants in Catholic Austria (above) came to the colonies to escape religious conflict in Europe.

late 1400s, a great demand for wool encouraged English landowners to raise sheep on a large scale. To create grazing areas for the sheep, landowners enclosed, or fenced off, land that until then they had rented out as small farms. "Sheep eat men" was the angry cry of evicted farmers, and riots broke out the year Jamestown was settled. Uprooted farmers roamed from countryside to town and from town to city looking for work.

At the same time, England's population was growing rapidly. As a result, an increasing number of people were in motion, looking for work, opportunity, and stability in their lives. In the average English village, three out of every four young men between the ages of fifteen and nineteen had to leave home to work in other households or businesses. It was no wonder that many people would risk the voyage to North America in the hope of a fresh start.

Many English also came to see North America as a haven from religious persecution. By law, everyone had to belong to the Church of England. But some remained Catholics. Others, called Puritans, believed in simpler, "purer" forms of worship— replacing the prayer book with the Bible, simplifying the service, and strictly observing the Sabbath. Depending upon the sympathies of the ruler, Puritans as well as Catholics were persecuted in the 1600s.

Puritan Colonies in New England

Most Puritans stayed within the Church of England and tried to change it. Some, however, followed the words of the Bible in the Second Book of Corinthians: "Come out from among them and be ye separate, saith the Lord." Thus they set up a separate church. For breaking with the official church, the Separatists were thrown into prison.

Many of the Separatists fled to the Netherlands. But they never felt at home there and worried that

Section 3-2

Objectives

- ***Answer the Focus Question.***
- *Explain how proprietary, royal, and self-governing colonies differed.*
- *Describe how representative government was established in the colonies.*

Introducing

THE SECTION

Ask students why they think people of today, as in the 1600s, leave their homelands and settle where language, customs, and environment may be very different. Ask students who are recent immigrants to discuss their families' motivations for coming to the United States.

Tell students that while the previous section dealt primarily with the profit motive for English colonization of North America, this section deals with some of the other factors that led Europeans to set up colonies in North America.

GTV Side 1

Chap. 9, Frame 23799

Settling Down, Moving On (Movie)

Search:

Play:

Developing THE SECTION

Analyzing Primary Sources

Mayflower Compact. Obtain a copy of the Mayflower Compact and read from it to students. Have them explain in their own words the rules contained in the document. **Ask:**

1. Why did the Pilgrims think it necessary to draw up such a document? **(They wanted a single written document that would spell put their rights and a governing agreement.)**
2. Why is the Mayflower Compact considered an important step toward self-government? **(It established a framework of organization for their community in the absence of a higher authority.)**

Thinking Critically

Evaluation. Under English common law, women were not allowed to sign documents such as the Mayflower Compact. Have students give their opinions as to whether the document was a democratic advance in spite of this restriction.

Backyard History

Attending a Town Meeting. If you live in an area of the country that still holds town meetings, have interested students attend one. Have them take notes on issues raised and decisions reached, then write a summary of the proceedings. They may share their experience with the rest of the class.

Social History

Captain John Smith wanted to serve aboard the *Mayflower* as a guide and advisor. He was turned down, Smith complained, "to save charges" because "my books and maps were much better cheap to teach them, than myself." He may have been right, for Smith's books and maps were indeed carried aboard the *Mayflower.*

Reduced student page in the Teacher's Edition

their children were growing up more Dutch than English. A small number of English Separatists, who became known as the Pilgrims, decided to build their own communities in North America. They joined a group planning to go to Virginia and were given permission by the London Company to settle north of Jamestown.

Pilgrims in Plymouth. On September 16, 1620, thirty-five Separatist men, women, and children set out from England on the *Mayflower*. With them were sixty-six non-Pilgrim "strangers," some of them indentured servants, who also intended to settle in Virginia. Storms blew the little ship far to the north of Virginia. Unable to sail south in the rough seas, the party was forced to land on Cape Cod.

Since they had permission to settle only in Virginia, the laws in their charter applied only to Virginia. Thus, as one "stranger" declared, "None had the power to command them," and they were free to do as they wished. But the Separatist leaders persuaded most of the men aboard ship to sign what is known as the Mayflower Compact. In the compact they agreed to form themselves into "a civill body politick" and promised to obey laws made by leaders of their own choosing "for the general good of the colony."

The Mayflower Compact was rooted in the Judeo-Christian idea of a covenant, an agreement in which God would see to the people's well-being in return for their allegiance. The idea of a covenant was later used by Puritans forming governments in Connecticut, New Hampshire, and Rhode Island colonies. It helped to establish the American tradition of democratic government that rests on the consent of the governed.

The Pilgrims established a government based on the Mayflower Compact. The signers of the compact met as the General Court, choosing the governor and council of advisors, enacting laws, and voting taxes. Eventually, the court became an assembly of representatives from the towns.

More important to the average settler, however, was the town meeting. Here residents met regularly to debate and vote on common solutions to problems and to elect "selectmen" to manage their affairs between meetings. They created other offices, such as highway surveyors, and appointed committees to deal with special questions. Later, Thomas Jefferson remarked that town meetings were "the best school of political liberty the world ever saw." Today, town meetings still form the backbone of government in many New England towns.

Puritans in Massachusetts Bay. Meanwhile, in England another group of Puritans, suffering from persecution and bad economic conditions, applied for and received a charter for a colony to be located north of Plymouth. In 1629 these Puritans, organized as the Massachusetts Bay Company, began to settle in New England.

The captain navigated with a compass and a backstaff, which roughly measured north-south progress. To determine east-west progress, he estimated the ship's speed and the effect of the current.

Learning From Art
Cross Section of the *Mayflower*

Connections: Literature
In his lengthy poem *Western Star*, Stephen Vincent Benét describes the settlement of Jamestown and Plymouth. Included are character sketches of people such as John Smith, Pocahontas, and individual Pilgrims.

They believed that God favored the move, saying, "God will be with us, and if God be with us, who can be against us?"

The Massachusetts Bay Company planned its colony as a community where Puritans would live together under God's laws. John Winthrop, the first governor of Massachusetts, hoped the colony would be an example for the rest of the world:

> *"We must . . . rejoice together, mourn together, labor and suffer together, always having before our eyes our commission and our common work. . . . For we must consider that we shall be like a City upon a Hill; the eyes of all people are on us."*

The Puritans were free to follow their religious beliefs because theirs was a self-governing colony, largely free of royal control. Their charter granted shareholders authority to govern the colony. But the charter, unlike other joint-stock company charters, did not require company headquarters to be in England. Thus, it was possible for the Puritans to transfer the company, the charter, and the whole government to Massachusetts.

Laws in Massachusetts were passed by the General Court, which gradually changed from a meeting of shareholders to a legislature with deputies to represent each town. In the 1640s the Massachusetts legislature became a **bicameral,** or two-house, assembly, with the deputies and advisors sitting separately, but with all decisions requiring a majority in each house. At first, only church members could vote for deputies, but both members and nonmembers could vote in town meetings. These developments were important steps in the expansion of democracy in the English colonies.

The expansion of New England. No sooner had the first colonists settled in Massachusetts Bay than they began to spread out into the rest of New England. Lured by what seemed to be unlimited empty land, people

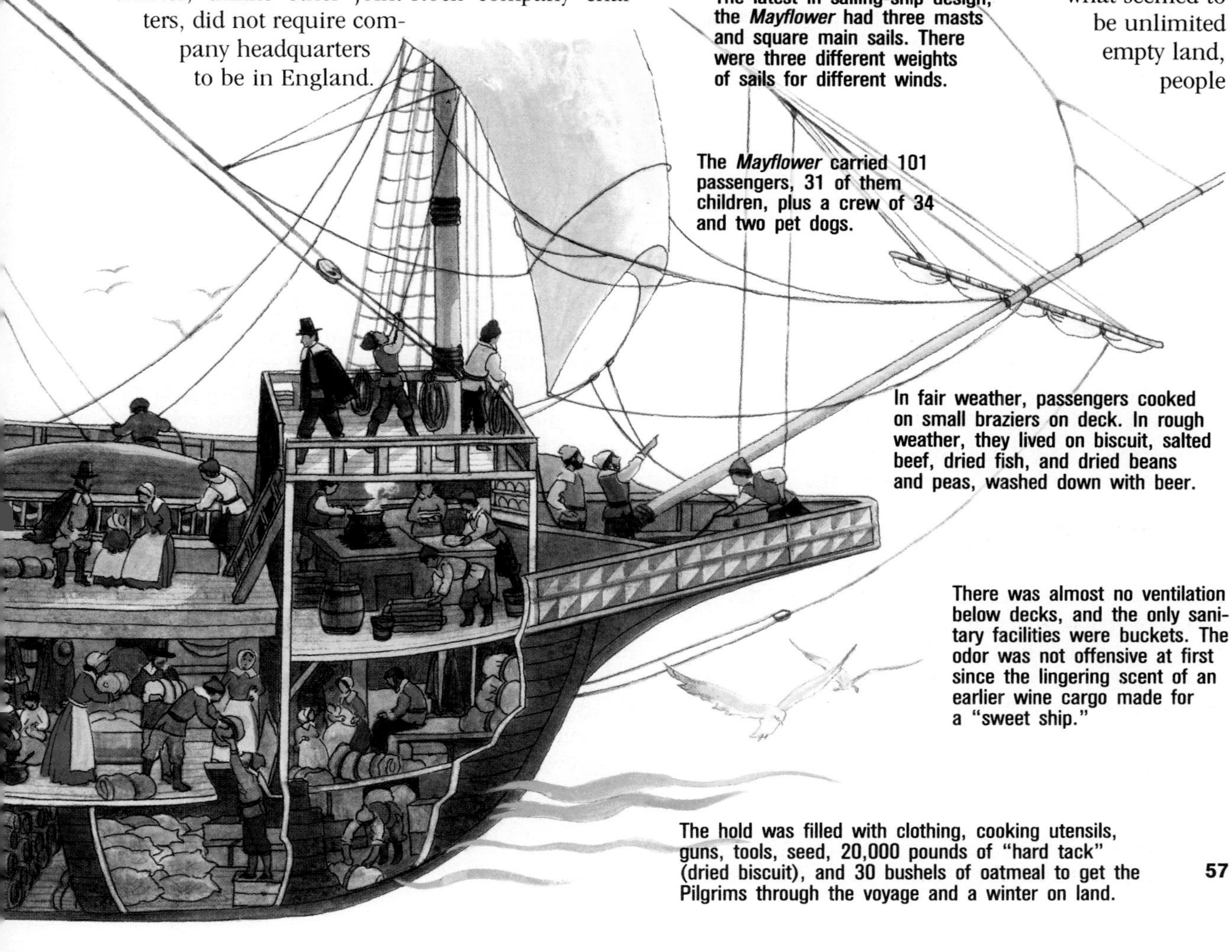

The latest in sailing-ship design, the *Mayflower* had three masts and square main sails. There were three different weights of sails for different winds.
The *Mayflower* carried 101 passengers, 31 of them children, plus a crew of 34 and two pet dogs.
In fair weather, passengers cooked on small braziers on deck. In rough weather, they lived on biscuit, salted beef, dried fish, and dried beans and peas, washed down with beer.
There was almost no ventilation below decks, and the only sanitary facilities were buckets. The odor was not offensive at first since the lingering scent of an earlier wine cargo made for a "sweet ship."
The hold was filled with clothing, cooking utensils, guns, tools, seed, 20,000 pounds of "hard tack" (dried biscuit), and 30 bushels of oatmeal to get the Pilgrims through the voyage and a winter on land.

Linking Past and Present

Writing. Refer students to the quotation on this page, in which John Winthrop uses the phrase "City upon a Hill" to describe his vision for Massachusetts. Tell them that Ronald Reagan quoted the phrase in a 1980 presidential debate.

Have students use reference materials to locate the debate and write a paragraph explaining what Reagan was referring to.

Analyzing Primary Sources

Puritan Attitudes. Before leaving England, some Puritans foresaw a moral dilemma for colonists in relation to Native Americans:

> *"By what right or warrant can we enter into the land of the Savages and take away their rightful inheritance from them and plant ourselves in their places?"*

Not long after settling in Massachusetts, however, the Puritans had begun to believe that they were chosen by God to subdue the "Savages" and inherit the land. When a smallpox epidemic ravaged the Indian population, John Winthrop remarked:

> *"If God were not pleased with our inheriting these parts, why did he drive the natives before us? And why doth he still make room for us by diminishing them as we increase?"*

Discuss how this attitude might influence future actions of settlers.

Connections: Religion

Anne Hutchinson, like Roger Williams, was banished from Massachusetts. Hutchinson had questioned the need to pray and do good works in order to receive God's favor. Deemed dangerous by some Puritan leaders, she was tried and convicted of heresy in 1637, and exiled from the colony.

Hutchinson and her family fled to Rhode Island, followed by thirty-five families. After her husband's death, she moved to New York, where Indians who had been defraued of their land thought she was an enemy and killed her and her family in 1643.

Active Learning

Cooperative Activity. Many of the products we take for granted today took enormous preparation time in colonial days. Have students work in small groups to research and present oral reports on the methods and materials colonists used to make such items as soap, shoes, cloth, bread, candles, barrels, and wheels.

Reports might be illustrated with flow charts, showing the steps involved. Discuss how the processes differ today.

Writing About History

Letters. The Middle and Southern colonies had no public schools. Schooling was usually privately funded. New York, for example, had English, Dutch, French, and Hebrew private schools. Have students write letters to officials of the Middle Colonies urging them to provide public education and giving reasons why everyone should have the opportunity for an education.

Reduced student page in the Teacher's Edition

moved, created farms, established towns, then moved again, establishing new farms and towns.

Some people moved in search of greater religious freedom. Although the Puritans had come to America to escape Anglican rule in England, they did not accept the idea of religious freedom. Puritans ridiculed people of other religious beliefs as the "Lord's debris." Government, they believed, should support the church, and people who disagreed with the church should be punished.

A young minister named Roger Williams, who arrived in 1631, was among the first to quarrel with Puritan leaders. He argued that laws that required church attendance made the church impure because sinners worshipped with God's elect. He also insisted that Native Americans, not the English king, had a rightful claim to American lands.

Williams was found guilty of holding "new and dangerous opinions" and was banished. He fled south, bought land from the Narragansetts, and in 1636 established the town of Providence in what is now Rhode Island.

In 1644 Williams received a charter establishing Rhode Island as a self-governing colony. Believing now that the purity of the church required complete separation of church and state, he rejected laws establishing a state religion and welcomed people of all faiths. Rhode Island settlers, he declared, had "as great liberty as any people . . . under the whole heaven."

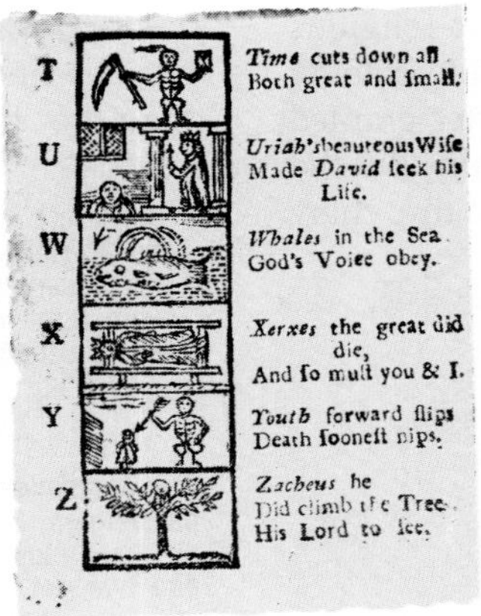

A New England reader.

Good farm land and the desire for fewer government restrictions led Thomas Hooker and his congregation to settle in Connecticut. In 1639 the General Court adopted the Fundamental Orders of Connecticut, setting up a government like Massachusetts' except voting was not limited to church members. Connecticut received a royal charter in 1662 but remained a self-governing colony.

In their search for new land, Massachusetts colonists also went north to New Hampshire and Maine. Massachusetts claimed both regions as part of its territory. But in 1680 the king declared New Hampshire to be a separate royal colony. Maine remained a part of Massachusetts until 1820.

Proprietary Colonies

In some cases, very wealthy individuals also sought to profit from resource-rich North America. Taking advantage of their connections with the king, several such individuals became owners of colonies. Established for a wide variety of reasons, these colonies lured diverse peoples looking for a fresh start in life.

A refuge in Maryland. George Calvert saw in America an opportunity to make great profits on tobacco. A Catholic, he wanted to start a colony where Catholics would have religious freedom. In 1632 King Charles I granted land on the Chesapeake Bay north of Virginia to his friend. Calvert died before receiving his charter, so it was granted to his son, the second Lord Baltimore.

Maryland was the first proprietary colony. In this type of colony, the proprietor, or owner, controlled all land and appointed the governor. However, the charter provided that laws must be passed with the "Advice, Assent, and [Approval] of the Free-Men of the . . . Province." These landholders were elected in a representative assembly like Virginia's House of Burgesses.

Many settlers in Maryland were wealthy Catholics. Many more, though, were Protestant laborers. Lord Baltimore began to fear that the Protestant majority would turn against the Catholics. At his request, the Maryland assembly passed the Toleration Act of 1649, giving religious freedom to Catholics and Protestants alike.

The Carolinas. Hoping to prevent the Spanish from advancing any farther into North America, in 1663 King Charles II gave a huge area of land between Virginia and Spanish Florida to eight "right trusty and right well-beloved cousins and counsellors." Almost from the first, Carolina was a divided colony. Settlers in the north established small farms. Then, around 1695 a special strain of rice was introduced that turned the southern part of the colony into a land of prosperous rice plantations worked by enslaved Africans.

Multicultural Perspectives

The first Jews to arrive in North America were "New Christians," Spanish Jews who had been forced to convert to Christianity. They were among the first Spaniards to come to Mexico, and some traveled north to what is now the southwestern United States.

The first avowed Jews arrived in New Amsterdam from Brazil in 1654. By the mid-1700s there were about 2,000 Jews in England's thirteen colonies, living mainly in New York, Philadelphia, Charleston, Newport, and Savannah. The Touro Synagogue in Newport, Rhode Island, dedicated in 1763, is the oldest synagogue in the United States. The Jewish people in Newport had feared that their faith might be lost if their children remained "uninstructed in our most holy and divine law."

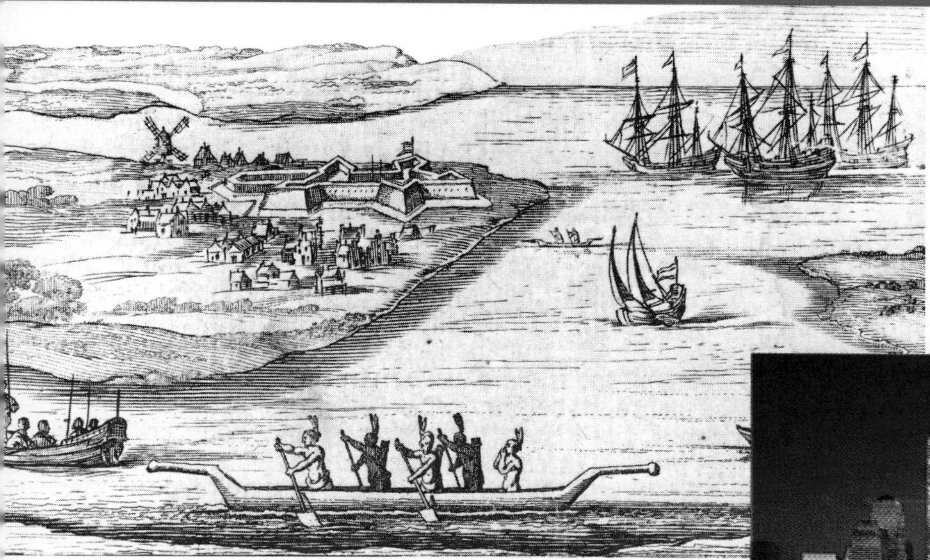

Iroquois in fur-laden canoes head for New Amsterdam to trade in the 1630s. Today, New York City is still a bustling center of trade, and home to a mix of diverse peoples.

The proprietors could not prevent Spanish attacks nor keep Carolina unified. In 1729 the Crown ended proprietary rule, and North and South Carolina became separate royal colonies, each with an elected assembly.

New York. The threat posed by Spanish Florida was not the only one to worry Charles II. The Dutch colony of New Netherland, which lay between New England and Maryland, was a barrier dividing the English colonies.

In 1664 Charles granted the territory to his brother, James, Duke of York. The duke's warships captured New Amsterdam, and the English soon conquered the remainder of the Dutch empire in North America. Four colonies—New York, New Jersey, Pennsylvania, and Delaware—were eventually carved out of New Netherland.

The "holy experiment" of William Penn. Like New England, Pennsylvania was colonized by people who refused to accept the doctrines of the Church of England. The proprietor of the new colony was William Penn, who received the land in 1681 as payment for a debt Charles II owed to Penn's late father. The following year the Duke of York transferred to Penn the territory known as Delaware, which remained a part of the colony of Pennsylvania until 1701.

Penn was a convert to the Religious Society of Friends, better known as Quakers, and viewed his colony as a "holy experiment," where Quakers and others "would be allowed to shape their own laws." His Frame of Government for Pennsylvania called for an elected assembly and gave religious freedom to all who believed in God. Settlers flocked to Pennsylvania from all over Europe. In 1684 Penn, satisfied with the results of his idealistic experiment, wrote, "I have led the greatest colony into America that ever anyone did upon private credit."

Georgia. Ideals also played a part in the establishment of Georgia, the last English colony. In 1732 King George II granted the land between South Carolina and Florida to a group of wealthy English people led by James Edward Olgethorpe. As a young man, Oglethorpe had watched a friend die in debtors' prison; his friend's only crime was being too poor to pay his debts. Oglethorpe wanted to save other debtors from jail. In Georgia, he hoped, they could become independent farmers. Oglethorpe also hoped that a colony in Georgia would protect the Carolinas from Spanish attacks.

Oglethorpe planned and established a community of small farms where slavery was forbidden, and no representative assembly was allowed. Unhappy with those rules, many of the colonists moved to South Carolina, where there was no limit on the amount of land or the number of slaves they could buy. As a result, by 1750 Ogelthorpe's rules had been abandoned. Two years later, Georgia became a royal colony.

Thinking Critically

Analysis. William Penn believed in dealing fairly with Native Americans. The land he was given by King Charles belonged to the Leni-Lape tribe, called the Delaware by the English. Penn made a treaty of friendship with the Leni-Lape and paid them for most of the land given him.

Ask: How did Penn's attitude toward Indians differ from other colonists'? How might the history of relations between the Indians and the English colonists been different if other colonists had adopted Penn's attitude?

GTV Side 1

Chap. 9, Frame 24153

The Thirteen Colonies, Mid-1700s (Map)

Search:

GTV Side 1

Chap. 9, Frame 24782

Colonial Regions, Mid-1700s (Map)

Search:

Active Learning

Role Play. Have interested students work in a group to re-enact the trial of John Peter Zenger. They should play the following roles: Zenger, Andrew Hamilton, the governor of New York, the governor's lawyer, witnesses, and two judges. The rest of the class can be the jury.

Writing About History

Editorials. Have students imagine that they are editors of New York City newspapers at the time of the Zenger trial. Ask them to write editorials either supporting or criticizing Zenger's acquittal. They should summarize the issue and express a clear point of view. Students may read their editorials in class.

Linking Past and Present

Discussion. Freedom of the press is an issue that will appear over and over again in American history. Ask students why they think this is so. Can they cite present-day examples of controversy over this issue?

Exploring Issues

ANSWERS

1. He feared that freedom of the press might stir up rebellion against the government.
2. A check on the power of the government.
3. Answers may include limits during times of war.

Social History

Elizabeth Timothy was the first woman publisher in the colonies. She took over her late husband's paper, the *South Carolina Gazette*. An estimated thirty colonial women published newspapers.

Reduced student page in the Teacher's Edition

Exploring Issues

FREEDOM OF THE PRESS

The Trial of John Peter Zenger

On August 4, 1735, New Yorkers crowded into a courtroom. John Peter Zenger, a printer, was on trial for publishing criticisms of the royal governor. Zenger's case had been the talk of New York for months. Yet as his trial began, few thought it would become a landmark in the history of freedom of the press in America.

Zenger had little hope of victory. The governor had hand-picked the judges. Zenger's lawyer had had his right to practice law taken away. But as the trial began, Andrew Hamilton, a famous Philadelphia lawyer, arrived to defend the printer.

The Zenger case rested on questions of justice and freedom. The royal governor, William Cosby, had abused his power by accepting bribes and interfering with elections. New York's only newspaper, controlled by the governor, dared not criticize him. Then, in 1733 Zenger started the *New York Weekly Journal*, the first American newspaper to be independent of government control. Week after week, the four-page newspaper boldly attacked the governor's actions.

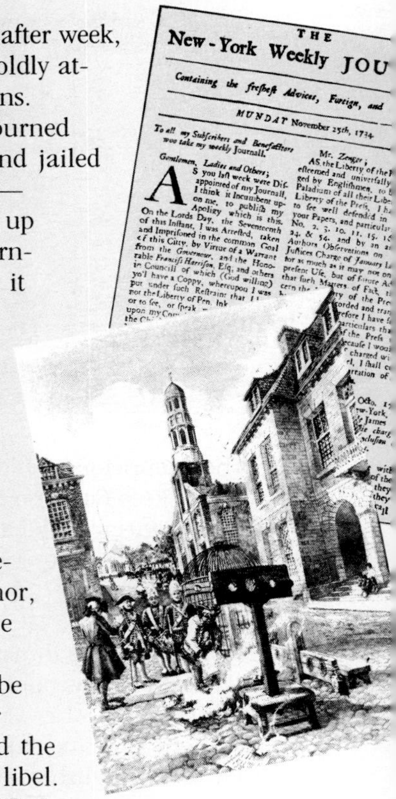

Furious, the governor burned copies of the newspaper and jailed Zenger for seditious libel—making statements to stir up rebellion against the government. Under English law, it did not matter whether the statements were true or false.

At the trial, Hamilton admitted that Zenger had printed the statements. However, the lawyer said, the critical question was not whether Zenger's statements attacked the governor, but whether they were true or false. If the statements were false, Zenger would be guilty of libel. But Zenger had printed the truth, and the truth could not be called libel. Hamilton told the court: "It is the truth alone that can excuse or justify anyone for complaining of a bad administration."

The judges warned Hamilton that his argument was against English libel law. But Hamilton asked the twelve jurors to ignore the opinion of the judges. He urged them "to hear with their own ears and to make use of their own consciences."

Colonial Government and English Rights

By the 1750s the colonists enjoyed the rights of a growing democracy. The basis of these rights could be traced to the *Magna Carta,* or "Great Charter," of England, which placed limits on the power of the king. Drawn up by the great nobles and signed by King John in 1215, the charter listed rights that even the monarch could not take away, such as the right to a fair trial. Although the Magna Carta was intended to protect only nobles, the rights it listed were eventually given to all English people, including the colonists.

The seeds of representative government had also been planted long before in England. In the mid-

The jury listened intently as Hamilton declared that people had the right to know what the government was doing and the right to protest the abuses of government. He concluded:

"The question before the Court . . . may in its consequence affect every freeman that lives under a British government on the main of America. It is the best cause. It is the cause of liberty . . . the liberty of both exposing and opposing arbitrary power . . . by speaking and writing truth."

Within ten minutes, the jurors reached their verdict: "Not guilty." Cheers filled the packed courtroom. The next day Zenger was released from jail and went back to publishing his newspaper.

Although the verdict freed Zenger, it did not change English law nor end government control of the press. However, Zenger's case inspired other colonists to fight for freedom of the press. When they created their own government many years later, they wrote that freedom into the law.

1. Why did Governor Cosby try to prevent freedom of the press?
2. What do you think is the role of freedom of the press in a democracy?
3. Do you think there should be limits to freedom of the press? Explain.

1200s the people won the right to a legislature, called Parliament, with two houses. The House of Lords drew its members from the nobility, or peers, while the House of Commons was made up of representatives who were elected by landowners.

In 1689 Parliament passed the English Bill of Rights, further limiting the power of the monarch. For example, the monarch could no longer collect taxes without Parliament's approval. The English Bill of Rights lists the rights of all English, not just nobles. These include the right to a trial by jury and the right to make a formal petition, or request, to the government.

As subjects of the English Crown, colonists in America believed that all the rights in the English Bill of Rights belonged to them. Some colonists went even further and demanded rights not yet recognized in England, such as freedom of the press.

Colonial assemblies. By the 1750s each colony had an elected assembly, which was looked on as a small parliament with the right to vote on laws and taxes. If a royal governor vetoed an assembly's laws, the assembly could punish him by refusing to vote funds for his salary. One stubborn governor of North Carolina went eleven years without receiving pay.

The English government did not think of the colonial assemblies as small parliaments. Although English monarchs could not veto an act of Parliament, they claimed the power to strike down any colonial law. So did colonial governors appointed by the Crown.

The experience of building colonies in North America drastically changed people. From the start, many looked on North America—not England—as their home, and on themselves as Americans. The English government, however, continued to see the colonies as a means to achieve mercantilist goals. These opposing views planted the seeds of political separation that would soon blossom into the demand for independence.

Section Review

1. Identification. Define *bicameral.*

2. Comprehension. List two problems that led English people to settle in England's colonies in North America.

3. Analysis. How did proprietary, royal, and self-governing colonies differ?

4. Evaluation. If you had been a colonist, would you have wanted a representative assembly? Give reasons for your answer.

Limited English Proficiency

Making Time Lines. Have students work in pairs to make time lines of some of the important developments on the path to representative government in North America. They should draw a vertical time line for the period 1600–1760, broken into 20-year time spans.

Events should include: the first session of the House of Burgesses in Jamestown (1619); Mayflower Compact (1620); representative assembly in Maryland (1630s), Fundamental Orders of Connecticut (1639), bicameral legislature in Massachusetts (1640s), Penn's Frame of Government (1680s), an elected assembly in each of the Carolinas (1729).

Section Review
ANSWERS

1. See definition of *bicameral* on text page 57.
2. Unemployment; religious persecution.
3. Proprietary: proprietor controlled all land and appointed governor; royal: governed by monarch's representative; self-governing: largely free from royal control with charter granting stockholders authority over colony.
4. Answers may include: in colonies where suffrage limited to white male landowners, an assembly might not have made any difference to some people. However, all colonists—at least, white males—could hope that eventually they would own land and thus have a voice in government.

Section 3-3

Objectives

- ***Answer the Focus Question.***
- *Analyze how patterns of racism began.*
- *Explain the relationship between cash crops, enslaved Africans, and the triangular trade.*

Introducing THE SECTION

Ask: Before you can predict what settlers will do upon arriving in the colonies, what do you need to know about them? **(their origins, political, religious, and social backgrounds; their goals)** How do you suppose the motives of the colonists affected their ways of living and treatment of other peoples?

Developing THE SECTION

Connections: Economics

Discussion. During colonial times, farm families were largely self-sufficient. One farmer wrote:

"I never laid out (besides my taxes) more than ten dollars a year, which was for salt, nails, and the like. Nothing to wear, eat, or drink was purchased, as my farm provided all."

Ask: Since most colonists lived on largely self-sufficient farms and plantations, why did cities grow up?

B · A · C · K · G · R · O · U · N · D

Social History
In 1750 one out of twenty colonists lived in a city. Philadelphia, Pennsylvania, the most advanced of these cities, boasted street lights, paved streets, a police department, a fire company, a newspaper, and America's first public library, hospital, and insurance company. Most of these were the contributions of Benjamin Franklin.

Franklin had come to Philadelphia at age seventeen and by the time he reached his fifties he had been a printer, newspaper publisher, inventor, scientist, diplomat, and postmaster general of the colonial postal system.

Reduced student page in the Teacher's Edition

3-3 Shaping New Patterns of Life

Focus: How did diversity affect life in the colonies?

In 1759 a young English minister named Andrew Burnaby spent two years traveling through the colonies and then went home to write a book about the future of England's outposts in America. Could the colonies ever unite? "Almost impossible," predicted Burnaby.

"Such is the difference of character, of manners, of religion, of interest, of the different colonies, that I think . . . were they left to themselves, there would soon be a civil war, from one end of the continent to the other."

By the time Burnaby visited America, each colony had developed its own distinct identity. Diversity was part of that identity. It made America, with its many cultures and peoples, unlike any place in Europe. But diversity often caused conflict, challenging the willingness of the colonists to treat all people with respect.

Different Colonies, Different Interests

"America is the land of work," said Benjamin Franklin, and most colonists worked at farming. They depended on Europe for the goods they needed and wanted but could not produce themselves—salt, tea, guns, ammunition, nails, tools, paint, glass, household items. Thus, growing just enough to live on was not enough. Colonists had to earn money to pay for imported goods, livestock, land improvements, and taxes. Different solutions to the need for money developed in the three major colonial regions.

Cash crops and plantations. The Southern Colonies, made up of Virginia, Maryland, the Carolinas, and Georgia, had a unique advantage—a warm climate almost year-round. Colonists there could grow crops prized by England that would not grow farther north. Virginia, it was said, was "founded on smoke." The tobacco of Virginia, Maryland, and North Carolina became the great **cash crop**—a crop raised to be sold for a profit—of colonial America.

Learning From Art A Colonial Street About 1760

To attract skilled craftspeople, a town or city often promised a house or land.

Due to the high cost of building materials, most homes were small. The front room often served as the owner's store, office, or workshop.

Street peddlers sold fish, eggs, produce, mintwater, buttermilk, and yeast. Grinders sharpened knives, razors, and scissors.

Connections: Health
Another business found in most colonial towns was the apothecary, or drugstore. Apothecaries often mixed natural ingredients to make their own medicines. Rhubarb relieved stomachache, chamomile flowers were a cramp remedy.

After 1695 rice became an important cash crop in South Carolina and Georgia. Later, in the 1740s, seventeen-year-old Eliza Lucas of South Carolina produced the first successful crop of indigo, a plant used to make blue dye. It, too, found a ready market in England. So did furs, lumber, and naval stores—tar, pitch, and turpentine.

Although many small farmers lived in the Southern Colonies, plantations dominated the economy. These large farms were organized for the production of cash crops and relied on a large labor force. Originally, plantations used indentured servants; later, they used enslaved Africans. The riverside location of plantations gave owners direct access to ocean-going ships that moved up and down the rivers, taking on crops and dropping off English goods. Access was so easy that few cities developed as centers of commerce.

Cash crops and commerce. With good land and climate, New York, New Jersey, Pennsylvania, and Delaware—the Middle Colonies—relied on grains as cash crops. During the 1700s huge wheat surpluses were milled into flour and exported to New England, the West Indies, Britain, and Europe. By 1750 grain was second to tobacco as the colonies' leading export.

Because of a harsh climate and rocky land, colonists in the New England Colonies—Massachusetts, New Hampshire, Rhode Island, and Connecticut—turned to the forests and the sea for products they could sell. Fishing grounds rich in cod, mackerel, and halibut were nearby. Dried and salted, New England fish became a major export. Whales supplied whale oil for lamps.

Fishing led to shipbuilding, and New England forests provided lumber, masts, pitch, and tar. In 1631 the first merchant ship, the *Blessing of the Bay,* was launched, and soon all the leading towns were building ships. Business increased so rapidly that after 1700 New England was selling ships in the Southern Colonies, the West Indies, England, Spain, and Portugal.

New England built its commercial success on what has been called the triangular trade, with Europe or Africa, the English colonies in the West Indies, and an American port as the three corners. On one route, New Englanders sold fish to the sugar planters of Barbados and Jamaica and, in return, bought sugar and molasses to make rum. Then they traded the rum for enslaved Africans on the African coast and took the slaves to the West Indies to sell to the planters. The profits were used to buy more sugar and molasses.

Trade rivalries were common among the colonies. Burnaby noted that

> *“Pennsylvania and New York have an inexhaustible source of . . . jealousy for the trade of [New Jersey], [and] Massachusetts Bay and Rhode Island are not less interested in that of Connecticut. The West Indies are a common subject of [rivalry] to them all.”*

Since land travel at night was risky, taverns and inns were vital. They became social and political centers where people learned news from travelers and discussed issues.

Cabinetmakers produced fine furniture using design books written by English furniture makers.

With no banks to deposit money in, colonists often converted their silver coin into silverware. The silver did not lose value and could be reconverted into coin by taking it to the mint.

Backyard History

Research. Have students do research for reports on changes in the local economy that have occurred since their city or town was founded. Suggest that they include both the original economic base (for example, fishing, cotton, timber) and its present economic base.

Connections: Geography

Discussion. Have students explain how geography affected the way colonial people made a living. Ask students to name products of the New England, Middle, and Southern colonies. Then refer them to the map on page 907. Ask them to compare the products of the three regions today with the products of the regions in colonial times. Why are there similarities? Differences?

Limited English Proficiency

Active Learning. Have students bring in pictures from magazines or newspapers showing people working at various kinds of jobs. Discuss how economic activities have changed and/or stayed the same since colonial times.

GTV Side 1

Chap. 10, Frame 27522

John Reynolds: Settling on the Pennsylvania Frontier (American Journal)

Search: Play:

Linking Past and Present

Research. Have interested students research and report on present United States imports and exports, United States trading partners, and status of balance of trade between the United States and its trading partners.

Thinking Critically

Analysis. Discuss the impact of the Navigation Acts by asking:

1. How did the acts reflect England's mercantilist goals? (forced American colonists to export their products either to England or other English colonies)

2. How did the acts benefit England? (ensured it a steady supply of raw materials at a relatively low price) The colonies? (provided a guaranteed market for their goods)

3. How did the acts work to the disadvantage of the colonies? (prevented them from selling their goods to the highest bidder and from buying goods at the lowest prices; prevented growth of manufacturing)

Geography Skills

ANSWERS

1. Boston; Charleston; New York or Philadelphia.
2. West Indies, Africa, Portugal.
3. Triangular trade routes:
(a) To Africa, to West Indies, to colonies. (b) To West Indies, to England, to colonies.
(c) To Portugal, to England, to colonies.

Reduced student page in the Teacher's Edition

Colonial Overseas Trade Routes

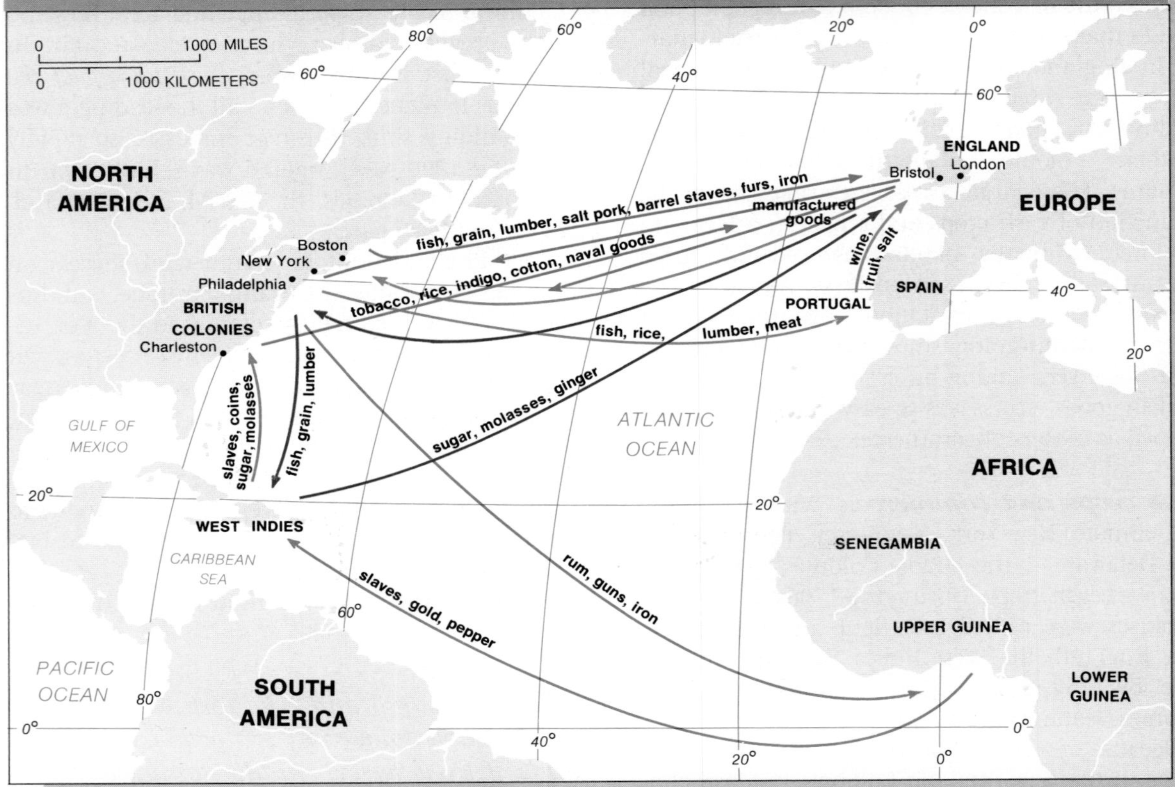

Geography Skills—Movement: Name an important trade center in New England. In the Southern Colonies. In the Middle Colonies. Where besides England did colonial ships sail? Describe three triangular trade routes.

The Navigation Acts. In the mercantilist system, colonial trade should have been only with England and its colonies. But the colonists carried on trade with foreign competitors, too. To make sure that English rather than foreign merchants profited from colonial trade, Parliament passed a series of laws called the Navigation Acts between 1660 and 1696. One of the first acts ordered that all goods imported into the colonies or exported from them be carried in English or colonial ships. The crews had to be 75 percent English or English colonists.

Other acts enumerated, or listed, goods, such as tobacco, cotton, indigo, sugar, rice, naval stores, and furs that colonists could export only to England or its colonies. Colonial traders got around this law by telling customs officials they were headed for another colony, then smuggling the goods into European ports. To close this loophole, Parliament passed an act forcing merchants to pay export duties, or taxes, before they left port.

The Navigation Acts served the economic needs of England and provided a sure market for colonial goods, but they angered many colonists. Virginians, as Burnaby discovered, "think it a hardship not to have an unlimited trade to every part of the world."

Global Connections

Colonial America and Europe, too, accepted witchcraft as a fact of everyday life. In Europe during the Middle Ages, witches were blamed for nearly every misfortune. Through the late 1600s, several hundred thousand Europeans convicted of witchcraft—most of them women—were put to death.

American colonists believed that witches were servants of the Devil and could destroy even whole communities if left unpunished. Massachusetts decreed in 1641 that witchcraft was punishable by death. In 1692 in Salem, fifty people confessed to being witches. Twenty were put to death.

Witch trials were held in North America into the 1700s. Virginia held one in 1706, North Carolina in 1712.

Connections: Religion

Reading Poetry. In *Leaves From Margaret Smith's Journal* (1849) and *Snow-Bound* (1866), poet John Greenleaf Whittier describes the Quaker experience. One or two students might enjoy reading aloud short selections from a Whittier poem describing Quaker life.

Connections: Literature

Reading a Play. Interested students might read *The Crucible*, Arthur Miller's 1953 play about the Salem witch trials.

People of Different Nations and Religions

As the colonies developed increasingly diverse economies, diversity among the settlers themselves increased, too. Until the 1680s most colonists had come from England. New England was settled mainly by English Puritan families that arrived during the "Great Migration" of the 1630s.

The majority of settlers in Virginia and Maryland were indentured servants, mostly single young men who had been arriving from England since the early 1600s. As more and more people were needed to work, 50,000 convicts—hardened criminals as well as people imprisoned for debt—were sent to Maryland and Virginia to serve their sentences as indentured servants. Growing numbers of captive Africans were also brought to these colonies to be sold as slaves.

After the 1680s an increasing number of migrants to the colonies came from Europe.

Religious diversity was typically American. Two of many groups are represented here by a Quaker meeting and a Jewish Torah. Religious feelings could be intense, inspiring Jonathan Edwards's fiery sermons and witch finders like Puritan Matthew Hopkins (below).

Throughout Europe, wars, poverty, and persecution drove people from their homes. For many, the lure of a better life and the promise of religious toleration in America was too powerful to resist. The majority of the newcomers were Protestants, but Jews and Catholics also came.

Most Europeans settled in the Middle Colonies. These colonies, Burnaby said, were made up of "people of different nations, different manners, different religions, and different languages." In New York the mix of religions was even more complex than that of ethnic groups. "Here," Governor Dongan reported in 1687,

66 *bee not many of the Church of England, [and] few Roman Catholicks, [but] abundance of Quakers—preachers, men and women, especially—singing Quakers, ranting Quakers, Sabbatarians, Anti-Sabbatarians, some Anabaptists, some Independents, some Jews; in short, of all sorts of opinions there are some, and the most part of none at all.* 99

William Penn heartily approved of religious freedom. To restrain or persecute anyone's choice of religion, he said, is to "rob the Almighty of that which belongs to none but Himself. . . . For He alone has authority over conscience."

⊙ **GTV** Side 1

Chap. 12, Frame 29544

Port Cities, Mid-1700s
(Animated Maps)

Search and Play:

Connections: Language

Using the Dictionary. Non-English settlers brought great diversity to the American colonies. Many words in their languages gradually became part of American speech.

Write the following words (Dutch and German) on the chalkboard: *boss, coleslaw, cookie, landscape, sleigh, sauerkraut, shoe, rifle, waffle*. Have students find these words in the dictionary and write down each word's original source, spelling, and meaning, and its present-day meaning if it differs from the original.

Ask students to name words from other languages that have become part of American speech. Remind them of Native-American words discussed in Chapter 2. Mention Spanish words for the land, such as *canyon, sierra,* and *mesa*.

Multicultural Perspectives

A group of German immigrants settled north of Philadelphia in an area they called Germantown. Their leader, Francis Pastorious, noted the settlers' many talents, which boded well for the community's success: *"There was a doctor of medicine with his wife and eight children, a French captain, a Low Dutch cakebaker, an apothecary, a glassblower, a mason, a smith, a wheelwright, a cabinetmaker, a cooper, a hatmaker, a cobbler, a tailor, a gardener, farmers, seamstresses, etc."*

Reduced student page in the Teacher's Edition

Not everyone agreed with Penn. English Protestants distrusted other nationalities, Catholics, and Jews. In the mid-1700s friction arose in Pennsylvania between the English and the growing number of Germans, who kept their own language and customs. Suspicious of the Germans, Benjamin Franklin asked, "Why should *Pennsylvania,* founded by the *English,* become a Colony of *Aliens,* who will shortly be so numerous as to Germanize us?"

Most of the tensions eased over time, primarily because most immigrants had a common European background. They also needed each other to help solve the problems they all faced in building settlements. Many colonists would have agreed with this letter printed in a Pennsylvania newspaper:

> *"What is it to me, when I am about to vote, whether the great grandmother of the candidate came from Germany or Ireland . . . whether he and his ancestors have dined oftenest on cabbage or potatoes? . . . I don't think one of those vegetables more calculated to make an honest man or a rogue than the other. All national prejudices are the growth of a contracted mind or silly head—it destroys all enquiry into the merit of a candidate."*

Patterns of Racism in the Colonies

In the early 1600s, most of what the people who settled in the English colonies knew about Native Americans was based on rumors of Spain's experience in the West Indies and Latin America. And the colonists had had no experience with Africans or the slavery that the Spanish and Portuguese had introduced in their American colonies.

By 1700, however, most of the English colonists had come to view Native Americans as dangerous enemies, to be pushed out of the way or, if they resisted, to be killed. By then, too, the colonists had established a system of lifelong slavery for Africans, justifying it by telling themselves that Africans were uncivilized and less than human. How did these patterns of **racism**—of believing that one's own race is superior to other races—begin? Why do they continue today?

"Eighty more white men in your boat? How do we know you won't send over four or five hundred before you're finished?"

Burr Shafer, *Through More History with J. Wesley Smith,* New York: The Vanguard Press, 1958

Different ways of life. When the English came to North America, Native Americans helped them adapt to the unfamiliar conditions they found. In fact, Indians played a vital role in the creation of every colony. As one historian has said, "Every European discoverer had Indian guides. Every European colonizer had Indian instruction and assistance."

As long as there was enough space for both peoples, and the leaders on both sides sought friendship, peaceful relations were possible. However, as more and more settlers arrived, they began to take over lands that the Indians considered their own. Conflicts arose. In fact, suspicion and conflict were almost inevitable among peoples whose ways of living were so different.

Most Native Americans did not have a tradition of living in one place permanently. Instead they moved within an area to find the greatest food supplies. In spring the villagers planted crops, then moved to camps along river or seashore for a summer of fishing and collecting shellfish. In autumn they returned to their villages for the harvest and to hunt game and gather wild plants. To be mobile, families owned nothing that could not be stored or carried easily. They farmed, fished, hunted, gathered, and traded just enough to live comfortably.

Most Indians did not believe that the land belongs to the people, but that the people belong to the land. What they claimed were the fruits of the land—the crops planted, the animals hunted, the plants gathered. Thus, most places were named on

Connections: Art

A sketch of a beaver appears below. It was made by a French artist in 1701.

the basis of how they could be used, not ownership. For example, Wabaquasset, in Rhode Island, was the place where "flags or rushes for making mats" could be found; Abessah, in Maine, was the "clam bake place." Different groups could have different claims to the same land depending on how they used it.

The English lived differently. Heeding the Bible's command to "fill the earth and subdue it," they built permanent settlements, with fields, pastures, buildings, fences, and livestock. Thus, they believed, they "improved" the land. They also bought and sold the land itself and, as owners, could prevent others from trespassing on it.

Most of the English refused to recognize that Native American ways of living were as legitimate as English ways of living. John Winthrop, the governor of Massachusetts, wrote:

> *"As for the Natives in New England, they inclose noe Land, neither have any setled habytation, nor any tame Cattle to improve the Land by, and soe have noe . . . Right to those Countries."*

New Englanders believed that Native Americans could claim as property only the fields they planted. "The rest of the country," Winthrop said, "lay open to any that could and would improve it." Some colonists believed that they could take any Indian land because the English Crown had claimed it. To the English, the rest of the country was a "frontier"—a wilderness to be overcome. And the Native Americans were merely an obstacle to be removed.

As the colonists expanded into new territories, many Native American villages that once had welcomed the English now resisted. The result was a series of clashes that began in 1622 between the Powhatan Confederacy and Jamestown settlers, and would be repeated time and again.

Native American resistance was weakened, however, by diseases brought to America by Europeans.

The most important bond between Europeans and Native Americans was trade. Europeans wanted furs; Indians wanted guns, blankets, pots.

Settlement of the English Colonies

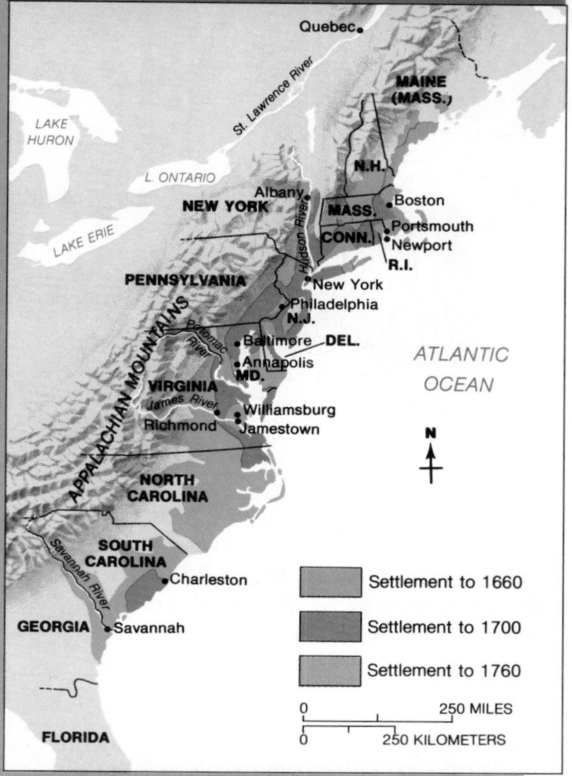

Geography Skills—Location. Where were the earliest English settlements established? Describe the extent of English settlement by 1760. What colonies still had large unsettled areas in 1760? What present-day states have boundaries that were set by 1760? In what colonies did settlers first begin to move into the Appalachians?

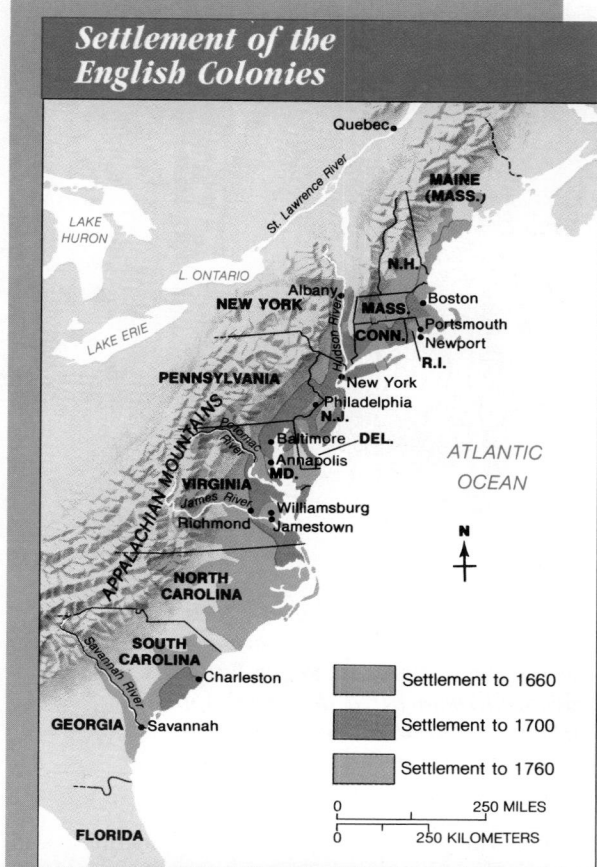

Active Learning

Paired Discussions. Assign half the students to assume the perspective of Europeans and half to assume the perspective of Native Americans in the early 1700s. Using information in the text, students will prepare to discuss in pairs their people's relationship to the land.

Give students about 15 minutes to prepare. Then, in pairs of "Europeans" and "Native Americans," have students describe to each other their people's relationship to the land. After all pairs have finished, ask several volunteers to share their discussions.

Geography Skills

ANSWERS

1. Virginia, Maryland, Penn., Conn., Rhode Island, Mass.
2. Most of the Atlantic Coastal Plain from northern Georgia to southern Maine.
3. S. Carolina, N. Carolina, Virginia, New Hampshire, Maine.
4. Rhode Island, Conn., Mass., except for Maine, Del., N.J.
5. N. Carolina, Virginia, Maryland, Pennsylvania, New York.

GTV Side 1

Chap. 11, Frame 28883

Native American Population: 1700 and 1760 (Population Clocks, 2 Frames)

Search:

Step:

Analyzing Primary Sources

Kwakiutl Song. Indians throughout North America found a multitude of uses for the trees that covered the land. Read to students from a portion of a Kwakiutl song about the all-purpose tree.

“Look at me, friend! I come to ask for your dress,
For you have come to take pity on us;
For there is nothing for which you cannot be used. . .
Long-life maker.”

Ask students to suggest how Native Americans used trees **(canoes, housing, medicines etc.)**. Then refer students to the large illustration on this page. Ask them to speculate about the feelings of the Indians, as they paddle past the fields of tree stumps.

Connections: Science and Technology

The word *canoe* comes from the Spanish word *canoa*, first used by Columbus in 1493 after a Carib Indian word, *kanu*. In the north, Native Americans made canoes from strips of birch bark. In the south, canoes were dugouts, made by shaping and hollowing large tree trunks. The Indians usually used fire to hollow their canoes. Dugouts ranged from six feet to twenty feet in length and could carry up to sixty people. Early white settlers learned to use the canoe to travel North America’s lakes and rivers.

Throughout the 1600s and 1700s, colonists fought to gain Native American lands for settlement. Roger Williams accused them of “a depraved appetite after . . . land in this wilderness.”

Whole villages were wiped out in epidemics, and the land quickly taken by colonists. Between 1600 and 1675, the total number of Native Americans in New England fell from more than 70,000 to fewer than 12,000.

Gradually less and less land remained free for Native Americans to use, and their earlier way of living became impossible. In 1642 Miantonomo, a Narragansett chief, clearly described the changes that occurred within a few years after English colonists settled near his people’s villages.

“Our fathers had plenty of deer and skins, our plains were full of deer, as also our woods, and of turkies, and our coves full of fish and fowl. But these English having gotten our land, they with scythes cut down the grass, and with axes fell the trees; their cows and horses eat the grass, and their hogs spoil our clam banks, and we shall all be starved.”

As a result of these early clashes between the English and the Native Americans, each side developed ideas about the other that would affect future relations. The colonists came to look on the tribes as dangerous and treacherous. The Native Americans came to see the Europeans as dangerous and greedy invaders demanding ever increasing amounts of land to farm.

The enslavement of Africans. In 1680 enslaved Africans represented less than 8 percent of the population of Virginia and Maryland; by 1710 the figure was 25 percent. By the time Burnaby visited Virginia in the 1750s, enslaved Africans made up almost 40 percent of the population. What had caused this great increase?

The fact was that to produce the crops—such as tobacco and rice—that supported their economy, the colonists required vast amounts of labor. For much of the 1600s the labor had been supplied by indentured servants. But in the mid and late 1600s the economy in England improved, and fewer indentured servants came to the colonies. Needing more workers for their expanding fields, planters in the Southern Colonies called for importing greater numbers of captive Africans. Thus the shift from indentured servants to African slaves began in earnest.

Multicultural Perspectives

In South Carolina, planters sought to buy enslaved Africans who knew how to grow rice. In contrast to Europeans, Africans on the West Coast of Africa had been cultivating rice for centuries. According to historian Peter H. Wood, "Hundreds of black immigrants were more familiar with the planting, hoeing, processing, and cooking of rice than were the European settlers who purchased them." African know-how, as well as labor, played a vital role in the development of rice as an important cash crop.

Dependence on slavery may have seemed like an economic necessity, but it was fast becoming a way of life that planters would resist changing. Burnaby recognized slavery as being a "cause of weakness." Speaking of the enslaved Africans, he said:

> *"Their condition is truly pitiful; their labor excessively hard, their diet poor and scanty, their treatment cruel and oppressive: they cannot therefore but be a subject of terror to those who so inhumanly tyrannize over them."*

Terror shaped the lives of both the planters and the enslaved Africans. To the planters, white indentured servants had been familiar in appearance; most spoke English and knew English ways. But Africans, arriving in larger and larger numbers, looked different and had unfamiliar languages and customs. Virginia laws in the late 1600s reflected the suspicion and fear many colonists felt:

> *"The frequent meeting of considerable numbers of negroe slaves under pretence of feasts and burialls is judged of dangerous consequence. . . .*
>
> *Noe master or Overseer Shall at any time . . . permitt . . . any Negro or Slave not properly belonging to him or them, to Remaine or be upon his or theire Plantation above the space of foure hours."*

Slavery was not permitted in England. Thus, the colonies made their own laws regarding slave labor. To enforce the laws, colonial militia often visited "all negro quarters and other places suspected of entertaining unlawful assemblies" in order to "take up" slaves who gathered together "or any other, strolling about from one plantation to another, without a pass from his or her master, mistress, or overseer." Fear also bred violence against slaves. Running away was punished by

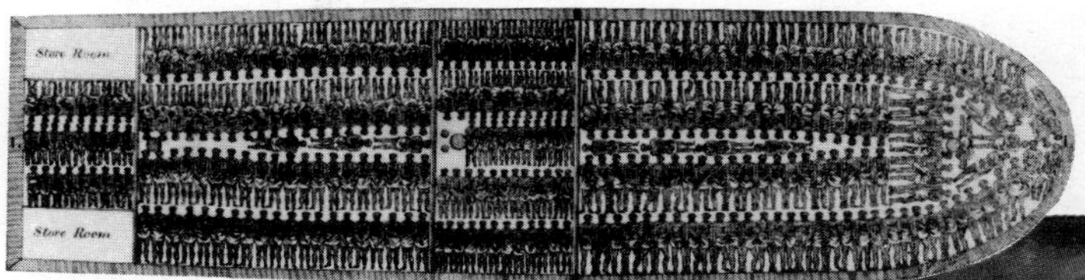

Captured Africans faced horrifying conditions. In most slave ships, the space for an individual was the size of a coffin.

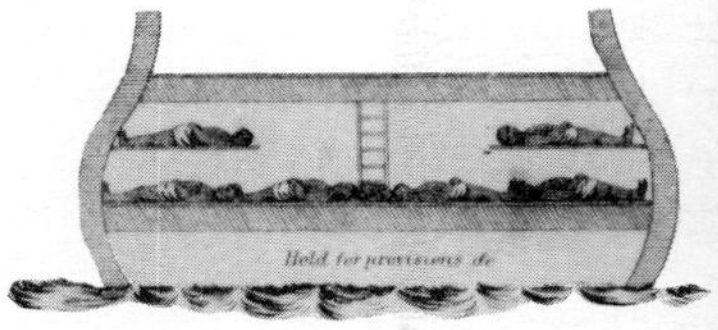

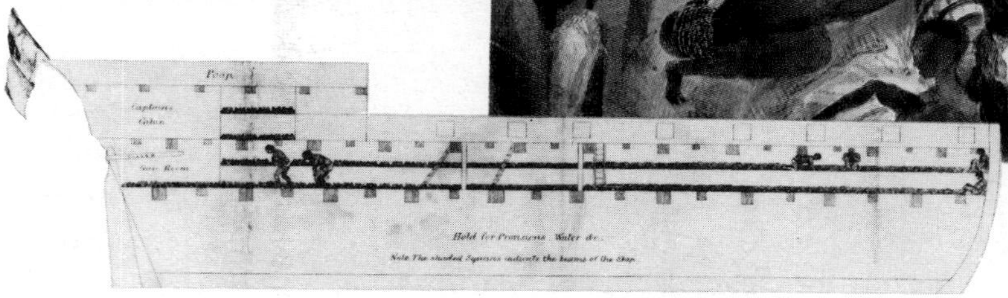

Africans often attempted mutiny or jumped overboard to drown rather than suffer enslavement.

Thinking Critically

Synthesis. Slave uprisings are difficult to document. Though over 250 have been identified, they were rarely mentioned, even by people who kept detailed diaries. Newspapers did not publicize such revolts.

Ask students to speculate about what might explain the silence. (People might have thought that news coverage would incite other slaves to revolt, for example.)

GTV Side 1

Chap. 13, Frame 34536

Olaudah Equiano: Kidnapped by Slave Traders (American Journal)

Search:

Play:

Writing About History

Persuasive Arguments. Colonial law books included complex slave codes that regulated all aspects of slavery. A Carolina slave code tried to justify slavery with these three arguments:

- Slave labor was essential to a plantation economy.
- People brought into the colonies as slaves had "barbarous, wild, savage natures."
- The tendency of such people to commit violent crimes made enslaving them essential to ensure the safety of others.

Have students write short essays, using information in the text to refute these justifications.

Connections: Language

A unique language evolved on the coastal islands off South Carolina and Georgia and the adjacent mainland. Called *Gullah* (possibly from *Ngola*, a people from Angola), it blended English with African languages brought in by enslaved Africans. Some words from this language, such as *goober* (peanut) and *gumbo* (a soup thickened with okra), have become a part of American speech.

whippings, mutilation, or death. In the 1690s Reverend Samuel Gray of Virginia reported that his "boy Jack" was dead, "an unfortunate Chance which I would not Should have happened in my family for three times his price. But . . . such Accidents will happen now and then." What kind of accident? The minister had found Jack, an escaped slave, and had beaten him to death. Gray never appeared before a court because a slave was legally considered property, not a person.

Like Gray, planters often thought of slaves as members of their family. But in that family slaves were treated as children, to be guided and disciplined by the father, the owner. Because slaves were thought to have no existence outside that family, they were given only first names. A particular slave

THE AMERICAN SPIRIT

Olaudah Equiano

Protesting Against Slavery

"I had never heard of white men or Europeans, nor of the sea," wrote Olaudah Equiano of his childhood years in Africa. However, that soon changed. Born in 1745 in present-day Nigeria, Equiano was only eleven years old when he and his sister were kidnapped by slave traders. The two were quickly separated, never to see each other again.

"I cried and grieved continually," Equiano remembered of that terrible time. "For several days I did not eat anything but what they forced in my mouth." Taken to the West African coast, he was sold to white slave traders and put on a slave ship bound for the West Indies. The voyage, known as the "middle passage," was a nightmare. Equiano was thrust into the hold, where slaves were chained closely together. Later he described his terrible experience:

"The closeness of the place, and the heat of the climate, added to the number in the ship, which was so crowded that each had scarcely room to turn himself, almost suffocated us. . . . The shrieks of the women, and the groans of the dying, rendered the whole a scene of horror almost inconceivable."

When the ship arrived in Barbados, Equiano was sold to a Virginia planter. An English sea captain then bought the boy and took him to England. On board ship Equiano, who was called Gustavus Vassa, was befriended by an American sailor who taught him to read and write English. Later he was sold to a Philadelphia merchant, whose ships carried sugar, rum, and slaves between the West Indies and North America.

Equiano was eventually able to buy his freedom. His roving nature kept him traveling, and he journeyed to Turkey, the Arctic, and Central America.

In 1789 Equiano published his life story, *The Interesting Narrative of the Life of Gustavus Vassa, the African.* A best seller, it went through eight editions in five years. By describing what it was like to be a slave, Equiano convinced many people to oppose the slave trade. He concluded:

"Surely this traffic cannot be good which violates the first natural right of humanity, equality and independency, and gives one person dominion over another which God would never intend."

Multicultural Perspectives

Groups of escaped slaves called Maroons established separate communities in Virginia as early as 1671. They were able to survive for years before being hunted down by white settlers and troops. Some fifty such communities existed nearly two hundred years before the Civil War.

Captured Africans were wrenched away from diverse cultures with powerful kingdoms and rich urban centers. Examples of remarkable West African art include a bronze plaque of a king of Benin, an Ashanti stool, and a Benin brass leopard.

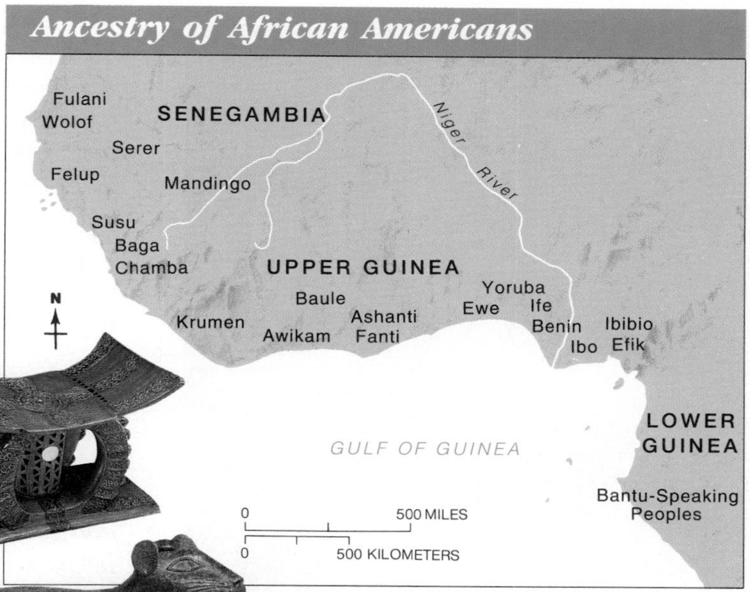

might be known as "Madam Creyke's Jack." Marriages among enslaved Africans were not recognized as legal, children born to them belonged to the owner, and family members could be sold away from each other.

Although slavery also existed in the New England and Middle colonies, colonists there did not consider it essential to their farming or commercial economies. However, Puritan merchants and ship captains prospered from their role as the primary link in the profitable slave trade, and slave markets thrived in New York and Philadelphia.

Creating an African-American culture. Some enslaved Africans resisted slavery by escaping, refusing to work hard, breaking tools, or openly rebelling. But rebellion and flight were difficult and the punishments severe. Most slaves adapted to their new conditions of life, creating an African-American culture of their own within the limits of the slave system—and they endured.

Slaves adopted family names, usually not those of their owners, to use among themselves. Despite the threat of separation, they married—often using African ceremonies—and raised children, passing on to them family beliefs and values. They struggled to keep families together and to reunite separated family members.

The slaves blended old and new ideas and ways of life. African religious beliefs mixed with the Christian religion. Slave owners may have sought to instill lessons of obedience in church, but slaves identified their plight with that of the Israelites in bondage in Egypt. Their spirituals rang with calls for freedom:

> *"Didn't My Lord deliver Daniel?*
> *He delivered Daniel from the lion's den,*
> *Jonah from the belly of the whale,*
> *An' the Hebrew children from the fiery furnace,*
> *An' why not every man?"*

African music, dance, songs, ceremonies, and folktales enriched African-American culture. Children listened to traditional tales of tricksters, such as Anansi the spider, who outsmarted stronger enemies, and of Africans who escaped slavery by flying home across the ocean.

Opposition to slavery. Aside from African Americans, the first people to oppose slavery openly were Quakers. They freed their own slaves, then

Thinking Critically

Analysis. Slaveowners often tried to justify slavery by pointing out that it also existed in African states. But there were significant differences between slavery in Africa and in the Americas. In the Ashanti kingdom of West Africa, for example, one person observed that a *"slave might marry, own property; himself own a slave; swear an oath; be a competent witness and ultimately become heir to his master."*

Have students contrast this treatment with what they know about the enslavement of Africans in the Americas. (American slavery was lifelong, destructive of family ties, and gave no hope for the future.)

B · A · C · K · G · R · O · U · N · D

Linking Past and Present

Research. Discuss with students the extent to which patterns of racism still exist today. Have students research evidence of institutional racism in our present-day society—hiring policies, college entrance examinations/ policies, housing patterns, and so on. They may present their findings to the class in written reports.

Section Review

ANSWERS

1. Definitions for the following terms are on text pages indicated in parentheses: *cash crop* (62), *racism* (66).
2. In late 1600s decline in number of indentured servants coming to colonies led southern colonists to import greater numbers of enslaved Africans; increasing numbers of migrants came to colonies from Europe instead of England.
3. Cash crops and enslaved Africans were vital products in New England's triangular trade. On one route, New Englanders traded cash crops in West Indies for sugar and molasses to make rum; rum traded for slaves on African coast; slaves taken to West Indies to sell to planters; and profits used to buy more sugar and molasses.
4. Possibly no enslaved Africans; no injustice toward Native Americans; Africans and Native Americans considered part of colonial society.
Linking Past and Present. Answers may include the effect of climate and land upon occupations and interests of settlers. Today, regional differences less marked because land and climate have less effect on occupations, especially in urban areas.

Connections: Music

Enslaved Africans composed songs to express joy and despair and to convey secret messages to one another. Often songs that opened on a note of sorrow ("Sometimes I feel like a motherless chile") ended in a rousing burst of confidence ("Sometimes I feel like/A eagle in de air . . . /Gonna spread my wings an'/Fly, fly, fly.") Songs such as *Jim Crack Corn, Go Down, Moses,* and *Nobody Knows the Trouble I've Seen* form a distinctive part of the African musical heritage.

Reduced student page in the Teacher's Edition

African-American Lemuel Haynes, a minister who preached to white congregations, spoke with such passion that an intolerant churchgoer "thought him the whitest man I ever saw."

called on others to do the same. Mennonites, another religious group, also opposed slavery, declaring in 1688:

" There is a saying that we shall do to all men like as we will be done ourselves, making no difference of what generation, descent, or color they are. . . . Here is liberty of conscience. . . . Here ought to be likewise liberty of the body. . . . Pray! What thing in the world can be done worse toward us than if men should rob or steal us away and sell us for slaves to strange countries, separating husbands from their wives and children. "

Even when they were free, African Americans led an uneasy existence because of racism. In some colonies, such as Massachusetts, they had some legal rights, such as the right to vote. In other colonies, however, they faced economic and political discrimination. And opportunities for success were limited. A French traveler to New England wrote:

" Those Negroes who keep shops never augment their business beyond a certain point. The reason is obvious. The whites . . . like not to give them credit to enable them to undertake any extensive commerce nor even give them the means of [a] common education. "

In the mid-1700s the Quaker John Woolman suggested one reason for the existence of racism. He wrote that

" placing on men the ignominious Title, SLAVE, dressing them in uncomely Garments, keeping them to servile Labor, in which they are often dirty, tends gradually to fix a notion in the Mind, that they are a sort of people below us in Nature, and leads us to consider them as such in all our Conclusions about them. "

Slavery in America began without a fixed plan. However, within just a short time it had become an accepted part of the social fabric of the colonies. By the end of the 1600s, new legal codes had institutionalized the holding of humans as property. Discrimination and racism went hand in hand with this new institution. It is a pattern that has continued to haunt America to the present day.

Section Review

1. **Identification.** Define *cash crop* and *racism*.

2. **Comprehension.** What factors led to increased diversity in the peoples living in the colonies?

3. **Analysis.** What is the relationship between cash crops, enslaved Africans, and the triangular trade?

4. **Synthesis.** If the colonists had respected African and Native-American ways of life, how might life in the colonies have been different?

Linking Past and Present. Jean de Crèvecoeur, a colonist, wrote that "the inhabitants of Massachusetts, the middle provinces, [and] the southern ones will be as different as their climates." In what way was this description true? Is it still true today? Give reasons for your answer.

Connections: Economics

Choosing a trade as an apprentice was not always easy, for master craftsmen did not want to train too many competitors. They, therefore, limited the number of apprentices by charging an entrance fee.

Social History

Benjamin Franklin was apprenticed in Boston to his half-brother James, a newspaper printer. Franklin wrote several anonymous articles, which he signed "Mrs. Silence Dogood" and slipped under the printshop door at night. Franklin's articles were well-received, but when he revealed his identity as the writer, his brother refused to print any more.

Benjamin Franklin (right), an apprentice printer, ran away because of harsh treatment.

young IN AMERICA

At Work

In England's American colonies, childhood ended early. By the age of eight, most children had begun working. Boys joined their fathers in the fields. Girls helped their mothers with cooking, spinning, and candlemaking. If the family ran a mill or a blacksmith shop, the children learned to help with the business.

Boys and girls also might be sent to live in other households, working as servants or apprentices for a specified period of time. An apprentice agreed to work under a skilled master in order to learn a trade—and perhaps reading and writing.

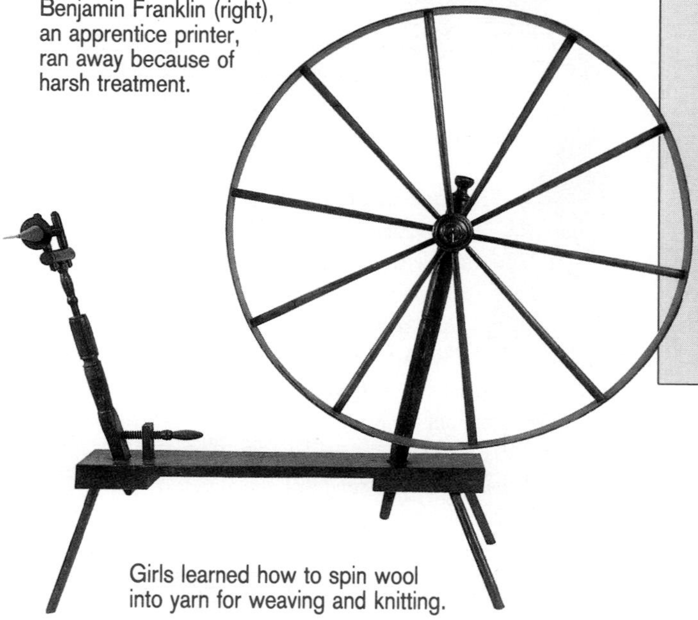

Girls learned how to spin wool into yarn for weaving and knitting.

This blacksmith also taught his apprentice fence mending and had to provide food, clothing, and lodging.

Orphans were often apprenticed until the age of twenty-one to crafts shops such as this New York pewterer's shop.

Writing About History

Reports. Have students write reports on one of the following, or other, colonial occupations: printer, blacksmith, saddler, silversmith, chandler, cooper, wainwright, miller. In their reports students should describe the kind of work the person did and the contributions this worker might have made to the economy of the colony. Suggest that they illustrate their reports with diagrams or drawings.

Analyzing Primary Sources

Letter to the Editor. A popular saying in the colonies was that anyone "that hath a trade hath an estate." Many of those with a trade or skills were women, often widows carrying on the family business. The following letter appeared in 1733 in the *New York Weekly Journal.*

"We, the widdows of this city have had a Meeting. . . . We are House keepers, Pay our Taxes, carry on trade, and most of us are she Merchants, and as we . . . contribute to the Support of Government, we ought to be Intituled to some of the Sweets ot it; but we find ourselves entirely neglected."

1. In what way to you think the women contributed to the support of government? **(paid taxes)**
2. What "sweets" of the government might the women have wished to enjoy? **(perhaps, the right to vote; serve in a government position)**

Section 3-4

Objectives

- ***Answer the Focus Question.***
- *Describe how France extended its claims in North America.*
- *Explain how European rivalries led to the end of French power in North America.*

Introducing

THE SECTION

Review with students what they have learned about the French and the English in North America. Remind them that both nations were empire builders. Ask why conflicts might arise between two such ambitious peoples. **(competition for wealth, power, land, markets for manufactured goods, sources of raw materials)**

Developing

THE SECTION

Multicultural Perspectives

Research. Have groups of students research and report on the French influence in North America. They might focus on a city such as New Orleans, St. Louis, or Detroit. Other groups might report on the Cajun people and their origins or how Louisiana's civil codes differ from civil codes in other states.

B · A · C · K · G · R · O · U · N · D

Global Connections
The wars in the colonies between 1689 and 1748 were named after the reigning British monarchs. In King William's War, which began in 1689, the French and their Indian allies attacked frontier settlements in New England and New York. At the same time, New England troops, British forces, and Iroquois warriors attacked New France. The war ended in 1697 with no clear winner. Queen Anne's War (1702–1713), however, was a victory for Great Britain. The treaty that ended the war gave Newfoundland, Nova Scotia, and Hudson Bay to Great Britain. Neither side gained any territory in the third war, King George's War (1744–1748).

Reduced student page in the Teacher's Edition

3-4 *The Struggle for North America*

Focus: How did Great Britain secure its American empire?

Three times between 1689 and 1748 Great Britain and France had gone to war. In 1754 another clash was brewing between them. A struggle for power in Europe may have seemed remote to the American colonies, but it had critical implications. In the end it would determine which nation would rule North America.

French Claims in America

In 1608, the year after Jamestown was founded, Samuel de Champlain sailed up the St. Lawrence River and built a fort at Quebec—the first French settlement in North America. Champlain's goal was not gold but something nearly as valuable—beaver fur for fashionable men's hats.

Champlain established a profitable fur trade with the Huron, thereby expanding French territory in eastern Canada. In the 1660s the French government tried to attract more settlers and encourage farming, but without success. New France remained a sparsely settled empire based solely on the fur trade.

Meanwhile, the French explored farther inland. Jacques Marquette (mahr-KEHT) and Louis Joliet (ZHŌ-lee-AY) traveled by canoe and on foot from the Great Lakes to the Wisconsin River and southward to the Mississippi River. Robert Cavelier, Sieur de La Salle (lah-SAHL), a fur trader, completed the journey down the Mississippi in 1682. He claimed for France "possession of that river, of all the rivers that enter it and of all the country watered by them." He called this vast region Louisiana in honor of his king, Louis XIV.

Following La Salle's voyage, the French built a line of forts and settlements from the Great Lakes to New Orleans. Louisiana, noted a government memorandum, would serve as an "advance guard against the English colonies."

Spotlight **on Politics**

How did England come to be known as Britain? In 1707 the Kingdom of England and Wales united with the Kingdom of Scotland to form the United Kingdom of Great Britain. From then on, the country was called Great Britain or simply Britain. By the mid-1700s, glorying in Britain's growing power in Asia and the Americas, the British were singing "Rule Britannia":

When Britain first, at heaven's command,
Arose from out the azure main;
This was the charter of the land,
And guardian angels sung this strain
"Rule Britannia, *rule the waves;*
Britons never will be slaves."

Conflict over the Ohio Valley. French fur traders were the first Europeans to reach the Ohio Valley, and France claimed it as part of New France. Pennsylvanians and Virginians, however, disputed France's claim, insisting that they owned the Ohio Valley because their charters granted them all land stretching west from their colonies. Pennsylvanians began crossing the Appalachian Mountains to establish fur-trading stations.

Traders were soon joined by **speculators,** people seeking big profits from risky investments. Virginia speculators had formed several land companies in the late 1740s, and the king granted them Ohio Valley territory, which they hoped to sell to settlers. Britain encouraged more land companies to claim valley territory, noting that "nothing

Multicultural Perspectives

In general, French relations with Native Americans was better in comparison to that of other colonial powers. Since the economy of New France centered around the fur trade, not agriculture, exploitation of Indian lands centered on the plentiful hunting grounds rather than choice agricultural sites. The French also recognized the close relationship Indians had with their lands and generally sought approval of land use. Native Americans were often employed as hunters or guides and many French traders and trappers adapted a life-style compatible with the Indians. French missionaries, on the other hand, did try to Christianize the Indians and transform the Indian cultures. Others relocated some Indian peoples and punished or enslaved those who rebelled.

can more effectively tend to defeat the dangerous designs of the French."

Alarmed, the French sent troops to take control of the Ohio Valley. By 1753 they had built a string of forts in what is now western Pennsylvania. They also whipped up fear among Native Americans in the region, warning that the English were trying to "rob you of your country."

The English colonists, in turn, became alarmed. Some urged the Iroquois, England's ally, to act against the French. Despite their own claims to the valley, the Iroquois stayed neutral, declaring:

"We don't know what you Christians, English and French together, intend. We are so hemmed in by both that we have hardly a hunting place left."

The governor of Virginia realized the French would not leave the Ohio Valley unless they were forced out. In 1754 he called out the militia, a group of citizens trained as soldiers, to challenge the French. Led by a twenty-two-year-old colonel named George Washington, 150 men crossed the Appalachian Mountains to the newly built French post, Fort Duquesne (doo-KAYN), in southwestern Pennsylvania. A large force of French and their Indian allies attacked the Virginians, and in a nine-hour battle, they drove them out of the valley.

"When we came [to the French fort], we were attacked by a body of French and Indians, whose number . . . did not exceed 300 men. Ours consisted of about 1,300 well-armed troops, chiefly of the English soldiers, who were struck with such a panic that they . . . broke and ran as sheep pursued by dogs; and it was impossible to rally them.

The general was wounded; of which he died three days after. Sir Peter Halket was killed in the field, where died many other brave officers. I luckily escaped without a wound, though I had four bullets through my coat, and two horses shot under me."

—George Washington on Braddock's Defeat

The Albany Plan of Union

Even before this defeat, delegates from seven colonies had been meeting in Albany, New York, to develop a plan "for their mutual defense" against the French. They also hoped to convince the League of the Iroquois, now made up of six tribes, to come to their aid if war with France broke out. However, they failed in both efforts.

In meetings with leaders of the Iroquois confederacy, the delegates promised to do something to keep land speculators from gobbling up confederation lands. Unconvinced, the Iroquois left the meetings without promising aid in return.

The Albany Congress also failed in its second goal. Benjamin Franklin offered a plan of union for the defense of the colonies. He suggested that the colonial assemblies send representatives to a "grand council," which would make treaties with the tribes, levy taxes for a colonial army, and oversee settlement in the western lands. The Albany delegates approved the plan, but not a single colonial assembly accepted it. The assemblies wanted to

George Washington returned from the war in 1758. Relieved, his mother wrote, "There was no end to my trouble while George was in the army, but he has now given it up."

Thinking Critically

Synthesis. Ask students to speculate about why the colonists rejected Franklin's plan of union. (Perhaps each colony concerned with own self interest; might have felt the plan infringed on individual rights of the colonies.)

Ask: How do you think England felt at the failure of the Albany Congress? Why? (probably relieved that the colonies could not agree among themselves)

Active Learning

Cooperative Activity. Divide the class into thirteen groups, each representing the members of a colonial assembly. The members of each assembly meet to discuss adoption of the Albany Plan, listing reasons for or against the plan from that colony's perspective. After the discussion, a representative or representatives of each group may present to the class the colony's reasons for supporting or opposing the Albany Plan.

B · A · C · K · G · R · O · U · N · D

Global Connections

The French and Indian War was part of a worldwide conflict between Britain and France known as the Seven Years' War. Involving nearly every nation in Europe, it extended from North America to India.

Thinking Critically

Analysis. Have students explain how the following events led to the French and Indian War: organization of Virginia speculators to sell land in the Ohio Valley to settlers, construction of French forts connecting Lake Erie and the Ohio Valley, sending Virginia militia to warn French that land they were fortifying belonged to the British.

Backyard History

Using Maps. Refer students to the maps on this page. **Ask:** What countries had laid claim to your region by 1763? How did the Treaty of Paris affect land claims in your region?

Geography Skills

ANSWERS

1. New France and Louisiana east of the Mississippi River (except New Orleans).
2. Louisiana west of the Mississippi (and New Orleans).

Reduced student page in the Teacher's Edition

keep the power to tax for themselves. "Everyone cries, a union is necessary," Franklin wrote, "but when they come to the manner and form of the union, their weak noodles are perfectly distracted."

European Claims in North America 1750

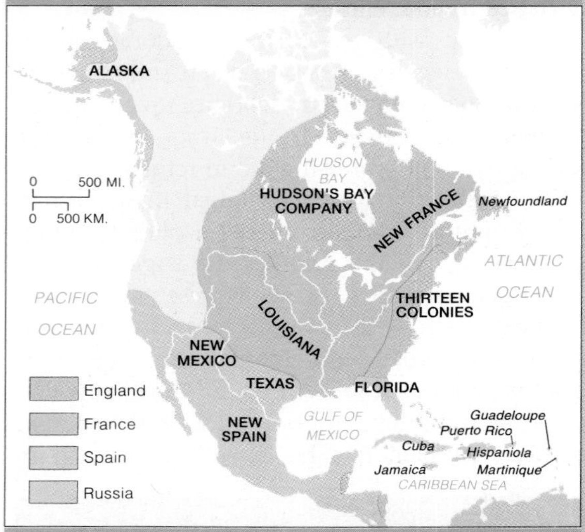

European Claims in North America 1763

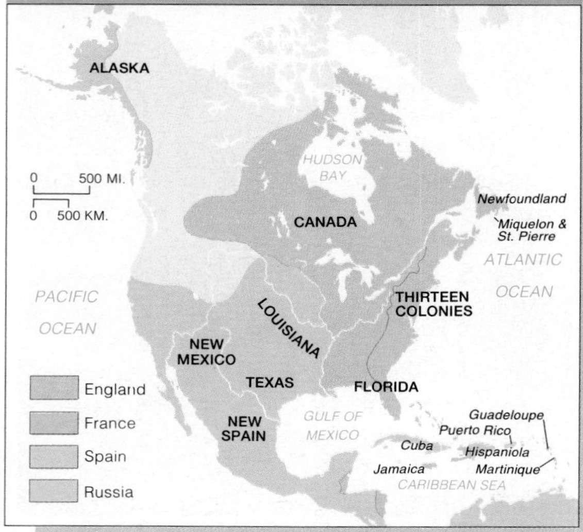

Geography Skills— Place. After the French and Indian War, what parts of France's holdings in North America were ceded to England? To Spain?

The French and Indian War

Meanwhile, the conflict in the Ohio Valley was about to become a full-scale war. In 1755, after Washington's defeat, Britain sent General Edward Braddock to drive the French out. Braddock marched on Fort Duquesne with 1,400 British and 450 colonial troops under Washington. Unfortunately, Braddock was the wrong man for the job.

Braddock was used to fighting on the open battlefields of Europe, where he could keep the enemy in view. He refused to listen when Washington explained that war in the American wilderness was based on surprise attacks, using the forest for cover. The result was a disaster. More than a thousand of the British were killed or wounded in an ambush. Braddock was mortally wounded.

The conflict, which colonists called the French and Indian War, soon spread. In 1756 Britain and France officially declared war on each other. They fought in Europe, Africa, India, and the West Indies, and on the high seas.

The first two years of the war went badly for the British in America. The French advanced southward, capturing British forts and building one of their own, Fort Ticonderoga, to strengthen their hold. Western New England and central New York were now open to attack. All the tribes north of the Ohio River became allies of France except those in the Iroquois confederacy. Some historians believe that if the French had been able to make allies of the Iroquois, they would have won the war.

From Defeat to Victory

Faced with defeat, in 1757 King George II and Parliament gave control of the war effort to one of Britain's most capable leaders, William Pitt. To win the war and seize New France, Pitt left the fighting in Europe to Britain's German allies. Then he hurled most of the British forces against the French in North America.

The climax came in 1759 when General Wolfe and 9,000 troops sailed up the St. Lawrence River toward Quebec, the heart of New France. Located on high, jagged cliffs above the river, Quebec was defended by 14,000 troops under the command of Louis Joseph, Marquis de Montcalm.

The city seemed secure, but Wolfe managed to scramble up a narrow path along the cliffs. When September 13 dawned, the astonished French found the British troops in control of the Plains of Abraham surrounding the city. In the battle that followed, both generals were killed, but the British won a decisive victory.

With the fall of Quebec, the French lost the war in North America. The following year, Montreal was captured and New France surrendered. In other parts of the world the fighting dragged on into 1762, as French forces crumbled on one battlefield after another.

The Treaty of Paris. The French and Indian War ended in February 1763 when a peace treaty was signed in Paris. Britain gained French Canada and all of Louisiana east of the Mississippi except for the city of New Orleans. From France's ally, Spain, Britain received Spanish Florida. To repay Spain for its aid, France gave it New Orleans and Louisiana west of the Mississippi.

Britain was now the most powerful nation in the world. The British navy ruled the seas, and the British army commanded Europe and North America.

American colonists felt a surge of pride in belonging to the British Empire. Some English leaders feared that the Americans might turn their thoughts to independence now that the French had been driven out. But Benjamin Franklin, expressing the view of many colonists, said that a union among the colonies "is not merely improbable, it is impossible," adding, "I mean without the most grievous tyranny and oppression."

Section Review

1. **Identification.** Define *speculators.*

2. **Comprehension.** Who claimed the Ohio Valley? What were their claims based on?

3. **Analysis.** What dispute led to the French and Indian War?

Data Search. Compare the maps on page 76. Which nation lost the most land as a result of the French and Indian War? Which nation gained the most land? With which nation might England's colonies have conflict in the future? Why?

Connections to Themes

Shaping Democracy

From today's vantage point, the new society that emerged in the thirteen colonies seems extremely unequal and unjust. However, white, male colonists found it a major step toward freedom, equality, and justice compared with the societies from which they had come.

In England and Europe, where social class divisions were firmly established, a person's opportunities were largely determined by birth. Landless farmers, for example, had little hope of improving their station in life. In North America, though, even indentured servants could hope eventually to become landowners.

Colonists enjoyed greater religious freedom, too. In Europe, religious differences divided the people of the continent. From the early 1500s through the mid-1600s, struggles between Catholics and Protestants had led to wars and persecution that had claimed thousands of lives.

The colonies provided a haven for religious groups that had known little but persecution in Europe. The hope of freedom to worship as they chose was an important motive for migrants to North America.

The idea that people of diverse religions, nationalities, and languages had an equal right to freedom and opportunity slowly took hold on American soil. The colonists excluded Native Americans and enslaved and free African Americans from this vision of equality. As time passed, however, excluded groups would claim that vision as their heritage, too.

Writing About History

War Reports. Have students imagine that they are colonial war correspondents, reporting on the French and Indian War. They are present at, and write articles about, the following events: the meeting of the Albany Congress, Braddock's march on Fort Duquesne, the British victory at Quebec, the signing of the Treaty of Paris. Articles should include important individuals, the course of action, and the significance of the events.

Limited English Proficiency

Making Time Lines. Have students work in small groups to make time lines of the major events of the French and Indian War from 1755 to 1763. As students suggest brief descriptions for each event, have one person from the group write them down beside each event.

Section Review

ANSWERS

1. Definition for the term *speculators* is on text page 74.
2. French claims based on French fur traders being the first to reach this area. Pennsylvanian and Virginian claims based on royal charters granting them the land. Indian claims based on their historic presence in the area.
3. War touched off by dispute over who owned the Ohio Valley—French had established a string of forts there; the English tried to drive them out.
Data Search. France lost most territory; England gained the most. Possible conflict with Spain as expansion moves westward.

Chapter Survey

ANSWERS

Using New Vocabulary

1. (c); Under mercantilism, trade was carried on between colonial and European merchants.
2. (a); Legislatures propose laws.
3. (b); Speculators bought land for profit.

Reviewing the Chapter

1. For money and power.
2. Colonies supplied raw materials for manufacturers and provided ready markets for those goods.
3. Jamestown in unhealthy location, first colonists expecting to find gold and were ill-prepared to support selves by farming and hard work, and colonial takeover of Indian lands led to clashes with Native Americans. Introduction of tobacco and colonists' right to own land put colony on firm footing.
4. House of Burgesses, first elected legislature in America, set precedent for self-government, though represented interests of only white adult male landowners, not population as a whole.
5. Both brought droves of people to North America.
6. Helped establish American democratic tradition of government based on consent of the governed.
7. New England: shipbuilding, fishing, whaling, shipping; Middle Colonies: grains; Southern Colonies: tobacco, indigo, rice.
8. Navigation Acts ordered that all goods imported or exported by colonies be carried in British or colonial ships; ships' crews had to be 75 percent English or English colonists; enumerated goods, like tobacco, cotton, indigo, sugar, rice, naval stores, furs could only be exported to England. Britain would not have to compete with other nations for colonial goods. The acts benefited England and provided a sure market for colonial goods.
9. Colonial takeover of Native-American lands, different ways of living; each side suspicious of the other.
10. Fewer indentured servants came to colonies as economic conditions improved in England. Laws institutionalized the holding of humans as property.
11. Quakers and Mennonites openly opposed slavery and called on others to do the same.
12. The French and Indian War was touched off by a dispute between the French and British over who controlled the Ohio

Chapter Survey

Using New Vocabulary

Match each numbered vocabulary term with its origin, then explain the connection between the origin and the vocabulary term.

Example: The origin of the term *veto* is the Latin word *vetare*, meaning "to forbid." To veto is to forbid a bill passed by the legislature from becoming a law.

1. mercantilism	(a) Latin: *legis*, the law + *latio*, proposing
2. legislature	(b) Latin: *speculari*, to view
3. speculators	(c) Latin: *mercans*, merchant

Reviewing the Chapter

1. Why did Europeans establish colonies in North America?

2. What was the role of the colony in a mercantilist economy?

3. Why did the Jamestown colony have such a struggle to survive? What finally put it on a firm economic footing?

4. What was the significance of the Virginia House of Burgesses for the future of American democracy? Whose interests did the burgesses represent?

5. What was the impact of each of the following on the colonies? (a) England's population boom in the 1600s (b) religious conflict in England in the 1600s

6. What role did the Mayflower Compact play in the beginnings of democracy in North America?

7. What were the main sources of income for the New England, Middle, and Southern colonies?

8. What were the major provisions of the Navigation Acts? Why were the Navigation Acts passed, and what effect did they have on trade?

9. What were the main causes of conflict between Native Americans and colonists? How were future relations between the two groups affected?

10. Why did the use of indentured servants give way to the practice of buying enslaved Africans in the Southern Colonies? How did laws contribute to the growth of slavery?

11. What role did religion play in opposition to slavery?

12. What were the causes and effects of the French and Indian War?

Thinking Critically

1. Application. Why can it be said that the English government did not have a general plan for establishing colonies in North America?

2. Evaluation. Do you think that conflict between the colonists and Native Americans was unavoidable? Give reasons for your answer.

3. Analysis. What role did close family ties and other African ways of life play in the way that Africans adapted to the harshness of slavery in North America?

History and You

1. The Pilgrims and Puritans came to North America with a mission: They wanted to establish communities in which they could worship as they wished. Do you think the American people today have a mission? Explain.

2. By 1750 people from many lands lived in the colonies. Find out about your ancestors. What countries did they come from? Why did they come to America? When? Compare their reasons for coming with those of the colonial settlers.

3. Gather information about the ways that colonists made a living. What colonial occupations no longer exist? When did they disappear? Why? What present-day occupations do you think will cease to exist? Why?

Valley. The war ended with a peace treaty making Britain the most powerful nation in the world. Britain gained French Canada and all of Louisiana east of the Mississippi River except New Orleans. Britain also received Spanish Florida from Spain, France's ally.

Thinking Critically

1. Absence of a plan suggested by diversity of kinds of colonies and of reasons for their establishment.
2. Students might argue that, given colonists' predominant view of Native Americans as uncivilized and colonists' relentless westward expansion, clash was inevitable. Students could also argue that if all colonists had dealt fairly with Indians, conflict might have been avoided.
3. Africans adapted by blending old and new ideas ways of life into a distinct Africa-American culture.

History and You

1. Students may consider: search for international peace, establishment of colonies in space, encouragement of spread of democratic institutions, control of racism and human rights abuses, preservation of world's animal life and habitats.
2. Answers will vary.
3. Answers regarding present-day occupations will vary. Students should consider effect of machines and computers on occupations today.

Applying Thinking Skills

1. Snake represents separate English colonies; initials represent names of colonies.
2. New England, New York, New Jersey, Pennsylvania, Maryland, Virginia, North Carolina, South Carolina.
3. Union of the colonies.
4. Answers will vary. Cartoon based on myth that if pieces of dead snake were rejoined quickly, snake would live.
5. Yes; Albany Plan called for permanent union of colonies for their mutual defense.

Applying Thinking Skills

Interpreting Political Cartoons

The political cartoon below was created by Benjamin Franklin in 1754, shortly after war had broken out between French and English colonists. Many historians think this was the first political cartoon to appear in an American newspaper. It was printed in the *Pennsylvania Gazette* soon after delegates from many of the English colonies had gathered at the Albany Congress to discuss whether they should fight together against the French. Study the cartoon and then answer the questions that follow.

1. In this cartoon, what does the snake stand for? How can you tell?

2. What does each abbreviation stand for?

3. What do you think Franklin's message was?

4. Do you think this cartoon communicates Franklin's message effectively? Explain why or why not.

5. Does this cartoon support the Albany Plan of Union? Give reasons for your answer.

Writing About Issues

The Issue: Should cigarette advertising be banned completely?

Beneath the glossy poster for a recent Virginia Slims Tennis Championships appeared the following message: "SURGEON GENERAL'S WARNING: Smoking Causes Lung Cancer, Heart Disease, Emphysema, and May Complicate Pregnancy."

In 1971 Congress banned advertising for cigarettes on radio and television in order to severely limit the number of ads that could be seen or heard by adolescents. However, opponents of cigarette advertising were not satisfied. The ban did not apply to magazines, newspapers, or billboards. The next year, in order to avoid a complete ban on advertising their products, tobacco companies agreed to place warnings on all of their cigarette advertisements.

Critics of cigarette advertising argue that health warnings do not discourage teenagers from starting the habit. They point to estimates that 20 percent of high school seniors smoke. These young smokers are bombarded by ads everywhere, from billboards to sporting events, they say. Only a total ban on ads will help keep them from starting to smoke in the first place.

Tobacco companies declare that their right to advertise is protected by the First Amendment's guarantee of free speech. They also claim that they are aiming their advertising at the adult market. Their goal they say, is not to create new smokers, but to cause existing adult smokers to change brands. "The fact is," writes Frank Resnik, chairman of Philip Morris U.S.A., "cigarette consumption is rising most strongly in [Eastern European] countries, where cigarette advertising has been unknown for decades."

Do you think that cigarette ads should be prohibited? Find a magazine or newspaper that carries cigarette ads. Write a letter to the publisher that expresses your view on the subject. Be sure to explain your reasons.

Unit 1 Survey

ANSWERS

Making Connections

1. Agree: Improved navigation and desire for trade would have led Europeans to the Americas eventually. Disagree: The Portuguese did not go near the Americas; only Columbus was bold enough to sail westward.

2. Spain planted colonies in the Caribbean and southern North America for wealth, power, and to spread their faith; brought Africans as forced labor and treated Native Americans as near-slaves. England planted colonies on the North Atlantic Coast where "needy people might settle," for wealth and power, and as markets for goods; imported enslaved Africans and clashed with Indians over land.

3. Southern Colonies: Year-round warm climate, broad coastal plain, navigable rivers supported plantation agriculture; few cities. Enslaved Africans worked plantations. Middle Colonies: Land and climate good for grains; flour mills. Diverse peoples settled. New England: Harsh climate, rocky soil; New Englanders turned to forests and sea; many large seaports.

4. Church and state were closest in New England colonies established by religious groups. Toleration was greatest in Pennsylvania, with freedom for all believers in God. Answers may include Maryland and Rhode Island.

5. Answers may include the Mayflower Compact, town meetings, Massachusetts' bicameral legislature, House of Burgesses, Fundamental Orders of Connecticut.

6. Diverse groups of Native Americans, Europeans, and Africans, and diverse religious groups, such as Puritans, Catholics, Quakers, Jews.

Using the Time Line. 1400s: Europeans began to explore, set trade routes. 1500s: They reached far corners of the globe; Spain colonized North America. 1600s: Other Europeans colonized North America.

Projects and Activities

1. Students should review the geography feature, page 44.

2. Explorers and their backers were spurred on by first-hand accounts of other explorers, who also passed on technical data and sailing directions. Geographers pieced together an accurate picture of the world from the explorers' records, which in turn aided other explorers.

Using the Time Line. For each event mentioned students should include information about who was affected and how.

Unit Survey

Making Connections

1. Agree or disagree with this statement: The times were right for Europeans to find the Americas. If Columbus had not, somebody else would have. Give evidence for your position.

2. Compare the Spanish and English colonies in North America in terms of the search for opportunity, areas settled, slavery, and relationships with Native Americans.

3. How did geography affect the pattern of settlement in the three regional groups of English colonies? How did these patterns of settlement influence local political organization?

4. Compare the relationship of church and state in the various English colonies. Where was religious toleration greatest? Why?

5. In the English colonies, which practices provided a basis for the growth of democracy?

6. Describe the diversity of peoples living on the North American continent by 1760.

Using the Time Line. Review the events on the time line, then write a paragraph for each century—1400s, 1500s, 1600s—describing its main characteristics based on these events.

Projects and Activities

1. Work in groups of five. With your group, make a shopping list for a breakfast, lunch, and dinner for one day. Then do research to find the origin of each food. Which foods were introduced into the Americas from other continents? Which foods were native to the Americas? Make a poster to share your information on at least ten foods with the class.

2. In the mid-1400s Johannes Gutenberg invented a practical form of movable metallic type, which made mass printing of books possible. The development of printing contributed to a spread of knowledge. Do research to find out how this development affected European exploration. How did the voyages of the explorers contribute to the exchange of knowledge? Write a report on your findings.

Using the Time Line. The practice of coffee drinking spread from Ethiopia to Arabia by 1200, to Turkey by 1500, to Italy by 1600, and then to the rest of Europe. Coffee houses sprang up as places where people met to exchange news and views. Write a dialogue between three people meeting in a coffee house in the early 1700s. The people exchange news about at least five events listed on the time line and discuss the impact of those events.

Milestones	1400	1495
Political and Economic	• Norse settlement in N. America ends • Inca establish rule in Peru • Portuguese settle Azores Islands • Portugal/Benin trade	• Treaty of Tordesillas • Moctezuma becomes Aztec ruler • Cortés conquers Aztecs • Pizarro conquers Incas
Social and Cultural	• Italian Renaissance begins • First book printed in English • Perspective drawing develops, Italy • Modern English language develops • Hohokam people disperse	• First Africans in West Indies • Las Casas protests Spanish treatment of Indians
Technological and Scientific	• First hand guns, harquebuses, develop • First navigation school, Portugal • Movable type, Gutenberg	• Columbus sights N. America • First world globe, Martin Behaim • German mapmaker suggests the name "America"

Assessment

To encourage historical empathy, stress that the seventeenth-century characters should hold values and beliefs consistent with the time and place in which they live. Let students know that the two characters from the same century do not always have to agree with each other.

You may wish to allow groups time to meet, plan, and divide their work so that students can do research into the roles they will play. Then the groups can meet again to write their scripts.

Assessment: Demonstrating What You Know

Writing a Script

Two Americans from the twentieth-century travel back in time and meet two people from seventeenth-century Europe. The twentieth-century time travelers see a chance to influence the European exploration of the Americas. If they are persuasive enough, they might change the outcome of early encounters between European explorers and Native Americans. The twentieth-century Americans give the Europeans at least five guidelines for exploration. They base their guidelines on modern-day ideas of unity and diversity, democracy, and opportunity. The Europeans respond that they are from a different century and therefore have different views.

Work in groups of four to write a script of the conversations that take place in this meeting of people from two different centuries. When your script is complete, read it aloud to the class, with each member of the group taking one of the roles. The conversation is to take place in four parts:

1. The four characters meet and introduce themselves, telling who they are, where they come from, what they do, and so forth.
2. The modern time travelers present their guidelines for exploration.
3. The people of the seventeenth century react to the guidelines. They explain their own goals, actions, and values.
4. The group discusses what aspects of the guidelines they can all agree on, what they cannot agree on, and why.

Evaluation Criteria

Your work will be evaluated according to how well you meet the following criteria.

- **Completing the task**. Your group creates a character for each person and writes a script that includes the guidelines, a likely response, and a comparison of the two points of view.
- **Knowing history**. You base the guidelines on modern views, supported by information from the text or other sources. You demonstrate your knowledge of European exploration by supporting the seventeenth-century response with examples from the text or other sources.
- **Thinking critically**. You analyze the goals and motives of the early European explorers. You compare common seventeenth-century views of exploration with twentieth-century views.
- **Communicating ideas**. Each character's position is clear. Your evidence is persuasive.

1590 **1685** **1780**

- Spain settles St. Augustine
- Mayflower Compact
- English Bill of Rights adopted
- League of the Iroquois formed
- First of the Navigation Acts
- John Zenger trial
- England settles Jamestown
- Pueblo Indian Revolt
- French and Indian War
- France settles Quebec
- France claims Mississippi Valley

- Horse introduced into N. America
- First Africans in English colonies
- Mother Goose published, Boston
- Protestant Reformation begins
- Harvard College founded
- First *Poor Richard's Almanac*
- First book printed in the English colonies
- First Jewish immigrants, New Amsterdam

- Portuguese ships reach Japan
- *A Description of New England*, John Smith
- First smallpox inoculations, Lady Montagu
- Practical navigation map, Mercator
- Pascal devises the adding machine
- First modern atlas, Ortelius
- Torricelli invents the barometer
- Franklin invents lightning rod
- Dutch develop the telescope
- La Salle explores the Mississippi

Scoring

To create a scoring system, or rubric, assign an achievement scale to each of the evaluation criteria. For example, you might evaluate "Knowing history" on a scale of 0 to 4 as follows.

4—Exemplary response: five or more guidelines for exploration are provided, at least one for each theme—balancing unity and diversity, shaping democracy, the search for opportunity. The guidelines are supported by statements that reflect twentieth-century thinking. Responses of seventeenth-century characters reflect goals and beliefs that are supported by examples from the text or other sources.

3—Good response: at least five guidelines, at least one for each theme; some incomplete, unclear, or incorrect information.

2—Adequate response: at least five guidelines but may not address all themes; distinctions between the two centuries unclear.

1—Poor response: at least three guidelines but does not address all three themes; no distinction between the two centuries; motives and goals of the European explorers unclear; statements not supported with evidence.

0—No response/inadequate response.

Follow-up Activities

Class discussion. Compare the groups' guidelines for exploration and the reasoning behind them.

Essay. Some people think of Columbus Day as a day of celebration; others suggest that it should be a day of mourning. How do you think Columbus Day should be recognized? Explain.

Unit **2**

Objectives

- Explain how disagreements with Britain's economic policies helped lead to the American Revolution.
- Identify early challenges to the narrowly defined view of the American identity.
- Discuss how weaknesses in the Articles of Confederation led to calls for a stronger national government.
- Describe conflict and compromise among delegates to the Constitutional Convention.
- Discuss the flexibility of the Constitution and how its principles affect the daily life of citizens.
- Trace the political and economic development of the U.S. under the presidencies of George Washington and John Adams.

Introducing

THE UNIT

In 1763 Britain's battle with France for supremacy in North America ended with the British acquisition of the North American mainland east of the Mississippi River. Britain's dominance, however, was soon tested by its thirteen American colonies. Refusing to be taxed by a parliament in which they were not represented, the colonies declared their independence from Britain and won it on the battlefield. The newly born United States established a successful form of union under the Constitution, dealt with financial problems, and steered a neutral course in foreign affairs.

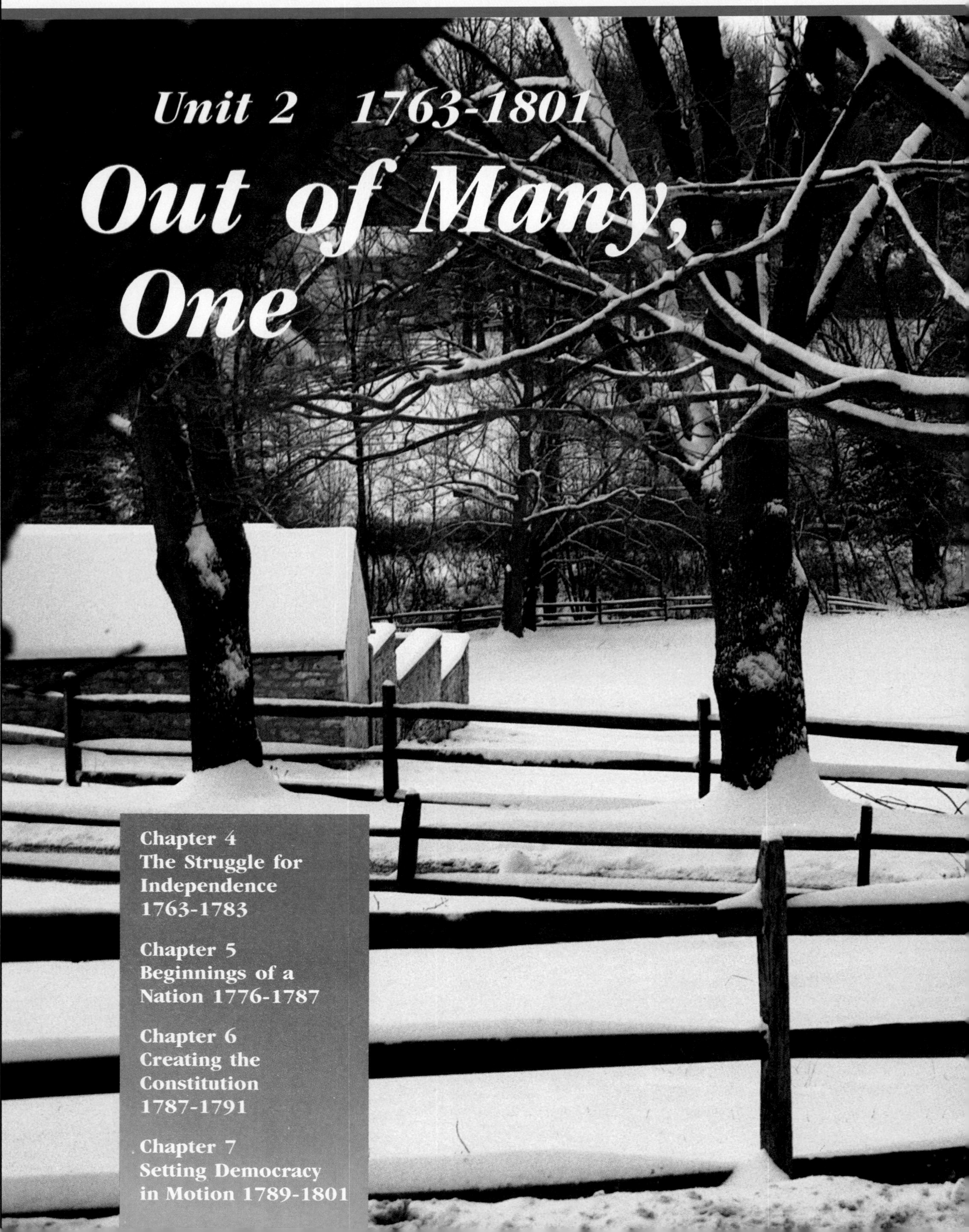

Unit 2 1763-1801

Out of Many, One

About the Speaker

During the Revolutionary War and after, Patrick Henry served as governor of Virginia. In 1788 he at first opposed ratification of the Constitution because he thought it endangered the rights of individuals and states. Eventually he accepted it for adoption after the addition of the Bill of Rights.

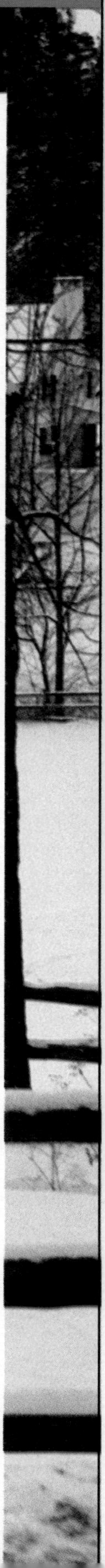

History Through Literature

He is by far the most powerful speaker I ever heard. Every word he says not only engages but commands the attention." So said an admirer of Patrick Henry (1736-1799), the distinguished political leader from Virginia. As early as 1763 Henry had denounced the king as a tyrant, a point of view shared by only a small minority of colonists at that time. By the time the colony of Virginia elected Henry to the first Continental Congress, the fiery patriot leader was outspoken in his attacks on British policy.

Unfortunately, many of Henry's speeches were not recorded at the time they were given. Still, some were reconstructed based on the memory of eyewitnesses. The following excerpt is a reconstruction by Henry's early biographer, William Wirt. Henry delivered the speech in 1775 to the Virginia Convention, which met in defiance of royal orders to disband. His words electrified his listeners and soon became a rallying cry for revolution.

from

"Give Me Liberty or Give Me Death"

Patrick Henry

Mr. President, it is natural to man to indulge in the illusions of hope. We are apt to shut our eyes against a painful truth and listen to the song of that siren, till she transforms us into beasts. Is this the part of wise men, engaged in a great and arduous struggle for liberty?

Is it that insidious smile with which our petition has been lately received? Trust it not, sir; it will prove a snare to your feet. Suffer not yourselves to be betrayed with a kiss. Ask yourselves how this gracious reception of our petition compares with those warlike preparations which cover our waters and darken our land. Are fleets and armies necessary to a work of love and reconciliation? Have we shown ourselves so unwilling to be reconciled that force must be called in to win back our love? Let us not deceive ourselves, sir. These are the implements of war and subjugation—the last arguments to which kings resort. I ask gentlemen, sir, what means this martial array, if its purpose be not to force us to submission? Can gentlemen assign any other possible motive for it? Has Great Britain any enemy in this quarter of the world to call for all this accumulation of navies and armies? No, sir, she has none. They are meant for us; they can be meant for no other. They are sent over to bind and rivet upon us those chains which the British Ministry have been so long forging.

Guided Reading

Discussion. Oratory is skill and eloquence in public speaking. Patrick Henry, considered the greatest orator of the American Revolution, inspired the colonists to unite to resist British rule.

As students read Henry's persuasive speech, have them look for ways that he emphasized his points. How did he capture the attention of his audience? **(skilled use of questions, repetition, invoking of patriotic images, emotional appeal)**

Vocabulary Building

Discussion. Knowing the following terms will help students understand Patrick Henry's speech: *arduous* (difficult), *insidious* (deceitful; treacherous), *subjugation* (the act of conquering), *supplication* (the act of requesting), *remonstrated* (argued), *prostrated* (lay in a face down position), *interposition* (intervention), *adversary* (opponent), *supinely* (passively), *vigilant* (alert to danger), *extenuate* (make less serious).

Writing About History

Persuasive Speech. Have students imagine that they are a speaker at the Virginia Convention who does not agree with Patrick Henry. They are to write a speech in opposition to Henry's remarks. First, they should list the arguments against Henry's ideas. Then they can write the speech, using some of the persuasive devices Henry used to strengthen his arguments—repetition, emotional appeal, questions, and so on. Students can present their speeches to the class, speaking slowly, clearly, and forcefully.

And what have we oppose to them? Shall we try argument? Sir, we have been trying that for the last ten years. Have we anything new to offer upon the subject? Nothing. We have held the subject up in every light of which it is capable; but it has been all in vain. Shall we resort to entreaty and humble supplication? What terms shall we find which have not been already exhausted? Let us not, I beseech you, sir, deceive ourselves longer. Sir, we have done everything that could be done to avert the storm which is now coming on. We have petitioned; we have remonstrated; we have supplicated; we have prostrated ourselves before the throne and have implored its interposition to arrest the tyrannical hands of the Ministry and Parliament. Our petitions have been slighted; our remonstrances have produced additional violence and insult; our supplications have been disregarded; and we have been spurned, with contempt, from the foot of the throne. In vain, after these things, may we indulge the fond hope of peace and reconciliation.

There is no longer any room for hope. If we wish to be free; if we mean to preserve inviolate those inestimable privileges for which we have been so long contending; if we mean not basely to abandon the noble struggle in which we have been so long engaged, and which we have pledged ourselves never to abandon, until the glorious object of our contest shall be obtained; we must fight! An appeal to arms and to the God of hosts is all that is left us!

They tell us, sir . . . that we are weak, unable to cope with so formidable an adversary. But when shall we be stronger? Will it be the next week or the next year? Will it be when we are totally disarmed, and when a British guard shall be stationed in every house? Shall we gather strength by irresolution and inaction? Shall we acquire the means of effectual resistance by lying supinely on our backs and hugging the delusive phantom of hope,

(Background) Valley Forge, Pennsylvania; (above) Patrick Henry; masthead of the Massachussetts Spy, *with united colonies menacing the British griffin; (opposite) "The Yankey's return from Camp," from a 1775 broadside.*

84

until our enemies shall have bound us hand and foot? Sir, we are not weak if we make a proper use of those means which the God of nature has placed in our power. Three millions of people armed in the holy cause of liberty and in such a country as that which we possess are invincible by any force which our enemy can send against us.

Besides, sir, we shall not fight our battles alone. There is a just God who presides over the destinies of nations, and who will raise up friends to fight our battles for us. The battle, sir, is not to the strong alone; it is to the vigilant, the active, the brave. Besides, sir, we have no election. If we were base enough to desire it, it is now too late to retire from the contest. There is no retreat but in submission and slavery! Our chains are forged. Their clacking may be heard on the plains of Boston! The war is inevitable— and let it come!! I repeat, sir, let it come!!!

It is vain, sir, to extenuate the matter. Gentlemen may cry, peace, peace; but there is no peace. The war is actually begun! The next gale that sweeps from the north will bring to our ears the clash of resounding arms! Our brethren are already in the field! Why stand we here idle? What is it that gentlemen wish? What would they have? Is life so dear or peace so sweet as to be purchased at the price of chains and slavery?

Forbid it, Almighty God— I know not what course others may take; but as for me, give me liberty, or give me death!

Taking a Closer Look

1. *What course of action does Patrick Henry seek to motivate colonists to take?*

2. *Why does Henry see war as inevitable? How does he view the consequences of continued British rule?*

3. *What makes Henry's speech a persuasive call to action? Support your answer with specific examples of words or phrases from his speech.*

Taking a Closer Look

ANSWERS

1. Patrick Henry's speech is a direct call for war, a war for liberty against what Henry sees as the tyranny of British rule.
2. There is no alternative but war; other attempts to end British tyranny have failed. He sees the alternative as complete subjugation of the colonies.
3. Answers will vary. Henry presents a strong argument and supports it with emotional eloquence: "Give me liberty or give me death," or the question, "Is life so dear or peace so sweet as to be purchased at the price of chains and slavery?" Students may also mention that Henry addresses all the possible courses of action open to the colonies and carefully refutes all but one, war. He also uses persuasive devices such as rhetorical questions, emotional appeal, repetition.

Chapter 4

The Struggle for Independence

Planning Guide

	Student Text	TWE Lesson Plans	Support Materials
SECTION 1	**Section 4–1** (1–2 Days) **"The Sole Right to Lay Taxes,"** pp 88–93 Review/Evaluation Section Review, p 93	**Introducing the Chapter:** Taking Action—Class Activity, 30 minutes, p 85B **Teaching the Main Ideas:** Patriotic Slogans—Class Activity, one class period, p 85B	★ **Read to Remember,** Section 1 ● **Section Activities,** Section 1 Δ **Enrichment Activities,** Section 1 Δ **Readings** ● **Tests and Quizzes,** Section 1 Quiz
SECTION 2	**Section 4–2** (1–2 Days) **The Path to War,** pp 94–100 Review/Evaluation Section Review, p 100	**Teaching the Main Ideas:** Why Not Compromise?—Individual Activity, one class period, p 85C **Reinforcement Activity:** Two Points of View—Individual Activity, one class period, p 85C	★ **Read to Remember,** Section 2 ● **Section Activities,** Section 2 Δ **Readings** ● **Tests and Quizzes,** Section 2 Quiz
SECTION 3	**Section 4–3** (1 Day) **The Break With Britain,** pp 100–106 The American Spirit: Mercy Otis Warren, p 102 Review/Evaluation Section Review, p 106	**Enrichment Activity:** Our Political Heritage—Individual Activity, 3 days student preparation, p 85C	★ **Read to Remember,** Section 3 ● **Section Activities,** Section 3 Δ **Enrichment Activities,** Section 3 Δ **Readings** ● **Tests and Quizzes,** Section 3 Quiz
SECTION 4	**Section 4–4** (1–2 Days) **Fighting for Independence,** pp 107–113 Connections to Themes: Shaping Democracy, p 113 Review/Evaluation Section Review, p 113 Chapter 4 Survey, pp 114–115 Skills, pp 114–115 Using New Vocabulary Thinking Critically Using Geography Applying Social Studies Skills: Analyzing Line Graphs Writing About Issues	**Evaluating Progress:** Revolution, Rebellion, or Anarchy?—Individual Activity, one class period, p 85C	★ **Read to Remember,** Section 4 ● **Section Activities,** Section 4 ● **Geography Activities,** Section 4 Δ **Readings,** Jacob Francis ● **Tests and Quizzes,** Section 4 Quiz, Chapter 4 Test (Forms A and B) **Additional Resources** Δ **Twentieth Century Issues: Links to the Past** ● **Active Learning** Δ **GTV Videodiscs** Δ **Transparencies and Activity Book** ● **Testing Software** ★ **Chapter Summaries** **Key:** ★ **For Extra Support** ● **For All Students** Δ **For Enrichment**

Overview

Serious quarrels between Great Britain and its North American colonies began to develop in 1763. At the heart of the conflict was the issue of power. The colonists, growing more and more conscious of their separate identity, felt that the British government was ignoring their right to representative government. Britain, however, saw the colonies as just one part of its vast mercantile empire, to be ruled as the king and Parliament saw fit.

Colonial protests grew with each attempt by the British government to control settlement and commerce and to levy taxes. In reaction to Parliament's passage of the "Intolerable" Acts, delegates from the colonies met for the First Continental Congress. When the Congress's grievances were not resolved and fighting broke out in Massachusetts, delegates to the Second Continental Congress created an army and, in 1776, proclaimed independence.

At first, the revolutionary war went badly for the Americans. British forces, however, could not maintain their advantage when France and Spain provided vital aid to the Americans. In the Treaty of Paris which ended the war, Britain recognized the independence of the United States and agreed to an extensive territory for the new nation.

Activity Objectives

After completing the activities, students should be able to

- identify issues that caused conflict between Britain and its North American colonies.
- explain how the failure to compromise led to war between Britain and the American colonists.
- identify the causes of British policies and their effects on the American colonists.
- evaluate the concept of revolution.
- explain how the principles of the Declaration of Independence apply to the United States today.

Introducing the Chapter

Taking Action

This class activity requires about 30 minutes.

Chapter 4 focuses on the issues that led the American colonists to declare independence from Great Britain. It will help students to understand the nature of the dilemma of the colonists if they first consider ways to remedy grievances against their government.

Ask students to imagine themselves fifteen years from now and to listen to the following description of their lives.

> *Although you work hard, your income has increased little in the last three years. Meanwhile, for three straight years the property tax on your home has increased. This year the sales tax also increased. You wonder what you are getting in return for your tax dollars—crime is on the rise, the roads have potholes, the courts are overloaded with cases.*
>
> *You are also fed up with politicians. They seem out of touch with your needs and concerns. All they do is pass laws that interfere with your life, requiring air bags in all cars, banning smoking in restaurants, regulating hiring policies in businesses.*

Without discussion, ask students to spend five minutes writing a response to the following questions: How do you feel about government based on this description? What actions can you take to remedy your grievances?

Ask students to share their opinions. Write their suggestions for action on the chalkboard. These may include writing letters to government officials, voting for new officials or programs, forming advocacy groups, taking part in demonstrations, and running for office.

If a student suggests revolution, ask how many in the class would become revolutionaries and why. If no one mentions this alternative, suggest it and discuss whether revolution would be an appropriate way to bring about change. Conclude by pointing out that in the 1760s the colonists were asking themselves similar questions.

Teaching the Main Ideas

Section 4-1: Patriotic Slogans

This class activity requires one class period, or it may be assigned as homework and shared in class the following day.

In Section 4-1 students are introduced to the slogan, "No taxation without representation," coined by the Patriots after Parliament enacted the Stamp Act. The following activity engages students in creating slogans that summarize the colonists' views of other critical events between 1763 and 1773.

Before class begins, write the following events on the chalkboard: Proclamation of 1763, Sugar Act, British use of writs of assistance, Currency Act, Quartering Act, Townshend Acts, British suspension of New York assembly, Boston Massacre, the Tea Act.

Begin the activity by reciting the slogan: "No taxation without representation." Ask students to explain what British actions prompted the slogan. Discuss how slogans help to create awareness of issues and unite people. Ask students to cite some current slogans that serve these purposes, for example, "Say No to Drugs" or "Don't Drink and Drive."

Divide the class into groups of three and assign each group one of the events written on the chalkboard. Direct the groups to spend 15 minutes creating a slogan that summarizes the colonists' view of the event. Distribute poster paper and markers for students to use in making signs featuring their slogans.

Direct the groups to display their signs. Have the class identify the event referred to by each slogan. Conclude by having students identify the issues that led to conflict between Britain and its American colonists. (Answers may include settlement of western lands, taxation without representation, abuse of power by government officials.)

Teaching the Main Ideas

Section 4-2: Why Not Compromise?

This individual activity requires one class period, or it may be assigned as homework and shared in class the following day.

This activity is designed to help students consider whether the American War of Independence could have been prevented by compromise.

Begin the activity by reviewing the events preceding passage of the Coercieve, or Intolerable, Acts and the provisions of the acts described in Section 4-2. Then ask students to speculate about what might have happened if Britain had tried to compromise with the colonists, passing *Tolerable* Acts rather than *Intolerable* Acts.

Have students imagine that they are members of Parliament in 1774 who are charged with the task of writing legislation to deal with problems in the colonies in order to avert further conflict. The legislation should address both Britain's need for greater revenue and the colonists' desire to have a voice in their own affairs.

Have students present their legislation to the class. Discuss the likelihood of the king, Parliament, and colonial leaders accepting the acts. Then direct the class to draft new legislation, incorporating the acts that seem to have the best chance of being accepted by all sides.

Conclude by having the class consider chances for compromise while the Second Continental Congress was meeting. Ask students what George III did after the Battle of Bunker Hill that made compromise more difficult. (He refused to read the Olive Branch Petition, declared the colonies to be in a state of rebellion, and closed the colonies to all trade.) What actions of the Patriots made compromise more difficult? (They seized Fort Ticonderoga, created the Continental Army, and marched on Canada.)

Reinforcement Activity

Section 4-2: Two Points of View

This individual activity requires one class period.

This creative writing activity is designed to help students review the major events from 1773 to 1775 and compare British and American reactions.

Tell students that they are to write a series of letters from the point of view of either pro-British merchants in Boston or Patriot merchants in Boston. The letters should be written to relatives or friends in Britain on the following dates: December 1773, October 1774, July 1775, and March 1776. In the letters students should describe the major events that have occurred in the colony and their views on Parliament, George III, and Patriot leaders.

Ask volunteers to read their letters to the class. Compare pro-British and Patriot reactions to the Intolerable Acts, the First Continental Congress, fighting at Lexington and Concord, the Second Continental Congress, the Battle of Bunker Hill, the Olive Branch Petition, the American defeat in Canada, and the British defeat in Massachusetts. Conclude by discussing how such reactions reflected the widening breach between Britain and the American colonists and by speculating about the possibility of compromise in early 1776.

Evaluating Progress

Section 4-4: Revolution, Rebellion, or Anarchy?

This individual activity requires one class period, or it may be assigned as homework.

This activity is designed to assess students' understanding of the events and issues in the American War of Independence through their ability to identify revolutionary actions.

Before class, write the following terms and definitions on the chalkboard.

- *Revolution:* overthrow of a government by those governed and usually by forceful means, with another government taking its place.
- *Rebellion:* armed resistance to one's government; seeks to modify or change the existing system.
- *Anarchy*: complete absence of government.

Remind students that in Chapter 4 the actions of the colonists are described as revolutionary. Point out that some historians argue that colonial actions might be more accurately described as rebellion or anarchy. Call students' attention to the definitions on the chalkboard.

Direct students to write an essay answering the question: *Was the American War of Independence a revolution, a rebellion, or anarchy?* Essays should include an introduction, a body with the main points supported by arguments and examples, and a conclusion.

Criteria for evaluation should include clearly expressed answers and convincing examples to support them. Although there is no right answer to the question, the following points may be included: *Revolution*—colonists' actions were based on the political beliefs expressed in the Declaration of Independence. *Rebellion*—colonists' actions resulted in few changes other than ending English rule. *Anarchy*—colonists' actions were disorganized, and many colonists did not support the war.

Enrichment Activity

Section 4-3: Our Political Heritage

Students need at least three days outside of class to complete this individual activity.

In Section 4-3 students learn the historic importance of the Declaration of Independence. This activity helps students to recognize that the principles of the Declaration remain the cornerstone of American democracy.

Begin the activity by having a student read aloud the Preamble (the first two paragraphs) of the Declaration of Independence (page 912 of the text) as other students follow along in their texts. Help students identify the four principles stated in the Preamble as you write them on the chalkboard—equal rights, unalienable rights, government by consent of the governed, the right to overthrow the government and establish a new one. Discuss whether these principles still apply in the United States today.

Have students find evidence in newspaper and magazine articles of the influence of the principles of the Declaration of Independence today. Students should find at least one article for each of the four principles.

Direct students to post their articles on the bulletin board, organizing them according to the principle reflected in each article. Have the class note the distribution of articles and generalize about the application of the Declaration's principles today. Students probably will have found few if any articles on the right to overthrow the government. Conclude by discussing why this principle seems to be less of an issue today than it was in 1776.

Bibliography and Audiovisual Material

Teacher Bibliography

De Crévecoeur, J. Hector. *Letters from an American Farmer.* 1782. Reprint. Magnolia, MA: Peter Smith Publisher, 1990.

Depauw, Linda Grant. *Founding Mothers: Women of America in the Revolutionary Era.* Boston: Houghton Mifflin, 1975.

Hofstadter, Richard. *America at 1750: A Social Portrait.* New York: Alfred A. Knopf, 1971.

Kaplan, Sidney. *The Black Presence in the Era of the American Revolution, 1770–1800.* Washington, D.C., Smithsonian, 1973.

Middlekauff, Robert. *The Glorious Cause: The American Revolution, 1763–1789.* New York: Oxford University Press, 1982.

Tuchman, Barbara W. *The First Salute.* New York: Alfred A. Knopf, 1988.

Student Bibliography

Cooper, James F. *The Last of the Mohicans.* New York: Dutton, 1962.

Dann, John C., ed. *The Revolution Remembered: Eyewitness Accounts of the War for Independence.* Chicago: University of Chicago Press, 1983.

Edmonds, Walter D. *Drums Along the Mohawk.* Boston: Little, Brown, 1936.

Fast, Howard. *April Morning.* New York: Bantam Books, 1962.

Norton, Mary Beth. *Liberty's Daughters: The Revolutionary Experience of American Women, 1750–1800.* Boston: Little, Brown, 1980.

Quarles, Benjamin. *The Negro in the American Revolution.* New York: Norton, 1973.

Roberts, Kenneth. *Oliver Wiswell.* New York: Fawcett Book Group, 1981.

Films, Videocassettes, and Videodiscs

American History—Birth of a Nation Series. AIMS Media. Videodiscs.

American Revolution. 16 min. EBEC. Movie.

American Revolution Series: The Background Period. 10 min. Coronet/MTI. Videocassette.

American Revolution Series: The War Years. 10 min. Coronet/MTI. Videocassette.

Filmstrips

America: Colonization to Constitution: Road to Independence. National Geographic Society.

Black People in the Revolution. EBEC.

Where Historians Disagree Collection: Origins of the American Revolution. Random House Media.

Women in the American Revolution. Multi-Media Productions.

Computer Software

Revolution '76. Apple or IBM. Britannica Software.

Revolutionary Wars: Choosing Sides. Apple. Tom Snyder Productions.

U.S. History: American Revolution. Apple. Focus Media.

Washington's Decision. Apple. Educational Activities, Inc.

Chapter 4

Objectives

- Explain why quarrels broke out between Britain and its American colonies.
- Discuss how the colonists' resistance to British laws led to war.
- Explain why the colonies declared their independence.
- Analyze why the United States won the Revolutionary War.

Introducing THE CHAPTER

For suggestions on introducing Chapter 4, refer to page 85B in the Teacher's Edition.

Developing THE CHAPTER

For activities and teaching strategies to help you reinforce and enrich chapter content see pages 85B–85D in the Teacher's Edition.

B · A · C · K · G · R · O · U · N · D

Chapter Opener Illustrations

John Trumbull's *Declaration of Independence* includes 48 of the 56 signers of the document. The portion of Trumbull's painting below shows John Adams, Roger Sherman, Robert R. Livingston, Thomas Jefferson, and Benjamin Franklin standing before John Hancock.

Defiant colonists united to tear down statues of George III and replace them with liberty poles, as shown below in the painting by John McRae.

Britain hoped to quickly destroy the ill-equipped Continental Army. Congress specified that uniforms were "as much as possible" to be brown with different color facings to distinguish regiments. Early in the war, however, uniforms were the exception, not the rule.

Reduced student page in the Teacher's Edition

Chapter 4 1763-1783

The Struggle for Independence

"Yankee Doodle," written in 1755, was sung by Patriot troops throughout the war. British troops heard it so often that General Gage is said to have exclaimed, "I hope I shall never hear that tune again!"

Women, too, helped the war effort. Robert Shurtleff—Deborah Sampson disguised as a man—was shot in the leg. Fearing discovery of her identity, she removed the musket ball herself and went back to fight. Her watercolor portrait appears below.

Paul Revere placed a lantern in the steeple of Boston's North Church to warn the Patriots of the British march toward Lexington and Concord.

American Voices

In the early days, most colonists in the English colonies saw themselves as loyal subjects of the Crown. But in 1766, when the British Parliament questioned Benjamin Franklin about colonial reaction to the Stamp Act, his answers showed that the colonists' feelings had changed.

> "Q. *Do not you think the people of America would . . . pay the stamp duty, if it was moderated?*
> A. *No, never, unless compelled by force. . . .*
> Q. *What was the temper of America towards Great Britain before the year 1763?*
> A. *The best in the world. They submitted willingly to the government of the Crown. . . .*
> Q. *And what is their temper now?*
> A. *O, very much altered. . . .*
> Q. *What used to be the pride of Americans?*
> A. *To indulge in the fashions and manufactures of Great Britain.*
> Q. *What is now their pride?*
> A. *To wear their old clothes over again, till they can make new ones.*"

Far from their home country, the colonists had begun to develop their own economic and political institutions and to develop a new sense of who they were and where their loyalties lay. England, however, continued to view the American colonies as just one part of an empire that provided a market for its goods and that king and Parliament had the right to rule.

Presenting the Declaration of Independence; raising the Liberty Pole; drawing of American soldiers; sheet music for "Yankee Doodle"; Deborah Sampson, disguised Patriot soldier; Patriot lantern.

Analyzing Primary Sources

American Voices

Many historians consider Benjamin Franklin to be the ablest and most successful American diplomat ever sent abroad. He spent the years between 1764 and 1775 in England as an agent for the colony of Pennsylvania.

In February 1766 Franklin appeared before the House of Commons to answer questions about the Stamp Act. The excerpt on this page represents only a few of the 174 questions that Franklin answered. Ask students:

1. Do the British seem willing to moderate their demands at this time? **(yes)** Do the American colonists? **(no)**
2. What change in colonial attitude does Franklin report? **(Colonists now challenge government; do not copy British fashions nor buy their goods.)**
3. How could this change harm Britain? **(reduce demand for its products in colonies)**

GTV Side 1

Chap. 15, Frame 35698

Laying Down the Law (Movie)

Search:

Play:

Section 4-1

Objectives

- ***Answer the Focus Question.***
- *Discuss how Britain tried to strengthen its control of the colonies.*
- *Explain why the American colonists objected to the Stamp Act, the Townshend Acts, and the Tea Act.*

Introducing

THE SECTION

Write on the chalkboard the following words of John Adams: "*The revolution was complete, in the minds of the people, and the union of the colonies, before the war commenced.*" Ask students to explain what Adams meant. **(Colonists changed from being loyal subjects to something new—Americans.)**

Have students compare Adams's words with the answers of Benjamin Franklin (page 87) about colonial attitudes. **(Both men agreed that attitudes and practices changed.)**

Students will be reading about new British policies that caused these changes. Have students speculate about what these changes might be **(political, social, economic).**

B · A · C · K · G · R · O · U · N · D

Time Line Illustrations

1. Chief Pontiac tried to unite Indian tribes of the Great Lakes area and the Ohio and Mississippi valleys against white encroachment on Indian lands. In 1763 he led a series of attacks on British forts.

2. The *Pennsylvania Journal* ceased publishing in protest of the Stamp Act. The skull and crossbones stamp appeared on the last edition, warning of the effects of the stamp tax.

3. Coffin symbols refer to the first four victims of the Boston Massacre—Samuel Gray, a ropemaker; Samuel Maverick, an apprentice joiner; James Caldwell, a seaman; and Crispus Attucks, who had long before escaped slavery to become a seaman.

4. African Americans, both slave and free, played an important part in the war effort. The painting of a free black

Reduced student page in the Teacher's Edition

CHAPTER TIME LINE

1763 - 1783

1765 Stamp Act

1773 Tea Act

1763 | 1767 | 1771

1770 Boston Massacre

1763 Pontiac's Rebellion

1767 Townshend Acts

4-1 "The Sole Right to Lay Taxes"

Focus: What quarrels broke out between Britain and its American colonies?

The year was 1765. An angry crowd gathered in Boston. A ship had arrived from Britain with news that Parliament had passed a law to tax the colonists. Soon, a speaker warned, the colonies would be enslaved by taxes. His listeners shouted their agreement. As English citizens, they believed they could be taxed only by their own consent given through their own representatives.

Conflict Over Western Lands

By 1765 a serious rift was developing between Britain and its American colonies. The colonists grumbled that the British were ignoring their rights and interests. The king and Parliament, on the other hand, assumed that they had the authority to rule the American part of the empire as they saw fit.

The first serious quarrel broke out in 1763, as a result of an Indian uprising in the lands west of the Appalachian Mountains. After the French surrendered to the British in February, settlers had once again begun flowing into lands belonging to the Seneca, Delaware, Shawnee, and others.

In May, Indian resentment boiled over. Pontiac, an Ottawa chief, spoke passionately against the British to other tribes:

"When I go see the English commander and say to him that some of our comrades are dead [killed by settlers], instead of be-

sailor was done in 1779. He was probably a member of the crew of the *General Washington,* the ship in the background.

5. The Treaty of Paris, ending two years of peace negotiations, was signed September 3, 1783. Note the signatures of Benjamin Franklin, John Jay, and John Adams.

6. The French officer Marquis de Lafayette volunteered to serve as a major general in the American army and helped lead American and French forces to victory at Yorktown.

1774 Intolerable Acts

1775 Battles of Lexington and Concord

1776 Declaration of Independence

1778 Continental Army enlists enslaved African Americans

1781 American-French victory at Yorktown

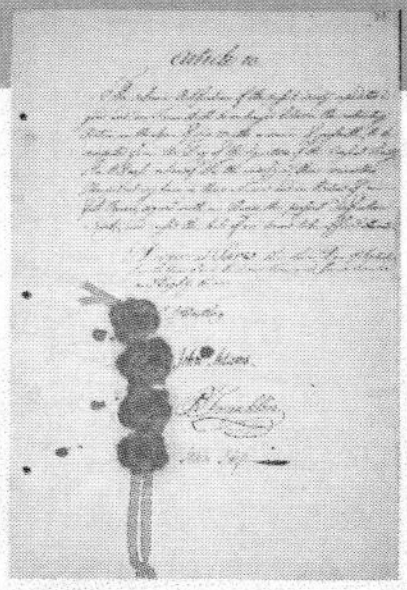

1783 Treaty of Paris

1775 — 1779 — 1783

waiting their death as our French brothers do, he laughs at me and at you. If I ask for anything for our sick, he refuses. . . . You can well see that they are seeking our ruin. Therefore, . . . we must all swear their destruction and wait no longer. . . . They are few in number, and we can accomplish it. ”

Pontiac's appeals moved eighteen tribes to form an alliance, with himself as their leader. In the course of a year, traveling over 1,000 miles, they captured eight of the eleven British forts and killed many settlers west of the Appalachian Mountains.

The alliance was broken when French supplies failed to arrive. However, Pontiac's Rebellion had nearly succeeded. George III and Parliament decided that the way to keep the peace was to reserve the newly acquired lands for the tribes.

Accordingly, in October 1763 the king proclaimed that all lands beyond the Appalachians were closed to "any purchases and settlements." But the Proclamation of 1763 was designed to do more than keep the peace. It would stop colonists from moving westward, away from British control.

The colonists reacted with anger. They had fought and died for this land, and they thought Britain was unfair in closing it to them. Even then, colonists were looking west, imagining a better life beyond the mountains. Denying it to them was like slamming a door in their faces.

A further source of resentment was the British decision that to defend its empire it must keep an army of 10,000 soldiers in the colonies. The colonists protested to Parliament, asking why an army was needed in peacetime. But Britain expected help, not complaints, from its colonies.

Grenville Taxes the Colonies

Britain's wars with the French and with Pontiac's alliance had ended in victory, expanding its empire and strengthening its control over the western lands. However, victory had proved costly, doubling the national debt. Where was the money to come from? In Britain, citizens had already rioted over a new tax intended to raise revenue.

George Grenville, the new prime minister, thought the colonies should bear some of the costs.

Developing

THE SECTION

Analyzing Primary Sources

Proclamation of 1763. The main points of the Proclamation of 1763 appear below. Read them to students. Then ask the questions that follow.

“ *In so much as it is in our interest and in the interest of our colonies that the several nations of Indians who live under our protection should not be disturbed in the territories that are reserved to them as hunting grounds; we do therefore . . . declare it to be our royal will that no governor in any of our colonies . . . grant warrants of survey or pass any patents for lands beyond the bounds of the stated proclamation line.* ”

1. Why was the proclamation issued?
2. As a Native American, how might you have reacted to the statement that the Indian nations lived under British "protection"?
3. What does this phrase indicate about the status of Native Americans in 1763?
4. How would it benefit the British to have good relations with Indian tribes at that time?

GTV Side 1

Chap. 15, Frame 38609

Proclamation of 1763 (Map)

Search:

Connections: Politics
The office of prime minister did not exist in the 1700s though the term is often used. George Grenville was not a prime minister in the present-day sense. The key position in government was the person who held the most power in the House of Commons, "the minister of the House of Commons." This person was usually chosen by the King to be the principal minister, the head of the Treasury. The title *prime minister* did not become official in England until 1905.

Active Learning

Song Lyrics. The Daughters of Liberty boycotted English products and sang protest songs. Read these lyrics to a portion of one such song. Ask students what women did to hurt the British economy.

"First, then, throw aside
your topknots of pride,
Wear none but your own
country linen,
Of Economy boast, let
your pride be the
most,
To show clothes of your
own make and
spinning."

Have students write lyrics to a song in support of a present-day movement they feel strongly about; for example, preservation of the world's resources.

Reduced student page in the Teacher's Edition

After all, they were benefiting from British protection. Up to this time, the customs duties that Britain levied had been designed simply to encourage the colonies to trade only with Britain. Thus, goods brought in from Britain were charged lower duties than goods imported from other nations. Duties often went uncollected, however, for the colonists were expert at smuggling goods into the colonies.

To raise money and at the same time discourage smuggling, Grenville took a bold step. In April 1764, at his urging, Parliament passed the Sugar Act, which added or increased duties on foreign imports such as sugar, wine, cloth, and coffee. It also reduced an earlier duty on molasses in the hope that the colonists would actually pay it instead of smuggling molasses from the French West Indies.

To halt smuggling, customs collectors were allowed to use **writs of assistance,** legal documents that permitted them to search any building in which illegal goods might be hidden. Accused smugglers were to be tried before a British judge in British admiralty courts instead of before juries of their fellow colonists. The right to a trial by a jury of their peers, long cherished by British citizens, was thus denied the colonists.

That same year Parliament passed the Currency Act, forbidding colonial legislatures to print paper money. All duties and debts that colonists owed British creditors would now have to be paid with gold and silver, always in short supply. The colonists soon were having trouble transacting their daily business.

When Parliament levied taxes in the form of stamps in 1765, colonists responded with protests and then with rioting. All the stamp distributors resigned to save their lives and property.

Next, Parliament found a way to reduce the cost to Britain of maintaining its troops in the colonies. In March 1765 it passed the Quartering Act, which required colonial legislatures to provide royal troops with barracks and supplies.

Britain's efforts to raise money enraged the colonists. James Otis, a leader of the Massachusetts assembly, said of the Sugar Act:

> *"One single act of Parliament has set the people a-thinking in six months more than they have done in their whole lives before."*

The Stamp Act

On October 31, 1765, a Pennsylvania newspaper attacked Britain's newest attempt to raise revenue—the Stamp Act.

> *"I am sorry to have to tell my readers that as the Stamp Act will have to be enforced after the first of November (the fatal tomorrow) the publisher of this paper is unable to bear the burden. I have decided it is better to stop printing for a while and to think about ways we can find to avoid the chains forged for us, and to escape this slavery."*

Under the Stamp Act, written materials such as newspapers, contracts, birth certificates, diplomas, and advertisements had to be printed on a special stamped paper. To get the paper, colonists must pay a tax to local British agents. People who violated the Stamp Act would be tried in admiralty courts. Again, the colonists charged, basic rights of British citizens were being violated.

Most colonists realized they were not taxed more than people in Britain, who also paid a stamp tax. What they objected to was the *way* the tax had been imposed on them.

Connections: Language

The Patriots used boycotts to protest the Stamp and Townshend acts. The term *boycott* has an Irish origin. C. C Boycott was a British army officer who lived in the 1800s. He treated Irish tenants so badly that they decided to ostracize him. The colonists, of course, did not use the term *boycott* to describe their actions.

They believed that only representatives they themselves elected— the delegates to their colonial assemblies— should be able to levy taxes on them. The colonists did not elect representatives to the British Parliament. Therefore, although Parliament claimed to represent all British subjects, the colonists felt it had no right to tax them.

Previous acts of Parliament had caused outbursts of indignation. But the Stamp Act, which touched nearly everyone, raised the protests to an important new level: the colonists began to unite.

"No taxation without representation." From New Hampshire to Georgia, a small but determined minority of colonists calling themselves **Patriots** set to work to rally public opinion against Britain. In town after town they formed groups called the Sons of Liberty and the Daughters of Liberty. Patriot merchants refused to trade with Britain. Women in the liberty groups organized a **boycott** of British goods, urging other colonists not to buy or use them. In every colony, people took up the rallying cry "No taxation without representation!"

The Virginia House of Burgesses declared that it alone had the "sole exclusive right and power to lay taxes . . . upon the inhabitants of this colony." Massachusetts, mirroring this mood, called on other colonies to attend a Stamp Act Congress. In response, representatives from nine colonies met in New York in October 1765.

At the Congress the delegates resolved that

" it is inseparably essential to the freedom of a people, and the undoubted right of Englishmen, that no taxes be imposed on them but with their own consent, given personally or by their representatives. "

Delegate Christopher Gadsden of South Carolina put the new spirit of unity into words: "There ought to be no New Englanders, no New Yorkers, known on the continent, but all of us Americans." In the same spirit, the Congress sent Parliament a petition urging repeal of the Stamp Act.

The stamp tax petition reached an England already divided over the tax issue. The American boycott had hurt English merchants. Within a few months, exports to the colonies had fallen nearly 40 percent.

In March 1766 Parliament repealed the Stamp Act. As a goodwill gesture, it even reduced the duty on molasses. On the same day that it repealed the Stamp Act, however, Parliament passed the Declaratory Act, which upheld its power to make laws for the colonies "in all cases whatsoever." The basic disagreement between Parliament and the colonists over who had the power to govern them had not been resolved, and more trouble lay ahead.

The Townshend Acts

One year later Britain was still tormented by money problems and declining business activity. To give Britons economic relief, Parliament cut their land taxes. To make up for the lost revenue, the new finance minister, Charles Townshend, made the mistake of following Grenville's example. He turned to the colonies.

In June 1767 Parliament passed the Townshend Acts, which levied new duties on imports and set up a customs board in Boston to make sure that duties were collected. Once again the colonists protested. In a series of essays, John Dickinson, a Philadelphia lawyer, took the lead in expressing their point of view. The colonies, he wrote, were willing to accept duties that regulated trade, but they refused to accept taxes disguised as duties.

Colonial merchants knew that the best way to convince Britain to reconsider its policies was to "touch the pocket nerve." They banded together to refuse to import British goods until the Townshend Act was repealed. Women organized spinning bees to make cloth. Tea was smuggled in or brewed from raspberry leaves.

Linking Past and Present

Discussion. With the passage of the Stamp Act, the slogan "No taxation without representation" became a rallying cry for Patriots.

Ask: How do slogans become rallying cries? Can students think of some slogans used today? **("Just Say No to Drugs," "Don't Drink and Drive," and so on.)** What issues do these slogans summarize?

Analyzing Primary Sources

Gadsen's Speech. Refer students to Gadsen's words spoken to the Stamp Act Congress.

Ask: What was important about Gadsen's words? What relatively new idea did they suggest? **(Even many years after the Revolution, some Americans thought their primary allegiance was to their states.)**

Limited English Proficiency

Cooperative Activity. Lead students to identify the colonists' growing list of grievances against Britain, from those that resulted from the Proclamation of 1763 through the Tea Act. Then have students work in small groups to write brief descriptions of each event or act of Parliament that aroused colonial opposition.

Dates should be included as well as any actions the colonies took to protest or remedy their grievances. Allow ample time for class discussion so that students can share their lists and descriptions.

Connections: Art

Analyzing the Visual. Art used in the service of a cause is propaganda. Have students study the engraving of the Boston Massacre by Paul Revere.

Ask: How does the engraving differ from the description of the event in the text? **(Jeering by the crowd is not depicted.)** How does Revere appeal to the emotions of the observer? **(showing unarmed colonists as innocent victims of murderous British troops)** Can this engraving be called propaganda? Why?

Social History

The term "Sons of Liberty" had originally been used by the Irish MP Colonel Isaac Barré in a speech against passage of the Stamp Act in the House of Commons in February 1765. Barré, who had served in the French and Indian War, opposed taxation of England's American colonies.

In this engraving Paul Revere condemned the British for the Boston Massacre. News of the incident sent shock waves through the colonies. The dead, including Crispus Attucks (above), became Patriot martyrs.

> *The people had sticks. And as the soldiers were pushing with their guns, they struck their guns. . . .*
>
> *One of these people, a stout man with a long cordwood stick, threw himself in, and made a blow at the officer. . . . The stout man then turned round and struck the soldier's gun. He knocked his gun away and struck him over the head.*
>
> *The stout man cried, "Kill the dogs. Knock them over." This was the general cry. The people then crowded in. . . .*
>
> *I turned to go, when I heard the word "fire." I thought I heard the report of a gun. I then saw the soldier swing his gun and fire it. . . . I thought and still think it was Crispus Attuck who was shot.*
>
> —*Testimony of Andrew, an enslaved African American, at the trial of the British soldiers after the Boston Massacre.*

Meanwhile, Parliament suspended the New York assembly for its defiance of the Quartering Act. New York had refused to raise money to supply British troops, claiming that the act was a tax. If New York's assembly could be suspended, colonists realized, no assembly was safe. Without assemblies, representative government would be dead.

The Boston Massacre

In late 1768 two regiments of British soldiers made Boston their headquarters. Throughout 1769 an uneasy standoff prevailed between soldiers and citizens. Then, on March 5, 1770, a violent incident shocked the city. A crowd led by Crispus Attucks, who had long before escaped slavery to become a seaman, gathered at the Boston customshouse, jeering and throwing snowballs at British guards. Tempers exploded and the troops fired. When the smoke cleared, three colonists, including Attucks, lay dead. Two more were fatally wounded.

The British commander and eight soldiers were arrested and charged with murder, but they got a fair trial. Two of the colony's best lawyers, Patriots John Adams and Josiah Quincy, undertook the defense of the British. The two lawyers argued that

Multicultural Perspectives

The name of Attucks endured after the War for Independence. African-American military companies took the name of Attucks Guards. Boston blacks held a Crispus Attucks Day annually from 1858 to 1870. In 1888 a Crispus Attucks monument was erected on the Boston Common.

the crowd had provoked the shooting. Two soldiers were given light punishment, and the commander and six soldiers were acquitted.

While John Adams focused on the importance of a fair trial, his cousin, Samuel Adams, a fierce critic of England, saw the "Boston Massacre" as a symbol of British tyranny. For years to come, in speeches and pamphlets, he would remind the colonists of that fateful event. These reminders fed the fire of liberty, wrote one Patriot, "and kept it burning with an incessant flame."

Forming Committees of Correspondence

Meanwhile, in London, a new prime minister, Lord North, had decided that the Townshend Acts were a mistake. They had brought little money in duties. Worse still, British trade to major colonial ports had been cut in half by the boycott. Parliament repealed the Townshend Acts and allowed the Quartering Act to expire.

But even as he sought to calm the colonists, Lord North made sure to assert Parliament's right to tax them. Accordingly, he kept one Townshend tax on the books—the duty on tea.

After two years of relative calm, several incidents again inflamed colonial resentment. In June 1772 the British warship *Gaspee* went aground off Rhode Island while chasing a suspected smuggler. A crowd boarded the hated ship, chased off the crew, and burned the *Gaspee.*

Britain appointed an investigating commission, and rumors quickly spread that anyone arrested would be sent to England for trial—another threat to the colonists' cherished right to trial by a jury of their peers. The commission could find no evidence, however, and no one was arrested.

Shortly after the *Gaspee* incident, Massachusetts citizens learned that the salaries of the governor and judges would now be paid from customs revenues rather than by the Massachusetts assembly. Thus, the assembly had lost its one power over the governor and judges—"the power of the purse."

In these incidents Samuel Adams saw a golden opportunity to unite the colonists against Britain. At his urging, the Boston town meeting appointed a "committee of correspondence" to keep in touch with other towns, sharing their grievances. Adams's idea spread quickly. By August 1774 all the colonies were linked by committees of correspondence.

The Tea Act

In May 1773 Parliament again misjudged the colonists' state of mind when it passed the Tea Act. The purpose of the act was to help the British East India Company. Instead, it further fanned the flame of colonial discontent.

For years, British wholesale merchants had bought tea from the East India Company and sold it to colonial wholesalers, who then sold it to shopkeepers. By the time the tea reached the shops, its price was so high that most colonists preferred to buy cheaper tea smuggled from Holland.

Under the Tea Act, the East India Company could sell directly to colonial retailers, avoiding all wholesale costs. The act also removed all but the Townshend duty on British tea exported to the colonies. Now the price of East India Company tea was lower than that of smuggled tea.

Howls arose from wholesale merchants, who complained that the Tea Act was ruining their business. Before long, they warned, the East India Company would control all tea sales in the colonies. And what, the merchants asked, would keep the British from controlling other colonial businesses as well? The Tea Act set off a chain reaction that was to end in open rebellion.

Section Review

1. Identification. Define the terms *writs of assistance, Patriots,* and *boycott.*

2. Comprehension. Explain why the British government issued the Proclamation of 1763.

3. Analysis. Describe the following acts and colonists' reactions to them: (a) the Stamp Act (b) the Townshend Acts (c) the Tea Act.

4. Synthesis. Write a slogan that summarizes the colonists' view of the use of British admiralty courts to try smugglers.

Writing About History

Letter. John Adams outraged many colonists by defending the British soldiers who were involved in the Boston Massacre. Have students write letters to Adams condemning or supporting his behavior and giving reasons for their opinions.

Thinking Critically

Evaluation. As a result of the Tea Act, the price of East India Company Tea was lower than that of smuggled tea. **Ask:** Why did the colonists protest this act? (Merchants claimed it was ruining their business. Colonists feared a monopoly of all tea and eventually other businesses.) Were the colonists justified in their assumptions?

Section Review

ANSWERS

1. Definitions for the following terms are on text pages indicated in parentheses: *writs of assistance* (90), *Patriots* (91), *boycott* (91).
2. To keep peace with Indians and keep colonists under British control.
3. (a) Provided that certain written materials be printed on stamped paper on which taxes were to be levied; colonists boycotted British goods (b) Levied duties on imports; colonists boycotted imports or smuggled them in (c) Empowered East India Company to bypass wholesalers and sell directly to retailers; set off chain reaction that led to open rebellion.
4. Slogans should express the importance to colonists of the right to trial by jury of peers.

Section 4-2

Objectives

- ***Answer the Focus Question.***
- *Describe colonists' response to the Intolerable Acts.*
- *List three actions taken by the First Continental Congress.*
- *Explain the significance of the battles of Lexington and Concord.*

Introducing

THE SECTION

The Boston Tea Party had the effect of hardening the British government's position. The harsh Intolerable Acts spread the spirit of resistance. Despite strained relations, the Patriots still professed their desire to remain within the British Empire.

Ask: Why did the Patriots hold on to this position? **(Answers may include trade, protection in clashes with Indians and foreign countries, cultural ties, loyalty to the Crown.)**

Brainstorm with students what the colonists wanted from Britain. How could these goals be achieved? What form of government would be needed to carry out these goals? Was revolution inevitable?

B · A · C · K · G · R · O · U · N · D

Connections: Music

This song was written for the Boston Tea Party, probably to rally the Patriots.

“Rally Mohawks! Bring out your axes
And tell King George we'll pay no taxes
on his foreign tea;
His threats are vain, and vain to think
To force our girls and wives to drink
His vile Bohea [tea];
Then rally, boys, and hasten on
To meet our chiefs at the Dragon [inn].”

4-2 The Path to War

Focus: How did the colonists' resistance to British laws lead to war?

When the first shiploads of East India Company tea arrived in the colonies in late 1773, the Sons of Liberty were ready. In Charleston, South Carolina, Patriots locked up the tea in a warehouse. In New York and Philadelphia they forced ships' captains to turn back without unloading. In Annapolis, Maryland, they burned a ship carrying tea.

In Boston, ships' captains tried to turn back, but the governor insisted the tea be landed. The Sons of Liberty ended the standoff. They boarded the ships and dumped the tea into the harbor, and “next morning tea lay strewn like sea weed along Dorchester beach!” The Boston Tea Party became the symbol of the colonists' determination to resist British tyranny. John Adams wrote:

> *“The die is cast: The people have passed the river and cut away the bridge. . . . This is the grandest event which has ever yet happened since the controversy with the British opened!”*

As a warning to people who might import tea, Patriots tarred and feathered the Boston commissioner of customs and forced tea down his throat.

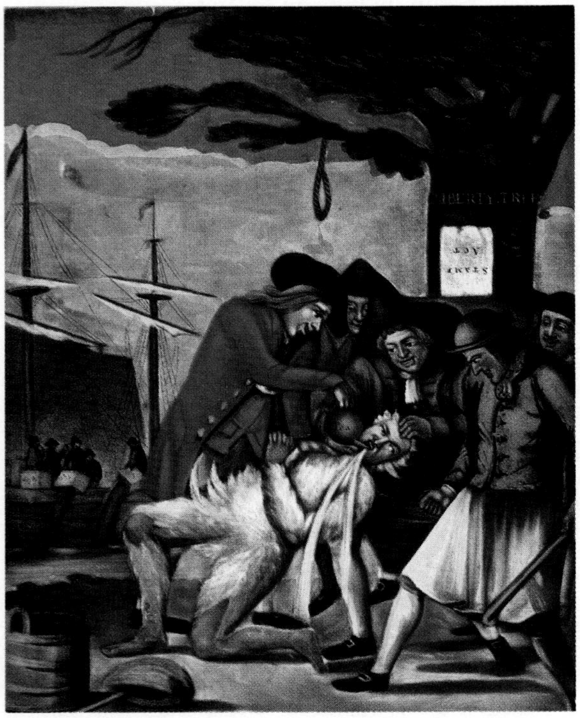

The Intolerable Acts

After the Boston Tea Party, frustrated colonists began to direct their resentment against British officials. In January 1774 a customs officer was attacked in Boston. An eyewitness recounted:

> *“He was stripped stark naked, . . . his body covered all over with tar, then with feathers, his arm dislocated in tearing off his clothes. He was dragged in a cart with thousands attending, some beating him with clubs and knocking him out of the cart, then in again.”*

The Boston Tea Party and the attacks on officials outraged the British government. Parliament decided to punish Massachusetts and give warning to the other colonies at the same time. Thus, in 1774 Parliament passed the Coercive Acts. Furious colonists dubbed the laws the “Intolerable Acts.”

One of the Intolerable Acts, the Boston Port Act, closed the harbor until the tea was paid for, cutting off the city's lifeline of trade. The Administration of

Steps Toward the American Revolution 1763 – 1774

Year	Event
1763	**Proclamation of 1763:** Prohibits settlement west of the Appalachians and trading in the area without a license
1764	**Sugar Act:** Lowers taxes on molasses, with revenue to pay colonial government officials; puts new tax on wine and coffee
	Currency Act: Prohibits colonies from issuing paper money; requires all debts to be paid in gold
1765	**Stamp Act:** Requires all written materials to be printed on stamped paper; revenue from stamped paper to be used for government salaries and defense
	Quartering Act: Requires colonists to house and feed British soldiers if ordered to
1766	**Repeal of Stamp Act:** Repeals Stamp and Sugar acts
	Declaratory Act: Affirms Parliament's right to tax the colonies
1767	**Townshend Acts:** Taxes tea, lead, glass, and paper; establishes customs board in Boston; suspends New York legislature; legalizes writs of assistance
1770	**Repeal of Townshend Acts:** Repeals all Townshend Acts except tax on tea
1773	**Tea Act:** Requires that only the East India Company may import and sell tea
1774	**Intolerable Acts:** Closes Boston port until destroyed tea paid for; suspends town meetings; appoints military governor of colony; permits trials of government officials to be in England; Quebec Act extends territory of Quebec south to Ohio and Mississippi rivers

Justice Act protected Crown officials by permitting them to be tried in England for offenses committed in the colonies. And a new Quartering Act forced people to house troops in their homes if barracks, taverns, or deserted buildings were not available.

A fourth measure, the Massachusetts Government Act, revoked most of the colony's independent rights. The Crown would now control appointments of the governor's council, judges and juries, and many other officials who had previously been elected. Town meetings, the birthplace of Samuel Adams's committees of correspondence, could now meet only with the governor's consent.

Parliament also passed the Quebec Act, extending Canada's boundary south to the Ohio River, an area in which Pennsylvania, Virginia, and Massachusetts all claimed land. Colonists accused Britain of trying to punish them by cutting them off from western expansion.

The Intolerable Acts shocked the colonies. Committees of correspondence spread news of Boston's plight from town to town. From as far as South Carolina, supplies rolled into Boston. The committees adopted resolutions calling the acts "oppressive and tyrannous" and urged the colonies to send delegates to a continental congress to decide what to do.

In Virginia, the governor disbanded the House of Burgesses for protesting the Intolerable Acts. The burgesses gathered at the Raleigh Tavern where they, too, called for a congress of the colonies.

Again Parliament had blundered. Instead of crushing the defiance in Massachusetts, the Intolerable Acts had made the colony a martyr and had spread the spirit of the Boston Tea Party. Throughout the colonies people were following the example of John Adams. He asked a Massachusetts innkeeper for a cup of tea,"provided it has been honestly smuggled." Replied the innkeeper, "We have renounced all tea in this place." Adams approved. "Tea must be universally renounced," he said. "I must be weaned, and the sooner, the better."

Developing
THE SECTION

Writing About History

Newspaper Reports. Have students write two newspaper reports on the Boston Tea Party: one that would appear in a British newspaper and one that would appear in a colonial newspaper. The reports should include reasons for the "tea party," descriptions of the event, responses of the citizens and government officials, and commentary on the results.

Ask several students to read their reports to the class.

Thinking Critically

Evaluation. John Adams, who had denounced the Boston Massacre, wrote in his diary after the Boston Tea Party: *"There is a dignity ... in this last effort of the Patriots that I greatly admire."* Benjamin Franklin termed the Boston Tea Party an act of violent injustice and recommended that the shipowners be reimbursed.

Ask students to speculate about why Adams changed his view toward violence. How might they account for the viewpoint of Franklin? With whom do they agree? Why?

Limited English Proficiency

Building Vocabulary. Lead students to understand the difference in meaning between *coercive* (use of force to do something) and *intolerable* (unbearable). Ask how the term "Coercive Acts" suggests the view of a ruler and "Intolerable Acts" the view of disatisfied subjects.

Connections: Literature

Discussion. Harriet Spofford, poet and novelist (1835–1921), ended a poem about the closing of the Boston port in this way: *"And that great day the Port Bill passed/Made us a nation hard and fast."* Discuss with students what she meant. **(The Intolerable Acts united the colonies in defiance of Britain.)**

Connections: Politics

Georgia did not send delegates to the First Continental Congress because it feared loss of British help putting down a Creek Indian uprising in the colony. Boston was distant, and the Indians close by.

The First Continental Congress

In September 1774 all the colonies except Georgia sent delegates—fifty-six in all—to the First Continental Congress in Philadelphia. The delegates represented a cross section of colonial opinion. They would have to find a way to agree if they were to be successful in speaking with the "united voice of America."

One group at the Congress, the **radicals,** took an extreme position. They called for all colonial trade with Britain to stop until the Intolerable Acts were repealed. Among the radicals were the Adams cousins—John and Sam—from Massachusetts. From Virginia came the fiery speakers Patrick Henry and Richard Henry Lee, members of the House of Burgesses. Also a member of this group was Christopher Gadsden, a well-known South Carolina plantation owner.

Other delegates, including Virginia planter George Washington and Pennsylvania lawyer John Dickinson, were **moderates.** They hoped to achieve gradual change through compromise with Britain. Washington, however, was not optimistic. "Shall we . . . whine and cry for relief," he wrote, "when we have already tried it in vain?"

Taking action. After weeks of heated debate, the delegates drew up a list of resolves, which they passed on October 14. The resolves demanded an end to the Intolerable Acts and denounced Britain's attempts to raise money by taxing the colonies.

The delegates also passed a Declaration of Rights, which drew on ideas that Virginia legislator Thomas Jefferson and Pennsylvania lawyer James Wilson had published in recent pamphlets. Jefferson and Wilson restated the colonists' claim that Parliament had no right to tax or make laws for the colonies. The colonies, they also argued, owed allegiance to the Crown but would not accept acts of Parliament that violated their rights.

On October 18 the Congress formed the Continental Association. Delegates pledged that their colonies would refuse to import goods from Britain. To enforce the agreement, local committees would publish the names of violators, boycott them, and seize any goods they imported.

The First Continental Congress adjourned on October 26 after agreeing to meet again on May 10, 1775, if colonial grievances had not been resolved. Already, people in Massachusetts were preparing for war. Special militia units called **minutemen** were formed to "come in at a moment's warning" to defend the colony. Commenting on the work of the Congress, John Adams later wrote:

> *"The revolution was complete, in the minds of the people, and the union of the colonies, before the war commenced."*

Some members of Parliament were sympathetic to the colonists. William Pitt, a leading statesman, proposed removing the troops from Boston and repealing the Coercive Acts. However, George III took the Congress's actions as open defiance and refused to yield. And Parliament, by a large majority, declared Massachusetts to be in a state of rebellion.

Today North Bridge in Concord looks much as it did on April 19, 1775, when minutemen drove the British back and, in the words of Ralph Waldo Emerson's poem, "Concord Hymn," they "fired the shot heard round the world."

Lexington and Concord

In the course of the winter, Britain began military preparations. General Thomas Gage, the royal governor of Massachusetts, received orders from London to carry out the Coercive Acts by force if necessary. Sure that such efforts would lead to war, Gage delayed. But when he learned that the Patriots had a secret store of weapons in Concord, he decided to act.

In order to take the colonists by surprise, Gage ordered British troops to march by night from Boston to Lexington. The next morning they would continue to Concord to seize the weapons. The soldiers may also have had orders to capture Patriot leaders Samuel Adams and John Hancock, who were in Lexington.

As the British soldiers marched into Lexington on April 19, 1775, early morning mists rose from the village green. There, facing the British, stood Captain John Parker and an uneven line of seventy armed minutemen. Paul Revere and William Dawes had ridden all night from Boston to rouse them. The British surprise had failed.

The British major ordered the minutemen to go home. Captain Parker, seeing his men greatly outnumbered, also commanded them to withdraw. But in the confusion someone fired a shot. Within seconds, bursts of gunfire erupted from both sides of the green. When the minutemen retreated, they left eight dead on the field.

The British marched on to Concord where they exchanged fire with minutemen at North Bridge. This time the British retreated and turned back toward Boston. Their march quickly turned into a race for safety. Militia from a dozen towns had been alerted. Hidden behind trees and stone fences along the British route, the minutemen fired into the orderly ranks of red-coated soldiers. The British could only shoot back blindly at puffs of gun smoke and then flee. Finally, they reached Lexington. Saved by the arrival of fresh troops, the British continued on to Boston. But 273 redcoats had been killed or wounded or were missing. Patriot casualties numbered only 93.

Knowing that the day's fighting was only the beginning, the Massachusetts Provincial Congress called out 13,600 troops and asked other colonies for help. Supporters from Connecticut, Rhode

Connections: Music

Discussion. On July 4, 1837, the Concord Hymn, by Ralph Waldo Emerson, was sung at the completion of a monument to the battle of Concord. Read to students the first stanza of the hymn:

“By the rude bridge
that arched the flood,
Their flag to April's breeze
unfurled,
Here once the embattled
farmers stood,
And fired the shot heard
round the world.”

Ask: In what way was “the shot heard round the world”? **(revolt of colony against parent country, influenced the French Revolution, revolt of South American colonies from Spain, among others)** Could the last two lines also be used to describe the action at Lexington? Explain.

Multicultural Perspectives:

Analyzing Poetry. Lemuel Haynes, an African-American minuteman during the Revolution, became a minister after the war. Inspired by the key events in Lexington on April 19, 1775, he wrote the following poem:

The Battle of Lexington

For liberty each Freeman strives
As it's a Gift of God
And for it, willing yield their Lives
And Seal it with their blood.

Twice happy they who thus resign
Into the peaceful Grave
Much better those in Death Consign
Than a Surviving Slave.

This motto may adorn their Tombs
(Let Tyrants come and view):
"We rather seek these silent Rooms
Than live as slaves to you."

Ask: What are Haynes's grievances? **(That slaves deserve freedom; their lives are so miserable that they would be twice as happy dead as alive.)** According to Haynes, under what circumstances is death preferable to life? **(Death is preferable to slavery.)** How might this poem be interpreted to mean that Americans were slaves to King George III or that African Americans were slaves to both the king and slaveholders?

Multicultural Perspectives

Peter Salem almost missed the Battle of Bunker Hill. It was declared in May 1775 that only free blacks would be accepted as soldiers. Although Salem had fought earlier at Concord, he fell under this ruling. Some slaveowners freed their slaves so they could fight, and Peter Salem was one of them. Salem joined a Massachusetts regiment just in time to fight at Bunker Hill, and later at Saratoga and Stony Point. Peter Salem remained in the Continental Army until the end of the war and then he settled down near Leicester, Massachusetts.

Reduced student page in the Teacher's Edition

Island, and New Hampshire rushed to join the Patriot camps ringing Boston. The British were under siege.

Three weeks later, on May 10, Ethan Allen's Vermont "Green Mountain Boys," and militiamen under Colonel Benedict Arnold, captured a supply of weapons at British-held Fort Ticonderoga, in northeastern New York. News of the successful raid swept through the colonies as rapidly as had tales of Lexington and Concord.

Second Continental Congress

On the day of the raid, delegates gathered in Philadelphia, as planned, for the Second Continental Congress. Banners proclaiming "Liberty or Death" fluttered overhead. There was no question that the colonies were at war with Britain. Now order must be brought to the scattered militias.

From the New England militias that surrounded Boston the delegates created the Continental Army. They voted to raise more companies from Pennsylvania, Virginia, and Maryland to join the troops at Boston.

John Adams proposed George Washington of Virginia as commander in chief. Washington had fought in the French and Indian War and, said Adams, had "an easy, soldierlike air." He was a true Patriot, but as a moderate he was acceptable to all the delegates. Adams also realized that Washington's leadership would assure the support of Virginia and the other southern colonies. The Congress approved Washington's appointment on June 15.

The Battle of Bunker Hill

Before Washington could reach his troops in Boston, more blood was shed. Throughout May, Patriots had been flocking to the defense of Boston. Meanwhile, three British generals—Henry Clinton, William Howe, and John Burgoyne—had brought in reinforcements to assist General Gage.

After dark on June 16, Massachusetts Patriots sent Colonel William Prescott to fortify Breed's Hill, overlooking Boston. Shortly after noon the next day, 2,400 British soldiers under General Howe prepared to drive the 1,600 defenders from the hill.

As British troops successfully stormed American fortifications on Breed's Hill, Peter Salem (far right) probably shot Major John Pitcairn (center right), who had led British troops at Lexington.

Social History
Artist John Trumbull (see illustrations on page 86 and below) was a member of a family that was very active in the Revolution. Trumbull himself served as an officer in the war. His father Jonathan Trumbull—governor of Connecticut—offered his home to the American War Office and sent 300 head of cattle to the starving troops at Valley Forge. The artist's mother, Faith, raised money and gathered clothes for the Patriot cause.

Thinking Critically

Analysis. A British textbook explains the King's obstinate position:

"The British government was [stubbornly] convinced ... that a dominant minority in the colonies was aiming at independence, and that either British authority must be reasserted in the colonies, or else the whole fabric of empire would dissolve and Britain sink back into the role of a minor power."

Ask: What assumptions did the British make? Were they correct? (assumed that only a minority of colonists wanted independence) Can students see a parallel with countries in more recent history?

While townspeople watched from nearby hills and rooftops, Howe sent his force on a frontal attack up Breed's Hill. Weighed down by heavy packs, the British were driven back by intense fire from Prescott's troops. British officers rallied their troops and once more they attacked. To conserve ammunition, the Americans waited until the enemy came close, in some cases to within a hundred feet. Then they opened fire and drove the British forces back with "a continued sheet of fire."

Astounded at the Americans' strength but determined to win, Howe ordered a third assault. His troops, who had dropped their packs and been strengthened by reinforcements, charged up the hill. By now the Americans had run out of ammunition, and the main force retreated. Some fought on, using their muskets as clubs, but the British could no longer be stopped. After capturing Breed's Hill, the British went on to seize a second garrison at Bunker Hill. The day's fighting became known as the Battle of Bunker Hill.

The British victory at the Battle of Bunker Hill was a costly one for them. Whereas American losses were slight, nearly half the redcoats were killed or wounded. The colonists rejoiced. They had stood up to a professional army, giving more punishment than they received. Two weeks later, George Washington arrived to turn the enthusiastic but untrained militias into an army.

The Olive Branch Petition

As bloodshed widened the breach between the colonies and Britain, moderates in the Continental Congress again urged a compromise. In early July the delegates sent the "Olive Branch Petition" to George III. They pledged loyalty to the king and asked him for a peaceful resolution of colonial grievances, which they blamed on Parliament.

In November the delegates received their answer. The king had refused to read their petition. He declared the colonies to be in a state of rebellion. In December the king closed the colonies to all trade and commanded that American ships under sail be seized. Far from frightening Congress into submission, the king's actions unified it. And Congress was now truly representative of all the colonies, for in September, Georgia, too, had sent delegates.

The Revolutionary War 1775-1776

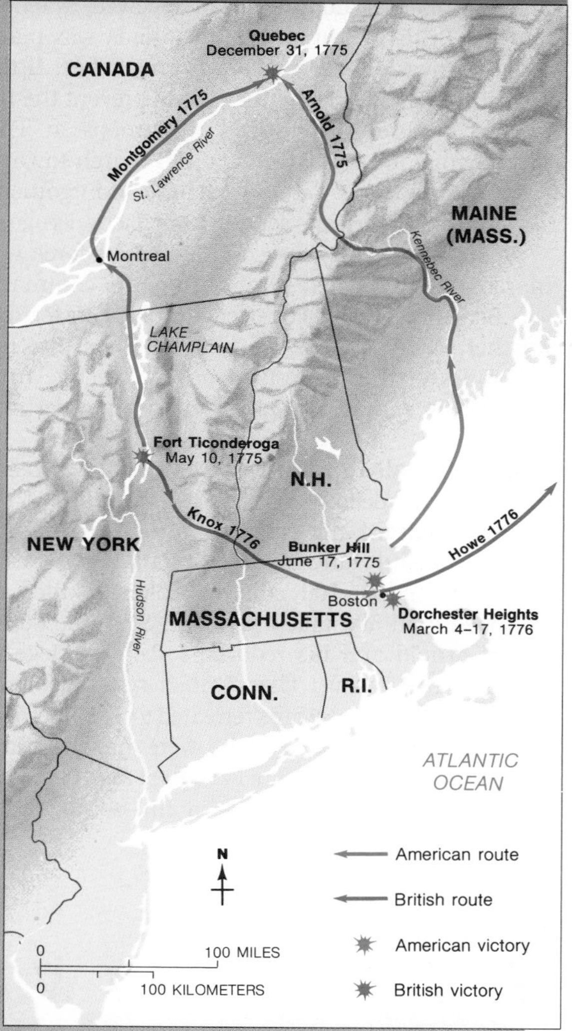

Geography Skills—Movement: By what routes did Americans invade Canada? How did geographic features influence the routes they followed?

While Congress was waiting for the king's reply, it had continued preparations to defend the colonies. It had also seized a chance to act against the British. In the fall of 1775, American troops marched toward Canada.

Geography Skills

ANSWERS

1. Montgomery: Fort Ticonderoga to Quebec. Arnold: From near Boston to Quebec.
2. Montgomery went by way of Lake Champlain and the St. Lawrence River. Arnold went by way of the Kennebec River, then over the mountains.

Section Review

ANSWERS

1. Definitions for the following terms are on text pages indicated in parentheses: *radicals* (96), *moderates* (96), *minutemen* (96).
2. Closed Boston Harbor until tea paid for, permitted Crown officials to be tried in England for offenses committed in colonies, compelled colonists to quarter British troops if other buildings not available, revoked most of Massachusetts' independent rights. Colonists sent supplies to Boston and called for a continental congress.
3. Answers may include: resolutions demanding an end to the Intolerable Acts and denouncing Britain's taxation of the colonies, passage of the Declaration of Rights, formation of the Continental Association.
4. No question now that colonies were at war with Britain.
5. Nearly half the British troops were killed or wounded.

Defeat in Canada, Victory in Massachusetts

The Continental Congress had received a report that the British commander in Canada was planning an invasion of New York from Quebec. If the Americans acted quickly, they could prevent the invasion. Congress authorized the troops at Fort Ticonderoga to invade Canada and march to Quebec. Led by young General Richard Montgomery, about 1,200 Americans set out from Ticonderoga.

At the same time, a second American force was marching on Quebec from Maine. In command was Benedict Arnold. For over a month, in terrible weather, Arnold drove his 1,100 soldiers through 350 miles of thick forest. At one point, the army survived by eating a mash of talcum powder and shoe leather.

Arnold finally joined with Montgomery outside Quebec in the dead of winter. On December 31, in a raging blizzard, the American forces attacked the city. The assault failed, leaving Montgomery dead, Arnold wounded, 100 colonial soldiers killed or wounded, and 300 taken prisoner. Still, the determined Arnold and his reduced force laid siege to the city until spring. Then British reinforcements arrived, and the Americans retreated to Ticonderoga.

Meanwhile, the Americans were having better success in Boston. Early in 1776 they assembled artillery on Dorchester Heights, a hill south of the city. The British, already short of supplies, feared that they would soon be overpowered. On March 26 General Howe, now in command of the British troops in Boston, fled by sea to Halifax, in Canada. New England was now free of the British army.

After the colonies' disastrous defeat at Quebec, the British retreat thrilled the Patriots. In a letter to her husband, John, Abigail Adams wrote of her amazement that the Americans had peacefully regained "a town which we expected would cost us a river of blood." She continued, "Every foot of ground which they obtain now they must fight for, and may [they buy it at] a Bunker Hill price."

Section Review

1. **Identification.** Define *radicals, moderates,* and *minutemen.*

2. **Analysis.** Describe the Intolerable Acts and the colonists' response to them.

3. **Comprehension.** List three actions taken by the First Continental Congress.

4. **Synthesis.** In what way were the battles at Lexington and Concord a turning point in the quarrel between Britain and its American colonies?

5. **Application.** General Howe described his victory at Bunker Hill as "too dearly bought." Explain what he meant.

4-3 *The Break With Britain*

Focus: Why did the colonies declare their independence?

It was now 1776. In the thirteen years since the Proclamation of 1763, blunders by the Crown and Parliament had driven the colonies closer together and widened the rift with Britain. However, although most colonists resented Parliament's oppressive acts, they were divided by issues of loyalty and independence. Even their flag reflected the uncertainty. Thirteen stripes stood for the colonies, but the Union Jack of Britain held its place in the corner. As Washington trained his troops outside Boston, he still raised his cup each evening in a toast to the king.

Global Connections

The influence of the Declaration of Independence has spread throughout the world. Jefferson drew on it to help Lafayette draft France's 1789 Declaration of the Rights of Man and Citizen. Leaders of revolts in the Spanish colonies were motivated by its principles. In the twentieth century, India's nation builders copied the Declaration's ideals. Later it influenced nationalist leaders in Africa and Asia in their drives for independence.

Section 4-3

Objectives

- ***Answer the Focus Question.***
- *Explain how the Declaration of Independence justified colonists' right to establish a new government.*
- *List American and British advantages and disadvantages in the war.*
- *Explain why African Americans fought in the War for Independence despite the existence of slavery.*

Introducing

THE SECTION

Tell students that the name "United States of America" was first used officially in the Declaration of Independence. During the Revolution, "United Colonies" was used rather than "United States." George Washington wrote "U.S." in 1791, and within a few years "U.S.A." came into use.

GTV Side 1

Chap. 17, Frame 44976

The American Revolution (Movie)

Search:

Play:

Paine's *Common Sense*

> *"In the following pages I offer nothing more than simple facts, plain arguments, and common sense. . . . There is something very absurd in supposing a continent to be perpetually governed by an island. . . . England [belongs] to Europe. America to itself."*

Thomas Paine wrote these words in 1776 in a small pamphlet titled *Common Sense.* Paine, a recent immigrant from England, put into words what a growing number of Americans were daring to consider—separation from England. Paine attacked King George, calling him a "royal brute" who menaced American freedom. Within only a few months, 100,000 copies of *Common Sense* had been sold in the colonies. From Massachusetts to Georgia, colonists were influenced by its simple but powerful message.

The mood in the Second Continental Congress and the colonial governments was swinging toward independence. John Adams noted that "Britain has at last driven America to the last step, complete separation from her." Beginning with North Carolina and Virginia, the colonies advised their delegates in the Congress to vote for independence.

On June 7, 1776, Richard Henry Lee of Virginia offered a resolution to Congress:

> *"That these United Colonies are, and of right ought to be, free and independent States . . . absolved from all allegiance to the British Crown, and that all political connection between them and the State of Great Britain is, and ought to be, totally dissolved."*

The Declaration of Independence

After three days of debating Lee's resolution, Congress formed a committee to write a declaration of independence—a document announcing that the colonies were breaking all ties with Britain and establishing an independent nation. Entrusted with the task were Thomas Jefferson, Benjamin Franklin, John Adams, Robert Livingston, and Roger Sherman. Jefferson, who had often written on behalf of the Patriot cause, was chosen to do the actual writing of the document.

Jefferson had studied the ideas of John Locke, a philosopher who argued that there is a contract between the government and the people. If government violates the people's natural rights, they can rebel and set up another government.

Jefferson applied Locke's theory to the declaration. All people, Jefferson wrote, have certain natural or God-given rights such as "life, liberty, and the pursuit of happiness." If a government does not protect these rights, it loses its right to govern.

Jefferson went on to explain why the colonists were taking up arms and demanding independence. He listed, under twenty-eight headings, the abuses by King George. In the last section of the declaration, Jefferson pointed out that the colonists had tried, and failed, to convince Britain to set right these wrongs. Therefore, the representatives of

Spotlight On People

Years later, John Adams recalled how Jefferson was chosen to write the Declaration of Independence:

The committee met, discussed the subject, and then appointed Mr. Jefferson and me to make the draught [draft]. . . . Jefferson proposed to me to make the draught.

I said, "I will not.". . .

"Why?"

"Reason enough."

"What can be your reasons?"

"Reason first—You are a Virginian, and a Virginian ought to appear at the head of this business. Reason second—I am obnoxious, suspected, and unpopular. You are very much otherwise. Reason third—You can write ten times better than I can."

"Well," said Jefferson, "if you are decided, I will do as well as I can."

Developing
THE SECTION

Writing About History

A "Declaration of Independence." Interested students might research and find information about a people in the world today who desire their independence. Students can then imagine they are in this situation and write a "Declaration of Independence" addressing their reasons for wanting to be independent.

Thinking Critically

Analysis. Have students speculate on what the Declaration of Independence meant by "all men." What implications did the phrase have in the minds of the signers? (They had in mind white male landowners only.) What does it mean today? (The meaning of "all men" has been expanded to include African Americans, Native Americans, women and others who were once left out.)

Chapter Connections

Jefferson's conflict regarding African Americans is discussed in further detail in Chapter 5.

Social History

The first publisher of the Declaration of Independence was Mary Katherine Goddard, who was also America's first woman postmaster. Members of Congress asked her to print the Declaration in 1776 so that citizens in every state could read it.

Reduced student page in the Teacher's Edition

the United States of America, acting by the "authority of the good people of these colonies," solemnly declared their complete independence from Great Britain.

Congress debated and made some changes in what Jefferson had written. Of concern to South Carolina and Georgia was the statement that George III had violated the "most sacred rights of life and liberty of a distant people, . . . captivating them into slavery in another hemisphere." Did that imply that the slaves should be freed? To ensure South Carolina and Georgia's support for the declaration, this statement was struck out.

The ownership of slaves belied Jefferson's claim that "all men are created equal." Yet, as the years passed, the meaning of "all men" would be expanded to include African Americans, Native Americans, women, and others who were once left out.

On the evening of July 4, 1776, the delegates voted overwhelmingly to approve the Declaration of

THE AMERICAN SPIRIT

Mercy Otis Warren

Writing for the Revolution

"These Yankee dogs . . . divert themselves by firing at us, as at a flock of partridges. A man can scarcely put his nose over the entrenchments without losing it."

Mercy Otis Warren put these words into the mouth of a British soldier in a satirical play. It was one of many plays that she wrote to rally public opinion to the Patriots by making fun of the British.

Mercy Otis Warren had a keen wit and lively imagination. She and her husband, James Warren, were deeply involved in the Patriot cause. Their home in Plymouth, Massachusetts, was a meeting place for opponents of British policy, including Samuel Adams and John Adams. "By the Plymouth fireside," she

Courtesy, Museum of Fine Arts, Boston

wrote, "were many political plans originated, discussed, and digested."

Performances of plays were prohibited in Massachusetts. Yet it was mainly as a playwright that Mercy Otis Warren made her own contribution to the American Revolution.

Her first play, *The Adulateur*—"The Flatterer"—appeared anonymously in a Boston newspaper in 1772. The villain was a tyrant named Rapatio who hoped to crush "the ardent love of liberty" in an imaginary country's "freeborn sons." Everyone recognized the character as the royal governor of Massachusetts, Thomas Hutchinson.

In the next play, *The Group,* published in 1775, Warren disguised evil Massachusetts Loyalists under such names as Judge Meagre, Brigadier Hateall, and Hum Humbug.

Mercy Otis Warren's plays delighted Patriots, who eagerly passed them from hand to hand, and she continued to provide new works for them. In the late 1770s she also began writing a three-volume *History of the Rise, Progress and Termination of the American Revolution,* vividly describing the people and events she had known firsthand.

Throughout the revolution, the British faced not only the ready gunfire of the American army but also the satirical pen of Mercy Otis Warren. In her hand, they found, it could be as piercing as a Patriot bullet.

Connections: Religion
Almost all Quakers disapproved of the violence of the American Revolution, and many tried to stay out of the war. Shortly before the British captured Philadelphia in 1777, Patriots seized Quakers who were suspected of disloyalty to the American cause and confined them in outlying towns.

Independence. In the weeks that followed, the declaration was read in the streets of every town and village. A newspaper described the reaction in New York City:

> *" It was received everywhere with loud cheers, and demonstrations of joy. And tonight the statue of King George III has been pulled down by the Sons of Liberty. The lead with which the monument was made is to be run into bullets—a just end to an ungrateful Tyrant! "*

Thirteen British colonies had now become thirteen American states.

The full text of the Declaration of Independence will be found on pages 898-899.

Loyalists and Patriots

Although the Declaration of Independence inspired widespread celebration, there were people in every colony who opposed it. Families and friends were often divided in their loyalties. Out of a total population of 2.5 million people, about 1 million were Patriots, while another million refused to take sides. **Loyalists,** those loyal to the Crown, numbered about 500,000.

American Voices

> *" A Tory is a thing whose head is in England, and its body in America, and its neck ought to be stretched. "*
>
> —Popular American Definition

Who were the Loyalists? Not surprisingly, colonists who held office under the Crown often stayed loyal. Benjamin Franklin's son William, the royal governor of New Jersey, was a confirmed Tory—another name for Loyalist. Among the Loyalists, too, were many wealthy merchants, planters, and Anglican ministers who had prospered under British rule. Support for the king also existed in the middle and lower classes.

Loyalists could be found in every state. In Patriot centers like Virginia, Massachusetts, and Connecticut, they made up less than 10 percent of the population. However, half the population of New York was Loyalist, and in the Carolinas and Georgia they were in the majority.

Eventually, about 60,000 Loyalists fought with the British. Before the struggle ended, another 100,000 had fled to Canada or England. State governments considered the Loyalists who fled to be traitors to the infant country, and seized and sold their property.

British Strengths and Weaknesses

The colonists had declared their independence. But the question remained whether they could successfully defy Great Britain. As they weighed the factors that would mean victory or defeat—ships, soldiers, leadership, experience, ability to produce weapons, and the like, Americans must have felt at a distinct disadvantage. Didn't Britain boast the most powerful navy in the world? Wasn't its large army well-disciplined and experienced from the long war with France? In addition, didn't most of the tribes of the strong League of the Iroquois side with the British?

Although these factors seemed to give the British the upper hand, they might not all work to Britain's advantage on American soil. For example, British soldiers were skilled at fighting "on equal terms," since battles in Europe were fought face to face in open fields, much like a gigantic, deadly board game. In America, however, the British were fighting an enemy that did not follow European rules.

Colonial warfare was guerrilla warfare, as the British had discovered at Lexington and Concord. When armies marched in Europe, farmers and townspeople stayed out of the way. In the colonies the farmers and townspeople *were* the army. As columns of British soldiers marched through forests and towns, bands of militia appeared, attacked, and disappeared just as quickly. One British officer summed it up: "The Americans are nowhere and they are everywhere."

Analyzing Primary Sources

Jefferson on Slavery. Tell students that although Jefferson owned slaves, he included in one of the first drafts of the Declaration of Independence the following passage opposing slavery:

> *" [George III] has waged cruel war against human nature itself, violating the most sacred rights of life and liberty of people who never offended him, capturing and carrying them into slavery in another hemisphere, or into a miserable death during their transport here. . . . he has prevented every attempt to prohibit this horrible business.*
>
> *He is now encouraging those very people to take up arms against us, and grant the freedom which he took from them, thus paying off former crimes committed against the liberties of one people, with crimes which he urges them to commit against the lives of another. "*

Ask: What charges did Jefferson make against the King? Do you think this passage should or should not have been included in the final document? Why?

Limited English Proficiency

Cooperative Activity. Have students work in small groups to make charts identifying contributions to the war effort by women and racial or ethnic groups. The text, margin notes, and reference books can be used for information.

Encourage students to research the role of their own racial or ethnic group in the war and share this information with the group.

Linking Past and Present

Foreigners who helped the Patriot cause have been remembered in American place names. Today, thirty-six towns, eighteen counties, one college, and countless streets, avenues, parks, and monuments bear the name of Lafayette. La Grange, the name of his chateau outside Paris, has been adopted by thirteen cities.

Casimir Pulaski and Thaddeus Kosciusko, also distinguished themselves in the Revolutionary War. At least fifteen towns and counties in the United States are named in honor of these two citizens of Poland.

Reduced student page in the Teacher's Edition

Supplying the British army was a nightmare. Everything had to be sent across an ocean— arms, uniforms, tents, cooking equipment, food, wagons, and horses. Food often spoiled on the Atlantic crossing. As the army moved inland, away from ports and supply ships, problems worsened.

Throughout 1775 and 1776 British generals begged for more soldiers. But the recruiting officers were having trouble. Many Britons did not like the idea of fighting a "civil war" against fellow British subjects. In early 1776 Britain was finally able to fill out its army by buying the services of mercenaries— professional soldiers for hire. Eventually, 30,000 mercenaries, mainly from the German state of Hesse-Kassel, boarded ships for the colonies.

Sympathy for the Patriots led several high-ranking British officers to resign. In London, Edmund Burke, a member of Parliament, spoke eloquently on behalf of the Americans. He proposed an end to coercive laws. Burke argued that the colonists were simply acting out the traditions of English politics as the English had always done. He declared, "The temper and character which prevail in our Colonies are, I am afraid, unalterable."

Burke's words, however, had no effect on the king or his ministers. They pushed ahead with their plans to put down the rebellion and to teach the colonists an unforgettable lesson. Most members of Parliament were confident of success. They knew that the Americans had nothing to rely on but a tiny navy, a one-year-old army, and ill-trained local militias.

American Strengths and Weaknesses

"Never has such a rabble been dignified by the name of army," declared George Washington when he took command of the American forces in Boston. Washington faced the huge task of turning a collection of independent militias— made up of farmers, shopkeepers, lawyers, ministers, and every other occupation known in the colonies— into the Continental Army.

The rough-and-ready Continental Army inherited weaknesses from the militias. There was little discipline. Officers were elected by the soldiers, who often simply ignored their orders. Most militia members had greater allegiance to their home states and towns than to the Continental Army. Some of Washington's best officers were volunteers from Europe, such as the Marquis de Lafayette, a nobleman from France, who was made a major general when he was twenty.

Washington also had trouble keeping citizens in the army long enough to make them into good soldiers. Men signed up only when they were needed, and went home when the battle was over. Washington had, on average, no more than 10,000 soldiers in his army. Often local militias had to back up the army troops.

But these weaknesses also gave the Continental Army its strength. The soldiers were fighting on their own soil, for their homes, and for their freedom. The British were fighting far from home, with no cause in their hearts. They faced not only enemy soldiers but outraged civilians who firmly supported their army.

Learning From Art
British and American Styles of Warfare, 1775

It took a British soldier three hours a day to wash his white breeches, powder his hair, and clean his metal trim and belts.

Massachusetts militiamen wore all kinds of civilian clothes— there were no uniforms. They carried muskets of every sort.

Multicultural Perspectives

Both the British and the Americans sought Native-American help in the war. The large majority of Indians sided with the British, who supplied vital trade goods and tried to stop colonial encroachment.

The powerful League of the Iroquois was also drawn into the war. Its unity was shattered when the Mohawks, Cayugas, Senecas, and Onondogas supported the British, while the Oneidas and Tuscaroras sided with the Americans.

Analyzing Primary Sourves

Guerrilla War Tactics. Read to students the following statement by a British soldier regarding American guerrilla tactics:

> *"Never had the British army so ungenerous an enemy to oppose; they send their riflemen five or six at a time who conceal themselves behind trees, etc., till an opportunity presents itself of taking a shot at our advancing sentries, which done they immediately retreat. What an unfair method of carrying on a war!"*

Ask: How does this soldier's statement reflect differences in warfare in Europe and America?

American women played a vital role in the Patriot cause. Many women, including Abigail Adams, took over family farms and businesses while the men were at war. Others cared for the wounded, raised money for supplies, sewed uniforms, and melted lead into bullets. The Daughters of Liberty continued the boycott of British goods.

Martha Washington was one of many women who followed their soldier husbands to camp, where they cooked, sewed, and helped out with the camp work. A few became spies or took up arms. Sally St. Clair and Deborah Sampson dressed in men's clothing and marched off to battle. Margaret Corbin replaced her fallen husband at his artillery post. Sixteen-year-old Sybil Ludington rode 40 miles through the night to summon troops to fight the British in Connecticut.

War at sea. At first glance, the Americans' chances at sea appeared bleaker. The Continental Navy barely existed: just thirteen warships in all, each operating alone. But these few ships were commanded by daring, able captains. The most successful was John Paul Jones.

However, the greatest success was achieved by **privateers**—privately owned ships authorized by the government to attack and capture enemy ships. Lured by rich prizes, hundreds of sea captains made privateering a wartime career. They raided British ships on both sides of the Atlantic, capturing millions of dollars' worth of supplies.

Despite some important advantages on land and sea, the Americans were seriously hampered by a lack of funds. The Continental Congress had to beg the states for supplies, troops, and money, but it had no power to force them to contribute or to levy taxes to pay for the war. Meanwhile, the states had their own economic problems, and each seemed to think the other states should do more. At best, states supplied their own soldiers. But the army was always poorly paid and undersupplied.

Haym Salomon, a Jewish immigrant from Poland, took on the lonely task of raising money for Congress. Salomon, a banker, raised thousands of dollars and negotiated loans from France. However, as the bills mounted, Salomon gave his own fortune to Congress. He died penniless.

Another problem was **profiteering** by merchants who made fortunes by charging high prices for food and other supplies. Spoiled meat and shoes that fell apart were constant nuisances the army had to endure. "No punishment," wrote Washington, "is too great for the person who can build greatness upon the country's ruin."

Seventeen separate commands were given to British soldiers to load and fire their muskets. Standing in close ranks, they fired by platoons.

The chief weapon of both sides was the musket with its attached bayonet. Some Americans used the "Pennsylvania" rifle, the most accurate weapon at long ranges, but it could not be equipped with a bayonet and took far too long to reload.

Unused to taking orders, militiamen often left their guardposts before being relieved and crept out beyond the line of sentries to take shots at the British.

Section Review

ANSWERS

1. Definitions for the following terms are on text pages indicated in parentheses: *Loyalists* (103), *privateers* (105), *profiteering* (105).

2. If a government does not protect the unalienable rights of all people.

3. American advantages: fighting guerilla warfare on home ground, fighting for a cause they believed in, receiving civilian support; disadvantages: undisciplined army fighting a far more powerful and experienced force, lack of funds to supply troops. British advantages: powerful navy and experienced army, support from League of the Iroquois; disadvantages: opposition in Britain to the war, difficulty in maintaining supply line, coping with guerilla warfare.

4. Answers may include that the Continental Army did not accept slaves until British forces enlisted them. British recruitment as well as shortage of troops in the Continental Army led to recruitment of both slave and free African Americans.

Multicultural Perspectives

James Armistead, a twenty-one-year-old slave, was assigned to spy on Benedict Arnold's camp. Armistead offered his services as a servant and guide and in return was promised his freedom after the war. When Cornwallis suddenly disappeared with his troops, Armistead forwarded the location—Yorktown—to Lafayette.

Multicultural Perspectives

The eight African Americans who signed the Massachusetts petition were Prince Hall, organizer of the African Lodge of Freemasons; Lancaster Hill; Peter Best; Bristol Slenzer; Jack Pierpont; Nero Funelo; Newport Sumner; and Job Lock. Petitions were also presented to legislatures in Connecticut and New Hampshire in 1779.

Reduced student page in the Teacher's Edition

The Revolution—for Whom?

In 1777 eight African Americans, most of them free men, presented a petition to the Massachusetts legislature. Calling for an end to slavery, it stated:

> *“Your petitioners . . . have in common with all other men a natural . . . right to that freedom which the Great Parent of the universe has bestowed equally on all mankind.”*

African Americans took the words of the Declaration of Independence seriously. It seemed to them hypocrisy that slavery should exist while the states fought a war for liberty. African Americans took part in every major battle of the war because they viewed the declaration as a crucial opportunity to attain freedom and equality.

Early in the war, black Patriots took part in the fighting at Concord, Fort Ticonderoga, and Bunker Hill. But late in 1775 Congress and General Washington decided not to enlist them in the Continental Army. There was a fear that slaves who tasted freedom might rebel against the system of slavery.

Master spy James Armistead received this letter of praise from Lafayette.

Desperate for soldiers, the British did not hesitate. The royal governor of Virginia promised freedom to slaves who fought for the king. At the end of the war, more than 15,000 freed slaves left the country with the British, including three who had belonged to George Washington.

In January 1776 Washington, noting the British recruitment and facing a shortage of troops, finally decided to enlist free African Americans. Two years later, he began to accept slaves in the army as well, promising them freedom after the war.

About 5,000 African Americans served in the Continental Army, fighting in regiments from every state but Georgia and South Carolina. Less reluctant than other soldiers to sign up for long enlistments, African Americans generally served for three years or more. Many served throughout the entire war. Another 2,000 African Americans joined the navy, which had accepted them from the beginning. Watching a black regiment in action, a white soldier affirmed their role in the Patriot cause:

> *“Had they been unfaithful, or given way before the enemy all would have been lost. Three times in succession they were attacked, . . . and three times did they successfully repel the assault and thus preserve our army from capture. They fought through the war. They were brave, hardy troops. They helped gain our liberty and independence.”*

Section Review

1. Identification. Define *Loyalists, privateers,* and *profiteering.*

2. Analysis. According to the Declaration of Independence, under what circumstances do people have a right to set up a new government?

3. Comprehension. List the American and British advantages and disadvantages in the war.

4. Evaluation. Do you think that military need determined whether African Americans were allowed to fight in the war? Why or why not?

Citizenship

Since 1984 Maurice Barboza has been trying to establish a memorial to African-American Patriots. To gather support, Barboza started a volunteer organization—The Black Revolutionary War Patriots Foundation. The memorial is to be located between the Washington Monument and the Lincoln Memorial in Washington, D.C.

Barboza's next challenge is to raise the $4 million needed to build the memorial. *"These black patriots fought a dual battle for independence,"* Barboza says. *"They fought for independence from the British . . . but they were also fighting for their own independence from slavery."*

4-4 Fighting for Independence

Focus: Why did the United States of America win the war against Britain?

On June 29, 1776, an American soldier looked out a second-story window on New York City's Staten Island. To his amazement, he saw that "the whole bay was full of shipping. I declare I thought all London was afloat."

General William Howe and his British troops had returned from Halifax. Three days later, as Congress was debating the Declaration of Independence, the British landed unopposed on Staten Island. Shortly after, Howe's brother, Admiral Richard Howe, sailed in with a huge British fleet.

The British Capture New York

The British planned to make their headquarters in New York City. New York had the finest port and a strong Loyalist population, and was strategically located midway between New England and the southern states.

Washington had expected the British to move into New York. In April he had moved the Continental Army there from Boston and had fortified Manhattan Island and Long Island. Still, the army was badly outnumbered. The British force included 32,000 experienced troops. The Americans faced them with barely 20,000 soldiers, mostly ill-trained militia. This was one of the largest forces Washington would be able to piece together during the war.

On August 27 Howe attacked the Long Island fortification, keeping it under siege for two days. The Americans lost 1,500 in casualties. Under cover of darkness and fog, Washington moved his remaining troops to safety on Manhattan, but Howe began to close in. Washington, realizing he would be trapped, abandoned Manhattan on September 13 and retreated into New Jersey. Aware of the weakness of his forces, Washington told Congress:

> *"We should on all occasions avoid a general action or put anything to the risk, unless compelled by a necessity, into which we ought never to be drawn."*

Boosting Morale: Trenton and Princeton

By December 1776 Washington's troops, badly battered by rear guard skirmishes with the British army, had crossed the Delaware River into Pennsylvania. The British withdrew to New York for the winter, leaving several garrisons in New Jersey.

At this point in the war, American despair matched the dark of winter. The months of retreat had worn down the army. Congress had fled Philadelphia without providing fresh troops to replace the soldiers whose

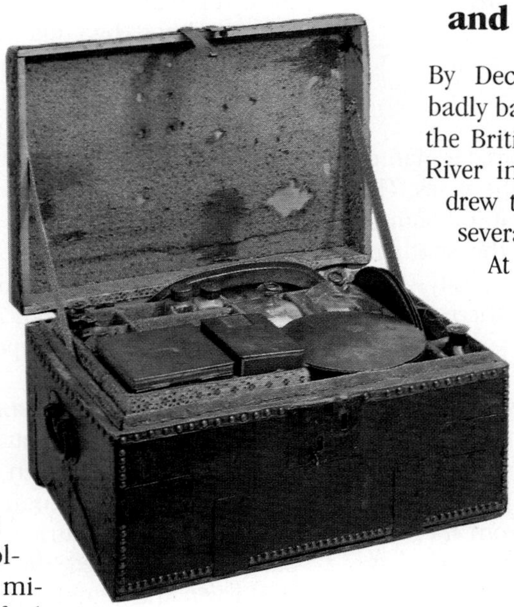

The mess chest that Washington used during the war held tin plates, pots, bottles, and knives and forks.

Section 4-4

Objectives

- ***Answer the Focus Question.***
- *Explain why the Battle of Saratoga was a turning point in the war.*
- *Analyze why British strategy in the southern states failed.*
- *List the terms agreed to in the Treaty of Paris of 1783.*

Introducing

THE SECTION

Today everyone knows that the colonists were victorious in the Revolutionary War. But did victory seem certain in 1776?

Refer students to the quotation from Thomas Paine's *The Crisis* on text page 108. Ask them to recall from previous sections why, by December 1776, "these are the times that try men's souls"? **(defeats in Canada and New York; Patriot troops ill-fed, poorly clothed, undersupplied; Congress short of money)**

Ask students to speculate on why the Americans were victorious despite such bad conditions. Have them review their answers after reading this section.

Global Connections

The Revolutionary War was in reality a world war. After France declared war on Britain, Spain soon followed. The Dutch, too, were drawn into the hostilities after recognizing American independence. Neutral countries in Europe, including Russia, Prussia, Sweden, Denmark, Portugal, and Turkey formed the League of Armed Neutrality to protect their commerce from British blockades. Members of the league did not declare war, but they assumed an unfriendly attitude toward Britain.

Developing THE SECTION

Active Learning

Predicting. Have students form groups to review the battles in the War for Independence from 1776 to 1778. On the basis of these battles and their results, each group should predict which side—the Patriots or the British—will eventually win the war.

Caution students that all battles were not equally important and they must decide which ones had the most impact. (For example, the Battle of Saratoga was significant because it led to an open alliance with France and Spain.)

Have each group choose a representative to present its reasoning and conclusions to the class.

Thinking Critically

Synthesis. Refer students to the map on this page. Have them find on the map the route Howe would have taken had he not gone to Philadelphia. How might the British campaign to control the Hudson have fared if Howe had acted according to plan?

enlistments were running out and the many others who deserted. Thomas Paine captured the mood when he wrote in *The Crisis*:

> *“These are the times that try men's souls. The summer soldier and the sunshine patriot will, in this crisis, shrink from the service of their country; but he that stands it* now *deserves the love and thanks of man and woman.”*

Washington knew he had to take action before his entire army melted away. In a daring move he led his soldiers on Christmas night back across the ice-clogged Delaware River and into New Jersey. At Trenton, the Continental Army surprised and captured an entire garrison of Hessian mercenaries while losing only four men.

A week later Washington pushed deeper into New Jersey. In a fierce battle he forced the British to withdraw from Princeton. The battles at Trenton and Princeton drove the British from much of New Jersey. Equally important, they boosted American morale. Washington's successes, however, had exhausted the ragged Continental Army. He had to pull his troops back to the hills around Morristown, New Jersey, and settle down for the winter.

Saratoga—the Turning Point in the War

In 1777 the British government approved a plan to isolate New England from the rest of the states. The Hudson River provided an excellent natural boundary. The British already controlled the southern part of the Hudson River at New York City. Now they decided to gain control of the northern part by capturing the city of Albany.

To carry out their plan, the British devised a three-pronged attack. The main army, under General "Gentleman Johnny" Burgoyne, would march south from Canada, across Lake Champlain, and down the Hudson. Lieutenant Colonel Barry St. Leger would lead a flanking army from the west, along the Mohawk River. From New York City, General Howe's forces would move north up the Hudson. All three armies were to meet at Albany.

Burgoyne and St. Leger set off, but Howe decided to capture Philadelphia, the Patriot capital. Sailing up Chesapeake Bay into Pennsylvania, Howe routed Washington's forces at Brandywine Creek. He occupied Philadelphia on September 26, welcomed by that city's many Loyalists. Congress, having returned to Philadelphia in March, once again fled.

Washington tried to secure the area around the city, but finally had to withdraw. He and his troops made their winter camp at Valley Forge, 25 miles to the west.

Despite his victory, Howe had set his own trap. Ignoring the plan to divide the states, Howe stayed in Philadelphia, enjoying the company of wealthy Loyalist families. Indeed, when Benjamin Franklin heard that Howe had captured the city, he said, "No, Philadelphia has captured Howe."

Meanwhile, the two British armies to the north were running into trouble. St. Leger's force, made up mainly of Loyalists and Iroquois, stopped to besiege Fort Stanwix. The Americans sent a relief force to Stanwix under Benedict Arnold. St. Leger, who had gone only a third of the way to Albany, was forced to turn back.

Burgoyne, traveling south from Canada, had an early victory at Fort Ticonderoga. As he struggled farther south through New York's dense forests, though, his forces were continuously attacked by local militias. By October 1777 Burgoyne was desperate. Almost half his troops had been killed or wounded, and he now realized that Howe would not be coming to his aid.

Battered by American attacks on his right and left flanks, Burgoyne was then attacked head-on by Benedict Arnold. The besieged British forces halted at the town of Saratoga. For five days American troops under General Horatio Gates leveled a constant fire at them. On October 17 Burgoyne surrendered his entire army of almost 6,000 soldiers. It proved to be the turning point in the war.

Alliance with France. American spirits soared with the victory at Saratoga. Across the Atlantic in Paris, American agents led by Benjamin Franklin had been urging Britain's old enemy, France, to aid the Patriots. The smashing victory at Saratoga convinced the French that Americans could win the war. In February 1778 the French signed a treaty of alliance, recognizing American independence and declaring war on Great Britain. The two nations also agreed to give each other special trade privileges.

France's help came in the nick of time. Now Britain had another enemy to fight, and French supplies would enable Washington to continue the war. The French navy and well-equipped French troops would also be of great assistance.

Vital help also came from Spain, which joined the war against Britain in June 1779. The governor of Louisiana, Bernardo de Gálvez, opened the port of New Orleans to Americans, seized British ships, and sent supplies to American troops. With an army of Spaniards, free African Americans, and Indians, Gálvez captured British forts along the Mississippi and the Gulf of Mexico. His capture of a British army at Pensacola, Florida, in 1781 prevented British forces from combining against Washington.

Valley Forge and Monmouth

Meanwhile, during the brutal winter at Valley Forge, more than 3,000 of Washington's soldiers had died from cold, starvation, and smallpox. Joseph Martin, a seventeen-year-old private, noted in his diary that by December 1777, "the army was not only starved but naked."

Washington feared that the army would "starve, dissolve, or disperse." It is a tribute to his greatness as a leader that his soldiers maintained their faith in him. Their training had also been improved by a former Prussian general, Baron von Steuben, who drilled them through the winter. By June they were ready to follow Washington into battle.

The British army had remained in Philadelphia for the winter. In May, Howe was replaced by General Henry Clinton. Hearing that the French fleet was heading for North America, Clinton decided to move the British troops back to New York City. Washington's army set off in pursuit.

American advance forces met the British at Monmouth Court House in New Jersey on June 28. Faced by British reinforcements, the Americans had begun to withdraw just as Washington and the main army arrived. In a rage as blistering as the day's heat, Washington turned the American retreat into a relentless attack and victory. That night, the British slipped away to New York. Washington followed and encamped on the hills above the city to await French reinforcements.

Little was accomplished for the rest of 1778. As winter approached, Washington again settled his army in Morristown, New Jersey. Here the unpaid, ill-fed troops suffered through a winter as harsh as at Valley Forge. With profiteering driving costs of supplies skyward, and Congress unwilling or unable to act, morale was again at rock bottom.

The Revolutionary War 1776-1778

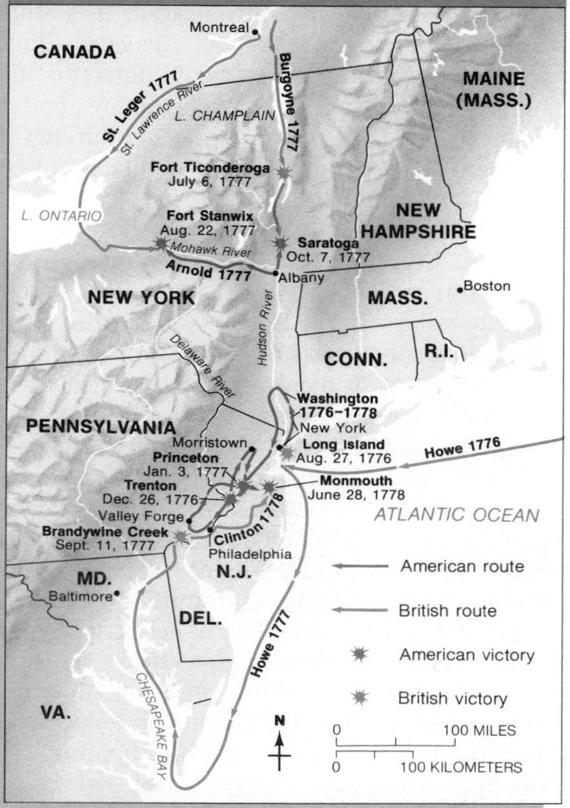

Geography Skills—Movement: Where were British forces from Canada blocked? What might have happened if the British had not been stopped at Trenton?

Continental Army musket

Writing About History

War Report. Have students write one of the following:

- Imagine that you are a member of the congressional Board of War. Then write a report for Congress analyzing the American position at the end of 1777. The report should include: the status of the war; the state of the army and the navy; enlistment, money, and supply problems.
- Imagine that you are the British Secretary of War. Then write a report for Parliament analyzing the British military position at the end of 1777. The report should include: the status of the war; the state of the army, supplies, and support of the Loyalists.

Geography Skills

ANSWERS

1. Fort Stanwix, Saratoga.
2. American loss of Pennsylvania and upper New Jersey.

Social History

Discussion. George Washington commented to Congress at the start of the war, "*I do not think myself equal to the command I am honored with.*" Ask students what they think of this comment, in light of later events. What leadership abilities did Washington display?

Multicultural Perspectives

Elizabeth Freeman, an enslaved African American, took the words of the Declaration of Independence seriously. In 1781 she left her master's house in western Massachusetts to sue for legal freedom. When asked by her lawyer what gave her the idea, Freeman replied that she had overheard a town panel preparing a resolution that all people are born free and equal. She felt that this applied to her, too. The jury ruled in her favor.

Thinking Critically

Application. With students, begin a list on the chalkboard of military tactics described in this section. Such a list might include: *fortify, retreat, besiege, flank, divide and conquer, guerrilla warfare, head-on attack, blockade.*

Discuss military tactics by asking: What tactics were used at Long Island and Manhattan Island? (Americans fortified and retreated; British besieged.) At Saratoga? (British plan was to divide and conquer. Americans used guerrilla tactics to attack Burgoyne on right and left flanks; Benedict Arnold attacked head-on.) At Monmouth? (British retreat) At Kings Mountain? (guerrilla tactics) At Yorktown? (blockade)

Writing About History

Journal. Have students imagine they are colonists and write journal entries describing an event studied so far in this chapter. Suggest that students include opinions and interpretations of events whenever appropriate.

Suggested topics: joining Sons or Daughters of Liberty, witnessing the Boston Massacre, participating in the Boston Tea Party, working for Committee of Correspondence, participating in a particular battle.

Reduced student page in the Teacher's Edition

War in the Southern States

The British failed to take advantage of the weakness of Washington's army. Instead, they shifted their attention south where, General Clinton claimed, Loyalist support would turn the tide. Clinton planned an offensive to capture southern seaports, bring in troops, and sweep through the southern states where the large population of Loyalists would join them.

In December 1778 the British navy landed in Savannah, Georgia. Local militia, caught between the navy and a rear guard of British infantry, quickly collapsed. The British then stormed farther into Georgia and reestablished a royal government. Throughout 1779 the Americans repeatedly tried, but failed, to retake Savannah.

Early in 1780 the British struck the major southern port, Charleston. Clinton sailed south from New York to lead a massive army of 14,000 against the city, swamping the 5,000 American defenders. His victory won, Clinton returned to New York, leaving General Charles Cornwallis in command. Charleston was the worst Patriot defeat of the war.

In October Congress appointed Nathanael Greene as head of the southern army. An outspoken general who had risen from the ranks, Greene adopted a hit-and-run, guerrilla fighting style. Guerrilla tactics had already stopped Cornwallis at the border between South and North Carolina. Assailed by Patriot bands led by such wily commanders as Francis "Swamp Fox" Marion, Cornwallis sent a Loyalist force out to cover his flank. At Kings Mountain, South Carolina, a Patriot militia caught the Loyalists and crushed them.

Britain's southern strategy was faltering. Clinton had not counted on the fierce bands of Patriots and their guerrilla tactics. There were far more Patriots taking up arms than Loyalists. By the end of 1780, Clinton's southern offensive had collapsed.

The Americans continued to strike at Cornwallis. In January 1781 at Cowpens, South Carolina, they routed his forces. By March, when the armies clashed at Guilford Court House, Cornwallis had had enough. Although he won the battle, he had lost more than a quarter of his army. He pulled his troops back to Wilmington, North Carolina.

In Virginia a British force was having more luck. Benedict Arnold, a Patriot hero, had turned traitor. Now, as a general in the British army, he was leading raids against the Americans throughout the state. In May, Cornwallis marched into Virginia to join Arnold. The British raids continued into summer, but American strength was growing.

By August 1781 the American troops, led by the Marquis de Lafayette and Baron von Steuben, had followed Cornwallis to the city of Yorktown on Virginia's coast. Cornwallis felt secure in Yorktown because he now had a sea link to General Clinton in New York. What he had not bargained for was the arrival of the French fleet.

Victory at Yorktown

In New York, Washington at last received the French reinforcements he needed for an attack on Clinton. But new information changed Washington's mind. He had learned that the French fleet under Admiral de Grasse was headed for Chesapeake Bay. At the mouth of Chesapeake Bay lay Yorktown—and Cornwallis. Washington seized the opportunity.

On August 20 Washington and his French allies—5,000 soldiers under the Comte de Rochambeau (RŌ-shahm-BŌ)—set out on an overland march south. Ten days later, right on schedule, de Grasse and the French fleet arrived to blockade Yorktown. The British navy sped south to rescue Cornwallis but was soundly beaten by de Grasse.

The French then sailed north up Chesapeake Bay to Baltimore. They picked up Washington and Rochambeau and their troops and sailed south to Williamsburg, just outside Yorktown. There the allied armies were joined by Lafayette. On September 28 the force of 17,000 marched on Yorktown.

Cornwallis and his army of 9,000 British and Hessians were trapped. The Americans and French besieged Yorktown for three weeks. A jubilant American wrote of Cornwallis, "We have got him handsomely in a pudding bag."

On October 19, 1781, Cornwallis surrendered. The British soldiers stacked their weapons on the ground, then marched back to their camp. They were flanked on the right by the Americans, and on the left by the French. The British band, it is said, played a popular song, "The World Turned Upside Down." The Americans sang "Yankee Doodle."

The Revolutionary War 1778-1781

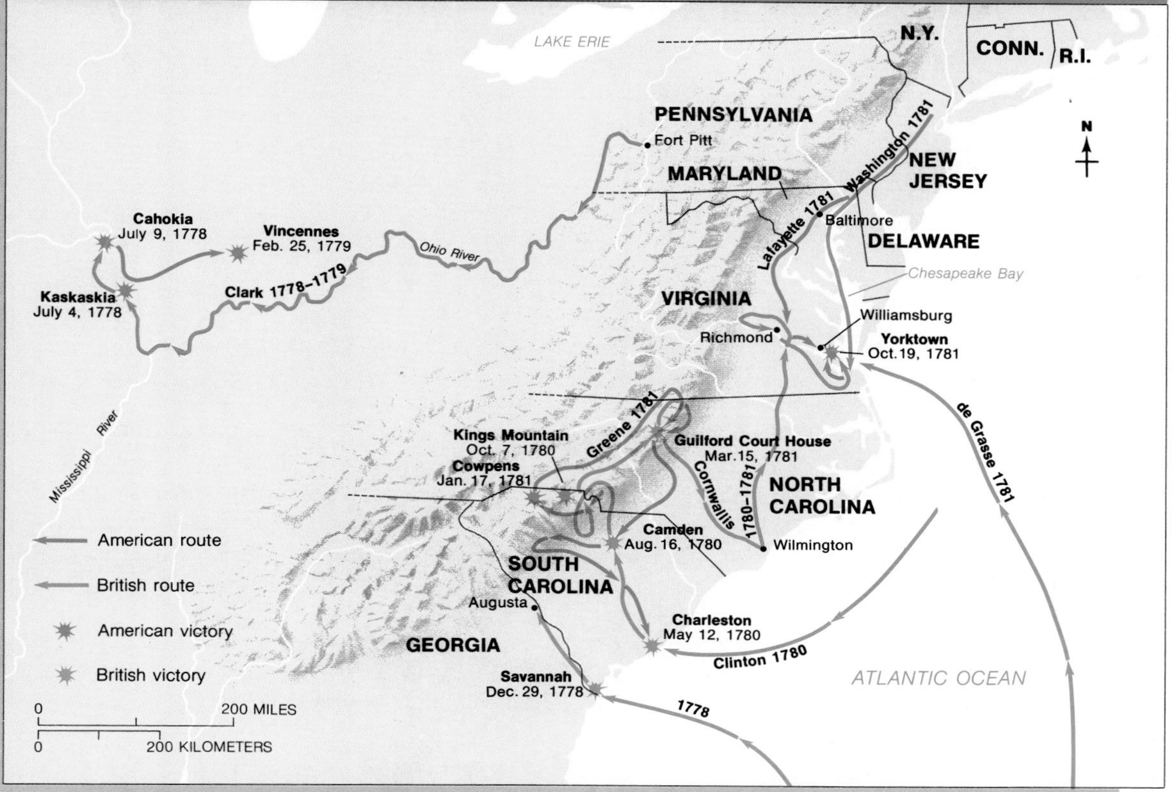

Geography Skills—Movement: Trace Cornwallis's route—and his successes and failures—from Charleston to Yorktown. What three forces came together against Cornwallis at Yorktown? George Rogers Clark led a small band to victories that helped settle the western and northern boundaries of the United States after the war. In what geographic area did Clark fight?

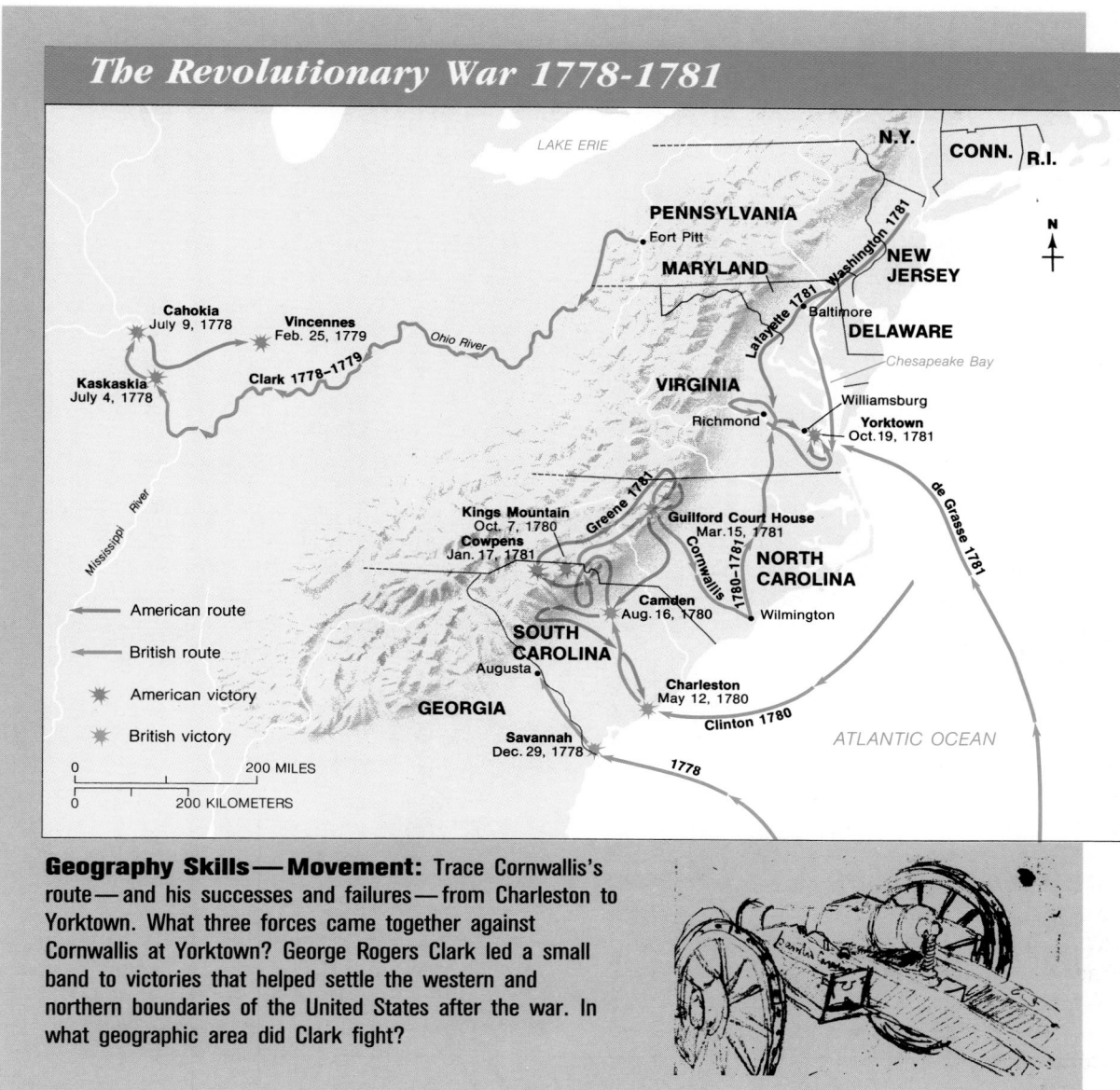

Peace

Washington hurried back to New York to keep an eye on Clinton's troops. With Cornwallis's surrender, however, the war in North America was over.

In March 1782 Lord North, the British prime minister, resigned. The new government quickly sent a peace commissioner to Paris to begin talks with the Americans. The Congress had instructed the American negotiators—Benjamin Franklin, John Adams, John Jay, and Henry Laurens—to consult fully with the French commissioners during peace negotiations.

However, the Americans worried that the French might block American claims to the western lands, despite the treaty of alliance. They began separate talks with the British and worked out a preliminary peace treaty in November.

Geography Skills

ANSWERS

1. Cornwallis succeeded in taking Charleston, won at Camden, lost patrols at Cowpens and Kings Mountain, won but with heavy losses at Guilford Court House, withdrew to Wilmington, marched to Richmond, then to Yorktown, where his troops were defeated.
2. Lafayette, Washington, and de Grasse came together against Cornwallis at Yorktown.
3. The Northwest.

Thinking Critically

Evaluation. The morality of writing a preliminary peace treaty without France was a point of controversy. What instructions did the American delegates have? (consult fully with the French)

Ask students to speculate on why France would not want the United States to get the western lands. (United States might be too powerful.) In light of the French view, do they think the delegates were justified in their actions? Why or why not?

Thinking Critically

Analysis. The peace treaty was looked upon in Britain as "dishonorable surrender" while the majority of Americans were pleased with it.

Ask: Why might the British feel this way? (British gave more than was necessary.) Why did the British make concessions? (to counter-balance United States against France and Spain) Why would Americans be happy? (received generous land grant and fishing rights, vague terms for repaying Loyalists) To what issue might Americans object? (points relating to the Loyalists)

Geography Skills

ANSWERS

1. From the Atlantic coast to the Mississippi; Great Lakes to Florida.
2. Britain, Spain, France.
3. Appalachians.
4. New Orleans.
5. Spain.
6. Most likely Great Britain and Spain.

Backyard History

A Walk Through History. If possible, have students walk through a cemetery and record the name, and birth and death dates of persons who lived during the Revolutionary War (1775–1783).

They should note if a tombstone makes any reference to the position a person held in the army or navy or service in any other capacity. Students can share their findings with the class.

Social History

At the formal ceremony of surrender, Cornwallis could not bring himself to hand over his sword in person. It was ceded by General Charles O'Hara, his second-in-command, to General Benjamin Lincoln, a general subordinate to Washington.

North America After Treaty of Paris 1783

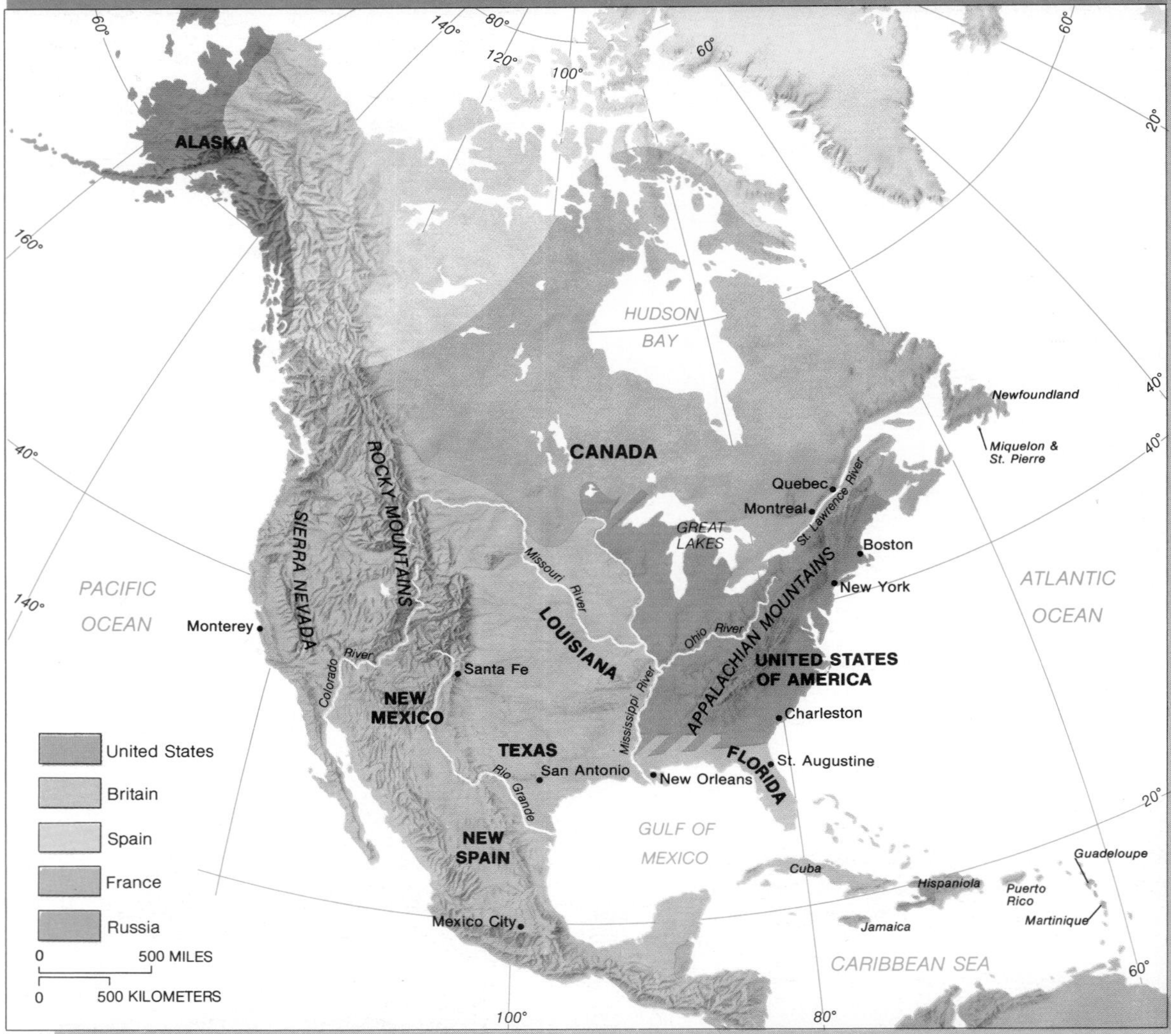

Geography Skills—Location: Describe the boundaries of the United States established by the peace treaty ending the Revolutionary War. What European nations had interests in North America in 1783? Name the geographical barrier that separated the eastern and western parts of the United States. If you lived and farmed to the west of this barrier, in what port city would you probably sell your crops? To which nation did that port belong? From your answers to these questions, predict the European nations that the United States would be dealing with after 1783.

Most importantly, the British recognized American independence. American boundaries would stretch from the Atlantic to the Mississippi, and from the Great Lakes south to Florida. The Mississippi River would remain open to both American and British shipping, and Americans could still fish off the coast of Canada. Britain also agreed to withdraw its forces from American territory.

In turn, the Americans pledged that the Congress would "recommend" that the states allow Loyalists to sue for recovery of their lost property. Without direct authority over the states, there was little else the Congress could do. Both sides agreed that citizens of either country could try to collect debts owed by citizens of the other country. This meant chiefly that British exporters could try to collect old debts from American merchants.

The Treaty of Paris was sent to the Congress, which ratified it on April 15, 1783. The "shot heard round the world" had touched off a war that lasted for six years. The peace negotiations took another two years. As Benjamin Franklin, America's representative at the Paris signing, observed: "There never was a good war or a bad peace." But there had never before been a war like this one, in which a group of citizens threw off their colonial overlords and established a self-governing nation.

Section Review

1. Comprehension. What were the results of the battles at Trenton and Princeton?

2. Evaluation. Do you agree or disagree that without the victory at Saratoga the Americans would have lost the war? Explain.

3. Analysis. Why did British strategy in the southern states fail?

4. Comprehension. What terms did Britain agree to in the Treaty of Paris of 1783? What terms did the Americans agree to?

Linking Past and Present. Study a map of your area to find out if there are any places named after revolutionary war battles or heroes. If revolutionary war battles took place in your state, gather information about them. How did they affect the outcome of the war?

Connections to Themes

Shaping Democracy

Even before independence was declared, years of conflict with England had made colonists distrustful of a strong central government. This distrust was to have a powerful influence on the shaping of American democracy.

The conflict over taxation involved far more than a question of who would pay the huge costs of England's empire in America. At the core lay the issue of where power lay. To King George and most members of Parliament, the issue was easily resolved: all power came from the center, that is, from Parliament and the king. The colonists, however, saw the matter differently. They insisted on their right to govern their own affairs.

Most English leaders scoffed at the colonists' demands. Twice before in the 1700s, the people of Scotland had resisted England's authority. Both times the matter had been settled by military force. To the king and Parliament, the problem in the colonies seemed similar. King George insisted that the colonies would never be freed "from their dependency upon the supremacy of England."

In fact, the Americans did win their independence—the first colonial people to win the right to govern themselves. However, the question of where power was to lie was not settled by the victory at Yorktown. It was transformed into the issue of how power should be divided between the governments of the states and the national government. The future of the new nation would be shaped by the efforts of Americans to resolve that issue.

Writing About History

Epitaphs. Epitaphs are inscribed on tombstones. These verses and sayings tell you something about peoples' lives.

Have students write epitaphs for significant people in the chapter. They may use the following epitaphs as models:

"Here lies Josiah Trent, 1745–1778, loving husband, gallant Patriot, who died fighting for his country, mourned by all who love him."

"Here lies Sophia Edgecomb, 1730–1805, a woman of wit and learning, author of ten plays, two books of essays, and many poems. Her spirit lives on in her writing."

Have students share the epitaphs they have written and explain why they wrote what they did.

Section Review

ANSWERS

1. Drove British from much of New Jersey and boosted American morale.
2. Students may argue, for example, that without the victory France might not have joined the Americans against Britain.
3. British counted on Loyalist support in the South, but there were far more Patriots than Loyalists. Also, Britain had not counted on Patriots' guerilla tactics.
4. Britain recognized America's independence, certain boundaries, and agreed to withdraw troops. America agreed to vague terms concerning Loyalists' rights to sue to recover property and to collect debts.
Linking Past and Present. Answers will vary depending on where students live.

Chapter Survey

ANSWERS

Using New Vocabulary

1. b. Patrick Henry as a radical favored cutting off all trade with Britain until repeal of Intolerable Acts.
2. c. Franklin, as royal governor of New Jersey, remained loyal to Britain.
3. d. George Washington was a moderate who favored compromising with Britain.
4. a. Abigail Adams supported the Patriot cause by assuming her husband's role while he was away.

Reviewing the Chapter

1. Britain needed money and wanted to avoid the expense of future wars with Indians.
2. (a) These acts imposed taxes to raise money instead of to regulate trade. (b) Refused to accept taxes disguised as duties.
3. To uphold its power to make laws for the colonists. So that colonists would not think they could control Parliament.
4. Britain enacted Stamp Act. Colonists claimed this was taxation without representation. The Olive Branch Petition was an attempt at compromise for a peaceful resolution of colonial grievances. Stamp Act repealed; George III refused to read Olive Branch Petition and declared colonies to be in rebellion.
5. Answers may include: boycott of British goods; petitions (Stamp Act Petition and Olive Branch Petition); written opposition (Thomas Paine's pamphlet *Common Sense*); disobedience (New York Assembly refused to raise money to supply British troops in 1766); property damage (Boston Tea party); hostile acts (harassment of British soldiers in Boston, tarring and feathering British customs officer).
6. (a) There is a contract between government and the people; government should protect natural rights of people; people have right to create new government if peaceful attempts to correct abuses have failed. (b) Meaning of equality for all now includes African Americans, Native Americans, women, and others once left out.
7. (a) Protests raised to new level because Stamp Act affected all colonists. (b) Colonists feared suspension of all assemblies. (c) Acts so oppressive that spirit of defiance

Reduced student page in the Teacher's Edition

Chapter Survey

Using New Vocabulary

Match each numbered vocabulary term with the person most closely related to it. Some terms may apply to more than one person. Then explain how the term and the person in each pair are related.

1. radical	a. Abigail Adams
2. Loyalist	b. Patrick Henry
3. moderate	c. William Franklin
4. Patriot	d. George Washington

Reviewing the Chapter

1. Why did Britain try to tighten control of its American colonies?

2. (a) How did taxes levied under the Sugar, Stamp, and Townshend acts differ from taxes that the colonists had paid before? (b) Why did the colonists protest against each of the acts?

3. Why did Parliament pass the Declaratory Act? Why did Parliament keep the tax on tea when it repealed the other Townshend duties?

4. What events led to the petition by the Stamp Act Congress and the Olive Branch Petition? What was the response to each?

5. Between 1763 and 1776, the colonists used many methods to protest against British policies. Describe five of these methods.

6. (a) Explain three principles of government that are stated in the Declaration of Independence. (b) In what way has the meaning of the declaration changed since the 1700s?

7. Explain how each of the following events increased unity in the colonies: (a) passage of the Stamp Act (b) suspension of the New York assembly (c) passage of the Coercive Acts (d) the battles at Lexington and Concord.

8. Put the following events in chronological order and explain how each event led to the next: the First Continental Congress, the Tea Act, the Intolerable Acts, the Boston Tea Party.

9. Compare the advantages and disadvantages of Britain and the colonies in the American Revolutionary War.

Thinking Critically

1. Application. How do citizens today protest government policies? In what ways are these similar to and different from the colonists' protests against British policies?

2. Evaluation. One historian has said that the political separation between Great Britain and its American colonies was unavoidable. Do you agree or disagree? Give reasons for your answer.

Using Geography

The map below shows the routes British troops and Patriots Paul Revere and William Dawes traveled before the battles at Lexington and Concord. Use the map to answer the questions.

1. The Patriots expected a British attack and watched all around Boston to report any suspicious moves by British troops. Which would be likely places to watch? Why?

2. Describe the route that the British troops traveled.

3. Which routes did Paul Revere and William Dawes take?

4. Why do you think both Revere and Dawes were sent to warn the Patriot leaders?

Lexington and Concord 1775

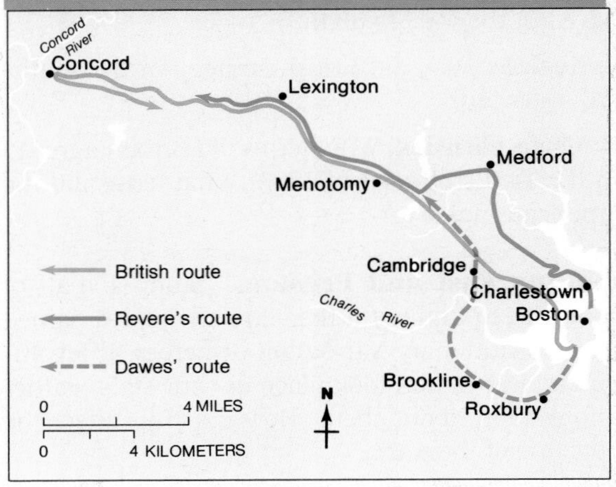

spread. (d) Battles forced colonists to realize they were at war with Britain.

8. Tea Act angered colonists, so they dumped tea into Boston Harbor. British so angry at Boston Tea Party, they passed Intolerable Acts. Colonists responded by holding First Continental Congress.

9. American advantages: guerrilla warfare tactics, fighting for a cause they believed in, civilian support; disadvantages: undisciplined army fighting a powerful and experienced force, lack of funds to supply troops. British advantages: powerful navy and experienced army, support from League of the Iroquois; disadvantages: coping with guerrilla warfare, opposition in Britain to the war, difficulty maintaining supply line.

Applying Social Studies Skills

Analyzing Line Graphs

How did colonial imports of tea reflect the colonists' responses to the tax policies of the British Parliament? The line graph below provides information to answer that question. The graph shows changes in colonial tea imports from Britain between 1761 and 1775. The questions that follow and information in your text will help you analyze the graph.

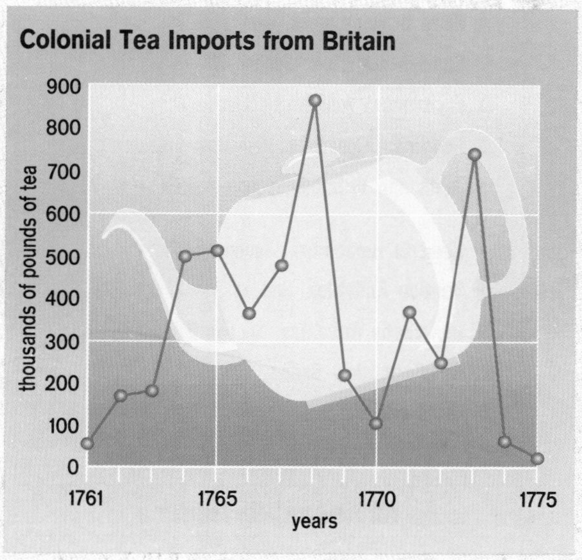

1. What do the numbers on the horizontal and vertical scales of the graph represent?

2. In what year did the amount of tea imported from Britain first exceed 500,000 pounds?

3. Britain passed the Stamp Act in 1765. How did the colonists' response to the act affect tea imports during the next year?

4. What was the effect on tea imports when Parliament repealed the Stamp Act in 1766?

5. In 1768, responding to the Townshend Acts, the colonists agreed not to import certain British goods, including tea. How are the effects of this agreement shown on the graph?

6. Use the graph to explain how the colonists' response to the 1773 Tea Act affected imports of tea.

Writing About Issues

The Issue: *Should a police officer be permitted to conduct certain searches without a search warrant?*

Recently, while selling tickets for a charity, a police officer noticed a suspicious smell wafting out from behind an apartment door. The officer, without a search warrant, forcibly entered the apartment, where he spotted a lit marijuana "joint." The occupant was arrested and found guilty of possession of the illegal drug.

The Fourth Amendment to the Constitution guarantees individuals the right to be free from "unreasonable searches and seizures" and requires that a warrant be obtained before searches are conducted. Nevertheless, the courts have ruled that in some cases searches may be "warrantless"— that is, made without obtaining a warrant. Such cases include emergencies and situations in which evidence of a crime is observed or permission to search is given, or when delay would prevent an investigation.

Many people believe that police should have even broader powers to conduct warrantless searches. They say that guilty people are too often set free because evidence against them was obtained without a warrant and must be excluded from the trial. "To exclude such evidence," wrote a Supreme Court justice, "would punish law enforcement officers whose conduct is objectively reasonable."

Defenders of a strict reading of the Fourth Amendment believe that requiring search warrants is the only sure way to prevent authorities from abusing their power to search individuals. Without the need to obtain a warrant from an impartial court, they say, officials could use almost any excuse to intrude into personal matters. "It is better one hundred guilty persons should escape," Benjamin Franklin wrote in 1785, "than that one innocent person should suffer."

What do you think? Write an essay explaining your opinion on warrantless searches. Give reasons why you hold this view.

Thinking Critically

1. In making comparisons, students may consider petitions, boycotts, pamphlets, committees of correspondence, group meetings, and destruction of property.

2. Students who agree may argue that geographical distance and conflicting economic interests made separation inevitable. Those who disagree can point to Canada, which is still a member of the British Commonwealth.

Using Geography

1. Charlestown and Roxbury; any places where British might cross over and march inland from Boston.

2. Northwest, from near Boston by Cambridge, then by Menotomy to Lexington and Concord.

3. Revere left Boston, through Charlestown, northwest to Madford, then by Menotomy, through and past Lexington. Dawes went south from Boston to Roxbury and Brookline, north to Charlestown, northwest to Menotomy.

4. If one captured by British, other might get through.

Applying Social Studies Skills

1. Years; thousands of pounds of tea.

2. 1765.

3. Dropped sharply.

4. Tea imports rose.

5. Sharp drop in imports.

6. Tea imports dropped sharply.

Chapter 5

Beginnings of a Nation

Planning Guide

	Student Text	TWE Lesson Plans	Support Materials
SECTION 1	**Section 5-1** (1-2 Days) **Congress and the States,** pp 118-122 Geography—Location: The Northwest Survey System, p 123 Review/Evaluation Section Review, p 122	**Introducing the Chapter:** An Identity Crisis—Class Activity, 30 minutes, p 115B **Evaluating Progress:** Reacting to British Tyranny—Individual Activity, one class period or homework, p 115C	★ **Read to Remember,** Section 1 ● **Section Activities,** Section 1 Δ **Enrichment Activities,** Section 1 Δ **Readings,** Articles of Confederation ● **Tests and Quizzes,** Section 1 Quiz
SECTION 2	**Section 5-2** (1-2 Days) **Seeking a National Identity,** pp 124-129 The American Spirit: Abigail Adams, p 127 Review/Evaluation Section Review, p 129	**Teaching the Main Ideas:** Challenging the Narrowly Defined "American Identity"—Cooperative Activity, one class period, p 115B	★ **Read to Remember,** Section 2 ● **Section Activities,** Section 2 Δ **Enrichment Activities,** Section 2 Δ **Readings,** Constantia, Benjamin Franklin ● **Tests and Quizzes,** Section 2 Quiz
SECTION 3	**Section 5-3** (1-3 Days) **The Country Adrift,** pp 130-133 Connections to Themes: Balancing Unity and Diversity, p 133 Review/Evaluation Section Review, p 133 Chapter 5 Survey, pp 134-135 Skills, pp 134-135 Using New Vocabulary Thinking Critically Using Geography Applying Social Studies Skills: Analyzing Maps and Graphs Writing About Issues	**Teaching the Main Ideas:** "E Pluribus Unum"—More Hope Than Reality—Cooperative Activity, one class period, p 115C **Reinforcement Activity:** Assessing the Articles of Confederation—Class Activity, 30 minutes, p 115C **Enrichment Activity:** The Human Drama of Shays' Rebellion—Individual Activity, homework, p 115C	★ **Read to Remember,** Section 3 ● **Section Activities,** Section 3 ● **Geography Activities,** Section 3 Δ **Readings,** Joel Barlow ● **Tests and Quizzes,** Section 3 Quiz, Chapter 5 Test (Forms A and B) **Additional Resources** ● **Active Learning** Δ **Transparencies and Activity Book** ● **Testing Software** ★ **Chapter Summaries** **Key:** ★ **For Extra Support** ● **For All Students** Δ **For Enrichment**

Overview

Chapter 5 explores the political, social, and economic issues that faced the fledgling nation during the American War of Independence. States quickly formed governments based on the foundation of representative government laid by their colonial charters. However, forming a national government proved to be a much more difficult task. In the midst of war, the states agreed on a loose alliance under the Articles of Confederation.

Recognizing the political and economic conflicts between states, many leaders hoped to foster a sense of national identity as "Americans." However, since most political leaders in the Continental Congress and state governments were English-Americans, they narrowly defined that identity in terms of their own racial and cultural heritage. Nevertheless, there were early challenges of this narrow view of American society.

Although the Articles of Confederation unified the states in the war effort and resolved some issues concerning western land claims, they failed to resolve state conflicts over trade, currency, and taxes. Meanwhile, the Congress was too weak and divided to take decisive action in foreign policy. By 1787 it was clear that the Articles needed to be revised if the young nation was to survive.

Activity Objectives

After completing the activities, students should be able to

- describe the grievances of groups excluded from a national, "American" identity.
- create visual images reflecting the contrast between the ideal of national unity and the reality of conflict between the states.
- describe economic and political problems that prompted many Americans to favor a stronger national government.
- compare colonial and state governments, explaining the reasons for the differences.
- identify problems that motivated farmers to join Shays' Rebellion.

Introducing the Chapter

An Identity Crisis

This class activity requires about 30 minutes.

This activity addresses the theme of balancing unity and diversity by helping students understand why seeking a national identity was a challenge from the very beginning. Ask students to assume that they are living in one of the thirteen states in 1776, soon after the signing of the Declaration of Independence. They have pledged their loyalty to their particular state and live under its government. As a result they think of themselves as Virginians, New Yorkers, or Pennsylvanians rather than as Americans. After the signing of the Declaration, they are being encouraged to consider themselves Americans.

Ask students to define "American" as they would have defined it in 1776. Allow about five minutes for them to individually complete their definitions. Then encourage them to share their answers with the class. List on the chalkboard the major themes included in their definitions.

In a discussion of their definitions, ask students to consider how average citizens of states in 1776 would have answered the following questions:

- Should citizens pledge their first loyalty to their state or to an alliance of states?
- In what ways might a national government be more (less) beneficial to individual citizens than a state government?
- Is there an "American" identity?

Save the responses and have the class reassess their answers after they have finished reading the chapter.

Teaching the Main Ideas

Section 5-2: Challenging the Narrowly Defined "American Identity"

This cooperative activity can be assigned in class or as homework. If done in class, it will require most of one period.

This activity is designed to help students understand and empathize with the various groups of people who were denied political power and who faced discrimination based on race, culture, or sex in the early years of our country.

Begin by emphasizing to students that the point of view of English-American men was dominant in the formation of the Confederation government, not because they were "right" but because they held most of the political and economic power. Their interests in protecting their land, wealth, religious freedom, and political power influenced their perceptions of who should be considered "Americans" and what rights they should or should not have.

Explain to students that in this activity they will have a chance to speak out for groups of people who had little or no voice in government. Divide the class into pairs and direct each pair to choose one group mentioned in Section 5-2 to represent: Native Americans, African Americans, women, men without property, or white but non-English groups such as German Americans.

Explain that a common form of persuasion in the early days of the nation was the broadside—a large sheet of paper on which was printed a political message or advertisement. Broadsides were posted in public places and read by people who often had few other sources of information. Direct each pair to prepare a broadside arguing that their group be represented among those citizens granted voting rights and cultural acceptance. Point out that students may want to argue that all people should be granted equal rights or only that the group they represent should be accorded these rights. Remind them that not all people could read the English language. Therefore they should consider other racial and cultural groups as they prepare their messages. Visually representing their ideas might help to overcome the language barrier.

Display the completed broadsides and have students assess the persuasiveness of the messages. Which broadsides considered the traditions of other racial and cultural groups? Conclude with a discussion of the recurring concepts and values illustrated in the broadsides.

Teaching the Main Ideas

Section 5-3: "E Pluribus Unum"—More Hope Than Reality

This cooperative activity requires one class period, or it may be assigned as homework.

After students have finished reading Section 5-3, use this activity to reinforce their understanding of the significant political differences that existed between the states in 1776. Remind students of the national motto, "E pluribus unum" ("Out of many, one"), which was adopted in 1782. Review information from the chapter that points out the serious disagreements which existed between the states in 1782 and list them on the chalkboard. Help students recognize that the motto was more hope than reality when adopted.

Divide the class into groups of three and distribute drawing paper and marking pens. Assign half the groups the task of creating a seal or logo to illustrate the *hope* of the motto "E pluribus unum." Refer these groups to state seals and company logos for ideas. Assign the other groups to illustrate the *reality* of "E pluribus unum" in 1782. Refer these groups to the Franklin drawing on page 79 of the text as an example of political disunity among the states.

When the seals or logos are completed, have the groups present them to the class. Ask students to reflect on the images and consider how "average Americans" in 1782 might have felt about the prospect for a truly unified country. Conclude by pointing out the national seal and the "E pluribus unum" motto on our one-dollar bills. Ask if students think the motto reflects reality today in our nation.

Reinforcement Activity

Section 5-3: Assessing the Articles of Confederation

This class activity requires about 30 minutes.

This activity will reinforce students' understanding of why the Articles of Confederation did not unify the states into an effective nation. Students will analyze economic problems that the Confederation government seemed powerless to solve.

Before beginning the activity, draw two columns on the chalkboard with the labels: *Cause* and *Effect*. Write the following statements under *Effect*. Do not write the causes listed in parentheses.

- *The nation has an unfavorable balance of trade.* (Britain bans United States from trading in British West Indies. The United States spends more on imports than it receives for exports.)
- *Britain shows disrespect for the American government.* (Congress helpless in face of trade restrictions; no power to impose tariffs on Britain.)
- *The nation cannot pay its war debts.* (States do not provide money for national debt—more concerned with paying their own debts.)
- *The nation suffers from inflation.* (Congress and states print money not backed by gold or silver; money declines in value; prices rise.)
- *Groups of farmers break up court sessions in Massachusetts.* (Farmers, taken to court because of inability to pay debts or high taxes, try to prevent judges from foreclosing and sending debtors to prison.)

Have students copy the two-column chart. Then have them review Section 5-3 to find one or more causes for each effect listed and write them in the left column. Discuss their finished charts by asking why many Americans called for a stronger national government. Conclude by asking students what solutions they think the American leaders participating in the convention in 1787 could pose to solve the problems faced by their young nation.

Evaluating Progress

Section 5-1: Reacting to British Tyranny

This individual activity can be used as an in-class or take-home evaluation.

This evaluation activity is designed to assess students' understanding of the extent to which the organization of the state governments after 1776 was a reaction to British rule and tyranny.

Direct students to create a chart with three vertical columns labeled *Colonial, State,* and *Reason for Change,* and four horizontal rows labeled *Governors, Judges, Legislatures,* and *Individual Rights.* Have them fill in short phrases characterizing the nature of these aspects of colonial and state governments and explaining the changes. For example, colonial governors might be described as "usually appointed by king or Parliament," and "often ignored people's will." State governors might be described as "more answerable to people, often appointed by legislature." The reason for this change could be summarized as "to prevent governors from ignoring the people's will."

Criteria for evaluating students' work should be accuracy in identifying characteristics and logic in explaining the changes.

Enrichment Activity

Section 5-3: The Human Drama of Shays' Rebellion

This individual activity may be assigned as homework to be shared in class the next day.

After reading Section 5-3, students will be familiar with Shays' Rebellion and its role in spurring greater support for revising the Articles of Confederation. This activity will enrich students' understanding of the human drama of Shays' Rebellion and why it is considered a critical event in the early history of our country.

Introduce the activity by having students recall information about Shays' Rebellion. Challenge them to think about how the conditions prompting the rebellion affected individual farmers. Then have them each write a short story to describe one such individual drama. The characters in their stories are to be fictional, but events should be grounded in historical fact. Stories should begin with farmers returning home from service as a Patriots in the War of Independence, and conclude with Shays' Rebellion. The stories should include descriptions of events as well as thoughts about the farmers' situation and what the state and national government should do to alleviate it.

Have students form groups of four and exchange stories to read and discuss their concluded stories. Did the activity help them to empathize with the farmers? Do they believe that the government's reaction to the farmers' protest was hypocritical in light of the recent war against the British? Why or why not? What do they think were the most important lessons of the rebellion?

Bibliography and Audiovisual Material

Teacher Bibliography

Kenyon, Cecilia M., ed. *The Antifederalists.* Boston: Northeastern University Press, 1985.

Middlekauff, Robert. *The Glorious Cause: The American Revolution, 1763–1789.* New York: Oxford University Press, 1985.

Morris, Richard B. *The Forging of the Union, 1781–1789.* New York: HarperCollins, 1987.

Williams, Selma R. *Demeter's Daughters: The Women Who Founded America, 1587–1787.* New York: Atheneum, 1976.

Student Bibliography

Akers, Charles W. *Abigail Adams, An American Woman.* Boston: Little, Brown, 1980.

Bowen, Catherine Drinker. *The Most Dangerous Man in America: Scenes from the Life of Benjamin Franklin.* Boston: Little, Brown, 1986.

Craven, Wesley F. *The Legend of the Founding Fathers.* Westport, Conn.: Greenwood Press, 1983.

Hilton, Suzanne. *We the People: The Way We Were.* Philadelphia: Westminster Pres, 1981.

Morris, Richard B. *The Making of a Nation.* New York: Time-Life, 1974.

Page, Elizabeth. *The Tree of Liberty*. New York: Holt, Rinehart, and Winston, 1939.

Wills, Garry. *Inventing America: Jefferson's Declaration of Independence.* Garden City, NY: Doubleday, 1978.

Films, Videocassettes, and Videodiscs

American Revolution Series: The Postwar Period. 11 min. Coronet/MTI. Videocassette.

"A Little Rebellion Now and Then": Prologue to the Constitution. 30 min. Churchill Media. Videocassette or movie.

Patrick Henry's Fight for Individual Rights. 29 min. EBEC. Videocassette.

The Postwar Period. 11 min. Coronet. Movie.

Remaking Society in the New Nation. 20 min. EBEC. Videocassette.

Filmstrips

American Heritage Media Collection: The Making of the Nation. Westport Media.

Creating a Federal Union (1783–1791). Guidance Associates.

Where Historians Disagree Collection: The Background of the Constitution. Random House Media.

Computer Software

The Great Knowledge Race—U.S. History Package: Series 2. Apple. Focus Media.

Objectives

- Explain how the first national government of the United States was organized.
- Explain why the American identity was narrowly defined in the early years of the nation and how this view was later challenged.
- Trace the early efforts of many Americans to strengthen the national government.

Introducing
THE CHAPTER

For suggestions on introducing chapter 5, refer to page 115B of the Teacher's Edition

Developing
THE CHAPTER

For activities and teaching strategies to help reinforce and enrich chapter content, see pages 115B–115D in the Teacher's Edition.

Chapter Opener Illustrations
Rufus Hathaway. *A View of Joshua Windsor's House*. This painting shows the home and wharf of a prosperous fishing merchant in Duxbury, Massachusetts in 1795. New England towns prospered on shipbuilding and the export of cod, mackerel, and clams.

Pennsylvania Farmstead with Many Fences. Further inland, German families dotted the Pennsylvania countryside with tidy, well-managed farms, raising grain crops.

Francis Guy. *Tontine Coffee House*. The nation's commerce was centered on the east coast, in New York City. Merchants and shippers met every day at the corner of Wall Street in Manhattan to transact business.

Note the word "Congress" stitched on the hat of the

Chapter 5 1776-1787

Beginnings of a Nation

Courtesy, Museum of Fine Arts, Boston

Continental Army soldier. One soldier wrote, "I was confirmed in the habit of considering America as my country and Congress as my government." Although blue uniforms had been ordered for all services, the typical field uniform consisted of a cloth or deerskin hunting shirt and fitted leggings. The pigskin hunting bag held flints and bullets, and a powder horn.

Chapter Connections

Events in Chapter 5 were occurring at the same time as events in Chapter 4. Also, the three sections of Chapter 5 are essentially concurrent with each other. Section 5-1 has a political focus, Section 5-2 is social, and Section 5-3 is largely economic.

American Voices

While fighting to break free of their colonial past, the Patriots also struggled to set a course for their future. Even before the break with Britain, Americans asked themselves what would take the place of the colonial governments. Abigail Adams, writing to her husband while he attended the Second Continental Congress in 1775, expressed her fears for the future:

> *"If a form of government is to be established here, what one will be assumed? Will it be left to our assemblies to choose one? And will not many people have many minds? . . .*
>
> *The building up of a great empire may now I suppose be realized. . . . Yet will not ten thousand difficulties arise in the formation of it? . . .*
>
> *If we separate from Britain, what code of laws will be established? How shall we be governed so as to retain our liberties? Can any government be free which is not administered by general stated laws? Who shall frame these laws? Who will give them force and energy? . . .*
>
> *When I consider these things . . . I feel anxious for the fate of our monarchy or democracy or whatever is to take place."*

The need for new governments would mean new loyalties. But what would those loyalties be? Most Patriots were first and foremost Virginians, New Yorkers, Pennsylvanians—not Americans. Indeed, who could say what it meant to be an "American"? Casting off colonial rule meant facing the question of whether they could become a nation.

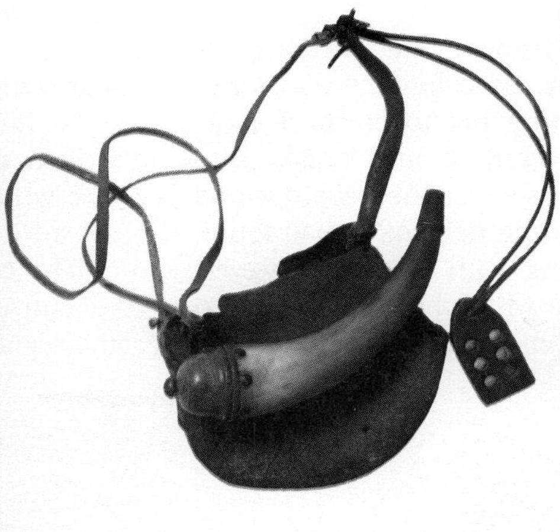

Pennsylvania farm; commercial street in New York City; New England coastal scene; hunting bag and powder horn; Continental soldier.

Analyzing Primary Sources

American Voices

Abigail Adams is considered one of the great letter writers of all time. While Abigail and her husband John Adams were almost continually separated during the War for Independence, their letters—many of which still exist—overcame the distance separating them.

1. What problem does Abigail Adams foresee in the formation of a government by the states? **(Each state will have different ideas.)**
2. What fears does she have about the American people? **(They might not like restraints necessary to preserve order.)**
3. Abigail Adams asks: "Can any government be free which is not administered by general stated laws?" How would you answer this question?

Section 5-1

Objectives

- ***Answer the Focus Question.***
- *Explain how the new state constitutions reflected the colonists' reaction to British rule.*
- *Evaluate whether the Articles of Confederation effectively settled the dispute of states' rights vs. a strong national government.*
- *Describe how the Northwest Ordinance provided for government in the western lands.*

Introducing
THE SECTION

Remind students that when the Revolutionary War broke out, the newly independent states formed governing bodies from the old colonial assemblies. Despite wartime difficulties, each state worked to adopt a constitution.

Ask: How might problems faced by Americans under British rule affect the design of a new government? **(Students might reply that representatives would be careful of giving too much power to a central government.)**

B · A · C · K · G · R · O · U · N · D

Time Line Illustrations
1. John Hancock boldly affixed his signature to the Declaration of Independence.
2. On June 14, 1777, the Continental Congress resolved that "the Flag of the United States be 13 stripes alternate red and white, and the Union be 13 stars white in a blue field representing a new constellation." Though there was no official arrangement for the stars the most popular design, had alternating rows of 3, 2, 3, 2, and 3 stars.
3. On June 20, 1782, Congress adopted the seal still used today. In the eagle's beak is a scroll on which is written *E Pluribus Unum*—out of many, one.
4. As thousands of Americans spread westward across the Appalachians, Congress established a way to survey and

Reduced student page in the Teacher's Edition

CHAPTER TIME LINE

1776 - 1787

1777 Articles of Confederation drafted

1781 Articles of Confederation ratified

1775 | 1780

1776 **Jul 4** Declaration of Independence adopted
First state constitutions drafted

1780 Pennsylvania becomes first state to abolish slavery

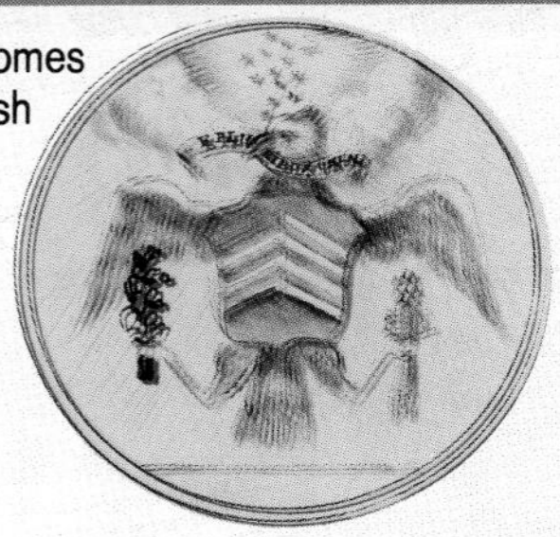

5-1 Congress and the States

Focus: How did Americans preserve their tradition of government by consent of the people?

In the letter quoted on page 117, Abigail Adams mentioned that the new American government might be a monarchy. For most Patriots, however, another monarchy was unthinkable. They believed that the ideal form of government was a **republic,** a government run by representatives elected by the people.

The seeds of self-government were, of course, already firmly planted in the colonial legislatures. The Patriots were fighting not to create a completely new type of government but to make sure that government by consent of the people would never be uprooted from the rich soil it had found in America. In breaking with Britain, however, they still had to decide what changes, if any, to make in the former colonial governments.

Turning Colonies into States

The Continental Congress saw that stable governments would be needed throughout the war and beyond. A month before the signing of the Declaration of Independence, Congress was laying the groundwork by urging each colony to create a state government. By doing so, each would be claiming **sovereignty,** the power to control its own affairs.

By the end of 1776, most states had produced written **constitutions,** or plans of government. The writers built these plans upon the framework already found in the colonial charters.

The colonial governments had had legislative, executive, and judicial branches. Of the three, only the legislatures typically had members elected by then divide large areas of land for settlement. The direction of boundary lines was measured with a compass like the brass model below. After peering at a distant landmark through the sights, the surveyor noted its bearing by reading the compass needle.

5. Colonial churches were used for community gatherings as well as religious services.

6. The engraving of Daniel Shays was published in "Bickerstaff's Boston Almanac for 1787."

Developing

THE SECTION

Thinking Critically

Analysis. When the War for Independence was over, writer Mercy Otis Warren said that America was "as a child just learning to walk." **Ask:** In what ways might a new nation be like a child? What skills might it have to master? (The new nation had many things to learn; for example, how to govern itself.)

Limited English Proficiency

Building Vocabulary. Ask students to speculate about what rights might be guaranteed in a bill of rights. What are civil rights or civil liberties? Point out the connection between the words *civil* and *citizen*.

1783 Treaty of Paris with Great Britain

1785

1785 Land Ordinance

1786 Virginia Statute of Religious Freedom

Annapolis meeting calls for constitutional convention

1787 Northwest Ordinance

Shays' Rebellion crushed

1790

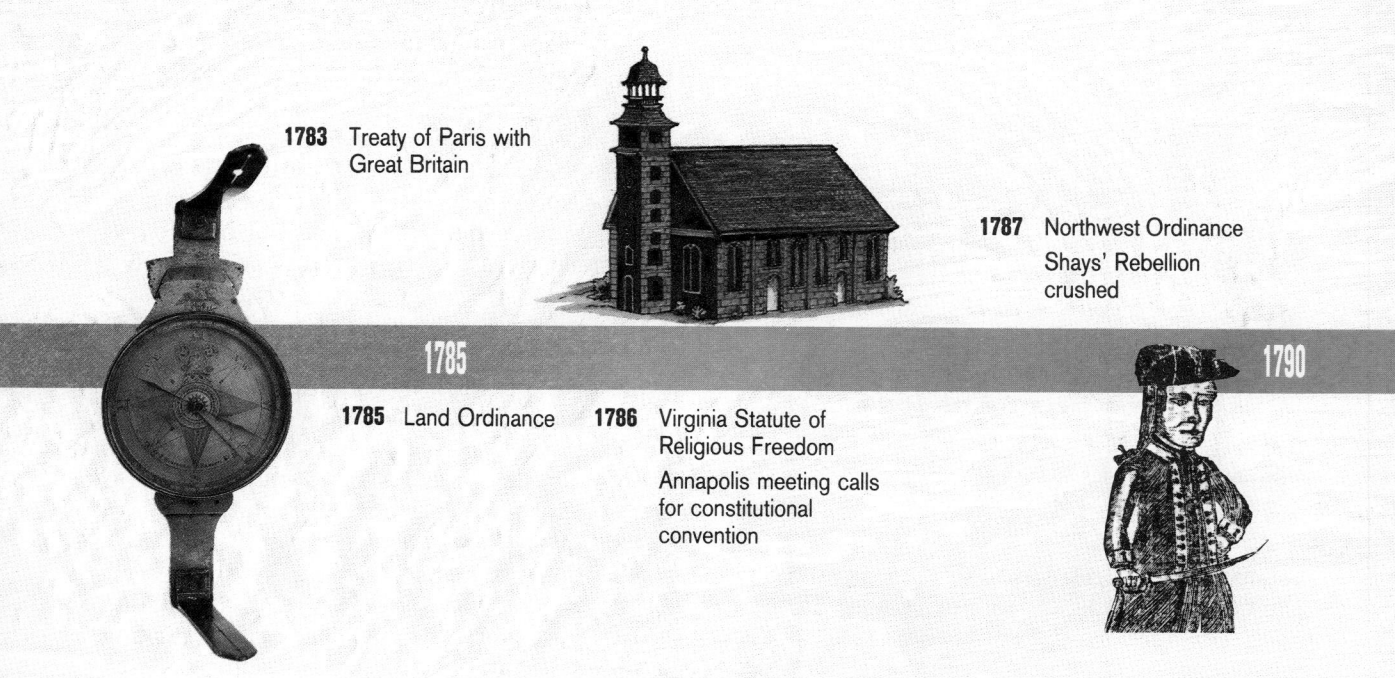

the people. Governors and judges were usually appointed by the king or Parliament—and they often ignored the people's will. The memory of such tyranny was fresh in the minds of the writers of the new state constitutions. They wanted to make sure that the main source of government power would be the consent of the people.

Not surprisingly, then, most state constitutions increased the legislature's power, while making the judicial and executive branches more answerable to the people. Judges would now be selected by the voters, and in many states the governor was to be appointed by the legislature and could do nothing without its advice and consent. Pennsylvania's first constitution did not even provide for a governor. The citizens of one town declared, "We do not want any goviner but the Goviner of the Univarse."

The legislatures were made even more responsive to the people. In the colonial governments, the upper house had usually been appointed by the governor or the king. In most states, now, the upper house was to be elected by the lower house—the people's representatives.

Most state constitutions included a **bill of rights,** a list of rights and freedoms guaranteed to the people. The belief that all people have rights no government may take away was deeply rooted in the English tradition. The idea of stating them in a written plan of government, however, was distinctly American. State constitutions also spelled out rights that English law did not guarantee. One was freedom of religion—the idea that each person was free to practice any religion, or no religion at all. Freedom of the press, another right that grew out of the colonists' experience, was also protected.

The Articles of Confederation

Before the signing of the Declaration, John Hancock had said that "the members of the Continental Congress must hang together," to which Benjamin Franklin responded, "Yes, we must indeed all hang together, or most assuredly we shall all hang separately." A call for united action, however, was not the same as uniting Americans under one government. Were the states fighting the war as thirteen countries or as one?

Most Americans recognized the need for a central government to direct the war effort and

Multicultural Perspective

A Shawnee chief comments: *"If the United States were such lovers of peace as you describe them to be, they would have chosen for their coat of arms something more appropriate as an expression of it. There are, for instance, many agreeable and harmless birds.*

But what is the eagle? He is the largest of all birds! He is the enemy of all birds. His head, his eyes, his beak and his long crooked talons declare his strength and hostility!

You have not only put one of the instruments of war, a bundle of arrows, into one of his hands (claws), and rods in the other, but have painted him in the most fearful guise, and in the posture of attack upon his prey."

Writing About History

Editorial. Have students write one of the following editorials and then share them in class. Compare the viewpoints of the states and discuss how the congressional compromise might affect the government's ability to act.

- Students assume that they own a newspaper in a small state, such as Delaware. They write an editorial opposing population as a basis for representation in Congress under the Articles of Confederation. Then they write a second editorial supporting the compromise of the delegates in Congress.
- Students assume that they own a newspaper in a large state, such as New York. They write an editorial opposing an equal vote in Congress for all states under the Articles. Then they write a second editorial supporting the compromise of the delegates in Congress.

Reduced student page in the Teacher's Edition

Spotlight on National Symbols

In 1782 Congress voted to make the eagle the national symbol. Benjamin Franklin opposed the choice, calling the eagle "a bird of bad moral character" because it steals food from other birds. Franklin also thought the eagle was too common. For a national symbol, he suggested a uniquely American bird: the turkey.

conduct foreign relations. No state constitution claimed the right to declare war or make treaties. Each state, however, did want to keep control of its internal affairs—particularly through the powers to tax and to regulate trade. British rule had left many Americans fearful of giving those powers to a central government that might interfere with their rights.

These fears were reflected in the Articles of Confederation and Perpetual Union, a constitution proposed by a committee of Congress in 1776. The plan provided only for a legislature—Congress. There would be no executive or judicial branches, which the states saw as threats to their sovereignty. The words *perpetual* and *confederation* showed that the union was to be permanent but also loose. Instead of a central government with complete sovereignty—like those in England and France—it proposed an alliance of independent states.

A loose alliance. For a year Congress debated the proposal. As the Revolutionary War raged on, the delegates argued over how states were to be represented in the legislature. The large states demanded that representation be based on state population, while the small states insisted that each state have an equal vote. Finally, the delegates agreed that each state would have one vote. Major decisions would require approval by nine states. Amendments, or changes, to the Articles of Confederation would require approval of all thirteen states.

Under the Articles, Congress's powers were limited mainly to areas directly related to the war. It could wage war, make peace, make treaties, and request troops and money from the states. It could coin and borrow money, set standards for weights and measures, and set up a postal service. However, it was denied the power to levy taxes or to regulate trade through **tariffs,** taxes laid on imports or exports.

The Articles also limited the power of Congress to enforce its decisions. It could not force states to abide by treaties made by Congress. Nor could it require them to contribute money or troops to the war effort. In effect, instead of issuing orders, Congress would have to beg for cooperation. The Articles were intended to create only "a firm league of friendship" between sovereign states.

After Congress adopted the Articles of Confederation in 1777, it took until 1781 for all the states to **ratify,** or approve, the plan. The main stumbling block was the land west of the Appalachians. Seven states had claims—often overlapping—that dated back to colonial charters. Their agreement to cede, or yield, their claims to Congress, together with the need for a united war effort, paved the way for the Articles. Not until 1802, though, were all the claims east of the Mississippi ceded.

Moving Westward

Long before the war, colonists had pushed westward, as farmers and hunters looked for new opportunities. Despite Britain's attempt to curb westward movement by the Proclamation of 1763, settlers had begun trickling over the Appalachians. Many were guided by explorers like Daniel Boone. In 1775 Boone and others connected several trails to form the Wilderness Road, which cut through the Cumberland Gap to Kentucky. This would open the West to thousands of new settlers.

After the war, the westward trickle became a torrent as the young nation, under the 1783 Treaty of Paris, took over British claims extending to the Mississippi. By wagon, on foot, or on river barges called flatboats, pioneers moved into the western parts of New York, Pennsylvania, and Virginia, and into what would become Kentucky, Tennessee, Ohio, Indiana, and Illinois.

Multicultural Perspectives

The 1783 Treaty of Paris did not address the issue of Native Americans and the lands they occupied. When England ceded its lands to the Americans, no provisions were made for its faithful allies. John Jay stated the American position: "We claim the right of preemption," the right to buy Indian lands.

However, Congress did not recognize the Indians' right to keep their lands indefinitely. A new coalition of Indians formed in the eastern woodlands to defend their lands and way of life. This new alignment asserted that the Ohio River was to be the boundary between whites and Indians. But territory controlled by the Indians shrank immensely as the United States expanded westward.

Connections: Geography

Comparing Maps. Have students compare the map on this page with a present-day map of the United States to determine what states were created from the original thirteen states' cessions of territory.

Western Land Claims 1782-1802

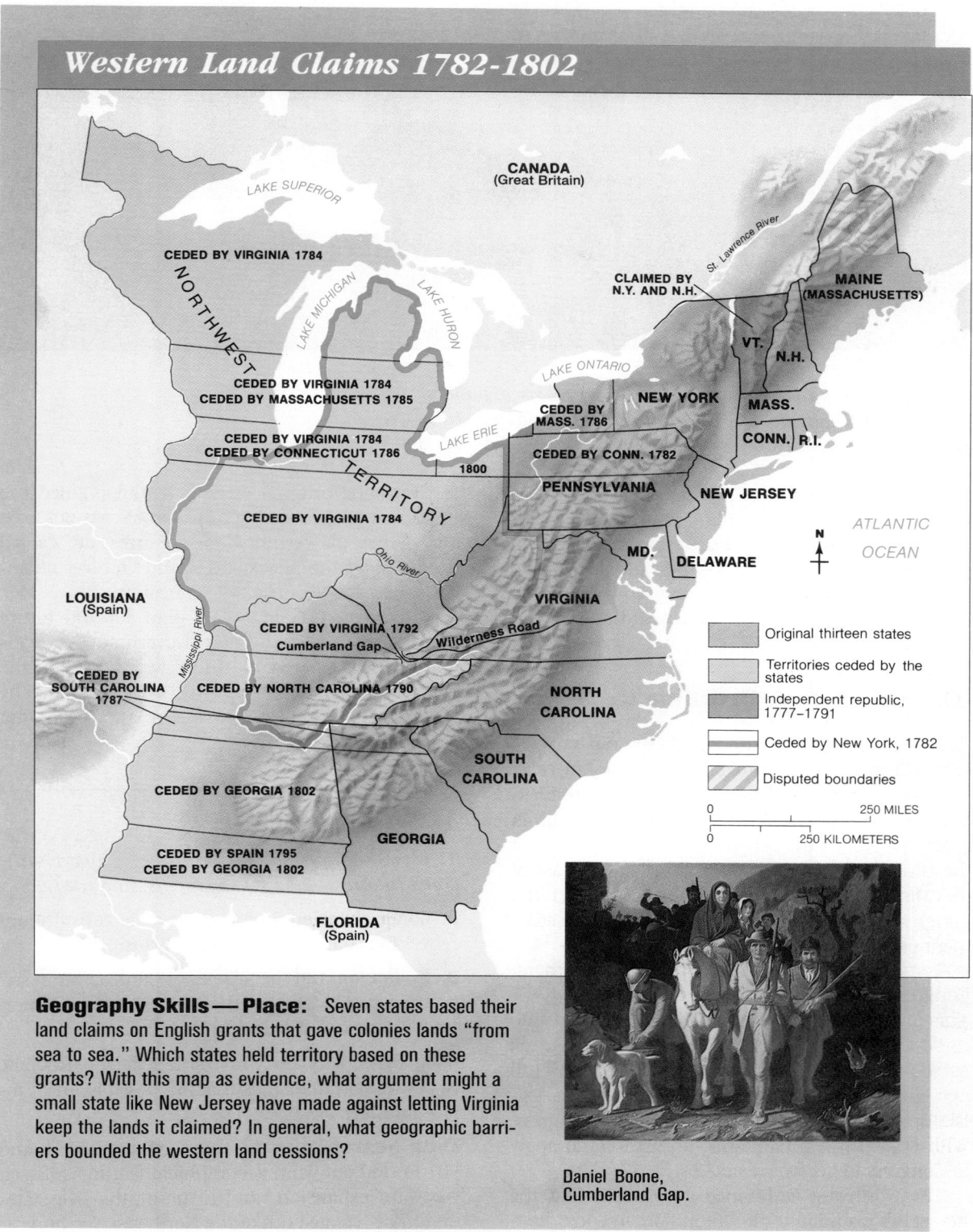

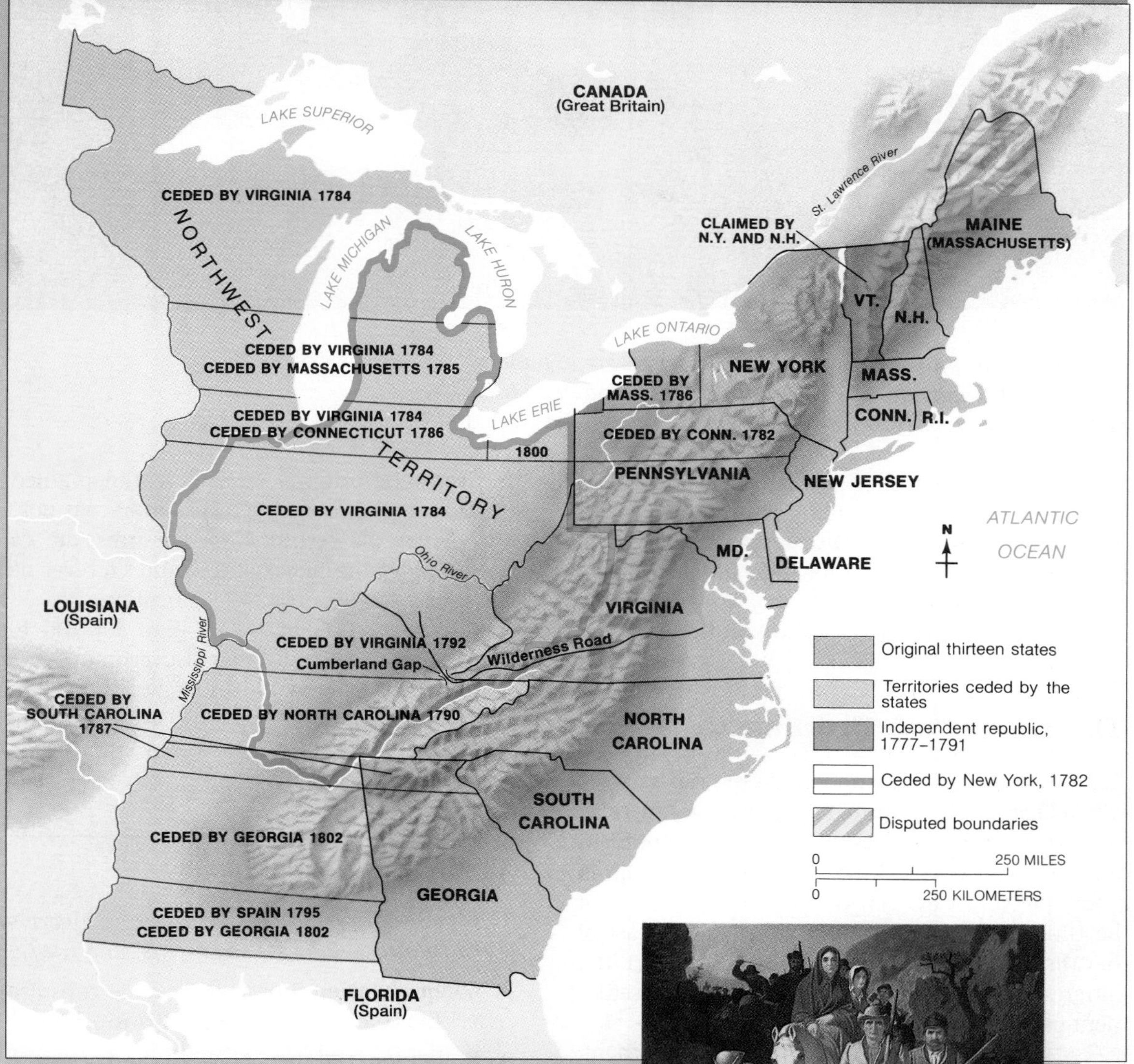

Daniel Boone, Cumberland Gap.

Geography Skills — Place: Seven states based their land claims on English grants that gave colonies lands "from sea to sea." Which states held territory based on these grants? With this map as evidence, what argument might a small state like New Jersey have made against letting Virginia keep the lands it claimed? In general, what geographic barriers bounded the western land cessions?

Geography Skills

ANSWERS

1. Georgia, South Carolina, North Carolina, Virginia, Connecticut, Massachusetts, New York.
2. Virginia would become too large and powerful.
3. Mississippi River, Great Lakes, Appalachian Mountains.

Section Review
ANSWERS

1. Definitions for following terms are on text pages indicated in parentheses: *republic* (118), *sovereignty* (118), *constitutions* (118), *bill of rights* (119), *tariffs* (120), *ratify* (120).
2. Most state constitutions increased legislatures' powers, made judicial and executive branches more answerable to the people, and included a bill of rights.
3. Students may answer that the Articles made the union permanent but provided for a very loose union, making states virtually independent.
4. The Northwest Territory would be a large region in which slavery would be banned and representative government would protect individual freedoms.
Data Search. Mountains may have hindered expansion, rivers may have provided transportation. States include Michigan, Wisconsin, Ohio, Indiana, Illinois.

B · A · C · K · G · R · O · U · N · D

Chapter Connections

Point out to students that as the United States acquired more territory (such as the Louisiana Purchase) the question of which territories and new states should allow slavery and which should be free became a burning issue dividing the North and South. Students will discover the consequences of this issue when they study Chapters 11, 12, and 13.

As Americans moved west, a network of roads expanded, dotted with roadside inns. A common sight outside inns was the canvas-covered Conestoga wagon.

"The woods are full of new settlers," one traveler wrote. "Axes are resounding and the trees literally falling about us." The westward movement brought new opportunities for these pioneers, but it proved tragic for Native Americans, who were pushed off their lands despite treaties with Congress.

The Northwest Ordinance

Congress had neither enough power nor enough will to keep settlers from taking Native-American lands. However, the states did give it clear authority to oversee settlement of the West. In 1784, Virginia ceded the Northwest Territory—the area north of the Ohio River, west of Pennsylvania, and east of the Mississippi. In the Land Ordinance of 1785, Congress planned for the orderly sale and settlement of the area.

To help establish representative government, Congress passed the Northwest Ordinance in 1787. This law called for the territory to be divided into no fewer than three and no more than five areas. As soon as 5,000 "free male inhabitants of full age" lived in an area, the people could elect a legislature and send a nonvoting delegate to Congress. With 60,000 free inhabitants, an area could apply to Congress to become a state.

The Northwest Ordinance guaranteed that the new states would join the Union "on an equal footing with the original states." It also planted two important seeds of democracy: slavery was not to be allowed in the territory nor in any state carved from it, and the new states would "forever be encouraged" to support public education.

Congress had laid out a plan for the future growth of the United States. Government by consent of the people would move westward with the pioneers. Jefferson, expressing a view shared by many, had a vision of the western lands becoming "an Empire for Liberty."

Section Review

1. Identification. Define *republic, sovereignty, constitutions, bill of rights, tariffs,* and *ratify.*

2. Comprehension. How did the state constitutions reflect the colonists' reaction to British rule?

3. Evaluation. Did the Articles of Confederation settle the issue of whether the United States of America was one country or thirteen? Explain.

4. Analysis. Why do you think Jefferson saw the Northwest Ordinance as making possible an "Empire for Liberty"?

Data Search. Use the maps on pages 121 and 901 to find out what geographical features affected westward expansion, and to name the five states eventually created out of the Northwest Territory.

Geography

A KEY TO OUR PAST

Location: The Northwest Survey System

At the end of the Revolutionary War, the new nation was deeply in debt, but where was the money to come from? The best solution seemed to be to sell land in the Northwest, but there was no procedure for the orderly division of new lands. At the time, settlers simply claimed the land they wanted. Their claims often had odd shapes because they drew boundary lines to exclude swamps, steep slopes, and other unusable land.

The description of a land claim could be confusing. A typical description read, "Start at the granite boulder. Run a line southeast to the old chestnut stump. Turn at an angle of 45 degrees and run a line to the old barn," and so on. After several generations, however, the boulder might have been moved or the barn burned down. So people often argued about boundary claims.

To avoid such problems, Congress passed the Land Ordinance of 1785. The land was surveyed and divided into areas called townships, each 6 miles square. Each township was further divided into 36 sections of 1 square mile each, 640 acres to a section. Four sections in each township were set aside for the national government, and one was reserved to maintain public schools. The remaining sections were sold to settlers.

To lay out boundaries, geographers had to survey, or measure, areas of land to determine their **absolute location,** or exact position. They used lines of latitude and longitude, like those on a map, to divide the townships into a pattern of square sections. It is not known who invented this American system of surveying, but one engineer said, "No man in particular was the originator. It was a result of growth and development founded on the principles of self-government, formulated into a law after long sectional controversy, and put into practice because necessity required it."

This survey system was later used in territories and states across the nation. An engineering chief in the Bureau of Land Management once observed, "Fly across the heartland of the United States today and you will see below a vast checkerboard, with fields and roads and cities laid out in a precise north-south, east-west arrangement. Practically the only features that don't run by the compass are the ridges and valleys and streams."

Land Ordinance Survey System

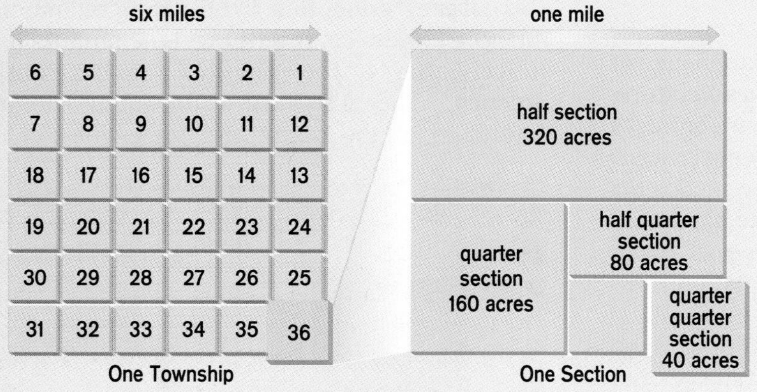

1. Why did Congress create the Northwest survey system?
2. What is the relationship between a township and a section?
3. Contrast political boundaries of countries around the world with those of states west of the Appalachian Mountains. Explain how the Northwest survey system might account for these differences.

Backyard History

Research. Have students find out how and when the land in their community was divided and whether there were boundary disputes. They should also discover how and when land was set aside for public schools, parks, and other special purposes, and what zoning regulations now apply.

Connections: Science and Technology

Reporting. Have students research and make oral or written reports about different kinds and methods of surveying, including such surveying tools as the transit and the invar tape.

Geography: A Key to Our Past

ANSWERS

1. To provide an orderly way to lay out boundaries for sale of new lands.
2. A township—six miles square—contained 36 sections, each one-mile square.
3. Most boundaries in the world do not follow any set patterns; many are formed by natural features like rivers. The Northwest System, dividing land into square sections, accounts for the precise checkerboard arrangement.

Section 5-2

Objectives

- ***Answer the Focus Question.***
- *Describe how Native Americans and African Americans were treated in colonial North America.*

Introducing THE SECTION

Benjamin Franklin described racial differences almost like a chain of color, with white on one end and black on the other:

“The Number of purely white People in the World is proportionately very small. All Africa is black or tawny [tan]. Asia chiefly tawny. America (exclusive of the new Comers) wholly so. And in Europe, the Spaniards, Italians, French, Russians, and Swedes are generally of what we call, swarthy [dark] Complexion; as are the Germans also, the Saxons only excepted, who with the English make the principal Body of White People on the face of the Earth.”

Ask: Why might Franklin have made these distinctions? What does it tell about the view of American leaders regarding the American identity?

As students read this section they should look for how English Americans narrowly defined the American identity.

B · A · C · K · G · R · O · U · N · D

Connections: Language
Noah Webster believed that Americans should speak and write English the same way. He saw, for instance, that a place for travelers to stay was called an “inn” in Connecticut but an “ordinary” in Virginia. In New England the word *clever* meant “shrewd,” but in the Southern states it meant “courteous.” In his dictionary, Webster included definitions of new words born from the American experience—such as *hickory*, *bullfrog*, *handy*, *skunk*, and *applesauce*.

Reduced student page in the Teacher's Edition

5-2 Seeking a National Identity

Focus: How was the American identity narrowly defined by English Americans, and how was that view challenged?

Although each state considered itself basically independent, many Patriot leaders encouraged people to think of themselves not mainly as citizens of states but as “Americans.” In the words of Alexander Hamilton, they were urged to “think continentally.”

Could the citizens of different states learn to see themselves as part of one **nation,** a group of people with a feeling of unity based on sharing a common land and a common past? George Washington knew that forming a government and winning the war had not necessarily united the people as a nation. As the defeated British troops sailed for England, Washington foresaw the challenge. “We are placed among the nations of the earth,” he said, “and have a character to establish.”

But what would this character be? The former colonists shared a common land, but what about a common past? Did they share a language, race, or culture? Did they share political beliefs and struggles? What common experiences might define what it meant to be an American?

A Narrow View

Many pointed to the struggle for independence as being part of the “American” past, but the people did not share a common culture, language, or race. Many came from different European cultures and spoke different languages. Those forced to come from Africa as slaves also represented a variety of cultures and languages. There were also the Native Americans, whose cultures had flourished long before the coming of the Europeans. What would be their relationship to the new nation?

European countries like France and England each had a dominant language and culture. Many European Americans thought that the same should be true of the United States. But what should their language and culture be?

The answer seemed obvious to most Patriot leaders. The English outnumbered other cultural and racial groups in the United States, making up about 60 percent of the white population. With the political and economic power in their hands, they felt they had the right to say that *their* language and culture were most “American.”

An “American” Language and Culture?

In looking for a way to bind people together as Americans, many leaders focused on the English language. How, they asked, could Americans ever hope to become one people without speaking the same language? Noah Webster, who later put together an American dictionary, declared that “a national language is a bond of national union.” He Americanized British spellings and predicted that American English would be better than British English.

Many English Americans hoped not only for a common language but also for a uniquely American culture. Writers and artists did indeed promote American pride. Poets celebrated the land itself, as in Joel Barlow's “The Vision of Columbus Praising America.” They also sang of the young country's future, as in the poetry of Phillis Wheatley, an

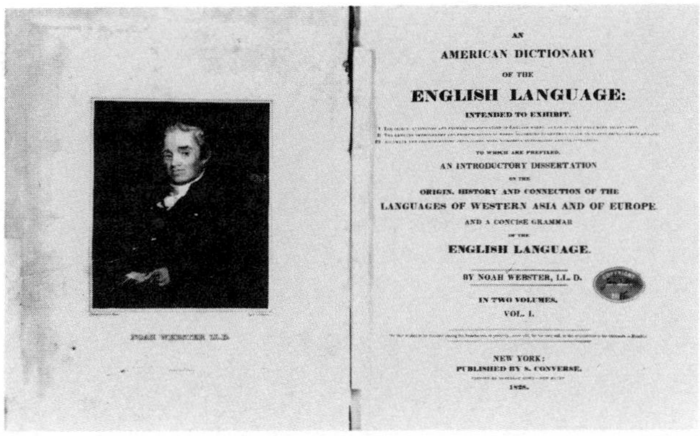

Connections: Literature

Jupiter Hammon was the first black poet to be published in America. His first poem appeared in 1761 when he was a slave for the Lloyd family in New York. Though they never met, Hammon wrote a poem honoring Phillis Wheatley in 1778: "An Address to Miss Phillis Wheatley, Ethiopian Poetess of Boston."

African American. History books like Mercy Otis Warren's three volumes on the Revolution encouraged a sense of a shared American past. Patriotic feelings were stirred by John Trumbull's Revolutionary War scenes and Charles Willson Peale's portraits of Washington and other war heroes.

These works of art and literature, however, were "American" only in being *about* America. Their style still imitated English traditions. Although promoting English as the national language, Webster worried that "an astonishing respect for the arts and literature of their parent country, and a blind imitation of its manners, are still prevalent among Americans." The question of what, if anything, was truly unique about American culture remained unanswered as long as English culture continued to dominate, leaving out the traditions of other racial and cultural groups.

In believing that their culture was superior and more American than others, English Americans reflected a common human prejudice: assuming that people whose race or culture are different from one's own are therefore inferior. People of other European ancestry could try to avoid the effects of this English-American prejudice. By adopting English customs and learning the English language, they could become **assimilated,** or absorbed into the dominant group. Perhaps they expected greater opportunities if they "fit in" with English-American society. As a French settler, Hector St. John de Crèvecoeur (KREV-KOOR), noted:

> *"What attachment can a poor European have for a country where he had nothing? The knowledge of the language, and love of a few kindred as poor as himself, were the only cords that tied him; his country is now that which gives him land, bread, protection, and consequence [importance]."*

Although some groups—such as German communities in Pennsylvania—were determined to preserve their own language and culture, the pressure to be assimilated was great. A traveler from Sweden said that he "found in this country scarcely one genuine Swede left. . . . The English are evidently swallowing up the people."

The English were not "swallowing up" Native and African Americans, however. These groups—like Hispanic and Asian Americans later—did not fit the English-American view of the "American" identity because that view was partly based on race. They were victims of the prejudice shared by many English and European Americans that white people were superior.

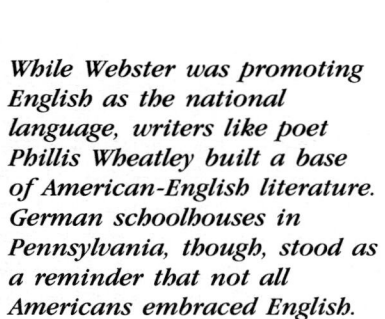

While Webster was promoting English as the national language, writers like poet Phillis Wheatley built a base of American-English literature. German schoolhouses in Pennsylvania, though, stood as a reminder that not all Americans embraced English.

Developing

THE SECTION

Multicultural Perspectives

Analyzing Primary Sources. Part of a poem by Phillis Wheatley appears below. Read it to students.

"I, young in life, by seeming cruel fate
Was snatch'd from Africa's fancy'd happy seat:

What pangs excruciating must molest,
What sorrows labour in my parent's breast?

Steel'd was that soul and by no misery mov'd
That from a father seiz'd his babe belov'd:

Such, such my case.
And can I then but pray
Others may never feel tyrannic sway?"

Ask: What personal experience was Wheatley relating? **(her abduction into slavery)** How did she say African families felt when their families were split by slavery? **(miserable, sorrowful, in great pain)** What did Wheatley mean when she said: "I then but pray/ Others may never feel tyrannic sway?" **(She hopes no other Africans will experience such cruelty.)**

Analyzing Primary Sources

Red Jacket. Red Jacket, a Seneca chief, worked his entire life to preserve the ancient customs of his people against attempts by whites to force their culture on the Seneca. Because of his activism, in the 1790s he came to be called by his Indian name Sagoyewatha (He Keeps Them Awake). Protesting Seneca land sales, the chief said:

"We stand a small island in the bosom of the great waters. . . . They rise, they press upon us and the waves will settle over us and we shall disappear forever. Who then lives to mourn us, white man? None."

Ask: To whom is Red Jacket referring with the words "the great waters"? **(white settlers)** What does Red Jacket think will happen to Native Americans as more white settlers move onto Indian land? **(Native Americans will disappear.)**

Connections: Religion

In 1787 two free African-American clergymen, Richard Allen and Absalom Jones attended services at a mixed-race church in Philadelphia. Allen and Jones refused to go to the balcony reserved for African Americans, so they were removed from the service. The two men then organized the Free African Society, a beneficial and mutual aid association. Allen later went on to found the Bethel African Methodist Episcopal Church and Jones became pastor of the African Protestant Episcopal Church. (The incident referred to here is described in the primary source on page 20 in *Readings in Literature and Primary Sources* in the Teacher's Resource Package.)

African Americans: Cultures Suppressed

In order to justify slavery, many whites had convinced themselves that blacks could not be assimilated. For if it was accepted that blacks could in theory become members of "American" society, then how could it be right to treat most of them as property rather than as people?

The heritage of African-American churches lives on today, as in this African Methodist Episcopal Church congregation in Los Angeles.

Meanwhile, in order to strengthen their control, slaveholders suppressed African cultures. They tried to create a sense of inferiority by banning African languages, religions, and art such as sculpture and metalwork. Drums were forbidden for fear that they could send messages about plans for slave revolts.

Although African Americans represented many different peoples and cultures, European Americans labeled them all "Negroes," from the Spanish word for "black"—as if their only identity was in the color of their skin. Discouraged from taking pride in their rich African cultures, they were also denied a place in the new "American" society.

As European Americans suppressed African cultures, they claimed they were trying to "civilize" blacks by teaching them Christian beliefs. Many

In the late 1700s many African-American churches were organized. Philadelphia's African Episcopal Church and others became centers of community life.

blacks did become Christians, not because they thought they needed to be "civilized," but because in Christianity they found a source of strength and hope. They became Christians in spite of the "Christianity" practiced by slaveholders.

By the late 1780s blacks, both slave and free, were organizing their own churches. These became the only places where blacks could legally gather in large groups, and so became centers of community life, fostering hope and pride.

Conflict With Native Americans

Self-interest also shaped European-American views of Native Americans, but in a different way. Many wanted to believe that Indians could join "American" society by adapting to "civilized" farming and becoming Christians. Congress favored assimilation and called for "utmost good faith" in dealings with Native Americans, hoping this policy would prevent conflict.

Settlers, however, were more interested in good soil than in good relations. As they kept taking Native-American lands, and as Native Americans

THE AMERICAN SPIRIT

Abigail Adams

The Pen of a Patriot

One day in 1775, after news of a patriot defeat, Abigail Adams wrote from Massachusetts to her husband in Philadelphia, "We are in no ways dispirited here. . . . If our men are all drawn off and we should be attacked, you would find a race of Amazons [women warriors] in America." This was a woman of strong spirit.

Born in 1744, the daughter of a Protestant minister, Adams was raised with little formal schooling. But her home was filled with conversation and books, and she eagerly sought knowledge about the world beyond her door.

In 1764 she married a young lawyer named John Adams. During the next ten years, while he established himself in law and politics, the

couple had five children. Then, in August 1774, John Adams set out for Philadelphia as a member of the Continental Congress.

With her husband away, Abigail avidly wrote letters that offer a colorful record of life in America. By mail, she engaged in political debates with her husband. She also wrote to her friend Mercy Otis Warren and others, such as James Madison and Thomas Jefferson.

She wrote passionately of the causes that mattered to her. Once, while her husband was a member of Congress, she urged him to "remember the ladies, and be more generous and favorable to them than your ancestors." On another occasion, she related that she had taught her free servant to read and write and had overcome the neighbors' objections by demanding, "Merely because his face is black is he to be denied instruction?"

Abigail Adams sacrificed her own comfort in the cause of freedom. At the height of the Revolutionary War, she summed up her feelings: "Difficult as the day is, cruel as this war has been . . . I would not exchange my country for the wealth of the Indies, or be any other than an American though I might be queen or empress of any nation."

rejected "white" ways, Congress's goals of peace and assimilation appeared increasingly unrealistic. Native-American and European-American cultures seemed destined to remain separate.

No Voice for Women

White women were considered to be Americans, of course, but their part in society was defined largely by white men. Jefferson expressed the common view of women's role in "shaping" public policy when he hoped that "our good ladies are contented to soothe and calm the minds of their husbands returning ruffled from political debate."

Women themselves were getting "ruffled" over the fact that they were given no voice in government. Abigail Adams, an early champion of women's rights, commented to her husband, "Remember, all men would be tyrants if they could." However, her interpretation of the words "all men are equally free" as "all people are equally free" was not shared by her husband nor by most other leading statesmen of the day.

Thinking Critically

Evaluation. Hold a class discussion on the following proposition: Women in colonial North America did not need the right to vote because their husbands had it. Women could make known their political views to the men, whose votes would reflect the influence of their wives.

Multicultural Perspectives

The system of slavery in the United States was based largely on the assumption of white superiority. Many white people had so convinced themselves of their superiority that they misinterpreted slave resistance. They labeled slaves as "lazy" and "stupid," failing to recognize that slaves had no incentive to work hard and often "played dumb" to avoid doing the will of slaveholders.

Active Learning

Cooperative Activity. One American pointed out the irony of white southern colonists criticizing the British government for denying their freedoms and rights while *"continuing this lawless, cruel, inhuman, and abominable practice of enslaving your fellow creatures."*

Refer students to the Declaration of Independence on pages 912—913, especially the section that lists abuses by the king. Then divide the class into small groups to rewrite this section from the point of view of enslaved Africans living in Virginia. Their documents should reflect protests against slave owners.

As a class, discuss the contradiction of signers of the Declaration continuing to own slaves even while demanding liberty from England.

Reduced student page in the Teacher's Edition

Toward a Broader National Identity

The Revolution did not change the status of African Americans, Native Americans, or women because most white men saw the war solely as a struggle to protect *their* rights and *their* freedom from tyranny. "Freedom" to them mainly meant freedom from being taxed by the government without their consent.

Despite the claim in the Declaration of Independence that "all men are created equal," most white Patriot leaders did not believe in equality for all. They wanted most of the political power to be in the hands of large property owners like themselves. People with little or no property, they believed, should have little or no voice in the government. John Adams, for instance, feared the effects of opening the door to equality:

> *"New claims will arise; women will demand a vote, lads from twelve to twenty-one will think their rights are not enough attended to, and every man who has not a farthing [a coin] will demand an equal voice with any other in all acts of state. It tends to prostrate [lower] all ranks to the common level."*

Adams and leaders like him assumed that their reasons for the Revolution were the only valid ones. However, their views were challenged by other Patriots, especially the thousands of African Americans and women who had also bravely put their lives on the line for liberty. These "forgotten" Patriots saw a broader meaning in the Declaration of Independence.

Meanwhile, there were already some signs that American society could provide freedom and opportunity for more than just white men with property. These signs included a movement to abolish slavery, an expansion of voting rights, and the principle of religious freedom.

Calls to abolish slavery. During the years leading up to the Revolution, African Americans, both slave and free, saw the glaring contradiction in white men crying out for liberty while denying it to black slaves. A slave in Concord, Massachusetts, had the following epitaph:

God
Wills us free.
Man
Wills us slaves.

I will as God wills,
God's will be done.

Here lies the body of JOHN JACK,
A native of Africa, who died March, 1773,
Aged about sixty years.

Tho' born in a land of slavery,
He was born free.
Tho' he lived in a land of liberty,
He lived a slave.

Death, the grand Tyrant,
Gave him his final emancipation
And set him on a footing with kings.

The Revolution's cry for liberty led many Americans, both white and black, to challenge slavery. Thomas Jefferson, for instance, opposed it in principle. In the southern states, though, slavery was closely tied to the economy. Like many southerners, Jefferson found himself balancing his moral beliefs against his economic interests. He continued to own slaves, telling himself that he would free them once he had gotten out of debt.

Opposition to slavery was stronger in the northern states, where the economy did not rely so heavily on slave labor. By 1780 Vermont and Pennsylvania had abolished slavery. In Massachusetts in 1781, a slave named Quock Walker sued for his freedom. He won the case, and the court declared that all slaves in the state should be freed. Mean-

Connections: Religion

Even though there was a movement toward religious freedom, many people continued to be intolerant of the beliefs of others. For instance, many Protestants continued to accuse Catholics of being more loyal to the Pope than to their country. Nevertheless, a principle had been firmly established: the American identity was not tied to any particular church.

The sight of slave auctions helped arouse support for the movement to abolish slavery. Such degrading treatment prompted an artist to create the powerful image and motto "Am I Not a Man and a Brother?" (facing page), which appeared frequently in anti-slavery literature.

while, some people not only called for an end to slavery but also objected to the narrow view of the American identity. A free African American named John Chavis declared, "I am Black. I am a true-born American and a revolutionary soldier."

Extending voting rights. Most states continued to allow only men who owned property to vote or hold political office. During and after the Revolution, however, property qualifications for voting were reduced almost everywhere. Some states extended voting rights further. In Massachusetts, free African Americans and Native Americans could vote, and for a time New Jersey allowed women to vote. These practices suggested that more people could eventually have a voice in government.

Religious freedom. The right to religious freedom took a firm hold during the early years of independence. Leading the way was Virginia's Statute of Religious Freedom, written by Jefferson. Under that law, citizens were no longer forced to pay taxes to support an "official" state church.

The recognition that a citizen could practice any religion—or no religion at all—and still be an American was an important sign. It suggested that American society could be seen as **pluralistic,** or made up of many different groups, each with its distinctive characteristics.

A crack in the mold. Most white Americans, however, continued to define the American identity largely in terms of race and cultural background. To them, America remained a "white man's country." People who would not, or could not, fit the narrow English-American mold were "outsiders."

Nevertheless, religious pluralism showed that such a narrow mold could be cracked. If people could accept that being American had nothing to do with belonging to a particular church, could they not also come to believe that it was not tied to any one race or cultural group? In seeking a national identity, Americans would continue to face that question.

Section Review

1. Identification. Define *nation, assimilated,* and *pluralistic.*

2. Comprehension. How and why was the American identity narrowly defined in the early years of the nation?

3. Analysis. In what ways were the African American and Native American cultures treated differently by most European Americans? In what ways were they treated alike?

4. Comprehension. What were some signs that there could eventually be a broader view of the American identity? Explain.

Linking Past and Present. What signs do you see today that the view of the American identity has become broader than it was in the 1780s? Explain.

Writing About History

Editorial. Unmarried New Jersey women who owned property were allowed to vote by their new state constitution. (This right was taken away in 1807.) The poem below appeared in a newspaper during that period. Have students write an editorial expressing their support or opposition to the ideas expressed in the poem.

"What we read in
days of yore, the
woman's occupation,
Was to direct the wheel
and loom, not to direct
the nation.

This narrow-minded policy by us hath met
detection;
While woman's bound,
man can't be free, nor
have a fair election."

Section Review

ANSWERS

1. Definitions for following terms on pages indicated in parentheses: ***nation*** (124), ***assimilated*** (125), ***pluralistic*** (129).
2. American identity defined in terms of English language, culture, and traditions. Americans of English lineage (majority of the population) assumed their culture was superior.
3. African Americans despised, suppressed. Native Americans looked down on, but not suppressed. Many favored assimilation of Indians. Both cultures kept separate from whites.
4. Growing opposition to slavery, extension of voting rights, guarantee of religious freedom.
Linking Past and Present. Growing respect for and interest in African-American and Native-American cultures and growing power of various rights groups.

Section 5-3

Objectives

- ***Answer the Focus Question.***
- *Identify economic problems created by the Articles of Confederation.*
- *Describe the problems that led to Shays' Rebellion.*

Introducing THE SECTION

Read and discuss with students the following quotation from Harriet Martineau: *"There are many soils and many climates included within the boundary line of the United States; many countries; and one rule cannot be laid down for all."*

Ask students to quickly scan the headings in this section, then list what they believe were the major challenges faced by Americans in the years between the end of the Revolution and the beginning of the Constitutional Convention.

Discuss the potential for so many states, with such diverse peoples, economies, and lifestyles to somehow unify under one rule, or constitution.

B · A · C · K · G · R · O · U · N · D

Connections: Economics
After the nation won independence, a variety of foreign coins and paper money circulated in the United States. On this page and the next are pictured, left to right: Continental $1 coin, Massachusetts 20 shilling bill, Continental half dollar bill, Rhode Island $2 bill, Massachusetts coin, New Jersey 12 shilling bill, New England coin, Continental penny.

Reduced student page in the Teacher's Edition

5-3 *The Country Adrift*

Focus: Why did many Americans believe that a stronger national government was needed?

At the First Continental Congress in 1774, Patrick Henry had declared, "The distinctions between Virginians, Pennsylvanians, New Yorkers, and New Englanders are no more. I am not a Virginian, but an American." This view was reflected in the national motto adopted in 1782: "E pluribus unum"—"Out of many, one." Such statements, however, reflected hope, not reality. As Congress was hampered by differences between the states, George Washington saw "one head gradually changing into thirteen."

An Unfavorable Balance of Trade with Britain

The root of most of Congress's problems was the economy, which was especially hurt by an unfavorable balance of trade with Britain. Though still buying American raw materials and manufactured goods, Britain banned American ships from trading in the British West Indies. Farmers, merchants, and fishers of the New England and Middle states lost their most important market.

At the same time, peace revived the American taste for British goods. British merchants rushed to sell goods at prices so low that American manufacturers could not compete. Soon, the United States was buying much more from Britain than it sold to that country. And it was paying for these goods with a dwindling supply of gold and silver.

One solution might have been to impose tariffs. Tariffs would raise prices of British goods, encouraging Americans to buy products made at home. However, Congress had no authority to set tariffs. States getting income from their own tariffs rejected proposals to give up that power to Congress.

Congress seemed helpless in the face of British trade restrictions. One Englishman scoffed, "It will not be an easy matter to bring the American States to act as a nation. They are not to be feared as such by us." Clearly, the young country would have to show more unity at home before it would be taken seriously abroad.

Problems in the West

Meanwhile, Congress was facing challenges from Britain and Spain in the western lands. It was unable to enforce the treaty ending the war with Britain because it could not force the states to pay debts owed to British citizens or to restore Loyalist property. For its part, Britain ignored American demands that British troops leave posts in the Northwest, saying that the posts would be held until British creditors were paid.

Spain also sensed the weakness of Congress and felt free to try to stop American westward expansion. In 1784 it closed the Mississippi to American settlers, taking away their only economical way to transport goods. It would only reopen the river to

The value of American currency dropped as the states and Congress created more money. People preferred coins, as bills were often not worth the paper they were printed on.

settlers who swore allegiance to Spain. Disgusted with Congress, many settlers were tempted to accept the offer. After traveling throughout the western lands, Washington noted that "the western settlers stand as it were on a pivot. The touch of a feather would turn them either way."

Members of Congress could not come to an agreement on how to deal with Spain. Those from the New England states cared little about the Mississippi and instead wanted to open up more overseas trade with Spain. Those from southern states refused to consider any treaty that let Spain control the Mississippi. Pulled in different directions, Congress found it almost impossible to set foreign policy.

American Voices

"A wagonload of money will scarcely purchase a wagonload of provisions."

—George Washington

Rivalries Between the States

The conflicting interests of the states also led to squabbles between state governments themselves. In general, each was looking out for itself, rather than for the country as a whole. Some even engaged in tariff battles. When New York taxed oysters from Massachusetts, Massachusetts struck back with a tariff on nails from New York.

Meanwhile, rivalries over land claims heated up. One British observer described Americans as having "no center of union and no common interest. . . . A disunited people till the end of time, suspicious and distrustful of each other." The ideal of "perpetual union" spoken of in the Articles of Confederation seemed destined to dissolve.

Debts and Worthless Currency

Each state was more concerned with its own debts than with the nation's. One member of Congress remarked that asking the states for money was like talking to the dead. Meanwhile, the states continued to deny Congress the power to levy taxes.

Congress was also unable to prevent a steep drop in the value of American currency. During the war, the Continental Congress had printed over $200 million in paper money, which it did not have enough gold or silver to back.

People soon lost confidence in these Continental dollars. In 1779 General Washington complained that "a wagonload of money will scarcely purchase a wagonload of provisions." Meanwhile, the states were printing their own money, and a dozen kinds of nearly worthless currency circulated along with the Continentals.

The increase in paper money led to **inflation,** a rise in prices which causes a decline in the value of money. A single national currency could have brought some order to the nation's finances, but Congress lacked the power to stop the states from printing their own money.

Shays' Rebellion

By the mid-1780s the country was in the grip of a **depression**, a long sharp decline in economic activity. Among those hardest hit were former Patriot soldiers, most of whom were farmers and laborers. In their pockets were papers from Congress, promising that they would be paid.

In Massachusetts, especially, small farmers were hurt by the economic downturn. During the war they had made great profits supplying the army. Now, faced with few peacetime buyers, they had to plow their crops back into the ground. But that ground, now producing little cash income, was taxed heavily.

Developing THE SECTION

Limited English Proficiency

Group Discussion. Have students cite the main weaknesses of the Articles of Confederation as you write them on the chalkboard. **(Government lacked power to levy taxes or set tariffs and had no executive branch to enforce laws nor a judicial branch to interpret them.)** Then have students meet in small groups to discuss how these weaknesses were reflected in each of the following problems:

1. The unfavorable balance of trade **(inability to impose tariffs allowed imports from Britain to be sold for less than American goods)**
2. Currency problems **(Congress could not prohibit states from issuing money; American currency lost value because no gold backing)**
3. Shays' Rebellion **(raised questions regarding ability of national government to maintain law and order)**

Active Learning

Debate. Have students work in teams to prepare a debate on Shays' Rebellion. One side can argue in favor of the farmers, explaining why they had a right to rebel. The other side can argue in favor of the government, explaining why it had a right to put down the rebellion. Both sides of the debate should make comparisons between Shays' Rebellion and the Revolutionary War.

Limited English Proficiency

Cooperative Activity. In our nation's history, Shays' Rebellion was not the only social movement composed mostly of veterans enduring post-war hard times. Have students work in pairs to research the "Bonus Army" of 1932. They should try to determine the causes of the Bonus Army's march on Washington and what happened to the veterans once they got to the nation's capital. Have them compare Shays' Rebellion with the Bonus Army's march on Washington.

Writing About History

Essay. Historians differ in their views of the Confederation period. In 1888, John Fiske's *The Critical Period of American History, 1783–1789* described the six years after the Revolutionary War as *"the most critical moment in all the history of the American people."*

In 1940 Merrill Jensen argued in *The Articles of Confederation* that this period was not as critical as previously thought—the nation's economy was expanding, states were successfully dealing with financial problems, and the central government was not inept. "*The fact that the Articles of Confederation were supplanted by another constitution,*" Merrill wrote, *"is no proof either of their success or of their failure."*

Have students write an essay supporting one of the two points of view of the Confederation period. They should provide evidence from the text to support their opinions. Discuss students' conclusions, comparing points of view.

B · A · C · K · G · R · O · U · N · D

Connections: Politics

Shays' rebellion had little focus. One of Shays' followers urged on the mob: "*My boys, you are going to fight for liberty. If you wish to know what liberty is, I will tell you. It is for every man to do what he pleases, to make other people do as you please to have them, and to keep folks from serving the devil.*"

George Washington noted that the national government had lacked the power to stop the rebellion: "*You talk . . . of employing influence to appease the present tumults in Massachusetts. . . .* Influence *is not* government. *Let us have a government by which our lives, liberties, and properties will be secured, or let us know the worst at once.*"

Despair led to bloodshed as Shays' Rebellion erupted in January 1787. As a present-day marker bears witness, within two months the rebellion had been crushed.

The legislature was determined to pay its debts, but not simply by printing nearly worthless paper money. Instead it voted for high taxes, to be paid in gold or silver coins.

Some farmers borrowed gold and silver to pay their taxes. When later they were unable to pay off their loans, creditors took them to court. The judges ordered that the farmers' crops, livestock, or land be sold to pay the debts. Many who failed to pay were jailed. "In 1786," one report said, "not a few of these poor creatures, blue with prison mold, were those who had fought for freedom."

Throughout the summer of 1786, farmers begged the legislature for help. They wanted a law permitting them to pay debts with their crops, and some also asked to have more paper money printed. Creditors, however, wanted to be repaid in gold or silver, not in paper money. When the legislature refused to help, some farmers took action. In county after county, angry groups broke up court sessions to prevent judges from ordering the farms sold or sending debtors to prison.

A former war hero named Daniel Shays emerged as the farmers' leader. In January 1787, he and 1,200 followers marched on the Confederation arsenal at Springfield to seize a supply of arms. In response, the governor called out the state militia. When Shays' force moved to take the arsenal, the troops opened fire, scattering the farmers and leaving four lying dead in the snow.

By the end of February, the rebellion had been crushed. Meanwhile, the nation's economy was recovering. But the rebellion had sent waves of uneasiness through the states. Congress had been unable to resolve the crisis, and many Americans believed that a stronger central government was needed to maintain order and solve the economic problems that had caused the uprising.

Toward a Constitutional Convention

Even before Shays' Rebellion, many Americans had seen the need for cooperation between the states to deal with economic problems. Officials from Maryland and Virginia, for instance, met in 1785 to work out an agreement on navigation rights. Encouraged by their success, they agreed to meet the following year and to invite representatives of the other states to discuss broader trade issues.

When the meeting took place in September 1786 at Annapolis, Maryland, delegates from only five states were present. James Madison of Virginia was there, as was Alexander Hamilton of New York. Both were young politicians who supported a strong national government.

No agreement could be reached because the meeting was only sparsely attended. However, the delegates—spurred by Madison and Hamilton—called for a new convention in Philadelphia the following May to discuss ways of strengthening the national government. During the winter, as news of Shays' Rebellion spread, many state legislatures agreed to send delegates, even though Congress had not approved the call for a convention.

Recognizing that the delegates were going to meet with or without its permission, Congress finally endorsed the convention in February 1787, instructing that it be "for the sole and express purpose of revising the Articles of Confederation." Only Rhode Island refused to participate. Benjamin Rush—Philadelphia physician, Patriot, signer of the Declaration of Independence—tried to encourage people to support the upcoming convention. He said that the Revolutionary War was only the "first act of the great drama" to be finished:

> *"Patriots of 1774, 1775, 1776—heroes of 1778, 1779, 1780! Come forward! Your country demands your services! . . . Hear it proclaiming, in sighs and groans, in its governments, in its finances, in its trade, in its manufactures, in its morals, and its manners, 'The Revolution is not over!'"*

Section Review

1. Identification. Define *inflation* and *depression.*

2. Comprehension. Explain how the unfavorable balance of trade with Britain hurt the nation's economy.

3. Analysis. Why did European countries have little or no respect for the American government under the Articles of Confederation?

4. Evaluation. What led to Shays' Rebellion? Do you think the rebellion was justified? Explain.

Connections to Themes

Balancing Unity and Diversity

What is an American? That question, raised even before the first shots were fired in the Revolutionary War, is still asked today. For how can a "government by the people" survive unless the people share a sense of purpose?

The American Revolution gave birth to a country quite different from those in Europe. Governments of countries such as France, England, and Spain were each built upon the foundation of an existing nation—with a language, culture, and history dating back centuries. In America, however, an independent government was created before the people had become a nation. Cultural differences and tensions between states made it difficult to inspire a sense of national unity.

Of course, Americans could look to a shared—though short—history. The Revolutionary War itself provided heroic people, symbols, and deeds. Americans could also claim a more distant past in such events as the Pilgrims' landing and Columbus's voyages. Writing and art also helped build a unifying tradition. Later generations have continued to celebrate the American past, finding more heroes and events to inspire patriotic pride.

A shared history was easier to identify then than a shared culture, and the same is true today. American culture remains a mingling of many cultures. In that mingling lies America's uniqueness, but also a continuing source of conflict. America's strength depends in part on respecting cultural differences while recognizing common beliefs.

Thinking Critically

Analysis. Refer students to the words of Benjamin Rush on this page. **Ask:** What did Rush mean when he said, *"The revolution is not over!"*? Do all revolutions involve armed conflict?

Section Review

ANSWERS

1. See definitions for following terms on text pages indicated in parentheses: *inflation* (131), *depression* (131).
2. Nation's gold and silver supply dwindled; buying power shrank; manufacturers and tradespeople sold fewer goods.
3. Rivalries between states weakened powers of Congress.
4. Farmers dissatisfied with legislature's inability to help solve debt problems brought on by depression. Led by Shays, they took action. Students' views will depend on how far they think people should go in dealing with a government that does not answer their needs.

Chapter Survey

ANSWERS

Using New Vocabulary

1. *Republic* and *nation* refer to large units of population. *Republic* is form of government. *Nation* is people who share common past and cultural heritage.
2. *Constitutions* and *bill of rights* refer to government. *Constitution* is general plan of government; *bill of rights* is more specific, lists rights and freedoms.
3. *Assimilated* and *pluralistic* describe how people of different backgrounds participate in larger group. *Assimilated* people give up old traditions, taking on ways of dominant group. In *pluralistic* society, traditions of different people coexist.

Reviewing the Chapter

1. Bicameral legislatures with increased power; elected judges; governor's power severely limited.
2. Wage war, make peace, make treaties, request troops and money from states, coin and borrow money, set standards for weights and measures, set up postal service. Lacked power to tax or enforce Congressional decisions.
3. Land Ordinance of 1785; Northwest Ordinance of 1787.
4. English settlers most numerous.
5. To strengthen control, slaveholders suppressed Africans by banning African languages, religion, and art.
6. Abolition of slavery followed revolutionary idea of liberty for all. Slavery not abolished in South where economy most dependent on it.
7. War debts, unfavorable balance of trade, inflation, lack of single national currency.
8. Congress lacked power to improve national economy, unable to maintain order.
9. Unable to oust British troops from Northwest because debts owed to British citizens unpaid; conclude trade agreement with Great Britain; prevent Spain from controlling Mississippi River.
10. To revise Articles of Confederation to strengthen national government.

Thinking Critically

1. To ensure orderly settlement and establishment of representative government in newly-formed states.
2. To ensure people considered themselves as one nation, not thirteen.

Reduced student page in the Teacher's Edition

Chapter Survey

Using New Vocabulary

The vocabulary terms in each pair listed below are related to each other. For each pair, explain what the two terms have in common. Also explain how they are different.

Example: *Tariffs* and *inflation* are both economic terms. Tariffs are taxes on imports or exports, while inflation refers to a rise in prices.

1. *republic* and *nation*
2. *constitutions* and *bill of rights*
3. *assimilated* and *pluralistic*

Reviewing the Chapter

1. What were three features of the state constitutions that limited government power? Explain.
2. What powers did Congress have under the Articles? What powers did it lack, and why?
3. How did Congress provide for the orderly settlement of the western lands?
4. Why did the English language and culture become dominant in American society?
5. How and why were African Americans deprived of their cultural heritage?
6. Why did some states take steps to abolish slavery? Why did others keep slavery?
7. Describe three of the economic problems facing the country after the Revolutionary War.
8. What weaknesses of the Confederation did Shays' Rebellion draw attention to? Explain.
9. Describe two foreign policy problems after the war and explain why they were difficult.
10. Why was a convention called to meet in 1787?

Thinking Critically

1. Analysis. Why was it important for Congress to control the development of the western lands?
2. Analysis. Why do you think many Americans believed a national identity was needed?
3. Analysis. Compare the efforts to promote cultural unity with the efforts to allow diversity. Which had greater influence? Explain.
4. Evaluation. Do you think efforts to limit the central government's power caused more harm than good in the young nation? Explain.
5. Evaluation. Alexander Hamilton called Congress "fit neither for war nor peace." Do you agree or disagree? Explain.

Using Geography

Match the letters on the map with the locations listed below. Explain the importance of each place during the nation's early years.

1. Mississippi River
2. Northwest Territory
3. Springfield, Massachusetts
4. Cumberland Gap
5. Annapolis, Maryland

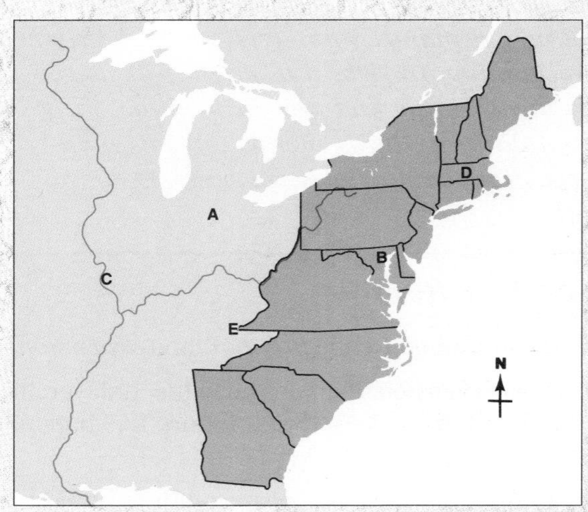

3. To promote cultural unity: English as national language; American art and literature imitated English traditions, leaving out other racial and cultural groups. Many Europeans chose to be assimilated. African cultures suppressed; efforts to assimilate Native Americans. Freedom of religion and end of state-supported churches allowed some diversity. So too, laws in Massachusetts that allowed free African Americans and Native Americans to vote and in New Jersey, women. Push for unity stronger than support for diversity.
4. Students might mention that central government's limited powers led to lost markets for farmers, flood of cheap imported goods that gave no incentive to American business, nonpayment of debts by individuals, downturn of economy.
5. Answers may include: Congress powerless to affect nations' domestic problems or establish effective foreign policy.

Using Geography

1. C, western border of United States claims.
2. A, eventually five new states carved out of area.
3. D, site of Shays' Rebellion, which focused attention on weakness of Confederation government.
4. E, pass in Appalachian Mountains through which Wilderness Road established to Kentucky.
5. B, site of 1786 conference of states to discuss trade issues.

History and You

Answers will vary depending on the state in which students live.

Applying Social Studies Skills

1. New England states; primarily settled by English.
2. African.
3. Graph more clearly shows large percentage of English colonists, thus why English was dominant language.

Writing About Issues

Answers will vary. Students should mention specific protest(s) against government actions or policies and use valid arguments to support their opinions.

History and You

The constitutions of the American states were the first written constitutions in the world. Find information on your state's earliest constitution and its present constitution. When was each one adopted? Compare what each says about voting requirements, qualifications for holding office, status of slavery, and individual liberties.

Applying Social Studies Skills

Analyzing Maps and Graphs

After studying the map and graph on the right, answer the following questions.

1. Which had the least cultural mix—the New England states, the Middle states, or the Southern states? Explain.

2. What was the second largest cultural group?

3. Which shows better why English was the dominant language—the map or the graph? Explain.

Writing About Issues

The Issue: *Is it ever right for Americans to use force against their elected governments?*

Shays' Rebellion brought into focus the question of whether citizens have a right to use violence against their elected governments. Shays and the other rebel farmers had resorted to force after the Massachusetts legislature denied their requests for changes in the tax laws. Samuel Adams and many other Patriot leaders condemned the rebels, insisting that Shays' Rebellion was different from the American rebellion against the British. Americans, they argued, did not have the right to use force against elected governments.

From the early years of our country to the present, citizens have at times used violence to protest government actions or policies. When, if ever, do you think violent protest is justified? Write a short speech explaining your opinion.

Settlement by Nationality 1790

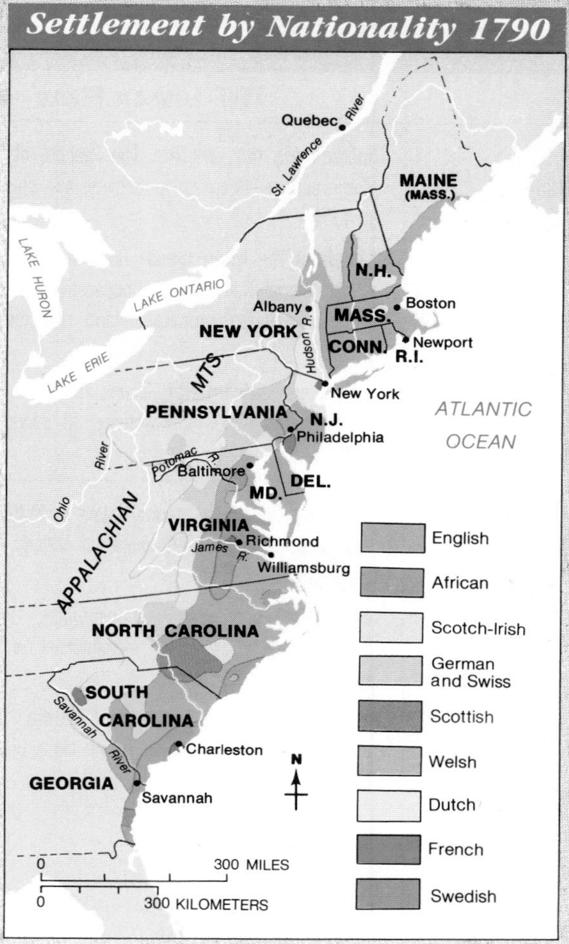

Population by Nationality 1790

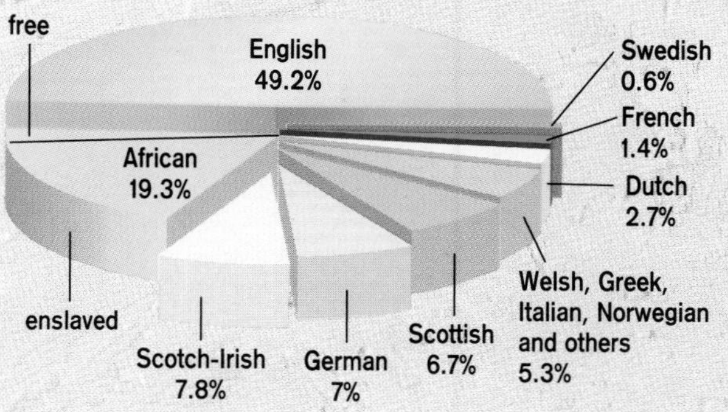

Chapter 6

Creating the Constitution

Planning Guide

	Student Text	TWE Lesson Plans	Support Materials
SECTION 1	**Section 6–1** (1–3 Days) **The Constitutional Convention,** pp 138–145 The American Spirit: James Madison, p 140 Review/Evaluation Section Review, p 145	**Introducing the Chapter:** The Process of Compromise—Cooperative Activity, one class period, p 135B **Teaching the Main Ideas:** Reporting on the Constitutional Convention—Cooperative Activity, one week student preparation and one class period, p 135B **Reinforcement Activity:** Issues and Compromises—Individual Activity, 30 minutes, p 135C	★ **Read to Remember,** Section 1 ● **Section Activities,** Section 1 Δ **Enrichment Activities,** Section 1 ● **Geography Activities,** Section 1 Δ **Readings,** Madison, Debate on Representation ● **Tests and Quizzes,** Section 1 Quiz
SECTION 2	**Section 6–2** (1–3 Days) **The Living Constitution,** pp 146–153 Connections to Themes: Shaping Democracy, p 153 Point of View: The Legacy of the Framers, p 154–155 Review/Evaluation Section Review, p 153 Chapter 6 Survey, pp 156–157 Skills, pp 156–157 Using New Vocabulary Thinking Critically Using Geography Applying Social Studies Skills: Interpreting Flow Charts Applying Thinking Skills: Comparing	**Teaching the Main Ideas:** Nation or State: Which should Be Stronger?—Cooperative Activity, one class period, p 135C **Evaluating Progress:** The Constitution: "The Supreme Law of the Land"—Individual Activity, one class period, p 135C **Enrichment Activity:** Who Are "We the People"?—Individual Activity, one class period, p 135D	★ **Read to Remember,** Section 2 ● **Section Activities,** Section 2 Δ **Enrichment Activities,** Section 2 Δ **Readings,** Alan Dershowitz, *Orlando* v. *Laird* ● **Tests and Quizzes,** Section 2 Quiz, Chapter 6 Test (Forms A and B) **Additional Resources** ● **Active Learning** Δ **GTV Videodiscs** Δ **Transparencies and Activity Book** ● **Testing Software** ★ **Chapter Summaries** **Key:** ★ **For Extra Support** ● **For All Students** Δ **For Enrichment**

Overview

The drama of the Constitutional Convention involves conflict and compromise among the delegates who met to frame a structure of government for their young country. Procedural matters were quickly settled, as was the decision not to revise the Articles of Confederation. After these early agreements, disputes erupted between small and large states and between slave and nonslave states. Issue by issue the delegates arrived at compromises on representation, presidential election, slavery, and division of powers.

Delegates left the convention with a plan of government to present to the states for ratification. Federalists and Anti-Federalists prepared arguments for and against ratifying the document. After long debates in the state conventions, the Constitution was ratified in 1790.

The amendment process and a flexible framework of general principles have enabled the Constitution to survive as the oldest written plan of government still in effect. Flexibility has also opened the door for debate on how constitutional principles should be applied to specific situations. Debates continue over the interpretation of such basic principles as federalism, separation of powers, checks and balances, protection of individual rights, and representative government. Twentieth-century case studies underscore issues relating to these principles.

Activity Objectives

After completing the activities, students should be able to

- describe the key events and personalities at the Constitutional Convention.
- compare the views of the Federalists and the Anti-Federalists.
- explain how the principles of the Constitution continue to affect the daily life of citizens.
- identify the major issues and compromises at the Constitutional Convention.
- describe the changing meaning of "We the People."

Introducing the Chapter

The Process of Compromise

This cooperative activity requires most of a class period.

Chapter 6 shows that the delegates were able to compromise on major issues in creating the Constitution. To help students appreciate the role of compromise in the convention, this introductory activity involves them in a group task that requires compromise.

Write the following items and prices on the chalkboard:

bicycle	$200	jacket	$70
charity donation	20	jeans	40
college fund	150	running shoes	80
compact disc	15	stereo repair	75
concert ticket	30	video game	40
dinner	20	watch	50

Tell students to imagine that they each have $200 to spend. Then ask them to choose which items from the list they would buy. Allow time for students to complete their lists.

Divide the class into groups of five. Ask each group to discuss its members' individual lists. Why did they choose certain items? Were there items they wanted to buy but decided against? Then direct each group to produce a group list of items they would buy for $150. Allow about 20 minutes for students to compromise. Then have a representative from each group read its list and write it on the chalkboard to make comparisons easier.

After a class discussion of their choices, challenge students to think about how their groups compromised in making their lists. Be sure students understand the meaning of the word *compromise*—a settlement in which each side agrees to give up a part of what it demands. Ask these questions about the process:

- How did the group get started?
- Was a leader appointed or did one emerge?
- How did the group work out disagreements?
- What problems were created by the requirement to produce only one list?
- Was everyone in the group satisfied with the list?
- What was most difficult about this group task?
- What can be gained or lost by compromise?
- What communication skills are needed to reach a compromise?

Review with the class some of the differing interests of the states represented at the convention. Then explain that Chapter 6 is about the compromises that enabled the framers to create the Constitution.

Teaching the Main Ideas

Section 6-1: Reporting on the Constitutional Convention

For this cooperative activity, allow a week for preparation and one class period for student presentations.

This activity, which can be used after Section 6-1 or at the end of the chapter, will help students carefully examine the events and personalities that dominated the Constitutional Convention.

Ask students to explain why delegates felt it necessary to hold the convention in secrecy. Then ask them to imagine that television was available during the 1780s and that the convention was a major news event even though cameras were not allowed in the meeting room. Tell students that they will pose as television reporters assigned to do a story on the convention.

Direct students to organize themselves into teams of four reporters to produce a news broadcast to present to the class. Their reports can cover one significant day in the convention or be a wrap-up at the convention's conclusion. Reports should include some background information on the delegates and the convention's setting in Philadelphia. They should summarize issues, arguments, and compromises and use direct quotations when possible. Emphasize that each report should end with an assessment of the job ahead for supporters and opponents of ratification of the Constitution.

After the groups present their reports, have the class assess them in terms of how well they identify major issues, recognize the delegates' ability to compromise, and explain compromises. Discuss how daily news coverage might have changed the outcome of the convention.

Teaching the Main Ideas

Section 6-2: Nation or State: Which Should Be Stronger?

This cooperative activity requires most of a class period.

This activity provides an opportunity to evaluate views of the Federalists and the Anti-Federalists concerning the Constitution. Students are to explain and defend either the Federalist or the Anti-Federalist positions in a "deliberate discussion" format.

Call on one or two students to briefly state the Federalist and Anti-Federalist positions on the Constitution. Divide the class into pairs and have each pair designate one partner to represent the Anti-Federalist point of view and the other to defend the Federalist position. Direct each student to write three to five statements summarizing the position he or she represents. Have members of the class briefly share and discuss their statements.

Direct students to move their desks to sit facing their partners. Describe deliberate discussion as a written dialogue in which one partner begins by writing a single, clear argument in favor of his or her beliefs. For example, the Federalist might write: "A strong national government can best represent the interests of all the people." That person then passes his or her statement to the partner. The partner responds (in writing) to the written statement. For example, the Anti-Federalist might respond: "A central government is too removed from citizens to understand their needs. Representatives should meet in a location close to the people whose interests they seek to protect." The partner then writes another argument. Repeat the process for about four rounds.

Conclude by discussing as a class the best arguments for each position. Ask students to consider what the Anti-Federalists would think if they returned to the United States today. Were their concerns justified?

Reinforcement Activity

Section 6-1: Issues and Compromises

This individual activity requires about 30 minutes.

In Section 6-1 students learn how conflicting views of government were resolved at the convention. This activity can be used to reinforce understanding of the key issues and compromises of the convention.

Remind students that the delegates faced many issues requiring compromise if a plan of government was to be created. Write the following issues on the chalkboard, excluding the answers:

- *How many representatives should each state have in the legislature?* (*Some options*: Each state's population would determine the number of its representatives in Congress; each state would have an equal number of votes. *Compromise*: Representation in the House would be based on state population; each state, regardless of population, would have two senators.)
- *Who will have the power to regulate the slave trade: the national government or the states?* (*Some options*: National government will regulate all trade and ban slave trade; each state will regulate its slave trade. *Compromise:* National government will regulate trade but cannot interfere with slave trade until 1808.)
- *How will slaves be counted in determining the number of representatives from each state?* (*Some options*: Each slave counted as a person; slaves will not be counted. *Compromise*: Each slave counted as three fifths of a person.)
- *Who will elect the President?* (*Some options*: President directly elected by citizens or by state legislatures. *Compromise:* Electoral College will elect President.)
- *Who will elect the members of Congress?* (*Some options*: Members directly elected by citizens or by members of state legislatures. *Compromise*: Citizens elected members of the House; state legislatures elect senators.)

Have each student copy the issues, leaving ample space between them to fill in information. Explain that for each issue students are to list two options proposed by delegates for resolving the issue and are to describe the compromise reached. Work through the first issue with the class.

Conclude by having students discuss which compromises are still in effect and which have been changed since 1787. (Compromises still in effect: representation in the House and Senate, election of President by Electoral College. Compromises that have been changed: counting a slave as three fifths of a person in determining state population; election of senators by state legislatures.)

Evaluating Progress

Section 6-2: The Constitution: "The Supreme Law of the Land"

This individual activity may be completed in class or assigned as homework.

As citizens, students need to understand that constitutional issues are still being raised today. In this activity students use newspaper and magazine articles to evaluate the role of the Constitution in daily life and to understand its continuing importance as "the supreme law of the land."

Ask students to find one newspaper or magazine article that describes a current event related to each of the following constitutional principles: federalism, separation of powers, checks and balances, and individual rights. For each article, students are to summarize the event reported and to describe how the constitutional principle involved could affect his or her life.

Students' work should be evaluated on the correct identification of the constitutional principles involved and on the accuracy in applying the principles to daily life.

Enrichment Activity

Section 6-2: Who are "We the People"?

This individual activity requires a class period.

Chapters 3 through 6 examine different dimensions of the country's early struggle for democracy and the associated questions of who was to be entitled to government-protected rights. This activity is designed to challenge students to clarify how the meaning of "We, the people of the United States" differs today from its meaning in 1787. Use the activity at the end of the chapter.

With students, read the Preamble to the Constitution on page 900. Explain that the Preamble is a statement of principles and the foundation upon which the Constitution's framers built our structure of government. Point out how clearly the Preamble states that the new government is to stem from the will of the people and to serve their interests. Emphasize, however, that the definition of "the people" in 1787 was different from its definition today.

Direct students to write an essay to answer three questions:

- To whom did the words "the people" refer in 1787?
- To whom do those words refer today?
- How have changes in the meaning of "the people" been reflected in the Constitution?

When students have completed their essays, ask them to explain their view of what effect the expansion of "We, the people" has had on the nation.

Bibliography and Audiovisual Material

Teacher Bibliography

1787: the Day-to-Day Story of the Constitutional Convention. Compiled by historians of the Independence National Historical Park. New York: Exeter, 1987.

Corwin, Edward S. *The Constitution and What it Means Today.* Princeton, NJ: Princeton University Press, 1979.

Rutland, Robert A. *The Birth of the Bill of Rights, 1776–1791.* Boston: Northeastern University Press, 1991.

Student Bibliography

Commager, Henry S. *Great Constitution.* New York: Macmillan, 1961.

Lurio, Eric. *The Cartoon Guide to the Constitution of the United States.* New York: Barnes and Noble, 1987.

Van Doren, Carl. *The Great Rehearsal: The Story of the Making and Ratifying of the Constitution of the United States.* New York: Viking Penguin, 1986.

Films, Videocassettes, and Videodiscs

Constitution of the United States. 22 min. EBEC. Movie.

The Living Constitution. 16 min. English/Spanish versions. AIMS Media. Videodisc.

The US Constitution: A Document for Democracy. 25 min. SVE. Videocassette.

Filmstrips

How A Bill Becomes A Law. Associated Press.

The U.S. Constitution in Action. Random House Media.

Computer Software

The Constitition and the Government of the United States. Apple. Educational Activities.

To Preserve, Protect and Defend. Apple. MECC.

Chapter 6

Objectives

- Identify the major issues debated at the Constitutional Convention of 1787.
- Describe how constitutional issues have arisen throughout American history.

Introducing THE CHAPTER

For suggestions on introducing Chapter 6, refer to page 135B in the Teacher's Edition.

Developing THE CHAPTER

For activities and teaching strategies to help you reinforce and enrich chapter content see pages 135B–135D in the Teacher's Edition.

Chapter Opener Illustrations
Benjamin Franklin's portrait, painted by Charles Willson Peale, appears below in a gilded frame. At age eighty-one, Franklin was the honored elder of the Constitutional Convention. He did not speak much at the convention, however, for he was ill with the gout and in much pain.

Long deliberations led to the moment when the Constitution was written out and ready to be signed. In the painting below, Thomas Rossiter, born thirty years after the convention, showed what that moment might have looked like. He painted George Washington in a place of lone dignity.

During the convention, delegates worked from printed copies of the latest draft of the Constitution. Changes were written in by hand.

Chapter 6 1787-1791

Creating the Constitution

Both the Constitution and the Declaration of Independence were signed in the meeting room of the Pennsylvania State House—now known as Independence Hall. The Assembly Room in the same building was the room in which the Articles of Confederation had been adopted.

The inkstand used during the convention had one container for ink and another for sand. The sand was used to help blot wet ink.

American Voices

During the summer of 1787 the American people stopped their national journey in midstream to re-examine their rules of government, the Articles of Confederation. As delegates gathered in Philadelphia for the Constitutional Convention, the governments of Europe awaited the outcome with curiosity and amazement. Some hoped for a failure and a resulting collapse of the young nation. Meanwhile, for many Americans Shays' Rebellion had aroused fears for their country's future. In a letter to James Madison in November 1786, George Washington expressed his hope that national loyalty would rise above local conflicts and interests:

"Let prejudices, unreasonable jealousies, and local interest yield to reason and liberality. Let us look to our national character, and to things beyond the present period. . . . Wisdom and good examples are necessary at this time to rescue the political machine from the impending storm."

Clashes between differing interests nearly did cause the convention to fail. But for all of the struggle involved in creating the Constitution and getting it approved by the states, it has endured for over two centuries with remarkably few changes. Not only has it served our nation well, but also it has become a model for constitutions of nations all over the world.

Portrait of Benjamin Franklin; delegates at the convention; the Constitution; Independence Hall; quill pen and silver inkstand used for signing the Constitution.

Analyzing Primary Sources

American Voices

Washington expressed these thoughts during the early stages of Shays' Rebellion. His fears were not shared by all leaders of the time. Patrick Henry was among those who accused nationalists of exaggerating the "crisis" to rally political support. Most historians, though, believe that genuine fears spurred Washington out of political retirement to preside over the convention.

1. What does Washington mean by "jealousies" and "local interest"? **(conflicting state interests over land claims, trade, and other matters)**
2. What are the "political machine" and "impending storm"? **(the national government; increasing clashes between Shays' rebels and the government)**
3. What might he mean by "look to our national character"? **(focus on common interests as Americans rather than conflicts between states, or between debtors and lenders as in the case of Shays' Rebellion)**

Section 6-1

Objectives

- ***Answer the Focus Question.***
- *Describe features of the Virginia and New Jersey plans.*
- *Identify what compromises were made at the convention.*
- *Discuss how the issues of presidential powers and slavery divided delegates to the convention.*
- *Explain why the states finally ratified the Constitution.*

Introducing

THE SECTION

Have students recall from Chapter 5 why some Americans feared a strong central government. **(could threaten individual freedoms)** Ask why many Americans came to think a stronger central government was needed. **(For example, a government could not function if unable to levy taxes or to enforce its decisions.)**

Tell the class that in this section they will learn how Americans came together to plan a strong central government.

B · A · C · K · G · R · O · U · N · D

Time Line Illustrations

1. A drawing of Independence Hall, formerly the Pennsylvania State House, where delegates met in the summer of 1787.

2. This *Portrait of William Paterson* was painted by Mrs. B.S. Church.

3. The "rising sun" chair was used by George Washington as president of the Constitutional Convention. On September 17, 1787, the delegates met for the last time to sign the Constitution. Franklin remarked to Madison that he had often looked at the sun painted on Washington's chair *"without being able to tell whether it was rising or setting.*

CHAPTER TIME LINE

1787 - 1791

Mrs. B.S. Church, *Portrait of William Paterson.*

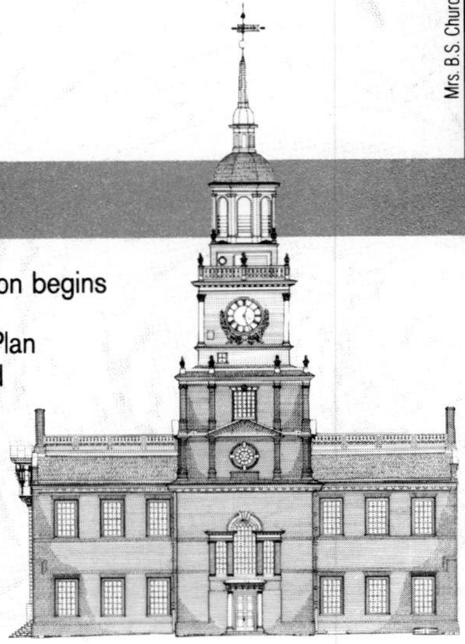

Jul 1787 Great Compromise

Jun 1787 New Jersey Plan proposed

1787

May 1787 Convention begins

Virginia Plan proposed

Sep 1787 Convention ends

6-1 The Constitutional Convention

Focus: What were the major issues at the convention?

The call for a convention to revise the Articles of Confederation was eagerly greeted by some but aroused suspicion in others. Patrick Henry, for one, feared the creation of a powerful central government that could threaten the freedoms for which the Revolution was fought. But those who welcomed the call believed that a stronger government was needed to keep order and guard against foreign threats.

A Profile of the Delegates

Seventy-three delegates were chosen, but only fifty-five actually attended. Some declined because of health, family, or business reasons. Others shared Patrick Henry's suspicions. In general, the delegates who finally gathered in Philadelphia during the summer of 1787 favored a strong national government. They represented every state except Rhode Island, which refused to send delegates.

Most notable among them was George Washington, who was greeted by a cannon salute and cheering crowds upon entering the city. Although his reputation stood to be tarnished if the convention failed, he was willing to take the risk. In accepting the invitation to lead Virginia's delegation he wrote, "To see this country happy is so much the wish of my soul."

Many delegates were veteran leaders of the struggle for independence. However, they were still young men. Half were in their thirties. Franklin, at the age of eighty-one, was the oldest. Notable by their absence were some giants of the American

But now, at length, I have the happiness to know that it is a rising and not a setting sun."

4. Hamilton, Madison, and Jay wrote the Federalist papers, a series of pro-Constitution newspaper articles in response to Patrick Henry and other Anti-Federalists.

5. In July 1788 New York celebrated the ratification of the Constitution in a grand manner. Five thousand men marched in a parade along with many elegant floats. The banner below was carried by the Society of Pewterers.

6. The printing press made constitutional issues more accessible to the public.

Jun 1788 Constitution ratified

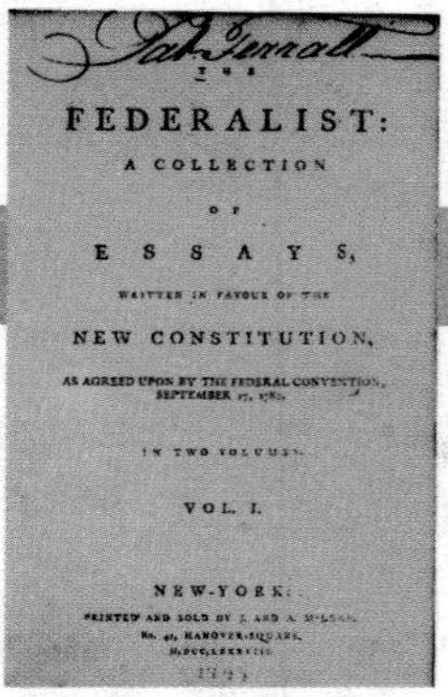

1788 — 1789 — 1790 — 1791

Oct 1787-Aug 1788 *The Federalist* papers published

Sep 1789 Bill of Rights proposed by Congress

Dec 1791 Bill of Rights ratified

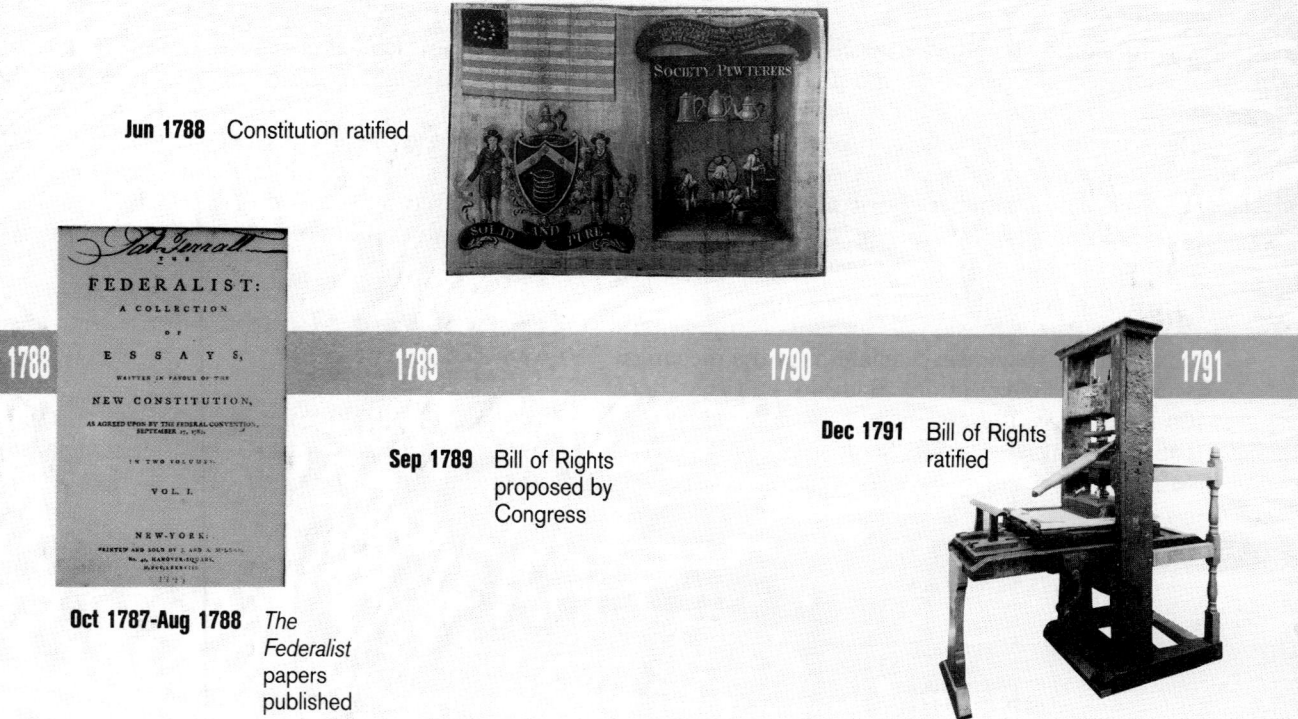

Revolution, particularly Thomas Jefferson and John Adams, who were in Europe serving as ambassadors of the United States.

Common ground. The delegates had much in common besides their ages and political experience. All were men and all were white, not surprising in a society that denied political and economic power to women and nonwhites. The delegates were also well-to-do and educated—over half had gone to college. They were lawyers, planters, merchants, physicians, and college professors. In general they represented the interests of merchants and large planters.

Most delegates believed that the Articles of Confederation were beyond mending. They agreed that the new government had to have the authority Congress lacked under the Articles: the power to levy taxes, to raise and support armed forces, to regulate commerce, and to make and enforce laws. They also accepted the principle of separating government functions into executive, judicial, and legislative branches to guard against abuse of power. There, however, the agreement ended.

Room for conflict. One sharp division was between those representing the states with small areas and populations and those representing states with the largest populations or potential for growth. The "large" states were Massachusetts, Virginia, Pennsylvania, North Carolina, South Carolina, and Georgia. The "small" states were Connecticut, New Jersey, Delaware, and Maryland.

The other main dividing line was between the southern states, which relied heavily on slave labor, and the northern states, whose economies were not so tied to slavery. The Carolinas and Georgia, states which faced a shortage of slaves, were particularly determined to preserve the slave trade. In short, there was plenty of room for conflict. One delegate noted, "We are neither the same nation nor different nations." Another described the convention as being "noisy as the wind."

Setting the Rules

The convention began on Friday, May 25, with the unanimous selection of George Washington as

Developing
THE SECTION

Thinking Critically

Evaluation. Was the selection of George Washington as chairperson of the convention vital to the successful outcome of the Constitutional Convention? Why or why not?

Multicultural Perspectives

Discussion. What groups were *not* represented at the Constitutional Convention? **(African Americans, Native Americans, women)** Discuss some of the issues related to these groups that were ignored or left unresolved by the convention and would have to be dealt with in later times. **(slavery, equal rights)**

GTV Side 2

Chap. 1, Frame 00005

A Fresh Start: The Constitution (Movie Segment)

Search and Play:

Thinking Critically

Analysis. Why was it important that the delegates hold their discussions in private, without reports of their conversations leaking to the public? (so they could speak freely, without pressure from the public)

Linking Past and Present

Discussion. Today, "sunshine laws" require government agencies to hold open meetings when public policies are discussed. By opening the meetings to "let the sunshine in," the laws discourage secrecy in government. Have students discuss the pros and cons of such laws.

B · A · C · K · G · R · O · U · N · D

Multicultural Perspectives

While the framers of the Constitution were debating issues in Philadelphia, free blacks in northern and southern cities were establishing self-help groups. One such group was the Free African Society established in 1787 by Absalom Jones and Richard Allen. They proposed that a society should be formed to help African Americans of "orderly and sober life to support one another in sickness and for the benefit of their widows and children." Money was given to those in need "provided this necessity is not brought on by their own improvidence." The society also paid for children's schooling and helped place them as apprentices in suitable trades.

Reduced student page in the Teacher's Edition

chairperson—the quickest decision that would be made over the next four months. The delegates next agreed on rules. Each could speak twice on a subject, and no one was to whisper, pass notes, or read while others spoke. Each state had one vote, regardless of its number of delegates, and decisions would be by majority vote of states present. The convention was free to reconsider earlier votes, which happened often during the summer.

To ensure the freedom to speak their minds and change their views, the delegates kept the meetings secret. Years later, James Madison said that "no Constitution would ever have been adopted by the convention if the debates had been public." The windows were nailed shut and guards were posted outside the doors. The private notes Madison made each night remain the best record of the convention.

An average of forty delegates attended the sessions. By and large, the secrecy rule was followed—even by talkative delegates like Franklin, who normally could not resist telling a good story.

Off to a Fast Start: The Virginia Plan

On May 29, with the rules agreed upon, the stage was set for debate—and the Virginia delegates were ready with a proposal. With the help of the

THE AMERICAN SPIRIT

James Madison

Architect of the Constitution

The slightly built delegate from Virginia knew exactly what he wanted to do at the Constitutional Convention. For the past year, James Madison had studied the strengths and weaknesses of ancient and modern confederations and republics. He was ready with a proposal for a new government. No delegate came to Philadelphia better prepared or argued more persuasively.

Madison's studious habits can be traced back to his childhood. Born in 1751, in Port Conway, Virginia, he was often ill as a child. But he had a healthy, inquisitive mind. By the age of eleven, he had read all of his father's books. He graduated from college in two years, often studying by candlelight late into the night.

After graduation, the brewing Revolution soon swept him into politics. Serving in his state's legislature and in the Continental Congress, he became convinced that the states should be united under a strong government.

With the gathering of delegates at the Constitutional Convention, his goal seemed within reach. Determined to record the birth of the new government, Madison did not miss a single session. He sat in the front row "for hearing all that passed" and each night wrote out an expanded version of his notes, a task that he later said "almost killed me."

While recording the events of the convention, he also played a major role in shaping them. Since the final document reflected many of the proposals he made, Madison has often been called the "architect of the Constitution."

The rest of Madison's life was dedicated to the Union he helped create. He served as Thomas Jefferson's Secretary of State and as President from 1809 to 1817. James Madison died in 1836, having outlived all the other delegates to the Constitutional Convention.

Pennsylvania delegates, they had created a plan based largely on Madison's ideas and now lost no time in springing it on the convention. Edmund Randolph introduced the Virginia Plan of Union by noting that the Articles of Confederation needed to be "corrected and enlarged." When he had finished speaking, though, it was clear that the plan called for replacing the Articles entirely.

In place of the loose confederation, the Virginia Plan recommended a strong national government with three separate branches, each with clearly defined powers. The delegates agreed to discuss the plan—a sign that the convention was on a course toward creating a whole new plan of government.

The Virginia Plan became the focus of the debates in the weeks ahead, during which the delegates followed a familiar pattern of postponing controversial issues and focusing first on areas of general agreement. The question of representation in Congress, an issue which divided the large states from the small, was too hot to be settled quickly. However, the convention approved the motion that "a national government ought to be established consisting of a supreme legislative, executive, and judiciary."

American Voices

"Though we cannot tell you what we are doing, we can tell you what we are not doing—we never once thought of a king."

—Convention Delegates

There was general agreement on having three branches of government, but how would they be organized? Most delegates thought that the legislature should be bicameral, with a House of Representatives and a Senate. The judicial branch would consist of a Supreme Court and lower courts. The delegates quickly agreed that the executive branch should be led by an elected official, not a monarch. To reassure a public fearful of tyranny, they announced, "Though we cannot tell you what we are doing, we can tell you what we are not doing—we never once thought of a king."

There was debate, however, over whether executive power should be in the hands of one person or a committee. The framers finally settled on a single leader with the title of President but limited the term of office to four years. Delegates fearing tyranny were also comforted by their belief that Washington would be the first President.

The people and power. The first week of June found the delegates returning to the issue of representation. The debate, which rocked the convention for more than a month, focused on two sides of a basic question: Who gets the power?

On the one side, the delegates argued over who should choose representatives to the new Congress—the people or the state legislatures? Madison said election by the people was "essential to every plan of free government," but Roger Sherman believed they were "constantly liable to be misled." Elbridge Gerry argued that "the evils we experience flow from the excess of democracy." Eventually a compromise was reached. Voters would elect members of the House, but the state legislatures would choose the senators.

The second side of the question—how many representatives each state would have in Congress—pitted large states against small. The Virginia Plan called for representation to be based on state population. This plan, which followed the principle of majority rule, favored the large states. The small states protested that the large ones would have an overwhelming majority in Congress. The small states lost their fight for equal representation in the House, but they kept pushing for equality in the Senate. When they lost on a six to five vote, their backs were to the wall.

Small-State Counterattack: The New Jersey Plan

Seeing the momentum going against them, the small-state delegates called for a day off on June 14. Deciding that the best defense was an offense, they prepared their own plan. William Paterson of New Jersey presented their proposal, known as the New Jersey Plan. It gave Congress the power to levy taxes and regulate foreign trade. However, each state—regardless of population—would still have one vote in Congress, whose members would be elected by the state legislatures.

Limited English Proficiency

Building Vocabulary. The framers were concerned about the distribution of *power* and *authority*. Help students define both terms and distinguish between the two concepts. **(Power is the ability to influence the behavior of others; authority is having the legal power to make decisions or laws.)**

Ask: What could give a state power? **(a large population, acording to the Virginia Plan)** What could give a state authority? **(equal representation in the Senate)**

As a follow up, have students bring in cartoons or drawings showing power and/or authority.

B · A · C · K · G · R · O · U · N · D

Connections: Politics

Just a few months before the Constitutional Convention, Shays' Rebellion demonstrated that a central government with a weak executive and little power to raise money or place an army in the field was vulnerable even to a small uprising by a poorly-armed mob. This challenge to the nation's existence convinced many who feared a strong executive branch to reconsider their positions.

Thinking Critically

Application. Discuss this proposition: The debate over slavery at the convention was political, economic, and social. Have the students offer evidence for this proposition using facts related on text pages 142-144.

Linking Past and Present

Research and Report. Ask a student to consult an encyclopedia about the electoral college and report back to the class, telling what the electoral college is, how someone today becomes a member of the college, and what the college does. Then ask the class to consider whether the electoral college is an example of democracy at work.

Writing About History

Journal. Have students imagine they are delegates to the Constitutional Convention. Ask them to write a journal entry telling their reaction to the Virginia and New Jersey plans. They should praise the good parts of each plan and criticize the bad parts. They should also offer some suggestions about how the two plans might be reconciled.

Reduced student page in the Teacher's Edition

Some supporters of the Virginia Plan called the New Jersey Plan a bluff. Charles Pinckney of South Carolina remarked, "Give New Jersey an equal vote [in the Senate], and she will dismiss her scruples and concur in the national system." Indeed, delegates from the small states did support a more powerful government. However, they threatened that if their states were not given a fair share of the power they would quit the convention. Without the small states' support, a new constitution stood little chance of success.

The large states, though, gave no ground. Randolph insisted that only a strong national government could gain the people's confidence. He declared, "The present is the last moment for establishing one. After this select experiment, the people will yield to despair."

After several days of heated debate, the New Jersey Plan went down to defeat and the convention formally voted against keeping the Articles of Confederation. Now there was no looking back, but stormy seas lay ahead. The small states dug in on their demand for equal representation in the Senate, and by the end of June the debate had become so fierce that Franklin proposed beginning each session with a prayer.

The Great Compromise

As the meetings moved into July, the delegates remained deadlocked. Unless they settled the issue of who would hold the power, they could hardly discuss what powers the government should have. The convention seemed to be close to collapse.

At the suggestion of Roger Sherman of Connecticut, a committee was formed to work out a compromise. It proposed that representation in the House be based on state population, but that each state have equal representation in the Senate.

A week of debate over the proposal brought the sides no closer. A frustrated Washington commented, "I almost despair of seeing a favorable issue [end] to the proceedings of our convention." Finally, on July 16, the compromise squeaked by in a five to four vote. It later became known as the Great Compromise because by meeting some demands of both the large and small states it avoided an almost certain failure of the convention.

How to Elect a President?

Although the Great Compromise kept the convention alive, it did not guarantee clear sailing. From late July through early September, delegates debated how the President should be elected. Many familiar issues arose: distrust of the average voter's ability to make good decisions, the desire of the small states to have an equal say in the choice, and disagreements over who could make the best selection: Congress, the voters, or the state legislatures.

The convention finally decided that each state legislature would choose electors who would meet as an electoral college to choose the President and Vice-President. Each state would have as many electors as it had members of Congress. This system settled the issue for the time being, but its flaws would become apparent in the years to come, giving rise to arguments over whether the electoral college is undemocratic.

The Three-Fifths Compromise

As debate over the interests of large and small states continued throughout the summer, conflict was also brewing between northern and southern states. It arose, as Madison noted, "from the effects of their having or not having slaves."

To get as many seats in Congress as possible, southern states wanted to count slaves as part of their population. Northern delegates argued that

Examining the Constitution

Although slavery is not specifically mentioned in the Constitution, acknowledgment of slavery appears in Article I, Section 2, which details the Three-Fifths Compromise; in Article I, Section 9, which alludes to the slave trade; and in Article 4, Section 2, which concerns fugitive slaves.

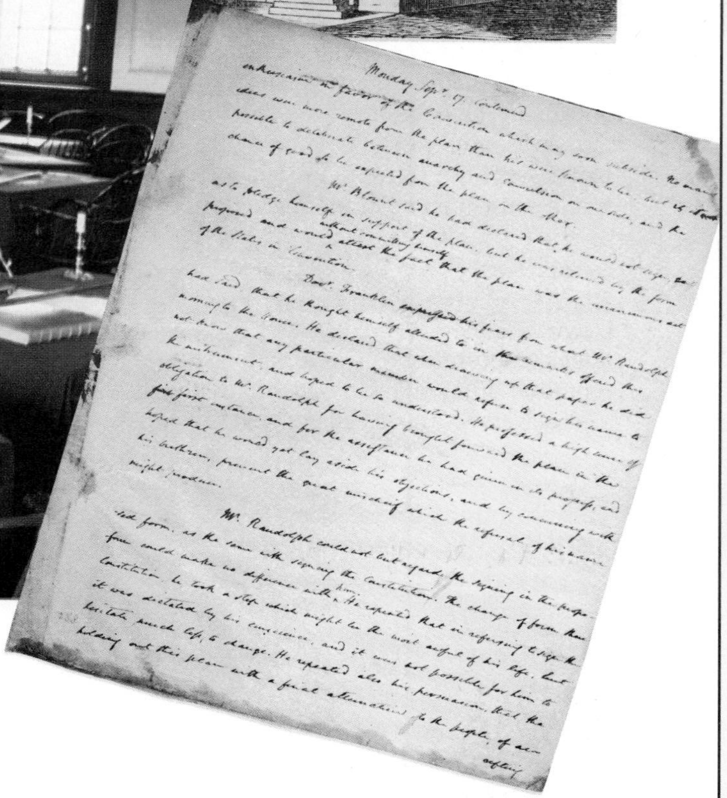

James Madison's notes, recorded each night in his room at a nearby inn (above right), are the best record of what took place in the convention meeting room (above).

the South could not have it both ways: either slaves were citizens and entitled to political rights, or they were property and could not be counted.

But the southern states did have it both ways. Since the South's support was needed, the delegates compromised. They agreed that each slave would count as three fifths of a person in figuring state populations. This arrangement became known as the Three-Fifths Compromise.

The slavery issue also surfaced in the debate over giving Congress the power to regulate trade. Northern merchants and manufacturers favored a national tariff policy to protect their businesses against foreign competition. Such tariffs, however, would do nothing for the largely agricultural southern states, which also feared that Congress might tax their exports of tobacco and other crops.

Delegates from the Carolinas and Georgia were particularly determined to prevent Congress from banning the importing of slaves. John Rutledge of South Carolina cut short a debate on the slave trade by warning that "the true question at present is whether the southern states shall or shall not be parties to the Union."

Analyzing Primary Sources

Remarks About the Constitution. Sojourner Truth (1797?-1883), a slave for half her life, became a leading speaker for abolition and women's rights. She is said to have remarked about the Constitution:

"Now I hear talk about the Constitution and the rights of man. I take hold of this Constitution. It is very long. I look for my rights, but there aren't any there. Then I say 'God, what ails this Constitution?' And you know what He says to me? God says, 'Sojourner, there is a little weasel in it.'"

Ask students what Sojourner Truth meant by her remarks. **(Equal rights granted by the Constitution did not apply to all people.)**

Active Learning

Role Play. Have students work in small groups to gather information to role play part of the Constitutional Convention. Students should play the roles of James Madison, George Washington, Edmund Randolph, Roger Sherman, Charles Pinckney, Elbridge Gerry, William Paterson, and John Rutledge.

They should prepare arguments on the main issues facing the convention: dividing power between the states and the national government, representation in Congress, the procedure for selecting government officials, and slavery.

Using the Visuals

Analyzing a Chart. Refer students to the chart on this page.

1. How does this chart show that the Constitution created a much stronger national government than had existed under the Articles of Confederation? **(Federal powers increased under the Constitution; for example, Congress given power to levy taxes and coin money.)**
2. Why did the convention think it necessary to increase the federal government's powers? **(to ensure domestic stability and encourage economic growth)**
3. What are the advantages of having only one form of national currency? **(makes trade easier by ensuring that value of currency is same in all states)**

Constitutional Heritage

The ratification of the Constitution rested on the promise of the Federalists to add a Bill of Rights to the document. Patrick Henry warned: *"The necessity for a Bill of Rights appears to me to be greater in this government than ever it was in any government before. . . . All rights not expressly reserved to the people are relinquished [given up] to rulers."* Henry was from Virginia, where the first American bill of rights, the Virginia Declaration of Rights, was written in 1776 by George Mason.

Virginia, which had a surplus of slaves, joined the North in pushing for a ban on a trade that Madison called "dishonorable to the American character." Many opponents of slavery, however, thought that the issue was not worth sacrificing the union for. Believing that slavery would soon die out on its own, most northern delegates shared Sherman's view that it was "better to let the southern states import slaves than to part with them."

Nothing divided the delegates more bitterly than the slavery issue. However, they eventually worked out a compromise that allowed the slave trade to continue. Congress could regulate trade and tax imports, but could not tax exports or end the importing of slaves before 1808. The compromise over the slave trade and the Three-Fifths Compromise helped save the convention, but they were to have tragic consequences in the years ahead.

Signing the Constitution

After compromising on the major issues—representation in Congress, election of the President, and slavery—the delegates carefully hammered out the rest of the government's framework, including the division of powers between the national and state governments. The men we call the framers produced a plan of government that is remarkably short—a blend of broad political ideals and practical common sense. A style committee smoothed out the wording and added flair, especially in the stirring words of the Preamble.

On September 17, 1787, the completed Constitution was read to the convention. Franklin then urged all the delegates to sign it. Most agreed with Franklin's assessment of the document. Thirty-nine delegates signed the Constitution, while three still refused to do so, mainly because it did not list individual freedoms and rights of citizens.

Now it was up to the people at the state level to approve or reject the convention's work. The delegates knew that the Constitution would meet strong opposition in the state legislatures, which stood to lose power under the new plan. Therefore, they specified that state ratifying conventions—not the legislatures—would decide whether it would become the law of the land. As soon as nine of the thirteen states ratified the Constitution, the new government would be created.

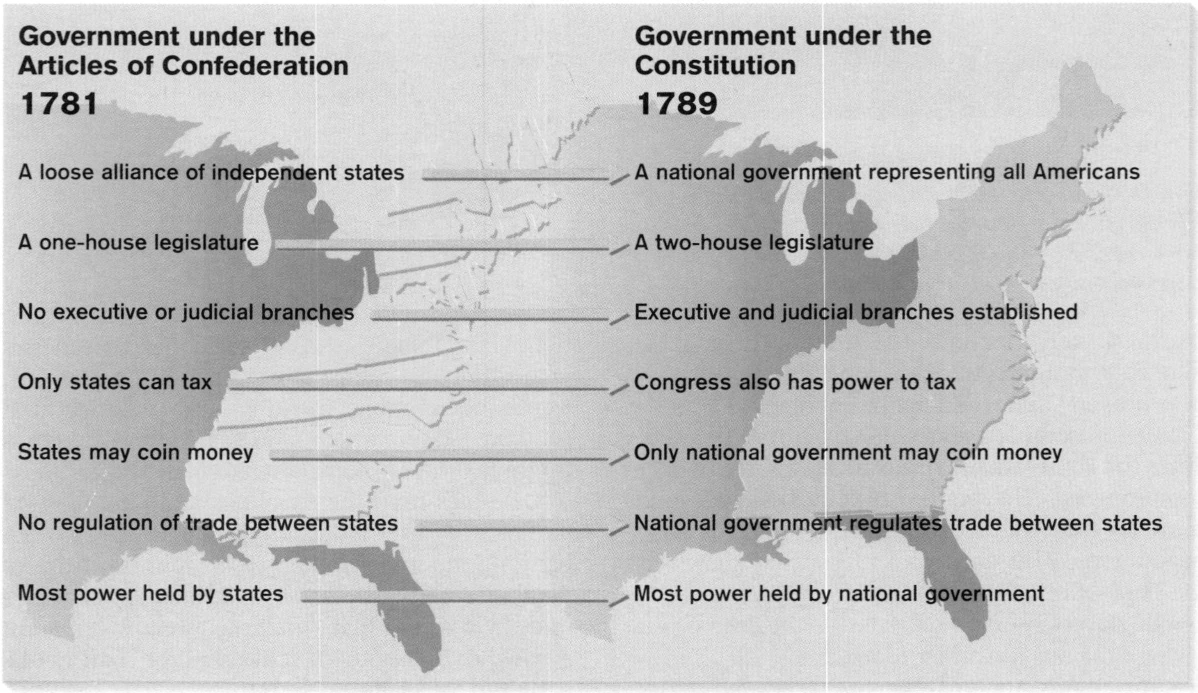
Government under the Articles of Confederation 1781
Government under the Constitution 1789
A loose alliance of independent states
A national government representing all Americans
A one-house legislature
A two-house legislature
No executive or judicial branches
Executive and judicial branches established
Only states can tax
Congress also has power to tax
States may coin money
Only national government may coin money
No regulation of trade between states
National government regulates trade between states
Most power held by states
Most power held by national government

Connections: Politics

The effort to ratify the Constitution received significant help from a series of eighty-five articles that appeared in New York newspapers with the signature "Publius." Publius was actually three people—James Madison, John Jay, and Alexander Hamilton. Later, these essays were collected and published in book form as *The Federalist.*

The Struggle Over Ratification

At the state ratifying conventions, feelings ran high. Supporters of the Constitution called themselves Federalists, to reassure those who feared that an all-powerful central government would swallow the states. They argued that the Constitution was the only alternative to chaos and disunion.

Opponents of ratification, who were labeled Anti-Federalists, claimed that it would weaken the state governments and undermine the "liberties of the people." In particular, they pointed out that the Constitution had no bill of rights.

The Massachusetts ratifying convention was typical of many. Delegates weighed the need for better trade regulation and more strength in foreign relations against the possible threats to state sovereignty and individual rights posed by the Constitution.

One delegate expressed the fears of many that the central government would "swallow up all us little folks." Mercy Otis Warren wrote a pamphlet criticizing the new plan for not specifically listing individual rights that the new government would protect. Only after delegates were promised a bill of rights did the Constitution squeak through in Massachusetts by a vote of 187 to 168.

By the end of May 1788, the approval of only one more state was needed. Washington wrote that "a few short weeks will determine the political fate of America." Then, in June 1788, New Hampshire ratified, making the Constitution the "supreme law of the land" among nine states.

It was not yet time to rejoice, however. The remaining four states had nearly 40 percent of the population. Without them—particularly without Virginia and New York—the new government stood little chance of success.

Virginia and New York. In Virginia, Patrick Henry spoke passionately against the Constitution, calling it "horridly defective." He warned that it would "destroy the state governments and swallow the liberties of the people." Among the Federalists, who were arguing just as forcefully for it, was an able young lawyer named John Marshall, who stoutly defended every article. Virginia finally ratified by a vote of 89 to 79.

In New York, Alexander Hamilton waited anxiously for news from Virginia to help him spur the mostly Anti-Federalist convention toward ratification. For several months Hamilton, Madison, and John Jay had been writing anonymous essays in New York newspapers to rally support. The essays were published as *The Federalist* in May 1788. Hamilton also made frankly emotional appeals. "A nation without a national government is, in my view, an awful spectacle."

Word of ratification by New Hampshire and then Virginia in late June won over some New York delegates. After weeks of bitter debate, the convention ratified, but by a bare three votes. Eleven states had now joined the Union. North Carolina finally ratified in November 1789, and Rhode Island in the spring of 1790. All thirteen states were now under the new constitution.

American Voices

"It will astonish our enemies, who are waiting with confidence to hear that our councils are confounded. . . . Thus I consent, sir, to this Constitution because I expect no better, and because I am not sure that it is not the best."

—Benjamin Franklin

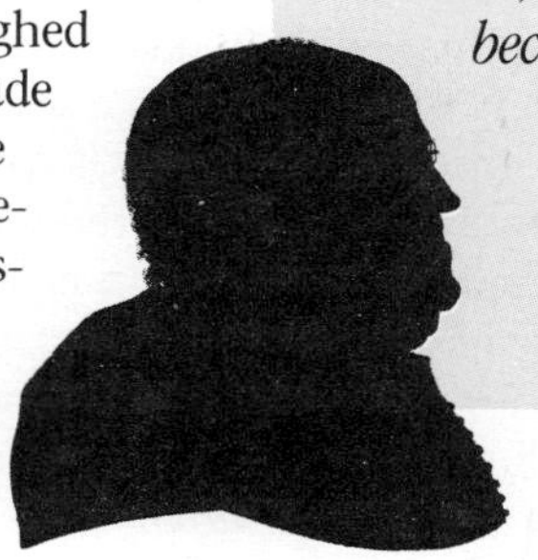

Section Review

1. Comprehension. Identify three important issues debated at the convention. Explain why each issue caused controversy.

2. Analysis. How did the Constitution differ from the Articles of Confederation?

3. Evaluation. Do you think the framers were right to compromise on slavery? Why or why not?

Linking Past and Present. Why do you think the framers did not trust the people to elect the President directly? If the framers were alive today, do you think modern elections would change their opinion? Why or why not?

Limited English Proficiency

Making Posters. Have students make posters celebrating the ratification of the Constitution. Each student should identify in the poster one aspect of the Constitution that he or she considers especially valuable or noteworthy.

Writing about History

Letter to the Editor. Have students write one of the following letters to the editor of a newspaper:

1. Write a letter supporting ratification of the United States Constitution. Explain why you think arguments against the Constitution are not valid. Describe the benefits to be gained from the document.

2. Write a letter opposing ratification. Explain why the new Constitution will not solve your state's problems. Explain why the states should remain sovereign.

Section Review

ANSWERS

1. Would people or state legislatures hold power? Large or small states? Conflict over slavery.
2. See chart on page 144.
3. Answers may include that Constitution could not have been ratified without compromises. With no compromise on slavery, many evils and future troubles could have been averted.
Linking Past and Present. All delegates educated, prosperous men; most distrusted less educated. With newspapers and TV today, students might argue that people are more well-informed about issues. Others may think a true picture of candidates and issues is not possible with "packaging and selling" candidates.

Section 6-2

Objectives

- ***Answer the Focus Question.***
- *Identify ways in which the United States Constitution is flexible.*
- *Compare the principle of separation of powers with that of checks and balances.*
- *Explain how the Constitution helps remedy abuses of political power and protects free speech.*

Introducing THE SECTION

Tell students that our Constitution has survived for over two hundred years because it is a "living" document that can respond to the needs of a growing and changing society. Ask students how the Constitution adjusts to changing times. **(through the amendment process)** When there is disagreement over interpretation of the Constitution who has the final say? **(the Supreme Court)**

In this section, students will read about several disagreements over the Constitution. The disagreements are presented as case studies, which are descriptions of situations or conflicts, the issues involved, and the decisions made.

B · A · C · K · G · R · O · U · N · D

Global Connections
Although the framers' plan was not the world's first constitution, up until this time most governments had unwritten constitutions based on custom or on the will of the monarch. Hamilton declared that the Constitution was a model of "establishing good government by reflection and choice" rather than by "accident and force." Indeed, the Constitution has set an example for many countries, including former colonies in Latin America and Africa when they gained their independence.

6-2 *The Living Constitution*

Focus: What constitutional issues have continued to arise throughout our nation's history?

The full text of the Constitution will be found on pages 914–935.

How much power is needed to govern a growing nation? How can the government be prevented from abusing its power? These questions faced the framers during that summer of 1787—and they continue to challenge Americans today. Our plan of government has been tested—at times to the breaking point—but continues to survive. Madison's prediction that it would "probably be still around" when the nation's population neared 200 million has been more than fulfilled. The Constitution lives on because the American people have put its principles into practice.

A Flexible Framework

Once called "the most remarkable work ever struck off by the mind of man," the Constitution stands today as the oldest written plan of government still in effect. The secret of its long life lies mainly in its flexible ability to adjust to changing times.

In large part that flexibility is found in the way the Constitution is written. The framers did not clutter it with hundreds of specific rules, for they knew that regulations appropriate for the 1780s might make little sense years later. Instead, they relied mainly on general principles stated in broad terms, so that later generations could "fill in the details" by applying those principles as they saw fit. As a result, the Constitution does not have to be changed in response to every new situation or problem the government faces.

The framers also provided for flexibility through a procedure for amending, or changing, the Constitution. That process, however, is designed to discourage hasty changes. An amendment must first be approved by two thirds of the members of each house of Congress, or by a convention called for by two thirds of the state legislatures. Next comes a higher hurdle. It must be ratified by three fourths of the states, either by their legislatures or by special ratifying conventions.

Amendments have indeed been rare. In more than two hundred years, thousands of proposals for amendments have been brought before Congress, but only twenty-six have become part of the Constitution. Why so few? Aside from the ratification hurdle, the main reason is that the Constitution's broad principles allow the government to adjust to changing times through custom and through laws passed by Congress.

Who decides whether government officials are abiding by the basic principles of the Constitution? Most historians agree that the framers intended this duty to fall on the judicial branch. In the early 1800s the Supreme Court first asserted its right of **judicial review,** the power to declare whether a law passed by Congress or an action taken by the executive branch is constitutional.

Strict vs. loose construction. Early in the nation's history, two views developed regarding how to interpret the Constitution. Some Americans have favored **strict construction,** the view that the government has only the powers that are specifically spelled out in the Constitution.

Other people believe that the government also has powers that are not directly stated in the Constitution but are suggested, or implied. This view is called **loose construction**.

Government officials—the President, members of Congress, and federal judges—have interpreted the Constitution strictly at some times and loosely at others. The Supreme Court's interpretations, however, are especially important, for the Court has the final say on constitutional issues in cases that come before it. A Court decision remains the law unless overturned by a later Supreme Court ruling or by an amendment to the Constitution.

Debates over strict versus loose construction and over what the framers really intended by some of the Constitution's clauses continue to this day. Even with a written constitution as a guide, shaping a democracy involves trial and error.

Disagreements have often centered on the following main principles: federalism, separation of powers, checks and balances, protection of individual rights, and representative government. The remainder of this chapter will provide brief case studies and overviews of these principles.

Federalism

Case Study: Wallace and Segregation

The year was 1963. The place was the University of Alabama. Governor George Wallace stood in the doorway of the administration building to prevent the enrollment of two African-American students. Wallace was refusing to obey a Supreme Court decision that made segregation in schools unconstitutional. When Deputy Attorney General Nicholas Katzenbach, representing the United States government, asked him to "step aside peacefully and do

In a tense test of the division between state and national power, Governor George Wallace confronted federal officials in 1963, apparently defying a law against segregation.

Federalism

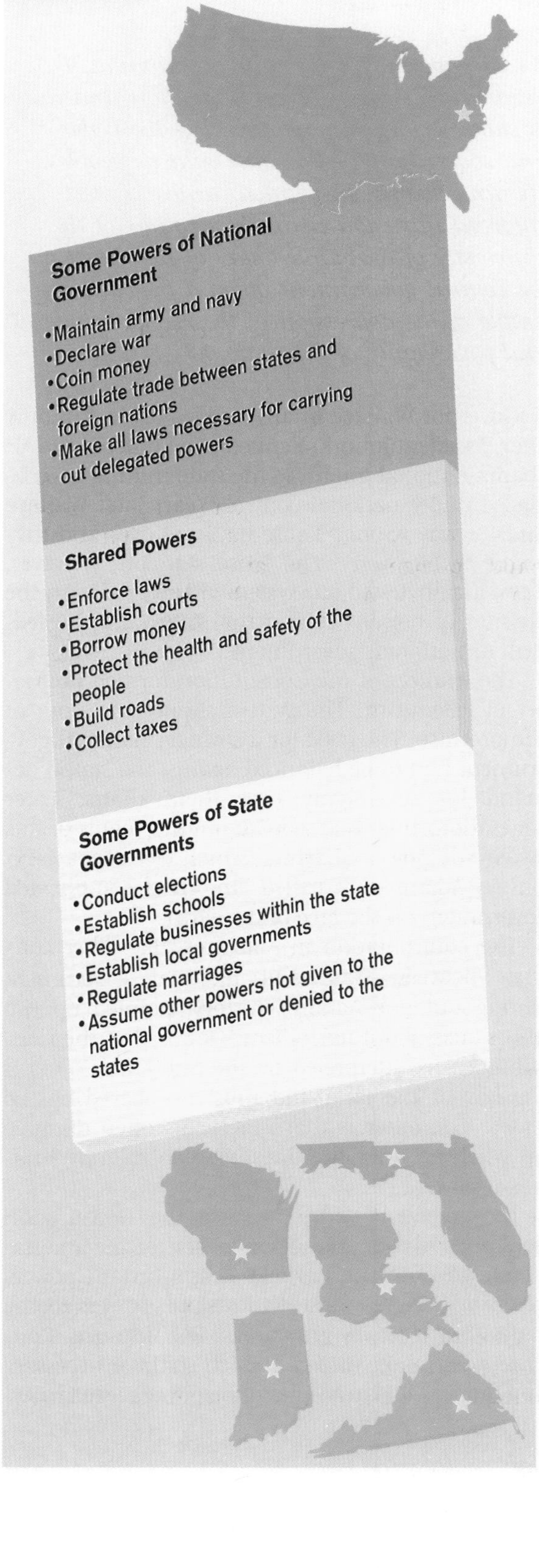

Some Powers of National Government
• Maintain army and navy
• Declare war
• Coin money
• Regulate trade between states and foreign nations
• Make all laws necessary for carrying out delegated powers
Shared Powers
• Enforce laws
• Establish courts
• Borrow money
• Protect the health and safety of the people
• Build roads
• Collect taxes
Some Powers of State Governments
• Conduct elections
• Establish schools
• Regulate businesses within the state
• Establish local governments
• Regulate marriages
• Assume other powers not given to the national government or denied to the states

Developing

THE SECTION

Using the Visuals

Analyzing a Chart. Refer students to the Federalism chart on this page.

1. How did the framers of the Constitution deal with the issue of federal and state government powers? **(divided powers between state and federal government)**

2. Why do you think the framers divided power this way? Cite ways in which powers given to state governments are different from those given to the federal government. **(State powers affect affairs of just one state; federal powers affect the whole country.)**

3. Why is only the federal government given power to declare war? **(There should be national action in matters of wider concern.)** Coin money? **(A national currency promotes a unified economic system and contributes to national unity.)**

4. What powers are shared by the states and federal government? **(for example, enforce laws, borrow money, collect taxes)**

5. Why are these powers shared? **(for example, allows states to solve local concerns)**

B · A · C · K · G · R · O · U · N · D

Linking Past and Present

Alabama Governor George Wallace's resistance to federal power is only one example in a long line of confrontations between the states and the federal government. In 1798, Thomas Jefferson stated that each state had a right to disregard—or nullify—federal laws. Many New Englanders opposed the War of 1812 and maintained that states had the right to leave the Union if no other remedies could be found for ending the war. In 1832, South Carolinians led by John Calhoun expressed their opposition to the economic policies of the federal government by resurrecting Jefferson's doctrine of nullification. The Civil War, 1861–1865, was fought over the issue of the federal government's authority over the states.

Writing About History

Essay. Have students reconcile the following apparent contradiction: On the one hand, many Americans want to protect their right to express themselves freely. On the other hand, many want to make their own values the law of the land, regardless of the values of others.

Thinking Critically

Evaluation. Have students discuss the problem of democratic rule of the majority versus the rights of individuals. Ask students to explain why the problem is built into democratic forms of government.

Reduced student page in the Teacher's Edition

your constitutional duty as governor," Governor Wallace responded:

> "*As governor of the state of Alabama, I deem it to be my solemn obligation and duty to stand before you representing the rights and sovereignty of this state and its peoples. The unwelcome, unwanted, unwarranted, enforced intrusion upon the campus of the University of Alabama today of the might of the central government offers a frightful example of the oppression of the rights, privileges, and sovereignty of this state.*"

Governor Wallace finally stepped aside, but only after President John F. Kennedy had ordered the Alabama national guard—the state militia—to be placed under national control. Years later Wallace said, "I was wrong. Those days are over and they ought to be over." The tense standoff, however, dramatically tested our system of **federalism,** the division of power between the states and the federal, or national, government.

The framers of the Constitution formed no theory of federalism. The system simply arose out of compromise. The need for a stronger national government had to be balanced against the states' demand for sovereignty over their affairs. Later generations have had to work out the details of this system of power sharing, which President John Quincy Adams once called "the most complicated government on the face of the earth."

The confrontation in Alabama, like other conflicts between state and national government throughout our nation's history, pointed up two main facts about federalism. One is that the Constitution, as interpreted by the Supreme Court, is the law of the land and must be obeyed by the states. The other is that Americans often disagree on where to draw the lines between state and national power.

Disagreements arise because the Constitution does not spell out all the powers of the state and national governments. Article 1 lists certain powers given to Congress and denies some powers to the states, but it leaves gray areas. For instance, Congress can "make all laws which shall be necessary and proper" for carrying out the powers listed in Article 1. This clause, often called the "elastic clause" because it gives Congress flexibility, has sparked debate over what is "necessary and proper."

Spotlight on Politics

At the Constitutional Convention, one debate on state versus national power was over the creation of a national army. The need for protection against foreign invasion was weighed against the possible threat to state sovereignty. When one delegate argued for limiting the size of the army to 3,000 soldiers, George Washington said he saw no problem with that—as long as the Constitution made it illegal for an enemy to attack the United States with more than 3,000 soldiers!

Meanwhile, there are many powers that the Constitution neither gives to the national government nor denies to the states. The Tenth Amendment says that such powers belong either to the states or to the people, a fact that the framers had considered to be obvious. However, the door is still left open for debate on how far the states' powers extend.

The 1963 showdown at the University of Alabama is a good case in point. Since the Constitution does not give the national government power to establish schools, that power rests with the states. But how much control should each state have in deciding how to run its schools? The Constitution recognizes that the needs and views of the majority of people in one state may differ from those in another. However, this has to be weighed against the national government's goal of applying the principles of the Constitution equally to all citizens.

Conflicts can also arise when states seek money from Congress to pay for local projects. Congress wants control over how its money is spent, but the states argue that they understand local needs better. In short, furthering the Constitution's goal to "promote the general welfare" of Americans involves seeking the right balance between the powers of the state and national governments.

Separation of Powers

Case Study: Bush and the Gulf Crisis

In August 1990 President George Bush ordered American troops to the Persian Gulf in response to Iraq's invasion of Kuwait. The President warned that if economic pressure seemed unlikely to push Iraq out of Kuwait, then military force would be used. Iraq was given a January 15, 1991, deadline, triggering a countdown that heightened debate over who has the power to take the nation into war. Some Americans argued that the President's role as commander in chief gave him that authority. Others said that the Constitution gives Congress alone the power to declare war.

Shortly before the deadline, Bush did ask for a vote in Congress, even though he did not believe that congressional approval was required. After vigorous debate, a divided Congress voted to support the use of military force. On January 16 the attack on Iraq was launched, and the nation was at war.

The Gulf conflict brought renewed attention to the principle of **separation of powers** — the division of government power into executive, legislative, and judicial branches. Intended to help prevent abuse of power, the principle seems at first glance to be clear-cut: Congress makes the laws, the President enforces them, the courts interpret them. However, as the Persian Gulf debate showed, the separation is not quite that simple — especially regarding the executive branch.

Questions arise over the President's powers because the Constitution describes them in brief, general terms. The presidency was completely new in a world dominated by monarchs, so the framers had

By sending troops to Saudi Arabia in 1990, George Bush triggered a debate over whether the Constitution gives the President power to take the nation into war.

Connections: Geography

Map Skills. Ask students to use a globe to locate the nations in the Middle East involved in the Persian Gulf War of 1991: Iraq, Iran, Turkey, Jordan, Syria, Israel, Kuwait, Saudi Arabia, the small states on the periphery of the Arabian Peninsula, and Egypt.

Connections: Politics

Discussion. Most Middle Eastern states are not democracies. Kuwait, Saudi Arabia, and Jordan are monarchies, Iran is an Islamic Republic. Discuss why the United States might want to defend nations with forms of governments so different from its own.

Active Learning

Taking a Survey. Have students conduct a survey to determine other people's views on this topic: Is it ever right for a President to initiate a military conflict without consent of Congress?

Encourage students to answer the question themselves, then ask this question of adults as well as young people in their families, at school, in their neighborhoood, etc. Each student should survey at least five people.

Compile the data and analyze results with the students. Compare the answers of class members and the out-of-class surveys.

Using the Visuals

Analyzing a Diagram. Refer students to the "Checks and Balances" diagram on this page.

1. What are the three branches of the federal government? **(legislative, executive, judicial)**
2. What powers does each branch have that limits the powers of the other two? **(For example, the House can impeach the President. If found guilty in a trial of the Senate, the President will be removed from office.)**
3. Why does the Constitution provide for these limits? **(to protect against abuse of power in the federal govenment)**

Analyzing Primary Sources

The Constitution. Refer students to the annotated Constitution starting on text page 914. Then have them cite the article and section that describes each of the powers listed in the "Checks and Balances" diagram on this page. **(Articles 1, 2, and 3)**

B · A · C · K · G · R · O · U · N · D

Connections: Politics

The acts of the various branches of the government are also checked and balanced by non-government institutions. The press, for example, monitors government actions and can urge the people to take political action. During the Watergate scandal, institutions of government might not have taken steps against the Nixon administration had not reporters like Robert Woodward and Carl Bernstein of the *Washington Post* uncovered the misdeeds of government officials.

Reduced student page in the Teacher's Edition

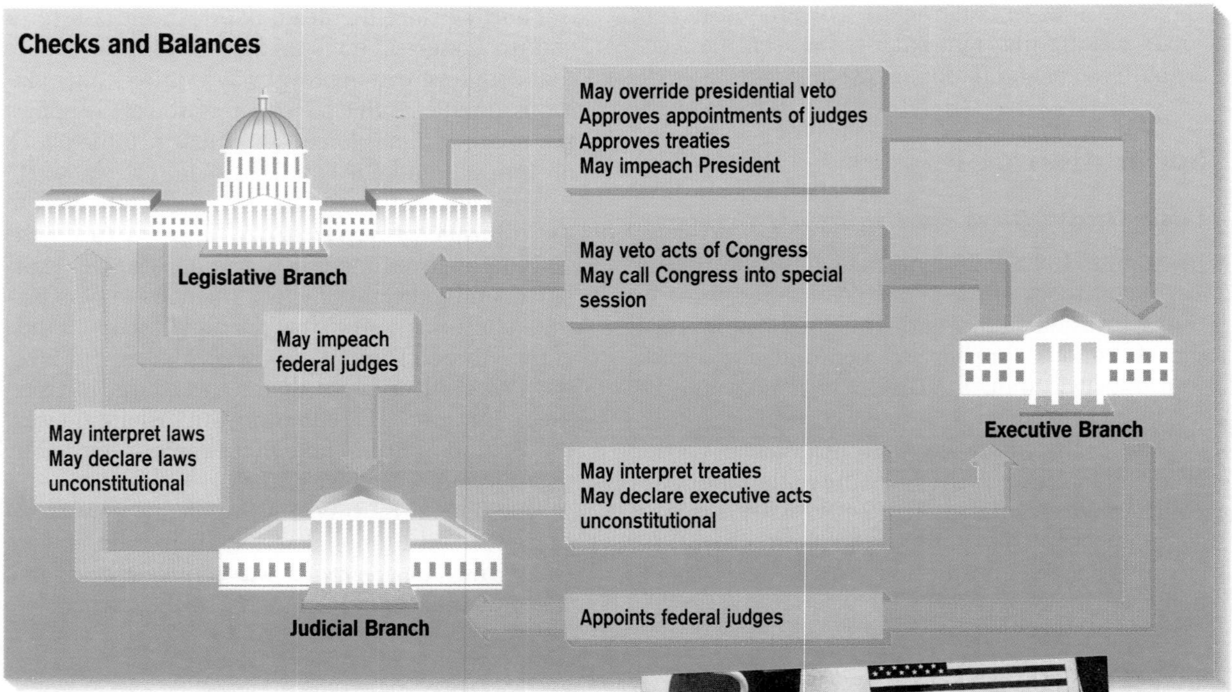

few guidelines. Furthermore, out of fear of tyranny, they did not want to place many specific powers in the hands of one leader. After being elected President, Washington commented, "My station is new; . . . I walk on untrodden ground." Indeed, examples set by Washington and his successors have largely defined how the President's duties are carried out under the Constitution.

As the country has grown, Presidents have taken on an ever greater leadership role, especially in shaping foreign policy. With the increasing responsibilities of the office, the limits of presidential power have often been loosely interpreted. Many Americans, however, believe that the presidency has become too powerful.

Debates also arise over the power of the judicial branch. In the view of some Americans, judges exercising judicial review often cross the line between interpreting the Constitution and making their own laws. Others, though, argue that the Constitution cannot remain supreme unless the courts determine whether laws, and actions taken by government officials, are constitutional.

In short, separation of powers does not mean that the three branches have completely separate roles. Government policies over the years have reflected the influence of all three. The continuing challenge is to keep any one branch from dominating the other two.

Facing likely impeachment, Richard Nixon resigned from the presidency in 1974. Despite his farewell "victory" sign, the real winner was the system of checks and balances.

Checks and Balances

Case Study: Nixon and Watergate

In 1974 Richard M. Nixon resigned from the most powerful office in the land, becoming the first President to do so. The events leading to his resignation had begun with the arrest of burglars in the Democratic party headquarters at the Watergate building in Washington, D.C. After newspaper reporters brought to light the fact that members of Nixon's reelection campaign staff had ordered the break-in, Congress began an investigation. The major question became: Did the President approve the break-in or the attempt to cover up the involvement of his staff?

Though shocked by the Watergate scandal, many saw in it proof that the system of **checks and balances** works—that the branches of government can limit each other's power. As the chart on page 150 shows, each branch acts as a watchdog on the other two. If Nixon had not resigned, he would probably have been **impeached**—accused of wrongdoing by the House—and then convicted and removed from office by the Senate. The message was clear: Under our Constitution no person is above the law.

The system of checks and balances reflects the framers' awareness that separation of powers alone cannot guard against abuse of power. They knew the weaknesses in human nature. Franklin noted the influence of "the love of power and the love of money." Madison declared, "If men were angels, no government would be necessary. If angels were to govern men, neither external nor internal controls on government would be necessary." A plan of government, he believed, best guards against tyranny by setting power against power so that no one person or group gains the upper hand.

Setting power against power, however, can have drawbacks. Some people argue that frequent use of the presidential veto interferes too much with the lawmaking process. Meanwhile, Congressional investigations are sometimes seen as unnecessary interference with the President's efforts to take decisive action, especially on foreign policy. The three branches face the challenge of balancing the need to make progress with the need to keep one branch from abusing its power.

Does freedom of speech give one the right to burn an American flag? Questions like this have made the Bill of Rights the most hotly debated part of the Constitution.

Individual Rights

Case Study: Flag Burning

Few cases that have come before the Supreme Court have gained as much national attention as a 1989 case on whether the Constitution permits a person to destroy the American flag. The case, involving a man who set a flag on fire, deeply divided the nine justices. In a five to four vote, the Court ruled that in this case burning the flag was a political statement protected by the Constitution's guarantee of freedom of speech.

The narrow vote reflected the difficulty of defining how much freedom an individual should have in our society. Madison once said that "every word of the Constitution decides a question between power and liberty." The answers the Constitution gives, though, are typically general. During the ratification debates, in fact, many Americans argued that the Constitution left far too much room for interpretation. Why, they asked, did it not include a bill of rights?

Limited English Proficiency

Cooperative Activity. Ask each student to find a magazine or newspaper article that describes a current event related to one of the three branches of government. Then have the class meet in small groups to share their articles and discuss how the events could affect their lives.

Thinking Critically

Application. Refer students to the Bill of Rights chart on this page. **Ask:** Which amendment offers you protection if a law enforcement officer insists that you tell what you know about a crime? (Fifth) Which amendment requires a police officer to obtain a search warrant before entering your home? (Fourth) Which amendment prohibits a judge from levying a $5,000 fine on a person convicted of shoplifting a $25 sweatshirt? (Eighth)

Connections: Music

Listening to Music. Ask students to collect examples of popular music that either defend the Bill of Rights freedoms or express unpopular opinions defended by the First Amendment. (for example, anti-war songs or particular songs from the Vietnam Era, etc.)

Writing About History

Linking Past and Present. Have students bring in articles from newspapers and news magazines that illustrate principles outlined in the Constitution.

Have them write a short paragraph for each article telling how it shows the Constitution in action. The articles can be part of a bulletin board display or a scrapbook that is added to throughout the school year.

Constitutional Heritage

In 1961 Clarence Gideon was charged with stealing food and money from a vending machine in a Florida pool hall. Though he pleaded innocent, he could not afford a lawyer. The court refused to provide him with one. He was found guilty and sentenced to five years in prison. Gideon spent hours in the prison library studying the Constitution. He learned that the right to have a lawyer is stated in the Bill of Rights. He wrote a letter asking the Supreme Court to hear his case. On January 14, 1963 all of the justices ruled that no court could deny a poor person the right to a lawyer. Gideon also won the right to a new trial in Florida, and he was found not guilty. It was a victory for thousands of Americans.

Reduced student page in the Teacher's Edition

The Bill of Rights 1791

Amendment	Subject
1st	Guarantees freedom of religion, of speech, and of the press; the right to assemble peacefully; and the right to petition the government.
2nd	Guarantees the right to possess firearms in a state militia.
3rd	Declares that the government may not require people to house soldiers during peacetime.
4th	Protects people from unreasonable searches and seizures.
5th	Guarantees that no one may be deprived of life, liberty, or property without due process of law; protects accused persons from double jeopardy and from being forced to testify against themselves.
6th	Guarantees the right to a trial by jury in criminal cases, and the right of the accused to question witnesses and be assisted by a defense lawyer.
7th	Guarantees the right to a trial by jury in most civil cases.
8th	Prohibits excessive bail, fines, and punishments.
9th	Declares that rights not mentioned in the Constitution belong to the people.
10th	Declares that powers not given to the national government belong to the states or the people.

The full text and an explanation of these amendments will be found on pages 925–927.

At first the Federalists argued that by limiting the government's power the Constitution was already, as Hamilton put it, "in every rational sense, and to every useful purpose, a bill of rights." Many Americans thought otherwise and tirelessly demanded more specific protections. To win ratification, the Federalists finally promised that the new Congress would propose a bill of rights. By 1791 ten amendments protecting individual rights had become part of the Constitution. Together they became known as the Bill of Rights.

The Bill of Rights has prompted more debate than any other part of the Constitution. The central issue usually boils down to individual rights versus the common good. For instance, the government must respect the rights of people accused of crimes, but at the same time it has a duty to protect the public's safety. And the cherished right of freedom of speech may have to be limited if using it unfairly damages the reputation of others or threatens their safety. In short, individual rights must constantly be weighed against the rights of society as a whole.

In 1920 the meaning of "We the People" widened to include women. Their years of struggle finally paid off when the Nineteenth Amendment gave them the right to vote.

The Right to Vote

Who should have a voice in electing the government has been another ongoing issue. Over the years the Constitution's flexibility has made it possible to widen the meaning of "We the People." The framers believed that only white men with property should be able to vote. As American society and attitudes have changed, though, constitutional amendments have ensured that voting rights will not be denied on the basis of race, color, sex, or wealth. In 1971 the Twenty-sixth Amendment lowered the voting age from twenty-one to eighteen.

Unless the right to vote is exercised, however, it does not guarantee a stronger voice in government. Through voting, the people make government accountable. In the words of George Washington:

"The power under the Constitution will always be in the people. It is entrusted for certain defined purposes, and for a certain limited period, to the representatives of their own choosing; and when it is executed contrary to their interests, or not agreeable to their wishes, their servants can and undoubtedly will be recalled."

To preserve government by the people, each generation faces anew the challenge of interpreting the Constitution and putting it into practice. As Thomas Jefferson once said, "The Constitution belongs to the living and not to the dead."

Section Review

1. Identification. Define *judicial review, strict construction, loose construction, federalism, separation of powers, checks and balances,* and *impeached.*

2. Comprehension. What makes the Constitution flexible?

3. Analysis. Compare the principle of separation of powers with that of checks and balances.

Data Search. After studying the diagram on page 150, identify some ways in which the executive and legislative branches check each other's power.

Connections to Themes

Shaping Democracy

The framers saw themselves as setting an example for other nations. Madison proclaimed, "We are teaching the world the great lesson that men do better without kings and nobles than with them." Hamilton declared that the Constitution was a model of "establishing good government by reflection and choice" rather than by "accident and force."

Indeed, the process of creating and ratifying the Constitution reflected the American faith in written plans of government based on the consent of the people. That faith, which can be traced back through the Articles of Confederation, the state constitutions, and the colonial charters, continues today. "We the People" are subject only to laws made by our elected representatives, not to military force or the inherited power of monarchs. The Constitution represents Americans' commitment to a government in which no one is above the law.

The Constitution has been a model for the constitutions of many nations and is the oldest written plan of government still in effect. Others have come and gone with revolutions and changes of leadership, and many have been democratic in name only. Ours has endured, largely because of its flexibility and the determination of the American people to apply its principles. It provides the framework for reshaping our government to meet new needs and conditions and to move further toward our ideals. In a very real sense, the United States Constitution represents endless unfinished business.

Citizenship

Cooperative Activity. Have students make a class chart showing the years in which African Americans, women, Native Americans, and eighteen-year-olds secured the right to vote. The chart should include the political means by which groups gained the vote (for example, the Twenty-sixth Amendment). Students can use encyclopedias as a source of information.

Section Review
ANSWERS

1. Definitions for the following terms are on text pages indicated in parentheses: *judicial review* (146), *strict construction* (146), *loose construction* (146), *federalism* (148), *separation of powers* (149), *checks and balances* (151), *impeached* (151).
2. The Constitution provides general principles stated in broad terms and provisions for amendment.
3. Separation of powers: divides power between executive, legislative, and judicial branches; checks and balances: each of the three branches given ways to limit the power of the other two.
Data Search. Executive branch: veto acts of Congress, call special sessions to pass particular legislation; legislative branch: impeach the President, override presidential vetoes.

Point of View

ANSWERS

1. John Hope Franklin most concerned about the framers' acceptance of slavery. By permitting slavery in writing the Constitution, he argues, framers contributed greatly to persistence of racial segregation and discrimination in the United States. He emphasizes that the framers should be held accountable for not living up to their ideals of freedom and equality.

2. Christopher and James Collier believe main legacy of framers is principle of government by the people. They argue that by making this principle the foundation of the Constitution, framers laid groundwork for freest, most prosperous nation on earth. The Colliers argues that framers' shortcomings should not be held against them because they were "so much people of their time."

3. Franklin and the Colliers agree framers should be admired for their commitment to ideal of political freedom. They

POINT OF VIEW

The Legacy of the Framers

Historians have written extensively about the framers of the Constitution and their legacy—the impact of their work on future generations. In the 1800s most agreed with Thomas Jefferson, who called the Constitutional Convention "an assembly of demigods," or godlike people. The Constitution they wrote was viewed as almost sacred. In this century, however, some historians have viewed the framers and their work more critically.

Betraying Ideals

" . . . The Declaration said 'all men are created equal.' 'Black men as well as white men?' some wondered. Every man had an inalienable right to 'life, liberty, and the pursuit of happiness.' 'Every black man as well as every white man?' some could well have asked. . . .

To be sure, some patriots were apparently troubled by the contradiction between their revolutionary philosophy of political freedom and the holding of human beings in bondage. . . . Patrick Henry, who had cried 'Give me liberty or give me death,' admitted that slavery was repugnant [hateful] to humanity; but . . . he continued to hold blacks in bondage. So did George Washington and Thomas Jefferson . . . and many others who signed the Declaration of Independence or the federal Constitution. . . .

We may admire [the framers] for their matchless service to a cause that captured the imagination of people around the world.

It does not follow, however, that we should admire them for . . . speaking eloquently at one moment for the brotherhood of man and in the next moment denying it to their black brothers . . . and for degrading the human spirit by equating five black men with three white men or equating a black man with a horse! . . .

Racial segregation, discrimination, and degradation are no unanticipated accidents in this nation's history. They stem logically and directly from the legacy that the founding fathers bestowed upon contemporary America. . . .

Their legacy to us in this regard cannot be cherished or celebrated. Rather, this legacy represents a continuing and dismaying problem that requires us all to put forth as much effort to overcome it as the founding fathers did in handing it down to us."

—From John Hope Franklin, *Race and History: Selected Essays 1938-1988.* Baton Rouge: Louisiana State University Press, 1989.

also agree that racism remains a persistent problem in the United States.

4. Answers will vary. Students should determine whether their overall evaluation of the framers' legacy should be positive or negative. One key judgment is whether framers should have gone further toward incorporating ideals of freedom and democracy into Constitution. Students whose judgment of framers is generally positive might argue that without a compromise on slavery, there would have been no Constitution and that at least framework for growth of democracy was laid. Those whose judgment is essentially negative may argue that framers' views cannot be excused as simply reflecting beliefs of time, for arguments of abolitionists were gaining strength during that period. They may also argue an ideal so basic as human freedom should not be compromised for sake of political unity—a "unity" eventually preserved only through military force in the Civil War.

Rising Above Themselves

“The American society that grew out of the Constitutional Convention is by no means perfect . . . But when we measure the United States against reality—the other nations of the world—we are amazed at how well it has worked, for it is certainly the most prosperous nation in the world, and a case can be made that it is the freest. . . . It is one of a very few nations in which it is virtually impossible to sustain for very long policies that the people do not want: the voice of the people, for better or worse, speaks louder in the United States than it does elsewhere.

Thus, without overlooking the . . . poverty and racism that continue to stain the American fabric, it is fair to say that the United States has gone a long way toward becoming what the men at Philadelphia wanted it to be: a prosperous, orderly nation in which no man need fear the arbitrary hand of a capricious government. . . .

The writers of the American Constitution were not angels. They . . . were so much people of their time that they could not see blacks were as human as they were. But withal, they rose above themselves far more than most men would have done in their place. And the generations of Americans who have grown up under the Constitution they struggled so hard to make are eternally in their debt.”

—From Christopher and James Collier, *Decision in Philadelphia: The Constitutional Convention of 1787.* New York: Random House, 1986.

1. What aspect of the framers' legacy most concerns John Hope Franklin?

2. What do the Colliers see as the framers' most important legacy?

3. What areas of agreement can you find between the writers of the two excerpts?

4. If you were writing an essay on the legacy of the framers, what would your main point be? Why?

Paintings of the delegates to the Constitutional Convention are typically glowing portraits. Historians' views, however, have been mixed—pointing to both good and bad effects of the document the framers created.

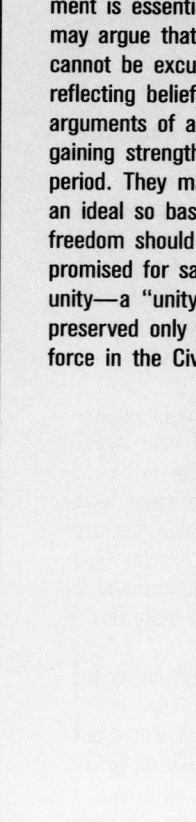

Chapter Survey

ANSWERS

Using New Vocabulary

1. Both refer to views of interpretation of Constitution. *Strict construction* is view that government has only powers specifically spelled out in Constitution; *loose construction* allows government implied powers.
2. Both are constitutional principles related to limitation of power. *Separation of powers* is division of power between three branches; *checks and balances* refer to each branch limiting the power of the other two.

Reviewing the Chapter

1. Delegates were white, prosperous, educated men who represented interests of merchants and large planters. Views often differed between representatives from "large" and "small" and southern and northern states.
2. Virginia Plan: stronger national government with three branches; executive to be single leader; two-house legislature, representation based on state population. Articles: no chief executive; unicameral legislature with each state having only one vote.
3. Large states got larger proportional representation in House, while small states got equal representation in Senate.
4. Three-fifths of all slaves counted as population for representation in Congress; no limit on import of slaves until 1808. Compromises made because delegates felt it more important to include slave-holding states in Union than ban slavery.
5. Federalists: Constitution only alternative to chaos and would not eliminate states' powers. Anti-Federalists: Constitution would destroy state governments and, lacking a Bill of Rights, fail to protect individual liberties.
6. Some power belongs only to federal government; some belongs only to states; others are shared by both. Federalism arose out of compromise: does a state's power affect the whole country or just the affairs of one state?
7. Representative government allows people to choose leaders who are responsive to will of people. The flexible framework of general principles can be applied to changing situations. Amendment process allows Constitution to be changed, but process is long and complicated enough to protect Constitution from being changed on a whim. Elastic clause provides flexibility for Congress to make necessary laws as needs of nation change.

Reduced student page in the Teacher's Edition

Chapter Survey

Using New Vocabulary

The vocabulary terms in each pair listed below are related to each other. For each pair, explain what the two terms have in common. Also explain how they are different.

1. *strict construction* and *loose construction*
2. *separation of powers* and *checks and balances*

Reviewing the Chapter

1. In what ways were the delegates similar in their backgrounds and beliefs? What were the main causes of conflict among them?
2. How did the Virginia Plan differ from the Articles of Confederation?
3. How did the Great Compromise meet demands of both large and small states?
4. What compromises did the delegates make on slavery and why?
5. Describe the main arguments for and against ratifying the Constitution.
6. Describe the system of federalism and explain how it arose.
7. Explain how the Constitution helps make possible the continuous reshaping of American democracy.

Thinking Critically

1. Evaluation. Do you think the Constitutional Convention should have been open to the public? Why or why not?
2. Analysis. Why do you think the Constitution allows both the national and the state governments to levy taxes?
3. Evaluation. In what sense do you think the Constitution is democratic? In what ways does it seem undemocratic? Explain.
4. Synthesis. If Patrick Henry were alive today, do you think he would feel that the national government has too much power? Explain.

History and You

Every ten years the federal government conducts a census, counting the population of each state to determine representation in the House of Representatives. Find out how the population of your state has changed since the beginning of the twentieth century and how these changes have been reflected in your state's congressional representation. Why do you think it is important for voters to fill out and return census forms?

Using Geography

Match each letter on the map with the correct state and describe that state's role in the creation and ratification of the Constitution.

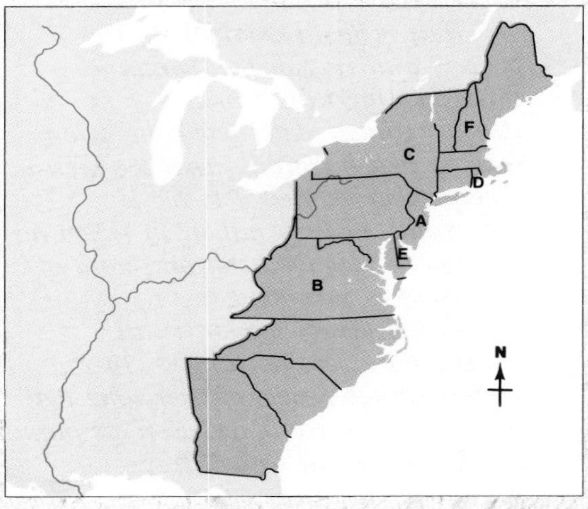

1. Rhode Island
2. Virginia
3. New Hampshire
4. Delaware
5. New York
6. New Jersey

Thinking Critically

1. Students may argue that common people should have had a greater voice in framing the Constitution, or that to bring about compromise, discussion and negotiation between a few people were required.
2. To prevent federal government from gaining too much power; to allow states to decide what taxes are necessary to meet their needs and how taxes should be levied.
3. Students may answer it is democratic in that it provides for representative government and for change if people voice a need for change. It is undemocratic in that large states have unequal representation in Senate and that passing amendments is slow, difficult process.
4. Patrick Henry would probably be appalled at the power of federal government today, but not all his predictions have come true. He opposed strong central government because it would destroy powers of states and not protect people's liberties. Even Henry would have to admit that federal government has done more to protect individual civil rights and freedoms than some of the states over the last 200 years.

History and You

Answers will vary by state.

Using Geography

1. Rhode Island: D, did not send delegates to Convention.
2. Virginia: B, proposed first plan for new government.
3. New Hampshire: F, ninth state to ratify Constitution.
4. Delaware: E, first state to ratify Constitution.
5. New York: C, one of largest states, ratification gave government chance of success.
6. New Jersey: A, proposed alternative plan of government.

Applying Social Studies Skills

1. Congress or national convention called by Congress.
2. State legislatures or special state ratifying conventions.
3. Four ways to propose and then ratify an amendment.
4. Most amendments proposed by Congress and ratified by state legislatures.
5. No; number falls short of three-fourths requirement.

Applying Thinking Skills

1. Vest power in an Executive.
2. Paterson's plan provides for Executive chosen by Congress, Hamilton's by Electors selected by states. Hamilton specifies executive powers, Paterson is more general.
3. Paterson suggests cautious attitude; Executive elected by Congress, forbidden to lead troops. Hamilton's plan suggests strong Executive.
4. Hamilton's plan; President has powers Hamilton proposes for Executive.

Applying Social Studies Skills

Interpreting Flow Charts

The flow chart below uses arrows and connecting lines to show the amendment process described in Article 5 of the Constitution. The chart shows the different routes that can be followed to propose and then ratify an amendment. Study the flow chart and then answer the questions that follow.

Amending the Constitution

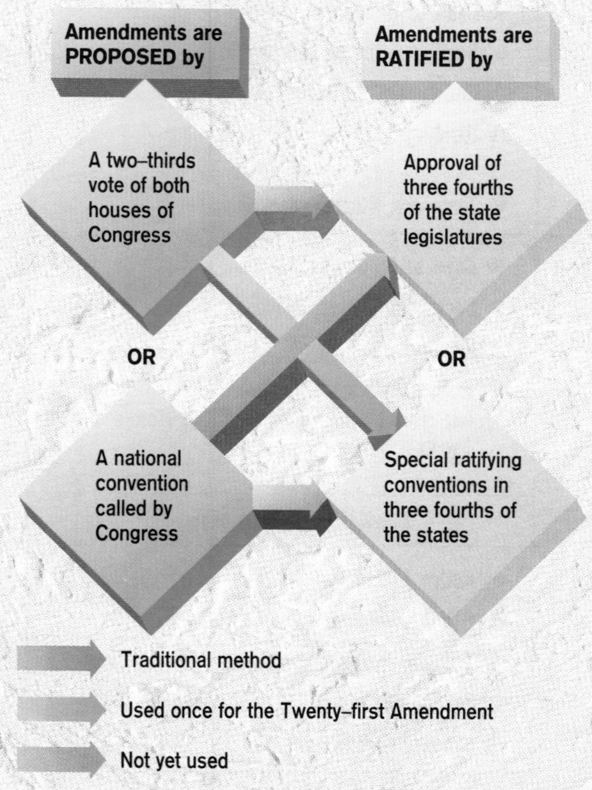

1. Who can propose amendments?
2. Who can ratify amendments?
3. How many different ways are there to propose and then ratify an amendment?
4. Which way has been used most often?
5. Would an amendment ratified by twenty-five states become part of the Constitution? Explain.

Applying Thinking Skills

Comparing

Comparing consists of identifying how objects or pieces of information are alike *and* how they differ. Below are two proposals for a federal executive that were offered to the Constitutional Convention—the first by William Paterson of New Jersey and the second by Alexander Hamilton of New York. Compare their proposals to find out their attitudes toward executive power. Then answer the questions that follow.

Paterson's Proposal: Congress should elect an Executive to consist of ____ persons to continue in office for ____ years, to be paid a fixed salary by the federal treasury, to be ineligible for reelection and to be removable by Congress on request of a majority of the Executives of the member states. The Executive should execute all federal laws, and direct all military operations but shall not take command of any troops or personally conduct any enterprise as General.

Hamilton's Proposal: The Supreme Executive Authority of the United States should serve during good behavior and should be elected by Electors chosen by the people of election districts in the States. The Executive shall have the power to veto bills passed by Congress, to direct war when it has been authorized, to make treaties with the advice and consent of the Senate, to appoint the heads of Finance, War and Foreign Affairs, and to nominate all other officers subject to the consent of the Senate.

1. In what ways were Paterson's and Hamilton's proposals similar?
2. In what ways did they differ?
3. Compare Paterson's and Hamilton's attitudes toward executive power.
4. Which proposal is most like the plan that was adopted by the Constitutional Convention? Explain.

Chapter 7

Setting Democracy in Motion

Planning Guide

	Student Text	TWE Lesson Plans	Support Materials
SECTION 1	**Section 7–1** (1–2 Days) **Launching the New Government,** pp 160–165 Review/Evaluation Section Review, p 165	**Introducing the Chapter:** Debating a site for the Capital—Class Activity, one class period, p 157B **Teaching the Main Ideas:** A Hearing on Hamilton's Policies—Class Activity, 2 class periods, p 157B	★ **Read to Remember,** Section 1 ● **Section Activities,** Section 1 ● **Geography Activities,** Section 1 Δ **Readings,** Δ **Enrichment Activities,** Section 1 ● **Tests and Quizzes,** Section 1 Quiz
SECTION 2	**Section 7–2** (1–2 Days) **Conflict at Home and Abroad,** pp 166–171 Review/Evaluation Section Review, p 171	**Teaching the Main Ideas:** The United States and Europe—Individual Activity, one class period, p 157C **Enrichment Activity:** Political Parties Yesterday and Today—Individual Activity, 30 minutes, p 157C	★ **Read to Remember,** Section 2 ● **Section Activities,** Section 2 Δ **Enrichment Activities,** Section 2 Δ **Readings,** ● **Tests and Quizzes,** Section 2 Quiz
SECTION 3	**Section 7–3** (1–3 Days) **Challenges to National Security,** pp 172–177 Exploring Issues—Freedom of Speech: The Arrest of Matthew Lyon, p 174 Connections to Themes: Shaping Democracy, p 177 Young in America: At School, pp 178–179 Review/Evaluation Section Review, p 177 Chapter 7 Survey, pp 180–181 Unit 2 Survey, pp 182–183 Skills, pp 180–181 Using New Vocabulary Thinking Critically Using Geography Applying Thinking Skills: Comparing, Interpreting Political Cartoons	**Reinforcement Activity:** Federalist and Republican Views—Paired Activity, 30 minutes, p 157C **Evaluating Progress:** If We Had Alien and Sedition Acts Today—Individual Activity, one class period, p 157C	★ **Read to Remember,** Section 3 ● **Section Activities,** Section 3 Δ **Readings,** ● **Tests and Quizzes,** Section 3 Quiz, Chapter 7 Test (Forms A and B), Unit 2 Test (Forms A and B) **Additional Resources** ● **Active Learning** Δ **GTV Videodiscs** Δ **Transparencies and Activity Book** ● **Testing Software** ★ **Chapter Summaries** **Key:** ★ For Extra Support ● For All Students Δ For Enrichment

Overview

Under President George Washington, the government of the United States was launched, with Congress creating departments within the executive branch and establishing a system of courts. In turn, Washington appointed people to serve in executive and judicial offices.

Serious economic questions faced the new government, particularly how to deal with national and state debts, whether to establish a national bank, and the wisdom of levying tariffs and excise taxes. Strong disagreements between the followers of Alexander Hamilton and Thomas Jefferson over the role of the federal government and the nature of democracy led to the rise of the Federalist and Republican parties.

Compounding domestic disagreements was the question of how to deal with foreign threats. Conflict between France and Great Britain in the aftermath of the French Revolution found Americans divided in their sympathies. Washington advocated a policy of American neutrality in foreign disputes and sought to secure the country's safety by forging treaties with Britain and Spain.

Foreign threats were revived during the Adams administration when France challenged the United States on the seas. Federalists who wanted to go to war with France feared the influence of pro-French foreigners as well as Republicans. They convinced Congress to pass the Alien and Sedition Acts. These laws engaged the Federalists and Republicans in another series of disputes over how American democracy was to be defined.

In 1800 Jefferson was elected President, and the Federalist era came to an end.

Activity Objectives

After completing the activities, students should be able to

- describe the main features of Hamilton's economic policy.
- describe the links between domestic politics and foreign affairs during Washington's administration.
- identify the political differences between Republicans and Federalists on major issues.
- evaluate provisions of the Alien and Sedition Acts.
- compare the functions of early political parties with today's parties.

Introducing the Chapter

Debating a Site for the Capital

This class activity requires one period.

In this activity students, in the course of choosing a permanent site for the nation's capital, experience the nature of the challenges facing the first Congress.

Tell students that one of the first issues facing the newly elected Congress in 1789 was where to locate a permanent national capital. Have them imagine that they are members of Congress. Discuss criteria they might consider in choosing a site—a central location, accessibility to population centers, availability of transportation, and an effort to avoid political rivalries among the states. Post the criteria for later reference.

Have students form small groups of three to five students. Direct each group to work independently to prepare a site recommendation for a national capital. They can use atlases and other available sources for research. Allow twenty minutes for preparation. At the end of the time, have each group present its choice to the class. Post and tally the recommendations.

After the presentations, take a class vote to determine the new site. Challenge students to be prepared, after reading Section 7-1, to explain how and why the first Congress chose Washington, D.C.

Teaching the Main Ideas

Section 7-1: A Hearing on Hamilton's Policies

This class activity requires two periods.

In Section 7-1 students learn that Alexander Hamilton's policies during Washington's first term set important precedents—and caused considerable dissension. The following activity will enable students to identify differing views on Hamilton's economic policies.

Ask students to explain some of the economic problems and issues facing the nation when Washington took office (national debt, state debts, need for a national banking system and for tariffs and taxes). Emphasize that as Secretary of the Treasury, Alexander Hamilton was charged with solving financial problems and setting the nation on a firm economic footing, but his proposals did not please everyone. Explain that, acting as members of the House of Representatives in the first Congress, the class will hold a mock hearing on Hamilton's proposals.

Divide the class into two groups: supporters of Hamilton's economic policy and opponents. Subdivide the first group of representatives into five groups and assign one group to write a speech describing and supporting Hamilton's overall view of the country's economic needs. Have each of the other four groups write a speech supporting one of Hamilton's economic policies: payment of national debt, assumption of state debts, establishment of a national bank, establishment of tariffs and excise taxes. Divide the second large group into five groups which will write speeches in opposition to Hamilton's overall view of the country's economic needs and his four specific economic policies.

Allow time for groups to write their speeches. Then call for the supporters to present their speech describing Hamilton's overview of the nation's economic needs. At its conclusion, call for the opposing view. Continue with speeches supporting and opposing the four points of Hamilton's economic policy.

After the speeches, allow some time for open debate. Conclude by discussing what might have happened and how the United States might have developed if the actions and policies proposed by the Republicans, rather than those advocated by Hamilton, had been adopted.

Teaching the Main Ideas

Section 7-2: The United States and Europe

This individual project takes one class period.

Outbreak of war between Great Britain and France widened the gap between Federalists and Republicans. In this activity students will prepare time lines showing the link between domestic politics and foreign affairs.

Have students review Section 7-2. Then ask them each to prepare a time line of economic and political events in the United States and Europe between 1791 and 1796. Direct them to list events in the United States on one side of the time line and events in Europe on the other.

Students should include the following events on the United States side of the time line: establishment of the *National Gazette*; appearance of political parties in elections, Proclamation of Neutrality, arrival of Citizen Genêt, British aid to Indians in the Northwest, embargo against Great Britain, Battle of Fallen Timbers, Treaty of Greenville, Washington's farewell address, election of Adams. On the European side of the time line, students should include: beginning of French Revolution, execution of French king, French call for revolution in Europe, war between France and Britain-Austria-Prussia-the Netherlands-Spain, British blockade of France, British seizure of American ships and sailors, and signing of Jay's treaty and Pinckney's Treaty.

When students have finished their time lines, review their work by having them work together to draw a class time line on the chalkboard. Discuss the time line by asking:

- *How did events in Europe affect the growth of political parties?* (Political divisions between pro-French Republicans and pro-British Federalists deepened with outbreak of war between Britain and France.)
- *What kinds of ties linked the United States to Europe?* (To France: political ties to its "democratic" revolution, and to treaties that had brought France to the support of the United States during the American Revolution. To Britain: economic ties based on crucial trade and, possibly, emotional ties to the "homeland" of most Americans.)

Reinforcement Activity

Section 7-3: Federalist and Republican Views

Students need at least 30 minutes to complete this paired activity.

The following activity, in which pairs of students draw political cartoons, reinforces understanding of the issues that dominated the administrations of Washington and Adams.

Tell students that they are to draw political cartoons for a Federalist or Republican newspaper of the period. The cartoons may take a stand on any of the following issues: Jay's Treaty, XYZ Affair, the "half-war," Alien and Sedition Acts, Kentucky and Virginia Resolutions, election of 1800. To stimulate creativity, point out examples of political cartoons in the text and in current newspapers and magazines. Discuss the use of symbols, satire, captions, and titles.

Direct students to display their completed cartoons, organizing them by topic. Have the class view the cartoons and comment on how accurately or inaccurately they think the cartoonists have reflected the view of the party they represented.

Evaluating Progress

Section 7-3: If We Had Alien and Sedition Acts Today

This individual activity may be assigned as homework and shared in class the following day.

This take-home activity is designed to assess students' understanding of the Alien and Sedition Acts through their ability to apply knowledge of the acts to present-day issues involving the government, especially the presidency, and immigration.

Remind students that the Alien and Sedition Acts were passed at a time when many Americans feared that foreigners and pro-French Americans were threatening the nation's security.

Tell students that in this activity they will complete a three-part writing project relating the Alien and Sedition Acts to present-day issues.

- First, they are to summarize in their own words the four laws known as the Alien and Sedition Acts.
- Second, they are to find two current newspaper articles: one that describes actions or statements that would have violated conditions of the Sedition Act, and one that describes an action or statement that in 1798 would have been regulated by the Alien Acts. For each article they should write a statement describing the link between the present-day events and the acts.
- Third, they are to write a response to the question: *Did the Alien and Sedition Acts violate the Constitution?* being sure to support the answer with examples.

Criteria for evaluating students' work should include accuracy of summaries, clearly expressed links between articles and the Alien and Sedition Acts, and convincing examples to support answers to the last question.

Enrichment Activity

Section 7-2: Political Parties Yesterday and Today

This individual activity requires half a class period.

This activity engages students in comparing the positive contributions of the early political parties with the functions of political parties today. Write on the chalkboard the following list of party functions: select candidates, set goals for government, provide leadership, play "watchdog" role in government, give citizens a voice in government, inform citizens, involve citizens in the political process.

Begin the activity by reminding students that the conflicts between Hamilton and Jefferson gave rise to two political parties. Emphasize that the nature and function of political parties were not legislated but instead emerged as the government and society of the young country developed. Point out that today we can identify more specifically the functions of political parties. Call students' attention to the functions listed on the chalkboard. Use examples from current local or national political events to illustrate and clarify each example.

Direct students to copy the list of party functions from the chalkboard onto their own paper. They are then to review Chapter 7, finding and writing down one or more examples to illustrate how each party function was fulfilled by the early Federalist and Republican parties.

Conclude by asking students to speculate about how the United States would be different today if political parties had not emerged. Then ask them how the country might be different if many, equally strong parties had emerged.

Bibliography and Audiovisual Material

Teacher Bibliography

Cunliffe, Marcus. *The Nation Takes Shape: 1789–1837.* Chicago: University of Chicago Press, 1960.

Dos Passos, John. *The Men Who Made the Nation.* Garden City, NY: Doubleday, 1957.

Hofstader, Richard. *The Idea of a Party System: The Rise of Legitimate Opposition in the United States, 1780–1840.* Berkeley: University of California Press, 1969.

Starkey, Marion. *Lace Cuffs and Leather Aprons: Popular Struggles in the Federalist Era, 1783–1800.* New York: Knopf, 1972.

Tunis, Edwin. *The Young United States: 1783–1830.* New York: Crowell, 1976.

Student Bibliography

Baldwin, Leland D. *Whiskey Rebels: The Story of a Frontier Uprising.* Pittsburgh: University of Pittsburgh Press, 1968.

Fisher, Louise. *President and Congress.* New York: Free Press, 1973.

Irving, Washington. *Life of George Washington.* New York: Sleepy Hollow, 1975.

Forester, C. S. *The Captain From Connecticut.* Boston: Little, Brown, 1941.

Johnson, Mary. *Lewis Rand.* Darby, PA: Arden Library, 1978.

Miller, John C. *The Federalist Era, 1789–1801.* New York: HarperCollins, 1963.

Richter, Conrad. *Awakening Land.* New York: Knopf, 1966.

Richter, Conrad. *The Light in the Forest*. New York: Amsco School Publications, 1970.

Smith, Barbara C. *After the Revolution: The Smithsonian History of Everyday Life in the 18th Century.* New York: Pantheon, 1987.

Films, Videocassettes, and Videodiscs

George Washington. 28 min. Coronet/MTI. Movie.

Profiles In Courage Series: John Adams. 50 min. Zenger Films. Videocassette.

Filmstrips

Our Political System. National Geographic Society.

Computer Software

U.S. Government. Apple. SEI Corporation.

Washington's Decisions. Apple. Educational Activities.

Chapter 7

Objectives

- Contrast the Federalist approach to government with that of the Republican.
- Cite domestic and foreign threats faced by the new nation.
- Explain how the United States faced the threat of war with France.

Introducing THE CHAPTER

For suggestions on introducing Chapter 7, refer to page 157B in the Teacher's Edition.

Developing THE CHAPTER

For activities and teaching strategies to help you reinforce and enrich chapter content, see pages 157B–157D in the Teacher's Edition.

Chapter Opener Illustrations

The site of the nation's capital was chosen by George Washington in 1791. The city's layout was designed by Pierre L'Enfant, a French engineer and architect who had fought with the Patriots and remained in the United States after the War for Independence. L'Enfant's drawing of Washington, D.C., adapted by Andrew Ellicott, was printed on a handkerchief. L'Enfant's plan showed the location of the Capitol, White House, and Mall. A contemporary view from the Lincoln Memorial of the Capitol and Mall also appears below.

Land for the new capital was surveyed by a six-man team that included Benjamin Banneker, a free African American from Maryland. A woodcut engraving of Banneker appears on the title page of the 1795 edition of the alma-

Reduced student page in the Teacher's Edition

Chapter 7 1789-1801

Setting Democracy in Motion

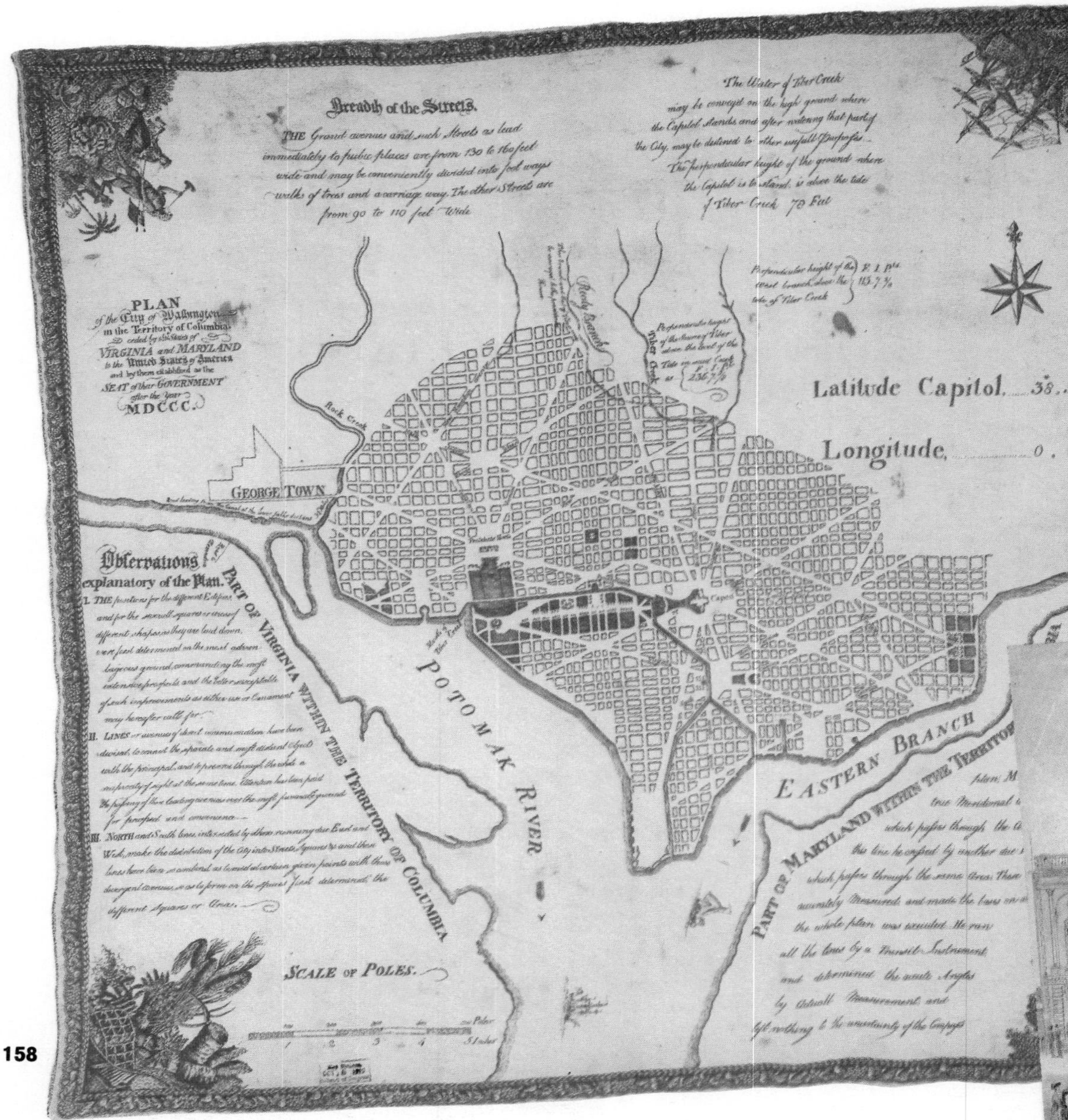

158

nac that he published annually for more than a decade. It offered weather data, recipes, medical remedies, and antislavery essays.

Washington held a competition for public building designs. The Capitol was designed with two wings—one for the Senate (below), the other for the House of Representatives.

Thomas Jefferson anonymously submitted plans for the White House that included a domed roof. However, his design was not chosen, and the White House today, unlike the Capitol, does not have a dome.

American Voices

In the spring of 1789, newly elected members of Congress made their way over mud-choked roads and swollen streams to New York City, the temporary home of the new national government. By fall, however, the First Congress was locked in debate over where the nation's permanent capital should be located.

"Mr. Thomas Hartley of Pennsylvania—Many persons wish it seated on the banks of the Delaware, many on the banks of the Potomac. I consider the Susquehanna as the middle ground. It will suit the inhabitants to the north better than the Potomac could, and the inhabitants to the south better than the Delaware would.

Mr. James Jackson of Georgia—Are the northern members to rule in this business? . . . I think the Potomac a better site.

Mr. Theodore Sedgwick of Massachusetts—It is the opinion of all the northern states, that the climate of the Potomac is unhealthy.

Mr. John Vining of Delaware—I am in favor of the Potomac. . . . I look on it as the center from which those streams are to flow that are to give life to the nation."

The issue at hand was more than the seat of government. It was also power. The Revolution had unified the colonists. But now the states seemed as separate from one another as they had been before the war, each defending its own interests. Furthermore, conflicts among the new leaders were turning the government into a political battlefield and threatening to upset the union. The new Constitution set up a form of government that was the first of its kind. But so far it was only on paper. How would it take shape? Would the experiment work?

L'Enfant's plan for Washington, D.C.; Senate wing of the Capitol, 1800; Benjamin Banneker's Almanac, 1795; view of Capital Mall today; Jefferson's contest entry for the President's house.

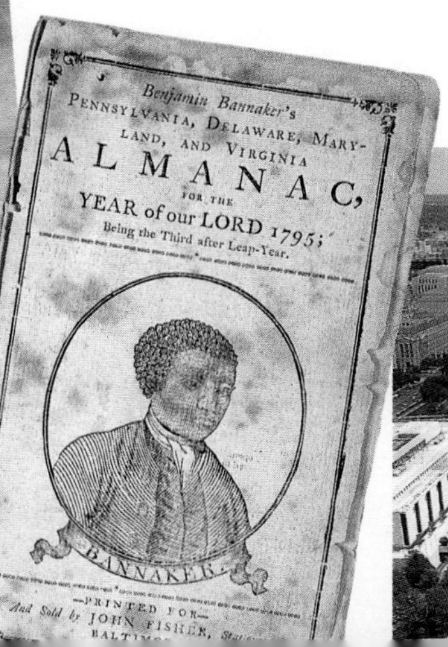

Analyzing Primary Sources

American Voices

Jealousy between sections of the nation was especially evident in the debates of Congress on the location of the national capital. Members of the House agreed that the capital should be centrally located for easy access to the Atlantic Ocean as well as to the western territory, but there the agreement ended.

Display a large map of the United States or refer students to the physical map of the United States on text pages 902–903.

1. Where is the Delaware River? The Potomac? The Susquehanna?
2. Why might James Jackson of Georgia prefer the Potomac River? **(closer to his southern state of Georgia)** Thomas Hartley, the Susquehanna? **(in his state of Pennsylvania)**
3. Explain the statement: The issue at hand was more than the seat of government. **(States closest to the capital might wield greater influence on government.)**
4. Make a generalization about which states supported situating the capital on the Potomac River site. **(Southern states for, New England against, Middle States divided)**

GTV Side 2

Chap. 1, Frame 04166

A Fresh Start: The Compromise Capital (Movie Segment)

Search and Play:

159

Section 7-1

Objectives

- ***Answer the Focus Question.***
- *Describe how Congress organized the executive and judicial branches of the new government.*
- *Explain the differences in the ways Thomas Jefferson and Alexander Hamilton envisioned the ideal American society.*

Introducing

THE SECTION

New nations face a number of problems. Have students preview the headings in this section and speculate about what problems the young republic encountered. **(deciding on form of national government, political disagreements about course of action, financial problems)** What similar and/or different problems do today's emerging nations face?

B · A · C · K · G · R · O · U · N · D

Time Line Illustrations

1. The first national bank of the United States was located on Third Street in Philadelphia. William Birch hand colored this engraving. The bank's architecture was known as Greek Revival—with graceful columns and marble front.
2. Miami chief Little Turtle, or Michikinikwa, was known as a brilliant leader of Northwest tribes. His warriors defeated United States forces in 1790 and 1791. When General Anthony Wayne strengthened forces, Little Turtle recognized the inevitability of defeat and counseled peace. The warriors chose a new leader and were defeated at Fallen Timbers in 1794. Little Turtle signed the Treaty of Greenville in 1795.
3. A detail from an American cartoon about the XYZ affair pictures the French government as a five-headed monster, crying out for money. The missing portion shows Americans—John Marshall, Elbridge Gerry, and Charles

Reduced student page in the Teacher's Edition

CHAPTER TIME LINE

1789 - 1801

1789 George Washington inaugurated

1790 Congress votes to assume state debts

1791 First Bank of the United States

1793 Citizen Genêt Affair

1794 Whiskey Rebellion
Jun Neutrality Act
Aug Battle of Fallen Timbers

1795 **Aug** Treaty of Greenville
Oct Pinckney's Treaty

1789 | 1791 | 1793 | 1795

7-1 Launching the New Government

Focus: How were the powers of the federal government to be defined?

On the morning of April 30, 1789, George Washington stood on a balcony overlooking New York City's Wall Street. Elected President by a unanimous vote of the electoral college, he had ridden north from Mount Vernon, retracing much of the route he had followed in his final assault on the British.

Now, wearing a suit of plain brown cloth given to him by a Connecticut mill, Washington took the oath of office. The huge crowd cheered mightily. In spite of the cheers, however, Washington confessed to a friend that he felt a bit like someone being led to his own execution.

Washington's feelings were understandable. The eyes of the world were on the new nation to see if self-government would work. Not only did Washington face the challenge of helping shape the new government, but he also faced pressing financial problems that threatened to rock the country. As a soldier and farmer, Washington had little interest in financial matters. With an empty treasury, huge debts to foreign nations and private creditors, and no means for collecting taxes, the new President saw an "ocean of difficulties."

Most Americans took comfort in the knowledge that Washington's hand was on the tiller of government. Even though colonial life, with its relative simplicity, was giving way to a larger and more complex society, Americans could still agree on one thing— their confidence in Washington's leadership. Washington and the First Congress turned their attention to shaping the new government.

Pinckney—coolly refusing the demands. (Entire cartoon is on text page 181.)
4. The Sedition Act of 1798 is housed in the National Archives, Washington, D.C.
5. Caleb Boyle painted Thomas Jefferson c.1800. Jefferson is pictured near the Natural Bridge on land he owned in Virginia.

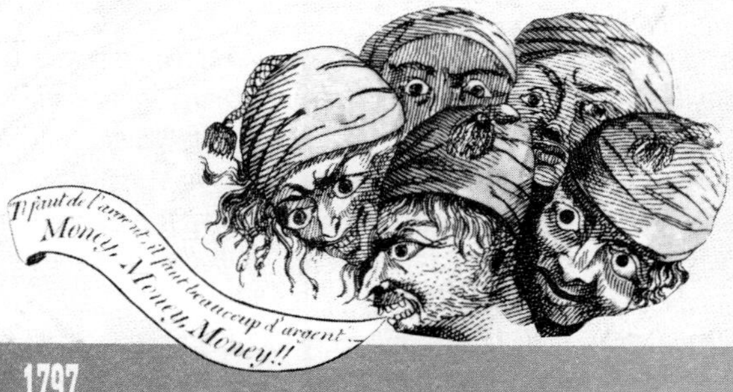

1798-1800 The "Half War"

1797 | 1799 | 1801

1797 The XYZ Affair

1798 **Jul** Alien and Sedition Acts
Dec Virginia and Kentucky resolutions

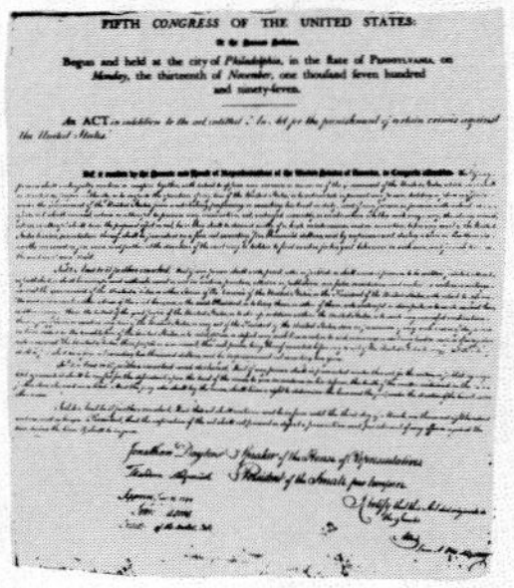
FIFTH CONGRESS OF THE UNITED STATES

1801 Election of Jefferson and Burr

Creating the Executive Branch

One of the first tasks facing Congress was organizing the executive branch of government. The Constitution provided a framework, but the details had to be filled in. President Washington and Vice-President John Adams had been unanimously elected to their positions. The next job was to establish executive departments and appoint qualified leaders to head them.

The Confederation Congress had created executive departments for foreign affairs, finance, war, and the postal service. Following that precedent, Congress created departments of State, Treasury, and War, and the lesser office of Postmaster General. President Washington's job was to appoint the department heads, along with almost a thousand minor federal employees.

For Secretary of State, Washington chose Thomas Jefferson, the American minister to France. He appointed lawyer-politician Alexander Hamilton to the position of Secretary of the Treasury, a key role, for the new nation was plagued with financial difficulties. Henry Knox, Washington's wartime artillery chief, became Secretary of War.

How these departments and their heads were to relate to Congress and to the President was not at all clear. Washington's own style of leadership helped shape these relationships. Washington did not attempt to lead Congress in making laws, nor did he make a habit of turning to Congress for advice. As he saw it, Congress was to make laws and the President was to enforce them. Before making decisions he often consulted with the department heads and Attorney General Edmund Randolph. This group of advisors came to be known as the President's **cabinet.** All other American presidents have relied on their cabinets for advice.

Creating the Judicial Branch

Along with creating a framework for the executive branch of government, Congress had to organize the judicial branch. The Constitution authorized a Supreme Court, but left it to Congress to decide what lower—or "inferior"—courts to create. Some congressmen wanted no inferior federal courts, preferring that state courts try federal cases. However, they were outvoted by those who wanted a

Developing THE SECTION

Linking Past and Present

Research. Today, the President leads a government that is much larger than the one in 1790. In 1790 the legislature was made up of 26 senators and 65 representatives. Today, there are 100 senators and 435 representatives.

Only four executive departments existed in 1789, employing about one thousand people. Today, there are fourteen executive departments with more than two million employees. Have students find out what these departments are and when they were established.

GTV Side 2

Chap. 2, Frame 05886

U.S. Pop. 1790/ Native American Pop. 1800 (Population Clocks, 2 Frames)

Search:

Step:

Linking Past and Present

Discussion. The role of the Supreme Court has changed significantly over the years. Have students contrast the Supreme Court as it began and as it is today. **(It has grown from six to nine members; justices formerly required to ride circuit, now stay in capital; judicial review added to its powers.)**

Multicultural Perspectives

Benjamin Banneker, a free African American from Maryland, was appointed to the Washington, D.C., surveying team by President Washington. He was the first black presidential appointee in the United States. Banneker had a photographic memory. When L'Enfant, the chief engineer of the capital city layout, resigned and took the plans back to France with him, Banneker was able to reproduce the plans from memory.

Reduced student page in the Teacher's Edition

complete federal system, with a Supreme Court, three circuit courts, and thirteen district courts.

In the Judiciary Act of 1789, Congress created a court system that was like a pyramid, with the thirteen district courts — one in each state — at the base. On the next level were three circuit courts, each of which heard appeals from a group of district courts in its region. Circuit courts also dealt with disputes between citizens of different states. Supreme Court justices were required to "ride the circuits," or travel to the circuit courts, which were comprised of one district judge and two Supreme Court justices.

At the top of the pyramid was the Supreme Court, staffed by a Chief Justice and five associate justices. The Supreme Court was to have the final say in cases involving federal laws and treaties and in conflicts between state law and federal law. The Judiciary Act also established the office of Attorney General to represent the United States in Supreme Court cases and to be legal advisor to the executive branch. John Jay was appointed Chief Justice, and Edmund Randolph became the Attorney General.

Hamilton vs. Jefferson

Even as the structure of the new government was being hammered out, serious disagreements were arising. In fact, open conflict erupted between two members of Washington's cabinet — Hamilton and Jefferson. This conflict was to flavor the period of Washington's presidency and beyond, and to give rise to political parties.

Hamilton and Jefferson were a study in contrasts. Hamilton presented an elegant image, handsome, suave, and fashionably dressed, but with a tough and commanding spirit. Jefferson was tall, gangly, and untidy, and possessed a great personal warmth. The differences between Hamilton and Jefferson went far deeper than appearances. The two men held vastly differing views of life in general and the role of government in particular.

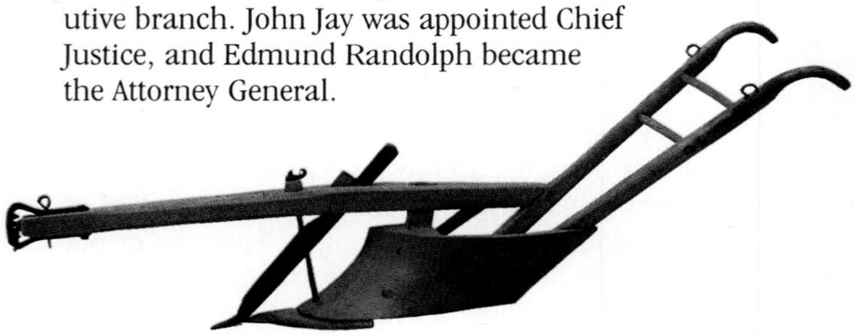

While most Americans in the 1790s were simple farmers, a growing number, including the Washingtons, lived like aristocrats. From left: "The Residence of David Twining, 1787," by Edward Hicks; plow invented by Thomas Jefferson; "Lady Washington's Reception," by Daniel P. Huntington.

Connections: Economics

Hamilton's Report on the Public Credit showed that in 1790 the young nation owed $11,710,738 to French and Dutch creditors and $42,414,085 in domestic debt, equivalent to a foreign debt of $2.4 trillion and a domestic debt of $8.7 trillion today. The interest payments on both debts were far behind. Yet, owing to Hamilton's economic policies, by 1794 the United States had an outstanding credit rating, higher than any country in Europe.

Hamilton distrusted the ability of the general population to rule itself. "The people are turbulent and changing," he wrote. "They seldom judge or determine right." If political power were given to the common people, Hamilton feared, issues would be settled by the will of the mob rather than through reasonable thought. He believed that a strong central government was necessary for the good of the nation as a whole, and that those with wealth and education were best fit to govern.

Hamilton viewed the world through the eyes of a business person. He saw a strong national government as essential to the orderly conduct of business, and he made advancing the interests of merchants, manufacturers, and bankers his goal. If those classes prospered, he believed, a vigorous economy would ultimately benefit less wealthy Americans.

Unlike Hamilton, Thomas Jefferson had great faith in the ability and right of all the people to play a vital role in government. "The influence over government," he wrote, "must be shared by all the people." Only when power—and the wealth that created it—was spread throughout the nation, he thought, would government be safe from corruption by any person or any group.

So, while Hamilton favored merchants and bankers, Jefferson was the champion of the farmers and landowners. He wanted as many people as possible to own property and to take part in government. In Jefferson's eyes, a nation of farmers—self-reliant economically and independent in their political views—would form a true republic. For this reason he trusted local government more than the federal government and was a strong supporter of the states as they grappled with the federal government for authority.

Facing the War Debt

The national debt. Opposing views first clashed over how to solve the nation's financial difficulties. The most pressing problem was the debt left over from the Revolution. The government had no money to pay its debts and run the country, and it had no credit. Hamilton, as Secretary of the Treasury, put together a plan for collecting revenue and building public credit.

In January 1790 Hamilton presented his Report on the Public Credit, which addressed the debt the nation had inherited from the Confederation—a whopping sum of $52 million. The money was owed to French and Dutch bankers and to United States citizens who had bought bonds during the Revolutionary War.

Hamilton believed that the war debt should be paid as soon as possible. If the United States did not honor its debts, he argued, its reputation would suffer both at home and abroad, and it would have difficulty borrowing money in the future.

Hamilton's plan was for the government to call in the old war bonds, which had lost value, and exchange them for new federal ones. The government would pay regular interest on these new bonds and redeem them at full value when due.

The problem was that many of the original bond holders had needed immediate money and had sold their bonds at a fraction of their full value—as little as twelve cents on the dollar. Speculators had bought the bonds, gambling that the government would survive and honor its debt. That gamble would pay off if the government redeemed the bonds at full value.

James Madison was suspicious of Hamilton's plan. He and others believed northern speculators might have inside information about Hamilton's proposals, since many New York financiers seemed to be the ones snapping up the bonds. Not surprisingly, many members of Congress also bought up all the bonds they could find. To make sure that speculators would not profit unfairly, Madison proposed that only the original bond holders be paid in full.

Hamilton argued that Madison's plan would be disastrous to the public credit. If speculators were denied the full value of the bonds that they had bought in good faith, it would be a "breach of contract." Lacking solid evidence that any of Hamilton's acquaintances were profiting from inside information, Madison could do little to stop the proposal from becoming law. Congress rejected Madison's plan and followed Hamilton.

State debts. In addition to the federal debt, the states had war debts totaling around $25 million. Hamilton recommended that the federal government assume, or take over, these debts. Then all

Thinking Critically

Analysis. Ask students why Jefferson favored the American farmer. What factors might have influenced his views? What groups did Hamilton favor? Why? Are there any similarities between Jefferson's and Hamilton's views? What are the differences? Are such differences healthy for a democracy? Why or why not?

Active Learning

Role Play. The conflict between Hamilton and Jefferson is reflected in their opinions of each other. Hamilton:

"[Jefferson] is activated by views, in my judgement, subversive of the principle of good government and dangerous to the Union, peace, and happiness of the country."

Jefferson:

"The ultimate object [of Hamilton's program] is to prepare the way for a change, from the present form of government to that of a monarchy."

Have students work in pairs—one student to play Hamilton and the other Jefferson—to restate the opinions in their own words and discuss similarities or differences.

Constitutional Heritage

Using the Constitution. Using the elastic clause in the Constitution, Hamilton persuaded Washington to approve the Bank of the United States. Have students turn to the Constitution at the back of the text and read Article 1, Section 8, especially noting the "elastic clause" and the Tenth Amendment. Then discuss the constitutionality or unconstitutionality of the national bank based upon their reading of Article 1. **Ask:** What kinds of federal legislation are passed today by Congress on the basis of the elastic clause? **(social welfare and business regulatory laws, for example)**

Thinking Critically

Analysis. Read to students the following statement by Jefferson concerning his views about establishing the Bank of the United States.

"To take a single step beyond the boundaries ...specially drawn around the powers of Congress is to take possession of a boundless field of power, no longer susceptible of any definition."

Ask students to describe Jefferson's views in their own words. (If Congress given power to establish bank, this could lead to unlimited actions by Congress.) What is Jefferson's main fear? (Government will gain unlimited power.) Do students agree or disagree with Jefferson? Why?

Linking Past and Present

Modern tax revolts are less violent than the Whiskey Rebellion. In June 1978, California voters passed Proposition 13, a measure that cut local property taxes by 50 percent. The tax revolt spread as other states passed similar measures.

Multicultural Perspectives

Disregard of treaties and growing encroachment by settlers on lands inhabited by Native Americans continued, even as the federal government was extending its power. With the Whiskey Rebellion, the government showed that it could enforce laws, *if* it wanted to.

Reduced student page in the Teacher's Edition

creditors would have a stake in supporting the federal government, for only a strong government could pay them.

Hamilton's proposal for assumption of state debts caused another great uproar. States that had already paid a large share of their debts were outraged at the idea of having to help pay other states' debts. Moreover, this plan would saddle the nation with an even larger debt, owed to a group of wealthy northerners.

Richard Henry Lee recalled a comment Patrick Henry had made about the power the Constitution gave to the central government: "I smelt a rat." Suspecting that Patrick Henry was right, Lee said he would rather that Virginia leave the Union than submit to the northern interests.

Desperate, Hamilton kept his assumption proposal alive by linking it to another heated controversy—where the national capital should be located. Northerners proposed New York City—the present capital—or Philadelphia. Southerners insisted on a southern site on the Potomac River.

Jefferson, fearing for the survival of the Union, asked Hamilton and Madison to come to dinner. Certainly, he thought, reasonable people could reach a reasonable compromise.

During the dinner, Hamilton agreed to support moving the national capital to Philadelphia for ten years and then giving it a permanent site on the Potomac between Virginia and Maryland. In return, Madison and Jefferson agreed to obtain enough southern votes to pass the assumption bill. The compromise was a success.

Hamilton's plan accomplished his purposes. With the bonds in the hands of a new wealthy class, Hamilton could foresee a source of capital for industrial development. However, the debate over the plan had also revealed a split between north and south that would persist and eventually threaten the nation's unity.

A National Bank

After the assumption bill passed, Hamilton plunged into his next major project. In December 1790 Hamilton proposed that Congress establish a national bank, modeled on the Bank of England. The federal government would provide one fifth of the bank's total capital of $10 million, and private investors would supply the rest by buying stock. These investors would also choose four fifths of the bank directors, thus controlling the bank.

The bank would serve the government as a financial agent, collecting taxes, keeping the government's cash safe, and lending the government money. In addition, the bank could print paper currency—backed by gold and silver—which people could use to pay taxes and which would keep trade flowing more smoothly. The bank could also lend money to help new businesses. Washington, however, was concerned that the measure might be unconstitutional and asked cabinet members for their written opinions.

The debate that followed brought into focus two opposing viewpoints that have continued to the present day—strict versus loose construction of the Constitution. Jefferson strongly urged Washington to veto the bill. In his view, the power to establish the bank was outside the powers of Congress and the President, as spelled out by the Constitution. Strict construction would thus prohibit this use of power.

In defending the bank, Hamilton used a loose construction. He argued that the "necessary and proper" clause of the Constitution applied to the bank, for the bank would be necessary to carry out tax collection. Thus, establishing a bank was one of the implied powers of Congress.

The President, swayed by Hamilton's arguments, signed the bill on February 25, 1791. Thanks to the bank, the United States established a thriving economy based upon a sound dollar. Almost as important as the bank bill itself, however, was the fact that for the first time Jefferson had personally stepped forward to oppose one of Hamilton's proposals. Hamilton began to suspect that a group of opponents—led by Jefferson—was forming to thwart his plans for the young nation.

Tariff Proposal Rejected

Next, Hamilton proposed to raise the tariff on imported goods. He believed that a high **protective tariff**—that is, a tax designed to discourage Americans from buying foreign goods—would encourage American industry to grow and prosper.

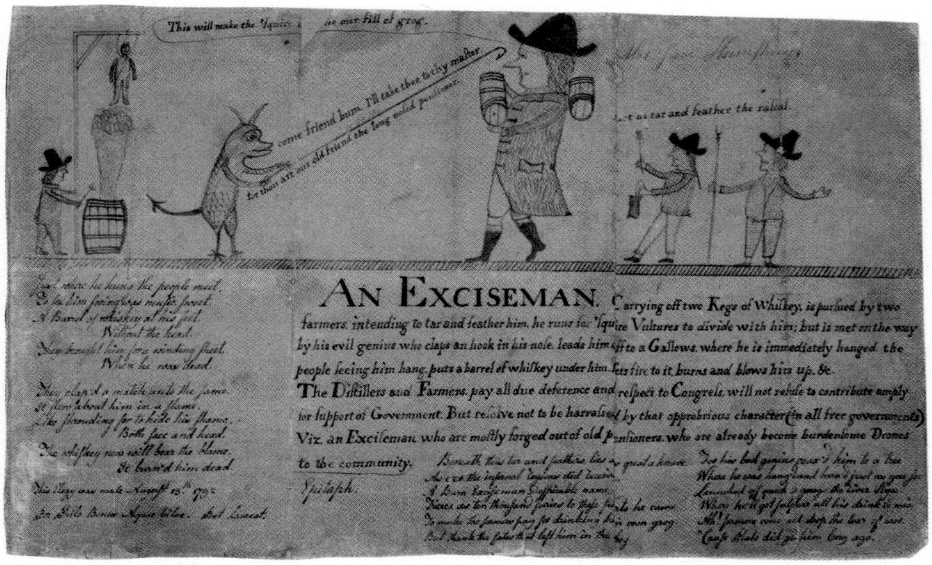

This cartoon shows the fate that many farmers wished for an exciseman — tar and feathers or hanging. The exciseman is carrying off whiskey on which farmers had not paid tax.

Both northern merchants and southern farmers opposed the plan. Merchants objected that the tariff would hurt international trade. Farmers feared that they would have to pay higher prices for the European manufactured goods they needed.

Convinced by these objections, Congress rejected the tariff. At this time Jefferson's vision of a largely agricultural America prevailed over Hamilton's desire to encourage industry. "For the general operations of manufacture," Jefferson advised, "let our work-shops remain in Europe."

The Whiskey Rebellion

The nation now had a bank and a plan to restore credit but it still needed income with which to pay off the national debt and meet the costs of government. Hamilton proposed an **excise tax** — a tax on goods produced, sold, and used within the country — to be levied on "spirituous liquors."

When the liquor tax passed in 1791, farmers of western Pennsylvania were outraged. Whiskey was their only marketable product and was used as a form of money. This tax would eat into their profits, and they refused to pay it. For three years they harassed tax collectors, and in 1794 they staged an armed rebellion.

President Washington saw the farmers' defiance as an attack on the federal government. At the urging of Hamilton, who feared mob rule, the President called out the militia. In November 13,000 troops marched into western Pennsylvania, but there was no real fighting. The farmers simply stayed at home. Only twenty prisoners were taken. Jefferson commented sarcastically that a rebellion "was announced and proclaimed and armed against, but could never be found."

Hamilton, however, was elated that the federal government had passed a crucial test, showing back-country westerners that its power reached across the Appalachians. Seven years earlier, the Confederation had been unable to act during Shays' Rebellion in Massachusetts. In the Whiskey Rebellion, by contrast, the new government had restored law and order and upheld its authority.

Section Review

1. Identification. Define *cabinet, protective tariff,* and *excise tax.*

2. Comprehension. Describe how Congress organized the executive and judicial branches of the new government.

3. Analysis. Explain the differences in the way Hamilton and Jefferson envisioned the ideal American society.

Writing About History

Book Report. Susanna Rowson made fun of the Whiskey Rebellion in her musical play *The Volunteers*, staged in 1795. She also wrote the first American best-seller, *Charlotte Temple*, a sentimental story published in London in 1791 and in Philadelphia in 1794. Two hundred editions of the book have been published. Rowson also wrote textbooks for a school she founded in Boston, the Young Ladies' Academy.

Have interested students read *Charlotte Temple* and write book reports expressing their opinions about the book and comparing it to present-day novels.

Section Review

ANSWERS

1. Definitions for the following terms are on text pages indicated in parentheses: *cabinet* (161), *protective tariff* (164), *excise tax* (165).
2. Executive: departments of State, Treasury, War, and Postmaster General, and leaders to head them; judicial: three-level court system with thirteen district courts, three circuit courts, Supreme Court; office of Attorney General to represent U.S. in Supreme Court cases and provide legal advice to executive branch.
3. Hamilton: political power in the hands of the wealthy and the educated, including merchants, manufacturers, and bankers; Jefferson: as many people as possible participating in government, with power in the hands of farmers and landowners.

Section 7-2

Objectives

- ***Answer the Focus Question.***
- *Describe the formation and goals of the first American political parties.*
- *Describe how France and Britain tested American neutrality.*
- *Cite ways that Washington tried to keep the United States out of international entanglements.*

Introducing

THE SECTION

Tell students that the Constitution said nothing about political parties. When political parties appeared, Washington warned that the "demon of party spirit" would tear the new government apart. In this section students will learn why he felt the warning necessary.

Reduced student page in the Teacher's Edition

7-2 Conflict at Home and Abroad

Focus: How would the new nation survive threats from at home and abroad?

The financial program that Hamilton so painstakingly created had a successful beginning. However, the political squabbles that it set off disturbed the President. Washington had hoped that with the ratification of the Constitution, the divisions between Federalists and Anti-Federalists would disappear. Like most Americans, he feared that factions would destroy national unity. To his dismay, he saw the divisions deepening. The American people seemed to be dividing into opposing groups, one group following Hamilton, and the other siding with Jefferson.

The Rise of Political Parties

Jefferson once said, "If I could not get to heaven except with a political party, I would not go there at all." Nonetheless he began to work with Madison to organize national opposition to Hamilton's followers, the Federalists.

Several months after Washington signed the bank bill, Madison and Jefferson set out to gain political support in the upcoming 1792 presidential election. Washington planned to retire after one term, and Jefferson and Madison hoped to attract votes for candidates representing the "republican interest," as opposed to the interests of the Federalists. Their followers were known as the Republicans.

Jefferson and Madison established an anti-Hamilton newspaper, the *National Gazette*, which was soon debating with the Hamilton-supported *Gazette of the United States*. Jefferson's supporters wrote violent attacks on Hamilton's policies, accusing him of trying to set up a monarchy, with "drawing rooms" and "stately nods instead of shaking hands."

Hamilton, using a variety of pen names, responded with editorials defending his actions and

A Federalist cartoon, "Mad Tom in a Rage," shows Jefferson as a brandy-soaked anarchist tearing down the pillars of government. Competing papers also reflected the growing rift.

Gazette United States

WEDNESDAY EVENING, JULY 8, 1795.

Notice is hereby given,

THAT the grantees of the Georgia Company have appointed William Urquhart, Esq. of Augusta, their agent for the purpose of receiving payments from the persons holding an interest in the said Company, and have authorised him to give receipts for the same: and, for the information of all concerned, the following Rule and Regulation of the Georgia Company is hereto subjoined.

JAMES GUNN,
M. McALLISTER, } Grantees.
GEO: WALKER,

RULE IV.

" If any person holding an interest in this Company, shall fail to pay punctually the full amount of the purchase money for the lands held by them, at and after the rate of two cents and one third of a cent per acre, or the balance which is or may be due on or before the seventh day of August, one thousand seven hundred and ninety five, to the Grantees, or their agents, every person or persons so holding an interest or shshare, and failing to pay as before mentioned, shall forfeit such interest or subshare, and the same ...

DELAWARE BRIDGE.

IN Pursuance of an act of the General Assembly of this Commonwealth, entitled " An act to authorize the Governor of this Commonwealth to incorporate a Company for erecting a Bridge over the river Delaware, at the borough of Easton, in the County of Northampton;" and also of the Legislature of the state of New Jersey, entitled " An act to empower the Governor of this state to incorporate a Company for erecting a Bridge over the river Delaware, at the township of Greenwich, in the County of Sussex, opposite the borough of Easton"

NOTICE is hereby given,

That Books will be opened to receive Subscriptions for the Stock of the said Company, at the times and places following, to wit :

In the City of Philadelphia, at the Counting House of Levi Hollingsworth, on Monday, the sixth day of July next, and on the two succeeding days—

In the Borough of Easton, at the House of Conrad Ihrie, sen. on the same three days;

And, in the State of New Jersey, at the House of Thomas Bullman, in the township of Greenwich, and County of Sussex, on the sixth and eighth days of July next; and ...

MISS

On WEDN... presented a Mi...

Overture,
Glee " Come all ...
Duett, " The W...
Recitation,
Catch " Mr. Sp...
Song, " The Sold...
Glee, " When S...
Glee, " Come li...
Song, " The ...
Concerto on ...
Duett, " To...

166

Even Americans who had cheered the French Revolution were horrified when it turned into a bloody "government by the guillotine."

accusing Jefferson of opposition to the Constitution and the administration of Washington. Newspapers chose sides and joined the battle.

The newspaper war and the repeated clashes between Hamilton and Jefferson in cabinet meetings bothered President Washington. He wrote to Jefferson, "I believe the views of both of you to be pure and well-meant. I have a great regard for you both, and wish that some line could be marked out by which both of you could walk." But there seemed to be no such line.

The political rift made Washington reconsider his plan to retire from the presidency. Hamilton and Jefferson, who could agree on little else, both urged the President to serve a second term, as did political leaders across the country. Although he wanted to return to the simpler life at his home at Mount Vernon, Washington agreed. No one opposed him for the presidency in 1792.

By the time of the election in December, the political factions had hardened into a more solid form—political parties. Hamilton's followers became known as the Federalist party, and Jefferson's the Republican party. Although Vice-President Adams sided with the Federalists, Jefferson was encouraged by the success of the Republicans in winning seats in Congress. Now Republican ideas would have a chance against Federalist ideas.

The Proclamation of Neutrality

The hope of preserving the unity of the young nation was not the only reason why Washington agreed to serve a second term. He was also concerned about foreign affairs.

Three years earlier, in 1789, revolution had broken out in France. Most Americans were delighted,

Developing THE SECTION

Linking Past and Present

Discussion. The Republican party formed by Jefferson and Madison was the forerunner of the present Democratic party. The present Republican party was formed in 1854. Ask students how the Republican party of today differs from Jefferson's Republicans. **(Present-day Republicans tend to be conservative, support large military expenditures, and favor business.)**

Global Connections

Research and Report. Have one student do research and report to the class about the causes and the beginning of the French Revolution. Have another student describe to the class the outcome of the Revolution.

Writing About History

Letter. Before Washington issued his Proclamation of Neutrality he put a series of questions to his cabinet. Pass out the following partial list of questions to students.

1. Shall a proclamation be issued for the purpose of preventing interferences of the Citizens of the United States in the War between France and Great Britain? What shall it contain?
2. Are the United States obliged by good faith to consider the Treaties made with France as applying to the present situation? May they either renounce them or hold them suspended till the Government of France shall be established?

Have students assume the identity of Jefferson, Hamilton, Knox, or Randolph, and write a letter to Washington presenting an answer to the questions.

Analyzing Primary Sources

Madison Speaks. James Madison said this about the Proclamation of Neutrality:

"The proclamation was in truth a most unfortunate error. It wounds the national honor, by seeming to disregard the stipulated duties to France. It wounds the popular feeling by a seeming indifference to the cause of liberty."

Ask a student to restate Madison's two objections to neutrality. Have students respond to Madison's statement.

feeling a kinship with the French in their struggle against monarchy. They put up liberty poles, wore French-style hats, and called each other "citizen," the democratic form of address popular in France.

However, as the revolution progressed, many Americans grew increasingly wary of the violence and frequent changes of leadership in France. The French king, Louis XVI, was beheaded in 1793, and some 20,000 French citizens were executed as enemies of the revolution. The new French republic alarmed European monarchs by calling for "a war of all peoples against all kings," and by 1793 France was at war with Austria, Prussia, Great Britain, the Netherlands, and Spain.

The violence in Europe shocked Americans and set off new disputes in the United States. Jefferson, Madison, and other Republicans were enthusiastic friends of the revolution, though horrified by its brutality. To them, the overthrow of monarchy was part of the struggle everywhere for democracy. With passion Jefferson said, "The liberty of the whole earth was depending on the issue of the contest and . . . rather than it should have failed, I would have seen half the earth devastated."

Republicans also stressed that the United States was legally bound to France. One of the treaties of 1778, which had brought French aid to the American fight for independence, had pledged "perpetual friendship and alliance."

The Federalists rejected this stand. Some feared that the spirit of mob rule would spread, threatening life, liberty, and property. Thus, the Federalists sided with Great Britain, which by contrast seemed stable, orderly, and well governed. In addition, Britain was a vital link in Hamilton's financial system, with most of the government's revenue coming from import duties on British goods. Supporting France would mean war with Britain, breaking the ties of trade.

Although both Hamilton and Jefferson saw danger in getting caught up in the war, each attempted to convince Washington to take sides. Instead, Washington chose a middle course—a policy of **neutrality,** or not taking sides. On April 22, 1793, he issued the Proclamation of Neutrality, declaring that the United States would "pursue a conduct friendly and impartial toward the belligerent powers," and warning individual Americans not to aid any of the warring nations. Washington's stand, however, did not silence public debate.

Learning From Art A Seaport About 1800

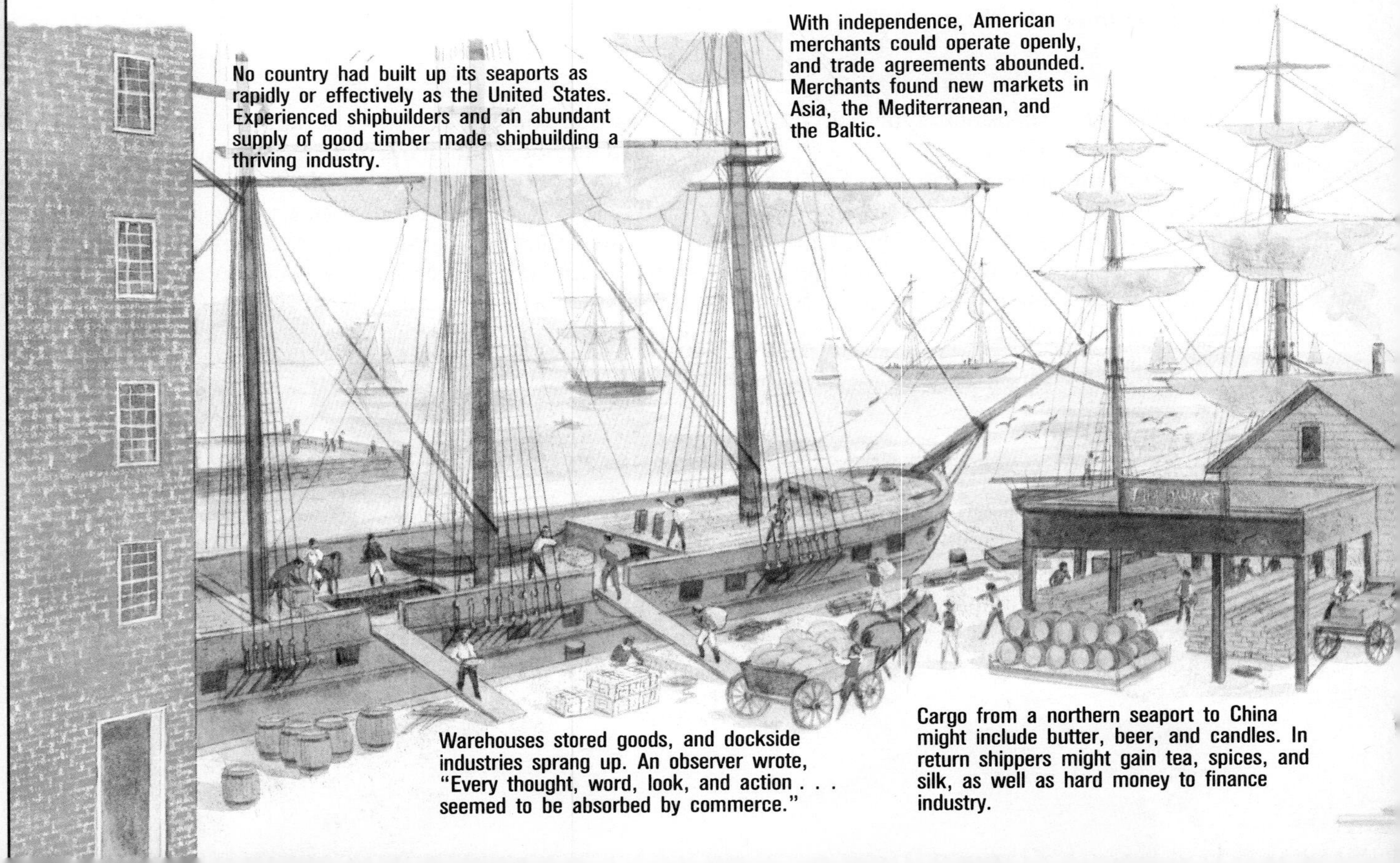

No country had built up its seaports as rapidly or effectively as the United States. Experienced shipbuilders and an abundant supply of good timber made shipbuilding a thriving industry.

With independence, American merchants could operate openly, and trade agreements abounded. Merchants found new markets in Asia, the Mediterranean, and the Baltic.

Warehouses stored goods, and dockside industries sprang up. An observer wrote, "Every thought, word, look, and action . . . seemed to be absorbed by commerce."

Cargo from a northern seaport to China might include butter, beer, and candles. In return shippers might gain tea, spices, and silk, as well as hard money to finance industry.

B · A · C · K · G · R · O · U · N · D

Global Connections
By the time Washington's cabinet demanded that the French government recall Genêt, the radical Jacobins had come to power. Genêt's arrest by his successor, Joseph Fauchet, might have ultimately led to a death sentence in France, where tens of thousands of people were being executed during the Reign of Terror. Washington granted asylum to Genêt, who became an American citizen and married the daughter of New York Governor George Clinton.

Social History
Service on British ships was so harsh that more than 2,000 sailors deserted each year. A captain had the power of life and death over his crew. A common form of punishment was whipping—30 or 40 lashes for an infraction. Another was keelhauling—dragging a sailor under the ship's keel from one side to the other until he nearly drowned.

Active Learning

Debate. The debate over support for the French Revolution highlights an issue that is important today—should the United States support democratic revolutions around the world? Ask students to state their opinions on this issue. What recent events can they think of that involve this issue? (Baltic states in Soviet Union, Kurdish rebels in Iraq, uprisings in Central America and China)

Divide the class into groups. Let each group choose one of the recent events identified in the discussion, divide into teams, then research and debate the issue of United States involvement.

Citizen Genêt

In early April 1793, Edmond Genêt (zheh-NAY), minister to the United States of the new French republic, landed in Charleston, South Carolina, to the cheers of pro-French Americans. His government had instructed him to gain American support for the French republic. Taking advantage of public enthusiasm, he also used the United States as a base for French action against its enemies.

In Charleston, Genêt recruited armies to free Louisiana and Florida from Spain. He also commissioned privately-owned American ships to attack British merchant ships along the American coast. As "Citizen" Genêt traveled north to the capital, he heard of the Proclamation of Neutrality, but he ignored it.

By early August, Thomas Jefferson, usually a supporter of the French, realized that Genêt wanted to drag the United States into war. He agreed with Washington that France must recall its minister.

Meanwhile, out of the political chaos in France, a new group had come to power and had sent another minister to the United States. The new minister had orders to arrest Genêt for "crimes" against the revolution. Washington, however, allowed Genêt to remain in the United States, where he wisely retired from politics. The whole affair prompted a surge of support for President Washington and his policy of neutrality.

Britain Angers the United States

In the meantime, Great Britain's actions were alarming even its firmest American supporters. Britain had declared a blockade of France in June 1793, planning to seize neutral ships that were carrying **contraband**— goods forbidden by law to be traded. At first only war supplies, such as ammunition and weapons, were contraband. But now the British, declaring food to be contraband, were seizing American trade ships bound for France and the French West Indies.

To make things worse, Britain was also seizing American sailors. Thousands of British sailors deserted each year and took jobs on American ships. Now British captains searching for contraband on neutral ships would also claim to be looking for these deserters. If an American sailor was suspected, he would be impressed, or seized and forced to serve in the Royal Navy. Many American citizens—both native-born and formerly British citizens—were "mistakenly" impressed.

Another source of friction was a string of forts that Britain still held in the Northwest Territory despite a promise to withdraw ten years earlier. Early in 1794 the American government learned that British officials had promised to help the Indians get rid of American settlers in the Ohio country. The British had even built a new fort in the area.

Outraged Americans thought Britain had overstepped its boundaries one time too many, and war fever swept the country. Americans volunteered for the militia, attacked British sailors, and harassed pro-British Americans. Congress exploded with anti-British legislation. It approved a two-month **embargo,** or ban on trade, against Britain. It also authorized a navy, voted for funds to build six ships, and passed a number of other defense measures. Washington, however, was steadfast in his opposition to war. He sent Chief Justice John Jay to England with orders to settle the disputes between the two countries.

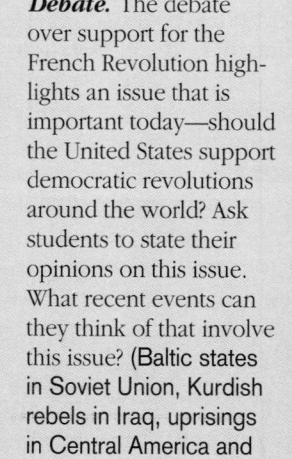

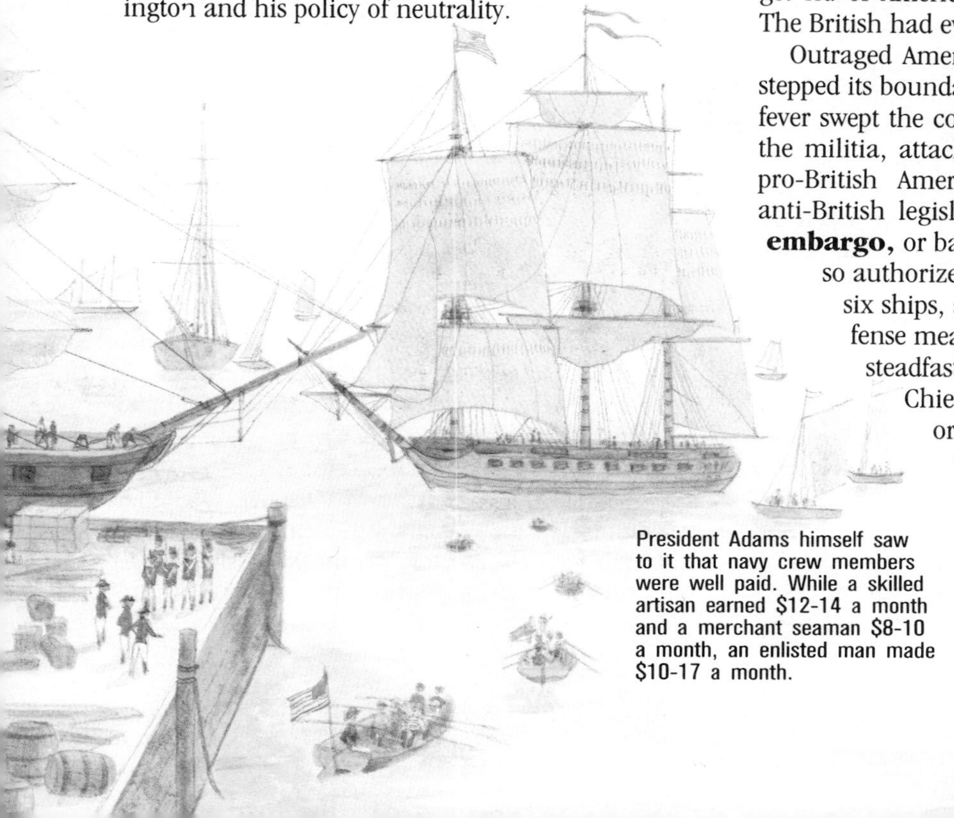

The six navy frigates authorized by Congress in 1794 were to protect the trade of the young nation. The navy would be expanded under the presidency of John Adams.

President Adams himself saw to it that navy crew members were well paid. While a skilled artisan earned $12-14 a month and a merchant seaman $8-10 a month, an enlisted man made $10-17 a month.

169

Using the Visuals

Analyzing an Illustration. Refer students to the illustration depicting General Wayne and Native Americans discussing the Treaty of Greenville. Ask students to tell in what ways it might be an accurate rendering of the event. In what ways might it be a romanticized rendering?

Thinking Critically

Analysis. Before Jay left for England to negotiate a treaty with Great Britain he was told that "Britain has all the cards." **Ask:** What evidence supports this statement? (United States with no real army or navy, economy dependent on British trade, United States' reluctance to join alliance against Great Britain) What group of people would object most to the treaty? Why? (white settlers, merchants, sailors, Republicans) Why was the treaty adopted even though it was so unpopular? (kept peace, removed British from continent and separated them from Native Americans)

Multicultural Perspectives

The Treaty of Greenville resulted from the Battle of Fallen Timbers. (The area where 2,000 Shawnee, Ottawa, and Chippewa Indians decided to take their stand was strewn with thousands of fallen trees.) After their defeat, Chief Little Turtle urged his fellow chiefs to negotiate the best treaty they could with Wayne, the "General-Who-Never-Sleeps."

Reduced student page in the Teacher's Edition

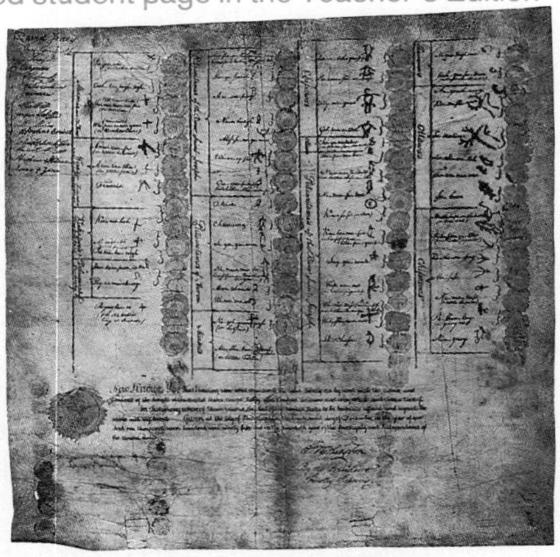

In the Treaty of Greenville (above), twelve tribes were forced to give up their Ohio lands and move west.

Jay's Treaty

Jay faced the daunting task of talking the British into withdrawing from the Northwest Territory and agreeing to pay for the seized American ships. He knew he had little bargaining power. The United States had no real army or navy to enforce an agreement, and its economy relied on British trade.

After five months of talks, the two sides finally signed a treaty. Britain promised to withdraw from its Northwest posts and pay Americans for seized ships. However the treaty made no mention of Britain's relations with Indian tribes in the region, nor did it include an agreement that Britain would give up seizing ships or sailors in the future.

Jay wrote to the President that the treaty "will doubtless produce fresh difficulties." But when the treaty was made public in March 1795, the uproar was louder than Jay had expected. Republicans called the treaty a sellout to Britain. Crowds burned "Sir" John Jay in effigy. When Hamilton tried to explain the treaty to a crowd in New York City, he was pelted with stones.

Nevertheless, Congress approved the treaty. Despite its flaws, it kept peace at a time when America was not prepared to wage war. The treaty also removed the British from the American frontier and separated them from their Indian allies.

Although the Northwest Ordinance of 1787 stated that Indian "land and property shall never be taken from them without their consent," white land hunters had been streaming into the fertile region north of the Ohio River. To protect them from attacks by the Miami, Shawnee, and other tribes fighting to defend their lands, the United States sent in troops under General Anthony Wayne.

In August 1794, after almost two years of fighting, Wayne won a decisive battle at Fallen Timbers. A year later the chiefs of twelve tribes were forced to sign the Treaty of Greenville. This treaty made the tribes cede most of the Ohio country to the United States government and move west, opening up the area to settlement. To the tribes the treaty represented a terrible loss. Yet the new nation saw the combined effect of Jay's Treaty and the Treaty of Greenville as securing the Northwest Territory.

Pinckney's Treaty

In the summer of 1794, Washington sent Thomas Pinckney to Spain to settle all boundary disputes between the two countries and gain the right to navigate the Mississippi River "in its whole length and breadth, from its source to the sea."

Pinckney signed a treaty in October 1795 that accomplished these goals. Americans could travel through Spanish territory on the Mississippi River and transfer their goods from river boats to ocean ships at New Orleans without paying duty. Spain

Global Connections

Washington, in his Farewell Address, warned against permanent alliances. The United States abandoned this policy when it established wartime alliances in World War I and World War II. In 1947 it began peacetime alliances: Rio Pact (Latin America), NATO, and various alliances with Asian countries.

Connections: Politics

In the 1796 election Hamilton did not want Adams in office, so he persuaded some Federalist electors to vote only for Thomas Pinckney and leave Adams's name off the ballot. Some of Adams's New England supporters, in turn, had decided to leave Pinckney's name off the ballot. As a result of these electoral strategies, Pinckney got fewer votes than Jefferson and Jefferson became Vice-President.

agreed to the 31st parallel as the boundary between the United States and Spanish Florida. Spain also promised not to support Indian attacks on American settlements.

Between them, the Pinckney and Jay treaties had successfully smoothed relations with Spain and Britain and thus helped establish the security of the new nation.

Washington's Farewell

Exhausted by political squabbles, Washington was set on retiring in 1797. He made this intention clear in his farewell address in September 1796. As "a parting friend," Washington warned against the "continual mischiefs" of party politics. Parties, especially those based on regions, would threaten the nation's unity. Washington also warned Americans against close political ties with other countries. While he encouraged trade, he urged Americans to "steer clear of permanent alliances with any portion of the foreign world."

During Washington's presidency, the new government had taken a number of important steps toward solving the problems that threatened its survival. While avoiding involvement in European wars, it had secured its borders, established credit abroad and at home, and held at bay internal threats to national unity.

Spotlight on Presidents

When Washington took office as the first President, no one knew how to address him. Some senators suggested "His Highness" or "His Elective Majesty." But James Madison and most representatives disapproved of such royal-sounding titles. After weeks of debate, the Senate gave up. Washington would be addressed simply as "Mr. President." Another precedent had been set.

Adams Elected in 1796

The Federalists finally settled on John Adams as their presidential candidate. To gain southern support, they chose Thomas Pinckney of South Carolina for Vice-President. The Republican candidates were Thomas Jefferson for President and New York's Aaron Burr for Vice-President.

When the framers of the Constitution established the electoral college, they did not foresee the rise of political parties. According to the Constitution at that time, each elector was to vote for two candidates. The candidate with the highest number of votes would become President, and the second highest, Vice-President.

When the electors cast their ballots, Adams won by a narrow margin—seventy-one to sixty-eight votes. However, electoral maneuvering by Adams and Hamilton, who disliked each other, resulted in Pinckney getting fewer votes than Jefferson. Thus, Jefferson became Vice-President.

The government now had a Federalist President and a Republican Vice-President. How would the new administration face internal divisions and external threats?

Section Review

1. **Identification.** Define *neutrality, contraband,* and *embargo.*

2. **Comprehension.** Why did Washington agree to serve a second term as President?

3. **Analysis.** How did the Federalists and the Republicans differ in their view of France and the French Revolution?

4. **Analysis.** How were Jay's Treaty, the Treaty of Greenville, and Pinckney's Treaty important in establishing the security of the new nation?

5. **Evaluation.** What dangers did Washington warn against in his Farewell Address? Why?

Linking Past and Present. Although the United States has many political parties, most Presidents have come from either the Republican or Democratic parties. Form a group to find out about "third parties" in the United States today. What are their origins and goals?

Limited English Proficiency

Making Charts. Have students work in small groups to make charts comparing the ideas of the Federalist party and the Republican party. Under each of two headings—"Federalists" and "Republicans"—have students list ideas about the role of the national government, the role of state governments, the importance of manufacturing and agriculture, and attitudes toward Great Britain and France.

Section Review

ANSWERS

1. Definitions are on text pages indicated in parentheses: *neutrality* (168), *contraband* (169), *embargo* (169).

2. Political rift between Hamilton and Jefferson.

3. Republicans supported France and the French Revolution. Federalists sided with Great Britain; feared mob rule.

4. Jay's Treaty: helped keep peace when the nation was too weak for war; removed British from frontier and Indian allies. Treaty of Greenville: Native Americans ceded most of Ohio territory to U.S. and moved west, opening area for white settlement. Pinckney's Treaty: settled boundary disputes between U.S. and Spain, gave Americans right to navigate the Mississippi, and prevented Spain from supporting Indian attacks on settlers.

5. Washington warned against "mischief" of party politics and entangling alliances. He thought growing factionalism and involvement in foreign wars could weaken the nation.

Linking Past and Present. Students might research parties such as Socialist, Communist, American Independent, Libertarian, Prohibition, Green.

Section 7-3

Objectives

- ***Answer the Focus Question.***
- *Explain how John Adams responded to the XYZ Affair.*
- *Describe the cause/effect relationship between the Alien and Sedition Acts and the Kentucky and Virginia Resolutions.*
- *Explain why the election of 1800 was decided in Congress.*

Introducing THE SECTION

Write the following words of Madison on the chalkboard:

"Perhaps it is a universal truth that the loss of liberty at home is to be charged to provisions against danger, real or pretended, from abroad."

Ask students to explain the quotation. Tell them, they will be studying how fear of foreigners, particularly the French, led to the suppression of individual liberties under the Alien and Sedition Acts.

B · A · C · K · G · R · O · U · N · D

Global Connections
American citizen George Logan, a peace-loving Quaker, made a trip to France at his own expense to negotiate an end to the "half-war." The Federalists resented his meddling and passed the the "Logan Act" of 1799. It forbade a private citizen to engage in unauthorized negotiations with foreign governments. The law in a modified form still remains.

Reduced student page in the Teacher's Edition

7-3 Challenges to National Security

Focus: How did the United States face the threat of war with France?

On March 4, 1797, John Adams stood in the crowded chamber of the House of Representatives and took the presidential oath of office. Like Washington, Adams had spent most of the last three decades striving to create the American nation. Also like Washington, Adams was uncomfortable with party politics and did not want to be a party leader.

However, Adams did not come into office with the popularity that Washington had had. He was not the unanimous choice of the nation, nor even of his own party, and he had won by only three electoral votes. Thus, he faced challenges in trying to hold his party—and the country—together.

Hoping to smooth divisions among the Federalists, Adams decided to retain the cabinet of Washington's second term. Only later did he discover that three department heads were loyal to Hamilton, now a private citizen practicing law.

Adams tried to follow Washington's lead and disregard political parties as much as possible. However, party politics were already firmly in place and fiercely divisive. As a result, the President rarely met with Vice-President Jefferson for consultation on public matters. "Party violence," Adams later recalled, "soon rendered it impracticable, or at least useless."

The XYZ Affair—"Not One Cent for Tribute"

Adams's first order of business was to face a hostile France. In his inaugural speech, Adams called for American neutrality. However, Jay's Treaty had infuriated France and made it deeply suspicious of an American-British alliance. To retaliate, France recalled its minister from the United States and refused to receive American minister Charles C. Pinckney. France then began seizing American ships. Determined to settle the dispute, Adams won Congress's approval to send a special commission to France for a fresh try at negotiation.

But shady dealings faced the commissioners, John Marshall, Elbridge Gerry, and Charles Pinckney. When they reached Paris in October 1797, the French foreign minister refused to receive them officially. Instead, he sent three of his agents—later known simply as Mr. X, Mr. Y, and Mr. Z—to call on them on the sly. The agents made three demands: an apology for Adams's anti-French remarks in Congress, an American loan to France, and a personal bribe of $250,000 for the French foreign minister. Enraged, Pinckney responded, "No! No! Not a sixpence!"

When news of the XYZ Affair reached the United States, it set loose a tide of anger against France. Federalists called for war. Their slogan, "Millions for defense, but not one cent for tribute," was heard across the nation.

With patriotism at a high, Congress prepared for war. It created the Department of the Navy and the Marine Corps and voted funds for new warships. It authorized the President to expand the army and called on George Washington to come out of retirement to lead it. Congress also repealed the 1778 alliance and trade treaties with France, which had been so important in the American Revolution.

The "Half War"

The full-scale war for which the United States prepared never came. Instead, an undeclared naval conflict sputtered along for two years, with American ships capturing French privateers.

Despite their initial enthusiasm, most Americans did not support open war, and they quickly tired of the expense of this "half war." Although Hamilton and his supporters continued to demand

Connections: Language

The term *xenophobia* comes from the Greek words *xenos*, meaning strange or foreign, and *phobia*, meaning fear. *Xenophobia* is the fear or hatred of strangers or foreigners. A wave of xenophobia swept the United States in the late 1700s.

The American vessel the Planter, right, is shown in close pursuit of a French privateer in the "half war."

a war with France, the Federalists were divided. Republicans, insisting that war was unnecessary, opposed most defense measures. And moderates thought it enough that the United States simply be prepared to defend itself.

The French government, moreover, had no intention of declaring war. Needing American trade, France now sought peace. In September 1798 France's foreign minister offered to receive an American representative in France.

Adams's cabinet — and the Federalists who followed Hamilton — pressured the President to fight, but he resisted. Instead, he proposed to the Senate that the United States send another mission to France. The Senate finally agreed to the plan, but Adams's victory widened the split in his party.

The American commission arrived in Paris in March 1800 to find a new government, ruled by General Napoleon Bonaparte. Napoleon was concentrating on strengthening his power in Europe and wanted to avoid trouble with the United States. In September he agreed to end the treaties of 1778, thus releasing the United States from the obligation to help France in war. As a compromise, the Americans dropped their claim for payment for seized American ships. Both countries accepted the principle of freedom of the seas — the right of trade ships to travel freely on the open seas.

To President Adams, peace was worth the party bickering and the personal attacks he had endured. He later wrote, "I desire no other inscription over my gravestone than: Here lies John Adams, who took upon himself the responsibility of the peace with France in the year 1800."

The Alien and Sedition Acts

Adams had managed to settle relations with France, but not before the XYZ Affair and the "half war" had stirred up suspicion and distrust in the nation. Federalists accused anti-war Republicans of being pro-French traitors who threatened national security. In addition, distrust increasingly fell upon foreigners, setting off the first major anti-alien scare in the nation's history. Since that time,

Developing THE SECTION

Writing About History

Position Paper. Foreign policy during the Adams and Washington administrations related to economic and political issues, such as the economic well-being of the country and concern about support for democratic ideals abroad. Cite the Persian Gulf as an example of the debate continuing into the present. Have students write short position papers outlining the most important issues the President and Congress should consider in foreign policy decisions. Then use the papers as a basis for discussion.

Active Learning

Writing Epitaphs. Have each student choose two or three persons described in this chapter, such as Washington, Jefferson, Hamilton, Jay, Pinckney, etc. Given the events these people experienced from 1789–1801, have students complete this statement for each character: "I desire no other inscription over my gravestone than ..."

Linking Past and Present

Discussion. The three Alien Acts applied to foreigners and reflected the wave of xenophobia that swept the country. Ask students why Americans were hostile to foreigners. Can they give other examples in American history of such hostility? The external threat of war with France made the Federalists suspicious of foreigners. What seem to be the causes of xenophobia today? Why is this a greater problem during wartime?

Thinking Critically

Evaluation. Both political parties engaged in publishing scandalous and malicious writings and in name-calling. Use the following questions to discuss the ethics of such practices: Is it ever justified to reveal a personal scandal about a candidate? Why or why not? Where should a newspaper draw the line?

Connections: Politics

Discussion. Contemporary political analysts claim that political campaigns today ignore issues in favor of gossip or character attacks. Do students agree or disagree? Have them cite examples to support their answers. Should a candidate's personal vices disqualify that person from holding political office? Why or why not?

B · A · C · K · G · R · O · U · N · D

Social History

Although the Sedition Act was unjust, it did make a significant contribution to freedom of the press—it established statutory support for truth as a defense against libel. Andrew Hamilton had used this argument as a defense in the John Peter Zenger trial in 1735. Even though laws of that time barred truth as a defense against libel, Zenger was freed.

The Sedition Act was in effect for two years; it expired in 1801. When Jefferson became President, he pardoned all those in jail for violation of the act and Congress restored the fines with interest.

Reduced student page in the Teacher's Edition

fear of aliens has cropped up repeatedly when the country has faced threats from abroad.

In 1798 the Federalists saw an opportunity to use anti-alien fears to stifle opposition to the war and undermine the strength of the Republicans at the same time. The Federalist-dominated Congress passed four laws known as the Alien and Sedition Acts. The first, the Naturalization Act, extended the time it took to become a citizen—from five to fourteen years. Since many foreign immigrants tended to vote Republican once they gained citizenship, this act was designed to cut off a major source of Republican votes.

The Alien Act gave the President the power to deport aliens "dangerous to the peace and safety of the United States." The Alien Enemies Act permitted the President, in wartime, to arrest, imprison, or deport all aliens from an enemy nation.

The Sedition Act, designed to silence Republican criticism, cut close to the bone of liberty. It stated that a person could be fined and jailed if found guilty of sedition, or conspiring to oppose the execution of the laws, or publishing "false, scandalous, or malicious" writings against the President, Congress, or the government of the United States. The Federalists in power could interpret these vague words as they liked.

Republicans and even many Federalists charged that the Sedition Act was a repressive measure that violated the constitutional guarantee of freedom of speech. Between 1798 and 1800, twenty-five people—none of them Federalists—were prosecuted under the act. Ten Republicans, including newspaper editors and printers and one member of Congress, were convicted, fined, and imprisoned.

Protesting the Alien and Sedition Acts

Jefferson and Madison saw the Alien and Sedition Acts as not just an attack on the Republican party but as a step toward tyranny. Since the federal courts were upholding these unjust laws, Madison and Jefferson turned to the state legislatures.

The two men acted secretly to draft resolutions approved by the states of Virginia and Kentucky. The Virginia and Kentucky Resolutions declared that the United States of America was a compact,

Exploring Issues

FREEDOM OF SPEECH

The Arrest of Matthew Lyon

In 1798 Congressman Matthew Lyon of Vermont was fined $1,000 and thrown in jail. He had been convicted under the Sedition Act of criticizing President John Adams and his administration.

While most Americans backed President Bush's decision to go to war against Iraq in 1990, protests occurred in many cities. These protestors are exercising their right to criticize the government.

Lyon described the "loathsome dungeon" he shared with horse thieves and pickpockets. "I was near four weeks without sight of fire, except my candle," he wrote, "in which time I suffered more with the cold than I had in twenty years before."

Federalists cheered Lyon's conviction, calling it "a noble triumph . . . over the unbridled spirit of opposition to government which is, at the present moment, the heaviest curse of America." But Lyon's own party, the Republicans, cried out against curbs on freedom of speech. "I know not which mortifies me most," Jefferson wrote, "that I should fear to write what I think or [that] my country bear such a state of things."

Before his arrest, Matthew Lyon had been known as one of President Adams's strongest critics. Lyon had long been sympathetic to the French Revolution with its cry of "Liberty, Equality, Fraternity." Then, when the XYZ Affair exploded in 1798, anti-French feeling swept the country. Many believed war was near. Some even suspected the Republicans of plotting to bring the French Revolution to America.

Republicans like Matthew Lyon thought that fear of war was exaggerated and that peace terms could be worked out. To the Federalists, such views seemed dangerous and unpatriotic. The Federalist Congress passed the Alien and Sedition Acts. The Sedition Act made it a crime to write or speak in a "scandalous or malicious" way against the government.

The Republicans protested the new law. "To laugh at the cut of a coat of a member of Congress will soon be treason," warned one.

The Federalists defended the Sedition Act. "It was never intended that the right to side with the enemies of one's country in slandering and vilifying the government and dividing the people should be protected under the name of Liberty of the Press," declared a Federalist newspaper.

Three months later, Matthew Lyon became the first person to be jailed under the Sedition Act. In a letter published in a Vermont paper, he had criticized President Adams for his "ridiculous pomp" and attacked his policy toward France.

In Congress, Republican leader Albert Gallatin charged that the real purpose of the act was to "enable one party to oppress another." He argued that Congressman Lyon had the right to express his opinions about President Adams. Thomas Jefferson agreed. "The basis of our government being the opinion of the people," he said, "the very first object should be to keep that right [to freedom of speech]."

As the French war scare ended, more Americans protested the Sedition Act. The people of Lyon's Vermont district were so angry over his conviction that they reelected him to Congress while he was still in jail. Support for the Republicans rose. In 1800 Thomas Jefferson was elected President, with Matthew Lyon himself triumphantly casting the deciding vote in the House of Representatives.

During Jefferson's term, the Sedition Act was allowed to expire. What Jefferson called "the reign of witches" was over. But the issue of freedom to criticize government policy in a time of national danger was not resolved. It has arisen whenever the government has felt threatened by opponents at home or abroad.

1. Why did the Federalists pass the Sedition Act? What arguments did the Republicans use against the Sedition Act?
2. Do you think the Sedition Act was necessary in 1798? Why or why not?
3. Are there ever times, such as a national emergency, when freedom of speech and the press should be limited? Explain.

Writing About History

Newspaper Articles. One of the themes in this chapter is the role of newspapers in reflecting and shaping public opinion. Divide the class into groups of five students each. Each group is to write several newspaper articles covering one or more events from 1789 to 1801. The articles must reflect the viewpoint of either the Federalists or Republicans. The articles can be collected and incorporated into several class newspapers.

Exploring Issues

ANSWERS

1. The Federalists passed the Sedition Act to protect the nation in a time of national danger. The Republicans argued that the Sedition Act enabled one political party to oppress the other and threatened freedoms guaranteed in the Bill of Rights.
2. Answers will vary. Students should consider public fears, the question of war with France, and the issue of national security.
3. Answers will vary.

Analyzing Primary Sources

A Self-Appraisal. John Adams said of himself:

“I am so well satisfied of my own principles, that I think them as eternal and unchangeable as the earth and its inhabitants . . . . I have never sacrificed my judgment to kings, ministers, nor people, and I never will.”

Read this passage to students and ask: What sort of man does Adams appear to have been? Do you think that Adams's character traits are an asset or a handicap for a President? What information from the text supports the quotation? **(He preserved peace despite his own party's cry for war and supported unpopular Alien and Sedition Acts.)**

Limited English Proficiency

Sequencing. Have students identify major events that occurred from 1789 to 1801, write the events on index cards, then organize the events in chronological order.

Using the Visuals

Discussion. Have students study the posters, especially noting the rays of sun, laurel wreath, and eagle associated with Washington, and Jefferson shown as wrinkled, with a candle that has gone out and a snake—symbol of treachery. **Ask:** What messages do these images convey? What is the point of view of the other poster? **(It shows Federalists as being pro-British; points out that candidates Jefferson and Clinton were Patriots in the War of Independence.)**

Connections: Politics

As Adams's term drew to a close, a slave revolt was planned by Gabriel Prosser. Several thousand enslaved Africans collected what arms they could and planned to march on Richmond, Virginia. The conspirators hoped that a capture of key points in the city would trigger a rebellion of some 300,000 slaves throughout the state. They were betrayed to the authorities, however, by two slaves who did not want their masters killed.

After a trial, Prosser and many of his followers were hanged. Federalist newspapers used the insurrection to embarrass Republicans who supported French revolutionary ideals yet held slaves.

or agreement, between states bound together by the Constitution. States, they said, had the right to judge whether or not measures passed by Congress were constitutional. Jefferson's Kentucky Resolutions went as far as to say that a state could **nullify,** or declare void and refuse to enforce, an act of Congress.

Jefferson and Madison's belief that the states had the right to judge whether Congress was going beyond its constitutional powers is known as the **states' rights** theory of the Constitution. This doctrine deeply troubled Hamilton. He warned that it could “destroy the Constitution of the United States.” Indeed the states' rights doctrine, when taken to its limit in the 1850s, contained the seeds of civil war.

The Election of 1800

As Adams's term drew to a close in 1800, the young nation had avoided war and was strong economically. However, political squabbling was still causing division and the dispute over the Alien and Sedition Acts had only widened the rift.

Adams ran for reelection, with Charles Pinckney as his running mate. Yet Adams's reputation had been damaged by the Alien and Sedition Acts.

Furthermore, many Americans saw the Federalists as warmongers. Moderate Federalists were now allying themselves with Jefferson. The disunity in the party was a public spectacle as Hamilton's criticism of Adams became increasingly vicious.

The Republican party, on the other hand, had grown stronger and more unified. It again nominated Thomas Jefferson for President and Aaron Burr of New York for Vice-President.

In December 1800, when the electoral votes were counted, Adams and Pinckney had been defeated. However, confusion arose over who was President. Because electors were to vote without distinguishing between President and Vice-President, Jefferson and Burr had drawn the same number of votes. In cases of ties, the House of Representatives decides the winner, with each state having one vote.

Everyone knew that the Republicans intended Jefferson as the presidential candidate, but some Federalists in the House were determined to cause problems by backing Burr. Then a surprising ally came to Jefferson's support—Alexander Hamilton. Hamilton knew and despised Burr from previous battles in rough and tumble New York politics. Therefore, he swallowed his pride and advised his fellow Federalists, “Jefferson is to be preferred. He is by far not so dangerous a man.”

The House remained deadlocked over the vote for six days and thirty-five ballots. Finally, on February 17, Jefferson was chosen President and Burr Vice-President. In 1804 the Twelfth Amendment would be added to the Constitution, providing separate balloting for President and Vice-President. This amendment was prompted by the rise of party politics, which had been unforeseen by the framers of the Constitution.

The spectacle of Hamilton jousting with his fellow Federalists over the Burr-Jefferson vote may have delighted the Republicans. But the equally embarrassing fact that Burr would not yield

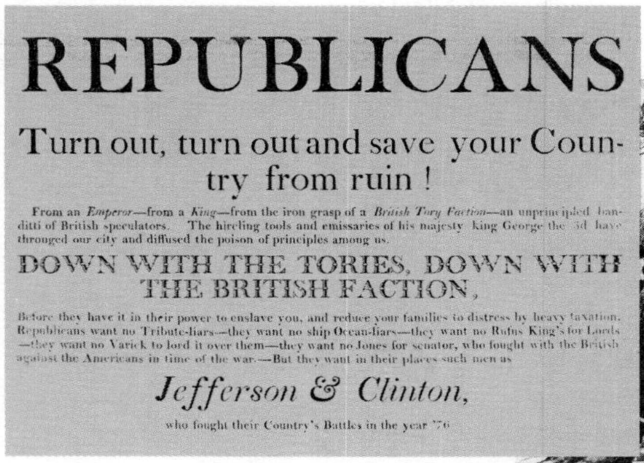

Campaign posters reflected bitter political rivalries.

to Jefferson gave them no comfort. There must have been times when both Hamilton and Jefferson remembered George Washington's warnings and doubted the wisdom of allowing political parties to develop.

Even though in 1800 many people viewed political parties as destructive, parties had already given the nation more than squabbles. They had provided Americans with clear choices between candidates and principles. They provided a way for those not in power to have a legitimate voice in opposing those in power. As one Maryland farmer wrote:

> *"On the preservation of parties public liberty depends. Whenever men are unanimous on great public questions, whenever there is but one party, freedom ceases and despotism commences."*

Parties had also encouraged the discussion of issues on the national level rather than as purely regional concerns.

In March 1801 the new President was inaugurated, and John Adams returned to private life. In his four years as President, Adams had strengthened the young nation and preserved peace with France, despite his party's cry for war. "In your administration," his son John Quincy Adams wrote him, "you were not the man of any party but the whole nation."

Section Review

1. Identification. Define *nullify* and *states' rights.*

2. Analysis. What French actions caused John Adams to send a special commission to France in 1797? What congressional actions resulted from the XYZ Affair?

3. Evaluation. Do you agree with John Adams that he "took upon himself the responsibility of the peace with France in the year 1800"? Explain.

4. Analysis. How were the Kentucky and Virginia Resolutions a response to the Alien and Sedition Acts?

5. Analysis. How did the election of 1800 show an unanticipated effect of political parties?

Connections to Themes

Shaping Democracy

Many Americans shared George Washington's suspicion of political parties. And, in fact, the parties that emerged in the 1790s showed divisions so deep that the new government seemed threatened.

For one thing, the parties held conflicting views of American democracy. The Federalist belief in a strong central government, with power in the hands of the wealthy and educated, convinced Republicans that they would transform the republic into a near-monarchy.

The Federalists were suspicious of the Republicans' faith in the judgment of the people and of their admiration of the French Revolution. "Let [Republicans] get into power," one Federalist wrote, and America would witness "the scenes which have rendered France a cemetery, and moistened her soil with the tears and blood of her inhabitants."

The two parties represented a geographical division, as well. In 1796 John Adams won only nine electoral votes in the South, while his opponent, Jefferson, won no votes in New England.

Many saw the election of 1800 as a test of the American democracy. Republicans cheered Jefferson's victory as having saved the nation from monarchy. But a leading Federalist declared, "Tis impossible that the Union can much longer exist." Could the young democracy survive the transfer of power from one party to the other? Two centuries later, political parties are still a central feature of American government and still play a role in shaping American democracy.

Section Review

ANSWERS

1. Definitions are on text pages indicated: *nullify* (176), *states' rights* (176).

2. French actions: withdrawing French minister from U.S., refusing to receive American minister Pinckney, and seizing American ships. Congressional actions: creating the Department of the Navy and the Marine Corps, voting funds for new warships, authorizing Adams to expand the army and calling on Washington to lead it, and repealing the 1778 alliance and trade treaties with France.

3. Answers may include that Adams withstood intense Federalist pressure to make war with France. Other students might point out that Adams prepared for war, was President during the "half war," and that France sought peace.

4. The Kentucky and Virginia Resolutions countered federal government's power by giving states right to nullify acts of Congress they considered unconstitutional. Jefferson and Madison drafted the resolutions in response to what they saw as federal tyranny in the Alien and Sedition Acts.

5. Jefferson and Burr, running for President and Vice-President on the Republican ticket, received an equal number of electoral votes, throwing the decision into the House of Representatives. Some Federalists in the House made problems by backing Burr instead of Jefferson.

Multicultural Perspectives

The first step toward formal education for Native Americans began in 1819 when Congress appropriated a "Civilization Fund" of $10,000 annually, obtained from the sale of Indian lands. This money went to church-sponsored private schools and so-called "Friends of the Indian" benevolent societies. Federally-administered schools, first funded by Congress in 1870, sought to educate Indians in the ways of white society. Children were removed from their families and forbidden to speak Native-American languages. Many of these schools, like the Carlisle School in Pennsylvania founded in 1879, were boarding schools that mainly taught boys trades such as carpentry and household tasks to girls.

This primer was published in the 1780s for the use of Mohawk students who wanted to learn to read their own language and English.

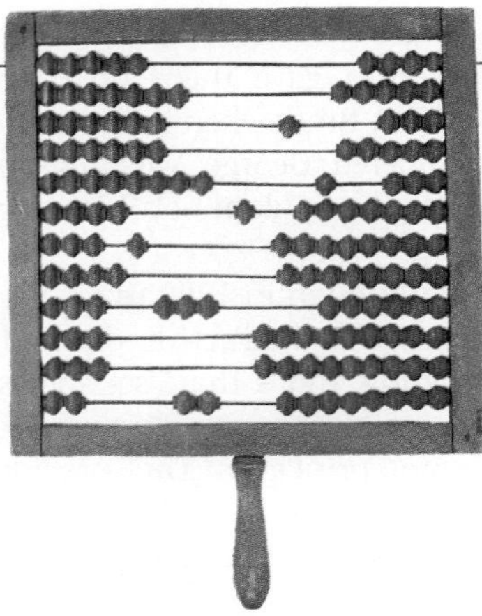

Students used an abacus, an ancient Asian device, to solve arithmetic problems.

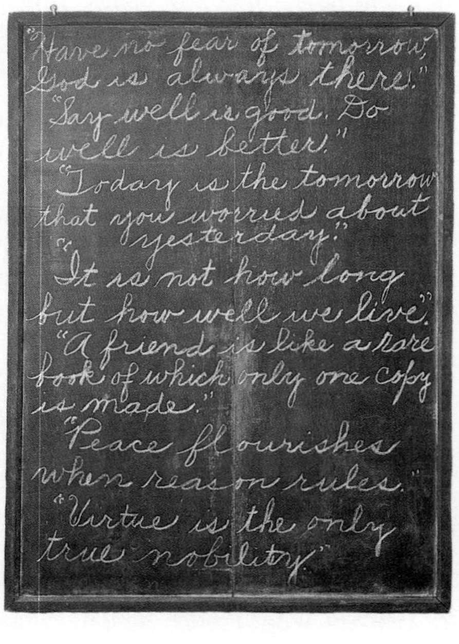

Chalkboards, made of slate, glass, or wood, became common in American schools in the early 1800s.

Girls practiced needlework on samplers. As adults they would make the sheets and clothing, and do other household sewing.

A few young women were able to attend private schools.

Multicultural Perspectives

Free African Americans in the cities established societies and organizations devoted to black education. One of the earliest, the Brown Fellowship Society, was organized in 1790. In 1829 Congressmen and citizens of Washington, D.C., founded the African Education Society for the purpose of teaching blacks academic, mechanical, and agricultural skills. In 1842 August Wattles and Samuel Emlen opened a school in Ohio for Native-American and African-American boys.

Social History

The hornbook is called such because the board was covered with a thin piece of clear horn through which a person could read. Some "hornbooks" were made of gingerbread. Students ate the letter of the alphabet they had learned.

Analyzing Primary Sources

Native Americans Speak. Ben Franklin recorded in the 1700s how some Native-American leaders rejected an offer of schooling:

> *"We have had some experience of it: Several of our young people . . . were instructed in all your sciences; but when they came back to us, they were bad runners; ignorant of every means of living in the woods; unable to bear either cold or hunger; knew neither how to build a cabin, take a deer, or kill an enemy; spoke our language imperfectly . . . they were totally good for nothing."*

Ask students what fault these Native Americans found with European style education. What did they deem more important?

young IN AMERICA

At School

Formal schooling was hard to come by in the new American nation. As in colonial times, children who learned reading and writing were usually taught by their families or tutors, or in private or church schools. Girls seldom received much education—it led, Governor John Winthrop of Massachusetts Bay Colony had believed, to insanity.

No state had a public school system. Schools were expensive to run and diverted children from essential farm work, it was thought. Besides, as one legislator exclaimed, "I hope you do not conceive it at all necessary that *everybody* should be able to read, write, and cipher."

By the 1830s, however, more and more Americans were calling for free public schooling. Democratic government, they declared, could work only if all citizens were educated.

At school and at play, children in the early 1800s dressed like adults.

A single teacher often taught all the grades in a one-room schoolhouse.

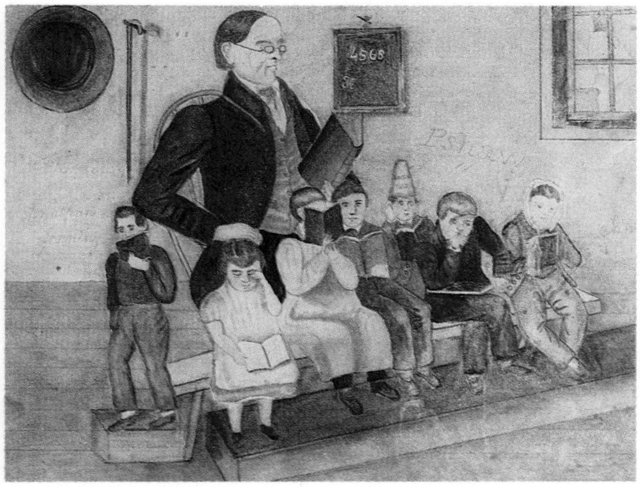

When children were learning to read, their first book was usually a hornbook.

Chapter Survey

ANSWERS

Using New Vocabulary

1. (c) Hamilton
2. (c) Hamilton
3. (a) Washington
4. (b) Jefferson

Reviewing the Chapter

1. Departments of State, War, Treasury. Washington conferred with department heads before making decisions, but did not try to lead Congress or ask Congress for advice.
2. Hamilton wanted central government to have power, and loose construction made it possible to find implied powers in Constitution. Jefferson opposed growth of federal power and favored strict construction of Constitution.
3. Jefferson had great faith in ability of average person to make wise decisions. Hamilton thought average person too easily swayed.
4. (a) National bank bill debate first time Jefferson openly spoke out against Hamilton. (b) *National Gazette* vehicle for Jefferson and Madison to publicize opposition to Hamilton's policies. (c) Public opinion divided over French Revolution, with Federalist opposition and Republican support intensifying party differences.
5. Jay's Treaty unpopular because it did not get the British to stop stirring up Indian tribes against white settlers. Nor did it stop British seizure of American ships or impressment of American sailors. Pinckney's Treaty gave white settlers direct benefits in form of right to travel on Mississippi River and right of duty-free deposit in New Orleans.
6. Jay's Treaty angered French and led them to block diplomatic relations with U.S. American commission sent to France to repair relations met instead with three French agents asking for bribe. XYZ Affair outraged Americans, and Federalists called for war against France. Instead of full-scale war, United States fought undeclared war at sea for two years. During "half war," Congress passed Alien and Sedition Acts to stem dissent.
7. Alliance with France ended by negotiation in 1800. In quest for European power, Napoleon did not want to be distracted by trouble with United States, so agreed to release United States from 1778 pledge to support France in time of war. United States dropped claim for payment of seized ships.

Thinking Critically

1. Since differences of opinion are bound to occur, political parties provide rallying points around which views can form.

Reduced student page in the Teacher's Edition

Chapter Survey

Using New Vocabulary

Match each numbered vocabulary term with an appropriate person. Then explain the connection between the person and the vocabulary term(s).

1. protective tariff	(a) Washington
2. excise tax	(b) Jefferson
3. neutrality	(c) Hamilton
4. states' rights	

Reviewing the Chapter

1. Name the first three executive departments Congress created and explain how Washington set the precedent for relations among the department heads, the President, and Congress.

2. Why did Hamilton favor a loose construction and Jefferson a strict construction of the Constitution?

3. Compare the views of Jefferson and Hamilton regarding the ability of the average person to participate in government.

4. How did each of the following contribute to the development of political parties?
(a) debate over the national bank bill
(b) establishment of the *National Gazette*
(c) public response to the French Revolution

5. Why did Americans dislike Jay's Treaty but welcome Pinckney's Treaty?

6. Explain how each event led to the next.
(a) Jay's Treaty (b) the XYZ Affair, (c) the "half war" (d) the Alien and Sedition Acts

7. With which European nation had the United States had a treaty of alliance since 1778? Why and how was this alliance ended?

Thinking Critically

1. Analysis. Washington warned against the dangers of political parties. What advantages can you see for a nation in having political parties?

2. Analysis. Using evidence from events described in this chapter, support Washington's opinion that neutrality was the best policy.

Using Geography

Match the letters on the map with the locations listed. Explain the importance of each during the administrations of Washington and Adams.

1. New York City	**4.** Ohio country
2. Washington, D.C.	**5.** New Orleans
3. Western Pennsylvania	**6.** Spanish Florida

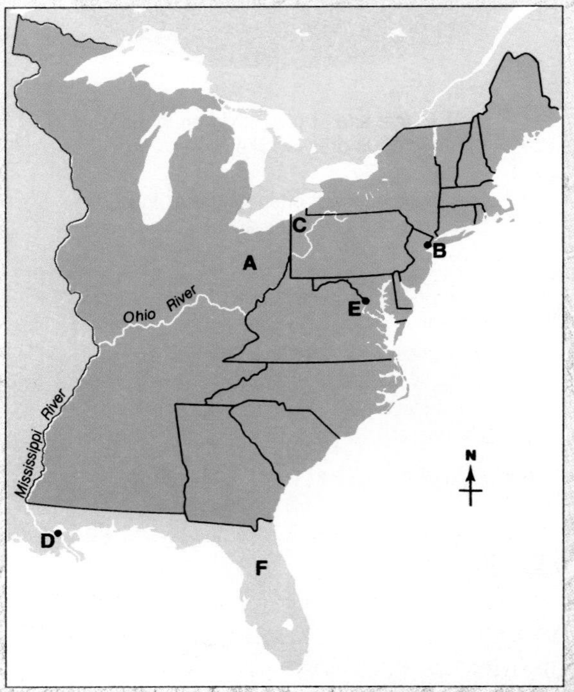

History and You

The Sedition Act of 1798 raised the question of how much diversity of opinion the nation can tolerate in times of threats from abroad. Form small groups to find out how the government has responded to this question in the twentieth century. As a class, discuss whether you think the United States seems to be getting more tolerant or more restrictive.

Organization provides strength of numbers to make sure that different positions are heard.
2. If United States had not followed policy of neutrality, it might have become involved in fighting Great Britain at sea over Northwest territory. It might have had to combat Spain in Southwest or Florida and might have gone to war with France. Foreign wars would have been financial burden on new nation and would have further stressed the newly-formed government.

Using Geography

1. B; nation's first capital
2. E; chosen as permanent capital, site was southerners' half of compromise on national debt
3. C; scene of Whiskey Rebellion, suppression of which demonstrated strength of new government
4. A; secured from Indians by Treaty of Greenville
5. D; owned by Spanish, who granted American right of deposit in Pinckney's Treaty
6. F; northern boundary set at thirty-first parallel by Pinckney's Treaty

History and You

Students should report on the Sedition Act passed during World War I under which dissenters were jailed, Japanese internment camps of World War II, and McCarthy investigations of Cold War. Protestors against Vietnam War met with tear gas from federal troops and called "bums" by President. Dissent of Persian Gulf War seemed to be well tolerated.

Applying Thinking Skills

Comparing

1. Both state that party spirit springs from people's natures.
2. Washington thinks party spirit the worst enemy of democracy; Jefferson thinks it is useful, each party checks the other.
3. Answers will vary.

Interpreting Political Cartoons

1. John Marshall, Elbridge Gerry, Charles Pinckney
2. Threat of war with France.
3. French agents demand for $250,000 bribe.
4. Anti-French sentiments; France depicted as five-headed monster.
5. Federalists; cartoon might have incited Americans to call for war with France—a Federalist position.
6. Might have been less inclined to favor France.

Applying Thinking Skills

Comparing

The following two quotations concern the rise of political parties in the early years of the nation. The first is an excerpt from George Washington's Farewell Address. The second is part of a letter written by Thomas Jefferson. Answer the questions that follow to compare the two men's views.

> *"Let me now . . . warn you in the most solemn manner against the baneful [harmful] effects of the spirit of the party . . . This spirit, unfortunately, is inseparable from our nature, having its root in the strongest passions of the human mind. It exists under different shapes in all governments . . . but, in those of the popular form [democracies,] it is seen in its greatest rankness [foulness] and is truly their worst enemy. . . . The common and continual mischief of the spirit of party are sufficient to make it in the interest and duty of a wise people to discourage and restrain it."*
>
> —from George Washington, "Farewell Address," September 17, 1796.

> *"In every free and deliberating society, there must, from the nature of man, be opposite parties, and violent dissensions [disagreements] and discords; and one of these [parties], for the most part, must prevail over the other for a longer or shorter time. Perhaps this party division is necessary to induce [cause] each to watch and relate to the people the proceedings of the other."*
>
> —from Thomas Jefferson, Letter to J. Taylor.

1. What evidence is there that the two men agree on the origins of "the spirit of the party?"
2. How do their views differ on the value of political parties in a democracy?
3. Which view do you agree with most? Why?

Interpreting Political Cartoons

Study the cartoon below. Between October 1795 and November 1799, the French government was headed by the Directory, an executive body of five people. The cartoon pictures the revolutionary French government as a five-headed monster. Use the cartoon to answer the questions below.

1. Who are the three men on the left?
2. What threat might the dagger symbolize?
3. Why does the five-headed monster say, "Money, money, money"?
4. Does the cartoon express pro-French or anti-French sentiments? Explain.
5. Do you think the cartoonist supported the Federalists or the Republicans? Explain.
6. How might the XYZ Affair have affected Republicans' attitudes toward France?

Unit 2 Survey

ANSWERS

Making Connections

1. Americans already thought of themselves as a distinct people. Those agreeing can cite opposition to British measures and such actions as the formation of committees of correspondence and Continental Congress. Those disagreeing can point to the large number of loyalists.

2. The dominant culture was English American, which many people assumed to be superior. Others tried to "fit in"; people who could not were judged inferior. Challenges to that view included German-American determination to preserve their language and culture, African-American preservation of African customs, Native-American refusal to assimilate, women's arguments that "all men are equally free" should read "all people are equally free."

3. Answers might include that by allowing dissenters to speak, rebellion is averted. Change can be peaceful.

4. Political parties came into being with Hamilton's and Jefferson's differing views. Jefferson's followers formed the Republican party; Hamilton's, the Federalist. Disadvantage: Parties encourage dissension and work against national unity. Advantage: They provide a voice for dissent, a check against tyranny by a single party.

Using the Time Line. Signs of hope may include the Declaration of Independence, Articles of Confederation, Stars and Stripes, Academy of Arts and Sciences, book on American agriculture.

Projects and Activities

1. Current Constitutional issues include freedom of speech, role of the press, access to economic opportunities, role of the government in the economy, states' rights, control of resources, right to privacy.

2. Discussions might include such topics as big government, foreign alliances, foreign aid, ways to deal with poverty, the homeless, crime.

3. Students should consider national security and the Alien and Sedition Acts, relations with other countries, and when and where the United States should go to war.

Using the Time Line. Events may include the Boston Tea Party, Continental Congress, American Revolution, postal system, Declaration of Independence, Constitution, Bill of Rights, U.S. mint, American architecture, art, and literature, Stars and Stripes, technological progress.

Unit Survey

Making Connections

1. In 1818 John Adams said, "The Revolution was effected [set in motion] before the war commenced. The Revolution was in the minds and hearts of the people." What did he mean? Do you agree or disagree? Give reasons.

2. What were the dominant views of race and ethnic background at the time of the American Revolution? What challenges did these views of diversity face in the early years of the Republic? Give examples.

3. The framers of the Constitution provided for conflict with such measures as checks and balances and federalism. What is the value of conflict in a democracy?

4. How and why did political parties arise in the United States? How are political parties a disadvantage? Of what value are they?

Using the Time Line. What events shown on the time line might have seemed signs of hope to many Americans—events that signalled progress in the search for opportunity or the growth of democracy? Explain each choice.

Projects and Activities

1. Name current issues that illustrate the following statement: The United States Constitution represents endlessly unfinished business. Choose one Constitutional issue, such as how much freedom the press should have. Do research to define the issue and arguments on both sides. Present this information in an oral report, concluding with a statement of your position and reasons supporting it.

2. Imagine Hamilton and Jefferson returning to life. Work in groups of four to prepare a discussion between these two leaders on the role of government and participation of "common people" in government. How would each man respond to changes that have taken place in government since his time? What recommendations do you think they would make?

3. As a class, re-enact the election of 1800. Discuss the issues and the candidates' views. Have each student vote and state a reason for his or her choice. Tally the results.

Using the Time Line. Between 1760 and 1800 the British colonies were transformed into a new nation. The former British subjects created a new American society. Work with a partner to make a poster depicting the development of this new nation and society. For your poster select at least eight events shown on the time line.

Milestones	1761	1771
Presidents		
Political and Economic	• Proclamation of 1763 • Boston Committee of Correspondence • Stamp Act • Townshend Acts	• Boston Massacre • Boston Tea Party • Intolerable Acts • Continental Congress
Social and Cultural	• Est. pop. English colonies 1,593,625 • Quakers begin to free their slaves • American styles in architecture developing • *The Colonial Housewife* cookbook published	• First Spanish mission in California • *Paul Revere* portrait by John Singleton Copley • Franklin begins his *Autobiography* • *Poems*, Phillis Wheatley
Technological and Scientific	• Conestoga wagons in use • Mastadon bones found in Illinois • First book on American agriculture • Mason-Dixon line survey • Medical school, Philadelphia	• Spaniards introduce grapes into California • Mental hospital founded, Williamsburg • Joseph Priestley discovers oxygen

182

Assessment

To prepare for the activity students might first develop brief time lines for the characters they create. Each time line should include the birthdate of the character and the dates of the five events the student will address.

Students should calculate the age of the character at each event. Journal entries should be dated and should mention the character's age at the time of the event being discussed.

Scoring

To create a scoring system, or rubric, assign an achievement scale to each of the evaluation criteria. For example, you might evaluate "Completing the task" on a scale of 0 to 4 as follows:

4—Exemplary response: more than five diary entries with full descriptions of five events; complete discussion of main issues surrounding each event; thoughtful evaluation of events.

3—Good response: five or more diary entries with adequate descriptions of five events; good discussion of issues surrounding each event; reasonable evaluation of events.

2—Adequate response: minimal description of five events; cursory explanations of issues; some evaluation of events.

1—Poor response: some diary entries unclear or missing; little understanding of issues; inadequate evaluation of events.

0—No response/inappropriate response.

Follow-up Activity

Class discussion. Tell students that it is now long after the journals would have been written. They might assume that the journals were written by their great-grandparents. Have students exchange journals and read to identify the single most important goal or purpose guiding the actions of the "great-grandparent." As students enumerate goals, list them on the chalkboard. Ask whether or not the list is representative of the goals of Americans in the years between 1763 and 1801. Are there any that should be added to the list?

Assessment: Demonstrating What You Know

Journal Writing

Imagine that the year is 1840. You have just reached the age of ninety, and you have been thinking over the events of your lifetime. You remember clearly the struggles of the Revolutionary War and the years that followed. So that future generations will know about those struggles, you are going to set down your memories in a journal, or personal record of events.

Decide what kind of person you are—for example, what gender, where you live, and what kinds of jobs you have had. Choose five of the following events in your life and write at least one journal entry for each. Describe each event and the issues surrounding it, including what others said and did, why, and how you reacted. Give your opinion of each situation.

1. Joining the Sons or Daughters of Liberty
2. Witnessing the Boston Massacre or the Boston Tea Party
3. Joining a Committee of Correspondence
4. Participating in a major battle of the Revolutionary War
5. Learning that your neighbor was a Loyalist
6. Hearing the Declaration of Independence read
7. Observing the Continental Congress creating the Articles of Confederation
8. Discussing with a writer in the early 1800s his or her newspaper article, "What is an American? Some Different Views"
9. Hearing Patrick Henry speak against the Constitution and Alexander Hamilton or Benjamin Franklin speak for it

Evaluation Criteria

Your work will be evaluated according to how well you meet the following criteria.

- **Completing the task**. You describe five events and issues and take a position on each.
- **Knowing history**. You base your descriptions on historical facts. You use information from the text or other sources to support your opinions.
- **Thinking critically**. You draw conclusions based on analysis of historical facts. The opinions expressed are reasonable for the times and the character you have created.
- **Communicating ideas**. The journal entries are interesting and creative. Descriptions of events and issues are clear. The opinions given are persuasive.

1781 | **1791** | **1801**

Washington | Adams | Jefferson

- American Revolution begins
- United Colonies postal system established
- Declaration of Independence
- Articles of Confederation proposed
- U.S./China trade opens
- Shays' Rebellion
- Northwest Ordinance
- Constitution
- Bill of Rights
- Rise of political parties
- First U.S. mint authorized, Philadelphia
- U.S. Proclamation of Neutrality
- Alien and Sedition Acts

- First antislavery society, Quakers
- First "Yankee Doodle" sheet music
- Woman suffrage (until 1807), New Jersey
- Congress adopts the Stars and Stripes
- *The American Spelling Book*, Noah Webster
- John Trumbull begins painting *Declaration of Independence*
- Benjamin Rush argues for education of women
- First U.S. census, pop. 3,929,214

- *Turtle*, first torpedo submarine, David Bushnell
- English expedition reaches Hawaii, James Cook
- American Academy of Arts and Sciences founded
- Franklin invents bifocal lenses
- John Fitch experiments with steamboat
- Samuel Slater builds textile mill
- Cotton gin, Eli Whitney
- Joseph Priestley migrates to U.S.

Unit 3

Objectives

- Explain how Thomas Jefferson influenced the westward expansion of the United States.
- Describe the expansion of democracy during the presidency of Andrew Jackson.
- Explain the connection between the spread of democracy and the growth of reform movements.
- Cite causes of the increasing tensions between the North and the South.

Introducing THE UNIT

The first half of the nineteenth century represented years of vast physical growth for the United States. Unit 3 describes how the nation surged westward with the Louisiana Purchase, the addition of Oregon, the annexation of Texas, and the Mexican Cession. Westward expansion, however, led to conflict with Native Americans whose lands were threatened by settlers from the East. The nation's expansion also fueled the growing sectional conflict between the North and the South regarding slavery.

Economic and political growth also characterized the period. The nation underwent a revolution in industry and transportation. Democracy expanded during the Jacksonian era, bringing with it other reform movements that sought to improve health care and education, limit or eliminate alcohol use, and expand rights of women and African Americans.

Unit 3 1801-1850

Building a Nation

About the Author
Herman Melville's first two books were successes, but readers found his third novel, *Mardi,* to be confusing, and Melville's popularity rapidly declined. Using the profits from his novels, Melville bought a farm in Massachusetts. Here he penned his most famous novel, *Moby Dick,* originally titled *The Whale.* Unable to understand the novel's complexity, readers responded negatively to it as well as to his next two works. As a result, Melville fell into debt. To support himself in his later years, he worked as a customs inspector at the Port of New York. Melville wrote several memorable poems on the Civil War, and one of his finest works, *Billy Budd,* was written near the end of his life. Melville died in 1891, his works largely unappreciated until their rediscovery by scholars in the 1920s. Since then, Melville has been recognized as one of the greatest American novelists.

History Through Literature

Herman Melville (1819-1891) drew on his rich life experiences to write his compelling novels and short stories. At eighteen Melville had sought adventure as a cabin boy in the thriving New England sea trade, and later he signed on as a seaman on a whaling ship. His years of sailing and his experiences living among peoples of the Pacific Islands gave him the material for *Typee* (1846), *Omoo* (1847), *Mardi* (1849), and *Moby Dick* (1851).

Moby Dick is a complex novel that operates on many levels. On one level, Melville tells an adventure tale, immersing the reader in the world of whaling. On another level, *Moby Dick* is a psychological study of Captain Ahab's obsessive search for a white whale called Moby Dick. On a symbolic level, the story explores good and evil and the search for truth.

In the following excerpt, Stubb is the second mate, and Daggoo, Queequeg, and Tashtego are harpooners. At the sighting of a whale, the crew swings into action, getting into smaller boats for the hunt.

from

Moby Dick

by Herman Melville

"There go flukes!" was the cry, an announcement immediately followed by Stubb's producing his match and igniting his pipe, for now a respite was granted. After the full interval of his sounding had elapsed, the whale rose again, and being now in advance of the smoker's boat, and much nearer to it than to any of the others, Stubb counted upon the honor of the capture. It was obvious, now, that the whale had at length become aware of his pursuers. All silence of cautiousness was therefore no longer of use. Paddles were dropped, and oars came loudly into play. And still puffing at his pipe, Stubb cheered on his crew to the assault.

"Ka-la! Koo-loo!" howled Queequeg, as if smacking his lips over a mouthful of Grenadier's steak. And thus with oars and yells the keels cut the sea. Meanwhile, Stubb retaining his place in the van, still encouraged his men to the onset, all the while puffing the smoke from his mouth. Like desperadoes they tugged and they strained, till the welcome cry was heard—"Stand up, Tashtego!—give it to him!" The harpoon was hurled. "Stern all!" The oarsmen backed water; the same moment something went hot

Guided Reading

Discussion. As students read this selection, have them note the dangers faced by the crew during the whale hunt. Have students speculate about why a whaling crew might put up with such dangers year after year.

Vocabulary Building

Discussion. Knowing the following terms will help students understand this selection from *Moby Dick*: *respite* (delay), *desperadoes* (dangerous, reckless individuals), *cleaving* (cutting; slicing), *canted* (tilted), *spasmodic* (characterized by a sudden, violent movement), *spiracle* (breathing hole), *vehement* (forceful; violent), *waning* (declining).

BACKGROUND

Multicultural Perspectives

The three harpooners who appear in this selection have different non-Western backgrounds. Queequeg is probably a Polynesian native of "an island far away to the West and South." Tashtego is a Native American from Gay Head, Massachusetts. Daggoo is an African American. These characters, with the other members of the *Pequod's* crew, symbolize all of humanity.

and hissing along every one of their wrists. It was the magical line. An instant before, Stubb had swiftly caught two additional turns with it round the loggerhead, whence, by reason of its increased rapid circlings, a hempen blue smoke now jetted up and mingled with the steady fumes from his pipe. As the line passed round and round the loggerhead; so also, just before reaching that point, it blisteringly passed through and through both of Stubb's hands, from which the hand-cloths, or squares of quilted canvas sometimes worn at these times had accidentally dropped. It was like holding a enemy's sharp two edged sword by the blade, and that enemy all the time striving to wrest it out of your clutch.

"Wet the line! Wet the line!" cried Stubb to the tub oarsman (him seated by the tub) who, snatching off his hat, dashed the seawater into it.[1] More turns were taken, so that the line began holding its place. The boat now flew through the boiling water like a shark all fins. Stubb and Tashtego here changed places—stem for stern—a staggering business truly in that rocking commotion.

From the vibrating line extending the entire length of the upper part of the boat, and from its now being more tight than a harpstring, you would have thought the craft had two keels—one cleaving the water, the other the air—as the boat churned on through both opposing elements at once. A continual cascade played at the bows; a ceaseless whirling eddy in her wake; and, at the slightest motion from within, even but of a little finger, the vibrating, cracking craft canted over her spasmodic gunwale into the sea. Thus they rushed; each man with might and main clinging to his seat, to prevent being tossed to the foam; and the tall form of Tashtego at the steering oar crouching almost double, in order to bring down his center of gravity. Whole Atlantics and Pacifics seemed passed as they shot on their way, till at length the whale somewhat slackened his flight.

"Haul in—Haul in!" cried Stubb to the bowsman! and, facing round towards the whale, all hands began pulling the boat up to him, while yet the boat was being towed on. Soon ranging up by his flank, Stubb, firmly planting his knee in the clumsy cleat, darted dart after dart into the flying fish; at the word of command, the boat alternately sterning out of the way of the whale's horrible wallow, and then ranging up for another fling.

The red tide now poured from all sides of the monster like brooks down a hill. His tormented body rolled not in brine but in blood, which bubbled and seethed for furlongs behind in their wake. The slanting sun playing upon this crimson pond in the sea, sent back its reflection into every face, so that they

[1]Partly to show the indispensableness of this act, it may be stated, that, in the old Dutch fishery, a mop was used to dash the running line with water; in many other ships, a wooden piggin, or bailer, is set apart for that purpose. Your hat, however, is the most convenient.

Taking a Closer Look

ANSWERS

1. A harpoon driven into the whale is attached to the upper part of the boat pursuing it. Then "dart after dart" is driven into the whale and the harpoon is "churned" into the whale until it dies.

2. The crew runs the risk of the boat capsizing from the struggle with the whale, or having the whale smash the boat.

3. The passage provides a glimpse of the excitement, hardship, and dangers of this life.

(Background) Connecticut lighthouse; (opposite page) scrimshaw of whaling ships; (right) model of a nineteenth-century square rigger, humpback whale breaching.

all glowed to each other like red men. And all the while, jet after jet of white smoke was agonizingly shot from the spiracle of the whale, and vehement puff after puff from the mouth of the excited headsman; as at every dart, hauling in upon his crooked lance (by the line attached to it), Stubb straightened it again and again, by a few rapid blows against the gunwale, then again and again sent it into the whale.

"Pull up—Pull up!" he now cried to the bowsman, as the waning whale relaxed in his wrath. "Pull up!—close to!" and the boat ranged along the fish's flank. When reaching far over the bow, Stubb slowly churned his long sharp lance into the fish, and kept it there, carefully churning and churning, as if cautiously seeking to feel after some gold watch that the whale might have swallowed, and which he was fearful of breaking ere he could hook it out. But that gold watch he sought was the innermost life of the fish. And now it is struck; for, starting from his trance into that unspeakable thing called his "flurry," the monster horribly wallowed in his blood, overwrapped himself in impenetrable, mad, boiling spray, so that the imperilled craft, instantly dropping astern, had much ado blindly to struggle out from that phrensied twilight into the clear air of the day.

And now abating in his flurry, the whale once more rolled out into view; surging from side to side; spasmodically dilating and contracting his spout-hole with sharp, cracking, agonized respirations. At last, gush after gush of clotted red gore, as if it had been the purple lees of red wine, shot into the frighted air; and falling back again, ran dripping down his motionless flanks into the sea. His heart had burst!

"He's dead, Mr. Stubb," said Daggoo.

"Yes; both pipes smoked out!" and withdrawing his own from his mouth, Stubb scattered the dead ashes over the water; and, for a moment, stood thoughtfully eyeing the vast corpse he had made.

Taking a Closer Look

1. *Describe how the whale is killed.*

2. *What dangers does the crew face during the whale hunt?*

3. *The American sperm-whaling industry employed more than 70,000 people during the years 1820 to 1850 and killed some 10,000 whales each year. What glimpse does this passage give about the life of a whaling crew?*

Chapter 8

The Growth of the Nation

Planning Guide

	Student Text	TWE Lesson Plans	Support Materials
SECTION 1	**Section 8–1** (1–2 Days) **The First Republican President,** pp 190–196 Review/Evaluation Section Review, p 196	**Introducing the Chapter:** Voices of the Early 1800s—Class Activity, 30 minutes, p 187B **Teaching the Main Ideas:** A Deed of Sale for Louisiana—Individual Activity, one class period, p 187B	★ **Read to Remember,** Section 1 ● **Section Activities,** Section 1 Δ **Readings,** Lewis and Clark ● **Tests and Quizzes,** Section 1 Quiz
SECTION 2	**Section 8–2** (1 Day) **The War of 1812,** pp 197–202 The American Spirit: Tecumseh, p 199 Review/Evaluation Section Review, p 202	**Reinforcement Activity:** War Letters—Individual Activity, homework, p 187C	★ **Read to Remember,** Section 2 ● **Section Activities,** Section 2 Δ **Enrichment Activities,** Section 2 Δ **Readings,** Star-Spangled Banner ● **Tests and Quizzes,** Section 2 Quiz
SECTION 3	**Section 8–3** (1–3 Days) **Revolution in Industry and Travel,** pp 203–208 Geography—Relationships Within Places: The Old Mill Stream, p 209 Point of View: The Lowell Factory System, pp 210–211 Review/Evaluation Section Review, p 208	**Evaluating Progress:** Mapping Sectional Differences—Cooperative Activity, 2 days student preparation and 2 half class periods, p 187C	★ **Read to Remember,** Section 3 ● **Section Activities,** Section 3 Δ **Enrichment Activities,** Section 3 ● **Geography Activities,** Section 3 Δ **Readings,** Matilda Joslyn Gage ● **Tests and Quizzes,** Section 3 Quiz
SECTION 4	**Section 8–4** (1–2 Days) **National Unity and Sectional Strains,** pp 212–217 Connections to Themes: Balancing Unity and Diversity, p 217 Review/Evaluation Section Review, p 217 Chapter 8 Survey, pp 218–219 Skills, pp 218–219 Using New Vocabulary Thinking Critically Using a Time Line Applying Social Studies Skills: Analyzing Maps Applying Thinking Skills: Identifying Arguments	**Teaching the Main Ideas:** Taking a Stand—Class Activity, one class period, p 187B **Enrichment Activity:** Outbreak of the Panic of 1819—Paired Activity, one class period, p 187C	★ **Read to Remember,** Section 4 ● **Section Activities,** Section 4 ● **Readings,** Monroe Doctrine ● **Tests and Quizzes,** Section 4 Quiz, Chapter 8 Test (Forms A and B) **Additional Resources** Δ **Twentieth Century Issues: Links to the Past** ● **Active Learning** Δ **GTV Videodiscs** Δ **Transparencies and Activity Book** ● **Testing Software** ★ **Chapter Summaries**

Key:
★ **For Extra Support**
● **For All Students**
Δ **For Enrichment**

Overview

Thomas Jefferson, the first Republican President, found his belief in limited government seriously challenged by pirate raids on American ships in the Mediterranean, the purchase of the Louisiana Territory, and quarrels with the Supreme Court, headed by Federalist John Marshall. Thus he changed little of substance in the government that he inherited from the Federalists.

Jefferson declared American neutrality in the war that broke out between Britain and France in 1803. However, he left his successor, James Madison, with the problems of ending British and French interference with American shipping, British impressment of American sailors, and British support for Tecumseh in the Northwest. In 1812 Congress declared war against Britain. After three years of inconclusive fighting, the United States and Britain signed the Treaty of Ghent, which did not settle issues that had led to the war.

A growing sense of American nationalism emerged in this era, buttressed by the war, the acquisition of Louisiana and Florida, nationalist decisions of the Supreme Court, and the growth of transportation and industry. Meanwhile, sectional differences, both economical and cultural, were intensified by the issue of extending slavery into the territories. The Missouri Compromise proved to be a landmark in the growth of southern sectionalism.

Activity Objectives

After completing the activities, students should be able to

- explain the pros and cons of the Louisiana Purchase.
- describe issues that Americans faced in the early 1800s.
- compare points of view about the War of 1812.
- compare the impact of industrialization and improved transportation on different sections of the country.
- trace the development of the Panic of 1819.

Introducing the Chapter

Voices of the Early 1800s

This class activity requires half a class period.

In this activity students use primary source materials from the chapter to hypothesize about events and issues facing Americans in the early nineteenth century.

Tell students that to introduce Chapter 8, you need the help of six volunteers who like public speaking or drama. Assign each volunteer one of the following primary sources in the chapter:

- Senator William Plumer, page 194 (Louisiana Purchase debate)
- Meriwether Lewis, page 198 (Lewis and Clark expedition)
- Frances Ann Kemble, page 206 (internal improvements)
- Charles Dickens, page 209 (Industrial Revolution)
- James Forten, page 212 (slavery)
- Thomas Jefferson, page 214 (Missouri Compromise)

As the volunteers prepare, direct the rest of the class to preview Chapter 8 by reading heads and subheads and looking at illustrations and maps.

Ask students to close their texts. In random order, call on the volunteers to read their assigned primary sources. After each reading, have the class hypothesize about the topic and discuss the feelings that it suggests. Emphasize the importance of carefully reading primary source materials in order to learn personal reactions to events and issues.

Teaching the Main Ideas

Section 8-1: A Deed of Sale for Louisiana

This individual activity requires a full class period, or it can be assigned as homework and shared in class the following day.

This activity will help students understand the importance of the Louisiana Purchase through preparation of a deed of sale for the transaction.

Explain to students that most purchases of land (property) are made with a deed of sale, or contract, between the seller and the buyer. The deed specifies the conditions of the sale. Ask students to imagine that the land on which their school is located is being sold. Have them describe conditions that might be specified in the deed of sale (date of deed, date of transfer of property, location, boundaries, price per acre and/or total price, structures on the property, rights to natural resources on the land). List the conditions on the chalkboard. If you have a sample deed, show it to students. Point out that deeds often include a surveyor's map of the property being sold.

Remind students that the Louisiana Territory was the first land that the United States considered buying. Ask students to imagine that they are members of Jefferson's staff responsible for drawing up a deed of sale for the purchase. The contract must include all the conditions listed on the chalkboard plus any other conditions they consider important. Encourage students to include a map that shows the location of the purchase, the major settlements, and natural resources. They may use encyclopedias and other available resources for research.

When assignments are complete, have students display or read their deeds of sale. Conclude by asking students what advice they would give to the Senate when it debates the purchase. Was the Louisiana Purchase a "good deal?" Why or why not?

Teaching the Main Ideas

Section 8-4: Taking a Stand

This class activity requires one period.

This activity gives students an opportunity to examine their opinions on some of the issues facing the nation in the early 1800s. In the activity, students acknowledge their opinions by "taking a stand."

Have students briefly review Chapter 8 to recall the important issues that faced Americans in the early 1800s. Tell them that they will have the opportunity to express their views on these issues.

Designate an imaginary line down the middle of the classroom. Define one end of the line as the "agree" position and the other as the "disagree" position. Define the midpoint as the "no opinion" position. Explain that you will read a statement about which students may agree, disagree, or have no opinion. They are to indicate their position by standing in the appropriate location along the imaginary line.

Read the statement: *A country must never pay ransom for the release of hostages.* Direct students to move to the position along the line that expresses their opinion on the statement. When all are in line, call on students in both the agree and disagree positions to explain their reasons for holding these opinions. Allow students in the "no opinion" position to move if they are persuaded by the explanations. Continue the procedure by reading some or all of the following statements:

- The power of judicial review allows the Supreme Court to rule over the other branches of government.
- A neutral nation should be willing to risk war in order to protect its right to trade freely with warring nations.
- It is the government's job to provide relief for the people in times of severe economic problems.
- The United States has the right to resist European interference in the Western Hemisphere to protect its interests and security.
- National problems should always be solved through compromise.
- Protective tariffs are necessary to protect American products and workers.

Conclude by asking students to identify issues from the early 1800s that are still issues today.

Reinforcement Activity

Section 8-2: War Letters

This individual activity may be assigned as homework.

The following creative writing activity reinforces students' understanding of different points of view about the War of 1812.

Review with students the causes of the War of 1812 described in Section 8-2. Ask them to identify the groups representing the four major views of the war—northern Federalists, westerners, southerners, and the War Hawks.

Assign one fourth of the students to represent each view of the war. Direct them to write a letter to a friend in another region of the country explaining their point of view and describing events to support their opinions.

When assignments are complete, ask at least two volunteers representing each viewpoint to read their letters to the class. Ask each volunteer whether he or she personally would have supported that point of view in 1812 and why or why not. Conclude the activity by taking a class vote to determine which viewpoint would have had the most support.

Evaluating Progress

Section 8-3: Mapping Sectional Differences

This cooperative activity requires about half a class period for students to plan projects, at least two days to collect and prepare information, and half a class period to present completed projects.

This activity, in which students create pictorial maps, is designed to assess students' understanding of the effect of industrialization and improved transportation on regional differences in the country.

Begin the activity by reviewing with students differences among the northern, southern, and western regions of the United States in the early 1800s. Point out that Section 8-3 describes how industrialization and the development of new forms of transportation deepened regional differences.

Organize the class into groups of four. Have each group create a pictorial map of the United States in the early 1800s that illustrates regional differences described in the text. Encourage groups to distribute tasks equally among members. Specify that each map must be drawn by hand and include the following features:

- the boundaries of the United States and the general boundaries of the North, the South, and the West
- important geographical features
- original drawings or photocopied pictures of types of economic activity, major products, workers, and forms of transportation important to each region
- original drawings of regional views of the tariff issue, shown as billboards, sign posts, slogans, cartoons, or other illustrations

Provide each group with poster paper and marking pens. To stimulate creativity, point out examples of maps in the text and reference books.

Display the maps and ask the groups to assess the major regional differences. Members of each group should be evaluated on the basis of the work done by the whole group. Criteria should include accuracy of the maps and a thoughtful summary of regional differences.

Enrichment Activity

Section 8-4: Outbreak of the Panic of 1819

This paired activity requires one class period.

The Panic of 1819 shook the nation's postwar mood of optimistic nationalism, causing sections to become narrowly interested in their own welfare and jealous of rival sections. In the following activity students trace the events that led to the Panic of 1819 by constructing a cause-and-effect diagram.

Have students review the Panic of 1819 in Section 8-4. Point out that the panic was not the result of a single cause. One event affected another, causing a chain reaction that led to a financial panic. Draw on the chalkboard the following model of a cause-effect chain reaction:

cause ⟶ *effect* ⟶ *cause* ⟶ *effect*

Divide the class into pairs and direct them to create a chain-reaction diagram to identify the sequence of events leading to the panic. Encourage students to use boxes or other graphics to show events and make the diagram interesting. Arrows are essential to show how one event relates to another.

Students should include the following events in their diagrams: postwar boom (European demand for American farm goods); rise in farm prices; rush to buy farm land; rise in land prices, encouragement of speculation through easy loans by state banks and Bank of the United States; bumper European crops in 1818 and reduction in cotton purchases by British textile mills; decreased demands for American farm goods and cotton; collapse of crop prices; financial panic; failure of banks, bankruptcy of farmers and merchants, bank foreclosures on homes, farms, businesses.

Display the completed diagrams and have the class view them. Conclude by asking pairs of students to speculate about how the Panic of 1819 might have been averted and to give reasons to support their views.

Bibliography and Audiovisual Material

Teacher Bibliography

Eisler, Benita ed. *The Lowell Offering.* New York: J. B. Lippincott, 1977.

Horsman, Reginald. *The Causes of the War of 1812.* New York: Octagon, 1970.

Snyder, Gerald S. *In the Footsteps of Lewis and Clark.* Washington, DC: National Geographic Society, 1970.

Student Bibliography

Chidsey, Donald B. *Lewis and Clark: The Great Adventure.* New York: Crown 1970.

Forester, C.S. *The Captain from Connecticut*. Boston: Little Brown, 1941.

Macaulay, David. *Mill.* Boston: Houghton Mifflin, 1983.

Marrin, Albert. *Eighteen Twelve: The War Nobody Won.* New York: Macmillan, 1985.

Phelan, Mary Kay. *The Story of the Louisiana Purchase.* New York: HarperCollins, 1979.

Films, Videocassettes, and Videodiscs

The War of 1812. 13 min. Coronet/MTI. Movie.

Inventors and the American Industrial Revolution. 14 min. Churchill Media. Videodisc.

The Industrial Revolution: Beginnings in the United States. 25 min. EBEC. Movie.

Western Man and the Modern World Series: The Industrial Revolution. 23 mins. New York Times. Videocassette.

Filmstrips

America's 19th Century Wars: The War of 1812. New York Times.

The Louisiana Purchase. Multi-Media Productions.

Computer Software

Industrialism in America: The Industrial Revolution Comes to the United States. Apple. Focus Media.

Interviews with History: Industrial America. Apple. Educational Publishing Concepts.

U.S. History Knowledge Race: Series 3. Apple. Focus Media.

Chapter 8

Objectives

- Describe how President Jefferson put Republican principles into practice.
- Cite the causes and effects of the War of 1812.
- Explain how changes in industry and transportation in the early 1800s affected the way Americans lived.
- Discuss how national unity both strengthened and weakened after 1817.

Introducing THE CHAPTER

For suggestions on introducing Chapter 8, refer to page 187B in the Teacher's Edition.

Developing THE CHAPTER

For activities and teaching strategies to help you reinforce and enrich chapter content see pages 187B–187D in the Teacher's Edition.

B · A · C · K · G · R · O · U · N · D

Chapter Opener Illustrations
Architect and engineer Benjamin Latrobe sketched the picture of Jefferson below. Jefferson wrote an epitaph for himself, *"Here lies Thomas Jefferson, Author of the Declaration of Independence, of the Statute of Virginia for Religious Freedom, and Father of the University of Virginia."*

The War of 1812 gave Americans a strong sense of loyalty to their nation. Feelings of patriotism were especially evident at the Fourth of July celebration in Philadelphia at Center Square in 1819.

Robert Fulton's *Clermont*, the first commercially successful steamboat, was 150 feet long, 18 feet wide, weighed 100

Reduced student page in the Teacher's Edition

Chapter 8 1801-1828

The Growth of the Nation

tons, and sailed 5 miles per hour. "Fulton's Folly," as critics called it, made river transportation faster and cheaper.

During the War of 1812, peace medals bearing the portrait of the President were given to Indians of the Northwest who were allies of the United States. Madison sent out medals of Jefferson, his predecessor, until his own solid silver ones were ready late in 1814.

Eli Whitney's cotton gin cleaned fifty times as much cotton in a day as a worker could by hand. Thus cotton became a profitable crop in the South—a cash crop.

American Voices

On March 4, 1801, Margaret Bayard Smith joined throngs of people in the unfinished capitol building in "Washington City," the new capital of the United States. There she watched President-elect Thomas Jefferson take the oath of office. Later that day she wrote to a friend:

> "*I have this morning witnessed one of the most interesting scenes a free people can ever witness. The changes of administration, which in every government and in every age have most generally been eras of confusion, villainy and bloodshed, in this our happy country take place without any . . . disorder. This day, has one of the most amiable and worthy men taken that seat to which he was called by the voice of his country.*"

Unlike Margaret Bayard Smith, many Federalists feared that Jefferson's victory marked the beginning of a decline, a descent to "blood and ashes." Yet the Federalists transferred power, according to law, to their bitter foe.

Jefferson regarded his coming to power as "the Revolution of 1800." However, neither he nor his Republican followers realized that his inauguration marked the beginning of a new political era—a period of Republican power that would last for twenty-eight years.

Sketch of Thomas Jefferson, 1801; Philadelphians celebrating the Fourth of July in 1819; Robert Fulton's steamboat the Clermont; *Madison peace medal given to Native-American allies in the War of 1812; a cotton gin.*

Analyzing Primary Sources

American Voices

Margaret Bayard Smith was a close observer of Jefferson's administration. She and her husband moved to Washington, D.C. in 1800, where her husband founded a newspaper, the *National Intelligencer.* A collection of her private papers, *The First Forty Years of Washington Society*, was published in 1906.

1. Why have changes in government been so frequently attended by "confusion, villainy and bloodshed"? How does the Constitution provide for a peaceful transfer of power? **(Refer students to Article 2 of the Constitution.)**

2. Why would Federalists consider Jefferson's election as a descent to "blood and ashes"? Why would Jefferson consider his coming to power as "the Revolution of 1800"? **(Refer to differences between Federalists and Republicans.)**

Section 8-1

Objectives

- ***Answer the Focus Question.***
- *Explain the power* Marbury *v.* Madison *gave to the Supreme Court.*
- *Explain how conflict with the Barbary States and the Louisiana Purchase tested Jefferson's Republican principles.*
- *Cite the effects of Lewis and Clark's expedition.*

Introducing

THE SECTION

When President John Kennedy invited all the American Nobel prize winners to dinner at the White House in 1962, he said, *"I think this is the most extraordinary collection of talent, of human knowledge, that has ever been gathered together at the White House, with the possible exception of when Thomas Jefferson dined alone."*

Ask students what Kennedy meant. **(Jefferson had many talents.)** As students read the section, have them find evidence to support Kennedy's opinion.

Time Line Illustrations

1. Pierre Dominique Toussaint L'Ouverture led an army of formerly enslaved Africans in a successful campaign to gain control of France's island colony of Saint Domingue (now called Haiti). After failing to regain control, France abandoned plans to build a new empire in North America.

2. In this cartoon about the War of 1812, President James Madison gives King George III a bloody nose. The cartoon celebrates the defeat of the British ship *Boxer* by the American ship *Enterprise* in 1813.

3. Jefferson called for an embargo of foreign trade in

Reduced student page in the Teacher's Edition

CHAPTER TIME LINE

1801 - 1828

1803 Louisiana Purchase
Marbury v. *Madison*

1812 War of 1812

1801 — 1807 — 1812

1801 Toussaint L'Ouverture: ruler of Saint Domingue

1804 Lewis and Clark expedition begins

1806 Tecumseh forms Indian confederacy

1807 Embargo Act goes into effect

8-1 The First Republican President

Focus: As President, how did Jefferson put Republican principles into practice?

Thomas Jefferson's inauguration fit the simplicity of the new federal city. "His dress," wrote one reporter, "was . . . that of a plain citizen." In his inaugural address, Thomas Jefferson tried to heal the wounds left by the recent election. He called upon all citizens to unite in accepting "the voice of the nation." Jefferson pleaded for an end to party strife. "Let us restore," he said, "that harmony and affection without which liberty and even life itself are but dreary things."

The new President then spoke of the Republican principles that would guide his administration. His government would protect the people's rights but "leave them otherwise free" to improve their lives as they saw fit. He would not raise taxes, because they "take from the mouth of labor the bread it has earned." Abroad, Jefferson called for "peace, commerce, and honest friendship with all nations, entangling alliances with none."

Once in office, Jefferson began to put Republicanism into practice, but he did not alter the basic machinery of government established by the Federalists. Nor did he change Hamilton's program to repay federal and state debts. The President did, however, reduce the number of federal officials and the size of the army and navy. He also persuaded Congress to repeal the excise tax on whiskey and a tax on property. For income, the government would depend primarily on import duties.

Finally, Jefferson allowed the hated Alien and Sedition Acts to expire. And at his urging, Congress repealed the Naturalization Act, eliminating the fourteen-year residence requirement and restoring the five-year requirement for citizenship.

1807. Alexander Anderson's cartoon shows the "ograbme" (embargo spelled backwards)—the American "Snapping-turtle"—catching a smuggler disobeying the Embargo Act.
4. Roads in the early 1800s were in terrible condition—rutted, potholed, frequently studded with stumps. In wet weather horses were sometimes belly-deep in mud.
5. The famous "Lowell Girls" worked at the water-powered textile mills in Lowell, Massachusetts.

1817 Congress considers building roads

1819 Florida ceded to United States
McCulloch v. *Maryland*

1820 Missouri Compromise

1822 Textile mill opens at Lowell, Massachusetts

1823 Monroe Doctrine

1825 Erie Canal opens

1817 — 1822 — 1828

The President and the Judiciary

It was in the judicial branch that Jefferson suffered the chief setback of his first term. During his last weeks in office, President Adams had made sure that the judiciary would remain in Federalist hands. He began by appointing John Marshall, a vigorous Federalist leader from Virginia, as Chief Justice of the Supreme Court.

Next, Adams rushed the Judiciary Act of 1801 through the outgoing Federalist Congress. This act improved the organization of the judicial branch and also created new court positions. On his last night in office, Adams busily signed commissions, appointing Federalists to the new posts. Republicans scornfully called these late-night appointees "midnight judges."

***Marbury* v. *Madison*.** Soon after taking office, Jefferson discovered a stack of Adams's commissions and ordered Secretary of State James Madison not to deliver them. One of the commissions belonged to William Marbury, whom Adams had appointed a justice of the peace. Marbury appealed to the Supreme Court to force Madison to deliver his commission. Section 13 of the Judiciary Act of 1789, Marbury claimed, gave the Court the power to require federal officials to perform their duties.

In 1803 the Supreme Court declared that Marbury indeed had a legal right to his commission. But in a critical turn, the Court also ruled that Section 13 of the Judiciary Act was unconstitutional and therefore void. Thus the Supreme Court had no power to force Madison to deliver Marbury's commission.

Marbury lost his appointment, but the Court's ruling in *Marbury* v. *Madison* established a precedent that gave the Supreme Court one of its more important powers—the power of judicial review. Judicial review is the power of the Supreme Court to decide whether a law is constitutional. The Court, as Marshall wrote in the decision, has the duty "to say what the law is."

The Barbary Pirates

Early in his first term, Jefferson's commitment to peace was sorely tested by the four Barbary States of North Africa. Pirates from Morocco, Algiers, Tunis,

Developing THE SECTION

Active Learning

Cooperative Activity. Judicial review is the power of the Supreme Court to decide whether a law is constitutional. Since 1803, over 1,000 state and local laws and over 100 federal laws have been overturned as a result of the Supreme Court's use of judicial review.

If the Supreme Court is in session, ask students to collect newspaper articles and editorials about current Supreme Court decisions. Have students work in small groups to select recent decisions overturning laws and report about them to the class. They should tell what the issue is, who the parties in the conflict are, and the effects of the Court's decision.

Linking Past and Present

Discussion. Why did Adams want the judiciary to remain sympathetic to Federalist ideas? On what basis do Presidents today appoint judges and justices? Bring into the discussion recent Senate/Presidential struggles over Supreme Court nominees.

Writing about History

Letter. Within twenty years of the signing of the Treaty of Paris in 1783, white settlers had pushed westward to the Mississippi River.

Discuss with students concerns settlers might have had at this time. **(desire for cheap land, conflicts with Native Americans, transportation problems, disputes with Spanish or French Mississippi, and the right to land goods at New Orleans)** What concerns might Native Americans have had as white settlers moved onto their land? **(takeover of Indian lands, loss of hunting and fishing rights, loss of ways of life)**

After the discussion, have students imagine they are a white settler or Native American writing a letter to Jefferson. This letter should express the person's concerns and suggest what actions Jefferson should take.

Connections: Art

Jefferson was a distinguished architect and inventor. His home at Monticello, near Charlottesville, Virginia, is one example of how his designs were influenced by ancient Roman buildings he saw on a visit to Europe. Jefferson's home is full of his inventions such as a revolving desk to provide quick access to papers, a hall clock with cannonball weights to mark off days of the week, and a system of air shafts for ventilation.

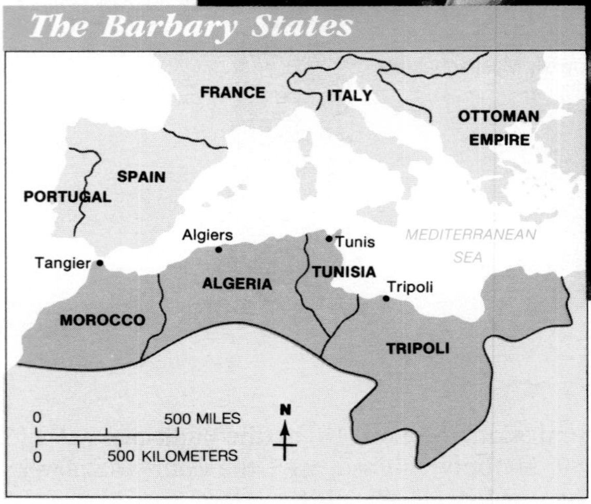

Efforts to protect American ships in the Mediterranean brought the United States into undeclared war with the Barbary States. Now the United States would pay tribute, vowed an officer, "through the mouth of a cannon."

and Tripoli prospered by seizing ships as they entered the Mediterranean Sea and holding the crews for ransom.

Presidents Washington and Adams had paid tribute to Barbary rulers in exchange for protection of American ships. While Federalists shouted "millions for defense, but not one cent for tribute," during the XYZ Affair in 1789, the United States was paying the Barbary States $100,000 a year. In 1801 the ruler of Tripoli demanded more money and declared war on the United States. Jefferson hated war, but he hated paying tribute even more. He sent warships to blockade Tripoli.

Two years later the U.S.S. *Philadelphia* ran aground on the coast of Tripoli while pursuing pirates. The captain and crew were captured and held for a ransom of $3 million. Rather than let the pirates have the *Philadelphia* intact, a young naval officer named Stephen Decatur led a raiding party into the heavily guarded harbor at Tripoli and set the *Philadelphia* afire.

In 1805 Tripoli made peace with the United States and stopped demanding tribute. In return, the United States ransomed the crew of the *Philadelphia* for $60,000. Nevertheless, Barbary pirates continued to plunder foreign ships. In 1815 American and European naval forces destroyed the pirate bases.

Looking Westward

Long before his presidency, Thomas Jefferson designed and built a home at Monticello, his Virginia plantation. He placed his new house on a hilltop, facing west. Stories about the land beyond the sunset had thrilled Jefferson as a child, and as President he continued to look westward with boyish enthusiasm.

Many Americans shared Jefferson's attraction to the West. In 1798 settlers organized the territory of Mississippi, which then included the present state

Global Connections

The United States' response to the slave rebellion on Saint Dominigue was ambivalent. It joined Great Britain in signing a trade agreement with Toussaint L'Ouverture but at the same time withheld diplomatic recognition. American and British naval squadrons contributed to L'Ouverture's final victory by blockading harbors and bombarding forts controlled by the French. In response to pressure from Napoleon, the United States cut off trade with Saint Dominigue in 1806.

Connections: Geography

Using a Map. Jefferson wrote to a friend, *"There is on the globe a single spot, the possessor of which is our natural and habitual enemy. It is New Orleans."* Have students conclude why possession of New Orleans was important by referring to the map on text page 195. What natural transportation system is located in roughly the center of the United States? **(Mississippi River)** How does New Orleans fit into this system? Why didn't farmers want to go overland? How does the issue of possessing New Orleans show the growing importance of the West?

of Alabama. Kentucky and Tennessee became states in time to help elect Jefferson President. Ohio entered the Union in 1803. Over the next six years Indiana, Michigan, and Illinois were organized as territories.

Beyond the Mississippi River, however, lay a vast land unknown to the inhabitants of the United States. Early in 1803, Jefferson persuaded Congress to fund an expedition to explore the western half of the continent. He placed two army officers—Captain Meriwether Lewis and Lieutenant William Clark—in charge.

To cross the continent, Lewis and Clark would have to travel through Louisiana Territory. Stretching from the Mississippi to the Rocky Mountains, this immense area had been claimed by France since the 1680s. As a result of defeat in the French and Indian War, France ceded Louisiana to Spain. But the French never forgot Louisiana and their dreams of empire in North America. In 1800 Napoleon Bonaparte, the French ruler, bullied Spain into returning Louisiana.

The key to Napoleon's plans for Louisiana was Saint Domingue, once France's richest colony in the Caribbean. For more than a century, enslaved Africans had toiled there to cultivate sugar cane for French planters. In 1794 a self-educated slave named Pierre Dominique Toussaint L'Ouverture (TOO-sahn LOO-vehr-tyoor) organized a rebellion. Using guerrilla tactics, Toussaint and his followers fought for seven years before gaining control of Saint Domingue.

In 1802 Napoleon sent 20,000 French troops to Saint Domingue to regain control. With the colony as his base, Napoleon dreamed of turning the Gulf of Mexico into a French pond and the Mississippi into a French stream.

Blocking French Plans

Napoleon's intentions alarmed Jefferson. American settlers west of the Appalachians shipped their crops down the Mississippi River and through the port of New Orleans, at the mouth of the river. If Napoleon gained control of New Orleans, he could stop American trade.

In April 1802 Jefferson asked Robert Livingston, the American minister in France, to find out if France would sell New Orleans to the United States. If France refused, Jefferson would consider an alliance with Great Britain, France's old enemy. "The day that France takes possession of New Orleans," he warned Livingston, "we must marry ourselves to the British fleet and nation."

The months slipped by with no answer from France. Westerners grew restless. A hotheaded young Tennessee lawyer named Andrew Jackson even organized a militia and offered to take New Orleans by force.

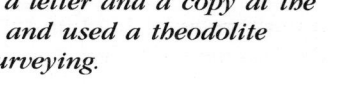

A man of wide interests, Jefferson was an architect, musician, and amateur scientist. He improved the polygraph (above), in which twin pens wrote a letter and a copy at the same time, and used a theodolite (left) for surveying.

Thinking Critically

Synthesis. Discuss with students how continual fighting in Saint Domingue led to the United States' purchase of the Louisiana Territory. (The revolt drained French resources; Napoleon realized he could not protect American possessions and decided to sell Louisiana.) What might have happened if Napoleon had decided not to sell the Louisiana Territory? Ask students to recall another incident in which European conflict benefited the Americans (Treaty of Paris ending French and Indian War).

Limited English Proficiency

Making Posters. Have students work in small groups to create posters and slogans either for or against the Louisiana Purchase. Posters in favor of the purchase might emphasize national security or expansion of American territory. Posters against the purchase might emphasize enormous cost of purchase or that the Constitution did not specifically grant power to make the purchase.

Reduced student page in the Teacher's Edition

Early in 1803, Jefferson sent James Monroe, ex-governor of Virginia, to France to assist Livingston. If Napoleon would not sell all of New Orleans, they were to bargain for just a part of the city where the United States could build its own docks and warehouses. If the French still refused to sell, the envoys were to go to London to seek a British alliance.

The Louisiana Purchase

While Monroe was traveling to France, Napoleon was rethinking his ambitions. In Saint Domingue the French had captured rebel leader Toussaint L'Ouverture, but his followers continued fighting. A deadly outbreak of yellow fever aided the rebellion. "Our death rate is dreadful," the commander of the French force wrote to Napoleon in 1802.

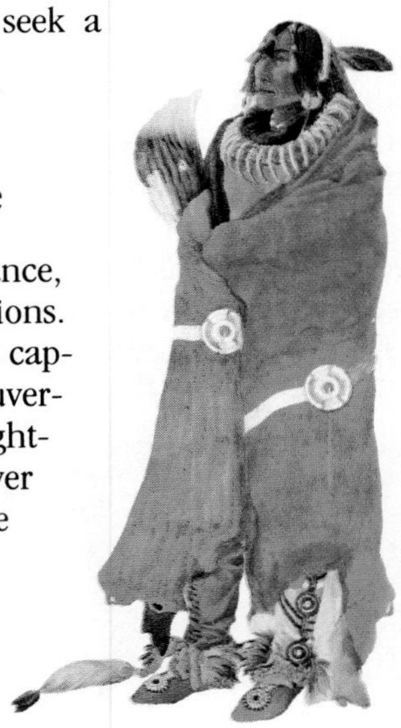

Mandan warrior.

Meanwhile, France had to face other hard facts. It was on the verge of war with Britain. The French navy, weakened by yellow fever, could not protect French possessions in America. If war came, Britain's fleet could seize New Orleans and even Louisiana. Thus Napoleon chose to deal with the Americans. "They only ask of me one town in Louisiana," he said, "but I already consider the colony entirely lost."

Monroe arrived in France hoping to buy a city. Instead France offered all of Louisiana for $25 million. Monroe and Livingston had no instructions covering such an offer, but this was an opportunity they could not resist. "We shall do all we can" to bring down the price, Livingston wrote to Secretary of State Madison, "but . . . we shall buy."

After weeks of bargaining, in a treaty signed on April 30, 1803, the United States agreed to buy all of Louisiana for about $15 million. Two weeks later, France and Britain went to war.

The purchase debate. Although its boundaries were vague, the Louisiana Purchase doubled the size of the United States. It added over 800,000 square miles of land and 200,000 Native Americans, French, and Spanish.

Jefferson gloried in the purchase of this vast territory, but the treaty posed a political problem. Republicans, who believed in strict construction of the Constitution, could find in that document no specific power to purchase foreign lands. A constitutional amendment would solve the problem, but the purchase had to be approved within six months.

With no time to lose, Jefferson swallowed his doubts and submitted the treaty to the Senate for approval. Opposition from the Federalists was fierce. Some abandoned loose construction ideals and opposed the treaty on constitutional grounds. Others feared for the future of the Union should the power of the East be diluted by the addition of such a large territory in the West. Senator William Plumer of New Hampshire argued:

> *"Admit this western world into the Union, and you destroy at once the weight and importance of the Eastern States and compel them to establish a separate, independent empire."*

After a long debate, the predominantly Republican Senate approved the purchase. On December 20, 1803, Louisiana became part of the United States. A delighted Tennessean wrote Jefferson:

> *"You have secured to us the free navigation of the Mississippi. You have procured an immense and fertile country: and all these great blessings are obtained without bloodshed."*

Most Americans agreed with this view, and in 1804 Jefferson was reelected by a landslide.

Lewis and Clark: Exploring the West

During the purchase debate, many questions had arisen about the true size of Louisiana. There was even speculation that a tribe of giants, mysterious

Connections: Geography

Spain was intensely interested in the Lewis and Clark expedition. The boundaries of Louisiana were vague and the expedition would be crossing territory claimed by Spain. The Spanish also feared that the headwaters of the Missouri might be close to Santa Fe, capital of their New Mexican domain. They observed the activities of Lewis and Clark at their camp near St. Louis and twice tried, but failed, to stop the expedition. These attempts were led by Pedro Vial, a Frenchman in the service of the Spanish Governor of New Mexico.

Writing about History

Report. While Lewis and Clark were exploring the western half of North America, the government dispatched Zebulon Pike to explore the sources of the Mississippi. Shortly after his return in 1806, Pike explored what is now Colorado and New Mexico. Students might want to read and write reports about the careers of these explorers.

The Louisiana Purchase 1803–1807

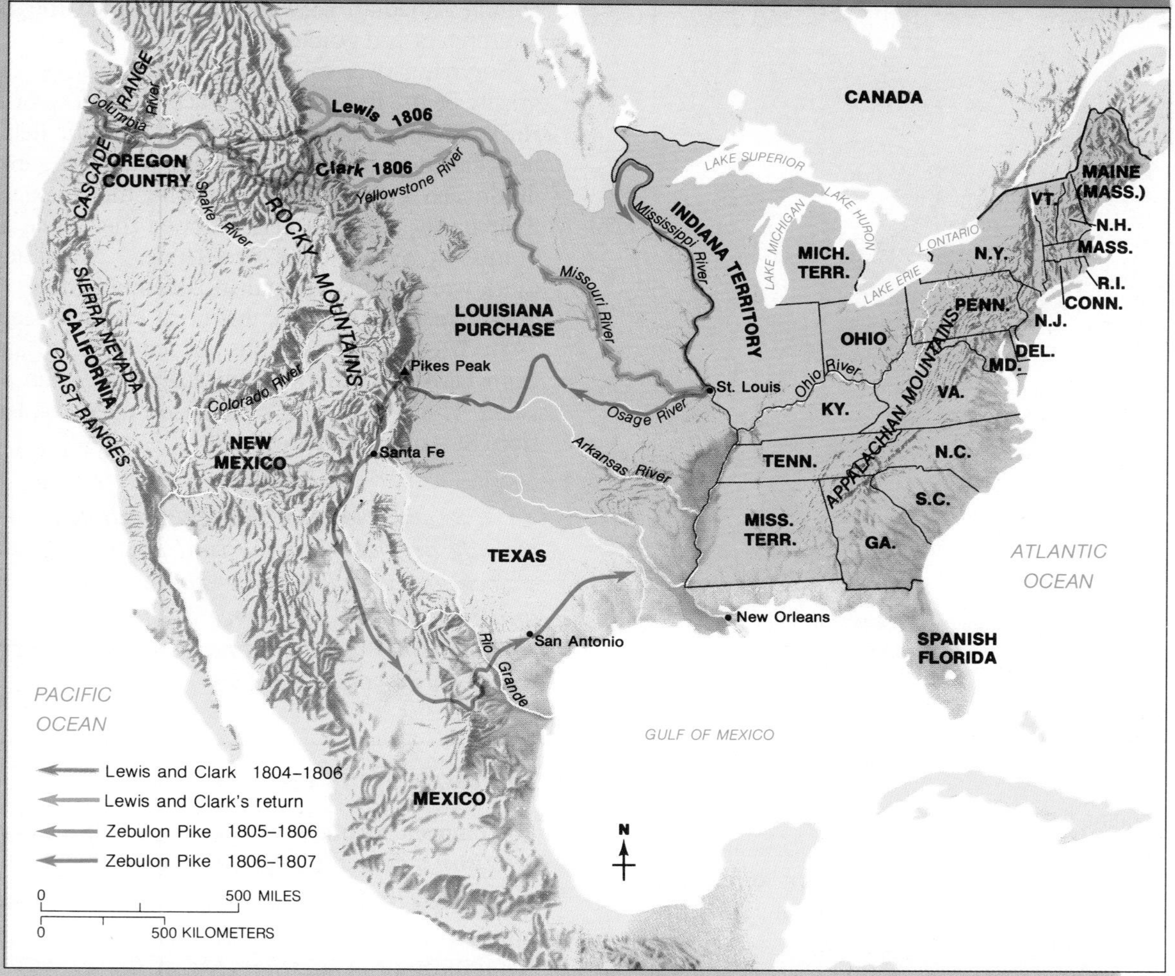

Geography Skills—Place. Writing as Lewis or Clark, make a report to President Jefferson on your trip from St. Louis to the Pacific Ocean. Describe the physical characteristics of the land. Recommend whether or not the United States should maintain an interest in Oregon. Explain why.

In the wake of Meriwether Lewis (right) and William Clark came other explorers, trappers, traders, miners, and settlers.

Geography Skills

ANSWERS

1. Students should list, and if possible, describe, the Missouri R., Yellowstone R., Rocky Mountains, and Pacific Ocean.
2. Recommendations may be negative (Oregon is too far from the United States to be of use) or positive (Oregon has rich farm land and access to the Pacific).

GTV Side 2

Chap. 4, Frame 09794

Lewis and Clark (Movie)

Search:

Play:

Section Review

ANSWERS

1. Judicial review.
2. Although Jefferson opposed war, he opposed paying tribute to the Barbary States and sent warships to Tripoli. Although a strict constructionist, he purchased the Louisiana Territory even though Constitution did not specifically authorize purchase of foreign lands.
3. Answers may include the French presence posed such a serious threat to United States trade and security that alliance with Britain was necessary.
4. Lewis and Clark successfully "penetrated the continent" and brought back information about western regions and resources, which encouraged other Americans to follow.

Linking Past and Present. The modern Republican party was formed in 1854 by groups opposed to slavery. It supported business interests and for many years was purely a party of the North. In recent years, Republicans have supported a strong military and opposed tax increases. Republicans tend to believe that state and local governments and non-governmental organizations should take more responsibility for social programs.

Connections: Health

As Lewis and Clark headed up the Missouri River, they noted the drastic decline of Native-American populations as a result of the spread of European diseases. Diseases that were minor in Europe, such as measles, chicken pox, and influenza, were killers in North America since the Indians had never encountered them and thus had built no immunity. Major diseases like smallpox were especially deadly. In present-day northeastern Nebraska, Lewis and Clark saw little trace of the once-powerful Omahas, who had been decimated in a smallpox epidemic in 1800, which reduced their population from about 700 to 300. The Poncas were also reduced to a remnant of their former strength by smallpox.

Reduced student page in the Teacher's Edition

William Clark drew a sketch of a salmon in his journal.

ancient towers, and a mountain of pure salt were to be found in the West. With Louisiana now in American hands, Lewis and Clark were free to explore this land and discover what it contained.

Jefferson instructed Lewis and Clark to explore the western rivers and to find a water route to the Pacific. The explorers were to establish friendly relations, and perhaps trade, with the Indian tribes they met. Above all, they were to gather knowledge. "Other objects worthy of notice," Jefferson wrote, "will be the soil and face of the country, the animals, the mineral production of every kind."

In May 1804 the expedition, which included Clark's African-American servant York, left St. Louis and headed up the Missouri River. The explorers traveled across Indian lands throughout the summer, meeting with tribal leaders, and finally made their winter camp in a Mandan village in what is now North Dakota. From there they shipped hides and skeletons of animals—and even a live prairie dog—back to Jefferson. In the spring, the expedition headed west again. A seventeen-year-old Shoshone woman named Sacajawea and her French-Canadian husband accompanied them as interpreters and guides.

Surviving river rapids, snakebites, hunger, and grizzly bears, the explorers reached the foot of the Rocky Mountains by late summer. With the help of her Shoshone people, Sacajawea guided the expedition across the mountains. With the Rockies at their backs, the explorers followed the Snake and Columbia rivers to the western sea. "Great joy!" Clark wrote in his journal in December 1805. "We are in view of the ocean, this great Pacific Ocean."

In Washington, months passed with no news from Lewis and Clark. Many feared they had perished. Then, in late 1806, Jefferson opened a letter from St. Louis. Lewis reported:

> *"It is with pleasure that I announce to you the safe arrival of myself and party at twelve o'clock today at this place with our papers and baggage. In obedience to our orders, we have penetrated the continent of North America to the Pacific Ocean."*

Section Review

1. Comprehension. What power did *Marbury* v. *Madison* give to the Supreme Court?

2. Analysis. How did conflict with the Barbary States and the Louisiana Purchase test Jefferson's Republican principles?

3. Evaluation. Jefferson said, "The day that France takes possession of New Orleans, we must marry ourselves to the British fleet and nation." Do you think Jefferson was correct? Give reasons for your answer.

4. Synthesis. Why might news of Lewis and Clark's expedition encourage Americans to move west?

Linking Past and Present. Jefferson's Republican party is not the same party that Republicans belong to today. Contact a local or state Republican party office and find out about the platform and origins of the modern party. Are its principles similar to those of Jefferson's party? Explain.

Connections: Literature
A poem published in July 1808 captured the growing frustration of Americans thrown out of work by the embargo:

Our ships all in motion,
Once whitened the ocean,
They sail'd and returned with a cargo;
Now doom'd to decay
They have fallen a prey
To Jefferson, worms, and Embargo.

Section 8-2

Objectives

- ***Answer the Focus Question.***
- *Explain the causes and effects of the Embargo Act.*
- *Describe how the War of 1812 affected Native Americans.*
- *Evaluate actions of the Hartford Convention.*

Introducing THE SECTION

Write the following quotations on the chalkboard:

" If we fail let us fail like men . . . and expire together in one common struggle, fighting for free trade and seamen's rights. "

" We will drive the British from our continent. They will no longer have an opportunity of intriguing with our Indian neighbors. "

" I therefore feel anxious not only to add the Floridas to the South, but the Canadas to the North of this empire. "

Have students identify the reasons for war in the quotations. Based on what they have studied, ask students to evaluate which reason had the most weight and why.

8-2 The War of 1812

Focus: What were the causes and effects of the War of 1812?

On June 22, 1807, the U.S.S. *Chesapeake* set sail from Virginia. As the American coast faded from view, a cry rang out from the lookout high in the ship's rigging. "Sail ho! Sail to starboard!"

That distant sail belonged to the British warship H.M.S. *Leopard.* Soon the two ships were within calling distance, and Captain James Barron invited a British officer to come aboard the *Chesapeake* and exchange mail. Once on board, however, the officer demanded to search the American ship for deserters from the Royal Navy. "Sir!" Barron exclaimed, "This is a national vessel of the United States." He would permit no one to search his ship.

The officer returned to his ship with Barron's message. In reply, the *Leopard* swung open its gunports and fired on the *Chesapeake.* Amid splintered rigging and timbers, twenty-one Americans lay dead or wounded. Unprepared for battle, Barron surrendered. The British boarded and seized four sailors. Only one was a British deserter. The other three were African American.

"Free Trade and Sailors' Rights"

In the early 1800s America found itself caught in a war between Britain and France. Because American merchants wanted to trade freely with both nations, the United States adopted a policy of neutrality when war began in 1803.

Illustration from a song: "The Impressment of an American Sailor Boy."

By 1806 the war was deadlocked. Desperate for victory, each side tried to cut off the other's trade. Britain clamped a blockade around Europe and banned all neutral trade in French-controlled ports. Napoleon struck back with a blockade of the British Isles. Both France and Britain began seizing American ships they claimed were illegally trading with the enemy. Even worse, the British navy began impressing—seizing and forcing into service—American sailors again.

Americans demanded revenge for the British attack on the *Chesapeake,* but Jefferson wanted to avoid war. His recent budget cuts had reduced the size of both the navy and the army. Instead, the President hoped that economic pressure might persuade both France and Britain to respect "free trade and sailors' rights."

Late in 1807 Jefferson persuaded Congress to pass the Embargo Act, halting all foreign trade. Under this law, no American ships could sail abroad and no foreign ships could enter American waters. The embargo would keep American ships and sailors at home, safe from being seized. As the embargo took hold, hundreds of ships rotted at dockside. Thousands of sailors lost their jobs, and many merchants and shippers faced ruin. New England's economy was hardest hit by the ban on shipping. Some New Englanders began talking about **secession**—withdrawal from the Union—if the "Dambargo" did not end soon.

One New Englander said that using an embargo was "like cutting one's throat to cure the nosebleed." Jefferson at

Global Connections

Americans referred to the French and the English blockades as the "Paper Blockade," because they felt that the blockades could not be enforced. The Embargo Act did, however, strangle American trade.

Social History

The Revolutionary War was etched in Clay's memory when British soldiers defiled his father's grave. Calhoun grew up in an area filled with the graves of American revolutionaries. These anti-British politicians saw war with Britain as a second War for Independence.

Developing

THE SECTION

Connections: Literature

Analyzing a Poem. The poet William Cullen Bryant, only fourteen at the time, wrote a satire on the embargo:

Go Wretch, resign the
Presidential chair,
Disclose thy secret
measures, foul or fair;
Go search with curious eye
for horned frogs
Mid the wild wastes of
Louisiana bogs;
Or where Ohio rolls his
turbid stream
Dig for huge bones, thy
glory and thy theme.

In analyzing the poem, lead students to realize that Bryant is criticizing government agents who are searching for goods that people are selling in violation of the embargo.

Connections: Economics

Discussion. Ask students why Jefferson wanted to avoid war. **(He felt country not prepared due to recent military budget cuts.)** What did Jefferson hope the embargo to accomplish? **(to stop British and French from harming American trade)**

How did the embargo affect the price of goods? **(Prices rose because goods in short supply.)** What might people have done to get around the embargo? **(smuggle goods)** Was the embargo successful? Why or why not? **(Embargo caused economic hardship for American sailors, merchants, shippers, and other citizens.)**

Reduced student page in the Teacher's Edition

last agreed. On March 1, 1809, three days before the end of his second term, Jefferson signed the Nonintercourse Act repealing the embargo. The new law allowed Americans to resume trade with all countries except Britain and France. It offered to reopen trade with those two nations when they stopped interfering with American shipping.

Drifting Toward War

Despite the unpopular embargo, the Republicans had won the presidential election of 1808. The nation's new President was James Madison, Jefferson's former Secretary of State. Madison hoped the Nonintercourse Act would force Britain and France to respect American neutrality. When it did not, he allowed the act to expire.

Madison then tried a new tactic. In 1810 he signed a measure lifting all restrictions on trade. To tempt Britain and France, Madison provided that if either nation agreed to respect American neutrality, the United States would cut off trade with the other.

Napoleon promptly agreed to Madison's terms but secretly ordered his navy to continue seizing American ships bound for Britain. Unfortunately, Madison trusted Napoleon's word, and he warned Britain to stop interfering with American shipping or lose American trade. When the British refused, the President banned all trade with Britain. Still, Britain refused to change its policies. Going to war, Madison began to think, was the only answer.

Tecumseh and the War Hawks. Since peace, though troubled, was more profitable to trade than war, most New Englanders did not welcome war with Britain. On the other hand, while most southerners and westerners lived far from the sea, they resented British abuse of American sailors. They also saw war as an opportunity to break British alliances with Indians and open up to settlement areas farther west.

For years, the steady stream of settlers into Indiana, Michigan, and Illinois had disturbed a powerful Shawnee chief named Tecumseh (tuh-KUHM-suh) and his brother, known as the Prophet. Tecumseh united tribes in the Mississippi Valley into a confederacy to defend their lands.

Alarmed, William Henry Harrison, the governor of Indiana Territory, led a militia to attack Tecumseh's capital of Prophetstown on Tippecanoe Creek. On November 7, 1811, however, the Indians struck first. Both sides suffered many dead and wounded, though neither could claim victory. In the ashes of Prophetstown, Harrison found British-made weapons—proof to westerners of British support for Tecumseh.

Several Republican newcomers to Congress from the South and the West shared this opinion. Dubbed "War Hawks" by the Federalists, Henry Clay of Kentucky and John C. Calhoun of South Carolina insisted that war with Britain would end Indian attacks and win Canada for the United States. Southern War Hawks also wanted Florida, which then belonged to Spain, Britain's ally.

On June 18, 1812, at the urging of Madison and the War Hawks, Congress passed a declaration of war against Great Britain. Two days before, the British government had finally repealed its restrictions of neutral trade, but word did not reach Washington until too late.

"Mr. Madison's War"

The United States was unprepared for war. The treasury was empty, and efforts to raise money met with only partial success. The army had only 7,000 troops and a handful of competent officers. Soldiers were desperately needed. For the first two years of the war, however, blacks who tried to enlist were barred from military service by the racial policies of the army and state militias. The navy had experienced officers and crews made up of blacks as well as whites, but only sixteen ships.

Lack of national unity also hampered the war effort. Northern Federalists bitterly denounced "Mr. Madison's war" as a "death blow to liberty." In the presidential election that autumn, anti-war feelings cost Madison every northern state except Vermont and Pennsylvania. The President won a second term only by carrying the South and the West.

Defeat in Canada. Growing dissent did not sway the War Hawks in the summer of 1812. They believed that the conquest of Britain's colony Can-

THE AMERICAN SPIRIT

Tecumseh

Defender of Indian Lands

"The once powerful tribes of our people," Tecumseh declared, were vanishing "before the . . . oppression of the White Man, as snow before a summer sun." Tecumseh, a Shawnee chief, issued this warning in 1811 when he was creating an alliance of tribes living east of the Mississippi. "The way," he insisted, "and the only way, to check and stop this evil, is for all Redmen to unite in claiming a common and equal right in the land, as it was at first and as it should be still."

Born in present-day Ohio in 1768, Tecumseh was still a boy when he fought alongside the British in the American Revolution. After the war, he led raids on pioneer settlements until the Indians suffered defeat at Fallen Timbers in 1794. Then Tecumseh withdrew to Indiana Territory where he lived peacefully. He attracted a following, however, by condemning the treaties that signed away Indian lands.

By 1805 Tecumseh and his brother Tenskwatawa, called the Prophet, had founded the community called Prophetstown. The town drew people from many tribes. In it Tecumseh saw the beginnings of a confederation. By 1809, a thousand warriors had joined him.

William Henry Harrison, the governor of Indiana Territory, respected Tecumseh, describing him as "one of those uncommon geniuses that spring up occasionally to produce revolutions." But Harrison watched Tecumseh's progress with alarm.

In 1811 Tecumseh went on a journey to promote a confederation among eastern tribes. In his absence, Harrison and his troops marched on Prophetstown. The Prophet ordered an attack on Harrison's camp at Tippecanoe Creek in Indiana. The Indians, however, were driven back.

The Battle of Tippecanoe disheartened Indians, and Tecumseh could never renew the Indian alliance. He continued to fight, however, joining the British in the War of 1812. Tecumseh was killed on Canadian soil in the Battle of the Thames during a cavalry attack led by Harrison.

ada was "a mere matter of marching." Canadians, the War Hawks assumed, would welcome liberation from British rule.

The first American to test this assumption was General William Hull. In July Hull invaded Canada from Fort Detroit. He then issued a proclamation promising "the invaluable blessings of civil, political, & religious liberty" to peaceful Canadians. Hull also warned that "no white man found fighting by the side of an Indian will be taken prisoner. Instant destruction will be his lot."

Hull's proclamation did not have the desired effect. Most Canadians felt that they already had liberty and did not want American interference. The warning to Canadians fighting with Indians also backfired. Tecumseh and his allies had already joined British forces in Canada.

Met with unexpected resistance, Hull soon retreated to Detroit. A few days later, Tecumseh's warriors and a large force of redcoats encircled the fort. Overmatched, Hull surrendered his army without firing a shot.

Thinking Critically

Analysis. Ask students why the war was called "Mr. Madison's war"? **(Federalists opposed to war; Madison appears to have blundered into the war.)** What could Madison have done to avoid war? Why was the United States unprepared for the war? **(Republican policy opposed defense spending.)** From the election results what can be inferred about support for the war? **(South and West supported it, North opposed.)** Why?

Active Learning

Debate. Divide the class into three groups representing the sections of the United States: the North, South, and West. Have students imagine they are members of Congress voting on a declaration of war with Great Britain. Issues to take into consideration are British seizure of ships and sailors and support of Native Americans, American desire for land in Canada and Florida, and national honor. Each group should research and discuss the position it will take on each issue before beginning the debate.

Limited English Proficiency

Using a Map. Have students work in small groups to study the map "The War of 1812" on this page. Direct each group to use the information on the map to make a chart showing battles in chronological order. Besides listing the battles, the chart should tell in which four regions—Great Lakes, northeastern New York State, Maryland and Virginia, and the Southwest—the battles were fought, and who won.

Ask students what the chart reveals about the war. **(For example, the United States had greater success in naval battles than in land battles.)**

Geography Skills

ANSWERS

The British blockaded all United States ports, and trade came to a halt.

Writing About History

Report. Although the War of 1812 was a draw militarily, a number of battles captured the imagination of Americans—Lake Erie, Thames, Plattsburgh, New Orleans—as did the exploits of such naval vessels as the *Constitution, Wasp, Essex, United States*. Have interested students read and write a report about one of these battles or exploits.

Multicultural Perspectives

Uriah Levy, born in Philadelphia of Jewish ancestry, served for many years as an officer in the United States Navy and fought in the War of 1812. During the war, Levy was captured and spent some time in a British prison. While maintaining a career in the navy, Levy also pursued other interests and managed to accumulate a fortune. He purchased Thomas Jefferson's house at Monticello to preserve it as a national monument.

Reduced student page in the Teacher's Edition

A large portion of this flag, which inspired Francis Scott Key to write "The Star-Spangled Banner," was torn away in "the perilous fight" at Fort McHenry in the War of 1812.

The War of 1812

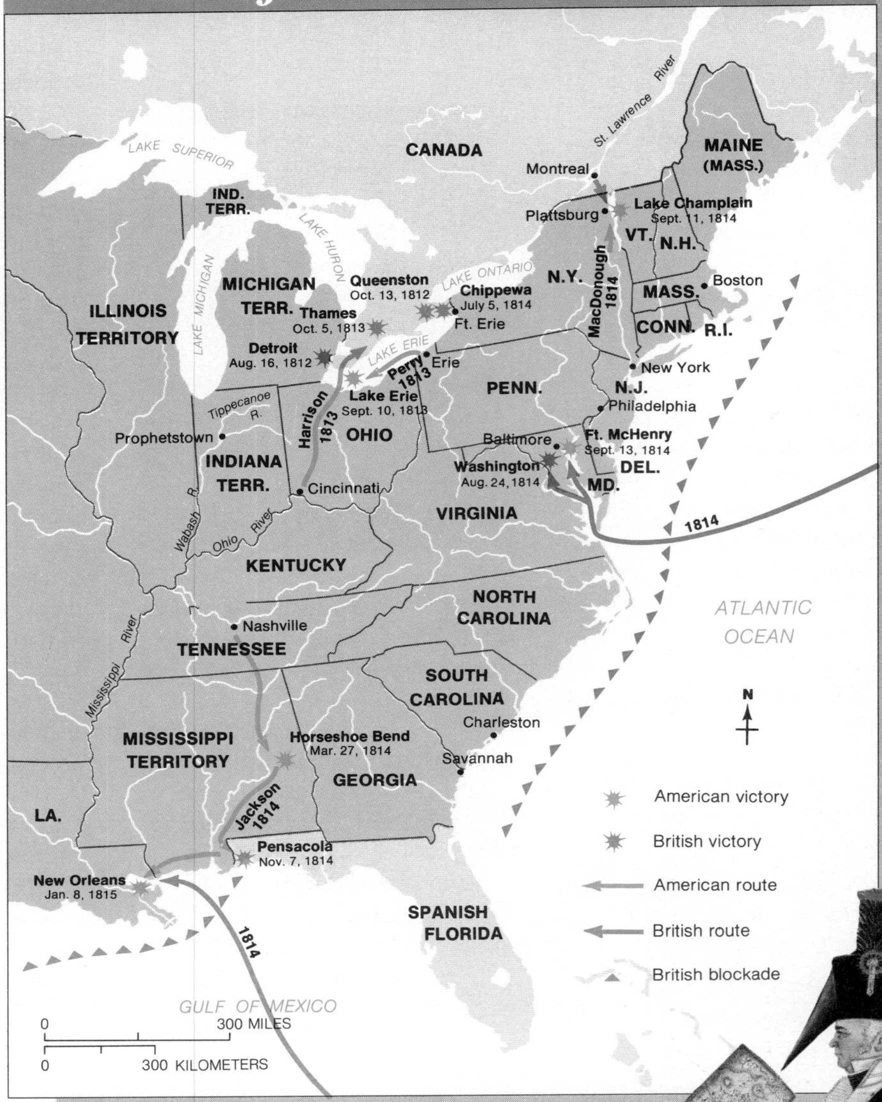

Geography Skills — Movement. In the early 1800s the United States depended chiefly on import duties for income. During the War of 1812, the nation slid into debt. Use the map to explain how the war contributed to financial problems.

A militia officer consults a map. Militias often refused to serve outside their states.

Global Connections

Captain David Porter, commander of the USS *Essex*, gave Great Britain a taste of its own medicine by raiding British commerce not only in the Atlantic but also in the Pacific. He sailed around Cape Horn and into the Pacific, and captured so many British whalers that he almost destroyed Britain's whaling industry in the area. British warships finally destroyed the *Essex*—and captured Porter in combat off Valparaiso, Chile.

Backyard History

Research and Report. Have students do research and write a report on one of two topics:

1. The Lewis and Clark expedition. Students should find out what states the expedition passed through, where the men camped, how long, and what they did.
2. The War of 1812. Students can do research on a particular battle in their state, and tell what took place, who won, and why.

Two more attempts to invade Canada were made in 1812. In both cases militia refused to cross the Canadian border, insisting that it was their duty only "to repel invasion."

A season of victory. Although the United States failed to conquer Canada, success at sea seemed likely for a time. American privateers harassed British shipping, and American warships captured or sank several British warships. Still, by 1813 the British fleet had blockaded the American coast, shutting off both overseas trade and coastal trade among the states.

The American navy had more success on the Great Lakes. To take control of Lake Erie, in 1813 Captain Oliver H. Perry built ships using local trees and iron scavenged from barn doors and gathered a crew of "blacks, soldiers, and boys." In a battle on September 10, Perry's forces demolished a British squadron. Perry sent the long-awaited message to General William Henry Harrison: "We have met the enemy, and they are ours!"

Perry's victory gave the United States control of Lake Erie and forced the British to abandon Detroit. It also encouraged General Harrison to invade Canada with 5,000 troops. On October 5, Harrison's force met and defeated a large British and Indian army beside the Thames River.

The Battle of the Thames was an important victory for the United States, but it was a tragedy for Tecumseh's confederacy. The Shawnee leader fell, and his dream of Indian unity died with him. The chiefs of six Mississippi Valley tribes signed a peace agreement with Harrison after the battle. Their long struggle to save their land was over.

Britain's Indian allies suffered another setback six months later. At Horseshoe Bend in Mississippi Territory, the Creeks were defeated by Tennessee militia under Andrew Jackson. They were forced to cede much of their land to the United States.

The British strike back. In April 1814 the British and their allies finally defeated Napoleon in Europe, and Britain began to send thousands more soldiers to the war in North America. British leaders planned a three-pronged attack. One British army would push south from Canada and another north from New Orleans, dividing the United States. At the same time, hit-and-run raids on coastal cities would keep citizens in a state of fear.

In August 11,000 British troops marched south from Canada along the shore of Lake Champlain.

The American navy scored its first triumph when the Constitution *defeated the British frigate* Guerrière *in August 1812. American guns disabled the foe in half an hour.*

Limited English Proficiency

Building Vocabulary. Discuss with students the concepts of *nationalism* (the doctrine that national interest comes before international considerations) and *patriotism* (loyal support of one's own country). Are they the same or different? Is nationalism always a good thing? Why did Americans feel a sense of nationalism after the War of 1812? **(fought to protect rights, stood up to Great Britain)**

Connections: Music

The song "Hail Columbia" competed with "The Star-Spangled Banner" throughout the nineteenth century as the national anthem of the United States. "Hail Columbia" reflected the patriotism that emerged during the XYZ Affair just as "The Star-Spangled Banner" expressed sentiments that emerged in the War of 1812. In 1931 Congress declared "The Star-Spangled Banner" the national anthem of the United States.

Section Review

ANSWERS

1. Definitions for the following terms are on text pages indicated in parentheses: *secession* (197), *nationalism* (202).
2. Britain's refusal to stop seizure of American ships and impressment of sailors made many Americans think that war was only way to redress wrongs.
3. Jefferson wanted to avoid war and hoped economic pressure would force Britain to respect neutral rights.
4. Britain's Indian allies suffered serious defeats and were forced to cede land to the United States.

Reduced student page in the Teacher's Edition

Their goal was to take control of the Hudson River, cutting off New England. Because the roads were so poor, the British used the lake to ferry supplies to the troops. Just below Plattsburgh, New York, an American naval squadron, commanded by Captain Thomas Macdonough, destroyed Britain's lake fleet. The British were forced to retreat.

Meanwhile, a second British force landed on the shores of Chesapeake Bay and marched toward Washington. On August 24 they captured the capital and burned the White House and other government buildings. All that was saved from the White House was a portrait of George Washington, which Dolley Madison had removed.

Andrew Jackson.

From Washington, the British sailed toward Baltimore, Maryland. On September 13 they began bombarding Fort McHenry, which protected the city. All day and night, rockets streaked across the sky, casting a red glare on black smoke. Bombs burst in midair, showering the fort with fragments of hot glowing metal.

Francis Scott Key, a Virginia lawyer, watched the spectacle from a British ship, where he had been arranging an exchange of prisoners. At dawn, he was thrilled to see that a tattered American flag still waved above the fort. Key put his feelings into a poem later set to music as "The Star-Spangled Banner." It became the national anthem.

The Hartford Convention. Despite the American victory on Lake Champlain and the standoff at Baltimore, dissent over the war grew. In New England, especially, many felt the war had brought the nation to the brink of collapse.

In December 1814 Federalist delegates from across New England met in Hartford, Connecticut, to discuss revising the Constitution. They proposed several amendments to increase New England's voice in government. They also declared that states had a duty to resist the national government when it threatened their rights. News of an American victory at New Orleans, however, abruptly ended the convention's work.

The Battle of New Orleans. While Federalists were meeting in Hartford, British troops prepared to attack New Orleans. Defending the city was General Jackson with a volunteer army of pirates, local militiamen, and two battalions of free blacks. On January 8, 1815, British troops charged Jackson's "backwoods rabble." Jackson's gunners unleashed a withering fire. Line after line of redcoats toppled "like blades of grass beneath the scythe," one officer wrote. After a second assault on Jackson's lines, the British withdrew.

Peace without victory. Although the Battle of New Orleans was the greatest American land victory of the war, it had no effect upon the outcome. Two weeks before the battle, American and British negotiators meeting in Ghent, Belgium, had signed a treaty ending the war.

The Treaty of Ghent did not settle the issues that had led to war— the rights of neutrals on the high seas and impressment of sailors. It simply restored the prewar boundaries between the United States and Canada.

Still, as a result of the war, **nationalism**— an intense feeling of national pride and unity— spread. "The people," wrote Treasury Secretary Albert Gallatin, "are more American. They feel and act more like a nation." Perhaps this new sense of nationalism was victory enough.

Section Review

1. Identification. Define *secession* and *nationalism*.

2. Comprehension. Explain how the *Chesapeake-Leopard* affair and others like it contributed to the American declaration of war.

3. Synthesis. Why do you think President Jefferson maintained the embargo in spite of the economic damage it was causing the United States?

4. Application. One historian has said that "the only real losers in the war [of 1812] were the Indians." Explain what she meant.

Section 8-3

Objectives

- ***Answer the Focus Question.***
- *Explain how the Industrial Revolution came to the United States.*
- *Discuss how the cotton gin made cotton a profitable crop.*
- *Cite similarities and differences in ways of life developed in 1800 by people in the West and the East.*

Introducing

THE SECTION

Ask students to name inventions important to them. **(television, jet planes, computers, for example)** How have these developments made a difference in their lives?

Tell students they will now read about inventions and developments important to people in the early 1800s. As students read, have them think about the long-range effects of these developments on people's lives.

8-3 Revolution in Industry and Travel

Focus: How did changes in industry and transportation in the early 1800s affect the way Americans lived?

To sailors lounging along the docks of New York City in 1789, Samuel Slater may have looked like any other newly arrived immigrant. This young Englishman, however, was an expert mechanic with plans for manufacturing American cloth.

Three years later, another mechanically minded young man could be seen walking along these docks. He was a Massachusetts tinkerer named Eli Whitney, who had invented a process for making nails more quickly than could be done by hand. Together, Whitney and Slater would trigger a revolution in the way Americans worked and lived.

Beginnings of Industry

In the United States, almost all of the goods people needed were produced in homes or small workshops. This was true in Britain until the mid-1700s, when English inventors developed machines that revolutionized the textile industry. The spinning jenny allowed one worker to spin a dozen threads at once, while power looms swiftly wove the thread into cloth. Because these machines were large and ran on water power, they were housed in factories built beside fast-flowing rivers.

This shift of manufacturing from homes and small workshops to factories with machines is known as the **Industrial Revolution.** From Britain, the Industrial Revolution spread to western Europe and the United States.

In 1790 Slater gained financial backing from Rhode Islander Moses Brown to reproduce a British spinning jenny. His textile mill in Pawtucket, Rhode Island, was the first successful factory in the United States. Thread from Slater's mills was woven into cloth by weavers working in their homes. By 1807 there were fifteen cotton mills spinning thread in Rhode Island.

In 1810 Francis Cabot Lowell, a Massachusetts merchant, visited British cotton mills and studied their power looms. When Lowell returned home, he built his own power loom and textile mill on the Charles River in Waltham, Massachusetts. Lowell's was the first American mill to combine spinning and weaving under one roof.

Francis Cabot Lowell's system replaced the home spinning wheel and loom. The Lowell mill in Waltham, one observer noted, "took your bale of cotton in at one end and gave out yards of cloth at the other, after goodness knows what digestive process."

203

Developing THE SECTION

Active Learning

Newspaper Advertisements. Have students design newspaper advertisements to attract workers to the Slater or Lowell mills. Remind students to decide who their audience is—women, farmers, newly-arrived immigrants—before creating the advertisement.

Social History

Catherine Littlefield Greene deserves some of the credit for the invention of the cotton gin. After the death of her husband, she took over the operation of their Georgia plantation. Greene provided lodgings there for Eli Whitney. In her conversations with him, Greene stressed the need for a machine that could separate cotton seeds from fiber. Through her encouragement and support, Whitney invented the cotton gin. (For more about Catherine Greene, see page 30 in *Readings in Literature and Primary Sources* in the Teacher's Resource Package.)

Reduced student page in the Teacher's Edition

Finding workers. Both Slater and Lowell had difficulty finding workers for their mills. Artisans, who worked at home or in small shops, were reluctant to give up their independence. Factories also held little appeal for farmers.

Slater solved his labor problem by hiring children to tend his simple spinning machines. Lowell hired young women from New England farms to operate the complicated power looms in his mill. Women and children had few other opportunities for paid work and so were willing to accept half the wages demanded by men. Later, factory owners would find inexpensive labor in the European immigrants entering the United States.

Lowell died in 1817, but the success of the Waltham mill spurred his partners to expand. In 1822 they built a new five-story mill on the Merrimack River and named it in honor of their late partner. In time, eighteen additional cotton mills would be built at Lowell, Massachusetts.

Eli Whitney's Cotton Gin

Textile factories, especially in Britain, created a huge demand for cotton. Where would the fiber come from? Eli Whitney answered that question while in Georgia in 1792.

At that time, southern planters were facing hard times. Prices for tobacco, rice, and indigo were dropping. As profits declined, so did the demand for slaves. Many southerners thought that slavery would soon vanish.

Visiting a plantation, Whitney listened to planters discuss cotton as a promising new crop and speculate about better ways to remove the seeds. The cost of handpicking the seeds out of raw cotton was too high, even using slave labor, to make cotton growing profitable.

Within ten days Whitney had built the first cotton engine, or "gin," which could clean fifty times as much cotton in a day as a worker could by hand. From small farmers to plantation owners, everyone began planting cotton. In ten years, cotton exports rose from 5 million pounds to 63 million pounds.

The cotton gin made the South the world's leading producer of cotton. Southern cotton fed the mills of Britain as well as those of New England.

Mass Production

Having made a great success with the cotton gin, Whitney took up another challenge—producing muskets by machine. Muskets had always been produced by gunsmiths, with each part individually crafted and fitted. Not only was this process slow and expensive, but a part made for one musket might not fit another. Whitney hoped to solve the problem by using **interchangeable parts,** parts that are so alike that one can be used in place of another.

In 1798 Whitney won a government contract to produce 10,000 muskets. He designed and built an arms factory in New Haven, Connecticut, on the principle of division of labor. Each worker was assigned to one or two simple operations. Using machine tools invented by Whitney, they produced thousands of identical musket parts.

Whitney's system of interchangeable parts marked the beginning of **mass production,** the manufacture of goods in large quantities, in the United States. In the years to come, the art of handcrafting would gradually give way to the business of large-scale manufacturing as Americans learned how to mass produce practically anything from clocks to carriages.

An "American System" to Build the Economy

The disruption of trade during Jefferson's embargo and the War of 1812 kept foreign rivals out of the American market. Without European competition, America's young industries flourished. After the war, however, British goods flooded the United States at prices so low that many American industries could not compete and closed.

This threat to America's new industries concerned President Madison as he drafted his annual message to Congress in late 1815. The war had

A computer programmer (opposite, top) creates patterns for knitting machines. Today American companies often have clothing produced in Asia and Latin America, where costs are lower, then sell it under their own labels.

Learning From Art
A Lowell Cotton Mill, 1820s

Unmarried women workers at Lowell mills lived in company boardinghouses with curfews and strict rules for visitors and church attendance.
Air in the mill was polluted with flying lint and fumes from whale-oil lamps that hung on each loom.
Workers tended looms by replacing spools of yarn and watching for broken threads as the rolls of cloth emerged.
Raw, baled cotton came in on the ground floor. After it had been untangled, it moved to the second floor to be spun into yarn, then to the next floor where the power looms wove it into cloth.
Water flowing into buckets caused the mill wheels to turn. Wooden gates controlled the amount of water and thus the speed of the wheels. The wheels were mounted on an axle, which was connected by gears and belts with the machinery it ran.
Most machinery was designed, built, and maintained in the mill's machine shop.
Lowell's mill produced a single product for a mass market; an inexpensive, sturdy cloth wide enough to cover a bed.

Thinking Critically

Analysis. People who made goods at home performed all the steps in the manufacturing process; people who made goods in factories performed only one. Have students discuss how this division of labor in factories might affect workers' attitudes toward the goods they produced. (Work could be boring and monotonous; some workers might take little pride in workmanship.)

Linking Past and Present

Discussion. Ask students how the factory system changed the way most goods were produced. Then have students contrast the two pictures on this page. **(For example, different power sources used to run machinery: computer uses electricity; mill machinery used water power.)** Just as the factory system altered the domestic system, how has the computer changed the factory system?

Backyard History

Investigating. Have students organize into committees to survey what internal improvements are necessary or desirable in their community. A representative of each committee can report to the class as a whole, which can then discuss who has primary responsibility for effecting the improvement—local, state, or federal government, or private citizens. Or is there joint responsibility?

Connections: Economics

Discussion. The issue of a protective tariff recurs in United States history. **Ask:** What are the advantages of a protective tariff? **(protect new or struggling industries; create jobs)** What are the disadvantages? **(higher prices; may lead to production of inferior goods; hurt world trade)** Why didn't the protective tariff work in 1816? **(imported goods still cheaper)** What policy does the United States generally promote today? **(free trade; some protective tariffs)**

Connections: Language

As settlers moved west, private companies began to build turnpikes. Spiked poles, or *pikes*, were placed across the roads at tollbooths. The pike was turned aside to let travelers pass after they had paid their toll, or fee for using the road.

Reduced student page in the Teacher's Edition

taught the value of self-sufficiency in a time of crisis. Now Madison was determined to protect new industries and strengthen the nation's economy—even if it meant setting aside cherished principles of limited government.

In his speech, Madison asked Congress to charter a new national bank to give the nation a uniform financial system. He also spoke of the need for the government to raise tariffs, or taxes, on imported goods and to build roads and canals.

Led by the most outspoken War Hawks—House Speaker Henry Clay and Representative John C. Calhoun—Congress created an economic system beneficial to all areas of the country. The "American System," as Clay called it, would make the nation as a whole more self-sufficient.

American Voices

"I like traveling by canal boats very much. The only nuisances are the bridges over the canal, which are so very low, that one is obliged to prostrate oneself on the deck of the boat, to avoid being scraped off it; and this humiliation occurs every quarter of an hour."

—Frances Ann Kemble

Creating a New National Bank

Money posed one of Congress's thorniest problems: there was simply too much in circulation. In the five years since the end of Hamilton's original Bank of the United States, the number of state banks had more than doubled. With no national currency, the banks printed their own paper money, called bank notes. Some banks redeemed their notes for gold or silver, but most did not. The result, Treasury Secretary Gallatin complained, was "a baseless currency varying every fifty miles and fluctuating everywhere."

In January 1816 Calhoun persuaded Congress to charter a second Bank of the United States for twenty years. The new bank would serve as a federal depository and would provide a uniform national currency. In addition, the bank would regulate credit. Farmers and manufacturers who borrowed money would receive a sound currency backed by gold and silver. Within a year the new bank had begun operating and in time opened twenty-five branches throughout the nation.

A Protective Tariff for the Nation

Next Congress considered a bill to raise tariffs on imports. Supporters of the bill argued that higher tariffs would encourage people to buy American goods by making imported goods more expensive. The tariff would stimulate the growth of industry and increase the export of American products while helping to rebuild the national treasury.

The mid-Atlantic states of New York, New Jersey, and Pennsylvania supported the tariff bill. These states all had new industries to protect. Western states also favored high tariffs, reasoning that fast-growing industrial cities in the East would become large markets for western farm products.

The tariff bill divided New Englanders. Merchants feared it would damage their profitable trade with Britain, while manufacturers welcomed protection from imports. In the South, where there was littlemanufacturing, Calhoun was one of the tariff's few supporters. Most southerners expected the tariff to raise the cost of the goods they imported without benefiting the southern economy in return.

Congress finally approved the nation's first protective tariff. The Tariff of 1816 set duties at about 20 percent of the value of imports that competed with major American manufactures. The added tax proved ineffective, however. Most imports still cost less than domestic goods, and the British continued to sell goods in the United States at the expense of struggling American industry.

Internal Improvements

President Madison's third request to Congress was the creation of a national transportation plan. Bad or nonexistent roads had interfered with the move-

Connections: Science and Technology

One of the most common sights on the National Road were Conestoga wagons. These wagons were first built about 1750 by German farmers in Pennsylvania's Conestoga Valley. The drivers were generally a boisterous, hard-drinking lot who smoked cigars, first known as Conestogas, then shortened to "stogies."

ment of troops and supplies during the war. Congress had voted funds for a National Road across the Appalachians in 1806, but progress on the highway had been slow.

In February 1817 Calhoun sponsored the Bonus Bill and called on Congress to fund a network of roads and canals. Calhoun pleaded for these "internal improvements" not only for military reasons, but also to unite the growing nation. "Let us then bind the Republic together," he said, "with a perfect system of roads and canals. Let us conquer space."

New Englanders and even southerners opposed Calhoun's bill. Good roads already crisscrossed New England, and in the South, rivers connected markets to the ocean. Calhoun managed to get his bill passed, but Madison vetoed it. Although the President had called for internal improvements, he had decided the Constitution did not permit the government to finance their construction.

Building roads. Work on the National Road continued despite the defeat of the Bonus Bill. By 1818 this "permanent turnpike" stretched from Cumberland, Maryland, to Wheeling, Virginia, on the Ohio River. By the 1830s it had pushed west to Ohio and, a decade later, into Illinois. Each day, wagons, families on foot, herds of cattle, and flocks of sheep crowded the road. Most were headed west.

State governments led the way in improving transportation to connect their cities and towns. In 1790 Pennsylvania chartered a private company to build a road between Lancaster and Philadelphia. People using the Lancaster Turnpike were charged a small fee, or toll, to pay the building costs.

The success of the turnpike sparked a flurry of toll-road building in New England and the mid-Atlantic states. But even with improved roads, hauling freight by wagon remained expensive. Canals offered a much cheaper alternative. A single horse or mule pulling a canal boat could haul as much freight as fifty animals could haul by wagon.

The Erie Canal. In 1817 New York Governor DeWitt Clinton proposed building a canal through the Mohawk River valley from the Hudson River to Lake Erie. When finished, the canal would link New York Harbor with the Great Lakes. Thomas Jefferson was not alone in thinking that cutting a 350-mile canal through the wilderness was "little short of madness." But construction began that summer on "Clinton's Big Ditch."

Besides carrying freight, the Erie Canal provided a safe, economical way for New Englanders and New Yorkers to move west into present-day Michigan and Wisconsin.

GTV Side 2

Chap. 9, Frame 24214

Getting Up to Speed: The Erie Canal and National Road (Movie Segment)

Search and Play:

B · A · C · K · G · R · O · U · N · D

Writing About History

Report, Diary, or Letter. Developments in transportation in the early nineteenth century provide good topics for research. Students can write a paper about: river boats, steamboats, turnpikes, or canals. Some students may write diary or journal entries about a trip down the Ohio or Mississippi rivers. Others might want to write a letter to a friend describing a trip on a steamboat, in a Conestoga wagon, or in a boat on the Erie Canal.

Connections: Science and Technology

After the success of the *Clermont*, steamboats were developed to navigate the treacherous shallows of western rivers like the Mississippi. River men built more powerful engines for western boats and replaced the heavy hulls and keels of eastern boats with flat platforms, which drew little water. The western steamboat, said one observer, is "an engine on a raft."

Social History

Rebecca Lukens owned a Pennsylvania ironworks that made iron plates for steamboat boilers. Lukens found adventure in ironworking. "The manufacture of iron is not a mere local or individual interest," she insisted, but a "chief element of progress."

Section Review

ANSWERS

1. Definitions for the following terms are on text pages indicated in parentheses: *Industrial Revolution* (203), *interchangeable parts* (204), *mass production* (204).
2. Labor force changed from mostly men to men, women, and children.
3. Reduced time needed to separate cotton from seeds, thus making cotton growing more profitable. Southerners came to believe that the use of slave labor was essential.
4. American system called for increased government action to establish national bank, levy protective tariffs, and build roads.
5. Students may answer booming economy in both regions; a feeling of optimism and of nationalism.

Reduced student page in the Teacher's Edition

New York State opened the Erie Canal in 1825. The cost of moving freight from Lake Erie to New York City dropped from over $100 a ton to less than $10. Westerners shipped farm products on the canal to eastern cities. Easterners sent factory goods to western farms. Traffic was so brisk that the canal paid for itself in just twelve years. New York City became the nation's largest commercial center.

The Erie Canal touched off a canal-building craze across the nation. Within twenty years, 3,000 miles of canals laced the country. Connecting the Great Lakes to the Ohio and Mississippi rivers, these waterways carried people and goods from the eastern seaboard to the Gulf of Mexico.

"Fulton's Folly." River travel was revolutionized by the steam engine. First perfected by James Watt of Scotland in the 1780s, the steam engine powered most British factories. American inventor Robert Fulton put the hissing engine to a new use—powering riverboats to move upstream as easily as down.

In 1807 Fulton built the *Clermont,* the first successful steamboat. Its huge paddle wheels slapping the water, "Fulton's Folly" amazed onlookers as it churned up the Hudson River against the current at a remarkable 5 miles per hour.

By the 1820s hundreds of steamboats paddled up and down the nation's rivers. Small river towns blossomed into major trade centers. On the lower Mississippi River, Memphis, Vicksburg, and Natchez prospered shipping cotton. Farther north, where the Missouri and Illinois rivers flow into the Mississippi, St. Louis grew into the West's transportation hub. On the Ohio River, Pittsburgh became a huge inland port, while Cincinnati shipped so much pork by steamboat that citizens nicknamed it "Porkopolis."

The Impact of Industrial Change

The rapid changes in industry and transportation touched each section of the United States differently. Factories in the North produced the machinery and goods needed by the South and the West. Textile mills sprang up throughout New England. Ironworks and machine shops multiplied in the mid-Atlantic states. Roads, canals, and rivers—used to transport raw materials as well as finished goods—were the very lifelines of these industries.

The rise of the textile industry in Britain had a dramatic impact on the South. As demand for cotton skyrocketed, southerners expanded their cotton fields westward to the Mississippi and beyond. As in the past, planters relied on slave labor. Instead of dying out, slavery came to be seen as an essential part of the South's "cotton kingdom."

The West remained an agricultural region, raising livestock and crops—especially wheat and corn—that easterners and Europeans wanted. As westerners specialized in these cash crops, they came to rely more and more on factory-produced clothing, furniture, and farm tools.

Steamboats and canals were vital to western settlement. Towns lived or died depending on how close they were to a waterway. A Richmond, Indiana, newspaper explained the value of a canal to a small western town in this way:

> *"With it our course will be upward, and without it our city will become a deserted village. . . . With it our streets will be the avenues of traffic; without, grass will grow upon the sidewalks. With it we will rival and outstrip surrounding towns; without it they will leave us in the background."*

Section Review

1. Identification. Define *Industrial Revolution, interchangeable parts,* and *mass production.*

2. Application. The Industrial Revolution led to changes in the American labor force. How did Slater's and Lowell's mills show these changes?

3. Synthesis. How did the cotton gin, which reduced hand labor in processing cotton, affect slavery in the South?

4. Comprehension. Why did Madison think the "American System" was contrary to Republican principles of limited government?

5. Analysis. The people of the West and the East developed different ways of life in the early 1800s. What similarites, if any, can you note?

Connections: Science and Technology
Pictured on this page is the first spinning mill in the United States, built in Pawtucket, Rhode Island, by Samuel Slater. While an apprentice in a British textile mill, he memorized the workings of the spinning machines that were revolutionizing the textile industry. In 1789 he sailed for the United States, disregarding Britain's law prohibiting the emigration of textile workers and the export of textile machinery or data. American state legislatures offered money to anyone bringing information about the new technology. The next year he reproduced from memory the British spinning machines, thus ushering in the American cotton textile industry.

Geography: A Key to Our Past

ANSWERS

1. Rushing water turns a mill wheel. This motion passes along a system of gears, belts, and rods to machines.
2. Lowell was built on banks of river in order to utilize water power for mills.
3. They built a series of canals to harness the power of the river.

Geography
A KEY TO OUR PAST

Relationships Within Places: The Old Mill Stream

"Although . . . it has been a manufacturing town barely one-and-twenty years, Lowell is a large, populous, thriving place. . . . The very river that moves the machinery in the mills—for they are all worked by water power—seems to acquire a new character from the fresh buildings of bright red brick and painted wood among which it takes its course."

In this way British writer Charles Dickens described Lowell, Massachusetts, in 1842. The most famous of all American mill towns, Lowell was the pride of American industry in the first half of the nineteenth century.

Lowell is an example of one of the fundamental themes in geography: **relationships within places,** or how people modify and adapt to natural settings. Lowell sprang up on the Merrimack River, where the 32-foot Pawtucket Falls provided power for Lowell's earliest mills. Soon Lowell's manufacturers added a series of canals to harness the enormous power of the river for even more mills.

Mills had dotted America's creeks and rivers even during colonial times. People searched for spots on streams where waterfalls, rapids, or water tumbling over a dam could provide power for mills. Then towns and cities grew up around the mills.

In one five-story Lowell mill, falling water turned two huge wheels. This motion was passed along a system of gears, belts, and rods. The wheels moved gears. The gears turned rods. The turning rods were connected by belts to other rods, which then also turned. These revolving rods ran all the looms and other machinery in the building.

By the end of the 1800s, steam power had largely replaced water power in factories. Today, powerful turbines create electricity which can be sent over great distances. People are freed from the necessity of situating factories along streams.

Today Lowell remains a textile center. Recently some of the old part of the city was restored so that people could see the water-driven mills on the Merrimack, where thousands of women and children made cotton and woolen cloth. The United States government has designated that part of the city a national historic park.

1. Explain in a few sentences how water can be used to power machinery.
2. How is Lowell an example of the relationship between people and the place they live?
3. How did people modify the natural setting of Lowell?

Linking Past and Present

Discussion. Women who worked in the Lowell mills lived in boarding houses provided by the company. They attended classes in the evening and church on Sunday, formed literary societies, and published a magazine (see Chapter 11). Ask students to speculate about why such working arrangements seldom exist today. What do employers offer today to attract and keep workers?

POINT OF VIEW

The Lowell Factory System

The Lowell factory system combined under one roof all the steps for making cotton fabric. Factory owners provided workers—mostly young, unmarried women—with food, clothing, lodging, and even moral guidance. At first considered a model of how employers should treat their employees, the Lowell system came under close scrutiny in the mid-1800s. The following excerpts—the first by English merchant James S. Buckingham, the second by American reformer Catherine Beecher, and the third a factory work song—provide different views of the system.

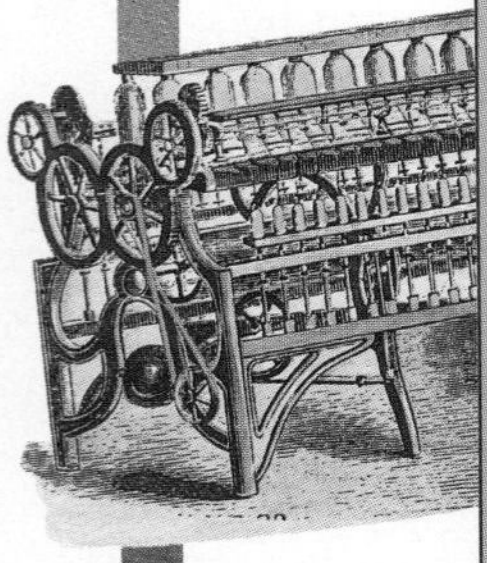

An early 1800s painting and a late 1800s photo reflect different views of working conditions.

Comfortable Conditions

“The greater number of the females employed here, are daughters of . . . farmers. . . . They do not leave their homes from want, but from . . . a desire to support themselves by their own labor. They rarely come to the factories till they are fifteen or sixteen, and there is a law prohibiting their being employed before they are fourteen. . . . When they come, they are in general amply provided with clothes, and every other requisite; and . . . are comfortably accommodated in one of the boarding houses belonging to the company. . . .

The hours of work are from six in the morning to seven in the evening in the summer; and from half past six to half past seven in the winter months, with the allowance of one hour to the two meals of breakfast at eight and dinner at one o'clock, supper being taken after their labors are over. On Saturdays the factories are closed at four o'clock, so that the labor is twelve hours a day on each day except Saturday, and then only nine. This is no doubt longer than it is desirable that any person should labor continuously. . . . But I have no doubt, that from the superior cleanliness, comfort, food, air, and healthful associations by which they are surrounded, their twelve hours' labor here do not produce more fatigue to them, than ten hours' labor do to the same class of factory girls in England. . . .”

—From James Buckingham, in *The Eastern and Western States of America,* Vol. I. London: Fisher, Son & Co., 1842.

B · A · C · K · G · R · O · U · N · D

Connections: Music

Folk music of the United States includes work songs—songs relating the experiences and struggles of workers from all professions and occupations. These songs may express misfortunes and tragedies of workers' lives: factory fires and accidents, coal mine disasters, railroad collisions, unemployment, hunger, hard times, and so on. The songs were usually set to traditional tunes, including gospel songs, hymns, and spirituals.

By the 1860s about 58 percent of workers in textile mills were women. Their dislike of working in the New England mills is expressed in the song below.

A Tight Timetable

"Let me now present the facts I learned by observation or inquiry on the spot [at Lowell]. I was there in mid-winter, and every morning I was awakened at five, by the bells calling to labor. The time allowed for dressing and breakfast was so short, as many told me, that both were performed hurriedly, and then the work at the mill was begun by lamplight; and prosecuted without remission till twelve, chiefly in a standing position. Then half an hour [was] allowed for dinner, from which the time for going and returning was deducted. Then back to the mills, to work till seven o'clock, the last part of the time by lamplight. Then returning, washing, dressing, and supper occupied another hour. Thus ten hours only remained for recreation and sleep. Now eight hours' sleep is required for laborers. . . . Deduct eight hours for sleep and only two hours remain for shopping, mending, making recreation, and breathing pure air. For it must be remembered that all the hours of labor are spent in rooms where lamps, together with from 40 to 80 persons are exhausting the healthful air. . . ."

—From Catherine Beecher, in *The Evils Suffered by American Women and Children*. New York: Harper and Brothers, 1846.

"Factory Girl"

"No more shall I work in the fact'ry,
Greasy up my clothes;
No more shall I work in the fact'ry
With splinters in my toes.

No more shall I hear the bosses say,
'Boys, you'd better dauf,'
No more shall I hear those bosses say,
'Spinners you'd better clean off.'

No more shall I hear the drummer wheels
A-rolling over my head,
When factories are hard at work,
I'll be in my bed.

No more shall I hear the whistle blow,
To call me up so soon;
No more shall I hear the whistle blow,
To call me from my home.

No more shall I see the super come,
All dressed up so proud;
For I know I'll marry a country boy
Before the year is out.

No more shall I wear the old black dress,
Greasy all around;
No more shall I wear the old black bonnet
With holes all in the crown.

Chorus:
Pity me my darling,
Pity me, I say;
Pity me my darling,
And carry me away."

—From *The Annals of America*, Vol. 10.

1. On what two major points did Buckingham and Beecher disagree?

2. In the song, what conditions does the factory girl find intolerable? What does she think will save her from factory life?

3. Some observers of the Lowell system referred to it as "paternalistic." What do you think they meant by this? Do you agree with their view? Why or why not?

4. The development of the Lowell system was part of the American Industrial Revolution. In your opinion, what was revolutionary about the Lowell system?

Point of View

ANSWERS

1. They disagree on the quality of the working conditions. Buckingham considers the conditions comfortable, while Beecher regards them as unhealthy. They also disagree on the workload, which Buckingham does not see as unduly harsh, given the working hours at factories in England. Beecher regards the hours as excessive.

2. She objects to the dirty conditions, the long hours, and the ragged clothing she must wear. She expects marriage to free her from factory work.

3. The system can be seen as paternalistic in the sense that the factory owners claimed to be taking care of the workers in the way a father takes care of children—telling them what to do and seeking what is supposedly best for them. Students' opinions will vary regarding the motives of the factory owners. Some may say that the owners felt that what was good for productivity was good for the workers as well. Others may argue that the owners were motivated mainly by self-interest.

4. Answers will vary. Students may point to the improved efficiency of factory operations, including rigid schedules. Another aspect that might be considered revolutionary is the housing of workers on the factory site.

GTV Side 3

Chap. 8, Frame 22071

New England Textile Centers, Late 1700s (Map)

Search:

Section 8-4

Objectives

- ***Answer the Focus Question.***
- *Discuss how the Supreme Court strengthened the power of the federal government.*
- *Explain why the Missouri Compromise was necessary.*

Introducing

THE SECTION

Ask students to give examples of nationalism they have studied in this chapter. **(pride after War of 1812, American System)** Into what sections was the United States divided? **(North, South, West)** What was the issue that would cause the most dissension? **(slavery)**

Tell students that in this section they will study the beginning of the tension between nationalism and sectionalism that ended in civil war.

B · A · C · K · G · R · O · U · N · D

Multicultural Perspectives

James Forten (see American Voices quote on this page) was born in 1766 to free African-American parents. He served as a powder boy aboard a Philadelphia privateer during the Revolutionary War. In later years, Forten became a wealthy businessman and turned his attention to the abolition movement and the movement for equal rights for all. In 1800 he worked to modify the Fugitive Slave Act of 1793 and to adopt *"such measures as shall in due course emancipate the whole of their brethren from their present situation."* When this movement was defeated, Forten became more determined than ever to change the attitude of unsympathetic Americans.

8-4 National Unity and Sectional Strains

Focus: How was national unity both strengthened and weakened after 1817?

As the Industrial Revolution was getting underway in the United States, Republican James Monroe—ex-governor of Virginia and Madison's Secretary of State—won the presidential election of 1816. The Federalist party, tarnished by its opposition to the War of 1812, made a dismal showing and fell apart over the next few years. In 1820 Monroe would be reelected to office unopposed, even without needing nomination. Americans, Monroe said, were becoming "one great family with a common interest."

After taking office, Monroe toured the northern states. No section welcomed him more warmly than Federalist New England. So many New Englanders turned out to cheer the President that a Boston newspaper proclaimed an "era of good feelings." Those feelings, however, would be sorely tested during Monroe's presidency by hard times and the slavery issue.

American Voices

"Has the God who made the white man and the black left any record declaring us a different species? Are we not sustained by the same power, supported by the same food, wounded by the same wrongs? And should we not enjoy the same liberty, and be protected by the same laws?"

—James Forten

The Panic of 1819

The first event to challenge the nation's optimism was a financial panic which grew out of the postwar boom. With the end of the Napoleonic Wars, Europeans had clamored to buy American grain, meat, tobacco, and cotton. Prices for farm products rose sharply, and American farmers rushed to expand production. Land prices soared as farmers and speculators scrambled to buy farm land on which to plant cash crops.

State banks encouraged speculation by making loans to anyone who needed cash to buy land or farm equipment. Instead of curbing the state banks, the Bank of the United States encouraged their easy credit policy.

The speculative bubble burst in 1819. European farmers had reaped bumper crops in 1818, and British textile mills had begun to buy less expensive cotton from India. With American foodstuffs and cotton no longer in demand in Europe, crop prices collapsed, causing a financial panic. Many state banks failed, while the national bank foreclosed on mortgages on homes, farms, and shops.

Traveling from Missouri to Washington in 1820, Senator Thomas Hart Benton heard the same story of despair everywhere. "No employment for industry—no demand for labor—no sale for the product of the farm—no sound of the hammer, but that of the auctioneer," he wrote. "Distress, the universal cry of the people; relief, the universal demand thundered at the doors of all legislatures, state and federal."

The Slavery Issue: "A Fire-Bell in the Night"

Meanwhile, the controversy over slavery, which had simmered for years, flared up. Slavery had been abolished in every state north of Delaware by 1804. Slavery had also been banned in the Northwest Territory. Then in 1818 the Missouri Territory—part of the Louisiana Purchase—applied for admission to the Union. Slavery had been legal there under French and Spanish rule. Now settlers hoped to legalize slavery in the new state.

Many northerners opposed slavery on moral grounds and were determined to keep it from spreading. They also disliked the Constitution's provision that allowed a southern state to include three fifths of its slaves in population counts for representation in Congress. Representative James Tallmadge of New York proposed an amendment to the Missouri statehood bill. Slavery would be gradually abolished in Missouri.

Southerners resented having slavery called into question. Congress, they said, did not have the right to interfere with slavery in a state. They also argued that under the Fifth Amendment slaveholders could not be denied the right to take their slaves into Missouri—that would be depriving them of property without due process of law.

The stormy debate was a landmark in the growth of **sectionalism,** or devotion to the interests of one section of the country over those of other sections. In defense of slavery, southerners became increasingly concerned with the division of power in Congress between the North and the South. The North with its larger population, had a majority in the House of Representatives, but the Senate was evenly divided. Southerners were convinced that without an equal number of senators, the South could not protect slavery.

The Missouri Compromise. Bitter wrangling caused the issue of Missouri statehood to spill over into the 1820 session of Congress. "It is a most unhappy question, awakening sectional feelings, and exasperating them to the highest degree," reported Henry Clay. "The words civil war and disunion are uttered almost without emotion."

Concerned over the prospect of endless disagreement, Clay worked out a compromise. Like Missouri, Maine had recently applied for statehood. Clay proposed that Maine be admitted to the Union as a free state and Missouri as a slave state. In addition, slavery was to be "forever prohibited" from

The Missouri Compromise 1820

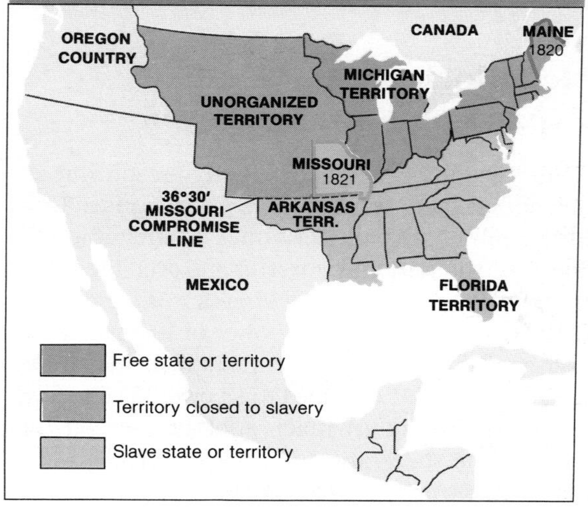

Expansion of the "cotton kingdom" increased demands for slave labor. The end of the foreign slave trade in 1808 gave rise to smuggling and a thriving domestic slave trade.

Developing

THE SECTION

Connections: Economics

Discussion. Ask how the government contributed to the Panic of 1819. **(by following easy credit policy and making loans to people or institutions with little or no qualifications)** What actions did the government take during the panic? **(foreclosed on mortgages on homes, farms, shops)** What does the government do today during a recession? **(provides unemployment benefits, creates jobs, tax breaks)**

Analyzing Primary Sources

James Forten Letter. In 1813 the Pennsylvania legislature was debating a bill to ban the entrance of free African Americans into the state. James Forten attacked this measure through five letters published in pamphlet form. A quotation from one of those letters appears as the "American Voices" selection on text page 212. Ask students to state Forten's views about differences between black Americans and white Americans. **(He believed in the equality of the races.)**

GTV Side 2

Chap. 15, Frame 45739

Missouri Compromise 1820 (Map)

Search:

Multicultural Perspectives

The Seminoles had long offered protection to escaped slaves. Often the two intermarried, and African Americans became active in tribal affairs. African Americans such as John Horse served as important advisors and negotiators for Seminole chiefs. The wife of Chief Osceola was an African-American woman, and blacks were actively involved in the Seminole Wars.

Thinking Critically

Analysis. Use Jefferson's quotation on this page as a basis for discussion. **Ask:** What do you imagine Jefferson's fears were? What does he mean when he states the compromise "is a reprieve only, not a final sentence"? What other issues are involved besides slavery? (representation, taxation, agriculture versus manufacturing)

Analyzing Primary Sources

Diary Entry. Uneasy about the Missouri Compromise, Secretary of State John Quincy Adams wrote in his diary:

" Perhaps it would have been a wiser . . . course to have persisted in the restriction upon Missouri, till it should have terminated in a convention of the states to revise the Constitution. . . . If the Union must be dissolved, slavery is precisely the question upon which it ought to break. "

Ask students how wise a course of action they think this would have been and why.

Active Learning

Reports. Have students report on one of the following African Americans who played an active role in the abolition movement of this period: James Forten, Elizabeth Freeman, Richard Allen, Paul Cuffe, Denmark Vesey.

the rest of the Louisiana territory north of latitude 36° 30′. This latitude line was the southern boundary of Missouri.

Congress approved the Missouri Compromise in March 1820. Northerners accepted the compromise because it banned slavery in most of the Louisiana territory. Southerners were satisfied that most of the region was prairie, too dry for growing cotton. More important, the balance of slave and free states had been maintained.

Thomas Jefferson was alarmed by this settlement. He wrote to a friend:

" This momentous question, like a firebell in the night, awakened and filled me with terror. I considered it at once as the knell [a bell signaling death] of the Union. It is hushed, indeed, for the moment. But this is a reprieve only, not a final sentence. "

McCulloch *v.* Maryland: Expanding National Power

While sectionalism plagued Congress during the Missouri debate, the Supreme Court, under Chief Justice John Marshall, continued to strengthen the power of the national government over the states. In the 1803 case of *Marbury* v. *Madison,* the Court had first asserted its power of judicial review over acts of Congress. Seven years later in *Fletcher* v. *Peck,* the Court extended this power to state laws.

In 1819 the Court made another decision that checked the states and built the power of the national government. *McCulloch* v. *Maryland* involved a high state tax that Maryland had imposed on the Baltimore branch of the national bank. The Court had to decide if the bank itself was constitutional, and if so, if a state had the power to tax it.

First, the Supreme Court upheld the power of Congress to charter the bank. The Court said that the Constitution implied this power when it allowed the government to tax, regulate commerce, and raise an army. All actions within "the letter and spirit of the Constitution," the Court decided, "are constitutional."

Then the Court declared that no state has the right to tax the national bank, arguing that "the power to tax involves the power to destroy." No state could be allowed to destroy an agency of the federal government. Therefore, the Maryland tax was unconstitutional. "The government of the United States," the Court concluded, "though limited in its powers, is supreme" over the states.

Assertive Foreign Policy

Although the War of 1812 had settled little, it did have a lasting impact on relations between the United States and Great Britain. The British finally accepted the United States as a nation. The United States, on its part, accepted Canada as a permanent part of the British Empire. By 1818 both nations were ready to deal with some of the issues unresolved by the Treaty of Ghent.

Border issues were settled fairly simply. The northern boundary of the Louisiana Purchase was fixed at the 49th parallel and ran westward to the Rocky Mountains. The United States and Britian decided to occupy Oregon jointly.

Gaining Florida. Monroe and Secretary of State John Quincy Adams turned next to problems with Spanish Florida. Seminole Indians from Spanish Florida were raiding across the Georgia border, and escaping slaves were taking refuge there. Angry Georgians demanded government action.

Monroe sent General Andrew Jackson to pursue the Seminoles but ordered him not to attack any Spanish fort. The headstrong general nevertheless captured the Spanish fort at St. Marks and destroyed Seminole settlements. He ordered the execution of two Seminole leaders as well as two British subjects who had helped the Seminoles. Finally Jackson seized the colony's capital, Pensacola, removed the Spanish governor, and replaced him with an American officer.

Spain had too few troops in Florida to repulse the American army so decided to bargain. In the Adams-Onís Treaty of 1819, Spain ceded Florida to the United States. In return, the United States promised to pay $5 million in claims filed against Spain for the border raids. The United States also gave up its claim to Texas, which it had considered part of the Louisiana Purchase. At last the United States had acquired all land east of the Mississippi.

The United States in 1822

Geography Skills — Place. Judging from the map, why did some Americans want Florida and why did Spain give it up? How many stars were on the American flag by 1822? Which states had been added to the Union since the Constitution was ratified?

The Monroe Doctrine. By the 1820s Spain had lost most of its empire in Latin America. For two decades, Latin American colonists had been fighting wars for independence. By 1821 Mexicans and most Central Americans had won their freedom from Spain. By 1825 colonists in Spanish South America, led by Venezuelan General Simón Bolívar and Argentine General José de San Martín would gain their independence.

Secretary of State Adams worried that European nations might try to help Spain regain its empire. The United States was carrying on a booming trade with northern Mexico, especially in present-day California and New Mexico, and feared it would be cut off if Spain regained control. Adams was also worried about Russia's attempt in 1821 to extend its claim on the Pacific Coast of North America south into Oregon. It was time, Adams advised the President, to inform Europe that further colonization in the Americas was not welcome.

In his message to Congress in December 1823, President Monroe issued a stern warning to the

Global Connections

Research and Report. To many, Simón Bolívar is *El Libertador*—the Liberator. He won independence for northern Latin America and became President of "Gran Colombia," the area now made up of Colombia, Venezuela, Ecuador, and Panama. He later became dictator of Peru. Interested students can find out more about Simón Bolívar, José de San Martín, and Agustín de Iturbide, who led the Mexican revolt. They can report their findings to the class.

Geography Skills

ANSWERS

1. Spanish Florida seems like an interruption in the United States coastline. Florida was difficult to protect because it was separated from other Spanish territory and "surrounded" by the United States.
2. 24 stars.
3. Maine, Vermont, Ohio, Indiana, Illinois, Missouri, Tennessee, Kentucky, Alabama, Mississippi, Louisiana.

Thinking Critically

Evaluation. Discuss with students how democratic the election of 1824 was. How were the presidential candidates chosen? (by caucus—closed meeting of a political group—or state legislature) How are candidates selected today? (national nominating conventions) Which do you think is more democratic? How democratic is it to have the President chosen by the Electoral College?

leaders of Europe. The warning became known as the Monroe Doctrine, although Adams wrote much of it. The doctrine stated that the American continents were closed to "future colonization by any European powers."

This announcement of American foreign policy also warned European nations not to impose their system of government in any part of the Western Hemisphere. Nor were European nations to interfere with the newly independent nations in Latin America "for the purpose of oppressing them, or controlling in any other manner their destiny." For its part, the United States vowed not to interfere with European affairs or with existing European colonies in the Americas.

Most of Europe derided the Monroe Doctrine as empty bluster. In fact, the United States did nothing to help the Latin American nations resist continued European interference. At home, however, Monroe's "America for the Americans" theme fit the nationalist spirit of the times.

Patriot armies led by Simón Bolívar won independence for Bolivia, Colombia, Ecuador, Peru, and Venezuela.

Spotlight on People

After the election of 1824, the Republican party faded away. At the same time, the era of the old fighters for independence was also drawing to a close.

On July 4, 1826, Americans were celebrating the fiftieth anniversary of the Declaration of Independence. At Monticello, his Virginia plantation, Thomas Jefferson lay dying. Hundreds of miles away in Massachusetts, John Adams was also close to death. The second and third Presidents had become fast friends in their old age. Both had hoped very much to see this special Independence Day.

As dawn broke, Jefferson asked a friend, "This is the Fourth?" When the friend said yes, Jefferson murmured, "Just as I wished." Adams, too ill to join the day's celebration, sent a toast: "Independence forever!" Both men died that day, their hopes fulfilled.

The Election of 1824: One-Party Politics

The following year brought another presidential election. As in 1820, only Republicans sought the office, but this year several candidates stepped forward, each representing a different section of the country.

Republicans in Congress met in caucus and nominated Secretary of the Treasury William H. Crawford of Georgia. Crawford did not have broad national support, however. New England Republicans nominated John Quincy Adams, whose reputation was widely respected.

In the West, the Kentucky legislature nominated Henry Clay, Speaker of the House of Representatives. Clay was the choice of many western states. The Tennessee legislature nominated Andrew Jackson. The Southwest was Jackson territory, but the hero of New Orleans had support in other regions, too. A teacher in Ohio described the passionate support in her state: "Strange! Wild! Infatuated! All for Jackson! . . . It is like an influenza."

Social History
John Quincy Adams was the only son of a President who also became President. In his first message to Congress Adams recommended a program of internal improvements, including national highways, canals, weather stations, and a national university. He argued that Congress should use the powers of government for the benefit of all the people. If it did not, it "would be treachery to the most sacred of trusts." But the nation was not yet ready to accept his ideas.

Jackson won the popular vote and carried 99 electoral votes. Adams was second with 84 electoral votes, Crawford third with 41, and Clay last with 37. But no candidate had a majority of votes in the electoral college.

In such a situation, the Constitution sends the election to the House of Representatives where each state may cast just one vote for one of the top three candidates. Now out of the race, Henry Clay convinced his supporters to vote for Adams. With this backing, Adams was elected President.

A few days later, Adams appointed Clay to be his Secretary of State, a position seen as a stepping stone to the presidency. Outraged, Jackson supporters charged that the appointment was a "corrupt bargain" between Adams and Clay.

The end of the Republican era. Adams's presidency was no less stormy than his election. Adams was a nationalist who hoped to expand internal improvements. By now, however, the postwar nationalist spirit was giving way to sectional concerns fostered by the Missouri Compromise. Adams could get none of his proposals through Congress.

During Adams's term in office, the Republican party split into two hostile camps. Adams and his supporters, now calling themselves National Republicans, were united by their belief in a strong national government. The other group took the name Democratic Republicans to signal their ties to the common people. They were united by little except their support for Andrew Jackson.

Jackson challenged Adams again in the election of 1828. Although Adams tried to run a campaign centered on issues, name-calling was the order of the day. The fierce contest brought twice as many voters to the polls as in 1824. Jackson soundly won both the popular and electoral votes. The Republican era had ended, one Adams backer said, in "a howl of raving Democracy."

Section Review

1. **Identification.** Define *sectionalism.*

2. **Comprehension.** What political situation made the Missouri Compromise necessary?

3. **Analysis.** How did the Supreme Court decision in *McCulloch* v. *Maryland* affect federal power?

Connections to Themes

Balancing Unity and Diversity

Americans viewed July 4, 1826, as a special day of celebration— it marked the fiftieth anniversary of the Declaration of Independence. To many, the growth of the nation seemed to be a sign that the United States enjoyed a "Divine blessing."

During those fifty years, the United States had more than doubled in size. Eleven new states had joined the Union, nine of them carved out of western lands. And many Americans confidently looked forward to extending the nation's western border in the future.

Westward expansion, however, led to conflicts with Native Americans whose lands were threatened by settlers from the East. Government officials wanted to keep peace with the tribes, but they also wanted to satisfy the demands of land seekers.

As early as 1803, with the addition of the Louisiana Purchase, President Jefferson hoped to solve this dilemma by persuading eastern Indians to exchange their lands for territory west of the Mississippi. President Monroe also adopted this policy. By 1830 the government had established a pattern for the future: the Indians must move or be destroyed.

Westward expansion caused increasing conflict between the North and the South, as well. The long simmering issue of slavery first came to a boil in 1819 over the question of extending slavery into lands beyond the Mississippi. As new lands were added to the nation and the views of the North and the South became more rigid, the issue would ultimately lead to secession and civil war.

Active Learning

Role Play. To explore what the theme of unity and diversity means today, students can role-play a TV panel show. One student can be the moderator. Others can be representatives of women's groups; various ethnic groups; labor unions; and business organizations. Each representative can report what unity vs. diversity means to the group. Still other students can be media reporters, putting questions to the panel.

Points to consider: What issues tend to divide Americans today? What tends to promote a sense of unity? How can unity be balanced against diversity?

Section Review

ANSWERS

1. Definition of *sectionalism* is on text page 213.
2. Missouri Territory applied for admission to Union. Northerners did not want slavery to spread. Southerners did not want to be prohibited from taking slaves into Missouri.
3. Extended power of federal government.

Chapter Survey

ANSWERS

Using New Vocabulary

1. (b) *Secession* means withdrawal of states from the union.
2. (c) *Nationalism* is patriotic pride in country.
3. (a) *Interchangeable parts* improved production of manufactured goods.

Reviewing the Chapter

1. Judicial review.
2. Napoleon's troops could not put down rebellion in Saint Domingue; his navy could not protect French possessions from British navy.
3. Federalists opposed purchase because not provided for in Constitution. Some easterners opposed, did not want to lose power to new western lands.
4. They did not find all-water route to Pacific; did explore western rivers and reach Pacific; established friendly relations with Indians.
5. Neutrality should have enabled American merchants to trade freely with both France and Britain, but each side seized American ships in effort to cut off the other's trade.
6. Embargo Act intended to pressure Britain and France into respecting free trade and sailors' rights. It devastated economy of New England but never succeeded in getting Britain and France to respect rights.
7. West and South resented British impressment of sailors, hoped to break British alliances with Indians and gain new lands for settlement, and to conquer Canada. Southerners hoped British defeat would cause Spain, Britain's ally, to cede Florida to U.S. New England opposed war because depended on trade.
8. North became manufacturing region; growth of textile industry led South to focus on cotton growing; West remained agricultural region.
9. North and South took opposing sides on issues of protective tariffs and spread of slavery. Missouri Compromise necessary to keep balance of slave and free states in Senate.
10. With Spain involved in European wars, its colonies in Latin America revolted and struggled for independence. Fearing other European countries would try to help Spain regain colonies, Monroe issued warning to stay out of Western Hemisphere.

Thinking Critically

1. Without War of 1812, there might have been more Indian resistance in West and less industrialization in Northeast. Country probably would not have made so much progress toward self-sufficiency. Nor

Reduced student page in the Teacher's Edition

Chapter Survey

Using New Vocabulary

Match each numbered vocabulary term with the lettered word or phrase most closely related to it. Then explain how the terms in each pair are related.

Example: *Sectionalism* is related to *sections* because sectionalism is devotion to the interests of one section of a country over those of other sections.

1. secession	(a) manufactured goods
2. nationalism	(b) states
3. interchangeable parts	(c) patriotic pride

Reviewing the Chapter

1. What power did the Supreme Court acquire through the precedent established by *Marbury* v. *Madison?*

2. Explain two reasons why Napoleon decided to sell Louisiana to the United States.

3. Some Americans opposed the Louisiana Purchase. Who were they and on what grounds did they base their opposition?

4. How well did Lewis and Clark meet the objectives of their expedition?

5. Explain the problem that neutrality posed for American merchants during the war between Britain and France that started in 1803.

6. What was the purpose of the Embargo Act? What were its effects at home and abroad?

7. Which two regions of the United States favored war with Great Britain in 1812? Why? Which region opposed war? Why?

8. How did the Industrial Revolution contribute to sectional differences in the United States in the early 1800s?

9. What were the political consequences of economic changes in the North and the South? Why was the Missouri Compromise necessary?

10. How did events in Europe affect Latin America? How did events in Latin America lead President Monroe to issue the Monroe Doctrine?

Thinking Critically

1. Synthesis. Although the War of 1812 settled few political differences between Great Britain and the United States, it affected many aspects of American life. How might the years from 1812 to 1828 have been different if the war had not been fought?

2. Analysis. As a European, compare the impressions created abroad by the Monroe Doctrine and the Missouri Compromise.

Using a Time Line

Match the events with the dates on the time line and list them in chronological order. Then answer the question below.

(A) Adams-Onís Treaty
(B) *Marbury* v. *Madison*
(C) Second Bank of the United States
(D) Monroe Doctrine
(E) *McCulloch* v. *Maryland*
(F) Louisiana Purchase
(G) Lowell's textile mill
(H) War between United States and Great Britain
(I) First protective tariff
(J) Missouri Compromise

What was happening to the power of the federal government during this period? Give examples.

History and You

The Supreme Court under Chief Justice John Marshall asserted its power to decide if state laws are constitutional. Find one recent example of the Supreme Court's use of this power. Briefly describe the case and the Court's decision.

would spirit of national unity have grown so much.
2. With Monroe Doctrine, the U.S. flexed its muscles to the world and warned against European meddling in western hemisphere. But Missouri Compromise showed sectional forces were competing with nationalism in the U.S. Without internal unity, United States' strength was questionable.

Using a Time Line

(A) 1819, (B) 1803, (C) 1816, (D) 1823, (E) 1819, (F) 1803, (G) 1810, (H) 1812, (I) 1816, (J) 1820.

Federal government, in general, is gaining power by acquiring land, through Supreme Court decisions, waging War of 1812, and announcing Monroe Doctrine. Rise of sectionalism as seen in Missouri Compromise threatens power of federal government.

History and You

Answers will vary.

Applying Social Studies Skills

1. 1800: Vermont, Pennsylvania, Maine; 1830: Kentucky, Ohio; 1860: Texas, Oklahoma, Minnesota.
2. Ship.
3. 600–900 miles.
4. 1860. Railroads.
5. Improved transportation increases distances people and goods can travel in any given period of time.

Applying Thinking Skills

1. South too dependent on North for manufactured goods, but the situation can and should change.
2. (a) Almost all other goods are purchased from North; (b) rich land allows South to raise crops other than cotton; (c) South has enough capital and water power for manufacturing.
3. South primarily agricultural; North industrial.

Applying Social Studies Skills

Analyzing Maps

The heavy lines on the map below show the distance that a New Yorker could reasonably expect to travel in one week in 1800, 1830, and 1860. Boundary lines show present-day states. Use the map to answer the following questions.

Travel in the 1800s

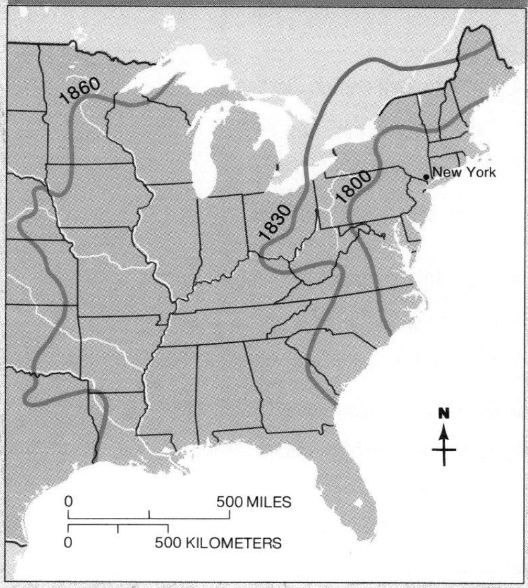

1. Which of the following states could a New Yorker reach in a week in 1800? In 1830? In 1860? Vermont, Texas, Georgia, Oklahoma, Minnesota, Pennsylvania, Kentucky, Maine, Ohio

2. In 1800 New Yorkers traveled by foot or horse on poor roads or by ship along the Atlantic Coast. Which mode of travel allowed them to travel farthest in a week?

3. By 1830 there were improved roads, canals, and steamboats. Estimate the maximum distance a New Yorker could travel in a week.

4. By what year could a New Yorker travel beyond the Mississippi in less than a week? What form of transportation would make this possible?

5. Summarize what the map shows about the effect of improved transportation.

Applying Thinking Skills

Identifying Arguments

An argument must present a claim as well as accurate, relevant reasons supporting that claim. Read the excerpt from the editorial below to identify the writer's argument. Then answer the questions that follow.

> *"That we have cultivated cotton, cotton, cotton, and bought everything else, has long enough been our [disgrace]. . . . If we have followed a ruinous policy and bought all the articles of subsistence instead of raising them, who is to blame? For what have we not looked to our northern friends? From them we get not only our clothes, carriages, saddles, hats, shoes, flour, potatoes, but even our onions and horn buttons. . . .*
>
> *Let us change our policy. . . . Let our farmers make and wear their homespun; raise in greater plenty corn and wheat, which will enable them to raise their own hogs, cattle, and horses; and let those who have capital and enterprise manufacture on a more extensive scale. There is nothing to prevent us from doing it. We have good land, unlimited water power, capital in plenty, and a patriotism which is running over in some places."*
>
> —Adapted from the *Georgia Courier,* June 1827

1. What is the writer's claim?

2. List three facts that the writer presents to support the claim.

3. What sectional differences between the North and the South are described in this editorial?

Chapter 9

Conflict and Reform

Planning Guide

	Student Text	TWE Lesson Plans	Support Materials
SECTION 1	**Section 9–1** (1–3 Days) **The Era of Andrew Jackson,** pp 222–229 Exploring Issues—States Rights: The Great Debate, p 228 Review/Evaluation Section Review, p 229	**Introducing the Chapter:** States' Rights vs. National Unity—Class Activity, 30 minutes, p 219B **Teaching the Main Ideas:** Debating Tough Issues—Class Activity, two class periods, p 219B **Enrichment Activity:** A Tragedy Told in the Oral Tradition—Individual Activity, homework, one class period for presentation, p 219D	★ **Read to Remember,** Section 1 ● **Section Activities,** Section 1 ● **Geography Activities,** Section 1 Δ **Readings,** *Worcester* v. *Georgia* ● **Tests and Quizzes,** Section 1 Quiz
SECTION 2	**Section 9–2** (1 Day) **Jackson and the Bank,** pp 230–233 Review/Evaluation Section Review, p 233	**Teaching the Main Ideas:** Political Cartoons—Individual Activity, homework, p 219C	★ **Read to Remember,** Section 2 ● **Section Activities,** Section 2 Δ **Reading,** Nicholas Biddle ● **Tests and Quizzes,** Section 2 Quiz
SECTION 3	**Section 9–3** (1–2 Days) **Pursuing the Perfect Society,** pp 234–239 The American Spirit: Margaret Fuller—A New View of Women, p 238 Review/Evaluation Section Review, p 239	**Reinforcement Activity:** A Less Than Perfect Society—Cooperative Activity, one class period, p 219C	★ **Read to Remember,** Section 3 ● **Section Activities,** Section 3 Δ **Enrichment Activities,** Section 3 Δ **Readings,** Declaration of Sentiments ● **Tests and Quizzes,** Section 3 Quiz
SECTION 4	**Section 9–4** (1–2 Days) **The Struggle to Abolish Slavery,** pp 240–243 Connections to Themes: Shaping Democracy, p 243 Review/Evaluation Section Review, p 243 Chapter 9 Survey, pp 244–245 Skills, pp 244–245 Using New Vocabulary Thinking Critically Using a Time Line Applying Thinking Skills: Interpreting Political Cartoons Writing About Issues	**Evaluating Progress:** "Mods" vs. "Rads"—Individual Activity, 30 minutes introduction, homework, p 219C	★ **Read to Remember,** Section 4 ● **Section Activities,** Section 4 Δ **Enrichment Activities,** Section 4 Δ **Readings,** Frederick Douglass ● **Tests and Quizzes,** Section 4 Quiz, Chapter 9 Test (Forms A and B) **Additional Resources** ● **Active Learning** Δ **GTV Videodiscs** Δ **Transparencies and Activity Book** ● **Testing Software** ★ **Chapter Summaries** **Key:** ★ **For Extra Support** ● **For All Students** Δ **For Enrichment**

Overview

Andrew Jackson's election as President in 1828 was hailed as a triumph for the common people, but critics condemned his "Kitchen Cabinet," the spoils system of political appointments, and Native American removal policies. When southern opposition to tariffs reached critical proportions, Vice-President John C. Calhoun invoked the doctrine of nullification. Jackson threatened passage of a Force Act but then agreed to a compromise put forth by Henry Clay to avoid deepening regional conflicts.

Determined to do away with the Bank of the United States, Jackson let its charter run out and deposited federal money in "pet banks." The resulting loose credit policies led to the Panic of 1837.

The Whig party, formed to oppose Jackson and the Democrats, used Jacksonian campaign techniques to elect William Henry Harrison in 1840. In fact, Jackson's appeal to the people and his use of presidential power had a lasting effect on American politics and the balance of power between President and Congress.

In the midst of governmental maneuvering between the 1820s and 1850s, several social reform movements grew in influence. Advocates of revival religion, utopian communities, public education, care of the mentally ill, and women's rights worked to promote their causes. No issue created more passionate feelings than slavery, however. As proslavery forces struggled to protect their economic and political interests, the Abolitionist movement gained momentum.

Activity Objectives

After completing the activities, students should be able to

- compare the viewpoints of states' rights advocates and national unity advocates in the early 1800s.
- describe how Andrew Jackson redefined the role of the President.
- compare proposed methods to end slavery.
- identify the social reform movements that arose or expanded their influence during the first half of the 1800s.
- explain the effects of Jackson's Indian removal policies.

Introducing the Chapter

States' Rights vs. National Unity

This class activity requires half a period.

The purpose of this activity is to heighten students' awareness of issues pitting states' rights against national interest. The activity points out that the controversy surrounding states' rights not only dominated the political scene during the twenty-year time period covered in Chapter 9 but continues today.

Introduce the activity by asking students to analyze the Pledge of Allegiance. Ask if they think the pledge speaks of the United States as a union or as a compact of independent states. Lead students in discussing their answers to the following questions:

- Do you think your community would be justified in passing a law that conflicted with the laws of your state?
- Do you think your state would be justified in passing a law that conflicted with a federal law?
- Would you rather have most of your tax dollars go to your community, your state, or the national government?

Conclude by challenging students to think about these questions as they read Chapter 9.

Teaching the Main Ideas

Section 9–1: Debating Tough Issues

This class activity requires two periods.

In this activity, students plan and hold a debate that will help them recognize the serious divisions that protective tariffs created between the North and West and the South.

Begin by briefly reviewing the information in Section 9–1 about protective tariffs and the doctrine of nullification. Emphasize that this issue created a major conflict between northern and southern legislators and began the movement toward southern secession. Tell students that they will participate in a mock senatorial debate on tariffs and nullification. They are to use information from the text to prepare for the debate, summarizing events and arguments that took place over a number of years.

Divide students into three groups—northerners, southerners, and westerners. Outline the debate format:

- First speaker presents the case for tariffs.
- Second speaker presents the case against tariffs.
- Each side presents up to five rebuttals.
- One speaker from each side delivers a final statement.

The same format is to be followed in debating the nullification doctrine. Every student should speak at least once during the two-part debate.

Point out that to represent regional perspectives the three regional groups will need to interact with each other to organize arguments for and against tariffs and nullification. Allow the remainder of the class period for groups to plan their strategies. Encourage them to include both intellectual and emotional arguments.

On the following day, begin the debate by having students, posing as senators, elect a president pro tempore to preside over the proceedings. End the debate about ten minutes before the end of the class period.

Bring the activity to closure by asking students to summarize intellectual and emotional highlights of the debate. Review the relevant text information from Section 9–1 and discuss how closely their debate paralleled events and arguments in the 1800s.

Teaching the Main Ideas

Section 9–2: Political Cartoons

This individual project may be assigned as homework.

This activity focuses on Andrew Jackson as President. Students create a cartoon to show how Jackson's presidency differed from that of his predecessors.

Have students browse through the text to find political cartoons featuring Presidents. You may also bring to class some present-day cartoons. Call attention to the use of labels, symbols, captions, and titles. Emphasize that a cartoon can use satire, stereotypes, and caricatures.

Suggest that Andrew Jackson was a good subject for cartoonists because he changed the role and image of the presidency. Have students describe, as you list on the chalkboard, some of the ways in which Jackson differed from his predecessors. Ask each student to create a political cartoon about an aspect of Jackson as President. Cartoons may be critical of Jackson or of his opponents.

Display students' completed cartoons. Encourage students to evaluate their effectiveness.

Reinforcement Activity

Section 9–3: A Less Than Perfect Society

This cooperative activity requires one class period.

This activity is designed to reinforce students' understanding that in the early and mid-1800s a number of social reform movements grew from insignificant to major influences in American life. To consider the impact and relationships of these movements, students create an organizational web.

Write the phrase "A Less Than Perfect Society" on the chalkboard. Ask students to review Section 9–3 in their texts. Discuss conditions in the early and mid-1800s that gave rise to reform movements.

Explain to students that their task is to create a graphic web to show the relationships between the various reform movements and their impacts on society. Explain that a graphic web is a way of organizing information visually. Illustrate a web by using the example below.

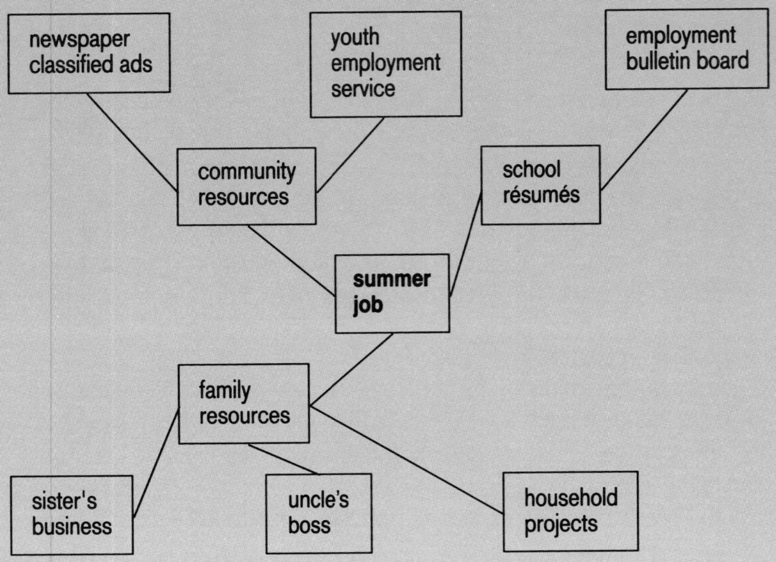

Divide the class into groups of three to prepare webs on poster paper. Encourage the groups to experiment with different visual "looks" for their webs but to make sure that they use specific information from the text and make their webs as complete and detailed as possible. Direct them to title their webs "A Less Than Perfect Society" and to keep the title in mind as they work.

Review the completed webs, making sure that all include religious revivals, utopias, free public education, care for the mentally ill, and women's rights.

Evaluating Progress

Section 9–4: "Mods" vs. "Rads"

This individual activity requires half a period of in-class introduction, but students can complete it out of class.

In this activity students reflect on Chapter 9 by analyzing different approaches to bringing about social change. Students summarize their reflections in position papers. Before class, write the following list on the chalkboard:

- Talk to slaveholders about the evils of slavery.
- Secretly teach slaves to read and write.
- Write pamphlets informing the public about the horrors of slavery.
- Organize a slave rebellion.
- Make speeches urging the abolition of slavery.
- Protect and hide escaped slaves.
- Sign petitions urging that slavery and the domestic slave trade be outlawed.
- Run for political office on an Abolitionist platform.
- Assassinate slaveholders.
- Campaign for an Abolitionist candidate.
- Give money to help the American Anti-Slavery Society.
- Organize committees to work for an end to slavery.

Ask students to imagine that it is 1830 and they have decided to take a stand against slavery. Call their attention to the twelve tactics listed on the chalkboard. Ask students to rank order the tactics in which they would engage, from 1 for most likely to 12 for least likely. When students finish, ask them to study their rankings and decide whether their personal approach tends to be more moderate (favoring slow, nonviolent change) or radical (favoring rapid change, even if it means violence).

Assign students to write position papers on the following topic: *Are radical or moderate tactics the most effective way to end slavery?* On the chalkboard write the format for their papers as follows:

- State the question.
- Summarize the arguments for and against both moderate and radical tactics.
- Discuss the strengths and weaknesses of arguments on both sides.
- State your personal answer to the question.
- Support your answer with arguments and evidence.

Evaluate student papers on aptness and specificity of examples. Expect the following points to be included.

Moderate position: advocates gradual change and cautious political action; tries not to alienate the South and risk secession.
Radical position: advocates an immediate end to slavery; sees change forced by the people because Congress is reluctant to act; accepts the possibility of violence in the interest of quick end to slavery.

Enrichment Activity

Section 9–1: A Tragedy Told in the Oral Tradition

This individual activity may be assigned as homework, with class time set aside for students to present their projects.

In this individual activity students use the Native American oral tradition to retell text information about the removal of Native Americans from their homelands during the Jacksonian era.

Introduce the activity by explaining that every culture transmits essential knowledge about its history, values, and traditions from one generation to the next. Point out that in Native-American culture, this knowledge has been transmitted orally through stories, legends, and songs. This oral tradition has handed down knowledge of survival techniques, tribal history, key beliefs, and details of sacred ceremonies. If you have examples of Native-American oral tradition, share them with the class.

Remind students that in Section 9–1 they read the tragic history of Native Americans forcibly removed from their homelands and moved to new, unfamiliar locations. Challenge students to review the text information and think about what events and feelings they would have wanted to pass along to future generations. Then ask them to prepare a story to be told in oral tradition form. Stories must include descriptions of life before, during, and after removal. Clarify that stories should be grounded in historical fact, but encourage students to make them more compelling with invented detail.

When assignments are complete, have students form groups of four to listen to each other's stories. Let each group select one story to present to the class.

Bibliography and Audiovisual Material

Teacher Bibliography

Hofstadter, Richard. *The American Political Tradition and the Men Who Made It.* New York: Alfred A. Knopf, 1973.

Tyler, Alice Felt. *Freedom's Ferment.* New York: Harper-Collins, 1962.

Walker, David and Henry Garnet. *Walker's Appeal & Garnets Address to the Slaves of the United States of America.* Reprint. Salem, N.H. Ayer & Co. 1969.

Walters, Ronald G. *American Reformers, 1815–1860.* New York: Hill & Wang, 1978.

Student Bibliography

Blos, Joan W.A. *A Gathering of Days: A New England Girl's Journal, 1830–32.* New York: Scribner, 1979.

Melville, Herman. *Moby Dick.* New York: Random House, 1991.

Thoreau, Henry David. *Walden.* Random House, 1991.

Films, Videocassettes, and Videodiscs

Black People in the Slave South. 11 min. EBEC. Movie.

Jacksonian Democracy. 39 min. EAV. Videocassette.

The Life of Sojourner Truth: Ain't I a Woman? 26 min. Coronet/MTI. Videodisc.

Filmstrips

Andrew Jackson: The People's President. Westport Media.

Andrew Jackson: Spirit of a New Democracy. Guidance Associates.

Chapter 9

Objectives

- Explain why some groups benefited from the democratic reforms in the Jackson era and others did not.
- Discuss how Jackson's war on the Bank of the United States reflected his view of democracy.
- Explain how religious revivals fueled reform movements in the attempt to improve society.
- Describe how the anti-slavery movement grew in the 1800s.

Introducing THE CHAPTER

For suggestions on introducing the chapter, refer to page 219B in the Teacher's Edition.

Developing THE CHAPTER

For activities and teaching strategies to help you reinforce and enrich chapter content, see pages 219B–219D in the Teacher's Edition.

B · A · C · K · G · R · O · U · N · D

Chapter Opener Illustrations
President-elect Jackson on the way to his inauguration. This print shows Jackson's immense popularity.

Robert Lindneux painted "The Trail of Tears" about a hundred years after the journey. In autumn of 1838, over 15,000 Cherokees started their forced march westward to Oklahoma, most of them on foot.

This almanac, one of the many anti-slavery publications of the time, attacks a fugitive slave law mandating the return of escaped slaves.

Reduced student page in the Teacher's Edition

Chapter 9 1828-1850

Conflict and Reform

The Shakers were founded about 1772 in Manchester, England, by Ann Lee. "Mother" Ann and eight followers emigrated to New York in 1774, and as their numbers grew, the Shakers formed communities. While formally known as the United Society of Believers in Christ's Second Appearing, community members were called Shakers because they shook with emotion during religious services.

A hornbook was a kind of textbook. A lesson was written on a piece of paper or parchment and attached to a wooden paddle, then covered with a transparent sheet of horn to protect the lesson. This hornbook was used to teach reading.

American Voices

In March, 1829, Andrew Jackson, nicknamed Old Hickory, was inaugurated President of the United States. After his speech at the Capitol building, Jackson mounted a white horse and rode to the White House, followed by a cheering mob of some 20,000 people. Margaret Bayard Smith described the tumultuous events at the reception:

> *"Country men, farmers, gentlemen, mounted and dismounted, boys, women and children, black and white. Carriages, wagons, carts all pursuing him to the President's house. . . . The President, after having been literally nearly pressed to death and almost suffocated and torn to pieces by people in their eagerness to shake hands with Old Hickory, had retreated through the back way. . . . Cut glass and china in the amount of several thousand dollars had been broken in the struggle to get the refreshments. . . . Ladies fainted, men were seen with bloody noses, and such a scene of confusion took place as is impossible to describe. Those who got in could not get out by the door again but had to scramble out of windows. . . . But it was the People's day, and the People's President, and the People would rule."*

Andrew Jackson represented the interests of ordinary people, whether northeastern city workers or western farmers. His followers had rowdy manners and a rambunctious approach to politics. They wanted national government that was fearlessly powerful in the face of the rich manufacturers, bankers, and plantation owners. Andrew Jackson shared their attitudes. The common people could depend on him to act in their interests as President of the United States.

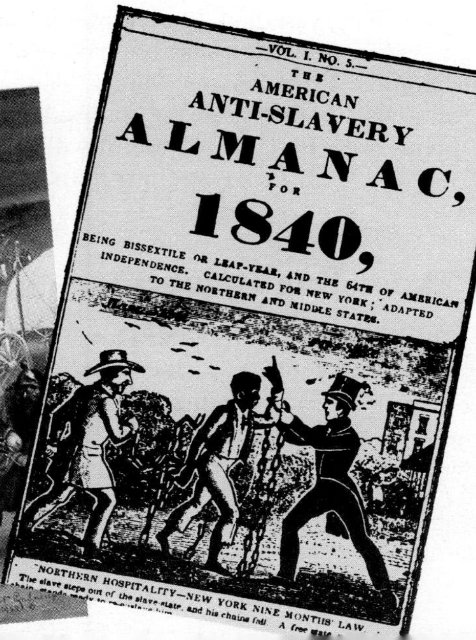

Andrew Jackson heading for his inauguration in 1829; "Trail of Tears," the forced migration of the Cherokees; abolitionist pamphlet; a Shaker community worshipping through dance; a sturdy wood "schoolbook."

Analyzing Primary Sources

American Voices

To the wealthy Eastern establishment, Andrew Jackson's arrival in Washington must have indeed looked like the invasion of a barbarian horde. Ask students:

1. What attitude does Margaret Bayard Smith have toward the events she is recording? To which social class does she probably belong? **(She was probably upper class.)**

2. Contrast this White House scene with the description of President Washington's way of life, evident in the illustration and caption on text page 162. How was Jackson's presidency likely to be different from Washington's? **(Jackson was likely to be less formal, not as devoted to ceremony; more likely to have favorable attitude toward the concerns of the "common man," especially westerners.)**

3. Have students review Margaret Bayard Smith's description of Jefferson's inauguration on page 189. In light of that description, what might have troubled her about Jackson's inauguration? **(She seems to have viewed the orderly transition of power to Jefferson as a sign that American democracy was more stable than other forms of government. Therefore, she was probably disturbed by the unruly celebration of Jackson's victory.)**

Section 9-1

Objectives

- ***Answer the Focus Question.***
- *Describe American Indian responses to the threat of forced migration.*
- *Discuss how different regions of the nation reacted to protective tariffs.*
- *Explain how the nullification crisis was settled.*

Introducing

THE SECTION

Have students consider what the concept of democracy meant in the United States of Jackson's day. Who was able to vote? **(white, male landowners)**

Ask students where in the country new states were likely to be formed. **(the West)** Were settlers in new states likely to be wealthy? Why or why not? **(No; they were usually poor people looking for opportunities, not the well-to-do and already established.)** Students will read more about western settlement in Chapter 10.

Finally, ask students to speculate about voting opportunities in the new western states. **(More white males might be eligible to vote because they now owned property.)** Who still could not vote? **(African Americans, Native Americans, and women)**

B · A · C · K · G · R · O · U · N · D

Time Line Illustrations

1. A wooden statue of Andrew Jackson made in 1834 for the ship *Constitution.*

2. A Whig flag emphasizing the log-cabin origin of their candidate William Henry "O.K." Harrison.

3. "Black Hawk and His Son, Whirling Thunder," shows the Sac chief, right, and his son, left. John Jarvis painted the portrait in 1833, while Black Hawk was a prisoner.

4. Angelina Grimké and her sister Sarah were reformers who wrote in favor of rights for women and the abolition of

Reduced student page in the Teacher's Edition

CHAPTER TIME LINE

1828 - 1850

1828 | 1832 | 1836

1828 "Tariff of Abominations"
Jackson elected President

1830 Indian Removal Act

1832 Jackson vetoes recharter of Bank of the United States
Black Hawk War

1833 American Anti-Slavery Society founded

1834 Whig party formed

1836 Proslavery "gag rule" passed in Congress

9-1 *The Era of Andrew Jackson*

Focus: What groups benefited most and benefited least from the spirit of democracy in the Jackson era?

In spite of the overwhelming excitement surrounding Andrew Jackson's election, not everyone was thrilled about the new President. Some feared the "reign of 'King Mob.' " Jackson's lack of formal education concerned public officials. John Quincy Adams called Jackson "a barbarian and savage who could scarcely spell his own name." Raised in the backwoods of the Carolinas, Jackson went to work in a law office at age seventeen. Even with the reputation of "the most roaring, rollicking, game-cocking, horse-racing, card-playing, mischievous fellow," he was made a lawyer at twenty.

By the time Jackson reached thirty he had also been a farmer, land speculator, merchant, war hero, and the first congressman elected from the state of Tennessee. Established political leaders did not know what to expect from this western President. The West had been growing rapidly. With Jackson's election, it now had political power. "My opinion," wrote Senator Daniel Webster of Massachusetts, "is that when he comes, he will bring a breeze with him. Which way it will blow I cannot tell. . . . My *fear* is stronger than my *hope.*"

Expanding Democracy

The breeze that worried Webster was the expanding spirit of democracy—the same breeze that had swept Jackson into office. Part of this change was the expansion of **suffrage**, or the right to vote. By slavery. They were criticized for stepping out of "woman's proper sphere."

5. Frederick Augustus Washington Bailey, who escaped slavery, changed his name to Frederick Douglass to avoid capture. Douglass lectured and wrote against slavery.

6. Actress Frances Kemble wore pantaloons in the United States in 1849. Two years later, the editor of a temperance journal, Amelia Bloomer, published an editorial on women's dress reform. Her name became synonymous with the garment she endorsed—bloomers.

1838 Trail of Tears

Angelina Grimké speaks on abolition

1848 Convention on women's rights at Seneca Falls

1840 1844 1848

1835-42 Second Seminole War

1844 "Gag rule" repealed

1847 Frederick Douglass founds *North Star*

1824 many states no longer had property restrictions, and all white adult males could vote. The total number of popular votes increased from 356,038 in 1824 to 1,155,350 in 1828, an increase that was a crucial factor in Jackson's election.

In addition to changes in suffrage, the process of elections was now more democratic. Until this time, state legislatures usually chose the electors who would vote for President. But by 1828 electors in all but two states were chosen by the voters.

Furthermore, since Jefferson's time, presidential candidates had been chosen by congressional leaders at a private party meeting called a **caucus**. In the 1820s voters condemned "King Caucus" as giving too much power to a select few. By 1832 party delegates were meeting in open national conventions to nominate candidates for President and Vice-President. Each party adopted a **platform**, or statement of their beliefs, to lure voters. Political power was being gradually pried from the hands of the few and spread out to the many.

By today's standards, those with the power of the vote were still a limited group. No states allowed women, American Indians, or slaves to vote, and only a few gave suffrage to free African Americans. As the breeze of democracy grew stronger, many Americans would awaken to these inequalities.

The Spoils System

Jackson used the executive office as no other President had. Defying tradition, he rarely met with his cabinet. Instead, he relied on unofficial advisors, whom his critics called the "Kitchen Cabinet."

Meanwhile, the new President removed about 10 percent of all officeholders and filled their jobs with his supporters, a practice his critics dubbed the **spoils system** after a supporter declared, "To the victor belong the spoils of the enemy." Jackson defended the spoils system as "rotation in office," and said:

> *"The duties of all public offices are . . . so plain and simple that men of intelligence may readily qualify themselves for their performance, and I cannot but believe that more is lost by the long continuance of men in office than is generally to be gained by their experience."*

Developing

THE SECTION

Connections: Politics

Discussion. The expansion of voting rights increased popular interest in politics. Campaigns also became more interesting with the use of slogans, songs, and posters. Ask students why they think elections held such popular appeal.

Linking Past and Present

Discussion. Ask students whether they feel that Jackson's faith in the ordinary person's ability to perform the duties of any public office was justified in the 1830s. How might the situation be different today? What might be the advantages and disadvantages of replacing many officeholders after the election of a new President?

GTV Side 2

Chap. 6, Frame 18450

The Advancing Frontier: The Near West (Movie)

Search:

Play:

Analyzing Primary Sources

Jackson on Indian "Removal." Have students discuss Jackson's statement on Indian "removal" by answering the following questions: What does language such as "relieve . . . of Indian occupancy" and "savage habits" suggest about Jackson's attitude toward Native Americans? What economic benefits did Jackson see states gaining from forcing Indians to relocate?

Writing about History

Newspaper Article. Have students imagine that they are working with Sequoyah on the first newspaper produced by American Indians. It is 1830, and President Jackson has ordered the relocation of all Indians living east of the Mississippi. Have students write one or more of the following: a news story written by a Native-American who witnessed the debates in Washington over Indian relocation; an editorial urging Native Americans either to resist or go along with the relocation; an open letter to President Jackson protesting the relocation policy.

Connections: Politics

During the nineteenth century, about 60 percent of congressional activities were devoted to Native-American issues.

Multicultural Perspectives

Ironically, the tribes being pushed out of the Southeast were called the "Five Civilized Tribes" because they had adopted many of the European-American ways of life and had already achieved much of what Jackson claimed would be the benefits to them of relocation. There remains today a large Cherokee reservation in North Carolina.

Reduced student page in the Teacher's Edition

The Indian Removal Act

Jackson's democratic intentions did not apply in his policy toward American Indians. The admission of new states and territories was bringing Indian lands within national boundaries. Westerners agitated for the speedy removal of tribes from the areas they wished to settle. Traditionally the government had dealt with the tribes as independent nations. Jackson, however, shared the westerners' view that negotiating with Indian tribes as nations was an "absurdity" and a "farce."

In 1830 Jackson took steps to satisfy his western supporters. In spite of some protest from northerners, Congress passed Jackson's Indian Removal Act in May, giving the President power to move Native Americans to land west of the Mississippi River. Jackson said:

"The consequences of a speedy removal will be important to the United States, to individual states, and to the Indians themselves. . . . [It will] perhaps cause [Indian tribes] gradually, under protection of the government and through the influence of good counsels, to cast off their savage habits and become an interesting, civilized, and Christian community."

In fact, several Indian tribes in the Southeast had decided that survival required adopting certain ways of white Americans. Surrounded by white settlers, five tribes—the Cherokees, Creeks, Choctaws, Chickasaws, and Seminoles—settled down on their ancestral lands, living in towns or on farms. Some even acquired cotton plantations and slaves. Many of them converted to Christianity and set up schools and churches. The Cherokee chief, Sequoyah, developed an alphabet so his tribe could write down and preserve its history.

But even adopting these ways did not protect Indian land. In spite of Jackson's talk of "civilizing," the truth was simple—white settlers still wanted the tribes' lands. The Indian Removal Act was used as a justification for taking the Native American lands they wanted. In 1834 Congress set up a special Indian territory west of the Mississippi in what is now Oklahoma.

Forced Migration and Resistance

Throughout the 1830s, Jackson's administration required Indian tribes to sign treaties ceding, or giving up, their lands. In the winter of 1831 the first forced migration—of the Choctaws—began. Private contractors hired by the government to supervise the trek ignored Indian needs. The Choctaws made the journey without warm clothing in freezing temperatures and heavy snows. Hundreds died of pneumonia and cholera. Alexis de Tocqueville, a French visitor, made this observation:

"It was then the middle of winter, and the cold was unusually severe; the snow had frozen hard . . . and the river was drifting huge masses of ice. . . . I saw them embark to pass the mighty river, and never will that solemn spectacle fade away from my remembrance. No cry, no sob, was heard among the assembled crowd; all were silent."

Indian resistance. Many Indians resisted removal. The Cherokees attempted a defense on legal grounds, claiming that earlier treaties with the federal government protected them. They had written a constitution in 1828, setting up an independent Cherokee nation within Georgia, but Georgia refused to recognize the Cherokee nation.

When missionaries defended Cherokee rights, they were arrested. The case of one was appealed to the Supreme Court. In *Worcester* v. *Georgia*, the Court upheld the Cherokee land claim and declared that Georgia law did not govern the Cherokee nation. Jackson is said to have commented, "[Chief Justice] John Marshall has made his decision, now let him enforce it." With no place left to appeal, the Cherokees ceded their eastern lands to the United States in 1835.

General Winfield Scott, in charge of the Cherokee removal, asked the troops to be kind, but they rarely were. One soldier wrote, "I saw the helpless Cherokee arrested and dragged from their homes. In the chill of a drizzling rain, I saw them loaded like cattle or sheep on 645 wagons." Nearly one fourth of the tribe died on the trail. The journey became known as the "Trail of Tears."

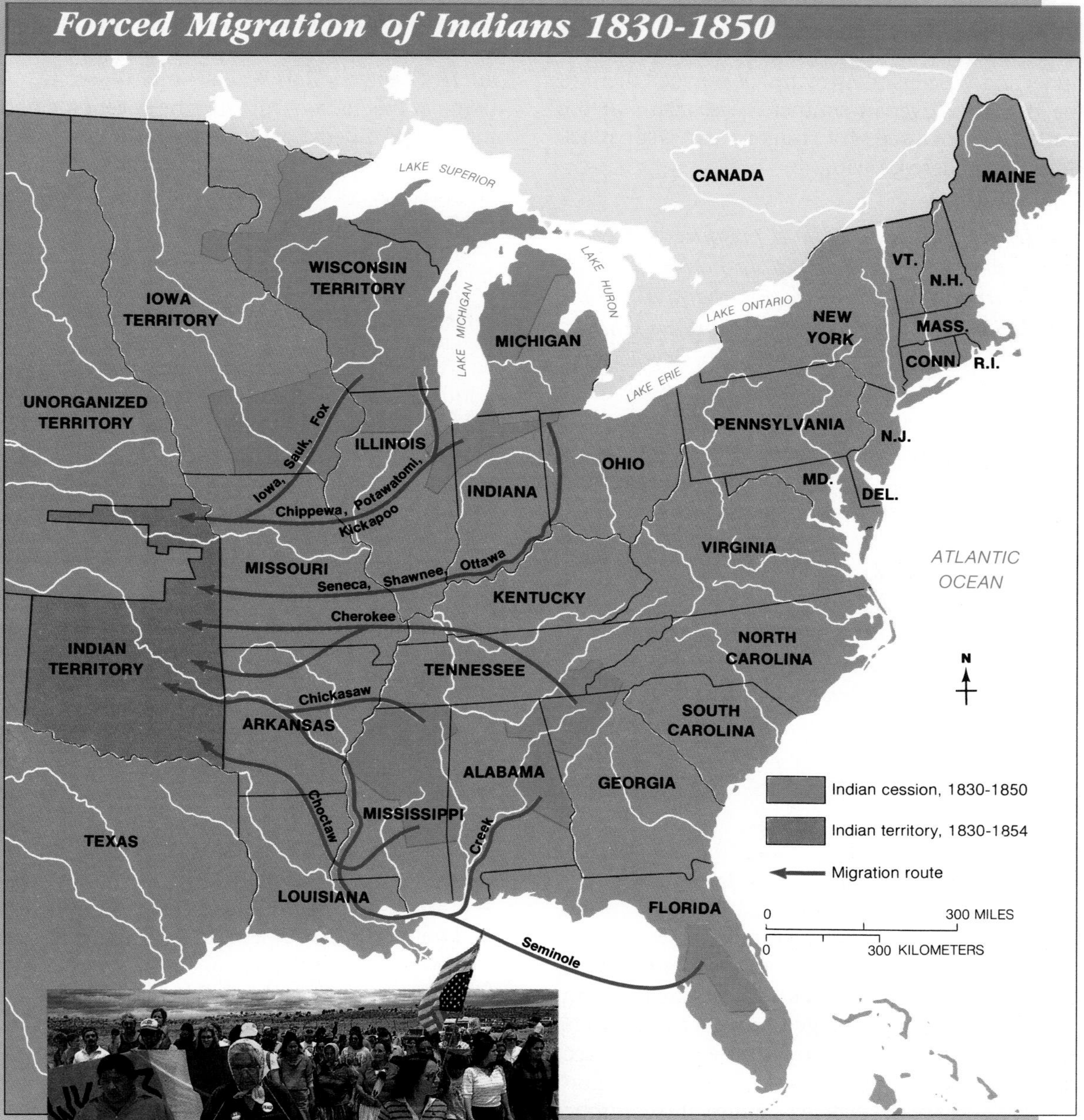

A 1986 Navajo protest shows that forced migration is still an issue.

Geography Skills—Movement. In the forced marches shown here, which people made the longest trek? Estimate the length of their journey. If you were to walk that far from your present location, what cities could you reach?

Analyzing Primary Sources

Cherokee Constitution. The Constitution begins:

“We, the Representatives of the people of the Cherokee Nation, in convention assembled, in order to establish justice, ensure tranquility, promote our common welfare, and secure to ourselves and our posterity the blessings of liberty . . . .”

Ask: How does this language compare with the Preamble to the Constitution of the United States? **(very similar in structure and vocabulary)**

Geography Skills

ANSWERS

Seminoles; approximately 1,100 miles; answers will vary.

GTV Side 2

Chap. 8, Frame 24207

Native American Population: 1800 and 1840 (Population Clocks, 2 Frames)

Search:

Step:

Multicultural Perspectives

Often traders would find a Native American who, in exchange for money, whiskey, and/or guns, was willing to sign a paper selling tribal land. In response, the Cherokee Nation made it an offense, punishable by death, for an individual to sell land belonging to the whole people. Many Native Americans thought they were simply allowing the whites use of the land. As Black Hawk recalled: *"I touched the goose quill to the treaty, not knowing, however, that by that act I had consented to give away my village."*

Thinking Critically

Evaluation. The use of tariffs to protect American industry from foreign competition remains a controversial issue today. Suppose, for example, that American car manufacturers feel that Japanese companies have an unfair advantage. They might propose that Congress enact a tariff raising the prices of Japanese cars.

Ask: Who would be likely to favor such protectionism? (auto workers, car companies) Who would likely oppose it? (consumer groups, foreign companies) Do you think tariffs are a good thing? Why or why not?

Reduced student page in the Teacher's Edition

As the government broke treaty after treaty and forced tribes westward, some Indians turned to armed resistance. In 1832 a group of Sac and Fox, led by Black Hawk, tried to regain their lands in Illinois and Wisconsin. Army troops pursued them to the Bad Axe River in southern Wisconsin. In the battle that followed, few Indians survived. Black Hawk surrendered, saying:

> *"[Black Hawk] is now a prisoner to the white men. . . . He has done nothing for which an Indian ought to be ashamed. He has fought for his countrymen, the squaws and papooses, against white men, who came year after year, to cheat them and take away their lands. You know the cause of our making war. It is known to all white men. They ought to be ashamed of it. Indians are not deceitful. The white men speak bad of the Indian and look at him spitefully. But the Indian does not tell lies. Indians do not steal.*
>
> *An Indian who is as bad as the white men could not live in our nation; he would be put to death, and eaten up by the wolves. . . . The white men do not scalp the head; but they do worse—they poison the heart. . . . Farewell, my nation! . . . Farewell to Black Hawk."*

Following the Black Hawk War, the Sac and Fox tribes were forced to cede eastern Iowa.

In Florida the Seminoles, led by Chief Osceola (os-ee-O-lah) and joined by escaped slaves, refused to move west and retreated into the swamps of the Everglades in 1835. Osceola was captured by army troops in 1837, but the fierce struggle continued for five years. In the end, many Seminoles were forced to surrender and were moved to Indian Territory. Hundreds, however, avoided capture and continued to live in the swamps, or Everglades.

By the early 1840s the Indian removal had been completed. Over 100,000 American Indians had been forced to migrate. The tribes were promised that the western lands would be theirs "as long as the grass grows, or water runs." But even as the Indians were getting settled on their new lands, pioneers were crossing the Mississippi.

The treatment of the American Indians by Jackson and Congress was condemned by Christian groups such as Quakers and Methodists. Individuals, especially in the Northeast, also protested. In an 1838 letter Ralph Waldo Emerson wrote, "The name of this nation, hitherto the sweet omen of religion and liberty, will stink to the world." But such criticism was not widespread. Meanwhile, other issues were drawing national attention—issues that threatened the country's unity.

The Tariff of Abominations

In 1827 an angry crowd gathered in Columbia, South Carolina. One speaker raised the question that burned in everyone's mind. "Is it worth our while," he asked, "to continue this Union of States, where the North demands to be our masters and we are required to be their tributaries?"

The issue was the protective tariffs that the government had placed on imported goods—each one driving a deeper wedge between the industrial North and the agricultural South. The tariffs were designed to protect American industry from British competition. The North, where most industry was located, clamored for such protection. Westerners hoped that with revenue from tariffs the nation could build roads out west. With the support of the western states, northerners in Congress had managed to drive the measure home.

Southern states had not developed as much industry as some had hoped, but remained dependent on cotton. Southerners sold cotton to Britain and bought British manufactured goods in return. However, when a depression hit in 1819, demand for cotton plummeted, as did cotton prices. Then, when tariffs raised the price of certain imported goods by as much as thirty-seven cents on the dollar, the South faced economic disaster.

Southerners argued that the tariffs protected the North at the expense of the South. The Constitution, they declared, provided no authority for such favoritism. When the Tariff of 1828 raised duties to an all-time high of forty-five cents per dollar, cotton states angrily labeled it the "Tariff of Abominations." Georgia, Mississippi, Virginia, and South Carolina passed resolutions attacking the tariff as "unconstitutional, oppressive, and unjust."

But even when treaties were honestly understood and negotiated with Native-American leaders, it hardly mattered; the pressure of white settlers led to renewed demands year after year.

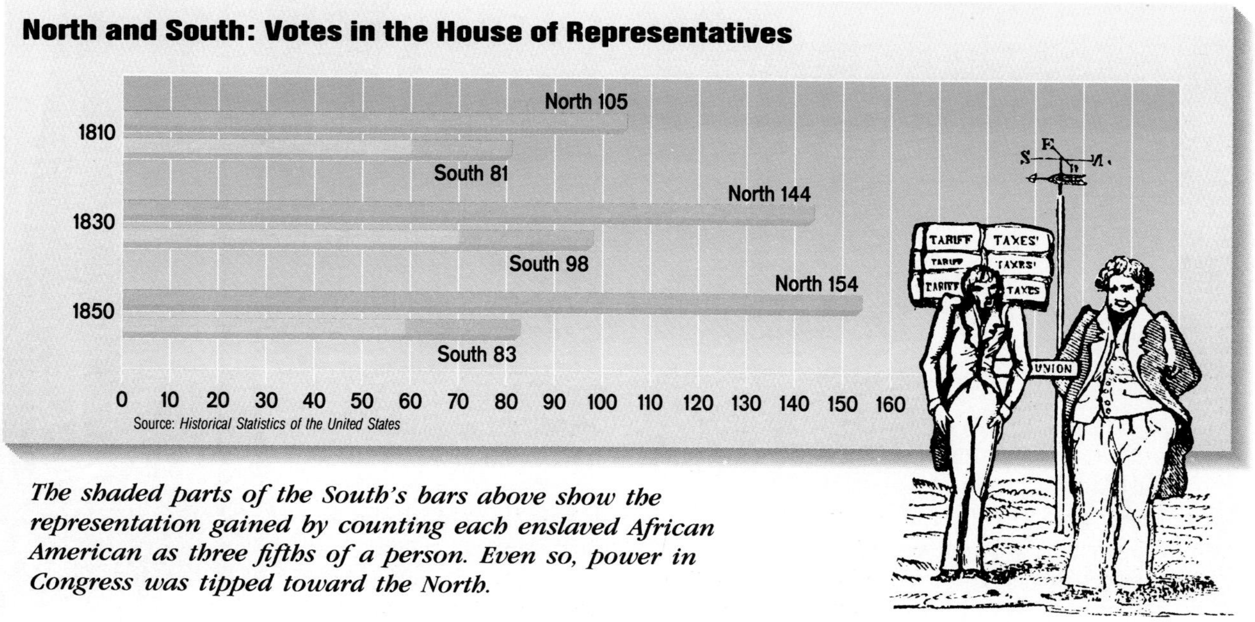

The shaded parts of the South's bars above show the representation gained by counting each enslaved African American as three fifths of a person. Even so, power in Congress was tipped toward the North.

Calhoun's Doctrine of Nullification

Vice-President John C. Calhoun of South Carolina was caught in the middle of the conflict. He had supported the first tariff, with hopes that southern industry would develop. Seeing his hopes dashed, Calhoun sought a peaceful solution. The answer that came to him was nullification.

Calhoun secretly penned a report, the "South Carolina Exposition and Protest," an argument for states' rights. Echoing the Kentucky and Virginia Resolutions of 1798, it asserted that the Union was a compact of independent states. If a state legislature judged an act of Congress unconstitutional, it had the right to nullify, or refuse to enforce, the act. The national government must then withdraw its act, unless three fourths of the states amended the Constitution to grant it such power.

Webster Defends the Union

The issue came to a head in January 1830. For six days, Daniel Webster, a strong nationalist from Massachusetts, and Robert Hayne of South Carolina debated in the Senate the powers of state and federal governments. Hayne's views were: Liberty first, Union afterwards. Webster summarized his view with the words, "Liberty and Union, now and forever, one and inseparable!"

President Jackson, a cotton planter himself, had said little about either the tariff issue or South Carolina's protest. At a dinner commemorating Jefferson's birthday, southerners forced the issue with the President. After many toasts to states' rights, Jackson was called upon. He stood, looked directly at Calhoun, and said, "Our federal Union. It must be preserved." Calhoun raised his glass and replied: "The Union. Next to our liberty, most dear. May we always remember that it can only be preserved by distributing equally the benefits and burdens of the Union." With this exchange, the political ties between Jackson and Calhoun were irreparably damaged.

The Nullification Crisis

Calhoun had hoped to run for President. Instead, with the rift between him and Jackson out in the open, he became the leading spokesman for the doctrine of nullification. Meanwhile, Jackson called for a revision of the tariff. In July 1832 Congress passed a new, lower tariff, which Jackson signed, sure that it would end southern discontent.

Limited English Proficiency

Analyzing a Bar Graph. Refer students to the graph on this page. Ask what the bars represent, and why some of the bars are in two colors. What does the dark orange in the bars representing the South show? **(representation in Congress based on counting an enslaved African American as three fifths of a person)** Which region would get the most votes in Congress if an issue divided representatives along North-South lines? **(the North)**

Active Learning

Preparing Arguments. Have students prepare index card summaries of the arguments used by Hayne and Webster in their famous debate. Each card can give one argument for or against states' rights, a possible objection, and an answer to the objection.

Example: *Anti-states' rights:* The Union cannot survive if any state can overturn any federal law. *Objection:* What happens if one part of the country is being hurt to benefit another? *Reply:* If the federal action is really unconstitutional, the Supreme Court can overturn it. If not, democracy requires obeying the will of the majority.

Connections: Politics

The passage of the Alien and Sedition Acts in 1798 (see page 174) had led to a confrontation between state and federal power. The Kentucky and Virginia resolutions asserted that if the federal government went beyond the powers specifically given to it in the Constitution, the states had the power to declare laws to be unconstitutional. The eventual repeal of the Alien and Sedition Acts made the issue dormant.

Exploring Issues

STATES' RIGHTS

The Great Debate

On January 19, 1830, Robert Y. Hayne of South Carolina, one of the ablest debaters in the Senate, rose to speak on the sale of public lands on the frontier. Then, almost as an aside, he went on to condemn the growth of federal power. "I . . . believe the very life of our system is the independence of the states," he declared. "I am opposed, therefore, in any shape, to all unnecessary extension of the power or the influence . . . of the Union over the states."

As Hayne spoke, Senator Daniel Webster of Massachusetts strolled through the Senate chamber. Alarmed by Hayne's words, he stopped to listen. The next day Webster took the floor to answer Hayne. It was the beginning of one of the most famous debates in Senate history.

The question of states' rights—whether the states or the federal government had final authority—was not new. It had arisen with opposition to the Sedition Act of 1798 and with opposition to the War of 1812. Now, in 1830, the southern states opposed a tariff but were forced to obey.

Webster began his answer to Hayne by discussing the issue of public lands, but then skillfully changed the subject. The real question, he said, was the fate of the Union. To him, the Union was "essential to the prosperity and safety of the States." Hayne's questions had bothered him. Did Hayne think the Union was to exist only "while it suits local and temporary purposes to preserve it; and to be sundered whenever it shall be found to thwart such purposes?"

Robert Hayne (top)
Daniel Webster

Over the next few days, Hayne responded in several brilliant speeches. If northern members of Congress valued the Union so much, he asked Webster, why had they passed a tariff that had brought "ruin and devastation" to the South? If this was the spirit of the government, he warned, "the seeds of dissolution are already sown, and our children will reap the bitter fruit."

To Hayne, the Union was a compact among independent states. Each state remained sovereign and could nullify any law it saw as violating its constitutional rights. To allow the federal government to interpret its own laws would be to allow tyranny.

As Hayne spoke, Webster sat nearby taking careful notes. The next day, impressive in a blue swallow-tailed coat with

Exploring Issues

ANSWERS

1. Hayne viewed Union as a compact among independent states in which each state could interpret the Constitution and set aside any national law that violated its rights. Webster believed United States was a federal union whose authority was the people, not the states.
2. Students may consider issue of minority rights or results of disobedience of federal laws.
3. Students may suggest environmental regulation, school funding, welfare administration, and management of public lands and natural resources.

The lower tariff, however, did not satisfy the people of South Carolina. Protest meetings shook the state. A convention called in November quickly adopted an ordinance, or a law, of nullification, declaring the tariffs of 1828 and 1832 null and void. The ordinance also declared that South Carolina would secede from the Union if the federal government forced it to collect the duties. To back the ordinance, the legislature voted money to buy arms and called for volunteers to fight.

Connections: Economics

John C. Calhoun's advocacy of states' rights can be traced back to 1811, when, as a first-term member of the House of Representatives, he described the Senate as "a diplomatic corps . . . sent here to protect states' rights." In his early career he supported the National Bank and a protective tariff as being good for the national economy. By the time he became Vice President in 1824, he had become concerned with what he saw to be the declining economic power of the South in the face of the North's growing industrial power. He now saw the tariff as helping northern industry at the expense of southern agriculture.

brass buttons, Webster began his famous reply. Steadily, hour after hour, he built his case. The great question, he said, was who had the right "to decide on the constitutionality or unconstitutionality of the laws." If each state could accept or reject federal laws as it pleased, the result would be chaos. The Union would fall apart like "a rope of sand."

The United States, Webster declared, was not a group of independent states but a federal union whose real authority was the people. "It is, sir, the people's constitution, the people's Government; made for the people; made by the people; and answerable to the people." If each state demanded sovereignty, the nation would be "rent with civil feuds, or drenched in blood." Webster ended his speech with a moving tribute to the Union: "Liberty *and* Union, now and forever, one and inseparable!"

In the years ahead, countless speakers quoted Webster. Thousands of schoolchildren, including a lanky frontier lad named Abraham Lincoln, memorized his final words. But the question of who had the final power, the federal government or the states, was far from settled.

1. How did Hayne view the relationship between the federal government and the states? How did Webster's view differ?
2. Do you think a state should have the right to disobey a federal law? Explain.
3. What are some of the issues today that involve state versus federal power? How do you think they should be decided?

Jackson, outraged, threatened to "hang every leader . . . of that infatuated people." Still, he moved cautiously. He asked Congress to reduce the tariff again. He also called on the people of South Carolina to reject nullification. "Disunion by armed force is treason," he warned. Then he alerted the armed forces.

In December 1832 Calhoun, having been elected a senator from South Carolina, resigned from the vice-presidency. Soon after, Jackson asked Congress to pass the Force Act giving him the power to use the armed forces to collect duties.

Henry Clay broke the deadlock. He proposed a compromise tariff that reduced the duties to a uniform 20 percent over the next ten years. Calhoun, torn between loyalty to his native state and to his beloved Union, readily accepted. Jackson, too, preferred this peaceful solution.

In early March, Congress passed the Tariff of 1833 as well as the Force Act, which Jackson had still demanded. South Carolina accepted the new tariff, but furiously nullified the Force Act. Slowly, though, cries for secession died out. Calhoun, exhausted, went home to his plantation to recover and to try to pacify South Carolina extremists. He feared, however, that "the struggle, so far from being over," had just begun.

Section Review

1. Identification. Define the terms *suffrage, caucus, platform*, and *spoils system.*

2. Comprehension. In what ways did the political process grow more responsive to a greater number of people in the 1820s and 1830s? What were some limits to participation?

3. Analysis. What were two American Indian responses to the threat of removal, and what effect did those responses have?

4. Analysis. How did the tariffs of 1816, 1824, and 1828 lead Calhoun to propose nullification?

5. Evaluation. What was Henry Clay's solution to the nullification crisis? Why did it work?

Linking Past and Present. Form a group and research recent protective tariffs on foreign goods. What countries have been affected? Why? Do you think tariffs are a good thing? Explain.

Data Search. Look at the graph on page 227. How might the South have used the figures for the years 1810 and 1830 in an argument against tariffs? How might the North have responded?

Section Review

ANSWERS

1. Definitions for the following terms are on text pages indicated in parentheses: *suffrage* (222), *caucus* (223), *platform* (223), *spoils system* (223).
2. Suffrage expanded greatly. By 1828 presidential electors were chosen directly by voters in almost all states. Rotation in office opened public office to more people. Women, Native Americans, enslaved African Americans denied vote; most states denied vote to free African Americans.
3. Cherokees attempted legal defense. Supreme Court upheld, but Jackson would not enforce; they were forcibly removed from land. Sac and Fox under Black Hawk battled U.S.; badly defeated, lost lands.
4. Tariffs raised price of goods, which South had to buy. When price of cotton plummeted, South suffered. Calhoun felt federal government overstepped its Constitutional powers and southern states had right to nullify tariffs.
5. Clay proposed tariffs be reduced to uniform 20 percent over next ten years. Compromise offered Calhoun, torn between loyalty to state and nation, a way out.
Linking Past and Present Answers will vary.
Data Search. The figures show the North with a majority in Congress. Southerners could argue that high tariffs were voted in by a self-serving northern majority and were not the best course for the whole country. Northerners could counter that their policies reflected the desire of their constituents and since the North's population was larger than the South's, high tariffs were the will of the majority.

Section 9-2

Objectives

- ***Answer the Focus Question.***
- *Cite steps Jackson took to destroy the Bank of the United States.*
- *State the effects of opposition to Jackson's actions.*
- *Explain the events that led to the depression of 1837.*
- *Explain why the Whig party was formed.*

Introducing

THE SECTION

Review the basic operations of banks in the early United States. The federal government issued hard money (silver and gold coins) but not bank notes. The nation's paper money supply consisted of notes issued by dozens of different state-chartered banks. Each was a promise to pay a specified amount in hard money.

Most banks kept only a small amount of hard money. If an economic panic caused a run on a bank, many depositors could not be paid. The Bank of the United States helped maintain sound currency by exchanging the notes it received for hard money; its own notes were accepted as trustworthy.

But the Bank of the United States was also a formidable competitor with the state banks and aroused their opposition. The end of the Second U.S. Bank led to a boom in state banking that contributed to economic growth and westward expansion, but the problem of providing a sound currency remained.

9-2 *Jackson and the Bank*

Focus: How did Jackson's war on the Bank of the United States reflect his view of democracy?

During his first term, Andrew Jackson had fought a defiant South Carolina. Perhaps his most hard-fought battle, however, was the one that dominated much of his second term. Andrew Jackson was at war with the Bank of the United States.

The bank was the brainchild of Alexander Hamilton. First chartered in 1791, it existed until 1811. Later, in 1816, the bank was given a second charter, to run for twenty years. But when the Panic of 1819 hit, many people, especially debtors, blamed the bank.

The majority of these debtors were westerners who had borrowed money to buy land and farm equipment or to start small businesses. Senator Thomas Hart Benton of Missouri, a leader of opposition to the bank, expressed their thoughts when he thundered:

> *“All the flourishing cities of the West are mortgaged to this money power. They may be devoured by it at any moment. They are in the jaws of the monster! A lump of butter in the mouth of a dog! One gulp, one swallow, and all is gone!”*

To its opponents, the Bank of the United States became known as "the Monster."

The Bank War

The Bank of the United States, which was controlled mainly by wealthy eastern investors, had great power. Since 1823 the financier Nicholas Biddle had run the bank as its president. The bank had maintained sound currency and spurred economic growth. Jackson, however, heard stories that the bank had interfered in state politics in the election of 1828. It had also lent money as a favor to influential people, including members of Congress. Furthermore, the government had appointed some of the bank's directors.

Jackson was convinced that the bank was the tool of the "rich and powerful." Like Jefferson, he feared the control of American wealth by a single class. Determined to protect democracy, Jackson decided to veto the recharter of the bank when its charter expired in 1836.

B · A · C · K · G · R · O · U · N · D

Multicultural Perspectives

The issue of slavery sometimes obscured the growing importance of free African Americans to American economic life. The Census of 1830 found that African Americans made up 18.1 percent of the total population. Of the total population of African Americans calculated in the census, 319,599, or 13.7 percent, were free. More than half of free African Americans lived in the South or in Washington, D.C.

By 1837 blacks in New York City owned $1.4 million worth of taxable real estate and had $600,000 deposited in savings banks. Free African Americans in Philadelphia owned smaller but still significant amounts.

Meanwhile Biddle's friends in Congress, Henry Clay and Daniel Webster, encouraged him to seek recharter of the bank in 1832—four years ahead of expiration. Webster was influenced by his financial interests in the bank. Clay planned to run against Jackson in the 1832 election and hoped that the bank issue would hurt Jackson's chances for reelection. Clay reasoned that if Jackson vetoed the recharter bill he would lose votes in the East.

Still, Jackson wasted no time in returning the bill to Congress with a stinging veto message. The Supreme Court had ruled, in *McCulloch* v. *Maryland*, that the bank was constitutional. Nevertheless, Jackson claimed that the bank was "unauthorized by the Constitution, subversive of the rights of the states, and dangerous to the liberties of the people."

Clay had miscalculated. Jackson's veto message appealed to voters. Running for the Democrats, as the Democratic Republicans were now called, Jackson carried 17 of the 25 states, receiving 219 electoral votes to Clay's 49. Jackson saw his reelection as a call from the people to destroy "the Monster."

In this 1836 cartoon, Andrew Jackson and allies battle the Bank of the United States, the "Many Headed Monster." The largest head is the bank's president.

> **American Voices**
>
> *"I have been for years in the daily exercise of more personal authority than any President habitually enjoys."*
>
> —Nicholas Biddle, president of the Bank of the United States

In a move to starve the Monster to death before the end of its charter, Jackson asked the Secretary of the Treasury to stop depositing the government's funds in the bank. When the Secretary opposed him, Jackson chose a new secretary. His new appointee also refused, and in 1833 Jackson replaced him with Roger B. Taney, who would do what Jackson wanted. Taney began depositing government funds in private, or "pet," banks in major cities.

In late 1833 and early 1834, Biddle fought back, reducing the bank's loans and tightening credit. He hoped the economic distress these moves caused would force Congress to recharter the bank. But Jackson held firm. The bank "is trying to kill me," he said, "but I will kill it." When its charter ran out in 1836, it was not renewed.

The Whigs Oppose Jackson

Jackson's critics claimed he misused presidential power, making and changing policy as he saw fit. In 1834 the National Republicans banded together to oppose him. Renaming themselves Whigs, they protested the actions of "King Andrew I," just as American Whigs had earlier opposed George III.

The Whigs attracted a wide variety of supporters: manufacturers, bankers and merchants, workers and conservative farmers in the North, and big planters in the South. It also included Democrats unhappy with Jackson's bank policy. The chief force binding the Whigs together was their distrust of Jackson.

The Whigs were unable to agree on a single candidate in the election of 1836, so they nominated three who had strong regional support in the West, the Northeast, and the South. They hoped to split the total vote, throwing the election into the House.

The Democrats nominated Jackson's choice for successor, Vice-President Martin Van Buren. Relying on Jackson's popularity, Van Buren pledged to "tread generally in the footsteps of President Jackson." He won, carrying fifteen of the twenty-six

Developing

THE SECTION

Thinking Critically

Application. Refer students to the Constitution to find where Congress is given the power to "coin money [and] regulate the value thereof" **(Article 1, Section 8, Clause 5)** and to "regulate commerce . . . among the several states" **(Article 1, Section 8, Clause 3).** Opponents of the national bank argued that the Bank was unconstitutional because Congress had only those specific powers mentioned in the Constitution. Ask students what part of the Constitution supporters of the bank turned to to justify their views. **(Article 1, Section 8, Clause 18, the "elastic clause")**

Using the Visuals

Analyzing a Political Cartoon. Refer students to the cartoon on pages 230–231. Tell them that the figures are Jackson, Van Buren, and a popular fictional character of the time, Major Jack Downing, and that the main head on the monster is Nicholas Biddle. Have students explain the action. **(Jackson is fighting the monster bank.)** What is the weapon Jackson uses? **(the veto)** What do the heads on the monster represent? **(the state branches of the bank)** What do Van Buren's words and actions indicate about his position? **(He is avoiding taking sides.)**

Limited English Proficiency

Discussion. Have students discuss whether they prefer a President who follows popular sentiment or one with strong beliefs who acts on them. Have each student suggest a word or phrase that identifies an admirable quality in a President.

Connections: Music

Analyzing a Song. Songs from the campaign of 1840 were far from kind. Here are two stanzas from a song that criticized Martin Van Buren. Ask students to identify the accusations made against the Democratic candidate.

He never was seen in a battle,
Where bullet and cannon shot flew;
His nerves would be shocked with the rattle
Of a contest like Tippecanoe!

But snug in his pretty silk stockings,
And dressed in his broadcloth all new,
He roasted his shins in a parlor—
Not fighting like Tippecanoe.

Connections: Economics

In New York City, depositors withdrew at least $1 million in gold and silver in just two days. The demand for hard money became so great that even pennies vanished from circulation. In order to provide small change, many businesses issued "hard times tokens" of copper or brass. A similar coin shortage developed during the Civil War.

Reduced student page in the Teacher's Edition

states, but he got only 25,000 more popular votes than his combined opponents.

As President, Martin Van Buren lived in the shadow of Andrew Jackson. At the inauguration, more people came to see "Old Hickory" than him, prompting Senator Benton to remark, "The rising was eclipsed by the setting sun."

The Panic of 1837

Jackson left Van Buren with the destructive results of his bank war. The trouble had started while Jackson was still President. With government funds deposited in "pet" banks, the Bank of the United States lost its power to regulate the nation's currency. "Pet" banks as well as new banks printed and loaned money that was not backed by gold or silver. Easy credit led to a spending spree and wild speculation in the purchase of public lands. In 1836 people bought over four times the acreage that had been sold two years earlier. Land prices were skyrocketing.

Jackson had tried to stop the speculation and resulting inflation. In 1836 he had issued a "Specie Circular," ordering the government to accept only specie—gold or silver coins—in payment for public lands. The land boom had stopped, but Jackson's order was to have a destructive effect.

Just as Van Buren took office in 1837, a financial crisis hit Britain. The United States had benefited from British loans of gold and silver. Now British banks were calling in these loans, forcing many American businesses into bankruptcy. In addition, Britain was the South's largest market for cotton, and when British demand dropped, cotton prices fell 50 percent. As a result, cotton brokers began to go out of business.

In May depositors rushed to withdraw their money from banks. The banks then suspended coin payments, and many banks simply failed. Land prices plunged as much as 90 percent. Nine in ten factories in the East closed and unemployment soared. The streets of cities swarmed with beggars, and many people struggled just to survive. By autumn, the United States was in a severe depression that would last for the next six years.

"Tippecanoe and Tyler, Too!"

Although many Americans blamed Van Buren for the depression, the Democratic convention renominated him for President in 1840. The Whigs, confident of victory, chose William Henry Harrison of Ohio as their candidate. Harrison, a military hero, had made a strong showing in the election of 1836 and had few political enemies. In order to gain anti-Jacksonian Democratic votes in the South, the Whigs chose Virginia legislator John Tyler for Vice-President. An ex-Democrat, Tyler had broken with Jackson over nullification.

The campaign of 1840 was the first presidential campaign to center more on slogans and name calling than on issues. Campaigns were beginning to be popular as a source of entertainment. The era of Jackson had launched the huge popularity of parades, picnics, barbecues, and a general party spirit of public involvement in a

campaign. Indeed, the Whigs had learned from Jackson's popularity as a man of the people and a military hero, and successfully adopted propaganda the Democrats had pioneered. Whigs portrayed Van Buren as an eastern aristocrat who ate with gold spoons and perfumed his whiskers. They blamed him for the depression and for not helping workers.

The Whigs painted Harrison as the "log-cabin candidate" and a greater military hero "than any other . . . now living." Whigs wore log cabin badges, handed out hard cider, and sang "Tippecanoe and Tyler, too," recalling Harrison's role in the famous battle. Few people cared that Harrison lived in a mansion on a 3,000-acre estate and that Van Buren was raised in poverty.

The good-time campaign swept Harrison into office with the largest voter turnout yet seen. Harrison carried 19 of 26 states, winning 234 electoral votes to Van Buren's 60. The Whigs also won majorities in both the House and the Senate.

Harrison did not live long enough to put Whig ideals into action. A month after he took office, he died of pneumonia. John Tyler, a Democrat at heart, was sworn in as President. Whigs were pleased when he kept Harrison's cabinet. They expected him to support their goals of internal improvements and a national bank. But to the Whigs' dismay, Tyler—who believed in states' rights and a strict interpretation of the Constitution—was set on following his own course.

Handkerchiefs, pins, pamphlets, and songsheets were just a few of the many items promoting William Henry Harrison as the "log cabin candidate" for President.

Within five months Tyler vetoed two Whig bills to create a new national bank. After the first veto, an armed mob marched on the White House, breaking windows and shouting insults. After the second, every cabinet member but one resigned in outrage. Tyler also vetoed every bill for internal improvements that Congress passed, believing that these measures gave the federal government too much control. The Whigs were outraged, and some even attempted to impeach him. A political loner, Tyler simply continued to follow his own independent course.

Shaping the Presidency

Jackson's successors followed his precedent—using presidential power to carry out their own policies, over and above carrying out the laws passed by Congress. For this reason Jackson can be said to have shaped the modern concept of presidential leadership. He sometimes supported a strict interpretation of the Constitution and sometimes disregarded Supreme Court decisions, such as on the constitutionality of the bank and on the status of the American Indian tribes. He sometimes supported nationalism and sometimes states' rights, depending upon his personal views on a question.

Most of all, Jackson and his party mastered the art of democratic politics. By catering to the popular sentiment they kept their party in power for most of the period until the Civil War.

Section Review

1. Comprehension. List three reasons why Jackson wanted to destroy the Bank of the United States. What steps did he take to achieve his goal?

2. Analysis. Why did Jackson's opponents unite against him? What was the result of this union?

3. Comprehension. What events led to the depression in 1837?

4. Evaluation. Do you think modern elections resemble the election of 1840? Why or why not?

5. Analysis. Explain how the Whigs won the election of 1840 and why some Whigs later tried to impeach John Tyler.

Active Learning

Campaign Speeches. The candidates of 1840 relied on party supporters to speak for them at local political rallies. Divide the class into Democrats and Whigs, and have students prepare brief speeches supporting their candidates. After students give their speeches to the class, evaluate the speeches with students, noting the major points raised and their political effectiveness.

Section Review

ANSWERS

1. Feared that the bank interfered in state politics, lent money to influential people. Government appointed some directors, compromising bank's independence. Jackson vetoed recharter bill, ordered Treasury to stop depositing government funds in bank.
2. They thought he had misused power and run the government as he willed. Result: formation of the Whig party.
3. Government funds deposited in "pet banks" offering easy credit led to wild land speculation. Prices soared. British banks called in loans, many American businesses went bankrupt. British demand for cotton dropped. When depositors tried to get money out of banks, banks went out of business.
4. Some students may mention that media advertisements of today try to grab attention, focus on a candidate's personality rather than qualifications and abilities, similar to tactics in the 1840 election.
5. Many Americans blamed Democrats for the depression. Whigs ran Harrison, a military hero. When Tyler became president he vetoed Whig bills for national bank and internal improvements.

Section 9-3

Objectives

- ***Answer the Focus Question.***
- *Describe opposition met by groups who wished to improve public education.*
- *Explain how reform movements set in motion the movement for women's rights.*

Connections: Religion
The established Presbyterian, Methodist, and Baptist churches in the United States owed much of their growth to an earlier period of religious revival called the First Great Awakening, which reached its peak in the mid 1700s. The later revival movement described in this section is sometimes called the Second Great Awakening.

Introducing

THE SECTION

The common features of the movements discussed in this section are dissatisfaction with society and an energetic idealism that turned toward increased religious faith and reform. Ask students to consider the following questions: Did the movement achieve its goals? Is the problem that the movement addressed an issue today? If so what present-day efforts have been made to solve this problem?

Reduced student page in the Teacher's Edition

9-3 *Pursuing the Perfect Society*

Focus: How did religious revivals and reform movements show a longing for a better society?

The democratic breeze that swept the United States during the Jacksonian era brought with it other movements that stirred Americans. Between the 1820s and the 1850s, Americans were zealous in their quest for the perfect society. This quest expressed itself in a variety of ways—from utopian communities that lived by their ideals to reformers who sought to correct injustice and transform the whole of American society.

Religious Revivals and Utopias

Religious faith spurred Americans in their drive to improve society. Around 1800, Protestant leaders launched a series of **revivals,** public meetings intended to renew commitment to Christian faith. For the next fifty years, waves of religious revivals swept the nation.

As the nationwide religious revival reached out to the West, Protestant churches sent ministers to preach at "camp meetings."

Religious awakening was especially fiery in the West. At "camp meetings," preachers preached to thousands, urging them to accept God's love and turn from the sin of a selfish life. Many people did change. As one minister reported:

> *“Drunkards, profane swearers, liars, quarrelsome persons, etc., are remarkably reformed. . . . Some neighborhoods, noted for their vicious and profligate manners are now as much noted for their piety and good order.”*

Revivals also kindled new movements aimed at establishing model communities. In New York state Joseph Smith, claiming that he had been given revelations from God, gathered followers into a community that became known as the Mormons. Ann Lee, called "Mother Ann," led English Shakers to the United States to escape religious persecution. The Shakers, who praised God in song and dance, attracted converts and established communities based on their beliefs. Eventually they spread to eight states.

Non-religious groups also sought to create perfect societies, or **utopias,** based on economic and social ideals. In some, members shared equally their possessions and the profits of their work.

Fruitlands and Brook Farm in Massachusetts were utopian communities. Fruitlands, which refused to "enslave" horses for farm work, faced starvation and failed within a year. Novelist Louisa May Alcott, whose father planned the experiment, later wrote, "Poor Fruitlands! The name was as great a failure as the rest." Brook Farm lasted several years, then collapsed from debt.

Connections: Literature

The word "utopia" comes from the Greek words meaning "no place." The word first appeared in 1516, in Sir Thomas More's *Utopia*, a tale of an ideal society based on justice and reason. Through his work, More criticized injustices of his time, such as poverty, unearned wealth, religious persecution, and war.

THE DRUNKARDS PROGRESS.
FROM THE FIRST GLASS TO THE GRAVE.

The reform movement included early efforts to discourage the drinking of alcohol. These two illustrations carry the same blunt warning.

However, a few of the more than fifty utopias did survive. A community at Oneida, New York manufactured silverware and other goods. In 1881 it reorganized as a corporation that is still active today.

Improving Public Education

Walking down a city street in the 1830s brought passersby face-to-face with an American problem: juvenile delinquency. Unschooled youth loitered in the streets, sometimes assaulting people, sometimes stealing, vandalizing, or setting fires. These youth were out of school because at the time of Jackson's presidency, public schools were still rare.

Before the 1820s most Americans had not considered free public education a responsibility of the government. However, with the expansion of democracy and the rise of reform movements, education became a target for change. In the 1830s educational reformers began to agitate for state-supported education. They saw education as the only way to protect the stability of democracy and to educate immigrants in what they saw as American values.

THE MARCH OF DEATH.

Horace Mann of Massachusetts led the way in educational reform. In 1837 he became secretary of the new state board of education. Mann disapproved of the tendency for one class in society to have all the wealth and education while the rest were trapped in poverty and ignorance. He was convinced that only educated citizens could make a democratic government work.

Mann's campaign succeeded. State funds for education were doubled, schools were improved, and the school year was extended to a minimum of six months. Teach-

Developing

THE SECTION

Thinking Critically

Evaluation. Many Americans today are concerned with the increasing number of young people who lack basic skills needed for citizenship or success in the work place. Ask students whether they think Horace Mann's belief in the connection between good schools and democracy is still valid today. Ask students for suggestions about improving the educational system.

Connections: Music

Analyzing a Song. The Shaker hymn "Simple Gifts" begins:

'Tis the Gift to be simple,
'Tis the Gift to be free,
'Tis the Gift to come down
Where we ought to be.
To turn and turn
Shall be our delight
Till by turning, turning,
We come round right.

Ask: What do these words suggest about Shaker beliefs?

Analyzing Primary Sources

Political Statement. A statement written in 1838 began:

❝ The undersigned, being of opinion that the action of the New-England Anti-Slavery Convention . . . inviting women to vote, debate, and aid generally as members of this body . . . is injurious to the cause of the slave by connecting it with a subject foreign to it; injurious as a precedent for connecting with it other *irrelevant topics.* ❞

Ask: Why did the writers oppose women's participation in the anti-slavery cause? Do you agree with the reasons given? Why or why not?

Connections: Literature
Among other works, Dorothea Dix threw herself into the vast task of creating what was perhaps the first encyclopedia written especially for children. Her husband-to-be scolded her for working too hard and forbade her to continue writing the encyclopedia. He said she should be satisfied "fulfilling the duties of my wife." Though heartbroken, she wrote to him breaking off the engagement and explaining that she could never give up her work and be the kind of wife he wanted.

ers' salaries were increased, and three schools were set up to train teachers.

Mann toured the country, spurring reformers in other states to fight for publicly supported schooling for all. Working class parents joined the movement, demanding schools for their children. "We want a *common* and *equal* education," a newspaper declared. "It is in the *interest of all*."

Such proposals sparked opposition. Taxpayers did not want to pay to educate "other people's children." Families often opposed compulsory attendance, when children could be working in fields or factories. Some believed that it was not necessary for everybody to read and write.

The spread of public schools. Despite such objections, states moved toward free public schooling. By the 1860s most northern states offered elementary education that was free and open to all white children. Separate—and inferior—schools were established for black children.

States also began to set up tax-supported high schools, which had been introduced by Massachusetts in 1821. The numbers of these schools grew slowly, since many private academies already existed to provide secondary education. However, by 1860 the nation had some 300 public high schools.

Help for the Mentally Ill

In 1841 when Dorothea Dix visited a prison near Boston, she saw mentally ill people treated as criminals. Outraged, she spent two years inspecting jails and poorhouses throughout the state. In 1843 she spoke to the Massachusetts legislature:

❝ Insane persons are confined within this Commonwealth in cages, closets, cellars, stalls, pens; chained, naked, beaten with rods, and lashed into obedience! ❞

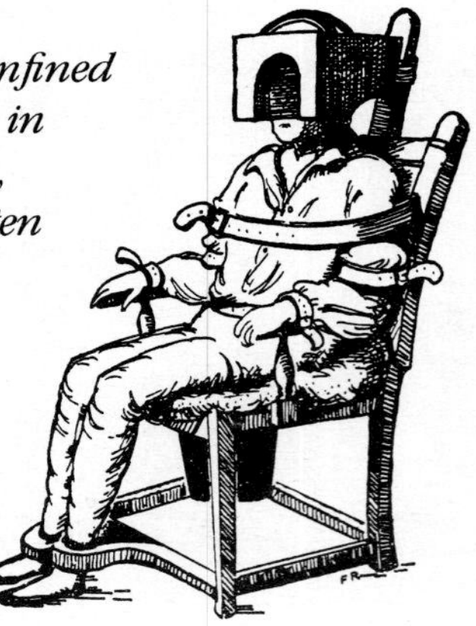

The "tranquilizing chair" was a misguided treatment for the mentally ill.

Dix's testimony convinced legislators to vote funds for a hospital for the mentally ill. She then traveled thousands of miles, visiting jails, planning hospitals, and winning support.

The Movement for Women's Rights

In 1838 Angelina Grimké stood before the Massachusetts legislature. She and her sister Sarah presented a petition by 20,000 women demanding an end to slavery.

Few members of the legislature had ever heard a speech by a woman. Grimké knew this, and made a plea not only to end slavery, but also to give women the right to be heard on any subject:

❝ These petitions relate to the great and solemn subject of slavery. . . . Because it is a political subject, it has often tauntingly been said, that women had nothing to do with it. . . . Are we bereft of citizenship . . . ? Have women no country? ❞

Women had been key participants in revival and reform movements. In church, women spoke out and formed societies devoted to social action. They crusaded for **temperance**, or moderation in the use of alcoholic beverages, and for the reform of education and of prisons and hospitals.

However, it was in the antislavery movement that women first took a major political role. And as women fought for the emancipation of slaves, they also saw the injustice in their own position in society and began to speak out against it. As Angelina Grimké said, "What then can woman do for the slave, when she herself is under the feet of man and shamed into silence?"

Grimké's call for political rights was rare at a time when women had a subordinate status to men in most areas of life. In some states, for example, when women earned wages, the money belonged to their husbands. Some state laws allowed husbands to beat their wives "with a reasonable instrument." Women had no right to vote, to own property, or to keep custody of their children after a divorce.

Multicultural Perspectives

African-American women banded together for social work and reform. Such organizations included the Colored Female Charitable Society in Boston and the Female Benevolent Society in Troy, New York, and Portland, Maine. By 1830 there were twenty-seven such benevolent and mutual aid societies in Philadelphia.

Social History

The entrance requirements at Mount Holyoke College were rigorous, and the women were expected to study hard as well as do the school's housework. One Thanksgiving, a student wrote, *"We all had the privilege of sleeping as long as we wished in the morning, provided we were ready for breakfast by 8 o'clock."*

Challenges to tradition: pant-like "bloomers" rather than dresses; women students at Oberlin College.

Women staged petition campaigns that forced some states to allow married women to own property. In 1860 New York gave women joint guardianship of children. It also granted them the rights to sue and to keep their own wages. However, progress was slow and opposition fierce.

Higher Education for Women

The common view was that women's education should make them better wives and mothers. They were seen as too frail to study the sciences. Girls found little opportunity beyond elementary school.

As the women's movement gained momentum, the doors to education started to open. The first high school for girls, Troy Female Seminary in New York, began classes in 1821. Established by Emma Hart Willard, it offered physics and geometry, subjects previously offered only to boys. In 1833 Ohio's Oberlin College became the nation's first coeducational college.

As higher education opened to them, women began to train for fields such as the ministry, journalism, and medicine. A determined young woman named Elizabeth Blackwell entered the medical school of Geneva College in New York and then graduated first in her class in 1849. Eight years later Dr. Blackwell opened the nation's first school

Spotlight on Women

Few women in the early 1800s received an education, and those who did had little choice about what to read. These excerpts from women's books show some attitudes of the time.

In the *Young Lady's Book of 1830:*

"In whatever situation of life a woman is placed from her cradle to her grave, a spirit of obedience and submission, pliability of temper, and humility of mind, are required from her."

In the book *Greenwood Leaves* (1850):

"True feminine genius is ever timid, doubtful, and clingingly dependent; a perpetual childhood."

Linking Past and Present

Discussion. Refer students to the Spotlight feature on this page. Ask them to explain what attitudes toward women are reflected in the excerpts. **(Women must be obedient, subservient, even-tempered, dependent, childlike.)** Have students compare these attitudes with attitudes toward American women today. What changes in women's rights have occurred since the 1850s? Compare recent methods used to attain these rights with those of the nineteenth century.

Active Learning

Posters and Songs. Have the class choose a cause—one covered in this section or another cause they believe in—and work in committees to create posters and songs supporting the cause. On a special class day—for example, Women's Rights Day—the posters can be displayed, and the students who wrote songs can perform them.

Social History
Lucy Stone was married to Elizabeth Blackwell's brother Henry, who actively supported her work. With his agreement, she kept her own last name, a practice common today but unheard of at the time. Women who adopted this custom become known as "Lucy Stoners."

Reduced student page in the Teacher's Edition

of nursing. Antoinette Brown, Blackwell's sister-in-law, was the first woman to attend Oberlin's theological school.

Women Organize

The successes of Blackwell and others were milestones, but by no means was every path open to women. In the 1840s Elizabeth Cady Stanton and Lucretia Mott decided that only an organized movement for women's rights could make real headway. They plunged into reform work, both for the causes of abolition and women's rights.

Stanton was moved by women's complaints to her father—a New York judge—that the law did not protect women's rights. Mott, a plain-speaking Quaker, would protest slavery with calm courage standing in front of a hostile crowd. When she challenged a speaker at one meeting, her husband,

THE AMERICAN SPIRIT

Margaret Fuller

A New View of Women

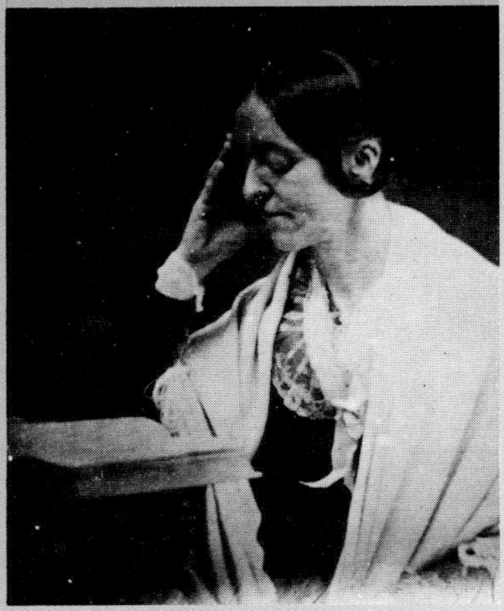

Even as a child, Margaret Fuller was different. Born in Massachusetts in 1810, she was reading Latin by the time she was six. In an age when women were expected to be pretty and helpless, she was brilliant, independent, and plain. "I made up my mind to be bright and ugly," she said.

While most women looked forward only to marriage, she wanted an education and a career. Yet no colleges admitted women, and there were few jobs open to them. Margaret Fuller tried teaching, writing, and editing a literary journal. She held a famous series of "Conversations" with Boston women, in which they discussed history, literature, and women's roles. Eventually she became the first woman on the staff of the New York *Tribune.*

During these years, her ideas about women developed. In 1845 she wrote *Woman in the Nineteenth Century,* a defense of women's rights in which she argued that women's natural talents were stifled. As her starting point she wrote, "there exists in the minds of men a tone of feeling toward woman as toward slaves. . . . We would have every arbitrary barrier thrown down. We would have every path open to Woman as freely as to Man."

Margaret Fuller argued that girls, like boys, should be encouraged to develop freely. "Some little girls like to saw wood, others to use carpenters' tools," she noted. When parents forbid such activities because they are "not proper for girls," their growth is stunted. In the same way, all jobs should be open to women. "Let them be sea-captains, if you will," she wrote.

While she never became a sea captain, Fuller did travel by ship to Europe in 1846 where she became a foreign correspondent for the *Tribune.* In Italy she met and married the Marchese Angelo Ossoli, and the two participated in the Italian revolution of 1848 to 1849. The couple and their young son were killed in a shipwreck on a voyage to the United States.

Many Americans found Margaret Fuller's ideas shocking. Yet she had planted a seed. That seed would sprout three years later, when the first women's rights convention at Seneca Falls proclaimed that "all men and women are created equal."

Connections: Politics
The issue of woman suffrage deeply divided the Seneca Falls convention and was ridiculed in newspapers. The *Oneida Whig* reported "the most shocking and unnatural incident ever recorded in the history of womaninity," while another newspaper ran the headline PETTICOATS VS. BOOTS.

Sojourner Truth spoke powerfully for abolition and women's rights.

James, advised him, "If she thinks thee is wrong, thee had better look it over again."

In 1848 Stanton, Mott, and Mott's sister, Martha Coffin Wright, called a convention at Seneca Falls, New York, to discuss women's rights. A large crowd of men and women gathered to hear Stanton read the Declaration of Sentiments, based on the Declaration of Independence. Stanton asked that women be given the rights of citizens, including the right to vote, an idea so radical at the time that even Lucretia Mott warned, "Why, Lizzie, thee will make us ridiculous!" Still, with the help of Frederick Douglass, a leading abolitionist, Stanton convinced the convention to accept the declaration.

After the Seneca Falls Convention, women set out on speaking tours to win support for the struggling movement. Susan B. Anthony devoted her life to the drive for women's rights. She and Stanton formed a close team. Stanton wrote fiery speeches that Anthony delivered in town after town. Henry Stanton remarked to his wife, "You stir up Susan and she stirs up the world."

Another tireless campaigner and abolitionist was Lucy Stone, a graduate of Oberlin College. Once, Stone refused to pay property taxes because "women suffer taxation, and yet have no representation." Government officials then took all her household goods— even her baby's cradle.

An important figure in both the abolition and women's rights movements was Sojourner Truth. Truth had been a slave for half her life. She gained freedom in 1827 and became a leading speaker for abolition and women's rights. At one women's convention, she listened to several male ministers dominate the discussion. Then she rose and said:

> *"That man over there says that woman needs to be helped into carriages and lifted over ditches. . . . Nobody ever helps me into carriages, or over mud-puddles or gives me any best place. And a'nt I a woman? . . . I have ploughed and planted and gathered into barns. . . . And a'nt I a woman? I could work as much and eat as much as a man, when I could get it, and bear the lash as well. And a'nt I a woman? I have borne thirteen children and seen most all sold off to slavery, and when I cried out . . . none but Jesus heard me! And a'nt I a woman?"*

The issue of slavery was to become the foremost concern of reformers. As the expansion of democracy and religious revivals continued to draw attention to a less-than-perfect world, the call for change grew louder and louder.

Section Review

1. Identification. Define *revivals, utopias,* and *temperance.*

2. Analysis. How did utopian communities reflect a quest for perfection?

3. Analysis. What groups were interested in improving education? What opposition did they meet?

4. Comprehension. How did reform movements help set the women's rights movement in motion?

5. Analysis. How were women's rights restricted? What improvements were made during the 1830s and 1840s?

Section Review

ANSWERS

1. Definitions for the following terms are on text pages indicated in parentheses: *revivals* (234), *utopias* (234), *temperance* (236).
2. They sought to live out their ideals of a "perfect" society. In some, members shared equally possessions and profits from work. One community refused to "enslave" horses for work.
3. People who saw education as a way to stabilize democracy and to educate immigrants in American values; working class people. Opposition came from taxpayers who did not want to spend public money to educate other people's children, and parents who wanted to put their children to work instead of in school.
4. Women had been active in reform movements, notably the antislavery movement. As they fought for emancipation, they came up against their own lack of rights to seek change.
5. In some states, husbands could keep wives' earnings and could beat them. Women could not vote, own property, or retain custody of children after divorce. Petition campaigns helped overturn some of these laws, and educational opportunities began to open up. Women organized.

Section 9-4

Objectives

- ***Answer the Focus Question.***
- *Cite contributions of Frederick Douglass, Harriet Tubman, and David Walker to the antislavery movement.*
- *Explain why there were different views on how to bring about the end of slavery.*

Introducing

THE SECTION

On the front line of the battle against slavery was the network of African-American men and women who organized and ran the Underground Railroad and mutual aid societies and fought the day-to-day struggle against slave owners and slave catchers. White abolitionists also played a key role in the struggle to end slavery.

Ask students to compare these efforts with other activities related to opposition such as colonial Committees of Correspondence, resistance movements in South Africa, and the Solidarity Union in Poland. What are some common features of successful struggles against oppression?

B · A · C · K · G · R · O · U · N · D

Multicultural Perspectives

One well-known early proponent of colonization was Paul Cuffe (1759–1817), a wealthy merchant mariner. Cuffe, whose father was a free African American and mother a Wampanoag Indian, grew up on the New England coast and advanced quickly in the business of sea trade. He also became a philanthropist and social activist, and his efforts led to a 1783 law which gave blacks in Massachusetts the right to vote. Still, his international reputation came from his efforts to colonize Sierra Leone. In 1815 Cuffe financed the voyage of thirty-eight free African Americans to start a settlement there, and returned convinced that colonization was the only solution to the bleak situation that black Americans faced.

Reduced student page in the Teacher's Edition

9-4 The Struggle to Abolish Slavery

Focus: How did the movement to abolish slavery gain strength in the early 1800s?

One Sunday in 1833, a young man stood on the shore of Chesapeake Bay. As he watched the passing boats, he observed:

> *"You are loosed from your moorings, and are free; I am fast in my chains and am a slave! . . . You are freedom's swift-winged angels, that fly round the world; I am confined in bands of iron! . . . O God, save me! God, deliver me! Let me be free!"*

The young man was Frederick Lewis Douglass, and he had been born into slavery. Slaves were forbidden to read and write, but Douglass taught himself. He escaped to freedom at the age of twenty-one and before he turned thirty, he had written his autobiography. The *Narrative of the Life of Frederick Douglass* revealed to the world what it was like to be a slave in the United States.

The Antislavery Movement

Some opposition to slavery had existed since the earliest days of the nation, but in the early 1800s an organized movement took shape. The steady pressure for change by African Americans was joined by the force of reform, and antislavery became the foremost movement of the reform era.

American Colonization Society. An early plan to end slavery came in 1817 with the founding of the American Colonization Society by northerners and southerners. The society urged slaveowners to free their slaves and send them to Liberia, a tract of land it had bought in West Africa. The society also sought to persuade free African Americans to migrate, believing that they would never fit into American society.

The colonization plan never took root. The society was short of funds, and most slaveowners opposed the plan. Most significant, however, was the fact that the plan did not reflect the wishes of African Americans. A convention of free blacks in New York City declared that America was their home, their country. Some of their fathers had fought and died for it, and they intended to die here, too.

Fighting Slavery. African Americans constituted a vital part of the antislavery movement. While blacks throughout the country risked their lives to end slavery, free blacks in the North were the least restricted in their actions. They organized antislavery societies, mutual-aid associations, and secret orders to help members of their community and shelter, clothe, and feed blacks who escaped from the South. A strong network developed, linking those who worked for change.

Free northern blacks and former slaves were also dedicated members of the Underground Railroad, a movement to help slaves escape. "Conductors" like Harriet Tubman and Jane Lewis risked their freedom and their lives by traveling south to guide slaves to freedom. Tubman, who escaped alone as a young woman, made nineteen trips, bringing more than 300 slaves out of bondage.

After his own escape from slavery in 1838, Frederick Douglass traveled throughout the North speaking against slavery. At first Douglass wrote for a white abolitionist newspaper, but in 1847 he founded his own paper, *North Star.* Rallying African Americans to the cause he declared:

> *"[Antislavery] is emphatically our battle; no one else can fight it for us. . . . Our relations to the [white] Anti-Slavery movement must be and are changed. Instead of depending upon it we must lead it."*

Multicultural Perspectives

The Underground Railroad was a testimony to human ingenuity as well as to courage. Henry "Box" Brown had himself shipped from Richmond, Virginia, to Philadelphia, crouching in an express box 2 feet, 8 inches tall, 2 feet wide, and 3 feet long. The journey took 26 hours. In another case, the light-skinned Ellen Craft disguised herself as an ailing planter. Her husband masqueraded as her slave, and the two managed to escape.

The Underground Railroad 1860

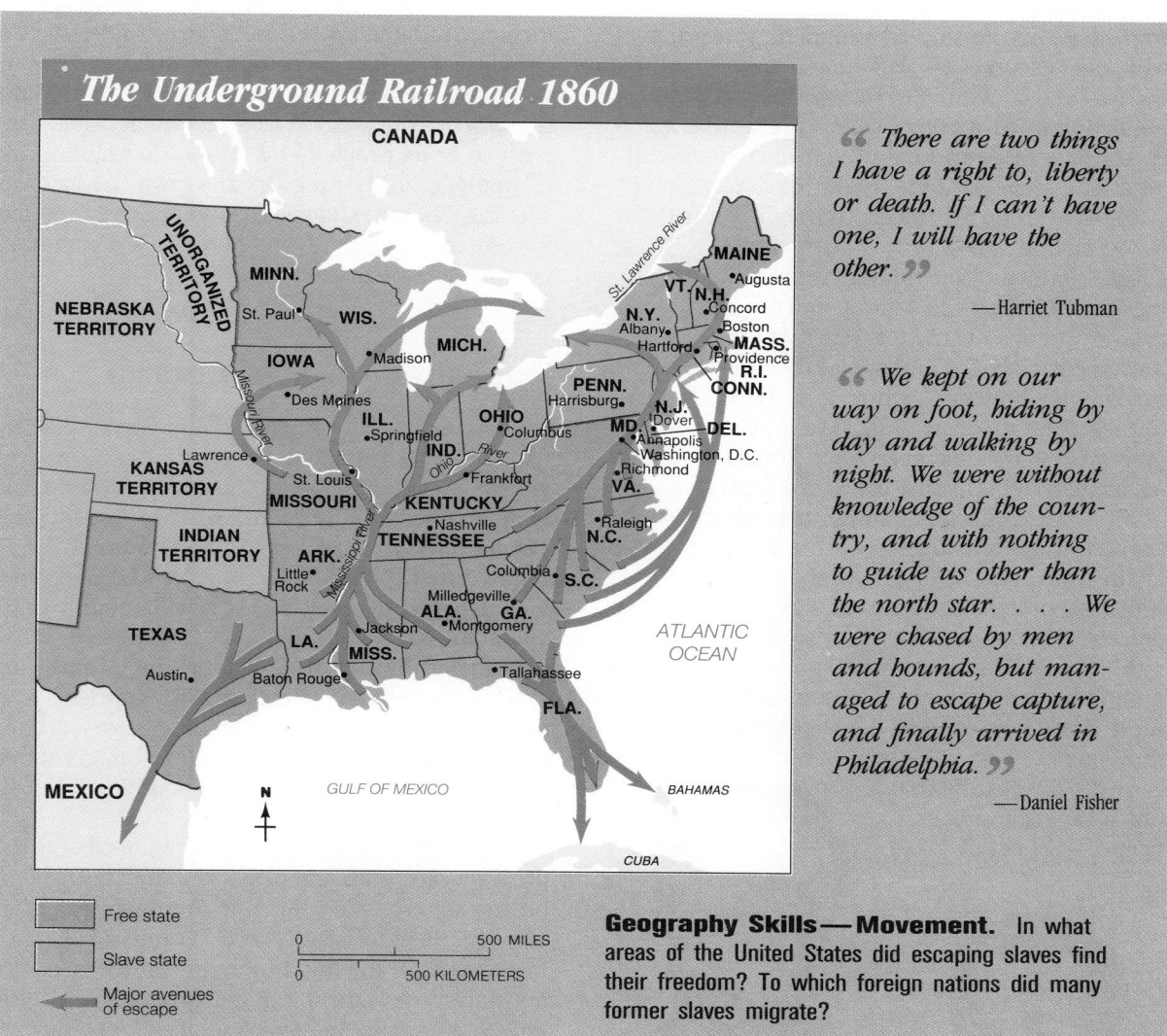

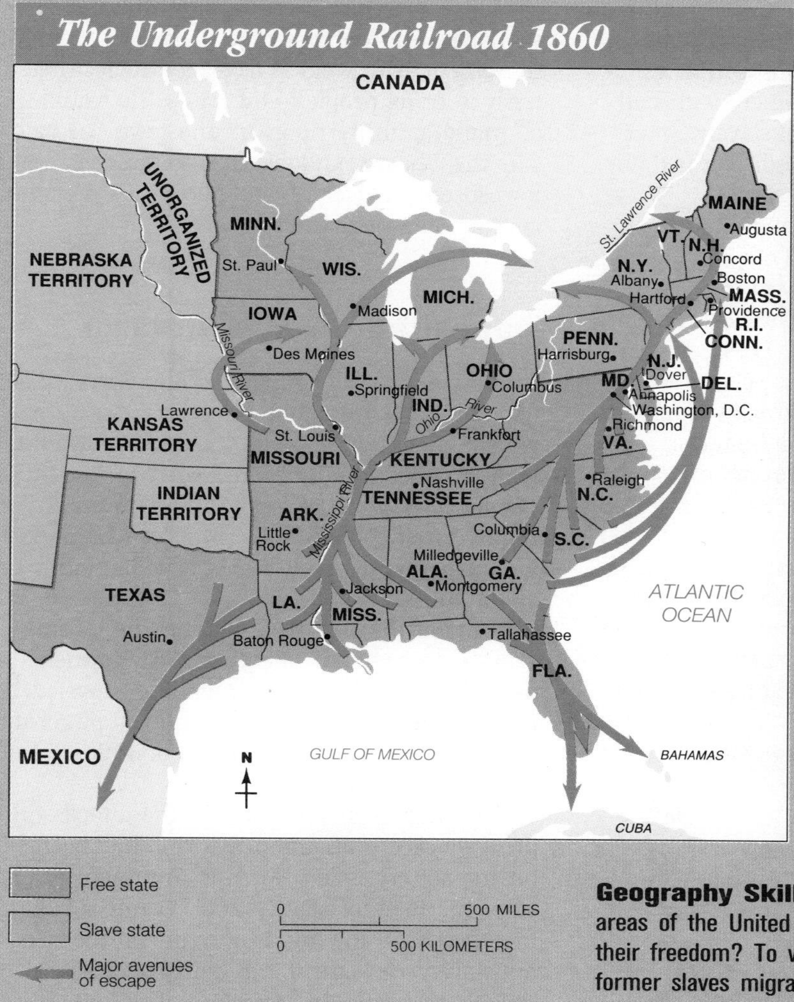

"There are two things I have a right to, liberty or death. If I can't have one, I will have the other."

—Harriet Tubman

"We kept on our way on foot, hiding by day and walking by night. We were without knowledge of the country, and with nothing to guide us other than the north star. . . . We were chased by men and hounds, but managed to escape capture, and finally arrived in Philadelphia."

—Daniel Fisher

Geography Skills—Movement. In what areas of the United States did escaping slaves find their freedom? To which foreign nations did many former slaves migrate?

Some African Americans called for violence as the only way to throw off slavery. In 1829, David Walker, a free black in Boston, published a pamphlet titled *Appeal to the Colored Citizens of the World,* in which he urged slaves to fight for their freedom.

The South reacted instantly in fear. Savannah's mayor demanded that the mayor of Boston arrest Walker. But Walker had not violated any law, so he could not be arrested. Many southern states made it a crime to circulate such pamphlets and forbade African Americans to meet in large groups or to travel without a white. Black sailors on ships docking in Georgia harbors were warned not to go ashore. Georgia also offered a reward of $10,000 to anyone who would deliver Walker alive, and $1,000 to anyone who would kill him. In the summer of 1830, Walker was found dead near his shop in Boston.

The American Anti-Slavery Society. The crusade against slavery became more visible when William Lloyd Garrison began his newspaper, *The Liberator,* in 1831. Garrison, a Massachusetts printer, became one of the most radical antislavery voices in the white community. He demanded an

Developing

THE SECTION

Analyzing Primary Sources

Speech by Frederick Douglass. The great African-American abolitionist leader Frederick Douglass gave an Independence Day address in 1852. An excerpt from the address follows:

"What to the American slave is your Fourth of July? I answer, a day that reveals to him more than all other days of the year, the gross injustice and cruelty to which he is the constant victim. To him your celebration is a sham . . . your sounds of rejoicing are empty and heartless; your denunciation of tyrants, brass-fronted impudence; your shouts of liberty and equality, hollow mockery; your prayers and hymns, your sermons and thanksgivings . . . are to him mere bombast, fraud, deception, impiety, and hypocrisy—a thin veil to cover up crimes which would disgrace a nation of savages."

Ask: How did Douglass use his listeners' own values to accuse them? Were these accusations likely to anger listeners, spur them to fight slavery, or both?

Geography Skills

ANSWERS

Northeast and Midwest. Canada, Mexico, and Caribbean Islands (Cuba and the Bahamas).

Analyzing Primary Sources

Poetry. In William J. Grayson's poem *The Hireling and the Slave*, he defends slavery by contrasting the free worker in the North and the southern slave:

"See the worn child compelled in mines to slave
Through the narrow seams of coal, a living grave,
Driven from the breezy hill, the sunny glade,
By ruthless hearts, the drudge of labor made. . . ."

By contrast, the life of the southern slave appears idyllic:

"And yet the life, so unassailed by care,
So blessed with moderate work, with ample care,
With all the good the starving pauper needs,
The happier slave on each plantation leads;
Safe from harassed doubts and annual fears,
He dreads no famine in unfruitful years;
If harvest hail from inauspicious skies,
The master's providence his food supplies . . ."

Ask: How does Grayson characterize free labor? In what way does Grayson define slavery? What aspects of slavery does he overlook?

B · A · C · K · G · R · O · U · N · D

Social History

In 1832 Prudence Crandall, headmistress of the Canterbury (Connecticut) Female Boarding School, admitted a seventeen-year-old African-American girl, Sarah Harris. The townspeople demonstrated against Sarah, and some of the town's families withdrew their daughters from the school. Defiantly, Prudence converted her school into an establishment for "young Colored Ladies and Misses." Despite a reign of terror against the school—and being jailed—Prudence stubbornly kept the school open. However, when the school was set on fire, she was finally persuaded to give up.

immediate end to slavery, thundering in print, "I will not excuse—I will not retreat a single inch—and I WILL BE HEARD." Garrison even publicly burned a copy of the Constitution as "a covenant with death and an agreement with hell" because it recognized the legality of slavery.

With a group of fifteen, Garrison formed the New England Anti-Slavery Society in 1831. When Great Britain abolished slavery throughout its colonies in 1833, Garrison's group and other small antislavery groups in America were swept into a major movement. Garrison and two wealthy New York silk merchants, brothers Arthur and Lewis Tappan, formed the American Anti-Slavery Society, which grew to 200,000 members. Six African-American leaders served on its first board of managers.

Meanwhile, the abolitionist movement gained support from revivalists who turned their fervor against slavery. Theodore Dwight Weld's faith led him to oppose the injustice of slavery with all his preacher's eloquence. While a student at Cincinnati's Lane Seminary, Weld preached abolition among his fellow ministry students, converting almost the whole student body to the antislavery movement.

In 1835 Weld and many of his Lane converts opened a school of theology at Ohio's Oberlin College. Under Weld's prodding, Oberlin agreed to admit blacks. Oberlin soon became the center of the western abolition movement, with Weld as its leader. He lectured tirelessly to bring people to the cause. He would speak as many as thirty times in one town, he said, to win the "hearts and heads and tongues" of the townspeople. Slavery, he told people, was a sin and contrary to American ideals of equality.

In 1827 Samuel Cornish (left) and John Russwurm started Freedom's Journal, *the first newspaper published by African Americans.*

Opposition to Abolitionism

In the years after the American Anti-Slavery Society was founded, anti-abolitionists staged a number of violent attacks on abolitionist speakers and free African Americans. A mob wrecked the presses of Garrison's *Liberator* and set his house on fire. In 1837 Elijah Lovejoy, an Illinois minister who published an antislavery paper, was shot dead by rioting anti-abolitionists.

Many of the riots were planned by leading citizens—professional men, property owners, and politicians—who opposed ending slavery. They feared a loss of economic and political power if free African Americans demanded economic, political, and social equality.

The murder of Lovejoy and the attacks on the press shocked even Americans who had been silent on the slavery issue. Now the argument went beyond the issue of slavery and became an issue of free speech. In the minds of many northerners, the antislavery movement was not just a moral crusade, but a matter of protection of civil liberties.

The free speech issue exploded in Congress. Abolitionists had launched a drive to outlaw slavery and the slave trade in Washington, D.C., and petitions were flooding Congress. Representatives from slave states were alarmed by the spread of the abolitionist movement. They did not want Congress to debate slavery. In 1836 the proslavery group pushed a "gag rule" through Congress, barring debate on antislavery petitions.

The gag rule aroused the wrath of former President John Quincy Adams, now a Massachusetts representative in the House. Adams was not an abolitionist, but he saw the gag rule as a violation of the right of petition. He doggedly fought the rule until it was repealed in 1844.

Multicultural Perspectives

J. W. Loguen, whose mother was an enslaved African American and father was her white owner, escaped to freedom, went to college, and became a minister in Syracuse, New York. When his former mistress wrote to him requesting $1,000 in compensation, Loguen's reply was published in *The Liberator*:

"You say, 'You know we raised you as we did our own children.' Woman, did you raise your own children for the market? Did you raise them for the shipping post? Did you raise them to be driven off, bound . . . in chains? Shame on you! . . . Before God and high heaven, is there a law for one man which is not a law for every other man?"

Limited English Proficiency

Evaluation. Have students form small groups, each to choose an outstanding advocate of human rights. A student from each group can present its choice to the class along with reasons for the selection. The class can vote to choose which person it thinks most outstanding.

The Anti-Slavery Society Split

Moderate abolitionists in the North condemned the radical stands of David Walker and William Lloyd Garrison. Like poet James Russell Lowell, they wished to end slavery but felt "the world must be healed by degrees." Moderates sought change through cautious political action.

However, Garrison and his followers continued to insist on immediate abolition. They were not willing to work through politics, since they believed that Congress would do nothing that might offend the slave states. These radical abolitionists also supported the participation of women in the movement and recommended African Americans as antislavery lecturers.

Moderate abolitionists feared that the visible involvement of African Americans and women would weaken the antislavery movement's appeal to a large number of Americans. In 1840 the moderate abolitionists—including Lewis Tappan—left the American Anti-Slavery Society in order to form their own group, the Liberty party.

In spite of the split in the abolitionist movement, the effort to end slavery gained a widening appeal—especially when it became linked to the question of westward expansion. Even northerners who had not been sympathetic to the cause began to support abolition because they feared what would happen if slavery were permitted in new territories and states. For them, the issue was economic—free workers would have a hard time competing with slave labor. The question of control of the frontier would continue to widen the split between North and South and inflame the debate over the future of slavery.

Section Review

1. Analysis. What events led to the formation of the American Anti-Slavery Society?

2. Comprehension. What contributions did David Walker, Harriet Tubman, and Frederick Douglass make to the antislavery movement?

3. Analysis. Explain how those who opposed slavery had different views on the question of how to bring about its abolition.

Connections to Themes

Shaping Democracy

People of devout Christian faith played key roles in the nineteenth-century reform movements. They led the way in improving education, health care, mental hospitals, and the prison system. The movement to limit, or to eliminate, alcohol use also had a solid core of church members. People of faith were zealous in their efforts to promote the rights of women and to end slavery in the United States.

The Christian church has had two impulses regarding social reform: to improve society slowly and to achieve social justice here and now. In the 1800s some established denominations had a tradition of close association with state governments. They tended toward a more gradual approach to change. Those with a tradition of dissent, such as the Congregationalists, Baptists, and Methodists, often led the way to radical reform.

Many Americans in the 1830s saw reform as both religious and democratic. Some intellectuals, whether or not they had a faith in God, had a religious-style impulse to reform society. Ralph Waldo Emerson expressed that passion by asking, "What is man for but to be a reformer?"

The zeal of reformers for their causes often caused friction. Abolitionists who demanded immediate emancipation of slaves stirred resentment in the South and opposition in the North. The conflict widened the gap between the regions—a gap that led to armed confrontation between the North and the South.

Section Review

ANSWERS

8

1. Widespread antislavery activity and Britain's abolition of slavery in its colonies led Garrison and the Tappan brothers to form the association. 2

2. Frederick Douglass called for abolition of slavery by speeches and through his newspaper, *North Star*. Harriet Tubman guided slaves to freedom by the Underground Railroad. David Walker published a pamphlet urging slaves to fight for freedom. 3

3. Moderates sought gradual cautious change; Garrison and followers wanted immediate abolition and, unlike moderates, wanted involvement of blacks and women. Some people, like David Walker, believed that violence was the only way to ultimately win freedom. 3

Chapter Survey

ANSWERS

Using New Vocabulary

1. (c) *Suffrage* is the right to vote.
2. (a) *Revivals* brought religious feeling back to life.
3. (b) *Utopias* are model societies, not like any place already existing.

Reviewing the Chapter

1. White male suffrage eliminated property qualifications for voting. Popular election of electors brought electing President closer to the voters. National political conventions opened candidate selection to all party delegates.
2. Jackson did not regard Indians as separate nations and wanted their land for settlers. He urged passage of Indian Removal Act.
3. Northerners supported protective tariffs because they would protect region's industries. Westerners supported tariff because revenue might be used for road building. Southerners opposed tariff because they did not want to pay tax on imported goods, did not want to fund improvements in other parts of country.
4. (a) Tariff of 1828 so angered southern states that Calhoun wrote the (b) "South Carolina Exposition and Protest," claiming states had right to nullify federal laws deemed unconstitutional. Congress passed the lower (c) Tariff of 1832, South Carolina passed (d) nullification ordinance voiding the tariff, and threatened to secede if government tried to collect duties. To preserve the Union, Congress passed both the (e) Force Bill and the (f) Tariff of 1833.
5. Jackson requested Treasury secretary to stop depositing federal funds in the bank.
6. Students should mention "pet" banks, wild speculation, high prices, bankruptcy of American businesses, drop in British demand for cotton, bank failures.
7. Temperance movement to ban alcohol. Public education movement to improve public schools and make education available to all children. Campaign to stop treatment of insane as criminals. Women's rights movement for education, property, and voting rights for women. Abolitionists wanted to end slavery.
8. Women could not vote, own property, or keep custody of children after divorce. They wanted to actively participate in the antislavery movement. Held a conference on women's rights and went on speaking tours.
9. *Liberator* made antislavery crusade more visible. British abolition of slavery encouraged American antislavery groups to expand efforts. Lane Seminary debate on slavery converted

Reduced student page in the Teacher's Edition

Chapter Survey

Using New Vocabulary

Match each numbered vocabulary term with its origin. Then explain the connection between the origin and the vocabulary term.

1. suffrage	(a) Latin: *re,* again + *vivere,* to live
2. revivals	(b) Greek: *ou,* not + *topos,* a place
3. utopias	(c) Latin: *suffragium,* a ballot

Reviewing the Chapter

1. Explain how each of the following allowed more participation in government: white male suffrage, popular election of electors, national political conventions.

2. Why did President Jackson favor a plan of forced migration for American Indians and how did he implement it?

3. Explain the position of the North, the South, and the West on the issue of protective tariffs.

4. Explain how each event led to the next. (a) Tariff of 1828 (b) "South Carolina Exposition and Protest" (c) Tariff of 1832 (d) South Carolina nullification ordinance (e) Force Bill (f) Tariff of 1833

5. How did Jackson quickly end the power of the Second Bank of the United States?

6. Describe the chain of events that led from the Bank War to the Panic of 1837 and explain how each event caused the one following it.

7. List four reform movements to improve society launched between 1820 and 1850. Explain the goal or goals of each movement.

8. Why and how did women begin an organized movement for their rights?

9. Explain how each of the following affected the abolitionist movement: the *Liberator,* British abolition of slavery, the Lane Seminary debate on slavery, the *North Star,* David Walker's *Appeal,* the murder of Elijah Lovejoy, the gag rule, the Liberty party.

Thinking Critically

1. Evaluation. Andrew Jackson said, "More is lost by the long continuance of men in office than is generally to be gained by their experience." Do you agree or disagree with him? Explain your answer.

2. Analysis. What connection do you see between the spread of democracy in the 1820s and 1830s and the growth of reform movements?

3. Analysis. Explain how the question of the abolition of slavery became linked with the issues of free speech and westward expansion. How did these links widen the gap between North and South?

Using a Time Line

Match each event in the list below with the correct date on the time line. Then explain the importance of the event. Write your answers in chronological order. (Some dates will have more than one event.)

(A) financial panic
(B) Indian Removal Act
(C) Tariff of Abominations
(D) Hayne-Webster Debate
(E) tariff reduced to 20 percent over ten years
(F) Jackson's election
(G) Force Act
(H) Seneca Falls Declaration
(I) Cherokee constitution
(J) American Anti-Slavery Society

History and You

Between the 1820s and the 1850s, the United States bubbled with movements to reform society. What reform movements exist today? What are their goals and what methods do they use to achieve these goals? Compare and contrast today's movements with those of the early nineteenth century.

most Oberlin students to abolitionism. *North Star* urged blacks to head antislavery movement, rather than follow lead of whites. David Walker urged blacks to fight for freedom, provoking harsher treatment of blacks in South. Elijah Lovejoy's murder made Americans see abolition as an issue of civil liberties. Gag rule banned discussion of slavery in Congress but raised issue of free speech. Liberty Party split off from American Anti-Slavery Society to form more moderate group.

Thinking Critically

1. Students who agree might argue for "house-cleaning" of appointed offices to bring in new ideas. Those who disagree might argue that rewarding political loyalty with government jobs opens the possibility of appointing incompetents.
2. As more people could vote, they gained a voice in public policy and began to see ways to change American society other than through government.
3. Southern attempts to gag abolitionists linked issue of slavery to that of free speech. Southern efforts to extend slavery to western territory linked the issue to westward expansion and convinced some that slavery must be abolished everywhere to keep it from spreading.

Using a Time Line

(C) 1828; (F) 1828; (I) 1828; (B) 1830; (D) 1830; (E) 1833; (G) 1833; (J) 1833; (A) 1837; (H) 1848

History and You

Answers may include environmental movement, goals: to stop pollution, promote conservation, and protect planet. Methods include informing public of problems, working for legislation, applying economic pressure to corporations, and staging protest demonstrations. Many methods are similar to those used in the early nineteenth century. The goal is different as is the tactic of using economic pressure on corporations.

Applying Thinking Skills

1. Andrew Jackson.
2. Jackson's veto of the rechartering of the Second Bank of the United States
3. Some felt Jackson used presidential power in excess of powers defined in Constitution.
4. Document calling for U.S. Bank; to destroy the bank before the end of its charter, Jackson ordered that government funds not be deposited in the bank.
5. Believes Jackson has abused his power.

Applying Thinking Skills

Interpreting Political Cartoons

Believing that President Andrew Jackson had overextended the powers of the presidency, the Whig party dubbed Jackson "King Andrew the First." Study the cartoon below and then answer the questions that follow.

1. Who is pictured in the cartoon?

2. What incident is referred to by the object in his left hand?

3. Jackson is shown stepping on the Constitution. Why?

4. What other object is Jackson stepping on? Explain the incident suggested by this action.

5. What is the cartoonist's point of view toward Jackson's use of power?

Writing About Issues

The Issue: *Should party hosts be held liable for the drinking and driving of their guests?*

The question of how much control government should have over people's personal choices arose with the reform movements of the early 1800s. Today, similar questions face Americans.

To celebrate his son's graduation from high school in 1983, C. Connor Murphy bought twelve half-kegs of beer and threw a party. When he realized that some of his son's friends were getting too drunk to drive, Murphy collected their car keys. But he missed one guest, Thomas Foley.

Driving home, Foley struck and killed classmate Christopher Ely. Ely's parents sued Murphy, charging that his negligence in serving alcohol to teenagers had led to Christopher's death. The Connecticut Supreme Court agreed, ruling that Murphy could be held liable for the death. Murphy was ordered to pay the Elys $750,000.

For years, courts have held restaurant and bar owners liable for accidents involving intoxicated customers. The Murphy case extended this responsibility to the home. Today more than twenty states have laws holding the hosts of social events liable for guests who drink. In most cases, these social-host-liability laws are limited to problems that arise from serving alcohol to minors.

Are such laws fair? Many people say no. They argue that it is the individual, not the host, who should be held responsible for his or her actions. Blaming hosts, they say, does nothing to solve the many problems associated with alcohol consumption in this country.

Others argue that these laws are both fair and necessary. Making hosts liable for their guests, they argue, may make them think twice about serving alcohol to minors. This, in turn, might help reduce the number of alcohol-related accidents and deaths among teenagers.

Choose one side of this issue and prepare notes for a class debate on the topic. Also, predict the arguments your opponent will make, and prepare points to use in response.

Chapter 10

The West: Crossroads of Cultures

Planning Guide

	Student Text	TWE Lesson Plans	Support Materials
SECTION 1	**Section 10–1** (1–2 Days) **Trails to the West,** pp 248–255 Review/Evaluation Section Review, p 255	**Introducing the Chapter:** A Report on Western Lands—Cooperative Activity, one class period, p 245B **Teaching the Main Ideas:** Packing a wagon—Cooperative Activity, one class period, p 245B **Teaching the Main Ideas:** Life on the Trail—Class Activity, one class period, p 245B	★ **Read to Remember,** Section 1 ● **Section Activities,** Section 1 Δ **Enrichment Activities,** Section 1 Δ **Readings,** Prudencia Higuera, Josiah Gregg ● **Tests and Quizzes,** Section 1 Quiz
SECTION 2	**Section 10–2** (1 Day) **Gone to Texas,** pp 256–259 Review/Evaluation Section Review, p 259	**Reinforcement Activity:** Time Line Card Sort—Cooperative Project, 30 minutes, p 245C	★ **Read to Remember,** Section 2 ● **Section Activities,** Section 2 Δ **Readings,** Herman Erenberg ● **Tests and Quizzes,** Section 2 Quiz
SECTION 3	**Section 10–3** (1–3 Days) **Manifest Destiny,** pp 260–265 Connections to Themes: The Search for Opportunity, p 265 The Creative Spirit: Hispanic Americans, p 266–267 Review/Evaluation Section Review, p 265 Chapter 10 Survey, pp 268–269 Unit 3 Survey, pp 270–271 Skills, pp 268–269 Using New Vocabulary Thinking Critically Using Geography Applying Social Studies Skills: Analyzing Maps Applying Thinking Skills: Recognizing Point of View	**Enrichment Activity:** To Go or Not to Go to War—Individual Activity, 30 minutes, p 245C **Evaluating Progress:** Help Wanted in the West—Individual Activity, one class period, p 245C	★ **Read to Remember,** Section 3 ● **Section Activities,** Section 3 Δ **Enrichment Activities,** Section 3 Δ **Readings,** Joint Resolution of Congress to Annex Texas ● **Tests and Quizzes,** Section 3 Quiz, Chapter 10 Test (Forms A and B), Unit 3 Test (Forms A and B) **Additional Resources** ● **Active Learning** Δ **GTV Videodiscs** Δ **Transparencies and Activity Book** ● **Testing Software** ★ **Chapter Summaries** **Key:** ★ **For Extra Support** ● **For All Students** Δ **For Enrichment**

Overview

In the early 1800s, Americans began to move west beyond the borders of the United States. Mountain men and traders led the way, and settlers followed in their paths. Pioneers headed to Oregon for the lush river valleys, to Utah to practice their religion, and to California for gold.

To escape a depression and to acquire new land for cotton, some American settlers cast their eyes on Texas. First Spain, then Mexico, encouraged the American settlers. But when strained relations led Mexico to try to enforce its rule over Texas, conflict ensued. The Texans emerged victorious and established the Lone Star Republic. In 1845 Texas was admitted to the Union as a state.

A widespread belief in manifest destiny—the idea that the United States was destined to occupy North America from coast to coast—spurred the nation's expansion. A peaceful agreement with Britain reconciled the northern border of the United States. Attempts to acquire Mexico's northern territories, however, led to war. As a result, the United States acquired California, New Mexico, Arizona, Utah, Nevada, and parts of Wyoming and Colorado.

Activity Objectives

After completing the activities, students should be able to

- consider questions prospective settlers faced in making their preparations.
- explain the the risks and hardships pioneers encountered on trails west.
- describe aspects of life in Texas and the Far West in the early 1800s.
- relate the sequence of events that led to the Lone Star Republic.
- describe the concept of manifest destiny and its impact on settlement of the Far West.

Introducing the Chapter

A Report on the Western Lands

This cooperative activity requires one and a half class periods.

This activity directs attention to American settlement in and acquisition of the Far West. Students report to Congress on the status of the Far West in 1825.

Have the class review the map "The United States in 1822" on page 215, identifying the boundaries of the United States and of neighboring areas and noting which boundaries in dispute. Remind students that Mexico had gained independence in 1821 and emphasize that western lands were populated by people of several cultures—Native American, Spanish, Mexican, British, and Russian.

Divide the class into three groups. Each group is to develop a "Report on the Lands to the West" to present to Congress in 1825 to help it make important foreign policy decisions. Each report should contain information about peoples, boundaries, landforms, resources, potential usefulness, and, if possible, climate. Students may use information found in Chapters 1 through 9 and maps on pages 899–907.

Students should advise Congress about its responsibilities to Americans who move into foreign lands and the position it should take in encounters between Americans and peoples of the Far West. Encourage students to list policy options and indicate their preference.

Have students present their reports to the class. After students have read the chapter, have them review their proposals to see how closely they parallel actual history.

Teaching the Main Ideas

Section 10–1: Packing a Wagon

This cooperative project requires one class period.

This activity makes pioneer travel come alive as students prepare a list of supplies that a pioneer family might have packed into a covered wagon about 1840.

Use masking tape to outline the dimensions of an average wagon bed—10 feet long by 4 feet wide—on the classroom floor. Emphasize that the people who traveled by covered wagon had to carry all their goods in a space equivalent to that marked off on the floor. Explain that the wooden sides of wagons were about 2 feet high, but the supports and canvas that covered the wagon allowed travelers to pack their belongings along the sides to a height of about 4 feet.

Divide the class into groups of five, each to represent a family moving from somewhere east of the Mississippi to a new home in the West. Direct the groups to plan a list of supplies for the journey and goods to help them establish new homes. They may also want to take family heirlooms.

Have the class evaluate the lists for sufficiency, appropriateness, and "fit" into the wagon bed. Ask students to consider what they would pack in the same amount of space for a cross-country move today. You can carry the activity further by having students actually pack the wagon space for either 1840 or 1990 travel.

Teaching the Main Ideas

Section 10–1: Life on the Trail

This class activity requires one class period.

Students draw conclusions about pioneer life on the trail by examining "artifacts" and other objects representative of those actually found at Oregon and Santa Fe trail sites.

Artifacts and other objects found at trail sites include grave markers (often inscribed "died of cholera"), old dolls, horns and skulls of buffalo or oxen, horseshoes and ox shoes, rusted kitchen utensils, heavy items of iron or steel such as anvils and forges, furniture, bellows, slabs of bacon, iron wagon tires and other wagon parts, empty cartridges, lead, and cavalry buttons. Provide seven of these objects for students to examine. If you are unable to find the actual objects, provide replicas or illustrations.

Challenge students to draw conclusions about life on the trail by studying the items. Divide the class into seven groups and give each group one object. Direct the groups to list words and phrases that describe how the artifact relates to life on the trail. For example, an anvil might represent hopes for a blacksmith business and also the items travelers had to discard—artifacts of their previous lives—to lighten the load. Wagon parts would indicate delay or the end of a journey when a wagon broke down.

Allow each group time to examine and describe an object, then rotate the objects to new groups. Each group should attach its list to the object. As groups rotate, they will add to the lists. Repeat the examination and description process until all groups have studied all seven objects.

Have students read the descriptive words associated with each object. Conclude by having a spokesperson for each group provide a one-sentence statement about the significance of one object. Write the sentences on the chalkboard and discuss with the class whether or not they provide a a complete picture of pioneer life on the trail.

Reinforcement Activity

Section 10–2: Time Line Card Sort

This cooperative project requires half a class period.

This activity reinforces understanding of the series of events that led Texas from Spanish control to statehood. Students create a time line of events from 1718 to 1837.

Prepare a set of 14 cards for every three students. Write one of the events below on each card in a set. Do not write the dates on the cards. Shuffle each set so that students do not receive the cards in chronological order.

- Spaniards establish San Antonio. (1718)
- Mexico becomes independent. (1821)
- Mexico confirms Stephen Austin's land grant. (1821)
- Mexico abolishes slavery. (1829)
- American population in Texas reaches 16,000. (1830)
- Santa Anna becomes dictator of Mexico. (1834)
- Mexican military rule is established in Texas. (1835)
- Texans block Mexican troops at Gonzales and Goliad. (1835)
- Texans capture San Antonio. (1835)
- Texas declares its independence from Mexico. (1835)
- The Alamo falls to Santa Anna's army. (1836)
- Santa Anna is defeated at San Jacinto. (1836)
- Republic of Texas is established. (1836)
- United States recognizes the Lone Star Republic. (1837)

Have students review Section 10–2 for about five minutes. At the end of the review period, have students put away their texts and form groups of three. Give each group a set of the cards and tell them that they have ten minutes in which to create a time line with the cards to show the order of events in Texas history from 1718 to 1837.

When finished, groups should check the accuracy of their time lines as you read the correct order of events. Encourage students to make and use time line cards in studying other historical periods.

Evaluating Progress

Section 10–3: Help Wanted in the West

This individual activity requires one class period, or it may be assigned as homework.

Have students exhibit their understanding of western life by creating "help wanted ads" for a newspaper. If students are not familiar with the format and style of employment ads, it might be helpful to bring in current examples.

Tell students that one nineteenth-century Nevada newspaper editor remarked, "American pioneers carry with them the press and the type, and wherever they pitch their tent, be it in the wilderness of the interior, among the snow covered peaks of the Sierra, or on the sunny sea beach of the Pacific, there too must the newspaper appear." These newspapers published local news; marriage, birth, and death notices; word of distant events; the editor's opinions; tall tales; and advertisements for goods, land, and jobs.

Have students brainstorm to list of the kinds of people whose skills were most likely needed in early Texas and the Far West. The list might include trappers, farmers, missionaries, guides, miners, and businesspeople.

Tell students to write classified advertisements for four different kinds of jobs likely to be found in Texas and the Far West from 1820 to 1850. Each ad should be written from a different location. In creating their ads, students should describe the environment, and the nature of the work, the skills and knowledge required of the worker, and the benefits such a worker could expect.

The ads, which may be imaginative, should be evaluated on the degree to which they reflect aspects of life in Texas and the Far West from 1820 to 1850, and on the creativity shown in making the jobs "attractive."

Enrichment Activity

Section 10–3: To Go or Not to Go to War

This individual activity requires about half a class period, or it may be assigned as homework.

This writing assignment is designed to help students understand the issues and conflicts that led to war between the United States and Mexico in 1848.

After students have read Section 10–3, explain that many Americans disagreed with their government's decision to go to war. Lead the class in discussing why the Mexican War was controversial, making sure that students consider the impact of slavery, border disputes, and manifest destiny. The following comments may help students view the war from different perspectives.

> *“The world beholds the peaceful triumphs of our emigrants. To us belongs the duty of protecting them. . . . The jurisdiction of our laws and the benefits of our republican institutions should be extended over [Americans] in the distant regions which they have selected for their homes.”*
>
> —President James Polk

> *“California will probably next fall away from the loose adhesion which . . . holds a remote province in a slight . . . dependence on the [capital]. Mexico never can exert any real government authority over such a country. A population will soon be in actual occupation of California, over which it will be idle for Mexico to dream of dominion.”*
>
> —Newspaper editor John L. O'Sullivan

> *“California, to become the seat of wealth and power for which nature has marked it, must pass into the hands of another race.”*
>
> —Anonymous

> *“America presents her ambitious plans for conquering all the American continent. . . . A war will give her a welcome pretense for possessing herself of all Mexico.”*
>
> —*Journal des Débats*, official French government paper

> *“A war of conquest is bad; but the present war had darker shadows. It is a war for the extension of slavery over a territory which has already been purged by Mexican authority from this stain and curse.”*
>
> —Abolitionist Charles Sumner

> *“Uncle Joshua always says, in nine cases out of ten it costs more to rob an orchard than it would to buy the apples.”*
>
> —Writer Seba Smith

Assign the following essay question: *Was the United States justified in going to war with Mexico?* Encourage students to consider manifest destiny, slavery, the aims and effectiveness of diplomacy, and the Mexican viewpoint on conflicts leading up to the war. Encourage students to supply supporting evidence to back the positions they take.

Divide the class into two groups—those who favored war and those who opposed it. Hold an open debate between the two sides, encouraging speakers to support their views with information from their essays.

Bibliography and Audiovisual Material

Teacher Bibliography

Armitage, Susan. *The Women's West.* Norman Oklahoma: University of Oklahoma Press, 1987.

Jackson, Donald D. *Gold Dust.* New York: Alfred A. Knopf, 1980.

Moquin, Wayne and Charles Van Doren, eds. *A Documentary History of the Mexican Americans.* New York: Bantam, 1978.

Ruiz, Ramon E. ed. *The Mexican War: Was It Manifest Destiny?* New York: Holt, Rinehart, and Winston, 1963.

Student Bibliography

Beckwourth, James P., as told to Thomas DiBonner. *The Life and Adventures of James P. Beckwourth.* Lincoln Nebraska: University of Nebraska Press, 1981.

Lavender, David. *The Great West.* Boston: Houghton Mifflin, 1965.

Richter, Conrad. *Sea of Grass.* New York: Alfred A. Knopf, 1937.

Films, Videocassettes, and Videodiscs

Life in a California Mission, 1790. 14 min. AIMS Media. Videodisc.

Life in America 1800. 16 min. AIMS Media. Videodisc.

Manifest Destiny. 30 min. PBS Video. Movie.

United States Expansion Series: Oregon Territory. 19 min. *Texas.* 21 min. Coronet/MTI. Movies.

Westward Expansion. 31 min. Guidance Associates. Videocassette.

Computer Software

American History Explorer Series: Westward Expansion. Apple. Mindscape, Inc.

The Explorer Series: The 49ers. Apple. Hartley Courseware.

The Fight For Texas. Apple. Focus Media.

Sante Fe Trail. Apple or IBM. Educational Activities, Inc.

Wagon Train 1848. Macintosh. MECC.

Chapter 10

Objectives

- Give reasons for the movement to the Far West in the early 1800s.
- Explain why American settlers in Texas rebelled against Mexico.
- Explain how a belief in manifest destiny led to an expansion to the Pacific Coast.

Introducing

THE CHAPTER

For suggestions on introducing Chapter 10, refer to page 245B in the Teacher's Edition.

Developing

THE CHAPTER

For activities and teaching strategies to help you reinforce and enrich chapter content, see pages 245B–245D in the Teacher's Edition.

B · A · C · K · G · R · O · U · N · D

Chapter Opener Illustrations
Independence Rock, a landmark along the Oregon Trail, overlooked Wyoming's Sweetwater River. Travelers tried to reach this spot by the Fourth of July in order to cross the mountains before the snow.

James Beckwourth, mountain man, lived with the Crow Indians from 1826 to 1837. He became a war chief of the Crow and often boasted of the battle honors that he won among his adopted people.

Founded in 1718, San Antonio was the capital of Spanish Texas. After Texas independence it became a busy commercial center. In the 1840's, a cathedral, hotel, and grocery, as well as the small shops seen in this view, surrounded the main plaza.

The *Wagon Road Guide* was published in 1858. Its cover

Reduced student page in the Teacher's Edition

Chapter 10 1820-1850

The West: Crossroads of Cultures

A VIEW from the SUMMIT of INDEPENDENCE ROCK,
exhibiting the Sweet-water river and Mountains, and
the Washington City Comp' corralled, at noon;
July 26, 1849.

was more romantic than factual since vast herds of buffalo had largely disappeared by the time the guide was published. Many guide books were inaccurate, written by promoters who had never been to the Far West.

Every item of a cowboy's dress had a useful purpose. Spurs were highly practical, and most cowboys rarely took them off. Most Mexican spurs had spiky rowels, or revolving wheels.

American Voices

The son of a slave, James Pierson Beckwourth grew up as a free man in St. Louis. In the 1820s he gave up city life for the life of a trapper, explorer, and guide in the Far West. In 1850 Beckwourth blazed a trail across the Sierra between Reno and the site of present-day California's Sacramento Valley. Thousands of settlers would follow his route. A year after Beckwourth's death in 1868, a railroad was built through the pass that still bears his name. In his autobiography Beckwourth described the discovery of the pass.

> "*We proceeded in an easterly direction, and all busied themselves in searching for gold; but my errand was of a different character; I had come to discover . . . a pass.*
>
> *It was the latter end of April when we entered upon an extensive valley at the northwest extremity of the Sierra range. . . . Deer and antelope filled the plains, and their boldness was conclusive that the hunter's rifle was to them unknown. We struck across this beautiful valley to the waters of the Yuba [River, which flows west]. From there we went to the waters of the Truckee. These flowed in an easterly direction, telling us we were on the eastern slope of the mountain range. This, I at once saw, would afford the best wagon-road.*"

Between the 1820s and the 1850s, adventurers like Beckwourth roamed country that seemed shrouded in mystery to most Americans. Tales of these mountain men's exploits drifted back across the continent. Such tales, with descriptions of remarkable landscapes, lured people westward, and pioneers began to follow the mountain men into western lands. The American settlement in the Far West would lead to discord within the United States and to conflicts between nations.

San Antonio Museum Association

Oregon Trail illustration by J. Goldsborough Bruff for U.S. government; James Beckwourth; East Side Main Plaza, San Antonio, Texas *by W.M.G. Samuel; an Oregon Trail guidebook; early California spur.*

Analyzing Primary Sources

American Voices

James Beckwourth (1798–1867) was born in Virginia, the son of an African-American mother and a white former Revolutionary War officer. In 1823 he joined his first fur-trading expedition with General William Ashley.

Ask: Which "errand" was more important, the discovery of gold or the discovery of a pass? Why? **(The pass was more important, because it would be useful to many people and provide Beckwourth a long-term business opportunity.)** How did Beckwourth know he had found a pass? **(He found a river that flowed west and then another that flowed east.)**

Have students look at a map of California and try to find Beckwourth's pass. **(located on State Highway 70 east of the junction with U.S. 395.)**

Chapter Connections

Tell students that events in Chapter 10 were occurring at the same time as the events they read about in Chapter 9.

GTV Side 2

Chap. 11, Frame 31769

Going to Extremes: The Far West (Movie)

Search:

Play:

Section 10-1

Objectives

- ***Answer the Focus Question.***
- *Cite achievements of individuals who participated in the westward movement.*

Introducing

THE SECTION

Have students review the explorations of Lewis and Clark (Chapter 8). Ask what resources Lewis and Clark found that might have attracted people to the Far West. **(fertile land, valuable animals such as the beaver)** What was needed before many were likely to travel to this area? **(a system of trails)**

Developing

THE SECTION

Understanding Geography

Using Maps. Is the "Great American Desert" really a desert? Have students answer this question by determining the main products of the states between the Missouri and the Rockies today (see map on text pages 906–907). Have them point out the part of the western lands that really is desert.

B · A · C · K · G · R · O · U · N · D

Time Line Illustrations

1. A California mission bell tower.

2. Flags of six nations have flown in the Texas winds. The lone star flag was adopted in 1839. The red, white, and blue stand for loyalty, strength, and bravery.

3. Between 1840 and 1870 nearly half a million people trekked about two thousand miles along the Oregon Trail to Oregon, California, and Utah. Wagon trains were outfitted in Missouri river towns, where pioneers camped in the spring while waiting for grass to grow on the plains to feed their animals.

4. People from many lands flocked to California to seek gold. This caricature of a German gold-seeker appeared in 1850. Note the cooking pot on his head, tools under his arms, pan and provisions over his shoulder, and weapons in his pocket.

Reduced student page in the Teacher's Edition

CHAPTER TIME LINE

1820 - 1850

1822 Becknell blazes Santa Fe Trail

1825 First Green River Rendezvous

1835 Texas War for Independence begins

1820 — 1827 — 1834

1823 Last California mission established

1830 Mormon Church founded

1833 Joe Walker crosses Sierras and sights Yosemite Valley

10-1 Trails to the West

Focus: Why did Americans venture west in the early 1800s?

In the early 1800s thousands of Americans ventured beyond the westernmost boundaries of the United States, which had been established by the Louisiana Purchase. Searching for new opportunities, they thought the vast, treeless plains that lie between the Missouri River and the Rockies were too dry for farming. Instead, they made their way beyond what they called the "Great American Desert" to the disputed territory of Oregon and the Mexican lands of California, Utah, and New Mexico. They saw these lands as their new frontier.

Remnants of the settlers' trails are still visible today. Here and there among lush fields of corn and wheat and across arid deserts run deep ruts carved more than a hundred and fifty years ago by countless wagons following the trails west.

Blazing the Santa Fe Trail

Some of the first Americans to move beyond the Louisiana Territory were traders seeking their fortunes in the Southwest. Zebulon Pike had published an account about his explorations in the Southwest and northern New Spain, and the Spanish towns he had visited there. His descriptions of Santa Fe's markets drew traders to the town. But the Spanish government was suspicious of the foreigners and threw them in jail. After Mexico won its independence from Spain in 1821, the Mexicans welcomed American traders.

Missouri trader William Becknell was one of the first to accept the welcome. He set out from Franklin, Missouri, in 1822, his three wagons piled with

5. On this campaign banner for the election of 1844, Polk is shown with vice-presidential nominee George M. Dallas. Dallas was chosen after Senator Silas Wright, an admirer of Van Buren, rejected the offer.

1836 Houston, Texas, founded

1846 Oregon boundary settled

1848 War with Mexico ends

1849 California gold rush begins

1836 — 1843 — 1850

1841 First wagon train on the Oregon Trail

1844 Polk calls for annexation of Oregon

cloth and household goods. Blazing a trail across a forbidding arid landscape, Becknell and his party drank mule blood to quench their thirst. When the weary Becknell finally reached Santa Fe, he sold his goods for huge profits.

Other traders heard about Becknell's good fortune and set out to follow his Santa Fe Trail. They found markets in Santa Fe and nearby Taos and brought back furs, hides, mules, and coins.

The Mountain Men

Fur trappers, often called "mountain men," led the way into the Far West. The fur trade was an important business in the early 1800s. Beaver pelts were especially prized, for men's beaver hats were very fashionable in both the United States and Europe.

The trappers were an independent and diverse group—Americans, French, Spaniards, Mexicans, and British. These mountain men hunted and trapped from Canada to Mexico and from the Missouri River to the Great Basin and beyond. Sometimes traveling together and sometimes alone, they roamed the West, working traps along streams and ponds and living mainly off the land they considered their "home in the wilderness."

Of course, their "home" was also home to American Indians. Some trappers and Indians met in friendship, and trappers often lived with Indians, occasionally becoming part of a tribe. Many mountain men gained their knowledge of trails and their mountaineering skills from the Indians, who knew the land. Many also adopted the values and life styles of the native peoples.

After months of trapping, the mountain men would paddle down the Missouri River to sell their furs in St. Louis, the center of the fur trade. Then in 1807 Manuel Lisa of St. Louis decided that it would be economical to meet the trappers partway. He built a trading post at the mouth of the Bighorn River, in present-day Montana, and hired his own crew of trappers. A year later, John Jacob Astor started the American Fur Company, and his posts soon dotted the Missouri River and its tributaries.

In the 1820s the Rocky Mountain Fur Company sent its trappers deeper into the mountains. Instead of setting up costly permanent trading posts, com-

Thinking Critically

Analysis. Discuss why people travel to set up new homes far from old ones. Have students cite reasons that people came to the American colonies. (for religious or political freedom, to gain land and/or business opportunities)

Encourage students to think back to Chapter 9 and suggest conditions in the East (such as the financial panic of 1837) that caused people to migrate westward. Have them suggest what conditions in the West might make people want to move there. (acquisition of new lands, discovery of valuable natural resources)

Connections: Economics

Discussion. **Ask**: What did the mountain men have to gain by being friends with Native Americans? **(knowledge of trails, mountaineering skills, safe passage through Native-American lands, knowledge of the best beaver locations, labor to help in trapping beaver)** What did Native Americans have to gain by making friends with mountain men? **(supplies such as guns and food, possible protection from white persecution)**

GTV Side 2

Chap. 11, Frame 33844

The Rocky Mountains, 1840s (Map)

Search:

Limited English Proficiency

Small Group Discussion. In 1848 George F. Ruxton described a beaver trapper's equipment. As you read the following description, have a volunteer write the items on the chalkboard. Then have students meet in small groups to discuss the usefulness of the items.

" . . . consists usually of two or three horses or mules—one for saddle, the others for packs—and six traps, which are carried in a bag of leather called a trap sack. Ammunition, . . . dressed [tanned] deerskins for moccasins . . . are carried in a wallet of dressed buffalo-skin, called a possible sack. . . . Over his left shoulder and under his right arm hang his powder-horn and bullet-pouch, in which he carries his balls, flint, and steel, and odds and ends of all kinds. Round the waist is a belt, in which is stuck a large butcher-knife in a sheath of buffalo-hide, made fast to the belt by a chain or guard of steel, which also supports a little buckskin case containing a whetstone. A tomahawk is also often added; and of course, a long, heavy rifle is part and parcel of his equipment. "

Writing about History

Diary. Have students research the lives of mountain men such as Jedediah Smith, William Sublette, Joe Walker, Jim Bridger, and Etienne Provost. Students can write an adventure that might be described in a mountain man's diary.

Connections: Geography
Zebulon Pike explored the West between 1805 and 1807. He later won fame for discovering the peak named after him—Pikes Peak (he himself called it simply Grand Peak). Pike explored the upper Mississippi River—to try to find the source—and later the Southwest.

Spanish authorities arrested him as a trespasser and possible spy when he entered New Mexico and took him and his men to Santa Fe. Released several months later, he brought back valuable information for the government. He lost his life in the War of 1812 while leading a successful advance on York (Toronto), Canada.

Reduced student page in the Teacher's Edition

pany traders met the trappers each summer at a designated spot in the mountains. At such a rendezvous (RAHN-day-voo), or meeting place, company trappers exchanged their fur pelts for supplies and wages. Independent trappers and bands of Indians were also welcome to trade, and the rendezvous became a boisterous social occasion that lasted several weeks.

In their search for furs, mountain men such as Joe Walker, Tom Fitzpatrick, Jedediah Smith, and James Beckwourth wandered high plains, explored passes in the Rocky Mountains and the Sierra Nevada, and trekked across blistering deserts. Some of them made their way into California and eventually settled there. Others wandered into the Oregon Country.

Then, around 1840, fashion changed, and gentlemen turned from beaver hats to tall silk ones. By then, too, beaver had been trapped almost to extinction. Most mountain men turned to trading, buffalo hunting, scouting for the army, or guiding others through the dense forests, towering mountains, and arid deserts of the West.

The mountain men portrayed in this painting by Alfred Jacob Miller wore buckskins—Native-American clothing made of deerskin.

The Oregon Trail

The mountain men's tales of Oregon's green valleys and lush forests trickled eastward, setting Americans to dreaming about the opportunities they might find there. Businesspeople imagined wealth in trade and fishing. Farmers were eager to plow the fertile soil. Missionaries felt a call to convert Native Americans to Christianity.

The first parties of American settlers to the Oregon Country were organized in 1832 and 1834 by Nathaniel J. Wyeth, who traveled with horses and mules. Among the pioneers who accompanied Wyeth on his second trip was Methodist minister Jason Lee. Once in Oregon, Lee explored the Willamette River Valley, chose a homestead, and established a mission and school.

Other missionaries soon followed. In 1836 Marcus Whitman, a doctor and Presbyterian minister, set out to prove that wagons could make the trip to Oregon. Traveling with a fur trade caravan, he and his wife soon had to abandon one of their

Multicultural Perspectives

Among those seeking new opportunities in Oregon was the family of George Washington Bush, a free African American. Bush helped guide a party along the trail in 1844. On arriving in Oregon, he was told that free blacks could not settle there. The whole wagon train had developed such respect and affection for Bush that they did not want to remain where he was not wanted. They chose to go north with him into British territory that is now Washington state. In 1845 the group became the first American settlers in the Puget Sound area.

Active Learning

Cooperative Activity. Have groups of students do research on wagon trains and then prepare a travel plan and a supply list for a wagon train. Travel plans might be for the Oregon Trail, the California Trail, the Mormon Trail, or others mentioned in the text.

wagons. The other also caused them trouble. "Wagon was upset twice," Narcissa Whitman noted in her diary one day. "It was a greater wonder that it was not turning a somersault continually." This wagon, too, was left behind in Idaho, and the missionaries finished their long journey on horseback.

In 1840 trappers found a route, the South Pass, that made wagon travel through the Rockies possible. Soon "Oregon fever" was sweeping the country. In 1841 the first wagon train—sixty-nine men, women, and children, with twelve wagons—set out on the Oregon Trail bound for "pioneer's paradise." Between 1841 and 1845 more than 10,000 "overlanders" trudged that trail.

From Missouri River towns—Independence, Kansas City, St. Joseph, Council Bluffs—the wagon trains started off in late April and early May. Timing was critical, for they had to cross the Rockies before the winter snows. The bulky wagons, which the pioneers called "prairie schooners," were usually pulled by sturdy, but slow, oxen.

The Oregon Trail stretched 2,000 miles through deserts, canyons, and mountain ranges. It took the pioneers at least four months, sometimes six, to reach the end of that trail. Along the way they had to conquer hunger, disease, numbing winter cold, and searing summer heat. Many of them died.

Tabitha Brown, who traveled to Oregon at age sixty-six, found the journey a nightmare. The wagon train's guide robbed the pioneers, leaving them lost in the wilderness. "We had sixty miles of desert without grass or water," she wrote, "mountains to climb, cattle giving out, wagons breaking, emigrants sick and dying."

Still, Brown and others endured. Once in Oregon, the now-hardy pioneers fanned out into the Willamette Valley, which is tucked in between the Cascades and the Coast Ranges just south of the Columbia River. They cleared land, built cabins, and laid out towns. Brown started a school for children orphaned on the trek west.

Growing American influence. Although under the Convention of 1818 the United States and Britain owned the Oregon Country jointly, most of the settlers were Americans. As the population increased, the settlers decided they needed a government. In 1843 they drew up a constitution

Spotlight on Daily Life

The first of the large caravans left Independence for Oregon in 1843, with 1,000 people, 5,000 cattle, and 120 wagons. Jesse Applegate, who led the section that included the cattle, noted these incidents in his diary, published as "A Day with the Cow Column."

4 A.M.	Rifle shot wakens caravan
5 A.M.	Round up cattle
6 A.M.	Breakfast Strike the tents; load the wagons
7 A.M.	Trumpet signals the march
12 P.M.	Lunch; caravan council meeting
1 P.M.	Resume march
4 P.M.	A baby is born
6 P.M.	Circle the wagons; pasture cattle
8 P.M.	Begin first night watch
10 P.M.	Hunting party returns with game

and a bill of rights that ensured religious freedom and trial by jury and banned slaveholding. They elected a governor and set up a legislature and a judicial system. All residents were expected to sign an oath of allegiance to the new constitution.

Meanwhile Oregon's Indians grew uneasy. Settlers were claiming their lands, and missionaries were trying to change their traditional ways of life. The clash of cultures led to an incident that was tragic for both settlers and Indians.

The Whitmans had built a mission, which had become a stopover for new settlers. In 1847 a party of settlers infected the mission's Indians with measles. In the epidemic that followed, more than half of the Cayuse tribe of 350 died, and the grieving survivors blamed the missionaries. Grief turned to anger. A small group of Cayuse attacked the mission, killing fourteen people including the Whitmans and setting fire to the buildings. Then the remnants of the Cayuse tribe fled their homeland and scattered into the mountains.

Connections: Health

Discussion. About one out of every seventeen pioneers who set out on the Oregon Trail was buried en route. Most of them died of disease. Going west was touted as a cure for ill health in the 1830s. Josiah Gregg, who wrote about his experiences on the Santa Fe Trail in *Commerce of the Prairies*, was virtually an invalid when he rode on his first wagon train but was healthy thereafter. *"The prairies have become very celebrated for their sanative [healthful] effect,"* he wrote.

Have students discuss which aspects of wagon train life might be healthful **(regular exercise, fresh air, simple diet)** and which might encourage disease **(poor sanitation, lack of fresh water, food, and vegetables).**

GTV Side 2

Chap. 11, Frame 35122

Trails West, Mid-1800s (Map)

Search:

Connections: Geography

Analyzing a Map. Explain to students that American settlement did not move regularly from east to west. Refer students to the map on text page 899. **Ask:** When did settlement reach the Mississippi River? **(lower Mississippi, by 1790; elsewhere, 1820–1850)** When did settlement reach the Far West? **(about 1850)** Besides Alaska, what was the last area settled? **(interior area between the Sierra-Cascades and the plains east of the Rockies)**

Multicultural Perspectives

The first settlers in the Los Angeles, California, area arrived on September 4, 1781. Forty-four people from eleven families were recruited in Mexico by Fernando de Rivera y Moncada for the original colony. Twenty-eight of the settlers were African Americans.

Global Connections

The Russians expanded southward along North America's west coast in order to hunt sea otters, which, like beavers, were valued for their pelts. They set up an outpost in Northern California at Fort Ross, which can still be seen.

Reduced student page in the Teacher's Edition

California

The next people to settle in California after the Native Americans were Mexicans from New Spain—a people of mixed Spanish and Indian ancestry. Claimed by Spain in the 1500s, California had remained largely unexplored for over two centuries. Then in the 1760s the British as well as the Russians, who claimed Alaska, began to expand southward. Alarmed, Spain set out to protect California from foreign powers.

In 1769 the government of New Spain sent an expedition to occupy California. In command was Gaspar de Portolá (POR-toh-LAH), accompanied by a priest, Father Junipero Serra (Hoo-NEE-peh-roh SEHR-ruh). From New Spain, the expedition headed north. When they reached San Diego Bay, Father Serra stopped to begin construction of Mission San Diego de Alcalá.

Between 1769 and 1823 Father Serra and his successors used Indian labor to build twenty-one missions from San Diego north to San Francisco. At each of these self-sufficient communities, priests worked to convert Indians to Christianity and teach them Spanish ways of life. Most Native Americans resisted these changes, but others were rounded up and forced to turn from their customary way of life. When Mexico won its independence in 1821, California became a Mexican province, and the mission system was doomed. Mission lands had been held in trust for the Native Americans by Spanish law, but Mexico broke up the lands into large *ranchos,* and granted them to favored settlers. The missions slowly fell into ruin. Mission Indians, left with neither land nor the protection of the Church, scattered. Some went to the hills, returning to old ways of life. Others herded cattle on the ranches formed from the mission lands.

A Californio

The California Trail

In the early 1820s ships from the United States began to call at ports in California. They came to trade with the Mexican settlers, or *Californios,* whose cattle and horses flourished on the open range. The traders bought cattle hides and cattle fat, called *tallow,* which was made into candles and soap. Many sailors found the *Californios'* ranch life to their liking and stayed.

A few American trappers found their way to California by an overland route. Twice, in 1826 and 1827, Jedediah Smith and some fellow mountain men wandered into California searching for furs. They explored the San Joaquin (wah-KEEN) and Sacramento valleys and returned home by blazing a trail east through the Sierra Nevada and the Great Salt Lake Basin. Other trappers soon followed, returning east with tales of California's "perennial spring and boundless fertility." Missourians John Bidwell and John Bartleson listened eagerly.

In 1841 the Bidwell-Bartleson expedition of thirty-four pioneers joined the first wagon train that set out on the Oregon Trail. They traveled with the train as far as Soda Springs, in Idaho, then headed south to California on their own. Plodding through the deserts of Utah and Nevada, they eventually abandoned their wagons and ate their oxen to survive.

When the party reached the towering Sierra Nevada, they plunged ahead on foot and horseback. Young Nancy Kelsey was the only woman in the group. Walking barefoot on blistered feet, Kelsey carried her infant child in her arms while she led her horse down steep cliffs.

The party made it through the mountains and emerged into California's San Joaquin Valley. This

Connections: Religion

Mormon beliefs make the tracing of family genealogy very important. Information that has been gathered about Mormons' ancestors is stored in the Granite Mountain Genealogical Vault, located about twenty miles east of Salt Lake City, Utah. The vault, carved out of solid rock in 1965 at a cost of more than two million dollars, contains more than 980,000 rolls of microfilm. It is the largest genealogical library in the world.

This meeting of settlers and Native Americans took place at Council Grove, Kansas, on the Santa Fe Trail.

journey and the others that followed opened the California Trail, and a small but steady stream of Americans began to flow into California.

The Mormon Trail

The California Trail was not the only one to branch off from the Oregon Trail. Another route angled through a high pass in the Rocky Mountains, then dropped down to the Great Salt Lake. This route, carved by the Mormons, a religious group, became known as the Mormon Trail.

The Mormon Church, or Church of Jesus Christ of Latter-Day Saints, was founded in New York in 1830 by Joseph Smith. Mormon leaders organized church members as a theocracy, or church-governed society. People were expected to work freely for the common good and, at first, businesses and personal property were considered the common property of the Church. By the 1840s many Mormons practiced polygamy, in which a man has more than one wife at the same time.

Many people reacted to these Mormon beliefs and practices with hostility. Driven out of communities in New York, Ohio, and Missouri, the Mormons fled to Illinois. On the banks of the Mississippi River they built the city of Nauvoo. By 1844 booming Nauvoo had almost 15,000 people. But anti-Mormon rioting erupted, and Joseph Smith and his brother were killed.

Brigham Young became the Mormons' new leader. As so many others had done, Young looked west for religious freedom and a new home. He determined to lead the Mormons beyond the Rockies, far away from their persecutors.

Early in the spring of 1846, the first groups left Nauvoo. Day by day, others followed until some 15,000 Mormons were on the move. In late fall most of them camped on the banks of the Missouri

Backyard History

Tracing a Family Tree. Suggest students trace as much of their own family trees as they can, interviewing parents and other relatives. If students and families are willing, encourage them to share stories about their ancestors. Experiences about westward migration or immigration from other countries would be especially interesting.

Limited English Proficiency

Using the Visuals. Have students study the picture of the wagon train on this page. What different activities are the people performing? How does each person help the train or individual family? What tools are the people using? What functions do the animals serve.

GTV Side 2

Chap. 11, Frame 36173

Mormon Migration, Mid-1800s (Map)

Search:

Geography Skills

ANSWERS

Whatever the site, a trapper would evaluate the fauna, a missionary would look for potential converts, a trader would look for commodities and customers, a miner for ores, and a settler for water and fertile land.

Connections: Economics

In the first phase of the movement to the Far West, meetings between pioneers and Native Americans along the Oregon Trail in the Platte River area were generally peaceful. Indians traded buffalo meat for tobacco, ironware, and travelers' worn-out clothing. Some enterprising Native Americans charged for ferry services across the wider rivers.

Reduced student page in the Teacher's Edition

Trails to the Far West

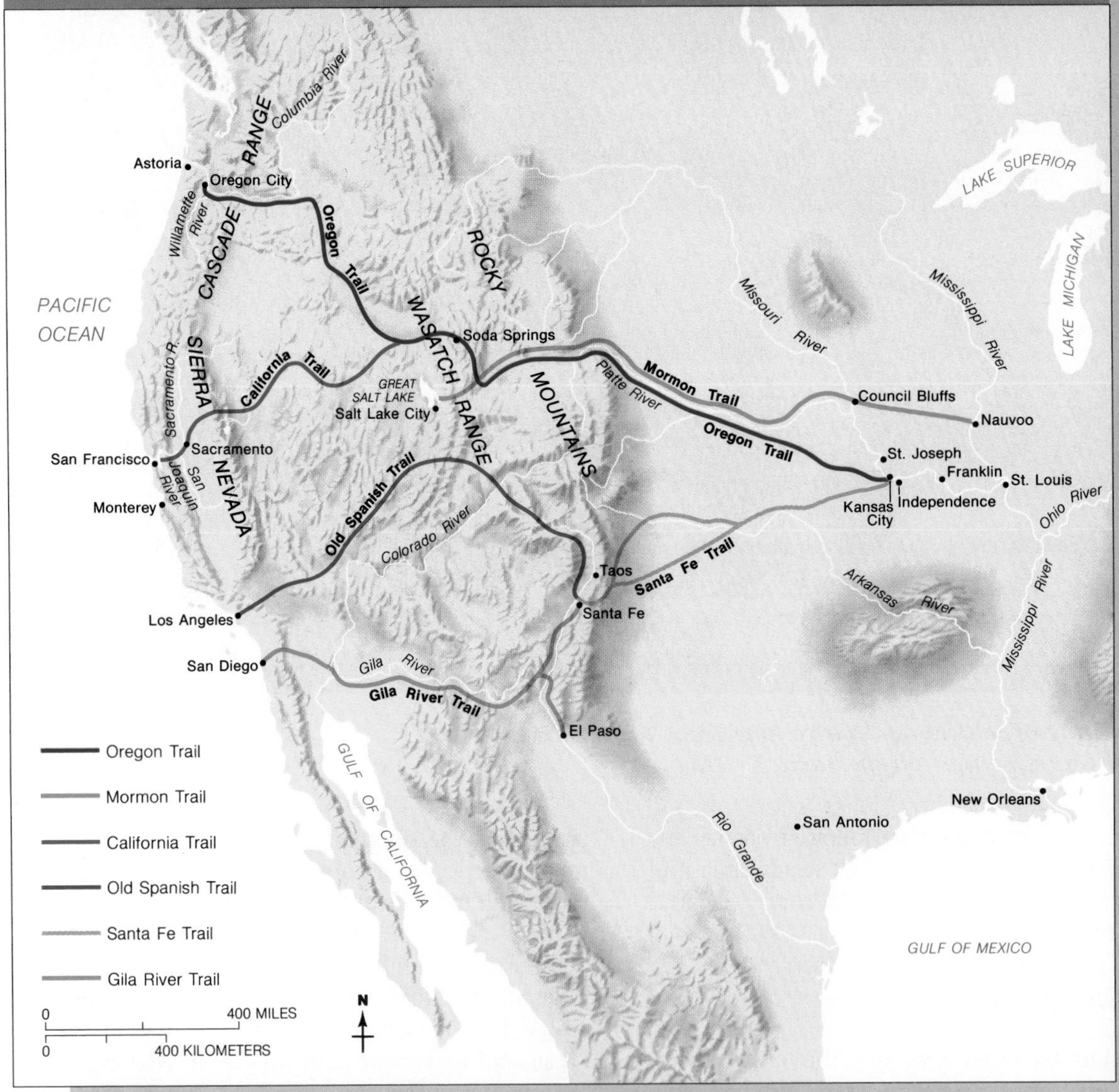

Geography Skills—Relationships Within Places. Each group of people evaluates a physical environment according to that group's traditions, purposes, and needs. Select a site at the end of any trail. In the mid 1800s, how might each of the following people have described the site's physical environment: a trapper, a missionary, a trader, a miner, and a settler?

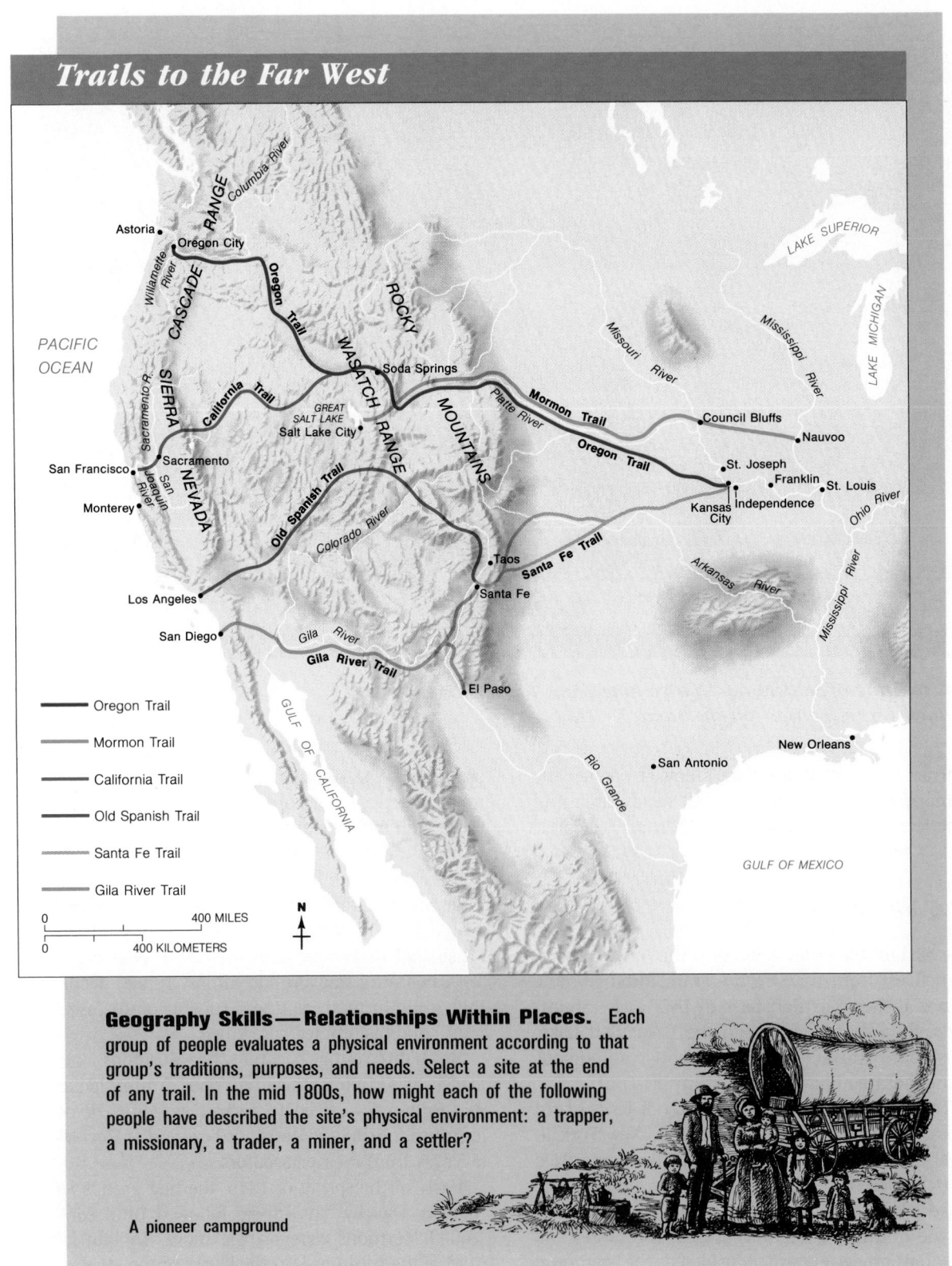

A pioneer campground

Connections: Geography

The Great Salt Lake is the remnant of a much larger freshwater lake, Lake Bonneville, which existed about 70,000 to 100,000 years ago. As the climate became drier, Lake Bonneville shrank until its shoreline fell below the level of its former outlet into the Snake River. Land speed record trials are run today on the Bonneville Flats, part of Lake Bonneville's dry bed.

Multicultural Perspectives

In July 1847, when the advance party of Mormons consisting of 143 men, 3 women, 2 children, and 73 wagons entered Salt Lake Valley, three men in the party were slaves. Their names were Oscar Crosby, Green Flakes, and Hark Lay. All were members of the Church of the Latter Day Saints. By autumn, more than fifty African Americans, some slaves and some free, had come to the valley.

In the 1850s Mormon converts from Europe completed their journey by walking 1,300 miles from Iowa City to Salt Lake City.

River. During that harsh, cold winter, hundreds died of hunger and disease. But when spring came, the survivors still looked westward with hope.

The first Mormon wagon train, with 148 people, resumed the journey in April 1847. It followed the north bank of the Platte River, then joined the Oregon Trail through the Rockies. From one mountain peak an advance party "looked out on the full extent of the valley where the Great Salt Lake glistened in the sunbeams."

The Great Salt Lake. When the wagons entered the valley in July, few places could have seemed less promising. The Mormons' new refuge was a dry, flat plain baked by the summer heat and populated chiefly by crickets, coyotes, and rattlesnakes. "I don't remember a tree that could be called a tree," one Mormon later said. Yet snow-fed streams from the surrounding mountains meandered across the plain, and the group offered prayers of thanksgiving.

The Mormons sowed crops, constructed complex irrigation systems, laid out a city, and prospered. Salt Lake City became a beacon for further migrations of believers. Within the next ten years, over ninety settlements arose in the valley, and Mormon outposts reached west to Nevada and California and north to Idaho.

After the United States acquired the region from Mexico in 1848, the Mormons applied to Congress for statehood. But the issue of polygamy proved to be a stumbling block. Instead, Congress made the area a territory in 1850 and gave it the name of Utah, after the Ute nation living there.

Section Review

1. Comprehension. What part did each of the following individuals play in the westward movement: William Becknell, Manuel Lisa, James Beckwourth, Joe Walker, Narcissa Whitman, John Bidwell, Brigham Young?

2. Comprehension. Study the map on page 254. In traveling from Missouri to Oregon, what landforms did the pioneers cross?

3. Analysis. What economic opportunities drew Americans westward? Explain at least three.

Linking Past and Present. It took up to six months to travel the 2,000-mile-long Oregon Trail, at a rate of about 11 miles a day. If you set off from your home on Monday morning and traveled westward at approximately 11 miles a day, where would you be on Friday night? Compare the difficulties of your trip with those the pioneers faced.

Section Review

ANSWERS

1. Bucknell blazed Santa Fe Trail. Manuel Lisa built trading post near mouth of Bighorn River. Beckwourth and Walker explored passes in Rocky Mountains and Sierra Nevada. Whitman and husband set up mission in Oregon that also served as stopover for travelers. Bidwell organized expedition over Oregon Trail to California. Young led Mormons from Missouri to what is now Utah, where they settled.

2. Crossed plains, Rocky Mountains, Wasatch Range, intermountain valleys and plateaus, rivers, Cascade Range.

3. Traders exchanged their goods for furs, hides, Spanish mules, gold and silver coins. Fur trappers brought back beaver pelts. Business people saw opportunities in trade and fishing. Farmers sought new fertile land.

Linking Past and Present. Note: Students living on the West Coast might calculate a trip in a different direction. Travelers of today have conveniences pioneers never had, such as advanced methods of transportation, paved roads, highways, restaurants, and motels.

B · A · C · K · G · R · O · U · N · D

Section 10-2

Objectives

- ***Answer the Focus Question.***
- *Explain why Americans began to settle in Texas.*
- *Describe the issues that prevented the United States from annexing Texas in 1836.*

Introducing

THE SECTION

Have students look at a map showing the United States as it was in the 1820s or 1830s. Point out the area of Texas. Then ask: What states are nearest to Texas? **(Louisiana, Mississippi, Alabama, etc.)** Were they slave states or free? **(slave states)** How might this have affected the settlement of Texas by people from the United States? **(Settlers would likely be slaveholders.)**

Connections: Language

Early Spanish visitors to the land that became Texas made friends with the local Caddo Indians. The Spanish called the Indians *Tejas* (TAY-hahs), from a Native-American word meaning "friends," and called the land by the same name. The spelling later was changed to Texas.

Reduced student page in the Teacher's Edition

10-2 Gone to Texas

Focus: Why did American settlers in Texas rebel against Mexico?

While many Americans sought land and opportunity in the Far West, others turned toward Texas. Some of the richest farmland in the West could be found there: vast prairies matted with buffalo grass, and rolling hills sprouting thick woods of cypress and pine.

Early Texas

Spain had claimed Texas in the early 1500s, but no Spaniards settled there for almost two centuries. As in California, it took a threat from outside to sting the Spanish to action. In the late 1600s, the French attempted to plant a colony in Texas. To protect Spain's claim from the French, Spanish priests, soldiers, and a few ranchers rode north from Mexico to occupy the area.

The Spanish built missions to bring Christianity to the Native Americans and presidios to defend the Spanish frontier. In 1718 seventy-two priests and soldiers established the mission and presidio of San Antonio, which soon became the capital of Spanish Texas.

The settlements did not prosper, however. Few Native Americans showed an interest in mission life. Although some Comanches became *vaqueros*—cowboys on Spanish ranches—most Comanches and Apaches had no wish to give up their nomadic ways, and they often raided Spanish settlements, driving off herds of horses.

By the early 1800s, Spain had new worries in Texas. Ignoring boundaries, Americans were drifting into eastern Texas. Some were troublesome fugitives, and some were thieves, who raided small Texas communities. Others were farmers, who settled along the Red River to farm land that was not legally theirs. The Spanish had forbidden such immigration but lacked power to enforce the ban.

Moses and Stephen Austin

Into this land came an American with big dreams, Moses Austin. The Connecticut-born Austin had settled in Missouri when it was Spanish territory, had pledged his loyalty to Spain, and had prospered. Now, though he was bankrupt, Austin hoped to find a new prosperity in Texas.

In December 1820 Moses Austin requested from the government of New Spain a grant of land in Texas, which he promised to settle with responsible Americans. Because the settlers would have a legal right to their land, he argued, they would defend Texas against illegal American immigrants.

Spanish officials agreed to Austin's proposal, promising to grant him 200,000 acres of his choice. Austin, however, died of pneumonia in June 1821. His last wish was that his son Stephen carry on in his place.

Stephen F. Austin chose an area along the Colorado and Brazos rivers. When Mexico won its independence from Spain in 1821, Texas became part of Mexico. The new Mexican government saw a chance to fill the land with settlers loyal to Mexico. It confirmed Austin's land grant. He could bring 300 American families into east Texas, and they would not have to pay for the land or pay taxes for six years. For their part, the settlers must become Mexican citizens. They must agree to obey Mexican laws, learn Spanish, and accept the Catholic religion. Also, they were forbidden to bring slaves into Texas.

Texas Fever

The Mexican government soon issued similar land grants to other settlers. "Texas fever" swept the Mississippi Valley, which was still suffering from the effects of Panic of 1819. Then in 1825, Mexican

Multicultural Perspectives

By 1825 there were 443 enslaved Africans and 1,347 white settlers in Austin. The constitution of Mexico had abolished slavery in 1824, but in Texas a system known as "contract labor" enabled slavery to remain an economic reality.

Sam Houston
Texas President

The Alamo

Lorenzo de Zavala
Vice-President

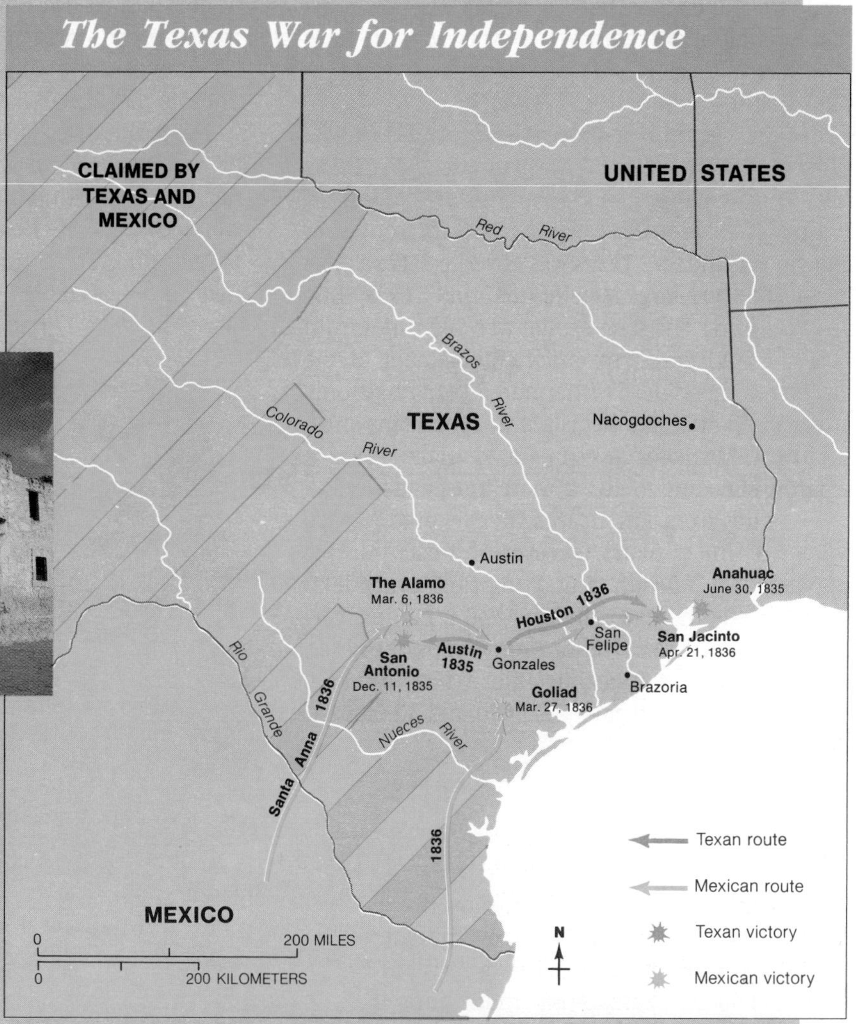

Geography Skills—Movement. Describe the movement of Santa Anna's troops across Texas in 1836.

laws changed, now allowing even more immigrants. Land agents poured into Texas seeking grants of land in return for promising to fill Texas with worthy settlers.

Advertisements for cheap land in Texas lured Americans, mostly southerners searching for good cotton land. Many brought their slaves. Free African Americans also arrived to start a new life. All over the South the words "Gone to Texas"—or just plain "GTT"—were scrawled on abandoned shacks and barns, and by 1830 some 16,000 Americans had settled in Texas, outnumbering Mexicans by at least four to one.

Tensions with Mexico

Most American settlers were loyal to the Mexican government at first, but relations soon soured. One issue that came between the American settlers and

Developing

THE SECTION

Limited English Proficiency

Building Vocabulary. Have students examine the map of Texas on this page. Point out that in addition to the state name (see note at the top of page 256), many other Texas place names are also Spanish. Have students find the following names in a dictionary: Brazos, Colorado, Rio Grande, Alamo, San Antonio, San Jacinto, Nueces. Have students explain what each place is, where it is, and what its name means in English. Speculate about why each place was so named.

Geography Skills

ANSWERS

Mexican border to San Antonio (Mexican victory at the Alamo), to Gonzales, to San Felipe, to San Jacinto (Texan victory)

GTV Side 2

Chap. 11, Frame 33525

Texas, Early 1800s (Map)

Search:

B · A · C · K · G · R · O · U · N · D

Analyzing Primary Sources

Letter. Mexican General Manuel Mier y Teran, after touring Texas in 1828 at his government's request, wrote to President Guadalupe Victoria:

“The whole population here is a mixture of strange . . . incoherent parts . . . numerous tribes of Indians, now at peace, but armed and at any moment ready for war . . . colonists of another people, more progressive and better informed than the Mexican inhabitants, but also more shrewd and unruly . . . honorable and dishonorable alike travel with their political constitution in their pockets. . . . The most of them have slaves, and these slaves are beginning to learn the favorable intent of the Mexican law toward their unfortunate condition and are becoming restless under their yoke, and the masters . . . are making that yoke even heavier.”

Ask: How did each of the groups mentioned contribute to the unrest in Texas? **(Native Americans might raid settlements; colonists might want to break away from Mexican rule; slaves might revolt against masters who, anticipating the event, might impose harsher conditions. Mexicans resented U.S. citizens and interested in protecting the rights of African Americans)**

Multicultural Perspectives

Not all Mexicans opposed the Texas Republic. Two of the fifty signers of the republic's "declaration of independence" were native Mexicans, and the first Vice-President of the republic—Lorenzo de Zavala—had been born in Mexico. Zavala's photo is on text page 257.

Social History

Sam Houston ran away from his home in Tennessee at age 15 and lived with a band of Cherokees. The chief of the band adopted Houston as his son. The group gave him the title Co-lo-neh, the Raven, identifying him as a man of honor and a leader of war parties.

Reduced student page in the Teacher's Edition

the Mexican government was religion. To own land, the Americans had to accept Mexico's national religion, although they did not actually have to practice Catholicism. Many settlers began to want their own churches, however.

Slavery was also a thorny issue. Mexico abolished slavery in 1829, but most Americans in Texas were southerners who had brought slaves along.

Besides religion and slavery, a third source of tension was the way Texas was governed. Texas was part of the very large state of Coahuila-Texas (KO-ah-WEE-lah). The state capital was 500 miles from Austin's land grant, so quick enforcement of the law was impossible. Furthermore, Texas had only one seat in the state legislature. Americans pressured the Mexican government to make Texas a separate state and to give it more independence.

Pressures from American settlers caused Mexico to fear a United States takeover of Texas. Mexico responded by encouraging Europeans and Mexicans to settle in Texas, and in 1830 it banned further American immigration. Americans, however, continued to cross illegally into Texas. By 1836 Texas was home to between 25,000 and 30,000 settlers, most of them Americans.

The Texas Revolution

The already tense situation was soon inflamed by changes in Mexico's government. In 1834 the president of Mexico, General Antonio López de Santa Anna, made himself dictator, setting off a series of rebellions across Mexico.

In June 1835 Texans intercepted a Mexican government messenger in San Felipe. From the dispatches he was carrying, they learned that Santa Anna had abolished the civilian government of Coahuila-Texas and was planning to lead an army into Texas to punish "the lawless foreigners." Texans began to prepare for warfare.

In October Texans marched to Gonzales (gohn-ZAHL-ehs), where they fired on Mexican troops to keep them from taking the city's sole cannon. With this shooting incident, the war began.

In late October Stephen Austin and a frontier fighter named Jim Bowie led Texas volunteers in a march on San Antonio. After a month's siege, Austin's troops captured the city, including the old San Antonio de Valero Mission, called the Alamo.

Representatives of the American settlements met at San Felipe to draft a declaration of independence and to set up a temporary government. They were loyal to Mexico, they declared, but not to Santa Anna. For commander of the army they settled on a newcomer to Texas, Sam Houston, who had been a congressman and a governor of Tennessee.

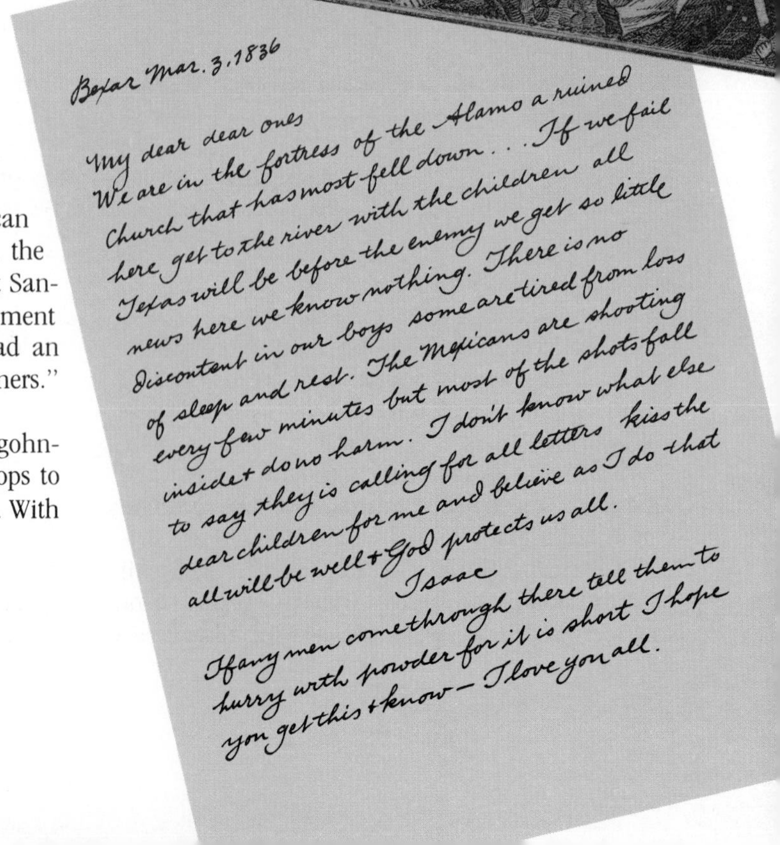
Bexar Mar. 3, 1836

My dear dear ones

We are in the fortress of the Alamo a ruined Church that has most fell down... If we fail here get to the river with the children all Texas will be before the enemy we get so little news here we know nothing. There is no discontent in our boys some are tired from loss of sleep and rest. The Mexicans are shooting every few minutes but most of the shots fall inside + do no harm. I don't know what else to say they is calling for all letters kiss the dear children for me and believe as I do that all will be well + God protects us all.

Isaac

If any men come through there tell them to hurry with powder for it is short I hope you get this + know— I love you all.

Reminders of the Alamo: a Crockett Almanack *page and a soldier's letter.*

"Remember the Alamo!"

In early February Santa Anna and more than 5,000 troops—most of them untrained—crossed the Rio Grande and headed for San Antonio. There, a small force of Texans waited in the Alamo. The old mission was now put to use as a fort, and Jim Bowie vowed, "We will rather die in these ditches than give it up to the enemy."

Over the following days, other Texans joined the small force at the Alamo. A young lawyer named William Travis arrived with twenty-five volunteers, among them Juan Seguín (seh-GEEN), a Mexican whose fighting for the Texans had earned him a place in the Texas army. Davy Crockett, pathfinder and former member of Congress, soon joined them. Then, on February 23 Santa Anna's troops arrived in San Antonio. Two days later, the Mexican cannons began their bombardment.

Travis sent out a message pleading for help from "the people of Texas and all Americans in the world." A few days later Seguín and his aide, Antonio Cruz, crossed enemy lines carrying a second call for help. Few reinforcements made their way through the Mexican lines, however. At dawn on March 6, 1836, Mexican soldiers swarmed over the walls, killing every defender of the Alamo.

The Lone Star Republic

Meanwhile, with the Alamo under seige, the Texans meeting in San Felipe had adopted a declaration of independence on March 2. They also drew up a constitution for the Republic of Texas.

Texans were defeated again a few weeks later when a thousand Mexican troops trapped some three hundred Texans near Goliad. Santa Anna ordered that all the Texans be executed.

As the Mexican army advanced, Houston's troops retreated. Finally, on April 21 Houston's army stopped near the San Jacinto (SAN hah-SEEN-toh) River. Screaming "Remember the Alamo! Remember Goliad!" the Texans turned on Santa Anna's army and won the battle, taking Santa Anna prisoner.

Before Santa Anna was released, he made two agreements with the Texans. One called for a truce and ordered all Mexican troops to leave Texas. In the other, he promised to support an independent Texas with a boundary at the Rio Grande. The Mexican Congress, however, would not recognize Texas as an independent nation, still considering it part of their territory. And for years, Texans and Mexicans were to clash over whether the boundary was the Rio Grande or the Nueces (NWEH-sehs) River, further north.

With victory at San Jacinto, Texans set about organizing a permanent government. In September 1836 voters approved the constitution drafted earlier that year. Like the United States, the Republic of Texas would have a president, a two-house legislature, and a supreme court. Sam Houston was elected president.

Texans also voted on another matter that September. By a large majority, they favored joining their territory to that of the United States. However, the American President, Andrew Jackson, refused to push for annexation, fearing it would lead to war with Mexico.

The issue of slavery was also on Jackson's mind. Texas wanted to enter the Union as a slave state, which would have upset the balance between slave and free states. Northerners, especially abolitionists, strongly opposed the admission of new slave states. Jackson thought that annexing Texas might tear apart the Union. Instead, on his last day in office in March 1837, Jackson recognized Texas as an independent nation.

Section Review

1. **Comprehension.** What problems did the Spanish encounter in trying to settle Texas?

2. **Comprehension.** What three issues caused friction between American settlers and the Mexican government?

3. **Evaluation.** In 1828 a Mexican official reported to his government: "Either the government occupies Texas now or it is lost forever." What argument might he have used to support his view?

4. **Analysis.** How did the actions of Antonio López de Santa Anna lead to war in Texas? Did Texans have a right to rebel?

5. **Comprehension.** Explain two issues that kept the United States from annexing Texas in 1836.

Active Learning

Brag Speech. Davy Crockett was famous for his backwoods wit, and stories attributed to him appeared in several books of the time. In one he bragged:

"I'm a screamer, and have got the roughest ... horse, the prettiest sister, the surest rifle and the ugliest dog in the district. I can run faster, dive deeper, stay under longer, and come out drier, than any chap this side the big swamp. I can outlook a panther [mountain lion] and out stare a flash of lightning, tote a steamboat on my back and play at rough and tumble with a lion."

Have students write or orally present their own "brag speeches."(African praise poems were presented as an enrichment activity in Chapter 3, page 47D.)

Section Review

ANSWERS

1. Spanish frustrated by Native Americans' refusal to accept Christianity and mission life, by illegal settlements of Americans.
2. Religion, slavery, and government representation.
3. Large numbers of Americans flooding into Texas and pressuring Mexican government to make Texas separate state.
4. Established military rule in Texas, which led to war. Texans had arguments with the government; religion, slavery, representation. Answers will vary as to whether they had right to rebel.
5. Jackson feared annexation would provoke war with Mexico, create conflict over admission of another slave state.

Section 10-3

Objectives

- ***Answer the Focus Question.***
- *Describe agreements that ended disputes over the annexation of Texas and the boundary of Oregon.*
- *Explain differing viewpoints of the causes of the Mexican War.*
- *Cite the terms of the Treaty of Guadalupe Hidalgo.*

Introducing THE SECTION

In 1783 French mountain man Jean Gasiot wrote to Spanish General Felipe de Neve:

“It is necessary to keep in mind that a new independent power exists now on this continent. It has been founded by an active, industrious, aggressive people. Their development will constantly menace the dominion of Spain in America and it would be an unpardonable error not to take all necessary steps to check their territorial advance.”

Ask: Who was the power that Gasiot referred to? **(the United States)** Was Spain able to do anything to restrain this power? **(no)** Can students think of anything that Spain—or Mexico, which later took over this land—could have done to restrain it?

B · A · C · K · G · R · O · U · N · D

Social History
Jessie Benton Frémont, the wife of John Charles Frémont, helped to write his famous books of exploration. Later in their lives, the writings by her provided the main support for their family. Jessie Frémont was the daughter of Senator Thomas Hart Benton of Missouri, who was quoted several times in Chapter 9. Frémont obtained leadership of his first expedition because of his wife's connections.

Reduced student page in the Teacher's Edition

10-3 *Manifest Destiny*

Focus: How did the United States expand to the Pacific Coast?

By the 1840s many Americans thought it was clear, or manifest, that the nation's destiny was to extend from the Atlantic to the Pacific. Some wanted to secure the nation's borders against foreign powers. Others imagined a railroad bringing goods from east to west for shipment to Asia. Still others thought it the duty of Americans to spread democracy across the continent.

Magazine editor John L. O'Sullivan put a name—**manifest destiny**—to this idea that the United States would and should extend across the whole continent. O'Sullivan wrote that it was "our manifest destiny to overspread the continent allotted by Providence [God] for . . . our yearly multiplying millions." Within less than a decade, the nation's boundaries had expanded all the way to the Pacific.

The Webster-Ashburton Treaty

One longstanding border dispute was settled during the presidency of John Tyler. Secretary of State Daniel Webster and Britain's Lord Ashburton worked out a treaty dividing disputed area between Maine and Canada. The Webster-Ashburton Treaty of 1842 added 7,000 square miles to Maine and set a boundary further west, between Lake Superior and the Lake of the Woods.

Annexation of Texas

President Tyler was an **expansionist**—someone with a policy of expanding a nation's territory or influence. Tyler had his eye on Texas. When Texas had become independent in 1836, it had applied to the United States government for **annexation,** or the joining of a new territory with one that is already organized as a country, a state, and so forth. Not wanting to stir up the slavery question or risk war with Mexico, Presidents Jackson and Van Buren had both declined to support the annexation.

Then, in 1843 Texas withdrew its request for annexation. Sam Houston hinted that Texas might form an alliance with Britain. Alarmed expansionists encouraged talks between the United States and Texas, and by April 1844 Tyler had a treaty to present to the Senate for approval.

However, the treaty provoked a hot debate over the slavery issue. John C. Calhoun, Tyler's Secretary of State, insisted that Texas must be annexed to assure the survival of slavery. Northern senators were outraged. Even Thomas Benton, a Missouri senator and a slaveholder, opposed the extension of slavery into lands taken from a country that had outlawed slavery. And some senators believed, along with Henry Clay, that "annexation and war with Mexico are identical."

Learning From Art
Cross Section of the United States

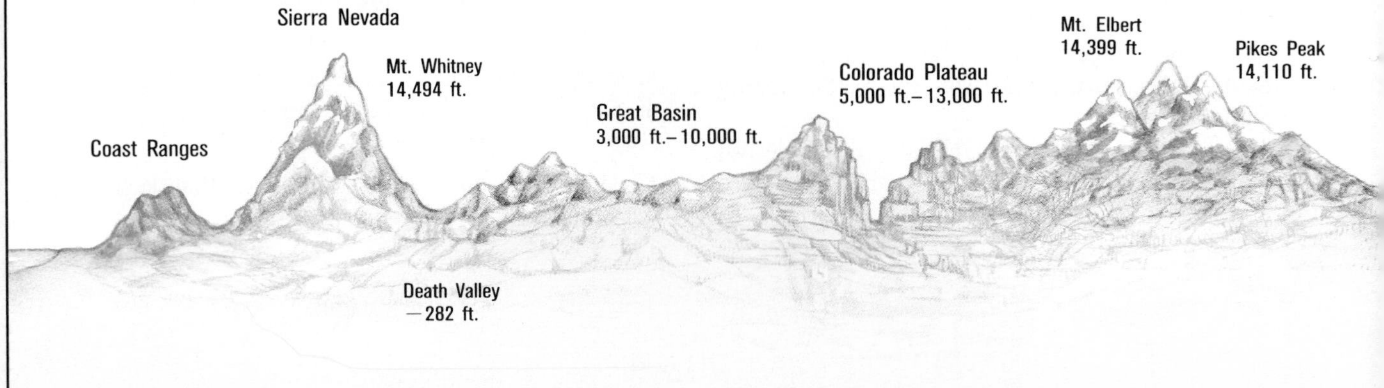

The election of 1844. While the Senate debated, political parties prepared for the election of 1844. The Whigs chose Henry Clay, who was against annexation of Texas without Mexico's consent. The Liberty party ran James G. Birney, who denounced the spread of slavery.

The Democrats chose James K. Polk, former governor of Tennessee, a congressman, and an expansionist. The Democratic platform called for occupation of Oregon as free territory and annexation of Texas as slave territory. In the election, Polk won 170 electoral votes to Clay's 105.

Outgoing President Tyler saw the election as a vote for annexation of Texas. Knowing that he could not get the needed two-thirds majority in the Senate to approve a treaty, he called for annexation by joint resolution of Congress, which required only a simple majority in both houses.

In February 1845 both houses approved a resolution inviting Texas to enter the Union as a state. Furthermore, the resolution extended the Missouri Compromise line of 36° 30′, thus permitting slavery in Texas. The Mexican minister to Washington called the annexation of Texas "an act of aggression, the most unjust . . . of modern history."

"Fifty-four Forty or Fight!"

A few days later Polk took office, expressing expansionist views in his inaugural address:

> *" The Republic of Texas has made known her desire to come into our Union. . . . I congratulate my country that by an act of the late Congress of the United States the assent of this government has been given . . . and it only remains for the two countries to agree upon the terms. . . .*
>
> *Our title to the country of Oregon is clear and unquestionable, and already are our people . . . occupying it. . . . To us belongs the duty of protecting them adequately. . . . The jurisdiction of our laws and the benefits of our republican institutions should be extended over them. "*

Texas entered the Union in December 1845. Meanwhile, Polk pressed Britain for all of the Oregon Country up to Russian Alaska at boundary line 54° 40′. His supporters adopted the slogan "Fifty-four forty or fight!" The British asked for a share of the Oregon Country extending as far south as the Columbia River. Earlier Presidents had offered to divide the Oregon Country at the 49th parallel, the boundary between the United States and Canada to the east. Polk had Secretary of State James Buchanan renew the offer of 49°.

The British were willing to compromise. American settlers outnumbered British fur traders in Oregon, and the fur trade was dying. In June 1846 the two nations agreed to make the 49th parallel the boundary between Canada and the United States west of the Rockies. In 1848 Congress officially organized Oregon as a territory.

The Break with Mexico

Although he did not mention California in his inaugural address, Polk confided to Secretary of the Navy George Bancroft that he intended to acquire it. In 1845 Polk sent Captain John C. Frémont to explore the southern Rockies. Frémont had already made two trips to the West, and his accounts had fired the imaginations of expanionists. Now it was rumored that he had a secret mission: If war broke out between Mexico and the United States, Frémont's armed force would be near California.

Polk's efforts to acquire California were complicated by Mexico's anger over Texas. In addition, the border between Texas and Mexico was still in

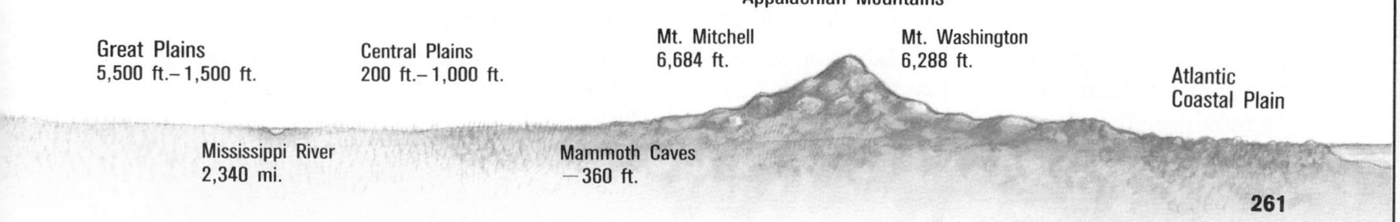

Developing

THE SECTION

Analyzing Primary Sources

Speech. Refer students to the excerpt from Polk's inaugural address on this page. **Ask:** On what grounds could Polk claim, "our title to the country of Oregon is clear and unquestionable"? How can the excerpt be understood as an expression of manifest destiny? **(Polk assumes United States has a God-given right to rule entire continent so as to spread its laws and "benefits of our American Institutions.")**

GTV Side 1

Chap. 1, Frame 04060

The Lay of the Land: Cross-Section of the Nation (Movie Segment)

Search and Play:

GTV Side 2

Chap. 5, Frame 17436

The Spirit of Manifest Destiny (American Journal)

Search:

Play:

Backyard History

Research. The flag of the short-lived California Republic, which was later modified to become the state flag of California, was designed and sewn by William Todd, a nephew of Abraham Lincoln's wife. The flag showed a red grizzly bear on a white background. The bear's head pointed toward a single red star (like the one on the Texas flag) in the flag's upper left corner. A red stripe and the words "California Republic" ran along the bottom of the flag.

Have students do research to discover the history of their own state flag and the meaning of its symbols.

Multicultural Perspectives

Discussion. The idea of manifest destiny looked different from the Mexican point of view. **Ask:** How did the idea of manifest destiny help explain the war with Mexico? If you were a Mexican in the 1840s, how might you have reacted to the American government's idea of manifest destiny? Explain.

Social History

A large part of the United States Army was made up of western adventurers, accustomed to fighting and taking what they wanted. General Winfield Scott admitted that they committed atrocities during the war: *"to make Heaven weep and every American of Christian morals blush for his country. Murder, robbery . . . have been common all along the Rio Grande."* A Mexican newspaper reported: *"the horde of banditti, of drunkards . . . vandals . . . monsters who bid defiance to the laws of nature . . . shameless, daring . . . thirsty with the desire to appropriate our riches."*

Reduced student page in the Teacher's Edition

dispute. In June 1845 Polk sent troops under General Zachary Taylor into the disputed area "on or near the Rio Grande" to support the Texas claim that the Rio Grande was the boundary.

Other issues also set the two countries at odds. During Mexico's revolt against Spain, Americans had sold supplies to Mexico on credit. In addition, American property had been destroyed and American lives lost in the revolution. The United States backed its citizens' claims for damage payments. But much like the United States after its revolution, Mexico, with little money in its treasury, had difficulty paying its debts.

Polk's offer. Polk hoped to settle the border dispute and acquire California in one agreement. In November 1845 he sent John Slidell to Mexico with his offer. If Mexico would accept the Rio Grande as the border of Texas, the United States would pay off Americans' claims against Mexico. Slidell was also to offer $5 million for New Mexico, and another $25 million for California. Enraged over the Texas annexation, Mexico refused to negotiate.

At the same time Polk harked back to the Monroe Doctrine to warn Europe not to interfere. In his message to Congress in December 1845, Polk declared that "the people of this continent alone have the right to decide their own destiny."

When Polk learned of the Mexican refusal, he ordered General Taylor to move closer to the Rio Grande. In late April 1846, Mexican cavalry crossed the Rio Grande and clashed with American soldiers. On May 11 Polk asked Congress to declare war. "Mexico," he declared, "has invaded our territory and shed American blood upon the American soil." Two days later, Congress agreed.

Not all Americans, however, supported the war. Northern Whigs and abolitionists considered it a plot by southerners to gain new land for slave states. Representative John Quincy Adams called it "a most unrighteous war" and voted against it.

American Voices

"In our judgment, those who have all along been loudly in favor . . . of the war . . . are not now rejoicing over peace but plunder. They have succeeded in robbing Mexico of her territory."

—Frederick Douglass on the Mexican War, 1848

War with Mexico

The American government had two war aims: to occupy the territories they had been trying to acquire from Mexico—New Mexico and California—and to invade Mexico itself, forcing a surrender. To occupy northern Mexico, General Stephen W. Kearny led an army westward from Missouri in June. Two months later, Kearny and his army reached New Mexico and occupied Santa Fe with little opposition.

Meanwhile, encouraged by Frémont, American settlers in northern California seized the small town of Sonoma. They declared the American settlements in California to be independent and lowered the Mexican flag, replacing it with the flag of the Republic of California.

In early July, a naval force under the command of John D. Sloat joined Frémont's "California Battalion," and the Americans swept first into northern California coastal towns and then, joined by General Kearny's group, they attacked towns in the south. Although *Californios* drove the American forces out of the southern towns for three months, in the end the Americans returned. By January 1847 the war in California was over.

Taylor marched his army out of Texas south into Mexico, where they captured the city of Monterrey in mid-September 1846. After an inconclusive battle at the ranch of Buena Vista (BWAY-nah VEES-tuh), near Monterrey, in February 1847, Mexico still refused to negotiate with the United States.

In early March 1847, an army led by General Winfield Scott invaded Mexico by sea, capturing Veracruz (VER-ah-KROOZ), on the east coast. Then Scott's army turned inland toward Mexico City. In a series of bloody battles, Santa Anna tried to stop Scott's forces. Finally, Americans stormed the fortress of Chapultepec, outside the capital. After another day's fighting, Mexico City itself fell, ending the war.

The United States in 1848

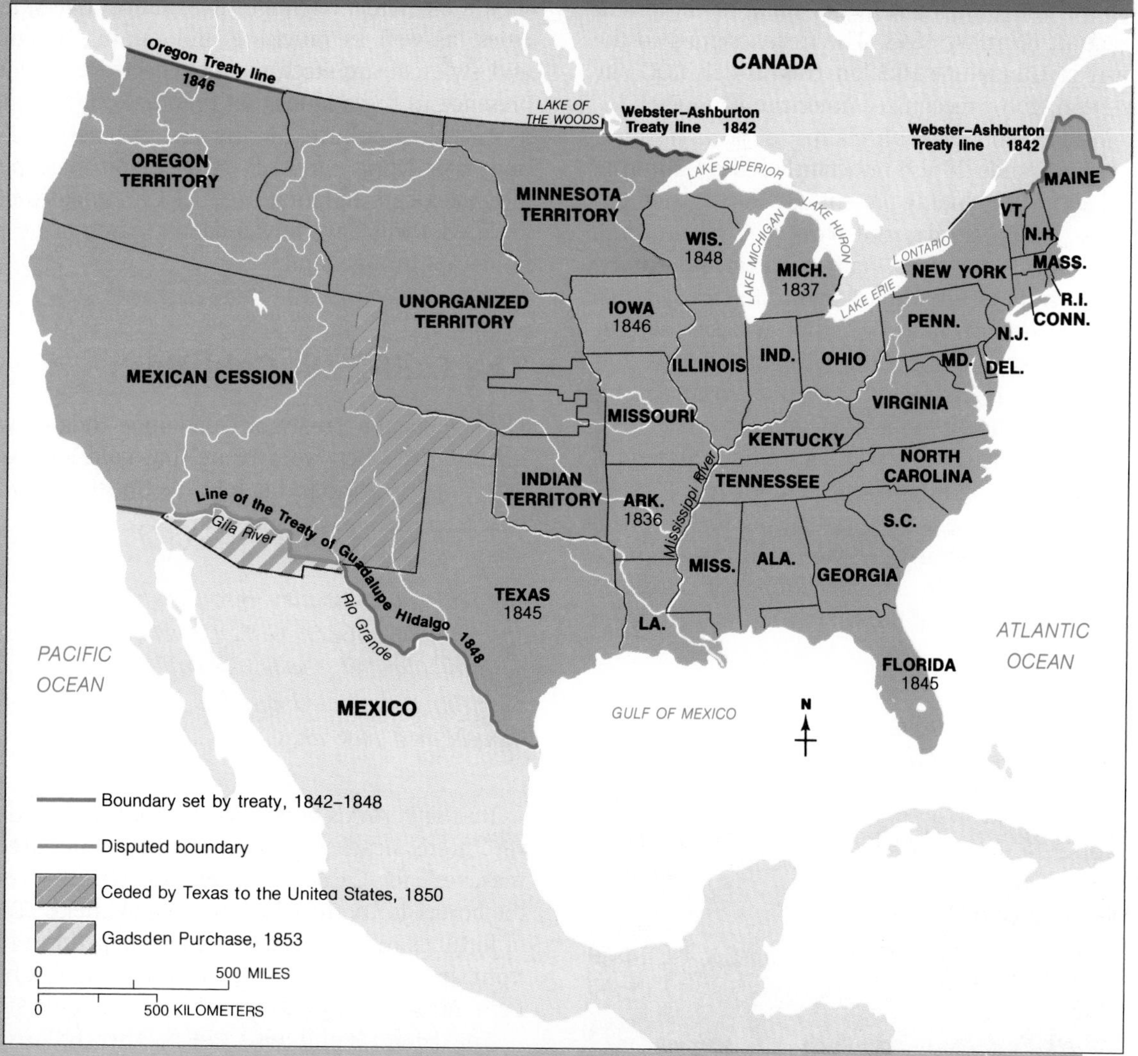

Geography Skills — Location. Compare this map with the map "The United States in 1822" on page 215. How much time has passed between the situations represented on the two maps? What areas did the United States acquire in those years? What boundary disputes were settled? What new states were added to the Union? Compare the extent of the United States in 1848 with the United States today.

This pioneer cabin was built of logs, with cedar shingles, stone fireplace, and a chimney of sticks.

Thinking Critically

Application. Have students offer evidence to support or refute the views of Polk and Adams quoted on page 262. (Polk's view: Mexico refused to negotiate; Adam's view: Mexico's prior claim to territory and prospect of extending slavery)

They might also do this for the two viewpoints described below in Carey McWilliams' book *North from Mexico:*

"To the Mexicans, every incident in Texas from the ... [early] raids to the Revolution of 1836 was regarded ... as part of a deliberately planned scheme of conquest. To the [white] Americans, the war was 'inevitable' having been provoked ... by the stupidity and backwardness of the Mexican officials."

Geography Skills

ANSWERS

1. 26 years.
2. Acquired Oregon Country, Texas, Mexican Cession, Gadsden Purchase.
3. Settled boundary with Canada at Maine, Minnesota, Oregon Territory.
4. New states: Wisconsin, Michigan, Iowa, Arkansas, Texas, Florida.
5. By 1848, the United States was as it is today but for Alaska and Hawaii.

Multicultural Perspectives

The majority of Hispanics in the United States are of Mexican descent. Only six countries have a larger Spanish-speaking population than the United States does. Starting with the largest, they are Mexico, Colombia, Argentina, Spain, Venezuela, and Peru.

Multicultural Perspectives

Many African Americans either owned or worked in the mines. The 1850 census in California recorded 962 African-American men. Moses Rodgers owned several mines and was a noted engineer and metallurgist. Robert Anthony owned what was probably the first quartz mill in California.

Active Learning

Role Play. Students can role-play a dialogue between Mexicans who remained in land ceded to the United States and those who left. Those who remained can give their reasons for staying and discuss treatment they received from other Americans. Those who left can explain reasons for leaving. Both groups can discuss which was the wiser decision.

Limited English Proficiency

Posters. Have students work in groups to create posters proclaiming the discovery of gold in California and inviting people from various countries to come and try their luck at prospecting. Some of the posters can be bilingual—in English and in the students' original language.

Connections: Geography

Using a Map. The California Gold Rush (1894) brought thousands of Easterners to California. Using the world map on text pages 904–905, have students determine the distance of overland and sea routes from New York City to San Francisco.

The overland trip took about six months to complete, while the record by the Yankee clipper ship *Flying Cloud*was 89 days, 8 hours. Have students compare the average miles per day for these two methods of transportation.

Ask: What other advantages did sea travel have for those able to afford it.

Reduced student page in the Teacher's Edition

The Treaty of Guadalupe Hidalgo

Mexico and the United States made their formal peace in February 1848. The treaty, signed in the town of Guadalupe Hidalgo (GWAH-dah-LOO-pay ee-DAHL-goh), recognized American conquests.

Mexico renounced all claims to Texas north of the Rio Grande. It also reluctantly ceded California and an area including present-day New Mexico, Arizona, Utah, Nevada, and parts of Wyoming and Colorado— altogether, half of Mexico's territory. In return, the United States agreed to pay $15 million and assume some $3 million in debts owed by Mexico to American citizens. The United States also guaranteed the religious, civil, and property rights of Mexicans living in the ceded area.

Five years later Mexico and the United States disputed the southern border of New Mexico. In 1853 James Gadsden, the American minister to Mexico, warned the Mexican government to give up the land or risk a fight. Mexico unhappily agreed to sell territory south of the Gila (HEE-lah) River for $10 million.

California's population soared as miners rushed in by land and by sea.

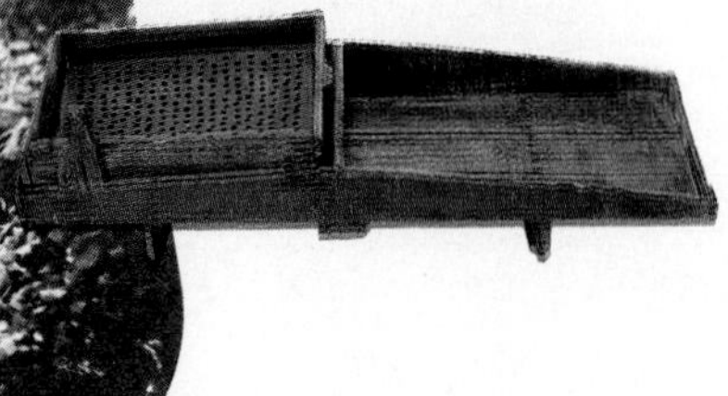

Some 80,000 Mexicans in the ceded territories now found themselves in a foreign land. Their ancestors, mainly Spanish and Indian, had made the West their home. Names of mountains, rivers, and cities, as well as ranching and mining practices and styles of architecture, all reflected their long presence in these lands. Yet they were now treated as an "alien culture." Many saw their land taken and their rights ignored. "Our unfortunate people," Mexican diplomat Manuel Crescencio Rejón declared, "will have to wander in search of hospitality in a strange land."

The California Gold Rush

The ink on the Treaty of Guadalupe Hidalgo was scarcely dry when word came that gold had been discovered in January at John A. Sutter's sawmill near Sacramento. One newspaper observed:

> *"The whole country resounds with the . . . cry of 'gold! GOLD! GOLD!' while the field is left half planted, the house half built, and everything neglected but the manufacture of shovels and pick axes."*

By 1849 crowds of people infected with "gold fever" were heading west, making "helter-skelter marches" for California. Mexicans streamed over the border to try their luck in the gold fields. Tales of fortunes made in a day brought hopeful miners from around the globe: Ireland, Germany, Chile, Peru, Australia, and China.

The demands of these "forty-niners" sent prices

Social History

A few women created opportunities for themselves in California by disguising themselves as men. Charlotte Parkhurst, who called herself "Charley," worked as a stagecoach driver and was famous for her ability to drive the coach at breakneck speed along narrow mountain trails.

Multicultural Perspectives

Thousands of people entered California, more than 80,000 in 1849 alone. The names of gold towns—China Camp, Mormon Diggings, Dutch Flat, Yankee Jims, Spanish Flat, French Corral—testify to their origins.

soaring. Coffee cost $4 a pound, flour $400 a barrel, and eggs $3 each—and miners paid in gold dust. Some people made their fortunes by selling food and other necessities to the miners. While Luzena Wilson's husband was searching for gold, she was starting her own hotel business in Nevada City, California.

> *"With my own hands I chopped stakes, drove them into the ground, and set up my table. I bought provisions at a neighboring store, and when my husband came back at night he found, amid the weird light of the pine torches, twenty miners eating at my table."*

The gold boom did not last long, and few made the fortunes that they had dreamed of. By 1852 the easily found ore was gone. What remained could only be mined by big companies with expensive equipment. However, many people found California to their liking and stayed on. The non-Indian population rose from 14,000 in 1848 to 225,000 in 1852. In 1849, looking forward to statehood, the people elected a constitutional convention to organize a state government for California.

Section Review

1. Identification. Define *manifest destiny, expansionist,* and *annexation.*

2. Comprehension. Describe the agreements that ended the disputes over the annexation of Texas and the boundary of Oregon.

3. Synthesis. Explain the causes of the Mexican War from the viewpoint of Americans in the mid-1800s. Explain the war from a Mexican viewpoint.

4. Comprehension. What were the terms of the Treaty of Guadalupe Hidalgo?

Data Search. Use the map on page 263 to estimate what portion of the present-day continental United States was gained in the Mexican Cession. About what portion of its territory did Mexico lose? What areas were added to the nation between 1845 and 1855? About what portion of the continental United States was gained in those years?

Connections to Themes

The Search for Opportunity

By the mid-1800s, trails to the West were marked by thousands of simple, shallow graves—silent reminders for those who came later that pioneering exacted a heavy price. Some pioneers were defeated by the hardships, but many more were convinced that the prize—the promise of new opportunity—was worth the price.

The dream took many forms: a farm or ranch in Texas or the lush river valleys of Oregon Country, or a business in a raw frontier town. For the Mormons, the dream was of religious freedom. In California, it was the lure of gold.

Even those who stayed behind caught the "westering fever," sharing a dream of the nation stretching "from sea to shining sea." Hundreds of thousands of square miles were acquired in little more than a decade. America's economic horizons suddenly seemed almost without limit, a vast frontier to settle and build, a single nation now larger than all of Europe, and most of it wide open, beckoning to those who dared.

But the nation's expansion also fueled the growing sectional conflict between North and South. For southerners, the survival of their region's way of life seemed to depend on extending slavery into the new lands. As forty-niners rushed to the gold fields of California, a southern Congressman warned the House of Representatives, "In the presence of the living God, if by your legislation you seek to drive us from the territories of California and New Mexico, I am for disunion."

Section Review

ANSWERS

1. Definitions for terms on text pages indicated in parentheses: *manifest destiny* (260), *expansionist* (260), *annexation* (260).
2. Joint resolution approved for annexation of Texas. Britain and United States agreed to 49th parallel boundary between Canada and Oregon.
3. American: Mexico owed money borrowed from Americans during revolt from Spain; American lives lost, property damaged. Mexican: America had taken Mexican territory, planned to take California.
4. Mexico renounced claims to Texas north of Rio Grande, ceded California and large western territory. United States agreed to pay $15 million, assume $3 million in debts owed by Mexico to Americans, and guarantee rights of Mexicans living in ceded area.
Data Search. One fourth. One half. Texas, Wisconsin, Iowa, Minnesota Territory, Indian Territory, Mexican Cessions, Oregon territory. One half.

GTV Side 2

Chap. 11, Frame 36687

California, 1849 (Map)

Search:

GTV Side 2

Chap. 11, Frame 37456

Settlement in the Far West, 1850 (Map)

Search:

Using the Visuals

Discussion. Refer students to the illustration of San Antonio on this page. Have them describe the scene and tell what it reveals about the Hispanic-American culture of the time.

Creative Spirit Illustrations

1. The view of San Antonio, painted in 1849 and dominated by the San Fernando Catherdral, was the work of G. M. Samuel, who later became town marshal.

2. Don José Andrés Sepúlveda owned an 80-mile square rancho south of Los Angeles. He lived on a lavish scale. His trousers were probably *calzoneras*, fitted pants whose bottoms flared out when unbuttoned.

3. The *bulto* of the Virgin Mary consists of a stick frame covered with plaster and cloth. The crescent moon on the skirt signifies purity.

Don José Andrés Sepúlveda's clothing, horse, and equipment reflect his Spanish heritage.

New Mexican iron workers excelled at elaborate Spanish-style designs, such as this gate.

Ladies' combs were often made from tortoise shell and studded with gems.

The Spanish who settled San Antonio in present-day Texas brought horses, cattle, sheep, and oxen for farming and ranching.

San Antonio Museum Association

Multicultural Perspectives

The Spanish, in a triangular relationship with Mexicans and Native Americans, helped lay the economic foundation of the American Southwest—mining, sheep (*churros*) and cattle raising, and irrigated farming. In 1800 Spanish colonel José Carrasco, guided by an Apache Indian, discovered the famous Santa Rita silver and copper mine in western New Mexico. It was here that the techniques of copper mining were first developed in the Southwest. The oldest irrigation systems are to be found in the Rio Grande Valley of New Mexico, where the Spanish were irrigating lands when the *Mayflower* landed at Plymouth. Edith Nicoll Ellison says: "*There are some arts of which a man becomes master in the course of three hundred years or more. Levelling land is one, irrigation is another. In both these arts the Mexican is at his best.*"

Connections: Art

Research. The Spanish adapted Native-American materials and tastes to their classic designs. For example, Spanish wooden furniture was often decorated with bright-colored mineral paints used by Native Americans. Yellows and greens were supplied by plants and roots; the browns came from iron ore; charcoal provided grays and blacks.

Have students use reference books to find examples of Native-American influence on Spanish arts and crafts. Students can share illustrations they find, or make their own drawings with captions and display them in class.

Santa Fe's Mission San Miguel, the nation's oldest mission church, reflects its Spanish-Indian heritage.

An Hispanic artist created this statue, or *bulto,* of the Virgin Mary.

THE CREATIVE Spirit

Hispanic Americans

In 1605 Juan de Oñate chiseled on a rock in present-day New Mexico *"Pasó por aquí"*—"passed by this way." The Spanish did more than pass by, however. They left a deep imprint on what is now the southwestern United States.

The Spanish brought not only their language and religion to the Americas, but also their arts, technology, and skills, which settlers and Native Americans adapted. Spaniards taught the Indians of the Southwest to weave wool and work iron, silver, and copper. They also introduced methods of sheep and cattle raising and irrigated farming that laid the basis for present-day agriculture in that arid region.

At the same time, traditional Spanish arts and crafts were being influenced by Indian taste and techniques. The blending of traditions created a rich Hispanic-American culture, evidence of which is clearly seen in the American Southwest today.

Leather for this trunk was a product of the cattle industry that began in Spanish California and Texas in the late 1700s.

Chapter Survey

ANSWERS

Using New Vocabulary

Manifest destiny was belief that U.S. was destined for (a) *expansion* to the Pacific. (d) *Annexation* of land was one way to extend the nation's (b) *borders.*

Reviewing the Chapter

1. (a) Desire for increased trade with Mexico. (b) Demand for fashionable beaver fur led trappers to explore paths and passes that opened area to settlement. (c) Rich farm land enticed Americans. (d) Missionaries tried to convert Native Americans to Christianity. (e) Economic depression, beginning in 1837, caused people to seek better life. (f) Mormons moved to Utah in search of religious freedom.
2. Theocratic nature of Mormon society, practice of considering all property church-owned, belief in polygamy. They moved west seeking religious freedom.
3. Many Texans did not accept Catholicism, insisted on keeping slaves, and felt they were inadequately represented in Mexican government. American efforts to buy Texas made Mexico fearful of annexation. Mexican military rule angered Texans into establishing their own government.
4. Issue of slavery; disapproval of Mexico. Compromise reached in Congress invited Texas to enter Union as state, allowed slavery in Texas.
5. Oregon first settled by Native Americans thousands of years ago. Nathaniel Wyeth and several missionaries traveled there in early 1830s. First wagons arrived in 1840; thousands followed; in 1848 Oregon was made territory after agreement with Great Britain.
6. (a) Mexico called annexation act of aggression. (b) U.S. and Mexico could not agree on southern border of Texas. (c) U.S. resented Mexico's failure to pay debts and pressured for claims for property damage.
7. Mexico gave up claims to Texas north of the Rio Grande and ceded other territory to the U.S.. The U.S. paid $15 million and assumed $3 million in debts owed by Mexico to American citizens.

Thinking Critically

1. Manifest destiny included belief that U.S. was fated to extend to Pacific regardless of Native American or Mexican claims on land, the desire to spread democracy, and desire to secure borders against Mexico and Britain.
2. Benefits: promised new opportunities for citizens; increased nation's size; vast natural resources; expanded world influence. Problems: gov-

Reduced student page in the Teacher's Edition

Chapter Survey

Using New Vocabulary

From the list below, select the three words whose meanings are related to the italicized vocabulary term and explain the relationships.

manifest destiny

(a) expansion	(d) annexation
(b) borders	(e) abolitionist
(c) containment	(f) culture

Reviewing the Chapter

1. Explain and give examples of how each of the following motivated Americans to move west. (a) trade (b) beaver fur (c) rich farm land (d) Native Americans (e) economic depression (f) religious freedom
2. List three reasons why many people reacted to Mormon beliefs with hostility. How did the Mormons respond to this hostility?
3. Explain the causes and the outcome of the Texas Revolution.
4. What obstacles blocked the annexation of Texas? How was annexation finally achieved?
5. Trace the development of American settlement of Oregon. How and when did Oregon become part of the United States?
6. How did each of the following cause tension between the United States and Mexico? (a) the annexation of Texas (b) the border between Texas and Mexico (c) American claims for damage payments
7. To what extent did the Treaty of Guadalupe-Hidalgo achieve the aims of the United States government in the Mexican War?

Thinking Critically

1. Synthesis. Why was the United States so eager to stretch its borders to the Pacific Ocean when much of the land it already owned—the land between the Mississippi River and the Rocky Mountains—was still unsettled?
2. Analysis. What benefits did land acquisition bring to the United States? What problems?
3. Synthesis. Write a statement about the annexation of Texas from the point of view of a Whig, a Liberty Party member, and a western Democrat in 1844. Then write statements for Andrew Jackson and John C. Calhoun on this issue.

Using Geography

Match the letters on the map to the locations listed below. Explain the importance of each place in the era of manifest destiny.

1. Great Salt Lake	5. Santa Fe
2. Gadsden Purchase	6. Sacramento
3. Nueces River	7. 49th parallel
4. San Jacinto	8. Independence

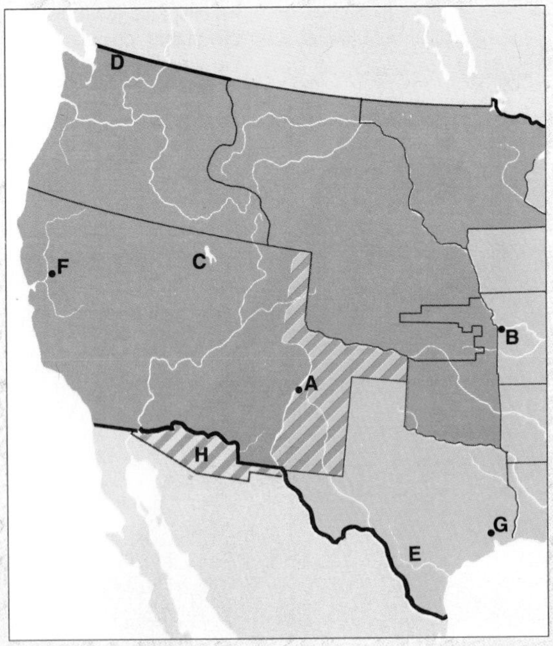

History and You

Using a road map, find out what highways follow the old Santa Fe, Oregon, California, and Mormon trails. What states do these trails cross? Do the towns that were "jumping-off places" still exist? What new cities have developed along the old routes?

erning new lands; slavery issue fueled sectional conflict.
3. Northern Whigs feared annexation would bring war with Mexico and opposed creation of new slave states. Liberty Party opposed spread of slavery. Western Democrats feared annexation would bring war with Mexico. Jackson favored expanding nation's territory but opposed annexation because it risked war with Mexico and sectional bitterness. Calhoun supported annexation to ensure survival of slavery and to increase southern political power.

Using Geography

1. C: Mormons settled here.
2. H: Land ceded by Mexico.
3. E: Mexico claimed southern border of Texas at this river.
4. G: Houston's army met Mexicans here.
5. A: Zebulon Pike's descriptions drew traders here.
6. F: Jedediah Smith explored near here; later, gold discovered nearby.
7. D: Agreed upon boundary between Canada and U.S. west of the Rockies.
8. B: Westward bound wagon trains left from here.

History and You

Sante Fe Trail: Interstates 35 and 25 (No interstates across Kansas parallel the trail.); Oregon Trail: Interstates 80 and 80 North; California Trail: Interstate 80; Mormon Trail: Interstate 80. Yes, the Missouri River towns still exist. Examples: Kansas City and St. Joseph. Examples of new, large cities: Reno, Boise, Lincoln, Omaha.

Applying Social Studies Skills

1. Missouri, Omaha, Arapaho, Pawnee, Cheyenne, Shoshone, Cayuse, Nez Percé, Spokane, Yakima, Chinook, Ute, Paiute.
2. Northwest.
3. Paiute, Ute, Shoshone.
4. Pawnee, Ute, Arapaho, Paiute, Miwok, for example.
5. Old Spanish Trail.
6. Lost their lands and ways of life, infected with diseases.

Applying Thinking Skills

1. Soldier.
2. Revenge.
3. Filisola sympathetic to Texans.
4. Defeat strengthened their resolve.

Applying Social Studies Skills

Analyzing Maps

Trails from Missouri westward crossed the homelands of many American Indian nations. Indians were also living in the lands where the pioneers settled. Use this map of Native American groups, information from the text, and the map on page 254 to answer the questions below.

1. Name six Indian nations whose lands the Oregon Trail passed through.

2. The settlers of which region met these Indians: Cayuse, Nez Percé, Spokane?

3. What Indians lived in the area settled by the Mormons?

4. Name five Indian nations travelers from Kansas to California could have met.

5. Name the trail described by the following set of directions: Travel from Santa Fe into land inhabited by the Apaches. From there travel into Navajo country. Then cross a river, heading into the land of the Paiute.

6. Discuss the effects of the westward movement of the 1830s and 1840s on American Indians.

Native-American Nations

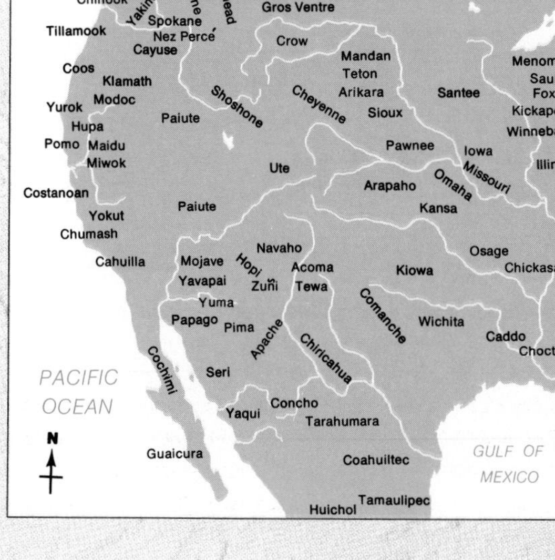

Applying Thinking Skills

Recognizing Point of View

How someone sees an event is colored by the person's *point of view,* that is, where the person stands in relation to the event. For example, an Indian might have viewed the arrival of a wagon train as a disturbance to game animals, while a mountain man might have seen it as an opportunity to apply for a job as a guide.

This account of the Alamo was written in 1849 by Vicente Filisola, a Mexican soldier:

> *"The Mexican troops were stationed at 4 o'clock, a.m., in accord with Santa Anna's instructions. The artillery . . . was to remain inactive, as it received no order. And furthermore, darkness and the disposition . . . of the troops . . . prevented its firing without mowing down our own ranks. . . .*
>
> *Our loss was very heavy. . . . Our own men were exposed not only to the fire of the enemy but also to that of our own columns attacking the other fronts. And . . . all shots that were aimed too low struck the backs of our foremost men. . . .*
>
> *In our opinion the blood of our soldiers as well as that of the enemy was shed in vain, for the mere gratification . . . and guilty vanity of reconquering Bexar [San Antonio] by force of arms. . . . The massacres of the Alamo, of Goliad, of Refugio, convinced the rebels that no peaceable settlement could be expected, and that they must conquer or die, or abandon the fruits of ten years of sweat and labor, together with their fondest hopes for the future."*

1. What was Filisola's role at the Alamo?

2. In the writer's opinion, what was Santa Anna's purpose in attacking the Alamo?

3. How do you think Filisola's point of view differed from Santa Anna's?

4. What point of view did Filisola think that the Texans had as a result of the battle?

Unit 3 Survey

ANSWERS

Making Connections

1. Nationalism: Albert Gallatin wrote, "The people . . . feel and act more like a nation"; the Star-Spangled Banner expresses that nationalism. Sectionalism: Northerners felt the war was against their interests, voted against Madison in 1812. The war led New Englanders to consider revising the Constitution.

2. Northerners opposed the Embargo Act, War of 1812, internal improvements, extension of slavery; were divided over protective tariffs. Westerners favored War of 1812, protective tariffs, internal improvements; were divided over extension of slavery. Southerners favored War of 1812, extension of slavery; opposed protective tariffs, internal improvements.

3. The new lands enabled cotton culture to expand, inflamed slavery debate, made Indian removal possible, increased demand for roads and canals. Without Louisiana, U.S. would have allied with Britain against France. Instead, westerners pressed for war with Britain to end attacks by Britain's Indian allies.

4. South maintained balance of slave and free states; North contained slavery.

5. Fearing competition with slave labor, northern workers supported abolition. Concern over division of power in Congress led northerners to support abolition and southerners slavery. Southerners who felt Congress had no right to interfere in state affairs were likely to be proslave. Northerners who resented the provision that allowed southern states to count slaves for representation in Congress supported abolition.

6. The western lands were public domain, some of which the government sold to raise revenue or gave away to encourage development. Alarm over destruction of nature and ideas about limiting use of resources arose in the mid-1800s and took hold slowly.

Using the Time Line. Answers will vary.

Projects and Activities

1. Answers will vary.

2. Answers will vary.

3. Women have gained the right to vote, own property, be legal guardians of their children. Women now have more choices of employment, earn fairer wages, and attend college. Conditions that are a matter of tradition—e.g., the role of women in religious institutions—change more slowly than conditions regulated by law.

Using the Time Line. Answers will vary.

Unit Survey

Making Connections

1. Explain the following statement: The War of 1812 planted the seeds of both nationalism and sectionalism. Give examples.

2. What political and economic issues divided regions of the country? What role did sectional interests play?

3. What impact did the acquisition of Florida and Louisiana have on foreign and domestic affairs?

4. In your opinion, who benefited most from the Missouri Compromise? Why?

5. How did economic and political issues affect support for abolition in the North? Explain.

6. The vast expanses of the West led Americans to think that the land had unlimited resources. What impact has this attitude had on the development of North American resources?

Using the Time Line. How are the War of 1812 and the writing of "The Star Spangled Banner" related? Find five additional pairs of connected events on the time line. Explain the relationship of the events in each pair.

Projects and Activities

1. Form into groups of five students, who take the roles of a Massachusetts merchant, an Indiana settler, a sailor, a Georgia slaveholder, and President Madison. Each character should argue for or against declaring war in 1812. If the decision had been up to your class, would the United States have declared war?

2. As a northern Whig, a member of the Liberty party, or a western Democrat, write a letter to the editor giving arguments for or against annexing Texas in 1844. Share your letter with the class so that the class can compile a master list of arguments for each position. Which position do you think is strongest? Why?

3. Read the Seneca Falls Declaration of Sentiments and Resolutions. With the class discuss which conditions have changed for women since 1848. Why have some conditions changed more easily than others?

Using the Time Line. Work in pairs. Write lyrics for a song that describes the nation's growth between 1800 and 1850. The lyrics might focus on growth in general or on one or two aspects, such as territorial expansion, or growth in government, industry, transportation, or efforts to extend democracy. Use at least six time line events in your song.

Milestones	1801	1813
Presidents	Jefferson	Madison
Political and Economic	• Louisiana Purchase • *Marbury* v. *Madison* • Tecumseh forms an Indian confederacy • Manuel Lisa opens fur trading post • War of 1812 begins	• First savings bank in U.S. • Florida Purchase • Missouri Compromise
Social and Cultural	• Library of Congress established • Movement for public schools begins • Congress outlaws African slave trade • The term "Uncle Sam" first used	• "The Star Spangled Banner" • First U.S. school for the deaf • Scots introduce golf in U.S.
Technological and Scientific	• First right and left shoes, William Young • United States Patent Office created • Lewis and Clark expedition begins • First practical U.S. Steamboat, *Clermont*	• First full-process cotton mill, Lowell • First machine-made paper in U.S. • Cast iron plow developed

Assessment

To help students think about how artifacts symbolize human activities, ask students for examples of items they would use today to represent each of the five topics listed.

Scoring

To create a scoring system, or rubric, assign an achievement scale to each of the evaluation criteria. For example, you might evaluate "Thinking critically" on a scale of 0 to 4 as follows:

4—Exemplary response: selections are appropriate for the times and topics; the collection is organized to make a meaningful statement about life in the early 1800s. Selections are grouped to express relationships. Students have used information from the text or other sources to formulate a general concept about each topic; the groups of items express these concepts. The collection is accompanied by a clear written analysis of the relationships between its elements.

3—Good response: selections are appropriate for the times and topics. Most selections are grouped to express relationships; some groups make a statement about the topic. The collection is accompanied by a good written analysis of the relationships between its elements.

2—Adequate response: most selections are appropriate for the times and topics; the collection hints at life in the early 1800s. Some items are grouped to express relationships. Groups may appropriately illustrate topics, but make no important statement about them. A written document explains choices.

1—Poor response: some items are appropriate, but the collection provides an inadequate picture of the 1800s. Few items are classified for meaning; the grouped items do not make a statement. Little or no written justification for choices is provided.

0—No response/inappropriate response.

Follow-up Activity

News story. Each student "opens" a time capsule—not the capsule he or she worked on. The student writes the headline and the first two paragraphs of a news story explaining the significance of the capsule.

Assessment: Demonstrating What You Know

Assembling a Time Capsule

It is 1850, and the people of your town have voted to put a time capsule in a vault beneath the statue in the town center. They want to help future generations of townspeople understand their past. The capsule will contain a collection of items that reflect the events, issues, and people of the years 1800 to 1850. A plaque on the statue's base will instruct future residents to open the capsule in the year 2000. You are on the committee to collect items for the capsule.

Work in groups of three. Each group will be a time capsule committee. Each committee will collect at least twenty objects, documents, and pictures for the capsule. (If necessary, you may draw pictures of some objects.) Each item must be accompanied by a written explanation of why it was chosen to represent life in the early nineteenth century. Before the collection is put into the capsule, display it for the class. Organize the items to show the relationships between them.

The mayor has instructed you to create a collection that represents all of the following topics.

1. Movement of people and goods: new places to go, new ways to get there
2. Expanding democracy, reforming society
3. Conflicts within the United States and between the United States and other countries
4. Growth in government and industry
5. Everyday life

Evaluation Criteria

Your work will be evaluated according to how well you meet the following criteria.

- **Completing the task**. Your group assembles at least twenty items and writes out reasons for each selection. You choose at least one item for each topic.
- **Knowing history**. The items your group selects are related to the topics and are appropriate for the time period. You base your selections on historical information from the text or other sources.
- **Thinking critically**. You explain clearly how each item relates to one of the topics. You arrange the items to show their relationship to each other and to the main topics so that whoever sees your collection will understand something about life in the early 1800s.
- **Communicating ideas**. You display the collection creatively to capture the interest of viewers. You use correct spelling and grammar.

1825 **1838** **1850**

Monroe | Adams | Jackson | Van Buren | Harrison | Tyler | Polk

- Mexico gains independence
- Monroe Doctrine
- First strike of women workers, Rhode Island weavers
- Indian Removal Act
- American Anti-Slavery Society formed
- Republic of Texas formed
- Trail of Tears begins
- "Manifest destiny" arises
- Mexican War begins
- Seneca Falls Declaration

- Sequoyah develops Cherokee alphabet
- German immigrants introduce gymnastics
- *Freedom's Journal*, first U.S. black newspaper
- *The American Dictionary*, Noah Webster
- Mount Holyoke, first U.S. women's college
- *Birds of America*, drawings of John J. Audubon
- *Autobiography*, Frederick Douglass

- Erie Canal completed
- First U.S. locomotive, Peter Cooper
- John Lane develops steel plow
- Cyrus McCormick patents reaper
- Photography introduced in U.S. from France
- Samuel F.B. Morse patents telegraph
- Sewing machine, Elias Howe

271

Unit 4

Objectives

- Explain how growing sectional differences and conflicts over states' rights led to the Civil War.
- Discuss strategies and major military actions of the North and the South during the war.
- Describe the struggles involved in the reconstruction of the South after the Civil War.

Introducing

THE UNIT

As the second half of the nineteenth century began, the United States confronted the growing force of sectionalism. The North and the South moved further and further apart over economic and political interests and the issue of slavery until the nation divided. Unit 4 deals with the causes and the consequences of the Civil War.

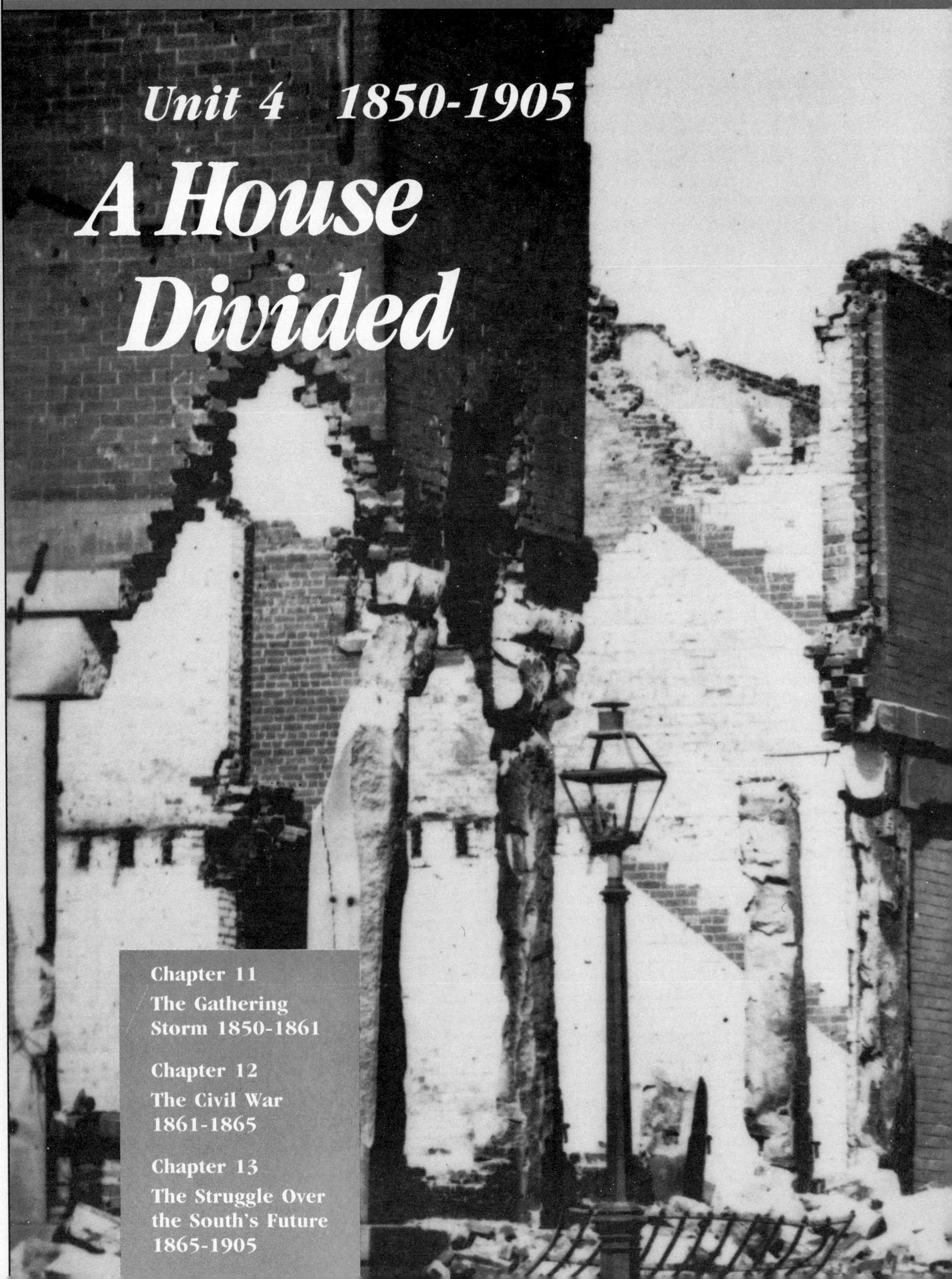

Unit 4 1850-1905

A House Divided

Connections: Literature
Stowe wrote *Uncle Tom's Cabin* not only to depict the evils of slavery in the South, but to suggest the complicity of the North in those evils. The novel's chief villain—Simon Legree, the overseer—is a northerner.

Guided Reading

Discussion. As students read the selection from *Uncle Tom's Cabin*, have them think about why Stowe's work influenced public opinion on *both* sides of the slavery issue.

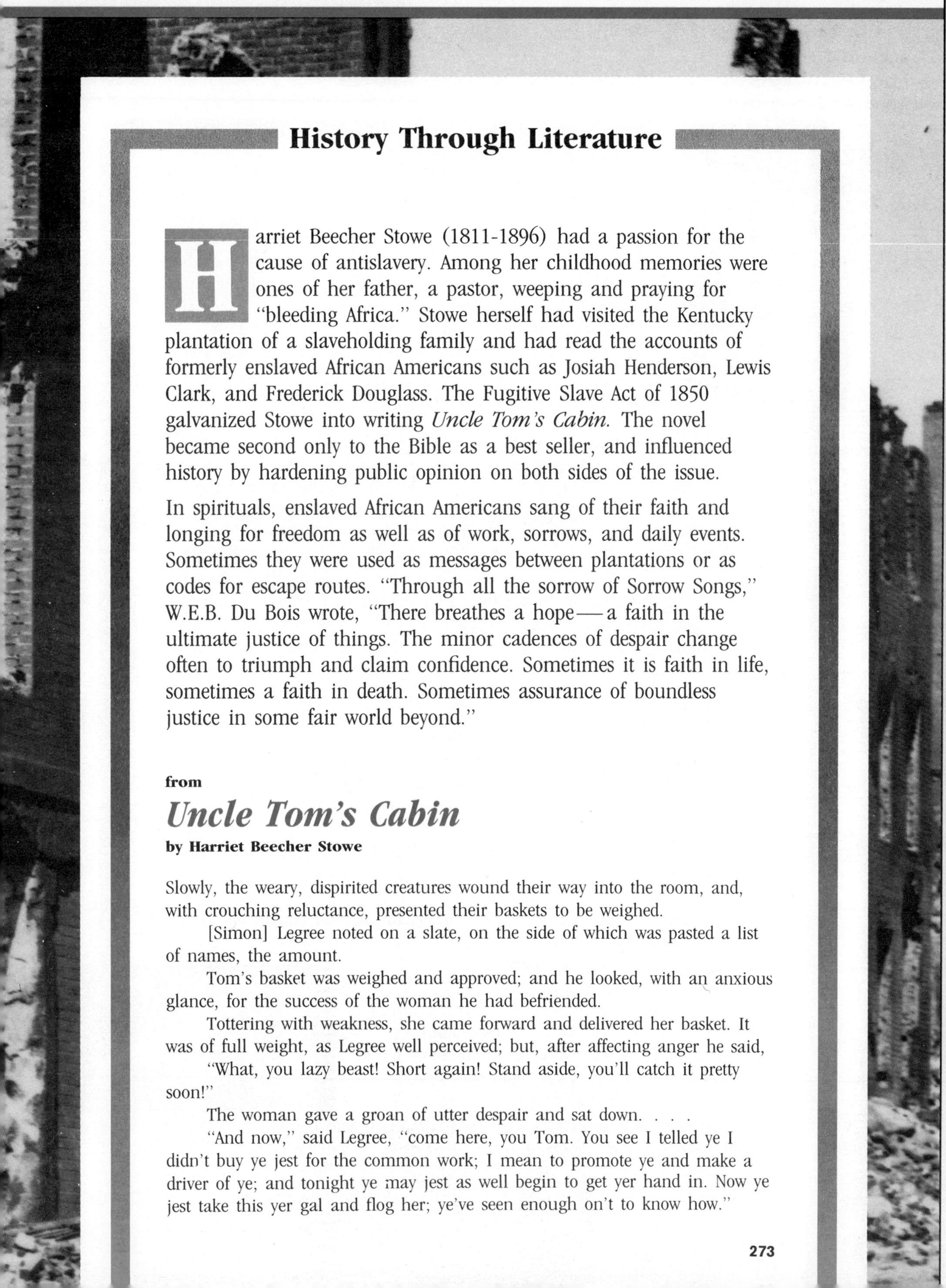

History Through Literature

Harriet Beecher Stowe (1811-1896) had a passion for the cause of antislavery. Among her childhood memories were ones of her father, a pastor, weeping and praying for "bleeding Africa." Stowe herself had visited the Kentucky plantation of a slaveholding family and had read the accounts of formerly enslaved African Americans such as Josiah Henderson, Lewis Clark, and Frederick Douglass. The Fugitive Slave Act of 1850 galvanized Stowe into writing *Uncle Tom's Cabin.* The novel became second only to the Bible as a best seller, and influenced history by hardening public opinion on both sides of the issue.

In spirituals, enslaved African Americans sang of their faith and longing for freedom as well as of work, sorrows, and daily events. Sometimes they were used as messages between plantations or as codes for escape routes. "Through all the sorrow of Sorrow Songs," W.E.B. Du Bois wrote, "There breathes a hope—a faith in the ultimate justice of things. The minor cadences of despair change often to triumph and claim confidence. Sometimes it is faith in life, sometimes a faith in death. Sometimes assurance of boundless justice in some fair world beyond."

from

Uncle Tom's Cabin

by Harriet Beecher Stowe

Slowly, the weary, dispirited creatures wound their way into the room, and, with crouching reluctance, presented their baskets to be weighed.

[Simon] Legree noted on a slate, on the side of which was pasted a list of names, the amount.

Tom's basket was weighed and approved; and he looked, with an anxious glance, for the success of the woman he had befriended.

Tottering with weakness, she came forward and delivered her basket. It was of full weight, as Legree well perceived; but, after affecting anger he said,

"What, you lazy beast! Short again! Stand aside, you'll catch it pretty soon!"

The woman gave a groan of utter despair and sat down. . . .

"And now," said Legree, "come here, you Tom. You see I telled ye I didn't buy ye jest for the common work; I mean to promote ye and make a driver of ye; and tonight ye may jest as well begin to get yer hand in. Now ye jest take this yer gal and flog her; ye've seen enough on't to know how."

273

"I beg Mas'r's pardon," said Tom, "hopes Mas'r won't set me at that. It's what I an't used to—never did—and can't do, no way possible."

"Ye'll larn a pretty smart chance of things ye never did know before I've done with ye!" said Legree, taking up a cowhide and striking Tom a heavy blow across the cheek, and following up the infliction by a shower of blows.

"There!" he said, "now will ye tell me ye can't do it?"

"Yes Mas'r," said Tom, putting up his hand to wipe the blood that trickled down his face. "I'm willin' to work night and day, and work while there's breath in me; but this yer thing I can't feel it right to do; and, Mas'r, I *never* shall do it—*never*!"

Tom had a remarkably smooth, soft voice, and a habitually respectful manner that had given Legree an idea that he would be cowardly and easily subdued. When he spoke these last words, a thrill of amazement went through everyone; the poor woman clapsed her hands and said, "O Lord!" and everyone involuntarily looked at each other and drew in their breath . . .

"What have any of you cussed cattle to do with thinking what's right? I'll put a stop to it! Why, what do ye think ye are? May be ye think ye're a gentleman, master Tom, to be a telling your master what's right and what an't! So you pretend it's wrong to flog the gal!"

"Think so, Mas'r" said Tom, "the poor crittur's sick and feeble; it would be downright cruel, and it's what I never will do, not begin to. Mas'r, if you mean to kill me, kill me; but as to my raising my hand agin anyone here, I never shall—I'll die first!"

Tom spoke in a mild voice but with a decision that could not be mistaken. Legree shook with anger; his greenish eyes glared fiercely and his very whiskers seemed to curl with passion; but like some ferocious beast that plays with its victim before he devours it, he kept back his strong impulse to proceed to immediate violence. . . .

"Ain't I yer master? Didn't I pay down $1,200 cash for all there is inside yer cussed black shell? Ain't yer mine, now, body and soul?" he said, giving Tom a violent kick with his heavy boot. "Tell me!"

"No! no! no! my soul ain't yours, Mas'r! You haven't bought it—ye can't buy it! It's been bought and paid for by one that is able to keep it—no matter, no matter, you can't harm me!"

"I can't!" said Legree with a sneer, "we'll see—we'll see! Here, . . . give this dog such a breakin' in as he won't get over this month! . . . The poor woman screamed with apprehension and all arose as by a general impulse while they dragged him unresisting from the place.

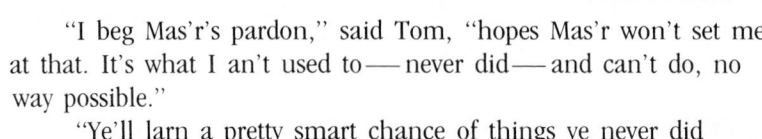

(Background) Richmond, Virginia, 1865; (above) **Uncle Tom's Cabin; *bales of cotton; (opposite) slave fetters and shackles.***

274

"Swing Low, Sweet Chariot"

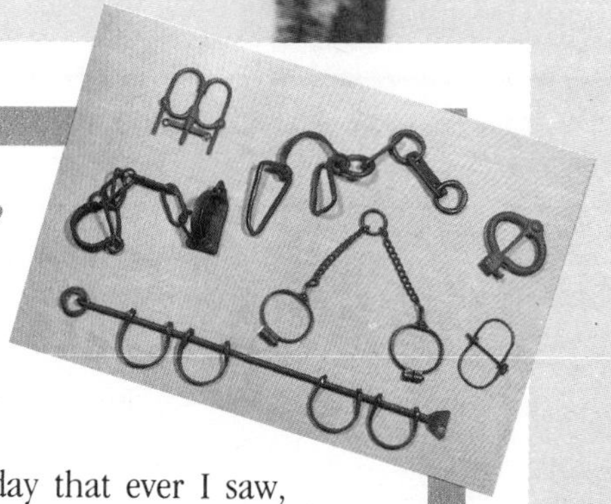

Chorus:
Swing low, sweet chariot,
Comin' for to carry me home.

I looked over Jordan and what did
I see,
Comin' for to carry me home?
A band of angels comin' aftah me,
Comin' for to carry me home.

If you git there before I do,
Comin' for to carry me home,
Tell all my frien's I'm a-comin', too,
Comin' for to carry me home.

The brightes' day that ever I saw,
Comin for to carry me home,
When Jesus washed my sins away,
Comin' for to carry me home.

I'm sometimes up an' sometimes
down,
Comin for to carry me home,
But still my soul feel heavenly-boun',
Comin' for to carry me home.

"Follow the Drinking Gourd"

When the sun comes back and the
first quail calls,
Follow the drinking gourd,
For the old man is a-waiting for
to carry you to freedom
If you follow the drinking gourd.

Follow the drinking gourd,
Follow the drinking gourd,
For the old man is a-waiting for
to carry you to freedom
If you follow the drinking gourd.

The river bank will make a
very good road,
The dead trees show you the
way,
Left foot, peg foot traveling on
Follow the drinking gourd.

The river ends between two hills
Follow the drinking gourd.
There's another river on the other
side,
Follow the drinking gourd.

Where the little river meets the great
big river,
Follow the drinking gourd.
The old man is a-waiting for to carry
you to freedom,
If you follow the drinking gourd.

Taking a Closer Look

1. *What does Simon Legree want Tom to do and why does Tom refuse?*

2. *Give three examples of possible hidden meanings in the lyrics of "Swing Low, Sweet Chariot" and "Follow the Drinking Gourd." Explain what the meanings might be.*

Guided Reading

Discussion. Tell students that many spirituals had a double meaning—they could be interpreted as merely religious songs or as expressions of slaves' desire for freedom. As students read the spirituals, have them look for their messages and hidden meanings.

Linking Past and Present

Discussion. Ask students if they would characterize these spirituals as protest songs. Why or why not? Have students name several recent protest songs. For what types of events or situations were they written? What messages do they convey?

Taking a Closer Look

ANSWERS

1. **Simon Legree wants Tom to whip "the woman he had befriended." Tom refuses the cruelty, stating that he, a slave, will "never!" whip another slave.**

2. **As a religious song, *Swing Low, Sweet Chariot* is about death—the chariot represents death; home symbolizes Heaven. As a song of freedom, the chariot represents the underground railroad; home symbolizes freedom in the North; the band of angels could be abolitionists. The Drinking Gourd is another name for the Big Dipper, a constellation which points to the North Star. Runaway slaves could always find North, the direction to free states, by literally following the path the Drinking Gourd made in the sky. The rest of the song gives almost precise directions.**

275

Chapter 11

The Gathering Storm

Planning Guide

	Student Text	TWE Lesson Plans	Support Materials
SECTION 1	**Section 11–1** (1–2 Days) **Life in the North and the South,** pp 278–287 The American Spirit: Frederick Douglass, p 286 The Creative Spirit: African Americans, p 288–289 Review/Evaluation Section Review, p 287	**Introducing the Chapter:** To Revolt or Not to Revolt—Class Activity, 30 minutes, p 275B **Reinforcement Activity:** Letters Between Cousins—Paired Activity, one class period, p 275C **Enrichment Activity:** Posters of Protest—Cooperative Activity, one class period, p 275D	★ **Read to Remember,** Section 1 ● **Section Activities,** Section 1 Δ **Enrichment Activities,** Section 1 ● **Geography Activities,** Section 1 Δ **Readings** ● **Tests and Quizzes,** Section 1 Quiz
SECTION 2	**Section 11–2** (1–2 Days) **Slavery in the West,** pp 290–294 Review/Evaluation Section Review, p 294	**Teaching the Main Ideas:** "Bleeding Kansas" in the News—Individual Activity, one class period, p 275B	★ **Read to Remember,** Section 2 ● **Section Activities,** Section 2 Δ **Readings** ● **Tests and Quizzes,** Section 2 Quiz
SECTION 3	**Section 11–3** (1–2 Days) **The Nation Divides,** pp 295–299 Connections to Themes: Balancing Unity and Diversity, p 299 Review/Evaluation Section Review, p 299 Chapter 11 Survey, pp 300–301 Skills, pp 300–301 Using New Vocabulary Thinking Critically Using Geography Applying Social Studies Skills: Analyzing Statistical Tables Thinking About History: Recognizing Point of View	**Teaching the Main Ideas:** Rail Tales Role-Play—Cooperative Activity, one or more class periods, p 275C **Evaluating Progress:** Civil War Cause and Effect—Individual Activity, one class period, p 275C	★ **Read to Remember,** Section 3 ● **Section Activities,** Section 3 Δ **Enrichment Activities,** Section 3 Δ **Readings** ● **Tests and Quizzes,** Section 3 Quiz, Chapter 11 Test (Forms A and B) **Additional Resources** Δ **Twentieth Century Issues: Links to the Past** ● **Active Learning** Δ **GTV Videodiscs** Δ **Transparencies and Activity Book** ● **Testing Software** ★ **Chapter Summaries** **Key:** ★ **For Extra Support** ● **For All Students** Δ **For Enrichment**

Overview

By the mid-1800s the economies and social structures of the North and South were developing along very different lines. Industrialization in northern cities created a demand for cheap labor that attracted rural Americans as well as immigrants from abroad. Attempts by workers to unionize met with fierce resistance, while immigrants as well as free blacks often suffered from discrimination. Meanwhile, the South continued to be largely agricultural, dependent on the cash crop of cotton and with a social hierarchy committed to preserving slavery.

In fact, the overriding issue of the period was the extension of slavery into the territories. Congress agreed to the Compromise of 1850, but that proved only a temporary solution. Another attempted solution was the Kansas-Nebraska Act. Based on the concept of popular sovereignty, it resulted in an eruption of violence in Kansas that helped give rise to the Republican party. With Abraham Lincoln as their candidate in 1860, the Republicans won the presidency, only to witness the immediate secession of seven southern states from the Union. The Confederate attack on Fort Sumter marked the beginning of the Civil War.

Activity Objectives

After completing the activities, students should be able to

- understand the concept of popular sovereignty and its effect on the conflict over extending slavery to the territories.
- identify causes and effects of events leading up to the Civil War.
- describe different viewpoints of northerners and southerners at mid-century.
- describe ways of life and attitudes of various social and economic groups in the North and the South.
- understand the grievances and goals of groups in the mid-1800s that faced discrimination and exclusion from the promises of democracy.

Introducing the Chapter

To Revolt Or Not to Revolt?

This class activity requires about 30 minutes.

This activity prepares students for the central issue of Chapter 11—slavery—by having them imagine themselves as slaves who are contemplating a revolt.

Begin by reading aloud the following description:

> *You are a slave who works in the fields on a cotton plantation. A year ago your wife and four children were sold to a planter in another state. You realized when you said goodbye to your loved ones that you would probably never see them again.*
>
> *Your daily life is hard. For twelve hours a day, six days a week, you work in the fields. During the workday you get only one break to swallow a few bites of cold food. Your master provides little more for your morning and evening meals.*
>
> *You have been forbidden to learn to read or write. During the past few weeks you have been accused of not working hard enough and of talking back to the master's wife. In both cases you received severe beatings.*
>
> *You have heard rumors that a slave revolt is being organized. The organizers promise to help all resisting slaves escape to the North. You know your life will get no better if you stay here, but you wonder what will happen if the revolt fails. Should you join the revolt?*

Without discussion, ask students to respond to the question in writing. Allow five to ten minutes for students to write their responses, then ask students to share what they have written. Record their reasons on the chalkboard under the headings *Yes–Revolt* or *No–Don't Revolt*.

Remind students of Patrick Henry's demand, "Give me liberty or give me death." Ask students if they think it is relevant to the situation of slaves in the United States in 1850. Conclude by acknowledging the difficulty of mounting a successful revolt when an entire society was organized to maintain slavery.

Teaching the Main Ideas

Section 11–2: "Bleeding Kansas" in the News

This individual activity requires one class period, or it may be assigned as homework.

This activity is designed to help students understand the concept and results of popular sovereignty by having them write newspaper articles reporting the passage of the Kansas-Nebraska Act and subsequent events.

With students, review the information in Section 11–2 on the Kansas-Nebraska Act. Emphasize that the act, based on the concept of popular sovereignty, prompted a bloody conflict. Explain that the task in this activity is to write two articles on the act and its effects. One article should be for a proslavery newspaper and the other, for an antislavery paper.

Remind students that news articles answer the questions who, what, when, where, why, and how. Also, although news articles are supposed to be objective, reporters and editors sometimes "slant" the news to support their points of view or appeal to their readers. Encourage students to lead off their articles with attention-getting headlines.

Post completed articles on two different sides of the classroom. Have students evaluate each others' work for accuracy in description of events and effectiveness in presentation of viewpoints. Conclude by recognizing how positions on both sides of slavery hardened with the passage of the Kansas-Nebraska Act.

Teaching the Main Ideas

Section 11–3: Rail Tales Role-Play

This cooperative activity requires one or more class periods.

This activity engages students in role playing a conversation among four strangers on a train ride in 1861. Students are to portray the travelers' viewpoints accurately and address relevant topics.

Before beginning the activity, write the following list of roles on the chalkboard:

- southern plantation owner
- northern abolitionist
- northern factory worker
- northern factory owner
- free African American
- fugitive-slave catcher
- adult daughter of a plantation owner
- poor white southerner hoping to start over in the West
- Republican candidate for Congress
- Democratic candidate for Congress

Remind students that in Chapter 11 they learned that people living in the North and the South in the mid-1800s not only held different points of view but had different reasons for their viewpoints. To illustrate these differences, students are to imagine themselves traveling by train in the spring of 1861 and striking up a conversation with three strangers in their compartment. In the course of the conversation they discover that each holds a different point of view on current events.

Divide the class into groups of four and point out the list of roles on the chalkboard. Each student may choose the specific role he or she will play, but each group must have equal representation of northern and southern views. Allow time for students to plan the topics—drawn from the chapter—that they will discuss in their conversations. Groups need not prepare scripts, but all members should be able to represent their roles convincingly.

Have each group role play its train ride conversation for the class. Encourage other students to discuss the accuracy and understanding evidenced in the role-plays.

Evaluating Progress

Section 11–3: Civil War Cause and Effect

This individual activity requires most of a class period, or it may be assigned as homework.

In this activity students draw on information from the entire chapter to construct diagrams illustrating cause and effect relationships.

Before students begin, put the following models of cause and effect diagrams on the chalkboard.

Single Cause and Effect:	cause → effect
Multiple Causes, Single Effect:	cause cause → effect cause
Single Cause, Multiple Effects:	effect cause → effect effect

Chain Reaction: cause → effect → cause → effect

Discuss the differences between the diagrams. Point out that while all the diagrams illustrate cause and effect relationships, some relationships are more complex than others. Illustrate two of the models with information from the chapter, as follows:

Multiple Causes	*Single Effect*
Inhumane working conditions Concern of skilled craftsmen Wage cuts, increased hours	Rise of labor unions

Chain Reaction:

Cause	*Effect*	*Cause*	*Effect*
Kansas-Nebraska Act	Conflict between pro- and anti-slavery forces	Formation of Republican party	Republicans elect Lincoln as President

Point out that the same action or event can sometimes be considered a causal agent and at other times an effect. For example, the Kansas-Nebraska Act was the effect of congressional compromise, but it was also the cause of a bloody conflict in the Kansas Territory.

Direct students to use information in Chapter 11 to create cause and effect diagrams. (Allow students to use their books, since this is an evaluation of their understanding of relationships rather than their recall of events.) Have them construct at least two diagrams for each of the four models, but encourage them to create as many diagrams as possible.

There is no one set of correct diagrams for this activity, but you should evaluate student work on the number of diagrams and the appropriateness of the connections they make.

Reinforcement Activity

Section 11–1: Letters Between Cousins

This paired activity requires a full class period.

In this activity pairs of students acting as "cousins" exchange letters designed to clarify the major differences between ways of life and attitudes in the South and the North in the mid-1800s.

Tell students that many Americans who lived in the North in the mid-1800s had relatives who lived in the South, and vice versa. Ask them to imagine themselves in 1860 as a young person whose favorite cousin lives in the other part of the country. Have students form pairs and decide which one will be the northern cousin and which the southerner. They will also need to decide on the social and economic roles of their families. For example, one cousin might be the daughter of a free African-American laborer and the other the son of an enslaved field hand on a small plantation. Or one cousin might be the son of a northern factory owner while the other's father owns a cotton plantation.

Have students review Section 11–1. Then tell them that they are to write letters to their "cousins" in which they describe their everyday lives and points of view on the events of the day and ask appropriate questions. The letters should be one to two pages long. When they finish, the cousins are to exchange their letters. Each cousin then writes a response. Continue the letter exchanges until each student has written three letters.

At the conclusion of the letter exchange, have students summarize the major differences between life and attitudes in the North and the South.

Enrichment Activity

Section 11–1: Posters of Protest

This cooperative activity requires one class period.

To enrich students' understanding of Section 11–1, this activity focuses on the groups of Americans who were generally exploited, discriminated against, or denied rights in the mid-1800s. Working in groups, students create posters to illustrate the grievances of these groups.

Review Section 11–1 with students and have them identify the four groups (factory laborers, immigrants, free African Americans, enslaved African Americans). Discuss how and why each group was exploited and/or discriminated against.

Divide the class into teams of three and assign each team to represent one of the "excluded" groups. Direct each team to create a protest poster that depicts the situation and grievances of the group it represents. Suggest that the posters might describe the feelings of the group's members, their treatment by others, their living conditions, and their specific goals. Encourage teams to create slogans and symbols and allow them to design more than one poster if they wish.

A the end of the period, have each team present its poster to the class. Hang the posters around the room and leave them up as the class studies the Civil War.

Bibliography and Audiovisual Material

Teacher Bibliography

Higham, John. *Strangers in the Land.* New York: Atheneum, 1967

Jacobs, Harriet A. *Incidents in the Life of a Slave Girl.* Cambridge: Harvard University Press, 1987.

Rose, Willie Lee. *A Documentary History of Slavery in North America*. New York: Oxford University Press, 1976.

Stampp, Kenneth M. *America in 1857: A Nation on the Brink.* New York: Oxford University Press, 1991.

Student Bibliography

Douglass, Frederick. *The Life and Times of Frederick Douglass.* Secaucus, NJ: Lyle Stuart, 1983.

Lester, Julius. *To Be a Slave.* New York: Scholastic, 1986.

Stowe, Harriet Beecher. *Uncle Tom's Cabin: Or Life Among the Lowly.* New York: Random House, 1991.

Films, Videocassettes, and Videodiscs

Agitation and Compromise. 30 min. PBS Video. Movie.

Civil War Series: Background Issues 1820–1860. 20 min. Coronet/MTI. Videocassette.

Crisis of Union. 30 min. PBS Video. Movie.

The Lincoln-Douglas Debates: The House Divides. 25 min. Coronet/MTI. Videodisc.

Filmstrips

The Civil War: Prelude to Conflict. National Geographic Society.

Walt Whitman: A Poet of the Civil War. Coronet/MTI.

Where Historians Disagree Series: Causes of the Civil War. Random House Media.

Computer Software

Interviews with History: Heading for Civil War. Apple. Educational Publishing Concepts.

Living American History Series: U.S. History II 1840–1875. Apple. Priven Learning Systems.

Conversations With Great Americans Series: Civil War and Expansion. Apple. Focus Media.

Chapter 11

Objectives

- Cite ways in which the North and the South were different in the middle of the nineteenth century.
- Discuss why compromise was crucial to preserving the Union in the 1850s.
- Explain how sectional differences over slavery led to the Civil War.

Introducing THE CHAPTER

For suggestions on introducing Chapter 11, refer to page 275B in the Teacher's Edition.

Developing THE CHAPTER

For activities and teaching strategies to help you reinforce and enrich chapter content, see pages 275B–275D in the Teacher's Edition.

B · A · C · K · G · R · O · U · N · D

Chapter Opener Illustrations
In his 1858 senatorial campaign Abraham Lincoln declared, "A house divided against itself cannot stand. I believe this government cannot endure permanently half slave and half free. . . . It will become all one thing, or all the other."

Enslaved African Americans haul cotton from the fields to the cotton gin. This photograph was taken by George N. Barnard near Charleston, South Carolina in the late 1850s.

New York City's Broadway in 1860, even then bustling with traffic.

The Fugitive Slave Act brought many northerners sympa-

Reduced student page in the Teacher's Edition

Chapter 11 1850-1861

The Gathering Storm

thetic to the antislavery cause into active opposition of slavery. This 1851 poster warned fugitive slaves in Boston against police and others enforcing the Fugitive Slave Act.

The Kansas-Nebraska Act of 1854 opened the possibility for settlers in those two territories to vote on whether to allow slavery there. On voting day in Kansas Territory, thousands of pro-slavery people from Missouri rushed across the border to help elect a pro-slavery legislature.

A steam locomotive, the DeWitt Clinton, traveled from Albany to Schenectady in New York state in under one hour. By 1860 there were over 30,000 miles of railroad track crisscrossing the United States.

American Voices

In 1854 sixteen-year-old Charlotte Forten, a member of a wealthy African-American family in the North, saw the capture of an escaped slave named Burns. A new law allowed escaped slaves to be captured in the free North and returned to their southern owners.

> *"Friday, June 2. Our worst fears are realized; the decision was against poor Burns, and he has been sent back to a bondage worse, a thousand times worse than death. . . . Today Massachusetts has again been disgraced. . . . With what scorn must that government be regarded, which cowardly assembles thousands of soldiers to satisfy the demands of slaveholders; to deprive of his freedom a man, created in God's own image, whose sole offense is the color of his skin!*
>
> *"Sunday, June 4. The sky is cloudless, the sun shines warm and bright, and a delicious breeze fans my cheek. How strange it is that in a world so beautiful, there can be so much wickedness; on this delightful day, while many are enjoying themselves in their happy homes, not poor Burns only, but millions beside are suffering in chains."*

By the 1850s the North and South were two different worlds, and the issue of slavery was becoming increasingly divisive. Factories dotted the North, and seemingly endless fields of cotton spread over the South. The needs of industry and the needs of agriculture were to underlie a great conflict.

In the West, lands were beckoning to settlers. New states would be carved from those lands. Should the states be slave or free? On the eve of the 1860s, this issue threatened to break the bonds that held the Union together.

Abraham Lincoln; field hands hauling cotton in South Carolina; New York City in 1860; Boston poster warning against slave catchers and kidnappers; the first steam train in New York; pro-slavery Missourians going to Kansas Territory to vote.

Analyzing Primary Sources

American Voices

In 1856 James Forten's granddaughter, Charlotte Forten, became the first African American to teach white children in Salem, Massachusetts. During the Civil War she volunteered to teach former slaves on the Union-occupied Sea Islands off the coast of South Carolina. Forten kept a journal between 1854 and 1864. After her death—in 1914—her *Journal* was published.

Ask: Why might Forten consider slavery worse than death? **(Compare death to the long-term physical pain and psychological degradation of slavery.)** How does Forten view Massachusetts as a result of the capture of Burns? **(Massachusetts considered itself the cradle of revolutionary ideas that produced the fight for "liberty and justice for all" in 1776. Now state authorities were helping return escaped slaves to bondage.)** How did the weather contrast with Forten's mood in her June 4 entry? **(It was a beautiful day, but she was depressed by thoughts about slavery.)**

GTV Side 2

Chap. 13, Frame 37962

One Nation, Still? (Movie)

Search:

Play:

Section 11-1

Objectives

- ***Answer the Focus Question.***
- *Explain how the development of transportation affected America's economic growth.*
- *Explain the relationship between the invention of the cotton gin and the growth of slavery.*
- *Analyze how slave revolts contributed to growing tension between North and South.*

Introducing THE SECTION

Have students relate what they know about the economic differences between the North and South in the mid-1800s. Point out the North had many more factories than the South, whereas the southern economy was dependent on agriculture, particularly cotton. Labor in the North was free, whereas southern plantations relied on slave labor.

Ask: How might these differences have affected the lives of the people in the two areas? **(Northern populations were more urban than in the South. The institution of slavery impacted all aspects of southern society.)**

B · A · C · K · G · R · O · U · N · D

Time Line Illustrations

1. The potato originated in South America and was introduced into Ireland in the mid-1500s. A large part of the Irish population came to depend on it for food. Between 1845 and 1847, blight ruined Ireland's potato crop, and as many as 2 million people died of starvation or disease. The potato famine spurred Irish emigration to the United States.

2. A pamphlet playing on nativist fears that immigrant labor might ruin American workers.

3. *Uncle Tom's Cabin* broadside. Harriet Beecher Stowe's novel aroused many northerners against the cruelties of slavery. In its first year of publication 300,000 copies were sold. Note the various editions available and the wide variety of prices. Before publication as a book, *Uncle Tom's Cabin*

CHAPTER TIME LINE

1850 - 1861

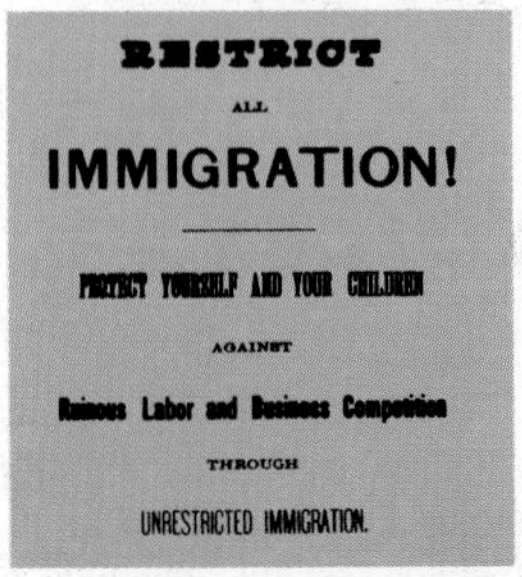
RESTRICT
ALL
IMMIGRATION!
PROTECT YOURSELF AND YOUR CHILDREN
AGAINST
Ruinous Labor and Business Competition
THROUGH
UNRESTRICTED IMMIGRATION.

1842 *Commonwealth* v. *Hunt* legalizes unions

1848 Free-soil party formed in opposition to slavery
Zachary Taylor elected President

1849 Know-Nothing party established

1841 — 1845 — 1849

1840s Potato blight in Ireland and crop failures in northern Europe

1850 Compromise of 1850

11-1 *Life in the North and the South*

Focus: By the middle of the nineteenth century, in what ways were the North and the South different?

By the 1850s factory and cotton field had become symbols of the different ways of life in the North and the South. In the North, new factories hummed to the tune of industry. In the South, life working on the land continued as rhythmically as the seasons.

Of course, factory and field were only symbols. Many northerners still earned their living by farming, and the South had some industry. Furthermore, North and South often worked together. Southern cotton fed northern mills, and Yankee ships moved southern crops to market. The two regions were bound together by the ties of commerce. But the North remained committed to free labor while the South remained dependent upon its "peculiar institution"—slavery.

Railroads and Steamboats: Engines of Commerce

Commerce could not exist without transportation. During the 1820s and 1830s canals, roads, and river-going steamboats had spurred the growth of trade and industry. Passenger and freight cars were pulled along rails by horses or mules. Then, in 1830, a New York inventor named Peter Cooper convinced the Baltimore and Ohio Railroad to hitch its cars to his steam-powered locomotive instead of to a horse. With this advancement the railroad era had begun.

Soon a railroad line stretched 130 miles westward from Charleston, South Carolina. In Pennsylvania, which soon took the lead in railroad was serialized in an antislavery newspaper, *The National Era*, in 1851 and 1852.

4. Contemporary artist Jacob Lawrence is noted for his works depicting significant episodes in African-American history. One series of paintings focuses on the abolitionist, John Brown. Brown was found "Guilty of treason and murder in the first degree," and was hanged in Charles Town, Virginia, on December 2, 1859.

5. The Confederate battle flag had stars for the eleven states that had seceded from the Union and for the governments of Kentucky and Missouri.

1852 Harriet Beecher Stowe publishes *Uncle Tom's Cabin*

1854 Kansas-Nebraska Act

Republican party formed as an antislavery party

1857 Dred Scott decision

1859 John Brown's raid on Harpers Ferry

1853 — 1857 — 1861

1860 Abraham Lincoln elected President

1860 Dec South Carolina secedes

1861 Apr 12 Confederate troops open fire on Fort Sumter; Civil War begins

building, lines brought coal straight from the mines to the blast furnaces of industry.

By 1840 over 400 railroads had laid some 3,000 miles of track, and cities from New England to Georgia had rail service. Then, in 1850 Congress began giving federal land to the states to build railroads in unsettled areas. The impact was enormous. Within five years Chicago, a small city with one railroad line, became the nation's busiest rail center, with nearly a hundred trains arriving or departing daily.

By 1860 over 30,000 miles of track linked cities of the eastern seaboard and reached westward like fingers to the Mississippi River. Almost 70 percent of the track was in the North, where railroads and industry depended on each other. Freight cars moved raw materials to factories and products to market, helping industry to grow. Still, not everyone welcomed the railroads. A critic cried,

> *"The railroad . . . is the Devil's own invention, compounded of fire, smoke, soot, and dirt, spreading its infernal poison throughout the fair countryside."*

While the railroads moved goods within the United States, ships carried American products across the sea, and America's merchant marine—ships used in commerce—grew tremendously. New England designers built clipper ships—swift, sleek sailing vessels that set speed records between ports in America, Europe, and Asia. With its fleet of sailing ships, the United States captured over half the highly profitable China trade by 1860.

However, steam power soon made sailing ships obsolete. Great Britain built a fleet of fast steamships with huge cargo holds and took the lead in ocean trade. The United States also built some steamships, but its infant steamship industry could not match that of Britain.

Nevertheless, improvements in America's transportation system spurred economic growth in the 1850s. Farmers in the Northwest supplied crops and livestock for the Northeast. Southern plantations prospered as the demand for cotton grew. The Northeast turned cotton into textiles and other finished goods for Americans in all sections of the country. It seemed that both raw materials and manufactured goods were in constant motion.

Developing
THE SECTION

Multicultural Perspectives

Discussion. The Plains Indians, through whose lands railroads eventually ran, referred to the locomotive as an "iron horse" or a "bad medicine wagon." ("Medicine" here means something like "spiritual power.") Discuss what each of these terms suggests about Native Americans' feelings toward the railroad. How might the railroad affect the way of life of Native Americans? **(open Native-American land for increased white settlement, for example)**

GTV Side 2

Chap. 9, Frame 28444

Getting Up to Speed: The Birth of Railroads (Movie Segment)

Search and Play:

Geography Skills

ANSWERS

North.

Backyard History

Research. Have students research the chief products of their area in the 1850s. What cities, towns, or posts were main centers of trade? Have them describe one or more main routes used in the 1850s in transporting products to a trading center in their area. Refer students to the Agriculture and Industry maps on pages 906–907, the Railroads in 1850 map on page 280, and encyclopedias. Students can also refer to state and local histories or—if appropriate—local historical societies.

Reduced student page in the Teacher's Edition

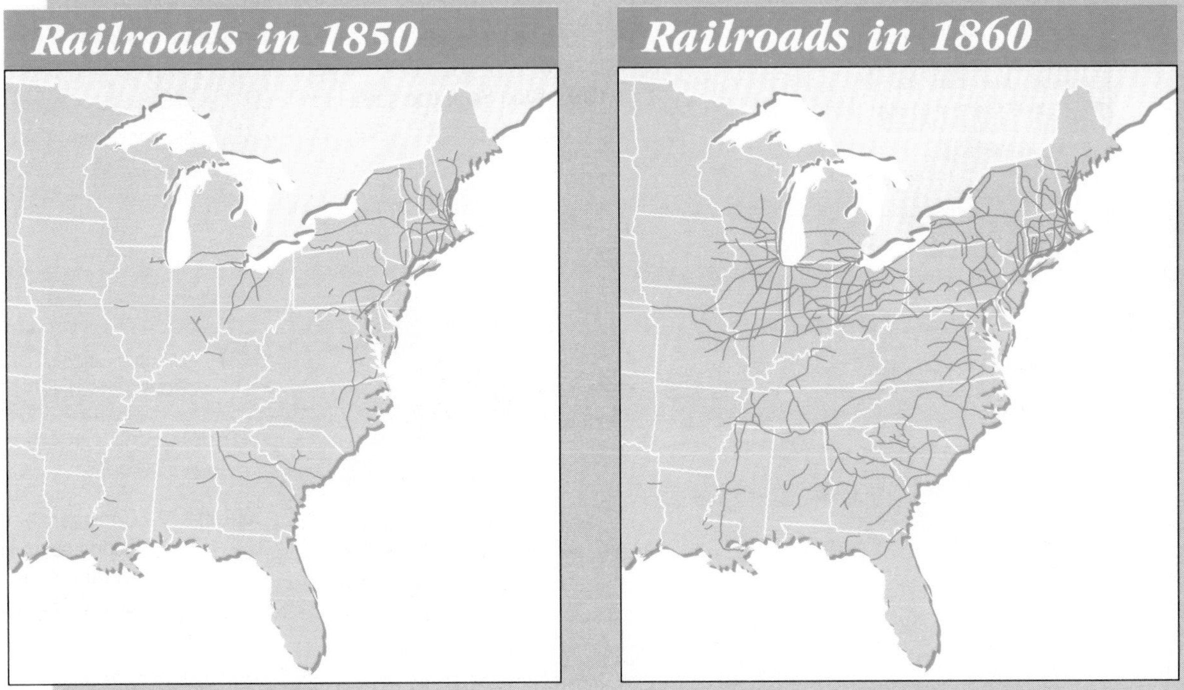

Geography Skills— Region. In which region— the North or the South— were more miles of new track laid between 1850 and 1860?

The Industrial North

Industrial expansion in the North brought economic growth and social change. Factories churned out goods such as cotton fabric, plows, clocks, rubber goods, shoes, and wool cloth. By 1860 the North boasted 74,058 factories. Work moved from the home to factories located in urban centers or in factory towns. Lowell, Massachusetts, for example, grew from a small farming village to a factory town of 30,000 built around busy textile mills.

At the time textile mills were growing rapidly, most American men either farmed or had a trade and scorned the idea of factory work. Thus, mill owners turned to rural areas to recruit young women to tend the machines. These women left

In this 1830 railroad-car race, the locomotive Tom Thumb *shows the potential of steam power over horse power.*

Social History
Some of the "Lowell girls" protested against harsh conditions in the mills. One was Sarah G. Bagley, who in 1845 formed the Lowell Female Labor Reform Association. Its aim was to limit the working day to ten hours and show the *"driveling cotton lords"* that *"our rights cannot be trampled upon with impunity."* The group signed up 304 members within five months of its founding.

Chapter Connections
Students will learn more about unions in Chapters 16, 22, and 26.

Thinking Critically

Evaluation. Early textile mills in New England resolved the problem of scarce labor by employing young single women, most of whom came from farm families.

1. What were the advantages and disadvantages of this source of labor from the perspective of the mill owners? (Advantages: might be seen as docile, could be paid less than men; disadvantages: unfamiliar with factory work, usually left factory after marriage) From the perspective of women workers? (Advantages: wages provided some independence, increased educational and occupational opportunities, provided opportunity for socialization with other women; disadvantages: lives regimented, damaged health.)

2. What other source of labor could be tapped as industry grew? (immigrants and children)

their parents to live in closely supervised boarding houses provided by the textile company. As one who had left home to work in a mill explained:

> *"I am almost nineteen years old. I must of course have something of my own before many more years have passed over my head. And where is that something coming from if I go home and earn nothing?"*

There was, however, a dark side to the work that first attracted the "Lowell girls." Long hours and low wages were commonplace. A newspaper article in 1836 exposed the harsh conditions:

> *"The operatives [machine operators] work thirteen hours a day in the summer time, and from daylight to dark in the winter. . . . So fatigued . . . are numbers of girls that they go to bed soon after receiving their evening meal"*

During the depression that began with the Panic of 1837, the already difficult working conditions grew worse in textile mills and in other factories, too. Managers sought to reduce expenses and increase production. They cut wages and made workers handle more looms or machines. But the long working hours remained the same. If workers complained, they were fired. Often managers would **blacklist** a fired worker, which meant that employers at other factories agreed not to hire that worker.

One factory manager summed up the prevailing view of labor. "I regard my work-people just as I regard my machinery. . . . When my machines get old and useless, I reject them and get new, and these workers are part of my machinery."

The Early Labor Movement

As industries grew, skilled workers such as printers, shoemakers, and carpenters realized that the old system of working for themselves in their homes was breaking down. Power-driven machines worked faster and more efficiently than they could. Since the future of craftspeople seemed to be as wage earners rather than business owners, many skilled workers tried to band together to protect their interests. These efforts to organize were the roots of the labor movement that continues today.

Some of the skilled workers formed political parties called Workingmen's parties and sought such changes as free education and an end to imprisonment for debt. Others formed craft unions, groups of people who tried to improve working conditions and wages in their trade. The first goal of the craft unions was to shorten the work day, which in 1830 averaged twelve and a half hours. To get a ten-hour work day, workers went out on **strike**— refusing to work until employers met their demands.

At the time, however, both strikes and unions were illegal. Workers involved in them could be fined and arrested. When twenty-one tailors went on strike in 1836, they were fined $1,150 for striking and for forming "an unlawful club or combination to injure trade."

During the depression of the late 1830s, craft union membership declined. But when the economy improved, many of the craft unions came back to life. The 1842 decision of the Massachusetts Supreme Court in *Commonwealth* v. *Hunt* further improved the status of craft unions by declaring that unions were legal organizations. Demands for the ten-hour day resumed, and this time spread rapidly among factory workers. As the 1840s drew to a close, many craft unions had won the ten-hour day, and by 1853 most northern states had passed laws upholding it.

Present-day union buttons worn by Iron Workers and United Farm Workers.

Using the Visuals

Analyzing a Graph. Refer students to the graph, "Immigration in the United States 1820–1860" on this page. Ask them to speculate about why immigration fell off so abruptly after 1860. **(probably because the Civil War made the United States a less attractive place for immigrants; also restrictions against immigration)**

Global Connections

Discussion. Immigration can be described as a process involving both "push" and "pull." Have students list the reasons immigrants in the early 1800s were forced—pushed—to leave their homelands **(crop failures, political turmoil in Europe)** and reasons they were attracted—pulled—to the United States **(low rates for passage, stories of economic opportunity)**.

Have students describe immigrants who came to the United States in this period **(Irish comprised almost half of immigrants and were mostly poor and unskilled farmers. Some other Northern Europeans were skilled artisans with money to move West.)** and ways they were perceived as being different from most native-born Americans of European descent. **(different traditions; for Irish and some Germans, Catholic faith; for Germans and Scandinavians, language)**

Connections: Science

The international potato blight that reached Ireland in 1845 was so devastating because one fourth of all the agricultural land in the country was used to raise potatoes. One writer noted: *"The smell of the potato rotting in the fields rose and mingled with the odors of death in the cottages and along the hedgerows."*

Reduced student page in the Teacher's Edition

However, the flurry of labor activity again died out. In 1857 another depression wiped out many unions. By 1860 less than 1 percent of American workers belonged to unions. Craftspeople were reluctant to give up their independence and accept the new industrial order by supporting unions. They held out, hoping for a return to the time when "every man was his own master." Meanwhile a new supply of cheap labor was flooding the market.

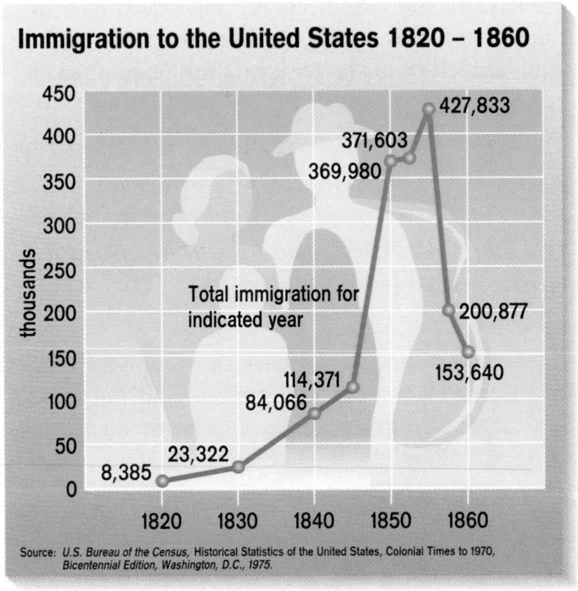
Immigration to the United States 1820 - 1860
thousands
450
400
350
300
250
200
150
100
50
0
1820
1830
1840
1850
1860
8,385
23,322
84,066
114,371
369,980
371,603
427,833
200,877
153,640
Total immigration for indicated year
Source: U.S. Bureau of the Census, Historical Statistics of the United States, Colonial Times to 1970, Bicentennial Edition, Washington, D.C., 1975.

A Tide of Immigrants

In 1783 George Washington had welcomed immigrants to the new nation, declaring, "The bosom of America is open to receive not only the opulent [wealthy] and respectable stranger, but the oppressed and persecuted of all Nations and Religions." However, American attitudes toward new arrivals have not always been so warm. Depending on their religion and the country from which they came, and depending on the economic and political conditions in the United States at the time, immigrants have, at various times, been viewed with suspicion—and even with hostility.

In 1798, fearing the influence of foreigners, Congress had passed the Naturalization and Alien Acts. In the 1850s a new political party emerged with a platform that once again called for laws that placed restrictions on immigration and naturalization.

Coming to America. The renewed suspicion of foreigners surfaced in part because such a huge wave of immigrants was pouring into the United States. From the 1830s through the 1850s, over 4 million immigrants landed at American ports. Almost half of them had fled from Ireland, where a blight had ruined the potato crop. Famine had swept the country, causing the death of as many as 2 million people.

Lured by cheap rates on ships bound for America, as well as by tales of jobs and opportunities, thousands of Irish men, women, and children fled their homeland. "All with means are emigrating. . . . Only the utterly destitute are left behind," noted one observer.

The typical Irish immigrant family was Roman Catholic, poor, and had known only subsistence farming as a way of life. This combination of factors caused them to be met with discrimination from the predominantly English Protestant population in America. The Irish had long been considered inferior by the British who ruled Ireland, and now Irish immigrants faced similar attitudes in the United States. One member of Congress revealed his contempt for the Irish when he said, "Their inferiority as a race compels them to go to the bottom [where they will] do the manual labor."

Irish immigrants packed the tenement buildings in slums in eastern cities, most notably New York, Philadelphia, and Boston. Able-bodied men, desperate for work, eagerly accepted low wages on construction gangs and in factories. Employers responded by lowering wages for all workers.

Workers who had been born and raised in the United States reacted angrily to the lower wages, and, in many cases, to replacement by immigrant labor. In one mill in Lowell, for example, less than 4 percent of the workers were foreign born in the mid-1830s. By 1860 more than 60 percent were.

Other groups of immigrants from northern Europe also flocked to America. Crop failures and political turmoil drove Germans to search for a new life in America. These immigrants were often skilled artisans or experienced farmers, as were most immigrants from Scandinavia and England. Many had enough money to move west in search of cheap land, business opportunities, and jobs.

In general, most immigrants settled in the Northeast and Northwest. Those who arrived in the South, unaccustomed to the hot, humid climate, usually moved north up the Mississippi River. As a result, it was in the northern United States that the flames of anti-foreign feelings ignited.

The nativist reaction. Many native-born Americans thought the newly-arrived immigrants posed a threat to native jobholders. They also feared the effect that these newcomers—with accents, languages, traditions, and sometimes religions different from their own—might have on what they saw as the "American way of life." Hostility to immigrants based on the belief that they threatened traditional American culture, institutions, and social order became known as **nativism.**

Nativists and immigrants viewed each other with suspicion and distrust. Nativists feared that the influence of priests and the Pope over Catholic immigrants might extend to the entire population of the United States. For their part, Catholic immigrants, mostly Irish, founded Catholic schools to protect their children from what they saw as Protestant indoctrination in public schools. Rioting broke out between Catholic immigrants and Protestant nativists, and Catholic churches and schools became the targets of vandalism and arson.

Reform movements also became a source of tension. Protestant reformers declared the use of alcohol in Irish and German communities to be evil. The Irish tended to view causes such as women's rights and temperance as "Protestant" issues and therefore unworthy of their support.

Tensions erupted in the political arena. The Irish-American community quickly became politically active, showing intense loyalty to the Democratic party. German Americans also expressed their concerns, such as abolition, through political channels. Meanwhile, nativist cartoons like the one on the previous page spread fear of foreigners.

In the 1840s nativists formed secret societies to keep immigrants out of politics and thus out of power. Members pledged to vote against any immigrant or Catholic candidate for office. One such society, the Supreme Order of the Star-Spangled Banner, spread throughout the country and by 1849 established itself as a political party, the American party. Because its members pledged to respond "I don't know" if questioned about party activities, it was dubbed the Know-Nothing party.

American Voices

"*As a nation we began by declaring that* "all men are created equal." *We now practically read it "all men are created equal,* except negroes." *When the Know-Nothings get control it will read "all men are created equal, except negroes,* and foreigners and Catholics."

—Abraham Lincoln, 1855

Multicultural Perspectives

Discussion. Mexicans in newly-acquired western lands also faced prejudice. Historian J.M. Guinn wrote of the Mexican Americans in California in the 1850s:

"*The Americans not only took possession of their [the Mexicans] country and its government, but in many cases despoiled them of their ancestral acres and their personal property. . . . They were often treated . . . as aliens and intruders, who had no right in the land of their birth.*"

Since the 1960s, many Mexican Americans in the Southwest have fought to regain land taken from their families in the 1850s. Ask students to consider whether either the federal government or private land owners have an obligation to compensate these families. Why or why not?

Multicultural Perspectives

A primary goal of early craft unions was to limit the supply of labor in order to maintain high wages. This goal, combined with the racism and sexism of the primarily white male craftworkers, acted to exclude most women and African Americans from union membership. Recruitment of African Americans as strikebreakers also contributed to a long-lasting hostility between the union movement and blacks.

Not all native-born Americans agreed with the views of the nativists. Still, many immigrants, attracted to the promise of democracy and freedom in the United States, found instead a society that sought to exclude them from that promise.

Free African Americans in the North

Recent immigrants were not the only people in the North to face resentment and exclusion. By 1860 approximately 250,000 free African Americans lived in the North. Yet in only a few New England states were they allowed to vote. If they found any work at all, African American men usually had to work as unskilled laborers or waiters, while women often worked as maids and laundresses. Frederick Douglass described the life of free African Americans as one in which they were

> *" . . . denied the privileges and courtesies common to others in the use of the most humble means of conveyance—shut out from cabins on steamboats, refused admission to respectable hotels, caricatured, scorned, scoffed, mocked, and maltreated by anyone."*

As was true with immigrants, African-American workers were often resented by white workers who had to compete with them for jobs. Furthermore, African Americans were barred from membership in most unions, and when white workers went on strike, employers quickly hired black workers to replace them. This practice heightened the bitterness of white workers toward African Americans.

Many free African Americans headed west, looking for a better life. But most discovered racism and discrimination in the West as well. In the early 1850s Iowa, Illinois, Indiana, and Oregon all had laws denying African Americans the right to settle there. In Oregon, African Americans could not own property or make contracts. In California they could not testify in court against whites.

The problems that workers, immigrants, and free African Americans faced were real. But people with the power to make changes tended to see these problems as merely a part of "progress," not as wrongs to be righted.

The Southern Economy

While the North moved to the clatter of the Industrial Revolution, the South was being shaped by different forces. In 1845 William Gregg, president of the company that owned the South's first cotton mill, urged South Carolina to develop more industry. "At every village and crossroad in the state," he wrote, "we should have a tannery, a shoemaker, a clothier, a hatter, [and] a blacksmith."

In fact, some manufacturing had begun in the South. By 1860 the region had

In a typical scene in a southern river port, bystanders, both black and white, await the arrival of a ship heavily loaded with bales of cotton. Cash crops, the back bone of the South's economy, were often shipped to market by riverboat.

Multicultural Perspectives

While subject to racism and discrimination, free African Americans in the North overcame tremendous obstacles, and made great contributions in a number of fields. In Ohio, David Clay advertised his plows, which could be made in any size and could plow depths of eight to twenty inches. The singing of Elizabeth Taylor Greenfield was compared to that of Jenny Lind and other famous sopranos of her time; Greenfield gave concerts in both the United States and Europe. Dr. Martin R. Delaney, graduate of the Harvard Medical School, performed outstanding service during a cholera epidemic in Pittsburgh.

Limited English Proficiency

Using the Visuals. Discuss with students the hierarchy of southern society discussed on this page and the next. With input from students, draw on the chalkboard a graphic overview of southern society: At the top, wealthy planters who were slaveholders, followed by white farmers who owned small farms and no slaves, poor whites, hill people of Appalachia, free African Americans, slaves.

Have students use the illustrations on pages 284–285 to discuss how ways of life within southern society differed.

over 20,000 small factories. Still, these factories produced only 15 percent of the nation's goods. The southern economy relied on agriculture. This dependence on cash crops—tobacco, rice, sugarcane, and cotton—had limits because intensive farming leached nutrients from the soil.

When it came to cash crops, cotton—which was especially hard on the soil—was king. Ever since Eli Whitney's invention of the cotton gin in 1793, more and more southern land had been turned over to cotton. Around 1800 most of the South's cotton was grown in South Carolina and Georgia. Then the soaring market for cotton and the depletion of the soil pressed southern farmers to expand to fertile lands in the West. The cotton kingdom spread to Alabama, Mississippi, Louisiana, and eventually Texas.

With improvements in the textile industry, more cotton cloth could be produced than ever before. Mills in the North and in Britain could use as much cotton as planters could grow. Between 1800 and 1850 the demand doubled, then doubled again. Cotton became America's major export, making up nearly two thirds of all exports.

The South's tiny minority of wealthy plantation owners relied on the labor of enslaved blacks. Another element of southern society, poor whites, scraped by on marginal lands.

Free Southern Society

Although many white farmers in the South wanted to own slaves, only about one fourth actually did. The South had a rigid class hierarchy. At the top were a small minority of wealthy planters, who owned estates of at least 800 acres with at least 20 slaves. Planters owned the richest land, reaped the profits of most of the South's cash crops, and wielded the greatest economic and political power.

Southern White Families Holding Slaves 1850

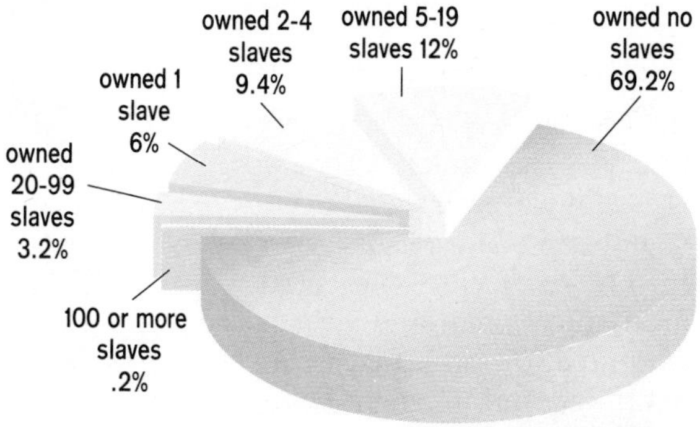

Multicultural Perspectives

In 1856 plans for a slave revolt were uncovered in Colorado County, Texas. According to Texans, enslaved African Americans planned to rebel, kill their masters, and, with the aid of native Mexicans, flee across the border to Mexico. Every Mexican in Colorado County was accused of being part of the plot and was ordered to leave the county immediately. More than two hundred slaves were arrested and punished. Two were whipped to death. Anti-Mexican sentiment swept through other towns, like Austin, where resolutions were passed against employment of Mexicans.

Thinking Critically

Analysis. Review material on Frederick Douglass from Chapter 9. Have students discuss if they agree with the words of Douglass, *"If there is no struggle, there is no progress."* Can students relate these words to "struggles" going on in the world today?

Finally, have students consider what Douglass might have meant when he said, *"Let us not forget that justice to the Negro is safety to the nation."* How does justice make a nation more secure? Explain.

Connections: Literature

Research. Have students read and report on slaves' lives. Biographies and autobiographies of such figures as Frederick Douglass, Sojourner Truth, and Harriet Tubman contain details of their lives as slaves. Other books of slave narratives include John F. Bayliss, ed., *Black Slave Narratives* (Collier, 1970); James Mellon, ed., *Bullwhip Days* (Avon, 1990); and Henry Louis Gates, Jr., ed., *The Classic Slave Narratives* (New American Library, 1987).

Reduced student page in the Teacher's Edition

In 1850 about 90 percent of all slaveholders were farmers who owned fewer than twenty slaves. The majority of these farmers owned fewer than five. Many "small" slaveholders labored side by side with slaves. That fact, however, in no way implied equality of slave and master.

About three fourths of southerners who worked the land were white farmers who owned small farms and no slaves. They grew their own food and a few acres of cotton or tobacco as cash crops. They were not rich, but they were not poor either. Many of these were staunch supporters of the slave system, for they hoped to one day own a slave or two and thereby "move up" in their status in society.

Poor whites made up about 10 percent of the population. Some settled on abandoned, worn-out lands and scraped by as best they could. Isolated from the rest of the South were the hill people of Appalachia, who lived by hunting, fishing, or herding wild cattle and hogs.

Some 250,000 free African Americans lived in the South. Among them were artisans, merchants,

THE AMERICAN SPIRIT

Frederick Douglass

Freedom's Voice

"Steal away . . . steal away . . . steal away to Jesus." The plaintive melody of the spiritual drifted over the Maryland plantation. The song was a secret signal telling slaves that someone was running away to the North, to freedom. This time it was eighteen-year-old Frederick Augustus Washington Bailey. His first run for freedom ended in a jail cell, but three years later, in 1835, he managed to reach New York through the Underground Railroad. To avoid capture, he kept only his first name and adopted the last name Douglass. Spelling the name with two s's gave it distinction.

As a boy, Frederick Douglass had learned to read and write in spite of laws that made such learning a crime for slaves. He came to believe that education was the key to freedom. As an adult, he gathered with other African Americans to discuss issues. He also joined forces with William Lloyd Garrison, a newspaper publisher and fervent abolitionist, and the two men became leading antislavery spokesmen.

In 1847 Douglass started his own newspaper, the *North Star,* naming it after the star that was the guiding light for runaway slaves. "I'll fight slavery with my pen as well as with my voice," he said. Douglass became increasingly well known and drew large crowds of people to his lectures.

When the Civil War broke out in 1861, Douglass published a stirring editorial—"Men of Color, to Arms!"—urging African Americans to enlist in the Union army and support the war. He also discussed the problems of slavery with President Lincoln on several occasions. He believed that freedom had to be fought for. "If there is no struggle, there is no progress," he argued. "Those who profess to favor freedom, and yet [discourage] agitation, are men who want crops without plowing up the ground."

After the war, Douglass served on government commissions and as minister to Haiti. His life was dedicated to seeking equal justice for all. As he once wrote, "Let us not forget that justice to the Negro is safety to the nation."

Connections: Religion

Nat Turner was born in 1800. Early in life, he came to believe that God had some special purpose in mind for him and that he was destined to lead his people out of bondage. Turner was inspired by a passage in the Bible: *"From that time began Jesus to show unto his disciples, that he must go unto Jerusalem, and suffer many things of the elders and chief priests, and scribes, and be killed."* There was a Jerusalem, Virginia, and it was here that Turner started his slave revolt.

Section Review

ANSWERS

1. Definitions for the following terms are on text pages indicated in parentheses: *blacklist* (281), *strike* (281) and *nativism* (283).
2. Ability to move large quantities of raw materials and finished products quickly stimulated growth of factories, increased shipment of goods overseas, and allowed for regional economic specialization.
3. Use of cotton gin made production of cotton more profitable, encouraging expansion of cotton cultivation and increased utilization of slave labor.
4. Made white southerners more nervous and determined to preserve their way of life, and northerners more convinced that slavery was an evil that should be abolished.
5. Students may cite nativist reaction to European immigrants; free African Americans in the North often could not vote, join unions, obtain good jobs, settle in certain areas, own property, testify against whites in court; free African Americans in South had virtually no legal rights; enslaved African Americans were treated as property.

and farmers, though most worked as servants, as hired farm workers, in factories, or in unskilled jobs in the cities. Laws severely restricted their freedom, imposing curfews, forbidding them from moving to other southern states, and preventing them from assembling without a white person present.

Slavery in the South

By 1860 some 4 million African-American southerners labored as slaves. Slaves could be found working in factories, on construction gangs, in mines, and as skilled artisans. But most labored on plantations.

Most plantation slaves were field hands. They worked the cotton fields in a gang system. Groups of thirty or forty men, women, and children plowed, hoed, planted, and harvested the cotton. They were supervised by a white overseer or by a fellow slave called the "driver." For crops like tobacco, rice, and sugar, a task system was used, with each slave assigned to a specific job. Some plantation slaves worked as carpenters or bricklayers. Household slaves cooked, cleaned, and waited on the slaveholding family.

Accounts of the treatment and living conditions of slaves vary. Some were treated almost like members of the family. On the other hand, "Scarce a week passed without [the overseer] whipping me," Frederick Douglass wrote of his days as a field hand. Whether or not a slave was beaten, the system of slavery did violence by depriving all slaves of what other Americans enjoyed— freedom. A North Carolina field hand said, "If I had my life to live over again, I would die fighting rather than be a slave."

Slave revolts. Although their chances of fighting to freedom were small, slaves did revolt. In 1822 an informer revealed plans for a revolt in Charleston, South Carolina. The leader, a free African American named Denmark Vesey, and thirty-five others were hanged. In 1831 Nat Turner led a band of slaves on a two-day sweep through the Virginia countryside, killing fifty-seven whites. The state militia tracked down Turner's band, killing between forty and one hundred blacks (accounts vary), many of whom had no connection with the revolt. Nat Turner himself was tried, convicted, and executed.

Slave revolts had a strong effect. Northern abolitionists saw them as further proof of the evils of slavery. Southern states, fearing more uprisings, passed stricter slave codes— laws designed to control both free blacks and slaves. The codes barred African-Americans from voting, moving freely from state to state, and meeting in large groups.

While there were white southerners who questioned and opposed the system of slavery, for the most part they defended the "peculiar institution." Overlooking the argument that it was immoral for one person to own another, many insisted that slavery was a positive good. They proudly pointed out that a slave was cared for for life— unlike a factory worker in the North. John C. Calhoun of South Carolina declared:

> *"Many in the South once believed it [slavery] was a moral and political evil. That folly and delusion are gone. We see it now in its true light, and regard it as the most safe and stable basis for free institutions in the world."*

The South's determination to maintain its tradition of slave labor became the issue that divided the North and the South. And when the question of the admission of new states arose, the issue of slave versus free labor came to a head.

Section Review

1. Identification. Define *blacklist, strike*, and *nativism.*

2. Comprehension. How did the development of transportation aid America's economic growth?

3. Analysis. Explain the relationship between the invention of the cotton gin and the growth of slavery.

4. Analysis. How did slave revolts contribute to the growing tension between North and South?

5. Application. Use examples from this chapter to illustrate racism and discrimination.

Limited English Proficiency

Holding an Art Show. Students whose families own art works, including reproductions, can bring them to class for an arts and crafts show. Each work should have a tag identifying the artist (if known) what it is, where it came from, and how long the work has been in the family. Students from other classes can be invited to view the show.

Connections: Religion

Harriet Powers was the wife of a Georgia farmer. Her quilt depicts, among other Biblical scenes: Adam and Eve and the serpent; Cain killing Abel; Cain in the land of Nod surrounded by bears; Jacob's Ladder; the Crucifixion; the Last Supper.

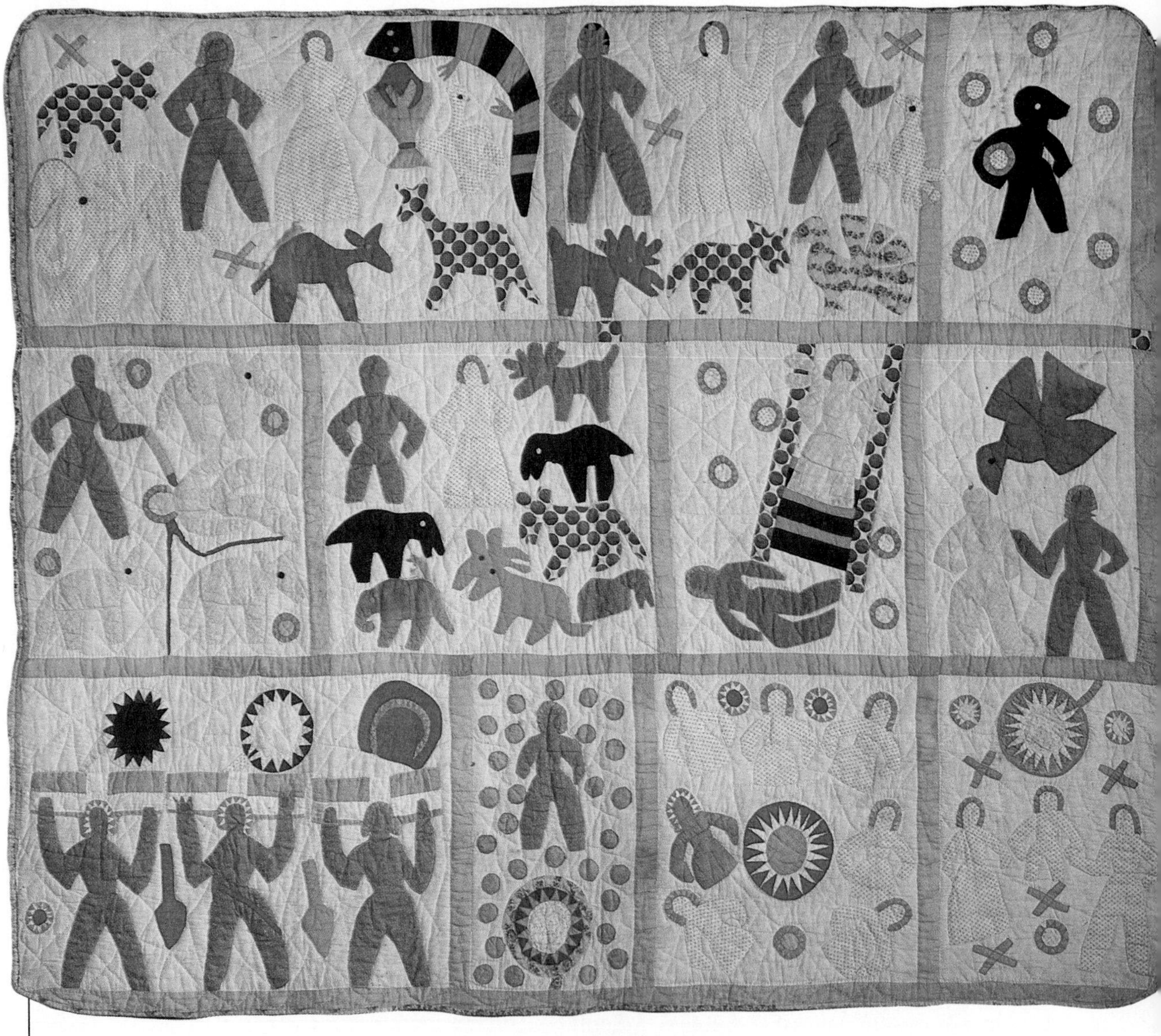

Harriet Powers's quilt of Bible stories combines American style with West-African techniques.

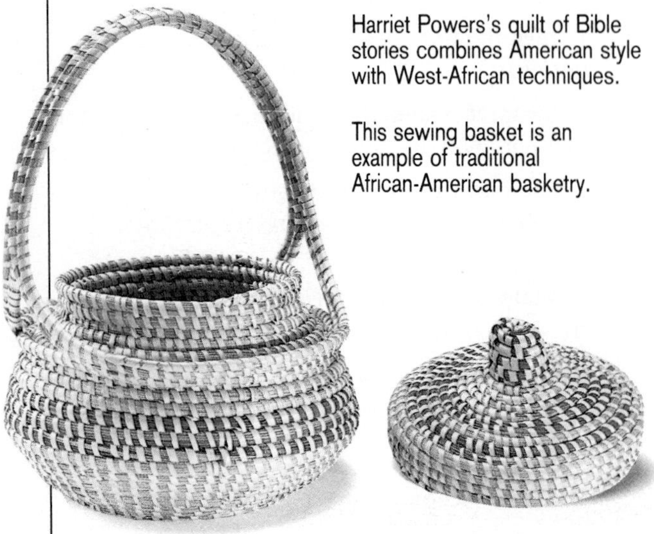

This sewing basket is an example of traditional African-American basketry.

This wrought-iron gate in Charleston, South Carolina, was made by enslaved Africans.

Connections: Art

Henry Ossawa Tanner was born in 1859 in Pittsburgh, Pennsylvania. His father was a bishop of the African Methodist Episcopal Church. From him Tanner learned the Bible stories he would later depict in his most famous paintings. Tanner loved to draw, and although it was not easy for an African American to succeed as a professional artist, he did not give up. Encountering prejudice in the United States, Tanner left for Europe in 1891. In Paris he found a new life and was soon recognized as an outstanding painter. *The Banjo Lesson* was painted from a drawing Turner made in the Ozarks before leaving the United States. His choice to leave was painful: *"I am sometimes sad,"* he wrote, *"that I cannot live where my heart is."*

Social History

Discussion. Enslaved Africans on plantations preserved African traditions in many skilled crafts and art forms. Often these traditions were incorporated into practical items made for use on the plantation, such as carved wood spoons, trays, buckets, and mortars and pestles. **Ask:** How do the knife box and the walking stick on this page reflect both a concern with design and aesthetics and skilled craftsmanship? **(Intricate design motifs include animals and geometric patterns; require great skill in carving)**

THE CREATIVE Spirit

African Americans

In his *Notes on Virginia,* written in 1784, Thomas Jefferson mentions an African musical instrument, "the Banjar [banjo], which they brought hither from Africa." Like the banjo, much of the cultural heritage that Africans carried with them became a familiar part of American life.

Despite efforts by slaveholders and others to suppress African culture, enslaved Africans showed great ingenuity in adapting their rich heritage to a new land. African-American music and dance, as well as the arts and crafts shown here, reflect both respect for tradition and a willingness to experiment. The results have significantly enriched the culture of the United States as a whole.

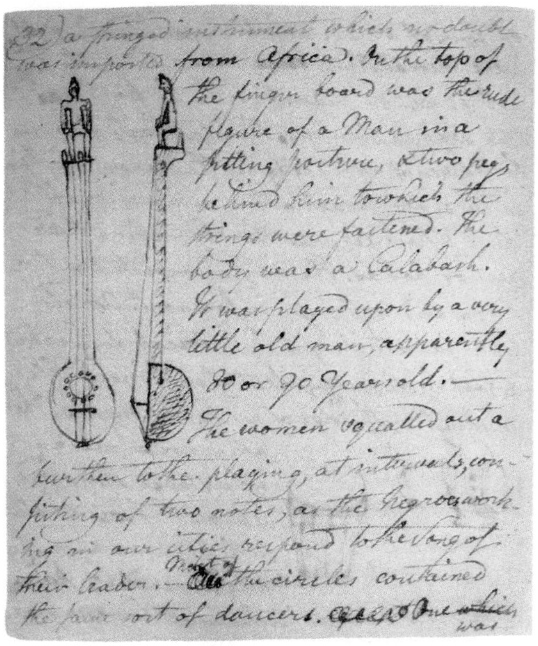
(32) a stringed instrument which no doubt was imported from Africa. On the top of the finger board was the rude figure of a Man in a sitting posture, & two pegs behind him to which the strings were fastened. The body was a Calabash. It was played upon by a very little old man, apparently 80 or 90 Years old. — The women squalled out a burthen to the playing, at intervals, consisting of two notes, as the Negroes working in our cities respond to the song of their leader. Most of the circles contained the same sort of dancers. One which was

Architect Benjamin Latrobe sketched and described an African instrument, probably a banjo, in 1819.

Henry Ossawa Tanner painted "The Banjo Lesson" in 1893.

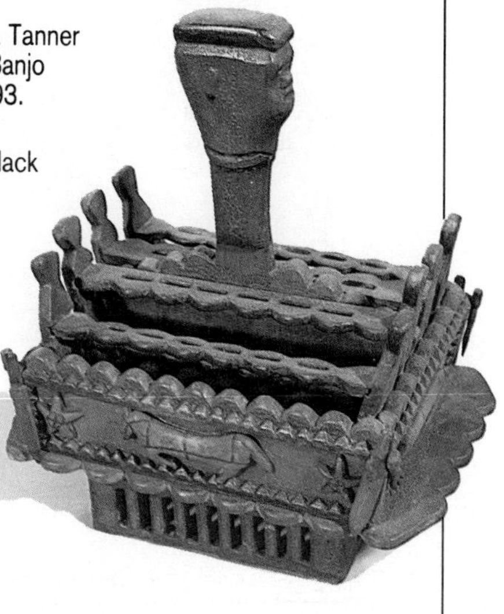

An unknown black artisan carved this elaborate knife box.

Animal carvings on this walking stick by Henry Gudgell in 1863 show his West-African heritage.

Section 11-2

Objectives

- ***Answer the Focus Question.***
- *List the terms of the Compromise of 1850.*
- *Explain how the Fugitive Slave Law further divided the North and the South.*

Introducing

THE SECTION

Have students review the acquisition of western lands following the Mexican War and the compromises that settled previous questions of slavery in western lands. Remind them that Mexicans generally were opposed to slavery and ask how such opposition might prove important if the question of slavery in the territories acquired from Mexico were to be settled by popular vote in the territories. Discuss why the question of allowing slavery in western territories was so important to the country as a whole.

Developing

THE SECTION

Social History

Discussion. Ask students what group they read about earlier in the chapter had views similar to those of David Wilmot **(nativists)**. How did the views of this group differ from Wilmot's? **(Nativists opposed immigrant labor even though immigrants were white.)**

Reduced student page in the Teacher's Edition

11-2 *Slavery in the West*

Focus: Why was compromise crucial to preserving the Union in the 1850s?

The differences between the North and the South came into sharp focus when war with Mexico broke out in May 1846. David Wilmot, a Representative from Pennsylvania, proposed a change to a House bill that set off arguments across the country. The bill provided funds to buy Mexican territory, and Wilmot proposed that it be altered so that "neither slavery nor involuntary servitude shall ever exist" in lands acquired during the war. The Wilmot Proviso passed in the House but not in the Senate. Still, the issue remained. Was slavery to be extended to new territories?

Senator John C. Calhoun of South Carolina denounced the Wilmot Proviso as unconstitutional. Slaves were property, he argued, and the Constitution protected property rights. Therefore, people could take their property wherever they pleased.

Many northerners argued just as fiercely against the extension of slavery onto free soil. Some, agreeing with abolitionists, condemned slavery as immoral and contrary to the principles of a free republic. Others, especially workers, opposed it because they feared competition from slave labor in western lands. David Wilmot agreed:

> *"I would preserve for free white labor a fair country . . . where the sons of toil, of my own race and color, can live without the disgrace which association with negro slavery brings upon free labor."*

Moderate proposals aimed for a compromise between protecting slavery and barring it altogether. One proposal, backed by President Polk, would extend the Missouri Compromise line to the Pacific, banning slavery north of the 36°30′ line, and allowing it south of the line. A proposal by Senators Lewis Cass of Michigan and Stephen A. Douglas of Illinois would give the people of each new territory the power to decide whether to allow or to ban slavery. This proposal became known as **popular sovereignty.**

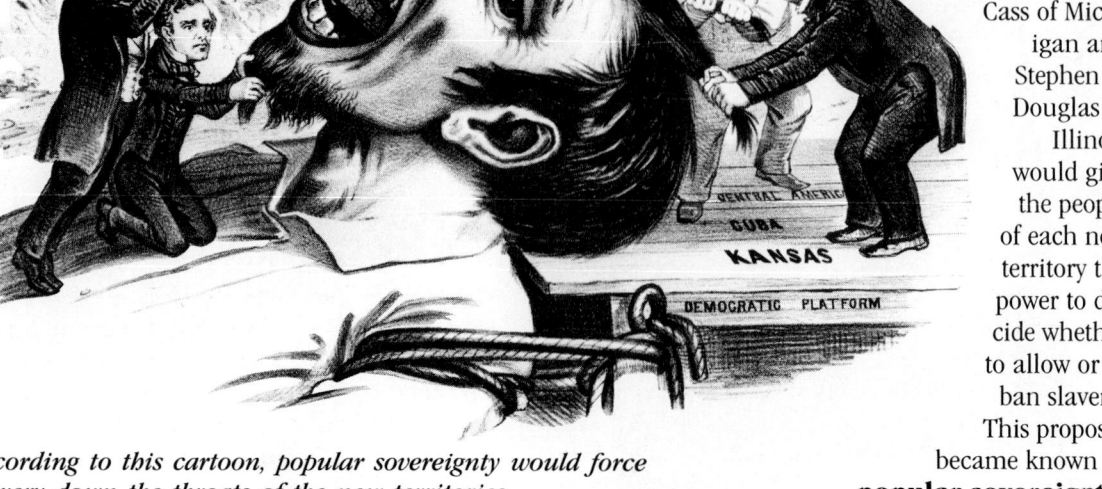

According to this cartoon, popular sovereignty would force slavery down the throats of the new territories.

Connections: Language

The antislavery Democrats led by Van Buren were called "barn-burners" from the story of the Dutch farmer who burned down his barn to get rid of the rats. Van Buren's followers were willing to burn down the "barn," or Democratic party, in order to get rid of the "rats," or proslavery Democrats.

The Election of 1848

The issue of slavery in the West was dividing the nation, so both major parties tried to avoid direct mention of it in the 1848 presidential election. Polk decided not to run again, and the Democrats chose another moderate, Senator Lewis Cass. The Whigs chose General Zachary Taylor, hero of the war with Mexico, a southerner, and a slaveholder.

Voters who opposed slavery were dissatisfied with both parties and formed their own party, the Free-Soil party. They nominated former President Martin Van Buren as their candidate. Under the slogan "Free Soil, Free Speech, Free Labor, and Free Men," the party opposed any extension of slavery.

The Free-Soil party showed surprising strength in the election, taking enough votes away from Cass to swing the key electoral votes toward Taylor. Thirteen Free-Soilers were elected to the House. Since the House had been evenly split between Democrats and Whigs, these Free-Soilers could wield some power by providing a majority to either side. Now Free-Soilers would keep the issue of slavery in the new territories alive in Congress. Democrats and Whigs could no longer avoid the question.

Congress Divided

The Congress that met on December 3, 1849, was deeply divided. It took fifty-nine ballots to elect a Speaker of the House acceptable to both northerners and southerners. When the question of statehood for California arose, the slavery issue erupted with a force that threatened the Union.

The admission of California as a free state would upset the balance of free and slave states in the Senate. Fearful of losing its political power, the South felt it needed to expand slavery into new territory to regain the balance. Throughout the South, state legislators, newspapers, and ordinary citizens spoke of secession if the government limited the spread of slavery. John C. Calhoun wrote in opposition to California's admission as a free state, "I trust we shall persist in our opposition until the restoration of all our rights or disunion, one or the other. . . ."

Other issues distressed the South as well. Many southerners deeply resented what they considered the nagging of Northern abolitionists and the demand for the end of slavery in the District of Columbia. Northern aid to escaped slaves also infuriated them.

The Compromise of 1850. Henry Clay of Kentucky, who had preserved unity in 1820 with the Missouri Compromise, once more thought of a plan to bridge differences. Clay, called the "Great Compromiser," offered concessions to both North and South. California would be admitted as a free state. Utah and New Mexico would become territories in which the slavery question would be decided by popular sovereignty. In the District of Columbia, the slave trade—but not slavery—would be abolished. In addition, Congress would not interfere with the slave trade between existing slave states, and a strict fugitive slave law would provide for the return of escaped slaves.

Clay's proposal touched off seven months of dramatic debate in the Senate. It was a time of brilliant speeches by the grand old debaters. John C. Calhoun—aging, ill, close to death—had to have a friend read his speech. He bitterly opposed Clay's plan. He warned that agitation over slavery would snap "the cords which bind these states together. . . . Nothing will be left to hold the states together except force."

Three days later, Calhoun was carried into the Senate chamber to hear Daniel Webster's speech. "Peaceful secession!" Webster thundered. "What states are to secede? What is to remain American? What am I to be? An American no longer? Where is the flag of the republic to remain?" He claimed that there was no need to exclude slavery from the territories—it would not prosper there anyway. Webster supported Clay's proposals.

President Taylor, furious at the South's threat of secession, opposed a compromise. Nevertheless, for months Clay and Webster, aided by Senator Stephen Douglas, worked to pass the proposals. Then, midsummer, President Taylor died. He was succeeded by Vice-President Millard Fillmore, who gave his support to Clay's plan. Finally, in September 1850, the plan passed Congress as a package of four laws. The laws became known as the Compromise of 1850. Most people thought that the question of slavery in the new territories had finally been settled.

Active Learning

Organizing Information. Have students work in small groups to make charts about the Compromise of 1850. Direct students to fill in information under these three headings: *Concessions to the North* (California admitted as a free state; Slave trade abolished in District of Columbia), *Concessions to the South* (Slavery permitted in District of Columbia; Congress would not interfere with slave trade between existing slave states; Strict fugitive slave law to provide for return of escaped slaves), and *Other Provisions* (Utah, New Mexico would decide slavery question by popular vote). Have groups come together and discuss whether they think this compromise favors the North or the South, or if it is evenly balanced.

GTV Side 2

Chap. 15, Frame 43529

The Gathering Storm (Movie)

Search:

Play:

Connections: Literature

Discussion. Harriet Beecher Stowe grew up in a deeply religious family: her father and her brother were ministers, and so was the man she married, Calvin Stowe. Mrs. Stowe claimed that the idea for *Uncle Tom's Cabin* came to her in a vision in church. She intended the book as a moral parable and a romance, not a realistic portrayal of slave life. When Stowe visited President Lincoln during the Civil War, Lincoln is said to have asked, *"Is this the little woman whose book made such a great war?"*

Ask: Why might Lincoln have thought that *Uncle Tom's Cabin* "made" the Civil War. Do you agree?

The Fugitive Slave Law

The Fugitive Slave Law, the part of the Compromise of 1850 that provided for the return of escaped slaves, proved to be almost universally hated in the North. In 1851, for example, a group of southern slave-catchers, hired to track down escaped slaves, arrived in Syracuse, New York. Citing the new law, they asked federal marshals to seize Jerry McHenry, who they claimed was an escaped slave.

People in Syracuse were shocked to see a man in chains marched through the streets to the federal courthouse. Led by abolitionist ministers, a crowd of more than 2,000 mobbed the courthouse and took McHenry from the marshals.

Ralph Waldo Emerson proclaimed the Fugitive Slave Law "a law which no man can obey . . . without the loss of self-respect." Some northern states passed "personal liberty laws" that denied state help to federal marshals attempting to capture escaped slaves. Southerners were outraged at the North's resistance to the law. They saw this resistance as a breach of the Compromise of 1850 and feared that abolitionists were gaining control of the North.

In 1852 Harriet Beecher Stowe published *Uncle Tom's Cabin,* a dramatic novel showing the plight of plantation slaves and attacking the moral evil of slavery. The novel caused a greater sensation than any work since Thomas Paine's *Common Sense.* It sold more than 300,000 copies the first year. Southern newspapers, claiming the novel gave a twisted view, pointed out that Stowe had no first-hand knowledge of slavery. Still, Stowe's work turned thousands against slavery.

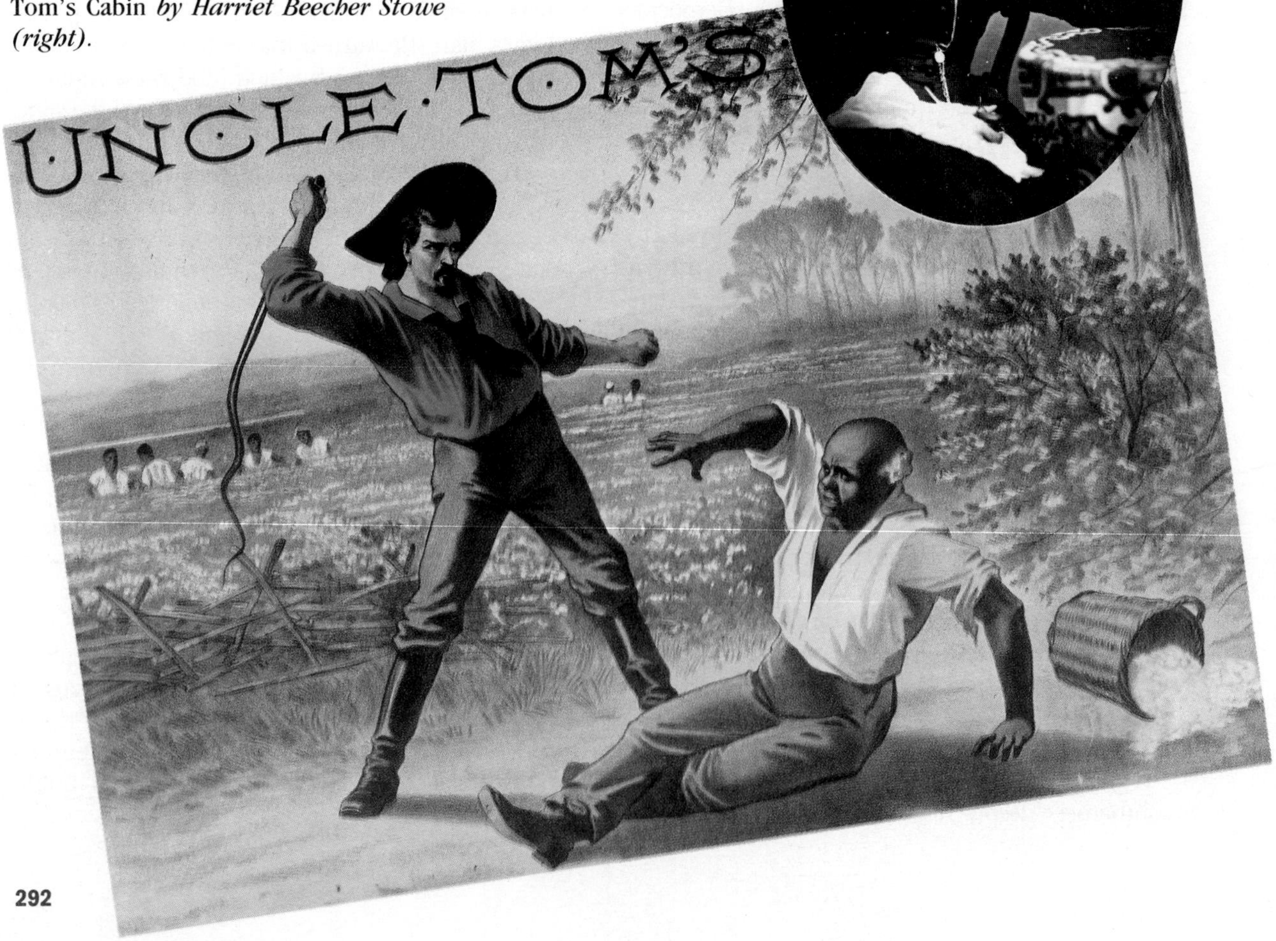

Dramatic posters drew thousands of Americans to plays based on Uncle Tom's Cabin *by Harriet Beecher Stowe (right).*

292

B · A · C · K · G · R · O · U · N · D

Connections: Politics
Stephen A. Douglas entered politics while still in his twenties. He was elected to the United States House of Representatives in 1843, becoming one of its youngest members. Three years later, he was elected to the Senate. Douglas's views of popular sovereignty brought criticism from both North and South. This criticism was sometimes expressed by burning him in effigy; hence Douglas's comment about being able to travel "by the light of my own effigies."

The Ostend Manifesto. In the election of 1852, Whig candidate General Winfield Scott was defeated by Democrat Franklin Pierce. Although a northerner, Pierce was thought to favor expanding slave territory. In fact, in 1854 three of his ministers met in Belgium and drafted the Ostend Manifesto, which suggested that the United States offer to buy Cuba. If Spain refused, it said, the United States should take Cuba by force. Pierce denied any part in the Ostend Manifesto, but northerners were horrified. The South, they charged, would risk even war to extend the boundaries of slavery.

"Bleeding Kansas"

"I could travel from Boston to Chicago by the light of my own effigies," joked Senator Stephen A. Douglas. At issue was his introduction of the Kansas-Nebraska Act in 1854, which provoked angry northerners to burn him in effigy.

The drama had begun as the nation entered the new year. Douglas supported a plan to build a transcontinental railroad from Chicago to the Pacific across unorganized territory. He thought that the railroad could be built only if the territory had some political organization, so he proposed a bill to establish the Nebraska Territory.

Southerners demanded that the territory be open to slavery. The area, however, was north of the Missouri Compromise line and therefore closed to slavery. As a compromise, Douglas proposed that two territories be created, Nebraska and Kansas, with each allowed popular sovereignty.

The Kansas-Nebraska Act passed in May 1854. It did away with the Missouri Compromise line, since the territories could opt to allow slavery north of 36°30′. Many northerners denounced the act. They were outraged that a restriction on the extension of slavery had been repealed.

After the act went into effect, both proslavery and antislavery people raced to settle the Kansas Territory. Many of these "settlers" stayed just long enough to vote for the territory's new legislature, which would decide whether slavery would be allowed. "We are playing for a mighty stake," a southern senator said. "If we win, we carry slavery to the Pacific Ocean."

The Missouri Compromise 1820

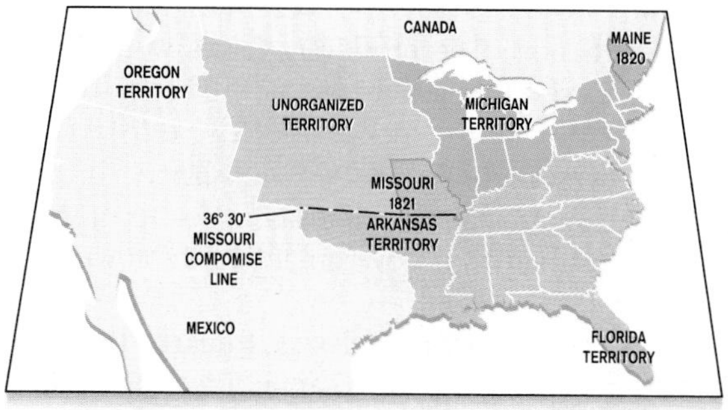

The Compromise of 1850

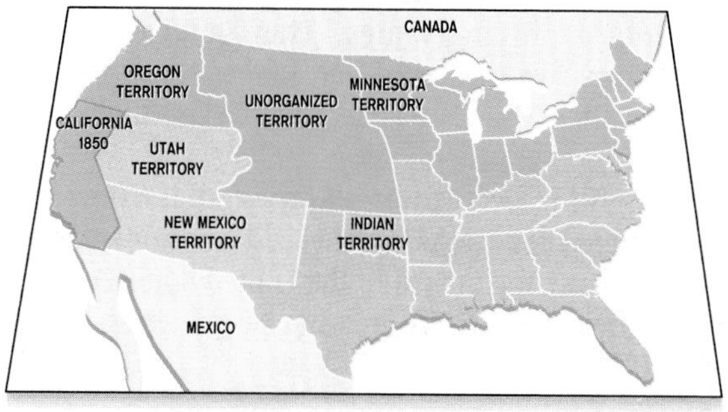

The Kansas-Nebraska Act 1854

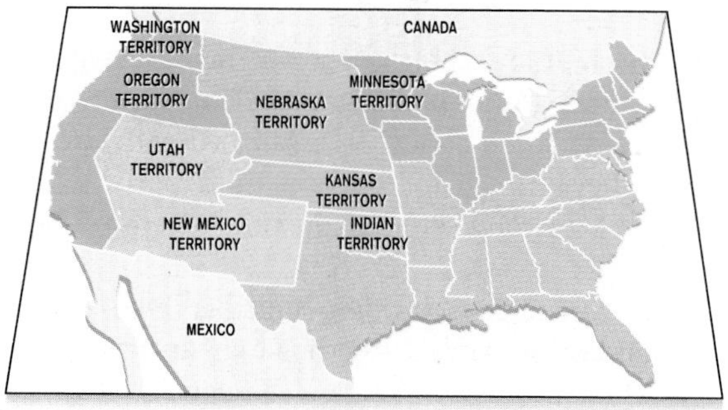

Free state or territory
Territory opened to slavery by Compromise of 1850
Territory closed to slavery
Territory opened to slavery by Kansas–Nebraska Act
Slave state or territory

Geography Skills—Region. Describe the status of slavery from 1820 to 1854 in each of the following regions of the present-day United States: Northeast, Southeast, Midwest, and Far West. Trace the spread of slavery during those years.

Geography Skills
ANSWERS

From 1820 to 1854, the Northeast consisted of free states; the Southeast, of slave states. The Midwest north of Missouri and Kentucky consisted of free states until 1854, when Kansas and Nebraska territories were opened to slavery. California, Oregon, and Washington territories were free territories, but Utah and New Mexico were opened to slavery in 1850.

GTV Side 2
Chap. 15, Frame 47240
Kansas-Nebraska Act 1854 (Map)
Search:

GTV Side 2
Chap. 15, Frame 46410
Compromise of 1850 (Map)
Search:

GTV Side 2
Chap. 15, Frame 45739
Missouri Compromise 1820 (Map)
Search:

Section Review

ANSWERS

1. Definition of *popular sovereignty* is on text page 290.
2. California admitted as free state; Utah and New Mexico territories to decide question of slavery by popular sovereignty; slave trade, but not slavery, to be abolished in District of Columbia; Congress not to interfere in slave trade between existing slave states; the Fugitive Slave Law would require return of escaped slaves.
3. Fugitive Slave Law, by forcing northern states to play active role in capture and return of escaped slaves to owners, increased sentiment for abolition in North. Southern hostility toward North grew when northern states refused to enforce law.
4. Continuation of the representational balance between free and slave states in Senate. Disrupting balance could have led to either northern or southern domination of the Congress.
5. Answers will vary. White Southerners probably justified in fear, given that most territories likely to become states not suitable for slave-based agriculture. Growing population and economic power of North also threatened balance of power.

On voting day, thousands of proslavery people rode from Missouri across the border into Kansas to cast their ballots. The proslavery forces won, and the new legislature passed laws to protect slavery. The legislature also expelled the few antislavery members who had been elected. Antislavery forces responded by proclaiming Kansas a free territory. They set up their own government in the town of Lawrence.

Both sides resorted to violence. In early 1856 a band of proslavery supporters rode into Lawrence, threw printing presses into the river, set the hotel on fire, and killed one man. Three nights later, John Brown, an antislavery activist, led a small band into a proslavery area. They dragged from their homes five men who had had nothing to do with the attack on Lawrence and hacked them to death.

The fighting between proslavery and antislavery groups raged for weeks, at the cost of more than 200 lives. Only the arrival of the United States Army created an uneasy peace in what people were now calling "bleeding Kansas."

The New Republican Party

While the Kansas-Nebraska Act was being debated in early 1854, groups of Whigs and Democrats were meeting across the country. Dissatisfied with their parties, they wanted to create a third party that would take a strong stand against the extension of slavery.

These conventions brought together Free-Soilers, abolitionists, and northern Whigs and Democrats. One convention, in Ripon, Wisconsin, vowed to form a new party if Congress passed the Kansas-Nebraska Act. In July 1854, this group of antislavery northerners formed the new party and adopted the name of Thomas Jefferson's party—the Republican party.

Republicans made a strong showing in the 1854 congressional elections, winning 108 seats in the House. The Whigs had practically disappeared as a party, and both great Whig leaders—Daniel Webster and Henry Clay—had died in 1852. With the Republicans wooing northern Democrats angry over the Kansas-Nebraska Act, the Democratic party faltered. But it still won 83 seats in the House. The anti-immigrant Know-Nothing party reached the peak of its power, winning 43 seats.

The presidential election of 1856 was a contest between parties on the rise and parties on the decline. The Republicans nominated John C. Frémont, western explorer and hero of California victories in the Mexican War. The Know-Nothings split over slavery. Northern members supported Frémont. Southern Know-Nothings and southern Whigs, meeting in separate conventions, chose former President Millard Fillmore. The Democrats chose James Buchanan of Pennsylvania, a former United States senator who had supported the Kansas-Nebraska Act and popular sovereignty.

The real contest was between the Republicans and Democrats. The Republicans, using the slogan "Free Soil, Free Speech, and Frémont," wanted to keep slavery out of the territories. The Democrats supported popular sovereignty as "the only sound and safe solution of the slavery question." Buchanan won a sound victory, carrying all of the southern states except Maryland, as well as five states in the North.

The election showed a new alignment in American politics. The Democrats had become primarily a party of the South, although they retained some areas of power in the North. The Republicans were purely a party of the North. By this time positions on both sides of the slavery issue had hardened. Now that the Democrats and Republicans represented separate sections of the country, the possibility of peaceful compromise was even more remote.

Section Review

1. **Identification.** Define *popular sovereignty.*
2. **Comprehension.** List the terms of the Compromise of 1850.
3. **Analysis.** Why did the Fugitive Slave Law drive a greater wedge between North and South?
4. **Analysis.** What was the basic principle of both the Compromise of 1850 and the Kansas-Nebraska Act and why was it important?
5. **Evaluation.** Do you think the South was justified in its fear of losing a balance of power in the Senate? Why or why not?

B · A · C · K · G · R · O · U · N · D

Multicultural Perspectives

Although he could not read or write, Dred Scott had learned much in his travels through several states. As his landmark legal case dragged on, he showed courage by seeing it through when he could have run away to freedom. Although Scott lost his case, which he said had brought him nothing but "a heap o' trouble," he was transferred to a new owner who freed him and his family two months later.

Section 11-3

Objectives

- ***Answer the Focus Question.***
- *Describe how the Dred Scott decision affected the Missouri Compromise.*
- *Compare the viewpoints of Abraham Lincoln and Stephen Douglas on the extension of slavery.*

Introducing

THE SECTION

Ask students whether slavery, or the right to forbid it, was addressed in the Constitution as it existed in 1857. Have them cite specific passages in the Constitution as evidence for their views. **(No specific mention of slavery; passing reference in Article I, Section 2, Clause 3; and "held to service" in Article IV, Section 2, Clause 3.)** Tell students that in this section they will find out how the Supreme Court interpreted the Constitution in its decision in the Dred Scott case.

11-3 The Nation Divides

Focus: How did sectional differences over slavery lead to the Civil War?

"To their decision, in common with all good citizens, I shall cheerfully submit, whatever this may be," vowed President James Buchanan in his inaugural address on March 4, 1857. He was referring to an upcoming Supreme Court decision that was to rock the nation.

The Dred Scott Decision

The Supreme Court case mentioned by Buchanan involved Dred Scott, a man who had been the slave of an army surgeon from Missouri. For four years Scott and his owner had lived in Illinois, a free state, and then in the free territory of Wisconsin where Scott had married his wife, Harriet. After their return to Missouri and the death of their owner, Scott sued the owner's widow for their freedom. His lawyers argued that the years living on free soil had made them free.

The case of *Dred Scott* v. *Sandford* reached the Supreme Court in March 1857. By a vote of seven to two, the Court ruled that black people—either free or enslaved—were not citizens of the United States and, therefore, did not have the right to sue in a federal court. Dred Scott thus would have to remain enslaved, subject to the laws of the state of Missouri.

The Supreme Court also declared the Missouri Compromise unconstitutional because it banned slavery in certain territories. Slaves were property, the Court held, and under the Fifth Amendment, persons could not be deprived of property without due process of law. Following this reasoning, the Court ruled that Congress could not forbid owners to take their slaves into free territories.

Southerners rejoiced at the Dred Scott decision, which opened all territories to slavery. The North was outraged at the decision. The Republican party had dedicated itself to preventing the extension of slavery. Now, it seemed, slavery could be extended throughout the territories. Frederick Douglass called the decision "an attempt to blot out forever the hopes of an enslaved people."

The decision was also a blow to Senator Stephen Douglas, who had hoped that popular sovereignty would settle the issue of slavery in the territories. Douglas had intended to promote popular sovereignty in his upcoming campaign for reelection.

The Lincoln-Douglas Debates

By 1858 northern Democrats were unhappy with their party and with their President. Buchanan had appointed a majority of southerners to his cabinet and had favored the admission of Kansas as a slave state. An opposition wing of northern Democrats broke away from the party and united under the leadership of Stephen Douglas. Douglas, who was running for reelection to the Senate in 1858, hoped that a solid victory would improve his chances to win the presidency in 1860.

Dred Scott and his wife, Harriet Scott.

Developing
THE SECTION

Linking Past and Present

Comparing. Debates between candidates still play a major part in presidential campaigns. Have students recall debates they have heard. Ask how these differ from the ones between Lincoln and Douglas. **(Present-day debates can be seen and heard by the whole country through radio and television.)** Have students discuss good and bad points of debates as a way to judge candidates.

Connections: Politics

Abraham Lincoln spent his early life in the backwoods of Kentucky, Indiana, and Illinois. Approaching a big-city audience, he usually appeared ill at ease. All this changed when he began to speak. A witness to a Lincoln speech in New York in February, 1860 thought:

"'Old fellow, you won't do; it's all very well for the Wild West, but this will never go down in New York.' But pretty soon . . . he straightened up, made regular and graceful gestures; his face lighted as with an inward fire; the whole man was transfigured. . . . Presently I was on my feet, cheering this wonderful man."

Reduced student page in the Teacher's Edition

Douglas was up against the Republican's candidate, Abraham Lincoln, a small-town lawyer from Springfield. Born in a log cabin in Kentucky, Lincoln had educated himself. Although he had served one term in the House of Representatives, Lincoln did not seem to be a rising politician.

As the underdog in the election, Lincoln challenged Douglas to a series of public debates. The two met seven times in different parts of Illinois for debates that were reported on throughout the country. Crowds gathered for each debate. Senator Douglas always arrived in grand style in a private railroad car. Lincoln arrived by regular train.

The opponents were a study in contrasts. The short, sturdy Douglas, known as the "Little Giant," was famous in the Senate as a brilliant debater with an aggressive style. Lincoln, on the other hand, was six feet four, lanky, and had a relaxed manner, often telling jokes to make a point. Beneath this manner, however, Lincoln was a shrewd politician. His law partner wrote that he "was a big—angular—strong man—limbs large and bony. His mind was tough—solid—knotty—gnarly, more or less like his body."

Both Lincoln and Douglas opposed slavery and wanted to maintain the Union at all costs. They proposed to do this in very different ways, however. In his opening campaign speech in June 1858, Lincoln sounded a note warning:

> *"A house divided against itself cannot stand. I believe this government cannot endure permanently half slave and half free. I do not expect the Union to be dissolved; I do not expect the house to fall; but I do expect it will cease to be divided. It will become all one thing, or all the other."*

Douglas, on the other hand, believed that the best way to protect the Union was to give each territory or state, rather than Congress, the power to make the decision about slavery.

At a debate in Freeport, Illinois, Lincoln challenged Douglas and the doctrine of popular sovereignty. Lincoln noted that in the Dred Scott case the Supreme Court had ruled that slavery could not be forbidden in territories. He asked, "Can the people of a United States Territory in any lawful way exclude slavery from its limits?"

Douglas's reply became known as the Freeport Doctrine. He claimed that although it was legal for an owner to bring a slave into any territory, citizens could refuse to enact laws protecting slavery. Without such slave codes, slavery simply could not exist.

With the Freeport Doctrine, Douglas lost southern support by suggesting a way to get around the Dred Scott decision and stop the extension of slavery. At the same time, Douglas angered northern abolitionists by dismissing the moral issue of slavery. Although Douglas defeated Lincoln and was reelected to the Senate, Lincoln had become a national figure and in two years would run for the presidency himself.

The Raid on Harpers Ferry

"This *is* a beautiful country," commented John Brown as he rode to his execution seated atop his coffin. He had been convicted of murder and treason for his part in an attack on the federal arsenal at Harpers Ferry, Virginia.

On October 16, 1859, John Brown, the abolitionist who had taken bloody revenge on proslavers in Kansas, had led a small band of followers to seize the arsenal. Brown planned to use the arsenal's weapons to arm the slaves of Virginia and bring about a mighty slave rebellion.

Brown and his raiders had no difficulty taking the arsenal. But news of the raid spread quickly, and local militia moved in, followed by federal troops under Colonel Robert E. Lee. Almost half of Brown's men were killed, and Brown and the survivors were taken prisoner.

Within a matter of weeks Brown and six raiders had been tried and convicted of murder, treason against Virginia, and conspiracy. All were hanged. The swift punishment, however, did not ease southern fears. Not since Nat Turner's slave revolt in 1831 had people in the South been so shaken.

Southerners found little comfort in the fact that no slaves had joined Brown, nor in northern newspapers' shocked reactions to Brown's raid. Indeed, their suspicions deepened when some northerners praised Brown's actions. Ralph Waldo Emerson even declared Brown "a new saint" who would "make the gallows as glorious as the cross."

Lincoln Elected in 1860

Approaching one of the most fateful elections of the century, the Democratic party met in Charleston, South Carolina, in April 1860. Southerners demanded a platform that promised to uphold slavery in the territories. But this demand was too much for the northern wing of the party, and the convention broke up.

Two months later Democratic delegates met again, this time in Baltimore, Maryland. The northern faction nominated Stephen Douglas for President and adopted popular sovereignty as a platform. Southern delegates stormed out of the convention. They met separately, nominated John C. Breckinridge of Kentucky, and adopted a pro-slavery platform.

"To his own soul he was right, and neither 'principalities nor powers, life nor death, things present nor things to come,' could shake his dauntless spirit or move him from his ground. . . . Those who looked for confession heard only the voice of rebuke and warning."

—Frederick Douglass, describing John Brown

Anticipating victory, the Republicans met in Chicago and nominated Abraham Lincoln. He was the only Republican who would have a chance against Douglas in the Midwest and who would satisfy both moderates and abolitionists.

The party's platform opposed the extension of slavery and condemned the Dred Scott decision. The Republicans also supported the building of a transcontinental railroad. They favored a new protective tariff, a homestead law to give western land to settlers, and immediate admission of Kansas to the Union as a free state.

In both the North and the South, some former Whigs, unhappy Democrats, and Know-Nothings still hoped to avoid the question of slavery. They formed the Constitutional Union party and nominated John Bell of Tennessee for President. Their platform supported the Constitution and the Union, and avoided any mention of slavery.

The split in the Democratic party gave Lincoln the election. Although he received only 40 percent of the popular vote, he won a solid majority of electoral votes. Douglas was close to Lincoln in popular votes, but carried only Missouri. Bell won Virginia, Kentucky, and Tennessee, while Breckinridge carried the rest of the South.

Abolitionist John Brown was hanged for raiding the Harpers Ferry arsenal in an attempt to arm slaves in Virginia.

Thinking Critically

Evaluation. John Brown's raid on Harper's Ferry was condemned by many in the North as well as in the South—Lincoln and Douglas both denounced him, the Republican party adopted a platform censuring the raid in 1860. To others, however, he became a "saint" and a martyr after his execution.

Ask: Should Brown be considered a criminal or a hero? How do his actions compare with recent examples of politically inspired "terrorism"? When, if ever, are such actions justified?

Writing About History

Speeches. Using information from the text and/or other sources, have students write campaign speeches for Lincoln and Douglas and present them to the class. Students should consider both the personalities and politics of the candidates.

Limited English Proficiency

Making Charts. Have students work in small groups to prepare charts of the 1860 election, showing each party, its candidate, what the party supported and opposed, and to which groups the party appealed.

While still in groups, have students discuss how Lincoln, the Republican party, and Douglas viewed slavery. Which section of the country would you expect to agree with Lincoln's view? Douglas's view? Why?

Thinking Critically

Evaluation. Ask students: What, if anything, would have been different if Lincoln had not sent the supply ship to Fort Sumter? Was there any way to avoid war by 1860? If so, what might it have been? (For example, Lincoln could have decided not to send supplies to Fort Sumter; Confederates could have decided not to attack the fort.) Why didn't these actions take place? (Lincoln did not want Confederates to control Union property; Confederates wanted to take control of the fort before reinforcements arrived.)

Writing About History

Editorials. Ask students to write editorials that might have appeared in a northern or southern newspaper, commenting on the Fort Sumter incident. As students read the editorials aloud, have the class decide whether they represent northern or southern points of view.

B · A · C · K · G · R · O · U · N · D

Social History

Mary Boykin Chesnut, wife of a military aide to Jefferson Davis, started a diary a few months before the firing on Fort Sumter. On the night of April 11, 1861 Mary Chesnut could not sleep. "Things are happening so fast," she wrote. Mary Chesnut loved the South and believed deeply in states' rights. "I was a rebel born," she wrote. Yet she branded slavery "a monstrous system." An early feminist, she also saw parallels between the lives of slaves and women.

All during the Civil War, Mary Chesnut kept her dairy. Published after her death, it documented southern life during these years, describing the battles and the balls, the gaiety and the destruction. From the beginning she felt a sense of doom. She knew she was watching "our world, the only world we cared for, literally kicked to pieces."

Reduced student page in the Teacher's Edition

Secession

Condemned in the South as a "half-witted village politician," President-elect Lincoln was viewed as a threat to the southern way of life. Alexander H. Stephens of Georgia wrote that in the South "the people run mad. They are wild with passion, doing they know not what. . . . The truth is our leaders and public . . . do not desire to continue the Union on any terms."

In South Carolina, the legislature called a statewide convention to vote on whether to secede. Southerners had threatened to leave the Union before. In the nullification crisis of 1832 they had claimed that the Union was a voluntary compact among states, and that any state could withdraw if it wished. Lincoln and most Republicans thought that now South Carolina was bluffing.

President Buchanan, serving the final months of his term, reacted cautiously. He warned that no state had the right to secede, but said that he had no constitutional power to force states to stay in the Union. Buchanan turned to Congress, asking for yet another compromise. Senator John J. Crittenden of Kentucky suggested that the Missouri Compromise line be restored and extended to the Pacific and that slavery be permitted in all states and new territories south of the line. But Republicans—including Lincoln—would not consider any plan that allowed the extension of slavery. The spirit of compromise was exhausted.

On December 20, 1860, the South Carolina convention voted unanimously to secede from the Union. By February 1861 Mississippi, Florida, Alabama, Georgia, Louisiana, and Texas had also seceded. Throughout the South, state troops seized federal forts, arsenals, and shipyards. Only a few forts were left in federal control.

In February, delegates from six of the seven states that had seceded met in Montgomery, Alabama, to form a new union—the Confederate States of America. They chose former Mississippi Senator Jefferson Davis as President, selected a flag of stars and crossed bars, and drafted a constitution modeled after the United States Constitution. This constitution, however, gave ultimate sovereignty to states and guaranteed the existence of slavery.

Spotlight on Politics

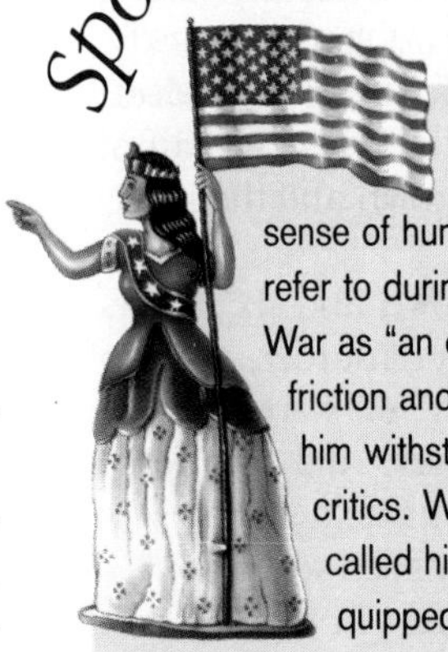

Lincoln was well known for his sense of humor, a quality that he would refer to during the troubled days of the Civil War as "an emollient [that] saves me much friction and distress." His humor helped him withstand frequent attacks by his critics. When Stephen A. Douglas called him a "two-faced man," Lincoln quipped, "I leave it to my audience. If I had another face, do you think I would wear this one?"

Fort Sumter

A month later, Lincoln took office as President of a shattered Union. Seven states had seceded, and the other southern states were discussing secession. Lincoln asked the Confederate states to return to the Union and repeated his promise not to forbid slavery where it already existed. He took a firm stand against secession, warning the Confederacy:

> *"In your hands . . . and not in mine, is the momentous issue of civil war. . . . You have no oath registered in Heaven to destroy the Government, while I shall have the most solemn one to 'preserve, protect and defend it.'"*

The day after he took office, Lincoln received a request from Major Robert Anderson for more troops and supplies to hold Fort Sumter, a federal fort in the harbor at Charleston, South Carolina. Lincoln's cabinet warned that if he sent a supply ship, the South would consider it an act of war. But Lincoln feared that surrendering Fort Sumter would be seen as recognition of the independence of the Confederacy.

For six weeks, Lincoln delayed. Tension mounted in the North, and the public and the press began to demand action. Lincoln at last decided to send food—but not troops—in an unarmed ship. He assured the governor of South Carolina that no troops would be sent without warning unless the fort was attacked.

That attack came. Confederate leaders took the sending of the supply ship as an act of war. Under orders from Jefferson Davis, General P.G.T. Beauregard demanded that Anderson surrender Fort Sumter. Anderson refused. At 4:30 in the morning on April 12, 1861, Confederate cannons opened fire. Anderson returned the fire. The supplies sent by Lincoln had to remain outside the harbor. On April 13, his ammunition exhausted, Anderson lowered the United States flag. He and his troops retreated to Union relief ships.

With the firing on Fort Sumter, all hope of preserving the union ended. The nation was now engaged in a civil war.

Section Review

1. Comprehension. What did the Supreme Court rule in the Dred Scott case? How did the decision affect the Missouri Compromise?

2. Application. With the Dred Scott decision, abolitionists jeered at the irony of the Supreme Court defending slavery in the name of the Bill of Rights. Explain this irony.

3. Analysis. Compare the viewpoints of Abraham Lincoln and Stephen Douglas on the extension of slavery.

4. Synthesis. Do you think that if President-elect Lincoln had accepted Senator Crittenden's compromise, war could have been avoided? Give reasons for your answer.

Connections to Themes

Balancing Unity and Diversity

The motto *e pluribus unum*—"one formed from many"— expresses both the unity and diversity of the American Republic: one nation created out of many states. Between 1800 and 1850, a sense of national unity had been growing, yet Americans still felt strong bonds to their state and region. In fact, because northern and southern states were developing in such different ways, it seemed as if two nations were emerging—an industrial, urban one in the North and an agrarian, slaveholding one in the South.

Most southern whites believed that their agricultural way of life, with its planter aristocracy, was far superior to the noisy, dirty cities and factories of the North. The region's writers developed elaborate arguments to justify the continued existence of slavery. The planters, they said, were in the tradition of earlier great Americans who owned slaves, including George Washington and Thomas Jefferson.

By the 1850s southerners were convinced that their entire way of life was threatened by the growing economic and political power of the North. If new slave states could not be carved out of the western territories, they feared, their region would become little more than a colony of the North.

To many in the South, therefore, the conflict over slavery forced them to face the question of loyalties: was their loyalty to their state and region stronger than their ties to the nation? The voters of eleven southern states answered by voting for secession from the Union.

Section Review

ANSWERS

1. Blacks, not being citizens, could not sue in federal court. Missouri Compromise was unconstitutional because deprived persons of property, i.e., slaves.
2. Bill of Rights designed to protect individual liberty from government interference, now being used to protect right of individuals to own others as slaves in any part of the Union.
3. Douglas opposed extension of slavery, but believed that each territory or state, not Congress, should be allowed to decide question. Lincoln believed that federal government should limit extension of slavery, and eventually slavery must be abolished for the Union to survive.
4. Answers may include: The Crittenden compromise might have delayed war, but would not have resolved long-standing economic, social and political differences between North and South—thus war probably inevitable.

Chapter Survey

ANSWERS

Using New Vocabulary

1. (b) *Employers' scare tactics* included *blacklist.*
2. (c) *Craft unions* might *strike*, refusing to work until demands are met.
3. (a) Those favoring *nativism* formed *Know-Nothing party* in 1849.

Reviewing the Chapter

1. Work moved out of homes into urban areas. Craft production increasingly replaced by industrial manufacturing. Northern politics became more identified with manufacturing interests; industry attracted immigrants, producing new political constituencies and hostilities.
2. Improve working conditions, increase wages, shorten working day. Craft unions illegal until 1842; employer scare tactics such as blacklist.
3. Based on cash crops, especially cotton. Only one fourth of white farmers owned slaves. Majority of white farmers, and 250,000 free African Americans in South did not own slaves.
4. North: California admitted as free state, slave trade abolished in District of Columbia; South: strict fugitive slave law, free slave trade in the South.
5. To win political support for establishing territorial government so transcontinental railroad could be built. Formed two territories, both with power to decide issue of slavery by popular sovereignty.
6. Fighting erupted between supporters of slavery and abolitionists after pro-slavery forces took control of territorial government.
7. Destroyed it by upholding right of slaveholders to bring slaves into free territories.
8. Douglas: Each territory or state, not Congress, be allowed to decide question of slavery. Lincoln: federal government should limit extension of slavery, eventually slavery must be abolished for Union to survive.
9. Democratic party split votes between Breckinridge, Bell, and Douglas. Southern states seceded, believing Lincoln threatened southern way of life.
10. Firing on Fort Sumter.

Thinking Critically

1. "Crimes" of trading and holding African Americans as slaves. Those thinking it could have been resolved might argue that people in both North and South were working to heal sectional differences—note various compromises. Those disagreeing might argue that feelings on both sides were too fierce to make resolution possible.
2. Lincoln was forced to de-

Reduced student page in the Teacher's Edition

Chapter Survey

Using New Vocabulary

Match each numbered vocabulary term with the lettered word most closely related to it. Then explain how the items in each pair are related.

1. blacklist (a) Know-Nothing party
2. strike (b) employers' scare tactics
3. nativism (c) craft unions

Reviewing the Chapter

1. How did the nature of work change in the Northeast between 1800 and 1850? How did this change affect the politics of the region?

2. What were the goals of early craft unions? What hindered their growth and development?

3. Describe the economy of the South. Who owned slaves? Who did not?

4. What were the terms of the Compromise of 1850? Which terms pleased the North? Which terms pleased the South?

5. Why did Senator Douglas propose the Kansas-Nebraska Act? What were its terms?

6. Why did the Kansas Territory become known as "Bleeding Kansas"?

7. How did the decision in *Dred Scott* v. *Sandford* affect the concept of popular sovereignty?

8. Contrast the arguments of Lincoln and Douglas on the issues of slavery and union.

9. Why did Lincoln win the election of 1860? What was the impact on the South?

10. What was the immediate cause of the outbreak of the Civil War?

Thinking Critically

1. Synthesis. John Brown's last words were, "I . . . am now quite certain that the crimes of this guilty land will never be purged away but with blood." What crimes do you think he meant? Do you think that the issue of slavery could have been resolved without war? Give reasons for your answer.

2. Synthesis. With or without resupply, Fort Sumter, in the heart of secessionist territory was bound to be taken. Why do you think Lincoln sent the supply ship loaded with food?

History and You

In the early nineteenth century, new technology transformed the way of life in the Northeast while it entrenched the traditional way of life in the South. What impact do you see technology having on the American work force today?

Using Geography

Study the map of the election of 1860 below, then answer the following questions.

1. Which states did Lincoln carry? Breckinridge? Bell? Douglas?

2. About what percentage of the electoral vote did Lincoln win? Of the popular vote?

3. Why are no votes shown for the territories?

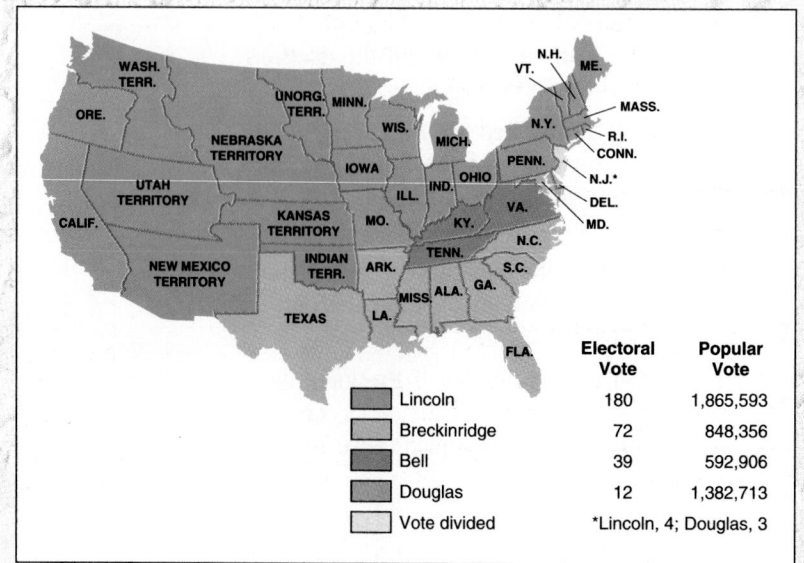

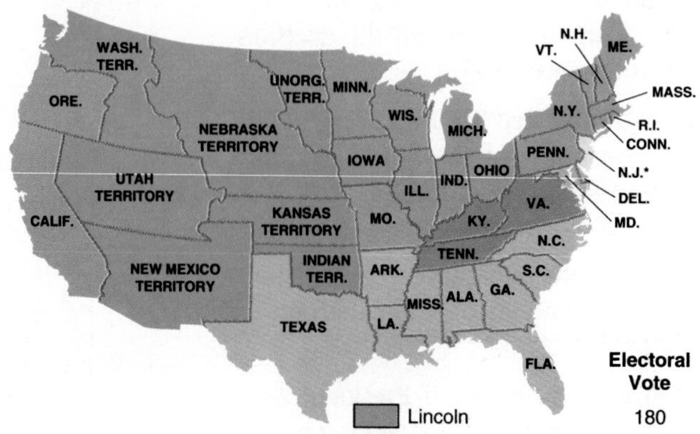

	Electoral Vote	Popular Vote
Lincoln	180	1,865,593
Breckinridge	72	848,356
Bell	39	592,906
Douglas	12	1,382,713
Vote divided		*Lincoln, 4; Douglas, 3

fend Fort Sumter or be seen as recognizing independence of southern states. Sending food, rather than troops, was not an aggressive act of war but did not back down to southern states.

History and You

Answers may include: high technology, robotics in industry, and importance of computers and telecommunications. These changes have made an economy based on service, not production, ushered in "information age."

Using Geography

1. Lincoln: CA, OR, MN, IA, WI, IL, MI, IN, OH, PA, NY, VT, CT, RI, MA, NH, ME. Breckinridge: TX, LA, AK, MS, AL, GA, FL, SC, NC, MD, DL. Bell: TN, KY, VA, Douglas: MO.
2. Electoral vote: 59% Popular vote: 40%
3. Territories did not have vote in the election.

Applying Social Studies Skills

1. factories, manufactured goods, farm land, railroad miles
2. The North. Could provide more military recruits. Part of free population of North engaged in economic activities necessary for war effort. South relied on slaves to carry out much of this work.
3. 15%. North could manufacture more arms and other supplies.
4. The North. Railroads allowed for rapid deployment of troops and supplies.
5. the North
6. Answers may include: population necessary to provide army with troops and supplies; factory production increases quantity and quality of arms and other war materials.

Thinking About History

1. Many Americans obsessed with building and selling things, and going places without consideration for how they should live their lives.
2. Railroads. Because railroads revolutionized transportation, making possible much of economic development of the time; also exploited workers.
3. People should stay at home and tend to own affairs.
4. Railroads dominate people's lives.
5. Opinions will differ. Comparisons can be made with the impact of computer technology and electronic media sources.

Applying Social Studies Skills

Analyzing Statistical Tables

Statistics are collections of information in the form of numbers. To analyze statistics it is helpful to organize them in some way. Sometimes statistics are displayed as graphs, but often the numbers are arranged in statistical tables.

The table below shows how national resources were split between the Union and the Confederacy. To analyze economic differences between the North and the South as the Civil War began, study the table. Then answer the questions.

Resources of the Union and the Confederacy as Percentages of the United States Total, 1861

	Union	Confederacy
Total population	71%	29%
Factories	85%	15%
Production of manufactured goods	92%	8%
Farm land	65%	35%
Railroad miles	71%	29%

Source: *Encyclopaedia Britannica*

1. What resources are being compared?

2. Which side had a greater free population? What importance might this statistic have in wartime? What factors might make the difference less important?

3. What percent of the total number of factories in the nation were in the South? What significance might this statistic have in wartime?

4. Did the North or South have more miles of railroad track? How could this resource be useful in wartime?

5. Which side had the overall advantage?

6. Which resources do you think might be most important during a war? Explain.

Thinking About History

Recognizing Point of View

Henry David Thoreau disliked the industrial society that he saw rapidly rising in the United States in the late 1800s. In fact, he viewed machines as unnecessary gadgets. In 1845 Thoreau withdrew to Walden Pond near Concord, Massachusetts, to live a simple life. In 1854 he published a book called *Walden* that told of his experiences and his views of nature and society. Read the excerpt below to identify his view of industrial society. Then answer the questions that follow.

"*Men think it essential that the* nation *have commerce, and export rice, and talk through a telegraph, and ride thirty miles an hour, without a doubt, whether* they *do or not; but whether we should live like baboons or like men, is a little uncertain. If we do not get out sleepers [railroad ties], and forge rails, and devote days and nights to the work, but go to tinkering upon our* lives *to improve* them, *who will build the railroads? And if railroads are not built, how shall we get to heaven in season? But if we stay at home and mind our business, who will want railroads? We do not ride on the railroad; it rides upon us. Did you ever think what those sleepers are that underlie the railroad? Each one is a man, an Irishman, or a Yankee man. The rails are laid on them, and they are covered with sand, and the cars run smoothly over them. They are sound sleepers, I assure you. And every few years a new lot is laid down and run over; so that, if some have the pleasure of riding on a rail, others have the misfortune to be ridden upon.*"

1. What fault does Thoreau find with many American people?

2. What industry does Thoreau use as an example in expressing his point of view? Why?

3. In Thoreau's view, how should people spend their time?

4. What does Thoreau mean when he says "We do not ride the railroad; it rides on us"?

5. Do you agree with Thoreau's point of view? Can it be applied to technological advances today? Explain.

Chapter 12

The Civil War

Planning Guide

	Student Text	TWE Lesson Plans	Support Materials
SECTION 1	**Section 12–1** (1–2 Days) **"To Arms! To Arms!"** pp 304–308 Review/Evaluation Section Review, p 308	**Introducing the Chapter:** Planning Military Strategy—Group Activity, one class period, p 301B **Teaching the Main Ideas:** Enlist Today!—Paired Activity, one class period, p 301B **Reinforcement Activity:** The Union vs. the Confederacy—Individual Activity, one class period, p 301C	★ **Read to Remember,** Section 1 ● **Section Activities,** Section 1 ● **Geography Activities,** Section 1 Δ **Readings** ● **Tests and Quizzes,** Section 1 Quiz
SECTION 2	**Section 12–2** (1–2 Days) **The Early Days of the War,** pp 308–313 Review/Evaluation Section Review, p 313	**Enrichment Activity:** Civil War Memorial—Individual Activity, homework, p 301C	★ **Read to Remember,** Section 2 ● **Section Activities,** Section 2 Δ **Readings** ● **Tests and Quizzes,** Section 2 Quiz
SECTION 3	**Section 12–3** (1–2 Days) **Societies at War,** pp 314–319 Exploring Issues—Presidential Power: Lincoln in the Civil War, p 318–319 Review/Evaluation Section Review, p 319	**Evaluating Progress:** Extra! Extra! Read All About It!—Cooperative Activity, one class period, p 301C	★ **Read to Remember,** Section 3 ● **Section Activities,** Section 3 Δ **Enrichment Activities,** Section 3 Δ **Readings** ● **Tests and Quizzes,** Section 3 Quiz
SECTION 4	**Section 12–4** (1–2 Days) **Ending the War,** pp 320–327 Geography—Relative Location: The Battle of Gettysburg, p 321 Connections to Themes: Shaping Democracy, p 327 Review/Evaluation Section Review, p 327 Chapter 12 Survey, pp 328–329 Skills, pp 328–329 Using New Vocabulary Thinking Critically Using a Time Line Applying Thinking Skills: Analyzing Cause and Effect Writing About Issues	**Teaching the Main Ideas:** Major Civil War Battles—Class Activity, one class period, p 301B	★ **Read to Remember,** Section 4 ● **Section Activities,** Section 4 Δ **Enrichment Activities,** Section 4 Δ **Readings** ● **Tests and Quizzes,** Section 4 Quiz, Chapter 12 Test (Forms A and B) **Additional Resources** ● **Active Learning** Δ **GTV Videodiscs** Δ **Transparencies and Activity Book** ● **Testing Software** ★ **Chapter Summaries** **Key:** ★ **For Extra Support** ● **For All Students** Δ **For Enrichment**

Overview

With the start of the Civil War, half of the crucial slave states of the Upper South—Virginia, Arkansas, Tennessee, and North Carolina—joined the Confederacy. The others—Delaware, Maryland, Kentucky, and Missouri—remained in the Union fold. The Confederates, fighting for independence, had the initial advantage of the best military officers and a defensive strategy but failed to gain British support. Northerners, fighting to preserve the Union, could count on a large population, extensive industry and transportation, and better finances, which would be invaluable in a long conflict.

Lack of decisive victories turned the Civil War into a long, bitter conflict. In 1861 and 1862 Union forces effectively blockaded the southern coast and took steps toward seizing control of the Mississippi River, but they failed repeatedly to capture Richmond, the Confederate capital. The Confederacy tried to hold all its territory but gambled without success on an invasion of the North in the hope that a decisive victory would persuade the Union to sue for peace.

The war affected Americans on both sides. Women played a vital role in businesses, aid organizations, and hospital work. The military stalemate and pressure from African Americans, both enslaved and free, persuaded President Lincoln to issue the Emancipation Proclamation and to enroll African Americans in the Union army. Thus the Union cause became a fight for human freedom as well as for national unity.

The Union achieved great victories in the East and on the Mississippi in 1863. With Ulysses S. Grant as supreme commander, Union forces went on to seize Georgia and the Carolinas, and to invade Virginia and capture Richmond. With General Robert E. Lee's surrender at Appomattox, the war ended.

Activity Objectives

After completing the activities, students should be able to

- explain why northerners and southerners were willing to fight in the war.
- describe the impact of major Civil War battles.
- compare the strengths and weaknesses of the Union and the Confederacy.
- explain how the war the war affected Americans on both sides.
- recognize the magnitude of the Civil War

Introducing the Chapter

Planning Military Strategy

This group activity requires one class period.

The following activity, in which students propose military strategies for Union and Confederate forces, will stimulate interest in reading about the Civil War in Chapter 12.

Begin the activity by reviewing the geographical, political, and economic features of the North and the South on the eve of the Civil War. Direct students' attention to the maps of railroads on page 280. Highlight the location of the Mississippi River and the boundary between the Confederacy and the Union (see the map on page 306).

Divide the class into teams of three and designate half the teams as Confederate generals and half as Union generals. Direct the teams to spend about 20 minutes developing a military strategy for their forces in the impending war. Inform the teams that at this stage the Union and the Confederacy have approximately the same number of troops. The Union has a small number of ships—and the potential to build or obtain more. The Confederacy has no ships and little shipbuilding capacity. Encourage students to review Chapter 11 in their planning.

Have the teams present their military strategies. Allow some time for the class to evaluate the merits and drawbacks of the plans. Encourage students to save their plans for comparison with the military strategies actually used in the Civil War.

Teaching the Main Ideas

Section 12–1: Enlist Today!

This paired activity requires most of a class period.

In Section 12–1 students learn that with the outbreak of war, volunteers rushed to join Union and Confederate forces. The following activity will help students understand why northerners and southerners were willing to fight in the war.

Begin the activity by discussing why people enlist in the armed forces. Ask students to speculate about the motivations of soldiers in the American War of Independence, the War of 1812, and the Mexican War. (Answers may include fighting for one's beliefs, patriotism, and desire for land.)

Divide the class into pairs and distribute poster paper and marking pens. Direct each pair to imagine that they are military recruiters during the Civil War who are responsible for creating posters to encourage civilians to enlist in either the Union or the Confederate armed forces. A poster should provide at least two motivations for enlistment. Encourage pairs to review Section 12–1 for ideas and to use persuasive language and eye-catching designs.

Direct the pairs to display their posters. Have the class comment on the most original and persuasive features.

Teaching the Main Ideas

Section 12–4: Major Civil War Battles

This class activity requires one period.

In this activity students come to understand the far-reaching effects of individual battles of the Civil War as they complete a summary chart.

Before class, set up a summary chart on the chalkboard. Across the top, put the following headings: *Battle, State, Date, Commanders, Casualties, Results.* Under the first heading, list the following battles:

- First Bull Run
- Forts Henry and Donelson
- Shiloh
- Seven Days
- Antietam
- Chancellorsville
- Gettysburg
- Vicksburg
- Chattanooga
- Wilderness
- Petersburg

Begin the activity by reminding students that Sections 12–2 and 12–4 describe battles in the East and along the Mississippi River between 1861 and 1865. To summarize information about major battles, students are to complete the chart on the chalkboard. Give each student responsibility for gathering information about one of the battles listed. Allow 15 minutes for them to compile data and then call on volunteers to fill in information on the chalkboard chart. Allow other students to challenge information that they believe is incorrect.

When students have completed the chart, ask them to use the information to answer the following questions:

- Was the Confederate strategy of fighting a defensive war successful? Why or why not?
- Would any change in strategy have allowed the Confederacy to win the war? Explain.
- Which battles showed the success of the Union's strategy in the war?
- What other battles might be added to the chart? Why?

Reinforcement Activity

Section 12–1: The Union vs. the Confederacy

This individual activity may be completed in class or assigned as homework.

This activity, in which students organize information in a chart, reinforces understanding of the strengths and weaknesses of the Union and the Confederacy.

Begin the activity by asking students how important military strength is in winning a war. Challenge them to describe other factors that also contribute to military success or failure. (Answers may include extensive industry and transportation, sound finances, unity of purpose.) Remind students that the American War of Independence is an example of a war that was not won by the side with greater military might.

Direct students to review Section 12–1 and organize the information in a chart comparing Union and Confederate strengths and weaknesses in the first year of the war. Students may use facts as well as graphics and symbols to create an interesting chart.

Have students examine each other's charts for accuracy and thoroughness. Conclude the activity by discussing what events might affect the strengths and weaknesses of each side. Students should give reasons to support their opinions. (One example: aid from Great Britain might have strengthened the Confederacy.)

Evaluating Progress

Section 12–3: Extra! Extra! Read All About It!

This cooperative project requires one class period.

In Section 12–3 students learn how the Civil War affected Americans on both sides. Use this creative writing activity to evaluate students' understanding of life on northern and southern home fronts during the war.

Before class, write the following topics on the chalkboard:

- African Americans
- Emancipation Proclamation
- women and the war
- economic effects of war
- during the war

Begin the activity by reminding students that the first three sections of Chapter 12 describe not only the military progress of the Civil War but also the effect of the war on civilians. Point out that newspapers were an important source of information for northerners and southerners. Newspapers, especially in the North, sent war correspondents into the field and received their reports by telegraph.

Divide the class into teams of five and assign an equal number of teams to southern and northern newspapers. Have the teams imagine they are news reporters and direct them to create the front page of a newspaper. They are to prepare articles, using information in the text, on the topics listed on the chalkboard. They are also to include headlines, original or photocopied pictures, and bylines. Students may also want to design a newspaper masthead. Encourage teams to divide the work equally among all members.

When the projects are finished, have northern and southern reporters exchange their front pages for review. Conclude by discussing the difference in viewpoints on each topic.

Evaluate students' newspapers on accuracy of description of events, use of the appropriate point of view, and specific examples.

Enrichment Activity

Section 12–2: A Civil War Memorial

This individual activity may be completed in class or assigned as homework.

This activity engages students in designing a Civil War memorial that represents the feelings of supporters of the Union or the Confederacy.

Begin the activity by explaining that people in many societies, including ours, create memorials to help people remember the soldiers who served in wars. Ask students to describe war memorials they have seen or show them the Marine Corps War Memorial on page 636 and the Vietnam Veterans Memorial on page 774.

Have students imagine that they are artists who have been commissioned to design a Civil War memorial. They may choose either the Confederate or the Union forces, but their design should reflect the feelings of the people on the side they choose. The memorial may take any form but should stand as a reminder to future generations of the magnitude of the Civil War.

Display the completed designs. Have the class determine which side is reflected in each design. Conclude by discussing an appropriate design to memorialize both sides in the Civil War.

Bibliography and Audiovisual Material

Teacher Bibliography

Chester, Thomas Morris. *Thomas Morris Chester, Black Civil War Correspondent: His Dispatches from the Virginia Front.* Edited by R.J.M. Blacket. Baton Rouge: Louisiana State University Press, 1989.

Commager, Henry S., ed. *The Blue and the Gray: The Story of the Civil War as Told by Participants.* 2 vols. (New American Library.) New York: NAL Dutton, Inc., 1973.

Foner, Jack D. *Blacks and the Military in American History: A New Perspective.* New York: Praeger, 1974.

McFeely, William S. *Grant: A Biography.* New York: Norton, 1982.

McPherson, James M. *Battle Cry of Freedom: The Civil War Era.* New York: Oxford University Press, 1988.

Quarles, Benjamin. *The Negro in the Civil War.* New York: De Capo Press, 1989.

Sandburg, Carl. *Abraham Lincoln: The Prairie Years and the War Years.* New York: Harcourt, Brace, 1974.

Woodward, C. Vann, ed. *Mary Chesnut's Civil War.* New Haven: Yale University Press, 1981.

Student Bibliography

Catton, Bruce. *The Civil War.* (American Heritage Library.) Boston: Houghton Mifflin, 1985.

Crane, Stephen. *The Red Badge of Courage.* New York: Bantam, 1981.

Eaton, Clement. *Jefferson Davis.* New York: The Free Press, 1977.

Higginson, Thomas W. *Army Life in a Black Regiment.* New York: W.W. Norton, 1984.

Mitchell, Margaret. *Gone with the Wind.* New York: Avon, 1976.

Sherman's March. Civil War Series. Alexandria, VA: Time-Life Books, 1986.

Films, Videocassettes, and Videodiscs

The Civil War. Time Life Entertainment/PBS Video. Videotapes.

The Civil War: A House Divided. 25 min. McGraw-Hill. Movie.

The Civil War: Union at Risk. 25 min. Britannica.

Civil War Series: First Two Years. 20 min. Coronet/MTI. Movie.

The Events Which Led To The Emancipation Proclamation. 15 min. Life Video. Videocassette.

Lincoln's Gettysburg Address. 15 min. Oxford Films. Videocassette

Filmstrips

The Civil War: A People at War. National Geographic Society.

The Civil War: Darkest Hour; Then Peace. SVE.

Women In The Civil War. Multi-Media Productions.

Computer Software

American History Keyword Series: Civil War. Apple. Focus Media.

Civil War. Apple. Hartley Courseware.

Civil War. Apple. Heizer Software.

Lincoln's Decisions. Apple. Educational Activities.

Chapter 12

Objectives

- Describe how the Union and the Confederacy prepared for war.
- Cite events in 1861 and 1862 that caused the Civil War to be a long, bitter conflict.
- Discuss how the Civil War affected northern and southern societies.
- Explain how the Union finally defeated the Confederacy.

Introducing THE CHAPTER

For suggestions on introducing Chapter 12, refer to page 301B in the Teacher's Edition.

Developing THE CHAPTER

For activities and teaching strategies to help you reinforce and enrich chapter content, see pages 301B–301D in the Teacher's Edition.

Chapter Opener Illustrations
Confederate pickets warm themselves over a small fire outside of Fredericksburg, where a fierce battle in December 1862 blocked the Union's march on Richmond.

A contemporary photo by David Muench shows East Cemetery Hill in Gettysburg, Pennsylvania.

Confederate General "Stonewall" Jackson inspired such loyalty that one observer said his men would "meet death for his sake, and bless him when dying."

By the spring of 1865 Richmond, capital of the Confederacy, lay in ruins. Upon surveying the damage, one Confederate soldier wrote: "The old war-scarred city seemed to prefer annihilation to conquest."

Reduced student page in the Teacher's Edition

Chapter 12 1861-1865

The Civil War

The green regimental flag of the 1st Arkansas displays the names of the engagements in which it was involved. At Chickamauga, an Indian word meaning "river of death," the rebel regiment pressured Major General Thomas's Federals. Thomas was later called "the Rock of Chickamauga" for withstanding the numerous assaults.

Social History

In 1862 Theodore Upson enlisted in the Union army. When asked by his father why he insisted on enlisting, Theodore replied, *"Father, we must have more soldiers. This Union your ancestors and mine helped to make must be saved from destruction. I can go better than some others. I don't feel right to stay home any longer."*

American Voices

On April 12, 1861, the North and the South went to war. Northerners put on the blue uniform of the United States Army. Southerners wore the gray of the Confederate States of America. For thousands of Americans, the war brought a special tragedy. Family ties and friendships did not stop at state borders. Theodore Upson, an Indiana teenager, glimpsed what was to come. This would be a war of American against American.

"Father and I were husking out some corn when William Cory came across the field and said, 'Jonathan, the Rebs have fired upon and taken Fort Sumter.' Father got white and couldn't say a word.

We did not finish the corn and drove to the barn. Father left me to unload. . . . After I had finished I went in to dinner. Mother said, 'What is the matter with Father?' He had gone right upstairs. I told her what we had heard. She went to him. After a while they came down. Father looked ten years older.

We sat down to the table. Grandma wanted to know what was the trouble. Father told her and she began to cry. 'Oh, my poor children in the South! Now they will suffer! I knew it would come!' . . .

Mother had a letter from the Hales. Charlie and his father are in their army. I wonder if I were in our army and they should meet me would they shoot me. I suppose they would."

What Theodore Upson could not foresee was that this conflict would grow into the nation's bloodiest war. More Americans lost their lives in this war than in all of the country's other wars combined. The war would also cause vast change, destroying slavery and secession and changing the United States from a loose union of states under a weak central government into a new nation led by a strong central government. Before 1861 Americans said, "The United States *are*—." After 1865, they were to say, "The United States *is*—."

Confederate soldiers warming their hands; Gettysburg National Cemetery; Confederate General Thomas J. "Stonewall" Jackson; Richmond in ruins; flag of the 1st Arkansas Regiment; Confederate and Union bullets.

Analyzing Primary Sources

American Voices

Theodore Upson, living on a farm in Indiana, described in his journal his family's despair upon hearing the news of Fort Sumter. The selection on this page is from the *Journal of Theodore Upson.*

1. How did Theodore's father respond to the news of the fall of Fort Sumter? **(He withdrew in silence.)**
2. Upon hearing the news, Theodore's grandmother stated, "I knew it would come!" To what was she referring? **(war between the South and North)**
3. What is the tragedy reflected in the last three lines of the quotation? **(Families and friends might end up fighting against each other.)**

GTV Side 2

Chap. 16, Frame 50040

The Civil War (Movie)

Search:

Play:

303

Section 12-1

Objectives

- ***Answer the Focus Question.***
- *Compare advantages of the North and the South in the Civil War.*
- *Explain how business people on both sides were affected by the war.*

Introducing

THE SECTION

Before the Confederate bombardment of Fort Sumter, few people knew what to do about the secession of seven southern states from the Union. Some northerners even counseled letting the "sisters depart in peace." However, when Confederate cannons fired on Fort Sumter, northerners united behind President Lincoln in a determination to preserve the Union, by military force if necessary.

Ask students to imagine that they are leaders in the North or the South. What kinds of things would they have to consider before they could launch a military campaign? **(for example, how to recruit and equip soldiers)**

B · A · C · K · G · R · O · U · N · D

Time Line Illustrations

1. Robert E. Lee's sword symbolizes the era of cavalry charges. General Grant allowed Lee to keep his sword during surrender ceremonies at Appomattox Court House.

2. In 1863 the North began enlisting African-American soldiers. Sergeant J.L. Balldwin, Company G, 56th Colored Infantry, posed for this picture.

3. This photograph from the Confederate Museum pictures three Confederate soldiers from Braxton Bragg's Army of Tennessee.

4. The new Gatling gun, a machine gun that fired about 200 bullets per minute, was tested by the Union army at Petersburg. Other innovations, like the long-range rifle, made cavalry charges obsolete and trenches necessary.

Reduced student page in the Teacher's Edition

CHAPTER TIME LINE

1861 - 1865

1861 Apr Lincoln and Davis call for volunteers

1863 Jan Emancipation Proclamation
African Americans enlist in Union army

1861 — 1862 — 1863

1861 Jul First Battle of Bull Run

1862 Sep Battle of Antietam

1862 May Lee takes command of Army of Northern Virginia

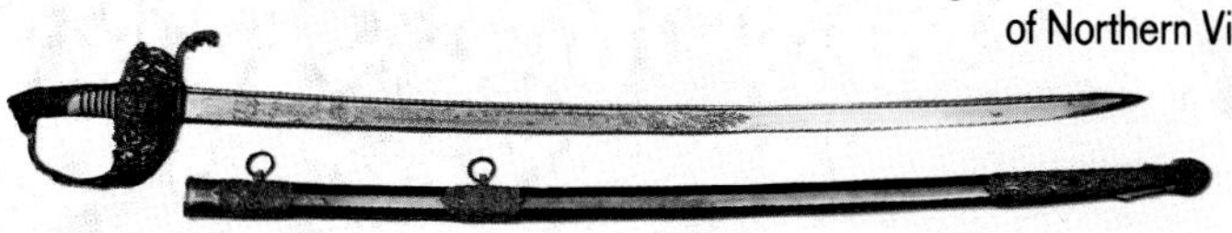

12-1 "To Arms! To Arms!"

Focus: How did the Union and the Confederacy prepare for war?

"War! and volunteers are the only topics of conversation or thought. I cannot study. I cannot sleep, I cannot work, and I don't know as I can write."

So wrote an Ohio college student after hearing of the Confederate attack on Fort Sumter. On April 15, one day after the fort surrendered, the North and the South prepared for war. President Lincoln called on the free states to supply 75,000 militia for three months to maintain the Union and ordered a blockade of southern seaports. Confederate President Jefferson Davis asked for a volunteer army of 100,000 soldiers to defend the South.

North and South, volunteers rushed to join the cause. Northerners were fighting to preserve the Union. As a New England officer wrote to his wife:

"I know . . . how great a debt we owe to those who went before us through the blood and sufferings of the Revolution. I am willing—perfectly willing—to lay down all my joys in this life, to help maintain this government, and to pay that debt."

Southerners were fighting for independence. They wanted a government of limited powers that protected the right to own slaves. A Confederate officer declared:

5. When Lincoln ran for reelection in 1864, he had little hope of winning. However, Union victories restored voters' faith in him and gave him the election.

Social History

Robert E. Lee graduated from West Point in 1829 and began his career as an army engineer. During the Mexican War he specialized in scouting work. Lee was praised highly in official reports: *"success in Mexico was largely due to the skill, valor, and undaunted courage of Robert E. Lee . . . the greatest military genius in America."*

1863 Jul Battles of Gettysburg and Vicksburg

1864 Jun Union siege of Petersburg begins

1865 Apr Confederacy surrenders

1864

1865

1864 Sep Union forces seize Atlanta

1864 Nov Lincoln reelected

1863 Nov Battle of Chattanooga

"We were wronged. Our properties and liberties were about to be taken from us. It was a sacred duty to rebel."

Both sides predicted a short, easily won war. Most northerners thought of it as a "six months' war." Southerners felt sure they would defeat the North in a few battles. One even promised to wipe up all the blood spilled with his handkerchief.

Taking Sides: The Upper South

Sandwiched between the Union and the Confederacy were the eight slave states of the Upper South (see map, page 306), which had not yet decided whether to secede. Their decisions would have an important effect on the outcome of the war.

These eight states had more than half of the South's population and food crops—and three fourths of its factories. Many of the best military officers also came from the Upper South.

The railroads and rivers in these states were of strategic importance to move supplies and troops. The Baltimore and Ohio Railroad, the major link between East and West, ran through Maryland and western Virginia. The Ohio River flowed along the northern border of Kentucky, and the Mississippi along the eastern border of Missouri. These rivers would provide a barrier or a path of invasion, depending on which side controlled them.

Virginia, Arkansas, Tennessee, and North Carolina had held conventions on secession soon after Lincoln's election but had decided either not to secede or to wait. After the outbreak of war at Fort Sumter, however, all four states left the Union to join the Confederacy.

Robert E. Lee, considered the best officer in the United States Army, symbolized the plight of many in these states. Lee disliked slavery and had spoken against secession. But when Virginia joined the Confederacy, he changed his mind. "I cannot raise my hand against my birthplace, my home, my children," he decided. Lee declined Lincoln's offer of command of the Union forces and resigned from the army.

These four states almost doubled the population of the Confederacy—and furnished thousands of

Developing

THE SECTION

Thinking Critically

Analysis. Refer students to the words of the Union officer on page 304 and of the Confederate officer on this page. **Ask:** What connection does the New England officer make between the Civil War and the American Revolution? (The Revolution established a government which the officer would fight to preserve.) What similarity might the Confederate officer see between the Confederates of 1861 and the American revolutionaries of 1776? (The southerners were also fighting for independence.)

Active Learning

Presentation. Both northern and southern morale would be tested by war. **Ask:** Why are strong leaders important in a crisis? What qualities are valuable for leadership?

Divide the class into four groups. Assign each group a Civil War leader: Lincoln, Davis, Grant, or Lee. Each group must put together an "Up Close and Personal" presentation on their leader for the class which includes: a short biography of the leader, an interview with the leader discussing his thoughts on the war, and a chart assessing the leader's strengths and weaknesses.

Thinking Critically

Analysis. When Lincoln called for volunteers from state militias on April 15, 1861, the governor of Kentucky said his state *"will not furnish a single man for the purpose of coercion... but fifty thousand if necessary for the defense of our rights and those of our southern brothers."*

Lincoln promised Kentucky that it could keep its slaves, and pro-Union forces gained the upper hand. However, Lincoln intervened much more quickly and forcefully in Maryland. **Ask:**

1. Why do you think Lincoln's strategy differed from state to state? (because of the need to protect Washington, D.C.)
2. What does Lincoln's promise to Kentucky reveal about his goals? (that the preservation of the Union was the top priority)

Geography Skills

ANSWERS

South Carolina, Mississippi, Florida, Alabama, Georgia, Louisiana, and Texas; seceded from the Union first, before Confederate attack on Fort Sumter.

Multicultural Perspectives

Estevan Ochoa was born in Mexico in 1831. His family had come from Spain to Mexico in the days of Cortés. As a young man, he lived for a time in Independence, Missouri, where he learned the English language. Ochoa returned to the Southwest in 1859 by way of the Santa Fe Trail, where he organized a chain of stores and a pack train of mules to supply them. When Confederate troops seized Tucson during the Civil War, Ochoa was given the ultimatum of either taking an oath of allegiance to the Confederacy or of leaving Tucson. He chose to leave. Later he returned and became a member of the territorial legislature and mayor of Tucson.

Reduced student page in the Teacher's Edition

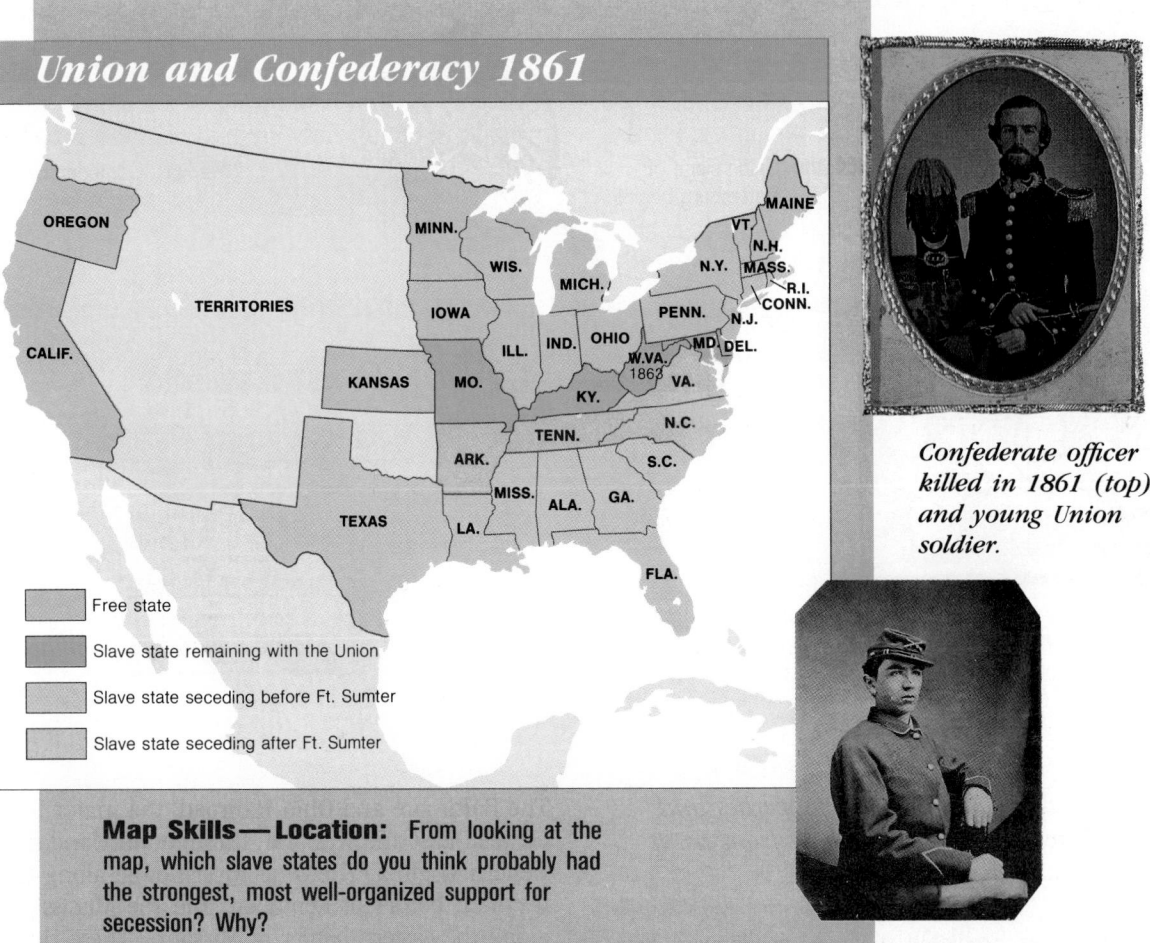

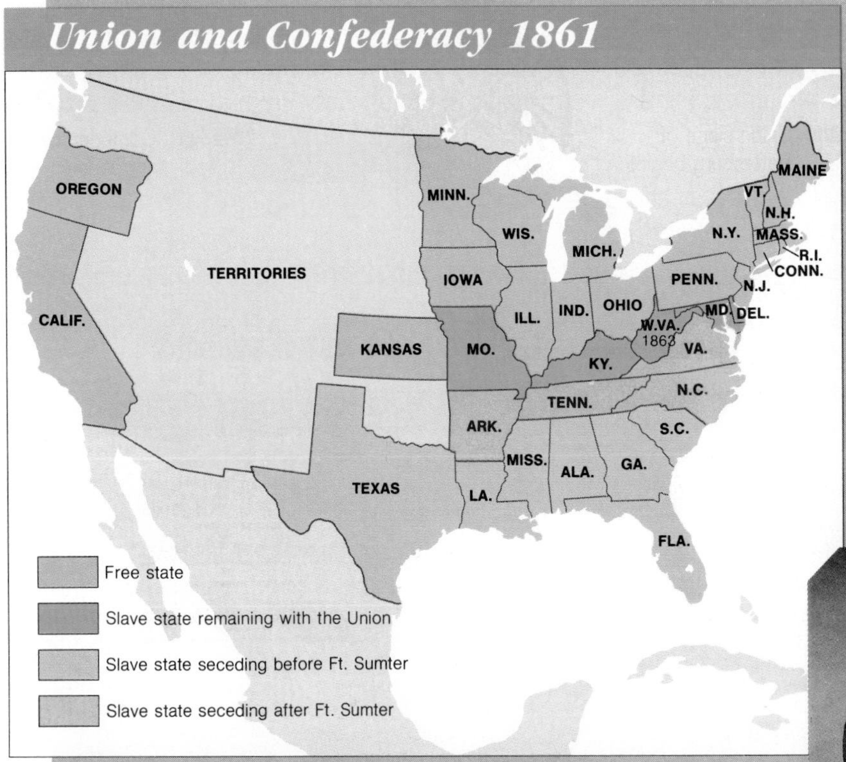

Confederate officer killed in 1861 (top) and young Union soldier.

Map Skills—Location: From looking at the map, which slave states do you think probably had the strongest, most well-organized support for secession? Why?

soldiers for southern armies. The Confederate Congress chose Richmond, Virginia, as its new capital, and the government moved there in June 1861.

Slave States in the Union. Of the other slave states, Delaware unanimously rejected secession. Virginia's western counties refused to recognize their state's secession and declared their loyalty to the Union. They formed the new state of West Virginia and joined the Union in 1863. However, in Maryland, Kentucky, and Missouri, unionists and secessionists struggled bitterly for control.

It was crucial for the Union to control Maryland which surrounded Washington, D.C., on three sides. When a pro-secession mob attacked a Massachusetts regiment passing through Baltimore in April 1861, Lincoln sent troops to keep order. He also suspended the right of ***habeas corpus***, the right of a person to appear in court so a judge can decide whether the person is being imprisoned lawfully. The Constitution allows this right to be suspended only in cases of rebellion or invasion. Pro-Confederate leaders were jailed without trial. In the fall a pro-Union governor was elected, and Maryland stayed loyal to the Union.

Kentucky at first declared its neutrality in the war. But when fighting broke out between Confederate and Union forces, Kentucky sided with the Union. In Missouri, conflict between unionists and seccessionists grew so intense that Lincoln put the state under **martial law,** rule by military rather than civil authorities.

Connections: Economics

Federal expenditures rose tremendously from $66.6 million in 1861 to $474.8 million in 1862, and up to $1,297 million in 1865. This peak was not equaled again until the United States entered the First World War. Personal income taxes brought in about 20 percent of the total federal revenue in 1865. After the war, new federal expenditures, like veterans' benefits, kept the budget far above the prewar level.

Limited English Proficiency

Building Vocabulary. Help students understand the following terms: *war bond, greenback*, and *inflation*. **Ask:** Why couldn't war bonds finance the war? **(people had little gold or silver to buy bonds)** Why was the South faced with runaway inflation? **(Government printed excessive amount of paper money not backed by gold or silver.)**

Union and Confederate Strengths

If numbers told the whole story, the Confederate cause looked hopeless. The Union had a population of 22 million. The Confederacy had only 9 million people. Of these, 3.5 million were enslaved. However, at first the Confederate army easily filled its ranks with volunteers. Thus, the South's smaller population made little difference.

Confederate leaders felt they had many advantages for a short, defensive war. To win, they needed only to push back invading Union forces, which would require fewer troops than the North would need to conquer the Confederacy. Union troops also would have greater distances to travel, and their long supply lines would be vulnerable to attack.

The North had its own advantages. In this war, railroads would be vital. The Union had more than twice as many miles of track as the Confederacy. Supplying troops with war materials was also crucial, and more than 80 percent of the nation's factories and most of its coal and iron were in northern states. Even in farm production the northern states outstripped the southern states.

In addition, most shipping and shipbuilding was in the North. Although in 1861 the Union navy had only 42 ships, it bought merchant ships, armed them, and sent them to blockade southern ports. Eventually the Union navy grew to 650 vessels. In 1861 the Confederate navy secretary had not a single ship to command.

Financing the War

Before 1861 most Americans' contact with their national government was limited to using the post office. That situation would change dramatically, especially in the North, as the government expanded its powers in order to fight the war.

At first, the Union government raised duties on imports and sold war bonds to finance the war. In 1861 Congress also passed the nation's first federal income tax and created an internal revenue bureau to collect it.

When bond sales and taxes failed to raise enough money, Congress imposed taxes on everything from liquor to newspaper ads. It also passed an act enabling the government to print money. Eventually, the Union printed $450 million of the new green federal bank notes. Since these "greenbacks" were not backed by gold or silver, they lost half their value during the war, due to inflation.

The government also set up new federal banks and required them to invest part of their capital in war bonds. The banks could then issue paper money up to 90 percent of the value of the bonds they bought. This federal money became the standard currency of the nation, driving money issued by state banks out of circulation.

Confederate finances. The Confederate government, too, resorted to duties, taxes, and war bonds to raise money. But it had less success than the North. With trade choked by the Union blockade, import duties yielded scant income. Strong opposition from citizens discouraged the government from imposing high taxes. And southerners, like northerners, had little gold or silver to buy bonds.

When the government could not borrow enough money to pay its bills, it turned to the printing press. About $2 billion in paper money flooded the South, and the Confederacy was soon faced with runaway inflation. Salt, the only means of preserving meat, soared in some places from $2 a bag before the war to $60 by late 1862.

Spotlight on the Civil War

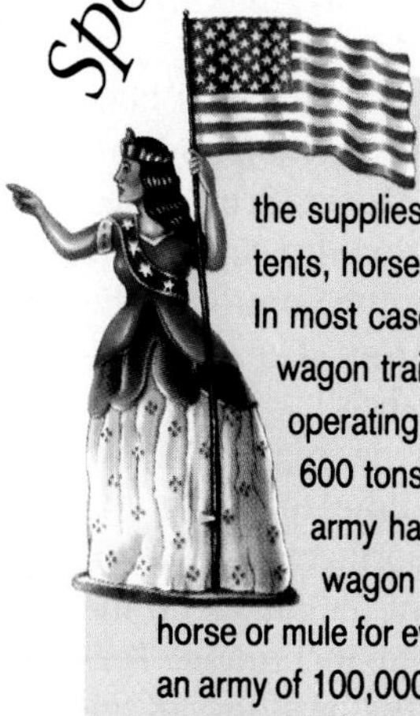

How did an invading army get the supplies—shoes, canteens, blankets, tents, horses, horseshoes—that it needed? In most cases, it established supply lines of wagon trains or railroads. A Union army operating in enemy territory consumed 600 tons of supplies each day. Such an army had to have, on average, one wagon for every forty soldiers and one horse or mule for every two or three soldiers. Thus, an army of 100,000 troops needed 2,500 supply wagons and at least 35,000 horses or mules.

Social History
The soldiers in the Union army were young—800,000 were 17 years of age or younger; 100,000 were under 15. While most could shoot reasonably well, it took time for them to learn military routines. To teach them to march, sergeants tied a stalk of hay to each man's left shoe and a wisp of straw to the right. As the soldiers set out, they would chant "hay foot, straw foot, hay foot, straw foot . . ."

Section Review

ANSWERS

1. Definitions for following terms are on text pages indicated in parentheses: *habeas corpus* (306), *martial law* (306).
2. Answers include food crops, factories, railroads, rivers, experienced military officers.
3. North's advantages: greater population, twice as many miles of railroad track, larger navy and merchant fleet, most of the factories, coal, and iron, more farm production. South: volunteers eager to fight, experienced military officers, shorter supply lines, need only repel rather than conquer territory.
4. The South needed only to push back invading Union forces. If it could be done quickly, the Union would not have time to amass large numbers of troops and supplies.
5. Businesses based on trade between North and South hurt. Export of southern cotton halted. Businesses selling to military prospered.

Reduced student page in the Teacher's Edition

Southern leaders hoped to force the British into aiding the Confederacy. Convinced that Britain was dependent upon southern cotton, the Confederacy banned cotton exports in 1861. Rather than lose its cotton supply, Confederates believed, Britain would recognize the South's independence and perhaps offer help.

The Confederate strategy failed because Britain found new sources of cotton in India and Egypt. Also, British trade with the Union in grain and military supplies was booming, and Britain was reluctant to endanger it by supporting the Confederacy.

Section Review

1. **Identification.** Define *habeas corpus* and *martial law.*

2. **Comprehension.** Name four resources of the Upper South that both the Union and the Confederacy needed in the war.

3. **Comprehension.** Compare the advantages of the North and the South early in the war.

4. **Analysis.** A Confederate said, "What we have to do must be done quickly. The longer we have them to fight the more difficult they will be to defeat." What do you think he meant?

5. **Synthesis.** How might business people on both sides have been affected by the war?

12-2 The Early Days of the War

Focus: What events in 1861 and 1862 caused the Civil War to become a long, bitter conflict?

In the Union and Confederate capitals, Presidents Lincoln and Davis planned their strategies. Davis set out to fight a defensive war. The South would try to hold all its territory, making the war so costly that the North would give up.

Lincoln approved General Winfield Scott's plan for a limited war to put down the rebellion and win back the loyalty of southerners. It was Scott's idea to seal the South off from much-needed supplies by blockading its seaports and gaining control of the Mississippi. Then the Union army, like an anaconda snake, would crush the rebels.

Scott's "Anaconda Plan," as newspapers scornfully called it, depended on time to make the blockade effective. But many northerners believed the war could be won with an all-out attack on the Confederate capital. "Forward to Richmond! Forward to Richmond!" screamed the headlines of the *New York Tribune.* The public picked up the cry. Under pressure, Lincoln agreed to the attack.

The First Battle of Bull Run

In July 1861 General Irvin McDowell led 30,000 Union troops out of Washington, across the Potomac, and into Virginia. Civilians followed on horses and in carriages, hoping to see the fighting.

About 25 miles from Washington, the Union columns met 30,000 Confederate troops under General P.G.T. Beauregard, the Confederate hero of Fort Sumter. They were camped at the town of Manassas Junction, near a stream called Bull Run.

The Union troops attacked, but Confederate General Thomas J. Jackson—"standing like a stone wall"—kept his brigade's line firm. From that time on, Jackson was known as "Stonewall" and his troops as the Stonewall Brigade. Reinforcements arrived and the Confederates counterattacked, letting loose the piercing "rebel yell."

Panic shot through the Union soldiers. Almost the entire Union army bolted, scrambling in haste

Connections: Science and Technology
Horace L. Hunley developed a cigar-shaped submarine and brought it to Charleston in 1863. Several disastrous trials led to the deaths of Hunley and twenty others. On February 14, 1864, the submarine attacked the Union sloop *Housatonic* in Charleston Harbor. In a tremendous explosion, the Union ship, as well as the *H.L. Hunley* and her crew, sank.

to get back to Washington. The Confederates, surprised and confused, did not follow.

The Union army's disastrous retreat ended the North's dream of a short, heroic war. Meanwhile, the South's confidence that it would win the war soared.

In the week after Bull Run, Lincoln called for the enlistment of a million men to serve for three years. He appointed the dashing General George B. McClellan to take command of this new force, named the Army of the Potomac, and turn it into a superb fighting machine.

Lincoln also outlined future strategy. The navy would make the blockade effective. Meanwhile, Union forces would seize the Mississippi and prepare for a new invasion of Virginia. The Union, Lincoln was beginning to see, could win only by destroying Confederate armies.

The War at Sea

The blockade played an important role in the Union's ultimate victory. Eventually, 150 Union ships were patrolling the Confederate coastline at any one time. The Union navy tightened the blockade by taking almost every harbor of importance on the South's Atlantic coast. In the course of the war, the blockade reduced the South's ocean trade to less than a third of normal.

The Confederacy soon became desperate for all kinds of supplies. Daring sea captains in swift, small ships ran the blockade. Their ships, however, were built for speed, not for carrying the large cargoes that the South needed during wartime.

The Confederates' one hope was to break the blockade with ironclad warships. When Union forces had abandoned the navy yard in Norfolk, Virginia, they had sunk the steam-powered U.S.S. *Merrimac.* The Confederates raised the *Merrimac,* covered its sides with iron plate, and attached an iron ram to the prow to batter wooden warships.

On March 8, 1862, the *Merrimac,* renamed the *Virginia,* lumbered into Chesapeake Bay. Within a few hours, it had destroyed two Union ships and run a third aground.

The Union navy, however, had its own ironclad, the *Monitor.* On March 9 the two ships met in a noisy five-hour battle. Neither ship could sink the other, but the battle dashed southern hopes that the *Virginia* could help blockade runners reach the open sea.

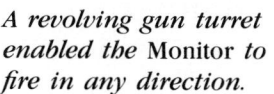

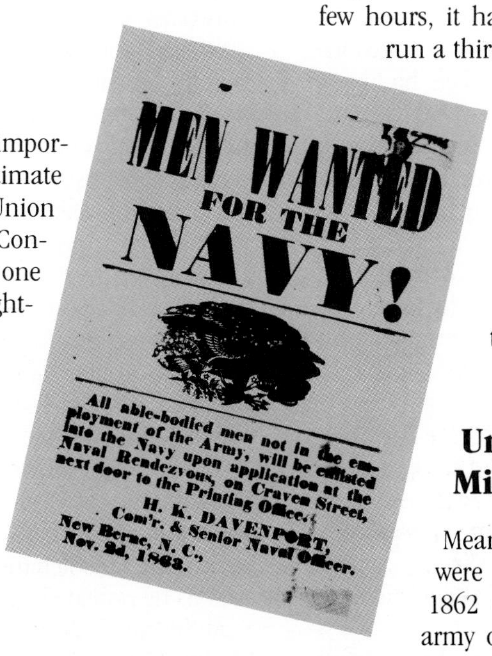

A revolving gun turret enabled the Monitor *to fire in any direction.*

Union Victories on the Mississippi

Meanwhile, Union forces to the west were meeting with success. In early 1862 General Ulysses S. Grant led an army of 15,000 soldiers south into Tennessee. They were heading for the Mississippi River, but first they would have to take Confederate forts on the Tennessee and Cumberland rivers. With the help of Union gunboats, Grant easily captured Fort Henry on the Tennessee River.

Grant pushed on to Fort Donelson on the Cumberland. After four days of siege, the Confederate commander asked for an armistice. Grant demanded—and got—"an unconditional and immediate surrender." After that, U.S. Grant was known as "Unconditional Surrender" Grant.

Section 12-2

Objectives

- ***Answer the Focus Question.***
- *Describe the strategies of the North and the South for winning the war.*
- *Discuss the effect of the Battle of Antietam on the war.*

Introducing
THE SECTION

No one expected a long war. Most northerners agreed with Philadelphian Sidney George Fisher: *"I cannot imagine that the South has resources for a long war or even a short one."*

Ask: Which side had the advantage at the start of the war? Why?

Developing
THE SECTION

Thinking Critically

Analysis. Ask students to compare the strategies of the Union and the Confederate navies. (Northern navy blockaded southern ports; Confederates tried to break the blockade with ironclad ships.) Was the northern strategy significant to the outcome of the war? Why or why not? (The South lost its northern markets and reduced its trade with Europe; could not get needed supplies.)

Connections: Geography
When historians of the Civil War refer to "the West" they usually mean the western theater of the war—the Mississippi River valley. While only skirmishes and small battles were fought from New Mexico to California, the Confederates did attempt to invade New Mexico from Texas. Their purpose was eventually to reach the Pacific, where they hoped to find sympathizers and a trade route that couldn't easily be blockaded. Also, the Confederates hoped to find recruits in New Mexico.

Thinking Critically

Analysis. Some Native Americans chose sides during the war too. Most of the Plains Indians and a rival group among the Cherokees, led by Chief John Ross, favored the Union cause. Three regiments of Native Americans fought for the Confederacy. Ironically, they were members of five tribes— the Cherokees, Chickasaws, Choctaws, Creeks, and Seminoles— who had been driven westward a generation earlier by southerners. One Cherokee chief, Brigadier-General Stand Watie, was so loyal to the southern cause that he did not formally surrender until a month after the war was over.

Ask: Why might Native Americans have chosen to fight for the North or the South? (hoped to be treated better by the Confederates than they had by the federal government; hoped to get land back if South won the war)

Forts Henry and Donelson had been the outposts of the Confederate western defense. With their surrender, General Albert Sidney Johnston withdrew his southern army farther south to Corinth, a major railroad center near the Tennessee-Mississippi border.

Shiloh. Grant continued to advance south along the Tennessee River. But on the morning of April 6 he was surprised by Johnston near a country church called Shiloh. The fighting raged fiercely all day, and the Union line barely held. Some of Grant's officers advised retreat. Grant replied, "Retreat? No. I propose to attack at daylight and whip them." The next day, with reinforcements, Grant attacked. The Confederates withdrew to Corinth, but Union troops were too exhausted to pursue.

The Battle of Shiloh left the Union in control of Kentucky and much of Tennessee, but it was the costliest battle that Americans had ever engaged in. On each side, more than 10,000 soldiers had been killed or wounded. Among the dead was General Johnston. Many northerners called for Grant's removal because of the losses. But President Lincoln replied, "I can't spare this man— he fights!"

Meanwhile, a powerful Union naval force under Flag Officer David G. Farragut struck northward from the Gulf of Mexico. In late April the force captured New Orleans. Then part of Farragut's fleet moved upriver and took Baton Rouge, Louisiana, in early May.

A few weeks later, Union troops drove the Confederates out of Corinth. Next, a joint force of army troops and gunboats took Memphis, Tennessee. By June the only forts on the Mississippi still in southern hands were Vicksburg and Port Hudson. Southern resistance, however, stalled the Union advance for the rest of 1862.

Writing in her diary during April and May, Mary Boykin Chesnut of South Carolina reflected southern despair at these losses:

“Battle after battle— disaster after disaster. . . . How could I sleep? The power they are bringing to bear against our country is tremendous. . . . New Orleans gone— and with it the Confederacy. Are we not cut in two? The Mississippi ruins us if lost.”

Confederate Victories in the East

In the East, McClellan drilled the Army of the Potomac long after it was sharp and well disciplined. Through the fall and winter of 1861-1862, Lincoln could not get McClellan to go on the offensive. Fed up, Lincoln wrote: "My dear McClellan: If you don't want to use the army I should like to borrow it for a while. Yours respectfully, A. Lincoln."

Finally, in March 1862, McClellan led his army against Richmond. Instead of going overland, his force of 100,000 soldiers moved by ship through Chesapeake Bay and landed on the Virginia Peninsula below Richmond. Fearing that the Confederates had more troops than he did, McClellan advanced cautiously up the peninsula. This gave the Confederates time to bring General Joseph E. Johnston's whole army to Richmond.

When McClellan's forces finally approached the capital, Johnston struck. At the Battle of Seven Pines, near the Fair Oaks Station, Johnston stopped the Union advance, but casualties on both sides were high. Johnston himself was severely wounded, and General Robert E. Lee took command.

Lee's first move was to keep reinforcements in Washington from reaching McClellan. Lee sent Stonewall Jackson to raid the Shenandoah Valley of western Virginia in order to make northerners think Washington was threatened. McClellan never got his reinforcements. Jackson escaped the Union troops and joined Lee at Richmond.

In late June, Lee launched an offensive to drive McClellan out of Virginia. For a week the Confederate Army of Northern Virginia struck again and again, but McClellan inflicted heavy casualties even as he retreated.

At the end of these battles, called the Seven Days' Battles, McClellan was on the banks of the James River, protected by Union gunboats. The Confederates withdrew. They had not crushed McClellan as hoped, but they had stopped the Union drive toward Richmond.

Second Bull Run. McClellan's troops were evacuated by sea to northern Virginia, where they were to join another force under General John Pope. The combined armies, under McClellan's command, would then march on Richmond.

Multicultural Perspectives

David G. Farragut, of Spanish descent, was born in 1801 near Knoxville, Tennessee. His father, George Farragut Mesquida, was a Spanish soldier in North America who fought in the War of Independence. The younger Farragut entered the navy when he was nine years old and at age thirteen served aboard the USS *Essex* in the War of 1812. In honor of his outstanding service in the Civil War, Farragut was promoted to the rank of admiral. He was the first full admiral in the U.S. Navy.

Geography Skills

ANSWERS

1. Grant captured Forts Henry and Donelson on the Tennessee and Cumberland rivers, moved south to Shiloh, and took Memphis and Vicksburg on the Mississippi. Farragut moved from the Gulf of Mexico up the Mississippi to capture New Orleans and Baton Rouge.

2. Lee moved from Richmond to Manassas (Bull Run) to Maryland.

The Civil War 1861–1862

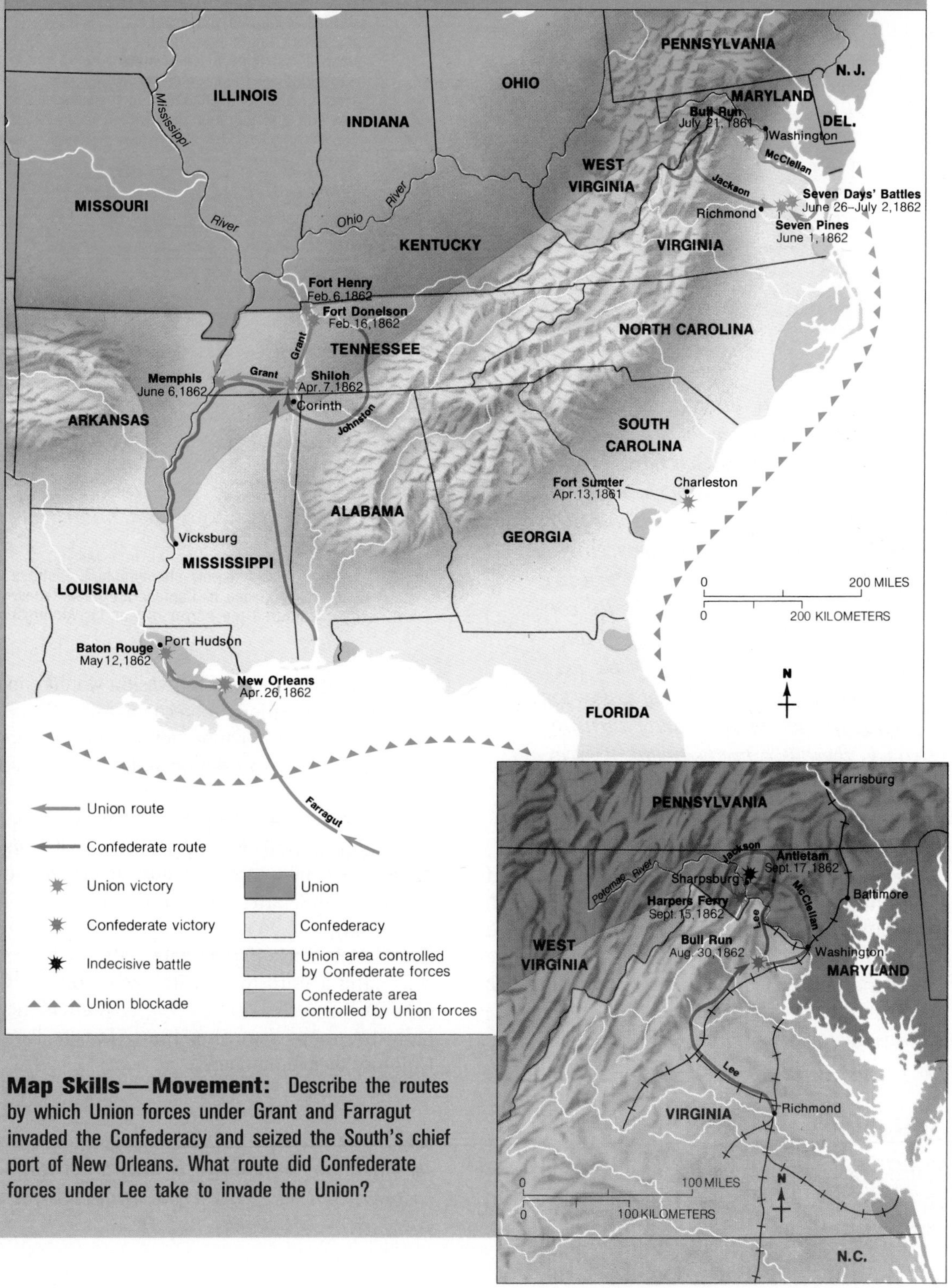

Map Skills—Movement: Describe the routes by which Union forces under Grant and Farragut invaded the Confederacy and seized the South's chief port of New Orleans. What route did Confederate forces under Lee take to invade the Union?

Writing About History

Diary Entry. Ask students to imagine that they were on the battlefield of Antietam when *"the mental strain was so great that . . . the whole landscape for an instant turned slightly red."* Have them write a diary entry from the point of view of a Confederate or a Union soldier, describing the battle and how they felt. Students can refer to the text and illustrations on pages 312–313. Have students compare diary entries. How do they reflect the common experiences of war?

B · A · C · K · G · R · O · U · N · D

Connections: Science and Technology

High casualties at Antietam and other battles were due in part to the development of more effective guns. Civil War soldiers were the first to use rifles that spun bullets through the air thus increasing their range. With an effective range of 300 to 400 yards, defenders firing rifles inflicted huge casualties on troops charging in close formation. Sharpshooters could pick off horses at distances up to half a mile. Marksmen singled out enemy officers, which helps explain the high casualty rate among generals.

Reduced student page in the Teacher's Edition

Learning From Art
The Battle of Antietam, 1862

McClellan learned the exact position of Confederate forces when a lost copy of Lee's orders was found by Union soldiers. McClellan's delay in attacking enabled Lee to discover the loss and pull together his divided army at Sharpsburg.

The Civil War was the first war to be extensively photographed. Pictures like the one of Confederate dead (above left) captured the horror of war for Americans at home.

> *"We heard all through the war that the army 'was eager to be led against the enemy.'. . . But when you came to hunt for this particular itch, it was always the next regiment that had it. The truth is, when bullets are whacking against tree-trunks and solid shot are cracking skulls like egg-shells, the consuming passion in the breast of the average man is to get out of the way. Between the physical fear of going forward and the moral fear of turning back, there is a predicament of exceptional awkwardness."*
>
> —David L. Thompson, 9th New York Volunteers

Lee decided to strike Pope before McClellan joined him. Leaving a small force at Richmond, Lee and Jackson hurried north. On August 29 and 30 the two forces clashed at Manassas Junction, the site of the Battle of Bull Run a year before. The outcome of the Second Battle of Bull Run was the same as the first—a Confederate victory.

Antietam—A Turning Point

Still on the offensive, Lee invaded western Maryland early in September 1862. His immediate goal was to persuade Maryland to join the Confederacy. He also hoped a successful invasion would encourage European nations to recognize the Confederacy. It might also cause northerners to support antiwar candidates in the upcoming congressional elections.

Lee sent Jackson with part of the army to capture the Union arsenal at Harpers Ferry. With his remaining 50,000 troops, Lee took up a defensive position at Antietam (an-TEE-tahm) Creek near Sharpsburg.

On September 17 McClellan attacked—once, twice, and a third time. With each blow the Confederate line reeled and then held, strengthened finally by troops returning from Harpers Ferry. A Union soldier remembered:

> *"The air was full of the hiss of bullets and the hurtle of grapeshot. The mental strain was so great that . . . the whole landscape for an instant turned slightly red."*

Social History

The battle on September 17, 1862 was called Antietam in the North and Sharpsburg in the South. The casualties numbered four times the total suffered by American troops at Normandy during World War II. More than twice as many Americans lost their lives in one day as fell in combat in the War of 1812, the Mexican War, and the Spanish-American War *combined.*

Limited English Proficiency

Making Campaign Maps. The Union forces usually named battles after geographic features. The Confederates, however, named battles after the nearest town. Thus, the Battle of Bull Run became for the Confederates the Battle of Manassas, and the battle of Antietam, the Battle of Sharpsburg.

In small groups, have students make campaign maps for each of the battles studied in this section. Have half the groups make them for the Confederacy, half for the Union, using the correct names.

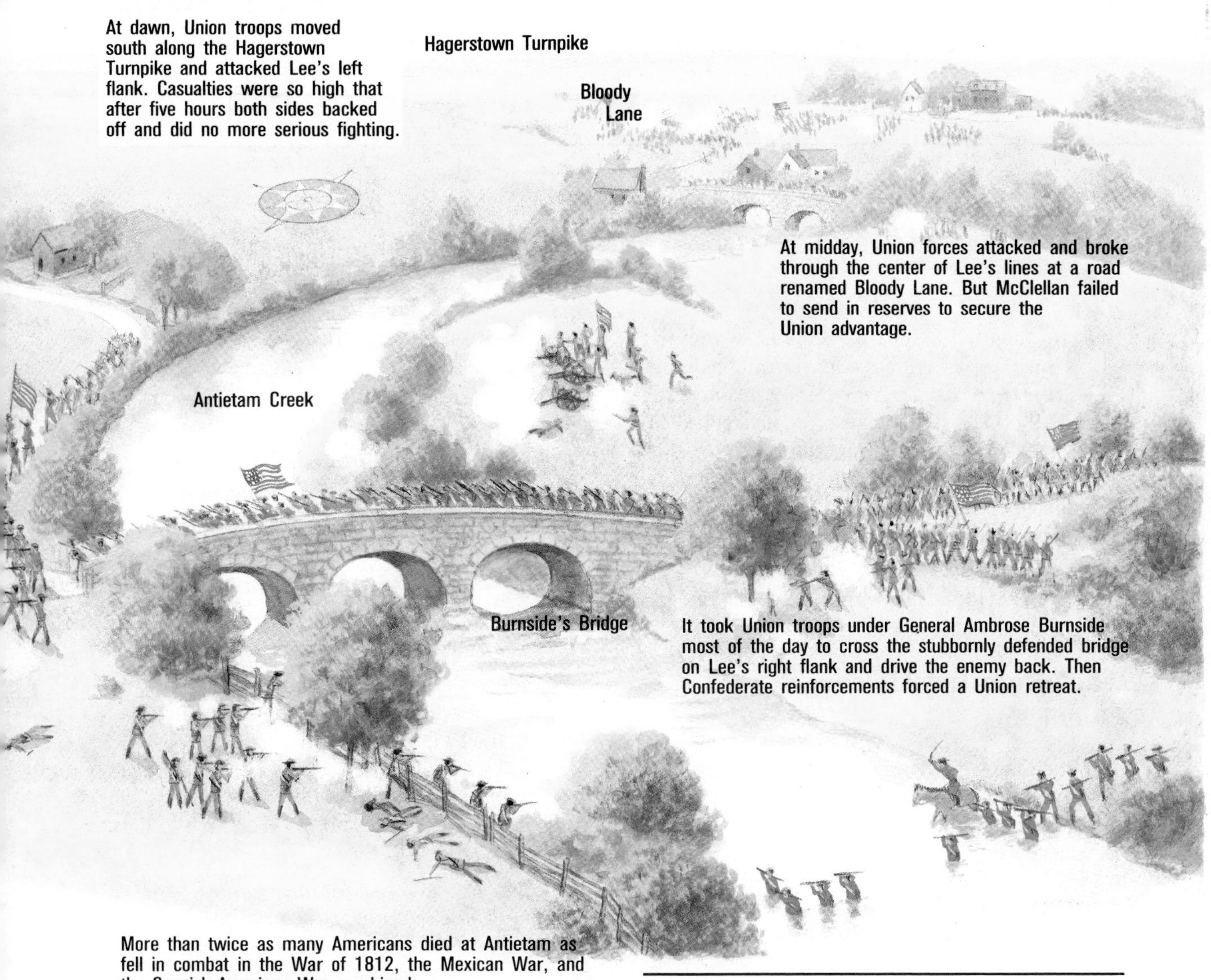
At dawn, Union troops moved south along the Hagerstown Turnpike and attacked Lee's left flank. Casualties were so high that after five hours both sides backed off and did no more serious fighting.
Hagerstown Turnpike
Bloody Lane
At midday, Union forces attacked and broke through the center of Lee's lines at a road renamed Bloody Lane. But McClellan failed to send in reserves to secure the Union advantage.
Antietam Creek
Burnside's Bridge
It took Union troops under General Ambrose Burnside most of the day to cross the stubbornly defended bridge on Lee's right flank and drive the enemy back. Then Confederate reinforcements forced a Union retreat.

More than twice as many Americans died at Antietam as fell in combat in the War of 1812, the Mexican War, and the Spanish-American War combined.

The toll of that long, bitter day's battle was more than 17,000 wounded and almost 6,000 dead. Nearly a third of the Confederates who had marched into Maryland were casualties. Antietam was the bloodiest day of the war. When McClellan did not attack the next day, Lee led his battered troops back to Virginia. McClellan's almost equally battered soldiers did not pursue them.

The Battle of Antietam was not decisive, but it was a turning point in the war. The battle shattered the Confederate invasion of the North. It forestalled European recognition of the Confederacy. And it set the stage for Lincoln to issue the Emancipation Proclamation.

Section Review

1. Comprehension. What was the South's strategy for winning the war?

2. Analysis. How do you think the outcome of the First Battle of Bull Run might have affected McClellan's campaign in Virginia?

3. Synthesis. How might the course of the war have been changed if the South had won a decisive victory at the Battle of Antietam?

Data Search. Use the map on page 311 to answer the following questions. What was the approximate distance between the Union and Confederate capitals? How did this distance affect the strategies of the Union and the Confederacy? Give at least one example.

Section Review

ANSWERS

1. Fight a defensive war.
2. It might have made McClellan overly cautious (as he turned out to be), unwilling to risk another defeat like Bull Run.
3. South might have invaded other parts of North such as Washington D.C., Maryland might have joined Confederacy. Britain or France might have recognized Confederacy, increasing pressure for peace.
Data Search: The two capitals are about 100 miles apart. Each side tried to take or threaten the security of the other's capital, as at the first Battle of Bull Run.

Section 12-3

Objectives

- ***Answer the Focus Question.***
- *Discuss the Emancipation Proclamation as a success and as a failure.*
- *Explain how industrialization helped lead to the North's victory.*

Introducing
THE SECTION

African Americans played an active role in the Civil War, overcoming white resistance to fight bravely, skillfully, and in increasing numbers as the war progressed. A popular camp song expressed the attitude of many black soldiers:

> *"So, rally, boys, rally, let us*
> *never mind the past;*
> *We had a hard road to travel,*
> *but our day is coming fast,*
> *For God is for the right, and*
> *we have no need to fear,*
> *The Union must be saved by*
> *the colored volunteer."*

Ask: What obstacles would black soldiers have to face?

B · A · C · K · G · R · O · U · N · D

Multicultural Perspectives

In August 1863 Lincoln wrote to Grant that enlisting African-American soldiers *"works doubly, weakening the enemy and strengthening us."* In December 1863 he declared *"it is difficult to say they are not as good soldiers as any."* In August 1864 he said, *"Abandon all the posts now garrisoned by black men, take 15,000 [black] men from our side and put them in the battlefield or cornfield against us, and we would be compelled to abandon the war in three weeks."*

Reduced student page in the Teacher's Edition

12-3 Societies at War

Focus: How did the Civil War affect Americans on both sides?

On August 19, 1862, abolitionist editor Horace Greeley criticized President Lincoln in the *New York Tribune* for not freeing "the slaves of the Rebels." Lincoln promptly replied to Greeley's editorial. "My paramount object in this struggle *is* to save the Union," he wrote, "and is *not* either to save or destroy slavery." Soon, however, pressure from blacks, abolitionists, generals, and Congress convinced Lincoln that abolishing slavery was essential to preserving the Union.

What Role for African Americans?

From the moment the war began, abolitionists and certain military commanders had called for allowing African Americans to enlist as soldiers. In fact, free blacks had been flocking to recruiting centers. In Cleveland, Ohio, blacks had organized a military corps, declaring they were ready to do battle "as in times of '76 and the days of 1812." G. P. Miller, a black doctor in Michigan, wrote to the Secretary of War, offering to raise

> *"five to ten thousand free men to report in sixty days to take any position that may be assigned us (sharp shooters preferred). . . . If this proposition is not accepted, we will if armed & equipped by the government fight as guerrillas."*

Such offers were turned down because Lincoln feared the reaction in the slave states that had stayed in the Union.

Frederick Douglass was outraged. "Colored men were good enough to fight under Washington," he thundered, "but they are not good enough to fight

The 107th U.S. Colored Infantry saw action in the Carolinas. Desperate for soldiers, the Confederacy decided to use black troops just as the war was ending.

Linking Past and Present

Juneteenth, a holiday now widely celebrated in African-American communities, commemorates June 19, 1865, when Union troops arrived in Galveston, Texas, to enforce the proclamation enacted two and one half years earlier. Legend states that slave owners fleeing to east Texas to avoid emancipation did everything in their power to keep word of the proclamation from their slaves, including murdering messengers. According to history professor James Todd, "It's a celebration not just of freedom, but of word-of-mouth communication. It's a reminder to be wary of official channels like: It's Juneteenth, brother—Time to be mindful."

under McClellan." As the war went on, African Americans—by their actions as well as their words—stepped up the pressure for both abolition and military service for blacks.

For example, as Union forces invaded the South, enslaved blacks began to escape to Union camps. Most commanders returned them to their owners. But General Benjamin F. Butler, in command of Fortress Monroe in Virginia, took a different approach. In May 1861 he declared that escaped slaves were "contraband of war" because they had built fortifications and hauled supplies for Confederate armies. Instead of returning the slaves, Butler gave them work and paid them wages. Ultimately, nearly 200,000 escaped slaves were working for the Union as carpenters, cooks, scouts, and teamsters.

Some military commanders, like Generals John C. Frémont and David Hunter, tried to free all slaves in the areas under their control. Abolitionists were furious when Lincoln revoked their orders. Freeing the slaves, they argued, would deprive the South of a labor force that was vital to its war effort. Congressman George W. Julian of Indiana told the House of Representatives:

> *"[The 4 million enslaved African Americans] cannot be neutral. As laborers, if not as soldiers, they will be the allies of the rebels, or of the Union. . . . Suppression of the rebellion will be an empty mockery . . . if slavery shall be spared to canker [eat at] the heart of the nation anew."*

In March 1862 Congress adopted General Butler's contraband policy, forbidding the army to return escaped slaves. Later that spring and summer, Congress also abolished slavery in the District of Columbia and in all of the territories and gave the President the power to enroll African Americans in the army.

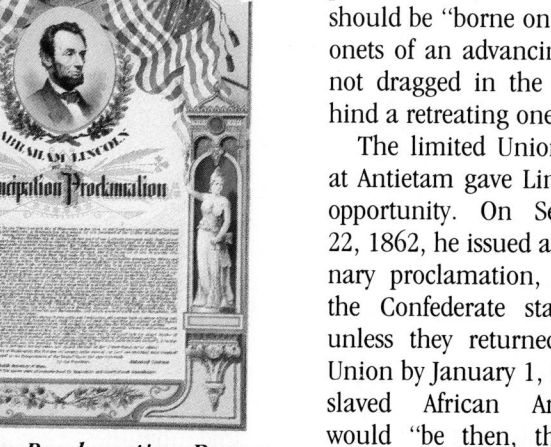

Emancipation Proclamation Banner

The Emancipation Proclamation

As the war dragged on, Lincoln became convinced that emancipation was "a military necessity, absolutely essential to the preservation of the Union." In July 1862 he presented a plan for emancipation to his cabinet. Secretary of State William Seward urged him to wait until the North had won a battle. The proclamation, Seward said, should be "borne on the bayonets of an advancing army, not dragged in the dust behind a retreating one."

The limited Union victory at Antietam gave Lincoln his opportunity. On September 22, 1862, he issued a preliminary proclamation, warning the Confederate states that unless they returned to the Union by January 1, their enslaved African Americans would "be then, thenceforward, and forever free."

The Confederate states ignored the warning. On New Year's Day, Lincoln issued the Emancipation Proclamation. It stated that all slaves in states in rebellion were from that moment "forever free." Lincoln believed that he had no constitutional power to abolish slavery in loyal areas—the slave states still in the Union and Confederate areas occupied now by Union armies. Thus, the proclamation did not result in any slaves being set free immediately.

However, Lincoln saw the Emancipation Proclamation as an "act of justice" as well as a military necessity, and it was a giant step toward abolishing all slavery. As Lincoln signed the proclamation he said, "If my name ever goes into history, it will be for this act, and my whole soul is in it."

Not everyone in the North was as pleased as Lincoln. Racial prejudice was widespread, and by no means had all northern soldiers gone to war to free the slaves. Nevertheless, throughout the North, the feeling was growing that the Union cause was now more noble. The war had become a fight for human freedom as well as for national unity.

Developing
THE SECTION

Thinking Critically

Analysis. The Emancipation Proclamation had several purposes. Discuss these purposes. Have students comment on Lincoln's timing in issuing the proclamation. **Ask:** Why did Lincoln issue the proclamation at that particular time? (consider the Battle of Antietam) What were the results? (Students should consider its effects on members of Congress, abolitionists, northern blacks, the Confederacy, and foreign nations; also the Union cause and Union morale.)

Limited English Proficiency

Discussion. Have students view a videotape of the 1989 film *Glory*, about the 54th Massachusetts Infantry. As students view the videotape have them consider what obstacles the black soldiers had to overcome to participate in the war. Ask them to note how they overcame these obstacles.

Tell students that a monument was built commemorating the 54th Massachusetts and its white officers. An inscription on the monument reads: *"Together they gave to the nation and the world the undying proof that Americans of African descent possess the pride, courage, and devotion of the patriot soldier."*

Multicultural Perspectives

In the summer of 1862 Union General Benjamin Butler questioned 1,400 freed African Americans in New Orleans about their willingness to fight. One answered: *"General, we came from a fighting race. Our fathers were brought here because they were captured in war, and in hand to hand fights, too. We are willing to fight."* Butler formed the First Louisiana Native Guards, which was the first regiment of black soldiers officially recognized by the Union army.

Reduced student page in the Teacher's Edition

Fighting for Freedom

The Emancipation Proclamation opened the way for free African Americans to enlist in the Union armies. Some blacks were already soldiers in the 1st South Carolina Volunteers, the Native Guards of Louisiana and the Kansas Colored Volunteer Regiment—all formed by commanders without government permission. But with the proclamation, enlistment soared, especially in Union-occupied areas. Some 80 percent of the black troops were former slaves or free blacks from the South.

By the end of the war, about 186,000 blacks had fought in the Union armies and 30,000 in the navy. Black troops saw action in 450 engagements, 39 of them major battles. And sixteen black soldiers and four black sailors received the Congressional Medal of Honor for bravery.

Despite their proven bravery and willingness to serve, blacks suffered discrimination, especially in the army. They were confined to all-black regiments and assigned more than their share of building bridges, fortifications, and trenches.

In addition, black troops were paid as laborers, not as soldiers, and all received the same amount, regardless of rank. The 54th Massachusetts Infantry, which became famous for its courageous assault on Fort Wagner in South Carolina, refused to accept unequal pay. Corporal James Henry Gooding asked in a letter to President Lincoln: "The main question is, are we soldiers, or are we laborers? We have done a soldier's duty. Why can't we have a soldier's pay?" Finally, in 1864 Congress granted retroactive equal pay for all black soldiers.

The Civil War has been called "a war of self-emancipation" for African Americans. Corporal Thomas Long of the 1st South Carolina Regiment pointed out how blacks had, by their own efforts, won the right to be accepted as equals:

> *"If we hadn't become soldiers, all might have gone back as it was before; our freedom might have slipped through the two houses of Congress, and President Lincoln's four years might have passed by and nothing been done for us. But now things can never go back, because we have showed our energy and our courage."*

Known as the "Angel of the Battlefield," nurse Clara Barton also formed a bureau to search for missing soldiers.

Patriotism on the Home Front

"Before the War," Ralph Waldo Emerson wrote, "our patriotism was a fire-work thing . . . for holidays and summer evenings. . . . Now the deaths of thousands and the determination of millions of men and women show that it is real."

Women on both sides played a vital role in the war. They took over family farms and businesses while the men were away. Others took jobs in manufacturing and, for the first time, in government agencies. Still others formed organizations to aid sick and wounded soldiers and their families.

Northern women in the United States Sanitary Commission raised millions of dollars to train nurses, to supply hospitals, and to transport the wounded. Teacher Clara Barton started volunteer nursing groups. Reformer Dorothea Dix was appointed superintendent of nurses for Union forces.

In the South, where most of the fighting took place, women by the hundreds volunteered as nurses. Many used their homes as medical shelters. Defying prejudice against "refined ladies" working in military hospitals, Sally Louisa Tompkins set up one of the best small hospitals in Richmond.

Connections: Health

Because of the lack of medical knowledge at the time of the Civil War, wounded soldiers did not get the kind of medical treatment that in the twentieth century would be routine. Nearly one in every five wounded Confederate soldiers died of his wounds; so did nearly one in every six wounded Union soldiers. In the Korean War only one in every fifty American soldiers died of wounds; in the Vietnam War the proportion was one in four hundred. A soldier in the Civil War was eight times more likely to die of a wound and ten times more likely to die of disease than an American soldier in World War I.

Confederate spy Belle Boyd; Union doctor Mary Walker; Confederate nurse Anne Bell.

Nurses and doctors faced overwhelming problems. Hospitals lacked ways to treat water and sewage to prevent the spread of disease. Scientists had not yet discovered the importance of antiseptics in preventing infection. Twice as many soldiers died of disease as of combat wounds. Kate Cumming, a Confederate nurse, was appalled by what she saw:

> *“Nothing that I have ever heard or read had given me the faintest idea of the horrors witnessed here. . . . I sat up all night, bathing the men's wounds and giving them water. . . . We have to walk and . . . kneel in blood and water.”*

Black women and men, slave and free, often formed the core of nursing staffs in Confederate hospitals. Meanwhile, abolitionists Sojourner Truth and Harriet Tubman divided their time between nursing and scouting for the Union army.

Loretta Janet Valásquez, born in Cuba, enlisted in the Confederate army disguised as a man. After being found out twice, she became a spy. Another woman, "Franklin Thompson" of Michigan, served in the Union army. Elizabeth Bowser, a former slave, became a Union spy in Richmond. Rose O'Neal Greenhow headed a Confederate spy ring in Washington.

Economic Effects of War

The war affected the economies of the North and the South in different ways. The South suffered terribly. Invading Union armies destroyed crops and cut railroad lines, interfering with food shipments to cities and army camps.

The worst blow to the southern economy was the success of the Union blockade, which prevented the South from importing manufactured goods. Most Confederate industries lacked the capital and skilled workers to fill the needs of the army or civilians in a long war.

In contrast, the northern economy thrived on the demands of war. Nearly 5,000 miles of railroad track were laid. The sewing machine and the Blake-McKay machine for sewing shoes increased productivity. By 1863 industries were pouring out enough supplies to keep Union soldiers well clothed and armed.

The war also stimulated northern agriculture. Using machinery to fill the gap left when almost a million farmworkers joined the army, farmers were able to produce more grain than ever. One McCormick reaper could harvest as much as four to six farmworkers.

Active Learning

Cooperative Learning. In small groups, have students research one woman who helped the war effort. Students might consider Clara Barton, Dorothea Dix, Sally Louisa Tompkins, Kate Cumming, Sojourner Truth, Harriet Tubman, Elizabeth Bowser, Rose O'Neal Greenhow, Belle Boyd, and Mary Walker, (For additional Civil War figures, see the classified list of selected biographies in *Notable American Women: A Biographical Dictionary,* Volume III.)

Have groups present their findings in the form of interviews. One student in each group can be a news reporter, another the woman being interviewed.

Connections: Economics

Analysis. Ask students why they think the North "thrived on the demands of war." What businesses prosper during war? **(steel, for railroads and weapons for example)** What businesses suffered? **(non-essential items, and goods that use materials in scarce supply)** How do industries generally react to a labor shortage during wartime? **(seek new sources of labor, such as women)**

Limited English Proficiency

Building Vocabulary. Explain to students that in 1809 a *copperhead* meant a hostile person. In 1838 it meant a white person who lived with Native Americans. In the North, in 1862, it was the name for a northerner who sympathized with the South.

Writing About History

Letters to the Editor. Have students write letters to the editor of a northern newspaper either supporting or opposing the editorial attacking President Lincoln's suspension of the right of *habeus corpus*. The letter should use appropriate arguments discussed in the Exploring the Issues feature.

Active Learning

Debate. Supreme Court Justice Roger B. Taney (writer of the opinion in the Dred Scott case), acting as circuit judge, denied President Lincoln's right to suspend the right of *habeas corpus*. Taney claimed that only Congress could exercise that right. Lincoln refused to obey the ruling, citing his duty in time of crisis: *"Are all the laws but one to go unexecuted, and the government itself go to pieces, lest that one be violated?"*

Have students debate:

1. Was Lincoln right to suspend the right of habeas corpus?

2. Should the government be given more power in wartime than in time of peace?

B · A · C · K · G · R · O · U · N · D

Social History

Abraham Lincoln was born in 1809 in Kentucky. In 1832 he served briefly in the Black Hawk War against the Sauk and Fox Indians, but he never saw action. He said his biggest battle had been with the mosquitos. Although his military experience was slight, Lincoln took personal command of military strategy. He vowed *"not to shrink, not even to count the chances of [my] own life."*

Jefferson Davis was born in Kentucky in 1808 and served during the Mexican War as commander of the Mississippi Rifles. He had been a member of Congress and in the Cabinet. Davis accepted the presidency of the Confederacy because he felt it was his duty and vowed to *"redeem my pledge to the South by shedding every drop of blood in its cause."*

Reduced student page in the Teacher's Edition

Dissent on Both Sides

Opposition hampered both Jefferson Davis and Abraham Lincoln. Davis faced outspoken critics in the Confederate Congress and even lacked the full support of his cabinet. In addition, some state governments insisted strongly on states' rights. Their challenges to Davis's authority as President of the Confederacy weakened his power to conduct the war.

Jefferson Davis.

Lincoln, too, clashed with many of his advisors. Four of the seven members of his cabinet had been his rivals for the presidency, and most thought themselves better qualified to lead than Lincoln. Only later did many agree with Secretary of State Seward that Lincoln "is the best man among us."

Before the Emancipation Proclamation, Lincoln had faced opposition from abolitionists within his own party. After, he faced increasing opposition from an antiwar faction of the Democratic party, the Copperheads, who demanded a negotiated peace.

The draft. In both the North and the South nothing aroused wider opposition than conscription—or the draft—a system of selecting men for required military service. The Confederacy passed the first conscription law in American history in 1862. All white males between eighteen and thirty-five were liable for service for three years.

Loopholes, however, weakened the law. A draftee could escape service by paying $500 or hiring a substitute to serve for him. And slaveholders who owned at least twenty slaves were excused from the draft. Angry southerners protested that it was "a rich man's war but a poor man's fight."

In March 1863 the Union also resorted to a draft. There, too, a draftee could pay for a substitute or, for $300, be excused from service. Many northerners resented these provisions. Draft riots broke out in several cities, often combined with protests against emancipation. In New York City, mobs smashed African Americans' homes, lynched blacks caught on the streets, and burned down a black orphanage. At least 104 people died.

Despite resistance to the draft, the Union army filled its ranks. The Confederacy, however, grew more and more desperate for troops.

Exploring Issues

PRESIDENTIAL POWER

Lincoln in the Civil War

In 1863 several newspapers printed this bitter attack on President Lincoln:

> "*Q.*—*What is the meaning of 'law'?*
> *A.*—*The will of the President. . . .*
> *Q.*—*Have the people any rights?*
> *A.*—*None, except what the President gives.*
> *Q.*—*What is* habeas corpus*?*
> *A.*—*It is the power of the President to imprison whom he pleases.*"

The newspapers were calling Lincoln a dictator. Although most northerners would have disagreed, some—especially antiwar Democrats—believed that Lincoln was taking too much power into his own hands.

The Constitution gives Congress alone the power to declare war and to suspend the right of *habeas corpus* in cases of rebellion or invasion.When the Confederates attacked Fort Sumter in April 1861, Con-

Multicultural Perspectives

Native-born Americans and immigrants fought side-by-side in the war. Often the service of the immigrant marked his acceptance from alien to American citizen. Mike Scannell of Massachusetts, when called a "damned Yankee," was flattered. He replied to the rebel who called him such, *"Well, it is twenty years since I came to this country, and you are the first person who ever called me a Yankee."*

gress was not in session. Instead of waiting for Congress to meet, Lincoln declared an "insurrection" in the South, ordered a naval blockade, and called state militia into federal service. He also suspended *habeas corpus* in Maryland.

Lincoln pondered the issue of presidential power. The Constitution named the President "commander in chief of the army and navy." Thus, Lincoln believed, in wartime the President had the power to do whatever was necessary to save the nation.

By 1863 Lincoln had decided that the antiwar movement was hurting the war effort. He suspended *habeas corpus* for anyone who resisted the draft or was suspected of "affording aid to the rebels." The government also opened private mail and shut down newspapers.

During the presidential campaign in 1864, Lincoln's use of power became a major issue. "Crush the tyrant Lincoln before he crushes you," proclaimed one slogan. A newspaper asked, "By whom and when was Abraham Lincoln made dictator of this country?" Despite such protests, Lincoln was reelected and continued to use his "broader powers" during the war.

Senator John Sherman of Ohio may have best expressed the feelings of many northerners about the issue:

> *"I do not believe the President has the power to suspend . . .* habeas corpus, *because that power is expressly given to Congress, and to Congress alone; I do not believe the President has the power to increase the regular army, because that power is expressly given by the Constitution to Congress alone."*

Nevertheless, Sherman supported Lincoln's actions. "I believe the President did right," he said. "He did precisely what I would have done if I had been in his place—no more, no less; but I cannot here, in my place, as a senator, under oath, declare that what he did was legal."

1. How did Lincoln exceed the powers of the President in 1861? How did he justify his actions?
2. Do you think there are times when Presidents should be able to take action on their own, even if it is unconstitutional? Give reasons for your opinion.
3. Other Presidents have made important decisions without consulting Congress. What examples, if any, can you note?

Section Review

1. Comprehension. How did enslaved African Americans affect the movement for abolition of slavery in the North?

2. Analysis. In what way was the Emancipation Proclamation a failure? A success?

3. Application. How did industrialization help lead to the North's victory in the Civil War? Give at least one example.

Linking Past and Present. Gather information about conscription after the Civil War. When has the draft been used? How did Americans react? What system is in operation now?

Exploring Issues

ANSWERS

1. Suspended writ of *habeas corpus*, increased regular army, declared an "insurrection" in the South; suggested that as commander in chief he had power to do whatever was necessary to save nation.
2. Students might consider speed with which President can act alone in times of crisis.
3. Answers may include Johnson during the Vietnam War.

Section Review

ANSWERS

1. Enslaved Africans escaped to Union camps. Abolitionists argued that freeing slaves would deprive the South of its labor force.
2. It did not result in immediate freeing of slaves. However turned war into fight for human freedom and opened way for African Americans to serve in Army and Navy.
3. Helped make up for loss of manpower on home front. Machinery for sewing clothes and shoes turned out these supplies. Machinery helped farmers bring in crops and supply food.
Linking Past and Present: Students may cite draft in two World Wars without loopholes for the rich, and in Korean and Vietnam wars, with some deferrals for college students, these deferrals having some similarity to Civil War loopholes: those who could afford to go to college could escape the draft. Some protest during Korean War, much during Vietnam War. Today there is no draft; young men and women are persuaded and invited to enlist.

Section 12-4

Objectives

- ***Answer the Focus Question.***
- *Explain why the Battle of Gettysburg was a turning point in the war.*
- *Compare Grant's campaign against Lee to campaigns of other Union generals.*

Introducing

THE SECTION

Have students review events of the first two years of the war. Tell the class that 1863 marked the turning point of the war. **Ask:** Which side seemed to be winning? Why?

B · A · C · K · G · R · O · U · N · D

Social History

McClellan's reluctance to engage the enemy was one of Lincoln's greatest problems. Though a skilled organizer and drillmaster, McClellan was a perfectionist who seemed not to understand that an army is never entirely ready and that some risks must be run to win a war. Believing that the Union army was outnumbered , he was overcautious—Lincoln accused him of having the "slows."

Reduced student page in the Teacher's Edition

12-4 *Ending the War*

Focus: How did the Union finally defeat the Confederacy?

The year 1862 ended with forces in Virginia deadlocked and the Union advance on the Mississippi stalled. Many northerners gave up hope of success. The new year, however, was to see another crucial turning point in the war, with the Confederates suffering crushing defeats in both the East and the West. For Lincoln, 1863 was to be a year spent searching for a general who could lead the Union to victory.

The Confederacy Falters

After the Battle of Antietam, Lincoln had urged General McClellan to attack Lee's retreating army. The cautious general had refused, and Lincoln replaced him with General Ambrose E. Burnside. In December 1862 Burnside's attempt to take Richmond was soundly defeated by Lee at Fredericksburg. Lincoln promptly replaced Burnside with General Joseph Hooker.

Hooker was also stopped by Lee, this time at Chancellorsville, in May 1863. Lee's brilliant victory, with little more than half as many troops as the enemy, came at great cost to the Confederacy. More than 1,600 Confederate soldiers were killed, including Stonewall Jackson who was mistakenly shot by his own troops.

Gettysburg. Buoyed by these victories, Lee planned to invade the North. He and Jefferson Davis hoped that a successful invasion would draw Union troops away from Vicksburg, one of the last two Confederate strongholds on the Mississippi. A decisive victory might also force the Union to negotiate for peace.

In June 1863 Lee led 75,000 troops northward across Maryland and into Pennsylvania. The Army of the Potomac moved forward to challenge him with 90,000 troops led by yet another new commander, General George G. Meade. The armies met at Gettysburg on July 1, 1863.

The Union troops established a line along Cemetery Ridge, just outside the town. The Confederate army drew up opposite them on Seminary Ridge, about a mile to the west. For two days the Confederates attacked the enemy's flanks, but the Union line held firm.

On the third day, Lee staked everything on an attack on the center of the Union line. Led by General George E. Pickett, 15,000 Confederates charged across the open fields. A Union officer described the scene:

> *"More than half a mile their front extends; . . . rank pressing rank, and line supporting line. The red flags wave, their horsemen gallop up and down; the arms . . . gleam in the sun, a sloping forest of flashing steel. Right on they move, as with one soul, in perfect order, without impediment [barrier] of ditch, or wall or stream, over ridge and slope, through orchard and meadow, and cornfield, magnificent, grim, irresistible."*

Union cannons and rifles responded with a withering fire. In half an hour it was all over. Scarcely half the Confederates who had gone forward returned.

Meade, who had lost more than a fourth of his army in the battle, did not counterattack. Lee gathered the remnants of his army and retreated into Virginia. He had failed both to win a victory and to relieve Union pressure on Vicksburg. In despair, Lee offered his resignation to Jefferson Davis, who refused to accept it. Lee's army went on to other successes, but it would never again have the power that it had had in Pennsylvania.

Geography

A KEY TO OUR PAST

Relative Location: The Battle of Gettysburg

The success of the Union army at the Battle of Gettysburg can be used to illustrate one of the basic concepts in geography: **relative location,** the relationship of one place to other places. A place can be said to have a *favorable relative location* if it meets the purposes of the people in that location.

At Gettysburg, on July 1, 1863, the Union army established a line that curled around Culp's Hill and Cemetery Hill and extended 2 miles south along Cemetery Ridge to a hill called Little Round Top. This location was relatively favorable for the Union's purpose, which was to defend its position. For one thing, being on high ground, the troops had a clear view of the fields below. Second, troops could be shifted quickly from one point to another in order to reinforce positions under attack. Finally, Cemetery Ridge was topped by stone walls, to which the troops added to protect themselves from enemy fire.

The Confederates occupied Seminary Ridge, lying parallel to the Union front and about a mile to the west. Seminary Ridge offered some cover by trees, but it was a less favorable relative location for the Confederates' purpose, which was to attack.

One of Lee's commanders, James Longstreet, studied the relative location of the Union line and decided that it was too strong to attack. Lee disagreed. The next day, his troops tried to break through the Union line at both ends. They gained the fields below Little Round Top and a foothold on Culp's Hill. But Union reinforcements shifted from one spot to another and the line held firm.

Lee decided that the next attack must be on the center of the Union line. Longstreet argued against advancing almost a mile across open fields toward troops that were well dug in behind walls and well supported by artillery. But again Lee disregarded the Union's favorable relative location.

At about 3 P.M. on July 3, 15,000 Confederate troops under General George Pickett charged forward. Many were mowed down by Union artillery as they crossed the open fields. The survivors vainly tried to scramble up Cemetery Ridge in the face of withering fire from in front of them and on their flanks.

"Pickett's Charge," as this assault is called, ended in disaster. More than 7,000 Confederate soldiers were casualties. "It's all my fault," Lee said as he rode among the stunned survivors. "It is I who have lost this fight." In fact, the Union's favorable relative location had made a Lee victory unlikely from the beginning.

1. What is relative location?
2. Why was the Union army's location at the Battle of Gettysburg a relatively favorable one?
3. How did the Union army improve upon its favorable relative location?

Gettysburg

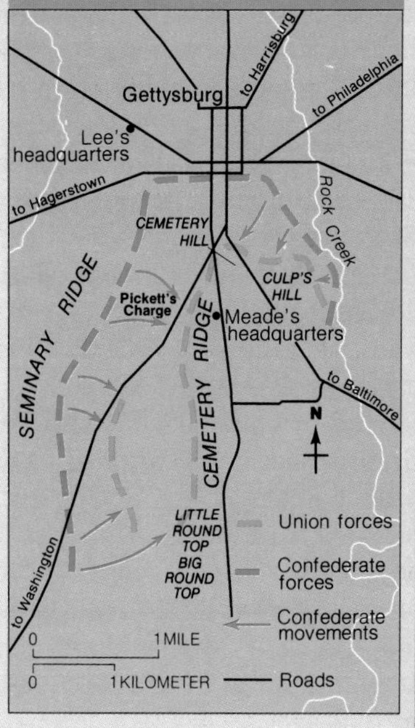

Developing THE SECTION

Connections: Geography

Discussion. Have students locate on the map the positions of the Union and Confederate forces at the Battle of Gettysburg. **Ask:** If Pickett's charge had succeeded, what effect might it have had on the Union forces? **(The Union forces would have been split; they might have retreated)**

Geography: A Key to Our Past

ANSWERS

1. **The relationship of one place to other places.**
2. **Union troops were positioned on high ground facing open fields.**
3. **Union army dug in behind stone walls.**

Analyzing Primary Sources

Gettysburg Address. Read to students the entire Gettysburg Address. **Ask:** What do you learn about Lincoln's viewpoint on government? What was his attitude toward the rights of states in relation to national government? **(Students may consider Lincoln's emphasis on maintaining a government subject to the will of the people as well as on maintaining the Union.)**

Linking Past and Present

Discussion. The Vicksburg campaign illustrates an important military principle—the use of combined forces. **Ask:** How did Grant use naval and land forces to subdue Vicksburg and almost every other city on the Mississippi? **(Naval forces maintained control of the river, overran enemy river forts, provided transportation and protection for troops being brought across river below Vicksburg. Land forces surrounded Vicksburg while gunboats bombarded it.)**

Combined military forces were also effective in later American wars, particularly in the Pacific campaign of World War II and the Persian Gulf War. Discuss how military technology has changed the relative importance of air, land, and sea military forces.

B · A · C · K · G · R · O · U · N · D

Multicultural Perspectives

Nearly 10,000 Hispanics fought in the Civil War. Some fought for the Union, others for the Confederacy. Cuban born Loretta Jane Velásquez, disguised as a man, joined the Confederate army in 1860. She fought in the battles of Bull Run, Ball's Bluff in Virginia, Fort Donelson in Kentucky, and at Shiloh.

Captain Frederico Fernández Cavada, another Cuban-born soldier, served as an engineer in the Union army. He also worked with hot-air balloons used to spy on Confederate

> *“We cannot dedicate—we cannot consecrate—we cannot hallow this ground. The brave men, living and dead, who struggled here have consecrated it far above our poor powers to add or detract. The world will little note nor long remember what we say here, but it can never forget what they did here. . . . It is rather for us to be here dedicated to the great task remaining before us—that from these honored dead we take increased devotion to the cause for which they gave the last full measure of devotion—that we here highly resolve that these dead shall not have died in vain—that this nation, under God, shall have a new birth of freedom—and that government of the people, by the people, for the people shall not perish from the earth.”*
>
> —from Abraham Lincoln's Gettysburg Address, given at the dedication of the Gettysburg National Cemetery, November 19, 1863

Vicksburg. While Lee's and Meade's forces battled at Gettysburg, Grant was finally subduing Vicksburg. Since mid-1862 he had been trying to capture the city, which was perched on cliffs above the Mississippi and partly surrounded by marshland. All attacks from the north had failed.

In March 1863 Grant tried a bold new plan. From Memphis he led 20,000 troops across the Mississippi and down its west bank to a point below Vicksburg. Union gunboats, which had slipped past Vicksburg's deadly cannons, ferried the troops to the east bank of the river. Grant's army drove eastward, defeating Confederate forces, then turned back west to attack Vicksburg.

After two attempts to storm the city had failed, Grant besieged, or encircled, it while Union gunboats bombarded it. For over six weeks Vicksburg held out. Civilians hid in caves for safety and ate dogs, cats, and mules for food. "We are utterly cut off from the world, surrounded by a circle of fire," one girl wrote in her diary. Finally, on July 4, 1863, the day after the battle at Gettysburg, the city surrendered.

The Battle of Gettysburg was fought at great human cost: 23,000 Union and 28,000 Confederate casualties.

Five days later, Port Hudson, the last Confederate stronghold on the Mississippi, gave up after a six-week siege. The Union now controlled the entire river, and the Confederacy was cut in two. Delighted, Lincoln declared, "Grant is my man and I am his for the rest of the war."

Although the war continued for almost two more years, the Union successes at Gettysburg and Vicksburg turned the tide toward Union victory.

Chattanooga. The third great Union victory in 1863 occurred at Chattanooga, a railroad center on the Tennessee River. In September a Union army under General William Rosecrans approached Chattanooga. Confederate forces under General Braxton Bragg evacuated the city and withdrew to Georgia. Rosecrans recklessly pursued them.

The two armies clashed near the stream of Chickamauga, an Indian name meaning "river of death." The Union forces reeled back to Chattanooga. The Confederates laid seige to the city.

A month later, Lincoln gave Grant command of all Union forces in the West—and the job of saving the starving Union army in Chattanooga. Grant assembled a mighty force and in late November swept down on the Confederates surrounding the city. After a two-day battle, the Confederates crumbled. With victory at Chattanooga, Union forces secured control of eastern Tennessee and prepared to move into Georgia.

troop movements. Cavada was captured at the Battle of Gettysburg and sent to Libby Prison in Richmond, Virginia. While there, he drew pictures on any paper he could find and wrote notes on margins of old newspapers and scraps of paper. After his release in 1864, Cavada wrote about the harsh conditions in the Confederate prison in a book called *Libby Life*.

Backyard History

Research. Have students research the status of their state during the Civil War. They can find out whether it was in the Union, the Confederacy, a border state, a territory, or not yet part of the United States. Have students share information about any of their ancestors who served in the war.

Geography Skills

ANSWERS

1. Vicksburg, Port Hudson, Murfreesboro, Chickamauga, and Chattanooga.
2. Answers may include rest of Pennsylvania, states north, east, and west of Pennsylvania, and Washington, D.C.

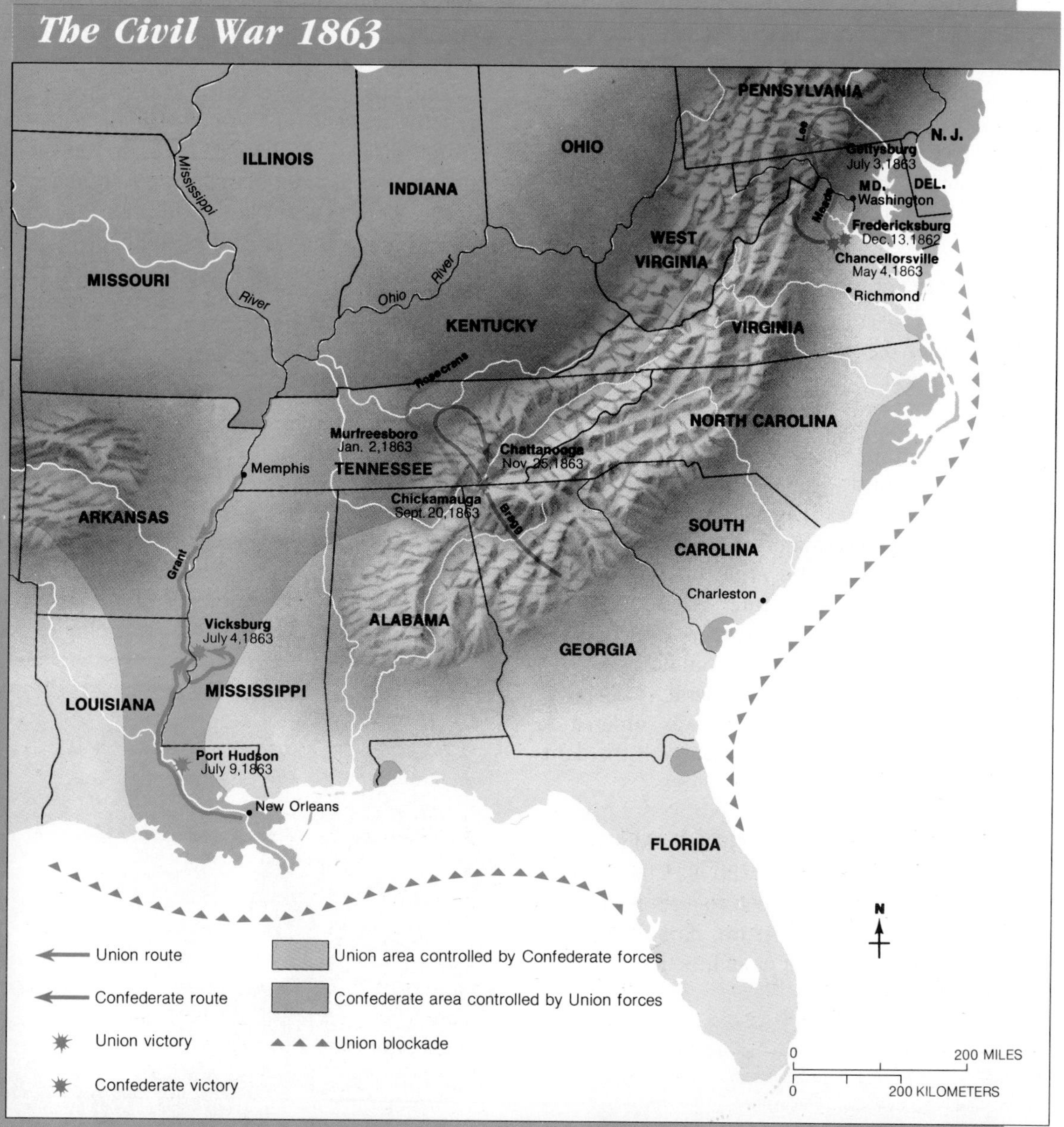

Map Skills—Location: Where did Union forces win victories to secure control of the entire Mississippi River valley? What areas might have been open to Confederate forces if they had not been stopped at the Battle of Gettysburg?

Sketch of the death of Union General John Reynolds near Gettysburg.

Thinking Critically

Analysis. Have students explain the concept of total warfare. **Ask:** How has total warfare made war more devastating? (Total warfare affects civilians. Cities as well as civilian homes, farms, animals, factories, and crops are destroyed.) Is there any way to wage war today and avoid total war? Have students cite arguments for and against total war. (Students might argue that it is immoral to destroy civilian property; or that the civilian enemy supports the military, therefore it is alright to attack civilian targets.)

Social History

Ulysses S. Grant graduated from West Point, fought in the Mexican-American War, and served in California and Oregon until resigning from the army in 1854. At the outbreak of the Civil War, he was commissioned colonel of the 21st Illinois Volunteer Infantry. Recalling his first assignment, an attack on a Confederate regiment, he wrote in his memoirs that he suddenly realized that the enemy *"had been as much afraid of me as I had been of him. This was a view of the question I had never taken before; but it was one I never forgot."* This was a lesson that many other Union commanders, such as McClellan, never learned.

Reduced student page in the Teacher's Edition

General Grant in Command

In March 1864 Lincoln changed generals for the last time, naming Grant supreme commander of Union forces. As early as the Battle of Shiloh, Grant had realized that the Confederates would not quickly collapse. As a result, he said, he "gave up all idea of saving the Union except by complete conquest." His strategy was simple:

> *"Find out where your enemy is. Get there as soon as you can. Strike at him as hard as you can and as often as you can, and keep moving on."*

Grant believed in total war—not just against armies, but against a people's resources and their will to resist.

Grant planned two major offensives at the same time. He would lead the Army of the Potomac against Lee's army and capture Richmond. Meanwhile, General William Tecumseh Sherman, in charge of all western armies, would destroy the Confederate forces under General Joseph E. Johnston in Georgia. Sherman was ordered to move into enemy country, "inflicting all the damage you can against their war resources."

Grant's pursuit of Lee. In early May, Grant invaded northern Virginia with 115,000 troops. They met Lee's army of 64,000 soldiers in the Wilderness, a dense forest. After two days of fighting, Grant's troops had heavier casualties than the Confederates. But Grant had told Lincoln that "whatever happens, there will be no turning back." Instead of retreating north, Grant turned south, toward Spotsylvania Court House.

There the armies clashed in five days of bloody trench warfare. Grant was once again battered but grimly pushed southward. In early June the two armies met at Cold Harbor, with similar results. Grant cut away again and headed for Petersburg, a key railroad center 20 miles south of Richmond. Lee moved to defend Petersburg, and Grant dug in to besiege the city. Lee would remain trapped at Petersburg for nine months.

Since the start of the Virginia campaign, there had been 65,000 Union casualties. Antiwar feeling soared in the North—and it was only four months before the presidential election. But Grant had inflicted a similar percentage of casualties on Lee and had him pinned down. Lincoln told northerners, "General Grant said, 'I am going through

The armies of Grant (left) and Lee burrowed in trenches at Petersburg, a tactic widely used in later wars.

The Civil War 1864–1865

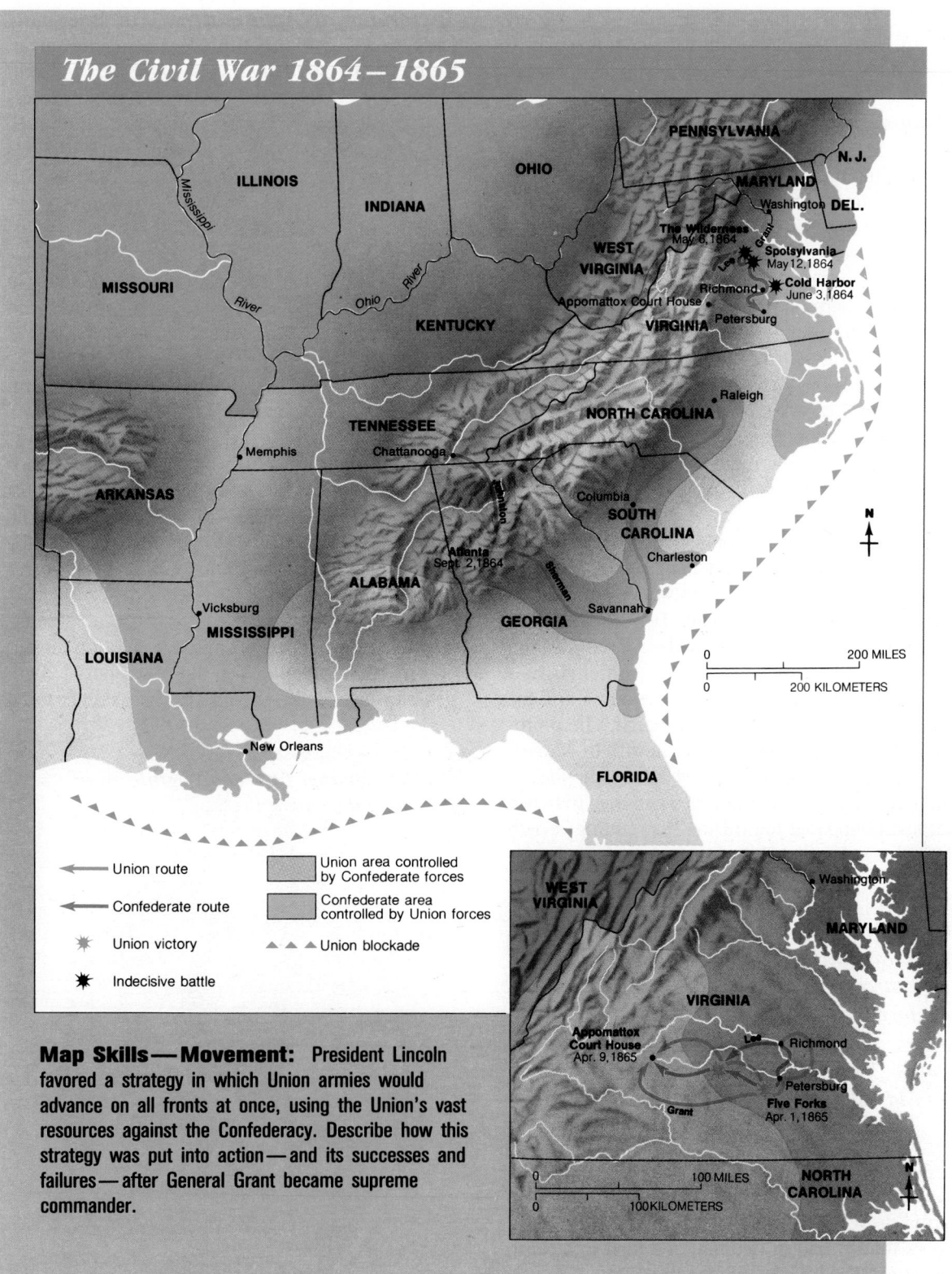

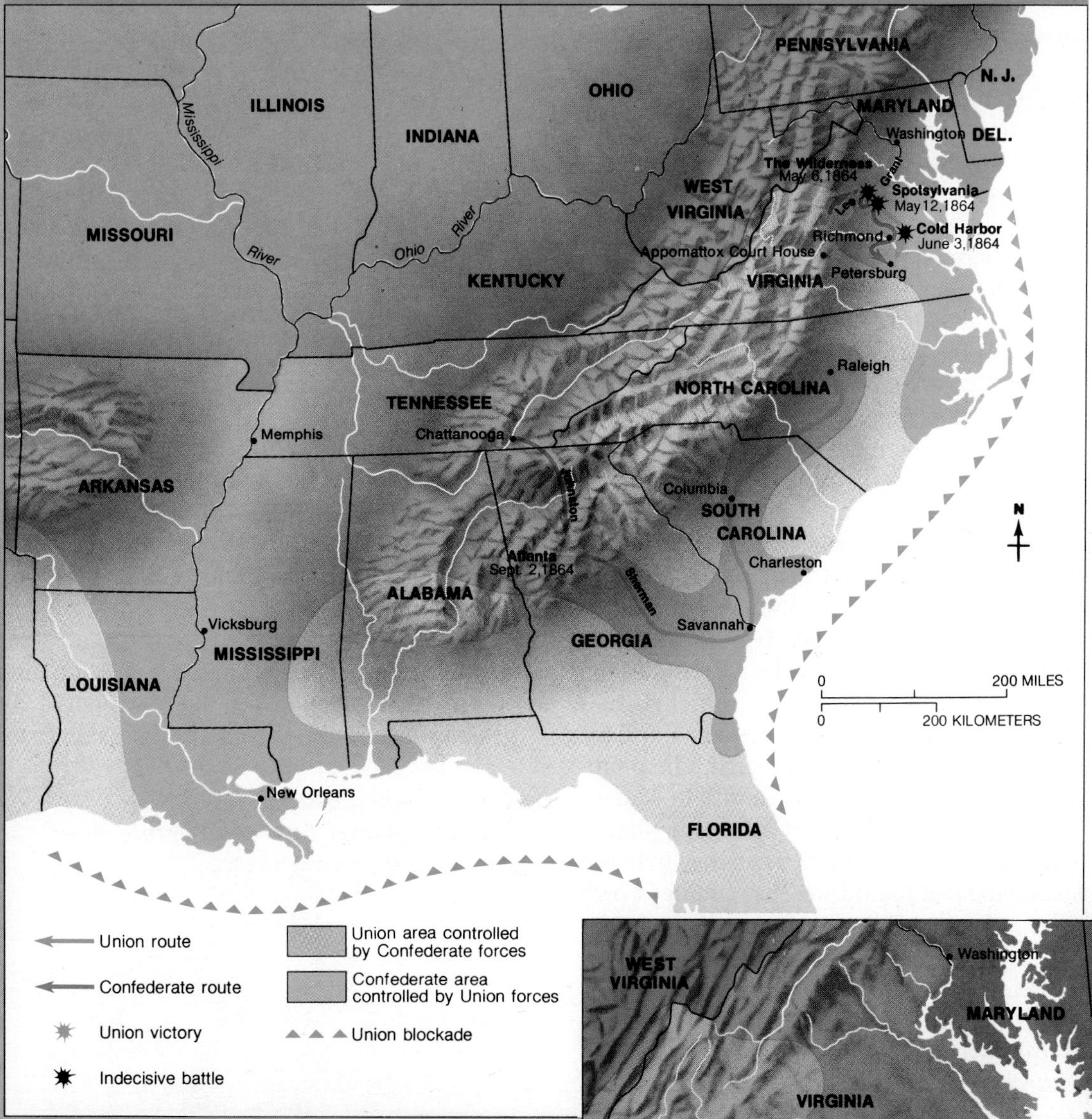

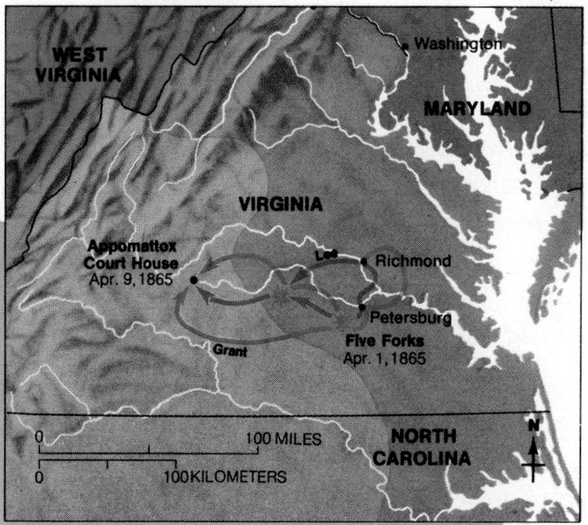

Map Skills—Movement: President Lincoln favored a strategy in which Union armies would advance on all fronts at once, using the Union's vast resources against the Confederacy. Describe how this strategy was put into action—and its successes and failures—after General Grant became supreme commander.

Geography Skills

ANSWERS

In one offensive, Grant moved south into Virginia against Lee, fighting but not winning Battles of the Wilderness, Spotsylvania, and Cold Harbor. He took Petersburg after a nine-month siege, then Richmond, and forced Lee to surrender at Appomattox Court House. Meanwhile, Sherman moved south into Georgia, took Atlanta, marched to the Atlantic coast and took Savannah, then moved north taking Carolinas and preparing to unite forces with Grant. Answers may also include ongoing Union blockade of Confederate coast.

Limited English Proficiency

Making a Chart. Work with the class to create a chart of the causes and effects of the Civil War. Discuss long-term causes, such as the issue of slavery; short-term causes, such as secession of southern states; short-term effects, such as devastation of South; and long-term effects, such as expansion of federal authority.

Connections: Health

The heavy fighting in 1864 filled prisoner-of-war camps to overflowing. The Andersonville camp in southwestern Georgia grew from 10,000 to 33,000 Union prisoners, many of them captives from Sherman's army and the fighting in Virginia. The Confederacy could barely feed and supply its own soldiers and citizens, let alone prisoners. During some weeks in the summer of 1864 more than 100 prisoners died every day in Andersonville due to disease, malnutrition, or exposure.

The Confederacy did not deliberately mistreat prisoners, but many northerners agreed with Secretary of War Edwin Stanton that *"there appears to have been a deliberate system of savage and barbarous treatment."* As Sherman's troops marched through Georgia they came upon several Anderson-

Reduced student page in the Teacher's Edition

on this line if it takes all summer.' . . . I say we are going through on this line if it takes three years more."

Campaign for Georgia. When Grant headed south, so did Sherman, with 98,000 troops against General Joseph Johnston's 65,000. The Confederates made the Union pay for every advance, but by mid-July Sherman was laying siege to Atlanta. Finally, the Confederates, now under General John B. Hood, abandoned the city, which Sherman occupied on September 2, 1864. Part of Sherman's forces followed Hood, later scattering his army.

American Voices

" We are going to be wiped off the face of the earth. . . . We have but two armies. And Sherman is between them now. "

—Mary Boykin Chesnut

The fall of Atlanta boosted Lincoln's reelection campaign. A war-weary public had been expected to elect the Democratic candidate, General George McClellan. But when the votes were counted, Lincoln and his running mate, Democrat Andrew Johnson of Tennessee, had won by a landslide.

Sherman now planned to march through central Georgia to destroy southern resources and the will to resist. "I can make the march," he promised Grant, "and make Georgia howl!" In November Sherman's troops destroyed all the supplies in Atlanta and set fire to the city. Then they marched almost unopposed toward the sea, cutting a path 60 miles wide. Eliza F. Andrews wrote of the results:

" There was hardly a fence left standing all the way from Sparta to Gordon. The fields were trampled down and the road was lined with carcasses of horses, hogs, and cattle that the invaders . . . had wantonly shot down. . . . Here and there, lone chimney stacks, 'Sherman's sentinels,' told of homes laid in ashes. "

Sherman reached the sea in December and crowned his campaign by taking Savannah. Then he set off north to join Grant. In early 1865 his army drove into South Carolina, destroying even more than it had in Georgia, and then into North Carolina. The two states fell to the Union.

Surrender at Appomattox. In Petersburg, Lee's troops could not hold out much longer. Grant's army was battering his defenses. In addition, raids by Union forces under General Philip H. Sheridan had destroyed Lee's food supplies in the Shenandoah Valley, and his troops were on scant rations.

When Grant's army broke through Confederate lines in early April, Lee escaped with 35,000 troops. On April 3 the Union army, headed by a black cavalry regiment, marched into Richmond.

Lee fled, with Grant in pursuit. But his escape route west was cut off by Sheridan's forces. Badly outnumbered and almost surrounded, Lee realized further fighting would be useless. On April 9, 1865, he met Grant at the village of Appomattox Court House to offer his surrender.

Grant wrote out generous terms. Lee's soldiers could go home if they promised to fight no longer, and all soldiers could keep their own horses. Both generals signed the document, then saluted each

War correspondent Thomas Morris Chester reported from the Virginia front for the Philadelphia Press.

ville escapees. They were shocked at their skeletal appearance and *"infuriated at the thought of them starving in the midst of plenty."* Henry Wirz, officer in charge at Andersonville, was the only person after the war to be tried and executed for war crimes.

other. The bloodiest war in the history of the nation, with more than 620,000 Union and Confederate dead, had ended.

Grant introduced Lee to his staff. To Grant's military secretary, Ely Parker, a Seneca Indian, Lee said, "I am glad to see one real American here." Parker replied, "We are all Americans."

At a ceremony three days later, Confederate troops marched up to stack their weapons and surrender their flags. In charge, General Joshua Chamberlain watched the Confederates come forward. As they approached the Union line, Chamberlain gave an order and a bugle rang out. Instantly his troops shifted to "carry arms," the salute of honor. Surprised, Confederate General John B. Gordon dipped his sword in salute and ordered his troops to carry arms, too.

Chamberlain was deeply moved. "On our part not a sound of trumpet more; nor roll of drum; not a cheer, nor word, nor whisper," he wrote. "Here pass the men of Antietam . . . and Cemetery Hill at Gettysburg; these survivors of the terrible Wilderness." As the lines passed by, he thought, "It is by miracles we have lived to see this day."

Section Review

1. **Comprehension.** Why was the Battle of Gettysburg a turning point in the war?

2. **Synthesis.** Why might civilians be in as much danger as soldiers in a total war?

3. **Analysis.** What made Grant's campaign against Lee different from those of other Union generals?

4. **Evaluation.** What do you think Confederate soldiers thought of Grant's terms of surrender? Why?

5. **Analysis.** What do you think Ely Parker meant when he said, "We are all Americans"?

Reelection cartoon: "Long Abraham Lincoln a Little Longer."

Connections to Themes

Shaping Democracy

The Civil War provided answers—written in blood—to long-standing issues in the United States. From the nation's earliest days, Americans had debated whether a state could secede from the Union. The Civil War resolved that question. The Union was permanent: sealed at the cost of enormous human suffering.

The war also determined that the nation could not, as Lincoln had warned, "endure permanently half slave and half free." The Emancipation Proclamation led to liberty for 4 million African Americans. Thus the Civil War is often called the "Second American Revolution."

But what of the future of the former slaves? In 1865 a black Union soldier recognized his former master among Confederate prisoners he was guarding. The soldier called out, "Hello massa; bottom rail on top this time!" How would the new relationship work out? Would white Americans, North and South, accept African Americans as equals?

Americans faced another critical issue in 1865. How could they restore a sense of national unity after four years of ferocious war? Lincoln hoped to reconstruct the nation in ways that would spare the defeated South undue hardship. In 1864 he had met with Grant and Sherman to discuss the terms of surrender. "Let 'em up easy," Lincoln instructed his two generals.

But radical elements in both the North and the South were yet to be heard from. Adjustment to the postwar nation would produce new struggles for the South and especially for freed African Americans.

Active Learning

Cooperative Activity. Have the class brainstorm a list describing the "state of the Union" at the end of the war. (Consider the physical damage in the South, and military occupation, the fate of free blacks, reintegration of veterans into civilian society, need to establish loyal southern governments, and so on.)

Have students form small groups to discuss plans for recovery after the war. Each group should consider one of the items from the class list they created, suggest solutions for the problems, and present their plan for Reconstruction to the class.

Section Review

ANSWERS

1. **Lee failed to win a victory and to relieve pressure on Vicksburg. He also suffered such heavy losses that his army was never again so powerful.**
2. **Total war is waged on civilians as well as soldiers. Their property might be totally destroyed. Note Eliza Andrews's words on page 326.**
3. **Grant refused to retreat despite defeats and heavy casualties.**
4. **They might have thought the terms surprisingly generous considering the bitterness of the war and the casualties suffered by northern forces.**
5. **Answers may include that they were all citizens of the same country.**

Chapter Survey

ANSWERS

Using New Vocabulary

In times of extreme *civil unrest, military authority* replaces *civilian government* to preserve *law and order.* This practice is called *martial law.*

Reviewing the Chapter

1. Had more than half of South's people, food crops, factories; home of many of best military officers; rivers, railroads provided strategic links to West. Virginia, Arkansas, Tennessee, North Carolina became Confederate; Maryland, Missouri, Kentucky, Delaware stayed in the Union.
2. (a) North had 22 million people, South had 9 million, 3.5 of these enslaved. (b) South had advantage in fighting defensive war because had shorter supply lines. (c) North had four fifths of nation's factories, more natural resources, and more miles of rail track. (d) North had small navy, bought and equipped merchant ships to enforce blockade. South started war with no navy. (e) North raised more money from taxes and import duties, and suffered less from inflation.
3. South planned to defend its territory, making war so costly that North would give up. North sought to blockade South to cut off supplies, control Mississippi River, capture Richmond, and crush Confederates.
4. Union took Fort Henry on Tennessee River, Fort Donelson on Cumberland River, defeated Confederates at Shiloh; navy captured New Orleans, Baton Rouge in 1862. Union gained complete control of Mississippi when Vicksburg fell to Grant on July 4, 1863 and Port Hudson surrendered on July 9.
5. (a) Blocked advance of Union troops toward Richmond. (b) Prevented reinforcements from reaching McClellan. (c) Pushed McClellan back to banks of James River.
6. Battle stopped Confederate invasion of North, kept European nations from recognizing Confederacy, gave Lincoln opportunity to issue Emancipation Proclamation.
7. Slaves in Confederate states forever free; slaves in Union states or in Confederate areas occupied by Union armies not freed. Mixed reception in North: because of racism, some did not want to fight for emancipation; most felt fighting for freedom ennobled the war. South ignored the proclamation.
8. North: abolition, resistance to draft, antiwar movement of Copperheads. South: states' rights, resistance to draft and high taxes.
9. South no longer invaded North, Union in control of Mississippi; pushed on to capture Chattanooga, then able to

Reduced student page in the Teacher's Edition

Chapter Survey

Using New Vocabulary

From the list below, select the four words or phrases whose meanings relate to the underlined vocabulary term. Explain how they are related. Example: The meaning of the term *legal right* is related to the vocabulary term *habeas corpus* because habeas corpus is the legal right to appear in court and be charged with a crime before imprisonment.

<u>Martial Law</u>

(a) military authority
(b) blockade
(c) law and order
(d) greenbacks
(e) civilian government
(f) civil unrest

Reviewing the Chapter

1. Why were the states of the Upper South of value to both the Union and the Confederacy? Which of these states joined the Confederacy? Which stayed with the Union?

2. Compare the North and the South in the Civil War in terms of the following resources. (a) population (b) supply lines (c) industry (d) sea power (e) finances

3. Compare the military strategy of the South with that of the North.

4. How did the Union army gain control of the Mississippi River?

5. Explain how each of the following military actions helped Confederate forces to hold Richmond. (a) the Battle of Seven Pines (b) Stonewall Jackson's raids in the Shenandoah Valley (c) the Seven Days' Battles

6. What were the effects of the Battle of Antietam?

7. State the provisions of the Emancipation Proclamation. How was it received in the North? In the South?

8. During the Civil War, what issues brought about conflict in the North? In the South?

9. How did the course of the war change after the Battles of Gettysburg and Vicksburg?

Thinking Critically

1. Application. General Sherman's march through Georgia represented what is called a "scorched earth policy." What do you think this means? Use examples from the chapter to explain your answer.

2. Synthesis. What might have happened if Great Britain had come to the aid of the South in the Civil War? Describe what you think the effects and the possible outcome of the war might have been.

3. Synthesis. Why do you think General Grant's terms of surrender at Appomattox were so generous? If you had been in his place, what terms would you have offered? Why?

History and You

Opposition to the draft flared in this country in the 1860s and again in the 1960s during the Vietnam War. Compare the provisions for exemption in the Union and Confederate draft laws with those in the Selective Service Act in effect in the 1960s. How could young men avoid service? Why did people protest in each case? What role did race play in the draft systems and in the protests?

Using a Time Line

Match each date on the time line with the correct battle or battles in the list below. Write your answers in chronological order and explain the importance of the event.

(A) Chancellorsville
(B) Second Battle of Bull Run
(C) Chattanooga
(D) Atlanta
(E) Fredericksburg
(F) Chickamauga
(G) Shiloh

Apr 1862 | Aug 1862 | Dec 1862 | May 1863 | Sept 1863 | Nov 1863 | Sept 1864

concentrate on Georgia and Richmond.

Thinking Critically

1. Destroy everything useful to the enemy; cite Atlanta, march through Georgia.

2. Confederacy might have won with British aid. Country would have split with South becoming client state to British.
3. Grant's terms were generous because he and Lincoln wanted to reunite the nation quickly.

History and You

During Civil War men could avoid draft by paying money or hiring a substitute. During Vietnam War, students could receive college deferment until graduation.

Anti-draft riots in Civil War took place in New York and other cities. Draft cards burned in opposition to Vietnam War.

Former slaves and free African Americans volunteered for Union army. During Vietnam War African Americans drafted in numbers higher than their percentage of population.

Using a Time Line

(G) Shiloh, Apr 1862. (B) Second Battle of Bull Run, Aug 1862. (E) Fredricksburg, Dec 1862. (A) Chancellorsville, May 1863. (F) Chickamauga, Sept 1863. (C) Chattanooga,Nov 1863. (D) Atlanta, Sept 1864.

Applying Thinking Skills

1. Agree: South could not manufacture or import enough war materials. The North could lose more men and still have larger army. Disagree: Southern cause had popular support. South had many of the best military officers. South required fewer troops and did not have to maintain long supply lines.
2. Students should recognize that both North and South suffered from lack of unity. Davis faced opposition in congress and his cabinet, and from some states; Lincoln faced opposition in his cabinet, and from abolitionists and Copperheads. The draft created widespread opposition in both the North and South.
3. Students will probably agree that Lincoln turned out to have greater abilities as a war leader than Davis. Students should recognize that the South had abler military commanders in the first year or two of the war, but that the North acquired military commanders, such as Grant, with the determination necessary to win the war.
4. Students should recognize that the results of several critical battles—Antietam in 1862, Gettysburg, Vicksburg, and Chattanooga in 1863, and the capture of Atlanta in 1864—could easily have been different.
5. Answers will vary.

Applying Thinking Skills

Analyzing Cause and Effect

What was the major cause of the defeat of the Confederacy? Historians have debated that question for years. Study the list of causes below. Then use the questions that follow and information from the chapter to help you analyze cause and effect with respect to the outcome of the Civil War.

Cause 1: The South faced overwhelming odds.

Cause 2: The South was greatly weakened by internal divisions, or lack of unity.

Cause 3: The South suffered from weak civilian and military leadership.

Cause 4: The South was defeated primarily by events on the battlefield.

1. Some historians disagree with the first cause. They argue that other peoples have won independence against great odds, for example, the American Patriots of 1776. Give reasons for agreeing or disagreeing with the view that the South could not win the war because it faced overwhelming odds.
2. Compare internal divisions in the North and the South. Do you think lack of unity was an important cause of the South's defeat? Why or why not?
3. Some historians think that the North's military and civilian leaders were superior to those in the South. Do you agree? Give reasons for your answer.
4. Do you think that events on the battlefield played the most important role in the outcome of the war? Explain your answer.
5. Which of the four causes above do you think were most important to the defeat of the South? The least important? What other causes, if any, would you add? Why?

Writing About Issues

The Issue: *Should Civil War battlefields be protected?*

Today many famous Civil War battlefields are in danger of being swallowed up by urban growth. According to Edwin Bearss, chief historian of the National Park Service, some of the nation's greatest urban development is occurring around Gettysburg, Petersburg, and Appomattox. Urban growth also threatens other Civil War sites, from Cypress Hills National Cemetery in New York to Byram's Ford Historic District in Missouri.

The first military parks in the United States were established in the 1880s at Gettysburg, Shiloh, Vicksburg, and Chickamauga/Chattanooga. The parks were located near Civil War cemeteries to honor the dead and to preserve open land for military training exercises, a practice still in effect today.

In 1902 Congress began to create "ribbon parks"—strips of battlefields preserved along highways. The battlefield beyond a strip remained farm land. Bearss explains, "The idea worked fine for that era. Nobody then could envision what was coming in terms of population expansion."

Today many Americans, including historical preservationists, farmers, and the army, are rallying to "Save our Civil War battlefields." Environmental groups consider these sites to be vital open land. Some people want to preserve the battlefields out of a sense of racial or cultural pride. A move is underway to save four sites where African Americans and/or Native Americans played a significant role: Blakely Battlefield in Alabama, Port Hudson in Louisiana, New Market Heights in Virginia, and Honey Springs in Oklahoma.

Should Civil War battlefields be protected? Take a position on this issue. Then make notes of your main arguments, which you will present in a two-minute speech to the class. Make notes of opponents' arguments so that you can reply to them in a one-minute rebuttal.

Chapter 13

The Struggle Over the South's Future

Planning Guide

	Student Text	TWE Lesson Plans	Support Materials
SECTION 1	**Section 13-1** (1-2 Days) **Rebuilding the Union,** pp 332-335 Point of View: A Civil Rights Debate, pp 336-337 Review/Evaluation Section Review, p 335	**Introducing the Chapter:** Reconstructing the Union—Cooperative Activity, 30 minutes, p 329B **Teaching the Main Ideas:** From Slavery to Freedom—Cooperative Activity, one class period, p 329B	★ **Read to Remember,** Section 1 ● **Section Activities,** Section 1 Δ **Readings,** C. Forten, Mississippi Black Codes ● **Tests and Quizzes,** Section 1 Quiz
SECTION 2	**Section 13-2** (1-2 Days) **The South Under Reconstruction,** pp 338-342 Review/Evaluation Section Review, p 342	**Evaluating Progress:** Goals and Results—Individual Activity, one class period, p 329C **Reinforcement Activity:** Equality: Some Then None—Individual Activity, homework, p 329C	★ **Read to Remember,** Section 2 ● **Section Activities,** Section 2 Δ **Enrichment Activities,** Section 2 ● **Geography Activities,** Section 2 Δ **Readings,** J.L. Hunnicutt ● **Tests and Quizzes,** Section 2 Quiz
SECTION 3	**Section 13-3** (1-2 Days) **The "New South,"** pp 343-347 Connections to Themes: Shaping Democracy, p 347 Review/Evaluation Section Review, p 347 Chapter 13 Survey, pp 348-349 Unit 4 Survey, pp 350-351 Skills, pp 348-349 Using New Vocabulary Thinking Critically Using a Time Line Applying Social Studies Skills: Using Maps and Graphs Applying Thinking Skills: Recognizing Point of View	**Teaching the Main Ideas:** Citizenship and Suffrage—Cooperative Activity, one and a half class periods, p 329C **Reinforcement Activity:** Equality: Some Then None—Individual Activity, homework, p 329C **Enrichment Activity:** Views of Change—Individual Activity, homework, p 329C	★ **Read to Remember,** Section 3 ● **Section Activities,** Section 3 Δ **Enrichment Activities,** Section 3 Δ **Readings,** *Plessy* v. *Ferguson* ● **Tests and Quizzes,** Section 3 Quiz, Chapter 13 Test (Forms A and B), Unit 4 Test (Forms A and B) **Additional Resources** ● **Active Learning** Δ **GTV Videodiscs** Δ **Transparencies and Activity Book** ● **Testing Software** ★ **Chapter Summaries** **Key:** ★ **For Extra Support** ● **For All Students** Δ **For Enrichment**

Overview

With the end of the Civil War, Americans faced the issues of how to restore the Confederate states to the Union and whether the President or Congress would direct Reconstruction. President Andrew Johnson planned a quick reconciliation and had no commitment to equal rights for freedmen. Dissatisfied with this plan and events in the South, Congress opposed the President, impeached him, and gained control of Reconstruction.

Congress put the Confederate states under military rule. In order to be readmitted to the Union, the states established new state governments that guaranteed African-American suffrage and ratified the Fourteenth Amendment. Opposition to Congress's efforts to bring about political and social change erupted. Violence against African Americans and their supporters broke out on a larger and larger scale, strengthening northern weariness with Reconstruction. By 1877 white southerners had regained control of their state governments.

Reconstruction did not provide African Americans with genuine equal rights and opportunities. Most freedmen were forced to become sharecroppers, living forever in debt. After Reconstruction southern states disenfranchised black voters and created systems of rigid segregation. Terrorism and violence were widespread. In reaction, black leader Booker T. Washington advised temporary acceptance of discrimination and concentration on economic goals. In contrast, W.E.B. Du Bois advocated political action to promote political and social equality.

Activity Objectives

After completing the activities, students should be able to

- identify problems that the freedmen faced.
- trace events that affected citizenship and suffrage for African Americans between 1787 and 1869.
- compare conditions of African Americans during and after Reconstruction.
- describe Congress's goals for Reconstruction and results.
- analyze views of how to effect political and social change for African Americans.

Introducing the Chapter

Reconstructing the Union

This cooperative activity requires one class period.

In this activity students, in the course of planning Reconstruction, experience the nature of the problem facing Americans.

Before class write on the chalkboard the following questions:

- How would the Confederate states be restored to the Union?
- How would the economic life of the South—its agriculture, industry, and labor system—be rebuilt?
- What would be the new relationship between black and white southerners?

Begin the activity by having students describe the problems that faced Confederate states at the end of the Civil War. Then have students speculate about how the states could be restored to the Union and who could decide, the President or Congress. Point out that the President controls the armed forces and has the power to pardon. However, Congress has the right to admit new states, make rules for territories, and judge the qualifications of its own members.

Divide the class into groups of four and call attention to the three questions on the chalkboard. Direct groups to spend 20 minutes creating a plan for Reconstruction based on these questions.

At the end of the time, have volunteers read their plans, and write recommendations on the chalkboard. Take a class vote to determine which plan might have the best chance of success and discuss reasons why. Challenge students to be prepared, after reading Sections 13–1 and 13–2, to compare this plan with actual Reconstruction policy.

Teaching the Main Ideas

Section 13–1: From Slavery to Freedom

This cooperative activity requires one class period.

In Section 13–1 students learn about the problems that the freedmen faced at the end of the Civil War. The following activity will enable students to identify ways that government could help the freedmen.

Begin the activity by asking students to describe the situation of the freedmen at the end of the Civil War. Have students consider problems that the formerly enslaved people might face, such as lack of money, property, education, jobs, food, and medical care. Point out that Congress established the Freedmen's Bureau in 1865 in order to provide "provisions, clothing, and fuel" to relieve "destitute and suffering refugees and freedmen and their wives and children."

Divide the class into groups of three or four. Have the groups imagine that they are state officials of the Freedmen's Bureau who are responsible for providing services to help the freedmen in their transition from slavery to freedom. Groups are to write a description of the services that they think are most needed and then create a directory listing the services. If students are unfamiliar with service directories, you may wish to show them local or state government examples in the telephone book.

Display the completed directories. Have the class view the directories and identify the services that were most often included. Conclude by evaluating the merits of those services as well as the services less frequently included.

Teaching the Main Ideas

Section 13–3: Citizenship and Suffrage

This class activity requires one class period.

With the Thirteenth, Fourteenth, and Fifteenth Amendments, Congress hoped to make African Americans a part of "We the People." In this activity students will prepare time lines showing events in the eighteenth and nineteenth centuries that affected citizenship and suffrage for African Americans.

Begin the activity by telling students that up until Reconstruction the states had the power to decide who could be a citizen, and most states—both northern and southern—denied citizenship to African Americans. The Fourteenth Amendment took that power away from the states and also specifically requires the states to respect citizens' rights. Thus, it has often been called the "second Bill of Rights."

Ask students to prepare a time line of events between 1787 and 1869 that affected citizenship and suffrage for African Americans.The time lines are to include the following events: Three-Fifths Compromise, Missouri Compromise, Dred Scott Decision, Thirteenth Amendment, Fourteenth Amendment, and Fifteenth Amendment. Students are to give a date for each event and briefly describe how it affected African-American citizenship or suffrage.

When students have finished their time lines, review their work by having them work together to draw a class time line on the chalkboard. Discuss the time line by asking:

- *In what way could African Americans consider the Reconstruction amendments a failure?* (Although the Constitution now banned slavery and promised equal treatment, it could not automatically ensure the latter. The struggle for citizenship and voting rights had only begun.)
- *Historian George Brown Tindall called the Thirteenth, Fourteenth, and Fifteenth amendments "an enduring legacy" of Reconstruction. What do you think he meant?* (The amendments were "not dead but dormant, waiting to be warmed back into life." They would be used in the twentieth century, especially in the African-American civil rights movement in the 1950s and 1960s, to ensure equal rights.)

Reinforcement Activity

Sections 13–2 and 13–3: Equality: Some Then None

This individual activity may be assigned as homework and shared in class the following day.

The following activity, in which students draw cartoon strips, reinforces understanding of the events that shattered African-American dreams of living in a society based on the ideals of equal rights and opportunities for all.

Before class write the following events on the chalkboard: *Thirteenth Amendment, Freedmen's Bureau, Reconstruction Act, return to "white man's rule," and passage of Jim Crow laws.* Have students describe the impact of each event on formerly enslaved African Americans.

Direct students to create cartoon strips that show the responses of African Americans to one or more of the five events. Emphasize that cartoon strips are used not only to entertain but also to comment about events or states of affairs. Each strip includes a series of panels, with characters' words printed in "balloons." To stimulate creativity, you may want to point out examples of comic strips with political messages in current newspapers and magazines. Discuss the use of symbols, satire, and titles.

Direct students to display their completed cartoon strips. Have the class view the cartoon strips and comment on how accurately or inaccurately they think the cartoonists reflected events and the views of African Americans. Conclude by hypothesizing about the emotions African Americans might have felt during and after Reconstruction.

Evaluating Progress

Sections 13–2 and 13–3: Goals and Results

This individual activity requires most of a class period, or it can be assigned as homework.

In this activity students use an organizational pattern called a *Big T* to draw conclusions about the results of Reconstruction.

Have students create a large *T* by drawing a vertical line down the center of a piece of paper and a horizontal line across the top. Have them label the left side *Goals of Reconstruction* and the right side *Conditions After Reconstruction.* Tell students they are to use the Big T to identify Congress's Reconstruction goals and the situation in the southern states after Reconstruction. They may use their texts to review Sections 13–2 and 13–3 and should list as much information as possible. To illustrate, suggest that under *Goals of Reconstruction* they might write *black male suffrage,* and under *Conditions After Reconstruction* they could write *poll taxes deny vote to blacks.*

Review projects by having students identify events that they think had the most important effect on Reconstruction and its aftermath. Ask them to speculate about the effect of white racism in the United States on acceptance of African Americans as equals. Conclude by discussing whether Reconstruction ever had a real chance of success.

Criteria for evaluating students' work should include accuracy of information and clearly expressed links between entries. Topics that students should use in their Big Ts include: equality, suffrage, new state governments, return to "white man's rule," the election of 1876, and efforts to reverse Reconstruction.

Enrichment Activity

Section 13–3: Views of Change

This individual activity may be assigned as homework and shared in class the following day.

In this activity students reflect on Chapter 13 by analyzing different approaches to bringing about change.

Begin the activity by having students describe the conditions of growing discrimination and violence that African Americans faced after Reconstruction. Ask them to speculate about how they would try to deal with such conditions and bring about change.

Have students imagine that it is 1903 and they have decided to take a stand against discrimination and segregation. Direct them to write short position papers on the following topic: *Are Booker T. Washington's tactics or W.E.B. Du Bois's tactics the most effective way to end discrimination and segregation?*

On the chalkboard write the format for their papers as follows:

- State the question.
- Summarize the arguments of Booker T. Washington and W.E.B. Du Bois.
- Discuss ways in which you agree or disagree with both arguments.
- State your personal answer to the question, providing supporting arguments and evidence.

Ask volunteers to read their position papers and have the class evaluate the arguments presented. Point out that in spite of Washington's cautious position, he worked behind the scenes against disenfranchisement and other forms of discrimination. Conclude by discussing which tactics or combination of tactics might have been most effective at that time and why.

Evaluate student papers on aptness and specificity of examples. Expect the following points to be included in satisfactory papers: Washington advocated hard work and self-help to improve African Americans' place in society; he tried not to alienate white Americans. Du Bois took a more radical position, demanding an immediate end to discrimination and segregation; he called for protest in order to force the government to act.

Bibliography and Audiovisual Material

Teacher Bibliography

Du Bois, W.E.B. *Black Reconstruction in America, 1860–1880.* New York: Atheneum, 1969.

Foner, Eric. *Reconstruction: America's Unfinished Revolution, 1863–1877.* New York: Harper and Row, 1988.

Franklin, John Hope. *Reconstruction After the Civil War.* Chicago: University of Chicago Press, 1962.

Litwack, Leon F. *Been in the Storm So Long: The Aftermath of Slavery.* New York: Random House, 1980.

Woodward, C. Vann. *Reunion and Reaction: The Compromise of 1877 and the End of Reconstruction.* New York: Oxford University Press, 1991.

Student Bibliography

Chopin, Kate. *The Awakening and Selected Stories.* New York: Penguin, 1984.

Douglass, Frederick. *My Bondage & My Freedom.* Champaign: University of Illinois Press, 1988.

Stampp, Kenneth M. *The Era of Reconstruction, 1865–1877.* New York: Random House, 1967.

Sterling, Dorothy, ed. *The Trouble They Seen: Black People Tell the Story of Reconstruction.* Garden City, NY: Doubleday, 1976.

Films, Videocassettes, and Videodiscs

Civil War Series: Postwar Period. 20 min. Coronet/MTI. Movie.

Industrialization: The Progressive Era: Reform Works in America. 23 min. Britannica. Videocassette.

Rebuilding the American Nation (1865–1890). 23 min. Guidance Associates. Videocassette.

Reconstructing The South. 30 min. PBS Video. Movie.

Filmstrips

America Divided: The Civil War and Reconstruction: Reconstruction. 60 min. EBEC.

The Civil War: A Nation Restored. National Geographic Society.

Computer Software

The U.S. History Package—U.S. History, Growth of a Nation: Modern Times. Apple. Focus Media.

13

Objectives

- Describe the conflict between Andrew Johnson and Congress over plans for Reconstruction.
- Explain how Reconstruction changed the South.
- Cite how African Americans were affected by the end of Reconstruction.

Introducing THE CHAPTER

For suggestions on introducing Chapter 13, refer to page 329B in the Teacher's Edition.

Developing THE CHAPTER

For activities and teaching strategies to help you reinforce and enrich chapter content, see pages 329B–329D in the Teacher's Edition.

Chapter Opener Illustrations

Photographers were on hand at the end of the Civil War to record the devastation in the South, such as the burned-out buildings of Charleston below. Fire swept the city in 1861 and Union artillery pounded it from 1863 on.

With the ruins of Richmond in the background, a group of former slaves pose alongside a canal.

Succeeding to the presidency after Lincoln's assassination, Andrew Johnson favored a policy toward the defeated South of punishing only the Confederacy's leaders. His views clashed with those of congressional Republicans seeking harsher measures.

William E. B. Du Bois, born shortly after the Civil War in a small Massachusetts town, emerged as an outspoken

Reduced student page in the Teacher's Edition

Chapter 13 1865-1905

The Struggle Over the South's Future

leader of African Americans in the 1890s. He asked African Americans to fight discrimination and prejudice and demand their political rights.

Northerners who moved to the South after the war were often called carpetbaggers because of the cloth suitcases they carried. The name suggested that they had come to grab what they could in a short time and then go home.

American Voices

The year 1865 saw the Thirteenth Amendment become part of the Constitution, thereby legally ending slavery in the United States. That year former slaves held conventions across the South to discuss their future as a free people. From the Charleston convention came this plea to the white people of South Carolina.

> *"Thus we would address you—not as Rebels and enemies, but as friends and fellow countrymen, who desire to dwell among you in peace, and whose destinies are interwoven and linked with those of the whole American people. . . . We ask for no special privileges, or peculiar favors. . . . We simply ask that we shall be recognized as men; that there be no obstructions placed in our way; that the same laws which govern white men shall govern black men. . . .*
>
> *We trust the day is not too distant when . . . we shall realize the great truth that 'all men are endowed by their Creator with certain inalienable rights' and that although complexions may differ, a 'man's a man for [all] that.'"*

The end of the war brought with it the task of binding the Union together again and rebuilding the devastated South. The nation also faced the question of whether it could heal the wounds of war and at the same time move closer to its ideals of liberty, equality, and justice.

Charleston, South Carolina, 1865; Richmond, Virginia, 1865; President Andrew Johnson; civil rights leader W. E. B. Du Bois; carpetbag.

Analyzing Primary Sources

American Voices

This speech comes from the "Address of the State Convention to the White Inhabitants of South Carolina." **Ask:** What rights are the former slaves asking for? **(equality, respect, economic opportunity)** What point does the speaker make to reassure whites? **("We ask for no special privileges, or peculiar favors . . . ")** How might a southern white respond to this plea? What American document does the speaker quote from in this speech? **(Declaration of Independence)**

If a group of African Americans were to speak before Congress today, what issues might they address? **(Some possible answers include equality, non-discrimination, protection from crime, job training, affirmative action, better schools, affordable housing.)**

Section 13-1

Objectives

- ***Answer the Focus Question.***
- *Describe the response of African Americans to the ending of slavery.*
- *Explain how southerners and northerners responded to Johnson's Reconstruction plan.*
- *Cite provisions of the Fourteenth Amendment.*
- *Compare Congress's Reconstruction plan and the President's.*
- *Identify reasons for Johnson's impeachment.*

Introducing

THE SECTION

Discuss with students the problems faced by Lincoln and Johnson after the war, such as loss of lives, destruction of property, freed slaves, lack of money, opposition of Confederate leaders. Refer students to Lincoln's second inaugural address and ask them to explain what type of peace, lenient or harsh, is implied. **(generous, "With malice toward none, with charity for all. . . . ")**

State the following proposition: A lenient peace plan is better than a harsh one. **Ask:** What is the evidence for and against the proposition?

B · A · C · K · G · R · O · U · N · D

Time Line Illustrations

1. A reward poster for the apprehension of John Wilkes Booth, Lincoln's assassin.

2. Johnson's impeachment drew large crowds. Visitors had to show tickets of admittance to the Senate gallery.

3. When given the vote, African Americans eagerly participated in the electoral process. Here they are depicted in an 1867 election in Washington, D.C., not only voting but serving as polling judges.

4. A Rutherford B. Hayes campaign medal.

Reduced student page in the Teacher's Edition

CHAPTER TIME LINE

1865-1905

1865 Apr Abraham Lincoln assassinated
Dec Thirteenth Amendment ratified

1868 Feb–May Andrew Johnson impeached and acquitted
Jul Fourteenth Amendment ratified

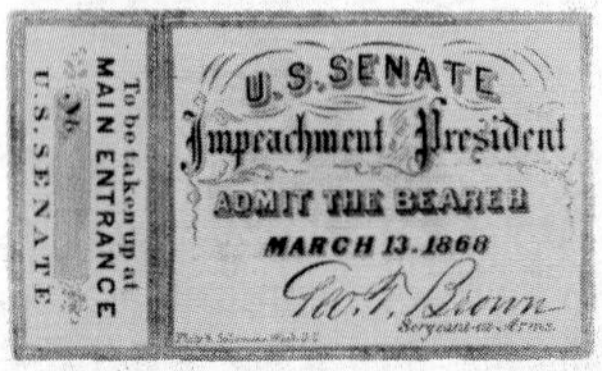

1865 · 1870 · 1875

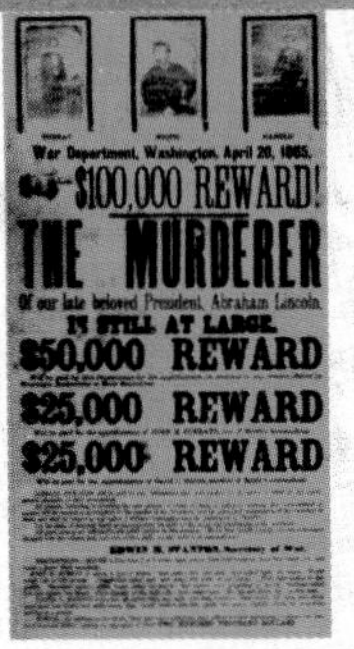

1867 Reconstruction Act passed

1870 Fifteenth Amendment ratified

1877 Reconstruction ends after Hayes' inauguration

13-1 *Rebuilding the Union*

Focus: How did the nation move toward reunion after the Civil War?

The national nightmare of secession and civil war had taken a terrible toll. Over half a million soldiers died: about 360,000 Union and 258,000 Confederate. Thousands more were wounded. The tragedy weighed heavily on Abraham Lincoln as he gave his second inaugural address in March 1865. He ended by calling for a generous peace:

> *"With malice toward none, with charity for all, with firmness in the right as God gives us to see the right, let us strive on to finish the work we are in, to bind up the nation's wounds . . . to do all which may achieve . . . a just and lasting peace."*

The nation was never to know how Lincoln planned to bring about such a peace. Six weeks after his inauguration and five days after the Confederate surrender at Appomattox, the President was fatally shot while attending a play at Ford's Theater. His assassin, John Wilkes Booth, thought he could save the Confederacy by murdering Union leaders. Booth escaped after the assassination, but he was tracked to a barn in rural Virginia where he was killed, shot either by himself or his pursuers.

Lincoln's death rocked the nation. "Never before that startled April morning," wrote poet James Russell Lowell, did so many "shed tears for the death of one they had never seen, as if with him a friendly presence had been taken away from their lives, leaving them colder and dark."

5. A cotton plant, the South's primary crop.
6. Booker T. Washington was born into slavery in Franklin County, Virginia in April 1856.
7. A cartoon showing "Jim Crow" in action. An African American is ordered off the "white" section of a train. The Court's ruling in *Plessy* v. *Ferguson* declared such laws constitutional.

Connections: Literature
Poet Walt Whitman wrote, *"Of all the days of the war, there are two . . . I can never forget, . . . the day of that first Bull Run defeat, and the day of Abraham Lincoln's death."* This excerpt is from Whitman's poem "When Lilacs Last in the Dooryard Bloomed," an elegy for Lincoln.

1880s First "Jim Crow" segregation laws

1881 Booker T. Washington founds Tuskegee Institute

1905 W. E. B. Du Bois and other African-American leaders launch the Niagara Movement

1880 — 1890 — 1905

1890 Poll tax used to exclude black voters in the South

1896 *Plessy* v. *Ferguson*

The Defeated South

The responsibility for restoring the defeated South to the Union passed to Vice-President Andrew Johnson. A southerner who had remained loyal to the Union, Johnson blamed the war on a "slavocracy" of wealthy planters who should be "punished and impoverished."

After taking office, President Johnson sent Supreme Court Chief Justice Salmon P. Chase on a tour through the South. Accompanying Chase was a reporter named Whitelaw Reid. As the travelers moved south, vast scenes of desolation confronted them. Wherever the great armies had marched and fought, towns had been leveled and farms turned into wasteland. Industrial and farm buildings, crops, livestock, and miles of railroad had been laid waste.

Equally devastating to white southerners was the fact that their entire social order had been swept away. Planters were in a state of shock. Without slaves, many did not know how they could go on. A Georgia planter told Reid, "I never learned a trade. . . . There's nothing else that I know anything about, except managing a plantation."

The Freedmen

Formerly enslaved people, now called **freedmen** (a term that applied to both men and women), welcomed the end of the old social order. Many thousands took to the road to search for loved ones sold away from them during slavery, or simply to experience their new freedom to travel. Most, however, remained on the plantations, where they had homes and could farm the land as free laborers.

When Whitelaw Reid talked with whites about the freedmen, he was told that "the poor, shiftless creatures will never be able to support themselves." A visit to the Sea Islands of South Carolina convinced him that this was not true. The Sea Islands had been captured by Union forces early in the war. When the planters fled to the mainland, their plantations were turned over to freedmen to farm.

By 1865 the Sea Island farmers had built a bank, churches, and schools. Teachers there told Reid that they saw no difference "in the facility [ease] with which these students and ordinary white children . . . learn to read." Reid left certain that "the question about [former] slaves being self-supporting is a question no longer."

Developing
THE SECTION

Social History

Discussion. There was no federal agency to help returning soldiers. Various bureaus of the army and navy simply shut down after April 1865, and more than three quarters of a million volunteers found their own way home. Have students speculate about the problems they might have encountered on their return.

Analyzing Primary Sources

Letter. This excerpt is from a letter written by Jourdon Anderson to a former master who had asked Anderson to work for him:

"And we have concluded to test your sincerity by asking you to send us our wages for the time we served you. This will make us forget and forgive old scores . . . I served you faithfully for thirty-two years and Mandy twenty years. At $25 a month for me, and $2 a week for Mandy our earnings would amount to $11,680 . . . please send the money by Adams Express."

Ask: To what "old scores" might the letter be referring? Do you think the writer really expected to be paid? If not, what message is he communicating to the former master? (The letter from which this excerpt was taken appears on page 51 of *Readings in Literature and Primary Sources* in the Teacher's Resource Package.)

Connections: Politics

The Radical Republicans were led by two strong-willed lawmakers—Thaddeus Stevens of Pennsylvania and Charles Sumner of Massachusetts. Stevens, a member of the House of Representatives, had long supported equal rights for African Americans. He argued *"There can be no state rights against human rights."*

Senator Charles Sumner insisted that African Americans be given full rights as citizens. *"I am for Negro suffrage in every rebel state. If it be just, it should not be denied; if it be necessary, it should be adopted; if it be a punishment to traitors, they deserve it."*

Active Learning

Making Commercials. Today, many public issues are fought out on television. Ask students to assume television existed in President Johnson's day. Have them work in groups to plan television commercials supporting either Johnson or Congress in the struggle over Reconstruction. The commercials can include graphics (such as a poster), slogans, and skits.

Issues students should consider: Who should control Reconstruction, the President or Congress? What rights did people freed from slavery possess? Was Johnson being too easy on the South? Was Congress being too hard?

Linking Past and Present

Discussion and Research. The Senate, on April 9, 1866, overrode the President's veto of the Civil Rights Act. It was the first override of a presidential veto. **Ask:** Why did Congress override the veto? **(to protect freedmen's rights)** What was the larger issue involved? **(control of Reconstruction.)**

Have students research to find out if there have been any overrides of presidential vetoes during the past two administrations. What issues were involved and what was the outcome?

Reduced student page in the Teacher's Edition

In Savannah, Georgia, freedmen pressed Chief Justice Chase to support giving black men the right to vote. When Chase voiced his fear that black voters might be deceived by white politicians, one of the freedmen replied:

> *"We always knows who's our friends and who isn't. . . . Because, sir, some of our people stand behind these men at the table, and hear 'em talk. . . . We know 'em from skin to core."*

President Johnson's Plan

In May 1865 President Johnson announced his plan for **Reconstruction**—the restoration of the Confederate states into the Union. Under Johnson's plan, a state could rejoin the nation once it had written a new state constitution, elected a new government, repealed its act of secession, agreed not to repay Confederate war debts, and ratified the Thirteenth Amendment.

A vocal group of congressional Republicans, called "Radicals," pressed the President to require the states to give black males the right to vote. However, Johnson refused, insisting that "white men alone must manage the South."

As spring turned into summer, the despair of defeat among white southerners began to give way to hope. The President's Reconstruction plan gave them the power to shape their own future. By fall, new governments—most of them led by former Confederate officials—had been elected in all eleven southern states.

The new state legislatures turned to the task of recovery. Most made plans to build free public schools, but for whites only. One Louisiana lawmaker said his state had no duty to educate "any but the superior race of man—the white race."

Southern legislatures also passed laws known as "black codes" to clarify the status of freed men. The black codes allowed them to own property, marry, and sue. But they kept political power in white hands, denying blacks the right to vote, serve on juries, or bear arms. The codes also restricted freedmen mainly to farm work, a great help to planters looking for farm laborers.

Johnson vs. Congress

By late 1865 President Johnson believed that the work of Reconstruction was finished. Many northerners and black southerners, though, were upset to see former Confederates regaining power, and they viewed the black codes as a giant step backwards toward slavery. "The [South's] rebellion has not ceased," warned abolitionist Wendell Phillips. "It has only changed its weapons."

For the next two years, the President and Congress were locked in a power struggle for control of Reconstruction. An early battle was over the Freedmen's Bureau, an agency that Congress set up at the end of the war to help African Americans move from slavery to freedom. It provided food and medical care to the needy, white as well as black, and organized schools for African Americans.

In 1866 Johnson vetoed a bill to extend the life of the Freedmen's Bureau. He argued that the Constitution did not allow

To educate people freed from slavery, the Freedmen's Bureau founded 4,300 schools in five years.

Connections: Politics

In 1875 Andrew Johnson returned to Washington, D.C. as a senator from Tennessee, an office he had held before becoming Vice-President. When he entered the Senate chamber, there was at first an embarrassed silence. Then other senators came up to shake his hand, and a Senate page presented him with flowers.

Multicultural Perspectives

The Cherokees, Creeks, Choctaws, Chickasaws, and Seminoles had fought as allies of the Confederacy. After the war they were required to abolish slavery, which existed in some of the tribes. They were also forced to give up sections of their land in Indian Territory (present-day Oklahoma).

Active Learning

Small Group Activity. Divide the class into groups. Each group should come up with two arguments for and two arguments against removing President Johnson from office. Have each group present their arguments to the class. Then the class can vote on Johnson's guilt or innocence.

the creation of a federal agency to help the needy. He also vetoed a bill giving freedmen **civil rights,** rights as full citizens to equal opportunity and equal treatment under the law. Congress, however, stood firm. It overrode Johnson's vetoes, and the Freedmen's Bureau Act and the Civil Rights Act became law.

The Fourteenth Amendment. For some Radical Republicans, this victory was not enough. They feared that the Supreme Court, which had denied blacks citizenship in the Dred Scott case, might overturn the Civil Rights Act. Therefore, they pushed through Congress a constitutional amendment to grant citizenship to "all persons born or naturalized in the United States."

Besides making African Americans citizens, the proposed Fourteenth Amendment guaranteed to all persons "the equal protection of the laws." It said that no state could deprive a person "of life, liberty, or property without due process of law."

As the state legislatures debated the proposed amendment, the 1866 congressional elections were approaching. President Johnson decided to take his fight with Congress to the people by making a speaking tour of northern cities.

The tour backfired. Wherever Johnson spoke, his message turned voters against him. In November the Republicans won a two-thirds majority in both houses of Congress. The Radicals now felt that they were "masters of the situation."

Congress in control. In March 1867 Congress passed its own Reconstruction Act over President Johnson's veto. The plan disbanded the new southern governments and put the southern states under military rule. The army was to register as voters any southerners—black or white—who had been loyal to the Union. To be readmitted to the Union, each state had to adopt a new constitution guaranteeing black male suffrage, elect a new government, and ratify the Fourteenth Amendment. Former Confederate soldiers and officials in Confederate states could not hold office.

To keep Johnson from interfering with this plan, Congress passed two laws designed to reduce his power. The Command of the Army Act limited the President's powers as commander in chief of the military. The Tenure of Office Act banned the President from firing certain appointed officials without the Senate's consent.

Johnson believed that both these laws were unconstitutional. In February 1868 he tested the Tenure of Office Act by firing Secretary of War Edwin M. Stanton. The House promptly voted that Johnson be impeached.

That spring the President went on trial before the Senate. Johnson's lawyers argued that his only crime had been to take actions that were unpopular. Seven Republican senators agreed. As a result, the Senate was one vote short of the two-thirds majority needed for the removal of the President.

Johnson finished his term in office, but his power was broken. The long and bitter struggle for control of Reconstruction was over.

American Voices

"To make free labor successful, it is necessary that the laborer shall be treated fairly. . . . Give to the freedman justice, and we believe he will work better as a freedman than he did as a slave."

—Freedmen's Bureau agent John Bryant

Section Review

1. Identification. Define *freedmen, Reconstruction,* and *civil rights.*

2. Comprehension. Describe Johnson's Reconstruction plan. Why did many white southerners support his plan? Why did most northerners oppose it?

3. Analysis. How did Congress's plan differ from the President's?

Linking Past and Present. Power struggles between Congress and the President are part of the American political system. Check newspapers or magazines for reports of current conflicts between these two branches of government. Describe one.

Section Review

ANSWERS

1. Definitions for the following terms are found on text pages indicated in parentheses: *freedmen* (333), *Reconstruction* (334), *civil rights* (335).
2. State could rejoin Union if adopted new state constitution, elected new governor, repealed secession, agreed not to repay Confederacy war debts, ratified Thirteenth Amendment. White southerners supported plan because kept power in their hands. Many northerners objected did not give freedmen voting rights.
3. President believed southern white men must manage Reconstruction while Congress believed federal government and freed African Americans should participate. Congress wanted to extend life of Freedmen's Bureau and declare freedmen full citizens. President did not believe he had Constitutional authority to do so.
Linking Past and Present Choice of conflicts will vary.

Citizenship

Most observers agreed that Elliott's arguments were stronger than those of Stephens. After futher debate and discussion in Congress, the Civil Rights Act of 1875 was passed. Its key passage declared, *"all persons within the jurisdiction of the United States shall be entitled to the full and equal enjoyment of the accommodations, advantages, facilities, and privileges of inns, public conveyances on land or water, theaters, and other places of public amusement; subject only to the conditions and limitations established by law, and applicable alike to citizens of every race and color, regardless of any previous condition of servitude."*

Eight years later, though, the Supreme Court declared the law unconstitutional, saying that Congress had no authority to regulate the social customs of any state. For decades

Thinking Critically

Evaluation. In opening their speeches, both Stephens and Elliott stress that their arguments were not influenced by any bias. In the opening of Elliott's speech (not included in the excerpt here), he says *"I regret that the dark hue of my skin may lend a color to the imputation (charge) that I am controlled by motives personal to myself in my advocacy of this great measure of national justice."*

Have students note how Stephens stresses that his own view is not affected by bias (first paragraph of excerpt). Have them discuss what types of people would likely have doubted Stephen's claim and why. What types would likely have doubted Elliott's claim and why?

Using the Visuals

Analyzing Primary Sources. The painting of Elliott delivering his speech displays a passage not included in the excerpt: "What you give to one class you must give to all; what you deny to one class you shall deny to all." Have students discuss the relation of this statement to the Fourteenth Amendment.

Reduced student page in the Teacher's Edition

POINT OF VIEW

A Civil Rights Debate

In 1874 Congress debated a civil rights bill aimed at ensuring equality for African Americans by prohibiting discrimination in public places. Alexander Stephens of Georgia, former vice president of the Confederacy, argued that the federal government did not have the constitutional power to take such action. Among those who favored passage was Robert Brown Elliott, an African-American lawyer and representative from South Carolina. Stephens's speech and Elliott's response drew national attention to the issue of civil rights.

A Question of Authority

"My opposition to this bill springs from no prejudice, in the slightest degree, against any man, woman, or child within the limits of the United States, on account of race or color or previous condition of servitude. . . .

I am opposed to the passage of this measure, or any one kindred to it, even if any of the rights proposed to be secured by it were properly just in themselves, because of the want [lack] of the necessary power, under the Constitution. . . . I presume that it will not be assuming too much to take it for granted that it will be admitted by every member of the House that the powers of Congress are specific as well as limited. . . . Where then is the power to be found which authorizes the passage of this measure? The power under which it is claimed, as I understand it, is derived chiefly from the first and fifth sections of the Fourteenth Article of Amendment. . . .

As to the first section . . . , all I have to say here is that it very clearly appears from its words that it has but two objectives. These were, first, to declare the colored race to be citizens of the United States, and of the States, respectively, in which they reside; and, secondly, to prohibit the States, severally, from denying to the class of citizens, so declared, the same privileges, immunities, and civil rights which were secured to the citizens of the several States, respectively, and of the United States, by the Constitution as it stood before citizenship to the colored race was declared by this amendment. . . .

Neither of these amendments confer, bestow . . . any rights at all to citizens of the United States, or to any class whatever. . . .

Interference by the Federal Government, even if the power were clear and indisputable, would be against the very genius and the entire spirit of our whole system. If there is one truth which stands out prominently above all others in the history of these States, it is that the germinal and seminal [basic] principle of American constitutional liberty is the absolute unrestricted right of State self-government in all purely internal municipal affairs."

—From Alexander Stephens, in the *Congressional Record,* January 5, 1874 after the Court's ruling, the federal government did little to protect civil rights. Only as a result of the civil rights movement of the 1950s and 60s did the political climate change enough to spur the passage of the Civil Rights Act of 1964, provisions of which were upheld by the Supreme Court.

"Justice Demands It"

"There are privileges and immunities which belong to me as a citizen of the United States, and there are other privileges and immunities which belong to me as a citizen of my State. The former are under the protection of the Constitution and the laws of the United States, and the latter are under the protection of the constitution and laws of my state. But what of that? Are the rights which I now claim—the right to enjoy the common public conveniences of travel on public highways, of rest and refreshment at public inns, of education in public schools, of burial in public cemeteries—rights which I hold as a citizen of the United States or of my State? . . . Is not the denial of such privileges to me a denial to me of the equal protection of the laws? For it is under this clause of the Fourteenth Amendment that we place the present bill, no State shall "deny to any person within its jurisdiction the equal protection of the laws."

No matter, therefore, whether his rights are held under the United States or under his particular State, he is equally protected by this amendment. He is always and everywhere entitled to the equal protection of the laws. All discrimination is forbidden; and while the rights of citizens of a State as such are not defined or conferred by the Constitution of the United States, yet all discrimination, all denial of equality before the law, all denial of the equal protection of the laws, whether State or national laws, is forbidden.

Never was there a bill which appealed for support more strongly to

Robert B. Elliott of South Carolina defends a civil rights bill in Congress.

[the] sense of justice and fairplay. . . . The Constitution warrants it; the Supreme Court sanctions it; justice demands it."

—From Robert Brown Elliott, in the *Congressional Record,* January 6, 1874

1. What were Representative Stephens's main reasons for opposing the bill?

2. What were Representative Elliott's chief arguments in favor of the bill?

3. Imagine that you and your friends formed a social club and chose to exclude members of the opposite sex from joining. Do you think that Congress should be able to pass a law forbidding you to do so? Why or why not?

4. If you had been a member of Congress in 1874, how would you have voted on the civil rights bill? Which position do you think is constitutionally correct?

Point of View

ANSWERS

1. Stephens argues that the Constitution gives Congress no authority to pass such a law—that the purpose of the Fourteenth Amendment was only to guarantee citizenship to African Americans, not to declare what rights citizens should have. Furthermore, he says, by imposing a civil rights law on the states Congress would be violating the basic American principle of state self-government in internal affairs.

2. Elliott emphasizes that the Fourteenth Amendment is intended to outlaw all discrimination and unequal treatment, whether by the national government or by state governments. The proposed civil rights bill simply spells out very basic rights that must be guaranteed to ensure the equal treatment intended by the Fourteenth Amendment. It is irrelevant, he argues, to debate which rights are protected by the United States Constitution and which by state constitutions. Rather, he stresses that the issue is a simple matter of justice.

3. Answers will vary. Under current law, private social clubs may still discriminate under certain conditions.

4. Answers will vary.

Section 13-2

Objectives

- ***Answer the Focus Question.***
- *State the purpose of the Fifteenth Amendment.*
- *Explain how Reconstruction ended.*

Introducing THE SECTION

Have a student read aloud the words of Senator Yates. Ask why he believed suffrage was the answer to equality for African Americans. **(African Americans would elect people who would protect their rights and interests.)** Have students explain Yates's reference to Moses. **(Moses freed the Jews from bondage in Egypt.)** Do students believe that giving freedmen the vote solved all their problems? Why or why not?

Developing THE SECTION

Writing About History

Biographical Report. Have students write biographical reports on African-American politicians who gained office during Reconstruction; for example, Senators Blanche K. Bruce and Hiram Revels, Mississippi; Representatives Robert Smalls and Robert Elliott, South Carolina; Representative John R. Lynch, Mississippi, Representative James T. Rapier, Alabama. The reports should include the leader's early life, political career, and legislative accomplishments.

Reduced student page in the Teacher's Edition

13-2 The South Under Reconstruction

Focus: How did Reconstruction change the South?

Radical Republicans believed that the Civil War had created a "golden moment" in American history, a rare opportunity to shape a more "perfect republic" out of the chaos of war. Senator Charles Sumner hoped to use this moment to make the ideals of the Declaration of Independence "fundamental law." Senator Henry Wilson dreamed of building a society based on "equality among citizens— equality in the broadest sense."

Republican leaders saw suffrage for black men as the key to such equality. They were certain that once freedmen could vote, the former slaves would use the power of the ballot to protect their rights and interests. As Senator Richard Yates said:

> *"The ballot will finish the Negro question; it will settle everything connected with this question. . . . We need no vast expenditures, we need no standing army. . . . The ballot is the freedman's Moses."*

Congress's plan for Reconstruction was a bold experiment to shape a democracy in which African Americans would be part of "We the People."

This print celebrates the ratification of the Fifteenth Amendment, which declared that voting rights cannot be denied because of race. The smaller images also reflect views of the benefits of freedom and citizenship.

Multicultural Perspectives

Hiram Revels was the first African American to serve in the United States Senate. From 1870 to 1871 he served the unfinished term of Jefferson Davis. Revels is pictured below in 1872 with six black members of the House of Representatives: Robert C. DeLarge, Joseph H. Rainey, and Robert Brown Elliott of South Carolina, Jefferson Long of Georgia, Benjamin S. Turner of Alabama, and Josiah T. Walls of Florida.

New Voters in the South

Under the Reconstruction Act, the army returned to the South in 1867 and began registering three groups of voters. The largest consisted of freedmen. The smallest was made up of northerners—teachers, Freedmen's Bureau agents, and business people—who had moved to the South after the war. Resentful white southerners called the newcomers **carpetbaggers,** after a common type of traveler's handbag, and accused them of seeking to "fatten on our misfortunes." Like the freedmen, these northern carpetbaggers registered as Republicans.

The third group to be registered was made up of white southerners who had not supported the rebellion. Many were poor farmers from the back country who had always disliked planters and slavery. White southerners who joined the Republican party and worked with freedmen and carpetbaggers were called **scalawags** by former Confederates, who scorned them as traitors to the South.

The army registered 703,000 black and 660,000 white voters in time to participate in the 1868 presidential election. The Republicans nominated Union war hero Ulysses S. Grant. The Democrats chose former New York governor Horatio Seymour, a strong opponent of Congress's Reconstruction policies. On election day, an African-American voter wrote in his diary:

"The Great Epoch in the history of our race has at last arrived. Today the colored citizens of these southern [states] are casting their votes for presidential candidate U.S. Grant. . . . Their votes are going in like snowflakes, silently and surely."

Seymour probably won a majority of white votes, but the votes of 500,000 African Americans swung the election to Grant.

The Fifteenth Amendment. In an effort to safeguard black voting rights, Republicans in Congress proposed a constitutional amendment in 1869. This amendment said that a citizen's right to vote "shall not be denied . . . on account of race, color, or previous condition of servitude." A year later, upon learning that the Fifteenth Amendment had been ratified, abolitionist William Lloyd Garrison wrote:

"Nothing in all history [equals] this wonderful, quiet, sudden transformation of four million human beings from . . . the auction block to the ballot box."

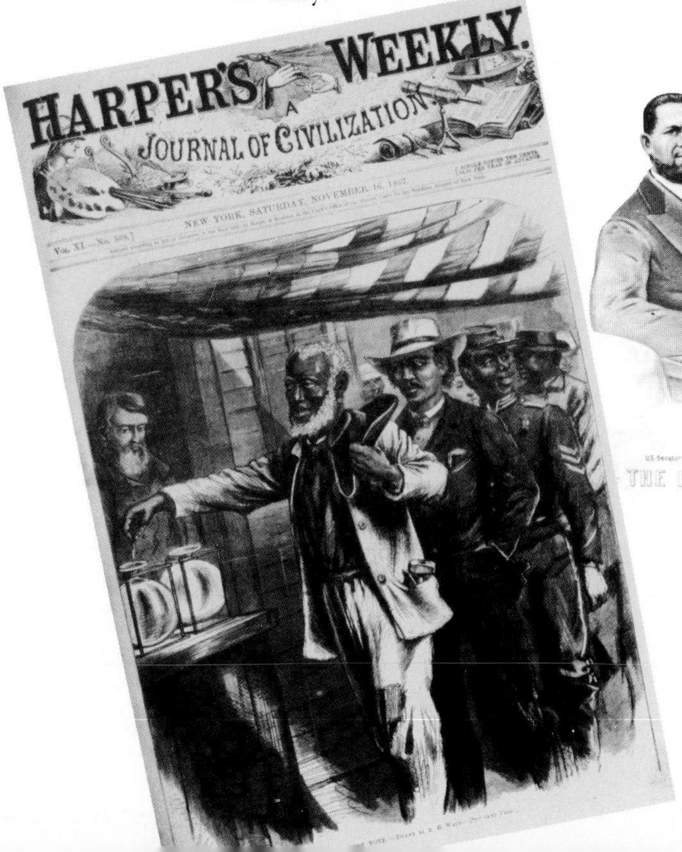

From 1868 to 1876, voters elected sixteen African Americans to Congress and many more to state and local governments in the South.

Active Learning

Cooperative Activity. Divide the class into groups of four. Students should pretend that President Johnson has been ousted, Benjamin Wade has become President, and they are members of the Fortieth Congress. Have each group write a plan for Reconstruction.

Points to be considered: How states should be treated (conquered provinces or wayward states); treatment of Confederate leaders (lenient, confiscate property, jail, exile); voting rights for freedmen; role of the federal government in rebuilding the South. Have each group choose a spokesperson to present the plan to the class.

Thinking Critically

Analysis. Northerners and southerners held differing viewpoints on carpetbaggers and scalawags. Ask students to contrast these two views. (Northerners viewed carpetbaggers as liberators and entrepreneurs and scalawags as allies. White southerners viewed carpet-baggers as outsiders and exploiters and scalawags as traitors.)

Ask: What factors influenced these points of view? (position on the war, attitude toward change, suspicion of outsiders) Was stereotyping involved? Explain.

Thinking Critically

Evaluation. Have teams of students debate this proposition: Radical Reconstruction has been falsely represented as a failure. Students should identify evidence to support their position.

Ask: What were the positive aspects of Radical Reconstruction? (Fourteenth Amendment, public schools and hospitals established, rebuilt infrastructure, women's property rights established, laws against child abuse) Negative? (high taxes, government corruption)

Each team can conclude by writing a paragraph responding to the proposition, citing three pieces of evidence to support its position.

Using the Visuals

Interpreting a Cartoon. Refer students to the Thomas Nast cartoon on this page. **Ask:** What is the topic of the cartoon? **(campaign of terror against blacks)** According to the cartoon, how successful was violence against African Americans? **(successful; African-American couple and child huddled for protection)** What two groups does the cartoonist feel are responsible for the acts of violence? **(White League, KKK)** What is Nast's point of view? **(Nast is against these acts of violence. Note the caption: "Worse than slavery.")**

B · A · C · K · G · R · O · U · N · D

Social History

While African Americans were being terrorized by the Ku Klux Klan, the Chinese on the West Coast were subjected to discrimination and anti-Chinese riots. The Fourteenth Amendment and Civil Rights Act passed to protect freedmen, applied to the Chinese as well and with the same feeble results. Also, Native Americans were dispossessed of their lands bit by bit and by 1885 almost every Native American had been pushed onto a reservation.

Reduced student page in the Teacher's Edition

New State Governments

Meanwhile, the South's new voters turned to the task of rebuilding their state governments. In 1868 black and white delegates attended conventions where they drew up new state constitutions based on universal male suffrage. Once the constitutions were approved, elections were held to fill all state offices. The results cheered the Republican party. The new state governments were dominated by Republican officeholders, black and white. By 1870 all the defeated states had met Congress's requirements and had been readmitted to the Union.

The new state governments undertook ambitious programs of rebuilding and change. Public schools and public hospitals were finally established in the South. Lawmakers expanded women's property rights and passed laws to protect children from abuse. To pay for new programs and to rebuild roads, railroads, and bridges, most legislatures raised taxes. Whenever taxes increased, so did opposition to "Republican rule."

Many southerners blamed rising taxes on government extravagance and corruption. Anti-Republican newspapers fueled these charges with stories of high salaries, money spent on projects never built, and bribe-taking public officials.

Abuses did occur, but the misdeeds of southern governments were minor compared with the corruption that plagued the rest of the nation in those years. Historian John Hope Franklin notes that no section or party had a "monopoly on public morality" after the war, and that "corruption was bisectional, bipartisan, and biracial."

Return to "White Man's Rule"

As Republicans struggled to bring about political and social change in the South, conservative white southerners were working to drive them out of office. As early as 1866 whites had begun to organize secret societies, such as the Knights of the White Camelia and the Ku Klux Klan, to return the South to "white man's rule." Prospective Klan members were asked: "Are you opposed to Negro equality, both social and political? Are you in favor of a white man's government in this country?"

Violence was the main weapon these societies used against African Americans and their white supporters. Acting at night, Klansmen donned long, hooded robes and rode across the countryside spreading terror. They set the night sky ablaze with burning crosses, a grim warning to all who dared to defy them. Warnings were followed by beatings, and beatings by murder.

In 1870 and 1871 Congress responded to the violence by passing the Force Acts, authorizing the President to use military force in lawless areas. The violence, however, did not stop. One reason was that few of the thousands of people arrested under the Force Acts were ever convicted. Furthermore, even though pressure from Congress caused the Klan and the Knights of the White Camelia officially to disband, small local groups with harmless-sounding names like "Mother's Little Helpers" and "Allendale Mounted Baseball Club" continued to terrorize black voters.

The campaign of terror helped turn the tide back toward white rule. However, an even more important factor was that the North lost interest in Reconstruction. By the 1870s new issues such as corruption had distracted northerners from the South and its problems.

A Thomas Nast cartoon attacks tools of terror used by those who wanted "white man's rule" in the South.

Connections: Politics

In the election of 1875 whites in Mississippi openly advocated the use of threats and force to oust their state Reconstruction-established administration. A white militia made a show of force, parading through African-American areas. Political meetings were broken up. African Americans were killed in riots. On election day, many African Americans stayed away from the polls, and the white supremacists won.

Limited English Proficiency

Making Charts. Have students work in small groups to make charts of Reconstruction legislation. Each chart should have three headings: *Year, Law, Provisions*. The first entry should be 1865, Thirteenth Amendment, Prohibits slavery in the United States. The last entry can be 1872, Amnesty Act, Allows Confederate veterans to hold office and supporters of the Confederacy to vote. Groups can share their charts with the rest of the class and fill in any missing items.

The Election of 1876

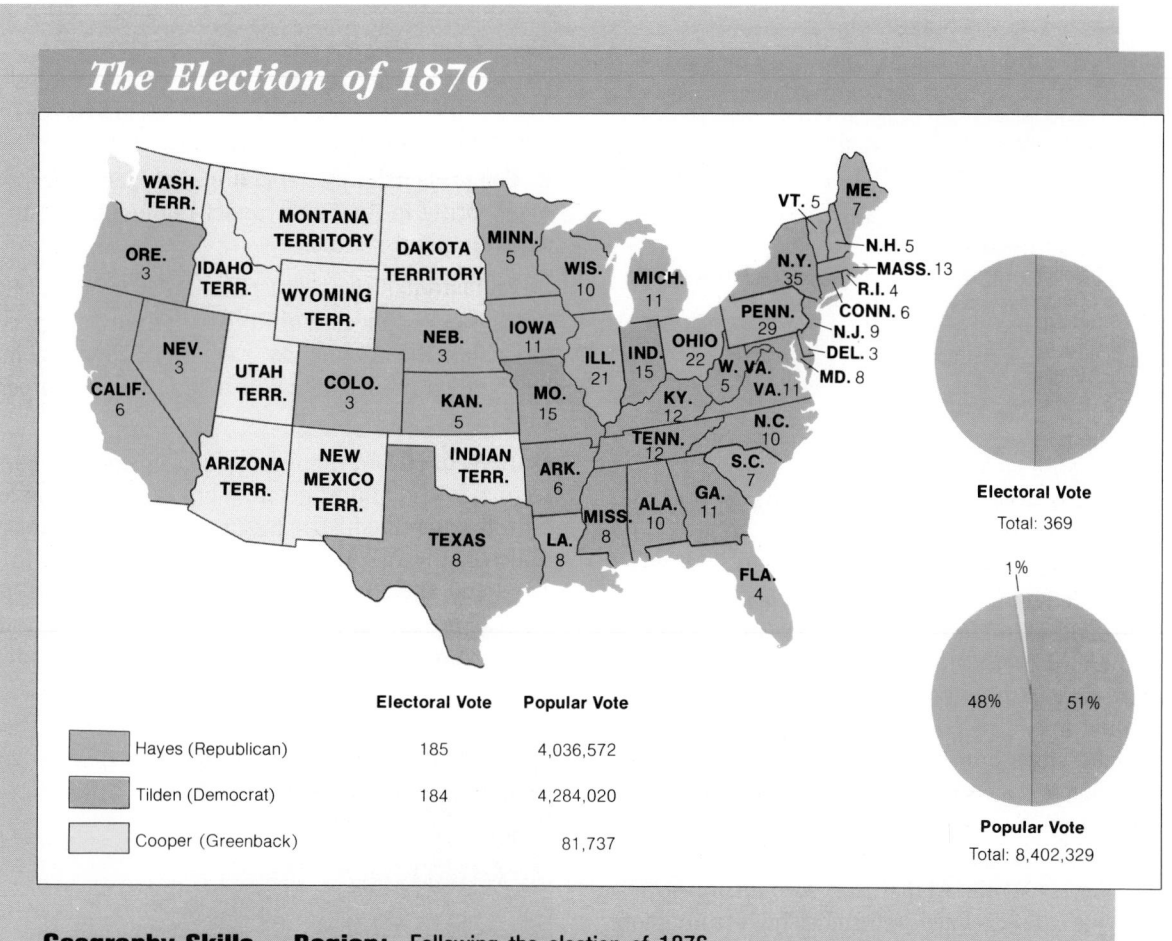

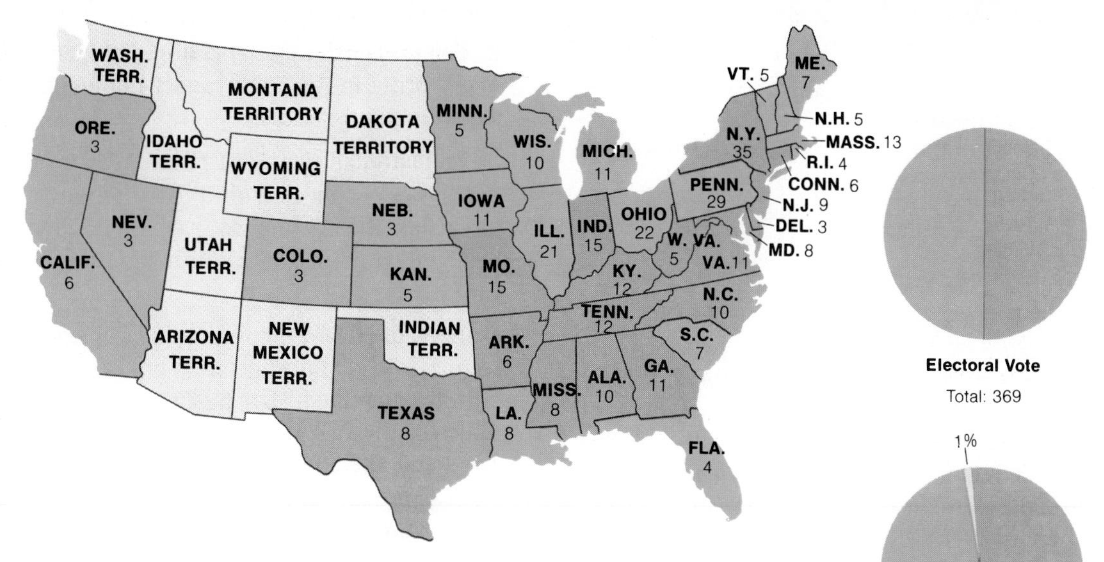

	Electoral Vote	Popular Vote
Hayes (Republican)	185	4,036,572
Tilden (Democrat)	184	4,284,020
Cooper (Greenback)		81,737

Geography Skills—Region: Following the election of 1876, many observers of the major political parties began referring to the "Solid South." Based on the election results, what do you think this term meant? In what sense was it premature?

Geography Skills

ANSWERS

Most of the southern states voted for the same political party—the Democrats. Louisiana, South Carolina, and Florida did not vote with the rest.

As northerners wearied of Reconstruction, the Radicals lost influence in Congress. In 1872 Congress passed the Amnesty Act, allowing almost all Confederate veterans to hold offices and allowing former supporters of the Confederacy to vote. Under the banner of the Democratic party, southern whites regained control of state and local government. To freedman Henry Adams it seemed that "the whole South . . . had got back into the hands of the very men that held us as slaves."

South Carolina was among the last states to return to "white man's rule." Democrats took control in 1877 after an election described by a white Carolinian as "one of the greatest farces [jokes] ever seen." Democratic senator Ben Tillman admitted that his party had "stuffed the ballot boxes." "We are not ashamed of it," he said. "This is a white man's country, and white men must govern it."

The End of Reconstruction

The year 1876 was the hundredth anniversary of the Declaration of Independence, and most Americans were yearning for an end to the strife of Reconstruction. "Let us see to it, North and South,"

B · A · C · K · G · R · O · U · N · D

Thinking Critically

Analysis. Have students compare disputed elections of 1824 (Chapter 8, pages 216-217) and 1876. (Candidate with greatest popular vote did not win; election decided by Congress; claims of corruption and cheating.) Have them explain the phrases "corrupt bargain" (1824) and "stolen election." (In 1824 Jackson supporters claimed corrupt bargain struck between John Quincy Adams and Henry Clay to give former the Presidency. In 1876 the Democrats claimed election was stolen from Samuel J. Tilden by the commission giving all 20 disputed electoral votes to Hayes.)

Multicultural Perspectives

In 1866 the army established the Ninth Cavalry, one of the four all-black military units operating in the West. These troops were named "Buffalo Soldiers" by Native Americans against whom they fought. The Indians saw a resemblance between the African-American soldiers' hair and the buffalo's dark coat. Also, the Indians considered the buffalo a sacred animal, and honored blacks by linking them with it. At least fourteen of these Buffalo Soldiers went on to win the Congressional Medal of Honor.

Reduced student page in the Teacher's Edition

The Nation Reunites

	Readmitted to the Union	Reconstruction government ended
Tennessee	1866	1869
Alabama	1868	1874
Arkansas	1868	1874
Florida	1868	1877
Louisiana	1868	1877
North Carolina	1868	1870
South Carolina	1868	1877
Georgia	1870	1871
Mississippi	1870	1875
Texas	1870	1873
Virginia	1870	1870

wrote *Scribner's Monthly Magazine,* "that the Centennial heals all the old wounds." Many northerners wanted to "let the South alone."

The centennial was also a presidential election year. The Republicans nominated Ohio governor Rutherford B. Hayes, a Civil War general. Democrats staked their hopes on New York Governor Samuel J. Tilden. Early election returns seemed to indicate victory for Tilden. He had won 184 electoral votes, just one short of the total needed for election. Hayes had only 165 electoral votes, but 20 votes from four states were in dispute.

Congress set up a bipartisan commission to investigate the disputed returns. The commission awarded all twenty electoral votes to Hayes, giving him just enough to win. Democrats fumed over what they called "the stolen election" and threatened to block Hayes's inauguration. To soothe their feelings, Hayes agreed to remove the few remaining federal troops from the South.

The inauguration of President Hayes in 1877 marked the end of Reconstruction. It was welcomed by white northerners weary of the war and its bitter aftermath and eager to move forward as one nation. Meanwhile, conservative white southerners were glad to have their state governments firmly under their control again.

However, African Americans—and many whites, both northern and southern—were left feeling sad and disillusioned. Their dream of expanding democracy and creating a society based on the ideals of equal rights and opportunities for all had been shattered.

Section Review

1. Identification. Define the terms *carpetbaggers* and *scalawags.*

2. Comprehension. What changes did state governments bring to the South under Congress's Reconstruction plan?

3. Evaluation. African-American scholar W. E. B. Du Bois called the end of Reconstruction "a victory for which the South has every right to hang its head." Explain what Du Bois meant. Do you agree? Give reasons.

Data Search. To many freedmen, Reconstruction seemed to end almost before it began. Use the table on this page titled "The Nation Reunites" in order to determine (a) the number of years between the war's end and the readmission of all the southern states, and (b) which states spent the fewest and the most years under Republican rule after Reconstruction began in 1867.

In 1877 President Rutherford B. Hayes ordered withdrawal of the last federal troops from the South.

Section Review

ANSWERS

1. Definitions for the following terms are on text pages indicated in parentheses: *carpetbaggers* (339), *scalawags* (339).
2. State legislatures were dominated by Republicans, including white northerners settling in South, white southerners, and African Americans. Public schools and hospitals built, taxes raised, and women given property rights.
3. Agree: Reconstruction brought about improved schools, hospitals, property rights for women, improved treatment of African Americans. Disagree: the treatment of formerly dominant whites.
Data Search. (a) five years (1865–1870) (b) fewest years: Tennessee (two years: 1867–1869); most years: Florida, Louisiana, and South Carolina (ten years: 1867–1877).

Multicultural Perspectives

During this post-Civil War period a small group of African-American women—Ida B. Wells, Mary Church Terrell, and Fannie Barrier Williams—emerged as leaders. Caroline V. Still was one of the first African-American woman doctors while Charlotte Ray became the first African-American woman lawyer.

13-3 The "New South"

Focus: What happened to African Americans in the South after Reconstruction?

With Reconstruction over, southern Democrats began to talk of building a "New South." According to one paper, the South would soon be "thrilling with new life . . . her cities vast hives of industry." While awaiting the creation of this New South, however, most southerners were living in poverty.

Tenants and Sharecroppers

After the war, life was hard in the South for both blacks and whites. The union victory had freed blacks but left them penniless. Most freedmen desperately wanted land of their own to farm but had no money to buy it. A few Radical Republicans talked of breaking up large plantations and giving every freedman "forty acres and a mule." However, most other Republicans resisted this idea as a violation of the property rights of plantation owners. And so the freedmen were left to find whatever work they could get.

Most whites were not much better off than the former slaves. They had lost what little they had in the war and now had to compete with freedmen for work. Even the once-wealthy planters were in trouble. They had land but no money, and without money they could not hire workers to make their land productive.

The solution for many planters was to divide

Many blacks became tenant farmers in the hope of one day owning land. Instead, they were caught in a cycle of debt created by harsh working conditions, low crop prices, and dishonest landowners and merchants.

Section 13-3

Objectives

- ***Answer the Focus Question.***
- *Explain how Jim Crow laws set up segregation.*
- *Compare the views of Booker T. Washington and W.E.B. Du Bois.*

Introducing THE SECTION

Have students read aloud the first paragraph on this page. Discuss the optimistic newspaper prediction for the "New South." Ask students what they know about the South that might work against this prediction. **(agrarian based, war damaged, economic dislocation, political turmoil)**

Ask: If you were a southerner, what would you want the "New South" to be? How would you achieve this? Explain that students will examine the "New South," which in many ways came to resemble the old South before Civil War.

Developing THE SECTION

Connections: Economics

Discussion. Discuss the practice of sharecropping by asking: What is the economic advantage to the plantation owner? **(does not have to pay wages, sells supplies and food)** To the sharecropper? **(provides employment, can borrow, if prices good can get ahead)** How was it a kind of bondage? **(sharecropper always in debt)** Why? **(crop prices generally low; owners often cheated sharecroppers.)** Was there any alternative available at the time? **(land redistribution)**

Backyard History

Interview. Jim Crow laws existed in many parts of the United States until struck down in the 1950s and 1960s. Have students conduct an interview with someone in their family or community who remembers these laws. Some possible questions: What were the laws? What were the penalties for violation? How strictly were the laws enforced? How did the person feel about the laws? Have students share their findings with the class or produce a book or video of the interviews.

B · A · C · K · G · R · O · U · N · D

Connections: Literature

The editor of the Charleston *News and Courier* was among many white southerners who protested the treatment of African Americans. Amos T. Akerman, Attorney General in Grant's cabinet, was outspoken in his defense of African-American rights. George Washington Cable of New Orleans wrote *Silent South*, one of the most radical indictments of southern racial policies for its time. Lewis H. Blair of Richmond wrote *The Prosperity of the South Dependent upon the Elevation of the Negro*, an attack on the twin notions of white superiority and black inferiority.

Reduced student page in the Teacher's Edition

Spotlight on Injustice

An experience of three Louisiana sharecroppers pointed to the problem of unjust landowners:

> "We worked, or made a contract to work, and make a crop on shares on Mr. McMoring's place, and worked for one third of the crop, and he was to find us all provisions; and in July 1875, we was working alone in the field, and Mr. McMoring and McBounton came to us and says, 'Well, boys, you all got to get away.' . . . The two white men went and got sticks and guns, and told us that we must leave the place; and we told them that we would not leave it because we don't want to give up our crop for nothing; . . . we wanted justice, but he would not let us have justice; . . . All the time that we were living and working on the place they would not half feed us; and we worked for them as though we were slaves, and then treated like dogs all the time."

their land into small parcels and rent them out to **tenant farmers**— farmers who rented their land from a landlord. Some tenant farmers were able to pay the rent in cash after selling their crops. However, most ended up as **sharecroppers**— tenants who paid their rent by giving the landowner a share of their crop instead of cash. Often that share came to as much as half of the crop.

For black and white sharecroppers alike, this system created a new kind of bondage: a lifetime of debt. Most had to borrow money to buy seeds and supplies and to feed their families until harvest time. If crop prices were good, they might be able to pay off their debts and get ahead. But crop prices were generally low after the war. Furthermore, landowners and merchants often cheated sharecroppers. Most sharecroppers never made enough money to escape from debt.

Reversing Reconstruction

Democrats working to undo Reconstruction largely ignored the problem of poverty. They slashed taxes and state spending. Public education, which one Democratic governor labeled a "luxury," was hard hit. Louisiana spent so little on education between 1880 and 1900 that the percentage of whites who could read actually dropped.

Democrats also moved to eliminate the source of the Republicans' remaining political power: black voters. One method was to refuse to count ballots cast by African Americans. One black voter said:

> *"We are in a majority here, but you may vote till your eyes drop out or your tongue drops out, and you can't count the colored man in one of them boxes. There's a hole gets in the bottom of the boxes some way and lets out our votes."*

In the 1890s the southern states found new ways to deny the vote to blacks. They required voters to pay a **poll tax**— a fixed tax levied on each adult. Voters also had to pass a literacy test.

In theory, these new requirements for voters applied equally to blacks and whites, but most blacks were too poor to pay the poll tax. Furthermore, many states included a "grandfather clause." Any man whose father or grandfather had been eligible to vote on January 1, 1867, did not have to pay the poll tax or pass a literacy test. Since only whites had been eligible to vote on that date, white voters were protected by the grandfather clause.

African Americans asked the federal courts to protect their voting rights. But the Supreme Court ruled in *Williams* v. *Mississippi* that the new laws did not violate the Fifteenth Amendment because they did not "on their face discriminate between races." Not until 1915 did the Court declare that the grandfather clause was unconstitutional.

Jim Crow laws. During Reconstruction, many southern states had passed laws to punish railroads, hotels, or theaters that denied "full and equal rights" to any citizen. Such laws were repealed after 1877 and were gradually replaced with

Multicultural Perspectives

Despite the negative effects of Jim Crow, some gains were made in education. African-American students pursued learning at all-black universities such as Howard, Atlanta, Fisk, and Hampton Institute. Booker T. Washington began the Tuskegee Institute to teach young African Americans farming skills and trades. Carter G. Woodson received a doctorate from Harvard. He published many books on black history, founded the *Journal of Negro History*, and was the originator of Black History Week, observed every February.

Jim Crow laws, laws calling for **segregation**—or separation—of the races in public places. Jim Crow laws got their name from a black song-and-dance character created by a white entertainer in the 1830s. The name suggested a negative image of African Americans.

Not all whites supported Jim Crow laws. When a segregation law was proposed in South Carolina, the editor of the Charleston *News and Courier* tried to show how silly it was by taking segregation to ridiculous extremes:

> *"If there must be Jim Crow cars on railroads, there should be Jim Crow cars on the street railways . . . Jim Crow waiting saloons [rooms] . . . Jim Crow eating houses . . . Jim Crow sections of the jury box, and a . . . Jim Crow Bible for colored witnesses to kiss."*

What seemed so foolish would soon be common across the South—even the Jim Crow Bible.

Plessy v. Ferguson. African Americans again looked to the courts to protect their rights—only to see their hopes crushed, most notably in an 1896 Supreme Court decision, *Plessy* v. *Ferguson*. The case involved a black man named Homer Plessy who had refused to leave a "whites only" railroad car. Plessy argued that the state law requiring segregated cars violated his right to "equal protection of the laws" under the Fourteenth Amendment. The Court, however, ruled that blacks could be separated from whites as long as the facilities available to both groups were equal.

Justice John Marshall Harlan, a former slaveholder, was the only member to disagree with the decision. "Our Constitution," he declared, "is colorblind, and neither knows nor tolerates classes among citizens." Justice Harlan predicted that the Court's approval of "separate but equal" facilities would be as harmful as the 1857 Dred Scott decision that slaves were property.

American Voices

> *"Though slavery was abolished, the wrongs of my people were not ended. Though they were not slaves, they were not yet quite free. No man can be truly free whose liberty is dependent upon the thought, feeling, and action of others."*
>
> —Frederick Douglass

Harlan was right. *Plessy* v. *Ferguson* triggered a flood of new Jim Crow laws. And despite the doctrine of "separate but equal," schools, parks, and other facilities for blacks were inferior. Charles Harris, a Union veteran and former member of Alabama's legislature, wrote:

> *"We obey laws; others make them. We support state educational institutions whose doors are virtually closed against us. We support asylums and hospitals, and our sick . . . are met at the doors by . . . unjust discriminations. . . . From these and many other oppressions . . . our people long to be free."*

African-American Responses

It took great courage for African Americans to protest against segregation and the denial of their voting rights. Between 1882 and 1903 mobs lynched, or hanged, some 3,000 blacks in the South, mostly for challenging white rule. African-American newspaper editor Ida B. Wells-Barnett called on the federal government to take action against "the national crime of lynching." But her antilynching crusade fell on deaf ears.

Discouraged, many thousands of African Americans chose to leave the South after Reconstruction ended in 1877. In April 1878 two hundred freedmen emigrated to Africa. A year later, a freedman named Benjamin "Pap" Singleton organized the "Exodus of 1879," a migration of freedmen to Kansas. Life on the plains was not easy for the "exodusters," but as one of them said, "we had rather suffer and be free."

Most freedmen, however, chose to remain in the South. There, at least, they had the support of their families and a close-knit African-American community.

Linking Past and Present

Discussion. The decision in *Plessy* v. *Ferguson* was overturned in 1954 by *Brown* v. *Board of Education*. The Supreme Court ruled that "separate but equal" facilities were inherently unequal because they generated in black children *"a feeling of inferiority . . . that may affect their hearts and minds in a way unlikely ever to be undone."* This decision led to a flood of cases challenging Jim Crow Laws. **Ask:** How might "separate but equal" in theory prove to be very unequal in practice? **(Students might cite schools, other public facilities.)**

Limited English Proficiency

Campaigning Against Jim Crow. Students can work in groups to create posters and slogans against the "separate but equal" ruling and the flood of Jim Crow laws that resulted.

Thinking Critically

Analysis. Discuss with students the options open to freedmen other than remaining in the South. What were the advantages of moving North? (industrial jobs, less prejudice) Disadvantages? (separation from family and community) Why did most African Americans resist emigrating to Africa? (separation from family and community, distance, alien culture)

Active Learning

Cooperative Activity. Divide the class into five teams, each representing a different group—African Americans in the South; Mexican Americans in the Southwest; Women's Christian Temperance Union; Chinese Americans in California; Irish miners in Pennsylvania. Each team is to research the status of their group in approximately 1876. Teams should research the problems faced by the group, its goals, and contributions to the society at large. One student from each team should present its findings in a panel discussion format.

Multicultural Perspectives

In public, Booker T. Washington always supported accommodation in order to "cement the friendship of the races and bring about hearty cooperation between them." Given the retreats of the Republicans, the North, and the Supreme Court on equal rights, Washington believed that this was the only policy which could be really effective. In private, however, he worked to stop racial discrimination. For example, he raised funds to challenge cases in the federal courts against disfranchisement and Jim Crow laws, and argued against discrimination in the allocation of funds to white and black schools.

Reduced student page in the Teacher's Edition

Visions of hope and change. Two new leaders emerged from the black community in the 1890s, each with his own vision of hope and change. Booker T. Washington, a former slave from Virginia, was a teacher who became head of a new college for African Americans, the Tuskegee Institute in Alabama. Washington urged blacks to think less about the injustices they suffered and more about improving their education and industrial skills. He argued that

"friction between the races will pass away . . . as the black man, by reason of his skill, intelligence, and character, can produce something the white man wants."

African Americans who thought Washington was too willing to accept segregation found an outspoken leader in William E. B. Du Bois (doo BOYS). Born in Massachusetts, Du Bois grew up to be a brilliant scholar, first as a student at Harvard University and then as a teacher at Atlanta University. Unlike the more cautious Washington, Du Bois urged blacks to stand up against discrimination and to demand equality.

In 1905 Du Bois met with African-American leaders in Niagara Falls, New York, to form "a permanent national forward movement." A year later the Niagara Movement met at Harpers Ferry—where in 1859 John Brown had launched his uprising against slavery—to outline the task ahead. Du Bois spoke for everyone there when he said:

To educate freedmen and their children, twenty-nine colleges were founded in the South in the late 1800s. Members of the 62nd U.S. Colored Infantry gave $5,000 to help found Lincoln University. These photos reflect the long, proud tradition of the Fisk University Jubilee Singers, whose concerts raise money for their school while sharing African-American music with the world.

Connections: Science and Technology

George Washington Carver spent his life teaching agricultural chemistry at Tuskegee Institute. He developed hundreds of products from the peanut and sweet potato (including peanut butter). His research had a direct influence on the shift of southern agriculture from single-crop to diversified farming.

Multicultural Perspectives

William E. B. Du Bois received his undergraduate degree from Fisk University, Nashville, Tennessee in 1888. While at Fisk, Du Bois was the editor of the student newspaper, *The Fisk Herald.* In 1895 he became the first African American to receive a graduate degree at Harvard University.

Linking Past and Present

Research. On January 29, 1901 George H. White, the last African-American congressman from the South, gave his farewell speech. The first African-American senator since Reconstruction was Edward Brooke of Massachusetts, who served from 1967 to 1979. Have students research the election of other African Americans to national offices. How many black politicians hold national offices today?

"We claim for ourselves every single right that belongs to a freeborn American, political, civil, and social; and until we get these rights we will never cease to protest and assail the ears of America."

Section Review

1. Identification. Define *tenant farmers, sharecroppers, poll tax,* and *segregation.*

2. Comprehension. How did southern Democrats undo the work of the Reconstruction governments?

3. Analysis. In what ways were African Americans worse off in 1900 than they were when Reconstruction ended?

4. Evaluation. If you had been an African American in the late 1800s, which leader would you have supported—Booker T. Washington or W. E. B. Du Bois? Why?

Connections to Themes

Shaping Democracy

By 1865 most white northerners had come to agree with African Americans and white abolitionists that a nation founded in the name of freedom could not tolerate slavery. A tragic wrong—the compromise over slavery at the Constitutional Convention in 1787—was righted by the Thirteenth Amendment.

A commitment to freedom, however, was not the same as embracing the ideal of equal rights. After the war Congress had tried to make men equal as well as free. However, its Reconstruction plan was short-lived, and even the Fourteenth and Fifteenth amendments could not end the pattern of segregation and discrimination. Meanwhile, equal rights were also being denied to Native Americans, Hispanics, and women of all races.

To most white northerners as well as southerners, American "democracy" was still a white man's government. This narrow view had changed little since the Constitutional Convention. The undoing of Reconstruction reinforced a lesson to those struggling for equal rights: they could not rely on the good will of those in power.

In short, the reshaping of American democracy toward ensuring equal rights would come about mainly through the ceaseless efforts of the people who were denied those rights. Their efforts, which achieved results in the woman suffrage movement of the early 1900s and the civil rights movement of the 1950s and 1960s, continue to this day.

Section Review

ANSWERS

1. Definitions for the following terms are on text pages indicated in parentheses: *tenant farmers* (344), *sharecroppers* (344), *poll tax* (344), *segregation* (345).

2. Slashed taxes and state spending, set up a poll tax and literacy test for voting, passed Jim Crow laws that segregated whites and African Americans.

3. At the end of Reconstruction they had political rights and representation. By 1900 had almost as few rights as under slavery.

4. Answers will vary. Supporters of Washington might say his tactics were more likely to bring immediate improvement. Those who support Du Bois can argue that nothing short of full equality was acceptable and that it was his efforts that led to the great strides made in civil rights in the 1950s and 1960s.

Chapter Survey

ANSWERS

Using New Vocabulary

1. *Freedmen* former slaves; many became *sharecroppers,* tenant farmers paying rent with a percentage of harvest. Not all freedmen sharecroppers, and not all sharecroppers former slaves; some were white.
2. *Carpetbaggers* northerners who moved south after Civil War; *scalawags* white southerners who joined Republican party. Both supported reconstructed state governments.
3. *Poll tax* fee paid in order to vote; *segregation,* separation of races. Both used to reverse Reconstruction.

Reviewing the Chapter

1. Freedmen could own property, sue and be sued, marry, but could not vote, serve on juries, bear arms; mostly limited to farm work. Purpose to keep African Americans subject to whites.
2. Bills passed by Congress, vetoed by President, veto overridden by Congress. Beginning of open confrontation between Congress and President over control of Reconstruction.
3. Johnson wanted to keep whites in control, restore rebel states to Union as quickly as possible; states had to write new constitution, agree not to pay Confederate debts, ratify 13th Amendment. Congress wanted to promote equality in South, suffrage for blacks; put states under military rule, would not readmit states to Union until adopted new constitution guaranteeing black suffrage, elected new government excluding former Confederates, ratified 14th Amendment.
4. Congress passed laws controlling Reconstruction, overrode Presidential vetoes.
5. Voters were freedmen, carpetbaggers, scalawags, officeholders were both white and African American loyal to Union. Wrote new state constitutions including universal male suffrage, built schools and hospitals, laws protecting women and children; shortcoming: rising taxes, some corruption.
6. To protect black voting rights.
7. Secret societies bent on intimidating black voters, northerners lost interest in Reconstruction, Amnesty Act of 1872 allowed former Confederates to hold government office, they built up Democratic party to recapture political power in south. Disputed election of 1876 resolved by Hayes's promise to remove last federal troops from South, thus ending Reconstruction.
8. Intimidation by violence, poll tax, literacy requirements for voting.
9. Legal justification of "separate but equal" facilities. In

Reduced student page in the Teacher's Edition

Chapter Survey

Using New Vocabulary

The vocabulary terms in each pair listed below are related to each other. For each pair, explain what the two terms have in common. Also explain how they differ.

1. freedmen, sharecroppers
2. carpetbaggers, scalawags
3. poll tax, segregation

Reviewing the Chapter

1. What restrictions did the black codes place upon African Americans? What was the purpose of the codes?
2. What was the importance of the Freedmen's Bureau Act and the Civil Rights Act?
3. Contrast the goals and methods of the plans for Reconstruction put forward by President Johnson and by Congress.
4. How did Congress gain control of Reconstruction?
5. Describe the new state governments formed under congressional Reconstruction. Who were the voters and officeholders? What were their accomplishments and shortcomings?
6. What was the purpose of the Fifteenth Amendment?
7. What factors led to the end of Reconstruction?
8. After Reconstruction, what methods did southern whites use to keep African Americans from voting?
9. What was the significance of the *Plessy* v. *Ferguson* case?
10. Contrast the methods of working for change proposed by Booker T. Washington and W. E. B. Du Bois.

Thinking Critically

1. Analysis. Why do you think that President Johnson believed "white men alone must manage the South"?
2. Synthesis. Give examples of the political, economic, and social treatment of African Americans by whites in the South after Reconstruction. Use these examples to make a generalization about life in the South for blacks between 1877 and 1900.
3. Analysis. What factors do you think motivated white behavior in the South after Reconstruction? Give evidence to support your answer.

History and You

If Booker T. Washington and W. E. B. Du Bois were to come back to life today, what progress would they see for African Americans? What problems? Do you think either one would have changed his view? Explain.

Using a Time Line

Match each date on the time line with the correct event in the list below. Write your answers in chronological order and explain the importance of each event.

(A) Rutherford B. Hayes elected President
(B) Niagara Convention held
(C) Fourteenth Amendment proposed
(D) last southern states readmitted to the Union
(E) Amnesty Act passed
(F) Reconstruction Act passed
(G) *Plessy* v. *Ferguson* decision
(H) Ulysses S. Grant elected President

1867 1870 1876

1866 1868 1872 1896 1905

fact, facilities for African Americans vastly inferior to those for whites.
10. Washington focused on education and economic improvement; Du Bois argued for first winning political rights.

Thinking Critically

1. Johnson white southerner, raised in racially stratified environment.
2. Political—lost right to vote; economic—mostly limited to sharecroppers; social—faced radical segregation in public life. In general, African Americans forced to remain second-class citizens.
3. Racism; desire to regain political power; desire to rebuild southern economy on basis of cheap black labor.

Applying Social Studies Skills

Using Maps and Graphs

The election of 1876 was one of the closest in American history. Use the map and graphs on page 341 and the following questions to analyze the results of the election.

1. In which section of the country did most states vote Republican? Why?

2. In which regions did Tilden have the most support?

3. In 1876 three southern states had Reconstruction governments. Which were they? How is this fact reflected in the map?

4. How did the popular vote compare with the electoral vote?

5. How was the election unusual in terms of popular vote, electoral vote, and the winner?

Applying Thinking Skills

Recognizing Point of View

The first account below is taken from testimony a white newspaper editor gave to a committee of Congress in 1866. The second is from a speech that an African-American member of Georgia's legislature made in 1868. Examine each account to identify the speaker's point of view. Then answer the questions that follow.

“I think if the whole regulation of Negroes, or freedmen, were left to the people of the communities in which they live, it will be administered for the best interest of the Negroes as well as of the whites. I think there is a kindly feeling towards the freedmen. . . . The sentiment prevailing is that it is for the interest of the employer to teach the Negroes, to educate their children, to provide preachers for them, and to attend to their physical wants. . . .

I think there is a willingness to give them every right except the right of suffrage. . . . They will eventually be endowed with that right. It is only a question of time; but it will be necessary to prepare for it by slow and regular means, as the white race was prepared. I believe everybody unites in the belief that it would be disastrous to give the right of suffrage now.”

—James D. B. DeBow

“We are told that if black men want to speak, they must speak through white trumpets; if black men want their sentiments expressed, they must be . . . sent through white messengers. . . .

The great question, sir, is this: Am I a man? If I am such, I claim the rights of a man. Am I not a man because I happen to be of a darker hue than honorable gentlemen around me?

We have pioneered civilization here; we have built up your country; we have worked in your fields, and garnered your harvests for two hundred and fifty years! And what do we ask of you in return? Do we ask you for compensation for the sweat our fathers bore for you—for the tears you have caused, and the hearts you have broken, and the lives you have curtailed, and the blood you have spilled? Do we ask retaliation? We ask it not. We are willing to let the dead past bury its dead; but we ask you now for our rights.”

—Henry McNeal Turner

1. How did the speakers differ on the issue of black rights? What arguments did each speaker give for his position?

2. How might the background of each speaker have affected his point of view on black rights?

3. Each speaker attempted to express not only his own point of view but also the point of view of a large group of people. Do you think that all white southerners agreed with DeBow or all black freedmen with Turner? Explain.

History and You

Progress: End of segregation, Civil Rights, and Voting Rights acts, black participation in politics on many levels, growth of black middle class; greater social integration. Problems: De facto segregation, ghettos beset with drugs, crime, violence; lack of education and job opportunities. Du Bois might note that even with rights guaranteed by law, problems facing African Americans are great; might advocate political process to get more job training. Washington might still argue in favor of education to gain economic improvement.

Using a Time Line

(c) 1866, (f) 1867, (h) 1868, (d) 1870, (e) 1872, (a) 1876, (g) 1876, (b) 1905

Using Maps and Graphs

1. North, Republican party was party of the Union in Civil War.
2. South, "border states"
3. Florida, Louisiana, South Carolina. Only Southern states to vote Republican.
4. Tilden won 51% of the popular vote, 49.9% of the electoral vote.
5. Popular vote winner lost in electoral votes and lost the election.

Applying Thinking Skills

1. DeBow: African American rights should be left to community, and African Americans would be given equal rights, except that of voting, because it was in community's interest.Turner: immediate equality for African Americans after 250 years of slavery.
2. DeBow white newspaper editor with paternal attitude and probable interest in maintaining community as it was. Turner former slave and then member of Georgia legislature.
3. Answers may include that some white southerners disagreed with DeBow, some sympathetic to African Americans, others not. Probably fewer freedmen disagreed with Turner but some demanded more radical change, others more cautious.

Unit 4 Survey

ANSWERS

Making Connections

1. Development of canals, roads, steamboats, and railroads facilitated the movement of coal and other raw materials from sources to factories and products from factories to market. Growth of northern mills increased demand for southern cotton.

2. Southerners might have noted that taxation triggered the Revolution; taxation meant government taking of private property. For many southerners abolition of slavery also meant government interference with private property. A northerner might have pointed out that the Revolution was fought for the right to representative government, but secessionists were unwilling to abide by majority rule.

3. One view is that the Union needed African-American soldiers, Lincoln needed the support of abolitionists, blacks, Congress. The Emancipation Proclamation lacked provisions for integrating blacks into southern society, which made reconciliation of North and South more difficult.

4. The Civil War has been called the first modern war for the use of such modern technology as railroads and telegraph and because it was a total war. It differed from previous U.S. wars in that it was a civil war. Also, there were huge casualties.

Using the Time Line. Students should note that during and shortly after the Civil War African Americans made political gains, e.g., the Emancipation Proclamation. (Students might also note the thirteenth, fourteenth, and fifteenth amendments.) With the end of Reconstruction—when federal troops left the South—African Americans began to suffer political losses, e.g., Jim Crow, grandfather clauses, the failure of the Civil Rights Act of 1875 and the Force Bill.

Projects and Activities

1. Goals and strategies will vary. Free-Soilers and abolitionists opposed slavery and extension of slavery. Northern Democrats opposed slavery and favored popular sovereignty. Whigs compromised. (They nominated a slaveholder, Taylor; Clay, a Whig, offered concessions to North and South to preserve unity.)

2. Answers will vary.

3. Answers will vary.

Using the Time Line. Their works all contain specific references to the war. (Washington's autobiography is *Up from Slavery.)*

Reduced student page in the Teacher's Edition

Unit Survey

Making Connections

1. How did technological developments spur economic growth in both the North and the South before the Civil War?

2. In January 1861 Robert E. Lee wrote to his son, "Secession is nothing but revolution." What similarities might Lee have drawn between Confederate secession and the American Revolution? What differences might a northerner have noted?

3. Why did the Union's goal in the Civil War expand from preserving the nation to abolishing slavery? How did this shift affect Reconstruction?

4. Historians have called the Civil War the first modern war. In what ways was it modern? How was it different from previous wars the United States had fought?

Using the Time Line. Use the time line to trace the gains and losses in political status of African Americans over the last half of the nineteenth century. Refer to six events and explain in what way each represents a political gain or loss. What trend do you detect as the century came to an end?

Projects and Activities

1. Work in teams of four, with each team made up of the following characters: Free-Soiler, abolitionist, northern Democrat, and northern Whig. First, the characters speak for the interests of the group they represent, then together the team decides on the goals of the new Republican party. Finally, the team develops a strategy for carrying out its goals.

2. Form groups of three, each group to do research on one Civil War battle. Presenting in the order in which battles were fought, groups briefly describe dates, locations, and outcomes to the rest of the class and mark the battle locations on a large map.

3. Imagine yourself as a southerner who was sixty years old in 1900. Write or act out your life story, describing changes you have seen and their affect on you. Predict what politics, the economy, and society will be like in the next sixty years. End with advice to your grandchildren on how to lead their lives.

Using the Time Line. Work in groups of four to investigate and report on how one of the following people was affected by the Civil War: Winslow Homer, Walt Whitman, Mark Twain, Stephen Crane, Booker T. Washington. If possible, display or read selections from their works.

Milestones — 1850 — 1864

Presidents	Taylor	Fillmore	Pierce	Buchanan	Lincoln	Johnson	Grant

	1850	1864
Political and Economic	• Compromise of 1850 • Kansas-Nebraska Act • Dred Scott Decision • S. Carolina secedes • Civil War begins	• Emancipation Proclamation issued • First "black code," Mississippi • Reconstruction begins
Social and Cultural	• "Swanee River," Stephen Foster • *Uncle Tom's Cabin* published • "Dixie" written • First American war photos, Mathew Brady	• Walt Whitman publishes *Drum Taps* • *Prisoners from the Front,* Winslow Homer • First national Memorial Day
Technological and Scientific	• Railway links New York-Chicago • Overland stage west • Coast-to-coast telegram • Army Balloon Corps	• Railway sleeping car, George Pullman • First successful typewriter • Railway air brake, G. Westinghous • First transcontinental railroad

Assessment

A scored discussion may be conducted in a fishbowl format, that is, participants sit in a circle in the center of the room, the rest of the class in a larger circle around them.

First-time participants in scored discussion may experience anxiety. To build confidence, have students practice discussions, limiting practices to small groups, simple topics, and short periods of time. Students may also practice scoring.

Before a scored discussion, give participants time for research. Require them to bring notes to the discussion. Tell them they must all be prepared to discuss every agenda item.

Scoring

Students receive points each time they participate appropriately in the discussion. You might score the discussion yourself, or you might have the class score it, assigning each listener one or two participants, then averaging the results.

Develop a scoring sheet listing the behaviors for which points will be awarded. Place tally marks by participants' names for points earned. You might deduct points for negative behavior, such as inattention, interrupting, or monopolizing. A scoring sheet might include the following behaviors:

Completing the task: prepared: has research notes for all topics (4 points); making a relevant contribution (1 point)

Knowing history: using factual information (2 points); using evidence to support a position (2 points)

Thinking critically: taking a position (2 points); asking a clarifying question (1 point); recognizing a contradiction (2 points); making an analogy (2 points); recognizing an irrelevant comment (2 points)

Communicating ideas: listening to others throughout the discussion (4 points); drawing another person into the discussion (1 point); moving the discussion along (1 point)

Follow-up Activity

Letter writing. Have students write a letter to the TV station imagined in the activity, telling the TV producers which analysis (besides their own) of the causes of the war was most convincing and why.

Assessment: Demonstrating What You Know

Scored Discussion

A national television network will broadcast a drama series set during the Civil War. The network has planned other programs to stimulate interest in the series and help viewers understand its background. Because you are an expert on the Civil War, the network has invited you to take part in a televised discussion of the causes of the war.

To help you plan for your appearance on the TV program, the director has sent you the following agenda for the four-part discussion.

1. *Events that led to war.* Be prepared to recount events that hardened feelings on both sides.

2. *Behind the events: the root causes of the war.* What were the major issues behind the conflicts?

3. *Different explanations of the causes of the war.* Even if two people agreed that a certain issue was driving the North and South apart, they might give different explanations of how or why. Identify people who voiced opinions on issues before the war and explain their positions.

4. *What do* you *think was the main cause of the war?* Be prepared to state your own position on the war's causes and give your reasons.

Work in groups to enact the TV program. Each group will discuss the causes of the Civil War for about twenty minutes, following the director's agenda. Meanwhile, the rest of the class will act as an audience.

Evaluation Criteria

Your work will be evaluated according to how well you meet the following criteria.

- **Completing the task**. You participate in the discussion, contributing constructive comments on each agenda item.
- **Knowing history**. You include facts in your discussion, and you use historical information as evidence to support your opinions.
- **Thinking critically**. Your comments are relevant. You ask other speakers questions that help to clarify issues and move the discussion along. You take positions based on evidence.
- **Communicating ideas**. You express yourself clearly. You listen to the other speakers, and by your comments and questions help to draw them into the discussion. You disagree without making a personal attack. (You may be given a lower score for interrupting, monopolizing the discussion, or attacking another speaker.)

1878 **1891** **1905**

Hayes | Garfield | Arthur | Cleveland | Harrison | Cleveland | McKinley

- First African-American congressmen
- Federal troops leave South
- "Jim Crow" railroad law, Tennessee
- Civil Rights Act of 1875 made unconstitutional
- Force Bill to protect minority voting rights fails in the Senate
- *Plessy* v. *Ferguson*
- First grandfather clause, Louisiana

- First professional baseball team, Cincinnati Red Stockings
- College football develops
- National Baseball League formed
- Tuskegee Institute chartered
- *Huckleberry Finn*, Mark Twain
- *The Red Badge of Courage*, Stephen Crane
- Gettysburg National Park established

- Machine lubrication system, Elijah McCoy
- First steel bridge spans Mississippi
- Edison patents phonograph
- Edison Electric Light Co., New York
- Kodak box camera, George Eastman
- Safety bicycles first made in U.S.
- Edison builds first film studio, New Jersey
- Gasoline-driven car patented, Duryea

Objectives

- Explain how actions of new settlers and the United States government changed the way of life of Native Americans west of the Missouri River.
- Describe how industrialization affected American workers and farmers.
- Discuss social, political, and economic problems largely ignored by politicians of the Gilded Age.

Introducing
THE UNIT

As Reconstruction ended, the United States entered a period of vast economic growth. People moved westward in increasing numbers, taking Native-American lands and turning the plains into farms, ranches, and towns.

The nation underwent rapid industrialization which spurred new inventions, industries, and forms of business; transformed cities into manufacturing centers; and put to work immigrants who poured into the country in the late nineteenth and early twentieth centuries.

By 1890 the United States had the greatest industrial economy in the world. Farmers and workers, feeling powerless in the economy, organized to make industrial United States responsive to their needs.

Unit 5 1850-1910

New Horizons

About the Author

Edna Ferber was one of the most successful writers of her time. Born in Kalamazoo, Michigan, in 1885, she was raised in Appleton, Wisconsin. Ferber wrote *So Big,* winner of the 1925 Pulitzer Prize for fiction; *Saratoga Trunk* (1941); *Giant* (1952); and *Ice Palace* (1958). All of these books, as well as her plays *The Royal Family* and *Dinner at Eight,* were made into films.

Guided Reading

Discussion. As students read this selection from *Cimarron*, have them note the characteristics of the pioneer women as portrayed by Ferber. How important a role did women play in settling the West? Why?

Vocabulary Building

Discussion. Knowing the following terms will help students understand this selection from *Cimarron*: *fracas* (commotion), *calico* (printed cotton material), *alkali* (mineral salt), *hombre* (man), *parching* (thirsty).

History Through Literature

The life of Edna Ferber (1885-1968) did not turn out the way she thought it would. Her acting ambitions ended when her father went blind. The seventeen-year-old Ferber had to take a job as a journalist in order to support her family. She threw the manuscript for her first novel in the trash, but her mother rescued it and sent it to a publisher. Soon Ferber's writing career expanded to include plays as well as novels such as *So Big, Giant,* and *Show Boat,* that depicted American life in the late 1800s.

In *Cimarron,* Edna Ferber tells the dramatic story of the land rush in the Oklahoma Territory in 1889. The novel portrays the energy of people hungry for land and eager for a new start in life. It centers on the rambunctious and wild Yancy Cravat and his genteel, strong willed, and influential wife Sabra. In this excerpt Yancy describes the "unnamed women" of the West—"Women with iron in 'em," Yancy says. He recognized their unrecorded role in history, observing, "If it's ever told straight you'll know it's the sunbonnet and not the sombrero that has settled this country."

from

Cimarron

by Edna Ferber

"Well, the Border at last, and it was like a Fourth of July celebration on Judgment Day. The militia was lined up at the boundary. No one was allowed to set foot on the new land until noon next day, at the firing of the guns. Two million acres of land were to be given away for the grabbing. Noon was the time. They all knew it by heart. April twenty-second, at noon. It takes generations of people hundreds of years to settle a new land. This was going to be made livable territory over night—was made—like a miracle out of the Old Testament. . . .

There wasn't a drink of water to be had in the town after the first twenty-four hours. There we were, thousand and thousands of us, milling around the Border like cattle, with the burning sun baking us all day, nowhere to go for shade, and the thick red dust clogging eyes and nose and mouth. No place to wash, no place to sleep, nothing to eat. Queer enough, they didn't seem to mind. Didn't seem to notice. They were feeding on a kind of crazy excitement, and there was a wild light in their eyes. They laughed and joked and just milled around, all day and all night and until near noon next day. If you had a bit of food you divided it with someone. I finally got a cup of water for a dollar, after standing in line for three hours, and then a woman just behind me—"

"A woman!" Cousin Armita Greenwood (of the Georgia Greenwoods). And Sabra Cravat echoed the words in a shocked whisper.

"You wouldn't believe, would you, that women would go it alone in a fracas like that. But they did. They were there with their husbands, some of them, but there were women who made the Run alone."

"What kind of women?" Felice Venable's tone was not one of inquiry but of condemnation.

"Women with iron in 'em. Women who wanted land and a home. Pioneer women."

From Aunt Cassandra Venable's end of the table there came a word that sounded like, "Hussies!"

Yancey Cravat caught the word beneath his teeth and spat it back. "Hussies, heh! The one behind me in the line was a woman of forty—or looked it—in calico dress and a sunbonnet. She had driven across the prairies all the way from the north of Arkansas in a springless wagon. She was like the women who crossed the continent to California in '49. A gaunt woman, with a weather-beaten face; the terrible neglected skin"—he glanced at Sabra with her creamy coloring—"that means alkali water and sun and dust and wind. Rough hair, and unlovely hands, and boots with the mud caked on them. It's women like her who've made this country what it is. You can't read the history of the United States, my friends" (all this he later used in an Oklahoma Fourth of July speech when they tried to make him Governor) "without learning the great story of those thousands of unnamed women—women like this one I've described—women in the mud-caked boots and calico dresses and sunbonnets, crossing the prairie and the desert and the mountains enduring hardship and privation. Good women, with a terrible and rigid goodness that comes of work and self-denial. Nothing picturesque or romantic about them, I suppose—though occasionally one of them flashes—Belle Starr the outlaw—Rose of the Cimarron—Jeannette Daisy who jumped from a moving Santa Fé train to stake her claim—but the others—no, their story's never really been told. But it's there, just the same. And if it's ever told straight you'll know it's the sunbonnet and not the sombrero that has settled this country."

"Talking nonsense," drawled Felice Venable.

Yancy whirled on his high heels to face her, his fine eyes blazing. "You're one of them. You came up from the South with your husband to make a new home in this Kansas—"

"I am not!" retorted Felice Venable, with enormous dignity. "And I'll thank you not to say any such thing. Sunbonnet indeed! I've never worn a sunbonnet in my life. And as for my skin and hair and hands, they were the toast of the South, as

I can prove by anyone here, all the way from Louisiana to Tennessee. And feet so small my slippers had to be made to order. Calico and muddy boots indeed!"

"Oh, Mamma, Yancey didn't mean— he meant courage to leave your home in the South and come up— he wasn't thinking of— Yancey, do get on with your story of the Run. You got a drink of water for a dollar— dear me!— and shared it with the woman in the calico and the sunbonnet. . . . "

He looked a little sheepish. "Well, matter of fact, it turned out she didn't have a dollar to spare, or anywhere near it, but even if she had it wouldn't have done her any good. The fellow selling it was a rat-faced hombre with one eye and Mexican pants. The trigger finger of his right hand had been shot away in some fracas or other, so he ladled out water with that hand and toted his gun in his left. Bunged up he was, plenty. A scar on his nose, healed up, but showing the marks of where human teeth had bit him in a fight, as neat and clear as a dentist's signboard. By the time I got to him there was one cup of water left in the bucket. He tipped it while I held the dipper, and it trickled out, just an even dipperful. The last cup of water on the Border. The crowd waiting in line behind me gave a kind of sound between a groan and a moan. The sound you hear a herd of cow animals give, out on the prairie, when their tongues are hanging out for water in the dry spell. I tipped up the dipper and had downed a big mouthful—filthy tasting stuff it was too. Gyp water. You could feel the alkali cake on your tongue. Well, my head went back as I drank, and I got one look at that woman's face. Here eyes were on me— on my throat, where the Adam's apple had just given that one big gulp after the first swallow. All bloodshot the whites of her eyes, and a look in them like a dying man looks at a light. Her mouth was open, and her lips were all split with the heat and the dust and the sun, and dry and flaky as ashes. And then she shut her lips a little and tried to swallow nothing, and couldn't. There wasn't any spit in her mouth. I couldn't down another mouthful, parching as I was. I'd have seen her terrible face to the last day of my life. So I righted it, and held it out to her and said, 'Here, sister, take the rest of it. I'm through.' "

Taking a Closer Look

1. *Why were people from all parts of the United States lined up in Oklahoma?*

2. *Describe the women Yancy saw.*

3. *How do the women at the land rush differ from Sabra and her relatives?*

(Background) Little Big Horn, Montana; (opposite) pioneer woman gathering cow chips for fuel; (above) pioneer family.

Taking a Closer Look

ANSWERS

1. They are lined up to claim land in the Oklahoma territory, once the signal—a gunshot—is given.
2. The women Yance saw had "iron in them"; they were "pioneer women." They have weather-beaten faces, rough skin, "unlovely hands," and "the rigid goodness that comes of hard work and self-denial."
3. As Sabra's aunt and mother point out, she and her daughter are much more delicate and refined in appearance. They also think they are more respectable. Sabra's aunt calls the other women "hussies."

355

Chapter 14

Forces Shaping a New West

Planning Guide

	Student Text	TWE Lesson Plans	Support Materials
SECTION 1	**Section 14–1** (1–3 Days) **The Plains Indians,** pp 358–365 Review/Evaluation Section Review, p 365	**Introducing the Chapter:** Attitudes Toward Native Americans—Class Activity, 30 minutes, p 355B **Teaching the Main Ideas:** On Trial—The United States Government—Class Activity, two class periods, p 355B **Enrichment Activity:** Plains Pictographs—Cooperative Activity, one class period, p 355C	★ **Read to Remember,** Section 1 ● **Section Activities,** Section 1 Δ **Readings** ● **Tests and Quizzes,** Section 1 Quiz
SECTION 2	**Section 14–2** (1–2 Days) **The Booming West,** pp 365–370 Geography—Place: The Saga of a Mining Town: Place, p 371 Review/Evaluation Section Review, p 370	**Teaching the Main Ideas:** The West Today—Individual Activity, homework, half class period, p 355C **Evaluating Progress:** Mural of the Booming West—Cooperative Activity, one class period, p 355C	★ **Read to Remember,** Section 2 ● **Section Activities,** Section 2 Δ **Readings** ● **Tests and Quizzes,** Section 2 Quiz
SECTION 3	**Section 14–3** (1–2 Days) **The Prairie Farmers,** pp 372–377 Connections to Themes: The Search for Opportunity, p 377 Review/Evaluation Section Review, p 377 Chapter 14 Survey, pp 378–379 Skills, pp 378–379 Using New Vocabulary Thinking Critically Using a Time Line Applying Thinking Skills: Detecting Bias Writing About Issues	**Reinforcement Activity:** Prairie Farming—Individual Activity, Homework, p 355C	★ **Read to Remember,** Section 3 ● **Section Activities,** Section 3 Δ **Enrichment Activities,** Section 3 ● **Geography Activities,** Section 3 Δ **Readings** ● **Tests and Quizzes,** Section 3 Quiz, Chapter 14 Test (Forms A and B) **Additional Resources** Δ **Twentieth Century Issues: Links to the Past** ● **Active Learning** Δ **GTV Videodiscs** Δ **Transparencies and Activity Book** ● **Testing Software** ★ **Chapter Summaries** **Key:** ★ For Extra Support ● For All Students Δ For Enrichment

Overview

In the 1850s and 1860s American settlers looked to lands that earlier pioneers had passed over—the plains. Settlement of the plains brought pioneers into conflict with the Native Americans who lived there. Native Americans resisted the devastation of their hunting grounds and the loss of their lands and way of life. Warfare erupted on the plains. The United States government's solution was to try to separate Native Americans and settlers by confining Native Americans to reservations. However, most Native Americans fought against confinement, too, and conflicts grew more intense.

The first transcontinental railroad linked the West and the East in the 1860s, providing a feasible way to transport range cattle to eastern markets and settlers to western lands. Increased settlement and barbed wire fences eventually "tamed" the open range and brought an end to cattle drives. Gold and silver strikes brought even more settlers, and boom towns arose across the West.

Lured by the Homestead Act and railroad advertising, which was often false, increasing numbers sought opportunity in prairie farming. Overcoming great hardships, settlers developed new ways of farming, and homesteads and towns sprang up on the prairies and plains.

Activity Objectives

After completing the activities, students should be able to

- evaluate the consequences to Native Americans of the settlement of the plains.
- explain the influence of the West on national consciousness.
- describe the realities of prairie farm life.
- identify economic opportunities that lured settlers west and conflicts that arose among them.
- recognize how pictographs preserve the heritage of plains Indians.

Introducing the Chapter

Attitudes Toward Native Americans

This class activity requires half a class period.

This activity heightens awareness of the role of cultural prejudice and ethnic stereotyping in the settlement of the plains.

Tell students that the following comments were made by commissioners of Indian affairs, in the period between 1850 and 1873. These men were all considered humanitarians, generally sympathetic to the plight of Native Americans. Many moderate Americans agreed with them. Yet their comments reveal cultural prejudices. Read each comment to the class.

“*It is indispensably necessary that [Native Americans] be placed in positions where they can be controlled and finally compelled by sheer necessity to resort to agricultural labor or starve. . . . There should be assigned to each tribe, for a permanent home, a country adapted to agriculture, of limited extent and well-defined boundaries.*”

—Luke Lea, Commissioner of Indian Affairs

“*Sums of money shall be paid to the . . . tribes, or expended for their use and benefit under the direction of the President of the United States, who may from time to time determine . . . what proportion of the annual payments . . . shall be . . . expended for their [Native Americans'] moral improvement and education; for such beneficial objects as in his judgment will . . . advance them in civilization; for buildings, opening farms, fencing, breaking land, providing stock, agricultural implements, seeds, etc.*”

—George Manypenny, Commissioner of Indian Affairs

“*Inasmuch as the progress of our industrial enterprise has cut these people [Native Americans] from modes of livelihood entirely sufficient for their wants and for which they were qualified, . . . and has left them utterly without resource, they have a claim . . . to such assistance as may be necessary to place them in a position to obtain a livelihood by means . . . compatible with civilization.*”

—Francis A. Walker, Commissioner of Indian Affairs

Ask the following questions about each comment and list the answers on the chalkboard:

- What kinds of activities does this person believe to be worthwhile?
- What assumptions does he make about Native Americans?
- How does he think Native Americans should change?
- How does he recommend bringing about this change?

Have students compare the attitudes of the three commissioners and then predict how Native Americans would have responded. Point out that in Chapter 14 students will read about conflicts between white settlers and Native Americans. Ask them to consider as they read how misunderstandings and stereotypes led to injustices.

Teaching the Main Ideas

Section 14–1: On Trial—The United States Government

This class activity requires two class periods.

In this activity students consider the role of the United States government in nineteenth-century conflicts between settlers and Native Americans.

After students have read Section 14–1, ask them to consider what arguments Native-American nations might have used in a lawsuit against the federal government for its treatment of them. Students will serve as law clerks gathering evidence to be used in a mock trial.

On the chalkboard write the following statement:

The United States government is accused of (1) willfully attempting to deny Native Americans use of their rightful land and (2) willfully attempting to deny Native Americans their right, as guaranteed by the First Amendment, to practice their religion and follow their cultural traditions.

Students will prepare the case against the government by gathering evidence from Section 14–1. Divide the class into nine groups and assign each group one of the following topics to research: treaties, cultural stereotyping, conflict between the values of settlers and Native Americans, reservation system, Sand Creek massacre, Custer, killing of buffalo, Battle at Wounded Knee, Dawes Act. Each group is to prepare an oral statement to support the case against the government. Allow one class period for the groups to find and organize their evidence.

On the following day, conduct the plaintiff's side of the mock trial. Read the charges, then ask each group to deliver its evidence. After all nine groups have presented, engage students in a discussion of the case. Ask what arguments the United States government might have used to defend its actions in such a trial.

Teaching the Main Ideas

Section 14–2: The West Today

Preparation of this individual activity is to be done as homework; half a class period is required for presentations.

This activity is designed to increase understanding of how romantic images of the "Old West" not only influenced settlers in the late 1800s but continue to shape ideas today.

Tell students that the story of the "Old West" is part of our national myth; many of our notions have been formed by poems, paintings, stories, songs, and films, rather than by historical fact. Point out that modern advertising often calls upon our romantic notions of the West to sell products. Challenge students to discover how words and images associated with the West are used to influence us.

Brainstorm to create a list of words associated with the "Old West," for example, horse, cowboy, gun, sheriff, adventure, wild, and tough. Assign students the task of finding pictures and statements from current magazines and newspapers that illustrate the images these words create. Direct students to organize the pictures and statements to complete the following sentence: *"Today, the Old West is portrayed as a place of . . . ."*

Have students read their statements and show their pictures. Discuss the portrait of the West that emerges and why advertisers have created such a portrait. Have the class evaluate the accuracy of the portrait.

Reinforcement Activity

Section 14–3: Prairie Farming

This individual activity may be assigned as homework.

To understand the accomplishments of plains farm families, students write narratives describing farm life.

Review with students how and why advertising was used by territorial and state governments, and railroads to encourage people to move west to the plains and buy land on the plains. Point out that immigrants and easterners had no way of assessing the accuracy of such advertising, which sometimes made extravagant promises. Discuss the feelings pioneers must have had when they discovered they had been misled.

Have each student imagine himself or herself to be a prairie farmer writing a letter to a relative in the East. The farmer moved west after seeing a handbill that advertised lush, fertile land—a paradise. Upon arriving, the farmer found the land to be dry, almost a desert. Water is a good distance away, there is no wood or building material, infestations of insects are a plague in the summer, prairie fires are a threat in the fall, blizzards are a danger in the winter, and isolation and loneliness are problems all the time. Now after a year on the plains, the farmer describes in the letter the false advertising claims and the realities of prairie farming.

Encourage students to trade letters, each reading at least two or three besides his or her own. Then discuss how students might have reacted to such a situation. Would they have found it discouraging or challenging? Why?

Evaluating Progress

Section 14–2: Mural of the Booming West

This cooperative activity requires one class period.

In this activity students work in groups to create murals picturing life in the "Booming West."

Have students identify five occupational groups discussed in Section 14–2 (railroad workers, cowhands, ranchers, farmers, miners, merchants and other business people, law enforcers). Point out that many of the people who migrated to the West in the late 1800s earned their livelihood in one of these occupations and that each group was made up of people from many different cultural backgrounds.

Divide the class into groups of three or four and provide each group with large sheets of paper. Direct each group to create a mural depicting everyday life in the West in the late 1800s. Each mural is to include five or more of the occupational activities discussed in Section 14–2. Murals are to be primarily illustrative but may include some words. Explain that the murals should show interactions—which may be positive or negative—between the occupational groups.

Display the murals and discuss the activities portrayed. Evaluate murals on comprehensiveness and accuracy in depicting occupations and in showing cooperation and conflict between occupational groups in the "Booming West."

Enrichment Activity

Section 14–1: Plains Pictographs

This cooperative activity requires one class period.

The activity engages students in the Plains Indian tradition of drawing pictographs on buffalo hides to chronicle their peoples' history. If students are unfamiliar with Plains Indian art, you may wish to provide photographs of pictographs.

Begin the activity by explaining that Plains Indians did not have a written language. Their culture was passed from generation to generation orally. However, they did record their history with pictographic symbols on buffalo hides which were easily carried as the people moved from place to place. The pictographs served as a visual code to past events. On long winter evenings, a chronicler would haul out a hide inscribed with pictographs to serve as a reminder as people reminisced about the past. In this way, the past would come to life over and over again.

Generally pictographs depicted major events that had affected the whole group rather than personal experiences, although occasionally a personal experience of great importance was recorded. The pictures were not intended to be realistic. Images were drawn without regard for perspective and most humans were shown in profile.

Pictographs usually consisted of concrete images—humans, animals, objects, and geographical features, for example—set down as a record of an event. Certain images recurred. For example, in Kiowa chronicles, events happening in the winter were placed above a blade of dry grass and events happening in the summer were drawn above the image of the sacred lodge in which the sun dance took place.

Divide the class into groups of three and direct each group to choose a significant event discussed in Section 14–1. Their task is to devise a series of pictographs telling the story from the Native-American perspective.

When the projects are finished, have the class guess which event each series of pictographs portrays. Conclude by discussing the role that pictographs had in preserving the heritage of Plains Indians.

Bibliography and Audiovisual Material

Teacher Bibliography

Brown, Dee. *The Gentle Tamers: Women of the Old Wild West.* Lincoln: University of Nebraska Press, 1981.

Collier, Peter. *When Shall They Rest? The Cherokee's Long Struggle with America*. New York: Holt, Rinehart, and Winston, 1973.

Durham, Philip, and Everett L. Jones. *The Negro Cowboys.* Lincoln: University of Nebraska Press, 1983.

Farr, William E. *The Reservation Blackfeet, 1882–1945.* Seattle: University of Washington Press, 1984.

Student Bibliography

Brown, Dee. *Bury My Heart at Wounded Knee.* New York: Holt, Rinehart, and Winston, 1981.

Cabeza de Baca, Fabiola. *We Feed Them Cactus.* Albuquerque, New Mexico: University of New Mexico Press, 1954.

Cather, Willa. *O Pioneers!* Boston: Houghton Mifflin, 1941.

Ferber, Edna. *Cimarron.* New York: Doubleday, 1951.

McLuhan, T. C. *Touch the Earth.* New York: Simon & Schuster, 1971.

Sandoz, Marie. *Cheyenne Autumn.* New York: Avon, 1964.

Stratton, Joanna. *Pioneer Women: Voices from the Kansas Frontier*. New York: Simon and Schuster, 1982.

Films, Videocassettes, and Videodiscs

Broken Treaties. 34 min. Coronet/MTI. Videodisc.

Life in a Gold Mining Camp 1850. 18 min. AIMS. Videodisc.

Railroads and Westward Expansion (1865–1900). 16 min. BFA Educational Media. Videocassette.

Technology in America: The Age of Invention. 18 min. Coronet/MTI. Movie.

Westward Movement. United Learning. 5 Videocassettes.

Filmstrips

Growing Up With America: Growing Up On The Way West. SVE.

Progressives, Populists and Reform in America. 32 min. 2 filmstrips. Guidance Associates.

Computer Software

American History Keyword Series: Westward Ho! Apple. Focus Media.

The Indian Wars. Apple. Heizer Software.

The Time Tunnel—American History 1860–1920. Apple. Focus Media.

Chapter 14

Objectives

- Explain how the lives of the Plains Indians were changed by the arrival of settlers.
- Identify economic factors that helped shape life in the West.
- Cite characteristics of farm life on the Great Plains.

Introducing THE CHAPTER

For suggestions on introducing Chapter 14, refer to page 355B in the Teacher's Edition.

Developing THE CHAPTER

For activities and teaching strategies to help you reinforce and enrich chapter content, see pages 355B–355D in the Teacher's Edition.

Chapter Opener Illustrations

George Catlin painted this portrait of a Wichita woman, She Who Bathes Her Knees, in 1832. Catlin set out to preserve on canvas Native American customs before they were changed forever by the meeting of Indians and settlers.

Alfred Jacob Miller was the first European American artist to paint scenes along the route that would become the Oregon Trail. About 1837 he painted this picture of Fort Laramie, a trading post in eastern Wyoming 75 miles north of present-day Laramie. Several Native American tribes frequented this fort, trading furs and skins for guns and powder.

About 1877 Howling Wolf, a Cheyenne, sketched a corn patch and the kind of domed wigwam to be found in semi-

Reduced student page in the Teacher's Edition

Chapter 14 1850-1910

Forces Shaping a New West

permanent prairie settlements. At the time Howling Wolf was at Fort Marion, in St. Augustine, Florida, where the U.S. government imprisoned the Plains warriors considered to be the greatest threat. The prison's supervisor, Lieutenant Richard Henry Pratt, encouraged his charges to earn money by selling illustrations depicting their experiences.

Nomadic Plains Indians, following large buffalo herds, often had to pack and move in a great hurry. The family below moved from Fort Keogh, Montana. The cage kept children from falling off the platform.

Music was central to the Plains Indian culture. Instruments like the buffalo effigy drum, made from buffalo hide, were used in sacred dances.

American Voices

Iron Teeth, a Cheyenne woman, was born in 1834. When Iron Teeth was young, her homeland was barely touched by the pioneers trudging across the Great Plains to Oregon and California. The United States government had promised it forever to the Indians.

> *"We used to plant corn, when I was a little girl. With sharpened sticks we punched holes in the ground, dropped in the grains of corn, went hunting all summer, then returned to gather our crops. . . .*
>
> *The first issue of government presents to the Cheyenne was when I was fifteen years old. . . . We were given beef, but we did not eat any of it. Great piles of bacon were stacked on the prairie and distributed to us, but we used it only to make fires or to grease robes for tanning. . . .*
>
> *Soldiers built forts in our Powder River country when I was about thirty-two years old. The Sioux and the Cheyenne fought against them. After a few years, peace was made. The Cheyenne settled at the White River agency, in our favorite Black Hills country. This was to be our land forever, so we were pleased. But white people found gold on our lands. They crowded in, so we had to move out. . . . The only thing we could do was go to other lands offered to us. We did this."*

By the 1860s, railroad tracks were creeping across the vast plains. Soon a new generation of pioneers had begun arriving in search of opportunity. They found grass that could fatten cattle and sheep, soil that could be farmed, and hills that could be mined for gold and silver. This land that was home to the Plains Indians was seen by the newcomers simply as promising territory to tame.

A Wichita Woman; Fort Laramie, Wyoming, about 1850; sketch of corn made about 1880 by Howling Wolf, a Cheyenne; Indian family in Montana; buffalo drum used for religious dances.

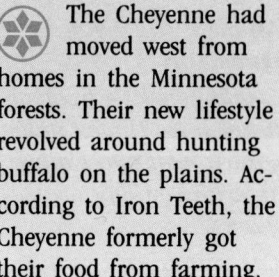

Analyzing Primary Sources

American Voices

The Cheyenne had moved west from homes in the Minnesota forests. Their new lifestyle revolved around hunting buffalo on the plains. According to Iron Teeth, the Cheyenne formerly got their food from farming.

In addition to beef and bacon, the Cheyenne also received other government issues: "The green coffee," Iron Teeth said, "looked to us like some new kind of berries. We boiled these berries just as they were, green, but they did not taste good."

Ask: How useful were the government's presents to the Cheyenne? **(Presents included goods but not information about their use.)** How did the United States government go back on its word to the Cheyenne? **(by building railroads and settling on land promised to them)**

GTV Side 3

Chap. 1, Frame 05100

The State of the Union, 1876: Looking West (Movie Segment)

Search and Play:

GTV Side 3

Chap. 3, Frame 08323

A World of Change (Movie)

Search:

Play:

Section 14-1

Objectives

- ***Answer the Focus Question.***
- *Identify various treaties between the United States government and Native-American groups on the Plains.*
- *Cite causes and results of wars between American Indians and the United States government from 1869–1890.*

Introducing

THE SECTION

Have students refer to text page 27 to recall early ways of life on the plains. Then have students use the illustrations on pages 356, 357, and 361 to elaborate. Students should note both settled and nomadic ways of life, as well as the addition of the horse.

In the first half of the nineteenth century, American settlers looked to the Far West and to Texas. Have students use the map on text page 254 to explain why American settlement of the Far West stirred the government's interest in controlling Native Americans on the plains. **(To protect settlers on the trails to the Far West.)**

About mid-century, Americans began to show an interest in settling the Great Plains. Ask students to predict how this interest would alter the lives of the Plains Indians.

Time Line Illustrations

1. The rich Comstock Lode in Nevada's Washoe Mountains yielded this silver bar marked 999.5, indicating that it is nearly pure silver. Mining helped to open the West to settlement.
2. John Deere's plow, made in 1837 with slick smooth steel, was the first to break the prairie sod. Typical plows of the early 1800s often broke because of the heavy sod. New machinery, like this plow, increased productivity of farmers on the plains.
3. Sheet music of "The Midnight Flyer." In the 1800s, trains inspired many plays, novels, and songs. This march was dedicated to the Brotherhood of Locomotive Engineers.
4. The plight of the western tribes angered and disturbed many Americans. Sarah Winnemucca, daughter of a Paiute

Reduced student page in the Teacher's Edition

CHAPTER TIME LINE

1850 - 1910

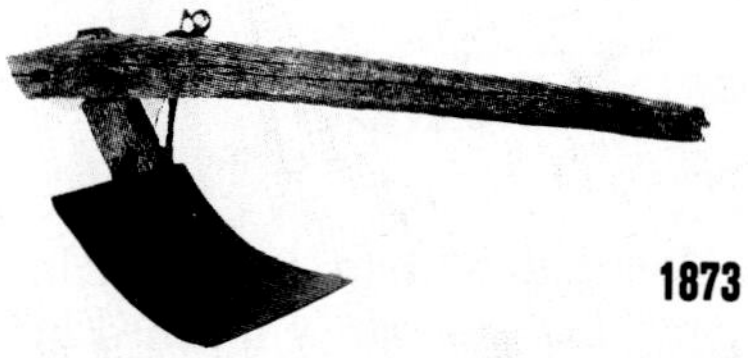

1873 Joseph Glidden patents barbed wire

1862 Homestead Act

1850 | 1862 | 1874

1851 Fort Laramie Treaty

1859 Comstock Lode discovered

1867 First cattle drive over the Chisholm Trail

1869 First transcontinental railroad completed

14-1 *The Plains Indians*

Focus: How were the lives of the Plains Indians changed by the arrival of settlers?

"A railroad, fellow citizens, is a machine, and one of the most beautiful and perfect of labor-saving machines. It well suits the energy of the American people. They love to go ahead fast, and to go with power."

So said one railroad booster. In the 1850s and 1860s people talked of laying track from the Missouri River to the Pacific—over 1,600 miles.

The railroad was to be a link in the American industrial chain. The West would ship raw materials to eastern factories. It would also be a profitable market for manufactured goods. The railroad's supporters promised that quick, reliable transportation between the East and the West would guarantee a bright economic future to all Americans.

But would railroads bring a better life to all the peoples of the continent? Railroads would require land—land that the government had promised to the Plains Indians. How would the coming of railroads affect these Native Americans?

The Fort Laramie Treaty

In the 1850s and 1860s, about 250,000 Native Americans—in dozens of different tribes—roamed the Great Plains, the mountains, and the Great Basin. Most of these tribes had lived in western North America for hundreds of years: the Arap-

chief, stirred the nation's conscience in her writing and lectures about the treatment of Native Americans.

5. The tipi was perfectly fitted to the housing requirements of the roving buffalo hunters. It was portable, easily erected, waterproof, and well ventilated by cleverly designed smoke flaps.

6. Advertisements like this one from the Independence, Kansas, entrepreneur who organized "The Grand Expedition" of May 7, 1879, encouraged settlers to move west, into lands once promised to the Indians.

1887 Dawes Act provides for division of Indian lands

1893 About 1,000 buffalo remain in U.S.

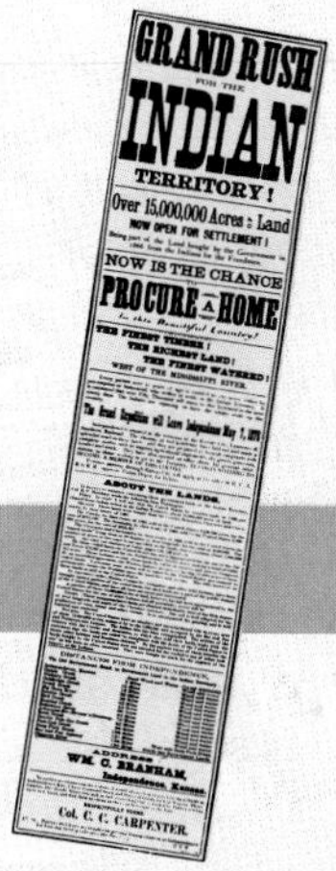

1886 — 1898 — 1910

1884 *Ramona* published

1890 Massacre at Wounded Knee

1896 Gold discovered on Klondike Creek

1907 Oklahoma admitted as a state

ahos, Kiowas, Comanches, Cheyennes, Osages, Pawnees, Blackfoot, Crows, and Sioux. Others had arrived more recently: the Cherokees, Creeks, Chickasaws, Choctaws, Seminoles, and Delawares.

Migration from the East disrupted the Native-American way of life. Pioneer trails stretched across Indian homelands. Gold seekers and pioneers trampled the buffalo range and killed thousands of the animals unnecessarily. Gradually, the government built forts along the trails to protect travelers from Native Americans seeking to drive them off Indian lands.

One official, Thomas Fitzpatrick, thought that the Plains Indians would rebel against the devastation of their hunting grounds. He called on the government to make treaties, as it had been doing for sixty years with the eastern tribes.

In 1851 government agents met with 10,000 Indians from 8 tribes in a great council near Fort Laramie, Wyoming. The result of the talks was the Fort Laramie Treaty, which gave the United States the right to build more roads and forts on the plains. In return, the United States would make annual payments to the tribes for fifty years. The treaty also defined the boundaries of each tribe's hunting grounds. The government's goal was to prevent conflict by keeping the settlers and the Native Americans apart.

A Path to War

The treaty proved a path to war, not peace. The government did not realize that individual Indians were not bound by the decisions of their chiefs. In order to survive, many Indian tribes followed the wandering buffalo as they always had, ignoring boundaries set for their hunting grounds.

Settlers, too, disregarded the Fort Laramie Treaty. When it was signed, few people expected that throngs of settlers would soon crowd the trails west. Lured by minerals, timber, and fertile soils, some of these settlers moved onto Indian lands. As greater numbers of people poured into the West, conflicts between settlers and Indians grew more frequent and more bitter.

The government tried to keep order by buying Indian land to resell to the settlers. In a series of

Developing

THE SECTION

Thinking Critically

Analysis. The notion that Native Americans should leave their homes for land far from areas occupied by white settlers may have begun with Thomas Jefferson, who advocated that the lands beyond the Mississippi should be reserved for them.

This notion was the seed from which the horrors of Andrew Jackson's Indian removal policy grew. Native-American nations were made to move from one kind of geographical region to another, and often the area they were moved to was not suitable in terms of food, clothing, or shelter.

Ask: How did Jefferson and Jackson believe they were permanently solving the white/Native-American problem? Why were they wrong?

GTV Side 3

Chap. 4, Frame 15097

Native American Population: 1890 and 1910 (Population Clocks, 2 Frames)

Search:

Step:

Active Learning

Cooperative Activity. Divide students into ten groups. Have each group research and report to the class on the cause, course, and outcome of an Indian War. Each group should make visual aids to accompany its presentations. Students can choose from the following:

The First Sioux War (1862-1864); Red Cloud's War (1866-1868); Hancock's War (1967); Sheridan's War (1868-1869); the Apache War (1871-1873); the Red River War (1874-1875); the Second Sioux War (1876-1877); the Flight of the Nez Percé (1877); the Flight of the Cheyenne (1878); the Geronimo Campaigns (1885-1886); the Ghost Dance Scare (1890).

Multicultural Perspectives

Great Britain dealt with Native American tribes as independent nations, making agreements with them by means of treaties. Following the same policy, between 1778 and 1871 the United States signed 370 treaties with the Native Americans. Under the Constitution, these treaties were as legally binding as United States agreements with France, Britain, or other nations.

However, most treaties made it clear that Native Americans did not enjoy the privileges of full sovereignty as did foreign nations. Through treaties the United States government forced Indians onto reservations and opened Native-American land to settlement. In 1871 the federal government stopped claiming to treat Indian tribes as independent nations; instead, its policy was to settle matters through agreements approved by both houses of Congress.

Reduced student page in the Teacher's Edition

treaties signed between 1853 and 1856, the government acquired 174 million acres, paying very little per acre. Some treaties established **reservations,** areas set aside for Indians. Some people saw the reservations as protection for Native Americans. Others saw them as a means of moving the Indians out of the way of the settlers. For most Native Americans the reservations were like prisons, and they fought against being confined there.

Wars for the plains raged from 1860 to 1890, often with bitter cruelty on both sides. In 1862 Chief Little Crow led angry Sioux warriors in an attack on settlers in southern Minnesota. The Sioux killed hundreds of men, women, and children, who they believed were a threat to the Sioux way of life.

Two years later a volunteer regiment swept into a Cheyenne and Arapahoe encampment at Sand Creek, Colorado, where the Indians thought that they were safely under the protection of a nearby army post. Although the Cheyenne chief, Black Kettle, raised an American flag and a white flag of surrender, the volunteers killed more than a hundred people, mainly women and children.

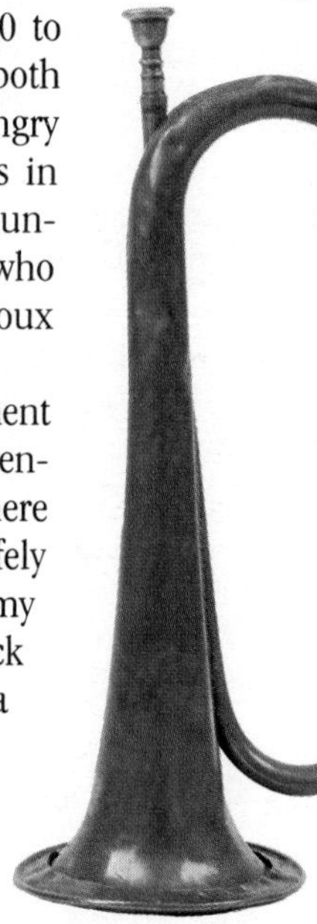
U.S. Army bugle

Red Cloud's War. In the struggle for the plains, Native Americans were rarely successful for long. But for years one Oglala Sioux chief, Red Cloud, successfully held off both soldiers and settlers. In 1863 Sioux warriors, led by Red Cloud, began to harass travelers on the Bozeman Trail, which crossed Sioux and Cheyenne hunting grounds to get to mines in Montana.

Government officials met with Red Cloud and other Sioux chiefs to discuss the trail. During the talks, troops rode in from the East, and their commanding officer announced plans to build forts along the trail. Red Cloud responded, "Before the Indians say yes or no, White Chief goes with soldiers to steal the road."

Red Cloud stormed out of the meeting. He later laid siege to the government-built forts. Finally, in 1868, the United States government agreed to give up the forts on the Bozeman Trail. The treaty that ended Red Cloud's war also established a reservation for the Northern Cheyenne and the Sioux that covered all of present-day South Dakota west of the Missouri River.

The Medicine Lodge treaties. To bring peace to the southern Great Plains, a second series of treaties was signed at Medicine Lodge Creek in Kansas. The Medicine Lodge treaties provided for new reservations in the Indian Territory—present-day Oklahoma—for the tribes of the southern Great Plains: Southern Cheyennes and Arapahos, Kiowas, Comanches, and Kiowa-Apaches.

The Medicine Lodge treaties did not bring peace, however. In Kansas and Colorado the army clashed with the Cheyenne, whose traditional lands extended beyond their reservation's boundaries. In November 1868 Lieutenant Colonel George Armstrong Custer became a hero to many when he led his cavalry in a surprise attack on a small group of Cheyenne led by Chief Black Kettle, the same chief who had been attacked at Sand Creek.

The Peace Policy

While settlers and miners were urging the government to protect them from Indians, reformers called for more humane treatment of Native Americans. In 1869 President Ulysses S. Grant responded by establishing a "peace policy." The aim of the policy was to place all Indians on reservations and teach them European-American ways. The policy was to be carried out by reservation agents chosen by church groups for their competence and good moral character.

Seeking to preserve their freedom and their way of life, many Plains Indians rejected the reservations and Indian agents. They were determined to remain free as long as there were buffalo to hunt. Old Lady Horse, a Kiowa woman, expressed the importance of the buffalo in their lives: "Everything came from the buffalo. Their teepees were made of buffalo hides; so were their clothes and moccasins. They ate buffalo meat."

Connections: Politics

In every war from 1860 to 1890 on each side people had many different opinions. Some white Americans objected to the federal government's policies and a substantial number of Native Americans refused to fight against government troops. Other Native Americans joined government forces as scouts.

Analyzing Primary Sources

The Comanche Oral Tradition. Traditional Plains Indians had no written language but they had a rich oral tradition. The following is an excerpt from a speech made by the Comanche chief Ten Bears at the Medicine Lodge Council in 1868:

“But there are things which you have said to me which I do not like. They are not sweet like sugar, but bitter like gourds. You said that you wanted to put us upon a reservation, to build us houses and make us medicine lodges. I do not want them. I was born upon the prairie, where the wind blew free and there was nothing to break the light of the sun. I was born where there were no enclosures and where everything drew a free breath. I want to die there and not within walls.”

Ask: Why was it difficult for Native Americans to live on reservations? **(not interested in confinement, used to living on open land, forced to give up their traditional way of life)** Do Native Americans believe in private ownership? Explain.

When artist George Catlin visited this village in 1834, the Comanches controlled a 240,000-square-mile area in northern Texas. By 1867 they were confined to a small Oklahoma reservation.

However, the buffalo had nearly vanished. Hunters had shot them for sport, and railroad crews had slaughtered them for food. When a way was found to tan buffalo hides for leather, hunters destroyed buffalo by the tens of thousands, taking the hides and leaving the meat to rot.

Many military leaders encouraged the buffalo slaughter. They thought that if the Indians were without food, it would be easier to force them onto reservations. General Philip Sheridan said, "Let them kill, skin, and sell until the buffalo is exterminated as it is the only way to bring about lasting peace and allow civilization to advance."

The Little Bighorn

The treaty that had ended Red Cloud's War promised the Indians exclusive rights to the land in and around the Black Hills of Dakota. But when gold was discovered in 1874, miners flocked to the region. In response, angry Sioux and Cheyenne warriors raided settlements in the Dakota and Montana territories.

In 1876 the government ordered all the tribes back onto their reservations, but thousands of Sioux and Northern Cheyenne refused. Under the leadership of chiefs Crazy Horse and Sitting Bull,

Linking Past and Present

Research. African Americans played key roles in the Indian Wars, serving the 9th and 10th United States Cavalry Regiments and the 24th and 25th United States Infantry Regiments. Native Americans called them Buffalo Soldiers because African Americans' hair reminded them of buffalo fur.

In spite of their exemplary service, African-American soldiers endured discrimination: their commissioned officers were white, they often were given the worst jobs, and they usually were sent to the worst posts on the frontier.

Have students research the percentage of non whites in the American army today. **Ask:** What jobs are African, Mexican, and Native Americans given? What opportunities? Is the military any different today?

Multicultural Perspectives

Ohiyesa was a Sioux, born in Minnesota in 1858. When Ohiyesa was fifteen, his father became convinced that the Indians were doomed unless they accepted white ways. He renamed his son Charles Eastman and sent him to a mission school in the Dakota Territory. At first, Charles wanted to run away. *"They might as well try to make a buffalo build houses like a beaver, as to teach me to be a white man."* Eventually, however, he became a doctor and at Wounded Knee worked desperately to save the victims.

He devoted the rest of his life to his people's cause. Although he believed most Indian problems were caused by land hunger and broken treaties, he tried to be a bridge between the two groups. *"I am an Indian,"* he said. *"Nevertheless, so long as I live, I am an American."*

Reduced student page in the Teacher's Edition

New technology met tradition at Little Bighorn. A Sioux painting shows Indians using guns as well as bows. Chief Crazy Horse (center) wore paint thought to provide protection.

National Museum of the American Indian S.I.

they gathered for a religious ritual at a bend in the Little Bighorn River in Montana Territory. Two hundred soldiers led by Lieutenant Colonel Custer had tracked the tribes to this point. Without warning, the cavalry attacked.

The assault proved a disaster for Custer and his men. His troops were isolated by Crazy Horse's forces and wiped out to a man. For the Indians, the Battle of Little Bighorn, which was also known as "Custer's Last Stand," stood as a great triumph. But it was to be their last victory in the struggle to save their lands.

The End of Indian Resistance

After the disaster at Little Bighorn, the government was under increasing public pressure to control the Indians. Indian attacks were interfering with mining, settlement, and the railroads. In fall 1876 government agents concluded yet another treaty, which took the mineral-rich Black Hills away from the Sioux. One anguished chief signed the treaty while holding a blanket in front of his eyes.

Meanwhile, the government increased its drive to force Plains Indians back to the reservations. The Sioux broke up into bands to evade the army. Sitting Bull escaped with some of his people into Canada. Crazy Horse and his followers remained on the plains and fought bitterly into the winter of 1877. Then, near starvation, they surrendered.

Other tribes also fled the reservations. The Nez Percé (NEHZ per-SAY) of Idaho, led by Chief Joseph, tried to reach freedom in Canada as Sitting Bull had done. The army stopped them just short of the Canadian border.

However, even in Canada Sitting Bull could not hold out much longer. Though land was plentiful, the buffalo were not. In desperation the Sioux sent hunting parties across the border into the United States in search of buffalo, but the buffalo were nearly gone. Finally, in 1881 Sitting Bull and his people returned to the United States and gave in to reservation life.

Wounded Knee

For many Native Americans, life on the reservation was a miserable fate. They had to depend on farming—a shameful occupation for hunters like the Sioux—and on meager government handouts. In their poverty, Indian children starved to death before their parents' eyes.

Connections: Religion

Discussion. Ask students to speculate about why so many Native Americans joined the Ghost Dance movement. Why might this movement have been so appealing in 1889?

Thinking Critically

Application. Susette La Flesche's Indian name was Inshta Theumba, which means "Bright Eyes." Although frightened of public speaking, she spoke to huge crowds in the East, testified before Senate committees, and discussed Indian issues with President Hayes.

"We are thinking men and women," she told her listeners. *"We have a right to be heard. Your government has driven us hither and thither like cattle."* **Ask:** How did La Flesche's determination help her to overcome her fear of speaking in public? Has conviction ever helped you overcome fear?

Hoping for a miracle to save them from destruction, some Native Americans embraced a religious movement called the "Ghost Dance." It began in 1889 when a Paiute leader named Wovoka described a vision that dead Indians would return with Christ and vast herds of buffalo would once more roam the prairie. The returning dead and the buffalo would drive away the whites. Indians who danced the Ghost Dance could see the world to come, and bulletproof "ghost shirts" with special markings would keep them from harm.

Worried that the spreading faith would provoke a Sioux uprising, government officials banned the Ghost Dance. They planned to arrest two Sioux leaders—Big Foot and Sitting Bull.

In December 1890, Indian police employed by the government surrounded Sitting Bull's cabin. When they tried to arrest the chief, a Sioux shot an officer. In the gunfire that followed, Sitting Bull was killed.

Ten days after Sitting Bull's death, the army found Chief Big Foot and his band of 350 men, women, and children. They were put under guard along the banks of Wounded Knee Creek in South Dakota. As soldiers were disarming the warriors, a shot was fired. In panic, the soldiers opened fire. A furious struggle left some 200 Sioux men, women, and children dead or dying, along with 25 soldiers. Some papers at the time labeled the battle a triumph over "Indian treachery," but others called it a brutal slaughter. Recently, historian Robert Utley has described this clash at Wounded Knee as "a tragic accident of war that neither side intended."

American Voices

"I am tired of fighting. It is cold and we have no blankets. The little children are freezing to death. Hear me my chiefs. I am tired. My heart is sick and sad. From where the sun now stands, I will fight no more forever."

—Chief Joseph of the Nez Percé

Legal Rights for Indians

While the army was crushing Indian resistance, one incident became a first step toward legal rights for Native Americans. In 1865 the government had guaranteed the small Ponca tribe a reservation along the Missouri River. But later it gave the same land to the Sioux. Realizing the mistake, officials decided to move the Poncas to Oklahoma.

The Poncas longed for their old home. When the son of Ponca chief Standing Bear died, the chief and thirty followers set out for their old homeland to bury the boy among his ancestors. Fearing a rebellion, the army arrested the group and imprisoned them in Omaha.

When the reasons for Standing Bear's journey became known, many people sympathized. Two Omaha lawyers volunteered to help. In 1879 the lawyers applied for a writ of *habeas corpus*, an order requiring law officers to bring an arrested person before a judge to decide if the person is being imprisoned legally. The government's attorneys argued that Indians did not have legal rights under the Constitution. The judge, however, decided that Indians were persons under the law—individuals with inalienable rights. The judge further found that the Poncas had broken no laws.

A Nebraska journalist, Thomas Tibbles, and the daughter of an Omaha chief, Susette La Flesche, took up the cause. La Flesche, who had been educated in white schools, defended Indian rights in fluent English. Standing Bear often joined the pair.

GTV Side 2

Chap. 7, Frame 23135

Sarah Winnemucca: Native American Activist (American Journal)

Search:

Play:

Active Learning

Debate. Have students discuss the rationale behind the Dawes Act: American Indians must be assimilated into American society in order to survive. Have them debate the pros and cons of the rationale.

Section Review

ANSWERS

1. The definition for the term *reservation* is on text page 360.
2. Answers may include that hunting grounds were limited by treaty, the buffalo herds on which some tribes depended were depleted, and settlers drove Native Americans off their lands.
3. Students might consider the following factors: the numbers of settlers and of soldiers; Indians' loss of hunting grounds and the depletion of the bison, leading to loss of food supply and way of life; the removal of Native Americans to areas with unfamiliar geographic characteristics; the separation of families and tribes; illnesses and deaths resulting from Indian removal policies.
4. Answers will vary. Those who think Native Americans treated fairly can argue that wants were to be provided for on reservations. Those who disagree can argue that whites had no right to confine Native Americans, who had occupied this land for centuries, and that Native Americans had a perfect right to defend their way of life.
Linking Past and Present. Answers will vary.

Reduced student page in the Teacher's Edition

A young writer named Helen Hunt Jackson heard Tibbles and La Flesche speak. She was so moved that she devoted her life to Indian causes. In *A Century of Dishonor* she told the story of the broken treaties. Her novel *Ramona* was a tale about California mission Indians. She hoped *Ramona* would help Native Americans as *Uncle Tom's Cabin* had helped blacks.

The Dawes Act

Public reaction to the Ponca case influenced changes in government policy. In 1887 Senator Henry L. Dawes of Massachusetts introduced a bill in Congress aimed at making Native Americans a part of American society.

Supporters of the Dawes Act believed that assimilation would solve the "Indian problem" once and for all. They argued that the government should stop dealing with Indians as tribes and start treating them as individuals, especially through individual rather than tribal land ownership.

Under the act, tribes were no longer to be recognized as legal groups and could not hold their reservation lands in common. Some land on reservations would be allotted to individual Native Americans. The remaining lands, totaling almost ninety million acres, were to be sold with the money being used for schools to teach Native Americans, pressuring them to abandon tribal ways and become United States citizens.

Most Native Americans, though, had no desire to adopt European-American ways. Meanwhile, speculators moved in quickly to buy up the land for as little as fifty cents an acre. In the decades to come, acres and acres of land would pass out of Indian hands.

National Museum of the American Indian S.I.

Sioux Chief Sitting Bull; a Pawnee "ghost shirt."

Under the Dawes Act, agents like Alice Fletcher surveyed Indian lands, dividing them among individual tribe members. Known as "the Measuring Woman," she was respected by Indians for her sensitivity to their cultures.

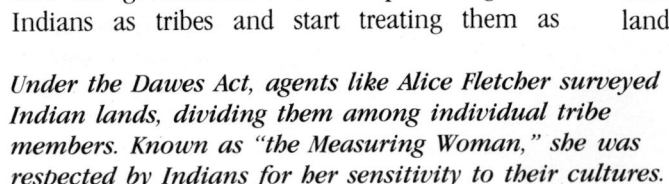

Multicultural Perspectives

Thousands of Chinese helped build the first American transcontinental railroad, working six days a week. One roadbed had to be gouged out of a granite cliff more than one thousand feet high. Chinese laborers were lowered down the rock face in wicker baskets. They drilled holes for explosives, lit the fuses, and then were swiftly hauled up before the powder blew. The expression "a Chinamen's chance" described the survival odds of the Chinese chosen to lay such dynamite charges.

Section Review

1. Identification. Define *reservation.*

2. Comprehension. How were the lives of Native Americans west of the Missouri River changed by the onrush of settlers? Give three examples.

3. Analysis. In the end, why were Native Americans unsuccessful in their efforts to resist the United States government?

4. Evaluation. Did the United States treat Native Americans fairly by placing them on reservations, or were the Native Americans justified in resisting this policy?

Linking Past and Present. Westerns are stories about the settlement of the West. Select a Western—a book, movie, or television program—that portrays the conflict between the government and Native Americans and tell whether it is true to life. Explain your answer.

14-2 The Booming West

Focus: How did economic opportunities shape life in the West?

The year the great Sioux leader Sitting Bull was born, Cyrus McCormick patented his reaping machine. When Sitting Bull was three, John Deere manufactured a plow with a hard steel blade. The new plow could cut through the tough soil of the plains with ease, and the reaper could harvest seas of wheat.

By the time Sitting Bull became chief of his tribe, longhorn cattle were being driven across the plains. The transcontinental railroad sliced across land that had once been Indian land. When Sitting Bull was forty, gold was discovered on Indian land in the Dakota Territory. The fate of Sitting Bull and all Plains Indians became tangled with the plow and the reaper, with the longhorn and the railroad, and with the quest for the earth's metals.

The Transcontinental Railroad

In the 1840s a newspaper editor wrote that a railroad could never be built across the continent. The barriers of mountains and rivers made construction too difficult and too costly, he declared. Nonetheless, in 1863 two railroad companies decided to build just such a line.

The Union Pacific Railroad planned to lay tracks westward from Omaha, Nebraska, while the Central Pacific Railroad worked eastward from Sacramento, California. To help finance the work, the federal government gave the companies long-term loans. It also gave land along the route, which was acquired in treaties with Indian tribes.

Union Pacific workers, mainly Irish immigrants, overcame blizzards and burning heat to lay track across the vast prairie. Of the 10,000 Central Pacific workers, 9,000 were Chinese. Many of them had been lured by pamphlets that the railroad companies had been circulating in China. One pamphlet read:

> *"Americans are very rich people. They want the Chinaman to come and will make him very welcome. There you will have great pay, large houses, and food and clothing of the finest description. You can write to your friends and send them money at any time, and we will be responsible for the safe delivery. . . . There are a great many Chinamen there now, and it will not be a strange country."*

Section 14-2

Objectives

- ***Answer the Focus Question.***
- *Describe the efforts of the nation to build a transcontinental railroad.*
- *Explain why cattle ranching became a big business.*
- *Name places where big mineral strikes occurred.*
- *Identify problems related to law and order in the West during the late 1800s.*

Introducing

THE SECTION

Ask: Was the West ever an unpopulated or unclaimed region? **(When settlers arrived in the West, Native Americans lived in every region and had developed a variety of sophisticated lifestyles.)** What other groups had settled in the Southwest and California? **(First Spaniards, then Mexicans.)**

Developing
THE SECTION

Connections: Geography

Using Maps. The route of the first transcontinental railroad roughly follows the 40th parallel. Have students describe the change in elevation along 40 degrees North latitude, using the physical map of the United States (pages 902–903). **Ask:** How did the topography affect the task of railroad construction? **(Students may compare their answers with the worm-eye view on pages 260–261)**

Geography Skills
ANSWERS

Reno—silver, location on the railroad; Denver—gold and silver, railhead; Cheyenne, Abilene, and Dodge City—cattle drives met the railroad; Omaha—major rail center, eastern and western lines converge.

Active Learning

Making murals. Have students do research in pairs on trains and the western towns that developed because of the railroads. Then have all students work to draw a mural showing several towns, their interdependence, and how they were linked together by the railroad.

Reduced student page in the Teacher's Edition

Railroads, Cattle Trails, and Mining Centers 1860-1890

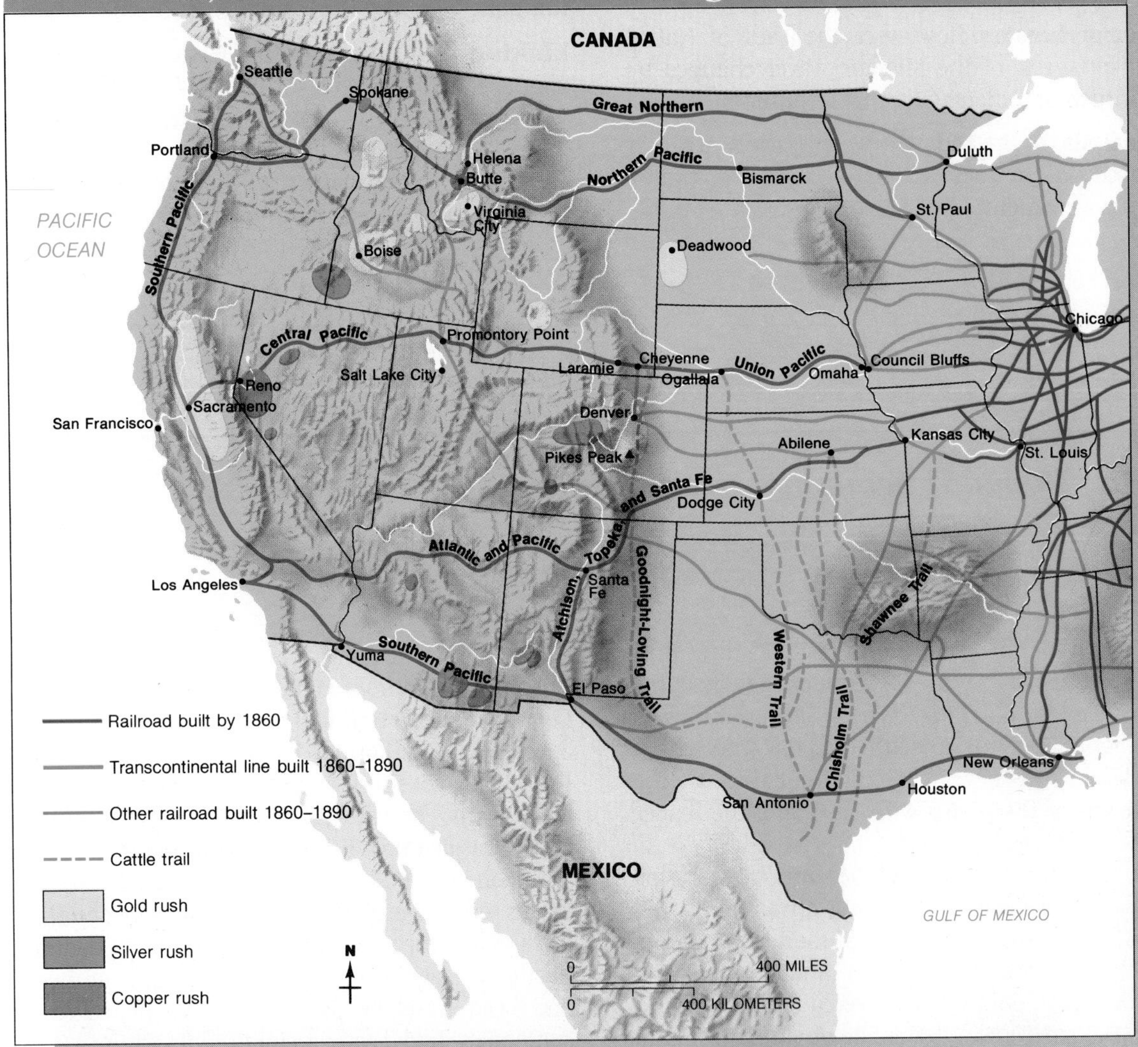

Geography Skills—Location.
Cities often grow as result of their location as centers of economic activity. What can you conclude about the reasons for the growth of the following cities: Reno, Denver, Cheyenne, Abilene, Dodge City, Omaha?

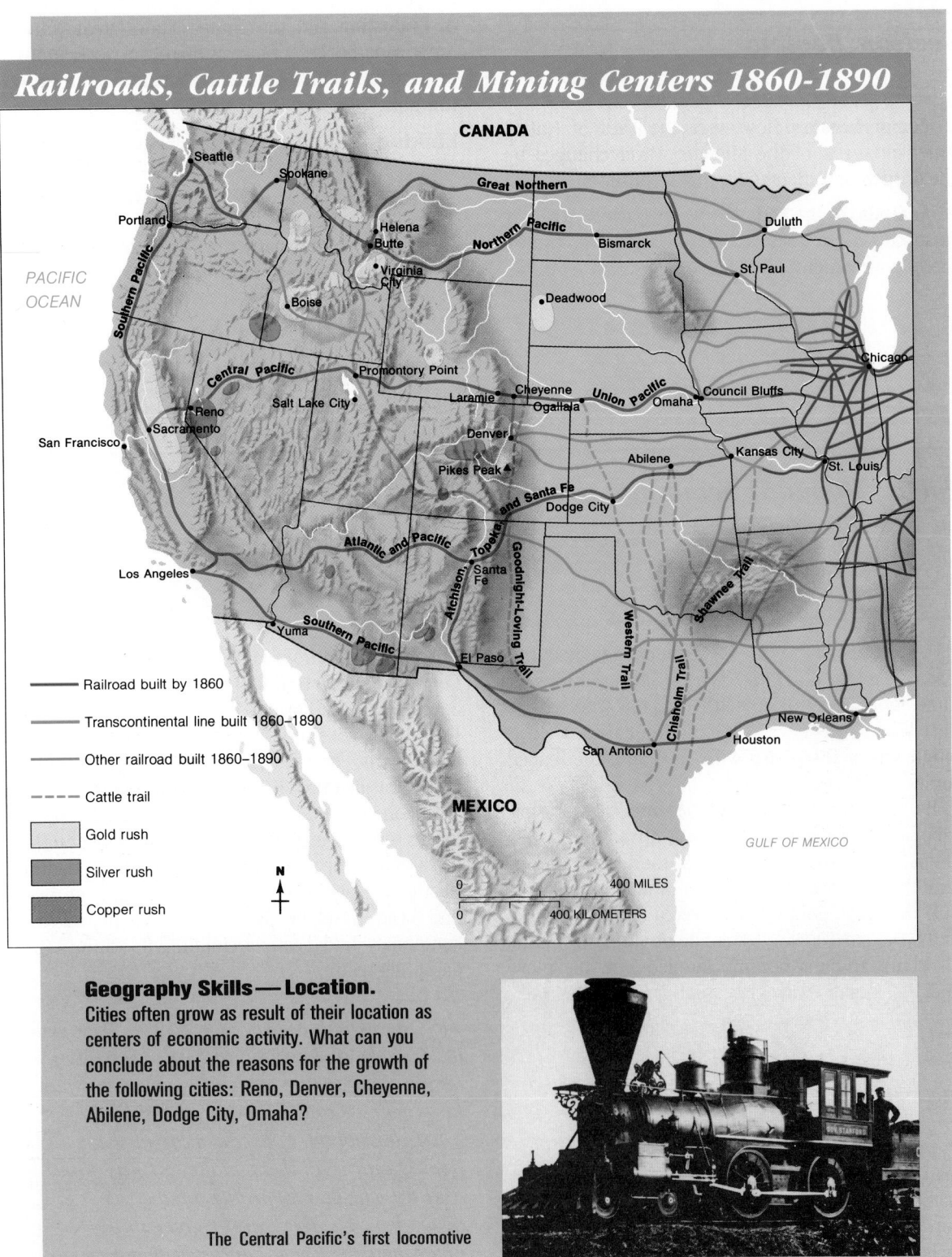

The Central Pacific's first locomotive

Social History

Leland Stanford, president of the Central Pacific Railroad, raised a silver hammer to strike in the golden spike linking the two rail lines. Engraved on the spike is the prayer: *"May God continue the unity of our Country as the Railroad unites the two great Oceans of the world."*

Writing About History

Biographical Report. Mary Fields was an African-American cowgirl in Cascade, Montana. She described her life: *"I was born in a slave cabin while Andrew Jackson was president. My first job out west was hauling freight for nuns. One night a pack of wolves attacked my wagon—I spent the whole night surrounded by wolves who I kept away from me with my revolver and rifle."*

Nearly one cowhand in three was either an African American or a Mexican; some of them were women.

Ask a few students to write brief biographies on the following cowboys or others: Henry Beckwith, John Wallace, Nat Love (Deadwood Dick). Have students report their findings to the rest of the class.

The promise of the pamphlets had little to do with reality. But the Central Pacific workers performed heroic tasks, dynamiting a route through the rugged Sierra Nevada. They worked even in the harsh winter, sometimes plowing through fifty-foot snowdrifts. In 1869, after six years of work, the two sets of tracks met at Promontory Point, in the Utah desert north of Salt Lake City. The last spike driven into the tracks was made of solid gold. Western author Bret Harte wrote:

> *"What was it the Engines said,*
> *Pilots touching, head to head,*
> *Facing on a single track,*
> *Half a world behind each back."*

A railroad network. Meanwhile, there was a flurry of railroad building in the East and the Midwest. Miles of track in the United States jumped from 30,000 in 1860 to over 166,000 in 1890—one third of the world's total.

The federal government supported the construction of three more transcontinental lines: the Southern Pacific; the Northern Pacific; and the Atchison, Topeka, and Santa Fe. A fourth line, the Great Northern, was built without government assistance.

To improve train scheduling the American Railway Association divided the nation into the four time zones we use today: Pacific, Mountain, Central, and Eastern. That way train schedulers knew what time it was throughout the country. Later the railroads agreed to lay tracks according to a standard gauge, or width, so that all trains could run on rails throughout the entire nation.

Cowboys and Ranchers

One important western product carried eastward by the new railroads was the longhorn steer. These cattle had roamed the Southwest when the land belonged to Mexico. American settlers adopted Mexican tools of ranching—the lasso, the saddle with a horn around which the lasso is anchored, chaps to protect ranchers' legs from cactus and sagebrush, and the branding iron.

A new American figure came to life on the open range—the "cowboy," a translation of the Spanish word *vaquero*. Many western cowboys were, in fact, Mexican. And about one in seven was black, mostly former slaves who had learned to rope and ride on Texas ranches. "It was the great West I wanted to see," wrote Nat Love, a former slave from Tennessee. "The wild cowboy, prancing horses of which I was very fond, and the wild life generally, all had their attractions for me."

After a few years on the range, most cowboys settled on their own ranches or headed back home. But the figure of the cowboy became part of a growing legend—the nation's new hero.

Typically, ranches were owned by men, with their wives and children sharing the work. But sometimes women ran ranches alone. Agnes Morley recalled how her mother learned the "role of cattle queen:"

> *"Cattle-raising on a grand scale was the Great Adventure of the hour. . . . Faced with the supervision of a well-stocked cattle range of a good many thousand acres, she rode and did her indomitable best to keep herself informed about what was happening to her livestock."*

Cattle drives. The growing eastern population demanded more beef than eastern herds could supply. Between 1867 and 1888 10 million head of cattle were headed north from Texas to Sedalia, Missouri, or Abilene or Junction City, Kansas. From there the steers were carried on cattle cars to Chicago stockyards to be butchered. The meat was shipped east in refrigerated cars.

GTV Side 3

Chap. 3, Frame 10830

Reaching Out: Rail Lines, Late 1800s (Animated Map)

Search and Play:

Thinking Critically

Analysis. How did railroads make mining easier? (Railroads could bring equipment and supplies to the mines and carry mining products to markets.) How did mining contribute to the development of railroads? (Mining gave railroads an economic incentive to build more lines.)

Connections: Literature

Reading. Bret Harte used humor and pathos in his stories of miners, sheriffs, pioneers, and gamblers. Recommend that interested students read "The Luck of Roaring Camp," "The Outcasts of Poker Flat," or other Harte stories.

Connections: Economics

The cattle industry was very profitable. A newborn calf, bought in Texas for $5, could be fattened for three to four years on public domain land and rounded up and driven to market for no more than $5 a head, including supplies, horses, salaries of about $300 per year, and food at eleven cents a day per cowboy. At the railheads, cattle could bring $45 a head. Foreign investments poured in. From Britain alone in the 1880s came $45 million.

Reduced student page in the Teacher's Edition

At spring and fall roundups, cowhands branded new calves and gathered mature animals for market. Here, a cowboy separates out a protective cow and her calf in order to brand the calf with the distinctive mark of its owner.

The long cattle drives began in the spring. For two or three months, two dozen or more cowboys herded up to 3,000 longhorns over the prairie, covering about 15 miles a day.

Cowboys spent the chilly nights swapping stories around a campfire. The peacefulness of the night camp, however, could shatter. Mattie Huffman, a fifteen-year-old girl who worked on her family's drive, wrote:

> *"A cow came up to the salt barrel near the camp; in taking a nibble of salt she in some way got a sack fastened on to her horns. Of course she went mad with fear and spread terror among the entire bunch by dashing among them. A stampede was on in no time. . . . It took about a week to get all the cattle together again."*

During the long drives, ranchers began to realize that the hardy buffalo grass that grew on the Plains Indians' hunting grounds was good for cattle. Soon, they were grazing their herds on the unclaimed public lands, or **public domain,** that stretched from Texas through the Great Plains to the Canadian border. To ship these longhorns to market, railheads sprang up at Dodge City in Kansas and at Laramie in Wyoming.

With plenty of open land, a steadily multiplying product, and ready transportation to market, cattle became a profitable business, attracting investors from the East and Britain. The new companies came to control huge spreads of land, and great cattle empires arose on the prairie. The powerful Prairie Cattle Company, for example, grazed 156,000 head of cattle on 5 million acres.

End of the Open Range

In the late 1880s, however, events spelled an end to the open range for cattle ranchers. Foremost was the rush of farmers into the cattle empire. The farmers unrolled barbed wire—patented in 1873—by the mile to mark off their property and keep out freely ranging cattle. Sheep ranchers also moved to the prairie. Cattle ranchers complained

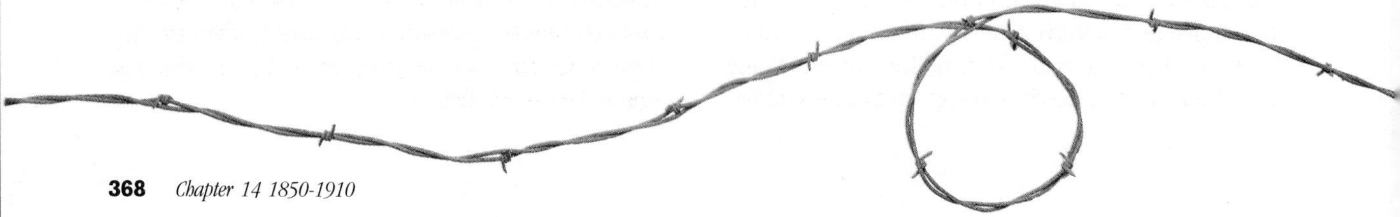

Connections: Language

The Spanish vaqueros developed much of the language used by the American cowboy. The lariat was known for centuries in Spain as *la reata,* lasso as *lazo.* To protect their legs while riding through thickets of brush and tall grass, Spanish cowhands wore heavy leather trousers called *chaparreras,* later shortened to "chaps." Cattle and horses were rounded up and kept in *corrals.* That term comes from a Spanish word meaning "ring" or "circle."

that longhorns would not drink from the same waterholes as the sheep, and that the sheep ate the grass down to the roots. Cattle ranchers and sheep ranchers fought bitter wars over range land.

The final blow to the open range fell in the winter of 1886-1887. Blizzards buried the grass under mountains of snow. Only about 10 percent of the cattle on the range survived. After that winter, many independent ranchers sold out to big companies. The cattle companies learned from the great blizzard that they could no longer depend on the open range. Thereafter, they drilled for water, stored feed, and like the farmers, fenced their land.

Texas Cowboy's Stampede Song

"I'm going to leave old Texas now.
They've no more use for the longhorned cow.
They've plowed and fenced my cattle range,
And the people there are all so strange.

I'll take my horse, I'll take my rope,
And hit the trail upon a lope.
I'll bid adieu to the Alamo,
And turn my head toward Mexico."

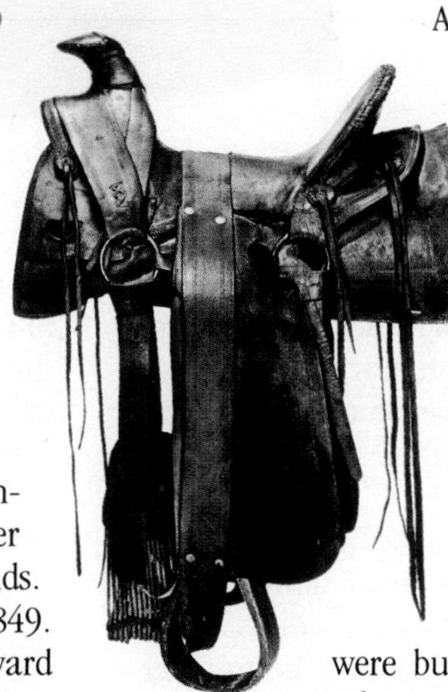

Mining Fever

While the grasslands of the West attracted ranchers and cowboys, discoveries of gold and other metals lured treasure seekers by the thousands. The first gold rush had been to California in 1849. When that strike ended, mining shifted eastward across the Great Basin to the Rocky Mountains. The first big gold strike there came near Pikes Peak in what is now Colorado. About 100,000 "yondersiders" from California and "greenhorns" from the East arrived in just six months in 1859.

Other strikes kept the mining fever burning. Gold and silver were found in Nevada, and copper gleamed in Montana. Gold was struck in Idaho, Wyoming, and the Dakota Territory. Prospectors poured into these areas. By 1870 Colorado, Nevada, Idaho, Montana, and Wyoming had been organized as territories.

A few prospectors found the fortunes they dreamed of, but large mining companies reaped most of the profits. For example, the wealth of silver and gold in Nevada's Comstock Lode was locked underground until a large company dug a mine in 1870. The company had money to pay for the latest engineering knowledge and machines that could bore through rock. In twenty years, the Comstock produced $306 million.

Still, individual prospectors continued to follow the strikes. Instead of fertile land, they sought minerals. Around such hopes, towns grew up.

Boom Towns

Amid deafening noise, writer Helen Hunt Jackson stepped off a stage coach in Garland City in the Colorado Territory late in 1877. She asked a bystander what was happening. "The building of the city," he said. "Twelve days ago there was not a house here. Today there are one hundred and five. And in a week there will be two hundred."

All over the West, towns were bursting into life. Some, grew up along railroads. Others were supply centers for the mines or were cowboy towns.

Many towns lived up to the "Wild West" image. According to Mark Twain, who visited it in the 1870s, the mining town of Virginia City was

"the 'livest' town . . . that America had ever produced. . . . There was a glad, almost fierce, intensity in every eye, that told of the money-getting schemes that were seething in every brain and the high hope that held sway in every heart."

369

Limited English Proficiency

Discussion. Ask students to explain what due process of law means. **(Accused persons must be treated fairly according to rules established by law.)** Have students recall the document that entitles American citizens to due process of law **(Constitution)**. In what ways did vigilante justice violate due process of law? **(no legally chosen jury, often no real defense attorney or witnesses; hasty, unexamined decisions made by a mob)**

Section Review

ANSWERS

1. Definitions for the following terms are on text pages indicated in parentheses: *public domain* (368), *vigilantes* (370).
2. Irish and Chinese immigrants had to cope with harsh winters, scorching summers, blizzards, raids by Native Americans, and the difficult terrain.
3. Since, in the East, there was a great demand for beef, considerable profits could be made by shipping cattle east. Prospect of establishing large and small ranches drew people westward.
4. Gold strikes in California, Montana, Colorado, Idaho, Wyoming, and the Dakota territory; silver in Nevada, Idaho, Colorado, Arizona, and New Mexico. Large mining companies, which had money to pay for engineering knowledge and machines, made greatest profit.
5. Answers will vary. Those agreeing can argue that the need for some kind of law and order outweighed the illegality of vigilante operations. Those disagreeing can argue that some of the actions were for the benefit of rich ranchers and directed against the poor.

Some of these towns kept on booming. Others grew more slowly into established communities. Still others turned quickly into "ghost towns" when the mines were no longer profitable. The same thing happened to some railroad towns. A shift in railroad company plans could turn one of these settlements into an "air town." A writer for *Harper's Monthly* described a place called Coyote, Kansas.

> *"On every side the dreary rolling plains lay up against the cloudless horizon. . . . Canvas saloons, sheet-iron hotels, and sod dwellings [were] surrounded by tin cans and scattered playing-cards. . . . In one short week not a house but that of the railroad section people remained."*

Frontier Justice

Sometimes towns boomed without government or law before a territory could be organized. When arguments arose or someone broke the unwritten code of behavior, punishment was swift. The worst crime on the range short of murder was horse theft, because it left a person on foot in harsh country. Horse thieves, robbers, and murderers were usually hanged—executed legally or illegally by "lynch law."

At best, a town might have a locally hired sheriff or a federal marshal. To keep order, lawmen like William Barclay "Bat" Masterson, James B. "Wild Bill" Hickok, and Wyatt Earp had to be tougher than the roughest pistol-toters in town.

In places where there were no peace officers or where they were ineffective, unofficial groups called **vigilantes** (vij-il-LAN-teez) sprang up to control lawlessness. Vigilante justice had none of the safeguards of due process of law. The innocent were sometimes punished, even put to death, with the guilty.

Often justice was handed out by cattle ranchers. Ranchers, who often competed for land and water, sometimes hired gunfighters like William "Billy the Kid" Bonney to settle their differences with their enemies. To control rivalries and to stop cattle rustling, ranchers formed stock-growers' associations.

Spotlight on Woman Suffrage

When it comes to suffrage for women, Wyoming can claim several "firsts." In 1869 the territorial legislature granted women the right to vote, hold office, and serve on juries—the first such law in the United States. Perhaps the men of the legislature had second thoughts. An attempt to repeal the law in 1871 failed by just one vote. Meanwhile, American women first served on a jury in 1870 in Laramie. In that same year Esther H. Morris became the territory's first woman officeholder when she was appointed justice of the peace of South Pass City, a gold town. When Wyoming entered the Union in 1890, it was the first state to allow women to vote.

These groups created informal rules for the range, often called "cow custom." Applying these "laws," the associations were often the only government for whole territories.

Section Review

1. Identification. Define *public domain* and *vigilantes*.

2. Comprehension. Who were the workers who built the first transcontinental railroad? What difficulties did they face?

3. Analysis. Explain why cattle ranching became a booming business and what role the ranches played in the settlement of the West.

4. Comprehension. Name four places where big mineral strikes occurred. Who made the greatest profits from mining? Why?

5. Evaluation. "Frontier justice was fair and just because formal laws and government had not yet arrived." Do you agree or disagree with this statement? Explain why.

Multicultural Perspectives

In 1906 Native Americans of Taos, New Mexico, had lands taken away from them that they considered sacred. The following statement was an appeal for help to regain control of the sacred Blue Lake area. It also illustrates the concept of place in geography, how a people's views of a place depend on their experience and beliefs. *"We have lived upon this land from days beyond history's records, far past any living memory deep into the time of legend. The story of my people, and the story of this place are one single story. No man can think of us without also thinking of this place. We are always joined together."*

Connections: Geography

Evaluation. Leadville was not the only place whose physical characteristics drew people in search of wealth. Ask students to report on the following gold and silver boom towns of the West: Helena, Montana; Virginia City, Nevada; Deadwood, South Dakota; Idaho City, Idaho. Have students compare and contrast the physical characteristics of these places.

Geography

A KEY TO OUR PAST

The Saga of a Mining Town: Place

The concept of **place** in geography includes the idea that one locality is distinguished from others by its physical characteristics, such as landforms and climate, and its human characteristics—the changes that people make in the landscape. Distinctive physical and human characteristics give each place its special flavor.

How people view a place in terms of its desirability and importance depends on their own needs and experiences, and their views may change over time. Several times, for example, people's changing views have altered circumstances in one place: a stony gulch cut by a stream running 10,000 feet high in the Colorado Rockies. In 1860 prospectors struck gold along the stream. Within a few months, 10,000 gold seekers had lined the gulch with their flimsy shacks. They called their new town Oro City. *Oro* is the Spanish word for gold.

This Colorado mining town flourished and faded several times, depending on the fortunes of the mines. The town's first life ended as suddenly as it had begun. When the placers (deposits of sand or gravel containing precious metals) ran out of gold, miners abandoned their shacks and moved on.

The town's second life began in 1875. Black sand that had been ignored by earlier miners turned out to be lead ore with a high silver content. News of the silver strike soon leaked out, and the mining town boomed again. But this time the settlers called it Leadville.

Over the next two years, Leadville became the richest city in the Rockies. One mine yielded $118,000 worth of silver in a twenty-four hour period. Owners of such mines became millionaires.

By 1880 Leadville boasted a population of 50,000 people. Simply finding a place to sleep was a problem. To keep up with the increasing demand for houses, thirty sawmills ran day and night, producing lumber.

Leadville attracted outlaws, gamblers, and gunslingers as well as miners, so brawls and shootings were commonplace. The citizens of Leadville finally posted a list of troublemakers with these words: "These and a great many others well known to us, have twenty-four hours to get out of the Leadville mining district. Do not fail to go."

Early in 1882, as the silver began to run out, Leadville faced yet another decline. Then, in the mid-1880s, silver prices tumbled and the country slid into an economic depression. Yet this time Leadville was not completely deserted. The mining of molybdenum, a mineral used to harden steel, kept the town alive. Leadville, Colorado, is much quieter today than in its noisy past, but it is home to almost 5,000 people and three active mines.

Leadville, Colorado in 1879, after discovery of silver-rich lead ore gave an old ghost town new life.

Section 14-3

Objectives

- ***Answer the Focus Question.***
- *Cite the major provisions of the Homestead Act of 1862 and some of its effects.*
- *Explain the lure Alaska had for settlers at the end of the 19th century.*

Introducing

THE SECTION

Have students use a dictionary and find phrases that begin with the word "prairie" such as "prairie dog" and "prairie schooner." Then have them draw a picture of the prairie from their findings.

B · A · C · K · G · R · O · U · N · D

Social History
The Homestead Act required the building of a house 12 by 12, but did not specify the units of measure. Wily land-sharks evaded the building regulation by erecting miniature cabins, 1 foot by 1 foot. Temporary shacks, some with wheels, were often moved from site to site to establish land claims.

Reduced student page in the Teacher's Edition

14-3 The Prairie Farmers

Focus: What was life like for the farmers who settled the Great Plains?

On his way to California's gold fields in 1849, Jasper Hixson took a good look at the land he was crossing—the Great Plains—and wrote in his diary:

> *"The land is too fertile and it possesses too many inducements for settlement to remain in possession of the Indians forever. Now that so many from the older states begin traveling over this fine land . . . they must write to their friends to 'Go West.'"*

Reports from pioneers like Hixson reached the East—and Europe—where farm land was in short supply. People responded, heading west to try prairie farming.

At first, homesteaders claimed the fertile river valleys on the fringes of the prairies. But that land filled up fast. Then, after the Civil War, homesteaders streamed into the lands farther west. They settled on the prairie's endless acres. It was not farming as they had ever known it, and many fled their lonely, treeless homesteads in despair. Yet others stayed and met the challenges, transforming grasslands into productive farms and solitary homesteads into thriving communities.

The Homestead Act

To encourage settlement on the plains, Congress passed the Homestead Act in 1862. Any citizen or immigrant who planned to become a citizen could claim 160 acres of public land. All a homesteader had to do was pay a small registration fee, build a house, improve part of the land, and live on it for five years.

Multicultural Perspectives

Many farmers from Norway, Sweden, and Denmark emigrated to the United States. By 1890, Minnesota had four hundred towns bearing Swedish names. Irish and German towns were scattered across Minnesota, Nebraska, and the Dakota Territory.

Between 1862 and 1900, 80 million acres were claimed under the Homestead Act. But only about 17 percent of this land was settled by homesteaders. Speculators bought much of it through various schemes and sold it off— often at high prices. Some farmers ended up paying sums as high as $6,000 for their homesteads.

Land for Sale

Railroad companies, which had been granted nearly 130 million acres of public domain land, wanted farmers to settle along their routes. They looked forward to the profits to be made from shipping farm crops east and bringing manufactured goods west. To attract settlers, the railroads sold them land at low prices. Soon towns sprang up at stops along the railroad lines.

Railroads spent millions on advertising to lure people to the prairies. They even had agents waiting in eastern seaports to meet immigrants and arrange their travel west. The Northern Pacific Railroad also had offices in England, Germany, Holland, and Scandinavia. Europeans came by the thousands. A Minnesota newspaper editor wrote,

> "It seems as if the Scandinavian kingdoms were being emptied into this state."

Territorial and state governments had land to sell, too. They persuaded newspapers to print glowing reports about the soil, the climate, the crops, and the people. Easterners were told to give their gardens a boost by ordering a sack of rich Minnesota soil. The Nebraska Immigration Association advertised in Europe: "Land for the landless! Homes for the homeless!"

The advertising attracted large numbers of people. Between 1870 and 1890 the populations of Kansas and Nebraska each grew by about a million people. The Dakota Territory, sparsely settled in 1870, was filled with over 500,000 newcomers within 20 years. By 1912 eight new plains states and four nonplains states had entered the Union.

> *"Chilled to the bones, starving and the wagon broken down. We'll stay here 'til the spring, hunting for game. Lord oh Lord, why did we come?"*
>
> —Mary Pearsal, 1851

By agreeing to farm 160 acres, this Montana man received them nearly free under the Homestead Act.

Developing THE SECTION

Backyard History

Research. Ask students why early residents of cities and towns on the prairies have been such dedicated boosters of their communities. Have students research the founders of their communities: who they were, where they came from, and why they settled there.

Thinking Critically

Evaluation. William Jennings Bryan, popular leader from Nebraska in the late 1800s and early 1900s, said, *"Destiny is not a matter of chance, it is a matter of choice; it is not a thing to be waited for, it is a thing to be achieved."*

Ask: How is this statement consistent with the actions of the homesteaders who came to Bryan's home state of Nebraska?

Writing About History

Report. Between 1890 and 1910, more than 25 African-American communities formed in Oklahoma. Beginning in the 1870s, vast numbers of African Americans moved from the South to states like Kansas in hopes of making a new life for themselves. They termed their journey an Exodus and called themselves "Exodusters." Nicodemus, Kansas, is the only such settlement that survives.

Have students research and write a one page report on the Exodusters. Have students answer the questions: Who led them? Where did they settle? What was their fate? Students can report their findings to the class.

Global Connections

In Europe war had become a way of life. Many Europeans from all regions of the continent emigrated to America, where they hoped to live free of military obligations and the uncertain fortunes of nations at war. Following is a partial list of European wars of the period: the Crimean War (1850s), involving: France, Russia, Great Britain; the Seven Weeks War (1866) involving Italy, Germany, Austria; the Franco-Prussian War (1870s); the Russo-Turkish War (1870s); the Greco-Turkish War (1890s).

Reduced student page in the Teacher's Edition

Homesteads on the Prairie

Unfortunately, the Homestead Act did not take into account the nature of prairie farming. In the East, where rainfall was plentiful, a 160-acre farm could produce enough crops to support a family. But prairie homesteaders found it hard to support themselves on such small farms. Many crops that thrived in the East would not grow well on the plains, where rainfall was scarce. One woman who moved to Kansas in 1879 wrote:

"Methods of farming, farm tools even, the western way of handling stock, all were so different from eastern ways that my father, who had always been successful with sheep, soon found his first venture in Kansas a disastrous failure."

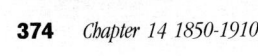

Homesteading the prairie tested the pioneers' courage and cleverness. Since there were few trees for timber, they learned to make houses of earth. Under the prairie buffalo grass lay a thick mat of roots. Homesteaders sliced up chunks of this sod with a special plow. With the sturdy sod bricks they built "soddie" houses, barnes, schools, and churches.

Most homesteaders found that they had to dig for their water, sometimes as deep as 300 feet. They erected windmills to pump the water to irrigate a few acres of vegetables. Large-scale irrigation, however, turned out not to be practical.

To use every drop of the scarce ground water, homesteaders tried "dry farming." With steel-tipped plows they dug until they reached soil that held some moisture. That moisture would rise through the plowed soil to reach the plants' roots. To keep the moisture from rising to the surface and evaporating, homesteaders packed the topsoil into a firm layer. With dry farming, farmers could grow grain crops like wheat, oats, and corn.

New machines mechanized labor. Steam-powered rigs drilled wells; threshers beat grain from its husks; binders gathered wheat into bundles. Such equipment, however, was expensive. Homesteaders could not afford to buy it unless they farmed large tracts. For most, plains farming remained a hard life and a risky business. Elinore Pruitt Stewart, a widow with one daughter, wrote:

"We had no money to hire men to do our work, so had to learn to do it ourselves. Consequently I learned to do many things which girls more fortunately situated don't even know have to be done. I have done most of my cooking at night, have milked seven cows every day, and have done all the hay cutting, so you see I have been working. But I have found time to put up thirty pints of jelly and the same amount of jam for myself."

Many people came to feel at home on the plains. In *O Pioneers!* Willa Cather, a writer who grew up on the prairie, wrote:

"It's a queer thing about that flat country. It takes hold of you, or it leaves you perfectly cold. A great many people find it dull and monotonous; they like a church steeple, an old mill, a waterfall, country all touched up and furnished, like a German Christmas card. . . . But when I strike the open plains, something happens. I'm home. I breathe differently."

The Last Land Rush

Throughout the nation's history, land had been a resource without limits. Settlers could always head west in search of new land. Now, by the late 1800s, the time of vast tracts of cheap land was drawing to a close. It seemed to people that the best of the country had been settled.

Connections: Science and Technology

Grassbound sod bricks were placed edgewise so the walls of a sod house were three to four feet thick. Sometimes the builder placed tar paper over the rafters before finishing the roof with a layer of sod bricks. Eventually grasses and sunflowers grew there. Sod houses were too heavy to be damaged by wind and too damp to be destroyed by fire.

Learning From Art Sod House About 1870

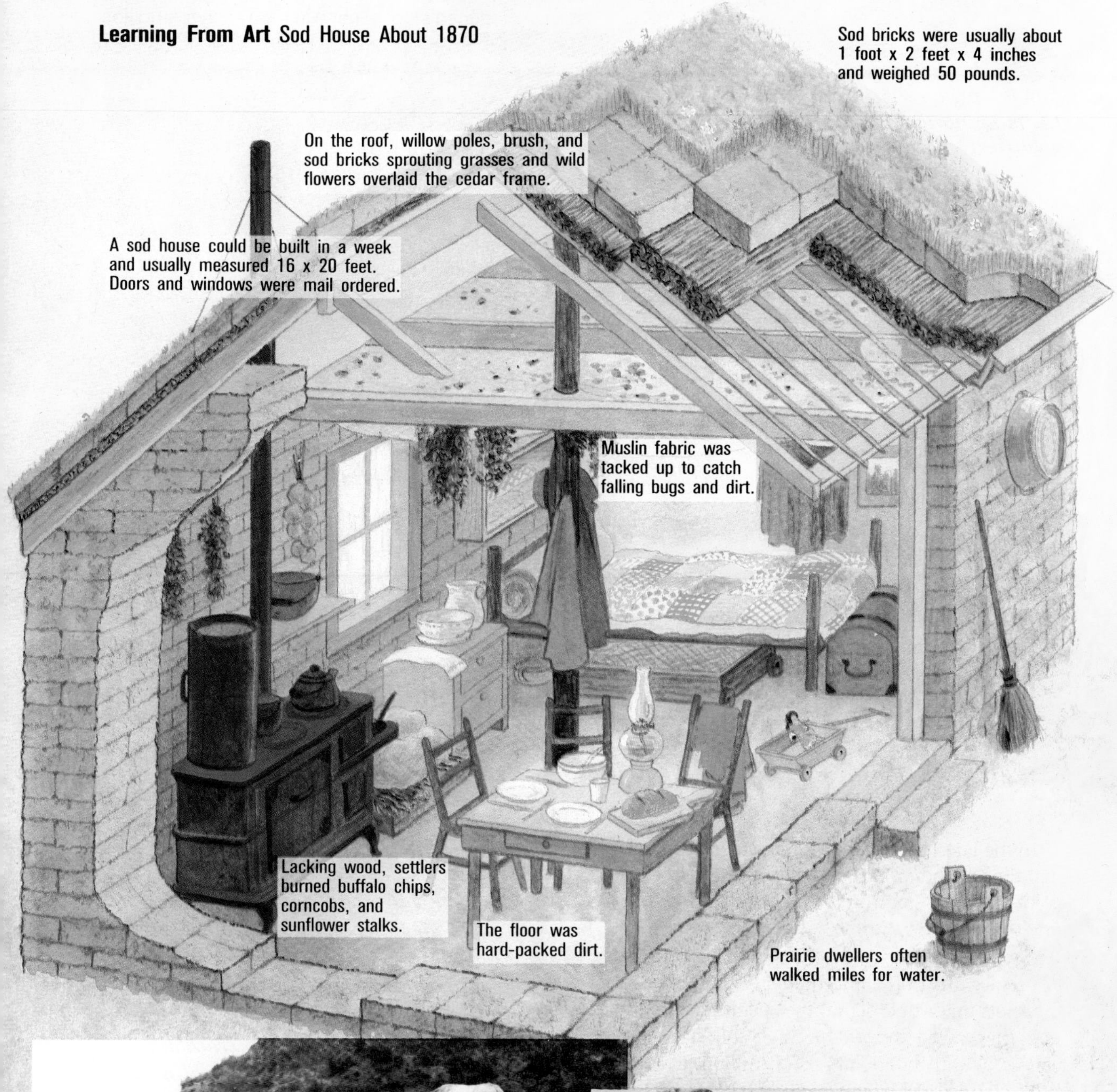

Sod bricks were usually about 1 foot x 2 feet x 4 inches and weighed 50 pounds.
On the roof, willow poles, brush, and sod bricks sprouting grasses and wild flowers overlaid the cedar frame.
A sod house could be built in a week and usually measured 16 x 20 feet. Doors and windows were mail ordered.
Muslin fabric was tacked up to catch falling bugs and dirt.
Lacking wood, settlers burned buffalo chips, corncobs, and sunflower stalks.
The floor was hard-packed dirt.
Prairie dwellers often walked miles for water.

Limited English Proficiency

Using the Visuals. Have students examine the picture on this page of a sod house and think about what life must have been like for a family of four or five living in such a structure. Have students imagine they are young persons living there.

Ask: What is it like? Where do you get supplies? **(Usually through mail order catalogues)** What are the winter months like in a sod house?

Connections: Literature

Assigned Reading. Laura Ingalls Wilder wrote many books about her family's experiences living on the homestead frontier. In one of them, *The Little House on the Prairie*, she describes how her parents constructed a sod house. Have a student get the book from the library, locate Laura's account of building a sod house, and read it to the class. Another student could read some experiences from Joanna Stratton's *Pioneer Women*.

Connections: Language

Discussion. *Sooners* were settlers who took land "sooner" than the time set for legally staking one's claim. *Boomers* were settlers and promoters who "boomed" or advocated, territorial settlement.

Ask: Where was the last land rush? **(the Cherokee Outlet)** How did the government obtain the land that it offered to the settlers? **(bought the land from the Cherokee)** Why did people participate in the land rush? **(People were land-hungry; they thought this was their last chance to buy good land.)** Would you have joined the land rush? Why or why not?

In 1896 the discovery of gold in Canada's Klondike region sent fortune seekers streaming north in the century's second "gold rush."

*"GOLD! We leapt from our benches. Gold!
We sprang from our stools.
Gold! We wheeled in the furrow, fired with the faith of fools.
Fearless, unfound, unfitted, far from the night and the cold,
Heard we the clarion summons, followed the master-lure—Gold!*

*Men from the sands of the Sunland; men from the woods of the West;
Men from the farms and the cities, into the Northland we pressed.
Graybeards and striplings and women, good men and bad men and bold,
Leaving our homes and our loved ones, crying exultantly—'Gold!'"*

—From *The Trail of Ninety-Eight* by Robert Service

In the late 1880s land-hungry settlers demanded that the Oklahoma District be opened to settlement even though it lay in the middle of Indian Territory. At noon on April 22, 1889, the government opened up the district to homesteaders. Thousands of people, lined up along the borders, awaited the gunshots that would signal the opening. At the signal, they raced forward to find and stake their claims. Within hours, almost 2 million acres had been claimed. Oklahoma gained close to 50,000 people in a single day.

In 1891 Sauk, Fox, and Potawatomi tribal lands in the Oklahoma Territory were offered to settlers. The following year, 3 million acres of the Cheyenne-Arapaho reservation in Colorado were settled.

Then, in 1893 the government bought from the Cherokee a strip of the Oklahoma Territory called the Cherokee Outlet. It, too, was opened to homesteaders. This last land rush took place at noon on September 16, 1893. Thousands of people gathered at the starting lines—100,000 on the Kansas border alone. One young pioneer, who was making the run by bicycle, watched the start:

"First in the line was a solid bank of horses; some had riders, some were hitched to gigs, buckboards, carts, and wagons, but to the eye there were only the two miles of tossing heads, and restless front legs. . . . While we stood, numb with looking, the rifles snapped and the line broke with a huge, crackling roar. That one thundering moment of horseflesh by the mile quivering in its first leap forward was a gift of the gods, and its like will never come again."

Alaska: A New Frontier

Much of America's expansion before the Civil War had been fueled by settlers' desire for land. Settlers crossed the frontier first, and government followed. But in 1867 the government acquired about

Linking Past and Present
From its earliest days as a Russian colony, Alaska had been considered a treasure house of natural resources. (Refer students to Chapter 2 for Native American cultures in this region.) The first Russians came there for furs, often inflicting violence on the Native Americans they found there. In the 1870s, outsiders came to Alaska to fish for salmon. Then, between 1880 and 1900, gold was discovered in Alaska, and towns were permanently established at Juneau, Fairbanks, and Nome.

During that period, more than $17.2 million in gold was mined in Alaska. After the gold craze wore off, timber became the resource people came to get. Today, oil from the North Slope is the most sought after commodity. Other resources include forests, fish, game animals, and large amounts of water.

Active Learning

Cooperative Activity. Divide students into three large groups. Have each group research one population of Alaska's Native Americans: Inuits, Tlingits, or Aleuts.

Have half of each group make posters portraying the traditional lifestyles of these people, while the other half makes posters illustrating the significant changes in lifestyle that occurred after the arrival of newcomers from the United States.

500,000 square miles of land without settlers demanding it. Secretary of State William H. Seward arranged the purchase of Alaska from Russia for $7.2 million. Alaska was called the "great land" by Indians who lived on the coastal Aleutian Islands. Easterners called it "Seward's folly," because they could see no use for this frozen land.

One young Californian, George Washington Carmack, wandered into Alaska and then over the border into Canada's Yukon Territory. In the summer of 1896 he found gold in a creek that flowed into the Klondike River. The news traveled quickly. Before the end of summer, a gold rush was on. A few years later gold was discovered in Alaska, too. Dreaming of fortunes, a stream of gold seekers set off for the Far North.

A wealth in gold, silver, copper, platinum, coal, timber, furs, and fish was eventually taken from Alaska's mines, forests, and rivers. But none could have guessed at the riches that would flow from Alaska's veins just over a hundred years later, after the discovery of "black gold," or oil, at Prudhoe Bay on the Arctic Coastal Plain. Enough oil is produced from Alaska's reserves every day to more than recover all of Seward's original purchase price. "Seward's folly"—the United States' last land frontier—has proved to be one of the soundest investments in history.

Section Review

1. Comprehension. Why did Congress pass the Homestead Act? How did it help settlers? What weaknesses did it have?

2. Comprehension. What part did railroads play in the development of the West?

3. Comprehension. Describe at least four problems that the homesteaders faced.

4. Synthesis. Do you think that a land rush was the best way to settle the plains? Why or why not? How would you have divided the land?

Data Search. Study the map on page 899 that shows changes in settlement from 1850 to 1890. Which states west of the Mississippi River were settled during each period shown on the map? Using information from the text, give reasons why settlers were attracted to each of these states.

Connections to Themes

The Search for Opportunity

The pioneers who crossed the Great Plains and the mountains to reach Oregon and California early in the nineteenth century labored six months or more on their hazardous journey. A few years later, however, the transcontinental railroad allowed settlers headed for the new West—the prairies, plains, and the Rockies—to reach their destination in a few days.

But other hardships awaited the people who went West in search of economic opportunity. Natural disasters such as drought, locusts, a hailstorm, a blizzard, or a prairie fire could destroy a crop and bankrupt a homesteading family in a single season. The newcomers also faced the dangers of outlaws, range wars, dishonest businessmen, and the resistance of Native Americans, who were fighting desperately to preserve their hunting grounds and their way of life.

Despite the uncertainties and violence of pioneer living, hopeful settlers dreamed that they could make a new life simply by taking hold of a piece of wilderness and taming it with their own hands. Success came to those who were quick witted, hardworking, or—often—just lucky. A few made fortunes from railroads, mines, or land speculation.

Most settlers, though, were not so successful. Meanwhile, for Native Americans the tragedy of broken treaties and stolen land continued. Still, the modest success of countless farms, ranches, and businesses added luster to the vision of the United States as the land of opportunity.

Section Review

ANSWERS

1. To encourage settlement of the plains; it enabled settlers to get land by living on it for five years. Speculators could acquire land and resell it at high prices.
2. Encouraged farmers to settle on land railroads had acquired through eminent domain by selling it at low prices.
3. Scarcity of water; difficulty of supporting oneself and family on a small farm; learning new ways of farming; lack of sufficient timber to build houses.
4. Land rushes drew vast numbers of settlers, but it was a disorderly method and allowed land grabs by the unscrupulous.
Data Search: To 1850: Iowa, Mo., Ark., La., Texas, N. Mex., Utah, Calif. To 1870: Okla., Kan., Neb., Colo., Nev., Wyo., Ore., Wash., Mont., S. Dak., Minn. To 1890: Ariz., Idaho, N. Dak. Settlers attracted to plains states for homesteading; to others for homesteading, mining, and agriculture.

Chapter Survey

ANSWERS

Using New Vocabulary

1. (c) *Public domain* is unclaimed government land.
2. (a) *Vigilantes* took law enforcement into their own hands in towns which had no organized police force.
3. (b) Government policy in setting up *reservations* was to separate Native Americans from settlers.

Reviewing the Chapter

1. Fort Laramie Treaty allowed government to build roads and forts in exchange for yearly payments to tribes. It also set boundaries for tribal hunting grounds, leaving Native Americans in home areas and allowing them to continue hunting way of life. Government continued to buy Native American land, make treaties, set up reservations, appoint agents, but Indians, unused to boundaries, disliked treatment by agents. Government tried to force tribes onto reservations, leading to conflict. Dawes Act tried to solve problem by no longer recognizing tribes, distributed land to individual Native Americans, sold land to raise money for schools to "Americanize" Native American children.
2. Some Native Americans complied. Others ignored boundaries, attacked settlers and miners, fought against confinement. Some went to Canada in search of buffalo and freedom, but eventually returned to reservation life. Many placed faith in "ghost dance" religion.
3. Thomas Tibbles and Susette LaFlesche successfully used court system to free Native Americans who had returned to tribal lands. Helen Hunt Jackson wrote *Ramona* to arouse sympathy for Native Americans; led to the Dawes Act.
4. Government gave railroad companies long-term loans and land.
5. Beef cattle were driven northward from Texas to railheads to be sent by train to slaughter houses in Chicago. From there beef was shipped in refrigerated rail cars to eastern cities.
6. Farmers who fenced open range with barbed wire, sheep ranchers whose animals ate grass down to roots, bad winter which killed 90 percent of herds.
7. Boom towns sprang up around mining strikes or railroad routes. When one was mined out or when railroad developed in other directions, boom towns could become ghost towns. Some towns had sheriffs or federal marshals. Those that did not might get vigilante justice, without the

Reduced student page in the Teacher's Edition

Chapter Survey

Using New Vocabulary

Match each numbered vocabulary term with the lettered word or phrase most closely related to it. Then explain how the items in each pair are related.

1. public domain	(a) law enforcement
2. vigilantes	(b) government policy
3. reservations	(c) government land

Reviewing the Chapter

1. Trace the development of the government's Indian policy from the Fort Laramie Treaty to the Dawes Act.

2. Describe Indian responses to government policies.

3. What methods did supporters of Indian rights use to plead their cause? How successful were they?

4. What government actions made possible the construction of the transcontinental railroad?

5. What were cattle drives? Why did they end at railheads?

6. What brought the cattle empire to an end?

7. Give three causes for the birth of boom towns. What might turn a boom town into a ghost town? How were western towns governed?

8. What was the purpose of the Homestead Act? What were the results?

9. Describe life for homesteaders on the Great Plains.

10. How did the settlement of Alaska differ from earlier American expansion?

Thinking Critically

1. Application. Settling the West brought various groups into conflict with each other over how to use the land. What were three of these conflicts? How were they resolved?

2. Analysis. How did technology change life on the Great Plains?

3. Synthesis. Women first gained the right to vote in several of the new western states, rather than in the more established East. What characteristics of the westward movement might have contributed to this expansion of democracy to include women?

Using a Time Line

Match the events below with the dates on the time line. Then list the events in chronological order and explain how each contributed to change in western North America in the second part of the nineteenth century.

(A) First transcontinental railroad completed
(B) Fort Laramie Treaty
(C) Pike's Peak gold rush
(D) Barbed wire patented
(E) Dawes Act
(F) First cattle drive on the Chisholm Trail
(G) The Homestead Act

1851 — 1859 — 1862 — 1867 — 1869 — 1873 — 1887

History and You

At the turn of the century, trains delivered freight and passengers to nearly every town in the country. How has that picture changed today? Find out what has happened to railroad service in your community since 1900. Do people who remember the railroad service of the past approve or disapprove of the changes?

protection of due process of law, or might follow "cow custom," rules of the range.
8. To attract settlers to plains. Homesteaders could claim 160 acres of public land by paying small registration fees, living on land for five years, building houses, and improving part of land. Most land claimed by speculators.
9. Lonely, hard work. Sod-houses made of sod, little rainfall, relied on windmills and dry farming methods. Plows and other machines essential but expensive.
10. Alaska's settlement primarily for commercial purposes (fur-trading and gold), rather than desire for land.

Applying Thinking Skills

Detecting Bias

The excerpts below reflect different views of Native Americans during the nineteenth century. Read them to identify each author's bias—slanted viewpoint. Then answer the questions that follow.

"There is not among the 300 bands of Indians one which has not suffered cruelly at the hands either of the government or the white settlers. This is especially true of the bands on the Pacific slope. These Indians found themselves of a sudden surrounded by and caught up in the great influx of goldseeking settlers, as helpless creatures on a shore caught up in a tidal wave. One of the federal government's strongest supports in breaking treaties with the Indians is the widespread sentiment among the people of dislike to the Indian, of impatience with his presence as a 'barrier to civilization,' and distrust of it as a possible danger.

There are hundreds of pages of . . . testimony on the side of the Indian; but it is . . . tossed aside and forgotten."

—From Helen Hunt Jackson, *Century of Dishonor.*

"If they, the Indians, stand up against the progress of civilization and industry, they must be relentlessly crushed. The westward course of population is neither to be denied nor delayed for the sake of all the Indians that ever called this country their home. They must yield or perish. . . . Whenever the time shall come that the roving tribes are reduced to a condition of complete dependence and submission, the plan to be adopted in dealing with them must be substantially that which is now being pursued in the case of the more [obedient] and friendly Indians."

—Adapted from the *Report of the Commissioner of Indian Affairs,* Washington, 1873.

1. Both authors agree on why Indians were poorly treated. What were those reasons?

2. Which account shows sympathy toward Indians? How is this evident?

3. List two biased statements in each selection. Explain how you know they are biased.

Writing About Issues

The Issue: *Should Congress fund a memorial to honor the Indians who died at the Battle of Little Bighorn?*

In 1990 Congress considered legislation to build a $2 million Indian memorial at Custer Battlefield National Monument, but it did not pass. At present, a large granite obelisk honors George Armstrong Custer and the men of the Seventh Cavalry who died there in 1876. White marble markers show where each of the 225 cavalrymen fell. The proposed memorial would honor the Cheyenne and Sioux who died defending their land.

The bill had strong support from Native Americans, including Barbara Booher, the first Native-American superintendent of the monument. When she arrived in 1989, signs referred to the cavalrymen as "fallen heroes" and the warriors as "hostile Indians." Most exhibits focused on the cavalry. Booher has worked to present a balanced view. "After all," she says, "Custer was only here for one afternoon. The Indians were here for years."

The bill was fought by Custer buffs and some historical associations. Jerry Russell, president of the Order of the Indian Wars, argued against building an Indian memorial because, he said, "They were the enemy."

Should public money be used to build a memorial to Native Americans who died in the Battle of Little Bighorn? Write your opinion in a letter to your representative. Address it to:

The Honorable (name of representative)
House of Representatives
Washington, D.C. 20515

Thinking Critically

1. Native Americans' life of hunting clashed with farmers, ranchers, miners; government used force to subdue Native Americans, confine to reservations. Cattle ranchers conflicted with sheep ranchers because sheep ate grazing lands down to roots. Range wars frequent. Sometimes stockmen's associations made rules to control territories. Ranchers clashed with farmers over fencing open range and water rights.
2. Railroads meant destruction of buffalo and Plains Indians' nomadic way of life. Steel plow, windmills, and barbed wire made farming possible on plains; railroads transported farm and ranch products eastward and brought manufactured goods. Towns grew up around railroad lines.
3. Women equal partners in struggle to set up life in West. Often did same work as men.

Using a Time Line

1. (B) 1851, **2.** (C) 1859, **3.** (G) 1862, **4.** (F) 1867, **5.** (A) 1869, **6.** (D) 1873, **7.** (E) 1887

History and You

Rail service has greatly diminished in importance, replaced by cars, trucks, airplanes.

Applying Thinking Skills

1. Native Americans viewed as standing in way of settlement and "civilization."
2. Jackson's excerpt; phrases such as "suffered cruelly," "helpless creatures," and government's "breaking treaties," as well as entire last sentence.
3. First and third sentences in Jackson excerpt and emotionally weighted phrases ("helpless creatures . . . caught up in a tidal wave"). The first two sentences of report, opposition between Native Americans and "progress and civilization," and righteous allusion to "westward course of population."

Chapter 15

The Age of Industry

Planning Guide

	Student Text	TWE Lesson Plans	Support Materials
SECTION 1	**Section 15–1** (1–3 Days) **Industry and Business,** pp 382–390 Review/Evaluation Section Review, p 390	**Introducing the Chapter:** A Letter of Introduction—Individual Activity, 30 minutes, p 379B **Teaching the Main Ideas:** Taking a Stand on Business Practices—Class Activity, one class period, p 379B **Evaluating Progress:** Charting Business Developments—Individual Activity, one class period, p 379C	★ **Read to Remember,** Section 1 ● **Section Activities,** Section 1 Δ **Readings,** R.S. Baker ● **Tests and Quizzes,** Section 1 Quiz
SECTION 2	**Section 15–2** (1–2 Days) **The Immigrants,** pp 391–396 Exploring Issues—Immigration: The Debate in Congress, p 394 Review/Evaluation Section Review, p 396	**Teaching the Main Ideas:** Congressional Hearing on Immigration—Group Activity, one class period, p 379C	★ **Read to Remember,** Section 2 ● **Section Activities,** Section 2 Δ **Enrichment Activities,** Section 2 Δ **Readings,** Chinese Exclusion Act, Rocco Corresco ● **Tests and Quizzes,** Section 2 Quiz
SECTION 3	**Section 15–3** (1–3 Days) **The Cities,** pp 397–403 The Creative Spirit: Inventors and Scientists, p 398–399 Connections to Themes: The Search for Opportunity, p 403 Review/Evaluation Section Review, p 403 Chapter 15 Survey, pp 404–405 Skills, pp 404–405 Using New Vocabulary Thinking Critically Using a Time Line Applying Social Studies Skills: Analyzing Bar Graphs Applying Thinking Skills: Identifying an Argument	**Reinforcement Activity:** Newspaper Stories—Individual Activity, homework, p 379C **Enrichment Activity:** Golden Door Board Game—Cooperative Activity, one class period, p 379D	★ **Read to Remember,** Section 3 ● **Section Activities,** Section 3 Δ **Enrichment Activities,** Section 3 ● **Geography Activities,** Section 3 Δ **Readings,** Jane Addams ● **Tests and Quizzes,** Section 3 Quiz, Chapter 15 Test (Forms A and B) **Additional Resources** ● **Active Learning** Δ **GTV Videodiscs** Δ **Transparencies and Activity Book** ● **Testing Software** ★ **Chapter Summaries** **Key:** ★ **For Extra Support** ● **For All Students** Δ **For Enrichment**

Overview

In the years after the Civil War, industry grew at a rapid pace. To raise money for expansion, business owners formed corporations. They also found ways to consolidate industries—primarily trusts and holding companies—in an effort to eliminate competition. Public resentment of the monopolies created by consolidation ultimately prompted the government to attempt to impose regulations on big business.

Large numbers of immigrants came to the United States to work in the growing industries, with newcomers from southern and eastern Europe settling mostly in the East, and immigrants from China and Japan mostly in the West. Religious prejudice, fear of foreign ideas, and resentment of job competition caused many Americans to respond to the immigrants with nativist attitudes and to demand legislation to restrict immigration.

As a result of immigration and industrialization, American cities grew rapidly. Problems such as crowded living conditions, lack of sanitation, and political corruption inspired reformers to call for improvement of political and social conditions in the cities.

Activity Objectives

After completing the activities, students should be able to

- identify conflicting views on business practices, competition, and the role of government in regulating business.
- describe the pressures for and against laws limiting immigration in the late 1800s.
- identify the major factors in the nation's industrial growth in the years after the Civil War.
- describe urban living conditions in the late 1800s.
- recognize the opportunities and hazards facing recent immigrants at the turn of the century.

Introducing the Chapter

A Letter of Introduction

This individual activity requires half a class period.

This activity is designed to heighten students' interest in the immigrant experience by having them write a letter of introduction to present themselves to a prospective employer in a new land.

Explain to students that in Chapter 15 they will read about the largest influx of immigrants in our nation's history. While we tend to think about immigrants in groups, each immigrant's story is unique. Point out that among immigrants in the late 1800s were many young people, some of whom arrived with their families and some by themselves.

Tell students that immigrants to the United States often carried a letter of introduction to present to prospective employers. Such letters, written in English, described the immigrant's reasons for immigrating, skills, abilities, personal characteristics, past experiences, and sometimes hopes and dreams. Have students imagine that they are planning to emigrate to another country. Direct them to write letters of introduction to help them get work.

Encourage volunteers to read their letters of introduction. Conclude by pointing out that immigrants of every era, including today, have faced problems of adjustment and discrimination, and that they have also displayed courage and tenacity.

Teaching the Main Ideas

Section 15–1: Taking a Stand on Business Practices

This class activity requires one period.

This activity gives students an opportunity to examine their opinions on some of the issues connected with business practices in the late nineteeth century. In the activity students acknowledge their opinions by "taking a stand."

Have students briefly review Section 15–1 to recall the people, events, and issues that dominated American business in the second half of the nineteenth century. Tell them that they will have the opportunity to express their views on important issues that faced Americans in the late 1800s.

Designate an imaginary line down the middle of the classroom. Define one end of the line as the "agree" position and the other as the "disagree" position. Define the midpoint as the "no opinion" position. Explain that you will read a statement about which students may agree, disagree, or have no opinion. They are to indicate their position by standing in the appropriate location along the imaginary line.

Read the statement: *If a business person is smart enough to drive his or her competitors out of the market, the competitors have no right to complain.* Direct students to move to the position along the line that expresses their opinion on the statement. When all are in line, call on students in both the agree and disagree positions to explain their reasons for holding these opinions. Allow students in the "no opinion" position to move if they are persuaded by the explanations. Continue the procedure by reading some or all of the following statements:

- A business should be able to do anything that is not against the law.
- It is fair for businesses to give discounts to regular customers.
- Owners have the right to lay off employees when profits drop.
- Owners have the right to lay off employees if they can find workers who will work for lower wages.
- The goal of business is to make as much money as possible.

- A business that can afford to do so should be allowed to undersell its competitors, even if that drives them out of business.
- Foreign companies should not be allowed to undersell American businesses.
- It is the government's job to regulate business activities.

Conclude by asking students to identify business issues in the late 1800s that are still issues today.

Teaching the Main Ideas

Section 15–2: Congressional Hearing on Immigration

This small group and class role-play activitiy requires a full period.

In this activity, students examine different responses to the immigrant experience and the impact of immigrants on the nation's economic and social life. Then they role play a congressional hearing on immigration policy.

Begin the activity by reminding students that in the late 1800s the continued influx of immigrants turned the question of limiting immigration into a major national issue. Tell them that they will role play a congressional hearing on immigration.

Divide the class into six groups. One group will serve as a congressional committee on immigration, which is conducting the hearing. Assign the other five groups the roles of people scheduled to appear before the committee: Chinese immigrants, members of the American Protective Association, California farmers, native-born factory workers, and Italian Catholic laborers.

Direct the groups who are to appear before the committee to review Section 15–2 to develop their position statements. Statements should reflect the beliefs and experiences of the people they represent. Encourage students to consider how each group might interpret its experiences and expectations in light of the three themes of the text: balancing unity and diversity, shaping democracy, and the search for opportunity. Students representing the congressional committee should review the section to determine what actions Congress took in response to the demands of the various groups.

Conduct the hearing by having the congressional committee call representatives from each of the five groups to state their positions. Encourage committee members to ask questions of the speakers. After all the statements have been heard, direct the committee to develop an immigration policy. The committee need not follow the historical decisions of Congress.

Conclude by comparing immigration issues in the late 1800s and early 1900s with today's issues.

Reinforcement Activity

Section 15–3: Newspaper Stories

This individual activity is to be assigned as homework.

This activity reinforces students' understanding of the plight of the urban poor in the late 1800s. Given headlines, students write news stories to raise readers' awareness of urban conditions during the period.

Review with students the causes and effects of the rapid growth of cities in the late 1800s and the conditions in which poor urban dwellers were forced to live. Remind them that the writings of reporters such as Jacob Riis brought the plight of these people to public attention.

Challenge students to imagine that they are newspaper reporters in the late 1800s who are outraged by the slum conditions and corruption in American cities. Ask them each to write an in-depth news story describing these conditions and calling on Americans to take action to improve the life of poor city dwellers. Students are to generate the stories from one of the following headlines:

- Urban Conditions Breed Disease
- Wealthy Flee Stinking City Centers
- Dead Dog Votes Twice
- City's Problems Do Not Fall on Deaf Ears

Emphasize that stories have greater impact if they use colorful details and encourage students to create fictional interviews. When the articles are finished, choose one of the headlines and ask students who wrote stories on that headline to read them. Compare the approaches and facts used in the stories.

Evaluating Progress

Section 15–1: Charting Business Developments

This individual activity requires one class period, or it may be assigned as homework.

This open-book activity assesses students' understanding of the growth of American industry and business after the Civil War by having them complete a summary chart.

Remind the class that Section 15–1 describes the rapid growth of American business and industry in the late 1800s. To summarize the information in the section, students are to set up a chart as follows:

	Name/Description	*Impact*
Industries Inventions Business leaders Organizational structures Philosophies		

Warn students to leave sufficient space to name and describe several examples of each topic listed in the left-hand column. Tell them to use their texts to complete the chart, explaining that they will be evaluated on comprehensiveness and accuracy.

Establish grading criteria based on your students' abilities. Charts should include most of the following information:

	Name/Description	*Impact*
Industries	steel railroads oil	cheaper railroad rails nationwide trade, increased industry energy for more industry
Inventions	railroad telegraph/ air brakes Pullman car refrigerator car Bessemer process oil refining process	safer transport comfortable travel safe food shipment cheaper, better steel cheaper energy
Business leaders	Macy/Woolworth Penney/Ward Wanamaker Rockefeller Carnegie Morgan	department and chain stores/cheaper, better merchandise catalog sales innovative use of advertising dominated oil industry consolidated steel industry role of banking in consolidating industries
Organizational structures	corporations trusts holding companies	could raise capital for expansion limited competition replaced outlawed trusts
Philosophies	free enterprise/ laissez-faire economics Gospel of Wealth Social Darwinism	private companies/little or no government regulation wealth carries social responsibilities economic competition without government regulation is natural

Enrichment Activity

Section 15–3: Golden Door Board Game

This cooperative activity requires one class period.

This project will help students understand the hardships and challenges facing immigrants to the United States at the turn of the century. In the activity students create "chance" cards for an immigration board game.

Explain to students that their task in this activity is to begin the development of a board game called *The Golden Door*. The game allows players to relive the experiences of immigrants who left their homelands and came to the United States seeking opportunity. Play will be directed by "chance" cards that players draw to determine whether they move forward or backward. The winner of the game is the player who leaves his or her homeland and achieves a better life in the United States.

Divide the class into groups of three or four and have them review text information on immigration. Point out that although experiences differed for each person, every immigrant faced challenges and obstacles.

Have students work with others in their groups to create a set of 20 chance cards for *The Golden Door* game. Each card is to describe an experience, positive or negative, that a turn-of-the-century immigrant might have had. Encourage students to use information from the text in creating their cards.

When finished, groups should share their five favorite cards with the class. Challenge students to finish developing the game by creating a game board and establishing rules of play.

Bibliography and Audiovisual Material

Teacher Bibliography

Brownstone, David M., and Irene M. Franck, ed. *Island of Hope, Island of Tears.* New York: Penguin, 1986.

Glaab, Charles N., and Theodore A. Brown. *A History of Urban America.* New York: Macmillan, 1983.

Handlin, Oscar. *The Uprooted.* 2nd ed. Boston: Little, Brown, 1973.

Shippen, Katherine. *Andrew Carnegie and the Age of Steel.* New York: Random House, 1964.

Student Bibliography

Alger, Horatio, Jr. *Making His Way: Frank Courtney's Struggle Upward.* Salem, NH: Ayer Company, 1975.

Asimov, Isaac. *The Golden Door: The United States from 1865–1918.* New York: Houghton Mifflin, 1977.

Bundles, A'Lelia P. *Madame C.J. Walker.* New York: Chelsea House, 1991.

Crane, Stephen. *Maggie: A Girl of the Streets.* New York: Bantam, 1986.

Ferber, Edna. *Saratoga Trunk.* New York: Fawcett, 1980.

Wharton, Edith. *The House of Mirth.* New York: Penguin, 1985.

Films, Videocassettes, and Videodiscs

Andrew Carnegie: The Original Man of Steel. 24 min. AIMS Media. Videodisc.

Expansion and Growth: Immigration in America's History. 11 min. Coronet/MTI. Videocassette.

The Industrial Revolution: Beginnings in the United States. 25 min. EBEC. Movie

Computer Software

Decisions, Decisions; American History Series: Immigration: Maintaining the Open Door; Urbanization. Apple. Tom Snyder Productions.

Industrialism in America. Apple. Focus Media.

The Time Tunnel—American History 1860–1920. Apple. Focus Media.

Chapter 15

Objectives

- Identify the growth and accompanying changes in industry between 1865 and 1910.
- Explain why immigration increased dramatically in the late 1800s.
- Describe the responses of United States citizens to increased immigration.
- Explain the effects of industrial growth on life in cities.

Introducing THE CHAPTER

For suggestions on introducing Chapter 15, refer to page 379B in the Teacher's Edition.

Developing THE CHAPTER

For activities and teaching strategies to help you reinforce and enrich chapter content, see pages 379B–379D in the Teacher's Edition.

B · A · C · K · G · R · O · U · N · D

Chapter Opener Illustrations

Edward Moran painted the dedication of the Statue of Liberty in New York Harbor in 1886. France gave the statue, entitled *Liberty Enlightening the World,* to the United States in 1884.

Many Chinese migrants traveled to the United States hoping to work there and return home rich in several years. In the 1860s laborers in South China might earn $3 to $5 dollars a month; in California they could work for the railroad and make $30 a month.

Two young bootblacks from New York posed for this photograph in 1896. By 1900, 1.5 million children in the

Reduced student page in the Teacher's Edition

Chapter 15 1865-1910

The Age of Industry

United States were working to help support their families.

Montgomery Ward sent mail order catalogs to rural families across the country advertising thousands of items, from barn nails to sunbonnets. By 1895 the catalog ran to 507 pages.

Thomas Edison invented the first practical phonograph in 1877. This 1908 Edison phonograph has a horn shaped like a morning-glory in full bloom.

Isaac M. Singer launched a successful ad campaign for his "new and improved" sewing machine. Singer was the first person to spend $1 million a year in advertising.

American Voices

Around 1900 Lee Chew wrote the story of his life. He had been born in China and had lived there until tales of a faraway place called America drew him halfway around the world. In the "country of American wizards" Lee Chew faced a new life.

> *"I worked on my father's farm till I was about sixteen years of age, when a man of our tribe came back from America. . . . The man had gone away from our village a poor boy. Now he returned with unlimited wealth, which he had obtained in the country of the American wizards. . . .*
>
> *"The wealth of this man filled my mind with the idea that I, too, would like to go to the country of the wizards. . . .*
>
> *"My father gave me $100, and I went to Hong Kong with five other boys from our place and we got steerage passage on a steamer, paying $50 each. Everything was new to me. . . . The food was different from that which I had been used to, and I did not like it at all. . . . When I got to San Francisco, . . . a few days' living in the Chinese quarter made me happy again. A man got me work as a house servant in an American family, and my start was the same as that of almost all the Chinese in this country."*

In the late 1800s millions of immigrants came to the United States seeking opportunity—jobs, land, fortunes, and freedom. They came from China and Japan, from Mexico, and from southern and eastern Europe. Within the United States itself, farmers were also leaving home to seek a better life in the rapidly growing cities.

In some ways, the United States that the immigrants found was the "country of the wizards" that Lee Chew sought. Almost like magic, inventors were transforming the nation. It was a noisy, busy age for the United States—an age of industry.

"The Unveiling of the Statue of Liberty," Edward Moran, 1886; immigrant ship from China; two young bootblacks, 1896; Montgomery Ward catalog; phonograph; ad for a Singer sewing machine.

Analyzing Primary Sources

American Voices

The Chinese who came to California in the 1800s were lured by rumors of gold and wealth. Even in far-off China, people called California *Gam Saan,* the "Gold Mountain," and those who set out for California were called *gam saan haak*—"travelers to the gold mountain."

1. Lee Chew indicated that his acquaintance returned to China from America with "unlimited wealth." Do you think this was true? What might it say about economic conditions in China? **(poor economic conditions)**

2. Lee Chew called Americans "wizards." What might he have meant by this term? **(Americans were clever to be able to create wealth.)**

3. What function did San Francisco's Chinatown play for Lee Chew? **(helped him maintain his Chinese culture)**

GTV Side 3

Chap. 6, Frame 21067

Immigrants Entering U.S.: 1871-1880, 1881-1890 (Population Clocks, 2 Frames)

Search:

Step:

Time Line Illustrations

1. This view of the Pennsylvania Steel Company in 1875 reveals the profound impact the use of steel had on the American landscape. The arrival of Bessemer plants, mills, and shops meant that long-lasting rails and machine parts could be mass produced at lower costs.

2. Alexander Graham Bell's telephone, invented in 1876, created an entirely new industry. By 1910 there were 5 million telephones in the United States.

3. Thomas Edison spent forty years experimenting before perfecting his vacuum lamp in 1879. He patented 1,093 inventions during his lifetime, including the mimeograph ma-

Section 15-1

Objectives

- ***Answer the Focus Question.***
- *Identify how the Bessemer process and the spread of railroads affected industrial growth in the United States.*
- *List three inventions and explain their impact on industrial growth in the 1800s.*
- *Explain the purpose of the Sherman Antitrust Act.*

Introducing

THE SECTION

Tell students that at the turn of the century novelist Frank Norris wrote *The Octopus*, a book about the struggles of the American wheat farmers in the last half of the nineteenth century. In the book, one of the characters makes the following prediction: *"Our century is about done. the great word of this [nineteenth] century has been 'production.' The great word of the [twentieth] century will be—listen to me, you youngsters—'markets.'"*

Norris's view of events was accurate. Industrial production in the United States soared in the last half of the nineteenth century. As the railroads moved goods to more people, the market for goods expanded, business boomed, new ways of life and business developed.

As students read this section, have them look for the social and political changes brought about by the rapid expansion of industry and business.

CHAPTER TIME LINE

1865-1910

1856 Henry Bessemer develops the Bessemer process for making steel

1876 Alexander Graham Bell invents the telephone

1879 Thomas Edison invents the first successful electric light bulb

1882 Standard Oil Trust formed

Chinese Exclusion Act

1860 · 1870 · 1880

15-1 *Industry and Business*

Focus: How did industry grow and change in the late 1800s?

The United States celebrated its hundredth birthday in 1876 with the grand Centennial Exposition in Philadelphia. The exposition showed how much the nation had changed since its birth and gave visitors a glimpse of the future.

About 8 million of the nation's 40 million people visited the Centennial Exposition. They saw firsthand that the United States was a nation of industry. In Machinery Hall the crowds passed row upon row of machines both for farming and manufacturing.

The giant of all the machines in the hall was the Corliss steam engine, which towered over thirty feet above the crowds. The great engine produced enough horsepower to run every machine at the exposition. One awed visitor reported:

> *"The Corliss engine does not lend itself to description. Its personal acquaintance must be sought by those who would understand its vast and almost silent grandeur. . . . In the midst of this powerful mechanism is a chair where the engineer sits reading his newspaper. Now and then he clambers up one of the stairways that cover the framework. He touches some irritated spot on the giant's body with a drop of oil. He then goes down again and takes up his newspaper. . . ."*

With a whir of machinery and a burst of inventiveness, the nation entered its second century.

chine, the electric voting machine, and the phonograph.

4. While in college, Jane Addams felt quite certain that she would study medicine and "live with the poor." Although ill health kept her from finishing medical school, Addams went on to found a settlement house, Hull House, and become a foremost American social reformer and peace worker. She received the Nobel peace prize in 1931.

5. This caricature from 1902 shows steel tycoon Andrew Carnegie carrying library buildings. He established more than 2,500 public libraries and several educational institutions.

1889 Jane Addams and Ellen Starr start Hull House

1901 J.P. Morgan forms the United States Steel Corporation

1905 Japanese Exclusion League founded

1890 — 1900 — 1910

1900 Carnegie publishes *The Gospel of Wealth*

1890 Sherman Antitrust Act

1886 Statue of Liberty dedicated

Industries Built on Steel and Rails

The Industrial Revolution had created the building blocks needed for modern industry in the United States: machines, steam engines, standardized parts, mass production, and the factory system. Now, between 1865 and 1890, these elements were to be brought together on a larger scale. Small shops and businesses developed into huge industries. The value of the nation's manufactured goods leaped from $2 billion to $9 billion.

Two of the nation's leading industries—steel and railroads—were vital links in the spread of American manufacturing. Steel gave industries a strong new building material, and railroads moved raw materials and goods to factories and markets.

The Bessemer process of making steel, developed in 1856, radically changed the steel industry. This process made it possible to use less coal, greatly cutting costs. It also sped production. What once took a day to produce now took only fifteen minutes. Soon steel was used in products from nails to barbed wire to bridge beams.

Railroad companies realized that steel would last longer than iron, and they began using steel rather than iron rails. By the mid-1880s almost all the rails laid were steel, which had become cheaper than iron.

Other developments improved railroad service. Granville T. Woods, an African-American inventor, devised a railway telegraph system that helped prevent collisions. George M. Pullman's sleeping cars made rail travel more comfortable, and George Westinghouse's air brakes made it safer. Gustavus F. Swift and Philip D. Armour developed refrigeration for railroad cars. Now beef could be safely shipped from midwestern slaughterhouses to butcher shops in the East.

Indeed, American industry moved on the nation's rapidly growing network of rails. Railroads carried iron ore from mines on the western rim of the Great Lakes to steel mills in Chicago, Cleveland, Buffalo, and Pittsburgh. Coal from the mines of Pennsylvania and West Virginia moved by rail to the same cities. The coal fired the blast furnaces that turned the ore into steel—steel for more tracks, engines, cars, and tools.

Developing

THE SECTION

Limited English Proficiency

Building Vocabulary. The first paragraph on page 383 lists the "building blocks" for modern industry: *machines, steam engines, standardized parts, mass production,* and the *factory system*. Before reading, have students provide definitions and examples of why these were needed for modern industry to develop.

The impact of railroads on industry illustrates important economic relations. Have students examine the following sentence, define italicized terms and, explain how they are related. "Railroads moved *raw materials* and *goods* to *factories* and *markets*."

GTV Side 3

Chap. 1, Frame 00005

The State of the Union: Centennial Expo (Movie Segment)

Search and Play:

GTV Side 3

Chap. 8, Frame 21664

The March of Industry (Movie)

Search:

Play:

Connections: Science and Technology

Reports. Have students prepare reports on inventions in the late 1800s that made rail traffic safer and more comfortable. They may choose a development mentioned in the text or one of the following: the automatic car coupler (1873), the air brake (1869), track circuit (1872). Students should identify who developed these innovations, how they work, and what effect they had on rail transportation. Students may want to update their reports by researching railroads of today and their relative importance to industry.

Active Learning

Designing Ads. Have students look through contemporary newspapers and magazines to locate advertisements for breakfast foods. Have them compare these ads to the ads on this page.
Ask: ***How are these advertisements similar? Different? Do you think the 1800s ads would be effective today? Why or why not?***
Now have two students work in small groups to design a contemporary ad for a product of the 1800s. Have them share their ads with the class.

Connections: Economics

From 1860 to 1900, American retailers developed the concept of market segments. A *market segment* is a group of consumers who retailers believe will be attracted by a particular level of price, quality, and service.

For example, the Marshall Field Department Store in Chicago appealed to the upper economic levels of consumers. Customers went there not only to buy goods but to have a social experience. They paid a high price for high quality goods and services.

Inventions Transforming the Nation

One measure of industry's vigor was the boom in inventions, which took over tasks once done by hand. Power-driven sewing machines could turn cloth into ready-made clothes. Machines plowed, sowed seed, harvested, and threshed wheat on the vast American prairies. Machines drilled deep wells for oil, gas, and water. Machines molded metal pots, printed newspapers, milled locomotive parts, and added and subtracted figures.

The new consumer. As people demanded more manufactured goods, production boomed and prices dropped. New items came on the market, and the buying and selling habits of the entire nation changed. The first department stores had opened in cities before the Civil War. Now they displayed the wide range of new goods for consumers. A.T. Stewart's Cast Iron Palace in New York set an example that was followed by R.H. Macy in New York, John Wanamaker in Philadelphia, and Marshall Field in Chicago.

The railroad boom made possible a new type of merchandising. Now that merchants could ship goods to locations across the country, they could take advantage of the fact that it was cheaper to buy goods from manufacturers in huge quantities. Frank Woolworth and J. C. Penney were among the first to see the possibilities, and their stores popped up nationwide. Thus the chain store was born. Soon city and town dwellers were shopping at a variety of department and chain stores.

Aaron Montgomery Ward realized that people living in the country were a market still untapped by large-scale merchandising. In 1872 he started a mail-order business, sending out a one-page list of items for sale. By 1874 his single sheet had grown to a seventy-two-page catalog. Soon Montgomery Ward had a rival— Sears, Roebuck and Company, a mail-order business that promised "Satisfaction Guaranteed or Your Money Back."

Department stores, chain stores, and mail-order businesses had to sell large quantities of goods in order to be profitable. Their owners also faced the question of how to sell to customers they would never meet in person. Advertising provided the answer to the concerns of the modern merchandiser. In 1879 John Wanamaker shocked his competitors by running a full-page newspaper ad. Slogans and colorful pictures soon abounded, and a new business— advertising— took off.

Corporations: Framework for Big Business

Before the Civil War, most American businesses were privately owned. As industry expanded, however, it needed large amounts of capital, labor, and equipment. Owners began to form **corporations,**

The first cold cereal was invented by Dr. John Harvey Kellogg for his patients. The cereal caught on and soon a rival, C. W. Post, who had once been a patient of Dr. Kellogg, engaged Kellogg's in the "corn flake wars."

People who had less to spend went to shop at F. W. Woolworth Store, where goods were piled in bins for consumers to pick through.

Montgomery Ward and Sears, Roebuck and Company sold to the vast rural communities. Since these people could not come to the store, Wards and Sears took the store to them in the form of mail-order catalogues.

Andrew Carnegie, Cornelius Vanderbilt, and John D. Rockefeller became leaders in the steel, railroad, and oil industries.

a type of business in which shares of stock are sold to investors who then own part of the business and share in its profits. Sale of stock brings in large sums of money to finance expansion of the corporation's business.

The corporation is created by a charter issued by the state government. It is an "artificial being" that can make contracts, own property, sue, and be sued. If the corporation fails, stockholders are protected by limited liability, meaning that they lose only the money they invested. They are not responsible for the corporation's debts, as are proprietors and partners if their business fails.

In certain industries, many corporations rushed headlong to do business and make profits. During the 1880s a thousand companies competed in the railroad business, and a thousand different plants were making steel. Most Americans welcomed such business competition. It was at the core of **free enterprise**— private companies freely competing with one another with little or no government regulation. However, in three major industries— railroads, oil, and steel— corporate leaders began to see that they could make greater profits if they could eliminate competition.

Competition Among Railroads

Railroading attracted many competing companies, which sometimes resorted to questionable business practices to survive. For example, in areas where a railroad had no competition, it would charge "all the traffic can bear." Where railroads competed for customers, they tried to charge less than their rivals. A railroad that won a rate war and drove its competitors out of business promptly raised its rates, and shippers had no choice but to pay them.

Other abuses included selling "watered" stock, not backed by railroad money or property. Some owners paid stockholders no **dividends,** or shares of the company's profits. Railroad directors offered **rebates** to large companies, promising to return part of the company's shipping costs in exchange for all of that company's business.

To protect themselves from going under, competing railroads sometimes formed a pool. All the companies in the pool agreed to share freight business, to set standard rates, and to divide profits. The pools did not always work. Members often ignored agreements and returned to cutthroat tactics to make a quick profit.

There was, however, another way to curb competition. Several companies could consolidate, or combine into one large company. Railroad lines could often be run more efficiently when consolidated. If the new company was successful, it could charge lower rates and pay higher stock dividends. Yet the consolidated railroads, taking advantage of the lack of competition, usually continued to offer rebates and charge variable rates.

Thinking Critically

Analysis. Have students identify the advantage of "limited liability" for investors. (involves less risk) **Ask:** How has "limited liability" for investors affected the success of American businesses? (encouraged investment, which provided needed capital for businesses to grow; encouraged competition and free enterprise) What disadvantages might "limited liability" create? (Corporations have used it to avoid responsibility for accumulated debts.) Why did major industrialists want to limit competition while consumers applauded it? (Industrialists had to work harder to make a profit; consumers enjoyed competitive prices.)

Limited English Proficiency

Building Vocabulary. Help students define the following terms used to describe business organizations: *partnership* (387), *corporation* (385), *pool* (385), *trust* (387–8), *holding company* (390).

Then have students place the terms on a continuum, or scale, starting from the simplest form and ending with the most complex.

After reading the section, students may discuss the different forms of organizations as a follow up. Discuss the *economic* advantages and disadvantages of each type of business organization. What are the *social* advantages and disadvantages of each?

Social History

Oral Report. Have interested students report to the class on the exploits of two of the most colorful swindlers and speculators of the nineteenth century: Jay Gould and Jim Fisk.

Students can include information on the takeover of the Erie Railroad from Cornelius Vanderbilt (1867–1872) and the attempt to corner the gold market (1869).

Students should gather information for their reports from other history books, encyclopedias, and biographical dictionaries.

Connections: Language

Railroads passed through some towns too small to warrant a regularly scheduled stop—hence the term "whistle stops." The conductor signaled the engineer that a passenger wanted to get off the train; the engineer responded by tooting the train's whistle.

Reduced student page in the Teacher's Edition

Regulating the Railroads

Abuses by railroads provoked cries of outrage from injured groups. Small shippers complained that the railroads discriminated against them, making it difficult for them to compete with large companies. Farmers, shippers, and business people who were threatened by the unfair rates demanded that government regulate railroads. By 1874 Illinois, Iowa, Minnesota, and Wisconsin had passed laws against discriminatory railroad practices.

The railroads argued that states had no legal right to regulate them, and the issue reached the Supreme Court. In 1877 the Court, in *Munn* v. *Illinois*, upheld an Illinois law regulating railroads. Yet nine years later the Court changed its view and ruled against state regulation. In *Wabash, St. Louis and Pacific Railroad Co.* v. *Illinois*, the Court ruled that states could not set the rates of railroads that crossed state lines. Only the federal government could regulate interstate commerce.

Pressure for federal regulation increased, and Congress responded by passing the Interstate Commerce Act in 1887. This act declared that rates of railroads crossing state lines must be "reasonable and just." It forbade rebates and pools. A five-member Interstate Commerce Commission (ICC) was created to enforce the act.

In practice, though, the ICC offered little relief. Railroads often ignored its rulings, forcing the commission to go to court. By 1897 sixteen cases had reached the Supreme Court, and the railroads had won fifteen of them.

The large photo shows Titusville six years after the first oil well was drilled there. Ramshackle drilling towns shot up almost overnight. Below, a modern oil rig.

Connections: Science and Technology
Before the tank car was invented in 1865, crude oil was transported from wells to refineries in barrels loaded onto railroad flatcars. After 1870, pipelines were built—by agonizingly slow means because most of the work was done by hand.

Thinking Critically

Analysis. A nineteenth-century newspaper humorist named Finley Peter Dunne had one of his favorite characters, Mr. Dooley, define a trust in this way: *"It's when you hand th' swag to someone else while th' police search yu."*

Ask: What does this definition mean? How might trusts have hidden illegal activities by complex organization?

Rockefeller's Oil Empire

Railroading was not the only industry affected by the drive toward consolidation. Perhaps the single most successful effort to establish control over an American industry was mounted by John D. Rockefeller, a shrewd businessman who came to dominate the oil industry.

In his twenties Rockefeller had started a partnership selling farm goods in Cleveland, Ohio. The Civil War boom helped him save several thousand dollars, and a visit to the oil fields of Pennsylvania gave him his opportunity.

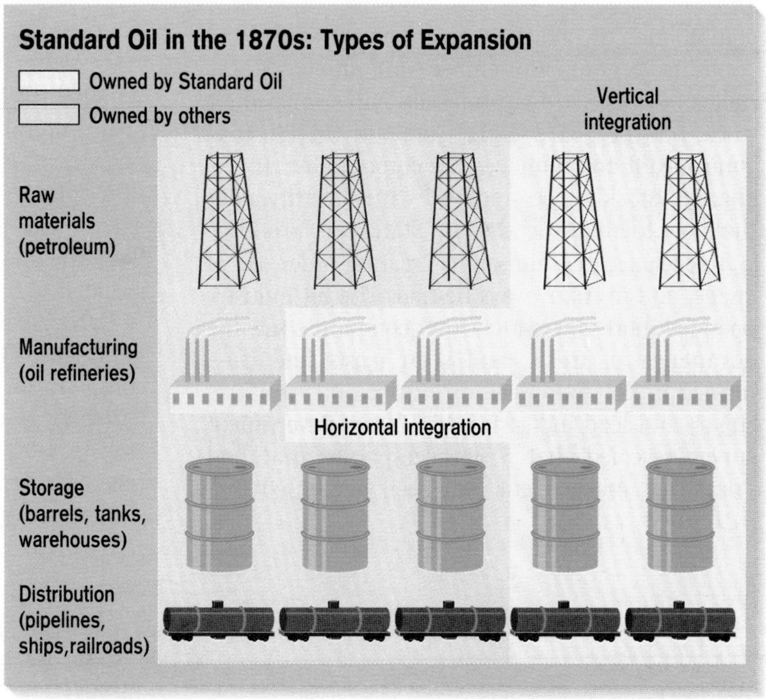

Vertical integration involves controlling each step of production in an industry; horizontal, controlling one area, such as refining.

Before the mid-1800s, oil had been little more than a nuisance to the farmers of western Pennsylvania. The smelly, greenish ooze ruined their water and splattered their cows. Shortly before the Civil War, however, a process had been discovered for refining oil into petroleum to fuel lamps and heaters. Soon oil was in demand, yet people did not know how to get enough of it out of the ground.

Then E. L. Drake drilled the first successful oil well near Titusville, Pennsylvania, in 1859. The frantic rush for "black gold" was on. By the end of the Civil War, wildcatters—prospectors for oil—were as common as prospectors for gold. Oil fields dotted Pennsylvania, Ohio, and West Virginia. Dozens of companies competed for wells, refineries, and markets.

John D. Rockefeller and his business partners were in the middle of the competition and bent on succeeding. Their goal was to drive their competitors out of the business.

The rise of the trust. In 1870 Rockefeller reorganized his partnership as a corporation, Standard Oil of Ohio, with stock worth $1 million. Because the railroads needed Rockefeller's business, he talked them into giving rebates to Standard and raising rates for rival refineries. He could then sell his oil for less than his rivals, forcing many of them out of business. By 1872 Standard Oil controlled 25 percent of the nation's oil refining. One independent refiner complained, "There was only one buyer on the market [Standard Oil] and we had to sell at their terms."

In a depression that began in 1873, many of the remaining oil refining companies failed. Rockefeller bought the bankrupt companies. Standard Oil was thus expanding in one area of the oil industry—refining. This type of expansion is known as horizontal integration.

During the 1870s Rockefeller extended his reach into the other areas of the oil industry. Standard bought ships, docks, and barrel companies, and even built its own pipelines. Controlling each step of production in an industry, from start to finish, is called vertical integration. By 1879 Standard controlled 90 percent of the refining business and almost all oil transportation. As a result, it had a **monopoly**—a single business with the power to control prices in its market.

In order to efficiently control the companies he had acquired, Rockefeller formed the Standard Oil Trust in 1882. A **trust** was a new form of business

GTV Side 3
Chap. 8, Frame 22751
Oil Fields 1900 (Map)
Search:

Backyard History

Research. The late 1800s were marked by the increased importance of industry over agriculture and a corresponding flow of population from rural to urban areas. Farming also expanded, but its growth depended increasingly on machinery, rather than human labor.

Have students do research to compare what life was like in their community before and after the age of industrialization. What kind of preindustrial economic activity existed? How did industrialization change the lives and work of local people? When did this happen?

Connections: Literature

Discussion. Use excerpts from one of Horatio Alger's books (*Ragged Dick*, *Tattered Tom*, *Luck and Pluck*) to illustrate the popular "rags to riches" explanation for the success of America's new tycoons.

Ask: Was Alger's viewpoint a realistic one? **(While a few of the new millionaires started in poverty, a study of 303 textile, railroad, and steel executives of the 1870s showed that 90 percent came from upper- or middle-class backgrounds.)** Which groups in American society were most apt to fit Alger's description? **(The wealthy industrialists were overwhelmingly white, Anglo-Saxon, Protestant men.)**

combination in which a single board of trustees controlled a group of member corporations. Stockholders of Standard's companies still owned their stock, but the board—the Standard Oil Trust—controlled it and managed the corporations. In exchange, stockholders received "trust certificates" that paid them dividends from Standard's profits.

Rockefeller saw himself as creating order out of chaos, and in many ways he had. The oil industry operated more efficiently. Other companies saw the advantages of trusts, and soon trusts had been formed in the cottonseed oil, linseed oil, whiskey, sugar, and lead industries. In 1904 a government survey revealed that 5,300 companies that had once been independent had been combined into 319 trusts.

Spotlight on American Ideals

"Go Slow and Sure, and prosper then you must
With Fame and Fortune, while you Try and Trust,"

advised Horatio Alger Jr. in novels like *Ragged Dick, Tattered Tom*, and *Luck and Pluck*. A whole generation of American boys grew up on Alger's "rags-to-riches" stories, their thoughts and dreams shaped by the adventures of Alger's heroes. Alger wrote over one hundred novels that traced the climb to success of clean-cut lads whose good deeds, intelligence, and hard work—along with a little luck—brought them fortune. In one example, the hero helps an old lady across the street. She turns out to be a wealthy widow, and rewards him by sending him to college.

Alger's novels were never considered well-written. Yet they reinforced the image of the United States as the land of opportunity—the place where dreams of power, wealth, and social status could come true.

Carnegie and Steel

While Rockefeller was creating his empire in oil, an immigrant from Scotland named Andrew Carnegie saw his future in steel. Although his first job, in a cotton mill, paid only $1.20 per week, Carnegie quickly rose to a position as manager for the Pennsylvania Railroad. He invested the money he made, and by the age of thirty was a wealthy man.

Carnegie recognized that railroads needed metal for tracks, locomotives, and bridges. He started a company to build bridges in 1864 and soon expanded it to include several plants producing iron. During a trip to England, Carnegie saw the Bessemer process for turning soft crude iron into hard steel. Carnegie moved into steel.

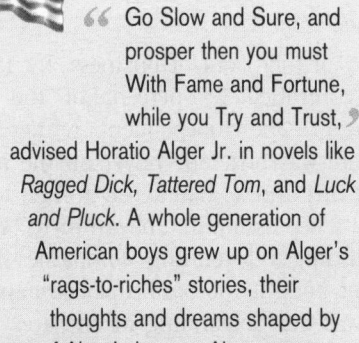

In 1873 Carnegie built the nation's largest Bessemer plant, the Homestead Steel Works. Like Rockefeller, Carnegie took advantage of railroad rebates to undersell his competitors. During the 1870s depression he bought failing companies in a process of horizontal integration.

Carnegie integrated his company vertically, too, buying freighters and railroads to ship his ore, and coal fields to supply his furnaces. He even leased part of Minnesota's ore-rich Mesabi Range. By 1900 the Carnegie Steel Company produced 25 percent of American steel.

Morgan and Banking

Money is the lifeblood of business, and by 1900 investment bankers controlled its flow. They acted as money managers for companies. They sold corporate stocks and bonds, arranged loans, and advised clients how to run their businesses.

J. Pierpont Morgan was a master of investment banking. He bought failing railroads and com-

Multicultural Perspectives

Madam C.J. Walker was born Sarah Breedlove in 1867 on a plantation in Delta, Louisiana. Plagued by hair loss as a young woman, she developed her own line of hair preparations. She said at the 1913 National Negro Business League Convention: *"The girls and women of our race must not be afraid to take hold of business endeavors. . . . I started eight years ago with one dollar and fifty cents and now I am giving employment to more than a thousand women."*

Madame Walker promoted black women's education and business participation, and spoke out against the lynching of blacks in the South—causes to which she also contributed large sums of money.

bined them into profit-making businesses. He encouraged businesses to form trusts, working to end the cutthroat competition he saw as wasteful.

Morgan helped put together many of America's trusts, including General Electric, American Telephone and Telegraph, and International Harvester. In 1901 he bought Carnegie's steel company for $492 million and combined it with steel companies he controlled, creating the mightiest trust of all, the United States Steel Corporation. It owned 1,000 miles of railroad track, 112 blast furnaces, and 78 ore boats, and employed 170,000 workers—most of whom worked twelve hours a day for wages that barely kept their families alive. Morgan took a fee of $150 million for his services.

C. J. Walker, the first black, self-made female millionaire, became a philanthropist and social activist. Her hair-care business fostered black enterprise. Below: the Walker Building, Indianapolis.

Walker Collection; Indiana Historical Society Library

No business venture seemed too large for Morgan. Even President Cleveland came to him for help in 1895. The United States, in the midst of a depression, needed a loan of $65 million in gold. Morgan, together with other bankers, made the loan and earned a profit of $18 million. A journalist wrote, "If a man wants to buy beef, he must go to the butcher. . . . If Mr. Cleveland wants much gold, he must go to the big banker."

Justifying Wealth

Morgan, Rockefeller, and Carnegie were just three of the many Americans who made fortunes from their businesses. There were over 4,000 millionaires in the United States in 1890. Many lived in a world of mansions, yachts, twelve-course dinners, and uniformed servants. As the gap widened between the very rich and the mass of Americans struggling to make a living, some captains of industry sought to justify their wealth.

The Gospel of Wealth. In 1900 Carnegie published *The Gospel of Wealth*, describing the growth of trusts and the wealth they created as "triumphant democracy." But he believed wealth carried with it a social responsibility. "The man who dies rich," he wrote, "dies thus disgraced."

Indeed, Carnegie spent his last years giving away most of his $400 million fortune "to help those who will help themselves." The money went to build libraries, universities, concert halls, and hospitals. He also set up foundations to serve the cause of international peace. Since his day, industrialists and corporations have been major supporters of American educational and cultural institutions.

Social Darwinism. How did business leaders justify killing off competition in a society committed to the idea that competition was healthy? Some turned to the leading scientific thought of the time—the theories of naturalist Charles Darwin.

Thinking Critically

Evaluation. Andrew Carnegie is admired both for building the nation's steel industry and for his philanthropy. He spent his final years giving away some $350 million. This money built 2,811 libraries, 7,689 church organs, Carnegie Hall in New York City, and several schools and museums.

Ask: What might be the motives behind such philanthropy? (a sense of social responsibility; a desire to repay society for the wealth it had enabled him to amass; a desire to influence the social, cultural, and intellectual values of the nation)

GTV Side 3

Chap. 8, Frame 23249

Iron Ore Deposits 1900 (Map)

Search:

GTV Side 3

Chap. 8, Frame 23590

Steel Centers 1900 (Map)

Search:

GTV Side 3

Chap. 8, Frame 22691

Coal Deposits 1900 (Map)

Search:

Connections: Politics

Far from being a serious obstacle to monopolies, the Sherman Antitrust Act aided business in a number of ways. Senator Sherman pointed out that it was designed to head off public calls for radical economic change. *"You must heed their appeal [to support the act] or be ready for the socialist, the communist, the nihilist. Society is now disturbed by forces never felt before."*

The Act proved harmless in attempts to break up the sugar trust, Standard Oil, and the tobacco monopoly. The Supreme Court used it to outlaw the 1894 railway worker's strike as a restraint of trade, and cited it in declaring a tax on high incomes unconstitutional.

Thinking Critically

Evaluation. Many people believe that the business tactics of Rockefeller, Morgan, and Carnegie were justified because they helped the United States rise to industrial leadership. Others argue that the three were "robber barons" who brought ruin to small businesses by unfairly controlling the market and the prices of the products.

Have students do research, using their textbooks and other sources, to determine whether these men were "heroes" or "villains." Hold a class discussion comparing various viewpoints and reasons.

Section Review

ANSWERS

1. Definitions for the following terms are on pages indicated in parentheses: *corporation* (385), *free enterprise* (385), *dividends* (385), *rebates* (385), *monopoly* (387), *trust* (387), *laissez faire* (390), *holding company* (390).

2. Made steel production cheap and quick, so railroads began using steel for rails. Railroads enabled people, raw materials, and manufactured goods to be moved faster and more easily.

3. Bessemer process, power-driven sewing machines, power drills, oil-refining process.

4. Corporations, holding companies, trusts; made businesses too powerful, eliminated competition, kept prices high and wages low, widened gap between rich and poor.

5. Reaction against trusts' abuses; businesses easily found ways around law such as "holding companies."

Reduced student page in the Teacher's Edition

Darwin observed that in nature, all living things are locked in a struggle to survive. He pointed out that over time the fittest organisms survive and pass their traits to their offspring. The English philosopher Herbert Spencer loosely applied Darwin's theory of evolution to society and business.

The philosophy of Social Darwinism soon took root in the United States. Social Darwinists believed that it was natural for companies to struggle for survival in the economic world and that government should not tamper with the process. In the struggle for survival, they argued, the fittest businesses would survive and would improve society. John D. Rockefeller adopted the idea, saying, "The growth of a large business is merely a survival of the fittest."

Social Darwinism fit with another guiding principle in American economics. A great number of people, including many in government, believed in **laissez-faire** (lehs-ay FEHR) economics—the idea that businesses should be free of government regulation. Government regulation, they thought, would hinder the natural laws of supply and demand.

American Voices

"Every contract, combination in the form of trust or otherwise, or conspiracy in restraint of trade or commerce among the several states or with foreign nations is hereby declared to be illegal."

—The Sherman Antitrust Act, 1890

The Sherman Antitrust Act

Public resentment rose as in industry after industry businessmen were killing competition, keeping prices high and wages low. Critics of big business blamed corporate leaders for business abuses and economic troubles. They called fast-rising business leaders "robber barons," after the medieval barons who grew rich on the labor of the peasants.

The public outcry against the abuses of the trusts awoke the political parties in the election year of 1888. Both Republicans and Democrats came out in favor of government regulation. Outgoing President Grover Cleveland said people were being "trampled to death beneath [the] iron heel" of trusts. Newly elected President Benjamin Harrison declared that trusts were "dangerous conspiracies against the public good."

In this atmosphere, Congress passed the Sherman Antitrust Act in 1890. The Sherman Act declared that any business combination, including trusts, operating "in restraint of trade" was illegal. The vague wording of the law, however, made it difficult to enforce.

Meanwhile, companies that were ordered to break up their trusts were avoiding regulation by shifting to a new form of business combination—the **holding company.** Whereas a trust controlled but did not own stock in other companies, a holding company owned stock in other corporations. A holding company held enough stock to control the policies of its flock of companies as effectively as did the trust.

The Sherman Antitrust Act, like the earlier Interstate Commerce Act, proved largely ineffective. And it would be years before government regulation had a significant influence on business practices. Still, a precedent had been set. The government was being asked to establish rules to ensure fairness in business and the economy.

Section Review

1. **Identification.** Define the terms *corporation, free enterprise, dividends, rebates, monopoly, trust, laissez faire*, and *holding company*.

2. **Analysis.** How did invention of the Bessemer process affect railroads? How did the railroads increase the pace of industrial growth?

3. **Evaluation.** List three inventions that led to the rapid growth of industry. Which do you think had the greatest impact on industry? Why?

4. **Analysis.** Describe three new forms of business organization developed between 1865 and 1890. What were the main objections to them?

5. **Analysis.** Why did Congress pass the Sherman Antitrust Act? Explain why it was not effective.

Connections: Geography

Until 1954 Ellis Island in New York Harbor was the port of entry for more than 60 million immigrants from Europe. New arrivals, who referred to it as "the isle of tears," often stayed there for days while being counted, medically examined, and sometimes given new, Americanized names.

At Angel Island in San Francisco Bay, thousands of Asian immigrants were detained in a grim, prison-like immigration center for days, weeks, and months before being allowed to begin life anew in the United States.

15-2 The Immigrants

Focus: Why did a flood of immigrants come to the United States in the late 1800s, and what was the response to immigration?

"America was in everybody's mouth. Businessmen talked of it over their accounts; the market women made up their quarrels that they might discuss it from stall to stall; people who had relatives in the famous land went around reading their letters for the enlightenment of less fortunate folk. . . . Children played at emigrating."

So wrote Mary Antin, who immigrated to Boston in May 1894 at age thirteen. Mary's home town in Russia was not the only place that was buzzing with tales of freedom and opportunity in the United States. All over southern and eastern Europe, and in China, Japan, Mexico, and the Mideast, people dreamed of a better life in the "magic land."

One of the largest tides of immigration the nation has ever known began in the early 1880s. During the next twenty years, almost 9 million people set foot on American soil for the first time. The twenty years after that brought 14.5 million more people. These immigrants came to the United States for the same reasons the first wave had come in the 1830s and 1840s. They were fleeing poverty, drought, high taxes, persecution, and a scarcity of jobs. They were seeking opportunity in a land, wrote a Polish girl, that had "plenty for all."

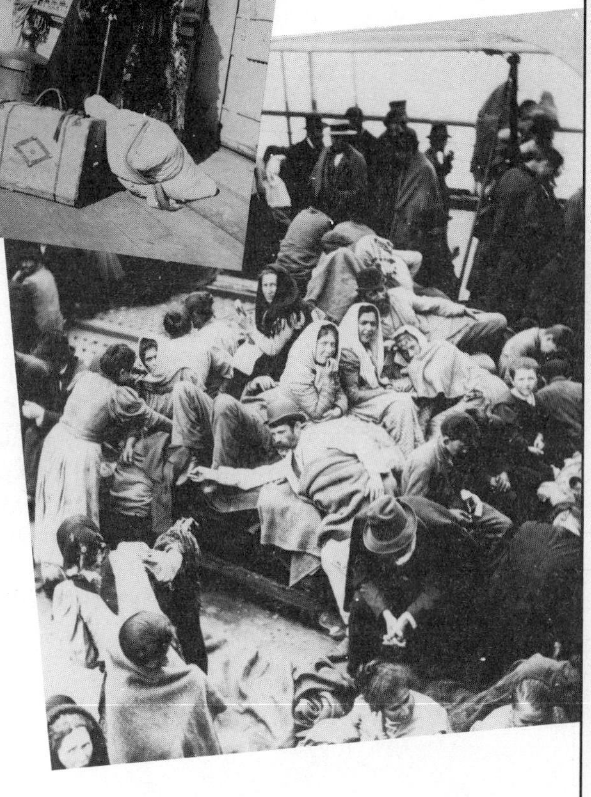

Italian family, Ellis Island; Chinese family, San Francisco; Russian immigrant, Ellis Island; steerage passengers on deck.

Section 15-2

Objectives

- ***Answer the Focus Question.***
- *Cite examples to illustrate the theme of balancing unity and diversity in the late 1800s.*

Introducing

THE SECTION

By the turn of the century about 15 million Americans had at least one parent who had been born abroad. Pulitzer Prize-winning historian Oscar Handlin wrote in the introduction to *The Uprooted*:

"Once I thought to write a history of the immigrants in America. Then I discovered that the immigrants were American history."

Ask students what he meant. Then tell them they will now read about the nation's response to the largest tide of immigration in United States history.

GTV Side 3

Chap. 5, Frame 15101

Making a Mark: The Impact of Immigration (Movie)

Search:

Play:

Developing
THE SECTION

Backyard History

Interviews. Ask students to question parents and grandparents about the first members of their families to come to the United States. **Ask:** Why did they come? What kind of welcome did they receive? How did they feel about their new home?

Using the Visuals

Analyzing a Graph. Refer students to the graph on this page. **Ask:**

1. Until the year 1900, which part of the world supplied most immigrants to the United States? **(northern and western Europe)**
2. Which year on the graph was the first in which more immigrants came to the United States from eastern and southern Europe than from northern and western Europe? **(1910)**
3. Which group of immigrants was usually the third most numerous from 1840 to 1910? **(those from the Americas)**
4. Where in the United States would Europeans, Asians, and Latin Americans be most likely to settle? Why? **(Europeans—east coast and Midwest; Asians and Latin Americans—west coast and Southwest; most likely to settle in the area closest to their point of arrival)**

B · A · C · K · G · R · O · U · N · D

Connections: Literature

The less glamorous side of the United States' new urban landscape was depicted by a school of authors who exposed the details of everyday life among the cities' middle and lower classes. Theodore Dreiser's *Sister Carrie* (1900) and Frank Norris's *McTeague* (1899) illustrate the struggle of middle-class people to stay above the poverty line. Upton Sinclair's novel *The Jungle* (1906) chronicled the wretched conditions faced by Chicago's immigrant packinghouse workers.

Reduced student page in the Teacher's Edition

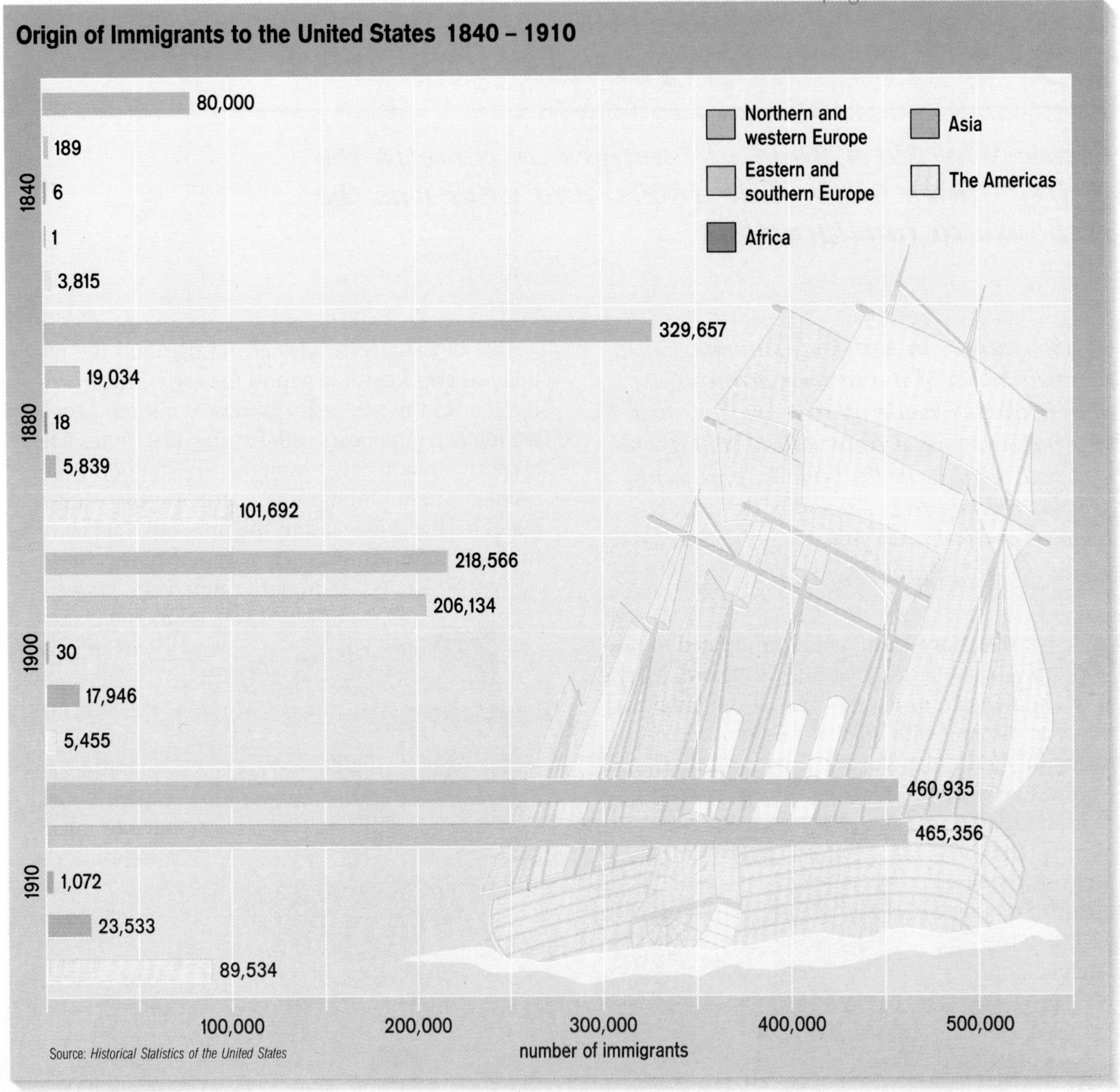

Immigrant Life

For the most part the newcomers settled in towns and cities, where industries offered jobs. By 1900 New York City had a foreign-born population of 1,260,924—more than a third of its total population. Some smaller factory towns had even larger percentages of foreign-born residents. In Lawrence, Massachusetts, most of the textile workers were immigrants, people of twenty-five nationalities who spoke forty different languages.

In cities, where people with the same language and customs clustered together, neighborhoods became known by such names as Little Italy, Second Warsaw, and Chinatown. The sculptor Jacob Epstein recalled growing up as the son of Jewish immigrants in New York City in the 1880s:

> *"My earliest recollections are of the teeming East Side where I was born. This Hester Street and its surrounding streets were the most*

densely populated of any city on earth. . . . I realize what I owe to its unique and crowded humanity. Its swarms of Russians, Poles, Italians, Greeks, and Chinese lived as much in the streets as in the crowded tenements. ❞

Many immigrants saw education as the key to future success. Public schools operated day and night in many cities, giving lessons in English and citizenship to immigrants and their children. Often, as the children learned English, they rejected their parents' language and old-country customs.

The immigrant boys below did hard labor all day and learned English at night. Day-school students pledge allegiance to the flag of their new country.

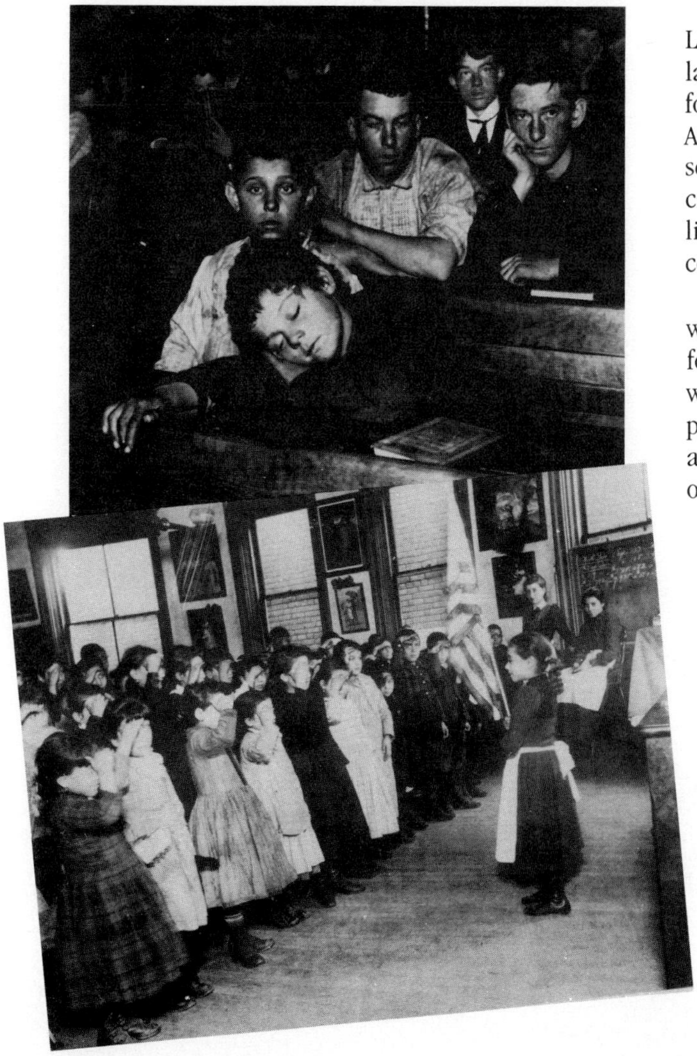

Most struggled to fit in with what they saw as "American." One immigrant girl wrote:

❝ *I can't live with the old world and am yet too green for the new. I don't belong to those with whom I was educated. I am one of the millions of immigrant children, children of loneliness, wandering between two worlds that are at once too old and too new to live in.* ❞

Some immigrants resented the process of assimilation, or absorbtion into the existing culture. They saw school as a threat to their religion and customs, and thought their children would be better off working. Still, old and new continued to mix, contributing to the complex, diverse society.

Nativist Feelings

Like immigrants before them, newcomers in the late 1800s faced nativist hostility. Their languages, food, and customs seemed strange to native-born Americans — many of whom, ironically, were descendants of earlier immigrants, as shown in the cartoon on page 395. Immigrants who were Catholic or Jewish met religious prejudice, while newcomers from Asia felt the effects of racism.

Many of the immigrants came from countries without democratic governments, where support for **communism, socialism,** and **anarchism** was beginning to spread. Communists thought that property should be owned by society as a whole, and wanted everyone to have an equal share of goods. Socialists wanted government to own major industries to protect the public from what they saw as the abuses of free enterprise. And anarchists wanted to do away with government entirely. Nativists charged that immigrants threatened American democracy by bringing these "foreign" ideas with them.

Also, many immigrants who were unskilled or without money needed jobs quickly. They accepted lower wages than native-born workers, and sometimes took the jobs of workers out on strike. American workers' fierce resentment of such competition fueled the growing nativism.

Limited English Proficiency

Building Vocabulary. Help students to cite three terms in the text that describe alternatives to capitalism—communism, socialism, anarchism. Have them use dictionaries to determine word roots of each term. What are some similarities and differences between the concepts?

Thinking Critically

Evaluation. Discuss the meaning of "assimilation" given in the text. (the process by which immigrants were expected to give up their culture and adapt, or be absorbed into the existing one) Refer students to the Jacob Riis photographs on this page.

Ask: Do the photographs illustrate the notion of "Americanization" —or assimilation? Is the process of old and new mixing the same as assimilation? Is the outcome of assimilation "a complex, diverse society"? (Assimilation implies that "foreign" cultures disappear producing homogeneity rather than diversity.)

GTV Side 3

Chap. 7, Frame 21070

Sadie Froun, Polish Immigrant (American Journal)

Search:

Play:

Writing About History

Biographical Reports. Have students research and write reports about the contributions of the following Chinese immigrants or descendents of immigrants: Ju Chin Chu (chemical engineer), Hiram L. Fong (U.S. Senator), Chen Ning Yang (physicist), Choh Hao Li (biochemist), Dong Kingman (artist), James Wong Howe (cinematographer), I. M. Pei (architect), Lin Yutang (writer), Jerry Tsai (financier).

Global Connections

Chinese immigrants came to the United States for many of the same reasons as Europeans: seeking greater economic opportunity and leaving behind social and political oppression and turmoil. Beginning in the early 1800s European nations imposed economic and political demands on China that caused upheavals in China's society and economy. In 1840 and 1858 the British (with French help in 1858) sent troops to maintain the opium trade and force China to trade with Western nations. Europeans intervened in the Taiping Rebellion in 1851 and their influence in China provoked the Boxer Rebellion in 1900, which eventually led to the collapse of the Ch'ing Dynasty.

Reduced student page in the Teacher's Edition

Immigrants from China

Beginning in 1849 thousands of Chinese immigrants entered California by way of Angel Island in the San Francisco Bay. Most were young men seeking fortunes in California's "golden hills," or simply jobs in the gold rush camps. They came from a wounded China, where crops were failing and civil war raged. Many planned only a temporary stay, promising their families they would work hard, send money home, and then return.

Set apart by appearance and customs, Chinese immigrants met with prejudice and discrimination from the beginning. Those who found gold had to pay a special miners' tax. In some places Chinese were not even allowed to stake claims.

Many Chinese immigrants started their own businesses, settling in San Francisco or in other urban areas. These communities became centers of intellectual and social life as Chinese immigrants sought to maintain their cultural identity. By the end of the 1860s the Chinese population in California had reached 48,000, and Chinese had become a vital part of the labor force in California's mining, construction, railroad, agriculture, clothing, and fishing industries.

Opposition to Chinese immigration. Chinese communities became known as models of order and industry. Yet, when a depression hit in 1873, nativist hostilities focused on the Chinese. Native-born workers, many without jobs, protested Chinese immigration, which was at the rate of about 4,000 per year. These angry workers formed the Workingmen's Party of California in 1877. Its leader, Denis Kearney, raged that the Chinese were stealing jobs from whites.

By July 1877 anti-Chinese feelings had reached a fever pitch. One night, groups of unemployed workers stormed through San Francisco's Chinatown, wrecking stores and homes. Soon Chinatown was burning. The rioting lasted for three days.

Anti-Chinese violence spread. In 1878 the Chinese in Truckee, California, were driven from the town. And in 1885, white miners in Rock Springs, Wyoming, drove 600 Chinese workers out of the town, killing 28 and setting fire to homes and shops. None of the miners were prosecuted.

Exploring Issues

IMMIGRATION

The Debate in Congress

In March 1896 Henry Cabot Lodge of Massachusetts addressed the Senate on the subject of immigration. He expressed concern about the number of immigrants arriving from southern and eastern Europe. Lodge believed that the newcomers, "whose thoughts and whose beliefs are wholly alien," threatened the way of life of native-born Americans. Moreover, he argued, they were "the most deadly enemy" of native-born workers, whose wages and standard of living would be forced down by the influx of low-cost labor.

Lodge had a plan to stop the flood of immigration. He proposed that immigrants be required to pass a literacy test to prove that they could read and write. Since northern European immigrants were more likely to be literate, such a test would "bear most heavily upon Italians, Russians, Poles, Hungarians, Greeks, and Asiatics."

Lodge's speech touched off a great debate on immigration. Representative Charles Buck of Louisiana disagreed with Lodge. An immigrant himself, Buck had come from Germany when he was eleven years old. "This country . . . has grown great by absorbing more than 40 million foreigners," he said. "We are big enough to take in all who want to come."

Representative Rowland Mahany of New York, an Irish immigrant, supported Buck.

Linking Past and Present

Paul Chow, a retired highway engineer, heads a foundation to restore Angel Island as a monument to the Asian immigrants detained there. Chow says: *"Every group has its story. This is ours. These were our heroes. They taught us how to survive; they sacrificed and suffered so my family and I could live a better life. I'm not saying this is a perfect country, but it's better than where they came from—despite discrimination, despite Angel Island, despite everything."*

"I would like to ask how many there are upon the floor of this House," he challenged "whose ancestors would have been admitted to this Republic" if there had been a literacy test. Lodge should not try to limit immigrants to people like himself, Mahany added. Samuel McCall of Massachusetts replied that the United States was not "an international soup kitchen for the benefit, primarily, of the rest of the world."

Congress passed the Lodge literacy bill by a large majority. Although most members of Congress did not want to stop all immigration, they were alarmed about slums, labor unrest, and the economic depression.

However, President Cleveland vetoed the bill. Until now, he said, Americans "have encouraged those coming from foreign countries to cast their lot with us and join in the development of our vast domain, securing in return a share in the blessings of American citizenship." This "generous and free-handed" immigration policy had worked for a hundred years, he declared, making the nation strong and prosperous.

Unlimited immigration continued until the end of the First World War, when a literacy bill became law. By 1924 restrictions had been passed that strongly favored northern European immigrants.

1. Why did Lodge and his supporters want to restrict immigration?
2. What reasons did Buck, Mahany, and Cleveland give in favor of immigration?
3. Do you think the United States today should admit all who want to enter? Why or why not? If you think there should be restrictions, what should they be?

This 1893 J. Keppler cartoon, "Looking Backward," ridicules nativism by showing what the newcomer can see—the shadows of the old-comers' immigrant fathers.

Active Learning

Simulation. Have the class reenact the Senate debate of 1896 on immigration. Divide students into four groups. Group 1 will research the benefits of immigration, Group 2 the liabilities. Group 3 will study the opinions of Lodge, Buck, Mahany, and Cleveland and choose members of their group to act as these senators during the debate. Group 4 will research how a bill reaches the Senate floor, and the rules for discussion. Students from this group can then act as moderators for the debate.

Exploring Issues

ANSWERS

1. They believed immigrants were taking jobs away from American workers during bad times; their low-cost labor would force down wages and standard of living of native-born workers; they threatened America's traditional way of life.
2. They argued that the United States had grown great by absorbing foreigners, that most members of Congress were descended from immigrants who would not have been able to pass a literacy test, and that Americans should not limit immigration to people like themselves.
3. Answers will vary.

Section Review

ANSWERS

1. Definitions are on pages indicated in parentheses; *socialism* (393), *communism* (393), *anarchism* (393).
2. Fleeing poverty, drought, high taxes, political persecution, and scarcity of jobs; attracted by stories of unlimited economic and social opportunity.
3. Examples should be of attempts at assimilation of immigrants, hostile nativist reactions to immigrants.
Linking Past and Present. For the most part, they are the same. People have been forced out of their homelands due to political upheavals and persecution (Southeast Asians, Central Americans, Russian Jews) and people come to the U.S. in search of greater economic opportunity.

B · A · C · K · G · R · O · U · N · D

Multicultural Perspectives

The following is a translation of the Chinese poem on the wall in the photograph below.

"From now on I am departing from this building.
All of my fellow villagers are rejoicing like me.
Don't say that everything within is western styled.
Even if it is built of jade it has turned into a cage.
Detained in this wooden house for several tens of days.
It is all because of the Mexican exclusion laws which implicated me.
It's a pity heroes have no way of exercising their prowess.
I can only await the word so that I can snap Tau Ti's sword.

“Detention is called 'awaiting review.'
No letter or message can get through to me.
My mind's bogged down with a hundred frustrations and anxieties,
My mouth balks at meager meals of rice gruel.
O, what can I do?
Just when can I go ashore?
Imprisoned in a coop, unable to breathe,
My countrymen are made into a herd of cattle!”

—from a Chinese folk rhyme

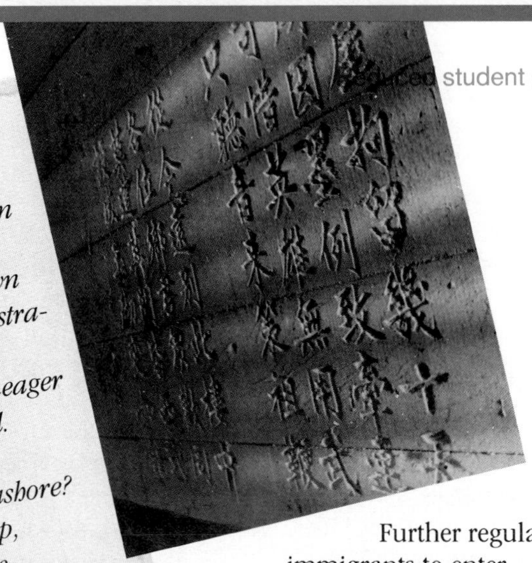

Asian immigrants were detained sometimes as long as a year. (Far left) "Detained on Angel Island." (Left) A poem on the wall at Angel Island.

Limiting Immigration

From the Golden Gate to Ellis Island, towns and cities echoed with nativist voices. Politicians heard, and the government responded. In 1882 Congress passed the Chinese Exclusion Act, banning the immigration of Chinese workers for ten years. Later laws renewed the ban.

Chinese exclusion had cut off a labor source for California farmers, who now demanded that the government admit Japanese workers. They came, many with their families, to work the farms, mines, and railroads. By 1900 there were 24,000 Japanese in the country.

Fears and prejudices erupted against Japanese immigrants, too. In 1905 the Japanese Exclusion League was formed. The following year San Francisco's school board proposed to place Japanese and Chinese students in a separate school.

The Japanese government was outraged, and President Theodore Roosevelt, eager to keep good relations with this growing world power, got involved. By the "Gentlemen's Agreement" of 1908, Japan agreed to limit immigration. San Francisco dropped its discriminatory law.

A flurry of restrictions affected all immigrants, not just Asians. The Contract Labor Act of 1885 barred entry to immigrants whose passage was paid by American employers. An 1891 law allowed illegal immigrants to be deported from the country. Further regulations made it harder for new immigrants to enter.

More anti-foreign groups formed. The American Protective Association formed in 1887 to protest against Catholic and southern and eastern European immigrants. The Immigration Restriction League demanded a ban on immigrants who could not read or write. Four such bills were vetoed before one became law in 1917.

At the height of nativist furor, in 1886, workers in New York City's harbor put in place the last bronze sections of the Statue of Liberty. The statue was a symbol of a different American attitude—a beacon of welcome and hope for immigrants. On the base would be a poem by Emma Lazarus:

“Give me your tired, your poor,
Your huddled masses yearning to breathe free,
The wretched refuse of your teeming shore.
Send these, the homeless, tempest-tossed to me:
I lift my lamp beside the golden door!”

Section Review

1. Identification. Define *socialism*, *communism*, and *anarchism*.

2. Comprehension. For what reasons did immigrants come to the United States in the late 1800s?

3. Application. Use examples from your reading to illustrate the theme of balancing unity and diversity in the late 1800s.

Linking Past and Present. Are the reasons why immigrants enter the United States today the same as they were in the late 1800s? Give examples to support your answer.

Connections: Geography
Chicago, Illinois, was the transportation hub of the nation, first as a crossroads of Native-American trails, then as a port where ships plying the Great Lakes docked. In the 1830s and 1840s a canal was built to link the Great Lakes with the Illinois and Mississippi rivers. From Chicago, transcontinental railroads reached westward. Later, the city's highway system radiated in every direction, making it a warehousing center of the nation. Today, the major airlines use Chicago's O'Hare Field as a hub for flights to cities across the nation and around the world.

15-3 The Cities

Focus: How did the growth of industry shape life in cities?

Immigrants were not the only people who poured into American cities in the late 1800s. Many farmers abandoned plow and soil for the jobs and excitement of urban centers. One young farmer was thrilled to go "from the farm to a new and shining world, a world where circuses, baseball games, and county fairs were events of almost daily occurrence." A few years later he moved on to a large city, where he saw another side of that shining world:

> *"With all my pay in my pocket, and my trunk checked, I took the train to Chicago. I shall never forget the feeling of dismay with which, an hour later, I perceived from the car window a huge smoke-cloud, which embraced the whole eastern horizon. . . . This I was told, was the soaring banner of the great and gloomy inland metropolis."*

That smoke cloud was also a signpost of the industry on which cities thrived. City populations swelled as people turned to factory work, and by the late 1880s many cities had sprawled into metropolises, or huge urban centers.

Cities in key locations grew fastest. There were port cities like San Francisco, New York, and New Orleans; river cities like Pittsburgh and St. Louis; and railroad hubs like Chicago and Memphis. All were crossroads where the flow of people and goods and money met.

By 1890 one person in three lived in a city of more than 8,000 people. And over 80 percent of all city dwellers lived in the Northeast and Midwest. Chicago, the world's grain and cattle center, had a population of 300,000 in 1870. The next year,

Louis Sontag's "The Bowery at Night, 1895," shows the glitter of turn-of-the-century New York.

Section 15-3

Objectives

- ***Answer the Focus Question.***
- *Evaluate the effect of political machines on city government.*
- *Describe actions that individuals and groups took to solve the political and social problems of the cities.*

Introducing THE SECTION

Refer students to the illustration on this page of busy Grand Street in New York City in 1895. Ask them to identify new developments that aided the growth of cities and changed American life—the electric streetcar, elevated railway, department stores, electric lighting.

Ask: How did these developments affect people's daily lives? **(New modes of transportation, for example, allowed people to live further from their jobs; they had easier and quicker access to stores.)** What kinds of problems might the rapid growth of cities create? What kinds of problems exist in cities today?

GTV Side 3
Chap. 10, Frame 25701
A New Life: The City (Movie)
Search:
Play:

Developing
THE SECTION

Connections: Science and Technology

Making a Graph. Tell students that between 1860 and 1890 more than 440,000 patents were issued. Have interested students research patent figures for ten-year periods for these years and present their findings in a bar or line graph. Refer students to the *Historical Abstracts of the United States* for their research.

Connections: Economics

Jan Matzeliger's machine brought about a 50 percent reduction in the price of shoes across the United States, doubled wages, and improved working conditions for those people dependent on the shoe industry for their livelihood. Matzeliger, unfortunately, died before he had a chance to realize any profits from his many patents.

Reduced student page in the Teacher's Edition

George Eastman sold his first Kodak camera with enough film for 100 exposures. Camera and film were returned to the factory for processing and reloading.

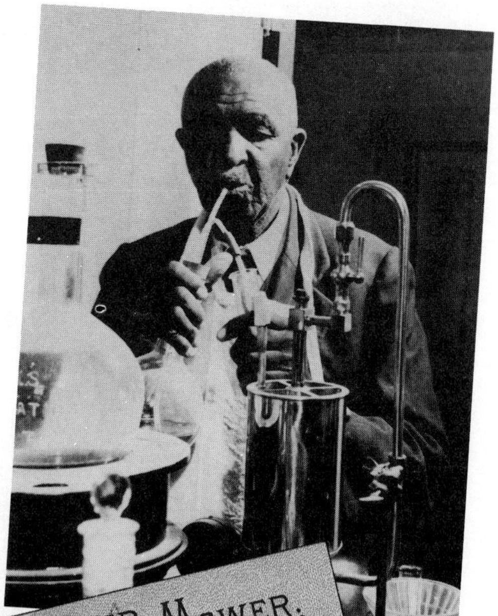

Agricultural chemist George Washington Carver developed hundreds of new products from southern farm crops and clays.

Jan Matzeliger revolutionized the shoe industry with a machine that attached the uppers of a shoe to the sole as smoothly as workers could by hand.

Using the new lawn-mowing machine, an 1870s advertisement assured readers, is child's play.

Garrett Morgan's experiences in driving an automobile led him to invent the three-way automatic traffic signal.

398

Connections: Science and Technology
When Mark Twain tried the new typewriting machine he wrote, *"One may lean back in the chair and work it. It piles up an awful stack of words on one page. It [doesn't] muss things up or scatter ink blots around."*

Connections: Science and Technology
In 1865 Maria Mitchell became head of the Astronomy Department at the newly-opened Vassar Female College in Poughkeepsie, New York. Her teaching ways were considered radically different from other instructors. She refused to report students absences, *"Given a small class and a teacher of any magnetism,"* she said, *"there need be no required attendance."*

Linking Past and Present

Discussion. Read to students the following first-hand account of telephone service by a resident in Indianapolis, Indiana at the turn of the century.

"When we got our telephone, that was quite a thing. If you needed to find out something, you didn't have to go on foot or hitch up a buggy or write a letter. You just used the telephone. . . . Whenever we used the phone, we tended to raise our voices. It seemed such a distance when you talked to somebody four or five blocks away."

Discuss with students what it would be like to live today without some of the conveniences, such as telephones and electric lights, that turn-of-the-century Americans found so amazing.

Experienced glider pilots, Orville and Wilbur Wright designed the wings, built the engine, and used modified bicycle parts for the first successful airplane in 1903.

THE CREATIVE Spirit

Inventors and Scientists

"Why, I could make anything a body wanted—it didn't make any difference what; and if there wasn't any quick new-fangled way to make a thing, I could invent one—and do it as easy as falling off a log." Thus said the Yankee in Mark Twain's 1889 novel, *A Connecticut Yankee in King Arthur's Court.* In the years after the Civil War, "new-fangled ways" invented by Americans made the United States the greatest economic power in the world.

Many of the inventions and scientific discoveries—new processes in steelmaking and refining, refrigeration, and electrical devices—were vital to the expansion of industry in the late 1800s. Almost all changed the lives of Americans. And before the end of the century, development of motion pictures and the internal-combustion engine would lay the foundations for new industries in the twentieth century.

Using one of the largest telescopes in the nation, astronomer Maria Mitchell pioneered research in sunspots, solar eclipses, and planetary surfaces.

©Michael Freeman

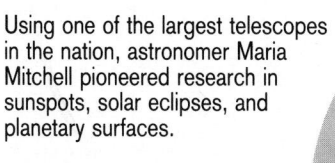

The 1874 Remington Number One, the first practical typewriter, introduced a keyboard layout that is still standard.

Active Learning

Cooperative Activity. Have students do research to make an illustrated time line of American inventions, beginning with the elevator brake (1852) and ending with the gasoline-powered automobile (1892). Encourage students to research the contributions of inventors from diverse backgrounds. Post the time line and pictures of inventors and inventions on the bulletin board.

Backyard History

Walking Tour. If you live close to an urban environment, plan a walking tour of the area. Plan visits to the self-contained communities of various ethnic groups. Draw attention to the specialized food shops, restaurants, churches, newspapers, and travel agencies that offer special trips to the "homeland."

Note also any signs of transition—and possible conflict—between newer and older immigrant groups. Visits to fire stations, police stations, and community centers will give students the opportunity to ask questions about the neighborhood's history.

more than half of the city's buildings were destroyed by fire and had to be rebuilt. Twenty years later, Chicago's population passed 1 million, making it the second largest city in the country.

Cities boomed all over the country. Mark Twain, who visited cities along the Mississippi River, reported that Minneapolis and St. Paul were alive with "newness, briskness, swift progress, wealth, intelligence . . . and general slash and go and energy." Perhaps that was the lure of the cities.

Inventors and Their Inventions

Much of the energy came from inventions. Some inventions solved existing problems. Some provided new and better ways of doing things. But they almost always changed the way people lived.

Most American cities had grown as "walking cities," small enough to cover on foot from one side to the other. As transportation improved, city borders expanded. By 1880 horse-drawn streetcars carried people beyond the old city limits. Then, in 1887, Frank J. Sprague installed a system of electric streetcars run on overhead trolley lines in Richmond, Virginia. Within three years, electric streetcars hummed in fifty-one cities. Americans could live farther and farther from their jobs. Cities spread outward, swallowing smaller towns.

Each new idea that succeeded spurred the growth of cities by creating new jobs, services, or products. A rich source of ideas was Thomas Alva Edison, who applied for over a thousand patents. Edison invented the phonograph and the motion picture camera and built America's first research laboratory in Menlo Park, New Jersey.

The "Wizard of Menlo Park" vowed to produce "a minor invention every ten days and a big thing every six months or so," and he did. Edison made the first successful electric light bulb in 1879. Then he took the first steps in making electricity common. Out of his laboratory came sockets for the light bulbs, switches, fuse boxes, underground cables, and the dynamo to produce electric current.

Electricity and the telephone. In 1882 Edison built the nation's first central power station in New York City. Soon other cities had stations. But Edison's electrical system, using direct current, could bring power only to nearby places. Then George Westinghouse, who had invented air brakes for railroads, introduced alternating current, a practical and inexpensive way to send electricity over long distances. By 1900 Westinghouse's electrical system was lighting 25 million electric bulbs.

Another inventor changed the way that people communicated. In 1876 Alexander Graham Bell invented the telephone, shown at the Centennial Exposition that year. Europeans scoffed at this "electrical toy," but most American cities had telephone service by 1880. By the end of the century, a giant web of telephones knit urban America together. Like Sprague's trolley and Edison's light bulb, Bell's telephone created a new industry. Thousands were employed as operators, assemblers, and installers—occupations that had not existed a few years earlier.

Such inventions not only created jobs and wealth, they also added to the magic of city life. One visitor to Chicago described the amazing Otis elevator, which served the new tall buildings called skyscrapers:

> *"The slow-going stranger . . . [is] loaded into one of those . . . baskets . . . and the next instant . . . up goes the whole load as a feather is caught up by a gale. The descent is more simple. Something lets go, and you fall from ten to twenty stories as it happens."*

City Problems

The cities' grand magic—skyscrapers, electric lights, telephones—was largely out of reach of the urban poor. One investigator in the city of Cleveland wrote the following report of a city dwelling:

> *"Three rooms, two adults and three children. No provisions for lighting; cooking, washing, and sleeping in the same room. In sheds, under stairways, rabbits, pigeons, and chickens breeding and at large. Privies [toilets] in foul, unsanitary conditions: surface and privy drainage upon alley where children are playing."*

Connections: Art
Photos from the collection of Jacob Riis appear in this chapter on page 393 and below left. The photo, below, of children playing in a tenement alley was taken in 1909 by Lewis Hine, another noted chronicler of the urban scene.

While some workers earned enough money to escape the noise, smoke, and filth and move away from the inner city, immigrants and those fleeing rural poverty poured into these run-down neighborhoods. They had to live closer to the docks, factories, and mills where they hoped to find work.

Almost every foot of ground in urban neighborhoods was used as living space. Thousands of people found shelter in ramshackle houses, subdivided into one room per family. Most lived in tenements—new housing hastily and cheaply constructed to relieve the housing shortage. Tenements were usually wood buildings four to six stories high. Some became extensions of the factory, with men, women, and children working in crowded rooms, sewing clothes or rolling cigars.

Sanitation was almost unknown. Many tenements had no water, except perhaps a faucet in the yard. Garbage piled up, rotting and rat-infested. Sewage ran in the gutters and ultimately dumped into rivers. Such conditions bred diseases such as typhoid and cholera, which spread quickly in crowded tenements. Due to lack of sanitation, claimed an 1882 report, half the children born in Chicago died before reaching five years of age.

Cities, which had grown with little planning, had to find a way to deal with these problems. At great expense, they began building sewage systems and water treatment plants and providing garbage disposal services. Boston spent 30 percent of the city's funds on such projects between the 1870s and 1890s. Over the years, most cities did make progress in health standards. By 1898, for example, 3,500 cities had public water works.

Political Machines

Cities trying to improve services were in a constant race against the influx of people. City officials were often slow to respond to the needs of the swelling ranks of the poor. In many cities political organizations called **political machines** sprang up, forming a link between the people and the city government.

Political machines were run by a "ring" of leaders headed by a "boss." Ring members were seldom elected officials. Instead, they gained power by exchanging favors with officials, who gave the machine the right to hand out city jobs, contracts, and political favors. In return, the machine promised to ensure the officials' reelection. Immigrants who had been helped by machine workers showed their gratitude by voting as the machine directed.

In poor neighborhoods, one observer noted, "souls and bodies were saved by the parish priest, the family doctor, and the local political [machine worker]." A machine worker listened to people's

Below left, children make paper roses to earn two to three dollars a week for their family. Below, children play in the alley of their tenement.

Thinking Critically

Synthesis. Have students work in small groups to propose possible solutions to city problems mentioned in the text—crowded and unsanitary conditions, unsafe housing, lack of public services. (They may consider: government regulation; more public housing; higher wages for workers; lower rents; educational programs to inform owners and renters of their legal rights; formation of citizen protection groups; changes in laws, for example, limiting the number of families per building; and so on.)

Have the groups share their ideas with the rest of the class.

Active Learning

Designing an Apartment. Many city dwellers in the late 1800s lived in overcrowded tenements. Have students design better conditions for low-income tenants.

Give students some guidelines to consider when designing a liveable apartment building: (a) all floors will be alike, so students need to draw only one floor, (b) family size will average seven persons, (c) all rooms should have at least one window, (d) recreational opportunities for children should be provided, (e) all rooms, doors, windows, stairways, and other elements should be clearly identified.

Limited English Proficiency

Linking Past and Present. Ask students to collect information from magazines, newspapers, and television reports about city problems and corruption in government today. Students might provide this information in conjunction with answering the Linking Past and Present question in the Section Review on page 403.

Writing About History

Using the Visuals. Using only the illustrations in this chapter, have students write one or two paragraphs about the advantages and disadvantages of industrialization and urbanization in the late 1800s. Have them share and discuss their opinions with the class.

Connections: Politics
One of the famous New York City workers who served the Tammany political machine was George Washington Plunkitt. Plunkitt saw the opportunity to make money from politics and he took it. But he also provided a service for the needy of his district. Here is a description of the kind of service he provided: *"6 A.M.: Awakened by fire engines passing his house. Hastened to the scene of the fire . . . to give assistance to fire sufferers, if needed . . . Found several tenants who had been burned out, took them to a hotel, supplied them with clothes, fed them, and arranged temporary quarters for them until they could rent and furnish new apartments."*

Reduced student page in the Teacher's Edition

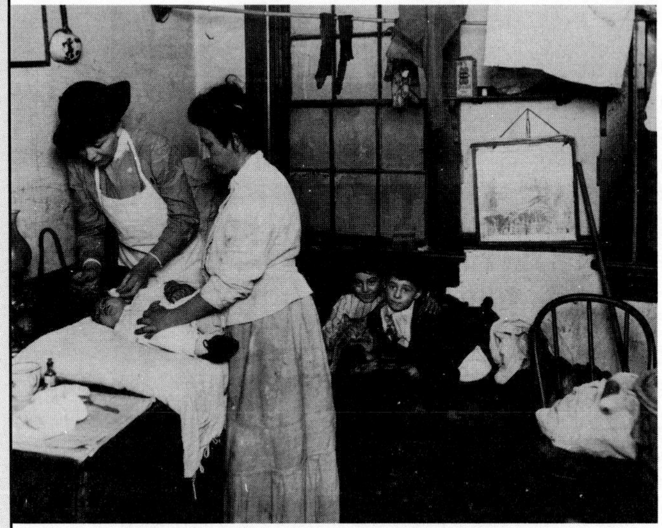

The Infant Welfare Society nurse, above, visited tenements to bring help to poor families. Jane Addams, below, was a pioneer in providing social services to the urban poor.

problems and helped bring about action. For example, if a landlord refused to heat a tenement, the worker would make the rounds of city hall and, within days, the landlord would be pressured into fixing the heating.

Although political machines helped make the voice of the poor heard in city hall, machines also bred corruption. Machine leaders made fortunes from bribes by job seekers, budding politicians, and companies who wanted contracts. They also corrupted the election process by delivering phony votes. One reporter uncovered voting lists with the names of "dead dogs, children, and non-existent persons."

The best known political machine was run by boss William Tweed in New York City. The Tweed Ring plundered the city treasury of at least $75 million, perhaps more. Finally, newspapers aroused the public, and reform politicians were elected. In 1871 Tweed and many of his ring were arrested.

Still, machines remained an important political element in New York and other cities. St. Louis was run by the Butler Ring, Minneapolis by the Ames Ring, and Philadelphia by the Gas Ring. Claimed one writer, "every little municipality in our whole land has to struggle with some 'boss' who has learned his trade or taken his cue from successful rascals in our larger towns."

Help for the Cities

In the 1880s and 1890s reformers began to tackle both the political and social problems of the cities. In 1887 a young woman named Jane Addams traveled to London where, in the midst of terrible slums, she found a ray of light—Toynbee Hall. This community center provided schooling, child care, and various forms of aid to the urban poor.

When she returned to the United States, Addams and a friend, Ellen Starr, decided to conduct their own "Toynbee Hall experiment." They bought an old building in Chicago and in 1889 opened their "settlement house," called Hull House. With other volunteers, mostly well-educated young women, they set to work. Jane Addams wrote of the experiment:

> *"From the first it was understood that we were ready to perform the humblest neighborhood services. We were asked to wash new-born babies, and to prepare the dead for burial, to nurse the sick, and to 'mind the children.'"*

Settlement workers taught classes in English, health, and nutrition. They helped people deal with city agencies. Addams even became a neighborhood garbage inspector and convinced the city to improve service. By 1895 there were fifty settlement houses in major cities in the United States.

Churches also tried to help the urban poor. Protestants dedicated themselves to the Social Gospel—a movement for the improvement of working and living conditions in the slums. Catholic parishes and Jewish synagogues set up schools, hospitals, and welfare agencies. The Salvation Army, established in 1880 to bring people back to a faith in Christ, joined in the welfare work. By the late 1880s it was running soup kitchens, employment agencies, and rooming houses for the poor.

While the efforts of individuals, churches, and synagogues made improvements in the lives of the urban poor, many early reformers saw that having government on their side would help bring about lasting change. Jane Addams had learned that charity work was "totally inadequate to deal with the vast numbers of the city's disinherited."

In 1890 Jacob Riis, a New York reporter and Danish immigrant, helped stir up the public in support of social reform efforts. In his book *How the Other Half Lives*, Riis described a tenement:

> *"This gap between dingy brick walls is the yard. That strip of smoke-colored sky up there is the heaven of these people. . . . What sort of an answer, do you think, would these tenement house dwellers give to the question, 'Is life worth living?'"*

Riis's writings and photographs influenced a New York politician named Theodore Roosevelt. When Roosevelt became governor of New York, he appointed a tenement house commission. Its report led to a state law that set strict building codes for tenements. In the years that followed, many more people would join the reform movement.

Section Review

1. **Identification.** Define *political machines*.

2. **Analysis.** Why was there rapid city growth in the 1880s and 1890s?

3. **Analysis.** Tell what effect each of these inventions had on cities and city life: electric streetcars, the central power station, alternating current, the telephone, the Otis elevator.

4. **Evaluation.** Agree or disagree with the following statement: Political machines helped extend democracy in America's cities. Explain your answer.

5. **Comprehension.** Name three individuals or groups that sought to change conditions for the urban poor. What actions did they take?

Linking Past and Present. How were the problems of cities in the 1880s and 1890s similar to problems cities have today? How were they different? Explain.

Connections to Themes

The Search for Opportunity

The decades following the Civil War offered economic opportunity on a scale unimaginable a generation earlier. Businesses now served a market stretching from coast to coast and growing at an amazing pace. Between 1850 and 1900, the nation's population tripled, increasing from 25 million to more than 75 million.

An abundance of natural resources, as well as power machinery, standardized parts, and factory production enabled the business owner to manufacture all the goods this growing market could absorb. And the development of corporations, trusts, and holding companies provided the money needed to operate on an ever-larger scale.

In addition, new inventions created new opportunities almost overnight. The harnessing of electricity gave birth to brand-new industries producing electric lights, telephone networks, phonographs, trolley cars, elevators, and films.

Yet these economic opportunities allowed a few to succeed at the expense of the many. In the space of a single generation, a few hundred corporate leaders had gained tremendous wealth and economic power. Meanwhile, millions of farmers and industrial workers found their standard of living plummeting.

Both workers and farmers saw the need to organize—to form unions and farm organizations and to influence political parties. Could their combined strength offset the awesome power wielded by business? Their struggles are part of the story of this new industrial age.

Section Review

ANSWERS

1. Definition for *political machines* can be found on text page 401.
2. Industrialization attracted workers to cities; cities were centers of transportation, and distribution.
3. Streetcars enabled people to travel longer distances; central power stations and alternating current made electricity available; telephone created new methods of communication and an industry; elevator encouraged construction of tall buildings.
4. Some may argue that they provided the poor with their only voice in city government. Others may argue that city bosses made democratic government impossible and fostered corruption.
5. Jane Addams started settlement house movement; Social Gospel groups sought to improve lives of urban poor; Salvation Army ran soup kitchens, unemployment agencies; Jacob Riis stirred demands for social reform.
Linking Past and Present: Similarities: high poverty rates, political corruption, poor city services, concentration of recent immigrant groups. Differences: decline of industry, inability of many urban poor to move from inner city, drug traffic.

GTV Side 3
Chap. 12, Frame 32453
The Price of Progress (Movie)
Search:
Play:

Chapter Survey

ANSWERS

Using New Vocabulary

1. Both describe an economic system based on competition among private companies; laissez faire indicates no government regulation.
2. Both were payments made by railroad companies: dividends were company profits paid to shareholders; rebates were refunds paid to large shippers.
3. Both forms of business organization: a trust controls a number of companies with the same board of directors but owns no stock in them; a holding company owns enough stock in a number of companies to control them.
4. Both are economic systems. A communist state owns all property and is supposed to distribute goods equally; a socialist state owns major industries to prevent abuses of free enterprise.

Reviewing the Chapter

1. With steel rails, laid many more miles of track; trains made safer; refrigerated cars made transport of perishable goods possible. Helped U.S. industry to expand by moving raw materials to factories and products to markets.
2. They made it possible to raise large amounts of money to finance expansion.
3. Horizontal integration means owning all the units in a given step of an industrial process, as in oil refineries. Vertical integration means that one company owns units for every step of an industrial process, such as oil wells, pipelines, refineries, and oil tankers.
4. State laws tried to regulate railroads, but not upheld by Supreme Court. Federal government set up ICC to control railroads, without much success. Sherman Antitrust Act passed to prevent monopolies but was also ineffective.
5. Chinese immigration was halted, but many came from southern and eastern Europe. Nation's largest tide of immigrants, but unlike earlier immigrants in origin, language, and religion.
6. Suspicion of different languages customs, foods, and race; resentment that new comers worked for lower wages; fear of people from nondemocratic countries and with radical political philosophies.
7. Began with Gold Rush in 1849; by 1860s, 75,000 Chinese in mining, construction, railroad, farming, clothing, and fishing industries; owned factories, laundries, hotels, restaurants. Chinese were banned in 1882, but Japanese came as farm workers, railroad workers, miners. 24,000 Japanese in America by 1900. San Francisco tried to segregate Asian school children. Gentlemen's

Reduced student page in the Teacher's Edition

Chapter Survey

Using New Vocabulary

The vocabulary terms in each pair listed below are related to each other. For each pair, explain what the terms have in common. Also explain how they are different.

1. free enterprise, laissez faire
2. dividends, rebates
3. trust, holding company
4. communism, socialism

Reviewing the Chapter

1. What changes took place in railroading in the second half of the 1800s? How did these changes affect the rest of American industry?

2. How did the formation of corporations promote the growth of industry?

3. Contrast horizontal and vertical integration of an industry. Give examples in 1890s' industries.

4. What efforts did government make to control the activities of large corporations in the 1800s? How successful were they?

5. How and why did immigration change after 1880?

6. List factors that contributed to nativism.

7. Summarize the history of immigration from Asia between 1849 and 1908. How many people came? What countries did most of them come from? Where did they settle? What actions were taken to help or discourage them?

8. What major problems did American cities face in the late nineteenth century?

9. What role did political machines play in large cities in the late 1800s?

Thinking Critically

1. Synthesis. "Captains of industry" argued that competition in industry was wasteful. They believed that consolidated companies were more efficient than numerous small, competing companies in the same industry. Present arguments supporting the opposite point of view, as if you were the owner of a small business.

2. Evaluation. Agree or disagree with the following statement: The concentration of wealth in the hands of the few poses a threat to democracy. Explain your reasoning.

3. Synthesis. Since colonial times Americans have tended to believe in the capacity of people to improve themselves and their way of life. In what ways was "progress" taking place in the period covered by this chapter? In what ways was it not?

History and You

The Sherman Antitrust Act was an early attempt by the government to regulate business. Today government regulation of industry is the subject of constant debate. Choose a business or industry in your area and determine to what extent it is regulated. Do you agree or disagree with its regulation? Defend your answer.

Using a Time Line

Match each date on the time line with the correct item in the list below. Write your answers in chronological order and explain the importance of each item.

(A) *Gospel of Wealth* published
(B) Centennial Exposition held
(C) Standard Oil of Ohio incorporated
(D) Interstate Commerce Commission established
(E) Homestead Steel Works built
(F) Chinese Exclusion Act
(G) Morgan makes loan to United States
(H) Statue of Liberty erected
(I) Ward's mail-order catalogue published
(J) Sherman Antitrust Act passed

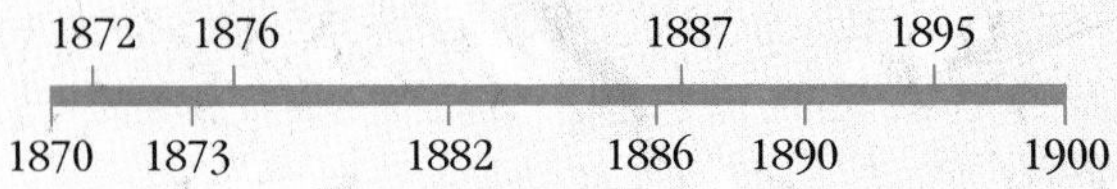

Agreement of 1908 ended segregation in exchange for Japanese ban on passports to workers without family in U.S.
8. Massive influx of people from farms and from foreign countries, seeking jobs in rapidly expanding industries. Inadequate housing, water, sanitation, education, public safety; political corruption.
9. Provided services for immigrants in exchange for votes; grew rich controlling the flow of city contracts for public works projects.

Thinking Critically

1. Consolidation can produce monopoly, driving out small businesses. Without competition, the public has no protection from price fixing or poor quality. Competition is more fair for small businesses and the consumer.
2. To agree, note that concentration of wealth allows a few individuals to make economic and political decisions affecting the nation. Owners of monopolies can determine prices and directly or indirectly control political decision-making. To disagree, note that democracy succeeded when public forced Congress to control the power of trusts through the ICC and the Sherman Anti-trust Act.
3. Industrialization represented "progress" by creating products, services, and opportunities. Inventions and business organizations solved problems and formed the basis for a better standard of living. But this "progress" did not reach many in America. A growing class of industrial workers and new immigrants were treated with hostility and discrimination and urban living conditions deteriorated.

Applying Social Studies Skills

Analyzing Bar Graphs

The years after the Civil War saw major population increases in the United States. The bar graph below shows rural and urban (towns or cities of 2,500 or more) population growth by decade. Use the graph and the text to answer the questions that follow.

1. In 1860 approximately what percent of the total population of the United States lived in urban areas? in rural areas?

2. In what year did the urban population first represent more than half of the total population?

3. Approximately how many more people lived in the United States in 1910 than in 1860?

4. Which population group—urban or rural—grew at a faster rate between 1860 and 1910? Explain how you know.

Rural and Urban Population 1860 – 1910

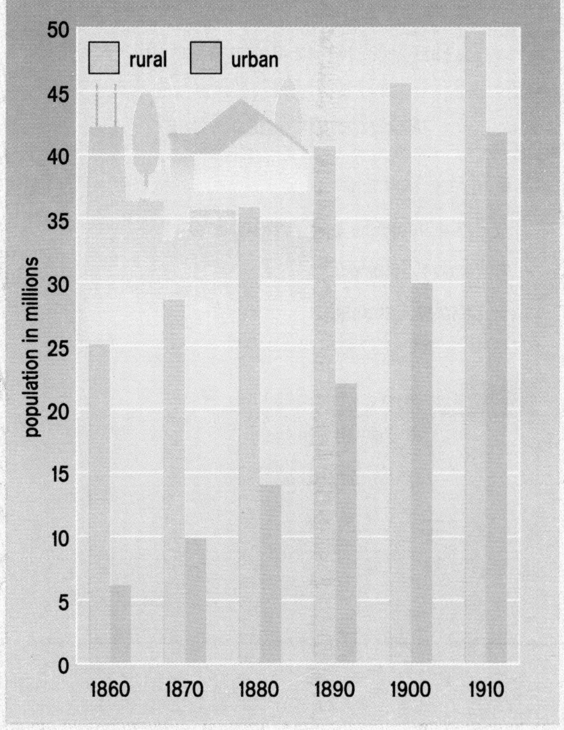

Source: *Statistical Abstract of the United States*

Applying Thinking Skills

Identifying an Argument

The account below is from the writings of Andrew Carnegie. It presents an *argument* in support of free enterprise, or the freedom of businesses to compete with each other for profit. An argument contains two basic elements. The *claim* is the main idea the author wants to persuade you of. The other basic element is the *reasons* supporting the claim. Reasons may be specific facts, rules, or generalizations. Read the account to find out what claim Carnegie wants to persuade you of and the reasons he gives for this claim. Then answer the questions that follow.

> *"The advantages of the law of free competition are greater than its costs. It is to this law that we owe our wonderful material development. Today the poor enjoy what before even the rich could not afford. What were luxuries for some are now necessities for all.*
>
> *The price we pay for this, no doubt, is great. We assemble thousands of workers in factory and mine. Rigid castes [social classes] are formed. Mutual ignorance breeds mutual distrust.*
>
> *While the law may be sometimes hard for the individual, it is best for the race, because it insures the survival of the fittest in every department. The law of competition is essential to the future progress of the race."*

1. What is the account about?

2. What is Carnegie's claim about free competition?

3. What reasons does Carnegie give to support his claim? What kind(s) of reasons does he use?

4. How does an argument differ from an explanation or description?

History and You

Answers will vary by locality. Commonly regulated industries include public utilities, transportation, food processing, pharmaceuticals.

Using a Time Line

(C) 1870, **(I)** 1872, **(E)** 1873, **(B)** 1876, **(F)** 1882, **(H)** 1886, **(D)** 1887, **(J)** 1890, **(G)** 1895, **(A)** 1900

Applying Social Studies Skills

1. 20%, 80%, **2.** 1890, **3.** 60 million, **4.** Urban

Applying Thinking Skills

1. The advantages of free competition.
2. Though hard on the individual ,it is best for all.
3. The availability of goods to all; survival of the fittest. Uses Social Darwinism as reason, appeals to patriotism for future of U.S.
4. Details are arranged to support a thesis or opinion and to persuade reader.

Chapter 16

Politics and Poverty in the Gilded Age

Planning Guide

	Student Text	TWE Lesson Plans	Support Materials
SECTION 1	**Section 16–1** (1–2 Days) **Corruption and Reform,** pp 408–412 Review/Evaluation Section Review, p 412	**Introducing the Chapter:** Voices of the Gilded Age—Class Activity, 30 minutes, p 405B **Enrichment Activity:** Gilded Age Cartoons—Individual Activity, homework, p 405D	★ **Read to Remember,** Section 1 ● **Section Activities,** Section 1 Δ **Readings,** Pendleton Civil Service Act ● **Tests and Quizzes,** Section 1 Quiz
SECTION 2	**Section 16–2** (1–2 Days) **The Rise of Organized Labor,** pp 413–421 The American Spirit: Mother Jones, p 417 Point of View: Labor Strikes, p 422–423 Review/Evaluation Section Review, p 421 Section Review, p 421	**Teaching the Main Ideas:** Strike!—Class Activity, one class period, p 405B **Evaluating Progress:** Agenda for Collective Bargaining—Paired Activity, one class period, p 405C	★ **Read to Remember,** Section 2 ● **Section Activities,** Section 2 Δ **Enrichment Activities,** Section 2 ● **Geography Activities,** Section 2 Δ **Readings,** Abraham Rosenberg, Sarah Comstock ● **Tests and Quizzes,** Section 2 Quiz
SECTION 3	**Section 16–3** (1–2 Days) **The Revolt of the Farmers,** pp 424–431 Connections to Themes: The Search for Opportunity, p 431 Review/Evaluation Section Review, p 431 Chapter 16 Survey, pp 432–433 Unit 5 Survey, pp 434–435 Skills, pp 432–433 Using New Vocabulary Thinking Critically Using Geography Applying Social Studies Skills: Analyzing Line Graphs Writing About Issues	**Teaching the Main Ideas:** On the Campaign Trail—Individual Activity, one class period, p 405C **Reinforcement Activity:** A Farmer's Plight: Cause and Effect—Individual Activity, one class period, p 405C	★ **Read to Remember,** Section 3 ● **Section Activities,** Section 3 Δ **Enrichment Activities,** Section 3 Δ **Readings,** Mary Lease ● **Tests and Quizzes,** Section 3 Quiz, Chapter 16 Test (Forms A and B), Unit 5 Test (Forms A and B), First Semester Test (Forms A and B) **Additional Resources** ● **Active Learning** Δ **Transparencies and Activity Book** ● **Testing Software** ★ **Chapter Summaries** **Key:** ★ For Extra Support ● For All Students Δ For Enrichment

Overview

Bribery and corruption were recurrent political issues in the United States after the Civil War. With the presidency weakened by Congress and the two major parties evenly divided, efforts to reform the federal bureaucracy failed time and again. Finally, in 1883, Congress approved legislation to develop an impartial federal civil service.

The costs of large-scale industrialization and uncontrolled business also became a major issue in the late 1800s. Seeking decent wages and working conditions, industrial workers unionized. However, hard times, government support of business, widespread fears of union members as revolutionaries, and violent conflicts between labor and management hindered the growth of the labor movement.

Farmers, faced with declining farm prices, also organized in the late 1800s in an effort to find political solutions to their problems. Their efforts culminated in the formation of the Populist party, which stressed unlimited coinage of silver, government action to redress grievances, and increased democracy. The party was destroyed as a result of the defeat of William Jennings Bryan, the Populist-Democratic candidate, in the presidential election of 1896.

Activity Objectives

After completing the activities, students should be able to

- summarize the benefits and risks of going on strike.
- describe Populist proposals to solve problems in the United States in the late 1800s.
- describe economic conditions that led farmers to organize in the late 1800s.
- evaluate the process of collective bargaining.
- identify types of corruption common in the Gilded Age.

Introducing the Chapter

Voices of the Gilded Age

This class activity requires half a class period.

In this activity students use primary source materials from the chapter to hypothesize about events and issues facing Americans in the late nineteenth century.

Tell students that to introduce Chapter 16, you need the help of 17 volunteers who like public speaking or drama. Assign each volunteer one of the following primary sources in the chapter:

- Mark Twain, page 408 (political corruption)
- Want ad by "two young ladies," page 410 (spoils system)
- Journalist, page 412 (civil service reform)
- Labor union member, page 413 (labor movement)
- Pennsylvania coal miner, page 414 (labor movement)
- Newspaper report, 1877, page 415 (child labor)
- Rose Cohen, page 416 (labor movement)
- Historian, page 417 (fear of revolution)
- Samuel Gompers, page 420 (the AFL)
- Hamlin Garland, page 424 (technology and farming)
- Kansas newspaper, page 424 (falling farm prices)
- Farmers' newspaper, page 426 (farm debt)
- Farm song, page 426 (farmers' protests)
- Mary Lease, page 428 (farmers' protests)
- Delegate to Texas People's party, page 429 (racism)
- *New York World,* page 430 (silverites)
- William Jennings Bryan, page 430 (free silver)

As the volunteers prepare, direct the rest of the class to preview Chapter 16 by reading heads and subheads and looking at pictures.

Ask students to close their texts. In random order, call on the volunteers to read their assigned primary sources. After each reading, have students hypothesize about the topic and discuss the feelings that it suggests. Emphasize the importance of carefully reading primary source materials in order to learn personal reactions to events and issues.

Teaching the Main Ideas

Section 16–2: Strike!

This class activity requires one class period.

In this activity students, in the course of deciding whether to call a strike, experience the dilemma facing union workers dissatisfied with their working conditions.

Have students imagine that they are members of a police officers' union. Tell them that collective bargaining between the union and city officials has failed. As a result, police officers will not receive an increase in their salaries or their health and vacation benefits for the second straight year. Have students discuss whether the union should strike. Then ask how many would be willing to picket if a strike were called. Discuss reasons why or why not. Then call for a strike vote.

Regardless of the outcome of the vote, point out that going on strike often creates additional problems and decisions for strikers. Ask the following questions and have students discuss each one from the point of view of a worker on strike.

- You voted *not* to strike, but the majority of union members voted to strike. Will you join the strikers or cross the picket line to go to work?
- A court injunction orders the strikers back to work. Will you obey the court order?
- Strikers who do not obey the injunction to return to work may be fined or go to jail. Will you continue to strike?

- The city is hiring new recruits to replace the police on strike. Will you go back to work?
- Close friends think you should return to work. You constantly argue about it. What will you do?
- The city offers members of the police union an increase in health and vacation benefits but not a salary increase. Will you continue to strike?
- The city offers members of the police union a 5-percent salary increase but not improved benefits. What will you do?

Conclude the activity by having students summarize the benefits and risks of going on strike.

Teaching the Main Ideas

Section 16–3: On the Campaign Trail

This individual activity requires a full class period, or it may be assigned as homework.

This activity will help students understand the importance of Populist solutions to American problems by preparing campaign speeches.

Begin the activity by reminding students that in the presidential elections of 1892 and 1896, the Populist party offered new proposals for political and economic reform.

Have students imagine that they are the Populist candidate for President in 1896. Direct them each to prepare a two-minute campaign speech to deliver before an audience of rural Americans. The speech should briefly describe Populist plans to solve problems facing Americans. Stress that the speech should be persuasive as well as informative.

Allow time for students to review information in Section 16–3 and write their speeches. Then have volunteers read their speeches while the class assumes the role of the audience. Conclude the activity by discussing the following questions:

- *Which Populist proposals would be of most interest to farmers?* (Answers may include government ownership of railroads and banks, government establishment of warehouses for crop storage, government loans to farmers, and a flexible money supply.)
- *Which proposals would be of interest to all Americans, not just farmers?* (Answers may include the graduated income tax, public ownership of railroads, banks, telephones, and telegraphs, direct election of senators, the secret ballot, and voting reforms.

To extend this activity, point out that Populist proposals were often derided as radical or outlandish. Yet within two decades, many of those measures were translated into law. Have students keep their speeches in order to compare Populist proposals with Progressive reforms described in Chapter 17.

Reinforcement Activity

Section 16–3: A Farmer's Plight: Cause and Effect

This individual activity requires a full class period.

The following activity, in which students create graphic organizers, reinforces understanding of events that affected farmers in the late 1800s.

Begin the activity by telling students that the life of a farmer has been described as a "roller coaster of ups and downs." Ask students why they think this description is accurate or inaccurate.

Write the following headings on the chalkboard: *Rising Farm Production, Falling Farm Prices, Rising Farm Debt.* Tell students to review Section 16–3 and identify events that fall under each of these headings. Then students are to create a graphic organizer that shows the interrelationships among the events. For example, students may use a series of boxes connected by arrows to show cause and effect chains, or they may stack boxes to show multiple causes of a single effect. (See the cause and effect diagrams in Chapter 11.) Diagrams may include the following information.

Rising Farm Production: new strains of wheat, new machinery to harvest crops or process products, planting more acres, concentration on cash crops, use of pesticides and fertilizers.
Falling Farm Price: overproduction for American market, foreign competition in the world market.
Rising Farm Debt: high cost of farm machinery, going into debt to buy farm machinery and seed, high freight costs, deflation, crop-lien system.

When students have finished their graphic organizers, review their work. Discuss the graphic organizers by asking whether farming has more "ups" or "downs." Conclude by discussing whether the government should give aid to farmers to ensure reasonable profits.

Evaluating Progress

Section 16–2: Agenda for Collective Bargaining

This paired activity requires most of a class period.

In Section 16–2 students learn about the rise of organized labor in the late 1800s. Use this paired activity to evaluate students' understanding of collective bargaining.

Begin the activity by reviewing with students methods used by unions to improve workers' working conditions. (These may include boycotts, strikes, collective bargaining, and slowdowns.) Remind students that collective bargaining is a process by which union and management representatives discuss and reach agreement about wages and working conditions. Before collective bargaining begins, each side usually prepares a list of goals or demands which are the basis for negotiation.

Tell students that in this activity they will prepare for and participate in a collective bargaining session. Divide the class into pairs and let each pair choose a union and a company to represent. Students may refer to Section 16–2 for examples or create imaginary unions and companies. One partner will represent the union, and the other, management. Direct students to complete the following four tasks:

- First, draw up separate lists of demands of union and management.

- Second, meet together to work out an agenda of the topics to be discussed at the first collective bargaining session.
- Third, hold a collective bargaining session, following the accepted agenda.
- Fourth, prepare separate reports stating which demands are and are not acceptable to both sides.

There are no correct answers in this activity, but students' work should be evaluated on the basis of appropriate demands and agenda topics, and realistic appraisals of areas of agreement and conflict.

Enrichment Activity

Section 16–1: Gilded Age Cartoons

This individual activity may be assigned as homework and shared in class the following day.

In the following activity students demonstrate their understanding of corruption in the Gilded Age by drawing political cartoons.

Before class write the following terms on the chalkboard: *corruption, spoils system, Crédit Mobilier, civil service reform.* Ask students to describe each term and explain how it relates to the Gilded Age. Emphasize that weak presidents, evenly divided political parties, and the belief that what was good for business was good for the nation hindered government efforts to deal with problems of corruption.

Tell students that they are to draw political cartoons about corruption in the Gilded Age. The cartoons may include presidents and their direct or indirect involvement in corruption. To stimulate creativity, point out the political cartoon on page 411 or other examples of political cartoons in the text and in current newspapers and magazines. Discuss the use of symbols, satire, captions, and titles.

Direct students to display their completed cartoons. Have the class view the cartoons and comment on how accurately or inaccurately they think the cartoonists have reflected events and views of the time.

Bibliography and Audiovisual Material

Teacher Bibliography

Hoexter, Corinne K. *From Canton to California: The Epic of Chinese Immigration.* New York: Four Winds Press, 1976.

Maddow, Ben. *A Sunday Between Wars: The Course of American Life from 1865–1917.* New York: Norton, 1979.

Peavy, Linda S. *Women Who Changed Things.* New York: Scribner, 1983.

Peterson, Florence. *Strikes in the United States 1880–1936.* St. Clair Shores, MI: Scholarly, 1988.

Shannon, Fred A. *The Farmer's Last Frontier: Agriculture 1860–1897.* Armonk, NY: M.E. Sharpe, 1977.

Student Bibliography

Doctorow, E.L. *Ragtime.* New York: Random House, 1991.

Garland, Hamlin: *Main Travelled Roads.* Columbus, OH: C.E. Merrill, 1970.

Harte, Bret. *The Luck of Roaring Camp*. Providence, RI: Jamestown Publishing, 1976.

Howells, William Dean. *Rise of Silas Latham.* New York: Random House, 1991.

Norris, Frank. *The Octopus.* New York: Penguin, 1986.

Twain, Mark and Charles D. Warner. *The Gilded Age: A Tale of To-Day.* New York: Dover, 1988.

Films, Videocassettes, and Videodiscs

The Farmer in a Changing America. 26 min. EBEC. Videocassette.

The End of an Era. 30 min. PBS Video. Movie.

Progressives, Populists and Reform in America (1890–1917). 32 min. Guidance Associates. Movie.

Filmstrips

The Growth of the Labor Movement. 37 min. 2 filmstrips. Guidance Associates.

Computer Software

The Time Tunnel—American History 1860–1920. Apple. Focus Media.

Chapter 16

Objectives

- Explain why political corruption became a major issues in the late 1800s.
- Relate how workers organized to improve working conditions and wages.
- List actions farmers took to improve their economic condition.

Introducing THE CHAPTER

For suggestions on introducing Chapter 16, refer to page 405B in the Teacher's Edition.

Developing THE CHAPTER

For activities and teaching strategies to help you reinforce and enrich chapter content, see pages 405B–405D in the Teacher's Edition.

B · A · C · K · G · R · O · U · N · D

Chapter Opener Illustrations

Socialists march in a New York May Day parade in the early 1900s. In 1886 American workers had turned out on May Day to demand the eight-hour day. As a result the Socialist International Congress chose May 1 as a world labor holiday.

This photograph of a sleeping newsboy, doubtless a homeless one, served as an enormously effective protest against child labor conditions.

This 1873 lithograph, showing the benefits of Grange membership, is called "Gift for the Grangers." The small scenes show aspects of farm life.

The African-American women stripping tobacco worked without backrests or breaks.

Reduced student page in the Teacher's Edition

Chapter 16 1865-1910

Politics and Poverty in the Gilded Age

Samuel Gompers played a major role in founding the American Federation of Labor and, except for one year, served as its president until his death in 1924.

This McKinley "gold bug" shows McKinley's stand on the gold-silver issue.

American Voices

Bessie Van Vorst, a writer in the late 1800s, wanted to find out for herself what life was like for women workers in the United States. Using a different name, she found work in a Pittsburgh pickle factory. Later she published her findings about work in this and other factories.

"I have become with desperate reality a factory girl, alone, inexperienced, friendless. I am making $4.20 a week and spending $3 of this for board alone. . . .

My shoulders are beginning to ache. My hands are stiff, my thumbs almost blistered. . . . Cases are emptied and refilled; bottles are labeled, stamped and rolled away. . . . Oh! the monotony of it, the never-ending supply of work to be begun and finished, begun and finished, begun and finished! Now and then someone cuts a finger or runs a splinter under the flesh . . . and still the work goes on, on, on! . . . Once I pause an instant, my head dazed and weary, my ears strained to bursting with the deafening noise. Quickly a voice whispers in my ear: 'You'd better not stand there doin' nothin'. If she catches you she'll give it to you.'"

The lives of working people in industrial America were often desperately hard. Even in prosperous times, they barely got by. But workers' efforts to unite and demand change led to such violent conflict with business owners that many feared the nation would be destroyed by class war.

Farmers, too, banded together to oppose "legislation tending to make the rich richer and the poor poorer." The late 1800s, then, saw both farmers and workers demanding changes to make the promise of opportunity a reality for all Americans.

Marchers in a labor parade, early 1900s; newsboy asleep on a tenement staircase; poster of the benefits of Grange membership, 1873; young woman stripping tobacco; Samuel Gompers; McKinley "gold bug" in election of 1896.

Analyzing Primary Sources

American Voices

Bessie Van Vorst cooperated with her husband's sister, Marie Van Vorst, in finding out about factory work for women. Bessie used the name "Esther Kelly" when she applied for work. Marie used the name "Bell Ballard." In 1903 the two women reported their findings in *The Woman Who Toils: Being the Experiences of Two Ladies as Factory Girls.*

Van Vorst's viewpoint might disappoint modern feminists, for she believed working women were, for the most part, willingly exploited by employers and that their proper sphere was at home serving as wives and mothers.

In the following years Bessie Van Vorst investigated child labor in textile mills in New Hampshire and Alabama. She published her findings in 1908 in *The Cry of the Children*.

1. Who was the person referred to as "she" in the last sentence? **(supervisor)**
2. What does the last sentence mean? **(If Bessie—Esther Kelly—did not work at a steady pace, the supervisor would give her a tongue lashing.)**
3. What other problems of factory work does Van Vorst mention? **(low pay, aches and pains, monotony, injury)**
4. Speculate about what women and other workers might do to try to improve working conditions. **(organize to demand better conditions)**

407

Section 16-1

Objectives

- ***Answer the Focus Question.***
- *Explain why corrupt practices were widespread in the Gilded Age.*
- *Describe what Presidents Hayes, Arthur, Cleveland, and Harrison did to bring about reform.*
- *Analyze the effect civil service reform had on the government.*

Introducing

THE SECTION

Point out to students that after the Civil War most people yearned for a period of calm, even at the expense of ignoring pressing social issues and disturbing rumors of corruption in high places. During the war, the economic potential of the nation had been redirected from satisfying consumer needs to meeting the requirements of two huge war machines. During the Gilded Age, the idealism that had motivated many Americans was exhausted. **Ask:** What might be the result of such exhaustion? **(an acquisitive society bent on acquiring wealth by any means)**

B · A · C · K · G · R · O · U · N · D

Time Line Illustrations

1. A lapel medal of General Ulysses S. Grant.
2. A broadside announcing a meeting of the United Labor party, a Pennsylvania offshoot of the Greenback movement.
3. A Grover Cleveland campaign matchbox for the 1884 election.
4. An artist's conception of the anarchist's cast iron, dynamite-filled bomb thrown at the Haymarket Affair in Chicago. This was the first time dynamite was used as a weapon in the United States.
5. Mary Lease, fiery orator for the Populist party, was known to some as the "Kansas Pythoness." She told farmers, "Wall Street runs the country."
6. Eugene Victor Debs, labor leader and leader of the Socialist party in its early years.
7. A William Jennings Bryan campaign button.

Reduced student page in the Teacher's Edition

CHAPTER TIME LINE

1865-1910

1869 Colored National Labor Union formed

1877 Great Railroad Strike

1883 Pendleton Act reforms civil service

1884 Cleveland wins presidential election

1865 | 1874 | 1883

1874 Corruption in Grant's Cabinet exposed

1875 Grange movement at its height

16-1 Corruption and Reform

Focus: Why did political reform become a national issue in the late 1800s?

The industrial growth of the late 1800s took place in an atmosphere of unbounded optimism, speculation, and get-rich-quick schemes. Americans rushed to take advantage of new opportunities to create wealth. This often led to illegal competitive practices and corruption. Some, like railroad owner Jay Gould, even bribed whole legislatures to get the laws needed to carry out their aims. Humorist Mark Twain wrote:

> *"Why, it is telegraphed all over the country and commented on as something wonderful if a [member of Congress] votes honestly and unselfishly and refuses . . . to steal from the government."*

In 1873 Twain described American life during this period in a novel called *The Gilded Age.* To Twain, American life after the Civil War glittered on the surface with economic growth and opportunities. However, underneath lay a society scarred by poverty, greed, and corruption. These years came to be known as the Gilded Age.

An Era of Weak Presidents

Government leaders failed to deal with the problems under the glittering surface, in part because most believed that what was good for business was good for the nation. However, politics also played an important part.

1886 Knights of Labor reaches greatest strength

Haymarket Affair

American Federation of Labor organized

1900 Debs: presidential candidate of Socialist party of America in 1900, 1904, 1908

1892 | 1901 | 1910

1892 Homestead Strike

Mary Lease: Populist party campaigner in presidential election

1894 Pullman Strike

1896 Bryan: Democratic and Populist candidate for President

Between 1868 and 1898 Americans elected seven Presidents. Except for Ulysses S. Grant, not one had enough support to win a consecutive second term. These Presidents were weak leaders who accepted the prevailing view that Presidents should *carry out* laws, not make them.

Even if a President had had a strong program, he would have had difficulty pushing it through Congress. Slim party majorities changed frequently. Thus, parties hesitated to take clear-cut stands on most of the controversial issues of the time for fear of alienating voters. They said nothing about curbing the growing power of big business or helping working people in their struggle for decent lives. At first, only one issue dominated this era: political corruption.

Scandals Under Grant

Corruption first became a major issue during the presidency of Ulysses S. Grant. Although honest himself, Grant appointed a number of people who used their offices to enrich themselves. The War and Treasury departments and the Post Office were rife with bribery. Even Grant's private secretary accepted bribes in return for inside information.

Perhaps the most widely publicized scandal involved Crédit Mobilier, a railroad construction company formed by the Union Pacific Railroad. The government paid Crédit Mobilier $94 million for work that only cost $44 million. The extra money went into the pockets of company officials. In 1873, to prevent a congressional investigation, Crédit Mobilier bribed members of Congress, including Vice-President Schuyler Colfax and Representative James A. Garfield, who was later to become President.

The spoils system. Reformers believed that the way to end corruption was to end the spoils system in the **civil service,** the body of government employees who are appointed rather than elected to their jobs. (Civil service does not include the military, the legislature, or the judiciary.)

President Jackson used the spoils system on a large scale, rewarding supporters with government jobs. At the time, the government employed

Developing

THE SECTION

Connections: Politics

Discussion. In 1875 the Whiskey Ring scandal became known. A conspiracy of distillers and revenue officials to defraud the government was uncovered and resulted in the disgrace of General O. E. Babcock, Grant's private secretary. A scandal in 1876 disclosed that Secretary of War William W. Belknap sold rights to trade on Indian lands—receiving up to $25,000 for each trading post in Indian Territory. Belknap was forced to resign from office.

Ask: What are the responsibilities of elected officials for the actions of those around them? What if they are unaware of those actions?

Limited English Proficiency

Drawing Political Cartoons. Have students work in pairs to produce political cartoons and slogans either supporting or attacking Hayes's record on civil service reform. The cartoons and slogans can take one of the following stands: Hayes has done much to reform the spoils system; he has not done nearly enough; he has done too much to eliminate the spoils system, which is the best way to give out government jobs. The cartoons and slogans can be displayed in the classroom.

Connections: Politics

Aware of the problems a President faced, Garfield apparently looked to serving as President with foreboding. He wrote: *"I am bidding good bye to a private life and to a long series of happy years which I fear terminate in 1880."*

After Guiteau shot Garfield, the assassin exclaimed, "I am a stalwart [a faction of the Republican party opposing Garfield] and Arthur is President now!"

Reduced student page in the Teacher's Edition

relatively few people, and many of the jobs were fairly simple. By the 1870s, however, the number of employees had soared, and the work often required special skills. Changing employees whenever a new President took office no longer made sense. And giving jobs to people merely because they were loyal invited incompetence and corruption.

Furthermore, after each election, officials were besieged by applicants for government jobs. While Lincoln was struggling to solve the secession crisis, he had to deal with "a swarm of miscellaneous people," one congressman reported, "as hungry and as fierce as wolves," all looking for jobs. In the 1870s prospective employees were even putting ads in Washington newspapers:

> *"WANTED—BY TWO YOUNG LADIES situations in Government office; will give first month's pay and $10 monthly as long as retained."*

In 1871 President Grant appointed a commission to reform the civil service. But four years later Congress, sneering at "snivel" service reform, rejected the commission's plan.

on Politics

There were endless stories of corruption in Congress during the Gilded Age. Collis P. Huntington, president of the Central Pacific Railroad, divided the members of the Senate in 1876 into the following three groups:

(1) the "clean": senators who would do what Huntington wanted without asking for favors

(2) the "commercial": senators who would do what Huntington wanted if paid for it

(3) the "communists": senators who resisted both his logic and his money

Hayes and Civil Service Reform

The election of 1876 set the pattern for most presidential elections in the Gilded Age. The Democratic party had regained control of the southern states. Since these states always voted Democratic, they were called the Solid South. New England remained a Republican stronghold. In other regions support was evenly divided. The result was a series of close elections.

In one of the closest elections ever, Democrat Samuel J. Tilden received more popular votes than Republican Rutherford B. Hayes. However, the election was disputed in four states. A special commission was formed, which finally declared Hayes the winner.

Both Hayes and Tilden had promised to reform the civil service. But when Hayes tried to make good on his promise, Republicans in the Senate rebelled. Calling him "a political dreamer," they refused to pass legislation. But Hayes did make some changes. He chose members of his Cabinet for their abilities, not for party loyalty. Several appointments went to reformers, and a southerner was chosen to head the Post Office.

Hayes also investigated charges of corruption among political appointees in the New York Customs House, which collected two thirds of the nation's duties on imported goods. When the collector, Chester A. Arthur, refused to carry out the President's commands, Hayes replaced him.

Hayes did not run for reelection in 1880, admitting that "I am not liked as President." True civil service reform would be left to his successors.

Reform Efforts by Garfield and Arthur

In 1880 the Republicans again captured the presidency. James A. Garfield from Ohio was an ideal candidate. He had been born in a log cabin, had risen from poverty to the Ohio Senate, and had served in the Civil War. Chester A. Arthur, the former head of the New York Customs House, became Vice-President.

Once in office, President Garfield was pestered daily by office seekers "lying in wait" for him. "It has been a steeple chase," he wrote, "I fleeing and

Connections: Politics

Belva Lockwood was also a candidate for President in 1884. A lawyer and the first woman admitted to practice before the Supreme Court of the United States, she was nominated by a group of women meeting in California as the National Equal Rights party. Lockwood's platform stressed equal rights for all, including African and Native Americans, and immigrants. She received about 4,000 votes in six states.

Linking Past and Present

Today, each state has a Federal Job Information Center which announces openings for civil service positions. Interested people submit applications and take a written examination. Results are published, and the applicants with the top three scores are considered for the job.

Linking Past and Present

Discussion. The election campaign of 1884 proved to be one of the most vicious in American history. Each party made use of embarrassing disclosures about the other's candidate. In addition, the Republicans "waved the bloody shirt," that is, they appealed to old Civil War emotions to equate the Democrats with the Confederacy. Republicans also appealed to nativist feelings by calling the Democrats the party of "rum, Romanism [Roman Catholicism], and rebellion," which was an insult to Catholics.

Ask: Are presidential campaigns today just as vicious as in 1884, less vicious, or more? Give reasons for answers.

Connections: Language

Discussion. The Mugwumps originally called themselves independents. Ask students if there are independents today. What part do they play in the two-party system?

Many politicians avoided taking stands on vital issues in order not to lose support from business interests. An 1889 cartoon attacked big business as the "bosses of the Senate."

they pursuing." On July 2, 1881, in a Washington railroad station, the President was assassinated by Charles J. Guiteau, an office seeker Garfield had refused to appoint.

Civil service reform. Shocked by the killing—and its cause—the public demanded action on civil service reform. Yet many doubted that the new President, Chester Arthur, would take the necessary steps. His lack of experience and his part in the New York Customs House scandal seemed a poor background for a reformer.

Arthur surprised everyone. But although he called for reform, Congress failed to pass a civil service law. Public anger against the Republicans mounted. In the 1882 congressional elections, the Democrats won sixty-two new seats in the House and even elected governors in the Republican strongholds of Pennsylvania and Massachusetts.

The setback shook Republicans. In January 1883 Congress finally passed the Pendleton Civil Service Act. It set up the merit system, a system of hiring and promoting people in the civil service on the basis of competitive examinations. New workers would be selected from among those with the highest scores. Once hired, they could not be fired for political reasons. They did not have to work for the political party or make payments in return for their jobs, as they had under the spoils system. At first, the act covered only about 10 percent of federal jobs. By 1940, however, 90 percent of all federal jobs were covered.

The election of 1884. Even with the passage of the Civil Service Act, corruption continued to be an issue in national politics. Opposition from anti-reform Republicans prevented Arthur's nomination for reelection in 1884. Instead, the party chose James G. Blaine, a former senator from Maine.

Reform Republicans refused to support Blaine, who had been involved in railroad scandals. The editor of the *New York Sun,* using an Algonquian word, referred to these Republicans as "little Mugwumps"—little men trying to be big chiefs. Regulars in the party joked that Mugwumps were unreliable Republicans with their "mugs" on one side of the fence and their "wumps" on the other.

The Democrats nominated Grover Cleveland, the reform governor of New York. The campaign was bitterly fought, and the election was extremely close. Cleveland gained thirty-seven more electoral votes than his rival. But his margin of victory in the popular vote was less than 30,000 votes.

Active Learning

Cooperative Activity. Divide the class into five teams, each representing a different group in the late 1800s: eastern factory owners, midwestern farmers, northern city workers, Republican senator from New York, Democratic representative from Georgia. Each team is to research their group's position regarding the tariff issue. One person from each group should present their position in a panel debate format.

Section Review

ANSWERS

1. Definition for *civil service* is on text page 409.
2. Answers may include: spoils system and bribes offered by large corporations, such as Crédit Mobilier, to government officials.
3. Answers may include: public demand for civil service reform after Garfield's assassination and election losses for Republicans in 1882.
4. Civil service reform provided that government workers be hired through competitive examination rather than patronage.
5. Agree: Answers may include that because tariffs lead to higher prices, they tax those who can least afford it. Disagree: Those who buy the most—the wealthy—pay the most.

Social History

Free-trade supporter Samuel Cox of New York injected a note of humor into an earlier debate over the tariff during Arthur's administration. Cox proposed taxing sunlight because it competed with gaslight. Thereafter he was known as "Sunset Cox."

Connections: Politics

Benjamin Harrison was the only grandson of a President to win the presidency himself. A campaign song of 1888 underlined the relationship: "Grandfather's Hat Fits Ben."

Reduced student page in the Teacher's Edition

Cleveland: A Middle Course on Reform

The first Democratic President in almost thirty years, Cleveland was besieged by Democratic office seekers. One journalist wrote,

> *“The Washington hotels are crowded, and office seekers are as thick as shells on the beach. The city will be overrun . . . until Cleveland has firmly established that civil service reform is to prevail.”*

Cleveland tried to steer a middle course between civil service reformers and party loyalists seeking jobs. He doubled the number of positions covered by the merit system but also rewarded thousands of party members with government posts.

On other issues, Cleveland showed his determination to do what he thought was right. Despite opposition from business, he approved the Interstate Commerce Act of 1887, which regulated railroads. Despite farmers' pleas, he vetoed a bill to help Texas farmers hit by drought. "Though the people support the government," he argued, "the government should not support the people."

American Voices

> *“What is the use of being elected unless you stand for something?”*
>
> —President Grover Cleveland

The tariff. In addition, Cleveland forced Congress to begin debate on lowering the tariff. During the Civil War, high tariffs had raised much needed revenue. But now the government was collecting more money than it spent. The Republicans supported high tariffs to protect industries from stiff foreign competition that would drive down prices and profits. But Cleveland saw high tariffs as a form of "unjust taxation." He charged that they raised the cost of goods to ordinary people while giving "immense profits" to manufacturers.

Democratic leaders, with an eye on the upcoming election, urged Cleveland to leave the tariff issue alone. But he was determined to act. The Democratic House passed a tariff bill, but the Republican Senate would not.

The Presidency of "Young Tippecanoe"

In the election of 1888, Cleveland was opposed by Republican Benjamin Harrison of Indiana. Harrison was the grandson of President William Henry Harrison, fondly remembered as "Old Tippecanoe." Shouting "Tippecanoe and tariff, too!" the Republicans campaigned for high tariffs. Although Cleveland received the most popular votes, Harrison won the majority of electoral votes.

As President, Harrison at first let the spoils system run rampant in non-merit jobs. In the postal service alone, 31,000 postmasters were replaced by party loyalists. Later, though, Harrison added to the growing list of government jobs filled through the merit system. He also bowed to public uproar over monopolies and trusts by signing the Sherman Antitrust Act in 1890. In that same year, a Republican Congress passed and Harrison signed the McKinley Tariff, pushing tariffs higher than they had ever been.

To many Americans, the McKinley Tariff was proof that the government had fallen under the control of powerful business leaders. And business agreed. "We own America," boasted Frederick Townsend Martin, a business tycoon. "We got it, [no one] knows how, but we intend to keep it."

Section Review

1. Identification. Define *civil service.*

2. Comprehension. Why were corrupt practices so widespread during the Gilded Age?

3. Application. Explain how the actions of ordinary Americans helped lead to the passage of the Civil Service Act.

4. Analysis. How did civil service reform change the way that government workers were hired?

5. Evaluation. Do you agree with Cleveland's view that high tariffs are a form of "unjust taxation"? Give reasons for your answer.

Connection: Economics
Henry George's own solution to economic ills was a single tax on land. He argued that it was unfair for land owners who made no productive contribution to receive great wealth from land that increased in value while many Americans remained poor. To remedy this problem, George proposed to levy taxes equal to the amount by which land values increased. This tax on land, he believed, would supply all the revenue the government would need. George's idea became very popular and even sparked single-tax movements in a number of countries. However, it was never adopted by the federal government.

16-2 The Rise of Organized Labor

Focus: What actions did workers take in the late 1800s to improve their wages and working conditions?

Political reform was an issue in the seven presidencies in the late 1800s. Overshadowing this issue, however, was the rapid, largely uncontrolled growth of the economy and the injustices against working people that resulted. In the 1870s the journalist Henry George wrote in *Progress and Poverty*:

> *"We plow new fields, we open new mines; . . . we girdle the land with iron roads and lace the air with telegraph wires; we add knowledge to knowledge, and utilize invention after invention . . . yet it becomes no easier for the masses of people to make a living. On the contrary, it is becoming harder."*

During the late 1800s and early 1900s, labor unions struggled to focus national attention on the desperate situation of workers.

Changes in the Work Place

During the 1880s the factory system of production became widespread in the United States. As the use of machinery and the size of factories increased, workers no longer had personal relationships with the people they worked for. A member of a labor union described the result:

> *"The men are looked upon as nothing more than parts of the machinery that they work. They are labeled and tagged, as the parts of a machine would be, and are only taken into account as a part of the machinery used for the profit of the manufacturer."*

Most factory jobs were monotonous and required little training or skill. One worker could easily be replaced by another. And there was an abundance of workers, swelled by the tide of immigration in the late 1800s.

The easy availability of workers meant that factories could pay low wages. As one manager declared, "If I wanted boiler iron I would go out on the market and buy it where I could get it cheapest, and if I wanted to employ men I would do the same."

To speed factory production and to cut costs, workers stood in one place and performed one task in the process of assembling a product. Thus, they learned little beyond their particular task.

Section 16-2

Objectives

- ***Answer the Focus Question.***
- *Describe the working conditions of workers.*
- *Explain how the railroad strike of 1877 mobilized workers.*
- *Compare the goals and methods of the AFL and the Knights of Labor.*
- *Explain why the Homestead and Pullman strikes set back labor's cause.*

Introducing

THE SECTION

Have students consider the positive and negative effects of industrialism on people's lives. **(Positive: made available low-cost manufactured goods, provided jobs; negative: unhealthy working conditions, long hours, low wages, led to overcrowded cities with unsanitary conditions)**

Have a student read aloud the passage by Henry George on this page. **Ask:** Who is the "we" George refers to? **(working people)** Why is it "becoming harder" for "the masses of people to make a living"? **(poor working conditions, low pay)**

Tell students that they will now find out how workers responded to the negative impact of industrialism.

Developing

THE SECTION

Writing About History

Journal Entry. Have students pick an individual from one of the pictures in this section and write a journal entry from this person's perspective. What would he or she be saying about what is happening to him/her and around him/her? Lead students to connect the individual to historical events discussed in the section.

Using the Visuals

Analyzing Photographs. Refer students to the photographs in this section. Tell them that photographers like Jacob Riis, Frances Johnston, and Lewis Hine documented what was taking place in slums, factories, and mines. **Ask:** What do the photographs show about working conditions in the late 1800s? In what ways was photography a more convincing medium than art or writing? What medium fulfills this function today? **(television)**

Backyard History

Survey. Have students make a survey of their community to identify factories. They should attempt to find out when the factories were built, what they manufacture, how many people work there, and what the working conditions of the factories are like.

Connections: Economics

Industrial work paid better than agricultural work. Unskilled industrial workers made about $360 per year and unskilled agricultural workers about $260 per year in the North at the turn of the century. In the South incomes were about one-fourth lower.

Reduced student page in the Teacher's Edition

Low wages meant that the average worker could not make enough money to support a family decently. A coal miner in Pennsylvania described his meager income and expenses in 1902:

> *"My wages were $29.47 for the two weeks, or at the rate of $58.94 per month. My rent is $10.50 per month. My coal costs me almost $4 per month. . . . When it comes down to groceries is where you get hit the hardest. Everybody knows the cost of living has been extremely high all winter. Butter has been 32, 36, and 38 cents a pound; eggs as high as 32 cents a dozen; ham, 12 and 16 cents a pound. . . . Flour and sugar did not advance, but they were about the only staples that didn't. Anyhow, my store bill for those two weeks was $11. That makes $22 per month. The butcher gets $5 per month. Add them all, and it costs me, just to live, $42.40."*

As in many other families, this miner's children went to work at about the age of ten instead of going to school. Spouses also added to the family income by taking in laundry or working in the fields.

Wages varied, depending on location, race, and gender rather than the job. For the same work, northern workers made more than southerners, whites made more than nonwhites, and men made more than women. As low as wages were for women in general, black women's wages were far

In 1900, 1.5 million children were working on farms and in factories to help support their families.

Global Connections

Great Britain, France, and Germany were also rapidly industrializing, and some thinkers and writers reacted against the unequal benefits of industrialization. The most influential was German-born Karl Marx. In 1848 he and his friend Friedrich Engels published the *Communist Manifesto*, urging workers to revolt and establish a society in which property would be owned in common and everyone would have an equal share of goods. By the 1870s "Marxian socialism" had become widespread.

Linking Past and Present

There was no system of social security for nineteenth-century workers. In a Pennsylvania coal mine disaster in 1869, 108 miners were killed. Without workers' compensation or survivors' insurance, their families were left destitute.

Thinking Critically

Synthesis. Today a law guarantees a minimum wage for most workers. Have students work out the monthly budget for a minimum wage earner. (factors: minimum wage per hour x 40 hours per week x 4.3 weeks; monthly cost of food, clothing, shelter, transportation, entertainment) Students should decide whether or not the minimum wage is truly a living wage. If not, what should the minimum wage be? Should it be different for different parts of the country? For adults and teenagers?

Some business people agree that without a minimum wage law there would be more jobs: small businesses could afford to hire more people. Is this a strong argument against the minimum wage? Why or why not?

Children who worked in mines and textile mills often lost thumbs and fingers in machine accidents.

lower. In fact, in many jobs, a black woman reported, "You never know what you are going to get; you just take what they give and go."

Working conditions. In many industries, working conditions were unhealthy or even dangerous. Factories often had poor lighting, heating, and ventilation. Even worse were the makeshift factories known as sweatshops. They were set up by "sweaters," contractors paid by large manufacturing companies to finish products begun in their factories.

Sweaters hired the cheapest labor possible, usually immigrant women and children, to do piecework, such as hand sewing or cigar making. Since sweatshop owners were paid by the number of finished products they delivered, they literally "sweated" the work out of employees by working them twelve to fifteen hours a day.

Mines were especially unhealthy and dangerous. In 1877 a newspaper described the working conditions for children in the sorting room of a coal mine:

> *"In a little room . . . forty boys are picking their lives away. . . . They work here, in this little black hole, all day and every day, trying to keep cool in summer, trying to keep warm in winter, picking away among the black coals, bending over till their little spines are curved, never saying a word all the livelong day."*

Connections: Economics

Discussion. The effort of workers to organize in the late 1800s was spurred in part by frequent hard times. The nation's economy goes through fluctuations in economic activity, called business cycles. In a major business cycle, prosperity, in which there is low unemployment and great demand for goods, gives way to a contraction, a slowdown marked by declining production and sales, and increased layoffs. Eventually the decline ends. Next comes expansion, a recovery in which production and employment increase.

If production has generally declined for six months, the contraction is called a recession. If it declines for a longer period, the contraction is called a depression. In 1873 and 1893 the United States experienced severe depressions, and there were milder depressions in 1867, 1883, and 1907.

Have students speculate about why an economy goes through a boom-bust cycle. **(Changes in amount of money spent on goods and services, and money supply will affect business cycles, for example) Ask:** If such a cycle is inevitable, what might be done to avoid downturns? Would such actions have any negative side effects?

Multicultural Perspectives

Isaac Myers was a caulker who became the spokesman of the 1,000 African Americans fired from a Baltimore shipyard after a strike by white workers protesting their employment. Under his leadership, African Americans raised money to purchase a shipyard and railway where 300 African-American caulkers and carpenters were employed. Myers founded a colored caulkers trade union, a Maryland state labor union, and later the Colored National Labor Union. Myers warned that unless black workers organized, *"in a few short years the trades will pass from your hands—you [will] become the servants of the servants, the sweepers of shavings, the scrapers of pitch and the carriers of mortar."*

Reduced student page in the Teacher's Edition

Organizing Workers

Craftspeople in small shops had some success in obtaining decent wages and working conditions. They could bargain personally with their employers on a fairly equal basis. And because they had skills, they were hard to replace. Unskilled workers did not have those advantages. To improve their status, they would have to organize.

Organizing millions of workers to demand better treatment was not easy. They were a diverse group which did not share the same ideas or sense of purpose. They only shared the same conditions.

In fact, most workers simply accepted existing conditions and tried to make the best of them. To many—especially the unskilled and poorly educated—protest seemed hopeless. However, about 20 percent of workers joined unions in the late 1800s in the hope of bettering their lives.

The first labor federations. The first successful unions had formed in the 1850s. They were craft unions, which organized workers who shared special skills—stone cutters, hat finishers, iron molders, machinists, and blacksmiths, for example.

In 1866 these unions united in a federation called the National Labor Union (NLU). The NLU sought social reform as well as specific goals for workers. It called for an eight-hour workday and aimed to organize all workers except the Chinese, who were accused of taking jobs from whites. The NLU was the first labor federation to claim that women should receive equal pay with men for equal work.

Despite the idealistic goals of the NLU, some of its member unions discriminated against black workers. As a result, African Americans founded their own Colored National Labor Union in 1869. Isaac Myers, a labor leader in Maryland, was elected president.

American Voices

"The men went out to their noon meal. Those who remained in the shop ate without hurry and read their newspapers. The boss kept his eye on us girls. We began last, ate hurriedly, and sat down to work at once. Betsy looked at the men and grumbled, 'This is what it means to belong to a union. You get a time to straighten out your bones.' "

—Rose Cohen

In 1873 a financial panic set off the worst depression that the United States had yet experienced. During the next four years, thousands of businesses failed, and more than half a million workers lost their jobs. Both federation's unions collapsed. But the original NLU did influence Congress to enact an eight-hour day for federal employees.

The Great Railroad Strike

Hard times may have killed the labor federations, but they inflamed railroad workers. In July 1877 the Baltimore and Ohio Railroad announced that it was cutting wages by 10 percent—the second such cut in eight months. Enraged, most of the railroad workers in Martinsburg, West Virginia, walked out. Then they blocked the tracks, refusing to let the trains run until the wage cuts were canceled

Other workers came to the support of the railroad strikers, and soon angry crowds of workers were attacking the railroads and fighting with militia in the cities of West Virginia, Pennsylvania, and Ohio. The local militia generally sided with the strikers, so federal troops were called in.

The strike quickly spread to Chicago, St. Louis, and Kansas City, and then on to San Francisco. Within a few days, 100,000 workers had walked off the job in the first nationwide strike. All the main railway lines were affected.

In every community, women rallied to support the strike. Describing the mothers and wives of workers in Martinsburg, a reporter for the *Baltimore Sun* wrote:

"They look famished and wild, and declare for starvation rather than have their people work for the reduced wages. Better to starve outright than to die by slow starvation."

Social History
Mother Jones enlisted other women as allies in her struggle to improve labor's lot. In the 1890s she went to Arnot, Pennsylvania, where she organized 3,000 women to march with mops and buckets to the mine head. There they attacked scab workers with their mops and beat on buckets to frighten away mine mules. Day and night, the women came to the mine ready to fight to keep the mine closed. Later, after the strikers and the women defeated the owners and the men went back to work, Jones gave her allies a simple, but appropriate honor. She said, "They were heroic women."

In cities in the Upper South, black and white workers went on strike together and prevented trains from moving. In St. Louis, the railroad strike developed into a **general strike**— a work stoppage by all the workers in the community. The general strike was so successful that it shut down all industry in the city.

In city after city, however, the strike was beaten back by police, militia, and federal troops. On August 5 the workers gave up. President Hayes wrote in his diary, "The strikers have been put down *by force*." More than one hundred workers had lost their lives.

Fear of revolution. The Great Railroad Strike stunned Americans. One historian observed:

> *"We had hugged the delusion [that] such social uprisings belonged to Europe and had no reason of being in a free republic where there was . . . an equal chance for all."*

For many people the strike raised the fear of a revolution like the one led by workers in Paris in 1871. The strike was called "un-American" and blamed on communist agitators. Such charges colored

THE AMERICAN SPIRIT

Mother Jones

"The Most Dangerous Woman in America"

A miner recalled his first encounter with Mary Harris "Mother" Jones: "She came right into the mine one day. . . . How she got in, I don't know; probably just walked in and defied anyone to stop her . . . [and] when she spoke, she carried an audience of miners with her."

For more than fifty years, from the 1870s through the 1920s, Mother Jones was on the scene wherever the tensions were greatest between labor and management. Most of her work was with coal miners, but she also helped metal miners, steelworkers, and women garment workers. And she led protests against child labor.

To the miners, she was a special friend. Newspapers called her "the most successful organizer and sustainer of strikes in the country." But mine owners and operators regarded her as "the most dangerous woman in America."

Born in Ireland in 1830, Mother Jones emigrated to Canada with her family. By the 1860s she was married to George Jones, a labor union organizer, and was raising a family in Memphis, Tennessee. In 1867 a yellow fever epidemic swept through Memphis, claiming the lives of her husband and four children. She moved to Chicago where she worked as a seamstress and became involved in labor's struggle to organize.

Mother Jones gained a large following during the railroad strike of 1877 and from then on traveled constantly. "I am always in the fight against oppression," she told a congressional committee in 1910. "Wherever a fight is going on, I have to jump there."

Often she worked as a paid organizer for the United Mine Workers. "My life work," she said, "has been to stir up the oppressed to a point of getting off their knees and demanding that which I believe is rightfully theirs." Mother Jones continued her crusade into her nineties. She died in 1930 at the age of one hundred.

Global Connections

Research. Have selected students research the Paris revolt of 1871, also known as the Paris Commune. They can report to the class why this revolt struck terror in the hearts of the rich and powerful in Europe and the United States.

Limited English Proficiency

Small Group Discussion. Have students work in small groups to discuss arguments for and against the general strike. Points to consider: Does a general strike do labor and the public more harm than good? **(It may provoke an extreme reaction from management and the government. It may turn the public against labor. On the other hand, it is a powerful weapon that may force management to capitulate.)** When is a general strike justified? Not justified? A spokesperson from each group can report what the group has determined and why.

B · A · C · K · G · R · O · U · N · D

Connections: Language

The *craft* union, made up of skilled workers in a particular craft or trade, was one approach that workers used to counteract the power of big business. Another approach, first used in the late 1800s, was the *industrial* union, which is made up of both skilled and unskilled workers in the same industry. The short-lived American Railway Union, founded by Eugene V. Debs in 1893, was an industrial union. Successful industrial unionism occurred after the formation of the Committee for Industrial Organization (CIO) in the 1930s.

Thinking Critically

Evaluation. Have students speculate about why the Knights of Labor excluded doctors and lawyers. **Ask:** If you were a leader of the union would you want to exclude these groups? Why or why not?

Writing about History

Newspaper Article. Have students imagine they are newspaper reporters who have interviewed Terence V. Powderly just after the successful strike against Jay Gould's railroads; now they are writing a newspaper profile about Powderly. In their profile they can present an account of Powderly's goals and favored methods, including how he and others transformed a secret fraternal lodge into a powerful mass union.

Thinking Critically

Evaluation. Ask students to debate the ethical question: Do strikers, such as those at the Haymarket Affair, or the defenders of the established order have the moral right to use violence to achieve their goals? Why or why not?

Reduced student page in the Teacher's Edition

many Americans' views of labor unions from then on. A prominent businessman summed up this view when he called for using armed force to end a strike. "Give the workingmen and strikers gun bullet food for a few days," he advised, "and you will observe how they take that sort of bread."

Toward Permanent Unions

In 1869 nine garment cutters from Philadelphia formed a secret society which they named the Noble Order of the Knights of Labor. Its founder, Uriah H. Stephens, believed that labor had to be unified to cope with the strength of business. Thus he called for an organization of both skilled and unskilled workers that "will include men and women of every craft, creed, and color."

The Knights survived the hard times of the 1870s. By the end of the decade it had a new leader, Terence V. Powderly, and had given up its secrecy in order to attract more members. Like the NLU, the Knights called for social reform as well as the eight-hour workday and equal pay for equal work by both sexes. All who had ever worked for wages could join except lawyers, doctors, bankers, and people who sold liquor. The Knights enrolled more women, both black and white, than any union before— and many unions after.

The Knights preferred boycotts to strikes as a way to put pressure on employers. Yet the Knights owed its greatest growth to strikes. In 1883 telegraphers organized by the Knights successfully struck Jay Gould's Western Union Telegraph Company nationwide. Two years later Knights working on the Gould railroads also struck successfully against wage cuts. These and other victories enabled the union to grow rapidly. In 1886 it had more than 700,000 members.

The Haymarket Affair. That year an incident occurred in Chicago that provoked widespread fear of labor unions and caused the Knights to decline rapidly. In early May nearly 200,000 workers na-

In a Labor Day parade in 1909, the Women's Auxiliary Typographical Union demanding "equal pay for equal work."

Connections: Politics

In 1893 three of the men convicted of the Haymarket bombing were pardoned by Illinois governor John Peter Altgeld. In his justification for the pardon, he cited the trial's unfairness—including the flimsiness of the evidence. Accounted one of the best governors in the history of Illinois, this German immigrant was criticized for his pardon, as in 1894 he was criticized for protesting President Cleveland's decision to have federal troops bust the Pullman strike.

Many years after Altgeld's death, Vachel Lindsay celebrated this now obscure figure in a poem. He called Altgeld "eagle forgotten."

The majority of the black members of the AFL in 1900 were in the United Mine Workers union.

The coal-mining industry was finally unionized by the United Mine Workers of America in 1890.

tionwide struck for an eight-hour day. Chicago became one of the centers of the movement. On May 3, strikers and police clashed, and four strikers were killed.

A small anarchist group called for a mass meeting the following night at Haymarket Square to protest the killings. The peaceful meeting was beginning to break up when police ordered the crowd to disperse. Then somebody threw a bomb at the police, killing seven. The police fired into the crowd, killing several and wounding thirty to forty.

The Haymarket bombing terrified Chicagoans. Police raided meetings of socialists, communists, and anarchists, and detained hundreds, beating many of them. In a trial marked by hysteria, seven anarchists were sentenced to death despite the lack of any evidence linking them to the bomb thrower, who was never identified. Six of the anarchists were German-speaking. The seventh, Albert Parsons, carried a membership card in the Knights of Labor.

Frightened Americans jumped to the conclusion that the Knights were anarchists. Employers used blacklists and arrests to drive workers out of the Knights. Managers of the Chicago, Burlington, and Quincy Railroad fired every worker who belonged to the union because the Knights "owe allegiance to somebody else, and not to the railroad." Meanwhile, African Americans and women began to leave the union, which had retreated from its stand on equality. Membership plummeted, and by 1900 the Knights of Labor was just a memory.

Gompers and the AFL. The Haymarket tragedy did not halt the growth of the labor movement. In 1886 delegates from thirteen national craft unions organized the American Federation of Labor (AFL). AFL unions worked toward common goals while retaining a large degree of independence. Each member union carried out its own business "without interference by the AFL."

With the exception of one year, Samuel Gompers served as president of the AFL from its start until his death in 1924. Born in London of Dutch-Jewish ancestry, Gompers came to the United States in 1863, when he was thirteen. A year later he became a member of the Cigarmakers' Union of New York and later made it a successful craft union.

Multicultural Perspectives

Research. Have students investigate the role played by the German immigrants in the Haymarket affair. Make sure they include information about August Spies and the newspaper called the *Arbeiter Zeitung*.

Linking Past and Present

Discussion. Throughout the nineteenth century, labor unions remained weak. No more than one or two percent of the work force and less than ten percent of industrial workers joined unions. In 1970 about 27 percent of the total labor force was unionized, but union membership has declined in recent decades.

Ask students to speculate about reasons for decline in union membership in recent years. **(Focus of our economy has changed from manufacturing to service; most employers aware of need for safe working conditions, and so on.)**

Active Learning

Making Picket Signs.
Discuss with students the aims of unions and some of the methods used to obtain them. (improving the conditions of working people; collective bargaining, strikes, for example) Ask students to explain the cause of the showdown between labor and management at the Pullman Company. Then have students make picket signs representing workers' complaints that led to the Pullman Strike. Display them in the classroom.

Writing About History

Editorial. At right is an emblem of the Industrial Workers of the World—the IWW. (Its enemies said the letters stood for "I Won't Work.") The IWW and its leaders believed that "one big union" including all workers regardless of race, sex, or skills could (in the words of its preamble) "do away with capitalism" and "carry on production when capitalism shall have been overthrown."

Have students research the history of the IWW, the life of its colorful leader, William D. "Big Bill" Haywood, and the strikes and other struggles in which it was involved. Have them assume they are newspaper people covering a city in which the "Wobblies" were active, such as Spokane, Washington; Fresno, California; or Missoula, Montana—and write an editorial either supporting or denouncing IWW activity.

Social History

The Homestead Strike resulted in a confrontation akin to class warfare, complete with well-armed, well-led workers, strikebreaking Pinkerton men, the use of a cannon by strikers against strikebreakers, and the flooding of the Monongahela River with oil and setting it afire to thwart an attack by boat.

Using the Visuals

The AFL union labels identify goods manufactured by its members. The federation urged shoppers to "look for the union label" and buy only union-made products.

Reduced student page in the Teacher's Edition

Elizabeth Gurley Flynn toured the nation for the Industrial Workers of the World (IWW). Formed in 1905, the IWW made a strong effort to organize female, black, Mexican, and Asian workers.

Whereas the NLU and the Knights had pushed for social reform, Gompers concentrated on the immediate economic problems of workers—wages, hours, and working conditions. The aim of the AFL, Gompers said, was to

❝ accomplish the best results in improving the conditions of the working people, men and women and children, today and tomorrow and tomorrow—and tomorrow's tomorrow. ❞

The AFL's chief means of obtaining its aim was **collective bargaining,** a process by which union and management representatives discuss and reach agreement about wages and working conditions. If collective bargaining failed, however, Gompers did not hesitate to use the strike to achieve objectives.

The AFL grew slowly at first, but by 1904 claimed 1,700,000 members. Not all workers were welcome, however, despite the AFL credo: "Working people must unite and organize, irrespective of creed, color, sex, nationality, or politics." Unskilled workers—including large numbers of women, African Americans, and immigrants—were largely barred from AFL craft unions. During the 1880s only the cigarmakers and the typographers accepted women. Others prohibited them from joining or refused to organize them.

Racist attitudes among member unions also prevented the AFL from carrying out its goal of including skilled black workers. By 1900 the AFL had given up trying to require its unions to admit blacks. And by refusing to open apprenticeship programs to young African Americans, many AFL unions kept blacks from learning the skills necessary to qualify them as skilled workers.

Opposition to Unions

Two violent incidents in the 1890s dealt the worst blows yet to the labor movement. The Homestead Steel Strike and the Pullman Strike set back the cause of unions for years to come.

The Homestead Strike. In 1892 the Carnegie Steel Company cut wages at its Homestead, Pennsylvania, plant. In July the Amalgamated Association of Iron, Steel, and Tin Workers—the strongest AFL union—called a strike. Instead of bargaining with the union, plant manager Henry Clay Frick decided to kill it. He locked the workers out of the plant. Then he hired 300 armed guards from the Pinkerton Detective Agency to enforce the lockout and to protect the new, nonunion workers he had hired to replace the strikers.

When the Pinkerton guards arrived, the unionists were waiting for them. Violence broke out, and seven guards and nine steelworkers were killed. The guards left, but the governor of Pennsylvania sent 8,000 militia to maintain order. The unionists watched as new workers, many of them African

Social History

George Pullman established Pullman town as a model community. His intention was to provide good housing and respectable surroundings in order to keep workers happy and productive. Furthermore, because he was a businessman, Pullman believed he could earn a nice profit from the rents collected in the community. The plan seems to have succeeded in boom times, but in the hard times of the early 1890s, profits at his factory plummeted and layoffs began. People not only lost their jobs, but also were turned out of their company-owned homes.

Active Learning

Small Group Activity. Divide the class into small groups to discuss whether the use of an injunction to end a strike is generally justifiable and, specifically, whether the injunction and the use of federal troops was justified in the Pullman Strike. Each group can prepare a position paper on the issue, which a spokesperson can read to the class.

Americans, arrived to take their jobs. Since the union barred blacks, strikebreaking was one of the few ways for them to get better paying jobs.

The strike dragged on until November, but by then the union was dead and thousands of workers had lost their jobs. Carnegie Steel had shown that with a private police force and the support of the government, it could break a strong union.

The Pullman Strike. In 1894 another violent showdown between labor and management occurred at Pullman, Illinois. Workers at the Pullman sleeping-car works were required to live in the company's town, paying higher rents than in nearby towns. They had to buy from company stores, where overcharging was so common that workers called them "pluck-me" stores.

After another financial panic hit the nation in 1893, the Pullman Company cut wages 28 percent. But it did not cut rents or store prices. Workers protested, but the company refused to bargain. In May 1894 the workers went on strike.

Many Pullman workers had joined the American Railway Union (ARU), founded the previous year by Eugene V. Debs. When the Pullman workers struck, 150,000 ARU workers across the country supported them by refusing to handle Pullman cars. By the end of June, shipping was tied up from California to Ohio.

In early July a federal court issued an injunction—or court order—based on the Sherman Antitrust Act. The court charged the strikers with interfering with interstate commerce and ordered them back to work. The strikers refused. President Cleveland sent federal troops to enforce the court order, and violence broke out.

By the time the strike ended on July 8, thirty-four lives had been lost. Debs was arrested for violating the injunction and sentenced to six months in jail. His union was so weakened that it dissolved three years later. After Pullman, courts would use injunctions widely to ban strikes on the grounds that they interfered with commerce and were therefore illegal.

Workers in 1990 used the strike to pressure employers into granting their demands.

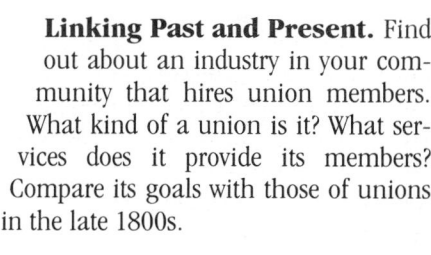

Debs spent his time in prison learning about socialism. He became the leader of the Socialist party of America, formed in 1901, and was its presidential candidate five times. Other workers, too, believing that more radical methods were necessary to oppose big business, called for the destruction of capitalist society. But the majority of organized workers still had faith in capitalism—they simply wanted to make it fairer and more humane.

Section Review

1. **Identification.** Define *general strike* and *collective bargaining.*

2. **Comprehension.** Describe the organization of the Knights of Labor and the AFL.

3. **Application.** Give at least three examples from the section of discrimination by organized labor in the late 1800s and early 1900s.

Linking Past and Present. Find out about an industry in your community that hires union members. What kind of a union is it? What services does it provide its members? Compare its goals with those of unions in the late 1800s.

Section Review

ANSWERS

1. Definitions for the following terms are on the text pages indicated in parentheses; *general strike*, (417), *collective bargaining*, (420).
2. The Knights of Labor was open to almost all who worked for wages; the AFL was a federation of craft unions, each made up of skilled workers.
3. Answers may include that NLU excluded Chinese, and discriminated against African-American workers; Knights of Labor retreated from its stand on equality for African Americans and women workers; Unskilled workers, including large numbers of women, African Americans, and immigrants, were banned from AFL unions.
Linking Past and Present Answers will vary.

Linking Past and Present

Discussion. Have students compare the arguments expressed in these sources with arguments voiced today regarding unions.

Thinking Critically

Synthesis. Have students discuss the pros and cons of unions. Which factors in employer-employee relations might union supporters tend to emphasize and why? Which ones might they tend to ignore and why? Which factors might union opponents emphasize or ignore and why?

Multicultural Perspectives

Discussion. As noted on pages 420–421, many strikebreakers at Homestead were African Americans. Have students discuss how the point of view of these workers might differ from the point of view of strikers at Homestead.

Social History

Members of the Industrial Workers of the world were called "Wobblies." They strongly believed in direct-action tactics such as strikes, boycotts, and sabotage. One of their most successful tactics was the talk-in, which was used after officials in various cities forbade the use of streets by union members for protest demonstrations. Wobblies preached from dozens of street corners in the hope that city officials would be forced to cancel their orders against street demonstrations when the jails became overcrowded. The tactic worked in two cities, but not in San Diego. There a band of vigilantes with approval from city officials drove the Wobblies from the city.

Reduced student page in the Teacher's Edition

POINT OF VIEW

Labor Strikes

In the struggle between labor and management, workers formed unions to protect what they saw as their rights. Employers portrayed unions as dangerous to public safety as well as to the nation's well-being. Here, a cartoon and editorial support management's point of view: that workers as well as the public would suffer from the unions' unjust demands and unreasonable actions. The Homestead Strike song is an example of how labor groups bolstered their spirits through ballads recounting the courage and determination of striking workers.

The Tyranny of Unions

"It is very hard to make the workingman understand this—that if he would exact [demand] justice from his employer, he must himself be just—that if he breaks the laws, he must not expect that the law will protect him in his assault upon the law-abiding. And this has been the teaching of the Knights of Labor, . . . of the Socialists and the Anarchists—that if a workman be dissatisfied with his work or with his wages, he is superior to all laws, civil, national, or moral.

The people have been patient and forbearing. They have been willing to believe that the working-folk were, as a rule, unfairly treated. They believe this no longer; and before long they must believe that the workingman is the enemy of peace, order, and industry. When they do believe this, and begin a war of reprisal [revenge], there will be even more distress and misery than we have yet seen. And this is what must surely come of the folly of men who have yielded up their independence, their self-respect, their very manhood, to the tyranny of 'organizers' [labor unions] who make their rich living out of over-worked women and half-starved children."

—From the editorial that accompanied the Keppler cartoon in *Puck* magazine, about 1880.

A Keppler cartoon, "Between Slavery and Starvation," shows a worker caught between the wolf of hunger and "union tyranny."

Connections: Music

Discussion. Students should review the discussion of the Homestead Strike on pages 420–421. Have them explain the song's statement that "a bunch of bum detectives came without authority."

Point of View

ANSWERS

1. Editorial states that strikes are illegal; unions are dangerous to public safety. Cartoon portrays worker as a slave to union tyranny.
2. The writer means that in order to demand fair treatment from employers, workers must first treat employers fairly. The statement is targeted against workers taking part in strikes or violent protests.
3. The song makes several points to justify the strikers' armed struggle: that they were being denied their rightful wages, that the workers faced the threat of losing their homes, that they needed to protect their families, and that the detectives sent to break up the strike were acting without legal authority.
4. Answers may include that violence is acceptable if nonviolent steps have proved unsuccessful and frustrated workers see no alternative way to achieve what is rightfully theirs. Others may argue in effect that "two wrongs do not make a right," that workers should continue nonviolent pressure on employers to bring about change in an orderly, lawful manner.

The Homestead Strike

"We are asking one another,
as we pass the time of day,
Why workingmen resort to arms [guns]
to get their proper pay,
And why our labor unions
should not be recognized,
Whilst the actions of a syndicate
must not be criticized.
Now, the troubles down at Homestead
were brought about this way:
When a grasping corporation
had the audacity to say,
'You must all renounce your union
and forswear your liberty
And we will give you a chance to live
and die in slavery.'

When a group of sturdy workingmen
started out at break of day,
Determination in their face
which plainly meant to say,
'No one shall come and take our homes,
for which we have toiled so long:
No one shall come and take our place;
no, it's here that we belong.'

A woman with a rifle
spied her husband in a crowd.
She handed him the weapon,
and they cheered her long and loud.
He kissed her and said, 'Mary,
you stay home until we're through.'
She said, 'No, when there is trouble,
my place is here with you.'

When a bunch of bum detectives came
without authority,
Like thieves at night, while decent men
were sleeping peacefully,
Can you wonder why honest hearts
with indignation burn,
Or why the worm that treads the ground,
when trod upon, will turn?
When they locked out men at Homestead,
then they were face to face
With a grasping corporation,
and they knew it was their place
To protect their homes and families,
and this was neatly done,
And the public will reward them
for the victories they won.

Chorus:
Oh, the man that fights for honor,
none can blame him.
May luck attend wherever he may
roam,
And no son of his will ever live to shame
him,
Whilst liberty and honor rule our
home."

—This workers' ballad was popular during the strike in Homestead, Pennsylvania, in 1892.

1. How do the editorial and cartoon criticize unions and strikes?

2. What does the editorial writer mean by saying that if a workingman "would exact justice from his employer, he must himself be just"?

3. According to the song, why did the strikers at Homestead believe that they were justified in using violence?

4. Do you believe that violence is ever justified in a strike? Why or why not?

Section 16-3

Objectives

- ***Answer the Focus Question.***
- *Describe how science and technology changed farming in the late 1800s.*
- *Evaluate the effect of easy credit and international competition on farmers.*
- *Analyze the importance of "free silver" to farmers and others.*

Introducing

THE SECTION

Inform students that because of new technology farmers throughout the country were producing larger harvests, but they were not prospering. Farmers often went into debt to buy new equipment to produce even more, but this, along with international competition, had the effect of driving prices lower and lower. High rates of indebtedness, low prices for crops, and the lure of cities all combined to draw people away from the farms. Rural people recognized these forces could destroy their way of life.

Tell students that they will now learn how farmers organized to combat such forces.

B · A · C · K · G · R · O · U · N · D

Connections: Economics
Many easterners were eager to loan money to farmers. A farm mortgage, they hoped, would be a good investment. The manager of an eastern loan company was busy in 1886:

"My desk was piled high every morning with hundreds of letters each enclosing a draft and asking me to send a farm mortgage from Kansas or Nebraska."

Reduced student page in the Teacher's Edition

16-3 The Revolt of the Farmers

Focus: What actions did farmers take in the late 1800s to improve their economic condition?

Workers who labored in mines and factories were not the only Americans affected by the growth of industry. Farmers, too, had trouble adjusting to the changes brought by industrialization.

In the 1830s a Michigan pioneer wrote, "We moved into a house of our own, had a farm of our own, and owed no one." That summed up the American dream of opportunity. But new inventions, nationwide transportation, and international competition changed the nature of farming. The Michigan pioneer of the 1830s would hardly have recognized his dream in the farm of the 1880s.

Technology and Farming

"As I look back over my life on that Iowa farm, the song of the reaper fills a large place in my mind. We were all worshippers of wheat in those days. Farmers thought and talked of little else between seeding and harvest, and you will not wonder at this if you have known and bowed before such abundance as we then enjoyed. . . . Our fields ran to the world's end."

Hamlin Garland was writing of his youth on a farm in the 1870s and 1880s. Wheat and the reaper were perfect symbols of farming in the prairie states. Science and machines were turning the small farm into a big business. Farmers were now planting new strains of wheat, developed in Europe and Asia, that could withstand the harsh prairie winters. And a new milling device was producing inexpensive, high-quality flour.

Meanwhile Cyrus McCormick, inventor of the reaper, developed a new machine called the combine. It handled every step of harvesting wheat. It cut, threshed, and even bagged the grain. By the 1880s giant combines rumbled through the fields, pulled by thirty to forty horses or mules.

Combines enabled farmers to plant more acres and obtain bigger harvests. And bigger harvests led to increased profits. However, the cost of such machinery was high. Farmers needed to make more money to pay for equipment, so they planted more acres. Farmers in the prairie states also began concentrating on growing a cash crop like wheat, hoping that prices would stay high.

In other parts of the country, farmers were also growing huge crops. In the South there were record-breaking harvests of cotton and good yields of wheat, corn, sugar, tobacco, and rice. Farmers in the West grew wheat, fruits, and vegetables. The Northeast churned out huge quantities of corn, milk, butter, fruits, and vegetables.

Machinery and science changed the nature of agriculture in these regions, too. A dairy centrifuge, marketed in 1880, separated cream from milk. Soon many dairy farmers were sending milk to creameries to be processed quickly and cheaply.

Meanwhile, researchers created pesticides to kill harmful insects, introduced fertilizers to enrich the soil, and found ways to combat plant diseases. One scientist saved California citrus groves by making use of ladybugs to eat pests.

Falling Farm Prices

Local boosters hailed the abundance created by farmers. "Do not be afraid of going into debt," a Kansas newspaper advised farmers on the Great Plains. "Do all you can for Belle Plaine regardless of money . . . and Belle Plaine will boom."

However, the farm boom did not last. As farmers grew more than the American market demanded,

Connections: Science and Technology
Cyrus Hall McCormick (1809–1884) was more of a perfecter than an inventor. Others had produced a machine much like his reaper. He himself developed a machine that his father had tinkered with for years. At the age of 38 McCormick went to Chicago where, with the sixty dollars he possessed, he set up a factory to produce reapers. Within two years he was a millionaire.

they tried to sell the rest abroad. But other countries—Australia, Canada, Russia, Argentina, Brazil—were also flooding the world market with their crops. Prices plunged. By 1893 cotton cost more to produce than the price it brought, and in some communities grain was so difficult to sell that farmers burned it as heating fuel.

The burden of debt. By the 1880s farmers were locked into a grim cycle: To pay off their debts, they needed to plant more crops, so they borrowed money and mortgaged more machinery and seed. Thus they fell deeper into debt to the banks and merchants.

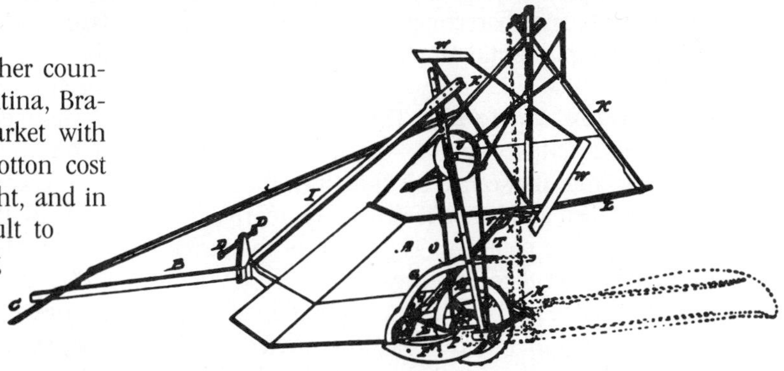

Thirty-four horses pulled this harvester combine through wheat fields in Oregon in the 1880s. They were soon replaced by steam engines and then internal-combustion engines.

Developing
THE SECTION

Connections: Science and Technology

Oral Report. Assign students to investigate and report to the rest of the class on each of the following technological advances in farming: twine binder, spring-tooth harrow, disk harrow, gang plow, corn shucking and fodder shredding machine, combine harvest thresher, centrifugal cream separator. Have students explain how the functions of these new machines were performed before their invention.

Connections: Economics

Discussion. For small farmers, technological advances were a mixed blessing. Farm machines increased production dramatically, but they also cost a lot. Between 1870 and 1900, the total value of farm implements and machinery increased from $102 per farm to $130.

To pay for these improvements, small farmers had to go into debt. But increased production led to surpluses which caused the wholesale prices of farm goods to decline 50 percent from 1866 to 1900. To pay their debts, farmers needed to produce more; thus they went further into debt to buy more machinery.

Have students discuss the proposition: The main problem of farmers in the late 1800s was overproduction.

Connections: Literature

Book Report. Interested students can read and report on Frank Norris's *The Octopus*. Published in 1901, the novel dramatizes the plight of wheat farmers who were at the mercy of the railroad that charged excessive freight rates for hauling wheat.

Backyard History

Oral Reports. The Grange still exists and has about 6,000 local groups in more than 40 states. Students who have relatives belonging to the Grange can interview them about a local group's goals and activities (without asking the member to reveal the groups secret activities) and then report back to the class.

Other students can write to the national organization— The Grange, 1616 H Street NW, Washington, DC 20006—to learn its goals and how it works to achieve them, and make oral reports.

Thinking Critically

Analysis. Have students cite similarities and differences between the Grange and early labor unions, such as the Knights of Labor.

B · A · C · K · G · R · O · U · N · D

Social History

The Grange movement was more than an economic and political organization. It was also a social, educational, and fraternal order. In 1872 Iowan Dudley W. Adams of the Union County Grange articulated what seemed to be a cry from deep within the American farmers' souls: *We have heard enough of this professional blarney about the honest farmer, the backbone of the nation. We have been too much alone. We need to get together to rub off the rough corners and polish down the symmetry. We want to exchange views and above all we want to learn to think."*

Reduced student page in the Teacher's Edition

Many farmers also owed the railroad companies that had sold them their land. And in the prairie states, where railroads had no competition, farmers had to pay high railroad rates. They also paid high prices to the grain merchant for handling the grain and storing it. One farmers' newspaper declared:

> *"There are three great crops raised in Nebraska. One is a crop of corn, one a crop of freight rates, and one a crop of interest [on loans]. One is produced by farmers who by sweat and toil farm the land. The other two are produced by men who sit in their offices and behind their bank counters and farm the farmers."*

Farmers were further hurt by deflation—a decline in the general level of prices—after 1865. A farmer who borrowed $1,000 in the late 1860s could have repaid that debt by selling 1,200 bushels of wheat. By the 1880s it took almost twice as many bushels to repay that same debt.

As costs rose, more independent farmers slipped into tenant farming and sharecropping, especially in the South. By 1910 one half of the tenant farmers in the country were southerners, many of them African Americans. Tenants and sharecroppers rarely had goods or lands to pledge for credit. To get credit they gave merchants a lien, or claim, on their crops. If they could not pay, the merchant took the crops in payment. Under the crop-lien system, tenants and sharecroppers piled up debts and lost hope of ever owning their own land.

Flight from the land. The farmers' troubles produced a bitter harvest—a migration away from the land. Between 1889 and 1893, thousands of farms failed and banks foreclosed on mortgages. In some prairie counties, 90 percent of the farms were sold or lost to foreclosures.

In that same period, half the population of western Kansas left the prairie, and other western states suffered similar losses. One wagon heading east carried a sign, "In God we trusted, in Kansas we busted." A sign on an empty Texas farmhouse said, "250 miles to the nearest post office—100 miles to wood—20 miles to water. . . . God bless our home! Gone to live with the wife's folks."

Farmers Organize

> *"When the banker says he's broke,*
> *And the merchant's up in smoke,*
> *They forget that it's the farmer feeds them all.*
> *It would put them to the test*
> *If the farmer took a rest,*
> *Then they'd know that it's the farmer feeds them all."*

In this song of the 1890s, farmers declared a revolt. The country, they reminded Americans, could not get along without farmers. And farmers were in trouble. Out of local groups, meeting to share problems, grew national organizations that sought political solutions to those problems. Finally, the movement fused into a new political party—the Populists—pledged to widespread reform.

The Grange protest. The farmers' movement began with the Patrons of Husbandry, a group better known as the Grange. Founded in 1867 by Oliver Kelley, the Grange sought to improve the lives of rural Americans.

The Grange grew especially strong in the Midwest, where it provided a welcome relief from the isolation of prairie farming. "New friendships are formed, and old ones strengthened," wrote a farmer in 1875. "The farmer is taught that the world does not end . . . at the boundaries of [the] farm." Men and women were equal members in the local Grange. The group held picnics and meetings and talked over common problems.

Grangers also started their own farm supply stores and formed cooperatives to run warehouses and granaries. Cooperatives were owned collectively by the members, who shared in the benefits and profits.

An admiring Kansas senator wrote of the Grange: "It lacks but one element of strength, and that will come in due time—namely, the uniting with other bodies of organized farmers in one great political movement."

Farmers' Alliances. The political movement was started by farmers in the South and the West who formed Farmers' Alliances. Like the Granges,

Social History

In 1891 Senator William A. Peffer of Kansas noted that in both the Grange and Farmers' Alliance *"women are equal with men. . . . Many of the best essays read and delivered in their meetings are prepared by women, and it is beginning to dawn upon the minds of men [that women] . . . are quite . . . capable of looking after the interest of men and women."*

the alliances were both social and political. Speakers toured farm areas, urging farmers to unite to solve their problems. Alliances published newspapers and magazines. Local branches held picnics. Cooperatives set up warehouses and stores.

The Farmers' Alliance in the South began as a ranchers' association in the 1870s. In the 1880s it merged with other southern farmers' groups. Some members tried to unite their group with the Colored Farmers' Alliance. However, racist attitudes destroyed these initial stirrings of unity.

The Farmers' Alliance in the Midwest was started in 1880 to "unite the farmers of America for their protection against . . . the tyranny of monopoly." The alliance flourished in the plains states, attracting thousands of indebted farmers.

In 1889 the three alliances met in St. Louis, Missouri. Prices for farm crops were plummeting, and the meeting rang with demands for government action. Farmers wanted lower taxes and more money in circulation. There was talk that the government should take over railroads. Farmers called for low-interest government loans.

In the congressional elections the next year, the alliances campaigned vigorously. Members of the southern alliance, running as Democrats, won control of eight state legislatures and elected three governors and forty-four congressmen.

The midwestern Farmers' Alliance distrusted both Democrats and Republicans, believing them to be controlled by business interests. So the plains farmers formed their own parties. In Minnesota,

Bountiful crops were offset by a falling market and natural disasters. In Kansas, Rosie Ise experienced a plague of billions of grasshoppers. They consumed every bit of greenery and clothes and curtains, and "flew into the water . . . and into kettles cooking on the stove."

Active Learning

Group Work. Divide the class into groups of four or five students. Each group should imagine it is a body of delegates to the meeting of Farmers' Alliances in St. Louis in 1889. Students can frame a set of goals for the alliances. They should note that Senator William Peffer of Kansas stated, *"One of the tenets of all these organizations is 'equal rights to all, special privilege to none.'"*

Using the Visuals

Analyzing an Illustration. Refer students to the poster titled "Gift for the Grangers" on text page 407. What benefits of Grange membership are depicted? **(social activities, for example)**

Linking Past and Present

Discussion. Have students consider how radical the Populist demands seem today. They can cite which demands have been adopted and argue for or against other demands. For example, should banks, railroads, telephones, and telegraphs be owned by the government?

Thinking Critically

Analysis. Refer students to Gillam's cartoon on this page. **Ask:**

1. To what does the cartoon compare the People's party? (A balloon made of patches)
2. What do the patches represent? (Various groups making up the party)
3. Tell students that the word patch also can mean "a clown or a fool." Does that meaning of the word apply in this cartoon? (Yes, cartoonist has a negative view of Populists.)
4. What does the cartoon suggest will happen to the party? (It will fall apart and sink.)
5. What is the cartoonist's point of view? (Hostile toward the party)

B · A · C · K · G · R · O · U · N · D

Social History

Kansas journalist William Allen White recalled, about Mary Lease: "*She could recite the multiplication table and set a crowd hooting and hurrahing at her will. One of her most famous sayings was '[the U.S.] is no longer a government of the people, by the people, and for the people, but a government of Wall Street, by Wall Street, and for Wall Street.'*"

Kansas, Nebraska, and South Dakota, these parties swept into state legislatures. Kansas, where the campaign reached fever pitch, even elected several members to Congress.

The fever was fanned by Mary Lease, preaching the farmers' plight throughout Kansas:

> *"The great common people of this country are slaves, and monopoly is the master. . . . Our laws are the output of a system which clothes rascals in robes and honesty in rags."*

The farmers were ready to unite in a single national party. At a meeting of Farmers' Alliances in May 1891, the People's party of the U.S.A. was launched. It soon became known as the Populist party.

The Populist Party

In the summer of 1892, a presidential election year, the first national convention of the Populist party met in Omaha, Nebraska. In their platform the Populists called for changes that farmers had been suggesting for years. Railroads, banks, and telephones and telegraphs should be owned and run by the government "in the interest of the people." The government should also set up warehouses where farmers could store their crops, and loan the farmers money until the crops were sold. To gain the support of city workers, the Populists called for an eight-hour workday.

The Populists supported taxes on personal income, rather than on land. They proposed the **graduated income tax**—a system by which people are taxed at a rate proportional to their income. In addition, they demanded that the government permit an unlimited amount of silver to be coined into money. Farmers had failed in their efforts to make the government increase the amount of paper money. They now wanted the federal government to enlarge the money supply by placing more silver in circulation.

The Populists also wanted people to be able to participate more directly in politics. They proposed that senators be chosen by the people, not by state legislatures, that votes should be by secret ballot, and that citizens should have the right to propose legislation and approve laws.

The Populist convention adopted the platform with cheers that "raged for 34 minutes."

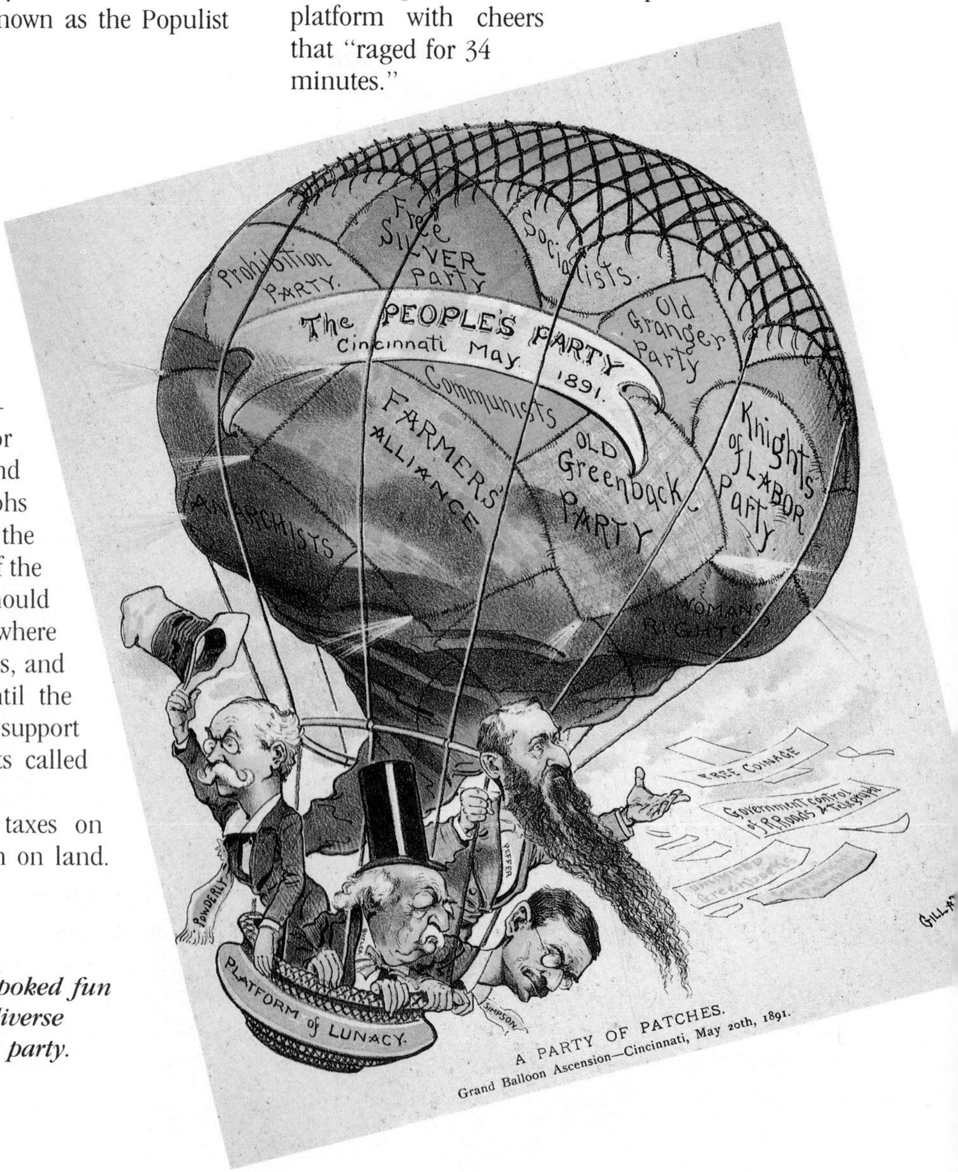

Cartoonist Bernard Gillam poked fun at the political views and diverse membership of the Populist party.

Connections: Politics
Grover Cleveland was the only President to have a split term of office. He won the presidency in 1884, but lost the election four years later to Benjamin Harrison. In 1892 Cleveland ran against Harrison again and won.

The convention then nominated a former Grange leader, James B. Weaver of Iowa, as the Populist presidential candidate.

The election of 1892. In the months that followed, populist leaders traveled the country roads, whipping up support and earning colorful knicknames. Jerry Simpson of Kansas, who had once scorned rich politicians who wore silk socks, became "Sockless Jerry." Mary Lease was known as the "Kansas Pythoness." Farmers joined the Populists by the thousands.

For a third party, the Populists made a remarkable showing in the election. Weaver won more than a million popular votes and twenty-two electoral votes, all from states west of the Mississippi. Over a dozen Populists were sent to Congress and Populist governors were elected in Kansas, North Dakota, and Colorado.

Nevertheless, Democrat Grover Cleveland won his second term, defeating President Harrison. In the South, many members of the southern alliance had voted Democratic, still hoping to reach power through that party. And city workers had simply ignored the Populist cause. Thus Populists emerged solely as the party of the plains farmers.

American Voices

"If we are equal, why does not the sheriff summon Negroes on juries? And why hang up the sign "Negro" in passenger cars? I want to tell my people what the People's party is going to do. I want to tell them if it is going to work a black and white horse in the same field."

—Delegate to Texas People's Party

The Depression of 1893

As Grover Cleveland took office in 1893, the nation was struck by its third depression within twenty years. People argued angrily over economic cures.

On one side were the "silverites," who wanted unlimited coinage of silver in order to increase the money supply. More money in circulation, they believed, would help people pay their debts, increase demand for products, and end the depression.

Standing firmly against them were business leaders, who opposed any measures that would allow debtors to pay off their loans in "cheap money." They were joined by conservatives in Congress and President Cleveland. All were defenders of the gold standard. Under the gold standard, a paper dollar was equal to a certain amount of gold and could be exchanged for it. There could be no more currency in circulation than there was gold in the nation's treasury to back that currency.

The debate over silver had gone on for twenty years. Until the Civil War, the country had followed a monetary policy of bimetallism. In other words, currency was based on both gold and silver. Under the Coinage Act of 1873, however, silver was no longer to be coined, leaving gold the sole standard. The money supply shrank, and deflation followed. People in debt, supported by western silver miners, had demanded that silver be coined again.

Buffeted between gold and silver backers, Congress passed the Bland-Allison Act of 1878 and the Sherman Purchase Act of 1890 to coin silver. But both laws limited the amount coined, and the money supply was not affected.

Breaking away from silver. President Cleveland was sure that the Sherman Purchase Act was at the root of the depression. Because of the act, the treasury was using up its gold to buy silver. In late 1893 Cleveland convinced Congress to repeal the act.

But the depression did not end. In fact, by 1894 it was worse. That year hundreds of the unemployed marched on Washington. One group, led by Populist Jacob Coxey, wanted the government to employ the jobless. When "Coxey's Army" reached the Capitol, they were arrested for trespassing.

The depression turned many voters against Cleveland. In the congressional elections that fall, thousands of voters flocked to the Populists. They elected 8 representatives to Congress and almost 500 to state offices. The voters also elected many Republicans and Democrats with Populist leanings. The discontent especially affected the Democratic party. It was split between silverites—mostly from the South and the West—and backers of gold and President Cleveland.

Limited English Proficiency

Making Time Lines. Divide the class into two groups—one to research major events described in the text that were occurring in the labor movement from 1866 to 1900, and the other to research events related to farmers' attempts to organize. Have the students include the dates that various organizations, such as unions and Farmers' Alliances, were founded and when strikes occurred, as well as any other pertinent dates.

When groups are finished with their research, construct a class time line from 1866 to 1900. Have students summarize reasons for attempts at organizing by workers and farmers.

Thinking Critically

Synthesis. Have students take a position as a silverite or as a supporter of the gold standard and defend it. For example, silverite view: free silver will increase the money supply, help people in debt, and stimulate the economy. Supporter of gold standard: coining more money will lead to inflation; buying of silver is depleting federal gold supply.

Writing About History

Campaign Platform. Have students take the position of a Populist candidate for President in 1896 and outline a platform. Suggest students use a formal outline procedure, with roman numerals for the main "planks" of the platform, and capital letters and arabic numerals for subordinate ideas. "Candidates" should include positions on labor, farmers, and money.

Thinking Critically

Application. Have students decide whom they would have voted for in 1896, Bryan or McKinley. Have them identify the issues they considered most important in the election and explain how the stands candidates took would have influenced their votes.

B · A · C · K · G · R · O · U · N · D

Connections: Literature

In 1900, even as the Populist party was collapsing, L. Frank Baum wrote a parable about the plight of farmers and industrial workers called *The Wonderful Wizard of Oz*. For Baum the Scarecrow represented the struggling farmer; the Tin Woodsman, the industrial worker; the Cowardly Lion, William Jennings Bryan; Dorothy, Everyperson; and the Wizard, President William McKinley. The Wicked Witches represented banks and corporations.

Dorothy and her friends went down the yellow brick road (the gold standard) to the Emerald City (Washington, D.C.) much as did Coxey's Army, seeking answers to their problems from Oz. Through deception, Oz sends Dorothy and her friends on wild goose chases and turns out to be a fraud.

Reduced student page in the Teacher's Edition

Bryan and "Free" Silver

By the presidential election of 1896 the silverites had gained control of the Democratic party. Cleveland was abandoned, and the party searched for a new candidate. The *New York World* noted:

> *"All the silverites need is a Moses. They have the brass bands and the buttons and the flags, they have the howl and the hustle, they have the votes. But they are wandering in the wilderness like a lot of lost sheep."*

The silverites found their leader at the Democratic convention—a two-term congressman from Nebraska named William Jennings Bryan.

Bryan electrified the convention with a speech that summed up the feeling of the silverites. Without silver, Bryan said, the farmers would be lost. Without farmers, the nation would be lost. In his famous "cross of gold" speech, Bryan thundered:

> *"You come to us and tell us that the great cities are in favor of the gold standard. I tell you that the great cities rest upon these broad and fertile prairies. Burn down your cities and leave our farms, and your cities will spring up again as if by magic; but destroy our farms and the grass will grow in the streets of every city in the country. . . .*
>
> *Having behind us the commercial interests and the laboring interests and all the toiling masses, we shall answer their demands for a gold standard by saying to them: You shall not press down upon the brow of labor this crown of thorns. You shall not crucify mankind upon a cross of gold."*

William Jennings Bryan
From Stefan Lorant's *The Glorious Burden*, Author's Edition.

The convention exploded into cheers, shouting for Bryan and "free" silver. The Democrats had taken over the Populist cause and made it their own.

McKinley Elected in 1896

When the Populist convention met, it was bitterly divided. Many wanted to support Bryan. Others argued that if they endorsed the Democratic candidate, the Populists would be doomed as an independent third party. The Bryan supporters won, and the Populist party endorsed him.

Bryan stormed across the country, traveling over 18,000 miles and making 600 speeches in 21 states. Meanwhile, the Republican candidate, Senator William McKinley of Ohio, stood on his front porch and spoke to audiences brought in by train for the occasion. McKinley said nothing to offend anyone, trusting that the smooth-running operation of the Republican party would get him elected.

The Republicans made their appeal to supporters of the gold standard. They counted not only on business support, but also on eastern Democrats—middle class Americans, such as lawyers, small business owners, and office workers—who feared the Populist influence on the Democratic platform.

Bryan gained the support of labor leaders Samuel Gompers and Eugene V. Debs. But many workers did not support Bryan. They were afraid that the Democratic policies would lead to inflation, which would decrease the value of their wages. And Republicans warned that business would be ruined and jobs would be lost if Bryan won.

The election all but destroyed the Populist party. On election day, only the farmers and the silver mining interests voted for Bryan. Theirs was a loud voice of protest. With 6.5

This placard supported William McKinley for President in the election of 1896. Voters spun the movable wheel on the placard to see the results of a McKinley victory—for example, "sound government, sound money, and prosperity."

million votes, Bryan carried almost as many states as McKinley. But those were the less populous states of the South and the West. McKinley, with 7 million votes, won all the industrial states in New England and the Midwest.

Section Review

1. **Identification.** Define *graduated income tax.*

2. **Comprehension.** How did technology and science change the nature of farming in the late 1800s?

3. **Evaluation.** Bankers and business people eagerly loaned money to farmers who wanted to expand production. Do you think this encouragement ultimately helped or hurt farmers? Give reasons for your answer.

4. **Analysis.** Why did the Populists make "free" silver a major issue?

5. **Synthesis.** How might history have been different if William Jennings Bryan had won the presidential election of 1896? Explain.

Connections to Themes

The Search for Opportunity

Between 1865 and 1910, the overwhelming power of big business cast a shadow on the vision of America as a land of opportunity for all. By gaining success for themselves, the nation's business leaders seemed to slam shut the doors of opportunity for others.

Both workers and farmers challenged the power of business. But by 1900 both seemed to have failed. Workers learned that government usually sided with the corporations and would even use military force to break strikes. The Farmers' Alliances and Populists had hoped to gain enough political power to bring about change, but their efforts also fell short.

However, the programs of the Populists had championed as never before the belief that government has the responsibility to regulate the economy to protect the public. Never before had this view been accepted by so many Americans.

A growing number of people began to see that economic injustices would continue as long as government was so closely allied with business. In the late nineteenth and early twentieth centuries, reform-minded journalists and politicians turned their energies to exposing the abuses of big business and demanding that government take action.

Their efforts, combined with the continuing struggles of workers and farmers, would lead the nation into a new era of reform. Reformers would insist that economic opportunity for all could be restored only by curbing big business and restoring political power to the people.

Using the Visuals

Analyzing an Illustration. Refer students to the McKinley placard on this page. **Ask:** What issues does the placard address? Compare McKinley's and Bryan's stands on these issues.

Section Review

ANSWERS

1. A definition for *graduated income tax* is on text page 428.
2. Development of new winter-resistant strains of wheat and invention of combine turned farming into big business. Farmers had to plant huge crops and concentrate on cash crops to pay for the machinery.
3. Answers may include that it enabled farmers to bring in bigger crops; it put farmers deeply into debt and led to foreclosures on many farms when farm prices fell.

Chapter Survey

ANSWERS

Using New Vocabulary

1. (b) Pendleton Act required exam for civil service workers.
2. (c) Gompers favored collective bargaining to resolve labor-management problems.
3. (a) General strike was a work stoppage involving all the workers in a community.

Reviewing the Chapter

1. Neither party would take controversial stand on an issue for fear of losing voters.
2. Spoils system had filled government jobs with people who were often unqualified and/or corrupt.
3. Wages were so low that people could barely afford to buy necessities, hours were long, and factory conditions were unhealthy and often dangerous.
4. Knights of Labor wanted social reform and eight-hour day, was open to all, and preferred boycotts to strikes. American Federation of Labor just for craft unions, favored collective bargaining over strikes, and barred unskilled workers along with large numbers of women, blacks, and immigrants.
5. Violence in strikes; fear of anarchy from Haymarket Affair.
6. Farmers faced poverty and loss of land due to high cost of loans, farm machinery, grain storage, and railroad shipping; falling crop prices; and deflation.
7. Farmers' movement started with Grange. Farmers in South and West formed Farmers' Alliances. Alliances met in St. Louis in 1889 to demand government action, influenced congressional elections in 1890, formed Populist party in 1891 and ran candidate for President in 1892. Some goals: government ownership of banks, railroads, and loans for farmers, eight-hour workday, graduated income tax, free silver coinage, direct election of senators, secret voting.
8. Populist position on silver issue adopted by Democrats. Populists threw their support to Democratic candidate, Bryan. Bryan's defeat spelled end of Populist party.

Thinking Critically

1. Farm families lived in isolation on plains, faced high prices for farm machinery, storage, and transportation but falling prices for crops. Life in industrial cities meant poverty for factory workers who lived and worked in crowded and often unsafe conditions and barely earned enough to survive. Farmers supported Populists who wanted govern-

Reduced student page in the Teacher's Edition

Chapter Survey

Using New Vocabulary

Match each numbered vocabulary term with the lettered word or phrase most closely related to it. Then explain how the items in each pair are related.

1. civil service	(a) work stoppage
2. collective bargaining	(b) Pendleton Act
3. general strike	(c) Samuel Gompers

Reviewing the Chapter

1. What effect did the evenly matched strength of Republicans and Democrats have on national politics between 1865 and 1899?

2. Why was civil service reform an important issue in the Gilded Age?

3. Describe the working conditions common to many factories in the late 1800s and early 1900s in terms of wages, hours, and health and safety.

4. Compare the Knights of Labor and the American Federation of Labor.

5. What events of the Gilded Age turned public opinion against labor unions?

6. Describe problems facing American farmers in the late 1800s and early 1900s and identify the factors that contributed to them.

7. Trace the development of the Populist party and list its goals.

8. What impact did the Populist party have on the election of 1896? What impact did the election have on Populists?

Thinking Critically

1. Analysis. Compare what was happening in 1890 in a farming town on the Kansas plains with life in an eastern industrial city such as Pittsburgh, Pennsylvania. Discuss economic and social concerns as well as political issues.

2. Evaluation. What was the importance of the strike in the early labor movement? Determine how many of the major strikes described in this chapter were successful. Give evidence of what they did or did not accomplish.

3. Application. How did racist and sexist attitudes prevent workers from uniting to improve their working conditions? Support your answer with examples from the chapter.

Using Geography

Study the map below, then answer the following questions.

1. Which regions supported McKinley?

2. Which regions supported Bryan?

3. How did the economy of a region affect the way its people voted?

4. Which parts of the country did not vote? Why not?

Election of 1896

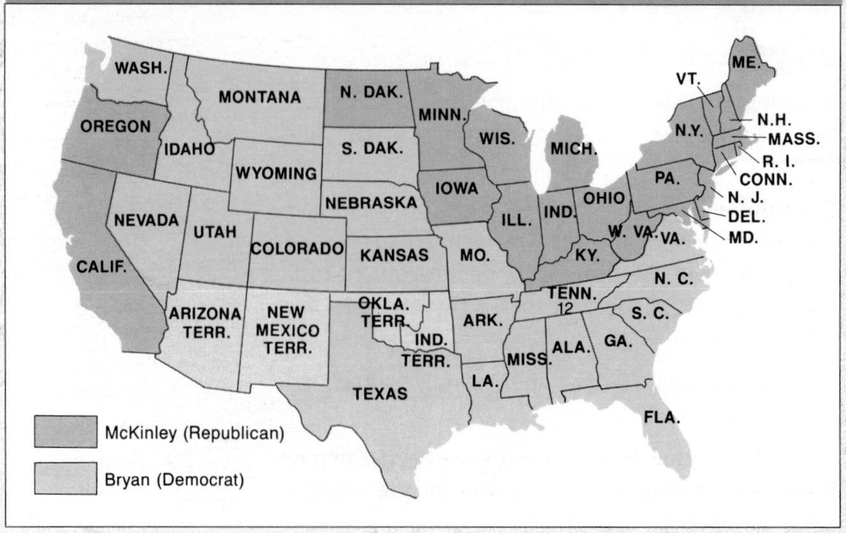

ment regulation and free silver. Urban workers opposed free silver for fear inflation would drive up cost of living.
2. Strikes were rallying points for labor but often turned public opinion against unions. Railroad strike of 1877, and Homestead and Pullman strikes all failed to win union demands. Use of court injunctions to ban strikes.
3. NLU excluded Chinese and discriminated against black workers. Knights of Labor retreated from its stand on equality. Unskilled women, African Americans, and immigrants banned from AFL; most skilled black workers also banned.

Applying Social Studies Skills

Analyzing Line Graphs

The line graph below shows price indexes for the years 1866 to 1890. The price index for any year represents the percent by which prices were higher or lower than the 1860 index of 100.

In the graph, the farm price index represents the level of prices that American farmers received for their crops. The general price index is the level of prices that farmers had to pay for equipment, clothing and other goods.

Use the graph to answer the following questions about the plight of American farmers in the late nineteenth century.

Farmers' Costs and Income 1866 – 1890

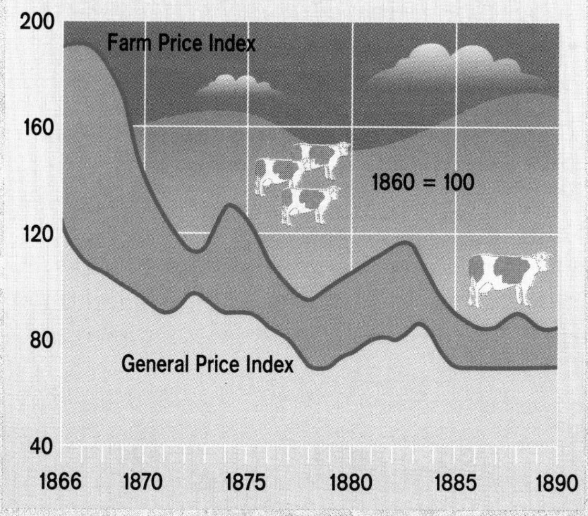

Source: *Historical Statistics of the United States*

1. Compare farm prices in 1866 and 1890. What factors contributed to the change?

2. If a farmer's income from the sale of crops was $1,900 in 1866, estimate the income from the same amount of crops in 1880. In 1890.

3. If the total price a farmer paid for goods in 1866 was $1,200, estimate how much the same goods would have cost in 1880. In 1890.

4. Based on your answers to questions 2 and 3, what would the farmer's profits be for 1866, 1880, and 1890? What does that tell you about the situation of American farmers in the late nineteenth century?

Writing About Issues

The Issue: *Should all groups have the right to hold demonstrations?*

Large crowds cheered Coxey's Army as it marched into Washington, D.C., in 1894 to demand help for jobless Americans. Government officials, however, believed that the march was a dangerous step on the road to revolution and had police arrest Coxey and scatter the marchers.

Under the First Amendment, citizens have the right to free speech and assembly as long as they are peaceful and do not violate the rights of other citizens. But what if a person or group expresses ideas that are very unpopular, or that might endanger individuals or society?

One of the most controversial cases on this issue occurred in 1977. That year members of the American Nazi party applied for a permit to march through Skokie, Illinois. Because many Skokie residents were Jews who had survived the horror of Nazi concentration camps, town officials passed laws to prevent the march. When the Nazis planned a rally to protest the laws, the county court ruled that the group could not hold a demonstration.

The Nazis challenged the court order, and a long court battle began. One side argued that the First Amendment does not protect people who want to destroy freedom and spread hatred. But the other side questioned this stand. If the government can deny freedom of expression to one group, they asked, what will prevent it from denying the right to other groups? As one person said, "The First Amendment has to be for everyone—or it will be for no one."

On June 15, 1977, the United States Supreme Court ruled that the American Nazis did have the right to freedom of expression under the First Amendment. Illinois courts later removed all laws banning Nazi marches and distribution of Nazi materials.

What do you think? Should all groups be allowed freedom of speech and assembly, even when their beliefs are very unpopular or encourage hatred and violence? Imagine that a newspaper has invited you to write an editorial on this issue. In your editorial combine the facts with a call for action.

Using Geography

1. Northeast, Great Lakes states, most of west coast.
2. South, central plains, Rocky Mountain states.
3. People in urban, industrialized areas voted McKinley and gold standard; people in farming and mining regions, hard hit by depression, voted Bryan and free silver.
4. Arizona, New Mexico, Oklahoma, Indian Territories. Territories could not vote in presidential elections.

Analyzing Line Graphs

1. Farm prices drop by more than half due to overproduction and overseas competition.
2. 1880–$1050; 1890–$850.
3. 1880–$800; 1890–$750.
4. 1866–$700; 1880–about $150; 1890–$100. Answers may include that farmers could make very little profit.

Unit 5 Survey

ANSWERS

Making Connections

1. Railroads disrupted Indians' way of life, provided jobs for Irish and Chinese immigrants, made cattle ranching profitable, and carried farmers, townspeople, and miners west. Speculators made great fortunes.

2. Good: spurred inventions, business, hard work; raised living standards. Harmful: damaged environment, encouraged ruthlessness, inhumane working conditions.

3. Homestead Act encouraged expansion. Land grants to railroads opened West to development. Interstate Commerce Act regulated railroad practices, and Sherman Antitrust Act, trusts, both ineffectively. Coinage, Bland-Allison, and Sherman Purchase Acts affected coinage of money.

4. Billington-Martin: growth of ranches and farms, towns and cities; wealth from ranching, mining, lumbering; spread of democracy; "taming of the wilderness" and fulfillment of manifest destiny. Nelson: Farms failed, mines played out, boom towns became ghost towns; westering settlers' destroyed Indian land; mining, lumbering, ranching ruined environment.

Using the Time Line. Innovations in transportation, industry, and building technology supported urban growth. Chisholm Trail, Yellowstone, Levi Strauss jeans, Pony Express, and barbed wire indicate development of the West.

Projects and Activities

1. Forces that shaped urban growth include nearby resources and markets, land and climate, inventions that created new industries, industrialization, immigrants, influx of rural people.

2. Robber baron would be interested in eliminating competition and making huge profits. Populist would oppose "the tyranny of monopoly" and high railroad rates. Union member would call for fair wages, hours, and conditions.

3. Reasons for immigration include religious persecution, wars, unrest, crop failure, famine, poverty. Eastern European Jews were oppressed; Scandinavians tasted poverty and shortage of farmland; Italians, political unrest and overpopulation.

Using the Time Line. The first generation might note urban growth, awareness of the Far West; second generation, development of big business, industry, and labor; third generation, growing knowledge of the "wide world," citing immigration, Columbian Exposition, start of radio, film.

Reduced student page in the Teacher's Edition

Unit Survey

Making Connections

1. Many groups of people were greatly affected by the coming of the railroad. Explain the impact of the railroad on at least four groups.

2. Explain in what ways competition in business and industry was good for the United States in the late 1800s. In what ways was it harmful?

3. The relationship of the federal government to the economy began to change during the Gilded Age. Explain how each of five separate actions by Congress affected the American economy.

4. Historians Ray Allen Billington and Martin Ridge described the history of the West as a "virtually unbroken chain of successes in national expansion." Historian Patricia Nelson Limerick said that "the West is the place where everybody was supposed to escape failure, but it didn't happen that way." What evidence might these historians use to support their views?

Using the Time Line. Using five or more events listed on the time line, explain reasons for rapid urban growth from 1850 to 1900. What five or more events indicate rapid population growth in the West? Explain.

Projects and Activities

1. Select a city from the political map of the United States on pages 900–901. Do research on that city's history from 1850 to the early 1900s. What geographic, economic, social, and political forces shaped its growth? Present your findings as a report or a poster.

2. Work in groups of four or five. Each group is to write the "Ten Commandments of Big Business" from the point of view of one of the following: a robber baron, a Populist, a labor union member. After each group reads its list to the class, compare the points of view.

3. In groups of five, do research to find out what was happening in the Scandinavian countries, eastern and southern Europe, China, and Japan which led to migration to the United States. Each group can make an annotated map of the world showing events causing emigration from each of these areas.

Using the Time Line. Invent three characters who might have lived between 1850 and 1910. These people are to represent three generations of the same family. Using events shown on the time line, write a sketch of the life of each character, showing how their lives differed from each other because of the times in which they lived.

Milestones	1850	1865
Presidents	Fillmore; Pierce; Buchanan; Lincoln	A. Johnson; Grant
Political and Economic	• Gadsden Purchase • Pikes Peak Gold Rush • Homestead Act • First department store	• Chisholm Trail opens • U.S. buys Alaska • National Grange organized • Yellowstone Park
Social and Cultural	• Levi Strauss first manufactures jeans • First kindergarten in U.S. • *The Song of Hiawatha*, Longfellow • *My Bondage, My Freedom*, Frederick Douglass	• *The Rocky Mountains*, Albert Bierstadt • First Horatio Alger story • *The Luck of Roaring Camp*, Bret Harte
Technological and Scientific	• Safety elevator, Elisha Otis • Plate glass developed • First oil well, Pennsylvania • Pony Express	• Congress authorizes metric system • First transcontinental railroad • Celluloid, the first plastic • Brooklyn Bridge

Assessment

Ask students where they have seen murals (public buildings) and what they usually depict (historical events, patriotism, heroism). Ask why murals are usually in public places (to teach, inspire, praise, reflect political values).

In the 1700s and 1800s, large wall paintings were popular in homes but were not often found in public buildings. John Trumbull's paintings in the Capitol were an exception. Murals at the Columbian Exposition (see Epilogue) aroused interest and prompted a flurry of mural painting in state buildings. Between 1910 and the New Deal, interest in murals declined.

Scoring

To create a scoring system, or rubric, assign an achievement scale to each of the evaluation criteria. For example, you might evaluate "Communicating Ideas" on a scale of 0 to 4 as follows:

4—Exemplary response: the scene immediately conveys the story of an individual or group in pursuit of opportunity in the years between 1850 and 1890. It suggests activity. All of the elements—main images, setting, details—contribute to the story. The symbols used enhance comprehension.

3—Good response: the scene suggests the story of an individual or group in pursuit of opportunity in the years between 1850 and 1890. The setting helps viewers understand the story. Details enhance the telling of the story.

2—Adequate response: the scene represents an appropriate individual or group but may offer minimal information. Some elements—setting, details, symbols—may not provide sufficient clues; the scene may have to be explained.

1—Poor response: the work may be unfinished, contain static images, lack a setting or details that provide context.

0—No response/inappropriate response.

Follow-up Activity

Class discussion. Have students discuss the following, citing examples from the mural. How do individual efforts affect national growth? How can national interests influence individual choices?

Assessment: Demonstrating What You Know

Creating a Mural

Your class has been hired to create a mural for the World's Columbian Exposition, to open in Chicago in 1893. Your mural will reflect the theme "The Search for Opportunity: 1850–1890."

With the class, make a list of situations in which people sought opportunity in those years. Consider, for example, railroads, homesteading, immigration, business, industry, labor organization, Plains Indians' ways of life. Each situation will be represented by one scene, which will tell the story of a person or a small group pursuing opportunity. Together, the scenes will make up the mural.

Before forming small groups to produce the scenes, agree on the size of the completed mural and calculate the size of the individual scenes. Establish a standard height for figures representing the average adult.

Form groups of two or three. Before you begin your illustration, consider these questions:

1. What situation are you representing?
2. Whom are you showing in that situation?
3. What is that person doing? Does the activity tell the story of a search for opportunity?
4. How does the person look? What clothing and hairstyle are appropriate for that person?
5. Where does the story take place? Will the setting tell the viewer something about opportunity?
6. What objects, images, or symbols will help the viewer understand the person's story?

Evaluation Criteria

Your work will be evaluated according to how well you meet the following criteria.

- **Completing the task**. You complete a scene for the class mural, following size guidelines set by the class. You and your partner or partners share ideas. Your scene portrays a search for opportunity in the years from 1850 to 1890.
- **Knowing history**. Your illustration represents the real struggles of many people. Details and setting are historically accurate, based on information from your text or other sources.
- **Thinking critically**. You use appropriate activities, objects, and settings to convey ideas. Your scene stands for real life events.
- **Communicating ideas**. You take into consideration that murals are usually viewed from several feet away, and you produce clear, bold images. Details are simple and can be seen from a distance. The scene tells a story.

1880 — 1895 — 1910

Hayes | Garfield | Arthur | Cleveland | Harrison | Cleveland | McKinley | T. Roosevelt

- The Great Railroad Strike
- Dawes Act
- Standard Oil trust
- Oklahoma Land Rush
- Wounded Knee
- AFL organized
- Brooklyn, Bronx, Queens become part of New York City
- U.S. Steel organized as a holding company

- Tennis introduced in U.S., Mary Outerbridge
- First Labor Day Parade, N.Y.
- First hockey league, Canada
- Statue of Liberty dedicated
- Ellis Island opens
- Columbian Exposition opens
- *The Call of the Wild*, Jack London
- *The Great Train Robbery*, first film with a story

- Barbed wire, Joseph Glidden
- First skyscraper, 10-story Home Insurance Building, Chicago
- Telephone, Alexander Graham Bell
- Bessemer I beams, steel beams for construction
- *Report on the Lands of the Arid Region*, John Wesley Powell
- Light bulb, Thomas Edison
- First transatlantic radio signal
- Rayon patented, Arthur Little

435

Unit 6

Objectives

- Identify the changes that the progressives sought to bring about.
- Explain how Presidents Roosevelt, Taft, and Wilson carried out a progressive agenda.
- Identify arguments for and against expansion beyond North America.
- Explain the effects of American expansion and of the Spanish-American War on U.S. foreign policy.
- Tell how the U.S. got involved in WWI and explain the effects of that war on Americans.

Introducing THE UNIT

During the second half of the nineteenth century, rapid industrialization stimulated a booming economy in the United States. However, waves of immigration and the rapid growth of cities created social problems and led to efforts at reform.

Meanwhile, the expansion of power abroad was a major theme in the U.S. Interested in foreign markets and territory, the U.S. reached outward, acquiring possessions in the Pacific and Caribbean and seeking commercial opportunities in China. Concern with Latin America led to continued American intervention in the Caribbean. When Europe plunged into WWI, the U.S. at first sought to maintain neutrality, but later joined the struggle and brought about the defeat of Germany.

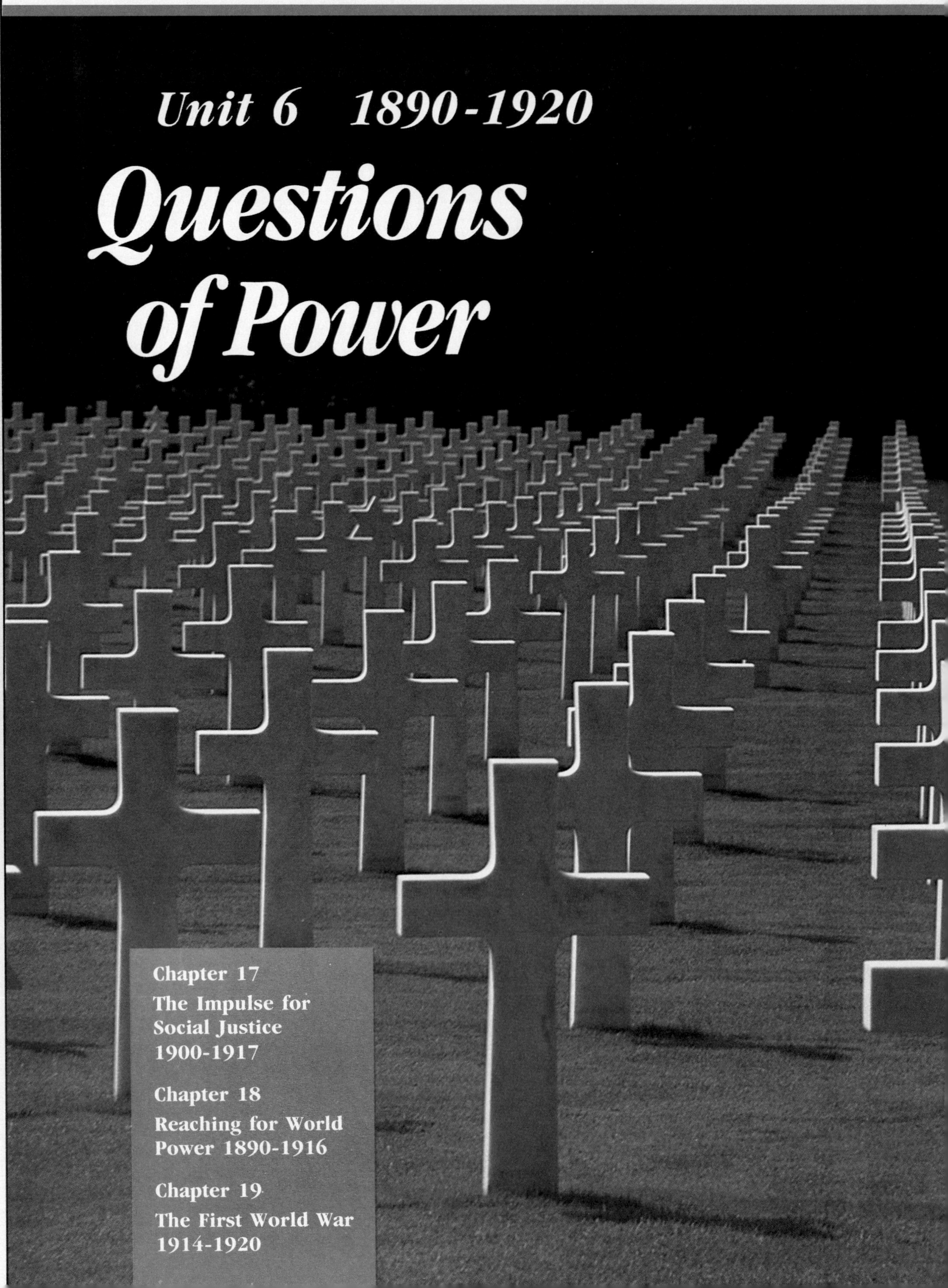

Unit 6 1890-1920

Questions of Power

Connections: Music

As American public opinion about the war in Europe shifted from watchful waiting to active participation, popular songs reflected the change. Before the declaration of war, many Americans had joined in the pacifist song "I Didn't Raise My Boy to Be a Soldier." Then, as United States involvement escalated, popular songwriters and entertainers "did their bit for the cause" by writing patriotic songs.

One such popular figure was George M. Cohan (1878–1942), prominent in American theater in the early 1900s. Cohan wrote dozens of plays and musicals, and directed, produced and starred in many of them. Several of his spirited songs—such as "You're a Grand Old Flag" and "I'm a Yankee Doodle Dandy"—had patriotic content. "Over There" became the most popular American patriotic song of World War I, and was later sung during World War II as well.

Guided Reading

Discussion. Direct students to pay attention to the patriotic language in the songs. What values do the songs emphasize? What imagery do the writers invoke? How does Dalton Trumbo take the same or similar images and call them into question?

History Through Literature

War erupted in Europe in 1914. When it was no longer possible to remain neutral, President Wilson asked Congress for a declaration of war in 1917. Appealing to American ideals, he described German actions as "warfare against mankind" and declared it the responsibility of the United States to fight for no less than "the ultimate peace of the world and for the liberation of its people." Like Wilson, songwriters in the early phases of the war sought to inspire both soldiers and civilians with the noble purpose of American participation in the war.

However, Allied victory in 1918 did not make the world safe for democracy. Nor did World War I prove to be the "war to end all wars." Bitter disillusionment replaced early optimism in the works of many writers. Among them was Dalton Trumbo (1905-1976). In his novel *Johnny Got His Gun,* the narrator is a blind and deaf quadriplegic wounded in the war. Trumbo, who also wrote screenplays, turned his book into an award-winning film in 1971.

"Keep The Home Fires Burning"

by Lena Guilbertford

They were summoned from the
hillside,
They were called in from the glen,
And the country found them ready
At the stirring call for men.
Let no tears add to the hardship
As the soldiers pass along,
And although your heart is breaking
Make it sing this cheery song.

Over seas there came a pleading,
"Help a nation in distress,"
And we gave our glorious laddies,
Honor bade us do no less.
For no gallant son of freedom
To a tyrant's yoke should
bend,
And a noble heart must answer
To the sacred call of "Friend."

Chorus

Keep the home fires burning,
While your hearts are yearning,
Though your lads are far away,
They dream of home.
There's a silver lining,
Through the dark cloud shining.
Turn the dark cloud inside out,
Till the boys come home.

437

"Over There"

by George M. Cohan

Johnnie get your gun, get your gun, get your gun,
Take it on the run, on the run, on the run,
Hear them calling you and me,
Ev'ry son of liberty.
Hurry right away, no delay, go today,
Make your daddy glad to have had such a lad,
Tell your sweetheart not to pine,
To be proud her boy's in line.

> Over there, over there,
> Send the word over there
> That the Yanks are coming,
> The drums rum tumming
> ev'rywhere,
>
> So prepare, say a prayer,
> Send the word to beware,
> We'll be over, we're coming over
> And we won't come back till it's over,
> Over there, over there.

Johnnie get your gun, get your gun, get your gun,
Johnnie, show the Hun you're a son of a gun,
Hoist the flag and let her fly,
Yankee Doodle do or die.
Pack your kit, show your grit, do your bit,
Yankees to the ranks from the towns and the tanks,
Make your mother proud of you
And the Red, White and Blue.

from

Johnny Got His Gun

by Dalton Trumbo

Did anybody ever come back from the dead any single one of the millions who got killed did any one of them ever come back and say by god I'm glad I'm dead because death is always better than dishonor? Did they say I'm glad I died to make the world safe for democracy? Did they say I like death better than losing liberty? Did any of them ever say it's good to think I got my guts blown out for the honor of my country? Did any of them ever say look at me I'm dead but I died for decency and that's better than being alive? Did any of them ever say here I am I've been rotting for two years in a foreign grave but it's wonderful to die for your native land? Did any of them say hurray I died for womanhood and I'm happy see how I sing even though my mouth is choked with worms?

(Background) American 3rd Army cemetery, Luxembourg; (this page) recruitment poster, World War I helmet; (opposite) "Soldier in WWI," by Sir William Orpen.

438

Connections: Literature

Dalton Trumbo published his novel *Johnny Got His Gun* in 1939, looking back at World War I at a time when many artists and writers were questioning the effectiveness of the government in meeting social needs. Because many film directors, actors, and writers took an interest in communism in the 1930s, this community came under suspicion by the House Un-American Activities Committee (HUAC) during the period of anti-Communist hysteria following World War II. Trumbo was one of the "Hollywood Ten," ten Hollywood screen writers and directors who were subpoenaed by HUAC in 1947. Like the others, Trumbo served a jail term for contempt of Congress. His career revived with the enormous success of the film *Spartacus*, for which he had written the screenplay.

Nobody but the dead know whether all these things people talk about are worth dying for or not. And the dead can't talk. So the words about noble deaths and sacred blood and honor and such are all put into dead lips by grave robbers and fakes who have no right to speak for the dead. If a man says death before dishonor he is either a fool or a liar because he doesn't know what death is. He isn't able to judge. He only knows about living. He doesn't know anything about dying. If he is a fool and believes in death before dishonor let him go ahead and die. But all the little guys who are too busy to fight should be left alone. And all the guys who say death before dishonor is pure bull the important thing is life before death they should be left alone too. Because the guys who say life isn't worth living without some principle so important you're willing to die for it they are all nuts. And the guys who say you'll see there'll come a time you can't escape you're going to have to fight and die because it'll mean your very life why they are also nuts. They are talking like fools. They are saying that two and two make nothing. They are saying that a man will have to die in order to protect his life. If you agree to fight you agree to die. Now if you die to protect your life you aren't alive anyhow so how is there any sense in a thing like that? A man doesn't say I will starve myself to death to keep from starving. He doesn't say I will spend all my money in order to save my money. He doesn't say I will burn my house down in order to keep it from burning. Why then should he be willing to die for the privilege of living? There ought to be at least as much common sense about living and dying as there is about going to the grocery store and buying a loaf of bread.

And all the guys who died all the five million or seven million or ten million who went out and died to make the world safe for democracy to make the world safe for words without meaning how did they feel about it just before they died? How did they feel as they watched their blood pump out into the mud? How did they feel when the gas hit their lungs and began eating them all away? How did they feel as they lay crazed in hospitals and looked death straight in the face and saw him come and take them? If the thing they were fighting for was important enough to die for then it was also important enough for them to be thinking about it in the last minutes of their lives. That stood to reason. Life is awfully important so if you've given it away you'd ought to think with all your mind in the last moments of your life about the thing you traded it for. So did all those kids die thinking of democracy and freedom and liberty and honor and the safety of the home and the stars and stripes forever?

You're goddam right they didn't.

Taking a Closer Look

1. *How do the songs appeal to both personal and national honor?*
2. *Why do you think Trumbo called his novel* Johnny Got His Gun?
3. *How might Woodrow Wilson have responded to the narrator of* Johnny Got his Gun?

Taking a Closer Look

ANSWERS

1. Both songs praise the intentions of the country in entering the war. "Keep the Home Fires Burning" portrays the country as answering the call of a friend in need. They appeal to personal honor in praising individual soldiers, "sons of liberty," or "glorious laddies," and parents and sweethearts are encouraged to suppress any sorrow and be proud of the soldiers. "Over There" makes joining up the honorable thing to do, to make parents proud and to be a part of a winning cause.
2. The title *Johnny Got His Gun* is an wry reference to Cohan's "Over There." While the song illustrates pre-war optimism, the book expresses post-war disenchantment.
3. Answers will vary. Students may want to mention Wilson's carefully thought out rationale for entering the war; the Fourteen Points, and Wilson's faith in democracy. In opposition the narrator calls these ideals "words without meaning." Wilson might answer that they do justify the nation going to war and sacrificing young lives.

Chapter 17

The Impulse for Social Justice

Planning Guide

	Student Text	TWE Lesson Plans	Support Materials
SECTION 1	**Section 17–1 (1–2 Days)** **The Progressive Movement**, pp 442–449 Young in America: At Play, pp 450–451 Review/Evaluation Section Review, p 449	**Introducing the Chapter:** Predicting Social, Political, and Economic Issues—Class Activity, 40 minutes, p 439B **Teaching the Main Ideas:** Initiating Reform Through Legislation—Cooperative Activity, two class periods, p 439B **Evaluating Progress:** Making Others Aware—Individual Activity, one class period, p 439C	★ **Read to Remember,** Section 1 ● **Section Activities,** Section 1 ● **Geography Activities,** Section 1 Δ **Enrichment Activities,** Section 1 Δ **Readings** ● **Tests and Quizzes,** Section 1 Quiz
SECTION 2	**Section 17–2 (1–2 Days)** **A Reform-Minded President**, pp 452–457 Exploring Issues—Labor Disputes: The Cloakmakers' Strike, p 454 Review/Evaluation Section Review, p 457	**Enrichment Activity:** What Would They Think Today—Individual Activity, introduction 20 minutes, homework, p 439C	★ **Read to Remember,** Section 2 ● **Section Activities,** Section 2 Δ **Enrichment Activities,** Section 2 Δ **Readings** ● **Tests and Quizzes,** Section 2 Quiz
SECTION 3	**Section 17–3 (1–2 Days)** **The Triumph of Progressivism**, pp 458–463 Connections to Themes: Shaping Democracy, p 463 Review/Evaluation Section Review, p 463 Chapter 17 Survey, pp 464–465 Skills, pp 464–465 Using New Vocabulary Thinking Critically Using a Time Line Applying Thinking Skills: Interpreting Political Cartoons Writing About Issues	**Teaching the Main Ideas:** Reform Today—Cooperative Activity, homework, half class period, p 439C **Reinforcement Activity:** Who Was the Most Progressive?—Cooperative Activity, one class period, p 439C	★ **Read to Remember,** Section 3 ● **Section Activities,** Section 3 ● **Tests and Quizzes,** Section 3 Quiz, Chapter 17 Test (Forms A and B) **Additional Resources** Δ **Twentieth Century Issues: Links to the Past** ● **Active Learning** Δ **GTV Videodiscs** Δ **Transparencies and Activity Book** ● **Testing Software** ★ **Chapter Summaries** **Key:** ★ For Extra Support ● For All Students Δ For Enrichment

Overview

The progressive reformers of the early twentieth century were mainly white, middle-class, urban citizens. Attacking many of the social ills that had arisen out of rapid industrialization, they focused on alleviating poverty, restoring free enterprise, and wresting the power of government from political machines and the influence of big business and returning it to the people. These reformers worked for such causes as woman suffrage, temperance, and abolition of child labor, as well as for changes in city and state government. African-American citizens also sought reform, concentrating on civil rights.

Filled with the progressive spirit, President Theodore Roosevelt, a Republican, sought to regulate trusts, increase government involvement in labor disputes, protect consumers, and conserve natural resources. William Howard Taft, Roosevelt's Republican successor, also supported reforms. Despite a dispute with progressives over the tariff, Taft proved even more of a trustbuster than Roosevelt.

Conflict between supporters of Roosevelt and supporters of Taft led to a split in the Republican party, with Roosevelt forming a third party—the "Bull Moose" party. Helped by this split, Democrat Woodrow Wilson won the presidency in 1912. He, too, backed progressive reforms, including further antitrust legislation, lower tariffs, and the Federal Reserve System, which gave government greater control of banking. During Wilson's presidency, two progressive reforms were written into the Constitution as amendments—a graduated income tax and direct election of senators.

Activity Objectives

After completing the activities, students should be able to

- identify the major goals and methods of the progressives.
- compare progressive movements with present-day reform movements.
- compare the accomplishments of Presidents Roosevelt, Taft, and Wilson.
- analyze social issues of concern to progressives.
- evaluate the legacy of the early conservationists.

Introducing the Chapter

Predicting Social, Political, and Economic Issues

This class activity requires two-thirds of a class period.

This activity stimulates interest by asking students to check their own predictions against actual occurrences.

Tell students that between the Civil War and the turn of the twentieth century, the United States was transformed from an agricultural to an industrial society. This transformation produced both benefits and problems. By the early 1900s, large numbers of Americans were seeking reforms to correct the social, political, and economic problems that had arisen. Remind students that they studied the origins of many of these ills in Chapters 13, 14, 15, and 16.

Divide the class into groups of four or five. Have students use knowledge gained in their study of previous chapters to predict issues that would concern turn-of-the-century reformers. Ask each group to list five issues, citing events from the last half of the nineteenth century to support their choices.

Reconvene the class. Discuss the groups' choices and compile a class list. Select one or two students as scribes, to record the class's predictions so that when students have completed Chapter 17, they can compare their predictions to topics discussed in the text. (Remind students that the text may not include every possible reform issue.)

Tell students that about 1905 some reformers began to refer to themselves as progressives. Ask students what ideas they associate with the word *progressive* (forward-looking, making progress, improvement). Ask what this label tells about how the reformers saw themselves. When students have completed Chapter 17, ask if their assessment of the turn-of-the-century reformers was confirmed.

Teaching the Main Ideas

Section 17-1: Initiating Reform Through Legislation

This cooperative activity requires two class periods.

This role-playing activity encourages students to view social problems from the perspective of progressives by proposing legislation to alleviate problems.

Ask students to identify concerns of reformers in the early 1900s and list these issues on the chalkboard. The list may include corruption in government, poor working conditions and overlong work hours, child labor, slums, monopolies and trusts, impure foods and drugs, women's right to vote, lynching, new purposes and methods in education, alcoholism, juvenile justice, and the civil rights of African Americans and other ethnic groups.

Divide the class into groups of five. Explain that each group is to select one issue discussed in Section 17-1, identify a problem related to that issue, and propose a solution to the problem. Remind students that the progressives usually tried to bring about change through legislation. Each group should formulate its proposal as a city ordinance, a state law, or a federal law and provide reasons why the lawmakers should enact the proposed legislation.

Convene the class as a lawmaking body and have one or more representatives from each group present their proposal and arguments. After all proposals have been presented, inform the class that "legislative overload" will allow the governing body to accept only two proposals. Have the lawmakers vote for the two best proposals and discuss the reasons for their choices.

Teaching the Main Ideas

Section 17-3: Reform Today

Most of this class activity can be assigned as homework, but at least half a class period is required for discussion.

In this activity students collect and display information about present-day reform movements. This activity will be most effective if it is assigned when students begin reading Chapter 17 and is continued as students read the chapter.

Call on students to give examples of present-day efforts at reform. Then direct each student to find three newspaper or magazine articles that describe current reform efforts.

On the assignment's due date, divide the class into groups and have each group review their articles and place them into categories of reform. Then have the class as a whole decide on six or seven categories into which all the articles can be organized and display the articles accordingly. Encourage students to continue to add to the display.

Conclude the activity by asking students to compare the concerns of reformers today with the concerns of the progressives. How are they similar? Which issues were resolved as a result of progressive reforms? How have concerns changed?

Reinforcement Activity

Section 17-3: Who Was the Most Progressive?

This cooperative activity requires one class period.

In this activity students compare the accomplishments of Presidents Roosevelt, Taft, and Wilson as measured by a progressive yardstick. Students must have read the entire chapter before participating in the activity.

Remind students that three Presidents—Roosevelt, Taft, and Wilson—presided over the country during the progressive era. Ask them to indicate by a show of hands which of the three they believe most closely fulfilled progressive ideals. Divide the class into three groups based on their choices. If there are more than eight students in a group, subdivide the group.

Direct the groups to justify their choice for "most progressive president" by preparing a position statement. First, they are to establish a set of criteria for judging "progressiveness" that reflects the values of progressives. Then they are to give examples to prove that their presidential choice meets their criteria. Allow half a class period for students to develop criteria and identify examples.

Have each group read its position statement to the class. Direct other students to accept or challenge the criteria set by each group, then to accept or challenge the group's presidential choice. Conclude by summarizing the characteristics that defined a progressive politician in the early 1900s.

Evaluating Progress

Section 17–1: Making Others Aware

This individual activity can be assigned as homework; one class period is required for presentations.

In this activity students analyze social issues of concern to progressives by preparing and presenting public service announcements.

Begin the activity by discussing with students the nature and purpose of a public service announcement: a statement of a social problem, a proposed solution or action, and a call for participation. Encourage students to describe examples of public service announcements that they have heard on the radio or seen on television (drug prevention, automobile safety, AIDS, etc.). Explain that radio and television stations often broadcast worthy announcements without charge.

On the chalkboard write the following topics:

- education
- the "new" woman
- labor
- city, state, or federal government
- civil rights of ethnic groups

Divide the class into groups of four or five to prepare and present a one-minute radio or television announcement on one of the topics listed. Direct the groups to choose a topic, define an issue related to it, offer a stand on the issue or a solution to a related problem, and create an announcement to persuade others to accept their point of view. Tell students that their solutions should reflect the methods that progressives used.

Encourage students to capture attention with a succinct and striking statement or slogan. Groups presenting television announcements should provide one or more pictures or other graphics.

Have members of each group read or perform their announcement for the class. Ask the class what they would understand about a topic if all they knew about it came from the announcement. Does the announcement clearly state the issue? Why or why not?

Group performances should be evaluated on how accurately students state an issue and outline a solution and how convincingly they call for participation in a solution.

Enrichment Activity

Section 17-2: What Would They Think Today?

This individual activity requires half a class period for introduction; the remainder may be assigned as homework.

This activity engages students in evaluating the legacy of early conservationists. The activity may be extended by having students do research outside of the text to learn more about current efforts.

Remind students that President Roosevelt's ideas about natural resources and conservation were greatly influenced by Gifford Pinchot and John Muir. Review with students the ideas that these two men expressed about preservation of the environment and use of resources.

Have students imagine that they are either Pinchot or Muir, returned briefly to the United States in the present time. The two naturalists observe people's attitudes toward the environment and assess efforts to deal with it in the years since they died. Direct students to write a letter from the point of view of either man, summarizing his past recommendations and his observations about how his views are or are not being implemented today.

After students complete their letters, discuss with the class the influence Pinchot and Muir may have had on present-day environmental practices.

Bibliography and Audiovisual Material

Teacher Bibliography

Hofstadter, Richard. *The Age of Reforms: From Bryan to F.D.R.* New York: Random House, Inc., 1960.

Kraditor, Aileen S. *The Ideas of the Woman Suffrage Movement, 1890–1920.* New York: W.W. Norton & Co., 1981.

Painter, Nell Irvin. *Standing at Armageddon: The United States, 1877–1919.* New York: W.W. Norton & Co., 1987.

Pinchot, Gifford. *Breaking New Ground.* Covelo, CA.: Island Press, 1987.

Singer, Ray. *Age of Excess: The United States from 1877–1914.* Prospect Heights, IL.: Waveland Press, Inc., 1989.

Steffens, Lincoln. *The Autobiography of Lincoln Steffens.* 2 vols. San Diego: Harcourt Brace Jovanovich, Inc., 1968.

Thelen, David. *Robert M. LaFollette and the Insurgent Spirit.* Madison: University of Wisconsin Press, 1986.

Student Bibliography

Dreiser, Theodore. *The Titan.* New York: NAL/Dutton Co., 1965.

Du Bois, W.E.B. *Souls of Black Folk.* New York: Bantam Books, Inc., 1989.

Fox, Stepehen R. *John Muir and His Legacy: The American Conservation Movement.* Boston: Little, Brown & Co., 1981.

Gilman, Charlotte Perkins. *Her Land: A Lost Feminist Utopian Novel.* New York: Pantheon Books, 1979.

Sinclair, Upton. *The Jungle.* New York: NAL/Dutton Co., 1989.

Steffens, Lincoln. *The Shame of the Cities.* New York: Hill & Wang, 1957.

Terrell, Mary Church. *A Colored Woman in a White World.* Salem, N.H.: Ayer Co. Publishing, Inc., 1980.

Van Voris, Jacqueline. *Carrie Chapman Catt: A Public Life.* New York: Feminist Press, 1987.

Films, Videocassettes, and Videodiscs

American Heritage Media Collection: The Confident Years. 35 min. Westport Media. Videocassette.

Technology in America: The Age of Material Progress. 18 min. Coronet Film and Video. Videocassette.

Theodore Roosevelt. 26 min. MCGH. Movie.

Woman in American Life series: 1880–1920: Immigration, New Work and New Roles. 16 min. National Women's History Project. Videocassette.

Woodrow Wilson. 26 min. MCGH. Movie.

Filmstrips

Famous American Presidents: The Life of Theodore Roosevelt. 7 min. 1 filmstrip, cassette. SVE.

Leaders in Social Reform. 4 color filmstrips, 4 cassettes, guide. Encyclopaedia Britannica.

Chapter 17

Objectives

- Describe the aims and methods of the progressives.
- Explain the progressive reforms advocated by Roosevelt.
- Relate the accomplishments of the progressives during the Taft and Wilson administrations.

Introducing THE CHAPTER

For suggestions on introducing Chapter 17, refer to page 439B in the Teacher's Edition.

Developing THE CHAPTER

For activities and teaching strategies to help you reinforce and enrich chapter content, see pages 439B–439D in the Teacher's Edition.

B · A · C · K · G · R · O · U · N · D

Chapter Opener Illustrations

The first bicycle was invented about 1790 by a Frenchman. Bicycles—high-wheelers—were first made in the U.S. in 1878. In 1885 the safety bicycle was invented in England. By 1897, 4 million Americans were riding bicycles.

In this 1901 painting Maurice Prendergast depicts playground activity at New York City's East River. Many progressive reformers urged the construction of city parks and playgrounds as antidotes to the overcrowding, filth, ugliness, and despair of industrial cities.

The Triangle Fire killed 146 workers. Doors had been locked from the outside to prevent workers from leaving the building. After the tragedy, New York City passed laws to upgrade building codes and to outlaw locking the doors of

Reduced student page in the Teacher's Edition

Chapter 17 1900-1917

The Impulse for Social Justice

Maurice Prendergast: *The East River* (1901)

workplaces from the outside.

Theodore Roosevelt became President as the nation entered the twentieth century. He was the youngest—and probably the most energetic and most athletic—U.S. President. Confident and assertive, Roosevelt generated excitement and stirred enthusiasm in others.

Ben Shahn's mural shows members of the Women's Christian Temperance Union, protesting in front of a saloon.

Wilson's 1912 campaign button described him as "The Man of the Hour" because he supported programs of current concern such as the regulation of big business and reform of United States monetary policies.

American Voices

In 1911 a fire raged through New York's Triangle Shirtwaist Company. The women who worked there were trapped in the blazing building because stairways were narrow, fire escapes had collapsed, and exits were locked. Social worker Frances Perkins witnessed the scene:

> "*We saw the smoke pouring out of the building. We got there just as they started to jump. . . . They came down in twos and threes, jumping together in a kind of desperate hope.*
>
> *The life nets were broken. The firefighters kept shouting for them not to jump. But they had no choice; the flames were right behind them. . . .*
>
> *Out of that terrible episode came a self-examination . . . in which the people of this state saw for the first time the individual worth and value of each of those 146 people who fell or were burned . . .*
>
> *There was a stricken conscience of public guilt and we all felt that we had been wrong, that something was wrong with that building which we had accepted or the tragedy never would have happened.*"

"Out of the ashes of the tragedy," wrote Perkins, "rose the Factory Investigating Commission. It led the state legislature to pass tough protective laws." In the early 1900s, all across the United States, people were moved to correct injustices. This stirring flowered into a nationwide reform movement known as progressivism.

Demorest touring bike; New York at the turn of the century; Triangle Shirtwaist Factory fire, New York, 1911; Theodore Roosevelt; W.C.T.U. parade, from a mural by Ben Shahn; Wilson campaign button.

Analyzing Primary Sources

American Voices

Frances Perkins was a New York progressive who headed the New York State Industrial Board from 1926 to 1929. She went on to become the Secretary of Labor in Franklin D. Roosevelt's administration, the first woman to hold a cabinet position.

1. Why did the women jump to their deaths? **(trapped; stairways were narrow, fire escapes had collapsed, and exits were locked)**
2. Why was there "a stricken conscience of public guilt" after the fire? **(accepted faulty building)**
3. Why didn't state or federal governments have stricter building codes? **(laissez-faire philosophy)**
4. How much did the interpretation of the Constitution have to do with incidents such as this? **(strict interpretation—limited role of government)**
5. What good result came out of this disaster? **(laws to regulate safety conditions)**

Section 17-1

Objectives

- ***Answer the Focus Question.***
- *Describe the aims and methods of the progressive educators, muckrakers, and women suffragists.*
- *Relate reforms that progressives accomplished on state and local levels.*
- *List the goals of the NAACP.*

Introducing

THE SECTION

Ask students the following questions, drawing upon prior knowledge. What were some of the problems facing cities after the Civil War? Factories? How did the aftermath of the Civil War play a part? Industrialization? Are there any other factors that may have caused these problems?

Tell students that in this section they will study how a group of middle class reformers—progressives—concentrated on improving social problems through political reforms.

B · A · C · K · G · R · O · U · N · D

Time Line Illustrations

1. In 1904 Debs ran for President as candidate for the Socialist party. Socialists adopted many programs of the populists, but they also advocated public ownership of the means of production and distribution, and the destruction of capitalism. American voters rejected the most radical of the socialist programs and gave Debs only 2.98 percent of the popular vote.

2. Sinclair's 1906 exposé of the meat-packing industry captivated the American people and was made into a film. Sinclair became a socialist and ran for the House and Senate and for governor of California. His political career was never as successful as his writing career.

3. California's redwood forests became a symbol of the need to preserve the nation's resources.

4. Published by the NAACP, *The Crisis* magazine spread

CHAPTER TIME LINE

1900 - 1917

1906 *The Jungle* published; Pure Food and Drug Act

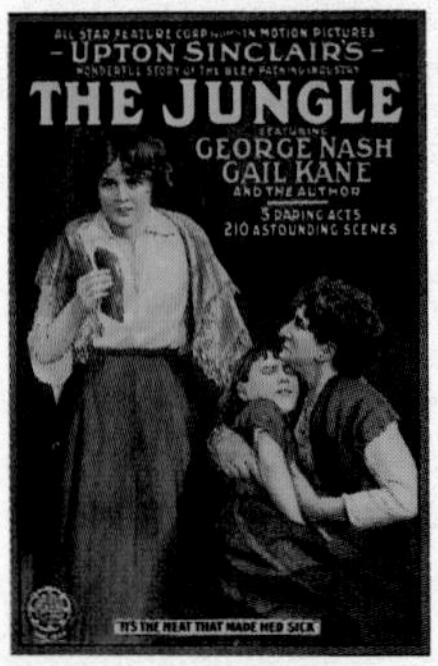

1902 Coal miners' strike begins in Pennsylvania

1900 — 1904 — 1907

1901 Socialist Party organized

1904 National Child Labor Committee formed

1908 White House Conservation Conference

17-1 The Progressive Movement

Focus: What changes did the progressives want to make and how did they expect to bring them about?

At the opening of the twentieth century, the economy was booming, and new technology flourished. The rapid industrialization that brought such progress, however, also created serious social problems. Wealth and power were concentrated in the hands of a few, and poverty and political corruption were widespread.

As people became aware of these problems, a new reform movement was born. Unlike populism, which had been a movement of farmers grown desperate as the economy sank into depression, the new reform movement arose in the cities among the prosperous middle class. These people were confident that they could achieve social progress through political reform. They became known as progressives.

Progressivism

Progressivism was a combination of many small movements. Most progressives concentrated on a specific concern—woman suffrage, child labor, education, alcohol, or the power of giant corporations. However, in general they focused their efforts on three aims: helping the poor by improving working conditions and cleaning up slums, prying government out of corruption's grip and returning it to the people, and ending business abuses that brought wealth to the few and destroyed free enterprise.

The muckrakers. Journalists first sounded the alarm. In 1900 alone more than 150 magazine articles exposed the threat that trusts posed to Amerinews of the plight of African Americans and was, from 1910 to 1932, edited by W.E.B. DuBois. The magazine reflected DuBois's position that blacks should militantly struggle for equality.

5. Like the Republicans and Democrats, the Progressive party of 1912 had an animal, the bull moose, as its symbol. This cartoon reflects the dominance of the Progressive or Bull Moose party by Theodore Roosevelt.

6. Perhaps Wilson's most enduring domestic achievement as President was the establishment of the Federal Reserve System. The Federal Reserve issues paper currency called Federal Reserve notes. A serial number, letter, and seal all appear on the notes. This is how the seal looked on a 1914 Federal Reserve note.

1909 NAACP formed

1913 **Feb** Sixteenth Amendment permits income tax
Dec Federal Reserve Act

1910 — 1913 — 1917

1911 Standard Oil Company dissolved

1912 Progressive, or Bull Moose, party formed

1914 Clayton Antitrust Act

1917 Prohibition amendment passes Congress

can society. In that year magazine publisher Samuel McClure asked writer Ida Tarbell to get the true story behind the Standard Oil trust. The result was a series of shocking articles that revealed Standard Oil's cutthroat practices. Tarbell wrote:

> *“Mr. Rockefeller has systematically played with loaded dice, and it is doubtful if there has ever been a time since 1872 when he has run a race with a competitor and started fair. Business played in this way loses all its sportsmanlike qualities. It is fit only for tricksters.”*

McClure's Magazine also featured articles on police corruption written by Lincoln Steffens and on dishonest mine workers' union leaders by Ray Stannard Baker. In an editorial, McClure wrote, "Capitalists, workers, politicians, citizens—all breaking the law, or letting it be broken. Who is left to uphold it? . . . There is no one left," he continued, "none but all of us."

The stories in *McClure's* caused a sensation. Other magazines rushed to print their own exposés. Journalists investigated lynching, false advertising, bribery in the Senate, and a host of other evils.

In 1906 Theodore Roosevelt compared investigative reporters to a character in John Bunyan's *Pilgrim's Progress* who did nothing but rake filth and muck, never looking up. Such people, said Roosevelt, "are often indispensable to the well-being of society, but only if they know when to stop raking the muck." The name "muckrakers" took hold. The muckrakers rarely offered solutions, but they made Americans aware of society's ills.

Progressive Education

Many progressives thought that the best way to reform society was through its schools. Public education had grown rapidly since the Civil War. Between 1870 and 1900, the number of children who attended school had increased from 57 percent to 72 percent. And most of these students attended tax-supported public schools.

Developing

THE SECTION

Linking Past and Present

Discussion. Refer students to Roosevelt's quotation on this page. Tell them that Roosevelt went on to say a person who continually searches for faults was *"not a help to society, not an incitement to good, but one of the most potent forces of evil."* **Ask:** Was Roosevelt justified in his opinion? Explain. Do we have anything similar to muckrakers today? When do such people help or when do they harm our society?

Thinking Critically

Synthesis. In 1906 the National Woman Suffrage Association petitioned the President and Congress for a Constitutional amendment, but it was unsuccessful as were several later petitions.

Ask: Why do you think woman suffrage came later than other reforms women supported? (Politics still considered male domain, women were to be more interested in moral causes.) Why did western states tend to give the vote to women earlier than eastern and southern states? (Women scarcer in the West so were more valued. In the West more likely all hands were needed to survive, so women's contributions were viewed as essential.)

Multicultural Perspectives

Few muckrakers dealt with racial discrimination. One notable exception was Ray Stannard Baker, whose *Following the Color Line* reported on segregation and racial discrimination in the United States. Another was Narcisco Gonzales, who founded *The State*, a South Carolina newspaper in 1891. His editorials condemned child labor and lynching, and supported women's right to vote.

Limited English Proficiency

Building Vocabulary. Help students define the idiom "grass-roots campaigns" used on this page. Ask students how they think the term originated and have them use it in another context. **(Term refers to the common people, especially of rural or nonurban areas, hence "grass.")**

Reduced student page in the Teacher's Edition

Progressives had new ideas about the purpose of education. It was not only to prepare an individual to earn a living, they said, but also to prepare the student to play a constructive role in a democratic society.

Traditional teaching methods had stressed memorization. To show what they had learned, students recited lessons in arithmetic, history, and geography. But progressive educators like John Dewey believed that children learned best by participating in a wide variety of experiences. In laboratories, kitchens, gymnasiums, and gardens—as well as in classrooms—students would work on projects, learning at their own pace. In the process they would learn to think for themselves and to take responsibility for their community.

These progressive ideas had a strong influence on education, even outside the borders of the United States. They would remain the strongest influence in American education throughout the first half of the twentieth century.

"The New Woman"

The drive to reform education found strong support among women. In fact, women had taken an active role in every reform movement in the nation's history. They had worked to establish public education in the first place. They had been abolitionists and had founded the first settlement houses for tenement dwellers. Now women plunged into the progressive movement, too.

The so-called "new woman" of the progressive years was from the middle or upper class. She had been freed from day-long housework by canned foods, factory-made clothing, and labor-saving devices. Many women used their new free time to join clubs that focused on special issues such as education, child labor, and temperance.

American Voices

"A Congressman is a green toad on a green tree, a brown toad on a brown tree. He reflects his constituents."

—Carrie Chapman Catt

The temperance movement drew many progressives who believed that outlawing liquor would reduce crime and poverty. The Women's Christian Temperance Union (WCTU) attracted hundreds of thousands of members. Following president Frances Willard's motto, "Do everything," the WCTU did more than campaign against liquor. It set up reform schools for girls, gave textbooks to schools, and worked for causes from suffrage to public drinking fountains.

Liquor still flowed, however, in states where it was legal, and into states where it was banned. The WCTU began to argue that nationwide action was needed if liquor was to be outlawed effectively.

Woman suffrage. Another cause to which many women were deeply committed was woman suffrage. Progressive women saw that if they could vote, they could advance progressive causes by helping to elect reform candidates.

The new leader of the woman suffrage movement was Carrie Chapman Catt. Catt had risen through the Iowa school system, from teacher to principal to superintendent of schools, the first woman to hold such a high position in school administration. She mapped out a new strategy for the suffrage movement. Instead of trying to win support from the President and Congress, Catt advocated building support at the local and state levels through grass-roots campaigns.

Catt and her followers applied the new strategy in New York. There, Harriot Blatch, daughter of Elizabeth Cady Stanton, organized parades and rallies and formed the first suffrage group to include working-class women. Suffrage bills were defeated two times—once by the state legislature, and once by the voters. But with constant publicity, thousands of meetings, millions of leaflets, and a million signatures on a petition, the women of New York finally gained the vote in 1917.

Protecting the Worker

Meanwhile public-spirited women were joining their male counterparts in advancing another progressive cause: making the work place safer. Millions of workers yearned for better pay, shorter

Social History

Leaders like Carrie Chapman Catt pictured on page 447 argued that women, due to their role as mothers and wives, were more moral and pure than men, making them better able to straighten up the mess that men had made in politics. While this view increased support for suffrage, it also reinforced the prevailing stereotype of women.

Connections: Politics

In 1913 attorney Alice Paul organized the National Woman's Party, which worked for women's rights including suffrage. She later wrote the first version of the Equal Rights Amendment, which she submitted to Congress in 1923.

Writing About History

Newspaper Article. Muckraking articles helped ignite the progressive movement. Have students write an article about a condition in business or government (local, state, or national) that they think should be changed. They should include facts, not just opinions, to support their positions.

Suggested topics: homelessness, child abuse, poverty among single parents, crime, drugs, savings and loan failures, drunk driving, pay and job discrimination, toxic wastes.

In the progressive era woman suffrage groups encouraged physical fitness, while enlightened factory owners provided humane conditions for their women workers.

hours, and safer working conditions. Writer Robert Hunter sympathized with their situation. In his 1904 book, *Poverty,* he wrote:

> *" On cold, rainy mornings, at the dusk of dawn, I have been awakened, two hours before my rising time, by the monotonous clatter of hobnailed boots on the plank sidewalks. . . . Heavy, brooding men; tired, anxious women; thinly dressed, unkempt little girls; and frail, joyless little lads passed along, half-awake, not one uttering a word as they hurried to the great factory. "*

Whereas unions used strikes and collective bargaining to protect workers, the progressives tried different tactics. They believed that the solution lay in pressing government to pass protective laws.

One of the first goals was to end child labor. In the early 1900s, nearly 1.5 million children under sixteen years of age toiled in America's factories and mines. They worked ten to thirteen hours a day, earning as little as sixty cents a day.

"March of the Mill Children." In 1901 an Alabama minister, Edgar Murphy, organized the Child Labor Committee to demand government action. The committee had an ally in "Mother" Jones, the famous labor activist. In 1903 Mother Jones organized 300 child workers from Pennsylvania textile mills for a march to the home of President Theodore Roosevelt in New York. Leading the march were children carrying signs that said, "We Want to Go to School" and "Prosperity, Where Is Our Share?"

Thousands witnessed this "March of the Mill Children." As their cries for reform joined the voices of the muckrakers, the social workers, and others, the campaign began to produce results. Pennsylvania, New Jersey, and New York soon passed child labor laws. Between 1902 and 1909, laws limiting or banning the hiring of children were passed in twenty-three states.

Thinking Critically

Analysis. Read aloud or write on the chalkboard this description of city governments by Lincoln Steffens:

"Corruption was not merely political, it was financial, commercial, social, the ramifications of boodle (bribery) were so complex, various, and far reaching that one mind could hardly grasp them."

Ask: What is the tone and main idea of this quotation? Why would the tasks of reforming the cities seem almost impossible? Would getting rid of corrupt politicians do the job? What else would have to be done?

Linking Past and Present

Discussion. Have students study the "parade" of reformers across the bottom of these pages. **Ask:** What reforms are represented? What adjectives would you use to describe the spirit (feelings) of the reformers?

If students were to plan a "parade" representing the same sort of spirit of reform today, what issues would they address? Who would they include?

Connections: Politics

Cities grew rapidly in the early part of the century. American municipal governments had not been set up to handle traffic, sanitation, crime and fire safety problems on such a large scale. Brand Whitlock, a disciple of Samuel M. Jones who became mayor of Toledo after Jones's death in 1904, wrote: *"The American city is not fundamentally democratic, because it is governed from without. . . . Cities are ruled by legislatures from the State capital; they are governed, that is, by men from the country who know nothing of city problems or city life, and have no real conception of just what cities need. In league with them . . . are the public utility corporations and political machines. The first requisite, therefore, for municipal reform, is home rule."*

Reform in City Hall

As progressives turned to city and state governments, they often found that these governments were inefficient and corrupt. Political machines ran many cities and states, and government officials too often put their own interests ahead of the interests of the public. Disgusted, reformers vowed that the citizens themselves would take action. In city after city, progressives formed civic groups to demand improvements, such as police protection and better lighting systems. They also worked to rid cities of political machines.

Toledo, Ohio, was one of the first to be touched by reform. In 1897 Toledo voters elected reformer Samuel M. Jones as mayor. Jones hung a sign in his office bearing the Golden Rule: "Do unto others as you would have them do unto you."

When Jones took office, Toledo's public utilities—trolleys, waterworks, electric plants, telephones—were almost all privately owned. They charged high rates but gave poor service. Jones believed that services "necessary to the welfare of the whole family [city] . . . can only be successfully operated by the family." He fought to place public services under city control.

In San Francisco, New York, Jersey City, St. Louis, and Cleveland, other progressive mayors also battled corruption. However, reform meant more than a new mayor. In some cases it meant changing the form of government itself. Galveston, Texas, for example, devised a new government in 1900, after a flood ruined the city. The task of rebuilding was placed in the hands of a group of elected commissioners instead of a mayor. Under this **commission system,** each commissioner was responsible for a separate function, such as safety, finance, or public health. Some 200 cities soon adopted the commission system.

In 1914 Dayton, Ohio, adopted a council-manager form of government. An elected city council made policy but hired a professional executive, a **city manager,** to manage day-to-day business. Because the manager was not elected, he or she was free from political pressures. This system spread to hundreds of cities.

Reform in the Statehouse

Progressives too often found their attempts to improve city government blocked by the state. Thus they broadened their goals to include defeating state political machines, some of which were in the hands of powerful interest groups.

Wisconsin's legislature was controlled by a political machine which was, in turn, controlled mainly by railroads and lumber companies. The machine's fiercest opponent was Robert M. La Follette, a lawyer with strong convictions and determi-

Senator Robert La Follette (left) championed railroad regulation and conservation. Wealthy reformers and working-class labor leaders together formed the National Women's Trade Union League.

446

Connections: Politics
La Follette was a district attorney and then served three terms in Congress, being defeated in 1890. In 1891 Sen. Philetus Sawyer, a millionaire in the lumber industry and boss of Wisconsin's Republican party, offered La Follette a bribe. La Follette reported the bribe to the newspapers. Sawyer, who denied the charge, tried unsuccessfully to destroy La Follette's political career. La Follette was elected governor in 1900, 1902, and 1904. In 1906 he was elected to the Senate. In 1924 he ran for President as a Progressive.

nation to match. La Follette ran for governor of Wisconsin twice. Twice, the machine helped to defeat him. Unfazed, "Battling Bob" ran a third time in 1900. This time he swept into office on the progressive tide. He wanted, he said, to "go back to the first principles of democracy. Go back to the people."

Through three terms, Governor La Follette fought the Wisconsin machine. The machine usually nominated candidates for public office at a party convention attended mainly by machine followers. La Follette dealt the system a major blow by establishing the **direct primary,** an election in which candidates for public office are chosen by a direct vote of the people.

In 1906 La Follette moved on to the United States Senate. But his reform movement continued. For example, Wisconsin accepted La Follette's proposal of a graduated personal income tax. "Battling Bob," said Theodore Roosevelt, had turned Wisconsin into a "laboratory of democracy."

Reform in other states. Wisconsin's successes inspired progressives in other states. New Yorkers elected Charles Evans Hughes governor after he exposed corruption in that state's insurance companies. Californians chose Hiram Johnson because he would fight the powerful Southern Pacific Railroad, which had a grip on state government.

Behind the political reforms lay one main goal: to give people greater participation in government. By 1916 most states had adopted at least one of the reforms described in the chart on page 448.

States also adopted social reforms. In some states, workers' compensation laws provided income for workers injured on the job. Other new laws protected children. For example, children who committed crimes had always been treated like adults in court and in jail. Jane Addams and others pressed for more humane treatment of juvenile offenders. In 1899 Illinois set up special juvenile courts, and the idea spread to other states.

Even when states did pass reform laws, however, they were not always enforced. Florence Kelley, a social worker at Hull House, described a large sign put up by reformers in Philadelphia in 1907:

> *"Pennsylvania—*
> *Children employed, 40,140.*
> *Children Illegally Employed, 3,243.*
> *Prosecutions, 22."*

"The next step which we need to take," wrote Kelley, "is to insist that this is a national evil, and we must have a national law abolishing it." Having grappled with reform in city halls and state houses, the progressives were now setting their sights on Congress and the White House.

The NAACP fought lynching by taking legal action and by arousing public opinion. Carrie Chapman Catt organized woman suffrage campaigns both in the United States and abroad.

Analyzing Primary Sources

Florence Kelley. Discuss the quotation by Florence Kelley on this page. **Ask:** Why does Kelley insist that illegal employment of children "must be considered a national evil"? Why does she call for a national law to deal with illegal employment of children? Based on this quotation, what view of the federal government does she support? **(Students should note that Kelley, and other progressives, looked to the national government to solve economic and social problems that the state governments could not or would not remedy.)**

Active Learning

Cooperative Activity. Have the class list problems facing children today. The list will probably include poverty, child abuse, education, child labor, drugs, child care, peer pressure, one-parent families. Then divide the class into groups of four. Each group is to write a reform program to remedy at least two problems.

After completing the activity, the groups can present their programs to the class. Discussion of their recommendations should follow, and the class can arrive at a consensus for a reform program for each problem addressed.

Using the Visuals

Building Vocabulary. Refer students to the chart on this page. Discuss the role of the citizen in each process. Have them summarize in a one-sentence statement the apparent purpose behind all these reforms. What do they have in common? **(Each gives people greater participation in government.)**

Thinking Critically

Synthesis. Tell students that one of the ironies of this period is that it was a time of reform but lynching of African Americans reached a high of 79 in 1915 and riots erupted among some African Americans in Georgia, Texas, and Illinois. The first lynching of an African American outside of the South occurred in August 1911 in Pennsylvania.

Ask: Why would these acts of violence occur in the North? Why did progressives in both the Democratic and Republican parties tend to ignore these incidents?

Linking Past and Present

Debate. A major issue among African Americans in the early part of the century was segregated vs. integrated education for blacks. Today, groups such as the NAACP uphold the demand for integrated education, but others call for segregated all-black schools that emphasize the history and culture of African Americans. Have students research these viewpoints and debate them.

Multicultural Perspectives

African-American publisher William Monroe Trotter stirred opposition to Booker T. Washington. In his Boston newspaper, the *Guardian*, he charged that Washington was too complacent about worsening racial conditions and hypocritical for emphasizing economic over political gains for others while enjoying considerable political power himself.

Social History

Boxer Jack Johnson defeated Tommy Burns in 1908 to become the first African American to be world heavyweight champion. Some enraged white Americans urged former champion Jim Jeffries out of retirement in 1910 to reclaim the title. The bout reflected the racial tensions of the times; Johnson's defeat of Jeffries set off race riots. Johnson retained the title until 1915.

Reduced student page in the Teacher's Edition

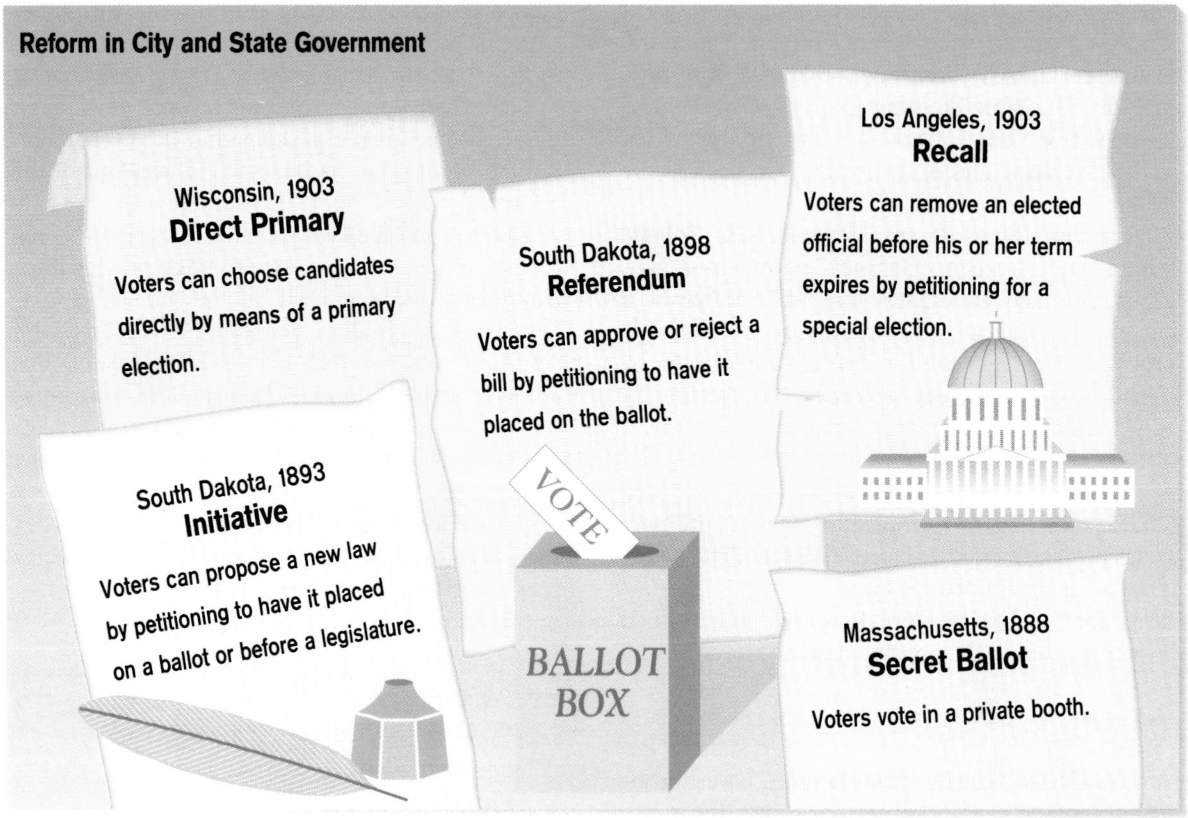
Reform in City and State Government
Wisconsin, 1903
Direct Primary
Voters can choose candidates directly by means of a primary election.
South Dakota, 1898
Referendum
Voters can approve or reject a bill by petitioning to have it placed on the ballot.
Los Angeles, 1903
Recall
Voters can remove an elected official before his or her term expires by petitioning for a special election.
South Dakota, 1893
Initiative
Voters can propose a new law by petitioning to have it placed on a ballot or before a legislature.
VOTE
BALLOT BOX
Massachusetts, 1888
Secret Ballot
Voters vote in a private booth.

African Americans Unite

Concerned with government corruption, business abuses, and unsafe working conditions, most progressives ignored the plight of African Americans. Thus, blacks looked to their own leaders—notably Booker T. Washington and W.E.B. Du Bois.

In his 1903 book, *The Souls of Black Folk*, Du Bois wrote of the despair of African Americans:

> *"One ever feels his two-ness—an American, a Negro; two souls. . . . He simply wishes to make it possible . . . to be both a Negro and an American, without being cursed and spit upon by his fellows, without having the doors of opportunity closed roughly in his face."*

Those doors had been slammed by Jim Crow segregation laws in the South and by similar discrimination in the rest of the country.

Although they both wished to foster opportunity for African Americans, Washington and Du Bois followed very different paths. If blacks work for economic independence and moral self-improvement, Washington predicted, "the time will come when the Negro . . . will be accorded all the political rights which his ability, character, and material possessions entitle him to."

Du Bois acknowledged Washington to be "the most striking figure in the history of the American Negro since 1876." But he criticized Washington for his passive methods, for being willing to postpone black political rights, and for accepting segregation. Speaking for members of the Niagara Movement in 1905, Du Bois declared:

> *"We want full manhood suffrage and we want it now. . . . We want the Constitution of the country enforced. . . . We want our children educated. . . . We are men! We will be treated as men. And we shall win."*

Global Connections

The Mexican Revolution, which occurred at this time, changed the character of the American Southwest. The majority of immigrants who fled the chaos involved in the revolution were agricultural workers. They provided the cheap labor that southwestern agriculture and industry so badly needed. Some found jobs in mining and railroads, but the majority were farmers. Like their African-American counterparts they encountered prejudice and were trapped by low wages and a system of debt peonage.

Despite such appeals, blacks continued to suffer unjust and violent treatment. Most victims of the lynchings that plagued the country were black. And when African-American newspaper editor Ida Wells-Barnett charged whites in a lynching of three blacks, her presses were wrecked and her life threatened. She courageously continued her crusade, however, writing and speaking against lynching and other injustices to blacks.

W.E.B. DuBois edited **The Crisis** *"to set forth those facts and arguments which show the danger of race prejudice."*

In 1908 a lynch mob terrorized a black neighborhood in Abraham Lincoln's home town, Springfield, Illinois. Shocked, progressives Jane Addams and John Dewey and muckrakers Lincoln Steffens and Ray Stannard Baker offered their help. Du Bois and other African Americans welcomed this support. The mixed group called for a new organization, saying, "If Mr. Lincoln could revisit this country in the flesh, he would be disheartened."

In 1909—on the hundredth anniversary of Lincoln's birth—the group formed the National Association for the Advancement of Colored People (NAACP). The Niagara Movement, which had seemed too radical to many people, was absorbed into the NAACP, and W.E.B. Du Bois served on the organization's first board of directors. The NAACP's goals were to stamp out lynching, work through the courts to protect the civil rights of African Americans, campaign for state and federal laws enforcing these rights, and educate the public about race relations.

In 1916 Joel Spingarn, chairman of the NAACP, called a conference. There, conservative and radical African-American leaders hammered out their differences, agreeing on education and political rights as their goals. By the end of the decade, the NAACP was firmly established as a nationwide organization, with more than 90,000 members. Today, with 400,000 members, it is still an important voice for the rights of black Americans.

Intelligent and energetic, Mary Church Terrell was a leader in the woman suffrage movement and helped to organize the NAACP.

Section Review

1. Identification. Define *commission system, city manager, direct primary, initiative, referendum, recall,* and *secret ballot.*

2. Comprehension. Explain three major aims of the progressive movement. What was the chief means by which the progressives expected to bring about changes?

3. Analysis. What was the relationship of each of the following to the progressive movement: muckrakers, John Dewey, NAACP, woman suffrage supporters, Mother Jones?

4. Synthesis. Based on your reading, create a believable progressive. Include the person's chief concern, why he or she became concerned, and how he or she expects to remedy the situation.

Linking Past and Present. Do research to compare your high school curriculum with the typical high school curriculum in 1900. How might you explain the changes that have occurred?

Writing About History

Biography. The progressive movement produced a number of prominent and influential women. Have students write biographical reports on one of the following: Ida Tarbell, Jane Addams, Frances Willard, Frances Perkins, Carrie Chapman Catt, Mother Jones, Ida Wells Barnett, Florence Kelley, Lillian Wald, Julia Lathrop. Students can share their information with the class.

Section Review

ANSWERS

1. Definitions are on text pages indicated in parentheses: *commission system* (446), *city manager* (446), *direct primary* (447), *initiative* (448), *referendum* (448), *recall* (448), *secret ballot* (448).

2. Helping the poor by improving working conditions and cleaning up slums; wiping out corruption in government; ending business abuses. Chief means: political reforms.

3. Muckrakers: investigated and wrote to expose evils of society; Dewey: advocate of progressive education; NAACP: fought for African-American equality; woman suffrage supporters: fought to get vote for women, who would support other progressive causes; Mother Jones: fought to better workers' conditions

4. Answers will vary. The person could be chiefly concerned about government reform, education, women's rights, African-American rights, or working conditions; could be a worker or union organizer, a woman seeking the vote, an African American, or an educator; could hope to achieve goals through NAACP, militant unionism, the ballot, political organizations, improving education.

Linking Past and Present: Answers will vary.

Linking Past and Present

Discussion. Have students compare the clamp-on roller skates shown on this page with skates of today. Have the use of skates changed over time? **(Skates today are a means of transportation as well as recreation.)**

Connections: Science and Technology

Few toys are ever made of glass because of their fragility. Marbles are the exception. The swirl designs inside the marbles illustrated were made by glassmakers heating and twisting bundles of long, colored glass rods, called canes, and then enclosing them in clear glass. Today, most marbles are made by automated machinery.

Reduced student page in the Teacher's Edition

Created in 1889, the Flexible Flyer was a steerable sled with runners of flexible steel.

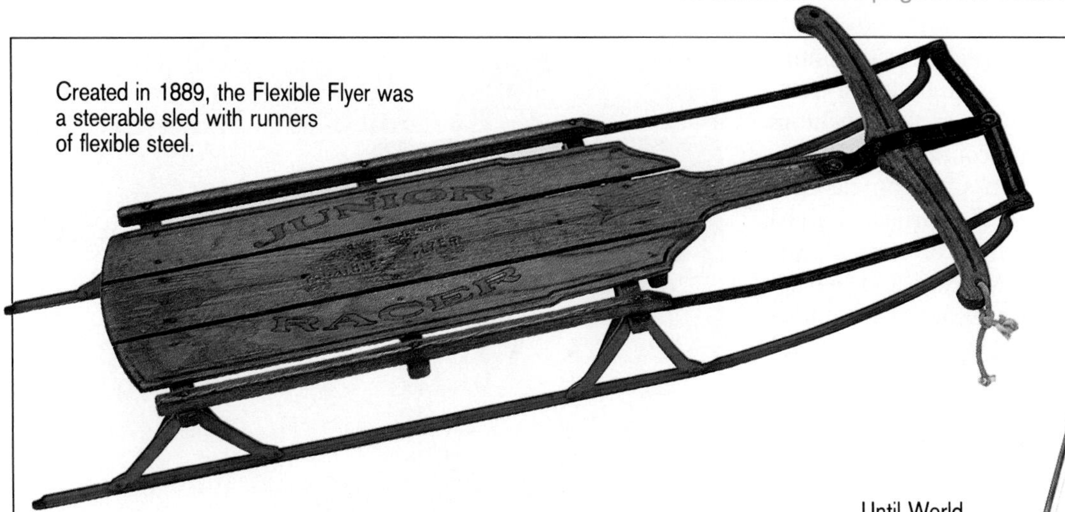

Going to the circus was more popular in the early 1900s than ever before —or after.

Until World War I, most marbles were imported from Germany.

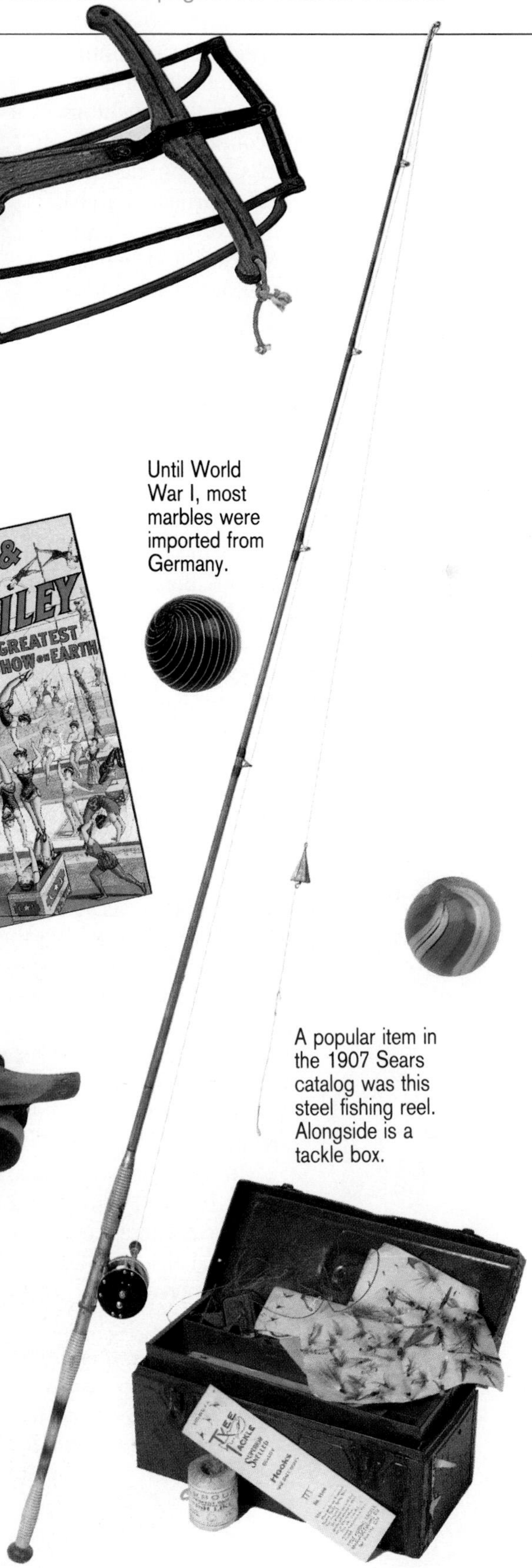

A popular item in the 1907 Sears catalog was this steel fishing reel. Alongside is a tackle box.

Jumping rope, playing checkers, and skating were favorite pastimes. Skaters used clamp-on roller skates with wooden wheels.

450

Connections: Literature

Ben Hur, written by Lew Wallace, was published in 1880. It sold 250,000 copies between 1880 and 1890; one million copies between 1890 and 1900, and eventually between four and five million by 1970. In 1896 it was the most widely circulated book in eight out of ten libraries. Sears, Roebuck, and Company sold over one million copies through their catalog.

Mary Roberts Rinehart, author of *The Circular Staircase,* was born in 1876 in Pittsburgh, Pennsylvania, where she studied nursing. Her first mystery novel was published in 1908, the last in 1953.

Multicultural Perspectives

Research. Jackie Robinson broke the color barrier in modern major league baseball when he was signed by the Brooklyn Dodgers on April 10, 1947. By the 1970s African Americans played on every team in the league as did players from Puerto Rico, the Dominican Republic, Venezuela, and other parts of Latin America.

Have interested students research African-American and Hispanic-American baseball players who have been voted into the Baseball Hall of Fame, such as Satchel Paige and Juan Marichal.

young IN AMERICA

At Play

In the half century after the Civil War, Americans went sports mad. College football gained enormous popularity, and baseball became the "national pastime." New sports, such as basketball and volleyball, were invented. Roller skating was the rage. And bicycling, especially on Sunday, turned into the greatest craze of the 1890s despite preachers' warnings that "you cannot serve God and skylark on a bicycle."

New toys and games were also created during these times. Children played with teddy bears—named after Teddy Roosevelt—and the first die-cast toy cars. They delighted in the first chemistry sets and board games, such as Parcheesi. But older pastimes, many of which are shown here, remained well loved.

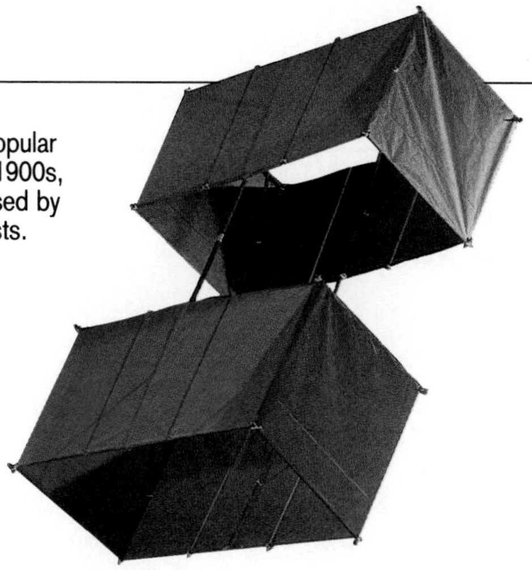

Box kites, popular in the early 1900s, were also used by meteorologists.

Thousands read religious novels like *Ben Hur* and mysteries like *The Circular Staircase.*

Photographs seen through a stereoscope had a three-dimensional effect.

By 1900 the National and American baseball leagues had been formed. Excluded from play, African Americans organized their own professional teams, leagues, and world series.

Section 17-2

Objectives

- ***Answer the Focus Question.***
- *Explain Roosevelt's attitude toward trusts and describe what actions he took to regulate them.*
- *Describe what measures Roosevelt supported with regard to labor disputes, regulation of railroads, regulation of food and drugs, and conservation.*
- *Evaluate Roosevelt's accomplishments as a progressive.*

Introducing
THE SECTION

Have students refer to the picture of Theodore Roosevelt on this page and on page 457. Ask students their impressions of the man **(enthusiastic; dynamic, for example).** Then have students read the short quotation on the page. **Ask:** Does the quotation support your perceptions of Roosevelt? Why would a man with Roosevelt's personality and philosophy be suited for the progressive movement? Would Roosevelt's philosophy fit in with the ways of living today? Tell students they will study how Theodore Roosevelt put his distinctive imprint on progressive reforms.

B · A · C · K · G · R · O · U · N · D

Connections: Politics

The Sherman Antitrust Act was passed by Congress in 1890. Until Roosevelt's time the act, which outlaws "combination . . . , or conspiracy, in restraint of trade or commerce," had usually been invoked against labor unions, seldom against business. In the few cases that were prosecuted, courts had interpreted the law in favor of big business. In the first case to reach the Supreme Court—*United States* v. *E.C. Knight Co.*—the Court ruled that manufacturing was not commerce, so the Sherman Act did not apply to E.C. Knight, which monopolized sugar refining. Roosevelt said that with such laissez-faire interpretation the *"courts . . . had for a quarter of a century been . . . the agents of reaction and by conflicting decisions . . . had left both the Nation and the States well-nigh impotent to deal with the great business combinations."*

Reduced student page in the Teacher's Edition

17-2 A Reform-Minded President

Focus: What progressive reforms did the federal government carry out under Theodore Roosevelt?

"Get action; do things; be sane; don't fritter away your time; create, act, take a place . . . and be somebody; get action."

Theodore Roosevelt advised others to live an active life, and he followed his own creed. A dynamic leader, he brought new energy to a White House that had been occupied by a series of cautious Presidents.

When President McKinley defeated Bryan and the Democrats for a second time in 1900, Roosevelt was his running mate. Then, in September 1901, only six months into his second term, McKinley attended a public reception in Buffalo. A man later judged to be insane fired two bullets from a hidden revolver. McKinley died eight days later, and Roosevelt found himself President.

Roosevelt: A Man of Action

Roosevelt, the son of a wealthy family, was a man of action. Sickly as a boy, he turned himself into an athlete and outdoorsman. He boxed, rode horses, played tennis, climbed mountains, and explored jungles. He toured Europe and the Middle East. Yet he also loved quieter pursuits—history, literature, and science. As he studied and thought, he developed a strong moral code. His religion, he said, consisted of "good works," and he decided early in his life to devote himself to public service.

At age forty-two, Roosevelt was the youngest man ever to be President. But he came to the office as an experienced leader. He had been police commissioner of New York City, a member of the United States Civil Service Commission, Assistant Secretary of the Navy, and governor of New York.

Members of the press make notes as a vigorous Theodore Roosevelt delivers a speech. "No President has ever enjoyed himself as much as I have," he said later.

Trustbusting

Roosevelt relished being President at a time when change was sweeping the country. He was eager to plunge into domestic policy and the progressive drive for social justice.

When Roosevelt took office, one of his first priorities was to loosen the stranglehold that trusts had on American business. But although he gained a reputation as a "trustbuster," his goal was to regulate the trusts, not to break them up. In his first annual message to Congress, in December 1901, he said:

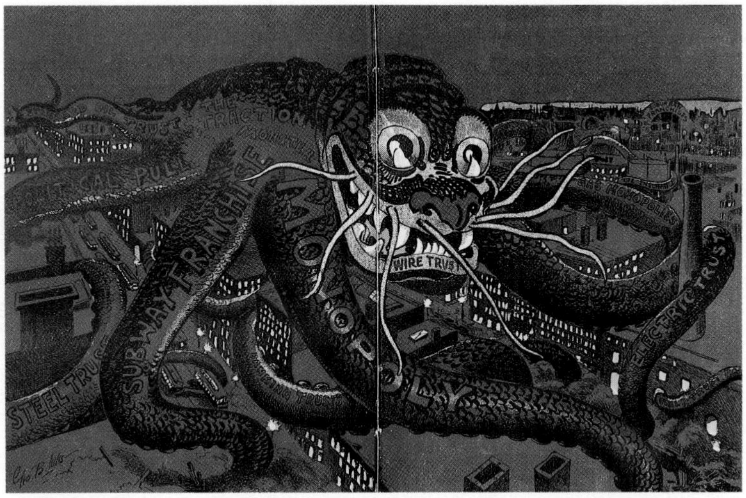

George Luks's cartoon "The Menace of the Hour" expressed the public view of trusts as hideous monsters.

> *"The captains of industry . . . have, on the whole, done great good to our people. Without them the material development of which we are so justly proud could never have taken place. . . . [But] there is a widespread conviction in the minds of the American people that the great corporations known as trusts are . . . hurtful to the general welfare. . . . [This opinion is] based on the conviction that . . . concentration should be, not prohibited but supervised and within reasonable limits controlled; and in my judgment this conviction is right."*

To control trusts, Roosevelt decided to apply the Sherman Antitrust Law of 1890. Most previous government attempts to enforce the law had been blocked by the courts. But Roosevelt was determined. He ordered his attorney general to file suit against the Northern Securities Company, a huge holding company created in 1901 by the merger of three railroads — the Northern Pacific, the Great Northern, and the Chicago, Burlington, and Quincy. The company had a monopoly on such a large part of the national railroad system that it had nearly eliminated all competition in transportation services.

Northern, headed by financier J. P. Morgan, fought the suit. In 1904, however, the Supreme Court upheld the government's view and broke up the holding company. Wall Street, the nation's financial center, was outraged. *The Detroit Free Press* commented sarcastically: "Wall Street is paralyzed at the thought that the President of the United States could sink so low as to try to enforce the law."

The successful enforcement of the Sherman Antitrust Act put other trusts on notice. The government went on to file forty-four suits against such giants as the beef, tobacco, and oil trusts.

Meanwhile, at Roosevelt's request, Congress created a new cabinet-level department — the Department of Commerce and Labor. The department would include a Bureau of Corporations to supervise the conduct of big business.

The Coal-Miners' Strike

Roosevelt also made government a force in settling labor disputes. The federal government had intervened in disputes in the past, but usually by sending troops to control the strikers. When more than 140,000 Pennsylvania coal miners walked off the job in the spring of 1902, Roosevelt took a different approach.

The miners' hours were long, their pay low, and their work dangerous. They were striking in order

Developing
THE SECTION

Thinking Critically

Evaluation. Refer students to the statement on this page by Roosevelt concerning trusts. **Ask:** What is Roosevelt's view of big business? (supported business) How does Roosevelt believe trusts should be "busted"? (regulate them) Why might some big businesses have supported government interference? (Reforms satisfied public protest, regulation and quality control drove many small producers out of business, gave business a greater say in politics.) Discuss whether present government regulation hurts or helps big business.

Connections: Economics

Debate. Have students debate: Big corporations are a threat and should be broken up. A good example is AT&T. Did the break up of AT&T benefit the consumer? Students should consult the *Readers Guide to Periodical Literature* for information on this topic.

Active Learning

Cooperative Activity. Divide the class into teams of six to negotiate work issues. Three students of each team are to represent labor and three are to represent management. Each team is to select one of the industries students have studied: for example, mining, textiles, oil, steel, meatpacking.

Each team will have four issues to discuss: hours, wages, working conditions, open shop. Allow the labor and management sides of each team to meet separately to discuss what position they will take on each issue.

Have students come back into their teams to negotiate the issues. After negotiations are ended, teams should present their results to the class.

Social History

Lincoln Steffens gave his view of how the slogan "A square deal all around" came into being. The journalist, in a conversation, reproached the President, "You don't stand for anything fundamental. All you represent is the square deal." "That's it," Roosevelt jumped up and shouted, "That's my slogan: the square deal." What was intentionally a put-down became an effective campaign slogan.

Connections: Music

During this period of strikes, a number of songs were written to raise the spirits of weary strikers. The most popular songwriter was Joe Hill, a member of the radical International Workers of the World (IWW). His most popular song was "Hallelujah, I'm a Bum", but "There is Power in a Union" had a rousing chorus for picket marchers:

to call attention to their demands for a raise and an eight-hour day. They also wanted management to recognize and bargain with the United Mine Workers union, led by John Mitchell.

Management refused to negotiate. The strike dragged on through the summer and fall. As winter and cold weather approached, the nation's coal supplies dwindled. "The situation became so grave that I felt I would have to try . . . something," explained Roosevelt.

On October 1 Roosevelt invited the owners and union leaders to the White House to discuss their differences. Mitchell agreed to arbitration, but the mine owners refused to "deal with outlaws" and demanded that federal troops be sent in to put down the strike.

Furious at the owners, Roosevelt threatened instead to send federal troops to seize and run the mines. The owners backed down and agreed to federal arbitration, and the miners went back to work. In March 1903 the arbitration board announced its verdict. The miners were given a 10-percent raise in pay and a nine-hour day. But the union was not to be given formal recognition.

The nation had coal in time for winter. Later, Roosevelt said that he had simply been trying to give both miners and owners a "square deal." The phrase caught on as a description of Roosevelt's administration.

The Square Deal

In the election campaign of 1904, Roosevelt was determined to become "President in his own right." His Democratic opponent, Judge Alton B. Parker, a conservative from New York, campaigned against government interference in the economy. Roosevelt was careful to say nothing to anger corporate leaders. Even his campaign button spoke to all Americans with the slogan "A square deal all around."

Roosevelt triumphed, winning by the largest margin in history. He saw his victory as a vote against laissez-faire views, and he vowed to continue his progressive reforms.

First on Roosevelt's square-deal program was regulation of railroads. Railroad companies were still being accused of charging most shippers un-

Exploring Issues
LABOR DISPUTES

The Cloakmakers' Strike

At two o'clock on July 7, 1910, the streets of New York City's garment district began to fill with workers. They streamed out of dingy workrooms where they spent their days cutting and stitching cloaks and suits. Before the day was over, more than 60,000 cloak and suitmakers had left their jobs. It was the beginning of a long and bitter strike that would make history.

Conditions were harsh. The workers—mainly new Jewish and Italian immigrants—labored in crowded, poorly lit shops that were often infested with rats and cockroaches. During the slow season, the workers sat at their jobs nine or ten hours a day. In rush periods they worked up to sixteen hours. Wages were barely enough to live on. Men earned from $10 to $20 a week, women as little as $3 or $4. Out of their salaries, they bought their own machines and supplies.

The workers were striking for higher wages, a forty-eight-hour week, and extra pay for overtime. More important, they wanted the right to have the cloakmakers' union speak for them.

At first, most manufacturers refused to deal with the union. They told workers that "employers were their best friends." As the days wore on, however, the employers were losing millions of dollars in business. By late July they were ready to talk.

There is pow'r, there is pow'r
In a band of workingmen,
When they stand hand in hand,
That's a pow'r, that's a pow'r
That must rule in every land—
One Industrial Union Grand.

In 1915 Joe Hill was accused of killing a Salt Lake City grocer. Despite a lack of direct evidence linking him with the crime, Hill was found guilty. Although the governor of Utah received thousands of letters of protest, Hill was executed by firing squad. Before his death, Joe Hill wrote, *"Don't waste any time in mourning. Organize."*

Louis Brandeis, a brilliant Boston lawyer who would later become a Supreme Court justice, was called in to bring the two sides together. With Brandeis' help, labor and management settled wage and hour questions. But then they reached a deadlock.

The workers demanded a closed shop, in which only union members could be hired. The employers insisted on an open shop, where they would be free to hire anyone they pleased. The open shop, they argued, gave every person the freedom "to work for whom he will for such prices as he is willing to accept."

The strikers disagreed. "Should we accept your proposition," said one union leader, "that is, having non-union [people] working hand-in-hand with us, then we will lose our organization, as every organization was lost that went into deals like you are trying to make us go into."

Brandeis proposed a compromise. He called it the "preferential union shop." Under this plan, management would hire union people first and non-union workers only if no qualified union members were available.

At first union members feared employers would use the plan to break the union. It was merely "the open shop with honey," said one. However, in September the union accepted the Brandeis plan. Although the workers had not won a closed shop, the agreement gave them higher wages, a fifty-hour week, and extra pay for overtime. It also set up a board to inspect sanitary conditions and worker-management committees to settle disputes. The workers agreed to take their complaints to these committees instead of striking. Both sides agreed to the preferential union shop.

As word spread, garment workers poured into the streets. "Men and women, young and old, hugged and kissed and congratulated each other," one striker remembered. Although the issue of the open and closed shop was only temporarily settled, a vital process had been established. In one of the first instances of collective bargaining in American history, management and organized labor had sat down together to work out their differences.

1. What were the main issues in the strike?
2. The issue of the open and closed shop is still debated. Describe the open shop, closed shop, and preferential union shop. Which do you think is best for labor? For management? For the public?
3. How does collective bargaining work? Is it effective? Why or why not?

Louis Brandeis was known as the "people's attorney" because he believed modern business must be concerned with working conditions as well as profit.

Linking Past and Present

Discussion. Tell students that the current relationship between labor and management is characterized more by cooperation and compromise than by conflict. If collective bargaining fails, an outside party often steps in to solve the problem. In *conciliation* a third party encourages both sides to keep negotiating. In *mediation* a third party suggests solutions to the problem. In *arbitration* both sides agree to abide by a third party's decision.

Have students describe a recent management-labor dispute in their community or on a national level. **Ask:** How was it settled? Was collective bargaining used or did a third party become involved?

Exploring Issues

ANSWERS

1. Higher wages, a 40-hour week, extra pay for overtime, recognition of union as bargaining agent.
2. Open shop: employment open to everyone; closed shop: only union members hired; preferential union shop: non-union workers hired if union workers unavailable. Answers to latter parts of question will vary.
3. The union representing the workers bargains with the employer to set pay and working conditions. Answers will vary to latter part of question. Those thinking it is effective can argue that it limits bargaining to two parties, management and the union, rather than having management bargain with each individual worker. Those disagreeing can argue that it limits individual workers' freedom and choices.

Linking Past and Present

Discussion. Pinchot identified the conservation movement with three principal goals: (1) to develop natural resources and make the fullest use of them for the present generation; (2) to prevent waste, and (3) to develop and preserve our natural resources for the benefit of the many, and not merely for the profit of the few.

Ask: Have we lived up to these goals? Have any other goals been added today? How do these goals compare with Muir's idea of preservation?

Limited English Proficiency

Building Vocabulary. Two different philosophies on the environment are termed *conservation* and *preservation.* Help students identify the roots of these words and define how they differ.

Backyard History

Guest Speaker. Invite someone from the local chapter of the Sierra Club or another environmental organization to discuss conservation/preservation efforts in your area.

Writing About History

Travelogue. Have students find out about one of the national parks. (Information might be found at a library, obtained from a travel agency or based on personal experience.) Then have students write a travel feature about the park. What would one see and do there?

Social History

In 1867 John Muir, founder of the Sierra Club, was temporarily blinded in an industrial accident. The experience changed his life, and he decided to pursue nature studies. He began a 1000-mile walk from his Wisconsin home to the Gulf of Mexico that year. In 1868 he traveled to California, where he studied the Sierra Nevada especially the Yosemite Valley. He became a professional writer, naturalist, and rancher.

Reduced student page in the Teacher's Edition

Roosevelt's aides reported on "meat shoveled from filthy wooden floors, piled on tables rarely washed, pushed from room to room in rotten box carts."

reasonably high rates while at the same time giving large rebates to favorite customers. The President's plan was to strengthen the Interstate Commerce Commission (ICC).

Roosevelt's ICC proposals survived an eighteen-month battle in Congress. In June 1906 Congress passed the Hepburn Act, which allowed the ICC to set a ceiling on railroad rates. It also expanded the ICC's jurisdiction to include railroad terminals, bridges, ferries, oil pipelines, and sleeping-car companies. The Hepburn Act represented a major expansion of federal power to regulate an industry.

Regulating foods and drugs. In the meantime, *The Jungle*, a novel by muckraker Upton Sinclair, had called the nation's attention to abuses by the meatpacking industry. To kill rats, Sinclair wrote, "the packers would put poisoned bread out for them; they would die, and then rats, bread, and meat would go into the hoppers together." Out of that, sausage was made for "the public's breakfast."

Roosevelt doubted some of Sinclair's charges, but he ordered an investigation of meatpacking practices. The report so shocked him that he demanded congressional action. In June 1906 Congress passed the Meat Inspection Act, which established sanitation regulations for the meatpacking industry and federal inspection of meat sold across state lines.

Congress also passed the Pure Food and Drug Act, which prohibited "the manufacture, sale, or transportation of adulterated or misbranded or poisonous or deleterious [harmful] foods, drugs, medicines, and liquors." It also forbade misleading advertising for products that promised cures for everything from freckles to baldness.

Conservation of Natural Resources

At the turn of the twentieth century, some farsighted Americans were beginning to worry about the fate of the nation's resources. Under existing laws, public lands were quickly passing into private hands. Three quarters of the nation's forests were being logged, and careless farming was destroying the topsoil. Mining and manufacturing were scarring the land and ruining waterways.

Roosevelt, an avid outdoorsman, had an intense interest in protecting wilderness areas. Two earlier Presidents, Harrison and Cleveland, had set aside forest areas as reserves. Now, Roosevelt, encouraged by his chief of the United States Forest Service, Gifford Pinchot, forged a national policy to promote **conservation**— protecting resources and managing them wisely for such uses as lumbering and irrigation.

Roosevelt was also deeply influenced by naturalist John Muir. Muir's ideas about wilderness were different from Pinchot's. Muir was a staunch believer in **preservation**— keeping some wilderness areas in their natural state. Muir warned:

> *"God has cared for these trees, saved them from drought, disease, avalanches, and a thousand straining, leveling tempests and floods; but he cannot save them from fools— only Uncle Sam can do that."*

In 1903 Roosevelt and Muir camped for three days in the Yosemite Valley. Afterward the President declared: "I hope for the preservation of the groves of giant trees simply because it would be a shame to our civilization to let them disappear."

In 1908 Roosevelt called political leaders to the White House Conservation Conference. "The time

Connections: Politics

Gifford Pinchot was the driving force behind the conservation movement. It was he who first applied the term "conservation" to what were at the time new ideas about public lands. Pinchot favored public control of the nation's resources. He was opposed by people who disliked any expansion of government power and by speculators and entrepreneurs who would profit by unrestricted private development of minerals, forests, grasslands, and water.

John Muir, (here with Roosevelt at Yosemite), rallied support for preserving wilderness areas. Today the National Park Service manages more than 300 sites.

has come to inquire seriously what will happen when our forests are gone," he said, "when the coal, the iron, the oil, and the gas are exhausted, when the soils . . . [are] washed into the streams." The conference led to the creation of the National Conservation Commission, devoted to protecting the nation's natural resources.

The End of Roosevelt's Term

Toward the end of his second term, Roosevelt's popularity was strained by a sudden economic depression. Throughout 1907 stock prices fell and production of goods slowed. In October, a crisis struck the financial community. Banks, low on funds, could not make loans. Some simply closed their doors. Several companies went bankrupt.

Then J. P. Morgan, the longtime "Doctor of Wall Street," took charge. Morgan bailed out a failing company, then a bank, then the city of New York. He made or arranged loans and also directed the flow of federal loans arranged by Roosevelt.

Corporate leaders blamed the depression on Roosevelt's regulatory reforms. Roosevelt, in turn, blamed "certain malefactors [evil doers] of great wealth," who wished to "discredit the policy of the government." Joining in the chorus of blame, some progressives argued that the President's regulations did not go far enough. Despite the numerous antitrust suits, they noted, there were more trusts in 1908 than when Roosevelt had taken office.

To many progressives, however, Roosevelt was still a hero. He had prodded Congress to pass national conservation laws, to regulate corporations, and to protect public health. La Follette, now a senator, said that Roosevelt had "made reform respectable in the United States."

Section Review

1. Identification. Define *conservation* and *preservation*.

2. Comprehension. List four situations that led Roosevelt to press for federal regulation. What regulations resulted in each case?

3. Analysis. Compare Roosevelt's views of large corporations with the views of those who believed in laissez faire, that is, letting businesses run themselves without government intervention.

4. Evaluation. Roosevelt once said, "The object of government is the welfare of the people." Did Roosevelt act to promote the welfare of the people? Provide evidence for your answer.

Section Review

ANSWERS

1. Definitions are on text pages indicated: *conservation* (456), *preservation* (456).
2. Unfair railroad practices: Hepburn Act; Upton Sinclair's *The Jungle*: Meat Inspection Act and Pure Food and Drug Act; despoliation of natural resources: National Conservation Commission; big business abuses: Department of Commerce and Labor.
3. Advocates of laissez faire believe business should be absolutely free from government regulation. Roosevelt believed regulation necessary to end abuses.
4. Students might agree he did, citing his enforcement of Sherman Act, intervention in coal miners' strike, regulation of food industry, creation of National Conservation Commission, and final message to Congress proposing 8-hour day, abolition of child labor, and workers' compensation act.

GTV Side 3

Chap. 15, Frame 42746

Protected Lands 1901-1909 (Animated Map)

Search and Play:

GTV Side 3

Chap. 15, Frame 37503

A Progress Report: Early Conservation (Movie)

Search:

Play:

Section 17-3

Objectives

- ***Answer the Focus Question.***
- *Evaluate Taft's accomplishments as a progressive.*
- *Contrast Roosevelt's and Wilson's attitudes toward monopolies.*
- *Identify the Federal Reserve Act, Federal Trade Commission, and Sixteenth and Seventeenth Amendments.*

Introducing THE SECTION

Have students read the first paragraph and study the cartoon on this page. **Ask:** Who does the elephant represent? **(Taft)** Who is he talking to on the telephone? **(Roosevelt)** What do you suppose they are discussing?

Tell students Roosevelt picked Taft as his successor but progressives felt betrayed by Taft. This caused a rift in the Republican party which paved the way for reform-minded Democrat Woodrow Wilson to win the election.

Reduced student page in the Teacher's Edition

17-3 *The Triumph of Progressivism*

Focus: How did Presidents Taft and Wilson extend progressivism?

Roosevelt backed the jovial, 300-pound William Howard Taft as his successor, promising that Taft would carry on "my policies." The Republican convention followed Roosevelt's wishes and nominated Taft. The Democrats turned for a third time to William Jennings Bryan. Both men ran on a progressive platform. But Bryan had apparently lost his vote-getting appeal. The campaign, wrote a newspaper, was "loaded down with calm." Taft won comfortably. Confident that Taft would follow his policies, Roosevelt went off to Africa to hunt game.

Taft and the Republican Split

Taft, known as a kindly, easygoing man, had been an able governor of the Philippines and Secretary of War in Roosevelt's cabinet. But he proved to be a poor politician. He began by alienating many of his progressive supporters with his handling of the extremely controversial issue of the tariff.

Taft had promised midwestern progressives that he would lower tariffs, and he called a special session of Congress for that purpose. However, eastern conservatives favored high tariffs to protect their industries from foreign competition. In Congress they weighed the tariff down with some 800 amendments, actually increasing rates on hundreds of imports.

Progressives were furious and called on Taft to help kill the bill. But Taft, reluctant to cross the conservatives, held back. Then he made matters worse. When the Payne-Aldrich Tariff bill came to his desk in 1909, he not only signed it, he called it "the best tariff bill that the Republican party has ever passed."

Progressives felt betrayed. The tariff issue drove a wedge between progressives and Taft. It also created a split between conservatives and progressives in the Republican party.

The wilderness. A feud between two of Taft's officials caused a further break between the President and the progressives. Gifford Pinchot, chief of the United States Forest Service, and Richard Ballinger, Taft's Secretary of the Interior, clashed over wilderness areas in Wyoming and Montana.

Under Roosevelt, these areas had been set aside as protected federal lands. Then, in mid-1909, Ballinger reopened the lands for sale to private interests. When Pinchot wrote a letter to Congress calling Ballinger's actions "a national danger," Taft fired him for disloyalty. Although a congressional investigation concluded that Ballinger had done nothing illegal, progressives labeled Taft and Ballinger "despoilers of the national heritage."

Taft's Progressivism

Despite the progressives' distrust of him, Taft remained true to his own progressive convictions. When Ballinger resigned, the President replaced him with a strong conservationist. Taft eventually set aside more public lands as forest reserves than Roosevelt had.

B · A · C · K · G · R · O · U · N · D

Connections: Politics
In 1912 Taft appointed Julia Lathrop director of the newly-established federal Children's Bureau. She became the first woman to head a federal agency.

Connections: Politics
Taft had not much wanted to be President. A former lawyer and federal judge, his dream was a place on the Supreme Court. Appointed by President Harding, Taft did serve as Chief Justice of the Supreme Court from 1921 to 1930.

Developing
THE SECTION

Thinking Critically

Synthesis. At no time in United States history was there greater acceptance of socialism than in the early 1900s. Within five years socialist mayors were elected in Milwaukee; Butte, Montana; Berkeley, California; and Schenectady, New York. Outdoing his showing in two previous elections, Debs won his biggest share of the votes in 1912.
Ask: Why do you think socialism had such an appeal at this time?

Taft also called for increased regulation of industry. The Mann-Elkins Act of 1910, which he proposed and nursed through Congress, expanded the power of the Interstate Commerce Commission (ICC) over the railroads and it extended to regulate telephone and telegraph companies.

Taft was twice the trustbuster that Roosevelt had been. His attorney general used the Sherman Act to file ninety suits against monopolies—twice as many in four years as there were in Roosevelt's seven years. When corporate leaders complained, Taft replied, "We are going to enforce that law or die in the attempt."

Under Taft, new laws ensured safer conditions in mines and railroads. Federal workers were given an eight-hour day. The new Department of Labor formed a Children's Bureau to look into child labor. Despite his actions, however, Taft had started his term at odds with the progressives, and they refused to give him full credit for his reforms.

Roosevelt's New Nationalism

In mid-1910, Roosevelt returned from Africa to a hero's welcome. He immediately blamed Taft for having "twisted around" his policies and split the Republican party. On a speaking tour of the West, he called for a New Nationalism. This program, he said, would give government new powers to guard the American people. The President should be "the steward of the public welfare," according to Roosevelt, and Congress should supervise industry and revise the tariff.

Roosevelt's views further split the Republican party. In the congressional elections of 1910, the Democrats gained control of the House while the Republicans barely held on in the Senate. Everyone began preparing for the 1912 presidential race.

The Election of 1912

A number of candidates entered the presidential race in 1912, all of them progressives of one kind or another. The Socialist candidate was Eugene V. Debs—union leader and co-founder of the Socialist Party of America. The Socialist party was committed to correcting injustices in society through government ownership of major businesses and industries. Modeled after parties in Britain and Germany, the American Socialist party aimed to bring about government ownership gradually and peacefully.

Socialism drew its support largely from dissatisfied workers. Although socialism did not gain widespread support, partly because of the American tradition of respect for private property, it was strong in several industrial cities.

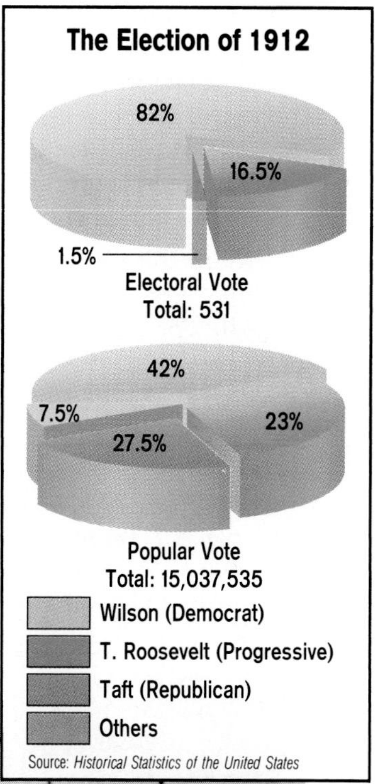

William Howard Taft (far right) shown here at Wilson's inauguration, later said that he was happiest as Chief Justice of the Supreme Court.

Multicultural Perspectives

W.E.B. Du Bois and William Trotter, an associate of Du Bois in the Niagara Movement, supported Wilson for President in 1912, but they soon regretted it. Wilson rejected a proposal to appoint a National Race Commission to study the social and economic status of African Americans. He also appointed white foreign service officers to Haiti and Santo Domingo, among the few consular posts open to blacks by custom and practice.

Active Learning

Writing a Campaign Speech. Divide the class into four groups. Let each group represent the campaign staff of one of the four candidates in the election of 1912. Have groups research their leader's position on the following issues: trust-busting, regulation of industries, conservation, woman suffrage, child labor laws, and unions. Each staff is to write a campaign speech to be delivered in front of the class by a student representing the candidate.

Connections: Politics

Discussion. Tell students that Woodrow Wilson addressed a joint session of Congress on April 8, 1913, urging lower tariffs. He was the first President since John Adams to do so. One irate critic remarked, *"I am sorry to see revived the old Federalistic custom of speeches from the throne."*

Ask: What did the critic mean by the remark? **(Federalists favored strong central government with power in the hands of the wealthy and educated, even to the point of trying to suppress opposition. Some people accused them of wanting to establish a near monarchy. In comparing Wilson with the Federalists, the critic was accusing Wilson of behaving as a would-be king. The critic was probably concerned that Wilson was trying to dominate Congress. However, unlike the Federalists, Wilson believed in limited government; he proposed removing or lowering protective tariffs; he broke up trusts.)**

Reduced student page in the Teacher's Edition

The Republican party splintered, with Taft, Roosevelt, and La Follette all trying to win the nomination. It became a two-way race when La Follette, in ill health, withdrew. At the party's convention, Taft won the nomination.

Unwilling to accept defeat, Roosevelt and his supporters formed a new party—the Progressive party. Announcing, "I feel as fit as a bull moose," Roosevelt accepted the nomination of the party, which became known as the "Bull Moose" party.

The Democrats chose New Jersey's reform governor, Woodrow Wilson—former history professor and president of Princeton University. Described by some people as "aloof," he was nevertheless well-respected. He felt destined to carry out some important mission. "I should be complete," he wrote, "if I could inspire a great movement." In 1912 Wilson named his movement New Freedom.

The campaign was a heated battle over how to reform trusts. Roosevelt insisted that monopolies were not harmful if they were regulated by a powerful federal government. Wilson claimed that monopolies were "intolerable" because they strangled free enterprise. His solution was to break up the trusts and to lower the tariff that gave them an advantage over small businesses. Roosevelt's New Nationalism would increase government power, while Wilson's New Freedom would limit it.

Wilson had two advantages. Virginia-born, he could count on the support of the South. More important, the Republicans were split. Wilson sailed to victory, but the biggest winner of the election was an idea—progressive reform.

After the Sixteenth Amendment passed, incomes over $3,000 were taxed at a rate of 1 percent. People with incomes over $20,000 paid an additional 1 to 6 percent, according to a graduated scale.

Wilson's New Freedom

The first goal of President Wilson's New Freedom was to lower the tariff. Lowering or removing protective tariffs, he said, would force American businesses to compete. Where Taft had failed, Wilson was determined to succeed.

He conferred with Congressman Oscar Underwood, an authority on tariff reform. Underwood proposed a bill that would reduce the average tariff by 11 percent. It would also remove all duties from imported goods that competed with goods manufactured by the trusts, for example, steel.

Into the capital swarmed **lobbyists**—people acting on behalf of special interests in order to influence legislation. The lobbyists demanded that high duties be restored on imported wool, sugar, and cotton. Wilson appealed to the public. He forcefully argued that lobbyists were spending "money without limit" to support special interests, while no lobby protected the interests of the public.

Public concern, and a judiciary committee investigation into lobbying, moved the Senate to pass the Underwood Tariff Act in October 1913. The bill lowered the tariff rate by an astonishing 21 percent. This success, said a London newspaper, boosted Wilson "from the man of promise to the man of achievement." Encouraged, Wilson moved on to his next task—banking and currency reform.

The Federal Reserve Act

The nation's banking system was outdated. Individual banks simply estimated what the demand for cash might be and kept enough money on hand to meet that estimate. But estimates could be

Constitutional Heritage

A federal tax on individual incomes would make up for the loss of revenue due to the lowered tariffs. Americans first experienced a federal income tax during the Civil War, when a 3 percent tax was levied on incomes over $800. Congress abolished this tax in 1872, and for revenue the federal government relied on excise and import taxes. In 1894 Congress passed a bill that included a provision for a tax of 2 percent on individual incomes over $4,000, but the Supreme Court declared it unconstitutional in 1895 because of a constitutional requirement that a direct tax be divided among the states according to their population (see Article 1, Section 9, Clause 4 of the Constitution). The Sixteenth Amendment removed this requirement.

wrong, as they had been in the Panic of 1907, when people suddenly demanded cash and many banks ran out of currency.

Bankers, business people, and political leaders all agreed that the banking system must be made more stable, but they disagreed as to how. Conservatives wanted a central bank controlled by bankers. Progressives demanded government control over the banking system. Wilson decided that only government control could create stability and make banks serve "individual enterprise and initiative." He threw his support behind the progressives in Congress, and on December 23, 1913, the Federal Reserve Act was passed.

The act divided the country into twelve Federal Reserve districts, each with a Federal Reserve bank. The Federal Reserve bank in each district would not serve businesses or private citizens directly. It would be strictly a bank for national banks and other banks that chose to join the system. The President would appoint a Federal Reserve Board to coordinate this new banking system.

To make sure that member banks had enough money to meet demands, the Federal Reserve set a minimum amount that local banks must keep on deposit with their district bank. The district bank could supply local banks with currency and low-cost loans.

By controlling the amount of money it loaned, the district bank could increase or decrease the district's money supply. Thus the Federal Reserve could discourage or encourage borrowing and spending, according to the needs of the times. The system encouraged small businesses by ensuring that money was available for business loans.

The Sixteenth and Seventeenth Amendments

In the same year that the Federal Reserve system was established, two progressive reforms made their way into the Constitution. The Sixteenth Amendment allowed Congress to levy taxes on incomes. Progressives thought that an income tax would raise money to pay for social reforms such as workers' compensation.

The Seventeenth Amendment provided for the direct election of senators by the people, rather than by state legislatures. During recent years, the Senate had consistently been slower than the House to consider reform. Progressives hoped that if the election of senators depended on the people, the Senate would react more favorably to reform.

Tackling the Trusts

Wilson had promised to break up trusts and rescue free enterprise. In 1913 he called for a new antitrust law to cover abuses not already covered by the Sherman Antitrust Act. In response, Congress passed the Clayton Antitrust Act, banning certain practices that discouraged competition. For example, under the act one company could not buy

Spotlight on the Movies

The earliest motion picture capital was not Hollywood, but New York City, along with nearby New Jersey, where Thomas Edison had his laboratory. In 1909 Edison formed the Motion Picture Patents Company to enforce his patents on movie equipment and processes, eliminate competition, and create a monopoly on movie production.

Independent producers battled the Patents Company and each other both in and out of court. Lawsuits, spying, and outright sabotage followed. Equipment disappeared, mysterious accidents happened, and fires broke out.

To escape the monopoly and the disruptive movie wars, some film makers sought refuge in far-distant California. But the conflict followed them. Cecil B. de Mille was shot at twice as he directed his first movie in 1913. Nevertheless, by the following year, fifty-two movie companies were taking advantage of the area's sunny skies and varied scenery. The movie industry had moved to Hollywood to stay.

Connections: Economics

Discussion. Discuss with students how the Federal Reserve influences the economy. **Ask:** How can the Federal Reserve encourage borrowing and spending? **(increasing a district's money supply)** How does the Federal Reserve increase a district's money supply? **(lowering amount bank must keep on deposit; low cost loans by lowering interest rates)** If there is an inflationary period what would the Federal Reserve most likely do? **(raise minimum deposit amount; raise cost of loans)** In a depression what does the Federal Reserve want to encourage? **(borrowing and spending)**

Limited English Proficiency

Building Vocabulary. Discussion of the Federal Reserve Act requires knowledge of several terms associated with economics. Help students to define the following terms and use them in a different context: *demand, currency, deposit, loans, money supply.*

Linking Past and Present

Research and Report. Refer students to the Spotlight feature on this page. Tell them that from about 1915 to the late 1940s, each movie studio, for the most part, controlled three aspects of the motion picture business: the production, the distribution, and the exhibition of films.

Have a group of students do research and explain to the class how these three aspects of the business are conducted today. What controversies have arisen in recent years over possible monopolies in the movie business?

B · A · C · K · G · R · O · U · N · D

Thinking Critically

Analysis. Tell students that labor leaders referred to the Clayton Act as "Labor's Magna Carta." **Ask:** What provisions in the act caused such praise from labor? (Unions could not be considered illegal under antitrust laws; not prosecuted for lawful strikes and picketing.) How could declaring a strike illegal hurt a union? (discourage workers from joining unions)

Linking Past and Present

Drawing Up a Code of Ethics. Exposing injustice and checking the power of big business were the goals that lay behind many progressive reforms. Refer students to the advertisements at the bottoms of these pages. Discuss how they might have misled the public. **(promise miracle cures, no listed ingredients)**

Ask: Today what are some federal regulations intended to ensure ethical advertising? Are they effective? **(Ads, for example, may not say that a medicine can cure a disease when in fact it contains only sugar and alcohol. Agencies like the Food and Drug Administration and the Consumer Product Safety Commission watch for truthful labels and honest advertising for food and drugs, toys, tools, children's clothes, household appliances.)**

Have students draw up a code of ethics for advertisers today, according to the goals of the progressives.

Connections: Economics

Henry Ford carried the movement toward improving the status of workers a step further when he started paying his workers five dollars a day. The pay increase cost the Ford Motor Company ten million dollars a year, but increased productivity cut costs in half, and the publicity increased sales. *"The payment of five dollars a day for an eight hour day was one of the finest cost-cutting moves ever made,"* Ford later remarked.

Reduced student page in the Teacher's Edition

stock in — and therefore, control — a competing company. One person could not serve on the board of directors of two competing firms at the same time. These measures kept one group of people from controlling all the companies in the same business.

Labor leaders, remembering how the Sherman Antitrust Act had been used against unions in the 1890s, had demanded that unions be exempt from antitrust laws. The Clayton Act declared that unions could not be declared illegal under antitrust laws. The act also protected unions from prosecution if their activities, such as strikes and picketing, were lawful.

Wilson realized that no antitrust law could possibly define all business abuses. He threw his support behind a bill to establish a trade commission to deal with new problems that came up. In the autumn of 1914, Congress created the Federal Trade Commission (FTC). The FTC could monitor businesses involved in interstate trade to ensure fair competition and could order companies to stop unfair practices. The FTC also worked to protect consumers from misleading practices such as false advertising.

Progressives had high hopes for the trust regulation, and they congratulated Wilson on another victory. These laws, said Wilson, would help small business succeed as easily as big business did, and would "kill monopoly in the seed."

Wilson's Reform Bills

Wilson believed that social reform was the responsibility of the states. However, progressives pressed him to support social legislation if he wanted to be reelected in 1916.

In response, Wilson encouraged Congress to pass an array of reform bills. For example, the Seamen's Act, sponsored by Senator La Follette, regulated conditions in the merchant marine. The Adamson Act gave railroad workers the eight-hour day. Congress also passed a child labor act, limiting the number of hours children could work.

Wilson signed a bill creating the National Park Service, largely owing to the work of Stephen T. Mather, who became its first director. In setting the policy "that the national parks . . . be maintained . . . for the use of future generations," Mather was breaking new ground. No other nation except Canada had national parks.

Pointing to the tariff, banking, and trust bills, and this latest burst of reform, Wilson proudly summed up the accomplishments of his first term:

> *"This record must . . . astonish those who feared that the Democratic party had not opened its heart to comprehend the demands of social justice. We have in four years come very near to carrying out the platform of the Progressive party as well as our own; for we also are progressives."*

Drug companies kept the formulas for their "miracle cures" a secret. One such cure consisted of whiskey, water, pepper, and burnt sugar.

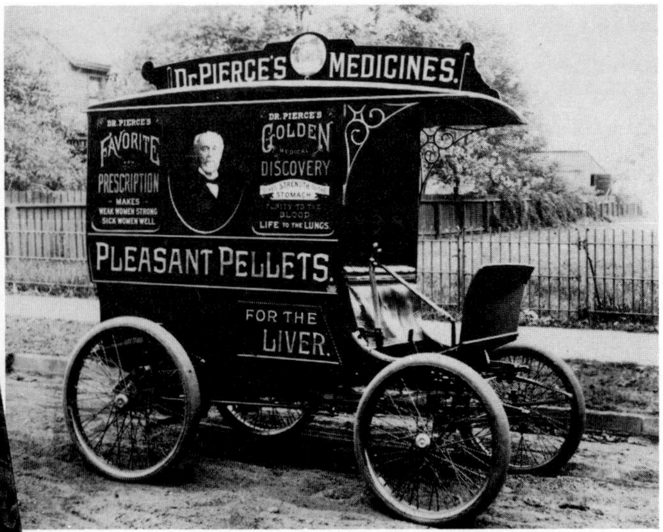

Connections: Economics

There are two basic views about government intervention in the economy. *Liberals* often favor government action to provide equality, justice, and the health of the people. In contrast, *conservatives* believe most problems are best solved by individuals, private business, and the market.

Section Review

1. **Identification.** Define *lobbyists.*

2. **Comprehension.** How did Presidents Taft and Wilson each extend progressivism in the federal government in relation to monopolies? Labor? Conservation?

3. **Analysis.** Compare the New Freedom and the New Nationalism.

4. **Comprehension.** What was the purpose of each of the following: Federal Reserve Act, Sixteenth Amendment, Seventeenth Amendment?

Data Search. Examine the graph "The Election of 1912" on page 459 to answer the following questions. How many electoral votes did Eugene Debs win? How do you know? What percent of the popular vote did Taft and Roosevelt win altogether? What might have happened if Roosevelt had not run?

At a time when ads for Lydia Pinkham's Compound encouraged women to write to Mrs. Pinkham for medical advice, she had been dead for 20 years.

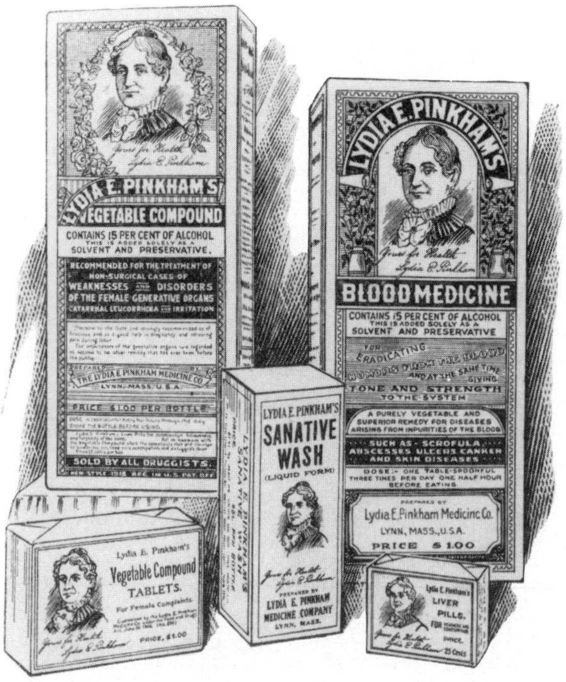

Connections to Themes

Shaping Democracy

Throughout the nineteenth century, the majority of Americans held the laissez-faire view that a democratic government does not have the right to interfere in the workings of the free enterprise system. By the opening of the twentieth century, however, workers through their labor unions and farmers through the Populist party had already challenged that belief.

The progressives, too, questioned long-held assumptions about free enterprise and laissez faire. They claimed that some businesses had grown too powerful—strangling free enterprise and creating a number of economic and social ills. Progressives thought the only force strong enough to change the situation was government.

The progressives were more successful than the unions and the Populists had been in forcing government to act to correct the nation's ills. Some of the reforms they pushed through are a part of our democracy today—measures that regulate business, limits on child labor, the graduated income tax, the Federal Reserve System, and protection of natural resources.

The progressives did not create a perfect society, and some of their reforms were failures. But they firmly established the idea that government intervention is necessary to balance the interests of different groups in American society. From that point on, the American people would increasingly turn to government in times of economic and social troubles.

Section Review

ANSWERS

1. See definition for *lobbyists* on page 460.
2. Monopolies: Taft used Sherman Act to file suits against monopolies; Wilson called for new antitrust law, and Congress passed Clayton Act and created FTC. Labor: Taft had laws passed setting up safer conditions in mines and on railroads, had Children's Bureau look into child labor, and set 8-hour day for government workers; under Wilson, Congress passed acts regulating conditions in merchant marine, giving railroad workers an 8-hour day, and limiting children's work hours. Conservation: Taft set aside lands as forest preserves; Wilson signed bill creating National Park Service.
3. New Nationalism called for giving government power to supervise industry and regulate the economy. New Freedom promised to break up trusts and lower the tariff.
4. Federal Reserve Act aimed to ensure stability of banks by controlling money supply. Sixteenth Amendment raised money for reforms. Seventeenth Amendment provided for election of senators by direct vote; its purpose was to elect reform-minded senators.
Data Search. None. Graph shows that only Wilson, Roosevelt, and Taft won electoral votes. 50.5 percent; Taft might have won.

Chapter Survey

ANSWERS

Using New Vocabulary

initiative, referendum—voters propose or approve laws; *direct primary, secret ballot*—election reforms; *city manager, commission system*—forms of city government; *conservation, preservation*—protection of natural resources.

Reviewing the Chapter

1. Muckraking journalism; organizations, marches and rallies.
2. (a) Education, end child labor, temperance, suffrage; (b) better pay, shorter hours, safer conditions, end child labor; (c) economic independence, political rights, an end to segregation, discrimination, lynching. People organized, spread information, demonstrated, took political action, took legal action, campaigned for new state and federal laws.
3. Public ownership of utilities; new forms, such as city manager and commission system. State legislatures often blocked city reforms.
4. Direct primary, initiative, referendum, recall.
5. Believed trusts not necessarily bad; should be regulated rather than broken up.
6. Previous Presidents had used federal troops against workers. Roosevelt threatened to use troops to run the mines, taking aim at mine owners rather than workers.
7. Demanded laws establishing federal regulation and inspection of meatpacking and prohibiting adulteration, misbranding, and misleading advertising of food and drugs.
8. Suits against monopolies, railroad regulation, Children's Bureau, safety conditions in mines and railroads, eight-hour day for federal workers.
9. Republicans split between conservatives and Progressive (Bull Moose) party; Wilson had support of the South.
10. (a) Passed Underwood Tariff, lowering rates by 21 percent; (b) set up Federal Reserve System to stabilize banking; (c) passed Clayton Antitrust Act to prevent business practices that blocked competition; (d) Clayton Act protected unions; Seaman's Act protected merchant marine; Adamson Act gave railroad workers eight-hour day; child labor act limited working hours for children.

Thinking Critically

1. Roosevelt believed trusts not harmful if regulated by federal government, for example, regulation of railroad rates. Possible advantage: protection of con-

Reduced student page in the Teacher's Edition

Chapter Survey

Using New Vocabulary

Think about the meaning of each vocabulary term below. Then group the terms with related meanings into pairs and explain the relationship between the words in each pair.

Example: *Populism* and *progressivism* were both political movements for reform through government action. Both fit into the category "political movements."

1. direct primary
2. city manager
3. initiative
4. secret ballot
5. conservation
6. commission system
7. preservation
8. referendum

Reviewing the Chapter

1. What were three ways that information about progressive causes was spread?

2. Throughout the progressive era, private citizens worked hard to influence public affairs. Name one goal and describe one method used by each of the following: (a) women's groups, (b) nonunion workers, (c) African-American leaders.

3. What reforms did progressives make in city government? What caused progressives to shift their attention from city to state government?

4. What reforms did progressives make in state government?

5. What was Theodore Roosevelt's view of the trusts? What did he think government should do about them?

6. How was Roosevelt's handling of the coal-miners' strike in 1902 a break from the way previous Presidents had handled strikes?

7. What actions did Roosevelt take to protect consumers?

8. List three examples of President Taft's progressive accomplishments.

9. Why did Democrats win the election of 1912?

10. What impact did the Wilson administration have on (a) tariffs, (b) the banking system, (c) trusts, (d) workers?

Thinking Critically

1. Analysis. Compare Roosevelt's idea of big government with Wilson's idea of limited government. Give examples and describe advantages and disadvantages of each viewpoint.

2. Synthesis. Assume the role of one of the following people and write a position statement on the Clayton Antitrust Act from that person's point of view. (a) President Wilson (b) a labor union member (c) the owner of a small business (d) a leading industrialist

3. Evaluation. "Go back to the first principles of democracy. Go back to the people," advised Robert La Follette on the issue of government reform. La Follette expressed the progressives' complete faith in the people to do what was right. Do you agree or disagree with this assumption? Defend your answer.

Using a Time Line

Match each date in the time line with the correct event. Write your answers in chronological order and explain what part each event played in the progressive movement.

(A) formation of NAACP
(B) addition of Seventeenth Amendment
(C) publication of articles on Standard Oil
(D) establishment of Federal Trade Commission
(E) March of the Mill Children
(F) passage of Hepburn Act
(G) woman suffrage in New York
(H) White House Conservation Conference

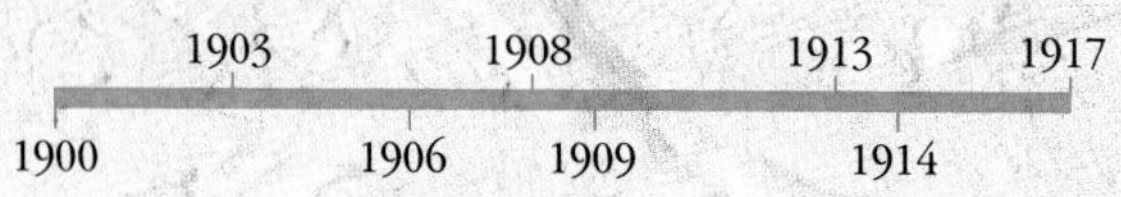

sumer by controlling costs of transportation of goods. Possible disadvantage: growth of bureaucracy which could be very inefficient, subject to industry pressure or bribery. Wilson wanted to break up trusts to promote competition and small businesses, for example, Clayton Antitrust Act. Possible advantage: providing a "more level playing field" for small businesses. Possible disadvantage: loss of economies of scale.
2. (a) Excellent law because it promotes competition and strengthens free enterprise. (b) A big boon to unions because it allows us to use strikes and picket lines in a lawful manner. (c) It limits monopolies and trusts. (d) A terrible law, sets us back decades, interferes with efficiency of vertical and horizontal integration in an industry; will end up costing consumers more through inefficient production.
3. Answers may include that individuals may not measure up to this standard, but on the average people are trustworthy, want honesty and accountability in government. On the other hand, many people don't want to get involved in government. Low voter turnout shows people not committed to doing "the right thing" all the time.

History and You

Do research to find a political reform made in your state during the progressive era. Some possibilities are the direct primary, the initiative, the referendum, and the recall. Find out the names of the people responsible for the law. Does the law still exist? If so, how does it affect government in your state today?

Applying Thinking Skills

Interpreting Political Cartoons

Theodore Roosevelt believed that big business combinations were "bad" if they misused power. Roosevelt's approach to these "bad" trusts was to increase the government's power to regulate business and stop abuses. Study the cartoon below and answer the questions that follow.

1. Who is the man in the cartoon?

2. Why is he portrayed as a hunter?

3. What has happened to the "Bad Trusts"? How are the "Good Trusts" treated?

4. Explain how the cartoon supports this statement by Roosevelt: "We do not wish to destroy corporations, but to make them serve the public good."

Writing About Issues

The Issue: *What kinds of child labor laws do we need today?*

Most young people in the labor force today work in fast food restaurants, supermarkets, and movie theaters. Relatively few work under the terrible conditions that led to the first child labor laws. Nevertheless, the laws still exist, and government still tries to enforce them.

In 1990 the United States Department of Labor conducted Operation Child Watch, a three-day sweep of selected businesses suspected of violating child labor laws. The investigation found 7,000 children who were illegally employed.

People who believe that child labor laws are still needed today cite Operation Child Watch as proof that young workers are still being exploited. While the investigation was under way, a young man testified before Congress that, at age thirteen, he lost his leg in a drying machine while working at a car wash. "It is shocking," said California Representative Tom Lantos, "that thousands of youngsters are jeopardizing their education, health, and safety by working too many hours, too late at night, and in dangerous, prohibited occupations."

People who remain unconvinced of the need for child labor laws argue that holding a job teaches children responsibility. Furthermore, they say, most children work because they want to, not because their families need their income. A New Yorker who illegally employed his fifteen-year-old nephew in a small factory argued that if the boy was not working he would be "walking the streets doing nothing. He would fall into a bad gang." A group of fourteen- and fifteen-year-olds in Maryland pleaded with government officials to let them keep their jobs frying chicken in vats of boiling grease. The young people said that they were working to earn money to buy clothes and cars.

What do you think? Should minors be restricted as to how long and where they work? Should age be a factor in making a determination? Write a letter to your representative in Congress, stating your views on child labor laws.

Using a Time Line

(C) 1900, **(E)** 1903, **(F)** 1906, **(H)** 1908, **(A)** 1909, **(B)** 1913, **(D)** 1914, **(G)** 1917

History and You

Answers will vary by state.

Applying Thinking Skills

1. Theodore Roosevelt.
2. Roosevelt was noted for his exploits as a hunter. It is appropriate that his actions against trusts be likened to his hunting exploits.
3. Bad trusts are slain, good ones spared.
4. Only the "bad trusts"— those that act against the public good—are destroyed.

Chapter 18

Reaching for World Power

Planning Guide

	Student Text	TWE Lesson Plans	Support Materials
SECTION 1	**Section 18-1 (1 Day)** **Eyes Toward Expansion,** pp 468–472 Review/Evaluation Section Review, p 472	**Introducing the Chapter:** A Question of Power—Class Activity, 30 minutes, p 465B **Evaluating Progress:** Cartoon Views on Expansionism—Individual Activity, one class period, p 465C	★ **Read to Remember,** Section 1 ● **Section Activities,** Section 1 ● **Tests and Quizzes,** Section 1 Quiz
SECTION 2	**Section 18-2 (1-2 Days)** **The Spanish-American War,** pp 473–477 The American Spirit: Joseph Pulitzer, p 474 Review/Evaluation Section Review, p 477	**Teaching the Main Ideas:** A Human Time Line—Cooperative Activity, 30 minutes, p 465B	★ **Read to Remember,** Section 2 ● **Section Activities,** Section 2 Δ **Enrichment Activities,** Section 2 Δ **Readings** ● **Tests and Quizzes,** Section 2 Quiz
SECTION 3	**Section 18-3 (1-2 Days)** **A Stronger Arm in Asia,** pp 478–482 Review/Evaluation Section Review, p 482	**Teaching the Main Ideas:** A Debate on Foreign Policy—Group Activity, one class period, p 465C **Reinforcement Activity:** Letters of Protest—Individual Activity, homework, p 465C	★ **Read to Remember,** Section 3 ● **Section Activities,** Section 3 Δ **Readings** ● **Tests and Quizzes,** Section 3 Quiz
SECTION 4	**Section 18-4 (1-2 Days)** **Stepping into Latin America,** pp 482–489 Geography—Relationships Within Places: The Building of the Panama Canal, p 485 Connections to Themes: Shaping Democracy, p 489 Review/Evaluation Section Review, p 489 Chapter 18 Survey, pp 490–491 Skills, pp 490–491 Using New Vocabulary Thinking Critically Using Geography Applying Thinking Skills: Detecting Bias Writing About Issues	**Enrichment Activity:** Foreign Policy Then and Now—Individual Activity, one class period, p 465C	★ **Read to Remember,** Section 4 ● **Section Activities,** Section 4 ● **Geography Activities,** Section 4 Δ **Enrichment Activities,** Section 4 Δ **Readings** ● **Tests and Quizzes,** Section 4 Quiz, Chapter 18 Test (Forms A and B) **Additional Resources** ● **Active Learning** Δ **GTV Videodiscs** Δ **Transparencies and Activity Book** ● **Testing Software** ★ **Chapter Summaries** **Key:** ★ **For Extra Support** ● **For All Students** Δ **For Enrichment**

Overview

By the 1890s, expansionists were arguing that the United States had to become a colonial power to protect its economic interests and become the equal of the European powers. Opponents of expansionism, however, argued that controlling other lands ran contrary to American ideals. As public opinion tilted toward the expansionists, Congress approved construction of a modern steel navy to protect American trade and enforce the Monroe Doctrine.

An opportunity for the United States to test its military power soon presented itself in Cuba, where Cuban rebels were fighting for independence from Spanish colonial rule. With many Americans already sympathetic to the rebels, expansionists pushed for intervention, hoping to gain increased influence in Latin America. By emerging victorious in the Spanish-American War, the United States became a world power. The terms of the peace treaty called for Spain to relinquish control of Cuba, Puerto Rico, the Philippines, and Guam.

After the treaty was ratified—over the protests of anti-expansionists—the United States had firm footholds in two strategic areas: Asia and the Caribbean. It then proceeded to carry out a more assertive foreign policy in both regions. That self-confidence was reflected in Asia through the declaration of the "Open Door" policy of free trade with China. Meanwhile, United States policy in Latin America was marked by repeated military and economic intervention in the affairs of Latin American nations.

Activity Objectives

After completing the activities, students should be able to

- describe the sequence of key events before and during the Spanish-American War.
- compare arguments for and against overseas expansion.
- examine the effects of expansionism on indigenous populations.
- create political cartoons to express opposing views on expansionism.
- demonstrate an understanding of the "big stick," "dollar," and "moral" diplomacies.

Introducing the Chapter

A Question of Power

This class activity requires half a class period.

This activity underscores the significance of the 1890s and early 1900s for United States foreign policy.

Tell students that Chapter 18 traces the transition from an essentially isolationist foreign policy to the increased involvement in world affairs that has characterized United States foreign policy throughout most of the twentieth century. Write the phrase *World Power* on the chalkboard. Ask students what characteristics make the United States a world power today and write them on the board. (Answers may include such strengths as powerful armed forces, extensive trade and foreign investment, a large population, the ability to politically and economically influence regions and people beyond our borders.)

After exploring the "qualifications" for being a world power, ask students what they see as its advantages and disadvantages. Write the answers on the board. (Some advantages might be national security, international prestige, and a strong economy. Some disadvantages might be the expense of supporting a large military force, ill will caused among other countries, and entangling alliances.)

After discussing the status of the United States as a world power today, direct students to assess its status in the 1880s. Could it have been considered a world power then? (Students may note that territorial expansion across the continent, a growing population, and expanding industry all gave the nation a potential to become a world power. However, the nation was not in a position to significantly influence other nations. It was weak militarily and had been preoccupied with domestic affairs, including recovery from the Civil War.)

Conclude by having students discuss why the United States did not become extensively involved in international affairs during its first century. Then have them speculate what might bring about a change in this isolationist attitude. Ask them to keep their predictions in mind as they read the chapter.

Teaching the Main Ideas

Section 18-2: A Human Time Line

This cooperative activity requires half a class period.

In this activity students review the series of key events before and during the Spanish-American War by creating a human time line. Before class write each of the events listed below on a separate large index card or half sheet of paper. The events are listed in chronological order.

- Cubans rise in revolt against Spain
- General Weyler puts Cubans in reconcentration camps
- Yellow journalism whips up support for war
- Expansionists begin urging intervention in Cuba
- The *Maine* explodes
- Spaniards investigate the *Maine* explosion
- McKinley offers to arbitrate between Spain and the Cuban rebels
- Roosevelt secretly cables Dewey
- Congress declares war
- Dewey blockades the Spanish fleet
- Battle of San Juan Hill

- Spaniards in Cuba surrender
- American troops join Aguinaldo's rebels
- Spain signs truce
- Peace treaty signed

To do the activity, pairs of students will use separate event cards. If you have more than 30 students, group some into trios. If you have fewer than 30 students, delete cards naming less significant events.

Begin the activity by explaining that today students will illustrate the Spanish-American War chronology by creating a human time line. Randomly distribute event cards among pairs of students. Direct pairs to reread text information about the event named on their card and to write a paragraph explaining the event under the heading on the card. Their paragraph should include a date, or approximate date, for the event. When the paragraphs are written, have students put away their texts.

Designate starting and ending points for the human time line and have the pairs whose events begin and end the chronology stand in those positions. Direct the rest of the pairs to decide among themselves where along the time line they should stand to create an accurate chronology. Check the accuracy of their time line with the chronological listing of events provided above.

Teaching the Main Ideas

Section 18-3: A Debate on Foreign Policy

This group activity requires one class period and out-of-class preparation time.

In this activity students look at the issue of expansionism from different points of view. Students should complete Section 18–3 before beginning the group discussions.

Divide the class into groups of three. Tell them that they will participate in hypothetical early 1900s discussions about what policy the United States should follow in the Philippines. Within each group, one student will represent the expansionist viewpoint, one the anti-expansionist viewpoint, and the third the viewpoint of a Filipino. Students should come prepared with notes listing arguments in support of their viewpoint and arguments to refute opposing viewpoints.

Allow 30 minutes for the group discussions. First, the member representing the expansionists has five minutes to state and support that viewpoint, while the other group members briefly list the key arguments made. Next, the other two members have five minutes between them to respond to the points made by the expansionist. The procedure is then repeated for the other two viewpoints.

Following the discussion, select members of various groups to summarize the key arguments of each viewpoint. To check whether students listened carefully during the discussions, randomly select students to summarize viewpoints other than the one they represented. List the key arguments on the board. Conclude by asking students to note what assumptions, beliefs, and interests are reflected in the arguments for each point of view.

Reinforcement Activity

Section 18-3: Letters of Protest

This individual activity may be assigned for homework.

Designed to reinforce students' understanding of the effects of expansionism on indigenous populations, this activity requires students to write personal letters of protest from an Hawaiian, Filipino, Cuban, or Puerto Rican.

Review with students the actions taken by the United States in Hawaii, the Philippines, Cuba, and Puerto Rico. Point out that the people of these lands experienced dramatic changes in their lives as a result of foreign policy decisions by the United States.

Ask students to imagine what it might have been like to be an Hawaiian, Filipino, Cuban, or Puerto Rican during intervention by the United States in their lands. Direct them to assume the role of a person from one of these lands and to describe that person's feelings by writing a one- to two-page letter to the editor of the *New York Times*. Their letters should explain the situation in their land and express their personal opinions about United States intervention.

On the day their assignment is due, volunteers should be encouraged to read their letters aloud. Then have students summarize the attitudes toward United States expansion expressed in the letters.

Evaluating Progress

Section 18-1: Cartoon Views on Expansionism

This individual activity requires one class period.

To evaluate students' understanding of different viewpoints on expansionism, this activity involves them in drawing two political cartoons, one supporting expansionism and the other opposing it.

Evaluate students' work on the clarity with which their cartoons depict arguments for and against expansion and on their inclusion of key cartoon elements such as symbols, satire, dialogue, and captions or titles.

Enrichment Activity

Section 18-4: Foreign Policy Then and Now

This individual activity requires one class period or can be done as homework.

In this activity students demonstrate an understanding of three foreign policy approaches described in the chapter by applying them to a present-day problem, the destruction of tropical rain forests. They then evaluate the advantages and disadvantages of each approach.

Introduce the activity by writing the terms *big stick diplomacy, dollar diplomacy,* and *moral diplomacy* on the chalkboard, briefly reviewing the differences between these three approaches. Point out that they are still applied to various foreign policy issues today. Ask students to give some recent examples.

Explain that one issue today is the destruction of tropical rain forests in Latin America and Southeast Asia. Point out that these forests are being rapidly cut down at the rate of one acre per minute to provide a source of hardwood and to increase land available for grazing and farming. Some destruction is done by large companies, and some is done by native peoples who have no other way to support themselves. The result is that local environments are destroyed, natural resources found only in rain forest ecosystems disappear, and one of the earth's best defenses against global warming is eliminated.

Direct students to assume the role of a foreign policy advisor to the President. The President has asked for a report summarizing how each of the three approaches might be applied to the rain forest problem. The report is to include an assessment of the possible advantages and disadvantages of each approach, concluding with a recommendation on which approach, or combination of approaches, to take and why. The activity might be followed up by asking some students to read their recommendations to the class, stimulating class discussion on the relative merits of the three approaches in influencing other nations.

Bibliography and Audiovisual Material

Teacher Bibliography

Gatewood, Willard B., Jr. *Smoked Yankees and the Struggle for Empire*. Fayetteville: University of Arkansas Press, 1987.

Gould, Lewis L. *The Spanish-American War and President McKinley*. Lawrence: University Press of Kansas, 1982.

LaFeber, Walter. *The New Empire: An Interpretation of American Expansion, 1860–1898*. Ithaca: Cornell University Press, 1967.

Mahan, Alfred T. *Influence of Sea Power Upon History*. New York: Dover Publications, Inc., 1987.

Pearce, Jenny. *Under the Eagle: U.S. Intervention in Central America and the Caribbean*. Boston: South End Press, 1982.

Student Bibliography

Dunbar, Paul L. *Lyrics of a Lowly Life*. Salem, N.H.: Ayer Co. Publishers, Inc., 1969.

McCullough, David. *The Path Between the Seas: The Creation of the Panama Canal, 1870–1914*. New York: Simon and Schuster, Inc., 1978.

Moody, William Vaughn. *Poems and Plays*. 2 vols. New York: AMS Press, reprint of 1912 edition.

Roosevelt, Theodore. *Autobiography of Theodore Roosevelt*. New York: Da Capo Press, 1985.

Films, Videocassettes, and Videodiscs

A Man, A Plan, A Canal: Panama (Nova Series). 57 min. Coronet/MTI. Film.

History of the Twentieth Century: (1900–1909). 60 min. ABC Video. Videocassette.

The Monroe Doctrine Applied: U.S. Policy toward Latin America. 16 min. Guidance Associates. Videocassette.

Progressives, Populists and Reform in America (1890–1917). 32 min. Guidance Associates. Videocassette.

Filmstrips

The Building of the Panama Canal. 3 color filmstrips. Multi-Media Productions.

The Philippine-American War. 1 filmstrip. Multi-Media Productions.

The Spanish-American War. 30 min. 2 color filmstrips. Multi-Media Productions.

Where Historians Disagree Collection: Populism. 2 filmstrips. Random House Media.

Computer Software

American History: Becoming a World Power (1865–1912). Apple. Micro Learn/Word Associates.

The Great Knowledge Race; U.S. History Package: Series 4. Apple. Focus Media, Inc.

Chapter 18

Objectives

- Summarize the main arguments for and against overseas expansion.
- Cite the causes of the Spanish-American War.
- Analyze the annexation of the Philippines and its effects on United States policy toward Asia.
- Describe the effects of United States intervention in Latin America.

Introducing
THE CHAPTER

For suggestions on introducing Chapter 18, refer to page 465B in the Teacher's Edition.

Developing
THE CHAPTER

For activities and teaching strategies to help you reinforce and enrich chapter content, see pages 465B–465D in the Teacher's Edition.

Chapter Opener Illustrations

The victory of Dewey's steel fleet over the Spanish Pacific fleet at Manila Bay encouraged the belief that the United States needed a world-wide system of naval bases and colonial possessions to become a world power.

In the 1880s and 1890s the United States built a new steel naval fleet. Roosevelt sent it on a world tour to display American might. This painting depicts the Great White Fleet's triumphant entry into San Francisco Bay at the end of the tour.

Cartoonist Charles Macauley saw Theodore Roosevelt as a militarist whose policies had made the United States into an international bully.

The Panama Canal was a major undertaking of Roose-

Reduced student page in the Teacher's Edition

Chapter 18 1890-1916

Reaching for World Power

NIGHT SPECIAL. NEW YORK JOURNAL

WAR SURRENDERS! DEWEY'S FLEET TAKES MANILA.

WASHINGTON GETS NEWS OF THE CITY'S FALL

velt's administration. His goal was to link the Atlantic and Pacific oceans to provide easy access for United States naval and merchant fleets.

Theodore Roosevelt participated in the Spanish-American War of 1898 as colonel of the "Rough Riders" a volunteer regiment. He is pictured in his field tent, writing a letter home.

This painting shows a Japanese artist's view of Commodore Matthew Perry, who led a naval expedition to Japan in 1853 and negotiated a treaty that permitted trade between the United States and Japan.

American Voices

In the late 1800s the nation began to plunge into world affairs, looking outward to new markets and control of foreign territory. Speaking to the Republican convention in 1900, vice-presidential candidate Theodore Roosevelt reflected the growing willingness among Americans to reach for a new role as a world power:

> *"We stand on the threshold of a new century big with the fate of mighty nations. It rests with us now to decide whether in the opening years of that century we shall march forward to fresh triumphs or whether at the outset we shall cripple ourselves for the contest. Is America a weakling, to shrink from the work of the great powers? No. The young giant of the West stands on a continent and clasps the crest of an ocean in either hand. Our nation, glorious in youth and strength, looks into the future with eager eyes and rejoices . . . to run a race."*

The country did indeed join the race for empire, looking south to Latin America and west toward Asia. The reach for world power, however, raised the question of whether it was right for the United States to take control over people and lands beyond its borders.

Headline hailing naval victory over Spain; the Great White Fleet; cartoon on Roosevelt's foreign policy; Panama Canal dam; Roosevelt as army colonel; Japanese painting of Matthew Perry.

Analyzing Primary Sources

American Voices

Have students recall the doctrine of manifest destiny and the acquisition of Oregon, Texas, and California and other formerly Mexican lands in the 1840s (Chapter 10).

1. How do Roosevelt's words show that the doctrine has been revived? **(Roosevelt's words indicate interest in extending the nation's power beyond its borders.)**
2. What emotional phrases does Roosevelt use to downplay anti-expansionism? **("cripple ourselves," "weakling," "shrink from")**
3. What do you imagine was the reaction of the majority of Americans to this speech? Why?

GTV Side 3
Chap. 17, Frame 45012
The Limits of Power (Movie)
Search:

Play:

Section 18-1

Objectives

- ***Answer the Focus Question.***
- *Analyze the importance of naval power to the proponents of expansionism.*
- *Explain why expansion led to conflicts in the Pacific and the Caribbean.*

Introducing

THE SECTION

Review with students the meaning of the phrase *manifest destiny* as it had been applied in the United States in the 1840s (Chapter 10). Review the reasons why many Americans believed in manifest destiny. **(They wished to spread liberty and democracy across the continent.)**

Then explain that in the 1890s expansionists began seeing the manifest destiny of the United States not merely in terms of the North American continent but in terms of the world.

B · A · C · K · G · R · O · U · N · D

Time Line Illustrations

1. This 1893 image is from a Currier and Ives engraving of the armored steel cruiser *New York*, one of the new steel ships created for the United States Navy.

2. The canteen was used by American soldiers during the Spanish-American War; they needed all the water they could get to avoid dehydration. The first troops sent to tropical Cuba wore woolen uniforms made for the harsh winters of the Great Plains.

3. This magazine cover depicts General Adna R. Chaffee, who led the American troops sent to China to combat the Boxer siege of the Peking diplomatic missions.

4. The New York *Globe* depicted the President as a militarist whose achievements were based more on his use of

Reduced student page in the Teacher's Edition

CHAPTER TIME LINE

1890-1916

1899 **Feb** Philippines annexed
Feb Filipino revolt (through mid 1902)
Sep Open Door policy in China proposed

1895 **Feb** Cuban revolt begins

1890 — 1895 — 1900

1890 Congress votes funds to build up navy

1898 **Apr-Aug** Spanish-American War
Jul Hawaii annexed

1900 **Jun-Aug** Boxer Rebellion in China

18-1 Eyes Toward Expansion

Focus: What were the arguments for and against expansion?

By the 1850s the vision of manifest destiny had been fulfilled: the country stretched "from sea to shining sea." Over the next three decades, that expansion was enough for most Americans. Preoccupied with healing the wounds of the Civil War and adjusting to industrialization, they had little interest in acquiring land outside of North America.

As the reunited nation became an industrial giant, however, a growing number of politicians, military leaders, and scholars came to believe that the country must look beyond its borders. They pointed to the need to protect economic interests. More importantly, they felt that national pride required the United States to flex its muscles, staking out a place in the world as an equal of the European powers. To these expansionists, the nation had a "new Manifest Destiny"—to extend its power across the Pacific Ocean and around the Caribbean Sea.

Arguments for an Expansionist Policy

Among the voices calling for expansion was that of Senator Henry Cabot Lodge. In 1892 he declared:

> *"We have a record of conquest, colonization, and territorial expansion unequalled by any people in the nineteenth century. We are*

the "big stick" than on international negotiations.

5. Following the Mexican Revolution, many Mexican farmers supported General Francisco "Pancho" Villa, who pledged land reform. Villa soon became a focus of United States policy toward Mexico.

6. Roosevelt's image appears on this medal, commemorating the completion of the Panama Canal in 1914. He had left office more than six years before. The reverse side of the medal shows the canal.

1904 Building of Panama Canal begins

Feb Panama Canal Treaty ratified

1914 **Aug** Panama Canal opens

1905 — 1910 — 1915

1905 **Sep** Treaty ends Russo-Japanese War

1907 Great White Fleet tours the world

1910 Mexican Revolution

1916 **Mar** Wilson sends troops into Mexico

not to be curbed now. . . . Commerce follows the flag, and we should build up a navy strong enough to give protection to Americans in every quarter of the globe. . . . The great nations are rapidly absorbing for their future expansion and their present defense all the waste places of the earth. It is a movement which makes for civilization and the advancement of the race. As one of the great nations of the world, the United States must not fall out of the line of march. ❞

Lodge's statement reflected several main arguments. One was that European countries were already spreading their tentacles and gaining power. The 1880s had seen them scramble for African colonies as part of a policy of **imperialism**— the effort to dominate the trade and government of other lands. Expansionists like Lodge believed that the United States must either join the imperialist race or end up a second-rate power.

Some argued that expansion was morally right, that white Americans had the duty to spread democracy and Christianity in order to "civilize" nonwhite and non-Christian people. This racist belief in white superiority was shared by European imperialists, but no one expressed it more bluntly than the Reverend Josiah Strong:

❝ *God, with infinite wisdom and skill, is training the Anglo-Saxon race for an hour sure to come in the world's future. . . . And can anyone doubt that the result of this competition of races will be the 'survival of the fittest'? . . . Is there room or reasonable doubt that this race . . . is destined to dispossess many weaker races, assimilate others, and mold the remainder, until in a very true and important sense it has Anglo-Saxonized mankind?* ❞

Strong's views clearly reflected the "survival of the fittest" theory of social Darwinism. He argued that Americans— and specifically white, Anglo-Saxon Americans— were the fittest and therefore were destined to build a great empire.

Developing

THE SECTION

Limited English Proficiency

Building Vocabulary. Help students to interpret the following idioms, examining the positive or negative connotations implied in their use.

1. Expansionists felt national pride required the United States to *flex its muscles*. (page 468)
2. European countries were already *spreading their tentacles*. (page 469)

Global Connections

Making a Chart. Have students look in a historical atlas or a world history text to determine which European nations had colonies in Asia, Africa, and the Pacific Islands. Ask them to make a chart of European nations and their colonies up to 1900.

Analyzing Primary Sources

Josiah Strong. Read aloud the quote from Reverend Strong on this page.

Ask: Who is described as the fittest? **(Anglo Saxons)** What will happen to "weaker races"? **(dispossessed, assimilated, molded)** What effect will this have on "mankind"? **(All will become Anglo-Saxonized.)** What racist beliefs was Strong supporting? **(God made whites to be the strongest race, for example.)**

Can students cite examples of defenders of such racist beliefs today? **(neo-Nazis or Aryan groups, for example)** What dangers do students see in these views?

Analyzing Primary Sources

Anti-Expansionist.

“We cannot set our house in order if we must spend our energies in its defense or in attacks upon a neighbor. . . . There is one unvarying demand in all the forward policy and that is for ships, soldiers, and money . . . To make it effective no one can tell the cost. This means heavy taxation.”

Ask: What two arguments is the speaker using against expansion? **(Improvements within the nation cannot be made if the country is occupied with expansion outside the nation, expansionism financed with heavy taxes.)** How similar were arguments against the Persian Gulf War in 1990? **(some similarities: financing the war, helping those within the country rather than dealing with problems in foreign lands)**

Thinking Critically

Analysis. Captain Mahan argued that every great nation in history grew through naval power. He said that the United States needed more merchant ships to carry its goods to other nations and a larger navy to protect the ships.

Ask students what effect Mahan's ideas might have on each of the following: the shipbuilding industry (help the industry by creating a demand for more ships); the United States Navy (expand and strengthen the navy); factory owners (open up world markets for manufactured goods).

Connections: Language

People known as “Continentalists” believed that the United States should not expand beyond its continental limits. They were morally opposed to acquiring territories without the inhabitants' consent, feared foreign entanglements, and felt the nation could not absorb people of foreign lands.

Reduced student page in the Teacher's Edition

The desire for economic gain was another motive for expansion. Unlike the European powers, the United States did not have a great need for raw materials. However, expansionists did want to ensure that the nation got a fair share of foreign trade, especially with China. In saying that commerce follows the flag, Lodge was calling for American military power to protect American trade and investments overseas.

The Case Against Expansion

Calls for expansion did not drown out the voices of Americans who opposed raising the flag over foreign soil. Perhaps the strongest anti-imperialist argument was that taking control of other lands by force flew in the face of American ideals. Carl Schurz, an editor and political leader, argued that the price of expansionism was that “our old democratic principle that governments derive their just powers from the consent of the people will have to go overboard.” Also, ignoring the rights of people in other lands would invite their rebellion.

Anti-imperialists also pointed to the economic burden of building and protecting an empire. Taxes would have to be raised, Schurz warned, and “every American worker, when at his toil, will have to carry a soldier or sailor on his back.”

There was also the racist view that America was a “white man's country” and that nonwhite peoples in other lands could never become assimilated as Americans. Actually, many expansionists shared this deep fear of “tarnishing” white society.

Lodge declared, “We desire no extension to the south, for neither the population nor the lands of Central or South America would be desirable extensions to the United States.” Such statements also reflected an arrogant assumption by European Americans that people elsewhere would welcome living under the American flag.

A Plea for Naval Power

Although by the 1880s expansionist goals were taking hold within the circles of government, they still lacked widespread public support. Also, the country did not have the military muscle to carry them out. The vision forming in the minds of Lodge and other leaders depended upon the country building a stronger navy.

The boasts of some politicians that the United States could “lick all creation” were hollow. Following the Civil War, the United States Navy had entered a period of decline. Congress had set aside so little money for shipbuilding that by 1880 the American fleet ranked only twelfth in the world. Indeed, when an American admiral tried to intervene in a war between Chile and Bolivia, the Chilean navy threatened to sink all his ships—and could have easily done so.

The picture of American weakness at sea, however, was soon to change—particularly through the influence of Captain Alfred T. Mahan, an instructor at the Naval War College. Pointing to Great Britain as an example, Mahan argued that sea power can make or break nations because it protects commerce, a country's lifeblood.

Mahan, like other expansionists, believed that the country's future greatness depended upon using naval power to achieve two main goals: dominance of the Pacific trade routes and enforcement of the Monroe Doctrine. Unless the United States had strength at sea, he warned, other world powers would control the Pacific and defy the Monroe Doctrine by seeking control of Latin America. United States trade would ultimately suffer, and with it, the nation's security.

Captain Alfred T. Mahan helped convince government leaders that prosperity depended on building a powerful navy.

Multicultural Perspectives

Polynesians settled in Hawaii about 2,000 years ago. They were joined by the Tahitians around A.D. 1200. Nearly 300,000 people lived on the islands in 1778 when British explorer James Cook arrived. In the 1800s many Chinese and Japanese laborers came to the islands. By 1920 Hawaiians made up 16.3 percent of the population, Europeans 7.7, Chinese 9.2, Japanese 42.7, Portuguese 10.6, and Filipinos 8.2. Other groups, including Koreans and Samoans, made up 5.3 percent. Today, only about 15 percent of the people are of Hawaiian ancestry, nearly 50 percent are of European ancestry, and about 25 percent are of Japanese ancestry.

Active Learning

Debate. Divide students into two groups—expansionists and anti-expansionists. Have students present a debate on the role of the United States in world affairs. Expansionists should consult the writings of Senator Albert Beveridge, Captain Alfred Mahan, Theodore Roosevelt, Secretary of State John Hay, minister Josiah Strong. Anti-expansionists should read the statements of William Jennings Bryan, Senator George Hoar, Grover Cleveland, Mark Twain, Samuel Gompers.

Ships in Honolulu harbor were signs of growing foreign control over Hawaii. In 1893 Queen Liliuokalani tried to free the economy from American sugar planters.

Politicians who shared Mahan's views labored to gain congressional support for his recommendations. In 1890 Congress finally approved funds to build a navy of steel ships strong enough to defeat the fleets of European nations.

Looking to the Pacific

Mahan believed that naval bases in the Pacific were essential to the nation's foreign trade. Steam-powered ships needed bases as refueling stops on the long trips to markets in Asia. If the United States did not act soon, he warned, European powers would get all the good ports. As an example of European aggressiveness, he pointed to the Samoan Islands.

The Samoan harbor of Pago Pago had long provided shelter and supplies for American ships crossing the Pacific. But in the 1870s Congress had rejected a proposal to annex Samoa as smacking of imperialism. By the late 1880s Germany and Great Britain were eyeing the islands. When a civil war broke out there in 1889, warships from the three countries all moved to intervene. The three powers finally agreed to joint control of the islands, but only after a violent hurricane had destroyed most of their warships. To Captain Mahan the lesson was clear: such "dangerous germs of quarrel" would spread in the future, and the American navy must be ready for them.

Conflict over Hawaii. "As regards Hawaii, I take your views absolutely," Assistant Secretary of the Navy Theodore Roosevelt wrote to Mahan in 1897. "If I had my way we would annex those islands tomorrow." When Roosevelt wrote these words, the expansionist tide was swelling, and annexation of those stepping stones to the Far East was not far off.

Strong American interest in Hawaii dated back to the early 1800s, when Christian missionaries arrived. Their descendants built successful careers as sugar planters and traders, ignoring the impact on the land and culture of the Hawaiian people. By the late 1800s the planters were badgering Congress to annex the islands so that they would get the same trade protections as planters in the United

Limited English Proficiency

Building Vocabulary. Help students to interpret the following idioms, examining the positive or negative connotations implied in their use:

The expansionist *tide was swelling*, and annexation of those *stepping stones* to the Far East was not far off. (page 471)

GTV Side 3

Chap. 17, Frame 47825

Hawaiian Islands 1893 (Map)

Search:

Writing About History

Letter. Have students imagine that they are one of the following people in the 1800s: an American missionary in Hawaii, an American sugar planter in Hawaii, an American navy or merchant ship captain whose ship often visits Pearl Harbor, a native Hawaiian, or a Japanese person living in Hawaii.

Have them write a letter to a friend, describing their feelings and opinions about the annexation of Hawaii. Ask some students to read their letters aloud to the class.

Connections: Language
In the mid-1800s Canadians and Americans were arguing over fishing and seal-hunting rights. American newspapers fanned the flames of the conflict. The Detroit *News* rephrased a popular British song of the 1870s to suggest that Americans and Canadians might go to war. In the song the words "by jingo" were used. The dispute was peacefully settled, but the word *jingo* was remembered. *Jingoism* came to refer to intense national pride and support of a warlike foreign policy. By the 1890s *jingoism* flourished in the American press.

Section Review

ANSWERS

1. Definition for *imperialism* is on text page 469.
2. For: to compete with European imperialist nations to be a first-rate power; "civilize" non whites, non-Christians; increase foreign trade. Against: opposed American ideal of government by consent of governed; higher taxes to build, protect empire; the racist argument that nonwhite people could not be assimilated.
3. Goals: dominance of Pacific trade routes and enforcement of Monroe Doctrine. They argued that only naval power could keep other nations from controlling Pacific and Latin America.
Linking Past and Present
The arguments of those opposed to Persian Gulf War were largely moral and economic: that the United States was not justified in using force and that the war would be extremely costly. In this respect the arguments were like the moral and economic arguments against expansion.

Reduced student page in the Teacher's Edition

States. Annexation would also help them get a firm grip on the islands in the face of a growing Hawaiian native movement.

In 1891, while the debate over annexation continued in the United States, Hawaii's throne passed to a strong-willed new ruler, Queen Liliuokalani, (lih-LEE-oo-oh-kuh-LAH-nee). Determined to restore power to the Hawaiian monarchy, she rallied support with the slogan "Hawaii for Hawaiians." The white planters reacted by staging a successful revolt. Aided by American marines, they set up a provisional, or temporary, government. The queen had little choice but to surrender.

The leaders of the provisional government soon asked to be annexed, but their appeal was rejected. They then declared independence and established the Republic of Hawaii. Meanwhile, American expansionists continued to push for annexation. If the United States did not do so, they argued, another country would.

American Voices

"If I had my way we would annex those islands [Hawaii] tomorrow."

—Theodore Roosevelt

Defending the Monroe Doctrine

While looking across the Pacific, expansionists also wanted to keep European powers out of Latin America. They called upon the government to vigorously apply the Monroe Doctrine. First stated in 1823, the doctrine had warned Europeans not to try to set up new colonies in the Americas. Over the years the United States broadened it, warning European nations not to use force against independent nations in the Americas. But those warnings were seldom backed by action.

Aware that Europe and Latin America had never formally recognized the Monroe Doctrine, Captain Mahan stressed the need for sea power to enforce it. He was sure that European powers would seek a greater foothold in Latin America, particularly when the long-planned canal between the Atlantic and Pacific oceans became a reality. Only if it had a strong fleet and naval bases in the Caribbean could the United States keep European nations from moving in.

Showdown in the Caribbean. As the fleet expanded during the 1890s, the government felt ready for any conflict in the Caribbean. And in 1895 it got one when a dispute erupted between Great Britain and Venezuela over the boundary between that South American nation and the British colony of Guiana. When Great Britain refused Venezuela's request that the issue be settled through arbitration—a binding decision made by a neutral third party—President Grover Cleveland felt that he had to enforce the Monroe Doctrine.

Cleveland's Secretary of State, Richard Olney, sent a challenging note to Great Britain. He declared that the United States would not permit Britain to take action against Venezuela, boldly insisting that "the United States is practically sovereign on this continent." Congress then created a commission to settle the boundary dispute.

The enraged British government, resenting this challenge to its power, prepared for war. Just then, however, a conflict with Germany over colonies in Africa diverted Britain's attention. The threat of war evaporated, much to the relief of the majority of Americans, who were not convinced that Venezuela's border was worth fighting over. Nevertheless, the showdown was seen by many Americans as a victory for the Monroe Doctrine and justification for a more active role in Latin America.

Section Review

1. Identification. Define *imperialism.*

2. Comprehension. Describe the main arguments for and against overseas expansion.

3. Analysis. Explain why expansionists believed that a stronger navy was needed in order to reach their two main goals.

Linking Past and Present. Compare the views of anti-expansionists in the 1890s with the views of Americans who opposed the Persian Gulf War with Iraq in 1991.

Connections: Economics
Economics played a role in Americans' concern about the conflict in Cuba. By the mid-1890s Americans had about $50 million invested there. United States trade with Cuba amounted to about $100 million a year.

Section **18-2**

Objectives

- ***Answer the Focus Question.***
- *Analyze why the Spanish-American War was a turning point in American history.*
- *Evaluate United States' motives in going to war.*

18-2 The Spanish-American War

Focus: Why did the United States go to war with Spain?

The showdown with Britain over Venezuela reflected a new posture. The United States was ready to test its strength against any world power that challenged its interests in Latin America. A challenge soon came in Cuba, a Spanish possession in the Caribbean.

Growing Tensions Over Cuba

Cuba and Puerto Rico were Spain's last two Latin American colonies. In February 1895, Cubans—many of whom had long struggled against Spanish rule—rose again in revolt. Spain sent General Valeriano Weyler to crush the rebellion. He herded men, women, and children into "reconcentration camps" to shut off peasant support for the rebels. Hundreds of thousands of captives died from hunger and disease.

American newspapers, especially the New York *Journal* and the New York *World,* tried to outdo each other with sensational accounts of the rebellion. Headlines screamed that "Mad Dog Weyler" was "feeding prisoners to sharks." This emotional reporting, known as "yellow journalism," whipped up support for the rebels.

Expansionists, who had long sought to annex Cuba and Puerto Rico, called for the United States to intervene. They were joined by business leaders who had invested in Cuban sugar plantations. In this highly charged atmosphere, only a spark was needed to ignite the fire of war.

***"Remember the* Maine!"** At 9:40 p.m. on February 15, 1898, an American stepped into a small cafe in Cuba's capital city of Havana. Suddenly, as he recalled,

> *"The city shook to a terrific explosion. Amid a shower of falling plaster every light in the place went out, as did every other electric light in the city."*

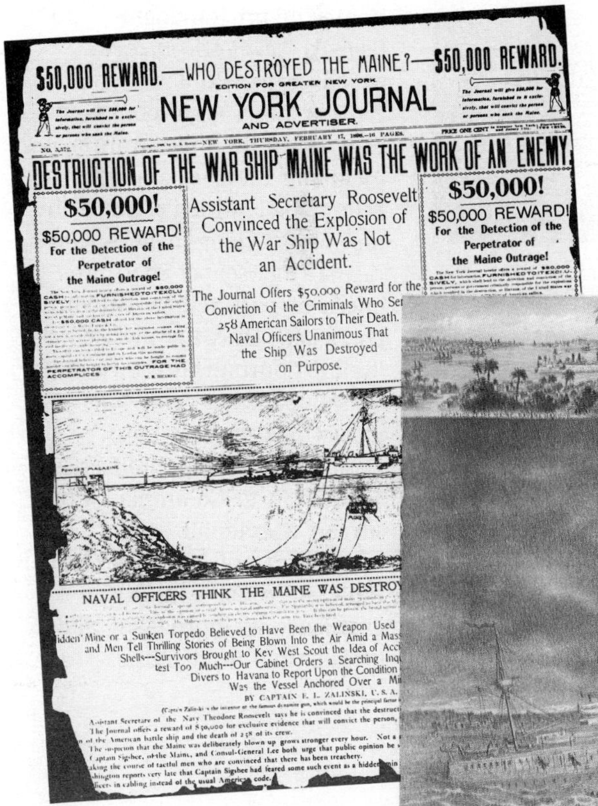
$50,000 REWARD.—WHO DESTROYED THE MAINE?—$50,000 REWARD.

EDITION FOR GREATER NEW YORK.

NEW YORK JOURNAL AND ADVERTISER.

DESTRUCTION OF THE WAR SHIP MAINE WAS THE WORK OF AN ENEMY.

$50,000!
$50,000 REWARD!
For the Detection of the Perpetrator of the Maine Outrage!

Assistant Secretary Roosevelt Convinced the Explosion of the War Ship Was Not an Accident.

The Journal Offers $50,000 Reward for the Conviction of the Criminals Who Sent 258 American Sailors to Their Death. Naval Officers Unanimous That the Ship Was Destroyed on Purpose.

$50,000!
$50,000 REWARD!
For the Detection of the Perpetrator of the Maine Outrage!

NAVAL OFFICERS THINK THE MAINE WAS DESTROY

Hidden Mine or a Sunken Torpedo Believed to Have Been the Weapon Used ... and Men Tell Thrilling Stories of Being Blown Into the Air Amid a Mass ... Shells—Survivors Brought to Key West Scout the Idea of Acc... test Too Much—Our Cabinet Orders a Searching Inq... Divers to Havana to Report Upon the Condition ... Was the Vessel Anchored Over a M...

BY CAPTAIN F. L. ZALINSKI, U. S. A.

When the* Maine *exploded in Havana harbor, Americans quickly blamed Spain, despite not having proof.

Introducing
THE SECTION

When he became President, McKinley announced, *"We want no wars of conquest."* But eventually pressure for war with Spain became too great for him to withstand.

Have students read the section to find out why McKinley gave in to expansionists' pleas for war and how the Spanish-American War made the United States a world power.

Social History
Ironically, William R. Hearst began his journalism career as a reporter on Pulitzer's New York *World.* Then he took over his father's newspaper, the San Francisco *Examiner.* To break into the New York market, Hearst bought the New York *Morning Journal.*

Developing
THE SECTION

Multicultural Perspectives

Discussion. Lola Rodriguez de Tió was a Puerto Rican woman who spoke out in the late 1800s for freedom from Spain. Forced to leave her homeland, she fled to Cuba and then to New York, where she published several books of poems. She spoke of freedom in this poem:

"Freedom comes if
you want it,
Be you called a man or
a woman,
If you can aspire to
justice
If you can recognize
duty.

Deny all that you like
If denying is your
misfortune,
But do not deny me three
things:
Spirit, God, and
nation."

Ask: What did the poet mean by valuing "Spirit, God, and nation"? Why might those values be particularly important to a person?

Reduced student page in the Teacher's Edition

The battleship U.S.S. *Maine,* sent to protect Americans in Cuba, had exploded, killing 260 sailors and marines. When the news reached New York *Journal* publisher William Randolph Hearst, he reportedly declared, "This means war!"

A Spanish investigation concluded that the explosion might have been caused by an accidental fire in one of the ship's engines. Most Americans, though, agreed with Theodore Roosevelt's opinion. "The *Maine* was sunk by an act of dirty treachery on the part of the Spaniards," he said. The battle cry "Remember the *Maine!*" resounded throughout the country.

"A Splendid Little War"

President William McKinley, hoping to avoid a war over Cuba, offered to arbitrate the dispute between Spain and the rebels. As Spain hesitated, however, he bowed to pressure from Congress and the public, which largely supported a fight to gain freedom for Cuba. In April he asked for a declaration of war. When declaring war, Congress also passed a resolution recognizing Cuban independence. To calm fears of anti-expansionists, it added the Teller Amendment, stating that the United States would not annex Cuba.

THE AMERICAN SPIRIT

Joseph Pulitzer

The Father of Yellow Journalism

Seventeen-year-old Joseph Pulitzer wanted to be a soldier, but the Austrian Army, the French Foreign Legion, and the German navy all rejected the lanky, near-sighted Hungarian boy. Then Pulitzer met an American recruiter in Germany who was scouting for troops for the Union in the Civil War. He signed Pulitzer up.

After the war Pulitzer looked for work in St. Louis. With so many former soldiers in the market, jobs were hard to find. Pulitzer was talked into paying for steamboat passage by the promise of a job in Louisiana. When the boat broke down outside St. Louis, a newspaper in the city published Pulitzer's account of the swindle and gave him a job.

Soon Pulitzer owned the St. Louis *Post-Dispatch.* Like many newspapers of the time, it printed news that embarrassed prominent citizens by exposing their shady business deals. Pulitzer claimed, "More crime, immorality, and rascality is prevented by the fear of exposure in the newspapers than by all the laws ever devised."

In 1883 Pulitzer bought the *World,* a New York City newspaper. Readers were soon drawn to Pulitzer's often sensational stories. One of his first headlines blared: "A FORTUNE SQUANDERED IN DRINK."

The *World* faced competition from William Randolph Hearst's New York *Journal,* which copied Pulitzer's style. Pulitzer hired a cartoonist and began printing "the funnies," including the cartoon "The Yellow Kid," which marked the first use of color in newspapers. Hearst's newspaper soon produced its own yellow cartoon character. Thus the phrase "yellow journalism," meaning sensationalism intended to attract readers, was born.

Upon his death, Pulitzer left $2 million to Columbia University for a graduate school of journalism and to create the Pulitzer Prizes, awarded for excellence in journalism, literature, drama, and music.

Social History

The American victory at Manila Bay made Dewey a national hero, and he was later touted as a presidential candidate. The Topeka *Daily Capital* published this poem:

"Oh dewy was the morning
Upon the first of May,
And Dewey was the Admiral,
Down in Manila Bay.
And dewy were the Spaniards' eyes,
Them orbs of black and blue;
and dew we feel discouraged?
I dew not think we dew!"

Active Learning

Cooperative Activity. Have students imagine that they are members of Congress in 1898, just prior to the Spanish-American War. With a partner, have them develop a pamphlet to either persuade others to go to war or to resist the war effort. Arguments should revolve around issues of Spain's domination of Cuba and the proper role of the United States in the hemisphere: whether it was going to war to extend its control and, if so, did it have the right to do this.

African-American soldiers and Roosevelt's "Rough Riders" played key roles in the Battle of San Juan Hill. Also shown are Roosevelt's insignia and a Native-American Rough Rider. Few horses were used, though, for most could not fit on the crowded transport ships to Cuba.

Although the government portrayed the war mainly as a struggle to liberate Cuba, American expansionists were clearly more interested in taking over what was left of Spain's empire. Their goal helps to explain why the war began not in Cuba but halfway around the world in the Philippines.

Victory in the Pacific. The golden opportunity to strip Spain of the Philippines was not lost on Assistant Secretary of the Navy Theodore Roosevelt. Even before war was declared, he had begun to lay the groundwork for an American foothold in the Far East. Impatient with the cautious Secretary of the Navy, whom he regarded as suffering from the "slows," Roosevelt secretly cabled Commodore George Dewey in Hong Kong. Dewey was instructed to prepare to attack Spain's Pacific fleet in the Philippines.

On April 30, 1898, just eleven days after Congress declared war on Spain, Dewey's fleet steamed into Manila Bay. The United States' modern steel navy easily defeated the Spanish warships. Dewey then waited for reinforcements while his ships blockaded the bay.

After American troops arrived in June and July, they were joined by Filipino rebels led by Emilio Aguinaldo (AH-gwee-NAHL-doh). The rebels believed that the United States could help them gain independence. On August 13, 1898, the combined American and Filipino forces attacked Manila, the Philippine capital. The Spaniards surrendered, and Spain's rule of the Philippines was ended.

Victory in the Caribbean. News of Dewey's quick victory over the Spanish fleet electrified the nation and boosted support for the war. To aid the

Active Learning

Cooperative Activity. Divide the class into six small groups. Assign each group one of the following incidents to research for newspaper reports: Weyler's reconcentration camps; sinking of *Maine;* declaration of war; Battle of Manila Bay; Battle of San Juan Hill; the peace settlement.

Each group will produce the front page of a newspaper and present it to the class. The page ought to include a catchy headline on the incident, the lead article, and appropriate graphics such as maps and illustrations. You may wish to have each group do two versions: one reflecting objective journalism and the other "yellow journalism."

Social History

On April 30, 1898, Theodore Roosevelt placed the following order with the Brooks Brothers clothing store: *"Can you make so I shall have it here by next Saturday a blue cravennat regular lieutenant-colonel's uniform without yellow on collar, and with leggings? If so make it."*

Connections: Literature

Stephen Crane, the author of *The Red Badge of Courage*, served as a war reporter in Cuba. When Crane wrote his Civil War novel about fear and courage under fire, he had never seen a battle. But after witnessing his first battle in the Spanish-American War, Crane believed he had imagined war truly. "*The Red Badge*," he said, "*is all right.*"

Reduced student page in the Teacher's Edition

Cuban freedom fighters, 17,000 regular troops and volunteers landed in June near the Spanish stronghold at Santiago. By July 1 victories on the outskirts of Santiago had enabled the Americans to place artillery on hills overlooking the city.

Most widely reported in the newspapers was the decisive Battle of San Juan Hill. It began with a force of 8,000 Americans pinned down by withering Spanish gunfire. Among them was Theodore Roosevelt, who had resigned his government post to lead a volunteer regiment called the Rough Riders. The Rough Riders joined with African-American troops from the elite 9th and 10th Cavalry regiments, relentlessly charging up a slope despite heavy casualties. Recalled one reporter:

> *"They walked to greet death at every step, many of them, as they advanced, sinking suddenly or pitching forward and disappearing in the high grass, but others waded on, stubbornly, forming a thin blue line that kept creeping higher and higher up the hill. . . . The fire of the Spanish riflemen, who still stuck bravely to their posts, doubled and trebled in fierceness, the crests of the hills crackled and burst in amazed roars. . . . But the blue line crept steadily up. . . ."*

While agreeing that the charge was brave, many observers saw it as foolish. One American officer later noted, "If we had been in that position and the Spaniards had come at us, we would have piled them up so high the last man couldn't have climbed over." Fortunately, most of the Spanish bullets sailed over the heads of the attacking troops, or the casualties might have been much higher than the 200 killed and 1,100 wounded.

As American troops laid siege to Santiago, a squadron of American ships bottled up the Spanish fleet in the harbor. When the Spanish ships tried to fight their way out on July 3, they were sunk or run aground. The 24,000 Spaniards in Santiago were now trapped, for American ships commanded the harbor and American soldiers encircled the city. On July 17 the Spaniards surrendered.

Shortly afterward, an American force landed on the nearby island of Puerto Rico. After a brief fight it fell, and Spain signed a truce on August 12, 1898. In less than four months, the United States had won what Secretary of State John Hay called "a splendid little war, begun with the highest motives, carried on with magnificent intelligence and spirit, favored by that Fortune which loves the brave."

Spotlight on Politics

Wartime exploits can be a springboard to political success. Witness these notes from the diary of Secretary of the Navy John Long, dated April 25, 1898:

> *"My Assistant Secretary, Roosevelt, has determined upon resigning, in order to go into the army and take part in the war. He has been of great use; a man of unbounded energy and force, and thoroughly honest, which is the main thing. . . . He has lost his head to this unutterable folly of . . . running off to ride a horse and, probably, brush mosquitoes from his neck. . . . He thinks he is following his highest ideal, whereas, in fact, as without exception every one of his friends advises him, he is acting like a fool. And, yet, how absurd all this will sound if, by some turn of fortune, he should accomplish some great thing and strike a very high mark."*

After the war Long added:

> *"P.S. Roosevelt was right and we his friends were all wrong. His going into the army led straight to the Presidency."*

The Peace Settlement

When the truce was signed in President McKinley's White House office, one of his aides walked over to a large globe and remarked, "Let's see what we get by this." The answer would be found in the final

Multicultural Perspectives

The term "Spanish-American War" is misleading in that Filipino and Cuban freedom fighters played key roles in freeing their people from Spanish rule. Cubans were inspired by José Martí. Exiled from Cuba for his revolutionary writings and activities, Martí lived in the United States from 1880 to 1895. After returning to join the 1895 revolt, he was killed by Spanish soldiers. His memory, however, inspired Cubans' quest for independence.

Geography Skills

ANSWERS

The island territories were small in square miles but provided the United States with naval (and later, air) bases all across the Pacific, making it a major power in the region.

The United States in the Pacific 1865-1900

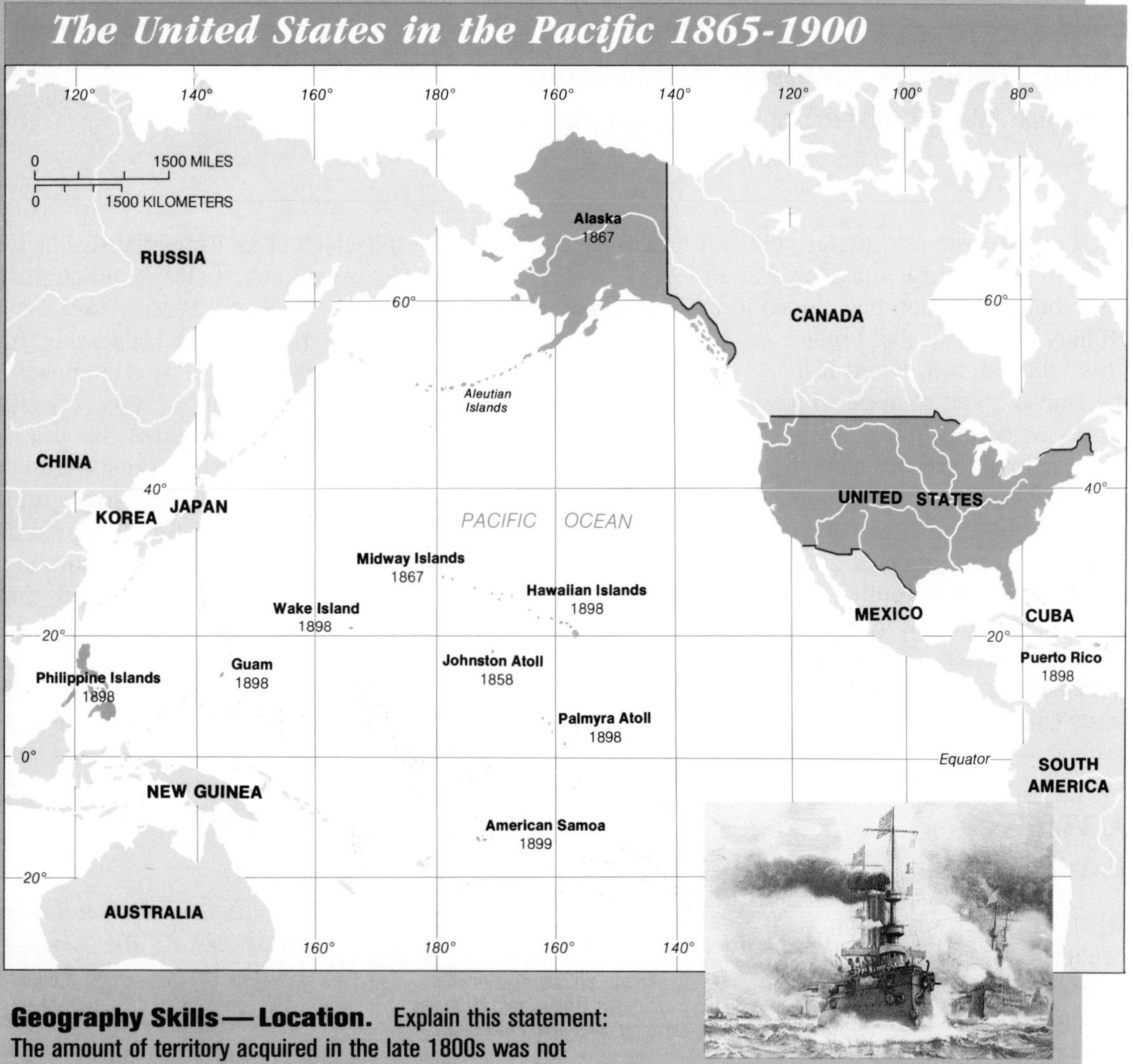

Geography Skills — Location. Explain this statement: The amount of territory acquired in the late 1800s was not great, yet the lands were important strategically.

peace treaty, signed December 10, 1898. The treaty required Spain to surrender Cuba, leaving the island in the hands of American forces. The Philippines and Puerto Rico were also turned over, along with the South Pacific island of Guam.

The treaty clearly reflected expansionist goals. Yet it could not go into effect unless Congress ratified it. Most Americans had strongly supported a war to free Cuba. Would Congress — and the public — now support a peace agreement that would create an overseas empire?

Section Review

1. **Comprehension.** What were some causes and effects of the Spanish-American War?

2. **Application.** How does the Spanish-American War illustrate the strength of public opinion in a democratic society?

3. **Evaluation.** Reread the statement on the facing page about the "splendid little war." Which parts do you agree with? Disagree with? Explain.

Section Review

ANSWERS

1. Causes: expansionists' desire to annex Puerto Rico and Cuba; sinking of the *Maine*; treatment of Cubans; newspaper support for rebels. Effects: U.S. control of Philippines, Puerto Rico, Guam, Cuba.
2. McKinley hoped to avoid war but was forced into it by public and congressional demands for war.
3. Answers will vary. Students should recognize that American motives were mixed, combining imperialism with concern for Cubans, and that the San Juan Hill charge was foolhardy.

GTV Side 3

Chap. 17, Frame 48262

U.S. and British Dominance 1900 (Map)

Search:

GTV Side 3

Chap. 17, Frame 46720

Spanish-American War and Trade Influence (Animated Maps)

Search and Play:

Section 18-3

Objectives

- ***Answer the Focus Question.***
- *Explain why some Americans opposed annexing the Philippines.*
- *Describe the Open Door policy.*
- *Explain how Roosevelt's intervention in the Russo-Japanese war was part of United States expansion.*

Introducing

THE SECTION

McKinley, who had been reluctant to go to war, said at the war's end,

> *"And so it has come to pass in a few short months we have become a world power; and I know . . . with what added respect the nations of the world now deal with the United States."*

Yet the war left the nation sharply divided. Ask students how the expansionists probably felt about the war's outcome. **(delighted to receive new territories)**

Tell students that a small but vocal group of Americans opposed annexing territory and that the argument between these two groups soon centered on the Philippines. What happened on those islands would set the foreign policy course that the United States was to steer.

B · A · C · K · G · R · O · U · N · D

Social History
Those who opposed annexation formed an Anti-Imperialist League. The group attracted such people as Andrew Carnegie, Samuel Gompers, Mark Twain, Jane Addams, Grover Cleveland, and William Jennings Bryan.

Reduced student page in the Teacher's Edition

18-3 A Stronger Arm in Asia

Focus: How did gaining the Philippines affect United States foreign policy in Asia?

For expansionists, the greatest fruit of victory in the Spanish-American War was the foothold the nation had gained in the Far East. Military bases in the Philippines, they argued, would help the United States compete with European powers and a newly industrialized Japan for control of trade with China. Such arguments were countered by a small but vocal group of anti-expansionists. The conflict between the two groups soon centered on the issue of whether or not Congress should ratify the treaty ending the war.

A cartoon shows presidential candidates Bryan and McKinley clashing over the Philippines.

A Victory for Expansionism

When the treaty was sent to the Senate for ratification early in 1899, it set off a fierce debate. No provision of the treaty was more controversial than the annexation of the Philippines. Labor leaders joined the fight against annexation, arguing that it would lead to a flood of cheap labor. The most compelling argument, though, was that it was contrary to American principles of freedom and self-government. As Mark Twain declared,

> *"It should, it seems to me, be our pleasure and duty to make those people free and let them deal with their own domestic questions in their own way. And so I am an anti-imperialist. I am opposed to having the eagle put its talon on any other land."*

Despite the efforts of anti-imperialists, the treaty was ratified on February 6, 1899, although by a margin of only two votes. It was, said Senator Henry Cabot Lodge, the "hardest fight I have ever known."

The public was less closely divided. Clearly the war had added to the expansionist momentum. For example, during the war the Senate approved the annexation of Hawaii on the strength of arguments that it was needed as a "halfway station" to the Philippines.

Why had the tide shifted toward greater support for expansionism? Historian George F. Kennan suggests that the American people may have felt

> *"an urge to range themselves among the colonial powers of the time, to see our flag flying on distant tropical isles, to feel the thrill of foreign adventure and authority, to bask in the sunshine of recognition as one of the great imperial powers of the world."*

In short, the "rational" arguments for expansion were only part of the picture. Perhaps, as Kennan notes, a growing number of Americans "simply liked the smell of empire."

By the time of the presidential election of 1900, President McKinley—who had once called forced annexation "criminal aggression"—was swimming with the expansionist tide. His opponent,

Multicultural Perspectives

The Anti-Imperialist League adamantly opposed the war against the Filipino rebels. At home and abroad, African Americans played a leading role in denouncing the war. Many black soldiers sympathized with Filipinos, who were looked down on by white troops.

One black soldier wrote: *"I was struck by a question a Filipino boy asked me . . . 'Why does the American Negro come . . . to fight us where we are a friend to him and have not done anything to him. He is all the same as me and me all the same as you. Why don't you fight those people in America who burn Negroes, that make a beast of you?'"*

William Jennings Bryan, campaigned under the Democrats' anti-imperialist slogan, "A Republic Can Have No Colonies." However, a healthy economy helped McKinley's campaign, and the Republican slogan, "Don't Haul Down the Flag," was well received. McKinley won the election by a bigger vote than he had received in 1896.

Next Steps in the Philippines

While Americans were debating the treaty, Filipinos led by Emilio Aguinaldo had set up their own government. They expected the United States to recognize their independence. When Aguinaldo realized that the islands were to be annexed, he led a revolt against American rule.

For three years Aguinaldo's 80,000 freedom fighters waged a war of resistance against some 70,000 American soldiers. Finally, in the spring of 1901, Aguinaldo was captured. In captivity he called upon his fellow Filipinos to put down their arms. The organized fight was over—at a cost of more than 20,000 lives. Meanwhile, in the United States, the same newspapers that had provided such lurid descriptions of Spanish brutality in Cuba practically ignored the brutal suppression of the Filipinos by the American troops.

In July 1901 the government of the Philippines passed from the American military to a civil commission headed by William Howard Taft, who became the islands' governor. The efficient Taft quickly set about building a government for the Filipinos. They were promised that in time they could have self-rule, but for the present they were labeled "unfit for self-government."

Under the commission, the people of the Philippines were gradually given a greater role in government. Eventually, three Filipinos joined the commission. Under its direction, roads and schools were built and farmers were given lands previously held by the Catholic Church.

In 1902 Congress passed the Organic Act, which made the Philippines an unorganized territory. The act extended the commission's work and gave encouragement to Filipino self-rule. Filipinos were allowed to elect the lower house of the legislature, while the commission became the upper house.

The islands inched toward independence. In 1916 Congress took a major step by passing the Jones Act, under which Filipinos

No sooner were Filipinos free from Spain than they took up arms against American rule. Since independence in 1946, many have opposed the continued American military presence, as in this 1980s protest.

Developing THE SECTION

Active Learning

Drawing Political Cartoons. Discuss with students the political cartoons regarding expansionism on pages 478 and 480. Then, considering the words of Mark Twain and George Kennan (on page 478), have each student draw a cartoon that expresses a point of view toward the annexation of the Philippines. Have students share these with the class.

Using the Visuals

Discussion. Refer students to the illustration of the Filipino protestors on this page. One of the protest signs is written in Tagalog, the Filipino language. "Sumulong Ka AnakPawis" roughly translates as "Move ahead hard workers." Have students speculate about what this means in the context of the protest.

GTV Side 3

Chap. 14, Frame 36690

From the "Sewing Machine Advance," 1908 (American Journal)

Search:

Play:

Linking Past and Present

On July 4, 1946, Filipinos were granted full independence. In 1950, in exchange for economic and military aid, the Philippine government agreed to let the United States establish two major military bases. In 1988 the United States gave the Philippines $962 million in aid in return for permission to continue using the bases until 1991. The Philippine legislature voted in 1991 not to renew the leases for the military bases.

Connections: Language

Because westerners had difficulty writing Chinese characters in the Roman alphabet, the western press began using a journalistic spelling of the capital—Peking. In 1979 the

Thinking Critically

Analysis. Help students analyze the cartoon on this page by asking:
1. What do the characters represent? (United States and other imperialist nations)
2. What is significant about Uncle Sam's position and the key he leans on? (United States intent to keep trade with China open to all nations)
3. Why is the Chinese figure smiling? (The Open Door policy helped China's independence.)
4. What is the cartoonist's point of view toward United States diplomacy in the 1890s? (approves of the Open Door policy)

Limited English Proficiency

Tracing Cause and Effect Relationships. Read with students the first paragraph under the heading: "The Open Door Policy" and help them diagram how the growth of Japanese industry resulted in greater European attempts to create spheres of influence. (Industry—need for raw materials, markets—war with China to control Korea—Chinese defeat—realization of China's weakness—increased European spheres of influence.)

Reduced student page in the Teacher's Edition

were granted full civil rights and the power to elect both houses of the legislature. The governor was still to be an American, however. Another thirty years would pass before the Filipinos were finally granted their independence.

Japan: A Rising Sun

By taking over the Philippines, the United States became a major force in the imperialist competition in Asia. Another relative newcomer to the scene was Japan. From the 1600s to the mid-1800s, Japan had shunned contacts with other nations. Then, on July 8, 1853, an American naval squadron led by Commodore Matthew Perry dropped anchor in Tokyo Bay. Through naval power and his diplomatic skill, Perry negotiated a treaty that permitted trade between the United States and Japan.

Perry's move opened the door to further contact between Japan and other nations. Then, in 1868 Japan embarked upon an ambitious policy of industrialization along western lines. American and British experts gave advice, while German military officers trained a modern Japanese army. Within thirty years Japan had moved from a farming society to an industrial economy, the first Asian country to do so.

This cartoon reflects the American view that the United States played a major role in guaranteeing all nations an "open door" to trade with China.

The Open Door Policy

As Japan's industry grew, so too did its desire for markets, raw materials, and land for its growing population. In 1894, it went to war with China in an effort to take control of Korea. Japan quickly scored a stunning victory with its modern military forces. Although the peace agreement did not gain Japan much territory, it did underscore China's military weakness. European powers, along with Japan, moved quickly to carve China into their own **spheres of influence**— areas in which each nation had claimed exclusive rights to trade and to invest.

President McKinley and Secretary of State Hay recognized that control of the Philippines would do little good if the new spheres of influence closed off free trade with China. In the fall of 1899, Hay sent letters to the nations involved in China, urging them to follow an **Open Door policy,** in which Chinese ports would remain open to trade of all nations. Despite a cool response, Hay boldly declared the Open Door policy to be in effect.

In China, at about this same time, a secret society that opposed all "foreign devils" was gaining in strength. In June 1900 its members, nicknamed "Boxers" because of their skill in martial arts, killed more than 200 foreigners. Other foreigners sought refuge in foreign diplomatic offices in Beijing, where they were besieged by the Boxers. Troops from Russia, Britain, Germany, and Japan quickly converged on Beijing to fight the Boxers.

The United States feared that the European powers and Japan might use the Boxer rebellion as an excuse to seize Chinese territory. Seeking a hand in settling the crisis, McKinley, too, sent troops to China. Meanwhile, John Hay wrote a second Open Door letter urging that both China's territory and its government be preserved. Fortunately, the powers were unwilling to risk a war over China. Whether the Open Door policy would be respected in the future, however, remained a question.

Uneasy Relations with Japan

A major challenge to the Open Door policy was not long in coming. Both Japan and Russia had designs on Korea and on China's northeastern province of Manchuria. In February 1904 Japan

People's Republic of China started using Pinyin a new system of translating Chinese characters into the Roman alphabet. Thus Peking became Beijing. In the map on this page the old system of translation is used, with the words in Pinyin spelling in parentheses.

Multicultural Perspectives

Japanese-American relations after the war soured due in part to treatment of Japanese in California. In 1906 the San Francisco school board ordered the segregation of Japanese students. Japan was outraged. In response, Roosevelt met with the school board and they agreed to rescind the segregation order if the government restricted Japanese immigration.

Thinking Critically

Analysis. Refer students to the map "Foreign Influence in China 1900" on this page. **Ask:**

1. What are spheres of influence? (areas in which each nation had exclusive rights to trade and to invest)
2. What is the difference between spheres of influence and possessions? (Possessions are governed by the foreign countries which control them.)
3. Why didn't foreign countries take over the interior of China? (country too vast; ports and waterways gave access to interior and trade centers)
4. What conclusion can be drawn about the absence of a sphere for the United States? (United States arrived late as foreign power.)

Foreign Influence in China 1900

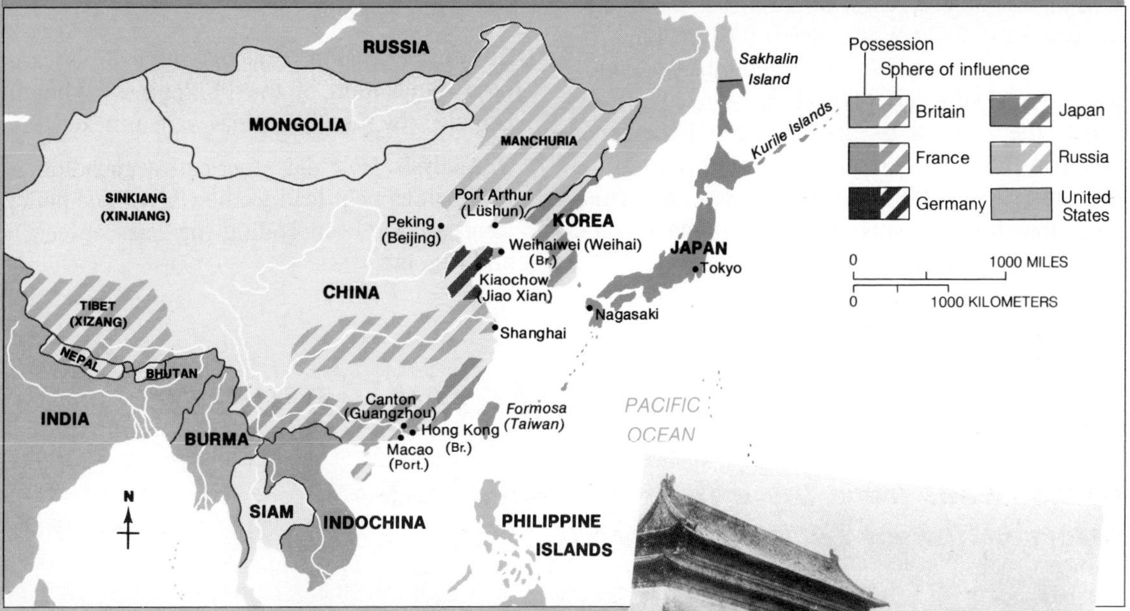

Geography Skills—Region. Use the map to describe the extent of foreign influence in China and to explain why the United States favored an Open Door policy.

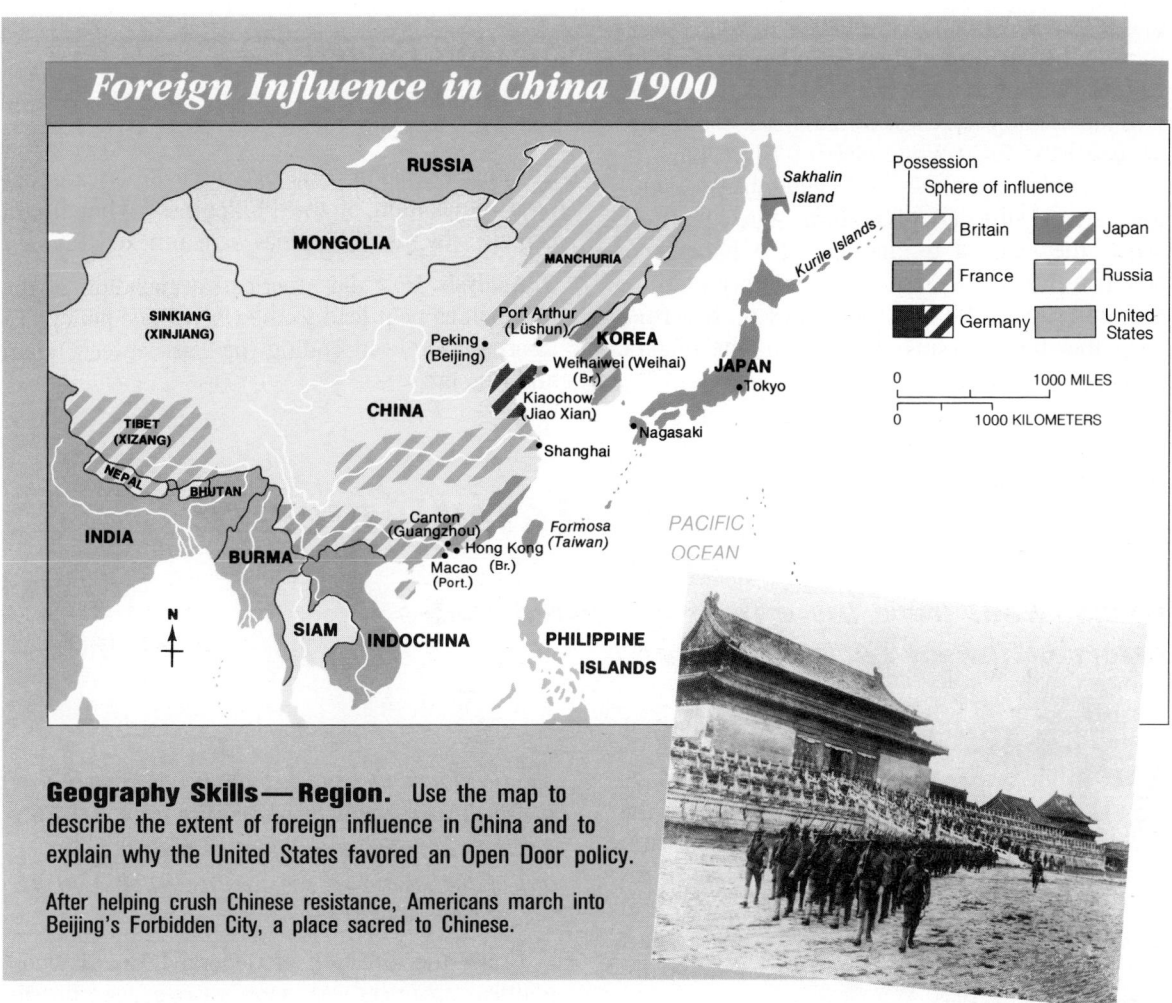

After helping crush Chinese resistance, Americans march into Beijing's Forbidden City, a place sacred to Chinese.

launched a surprise attack on the Russian naval base at Port Arthur, Manchuria. The attack destroyed much of the Russian fleet and triggered the Russo-Japanese War.

As the war progressed, Japan scored victory after victory. Theodore Roosevelt—who had become President when McKinley was assassinated in 1901—worried that Japan might win the war and then develop an interest in the Philippines. He thought that the Japanese might look upon "Russians, English, Americans, and Germans . . . simply as white devils inferior to themselves" and might try to "beat us in turn." Indeed, the Japanese victories marked the first time an Asian nation had defeated a major European power.

Therefore, when a nearly exhausted Japan asked for the President's help to end the war, he eagerly accepted. Under Roosevelt's guidance, emissaries from Russia and Japan met at Portsmouth, New Hampshire, in 1905. Japan, acknowledged as the victor, received recognition of its claims in Korea and part of Russia's Sakhalin Island. Russia agreed to withdraw its troops from Manchuria. Roosevelt did, however, get Japan to give up its demand that Russia pay a huge indemnity for Japanese losses. For his efforts in helping to negotiate the treaty, Roosevelt received the Nobel Peace Prize.

After the war, relations between the United States and Japan remained uneasy. Japan resented the discrimination suffered by Japanese immigrants in California, and there was talk on both sides of the Pacific of the possibility of war between the United States and Japan. Deciding to display American power as a warning, in December 1907 Roosevelt

Geography Skills

ANSWERS

European powers and Japan exerted influence over about one-fourth of China, including nearly all of its seacoast and therefore its trade. The United States favored the Open Door policy because it did not have a sphere of influence in China.

Section Review

ANSWERS

1. Definitions for the following terms are on text pages indicated in parentheses: *spheres of influence* (480), *Open Door policy* (480).
2. Some feared it would lead to an influx of cheap labor; others thought annexation contrary to the American ideal of self-government. Most were for expansion and annexation; it offered strategic location for United States penetration of Asia.
3. McKinley recognized that annexation would do little good if spheres of influence closed free trade with China. He urged an Open Door policy in which trade with Chinese ports would be open to all nations. Roosevelt was motivated by the possibility that a Japanese victory might lead Japan to become interested in the Philippines.

sent a "Great White Fleet" of sixteen white battleships to the Pacific and then on to Japan, ready for "a feast, a frolic, or a fight."

If Japan had been eager for a fight, it could have destroyed the Great White Fleet in Tokyo Bay. Instead, it welcomed the ships. In 1908 the two countries signed the Root-Takahira Agreement, by which they agreed to maintain the balance of power in the Pacific, respect one another's territories, and support China's independence. Nevertheless, the two growing powers in the Pacific continued to eye each other warily.

Section Review

1. Identification. Define *spheres of influence* and *Open Door policy.*

2. Comprehension. Why did some Americans oppose annexation of the Philippines? What might explain why the Philippines were annexed anyway?

3. Analysis. How did American annexation of the Philippines help lead to the Open Door policy? To Roosevelt's role in ending the war between Japan and Russia?

18-4 Stepping into Latin America

Focus: What were the effects of United States intervention in Latin America?

While the United States faced the challenge of strong rivals in Asia, it also feared the emergence of European rivals in Latin America. A key factor in keeping the Europeans out, policymakers believed, was to keep order and stability in Latin America. A good place to start seemed to be the territories stripped from Spain: Cuba and Puerto Rico.

Governing Cuba and Puerto Rico

Governing Cuba became a thorny matter. The Teller Amendment forbade annexation, and warfare had left much of the island a scorched ruin. President McKinley gave the following orders:

"Go down there to get the people ready for a republican form of government. . . . We want to do all we can for them and to get out of the island as soon as we safely can."

Under the direction of General Leonard Wood, political prisoners were soon set free, food distributed, roads and schools built, and yellow fever

A 1901 cartoon shows the U.S. "protecting" Latin America by keeping its rivals "cooped up" in Europe.

B • A • C • K • G • R • O • U • N • D

Global Connections

In November 1906 President Roosevelt and his wife paid a visit to the Canal Zone to see the progression of the project. It was the first time in the country's history that an American President had traveled outside the United States while in office.

brought under control. In response to Cuban calls for self-government, General Wood arranged for a constitutional convention in 1900. The convention prepared a plan of government that closely resembled the United States Constitution.

To guard against future European intervention in Cuba, Congress added the Platt Amendment, which prohibited Cuba from making treaties that threatened its independence and from taking on heavy debts. The United States also reserved the right to lease naval bases and intervene to maintain order in Cuba. In effect, Cuba became a **protectorate,** a nation protected and controlled by another nation. When the Cubans grudgingly agreed to the Platt Amendment, President Theodore Roosevelt removed American soldiers from the island.

Cuban anger at American interference was reinforced by repeated American military interventions, first in 1906 and then three more times before the Platt Amendment was repealed in 1934. The resentment lingered into the 1950s, when Fidel Castro led a successful revolution against the Cuban dictator Fulgencio Batista, who had formed close ties with American sugar growers on the island. To free the economy from "Yankee imperialists," Castro began taking control of the sugar plantations. Relations between Cuba and the United States have remained strained to this day.

The relationship with Puerto Rico has not been quite so rocky, largely because many Puerto Ricans accepted rule by the United States. By 1900 the American army's rule had been replaced by an elected legislature and a territorial governor appointed by the President of the United States.

In 1917, Puerto Ricans were granted American citizenship. In 1947 they voted on whether they wanted independence, statehood, or commonwealth status. The majority voted to become a commonwealth—responsible to Congress but with powers of self-government. The issue is still alive, however, with some Puerto Ricans favoring complete independence, some favoring the status quo, and others calling for statehood.

American Voices

"I took the Canal Zone and let Congress debate. And while the debate goes, so does the canal."

—Theodore Roosevelt

"Taking" the Panama Canal

With an empire that now included colonies in the Caribbean and the Pacific, United States policymakers thought it was critical to control any canal that cut between the two oceans. An obstacle was an earlier treaty in which Britain and the United States had agreed to joint control of any future canal. Now, preoccupied with events in Europe and Africa, Britain agreed to let the United States proceed independently with a canal.

Two possible routes were considered: through Nicaragua or across Panama. Supporters of the Panama route prevailed, and in 1902 Congress authorized President Roosevelt to secure the right to dig a canal. However, Panama was part of Colombia, which asked for more money than the United States government was willing to pay.

Fearful that the Nicaraguan route might be chosen, some Panamanians planned a revolt against Colombia. The rebels had an ally in a Frenchman named Philippe Bunau-Varilla (fil-EEP BOO-now var-EE-yah), a representative of the company that owned the rights to the Panama route. He spoke secretly to Roosevelt and Hay on behalf of the rebels. Although Roosevelt did not commit himself, Bunau-Varilla believed that the United States would support a revolt. In fact, Roosevelt had written to a friend,

"I should be delighted if Panama were an independent state or made itself so at this moment; but for me to say so publicly would amount to an instigation of a revolt, and therefore I cannot say it."

The U.S.S. *Nashville,* an American warship, arrived at Panama on November 2, 1903. "Coincidentally" the revolt took place the next day. While American marines from the ship prevented Colombian soldiers from entering the country, the ragtag rebel army won a quick victory.

Section 18-4

Objectives

- ***Answer the Focus Question.***
- *Describe the Roosevelt Corollary to the Monroe Doctrine.*
- *Contrast Roosevelt's big stick diplomacy, Taft's dollar diplomacy, and Wilson's moral diplomacy.*
- *Describe United States intervention in Latin American affairs.*

Introducing

THE SECTION

The United States tried many kinds of diplomacy in dealing with Latin America. As students read, have them note differences between Roosevelt's "big stick diplomacy," Taft's "dollar diplomacy," and Wilson's "moral diplomacy."

Ask: Why was the United States concerned about Latin America? **(proximity to the United States, source of raw materials, Panama Canal)**

Developing

THE SECTION

Limited English Proficiency

Building Vocabulary. Help students define and compare the three forms of government voted on by Puerto Ricans in 1947: *independence, commonwealth, statehood.*

Ask: How do the powers of government differ? What advantages or disadvantages does each offer?

Connections: Politics

Discussion. Discuss with students the means Roosevelt used to obtain a treaty to build the canal through Panama. Refer students to his boast on text page 483. Just what role did Roosevelt play in the revolt? **(Panamanians knew he would support them; sent USS *Nashville* to Panama; prevented Colombian troops from entering country; signed rush order treaty)** What criticism can be made of Roosevelt's actions during this affair?

Thinking Critically

Evaluation. Have students research and then compare provisions of the Hay-Varilla Treaty and the canal treaty approved by the Senate in 1978.

Ask: What did the United States relinquish in the newer treaty? Why was there so much opposition to it? (nationalism; United States built the canal; still useful; appeasement; viewed as American possession) What arguments could be used to justify the 1978 treaty? (no longer militarily defensible; can't handle all ships; Panamanian nationalism) Do you approve or disapprove of the 1978 treaty? Why?

Multicultural Perspectives

Cuban-born doctor Carlos Juan Finlay studied medicine in Philadelphia, Pennsylvania. In 1881 he first proposed that yellow fever was spread by a certain type of mosquito. In 1900 Major Walter Reed headed the American Yellow Fever Commission that was sent to Havana to find the cause of the deadly disease. Reed consulted with Finlay about his research and concluded, after experiments of his own, that yellow fever was indeed spread to humans by mosquito.

Reduced student page in the Teacher's Edition

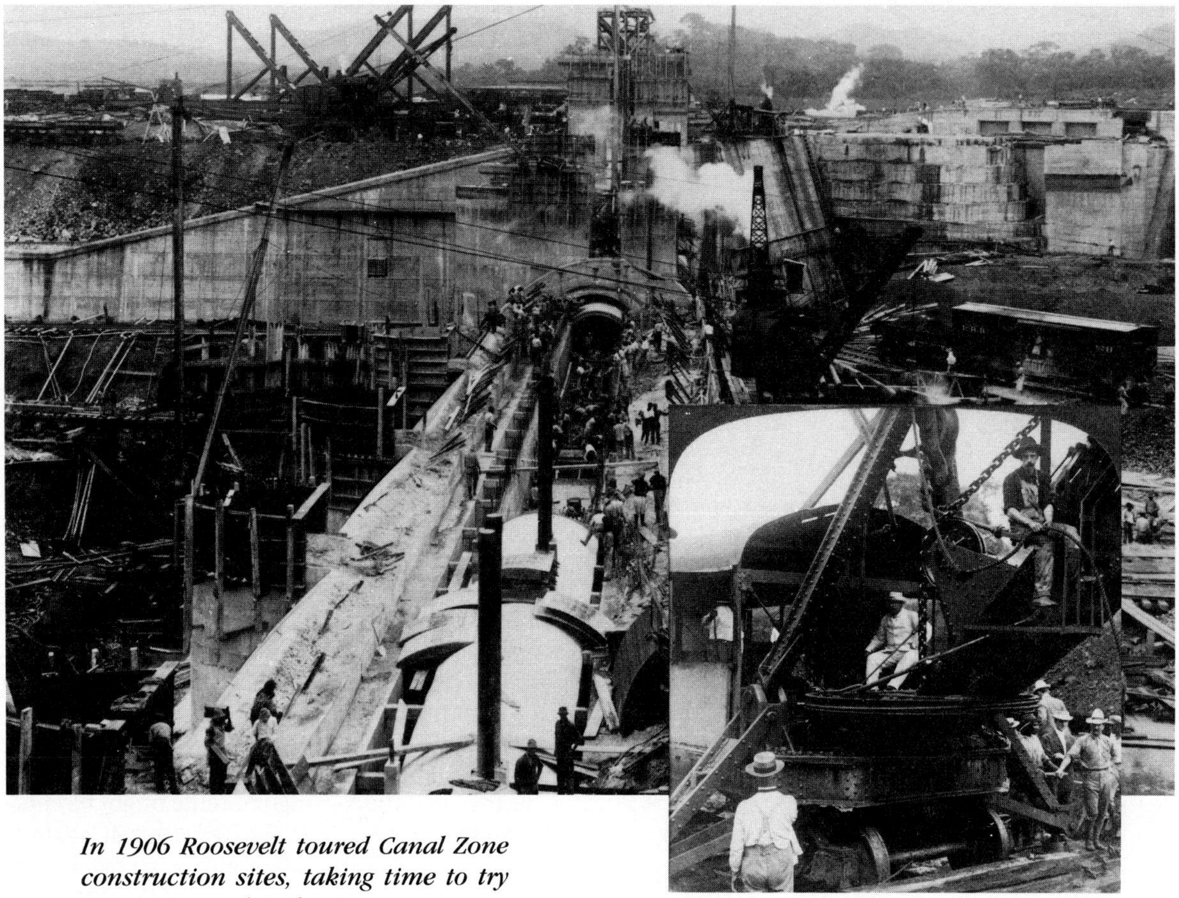

In 1906 Roosevelt toured Canal Zone construction sites, taking time to try out a steam shovel.

The United States promptly signed a treaty with Panama's new minister, Bunau-Varilla. The Hay-Varilla Treaty guaranteed Panama's independence and gave the United States control of a canal zone ten miles wide. The United States agreed to pay Panama $10 million plus an annual fee of $250,000—the same terms originally offered to Colombia.

Although Roosevelt denied helping to arrange the Panamanian revolt, suspicion persisted. Anti-imperialists charged that the Roosevelt Administration "approved and aided, if it has not instigated, a revolt in Panama." However, the President had wide public support, and the Senate approved the Hay-Varilla Treaty. Roosevelt, who was eager to "make the dirt fly," later boasted, "I took the Canal Zone and let Congress debate. And while the debate goes, so does the canal."

Opened in August 1914, the canal was hailed as one of the greatest engineering feats in the world. As the years passed, few Americans questioned the importance of the Panama Canal to the nation's well-being. But one historian noted that the canal episode marked the beginning of what was to become, in fact, a "Bad Neighbor" policy toward Latin America.

"Big Stick" Diplomacy

The month he became President, September 1901, Roosevelt gave a speech at a state fair.

"There is an . . . adage which runs, 'Speak softly and carry a big stick: you will go far.' If the American nation will speak softly and yet build and keep at a pitch of the highest training a thoroughly efficient navy, the Monroe Doctrine will go far."

Connections: Health
During the French period of canal building, the French hospital in Panama City was unknowingly spreading yellow fever. The French used crockery rings filled with water to protect plants on the hospital grounds from the ravages of the umbrella ant. But these pots served as perfect breeding grounds for the yellow-fever mosquito. Under Gorgas, who worked at the same hospital, all stagnant water was eliminated as breeding grounds.

Geography
A KEY TO OUR PAST

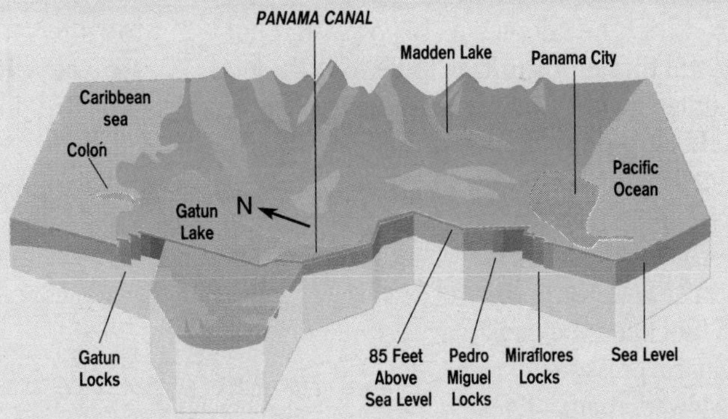

Relationships Within Places: The Building of the Panama Canal

To improve our way of living, we sometimes radically alter the environment. Such was the case with the building of the Panama Canal. What was once lush rain forest and humid swamps is now a major water route for nearly 15,000 ships each year. The story of what it took to bring about this change is a legend in the history of engineering and construction.

As an isthmus, or narrow strip of land bounded by water on each side, Panama was a promising location in which to cut a water route. The canal, a 51-mile waterway built between 1904 and 1914, is a dramatic short cut between the Atlantic and Pacific oceans. By using the canal rather than going around the southern tip of South America, a ship traveling from New York City to San Francisco can shorten its voyage by almost 8,000 miles.

Although Panama is a narrow strip of land, building the canal was still a monumental task. Before actual construction of the canal could begin, the varied landscape had to be rearranged. As one observer noted, "It was necessary to cut a passage through a mountain range near the Pacific end and erect a lower mountain range or ridge at the Atlantic end. A mountain had to be moved, not by faith, but by dynamite, steam shovels, and railway trains, and set up 30 miles away."

Because of differences in elevation along the canal route, a series of locks, or closed chambers, were built. After a vessel floats into a lock, water floods in or is emptied through a gate at either end, raising or lowering a ship to the next step of its passage. The question at the outset was where to get water to fill the locks. Because Panama has no large natural lakes, three artificial ones were created: Miraflores, Madden, and Gatun lakes. Completed in 1913, Gatun Lake was the world's largest artificial lake, covering approximately 164 square miles.

At the peak of construction more than 43,000 workers, three fourths of them blacks from the British West Indies, were employed. The greatest threat to workers was not accidents but the diseases of yellow fever and malaria. Under the supervision of Colonel William Gorgas, thousands of acres of swamps were cleared of mosquitoes, which carry these deadly diseases.

Nevertheless, "the total price in human life," says historian David McCullough, "may have been as high as 25,000, or 500 lives for every mile of the canal." In short, what has been called "The Greatest Engineering Feat of All Time" came about only at great cost and sacrifice.

1. What geographical challenges did the builders of the Panama Canal face? How were they overcome?
2. If the Panama Canal did not already exist, do you think it would be built today? Explain your reasons.

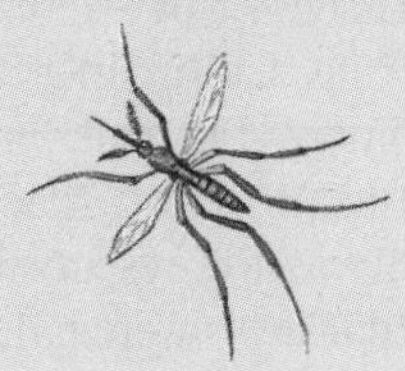

Writing About History

Journal Entry. Give students an option for a writing assignment: Compose a diary entry describing a day in the life of a worker building the canal or describing a trip through the Panama Canal today. Students may want to do further reading before completing the assignment.

Geography: A Key to Our Past

ANSWERS

1. Cut path through a mountain range near the Pacific, set up a lower range near the Atlantic. Used dynamite and steam shovels; used trains to move the earth that was dug out. To adjust for difference in elevation, locks were built. To get water for the locks, three artificial lakes were created.
2. Can argue that it would still be useful and much easier to build with modern technology. Others can argue that with shipping being done by air, the canal would not be as useful.

Thinking Critically

Analysis. How was Roosevelt's big stick policy implemented by the Roosevelt Corollary? (Corollary gave United States the right to intervene in Latin American countries.) How did the Corollary express change in the role of the United States in Latin America? (provided a justification for intervention) Why did some Americans object to it? (disliked increased intervention in other countries' affairs)

Have students identify areas in Latin America where Roosevelt used the big stick policy. (Venezuela 1902-03; Panama 1903; Dominican Republic 1905; Cuba 1906)

Limited English Proficiency

Building Vocabulary. Help students define the following terms: *confrontation*, *arbitration*, *intervene*. Then have them explain their relationship in the context of the dispute between the United States, Europe, and Venezuela in 1902. (The ***confrontation*** **between the United States and European nations who sought to** ***intervene*** **in Venezuela was avoided through** ***arbitration*** **of the dispute.)**

Connections: Economics

By the early 1900s the United Fruit Company, an American firm operating in Central America and the Caribbean, controlled 77 percent of the world's banana exports. It had holdings in Jamaica, Costa Rica, Nicaragua, Colombia, the Dominican Republic, Cuba, Panama, Honduras, and Guatemala. It built private railroad lines to service its plantations and operated a fleet of ships.

Often called "the Octopus," the United Fruit Company has been criticized for acquiring vast amounts of land at ridiculously low prices, creating a monopoly, and interfering in the domestic affairs of host countries.

Reduced student page in the Teacher's Edition

Roosevelt's message was a version of a West African proverb, which he adopted as his own. His policy of using the threat of military force to influence political events in other countries became known as **big stick diplomacy.** Within a few years he had put it into action in the Caribbean.

Big stick diplomacy was tested in December 1902. Britain, Germany, and Italy sent warships to blockade the coast of Venezuela to pressure it to repay debts owed them. They had tried negotiating with Venezuela's ruler, Cipriano Castro, but he had refused to pay the long-overdue debts. Mindful of the Monroe Doctrine, the three countries got Roosevelt's approval before using force. When German ships shelled a Venezuelan fort, however, the American public reacted angrily, branding it a brutal attack.

> **American Voices**
>
> *"The force of America is the force of moral principle."*
>
> —Woodrow Wilson

The incident drew to a close when Castro and the European powers—who were eager to avoid a confrontation with the United States—agreed to arbitration. The three European countries withdrew their warships and submitted their claims to the International Court in the Netherlands.

The incident had significance for both Latin America and the United States. Latin Americans feared that armed intervention might be repeated. The United States was pleased that the Monroe Doctrine had been respected, but worried that European nations might again attempt to intervene.

In early 1904 Venezuela's island neighbor, the Dominican Republic, found itself in a similar situation. It owed Europeans over $20 million but was paralyzed by civil war and nearly bankrupt. The possibility arose that European warships would again appear in the Caribbean.

By May, Roosevelt had decided that it was time to defend American interests in the Western Hemisphere. "If we intend to say 'Hands off' to the powers of Europe," he wrote, "sooner or later we must keep order ourselves" by exercising "international police power" in Latin America. In other words, since the Monroe Doctrine barred other powers from intervening in Latin America, Roosevelt was saying that it was the responsibility of the United States to see that debts were paid.

The assertion that the United States had a right to intervene in Latin America was called the **Roosevelt Corollary** to the Monroe Doctrine. It signaled a major shift in American foreign policy.

Taft's Dollar Diplomacy

The Presidents who followed Roosevelt inherited a delicate situation in the Western Hemisphere. Increasingly, the Roosevelt Corollary led the United States to intervene in Latin America. Latin Americans came to view the "Colossus of the North" as more of a threat than a protector.

William H. Taft, home from his term as governor of the Philippines, was elected President in 1908. Taft's policy, known as **dollar diplomacy,** aimed at influencing events by "substituting dollars for bullets." In Taft's mind, American investments abroad would profit the United States and help China and Latin America gain stability and peace.

Nicaragua, like other Latin American countries, had borrowed heavily from Europeans. After a year-long revolution, a new president, Adolfo Díaz (DEE-ahs), asked the United States for help in sorting out his country's finances.

A treaty was drawn up in which the United States agreed to lend Nicaragua enough money to pay its debts. To protect the loan, the United States would operate Nicaragua's customhouses. When the Senate refused to approve the treaty, Taft encouraged American bankers to make the loan, and he appointed an army officer to collect the duties.

Many Nicaraguans heartily disliked American control of their finances. Revolt broke out against Díaz in August 1912. At Díaz's request Taft sent marines, on the grounds that American economic interests had to be protected. The marines remained in Nicaragua until 1933. They managed to keep elected governments in power, but little was done to improve living conditions in the impoverished country. Indeed, intervention in Nicaragua served mainly to increase resentment of the United States throughout much of Latin America.

Connections: Politics
Latin America's political response to foreign intervention was embodied in two doctrines. The Calvo Doctrine stated that recovery of debts does not justify armed intervention and ruled out international interference altogether. The Drago Doctrine also argued against the use of armed intervention to collect public debts but accepted arbitration.

Wilson's Moral Diplomacy

Woodrow Wilson, who succeeded Taft in 1913, replaced dollar diplomacy with **moral diplomacy,** a policy based on his idea that "the force of America is the force of moral principle." Wilson thought moral diplomacy would spread the ideas of human rights, democracy, and world peace. In Latin America his goal was to "prove ourselves their friends . . . upon terms of equality and honor."

Wilson hoped to end the seemingly endless revolutions in Latin America and promote democracy. However, he continued to use the marines to maintain governments in power and protect America's economic interests. In fact, Wilson intervened even more often than had Roosevelt and Taft.

Wilson sent the marines to Haiti in 1915 and to the Dominican Republic in 1916. He kept a force in Nicaragua and sent another to Cuba. American newspapers became accustomed to reporting that "the marines have landed and have the situation well in hand." Moral diplomacy, although well-intentioned, had the same effect as earlier forms of diplomacy: a growing number of United States protectorates and resentful Latin Americans.

Intervention in Mexico. Wilson's moral diplomacy faced perhaps its toughest test in Mexico.

A cartoon shows Wilson scolding Mexico over its political unrest.

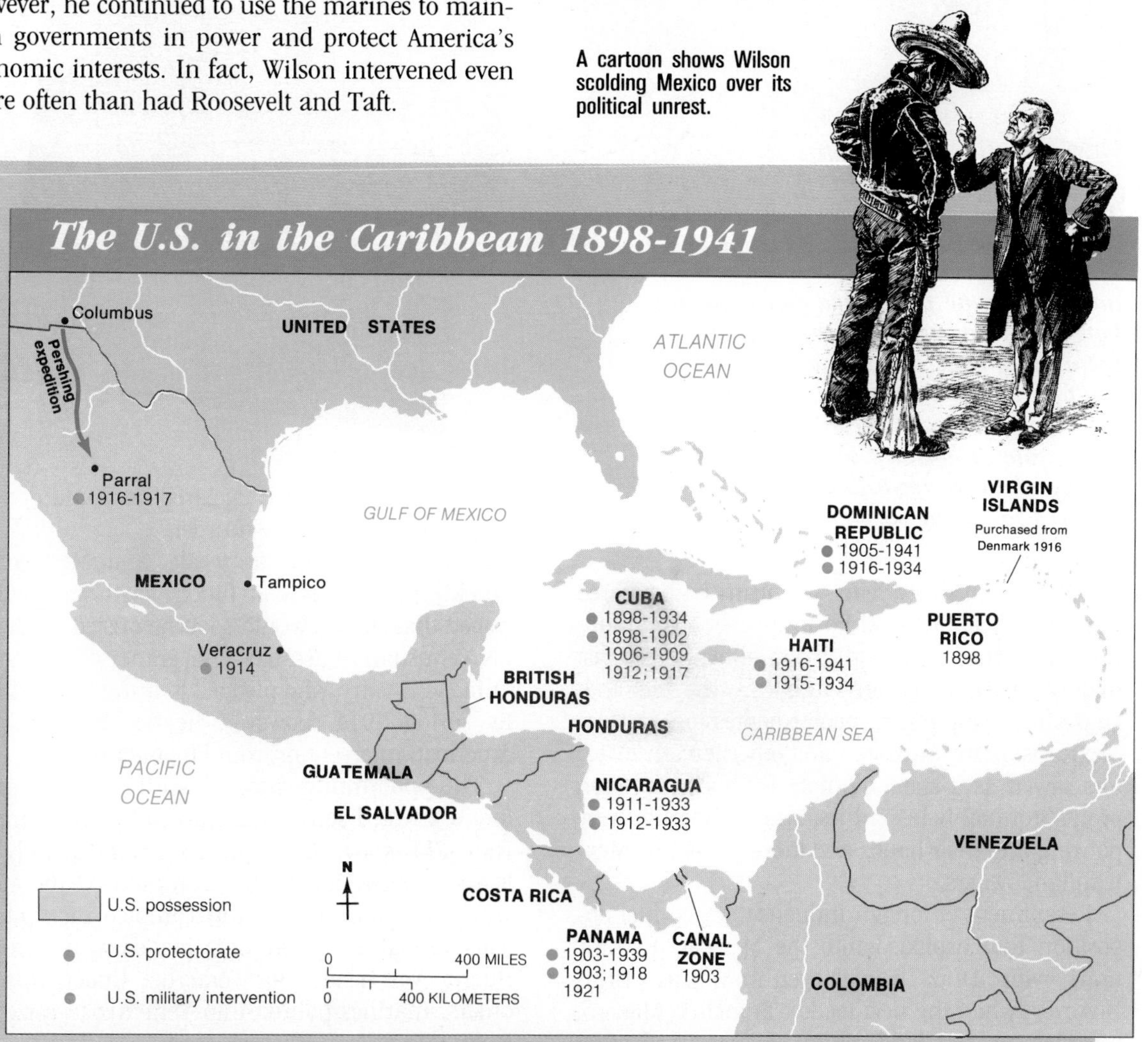

Geography Skills—Movement. Which Caribbean and Central American governments have been managed in part by the United States? Which lands have been claimed by the United States?

Connections: Geography

Discussion. Refer students to the map on this page and point out the location of Guantanamo Bay. The United States still retains a naval base there despite Cuban pressure to relinquish it.

Discuss the strategic importance of Guantanamo. Why has the United States been reluctant to give up the base? **(still important naval base for protecting our interests in Caribbean)**

Writing About History

Editorial. Discuss the differences in the evolving relationships between the United States, Puerto Rico, and Cuba. Have students write a short editorial as a Cuban arguing for or against improving relations with the United States, or as a Puerto Rican supporting independence, statehood, or commonwealth status.

Geography Skills

ANSWERS

1. Dominican Republic, Cuba, Haiti, Nicaragua, Panama.
2. Virgin Islands, Puerto Rico, Canal Zone.

GTV Side 3

Chap. 17, Frame 48620

The U.S. in the World 1900: Trade (Animated Map)

Search and Play:

Multicultural Perspectives

American demand for inexpensive labor and, to a lesser extent, social disruptions of the Mexican Revolution led to the first large-scale migration of Mexicans to the United States. Mexican workers were recruited to lay tracks for the Southern Pacific and Santa Fe railroads in the Southwest. They played a major role in increasing production of southwestern crops—cotton, sugar beets, and fruits and vegetables. They also worked in industries in parts of the Northwest and the Midwest. (See Chapter 20.)

Thinking Critically

Drawing Cartoons. Have students draw a political cartoon supporting or attacking the sending of United States marines to Veracruz. A cartoon in support might show the threat of a German ship loaded with arms for General Huerta. A cartoon in opposition might contrast the phrase "moral diplomacy" with the reality of military might as indicated by photographs on this page.

Multicultural Perspectives

Oral Report. The political and social struggles going on in Mexico made profound impressions upon Mexicans living in the United States. Three prominent men are remembered by Mexican Americans today: Francisco Madero, Emiliano Zapata, Francisco "Pancho" Villa. Have three students research and present oral reports on these men.

Limited English Proficiency

Making Charts. Have students work in small groups to make charts summarizing the results of United States intervention in the following areas in the period described in this chapter: Cuba, Puerto Rico, the Philippines, Panama, Nicaragua, Mexico. **(Example: For Cuba, students might list as results: Spain surrendered claim to Cuba; Cuba became a protectorate of the United States.)**

Reduced student page in the Teacher's Edition

Intervention by the United States has a long history of arousing the anger of Latin Americans. Protests against military action in Veracruz, Mexico (1914) and Panama (1989) sounded the same note: a nation's sovereignty should not be violated, regardless of the motives for doing so.

For more than thirty years, Mexicans had suffered under the dictatorship of Porfirio Díaz. A small upper class owned almost all the land, while the vast majority lived in poverty. Ignoring the fact that Díaz's iron rule meant brutal oppression to most Mexicans, many American and other foreign investors saw it as a stable climate for business. Soon profits from oil fields, mines, and textile mills were pouring into their hands and those of wealthy Mexican landowners.

Resentment of foreign influence helped fuel opposition that exploded into the Mexican Revolution, with Díaz being overthrown in 1911. However, when the new leader, Francisco Madero, was slow to start land reform, farmers and other workers rose up. In the turmoil, General Victoriano Huerta (WEHR-ta) seized power in 1913 and had Madero shot. Supported by wealthy landowners, Huerta seemed little different from Díaz. Meanwhile, President Wilson declared he would not recognize "government by murder."

Huerta's control was weak, and Mexico was quickly plunged into a bloody civil war. Wilson hoped that Huerta would soon be ousted by Generals Venustiano Carranza and Francisco "Pancho" Villa (VEE-yah), who pledged to bring land reform. By spring 1914, however, he decided that only American intervention could topple Huerta.

The opportunity came in April, when Huerta's forces arrested some American sailors in Tampico (tam-PEE-koh). Although they were quickly released, Wilson put the navy on alert off the Mexican coast. Shortly after the Tampico incident, he learned that a German ship loaded with arms for Huerta was headed for Veracruz. Under Wilson's orders, marines poured into Veracruz to seize the town, killing over 400 Mexicans.

The intervention backfired, as protest swept across Mexico—even in Carranza's stronghold. Although tensions were slow to ease, the crisis passed. By then Huerta's power was badly eroded and he resigned in July 1914, being succeeded by Carranza. Villa, however, turned against his former ally, leaving Wilson unsure about whom to recognize. After briefly supporting Villa, he tried a neutral policy of "watchful waiting" and then finally recognized Carranza in October 1915.

Furious, Villa began a series of attacks against Americans, hoping to gain popular support by forcing the United States to take some action against him. Early in 1916 his troops killed eighteen American engineers. A few weeks later they burned the town of Columbus, New Mexico, leaving nineteen Americans dead.

In March 1916, after Carranza agreed to let American troops cross the border to pursue Villa, an expedition under General John J. Pershing began the search. When Pershing's troops pushed deep into Mexico, though, Carranza decided that they had far exceeded the agreement and demanded an end to the "invasion." As tensions between the two countries increased, Wilson finally ordered the troops home in 1917.

Once again, by meddling in the affairs of a sovereign nation, the United States had talked itself into a self-defeating policy. While trying to protect American interests, and while claiming to be supporting an independent, democratic government in Mexico, it had managed to arouse the suspicion and ill will of a Latin American neighbor.

Section Review

1. Identification. Define *protectorate, big stick diplomacy, Roosevelt Corollary, dollar diplomacy,* and *moral diplomacy.*

2. Comprehension. How did the Roosevelt Corollary change the Monroe Doctrine? What effect did the corollary have on relations between the United States and Latin-American nations?

3. Analysis. Compare and contrast Roosevelt's big stick diplomacy, Taft's dollar diplomacy, and Wilson's moral diplomacy.

Data Search. Explain how the map on page 487 can be used to support the following statement: "The United States intervened extensively in Latin American countries during the first half of the twentieth century."

Connections to Themes

Shaping Democracy

Many expansionists viewed the nation as being in a race with European powers—a struggle only the strong would survive. Anti-imperialists like William Jennings Bryan, however, argued that the United States did not need military conquests to establish its greatness. "For over ten decades our nation has been a world power," Bryan declared. "During its brief existence it has exerted upon the human race an influence more potent than all the other nations of the earth combined, and it has exerted that influence without the use of the sword or Gatling gun."

Expansionists, though, insisted that exercising power abroad was quite in keeping with American democratic ideals. In the words of President McKinley, Americans had the duty "to uplift and civilize" peoples they considered to be less fortunate. While this view helped expansionists justify the use of force, it led to anti-American feeling in Asia, Latin America, and other regions of the globe—a legacy that still lingers today.

Does the United States have the right, or the responsibility, to export its ideals to other parts of the world? And if so, can that goal be best achieved, as Bryan argued, by the influence of our example? Should the country use force, if necessary, in the name of freedom and democracy? These questions were debated during the Spanish-American War. They would come to the forefront again in 1914, when the world exploded into what became known as The Great War, and they continue to occupy Americans to this day.

Active Learning

Cooperative Activity. Ask students to name the Latin American nations discussed in this chapter. Have them form small groups to make time lines of significant events in one country's history since 1890.

Then have them use political cartoons, drawings, quotes from primary sources, and present-day newspaper and magazine articles to make a collage of that country's history.

Section Review

ANSWERS

1. Definitions for the following terms are on text pages indicated in parentheses: *protectorate* (483), *big stick diplomacy* (486), *Roosevelt Corollary* (486), *dollar diplomacy* (486), *moral diplomacy* (487).
2. Stated that the United States had right to intervene in Latin America; original doctrine simply warned against European intervention. The corollary led to active intervention in Latin American affairs and to Latin American hostility toward the United States.
3. Big stick policy advocated military intervention in affairs of other countries. Dollar diplomacy relied on investments in and loans to countries to influence their affairs. Moral diplomacy rested on assumption that American ideals would influence other nations.
Data Search. Map shows how often the United States intervened militarily or established protectorates in the Caribbean between 1898 and 1941.

Chapter Survey

ANSWERS

Using New Vocabulary

A (a) *colony* is a land whose government and economy are controlled by another country which practices *imperialism* and believes in (e) *expansionism.* An imperialist power may make its colony a (d) *protectorate* by taking over its government. One reason for doing so might be a (f) *civilizing mission*, the belief that it was spreading democracy and Christianity.

Reviewing the Chapter

1. For: economic gain, national pride, civilizing mission. Against: undemocratic in principle, economic burden, nonwhites could not be assimilated into American culture.

2. Naval power essential to national strength because it protects commerce; necessary if United States to dominate Pacific, enforce Monroe Doctrine. Provided rationale for building up navy and pursuing overseas expansion.

3. American Christian missionaries arrived in early 1800s; their children became wealthy planters and traders who staged revolt against native Hawaiian government, set up temporary government, and declared Hawaiian independence. United States annexed Hawaii during Spanish-American War to gain "halfway station" to Philippines.

4. Created American sympathy for Cuban rebels and desire for war after the *Maine* exploded.

5. Liberate Cuba, taking over remains of Spanish empire. Succeeded in gaining former Spanish colonies, but did not liberate Cuba, as the island was still under American control.

6. Aguinaldo assumed that because rebels helped Americans fight Spanish, Americans would help Filipinos gain independence. Bloody three-year war between rebels and Americans followed Spanish-American War. Philippines became territory of United States.

7. United States became major force in imperialist competition in Asia. Led to letters to nations involved in China urging open trade and preservation of China's government and territory.

8. Japan resented discrimination against Japanese immigrants in California.

9. Philippines annexed and governed by civil commission, in which Filipinos gradually took part; did not gain independence until 1946. Cuba

Reduced student page in the Teacher's Edition

Chapter Survey

Using New Vocabulary

From the list below, select the four words or phrases whose meanings relate to the underlined word and explain the relationships.

<u>imperialism</u>

(a) colony	(d) protectorate
(b) independence	(e) expansionism
(c) neutrality	(f) civilizing mission

Reviewing the Chapter

1. Describe the major arguments for and against American expansionism.

2. Explain how the ideas of Alfred T. Mahan affected American foreign policy.

3. Trace the history of American influence in Hawaii up to annexation.

4. What role did yellow journalism play in the Spanish-American War?

5. What were the goals of the Spanish-American War? How well were those goals accomplished?

6. How did Emilio Aguinaldo misjudge the American presence in the Philippines?

7. Explain how annexation of the Philippines led to a stronger American role in Asia.

8. Why did tensions arise between the United States and Japan?

9. Compare the status of the Philippines after the war with that of Cuba and Puerto Rico.

10. Why did United States foreign policy shift toward increasing intervention in Latin America?

Thinking Critically

1. Synthesis. Imagine that you were a reader of the New York *Journal* or the New York *World.* Write a letter to the editor supporting your view of the paper's coverage of the Cuban rebellion of 1895.

2. Analysis. Mark Twain criticized the annexation of the Philippines as playing "the European game." He wrote, "If it had been played according to the American rules, Dewey would have sailed away from Manila as soon as he had destroyed the Spanish fleet." Explain what Twain meant.

History and You

Find out the Panama Canal's status today, what role the United States plays there, and how Panamanians regard the United States.

Using Geography

Study the map below on the Spanish-American War in the Caribbean.

1. About how far did General Shafter have to transport his troops?

2. What strategy did Admiral Sampson use?

3. From studying this map and the text, explain how naval power contributed to the victory.

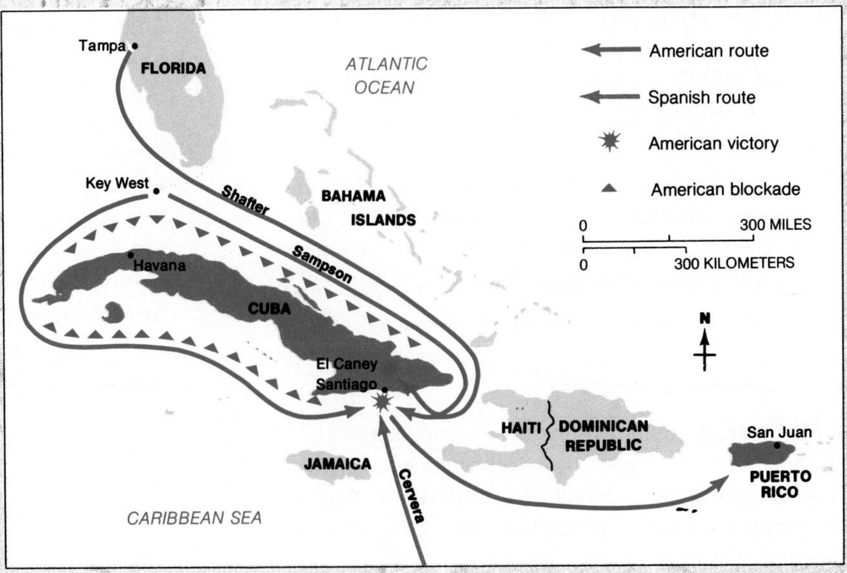

could not be annexed because of the Teller Amendment, but became a protectorate under Platt Amendment and as a result of military intervention. Puerto Rico annexed, people gained civilian government, citizenship, eventually became a commonwealth of the United States.

10. Roosevelt Corollary to Monroe Doctrine asserted right of United States to intervene in the affairs of Latin America.

Thinking Critically

1. Answers may include praise for exposing Spanish cruelties; criticism of exaggerations and warmongering.

2. By "European game," Twain means the policy of colonization of foreign lands. "American rules" refers to ideals of self-government and freedom.

History and You

Treaties in 1978 guaranteed neutrality of Canal Zone after year 2000, turned Canal over to Panama on December 31, 1999. United States still has about 8,000 employees in the Canal Zone. Following American invasion of Panama in 1989 to oust dictator Manuel Noriega, United States promised Panama $1 billion in aid to rebuild economy of Panama. Public opinion about United States divided—most people glad to be rid of Noriega, but wary of future United States intervention.

Using Geography

1. About 900 miles

2. Blockaded island of Cuba; trapped Cervera's fleet in Santiago harbor.

3. Dewey's attack in Manila Bay scored early naval victory and gave United States psychological edge; troop transport and naval blockades made possible success on land.

Applying Thinking Skills

1. Kipling refers to them as "sullen peoples/half devil and half child."

2. Americans are superior breed. Students can cite "white man's burden," "the best ye breed," and the last two lines of the second stanza.

3. It assumes white Americans are a superior race and that Filipinos are inferior and not fit to govern themselves. Note especially the reference to "sloth and heathen folly" near the end of the final stanza.

Applying Thinking Skills

Detecting Bias

A bias is a one-sided or slanted view that expresses a preference for or dislike of something. Some clues to bias include repeated use of emotionally charged words, exaggeration, opinions stated as facts, and presentation of only one side of an issue.

The excerpt below is from a poem written by British author Rudyard Kipling in support of American annexation of the Philippines. Read it to identify Kipling's bias, then answer the questions that follow.

"Take up the white man's burden—
Send forth the best ye breed—
Go, bind your sons to exile
To serve your captives' need;
To wait, in heavy harness,
On fluttered folk and wild—
Your new-caught sullen peoples,
Half devil and half child.

Take up the white man's burden—
In patience to abide,
To veil the threat of terror
And check the show of pride;
By open speech and simple,
A hundred times made plain,
To seek another's profit
And work another's gain.

Take up the white man's burden—
The savage wars of peace—
Fill full the mouth of famine,
And bid the sickness cease;
And when your goal is nearest
(The end for others sought)
Watch sloth and heathen folly
Bring all your hopes to nought. . . ."

—Abridged from *The White Man's Burden*, by Rudyard Kipling (1899)

1. What words does Kipling use to describe the Filipinos?

2. What is Kipling's perception of "Americans"? Give evidence from the poem.

3. In what way does the poem show bias?

Writing About Issues

The Issue: *Does freedom of the press guarantee the right to print any story?*

In 1898 William Randolph Hearst and Joseph Pulitzer, eager to sell newspapers, printed sensational and sometimes false accounts of Spanish atrocities during the Cuban revolt against Spain. Their newspapers had such power to shape public opinion that they helped push the United States toward war with Spain.

Over the years, controversy has arisen about the responsibility of the press. Questions are raised not only about *how* the press describes particular events but also about *what* topics and events it chooses to report on. For instance, in 1979 a magazine called *The Progressive* published an article describing how hydrogen bombs work. Although not a blueprint for assembling a bomb, the article did contain information useful to any country trying to develop one.

The article aroused spirited discussion. Some Americans charged the magazine with acting irresponsibly. "You evidently lack concern for the safety of our country and the world," said one angry citizen. Others, however, argued that *The Progressive* had done a public service by giving people information they need in order to be responsible citizens. "The important thing," wrote one reader, "is that you have raised the H-bomb issue in terms which can, possibly, make the arms race again a subject of political debate. No such debate is possible without facts."

What do you think? Does freedom of the press guarantee the right to print any story? Imagine that you have been invited to address a group of high-school newspaper editors on this matter. Write a speech that states your opinion and includes your reasons. You may want to consider such issues as national security and the possible invasion of privacy as well as the public's right to be informed.

Chapter 19

The First World War

Planning Guide

	Student Text	TWE Lesson Plans	Support Materials
SECTION 1	**Section 19-1 (1-2 Days)** **From Neutrality to War,** pp 494-500 Review/Evaluation Section Review, p 500	**Introducing the Chapter:** A Poem About War—Individual Activity, homework, one class period, p 491B **Teaching the Main Ideas:** To Be Or Not To Be Neutral—Class Activity, one class period, p 491B	★ **Read to Remember,** Section 1 ● **Section Activities,** Section 1 Δ **Enrichment Activities,** Section 1 Δ **Readings** ● **Tests and Quizzes,** Section 1 Quiz
SECTION 2	**Section 19-2 (1-2 Days)** **Mobilizing for War,** pp 501-505 Point of View: To Fight or Not to Fight?, pp 506-507 Review/Evaluation Section Review, p 505	**Teaching the Main Ideas:** On the Home Front—Cooperative Activity, one class period, p 491C **Enrichment Activity:** Bringing Opposition View to Light—Individual Activity, homework, p 491C	★ **Read to Remember,** Section 2 ● **Section Activities,** Section 2 Δ **Readings** ● **Tests and Quizzes,** Section 2 Quiz
SECTION 3	**Section 19-3 (1-2 Days)** **The United States in the War,** pp 508-512 Review/Evaluation Section Review, p 512	**Reinforcement Activity:** World War I Newspaper—Cooperative Activity, introduction, homework, one class period, p 491C	★ **Read to Remember,** Section 3 ● **Section Activities,** Section 3 ● **Geography Activities,** Section 3 Δ **Readings** ● **Tests and Quizzes,** Section 3 Quiz
SECTION 4	**Section 19-4 (1-2 Days)** **The Diplomacy of Peace,** pp 513-517 Connections to Themes: Shaping Democracy, p 517 Review/Evaluation Section Review, p 517 Chapter 19 Survey, pp 518-519 Unit 6 Survey, pp 520-521 Skills, pp 518-519 Using New Vocabulary Thinking Critically Using a Time Line Applying Social Studies Skills: Interpreting Graphics Applying Thinking Skills: Identifying Unstated Assumptions	**Evaluating Progress:** Viewpoints on Peace—Individual Activity, one class period, p 491C	★ **Read to Remember,** Section 4 ● **Section Activities,** Section 4 Δ **Enrichment Activities,** Section 4 ● **Tests and Quizzes,** Section 4 Quiz, Chapter 19 Test (Forms A and B), Unit 6 Test (Forms A and B) **Additional Resources** ● **Active Learning** Δ **GTV Videodiscs** Δ **Transparencies and Activity Book** ● **Testing Software** ★ **Chapter Summaries** **Key:** ★ **For Extra Support** ● **For All Students** Δ **For Enrichment**

Overview

With the collapse of the delicate balance of power in Europe in 1914, war broke out between the Allies and Central Powers, who soon found themselves locked in a bloody stalemate. The United States proclaimed neutrality, but the American people were divided in their sympathies. Action by both Britain and Germany against neutral trade and shipping provoked Americans. However, when German U-boats sank the *Lusitania*, a shocked nation began making war preparations. Further German aggression in 1917 spurred President Wilson to ask Congress for a declaration of war against Germany.

Americans organized a military draft, raised money, mobilized resources, and converted industry to wartime production. Strong pro-war sentiments led, as in earlier times of national crisis, to suspicion and persecution of people thought to be traitors, and to attempts to limit their freedom of speech.

World War I was noted for trench warfare and the first military use of airplanes. American participation in the fighting helped defeat the Central Powers, although at the cost of an enormous number of deaths and injuries among both troops and civilians.

Months before the war ended on November 11, 1918, President Wilson had drafted a 14-point peace plan, which the Allies accepted with two major exceptions. Ironically, Wilson's partisan politics alienated Republicans and led Congress to reject both the Treaty of Versailles and membership in the League of Nations, the centerpiece of Wilson's hopes for lasting peace. Germany signed the Treaty of Versailles only after threats of renewed war, and later signed a separate treaty with the United States. The war was over, but lasting peace had not been assured.

Activity Objectives

After completing the activities, students should be able to

- describe the pros and cons of the United States policy of neutrality during the early years of World War I.
- understand the role of civilians on the home front during the war.
- summarize the goals of each of the Allies in drafting the Treaty of Versailles, and Germany's reaction.
- describe the military progress of the war.
- identify viewpoints and treatment of opponents of American participation in World War I.

Introducing the Chapter

A Poem about War

This activity requires individual homework and one class period for discussion.

In this activity, students write lines of poetry and then combine them in a collaborative poem about war. Begin by asking volunteers to share their knowledge and impressions of war in general and World War I in particular. Explain that before reading about World War I in Chapter 19, they will write a collaborative poem about war.

As a homework assignment have each student write one line of poetry. Encourage them, before they write, to talk with relatives and friends who have had wartime experiences. Suggest that their lines should describe a feeling, a sight, a sound, or a mood. Lines might begin with phrases such as, "I wish . . . ," "I never thought . . . ," "If I were . . . ," or "War is . . . ."

On the assignment's due date, collect the lines of poetry and write them on the chalkboard or an overhead transparency. Work with the class to decide on an order in which to arrange the lines. When the poem is finished, read it aloud and have students summarize its tone and the feelings and opinions it expresses.

Teaching the Main Ideas

Section 19-1: To Be Or Not To Be Neutral

This class activity requires one period.

In this activity, students imagine participating in a discussion of the United States policy of neutrality toward the war raging in Europe.

Prepare students for the activity by pointing out that the nation's official policy of neutrality in the European war stirred much debate among Americans. By 1917 many people wanted the United States to enter the war, while others held to the belief that absolute neutrality should be maintained no matter what the consequences.

Ask students to imagine that they are citizens who have gathered at a community meeting in early 1917 to debate the nation's neutrality policy. Divide the class in half and designate one half to argue the position that the United States should maintain neutrality. The other half is to argue that the United States should enter the war on the side of the Allies.

Direct students to review Section 19-1 to identify arguments and evidence to support their positions. As they review the section, have them identify hypothetical citizen roles to assume in the debate. Roles might include descendants of German, Irish, and English immigrants, pacifists, and business people. Allow about fifteen minutes for review and preparation.

Select one student to chair the meeting. Direct the chair to convene the meeting and call on speakers from each side to present their positions. All students should participate.

Conclude the activity by asking students to evaluate the presentations and give their personal opinions about whether or not the United States should have remained neutral during World War I.

Teaching the Main Ideas

Section 19-2: On the Home Front

This cooperative activity requires one class period.

In this activity, students experience the effects of war on the home front by forming committees to organize civilian war efforts. Begin by reminding students that during wartime, civilians often must take new jobs, face shortages of goods, and contribute to the welfare of soldiers and allied civilians. Ask the class to discuss how they, as civilians, might be affected if our country were to enter a protracted, large-scale war like World War I.

Tell students that to make the civilian role seem more real, you will assign them to committees that will develop plans for organizing a present-day civilian war effort. Write the following assignments on the chalkboard:

- *Scrap Committee.* List all scrap materials that could be recycled for use in making weapons and machinery. Develop a plan for collecting the materials.
- *Food Committee.* List all common foods made with sugar and wheat. Develop a rationing plan for limiting civilians' consumption of these foods so that military forces and civilians in war zones can be fed.
- *Slogan Committee.* Create slogans to encourage people to support conservation, rationing, and patriotism.
- *"Care" Package Committee.* List items to be sent to soldiers to cheer them up and make their lives more pleasant. Develop plans for assembling the items and sending the packages.
- *Civilian Relief Committee.* List items, such as clothing, household goods, and nonperishable foods, which people could make or collect to send to civilian war victims. Develop a plan for assembling and distributing the items.

Organize the class into five groups and have each group form one of the committees listed. Direct the committees to present their plans in writing.

Have committees read their completed plans to the class, and encourage other students to add ideas. Conclude the activity by asking students to interview their grandparents and other older acquaintances about civilian war efforts in which they participated.

Reinforcement Activity

Section 19-3: World War I Newspaper

Preparation for this cooperative activity requires half a class period. Students work on the project as homework and need one class period for completion and closure.

In this activity groups of students produce wartime newspapers. Describe the project before students read Section 19-3. Then preview the section by listing its major topics on the chalkboard: *The American Navy in Action, American Expeditionary Force, Trench Warfare, The German Advance, The Allies on the Offensive, Counting the Cost.*

Organize the class into six groups. Explain that after reading the section, each group will create a newspaper that includes news articles, feature stories, political cartoons, editorials, letters to the editor, ads, and perhaps an advice column and obituaries. Make issues of present-day newspapers available and encourage students to examine them to get ideas for their own papers. Allow groups to make their own individual assignments, but require each group member to contribute at least three items to the paper, including at least one news article based on one of the topics listed on the chalkboard.

Allow class time for students to assemble their articles into newspaper format on large poster sheets. Display the completed papers and ask students to compare the approach and information included by different reporters writing about the same topics.

Evaluating Progress

Section 19-4: Viewpoints on Peace

This individual activity can be completed in a class period or assigned as homework.

In this activity, students use the text, including maps, to develop position statements on the conditions of a peace treaty from the perspective of each of the four major Allies and Germany. Introduce the assignment by reminding students that at the end of World War I, when representatives of the four major Allied powers—the United States, Great Britain, France, and Italy—met to draft a treaty for Germany to sign, each nation had different goals.

Tell students that in this assignment they are to write proposals from the point of view of the foreign ministers of each of the four allied powers. They are to outline in writing the conditions their country demands be included in a peace treaty, stating the reasons for each demand, along with that country's vision of how its proposed peace plan will bring about a better future for the world. Position statements should also include a clear expression of each country's attitude toward Germany. When they finish their statements, students should prepare a German response to the four proposals.

Evaluation criteria should include accuracy in describing each country's conditions, logic in the supporting reasons provided, and perspective in expressing the victors' feelings toward Germany as well Germany's response to the victors' conditions.

Enrichment Activity

Section 19-2: Bringing Opposition Views to Light

This individual activity may be assigned as homework.

In the course of this activity—writing newspaper editorials—students gain a deeper awareness of opposition views and the treatment of the people who held them in the United States during World War I.

Introduce the activity by reminding students that not all Americans favored United States entry into World War I. For example, some Americans of German and Irish ancestry found it hard to sympathize with Britain, while pacifists argued against giving up American neutrality. Direct students to review Sections 19-1 and 19-2 to familiarize themselves with opposition views and the ways dissenters were treated.

Assign students the task of writing newspaper editorials. Each student should choose an individual or group that opposed American participation in the war and write an editorial from that viewpoint. The editorial should

- express the viewpoint and the reasoning behind it.
- describe any consequences, such as mistreatment or denial of rights, that the group or individual has suffered as a result of those views.
- attempt to influence readers either to support or reject the views.

After students complete the assignments, have them meet in groups to read each other's editorials. Ask each group to select one editorial to present to the class. Finally, discuss with the class the value and dangers of dissenting opinions during times of war. Do they believe that freedom of speech should be limited under wartime conditions? Why or why not?

Bibliography and Audiovisual Material

Teacher Bibliography

Barbeau, Arthur E., and Florette, Henri. *The Unknown Soldiers: Black American Troops in World War I*. Philadelphia: Temple University Press, 1974.

Coffman, Edward M. *The War to End All Wars: The American Experience in World War I*. Madison: University of Wisconsin Press, 1986.

Ferrel, Robert H. *Woodrow Wilson and World War I: Nineteen Seventeen to Nineteen Twenty-One*. New York: HarperCollins Publishers, Inc., 1986.

Kennedy, David M. *Over Here: The First World War and American Society*. New York: Oxford University Press, 1980.

Smythe, Donald. *Pershing: General of the Armies*. Bloomington: Indiana University Press, 1986.

Stone, Ralph. *Wilson and the League of Nations: Why America's Rejection?* Melbourne, FL.: Krieger Publishing Co., 1978.

Tuchman, Barbara. *The Guns of August*. New York: Bantam Books, 1982.

Vaughn, Edwin Campion. *Some Desperate Glory: The World War I Diary of a British Officer, 1917*. New York: Holt, 1988.

Student Bibliography

Dos Passos, John. *Three Soldiers*. New York: Carroll & Graf Publishers, 1988.

Hemingway, Ernest. *A Farewell to Arms*. New York: Scribner, 1987.

Kilmer, Joyce. *Trees and Other Poems*. Marietta, Ga.: Cherokee Publishing Co., 1989.

Remarque, Erich Maria. *All Quiet on the Western Front*. New York: Fawcett, 1987.

Stein, Gertrude. *Three Lives*. New York: Viking Penguin, 1990.

Films, Videocassettes, and Videodiscs

The Ordeal of Woodrow Wilson. 26 min. NBC. Videocassette.

World War I. 26 min. PROJP; MCGH. Movie.

World War I Series: Fighting on Two Fronts. 18 min. CORT. Movie.

Filmstrips

American Heritage Media Collection: World War I. 5 color filmstrips, 5 cassettes, guide. Westport Media.

Causes of World War I. 1 filmstrip. Guidance Associates.

Computer Software

The Tragedy of War: Attack on the Somme. 1 Apple diskette, backup, support materials, guide. Focus Media, Inc.

Chapter 19

Objectives

- Analyze factors leading to United States involvement in World War I.
- Describe United States mobilization for the war.
- Discuss the American experience in World War I.
- Explain why Wilson's actions as peacemaker aroused opposition in the United States.

Introducing THE CHAPTER

For suggestions on introducing Chapter 19, refer to page 491B in the Teacher's Edition.

Developing THE CHAPTER

For activities and teaching strategies to help you reinforce and enrich chapter content, see pages 491B-491D in the Teacher's Edition.

B · A · C · K · G · R · O · U · N · D

Chapter Opener Illustrations
Soldiers of the Yorkshire regiment (England) on the march in France are dramatically caught against the sunset.

War stamps raised money to pay for the war. This poster appeals to American women by comparing them to Joan of Arc, who rallied the French against English invading forces in the 1400s.

President Wilson campaigned for reelection in 1916, stressing domestic successes and keeping the United States out of World War I. "Preparedness," however, suggests the country was ready to defend itself.

Soldiers on the western front survived in cramped, filthy trenches. For a description of trench warfare, see text page 509.

Reduced student page in the Teacher's Edition

Chapter 19 1914-1920

The First World War

Joan of Arc Saved France
W.S.S.
WOMEN OF AMERICA
SAVE YOUR COUNTRY
Buy WAR SAVINGS STAMPS
UNITED STATES TREASURY DEPARTMENT

492

This scene of an armistice celebration, painted in 1918 by George Luks, shows the flags of many of the Allied nations. Luks (1867–1933) was a member of the Ashcan School, a group of American artists that emphasized a down-to-earth realism.

A gas mask was a necessary piece of combat gear. Both sides launched poison gas attacks, which killed thousands. The English soldier and poet Wilfred Owen described the experience of a gas attack: "*Gas! Gas! Quick, boys!—An ecstasy of fumbling, Fitting the clumsy helmets just in time.*"

American Voices

In June 1918, in a wooded patch of France that had once been a hunting preserve, Private Elton Mackin of the 5th Marine Regiment faced the guns of the German army. His regiment was on the advance, venturing into an area that seemed to have an invisible enemy.

> *"We left the firing line on our bellies snaking away into the trampled wheat. . . . From time to time, the Sergeant would motion us down while he surveyed the terrain ahead and to our right, where things were getting hot. . . .*
>
> *We began to fret some because we were really in no man's land, far . . . from our battalion line. . .*
>
> *Baldy, the most assured of us (none were at all brave) finally ventured to question, 'Hey, Sarge?' He got no answer—not even the grunt we expected. The Sergeant was full-length out of the ditch, snuggled down in a patch of shrubs and weeds; his chin rested on his folded arms, and he was peering under the brim of his helmet. His field glasses lay in front of him.*
>
> *'Hey, Sarge?' Baldy shook one foot to get his attention. There was no response. We knew better. We should not have left him there, but the evening star was glowing against the east and we were suddenly a bunch of lost, scared kids—a long way from home."*

American soldiers were getting their first taste of battle, in a war that had raged in Europe since 1914. At first the war had been called the "European War," but one by one nations from around the world were drawn in. In spring 1917 Americans crossed the Atlantic to join the fighting. This would be, they told each other, the "war to end all wars." Later, veterans recalled the "Great War." Finally when people realized that this war had not ended all wars, it became known as World War I.

Fresh troops advancing at dusk; war savings stamps poster; Woodrow Wilson campaign truck, 1916; in the trenches; "Armistice Night," by George Luks; gas mask.

George Luks: *Armistice Night* (1918)

Analyzing Primary Sources

American Voices

Many American young men went off to the "Great War" with visions of high adventure, gallantry, and opportunities for personal glory. The reality was far different. Have a student read Elton Mackin's account of a war episode to the class.

1. How does Mackin view himself and his comrades? **(*"a bunch of lost scared kids—a long way from home"*)**

2. Does his writing suggest a romantic, heroic vision of warfare? If not, what does it suggest? **(a group of ordinary people suddenly plunged into a life-and-death situation, coping as well as they can, but realizing their puniness in the scheme of things)**

Tell students that as they study this chapter, especially Section 3, they will learn more about what World War I was like for ordinary soldiers.

GTV Side 4

Chap. 1, Frame 00003

Modern Times (Movie)

Search:

Play:

Section 19-1

Objectives

- ***Answer the Focus Question.***
- *Explain why Europe was a "powder keg" on the eve of World War I.*
- *Analyze the effect of German submarine warfare on American public opinion.*

Introducing

THE SECTION

In 1914 Americans were spectators when war broke out, and most expected to remain so. In the summer of 1914 Wilson urged Americans not to show any favoritism:

> *"We must . . . put a curb upon our sentiments as well as upon every transaction that might be construed as a preference of one party to the struggle before another."*

Discuss with students what harm might result if Americans took sides in the war in Europe. **(American partisanship could lead to divisions in the U.S.; it could spoil the nation's possible role as a peace mediator; it could encourage the warring nations to seize American ships and goods.)**

Students will be reading about the events that led the United States to move from neutrality to involvement in World War I and about the role the United States played in that conflict.

B · A · C · K · G · R · O · U · N · D

Time Line Illustrations

1. Dress uniforms on both sides reflected the pomp of empires with long histories. The eagle emblem on the German helmet was introduced into Germany by the ancient Romans.

2. The *Lusitania* was the pride of the British Cunard fleet. When a German U-boat sank it on May 7, 1915, with the loss of 128 American citizens, Americans were outraged.

3. President Woodrow Wilson, in a ceremonial top hat and tail coat, doffs his hat to a crowd.

4. This famous recruitment poster in which Uncle Sam practically reaches out to nab a recruit was painted by the well-known illustrator James Montgomery Flagg.

5. A crowd in Times Square, New York City, on November 7, 1918, celebrated a premature report of the armistice.

Reduced student page in the Teacher's Edition

CHAPTER TIME LINE

1914-1920

1916 Wilson seeks support for a defense plan

1915 **May** German U-boat sinks the *Lusitania*

1914 | 1915 | 1916

1914 **Jun** Archduke Francis Ferdinand and his wife assassinated

Jul-Aug Allies and Central Powers prepare for war

19-1 From Neutrality to War

Focus: How did the United States move from a policy of neutrality to one of active involvement in the European war?

It was Sunday, June 28, 1914. Americans who relaxed with the Sunday comics laughed at the pranks of the Katzenjammer Kids and Buster Brown. Sports fans read news of the first African-American heavyweight boxing champion, Jack Johnson. The front page reflected the nation's concerns in headlines like "Suffragettes March on Capitol" and "Plain Facts About Tariff."

Something else happened that Sunday, but it occurred thousands of miles away and seemed to have little to do with the United States. Still, on Monday *The New York Times* splashed the news over half the front page: "HEIR TO AUSTRIA'S THRONE IS SLAIN WITH HIS WIFE BY A BOSNIAN YOUTH TO AVENGE SEIZURE OF HIS COUNTRY."

Roots of World War I

Few Americans knew of Bosnia, a possession of Austria-Hungary on the mountainous Balkan Peninsula of southeastern Europe. The tiny Balkan countries had feuded for centuries over territorial claims and had been dominated by land-hungry neighbors—Austria-Hungary, the Ottoman Empire (now called Turkey), and Russia. In fact, the war-torn peninsula had earned the nickname "the powder keg of Europe."

Europe itself was a powder keg. A fierce sense of nationalism had been growing since the mid-1800s. Some countries exhibited nationalism by building up their armies and fighting over na-

6. This scene depicting the signing of the peace treaty at Versailles was painted by the British artist Sir William Orpen. President Wilson is second from left. To his left is Prime Minister David Lloyd George of Great Britain. To Wilson's right is Premier Georges Clemenceau of France.

1917 Feb "Zimmermann note"

Apr The United States declares war

May Selective Service Act

1917 Nov Bolshevik revolution in Russia

1918 Mar Treaty of Brest-Litovsk

Nov Germany signs armistice

1919 Jun Treaty of Versailles

1920 Treaty of Versailles defeated in U.S.; separate peace with Central Powers

1917 — 1918 — 1919 — 1920

tional boundaries. Germany had annexed French provinces. Austria-Hungary had brought Italians as well as Slavic peoples under its rule. Great Britain, France, and Germany had expanded their empires to Africa, Asia, and the Pacific. Conquest and competition heightened the tension in Europe.

In the midst of this atmosphere of fear and suspicion, alliances began to form. Although Germany had greatly increased its strength since it unified under Chancellor Otto von Bismarck in 1871, it searched for allies to help protect its territory. It found those allies in Austria-Hungary and Italy, both of which shared Germany's fears of other European powers. In 1882 the three nations formed the Triple Alliance.

Britain, France, and Russia were aware of the threat to them from the powerful Triple Alliance. Furthermore, Russia was a rival of Austria-Hungary for control of the Balkans. France had suffered humiliation at the hands of German troops who annexed French territory. The British believed that their safety in Europe depended on keeping any one state from gaining too much power. Although the three nations were not without disputes among themselves, they formed their own alliance, the Triple Entente (ahn-TAHNT).

Peace in Europe now hinged on a precarious **balance of power,** a situation in which the power of rival nations or alliances is roughly equal. As the German ambassador to France said in 1914, "Peace remains at the mercy of an accident."

Outbreak of War

The gunshot on that Sunday in June 1914 lit a match to the powderkeg and exploded the balance of power in Europe. Austria-Hungary blamed Serbia for the assassination, and on July 28, with encouragement and support from Germany, declared war on Serbia. Now the elaborate system of alliances began to come into play.

Within weeks, the five major European nations were at war. Russia, France, and Britain sided against Germany and Austria-Hungary and then, like falling dominoes, other nations joined the war. Japan declared war on Germany, seeking German claims in the Pacific and China. The

Developing THE SECTION

Linking Past and Present

Research. Ask students to explain the term nationalism and give examples of how some countries exhibited nationalism in the 1800s. Have students recall strong nationalistic movements in the 1990s. The Baltic republics of Estonia, Latvia, and Lithuania, for example, gained independence from the Soviet Union as did other republics.

Have students research nationalistic movements in the 1990s and the conflicts that have resulted. What area of the world would be considered a "powder keg" today? Why?

Global Connections

Oral Report. Have students research the Congress of Vienna (1814–1815), ending the Napoleonic Wars, and the Treaty of Frankfurt (1871), ending the Franco-Prussian War. They can make oral reports explaining how these treaties influenced political conditions in Europe prior to World War I.

Active Learning

Drawing Cartoons. Have students draw political cartoons supporting either the Triple Alliance, the Triple Entente, or neutrality. The cartoons should convey a central idea, supporting details, and have a caption.

Analyzing Primary Sources

Letter From a German Soldier. Read to students this excerpt from a letter written by a German soldier to his sister in August 1914, eleven days after the German conquest of Belgium:

“No enemy can enter here without sacrificing one million men. . . . When 'volunteers to the front' is called out, all present themselves, the entire battery standing like a wall and each man wishing to be first. When we come back, it is always singing, no matter how tired we are.”

Ask: What is the mood of this soldier? How can you tell? **(optimistic; soldiers are always singing; men volunteer for duty)** What outcome does the soldier forsee for the Allies? Why? **(exorbitant loss of Allied lives; confidence of the German troops)**

Global Connections

Ironically Archduke Ferdinand had sympathy for the Balkan people. He was touring Bosnia in the hope that his presence would ease tension between Austria-Hungary and the Balkans. His assassin, Gavrilo Princip, was thought to be connected to the Black Hand, a Serbian terrorist group. In response, Austria-Hungary sent a drastic ultimatum to Serbia. The Serbs rejected a critical part of it. On July 28, 1914, Austria-Hungary declared war on Serbia.

Ottoman Empire and Bulgaria sided with Germany and Austria-Hungary. Italy broke with the Triple Alliance, hoping to grab from Austria-Hungary the Italian provinces under its control.

Now, replacing the alliances of peace were alliances of war. Germany, Austria-Hungary, the Ottoman Empire, and Bulgaria—in the center of Europe—became the Central Powers. Britain, France, Russia, Italy, and the twenty other nations that eventually joined them became the Allies.

Both sides counted on a quick victory—even by Christmas. But a few felt a grim foreboding. Sir Edward Grey, the British foreign minister, looked out his window at the street lamps. "The lamps are going out all over Europe," he said. "We shall not see them lit again in our lifetime."

Stalemate on the Western Front

Any hope for a quick victory soon died. In August the German army invaded its neutral neighbor, Belgium, and rolled on to the Marne River, near Paris. By the end of September, both sides had dug into a network of trenches on the western front.

Then the technology of warfare took control of events. The instruments of war in 1914 were better suited for defense than offense. Both sides had the weapons and skill to deflect enemy attacks, but neither had the ability to smash through a well-defended position. The two sides would find themselves in a bloody stalemate for nearly four years.

Archduke Ferdinand and his wife one hour before their assassination.

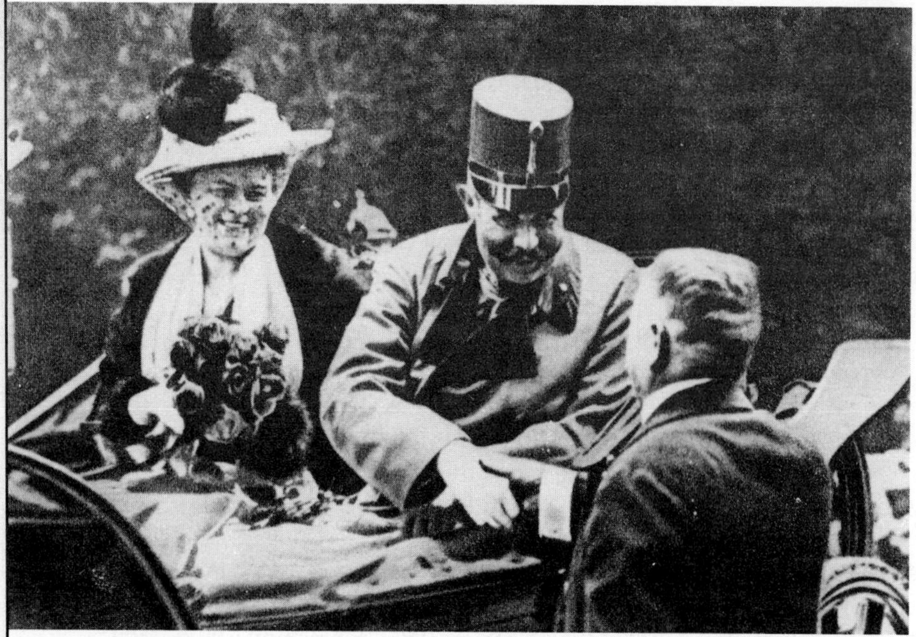

American Neutrality

On August 4, 1914, President Wilson issued a proclamation of neutrality and urged Americans to be "impartial in thought as well as in action." Ever since Washington had warned against "entangling alliances," Presidents had tried to avoid involvement in European in-fighting. Wilson feared that war would distract American attention from the domestic issues of reform and antitrust legislation to which he was so passionately committed.

Wilson did not see war in terms of glory and empire. He did, however, see a role for the United States in the war—as an impartial mediator who could bring peace to Europe.

Many Americans who supported neutrality nevertheless found it hard to be "impartial in thought." One third of Americans were immigrants or had immigrant parents. Many of them had relatives living in Europe. Not surprisingly, therefore, their sympathies were stirred by the memories of their countries of origin.

Some Irish Americans sided with the Central Powers because of their dislike for Britain, which ruled Ireland. German Americans made up the largest foreign-born group in the United States. Many of them felt a strong loyalty to Germany. Most Americans, however, sympathized with the Allies. For instance, even President Wilson, with his Scottish and English ancestry, could not really be completely impartial in thought.

Connections: Literature

The American novelist Henry James lived in England for much of his life. On the day after England declared war, he wrote to a friend, *"The plunge of civilization into this abyss of blood and darkness . . . gives away the whole long age during which we have supposed the world to be . . . gradually bettering."*

Backyard History

Researching Newspapers. Have students research their community's reaction to World War I. If your public library has a file of local newspapers that extends back to 1914, have students go there and read newspapers from the autumn of that year. (If your library does not have such material, you might ask editors of your local newspaper about their back files.)

If national as well as local papers are available, have students compare issues with the same date and note differences in reaction in editorials, letters to the editor, political cartoons, and so on. Have students share their findings in class. Speculate about reasons for differences in coverage.

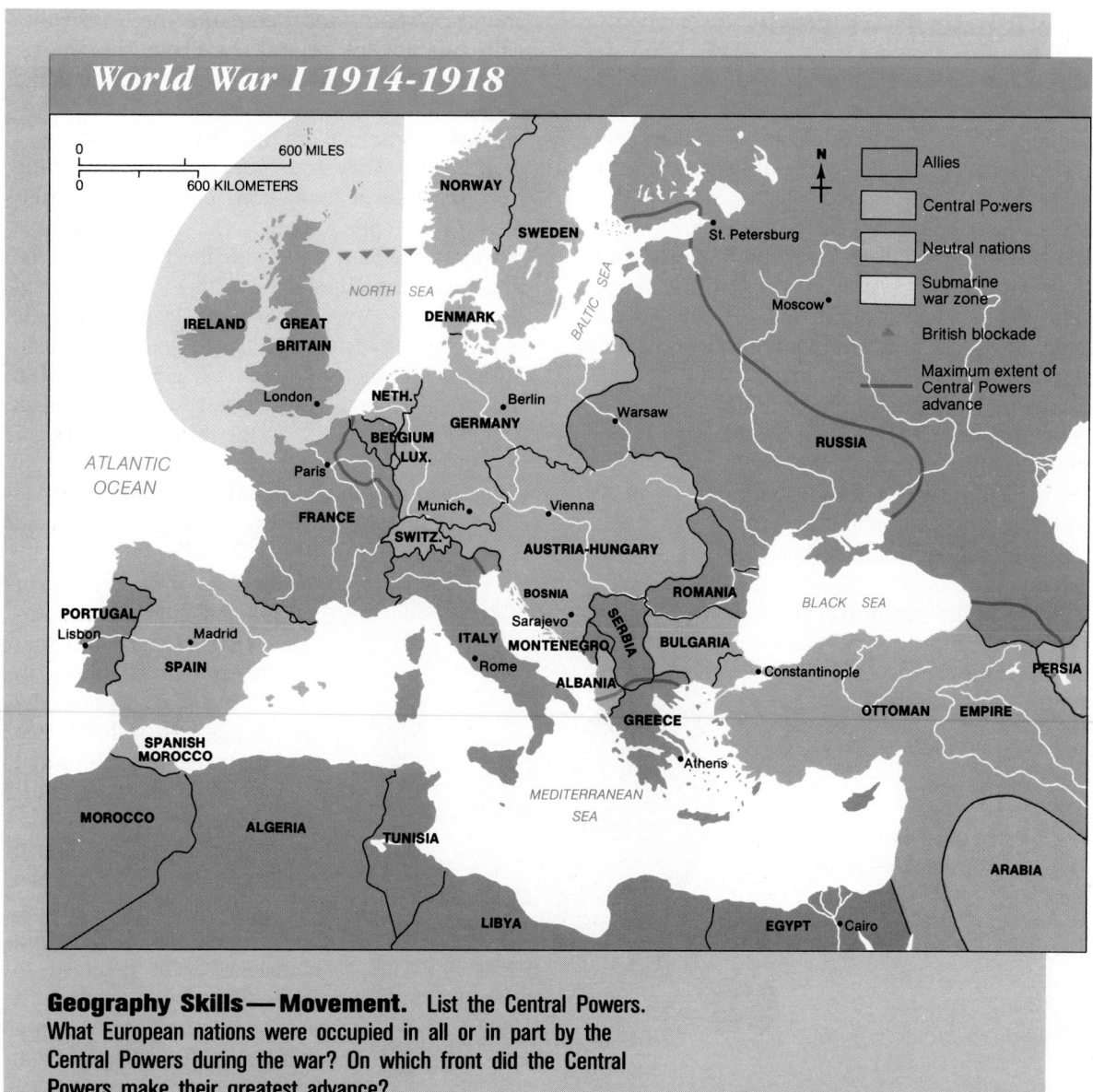

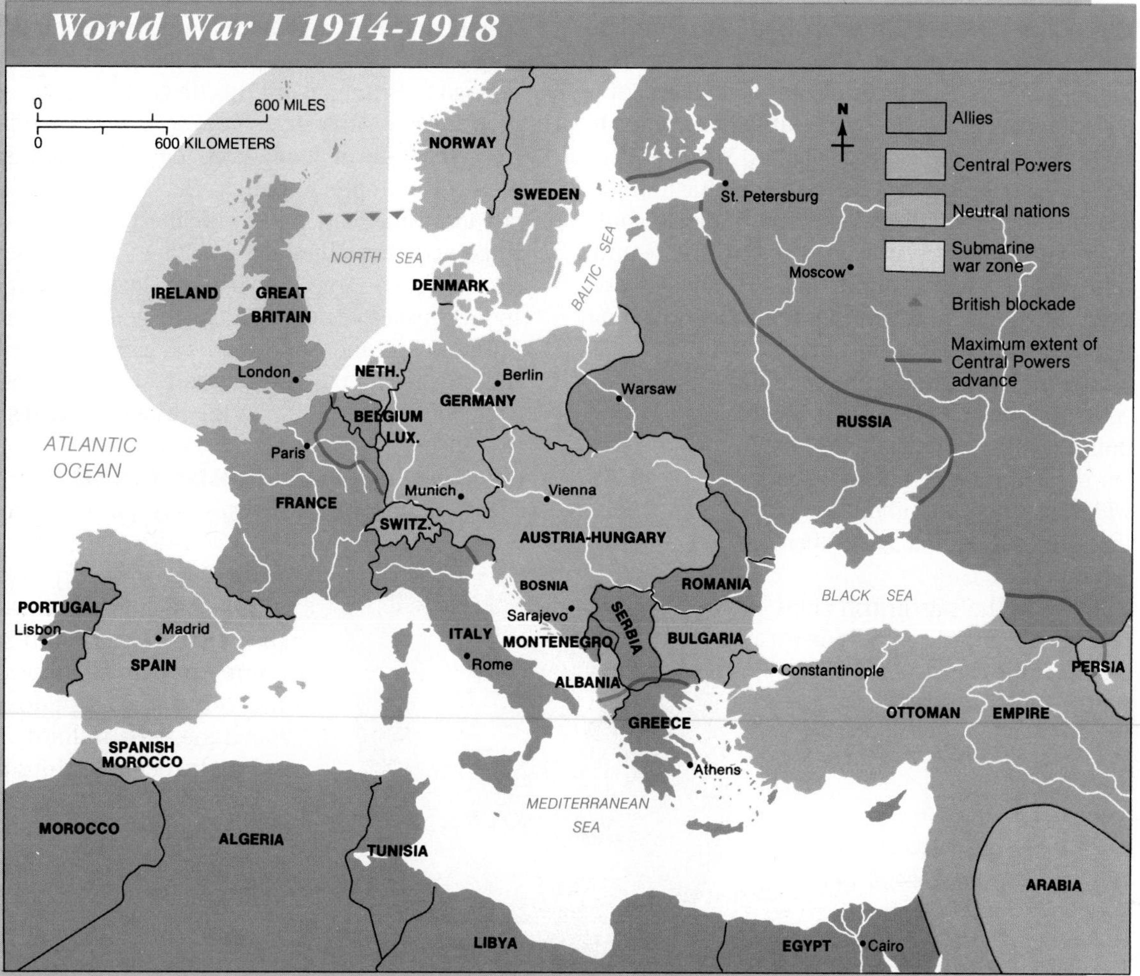

Geography Skills — Movement. List the Central Powers. What European nations were occupied in all or in part by the Central Powers during the war? On which front did the Central Powers make their greatest advance?

Geography Skills

ANSWERS

1. Germany, Austria-Hungary, Bulgaria, Ottoman Empire.
2. Belgium, France, Italy, Montenegro, Albania, Serbia, Greece, Romania, Russia.
3. Eastern front.

Propaganda

Noting the diversity of American opinion, both Britain and Germany tried to whip up support for their cause. They flooded the nation with propaganda by mail, telegraph, and a new invention—the radio. From Allied sources Americans heard of mass murder and mutilation by German troops in Belgium and France. The Germans told of similar horrors committed by the French and British. When Britain cut Germany's transatlantic telegraph lines, it gained an advantage in the propaganda war.

Still, sympathizing with one side was far different from going to war in support of that side. Moving Americans from a neutral stance to active participation would take more than propaganda.

Chapter Connections

Discussion. Ask students to recall another time in our nation's history when Britain had tried to cut off American trade with its enemies. **(See Chapter 7, pages 169–170. In 1793 Britain had declared a blockade of France, seized neutral ships, and even impressed American sailors. Opposed to war, Washington tried to negotiate dispute; led to signing of Jay's Treaty. See also Chapter 8, pages 197–198. In the early 1800s both Britain and France had seized American ships they claimed were trading illegally with the enemy. The British also had impressed American sailors. The dispute between Britain and the United States led to the War of 1812.)**

Connections: Science and Technology

At the beginning of the war, airplanes were mostly used for observing enemy forces. After a Dutch inventor developed a synchronizing gear that allowed machine guns to fire between blades of the propellers, air warfare began.

Reduced student page in the Teacher's Edition

The Blockade of Trade

The stalemate on the western front was draining both Germany and the Allies. Every day some 7 million soldiers went through tons of food and military supplies. Each side was grimly determined to stop the other from getting supplies. Whoever controlled the seas and the ports had a lifeline to trade. Under international law, neutral nations could trade with countries at war as long as the neutral ships did not carry contraband—forbidden cargoes like guns and ammunition. Neutral ships could be searched, but only at sea.

The major neutral country trading with Europe was the United States. Both the Allies and the Central Powers tried to cut off American trade with their enemies without turning the United States against themselves.

Early in the war British ships began stopping neutral merchant ships headed for Germany, or even for Germany's neutral neighbors—the Netherlands, Sweden, and Denmark. The British illegally brought the neutral ships into Allied ports, searched them, and seized even noncontraband cargoes like food. The United States quickly complained to Britain about this illegal blockade.

American industry, however, was profiting from the sale of food, steel, oil, and other supplies to Europe. Although the British blockade cut into American trade with the Central Powers, trade with the Allies soared. When the Allies ran short of cash, American bankers loaned them the money to keep buying American goods. American business and industry became increasingly tied to the Allied nations. The Germans decided to break the British blockade.

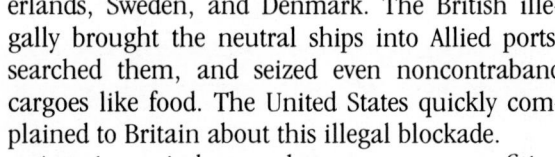

The poster at right may have been designed as an ad for a German book or movie. It reads, "The U-boats are out!" Below, a surfaced U-boat.

Submarine Warfare

The seas of Europe soon grew dangerous. In November 1914 both Britain and Germany planted mines in the North Sea. Britain declared the sea a military area and warned neutral ships that they would be safe only under Allied protection.

Germany could not match Britain's mighty navy, but it did have a tiny fleet of submarines, called U-boats. Small and light, submarines were designed to travel underwater unseen. A submarine could close in on a surface ship, fire a torpedo, and slip away.

Americans protested that submarine attacks violated international law. The law stated that a warship must warn a merchant ship before firing on it, and must rescue passengers and crew after sinking it. Slow on the surface, submarines could not give warning without endangering themselves. Furthermore, they had no room to carry survivors.

Global Connections
When the *Lusitania* left New York City, it was carrying not only passengers but also a large cargo of munitions for British use. After the ship was sunk, Secretary of State William Jennings Bryan blamed England as well as Germany. *"Germany has a right to prevent contraband going to the Allies,"* Bryan wrote, *"and a ship carrying contraband should not rely on passengers to protect her from attack—it would be like putting women and children in front of an army."* When Wilson refused to take Bryan's advice and protest the British blockade as well as the German sinking of the *Lusitania*, the Secretary of State resigned.

Thinking Critically

Evaluation. Refer students to the *Notice!* accompanying the *Lusitania* ad on this page. **Ask:** Why do you think travelers ignored the warning? (Travelers probably didn't believe the ad; they felt the British could protect them.) Remind students that the ship was carrying contraband, including ammunition. Was Germany justified in sinking the *Lusitania?* Why or why not?

In February 1915 Germany announced a war zone in the waters around Britain. Enemy ships would be sunk on sight. Even neutral ships might be sunk, Germany warned, because British ships might disguise themselves with neutral flags. Wilson protested. If an American ship was sunk or an American killed, the United States would consider it a violation of neutrality. Germany, in turn, warned Americans not to travel on enemy ships.

While warnings were being exchanged, Colonel Edward M. House was trying to negotiate a peace settlement. House, Wilson's advisor and closest friend, shuttled from London to Paris to Germany and back again. "Everybody seems to want peace," he wrote home, "but nobody is willing to concede enough to get it."

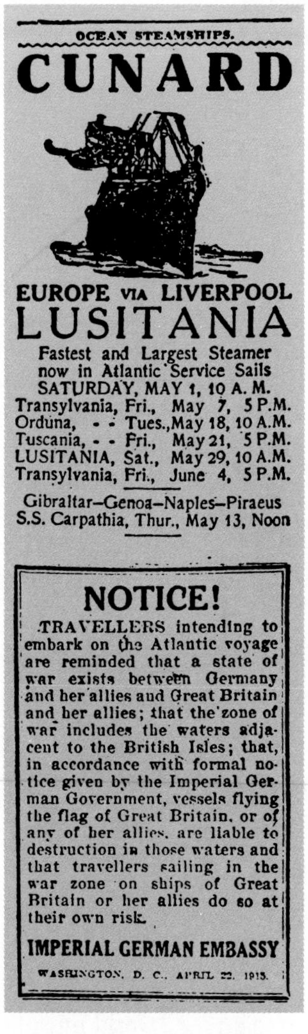

New York newspapers printed this German warning before the Lusitania sailed.

The Lusitania

On May 1, 1915, the *Lusitania*, a British luxury liner, sailed from New York bound for England. Passengers, seemingly unaffected by the knowledge that they would sail through a war zone, enjoyed six days of dining and dancing. Then, on May 7, just off the coast of Ireland, German torpedoes ripped into the *Lusitania*. Within minutes it rolled over and sank, taking with it 1,198 men, women, and children—128 of them American citizens.

Americans were outraged, and some cried war. Still, President Wilson said that the United States must remain an example of peace. He sent a letter of protest to Germany and asked for compensation for damages. Germany replied that the *Lusitania* had carried arms and that Americans had been warned to stay home. It apologized and offered to pay damages, but refused to abandon submarine warfare.

The Preparedness Campaign

The *Lusitania* incident convinced Wilson that the United States should be prepared to defend itself. He toured the country to gain support for building up the army and navy. But most Americans, still hoping for peace, failed to support the plan, which they saw as inching the nation toward war. Responding to public hesitation, Congress refused to act on Wilson's plan.

Then, after Germany agreed not to sink unarmed passenger vessels, a U-boat torpedoed the French liner *Sussex* in March 1916. Several American passengers were injured. A furious Wilson sent an ultimatum to Germany. Unless Germany abandoned its warfare against merchant and passenger ships, the United States would sever diplomatic relations.

Germany pledged to give warning before sinking merchant ships but attached an impossible condition to its promise. The United States must force Britain to end its illegal blockade or Germany would feel free to change its policy. Wilson accepted Germany's pledge, but he replied that he could not accept the condition.

The *Sussex* sinking broke the deadlock in Congress over preparedness, and several defense measures were passed. The National Defense Act of 1916 more than doubled the size of the army. The Naval Appropriations Bill set shipbuilders to work. And a Council of National Defense was set up to prepare the nation's industry and resources in case of war.

As the election of 1916 approached, Wilson was in a quandary. He heard voters demanding "two inconsistent things, firmness and the avoidance of war." He chose a platform of reform and peace. The Democrats' slogan was "He kept us out of war." The Republicans also ran a peace candidate, Supreme Court Justice Charles Evans Hughes. Wilson defeated Hughes by a very narrow margin.

Connections: Politics

Using the Visuals. Discuss Wilson's reelection campaign by referring students to the photograph of the Wilson campaign truck on page 493.

1. Do the signs address themselves primarily to domestic or foreign issues? **(domestic)**
2. What two slogans concern the war? **("Peace with honor," and "Preparedness")**
3. How do these suggest Wilson's quandry about the war? **("Peace with honor" indicates his desire to stay out of the war; "Preparedness" indicates that the country is ready to go to war if it must.)**

Limited English Proficiency

Making a Time Line. Have students work in pairs to make a time line of events in Europe between June 28, 1914 and April 2, 1917, starting with the British blockade. When students have completed the time lines, ask which events were most important in drawing the United States into the war. Why? **(Answers may include the sinking of the *Lusitania* and the Zimmermann note. Both had exceptional impact on public opinion in the United States.)**

Section Review

ANSWERS

1. The definition for *balance of power* is on text page 495.
2. Answers may include fierce nationalism and expansionism, disputes over boundaries, the opposing Triple Alliance and Triple Entente.
3. Provoked hostility against Germany. Sinking of *Lusitania* led Wilson to send a letter of protest; sinking of *Sussex* led Wilson to threaten to break off diplomatic relations.
4. Answers may include that Wilson was a genuine peace candidate who strove to have the warring nations initiate peace talks and settle differences.
5. Answers may include Germany's announcement to resume unrestricted submarine warfare, Zimmermann note, and Russian Revolution. Wilson asserted United States wanted to "make the world safe for democracy."

Social History

American pacifists included Jane Addams and Henry Ford. Ford paid the expenses of about fifty men and women for a peace trip to Europe in 1915. After the United States entered the war, Ford's plants were converted to the manufacture of war materials.

Reduced student page in the Teacher's Edition

Cartoons such as the one above sought to stir American support for preparedness. But many Americans, including Henry Ford, continued to protest.

"I don't believe in preparedness. . . . Men and nations who carry guns get into trouble. If I had my way I'd throw every ounce of gunpowder into the sea."

—Henry Ford on Preparedness

Wilson tried one more time to lead the Europeans into peace talks. In January 1917 he proposed "a peace without victory," in which neither side would lose territory or gain power. But the Europeans felt they had fought too hard and too long to give up short of victory.

Congress Declares War

In February 1917 Germany, hopelessly stalled on the western front, announced that it would begin unrestricted submarine warfare again. It planned to break the British control of the seas with its fleet of U-boats—now numbering more than one hundred—and win before the United States joined the fight.

Wilson immediately cut off diplomatic relations, but he hoped that Germany would back down. In late February his hope died. Britain had gotten hold of a message from the German foreign minister, Arthur Zimmermann, to his minister in Mexico. The "Zimmermann note" suggested a German-Mexican alliance if the United States entered the war. "It is understood," the note added, "that Mexico is to reconquer the lost territory in New Mexico, Texas, and Arizona." Japan would also be included in the alliance.

When the press printed the note, Americans were at first unbelieving, then furious. Although Mexico rejected the offer, Americans in the West and Southwest—many of whom had opposed the war—now feared for their security. The public uproar against Germany increased when U-boats sank several American merchant ships.

Another barrier to joining the Allies fell when Russian revolutionaries overthrew dictator Czar Nicholas II and replaced the monarchy with a democratic government. With a democratic government in place, Russia became an acceptable ally in the minds of many Americans.

On April 2, 1917, with the unanimous backing of his cabinet, Wilson asked Congress to declare war against Germany. The United States, said Wilson, was not going to war for conquest or territory, but for the cause of human rights and the freedom of all nations. Then, in one phrase, Wilson expressed the heart of his war message: "The world must be made safe for democracy." On April 6 Congress voted to declare war.

Section Review

1. **Identification.** Define *balance of power.*

2. **Analysis.** What relationships among the nations of Europe made war likely?

3. **Analysis.** What effect did submarine warfare have on the American government and public opinion?

4. **Evaluation.** In your opinion, was Wilson genuinely a peace candidate in 1916? Explain.

5. **Comprehension.** What three events convinced Wilson that war was unavoidable? How did Wilson justify the United States going to war?

Global Connections

The democratic government in Russia lasted only eight months. It was overthrown by a wing of the radical Communist party. Alexander Kerensky, the overthrown premier, eventually moved to the United States where he became a staff member of the Hoover Institute on War, Revolution and Peace, at Stanford University in California.

19-2 Mobilizing for War

Focus: How did the United States prepare itself for war?

The Allies were overjoyed when they heard that the United States was entering the war. Parisians flew American flags, the British Parliament cheered President Wilson, and Allied soldiers on the western front managed smiles of hope. The Allies needed help desperately. Russia was in chaos after the revolution. Despair had driven some French units to mutiny. German U-boats were sinking Allied ships faster than the Allies could replace them.

The Draft

Large-scale **mobilization**— organization and preparation of people and resources for war— would have to be directed by the federal government, which would grow to meet the challenges of war. One major challenge was to build up the armed forces. In April 1917 the army numbered only 200,000 soldiers, most of them not yet trained. Wilson and Congress would have preferred to build up the army with volunteers, but they realized that volunteer enlistments could never fill the ranks. The alternative was conscription— the draft.

On May 18 Congress passed the Selective Service Act. The act required all men between the ages of twenty-one and thirty (and later, between eighteen and forty-five) to register for military service. From this pool, draftees were to be chosen by a lottery. Unlike the Civil War, buying a substitute was not an option.

Among those serving were some 360,000 African Americans, inspired by W.E.B. Du Bois's words: "Let us, while this war lasts, forget our special grievances and close ranks shoulder to shoulder with our fellow citizens." African Americans, however, met with discrimination in military service. One soldier wrote, "German prisoners were kinder than our white American comrades." African Americans were placed in segregated units that usually had white officers. Only after protests from groups like the NAACP were several hundred African Americans made officers.

The most famous black regiment, the 369th Infantry, was under enemy fire for a record-breaking

The African-American 15th Regiment parades up Fifth Avenue in New York. The Regiment was bound for an army training camp in New York State.

Section 19-2

Objectives

- ***Answer the Focus Question.***
- *Explain the changes mobilization caused in the work force.*
- *Relate how the government dealt with opposition to the war.*

Introducing

THE SECTION

Refer students to the word *mobilization* and its definition on this text page. Point out that mobilizing for war required many changes in the United States, and that the federal government took charge to accomplish those changes. Allow students time to preview the headings and illustrations in the section. Then have them speculate about how Americans were affected by mobilization.

1. How do you think young men were affected by mobilization? **(drafted)**
2. Women? **(took jobs of men who had been drafted)**
3. African Americans? **(With great need for labor, they were hired for jobs previously closed to them.)**
4. Farmers and business people? **(stepped up production to meet wartime needs)**

Developing
THE SECTION

Limited English Proficiency

Cooperative Activity. Refer students to the posters on this page. **Ask:** How do the posters promote ideas that helped the American cause? Then have students work in groups to create posters urging people to support the war effort. The posters might encourage purchase of Liberty Bonds, conservation of materials needed for war, more production of war goods. Each student should have one responsibility: researching information, writing a title, drawing illustrations, and so on. After the posters are done, have students explain how they promote certain ideas and values.

Global Connections

Discussion. As head of relief efforts for Belgium, Hoover made brilliant use of publicity to organize hundreds of local committees and to force the Allies to allow his relief shipments through. Trying to operate between the warring parties, he said, was *"like trying to feed a hungry kitten . . . confined behind bars with two hungry lions."*

1. Who were the "hungry lions"? **(Germany and the Allies)**
2. Why might the Allies not have wanted the relief shipments through? **(fear of the shipments being used by the Germans)**
3. Why might Germany not have wanted the shipments through? **(fear of some trick by the Allies)**

Constitutional Heritage

The food conservation campaign also gave new life to the movement to ban alcohol, as the grain used to make alcohol was needed to make bread. In December 1917 Congress passed the Eighteenth Amendment, prohibiting the manufacture, sale, and transportation of alcohol. However, the amendment was not ratified until after the war. It went into effect in January 1920. Meanwhile, in December 1917 Wilson ordered reductions in the alcohol content of beer and the amount of grain in malt liquor.

Reduced student page in the Teacher's Edition

191 days without losing a trench, retreating an inch, or surrendering a prisoner. Two African Americans, Henry Johnson and Needham Roberts, fought off a German attack and received France's highest combat honor, the Croix de Guerre. Despite such evidence of their combat effectiveness, only 10 percent of the African-American troops sent to France saw combat. Most were assigned noncombat tasks like cooking and moving equipment.

Raising Money

The massive mobilization eventually cost $36 billion. Congress passed two measures to raise the money. The Liberty Loan Act in April 1917 made it possible for the government to make loans to the Allies so they could buy food and supplies from the United States. The government could also borrow money by selling Liberty Bonds to the public. Politicians, artists, and film stars gave speeches, marched in parades, and held rallies to drum up support for bond drives. More than 21 million Americans bought bonds to support the war effort.

Congress also raised taxes by passing the War Revenue Act of October 1917. The act lowered the taxable level of income and raised tax rates. By enacting these measures and raising taxes on corporations and on goods like alcohol and tobacco, the government raised $10.5 billion.

Propaganda posters for Liberty Bonds and food conservation.

"Use All Left-overs"

The United States now had the huge responsibility of feeding the expanded armed forces as well as Allied troops and civilians. But American grain harvests had been poor for two years and food prices were rising. How could the country put food on the table for everyone? The government would have to take an active role in mobilizing resources to feed a vast number of people.

Wilson now set up the Food Administration to oversee the production and distribution of food, fuel, fertilizer, and farm machinery. To head the effort he appointed Herbert Hoover, a mining engineer who was living in London when the war started and had headed the relief efforts for Belgium. The American ambassador in London later wrote Wilson, "But for Hoover, Belgium would now be starved."

Hoover's Food Administration had authority to set prices on crops, determine which farm products would be sent to Europe, and punish people who

"A man who can't lend his government $1.25 per week at the rate of 4% interest is not entitled to be an American citizen."
—William McAdoo, Secretary of the Treasury, on Liberty Bonds

Connections: Economics

Once war mobilization got completely underway, the output of American industries was huge. Factories produced 9.5 million army overcoats, 34 million pairs of shoes, 3.1 million rifles, 5.4 million gas masks, and 22 million blankets.

Multicultural Perspectives

During the war, the demand for farm products increased, but farm workers were in short supply. Encouraged by the United States, thousands of Mexican workers crossed the border during the war to plant and harvest crops in the Southwest.

Writing About History

Interview. Students might like to know more about the career of Bernard Mannes Baruch (1870–1965), who was advisor to several Presidents. After researching him, they can present their findings in the form of an interview.

Questions they might ask Baruch: How did you move from a $3-a-week job to great wealth? Why were you known as a park bench advisor? **(Baruch cultivated the image of sitting on a park bench and giving advice to important people who came to him.)** What advice did you give to various Presidents?

Connections: Music

Discussion. Hundreds of songs were associated with World War I. Widely sung were "Over There," "K-K-K-Katy," and "Gee, How I Hate to Get Up in the Morning." **Ask:** What can you infer about Americans' attitude toward the war from these songs?

hoarded food or obtained unfair profits on food sales. But Hoover preferred to rely on voluntary efforts. He began a campaign to persuade Americans to adopt "food conservation." The campaign urged Americans to "use all left-overs."

The Allies most needed four basic foods—sugar, fats, meat, and wheat. Soon Americans at home were observing meatless Tuesdays, wheatless Mondays and Wednesdays, and porkless Thursdays and Saturdays. Crop prices were set high to encourage farmers to raise more food. The combination of reduced consumption and increased production was a great success, and the United States more than tripled its prewar shipments of basic foods to the Allied countries.

Industry Goes to War

"War is no longer Samson with his shield and spear," said Secretary of War Newton Baker. "It is the conflict of smokestacks now." Industry's smokestacks would have to burn night and day to produce enough rifles, artillery, ships, airplanes, and gas masks. Mobilizing industry for war was a task that required government power and effective leadership.

Congress had already set up the Council of National Defense to direct the overall war effort, but the council lacked the authority needed to get the job done. During 1917 and 1918 Congress expanded Wilson's powers to coordinate war-related agencies and to make wartime regulations.

Wilson created the War Industries Board in July 1917 to direct industrial production. As its head, he appointed Bernard Baruch, a stockbroker so at ease with the statistics and workings of business that Wilson called him "Dr. Fact." For two years Baruch worked at setting priorities for vital goods and making sure that they were delivered on time. He cut waste and saved labor by regulating the products and quantities that could be made. He also built new factories and converted old ones to wartime needs.

In some cases business owners cooperated voluntarily with Baruch's plans. Piano builders turned to making airplane wings. Corset manufacturers made belts and gas masks. The steel they would have used in corsets went to build trucks and guns. At other times, however, Baruch had to compel industrialists to cooperate. In one case he had the railroads stop service to automakers and the army seize their stockpile of steel in order to convince them to cut back on production of cars.

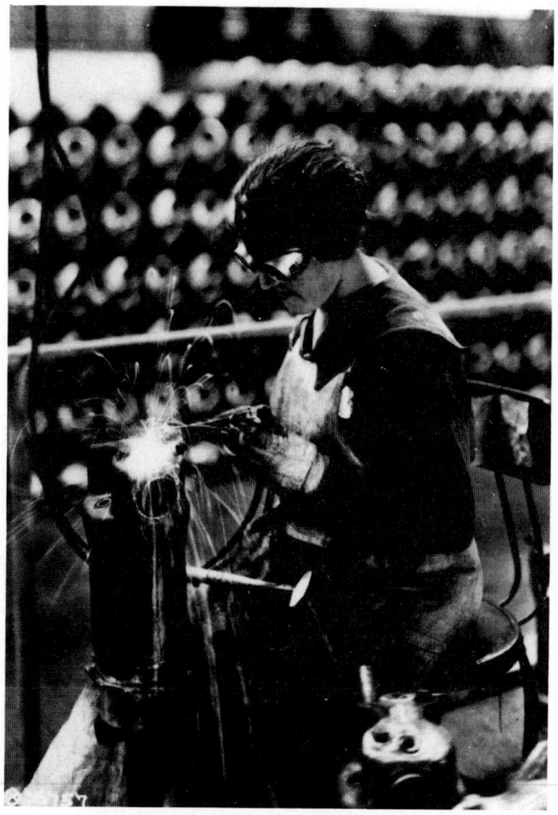

The women who moved into industry were paid less than men in the same jobs. The Department of Labor advertised the following: men, $2.24 to $2.64 per day; women, $1.36 to $2.24 per day.

Meanwhile, other agencies reached deep into American life. The Railroad Administration took over the country's railroads to move troops and supplies to seaports. The Fuel Administration increased the production of coal and oil and rationed the amount of fuel Americans could burn in their homes. The government even managed the clock when the Fuel Board established daylight-saving time, a practice that continues today. The extra hour of daylight at the end of the day enabled people to conserve energy by not turning their lights on until later.

B · A · C · K · G · R · O · U · N · D

Limited English Proficiency

Making a Chart. Have students work in pairs to make a chart about the mobilization effort. Direct each pair to make a two-column chart with the headings—Necessities for Mobilization, Government Response.

Ask students to cite what would have to be done to mobilize the nation for war and to fill in the first column of the chart with these responses: build army, mobilize industry and labor, conserve food and fuel, mobilize public opinion. Next have students use information from the text to fill in the second column.

When charts are completed, encourage students to realize that the mobilization effort brought people together to work for a common cause—preparing their country for war.

Active Learning

Debating Issues. Divide the class into two groups—Pacifists and Conscientious Objectors, and members of the Committee on Public Information. Have each group draw up arguments to support or oppose the following statement: Freedom of speech should be limited by the government in wartime.

After groups have prepared their arguments, hold a class debate. Have a spokesperson from each group cite the arguments for or against the statement. After the debate, discuss whether any opinions have changed and why.

Connections: Politics

Eugene Debs was put on trial for denouncing the war (see page 505). He refused to defend himself at his trial but spoke to the jury before it retired to deliberate: *"I have been accused of obstructing the war. I admit it. . . . I abhor war. . . . I have sympathy with the suffering, struggling people everywhere. It does not make any difference under what flag they were born."* On sentencing Debs, the judge denounced people *"who would strike the sword from the hand of this nation while she is engaged in defending herself against a foreign and brutal power."*

Reduced student page in the Teacher's Edition

Labor and the War Effort

America's dramatic increase in production would not have occurred without the dedication and cooperation of working people. Labor leaders, such as Samuel Gompers of the American Federation of Labor, pledged the support of labor.

Wilson set up the National War Labor Board in April 1918 to settle any labor disputes that might arise, and the War Labor Policies Board to set standard wages, hours, and working conditions. Labor leaders served on most of the war boards, including the Council of National Defense. The booming wartime economy made many jobs available, and union membership rose from 2.75 million in 1916 to 4.25 million in 1919.

The changing work force. When men moved from the factory to the military, women took their places. Women operated trolleys, directed traffic, delivered mail, cared for the wounded, worked in munitions factories, and served on war boards. Some 11,000 women did office work for the navy and 269 served in the marines. Women's involvement gave new strength to the struggle for woman suffrage, which Wilson at one point called "vital to the winning of the war."

Spotlight on Public Opinion

By the end of the war, George Creel's Committee on Public Information had become a mammoth propaganda agency, with more than 150,000 people in its service and a total operating cost of nearly $5 million. The committee used speeches, pamphlets, articles, movies, and posters to build public support for the war. One way the Creel Committee tried to whip up patriotic feelings was by encouraging people to sing the national anthem at public events. Today that tradition continues. Almost every athletic event opens with "The Star Spangled Banner."

Another major shift in the work force took place as African Americans found new opportunities in industry. The wartime labor shortage prompted northern business people to send recruiting agents to the South. The agents promised good wages and plenty of jobs, and 250,000 black southerners moved north between 1915 and 1917.

Many of the jobs that they filled had previously been closed to African Americans. Now they delivered goods and helped build ships. There were 26,648 African Americans employed as shipbuilders by the United States Shipping Board. They also worked in gas stations and garages, in the meat packing, steel, and auto industries, and for the railroads.

The African Americans who moved north sought escape from the low wages, discrimination, segregation, and lynching that were part of their lives in the South. While conditions were better in the North, African Americans still met with prejudice and, in some cases, violence. After anti-black rioting occurred in several cities in 1917, some 8,000 African Americans marched in silence in New York City. The signs they carried read:

> *"We are maligned as lazy and murdered when we work, and your hands are full of blood. Mr. President, why not make America safe for democracy?"*

Muffling Opposition and Mobilizing Support

There was a paradox in Americans fighting to make the world safe for democracy abroad while at home its benefits were denied to some citizens. The paradox came into sharp focus with the government's response to those who opposed the war.

Opponents ranged from individuals to groups like the peace societies and the Socialist party. Some opponents claimed they were willing to fight to defend the United States but wanted no part in this "European war of aggression." Others were **pacifists,** opposing the use of force under any circumstances. Still others attributed involvement in the war to the influence of profit-hungry bankers and industrialists who made loans to the Allies and turned out war supplies.

Social History

Some of the people prosecuted under the Sedition Act were suffragists who picketed the White House to protest that women did not have the right to vote. They were sentenced to several months in jail. Convinced that their sentences were unfair, the imprisoned suffragists went on hunger strikes and were forcibly fed. Wide publicity about their treatment, as well as women's war work, led many Americans to support woman suffrage.

In the May Day parade at right, workers protest the war as a profit-making venture of American capitalists. To some, the political ideology behind the war—human rights and freedom—was belied by limits at home that made protests like these illegal. Many labor leaders and Socialist party members were jailed for denouncing the war.

Fearing the effects of dissent, Congress passed the Espionage Act in June 1917. Anyone found guilty of helping the enemy, hurting recruitment, or causing disloyalty in the military could be fined up to $10,000 or imprisoned up to twenty years. The Trading with the Enemy Act outlawed trade with Germany and called for censorship of publications to other countries. The Sedition Act of May 1918 prohibited any "disloyal, profane, scurrilous, or abusive" speech about the government, Constitution, flag, or armed forces.

Constitutional protections had been sacrificed before in times of national emergency. The Alien and Sedition Acts of 1798 and Lincoln's suspension of *habeas corpus* during the Civil War are other examples of how wartime fears have led to limits on some of the nation's most cherished rights.

In 1919, in *Schenk* v. *U.S.*, the Supreme Court upheld the Espionage Act. It declared that there were situations—such as in wartime—in which freedom of speech could be limited. Although there is no evidence that opposition seriously threatened the war effort, nearly 900 people went to prison. Socialist leader Eugene Debs was sentenced to ten years in prison for denouncing the war.

At the same time that the government was suppressing opposition, it was also waging a campaign to win support. In April 1917 Wilson appointed newspaper editor George Creel to head the new Committee on Public Information to build and maintain public support for the war.

The committee's efforts sometimes backfired, creating anti-German hysteria that was turned against innocent German Americans. The governor of Iowa banned the speaking of German in public, or even on the telephone. Sauerkraut, a typical German dish, became known as "liberty cabbage." Some German Americans were abused when they appeared in public. These limitations on individual freedoms persisted, in spite of the fact that there was little disloyalty during the war.

Section Review

1. Identification. Define the terms *mobilization* and *pacifists.*

2. Comprehension. How did the United States mobilize soldiers, workers, industry, and opinion?

3. Synthesis. How might the growth of government during the progressive era have affected the mobilization for war?

4. Analysis. What opportunities did mobilization for war create for women and African Americans?

5. Evaluation. How was freedom of speech limited during the war? Do you think limiting speech was justified? Explain.

Section Review

ANSWERS

1. Definitions for the following terms can be found on text pages indicated in parentheses, *mobilization* (501), *pacifists* (504).
2. Selective Service Act passed; Congress created War Industries Board; Wilson set up National War Labor Board and the War Labor Policies Board; the Committee on Public Information established.
3. Provided precedents for greater government control of economy.
4. Both women and African Americans moved into jobs formerly closed to them. Many African Americans moved north, where in the main they suffered less discrimination.
5. The Espionage Act, Trading with the Enemy Act, and Sedition Act prohibited open opposition to the war. Answers may depend on whether students think the importance of civil liberties outweighs the effect that dissent might have on the war effort.

Using the Visuals

Discussion. Have students compare the points of view presented in the poster on this page, the political cartoon on page 500, and the Liberty Bond poster on page 502. **Ask:** What kind of impact were each intended to have? **(emotional)** What points do each focus on and what points do they ignore? **(All visuals sought to stir American support for either preparedness or involvement in war. They ignore dangers of involvement.)**

Reduced student page in the Teacher's Edition

POINT OF VIEW

To Fight or Not to Fight?

In April 1917, Congress declared that the United States would enter World War I. Whether it was right to go to war, however, remained an issue for each American to decide. There was no single "American" point of view, but supporters of involvement were quick to question the patriotism of those who refused to fight.

Some Americans swiftly took stands, while others struggled to form their opinions amid moral, emotional, and rational appeals from both sides. The following points of view include arguments expressed in writing and in pictures. As you examine each point of view, notice what it focuses on and what it pays little or no attention to.

The sinking of the Lusitania *inspired this military recruiting poster.*

What If . . . ?

"We are in this war because we were forced into it; because Germany not only murdered our citizens on the high seas, but also filled our country with spies and sought to incite our people to civil war. We were given no opportunity to discuss or negotiate . . . I believe that we are not only justly in this war, but prudently in this war. If we had stayed out and the war had been drawn or won by Germany, we should have been attacked . . . not directly at first, but through an attack on some Central or South American state to which it would be at least as difficult for us to send troops as for Germany. And what if this powerful nation, vowed to war, were once firmly established in South or Central America? What of our boasted isolation then?"

—James W. Gerard, American Ambassador in Berlin, 1917

Constitutional Heritage
For refusing to be drafted, Howard Moore was sentenced to 25 years in prison. Not until 1965, in the case *United States* v. *Seeger*, did the Supreme Court uphold the right of conscientious objectors to refuse military service on nonreligious grounds.

Citizenship

Discussion. Have students discuss whether there are situations where they would refuse to take part in an armed conflict in which the United States is involved.

MAY THE SPARKS NEVER REACH IT!
—Cesare in the New York *Sun*.

A cartoon refers to the fires of war in Europe.

Not a Sacred Call

"We are patriots who love our country and desire to serve her and those ideals for which she has stood . . . but we cannot believe that participation in war is the true way of service to America. . . . To us war, especially in its modern form, is not so much a sacred call to give one's self as it is a stern necessity to do all in one's power to kill others. . . ."

—Letter from the Fellowship of Reconciliation to the House Committee on Military Affairs, January 16, 1917

A Statement of Conscience

"I am not a member of any religious sect or organization whose creed forbids me to participate in war, but the convictions of my own conscience as an expression of my social principles forbid me from so doing. I hold that all war is morally wrong and its prosecution a crime. I hold life as a sacred thing and cannot bring myself to join in the slaughter of my fellow men. Moreover, I claim the same rights and considerations as are accorded under the law to members of a well-recognized religious sect or organization whose principles forbid their members to take part in war."

—Howard W. Moore, in a letter to his draft board, December 28, 1917

1. How are the points of view of Howard Moore and the Fellowship of Reconciliation similar?

2. How do you think James Gerard and Howard Moore might have criticized each other's point of view if they had met?

3. What does the "Enlist" poster emphasize about the *Lusitania* sinking and what does it ignore? Why?

4. In what ways are the cartoon and poster similar? In what ways do they differ?

Point of View

ANSWERS

1. Both hold that all war is morally wrong.
2. Answers will vary. Students may speculate that Gerard would have stressed to Moore that failure to fight would result in the loss of a greater number of lives in the long run and that therefore fighting back against aggression is necessary. Moore might have stressed that the deaths of American civilians on the high seas were a tragedy that cannot be reversed—that going to war would only compound the tragedy with the loss of more lives.
3. The "Enlist" poster stresses the deaths of innocent women and children in order to motivate men to join the army and fight the Germans. The poster's emotional appeal ignores the fact that the German government warned Americans against traveling on ships through the war zone and apologized for the loss of American lives. Since the poster is clearly intended to have an emotional impact to aid the recruitment effort, there was obviously no interest in acknowledging the German point of view.
4. Both the cartoon and the poster are intended to have mainly an emotional impact. However, the cartoon's purpose differs, stressing the dangers of American involvement in the war. The poster encourages involvement, while the cartoon expresses the wish that the war will never draw in the United States.

Section 19-3

B · A · C · K · G · R · O · U · N · D

Connections: Language
The word *doughboy* goes back to the Civil War, but its origin as a term referring to American soldiers is uncertain. It may come from the name of a round biscuit given to sailors or a round brass button on some Civil War infantry uniforms. It also may come from the practice of cleaning the white belts the infantry wore with pipe clay "dough."

Objectives

- ***Answer the Focus Question***
- *Analyze the effectiveness of American forces in the Allied war effort.*

Introducing THE SECTION

General Pershing wrote after the war, *"I am sure that each one of us silently wished that our Army might have been more nearly ready to fulfill the mission that loomed so large before us."* Soldiers of lower rank were also pessimistic about their lack of training. *"To have sent us to the front at that time would have been murder,"* wrote one American private. *"We were woefully ignorant of the basic principles of the soldier."*

Tell students that they will learn how American and Allied troops won the war.

Reduced student page in the Teacher's Edition

19-3 The United States in the War

Focus: What was the American experience in World War I?

On June 26, 1917, American troop and supply ships sailed into the small port of St. Nazaire on the west coast of France. The American commander of the operation described the effect of their arrival on the French:

> *"The population gathered along the quays looked on in whispering wonderment at the young khaki-clad strangers who had appeared, almost overnight, from over the seas. There was no cheering, no patriotic demonstration, only the respectful silence of the women and children, the old men and the broken soldiers."*

The American Navy in Action

That June day was the start of American military participation in the war. It also marked the navy's first success against the deadly U-boats, transporting troops and supplies through the German submarine zone. The use of convoys—guards of British and American destroyers and submarine chasers—worked beautifully throughout the war. More than 2 million soldiers and 4 million tons of supplies crossed the sea on this "bridge of ships." Only 24 out of 1,500 ships were sunk, and there was little loss of life.

The British and American navies also cooperated in the North Sea. They laid a barrier of over 50,000 mines, preventing U-boats from reaching the open sea. By October 1918 Allied shipping losses had declined by almost 90 percent. The United States Navy, with its 2,000 ships and 500,000 sailors, made up almost a third of the convoy escorts and laid 80 percent of the North Sea mines.

American Voices

> *"America has joined forces with the Allied Powers, and what we have of blood and treasure are yours. Lafayette, we are here."*
>
> —Colonel Charles D. Stanton of the American Expeditionary Force

American Expeditionary Force

On July 4, 1917, the French invited the American Expeditionary Force (AEF) to join in an Independence Day celebration. American and French officials and soldiers paraded through Paris, stopping at the tomb of the Marquis de Lafayette, who, with thousands of French soldiers, had come to help Americans during the Revolutionary War.

However, only a fraction of the AEF—about 14,000 troops—had reached France by July. These inexperienced soldiers, nicknamed "doughboys," were not ready for battle. The commander of the force, General John J. Pershing, rushed them to a training camp outside of Paris.

Pershing was every inch a soldier. Educated at West Point, he had fought in the Indian wars, the Spanish-American War, and the Philippines. Now he was determined to train the AEF as a distinct unit, separate from the other Allied armies. He resisted pressure from Britain to use Americans in British divisions, instead awaiting the arrival of the main body of the AEF. The doughboys would see little fighting in 1917, but their training with French units introduced them to trench warfare. The horrors of war in the trenches would prove an experience unlike any that American soldiers had ever faced.

Connections: Literature
Some of the nation's most powerful literature concerned World War I: Ernest Hemingway's *A Farewell to Arms*, John Dos Passos's *Three Soldiers*, William Faulkner's *A Fable*, and Lawrence Stallings and Maxwell Anderson's play *What Price Glory?*

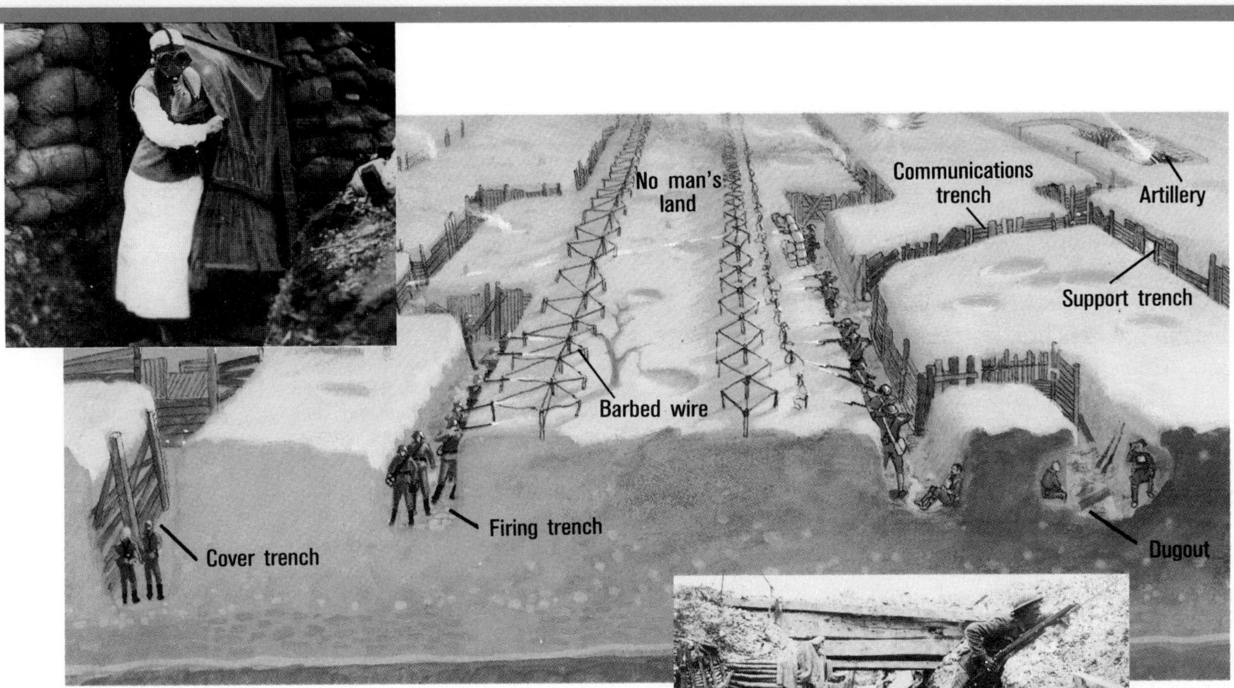

Learning From Art
Trench Warfare in World War I

Trench Warfare

“ Eventually I took shelter in a shell hole with two other men from the battalion; we were all wounded. I looked over the edge and could see the Germans in their trench again. I suddenly became very angry. I had seen my battalion mowed down by machine-guns and one of them trapped in the wire. I thought we were all doomed; I just couldn't see how any of us would get out of it alive. ”

This American soldier was describing warfare in the trenches of the western front. Each side tried to outflank, or go around, the other by extending its trenches. The soldiers hid by day and burrowed by night, eventually extending the trench line 600 miles from the North Sea to Switzerland.

The trenches were about 5 feet deep and 2 feet wide. Behind the front trenches stretched a network of supply and command trenches. A tangle of barbed wire in front of the firing line was set up to trap enemy attackers. Beyond that was "no man's land"—deadly open ground sometimes so narrow that soldiers could hear the voices of the enemy.

Front-line soldiers took shelter in dug-outs during enemy attack. Off duty soldiers rotated to rear trenches. (top left) An American army nurse in the trenches. Above, a soldier keeps watch while his comrades rest.

Each side used the newest weapons to try to break through the other's line. An attack began with hours of heavy artillery fire from howitzers and field guns. Then the attacking infantry charged across no man's land, hoping to get through holes in the barbed wire to the enemy's trench. But on both sides defensive fire power, especially from machine guns, usually won out. One American soldier wrote:

“ Bullets, millions of them, flying like raindrops. Rockets and flares in all directions. Shrapnel bursting the air and sending down its deadly iron. . . . Every minute looking to be gone . . . to the great beyond. A mad dash for fifty feet and then look for cover. ”

Developing
THE SECTION

Analyzing Primary Sources

Eyewitness Accounts. Have two students read aloud the eyewitness accounts of war by the two Americans on this page. **Ask:** What do the accounts reveal about the soldiers' reactions to war? **(anger, fear, disillusionment)** Do you think such feelings are typical of all wars or special to World War I? Explain.

Connections: Literature

Oral Report. Have interested students read and write a report on the English soldier and poet Wilfred Owen's well-known poem "Dulce et Decorum Est." The poem is a vivid description of poison gas warfare. Students should tell in their own words the soldiers' reactions to the attack, why the poet remembers the dying solders in his dreams, and why the poem refers to "The old Lie: Dulce et Decorum Est / Pro patria mori." **(The Latin is a famous line by the Roman poet Horace: "It is sweet and proper to die for one's country." The details of the poem make clear it is a lie.)**

Connections: Science and Technology

Reports and Bulletin Board Display. Have students do research and write reports about one of the new weapons used to fight World War I: poison gas, machine guns, submarines, aircraft (fighters and bombers), improved heavy artillery, tanks, bombs, and flamethrowers. Reports should include how the weapon was developed and its impact on warfare. Students can describe their findings in written reports, create drawings, or bring in pictures to make a bulletin board display.

Global Connections

Germany facilitated Lenin's return to Russia from Switzerland in the expectation that if he seized power, he would take Russia out of the war. The Treaty of Brest-Litovsk was harsh on Russia, forcing it to acknowledge the loss of Finland, Poland, the Ukraine, and the other new Baltic states, Estonia, Latvia, and Lithuania.

Social History

In 1916 American volunteers who had joined the French air service formed the Lafayette Escadrille. Several Americans, such as Eddie Rickenbacker and Billy Mitchell, became skilled at shooting down enemy planes and earned fame as "aces." After the United States entered the war, most of the pilots transferred to the AEF air service.

Reduced student page in the Teacher's Edition

A new, silent weapon was used by both sides—chemical weapons of chlorine and mustard gas. The clouds of gas floated down into the trenches, choking, blinding, and often killing anyone without a mask.

Enemy attacks were not the only threat to soldiers in the trenches. Isolated and exhausted in the dark, cold mud, the soldiers faced lice and rats as well as diseases such as dysentery, gangrene, "trench fever," and "trench mouth." The constant din of exploding artillery shells gave rise to a new mental disorder known as "shell shock."

Never before had so many people been killed so rapidly. When the Americans joined the conflict, millions of lives had already been lost. In one battle—which lasted six months—the German army advanced only four miles but lost more than 300,000 in casualties, while the French defenders lost more than 350,000. Once, 20,000 British soldiers were killed in a single day. American forces were to play a key role in fortifying the Allies against the German advance.

Learning From Art
New Weapons of War

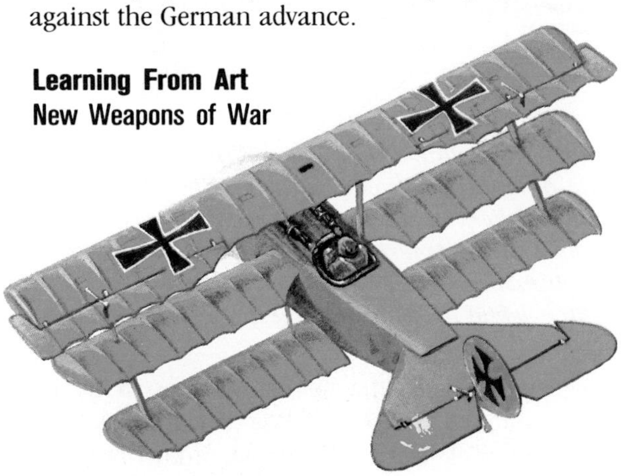

German Fokker Dr.I triplane, outfitted with machine guns.

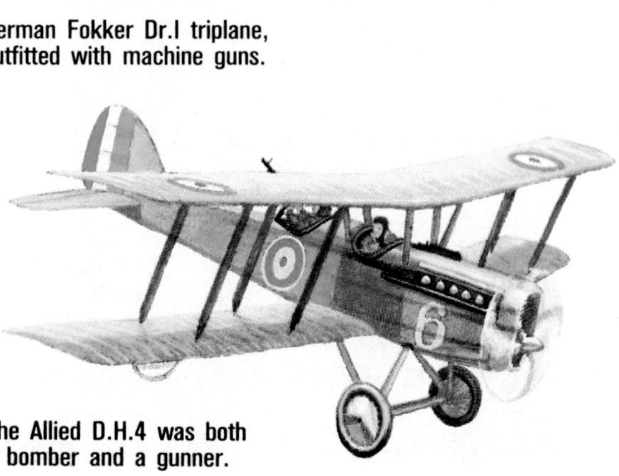

The Allied D.H.4 was both a bomber and a gunner.

MK IV tank first used in 1917. Tanks could tear through barbed wire and over trenches while gunning the enemy.

The German Advance

Germany gained the advantage on the southern and eastern fronts in the winter of 1917. On the southern front, German and Austrian troops crushed the Italians. Then, in November, the eight-month-old democratic government in Russia fell to the Bolsheviks, a wing of the radical Communist party. In March 1918 the Bolshevik leader, Lenin, signed the Treaty of Brest-Litovsk with Germany. Russia was out of the war.

No longer needed on the eastern front, the German army focused on a massive offensive in France. By the end of May they had reached the banks of the Marne River, only 50 miles from Paris. The AEF arrived just in time.

The doughboys entered the front at the town of Château-Thierry (shah-TOH teh-REE) and helped stop the German advance. Then they made their second offensive, to recapture a square-mile area known as Belleau (bel-LOH) Wood. "The air was full of red-hot nails," wrote a correspondent. After suffering nearly 10,000 casualties, the troops at last regained the territory. The Allies proceeded to force the German army into a northward retreat, regaining ground the Germans had held since 1914.

The 270,000 American troops suffered heavy casualties. But as one American wrote home, "Folks, we have them on the run."

Achieving the Armistice

By late summer over a million American soldiers had reached France, and thousands more arrived with each convoy. General Pershing and French General Ferdinand Foch made the plan of attack.

Social History

Some idea of the enormous cost of World War I can be gained from the fact that far more soldiers died in this war than in all the wars during the previous hundred years combined. In addition, 21 million men suffered wounds.

Foch would give Pershing artillery and air support at the town of St. Mihiel (SAN mee-YEL). In turn, Pershing and his army would join in an offensive around the Meuse River and the Argonne Forest.

For the attack on St. Mihiel, Pershing assembled 9 American and 3 French divisions, and some 3,000 field guns, 1,400 airplanes, and 267 tanks. Tanks had been developed by the British to cross land torn by shell holes. Airplanes had had to be adapted to warfare. At the war's outset, pilots had fired pistols at each other. Eventually planes were fitted with radios, bombs, and machine guns.

In the foggy predawn hours of September 12, 1918, the Americans launched heavy artillery at St. Mihiel. Airplanes supported the artillery by spotting the enemy and dropping bombs. Then, at 5:00 A.M., the tanks rolled into the German trenches, and by nightfall the infantry had routed the enemy. After three more days of mopping up, the Americans had successfully taken St. Mihiel and 16,000 prisoners.

Buoyed by their victory, the doughboys set out for the Meuse-Argonne front. Their goal was the Sedan railroad in northern France, the Germans' main line of supply and communication. Meanwhile, French, British, and Belgian troops would attack at other spots along the German line.

For forty-seven days, more than a million Americans struggled through the Argonne Forest, which was laced with barbed wire, German trenches, machine-gun nests, and bunkers. In the fog and rain the Germans were an invisible enemy.

Finally, in early November the weary Americans pushed through to Sedan and broke the German communications line. All along the western front, the Germans were crumbling under Allied blows. Germany's allies had already sensed defeat. Between late September and early November, Bulgaria, the Ottoman Empire, and Austria-Hungary each signed an **armistice,** or agreement to stop warfare until a peace treaty was signed. German military leaders now realized that the war was lost. On a cold, rainy day, November 11, 1918, they signed the armistice and the Great War ended.

Counting the Cost

The costs of the war horrified the world. Half the troops were killed, wounded, or missing. Over 5 million Allied troops and 3 million Central Powers troops died. Many millions of civilians, too, died of disease, starvation, and other war-related causes.

France and Germany suffered the greatest losses: one out of thirty people was killed in battle or died of battle wounds. American losses were far fewer, with close to 116,000 killed, and twice that many wounded or missing.

Dirigibles (above) and planes made aerial photos for reconnaissance possible. This one shows trenches, roads, and shell craters.

Active Learning

Cooperative Activity. Divide the class into teams of four to five students each. Each team should imagine it is a group of home-front relatives trying to cheer up a doughboy. The group can assemble an album of short letters, drawings, cartoons, and the like, letting the soldier know how much he is missed and giving the news from home. Each album should have an attractive cover. The completed albums can be displayed. Discuss how albums such as these might have affected soldier morale.

Writing About History

Newspaper Story. Have students research the forty-seven-day push through the Argonne Forest to Sedan. Then have them imagine that they are war correspondents for an American newspaper and write an account of one of the forty-seven days.

Limited English Proficiency

Using the Visuals. The aerial photograph on this page was taken in France in 1917. The wiggly white line is a trench. The small white splotches are shell craters. **Ask:** What is the purpose of military photographs? How are they used?

GTV Side 4

Chap. 1, Frame 02427

Modern Times: Technology and World War I (Movie Segment)

Search and Play:

Geography Skills

ANSWERS

1. From the North Sea to the Swiss border, mainly in northern France near the Belgian and German borders with some trenches in Germany.
2. Paris.
3. If Paris had fallen, it would have disrupted France's political and social structure and lowered French morale; the rest of France might have fallen. Cantigny, Belleau Wood, Château-Thierry, Argonne Forest, St. Mihiel, Sedan.

Section Review

ANSWERS

1. A definition for *armistice* is on text page 511.
2. Transported troops and supplies through German U-boat zone, convoyed ships, and laid most of North Sea mines.
3. Answers may include living in narrow trenches, barbed wire in front of the trenches, "no man's land," artillery attacks, use of poison gas, and prevalence of lice, rats, dysentery, and gangrene. Machine gun and artillery fire, poison gas, and prevalence of various diseases accounted for enormous casualties.
4. American forces helped stop German advance and forced Germans into northward retreat.
5. Defensive weapons, especially the machine-gun, led to stalemate in the trenches. New weapons—tanks and planes—were used in massive attacks on the enemy, causing heavy losses.

Connections: Literature

The lives of two of the United States' more promising poets were cut short by World War I. Alan Seeger (1888–1916), author of *I Have a Rendezvous with Death,* died while serving with the French Foreign Legion. Alfred Joyce Kilmer (1886–1918), author of "Trees," was killed while serving with the AEF.

Reduced student page in the Teacher's Edition

World War I: The Western Front 1918

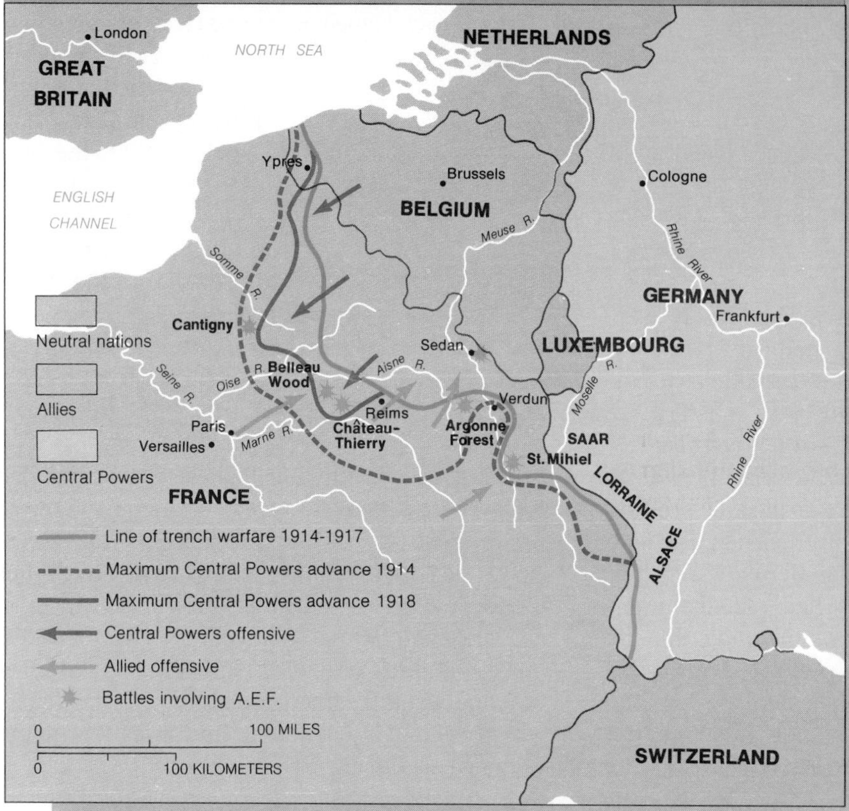

Geography Skills—Location. Describe the location of trench warfare. Toward which European capital were Central Powers offensives aimed? If the Central Powers had taken the capital, what effect might it have had on the war? In which battles did the A.E.F. take part?

For many of those left alive, memories would long remain. Novelist F. Scott Fitzgerald wrote about a group of friends visiting a battlefield years after the war. One says:

> *"See that little stream—we could walk to it in two minutes. It took the British a month to walk to it—a whole empire walking very slowly, dying in front and pushing forward behind. And another empire walked very slowly backward a few inches a day, leaving the dead like a million bloody rugs."*

Section Review

1. **Identification.** Define *armistice.*
2. **Analysis.** Why was the role of the American navy crucial in the war?
3. **Comprehension.** Describe trench warfare. Why was the loss of life so great?
4. **Analysis.** How did the arrival of American forces affect the Allies' war effort?
5. **Analysis.** How did new weaponry affect the way in which the war was fought?

Global Connections

The Ottoman Empire had massacred Armenians before—in 1894–1896 and in 1909. But during World War I, the Empire fiercely pursued a policy of eliminating its Armenian minority through massacre and deportation. Thousands of Armenian men conscripted into the Ottoman army were slain. Others were arrested, taken to remote areas and killed. Women, children and older men were deported, and in transit many lost their lives.

19-4 The Diplomacy of Peace

Focus: What role did President Wilson play in peacemaking after World War I, and what was the American response?

News of the armistice reached the United States at 3:00 a.m. Edith Wilson decoded the message and woke her husband: "The armistice is signed! The guns are still!"

While Americans joyfully celebrated, Wilson turned his attention toward the responsibilities that lay ahead. "Everything for which America has fought has been accomplished," he told a cheering crowd. Now the nation had a special mission, to "aid in the establishment of just democracy throughout the world."

The Fourteen Points

President Wilson had firm ideas about how a "just democracy" should be built. On January 8, 1918, even while the fighting still raged, Wilson had outlined his fourteen-point program to Congress.

The first five points were designed to remove the causes of conflict. First, nations would practice diplomacy openly and make no secret treaties. Second, ships would be allowed to move freely during peace and war. Third, tariff barriers would be removed to allow free trade. Fourth, nations would reduce their armaments. Finally, competing claims over colonies would be settled impartially, in the best interests of the colonial peoples.

Points six through thirteen dealt with the protection of national boundaries and with self-determination—the right of people to be independent or to decide what form of government to have. Wilson saw self-determination as crucial to protecting ethnic and national groups that had been oppressed under foreign rule.

One such group was the Armenians in the Ottoman Empire. In 1894, Muslim Turks had begun massacring thousands of Christian Armenians under their rule. Fearing that Armenians would

Wilson addressed self-determination of Armenians under Ottoman rule. These children's parents were killed by Turks.

Section 19-4

Objectives

- ***Answer the Focus Question.***
- *Identify Wilson's Fourteen Points.*
- *Evaluate the effectiveness of the Versailles Treaty in keeping the peace.*
- *Explain why Congress rejected the treaty and the League of Nations.*

Introducing

THE SECTION

Have students discuss the questions: What is a "just peace"? What should be the objectives of such a peace? How might these objectives be achieved? Tell students that in this section, they will be examining and evaluating the peacemaking process following World War I.

Developing
THE SECTION

Analyzing Primary Sources

Woodrow Wilson. In an address to the Senate on July 10, 1919, Wilson stated:

“*The United States entered the war upon a different footing from [other nations]. . . . We entered it not because our material interests were directly threatened . . . but because we saw . . . free government everywhere imperiled by the intolerable aggression of a power which respected neither right nor obligation.*”

How does Wilson contrast the United States with other nations? **(Other nations had selfish interests in entering the war, but the United States wanted to preserve democracy.)** Do Wilson's Fourteen Points support his statement? Why or why not?

Multicultural Perspectives

The first Pan-African Congress met in Paris at the same time as the peace conference. Organized by W.E.B. Du Bois, the congress passed resolutions calling on the new League of Nations to help the African people move from colonial rule to independence. Du Bois blamed World War I on the European nations' struggles to colonize Africa and Asia and predicted that African and Asian colonists would inevitably revolt. Permanent peace, therefore, required the expansion of self-government not only in Europe but also among the peoples of Africa and Asia.

The League of Nations paid little attention to the resolutions of the Pan-African Congress, and colonial powers opposed them. After World War II, Du Bois's prediction came true.

Reduced student page in the Teacher's Edition

support the Allies during the war, the Ottomans began the systematic destruction, or **genocide,** of the Armenian people. Some 1.5 million Armenians lost their lives in the slaughter.

To guard freedom and the right of self-determination, Wilson devised his fourteenth point, which he saw as the key to a permanent peace. It called for a "general association of nations." This League of Nations would have the power to guarantee the independence and territory of "great and small states alike."

Response to the Fourteen Points

As the war dragged on, the United States had continued to prosper while the economies of Europe neared collapse. With American economic and military power at new heights, it was clear that Wilson would have great leverage in the peace process. He was confident that he had the power he needed to put into practice his missionary diplomacy—the idea that the United States could actively bring free government to other nations.

Germany, recognizing Wilson's power, hoped that the Fourteen Points would ensure a generous peace. However, the Allies, in agreeing to an armistice based on the Fourteen Points, insisted on two exceptions. They would not accept the point that ensured freedom of the seas. They also demanded that Germany make **reparations,** or payment for war damages suffered by the Allies. Nevertheless, the war was brought to an end almost entirely on Wilson's terms.

Not all Americans were pleased, however. Many were suspicious that Wilson wanted to draw the country into an active role in the postwar world. The war had made them wary of involvement in the affairs and conflicts of other nations. Republicans feared that the Democrats would take all the credit for peace in the upcoming congressional election. Many of them also felt that Wilson's terms were too easy on Germany.

Political blunders. During the war, Republicans and Democrats had pulled together behind the nation's war policies. Now Wilson made blunders that would alienate Republicans from the peace process. He asked Americans to show the world their support for him by electing Democrats in November. Although many Americans approved of Wilson's program, they resented his appeal to party politics. Republicans won control of Congress in the election. They claimed that their victory showed that voters disapproved of Wilson's policies.

Wilson made two more blunders. To build his "association of nations," he decided to personally attend the peace conference in Paris. No President had gone to Europe while in office, and many people felt that the President's place was at home, facing domestic issues. Furthermore, a number of Americans opposed further involvement in Europe, calling for a return to isolationism.

Criticism grew stronger when Wilson named the delegation to the peace conference. Wilson included no leading Republicans, not even ex-President Taft or Justice Hughes, who had supported Wilson's plan for a League of Nations. By this omission Wilson missed an opportunity to create bipartisan support for his peace proposals. And even though the treaty would have to be ratified by the Senate, Wilson included no senators. He chose as delegates only loyal friends and advisors.

The Paris Peace Conference

Wilson went to the Paris peace conference in January 1919 with the loftiest intentions of creating a lasting world peace. But he found a different climate among Allied leaders. The three leaders who along with Wilson dominated the conference—British prime minister David Lloyd George, French premier Georges Clemenceau, and Italian prime minister Vittorio Orlando—each had interests in punishing Germany and dividing the spoils of war.

Lloyd George wanted to maintain Britain's naval superiority and crush Germany's naval power, and opposed Wilson's idea of "freedom of the seas." Clemenceau had lived through the German siege of Paris in 1871 and had seen overwhelming destruction as France became a scarred battlefield of the world war. He was bitterly determined to disarm Germany and to protect France by demanding a security line between them along the Rhine River. Orlando wanted to gain the territory secretly promised to Italy when it joined the Allies in 1915.

Global Connections

While statesmen met at Versailles to sign the treaty, some of the world's most prominent women met in Zurich, Switzerland, to promote a lasting peace. Jane Addams led the American delegation, which also included Florence Kelley of the National Consumers League, who had led the campaign against child labor; Alice Hamilton, a professor at the Harvard Medical School; and Jeannette Rankin, the first woman elected to Congress.

The conference formed the Women's International League for Peace and Freedom and elected Addams as its president. The League then denounced the Treaty of Versailles for the harsh terms imposed on the Central Powers and predicted the treaty would *"create all over Europe discords and animosities which can only lead to future wars."*

The Treaty of Versailles

Many of Wilson's Fourteen Points clashed with the Europeans' aims. The final peace treaty bore the marks of both Wilson's ideals and the Allies' demands. It included an agreement for a League of Nations, but it also redrew the map of Europe and severely punished Germany.

Mapmaking. The new borders were not drawn entirely along national lines. Italy, for example, received some territory that was home to Austrians. Never before, however, had Europe's political boundaries more clearly reflected the independence of national groups.

Poland gained independence. The former Russian territories of Finland, Estonia, Latvia, and

Geography Skills—Place. Compare this map with the map of Europe on page 497 to analyze changes in political boundaries that resulted from the war. Describe the break-up of the Ottoman Empire. What changes took place on the Balkan Peninsula? How did Russia change and what new nations emerged from Russian territory? In what ways were the boundaries of Germany changed?

Active Learning

Role Play. Divide the class into teams. Each team can research one of the areas affected by the Treaty of Versailles. Members of each team can role-play inhabitants of one of these areas and tell the class how the Treaty of Versailles affected their lives (for better or worse). They can also tell what they think of the treaty and whether—and why—they welcome their new independence.

Geography Skills

ANSWERS

1. Ottoman Empire became Turkey, Iraq, Syria, Lebanon, Palestine, Transjordan.
2. Balkan Peninsula: Serbia, Montenegro, and Bosnia became Yugoslavia; Bulgaria lost some land to Yugoslavia and Greece. Romania gained land from Austria-Hungary and the USSR.
3. Russia: Finland, Estonia, Latvia, Lithuania, and most of Poland emerged from Russia.
4. Germany: lost land to France, Denmark, and Poland; Polish Corridor separated two parts of Germany.

Chapter Connections

Central to the dispute over the League was Article Ten, which would require the United States to abandon its policy of unilateralism. This policy was powerfully voiced by George Washington in his Farewell Address when he warned the nation *"to have . . . as little political connection [with foreign countries] as possible"* and not to *"entangle our peace and prosperity in the toils of European ambition, rivalship, interest, humor or conceit."*

In 1919 Senator William Borah of Idaho, speaking against the League, once again stated this policy. He stated that *"If the United States joins the League we have forfeited and surrendered, once and for all, the great policy of no entangling alliances upon which the strength of this republic has been founded for 150 years."*

Reduced student page in the Teacher's Edition

Lithuania became independent. The territory of the Austro-Hungarian Empire was divided among seven countries: Austria, Hungary, Czechoslovakia, Yugoslavia, Poland, Romania, and Italy. United at last, as part of Yugoslavia, were Serbia and Bosnia with its large Serb population. Thus, Wilson's hope for national self-determination was partially realized.

Wilson kept Germany from being completely dismembered, but it still lost one eighth of its territory. German colonies and Turkish-ruled territories were distributed among France and Britain and other Allied powers as **mandates,** or temporary colonies. Each mandate was to be administered by an Allied nation until it was ready for self-rule and ultimately independence. Mandates included Iraq, Syria, Lebanon, and Palestine, as well as former German colonies in Africa and the Pacific Islands.

France regained Alsace-Lorraine and obtained control of Germany's Saar Valley, rich in coal. Clemenceau also received security for France: a buffer zone 31 miles wide along the Rhine, to be occupied by Allied troops for fifteen years.

The blow to Germany. The Europeans also took revenge, a move with serious consequences in the future. The treaty stripped Germany of its armed forces and submarines, and required it to pay for war damages and for disabled Allied soldiers and dependents of those killed. In effect, Germany would be forced to sign a blank check. (Later, the damages were fixed at a staggering $33 billion.) Finally, Germany had to accept full responsibility for causing the war.

In early May German delegates joined the conference at the palace of Versailles (ver-SI), just outside Paris. The Germans, expecting generous terms based on the Fourteen Points, read the treaty with dismay and refused to sign. Only after a threat of renewed fighting did Germany reconsider.

On June 28, 1919, Germany signed the Treaty of Versailles. But many doubted that Wilson's dream of a lasting peace had been achieved. As the Allied commander Ferdinand Foch

remarked, "This is not peace. It is an armistice for twenty years." Foch was right. Among the millions of Germans embittered by the treaty was a corporal recovering from blindness caused by mustard gas. Germany's humiliation would burn in the mind of Adolf Hitler for the rest of his life.

The League of Nations

Woodrow Wilson had finally agreed to the treaty's terms because he believed that any injustices could be corrected by the League of Nations. He pinned his hopes on the League to heal war wounds and keep the peace.

The League was to be devoted to maintaining peace. Members would pledge to reduce armaments and let the League settle disputes. If a member did go to war, the others would stop trade with — or even use force against — the aggressor. The key to peace-keeping was Article Ten of the League's covenant, pledging members to respect and preserve each other's independence against "external aggression." Yet the League had no way of enforcing the article.

Defeat of the Peace Treaty

Back home, Republican senators who opposed the League of Nations had taken a truer reading of the pulse of the American people than had Woodrow Wilson. Henry Cabot Lodge of Massachusetts especially objected to Article Ten. He was convinced that this article set the United States up to be drawn into European conflicts. Attempting to stay out of such conflicts had been a tradition in United States foreign policy since the Washington administration. How could this valued position be swept aside for the uncertain ideal of being the world's peace keeper? Opponents of the League began to fight the entire peace settlement.

Connections: Politics
Twenty-three Republican senators favored Lodge's proposals, and twelve would have accepted smaller changes. Forty-three of the forty-seven Democratic senators were in favor of the treaty. Had Wilson compromised, he would have been supported by a majority coalition.

Active Learning

Writing Speeches. Have students imagine that they are American politicians at the end of World War I. Divide the class into groups. Have each group research the provisions of the Covenant of the League of Nations and then write a speech arguing for or against American participation in the League of Nations. The speeches should suggest the consequences to the United States if it agrees to this provision. A representative from each group can present its speech to the class.

Desperate to save the peace treaty—and the League of Nations—President Wilson set out on a speaking tour of the nation. He traveled to twenty-nine cities and gave forty speeches in twenty-two days. After a speech in Colorado, Wilson suddenly collapsed from exhaustion and was hurried back to Washington. A few days later, a stroke left him half-paralyzed. From this point on Wilson communicated only through his wife. Edith Wilson made important decisions and used her judgment in communicating the President's messages.

Twice, an amended treaty came up for a vote in the Senate. Twice, Wilson, from his sickbed, refused to compromise and directed Democrats to vote against it. On May 20, 1920, the Senate defeated the treaty for the second, and final, time.

Five months later the United States concluded a separate peace with the Central Powers. In Geneva, the League of Nations began its struggle to keep the peace without the powerful United States.

On Armistice Day in 1923, a small crowd assembled outside the house of ex-President Wilson and a band struck up "Over There." As Wilson appeared, a member of the crowd called out sympathetic words about the Senate rejection of the League of Nations. Tears glinted in Wilson's eyes, but he turned his gaze to the veterans in the crowd and replied, "I am proud to remember that I had the honor of being the commander in chief of the most ideal army that was ever thrown together."

Section Review

1. Identification. Define *genocide*, *reparations*, and *mandates*.

2. Analysis. How did Wilson's Fourteen Points spell out his purpose of "establishing a just democracy throughout the world"? Why were they criticized?

3. Analysis. In what ways did the Treaty of Versailles differ from Wilson's proposals? Why did Marshall Foch say of the treaty, "This is not peace"?

4. Evaluation. Was the League of Nations set up to be an effective peace-keeping organization? Explain.

5. Comprehension. What led to America's rejection of the treaty?

Connections to Themes

Shaping Democracy

"This is the People's War," President Wilson declared as American troops headed for Europe in 1917, "a war for freedom and justice and self-government amongst all the nations of the world, a war to make the world safe for all the peoples who live upon it . . . the German people themselves included."

Americans entered the war in that crusading spirit, but they came away from it bitterly disillusioned. Warfare with twentieth-century weapons exacted a high price in human suffering, and it did not seem to "make the world safe." For the next twenty years, the nation would pursue a policy of isolation. Americans wanted nothing to do with "Europe's wars" or with a League of Nations that might drag them into conflicts.

Yet could Americans turn their backs when "freedom and justice and self-determination" were being overwhelmed by military conquest? The question would not go away, nor would Americans ever find a final answer. The use of force in World War II (1941-1945) and most recently in the Persian Gulf seemed to provide one answer. Some believed that noble causes could be advanced by military force. But other interventions—especially the war in Vietnam—were tragic contradictions. As the nation looks toward the twenty-first century, Americans still struggle to define the role of their democracy in an interdependent world.

Section Review

ANSWERS

1. Definitions for the following terms can be found on text pages indicated in parentheses: *genocide* (514), *reparations* (514), *mandates* (516).
2. Provided for removal of conflicts that might lead to war, protection of national boundaries, self-determination of peoples. Criticized for drawing United States too closely into affairs of other nations and being too easy on Germany.
3. Differed by not drawing up all boundaries along national lines, taking away one eighth of German territory, forcing Germany to assume full responsibility for war and pay huge damages. Foch believed war damages would embitter Germany, cause it once again to wage war.
4. Since League had no way of enforcing Article Ten, it could not effectively keep the peace.
5. Republican opposition led by Lodge; Lodge feared treaty, especially Article Ten, would embroil the United States in European conflicts.

Chapter Survey

ANSWERS

Using New Vocabulary

1. *Mobilization* and *armistice* are related to war.
2. *Reparations* and *mandates* part of the peace settlements.
3. *Balance of power* and *pacifists* relate to keeping the peace.

Reviewing the Chapter

1. Immediate cause: assassination of heir to Austrian throne. Long-term causes: nationalism, territorial expansion, alliances producing delicate balance of power.
2. Germany tried to block vital American trade with the Allies through submarine warfare.
3. Germany resumed unrestricted submarine warfare; Zimmermann note revealed German plan to offer Mexico United States territory in exchange for alliance; German subs sank several American merchant ships; Russian monarchy replaced by democratic government, making Russia an acceptable ally.
4. (a) Hoover headed Food Administration, directing production and distribution of food, fuel, fertilizer, and farm machinery. (b) Baruch headed War Industries Board, supervising industrial use of resources and production of war goods. (c) W.E.B. DuBois encouraged African Americans to join the military. (d) Samuel Gompers, head of AFL, assured labor's cooperation with wartime regulations.
5. Sold Liberty Bonds, lowered the level of taxable income, and raised taxes on personal and corporate income, alcohol, and tobacco.
6. Germans crushed Italians, no longer needed to defend eastern front; launched offensive which brought them within 50 miles of Paris.
7. Arrival of American troops helped stop German advance; Allied troops began pushing Germans northward, eventually cut main German supply and communications line and forced surrender.
8. Wilson wanted no secret treaties, freedom of the seas, free trade, reduced armaments, settlement of colonial claims in the interest of colonial peoples, protection of national boundaries, self-determination for all people, and League of Nations. Lloyd George did not want freedom of the seas or strong German navy. Clemenceau wanted Germany to be disarmed and a buffer zone. Orlando wanted land Allies secretly promised to Italy in 1915.
9. Germany lost Alsace-Lorraine, its colonies, and control of Saar Valley; had to accept full responsibility for causing war; had to pay reparations; and lost its armed forces and

Reduced student page in the Teacher's Edition

Chapter Survey

Using New Vocabulary

The vocabulary terms in each pair listed below are related to each other. For each pair, explain what the two terms have in common. Also explain how they are different.

1. mobilization, armistice
2. reparations, mandates
3. balance of power, pacifists

Reviewing the Chapter

1. What was the immediate cause of World War I? What were some of its long-term causes?
2. What part did United States trade play in American entry into the war?
3. Describe the chain of events which led the United States to declare war in April 1917.
4. How did each of the following contribute to the war effort? (a) Herbert Hoover (b) Bernard Baruch (c) W.E.B. DuBois (d) Samuel Gompers
5. How did the government pay the enormous costs of the war?
6. What disadvantages did the Allies face in early 1918?
7. How did the Allies succeed in defeating the Germans?
8. Summarize Wilson's Fourteen Points. Which points did the other Allied leaders disagree with? Why?
9. How did the Treaty of Versailles punish Germany?
10. Why did the Senate refuse to ratify the Treaty of Versailles?

Thinking Critically

1. Evaluation. Addressing Congress just before the United States entered the war, Wilson said, "The world must be made safe for democracy." What did he mean by this statement? Was Wilson's peace plan consistent with this statement? Explain your answer.
2. Synthesis. The Committee on Public Information recruited thousands of speakers known as "Four Minute Men." Imagine that you were one of these speakers and write a brief speech to build support for the war effort.
3. Analysis. In what ways did World War I advance the causes of democracy and economic opportunity at home? In what ways did it hinder progress in these areas?

History and You

During World War I, newspapers were a powerful factor in shaping public opinion. Today television plays that role as well. Prepare a discussion of the impact of television in reporting today. Discuss some of the differences in the effects of the two media.

Using a Time Line

Match each date in the time line to the correct event or events in the list below. Write your answers in chronological order and explain how each event affected the course of World War I.

(A) sinking of the *Sussex*
(B) assassination of heir to the Austrian throne
(C) treaty of Brest-Litovsk
(D) German invasion of Belgium
(E) American entry into war
(F) United States declaration of neutrality
(G) sinking of the *Lusitania*
(H) publication of Zimmermann note
(I) armistice with Germany
(J) start of German war zone around Britain

Jun 1914	Aug 1914	Feb 1915	May 1915	Mar 1916	Feb 1917	Apr 1917	Mar 1918	Nov 1918

submarines.
10. The treaty contained provisions for entangling the United States in European affairs, and Wilson refused to compromise.

Thinking Critically

1. Wilson meant causes of conflict must be removed to ensure human rights and freedom of all nations. Most students should agree his Fourteen Points were consistent with his statement; can cite points 1–5, removing causes of conflict; points 6–13, protecting self-determination; and point 14, providing for a League of Nations to ensure independence of all nations.
2. Speeches may include: depredations of Germans and Wilson's ideals that provided a rationale for American participation in the war.
3. Advancements: jobs were opened to women and African Americans; African Americans were encouraged to move north where they suffered less discrimination. Hindrances: freedom of speech limited, anti-German hysteria created, government increased controls on business, anti-black riots occurred.

History and You

Students should recognize that instantaneous television reporting of events leaves little time for journalistic reflection, so it is easy to convey incorrect information to millions of people very rapidly (for example, CNN's report that the Iraqi air force had been virtually destroyed on the first day of the war in the Persian Gulf). Television also tends to be far more superficial than print journalism, dealing in "sound bites" rather than measured responses.

Using a Time Line

(B) June 1914, (D), (F) August 1914, (J) February 1915, (G) May 1915, (A) March 1916, (H) February 1917, (E) April 1917, (C) March 1918, (I) November 1918.

Applying Social Studies Skills

1. Accept reasonable answers.
2. It might mean that U-boats are doing an effective job of winning the war.
3. A pro-German propaganda book or film celebrating the feats of a U-boat.
4. U-boats sank ships with American citizens on them.

Applying Thinking Skills

1. That a democracy is the most desirable form of government.
2. Wealthy control U.S., and war is being fought for their benefit.
3. He violated the Sedition Act.

Applying Social Studies Skills

Interpreting Graphics

A graphic is a symbolic representation of an object, idea, or relationship. We see graphics all around us — in logos, posters, advertising art, and illustrations. The graphic below, a poster designed by a German artist, may have been planned as an advertisement for a book or movie. The poster reads, "U-boats are out!" Study the poster and answer the questions that follow.

1. Describe what you see in the poster.

2. What might this poster mean in Germany?

3. What kind of book or movie might be titled "U-boote Heraus"?

4. Why would this poster have offended many Americans in 1915?

Applying Thinking Skills

Identifying Unstated Assumptions

An unstated assumption is an idea someone takes for granted as true but does not express directly. When an assumption underlies a claim, one must determine if the assumption is reasonable before accepting the claim as true.

Joseph Gilbert was one of many Americans who opposed the entry of the United States into World War I. In 1918 Gilbert expressed his opinion in the following statement. His remarks led to his arrest, and he was fined $500 and sentenced to a year in prison. As you read Gilbert's statement, think about his unstated assumptions about democracy and about who really controls the American government. Then answer the questions that follow.

"We are going over to Europe to make the world safe for democracy, but I tell you we had better make America safe for democracy first. You say, What is the matter with our democracy? I tell you what is the matter with it: Have you had anything to say as to who should be President? Have you had anything to say as to who should be the Governor of this state? Have you had anything to say as to whether we should go into this war? You know you have not. If this is such a great democracy, for Heaven's sake why should we not vote on conscription of men? We are stampeded into this war by newspaper rot to pull England's chestnuts out of the fire for her. I tell you, if they conscripted wealth like they have conscripted men, this war would not last 48 hours."

1. In the first sentence, what does Gilbert assume about democracy? How can you tell?

2. What are the unstated assumptions behind Gilbert's last sentence?

3. Why do you think this speech landed Gilbert in jail?

Unit 6 Survey

ANSWERS

Making Connections

1. Citizens pressed government to promote social welfare. Citizen pressure, fed by yellow journalism, led to the Spanish-American War. Wilson appealed to citizens to help win World War I.

2. The U.S. helped Cuba establish a constitution, but often interfered. U.S. extended benefits of citizenship to Puerto Ricans. Democracy was slow in coming to the Philippines. U.S. motives in Central America were chiefly economic.

3. Supervision of monopoly: Department of Commerce and Labor, Mann-Elkins Act, Clayton Antitrust. Intervention in labor disputes: Roosevelt's arbitration of coal strike. Regulation of industry: Meat Inspection Act, Pure Food and Drug Act. Modernizing banking: Federal Reserve Act.

4. Answers may include Jim Crow, denial of rights to African Americans and others, political power wielded by big business, party machines, denial of vote to women.

5. Answers may include Spanish-American War, annexation of Hawaii, Panama Canal, Open Door Policy, Roosevelt Corollary, sinking of Lusitania, World War I, Fourteen Points.

Using the Time Line. Answers may include Spanish-American War, annexation of Hawaii and the Philippines, Open Door policy, Roosevelt Corollary, interventions in Cuba and Mexico, World War I, Panama Canal.

Projects and Activities

1. Historical examples may include the U.S. entering World War I to make the world "safe for democracy" and Wilson's Fourteen Points. Students might also cite current concerns with human rights and aiding the hungry and the oppressed.

2. Poland: 1795: divided by Austria, Russia, Prussia. 1921: democratic constitution. 1926–1939: dictatorship. Czechoslovakia: Czechs, Slovaks, Germans. 1600s: Bohemia part of Austria; Slovakia part of Hungary. 1918–1935: democratic republic. Minority unrest. Yugoslavia: Bosnian Muslims, Croats, Serbs, Slovenes. 1400s: Austria, Hungary, Turkey ruled. 1918: Kingdom of Serbs, Croats, and Slovenes. 1921: constitutional monarchy. 1929: dictatorship. Ethnic fighting. Finland: 1100s: Sweden ruled. 1809: Russia conquered. 1917: independence. 1939: Soviet invasion. Latvia, Lithuania, Estonia: Denmark, Sweden, Poland, Germany, Russia ruled. 1918: independence. 1940: Soviet Union.

3. Using the Time Line. Projects will vary.

Unit Survey

Making Connections

1. How did the progressives' idea of citizen participation affect both domestic and foreign affairs between 1900 and 1920?

2. Spreading the benefits of democracy was often given as a reason for American actions as a world power in the late 1800s. Where were those benefits actually felt, and where was this reasoning used to justify economic expansion?

3. How did the relationship of the government to the economy change between 1900 and 1920? Use examples to support your answer.

4. Agree or disagree with the following statement: While the United States was fighting to make the world safe for democracy, it was not fully democratic at home. Give examples.

5. In 1892 the *New York Herald* suggested abolishing the Department of State since it had so little work to do. What events between 1890 and 1920 proved the newspaper to be wrong?

Using the Time Line. Choose at least six events on the time line that relate to the title of this unit, "Questions of Power." Explain the relationships.

Projects and Activities

1. Woodrow Wilson believed that moral principles should be the basis of American foreign policy. Prepare a position statement supporting Wilson's belief or a statement proposing a different basis for foreign policy. Use examples from Wilson's time as well as from the present to strengthen your argument. Debate this issue in class.

2. To identify European nations created after World War I, compare the maps of Europe on pages 497 and 515. Working in groups of four or five, do research and make a report to the class on one of the following: Poland, Czechoslovakia, Yugoslavia, Finland, the Baltic states (Latvia, Lithuania, Estonia). Include information about the ethnic groups that populate it; its history, including how it came to be part of the German, Austro-Hungarian, or Russian empire; its government between the two world wars; and what is happening there today.

Using the Time Line. Look at the newspaper front pages on text pages 466 and 473. Notice the number and style of headlines. Also notice that newspapers did not yet use photographs. Design a similar front page that includes news about at least three events on the time line. Do research into the events, if necessary.

Milestones	1890	1898
Presidents	Harrison; Cleveland	McKinley
Political and Economic	• Liliuokalani becomes queen of Hawaii • Homestead Strike • First Populist party convention • Pullman Strike	• Spanish American War begins • U.S. annexes Hawaii • U.S. annexes the Phillippines • Open Door policy proposed
Social and Cultural	• *How the Other Half Lives*, Jacob Riis • Carnegie Hall opens, New York City • Basketball invented, James Naismith • First Sunday comics, New York *World*	• "The Stars and Stripes Forever," John Philip Sousa • First Arabic newspaper in U.S. • "Maple Leaf Rag," Scott Joplin • First Chinese newspaper in U.S.
Technological and Scientific	• Battleship *Maine* launched • Zipper, W. Judson • Ferris wheel, George Ferris • Niagara Falls hydroelectric plant opens • Safety razor, King Gillette • First subway, Boston • Municipal water purification system, Lawrence, Mass.	

Assessment

Central America gained independence from Spain in 1821. Except British Honduras, the Central American countries joined Mexico in 1822–1823, then broke away. They tried to unite several times, but these unions always collapsed, and the countries remained independent. Discuss the characteristics of an independent country. How might such a country react to outside intervention?

Scoring

To create a scoring system, or rubric, assign an achievement scale to each of the evaluation criteria. For example, you might evaluate "Knowing history" on a scale of 0 to 4 as follows:

4—Exemplary response: cites several presidential acts as evidence of concern with justice; discusses U.S. policy in Central America between 1898 and 1918, citing expansionism, Platt Amendment, Roosevelt Corollary, "big stick," dollar, and moral diplomacies; displays knowledge of Monroe Doctrine and Fourteen Points.

3—Good response: cites more than one presidential act as evidence of concern with justice; describes U.S. policy in Central America between 1898 and 1918, including Roosevelt Corollary, "big stick," dollar, and moral diplomacies; cites Monroe Doctrine and Fourteen Points.

2—Adequate response: cites at least one presidential act as evidence of concern with justice; describes in general U.S. policy in Central America, citing at least Roosevelt Corollary, dollar and moral diplomacies.

1—Poor response: fails in more than one of the following: identifying justice concerns of each President; citing specific acts as evidence; describing U.S. policy in Central America between 1898 and 1918; citing specific policies as evidence.

0—No response/inappropriate response.

Follow-up Activity

Class discussion. Have the class as a whole consider student proposals for changes in United States policy and vote for the six they would have recommended in 1918.

Assessment: Demonstrating What You Know

Writing an Editorial

You are the managing editor of a newspaper in a Central American country. You have long been dissatisfied with United States policy toward your country. The year is 1918, and you have just read Woodrow Wilson's Fourteen Points. The ideals expressed in the Fourteen Points lead you to write an editorial in the form of a letter to Wilson. You appeal to his sense of justice and ask that the United States change its policies toward Central American nations.

In your editorial you cover the following points:

1. The ideals of each of the progressive Presidents—Roosevelt, Taft, and Wilson—as evidence of their concern for justice.
2. United States policies in Central America since the Spanish American War, including the Roosevelt Corollary, dollar diplomacy and moral diplomacy, and the probable goals behind these policies.
3. The effects of United States policies in Central America, including how Central Americans reacted to these policies.
4. The ideals expressed in the Fourteen Points compared to United States policies in Central America.
5. Recommended changes in United States policies toward Central America.
6. Reasons for your recommendations. Anticipate opposition and address the arguments that will probably be raised by your opponents.

Evaluation Criteria

Your work will be evaluated according to how well you meet the following criteria.

- **Completing the task**. You write an editorial as a letter to Wilson advocating changes in United States policies in Central America.
- **Knowing history**. You accurately summarize the Presidents' ideals and United States foreign policy in Central America based on historical information from your text or other sources.
- **Thinking critically**. You compare United States policies in Central America with policies toward Europe as expressed in the Fourteen Points. You evaluate the consequences of United States policies in Central America and formulate new policies calculated to bring about a desired effect. Your reasons are based on evidence.
- **Communicating ideas**. Your ideas are presented in a logical sequence. You state your positions clearly, using persuasive language.

1905 | **1913** | **1920**

T. Roosevelt | Taft | Wilson

- Roosevelt Corollary announced
- U.S. intervenes in Cuba
- Pure Food and Drug Act
- Mexican Revolution
- NAACP founded
- World War I breaks out
- U.S. intervenes in Mexico
- Puerto Ricans are made U.S. citizens
- U.S. enters World War I

- Ice cream cones introduced, St. Louis World's Fair
- First American Nobel Prize, T. Roosevelt
- "Memphis Blues," W.C. Handy
- First newsreel, Pathé News
- New York *World* begins publishing crossword puzzles
- *O Pioneers!*, Willa Cather
- First national child labor law
- *Chicago Poems*, Carl Sandburg

- Wright brothers first flight
- Panama Canal begun
- William Gorgas studies yellow fever
- White House Conservation Conference
- Peary and Henson reach North Pole
- First automobile service station, Pittsburgh
- Liquid-fuel rocket patented, Robert Goddard
- First Aero Squadron—8 airplanes
- First transcontinental telephone call

521

Objectives

- Describe the atmosphere and effects of racism, nativism, and labor unrest in post-World War I United States.
- Explain the boom in business in the 1920s.
- Discuss the causes and effects of changes in values in the 1920s.
- Explain why the economic boom came to an end and describe Hoover's attempts to end the Great Depression.
- Identify actions Roosevelt took to promote the nation's recovery.
- Describe Roosevelt's coalition of Democrats and the effects of his economic and social policies.

Introducing THE UNIT

The United States devoted much of the two decades following World War I to domestic concerns. Postwar economic dislocations, leading to widespread strikes and the Red Scare, were followed by the boom years of the "Golden Twenties." The frenzied economic growth, however, was short-lived. In 1929 the stock market crashed, and the United States slid into the Great Depression. Under the programs of the New Deal, the federal government attempted, with mixed results, to speed the recovery of the nation, provide relief for Americans, and prevent the occurrence of similar disasters in the future.

Unit 7 1919-1939

Prosperity and Depression

About the Author

John Steinbeck was born in Salinas, California, a region and landscape that had a profound effect on his writing. From that small farming community, Steinbeck enrolled in Stanford University but never graduated. He left school and traveled around the United States, writing, reading, and doing odd jobs for pay.

Many of the themes of Steinbeck's work—social injustice, the powerlessness yet dignity of the poor, and the tragic suffering of the dispossessed—come from the suffering he witnessed during the Great Depression of the 1930s. *The Grapes of Wrath* (1939), generally considered Steinbeck's greatest novel, won the National Book Award and the Pulitzer Prize. His other works include *Of Mice and Men* (1937), *Cannery Row* (1945), and *East of Eden* (1951). Steinbeck received the Nobel Prize for literature in 1962.

History Through Literature

A smothering dust storm opens *The Grapes of Wrath,* a novel by John Steinbeck (1902-1968). Like many Oklahoma farmers in 1939, the novel's Joad family is driven off the land by forces beyond their control: dust storms and drought, low crop prices, and the effects of the Great Depression. Fleeing to California in search of opportunity as migrant farm workers, the Joads encounter exploitation and violence instead.

Even during times of apparent prosperity, the plight of farmers was not a new problem in the United States. *The Grapes of Wrath* has been called "the *Uncle Tom's Cabin* of the twentieth century" because Steinbeck wanted to awaken the American conscience to the poverty and desperation of the dispossessed and to the social injustice they faced. In this selection, tenant families learn that they must leave their land.

from

The Grapes of Wrath

by John Steinbeck

The owners of the land came onto the land, or more often a spokesman for the owner came. They came in closed cars, and they felt the dry earth with their fingers, and sometimes they drove big earth augers into the ground for soil tests. The tenants, from their sun-beaten dooryard, watched uneasily when the closed cars drove along the fields. And at last the owner men drove into the dooryards and sat in their cars to talk out of the windows. The tenant men stood beside the cars for a while, and then squatted on their hams and found sticks with which to mark the dust.

In the open doors the women stood looking out, and behind them the children—corn-headed children, with wide eyes, one bare foot on top of the other bare foot, and the toes working. The women and the children watched their men talking to the owner men. They were silent.

Some of the owner men were kind because they hated what they had to do, and some of them were angry because they hated to be cruel, and some of them were cold because they had long ago found that one could not be an owner unless one were cold. And all of them hated the mathematics that drove them, and some were afraid, and some worshiped the mathematics because it provided a refuge from thought and from feeling. If a bank or finance company owned the land, the owner man said, The Bank—or the Company—needs—wants—insists—must have—as though the Bank or the Company were a monster, with thought and feeling, which had ensnared

Guided Reading

Discussion. Direct students' attention to the descriptions of the farm families and their environment and to contrast it with the descriptions of the bank and the "owner men." What language does Steinbeck use to contrast the two? How does Steinbeck communicate the power of the machine and the powerlessness of the farmers?

Vocabulary Building

Discussion. Knowing the following words will help students understand this selection: *augers* (tool with a spiral cutting edge for boring holes in the earth), *dooryards* (a yard into which the front door of a house opens), *ensnared* (trapped), *sties* (pigpens).

523

Linking Past and Present

Discussion. John Steinbeck's writing and the photography of Dorothea Lange are examples of art that revealed the plight of those who often lacked the power to reach a large number of people with their stories. Some people consider this art a form of social protest.

Have students discuss whether the themes of poverty and the dispossessed are relevant themes for artists and writers today. Ask them to cite current examples of art, music, writing, and photography that convey a message of social protest. What are the themes of this art? What might John Steinbeck write about if he were alive today?

Connections: Art and Technology

The 1930s saw the development of documentary photograpy as an art form. While photographs of the poor by Jacob Riis and Lewis Hine shocked the public and helped bring about social change in the late 1800s (see Chapter 15), innovations in technology during the 1920s and early 1930s added new creative possibilities for the camera. The invention of the small 35 mm camera in 1924 and the electronic flash in 1931 greatly broadened the range of subjects that a photographer could shoot. These developments also allowed the photographer to catch fleeting moments and emotions, the heart of the work of documentary photographers like Dorothea Lange (see photo below, biography on page 567). In addition to her Depression-era photos, Lange is well-known for her photographs of Japanese Americans interned during World War II (see page 637).

them. These last would take no responsibility for the banks or the companies because they were men and slaves, while the banks were machines and masters all at the same time. Some of the owner men were a little proud to be slaves to such cold and powerful masters. The owner men sat in the cars and explained. You know the land is poor. You've scrabbled at it long enough, God knows.

The squatting tenant men nodded and wondered and drew figures in the dust, and yes, they knew, God knows. If the dust only wouldn't fly. If the top would only stay on the soil, it might not be so bad.

The owner men went on leading to their point: You know the land's getting poorer. You know what cotton does to the land; robs it, sucks all the blood out of it.

The squatters nodded—they knew, God knew. If they could only rotate the crops they might pump blood back into the land.

Well, it's too late. And the owner men explained the workings and the thinkings of the monster that was stronger than they were. A man can hold land if he can just eat and pay taxes; he can do that.

Yes, he can do that until his crops fail one day and he has to borrow money from the bank.

But—you see, a bank or a company can't do that, because those creatures don't breathe air, don't eat side-meat. They breathe profits; they eat the interest on money. If they don't get it, they die the way you die without air, without side-meat. It is a sad thing, but it is so. It is just so.

The squatting men raised their eyes to understand. Can't we just hang on? Maybe the next year will be a good year. God knows how much cotton next year. And with all the wars—God knows what price cotton will bring. Don't they make explosives out of cotton? And uniforms? Get enough wars and cotton'll hit the ceiling. Next year, maybe. They looked up questioningly.

We can't depend on it. The bank—the monster has to have profits all the time. It can't wait. It'll die. No, taxes go on. When the monster stops growing, it dies. It can't stay one size.

Soft fingers began to tap the sill of the car window, and hard fingers tightened on the restless drawing sticks. In the doorways of the sun-beaten tenant houses, women sighed and then shifted feet so that the one that had been down was now on top, and the toes working. Dogs came sniffing near the owner cars and wetted on all four tires one after another. And chickens lay in the sunny dust and fluffed their feathers to get the cleansing dust down to the skin. In the little sties the pigs grunted inquiringly over the muddy remnants of the slops.

(Background) Solitary barn in a dry field; (this page) "Back, 1935," by Dorothea Lange; (opposite) old abandoned truck.

524

The squatting men looked down again. What do you want us to do? We can't take less share of the crop—we're half starved now. The kids are hungry all the time. We got no clothes, torn an' ragged. If all the neighbors weren't the same, we'd be ashamed to go to meeting.

And at last the owner men came to the point. The tenant system won't work any more. One man on a tractor can take the place of twelve or fourteen families. Pay him a wage and take all the crop. We have to do it. We don't like to do it. But the monster's sick. Something's happened to the monster.

But you'll kill the land with the cotton.

We know. We've got to take cotton quick before the land dies. Then we'll sell the land. Lots of families in the East would like to own a piece of land.

The tenant men looked up alarmed. But what'll happen to us? How'll we eat?

You'll have to get off the land. The plows'll go through the dooryard.

And now the squatting men stood up angrily. Grampa took up the land, and he had to kill the Indians and drive them away. And Pa was born here, and he killed weeds and snakes. Then a bad year come and he had to borrow a little money. An' we was born here. There in the door—our children born here. And Pa had to borrow money. The bank owned the land then, but we stayed and we got a little bit of what we raised.

We know that—all that. It's not us, it's the bank. A bank isn't like a man. Or an owner with fifty thousand acres, he isn't like a man either. That's the monster.

Sure cried the tenant men, but it's our land. We measured it and broke it up. We were born on it, and we got killed on it, died on it. Even if it's no good, it's still ours. That's what make it ours—being born on it, working it, dying on it. That makes ownership, not a paper with numbers on it.

We're sorry. It's not us. It's the monster. The bank isn't like a man.

Yes, but the bank is only made of men.

No, you're wrong there—quite wrong there. The bank is something else than men. It happens that every man in a bank hates what the bank does, and yet the bank does it. The bank is something more than men, I tell you. It's the monster. Men made it, but they can't control it.

Taking a Closer Look

1. *What claim do the tenants have to the land? Why are they no longer landowners?*

2. *Why are they being forced to leave?*

3. *Who or what is the monster? What adjectives does Steinbeck use to describe it? Why does Steinbeck use this image?*

Taking a Closer Look

ANSWERS

1. The tenants claim their land because that is where their families were born, and because they worked all their lives on their farms. They lost the land by taking loans from banks, and becoming tenant farmers.

2. The bank can make better short-term profits by forcing the tenants off the land to cheaply grow cotton with tractors.

3. The monster is the bank or the holding company, i.e., the economic system driving people from the land. Steinbeck uses adjectives such as "cold" and "powerful." Steinbeck uses this imagery to suggest the system's lack of humanity and its ability to devastate people's lives. Steinbeck also uses the monster to convey the powerlessness of people manipulated by forces beyond their understanding or control.

Chapter 20

The Twenties: Blowing the Lid Off

Planning Guide

	Student Text	TWE Lesson Plans	Support Materials
SECTION 1	**Section 20–1 (1–2 Days)** **Unrest in Postwar America,** pp 528–533 Review/Evaluation Section Review, p 533	**Introducing the Chapter:** Issues in the Twenties—Cooperative Activity, 30 minutes, p 525B **Teaching the Main Ideas:** Intolerance in the Twenties—Paired Activity, one class period, p 525B	★ **Read to Remember,** Section 1 ● **Section Activities,** Section 1 Δ **Enrichment Activities,** Section 1 Δ **Readings** ● **Tests and Quizzes,** Section 1 Quiz
SECTION 2	**Section 20–2 (1–2 Days)** **Government and Business,** pp 534–539 The Creative Spirit: Entertainers, pp 540–541 Review/Evaluation Section Review, p 539	**Teaching the Main Ideas:** Industrial Breakthroughs—Cooperative Activity, one class period, p 525C **Evaluating Progress:** Campaigning for Normalcy—Individual Activity, homework, one class period, p 525C	★ **Read to Remember,** Section 2 ● **Section Activities,** Section 2 ● **Geography Activities,** Section 2 ● **Tests and Quizzes,** Section 2 Quiz
SECTION 3	**Section 20–3 (1–2 Days)** **A Time of Changing Values,** pp 542–549 The American Spirit: Langston Hughes, p 548 Connections to Themes: Balancing Unity and Diversity, p 549 Review/Evaluation Section Review, p 549 Chapter 20 Survey, pp 550–551 Skills, pp 550–551 Using New Vocabulary Thinking Critically Using a Time Line Applying Social Studies Skills: Analyzing Bar Graphs Writing About Issues	**Reinforcement Activity:** People in the Twenties—Individual Activity, homework, one class period, p 525C **Enrichment Activity:** Individual Freedom and the Law—Individual Activity, homework, discussion 30 minutes, p 525C	★ **Read to Remember,** Section 3 ● **Section Activities,** Section 3 Δ **Enrichment Activities,** Section 3 Δ **Readings** ● **Tests and Quizzes,** Section 3 Quiz, Chapter 20 Test (Forms A and B) **Additional Resources** Δ **Twentieth Century Issues: Links to the Past** ● **Active Learning** Δ **GTV Videodiscs** Δ **Transparencies and Activity Book** ● **Testing Software** ★ **Chapter Summaries** **Key:** ★ **For Extra Support** ● **For All Students** Δ **For Enrichment**

Overview

The years just after World War I were characterized by economic problems and social unrest. The high cost of living led to union strikes throughout the country. Many Americans blamed the strikes on a communist conspiracy. Some bombings roused public fears of revolution, and the government organized raids on foreign organizations. In one episode of this Red Scare, two Italian anarchists, Nicola Sacco and Bartolomeo Vanzetti, were convicted of murder and executed despite claims that the trial was unfair.

Fear and unrest were also reflected in race riots and lynchings and suspicion of newcomers. These played a major part in the growth of a new, national Ku Klux Klan, based on racism and nativism, and restrictions on immigration. However, immigration from Latin America remained unrestricted to ensure an adequate labor force, and Mexican workers played a vital role in economic development in the Southwest.

Faced with social and economic problems, Americans turned for relief to Warren G. Harding, who won the presidency in 1920 by promising a return to "normalcy." He and his successor, Calvin Coolidge, followed pro-business policies which were credited with restoring prosperity to the nation. Industries, especially those based on the automobile, consumer goods, and entertainment, boomed. However, many Americans, especially those working on farms and in old industries, struggled to get by.

Traditional and new ideas clashed in the Twenties. Elders were shocked by the supposed wildness of the younger generation. Prohibition and the teaching of evolution in public schools sharply divided Americans. Writers questioned traditional American ideas and values.

No group more fully explored the failure of American values than African Americans. While the NAACP fought white injustice in the courts, black artists of the Harlem Renaissance dealt openly with their experiences as African Americans. Many African Americans found a source of pride in Marcus Garvey's "back to Africa" movement and demand for black power.

Activity Objectives

After completing the activities, students should be able to

- describe aspects of intolerance in the United States just after World War I and during the 1920s.
- summarize the impact of new industries on American life in the 1920s.
- describe the accomplishments of well-known people in the 1920s.
- explain the Republicans' view of normalcy.
- analyze the conflict between individual freedom and the law.

Introducing the Chapter

Issues in the Twenties

This activity requires half a class period.

In this activity students explore issues that Americans faced in the 1920s and compare them to issues that Americans face today.

Before class write the following headlines on the chalkboard:

- Jazz is banned in Zion, Illinois
- Quiet Tulsa erupts; 79 die in race riots
- Troops and planes battle coal strikers
- Interior chief Fall quits in oil scandal
- The "flapper" makes her daring debut
- Bryan defeated in bid to ban evolution
- Klan marches in capital
- Suffrage succeeds: women can vote
- U.S. deports 249 radicals to Soviet Russia
- Immigration is cut back
- Speakeasies flourish under eye of Prohibition
- Study sees crime getting out of hand
- New products to fit every need

Tell students that in the years after World War I Americans faced a series of changes so rapid as to be very disturbing. Some of these changes, like industrialization, had been going on for a long time. Others, such as conflict between traditional and new ideas and values, resulted from the war. Ask students to listen as you read each headline and to identify the issue.

Conclude the activity by asking students to identify the issues that still exist. Have students discuss why such issues are so difficult to resolve.

Teaching the Main Ideas

Section 20-1: Intolerance in the Twenties

This paired activity requires a full class period.

In Section 20-1 students learn that hard times and unrest led to increased intolerance in the 1920s. The following activity will enable students to identify kinds of intolerance that were widespread during those years.

Begin the activity by asking students to define *intolerance* (lack of tolerance of others' opinions, beliefs, or of persons of other races, background). Ask them for current examples of intolerance of others' opinions or beliefs. Point out that in the 1920s radicals, especially, socialists, communists, and anarchists, faced intolerance.

Divide the class into pairs and direct them to write the word *intolerance* down the left side of a piece of paper, leaving a line space between each letter. Students are to use each letter to begin a sentence that describes an aspect of intolerance in the 1920s. For example, a sentence for *"i"* might be, "Immigrants from southern and eastern Europe and Africa were discouraged from entering the United States."

Students should address the following aspects of intolerance in their sentences: hostility to labor unions, racial violence, the Red Scare, the growth of nativism, restriction of immigration, and discriminatory treatment of immigrants.

When students have finished their assignment, ask volunteers to read sentences for each letter. Conclude by discussing which aspects of intolerance in the 1920s still exist today. Why?

Teaching the Main Ideas

Section 20-2: Industrial Breakthroughs

This cooperative activity requires one class period, or it may be completed as homework.

In this activity students illustrate the impact of new industries on life in the United States in the 1920s. Assemble poster paper, markers, scissors, and magazines for groups to use in creating their projects, which may be completed out of class.

Tell students that many features of life that we take for granted today developed in the 1920s. Write on the chalkboard the following industries: automobile, airplane, electricity, chemistry, movie, radio. Divide the class into groups of three or four and have each group choose one industry, making certain that each industry is assigned to at least one group.

Direct each group to create a poster, a model, or a mobile to illustrate the impact of its industry on American life from the 1920s to the present. Provide materials for students to use and encourage them to do additional research.

Have each group to present its finished product to the class. Discuss which industry has had the most profound impact on American life. Conclude by challenging students to identify new industries that are changing American life today. (Two possibilities: the computer industry and the microwave industry.)

Reinforcement Activity

Sections 20-3: People in the Twenties

This individual activity may be assigned as homework and shared in class the following day.

The following activity, in which students create written interviews, reinforces understanding of important historical figures in the 1920s.

Begin the activity by asking students to name people they think should be included in history books in the future. Challenge them to think of people in a wide variety of fields, such as sports stars, musicians, writers, labor leaders, and political leaders. Have students discuss the criteria they used in making their choices.

Tell students to imagine that they are reporters, to choose a person discussed in Chapter 20, and to create a written interview with him or her. The interview should be in the form of questions and answers, and should focus on the interviewee's accomplishments and views. Encourage students to use quotations in the text and to find additional information about their subjects.

Have students summarize their interviews for the class by the significance of their subjects' accomplishments and views.

Evaluating Progress

Section 20-2: Campaigning for Normalcy

This individual activity may be assigned as homework and shared in class the following day.

This activity, in which students write campaign speeches, is designed to assess students' understanding of normalcy as put into practice by Republican Presidents Harding and Coolidge.

Have students imagine they are speech writers for President Harding. They are to prepare a two- to three-minute speech summarizing his goal of returning the United States to normalcy. Speeches should define normalcy and specify ways to attain it. Stress that the speeches should be lively and persuasive.

Have students present their speeches. Conclude by having students discuss how the policies of normalcy affected wealthy Americans as well as poor Americans.

Criteria for evaluating students' speeches should include accuracy and clearly expressed links between goals and means. The definition of normalcy should include a return to the pro-business polices of the late 1800s. Means of attaining normalcy may include less government regulation of business, more protection from foreign competition, and lower taxes for wealthy Americans.

Enrichment Activity

Section 20-3: Individual Freedom and the Law

This individual activity may be assigned as homework and shared in class the following day.

This activity engages students in analyzing the issue of government regulation of personal behavior of individuals.

Begin the activity by asking students to explain why prohibition became a national goal, and why the "noble experiment" failed. Point out that all societies need laws in order to protect the rights of their members and to function smoothly. However, it is difficult to know where to draw the line between necessary laws and laws that violate a person's individual freedom. To many Americans in the 1920s, prohibition went too far toward limiting individual freedom.

Poll the class on the following questions:

- Do you believe that prohibition violated personal freedom? Why or why not?

- Should the government regulate use of alcoholic beverages? If so, in what way?
- What criteria would you use to balance the rights of the individual and necessary laws?

Ask students to name present-day issues that represent conflict between individual freedom and the law. (Some issues are abortion, the drinking age, pornography, use of motorcycle helmets and seat belts, and drug use.)

Direct students to choose one of the issues mentioned and write a position paper. On the chalkboard write the format for their papers as follows:

- State the issue.
- Give at least two arguments for and two arguments against government regulation.
- Discuss strengths and weaknesses of arguments on both sides.
- State your personal view on the issue.
- Support your view with arguments and evidence.

Encourage students to consult reference books for information on their topics.

When students have finished their papers, take a poll of personal opinions on each issue and tally the results on the chalkboard. Conclude by discussing whether the class generally favors or opposes laws that regulate individual freedom. Where would students draw the line between necessary laws and laws that limit a person's individual freedom? Why?

Bibliography and Audiovisual Material

Teacher Bibliography

Allen, Frederick Lewis. *Only Yesterday*. New York: HarperCollins Publishers, Inc., 1986.

Baritz, Loren, ed. *The Culture of the Twenties*. New York: Macmillan Publishing Co., 1970.

Leuchtenburg, William E. *The Perils of Prosperity, 1914–1932*. Chicago: University of Chicago Press, 1958.

Lewis, David L. *When Harlem Was in Vogue*. New York: Oxford University Press, 1989.

Ross, Walter S. *The Last Hero: Charles A. Lindbergh*. New York: Woodhill Publishing Co., 1979.

Sinclair, Andrew. *A Social History of the Prohibition Movement*. New York: HarperCollins Publishers, Inc., 1964.

Student Bibliography

Anderson, Sherwood. *Winesburg, Ohio*. New York: Viking Penguin, 1988.

Cather, Willa. *My Antonia*. New York: David McKay Co., Inc., 1990.

Fitzgerald, F. Scott. *The Great Gatsby*. New York: Macmillan, 1988.

Hemingway, Ernest. *The Sun Also Rises*. New York: Macmillan, 1987.

Hughes, Langston. *I Wonder as I Wander: An Autobiographical Journey*. New York: Hippocrene Books, Inc., 1974.

Hurston, Zora Neale. *Their Eyes Were Watching God*. Champaign, Illinois: University of Illinois Press, 1978.

Lewis, Sinclair. *Main Street*. San Diego: Harcourt Brace Jovanovich, 1989.

McKay, Claude. *Harlem Glory*. Chicago: Charles H. Kerr Publishing Co., 1990.

Wright, Richard. *Native Son*. New York: HarperCollins Publishers, Inc., 1989.

Films, Videocassettes, and Videodiscs

American History Video: Warring and Roaring. 60 min. Mastervision. Videocassette.

The Reckless Years: (1919–1929). 39 minutes. Guidance Associates. Videocassette.

The Roaring '20s: Everybody Ought to Be Rich. Guidance Associates. Videocassette.

The Twenties. (A Walk Through the 20th Century with Bill Moyers Series). 57 min. PBS. Videocassette.

Filmstrips

The Big Red Scare of 1919–1920. 1 color filmstrip, cassette, guide. Multi-Media Productions.

Chapter 20

Objectives

- Analyze the causes of nativism and restrictions on immigration.
- Discuss the causes of the business boom.
- Describe changes in values in the 1920s.

Introducing THE CHAPTER

For suggestions on introducing Chapter 20, refer to page 525B in the Teacher's Edition.

Developing THE CHAPTER

For activities and teaching strategies to help you reinforce and enrich chapter content, see pages 525B-525D in the Teacher's Edition.

B · A · C · K · G · R · O · U · N · D

Chapter Opener Illustrations

The photograph, *"Couple in Raccoon Coats,"* is by James Van Der Zee, an African-American artist who recorded the history of Harlem for over fifty years.

Thomas Hart Benton completed *Contemporary America* in 1930. He depicted real people and situations, such as couples dancing, an audience at a movie house, and even himself (far right, toasting completion of his mural).

Ben Shahn used his paintings to comment on society in the late 1920s and early 1930s. Here he pictures men calling for the repeal of prohibition.

Three young women are arrested for wearing one-piece swimsuits in Chicago in 1922. Their bobbed hair and flippant attitudes were as controversial as their swimwear.

On radios like the one shown here, people listened to jazz, which first developed among African-American musi-

Reduced student page in the Teacher's Edition

Chapter 20 1919-1928

The Twenties: Blowing the Lid Off

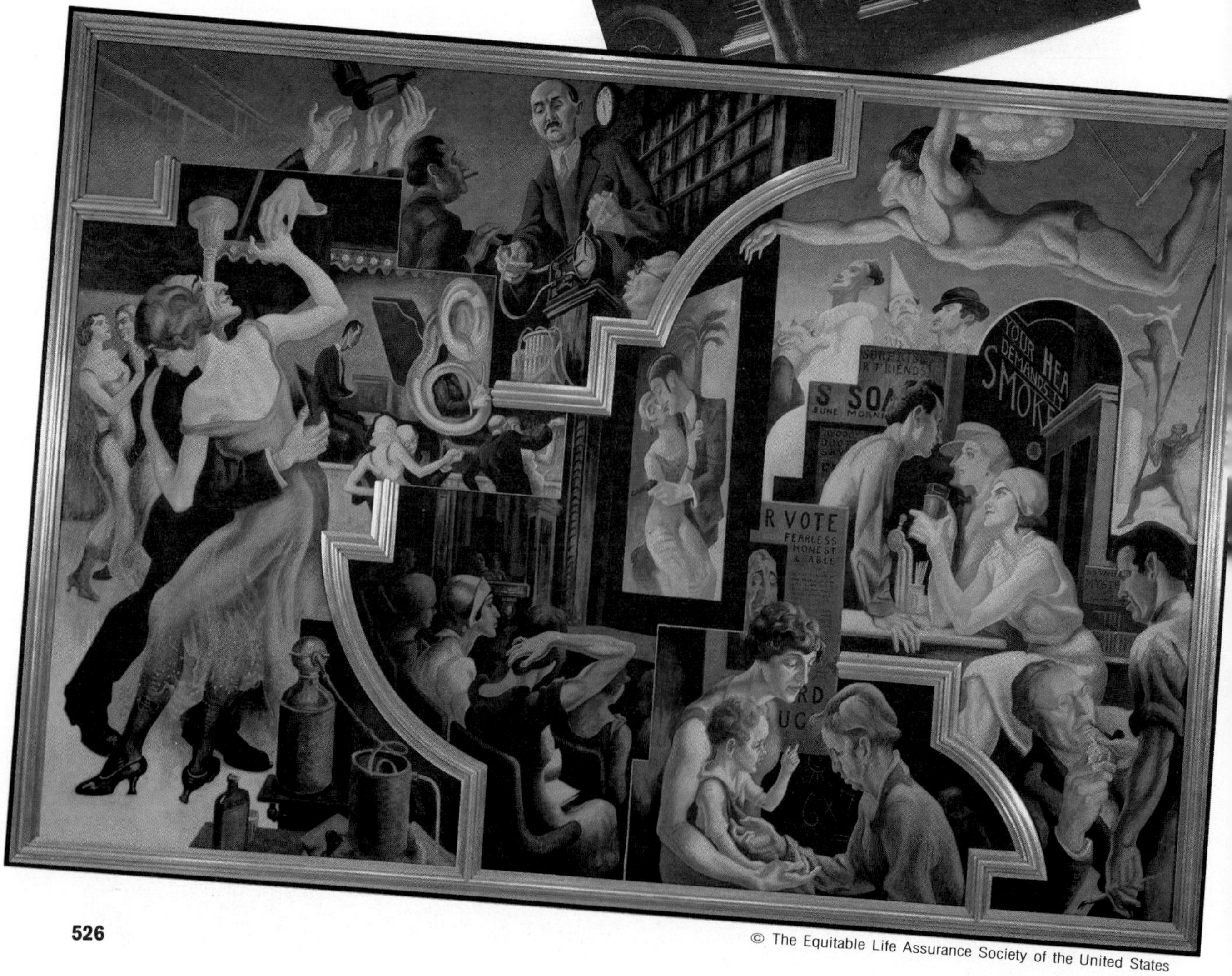

cians and quickly spread across the United States. Jazz became largely acceptable in white society only when Paul Whiteman adapted its sounds to his big band.

American Voices

In the 1920s James A. Rogers, a journalist for *The Messenger,* an African-American newspaper, reported on an exciting new kind of music. This music was "jazzed up" by musicians improvising melodies on the spot. The result, said Rogers, was a "new spirit of joy and spontaneity."

> *"The true spirit of jazz is a joyous revolt from convention, custom, authority, boredom, even sorrow—from everything that would confine the soul of man and hinder its riding free on the air. The Negroes who invented it called their songs the 'Blues.' . . . Jazz was their explosive attempt to cast off the blues and be happy, carefree happy, even in the midst of sordidness and sorrow. . . .*
>
> *Jazz reached the height of its vogue at a time when minds were reacting from the horrors and strain of war. Humanity welcomed it because in its fresh joyousness men found a temporary forgetfulness.*
>
> *Jazz is rejuvenation, a recharging of the batteries of civilization with . . . new vigor. It has come to stay."*

Like jazz, the years just after World War I were to be full of change and unexpected turns. Prosperity, science, and technology led to new ideas and ways of life. Immigrants and Americans from rural areas crowding into the cities were turning the United States into a predominantly urban nation of greater diversity than ever before.

Many Americans had difficulty adjusting to the dramatic changes taking place in these years. On every side they saw threats to traditional beliefs and ways of life. Conflict between the old and the new in America would be as much a feature of the Twenties as were the sounds of jazz.

James Van Der Zee photo of Twenties high style: raccoon coats and roadster; Thomas Hart Benton mural of Twenties; prohibition repeal march; young women arrested for wearing one-piece bathing suits in public; 1920s radio.

Analyzing Primary Sources

American Voices

James A. Rogers. As journalist, correspondent, and author of *Jazz at Home*, Rogers captured in words the spirit of the music that *"ranked with the movie and the dollar as a foremost exponent of Americanism."* During the 1920s jazz flourished throughout the United States and crossed the ocean to Europe.

Ask: According to Rogers, why did jazz become popular? **(made people happy; escape from hardships of reality)** Rogers predicted that jazz "has come to stay." Was he right? Why or why not?

GTV Side 4

Chap. 2, 05098

On the Move: Post-WW I Migration (Movie Segment)

Search and Play:

Section 20-1

Objectives

- ***Answer the Focus Question.***
- *Evaluate the fairness of the Sacco-Vanzetti trial.*
- *Describe the rebirth and growth of the Ku Klux Klan.*
- *Describe the quotas Congress set on immigration.*

Introducing
THE SECTION

Wartime unity did not last when the fighting ceased. New economic problems intensified long existing tensions, leading to domestic turmoil and violence. Review some of the prewar sources of conflict in the United States with students: the bitter history of the labor movement, racial tensions, fear and resentment of immigrants.

Explain that economic problems after the war led to strikes throughout the nation. Fear of communism led many Americans to link strikers with Russian revolutionaries. The revival of the Ku Klux Klan further affected the nation, intensifying racism and nativism.

B · A · C · K · G · R · O · U · N · D

Time Line Illustrations

1. This cartoon pokes fun at the fervor of members of the movement. In the cartoon, a woman is chasing a mouse labeled "Man's Supremacy," and her broom bears the banner "Votes for Women." The woman is saying "Scare *me*, will you?"

2. This 1918 poster shows an idealized woman about to smash a liquor bottle. Less ideal are the images of men, whom society identified as the foremost abusers of alcohol.

3. Marcus Garvey despaired of African Americans' future in racist American society. He urged African Americans to establish black economic independence and eventually to return to Africa to establish their own nation.

4. The Model T was noisy and uncomfortable, but was nearly indestructible. It could pass over rough and muddy roads suitable for horseback riders.

Reduced student page in the Teacher's Edition

CHAPTER TIME LINE

1919-1928

1920 Prohibition begins
Woman suffrage amendment ratified

1919 | 1921 | 1923

1919 Seattle general strike
"Red Summer" and "Red Scare"

1921 First immigration quota law

1922 NAACP supports anti-lynching bill
Claude McKay publishes *Harlem Shadows*
Ozawa v. *U.S.*

1923 Marcus Garvey's "Back to Africa" movement at height
Teapot Dome scandal
Business boom begins

20-1 *Unrest in Postwar America*

Focus: What events in 1919 and the early 1920s led to increased nativism and restrictions on immigration?

In 1919 a cartoon in *Life* magazine featured Uncle Sam speaking to a soldier returned from overseas. "Nothing is too good for you, my boy! What would you like?" he asks. "A job," replies the soldier. Four million ex-soldiers looking for work found the nation in economic distress.

When World War I ended, the government quickly canceled war contracts. Factories struggled to shift back to production of consumer goods. Many factories closed, and workers were laid off. At the same time, the cost of food, housing, and clothing was rising. Demand for goods exceeded supply, sending prices soaring. In 1920 prices were twice as high as in 1914.

Following the sacrifice of war, these economic problems made many Americans bitter. They had done their part, but victory had not brought the secure world they had worked and fought for.

Labor Strikes Raise Fears

The wartime truce between labor and management ended in 1919 as unions called for higher wages to keep up with rising costs. More than 4 million workers walked off their jobs that year. Instead of sympathizing with the workers' demands, however, many people greeted the strikes with suspicion.

In Seattle, when 35,000 shipyard workers went out on strike, other unions in the city decided to show their support in a general strike. Work in the city came nearly to a stop for four days.

5. Lindbergh's 1927 solo flight across the Atlantic caught the imagination of people around the world—he even had a new dance, the Lindy Hop, named after him.

6. Walt Disney's first cartoon character was originally named Steamboat Willie. Within a few years, Disney renamed him Mickey Mouse and added Donald Duck, Pluto, and Minnie Mouse to a growing family of cartoon characters.

1926 Ford Model T sells for $290

1928 First Mickey Mouse cartoon

1924 1926 1928

1924 Immigration Act of 1924

President Calvin Coolidge wins reelection

1925 Scopes trial

1927 Charles Lindbergh's solo nonstop flight across Atlantic

Execution of Sacco and Vanzetti

The Seattle general strike aroused the public's fear of radicals. The fear was intensified by what was going on in Russia. In 1917 the Russian Revolution had been taken over by Bolsheviks, radical communists who abolished religion and private property. The Bolsheviks—called "Reds" after their red flag—urged workers in the rest of the world to overthrow the ruling classes and establish communist governments.

Seattle's mayor, Ole Hanson, warned that the striking unions were tools of the Bolsheviks, bent on destroying the government. The general strike, he said, was aimed at "the overthrow of the industrial system; here first, then everywhere." Hanson called for federal troops to end the walkout.

Charges of Bolshevik control of labor destroyed support for striking steelworkers in Indiana, Illinois, and Pennsylvania, too. Such charges distracted attention from the terrible working conditions in the industry, where a twelve-hour workday and a seven-day work week were common. After four months, the steelworkers gave up the strike.

Anti-union feelings reached a climax with the police strike in Boston. Although no police officers were radicals, Bolsheviks were reported to be in control of the union. Massachusetts Governor Calvin Coolidge broke the strike by calling in state troops. He claimed that the police had no right to form a union in the first place. "There is no right to strike against the public safety by anybody, anywhere, any time," he declared. Coolidge's tough stand would win him the Republican vice-presidential nomination in 1920.

Regardless of whether these or other strikes were inspired by Bolsheviks, by the end of 1919 many Americans identified labor unrest with the threat of communism. Public hostility and, later, increasing prosperity, caused union membership to decline from 5 million to 3.5 million during the 1920s.

Racial Violence

The summer of 1919 also brought friction between races. In areas where African Americans and whites were competing for scarce housing and jobs, tensions exploded into riots. What NAACP secretary James Weldon Johnson called "the Red Summer" ("red" here meant blood) began with anti-black

Developing

THE SECTION

Analyzing Primary Sources

News Article. Read the following excerpt from an article concerning the steel strike of 1919 that was published in the Pittsburgh *Leader*:

"There is no good American reason for the strike. . . . The strike is not between workers and employers, but between revolutionists and America. . . . The strike is merely the diabolical attempt of a few Radicals to seize industry and plant Bolshevism in this country. . . . There is a strong possibility that the Huns had a hand in fomenting the strike, hoping to retard industrial progress in America."

1. According to the writer, who is primarily responsible for the strike? **(radicals)**
2. How does the writer exploit anti-German sentiment left over from World War I? **(suggesting that "Huns" participated in fomenting labor unrest in America)**
3. What other emotionally charged words does the author use? **(revolutionists, diabolical, Bolshevism, fomenting, retard)**
4. What evidence does the writer give to support the statement that the strike is an attempt to plant Bolshevism in America? **(none)**
5. Does the writer show a bias? Explain. **(yes, uses emotionally charged words, presents only one side of the issue; states opinion as fact)**

Limited English Proficiency

Building Vocabulary. In the 1920s the government attempted to discredit those individuals and organizations that called for fundamental reform of the economic and political order. Have students scan the section and list all the terms used to describe these people **(radicals, Communists, Bolsheviks, Reds).** Help them define the terms and discuss the accuracy of their application to Americans in the 1920s.

Writing About History

Point of View. Write on the chalkboard the following passage written by W.E.B. Du Bois in 1924: *"In 1924 as in 1899 I seem to see the problem of the [twentieth] century as the problem of the color line."* Discuss with students the meaning of the color line—the barrier of social, political, and economic restrictions imposed on African Americans or other nonwhites.

Ask students to write an essay in which they agree or disagree with Du Bois's statement, providing supporting evidence. Have students share their ideas in a class discussion.

Multicultural Connections

During the Red Scare the United States government allowed mass deportations of Mexican immigrants, not because they were suspected of being communists, but because they were accused of causing widespread unemployment. The first political movement among Mexican Americans began in 1921 with the formation of *Hijos de América* ("Sons of America") in San Antonio, Texas. Anti-Mexican attitudes and discrimination were intensifying, and repeated anti-Mexican attacks were especially violent in Texas. These attitudes led to congressional hearings in the mid-1920s on limiting Mexican immigration into the United States.

Reduced student page in the Teacher's Edition

riots in South Carolina, then spread to Washington, D.C., and other towns and cities.

The most serious riot occurred in Chicago in late July when whites stoned to death a young black swimmer who had strayed into the white section of a Lake Michigan beach. In the rioting that followed, 38 people were killed and more than 500 injured. During the next two months race riots erupted in Tennessee and Nebraska, and in Elaine, Arkansas, where black tenant farmers had tried to organize a union. In addition, that year eighty-three African Americans, including ten war veterans—some still in uniform—were lynched.

Unlike earlier incidents of white harassment, this time African Americans fought back. One black veteran declared, "We have been through the war and gave up everything, even our lives, and now we are going to stop being beat up."

Bolsheviks and the Red Scare

Many Americans blamed Bolsheviks for the wave of riots and strikes. Other events in 1919 seemed to confirm that Bolsheviks were plotting revolution in the United States.

In April—a time of communist-led uprisings in Germany and Hungary—the post office discovered forty bombs in packages addressed to prominent Americans. One bomb reached its goal, blowing up in the hands of a Georgia senator's maid. In June another bomb destroyed the front of Attorney General A. Mitchell Palmer's home.

Three months later the American Communist party was organized, and widespread fear of a communist revolution triggered a "Red Scare." Soon, all radicals and aliens had become suspect.

Many Americans approved of attacks on socialists, communists, anarchists, and Bolsheviks. In New York City, soldiers stormed the offices of a socialist newspaper and beat up everyone there, male and female. Some cities forced teachers to sign oaths declaring their loyalty to the government of the United States. In New York and Baltimore, teachers lost their jobs for teaching about Soviet Russia.

In the fall of 1919, Attorney General Palmer organized nationwide raids to round up suspected Reds. Nearly 6,000 people, many of them aliens, were arrested. Those who were aliens were deported, many without the benefit of a court hearing. The American citizens were handed over to state authorities. Investigations revealed that few of the people netted in the Palmer raids were Bolsheviks. Still, many of the suspects were held without warrants and denied legal counsel.

The unconstitutional treatment of aliens was not new in the United States. Fears that aliens were threatening the nation's security lay behind the Alien and Sedition Acts of 1798 and the anti-immigration proposals of the Know-Nothing party in the 1840s. However, most Americans recognized that they had more to fear from the suppression of liberty than from radical ideas. When, in January 1920, the New York legislature expelled five legally elected socialists, Americans from all political parties raised an outcry.

Ben Shahn: *Bartolomeo Vanzetti and Nicola Sacco* from the Sacco-Vanzetti series of twenty-three paintings (1931-32)

In 1921 Nicola Sacco and Bartolomeo Vanzetti were convicted of killing a paymaster and guard at a shoe factory and stealing $16,000. Demonstrators in the United States and abroad claimed that the Italian-born anarchists had not received a fair trial.

The dreaded communist revolution never broke out. Bombings tapered off, and strikes and race riots gradually declined. By the summer of 1920, the Red Scare had begun to die down.

The Growth of Nativism

Hostility toward newcomers to the United States was not put so quickly to rest, and the country experienced an upsurge of nativism. Immigrants from southern and eastern Europe, who had flooded the nation beginning in the 1880s, continued to arrive after the war. They were unwelcome competitors in a tight job market. And many Americans still suspected foreigners of being dangerous radicals trying to undermine faith in the American economic and political systems.

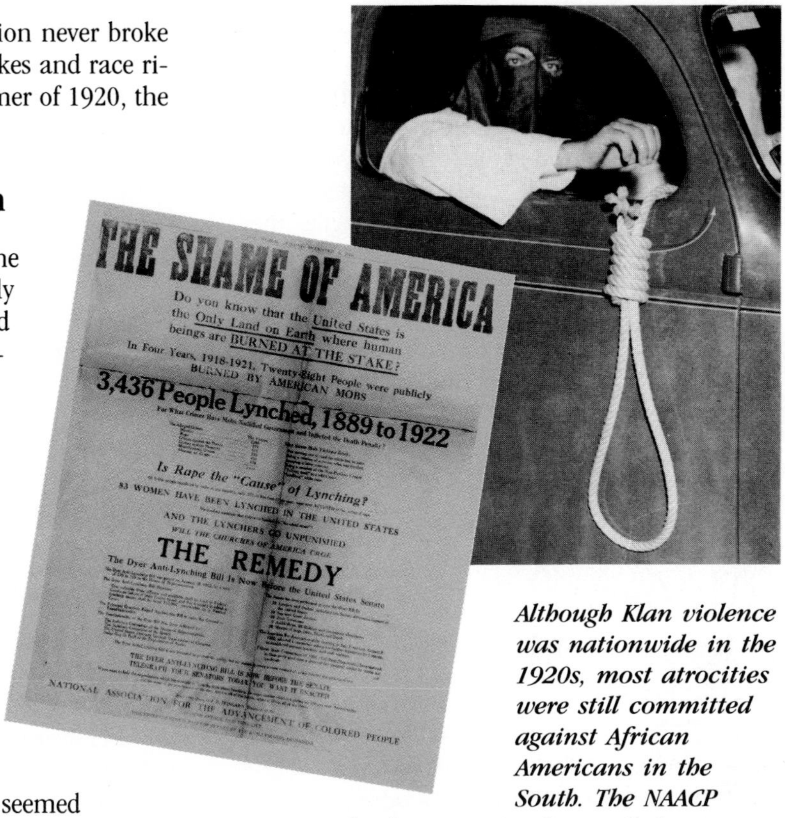

Although Klan violence was nationwide in the 1920s, most atrocities were still committed against African Americans in the South. The NAACP and other organizations called repeatedly for strong federal legislation to stop lynchings of blacks.

The Sacco-Vanzetti trial. A court case in the 1920s seemed to prove that radicalism—and perhaps crime, too—were foreign imports. In May 1920 two Italian-born anarchists, Nicola Sacco and Bartolomeo Vanzetti, were arrested for robbery and murder. The evidence against them was weak, but the two were found guilty and sentenced to death.

Critics of the verdict charged that Sacco and Vanzetti had been convicted for their beliefs and their Italian origin rather than for committing a crime. However, all legal appeals for a new trial failed. Just before Sacco and Vanzetti were executed in 1927, Walter Lippmann, an editor of the *New York World*, wrote:

" The Sacco-Vanzetti case . . . is full of doubt. The fairness of the trial raises doubt. The evidence raises doubt. The inadequate review of the evidence raises doubt. The Governor's inquiry has not appeased these doubts. The report of his Advisory Committee has not settled these doubts. . . . No man, we submit, should be put to death where so much doubt exists. "

The new Ku Klux Klan. The most discouraging symptom of nativism as well as racism in the 1920s was the revival of the Ku Klux Klan. The original Klan, which began in the South after the Civil War, had faded away after Reconstruction.

Reborn in Georgia in 1915, the new Klan was devoted to "100 percent Americanism," which it considered to be America's English, Protestant heritage. In addition to being hostile to African Americans, the Klan also opposed Catholics, Jews, foreigners, and any other individual or group it judged to be un-American or immoral. Membership was restricted to native-born white Protestants.

Appealing to racism and hostility to immigrants, the Klan swelled to 4 million members in the early 1920s and became a political power to be reckoned with. Klan members helped to elect senators from ten states and governors in eleven, including northern and western states such as Oregon, Colorado, Indiana, Oklahoma, and Maine.

Analyzing Primary Sources

Klan Terror. This selection is from "Fritz Rickman" by Melvin Tolson. Read it to students then ask the questions below.

" The scar Fritz Rickman received
The night Ku Klux riders
Drove all the Negroes out of Salem, Missouri,
Still shows on the back of his head.
He remembers the hooded figures in his bedroom,
The curses, threats, and vulgarities,
The cold muzzle of a fifty-four jammed against his temple. "

—From "Fritz Rickman," reprinted from *A Gallery of Harlem Portraits* by Melvin B. Tolson, by permission of the University of Missouri Press. © 1979 by the Curators of the University of Missouri.

1. How does this selection reflect racism? **(describes attacks by whites on African Americans)**
2. Cite examples of terror inflicted by the Klan. **(drove blacks from town, entered their homes, threatened them with guns, inflicted injury, cursed them)**
3. With whom does the poet sympathize? How do you know? **(African Americans; he cites the terror inflicted on them.)**

B · A · C · K · G · R · O · U · N · D

Global Connections

The Immigration Act of 1924 superseded the Gentlemen's Agreement of 1908, made by Japan to limit immigration. The Japanese people were outraged by the new law as well as by state laws limiting the right of the Japanese to own or lease farm land. On July 1, 1924, there were "Hate American" mass meetings in Tokyo.

Multicultural Perspectives

Just as with Chinese and Japanese workers, Mexican workers were met with intolerance and social rejection in the United States. Segregation was practiced in California public schools and in Texas theaters, stores, and public facilities. There were also repeated anti-Mexican attacks, many of them initiated by the Ku Klux Klan or other nativist groups.

Active Learning

Writing Cinquains. Have students write a cinquain, a five-line poem with a structure based on syllable count, on a topic discussed in this section. Write the following example on the board and discuss with students:

Line 1 2-syllable title	Strikers
Line 2 4 syllables that describe title	Hungry, fed up
Line 3 6 syllables that express action	Walkouts, protests, riots
Line 4 8 syllables that express feelings	Anger explodes, despair beckons
Line 5 2 syllables that refer to title	Workers

Chapter Connections

Discussion. Refer students to the Spotlight feature on this page. Have them comment on Will Rogers's attempt to define a "100 percent American." **Ask:** Is his definition of an American applicable today? Why or why not? Students can find out more about Will Rogers in the American Spirit feature on page 614.

Reduced student page in the Teacher's Edition

As the Klan gained public attention, its brutal tactics became hard to conceal. Hooded bands of Klansmen beat, tarred and feathered, burned, shot, and lynched their victims. Watching Klansmen in action in his hometown of Emporia, Kansas, editor William Allen White saw a parallel between their methods and those of the very Bolsheviks they hated. He wrote:

> *"It is a national menace, this Klan. It knows no party, it knows no country. It knows only bigotry, malice, and terror. . . . This Klan is preaching and practicing terror and force. Its only prototype is the Soviet of Russia."*

Spotlight on Americanism

What is a "100 percent American"? In 1925 cowboy humorist Will Rogers, from Oologah in the Indian Territory (now Oklahoma), tried to find out. He wrote:

> *"Here it comes out of the Corral. We got it caught; now it's throwed and Hog Tied; and we will pick the Brands and see what they are. The first thing I find out is there ain't any such animal. This American Animal that I thought I had here is nothing but the big Honest Majority, that you might find in any Country. He is not a Politician, He is not a 100 percent American. He is not any organization, either uplift or downfall. In fact I find he don't belong to anything. He is no decided Political faith or religion. I can't even find out what religious brand is on him. From his earmarks he has never made a speech, and announced that he was An American. He hasn't denounced anything. It looks to me like he is just an Animal that has been going along, believing in right, doing right, tending to his own business, letting the other fellows alone."*

When Indiana Klan leader David C. Stephenson was convicted for rape and murder in 1925, Klan influence began to decline. Membership plummeted. By 1930 fewer than 10,000 Americans still belonged to the organization.

Restricting Immigration

The 1920s saw an end to three centuries of unlimited immigration to the United States. The government had already ended immigration of laborers from China and Japan. The 1917 literacy bill had excluded immigrants who could not read or write.

Now, bowing to pressure from the Klan and from labor unions eager to protect jobs for their members, Congress began to pass laws setting quotas, or limits, on the number of immigrants who could enter the United States. The quotas favored immigration from northern and western Europe while discouraging southern and eastern Europeans and Africans. In 1929 a ceiling of 150,000 was put on the total number of people who could immigrate to the United States.

Asians suffered special discriminatory treatment. In 1922, in the case *Ozawa* v. *U.S.*, the Supreme Court confirmed that Japanese and other Asians could not become citizens because they were "not Caucasian." Two years later, the Immigration Act of 1924 barred immigration by "aliens ineligible to citizenship," meaning Asians. Meanwhile, state laws, notably in California, limited the right of the Japanese to own or lease farm lands. America had been "a dream of hope," one Japanese immigrant wrote in despair, but now it was "a life of tears."

Immigrants from the Americas. In order to ensure an adequate labor force, the government did not apply quotas to people from countries in the Western Hemisphere. Between 1900 and 1930, more than a million Mexicans came to the United States to find work. Most settled in the Southwest, where they were to play a vital role in the economy, building railroads, working mines, and dramatically expanding crop production. With Asian immigration barred and European immigration strictly limited, Mexican labor was essential to the

Connections: Politics

Octaviano A. Larrazolo was born in Chihuahua, Mexico, in 1859. When he was eleven years old he traveled to Arizona and later settled in New Mexico. Larrazolo became governor of New Mexico in 1916, and was later elected to the United States Senate.

Immigration Before and After Quota Laws

	From Northern and Western Europe	From Southern and Eastern Europe and Asia
Average annual number 1907-1914	176,983	685,531
Quotas under act of 1921	198,082	158,367
Quotas under act of 1924	140,999	21,847
Under provisions of 1929	132,323	20,251

Source: *Historical Statistics of the United States*

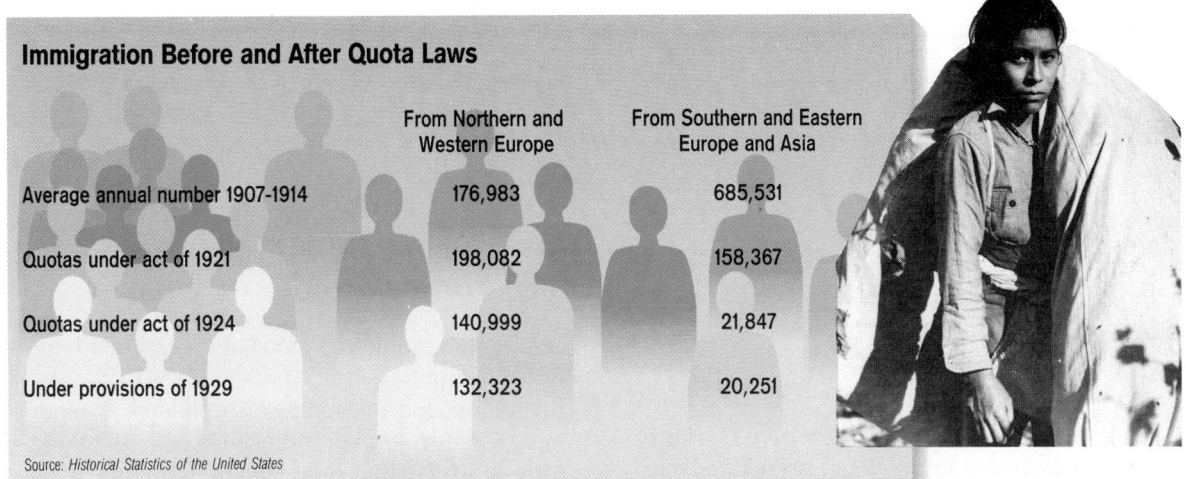

Beginning in the late 1800s, Mexican workers moved northward in response to growing demands for inexpensive labor in the southwestern part of the United States. They earned from fifty cents to two dollars or more a day. This was five to twelve times the usual wage in Mexico.

region's economic development.

Mexican labor became essential in other parts of the country, too. Mexican workers harvested beets in California, Colorado, and Michigan. They also worked in steel mills, packing plants, tanneries, and auto factories in Ohio, Illinois, Michigan, Pennsylvania and the Pacific Northwest. A California farmer said, "Mexicans scatter like clouds. They are all over America."

Section Review

1. Comprehension. What factors contributed to postwar America's fear of aliens?

2. Evaluation. As anarchists, Sacco and Vanzetti wanted to destroy the American system of government. Do you think they had the right to a fair trial under that system? Give reasons for your answer.

3. Analysis. What were some of the major causes of anti-black violence, including race riots and lynchings, during the 1920s?

4. Synthesis. How might the new immigration policy reinforce opposition to immigrants who were not from northern or western Europe?

Linking Past and Present. The immigration laws of the 1920s were the government's first attempt to use quotas to control immigration. Find out how immigration policy has changed since 1929 and describe the impact on patterns of immigration.

Section Review

ANSWERS

1. Mayor Hanson's accusation that the Seattle strike was Bolshevik inspired; the Russian Revolution; strikes blamed on radical immigrants; the Sacco-Vanzetti case; Ku Klux Klan activities; unemployment created fear that aliens would take jobs.
2. Answers may include that under the Constitution everyone has the right to a fair trial.
3. Racism, competition between races for scarce housing and jobs, rebirth of the Ku Klux Klan.
4. It might seem to give government sanction of bias against people from these areas.
Linking Past and Present: There have been fewer restrictions on immigration from particular countries. Most significant waves of immigration have been from Asia and Latin America.

Section 20-2

Objectives

- ***Answer the Focus Question.***
- *Analyze the causes and effects of the transportation boom.*
- *Describe the growth of other new industries.*
- *Analyze the causes of poverty among workers and farmers.*

Introducing

THE SECTION

The 1920s are commonly pictured as a time of prosperity and fun. There is some truth to this picture. Unemployment fell from 4.9 million in 1921 to 801,000 in 1926. However, beneath the surface, this era was not golden. Corruption tainted the federal government, economic policies favored big business interests, and financial gains for Americans were unevenly distributed.

B · A · C · K · G · R · O · U · N · D

Connections: Politics

In the presidential election of 1920, Americans were swayed by the image of Warren G. Harding. One journalist remarked that Harding *"looked more like a president than any president who ever lived."*

Harding's genial manner and handsome appearance made him popular. However, he worried about the job of President. He once said to a secretary, *"John, I can't make a thing out of this tax problem. I listen to one side and they seem right, and then . . . I talk to the other side and they seem just as right."*

Reduced student page in the Teacher's Edition

20-2 *Government and Business*

Focus: What caused business to boom in the 1920s?

"America's present need is not heroics, but healing; not nostrums [cure-alls], but normalcy; . . . not agitation, but adjustment; not surgery, but serenity."

In May 1920 Ohio Senator Warren G. Harding said what his audience wanted to hear. Tired of wartime crusades and postwar problems, Americans yearned for a return to prewar days.

The Election of 1920

In the 1920 presidential election, the first since World War I, the easy-going, likeable Harding became the Republican party's candidate for President. His running mate was Massachusetts Governor Calvin Coolidge, who had won respect for his handling of the Boston police strike. With Harding and Coolidge, the Republicans had merged warmth and strength—a combination that was sure to appeal to the troubled nation.

The Democrats were in disarray. The progressive coalition that had reelected Wilson in 1916 had dissolved over the war. As a result, it took the Democrats forty-four ballots to nominate James M. Cox, the former progressive governor of Ohio. For Vice-President, the party chose Franklin D. Roosevelt, the Assistant Secretary of the Navy.

Cox waged an active campaign, focusing on support for the League of Nations. Harding, campaigning from his front porch, stressed "back to normalcy" and was careful to avoid answering political questions.

There was a new element in this election. After more than seventy years of effort, women finally won the right to vote when the Nineteenth Amendment became law in August 1920. On election day, women joined other voters at the polls to give Harding an overwhelming victory.

Government Under Harding and Coolidge

Harding had caught the mood of the times, a longing for "normalcy." But what did normalcy mean? To Harding and his successor, Coolidge, it represented a return to the pro-business policies of government which had been absent from the White House since the death of McKinley.

Support for business. To deal with the economy, which was sliding into a depression, Harding relied on his Secretary of the Treasury, Andrew W. Mellon, a wealthy banker and aluminum manufacturer. Mellon believed that government could best end the economic decline by meeting the needs of business. And business, Mellon argued, needed less regulation, more protection from foreign competition, and lower taxes.

Harding could not dissolve the Interstate

Warren G. Harding won the presidency with a "back to normalcy" campaign.

Multicultural Perspectives

In the face of growing demands for reform, the Harding and Coolidge administrations began to evaluate the Indian program begun in the late 1880s with the Dawes Act. In 1923 a national advisory group was established to review Indian policy and recommend improvements. In 1924 Congress passed the Snyder Act, declaring all Native Americans to be citizens. (New Mexico, Arizona, and Maine, however, withheld the right to vote until after World War II.) The same year legislation was enacted to protect Pueblo lands. In 1928 an independent study known as the Meriam Report sharply criticized the terrible conditions in health, education, and economic welfare. As a result of government policy, by the 1920s Native Americans had lost nearly two thirds of the land they had owned in 1887.

Commerce Commission, the Federal Trade Commission, and other agencies that had been established to control business. However, he weakened them by appointing commissioners who were opposed to regulation.

Meanwhile, Mellon persuaded Congress to pass the Emergency Tariff Act in 1921 and the Fordney-McCumber Tariff in 1922. These acts raised tariffs on manufactured goods and farm products to the highest levels in the nation's history. Despite opposition, Mellon also convinced Congress to reduce the income taxes paid by the wealthiest Americans. Lower taxes, he argued, would allow the rich to invest more money in businesses, thus creating more jobs and ending the depression.

Mellon's policies seemed to work. By the end of 1922, the depression was over and the nation was entering a period of prosperity.

"Yes, Sir, he's my baby!" sang Big Business to President Coolidge.

Scandals in government. The successes of Harding's administration were soon overshadowed by a series of scandals. After taking office, Harding had appointed many of his friends from Ohio to federal posts. Unfortunately, his "Ohio Gang" often used their positions to line their pockets with bribes and money stolen from government agencies.

The worst corruption involved Albert B. Fall, Secretary of the Interior. Private oil companies paid Fall $400,000 for arranging to lease them two large oil fields, one in Elk Hills, California, and the other at Teapot Dome in Wyoming. After the Teapot Dome scandal was uncovered, Fall was convicted of accepting a bribe. He became the first cabinet officer in the nation's history to go to jail.

Depressed by rumors of his friends' corruption, Harding left Washington on a western speaking tour in June 1923. On August 2 in San Francisco, he suffered a stroke and died.

American Voices

"When I see a provision in this Mellon tax bill which is going to save Mr. Mellon himself $800,000 on his income tax and his brother $600,000 on his, I cannot give it my support."

—Congressman William P. Connery

"Silent Cal." In a Vermont farmhouse on August 3, John Coolidge, a local official, gave the President's oath of office to his son Calvin. The homey touch appealed to the nation. Americans saw in President Coolidge the virtues of small-town New England: common sense, honesty, hard work, and simple living.

A man of few words, Coolidge was nicknamed "Silent Cal." He acted quickly to remove corrupt officials from office. With that housecleaning done, he was content to let business keep the economy booming. As he tersely explained, "The business of America is business."

The business boom helped Coolidge win the presidential election of 1924. Divisions in the Democratic party helped, too. The Democratic candidate, John W. Davis, a lawyer from West Virginia, pulled in only half as many popular votes as Coolidge. Many Democrats voted instead for Senator Robert M. La Follette, the nominee of the new but short-lived Progressive party formed by workers and farmers. La Follette gained almost 5 million

Developing THE SECTION

Limited English Proficiency

Building Vocabulary. Using the quote by Harding on page 534, have students list those terms he used to describe the past and his promise for the future. Help students define the terms and discuss how the terms apply to the past. Then have students note as they read this section how they apply to this period.

Thinking Critically

Evaluation. Harding's administration in the 1920s, like Grant's in the 1860s and 1870s, was plagued by corruption and scandal. Have students review the administrations of both Presidents (text pages 409 and 535).

Ask: What kind of corruption occurred in each administration? **(bribes, stolen money)** Why? **(Appointed officials were greedy, dishonest.)** Are there ways that such corruption can be avoided? Why or why not?

Using the Visuals

Discussion. Refer students to Coolidge's maxim, "The business of America is business" and the cartoon on this page. **Ask:** Does the cartoon support or oppose Coolidge's attitude toward business? Explain. **(supports business; Coolidge playing music for big business to dance to)**

Analyzing Primary Sources

The Automobile Boom. Read to students the following comments made in 1929 about the automobile:

“*We don't spend anything on recreation except for the car. We save every place we can and put the money into the car. It keeps the family together.*”
“*No, sir, we've not got a car. That's why we've got a home.*”
“*I'll go without food before I'll see us give up the car.*”
“*We don't have no fancy clothes when we have the car to pay for. The car is the only pleasure we have.*”

Ask: What place does the car occupy in the lives of the speakers? How did it affect recreation and leisure? How did the arrival of the automobile affect American society?

Connections: Economics

Building Vocabulary. Have students identify and define the two measurements of economic growth that are used in “The Golden Twenties” section on this page. **(*gross national product:* the total dollar value of all services and goods produced in a country in a year; *average annual income:* the total amount of money earned in one year divided by the total number of people)**

Discuss the reality of these figures. Do students think all Americans were prosperous at this time? What do these measurements *not* show about the economy? **(distribution of income; differences in industries, regions)**

Social History

Because of the automobile, people in rural areas were no longer isolated. One interviewer asked a farm woman why she owned a car and not a bathtub. *“You can't go to town in a bathtub,”* she replied.

Reduced student page in the Teacher's Edition

Learning From Art
Auto Assembly Line, 1914

With the aid of a chain hoist, two workers lowered an engine, built on another assembly line, onto the frame of the car.

To see if each assembled gas tank was airtight, a worker filled the tank with compressed air, then put it in a water tank.

Two workers mounted the dashboard, with the steering wheel already in place, then hooked up the steering.

votes—the largest popular vote ever polled by a third-party candidate up to that time.

During the next four years, Coolidge continued the economic program begun under Harding. “Never before, here or anywhere else,” wrote the *Wall Street Journal,* “has a government been so completely fused with business.”

The Golden Twenties

The glow from the business boom led many people to call the decade the “Golden Twenties.” Between 1923 and 1929, industrial production rose more than 30 percent as machines took over jobs once done by hand. Industries also increased productivity by organizing work more efficiently. Efficiency experts, such as Frederick W. Taylor and Lillian Moller Gilbreth, studied every step in the creation of products to eliminate wasted time and materials.

One of the most important measures of economic health is the **gross national product** (GNP), the total dollar value of all final goods and services produced in a country in a year. Between 1922 and 1929, the GNP climbed from $74 billion to $104 billion. During those years the average annual income per person rose more than one third. Thus, more people had money to buy the new consumer goods that industries were producing.

The Transportation Boom

The most revolutionary new product of the time was the automobile. This advance in transportation not only fueled much of the business boom, but it also caused far-reaching changes in the American way of life.

Motor cars had been manufactured in the 1890s, but only the well-to-do could afford them. Then, in the early 1900s Henry Ford revolutionized the industry by designing a dependable car that “any American can afford.” The first Ford Model T came out in 1908, but at a price of $850 it was still too costly. Ford decided to mass produce Model Ts in order to lower the price. “Get the costs down by better management,” he advised. “Get the price down to the buying power.”

With help from an efficiency expert, in 1913 Ford developed an **assembly line,** a system in which a worker stands in one place and performs one task in the process of assembling a product. In Ford's assembly line, conveyors pulled a partly finished car from one workbench to the next until the car was completed. The assembly line cut production time from fourteen to six hours.

By 1926 the price of the Model T had dropped to just $290. By 1930 there were more than 23 mil-

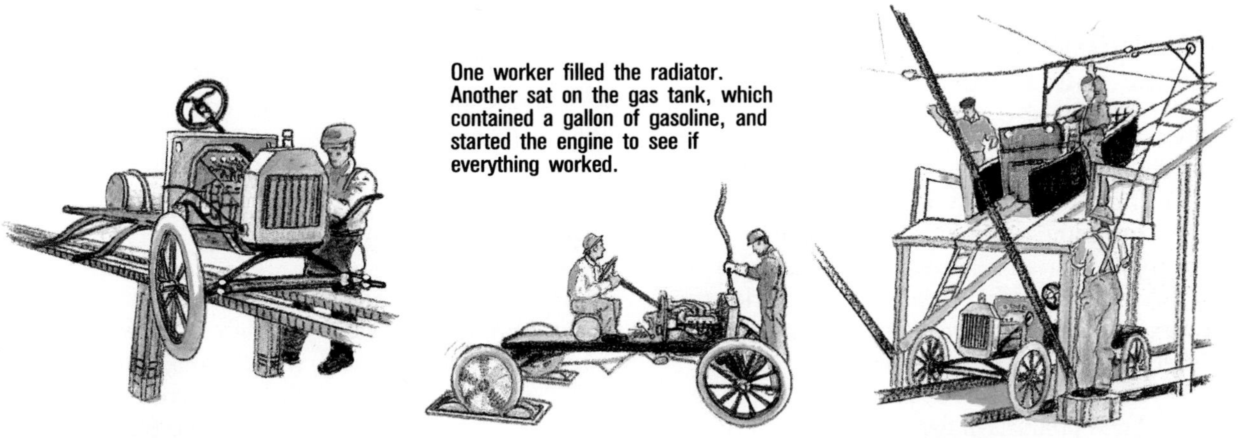

At this assembly point, a worker installed a radiator, brought to the main assembly line by ramp. Wheels with tires, were also installed.

One worker filled the radiator. Another sat on the gas tank, which contained a gallon of gasoline, and started the engine to see if everything worked.

Workers lowered the completed car body onto the chassis, which includes the engine, frame, wheels, and steering mechanism.

lion cars in the country, about one car for every five people. Ford Motor Company, along with General Motors Corporation and Chrysler Corporation, had put America behind the wheel.

Manufacturing motor vehicles, the largest industry in the country in the 1920s, spurred the growth of other industries. Steel, rubber, glass, and upholstery companies expanded production to supply auto bodies, tires, windows, and seat covers. Oil refineries quadrupled their output to meet the demand for gasoline. Highway construction boomed. Gas stations, roadside diners, motels, and suburbs sprouted along the new highways.

The airplane industry. Five years before the Ford Model T was developed, Wilbur and Orville Wright built the first successful airplane and made the world's first flight near Kitty Hawk, North Carolina. The airplane was a military weapon in World War I. In the mid-1920s the government contracted with private airlines to carry mail. Passengers sat on mail sacks.

When Charles A. Lindbergh made the first solo nonstop flight across the Atlantic in 1927, Americans lost their hearts to this shy new hero. Lindbergh's feat gave a great boost to the aviation industry. By 1930 there were thirty-eight domestic and five international airlines in operation in the United States. With the introduction of "coast-to-coast flights" and "comfort facilities" in cabins, airlines changed the way Americans traveled.

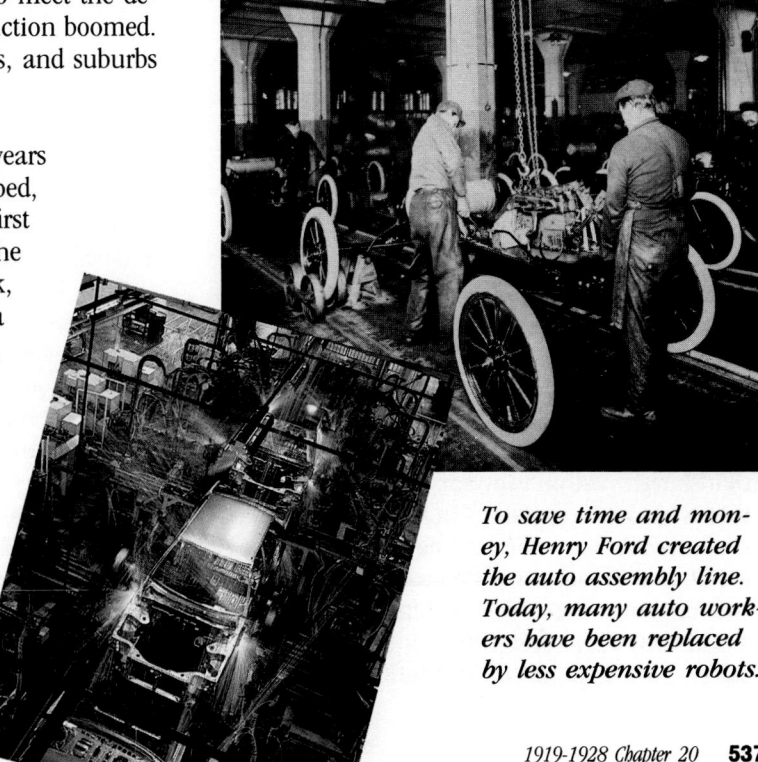

To save time and money, Henry Ford created the auto assembly line. Today, many auto workers have been replaced by less expensive robots.

Limited English Proficiency

Making an Illustrated Flow Chart. Discuss how the rapid growth of the automobile industry spurred the growth of other industries—steel, rubber, glass, highway construction, motels, and so on. Have students work in small groups to draw illustrated flow charts showing the interdependence of these industries.

Active Learning

Designing a Billboard. By 1930 millions of cars traveled thousands of miles of paved roads. On the highways advertisers showed their wares with the new outdoor billboard.

Have students imagine that they are copywriters in a 1920s advertising agency whose main client is the Ford Motor Company. They are to design a billboard advertising the Model T. Students should stress the affordability and convenience of the vehicle.

Writing About History

Research and Report. Many American pilots returned from World War I determined to use their skills in civilian life. Some became airmail carriers or established flying schools or passenger airlines.

Have students research an aviator such as Charles A. Lindbergh, Billy Mitchell, or Katherine Stinson, who tried to enlist as a pilot in World War I, but was refused because she was female.

Active Learning

Cooperative Activity. Have students discuss in small groups "the fantasy of American life" depicted in the entertainment industries of radio and movies. Then have them brainstorm images of both the fantasy of life in the Twenties and the reality of life for the majority of Americans outside the privileged elite.

To illustrate their images, have students use illustrations from contemporary magazines, newspapers, or drawings they have made. Have each group present their images to the class in collage form, depicting the clash between the fantasy and the reality.

Connections: Music

Discussion. Read the following excerpt from a New York newspaper review of 1924:

"The long-cherished dream . . . to see a colored musical comedy [Dixie to Broadway] *successfully playing in the very heart of Broadway is at last a reality. . . . That "art knows no color line" is substantiated by the conquest Miss Mills and her associates are making in a recognized Broadway house."*

Ask: What was the "long-cherished dream"? **(to have an African-American company performing on Broadway.)** In your opinion, does art "know no color line" today? Explain.

Social History

Sporting events also became big business during the Twenties. In baseball the strategy of the game was revolutionized by Babe Ruth's power hitting. Before Ruth, games were characterized by "hit and run" tactics such as bunts and stolen bases. When Ruth was chided about the fact that his $80,000-a-year salary was more than President Hoover's, he reportedly said, *"Well, I had a better year."*

Reduced student page in the Teacher's Edition

Breakthroughs in Other Industries

Other new industries also changed American life. As electric power companies linked regions, the price of electricity declined. By 1929 about two thirds of American homes were wired for electricity. More and more homes could use the new labor-saving appliances—toasters, irons, vacuum cleaners, washing machines, refrigerators. Companies like General Electric and Westinghouse took off.

Developments in chemistry also gave birth to a flock of new products in the 1920s. Chemist George Washington Carver turned surplus crops like sweet potatoes and peanuts into paste, shaving lotion, axle grease, ink, and instant coffee. The synthetics industry, led by Du Pont, used chemicals to make plastics, rayon, and cellophane.

Entertainment industries. Not every new industry turned out practical products. Entertainment became a major industry, too. American interest in movies had begun when Thomas Edison invented a way to make pictures appear to move. The first movie using modern film techniques to tell a story was *The Great Train Robbery,* produced in 1903. By the 1920s millions of Americans were flocking to the movies. In 1927 the first motion picture with electronic sound appeared and, a year later, the first Mickey Mouse cartoon.

Soon every large city and most small towns had theaters, and movies had become the nation's chief entertainment. Moviegoers copied the costumes, manner of speech, and conduct of their favorite stars. But movies did more than just set styles. To a surprising extent they replaced everyday reality with a fantasy image of American life not only for Americans but for people around the world.

Another new influence on millions of Americans was the radio. During the war, radio had been restricted to military use. In 1920 regular commercial broadcasts began at WWJ in Detroit and KDKA in Pittsburgh. Within two years more than 500 local stations were operating. In 1926 local stations were linked to form the first nationwide network, the National Broadcasting Company (NBC).

Throughout the Twenties, families clustered around their radio sets, listening to news reports, play-by-play accounts of baseball games, "live" band music, variety shows, comedies, dramas, and "soap operas." By the 1930s radio was also offering quiz shows, opera, and a weekly drama featuring the Lone Ranger.

Prosperity and Poverty

The 40 percent of American families who made more than $2,000 a year could buy the new products of the 1920s—radios, refrigerators, and automobiles. But the remaining 60 percent were struggling simply to pay for the basic necessities.

For workers in the coal and textile industries, the 1920s were hard times. Soft coal was being replaced by newer forms of energy: gasoline, natural gas, and especially electricity. The textile industry, which had fled New England for the South's cotton fields and cheap labor, faced heavy competition from rayon and other synthetic fabrics.

As old industries withered and new ones blossomed, workers scrambled to take advantage of what were being hailed as boom times. And, as usual, some groups had to struggle harder than others. In 1923, when the average worker made $30 for a 47-hour work week, women workers earned 23 cents per hour less than men. Low wages, however, did not stop women from pouring into factories and offices. By 1930 they made up 25 percent of the labor force.

Throughout the Twenties northern industry was a magnet to poor southern African Americans, especially sharecroppers. But the reality usually fell short of the dream. As in the past, blacks were the the last to be hired, the first to be fired, poorly paid, and barred from most unions.

To A. Philip Randolph, the editor of a magazine for blacks, unions offered African Americans the best hope for a fair wage. In 1925 he organized the Brotherhood of Sleeping Car Porters. Despite defeats, the brotherhood endured. Twelve years later the Pullman Company agreed to recognize the union.

Meanwhile, in a decade when America's business was business, almost 70,000 African Americans went into business for themselves. Among them were engineer Archie A. Alexander, who headed a firm that built bridges, including the Tidal Basin Bridge in Washington, D.C., and

Multicultural Perspectives

Kam Wai, a former migrant worker, said that in the 1920s, *"Chinese were just like Latins are now. You could see them all over the valleys, moving by the season."* After World War II, many Chinese left migrant farm work and were replaced by Mexican and Filipino laborers who continue to work in agriculture today.

Limited English Proficiency

Making a Chart. Have students work in small groups to make charts showing how certain groups like steelworkers, coal miners, farmers, and recent immigrants were affected by economic times in the 1920s. Have them indicate whether the group suffered or prospered and why. **(For example, steel workers prospered because the booming automobile industry relied on steel.)**

Eleven-Cent Cotton

"'Leven-cent cotton, forty-cent meat
How in the world can a poor man eat?
Pray for the sunshine, 'cause it will rain,
Things gettin' worse, drivin' us insane;
Built a nice house, painted it brown;
Lightnin' came along and burnt it down.
No use talkin', any man's beat
With 'leven-cent cotton and forty-cent meat.

'Leven-cent cotton, forty-cent meat,
Keep gettin' thinner 'cause we don't eat;
Tried to raise peas, tried to raise beans;
All we can raise is turnip greens.
No corn in the crib, no chicks in the yard,
No meat in the smokehouse, no tubs full of lard;
No use talkin', any man's beat
With 'leven-cent cotton and forty-cent meat."

—Bob Miller and Emma Dermer

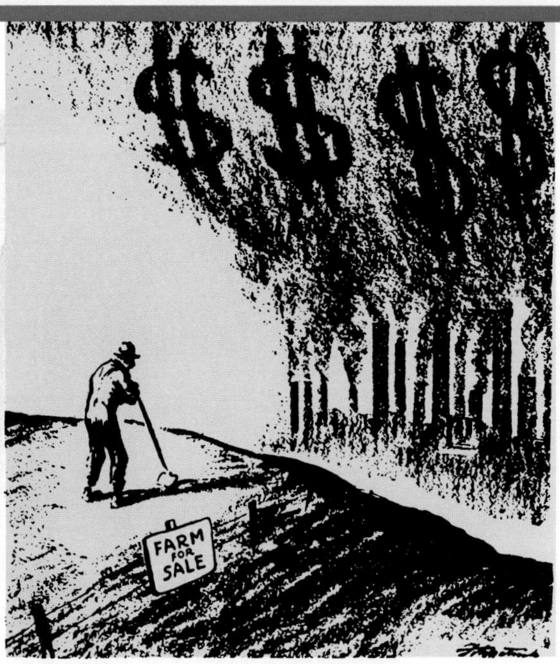

Cartoonist R. D. Fitzpatrick starkly portrayed the slump in agriculture while industry boomed in the Twenties.

inventor Garrett Morgan who produced an automatic traffic signal to cope with Americans' newest headache— traffic jams.

Hard times for farmers. During the war, the American farm economy had boomed, producing food crops for the Allies as well as the home front. Many farmers had borrowed heavily during those good times to buy more land and machinery. After the war, European demand for American farm products declined, but American farmers kept planting large crops, hoping to earn enough money to pay their debts.

Surpluses caused farm prices to collapse. Wheat that had sold for more than two dollars a bushel during the war was selling for sixty-seven cents by 1921. Between 1920 and 1924, more than 100,000 people lost their farms because they could not earn enough to pay their debts.

Hard times for farmers, of course, meant even harder times for farm workers. And among the hardest hit were Mexicans, Mexican Americans, and Asians, who earned the lowest wages and endured the worst health and housing conditions. As early as 1903 Mexican and Japanese sugar beet workers had formed a union and had gone on strike in Oxnard, California, to protest wage cuts.

The growers, with help from the police, crushed union activity among farmworkers, but strikes continued. In 1929 Mexican Americans in Texas formed the League of United Latin American Citizens (LULAC) to protect the economic and political rights of members. Eventually LULAC spread to more than thirty states.

Section Review

1. Identification. Define *gross national product* and *assembly line.*

2. Comprehension. How did the Harding and Coolidge administrations support business?

3. Evaluation. Did prosperity in the 1920s create the vast market for the automobile, or did the auto industry create the economic boom? Give reasons for your answer.

4. Synthesis. How might widespread poverty affect the demand for manufactured goods over time? Give reasons for your answer.

Section Review

ANSWERS

1. Definitions for the following terms are on pages indicated in parentheses; *gross national product* (536), *assembly line* (536).
2. Harding appointed commissioners opposed to regulation, established high tariffs, lowered taxes for wealthy. Coolidge continued these policies.
3. Those arguing auto sales created prosperity can point to the rising GNP after the Model T came down to $290. Those disagreeing can argue the GNP began to rise before then.
4. If people cannot afford to buy goods, demand drops, and so do sales and level of production; leading to layoffs and further economic decline.

GTV Side 4

Chap. 2, Frame 07880

Farm to Factory 1880-1930 (Map)

Search:

Linking Past and Present

Discussion. Refer students to the movie posters on this page. Explain that comedian Charlie Chaplin was famous for his character "the Tramp." Rudolph Valentino was considered to be the most popular and romantic American star of silent movies. In fact, when Valentino died in 1926 at age 31 almost 30,000 women attended his funeral.

Ask: How are characteristics of the movie stars of the 1920s similar to or different from movie stars of today?

Connections: The Arts

The Academy of Motion Picture Arts and Sciences, founded in 1927, presents awards annually for outstanding achievement in filmmaking. The first Academy Award for Best Picture was presented that year to *Wings,* a film about combat in World War I, starring Clara Bow and Buddy Rogers.

Connections: Science and Technology

The carbon microphone, pictured below, was manufactured in 1923 by Western Electric Company. This one was used at station WFLA in Tampa, Florida. The shape of the microphone has changed over the years, because of technical improvements and sometimes to camouflage it for a performer frozen with "mike fright."

First-rate big bands, like Cab Calloway's band, created their own versions of jazz.

Sound-effects experts provided realistic sounds for live radio broadcasts of dramas and comedies.

Jazz composer, musician, and band leader Duke Ellington gained international fame through his records and radio broadcasts.

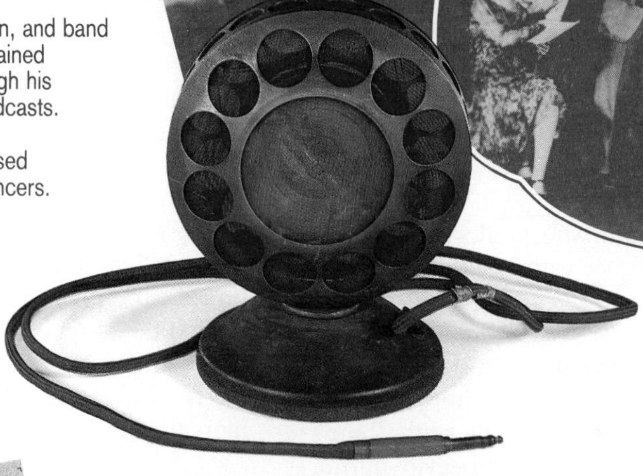

This microphone was used primarily by radio announcers.

Film stars Charlie Chaplin, Rudolph Valentino, and Gilbert Roland helped movie houses in 1925 sell 130 million admission tickets a week.

Multicultural Perspectives

Gilbert Roland, pictured on the previous page, was born Luis Antonio Alonso in Mexico in 1905. When Pancho Villa attacked his hometown of Ciudad Juárez in 1911, the family fled across the Rio Grande to El Paso, Texas. At the age of thirteen, Alonso hopped a freight train to California to become a movie star. He adopted the screen name Gilbert Roland by combining the names of movie stars John Gilbert and Ruth Roland. Over a long acting career, Roland spoke out against discrimination and was known to threaten to walk off a movie set rather than portray a Mexican character stereotypically or unrealistically.

Thinking Critically

Evaluation. The motion picture industry and radio broadcasting expanded rapidly in the 1920s, providing new forms of entertainment for Americans. Discuss with students the economic and social impact that movies and radio have had on life in the United States. Ask students to evaluate the impact of movies and radio in terms of benefits or harm.

THE CREATIVE Spirit

Entertainers

"Drum on your drums, batter on your banjos, sob on the long cool winding saxophones," wrote poet Carl Sandburg in 1920, "Go to it, O jazzmen." African-American musical styles were becoming a vital part of mainstream American music. Ragtime had taken the nation by storm in the late 1800s. Blues music grew in popularity in the early 1900s. In the 1920s the nation went jazz crazy.

During that same decade, new forms of entertainment also became wildly popular in the United States. New dances and dance marathons were the rage—ninety hours was the marathon record in 1923. Radio broadcasting began on a large scale, and movies took their place as Americans' favorite entertainment.

Eager customers across the nation snapped up sheet music and phonograph records of popular songs of the day.

This alto saxophone, now in a museum, belonged to famed musician Herman "Hymie" Schertzer.

Maude Russell and her "Ten Ebony Steppers" dance a number in "Just a Minute," one of many black shows that played on Broadway.

GTV Side 4

Chap. 4, Frame 14483

Getting to Know You: New Ways of Communicating (Movie Segment)

Search and Play:

Section 20-3

Objectives

- ***Answer the Focus Question.***
- *Explain why the 1920s are called the "Jazz Age."*
- *Explain why many Americans disobeyed the Volstead Act.*
- *Describe the controversy surrounding the Scopes trial.*
- *Discuss the roles played in the struggle for African-American rights by the NAACP, Urban League, and Marcus Garvey.*
- *Describe the Harlem Renaissance.*

Introducing

THE SECTION

Jazz appealed to many people. It expressed their desire to break with tradition, to be free from the restraints of the past. Jazz also expressed the mood of the 1920s. Like the shifting melodies of jazz, these years were filled with change.

Have students preview this section by looking at the headings and illustrations. What controversies arose in the 1920s? **(prohibition, Scopes trial, discrimination and violence against African Americans)** Describe the mood of the 1920s. **(rebellious, fun)**

B · A · C · K · G · R · O · U · N · D

Multicultural Perspectives

Jazz was not "invented" in the 1920s. Jazz had long been a part of African-American life in the South. The music traveled to Chicago and New York as African Americans moved north. It was new to, and became very popular among wealthy, young whites during the 1920s.

Reduced student page in the Teacher's Edition

20-3 A Time of Changing Values

Focus: What were the causes and effects of changes in values in the 1920s?

Nothing stood still in the Twenties. Farmers raced to plant, grow, and sell enough to live on. Workers crossed the nation for jobs. Business people rushed to put their newest dreams into production. Meanwhile youth lived faster and harder than Americans had ever lived before. Novelist F. Scott Fitzgerald recorded their way of life:

> *"We were tired of Great Causes. . . . Scarcely had the staider citizens of the republic caught their breath when the wildest of all generations, the generation which had been adolescent during the War, danced into the limelight."*

The recordings of Bessie Smith and King Oliver's Creole Jazz Band popularized the blues and jazz in the 1920s. Both forms of music arose in black communities.

A new age had begun. Fitzgerald called it the Jazz Age. Others would label it the Roaring Twenties, the era of wonderful nonsense, the ballyhoo years, and the aspirin age. During those years the new and old in America would come into sharp conflict.

The Sound of the Jazz Age

Jazz was the music of the 1920s, and its carefree form reflected the attitude of the people who enjoyed it. With roots in African rhythms, American folk songs, gospels, ballads, and ragtime music, jazz crossed wide cultural boundaries. Since jazz music was improvised—with tunes evolving as they were played—no two performances were ever quite alike.

Chapter Connections

Believing that alcohol contributed to crime and poverty, many women played an active role in getting prohibition passed. Their support for the ban on alcohol began in the progressive era, when the Women's Christian Temperance Union was formed (see Chapter 17, page 444).

Carrie Nation, was well-known for her violent efforts to stop the sale of alcoholic beverages. In 1890 Nation began to pray outside saloons. Later she began to smash them, first by throwing stones and other implements, then with hatchets.

Developing

THE SECTION

Active Learning

Writing Dialogue. Many slang words were coined during the 1920s, such as "gatecrasher," "lousy," "blind date," and "crush." Discuss the meanings of these terms, and ask if they are still used today.

In pairs, have students write a brief dialogue between friends, using the following terms and definitions from the Twenties. Have volunteers read their dialogues to the class.

all wet (wrong); *applesauce* (nonsense); *big cheese* (important person); *cake-eater* (ladies' man); *cat's meow* (anything wonderful); *cheeters* (eyeglasses); *copacetic* (excellent); *dogs* (feet); *flat tire* (dull, boring person); *heebie-jeebies* (the jitters); *botsy-totsy* (pleasing); *kisser* (mouth); *sheba* (young woman with sex appeal); *sheik* (young man with sex appeal).

Black musicians in New York's Harlem district dominated the jazz scene: composer Duke Ellington, blues singer Bessie Smith, trumpeter Louis Armstrong. The audience was white as well as black, rich as well as poor. Though mainly young, jazz listeners of all ages shared a common response to the music. "Jazz," said one fan, "is a release of all the suppressed emotions at once, a blowing off of the lid."

"Flaming Youth"

Young Americans, especially on college campuses, looked for excitement during the Twenties. They adopted any style that defied tradition. A wide gap stretched between them and their parents—a gap called the Great War—and it seemed to have swallowed up the prewar world. The most adventurous youth tried to live the words of poet Edna St. Vincent Millay:

> *"My candle burns at both ends;*
> *It will not last the night;*
> *But ah, my foes, and oh, my friends,*
> *It gives a lovely light."*

The title of a novel published in 1923 gave an enduring name to this generation: *Flaming Youth.*

Young women broke with the past by turning themselves into jazzy "flappers." They bobbed, or cut, their hair short and abandoned corsets for short dresses. They rolled their stockings below their knees and wore unfastened, flapping galoshes in place of shoes. They draped themselves with beads and bracelets and carried long cigarette holders and large compacts to hold rouge and lipstick. Young men wore raccoon coats and slicked down their hair to look like film idol Rudolph Valentino, star of *The Sheik.*

Decked out as daring sheiks and flappers, these jazz babies roared off in motor cars to clubs where they defied their parents by smoking cigarettes and drinking illegal beverages.

Prohibition and Evolution

The law against alcohol raised one of the most controversial issues in the 1920s. It was not just that many Americans were disobeying the law, but did the law violate the rights of individuals?

With passage of the Eighteenth Amendment during the war, Congress had made **prohibition**—the ban on the manufacture, sale, or transport of alcoholic drinks—a national goal. Early in 1919 the states ratified the amendment. Congress then passed the Volstead Act to enforce the ban.

Called the "noble experiment," prohibition failed almost from the start. For some

In 1936 Benny Goodman brought together for the first time black and white musicians in the same band: Teddy Wilson on the piano, Lionel Hampton on the vibraharp, and Gene Krupa on drums.

Thinking Critically

Analysis. Many female social reformers supported prohibition. One was Ella A. Boole, president of the National Woman's Christian Temperance Union (WCTU). In her testimony before a subcommittee of the United States Senate she claimed:

"The closing of the open saloon ... has resulted in better national health, children are born under better conditions, homes are better, and the mother is delivered from the fear of a drunken husband.... Savings-banks deposits have increased, and many a man has a bank account today who had none in the days of the saloon."

Ask: According to Boole, what "social evils" had prohibition helped cure? (domestic violence, poor health, poverty) Do you agree?

Connections: Music

Discussion. Many popular songs of the 1920s illustrated the defiance of prohibition:

"Mother's in the kitchen washing out the jugs;
Sister's in the pantry bottling the suds [beer]
Father's in the cellar mixing up the hops.
Johnny's on the front porch watching for the cops."

Discuss attitudes today toward drinking. Have students cite ads, billboards, song lyrics, and so on.

Connections: Language

"Bootleggers" were named for smugglers during the late 1800s who hid whiskey bottles in their boot legs when entering the dry states of Oklahoma and Kansas.

For every gallon of whiskey dumped by the small force of prohibition agents, a hundred gallons reached consumers through bootleggers. Speakeasies, hip flasks, and cocktail parties flourished during this era, and drinking by women increased.

Americans—especially young adults—defying prohibition was a form of rebellion. Others defied the new law because they thought it violated their right to live according to their own personal standards.

In New York alone, 15,000 pubs and bars closed, only to be replaced by an estimated 32,000 "speakeasies," small clubs that sold illegal alcohol. A 1929 guide to the city boldly reported that "five out of every seven cigar stores, lunchrooms, and beauty parlors are 'speaks' selling gin." Illegal liquor was not limited to cities, either. Smuggled in from Canada and Cuba, and from offshore ships, it could be purchased almost everywhere.

By the mid-1920s "bootlegging"—as the traffic in illegal alcohol came to be known—was a $2-billion business. Organized crime came to control the distribution of liquor, and violent gang feuds over territory alarmed the public. Gangster Al Capone, who ran a good part of Chicago, once asked:

"What's Al Capone done, then? He's supplied a legitimate demand. Some call it bootlegging. . . . I call it business. They say I violate the prohibition law. Who doesn't?"

The Federal Prohibition Bureau spent $12 million a year to enforce the Volstead Act. But the 3,000 agents working to stop the flow of liquor were simply outnumbered by the millions who drank it.

By the late 1920s many Americans had decided that prohibition had brought more harm than good. Crime had soared, and enforcement of the law was ineffective. In 1933 the Twenty-first Amendment was adopted, repealing prohibition.

The Scopes trial. Controversy also erupted over the teaching of a theory of evolution introduced by English naturalist Charles Darwin in 1859. According to Darwin, all plants and animals, including human beings, have evolved, or developed gradually, from simpler forms of life. Many Christians and Jews in the United States opposed this theory because it conflicted with their belief in God as the sole guiding force in the universe.

Social History

When the Tennessee legislature passed its law forbidding the teaching of evolution, the American Civil Liberties Union offered to finance the defense of any Tennessee teacher willing to test the law's constitutionality. John Thomas Scopes was the young high school biology teacher who volunteered and taught his students the theory of evolution. The Scopes trial attracted such crowds that the judge, fearing the courtroom would collapse, ordered the trial to be held outdoors.

Thinking Critically

Evaluation. The play *Inherit the Wind* was based on the Scopes trial. Playwrights Jerome Lawrence and Robert E. Lee wrote: "The stage directions set the time [of *Inherit the Wind*] as 'Not too long ago.' It might have been yesterday. It could be tomorrow." **Ask:** What do they mean? Do you agree? Do you believe that fundamentalists or any other group have the right to control what is taught to their children? To the children of others? If not, why? If so, under what circumstances?

When liberal biblical scholars tried to accommodate the idea of evolution and other recent scientific findings, members of some Protestant denominations united to preserve what they considered the basic ideas of Christianity. In 1910 they published a series of pamphlets, called *The Fundamentals,* setting forth basic Christian doctrines that should be accepted without question, including the absolute accuracy of the Bible.

The fundamentalists, as they came to be called, drew their support largely from rural areas, especially in the South. They found a leader in William Jennings Bryan, now in his sixties, but still a powerful and persuasive speaker. Bryan led a crusade to ban the teaching of evolution in the schools on the grounds that it contradicted the biblical story of creation. Governor Miriam "Ma" Ferguson of Texas took direct action herself, ordering the elimination of school textbooks supporting Darwinism. "I am not going to let that kind of rot go into Texas school books," she declared.

In 1925 Tennessee passed a law making it illegal to teach the theory of evolution in public schools. That year John T. Scopes, a high school teacher in Dayton, challenged the law by teaching the theory to his students. He was arrested and put on trial. Thousands poured into Dayton for the trial of Scopes, who was defended by Clarence Darrow, a famous criminal lawyer. Bryan aided the prosecution.

Darrow tried to show that Tennessee's law, in upholding the biblical story of creation and excluding a respected scientific theory, was out of touch with reality. By persistent questioning, he cast doubts on the soundness of Bryan's fundamentalist beliefs. But Bryan refused to yield.

The Darrow-Bryan debate over the truth of the Bible was merely a sideshow, however, for the judge ruled out the use of scientific testimony. The only issue before the court, he declared, was whether or not Scopes had taught evolution. No one denied that he had. Thus Scopes was found guilty and fined $100, although the conviction was later reversed because of a legal error.

The central legal question in the Scopes trial—whether Tennessee's law was constitutional—was not answered until 1968. That year the United States Supreme Court heard a case involving an "anti-evolution law" in Arkansas. The Court declared the law to be unconstitutional because it violated the First Amendment's ban on teaching religious doctrines in the public schools.

Linking Past and Present

Discussion. The controversy over teaching evolution in public schools is not over. There is still a movement to include the "creationist" theory in the classroom. Have students do research to find information in newspapers and books about the ongoing controversy. What do students think? Should both the scientific theory of evolution and the biblical story of creation be presented in the classroom, allowing students to make their own judgments?

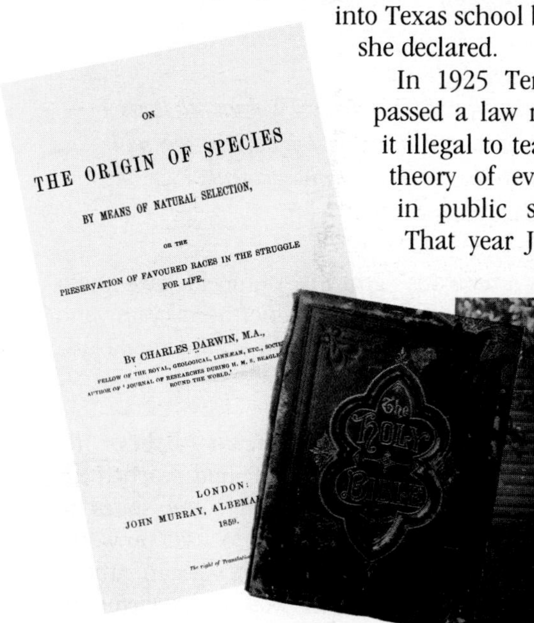

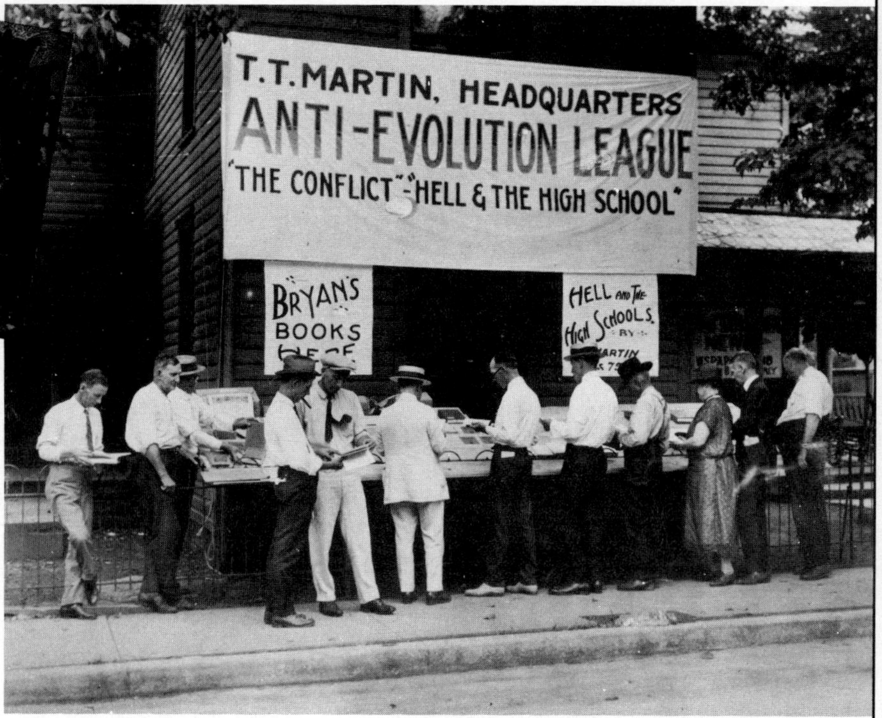

In the evolution controversy, not all theologians were on one side and scientists on the other. The Reverend Harry Emerson Fosdick argued, "Even in the Book of Genesis God made man out of the dust of the earth. . . . Evolution starts no lower."

Multicultural Perspectives

Research and Report. Over the years the NAACP has attempted to better the lives of African Americans through "litigation, legislation, and education." Have students research the many activities of the NAACP in the 1920s. They can use the library or contact a local chapter of the NAACP. Students can present their findings in oral reports to the class.

B · A · C · K · G · R · O · U · N · D

Connections: Literature

In 1931 F. Scott Fitzgerald wrote an article called "Echoes of the Jazz Age." He looked back at the Twenties and remembered the best of the age: "*Sometimes, though, there is a ghostly rumble among the drums, an asthmatic whisper in the trombones that swings me back into the early Twenties . . . and it all seems racy and romantic to us who were young then, because we will never feel quite so intensely about our surroundings any more.*"

"The Lost Generation"

Many of America's writers were critical of traditional American ideas and values, as reflected in prohibition and fundamentalism. As they tried to define the spirit of the Twenties, they showed the ways in which their generation of Americans had separated from the past.

F. Scott Fitzgerald set the tone for the decade in his novel *This Side of Paradise,* published in 1920. Only twenty-four years old at the time, Fitzgerald drew a brilliant picture of the aimlessness of postwar young people, who had embarked on the "greatest, gaudiest spree in history."

The war also numbed characters in the novels of Ernest Hemingway. Hemingway's *The Sun Also Rises* described the lives of American expatriates—Americans who chose to stay in Europe at the war's end. Sickened by the war and its slaughter, they did not feel at home in postwar America, with its glorification of business and wealth. One older expatriate writer, Gertrude Stein, said of Hemingway's generation, "All of you young people who served in the war, you are the lost generation."

F. Scott and Zelda Fitzgerald lived like the aimless, pleasure seeking young people in his early novels.

A New African-American Spirit

African Americans were also trying to find their voice in the 1920s. Between 1910 and 1930, over a million African Americans moved to northern cities in search of economic opportunity and to escape the restrictions of life in the segregated South. The vast movement had begun during the war when northern industries needed workers.

The "Great Migration" and the war, with its emphasis on making the world safe for democracy, raised new hopes among blacks. They looked forward to a future of equal opportunity and equal justice. During the war, W.E.B. DuBois had urged African Americans to "close ranks" and enlist in the war. Now, he wrote to returning soldiers:

> *"We return.*
> *We return from fighting.*
> *We return fighting.*
> *Make way for Democracy! We saved it in France, and by the Great Jehovah, we will save it in the United States of America, or know the reason why."*

African Americans' growing numbers gave them increasing political power in northern cities, and they stepped up their actions to protest racial discrimination and segregation.

Defending African-American rights. By 1919 membership in the NAACP had reached almost 100,000, despite efforts in some states to make it illegal. The organization focused on working through the courts to protect African Americans' civil rights. The NAACP won its first victory in 1915 when the Supreme Court ruled Oklahoma's grandfather clause unconstitutional because it deprived blacks of the vote. During the next decade the Court also ruled that laws upholding segregated housing were unconstitutional. Rulings like these marked the beginning of a long legal struggle that would lead to the Court's decision in 1954 to desegregate schools.

Meanwhile, the NAACP launched a campaign against lynching. A bill to make lynching a federal

Multicultural Perspectives

Marcus Garvey's call for black repatriation was preceded by Paul Cuffe in 1815—he transported thirty-eight blacks to Sierra Leone; Martin Delany in the mid-1800s—his study of the Niger Valley in West Africa included specific recommendations for black repatriation; and Henry McNeal Turner in the late 1800s and early 1900s.

Thinking Critically

Evaluation. Garvey called on African Americans to establish their own homeland in "mother Africa."

Ask: Was Garvey's goal realistic ? Why or why not? (Most African Americans rejected this narrow nationalism.) Do you think that black power advocates today who call for "a nation within a nation," are more practical? Explain.

Black southerners moved north, seeking equality and economic opportunity. Painting by Jacob Lawrence.

The Phillips Collection, Washington, D.C.

One-Way Ticket

"I am fed up
With Jim Crow laws.
People who are cruel
And afraid,
Who lynch and run,
Who are scared of me
And me of them.

I pick up my life
And take it away
On a one-way ticket—
Gone up North,
Gone out West,
Gone!"

—Langston Hughes

offense passed in the House in 1922, but southern senators blocked it in the Senate. Efforts to revive the bill failed all throughout the 1920s and 1930s.

The NAACP had greater political success when it joined with other groups in 1930 to block the Senate's confirmation of Judge John J. Parker to the Supreme Court. As a candidate for governor of North Carolina in 1920, Parker had described suffrage for African Americans as "a source of evil and danger."

While the NAACP stressed civil rights, the National Urban League concentrated on jobs, housing, and health needs of African Americans who had moved to northern cities. Co-founded in 1911 by Eugene K. Jones and George E. Haynes, one of the few black social workers in the nation, the league took as its motto "Not alms but opportunity." A major goal of the league was to open economic doors traditionally closed to blacks. In the 1920s the Urban League organized boycotts of stores that did not hire African Americans.

American Voices

"Garvey is giving my people backbones where they had wishbones."

—anonymous African-American woman

"Black power" and Marcus Garvey. The National Urban League and the NAACP stressed working closely with whites to achieve their goals. William Monroe Trotter, the founder of Boston's *Guardian* newspaper and a member of the Niagara movement, had a different approach, which later came to be called "black power." Trotter believed that African Americans must strive for equality on their own and stress their African, not American, heritage. Whites, he argued, could not be trusted to work for equal opportunity, political rights, and integration for blacks.

Marcus Garvey took Trotter's view even further in the 1920s. Born in Jamaica, Garvey came to New York City where in 1916 he started a "back to Africa" movement. Garvey believed that African Americans' only hope was to have their own homeland in "mother Africa." He asked:

"Where is the black man's government? Where is his king and his kingdom? Where is his president, his country, and his ambassador, his army, his navy, his men of big affairs? . . . I will help to make them."

GTV Side 4

Chap. 2, 06844

The Great Migration 1917 (Map)

Search:

Active Learning

Cooperative Activity. Divide the class into groups of four. Have each group choose a work from the Harlem Renaissance and create a presentation based on it for the class. Each creative activity should involve all members of the group and include some form of visual aids. (For example, groups may perform a piece of music, create a contemporary song or rap from a poem, act out a scene from a book of the period, or make a display of an artist's works.)

Thinking Critically

Evaluation. African Americans have made valuable contributions to music, literature, paintings, scholarship, and industrial invention. **Ask:** In which area do you think they encountered the least discrimination? (entertainment) In which areas do you think they encountered the most? (industry, scholarship) Why? (entertainers less threatening to job security, easier to patronize)

Reduced student page in the Teacher's Edition

Until an African homeland could be established, Garvey called on African Americans to set their own goals and achieve them by their own efforts, renouncing all work with whites. He exalted Africa and all things African. He also established an African Orthodox Church, which portrayed the images of God and Christ as black.

By the early 1920s Garvey's movement had thousands of supporters. Many bought stock in businesses Garvey organized to develop economic independence for African Americans. The movement was dealt a blow in 1925 when Garvey was convicted of mail fraud in connection with the sale of stock in one of his businesses. He was imprisoned and later deported to Jamaica.

Garvey's movement declined, but he had raised a critical issue—whether African Americans should create a separate society or work for an integrated one. He had also inspired many blacks with new pride in their African heritage. As one southern black woman said, "Garvey is giving my people backbones where they had wishbones."

The Harlem Renaissance. Out of new racial consciousness came a cultural movement, centered in the Harlem district of New York City, called the Harlem Renaissance. Every aspect of the arts was affected as artists, playwrights, actors, musicians, composers, and writers created dynamic new works in the 1920s.

THE AMERICAN SPIRIT

Langston Hughes

"The Drums of Life in Harlem"

"The sounds of jazz," Langston Hughes wrote, "are the drums of life in Harlem after dark." Hughes used those sounds to create a vibrant new poetry. When he was twenty-four years old, his first collection of poems, *The Weary Blues,* established his reputation as a major American writer.

Born in Missouri in 1902, Hughes grew up in northern cities, where he found that only the most menial jobs were open to African Americans. He worked as a dishwasher, janitor, porter, busboy. Determined to see the world, he signed on aboard a tramp steamer as a cook's helper and sailed for Africa. There he discovered "the Africa I dreamed about—wild and lovely, the people dark and beautiful." His experiences shaped his poetry and stories.

Hughes was always honest about racial injustice. "My poems are indelicate," he admitted. "So is life." He wrote about the tragedies of the "lower classes because they are the people I know best." He caught "the hurt in their lives, the monotony of their 'jobs,' and the veiled weariness of their songs."

Hughes gave voice to African-American pride and hope. His poem "The Negro Mother" proclaims: "God put a dream like steel in my soul." Again and again he affirmed that dream: "We have tomorrow/Bright before us/Like a flame."

From the 1920s to the 1960s, Hughes wrote poetry as well as novels, stories, plays, essays, history, and newspaper columns. Throughout his long career he remembered the people and music of Harlem in the 1920s: "I can still hear their laughter in my ears, hear the soft slow music, and feel the floor shaking as the dancers dance."

Multicultural Perspectives

Zora Hurston had only $1.50 and a stack of manuscripts to her name when she arrived in New York City in 1925. She had attended Howard University in Washington, D.C., but her real home was Eatonville, Florida.

Eatonville was a self-governing black town with a rich folk culture. Zora often sat on the porch of Joe Clarke's general store, listening to folk tales and to music played on the guitar and mouth harp.

In New York City she became known as a fine writer and extraordinary storyteller, who could entertain people for hours with Eatonville tales. As she came to understand the value of her heritage, she traveled to Eatonville and other southern towns to collect tales, songs, games, sermons, and sayings. The result was *Mules and Men,* the first popular book about black culture by an African-American scholar.

Writing About History

Essay. Have students write essays describing why the 1920s were called the Jazz Age. In their essays, students should explain what made these years unique, including information on music, attitudes of young people, prohibition, and literature.

Zora Neale Hurston

Black writing changed dramatically during this period, as writers dealt openly with their experiences as blacks. Poems in Claude McKay's book *Harlem Shadows* led the way in 1922, expressing defiance in the face of racial violence. McKay wrote: "Like men we'll face the murderous, cowardly pack,/Pressed to the wall, dying, but fighting back."

Another poet, Countee Cullen, celebrated his heritage in *Color* and other collections of poems. James Weldon Johnson wrote *God's Trombones,* celebrating the eloquence of black preachers. Zora Neale Hurston collected tales, songs, and sayings of blacks and published them in *Mules and Men.* Langston Hughes published more than twenty books of poetry and prose.

The Harlem Renaissance was part of the creative energy that flashed across America in the Twenties: writers, musicians, and filmmakers contributed. So did inventors, business people, and ordinary people. New ideas, new products, new forms of transportation and entertainment—all were changing the ways Americans thought and acted.

Section Review

1. **Identification.** Define *prohibition.*

2. **Analysis.** Why can jazz music be seen as a symbol of the 1920s? What characteristics did the music and the decade share?

3. **Comprehension.** Why did so many Americans disobey prohibition?

4. **Evaluation.** In 1928 Oscar De Priest of Chicago became the first black elected to Congress in the North. He told African Americans, "No one can really lead you but one who has been Jim Crowed as you have." Do you agree? Why or Why not?

Connections to Themes

Balancing Unity and Diversity

A nativist view of Americanism dominated thinking in the Twenties. Much of this nativism reflected the beliefs of rural Americans who feared that their way of life was disappearing. In fact, the 1920 census showed that for the first time more Americans were living in cities and large towns than in rural areas.

Rural Americans felt threatened by everything the city stood for—great diversity, fast-paced life, and acceptance of new ideas and technology. They clung to what they considered to be traditional American life, rooted in western- and northern-European ancestry and a strict Protestant faith. Intolerant of different people and customs, rural Americans tended to support prohibition and restrictions on immigration. Four million of them joined the Ku Klux Klan.

In the minds of many Americans, the diversity of immigrants posed the greatest danger to the nation. An immigrant, they believed, was likely to be an anarchist or communist, committed to overthrowing the nation's political and economic systems. A best-selling Klan book declared that "the Negro is not a menace to Americanism in the sense that the Jew or the Roman Catholic is a menace" because Jews and Catholics were subject to "foreign influence."

After World War II, the idea that "foreign influences" were undermining the American way of life would contribute to another, even greater Red Scare, led by Senator Joseph McCarthy.

Section Review

ANSWERS

1. Definition for *prohibition* is on text page 543.
2. As one fan put it, jazz is a "release of suppressed emotions." The decade was marked by fast cars, fast living, fast music, and a shedding of inhibitions.
3. For many, disobeying prohibition was an expression of rebellion. Others believed prohibition a violation of personal rights.
4. Those agreeing with De Priest can argue that no one who has not suffered discrimination can fully understand its injustice and that African Americans have a right to be led by their own. Those disagreeing can point to the role some whites have played in the fight for equality.

Chapter Survey
ANSWERS

Using New Vocabulary

1. (b) Harding wanted to increase GNP through government policies favorable to business.
2. (c) Ford introduced assembly line to reduce cost of manufacturing automobiles.
3. (a) Capone profited from selling bootleg liquor during prohibition.

Reviewing the Chapter

1. (a) Workers lost jobs in peacetime; shortages of goods raised prices; unions went on strike. (b) Americans blamed bolshevism for labor disputes and bombings. (c) Tension resulting from competition for scarce housing and jobs led to anti-black riots.
2. Used to promote nativism and racism, such as electing racist politicians, lynching or beating of African Americans.
3. By lowering taxes, raising tariffs, and reducing regulations on business. Appointment of regulatory commissioners against regulation, passage of highest tariffs on record, reduction of income tax paid by wealthy.
4. Automobiles provided mobility; airplanes speeded up delivery of mail; radio and movies provided new entertainment; refrigerators made housework easier.
5. Farmers produced food surpluses, lost their markets, went into debt. Farm workers were paid very low wages. Coal miners lost jobs as gasoline, natural gas, and electricity replaced coal. Textile workers lost jobs as synthetic fabrics gained in popularity.
6. Prohibition increased crime as people developed illegal channels for obtaining liquor. Alcohol-related crime led to the end of prohibition.
7. State of Tennessee represented biblical view of creation, while Scopes taught scientific theory of evolution; showed emergence of secular culture.
8. NAACP worked for political rights, Urban League worked for jobs and social opportunities; both groups sought integration within American society.

Reduced student page in the Teacher's Edition

Chapter Survey

Using New Vocabulary

Match each numbered vocabulary term with the appropriate person. Then explain the connection between the person and the vocabulary term.

Example: *General strike* could be associated with Ole Hanson because he called in federal troops to end Seattle's general strike in 1919.

1. gross national product	(a) Al Capone
2. assembly line	(b) Warren Harding
3. prohibition	(c) Henry Ford

Reviewing the Chapter

1. Explain how each of the following contributed to unrest in the United States after World War I: (a) economic conditions (b) political ideas from Europe (c) race relations.

2. The phrase "100 percent Americanism" was used during World War I to boost national pride against the Germans. For what purpose was this phrase used after the war?

3. How did Treasury Secretary Mellon plan to improve the economy? What actions of the Harding and Coolidge administrations furthered Mellon's goals?

4. How did technology change life for many Americans during the 1920s? Give at least five examples.

5. Which groups did not share in the prosperity of the 1920s? What factors contributed to their condition?

6. What effect did prohibition have on crime? What effect did crime have on prohibition?

7. Explain how the Scopes trial showed the clash of old and new values in the 1920s.

8. Compare the approaches taken to solve the problems of African Americans by the NAACP, the National Urban League, and Marcus Garvey.

9. Compare the "lost generation" with members of the Harlem Renaissance. What was each group looking for?

Thinking Critically

1. Synthesis. The Palmer raids pitted the right of individuals to free speech against the alleged need of the nation for security. What guidelines would you propose for the Attorney General to follow in investigating people who may pose a threat to the country?

2. Application. How would A. Philip Randolph and Henry Ford each have responded to Coolidge's famous maxim, "The business of America is business"?

3. Evaluation. Many Americans opposed prohibition as a violation of their personal freedom. The consumption of alcohol, they felt, should be an individual decision. Do you agree or disagree? Defend your answer.

Using a Time Line

Match each event in the list below with the correct date on the time line. Write your answers in chronological order, and explain the importance of each event.

(A) *Harlem Shadows* published
(B) Harding elected President
(C) Immigration restricted
(D) Ku Klux Klan revived
(E) Twenty-first Amendment adopted
(F) "Red Summer" occurred
(G) Sacco and Vanzetti executed
(H) Volstead Act passed

1915 — 1919 — 1920 — 1922 — 1927 — 1929 — 1933

History and You

Calvin Coolidge set a precedent by saying that no one had a right to strike against the safety of the public. Yet as labor unions gained strength, public employee groups did strike in the 1960s and 1970s. In 1981 air traffic controllers went on strike nationwide. Find out their goals, President Reagan's response, and the effect of his actions. Do you think public employees, such as police, firefighters, and trash collectors, have the right to strike? Give reasons to support your answer.

Marcus Garvey advocated separatism and return to Africa.

9. The "lost generation" were American writers alienated from traditional American values, seeking to lose themselves in the pursuit of pleasure. Harlem Renaissance writers were looking inward to find the meaning of the black experience in the United States.

Thinking Critically

1. Possible guidelines are: whether a person is committing criminal acts, threatening public safety, or merely expressing ideas.

2. Randolph: insist that the business of America is also "liberty and justice for all" citing inequality of wealth and discrimination. Ford: agree wholeheartedly.

3. Answers may differ depending on which students think more important, individual rights or rooting out a social evil.

Using a Time Line

(D) 1915, **(F) (H)** 1919, **(B)** 1920, **(A)** 1922, **(G)** 1927, **(C)** 1929, **(E)** 1933

History and You

Air traffic controllers wanted to reduce the immense stress of their jobs and improve air safety by shortening their work week. Reagan responded to their walkout by firing all air traffic controllers. The net effect was less experienced people in the control towers, longer work weeks as new people were being trained, and less airport safety. Student opinions will vary.

Applying Social Studies Skills

1. 2.9 percent
2. 67.2 percent
3. Buying power was very weak which hurt the economy.
4. Answers may include that the decade was very prosperous for wealthy, but the majority were not prospering.

Applying Social Studies Skills

Analyzing Bar Graphs

How many Americans shared in the prosperity of the 1920s? Study the graph below, which shows the distribution of income in 1929. Then answer the questions that follow.

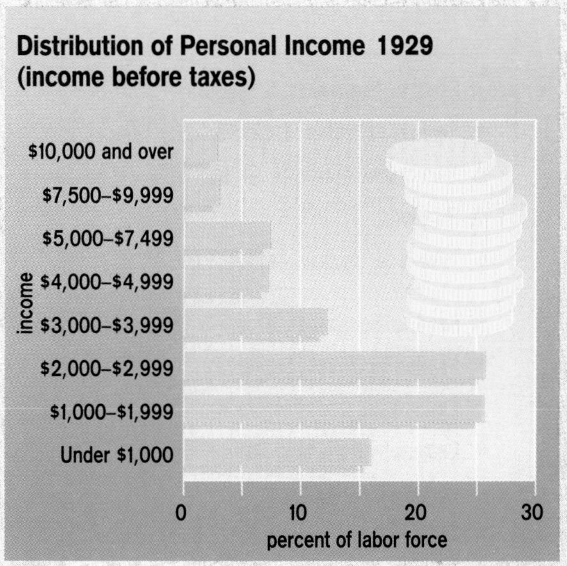

Source: *Historical Statistics of the United States*

1. What percent of the labor force in 1929 had an income of $10,000 or more per year?

2. In 1929 a family needed to earn approximately $3,000 in order to afford the necessities of life. What percent of the labor force had an income of less than that amount?

3. Based on this data, how would you describe the buying power of the majority of Americans in 1929? How might this buying power affect the growth of the economy?

4. Based on this data, do you think that the 1920s were, in fact, prosperous years? Give reasons for your answer.

Writing About Issues

The Issue: *Have recent inventions changed American life for better or for worse?*

> "*Good Luck, Mr. Ford. It will take a hundred years to tell whether you have helped us or hurt us, but you certainly didn't leave us like you found us.*"

Will Rogers was right—Henry Ford's Model T dramatically changed the way that Americans lived. It made Americans more mobile, enabling them to travel quickly and easily from suburban homes to city jobs, and from one end of the country to the other. At the same time, however, the automobile used great amounts of oil, a scarce resource, and polluted the air with toxic emissions.

Most of the inventions that have changed Americans' lives have had both positive and negative effects. In 1987 Robert J. Samuelson, an economist, listed ten inventions that had transformed American life since World War II. His list included television, jet travel, the birth control pill, air conditioning, automatic washers and dryers, antibiotics, and interstate highways.

Choose one of the inventions listed above and decide whether its impact has been mainly positive or mainly negative. Then write a paragraph stating your opinion and giving reasons to support your view. As an alternative assignment, you may write a paragraph about an invention that you think should be added to Samuelson's list. Then give reasons for your opinion.

Chapter 21

From Boom to Bust

Planning Guide

	Student Text	TWE Lesson Plans	Support Materials
SECTION 1	**Section 21–1 (1–2 Days)** **The "Good Times" Roll On,** pp 554–557 Review/Evaluation Section Review, p 557	**Introducing the Chapter:** Understanding Unemployment—Class Activity, 30 minutes, p 551B **Teaching the Main Ideas:** The Hard Sell in the 1920s—Cooperative Activity, one class period, p 551B	★ **Read to Remember,** Section 1 ● **Section Activities,** Section 1 Δ **Readings,** ● **Tests and Quizzes,** Section 1 Quiz
SECTION 2	**Section 21–2 (1 Day)** **The Crash on Wall Street,** pp 558–562 Review/Evaluation Section Review, p 562	**Teaching the Main Ideas:** Stock Market Pamphlets—Cooperative Activity, Homework, 30 minutes in class, p 551C	★ **Read to Remember,** Section 2 ● **Section Activities,** Section 2 Δ **Enrichment Activities,** Section 2 Δ **Readings,** ● **Tests and Quizzes,** Section 2 Quiz
SECTION 3	**Section 21–3 (2–3 Days)** **Years of Suffering,** pp 563–569 The American Spirit: Dorothea Lange, p 567 Connections to Themes: The Search for Opportunity, p 569 Point of View: Impacts of the Depression, pp 570–571 Review/Evaluation Section Review, p 569 Chapter 21 Survey, pp 572–573 Skills, pp 572–573 Using New Vocabulary Thinking Critically Using Geography Applying Social Studies Skills: Analyzing Statistical Tables Applying Thinking Skills: Evaluating Information	**Evaluating Progress:** Diagraming Cause and Effect—Individual Activity, one class period, p 551C **Reinforcement Activity:** A Letter of Despair—Individual Activity, 30 minutes, p 551C **Enrichment Activity:** The Bonus Army on the Big Screen—Cooperative Activity, one class period, p 551C	★ **Read to Remember,** Section 3 ● **Section Activities,** Section 3 Δ **Enrichment Activities,** Section 3 ● **Geography Activities,** Section 3 Δ **Readings,** ● **Tests and Quizzes,** Section 3 Quiz, Chapter 21 Test (Forms A and B) **Additional Resources** ● **Active Learning** Δ **Transparencies and Activity Book** ● **Testing Software** ★ **Chapter Summaries** **Key:** ★ **For Extra Support** ● **For All Students** Δ **For Enrichment**

Overview

The business boom continued during the late 1920s. Consumer confidence, encouraged by advertising, was high. Republicans took credit for the prosperity, and Herbert Hoover easily defeated Democratic candidate Alfred E. Smith in the presidential election of 1928.

Encouraged by the business boom, some people bought stock on margin, speculating that stock prices would continue to rise. However, there were generally unheeded signs that the economy was not as healthy as it appeared. These signs included a huge gap between the rich and poor, large debts owed by companies, weak banks, overproduction of crops and durable goods, and risky foreign loans. In light of these weaknesses, stock prices had risen to unreasonably high levels, and the bubble burst on October 29, 1929.

Most economists agree that the Great Crash did not cause the Great Depression, but neither was the crash merely a reflection of the economy's instability. It dealt a blow to consumer confidence, resulting in a drop in sales. Declining profits soon brought worker layoffs and plant closings. Hoover, a believer in laissez-faire economics, at first hoped that voluntary actions by businesses would bring recovery. Next he looked to local charities before finally supporting limited federal aid through loans. As private and government efforts failed to end the depression, frustrated voters blamed Hoover and gave Franklin D. Roosevelt a resounding victory in the 1932 election.

Activity Objectives

After completing the activities, students should be able to

- demonstrate an understanding of 1920s hard-sell advertising techniques.
- explain how and why stocks were bought on margin.
- describe the impact of the depression on families.
- identify cause-and-effect relationships relating to the stock market crash and the Great Depression.
- describe the social and political significance of the confrontation between the Bonus Army and the government.

Introducing the Chapter

Understanding Unemployment

This class activity requires half a class period.

This activity introduces students to the impact of the Great Depression on families. Before class write on the chalkboard the following questions:

- How would your family's life change if your bank closed and your family's savings were lost?
- How would unemployment affect your family?
- How would your life change if your family could no longer support you?

Begin the activity by telling students that unforeseen circumstances have caused an economic decline in your community and that 25 percent of its residents—including all of the class members' parents—have lost their jobs. Tell students to imagine themselves in this situation and to write responses to the questions. Allow a few minutes for their responses.

Divide the class into groups of four and have them discuss their responses. After about ten minutes of group discussion, reconvene the class.

Ask students to summarize the similarities and differences in their individual responses. Then help them reflect on the feelings generated by unemployment. Encourage them to identify personal qualities that help them deal with difficult times. Then tell the class that Chapter 21 will trace the movement from the boom of the 1920s to the despair and unemployment of the Great Depression.

Teaching the Main Ideas

Section 21-1: The Hard Sell in the 1920s

This cooperative activity requires one class period.

This activity engages students in designing a 1920s-style advertisement. Materials needed include white or colored construction paper, magazines and newspapers for samples and as sources of pictures, colored markers, scissors, and tape.

Before assigning the project, have students look at advertisements in magazines and newspapers. Ask them to identify the ads that catch their eye and analyze the most effective advertising techniques.

Explain to the class that one of the outcomes of the economic boom in the 1920s was the development of much bolder, more stylish, "hard-sell" advertisements in magazines and newspapers. Divide the class into pairs and ask them to review information in Section 21-1 on advertising and credit buying.

After their review, direct pairs to design a 1920s ad for a chain store or a new product. Point out that newspaper and magazine ads in the 1920s were often large drawings or photos with simple slogans. Stress that students' ads must use a hard-sell message and promote easy credit buying.

Display students' completed ads. Compare their finished products to identify commonly used techniques and ideas. Compare students' 1920s ads with present-day ads in style, message, and techniques.

Teaching the Main Ideas

Section 21-2: Stock Market Pamphlets

This cooperative activity may be assigned as homework. Allow about 30 minutes in class the following day to discuss.

In this activity students apply text information about stocks and buying on margin to create an informational pamphlet.

Begin the activity by reviewing the terms *stock, buying on margin, brokerage firm, "bull market,"* and *"bear market."* Tell students that these terms are still important in today's stock market.

Divide the class into groups of four or five. Ask the groups to imagine they represent a brokerage firm that is trying to encourage average citizens to buy stocks. Each group will create a pamphlet informing prospective buyers about stocks and buying on margin. Explain that the pamphlets should foster a "bull" outlook while explaining stocks and using diagrams to illustrate buying on margin. Suggest that each group create a firm name and logo for its pamphlet. The final product can be made by folding a sheet into thirds.

On the assignment's due date, display students' pamphlets. Ask volunteers to describe the major strategies they used to encourage investors.

Reinforcement Activity

Section 21-3: A Letter of Despair

This individual activity requires half a class period or may be assigned as homework.

This activity is designed to help students understand the desperate situation faced by many Americans during the Great Depression.

Begin the activity by challenging students to imagine themselves living at the beginning of the Great Depression, being homeless, without family income, and lacking adequate food and clothing. In this role, they are to write a letter to President Hoover expressing their view on what actions should be taken to relieve the plight of their families.

Encourage students to review Section 21-3 for information on Hoover's laissez-faire philosophy and his attempts to end the depression. Students' letters can criticize or support Hoover's policies, but they should refer specifically to his beliefs and actions.

When their letters are written, call on volunteers to read them. Discuss the persuasive techniques used.

Evaluating Progress

Section 21-3: Diagraming Cause and Effect

This individual activity requires most of a class period or may be assigned as homework.

In this activity students recall events from the entire chapter to construct diagrams illustrating cause-and-effect relationships. Write the following models for cause-and-effect diagrams on the chalkboard.

Single Cause and Effect:	cause → effect
Multiple Causes, Single Effect:	cause cause → effect cause
Single Cause, Multiple Effects:	effect cause → effect effect

Chain Reaction: cause → effect → cause → effect

Illustrate two of the models with the following information:

Multiple Causes	*Single Effect*
Gap between rich and poor Shaky corporate organization Weak banking system	Great Depression

Chain Reaction:

Cause	*Effect*	*Cause*	*Effect*
Holding companies borrow heavily.	Owners don't reinvest in their companies' products.	Product sales decrease.	Workers are laid off.

Direct students to use information in Chapter 21 to create cause-and-effect diagrams. Students should be allowed to use their books since this activity evaluates understanding of relationships rather than recall of events. Require them to construct one illustration for each of the four diagram models.

Students' work should be evaluated on the content of their diagrams and on the accuracy of connections they make.

Enrichment Activity

Section 21-3: The Bonus Army on the Big Screen

This cooperative activity requires one class period.

The activity is designed to underscore issues reflected in the Bonus Army protest and the government's response to it. Working in groups, students create a poster advertising a movie about the Bonus Army. They will need poster paper, markers, and samples of newspaper ads for movies.

Divide the class into groups of three. Explain that each group will be responsible for creating an ad for a movie about the Bonus Army. Point out that they must first create a story line for the movie to outline events it will feature and the message it will convey about American government and society. They must also create an appropriate title and choose actors for major roles.

From their story line, the groups should create a poster-size ad to promote the movie. Allow them time to study local movie ads. Point out pictures of intriguing scenes, catchy phrases or sentences highlighting human-interest aspects of the movie, and effective use of quotations from reviewers.

Display the completed posters and provide time for students to look at their classmates' work. Have them discuss what messages about American society and government the movie might try to convey to an audience.

Bibliography and Audiovisual Material

Teacher Bibliography

Bernstein, Irving. *The Lean Years*. New York: Da Capo Press, 1983.

Galbraith, John K. *The Great Crash of 1929*. Boston: Houghton Mifflin Co., 1988.

Meltzer, Milton. *Dorothea Lange: A Photographer's Life*. New York: Farrar, Straus & Giroux, Inc., 1978.

Sobel, Robert. *The Great Bull Market: Wall Street in the 1920s*. New York: W.W. Norton & Co., 1968.

Terkel, Studs. *Hard Times: An Oral History of the Great Depression in America*. New York: Pantheon Books, 1986.

Wilson, Edmund. *The Twenties: From Notebooks and Diaries of the Period*. New York: Farrar, Straus & Giroux, Inc., 1975.

Student Bibliography

Hellman, Lillian. *Six Plays by Lillian Hellman: The Children's Hour, Days to Come, The Little Foxes, Watch on the Rhine, Another Part of the Forest, The Autumn Garden*. New York: Random House, Inc., 1979.

Lewis, Sinclair. *It Can't Happen Here*. New York: NAL/Dutton, Inc., 1970.

Meltzer, Milton. *Brother, Can You Spare a Dime? The Great Depression, 1929–1933*. New York: New American Library, 1977.

Rawlings, Marjorie. *The Yearling*. New York: Macmillan Children's Group, 1988.

Saroyan, William. *My Name is Aram*. New York: Dell Publishing, 1991.

Steinbeck, John. *Grapes of Wrath*. New York: Viking Penguin, 1989.

Wilder, Thornton. *Our Town: A Play in Three Acts*. New York: HarperCollins Publishers, Inc., 1985.

Films, Videocassettes, and Videodiscs

The Crash of 1929. 60 min. PBS Video, Videocassette.

The Great Depression (1929–1939). 32 min. Guidance Associates. Videocassette.

Just Around The Corner. 52 min. Social Studies School Services. Videocassette.

Witness to History: The Great Depression. 9 min. Guidance Associates. Videocassette.

Filmstrips

Solving Some Social Problems: The Depression and the New Deal. 1 filmstrip, cassette. SVE.

The Great Depression. 2 color filmstrips, 2 cassettes, photocopy master, guide. Educational Enrichment.

Chapter 21

Objectives

- Analyze the causes of the business boom of the 1920s.
- Explain why the economic boom ended.
- Evaluate Herbert Hoover's attempt to end the Great Depression.

Introducing THE CHAPTER

For suggestions on introducing Chapter 21, refer to page 551B in the Teacher's Edition.

Developing THE CHAPTER

For activities and teaching strategies to help you reinforce and enrich chapter content, see pages 551B–551D in the Teacher's Edition.

B · A · C · K · G · R · O · U · N · D

Chapter Opener Illustrations

The cover of *Vanity Fair* magazine depicted the fat, confident market of the 1920s meeting with the thin, hobbled, tattered market of the 1930s. Note the use of stock market quotes for the cutouts.

The headlines in newspapers across the nation conveyed the desperation of the times, using words like "stampede" and "unexpected torrent."

During the Great Depression, some cities became ghost towns of hopelessness. This 1930 painting by Charles Burchfield, called *Rainy Night*, portrays ponderous, decaying buildings on a street in Buffalo, New York. Perhaps Burchfield saw American society in much the same way as he portrayed the buildings in his painting.

American workers swallowed their pride and stood in soup kitchen lines like this one. In the depth of the depression

Reduced student page in the Teacher's Edition

Chapter 21 1928-1932

From Boom to Bust

TWO CENTS

STOCK PRICES SLUMP $14,000,000,000 IN NATION-WIDE STAMPEDE TO UNLOAD; BANKERS TO SUPPORT MARKET TODAY

Sixteen Leading Issues Down $2,893,520,108; Tel. & Tel. and Steel Among Heaviest Losers

PREMIER ISSUES HARD HIT

Unexpected Torrent of Liquidation Again Rocks Markets.

about 25 percent of all American workers had no jobs and no money for food.

Rural poverty in Appalachia contrasts with this ad for a Pierce Arrow automobile, with its emphasis on youth, glamor, and prosperity. Note that the ad says little about the car itself.

American Voices

The 1920s were mainly years of glory for American business leaders. They received praise from writers like Edward E. Purinton, an efficiency expert and a popular lecturer. Purinton and others thought that business leaders offered the best example of art, science, education, and religion in action. They earned the spiritual reward of service to humanity. American business, thought Purinton, could bring about "the salvation of the world."

> *"What is the finest game? Business. The soundest science? Business. The truest art? Business. The fullest education? Business. The fairest opportunity? Business. The cleanest philanthropy? Business. The sanest religion? Business.*
>
> *You may not agree. That is because you judge business by the crude, mean, stupid, false imitation of business. . . .*
>
> *The finest game is business. The rewards are for everybody, and all can win. There are no favorites—Providence always crowns the career of the [person] who is worthy. And in this game there is no 'luck.' . . . The speed and size of your winnings are for you alone to determine; you needn't wait for the other fellow in the game—it is always your move. And your slogan is not 'Down the Other Fellow!' but rather 'Beat Your Own Record!' or 'Do It Better Today!'"*

The glory of business touched humble clerks just beginning their careers. It attracted the best efforts of sales representatives and advertising people. Like the executives, they were all players in "the finest game." The glory lasted as long as business boomed, but faded when business turned into a losing game.

Magazine cover with figures representing the stock market; October 19, 1929 New York Times *headline; Charles Burchfield's "Rainy Night"; soup kitchen line, a sign of urban poverty; rural poverty in Appalachia; a 1920s luxury car ad.*

Analyzing Primary Sources

American Voices

Edward Purinton wrote and lectured on the topics of health, psychology, efficiency, and business. His interest in efficiency is evident by the books he wrote: *Efficient Living* (1915), *Practical Course in Personal Efficiency* (1917), and *Personal Efficiency in Business* (1919).

1. What reasons did Purinton give for others not believing in the glory of business? **(They might equate all business with "bad" businesses.)**

2. What did Purinton mean by "the crude, mean, stupid, false imitation of business"? **(Purinton may have had in mind small, old-fashioned, inefficient, and perhaps unethical businesses.)**

3. Purinton offers a number of strong opinions in his statement. Does he give any facts to support his opinions? **(No)** Do any of his opinions seem questionable to you? **(Answers may include that his assertion that the speed and size of your winnings "are for you alone to determine" may seem naive. Many groups of people did not benefit from the business game.)**

4. What is the historical significance of Purinton's opinions? **(They represent an attitude toward business and business leaders that flourished in the 1920s.)**

Section 21-1

Objectives

- ***Answer the Focus Question.***
- *Contrast the public images and platforms of Hoover and Smith.*
- *Analyze the effect of the business boom of the 1920s on people's standard of living.*

Introducing

THE SECTION

Point out that despite the problems faced by farmers, textile and coal workers, and people facing racial discrimination, the 1920s were largely a prosperous time. Production and employment were high. Prices were stable. By the mid-1920s the United States as a whole was enjoying the highest standard of living the world had ever known.

B · A · C · K · G · R · O · U · N · D

Time Line Illustrations

1. Hoover's 1928 campaign button reflects the freedom from cares that many people felt before the Great Depression.
2. *Life* magazine's cover of March 1929, before the stock market crashed, shows how nearly everyone was interested in the ever-rising prices on the stock market.
3. Dorothea Lange's "White Angel Bread Line," depicting the crushed spirit of the man with the tin cup, contrasts starkly with the 1929 subject of *Life* magazine's cover.
4. Before the stock market crash the American banking system seemed rock solid, like the image of this child's toy bank. Afterwards, many Americans never again trusted financial institutions as they had before.

CHAPTER TIME LINE

1928-1932

1928 **Nov** Herbert Hoover elected President

1928 — 1929 — 1930

1929 **Oct 29** Stock Market Crash

1930 Bread lines begin to appear
Jun Hawley-Smoot Tariff Act passed

21-1 The "Good Times" Roll On

Focus: What contributed to the business boom in the 1920s?

While the nation's factories poured out new products, the Republicans looked on proudly. Their party had encouraged the quick growth of American business, and the economy overflowed with new cars, electric appliances, and hundreds of other items. Businesses turned increasingly to advertisements urging consumers to buy. And buy they did. Many people thought that the business boom would never end.

Hard-Sell Advertising

"Advertising is salesmanship in print," declared one ad writer around the turn of the century. By the 1920s, however, magazine and newspaper ads had been joined by billboards, electric signs, and radio commercials. Even airplanes bore sales messages. Meanwhile, company buildings that had once had only the firm's name carved in stone now blazed brand names and slogans in electric lights. The signposts pointing toward prosperity shone brightly against the night sky.

Radio was just beginning to play a major role in promoting the "American dream." Early radio stations did not allow commercials. Instead, corporations merely sponsored programs, much as they do today on public television and radio. But as consumerism grew, so did commercial messages. By 1928 sponsors were pouring more than $10 million a year into selling by radio. Their messages were direct, loud, and frequent.

5. Peter Arno rendered a cover for *The New Yorker* magazine that caught the spirit of the 1933 inaugural procession. Hoover left office a glum man, while Roosevelt entered the White House full of vigor.

1932 Reconstruction Finance Corporation begins lending money to businesses

May-Jul "Bonus Army" of jobless veterans camps out in Washington, D.C.

Nov Franklin D. Roosevelt elected President

1931

1932

1931 **Sep** Bank closings increase

Newspaper and magazine advertisements also grew bolder. Small, wordy ads gave way to stylish new ones featuring large drawings, photographs, and simple slogans that would stick easily in customers' minds. One typical ad screamed, "Thrift! Thrift! Thrift! Invest in an electric refrigerator." Meanwhile, salespeople also displayed an aggressive "hard sell" approach. Trainees were told to look prospective customers "straight in the eye," giving them little chance to think carefully before buying.

Buying on Credit

While assembly lines mass-produced products and advertising lured consumers, businesses made it easier to buy. Chain stores multiplied rapidly, making goods more easily available. Among the most popular and successful were the department stores, led by Sears Roebuck, Montgomery Ward, and J. C. Penney. Chain pharmacies such as Walgreen and Rexall also spread throughout the cities and suburbs. Meanwhile, Woolworth "five-and-ten-cent" stores crowded out local shops by selling small, useful articles at lower prices.

If the expansion of chain stores meant that consumers could more easily find what they were looking for, brand-name products assured them of quality. A new Ford, for instance, carried with it the company's reputation for building reliable cars.

Although buyers had confidence in the products, many did not have enough cash to pay for them, especially costly ones like cars and electric refrigerators. To pay cash for such "big ticket" items could mean saving for months or years. Eager to move merchandise, sellers increasingly offered **credit**—allowing a buyer to make a cash down payment followed by monthly payments with interest until the cost was paid off.

Credit purchases, a mere blip in total retail sales at the end of World War I, climbed to over $7 billion by 1929. The end of the decade saw 75 percent of the cars and 50 percent of the major appliances being bought with "a dollar down and a dollar forever." Because credit buying made it easier for many Americans to buy products, it helped keep business booming.

Developing

THE SECTION

Thinking Critically

Evaluation. The welfare of American business in the Twenties became dependent on creating consumer demand for new products. People were led to believe that their lives were incomplete without these new products.

Ask: What is materialism, as applied to a society and its values? (excessive concern with material possessions rather than spiritual or intellectual values) Did Americans become more materialistic in the 1920s? Do materialistic values weaken a society, or are they to be regarded as a normal aspect of human society? Is our society too materialistic today? Explain.

Linking Past and Present

Analyzing the Visuals. Refer students to the ads that appear on pages 553 and 557. **Ask:** What can you learn about society of the 1920s from these ads? **(People wanted products, like cars, to be elegant rather than simply useful; wanted time-saving products.)** Are these ads aimed at a particular audience? Explain. **(Probably people who want to gain social prestige by owning latest style; or those who desire more leisure time.)**

Have students bring in ads from current magazines. Discuss what the ads tell about society today.

Writing About History

Campaign Speech. Have students write a campaign speech for Herbert Hoover in which he claims that he is the right person for the office of President and that his opponent, Alfred E. Smith, is not. Party politics should be included in the speech: Republicans, having presided over a long period of economic expansion, have earned the right to continue in office.

Students may consult an encyclopedia or biographical dictionary for more information about the two candidates.

Connections: Politics

Research and Report. Ask students to prepare a report on a social issue that dominated the presidential election of 1928. Possible topics include: Alfred E. Smith's Catholicism, farmers' efforts to block the nomination of Hoover, or Democratic proposals for greater government regulation.

Limited English Proficiency

Using the Visuals. Refer students to the illustrations on this page. Have them cite evidence from the photos that indicates how technology in the 1920s differed from that of the 1990s. (for example, phonograph, cash register, electronics equipment)

Multicultural Perspectives

In 1923 George Sanchez was a teacher in a one-room country school near Albuquerque, New Mexico. He saw that the Mexican-American people of the Southwest had little share in the American dream. To Sanchez, education was both the problem and the cure. In *Forgotten People,* he showed that the schooling Mexican-American children received was not adequate. Their teachers were poorly trained and poorly paid. Often they did not speak Spanish. As a result, the dropout rate of students was alarming. Sanchez hoped to broaden American democracy to include his people. Through good schools, he believed, they could become a true part of the United States while preserving their special heritage. "*Democracy,*" Sanchez said, "*must not only be* thought—*it must be* done."

A Surge of Confidence

Accompanying the business boom was a general sense of progress in other areas. The nation seemed nearer than ever to conquering disease. Typhoid fever and diphtheria were disappearing. Babies born in 1900 had been expected to live forty-seven years on the average. By 1929 life expectancy had risen to fifty-seven years.

Meanwhile, public education had benefited from business success. Children whose parents had steady jobs within industry no longer had to drop out of school to help support their families. In 1900 only about 6 percent of all students had received high-school diplomas. By the late 1920s, more than 25 percent did.

Hoover Elected in 1928

Republicans took credit for the prosperity Americans were experiencing. They asked voters to keep the good times going by supporting their Grand Old Party, or GOP. Most voters did just that. The GOP held the majority of seats in Congress throughout the Twenties. Republican confidence was shaken briefly in the summer of 1927 when President Calvin Coolidge announced, "I do not choose to run for President in 1928." But a strong candidate was in the wings: Herbert C. Hoover.

Born in Iowa, Hoover had worked as an engineer, directing building projects all over the world. He became internationally famous for setting up food relief programs following World War I. These programs saved the lives of thousands of starving people throughout war-ravaged Europe.

With his high stiff collar and neatly parted hair, Hoover was the picture of a responsible business leader. Under President Harding he had run the Department of Commerce. Because of Hoover's involvement in business and a host of civic activities, one reporter jokingly called him "Secretary of Commerce and Under Secretary of everything else."

Hoover believed in laissez-faire economics—letting market forces set wages and prices with no interference by government. He asserted that after the war the Republican party had "restored the government to its position as an umpire instead of a player in the economic game." Most industry leaders agreed and strongly backed his campaign for President.

The Democrats chose as their candidate Alfred E. Smith, the four-time governor of New York. Born in the tenements of New York City, Smith had

In terms of technology, an electronics store of the 1920s could not begin to compare with one today. The basics of business remain the same, however. Stores still attract customers by offering product guarantees and easy credit.

Connections: Religion
Alfred E. Smith lost the presidential election of 1928, partly because he was a Catholic. Not until the election of 1960 did a Roman Catholic succeed in convincing Protestant Americans that he could put aside his religious loyalties in favor of his political and national duties.

Prior to the 1960 election, John F. Kennedy went before a convention of Baptist ministers in Dallas, Texas, to answer questions about his religion. Kennedy assured the ministers that, while he refused to give up his religion to become President, he would elevate his duty as President above his loyalty to Rome.

Among many public appearances in their 1928 campaigns, Herbert Hoover addressed an audience in Long Beach, California, and Al Smith threw out the first ball at a New York Giants game.

worked at several jobs, including selling fish, before entering politics. He had advanced quickly within the New York City Democratic organization, which was nicknamed "Tammany Hall."

Because Smith wore a brown derby hat, spoke with a strong New York accent, and smoked a big cigar, opponents labeled him a shrewd big-city politician who was not to be trusted. Meanwhile, his religion troubled many voters. Despite the nation's growing religious diversity since the 1830s, every President had been a Protestant. Smith was the first Roman Catholic to run for President, a fact that stirred anti-immigrant, nativist hostility.

Voters also had political reasons to doubt Smith. Although his party stood for prohibition, Smith personally hoped for repeal of the Eighteenth Amendment. Furthermore, Smith and the Democrats proposed greater government regulation of business, a view unpopular with Americans enjoying prosperity.

In trying to overcome voters' doubts, Smith faced an uphill battle. His biggest obstacle, though, was the apparent health of the economy, which Hoover credited to "the American system of rugged individualism" and the Republican party. It was hard to argue with success. Hoover won easily, gaining 444 electoral votes to Smith's 87.

Section Review

1. **Identification.** Define *credit.*

2. **Comprehension.** How were the public images of Herbert Hoover and Al Smith different? How were their stands on issues different?

3. **Evaluation.** Do you think advertising had a good or bad effect on the country in the 1920s? Explain.

4. **Synthesis.** How was the standard of living affected by the economy of the 1920s?

Linking Past and Present. Business continued to boom in the 1920s partly because of credit buying. Do such buying practices play too large a role in today's economy? Why or why not?

Analyzing Primary Sources

Campaign Speech. Read to students the following portion of a campaign speech by Hoover in October 1928.

> *"Business progress is dependent on competition. New methods and new ideas are the outgrowth of the spirit of adventure, of individual initiative, and of individual enterprise. Without adventure there is no progress."*

Ask: Where, according to Hoover, does improvement in business come from? **(adventurous individuals who take risks)** Point out the phrase "rugged individualism" on this page, What does it mean, in light of the quotation? **(open competition among individuals in business)** Speculate about the likely role of the federal government when the administration's philosophy is one of rugged individualism. **(limited government)**

Section Review

ANSWERS

1. Definition for the term *credit* is on text page 555.
2. Hoover's image was one of businesslike respectability, Smith's of a big-city politician. Hoover wanted a laissez-faire economy, Smith favored desired government regulation.
3. Advertising increased sales; encouraged people to buy what they perhaps did not need.
4. Business boomed, buying on credit was encouraged, the standard of living rose.
Linking Past and Present: Answers may include the increased number of bankruptcies today, caused in a large part by over-extended credit.

Section 21-2

Objectives

- **Answer the Focus Question.**
- *Explain the practice of buying stocks on margin.*
- *Evaluate whether or not the stock market crash was inevitable.*

Connections: Economics
In the early 1920s the volume of brokers' loans was around $1 billion. By early 1926 it had increased to $2.5 billion. In 1928 brokers' loans reached $4 billion on the first of June, $5 billion on the first of November, and at the end of the year were at $5.7 billion. By September 1929 they had risen to 8 billion.

Reduced student page in the Teacher's Edition

21-2 *The Crash on Wall Street*

Focus: What brought the economic boom to an end?

To Herbert Hoover, the prospects of continued business success raised grand hopes for the entire nation. He declared,

> ❝ *The poorhouse is vanishing from among us. We in America today are nearer to the final triumph over poverty than ever before in the history of the land.* ❞

Hoover's faith was shared by most business leaders and by those Americans who were benefiting from the nation's economic prosperity. With Republicans in power, investors felt confident, and their confidence had already spilled over into the stock market.

The Stock-Buying Spree

During the late 1920s an increasing number of Americans discovered that they could buy not only the products made by a company, but also a part of the company itself. As "partners in U.S. industry," ordinary people could purchase shares of stock in large corporations and receive a portion of a corporation's profits in the form of dividends.

Certificates of stock ownership were traded in several cities, but the chief market was the New York Stock Exchange. Founded in 1792, the Exchange was at the heart of Wall Street, the city's financial district.

Like merchants who set up chain stores, large New York brokerage firms opened branch offices. Now investors throughout the country found it easy to buy stock. Some brokers' offices looked like the barrooms of preprohibition days.

People entered through swinging doors and sat in mahogany chairs. While the latest stock prices were read off a ticker tape and posted on a board, brokers and clients swapped stories. By 1929, nearly 1,200 brokerage offices were scattered across the country.

Buying on margin. The 1920s are sometimes portrayed as a decade when everybody was buying stock. Actually, only about one family in twenty put money in the market. Most Americans could not afford to buy stock. Of those who could, many simply chose not to.

Among the people who bought stock, some made full payment in cash and held their shares as a long-term investment. However, a growing number of investors were eager to speculate, or take risks in the hope of making a quick profit.

Buyers willing to speculate often bought shares on margin, which was much like buying consumer goods on credit. A speculator got ownership of a company's stock without having to pay the full purchase price immediately. Instead, the speculator paid a cash down payment, or "margin," to a broker, who lent the balance of the cost to the purchaser at a high interest rate. Stockbrokers borrowed money from banks to cover these loans.

The speculator bet that the value of the stock would increase quickly. If the price did rise, the speculator sold the stock, paid off the loan, and reaped the benefit of selling the stock for more than its cost. If, on the other

A broker reads stock prices that are printed out on a ticker tape after being transmitted by telegraph.

Introducing

THE SECTION

Preview the section with students to find headings that indicate warning signs in the 1920s that an economic disaster was about to occur in the 1930s (for example, "A weak banking system," "Overproduction").

Have students state the ingredients of a healthy national economy (constant flow of goods—resulting in increased jobs, profits, and production) and encourage them to keep these in mind as they study this section.

Developing

THE SECTION

Chapter Connections

Discussion. Refer students to Hoover's words and the paragraph that follows. Based on Chapter 20, ask them which Americans benefited from the nation's prosperity and which did not. (Owners and investors in growing industries benefited; farmers, coal and textile workers, and people facing racial discrimination did not.)

Brokers thrived on the stock-buying spree. A March 1929 cartoon refers to the Federal Reserve's effort to make loans for stock purchases harder to get.

hand, the value of the stock dropped, the speculator sold the stock at a loss and had to pay back the balance of the loan out of personal funds. By the end of 1928, the risk for speculators looked reasonable because stock prices had been rising steadily for years and seemed likely to keep going up.

Dreams of wealth. In Wall Street's vocabulary a "bull" is someone who expects the market to rise; a "bear" is someone who expects it to fall. By spring of 1928 the bulls were dominating Wall Street. Radio Corporation of America (RCA), for example, was selling at just under $95 per share on March 3. By March 20, RCA shares were at $178.

Every surge in stock prices was described in glowing news stories. The public read about waiters and window washers who made fortunes in stocks. Lured by the promise of easy profits, people called, wrote, or visited brokers to buy shares on margin.

Speculators were encouraged by business leaders like John J. Raskob, who wrote "Everybody Ought to Be Rich," an article telling how investing as little as fifteen dollars a week in stocks could produce a fortune. Throughout the summer of 1929, speculators continued to dream of wealth. As industrialist Arthur Robertson later recalled,

> *"In 1929, it was a gambling casino with loaded dice. The few sharks taking advantage of the multitude of suckers. . . . I saw shoeshine boys buying $50,000 worth of stock with $500 down. Everything was bought on hope."*

Most speculators, however, did not see stocks as a gamble. It was confidence — not the chance to buy on margin — that spurred the buying spree. As economist Charles Dice noted in 1929, the people trusted big business:

> *"The common folks believe in their leaders. We no longer look upon the captains of industry as magnified crooks. Have we not heard their voices over the radio? Are we not familiar with their thoughts, ambitions, and ideals as they have expressed them to us almost as a man talks to a friend?"*

Thinking Critically

Analysis. An economist has referred to the market speculation beginning in 1928 and through most of 1929 as a "mass escape into make-believe." What did he mean? What was unreal about it?

Refer students to the comments of industrialist Arthur Robertson on this page. To what did he compare the speculation of 1929? Explain the comparison. (gambling casino with loaded dice)

Using the Visuals

Analyzing a Political Cartoon. Refer students to the cartoon on this page **Ask:** Who do each of the figures represent? **(The fat man sitting down represents American stock speculators. The waiter represents the Federal Reserve Board)** What is the waiter doing? Why? **(taking away the credit option for purchasing stocks; such a practice was too risky)** What is the cartoonist's point of view? How do you know? **(Stock speculation is a risky business that must be stopped, as evidenced by the gluttonous diner, tray full of food, indignant waiter.)**

Limited English Proficiency

Making a Graphic Organizer. Help students make a graphic organizer to show causes of the Great Depression. First, draw a circle and inside it write the words "Great Depression." Radiating out from this center circle, draw six lines, each connecting to a smaller circle. Label five of the small circles with one of the weaknesses of the American economy listed on pages 560–561. Label the sixth circle "The Great Crash." Discuss how the economy's weaknesses and the stock market crash were linked to the Great Depression.

Global Connections

In parts of Europe, economic depression began long before it did in the United States. The people of Germany, Austria, Italy, and Poland experienced devastating poverty. This was due largely to the huge demands made on their economies during World War I, to the loss of millions of lives during the war, and to huge reparations costs.

Germany and Austria attempted to lift their economies by printing new money, but this caused runaway inflation. Civilian industries in these countries had nearly disappeared because of wartime needs. There were few industrial jobs in war-ravaged Europe during the 1920s, while many Americans enjoyed "prosperity."

Reduced student page in the Teacher's Edition

Unseen Warning Signs

Big business was indeed confident, as were government leaders. Few people noticed signs that the economy was not as sound as it appeared. In more recent years, however, economists have suggested that the economy of the 1920s had some serious weaknesses. Among these were a great gap between the rich and other Americans, bad corporate organization, a weak banking system, overproduction of factory goods and farm produce, and risky foreign loans.

The gap between the rich and the rest. Very little of the profits from business trickled down to factory or farm workers in the form of higher wages. Nor were they passed on to consumers through lower prices. Most factory workers could not afford to buy the cars, appliances, and other luxury products they themselves were making.

One third of all personal income was earned by the wealthiest 5 percent of the population. However, long-term business growth could not rest on the rich, for even the wealthy set limits on how many cars, appliances, and other major consumer products they were willing to buy. Meanwhile, by investing heavily in stocks, they raised stock prices to unreasonable levels.

A shaky corporate organization. The business world was dominated by holding companies, which had borrowed heavily to buy up smaller companies. The holding companies used most of the profits from companies they owned to help pay off their huge loans. They had little money left to reinvest in the companies that produced the products or to increase the wages of workers.

Another problem was that dishonest business dealings, most of which were effectively hidden from the public, were widespread. Rather than making sound investments toward the long-term growth of their companies, many business leaders were simply looking for quick profits, mainly by speculating in stocks.

A weak banking system. Banks in the Twenties had almost complete freedom to invest depositors' funds as they chose. Those that made risky investments quickly went out of business. Since accounts were not insured by the government, when one bank went under depositors at other banks might easily panic and rush to withdraw their savings.

BROOKLYN DAILY EAGLE
And Complete Long Island News
WALL ST. IN PANIC AS STOCKS CRASH
Attempt Made to Kill Italy's Crown Prince
ASSASSIN CAUGHT IN BRUSSELS MOB; PRINCE UNHURT
Hollywood Fire Destroys Films Worth Millions
FEAR 52 PERISHED IN LAKE MICHIGAN; FERRY IS MISSING
PIECE OF PLANE LIKE DITEMAN'S IS FOUND AT SEA
High Duty Group Gave $700,000 to Coolidge Drive
STOCKS CRASH IN RUSH TO SELL; BILLIONS LOST

Normally, banks earn most of their profits by lending to businesses. But in the Twenties they increasingly found themselves lending to stockbrokers. The brokers' ability to repay loans depended on rising stock values. Thus, many banks relied heavily on the stock market.

Overproduction. Another unseen warning sign was that soaring stock prices were out of line with the actual growth in business. By early 1929 sales were leveling off, partly because many products, such as cars and stoves, were **durable goods**—products made to last a long time. Also, buyers saddled with monthly payments for a stove or a car rarely could afford another large item. As a result, factory surpluses grew, causing industries to cut back production and lay off workers.

Meanwhile, throughout the decade farmers had been plagued by crop surpluses and low prices. Many wanted the government to buy crops to keep prices up. Hoover rejected the idea of government interference, declaring:

"My fundamental concept of agriculture is one controlled by its own members, organized to fight its own economic battles and to determine its own destinies."

Risky foreign loans. The United States government had loaned some $10 billion to its allies during World War I and in the years that followed. The Allies had agreed to repay the loans gradually, over more than sixty years. Germany, meanwhile, was obliged to pay reparations to the Allies for war damages.

To repay their debts, European governments needed income. Since tariffs limited the money they could earn by selling products to the United States, they looked to private American investors for more than $12 billion in loans. These loans helped support the American economy because they made it possible for nations to buy American goods. However, by making loans to foreign countries facing economic hardship, American investors were taking a risk that the loans might not be repaid.

The Stock Market Crash

A few experts did notice warning signs and thought speculators were too optimistic. One, Edwin Lefevre, said "the American imagination has been responsible for the excesses witnessed in every bull market. We cannot be the most imaginative people on earth and not pay for it." On September 5, 1929, economist Roger Babson warned:

"Sooner or later a crash is coming, and it may be terrific. Factories will shut down . . . men will be thrown out of work . . . the vicious circle will get in full swing and the result will be a serious business depression."

Babson and others had predicted doom before, but on this day the market seemed to pay attention. It fell sharply in what became known as the "Babson Break." For the rest of the month and into October, stock prices were uneven but mostly down. Then, on the morning of October 24—"Black Thursday"—prices dropped rapidly. One newspaper reported that "fear struck the big speculators and little ones, big investors and little ones. . . . Losses were tremendous."

Hundreds of stunned investors gathered across from the New York Stock Exchange after the sharp drop in stock prices on October 24, 1929 (far left). Almost half a century later, on October 19, 1987, Wall Street experienced another crash—the biggest one-day drop in its history. As in 1929, the bubble burst after stock prices had risen to unreasonably high levels.

Writing About History

Letter. Have students imagine they are a stock broker before the crash and write a letter to a potential customer describing the advantages of buying stocks on margin. Have them use a "hard-sell" format, giving examples of people who made a large amount of money buying stocks on margin.

Then have students write a second letter after the stock market crash, explaining that the customer must cover his or her losses.

Backyard History

Interview. Some students may have grandparents who remember the stock market crash of 1929. Have these students talk to or write to their grandparents, asking them to tell their experiences during the tense days of the 1929 stock market crash. Have students take notes of the interview and share them with the class.

Linking Past and Present

Research. In 1987 the stock market experienced another crash. Ask students to research newspaper or magazine articles about the crash of 1987. Have them compare the eras of the 1987 and 1929 stock market crashes. Why didn't a depression come about after the 1987 crash? **(Both decades marked by booming stock market with record-setting prices, heavy borrowing—corporate raiders in 1987 borrowed up to 90 percent of purchase price of stocks. Safeguards from federal regulation make a depression today less likely.)**

Linking Past and Present.

Research. Have students research the Dow Jones Average to find out what it is and how it is reported in the news each day. Have students graph the Dow Jones Average for a week and find out whether it is a bull or a bear market.

Chapter Connections

Discussion. Review with students the Panic of 1837 discussed in Chapter 9, page 232. Ask them to compare the events that led to the depression of 1837 and the Great Depression. **(Both involved wild speculation, one in land, the other in stocks; soaring then plunging prices; business bankruptcies; bank closures; factory closings; unemployment.)**

Section Review

ANSWERS

1. Definition for the term *durable goods* is on text page 561.
2. People were encouraged to buy shares of corporations which made them, in a sense, partners.
3. Students should recognize that buying on margin enabled investors to buy stock they could not have otherwise afforded, but this practice helped weaken the shaky American economy.
4. Answers may include that government could have recognized warning signs and exercised control over the economy. However, the country was in no mood to heed warning signs or allow government to exercise control.

Connections: Economics

For an example of a rise in stock prices, consider the RCA Corporation. Between 1928 and 1929 the price of one share rose from $85 to $505. For an example of the devastating decline in stock prices, consider General Electric (GE). On September 6, 1929, the price of one share was $396. A few weeks after the crash it had dropped to $168.

Reduced student page in the Teacher's Edition

Spotlight on the Stock Panic

Early on October 24, a young shoeshiner named Pat Bologna walked into a brokerage office. Having invested his entire savings of $5,000 in stocks, he was looking for help in getting his money out of the market. He later described the frantic scene that convinced him no help was coming:

> *"Everybody is shouting. They're all trying to reach the glass booth where the clerks are. Everybody wants to sell out. The boy at the quotation board is running scared. He can't keep up with the speed of the way the stocks are dropping. . . . The guy who runs the board is standing at the back of the booth, on the telephone. I can't hear what he's saying. But a guy near me shouts, 'The son-of-a-gun has sold me out!'"*

To try to stop the panic selling, a group of bankers placed large orders for more than a dozen different stocks. The market promptly rebounded, making up some of the morning's losses. It held steady on Friday, and over the weekend the mood on Wall Street was hopeful. Many went to bed Sunday night with a recent *Wall Street Journal* "Thought for the Day" on their minds. The *Journal* had quoted Mark Twain: "Don't part with your illusions. When they are gone you may still exist, but you have ceased to live."

On Monday, however, the hopeful illusions vanished. Stock prices dropped sharply, and this time the bankers did not try to save the day. They were too busy trying to save themselves—selling their own stocks for whatever they could. Tuesday, October 29, was far worse. The *New York Times* reported that "stock prices virtually collapsed, . . . swept downward with gigantic losses in the most disastrous trading day in the stock market's history." Investor Sidney Weinberg recalled the crash's impact on Wall Street:

> *"It was like a thunderclap. Everybody was stunned. The Street had general confusion. They didn't understand it any more than anybody else. They thought something would be announced."*

Tuesday's disaster was followed by words of assurance from John D. Rockefeller. "Believing that fundamental conditions of the country are sound," he declared, "my son and I have for some days been purchasing sound common stocks." The market rallied for a few days but then sank again, reaching its low for the year. Investors and owners of companies lost billions. A few even committed suicide. Industrialist Arthur Robertson recalled:

> *"A cigar stock at the time was selling for $115 a share. The market collapsed. I got a call from the company president. Could I loan him $200 million? I refused, because at the time I had to protect my own fences, including those of my closest friends. His $115 stock dropped to $2 and he jumped out of the window of his Wall Street office. . . . On Wall Street the people walked around like zombies. . . . You saw people who yesterday rode around in Cadillacs lucky now to have carfare. One of my friends said to me, 'If things keep on as they are, we'll all have to go begging.' I asked, 'Who from?'"*

As the market plunged, so did the decade's high hopes for economic security. By the end of 1929, the dream of glorious opportunities just around the corner was dead.

Section Review

1. Identification. Define *durable goods.*

2. Comprehension. Explain how investors became "partners in U.S. industry."

3. Evaluation. Do you think that buying on margin was a good idea for most people? Explain.

4. Evaluation. Do you think the stock market crash could have been avoided? Why or why not?

Social History
The tragedy of the first years of the depression was that millions suffered for lack of food, clothing, and shelter, while the nation's farms and industries were faced with large surpluses. On this fact, Will Rogers commented, *"We are the first nation to starve to death in a storehouse that's overfilled with everything we want."*

21-3 Years of Suffering

Focus: Why did Hoover's policies fail to end the Great Depression?

After the crash, Wall Street was a place of shattered fortunes and ruined reputations. Bankers and stockbrokers who had once appeared to be business geniuses now seemed powerless and confused. Americans looking for economic leadership turned away from Wall Street and toward the White House.

In his public statements, President Hoover tried to be reassuring. Although the crash had wiped out billions in paper profits, it had not brought factory production to a halt. Furthermore, since 95 percent of all families had stayed out of the stock market, the average American did not lose a cent in the crash. What, then, plunged the country into more than a decade of economic downturn that became known as the Great Depression?

From the Great Crash to the Great Depression

Economists do not agree on what caused the lengthy period of mass unemployment, business failings, and plummeting prices that marked much of the 1930s. Furthermore, the relationship between the Great Crash of 1929 and the Great Depression that followed has remained a point of debate. Most modern economists do agree that the crash did not cause the depression. They believe that the economy's weaknesses would have brought about a depression even without the crash. Indeed, there is an old Wall Street saying: The stock market is like a dog's tail—its wagging is controlled by the economy.

Most economists also agree, however, that the crash had serious effects. It pushed an already shaky economy over the edge because it affected the very people who had previously had the most spending power and the largest savings. As those people cut their spending and looked for income to make up for their losses, their actions affected both the nation's and the world's economies.

Businesses soon saw their sales drop as Americans grew afraid to spend money and had trouble getting loans for credit purchases. As profits declined, workers were laid off and factories closed. Meanwhile, holding companies with huge loans to repay cut operating costs of the companies they owned. The crash also eventually hit the world economy because American investors, short of cash, stopped making their loans to European and Latin American countries, while calling for quicker repayment of previous loans.

The crash caused many Americans to reconsider their values. As the sign indicates, a former stock investor found that basic necessities did not include an automobile.

Section 21-3

Objectives

- ***Answer the Focus Question.***
- *Describe the effects of Hoover's economic policies following the crash.*
- *Compare the platforms of Hoover and Roosevelt in 1932.*

Introducing THE SECTION

Ask: What effect does the psychological state of a people have on the economy? **(If people feel prosperous, as many did in the 1920s, then their confidence encourages them to spend more vigorously.)**

The term "depression" relates both to economics and to psychology. Have students write out economic and psychological definitions of the term. How does an economic depression affect national and individual feelings of psychological well-being?

Developing THE SECTION

Active Learning

Making Cause-Effect Charts. Have students make charts illustrating the effects of the stock market crash on the economy. Direct them to use information from the fourth and fifth paragraphs on this page for their charts.

Using the Visuals

Analyzing Graphs. Refer students to the graphs on this page.

1. Was unemployment high or low in 1918–1919? Why? **(low; workers employed in wartime industries)**
2. Between what years did workers experience declining wages? **(1920–1922, 1929–1932)**
3. Is the following generalization supported by the two graphs? If so, how?— In years when unemployment increased by more than five percent, wages in manufacturing decreased. **(Yes. This holds for all the years of sharp increase in unemployment: 1921, 1930, 1931, 1932.)**
4. What might account for this correspondence of statistics in the graphs? **(Higher unemployment meant more job seekers competing for work and willing to accept lower wages. Wages also fell because employed workers, fearing loss of jobs, may have accepted pay cuts.)**

Limited English Proficiency

Building Vocabulary. Help students understand the difference between a *recession* and a *depression*. Have students identify the root words of these terms, and then define them in relation to the economy. **(*Recession*—from recede, to slope backward; a temporary decline in economic activity or prosperity. *Depression*—from depress, to lower, make less active; a long period of inactivity in business and trade, with widespread unemployment.)**

Reduced student page in the Teacher's Edition

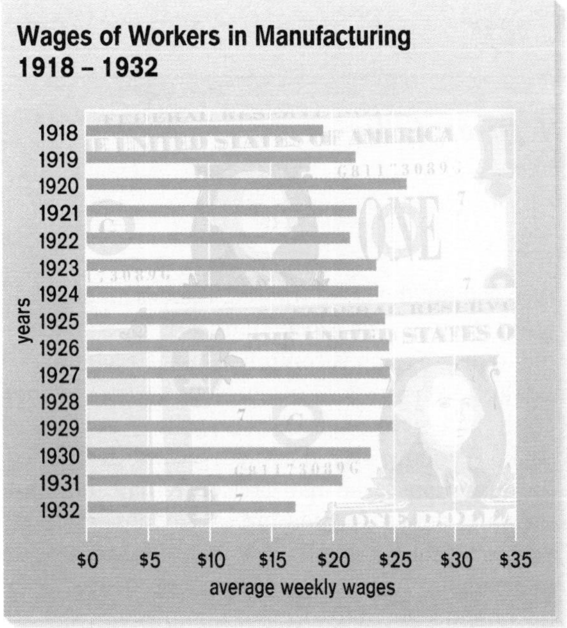

Source: *Historical Statistics of the United States*

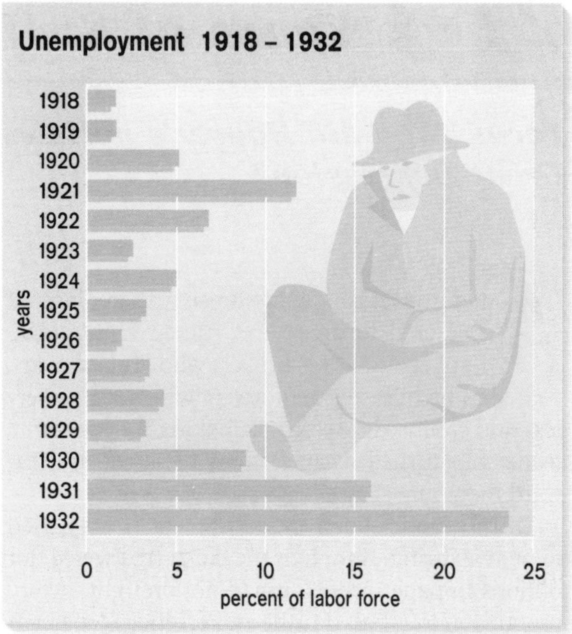

Source: *Historical Statistics of the United States*

Hoover's Plea to Business

In the early weeks following the crash, few business or government leaders foresaw a long economic downturn. Most thought that the nation was experiencing a normal part of the **business cycle,** a repeated series of "ups" of economic growth and "downs" of decline in business activity. After its "up," the economy was due for a "down."

Hoover's advisors believed that the economy was in a **recession,** a short decline, and would cure itself in a few weeks. They recommended that he take no action. Hoover, though, did not want the economy to drift downhill. While still believing that government should be "an umpire instead of a player in the economic game," he would ask the players to keep the game moving.

In November Hoover met with Henry Ford and other business leaders and urged them not to cut wages. He also talked with labor leaders, who promised not to seek wage increases. Before the year was over, Hoover asked businesses to maintain or even increase spending for new construction. He also requested state officials and Congress to speed up their spending for highway projects, public buildings, and other public works. Such projects provided much-needed jobs.

Recession's Impact on Industry

By and large, wages held steady through the summer of 1930. As soon as businesses felt the economic pinch, however, they cut wages and work hours. Historian Jeane Westin described some of the results:

> *"Women office workers in New York who previously earned forty-five dollars a week were taking home only sixteen dollars. . . . And black women in Alabama, working twelve-hour, six-day weeks in steamy laundries, made a pitiful $5.85."*

Afraid of losing their jobs, employees did not grumble too loudly. However, many found that their fears came true anyway. The first to be fired were usually unskilled laborers, followed by skilled workers, clerks, and then managers. At the time of the crash, about 1.5 million workers had been without jobs. That number jumped to more than 4 million in 1930. Factory closings became commonplace. Touring an idle automobile plant in Ohio, reporter Beulah Amidon saw what looked like a ghost town:

B · A · C · K · G · R · O · U · N · D

Multicultural Perspectives

By 1931 negative feelings in mainstream culture toward Hispanic Americans and other groups had grown. Many people felt that if immigrant workers went back to their native lands, then there would be more jobs for other Americans and the depression would soon end. The federal government established the Repatriation Program, especially aimed at Mexican Americans in southern California. The Los Angeles County Welfare Department offered free train rides back to Mexico between March 1931 and April 1934. Between 1929 and 1939 about 1.5 million Mexican Americans went to Mexico, many out of fear. Even those who were American citizens felt pressure to leave the United States.

Thinking Critically

Evaluation. Have students discuss the link between social attitudes about sex roles, race and employment. **Ask:** What social groups were likely to be the "last hired and first fired" in the United States in the late 1920s and early 1930s? Have these social attitudes changed much since the 1920s and 1930s? Explain.

“There was the same sense of suspended life, as I moved among silent, untended machines or walked through departments where hundreds of half-finished automobile bodies gathered dust while they waited for the next cleaning or finishing process.”

By the time the Great Depression hit bottom in 1933, over 13 million people—nearly one third of the labor force—would be unemployed. Hardest hit were African Americans, Hispanics, and other groups who even in boom times faced an economic struggle because of racism. One historian described the impact on blacks in Harlem:

“For virtually everyone in Harlem, the Great Depression was a traumatic experience. The economic crash had the same general impact as in the rest of America—massive unemployment, evictions, bank failures, loss of family savings, loss of business—but in every instance it was far more serious. Throughout most of the Depression the unemployment rate for Harlem blacks hovered between one-and-a-half and three times that of whites in New York City.”

As one African-American social worker later commented, "It was a depression because no whites and no blacks were working. The *whites* not working made it official."

Looking to Local Aid

Hoover soon had to accept the reality that voluntary cooperation from business would not pull the country out of the depression. And as the depression deepened, it became clear that unemployed people could not rely on their savings or on their family and friends for help. Even large savings were not a guarantee against hard times. As banks continued to fail across the country, more and more depositors lost their money.

Charities did their best to provide relief, distributing millions of dollars in food, clothing, and cash during 1930 and 1931. Hoover, who firmly believed that people should not learn to rely on the federal government for aid, applauded the charities for demonstrating the spirit of "mutual self-help through voluntary giving." He backed their efforts by setting up the President's Organization on Unemployment Relief (POUR). In advertisements POUR appealed to the public to give more money to charities like the Community Chest, the organization that would later become the United Way of America.

Voluntary giving might have been enough in better times. In these desperate days, though, charities could not hope to raise enough money to feed all the people who needed help.

When charities could not do enough, local governments stepped in. For instance, schools in New York City provided lunches, clothing, coal, and cash to needy families, and Detroit fed thousands of unemployed auto workers.

WORLD'S HIGHEST STANDARD OF LIVING
There's no way like the American Way

Margaret Bourke-White's photo of a breadline reflects the gap between a vision of prosperity and the reality faced by depression victims.

Connections: Music

Activity. Have the class listen to a recording of one of the hundreds of versions of the popular 1932 tune *Brother, Can You Spare a Dime.* Or read to students the following lyrics from the song.

*"They used to tell me I was building a dream,
And so I followed the mob
When there was earth to plough or guns to bear
I was always there, right on the job
They used to tell me I was building a dream
With peace and glory instead
Why should I be standing in line
Just waiting for bread?
Once I built a railroad, made it run,
Made it race against time
Once I built a railroad, now it's done
Brother, can you spare a dime?"*

Ask: What are some particular historical events referred to in the song? Why did the memory of these events cause bitterness in unemployed workers in the 1930s?

Connections: Literature

The mid-1930s were disastrous for many farmers. During the unrelenting drought of 1934 and 1935, entire families left their homes in the Midwestern Dust Bowl in search of a better life. Many ended up in California's migrant worker camps. Portraying the migration in his novel *The Grapes of Wrath*, John Steinbeck wrote:

"The people in flight streamed out on Highway 66, sometimes a little car, sometimes a caravan. . . . Fifty thousand old cars—wounded, steaming. Wrecks along the road, abandoned. What happened to them? . . . Where are they? . . . Did they walk? Where does the courage come from? Where does the terrible faith come from?"

Reduced student page in the Teacher's Edition

But the cost outpaced the ability of cities to raise taxes or to borrow. They could not deal with the effects of widespread unemployment.

Before the winter of 1932 was over, more than half the states had set up emergency relief programs. As needs kept increasing, though, many state and city officials pleaded for federal help. Gifford Pinchot, governor of Pennsylvania, declared that the welfare of working people was "a national responsibility and a national duty."

Hoover's Efforts: Too Little, Too Late

Although the call for federal aid grew louder, Hoover stood firm in his belief that direct relief would strike "at the roots of self-government." He warned of the danger to society if people began to rely upon "government charity in some form or other." Also, he did not want to throw the federal budget further out of balance by increasing government spending. He was open, however, to providing indirect aid.

One way to give indirect aid, Hoover thought, would be to protect manufacturers and farmers from foreign competition. In 1930 he signed the Hawley-Smoot Tariff Act, which raised import duties to an all-time high. However, the tariff ended up doing more harm than good. By making it harder for other countries to sell their products in the United States, the tariff left them with less income to buy American products or to pay back American loans. Thus both the American and the world economies sank deeper.

A form of indirect aid that helped somewhat was the creation in 1932 of a federal agency called the Reconstruction Finance Corporation (RFC). The RFC made loans of more than $1.5 billion to businesses. Hoover hoped they would have a trickle-down effect, creating jobs and increasing consumer spending.

Another good but inadequate step was the Emergency Relief and Construction Act, which gave the RFC up to $300 million for relief loans to the states. But many states needed more money than the RFC was willing to lend, and the program was largely ineffective.

"Migrant Mother," a photo by Dorothea Lange, became one of the most famous images of the despair that the depression brought to the lives of many.

Herbert Hoover tried to do more to help the economy than any previous President during a depression. Unfortunately, his efforts proved to be too little and too late.

People in Despair

"During the spring of 1930 bread lines began to appear . . . long lines of patient, hopeless, humiliated men shuffling forward slowly to receive a bowl of watery soup and a crust of bread from charity kitchens, Salvation Army halls, and local relief agencies. . . . You might go to the local poorhouse, your children to an orphanage. . . . You racked your brain to find out . . . what sin you committed to earn such a terrible punish-

ment. . . . Maybe capitalism was at fault, maybe democracy. You didn't make up your mind right away, but you were wondering. ❞

This description by historian Robert Goldston points to the despair felt by many victims of the Great Depression. Ashamed of being jobless, fathers deserted their families. Sons left home so they would not burden their parents. They joined thousands of drifters, young and old, begging for rides and food. As the depression deepened, many young women also became drifters. One was asked where she was going. "Going?" she snapped. "Just going."

The sense of helplessness is also reflected in writer Meridel Le Sueur's experience:

❝ *I am sitting in the city free employment bureau. It's the woman's section. . . . There are no jobs. Most of us have had no breakfast. Some have had scant rations for over a year. Is there any place else in the world where a human being is supposed to go hungry amidst plenty without an outcry, without protest, where only the bold steal or kill for bread? . . . We look away from each other. We look at the floor. It's too terrible to see this animal terror in each other's eyes.* ❞

The Bonus Army. Nowhere was desperation more evident than in the march of thousands of jobless veterans to the nation's capital in 1932.

THE AMERICAN SPIRIT

Dorothea Lange

Photographer of Despair

When the depression began, Dorothea Lange was a successful portrait photographer in San Francisco, California. However, her work seemed unimportant to her in such difficult times. From her studio window she often watched a bread line, where people without jobs waited for food. "I looked as long as I could," she remembered. Finally, grabbing her camera, she went outside to photograph the scene.

During the next years, Lange continued to photograph the victims of the Great Depression. Working mainly for the United States Farm Security Administration, she traveled throughout rural California, the South, and the Dust Bowl. She had a special rapport with the people she photographed. They trusted her and wanted her to know their stories.

Lange took her most famous photograph at the end of a month's tour of California migrant-labor camps. She was driving home, exhausted, when she glimpsed a crude sign, "Pea Pickers' Camp." Lange hurried on, but the sign stayed in her mind. Twenty miles beyond, she turned around and headed back toward the camp. "I was following instinct, not reason," she said.

At the camp she was drawn to a woman sitting in a ragged tent. The woman told Lange that the pea crop had frozen, so there was no work. She and her children were living on wild birds and frozen peas from the fields. "Migrant Mother"—the picture Lange took of this worn young woman with her hungry children—became the most published photograph of the time (see facing page). Through her art Lange brought home to all Americans the tragedy of the depression.

Connections: Literature

Discussion. From the library, have a few students obtain a copy of Studs Terkel's *Hard Times*. (Quotes from this book also appear in Chapter 22 of the text.) Terkel used a tape recorder to interview hundreds of Americans who had experienced the Great Depression. Have them choose several interviews to be read to the entire class.

Ask: Though times were hard during the Great Depression, what were some good things to come out of the experience for the American people?

B · A · C · K · G · R · O · U · N · D

Writing About History

Letter. Have students imagine themselves as leaders of the Bonus Army of 1932, encamped in Washington, D.C., hoping to influence lawmakers to grant them their World War I bonuses. Ask them to write a letter describing their economic condition back home, their dependence on the federal government for a ray of hope, and their hopes for the future.

Chapter Connections

Discussion. Review with students the discussion of "Coxey's Army" in Chapter 16, page 429. Have them compare reasons for the marches of the Bonus Army and Coxey's Army. **(The Bonus Army was made up of jobless veterans seeking benefits owed to them. Coxey's Army was composed of unemployed workers seeking employment of the jobless during depression of 1893.)** Compare the nation's economic health during Coxey's time and the late 1920s. **(depression)** Compare causes of the depressions. **(1893: falling farm prices, shrinkage of money supply, gold/silver issue, deflation)**

Social History

The leader of the troops sent to disband the Bonus Army village was the Chief of Staff of the United States Army, Douglas MacArthur. MacArthur was already a national hero of World War I. He later became one of the United States' leading World War II generals. In 1950 MacArthur again led American troops, this time in the Korean conflict.

In 1932, police attacked jobless war veterans who camped out in the nation's capital to demand their bonuses. Among other signs of desperation were "Hooverville" shacks in many cities.

Following World War I, Congress had agreed to give veterans bonuses, payable in 1945, but the veterans needed the money right away. Calling themselves the Bonus Expeditionary Force or Bonus Army, they came from every state and felt they had nothing to lose. Before leaving home one said, "I might as well starve there as here."

When they arrived in Washington, the veterans—some of whom had brought their wives and children—threatened to stay until their demands were met. They sought shelter in abandoned buildings, shacks, and even cardboard boxes and packing crates. Even when Congress refused their demands, about half stayed. On July 28, Hoover ordered that the Bonus Army be disbanded. Police swept veterans out of the abandoned buildings, and soldiers advanced on the outdoor camps. *Time* magazine described the scene:

> *"Cavalry and infantry, to the number of 1,000 men, began moving into Washington. . . . In their wake came five small tanks, a fleet of trucks. . . . Reaching the "affected area," troopers rode straight into hooting, booing ranks of the B.E.F. Veterans scrambled out of the way of swinging sabres, trampling hoofs. Steel-helmeted infantrymen with revolvers drawn advanced 20 abreast. Behind them came others with rifles lowered, bayonets prodding. Suddenly tear gas bombs began to pop on the street."*

Soldiers used tear gas to force out the veterans, then set fire to their shacks. Eventually the veterans were dispersed, but not before two were killed and dozens more seriously injured. One reporter reflected a sympathy shared by many:

> *"It was an experience that stands apart from all others in my life. So all the misery and suffering had finally come to this—soldiers marching with their guns against American citizens."*

Roosevelt Elected in 1932

The President's reputation had collapsed along with the economy. Groups of shacks that poor people built near city dumps were called "Hoovervilles," and the old newspapers that drifters huddled under at night were known as "Hoover blankets." An empty pocket turned inside out was a "Hoover flag." Hoover's use of force against the Bonus Army aroused even more bitter feelings about him. A writer recalled,

"By now, public hatred and contempt for Herbert Hoover had reached proportions possibly unique in the history of the Republic's opinions of its Presidents."

Although in 1932 Hoover ran for reelection, he was not expected to win. The Democrats nominated Governor Franklin D. Roosevelt of New York. Saying that the main issue was "a depression so deep that it is without precedent in modern history," Roosevelt promised "a new deal for the American people." He believed that the federal government should play a major role by providing "employment for all surplus labor at all times."

Hoover protested what he labeled "frivolous promises being held out to a suffering people." He warned that the Democrats were "proposing changes and so-called new deals which would destroy the very foundations of our American system." Such changes, he said, "would mean the growth of a fearful bureaucracy."

The voters could not be sure that Roosevelt had the answers, but most were convinced that Hoover did not. A hitchhiker's sign often seen during the fall of 1932 read: "If you don't give me a ride, I'll vote for Hoover!"

Voters gave Roosevelt a victory—one even more sweeping than Hoover's four years earlier. The electoral vote was 472 to 59. Unlike the last election, however, Americans were looking to the future with grave doubts about the economy rather than with hope for a thriving marketplace.

Section Review

1. Identification. Define *business cycle* and *recession.*

2. Comprehension. How and why did Hoover's economic policies change? What effect did they have?

3. Evaluation. Do you think it was fair to blame the depression on Hoover's policies? Explain.

Data Search. Two measures of a nation's economic health are its levels of unemployment and wages. Use the graphs on page 564 to explain how these measures reflected the shift "from boom to bust" between 1928 and 1932.

Connections to Themes

The Search for Opportunity

There were painful lessons for Americans in the transition from boom to bust. One of those lessons was that economic opportunity no longer depended only on the efforts of each individual. Instead, the economy was affected by unseen forces that no one fully understood.

Hardworking farmers discovered that the high production they struggled to achieve only led to a disastrous drop in their earnings. Factory and office workers learned that years of loyal labor would not spare them from layoffs or business failures. Even people who seemed to have achieved the heights of wealth and economic power could fall victim to the forces that led to the stock market crash and the depression.

Another lesson from those years was that gambling on the economy by playing the stock market created a bubble of prosperity that was easily burst. Americans did not learn this lesson thoroughly. Years later, in the 1980s, a new stock market scheme—the buying and selling of "junk bonds"—again led thousands to believe that they had found a foolproof way to "play the game of business."

A third lesson was that, in times of nationwide economic collapse, the national government would have to act. But what kind of action could rescue America from the depths of a depression? Could government programs prevent a recurrence of economic disaster? In 1932, desperate Americans could only hope that Franklin D. Roosevelt and his "new deal" had the answers.

Thinking Critically

Evaluation. Have students write brief evaluations of Herbert Hoover's career up to the election of 1932, in three parts: (1) Hoover's accomplishments in business and politics, (2) his problems from 1929 to 1932, and (3) the evaluation he deserves. When the writing is done, discuss with students how they evaluated Hoover.

Section Review

ANSWERS

1. Definitions for the following terms are on text pages indicated in parentheses: *business cycle* (564), *recession* (564).
2. Hoover's economic policy changed from laissez faire to encouraging business and labor to impose controls on themselves and get the economy going. He also created the Reconstruction Finance Corporation. The policy changes had little effect.
3. Opinions will vary. Some may argue that he did not create the conditions leading to the depression, and did his best to get the country out of it. Others may argue that Hoover did too little to get the country out of depression, and that his opposition to direct relief added to the people's misery.
Data Search. One graph shows unemployment rising sharply from 1929–1932. The other shows wages rising in the early 1920s, staying high until 1929, then falling sharply.

Connections: Literature
The statements by Dynamite Garland, Myrna Loy, and José Yglesias all come from Studs Terkel's *Hard Times*, an excellent collection of primary source accounts of the varying impacts of the Depression.

Reduced student page in the Teacher's Edition

POINT OF VIEW

Impacts of the Depression

The depression changed the lives of millions, uprooting many from their homes and separating families. However, many Americans barely noticed a difference. Those already poor had little to lose, while some people remained wealthy, having not relied heavily on stocks. Meanwhile, many people had jobs producing basic goods and services that were still in demand. The following points of view reflect different effects of the Depression.

Buying for the Future

“I began to do substitute teaching in Gary [Indiana] for about a year. But there really wasn't enough work because teachers weren't staying home sick . . . they couldn't afford it. Next I went to work at Montgomery Ward. Because I had college training, they thought I was smart enough to wrap packages. By this time, too, I met my husband. . . .

We rented in this building until we started buying it and eventually another one as well. One building helped pay for the other that way. . . . Many of our friends were doing the same thing. . . . Prices were down and property was cheap. It was the best time to buy security for the future.”

—An African-American woman named Pauline

Living in a Garage

“I remember all of a sudden we had to move. My father lost his job and we moved into a double garage. The landlord didn't charge us rent for seven years. We had a coal stove, and we had to each take turns, the three of us kids, to warm our legs. . . .

In the morning, we'd get out some snow and put it on the stove and melt it and wash around our faces. Never the neck or anything. Put on our two pairs of socks on each hand and two pairs of socks on our feet, and long underwear and lace it up with Goodwill shoes. Off we'd walk, three, four miles to school.”

—Dynamite Garland, waitress

The Golden Years

“When the Depression came, I had a very good job in Hollywood. . . . Everybody around me was working. You get up at five-thirty. . . . You're made up and ready at nine and work until six. They now call those The Golden Years of the Movies. Perhaps they were. People needed films, needed some diversion.”

—Myrna Loy, film and stage actress

A Certain Difference

"The Depression came imperceptibly. The realization came to me when Aunt Lila said there's no food in the house. My aunt, who owned the house we lived in, would no longer charge rent. It would be shameful to charge rent with $9 a week coming in. . . .

There was a certain difference between the Depression in my home town [Tampa, Florida] than elsewhere. There weren't dark, satanic mills. The streets were not like a city ghetto. There were poor homes that hadn't been painted in years. But it was out in the open. You played in the sunlight. I don't remember real deprivation."

—José Yglesias, author

A Broken Family

"While I was looking for a job, I left my two children with some friends; at least I thought they were friends. But they went to the law and said my children were neglected. When I asked, 'Why did you do that?' they said, 'We thought it would get you on relief and that would be a way for you to get money.'

I told [the judge] all the things I'd tried to do, all the things I'd done to keep them with me. But the judge said I had no established home and no money, and so he said, 'Young lady, I have no choice but to declare these as neglected children, and take them from you for their own welfare.'. . . I never saw or heard of them again."

—An anonymous woman from Michigan

Change in Chinatown

"Now I had been living out in the country for a while, but I came back [to Chinatown, San Francisco] around 1932 and the Depression changed a lot of things. You had guys going around from building to building selling meat. They sell pork for twenty-five cents, thirty-five cents a pound, cheaper than the butcher shop and you don't have to walk around, they come to you. Now during the Depression I was so broke, quite often I was with no money in my pocket. The most I ever had is maybe one or two dollars, the least was, well, normally I got ten, fifteen cents."

—A Chinese-American man named Fong

A Neighborhood Without Breadlines

"We didn't really feel the Depression. Everyone we knew had a job. Sure we saw breadlines, but not in our neighborhood. Everybody we knew pretty much had enough to eat."

—A Jewish-American woman named Pessy

1. In what ways was Pauline's experience different from that of most African Americans during the Depression?

2. Pick one of the points of view that is positive and explain what made it so.

3. Which person would you say was hurt most by the Depression? Explain.

4. What effect do you think being poor during the Depression might have had on people's points of view later in their lives?

Point of View

ANSWERS

1. Pauline's experience differed from those of most African Americans in that she was able to "buy security" for the future through real estate purchases. Most African Americans found that the Depression worsened their already bleak prospects for economic opportunity.
2. Answers will vary. The experiences of Pauline, Myrna Loy, José Yglesias, and Pessy all strike a positive note. Pauline notes the opportunities to buy real estate cheaply. Acting in Hollywood movies kept Myrna Loy steadily employed. Yglesias notes that, despite the poverty in his town, the atmosphere was better than living in what he saw as the dreary confinement of a city. He also does not recall any "real deprivation." Presumably he had enough food and adequate clothing and shelter. Pessy notes that there were no bread lines in her neighborhood.
3. Opinions will vary and should be supported with reasons. Students may note that the information is inadequate to give a full assessment of the depression's impact on these people. However, based on the short excerpts, they will probably feel that the person hurt most was the woman whose children were taken away from her. Unlike the experience of enduring temporary poverty and hunger, her pain was probably lasting.
4. Answers will vary. Students may speculate that the experience of "living with less" during the Depression could influence one's spending habits and attitude toward money and possessions later in life. People who lived through the Depression might tend to save more money in order to be prepared for emergencies. They might also take care not to waste what food they have.

Chapter Survey

ANSWERS

Using New Vocabulary

1. (b) Consumer makes a down payment to obtain *credit* from seller.
2. (c) Refrigerators are *durable goods.*
3. (a) Depression is a severe downturn in the *business cycle.*

Reviewing the Chapter

1. Advertising, chain stores, available credit, and confidence in the economy led to buying spree.
2. Republicans had overseen prosperity; the electorate did not support a Catholic candidate; Democrats proposed greater regulation of business.
3. A buyer orders stock with a broker and pays the broker only part of the price. The broker, with money from a bank, would loan the buyer the rest of the money. This was unsafe when the price of stock fell and the owner could not sell it. It hurt the buyer, the broker, and the banker.
4. Small number of Americans controlled the wealth of the nation; prosperity depended on the rich spending money. Holding companies did not reinvest profit. Banks made too many loans to stockbrokers, American investors made risky foreign loans, and both farmers and manufacturers produced more goods than they could sell at high prices.
5. Direct loss of money affected the small percentage of Americans who controlled the country's wealth. When they stopped spending money, the economy suffered. Americans in general were afraid to spend money. As profits fell, workers were laid off and factories closed.
6. Had loaned too much money to stockbrokers; unemployed people withdrew savings to live on; borrowers could not repay their loans.
7. It was meant to protect American industry and farmers from foreign competition by making imports more expensive. But when Americans did not buy foreign goods, other nations could not repay loans to U.S., which hurt American and worldwide economies.
8. Initially wanted the economy to recover on its own: asked business to maintain wages, labor to accept current wages, and local and state governments to increase spending. When this did not work, Hoover created the Reconstruction Finance Corporation which loaned money to businesses to create jobs which would provide money for consumer spending.
9. Nearly one third of Americans were unemployed. Many lost their homes, some husbands left their families because they could not support

Chapter Survey

Using New Vocabulary

Match each numbered vocabulary term with the lettered word or phrase most closely related to it. Explain how the items in each pair are related.

1. credit	(a) depression
2. durable goods	(b) down payment
3. business cycle	(c) refrigerators

Reviewing the Chapter

1. Explain the buying spree of the 1920s.
2. Why were Democrats at a disadvantage in the election of 1928? Give at least three reasons.
3. Why was buying stock on margin unsafe?
4. Describe the weaknesses of the American economy before the stock market crash of 1929.
5. Why did the crash have a disastrous effect?
6. Why did many banks fail in the early 1930s?
7. What was the intent of the Hawley-Smoot tariff? What was its impact?
8. What was Hoover's approach to recovery?
9. Describe the effects of unemployment.
10. Explain three or more factors that contributed to Roosevelt's election in 1932.

Thinking Critically

1. Analysis. Al Smith's campaign for President was hurt by his religion. What other forces were at work in American society during the 1920s which contributed to prejudice against him?
2. Evaluation. "Prosperity is more than an economic condition; it is a state of mind," wrote historian Frederick Lewis Allen. How did this description fit the economy of the 1920s?
3. Application. Hoover feared that direct relief from the government would strike "at the roots of self government." What did he mean? How did his actions attempt to avoid this problem?

History and You

Hoover wanted the national government to be "an umpire instead of a player in the economic game." Do you think Hoover's view would work today ? Why or why not?

Using Geography

Study the maps below to help you answer the following questions.

1. Compare the elections of 1928 and 1932 in terms of the number of states voting Democratic and the number voting Republican.
2. Name three states with large populations whose electoral votes shifted from the Republicans in 1928 to the Democrats in 1932.

Presidential Election of 1928

Presidential Election of 1932

them, some young people became drifters. People lost their self-respect in bread lines.

10. Hoover's policies had failed; use of force against Bonus Army made him even more unpopular; economy in terrible shape; Roosevelt promised employment and "new deal."

Thinking Critically

1. Resurgence of Ku Klux Klan, strong nativist feelings, "100 percent Americanism," fear of politician with any loyalty beyond the United States, such as to the Pope in Rome.

2. Confidence in the economy promoted consumer spending and investing in the boom years of the 1920s. After the crash, fear fed on itself, people held back on spending, the depression worsened.

3. Self-government depends on people making decisions for themselves; Hoover feared that direct relief would make people dependent on the government. His policies of "trickle-down" loans to businesses kept workers' wages coming from private industry.

History and You

Students should recognize the many ways government affects the economy today: makes foreign trade agreements; insures banks and savings institutions; and the Federal Reserve controls interest rates. Students may recognize that policies of Presidents Reagan and Bush reflected a more laissez-faire position.

Using Geography

1. 1928: 8 states Democratic, 40 Republican; 1932: 42 States Democratic, 6 Republican.

2. Answers will vary. Some possibilities: New York, Ohio, Illinois.

Applying Social Studies Skills

1. 1925–1932. Bread, eggs, milk, chuck roast, and navy beans. They are staples.

2. 1929. Prices went down each year after.

3. People could afford to buy less, demand fell, and so did prices. Additional necessary information: the price of items other than food that are in general use; wages; unemployment rates.

Applying Thinking Skills

1. Fact: "For weeks President Hoover did not act." Opinion: "Then he acted with inexcusable violence."

2. Strongly stated opinions such as "unforgivably stupid" and "any commander with an ounce of sense."

3. That Hoover made poor decisions in his assault on the Bonus Army. The bias is evident in both reasoned and unsupported opinions.

Applying Social Studies Skills

Analyzing Statistical Tables

One way of displaying statistics in an organized manner is in a statistical table. A statistical table is an arrangement of numbers in rows and columns. To determine the significance of the statistics, you must analyze the table, carefully examining each part of it. Use the statistical table below to answer the questions that follow.

Food Prices 1925 - 1932

	Bread 1 lb.	Eggs 1 doz.	Milk 1/2 gal.	Chuck roast 1 lb.	Navy beans 1 lb.
1925	9.3	55.4	27.8	22.8	10.3
1926	9.3	51.9	28.0	23.7	9.4
1927	9.2	48.7	28.2	25.2	9.4
1928	8.9	50.3	28.4	29.6	11.8
1929	8.8	52.7	28.8	31.4	14.1
1930	8.6	44.5	28.2	28.6	11.7
1931	7.7	35.0	25.2	22.7	8.1
1932	7.0	30.2	21.4	18.5	5.2

Prices given in cents

Source: *Historical Statistics of the United States*

1. What years are shown on the table? What foods are shown? Why do you think that these foods were chosen rather than, for example, steak and ice cream?

2. In general, in what year were the prices of these foods highest? What happened in each succeeding year?

3. What explanations can you think of for the answer to question 2? What additional information would you need in order to determine the effect of the change on American consumers?

Applying Thinking Skills

Evaluating Information

To decide whether you can trust a source of information, you must determine whether it is objective or biased. Evaluate this excerpt from an article published in 1932. Identify the point of view and decide whether the article reflects bias or unsupported opinions.

"From the time the Bonus Army encamped in Washington, all sensible people realized the situation might end in catastrophe. For weeks President Hoover did not act. Then he acted with inexcusable and wholly unnecessary violence.

If you grant that the ex-soldiers should have been removed from their rookeries on Pennsylvania Avenue, there was no reason for such frantic haste. It was outrageous that these men, many accompanied by their wives and children, should have been driven out with no place to go. It was unforgivably stupid and cruel to let the troops use full military equipment including tear gas bombs. Any commander with an ounce of sense would have sent in the police or infantry without bombs, bayonets, or ammunition.

There is absolutely no justification for what followed at Anacostia. Routing men, women and children out of bed, drenching them with tear gas, ruthlessly burning their poor shelters and then driving cripples, babies, pregnant women up a steep hill at bayonet point were the orders of someone seeking revenge. Thus did the government persecute those hungry and ragged men it sent fourteen years ago into the trenches at the risk of death."

—The *Washington Star*, July 15, 1932.

1. Give an example from the article of a statement of fact and of a reasoned opinion.

2. Is there evidence of bias? Explain.

3. What is the point of view expressed in this article? How do you know?

Chapter 22

The New Deal

Planning Guide

	Student Text	TWE Lesson Plans	Support Materials
SECTION 1	**Section 22–1 (1–3 Days)** **The First New Deal,** pp 576–584 Exploring Issues—The Role of Government in the Economy: the TVA, pp 582–583 Review/Evaluation Section Review, p 584	**Introducing the Chapter:** Problems and Solutions—Class Activity, one class period, p 573B **Teaching the Main Ideas:** Governments's Role in the Economy—Paired Activity, one class period, p 573B **Evaluating Progress:** Organizing New Deal Programs—Individual Activity, 30 minutes, p 573C	★ **Read to Remember,** Section 1 ● **Section Activities,** Section 1 ● **Geography Activities,** Section 1 Δ **Readings** ● **Tests and Quizzes,** Section 1 Quiz
SECTION 2	**Section 22–2 (1–2 Days)** **The Second New Deal,** pp 585–591 Review/Evaluation Section Review, p 591	**Reinforcement Activity:** A Fireside Chat—Individual Activity, one class period, p 573C **Evaluating Progress:** Organizing New Deal Programs—Individual Activity, 30 minutes, p 573C	★ **Read to Remember,** Section 2 ● **Section Activities,** Section 2 Δ **Enrichment Activities,** Section 2 Δ **Readings** ● **Tests and Quizzes,** Section 2 Quiz
SECTION 3	**Section 22–3 (1–2 Days)** **The Last Years of the New Deal,** pp 592–599 The American Spirit: Mary McLeod Bethune, p 593 Geography—Region: The Dust Bowl, p 597 Connections to Themes: The Search for Opportunity, p 599 Review/Evaluation Section Review, p 599 Chapter 22 Survey, pp 600–601 Unit 7 Survey, pp 602–603 Skills, pp 600–601 Using New Vocabulary Thinking Critically Using a Time Line Applying Thinking Skills: Determining the Strength of an Argument Applying Social Studies Skills: Analyzing Bar Graphs	**Teaching the Main Ideas:** A Mural of the Thirties—Class Activity, one class period, p 573C **Enrichment Activity:** Anti-New Deal Cartoons—Individual Activity, one class period, p 573D **Evaluating Progress:** Organizing New Deal Programs—Individual Activity, 30 minutes, p 573C	★ **Read to Remember,** Section 3 ● **Section Activities,** Section 3 Δ **Enrichment Activities,** Section 3 Δ **Readings** ● **Tests and Quizzes,** Section 3 Quiz, Chapter 22 Test (Forms A and B), Unit 7 Test (Forms A and B) **Additional Resources** ● **Active Learning** Δ **GTV Videodiscs** Δ **Transparencies and Activity Book** ● **Testing Software** ★ **Chapter Summaries** **Key:** ★ **For Extra Support** ● **For All Students** Δ **For Enrichment**

Overview

In 1933, at the height of the Great Depression, Franklin Roosevelt took office, promising immediate action. At Roosevelt's urging, during the first "Hundred Days" Congress passed measures meant to revitalize banking, big business and industry, and big agriculture. Congress also funded direct aid and work relief programs for the neediest of Americans. No one knew for certain if these early New Deal programs would foster recovery, but the energy and confidence of the New Dealers promoted optimism.

However, these first New Deal programs were greeted with mixed reactions. Some critics claimed that they were too extreme; others claimed that they were not radical enough to reform the economy or end the depression.

A second set of New Deal measures was aimed not so much at big business and agriculture but at more ordinary citizens—middle-class professionals, labor, and small farmers. This second New Deal included such fundamental economic reforms as social security.

The appeal of New Deal policies led to a new coalition of voters—African Americans, labor union members, and small farmers—a coalition that would play a role in Democratic party politics for decades to come. However, Roosevelt's popularity began to slip in 1937. A series of sit-down strikes, his controversial attempt to alter the federal court system, and a new economic decline all contributed to Roosevelt's loss of support. In Congress liberal Democrats faced Republicans and Democratic conservatives in a standoff, and no further major reforms were forthcoming.

Activity Objectives

After completing the activities, students should be able to

- discuss various views of the first New Deal.
- describe the impact of New Deal programs on diverse groups of people.
- explain key features of the New Deal.
- identify sectors of the economy addressed by specific New Deal programs.
- explain the views of Roosevelt's critics.

Introducing the Chapter

Problems and Solutions

This class activity requires one class period.

In this activity students, assuming the viewpoints of various people affected by the depression, define the nation's problems and propose solutions.

Begin the activity by telling students that when Franklin Roosevelt was elected President in 1932, 13 million workers were unemployed, families were hungry, banks were shaky, business stalled, and farmers were bankrupt. Roosevelt had promised a "New Deal," but he had not outlined specific plans.

Tell students to imagine themselves in the year 1932 as citizens who have been asked to present the newly-elected President with a list of complaints and suggestions for ending the depression. Direct each student to create a specific identity for himself or herself by assuming a name, age, and address, and developing a statement of personal belief about how to end the depression. Allow five minutes for students to create their characters.

Divide the class into groups of characters with common interests, for example, small farmers, bankers, workers, shopkeepers, and big business. Let the groups work for about fifteen minutes to compile a list of problems they have as a result of the depression and to offer one or two solutions. Encourage students to review Chapter 21 but ask them not to look at Chapter 22 for ideas.

When the groups have completed their lists, ask one or more members of each group to present their suggestions. Write suggestions on the chalkboard or poster paper and have students speculate about which suggestions might be most effective in resolving the country's economic crisis. Save the list for reference after the class has finished reading Chapter 22.

Teaching the Main ideas

Section 22-1: Government's Role in the Economy

This paired activity requires one class period.

In this activity students examine views of the role of government in ending the depression by engaging in a written dialogue.

Divide the class into pairs. Direct the pairs to select one of the following programs to discuss: AAA, NRA, relief programs, or TVA. Have each pair designate one partner to represent Roosevelt's viewpoint and the other to represent a position that a supporter of Herbert Hoover and the Republicans might have taken. Each student is to take several minutes to write down three to five major arguments central to the viewpoint that he or she represents. Some students may wish to review Chapter 21.

Explain that each pair will engage in a written dialogue of the two viewpoints. One partner begins the dialogue by writing a single, clear argument in favor of his or her views. The second partner writes an answer to the first partner's statement, then writes an argument for his or her position. The process is repeated for about four rounds. Direct the partner representing Roosevelt's opposition to write the first statement, allowing about five minutes writing time. The partner representing Roosevelt's views then responds in writing. To facilitate the dialogue, direct students to move their desks to face their partners if possible.

Conclude by discussing as a class the best arguments for each position. Call on students to summarize succinctly the views of Roosevelt and of his opposition on the role of government in ending the depression.

Teaching the Main Ideas

Section 22-3: A Mural of the Thirties

This class activity requires one or two class periods; part of the activity may be assigned as homework.

In this activity students, as part of the Federal Art Project, create a mural illustrating life during the New Deal era. Materials needed include a long roll of butcher or freezer paper, individual sheets of poster paper, colored markers, scissors, and tape or glue.

Discuss the nature and purpose of murals (large wall paintings, often created to beautify public places). Tell students that during the lifespan of the Federal Art Project, artists painted more than 2,500 murals on public buildings. Most of these murals were painted in a realistic style, many of them influenced by the style of Mexican artist Diego Rivera, and expressed pride in community life or concern over social problems. Point out that *Construction of a Dam* on page 575 is part of a large mural by William Gropper in the Department of the Interior building, Washington, D.C., and the industrial scene on page 588 is one of 27 large panels by Diego Rivera on the walls of the Detroit Institute of Arts.

Tell the class that they will create a mural depicting American experiences during the New Deal years. Each student will draw a section of the mural on a sheet of paper, then the separate sections will be assembled as one mural. Each student should review the chapter to identify a situation or experience to illustrate. Allow time in or out of class for students to create their illustrations.

Form a committee of students to mark off sections on the mural paper and assign a section to each student. When individual illustrations are completed, students should glue or tape them on their assigned section. Have the committee fill in blank areas with color or with a pattern made up of the initials of New Deal agencies.

Ask the class to evaluate the mural by considering how well it represents the New Deal years. What situations have been covered? What situations have been left out?

Reinforcement Activity

Section 22-2: A Fireside Chat

This individual activity requires one class period, or it may be assigned as homework.

The following activity, in which students write and deliver Roosevelt-style "fireside chats," reinforces students' understanding of key programs of the New Deal.

Explain that in the 1930s radio was not only entertainment but also a major source of information, much as television is today. Roosevelt made especially effective use of radio to inform and inspire. During his presidency, he gave at least 27 fireside chats over the radio; each broadcast usually dealt with a single issue. According to historian John Gunther, even though Roosevelt was speaking from prepared speeches, "he gave the impression . . . of speaking to every listener personally. . . . You could practically feel him . . . in the room."

Have students imagine that they are writing for Roosevelt and choose one New Deal program as the subject of a fireside chat. The speech should explain why the program is necessary and should inspire support. Students should plan a speech that would take three or four minutes to deliver.

When the speeches are written, ask each student to deliver his or her own or have volunteers read them. The talks should be clear, but conversational in tone. Conclude by comparing Roosevelt's fireside chats with present-day presidential television appearances.

Evaluating Progress

Sections 22-1, 22-2, 22-3: Organizing New Deal Programs

This individual activity requires at least half a class period.

This activity is designed to evaluate students' understanding of the scope of the programs implemented during the New Deal.

Remind students that Roosevelt's New Deal produced many different programs. Acknowledge that the numerous programs and agencies can be confusing. Explain that students will use a graphic organizer to organize New Deal programs according to the part of the economy each program was intended to assist, reform, or regulate. (Students were introduced to graphic webs in the Reinforcement Activity in Chapter 9.)

In the center of the chalkboard, write the heading *New Deal Legislation.* Surrounding the heading in four different quadrants, write *Unemployed, Big Agriculture and Small Farmers, Organized Labor and Industry,* and *Banking.*

Direct students to copy the headings on their papers, then identify under each heading the specific acts passed by Congress that relate to that heading. Tell students to use spokes, boxes, circles, or other graphics to organize the information and to write out the full names of the acts, not just the initials.

Final products should include most of the following: *Unemployed:* Federal Emergency Relief Act, Civil Works Administration, Public Works Administration, Civilian Conservation Corps, Works Progress Administration, National Youth Administration. *Agriculture:* Agricultural Adjustment Acts, Farm Credit Administration, Rural Electrification Administration, Bankhead-Jones Farm Tenant Act or Farm Security Administration. *Labor/Industry:* National Industrial Recovery Act, National Labor Relations Act or Wagner Act, Social Security Act. *Banking:* Emergency Banking Relief Act, Glass-Steagall Banking Act, Banking Act of 1935. Home Owner's Loan Corporation and Federal Housing Administration may also fall under banking. Some programs may be placed in more than one category.

Enrichment Activity

Section 22-3: Anti-New Deal Cartoons

This individual activity can be completed in one class period or assigned as homework.

This activity challenges students to summarize criticisms of Roosevelt and/or his New Deal programs by drawing political cartoons.

Ask student to recall critics of Roosevelt and the New Deal mentioned in Section 22-3. (Students should mention big business, Francis Townsend, Charles Coughlin, Huey Long, African Americans, critics of the court packing plan.) Discuss the views of the critics and why their criticisms did or did not change Roosevelt's policies and actions.

Direct students to draw a political cartoon criticizing Roosevelt or the New Deal from the viewpoint of one of the critics. Stimulate creativity by having students study examples of political cartoons in their text or current newspapers and magazines. Discuss the importance of symbols, satire, and titles or dialogue in cartoons.

Arrange a display of students' completed cartoons, organizing them by the subject of criticism. Have the class view the cartoons and then discuss whether or not the cartoonists have accurately represented the critics' views.

Bibliography and Audiovisual Material

Teacher Bibliography

Hunt, R. Douglas. *The Dust Bowl: An Agricultural and Social History*. Chicago: Nelson-Hall, Inc., 1981.

Leuchtenburg, William E. *Franklin D. Roosevelt and the New Deal, 1932–1940*. New York: HarperCollins Publishers, Inc., 1963.

McElvane, Robert S. ed. *Down and Out in the Great Depression: Letters from the Forgotten Man*. Chapel Hill: University of North Carolina Press, 1983.

McKinzie, R. *The New Deal for Artists*. Princeton: Princeton University Press, 1973.

Schlesinger, Arthur M., Jr. *The Age of Roosevelt*. 3 vols. Boston: Houghton Mifflin Co., 1959.

Sitkoff, Harvard. *A New Deal for Blacks: The Emergence of Civil Rights As a National Issue: The Depression Decade*. New York: Oxford University Press, 1978.

Student Bibliography

Dos Passos, John. *The Forty-Second Parallel*. New York: NAL/Dutton, Inc., 1983.

————. *Nineteen Nineteen*. New York: NAL/Dutton, Inc., 1983.

————. *The Big Money*. New York: NAL/Dutton, Inc., 1989.

Franklin D. Roosevelt: His Life and Times. Eds. Otis L. Graham, Jr., and Meghan Robinson Wander. G.K. Hall & Co., 1985.

Guthrie, Woody. *Bound for Glory.* New York: NAL/Dutton, Inc., 1983.

Roosevelt, Eleanor. *Autobiography of Eleanor Roosevelt*. New York: HarperCollins Publishers, Inc., 1961.

Steinbeck, John. *Of Mice and Men*. New York: Bantam Books, 1983.

West, Nathaniel. *A Cool Million*. New York: Farrar, Straus & Giroux, Inc., 1963.

Films, Videocassettes, and Videodiscs

American Chronicle Series: Between the Wars (1918–1939). AIMS Media. Videodisc.

American Documents—Roosevelt and the Fireside Chats: The New Deal Years. 27 min. Coronet/MTI. Videodisc.

Franklin D. Roosevelt: Part 1 The New Deal. 53 min. Coronet/MTI. Videocassette.

The Helping Hand (A Walk Through the 20th Century with Bill Moyers). 56 min. PBS. Videocassette.

The New Deal. 25 min. MCGH. Movie.

Witness to History: The New Deal. 15 min. Guidance Associates. Videocassette.

Filmstrips

The New Deal. 2 color filmstrips. Multi-Media Productions.

Chapter 22

Objectives

- Relate what Roosevelt did to promote recovery.
- Contrast the first and second New Deals.
- Explain why the New Deal coalition faltered.

Introducing THE CHAPTER

For suggestions on introducing Chapter 22, refer to page 573B in the Teacher's Edition.

Developing THE CHAPTER

For activities and teaching strategies to help you reinforce and enrich chapter content, see pages 573B–573D in the Teacher's Edition.

B · A · C · K · G · R · O · U · N · D

Chapter Opener Illustrations
Dorothea Lange was a noted photographic historian of the Great Depression. In this photograph of an unemployment line, taken from above, the contrasting sunlight and shadows seem to tell a story of former prosperity and present despair.

William Gropper was both a political cartoonist and a painter. His huge mural, *Construction of a Dam*, is found in the Department of Interior Building, Washington, D.C.

Garment workers display their posters during a walkout. The public was puzzled by the walkout: many Americans had no jobs at all.

Many Dust Bowlers migrated to California. This journey has been powerfully depicted in John Steinbeck's famous novel *The Grapes of Wrath*. Here a caravan of migrants stops for a moment along the road.

Reduced student page in the Teacher's Edition

Chapter 22 1932-1939

The New Deal

For this cotton picker in Arkansas, life in the Great Depression was even harder than in normal times.

Ben Shahn's lithograph depicts the despair of a Dust Bowl farmer. It was used to publicize the efforts of the government to aid such farmers and their families.

American Voices

Nearly 13 million workers in the United States were unemployed in 1933. Among those millions were Jessie Lopez De La Cruz, her brothers, and her grandmother. Once they had lived in Southern California. Now they were migrant workers, moving from farm to farm to harvest crops. They were joined by other desperate Americans, some from as far away as Oklahoma and Arkansas. Years later, Jessie Lopez De La Cruz remembered the Great Depression.

“In '33, we came up north to follow the crops because my brothers couldn't find any work in Los Angeles during the depression. I remember going hungry to school. I didn't have a sweater. I had nothing. I'd come to school and they'd want to know, 'What did you have for breakfast?' They gave us a paper, to write down what we had! I invented things! We had eggs and milk, I'd say, and the same things the other kids would write, I'd write. . . . You know: glasses of milk, and toast, and oranges and bananas and cereal. I'd never had anything. My grandmother couldn't work, we couldn't work, so we went hungry. One of my friends at school said, 'Jessie, why don't you eat with us?' And I said, 'I don't have any money.' . . . We weren't feeling sorry for ourselves: We didn't know there was anything better than we had. Everybody that came into the camp and stayed there lived the way we did.”

In 1933 President Franklin D. Roosevelt, confident and optimistic, launched the New Deal to encourage economic recovery and provide relief for the poor. To Americans like Jessie De La Cruz and her family, the New Deal programs offered action, aid, and most of all, hope.

Registering for benefits; William Gropper mural, Construction of a Dam; *garment workers on strike; Dust Bowl refugees; a cotton picker, 1935; poster by Ben Shahn.*

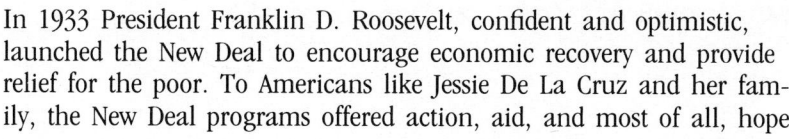

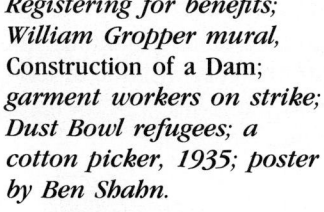

Analyzing Primary Sources

American Voices

The experience of Jessie Lopez De La Cruz suggests the severity of the Great Depression. Mexican Americans, who already suffered job discrimination, were especially hard hit. Jessie Lopez De La Cruz and her family had previously spent summers picking crops and living in crude migrant farm worker camps. Now they began a year-round life of migrant farm work.

1. How did Jessie Lopez De La Cruz respond to questions at school about breakfast? **(She invented menus.)**
2. Based on this account, did all the students in the school share the plight of Jessie Lopez De La Cruz? **(no; only children from camp)**
3. How did she respond to poverty and hunger? **(accepted it; no self-pity)**

GTV Side 4

Chap. 3, Frame 09811

Thinking Big: Depression and the New Deal (Movie)

Search:

Play:

Section 22-1

Objectives

- ***Answer the Focus Question.***
- *Explain why the AAA aroused opposition from some farmers.*
- *Describe how New Deal programs operated to increase employment.*

Introducing

THE SECTION

Have students read the excerpts from Roosevelt's first inaugural address on page 577.

Ask: What did Roosevelt say to combat the nation's fears? **(Students can point to the words about "fear itself" and his promise of action.)** What did he want from Congress? **(broad and sweeping emergency powers)** How would this change the presidency? **(make it more powerful)** Tell students they will learn how Roosevelt used his powers.

B · A · C · K · G · R · O · U · N · D

Time Line Illustrations

1. The symbol for the National Recovery Administration was the Blue Eagle; its slogan: "We Do Our Part." The NRA had broad powers to devise codes for industry. In 1935 the Supreme Court declared the NRA unconstitutional.

2. The Federal Theater Project used Works Progress Administration funds to bring theater to some 30 million people, to small and large cities, to towns and farming villages. Here a poster advertises a production by African Americans.

3. This political cartoon exemplified one criticism of Social Security—that by assigning everyone a number it would dehumanize people.

4. Roosevelt ran for reelection in 1936 and won handily.

5. Labor leader John L. Lewis broke with the American Federation of Labor in 1935 and was the moving force behind the establishment of the Congress of Industrial Organi-

Reduced student page in the Teacher's Edition

CHAPTER TIME LINE

1932-1939

1933 Mar Emergency session of Congress begins to enact New Deal

1935 May Works Progress Administration created

1933 — 1934 — 1935

1934 Indian Reorganization Act halts breakup of tribal lands

Southern Tenant Farmers' Union organized

1935 Aug Social Security Act

22-1 The First New Deal

Focus: What actions did Roosevelt take to promote the nation's recovery?

During the 1932 election campaign, Franklin D. Roosevelt had promised a "New Deal" to "forgotten" Americans "at the bottom of the economic pyramid." He had not proposed a definite plan for battling the depression. However, he had given the voters the impression that he was not afraid to try new solutions. "It is common sense to take a method and try it," he said. "If it fails, admit it frankly and try another. But above all, try something."

The public was impatient for the new President to take bold action against hunger, unemployment, and all the other urgent problems of the Great Depression. However, the nation had a long wait. Roosevelt could not be inaugurated until March 4, four months after his election. Although the new Twentieth Amendment to the Constitution provided that Presidents and newly elected members of Congress would take office in January, the amendment did not go into effect in time to speed Roosevelt's inauguration.

The Bank Holiday

While Roosevelt and the nation waited, the banking system began to collapse. The nation's banks held $41 billion in deposits early in 1933. The banks retained about $6 billion of that sum in cash. The remainder of the money was invested by bankers in home mortgages, business loans, and company stocks.

zations. In 1937 the Steel Workers Organizing Committee, an arm of the CIO, was recognized by U.S. Steel.

6. Marian Anderson, an African-American contralto, had an exceptionally beautiful voice. In 1939 the Daughters of the American Revolution denied her the use of their concert hall, Constitution Hall, in Washington, D.C. The District of Columbia school system also denied her the use of an auditorium. With Eleanor Roosevelt's support, she gave her concert anyway, singing on the steps of the Lincoln Memorial on Easter Sunday before a crowd of more than 75,000.

1936 Organized labor supports Roosevelt for reelection

Dec United Auto Workers sit-down strike at General Motors

1938 Economy slumps

1936 | 1937 | 1938 | 1939

1937 Court-packing controversy

Mar United States Steel recognizes John L. Lewis's steel workers committee

1939 Marian Anderson's Easter Sunday concert at Lincoln Memorial

John Steinbeck publishes *The Grapes of Wrath*

When the Great Depression began, homeowners could not keep up their mortgage payments. Businesses failed, and stock prices continued to decline. As the value of their investments shrank, more and more banks went out of business. Some depositors received part of their money back. Others received none.

When people lost confidence in their banks and demanded their savings in currency, banks began to run out of cash. In Michigan the situation became so grave that on February 14, 1933, the governor declared a "bank holiday." He closed all the banks in the state for several days in order to let them arrange to get more cash. As news of the Michigan closings spread, panicked depositors across the nation lined up to withdraw money from their banks.

Roosevelt Takes Over

The cold rain that fell on Inauguration Day that year matched the bleak mood of the nation. Some 5,000 banks had collapsed. Nearly every state had declared "bank holidays" or had at least set limits on the amount of cash a depositor could withdraw. With major industries operating at only a fraction of their capacity, a quarter of the nation's working people were unemployed. The world, said journalist Agnes Meyer, was "literally rocking beneath our feet."

In his inaugural address, Roosevelt attempted to calm the nation's fears. "First of all," he announced, "let me assert my firm belief that the only thing we have to fear is fear itself." Roosevelt went on to say, "The nation asks for action, and action now." If necessary, he said, he would ask Congress to grant him emergency power "as great as the power that would be given to me if we were in fact invaded by a foreign foe."

On March 5 Roosevelt announced a four-day national bank holiday. Then he called Congress into emergency session. His determination transformed the mood in Washington. Within days the government was charged with energy, like an army command post in wartime. From March 9 through June 16—known as the first "Hundred Days" of the new administration—Congress enacted more than a dozen major programs that gave meaning to Roosevelt's promised "New Deal."

Developing

THE SECTION

Global Connections

Discussion. At about the same time that Roosevelt became President, Adolf Hitler became chancellor of Germany. Both men had to cope with economic depressions. **Ask:** How did their approaches differ? **(Roosevelt worked within a democratic free enterprise system. Hitler set up a fascist dictatorship.)**

Thinking Critically

Evaluation. Critics of Roosevelt point out that he adopted policies that Hoover had instituted. Ask students to recall what measures Hoover took to stop the depression. (voluntary associations, established POUR, Reconstruction Finance Corporation, and Emergency Relief Construction Act) According to Hoover, who was to take the lead in dealing with the depression? (states) According to Roosevelt? (federal government) Why was Roosevelt more successful than Hoover? (Answers may include that Roosevelt projected confidence and decisive leadership; spent more money; made federal government more active.)

Linking Past and Present

Discussion. Comparisons have been made between the bank failures of the depression and the S&L failures of the late 1980s and early 1990s. **Ask:** Why did the S&Ls fail? **(Answers may include that basic reason was reckless lending policies, inadequate government regulation.)**

Using the Visuals

Analyzing a Graph. Refer students to the graph on this page. **Ask:** What generalizations can be made about the banking system prior to 1934? **(weak; unstable; large number of bank failures)** What can explain the large number of bank closures in 1933? **(run on banks; after bank holiday bad banks could not reopen)** Was Roosevelt successful in his bank policy? **(yes)** What evidence supports your answer? **(steep drop in bank failures in 1934)** Why did it become safer to keep money in reopened banks? **(banks sound, deposits insured)**

Connections: Economics

The Agricultural Adjustment Act shocked many people because it mandated the destruction of crops and animals. Henry A Wallace, the Secretary of Agriculture, went on the radio to defend it. He said that the act was *"a means of restoring the farmer's purchasing power"* and *"an effort to reduce those wastes of distribution which now cause food to pile up, unused, while people go hungry a hundred miles away."* He warned that *"unless, as we lift farm prices, we also unite to control production, this plan will not work for long. And the only way we can control production for the long pull is for you farmers to organize, and stick, and do it yourselves."*

Reduced student page in the Teacher's Edition

Ending the Bank Panic

On March 9 Congress hurriedly passed the Emergency Banking Relief Act. Now banks that the Treasury Department declared sound could reopen. On Sunday evening, March 12, Roosevelt made the first of a number of radio broadcasts that he called "fireside chats." He told the American people that banks would reopen the next day. Only banks in grave difficulty would stay closed. "I assure you," he said, "that it is safer to keep your money in a reopened bank than under the mattress."

By the end of the next week, three fourths of the nation's banks were again doing business. Congress then passed the Glass-Steagall Banking Act, which provided rules to keep bankers from speculating in unsound investments. The act also set up the Federal Deposit Insurance Corporation (FDIC), an agency that insures individual deposits in member banks for up to $5,000. These measures renewed public confidence in banks, and the frantic withdrawals stopped.

Recovery in Agriculture

Having restored confidence in the banks, Roosevelt and the Congress quickly turned to other severe problems. To bring about economic recovery and to provide immediate relief to the unemployed and the hungry, they launched an array of programs.

Two key pieces of legislation were geared to helping the groups on which the economy depended— industry and agriculture. To revitalize agriculture, Congress passed the Agricultural Adjustment Act. This act, carried out under Secretary of Agriculture Henry Wallace, was based on the idea that farmers could earn more by producing less. "We have been producing more of some crops than we consume or can sell in a depressed world market," said Roosevelt in a fireside chat. "The cure is not to produce so much."

The Agricultural Adjustment Administration (AAA) would pay farmers to produce less. Agricultural agents set out to convince farmers to destroy part of their existing crops, plant fewer acres, and limit the number of animals they raised. In 1933

In 1933, many worried depositors found bank doors closed.

Social History

Hugh Samuel Johnson (1882–1942) attended West Point, served with the army in Mexico in 1916, and was in charge of the draft during World War I. In 1918 he was made a Brigadier General. A New Deal colleague described him as "a blustering, flamboyant person." He was also energetic, flying around the country and persuading, cajoling, and bullying businessmen to sign the NRA codes.

Writing About History

Newspaper Article. As journalists working in the 1930s, have students write newspaper articles describing how the high unemployment rate might have affected one small town. Have them consider the effects on the town's merchants, banks, doctors and dentists, and schools, as well as on its inhabitants in general. They should consider the main source of income for the town, whether factory or farm.

Thinking Critically

Application. Private utilities challenged the constitutionality of TVA in the courts on the principal that it was using tax-backed money to compete with them in the energy market. The Supreme Court in 1939 ruled against the utilities companies. The Court's decision held that flood control, reforestation, and irrigation were the main purposes of TVA and electrical energy was a by-product.

One scholar of TVA refers to this interpretation as a "peculiarly fictitious legal fiction." Ask students to explain this statement. Then ask what students think was the main purpose of the TVA.

the agents persuaded farmers to destroy 10 million acres of cotton. In return, cotton farmers received more than $100 million. The AAA also arranged the slaughter of 6 million pigs to prevent a surplus of pork.

As production fell, however, farm prices rose. Between 1933 and 1934 wheat and cotton doubled in price. For the first time in years some farmers had money to pay debts and buy supplies.

In later years, the AAA arranged payments before crops were planted or farm animals bred. For example, in 1934 the AAA paid farmers to stop planting crops on acreage that was more than equal in size to the entire state of Illinois.

The new farm program helped to slow the ruinous cycle of surplus crops, falling prices, and farm bankruptcy. However, the program caused unexpected hardship to tenant farmers and sharecroppers, who were often evicted by farm owners trying to cut back on crop production.

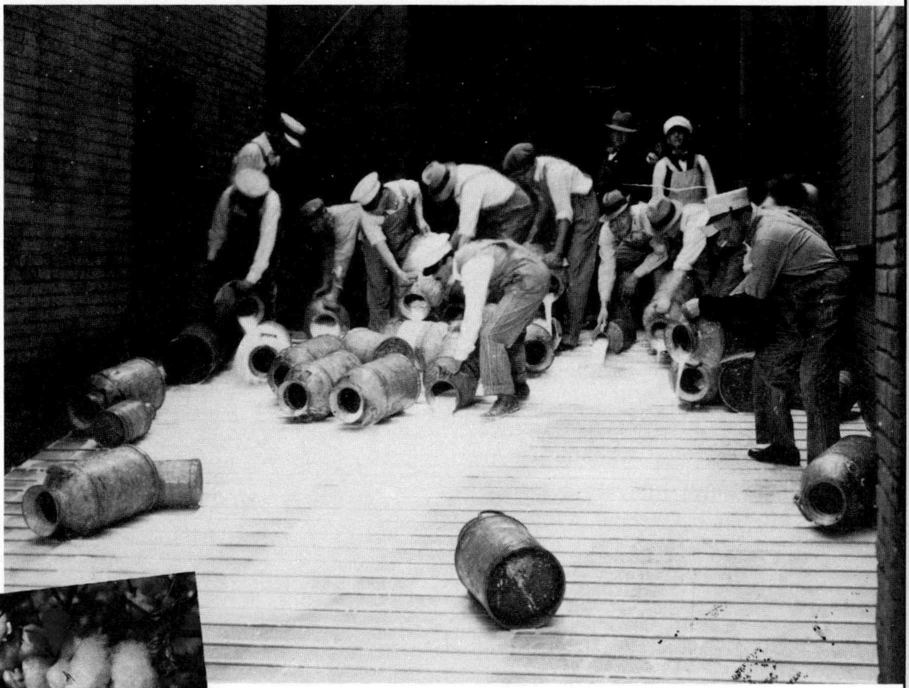

When farm prices plunged, desperate farmers and distributors destroyed products in protest rather than sell them at a loss.

Recovery in Industry

One of the most ambitious bills of the Hundred Days was the National Industrial Recovery Act, which established the National Recovery Administration (NRA). Planners of the NRA took as their model the cooperation in industrial planning that had gone on during World War I. Suspending antitrust laws, the NRA required industries to cooperate in drawing up codes to standardize production quotas, trade practices, and prices. When a code was approved by the President, it became law.

The act required that codes set maximum hours and minimum wages so no one business could gain an advantage by paying low wages for long hours. In theory, because of shorter hours, firms would hire more workers, and because workers earned higher wages, they would buy more goods. The act also guaranteed the right to organize.

Energetic cavalry veteran General Hugh S. Johnson worked with industries to draw up codes. Employers who signed codes could display the Blue Eagle, with the motto "We do our part." The Blue Eagle soon appeared on oil rigs and in coal mines, lumber mills, and small factories and shops.

Critics of the NRA. In 1933 people cheered the NRA. But by 1935 disappointment had set in, and critics were saying that NRA stood for "No Recovery Allowed." Small business owners charged that when the giants of industry cooperated to draw up codes, they were forming monopolies.

Employers were unhappy with the NRA provision that fostered unionization, while union leaders claimed that unions were making gains in only a few of the larger industries. African-American

Active Learning

Group Discussion. Gardiner C. Means, a New Deal official, told Studs Terkel, *"Had the NRA continued, it would have meant dangerously limiting the role of the market in limiting prices. ...The government handed industry over to industry to run... industry became scared of its own people. Too much power was being delegated to the code authorities... You might say NRA's greatest contribution to our society is that it proved that self-regulation by industry doesn't work."*

Divide the class into groups of five students each. Each group is to discuss the following issues: Should industry be regulated at all, other than by workings of the market? If so, who should regulate it: the government or industry itself? A representative of each group can report the group's findings to the class and explain the reasons for their opinions.

Social History

Despite the increase of women workers during the depression, job discrimination against women, especially married women increased. The federal government tolerated and even engaged in discriminatory pay practices. On WPA projects men were paid $5 per day, women received only $3.

Multicultural Perspectives

More than one hundred NRA codes had regional wage differentials. Southern workers, in many instances black, were paid less than people doing the same work elsewhere. NRA did not cover occupations in which most African Americans were engaged: farm labor and domestic service. In instances where equal pay was enforced, African Americans were often replaced by white laborers.

workers complained that price-fixing meant that the prices they paid for goods were increasing faster than the wages they earned. To one black writer, NRA meant "Negroes Ruined Again."

Finally, with more than five hundred codes, the whole system had become hopelessly complicated, leaving it open to the charge of too much government interference in business. Attempts by Congress to revise the NRA failed to please everyone. One lasting effect, however, stemmed from the clause guaranteeing employees "the right to organize and bargain collectively." For the first time, the government was backing organized labor, and union membership began to rise.

American Voices

"Franklin Roosevelt is no crusader. He is no tribune of the people. He is no enemy of entrenched privilege. He is a pleasant man who, without any important qualifications for the office, would very much like to be President."

—Walter Lippmann, 1932

Relief from Suffering

While the President and Congress tried to bring about recovery in agriculture and industry, they also faced the reality that some 13 million people were unemployed and hungry. Lewis Andreas, a Chicago doctor, told author Studs Terkel:

"People starved on the street . . . . Every day . . . somebody would faint on a streetcar. They'd bring him in, and they wouldn't ask any questions. . . . They knew what it was. Hunger. . . . People were flopping on the streets from hunger."

To deal with the immediate problem, Congress created the Federal Emergency Relief Administration (FERA). It channeled federal funds through state agencies, which helped the neediest with cash and groceries. However, FERA's very dynamic director, Harry L. Hopkins, thought direct relief might destroy people's self-reliance. He proposed a one-year work relief program, the Civil Works Administration (CWA). More than 4 million workers were hired to build and repair roads and teach in country schools, for example.

The PWA. In 1933 another work relief program got underway: the Public Works Administration (PWA), directed by Roosevelt's efficient Secretary of the Interior, Harold L. Ickes. The President expected PWA projects to provide jobs, stimulate business, and increase purchasing power. The PWA financed heavy construction, such as the completion of Boulder Dam in Nevada, which was to be carried out by private contractors. From 1933 through 1939 the PWA gave or loaned $6 billion for construction of lighthouses, bridges, sewer systems, and other construction. PWA dollars financed more than half of all the school buildings constructed during those years.

The CCC. The government also offered work relief to the 250,000 jobless young people roaming the country. To help these and other unemployed youth, Congress created the Civilian Conservation Corps (CCC). The CCC gave work to single men between the ages of eighteen and twenty-five, both blacks and whites.

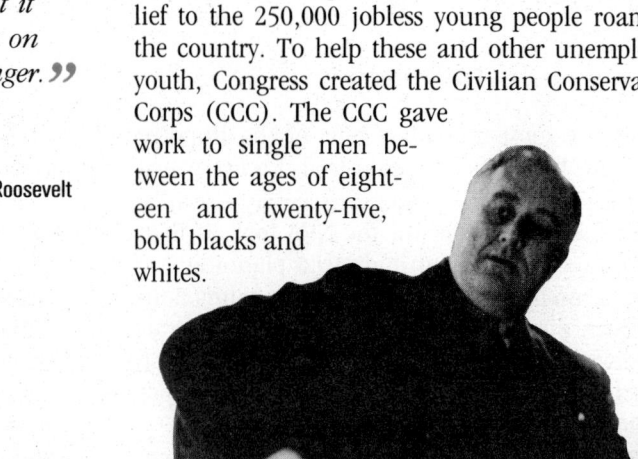

President Roosevelt at work

Connections: Economics
Before HOLC, mortgages would run usually for a number of years, at the end of which time the entire principal had to be repaid or the loan renegotiated. HOLC issued mortgages with uniform monthly payments that included both principal and interest. At the end of a time period the mortgage was paid off.

Connections: Geography
TVA was only one public power project the New Deal accomplished. Others include the Bonneville Dam on the Columbia River in Oregon and Washington and the Grand Coulee Dam in Washington.

Known as Roosevelt's "Tree Army," the CCC replanted national forests, cleared trails, restored historic sites, and battled forest fires. Workers were given room and board and paid $30 per month, part of which was sent home to their families.

The CCC was a great success. Blackie Gold told author Studs Terkel:

"We just dug trenches and kept planting trees. You could plant about a hundred an hour. . . . I really enjoyed it. I had three wonderful square meals a day. . . . You learned that everybody here was equal. There was nobody better than another in the CCC's. We never had any race riots."

Mortgage Relief

Also in need of immediate relief were the tens of thousands of people on the verge of losing their homes or farms because they could not keep up mortgage payments. By 1933 more than a thousand families were losing their homes each day.

By executive order, Roosevelt set up the Farm Credit Administration (FCA). It helped farmers borrow money to pay off their old mortgages. The new loans had lower interest rates than regular mortgages and could be repaid over a longer time. Eventually the FCA arranged refinancing for one fifth of all farm mortgages.

The Home Owners Loan Corporation (HOLC) did the same for townspeople, eventually refinancing one fifth of all home loans. In 1934 Congress also set up the Federal Housing Administration (FHA). The FHA insured home loans, guaranteeing creditors that if borrowers failed to repay, it would take over the property and the loan. Thus, creditors were more willing to loan to people of modest means.

The TVA

The depression had hit one area of the country especially hard. This was the Tennessee Valley, a rural area with a system of rivers that extends from the Great Smoky Mountains to the Mississippi.

During World War I the government built two explosives plants on the Tennessee River at Muscle Shoals, Alabama. It also started work on a dam to produce electricity. After the war Senator George W. Norris of Nebraska proposed that the government use the dam to provide low-cost electrical power for the people of the Tennessee Valley.

Norris's plan became part of the New Deal. Roosevelt and Congress created the Tennessee Valley Authority (TVA), which took over the dam and the two plants and sold power directly to homes and businesses. The TVA also planned additional dams for power and flood control. It was the first time the federal government had entered the energy business.

An article in *Harper's Magazine* described Roosevelt's view of the TVA:

"He revealed that he was thinking less . . . of the Tennessee River and its wasted electric energy than . . . of the Tennessee Valley and its wasted human energy. . . . They are rubbing hard on a modern sixty-watt Aladdin's lamp to make miracles happen in the Valley. They have the stupendous task of introducing not only electric lights but also electric appliances to people who scratch their fields with handmade plows [and] card their cotton for homemade quilts."

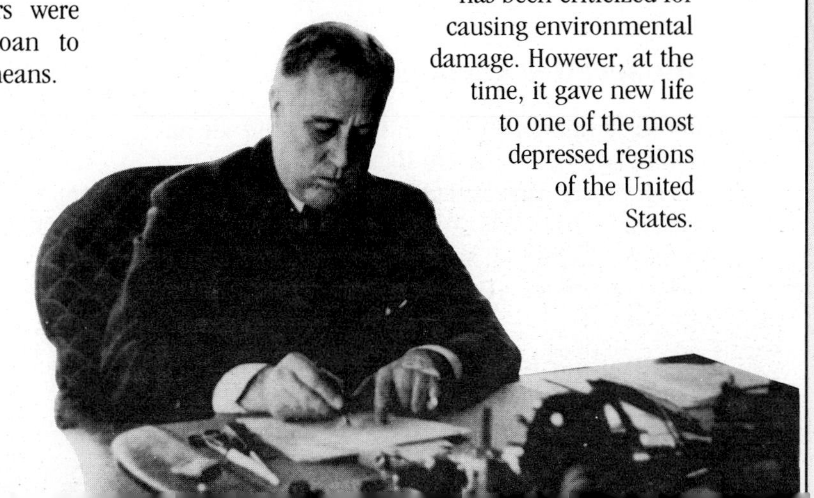

In recent years the TVA has been criticized for causing environmental damage. However, at the time, it gave new life to one of the most depressed regions of the United States.

Linking Past and Present

Discussion. With the CCC as an example, national leaders periodically propose some type of national service for young Americans. Have students give their opinions on such a plan. Is there a need for it? If so, what form should the service take? For how long? For what age group? Should it be for young women as well as young men?

Backyard History

Conducting an Interview. Students can interview a relative, friend, or neighbor who lived through the depression. Possible questions: How old were you? How did the depression affect your family? Did any member of the family participate in a New Deal program? What did you or your family think of President Roosevelt and the New Deal? Why? Students can share results with the class.

Thinking Critically

Application. Help students to see the relationship of the Agricultural Adjustment Act to a basic economic law. **Ask:** How did the effects of the Agricultural Adjustment Act illustrate the law of supply and demand? (If demand for food is greater than supply, prices will increase; if supply is greater than demand, prices will go down.) To avoid destruction of crops and animals in the future what alternatives were enacted? (pay farmers to plant fewer crops; raise fewer animals) Why were surpluses not distributed to needy Americans? (would further drive down farm prices)

Writing About History

Editorial. Have each student assume a role as the editor of a newspaper in the Tennessee Valley in the 1930s. Ask each to write an editorial opposing or favoring the creation of the Tennessee Valley Authority. The editorial should describe the Tennessee Valley Authority bill, note the controversy surrounding it, and provide reasons why Congress should defeat or pass the bill. Have students with different viewpoints read their editorials in class.

Connections: Science and Technology

In the message that Roosevelt submitted to Congress with his proposal for TVA legislation, he stated that the project *"transcends mere power development: it enters the wide fields of flood control, soil erosion, afforestation, elimination from agricultural use of marginal lands. . . . [It] leads logically to national planning for a complete river watershed, involving many states, and the future lives . . . of millions."*

Reduced student page in the Teacher's Edition

Exploring Issues

THE ROLE OF GOVERNMENT

The Tennessee Valley Authority

Harry Ransley, a member of Congress from Pennsylvania, was alarmed by the bill to create the Tennessee Valley Authority. This vast plan for the poverty-stricken Tennessee Valley would put government in the electric power business. "It is the entering wedge," he warned members of the House of Representatives in April 1933. "Continue along these lines and you will have a socialist government, destroying the initiative that has made this country great."

A representative from Tennessee, Gordon Browning, disagreed. "Members who are complaining about . . . putting the government into competition with private enterprise seem not to distinguish between what belongs to private enterprise and what belongs to the public." The electric power generated by the nation's rivers should not be used for private profit, Browning declared. "The little fellow who tills his farm on the hillside near the Tennessee Valley is just as much entitled to the use of this public resource for a reasonable charge as the man who runs a great manufacturing establishment."

When President Roosevelt was asked the political philosophy behind the project, he replied, "I'll tell them it's neither fish nor fowl. But, whatever it is, it will taste awfully good to the people of the Tennessee Valley."

The President's plan called for a public corporation, the Tennessee Valley Authority, "clothed with the power of government but possessed of the flexibility and initiative of a private enterprise." TVA would build dams on the Tennessee River to provide low-cost electric power to valley residents. It would use two World War I plants to make low-cost fertilizer. It would also establish projects to control flooding, to plant forests, and to conserve the soil.

TVA opponents believed government should stay out of business. When the government took over the railroads during World War I, it ran them very badly, claimed John Tabor of New York. "What can we expect if the government now tries to run power and fertilizer plants?"

John Rich of Pennsylvania argued that the government's job was to *regulate* business, not to own it. "If you want efficient business," he said, "it must not be controlled by politicians."

Others, however, pointed out that the state commissions set up to regulate private power companies had failed. Such commissions, said Senator George Norris of Ne-

Roosevelt's Advisors

Roosevelt was not alone in his efforts to lift the nation out of the depression. He turned to many others for advice. One circle of advisors was known as the "Brain Trust" because its members were university professors. This group—mainly government professor Raymond Moley, economist Rexford G. Tugwell, and law professor Adolf A. Berle, Jr.—helped shape New Deal programs.

One of the President's most important advisors was his wife, Eleanor Roosevelt. Since 1921, when polio left Roosevelt unable to walk, she had traveled the country as his "legs and ears." At the same time, she vigorously pursued her own concerns for people whose needs had often been overlooked,

Multicultural Perspectives

The precise impact of the Black Cabinet on the New Deal is difficult to determine. African Americans did have the ear and sympathies of Eleanor Roosevelt. She in turn exercised great influence on her husband. He, however, was reluctant to estrange elements of his constituency—especially the Democratic "Solid South"—by pressing strongly for African-American rights. She has said, *"When I would protest, he would simply say, 'first things come first, and I can't alienate certain votes I need for measures that are more important at the moment."* Historian Nancy Weiss has commented, *"The Black Cabinet was important to black people because it signified that the government was paying attention to them in ways that had never been the case before."*

Connections: Geography

Map Making. Have a group of students prepare a map of the Tennessee River and the area served by TVA electric power, with its principal dams. **Ask:** Which states benefit from the power? Why are the major dams located on the eastern part of the river?

Built on the Tennessee in 1925, Wilson Dam became part of the TVA.

braska, could no more control utility rates "than a fly could interfere with the onward march of an elephant." To him, the solution was public ownership.

Another supporter said, "I look upon the power in the river as I do the sunshine air, and the water of the . . . oceans. It is a right that is inherent to our peoples and should be used for the welfare of all people and not in the interests of a few."

To many supporters of TVA, the issue boiled down to the price of electricity. A representative from Tennessee pointed out that the people of his district were paying 10 cents a kilowatt-hour for electricity from a private company. In Canada, where the power company was publicly owned, the rate was 1.5 cents a kilowatt-hour. "Let us now insist," he urged, "that our people have a right to as low a rate as those people in Canada."

The battle over public versus private power ended temporarily when Congress approved creation of TVA. But the issues it evoked were far from decided. TVA brought low-cost electric power and fertilizer to one of the most depressed areas of the country. However, the question of what part the government should play in the economy is as controversial today as it was at the time of the TVA controversy in 1933.

1. Why did opponents of TVA think that the government should stay out of the electric power business?
2. What reasons did the TVA's supporters give for public ownership?
3. Who do you think should own such natural resources as rivers, forests, and coastlines? What rights should private business have to use or control them?

Exploring Issues

ANSWERS

1. Answers may include that government should not compete with private business; it would destroy individual initiative; government operation of business is inefficient.
2. Answers may include that commissions could not control utility rates; power resources belonged to all the people, not just to private businesses; only a government agency could provide cheap power.
3. Opinions will vary.

such as working women, sharecroppers, and youth. She also actively sought social justice for African Americans.

In part due his wife's urgings, President Roosevelt appointed many more African Americans to administrative positions than had any President before him. These officials met informally from time to time, becoming known as Roosevelt's "Black Brain Trust," or "Black Cabinet." Prominent members of the group included Mary McLeod Bethune of the National Youth Administration, Dr. Robert Weaver of the Public Works Administration, and William H. Hastie of the Department of the Interior. Although they could not erase racial injustice, they did win a fairer share of the benefits of the New Deal for African Americans.

Using the Visuals

Interpreting a Chart. The New Deal was based upon three R's—relief, recovery, and reform. Have students study the chart on this page and decide for each agency or program whether it was started for relief, recovery, or reform. Some agencies or programs may have had more than one purpose, so students should indicate the primary goal.

Section Review
ANSWERS

1. Congress passed Emergency Banking Relief Act. In fireside chat, Roosevelt assured Americans it was now safe to deposit money in banks.
2. Answers may include: AAA, paid farmers to produce less thus raising prices of crops; NIRA set maximum working hours and minimum wages and required industries to set production codes; FERA provided funds for the needy; CWA and PWA provided jobs; CCC, provided jobs for young people; FCA lent money to pay off farmers' mortgages; FHA provided money for home loans.
3. Answers may include: destroying crops would ultimately benefit farmers by bringing up prices, would help country out of the depression, would help set up a more rational system of crop production to prevent the market from being glutted.
4. Answers may include the CWA, the PWA, the CCC.
Linking Past and Present: Answers will vary.

B · A · C · K · G · R · O · U · N · D

Social History

Raymond Moley, a member of Roosevelt's original Brain Trust, spoke to Studs Terkel about the Hundred Days: *"During the whole '33 one-hundred days Congress people didn't know what was going on . . . couldn't understand these things that were being passed so fast. They knew something was happening, something good for them. They began investing and working and hoping again."*

Reduced student page in the Teacher's Edition

Highlights of the First New Deal 1933 – 1934

Date Signed	Agency or Program		Purpose	Status
March 1933	CCC	Civilian Conservation Corps	Provide employment for men 18-25 years of age	Ended in 1942
May 1933	AAA	Agricultural Adjustment Administration	Advise and assist farmers	Largely ended in 1936
	FERA	Federal Emergency Relief Administration	Provide direct relief to needy Americans	Ended in 1936
	TVA	Tennessee Valley Authority	Help develop resources of Tennessee Valley	Still in operation
June 1933	HOLC	Home Owners Loan Corporation	Help townspeople refinance mortgages	Ended in 1950
	NRA	National Recovery Administration	Revive American business	Ended in 1935
	PWA	Public Works Administration	Provide employment on public works	Ended in 1937
	FCA	Farm Credit Administration	Set up a credit system for farmers	Became part of Dept. of Agric. in 1939
	FDIC	Federal Deposit Insurance Corporation	Set up a system to guarantee individual bank deposits	Still in operation
November 1933	CWA	Civil Works Administration	Provide employment at federal expense	Ended in 1934
June 1934	SEC	Securities and Exchange Commission	Protect public and private investors in stocks	Still in operation
	FHA	Federal Housing Administration	Insure bank loans for home construction and repair	Still in operation

The End of the Hundred Days

Would New Deal programs bring recovery? At the end of Roosevelt's first hundred days, it was too early to tell. The programs that Congress approved had barely begun to be put in place. However, Roosevelt won wide praise from many Americans. "The admirable trait in Roosevelt is that he has the guts to try," said a Republican senator. A journalist noted that "Roosevelt the candidate and Roosevelt the President are two different men. The oath of office seems suddenly to have transfigured him from a man of mere charm and buoyancy to one of dynamic aggressiveness."

Roosevelt's optimism was contagious. The American public began to believe that the nightmare of the Great Depression might really end.

Section Review

1. Comprehension. How did Roosevelt end the bank panic?

2. Comprehension. Describe five programs of the first New Deal. How was each expected to help the nation recover from the depression?

3. Synthesis. What arguments might an agricultural agent have made to a farmer who did not want to destroy crops?

4. Application. Which New Deal programs were intended to increase employment?

Linking Past and Present. Gather information about current job programs for youth. Sources of information include school counselors, the library, and state and federal employment services.

Connections: Politics
Gerald L. K. Smith, Francis Townsend, and Father Charles E. Coughlin formed the Union party in 1936. The party's presidential candidate was Representative William Lemke of North Dakota. However, as the cartoon below suggests, dissension among its leaders over who was first among equals crippled the party.

22-2 The Second New Deal

Focus: How did the second New Deal differ from the first?

In spite of all the programs aimed at promoting recovery and relief, by the summer of 1934 many Americans were dissatisfied with the New Deal. Ernie Pyle, a reporter for the *Washington Daily News*, observed the national mood:

> *"Out all over the country the people with a little money are complaining because the government is spending so much on the people who have no money. . . . [T]he people with no money are complaining because the government doesn't give them more work."*

Some people thought that the New Deal, with its "alphabet agencies," was leading to too much government control. Other people wanted government to do still more to end the Great Depression.

Conservative Critics

Many people saw the New Deal as a threat to the relationship between individuals and the government. These conservative critics accused President Roosevelt of tampering with the Constitution.

Former General Motors board member John Raskob said business must "protect society from the suffering it is bound to endure if . . . no one should be allowed to get rich." He and others formed the American Liberty League "to defend the Constitution . . . [and] foster the right to work, earn, save, and acquire property."

The league warned that Roosevelt was leading the nation toward dictatorship and that his advisors were either impractical dreamers or communists. Although the league spent more than a half a million dollars publicizing its views, it never gained wide support. Businessmen were no longer the nation's heroes, as they had been in the 1920s. Now, ordinary people were likely to favor whatever wealthy businessmen were against.

Quick Cures

While conservatives attacked Roosevelt from one side, others offered more radical solutions. Three challengers in particular attracted attention with their plans to reform the economy and bring permanent relief to ordinary citizens.

Huey Long's friend Gerald L. K. Smith and others formed a third party in 1936.

The Townsend Plan. Dr. Francis E. Townsend, a retired physician, gathered many followers by offering "a quick cure for this depression." He wanted the government to pay a monthly pension of $200 to every citizen aged sixty and older who agreed to spend the entire amount every month. Such

Section 22-2

Objectives

- ***Answer the Focus Question.***
- *Explain the popularity of Townsend's, Coughlin's, and Long's ideas.*
- *Describe the WPA, the Wagner Act, and Social Security.*
- *Explain Roosevelt's victory over Landon in 1936.*

Introducing

THE SECTION

Have a student read aloud the observation by Ernie Pyle on this page. **Ask:**

1. What two groups, according to Pyle, are dissatisfied with the New Deal? Why? **(those with little money and those with no money; some thought too much money was being spent on relief and recovery programs, some thought not enough.)**
2. Read to the class Raymond Moley's statement in the margin note "Social History," on page 584. What people approved of the New Deal? **(those to whom it gave hope)**

Tell students they will now read about what critics of the New Deal said and proposed and what measures were part of the New Deal itself in the period following the Hundred Days.

Developing

THE SECTION

Connections: Literature

Book Report. Huey Long has received fictitional treatment in several novels. The most notable is Robert Penn Warren's Pulitzer-Prize winning *All the King's Men*, in which the main character, Willie Stark, is based on Long. Interested students might read Warren's novel and make written or oral reports on it.

Active Learning

Radio Panel Discussion. Have four students enact a radio panel discussion between critics of the New Deal. One student can be the moderator, the other three will portray Townsend, Coughlin, and Long, who will each discuss their solutions to the depression. The audience (class) should be divided into the elderly, farmers, workers, and veterans. They can question the panelists as to how they will be affected by their ideas.

Multicultural Perspectives

Father Divine, an African-American religious leader, refused to allow any of his followers to accept public relief, but he made sure that none went hungry. He served them at his restaurants for fifteen cents a meal. He sold them coal at cost and offered haircuts at his barber shops for three to five cents.

Reduced student page in the Teacher's Edition

spending, Townsend believed, would stimulate "every avenue of commerce and trade."

Economists pointed out that the Townsend Plan would require $24 billion each year, more than half the national income. However, over a thousand Townsend Clubs sprang up, and members collected over 10 million signatures on petitions favoring the plan.

The "Radio Priest." Father Charles E. Coughlin, a Catholic priest, reached his followers by radio. Coughlin had begun broadcasting from Detroit in 1926, and had soon attracted an audience of over 30 million listeners each week. By 1934 he was receiving more mail than any other American.

At first, Coughlin supported Roosevelt. However, he soon grew critical of the New Deal. Bankers, Coughlin believed, had brought ruin to working people. He called Roosevelt "the great betrayer" for not expelling bankers from positions of power.

As Coughlin's speeches became more bitter, his following slipped away. Later, his message became openly racist, and church officials ordered him to stop his broadcasts.

Huey "Kingfish" Long. A third major challenge to the President came from Huey Long of Louisiana. As governor and later as a senator, Long—known as the "Kingfish"—had built a powerful political machine. He also created a political organization that appealed to struggling farmers and workers. Its motto was "Share Our Wealth." Long proposed that the government impose heavy income and inheritance taxes on the wealthy and spend the money on the poor.

Every family should have a home, a car, and a radio, Long said. He called for a one-time payment of $5,000 and a minimum annual income of $2,500 for every family, free college educations for young people, and bonuses for veterans. Share-Our-Wealth clubs spread from Louisiana to other states, and by mid-1935 Long claimed 7 million followers.

Roosevelt broadcast 27 "fireside chats" over the new medium—radio.

Extending the New Deal

Although by mid-1934 most people still supported the President's efforts to solve the nation's problems, millions of working-class and middle-class Americans were becoming restless. Many agreed with a worker from Pennsylvania who wrote to Eleanor Roosevelt, the President's wife: "The forgotten man is still forgotten. . . . The New Deal and NRA has only helped big business."

For the 11 million unemployed, relief efforts did not seem adequate. In 1934, Martha Gellhorn, a federal relief investigator, told the President:

> *"They say to you quietly, like people who have been betrayed but are too tired to be angry, 'How does he expect us to live on that [amount of relief]?'"*

Labor unrest resulted in strikes during the summer, and the middle class showed more sympathy toward the striking workers than they ever had before. In Minneapolis, truckers went on strike, and workers throughout the city stopped work to show their support. When police tried to break the strike, two workers were killed and sixty-seven were wounded. In the funeral procession for one of the fallen strikers, tens of thousands of working-class and middle-class residents marched together. The governor ended the strike by stepping in on the side of the strikers.

A longshoremen's strike that closed all West Coast ports also led to bloodshed, with two strikers killed. And again, tens of thousands of supporters marched to the funeral. In San Francisco other workers struck to protest the violence against the longshoremen, and the city came to a halt. Finally, arbitration settled the dispute in the union's favor.

Meanwhile, farmers were organizing to call attention to rural poverty. In Arkansas, sharecroppers, tenant farmers, and small-business owners—both black and white—banded to-

Social History
The cartoon about Eleanor Roosevelt below was typical of jokes made about her in the 1930s and early 1940s. Other cartoons also depicted people encountering her in unlikely places. Radio comedians' gags celebrated her ubiquity.

Connections: Economics
The WPA and other New Deal programs pumped billions of dollars into the economy—a policy called "priming the pump," referring to the procedure of putting a little water into a pump to get it started. British economist John Maynard Keynes was a noted proponent of government spending money to get an economy moving.

Writing About History

Biography. Eleanor Roosevelt often went on fact-finding trips throughout the country, talking to Americans about their concerns. She established a standard of high visibility and activity for subsequent First Ladies. Have students research her life and then write an account of her activities and accomplishments.

Ask students about the role of First Ladies today. **(Some have initiated anti-drug and literacy programs, for example.)**

As the cartoon suggests, Eleanor Roosevelt seemed to be everywhere. Here, she observes working conditions in a West Virginia coal mine.

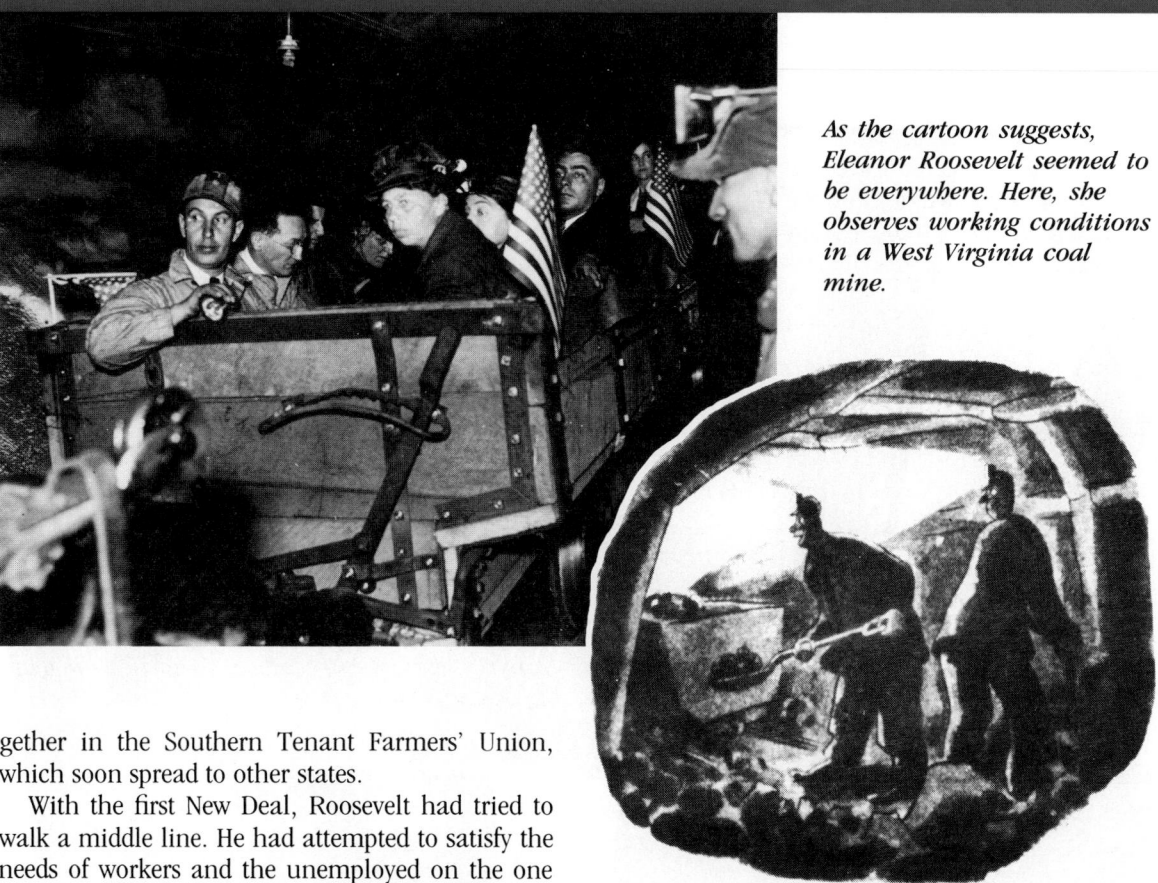

"For gosh sakes, here comes Mrs. Roosevelt!"
Drawing by Robt. Day; © 1933, 1961 The New Yorker Magazine, Inc.

gether in the Southern Tenant Farmers' Union, which soon spread to other states.

With the first New Deal, Roosevelt had tried to walk a middle line. He had attempted to satisfy the needs of workers and the unemployed on the one hand, and of big business and agriculture on the other. Now he found that he could not satisfy everyone. And he could not overlook the clamor from the shops, factories, and fields.

Whether from a deep desire to relieve the suffering of the depression's worst victims, or from a canny political instinct that they could offer him more votes, Roosevelt decided to focus his efforts on helping ordinary people. When Congress met in January 1935, the President outlined a new program of relief and reform that would guarantee the average individual a minimum of economic security. In the following months, Congress enacted this program, sometimes called "the second New Deal."

The Works Progress Administration

The most successful effort of the second New Deal was a massive work relief program managed through a new agency, the Works Progress Administration (WPA). The WPA reflected Roosevelt's belief in the importance of giving people meaningful jobs instead of direct relief payments or "make-work" tasks such as raking leaves. The goal, he said, was to "preserve not only the bodies of the unemployed, . . . but also their self-respect, their self-confidence and courage and determination."

Roosevelt named the former FERA director, Harry L. Hopkins, to manage the new agency. By mid-1936 WPA projects were employing 3,840,000 people at jobs ranging from road repair to office work to school teaching.

The WPA also found work for writers and artists. "They've got to eat just like other people," Hopkins said. WPA writers prepared state guidebooks, artists painted murals in government buildings, and actors presented plays in local parks and theaters. Historians trekked down back roads, notebooks and pencils in hand, to record people's personal experiences. One group collected folk songs and folk stories, for example, while another preserved the recollections of former slaves.

Active Learning

Drawing Political Cartoons. Critics of Roosevelt argued that his measures were ruining the free enterprise system with welfare programs and government control of business. Others maintained his programs were designed to aid and preserve the free enterprise system. Divide students into groups. Each group is to create a political cartoon either attacking the New Deal or supporting it. Discuss with students what alternatives were offered by opponents of the New Deal.

Backyard History

Oral Report. Artists employed by the Federal Art Project created 2,566 murals and 17,744 pieces of sculpture. These can be found in schools, hospitals, government buildings, and other public places. Have students find out if there are any such murals and sculptures in their area. They can report their location to the class as well as describe the works and provide photographs or other reproductions of them.

Thinking Critically

Analysis. Have students discuss the feelings evoked by the art works on this page. (optimism, dynamic quality) **Ask:** How do you think the artists felt to have their works on display? (proud, restored their confidence)

Connections: The Arts

The Federal Writers Project employed a number of writers who were to gain future distinction, among them Saul Bellow, John Cheever, Ralph Ellison, and Richard Wright. At its peak, the Federal Music Project employed some 15,000 musicians.

Multicultural Perspectives

Los Tres Grandes—Mexican painters José Clemente Orozco, Diego Rivera, and David Alfaro Siqueiros—painted murals in California, Michigan, New Hampshire, and New York in 1932 and 1933.

Reduced student page in the Teacher's Edition

The bold, realistic industrial scenes of Mexican muralist Diego Rivera (bottom) influenced many WPA artists. Sculptor Augusta Savage's La Citadelle—Freedom, *Dan Rico's* Testimonial *(below left), and Aimée Gorham's* CCC Men Fighting Forest Fires *reflect this realism.*

Social History
Movies were the most popular form of culture in the 1930s. They served as a form of escape through such genres as the gangster film, musicals, and "screwball" comedies. Movies that did tackle serious issues emphasized tradition. During the depths of the depression an average of 60 million to 75 million movie tickets were purchased each week.

With a budget that started at $5 billion and was frequently increased, Hopkins became known as "the world's greatest spender." But the WPA put millions of people to work and, through their wages, pumped more than $10 billion into the economy. The WPA also created a lasting legacy of public buildings and public art.

Perhaps the greatest contribution of the WPA was to help people keep up their skills and their spirits. Said one grateful WPA worker:

> *"My pride took an awful beating when I had to apply for relief, but I feel different about this. Here I am working for what I'm getting."*

The End of NRA

Just as the WPA was getting under way, the Supreme Court dealt the New Deal's recovery program a heavy blow. In the case of *Schechter* v. *United States*, the Court declared that the National Industrial Recovery Act, which had set up the NRA, was unconstitutional.

The Schechter brothers, who ran a poultry business in Brooklyn, New York, had been convicted of selling diseased chickens and breaking other NRA rules. When they appealed their case, the Court ruled unanimously that the NRA's system of codes gave the executive branch of the government powers that belonged to the legislative branch. Furthermore, said the Court, although the federal government has a right to regulate interstate commerce, it has no power to regulate commerce conducted entirely within a state.

The "sick chicken" case brought down the NRA. The Blue Eagle soon disappeared from the walls and windows of businesses.

A New Deal for Labor

The Court's decision might also have been a setback for organized labor, which had been protected and encouraged by the National Industrial Recovery Act. However, New York Senator Robert Wagner introduced a bill that restored and strengthened the rules protecting unions.

Spotlight on Entertainment

During the depression years, people turned to books, music, and movies as a relief from the uncertainties of everyday living. Here is a list of some entertaining diversions of the time.

1932—"Brother, Can You Spare a Dime?" by E.Y. Harburg and Jay Gorney becomes a sort of theme song of the depression.

1933—A Walt Disney cartoon, *Three Little Pigs*, provides a song that symbolizes the depression to many: "Who's Afraid of the Big Bad Wolf?"

1934—Donald Duck makes his first appearance.

1935—In the first major league baseball game to be played at night, the Philadelphia Phillies beat the Cincinnati Reds 2-1.

1936—Huddie Ledbetter (Leadbelly) and John Lomax publish the song "Goodnight, Irene."

1937—*Gone With the Wind*, published in 1936, wins a Pulitzer Prize.

1938—Orson Welles's radio broadcast of *War of the Worlds*, which describes an invasion of Earth by Martians, is so realistic that thousands panic.

1939—The movies *The Wizard of Oz* and *Gone With the Wind* open.

The Wagner Act, which Congress passed in July 1935, guaranteed workers the right to organize and join unions. Employers were now required to bargain with the unions and were barred from threatening workers with harm or firing them if they joined a union. A three-member National Labor Relations Board (NLRB) was created to monitor union elections and oversee collective bargaining.

The Wagner Act put the government firmly behind organized labor. With its passage, union membership soared—doubling within three years.

Thinking Critically

Evaluation. Have students discuss the Supreme Court's decision on NIRA. **Ask:** What reasons were given by the Court for declaring NIRA unconstitutional? **(gave executive branch legislative power; government has no right to regulate intrastate trade)** What objections might a New Dealer make to this decision? Do you think the Supreme Court's decision was justified? Explain.

Linking Past and Present

Discussion. Discuss the rise and decline of union membership in the United States. **Ask:** What would account for the rapid increase in union membership in the 1930s? **(Wagner Act put government behind organized labor.)** What rights did the Wagner Act guarantee to labor? **(collective bargaining; right to join union; could not be fired for organizing or joining a union)** Why is the right to collective bargaining so important? **(In negotiations with large businesses and corporations, organized groups of workers have more strength and influence than individual workers.)** Labor union membership has declined in recent years. What factors might account for this decline? **(Accept reasonable answers.)**

Linking Past and Present

Discussion. Have students discuss Social Security as it exists today. **Ask:** Why do most Americans not look upon Social Security as welfare? **(Workers put in money.)** What criticisms can be made of it? **(some workers excluded; doesn't help the really needy)** What demographic change has created a problem for Social Security? **(people living longer; declining birth rate; more money going out than coming in)** How did the government remedy the situation? **(increased taxes to be paid)** Why are Presidents reluctant to tamper with Social Security even though maintaining it at its present level may cause problems? **(Could be politically damaging, for example)**

Connections: Economics

Discussion. Have students explain what a graduated income tax is. **(The tax rate rises as income rises.)** Then have students discuss the Revenue Act of 1935. Why might some people consider it a "soak the rich" tax bill? **(The rich would be most affected by it).** Why would the rich object to an inheritance tax? **(They have the most wealth to pass on or inherit).**

Connections: Politics

In addition to serving as Secretary of Labor, Frances Perkins (1882–1965) was one of Roosevelt's most influential advisors. The two had developed a strong relationship when Roosevelt was governor of New York and appointed Perkins an industrial commissioner. Perkins stated that Roosevelt never let her down, and he in turn came to rely increasingly on her ability to get things done. In addition to the Social Security Act, Perkins played an important role in drafting NRA guidelines. As Secretary of Labor she created the Division of Labor Standards, expanded the Bureau of Labor Statistics, and encouraged states to establish their own labor departments.

Reduced student page in the Teacher's Edition

The Social Security Act

The Social Security Act followed hard on the heels of the Wagner Act. One of its strongest supporters was the Secretary of Labor, Frances Perkins—the first woman to be appointed to a President's cabinet. Roosevelt had known Perkins as the capable industrial commissioner for the state of New York. She agreed to accept the cabinet position only if Roosevelt would support a social insurance program to protect workers who lost their jobs or who retired.

Roosevelt had long favored such a plan. The depression had been especially hard on older Americans. Many had lost their savings in failed banks, and only 15 percent were covered by pension plans. Just eighteen states provided any kind of old-age assistance.

Roosevelt named a committee, headed by Perkins, to study the problem and pass their findings on to Congress. The result was the Social Security Act, signed into law in August 1935.

Workers covered by the act would receive retirement pensions when they reached age sixty-five. The money for the pensions would come from taxes on workers' wages and on employers' payrolls. The pension plan was not voluntary—every covered worker had to take part. Not every worker was covered, though. Farm workers and household servants, for example, were not included.

Under the Social Security Act the federal government would provide funds for dependent mothers and their children and for the blind. Perkins was satisfied that the act was a start toward giving workers "the greatest practical degree of economic security."

Other New Deal Measures

Three other major bills became law during the summer. One, the Banking Act of 1935, changed the Federal Reserve System, giving the government more power to regulate banks.

Labor Secretary Frances Perkins, shown meeting with steel workers, was asked by Roosevelt to draft the Social Security Act.

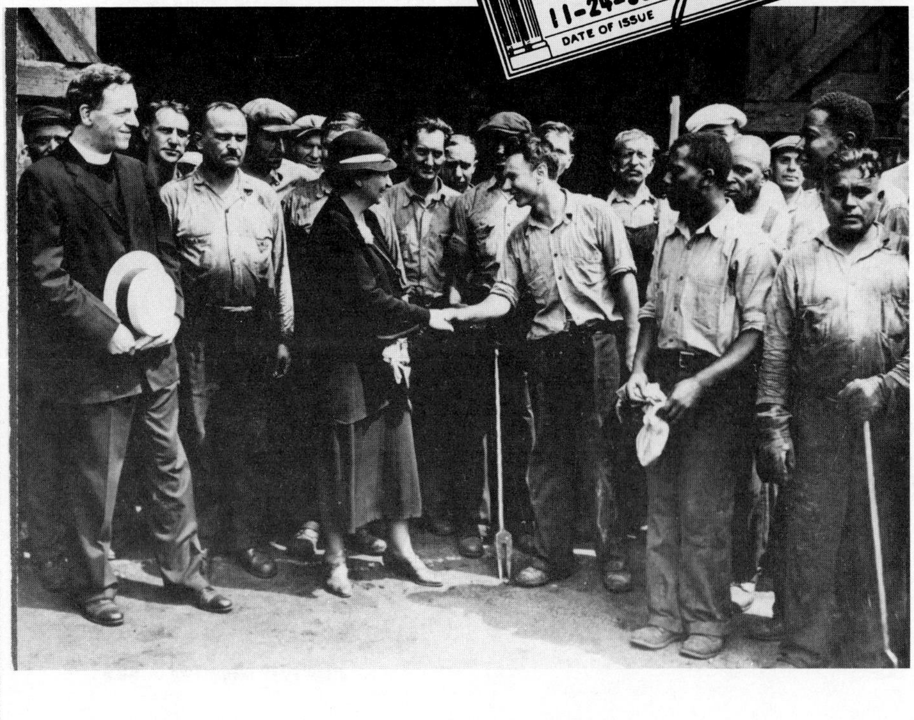

The Emergency Relief Appropriation Act, which set up the Rural Electrification Administration (REA), was to revolutionize rural life. At the time, barely 12 percent of all farm homes had electric service. The REA loaned money to electric companies to construct power lines in farm areas. By 1940 electricity was flowing to one third of all farm homes, and by 1945 to almost one half.

The Revenue Act of 1935 called for an inheritance tax and placed a graduated income tax on corporations. It was greeted with fury by people of wealth, including newspaper publisher William Randolph Hearst, who told his editors to use the term "Raw Deal" in place of "New Deal."

Highlights of the Second New Deal

Date Signed	Agency or Program		Purpose	Status
May 1935	WPA	Works Progress Administration	Provide employment in public works project	Ended in 1943
	REA	Rural Electrification Administration	Aid farmers to electrify homes	Became part of Dept. of Agric. in 1939
June 1935	NYA	National Youth Administration	Provide jobs and training for Americans 16-25 years of age	Ended in 1943
July 1935	NLRB	National Labor Relations Board	Guarantee rights of workers	Still in operation
August 1935	SSB	Social Security Board	Provide a sound social security system	Still in operation

Roosevelt Reelected in 1936

Despite bitter attacks by his critics, the President was still enormously popular. People believed that he was trying to help them. Confident of popular support, Roosevelt went on the offensive in his 1936 campaign. He lashed out at his opponents, especially rich conservatives who backed the American Liberty League:

"Never before in all our history have these forces [of selfishness and greed] been so united against one candidate as they are today. They are unanimous in their hate for me—and I welcome their hatred."

Roosevelt scarcely mentioned his Republican opponent, Governor Alfred M. Landon of Kansas, a former Bull Moose Progressive. Landon faced an uphill struggle. His party was linked in the public's mind with the crash and the early years of the depression. Moreover, the New Deal seemed to be working. Since the spring of 1935, a million more people had found jobs.

The emergence of a new third party briefly cheered the Republicans, who hoped that it would take votes away from the Democrats. The Union party, backed by Father Coughlin's National Union for Social Justice, nominated William Lemke of North Dakota as its candidate.

The Union party appealed to many followers of Father Coughlin, Dr. Townsend, and Huey Long. However, in September 1935 a political enemy shot and killed Long in the Louisiana capital, and Townsend, Coughlin, and Lemke were not well enough organized to run an effective campaign.

The President won an overwhelming victory, carrying every state but Maine and Vermont. Kansas newspaper editor William Allen White noted, "Landon went down the creek in the torrent."

Section Review

1. Analysis. Compare the proposals of Francis Townsend, Charles Coughlin, and Huey Long. Why do you think they gained so many followers during the depression?

2. Comprehension. Explain how Social Security works.

3. Analysis. Imagine that you are the owner of several large manufacturing plants in the 1930s. You claim that Roosevelt has turned away from helping big business in favor of helping ordinary people. How do you support your claim?

4. Synthesis. Before 1933, movies often portrayed government figures as ineffective, and wealthy businessmen as clever heroes. In the late 1930s, however, the opposite was true. How do you account for this change?

Thinking Critically

Application. Read to students Roosevelt's description of his philosophy: *"It is common sense to take a method and try it. If it fails, admit it frankly and try another. But above all, try something."* **Ask:** How did Roosevelt put this philosophy into action between 1933 and 1936? (Legislation from the first and second New Deals are examples.)

Section Review

ANSWERS

1. Townsend proposed government pay citizens monthly pensions; Coughlin wanted Roosevelt to expel bankers from positions of power; Huey Long proposed government redistribute wealth through taxation. Townsend's and Long's proposals gained followers through prospect of getting money from government. Coughlin's popularity rested on skill as a radio speaker and rabble-rouser.
2. Workers receive pensions at age 65; money comes from taxes levied on workers' wages and employers' payrolls.
3. Manufacturer could point to many government acts designed to help working people—social security, PWA, WPA, CCC—and scarcity of acts designed to help business.
4. Because government worked to help people recover from depression, government officials became more popular. Because business people seemed to be against New Deal and held to be responsible for depression, business became less popular.

Section 22-3

Objectives

- ***Answer the Focus Question.***
- *Explain why many African Americans supported Roosevelt.*
- *Explain the CIO's strategy for gaining recognition by management.*
- *Analyze the causes and effects of Roosevelt's major setbacks.*

Introducing THE SECTION

Write on the chalkboard *southern Democrats, northern liberals, African Americans, union members, farmers.* Tell students that by 1936 Roosevelt had united these groups into an alliance, or coalition. **Ask:** What is unusual about this alliance? **(contains groups that normally might seem antagonistic)** Why would southern Democrats support Roosevelt? **(traditional party; FDR soft on discrimination)** Northern liberals? **(liberal New Deal programs)** African Americans? **(benefited from some programs)** Union members? **(Wagner Act and New Deal programs)** Farmers? **(AAA & FSA)**

Tell students that they will study how the coalition fared in the late 1930s.

B · A · C · K · G · R · O · U · N · D

Connections: Music

While many African-American jazz singers and musicians prospered in the 1930s, African-American performers of the European classical tradition had a hard time gaining acceptance. No African Americans sang in any opera house in the United States before World War II. As a consequence, several African-American singers pursued careers principally in Europe. In 1955 Marion Anderson became the first African American to sing with the Metropolitan Opera. Baritone Robert McFerrin sang with the Met later that year. In recent decades such outstanding African-American performers as Leontyne Price, Jessye Norman, and Simon Estes have been much in demand by the United States's leading opera companies.

22-3 *The Last Years of the New Deal*

Focus: What groups helped create a new coalition of Democrats, and why did the coalition falter?

The election of 1936 marked the fourth time since 1928 that the Democratic party had increased its strength in Congress. As a result, President Roosevelt now had a mighty **coalition**, or alliance, of Democrats to work with. The coalition had been elected by longtime Democrats—southern conservatives and liberals in northern cities—as well as by voters newly attracted to the party by New Deal policies. Among the people from whom the Democratic party now drew its greatest strength were African Americans, union members, and small farmers.

African-American Voters and Roosevelt

Before the Great Depression, some 80 percent of all African Americans lived in the South. There the Democratic party controlled most state and local governments, using its power to maintain all-white rule.

To many blacks, the Republican party—the party of Lincoln—represented the old hopes of Reconstruction. Yet as a bold headline in the Baltimore *Afro-American* reminded its readers in 1936, "ABRAHAM LINCOLN IS NOT A CANDIDATE IN THE PRESENT CAMPAIGN." Black voters, especially in the North, shifted their support to the Democrats.

President Roosevelt's record with respect to black Americans was mixed. As a politician he wanted to keep the support of southern whites. Thus, for example, he failed to push for an anti-lynching bill in 1933, and he did nothing to end restrictions on the number of blacks who could participate in the CCC.

> ***American Voices***
>
> *"There must be equality before the law, equality of education, equal opportunity to obtain a job . . . and equality of participation in self-government."*
>
> —Eleanor Roosevelt, 1941

Including African Americans. However, the WPA and other New Deal programs offered work to thousands of blacks as well as whites. For the first time, many African Americans felt that the government included them, too. Said one black southerner, "They've talked more politics since Mister Roosevelt been in than ever before."

Roosevelt also invited blacks into his administration. One was Mary McLeod Bethune, a noted educator. Beginning in 1936 she directed the Division of Negro Affairs of the National Youth Administration (NYA), a program that aided youth between ages sixteen and twenty-five. Bethune became a member of Roosevelt's "black cabinet," an informal group of advisors working to reduce discrimination in New Deal programs.

Another strong voice urging fair treatment of blacks belonged to the President's wife, Eleanor Roosevelt. In one famous incident in 1939, the noted singer Marian Anderson was barred from giving a concert in a private hall in the capital because she was black. Mrs. Roosevelt joined a group of artists and politicians in sponsoring a free concert by Marian Anderson at the Lincoln Memorial.

On balance, then, African Americans came to see Roosevelt and the Democratic party as more likely to respond to their needs and protect their interests. It was at this time that a shift of party loyalty occurred among American blacks. By 1936 some 76 percent of African-American voters supported the Democrats.

Multicultural Perspectives

The WPA made funds available for unemployed writers to conduct oral interviews with 5,000 African Americans who had been enslaved. The interviews, called slave narratives, have provided historians with valuable perspectives on the era of slavery.

Multicultural Perspectives

Bethune-Cookman College, today, has over a thousand students. It is one of the leading African-American teacher-training institutions, and three fourths of its graduates enter the teaching profession.

Developing

THE SECTION

Backyard History

Research and Report. The WPA Writers' Project compiled a history of each state during the 1930s. Public libraries (except Alaska and Hawaii, which were not yet states) should have copies of their state's WPA history. Have interested students obtain and read copies of the history of their state and present oral or written reports about the information they find, emphasizing local history, if possible.

Labor and the Democrats

Another group of voters who swelled the Democratic coalition were members of labor unions. Armed with the Wagner Act, labor leaders during the Thirties had been actively organizing workers.

One of the most powerful figures in the labor movement was John L. Lewis of the United Mine Workers. Lewis believed that all workers had common concerns. Therefore, he wanted to create industry-wide unions by organizing unskilled workers along with skilled workers, and African-American and Hispanic-American workers alongside European-American workers.

Lewis and leaders of several other unions that belonged to the AFL formed the Committee for Industrial Organization to organize industrial unions. The AFL leadership, however, preferred to organize unions for skilled white workers only. After a bitter quarrel, the CIO broke with the AFL in 1936 and established a rival federation of unions, renaming it the Congress of Industrial Organizations (CIO).

Sit-down strikes. The CIO had its first great success in the automobile industry. On December 30, 1936, members of the United Auto Workers (UAW), a CIO union, took over several General

THE AMERICAN SPIRIT

Mary McLeod Bethune

"I Leave You Racial Dignity"

In 1935 Franklin Roosevelt asked Mary McLeod Bethune to head the Division of Negro Affairs of his National Youth Administration. Bethune had been a tireless worker for youth all her life.

The fifteenth of seventeen children born to poor sharecroppers, she was the only member of her family to go to school. After graduation, she taught in Georgia, South Carolina, and Florida. She was dismayed at the poor quality of schools for African Americans, however, and decided to found her own school.

She started, she said, with "faith and a dollar-and-a-half" in a rented shack next to a dump in Daytona, Florida.

Bethune and her students baked pies and sang in concerts to raise funds to keep the school going. It grew, and in 1926 merged with another school to become Bethune-Cookman College, today a teachers' college.

In Roosevelt's administration, Bethune was responsible for setting up youth training centers and distributing funds to schools for African Americans. But her influence extended far beyond her office. She convinced the President, for example, to issue passes to African-American journalists so they could cover White House press conferences for the first time. Roosevelt said of her, "Mrs. Bethune is a great woman. She always comes here on behalf of others."

Shortly before Bethune's death in 1955, *Ebony* magazine published "Last Will and Testament"— her legacy of hope to African-American youth:

"I leave you love. I leave you hope. I leave you the challenge of developing confidence in one another. I leave you a thirst for education. I leave you respect for the use of power. I leave you faith. I leave you racial dignity."

Limited English Proficiency

Small Group Discussion. Divide the class into small groups. Have each group discuss the following issues: Is it right for workers to use the sit-down strike? That is, are they entitled to occupy property they do not own? Is it right for management to use force to eject them? Do union workers have the right to require other workers to join the union? A spokesperson in each group can report what the group decided and why.

Chapter Connections

Discussion. Compare the problems of farmers in the 1930s with those of farmers in the 1880s and the 1920s. How were farm problems similar in all three decades? **(High production led to surpluses, which led individuals to plant more to make up for lower prices, which created greater surpluses and even lower prices.)**

Ask: Why do you think so few farmers accepted government pay for planting fewer crops? **(Answers may include that to individual farmers, *not* planting probably seemed at odds with their purposes.)** Restate the provisions of the new Agricultural Adjustment Act. What arguments would you predict over it?

(Answers will vary.)

Connections: Music

During the Flint sit-down strike the men in one of the plants organized a band and chorus to pass the time. One of the workers wrote a song:

When they tie a can to a union man
Sit down! Sit down!
When they give him the sack! They'll take him back.
Sit down! Sit down!
Sit down, just take a seat
Sit down, and rest you feet
Sit down, you've got em beat
Sit down! Sit down!

Reduced student page in the Teacher's Edition

Motors plants in Flint, Michigan. They staged a **sit-down strike,** a strike in which workers refuse to leave the work place until the company agrees to bargain with their union.

The workers knew that if management tried to remove them by force it risked damaging its own property. "We don't aim to keep the plants or try to run them," a union member explained, "but we want to see that nobody takes our jobs."

After six weeks, the two sides signed an agreement allowing the UAW to organize General Motors workers. Other auto makers quickly reached similar agreements with the union. At the same time, John L. Lewis's Steel Workers Organizing Committee won recognition from the giant United States Steel Corporation, and other steel companies followed suit.

The success of the General Motors strike set off a wave of sit-downs across the country. Alarmed by the takeover of private property, many people lost sympathy with the strikers. Roosevelt, too, disliked the strikes, but he would not call out federal troops to stop them, preferring instead to let management and labor negotiate. Many people blamed him for allowing the strikes to continue.

By the end of 1937, the number of sit-downs had declined. Two years later the Supreme Court outlawed them, ruling that they violated property rights. By then, however, CIO unions had organized much of American industry.

The success of the CIO tended to strengthen the Democratic party. Grateful to the party that had passed the Wagner Act and created the NLRB to oversee union growth, the CIO gave more than $750,000 to the Democrats' campaign fund in 1936. It also got out the vote. Hundreds of thousands of workers now voted Democratic.

Drought-damaged corn, Nebraska

Rural Voters

Rural voters were another source of strength for Democratic coalition. Troubled by the low farm prices they had received since the early 1920s and by one of the worst droughts in the nation's history, the rural voters judged the New Deal by the success of its farm policies. When the AAA was able to increase the prices of major crops, farmers changed their party loyalty from Republican to Democratic.

The Democrats worked hard to retain the farm vote. When the Supreme Court declared the AAA unconstitutional in January 1936, Congress quickly put new programs in place. The first congressional effort was a law that allowed the government to pay farmers for planting fewer crops. It failed, though, when not enough farmers took part.

Then, in 1938 Congress passed a new Agricultural Adjustment Act. Under this law, the federal government would try to control the wild swings in farm prices that had plagued farmers for decades. In years of good harvests the government would help keep farm prices up by buying surplus crops. It would store the crops and, in lean years, sell them to bring crop prices down. Thus, prices would stay close to **parity,** a level of prices that gave farmers about the same buying power they had in the good years, 1909 to 1914.

The new law helped only farmers who owned their land. To help farmers who rented land, Congress in 1937 passed the Bankhead-Jones Farm Tenant Act, setting up the Farm Security Administration (FSA). The FSA made long-term, low-interest loans to help tenant farmers and sharecroppers buy their own farms. The FSA also loaned money to farmers to improve their land.

Social History
One writer and editor reported, *"I inspected labor camps. The conditions were not to be believed. . . . The camps were filthy. We had a labor camp population of 175,000 in August and September [1938], the lowest season. In spring, they'd force people off relief rolls to take jobs at twenty cents an hour."*

Multicultural Perspectives
The depression deeply affected whatever economic gains Mexican Americans had achieved since 1900. Anti-Mexican feelings were already widespread in the Southwest, and job competition with Dust Bowl migrants intensified the situation. Some employers displayed signs that read "Only White Labor Employed," aimed at both Mexican Americans and African Americans.

Writing About History

Poem or Song. A number of poems and songs have been written relating the experiences and expressing the feelings of people who were driven from their land in the Dust Bowl. Have students imagine that they have lived through the Dust Bowl, and write a poem or song about how they feel.

The Dust Bowl. The new laws came too late for thousands of farmers, however. During the Thirties huge dust storms had begun sweeping over the Great Plains, burying crops, livestock, and farm buildings. The first large storm, "a wall of dirt," struck South Dakota in the fall of 1933. When it was over, said an observer, "fences, machinery, and trees were gone, buried." In a letter to Eleanor Roosevelt, reporter Lorena Hickok described one storm:

> *"The wind was blowing a gale. . . . We drove only a few miles and had to turn back. . . . It seemed as though the car would be blown right off the road any minute. . . . It was a truly terrifying experience. It was as though we had left the earth. We were being whirled off into space in a vast, impenetrable cloud of brown dust."*

The dust storms were caused by years of large-scale plowing followed by severe drought. During World War I, when crop prices were high, farmers had begun cultivating vast areas of the Great Plains. Then, for four years beginning in 1933, no rain fell. Dry, loose prairie soil was swept up by the wind. Dust storms battered the Dakotas, Nebraska, Kansas, Oklahoma, and the Texas Panhandle.

As the Great Plains turned into a "dust bowl," farmers and tenant farmers—unable to raise crops to pay what they owed—were evicted. Desperate families took to the road. By the late 1930s, more than a million migrants were on the move.

Lured by tales of abundant crops, the migrants traveled west, looking for work. However, most of the harvesting jobs lasted only a few weeks, wages were pitifully low, and conditions in the camps where migrant families huddled together were often miserable. "This is a hard life to swallow," said one migrant, "but I just couldn't sit back there and look to someone to feed us."

Many migrant workers of Mexican heritage were already in the West. Some were American citizens who had been forced to give up their own farms during the hard times. César Chávez, who later led the United Farm Workers union, remembered his feelings, as a child, when his family lost their land and became migrant farm workers:

> *"We had been poor, but we knew every night there was a bed there, and that this was our room. It was sort of a settled life, and we had chickens and hogs, eggs and all those things. But that all of a sudden changed. When you're small, you can't figure these things out."*

Stripped of its vegetation by poor farming practices, the plains soil was swept away by the wind.

GTV Side 4
Chap. 2, Frame 08040
On the Move: The Dust Bowl (Movie Segment)
Search and Play:

Multicultural Perspectives

Discussion. In 1938 John Collier, of the Commission of Indian Affairs, wrote:

> *“Our whole attitude toward the Indians has necessarily undergone a profound change. Dead is the centuries-old notion that the sooner we eliminate this doomed race . . . the better.”*

Have the class discuss whether, in fact, the attitude toward Native Americans has changed over the last few decades. They can cite attitudes expressed in books, television, plays, and movies.

Writing About History

Diary Entry. Have students assume the identity of a farm girl or farm boy and write a diary entry about one day in his/her life in the 1930s. Possible topics include: life after the REA provided electricity, the Dust Bowl, migrating west, life in a migrant camp, working in the fields.

Multicultural Perspectives

In an effort to improve their working conditions, Mexican Americans became increasingly active in the labor movement. The Cannery and Agricultural Workers Industrial Union organized and led the San Joaquin Valley (California) Cotton Strike in 1932–1933. In the El Monte Berry Strike of 1933, La Confederación de Uniones de Campesinos y Obreros Mexicanos was formally recognized by growers.

Reduced student page in the Teacher's Edition

Other migrants were Mexican citizens. During the Twenties, Mexicans had entered the United States easily because the demand for their labor was high. Now that jobs were scarce, thousands returned to Mexico, some voluntarily, but many more forced out by federal and state agencies.

John Steinbeck's novel *The Grapes of Wrath* brought the plight of migrant workers—especially Dust Bowl victims—to public attention. To try to stem the tide of migrants, the Farm Security Administration made small grants to families in the Dust Bowl region to help them stay on their lands.

Moving from place to place to harvest ripening crops, farm workers often lived in makeshift housing.

On the West Coast the FSA built camps that provided clean, safe living conditions for some 30,000 families. In addition, the Justice Department began to step in to protect the rights of migrant workers to speak freely and organize to demand better wages and working conditions.

A New Indian Policy

As the New Deal reached into rural America it touched the lives of Native Americans, too. Indians benefited from programs such as the AAA and the WPA. Furthermore, some measures for relief and recovery were specifically designed to aid Indians directly. For example, an Indian CCC was organized to make improvements on reservation lands.

More important, perhaps, was a major change in government policy toward Indians. For years, the government's policy had been to force Indians to give up tribal ways. Tribal lands were broken up and sold to individuals.

Now, however, President Roosevelt offered a New Deal to Native Americans. A sweeping new law, the Indian Reorganization Act of 1934, halted the breakup of tribal lands. It encouraged self-government on Indian reservations, allowed Native-American nations to manage their own economic affairs, and promoted the preservation of Indian customs and religions. Individual tribes were to vote on whether or not to accept the act or exclude themselves from it. Within two years 70 percent of the tribes voted for the plan.

Setbacks for Roosevelt

Despite his great victory in the election of 1936, by early 1937 Roosevelt's popularity had begun to slip, and his coalition in Congress showed signs of splintering. One cause of his problems was the series of sit-down strikes. Some people thought the strikers were Communists, while others simply considered the strikes unfair to employers. In any case, Roosevelt's failure to halt the strikes cost him support in Congress and in the nation.

A more direct cause of Roosevelt's problems was his attempt to change the federal court system. Claiming that the courts must be made efficient, in February 1937 the President sent Congress a plan to add judges and modify court procedures. He also proposed to add an extra justice to the Supreme Court for each justice who reached the age of seventy and did not retire. The plan limited the extra

Global Connections
The USSR eagerly imported prints of *The Grapes of Wrath* movie to show shortcomings of American capitalism. The showings backfired because Russian audiences were less impressed by the Joads' misfortunes than by the fact that they owned an automobile. Even the equivalent of a Ford jalopy was beyond reach of most Soviet citizens.

Geography

A KEY TO OUR PAST

Region: The Dust Bowl

On maps of the early 1800s, the words "Great American Desert" sprawl across the area of present-day Kansas, Nebraska, eastern Colorado and New Mexico, northern Texas, and Oklahoma. Early explorers identified the area as a **region**— any part of the earth's surface that people define according to a unifying set of natural or human characteristics. Because of the scarcity of wood and water, they declared the region unsuited for farming. Settlers heading west agreed and pushed on.

In the mid-1800s, however, Americans changed their minds. A Nebraska resident, Charles Dana Wilber, claimed, "There is not desert anywhere except by man's permission or neglect." He believed the saying "rain follows the plow."

People began to look at the area in a new way. They talked with excitement of a larger new region. The newly defined region, which they called the Great Plains, extended from Texas to Canada and from the hundredth meridian to the Rockies. People defined this region according to its smooth sea of short grass and its rainfall of from ten to thirty inches a year.

Homesteaders poured into the region, bringing their new iron plows, and grass that had anchored the soil for centuries vanished in "the great plow-up." New types of farm machinery cleared thousands of acres for wheat. Farmers called themselves "sodbusters" and boasted of "breaking the land."

Then in 1931 the moisture cycle changed. Less rain fell, wheat withered, and the soil became parched. Millions of acres lay vulnerable to the wind. With no sturdy grass to hold the soil, black clouds of dust filled the sky, and people took shelter, struggling to breathe. One Kansas woman said, "Our hair was gray and stiff, and we ground dirt between our teeth."

Gone forever was much of the fertile topsoil, borne eastward on the wind. In one day, 12 million tons of plains dust fell like snow in Chicago. The black blizzard hit East Coast cities two days later, then moved out to sea. Once again, people had defined a new region, to which a newspaper reporter gave the name the *Dust Bowl*.

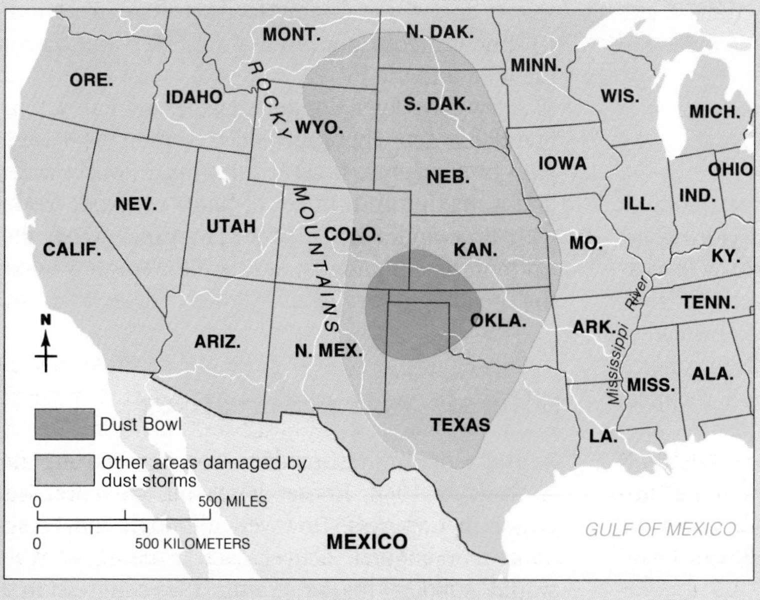

1. Define *region.*
2. How did people characterize the region they called "The Great American Desert"?
3. What features defined the Great Plains as a region? What features defined the Dust Bowl?
4. How did humans and nature create the Dust Bowl?

Geography: A Key to Our Past

ANSWERS

1. A part of the earth's surface with common natural and/or human characteristics.
2. Desert: food and water scarce, unsuited for farming; Great Plains: an area reclaimed and farmed by homesteaders.
3. Millions of dried up acres without grass cover; black clouds of dust driven by wind; lack of fertile topsoil.
4. Growing wheat caused the grass that anchored the soil to vanish. Lack of rain caused the soil to parch. Winds blew the topsoil off the land.

Limited English Proficiency.

Building Vocabulary. Write the terms *coalition, parity,* and *deficit spending* on the chalkboard. Have volunteers imagine that they are government officials at a press conference. Choose other volunteers to represent reporters who will ask questions that require the officials to use the listed terms in their responses. The officials should be sure to define each term and give examples to illustrate it.

Linking Past and Present

Discussion. The collapse of the economy in 1937 brought into focus a debate within Roosevelt's administration over whether to concentrate first on balancing the budget or on improving the economy by putting the unemployed back to work. At first Roosevelt favored balancing the budget, but the severity of the decline convinced him to try to stop it with a new spending program. **Ask:** What similar economic issues are hotly debated today? **(Balancing the budget, how much to spend on social programs, and who and how much to tax remain hot issues.)**

Connections: Economics

John Maynard Keynes (1883–1946) was an English economist who suggested ways for nations to avoid the extremes of the business cycle: periods of inflation and periods of depression. Roosevelt's decision to fight the recessions of 1933 and 1938 with deficit spending was in line with Keynes's policy of increasing government spending to avoid depression.

Frances Perkins explained the policy this way: *"A dollar spent on relief by the government was a dollar given to the grocer, to the wholesaler, and by the wholesaler to the farmer, in payment of supplies. With one dollar paid out for relief or public works or anything else, you have created four dollars' worth of national spending."*

Reduced student page in the Teacher's Edition

justices to a total of six. Thus, a President might increase the number of Supreme Court justices from nine to as many as fifteen.

The idea of tampering with the Supreme Court shocked members of Congress and upset voters. Few people believed that efficiency was Roosevelt's true motive. Recent Supreme Court decisions had dismantled major parts of the New Deal, such as the NRA and the first AAA. In upcoming cases the Court seemed likely to rule against the NLRB and the Social Security Act, too.

What Roosevelt really wanted, opponents declared, was to "pack" the court with justices who supported his New Deal policies. Such a plan, they warned, would destroy the Constitution's system of checks and balances. Roosevelt's court-packing plan split the Democratic coalition. Conservative Democrats joined Republicans in the fight to defeat it.

Arguing that his court plan was essential to save the New Deal, Roosevelt prepared to do battle. Events, however, weakened his case. Beginning in April the Supreme Court upheld the Wagner Act, thus saving the NLRB, and also ruled in favor of the Social Security Act and several other New Deal laws.

In August, Congress passed a bill that changed federal court procedures but did not give the President power to make extra appointments. Although Roosevelt lost his court-packing effort, he scored a partial victory. During his second term five Supreme Court justices retired or died, and he was able to appoint their replacements.

A New Economic Slump

The fight over the court plan distracted Roosevelt and weakened his power in Congress. During the spring and summer of 1937, no major new legislation was passed to cope with the depression. Then, in the fall, another problem appeared. Instead of continuing its steady improvement, the economy slumped badly. Sales slowed, production declined, and prices fell.

One cause of the decline was Roosevelt's decision to cut federal spending for work relief programs. Social-security taxes took effect at about the same time. These measures led consumers to reduce their spending.

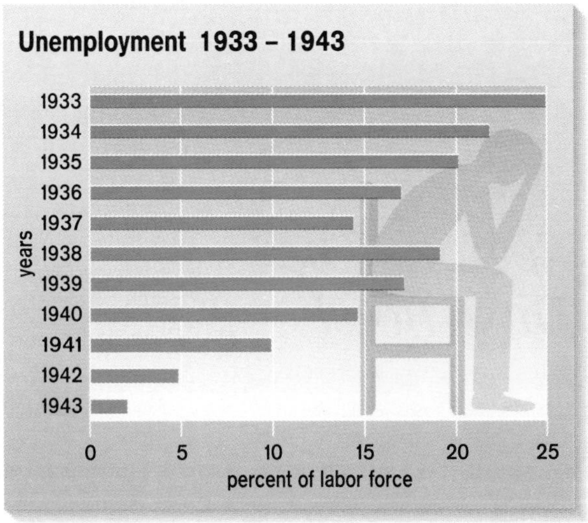

Source: *Historical Statistics of the United States*

Businesses, too, which were having to pay the higher wages won by unions as well as higher interest rates on loans, began to cut back. Just one year after the Flint strike, General Motors laid off 30,000 workers and put other workers on a three-day week. Across the nation, 2 million workers lost their jobs, and the unemployment rate soared to nearly 20 percent again.

In April 1938 Roosevelt decided to fight the decline with **deficit spending**— a policy in which the government spends more than it receives in taxes. The President convinced Congress to pump money into the economy to reverse the recession. In June Congress approved almost $2.5 billion for the WPA and the PWA.

A few days later Congress passed the Fair Labor Standards Act. This bill helped workers who were paid by the hour. It set a minimum hourly wage and a maximum number of hours per work week, with time-and-a-half pay for overtime. When the act took effect in August, it raised the wages— and the spending power— of 750,000 people.

Liberals vs. Conservatives

As the economy resumed its slow recovery in the summer of 1938, Roosevelt set out to recover his power in Congress. However, although the President campaigned actively for candidates who would support his programs, the congressional

Connections: Religion

The tasks of feeding the homeless and finding jobs for the unemployed led to religious groups to join together for mutual aid and cooperation. Catholic, Jewish, and Protestant organizations set up an Interfaith Committee on Welfare Activity.

Writing About History

Essay. Refer students to the quote by the defeated Democrat on this page. Have students write a short essay explaining the meaning of the statement and providing evidence to support the Democrat's conclusion.

elections that year proved a disappointment. The Democrats lost seven seats in the Senate and eighty in the House. As a defeated Democrat explained:

> *"The prosperity for which the American people have been yearning for more than a decade has failed to make its appearance. It is still around the corner."*

Despite their losses, the Democrats still had large majorities in both houses of Congress. The real power, however, was balanced between liberal Democrats on the one hand and Republicans and conservative Democrats on the other. Each group had some successes. The liberals passed a law that streamlined the executive branch. The conservatives passed the Hatch Act, barring most government workers from actively participating in political campaigns.

For the most part, though, liberals and conservatives faced each other in a standoff. Roosevelt, two years after his great election victory, could not push through further reforms. And conservatives could not undo the major programs he had already established.

In any case, by 1939 politicians on both sides were turning away from domestic worries. Increasingly, their attention was focused on the distant rumblings of war.

Section Review

1. Identification. Define *coalition, sit-down strike, parity*, and *deficit spending.*

2. Comprehension. How did the New Deal advance the cause of racial equality? Explain.

3. Analysis. Compare the methods and outcomes of the United Auto Workers strike against General Motors in 1936 with those of the truckers' and longshoremen's strikes in 1934.

4. Comprehension. Explain three setbacks that Roosevelt suffered between 1937 and 1939. How did they affect the future of the New Deal in Congress?

Data Search. Refer to the unemployment graphs in Chapters 21 and 22. Write a summary of unemployment from 1918 to 1943.

Connections to Themes

The Search For Opportunity

By 1933 millions of Americans found themselves living in a nation where economic opportunity had ceased to exist. In responding to the crisis, Roosevelt had two goals: to use the power of the federal government to stimulate the economy, and to provide protection for those being crushed by economic forces beyond their control.

The result was a vast array of government programs and agencies. Roosevelt justified this expansion of government:

> *"If private . . . endeavor fails to provide work for willing hands and relief for the unfortunate, those suffering hardship through no fault of their own have a right to call upon the government for aid."*

This statement reflected a major shift in American thinking—a recognition that the government has a responsibility to intervene in the economy when opportunity is seriously threatened. Today, most people accept such New Deal programs as social security, unemployment insurance, and aid to the disabled.

However, Americans are still debating how much government action is necessary. Roosevelt's critics charged that his programs destroyed initiative by encouraging people to become too dependent. In the 1980s this view inspired President Ronald Reagan to try to undo what he saw as excesses of the New Deal era.

Section Review

ANSWERS

1. Definitions for the following terms are on text pages indicated in parentheses: *coalition* (592), *sit-down strike* (594), *parity* (594), *deficit spending* (598).
2. Answers may include the New Deal programs offering work to all people, including African Americans; inviting African Americans into government; urging fair treatment for African Americans.
3. Truckers' and longshoremen's strikes marked by violence. UAW sit-down strike was relatively peaceful and ended in GM agreeing to recognize and negotiate.
4. Answers may include: reaction against sitdown strikes; the failure of attempt to pack Court; economic slump of 1937. With the loss of Democratic seats in Congress, power now balanced between New Dealers, on the one hand, and Republicans and conservative Democrats, on the other. Was harder to effect new reforms.
Data Search: 1918 unemployment about 2 percent; increased until 1921 then decreased and remained under 5 percent until 1929. Unemployment increased to 25 percent in 1933 then decreased to 2 percent in 1943.

Chapter Survey

ANSWERS

Using New Vocabulary

1. (c) Democrats in Congress were a *coalition* of different groups.
2. (a) United Auto Workers held *sit-down strike* at General Motors.
3. (d) *Parity* enabled farmers to achieve buying power.
4. (b) Roosevelt used *deficit spending* to pump money into the economy.

Reviewing the Chapter

1. Mortgage holders failed to repay loans, banks' investments lost value as businesses failed, stock prices dropped, depositors withdrew money. National bank holiday, Emergency Banking Relief Act, Glass-Steagall Banking Act, Federal Deposit Insurance Corporation.
2. AAA paid farmers to produce less and thus raise prices. NRA suspended antitrust laws, required industries to draw up codes standardizing production quotas, trade practices, prices.
3. Direct relief and work relief. PWA paid people to work on major construction projects. CCC put young men to work improving the environment. Relief payments and wages earned returned to the economy.
4. TVA built dams to provide flood control and produce hydroelectric power. "Miracles" were bringing electricity and modern means of production into one of the most primitive areas of the country.
5. 11 million people still unemployed, labor unrest, formation of farmers' organizations.
6. WPA put millions of people to work on public projects, pumped billions into economy. Wagner Act guaranteed workers right to unionize, led to doubling of union membership within three years. Social Security Act provided economic security for retired workers, dependent mothers and children, the blind.
7. African Americans abandoned Republicans because New Deal benefited them economically, Roosevelt sympathetic to their needs. Labor came to support Democrats because of pro-labor legislation like Wagner Act. Rural voters backed Democrats because of AAA's raising crop prices and federal loans to farmers.
8. (a) Dust Bowl ruined many farms on Great Plains; farmers migrated to California. (b) Migrant farm workers in West had competition from refugees from Dust Bowl. (c) Excess of farm workers forced many Mexican farm workers back to Mexico.
9. FDR cut federal spending for work relief, workers began contributions to Social Security and thus had less money to spend, businesses laid off workers to cut costs

Chapter Survey

Using New Vocabulary

Match each numbered vocabulary term with the appropriate person or group. Then explain the connection between that person or group and the vocabulary term.

1. coalition	(a) United Auto Workers
2. sit-down strike	(b) Franklin D. Roosevelt
3. parity	(c) Democrats in Congress
4. deficit spending	(d) farmers

Reviewing the Chapter

1. During the early years of the Great Depression, what conditions put banks in danger of failing? What steps did the federal government take to prevent bank failures?

2. How did the Agricultural Adjustment Administration and the National Recovery Administration seek to revive American agriculture and business?

3. Describe two kinds of relief that the first New Deal offered to needy Americans. How did these programs affect the economy?

4. What was the purpose of the Tennessee Valley Authority? What "miracles" was it supposed to work?

5. Explain the factors that led Roosevelt to undertake a second New Deal in 1935.

6. Describe three important programs set up under the Second New Deal. What was the impact of each one?

7. Which groups were newcomers to the Democratic party during the New Deal? Why did each group support the Democrats?

8. What effect did the Dust Bowl have on (a) Great Plains farmers (b) migrant farm workers in the West (c) Mexican farm workers in the United States?

9. Why did the economy go into a new slump in 1937? How did Roosevelt respond?

Thinking Critically

1. Analysis. In the presidential campaign of 1932, Hoover warned that the Democrats were proposing "changes and so-called new deals which would destroy the very foundations of our American system." What did Hoover mean? Do you think that Hoover's fears were justified? Why or why not?

2. Evaluation. Some historians think that the aims of the New Deal were not new. Instead, they say, these aims were similar to the goals of previous reform movements, such as populism and progressivism. Do you agree? Explain your answer.

3. Synthesis. What recommendations do you think a former WPA worker might make to someone interested in improving the welfare system today?

History and You

Find out which New Deal programs are still functioning today. Interview members of your family to find out which programs affect them. Explain how you and your family would be affected if these programs did not exist.

Using a Time Line

Match each date on the time line with the correct item or items in the list below. Write your answers in chronological order and explain the significance of each item. Where appropriate, explain the cause and effect relationship between items.

(A) 11 million people unemployed
(B) NRA established
(C) Roosevelt defeats Landon
(D) Farmers destroy 10 million acres of cotton
(E) PWA begins
(F) 13 million people unemployed
(G) *Schecter* v. *United States*
(H) AAA established

1933 — 1934 — 1935 — 1936

of higher union wages and higher interest rates on loans. Roosevelt responded with deficit spending.

Thinking Critically

1. Foundations Hoover referred to were free enterprise system. He feared government intrusion into economy would ultimately mean interference with protection of private property and individual freedoms. Hoover's fears largely unjustified; U.S. still has private property and individual rights.

2. Populists and progressives did not propose relief or recovery, did advocate reform through various forms of government regulation of business and in some cases, government ownership of businesses such as utilities.

3. Give people jobs. In that way, public projects could be undertaken, and people would retain their pride by working instead of taking a handout.

History and You

Answers may vary, but students should at least mention Social Security and FDIC. Other programs still in operation are Securities and Exchange Commission, Federal Housing Authority, National Labor Relations Board.

Using a Time Line

(B) (D) (E) (F) (H) 1933; **(A)** 1934; **(G)** 1935; **(C)** 1936.

Applying Thinking Skills

1. It is the beginning of "pure personal government," i.e., a dictatorship.
2. Roosevelt is already powerful because of "overwhelming victory" in 1936; Congress dominated by Democrats although 40 percent of voters repudiated New Deal.
3. Opinions will differ, depending on whether or not they think Roosevelt had ambitions to become a dictator.
4. Answers will vary, depending on what students think of Roosevelt and his plan.

Applying Social Studies Skills

1. Percentage of the labor force out of work
2. About 25 percent
3. Unemployment was decreasing.
4. Yes: unemployment again increased; No: unemployment had been decreasing for years before 1938.
5. Until World War II.
6. Answer will be 25 percent of class.

Applying Thinking Skills

Determining the Strength of an Argument

Before you accept or reject an argument, you should determine how strong or believable it is. To be considered strong, an argument at the very least must present a claim that is based on relevant reasons.

President Franklin Roosevelt's plan to reorganize the Supreme Court triggered a strong protest from newspaper columnist Dorothy Thompson. Examine Thompson's argument below to judge its strength. Then answer the questions that follow.

> *"If the American people accept this last audacity [rashness] of the President without letting out a yell to high heaven, they have ceased to be jealous of their liberties and are ripe for ruin.*
>
> *This is the beginning of pure personal government. Do you want it? Do you like it? Look around the world—there are plenty of examples (e.g., Hitler)—and make up your mind.*
>
> *The Executive is already powerful by reason of his overwhelming victory in November, and will be strengthened even more if the [Supreme Court] reorganization plan . . . is adopted. We have, to all intents and purposes, a one-party Congress, dominated by the President. Although nearly 40 percent of the voters repudiated [voted against] the New Deal at the polls, they have less than 20 percent representation in both houses of Congress. And now the Supreme Court is to have a majority determined by the President and by a Senate which he dominates.*
>
> *When that happens we will have a one-man Government. It will all be constitutional. So, he claims, is Herr Hitler."*
>
> —*Washington Star*, February 10, 1937

1. What claim does Dorothy Thompson make in her column about the court reorganization plan?

2. What facts does she offer to support her claim?

3. Do you think what Thompson says about Hitler is relevant to her argument? Why or why not?

4. If you had been in Congress, would Thompson's argument have persuaded you to vote against Roosevelt's plan? Explain your answer.

Applying Social Studies Skills

Analyzing Bar Graphs

Study the horizontal bar graph, "Unemployment 1933-1943," on page 598. Then answer the questions below.

1. What does each horizontal bar on the graph represent?

2. What percent of the labor force was out of work in 1933?

3. Describe the trend in unemployment from 1933 to 1937.

4. Do you think that people might have feared that a new depression was coming in 1938? Why or why not?

5. About how long did the Great Depression last?

6. If your class represented the work force of the United States, about how many of you would have been out of work in the worst year of the depression?

Unit 7 Survey

ANSWERS

Making Connections

1. Examples include the Red Scare, limits on immigration, Scopes trial, resurgence of Ku Klux Klan, fear of foreign influences as in the Sacco-Vanzetti case, some of the opposition to the New Deal.

2. Answers may include that "rugged individualism" is only part of the American experience; groups of people—families, neighbors, communities—have often supported each other in time of need. Depression was so severe no one could surmount it alone. New Deal projects contributed to the public good, which may have taken some of the sting out of receiving assistance.

3. Among the hardest hit were young people who had not yet held jobs, members of ethnic groups against whom others felt prejudice, older workers who were thought to be less effective, and workers not protected by unions. Families were shaken as people left home to find work or became discouraged. Health suffered because people could not afford food and medical care. People left school early to look for work. Local government had less to spend on services. Foreign trade slowed as people worldwide had less buying power.

Using the Time Line. Examples of events related to boom times are *The Great Gatsby,* the Charleston, armored cars, 4-wheel brakes, airmail, neon signs. Events related to "bust" times are stock market crash, Social Security Act, WPA projects, TVA, Boulder Dam.

Projects and Activities

1. Students might note the impact of World War I (simpler, less formal clothing), synthetics (rayon), mass-production (rapid change in women's styles), changing roles of women (hobble skirts in 1910, looser clothing and rising hemlines in the 1920s, slacks in the 1930s). Shoulders of men's suits went from natural to padded.

2. Articles will vary.

3. Silent films of the 1920s included westerns in which a strong hero and innocent heroine struggled against grave wrong. Silent comedies featured naive heroes who through grit and determination overcome obstacles to success. Films of the 1930s included gangster movies that explored the problems of prohibition, screwball comedies featuring independent women, and elaborate musicals that radiated the optimism needed to combat the depression.

Using the Time Line. Scripts will vary.

Unit Survey

Making Connections

1. Agree or disagree with the following interpretation of the 1920s and 1930s: Overwhelmed by rapid change, many people reacted to new ideas and diverse groups with suspicion and anger. Give examples.

2. "Rugged individualism," or succeeding only by one's own efforts, has long been considered an American value. Yet many Americans quickly accepted the government assistance introduced with the New Deal. How do you think people of the 1930s reconciled these ideas?

3. During the depression, as many as 13 million workers were unemployed. What groups were the hardest hit? Why? What effects do you think such massive unemployment had on family life, health, education, local government, foreign trade?

Using the Time Line. In general, the 1920s are said to be boom times and the 1930s, a "bust." List three events shown on the time line that are related to "boom" and three related to "bust." Explain the relationships.

Projects and Activities

1. Research clothing styles for both men and women in the 1910s, 1920s, and 1930s. What can you tell about the times from its popular styles? Make a poster displaying these clothes. Write a caption for each picture.

2. During the depression the WPA Writer's Project produced guidebooks for every state. Work in groups of three. Pick one aspect of your state to research, for example, agriculture, industry, population, recreation, or transportation. Find out what has changed in your state since the 1930s and what has not. Write an article for a new guidebook.

3. Many films from the 1920s and 1930s can be seen on videotape. As a class, view some of these films. Discuss what appealed to American viewers during those times. What values do the movies reflect? Consider such topics as speech patterns, roles of men and women, and roles of different social classes.

Using the Time Line. In the 1920s and 1930s radio was an important source of information and entertainment. Work in groups of three to write and perform a short radio comedy, drama, or news program. Base your program on five of the events shown on the time line.

Milestones	1919	1924
Presidents	Wilson; Harding	Coolidge
Political and Economic	• "Red Scare" • Sacco-Vanzetti case • Seattle general strike • *Ozawa* v. *U.S.* • Prohibition begins • Senate rejects League of Nations	• Immigration Act of 1924 • Snyder Act: all Native Americans are citizens
Social and Cultural	• Harlem Renaissance begins • National Negro Baseball League • First regular commercial radio broadcasts • Lincoln Memorial completed	• F. Scott Fitzgerald writes *The Great Gatsby* • Charleston dance craze • *Weary Blues*, Langston Hughes
Technological and Scientific	• Brinks uses armored cars • Hydraulic 4-wheel brakes, Loughead • First airmail, N.Y./Washington, D.C. • First helicopter flight	• First wirephoto transmission • Electric shaver, Jacob Schick • First neon sign, Cosmopolitan Theatre, N.Y. • Inlaid linoleum produced

Assessment

Ask what museums students are familiar with and what purposes museums serve (preserve special objects, research, education, pass on cultural history). Have students list different kinds of museums (art, natural history, science and technology, history, living history). Have them describe exhibits they've seen that were displayed in unusual or interesting ways.

Scoring

To create a scoring system, or rubric, assign an achievement scale to each of the evaluation criteria. For example, you might evaluate "Completing the task" on a scale of 0 to 4 as follows:

4—Exemplary response: floor plan shows more than five rooms and reflects thought about how the pattern of movement from room to room will affect the impact of the exhibit. For each room there is a detailed list of displayed items, grouped to show relationships, and a statement explaining the theme. Plans include vivid written and illustrative information about where and how items will be displayed.

3—Good response: floor plan shows five or more rooms and reflects thought about the relationship between the rooms. For each room there is a list of displayed items, which may be grouped to show relationships, and a statement describing the topic or theme of the room. Plans show where objects are placed and how they will be displayed.

2—Adequate response: includes a floor plan with five rooms. For each room there is a brief list of displayed items, a simple scheme for displaying the items, and a statement of the subject of the room.

1—Poor response: some elements of the project—floor plan with five rooms, list of items on display, plan for displaying the items, topic or theme statement for each room—are incomplete or missing.

0—No response/inappropriate response.

Follow-up Activity

Class discussion. If a museum-goer saw these exhibits, what would he or she learn about change in American life in the 1920s and 1930s?

Assessment: Demonstrating What You Know

Planning Museum Displays

Life in the United States changed greatly between the two world wars. Imagine that a federal commission is building a museum to help people today understand the changes that took place between 1919 and 1939, and the commission has appointed you to the planning committee.

Work in groups of five. Review the unit to identify significant events, people, ideas, and places. Classify these items to develop a list of topics. Each room will be devoted to one topic or theme—for example, the changing role of the worker or the impact of the automobile. Plan at least five.

Decide what you will display in each room to demonstrate its theme. Consider artifacts, documents, photographs, paintings, maps, sounds, music, models, interactive exhibits, and dioramas. For each room, write a statement summarizing the change illustrated by the displays. List the items in the room and explain why you have chosen each one.

Your final project will include the following items. Plan to display them in class.

1. A general floor plan for the museum
2. A room-by-room list of the items on display
3. A close-up plan of each room showing where and how the items are displayed
4. A theme statement for each room

Evaluation Criteria

Your work will be evaluated according to how well you meet the following criteria.

- **Completing the task**. Your floor plan includes at least five rooms, each based on one aspect of change. For each room you write a list of displays and a theme statement.
- **Knowing history**. The displays are based on historical information from your text or other sources. Theme statements are based on analysis of historical events and trends. The displays in each room support its theme.
- **Thinking critically**. You classify ideas, events, people, and places to identify historical themes. You analyze information about American life between 1919 and 1939 to draw conclusions about change and summarize your conclusions in concise statements.
- **Communicating ideas**. Viewers can readily understand your floor plans. The themes are clear and convincing. Your displays are attractive, creative, instructive, and varied.

1929 — 1934 — 1939

Hoover | F. D. Roosevelt

- Stock market crash
- Brotherhood of Sleeping Car Porters joins AFL
- Bonus Army march
- New Deal begins
- Indian Reorganization Act
- Social Security Act
- UAW sit-down strike, Flint, Mich.
- Court-packing controversy

- First animated talking picture, *Steamboat Willie*
- George Gershwin compose *An American in Paris*
- *The Maltese Falcon*, Dashiel Hammett
- Jane Addams wins Nobel Peace Prize
- WPA art project begins, influenced by Mexican muralists Diego Rivera and José Orozco
- Board game Monopoly introduced
- *Gone with the Wind*, Margaret Mitchell

- Charles Lindbergh's solo Atlantic flight
- First television transmission
- Empire State Building begun
- Planet Pluto discovered
- Amelia Earhart's solo Atlantic flight
- Yellow fever vaccine developed
- TVA begins development of Tennessee Basin
- Boulder Dam completed

603

Unit 8

Objectives

- Identify efforts nations made to secure lasting peace after World War I.
- Explain the economic and political factors that led to war.
- Tell how the United States moved from isolation and neutrality to active participation in World War II.
- Describe how the war affected Americans at home.
- Tell how the Allies defeated the Axis and describe the aftermath of the war.

Introducing THE UNIT

The United States emerged from World War I with a determination to avoid new foreign entanglements. However, efforts to guarantee world peace were thwarted by resentment of the Treaty of Versailles, economic concerns, and worldwide depression. Gradually the world divided into two camps—the Axis powers of Germany, Italy, and Japan, and the democracies of Britain, France, and the United States. Originally neutral in World War II, the United States moved slowly toward involvement. The Japanese attack on Pearl Harbor united Americans, and the United States and its allies waged a bitter struggle for four years before finally defeating the Axis powers.

Multicultural Perspectives

The detention center at Manzanar, California, held 10,767 detainees at its peak. Manzanar was one of ten permanent detention camps. Detainees were taken first to one or more of fifteen temporary detention camps and then to a permanent camp, where they stayed for more than three years.

Manzanar was designated a California state historical landmark in 1973. In addition to the bronze plaque on the gatehouse shown below, a stone obelisk on the site bears three Japanese characters reading I-REI-TOH. I stands for *nagusameru*, to console; REI for *tamashii*, or spirits; and TOH, meaning a monument. While former detainees make pilgrimages to many detention sites, the Manzanar Pilgrimage is the most consistent. It has occurred every year since 1969.

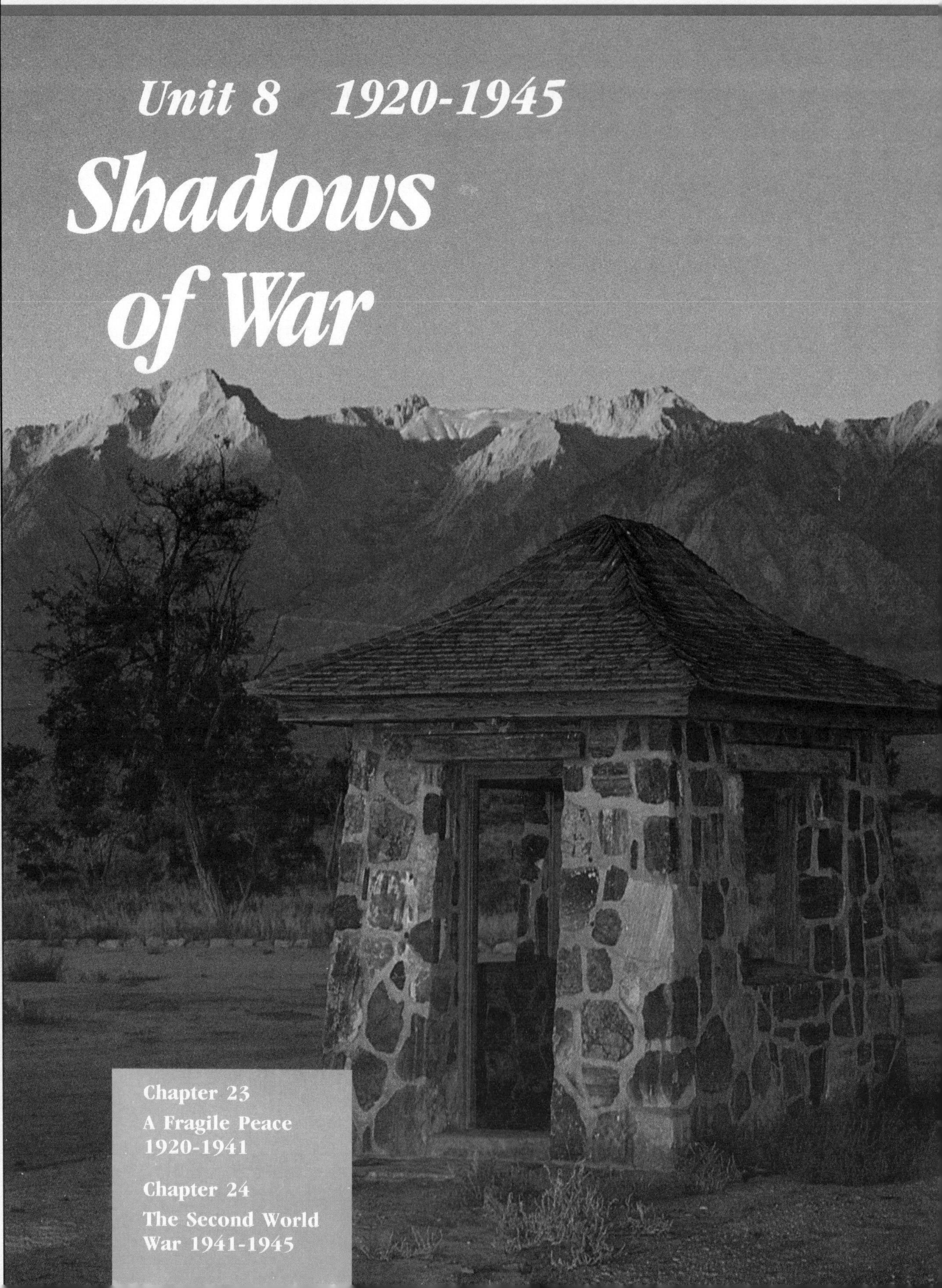

Unit 8 1920-1945

Shadows of War

ocial History
anne Wakatsuki Houston and her husband—the novelist mes D. Houston—used a tape recorder and the 1944 arbook from Manzanar High School to begin looking back her life in camp. With a grant from the University of lifornia at Santa Cruz they used recollections of the camp from family members to relive the devastating experience. *Farewell to Manzanar* has been adapted as a film for television and praised by TV critics.

Guided Reading

Discussion. An autobiography is an author's account of his or her own life. Autobiographies usually reveal the attitudes of the writer and give insight into his or her character, beliefs, and point of view. Direct students' attention to what the passage reveals about Jeanne Wakatsuki Houston's attitudes. How does the passage represent the point of view of a child? What do her observations about those around her and her environment reveal about the political climate of the time? How does she cope with circumstances beyond her control?

History Through Literature

On December 7, 1941, Japanese planes attacked the American naval base at Pearl Harbor, Hawaii, and the United States found itself at war. Soon Japanese Americans became the victims of anti-Japanese fears. Seven-year-old Jeanne Wakatsuki's family was forced to give up nearly everything and move three times, finally coming to Manzanar, one of the relocation centers in California that the government set up for people of Japanese ancestry. In *Farewell to Manzanar,* Jeanne Wakatsuki Houston tells of her family's experiences.

from

Farewell to Manzanar

by Jeanne Wakatsuki Houston

This was the first time I had felt outright hostility from a Caucasian. Looking back, it is easy enough to explain. Public attitudes toward the Japanese in California were shifting rapidly. In the first few months of the Pacific war, America was on the run. Tolerance had turned to distrust and irrational fear. The hundred-year-old tradition of anti-Orientalism on the west coast soon resurfaced, more vicious than ever. Its result became clear about a month later, when we were told to make our third and final move.

The name Manzanar meant nothing to us. . . . We didn't know where it was or what it was. We went because the government ordered us to. And in the case of my older brothers and sisters, we went with a certain amount of relief. They had all heard stories of Japanese homes being attacked, of beatings in the streets of California towns. They were as frightened of the Caucasians as Caucasians were of us. Moving, under what appeared to be government protection, to an area less directly threatened by the war seemed not such a bad idea at all. For some it actually sounded like a fine adventure.

Our pickup point was a Buddhist church in Los Angeles. It was very early, and misty, when we got there with our luggage. Mama had bought heavy coats for all of us. She grew up in eastern Washington and knew that anywhere inland in early April would be cold. I was proud of my new coat, and I remember sitting on a duffel bag trying to be friendly with the Greyhound driver. I smiled at him. He didn't smile back. He was befriending no one. Someone tied a numbered tag to my collar and to the duffel bag (each family was given a number, and that became our official designation until the camps were closed), someone else passed out box lunches for the trip, and we climbed aboard.

I had never been outside Los Angeles County, never traveled more than ten miles from the coast, had never even ridden on a bus. I was full of

605

Constitutional Heritage

How could Japanese Americans be so blatantly denied their Fifth Amendment right ("No person shall be . . . deprived of life, liberty, or property without due process of law.") and their Sixth Amendment right to a trial? The government used semantics to evade granting these rights. For example, even though Japanese Americans were held against their will in barbed-wire compounds, the government called the internment a "relocation" or "evacuation." Internment camps were called "relocation centers," temporary detention camps "assembly centers," and the prisoners "evacuees." Yet despite the official semantics, many government officials—including Presidents Roosevelt and Truman—made no bones about referring to the detention centers as "concentration camps."

excitement, the way any kid would be, and wanted to look out the window. But for the first few hours the shades were drawn. Around me other people played cards, read magazines, dozed, waiting. I settled back, waiting too, and finally fell asleep. The bus felt very secure to me. Almost half its passengers were immediate relatives. Mama and my older brothers had succeeded in keeping most of us together, on the same bus headed for the same camp. I didn't realize until much later what a job that was. The strategy had been, first, to have everyone living in the same district when the evacuation began, and then to get all of us included under the same family number, even though names had been changed by marriage. Many families weren't as lucky as ours and suffered months of anguish while trying to arrange transfers from one camp to another.

We rode all day. By the time we reached our destination, the shades were up. It was late afternoon. The first thing I saw was a yellow swirl across a blurred, reddish setting sun. The bus was being pelted by what sounded like splattering rain. It wasn't rain. This was my first look at something I would soon know very well, a billowing flurry of dust and sand churned up by the wind through Owens Valley.

We drove past a barbed-wire fence, through a gate and into an open space where trunks and sacks and packages had been dumped from the baggage trucks that drove out ahead of us. I could see a few tents set up, the first rows of black barracks, and beyond them, blurred by sand, rows of barracks that seemed to spread for miles across this plain. . . .

We had pulled up just in time for dinner. The mess halls weren't completed yet. An outdoor chow line snaked around a half-finished building that broke a good part of the wind. They issued us army mess kits, the round metal kind that fold over, and plopped in scoops of canned Vienna sausage, canned string beans, steamed rice that had been cooked too long, and on top of the rice a serving of canned apricots. The Caucasian servers were thinking that the fruit poured over rice would make a good dessert. Among the Japanese, of course, rice is never eaten with sweet foods, only with salty or savory foods. Few of us could eat such a mixture. But at this point no one dared protest. It would have been impolite. I was horrified when I saw the apricot syrup seeping through my little mound of rice. I opened my mouth to complain. My mother jabbed me in the back to keep quiet. We moved on through the line and joined the others squatting in the lee of half-raised walls, dabbing courteously at what was, for almost everyone there, an inedible concoction. . . .

(Background) Gatehouse at Manzanar; (opposite) Manzanar barracks in the 1940s; (above) War Relocation Authority pass for a leave from camp; identification tags.

As the months at Manzanar turned to years, it became a world unto itself, with its own logic and familiar ways. In time, staying there seemed far simpler than moving once again to another, unknown place. It was as if the war were forgotten, our reason for being there forgotten. The present, the little bit of busywork you had right in front of you, became the most urgent thing. In such a narrowed world, in order to survive, you learn to contain your rage and your despair, and try to re-create, as well as you can, your normality, some sense of things continuing. The fact that America had accused us, or excluded us, or imprisoned us, or whatever it might be called, did not change the kind of world we wanted. Most of us were born in this country; we had no other models. Those parks and gardens (built by camp residents) lent it an oriental character, but in most ways it was a totally equipped American small town, complete with schools, churches, Boy Scouts, beauty parlors, neighborhood gossip, fire and police departments, glee clubs, softball leagues, Abbott and Costello movies, tennis courts, and traveling shows. . . .

My sister Lillian was in high school and singing with a hillbilly band called The Sierra Stars—jeans, cowboy hats, two guitars, and a tub bass. And my oldest brother, Bill, led a dance band called The Jive Bombers—brass and rhythm, with cardboard fold-out music stands lettered J.B. Dances were held every weekend in one of the recreation halls. Bill played trumpet and took vocals on Glenn Miller arrangements of such tunes as *In the Mood, String of Pearls,* and *Don't Fence Me In.* He didn't sing *Don't Fence Me In* out of protest, as if trying quitely to mock the authorities. It just happened to be a hit song one year, and they all wanted to be an up-to-date American swing band. They would blast it out into recreation barracks full of bobby-soxed, jitterbugging couples:

"Oh, give me land, lots of land
Under starry skies above,
Don't fence me in.
Let me ride through the wide
Open country that I love. . . ."

Taking a Closer Look

1. *Describe living conditions at Manzanar when the Wakatsukis arrived.*

2. *What evidence is there that the Caucasians (whites) at Manzanar failed to understand Japanese-American culture?*

3. *What attitude did the families at Manzanar adopt to survive persecution?*

4. *The government isolated Japanese Americans out of fear that although most were American citizens, their race would make them loyal to Japan. What irony is there in Houston's description of the community created at Manzanar?*

Taking a Closer Look

ANSWERS

1. Conditions were poor and very bleak. Buildings were not finished, the housing was crowded and shabby. Dust storms pelted the residents.
2. For dinner they were served overcooked rice with canned apricots which Wakatsuki describes as almost inedible for the Japanese Americans, who would not eat such a combination.
3. The author describes how the Japanese Americans controlled their rage and despair in order to survive by focusing their attention on the present, attending to "busywork," and recreating a sense of normality.
4. The Japanese Americans tried to recreate a sense of normality in the camps which turned out to be much like normality for the rest of the country. They built parks, opened schools and churches, and played sports and music. Young men, such as Woody, wanted to join the military. They showed no signs of loyalty to Japan.

Chapter 23

A Fragile Peace

Planning Guide

	Student Text	TWE Lesson Plans	Support Materials
SECTION 1	**Section 23-1 (1-2 Days)** **The Search for Permanent Peace,** pp 610-615 The American Spirit: Will Rogers, p 614 Review/Evaluation Section Review, p 615	**Introducing the Chapter:** Keeping the Peace—Class Activity, 30 minutes, p 607B **Evaluating Progress:** Cartoon View of Peacekeeping—Individual Activity, homework, p 607C	★ **Read to Remember,** Section 1 ● **Section Activities,** Section 1 Δ **Readings** ● **Tests and Quizzes,** Section 1 Quiz
SECTION 2	**Section 23-2 (1-2 Days)** **A World Changed by War,** pp 615-620 Geography—Place: Japan Reaches Outward, p 621 Review/Evaluation Section Review, p 620	**Teaching the Main Ideas:** Fascism vs. Democracy—Individual Activity, 30 minutes, p 607B **Teaching the Main Ideas:** Time Lines of the Axis Powers—Cooperative Activity, one class period, p 607C	★ **Read to Remember,** Section 2 ● **Section Activities,** Section 2 Δ **Readings** ● **Tests and Quizzes,** Section 2 Quiz
SECTION 3	**Section 23-3 (1-2 Days)** **The Road to War,** pp 622-625 Point of View: Munich and Appeasement, pp 626-627 Review/Evaluation Section Review, p 625	**Teaching the Main Ideas:** Time Lines of the Axis Powers—Cooperative Activity, one class period, p 607C **Reinforcement Activity:** Stepping Stones to War—Cooperative Activity, one class period, p 607C	★ **Read to Remember,** Section 3 ● **Section Activities,** Section 3 Δ **Enrichment Activities,** Section 3 Δ **Readings** ● **Tests and Quizzes,** Section 3 Quiz
SECTION 4	**Section 23-4 (1-2 Days)** **The End of Isolation,** pp 628-633 Connections to Themes: Shaping Democracy, p 633 Review/Evaluation Section Review, p 633 Chapter 23 Survey, pp 634-635 Skills, pp 634-635 Using New Vocabulary Thinking Critically Using a Time Line Applying Thinking Skills: Recognizing Propaganda	**Reinforcement Activity:** Stepping Stones to War—Cooperative Activity, one class period, p 607C **Enrichment Activity:** Advising Roosevelt—Individual Activity, homework, p 607C	★ **Read to Remember,** Section 4 ● **Section Activities,** Section 4 Δ **Enrichment Activities,** Section 4 ● **Geography Activities,** Section 4 Δ **Readings** ● **Tests and Quizzes,** Section 4 Quiz, Chapter 23 Test (Forms A and B) **Additional Resources** Δ **Twentieth Century Issues: Links to the Past** ● **Active Learning** Δ **GTV Videodiscs** Δ **Transparencies and Activity Book** ● **Testing Software** ★ **Chapter Summaries** **Key:** ★ **For Extra Support** ● **For All Students** Δ **For Enrichment**

Overview

In the years after World War I, the United States took the lead in efforts to achieve a permanent peace. It negotiated treaties and pacts with European nations and Japan to limit the arms buildup and to "outlaw" war. Under the Good Neighbor Policy, the United States also made efforts to avoid interventionist policies in Latin America.

However, the war had shattered European economies, and with the onset of a worldwide depression in 1929, war reparations payments largely ended. Taking advantage of economic and political breakdown, fascist leaders rose to power in Germany, Italy, and Spain. Adolph Hitler played upon deep-seated German anti-Semitism to launch a policy of persecution of Jews. Meanwhile, an increasingly industrialized Japan began aggressive expansion.

Afraid of being drawn into conflict, the United States tried to isolate itself with a series of Neutrality Acts. Meanwhile, fascist Germany and Italy expanded their control, while other European nations attempted to appease them. When Germany invaded Poland in 1939, however, Britain and France declared war.

Although the United States remained officially neutral, President Roosevelt gave increasing amounts of financial and moral support to the Allies. Then, on December 7, 1941, Japan attacked Pearl Harbor, and the United States declared war.

Activity Objectives

After completing the activities, students should be able to

- distinguish between fascist and democratic forms of government.
- trace the major events in the histories of the Axis powers between 1920 and 1940.
- list events leading to American entry into World War II.
- explain how the United States and other nations attempted to secure peace after World War I.
- identify the major arguments for and against American policies of isolationism and interventionism.

Introducing the Chapter

Keeping the Peace

This class activity requires half a period.

This activity introduces students to several points of view about war and peace as expressed in quotations from well-known figures of the World War II era.

To introduce the activity, write the following quotations on the chalkboard, an overhead transparency, or a handout sheet.

"Ours is a world of nuclear giants and ethical infants. We know more about war than we know about peace; more about killing than we know about living."

—General Omar Bradley

"Mankind has grown strong in eternal struggle and it will perish through eternal peace."

—Adolph Hitler

"Peace is not only better than war but infinitely more arduous."

—George Bernard Shaw

Give students time to read and consider the three quotations, then ask volunteers to explain the meaning of each. Have students discuss the following questions:

- (Bradley) Why do we know more about war and killing? What could we do to learn more about peace and living?
- (Hitler) Is Hitler's perspective on war similar to Darwin's theory of evolution? What objections might Darwin make to Hitler's theory?
- (Shaw) Why is peace harder to achieve than war?

Ask students to spend a few minutes responding in writing to the following questions, giving reasons for their answers:

- Does our society glorify war?
- Is achieving peace an active or passive process?

Encourage students to reflect on the three quotations as they read the history of peacekeeping attempts after World War I.

Teaching the Main Ideas

Section 23-2: Fascism vs. Democracy

This individual activity requires half a period.

In this activity students use an organizational pattern called a *Big T* to sharpen their awareness of the differences between fascism and democracy. If you used the Evaluating Progress activity in Chapter 13, students will be familiar with a Big T.

Have students create a *T* by drawing a vertical line down the center of a piece of paper and a horizontal line across the top. Have them label the left side *Democracy* and the right side *Fascism*. Tell students they are to use the Big T to identify differences between the two political systems. They may use their texts to review Section 23-2 and should list as many characteristics in each column as possible. To illustrate, suggest that under *Democracy* they might write *allows two or more political parties*, and under *Fascism* they could write *allows only one political party.*

Topics that students should consider using in their Big Ts include: speech, religion, nationalism, attitudes toward war, racism, loyalty, opposition to government, role of press, role of leader, and control of business.

Conclude the activity by having students identify the distinctions between fascism and democracy that they consider most important. Ask them to suggest the conditions under which fascism might be appealing to the citizens of a country. Then have them identify indicators they could use to test for the rise of fascism in a society.

Teaching the Main Ideas

Sections 23-2 and 23-3: Time Lines of the Axis Powers

This cooperative project requires a full class period.

This activity engages students in creating time lines of major events in the Axis countries between 1920 and 1940. Provide index cards, preferably in three colors, for students to use in making their time lines.

Introduce the activity by reminding students that in the twenty years between 1920 and 1940, Germany, Italy, and Japan greatly strengthened their military and political positions in the world. Also point out that the histories of the three countries during those years are both separate and overlapping.

Divide the class into groups of three. Explain to the groups that to help them clarify the separate and intermingled histories of the Axis powers, they will create a time line for each country. On separate index cards they are to identify, date, and describe one historical event or action in one country between 1920 and 1940. For example, a card might read:

Country:	Italy
Year:	1927
Event:	Mussolini becomes dictator
Description:	Brought to power by military forces and Fascist control of the parliament

If you have provided index cards in three colors, suggest that students use a different color for each country. Direct them to use material in Sections 23-2 and 23-3 and to identify as many events and actions as possible.

When their cards are complete, groups are to arrange them by country in parallel time lines. Encourage students to compare and contrast the histories of the three countries during this time period. Then have them combine the three time lines into one and identify the years in which the three countries most interacted or took concurrent actions. To check the accuracy of the combined time lines, groups can check each other's work.

Reinforcement Activity

Section 23-3 and 23-4: Stepping Stones to War

This cooperative project requires one class period.

In this activity students reinforce their understanding of the steps that led the United States from neutrality to war by creating a flow chart of events.

Remind students that Sections 23-3 and 23-4 trace the events leading to American involvement in World War II. Organize students into groups of three and have them review the text, writing down the specific events discussed. (They should include Neutrality Acts, Spanish Civil War, German-Italian alliance, quarantine speech, *Panay* incident, Ludlow amendment, French and British declarations of war, buildup of American defenses, peacetime draft, Lend-Lease Act, the Atlantic Charter, Pearl Harbor.)

Provide poster paper and markers and direct each group to create a flow chart illustrating America's actions related to the European conflict and Japanese expansion between 1935 and 1941. Charts should reflect both chronology and relationships among events. Tell students that they may use arrows, lines, and other graphic means to show relationships.

Post the completed flow charts and provide time for the class to review them. Ask students to decide, by studying the charts, at what point the United States began to move away from neutrality in "spirit," and at what point it moved away from neutrality in action.

Evaluating Progress

Section 23-1: A Cartoon View of Peacekeeping

This individual project may be assigned as homework.

In this activity students demonstrate their understanding of the treaties limiting war and encouraging disarmament after World War I by creating cartoons to illustrate peacemaking attempts by the United States and other countries. If students have not previously created their own cartoons, bring examples to stimulate their creativity. Point out cartoonists' use of satire, stereotypes, and caricatures as well as titles and labels.

To introduce the activity, recall that after World War I the United States and other countries made several attempts to ensure world peace. Explain to students that their task in this activity is to prepare a political cartoon about one, several, or all of the treaties discussed in Section 23-1. The cartoons should reflect their personal opinions about these peacemaking efforts.

Students' cartoons should relate to one or all of the following treaties: Five-Power Treaty, Four-Power Treaty, Nine-Power Treaty, and the Kellogg-Briand Pact. Evaluate the cartoons on whether they correctly reflect treaty terms, make effective use of symbolism and other characteristics of cartoons, and show a point of view.

Enrichment Activity

Section 23-4: Advising Roosevelt

This individual activity is best assigned as homework.

In this activity students demonstrate their knowledge and opinions about pre-World War II events by writing a letter of advice to President Roosevelt.

On the chalkboard write the words *isolationism* and *interventionism* and ask students to review their definitions. Have students recall the United States's efforts to remain neutral in

European conflicts during the 1920s and 1930s and compare these actions with the nation's interventions in Latin America.

Tell students to imagine that they are advisors to President Roosevelt. Direct them to write a letter to the President, dated November 15, 1941, offering advice on how the country should respond to world events. The letter should begin with a review of the situation in Europe, Asia, and Latin America. Then it should present the advisor's personal opinion on whether the nation should follow a general policy of isolationism or interventionism in relation to those three areas of the world. Specific recommendations to support the proposed general policy should be made, including a recommendation on how to deal with Jewish refugees.

Conclude the activity by asking volunteers to read their letters. Discuss the recommendations and ask for a show of hands to determine how many students would have suggested military intervention in Europe and Asia before November 15, 1941, and how many would have advised refraining from intervention even after that date.

Bibliography and Audiovisual Material

Teacher Bibliography

Buchanan, A. Russell. *Black Americans in World War II.* Claremont, Ca.: Regina Books, 1977.

Dawidowicz, Lucy S. *The War Against the Jews, 1933–1945.* New York: Bantam Books, 1986.

Ferrell, Robert M. *American Diplomacy in the Great Depression.* Northford, Ct.: Elliots Books, 1957.

Offner, Arnold. *The Origins of the Second World War: American Foreign Policy and World Politics.* Melbourne, Fl.: Krieger Publishing Co., 1986.

Rauch, Basil. *Roosevelt: From Munich to Pearl Harbor.* New York: Da Capo Press, 1969.

Shirer, William. *The Rise and Fall of the Third Reich.* New York: Simon and Schuster, Inc., 1990.

Smith, Bradley F. *Adolf Hitler: His Family, Childhood and Youth.* Stanford, Ca.: Hoover Institute Press, 1967.

Student Bibliography

Arnow, Harriette. *The Dollmaker.* New York: Avon Books, 1985.

Greene, Bette. *Summer of My German Soldier.* New York: Bantam Books, 1984.

Hemingway, Ernest. *For Whom the Bell Tolls.* New York: Scribner, 1940.

Knowles, John. *A Separate Peace.* New York: Macmillan Publishing Co., 1987.

Wouk, Herman. *The Winds of War.* New York: Pocket Books, 1989.

Films, Videocassettes, and Videodiscs

American Chronicle Series: Prelude to War (1935–1939), Seeds of Discord (1933–1936). AIMS Media. Videodisc.

American Heritage Media Collection: The 20 & 30's. 35 min. Westport Media. Videocassette.

Between the Wars (1918–1941). 30-min. programs. Zenger Video. 8 videocassettes.

A Fragile Peace (1918–1929). 11 min. CORT. Movie.

The Inevitable War. 13 min. CORT. Movie.

The Life of Adolph Hitler. 101 min. Video Yesteryear. Videocassette.

Roosevelt: Manipulator-In-Chief. 24 min. LCA. Movie.

Filmstrips

Causes of World War II. 2 color filmstrips, 2 cassettes, guide. EAV.

Hitler and the Germans. 2 color filmstrips, 2 cassettes, guide. Multi-Media Productions.

Presidents of the United States Series: Part VI-2 Franklin D Roosevelt. 17 min. 1 filmstrip with cassette. National Geographic.

The United States as a World Power; from the 1890's to the 1970's: 1921 to 1945. 1 filmstrip with cassette. National Geographic.

Chapter 23

Objectives

- Explain how the United States and other nations tried to secure world peace.
- Analyze economic and political factors that threatened peace.
- Describe changes in United States policy of isolation and neutrality in the late 1930s.
- Analyze the factors that led the United States to declare war.

Introducing THE CHAPTER

For suggestions on introducing Chapter 23, refer to page 607B in the Teacher's Edition.

Developing THE CHAPTER

For activities and teaching strategies to help you reinforce and enrich chapter content, see pages 607B-607D in the Teacher's Edition.

Chapter Opener Illustrations

Hitler skillfully devised mass rallies to engender a sense of national purpose for his Nazi programs. This image shows thousands of German soldiers standing at attention at the National Socialist Party Congress on September 8, 1934.

Hitler and Mussolini established the Rome-Berlin Axis in 1936. In 1938 Hitler visited Rome and stood with Mussolini before huge crowds to demonstrate the solidarity of the Axis nations.

The 1935 Nuremburg Laws made the persecution of Jews legal in Germany. In 1938 Nazis began rounding up Jewish men, women, and children, and sending them to concentration camps.

Reduced student page in the Teacher's Edition

Chapter 23 1920-1941

A Fragile Peace

A pro-Japanese propaganda poster depicted Japan as an Asian colossus, in league with Nazi Germany and Fascist Italy. The poster, which evokes the samurai warrior tradition, was created in Italy during World War II.

Great Britain stood alone in 1940 against Nazi bombardment. In December firebombs fell on the old heart of London, destroying ancient buildings and landmarks, but St. Paul's Cathedral escaped almost unscathed. Volunteer firefighters put out every firebomb that hit the cathedral before serious damage was done.

American Voices

In 1938 German ruler Adolf Hitler took the first step toward annexing Austria to Germany. Dorothy Thompson, an American journalist in Europe, recognized that the world was threatened by dictators on a march of conquest, and she warned:

> "*Write it down. On Saturday, February 12, 1938, nazism started on the march across all of Europe east of the Rhine.*
>
> *Write it down that the world revolution began in earnest—and perhaps the world war . . . .*
>
> *And it never needed to have happened. One strong voice of one strong power could have stopped it.*
>
> *Tomorrow, one of two things can happen. Despotism can settle into horrible stagnation . . . . More likely the other law of despotism's nature—the law of perpetual aggressiveness—will cause it to move . . . onward, emboldened, and strengthened, by each success.*
>
> *To the point where civilization will take a last stand. For take a stand it will. Of that there is not the slightest doubt.*
>
> *Too bad that it did not take it this week.*"

In the United States, few heeded Dorothy Thompson's words. Sickened by the outcome of World War I, they had sworn that never again would they give their lives in someone else's war. World War I, however, had thrust the United States to the center of the world stage. Would Americans accept the leading role?

Nazi rally, 1934; Benito Mussolini and Adolf Hitler; women and children sent to concentration camp; pro-Japanese propaganda; London air raid.

Analyzing Primary Sources

American Voices

Dorothy Thompson reported the news from Europe for several large American newspapers. She was the first woman to broadcast news regularly for a radio network (NBC). Thompson was expelled from Germany on August 25, 1934, for her reports on Hitler's anti-Semitic campaign. She was married to novelist Sinclair Lewis.

1. Why did Thompson think February 12, 1938, was such an important date? **(Hitler annexed Austria, signaling his plan to extend his power outside Germany.)**
2. What two possibilities did Thompson foresee for Europe at that time? **(German control of Europe east of the Rhine or German aggression on an even wider front)**
3. What did she think would eventually happen? **("Civilization"—presumably the other European powers—would take a stand against Hitler, and a war would be fought.)**

After they study the chapter, ask students whether they agree with Thompson that war could have been prevented in the 1930s. What early actions might have been effective and why?

Section 23-1

Objectives

- ***Answer the Focus Question.***
- *Evaluate the successes of the Washington Naval Conference and the Kellogg-Briand Pact.*
- *Summarize changes in United States policy toward Latin American nations.*

Introducing

THE SECTION

Review the nature of the League of Nations and what Wilson had hoped to accomplish with the League. In addition, review why Congress refused to let the United States join the League. Point out that Britain and France had rejected key elements of Wilson's Fourteen Points and that Germany, as the defeated nation, was not allowed to join the League.

Ask: Could the League of Nations have been expected to prevent another world war? Why or why not? **(The League had little power to enforce its decisions and also had no influence over non-members, especially Germany and the United States)**

B · A · C · K · G · R · O · U · N · D

Time Line Illustrations

1. Before the attack on Pearl Harbor, significant numbers of Americans refused to take up arms against aggressors abroad. Students who attended a peace rally at the University of Chicago in 1937 carried signs, some of which read: "Build the Peace Council" and "Scholarships Not Battleships."

2. During the mid-1920s, recruitment into the military stressed travel and adventure rather than service to a nation on the brink of disaster. The young men who joined the marines in response to this poster served in Nicaragua, Haiti, and the Dominican Republic.

3. The Japanese flag reflected a vision of Japan as the "Land of the Rising Sun." The rising sun image also symbolized the growth of the Japanese empire in Asia and the Pacific.

4. The National Socialist Party of Germany (the Nazis)

Reduced student page in the Teacher's Edition

CHAPTER TIME LINE

1920-1941

1920 — 1924 — 1928

1921 **Nov** Washington Naval Conference

1925 Coolidge's "private war" in Nicaragua begins

23-1 The Search for Permanent Peace

Focus: What attempts did the United States and other nations make to secure lasting world peace?

In 1919, shortly after Germany's surrender ended World War I, President Woodrow Wilson made this solemn forecast:

> *"I can predict with absolute certainty that within another generation there will be another world war if the nations of the world do not concert [create] the method by which to prevent it."*

Over the next twenty years, as the United States rode a rollercoaster of prosperity and depression, few Americans gave much thought to Wilson's warning. The Depression convinced people that the government should focus on solving problems at home and leave Europe alone. Most Americans preferred a withdrawal from international affairs, a policy that became known as **isolationism.**

Still, the United States had emerged from the war as the world's leading economic power. Ties of trade linked the nation to many corners of the globe. It would not be easy for the United States to isolate itself from the rest of the world.

American Peace Efforts

Isolationist attitudes had been strong in the Senate when it turned down membership in the League of Nations by rejecting the Treaty of Versailles. Slowly, however, American distrust of the League began to adopted the swastika as its symbol in 1920. The original roots of the symbol, however, are in ancient cultures throughout the world. Swastikas can be found on Byzantine buildings, Buddhist inscriptions, Celtic monuments, and Greek coins. Yet the swastika's association with Nazism and anti-Semitism has made it a hated symbol of evil.

5. For the many Germans in the Sudetenland (Czechoslovakia), Nazism appealed to their German roots. This Sudeten German woman is overcome with emotion as she pays homage to the German armed forces marching into the border town of Cheb in 1938.

6. This image of the U.S.S. *Shaw* was photographed on December 7, 1941, during the Japanese attack on Pearl Harbor.

1931 Japan invades Manchuria

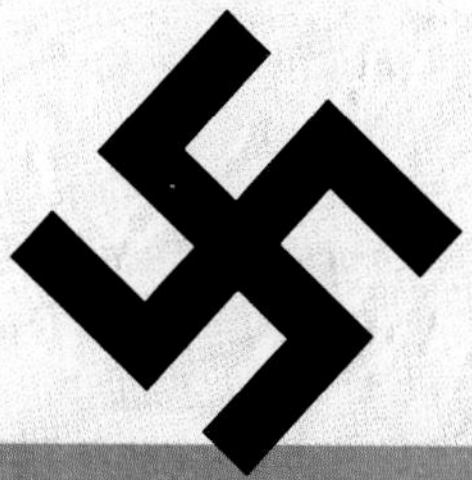

1938 **Mar** Germany annexes Austria
Nov *Kristallnacht*

1939 Germany occupies Czech capital and invades Poland

1932 — 1936 — 1941

1934 Hitler takes complete power in Germany

1935 Nuremburg laws in Germany deny citizenship to Jews
Italy invades Ethiopia

1940 **Apr** Germany invades Denmark and Norway
May Germany invades Belgium, the Netherlands, and Luxembourg
Jun France surrenders to Germany

1941 **Dec** Pearl Harbor

soften. Although the United States never joined the League, it did begin to cooperate with other nations in efforts to avoid future wars.

The arms race and disarmament. Most nations saw that the continued production of weapons was a serious threat to peace. And yet the war was scarcely over when an **arms race**— a peacetime competition to build more and better weapons— began.

Japan had emerged from World War I with troops in China's Shandong Peninsula and the eastern part of Siberia in Russia, and on several Pacific islands. The United States feared that Japanese expansion threatened its interests in China and the Philippines. Foreseeing a clash, both Japan and the United States launched huge shipbuilding programs.

The enormous cost of the naval buildup placed a crushing burden on taxpayers. Meanwhile, Great Britain, which had historically "ruled the seas," was still reeling from the war and knew it would be hard to compete. Thus, when President Harding suggested a disarmament conference, Japan, Great Britain, and six other nations agreed.

In November 1921 the delegates met in Washington, D.C., and hammered out several treaties. The Five-Power Treaty reduced the number of major warships. A tonnage ratio was established allowing 5 tons each for the United States and Britain, for every 3 tons for Japan, and 1.67 tons each for France and Italy. Britain, Japan, and the United States agreed to scrap a combined total of ships— almost 2 million tons.

In the Four-Power Treaty, Japan, Britain, France, and the United States agreed to respect each other's colonies in the Pacific. Japan, however, signed on the condition that the United States and Britain not fortify their Pacific island colonies, except Hawaii and a few British islands.

Other agreements eased tensions in Asia. In the Nine-Power Treaty, all nine nations agreed to uphold the Open Door policy and to "safeguard the rights and interests of China." In other negotiations, Japan promised to withdraw from China's Shandong Peninsula and from Russian Siberia.

The treaties were considered a triumph for President Warren G. Harding and Secretary of State Charles Evans Hughes, but they had major flaws. Naval limits applied only to heavy battleships, not

Developing

THE SECTION

Chapter Connections

Discussion. Did the United States follow a policy of isolationism at other times in its history? When? Why? **(For example, in 1796 George Washington warned against close political ties with foreign nations.)** What effect did conditions or events within the nation have in each case? In what period did the nation turn to expansionism? **(late 1800s)**

Limited English Proficiency

Building Vocabulary. Help students define the terms *arms race* and *disarmament*. Have students work in small groups to chart the several disarmament treaties, showing the terms and the flaws of each. For example: *Five-Power Treaty*—Terms: 1. Reduced number of battleships; 2. Ordered no new battleships built for ten years. Flaws: 1. Affected only battleships, not other kinds of ships; 2. Allowed Japanese navy to gain power in Pacific.

Ask: Were the treaties significant in spite of their flaws? Why or why not? **(The Five Power Treaty marked the first time in history that nations agreed to disarm.)**

B · A · C · K · G · R · O · U · N · D

Connections: Science and Technology
The treaties signed in 1921 emphasized battleships because they were very expensive and because most military leaders thought they would be the decisive weapon in any naval war. Submarines and aircraft carriers, which proved to be the most important naval weapons in World War II, were ignored. Air power in general was underrated, though a few leaders, such as Brigadier General William (Billy) Mitchell, insisted on its importance. In 1921 Mitchell staged a demonstration in which seven land-based bombers sank an "unsinkable" battleship in just over twenty-one minutes.

Thinking Critically

Analysis. Direct United States' investments in Latin American enterprises increased from almost $2 billion in 1919 to about $3.5 billion in 1929. **Ask:** From the Latin Americans' point of view, what were the benefits of this investment? (Jobs for Latin American citizens, a chance to develop industries that might not have been possible without foreign aid)

What were the drawbacks of heavy United States investments in their countries? (loss of control of their own economies; widening gap between rich—who usually benefited from the investments—and poor, and overreliance on a few crops or industries)

Reduced student page in the Teacher's Edition

to submarines and light surface ships. Japan's navy emerged as the most powerful in the Pacific, since the United States had to divide its navy between two oceans and Britain among three. In addition, the United States and Britain had agreed to leave most of their Pacific possessions undefended.

The Kellogg-Briand Pact. The weakness of the disarmament treaties as a means of ensuring peace caused governments to explore other paths. One idea was simply to make war a crime.

This idea appealed to the French foreign minister, Aristide Briand (bree-AHN). He and the new American Secretary of State, Frank B. Kellogg, drafted a proposal to outlaw war. In August 1928 delegates from fifteen nations met and signed the Kellogg-Briand Pact, which rejected war "as an instrument of national policy." Eventually, a total of sixty-two nations signed the pact.

Like the treaties signed at the Washington Naval Conference, the Kellogg-Briand Pact had no means of enforcing a nation's pledge to keep the peace. Indeed, most powers held on to their right to go to war in self-defense. It would only be a matter of time, most critics thought, before this ambitious attempt to outlaw war rang hollow.

In this 1928 cartoon, Peace remarries "This Wicked World" forever through the Kellogg-Briand Pact.

United States Interests in Latin America

As Americans sought ways to avoid armed conflict around the world, one area was a glaring exception: Latin America. Theodore Roosevelt's Corollary to the Monroe Doctrine in 1904 had promised the world that the United States would keep order in Latin America. Since then the United States had played an active role in Latin American affairs. By 1921, American troops were supporting the governments of the Dominican Republic, Haiti, and Nicaragua. By 1924 the United States was managing the treasuries of ten Latin American nations.

Business interests. A web of business ties linked the United States with Latin America. American companies had offices, factories, and mines there. Latin America was a good market for Yankee machines and automobiles. In return, the United States bought Latin American coffee, sugar, bananas, rubber, tin, copper, and oil. Clearly, political turmoil in Latin America threatened American investments, and intervention was one means of protecting those interests.

Charles Evans Hughes, Secretary of State to both Harding and Coolidge, often used the armed forces to preserve the stability of a nation so it could continue to pay back loans. Still, he tried to ease the growing tension between the United States and its neighbors by assuring them, "We covet no territory; we seek no conquest." Hughes and the leaders of the Dominican Republic worked out plans to hold elections there, and in 1924 United States troops left that nation. The next year United States troops also ended a thirteen-year occupation of Nicaragua, which had repaid its foreign debts.

Coolidge's "private war" in Nicaragua. No sooner had the marines left Nicaragua, though, than a rebellion led by generals, most notably General Augusto César Sandino, broke out. Fearing that unrest in Nicaragua might threaten the security of the Panama Canal, President Coolidge sent the marines back to restore stability. Sandino continued the revolt with a small but well-armed force supplied by communists in Mexico. Many Nicaraguans resented the presence of American marines and joined in support of Sandino's troops.

Multicultural Perspectives

As a side effect of the United States presence in Central America and the Caribbean in the 1920s, baseball became very popular in those regions. Now many major-league players in the United States come from Central America and the Caribbean, particularly the Dominican Republic.

Linking Past and Present

Research and Report. Have students do research on the civil war in the 1980s in Nicaragua and compare it and the United States' role in it with the situation in Nicaragua in the 1920s and early 1930s. (In the 1920s the communists were the rebels, while in the 1980s they were the ones in power. The war in the 1980s ended with a relatively democratic government, rather than a dictatorship.)

(Right) American Marines left Nicaragua in 1925 but were sent back in 1926 to put down a revolt led by Augusto César Sandino.

Beginning in the late 1970s the Sandinista party, named for Sandino, offered hope of reform to urban and rural workers.

Active Learning

Cooperative Activity. Divide the class into groups of six. Assign each student in the group one of the following roles:

1. An American diplomat in Nicaragua, under orders from Secretary of State Hughes.
2. A member of Sandino's forces.
3. A Nicaraguan member of the National Guard.
4. An American business person who owns factories and an office in Nicaragua.
5. A poor Nicaraguan farmer, sympathetic to Sandino.
6. An isolationist American assembly line worker.

Give students thirty minutes to develop their characters and define their interests. Each group must come up with a satisfactory compromise regarding United States' policy in Latin America. Have each group present its policy to the class.

The marines trained a Nicaraguan force, the National Guard, to help fight the rebels. In 1930 the National Guard captured Sandino and in 1934, after the marines withdrew, executed him. The head of the National Guard, General Anastasio Somoza, eventually assumed the presidency and became a cruel dictator, backed by the United States. The Somoza family would rule Nicaragua until 1979, when a rebel group that called itself the Sandinistas (after Sandino) came to power.

The intervention in Nicaragua set off protests in the United States and Latin America against Coolidge's "private war." Coolidge retorted that the United States was "not making war on Nicaragua any more than a policeman on the street is making war on passersby."

Dispute with Mexico. The United States also saw its economic interests in Mexico threatened in the 1920s. The Mexican Revolution had left bitter feelings on both sides of the border. To make matters worse, the new constitution limited foreign purchase of property in Mexico and gave the Mexican government the power to take over oil lands, some of which were owned by Americans.

Alarmed by Mexico's ties with Soviet communism and its aid to rebels in Nicaragua, American oil companies demanded that troops be sent to protect their property. However, most Americans favored nonintervention. In 1927 Congress voted to resolve the problem without the military.

That fall Coolidge named an old friend, Dwight W. Morrow, as ambassador to Mexico. As Morrow worked with the Mexicans to solve the dispute over oil rights, he proved to be a skillful diplomat. He also scored a victory by inviting newspaper columnist Will Rogers and aviator Charles Lindbergh to tour Mexico and give Americans a better picture of their next-door neighbor. Tensions eased, and Mexico let United States companies keep all oil lands they had owned before 1917. Both nations hoped that good will, rather than guns, would form the basis for future relations between the countries.

The Good Neighbor Policy

Americans saw the trend away from intervention as positive, and Coolidge's successors, Herbert Hoover and Franklin D. Roosevelt, hoped to extend this

Thinking Critically

Analysis. In his inaugural address on March 4, 1933, Franklin D. Roosevelt said:

"I would dedicate this nation to the policy of the good neighbor—the neighbor who resolutely respects himself and because he does so, respects the rights of others—the neighbor who respects his obligations and respects the sanctity of agreements in and with a world of neighbors."

Ask: What are the characteristics of a good neighbor? What types of policy might make a nation a good neighbor to other nations? At what point does Roosevelt's analogy break down?

Global Connections

One reason Roosevelt wanted so much to improve relations with Latin America was to increase hemispheric solidarity and security against the Nazi threat. At the Eighth Pan-American Conference in 1938, Secretary of State Cordell Hull tried to alert Latin American countries to the dangers of subversion by Axis agents. Many of the countries seemed to think Hull was exaggerating, and many had profitable commercial contracts with Germany that they did not want to lose. Later, at a meeting of foreign ministers in 1942, Hull got all the countries except Chile and Argentina to cut commercial and diplomatic ties with the Axis powers.

Reduced student page in the Teacher's Edition

good will to all of Latin America. Soon after winning the presidency in 1928, Hoover set off on a ten-week tour, assuring Latin Americans that the United States wanted to be "a good neighbor."

The Clark Memorandum. Hoover's administration gave proof of its good will toward Latin America with the Clark Memorandum in 1930. It said that the United States did not have the right to intervene militarily in Latin America.

The next year revolutions shook Panama, Cuba, and Honduras, but Hoover did not send troops. He also approved plans to remove marines from Nicaragua and Haiti. "I have no desire," he said, "for representation of the American government abroad through our military forces."

Roosevelt withdraws troops. President Roosevelt adopted Hoover's "good neighbor" slogan and further improved relations. He sent Secretary of State Cordell Hull to the Seventh Pan-American Conference in Uruguay. While there, Hull voted for a proposal that "no state has the right to intervene in the internal or external affairs of another."

In 1934 the United States and Cuba signed a treaty canceling the Platt Amendment of 1901, which had allowed the United States to intervene in Cuba to maintain law and order. In exchange for the cancellation, Cuba agreed that the United States could keep its naval base at Guantanamo Bay. In 1934 Roosevelt carried out Hoover's plan to withdraw the marines from Haiti. In 1936 the

Section Review

ANSWERS

1. Definitions for the following terms are on text pages indicated in parentheses: *isolationism* (610), *arms race* (611).
2. No. It applied only to battleships. It made Japan the dominant Pacific power since the United States and Britain had to divide their fleets and leave many possessions undefended.
3. Answers may include that the United States needed Latin America's raw materials and did not permanently take over these countries; or that United States operations in these countries was naked imperialism and violated their sovereignty.
4. It went further than earlier actions. American marines were deeply involved and fought openly against rebels, and a corrupt regime was set up.

THE AMERICAN SPIRIT

Will Rogers

The Cowboy Philosopher

When Will Rogers was growing up in Indian Territory, he was already known for his wit. "I never saw him get up in front of a class without making them laugh," a schoolmate remembered. Born in 1879, the eighth child of a prosperous rancher, Rogers was part Cherokee Indian. "My ancestors didn't come on the Mayflower," he said, "but they met the boat."

In his teens Rogers performed in roping contests, rodeos, and Wild West shows. Eventually he had his own vaudeville act, complete with a pony named Teddy. When Rogers added talk to his routine, he found that his audiences enjoyed his down-to-earth humor even more than his skill with a lasso. He poked fun at politicians and commented on the international scene. "I don't make jokes," he said. "I just watch the government and report the facts and I have never found it necessary to exaggerate." Soon he was doing radio shows, movies, and a newspaper column.

His warm humor made his name a household word in the 1920s and early 1930s. Like most Americans, he thought that the United States should stay out of world affairs. "We never lost a war and we never won a conference," he noted. "Who is the next country wants their affairs regulated?" he joked when he felt that the United States was too involved in Latin America. He traveled to observe the Japanese-Chinese war in Manchuria. "America could hunt all over the world and not find a better fight to keep out of," he warned.

On a trip to Alaska in 1935, Will Rogers was killed in a plane crash. The whole nation mourned his death. "A smile," said a friend, "has disappeared from the lips of America."

United States gave up its right, by an earlier treaty, to intervene in Panama.

Roosevelt's policy had its most severe test in 1938 when the Mexican government seized foreign oil holdings because of a labor dispute. Roosevelt resisted pressure by oil companies to intervene, and eventually Hull helped negotiate an agreement between the companies and the Mexican government.

After the marines left Haiti, the United States had no ground troops in Latin America for the first time since 1898. Roosevelt praised the "Good Neighbor Policy" in a speech:

> *" Throughout the Americas the spirit of the good neighbor is a practical and living fact. The twenty-one American republics are not only living together in friendship and in peace—they are united in the determination so to remain. "*

Nothing similar could be said for Europe and Asia. As military governments took power overseas, the United States would be torn between a historic desire to steer clear of foreign rivalries and the new responsibilities brought on by its economic power.

Section Review

1. Identification. Define *isolationism* and *arms race.*

2. Analysis. Was the Washington Naval Conference a success? Why or why not?

3. Evaluation. The nations that signed the Kellogg-Briand Pact reserved the right to defend themselves. Could United States military intervention in Latin America be called "self-defense"? Explain.

4. Synthesis. Why might Coolidge's "private war" have been condemned by some of the same people who backed earlier intervention in Latin America?

23-2 A World Changed by War

Focus: How did the economic and political situation in the world after World War I threaten peace?

Of the nations that fought in World War I, the United States had suffered the least economic hardship. Speaking in 1919, Woodrow Wilson had predicted:

> *" The financial leadership will be ours. The industrial primacy will be ours. The commercial advantage will be ours. The other countries of the world are looking to us for leadership and direction. "*

Wilson was right. In the 1920s, the United States became the world's banker. And as American economic influence grew, the nation found it increasingly difficult to remain aloof from political developments abroad.

The United States as a Creditor Nation

From earliest colonial days, Americans had been in debt to Europe. They had borrowed money to build farms, railroads, and industries. As World War I approached, though, the tables turned. Europeans needed money for military supplies. The United States not only repaid its debts, but loaned some $10 billion to the Allies. It also invested in foreign mines, steamships, and railroads, especially in the developing nations of Latin America. Between 1914 and 1919 the United States changed from a debtor nation owing $3.7 billion to a creditor nation that had loaned $12.5 billion.

A peaceful and productive Europe would have had little trouble repaying its loans after the war.

Section 23-2

Objectives

- ***Answer the Focus Question.***
- *Analyze the effect of high tariffs on efforts to repay Allied war debts.*
- *Describe the rise of fascism in Italy and Germany.*
- *Explain how Japanese expansion posed a problem for the United States.*

Introducing

THE SECTION

Have students speculate on the moods of Italy and Germany after the First World War—Italy, having gained little territory and suffering from war debts; Germany owing huge reparations.

Developing

THE SECTION

Connections: Economics

Discussion. Congress passed high tariffs, such as the Hawley-Smoot Tariff, in an attempt to protect American businesses from foreign competition. **Ask:** What was the effect of high tariffs on the world economy?

Using the Visuals

Discussion. Refer students to the photo and caption on this page. **Ask:** How does the photo illustrate inflation? Why should governments not print unlimited amounts of money? How did the devaluation of German money affect Germany's trade with other nations?

Writing About History

Journal Entry. Have students imagine that they lived in Italy, Germany, or the United States during the depression. Have them write a journal entry explaining why they would or would not support a radical (fascist, Nazi) solution to the economic problems of their country.

But two obstacles stood in its way. First, the war had shattered the economies of most European nations. Those countries that did have some industries left could barely afford to operate them. Second, Congress passed high protective tariffs, making it almost impossible for foreign nations to earn money by selling goods in the United States.

Therefore, the Allies' only hope of paying the United States was to collect reparations from Germany. In 1921 the Allies set German reparations at a whopping $33 billion. The German economy, however, was in tatters, and by early 1923 Germany gave up making payments. France and Belgium then sent troops to occupy Germany's Ruhr Valley and take over German mines.

The Dawes Plan. Meanwhile, an international commission was trying to find a way to help Germany. One commission member, American banker Charles G. Dawes, proposed an international loan that would allow Germany to again meet its reparations payments. British economist John Maynard Keynes noted how the plan actually worked: "The United States lends money to Germany, Germany transfers its equivalent to the Allies, the Allies pay it back to the United States government." In this way much of the money that circulated through Europe came from and ended up in American hands.

The Dawes Plan went into effect in September 1924, with American investors contributing over half the loan. However, when the American stock market crashed in 1929, American investment stopped and the delicate balance of payments was upset. By December 1933 Germany and all the Allies but Finland had stopped paying their debts.

Attempts to boost trade. When President Roosevelt assumed office, he took steps to lower tariffs and stimulate world trade. During the next seven years the United States signed trade agreements with twenty-one nations. The agreements won good will abroad but made little impact on the world economy. American industries still demanded protection, and tariffs on competing foreign goods remained fairly high. As parts of Europe— especially Germany and Italy— slipped deeper into depression, they began to turn toward more radical solutions to their problems.

The Rise of Fascism in Italy

"War and depression— ugly, misshapen, inseparable twins— must be considered together," wrote a senator in 1935. "Each is a catapult for the other." In Italy, war followed by depression gave rise to a major political upheaval and a terrifying dictatorship.

Although Italy was one of the victors in the war, it emerged bitter and divided, not having received the territory it wanted. The Italian economy was steadily declining, and jobless workers began to talk of communist revolution. Other Italians, searching for a new order, were drawn to **fascism,** a government system under the total control of a nationalist dictator and a single political party. Italian fascism emphasized anti-communism and supported the Roman Catholic Church, capitalism, and "law and order," thus winning the support of industrialists and the middle class. It also promised jobs to the unemployed.

German marks were so worthless by 1923 that they were more valuable as fuel than as currency.

Global Connections

Made chancellor on January 30, 1933, Hitler moved quickly to intimidate the opposition and gain total power. On February 27 the *Reichstag* (parliament) building was partly destroyed by a fire which was probably set by the Nazis. Hitler denounced the fire as a communist plot. In the "Red Scare" that followed, the president issued emergency decrees suspending the constitutional guarantees of free speech and free press, and Nazi troops were able to harass their opponents. On March 23 the German parliament gave the president dictatorial powers.

Writing About History

Essay. Herr Knoblauch, a middle-class German interviewed in 1932, said of Hitler: *"He spoke for two hours—I could have listened for two days. Every time I hear him I am all the more convinced that he alone can save us."*

Hitler preferred speaking to writing because listeners had less opportunity for critical thought during a speech. Have interested students write essays agreeing or disagreeing with Hitler's view: *"All epoch-making historical events have been produced not by the written but by the spoken word."*

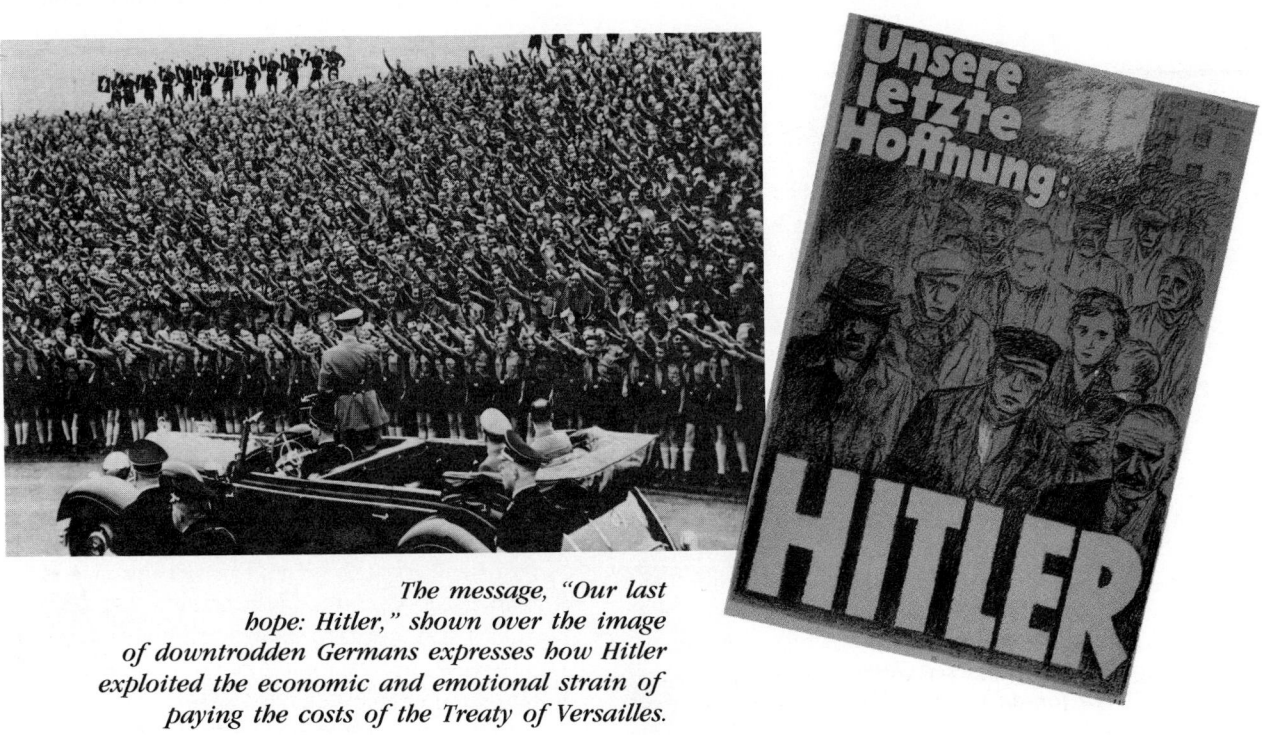

The message, "Our last hope: Hitler," shown over the image of downtrodden Germans expresses how Hitler exploited the economic and emotional strain of paying the costs of the Treaty of Versailles.

The Italian Fascist party denounced all other parties and hoped to eliminate them—by force, if necessary. The result would be a **totalitarian state,** in which the government controlled not only the economy, but also the political system. People would have no means of opposing the government, and no choice but to comply with its demands. The Fascist leader in Italy, Benito Mussolini, declared, "Nothing above the state, nothing outside the state, nothing against the state."

By 1921 Italian Fascists were attacking socialists and labor leaders, burning down union halls, and torturing and killing communists. A year later 50,000 of Mussolini's private army, the "Black Shirts," marched on Rome, seized control of the government, and installed Mussolini as the new prime minister. By 1924 the Fascists completely controlled parliament. Three years later Il Duce (EEL DOO-chay), or "The Leader," as Italians called Mussolini, ruled Italy as dictator.

As Italy's depression worsened in 1930, Mussolini provided jobs by building up the nation's armed forces. Italy, he promised, would soon be a mighty world power and the Mediterranean would be "an Italian lake."

Hitler Gains Control of Germany

Postwar chaos and economic crisis created fertile ground for fascism in Germany, also. Adolf Hitler, a World War I veteran, built the National Socialist (Nazi) party by promising desperate Germans that a new Germany could rise from the ashes of the old. By 1933 the Nazis were the nation's largest party, and Hitler was named the German chancellor, or prime minister. When the president died in 1934, the nation was in Hitler's hands.

Hitler moved swiftly to establish a fascist government he called the Third Reich. To manage public opinion, the Nazi party seized control of newspapers, film studios, radio stations, and schools. In defiance of the Treaty of Versailles, Hitler began a massive buildup of the German military. In August 1934 more than 42 million Germans—95 percent of Germany's registered voters—went to the polls. Some 38 million approved Hitler's seizure of power.

Legalized discrimination. Hitler's fascism was far more ruthless than the totalitarian politics of Italy. Hitler believed strongly in the racial supe-

Multicultural Perspectives

On April 1, 1933, the Nazis staged the first nationwide attack against German Jews—a massive boycott of Jewish businesses and professional offices. Throughout Germany stormtroopers were stationed at Jewish shops. The Star of David was painted across shop doors and windows. Posters read, "Germans! Defend yourselves! Don't buy from Jews" or simply "Jude."

Hans Levi, who considered himself a patriotic German and whose family had lived in Germany for centuries, was stunned. He recalled, *"I could see the writing on the wall. . . . Life would only get worse for Jews in Germany. It was then I knew I had to leave."* In 1934 Levi emigrated to the United States.

Thinking Critically

Evaluation. Hitler made Jews scapegoats for Germany's hardships. **Ask:** How do you think scapegoating Jews helped Hitler appeal to many Germans? (Suffering from economic and social upheaval, they were looking for someone to blame. Anti-Semitism was already widespread, so Germans could easily be led to blame Jews. Also, belief in German "superiority" consoled those who had little else to be proud of.)

Ask: Do you think Hitler's scapegoating prepared Germans to accept his use of violence against Jews? Why or why not?

Multicultural Perspectives

Oral Report. Jews who made important contributions to early twentieth century European culture include Marc Chagall (artist), Gustav Mahler and Arnold Schönberg (composers), Franz Kafka (writer), Sigmund Freud (founder of psychoanalysis), and Albert Einstein (theoretical physicist). Have students give biographical oral reports on these or other famous European Jews.

Reduced student page in the Teacher's Edition

The violence of Kristallnacht *left shop windows shattered. Jews were forced to wear the Star of David, and stars painted on shop windows had helped rioters identify Jewish-owned businesses.*

riority of Germans over other groups, such as Slavs and gypsies. He reserved a special hatred, however, for Jews, whom he considered to be an "inferior race."

Jews had long been discriminated against in Europe. In Germany, **anti-Semitism**—prejudice and discrimination against Jews—had increased during the late 1800s, as Jews began to enter the mainstream of economic and professional life. Although many of Germany's greatest scientists, artists, and business people were Jews, anti-Semites blamed Jews for all the evils in German society, including the disastrous depression after World War I.

Hitler played on Germans' hatred and fear of Jews. He portrayed them as national enemies who contaminated society and could never be truly German. He made Jews a scapegoat for all of Germany's hardships.

As dictator, Hitler made laws barring Jews from government service. Jews were also excluded from work in journalism and radio, from farming and teaching, and from practicing medicine. Grocery and butcher shops, bakeries, drugstores, and dairies would not sell to Jews. The Nuremberg laws of 1935 stripped Jews of their citizenship and forbade them to marry non-Jews. Jews over the age of six were ordered to wear a yellow Star of David on their clothing to set them apart in pubic.

The German people both permitted and took part in Hitler's extreme form of anti-Semitism. In the chaos of postwar Germany they sought, in the words of historian Fritz Stern, "a world with fixed standards and no doubts, a new national religion that would bind all Germans together." Hitler promised just that—a new Germany for "true" Germans and a new destiny as the greatest power in the world. As British prime minister Winston

Churchill observed, Hitler "called from the depths of defeat the dark and savage furies" asleep in the German people.

"Crystal Night." Tens of thousands of Jews fled Nazi Germany. But many nations, including the United States, would not ease their immigration restrictions, and refused to accept many of the Jewish refugees. In the fall of 1938 German policy toward Jews changed, and escape became nearly impossible. Emigration was halted and Jews were sent to concentration camps and to work as slaves in factories, fields, and mines.

Then, on November 9 the German government launched a nationwide assault against the Jewish population. Nazi officials instructed the state police to organize "spontaneous demonstrations" by the German people. The purpose of the demonstrations was to destroy Jewish shops and homes throughout the country. One instruction to police stations read:

"As many Jews, especially rich ones, are to be arrested as can be accommodated in the existing prisons. . . . Upon their arrest, the appropriate concentration camps should be contacted immediately, in order to confine them in these camps as soon as possible."

An official report to Nazi leaders claimed that at least 1,000 homes and shops and 200 synagogues had been destroyed. Over $1.2 million in windows were broken. Police arrested 20,000 Jews and reported 72 dead or wounded. Later estimates, however, put the number of looted shops at 7,500 and the number of dead closer to 1,000.

American Voices

"Jewish shop windows by the hundreds were systematically and wantonly smashed. . . . According to reliable testimony, the debacle was executed by S.S. men [Nazi party militia] . . . provided with hammers, axes, crowbars and incendiary bombs. . . . Ferocious as was the violation of property, the most hideous phase of the so-called 'spontaneous' action has been the wholesale arrest and transportation to concentration camps of male German Jews."

—Report by the American Consul in Leipzig, Germany

Kristallnacht, or "Crystal Night" as it was called after the glass from shattered windows, was only part of the Nazi plans for Germany's future. Already, Hitler was looking beyond Germany to neighboring regions. There he planned to expand his rule and build a mighty German empire.

Japan Threatens in the Pacific

On the other side of the world, a different form of dictatorship was arising in Japan. Instead of a political party seizing control, as in Italy and Germany, the Japanese military took power.

In September 1931 Japan defied the Washington disarmament treaties, the Kellogg-Briand Pact, the Open Door policy, and the Covenant of the League of Nations by sending troops into the Chinese province of Manchuria. Military leaders renamed the region Manchukuo, placed it under a puppet king, and began to develop mines and industries there. Now that they had a source of raw materials, the island-bound Japanese were ready to conquer China and the Pacific.

Secretary of State Henry L. Stimson sent a protest to Japan in January 1932. The United States, he said, did not recognize territory Japan gained "by the use of force." The League of Nations issued a similar protest. Yet though the world talked of limiting Japanese expansion, no one took action.

Encouraged by the weak world response, the Japanese military grew bolder. In 1933 Japan withdrew from the League of Nations. To silence opposition within the country, the military assassinated the premier of the civilian government and other important ministers. In further defiance of disarmament treaties, Japan began a military build up to prepare for an invasion of the rest of China.

Active Learning

Debate. Have students debate whether, given both the situation in Germany and the economic situation at home, the United States and other nations should have eased immigration restrictions for Jewish refugees in the 1930s.

Linking Past and Present

Discussion. Have students agree or disagree with this statement: Someone like Hitler could never come to power today in the United States.

Limited English Proficiency

Interpreting a Political Cartoon. Have students study the cartoon on this page. **Ask:** How are China and Japan represented in this cartoon? Why? **(China by a dragon—a symbol of that huge nation; Japan by a military officer because Japan was governed by the military)** What is the Japanese officer doing? **(cutting off part of the tail with a knife)** What does the basket contain? **(previously cut pieces of the tail)** What do the officer's actions symbolize? **(Japanese aggression)** What is the cartoonist's point of view? **(The cartoonist is against Japanese aggression.)**

Section Review

ANSWERS

1. Definitions for the following terms are on text pages indicated in parentheses: *fascism* (616), *totalitarian state* (617), *anti-semitism (618)*.
2. High tariffs made it almost impossible for Allied nations to earn money to repay war debts by selling goods in the United States.
3. The Fascists and Nazis seemed to offer strong governments that would end political chaos and the economic depression.
4. Germany halted Jewish emigration, sent Jews to concentration camps, and launched a nationwide assault on the Jewish population.
Linking Past and Present. Answers may include South Africa, Iraq, China (Tibet), and former nation of Yugoslavia.

Reduced student page in the Teacher's Edition

American response. Japanese expansion posed a problem for the United States. By the early 1930s the only Asian power strong enough to offset Japan was Russia, which the Bolsheviks had renamed the Union of Soviet Socialist Republics in 1922. The Soviet Union had a stake in curbing Japanese expansion, for its eastern provinces could be easy targets. However, the United States had not established diplomatic relations with the Soviets because the Bolsheviks opposed capitalism and democracy.

In November 1933, encouraged by business leaders who hoped for expanded trade, President Roosevelt officially recognized the Soviet Union. Although not much trade occurred, recognition sent an important message to Japan: The United States and the Soviet Union were willing to set aside their political differences to curb Japanese aggression.

The move was not a formal military alliance, but it did have military implications. Bolstered by the friendship of the Soviet Union, the United States could begin the process of granting independence to the Philippines without appearing to be handing the islands over to Japan.

By the mid-1930s the world seemed to have forgotten the lessons of World War I. With the United States and the Soviet Union sharing a common interest against an expansionist Japan in the Pacific, and with fascist governments in Germany and Italy bristling against their neighbors, the stage was set once again for war.

Spotlight on the Japanese Military

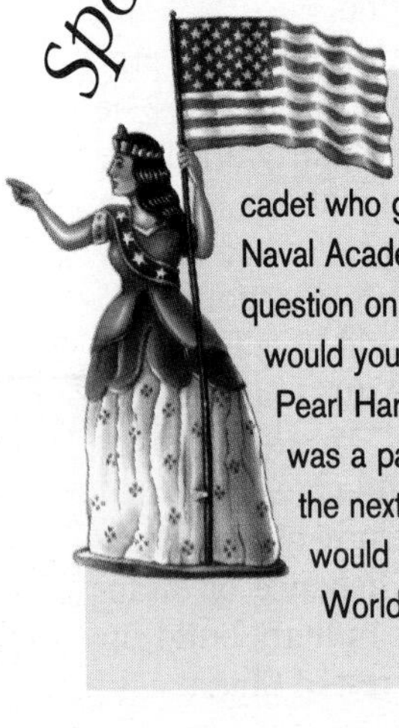

Beginning in 1931, every cadet who graduated from the Japanese Naval Academy had to answer the following question on his final examination: "How would you carry out a surprise attack on Pearl Harbor [Hawaii]?" The question was a part of the exam each year for the next ten years—until the event that would pull the United States into World War II.

THE SLEEPING GIANT BEGINS TO FEEL IT

This American cartoon condemns Japan's aggression in China, yet nothing was done to help China recover its northern provinces.

Section Review

1. Identification. Define *fascism, totalitarian state,* and *anti-Semitism.*

2. Comprehension. How did high tariffs in the United States affect the repayment of Allied war debts?

3. Analysis. How did conditions in Italy and Germany provide fertile soil in which fascism could take root?

4. Comprehension. Describe the change that took place in official Nazi policy toward German Jews in the fall of 1938.

Linking Past and Present. Research and report on a government today that holds a policy of discrimination against a racial, ethnic, religious, or national group within its borders. How does this compare to Nazi policy toward the Jews?

Geography
A KEY TO OUR PAST

Place: Japan Reaches Outward

According to Japanese legend, Earth was once nothing but a great ball of water with a rainbow arching over it. As the god Izanagi dipped his spear into the water and raised it toward the sun, sparkling drops of water became thousands of islands. When the god saw the beauty of these islands, he left heaven to live for awhile in the land that became Japan.

Japan, "Land of the Rising Sun," lies off the northeast coast of mainland Asia. It is composed of four large islands and thousands of smaller ones that are actually the tops of volcanic mountains rising steeply from the floor of the Pacific Ocean. Japan is so mountainous that only about 15 percent of its land can be farmed. Hidden in the hills and mountains are small quantities of minerals—coal, copper, lead, limestone, manganese, silver, tin, and zinc.

Japan's distinctive physical characteristics have had a strong effect on the economic and political activities of its inhabitants. For more than 200 years of its long history, from the early 1600s to the mid-1800s, Japan closed itself off from most of the world. Seas and oceans served as geographic barriers, enabling Japan to maintain this isolation. After Commodore Perry arrived to open Japanese ports to foreign trade, however, the Japanese government began looking to the industrialized world for new ideas and manufacturing methods. By the early 1900s, Japan was becoming a major industrial and military power.

In addition to its industrial expansion, Japan's population was also growing rapidly. However, the country lacked both the resources to support this population and the raw materials to build a modern industrial nation. Thus, the Japanese began to look outward, focusing first on Manchuria, a region in northeast China. Manchuria was rich in farmland and in the mineral resources that Japan lacked, especially the iron ore and coal necessary for the manufacture of steel.

Japan's leading citizens sought to justify the notion of invading another nation. A high-ranking army officer, Kingoro Hashimoto, said, "[T]here are only three ways left to Japan to escape from the pressure of surplus population: . . . emigration, advance into world markets, and expansion of territory. The first door . . . has been barred to us by the anti-Japanese immigration policies of other countries. The second door . . . is being pushed shut by tariff barriers. . . . What should Japan do when two of the three doors have been closed against her?"

Japan invaded Manchuria in 1931. England's Winston Churchill reacted with these words: "China is being eaten by Japan like an artichoke, leaf by leaf." Yet no country seemed willing to take military action to save China's northern provinces. Soon its natural resources were being converted into Japanese industrial materials, including weapons of war.

1. Describe the distinctive physical characteristics that make Japan a unique place.
2. How did these physical characteristics affect Japan's political activities in the 1930s?
3. Today, the Japanese have one of the world's largest merchant fleets. What change do you think this shows in their perception of the country's physical characteristics?

Global Connections

Research and Report. Have students do research to learn more about the history and traditional culture of Japan. Ask them to write a report on elements of culture such as the samurai code, that might have led the country toward a military emphasis.

Geography: A Key to Our Past

ANSWERS

1. Japan is composed of four large islands and many smaller ones. The land is mountainous, and only 15 percent of it can be farmed.
2. As Japan developed industrially, it lacked resources to support industrialization and its growing population. It reached out for what it needed, first invading Manchuria and then the rest of China.
3. They recognize that with limited resources and a large population they cannot be self-sufficient but must rely on extensive trade with other countries.

Section 23-3

Objectives

- ***Answer the Focus Question.***
- *Explain how the Neutrality Act of 1935 expressed United States isolationism.*
- *Analyze how the Neutrality Acts reflected change in the United States policy of isolation and neutrality.*
- *Relate the events that marked the outbreak of World War II.*
- *Explain the Soviet Union's role in the start of the war.*

Introducing THE SECTION

Ask students to recall what system of alliances existed in World War I. Ask them to think about what nations they would expect to be allies in the Second World War.

Developing THE SECTION

Thinking Critically

Evaluation. **Ask:** Was the Senate committee justified in placing the blame for the failure of neutrality on ammunition manufacturers and bankers? What other factors should be taken into account? (U.S. business interests abroad, submarine warfare, idea of defending human rights and freedom)

Global Connections

Not surprisingly, many African Americans protested against the Italian invasion of Ethiopia. Many communities raised funds for the defense of the African kingdom. Organizations were also established. New Yorkers organized the International Council of Friends of Ethiopia, and the executive secretary, Willis N. Huggins, pleaded Ethiopia's cause before the League of Nations.

Reduced student page in the Teacher's Edition

23-3 The Road to War

Focus: How did United States policies of isolation and neutrality change as Europe moved toward war?

In Europe and Asia, nations were grimly rearming. The disarmament and peace treaties of the 1920s were trampled underfoot. The League of Nations seemed paralyzed.

As militarist governments rose to power in the 1930s, the United States tried to steer a neutral course. "Is there a way to keep America out of war?" one senator asked. He warned:

> *"The world is . . . in that precarious condition in which the bad temper of a dictator, the ineptness of a diplomat, or the crime of a fanatic may let loose irremediable disaster."*

Fascist Aggression and American Neutrality

That war once again could seem so close despite efforts to prevent it raised disturbing questions. Americans asked how the nation had been drawn into World War I. The business magazine *Fortune* blamed the failure of neutrality on weapons manufacturers. Their aims, claimed the magazine, were to "(a) prolong war, (b) disturb peace."

In April 1934 a Senate committee headed by Gerald P. Nye of North Dakota began investigating the arms industry. The committee concluded that American arms merchants, bankers, and other "merchants of death" had reaped huge profits by selling arms and providing loans to the Allies. The United States had entered the war, charged the committee, so profiteers could make money. Americans easily accepted these charges during the depression, when bankers were already unpopular.

To keep profiteers from dragging the nation into another war, Congress passed the Neutrality Act of 1935. The act authorized the President to establish an arms embargo on nations at war. Meanwhile, President Roosevelt warned Americans that if they traveled on ships of belligerents—nations at war—they did so at their own risk.

The Neutrality Act was tested when Mussolini sent Italian troops into the African nation of Ethiopia in October 1935. Ethiopia was an independent nation sandwiched between two Italian colonies. By conquering Ethiopia, Italy would have a solid block of empire in Africa.

Roosevelt agreed with the League of Nations, which had promptly declared Italy the aggressor and banned all arms sales to Mussolini's government. But the Neutrality Act also prevented Americans from selling arms to Ethiopia. In February 1936 Congress further strengthened American neutrality. The Neutrality Act of 1936 forbade American firms to make loans or give credit for supplies to any nation at war.

The Spanish Civil War. While American isolationists tried to look the other way, the tide of fascism gained momentum. During the spring of 1936, Italy brutally crushed the last Ethiopian resistance, and German troops swept into the Rhineland, the buffer zone established on the French border after World War I. Although France remained secure for the time being, fascism was also flaring in neighboring Spain.

In July 1936 a civil war broke out in Spain. Nationalist rebels, led by Francisco Franco and aided by Mussolini and Hitler, wanted to install a fascist government. The Loyalists, fighting to save Spain's republican government, received supplies and technical advice from the Soviet Union.

The United States, Great Britain, and France had condemned Italy's aggression in Ethiopia. They now spoke out against the fascist revolt in Spain, but they feared that intervention would trigger world war. Although private funds were raised

Multicultural Perspectives

The Abraham Lincoln Battalion reflected the diversity of the American people. Volunteers included African, Japanese, and Native Americans, as well as Americans of Irish, German, Swedish, Polish, Italian, and Greek ancestry. Among the ranks were also Cuban and Canadian volunteers. For a period until his death, Oliver Law, an African American, commanded the "Lincolns."

Multicultural Perspectives

Hitler's prejudices were not limited to Jews. In the 1936 Summer Olympic Games in Berlin, Germany, Hitler refused to congratulate African-American athlete Jesse Owens, who won four gold medals. The Nazi newspaper *Der Angriff* ("The Attack") did not publish the victories of black athletes.

Hitler had vowed that Germany would prove Aryan superiority in the 1936 Olympic Games in Berlin. Instead, African-American track and field star Jesse Owens broke records and won four gold medals. At left, the German silver medalist gives a Nazi salute.

to help the Loyalists, and some 3,000 Americans formed a volunteer force—the Abraham Lincoln Brigade—to fight Franco, sympathetic governments did little but watch. After three years of fighting, Franco's forces crushed the Loyalists and set up a fascist dictatorship.

The Axis. Fascism's foothold in Europe was strengthened, too, when Italy and Germany formed an alliance in 1936. Mussolini had described the ties between the capitals of Rome and Berlin as the axis around which Europe would revolve. Thus the two nations became known as the Axis.

Evidence of growing axis power worried politicians in the United States. They regretted that the Neutrality Act had tied their hands in the Spanish Civil War. Seeking more flexibility, Congress passed the Neutrality Act of 1937. It retained an arms embargo but permitted belligerents to buy non-military supplies in the United States if they paid cash and carried the supplies away in their own ships. In this act, Congress also barred Americans from traveling on belligerents' ships.

A "Quarantine" on Aggression

The next threat to peace came not from Europe, but from Asia. In July 1937 Japanese and Chinese troops clashed on a bridge near Beijing, and the fighting quickly spread throughout eastern China.

President Roosevelt feared that the Neutrality Act of 1937 would help Japan and hurt China. Under the act's "cash-and-carry" clause, Japan could buy huge amounts of American supplies. To avoid this, Roosevelt announced that since Japan and China had not officially declared war, he would not authorize the cash-and-carry provision.

With storm clouds gathering in both Europe and Asia, Roosevelt felt that he must awaken Americans to the danger. The world was threatened by a "reign of terror," he warned in a speech that year. "Let no one imagine that America will escape." He compared the spread of aggression to a disease:

> *"When an epidemic of physical disease starts to spread, the community approves and joins in a quarantine of the patients in order to protect the health of the community against the spread of the disease."*

The "quarantine" speech raised doubts about Roosevelt's commitment to neutrality. In Congress, isolationists talked of impeaching the President.

Connections: Art

Discussion. Pablo Picasso, a Spanish painter living in France, painted his famous *Guernica* in 1937, in response to the bombing of a village of that name during the Spanish Civil War. Examine a reproduction of this painting with the class, and discuss the emotion it conveys and the meaning behind the symbols.

Active Learning

Debate. Have students choose which side they would have been on in 1939: (a) Americans who wished to stay out of the European conflict or (b) Americans who wished to help the Allies. In small groups, have students debate the advantages and disadvantages of the Neutrality Acts from their previously chosen standpoint.

Connections: Language

Understanding Metaphors. Refer students to the quote from Roosevelt on this page. Point out that Roosevelt used a metaphor—a figure of speech in which a word or phrase ordinarily used for one meaning is applied to another.

Ask: What, literally, is an epidemic? **(the rapid spread of a contagious disease)** What does *quarantine* mean literally? **(to isolate people who have an infectious disease)** According to Roosevelt, what is the disease needing to be quarantined? **(fascist aggression)** What action is implied by Roosevelt's use of *quarantine* as a metaphor? **(military intervention)**

Thinking Critically

***Analysis.* Ask:** In reaching a peaceful accord with an aggressor, is there a difference between compromise and appeasement? (appeasement implies giving in for the sake of peace; compromise requires that each side give up some of its demands in order to reach a settlement) Why might appeasement be criticized, while compromise is applauded?

Connections: Politics
The Hitler-Stalin pact startled the world, since fascism and nazism both were avowed enemies of communism and vice versa. In addition to wanting part of Poland, however, Stalin needed to buy time to rebuild the Soviet army, which his purges had gutted. He and the Allies also felt mutual distrust.

Analyzing Primary Sources

Roosevelt Letter. In 1936 Roosevelt wrote to the American ambassador in France: "*One cannot help feeling that the whole European panorama is . . . blacker than at any time.*" **Ask:** Cite evidence for Roosevelt's pessimism.

Active Learning

Cooperative Activity. Divide the class into groups of three. Each group will write a one-page summary of the attempts made by American Presidents to maintain the nation's neutrality in 1807-1811, 1914-1917 and 1935-1941.

Each individual in the group should study a particular time period. Together, they will discuss the similarities and differences in policies adopted and tactics employed. Their one-page summary must include an explanation of why they believe the attempts failed.

Reduced student page in the Teacher's Edition

Roosevelt reassured his critics by saying that he was only asking for "moral" condemnation of aggressors. Clearly, however, the President was warning Americans that they might have to do more than stand idly by in the face of spreading aggression.

The Sinking of the *Panay*

Fearing for the safety of American citizens in China, the United States began to evacuate them. Then, on December 12, 1937, Japanese war planes bombed several American oil tankers and the U.S.S. *Panay,* one of the evacuating ships. Two Americans were killed and several others wounded. The *Panay* sank. Americans were outraged over the attack. The Japanese, however, claimed it was an accident. They quickly apologized and offered to pay damages.

In Congress, the *Panay* incident prompted Representative Louis Ludlow of Indiana to propose a constitutional amendment. The amendment would require a national vote before Congress declared war, except in the case of invasion. According to a nationwide poll, over 70 percent of the American people favored such an amendment.

The Ludlow amendment was defeated by only twenty-one votes. The narrow defeat proved that isolationism was still a strong sentiment of many Americans.

The Outbreak of World War II

While Japan was tightening its hold on China, Hitler began a relentless attack on eastern Europe. In March 1938 Nazi troops swarmed into Austria. France and Britain protested in vain as Hitler annexed German-speaking Austria to his Third Reich.

Hitler's next target was the Sudetenland, an area of western Czechoslovakia where some 3 million Germans lived. When Hitler demanded the territory, the Czechs prepared to fight. France, Great Britain, and the Soviet Union agreed to support the Czechs. In September 1938 British and French leaders met with Hitler in Munich, Germany, where Hitler claimed that the Sudetenland was "the last territorial claim I have to make in Europe." Believing Hitler and hoping to avoid war, the British and French then urged Czechoslovakia to give up the territory.

In this case **appeasement**— the policy of giving in to the demands of a hostile power in order to keep peace— only postponed war. In March 1939, ignoring his promises, Hitler shattered hopes for peace when he sent troops to seize the Czech capital of Prague.

Blitzkrieg. Hitler next turned to Poland and demanded the Polish city of Danzig on the Baltic Sea. Having learned the lesson of Czechoslovakia, Great Britain and France pledged to support Poland if Germany attacked.

The Soviet Union's response was crucial to the situation. Bordering Poland, the Soviets with their huge army could thwart Hitler's plans. Great Britain and France knew that Joseph Stalin, the Soviet leader, had long distrusted Hitler. Thus the world was stunned in August 1939 when Germany and the Soviet Union signed a nonaggression pact. Publicly, each nation pledged not to attack the other. Privately, though, Germany and the Soviet Union agreed to divide Poland.

At 4:45 A.M. on Friday, September 1, 1939, a German battleship opened fire on Danzig. *Blitzkrieg,* Hitler's tactic of "lightning war," had begun. Ger-

The word "Munich" became a synonym for appeasement. Below, British Prime Minister Neville Chamberlain attempts to persuade Mussolini.

Global Connections

Hitler's philosophy of warfare emphasized the *blitzkrieg* because he wanted to avoid the long battles of World War I. He thought that the German economy and people could better withstand campaigns that were intense but short.

Connections: Science and Technology

Discussion. Have students review the kinds of weapons and tactics used in World War I and compare them with those used in the early phases of World War II. **(for example, relatively stationary trench warfare and poison gas in World War I versus the fast-moving attacks and bombing from the air in World War II)**

man dive bombers screamed down out of the skies, machine-gunning Polish troops. Bombs rained on Poland's airfields, destroying planes before they could get into the air. German tanks rumbled across the border.

Two days later Britain and France declared war on Germany. They could not save Poland, however, for within two weeks Soviet troops attacked from the east, and soon occupied the eastern third of Poland. On September 27, 1939, the Polish capital of Warsaw fell, and Poland soon surrendered. The country was divided between the Germans and the Soviets.

Debates Over American Neutrality

On the day that France and Britain declared war on Germany, President Roosevelt gave a fireside chat on the radio. The nation would remain neutral, he assured his listeners, "But I cannot ask that every American remain neutral in thought as well."

In a public opinion poll, 84 percent responded that they wanted the Allies—France and Britain—to win. As strong as the sympathies were, however, most Americans wanted no part of another European war. In spite of public opinion, Roosevelt saw help for the Allies as urgent. Germany's massive arms buildup left it bristling with armaments, while the Allies, with their lack of weapons, were vulnerable. Roosevelt called a special session of Congress to urge an amendment to the Neutrality Act that would lift the arms embargo for France and Britain.

For six weeks Congress rang with loud debate. If Americans sent arms to aid France and Britain, asked one senator, "will we—can we—if the hour of greater need should occur, refuse to send our armies?" President Roosevelt replied reassuringly that no one was suggesting sending Americans to "fight on the battlefields of Europe."

In November 1939 Congress passed the fourth Neutrality Act. Belligerents would be able to buy weapons on a "cash-and-carry" basis, but American ships would be forbidden from entering combat zones. Warring navies would also be forbidden from approaching within several hundred miles of the Americas.

No number of laws, though, could guarantee American neutrality. No speeches or promises could prepare Americans to watch passively the horrifying spectacle of blitzkrieg as it thundered across Europe.

Umbrella Road

In this 1940 cartoon, the Americas look with indecision on appeasement policy, represented by signs on Chamberlain's umbrellas.

A Copyright 1940 Herblock Cartoon

Section Review

1. **Identification.** Define *appeasement.*

2. **Analysis.** How did the Neutrality Act of 1935 reflect a distrust of the armament industry and bankers? What had caused that distrust?

3. **Comprehension.** When did it become clear that appeasement policy had failed?

4. **Evaluation.** Do you think that an earlier use of force against fascism might have averted world war? Why or why not?

5. **Analysis.** How do the four Neutrality Acts reflect gradual change in the United States' policy of isolation and neutrality?

6. **Comprehension.** What role did the Soviet Union play in the start of World War II?

Section Review

ANSWERS

1. Definition for *appeasement* is on text page 624.
2. Authorized the President to establish an arms embargo on nations at war; Senate committee charge that "merchants of death" had led America into World War I for profits.
3. When Hitler sent troops to seize the capital of Czechoslovakia.
4. Answers may include that early intervention, setting up a stable economy and government, could have prevented fascism's growth; or that Germany and Italy were simply too unstable for intervention to have prevented later war.
5. The 1935 act authorized the President to set up an arms embargo. The 1936 act forbade American firms to give loans or credit to warring nations. The 1937 act softened the previous ones, allowing belligerents to buy non-military supplies. The 1939 act permitted the sale of weapons, thus helping Britain and France.
6. Soviet Union signed a non-aggression pact with Hitler, freeing Germany to attack Poland without fear of Soviet reprisal.

Thinking Critically

Analysis. Have students explain the meaning of the political cartoon on this page showing a "Meeting of the Minds." (Through a sarcastic title and the depiction of Hitler's head as a cannon, the cartoonist portrays the Munich agreement as a concession in the face of military force rather than a product of rational agreement.)

Analyzing Primary Sources

Alexander Solzhenitsyn. Solzhenitsyn was arrested by Soviet authorities for "political crimes," sentenced to eight years in labor camps, and eventually exiled. Among his literary themes is an emphasis on the contrast between political ideals and reality.

Ask: How might Solzhenitsyn's experiences have influenced his point of view regarding the Munich agreement? Do you think Solzhenitsyn's criticism is fair?

Social History

Upon returning to London, Chamberlain was greeted by cheering crowds. To his announcement of "*peace in our time,*" the people responded, "*We thank you*" and "*God bless you.*" Chamberlain then said, "*And now I recommend you to go home and sleep quietly in your beds.*"

Reduced student page in the Teacher's Edition

POINT OF VIEW

Munich and Appeasement

On September 30, 1938, British Prime Minister Neville Chamberlain returned from Munich, Germany, waving a piece of paper which, he said, brought "peace with honor . . . peace for our time." Chamberlain has since been almost universally criticized. At the time, though, the voices of critics were drowned out by the many who cheered his policy of appeasing Germany to keep peace. Here are several points of view expressed back then—including Chamberlain's—and a more recent view.

Chamberlain and Hitler in a "Meeting of the Minds."

"The Road to Sanity"

"Before giving a verdict upon this arrangement, we should do well to avoid describing it as a personal or a national triumph for anyone. The real triumph is that it has shown that representatives of four great Powers can find it possible to agree on a way of carrying out a difficult and delicate operation by discussion instead of force of arms, and thereby they have averted a catastrophe which would have ended civilization as we have known it. . . .

My main purpose has been to work for the pacification of Europe. . . . The path which leads to appeasement is long and bristles with obstacles. The question of Czechoslovakia is the latest and perhaps the most dangerous. Now that we have got past it, I feel that it may be possible to make further progress along the road to sanity."

—Neville Chamberlain,
in a speech to Parliament

"A Bitter Cup"

"I find unendurable the sense of our country falling into the power, into the orbit and influence of Nazi Germany, and of our existence becoming dependent upon their good will or pleasure. . . .

We have sustained a defeat without a war, the consequences of which will travel far with us along our road. . . . We have passed an awful milestone in our history. . . . And do not suppose this is the end. This is only the beginning of the reckoning. This is only the first sip, the first foretaste of a bitter cup which will be proffered to us year by year unless, by a supreme recovery of moral health and martial vigor, we arise again and take our stand for freedom as in the olden time."

—Winston Churchill,
opposition leader in Parliament

The Price of Peace

“Let no man say that it would have been better to resist, and to fight it out ‘now rather than later,’ unless he himself would have given the order that would have sent young men marching into the dreary hell of war. Let no man say that the statesmen of Britain and France were out-traded in the bargain they have struck, until he has attempted to add the total of the price they might have had to pay . . . the price in death and destruction spread across the face of Europe; in whole cities laid waste by high explosives and seared with poison gas; in broken and mangled bodies of women and their children; . . . perhaps in the complete collapse of that civilization over a large part of Europe.

No man is wise enough to know whether too high a price has been paid for peace. But no man who is honest will attempt to pretend to himself that a high price has not been paid. It is a price which includes permission for Hitler to march into Czechoslovakia precisely on the day he said that he would march. It is a price which cedes land and resources solely under the plain threat that force would be used if this cession were not made. It is a price which may therefore put a premium on the use of similar threats of force in the future. It is a price which sacrifices the interests of a small, forsaken nation to the interests of its larger neighbors. It is a price which enormously increases the resources of the most aggressive and dangerous Power in Europe.”

—Editorial in the *New York Times,* September 30, 1938

“The Spirit of Munich”

“The spirit of Munich is not a thing of the past, it was more than a short episode. I would even venture to say that the spirit of Munich is predominant in the twentieth century. The entire civilized world trembled as snarling barbarism suddenly re-emerged and moved into the attack. It found it had nothing to fight with but smiles and concessions.

The spirit of Munich is an illness of the willpower of rich people. It is the everyday state of those who have given in to the desire for well-being at any price, to material prosperity as the main aim of life on this earth. Such people—and there are many of them in the world today—choose to be passive and to retreat, just so their normal lives may last a little bit longer, just so the move into austerity may not happen today. And as for tomorrow, it'll be all right, you'll see. . . . But it won't be all right! The price you have to pay for your cowardice will be all the worse. Courage and victory come to us only when we resign ourselves to making sacrifices.”

—Alexander Solzhenitsyn, exiled Russian writer, 1972

1. Compare the views of Chamberlain and Churchill on the Munich agreement.

2. Do you think the *New York Times* gave a balanced view? Explain.

3. What do you think Solzhenitsyn meant by saying “The spirit of Munich is not a thing of the past”?

4. What do you think the lesson of Munich should be for people today?

Point of View

ANSWERS

1. Chamberlain believed it was a victory for diplomacy and discussion over violence, and the foundation for peace in Europe. Churchill believed it to be a disaster and a sign that they had lost their courage and will to fight for freedom.
2. Opinions will vary. *The New York Times* tried to balance the risks of a destructive war (defending Czechoslovakia by force) against the risks of strengthening Hitler and encouraging similar threats in the future by giving in to his demands.
3. Solzhenitsyn meant that the same reluctance to confront unpleasant realities that led to appeasement in the 1930s operates in our world today whenever we refuse to sacrifice our present well-being in order to solve larger problems.
4. Opinions will vary. Some students may focus on the danger of giving in to aggression, others on the difficulty of knowing when to sacrifice their enjoyment of peace for higher principles.

Section 23-4

Objectives

- ***Answer the Focus Question.***
- *Explain the effects of Germany's invasion of the Netherlands, Belgium, Luxembourg, and France.*
- *List Roosevelt's actions that moved the United States away from strict neutrality.*

Introducing THE SECTION

Have students review their textbooks and then prepare a chart showing the strengths and weaknesses of both the Allies and the Axis powers at the start of the war. **(For example, the Germans had a much stronger air force than the Allies, but the Allies had more industries and resources to draw on.)**

Developing THE SECTION

Limited English Proficiency

Help students distinguish between *sitzkrieg* (sitting war) and *blitzkrieg* (lightning war).

Reduced student page in the Teacher's Edition

23-4 The End of Isolation

Focus: What circumstances led the United States to enter World War II?

During the winter of 1939-1940, the Allies mobilized for war. France fortified its eastern border against Germany, while Britain set up a tight naval blockade. Germany unleashed its submarines against British ships and mined British harbors. Beyond skirmishes at sea, however, Europe was eerily quiet.

The British called this time "the twilight war." The Germans called it the *sitzkrieg*, or "sitting war." Many people were deceived by the relative quiet. News writers in the United States began to refer to the "phony war."

The Fall of France

On April 9, 1940, Hitler shattered the winter lull. In a blitzkrieg as deadly as the earlier attack to the east, German troops now struck north and west. In one day the Germans occupied Denmark and key ports and airfields in Norway. By June Norway was overrun.

In May Hitler's troops stormed through the Netherlands, Belgium, and Luxembourg. British and French troops that had been sent to Belgium were forced to retreat. In late May and early June, some 340,000 French, British, and Belgian troops were rescued from Dunkirk in northern France.

Inspired by their new prime minister, Winston Churchill, the British mounted a daring rescue. While the Royal Air Force held off German bombers, the Royal Navy and hundreds of private boats from Britain ferried soldiers across the English Channel.

For France, however, the battle was nearly ended. The Germans swept south and pressed on toward Paris. In early June Mussolini declared war on France and Great Britain, and sent troops into France from the south. On June 22 the French surrendered to Hitler in the same railroad car in the same forest location where Germany had signed the armistice of 1918. Hitler had calculated his revenge carefully: he had the railroad car brought from a museum just for the occasion.

France was divided in two. Hitler's troops occupied the north and west. In the south, French leader Marshal Pétain (pay-TAN) established a fascist-type government at Vichy (vee-SHEE). However, thousands escaped France, and the fight against Germany continued both within France and from the outside. The headquarters of the Free French resistance movement was in London under General Charles de Gaulle (duh GOL).

Three million of the five million Parisians had fled before Nazi troops arrived in June 1940. The French surrendered rather than see the city destroyed.

Connections: Literature
Students might find compelling Anne Frank's *The Diary of a Young Girl,* the journal of a teenage German Jewish girl in hiding from the Nazis; and Paul Gallico's short novel *The Snow Goose* which is a story of heroism at Dunkirk.

Geography Skills

ANSWERS

1. Germany: 1936, armed forces to the Rhineland; 1938, Austria, Sudetenland; 1939, Czechoslovakia, Poland, Lithuania; 1940, Netherlands, Belgium, France, Luxembourg, Denmark, Norway.
2. USSR: 1939, Finland, Poland; 1940, Estonia, Latvia, Lithuania, Romania.

Thinking Critically

Evaluation. Refer students to Churchill's words on this page.
Ask: Do you agree or disagree with Churchill? How important was the survival of Britain to the overall outcome of the war? (Britain an important ally in the fight for democracy; Roosevelt and Churchill worked closely together, especially in their talks with Stalin)

Aggression in Europe 1935-1940

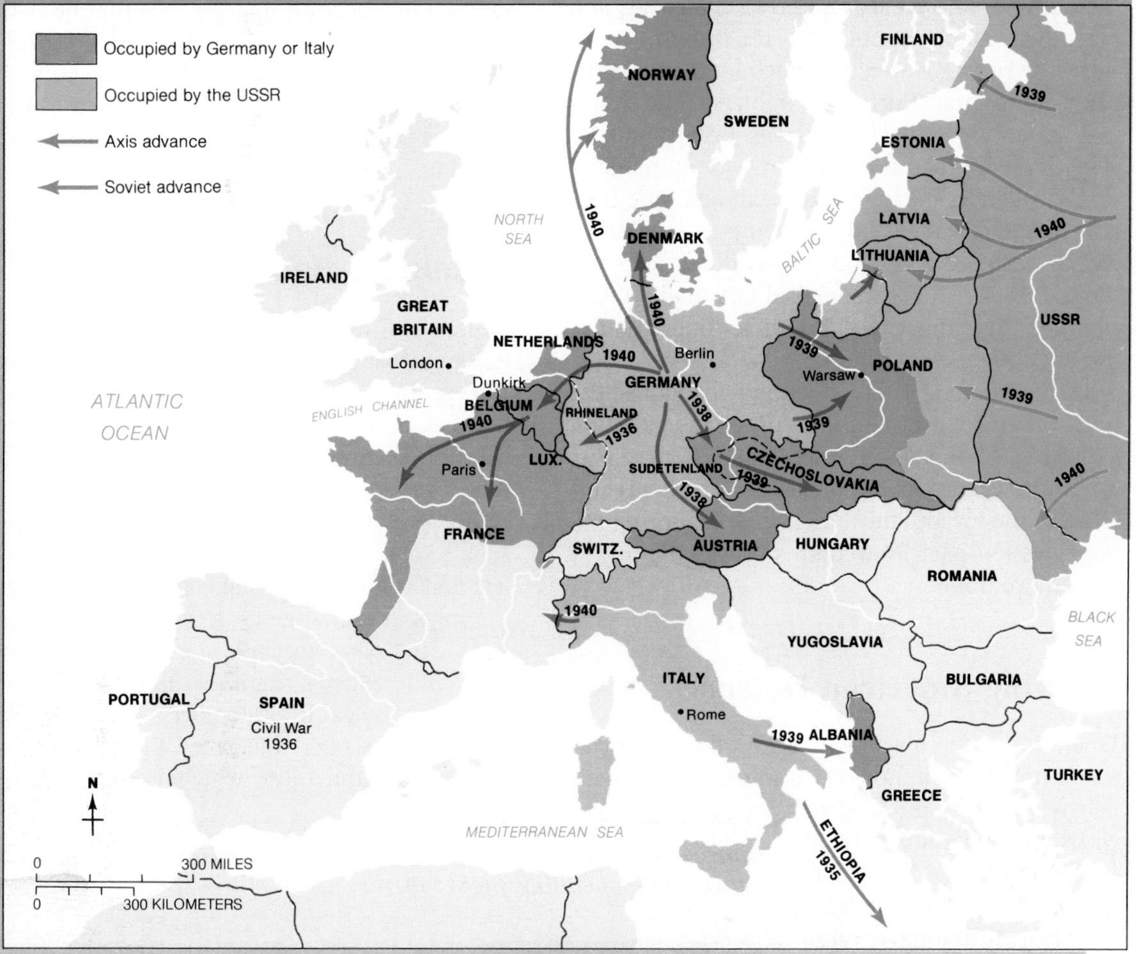

Geography Skills—Movement. Use information on the map to prepare a time line of German expansion from 1936 to 1941. In addition, describe the expansion of the Soviet Union in 1939 and 1940.

The Battle of Britain

Britain now stood alone against the Axis powers. Prime Minister Winston Churchill, an eloquent and courageous leader, rallied his nation:

> *"The Battle of France is over. I expect that the Battle of Britain is about to begin. . . . Hitler knows that he will have to break us in this island or lose the war. If we can stand up to him, all Europe may be free and the life of the world may move forward into broad, sunlit uplands. But if we fail, then the whole world, including the United States, including all that we have known and cared for, will sink into the abyss of a new Dark Age."*

GTV Side 4
Chap. 4, Frame 18960
Getting to Know You: Into World War II (Movie Segment)
Search and Play:

Active Learning

Preparing a Radio Broadcast. Have a group of students do research on the Battle of Britain (they might read "Remembering the Blitz" in *National Geographic*, July 1991) and together prepare and deliver a radio broadcast from Britain, describing the bombing and asking for help from the United States.

Thinking Critically

Evaluation. Have students compare United States preparedness for war in 1940 with its preparedness in 1916. **Ask:** Why are democratic societies less prepared for war than totalitarian ones? What part does the military play in totalitarian nations? (Totalitarian regimes often gain power with military might and are dependent on the military to maintain control within their own countries.)

Connections: Science and Technology

Another of Britain's strengths against Germany was the systematic use of radar. RADAR stood for Radio Detecting and Ranging. It was developed in Britain in the late 1930s by Robert A. Watson-Watt, Arnold (Skip) Wilkins, and others.

Radio transmitters send out "loud, short, sharp radio bangs," while receivers listen for the echoes of the "bangs." If an object such as a plane gets in the way of the waves, it changes the echoes. The result, displayed on a cathode ray screen, shows both where the object is and how far away it is.

Reduced student page in the Teacher's Edition

Hitler, meanwhile, boasted that Nazi troops would be in London within three months. To prepare for the invasion, in August 1940 Hitler sent the German air force to bomb British airfields and ports. German planes outnumbered Britain's small Royal Air Force, yet were no match for the fast British Spitfire and Hurricane fighters. The Nazis switched to night attacks. However, Britain had developed radar and could intercept German planes.

In September the Germans began bombing British cities, especially London, hoping to demoralize civilians. Cities were shattered and burned, and thousands of civilians were killed in London alone. In what Churchill called Britain's "finest hour," the British refused to submit.

By the spring of 1941, Hitler had abandoned the invasion of Great Britain and turned his attention eastward. Fearing Soviet ambitions in Eastern Europe, and seeking control of Soviet wheat fields and oil wells, he invaded the Soviet Union, ignoring the nonagression pact. Now Germany was fighting a war on two fronts.

Building American Defenses

When the Nazi blitzkrieg began, the American mood turned grim. Americans worried about their defenses. If Britain fell, the Nazis would dominate the Atlantic. In the late 1930s Congress had voted funds to build up the army and navy. Yet by 1940 the armed services had only 350 tanks, 2,806 outmoded airplanes, and combat equipment for just 75,000 soldiers.

In May President Roosevelt asked Congress for an all-out buildup of the armed forces. Over the next five months Congress voted some $17 billion for defenses. Plans were made for a two-ocean navy, and factories tooled up to make fighter and bomber planes and military weapons.

Meanwhile, Congress began debating a bill for a peacetime draft. Men had been drafted during the Civil War and World War I, but never in peacetime. Support for the draft increased during the Battle of Britain, and in September the Selective Training and Service Act became law. Men between the ages of twenty-one and thirty-five would have to register, and 2 million would be selected for military training.

A Helping Hand for Britain

While the United States was building up its defenses, Great Britain was suffering heavy losses. During the summer of 1940, attacks by Nazi submarines and bombers left the British desperately short of destroyers. Churchill begged Roosevelt for fifty "over-age" United States destroyers.

Roosevelt was certain that Congress would block such a sale, but his Attorney General pointed out a legal alternative. Roosevelt could *give* Great Britain the ships in exchange for a 99-year lease on naval bases in Newfoundland and the Caribbean. Churchill eagerly agreed, and Roosevelt announced the deal in September.

Roosevelt's offer intensified the debate between isolationists and those who favored intervention.

Courageous Londoners took shelter in the subway during air raids, often spending nights there.

Members of the isolationist America First Committee argued that Hitler posed no threat to the nation. They opposed any kind of aid to Great Britain, certain that it would force the United States into war.

Members of the Committee to Defend America by Aiding the Allies, on the other hand, were delighted that Roosevelt had abandoned strict neutrality. Only by helping Great Britain defeat Hitler, they argued, could Americans avoid war.

Amid all the controversy over the European war came the presidential campaign of 1940. Roosevelt ran for an unprecedented third term, declaring, "Your President says this country is not going to war." Although his opponent, Wendell Willkie, ran close in the popular vote, Roosevelt swept the electoral vote 449 to 82. He interpreted his victory as a vote of approval for more aid to Great Britain.

American Lend-Lease

By late 1940 Britain, which had been buying arms and supplies "cash-and-carry" from the United States, was short of cash. Roosevelt wanted to continue to help the British, certain that the fate of the United States was tied to that of Britain.

In December 1940 Roosevelt called a press conference and outlined a simple way to aid Britain. "Let me give you an illustration," he said:

> *"Suppose my neighbor's home catches fire. . . . If he can take my garden hose and connect it up with his hydrant, I may help him to put out his fire. Now, what do I do? I don't say to him before that operation, 'Neighbor, my garden hose cost me $15; you have to pay me $15 for it.' I don't want $15—I want my garden hose back after the fire is over."*

Roosevelt proposed that the United States lend arms and supplies to the British, who would return or replace them after the war.

Roosevelt submitted his plan to Congress in January 1941. Isolationists mounted fierce opposition, but Congress passed the bill in March. Under the Lend-Lease Act, the President could lend, lease, or sell war supplies to any nation whose defense was vital to the United States. Roosevelt signed the bill into law and approved a list of supplies for immediate shipment to Britain. With the news of the law, the British raised American flags over the bomb-cratered streets.

U.S. Help in the Atlantic

During the spring and summer of 1941, Roosevelt faced a problem that went with Lend-Lease. American supplies would be of no help unless they could reach Britain. But Hitler, to cut the flow of American aid, was sending Nazi planes and "wolf packs" of submarines into the Atlantic.

To help Britain in the Atlantic, Roosevelt ordered navy patrols to broadcast the location of German ships to the British. He also stretched the American safety zone, first defined in the 1939 Neutrality Act, far out into the Atlantic. In July, with Iceland's permission, he sent American marines to join British troops in occupying that strategic island, which at the time was a kingdom united with Denmark. The United States Navy would now escort supply ships as far as Iceland.

The Atlantic Charter. In August Roosevelt met Churchill for what one reporter called "the greatest fishing trip that any President . . . had ever undertaken." In secret talks aboard a cruiser off Newfoundland, they drew up the Atlantic Charter, a statement of Allied goals "for a better future for the world." They pledged to seek no territory and to support national self-determination, "the right of all peoples to choose the form of government under which they will live."

Roosevelt also insisted that the charter confirm that the allies were fighting to preserve the "Four Freedoms"—freedom of speech and religion, and freedom from want and fear. Like Wilson's Fourteen Points, the Atlantic Charter gave Americans the sense that they had a stake in a European war.

In September a German submarine fired on an American destroyer that had been tracking it. Although the destroyer was not hit, Roosevelt ordered the navy to "shoot on sight" all German and Italian warships in the American convoy zone. The United States—without a formal declaration—had entered the war in the Atlantic.

Analyzing Primary Sources

Roosevelt. Refer students to Roosevelt's words on this page. Ask them to explain the analogy of the garden hose with arms and supplies. Have students evaluate the appropriateness of the analogy. **Ask:** Were very many of the arms and supplies used in war likely to be returnable? Could they be replaced if a country's economy was damaged by war, as happened after World War I?

Linking Past and Present

Discussion. Cite the Four Freedoms the Allies were fighting for—freedom of speech and religion, freedom from want and fear. **Ask:** Does one country today provide its citizens with all of these freedoms? Which freedoms exist in the United States? To what degree? **(Remind students that the presence or absence of the freedoms is often relative; that is, probably no country exists in which all citizens are completely free from want or fear, but the percentage of citizens who feel want or fear is much larger in some countries than in others.)**

Active Learning

Cooperative Activity. Have students work in groups to prepare reports on the attack on Pearl Harbor, including quotations from as many eyewitnesses as possible (for example American sailors, Hawaiian civilians, Japanese Americans living in Hawaii, and Japanese pilots). They may also include recollections by people who heard about the attack on the radio. Groups might present the reports orally, with different students reading the various first-hand accounts.

Geography Skills

ANSWERS

Time lines should include the following dates and actions related to Japanese expansion: 1931, occupied Manchurian coastal regions; 1932, occupied Manchurian interior; 1937, occupied parts of China; 1938, moved further into China; 1940, took northern Indochina; 1941, occupied the rest of Indochina, attacked Hong Kong, Philippines, Malaya, Guam, Wake and Midway islands, Hawaiian Islands.

B • A • C • K • G • R • O • U • N • D

Social History

Some Americans in the 1930s observed that the scrap metal that the United States was then selling to Japan could be used by the Japanese military. A soldier named Curtis Ewing stationed in Australia in 1942, escaped just in time when a Japanese plane dropped a bomb on the jeep in which he was riding.

Afterward, Ewing looked at the fragments of the bomb and to his amazement, found one with the name "Ray Ewing" on it. Ray was Curtis Ewing's father. Years before, the name had been stenciled on the engine block of the Ewing family car. The car later had been sold for junk, and the metal had gone to Japan—and found its way back to Curtis Ewing.

Reduced student page in the Teacher's Edition

Aggression in Asia 1931-1941

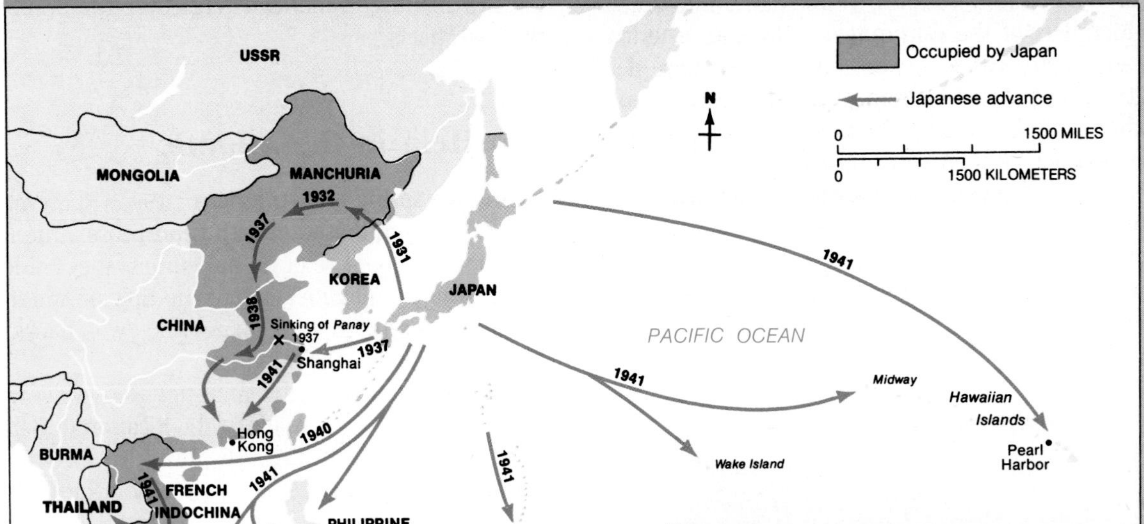

Geography Skills—Movement. Use information on the map to prepare a time line of Japanese expansion from 1931 through 1941.

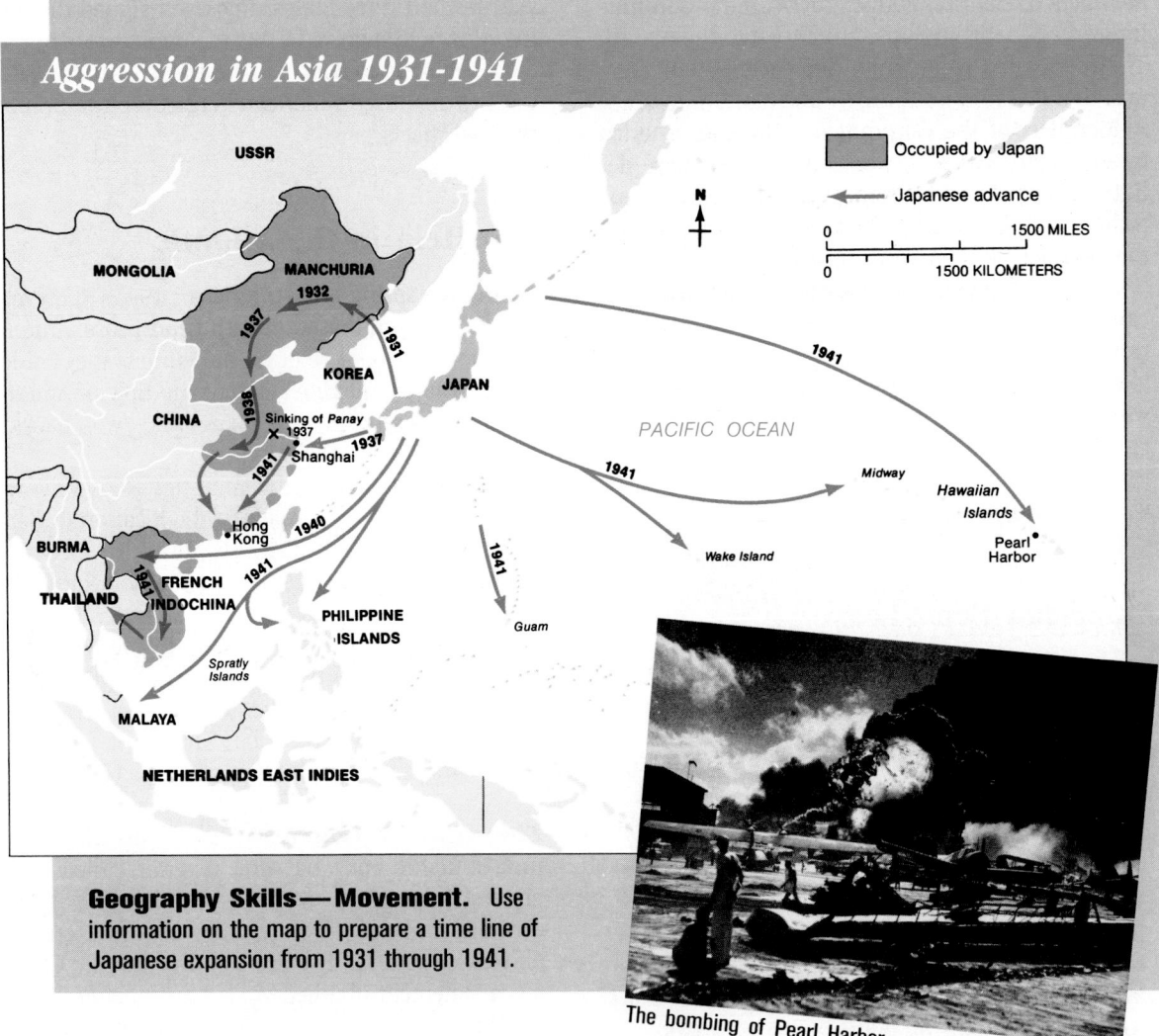

The bombing of Pearl Harbor

Japan on the Move

A year earlier, in September 1940, Japan had signed the Tripartite Pact with Germany and Italy, formalizing its role as the third Axis power. The three recognized each other's conquests and pledged to declare war on the United States if it went to war against any Axis power.

Japan, meanwhile, slashed through Asia, seizing French bases in Indochina. Cautiously, Roosevelt adopted a policy of "slowing Japan up." The United States declared an embargo on material critical to war, such as machine tools, chemicals, scrap metal, and oil. It also increased aid to China and fortified bases on the Philippines and Guam.

Japan and the United States continued to meet in negotiations, despite their crumbling relations. According to Secretary of State Cordell Hull, the talks went "around and around the same circle." Japan wanted the United States to cut off aid to China and to end the embargo. Hull asked Japan to renounce the Tripartite Pact and withdraw from China and French Indochina.

In November, American intelligence officers broke a Japanese code. They learned that Japan was planning an attack, though they did not know where. "War warnings" were sent to American naval bases in Hawaii and the Philippines. However, most people doubted that Japan would risk an attack, which could unify Americans in favor of war.

Pearl Harbor. On Sunday, December 7, 1941, the telephone rang on President Roosevelt's desk. The caller was Secretary of the Navy Frank Knox, who read a message he had just received from Hawaii: "Air raid, Pearl Harbor—This is no drill."

At 7:55 A.M. some 360 Japanese bombers had whined out of the sky. In the surprise attack, nineteen American ships were sunk or damaged, 149 planes were destroyed, and 2,403 soldiers and civilians were killed, with another 1,178 wounded. Three American aircraft carriers at sea escaped attack, but American bases on Midway, Wake, Guam, and the Philippines were badly hit.

The following day a grim President Roosevelt addressed Congress:

> *"Yesterday, December 7, 1941—a date which will live in infamy—the United States of America was suddenly and deliberately attacked by naval and air forces of the Empire of Japan."*

Within an hour Congress had declared war on Japan. Three days later Germany and Italy declared war on the United States, and Congress unanimously voted to go to war against the Axis.

Roosevelt told the American people, "We are now in this war. We are all in it all the way. Every single man, woman and child is a partner." Twenty-three years and twenty-six days after the end of World War I, the United States entered World War II.

Section Review

1. Comprehension. Describe what happened when Germany broke its *sitzkrieg* in 1940.

2. Analysis. What was the effect of the Battle of Britain on United States foreign policy?

3. Evaluation. Was the Atlantic Charter essential to convince the United States to join the war?

4. Evaluation. At what point do you think American foreign policy ceased to be neutral? Support your answer.

Data Search. Using the map on page 629, describe how the German invasion of France avoided France's heavily fortified eastern border.

Connections to Themes

Shaping Democracy

"If Europe will leave us alone," Woodrow Wilson's military advisor had said in 1920, "I think we better stay on our side of the water and keep alive the spark of civilization. . . ." That isolationist view was shared by the overwhelming majority of Americans during the 1920s and 1930s. Both Congress and the public were convinced that the best way to safeguard American democracy was to avoid trouble in other parts of the world.

Some Americans, including Franklin Roosevelt, understood that the nation could no longer remain an island of democracy in a world in which distances seemed to be shrinking with the increasing speed of travel. Their warnings were not heeded. Isolationists insisted that the military conquests of Germany and Japan were not a threat to this country. Even as Hitler's blitzkrieg stormed across Europe in 1940, Charles A. Lindbergh, an American aviation hero and a leading isolationist, declared, "Our dangers are internal. Nobody wishes to attack us, and nobody is in a position to do so."

The Japanese attack on Pearl Harbor exploded that myth. A Japanese fleet had crossed the Pacific Ocean undetected to launch its deadly air strike on Hawaii. That surprise attack shocked Americans into a new awareness. They had entered a global age, and the oceans no longer isolated them from the rest of the world. Suddenly, entering the war was not a matter of settling Europe's problems; it was a matter of saving American democracy.

Writing About History

Evaluation. Historians have long disagreed about how much the American military and President Roosevelt knew about the planned attack on Pearl Harbor. There is also disagreement about why no action was taken to prevent the attack.

Some historians say that American leaders underestimated Japanese desire or ability to carry out the attack; others say that Roosevelt let the attack happen so he could overcome the isolationists and bring the United States into the war. Have students research these opposing viewpoints and write a persuasive paragraph summarizing their own conclusions.

Section Review

ANSWERS

1. Germany overran Denmark, Norway, the Netherlands, Belgium, and Luxembourg and drove deep into France, occupying half of it.
2. Roosevelt began building U.S. armed forces and abandoned neutrality to help Britain.
3. Charter was essential in massing pro-war opinion and providing a philosophical basis for intervention.
4. Loan of fifty destroyers to Britain, the Lend-Lease Act, or the Atlantic Charter.
Data Search: Pushed into France through Belgium and Luxembourg

GTV Side 4

Chap. 4, Frame 19145

Aggression in Europe and Asia (Animated Maps)

Search and Play:

Chapter Survey

ANSWERS

Using New Vocabulary

1. (b) In spite of a policy of *isolationism* the United States joined the *arms race* to protect interests in Asia.
2. (c) *Fascism* was one form of *totalitarian state.*
3. (a) *Kristallnacht* was one result of Hitler's *anti-Semitism.*

Reviewing the Chapter

1. Five-Power Treaty reduced number of battleships, arms and agreed to respect Pacific colonies, easing tension among participating countries in Asia. Treaties did not address problems of submarine and light surface warships. Left Japan with the most powerful navy in Pacific, and British and American island possessions undefended.
2. Harding and Coolidge used military forces to maintain stability and protect business interests in Latin America. Coolidge sent marines back to Nicaragua to train National Guard to fight rebels. Hoover's Clark Memorandum said United States had no right to intervene militarily in Latin America. Roosevelt canceled Platt Amendment, withdrew troops from Haiti, issued Good Neighbor policy.
3. United States kept tariffs high, which discouraged trade and made it difficult for Allies to repay war debts. Dawes plan loaned money to Germany so it could pay Allies, who then paid back United States loans. United States crash led to depression in Europe because it stopped this flow of cash.
4. Economic hardship and postwar bitterness made fascist promises of power and glory appealing. Mussolini and Hitler used violence to seize control of government. Lack of opposition from the world after invasion of Manchuria strengthened Japanese military.
5. Used anti-Semitism and hatred of all foreigners to create scapegoats for Germany's economic woes and build support for Nazis.
6. (a) Blamed arms sellers for dragging United States into World War I, led to passage of Neutrality Act of 1935 to keep United States out of another war. (b) led to Neutrality Act of 1936. (c) made United States want to block fascists, so passed Neutrality Act of 1937 which allowed cash-and-carry sales of nonmilitary supplies to warring nations. (d) revealed isolationist feeling in the United States
7. Nazi troops invaded Austria, Germany annexed it; Hitler asked for and got Sudetenland from Czechoslovakia; Nazi troops seized Prague.
8. Germans invaded Poland, France fell to Nazis, Battle of Britain, German invasion of

Reduced student page in the Teacher's Edition

Chapter Survey

Using New Vocabulary

Match each vocabulary term in the first column with the related term in the second column and explain their relationship.

1. isolationism	(a) *Kristallnacht*
2. fascism	(b) arms race
3. anti-Semitism	(c) totalitarian state

Reviewing the Chapter

1. What did disarmament treaties of the 1920s accomplish? What problems did the treaties fail to solve?

2. How did the Latin American foreign policy of Harding and Coolidge differ from that of Hoover and Roosevelt? Give examples to support your answer.

3. What were American policies in the 1920s regarding world trade and Allied war debt? What effect did the American stock market crash have on Europe? Why?

4. How did totalitarian regimes come to power in Italy and Germany? What encouraged the rise to power of the military in Japan?

5. Explain the role of racism and anti-Semitism in Hitler's consolidation of power within Germany.

6. How did each of the following affect American isolationism? (a) the Nye Committee (b) the Italian invasion of Ethiopia (c) the Spanish Civil War (d) the sinking of the *Panay*

7. Trace the steps by which Hitler expanded German territory in eastern Europe before the outbreak of war.

8. What events led to the build-up of American defenses? What kinds of defenses were undertaken?

9. In what ways did the United States help Great Britain? Why was Britain so vital to American security?

10. What actions by Japan and the United States led to deterioration of relations between the two nations in 1940 and 1941?

Thinking Critically

1. Synthesis. What reasons can you suggest to explain why the allied powers did not stop Hitler's rearmament of Germany in the early 1930s?

2. Application. Journalist Dorothy Thompson wrote that one feature of dictatorship was "perpetual aggressiveness." What did she mean? How did events in the 1930s support her statement?

3. Evaluation. The Battle of Britain began in July 1940. Which policy would you have supported for the United States: strict neutrality or intervention to help Britain? Defend your position.

History and You

In the 1920s nations tried to disarm in order to preserve peace. What is the United States doing today for the cause of peace? Do you think such efforts can be successful? Explain.

Using a Time Line

Match dates on the time line with the correct events in the list below. Write your answers in chronological order and explain the impact of each event on World War II.

(A) Pearl Harbor attacked
(B) Sudetenland given to Germany
(C) Manchuria invaded by Japan
(D) Mussolini becomes dictator of Italy
(E) Spanish Civil War begins
(F) German voters confirm Hitler's power
(G) Germany attacks Poland

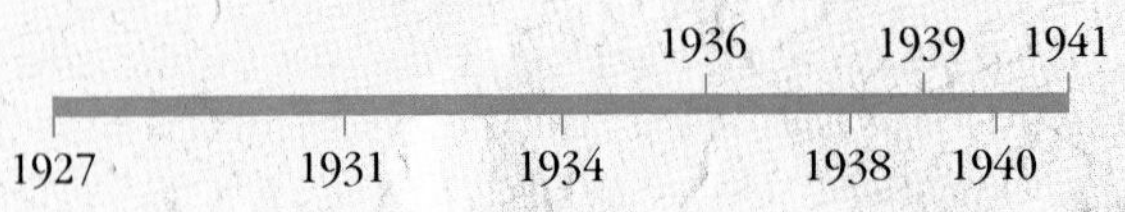

USSR. Defenses included enlarged navy, more aircraft, military weapons, and a draft.
9. Gave Britain old ships in exchange for lease on naval bases; lend-lease allowed United States to lend, lease, or sell war supplies to Britain. If Britain fell, Germany would control Atlantic, which would leave United States vulnerable to attack.
10. Japan became one of Axis powers, invaded French Indochina; United States tried to slow up Japanese war effort by embargo on war materials; Japanese attacked Pearl Harbor.

Thinking Critically

1. Answers may include: allied powers were divided among themselves, and had internal problems to cope with. Some saw an armed Germany as a buffer against the Soviet Union, which they thought the greater menace. Some did not want to get involved in any war, no matter how justified.
2. Dictatorships had to perpetually battle with and triumph over external enemies to maintain popular support and power. Japan invaded Manchuria, China, French Indochina; Germany invaded Austria, Czechoslovakia, Poland, Denmark, Norway, Belgium, France, Soviet Union.
3. Those favoring neutrality can argue that United States should stay out of war until directly threatened by German attack in North Atlantic. Those favoring intervention can argue that helping Britain might prevent an attack on United States.

History and You

Answers will vary according to current events and student opinions.

Using a Time Line

(D) 1927, **(C)** 1931, **(F)** 1934, **(E)** 1936, **(B)** 1938, **(G)** 1939, **(A)** 1941.

Applying Thinking Skills

1. Name-calling ("murder-hungry beast"); glittering generalities ("German sword," "clean weapons," "chivalrous manner"); card-stacking ("Winston Churchill . . . " ignores the fact that Germany is dropping bombs on Britain).
2. Rage, national pride, indignation and desire for revenge.
3. Answers will vary.
4. In order to guard against specious arguments and appeals. Safeguards include free speech and free press, so that all sides of a questions can be presented and people trained to recognize propaganda devices.

Applying Thinking Skills

Recognizing Propaganda

Propaganda is a campaign to influence ideas, opinions, or actions. Propaganda may be used to promote worthy causes, such as raising money for a library, or unworthy causes, such as winning support for a dictator.

Whatever the cause, propagandists tend to use catchy slogans and vivid symbols to appeal to emotions rather than reason. To give greater weight to their message, some propagandists conceal their true purpose, tell one side of the story, and distort the truth. Knowing how propaganda works will help you to recognize it—an important step in deciding how to react to it. The following techniques are common.

In *card-stacking,* propagandists present only facts that support their cause. They may exaggerate some facts and hide others. For example, a candidate for city office may claim, "My opponent voted against a proposal for city parks," without mentioning that the opponent supported an alternative proposal.

A technique known as *just plain folks* is based on the fact that people are more likely to trust others who are like themselves. Therefore, propagandists often try to portray themselves as "just ordinary folks like you." People who deliver the propagandists' messages dress, speak, and act in ways the audience identifies with.

The *bandwagon* approach encourages people to do something because "everyone else is doing it." An advertiser may try to make buyers feel that they must own a certain brand of shoes because everyone else does. They hint that people do not buy the product will feel left out. In an other example, people may be encouraged to support a government policy not because it is wise, but because it is popular.

Name calling attaches negative labels to an opponent or "enemy." Comments like "He is a cry baby," "she is a bleeding heart," and "they are soft on crime" may be used to put down political opponents. Popular support for a war effort may be increased by calling the enemy "criminal," "barbaric," and "another Hitler."

Glittering generalities—vague but catchy statements—have a strong emotional appeal. By using words like "freedom" and "justice," for example, propagandists can gain wide acceptance without providing hard facts. Their arguments are hard to prove or disprove. Many people would agree with the statement "I stand for freedom and the American way," yet they would not really know what "way" the speaker stands for.

With *transfer* propagandists connect their views to a respected person or group. The hint that respected authorities approve may make a message or cause seem more legitimate. "Four out of five doctors use this product" and "This plan follows in the tradition of Abraham Lincoln" are both examples of transfer.

The Nazis made widespread use of propaganda to gain power. Look for examples of propaganda techniques in these excerpts from German newspapers. Then answer the questions.

> *"[Britain] has shown itself to be a murder-hungry beast which the German sword will liquidate in the interest not only of the German people but of the whole civilized world."*
>
> —*Borsen Zeitung,* Sept. 19, 1940

> *"Germany is waging war with clean weapons and in a chivalrous manner."*
>
> —*Diplo,* Sept. 20, 1940

> *"Winston Churchill again yesterday gave British airmen the order to drop their bombs on the German civilian population and thus continue their murder of German men, women, and children."*
>
> —*Nachtausgabe,* Sept. 23, 1940

1. Which propaganda techniques are being used in each of these German articles?

2. What emotions do you think each of these newspaper pieces was intended to appeal to?

3. Totalitarian governments are masters of propaganda. Propaganda, however, also exists in our society. Describe six television commercials and explain which techniques they use.

4. Why is it important to recognize propaganda? What safeguards has a free society against it?

Chapter 24

The Second World War

Planning Guide

	Student Text	TWE Lesson Plans	Support Materials
SECTION 1	**Section 24-1 (1-2 Days)** **Mobilizing for Global War,** pp 638-645 Young in America: On the Home Front, pp 646-647 Review/Evaluation Section Review, p 645	**Introducing the Chapter:** Mobilizing for War—Cooperative Activity, 30 minutes, p 635B **Teaching the Main Ideas:** Could Internment Happen Again?—Class Activity, one class period, p 635B **Evaluating Progress:** A Letter to the President—Individual Project, 30 minutes, p 635C	★ **Read to Remember,** Section 1 ● **Section Activities,** Section 1 ● **Geography Activities,** Section 1 Δ **Readings** ● **Tests and Quizzes,** Section 1 Quiz
SECTION 2	**Section 24-2 (1-2 Days)** **Winning the War in Europe,** pp 648-655 Review/Evaluation Section Review, p 655	**Teaching the Main Ideas:** Advising the President—Cooperative Activity, one class period, p 635C **Reinforcement Activity:** Allied Strategy—Cooperative Activity, one class period, p 635C	★ **Read to Remember,** Section 2 ● **Section Activities,** Section 2 Δ **Enrichment Activities,** Section 2 Δ **Readings** ● **Tests and Quizzes,** Section 2 Quiz
SECTION 3	**Section 24-3 (1-2 Days)** **The War in the Pacific,** pp 656-663 Exploring Issues—Using Nuclear Weapons: The Atomic Bomb, pp 660-661 Connections to Themes: Shaping Democracy, p 663 Review/Evaluation Section Review, p 663 Chapter 24 Survey, pp 664-665 Unit 8 Survey, pp 666-667 Skills, pp 664-665 Using New Vocabulary Thinking Critically Using a Time Line Applying Social Studies Skills: Interpreting Graphics	**Reinforcement Activity:** Allied Strategy—Cooperative Activity, one class period, p 635C **Enrichment Activity:** "Support the War" Posters—Cooperative Activity, one class period, p 635D	★ **Read to Remember,** Section 3 ● **Section Activities,** Section 3 Δ **Enrichment Activities,** Section 3 Δ **Readings** ● **Tests and Quizzes,** Section 3 Quiz, Chapter 24 Test (Forms A and B), Unit 8 Test (Forms A and B) **Additional Resources** ● **Active Learning** Δ **GTV Videodiscs** Δ **Transparencies and Activity Book** ● **Testing Software** ★ **Chapter Summaries**

Key:
★ **For Extra Support**
● **For All Students**
Δ **For Enrichment**

Overview

The United States used all of its productive capacity and civilian work force to mobilize for war. Under government control, industry converted to war production, scarce goods were rationed, and wage and price limits were established. As a result of wartime conditions, millions of people moved to serve in the military or find jobs, and women took jobs previously reserved for men.

Wartime conditions fanned racism. Violence erupted between white and black Americans and between white and Mexican Americans. Despite concerted African-American efforts, most African Americans continued to face segregation and discrimination in the armed forces as well as at home. As a result of racism and war hysteria, the government violated the rights of more than 120,000 Japanese Americans by confining them without cause in internment camps.

Allied strategy concentrated on defeating Germany first. With victories in North Africa and Russia in 1943, the Allies went on the offensive, invading Sicily and Italy. British and American forces invaded France and advanced toward Germany in 1944, while Russian forces pushed toward Germany from the east. The Allies opened German death camps and were stunned by their first sight of the Holocaust. Close to victory, Allied leaders met at Yalta in early 1945 and made plans for postwar Europe. Invaded from the east and the west, Germany surrendered in May 1945.

In the Pacific, the United States did not stop Japan's offensive until the Battle of Midway in 1942. Adopting an island-hopping strategy, American forces slowly advanced through the South and Central Pacific. Continued fierce resistance at Iwo Jima and Okinawa convinced American leaders that they were in for a desperate fight in Japan, and they decided to use newly developed nuclear weapons. Japan surrendered in September 1945, after the United States dropped atomic bombs on Hiroshima and Nagasaki.

Activity Objectives

After completing the activities, students should be able to

- analyze the effect of racism and wartime hysteria on the treatment of Japanese Americans.
- describe agreements about postwar Europe made at the Yalta Conference.
- summarize Allied strategy in Europe and the Pacific.
- recognize the extent of racism on the home front.
- explain how the government encouraged participation in the war effort.

Introducing the Chapter

Mobilizing for War

This activity requires half a class period.

In this activity students, by analyzing how to cope with shortages of goods, experience the nature of the challenges facing Americans at home in World War II.

Remind students that in World War I the United States had responsibility for feeding American armed forces as well as Allied troops and civilians. To feed such a vast number of people, the Food Administration persuaded Americans to adopt "food conservation." World War II, which involved many more Americans for a much longer period of time, required even greater commitment and sacrifice.

Tell students to consider how shortages of goods would affect their lives. Write the following goods on the chalkboard: red meat, wheat, sugar, fats, nylon, gasoline. Divide the class into six groups and assign each group one of the goods. Give each group ten minutes to list ways that they would be affected by limited supplies of that good.

Post each group's list on the chalkboard and encourage other class members to add to the lists. Have students speculate about how they would cope with limited supplies of these goods during a long, large-scale war like World War II. Leave the lists posted while students study Chapter 24 and refer to them when appropriate.

Teaching the Main Ideas

Section 24-1: Could Internment Happen Again?

This class activity requires a full class period.

This activity engages students in debating the likelihood of future government violations of the human rights of Americans as occurred in the internment of Japanese Americans in World War II.

Remind students that during World War II the government forced more than 120,000 Americans of Japanese ancestry from their homes into internment camps. Two thirds of these people were American citizens. This drastic step was supposedly taken as a precautionary defense measure, but today most evidence indicates that the root cause was racism and war hysteria. Do students think such a violation of human rights could happen again?

Write on the chalkboard the following proposition for debate: *An internment like that of Japanese Americans during World War II could never happen again in the United States.*

Divide the class into two groups. The affirmative team is to argue in support of the proposition, and the negative team is to argue against the proposition. Direct each team to appoint a captain to lead a discussion about arguments to use in the debate. The captain should also assign a pair of students to develop supporting evidence for each argument. Other students should prepare responses to objections that may be raised by the opposing team.

Begin the debate by giving the affirmative team 15 minutes to present its arguments. Then give the negative team the same amount of time to present its arguments. Give 10 minutes to each team for rebuttal.

Conclude the activity by asking the class to identify the best arguments and supporting evidence for and against the proposition. Ask students if they think it is possible for democracy to exist in a war involving total national commitment. Why or why not?

Teaching the Main Ideas

Section 24-2: Advising the President

This cooperative activity requires a full class period.

At the Yalta Conference the Big Three reached significant agreements about postwar Europe. In this activity students describe the agreements and the different goals of the United States, Great Britain, and the Soviet Union.

Prepare students for the activity by having them read aloud or review the subsection entitled "The Yalta Conference." Emphasize that although the Big Three—Roosevelt, Churchill, and Stalin—were determined to secure peace, each had different wartime goals.

Have students imagine that they are foreign affairs experts responsible for advising President Roosevelt about issues to be discussed at the Yalta Conference. Write the following issues across the top of the chalkboard:

- How will Germany be governed after the war?
- How can the United States ensure that the Soviet Union will join the war against Japan?
- How will the eastern European countries liberated by Soviet armies establish governments of their own choosing?
- How will Poland establish a government free from Soviet control?

Divide the class into groups of four and direct each group to prepare a position paper suggesting ways for the President to deal with these issues. Groups should also describe how their suggestions are likely to be viewed by Churchill and Stalin. Encourage students to use their texts as well as reference books in preparing their papers.

When the papers are complete, have the groups record their suggestions under the appropriate issues on the chalkboard. Ask the class to compare recommendations. Conclude the activity by asking the following questions:

- The Yalta agreements were later attacked for paving the way for Soviet domination of eastern Europe? Do you agree? Why or why not?
- One historian has written that "preventing Soviet control of eastern Europe would have required force—a course of action that the American and British publics would have opposed." Do you agree? Why or why not?
- How would you describe the Yalta agreements? Why?

Reinforcement Activity

Sections 24-2, 24-3: Allied Strategy

This cooperative activity requires a full class period.

The following activity, in which groups of students write military reports, reinforces understanding of overall Allied strategy.

Review with students the three theaters of war in World War II: Europe, North Africa, and Asia and the Pacific. Have students discuss the geographical problems each theater posed for Allied forces. Have them also consider problems the United States faced in moving troops and supplies to war zones.

Have students imagine that they are President Roosevelt's—and President Truman's—military advisors. Divide the class into five groups of advisors and direct each group to write an end-of-the-year military report for one of the following years: 1941, 1942, 1943, 1944, 1945. On the chalkboard write the format for their reports:

- Summarize Axis advances and areas of control. (See Chapter 23 if necessary.)
- Summarize Allied military campaigns that took place in each theater of war and the results.
- Make plans for next year's military campaigns in each theater. (Reports for the year 1945 should note Allied occupation of Germany and Japan.)

Responsibility for gathering information about Allied military campaigns in each theater of war should be divided among group members. Groups may also want to have one or more members make maps or charts.

Have groups present their reports to the class. Encourage students to ask questions and challenge plans. Conclude the activity by asking students what might have happened if the Allies had not been determined "to pay whatever price necessary" to gain ultimate victory.

Evaluating Progress

Section 24-1: A Letter to the President

This individual activity requires half a class period, or it may be assigned as homework.

This activity is designed to assess students' understanding of racism in the United States in World War II.

Remind students that Americans of all backgrounds pitched in to support the war effort, serving in the armed forces, working in war industries or agriculture at home, and helping to conserve scarce goods. Yet the experiences of African, Hispanic, and Japanese Americans showed that, even in the course of a struggle to defeat a racist nation overseas, racism persisted in American society.

Ask students to imagine that it is 1945 and they have decided to write the President to express their outrage at racism and discrimination in the United States. Letters should include a statement about one's beliefs, examples of racism in the armed forces and on the home front during the war, and suggestions for presidential action. Encourage students to review Section 24-1.

Criteria for evaluating students' work should include clearly expressed opinions and suggestions and accurate, convincing examples.

Enrichment Activity

Section 24-3: "Support the War" Posters

This cooperative activity requires a full class period.

In this activity students create posters to encourage Americans' support for the war effort. Provide poster paper and colored markers for students.

Begin the activity by asking students to list ways that Americans on the home front contributed to the war effort (joining the work force, reducing consumption of scarce goods, giving blood, recycling scrap materials, donating clothing, buying war bonds, growing food). Tell students that after the United States entered World War II, the government encouraged civilians to participate in the war effort. As the war dragged on, however, civilian commitment was more difficult to sustain.

Divide the class into groups of three and have each group design a poster to encourage civilians in early 1945 to remain committed to the war effort. The posters should be patriotic and focus on specific aspects of the war effort. To stimulate creativity, have students look at the wartime posters on pages 637, 638, 640, and 665. Allow students at least half the class period to create their posters.

Direct groups to display their posters. Have the class comment on how accurately the posters reflect different aspects of the war effort. Conclude by having students identify wartime activities that would be most difficult to sustain over a long period of time. Students should provide evidence to support their arguments.

Bibliography and Audiovisual Material

Teacher Bibliography

Divine, Robert A. *Roosevelt and World War II*. New York: Viking Penguin, 1970.

Gilbert, Martin. *The Holocaust: The History of the Jews in Europe During the Second World War*. New York: H. Holt & Co., 1986.

Hartmann, Susan. *The Home Front and Beyond: American Women in the 1940s*. Boston: G. K. Hall & Co., 1983.

Hosokawa, Bill. *Nisei: The Quiet Americans*. New York: William Morrow, Inc., 1969.

McGuire, Philip. *He, Too, Spoke for Democracy: Judge Hastie, World War II and the Black Soldier*. Westport, Ct.: Greenwood Publishing Group, Inc., 1988.

Terkel, Studs. *The Good War: An Oral History of World War Two*. New York: Pantheon Books, 1984.

Wright, Gordon. *The Ordeal of Total War.* New York: Harper Torch Books, 1968.

Student Bibliography

Frank, Anne. *Diary of a Young Girl*. New York: Doubleday, 1989.

Hargrove, Marion. *See Here, Private Hargrove*. New York: AMS Press, 1942.

Hersey, John. *Hiroshima*. New York: Random House, 1989.

Maulden, Bill. *Bill Maulden's Army: Bill Maulden's Greatest World War II Cartoons*. Novato, Ca.: Presidio Press, 1983.

McGuire, Philip. *Taps for a Jim Crow Army: Letters from Black Soldiers in World War II*. Santa Barbara, Ca.: ABC-Clio, Inc., 1983.

Pyle, Ernie. *Here Is Your War*. New York: Dorset Press, 1990.

Shaw, Irwin. *The Young Lions*. New York: Dell Publishing Co., 1984.

Teraskai, Gwen. *Bridge to the Sun*. Newport, Tenn. Walestone, 1986.

Wiesel, Elie. *Night*. New York: Bantam Books, 1982.

Wilder, Thornton. *The Skin of Our Teeth*. New York: Harper-Collins Publishers, Inc., 1985.

Films, Videocassettes, and Videodiscs

American Chronicle Series: The Darkest Hour (1939–1941), The Turning Point (1941–1944), End of the Ordeal (1943–1945). AIMS Media. 3 Videodiscs.

Hiroshima and Nagasaki. 20 min. Zenger Video. Videocassette.

Holocaust: In Dark Places. 90 min. Mastervision. Videocassette.

On the Home Front (1941–1945). 114 min. Social Studies School Services. Videocassette.

Filmstrips

Home Front, World War II. 2 color filmstrips, 1 cassette, guide. Multi-Media Productions.

Hiroshima Decision: Was the Use of the A-Bomb Necessary? 1 color filmstrip, cassette, 10 photo aids, guide. Zenger.

Relocation of Japanese-Americans: Right or Wrong? 2 filmstrips, 2 cassettes, 10 photo aids, guide. Zenger.

Computer Software

Axis or Allies? 2 Apple diskettes, backups, guide. Focus Media.

The War in the Pacific. 2 Apple diskettes, backups, guide. Focus Media.

Chapter 24

Objectives

- Analyze the effects of mobilization on the United States economy and the American people.
- Describe how the Allies won the war in Europe.
- Explain how the Allies defeated Japan.

Introducing THE CHAPTER

For suggestions on introducing Chapter 24, refer to page 635B in the Teacher's Edition.

Developing THE CHAPTER

For activities and teaching strategies to help you reinforce and enrich chapter content, see pages 635B–635D in the Teacher's Edition.

B · A · C · K · G · R · O · U · N · D

Chapter Opener Illustrations

A segregated training base for African-American pilots was established near the Tuskegee Institute. During 200 missions the "Tuskegee Airmen" protected the bombers they escorted so well that not a single one was lost. Collectively, they won a Presidential Unit Citation, and individual pilots won 150 Distinguished Flying Crosses.

On February 23, 1945, American troops took Mt. Suribachi on the island of Iwo Jima and raised the American flag. The photograph is of the Marine Corps War Memorial in Arlington, Virginia. It was designed by Felix de Weldon after a photograph by Joseph Rosenthal.

Japanese Americans living on the West Coast of the United States suffered a violation of their human rights when they were interned during the war. These children were two of thousands sent to internment camps.

Reduced student page in the Teacher's Edition

Chapter 24 1941-1945

The Second World War

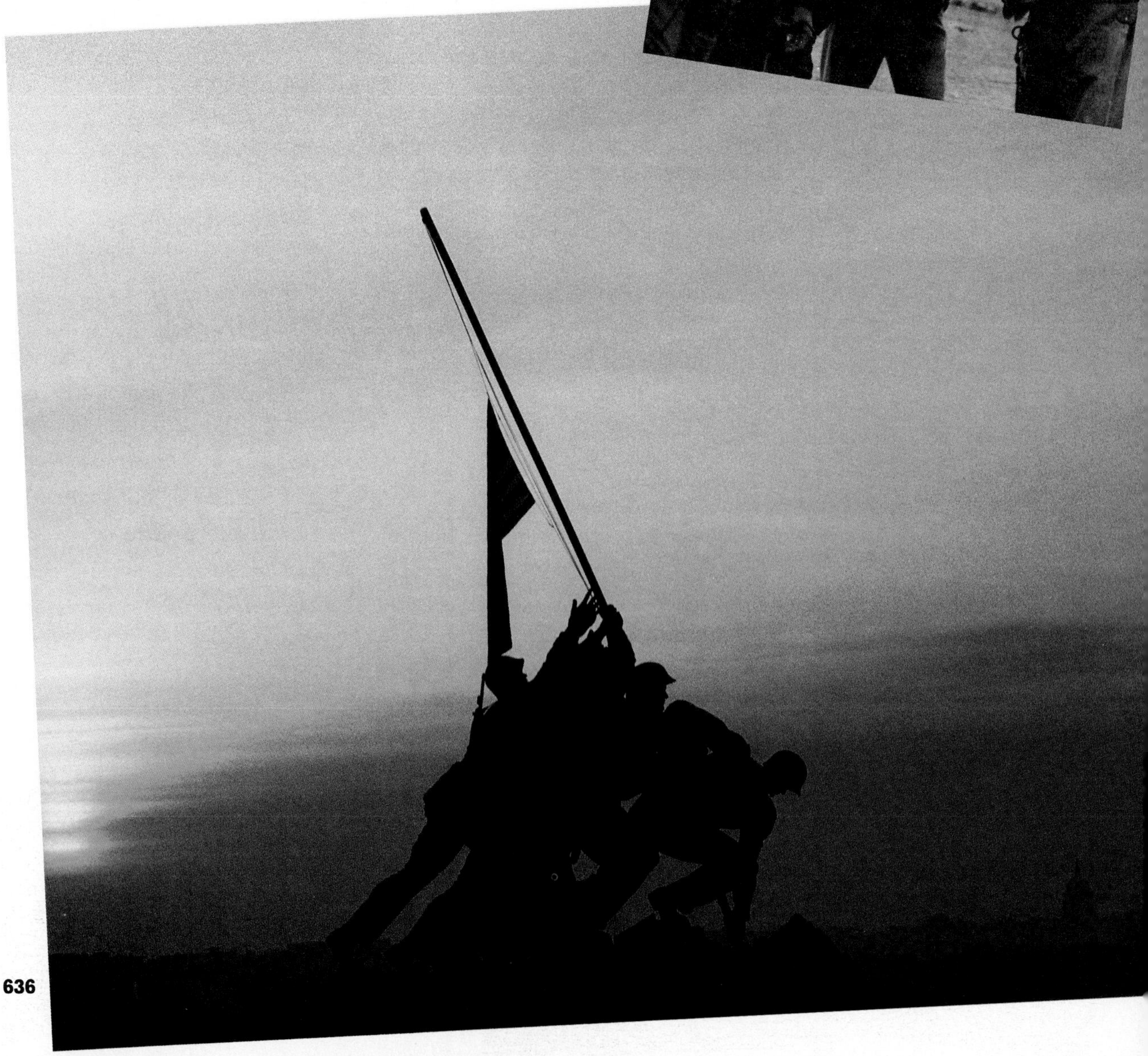

636

Starting in 1942, almost 2,000 women came to Avenger Field, Sweetwater, Texas, to become Women's Air Force Service Pilots (WASPs). They flew everything from giant B-17 and B-29 bombers to the P-51 Mustang fighter.

The December 7, 1941, attack on Pearl Harbor galvanized the American war spirit. The United States government called on Americans to avenge the attack.

In 1945 American troops saw the horrors committed by the Nazis against Jews and other groups. At Camp Gusen in Austria and elsewhere, Allied soldiers found thousands of people like this man, starved, naked, nearly dead, and evidence that millions of others had been murdered.

The Purple Heart is a military decoration awarded to any member of the American armed forces wounded in action. During World War II over 600,000 Americans received the medal.

American Voices

From the bombing of Pearl Harbor to the final surrenders of the Axis powers, more than 15 million Americans served in a long, harsh war that took them to nearly every part of the world. In thousands of letters home, these young men and women told stories of both courage and fear. The pilot who wrote the following letter was one of the "Tuskegee Airmen"—African-American fighter pilots who gained fame for their exploits over Africa and Europe. He won the Distinguished Flying Cross for bravery on the mission he describes here.

"We were flying the best fighters in the war, the North American Mustang (Army P-51). . . . I saw a German plane flying along slightly above me and in front of me. . . . I started to follow him, but I saw a German 109 fleeing an American P-51, who in turn was being followed by a German 109. I stopped my pursuit . . . to attempt to rescue the American pilot who evidently didn't realize his plight. The minute I opened up on the German plane, he stopped his chase of the American plane, and attempted to get away. . . . I overtook him and held my fire until about 75 yards out when I opened up with all four of my fifty cal. machine guns. The German plane lit up like a Christmas tree. . . . As I passed under the burning 109, the pilot bailed out."

The consequences of World War II would be devastating. More people would be killed and more property destroyed than in any previous war. Civilian deaths would be even greater than military deaths. And at war's end, the United States and the Soviet Union would emerge as the two most powerful nations in the world.

American fliers in Italy; Marine flag raising on Iwo Jima; Dorothea Lange photo of children awaiting internment; woman student pilot; World War II poster; starved concentration camp survivor; the Purple Heart medal for wounds in action.

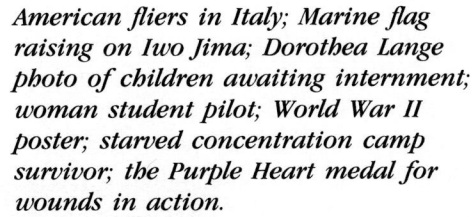

Analyzing Primary Sources

American Voices

During World War II thousands of African-American soldiers and sailors wrote letters to the National Association for the Advancement of Colored People (NAACP) and to the black press about their experiences in training camps and on fighting fronts. Some wrote bitterly of discrimination. Others, like the pilot quoted here, described battles, honors received, and promotions (he became a captain).

1. How does the quotation show the confusion of aerial battle? **(The American pilot who the airman rescued didn't even know he was being pursued by a German plane.)**

2. What supporting evidence does the pilot provide for his statement that the North American Mustang was the best fighter in the war? **(He was able to overtake the German plane and shoot it down.)**

3. Why did the pilot receive the Distinguished Flying Cross? **(He risked his life to pursue and shoot down the German plane.)**

GTV Side 4

Chap. 6, Frame 22643

Echoes of War (Movie)

Search:

Play:

Section 24-1

Objectives

- ***Answer the Focus Question.***
- *Identify the government's role in production, price controls, and rationing.*
- *Relate how African Americans fared in the armed forces.*
- *Explain what the government did to combat discrimination.*
- *Analyze why the government violated the rights of Japanese Americans during the war.*

Introducing

THE SECTION

Enemies as well as allies knew the entry of the United States radically changed the war. Six months before Pearl Harbor, Japanese admiral Osami Nagano, recognizing the United States' untapped industrial and military potential, had warned: *"As for war with the United States, although there is now a chance of achieving victory, the chance will diminish as time goes on. By the later half of next year it will already be difficult for us to cope with the United States: after that, the situation will become increasingly worse."*

Have students keep this statement in mind as they read later about events in the Pacific war. How accurate were Admiral Nagano's fears?

B · A · C · K · G · R · O · U · N · D

Time Line Illustrations

1. In 1941 A. P. Randolph, president of the Brotherhood of Sleeping Car Porters, threatened Roosevelt with a mass march on Washington to protest discrimination against blacks in defense industries and government employment. Roosevelt gave in to Randolph's demands and issued an executive order establishing fair employment practices.
2. During the war many women served in auxiliary units of the armed forces: WAVES (Navy), WAACS (Army), WAFS (Air Corps), SPARS (Marines).
3. Most goods and resources for civilian consumption were scarce during the war. To ensure that each person would be able to buy a fair share of scarce goods, the government issued ration stamps. Most rationing ended in 1945.
4. This image shows the most famous landing in history, the Allied attack on the beaches of Normandy on D-Day,

Reduced student page in the Teacher's Edition

CHAPTER TIME LINE

1941-1945

1942 Jan Tire rationing in effect

Feb Internment of Japanese Americans

May Women in the armed forces

Jun Battle of Midway

1941 — 1942 — 1943

1941 A. P. Randolph challenges discrimination in war industries

1943 Feb Victory at Battle of Stalingrad

May Allied victory in North Africa

Jun Race riots: Detroit, Los Angeles

24-1 Mobilizing for Global War

Focus: How did mobilization affect the nation's economy and the American people?

After the war, Winston Churchill recalled December 8, 1941, the day the United States formally entered World War II:

> “*Some said [the Americans] were soft, others that they would never be united. . . . [But] the United States is like a gigantic boiler. Once the fire is lighted under it there is no limit to the power it can generate.*”

The Japanese attack on Pearl Harbor had ignited America, ending the debate on neutrality and uniting the nation. The United States, as Churchill said, was now "in the war, up to the neck and in to the death."

Fortunately, the United States was better prepared for war than it had been in 1917. The draft was already in effect. Even the economy was partially mobilized by lend-lease and defense needs. Now, to direct the war effort, the government took charge of the economic life of the nation.

Industry Goes to War

Hermann Göring, commander of the German air force, once scoffed, "The Americans can't build planes—only electric iceboxes and razor blades." Göring was wrong. American industry would not only build planes, it would also produce the world's most powerful military machine. Less than two

June 6, 1944. The Allies assembled some 4,500 ships and 10,000 aircraft for the invasion. On the first day more than 170,000 American, British, and Canadian troops landed.
5. World War II ended in August 1945, after the United States dropped atomic bombs on Hiroshima and Nagasaki, Japan. The bombs completely destroyed large parts of the cities and brought death or injury to hundreds of thousands of Japanese civilians.

1944

1944 Jun D-Day

Jul First Allied view of Nazi death camps

Oct Battle of Leyte Gulf
American forces land in Philippines

Dec Battle of the Bulge

1945

1945 Feb Yalta Conference

May Germany surrenders

Aug Atomic bombs dropped on Hiroshima and Nagasaki
Japan surrenders

years after Pearl Harbor, the United States would be producing more war equipment than Germany, Japan, and Italy combined.

In January 1942 Roosevelt set up the War Production Board (WPB) to supervise the conversion of American industry from peacetime goods to war materials. Automobile makers switched to producing tanks, shirtmakers made mosquito netting, and refrigerator manufacturers produced ammunition.

The WPB set high production goals. The aircraft industry had produced 6,000 planes in 1939. For 1942, the WPB set a goal of 60,000. By 1944 the industry was producing 96,000 planes a year.

Shipbuilding gains were also impressive. By using prefabricated construction and electric welding, industrialist Henry J. Kaiser cut the time needed to build Liberty cargo ships from 241 days to 22 days. So fast were the shipbuilders that a joke was told of a woman who stepped up with a champagne bottle to christen a new ship. The keel, however, had not been laid. "What shall I do now?" she asked Kaiser. "Just start swinging," he said.

The government urged farmers to increase production to feed American and Allied troops. As a result, the farm economy, which had suffered hard times since World War I, boomed. With so many men in the military, farm workers were desperately needed. Thousands of Native-American families left the reservations to work on farms and ranches. In 1942, after Mexico had declared war on the Axis, it agreed to provide the United States with temporary agricultural workers. More than 375,000 *braceros,* as they were called, worked in twenty-one states, producing and harvesting crops.

The end of the depression. Mobilization for war ended the Great Depression by creating plentiful jobs. To replace the workers who joined the military, millions of women, youth, and elderly citizens went to work. Old barriers to women in the workplace fell as women took all sorts of jobs previously reserved for men. Unemployment plunged and personal income more than doubled.

Now that Americans had money to spend, there was nothing to spend it on. At a time when most factories were producing war materials, the demand for cars and other consumer goods was rising at a rate that threatened to send prices soaring.

Developing THE SECTION

Active Learning

Making Charts. Before students read the section have them prepare charts on the mobilization of the United States. The charts should have seven headings: Human Resources, War Production, Labor, Consumption Controls, Inflation Controls, War Finances, and Civil Rights. Ask students to complete the charts as they read, listing agencies and actions in the appropriate columns.

Ask: Based on your charts, was World War II a total war? (Review the meaning of total war, stressing equal importance of the home front and the fighting front.) Describe the government's role in mobilization. How do you think the nature of the United States's entry into the war helped to mobilize Americans? (Japanese attack on Pearl Harbor probably affected American unity and created anger.)

GTV Side 4
Chap. 6, Frame 22645
Echoes of War: Mobilization (Movie Segment)
Search and Play:

B · A · C · K · G · R · O · U · N · D

Analyzing Primary Sources

Edward R. Murrow. News commentator Edward R. Murrow said to Americans in 1942:

“We are the only people fighting this war with plenty of food, clothing, shelter, with an undamaged productive system. . . . We aren't tired, and Europe is—all of it.”

Have students use information in this section to agree or disagree with this view.

Limited English Proficiency

Building Vocabulary. Have students define *rationing*. Then discuss whether rationing could occur in the United States today.

Linking Past and Present

Discussion. Refer students to the poster on this page. Today, too, people are conserving resources as part of an effort to preserve the environment. Discuss where and how such materials are recycled in the students' community. Have them find posters, or advertisements in magazines and newspapers calling on people to do their part. Ask students if they think today's environmental challenges require a level of commitment and effort comparable to that in wartime. Why or why not?

Social History

Some 25,000 women pilots applied to join the Women's Air Force Service Pilots (WASPs). These women filled positions previously held by male civilian contract pilots, at a fraction of the cost. When the men complained to Congress, the WASPs were deactivated in 1944. The WASPs appealed for veteran's benefits but were denied them until 1978. It was only then that Congress admitted that the 800 surviving WASPs were entitled to benefits routinely granted to veterans.

Rationing and Price Controls

In 1942 the government established the Office of Price Administration (OPA) to halt inflation. Eventually, the OPA put ceilings, or limits, on wages and prices for almost all products, and on rents in areas important to defense industries.

On several occasions the government took control of an industry when unions or management threatened to defy wage or price controls. For the most part, though, labor and management cooperated to ensure full production, negotiating problems through the War Labor Board (WLB).

With prices frozen, the OPA set up a system of **rationing**—limiting the amount of scarce goods that each person could buy—to ensure fair distribution. Ration boards gave every citizen ration stamps, which had to be used to purchase such items as car tires, sugar, coffee, red meat, gasoline, and shoes.

Pitching in to support the war effort became a matter of pride and patriotism for Americans. To save cloth, they bought skirts made without pleats and men's suits without pockets or cuffs. People drove slower and organized car pools to conserve gasoline. "The empty seat," posters warned, "is a gift to Hitler."

Across the nation, people collected tons of paper, rags, metal, and rubber to be used in war production. They gave blood, donated clothing, sold war bonds, and planted more than 20 million "victory gardens" to grow their own food. After all, people reminded each other, "don't you know there's a war on?"

The Armed Forces

In the course of the war, some 15 million men served in the armed forces, including 10 million draftees. Although women did not have to register for the draft, more than 300,000 of them joined the women's branches of the army, navy, marines, and air force. They worked as mechanics, radio operators, airplane spotters, and clerks. They also flew planes from factories to military bases and towed targets for aerial gunnery practice.

Save waste fats for explosives
TAKE THEM TO YOUR MEAT DEALER

The war effort required full employment and conservation. Six million new women workers prevented a labor shortage. Consumers learned to "buy wisely [and] cook carefully."

Americans of all backgrounds swelled the military, including 25,000 Native Americans. Half a million Hispanics — most of them Mexican Americans — also served, as well as nearly 900,000 African Americans.

Campaigning against segregation. Even before the war began, African-American organizations and the African-American press had launched a campaign to end discrimination in the armed forces. Judge William H. Hastie, the first black to be appointed a federal judge, vowed:

> *“We will be American soldiers. We will be American aviators. We will be American laborers. We will be anything that any other American should be in this whole program of national defense. But we won't be black auxiliaries.”*

As a result of this campaign, the draft bill that was passed in 1940 banned “discrimination against any person on account of race or color” in the selection process. Equal treatment in the draft did not mean an end to discrimination in the armed services, however. The military's policy of segregation remained unchanged.

In fact, bowing to pressure from the army and navy, Red Cross blood banks refused to accept blood donations from African Americans “on the score that white men in the service would refuse blood plasma if they knew it came from Negro veins.” Ironically, Dr. Charles R. Drew, the scientist who pioneered blood preservation and was the director of the American Red Cross Blood Bank in New York City, was an African American.

Eventually, African Americans served in every branch of the armed forces and in every theater of the war. But most served in strictly segregated labor units. Observing the treatment of black soldiers in a New York army camp, a white private saw a parallel between the United States and the very nations it was fighting:

> *“Negro draftees are segregated from the minute they come into the camp. . . . The whole picture is a very raw and ugly one. It looks, smells, and tastes like fascism.”*

Black officers fared better than enlisted men. With the exception of air force pilots, who were trained at a separate flight school at Tuskegee, Alabama, they attended integrated officer candidate

Women and young people took jobs of all sorts, including work on railroads and in aircraft plants and shipyards. Women also served as armed guards at some military bases, learning to use anti-aircraft and riot guns.

Multicultural Perspectives

Discussion. General Dwight Eisenhower, who approved integrated infantry units during the war, stated that he did not “differentiate among soldiers.” Ask students to compare this view with the general policy of American armed forces during the war, citing examples. Discuss the history of this policy, reviewing treatment of African-American troops in the Civil War and World War I.

Connections: Language

Wartime Slang. Write the following words on the chalkboard: *blitz, quisling, flak, GI, snafu, ack-ack.* Tell students that these are World War II slang words that have become part of our language. *Snafu,* for example, is a wartime acronym for “situation normal, all fouled up.” Ask students to find derivations of the other words by checking the dictionary or by asking friends or relatives who remember World War II.

GTV Side 4

Chap. 6, Frame 23882

Echoes of War: Women in the Workforce (Movie Segment)

Search and Play:

Linking Past and Present

The worst home-front disaster of the war, the Port Chicago explosion killed 320 seamen, two thirds of them black. The fifty men who refused to go back to work after the explosion were tried, convicted, and sentenced to fifteen years in prison. Through the tireless efforts of Thurgood Marshall and NAACP leaders, in January 1946 most of the men were released from prison. In 1991 the House Armed Services Committee recommended that Congress order the Secretary of the Navy to review the Port Chicago convictions because they may have been influenced by racial prejudice. In 1992 Congress approved legislation for a national monument to commemorate the disaster.

Reduced student page in the Teacher's Edition

schools. Racist attitudes, however, limited opportunities for assignment and promotion. Benjamin O. Davis was the only African American among the 776 generals during the war.

Segregation sometimes led to conflict between black and white troops. Some black soldiers responded with bitterness and despair. Others fought back or found other ways to protest. In a widely publicized event, fifty black ammunition loaders were put on trial for refusing to go back to work under the same unsafe conditions that had sparked an explosion at Port Chicago, California, in 1944.

Thurgood Marshall, chief counsel for the NAACP and a future Supreme Court justice, called for an investigation of the navy. He wanted to know why only African Americans were assigned to loading ammunition and why they were not given training in the safe handling of explosives. The outcry so embarrassed navy officials that they began to take steps toward ending segregation.

With few exceptions, the 4,000 black servicewomen—even the officers—were segregated and given the most menial work to do. Representative Helen Gahagan Douglas of California could have been speaking for black servicewomen as well as servicemen when she paid tribute to the black soldier, who "fought and shed his blood for a freedom which he has not been permitted fully to share."

Racial conflict during the war is shown in "Zoot Suit Riots," part of a mural created by Judith Baca and young Los Angelenos in the 1970s and 1980s.

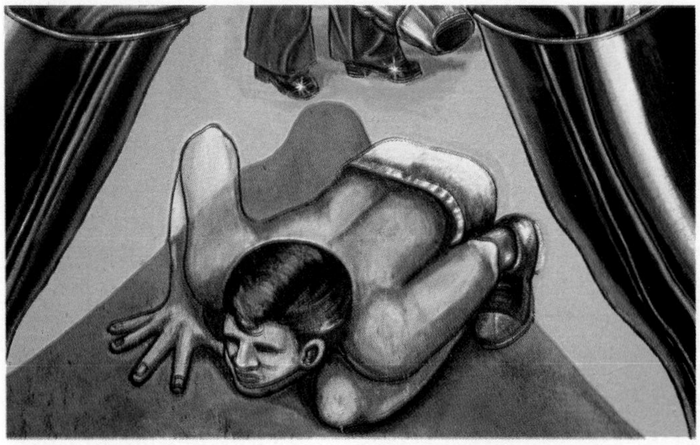

Confronting Racism

The greatest internal migration in the nation's history took place during the war. Some 27 million people moved, pursuing jobs or serving in the military. More than a million people flocked to shipyards and aircraft plants on the Pacific Coast alone. The demand for labor revived migration of blacks from the South, which had declined during the depression. Now large numbers of African Americans headed north and west in a "Second Great Migration," which would continue through the 1960s and involve more than 5 million people.

Towns and cities, swelling with migrants, faced urgent demands for schools, hospitals, and especially housing. With building materials unavailable, housing shortages were a problem throughout the war. In addition, older residents often resented newcomers, especially of different races and religions. Racism, fanned by wartime conditions, sometimes exploded into violence.

In 1943 alone there were more than 200 incidents of racial violence. The most serious occurred in Detroit, where rioting was halted only after the President sent in army troops. Thirty-four people were killed.

Violence also erupted between whites and Mexican Americans. In Los Angeles in 1943, white soldiers and sailors roamed the streets attacking young Mexican Americans who wore "zoot suits," suits cut loosely for ease in dancing. "Zoot suit riots" spread to other parts of the country just at a time when President Roosevelt was holding meetings with President Avila Comacho of Mexico, an ally in the war.

Both presidents were assured that the riots were "non-racial." But if this were true, Dan G. Acosta asked in a letter to the Los Angeles press,

> *"Why are we consistently called hoodlums? Why is mob action encouraged by the newspapers? Why did the city police stand around saying very nonchalantly that they could not intervene and even hurrahed the soldiers for their 'brave' action?"*

Multicultural Perspectives

After the Japanese attack on Pearl Harbor, China and the United States became allies. As a result, in 1943 Congress repealed the exclusion acts that had kept Chinese immigrants out of the United States since 1882. New legislation, based on national-origins quotas, allowed a limited number of Chinese as well as Filipinos and Asian Indians to immigrate to the United States each year. Passage of the War Brides Act in 1945 allowed Asian wives and children of American servicemen to enter the United States as nonquota immigrants.

A picketer for the Negro Labor Relations League protests job discrimination. The government ban on discrimination did not apply to non-war work.

Draftee's Prayer

Dear Lord, today
I go to war:
To fight, to die,
Tell me what for?
Dear Lord, I'll fight,
I do not fear,
Germans or Japs;
My fears are here.
America!

—African-American newspaper, 1943

Fighting prejudice. Even before the United States entered the war, African Americans had begun to challenge all forms of discrimination. In January 1941 A. Philip Randolph, head of the Brotherhood of Sleeping Car Porters, had called for a march on Washington to protest against the exclusion of blacks "from defense industries and their humiliation in the armed forces." Thousands were ready to show up.

President Roosevelt headed off the protest by issuing Executive Order 8802, which forbade racial discrimination in defense industries and government jobs. To enforce the order, Roosevelt established the Fair Employment Practices Commission (FEPC) to investigate discrimination. As a result, some 2 million African Americans were working in war plants by the end of 1944.

During the war, African Americans launched a campaign for the "Double V"—victory at home and abroad—thus linking the war against fascism to the struggle against racism at home. Membership in the NAACP soared to 450,000.

While the NAACP focused on legal challenges, a new group was formed to fight segregation through nonviolent action. The Congress of Racial Equality (CORE), founded in 1942 by James Farmer and a Quaker social-action group, staged its first sit-in at a segregated Chicago restaurant. Denied service, CORE members simply sat there, refusing to leave until they were served.

Mexican Americans also fought discrimination. The Elizalde Anti-Discrimination Committee, formed in 1946, was made up of veterans. "Mexican-American soldiers," said Marine Corps veteran Balton Llanes, "shed a quarter of the blood spilled at Bataan. . . . What they want now is a decent job, a decent home, and a chance to live peacefully in the community." The Elizalde Committee, like CORE and NAACP, and other anti-discrimination groups, laid the foundation for even greater civil rights efforts after the war.

Japanese-American Internment

"'Where was I on December 7, 1941?' I was helping on the family farm. . . . It wasn't until after five that I went home. That was when I first heard about the Japanese attack on Pearl Harbor. My reaction was one of shock . . . and then fear about what public reaction toward us would be like."

Nineteen-year-old Mikiso Hane had reason to be concerned. For Japanese Americans growing up in California, he wrote, "racial bias and discrimination were facts of life that we had been conditioned to live with since childhood." Racism against Asians had existed in America since the mid-1800s.

Multicultural Perspectives

Discussion. Ask students how President Roosevelt's Executive Order 8802 and the Fair Employment Practices Commission set a precedent for future government action against racial discrimination. Also ask students how the different emphases of the NAACP and CORE complemented each other. Have students research similar efforts by Mexican Americans.

Writing About History

Diary Entries. Have students imagine that they were Japanese-American children in 1942. Have them write diary entries describing their reactions to the news about Pearl Harbor, the loss of the family's home and property, the journey to an internment camp, and life at the camp. Students can research primary and secondary sources to find information about these topics. Ask students whether they think that such an internment could ever happen again. Why or why not?

Citizenship

Discussion. Tell students that Japanese Americans protested Executive Order 9066 by bringing suit against the government for violating their civil rights. **Ask:** Which civil rights were violated? **(Answers may include the right to due process of law, the right to a speedy and fair trial, and protection from cruel and unusual punishment.)**

Analyzing Primary Sources

Justifying Internment. General John DeWitt, head of the Western Defense Command, said:

> *"A Jap is a Jap. . . . It makes no difference whether he is an American citizen or not. . . . I don't want any of them. . . . There is no way to determine their loyalty. . . . The very fact that no sabotage has taken place to date is a disturbing and confirming indication that such action will be taken."*

Ask students whether they think the general's attitude is reasonable. Why, by and large, weren't similar fears expressed about German Americans or Italian Americans? **(Issue was racism made worse by hysteria.)**

Multicultural Perspectives

In Italy and France, the 442nd Regimental Combat Team, which included the famed 100th Infantry Battalion, fought in the fierce battles of Monte Cassino and the Vosges, taking heavy casualties. The Nisei troops won more than 3,600 Purple Hearts, 350 Silver Stars, 810 Bronze Stars, 47 Distinguished Service Crosses, and other medals.

Reduced student page in the Teacher's Edition

Now, in reaction to Japan's attack on Pearl Harbor, the United States started a process that would destroy the lives of thousands of Japanese Americans and test the limits of Americans' commitment to the Constitution.

The shock of the Pearl Harbor attack created an atmosphere of hysteria on the West Coast. Within hours there were rumors that the Japanese fleet was approaching. Alarm and confusion raged in the army, which was now responsible, due to the naval losses at Pearl Harbor, for defending the coast. California alone had 80 percent of the aviation industry, all within the range of naval guns.

General Joseph W. Stilwell, in command of the defense of California, frantically called the War Department demanding ammunition. When the officer in Washington promised to do "the best we can," Stilwell roared, "The best you can! Good God, what . . . am I supposed to do? Fight 'em off with oranges?"

As fears mounted, so did racist suspicions that the Japanese Americans on the West Coast were traitors eager to help Japan invade the United States. Government officials and the press fanned the flames. Walter Lippmann informed readers that the entire Pacific Coast was "in imminent danger of a combined attack from within and without." General John L. DeWitt, the army's West Coast commander, saw no distinction between Japanese in Japan and Japanese Americans in the United States. They were all members of an "enemy race."

American Voices

> *"I was scared. Here I was, bucking the whole government and military. But I must have had enough confidence as an American citizen to test our democratic nation. I was classified as a prisoner-of-war, an enemy alien, so I didn't have anything to lose."*
>
> —Fred Korematsu

Roosevelt accepted the advice of the War Department. On February 19, 1942, he signed Executive Order 9066, authorizing military officials to exclude "any or all persons" from areas designated "military zones." Under this order, all Japanese on the West Coast, including American citizens of Japanese descent, were to be evacuated and confined in internment camps. Canada and most Latin American governments adopted similar measures against residents of Japanese ancestry.

At the time Roosevelt signed the order, there was no evidence of disloyalty among Japanese Americans—and none would ever be found. In fact, a prewar investigation carried out by the Office of Naval Intelligence had shown the overwhelming loyalty of Japanese Americans.

Internment camps. During 1942 about 110,000 Americans of Japanese ancestry were forced from their homes into so-called relocation centers scattered from the California desert to the Arkansas swamps. Two thirds of these people were Nisei (NEE-say)—children born in the United States of Japanese parents and thus American citizens. Families had little time to settle their affairs. Kisaye Sato recalled:

> *"We only had 48 hours to get out of our homes. They came in truckloads to buy our things. We had to get rid of our furniture and appliances for whatever the people would pay. They took terrible advantage of us."*

Both Kisaye Sato and Mikiso Hane and their families were sent to the internment camp in Poston, Arizona, a barren desert where summer temperatures reach 120 degrees. Eventually 20,000 Japanese Americans were interned at the Poston camp. Mikiso Hane recalled:

> *"For the next several months we struggled with the heat, the sandstorms, the scorpions, the rattlesnakes, the confusion, the overcrowded barracks, and the lack of privacy."*

Most Japanese Americans remained in the camps for more than three years, enduring their imprisonment with dignity. Others fought back through strikes, petitions, mass meetings, and riots.

Connections: Literature

Tule Lake was the toughest of the ten internment camps. Japanese shipped there were asked if they were willing to serve in the American military. They said "no." They were also asked to swear unqualified allegiance to the United States, which had put them in internment camps. They said "no" again. They were known as the "no-no's." The following quotation is from *No-No Boy*, a novel by John Okada, a Nisei. *"When one is born in America and learning to love it more and more every day without thinking about it, it is not an easy thing to discover suddenly that being American is a terribly incomplete thing if one's face is not white and one's parents are Japanese of the country Japan which attacked America."*

Interned in Colorado, the Hirano family posed with a photograph of a son serving in the 442nd Regimental Combat Team, made up of Hawaiian and mainland Nisei. The 442nd's shoulder patch showed a torch of liberty. Its motto was "Go for broke!"

More than a thousand young men, whose parents remained in the camps, volunteered and were accepted for military service. Japanese Americans fought with valor in Europe. The Nisei 442nd Regimental Combat Team suffered more casualties and won more medals than any other army combat brigade in United States history. Thousands of other Japanese Americans served as interpreters and translators for American forces in the Pacific. Speaking for many soldiers, Mike Masaoka later said, "We had to purchase the right to live as Americans, not only for ourselves, but for our children's children."

In 1944 the Supreme Court upheld the policy of internment in the case of *Korematsu* v. *United States.* But Justice Frank Murphy had serious doubts about the action. The exclusion order, he said, toppled into "the ugly abyss of racism."

In 1983, at Japanese-American insistence, a congressional committee investigated internment. It concluded that "race prejudice, war hysteria, and a failure of political leadership" on the part of President Roosevelt and his advisors had resulted in a "grave injustice" to Japanese Americans.

That year the forty-year-old verdict in the Korematsu case was overturned when United States District Judge Marilyn Hall Patel ruled that the mass evacuation and internment were "based upon . . . unsubstantiated facts [and] distortions." The case, Patel said, served as a "signal of caution" that the government must "protect all citizens from the . . . prejudices so easily stirred up" by war.

In 1988, forty-six years after the internment order, Congress passed a bill formally apologizing to the nation's Japanese-American citizens. The bill also granted a payment of $20,000 to each of the estimated 60,000 survivors of the internment camps as recognition of the violation of their human rights and the harm done to them.

Section Review

1. **Identification.** Define *rationing*.

2. **Analysis.** How did the role of the federal government in the economy expand during World War II?

3. **Comprehension.** Why did World War II bring an end to the Great Depression?

4. **Evaluation.** In 1939 an NAACP newspaper warned, "Judging from prevailing Jim Crow practices in the armed forces of the United States today, the next war . . . will see the same gross maltreatment of the Negro soldiers seen in the world war." Do you think that warning was accurate? Give reasons for your opinion.

5. **Analysis.** Judge Marilyn Hall Patel said that the government must "protect all citizens from the . . . prejudices so easily stirred up" by war. What do you think she meant?

Citizenship

Discussion. The 1988 congressional apology to Japanese Americans was not the first time restitution was granted by legislation. In 1825 Thomas Cooper was granted restoration of $400 plus interest for a fine he had incurred in 1800 for violating the Sedition Act. (Chapter 7) **Ask:** What value does such compensation have for individuals involved and society in general?

Section Review

ANSWERS

1. Definition for the term *rationing* is on text page 640.
2. Government supervised war production, set ceilings on wages and prices, established system of rationing, and solved labor-management problems.
3. Full production in defense plants provided jobs. Many young males drafted, taking them out of job market, increasing employment rate.
4. Widespread segregation in military, use of African Americans in the navy for the dangerous work of ammunition loading and in military for most menial work. If disagree can point to integrated officer candidate schools.
5. Wartime fears and hysteria intensified racism, which can lead to unconstitutional actions.

GTV Side 4

Chap. 6, Frame 23271

Echoes of War: Japanese-American Internment (Movie Segment)

Search and Play:

Linking Past and Present

Discussion. Movie stars and other celebrities contributed to the war effort by entertaining troops overseas and heading up war bond drives on the homefront. In one marathon radio broadcast, singer Kate Smith convinced listeners to buy $39 million in war bonds.

Ask students to cite movements and causes that are supported by celebrities today. What are some kinds of events that celebrities publicize? How do stars' names help a cause?

Connections: Economics

Among items in short supply were shoes—due to the shortage of leather, Americans were limited to three pairs a year; textiles—men's trouser cuffs and frills on women's dresses vanished; hemlines became shorter; coffee—some people rebrewed coffee grounds; gasoline—when shortages were critical, lines of cars streamed behind gasoline tankers to service stations; nylon and silk stockings—women used leg makeup and some even painted on seams; reading materials—books were printed in small type to use less paper and some magazines limited their circulations; tires—one enterprising man made a retread from the soles of old shoes.

Residents of Detroit, Michigan, waited in a long line at a sugar rationing board. Each person in a family, including the children, received a ration book.

WAR RATION BOOK TWO

Volunteering for civilian-defense, students were trained to spot enemy aircraft and put out fires in case of bombing raids.

Work on a farm...
this Summer
JOIN THE U.S. CROP CORPS
SEE YOUR U.S. EMPLOYMENT SERVICE OR YOUR LOCAL COUNTY AGENT

Young people helped cultivate and harvest crops. Like these children in Chicago, they also recycled scrap materials.

Hasten the Homecoming
BUY VICTORY BONDS

In classrooms, students used their allowances to buy government bonds that raised money to pay for the war. A greater war effort, this Norman Rockwell poster urged, would bring the war to a swifter end.

FOR RENT

646

Social History

The war brought new experiences and traumas to American children. Many fathers were away in the armed forces, and many mothers were working outside the home for the first time. Children were placed in child-care centers, when available. More common were "latchkey" children—children left alone at home after school hours. Among older children juvenile delinquency increased sharply.

Active Learning

Cooperative Activity. Propaganda was used to urge Americans to support the war effort. Propaganda is the communication of ideas to further a cause or damage an opposing one. Propaganda appeals to people's emotions.

Have students work in small groups to prepare oral presentations on the role of propaganda in mobilizing American support for the war. Have them describe types of propaganda, such as posters, political cartoons, speeches, and patriotic songs. Where appropriate, students can bring in examples of some of these, including recordings of songs and speeches, newspaper articles, movies, and the like, and explain why they were effective.

With gas rationed and a 35-mph speed limit, people drove only when necessary.

young IN AMERICA

On the Home Front

For most Americans, World War II was a time of achievement as well as anxiety. More than 15 million wore a uniform—four times the number who had served in World War I. For families, pride in having a relative in the service contended with the constant fear of receiving a dreaded telegram from the War or Navy Department: "I regret to inform you . . ." Many children grew up without knowing their fathers, and an unprecedented number of women, including mothers, took jobs in war industries.

Young people pitched in with gusto to help with the war effort. They, too, worked in war industries and on farms. Guided by the motto "Use it up, wear it out, make it do, or do without," they conserved scarce wartime materials. They also knit socks for soldiers overseas, rolled bandages, and prepared packages of clothing to send to children in war-devastated lands.

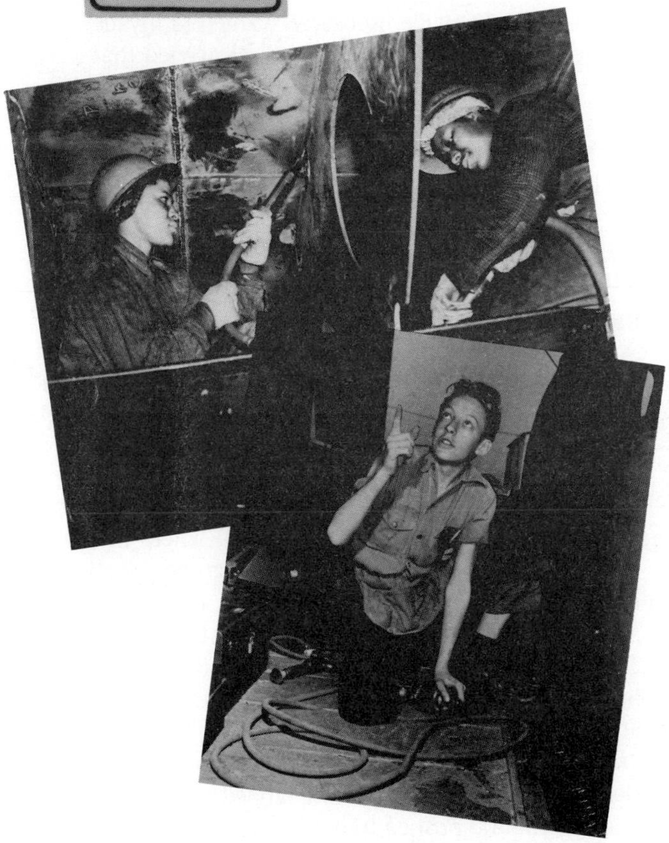

Many young people took assembly-line jobs in aircraft plants and shipyards (above). Students at Mount Holyoke College (below) organized a "land army" to grow enough food to feed students and servicewomen training at the college.

Section 24-2

Objectives

- ***Answer the Focus Question.***
- *Evaluate the agreements made by the Big Three at Yalta.*
- *Describe the Holocaust.*

Introducing THE SECTION

In early 1942 it looked as though the Axis in Europe was close to total victory. In western Europe only Great Britain held out against Hitler, and the British had few resources left. Although the Germans had been slowed down by the Russian winter and stubborn Soviet resistance, their army was ready to strike another powerful blow. German U-boats had a stranglehold on the sea lanes between the United States and Britain, and between Britain and the Soviet Union.

Have students take the role of Allied military advisors. Given limited resources, what were to be the priorities? How could an Allied offensive be started, and how could the Soviets be effectively aided? The campaigns discussed in this section should be seen in the context of these overriding strategic needs.

B • A • C • K • G • R • O • U • N • D

Social History

When World War II began, Margaret Bourke-White was already a well-known photographer. During the Great Depression her haunting pictures of the Dust Bowl brought her fame. Born in 1904 in New York City, she dreamed as a child of traveling around the world. In college she discovered her talent for photography. In 1941 Bourke-White was the only foreign photographer to cover the German attack on Moscow. In the spring of 1945, while working for *Life* magazine, she was with General George S. Patton's troops when they discovered Nazi concentration camps. Though heartsick at what she saw, she photographed it all, because she wanted the world to know the full horror.

Reduced student page in the Teacher's Edition

24-2 *Winning the War in Europe*

Focus: How did the Allies defeat Italy and Germany?

When the United States entered World War I in 1917, Americans sent off the doughboys with banquets and parades. Most people believed, with President Wilson, that the nation was fighting to make the world "safe for democracy." In December 1941 there were no parades. World War II, warned President Roosevelt, would be "the survival war."

The Allies Plan Strategy

Soon after the Pearl Harbor attack, Prime Minister Churchill and President Roosevelt met to determine a common war plan. They agreed to concentrate on defeating Germany first. Nazi forces in western Europe and in the Atlantic posed a more direct threat than Japan. The two leaders also knew that Germany, with its industrial power, had the greatest potential for inventing new, devastating weapons. "Defeat of Germany," Churchill said, "will leave Japan exposed to overwhelming force, whereas the defeat of Japan would not by any means bring the world war to an end."

Roosevelt and Churchill also consulted with Joseph Stalin, the leader of the Soviet Union, now an ally. Suspicion marred relations among the "Big Three," laying a basis for future difficulties.

Roosevelt and Churchill had little reason to trust Stalin. He had, after all, signed the nonaggression pact with Hitler. He had also seized eastern Poland, parts of Finland and Romania, and the Baltic countries of Estonia, Latvia, and Lithuania. For his part, Stalin suspected that his allies were failing to give him enough help in hopes that Russia would "bleed to death" in its struggle against German invaders on the Russian front.

The Big Three did agree that the Allies should invade western Europe. A second fighting front would give Stalin's forces relief by forcing Germany to divide its troops. However, Roosevelt and Churchill differed about where and when an invasion should take place. Roosevelt wanted to invade France as soon as possible. Churchill argued that such an invasion would be disastrous because the Allies did not yet have enough troops and supplies. Churchill convinced Roosevelt that they should begin in North Africa.

Turning the Tide in Africa and Europe

The British in North Africa were in desperate need of help. German forces under General Erwin Rommel, the "Desert Fox," threatened to take Egypt and the Suez Canal, a vital Allied supply route.

In October 1942 British troops took the offensive against the Germans at El Alamein. Their new commander, General Bernard L. Montgomery, had issued an ultimatum: "From now on the Eighth Army will not yield a yard of ground to the enemy. Troops will fight and die where they stand." The British triumphed, driving Axis forces out of Egypt and back toward Tunisia.

In November British and American troops under General Dwight D. Eisenhower landed in Morocco and Algeria and pushed into Tunisia. By May 1943 the Germans were trapped by Eisenhower's forces to the west and Montgomery's troops to the east. The Axis army surrendered on May 13, leaving all of North Africa in Allied hands. Now the Allies had bases from which to invade southern Europe.

Russian counterattack. On the eastern front, German forces had orders from Hitler "to crush Soviet Russia in a quick campaign." Unprepared, Soviet forces, aided by civilians, fought desperately. They finally stopped the German advance at Leningrad and Moscow in the winter of 1941-1942. At the front, American photographer Margaret Bourke-White wrote, "We drove through plains scattered with helmets of the dead and battlefields that looked like the end of the world."

Connections: Literature

War correspondent Ernie Pyle followed the war from the front lines in North Africa and Italy to the D-Day invasion, describing the daily lives of ordinary soldiers. His vivid war reports were republished in book form in *Here Is Your War*. In 1944 he was awarded the Pulitzer Prize for general correspondence. In April 1945 Pyle was killed fighting on Okinawa.

Spotlight on War

Great Britain had a weapon so secret that only the highest commanders knew about it. Ultra was the name of a machine that could break the German military code for secret messages.

Ultra played an important role in the Battle of Britain in 1940-1941, helping the British predict the targets of the German air force and the number of aircraft that would be involved. Ultra helped General Montgomery defeat the Germans in Egypt in 1942 by revealing Rommel's plan of attack. During the Battle of the Atlantic the British broke the German U-boat code and could tell their sub-hunters where to look for German prey. The British were so cautious in their use of Ultra that the Germans never discovered that their code had been broken.

In the spring of 1942, the Germans launched a major new attack toward Soviet oil fields and the city of Stalingrad in south central Russia. Despite heavy bombing, the Soviets held off the Germans, fighting hand-to-hand amid the ruins of the city. Then, in November 1942 the Red Army struck back with everything it had—tanks, cannon, infantry, and even mounted horsemen.

The battle continued throughout the cold, bleak winter. Thousands of German soldiers froze or starved to death. Finally, on February 2, 1943, the last German troops in Stalingrad surrendered. Although about 400,000 Soviets had died, the Battle of Stalingrad marked a turning point in the war. It halted Germany's eastward advance in Europe, and it proved that the Soviets were a force to be reckoned with.

Demand for unconditional surrender. In January 1943, with the tide of the European war turning in favor of the Allies, Roosevelt and Churchill met in Casablanca, Morocco, to decide where to strike next. Stalin, who would not leave Russia at that critical time, again urged his allies to open a second front in Europe.

The United States and Britain still lacked the necessary equipment, especially landing craft, for an invasion from England. Thus, Roosevelt agreed with Churchill's plan to attack "the soft underbelly of the Axis" by invading Sicily. The capture of that island would divert the Germans from the Russian front and open the way for the Allies to take all of Italy.

The two leaders also agreed to insist on the unconditional surrender of their enemies. Wilson's Fourteen Points had led the Germans to sign the armistice of 1919 with false hopes of easy terms for peace. Roosevelt wanted no misunderstanding this time. "Every person in Germany," he said, "should realize that this time Germany is a defeated nation."

Invasion of Italy

Before dawn on July 10, 1943, some 160,000 British and American troops splashed ashore on Sicily. In a relentless thirty-eight-day campaign, the Allies swept the German and Italian defenders from the island. The most important result of the invasion was its effect on the Italians. Fed up with the war, they forced Mussolini to resign. The new government began peace talks with the Allies and surrendered in September. The Germans, however, were determined to fight the Allies for control of Italy.

In early September British and American forces landed in southern Italy and struggled up the mountainous Italian Peninsula toward Rome. The Germans made them pay for every mile gained. War correspondent Ernie Pyle wrote:

> *"The hills rise to ridges of almost solid rock. You can't go around them through the flat peaceful valleys, because the Germans look down upon you and would let you have it. So you have to go up and over. . . . Each division has hundreds of horses and mules to carry it beyond the point where vehicles can go no farther. On beyond the mules' ability, mere men . . . take it on their backs."*

Developing THE SECTION

Active Learning

Role Play. Although allies, the United States, Great Britain, and the Soviet Union saw the war situation differently. Have students take the roles of Roosevelt, Churchill, and Stalin as they discuss war strategy in early 1942. What were the most urgent priorities for each leader? What compromises might be possible?

Connections: Geography

Analyzing a Map. Have students look at a map of Italy showing geographical features. Ask students what obstacles an Allied drive into Italy would face. What natural "choke points" could defenders take advantage of?

Social History

Discussion. Pilots often gave their planes fanciful names such as "Memphis Belle" and painted pictures and slogans on them. Ask students why they think they did this. What small things helped make the terror of war bearable?

Connections: Science and Technology

Discussion. Weather forecasting is not an exact science even today, and World War II meteorologists had no weather satellites for getting the "big picture." Weather reports came by radio from meteorologists in lonely outposts and ships far away at sea, sometimes on the Arctic ice. One advantage the Allies had was that prevailing west winds meant that the weather in England today was likely to be that in France tomorrow. **Ask:** Why was an accurate weather forecast crucial for the success of the D-Day invasion?

Connections: Science and Technology
World War II was the first war in which radar and electronic countermeasures played an important part. The Allies developed sonobuoys—floating sonar detectors that could be dropped from aircraft to track submarines. Submarines in turn tried to use their radar to detect approaching planes. The dilemma of radar and sonar is that their use might detect the enemy, but it also exposed you to detection. The submarine war became a deadly game of cat and mouse. (The film *Das Boot* gives a realistic depiction of the cramped life aboard a submarine and the terror of depth-charge attacks.)

Reduced student page in the Teacher's Edition

By early November the Germans had stopped the Allies near Monte Cassino, 75 miles south of Rome. To break German resistance, American forces landed on the beaches at Anzio, behind the enemy's lines. It took four months of some of the most brutal fighting of the war for the Americans to break out and smash German defenses.

The Allies liberated Rome in June 1944, then slowly but steadily pushed the German troops northward. German forces finally surrendered on May 2, 1945. A few days before, Mussolini had been captured and shot by Italian resistance fighters.

Closing in on Germany

In November 1943 American and British armies were inching toward Rome, and Soviet armies were driving the Germans off Russian soil. That month all three Allied leaders met at Teheran, Iran, to plan their next move. Churchill and Roosevelt assured Stalin that the invasion of France, called Operation Overlord, would take place by the summer of 1944.

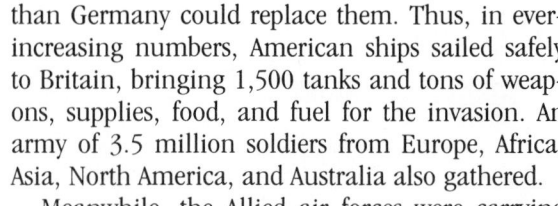

"Joe, yestiddy ya saved my life an' I swore I'd pay ya back. Here's my last pair of dry socks."

Stalin, in turn, promised to start a Soviet offensive to coincide with the invasion. He also pledged to join the war against Japan after Germany's defeat. To both Roosevelt and Churchill, this promise was important for a speedy ending of the war.

Command of the sea and air. One of the most important steps in preparing for Operation Overlord was to ensure the safe arrival of American supplies and troops in Britain. In the first four years of war, German submarines had destroyed so many tons of Allied shipping that Germany came close to cutting Britain's lifeline to North America. "The only thing that ever really frightened me during the war," Churchill admitted, "was the U-boat peril."

By mid-1943 the tide had begun to turn, however. Using radar, depth charges, and bombs, the Allies destroyed submarines both above and below the surface. The Allies began sinking U-boats faster than Germany could replace them. Thus, in ever-increasing numbers, American ships sailed safely to Britain, bringing 1,500 tanks and tons of weapons, supplies, food, and fuel for the invasion. An army of 3.5 million soldiers from Europe, Africa, Asia, North America, and Australia also gathered.

Meanwhile, the Allied air forces were carrying the war into Hitler's "Fortress Europe." Beginning in 1942, they carried out daily bombing raids on German military and industrial targets. As in the earlier German air raids on Britain, they also bombed cities. By the end of the war, German cities, factories, and railroads were in ruins, and thousands of civilians had been killed.

The German air force suffered such heavy losses that it could no longer challenge every Allied raid. On D-Day, the day of the invasion of France, General Eisenhower, the supreme commander, would be able to promise his troops, "If you see fighting aircraft over you, they will be ours."

The Allied Invasion of France

It was 4:15 A.M. on June 5, 1944. In southern Britain, the wind was howling and rain fell in sheets as the commanders of Operation Overlord gathered to hear a forecast of the next day's weather. On the basis of that prediction, Eisenhower would decide whether to launch the largest seaborne invasion in history. A fleet of 4,500 ships carrying 170,000 men was ready, with some units already at sea. More than 10,000 airplanes stood waiting on runways.

Amid the storm, the forecaster offered "a gleam of hope." The next day, June 6, he said, there would be a break in the rain for perhaps thirty-six hours, and the waves would not be high. To postpone the attack meant waiting another month before first light and low tides would again coincide. Yet a miscalculation now could mean huge casualties and perhaps defeat. "I sat silently reviewing these things, maybe 35 or 45 seconds," wrote Eisenhower later. "I just got up and said, 'O.K., we'll go.' "

Connections: Health

German, French, British, and American scientists developed sulfa drugs in the 1930s. Their use for all sorts of infections saved many lives in World War II. The British also developed penicillin in the late 1930s and it was used in the treatment of war wounds. Charles Drew, an African-American medical doctor and teacher of surgery, helped develop chemical methods of preserving blood from donors until it was needed. He also worked to set up a blood bank that could stockpile different types of blood and provide them on demand.

War in Europe and Africa 1942-1945

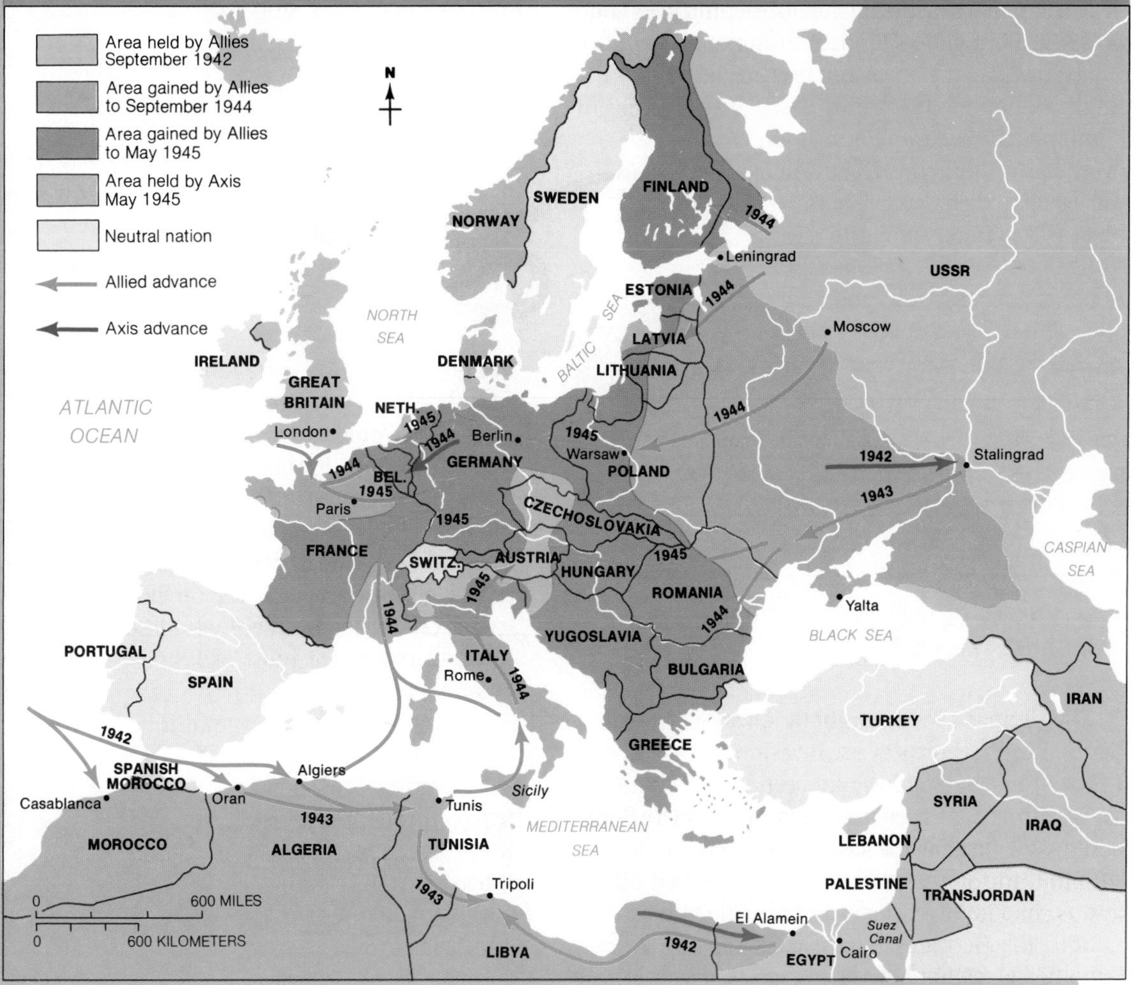

Geography Skills—Movement. At the lowest point in the war for the Allies, what parts of Europe did the Axis control? In the Allied campaign to drive back the Axis, where did the Allies make their first advances? In general, the Allies advanced on the Axis from three directions. What three areas were the springboards for those advances?

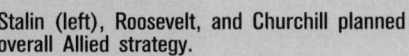

Stalin (left), Roosevelt, and Churchill planned overall Allied strategy.

Connections: Geography

Discussion. Churchill described Hitler's Europe as a crocodile—its underbelly rested on the Mediterranean and its snout pointed toward the USSR. **Ask:** How could this description explain the Allied advances from 1942 to 1945? **(invasion of Sicily and Italy would divert Germany from the Russian front)**

Geography Skills

ANSWERS

1. All of Europe but the neutral nations and Great Britain.
2. In North Africa.
3. North Africa, Russia, from Great Britain through France.

Writing About History

War Report. D-Day was one of the most dramatic scenes in world history. Have students take the role of war correspondents going ashore with the troops to write reports on the action. Reports could include the trip aboard the vast invasion fleet, "hitting the beach," the bloody fighting at Omaha Beach, and interviews with soldiers.

Multicultural Perspectives

About 500 African Americans were among the troops who went ashore at Omaha Beach on D-Day. The 761st Tank Battalion was the first African-American armored unit to enter combat in the war. Later, Major General M. S. Eddy said that this unit *"entered combat with such conspicuous courage and success as to warrant special commendation."* Ten tanks from the battalion were chosen to be in the honor guard at the German surrender in Austria.

Reduced student page in the Teacher's Edition

D-Day. The target of the invasion was 60 miles of beach in a region of northern France called Normandy. Airborne forces parachuted behind the beaches during the night to seize airfields and bridges. Silent gliders landed equipment.

Meanwhile, the invasion fleet sailed across the English Channel. Just before dawn, warships began bombing the coast. Planes screamed overhead in bombing runs. Then the troops, each loaded with almost 70 pounds of battle gear, spilled out onto the beaches. Robert Capa, the only photographer with the first troops, wrote:

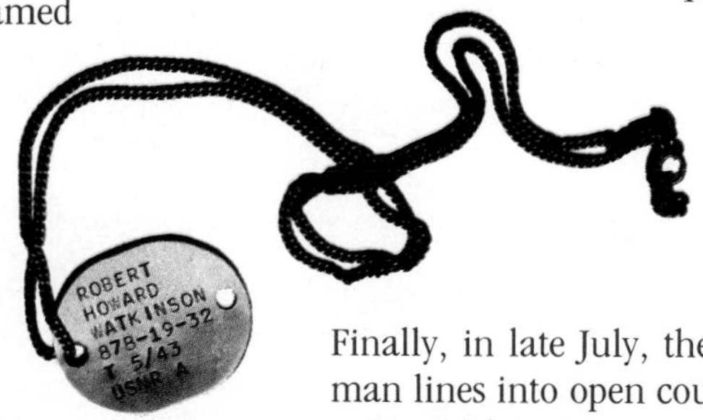

" Bullets tore holes in the water around me and I made for the nearest steel obstacle. . . . Fifty yards ahead of me, one of our half-burnt amphibious tanks offered me my next cover. . . . Between floating bodies I reached it, paused for pictures and gathered my guts for the last jump to the beach. "

The Germans were caught by surprise. The Allies had led them to expect an invasion farther north. In addition, the weather had been so bad that German patrols had been canceled on June 5. Rommel, whose army defended the French coast, was so sure that the storm would prevent an Allied attack that he had gone home for his wife's birthday.

Still, the Germans fought back fiercely. At one landing site, code-named Omaha Beach, American troops got caught in mined water and then had to make it across a beach exposed to German crossfire before they could huddle under a seawall. Omaha was secured, but more than 90 percent of the American casualties occurred there.

Total Allied casualties were high—about 10,000 soldiers—but all landing beaches were secure by the end of D-Day. During the next three weeks the Allies landed a million troops and tons of equipment, food, and supplies in Normandy.

Breaking out. The Allies slowly fought their way inland through marshes and across fields enclosed by thick hedges. German troops, ordered by Hitler to contest every inch of land, put up fierce resistance. To Samuel Fuller, a corporal in the 1st Infantry Division, those weeks passed in a sickening blur:

" You're out of control. You shoot at anything. Your eyes hurt. Your fingers hurt. You're driven by panic. We never looked at the faces of the dead, just at their feet—black boots for Germans, brown for G.I.s. "

Finally, in late July, the Allies broke through German lines into open country.

In mid-August an American-French invasion force landed on France's Mediterranean coast and advanced northward. French resistance fighters joined the advancing Allies. On August 25 American and Free French forces liberated Paris. A provisional government was set up under Free-French leader Charles de Gaulle. By mid-September the Allies had control of most of France, Belgium, and Luxembourg.

Meanwhile, in June Stalin launched his offensive. Soviet armies burst into Axis-controlled eastern Europe. They forced Romania and Bulgaria out of the war and helped to free Yugoslavia from German control. Soviet forces also swarmed across the border into German-held Poland.

The Battle of the Bulge. Hopes of a quick victory in Europe soared as the Allies on the western front reached the German border. However, in December 1944 four German armies suddenly

Connections: Science and Technology

By 1944 Allied air power was so overwhelming that German units could not move during daytime without encountering devastating attacks. Yet Germany had developed a revolutionary new plane—the jet-powered Me-262. This plane flew about 100 mph faster than the fastest Allied fighters. But Hitler insisted on concentrating on developing a jet bomber, and the Me-262s proved to be too few and too late to influence the outcome of the war. Germany also developed the first "cruise missile" (the V-1) and the first ballistic missile, the V-2, for which there was no defense.

Thinking Critically

Analysis. Some people feel in retrospect that the United States and Great Britain should have taken a harder line against Stalin in the hope of reducing Soviet influence in Eastern Europe in the postwar world. Ask students whether they agree. What advantages and disadvantages might such a course have had?

counterattacked American forces in the Ardennes Forest. The Germans broke through and advanced 50 miles in Belgium, creating a bulge in Allied lines.

Americans grimly dug in to stop the German advance in this so-called Battle of the Bulge. Typical of Allied determination was General Anthony C. McAuliffe, whose 101st Airborne Division was encircled at Bastogne. When the Germans demanded his surrender, McAuliffe replied, "Nuts!" In two weeks the Americans stopped the German advance.

A fourth term for Roosevelt. In 1944, with the Allies on the offensive in Europe, Roosevelt ran for a fourth term. Although his health was failing, he felt the nation should not change leaders during the war. In this situation, selection of the vice-presidential candidate was critical, and Roosevelt chose Senator Harry S Truman of Missouri. As head of the Senate committee investigating the nation's defense program, Truman had gained a reputation for hard work and capable leadership.

The Republicans pinned their hopes on Governor Thomas Dewey of New York, but he had little ammunition for his campaign. With the Nazis on the run, Roosevelt won another one-sided victory.

The Yalta Conference

Roosevelt was eager to make plans for the postwar world. With victory within reach in Europe, he met Churchill and Stalin at Yalta, a town in southern Russia, in February 1945. The leaders completed plans, begun earlier, for a new peace-keeping organization, the United Nations. Then they agreed that after its surrender Germany would be divided into four zones. The United States, Britain, the Soviet Union, and France would each have control of one zone.

At the time, American commanders were predicting many more months of hard fighting against Japan. At Roosevelt's urging, Stalin promised to join that war within three months of Germany's defeat.

D-Day forces secured five beachheads, then prepared to advance on Paris.

Limited English Proficiency

Building Vocabulary. Refer students to the term *Holocaust* on this page. The term derives from the Greek word *holokaustos*, meaning "burnt whole." Ask students how this derivation relates to the term as defined in the text. **(Germans wished to destroy all Jews, as a fire totally destroys.)**

Global Connections

Discussion. Ask students what "grave difficulties" they think Churchill foresaw in the Soviet actions in eastern Europe. **(spread of communism)** Did his predictions come true? Tell students that these problems will be the focus of Chapter 25.

Analyzing Primary Sources

A Holocaust Survivor. The Holocaust Oral History project in San Francisco has recorded over 900 accounts by Holocaust survivors. One survivor, Linda Breder, 67 years old, spoke before the cameras: *"My only reason to survive was to make sure that the whole world knows of the suffering. . . . To all of us [survivors], it means life after death, and that the memories of those who suffered and were killed will never be forgotten."*

Ask: To what does Breder attribute her survival? **(the will to let others know of the Holocaust)** Do you think the oral testimony of Holocaust survivors might be more powerful than written accounts? Why? How might these accounts help fight anti-Semitism and racism today?

Connections: Literature

Although millions died in Nazi concentration camps, some people survived to tell the world of the horrors they experienced. Elie Wiesel, a Holocaust survivor, was awarded the 1986 Nobel Peace Prize in recognition of his life's work as a chronicler of the Holocaust. In *Night,* Wiesel gives an account of the Holocaust as witnessed by a fifteen-year-old boy.

Reduced student page in the Teacher's Edition

In return, Roosevelt and Churchill agreed that the Soviet Union could take the southern half of Sakhalin Island and the Kurile Islands from Japan.

The Big Three also reached agreements about eastern Europe. By this time Soviet armies were in control of large areas that they had liberated from the Germans. Poland was now completely occupied by the Soviets. Roosevelt and Churchill accepted Stalin's proposal that the Soviet Union keep much of the Polish territory it had occupied in 1939, and give Poland territory from Germany.

Stalin had already set up a temporary Polish government under Soviet control. Roosevelt and Churchill demanded that he enlarge the government to include democratic leaders from Poland itself and the Polish government in exile in London. Stalin agreed and joined his allies in a pledge to support the right of the liberated peoples in eastern Europe to establish governments of their own choosing.

Roosevelt did not live to see the outcome of the Yalta agreements. On April 12, 1945, he died of a cerebral hemorrhage, and Vice-President Truman took his place. Since Yalta, however, Roosevelt and Churchill had realized that the Soviet Union was doing nothing to make the Polish government more democratic. Worried, Churchill foresaw "grave difficulties" if Soviet power came to dominate Europe.

American Voices

"So much depends in the future on how we learn to live together. Do you think it will be possible for the United States and the USSR to see things in similar ways?"

—Roosevelt to Stalin, 1943

Victory in Europe

The collapse of Germany came less than a month after Roosevelt's death. Russian forces had completed their sweep through Poland and poured into Germany from the east. Advancing all along the western front, the Allies had cleared the Germans out of the Netherlands and had swept into northern and central Germany. Hitler ordered his soldiers to fight to the death, but thousands surrendered.

By April 25 Soviet troops had surrounded Berlin. Five days later, Hitler committed suicide. On May 7, 1945, the head of the German military agreed to unconditional surrender. After six years of war, the Allies had finally achieved victory in Europe.

The Holocaust

The most shocking part of the Allied victory was seeing the **Holocaust**— the extermination of more than 6 million European Jews by the Nazis. During the war, underground groups had gathered growing evidence of Germany's genocide against Jews. Reports appearing in American newspapers as early as 1942 were ignored or never completely believed, however. Remembering false "atrocity tales" from World War I, many Americans were skeptical. In addition, horror stories from the Nazi camps seemed beyond belief.

The extent of the atrocities was found to be true, however. Allied forces liberating survivors of concentration and death camps in Germany and eastern Europe found mass graves and uncovered evidence of the Nazis' methods of mass murder. American photographer Margaret Bourke-White was with the American Third Army when it reached Buchenwald in Germany in April 1945. She wrote:

"I saw and photographed the piles of naked, lifeless bodies, the human skeletons in furnaces, the living skeletons who would die the next day because they had to wait too long for deliverance, the pieces of tattooed skin for lampshades. . . . Buchenwald was more than the mind could grasp."

Mass killing of Jews began in 1941 with the German invasion of Russia. Death camps were established in Poland a year later, with trainloads of Jews brought from all over occupied Europe.

The horror of the camps was not only the vast number of people who died, but also the Nazis' cold-blooded use of bureaucracy and technology to round up and kill their victims. As a "final solution to the Jewish problem," the Nazis had forced Jews into ghettos in cities, transported them to death camps where they were shot or killed by poison gas, and burned their bodies in huge furnaces.

Jews were not the only victims. More than 5 million political opponents of the Nazis, and other people Germans considered inferior— including Gypsies, homosexuals, and the physically and mentally handicapped—were also put to death.

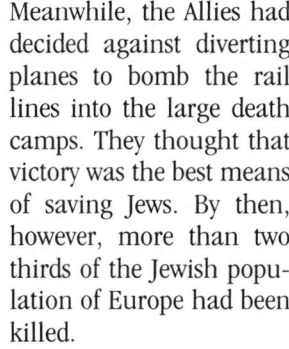

As the truth about the Holocaust broke upon the world, people began to ask themselves why more had not been done to save the victims. Early in the war, many nations had refused to accept refugees desperate to flee Germany. In the United States, President Roosevelt failed to press Congress to relax immigration restrictions. He feared stirring up anti-Semitism at home.

Not until 1944 did Roosevelt set up the War Refugee Board, which rescued 200,000 European Jews. Meanwhile, the Allies had decided against diverting planes to bomb the rail lines into the large death camps. They thought that victory was the best means of saving Jews. By then, however, more than two thirds of the Jewish population of Europe had been killed.

Section Review

1. **Identification.** Define *Holocaust.*

2. **Comprehension.** Why were the Allies eager to win victories in Africa and the Soviet Union?

3. **Analysis.** On what factors did the successful launching of Operation Overlord depend?

4. **Evaluation.** Do you think that Roosevelt and Churchill's decisions at the Yalta Conference were based on a realistic appraisal of the military situation? Give reasons for your answer.

5. **Synthesis.** Speculate about why guards and other workers in death camps carried out their orders to execute prisoners.

Thinking Critically

Evaluation. Divide the class into small groups to discuss whether the Holocaust was a terrible but isolated event, or something that could happen again. How did the anti-Semitic nature of the Holocaust make it uniquely terrible? Ask students if they know of races or ethnic groups who have been victims of *genocide*—the attempt to kill an entire ethnic group. (Some examples are the Armenians in Turkey during World War I, Cambodians under Pol Pot during the 1970s.) What can be done to prevent future genocides?

Section Review

ANSWERS

1. Definition for the term *Holocaust* is on text page 654.
2. Victory in Africa gave Allies bases from which to invade southern Europe. Victory in Soviet Union halted Germany's eastward advance in Europe, led to Soviet offensive.
3. Safe arrival of American troops and supplies in Britain; weakening German air force; favorable weather; coordinating forces.
4. Opinions that it was realistic may note that the Soviet Union already occupied most of eastern Europe, and the United States and Britain expected to need Soviet help in war against Japan. However, given Stalin's previous behavior, it was hardly realistic to expect he would allow self-determination in eastern Europe.
5. Extreme anti-Semitism of many Germans; the high value Germans gave to absolute obedience; the desire to stay alive.

Section 24-3

B · A · C · K · G · R · O · U · N · D

Connections: Science and Technology
American code breakers used a clever trick to find out about the Japanese plans for Midway. The Japanese used code letters such as AF to refer to the objective of their next attack. But where was "AF"? The Americans sent out an uncoded radio message saying that Midway was running short of water. Soon a coded Japanese message was intercepted. It said "AF short of water." Now the Americans knew that Midway was the objective.

Objectives

- ***Answer the Focus Question.***
- *Evaluate the importance of the Battle of Midway.*
- *Analyze how the Pacific war differed from the war in Europe.*

Introducing

THE SECTION

Point out to students that the Allied strategy in the Pacific involved three overall objectives: recapturing the Philippines, severing Japan's lines of communications, and establishing of bases from which an attack on Japan could be made. Have students keep these objectives in mind as they read the section.

Reduced student page in the Teacher's Edition

24-3 The War in the Pacific

Focus: How did the Allies defeat Japan?

Like the war in Europe, the war in the Pacific was a long, hard struggle against a mighty enemy. By mid-1942, Japan had gained control of much of eastern and southern China, all of Southeast Asia, and most of the Pacific islands west of Midway, including American-held Guam and Wake.

By then, too, after a desperate three-month stand, American and Filipino forces in the Philippines had had to surrender to the Japanese. General Douglas MacArthur, commander of American forces, left the Philippines, vowing, "I shall return," but his promise rang hollow in the face of such overwhelming defeats.

Slowly, however, the Allies began to gain ground. On the Asian mainland they helped Chinese forces fight the Japanese. They also fought to recapture Burma and reopen the Burma Road connecting British India with China. For three years American pilots known as the Flying Tigers were the sole lifeline supplying Allied forces in China, flying from India on a hair-raising route across the Himalayas, the world's highest mountains.

The main American thrust, however, was in the Pacific. American forces launched dozens of invasions like D-Day to take far-flung islands held by the Japanese.

From Pearl Harbor to Midway

On April 18, 1942, just four months after Pearl Harbor, General James H. Doolittle led a group of B-25 bombers in a raid on Tokyo. Taking off from an aircraft carrier in the Central Pacific more than 600 miles east of Japan, the planes dropped their payloads on the Japanese capital. Although the raid did little damage, it raised American morale and proved that Japan was not invincible.

Japan's next step was to extend its defenses by advancing into the South Pacific, cutting Australia off from the Allies and striking again at Hawaii. That decision would lead to Japan's first defeats in the war.

On May 7 and 8, 1942, in the Coral Sea near New Guinea, an American naval force stopped a Japanese fleet that was advancing on Australia. Unlike any naval engagement in history, this one was fought entirely by planes launched from aircraft carriers. The ships were never within sight of each other. Neither side won a clear victory, but the

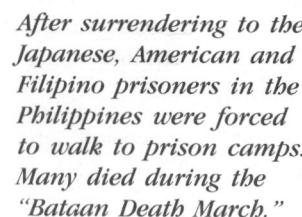

After surrendering to the Japanese, American and Filipino prisoners in the Philippines were forced to walk to prison camps. Many died during the "Bataan Death March."

Multicultural Perspectives

The Navajo code talkers also "scrambled around" their Navajo words as an added precaution. Even if the Japanese found someone who knew Navajo, the messages would still make little, if any, sense. The Japanese never broke the code, however, and several of the Navajo were awarded Purple Hearts for their valor under fire.

Developing

THE SECTION

Active Learning

Making Charts. Have students start a chart that lists the successive goals of American forces in the Pacific and the reasons why each goal was important. For example:

Goal—Coral Sea; **Why Important**—Prevent Japanese advance toward Australia.
Goal—Midway; **Why Important**—Keep Japanese out of central Pacific; destroy a major Japanese fleet.

Battle of the Coral Sea checked the Japanese threat to Australia.

Less than a month later, Japanese naval commander Isoroku Yamamoto moved on Midway Island, a stepping stone to Hawaii. Learning of the planned attack when code breakers cracked the Japanese naval code, Admiral Chester W. Nimitz reinforced Midway with planes and aircraft carriers. In the battle, Japan lost four aircraft carriers, a third of its airplanes, and the lives of more than 3,000 men. The Battle of Midway ended the Japanese advance. It proved to be a turning point of the Pacific war.

American Voices

"Navajo Marines transmitted and received messages, orders, vital information. The Japanese ground their teeth."

—American newspaper

Leapfrogging to Japan

After Midway, American military leaders worked out a strategy for defeating Japan. From Australia, Allied forces under General MacArthur would advance across the South Pacific, taking New Guinea and the Philippines. Forces under Admiral Nimitz would take Japanese-held islands in the Central Pacific. Nimitz would then join MacArthur in the Philippines for the final assault on Japan.

The American strategy also called for "island hopping," or "leapfrogging." In their drive toward Japan, American forces would bypass some islands defended by the Japanese and take others. American planes based on these islands could keep Japanese ships from supplying the bypassed outposts, rendering them useless.

Lessons of Guadalcanal. In August 1942 American marines began to clear the southern route to Japan. Their first target was Guadalcanal in the Solomon Islands, where the Japanese were building an airbase from which to attack Allied ships. Matted with rain forests, Guadalcanal taught the Americans about jungle warfare. There was steaming heat, malaria, snakes, and rains heavy enough to drown a wounded soldier.

Guadalcanal also taught Americans about the tenacity of Japanese soldiers. Eugene B. Sledge, with the 1st Marine Division, wrote:

> *"The Japanese fought by a code they thought was right:* bushido. *The code of the warrior: no surrender. You don't really comprehend it until you get out there and fight people who are faced with an absolutely hopeless situation and will not give up. . . . To be captured was a disgrace."*

Both Japan and the United States poured reinforcements into Guadalcanal in one of the fiercest battles of the war. Finally, in February 1943 the Japanese evacuated what they now called the "Island of Death." Then MacArthur's forces moved on to the northern Solomons.

American communication in the Pacific was aided by a special unit of Navajo marines who served as "code talkers." The Navajo language was as good as a secret code, for only twenty-eight non-Navajo spoke it. A newspaper described the code talkers in action:

> *"Huddled over their radio sets in bobbing assault barges, in foxholes on the beach, in slit trenches, deep in the jungle, the Navajo marines transmitted and received messages, orders, vital information. The Japanese ground their teeth."*

While MacArthur's forces attacked the Japanese in northern New Guinea, Nimitz's forces struck at Makin and Tarawa in the Gilbert Islands. Once captured, these islands became bases for bombing raids on the Marshalls, the next step "up the ladder" to Japan. By the end of February 1944, the Marshalls were in Allied hands, and Nimitz's troops went on to the Mariana Islands, which were within bombing distance of Japan.

Flying Tigers insignia

Connections: Geography

Discussion. Ask students why the Japanese desperately defended Leyte Gulf and the Philippines. How did Allied control of the Philippines and the surrounding seas threaten Japan? **(provided air bases closer to Japan, made it easier to cut off supplies coming to Japan from the Asian mainland and southeast Asian islands)**

Multicultural Perspectives

About 500,000 Hispanic Americans served in the armed forces in World War II. A higher percentage of Hispanics took part in overseas combat than any other ethnic group in the United States. They also received more combat medals than any other ethnic group in the nation. Twelve Hispanic Americans received the Congressional Medal of Honor, including Technical Sergeant Cleto Rodriguez for his brave role in the Philippines and José López, who held back a German counterattack during the Normandy invasion.

Reduced student page in the Teacher's Edition

By August, American forces had occupied Saipan, Tinian, and Guam, the three most important islands in the Marianas. From Guam, once more in American hands, a radio operator happily tapped out a message to Pearl Harbor: "This news is from Radio Guam. Nothing heard from you since 1941. Greetings."

Liberating the Philippines. In October 1944 Central Pacific forces under Nimitz and South Pacific forces under MacArthur converged on the Philippine island of Leyte (LAYT-ee). Wading ashore after troops had stormed the beaches, MacArthur announced, "People of the Philippines, I have returned. . . . Rally to me."

The Japanese risked what was left of their fleet to drive MacArthur out again. For three days, Japanese and American ships clashed in the Battle of Leyte Gulf, the largest naval battle in history.

As the tide turned against them, the Japanese unleashed a desperate new weapon, *Kamikaze* pilots. They were named for the "Divine Wind," a typhoon that had saved Japan in the thirteenth century by destroying an invading armada. Kamikaze pilots deliberately crashed their explosive-laden planes into American warships. As one pilot explained before his suicide mission, "I am nothing but a particle of iron attracted by a magnet—the American aircraft carrier."

Planes with folded wings line the deck of an American carrier.

When the Battle of Leyte Gulf was over, Japan had lost most of its aircraft and nearly all of its warships. However, it took the Americans and 250,000 Filipino guerrillas months of hard fighting to dislodge Japanese ground troops in the Philippines. Finally, in March 1945 the Americans and Filipinos captured the war-torn capital of Manila.

Victory in the Pacific

By early 1945 the Allies had won command of the sea and the air in the Pacific. American submarines were sinking ships that tried to bring vital supplies to Japan, and American planes were bombing Japanese industries. Americans also began to drop incendiary bombs on cities. Igniting on impact, the bombs spread fire everywhere. Despite widespread destruction and heavy civilian casualties, the Japanese continued to resist.

In February Nimitz's forces invaded the small island of Iwo Jima, hoping to use its airfield as a bomber base. It took the Americans nearly six weeks of bitter fighting to secure the 8-square-mile island, at a cost of 25,000 casualties, with almost 7,000 dead.

The successful fight for Okinawa, the last stepping stone to Japan, was even bloodier. Desperate Japanese counterattacks caused heavy American losses. Kamikaze planes came in by the hundreds. Japan also sent its last remaining warships—with fuel for only a one-way trip—into the battle. By the time the two-month struggle ended in late June, the Americans had suffered 50,000 casualties. More than 100,000 Japanese were killed.

In spite of Japan's staggering losses, Allied commanders worried about the risks of invading Japan itself. They suspected that the Japanese would fight to repel an invasion of their homeland with the same fury that had made the conquests of Iwo Jima and Okinawa so costly.

War in the Pacific and Asia 1942-1945

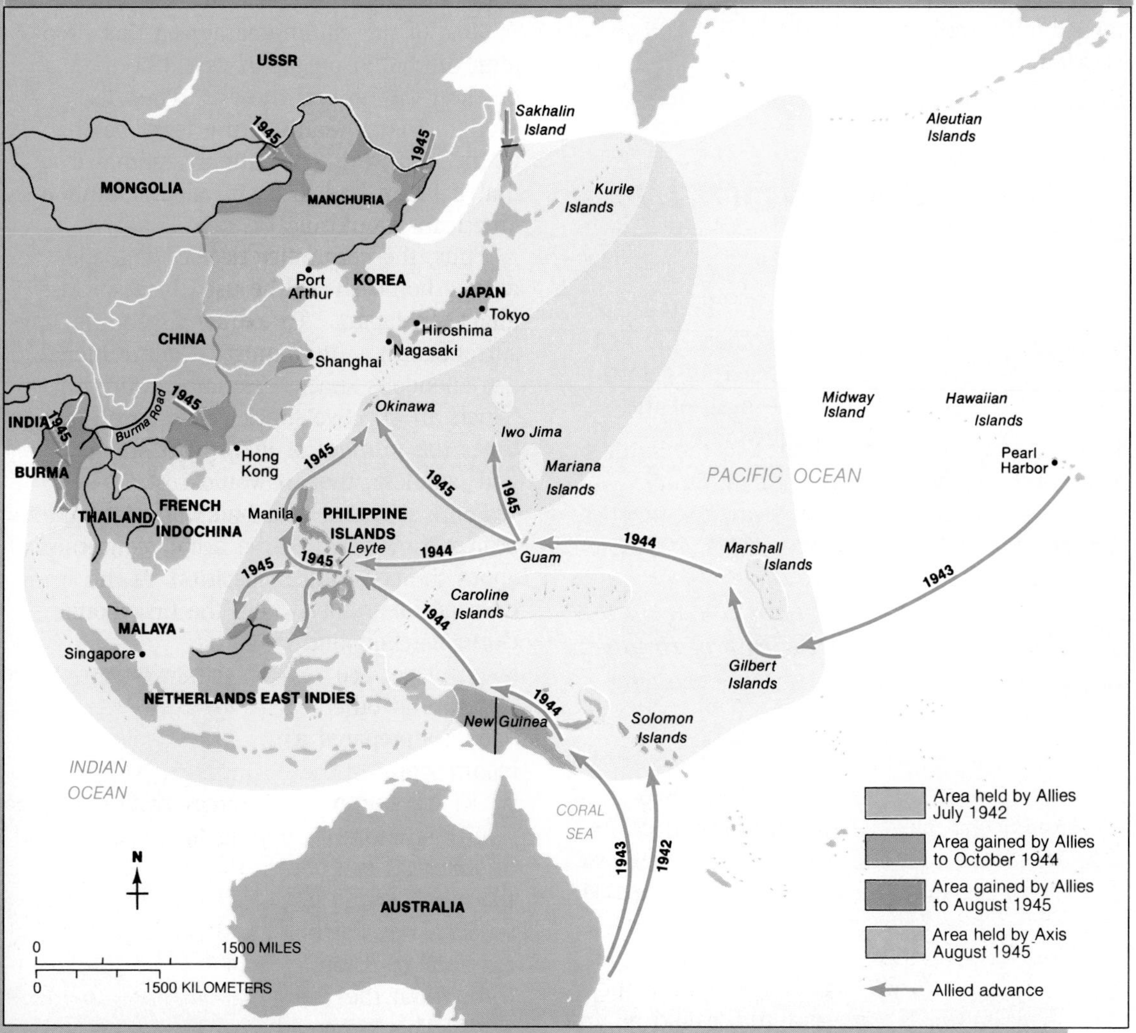

Geography Skills—Movement. From what two sites did the Allies start their two-pronged advance across the Pacific in 1942? Briefly describe the progress of this advance year by year. What territories had the Allies regained by the last year of the war? What territories were still held by the Axis?

Insignias: China-Burma-India theater of war (upper left), Pacific Ocean area (left), and Southeast Asia.

Geography Skills

ANSWERS

1. Hawaii, Australia.
2. 1942, Solomon Islands; 1943, Gilbert Islands, New Guinea; 1944, Guam, New Guinea, Philippine Islands; 1945, Philippine Islands, Netherlands East Indies, Okinawa, Iwo Jima.
3. Solomons, Gilberts, New Guinea, much of the Philippines; some of the East Indies, most of Burma, some of China, some of Manchuria, part of Sakhalin Island.
4. Marshalls, Carolines, Marianas, most of the East Indies, Thailand, Indochina, large parts of China, Manchuria, Korea, part of Sakhalin Island.

Linking Past and Present

Research. American officials in 1991 were concerned that Iraqi dictator Saddam Hussein was continuing to try to develop nuclear weapons despite his defeat in the Gulf War. Have students do research on the problem of the control of nuclear technology today.

Thinking Critically

Analysis. Why would an invasion of Japan have cost so many lives? How would it have been different from the D-Day invasion? How many islands would have been involved?

Multicultural Contributions

The story of nuclear fission and the atomic bomb involves an international cast of characters. Ironically two key figures, Albert Einstein and Max Born, were Jews who fled from Nazi Germany. When another great physicist, Enrico Fermi, went to Stockholm in 1938, with his Jewish wife to collect the Nobel Prize for work in nuclear fission, the couple went on to the United States rather than return to Mussolini's Italy and its Hitler-style anti-Semitism.

The generation of scientists who made the atomic breakthrough were keenly aware of the destructive potential of their discoveries. Many agreed to work on an American atomic bomb only because they were afraid that Hitler would get one first.

Reduced student page in the Teacher's Edition

Exploring Issues

USING NUCLEAR WEAPONS

The Atomic Bomb

On July 16, 1945, scientists in the top-secret Manhattan Project exploded the first atomic device in the New Mexican desert. J. Robert Oppenheimer, the head of the project, recalled his thoughts as he watched the explosion from a bunker:

> *"A few people laughed, a few people cried, most people were silent. There floated through my mind a line from the* Bhagavad-Gita *[a sacred work of Hinduism]: 'I am become death, the shatterer of worlds.'"*

For more than two years, thousands of Americans had worked frantically to create a successful atomic bomb in the belief that Germany was developing a weapon capable of deciding the war. "There was the feeling," one scientist said, "that the Germans had a four years' head start on us. If they were as good as we were, that would be an end of the United States."

In May 1945, even before the atomic bomb was tested, Secretary of War Henry Stimson had organized a committee of government officials and scientists to decide how to use it. Some of the scientists favored a demonstration of the bomb in an uninhabited area. After seeing this "enormous nuclear firecracker," one scientist said, the Japanese might surrender. Oppenheimer, however, doubted that a harmless demonstration would "convince the Japanese they ought to throw in the sponge."

Most of the committee agreed that dropping the bomb on Japan would be the quickest way to end the war. They also thought that it would cause fewer deaths in the long run. The military estimated that if Japan had to be invaded, a million Americans would die.

Thus, the committee decided that the atomic bomb should be used in a surprise attack on Japan. "To extract a genuine surrender . . . they must be administered a tremendous shock," explained Stimson. "Such an effective shock would save many times the number of lives, both American and Japanese, than it would cost."

Some scientists who had worked on the project, however, became deeply concerned about the committee's decision. At the Chicago laboratory where the first atomic chain reaction had taken place, Leo Szilard and other scientists prepared a report opposing the use of the bomb.

The scientists argued that use of the bomb would send "a wave of horror and repulsion" throughout the world. They proposed "a demonstration of the new weapon before the eyes of the representatives of all the United Nations, on the desert or a barren island."

The ruins of Nagasaki, Japan

The "Chicago report" forced the committee to reconsider its decision. Again, however, it rejected a demonstration.

One member of the committee did change his mind. Undersecretary of the Navy Ralph Bard came to believe that Japan was so weak that it might surrender with just a warning about the bomb's destructiveness. General Dwight D. Eisenhower agreed, believing that "Japan was already defeated." However, the committee's decision had been made.

1. Why did the committee recommend a surprise atomic attack on Japan?
2. Why did scientists at the Chicago laboratory oppose using the atomic bomb? What did they suggest instead?
3. Do you think the United States should have used the atomic bomb? If not, what alternatives would you suggest?

The atomic bomb. On July 17, 1945, Truman met Churchill and Stalin in Potsdam, Germany, to discuss plans for postwar Europe and map strategies for the final defeat of Japan. The day after he arrived, Truman received a cable from the United States that read, "Diagnosis not yet complete, but results seem satisfactory." Truman understood the message: the United States had successfully tested an atomic bomb.

Since 1939, when nuclear fission was discovered in Germany, scientists in every major industrial nation had been aware of the possibility of producing an extremely powerful explosion by splitting the atom. Fearful that Germany would take the lead, President Roosevelt had set up the top-secret Manhattan Project in 1942 in order to develop atomic weapons.

Once the bomb was a reality, atomic scientists and Truman's advisors debated whether the United States should use such a powerful weapon. By using the bomb, the United States could end the war without invading the Japanese islands, and without the help of Stalin, whom President Truman heartily distrusted.

Truman made up his mind quickly. "I regarded the bomb as a military weapon," he wrote later, "and never had any doubt that it should be used." Both Britain, which had worked with the United States on the bomb, and the Soviet Union, which was already secretly working on its own atomic weapons, approved Truman's decision.

On July 26 the Allied leaders issued an ultimatum to Japan to surrender before August 3 or face "prompt and utter destruction." In Japan the government, torn between surrendering unconditionally and continuing the struggle, allowed the deadline to pass.

"A rain of ruin." At precisely 8:15 A.M. on August 6, 1945, a B-29 bomber named the *Enola Gay* dropped an atomic bomb on Hiroshima, the site of numerous war plants and a major assembly point for convoys. Military strategists believed its destruction "would most adversely affect the will of the Japanese to continue the war."

Forty-three seconds later, a flash appeared in the air above the city and grew larger and larger. From his tail-gunner's seat, Sergeant George Caron reported the scene:

Exploring Issues

ANSWERS

1. The committee believed that a surprise atomic attack on Japan would be the quickest way to end the war and would cause fewer deaths in the long run.
2. The Chicago group opposed using the bomb because it would send a "wave of horror and repulsion" around the world. They urged a demonstration in an unpopulated area.
3. Answers will vary.

Active Learning

Making a Time Line. In pairs, have students make a time line of the Allied campaign in the Pacific from June 1942 to August 1945. Below the time line students should describe how one event affected the other.

In a class discussion ask students how fighting in the Pacific differed from fighting in Europe. (Most fighting in the Pacific took place in jungles and was characterized by amphibious landings on small islands. Thus, naval superiority was vitally important.)

GTV Side 4

Chap. 6, Frame 23271

Echoes of War: Japanese-American Internment (Movie Segment)

Search and Play:

Writing About History

Eyewitness Account. Captain William S. Parsons, Manhattan Project's chief ordinance officer, described the men on board as "amazed and speechless." He said, *"One of them simply stared and softly murmured a single, 'My God.'"*

Have students write an account of the reactions of an American on the home front to the first use of the atomic bomb, until then held secret. What feelings were uppermost? Awe of the power of a bomb (with an explosive force of 20,000 tons of TNT)? Fear of the consequences of its use?

Thinking Critically

Evaluation. The destruction and loss of life in Hiroshima and Nagasaki were terrible, but comparable to the firebombing of Tokyo and Dresden earlier in the war. Ask students whether they think there are significant moral differences between the nuclear and non-nuclear attacks. What alternative might there have been to using the atomic bombs or invading Japan at the cost of many American lives?

"A column of smoke rising fast. It has a fiery red core. Here it comes, the mushroom shape. . . . It's like a mass of bubbling molasses. It's nearly level with us and climbing. . . . The city must be below that."

Found in the ruins of Hiroshima, this watch shows the effects of the atomic explosion.

The heat in the fireball above the city was later calculated at 540,000 degrees Fahrenheit. At ground zero, directly below the explosion, a hospital was vaporized. Within 1,000 yards of ground zero, the surface of granite building stones melted; 2 miles away, wood buildings burst into flame.

The explosion killed between 80,000 and 100,000 people. Many survivors were so badly burned that their skin peeled off in large strips. Even people who appeared unhurt began to die—the first victims of radiation sickness. A young woman who survived wrote:

"I felt I had lost all the bones in my body. . . . I passed out. By the time I woke up, black rain was falling. We thought it was oil, the B-29s coming back to drop oil on us to burn us up. I couldn't see. I thought I was blind, but I got my eyes open, and I saw a beautiful blue sky and a dead city. Nobody is standing up. Nobody is walking around."

The black drops that were pelting people were not oil but rain polluted with deadly radioactivity. Eventually, the number of deaths that resulted directly from the bomb was set at 140,000.

In the United States, Truman warned Japan to surrender or "expect a rain of ruin from the air, the like of which has never been seen on this earth." Japan did not reply. On August 8 the Soviet Union declared war on Japan and invaded Manchuria. Soviet troops also moved toward Korea.

Still Japan did not surrender. On August 9 the United States dropped an atomic bomb on Nagasaki, a shipbuilding center. The city was destroyed, and between 35,000 and 70,000 people were killed.

That night Emperor Hirohito said that Japan should surrender on the sole condition that the Allies would allow him to remain as ruler. "The time has come," he said, "when we must bear the unbearable." The United States agreed to let the emperor keep the throne under the authority of an Allied supreme commander. The surrender of Japan became official on September 2, 1945.

Aftermath of War

Japan's surrender ended the deadliest conflict in human history. World War II claimed the lives of more than 55 million people, over half of them civilians. Of the civilians, 11 million, including 6 million Jews, were ruthlessly exterminated in German concentration and death camps. The Soviet Union suffered the greatest civilian losses of any country: nearly 20 million dead—one tenth of the nation's population—and 25 million left homeless. At least 10 million civilians in China died.

The destruction was almost as appalling. Air raids, land battles, and street fighting had left hundreds of cities in ruins. Stalingrad and the Polish capital of Warsaw were almost completely flattened. Fire storms sparked by incendiary bombs consumed the ancient, beautiful city of Dresden, Germany, which had little military importance. Atomic bombs leveled Hiroshima and Nagasaki. So much of Berlin was destroyed that engineers estimated it would take fifteen years simply to clear all the rubble.

The fighting also destroyed manufacturing, agriculture, and transportation systems. In 1946 Western Europe's production of coal, iron, and steel was less than one third the 1939 output. Agriculture suffered even more severely. The little that was grown could not be distributed because railways had been destroyed. In 1947, drought followed by a harsh winter ruined crops and led to widespread famine. Europe, declared Winston Churchill, was "a rubble heap."

Global Connections
The Japanese probably believed that the United States had many atomic bombs left in its arsenal. In fact, there were only two remaining. These were scheduled to be dropped on August 13 and 16 if Japan did not surrender.

Meanwhile the roads in Europe were jammed with millions of starving, homeless people, uprooted by the war. People who had been forced to work in Germany during the war as well as Jewish survivors of death camps tried to make their way home or find another haven. On the road, too, were Germans fleeing from formerly Nazi-held areas of eastern Europe and Russians moving westward to territories now occupied by Soviet armies.

New threats. In proportion to population, the United States, with 400,000 dead, suffered less than either its allies or its enemies, and American territory escaped the devastation that confronted Europe and Asia. In fact, at war's end, the United States was the strongest nation on earth, both economically and militarily.

General MacArthur spoke for many when he said, "It is my earnest hope . . . that a better world shall emerge out of the blood and carnage of the past." However, the rejoicing and the hope were overshadowed by two new threats. First, the existence of atomic weapons imperiled the world's security. Second, the Soviet Union, having emerged from the war with new territory and influence, was flexing its muscles in both Europe and Asia.

During the war the United States and the Soviet Union had been uneasy allies. Now, two superpowers, they stood facing each other across the ruins.

Section Review

1. Evaluation. Do you agree or disagree that the Battle of Midway was critical to American victory in the Pacific war? Explain.

2. Comprehension. What was the American strategy for defeating Japan?

3. Analysis. How did the Pacific war differ from the war in Europe? What was common to each?

4. Synthesis. Why can Truman's decision to use the atomic bomb be viewed as the most important decision of the war?

Linking Past and Present. The Allied scientists who developed the atomic bomb greatly underestimated its destructive power. Gather information about the biological effects of radiation that have been discovered since the war.

Connections to Themes

Shaping Democracy

The Japanese attack on Pearl Harbor had a radical effect on American attitudes. In a single day, the nation discarded isolationism. As Americans went to war again, they may have felt less idealism than in 1917, but they were united in a firm determination to rid the world of fascist dictators. A poet summed up the national mood: "It is but one more task that must be done/ To quench the flame that would engulf the world."

Thirty months later, on the eve of D-Day, General Eisenhower sent a message to his troops expressing the nation's sense of mission in this war. "The hopes and prayers of liberty-loving people march with you," he said. "In company with our brave Allies . . . on other fronts, you will bring about the destruction of the German war machine, the elimination of Nazi tyranny over the oppressed peoples of Europe, and security for ourselves in a free world."

As victory drew near, the American people and their leaders accepted a new reality: there could be no return to isolationism in this global age. Indeed, the United States had already taken the lead in creating a new international organization—the United Nations.

Americans were eager to turn their backs on war. Within three years, however, the world would again be divided into two armed camps, and the free world would once again look to the United States for leadership in helping to preserve and extend freedom and democracy throughout the world.

Section Review

ANSWERS

1. Answers may include that Midway stopped the Japanese advance and destroyed four aircraft carriers and a third of Japanese planes; or that the United States, with its vast industrial base and store of resources would have won the war anyway.
2. Forces under MacArthur would take New Guinea and the Philippines. Forces under Nimitz would take the islands in the central Pacific. The two forces would converge for a final assault on Japan.
3. Differences: war in the Pacific was fought as much by sea as by land and used "leap-frogging," while in Europe, forces advanced steadily; the Pacific war depended primarily on American forces, while the European war depended on American, British, Russian forces; in the Pacific, the military had to contend with jungle conditions—extreme heat, malaria, and snakes; tanks were more important in Europe. Both parts of the war involved terrific casualties and slow arduous advances. Air power was important in both.
4. The decision involved the use of the most destructive weapon yet known. It also raised the possibility that atomic warfare would dominate future wars and the fear that all humanity might be destroyed.
Linking Past and Present: Answers will vary.

Chapter Survey

ANSWERS

Using New Vocabulary

The *Holocaust* was the (a) extermination or (e) genocide of European Jews by the Nazis. It was carried out by means of (d) atrocities at concentration camps like (c) Buchenwald.

Reviewing the Chapter

1. Wartime production ended the depression, introduced government regulation of production, and introduced rationing.
2. Bought war bonds, participated in scrap drives, participated in rationing and conscription programs.
3. Racial tension increased as members of different groups interacted at work and often competed for scarce housing. Struggle against racism increased as racial and ethnic groups demanded equal treatment for equal service to their country in the military.
4. Government violated the rights of Japanese Americans by putting them in internment camps in response to racist suspicions heightened by war hysteria.
5. Needed to protect access to Suez Canal, a vital supply line. After German defeat, Allies invaded southern Europe (Italy) from North Africa to force Germans to fight on two fronts.
6. Churchill, Roosevelt, Stalin. Agreed on Allied invasion of western Europe. Churchill and Roosevelt distrusted Stalin and vice versa, disagreed among themselves on timing of invasion.
7. Allies' capture of Sicily in July-August 1943 led Italians to force Mussolini from office. Invasion of Italian mainland began in September 1943. Allied forces pushed slowly northward, stopped by Germans at Monte Casino in November. Infusion of American troops from Anzio beaches turned the tide. Rome liberated in June 1944, but German forces kept on fighting in Italy until May 1945.
8. Plans for United Nations, division of Germany into four occupation zones; Stalin promised to enter fight against Japan after Germany defeated in exchange for islands; USSR to keep Polish territory and to set up more democratic governments in Poland and eastern Europe. Significant because agreements set up problems of postwar world, as well as international peacekeeping organization.
9. Allied forces under MacArthur would advance across South Pacific while forces under Nimitz would take enemy islands in Central Pacific. Forces would unite in Philippines for final assault on Japan. Forces would use strategy of island hopping.
10. Supplying islands difficult because islands easily attacked.

Chapter Survey

Using New Vocabulary

From the list below, select the four words or terms whose meanings are related to the underlined vocabulary term and explain the relationship.

Holocaust

(a) extermination
(b) OPA
(c) Buchenwald
(d) atrocities
(e) genocide
(f) Churchill

Reviewing the Chapter

1. Describe at least three ways in which American entry into World War II changed the economy.

2. In what ways did Americans show their willingness to support the war effort?

3. How did wartime increase both racial tension and the struggle against racism?

4. How did the government violate the rights of Japanese Americans during the war? What proved to be the basic cause of such drastic action?

5. Why did the Allies need to defeat the Germans in North Africa? How did their victory fit into Allied strategy for Europe?

6. Who were the "Big Three"? On what did they agree in the early years of the war? On what did they disagree?

7. Describe the Allied campaign in Italy. Why did it continue after Italy surrendered?

8. What were the outcomes of the Yalta Conference? Why were they significant?

9. Describe the Allied strategy in the Pacific.

10. What problems did geography pose for Allied forces in the Pacific?

Thinking Critically

1. Application. Roosevelt called World War II "the survival war." What did he mean? Do you agree? Why or why not?

2. Synthesis. Form a hypothesis about the relationship between changes in ways of life and times of war. Support your hypothesis with evidence from this chapter.

3. Evaluation. A historian concluded that "the Allies had written [European] Jews off as wartime casualties." Based on the information in this chapter, do you think her conclusion is valid? Give reasons for your answer.

4. Analysis. Bradford Perkins, a soldier who would have taken part in the invasion of Japan, later wrote, "News that . . . an atomic bomb had been dropped on Hiroshima filled us all with a sense of relief. . . . I do not believe that any American politician could have withstood the protest if he had blocked its use." What do you think Perkins meant?

Using a Time Line

Match each event in the list below with the correct date on the time line. Write your answers in chronological order and explain the importance of each event.

(A) D-Day
(B) Battle of Midway
(C) end of Battle of Stalingrad
(D) Battle of Leyte Gulf
(E) Victory in Europe
(F) Battle of the Coral Sea
(G) invasion of Sicily
(H) Japanese surrender

May 1942	June 1942	Feb 1943	Jul 1943	June 1944	Oct 1944	May 1945	Sept 1945

History and You

The introduction of atomic weapons led to a new arms race and the potential to destroy the entire world. In response, concerned citizens began to join together to oppose nuclear weapons. Find out when and how the anti-nuclear movement started and what activities, if any, it has conducted in your community in recent years.

Jungle conditions—heat, humidity, dangerous animals and insects—made fighting difficult.

Thinking Critically

1. Roosevelt meant that this would be a fight to the death. Students who agree might cite power of German industry and military, Hitler's determination to destroy peoples he considered inferior, Japanese code of fighting with no surrender.
2. Answers may include: mobilization for war causes major changes in ways of life. Examples: movement of women into jobs previously reserved for men; mass migration; and heightened racism as a result of wartime conditions, which led to violence in Detroit and Los Angeles, and to internment of Japanese Americans.
3. Answers may include: U.S. ignored or never really believed reports of genocide and refused to accept Jewish refugees, and the Allies decided not to bomb death camps.
4. Answers may include: willing to use any weapon to end the war as soon as possible.

Using a Time Line

(F) May 1942; **(B)** Jun. 1942; **(C)** Feb. 1943; **(G)** Jul. 1943; **(A)** Jun. 1944; **(D)** Oct. 1944; **(E)** May 1945; **(H)** Sep. 1945

History and You

Students should research the origins of the Committee for a Safe Nuclear Policy (SANE) in the 1950s and the activities of its offshoot, the nuclear freeze movement of the 1980s.

Applying Social Studies Skills

1. The Revolutionary War and World War II.
2. Both images are of soldiers in ranks; in contemporary gear and in revolutionary uniforms.
3. Artist wanted people to see parallel between Revolutionary War and World War II; to inspire morale.
4. Artist is saying both wars were fought for liberty. Answers will vary.
5. Poster shows the two working together on the war effort.
6. Draw attention to the interdependence of the home front and the battle front.
7. Poster shows a woman working at an industrial job which women did not often do before the war.
8. Answers may include: women felt empowered, overworked, enjoyed the financial independence of their own job.
9. One of busy and hard-working women.
10. Poster ideas may include: high production goals in war industries or on farms, support for the war on home front, and ending racial conflict.

Applying Social Studies Skills

Interpreting Graphics

Patriotic graphics, such as recruiting posters, are widely used in wartime to inspire unity and encourage participation in the war effort. The graphics on this page, posters designed by American artists, were displayed in the United States during World War II. Study the posters and then answer the questions.

1. What wars are referred to on the poster below?

2. What images are used on the poster? How are the images similar? How are they different?

3. How do you think the artist wanted people to respond to the poster? Why?

4. What do you think the artist is implying about the purpose of the two wars? Do you agree or disagree with this view? Give reasons for your answer.

5. On the poster above, *WOW* stands for "Women Ordnance Workers," who made weapons. What relationship does the poster show between the woman and the soldier?

6. What do you think is the purpose of the poster?

7. How does the poster reflect changes in American life that occurred during the war?

8. Speculate about how women were affected by their wartime work.

9. The "WOW woman," "Rosie the Riveter," and "Jenny on the Job" were popular images of women who joined the labor force during the war. What image of women did these models project?

10. Consider the wartime concerns of government discussed in this chapter. Give at least one example of a poster that you would create to respond to one of those concerns.

Unit 8 Survey

ANSWERS

Making Connections

1. Nationalism, arms races, and expansionism make an explosive combination. Analysis of the causes of war will vary. Militarism, suspicion, international rivalries, nationalism, severe economic problems, bitterness over the consequences of World War I all contributed to World War II.
2. Answers may include high tariffs, disillusionment with the outcome of World War I, rejection of the League of Nations, Nye committee, preoccupation with domestic problems, Ludlow amendment, the Neutrality Acts. The United States was linked to other nations through disarmament treaties, business ties, trade, investments, loans, and an interest in mutual security.
3. Students who agree may cite Japan's invasion of Manchuria and China, its alliance with Germany, seizure of territory in Southeast Asia, unwillingness to compromise in negotiations. Students who disagree may cite the Four-Power Treaty and the Nine-Power Treaty and suggest a stronger U.S. alliance with the Soviet Union.
4. Answers may include internment of Japanese Americans, segregation in the armed forces, trial of African-American ammunition loaders, racial violence including the Detroit riots and zoot suit riots, and establishment of FEPC. Students may also mention public awareness of the contribution made by members of various ethnic groups to the war effort.
Using the Time Line. Answers will vary.

Projects and Activities

1. Students should keep in mind that the goal of both committees was to keep the United States out of the war.
2. Answers may include the establishment of the Nazi party, its seizure of communications and schools, German military build-up, the 1934 election, Nuremberg laws of 1935, *Kristallnacht,* alliance with Italy, and the invasions of Austria, Czechoslovakia, and Poland.

Using the Time Line. Maps will vary.

Unit Survey

Making Connections

1. What did nations learn about the causes of war as a result of World War I? Why did recognition of these causes fail to prevent another world war?

2. Provide evidence that American public opinion strongly favored isolationism in the 1930s and early 1940s. Why was isolationism so strong? Explain the changes behind the following statement: At the end of World War II there could be no return to isolationism.

3. Writer Kenneth C. Davis has said that "a clash between Japan and the United States and other Western nations over control of the economy and resources of the Far East and Pacific was bound to happen." Do you agree or disagree? Give evidence to support your views.

4. What experiences during World War II made many Americans more aware of racism in the United States?

Using the Time Line. On the time line find ten events that are related to World War I or II. List the events in chronological order and explain what each has to do with either war.

Projects and Activities

1. Work in groups of six. Within each group, three people are to represent the America First Committee and three the Committee to Defend America by Aiding the Allies. Become familiar with the ideas and reasoning of the two committees, then debate intervention in the war. Assume the debate takes place during the Battle of Britain.

2. With the class, discuss whether it would have been possible to stop Hitler's consolidation of power. Identify significant milestones on Hitler's road to power—such as his rebuilding of the German military in defiance of the Treaty of Versailles—and analyze what, if anything, the Allies could or should have done. As a follow-up, do research to find out why these steps were not taken.

Using the Time Line. Draw a large map of the United States. From the time line choose ten domestic events and do research to find out where they happened, if you do not know. Make a descriptive label for each event. Place the label on the map at the location associated with the event. For example, a film might be associated with Hollywood and federal government decisions with Washington, D.C. Include illustrations on your map for at least five of the events.

Milestones	1920	1926
Presidents	Harding; Coolidge	Coolidge; Hoover
Political and Economic	• Washington Naval Conference • U.S. troops leave Germany • U.S. Steel agrees to 8-hour day • Dawes Plan	• U.S. establishes relations with Canada independent of Britain • Kellogg-Briand Pact
Social and Cultural	• First burial, Tomb of Unknowns, Arlington • First hamburger stand, Wichita • Armistice Day proclaimed a holiday • First World Series broadcast	• Gertrude Ederle swims English Channel • *Ben Hur* stars Ramon Novarro • Babe Ruth hits 60 home runs
Technological and Scientific	• Einstein lectures on relativity at Columbia • Radar develops • Technicolor process, Herbert Kalmus • Frozen foods, Clarence Birdseye	• *National Geographic* publishes first color underwater photo • Iron lung invented • First yogurt dairy in U.S.

Assessment

Ask students to recall the issues that occupied Americans in the 1920s and 1930s. How did most Americans view the rest of the world? What did they think their nation's involvement in international affairs should be? How did United States involvement in world affairs change between 1920 and 1945? Tell students that their charts will reflect United States foreign policy during that period of changing views.

Discuss the purpose of charts—to organize data and present it visually so that information and relationships are understood quickly. Students might bring in examples of successful charts and discuss their characteristics.

Scoring

To create a scoring system, or rubric, assign an achievement scale to each of the evaluation criteria. For example you might evaluate "Communicating Ideas" on a scale of 0 to 4 as follows:

4—Exemplary response: visually, information is organized clearly and logically; devices such as labeling, lettering, symbols, color, spacing, rows, and columns optimize understanding; essay includes a clear position statement supported by convincing arguments.

3—Good response: visually, information is organized effectively for understanding; design devices contribute to understanding; essay includes a clear position statement backed by some sound reasons.

2—Adequate response: information is organized in an understandable way; some design devices are used to aid understanding; essay takes a position backed by one or two satisfactory reasons.

1—Poor response: lacks coherent organization; no devices are applied to enhance understanding; lacks an essay and/or position statement with supporting reasons.

0—No response/inappropriate response.

Follow-up Activity

Cartoon. Have students create political cartoons commenting on the contrast between the role of the United States in world affairs in the 1920s and the position in which the nation found itself in 1945.

Assessment: Demonstrating What You Know

Making a Presentation Chart

When World War II was over, the United States suddenly found itself in a stronger position among nations. This new position would revolutionize United States foreign policy.

Assume that you are a junior member of the State Department in 1945 and one of several people called upon to review United States foreign policy of the past twenty-five years. You will present your review to department officials for them to consider as they are working out new foreign policies.

Work in groups of four to plan and present your review. For your presentation, make a chart to show major trends in United States foreign policy between 1920 and 1945. Look back over Unit 8, noting broad policies, such as isolationism, and related events, such as treaties or deployment of troops. List the broad policies and related events on your chart. Briefly describe each policy or event, explain its goals, evaluate its success or failure, and draw conclusions about what lessons you think the nation learned from the experience.

To make it easier for your audience to follow the main threads of foreign policy, group policies and decisions in some way. You might, for example, list policies and decisions according to basic principles, such as isolationism. Or you might group items chronologically, by regions, such as Europe, Asia, and Latin America, or by success and failure.

Evaluation Criteria

Your work will be evaluated according to how well you meet the following criteria.

- **Completing the task**. You make a chart describing United States foreign policy from 1920 to 1945, its successes and failures, and the lessons learned from these successes and failures.
- **Knowing history**. You accurately identify broad policies and the related events based on historical information from your text or other sources.
- **Thinking critically**. You classify events and decisions according to a scheme that helps your audience see relationships and recognize major trends in foreign policy. You make reasoned judgments about the causes and effects of policies.
- **Communicating ideas**. Your chart is well organized. You make use of devices such as design, lettering, and color to help viewers understand the information on the chart.

1933 **1939** **1945**

F.D. Roosevelt | Truman

- Good Neighbor Policy
- U.S. recognizes USSR
- Hitler takes power in Germany
- Japan invades China
- Munich Conference
- *Kristallnacht*
- World War II begins
- Lend Lease Act
- U.S. enters World War II
- Executive Order 9066
- World War II ends

- Prohibition ends
- *King Kong* opens
- *Life* magazine's first cover photo, Fort Peck Dam by Margaret Bourke-White
- "God Bless America" introduced, Irving Berlin
- *The Grapes of Wrath*, John Steinbeck
- Sugar, coffee, gasoline rationing
- *Here is Your War*, Ernie Pyle

- "Walkie Talkie," Signal Corps
- *A Field Guide to Birds*, Roger Tory Peterson
- Nylon patented
- Golden Gate Bridge opens
- First radio telescope, Grote Reber
- Seaborg and McMillan discover plutonium
- Xerox process patented, Chester Carlson
- Atomic bomb

Unit 9

Objectives

- Discuss the origins of the Cold War and its impact on foreign policy.
- Describe the effects of rapid technological change on labor, industry, the environment, and ways of living.
- Explain how visions of reform during the Kennedy-Johnson years led to social changes and conflicts.
- Explain how turmoil in the Middle East, Latin America, and Asia affected the U.S.
- Trace the growth and development of the civil rights movement in the 1950s and 1960s.
- Discuss causes and effects of the Vietnam War.

Introducing THE UNIT

Following World War II Americans experienced rapid change. Rivalry between the United States and the Soviet Union developed into the Cold War, which threatened the precarious stability of a recently shattered world. The Cold War led to armed conflict in Korea and in Vietnam as the United States attempted to check Communist expansion.

Technological innovations made television, suburbs, freeways, computers, and the space program part of the American scene. Social upheaval brought change, too. Both the civil rights movement of the 1960s and the anti-Vietnam War movement of the 1970s challenged old notions of American society.

Connections: Geography

The photograph shows a street in Harlem. This New York City community was once a sleepy rural village, its shacks built of bits and pieces. In the 1870s Harlem's shacks were toppled and replaced with luxurious homes and apartments; the area became fashionable. The coming of subways to Harlem in the 1890s triggered a wild real estate boom. However, overdevelopment and high rents eventually led to a high vacancy rate. Faced with financial ruin, landlords began to rent to African Americans, who were willing to pay the high rates because it was one of the few places in the United States where they could rent or buy comfortable homes. Custom kept them out of housing elsewhere. By the 1920s Harlem had become a predominantly African-American community and the center of African-American cultural, political, and intellectual life.

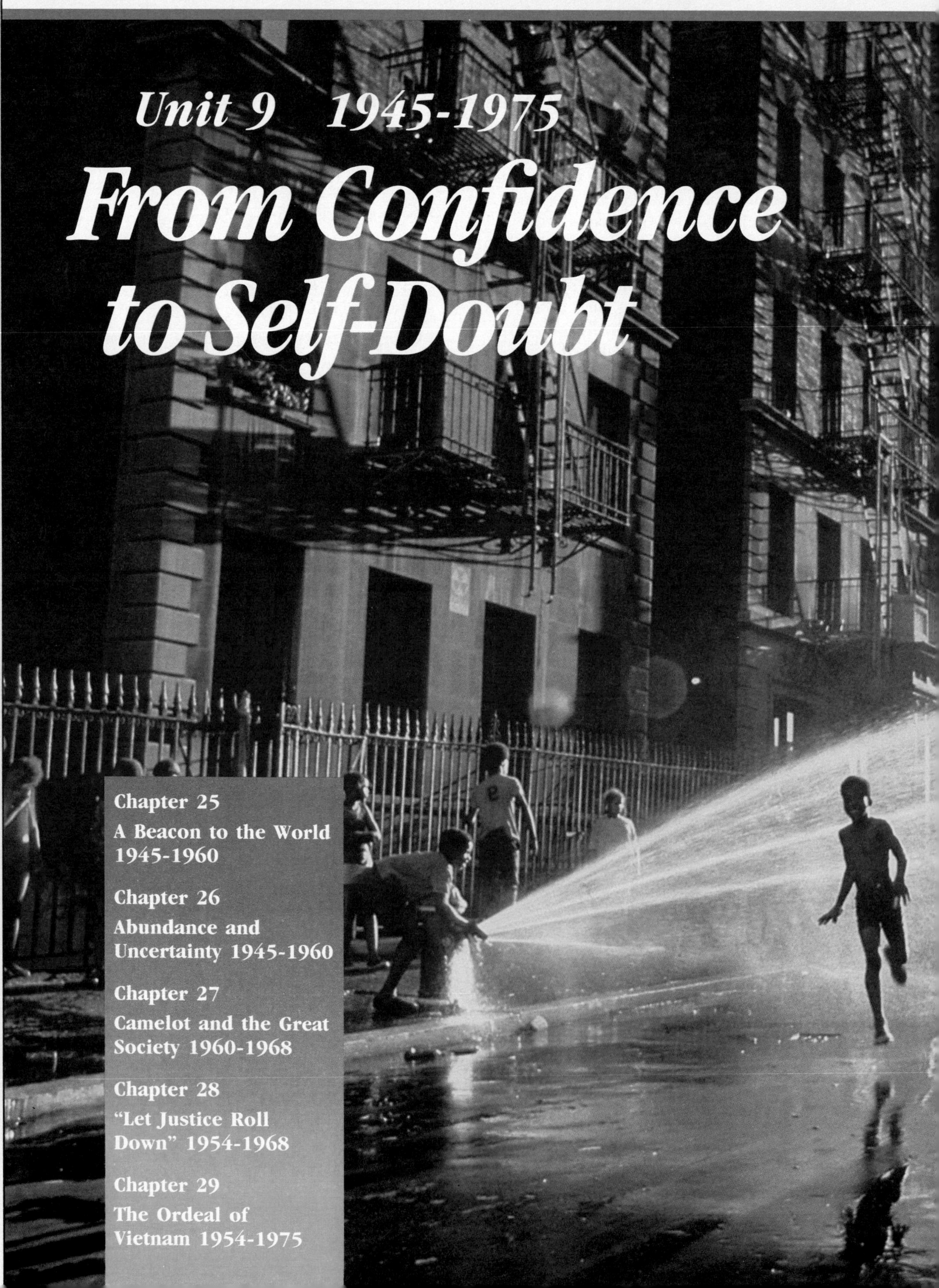

Unit 9 1945-1975

From Confidence to Self-Doubt

About the Author

Langston Hughes was a prolific writer in verse and prose. Interested students might like to read his poems. Students might also enjoy *Simple Speaks His Mind*, a collection of newspaper columns both humorous and serious, in which Jesse Simple, an African American, serves as Hughes's spokesman, and his autobiography, *I Wonder As I Wander: An Autobiographical Journey.*

Hughes wrote with ironic humor and sadness rather than anger. He did change with the times, however. While his earliest volumes of poetry included a few poems of protest and social comment, his last work, *The Panther and the Lash*, was more militant. In this work he warned whites that "you're the one will have the blues."

Vocabulary Building

Discussion. Knowing the following terms will help students understand Langston Hughes's poem: *connive* (scheme underhandedly), *bartered* (traded goods or services), *serf* (in a feudal system, peasant bound to the land), *furrow* (narrow groove made by a plow), *lea* (meadow), *foundry* (place where metal is cast), *leeches* (those who, like the bloodsucking worms, cling to others to get what they can), *graft* (taking advantage of one's political position to get money dishonestly).

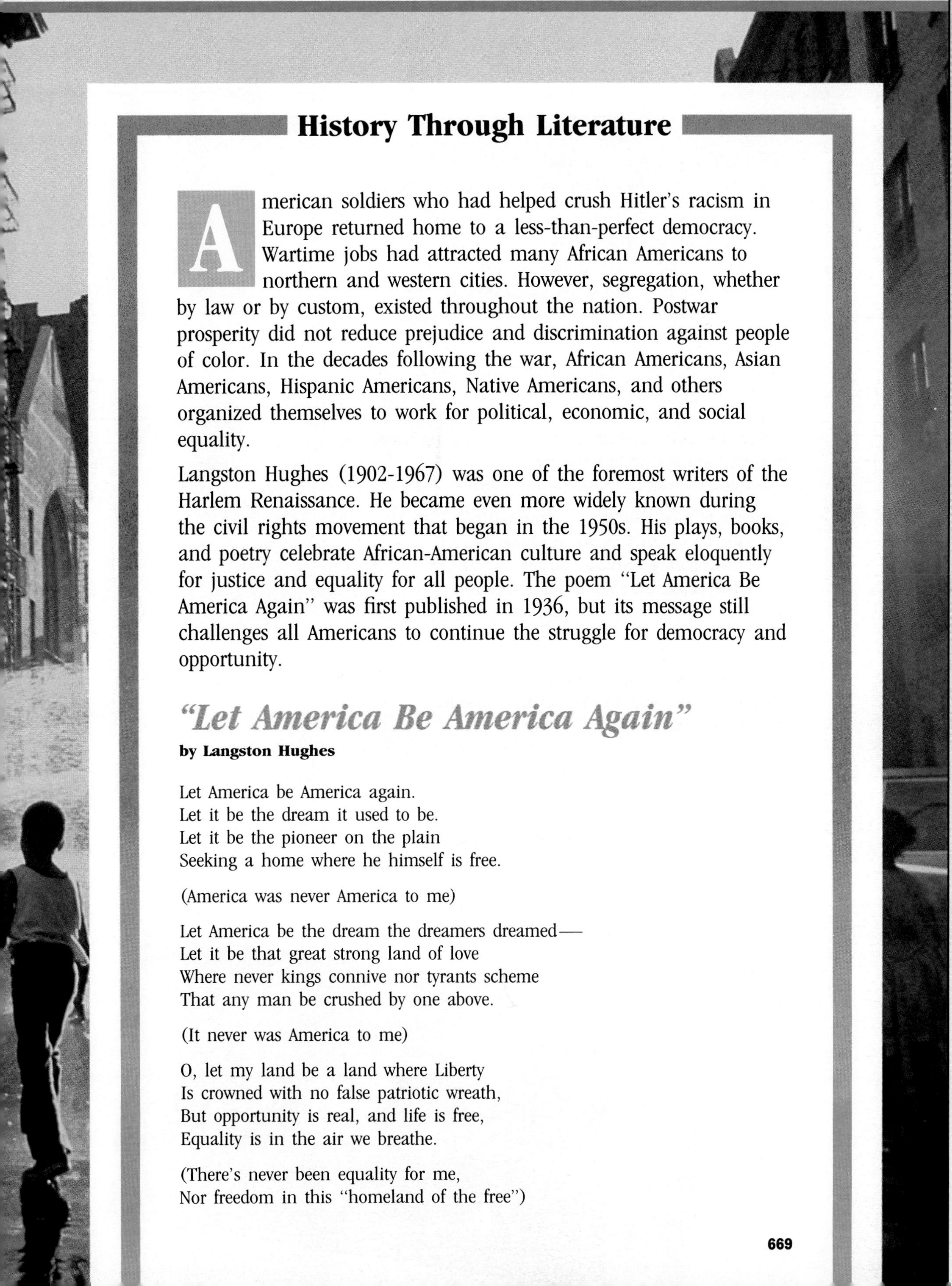

History Through Literature

American soldiers who had helped crush Hitler's racism in Europe returned home to a less-than-perfect democracy. Wartime jobs had attracted many African Americans to northern and western cities. However, segregation, whether by law or by custom, existed throughout the nation. Postwar prosperity did not reduce prejudice and discrimination against people of color. In the decades following the war, African Americans, Asian Americans, Hispanic Americans, Native Americans, and others organized themselves to work for political, economic, and social equality.

Langston Hughes (1902-1967) was one of the foremost writers of the Harlem Renaissance. He became even more widely known during the civil rights movement that began in the 1950s. His plays, books, and poetry celebrate African-American culture and speak eloquently for justice and equality for all people. The poem "Let America Be America Again" was first published in 1936, but its message still challenges all Americans to continue the struggle for democracy and opportunity.

"Let America Be America Again"

by Langston Hughes

Let America be America again.
Let it be the dream it used to be.
Let it be the pioneer on the plain
Seeking a home where he himself is free.

(America was never America to me)

Let America be the dream the dreamers dreamed—
Let it be that great strong land of love
Where never kings connive nor tyrants scheme
That any man be crushed by one above.

(It never was America to me)

O, let my land be a land where Liberty
Is crowned with no false patriotic wreath,
But opportunity is real, and life is free,
Equality is in the air we breathe.

(There's never been equality for me,
Nor freedom in this "homeland of the free")

Using the Visuals

Discussion. Explain to students that in 1965, in many parts of the United States, African Americans were still prevented from exercising their right to vote. The people in the photograph on this page were marching from Selma, Alabama, to the state capital, Montgomery, to present Governor George Wallace with a petition for African-American voting rights. State police used clubs and tear gas to stop the march, but a federal court ordered the state to allow the march to continue.

Ask: What does the mood of the marchers appear to be? Why do you think that they feel that way? **(buoyant; possibly pleased to be taking action, hopeful about the results)** What shows that the marchers are critical of the United States and patriotic at the same time? **(marching in order to protest, but marching under the American flag)** In what ways do they reflect Langston Hughes's ideas? What lines of the poem would make the best caption for this photograph? Why? **(Hughes seeks change, is saddened by and critical of aspects of American life, especially those that thwart the people he sees as the true builders of America. However, the change he seeks is not destructive; it is to make America a better place. Answers will vary.)**

Connections: Literature

A man of broad interests and talents, Langston Hughes was interested in the achievements of other African Americans. Among the nearly fifty works he wrote or edited before his death in 1967 are several about African-American history and culture: *A Pictorial History of Blackamericans*, *The Book of Negro Folklore*, and *The Book of Negro Humor*. He encouraged African-American writers and saw to it that the world was made aware of their talents. His book *The Poetry of the Negro*, edited with Arna Bontemps, includes poems by Countee Cullen, Pauli Murray, Gwendolyn Brooks, Ossie Davis, LeRoi Jones, Ishmael Reed, and Julian Bond, among others.

Say who are you that mumbles in the dark?
And who are you that draws your veil across the stars?

I am the poor white, fooled and pushed apart,
I am the Negro bearing slavery's scars.
I am the red man driven from the land,
I am the immigrant clutching the hope I seek—
And finding only the same old stupid plan
Of dog eat dog, of mighty crush the weak.

I am the young man, full of strength and hope,
Tangled in that ancient endless chain
Of profit, power, gain, of grab the land!
Of grab the gold! Of grab the ways of satisfying need!
Of work the men! Of take the pay!
Of owning everything for one's own greed!

I am the farmer, bondsman to the soil.
I am the worker sold to the machine.
I am the Negro, servant to you all.
I am the people, humble, hungry, mean—
Hungry, yet today despite the dream.
Beaten yet today—O, Pioneers!
I am the man who never got ahead,
The poorest worker bartered through the years.
Yet I'm the one who dreamt our basic dream
In that Old World while still a serf of kings,
Who dreamt a dream so strong, so brave, so true,
That even yet its mighty daring sings
In every brick and stone, in every furrow turned
That's made America the land it has become.
O, I'm the man who sailed those early seas
In search of what I meant to be my home—
For I'm the one who left dark Ireland's shore,
And Poland's plain, and England's grassy lea,
And torn from Black Africa's strand I came
To build a "homeland for the free."

The free?

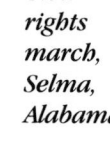

Civil rights march, Selma, Alabama.

670

Connections: Art

The picture of the two young women, below, is the work of photojournalist Charles Moore. A native of Alabama, Moore began his career on a Montgomery newspaper just as that city's African-American citizens ended their bus boycott. (See pages 758–759.) In 1958 Moore began to document the emerging civil rights movement, with Montgomery's Dexter Avenue Baptist Church as its center and Martin Luther King, Jr., not yet well known, as its leader. For the next seven years Moore placed himself in danger in order to photograph freedom marches, voter registration drives, prayer meetings, Ku Klux Klan meetings, and numerous confrontations. Many of these photographs were first seen in *Life* magazine. Moore's photographs are collected in *Powerful Days: The Civil Rights Photography of Charles Moore.*

Who said the free? Not me?
Surely not me? The millions on relief today?
The millions shot down when we strike?
The millions who have nothing for our pay?
For all the dreams we've dreamed
And all the songs we've sung
And all the hopes we've held
And all the flags we've hung,
The millions who have nothing for our pay—
Except the dream that's almost dead today.

The march on Washington, 1963.

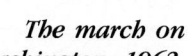

O, let America be America again—
The land that never has been yet—
And yet must be—the land where *every* man is free.
The land that's mine—the poor man's, Indian's, Negro's, Me—
Who made America,
Whose sweat and blood, whose faith and pain,
Whose hand at the foundry, whose plow in the rain,
Must bring back our mighty dream again.

Sure, call me any ugly name you choose—
The steel of freedom does not stain.
From those who live like leeches on the people's lives,
We must take back our land again,
America!

O, yes,
I say it plain,
America never was America to me,
And yet I swear this oath—
America will be!

Out of the rack and ruin of our gangster death,
The rape and rot of graft, and stealth, and lies,
We, the people, must redeem
The land, the mines, the plants, the rivers,
The mountains and the endless plain—
All, all the stretch of these great green states—
And make America again!

Taking a Closer Look

1. *According to the poem, what is the dream of America? What is the reality?*

2. *Who is the narrator of the poem?*

3. *What does Langston Hughes want? If he were alive today, what suggestions do you think he would make for achieving that goal?*

(Background) Harlem evening, 1950s.

Taking a Closer Look

ANSWERS

1. The dream is of a "great strong land of love," equality, and opportunity for all. The reality is of inequality for African Americans, Native Americans, and immigrants; of greed and oppression.
2. The narrator takes a number of identities; poor white, Native American, African American, and immigrant. Hughes represents the underclass and poor through American history.
3. Hughes wants his dream to become reality. Answers to the second part may vary.

Chapter 25

A Beacon to the World

Planning Guide

	Student Text	TWE Lesson Plans	Support Materials
SECTION 1	**Section 25–1 (1–2 Days)** **From Cool Cooperation to Cold War,** pp 674–681 The American Spirit: Eleanor Roosevelt, p 680 Review/Evaluation Section Review, p 681	**Introducing the Chapter:** The Postwar Years: What Do You Know?—Cooperative Activity, one class period, p 671B **Teaching the Main Ideas:** Linking Past and Current Events—Individual Activity, homework, one class period, p 671B **Evaluating Progress:** A Briefing for the Senator—Individual Activity, homework, p 671C	★ **Read to Remember,** Section 1 ● **Section Activities,** Section 1 Δ **Readings** ● **Tests and Quizzes,** Section 1 Quiz
SECTION 2	**Section 25–2 (1–2 Days)** **Pursuing the Containment Policy,** pp 682–689 Review/Evaluation Section Review, p 689	**Teaching the Main Ideas:** Investigating the Dismissal of MacArthur—Class Activity, one class period, p 671C	★ **Read to Remember,** Section 2 ● **Section Activities,** Section 2 Δ **Enrichment Activities,** Section 2 ● **Geography Activities,** Section 2 Δ **Readings** ● **Tests and Quizzes,** Section 2 Quiz
SECTION 3	**Section 25–3 (1–2 Days)** **Threatening "Massive Retaliation,"** pp 689–695 Connections to Themes: Shaping Democracy, p 695 Review/Evaluation Section Review, p 695 Chapter 25 Survey, pp 696–697 Skills, pp 696–697 Using New Vocabulary Thinking Critically Using Geography Applying Social Studies Skills: Analyzing Bar Graphs Writing About Issues	**Reinforcement Activity:** Foreign Policy Poster—Cooperative Activity, one class period, p 671C **Enrichment Activity:** Creating a Foreign Policy—Individual Activity, one class period, p 671C	★ **Read to Remember,** Section 3 ● **Section Activities,** Section 3 Δ **Enrichment Activities,** Section 3 Δ **Readings** ● **Tests and Quizzes,** Section 3 Quiz, Chapter 25 Test (Forms A and B) **Additional Resources** Δ **Twentieth Century Issues: Links to the Past** ● **Active Learning** Δ **GTV Videodiscs** Δ **Transparencies and Activity Book** ● **Testing Software** ★ **Chapter Summaries** **Key:** ★ For Extra Support ● For All Students Δ For Enrichment

Overview

The end of World War II brought new opportunities for peace with the establishment of the United Nations. However, longstanding political and economic differences between the United States and the Soviet Union, mutual distrust during the war, and new conflict between the two allies over Soviet domination of Eastern Europe and over the administration of Germany led to the Cold War.

To prevent the spread of communism, the Truman administration adopted a policy of containment. As part of that policy, the Marshall Plan was implemented to give massive aid to Western Europe, and the North Atlantic Treaty Organization was formed to create an American-Western European military alliance. In the tense postwar world, conflict in the Middle East, the Berlin Airlift, the Communist victory in China, and the Korean War intensified the Cold War.

The Eisenhower administration attempted to take a harder line against communism, but returned to a policy of containment when faced with the risk of war in Indochina and Europe. Tentative reconciliation between the United States and the Soviet Union evaporated when an American spy plane was shot down over the Soviet Union.

Activity Objectives

After completing the activities, students should be able to

- relate current events to post-World War II policies
- analyze the significance of Truman's decision to dismiss MacArthur.
- describe foreign policy during the Eisenhower administration.
- explain the policy of containment established by the Truman administration.
- analyze foreign policy options between 1945 and 1960.

Introducing the Chapter

The Postwar Years: What Do You Know?

This activity requires most of a class period.

This activity is designed to assess students' knowledge of post-World War II history before they read Chapter 25.

Before class prepare materials for the activity by writing on separate sheets of paper each of the following topics: Harry Truman, United Nations, containment, Cold War, Berlin Airlift, NATO, Korean War, Douglas MacArthur, Dwight Eisenhower, massive retaliation, domino theory, *Sputnik I*, U-2 incident.

Tell students that you are interested in learning how much they know about the years 1945 to 1960. To find out, you will circulate thirteen sheets of papers, each with a person, an event, or a policy important in the post-World War II years. As each paper comes to students, tell them to write what they know about the topic on the page and initial their statements. Have students read the statements written by other students and put a question mark beside those that they think are inaccurate. Each student should respond to each topic.

When students have finished their comments, read each paper and discuss the statements. Clarify statements that have been questioned. Conclude the activity by having students assess their knowledge of and misconceptions about the United States during the postwar period.

Teaching the Main Idea

Section 25-1: Linking Past and Current Events

This individual activity may be assigned as homework. Set aside a full class period the following day for students to complete their work.

In this activity students will use newspapers and news magazines to identify and analyze current events that were affected by postwar policies.

Begin the activity by asking students to brainstorm to create a list of countries with which the United States currently has relations of cooperation or conflict. Write students' responses on the chalkboard. Have students review Section 25–1 to determine which relations stem from events that occurred between 1945 and 1960.

Assign students the task of collecting two articles in newspapers or news magazines about the countries listed on the chalkboard. Students are to read the articles and highlight the events, people, or ideas with links to the postwar period.

On the assignment's due date, have students organize their articles by countries. Divide the class into pairs and assign each pair one of the countries. Direct the pairs to write a brief summary of the articles and then post the articles and their summary on a poster sheet. Conclude by having the pairs give brief statements about how current events in the countries relate to post-World War II history.

Teaching the Main Ideas

Section 25-2: The Dismissal of MacArthur

This class activity requires one class period.

In this activity students analyze the issue of civilian control of the military by simulating a Senate hearing on Truman's dismissal of MacArthur.

Begin the activity by asking one or two students to summarize events in Korea that led President Truman to fire General MacArthur. Encourage students to take notes as others speak. Explain that in this activity students will simulate a Senate investigation of the dismissal.

Select seven students to serve as a Senate committee inquiring into Truman's decision to dismiss MacArthur. Direct the committee to prepare questions to be addressed at the hearing. Divide the rest of the class into two groups, one representing Truman's advisors and the other representing Americans who support MacArthur. Have the opposing sides prepare a list of reasons why they believe the dismissal was or was not justified.

Allow 20 minutes for the groups to prepare. Make certain that Truman's advisors address the constitutional right of the President to control the military and direct foreign policy, and that the pro-MacArthur group emphasizes the policy of containment and American fears about the expansion of communism.

Convene the hearing and let both sides present their arguments. Then have the Senate committee ask questions and summarize each side's major points. After deliberation, the committee should state its view of Truman's action.

Have students discuss the relationship between the President as commander in chief and the armed forces. Challenge students to state reasons for civilian control of the military. Compare civilian-controlled governments with governments currently controlled by military leaders. Conclude the activity by having students explain how they feel about Truman's dismissal of MacArthur and why.

Reinforcement Activity

Section 25-3: Foreign Policy Posters

This cooperative activity requires one class period.

The following activity, in which students create posters, reinforces understanding of the foreign policy of the Eisenhower administration. Provide poster paper and colored markers for students.

Ask students to describe Secretary of State John Foster Dulles as he is characterized in Section 25–3. List on the chalkboard and review with students the foreign policy toward communism that Dulles championed, such as the quest to end communism, "ideas as weapons," covert operations, massive retaliation, and brinksmanship.

Divide the class into groups of three. Assign each group one of the foreign policy options listed on the chalkboard. Tell students they are to create a poster illustrating their assigned policy. Students may use symbols, pictures, or caricatures. Encourage them to give their posters a title but to use words sparingly in the design. Challenge students to create posters that are clear enough for viewers to understand without reading the section.

Have groups display their posters. Ask the class to view the posters and comment about how accurately they reflect Dulles's policies. Conclude by having students decide which policies were most appropriate between 1945 and 1960 and which would be most appropriate today. Why?

Evaluating Progress

Section 25-1: A Briefing for the Senator

This individual activity may be assigned as homework.

This written activity is designed to assess students' understanding of the policy of containment.

Remind students that following World War II, the Truman administration established a policy of containing communism. Have students imagine that they are aides to a senator on the Foreign Relations Committee. They have been asked to prepare a briefing paper about whether the United States should follow a policy of containment toward Country A—an imaginary country. Read or write on the chalkboard the following information.

Country A is seen as a political and economic rival of the United States. Its political system is very different from the American system. Recently Country A has been "courting" countries that are trading partners of the United States by offering to give foreign aid and sell military weapons to them. In these economically competitive times, Country A seems to be on the verge of attracting some of these countries to trade with it instead of the United States.

On the chalkboard write the format for students' briefing papers as follows:

- Describe the policy of containment.
- Describe how containment could be applied to Country A.
- Analyze the costs and benefits of applying containment to Country A.
- State your personal recommendation and supporting arguments.

Criteria for evaluating students' papers should include accuracy of descriptions and application of principles of containment, and convincing examples to support arguments.

Enrichment Activity

Section 25-3: Creating a Foreign Policy

This individual activity requires one class period, or it may be assigned as homework and shared in class the following day.

This activity engages students in writing their own foreign policy for an historical event.

Begin the activity by asking students to list as many foreign policy options as possible. Write their responses on the chalkboard. (Options may include defense; military, political, or economic alliances; diplomacy, including summit meetings and foreign aid; trade measures, such as tariffs, boycotts, limiting exports, and selling weapons on favorable terms; and intelligence.) Have students identify situations in Chapter 25 in which some of these options were used.

Tell students they will have the chance to rewrite history by choosing an event in the chapter and writing a paper describing the foreign policy they would use in reaction to it. The papers should summarize the event and the response, which may be an option listed on the chalkboard or one that students develop. Require students to find additional information about the country they choose, focusing on its history, geography, economic system, and industrial development.

Write the following criteria on the chalkboard for students to use in evaluating their foreign policies:

- Does the United States have sufficient resources to carry out the policy?
- How will the policy affect other nations?
- Will the American people support the policy?
- Do the potential benefits outweigh the risks?
- Will the policy be in the best interests of the United States?

When students have finished their papers, group together students who have written about the same situations or countries. Have them compare their policies in terms of effectiveness and then construct one compromise policy. How do group members think this policy is more effective than the one actually used? Why?

Bibliography and Audiovisual Material

Teacher Bibliography

Donovan, Robert J. *Conflict and Crisis: The Presidency of Harry S Truman, 1945–1948*. New York: W. W. Norton & Co., 1979.

Gaddis, John. *The United States and the Origins of the Cold War, 1941–1947*. New York: Columbia University Press, 1972.

LeFeber, Walter. *America, Russia and the Cold War, 1945–1971*. New York: Alfred A. Knopf, Inc., 1985.

Manchester, William. *The Glory and the Dream*. New York: Bantam Books, 1984.

————. *American Caesar: Douglas MacArthur*. New York: Dell, 1978.

Ridgway, Matthew. *The Korean War*. New York: Da Capo Press, 1986.

Truman, Harry S. *Memoirs of Harry S Truman: Years of Trial and Hope*. New York: Da Capo Press, 1987.

Student Bibliography

Condon, Richard. *Manchurian Candidate*. New York: Armchair Detective Library, 1991.

Heller, Joseph. *Catch 22*. New York: Dell, 1985.

LeCarre, John. *The Spy Who Came in from the Cold*. New York: Bantam Books, 1984.

Salinger, J. D. *Catcher in the Rye*. Boston: Little, Brown & Co., 1991.

Shute, Nevil. *On the Beach*. New York: Ballantine Books, Inc., 1983.

Films, Videocassettes, and Videodiscs

America and the World Since World War II: 1945–1960 Volume 1 & 2. 52 min. each. ABC News. 2 videocassettes.

The Cold War: The Early Period (1947–1953). 19 min. MCGH. Movie.

Eleanor Roosevelt. 26 min. Coronet Film and Video. Videocassette.

First Lady of the World: Eleanor Roosevelt. 25 min. AIMS. Movie.

Modern U.S. History: From Cold War to Hostage Crisis: Unit 1 (1945–1960). Guidance Associates. Videocassette.

Filmstrips

The 1950s: American Decades Series. 6 color filmstrips, 3 cassettes, guide. United Learning.

McCarthyism: Era of Fear. 2 color filmstrips, 2 cassettes, guide. New York Times.

Computer Software

The U.S. History Package: American Foreign Policy. 1 Apple diskette, backup, guide. Focus Media.

Chapter 25

Objectives

- Analyze why American-Soviet relations changed after World War II.
- Relate how Truman's policy of containment was implemented.
- Compare Eisenhower's policy toward communism with Truman's.

Introducing THE CHAPTER

For suggestions on introducing Chapter 25, refer to page 671B in the Teacher's Edition.

Developing THE CHAPTER

For activities and teaching strategies to help you reinforce and enrich chapter content, see pages 671B–671D in the Teacher's Edition.

B · A · C · K · G · R · O · U · N · D

Chapter Opener Illustrations

Every year *Time* magazine names its man [or woman] of the year. In 1958 it chose Nikita Khrushchev because under his leadership the USSR ushered in the space age.

The Soviet Union and the United States stockpiled nuclear missiles such as the ICBM. The prospect of such missiles being launched, and the threat of nuclear war haunted the citizens of many nations.

With the Marshall Plan, the United States undertook the most massive government-sponsored aid program in history. Here sacks of grain are being delivered to London.

The United States came to the aid of South Korea after it was invaded by Communist North Korea. This combat photograph has contrasted two opposing movements: United States soldiers toward the front and Korean refugees toward safety.

Reduced student page in the Teacher's Edition

Chapter 25 1945-1960

A Beacon to the World

A contemporary claimed that Marshall Plan aid was directed "not against any country or doctrine but against hunger, poverty, desperation and chaos." The Marshall Plan emblem affirms this humanitarian objective.

American Voices

In 1945 Eleanor Roosevelt became a member of the United States delegation to the United Nations, which had been created to build peace. Her husband, Franklin D. Roosevelt, had laid the groundwork for this world organization, and now she was among the leaders trying to make it work. She described her experiences in her diary and letters.

> *"February 6, 1946. Committee meeting was one long wrangle. Finally at 1:00 I asked for a vote. The Russians, who always play for delay, asked for a subcommittee to try to get a resolution we could agree upon. It is hopeless as there are fundamental disagreements. . . . At 3:10 we sat down in the subcommittee at Church House and we got up at 6, having agreed on 25 lines!*
>
> *February 13. Yesterday we fought the whole battle over again in the Assembly. . . . The Russians are tenacious fighters. When we finally finished voting at 1 a.m. last night, I shook hands and said I admired their fighting qualities and I hoped some day on that kind of question we would be on the same side, and they were cordiality itself!"*

Eleanor Roosevelt found that talks between the Americans and the Soviets often turned into "one long wrangle." It was a fitting description, for the United States and the Soviet Union were to come into conflict repeatedly in the postwar world.

Time *magazine's 1958 "Man of the Year," Nikita Khrushchev;* Titan-2 *intercontinental ballistic missile; first Marshall Plan shipment to London; South Korean women fleeing the war as American troops move to the front; Marshall Plan emblem.*

Analyzing Primary Sources

American Voices

Although Eleanor Roosevelt did not support military action against the Soviet Union, neither did she trust that nation. On the whole she agreed with Truman's anti-Soviet policy. She answered Soviet delegates' charges of injustice in the United States by suggesting that both countries submit to investigation of their social conditions. The Soviets rejected this idea.

1. What blocking tactics did the Russians use in the United Nations, according to Roosevelt? **(delay, repetition of points, tenacity)**
2. What sorts of things might the United States and the Soviet Union disagree about? **(Answers may include: division and governing of conquered countries and territories, structure of the United Nations, economic policies)**
3. If Eleanor Roosevelt were alive today, do you think she would experience the same frustrations? **(perhaps not, since the Cold War has largely diffused)**

Section 25-1

Objectives

- ***Answer the Focus Question.***
- *Describe the United Nations and its functions.*
- *Analyze the roots of the tension between the United States and the Soviet Union.*

Introducing

THE SECTION

Refer students to the opening paragraph. **Ask**: Why might Eleanor Roosevelt think that Harry Truman, as President, was "in trouble." **(He faced the question of whether to use the atomic bomb against Japan, how to deal with postwar problems at home, and how to deal with the Soviet Union.)**

Read to students one historian's comment on Truman: *"During the next few years this strange little man . . . would make and enforce a series of decisions upon which, for better or worse, our world now rests, or shakes."* Tell students they will be reading about what decisions Truman made and how he enforced them.

B · A · C · K · G · R · O · U · N · D

Time Line Illustrations

1. The official emblem of the United Nations was approved on November 20, 1946, by the General Assembly. The design shows a projection of the world map centered on the North Pole extending to the sixtieth degree south latitude. The map includes all lands except the Antarctic continent and is encircled by olive branches. Usually the emblem is printed in gold on a field of smoke blue, with all water areas in white.

2. Mao Zedong led the Chinese Communists to victory over Chiang Kai-Shek's corrupt regime in mainland China. A tough, ruthless leader, Mao eventually broke with his ally and supporter, the Soviet Union.

3. The Korean War pitted South Korea—whose flag depicted traditional Buddhist symbols—against North Korea—whose flag depicted the red star of communism.

Reduced student page in the Teacher's Edition

CHAPTER TIME LINE

1945-1960

1945 **Oct 24** UN Charter goes into effect

1949 **Apr** NATO formed
Sep Soviets test atomic bomb
Oct Communists come to power in China

1945 — 1948 — 1951

1947 Truman Doctrine announced

1948 Marshall Plan begins
Berlin Airlift (through May 1949)

1950 Korean War begins

25-1 From Cool Cooperation to Cold War

Focus: How and why did the American-Soviet relationship change following World War II?

When Franklin Roosevelt died on April 12, 1945, Harry Truman was called to the White House. Eleanor Roosevelt put her arm around his shoulders and said simply, "Harry, the President is dead." Stunned, Truman asked, "Is there anything I can do for you?" She replied, "Is there anything *we* can do for *you?* For you are the one in trouble now."

Truman's troubles would go beyond the weighty decision to drop the atomic bomb. The war's end brought other challenges, which some thought he was ill-prepared to meet. Noting his lack of foreign policy experience, critics considered him unlikely to emerge from Roosevelt's shadow. They were wrong. A determined leader whose favorite sayings were "The buck stops here" and "If you can't stand the heat, get out of the kitchen," Truman was to play a major role in shaping the postwar world.

That role, though, would have to be shared with the Soviet Union, second only to the United States in power. During the war the United States and Great Britain had formed an uneasy alliance with the Soviets to defeat the Axis powers. Could they now cooperate in peacetime?

Dealing with the Defeated Axis

A major decision facing the Allies was what to do with the defeated nations, particularly Germany and Japan. The Americans, Soviets, British, and French divided Germany into four occupation

4. Egyptian President Nasser sought to unite all Arabs under Egyptian leadership. When Egypt and Syria merged in 1958 as the United Arab Republic, Nasser was its President. Two years previously, he had touched off an international crisis by seizing the Suez Canal.

5. *Sputnik*, a symbol of Soviet technological and scientific advancement, was a blow to the United States' national pride. It spurred many to reevaluate the quality of scientific education in the United States.

6. Khrushchev and Eisenhower chat during the Soviet leader's visit to the United States in September 1959. They agreed that the following year they would hold a summit meeting in Paris and then Eisenhower would visit the Soviet Union. The U-2 incident (see page 695) cut short the summit, and Eisenhower's visit never took place.

1956 Suez Crisis

1954 1957 1960

1953 Korean War ends

1954 Vietnam is divided

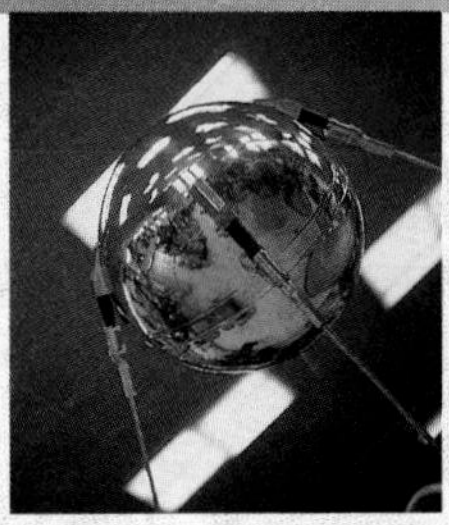

1957 Soviets launch *Sputnik*

1959 Castro comes to power in Cuba

1960 U-2 incident ruins U.S.-Soviet summit meeting

zones. They also divided Berlin, the German capital, located deep inside the Soviet zone. The Allies agreed to disarm Germany and treat it as one economy, sharing supplies among the zones.

It soon became clear, though, that Soviet and American aims differed. Having suffered horrendous casualties, the Soviets wanted to keep Germany weak. They shipped German equipment, crops, and even workers to the Soviet Union. Truman, on the other hand, wanted to get Germany quickly back on its feet to avoid burdening American taxpayers with long-term relief costs.

Increasingly suspicious of Soviet intents, Truman made sure that occupied Japan was governed only by American policies, enforced by troops under General Douglas MacArthur. American forces disarmed Japan, sweeping military leaders from power. Japan was stripped of all conquered territories, leaving its home islands the only remnant of a once-mighty empire. As in Germany, however, American policy soon stressed rebuilding.

The groundwork was also laid for democracy in Germany and Japan. Although the Soviets kept an iron grip on eastern Germany, in the western zones Britain, France, and the United States planned for free elections. Meanwhile, American leaders dramatically changed Japan's government, creating a constitution that guaranteed free elections, voting rights for women, labor unions, and land reform.

War crimes trials. Another American policy was to bring to justice Axis leaders suspected of committing war crimes. During 1945 and 1946 the Allies held trials in Nuremberg, Germany. Twenty-two key Nazi leaders were charged with "crimes against humanity" and "crimes against the peace," particularly associated with the Holocaust.

During the first months, testimony by survivors and other witnesses revealed slave labor, inhumane medical experiments, forced starvation, and mass murder. The judges refused to accept arguments that the defendants had just followed orders and that other nations had committed similar acts. They convicted nineteen defendants, sentencing twelve to death and seven to prison terms.

The Nuremberg trials made the world aware of the horrors of the Holocaust and other Nazi war crimes. Trials in Japan received less attention but also made the point that soldiers and civilians have a moral duty to disobey inhumane orders and laws.

Developing

THE SECTION

Limited English Proficiency

Discussion. The two sayings quoted on page 674—"The buck stops here" and "If you can't stand the heat, get out of the kitchen"—were popular with many Americans. Have students explain their meaning. **Ask:** What do sayings suggest about Truman? **(Take-charge, responsible person)**

Connections: Geography

Completing a Map. Have small groups of students work together to research how territory in Europe was divided after World War II. Then have them color and label outline maps showing the following: U.S., British, French, and Soviet occupation zones; areas annexed by the Soviet Union (including the Baltic states) and by Poland; and the areas ceded to France, Yugoslavia, and Greece by Italy.

Ask: What country other than Germany was also divided into four zones? **(Austria)** When did occupation of Germany and Austria end? **(1955)**

Thinking Critically

Evaluation. The concept of genocide was first introduced at the Nuremberg trials. Students can discuss how this concept is applied. They can also discuss the issue raised at the time and since then: should only the losers in a war be judged?

Connections: Politics
Internationalists feared that isolationists in Congress would block membership in the United Nations just as they had done with the League of Nations. However, on January 10, 1945, Senator Vandenberg, a former isolationist, stated "I do not believe that any nation hereafter can immunize itself by its own exclusive action." Vandenberg played a major role in getting Republican senators to ratify the United Nations charter. He served as a delegate to the San Francisco meeting in 1945 and the following year was a delegate to the Paris Peace Conference.

Linking Past and Present

Research. Even today, Nazi war criminals continue to be hunted down and extradited when found in other countries. Have students research the search for, and discovery of, Nazi war criminals. Discuss whether at this point in time (more than 45 years later) these individuals should still be pursued.

Global Connections

Discussion. Recall with students why Congress voted against the League of Nations after World War I. **(Isolationists feared being drawn into another war. Ask:** Why in 1945 was isolationism no longer considered a possible course in this country? **(Answers may include the atomic bomb, strong alliances formed during the war, the shattered state of Europe.)**

Active Learning

Cooperative Activity. Divide the class into two groups to debate the topic: "The United Nations has helped to keep world peace." Each student should be responsible for researching an activity of the United Nations since its organization in 1945. All students should participate in planning the debate points.

Reduced student page in the Teacher's Edition

The trials did arouse some controversy. Critics questioned their fairness, noting that no investigations focused on Allied actions such as the firebombing of Dresden. Although few doubted the guilt of those convicted, some questioned whether it was fair to judge only the losers of a war.

The Birth of the United Nations

The devastation of world war spurred the creation of an international peacekeeping organization, the United Nations (UN). To a great extent, the UN sprang from the heart of Franklin Roosevelt, who admired Wilson's quest for peace with the ambitious but ineffective League of Nations.

In 1944 American, British, Soviet, and Chinese representatives met at Dumbarton Oaks, near Washington, D.C. to discuss plans for the UN. They scheduled a meeting for April 1945 in San Francisco to draw up the UN charter, or constitution.

Roosevelt did not live to see his vision become reality, but Truman opened the meeting on April 25 as scheduled, with a speech to 800 delegates from 50 nations. Eight weeks later the charter was completed, and by October it had been ratified by the member nations. The vote in the Senate was an overwhelming 89 to 2. Senator Arthur Vandenberg, an isolationist before the war, echoed the feelings of other UN supporters:

> *"World War III is too horrible to contemplate. It clearly threatens the end of civilization. Here is our chance to try to stop this disaster before it starts."*

The charter begins "We the people of the United Nations [resolve] to live together in peace," pointing to the goals of peacefully settling international disputes and stopping aggression. The UN is also committed to promoting human rights and relieving hunger and poverty.

UN organization. Each member nation sends a representative to the General Assembly—a "town meeting of the world" where international issues are discussed. Although the Assembly cannot enforce decisions, it can recommend action to the Security Council, where the real power rests.

The Security Council is the peace-keeping body, with a core of five permanent members: the United States, Britain, Russia, China, and France. Commonly called the "Big Five," they are joined by ten members elected by the Assembly for two-year terms.

The Security Council can call on UN members to take measures against an aggressor nation, such as suspending diplomatic relations, participating in boycotts, or even taking military action. Any one of the Big Five, however, can veto the use of force. The veto, which both the United States and the Soviet Union insisted upon, has hampered the UN's ability to stop aggression.

Working with the General Assembly and the Security Council are four other bodies. The Secretariat handles administrative work. The International Court of Justice, or World Court, decides cases submitted by members and advises the UN on legal matters. The Trusteeship Council supervised former colonies lost by defeated nations in the two world wars, helping them move toward independent government. The Economic and Social Council supports agencies working to improve health, education, and other areas of human welfare.

Spotlight on European Relief

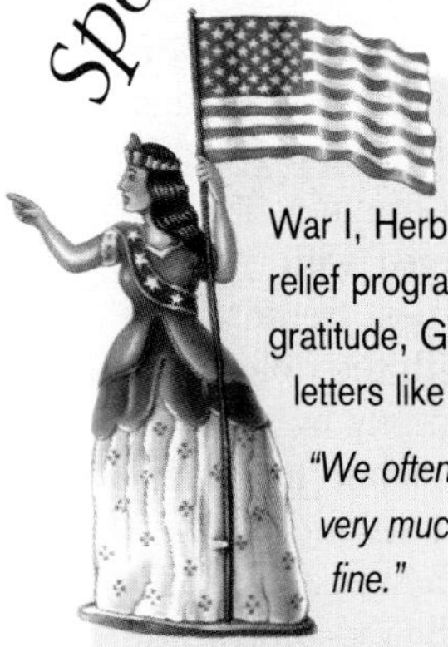

As he had done after World War I, Herbert Hoover helped coordinate relief programs in Europe. To express their gratitude, German schoolchildren wrote him letters like the following:

"We often get sweet foods, which I like very much. But even the vegetables are fine."
—Helga Steinitzke

"With your many efforts, you might have saved many children from death."
—Perth Welzel

"Our mom is very happy. Because now we save some bread. Everybody likes to go to school now."
—Sofie Held

Connections: Literature

Many Jews who settled in Palestine were Zionists who sought to establish a Jewish state. Theodor Herzl, an Austrian journalist, became a forceful exponent of Zionism after concluding that anti-Semitism could not be eliminated until Jews had a nation of their own. Interested students can learn more by reading his book *The Jewish State*.

Global Connections

The Balfour Declaration of 1917 was issued by Britain and affirmed the right of Jews to establish a homeland in Palestine. The meaning of the declaration, however, was interpreted differently by Arabs and Jews. Jews thought it pledged Britain's support for their goal and Arabs claimed it allowed for such a homeland only if they (the Arabs) agreed to it.

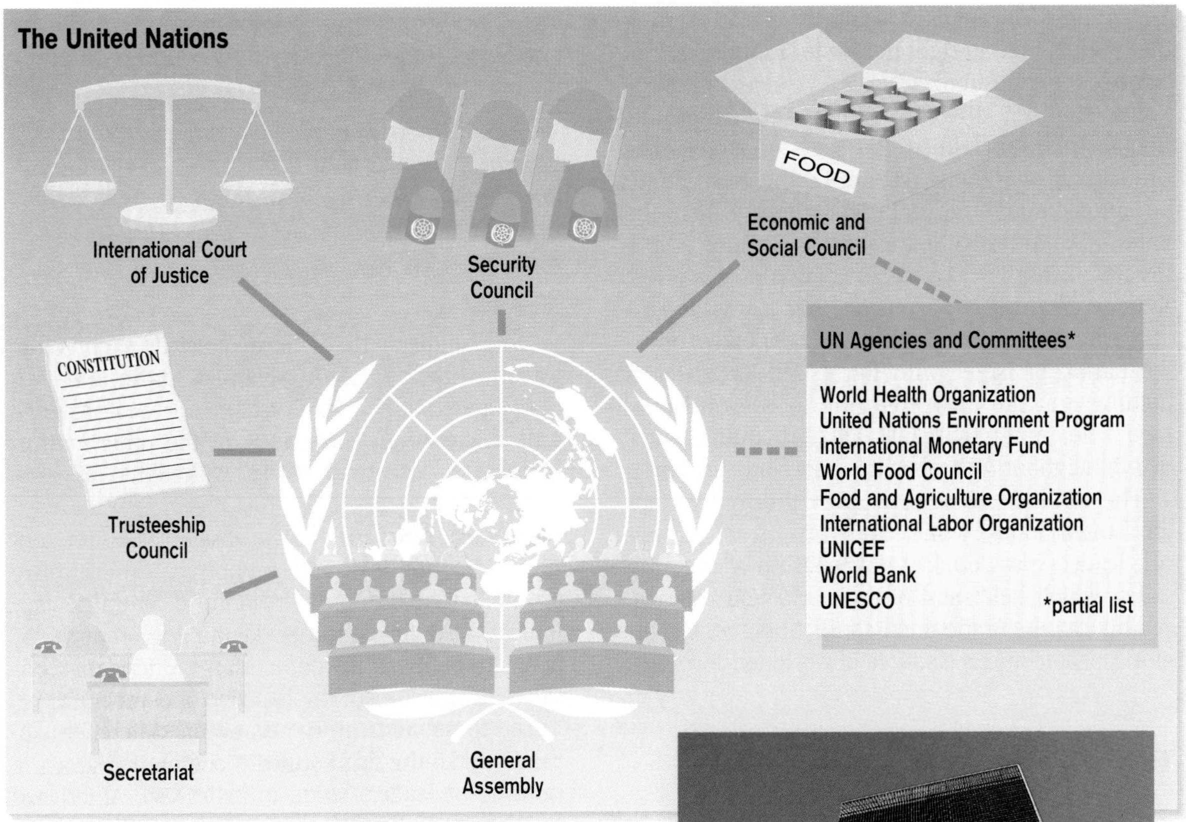

UN headquarters (right) is in New York City. A second headquarters is in Geneva. The International Court meets at The Hague in The Netherlands. The Atomic Energy Agency is in Vienna, UNESCO is in Paris, and the Food and Agriculture Organization is in Rome.

The most pressing need facing the new UN was emergency aid to war-ravaged nations. Between 1945 and 1947 the UN Relief and Rehabilitation Administration (UNRRA) rushed 22 million tons of food, clothing, and supplies to Europe and Asia.

Seeking Peace in Palestine

The war had struck a death blow to colonialism by removing or weakening European control over colonies and mandates in the Middle East, Asia, and Africa. The door was opened to independence movements, presenting peacekeeping challenges.

One hot spot was the Middle Eastern land of Palestine, which the League of Nations put under British control after World War I. Although the Jewish homeland in ancient times, it was conquered by Arabs, becoming home to an Arab majority for centuries. In the late 1800s, as Jews sought to reclaim the land of their ancestors, conflict arose between the two groups in Palestine. It increased when thousands of Jewish refugees from Europe arrived during the 1930s and after the war.

Unable to deal with the turmoil, Britain finally asked the UN to settle the problem. Moved by sympathy for Holocaust victims, the General Assembly voted in 1947 to divide Palestine into Jewish and

Writing About History

Written Report. Assign groups of students to do research and write reports on some of the functions and accomplishments of agencies overseen by the United Nations, for example UNESCO (United Nations Educational, Scientific, and Cultural Organization), UNICEF (United Nations International Children's Fund), and WHO (World Health Organization).

Using the Visuals

Interpreting a Diagram. Refer students to the diagram of the United Nations on this page. **Ask:** What are the six major bodies of the UN? **(General Assembly, Security Council, Secretariat, International Court, Trusteeship Council, Economic and Social Council)** Which body is central to the other five? **(General Assembly)** Which two major organizations are responsible for maintaining peace and settling disputes? **(Security Council, Court of Justice)**

GTV Side 4

Chap. 6, Frame 27912

Echoes of War: The Birth of the U.N./ End of Isolation (Movie Segment)

Search and Play:

Linking Past and Present

Oral Report. Have students do research and report on the relationship between Israel and neighboring Arab countries in the Middle East today (including the question of the Palestinian Arab refugees). They can explain how this relationship developed from the situation described in the text.

Global Connections

Discussion. Have students discuss what they think the United Nations and/or the United States should have done about Palestine and why.

Active Learning

Skits. Have groups of students present skits that indicate the deterioration of United States-Soviet relations. One skit might show Soviet and United States soldiers talking to each other in 1945, 1947, and 1948. Another skit could present diplomats from the two countries meeting in 1945 and 1947. A third skit could portray how the opinions of ordinary Americans changed regarding the Soviet Union from 1945 to 1948.

Multicultural Perspectives

Ralph J. Bunche headed the department of political science at Howard University in Washington, D.C. He headed the Africa section of the Office of Strategic Services during World War II. Bunche joined the State Department in 1944 and the UN Secretariat in 1946. In addition to his work on the Arab-Israeli armistice, he was principal director of the UN's Trusteeship Division. In the 1950s and 1960s he was an undersecretary of the United Nations and accompanied UN peacekeeping forces to various troubled parts of the world.

Bunche's work as a mediator won him the Nobel Peace Prize in 1950. He was the first African-American to be so honored. He was also given the NAACP's Spingarn Medal in 1949 and the Medal of Freedom, the highest United States civilian award, in 1963.

Reduced student page in the Teacher's Edition

Arab states. The Arabs rejected the plan, arguing that the UN had no right to give Jews land that had belonged to Arabs for centuries.

On May 14, 1948, as Britain pulled out its troops, Jews proclaimed the state of Israel. The United States promptly recognized the new nation, but almost every Arab state sent troops to help the Palestinian Arabs battle the Israelis. In July 1949 a UN team led by American diplomat Ralph J. Bunche arranged an armistice, but it was an uneasy truce. Most of Palestine was now taken up by the nation of Israel, with Egypt and Jordan each holding an Arab area. Refusing to live under Israeli rule, more than 600,000 Palestinian Arabs fled to neighboring Arab states, especially Jordan.

The conflict was a particularly thorny issue for the United States. While supporting Israel, American leaders also sought the friendship of the Arab states, which held most of the world's oil reserves. To this day the Arab-Israeli conflict plagues the region's people and is a source of world tension.

From Yalta to Potsdam

In its early efforts, the UN faced a major obstacle to international cooperation: growing tension between the Soviet Union and the United States. During the war that tension had only simmered below the surface, and as peace approached many Soviets and Americans had even looked to the future with hope. On April 28, 1945, the American armed forces newspaper gave a glowing account of the first Soviet troops the Americans met in Germany:

> *"Russian soldiers are the most carefree bunch. . . . They would best be described as exactly like Americans, only twice as much. . . . You get the feeling of exuberance, a great new world opening up."*

The soldiers may have greeted each other warmly, but the meeting between Stalin and Truman later that year at Potsdam was cool. As each grew increasingly suspicious of the other's aims, hopes for a "great new world" withered.

Roots of tension. The deepest roots of tension were political and economic. Communism prohibited the economic freedom so central to capitalism. Also, Soviet leaders kept a grip on power by denying political freedom. Many Americans considered communism the opposite of democracy.

Did these political and economic differences actually make the two countries enemies? A growing number of leaders came to believe so. Americans suspected the Soviets of encouraging Communist

David Ben Gurion (in suit), first prime minister of Israel, takes over from the British. (Right) For negotiating an Israeli-Arab armistice, American Ralph Bunche won a Nobel Peace Prize.

Global Connections
Winston Churchill had always been suspicious of the Soviet Union's motives. In November 1943 Churchill told one of his ministers of state, *"Germany is finished. . . . The real problem now is Russia. I can't get the Americans to see it."*

Connections: Geography
The Russians had wanted a warm-water port for hundreds of years because their ports on the Baltic generally freeze and become unusable in the winter. Also, control of Turkey would have given the Soviet Union control of the eastern Mediterranean.

Linking Past and Present

Oral Report. Have individual students or groups choose particular countries in the former Soviet bloc. They can present oral reports on changes in their governments, economies, and relationships with other nations since 1988.

Analyzing Primary Sources

Joseph Stalin. When Truman insisted that free elections be held in Eastern Europe, Stalin refused, explaining, *"Any freely elected government in these countries will be an anti-Soviet government and we cannot allow that."*

Ask students what this quotation implies about the following issues: Soviet security concerns, Eastern European feelings toward the Soviet Union, the Soviet Union's willingness to compromise, the Soviet Union's confidence in other nations accepting its ideals, the possibility of Eastern Europe being free of Soviet domination, and the chances for cooperation between the Soviet Union and the United States.

movements in the United States and elsewhere. The Soviets never forgot that American troops had aided anti-Communists in the civil war in Russia from 1918 to 1920. They also thought that the United States was seeking to expand its influence in order to gain capitalistic profit.

Distrust was deepened by strategic moves during World War II, particularly the 1939 Nazi-Soviet Pact and the British-American decision to delay the attack on the western front until 1944. The Soviets saw their pact as a defensive step to buy time, but to American leaders it was a sign that Stalin could not be trusted. Roosevelt had bowed to Churchill's opinion that an earlier attack on the western front would be disastrous, but Stalin saw the delay as an attempt to bleed Soviet forces battling the Germans in the east. It is not surprising, therefore, that clouds of suspicion began to gather after the war.

The mistrust with which Americans and Soviets viewed each other was intensified by anxieties over the rapid development of nuclear weapons.

The Soviet bloc. At Yalta, Roosevelt had hoped that the Soviets would allow free elections in Eastern Europe, though the Yalta agreements did not require them. Truman, however, openly distrusted the Soviets, an attitude that deepened when Stalin refused to allow elections in Poland.

From the Soviet Union's viewpoint, the Yalta agreements acknowledged its need for a buffer zone on its western border. After annexing Latvia, Lithuania, and Estonia, the Soviets swept much of Eastern Europe into their orbit. Eastern European nations under Soviet-backed Communist parties became known as the **Soviet bloc**.

Flexing muscles in the Middle East. Like the United States, the Soviet Union had strategic interests in the oil-rich Middle East. During the war British and Soviet troops were stationed in Iran to protect the oil fields. After the war, though, the Soviets refused to leave. Instead, they demanded partial control of Iranian oil production, which was largely in British hands. Pressured by the United States, the Soviets pulled out in 1946, but only after receiving control of an Iranian oil company.

The Soviets also sought ports along the Turkish straits connecting the Black Sea with the Mediterranean. They pressed Turkey to lease naval bases and demanded two Turkish provinces along the Soviet border. Only after Britain and the United States protested did the Soviets back down.

Getting Tough with Communism

Truman believed that all this muscle-flexing was a sign that the Soviet Union wanted to expand its influence. Privately he remarked that he was "tired of babying the Soviets." His view was shared by Churchill, who in describing the Soviet bloc declared that "an iron curtain has descended across the continent." Both men thought that the Soviets were seeking a Communist empire.

Many Americans, however, were still optimistic about having good relations. To convince them otherwise, Truman followed recommendations made by George F. Kennan, a Soviet expert in the State Department. Kennan believed that the Soviet

Analyzing Primary Sources

George Kennan. Refer students to Kennan's words on this page. **Ask:** What does Kennan see as the root of the cold war? **(Soviet Union's desire to expand its power worldwide)** How does Kennan think the United States should react to Communist aggression? **(The United States should contain Soviet expansion)**

Limited English Proficiency

Interpreting a Political Cartoon. Refer students to the cartoon on the next page. **Ask:** What three symbols does this cartoon use? What do they represent? **(a blindfolded Uncle Sam for the United States, a money bag for foreign aid, a log for United States foreign policy)** What does the cartoon suggest? **(that giving such aid and involving the United States in these nations' affairs is as risky as a blind person walking on a log over water)**

Multicultural Perspectives

Not all Americans agreed with the government's "Cold War" view of the Soviet Union. Paul Robeson, a popular African-American actor and singer, believed that the Soviet Union offered at least some of the answers to the inequality and racism that African Americans suffered in the United States. He was investigated during the McCarthy era (see Chapter 26) for his pro-Soviet views. He lived in the Soviet Union and Eastern Europe for a while in the late 1950s and early 1960s but returned to the United States permanently in 1963.

Multicultural Perspectives

In 1938, Eleanor Roosevelt attended a conference on human welfare in then-segregated Birmingham, Alabama. The delegates were seated in two groups—

Reduced student page in the Teacher's Edition

Union intended to "make sure that it has filled every nook and cranny available to it in the basin of world power." He argued for "a long-term, patient but firm and vigilant containment of Soviet expansive tendencies."

This policy of **containment** would focus on keeping communism within its current borders. The United States was prepared for limited wars, or local fights, against Communist rebels but would avoid direct confrontation with the Soviets.

Some critics considered containment an overreaction. Soviet moves, they argued, were efforts to protect national security, not attempts to spread communism. Noting that the Soviets were burdened with postwar recovery, they saw little sign of expansionism. Other critics wanted communism crushed. Their views, though, were out of tune with the mood of the general public, which was not yet convinced of even the need for containment.

Birth of the Cold War. To rally support for containment, Truman focused attention on a rebellion by Greek Communists. Britain, which had been helping Greece's right-wing government fight

THE AMERICAN SPIRIT

Eleanor Roosevelt

First Lady of the World

"All my life I have been physically afraid of doing anything myself," Eleanor Roosevelt once confessed. "It took me years to get enough confidence to drive or to feel that I could hold any opinion." She never stopped fighting that fear but overcame it enough to become perhaps the most energetic and influential of all First Ladies.

Like her husband, Franklin, Eleanor was born into the aristocratic Roosevelt clan—a niece of Theodore Roosevelt, from whom she gained a strong commitment to social reform. Married in 1905 to her distant cousin Franklin at the age of twenty, she spent the next 25 years raising five children. She also developed into an excellent public speaker, a persuasive writer, and an important political ally for her husband. Above all, she became a social reformer, working tirelessly on any project that could lead to greater equality, especially for African Americans. A black newspaper editor wrote that "she gave all Americans of all races and colors a living example of what interracial relations should be."

Eleanor Roosevelt never hesitated to criticize the New Deal or the President when she felt it was warranted. She gave speeches and radio addresses, held news conferences, and wrote a popular newspaper column. No other First Lady has had such a powerful influence on national affairs.

After Franklin's death in 1945, Eleanor turned her energies to the new United Nations. From 1946 to 1948 she chaired the UN Commission on Human Rights, facing the seemingly impossible task of drafting a declaration acceptable to all fifty-eight member nations. With remarkable tact, patience, and skill, she succeeded in working out the Universal Declaration of Human Rights, which she said, "may well become the international Magna Carta." Eleanor Roosevelt died in 1962 at the age of 78. Thousands of tributes to her were written, including one that seemed especially fitting: "She would rather light a candle than curse the darkness."

according to race. Mrs. Roosevelt sat on the African-American side and refused to move. When police threatened to break up the meeting, Mrs. Roosevelt had her chair placed in the center aisle, which separated the white from the black delegates.

Global Connections

Perhaps the first large meeting of Third World leaders was the Afro-Asian Conference, held at Bandung, Indonesia in April 1955. Representatives of twenty-three independent Asian states and four African ones (as well as two others that were about to become free) attended. Indonesian President Sukarno called it *"the first inter-continental conference of colored peoples in the history of mankind."*

Cartoonist Fred Seibel expressed the uncertainty of many Americans who wondered where the new foreign policy would lead them. Aid to Greece included military advisors.

the rebels, had said in February 1947 that it could no longer afford to keep troops in Greece and Turkey. Truman decided the United States should take over the British role. Arguing that a Communist takeover of Greece or Turkey would threaten world peace and American security, he declared:

> *“I believe that it must be the policy of the United States to support free peoples who are resisting attempted subjugation [conquest] by armed minorities or by outside pressure.”*

Soon labeled the Truman Doctrine, this statement publicly announced the containment policy.

Truman and his advisors saw the Soviet hand in any Communist uprising, even when there were no fingerprints. Such was the case in Greece, where the Soviets had not offered aid to the rebels. Still, by raising the specter of Soviet expansionism, Truman aroused public support. Congress approved $400 million in aid for the Greek government.

Containing communism was not the same as promoting democracy. Indeed, American aid to Greece had propped up a military dictatorship. For better or worse, however, the United States was embarking on a campaign that prompted Bernard Baruch to declare in April 1947, "Let us not be deceived. Today we are in the midst of a cold war."

By **Cold War** Baruch meant the state of tension between the Soviet Union and other Communist countries on one side and the United States and other non-Communist countries on the other. As nations took sides, this war of world views soon overshadowed the UN vision of cooperation.

Some developing countries, especially in Asia, Africa, and the Middle East, did not align themselves with either world view. They became known as **third world** countries. As the Soviet Union and the United States pursued their own security and economic interests, they often showed little understanding of third world viewpoints or respect for the sovereignty of third world nations.

Section Review

1. Identification. Define *Soviet bloc, containment, Cold War,* and *third world.*

2. Comprehension. Describe the major challenges facing the UN after the world war.

3. Analysis. Explain why the American-Soviet relationship changed from "cool cooperation" to "Cold War."

4. Evaluation. Who do you think was to blame for starting the Cold War—the United States, the Soviet Union, or both? Explain.

Connections: Language

Discussion. Have students describe the feelings invoked by the metaphors "cold war" and "iron curtain." Suggest why these metaphors might have been used, and discuss whether they seem appropriate. You might also have students make up metaphors to describe the relationship between the United States and the Soviet Union and/or the situation in Eastern Europe today.

Section Review

ANSWERS

1. Definitions for the following terms are on text pages indicated in parentheses: *Soviet bloc* (679), *containment* (680), *Cold War* (681), *third world* (681).
2. Answers may include: aid to war-ravaged countries; conflict in Palestine; growing conflict between United States and the Soviet Union.
3. Basic distrust between the two countries—due to political and economic differences and United States' slowness in opening up a second front. Distrust grew when eastern European nations were forced to become part of Soviet bloc, and Russians were slow to leave Iran and tried to get naval bases in Turkey.
4. Those thinking the United States responsible can point to containment and statements of Kennan and Baruch. Those thinking Soviets responsible can point to its actions in Eastern Europe, Iran, Turkey. Those thinking both nations responsible can point to actions on both sides.

Section 25-2

Objectives

- ***Answer the Focus Question.***
- *Evaluate the objectives and methods of the Marshall Plan.*
- *Identify the purpose of NATO.*
- *Explain how the United States become involved in the Korean War.*
- *Explain how the Truman Doctrine was implemented.*

Introducing
THE SECTION

Have students compare three possible policies in regard to world communism—containment, all-out war (attempt to destroy communism), and doing nothing (isolationism)—in terms of their effectiveness in promoting democracy. Encourage students to suggest other policies or approaches that they think might have been tried and describe their possible effects.

B · A · C · K · G · R · O · U · N · D

Connections: Politics
The National Security Council directs the activities of the Central Intelligence Agency. The director of the CIA is appointed by the President and confirmed by the Senate. The agency's mission is to collect and evaluate data related to national security as well as carry out undercover activities. Initially it was to function only in foreign affairs, but it was authorized to collect information inside the United States in 1981.

Connections: Economics
The Marshall Plan continued for four years and cost $13 billion. As a result of the plan, the standard of living in Europe rose, and European demand for American goods increased.

Reduced student page in the Teacher's Edition

25-2 *Pursuing the Containment Policy*

Focus: How did the United States under Truman try to contain communism?

"It is possible to fix the time and place when the flag of world leadership began to pass from the dying British Empire to the United States."

So writes historian William Manchester about February 21, 1947, the day the British ambassador urgently reported that his country could no longer help Greece and Turkey. By responding to the British plea with the policy of containing communism, President Truman defined the course that American leadership would take. In effect the United States saw itself as a beacon to the world, a light of democracy against the darkness of communism.

How and where, though, would containment take place, and at what cost in aid and lives? Critics who considered the policy too broad warned that it would trigger a series of "hot wars," with American forces putting out countless Communist "brush fires" around the world. Our "first team," they predicted, would be gradually worn down in battles with Communist "third teams" composed of Soviet-supported rebels.

Indeed, as the containment policy took hold, military preparedness became a Cold War watchword. Congress passed the National Security Act in July 1947, unifying the armed forces under the Department of Defense and the heads of the Army, Navy, Air Force, and Marines as the Joint Chiefs of Staff. To further inform the President on security issues, the Act also created the National Security Council (NSC) and the Central Intelligence Agency (CIA).

Truman and the Marshall Plan

Though stressing preparedness, Truman wanted to avoid war. Believing that communism was best contained by economic aid, he declared,

"The seeds of totalitarian regimes are nurtured by misery and want. They spread and grow in the evil soil of poverty and strife. They reach their full growth when the hope of a people for a better life has died. We must keep that hope alive."

The Marshall Plan, or European Recovery Program, rushed aid after 16 European nations drew up a recovery plan. The 209 tractors unloaded at the French port of Le Havre were part of the aid.

Social History
For months Berliners lived with the sound of planes ringing in their ears. One plane landed every three minutes. So many planes were in the air that a plane not able to land on the first try had to return to its home base.

One pilot, Lt. Gail Halvorsen, won the hearts of Berlin's children by dropping candy and gum. He identified his plane for them by waggling its wings as he flew over. They soon called him "Uncle Wigglywings" or "The Chocolate Flier." He solved the problem of making parachutes for the small drops by using handkerchiefs.

Nowhere was hope more in danger of dying than in Europe. During the harsh winter of 1946-1947, blizzards raged, leaving food and fuel shortages in their wake. Like most Americans, Truman had not at first seen a need for long-term relief. Early in 1947 Congress had even cut off UNRRA funds in the belief that the aid was helping Communists. Now, though, it seemed that Western Europe would collapse into chaos without continued aid.

In June Secretary of State George Marshall proposed a bold, innovative plan to get Europe back on its feet. If European nations worked out a joint plan for recovery, he promised, the United States would cover most of the cost. He proposed massive aid in money, food, fuel, and machinery.

Although Marshall said that "our policy is directed not against any country or doctrine," an underlying goal was to thwart the spread of communism. Spurred by news in February 1948 that Soviet-backed rebels had taken control of Czechoslovakia, Congress passed the Marshall Plan in March. Between 1948 and 1952, $13 billion in aid poured into Europe. Slowly, prosperity returned as entire cities were rebuilt, railroads were repaired, and new factories sprang up. In France and Italy the threat of Communist victory evaporated.

The Marshall Plan was a dramatic success, in contrast to the post-World War I policy of punishing defeated nations. Punishment had sown seeds of despair on which dictatorships later thrived, but the Marshall Plan brought recovery and hope.

Berlin was already suffering shortages of food and fuel when the Soviets announced a blockade. In 318 days American and British planes flew in 2.3 million tons of supplies.

The Berlin Airlift

In Germany, the United States, Britain, and France merged their occupation zones to prepare for the Marshall Plan. Then, in June 1948 they announced plans to form a democratic government in western Germany. Protesting this "violation" of four-power control, the Soviets proceeded to truly violate that principle. Soviet troops blocked all the routes between western Germany and Berlin, confident that the blockade would gain them complete control of Berlin.

It was a test of wills. The governor of the American zone promptly cabled: "If we plan to hold Europe against communism, we must not budge." To keep Berlin from falling into Soviet hands, the three powers decided to fly in food and supplies for western Berlin's 2.1 million residents.

Thus began a monumental effort known as the Berlin Airlift. Day after day, transport planes roared into the city at rooftop level, landing every three minutes. In May 1949 the Soviets finally lifted the blockade, allowing West Berlin to again receive goods along the single highway connecting it to West Germany. It was a dramatic victory in a Cold War "battle."

On May 23, 1949, the independent West German Federal Republic was created, with its capital at Bonn. Five months later the Soviets organized the East German Democratic Republic, with East Berlin as its capital. Cold War fighting had caused one country to be carved into two: West Germany and East Germany.

Developing

THE SECTION

Thinking Critically

Analysis. Have students compare the Truman Doctrine and the Marshal Plan to identify similarities and differences regarding (a) their adoption (b) their goals, and (c) means of implementing them.

Ask: Why was the United States eager to help Europe recover from the war, to create West Germany, and to make sure Western powers kept control of their sectors of Berlin? (Refer to Truman's quote on page 682. If countries had hope of recovery, they might not turn to communism. At the same time he wanted to ensure that all of Germany did not fall into Soviet hands.) Was the United States' foreign policy based on humanitarian concern, political strategy, or both?

Writing About History

Diary Entries. Have students do research to find out more about the Berlin Airlift. One book they might read is Richard Collier's *Bridge Across the Sky*. Then have them describe the airlift in diary entries that could have been written by a Berlin citizen or an American pilot.

Connections: Geography

Drawing a Map. Have students do research to discover the present independence status and alignment of each country shown on the map on this page. They can then redraw the map to show what they have learned.

Connections: Politics
Senator Robert Taft was an isolationist before World War II. In 1949 he was still wary of the close ties with other nations. Speaking against ratifying the NATO treaty, he said, *"If one of the nations of the pact provides [makes] an attack, even by conduct which we disapprove, we would still apparently be bound to its defense. By executing a treaty of this kind, we put ourselves at the mercy of the foreign policies of eleven other nations, and do so for a period of twenty years. The charter is obviously aimed at possible Russian aggression against Western Europe, but the obligation assumed is far broader than that."*

Geography Skills

ANSWERS

1. The East (Warsaw Pact and other communist nations): USSR, Bulgaria, Romania, Hungary, Poland, Czechoslovakia, Albania, Yugoslavia, East Germany.
2. The West (NATO and other western nations traditionally aligned with the free world): Great Britain, Ireland, Norway, Denmark, Sweden, Finland, Netherlands, Belgium, West Germany, France, Luxembourg, Switzerland, Austria, Italy, Portugal, Spain, Greece, Turkey.

Reduced student page in the Teacher's Edition

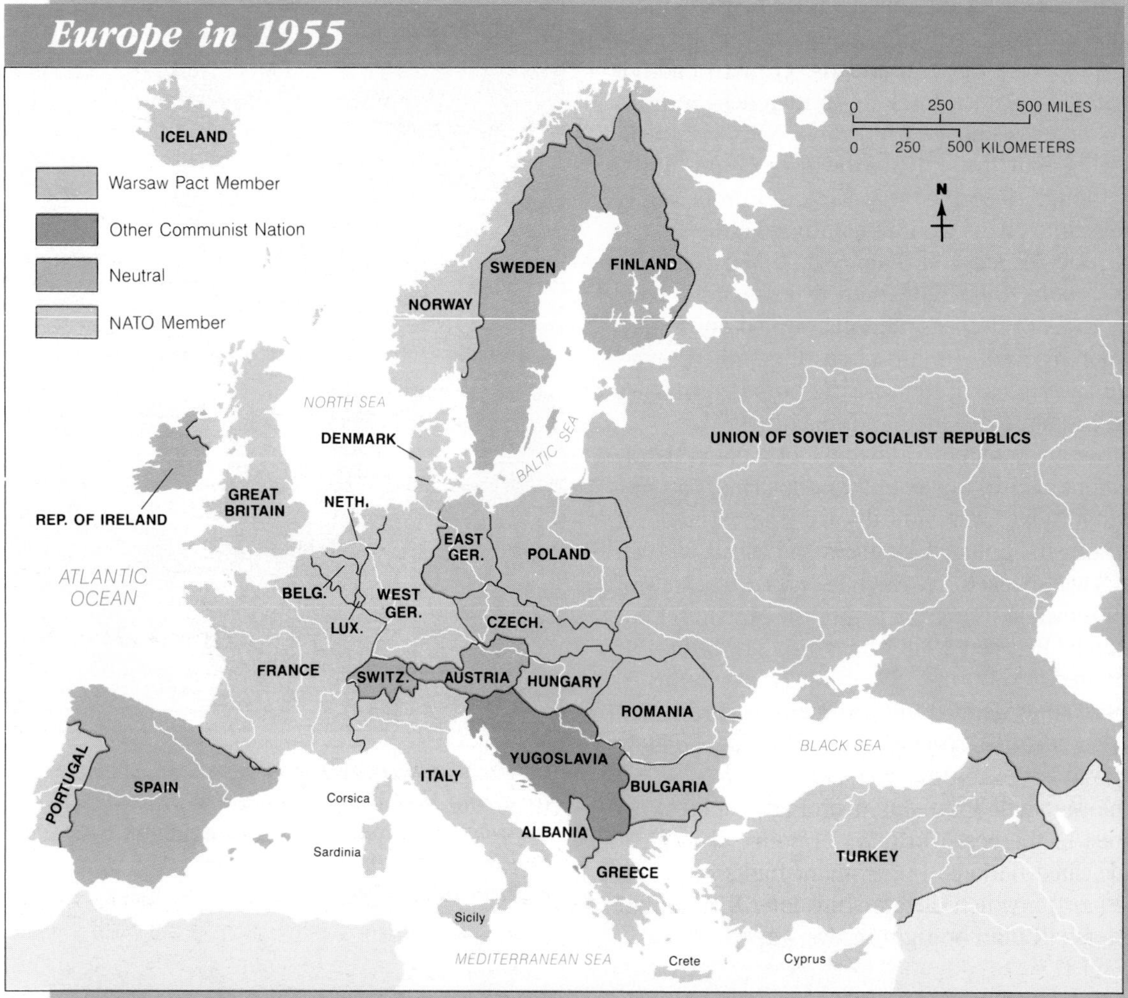

Geography Skills— Region. With the Cold War, Europe came to be seen as divided into two political regions— the East and the West. What countries made up each region?

NATO: A Sword and a Shield

Western Europeans had watched Soviet moves with increasing alarm. In March 1948, Britain, France, Belgium, Luxembourg, and the Netherlands signed the Brussels Pact, pledging military aid to any member attacked by the Soviet bloc. Without the United States, though, the alliance would be weak.

In 1948, after winning his second term, President Truman announced plans for an American-European alliance. In April 1949, twelve nations formed the North Atlantic Treaty Organization (NATO). An attack on one would be considered an attack on all. Signing were the United States, the Brussels Pact nations, Canada, Italy, Portugal, Denmark, Norway, and Iceland. Greece and Turkey joined in 1952 and West Germany in 1955.

When sent to the Senate for ratification, the treaty raised familiar concerns that the United States might be forced into a war. Truman's new

Global Connections

The Chinese Republic was established in 1912. It got off to a shaky start under Yuan Shih-k'ai, then was effectively divided among feuding warlords at his death. In 1924 the nationalist Kuomintang, founded by Sun Yat-sen, allied itself with the Communists, but Chiang Kai-shek, an aide of Sun's who came to power after the latter's death, began to attack Communists in 1927. As World War II ended, the Communists, led by Mao Zedong, gained power in the countryside.

Active Learning

Debate. NATO was formed in response to American-Soviet conflicts. Although some Americans saw NATO as a means of protecting free nations, others saw it as an opening to another war. NATO was established only after stormy debates in the Senate.

Have students debate, as though they were senators at the time the NATO treaty was presented to Congress, the issue of whether or not NATO should be established.

To prepare for the debate have students consider the pre-NATO activities of the United States and the Soviet Union and the purpose of NATO. The overall foreign policies of the United States and the Soviet Union should also be considered.

Secretary of State, Dean Acheson, assured the senators that Congress held the power to declare war, but he went on to warn:

> *"We have learned our history lesson from two world wars in less than half a century. If the free nations do not stand together, they will fall one by one."*

In July the Senate overwhelmingly approved the treaty, the nation's first military alliance with Europe since the treaty with France during the Revolutionary War.

At the first NATO meeting members decided to build a defensive force in order to deter the Soviet Union from attacking Western Europe. American atomic weapons, NATO's "sword," would provide protection for at least ten years, the time the NATO nations thought it would take the Soviets to unlock the atom's secret. In the meantime, NATO would have time to build a "shield," a ground force to counter the Soviet army.

Late in September, though, a plane detected radioactivity over the Soviet Union. The conclusion was shocking and inescapable: the Soviets had exploded an atomic bomb. Upon being informed, Truman asked, "Are you sure? Are you *sure?*" Then he said, "This means we have no time left."

Congress quickly voted $1 billion to arm NATO. Four months later Truman announced plans to build a hydrogen bomb, potentially a thousand times more powerful than the atomic bomb. Fearing an arms race, one physicist noted, "There is only one thing worse than one nation having the atomic bomb—that's two nations having it."

In 1950 American weapons and troops poured into Europe to strengthen NATO, and General Dwight D. Eisenhower was named its Supreme Commander. Reflecting the fact that NATO had become the focus of containment, Truman declared that "the defense of Europe is the basis for the defense of the whole free world."

In 1955, as a counterforce, the Soviet bloc formed the Warsaw Pact. It included the Soviet Union, Albania, Bulgaria, Czechoslovakia, East Germany, Hungary, Poland, and Romania. Once again Europe was divided into two hostile camps, armed and ready for conflict.

Communist Victory in China

The news of a Soviet atomic bomb was not all that jolted Americans early in the Cold War. The year 1949 also saw Communists sweep to power in China. Led by Mao Zedong (MOW DZUH-DOONG), they emerged victorious from a civil war with the Nationalists, led by Chiang Kai-shek.

Even though Chiang's government was brutal and corrupt, the United States had supported him, preferring a non-Communist leader to a Communist takeover. Mao's forces, however, had gradually gained ground, winning the support of the majority of the Chinese people, so that only massive military aid would keep Chiang in power.

Truman had foreseen a military nightmare, a view shared by General MacArthur, who had commented that "anyone who commits the American Army on the mainland of Asia ought to have his head examined." A land war in China could require hundreds of thousands of troops and lengthy supply lines. When Truman did not send troops, Chiang had bitterly accused the United States of ensuring a Communist victory.

A parade fills the streets of Shanghai in 1949 to greet the Communists.

Limited English Proficiency

Making a Time Line. Have students work in pairs to draw time lines that begin with 1945 and end with 1955. On the time lines have students write the dates and names of each of the following: Truman Doctrine, Marshall Plan, NATO, Warsaw Pact.

Once the students have placed each item on the time line, they should then add the threat(s) or conflicts, with appropriate dates, that led to each. Have students write a brief statement explaining how each conflict served as an impetus to the creation of each of the five items.

Global Connections

"Charlie" Soong, a Chinese man who grew up in the United States, founded a family that played a major role in the history of modern China. Soong came to this country in 1878, became an apprentice to a Chinese merchant, ran away to sea, and became a crewman on a U.S. ship. The ship's captain helped him get an education.

In 1886 Soong returned to China and raised a family. His son T.V. Soong held important posts in the Chinese Nationalist government. One of his daughters, Qingling, married Dr. Sun Yat-sen, the leader of the 1911 revolution against China's Manchu emperors. Another, Meiling, married Chiang Kai-shek, the leader of Nationalist China.

Thinking Critically

Analysis. Should the United States have recognized the government of the People's Republic of China in 1949? Tell students that the United States finally recognized the People's Republic of China in 1979. Have students speculate about why this happened.

Limited English Proficiency

Cooperative Activity. Refer students to the statement of the Truman Doctrine on page 681. Have them discuss its meaning in small groups and consider whether they would have supported or opposed it and why. Based on the discussion, the group can make a poster supporting or opposing involvement in the Korean War.

Reduced student page in the Teacher's Edition

American Marines advance in Korea in 1950. The United States provided half the ground troops in the Korean War.

Ousted in 1949, the Nationalists fled to the island of Taiwan (TI-WAHN). In October the Communists proclaimed the People's Republic of China, which Westerners labeled Red China. Twenty-five nations recognized the People's Republic, but the United States still regarded the Nationalist regime as China's legal government. With American support, the Nationalists continued to hold China's seat on the Security Council.

In 1950 Mao signed a treaty with the Soviets, allying 600 million Chinese to the Soviet Union. Dismayed, some Americans accused Truman of being "soft on communism" and of allowing China to "pass into the Soviet orbit." Others pointed to the corruption and inefficiency of Chiang's regime as reasons for the Communist victory.

A Defense Line in Asia

The Communist victory in China raised the question of how far the United States would go to contain communism. Few questioned the importance of Western Europe to American security, but Asia was another matter. Even during the civil war in China, American military leaders did not see a Red victory as a serious threat.

Similarly, policymakers displayed lukewarm interest in China's neighbor, Korea. In 1945 the United States and the Soviet Union had divided Korea into two zones along the 38th parallel. They promised to create a unified, independent Korea but could not agree on a plan. Therefore, in 1948 two governments were formed: the Republic of Korea, or South Korea, and the Democratic People's Republic of Korea, or North Korea. Despite their names, neither country was truly democratic.

In late 1949 and early 1950 North and South Koreans skirmished along their border. To American leaders, though, the 38th parallel was not yet a crossroads in the Cold War. As late as April 1950, they had announced a defense line from Alaska to Japan to the Philippines. The protected area did not include either Taiwan or Korea.

Truman, however, stung by public criticism over the "loss" of China, decided on a new policy: to resist Communist threats anywhere in the world. For some reason, though, this policy was not made public. As far as Soviet and North Korean leaders knew, South Korea was being left to fend for itself.

American Voices

"Anyone who commits the American Army on the mainland of Asia ought to have his head examined."

—General Douglas MacArthur, in 1949

The Korean War

Korea burst into American headlines early on June 25, 1950. North Korean troops stormed across the 38th parallel with their Soviet tanks and artillery, shattering the lightly armed South Korean forces and driving them southward.

Truman asked for an emergency session of the UN Security Council, which called for a cease-fire and the withdrawal of North Korean troops to the 38th parallel. The Soviets would have vetoed the resolution, but they were boycotting the Council because China's seat in the UN was held by a Nationalist.

Global Connections

Korea was divided following its liberation from Japan. Soviet presence in Korea grew out of ideas about international trusteeship encouraged by President Roosevelt, who hoped to see the United States and the Soviet Union cooperate first in ousting Japan from the area and then in preparing Korea for self-government. The required cooperation never materialized.

Truman ordered American forces to assist the South Koreans, an action cheered by Congress, the American public, and much of the non-Communist world. The Security Council urged United Nations members to help repel the attack, but the majority of the UN forces were American troops. Though officially part of a United Nations "police action," they were in effect fighting an American war to contain communism.

A seesaw conflict. Under MacArthur's command, UN troops marched into Korea in the summer of 1950. Having no tanks or heavy artillery, they were quickly pushed back to Korea's southeastern tip. There, as fresh troops and weapons arrived in August, the defense line held.

Now MacArthur took the offensive with a daring plan: an attack behind enemy lines at Inchon, near the 38th parallel. "We shall land at Inchon," he declared, "and I shall crush them." In a surprise attack American marines landed at Inchon on September 15 and then pushed inland to free Seoul (SŌL), the South Korean capital. By October UN troops were poised along the 38th parallel.

Having swept the invaders from South Korea, MacArthur got Truman's approval to push into North Korea. As his army marched north, China warned that it would not "stand idly by," a threat that both Truman and MacArthur considered a bluff. By November MacArthur reached the Yalu River separating North Korea from China. Soon the triumphant general was promising to "have the boys home by Christmas."

However, on November 26 more than 300,000 Chinese troops swept down upon UN forces. Injecting humor into a desperate situation, a Marine colonel told his troops, "The enemy is in front of us, behind us, to the left of us, and to the right of us. They won't escape *this* time." Instead, it was the UN forces that found themselves in rapid retreat along an icy road the troops called "nightmare alley." Violent snowstorms took as many lives as did Chinese grenades and machine guns.

UN forces were driven back into South Korea, pursued by what a stunned MacArthur called a "bottomless well" of Chinese soldiers. MacArthur and his staff had fallen victim to inaccurate intelligence reports, for early in November thousands of Chinese had slipped into the steep gorges of North Korea, unseen by UN patrols.

The setback confronted Americans with a dreadful reality. As MacArthur reported, UN forces were "facing the entire Chinese nation in an undeclared war." In his private notes Truman wrote, "I have worked for peace for five years and six months and it looks like World War III is near."

The Korean War 1950-1953

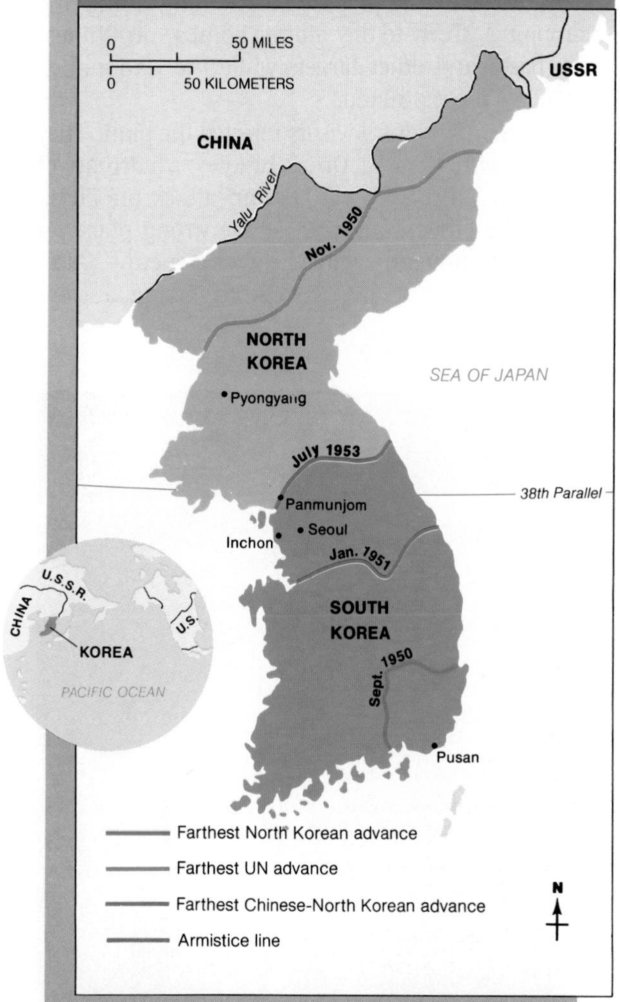

Geography Skills—Movement.
Describe the four stages of the Korean War in terms of the advances, retreats, and extent of territory held by Communist and UN forces.

Linking Past and Present

Discussion. Both the Korean War and the 1991 Gulf War were technically United Nations' "police actions" but in fact the United States directed the war effort and provided a majority of the troops. Have students compare the two wars in terms of United Nations (other than United States) participation and reasons for UN intervention, including U.S. reasons for supporting the intervention. Finally, have them discuss the extent to which they think each war was an international effort and (if they think it was not) whether it was necessary or acceptable to call it one.

Analyzing Primary Sources

Harry Truman. Refer students to Truman's assertion on this page: *"I have worked for peace for five years and six months and it looks like World War III is near."* Have them consider which of Truman's actions support his statement that he worked for peace **(for example, sought a cease-fire order from the United Nations).** Which actions seem to contradict it?

Geography Skills

ANSWERS

1. North Koreans advance to the southeastern tip of the peninsula by September 1950.
2. United Nations troops drive the North Koreans back nearly to the Yalu River by November.
3. Chinese join the North Koreans in shoving UN forces to a line south of Seoul.
4. Armistice line established midway on peninsula.

Constitutional Heritage

Discussion. Who had the right to make the military decision in the Truman-MacArthur controversy? Why is the President the commander in chief of the armed forces? What gives the President that power? **(the Constitution)** Why is that power important in a democracy?

Multicultural Perspectives

African-American soldiers in the Korean War were able to serve in integrated units for the first time, as a result of President Truman's 1948 order commanding "equality of treatment and opportunity" for all races in the American military. Two African-American soldiers who gave their lives in the war, Private First Class William Thompson and Sergeant Cornelius H. Charlton, were awarded the Medal of Honor posthumously.

One fighting unit, the 65th infantry, was made up entirely of Puerto Ricans. Flying ace Colonel Manuel J. Fernández flew 125 combat missions. Nine Hispanic Americans were awarded Congressional Medals of Honor for heroism in the Korean conflict.

Section Review

ANSWERS

1. Agree: Marshall Plan helped nations that badly needed help, avoiding economic chaos that followed World War II; provided a bulwark against totalitarianism. Disagree: very expensive.
2. Purpose was to provide for the common defense of member nations against an attack by the Soviet bloc. Its sword was atomic weapons, its shield a ground force.
3. Became involved when Communist North Korean forces drove beyond the 38th parallel into South Korea. Truman, resolved to resist Communist aggression everywhere, had American troops assist South Korea. The effects were American participation in a long, and not altogether popular, costly war and the Republican presidential victory in 1952.
Data Search: Sept 1950: North Korea advanced far south; Nov 1950: UN forces advanced far north; Jan 1951: North Korea and China again advanced south; Nov 1951: armistice line at 38th parallel.

Reduced student page in the Teacher's Edition

The MacArthur controversy. Admitting that "we face an entirely new war," MacArthur argued that the only path to victory was to attack China directly. He proposed blockading China and dropping "thirty to fifty atomic bombs" on Chinese air bases and other targets while the Nationalists attacked the mainland.

Truman and his advisors rejected the plan. They agreed with General Omar Bradley, chairman of the Joint Chiefs of Staff, that an attack on China would be "the wrong war, at the wrong place, at the wrong time, and with the wrong enemy." Also, it might draw in the Soviets, triggering a third world war.

Truman and MacArthur meet on Wake Island in October 1950. Later, after they clashed over Korean War strategy, Truman fired MacArthur.

The President returned to the goal of driving the Communists out of South Korea. UN troops regrouped and by March 1951 had pushed the Communists back into North Korea. MacArthur, however, publicly threatened to attack China and sent a letter to Congress stating that "there is no substitute for victory."

Convinced that the general's actions were ruining efforts to arrange a truce, Truman fired him on April 11. "MacArthur left me no choice," he later wrote. "I could no longer tolerate his insubordination." Many Americans were outraged at Truman's action. Pro-MacArthur telegrams flooded the White House, and upon arriving home he was welcomed as a hero.

When Congress inquired into the dismissal, Truman's advisors argued that the general had challenged the President's constitutional right to control the military and direct foreign policy. Congress upheld Truman's decision, and the controversy slowly died down. In the meantime, however, the President had suffered political damage, and the general public remained frustrated with the Korean War stalemate.

Eisenhower Elected in 1952

In July 1951 UN representatives and the Communists began cease-fire negotiations. Clouded by suspicion on both sides, the talks dragged on. Meanwhile, the fighting continued.

When Americans went to the polls to elect a new President in November 1952, the Korean War was a major issue. Truman had decided not to run for reelection, but the Democratic candidate, Governor Adlai E. Stevenson of Illinois, supported his policy of limited war. Republican candidate Dwight D. Eisenhower, riding on his popularity as a World War II hero, roused support by declaring "I shall go to Korea." He did not say what he might do once he got there.

The voters, confident that "Ike" would end the war and salvage American pride, swept him to victory. Eisenhower visited the battle front in December, before taking office as President, but admitted to finding no solutions.

Seven more months of talks finally produced an armistice on July 27, 1953, which divided Korea

Linking Past and Present
The Voice of America, established in 1942, still operates today. Each week it broadcasts in English and about forty other languages to an estimated 110 million people. Programs originate in Washington D.C., and are relayed to stations in Europe, Asia, and the Middle East.

along the battle line, which was roughly the 38th parallel, with a demilitarized zone between North Korea and South Korea. However, no permanent peace treaty was signed.

Neither side could claim victory in the conflict, which had claimed the lives of 54,000 Americans and more than a million Chinese and Koreans. Some $18 billion in American aid had been funneled into an undeclared war—one that set a precedent for a much longer intervention: the Vietnam War.

Section Review

1. Evaluation. If you had lived in the 1940s, would you have supported the Marshall Plan? Explain.

2. Comprehension. What was NATO's purpose? What were its "sword" and "shield"?

3. Analysis. Why did the United States become involved in the Korean War? What were the effects?

Data Search. Explain how the map on page 687 shows that the Korean War was a "seesaw conflict."

25-3 *Threatening "Massive Retaliation"*

Focus: How did the policy toward communism under Eisenhower compare with Truman's policy?

Dwight D. Eisenhower won the presidency, in good part, by pledging to end the Korean War. "A soldier all my life," he told voters, "I have enlisted in the greatest cause of my life—the cause of peace." To guide foreign policy, though, Eisenhower chose a man with a sharp tongue and an abiding hatred and distrust of communism: John Foster Dulles.

While Truman had declared "*I* make foreign policy," Eisenhower gave Dulles considerable control, more than any previous Secretary of State. Dulles showed a talent for expressing policies in dramatic phrases that the more moderate Eisenhower often had to soften.

The Dulles Approach

For Dulles, the Cold War was a moral conflict pitting the forces of good against the evil of communism. He labeled containment a "negative, futile, and immoral policy" because it allowed communism to exist. Instead, he wanted to liberate people from communism. One method was to use "ideas as weapons" through Voice of America radio broadcasts urging people in the Soviet bloc to overthrow their governments.

The struggle against communism also involved the CIA, which since its founding in 1947 had moved beyond intelligence gathering and into **covert operations,** secret activities to undermine governments considered unfriendly to American interests. Truman had given lukewarm support to such activities, but under Eisenhower and Dulles the CIA took on a more aggressive role.

The intensified campaign against communism included not only increased covert activity but also overt threats. In January 1954 Dulles announced a new military policy. Instead of relying on limited war, as in Korea, the United States would "retaliate, instantly, by means and at places of our choosing." This thinly veiled threat to attack the Soviet Union or China with nuclear weapons became known as the policy of **massive retaliation.**

According to Dulles, nuclear weapons not only presented a stronger military threat than troops and tanks but also cost the taxpayers less, giving "more bang for the buck." In departing from the strategy of limited war, the government could save money by cutting back the armed forces.

Section 25-3

Objectives

- ***Answer the Focus Question.***
- *Explain Dulles's approach to the Cold War.*
- *Analyze how events in Asia and Europe increased international tension.*
- *Explain how events in Latin America intensified the Cold War.*

Introducing

THE SECTION

Discuss why someone might have felt (as John Foster Dulles did) that communism was a moral as well as a political issue. Have students discuss whether they agree or disagree with this point of view and why.

Developing
THE SECTION

Active Learning

Drawing Political Cartoons. Have students discuss whether or not they agree with the domino theory. Why might the fall of one country to communism lead to the fall of another? (Communist insurgents might use the first country as a base for invading the second, for example.) Why might the fall of one not lead to the fall of another? (Social conditions in the two countries might be different; ability to resist Communist attack might be different.) Have students draw political cartoons reflecting their views of the domino theory.

Global Connections

Discussion. Have students discuss whether the United States could have taken any action in Vietnam at this time that would have prevented the later war. If so, what?

Nuclear weapons, however, proved to be far from cheap. By 1953 both the Americans and the Soviets had added the awesome hydrogen bomb to their arsenals. With scientists working on even more powerful bombs, the two nations found themselves locked in an expensive arms race.

Brinkmanship. Dulles believed that the threat of massive retaliation would ensure peace. Noting that the United States had frequently been brought to the verge of war by the actions of others, he favored taking the initiative by risking war in order to avoid war. In a *Life* magazine article, he explained his view:

> *"You have to take chances for peace, just as you must take chances in war. . . . The ability to get to the verge without getting into the war is the necessary art. If you are scared to go to the brink, you are lost."*

Americans were shocked and unsettled by Dulles's view, which newspapers labeled "brinkmanship." In foreign policy, though, as in other areas, actions speak louder than words. Would the United States truly risk nuclear war to force the Communists to back down?

Inaction in Indochina

Dulles's strategy was soon tested in the French colony of Indochina, which included Laos, Cambodia, and Vietnam. French forces were being challenged by nationalist rebels, some of whom were Communists. The fighting centered in Vietnam, where nationalists led by Ho Chi Minh called themselves the Vietminh.

American policymakers saw the rebellion as Communist expansionism and approved aid to the French, paying 80 percent of the war costs. Still, by March 1954 French forces were losing their grip. They desperately pleaded with the United States to drop atomic bombs on the rebels.

American Voices

> *"If you are scared to go to the brink, you are lost."*
>
> —John Foster Dulles

Arguing that the fall of Vietnam could lead to the loss of all the Southeast Asian countries, Eisenhower declared, "You have a row of dominoes set up, and you knock over the first one, and what will happen to the last one is the certainty that it will go over very quickly." This view that the fall of one country to Communists would lead to the fall of others was called the **domino theory.** Though supported by little evidence, it was accepted as truth by American policymakers.

Despite the domino theory and Dulles's tough brinkmanship talk, none of America's allies were willing to join in fighting the Vietminh. Therefore, Eisenhower did not intervene, a decision that sealed the French defeat. A multinational conference divided Vietnam in half, with a Vietminh government in the north and a pro-Western one in the south. Elections were to take place in two years to unite the country, but the south never held them. Vietnam remained split, setting the stage for heavy American intervention a decade later.

Brief "Peaceful Coexistence"

After sizing up the Indochina situation, Eisenhower had exercised caution, an attitude seemingly shared by the new Soviet leader, Nikita Khrushchev (nuh-KEE-tuh Kroosh-CHAWF), who came to power after Stalin's death in 1953. In 1955 Khrushchev began speaking of "peaceful coexistence," or nonmilitary competition. Cold War ice seemed to crack further in June 1956, when word spread of a speech Khrushchev had made at a secret session of the Communist Party. Denouncing Stalin as a brutal dictator, he seemed to promise greater freedom and independence within the Soviet bloc.

In Poland people responded by demonstrating against the Communist party and demanding greater freedom. Khrushchev reacted moderately to these protests, giving limited self-rule to the Poles, who in turn reaffirmed their alliance with the Soviet Union.

Waves of restlessness also swept through Hungary, with riots breaking out in the capital of

BACKGROUND

Global Connections

Oil was discovered in what is now Iran in 1908. Subsequently, foreign corporations, mostly British and American, acquired rights—called *concessions*—to develop the land for oil production. After World War II, oil became increasingly important to the industrialized nations, and nationalists began to challenge foreign control of oil deposits.

In 1951 the Iranian parliament (Majlis) voted to nationalize the oil industry. The prime minister refused to enforce the law and was replaced by nationalist leader Mohammed Mossadegh. In a power struggle, Mossadegh forced the shah into exile. However, with CIA help, the shah was returned to power in 1953, and Mossadegh was arrested.

In the 1950s Soviets crushed East German and Hungarian (left) revolts. In 1989, with Soviet support withdrawn, Communist regimes in Eastern Europe crumbled. Here, Romanians remove a statue of Lenin.

Budapest and quickly spreading. The Hungarian people, though, wanted more than limited self-rule. Urged on by the Voice of America, they were seeking freedom from communism. They declared their independence and withdrew from the Warsaw Pact in November.

In response, Soviet tanks and troops rolled into Hungary. Rebels armed with little more than rocks and rifles tried in vain to stop the tanks while others used Radio Budapest to broadcast pleas for help to the outside world. The UN and United States, however, offered only words. Eisenhower urged the Soviets to withdraw, but neither he nor Dulles was willing to intervene and risk war. The revolt was crushed, leaving brinkmanship once again looking like "bluffmanship."

Meddling in the Middle East

When the Hungarian revolt failed, the Cold War line in Europe between NATO and the Warsaw Pact was left untouched. Meanwhile, in the sands of the oil-rich Middle East, Cold War lines had not been drawn, but both superpowers were trying to extend their influence.

Suspecting that Soviet spies were at work in the region, Eisenhower and Dulles turned the CIA loose to plot its own covert operations. The CIA made its boldest move in Iran, which had nationalized Western oil companies and, to American eyes, seemed likely to align with the Soviets. In 1953 CIA agents helped the Shah of Iran overthrow the government in a coup that returned control of oil to Western companies. However, the CIA's involvement left many Iranians bitterly resentful of what they saw as American imperialism.

Outside of Iran, most of the region's oil was in Arab lands. Egyptian leader Gamal Abdel Nasser was seeking to unite those lands into one nation. A fierce nationalist who wanted Arabs to step out of the shadow of foreign nations, Nasser did not take sides in the Cold War. He cleverly played one side against the other as he worked to create a strong Arab nation that could crush Israel.

In 1955 the United States offered to help Egypt finance a dam at Aswan on the Nile River. In July 1956, however, after Egypt stepped up trade with the Soviet bloc, an annoyed Dulles declared that Nasser could "go to Moscow" for the money, and withdrew the offer. Furious, Nasser nationalized the Suez Canal, which had been operated by a

Writing About History

Diary Entry. Two hundred thousand Soviet troops and 2,500 tanks invaded Budapest, Hungary, on November 4, 1956. Before the revolt was put down, 32,000 people were killed and 195,000 fled their homeland.

Students can research the Hungary uprising and then write a diary account of one or two days during the uprising from the point of view of a Hungarian or a Soviet soldier involved in it.

Global Connections

Discussion. **Ask:** Why did the United States intervene in the takeover of South Korea but not in the takeover of Hungary? Should the United States have intervened in the Hungarian situation? Why or why not?

Thinking Critically

Evaluation. Explain that nationalization means government takeover of private property or business, with or without compensation. Have students discuss whether nationalization is justified. (Nationalization might be justified if a government could run an industry more efficiently than private enterprise or if a foreign company was unfairly exploiting a country's workers or resources; or unjustified if it interfered with a free market or made business less efficient.)

Limited English Proficiency

Cooperative Activity. Have students imagine they are advisors to President Eisenhower. Have them meet in small groups to suggest an appropriate policy for the Suez Crisis or the situations in Lebanon, Guatemala, or Cuba. Ask them to give reasons supporting the policy they would suggest to the President. Each group can share their ideas with the class.

Geography Skills

ANSWERS

Students might speculate that: **1.** A Communist Korea would give China a friendly neighbor. **2.** Hungary was part of the Soviet bloc, and Soviets wanted to keep it that way. **3.** United States saw Iran as a major power in the Middle East, important for its oil and transportation routes, and wanted to be an influence there. **4.** Central location of Lebanon relative to the sea lanes and oil wells of the Middle East would prompt the U.S. to want to keep it stable. **5.** United States interest in Guatemala was prompted by the nation's policy of excluding communism from the Western Hemisphere. **6.** Berlin was a thorn to the Communists; gaining all of Berlin would have eliminated western presence in East Germany.

Connections: Science and Technology

The Aswan Dam was finally completed in 1970. It allows the annual Nile floods to be controlled for the first time in history. One problem faced by the builders of the dam was that it would have submerged the temple complex of Abu Simbel, built by the pharaoh Ramses II, who ruled between about 1304 and 1237 B.C. The complex includes four huge (67 feet high) statues of Ramses. Between 1964 and 1966, in work sponsored by UNESCO, the temples and statues were completely cut apart into giant blocks, then moved to higher ground and reconstructed.

Reduced student page in the Teacher's Edition

Cold War Trouble Spots 1947-1960

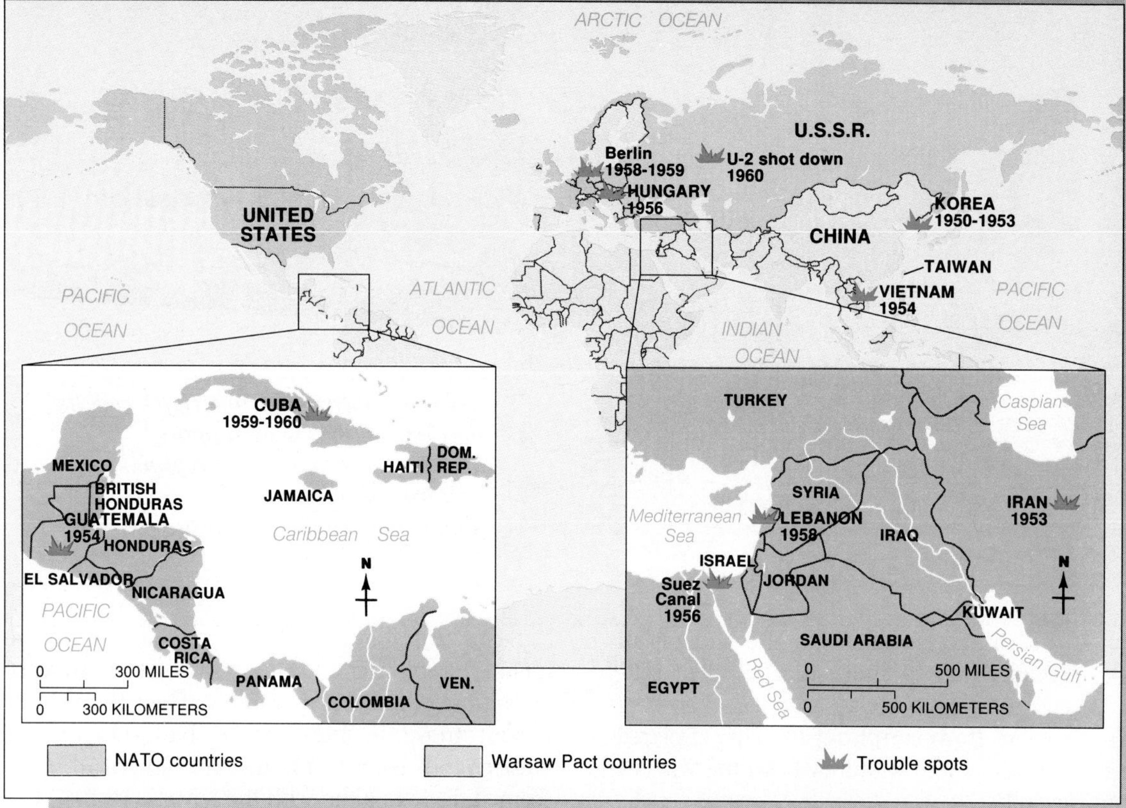

Geography Skills—Location. Study the map to determine how in each case relative location influenced a country's decision: China's intervention in Korea; Soviet response to Hungarian revolt; U.S. support of Iranian coup; U.S. assignment of marines to Lebanon; U.S. support of overthrow of Guatemalan government; Soviet ultimatum on Berlin.

British-French company. In addition to declaring that Egypt was taking control of the canal, he said that canal tolls would finance building the dam.

Fearing that Egypt would bar them from the canal, Britain and France secretly plotted with Israel to overthrow Nasser. On October 29, 1956, Israeli troops swept into Egypt, attacking bases from which Arabs had been raiding Israel. Britain and France, claiming that the fighting threatened the canal, launched their own attacks and by early November controlled the key waterway.

Eisenhower and Dulles were enraged by the attacks, which violated the UN Charter and, they feared, opened the door to increased Soviet influence in Egypt. Under American and Soviet pressure, the British and French pulled out. The Israelis pulled out early in 1957.

Many Arabs saw the conflict, labeled the Suez Crisis, as a triumph of nationalism because the old colonial powers had been swept from the Middle East. The Soviets, seeing it as an opportunity to expand their influence, sent aid to Egypt and Syria.

Global Connections

The Organization of American States includes 31 Latin-American nations, as well as the United States. The OAS advocates international law and economic cooperation. It also proclaims that an aggression against one member nation is an aggression against all. The OAS functions through a number of bodies, the most important of which is the Permanent Council, located in Washington, D.C. One of its agencies, the Inter-American Rights Commission, investigates violations of human rights in Latin America.

A return to containment. In the Middle East, as elsewhere, both superpowers continued to view third world nations as pawns in the Cold War. In January 1957 Eisenhower said, "The existing vacuum in the Middle East must be filled by the United States before it is filled by Russia." In March Congress approved a plan that became known as the Eisenhower Doctrine. It authorized the President to give aid to Middle Eastern nations resisting attack by "any nation controlled by international communism."

The Eisenhower Doctrine, which assumed that the Soviets were pulling the strings on all Communist activity, was first put into practice in 1958. In July the pro-Western government of Iraq was toppled by rebels suspected of receiving help from Egypt and Syria. Lebanon and Jordan, fearing they might be targeted for revolts, asked for help.

Eisenhower swiftly sent 5,000 marines to Lebanon and convinced Britain to send troops to Jordan. After Egypt and Syria pledged not to intervene, the troops withdrew. The United States had demonstrated willingness to engage in limited war, a threat more easily carried out than massive retaliation. Meanwhile, the quest to end communism was quietly dropped in favor of containment.

Tense Relations with Latin America

In the early days of efforts to counter communism, American policymakers saw little danger in Latin America. As a result, less than 3 percent of American foreign aid went to the region, mostly to support right-wing dictators. Starting in 1954, however, the picture began to change rapidly.

In 1950 the United States had joined the Organization of American States (OAS), founded to settle regional disputes and to maintain peace and security. In March 1954, after prodding by the United States, the OAS declared communism a threat to the Americas. Two months later, when Czechoslovakia shipped arms to Guatemala, Dulles accused the Czechs of trying to "endanger the peace of this hemisphere." Citing the domino theory, the United States sent arms to Honduras and Nicaragua.

Next, in June, CIA-backed rebels overthrew the elected Guatemalan government and set up a dictatorship. Boiling with resentment of American neglect, on the one hand, and anger over interference on the other, Latin Americans showered Vice-President Richard Nixon's car with rocks and eggs when he visited the region in 1958.

The Cuban revolution. In January 1959 rebels led by Fidel Castro overthrew Cuban dictator Fulgencio Batista (bah-TEES-tah). Arguing that American businesses had profited from ties with Batista, Castro nationalized American sugar plantations, paying the owners almost nothing. As he jailed or shot opponents and suspended civil liberties, relations with the United States soured further.

In 1960 Castro signed a trade agreement with the Soviet Union. When the United States reacted by blocking Cuban sugar imports, he moved further toward the Soviet camp.

Soon Castro was boasting of spreading communism to other Latin American countries. Eisenhower, fearing that anti-American feelings could fuel Communist expansion, approved $500 million

Unemployment and a wide gulf between the rich and the poor led many Cubans to support Fidel Castro.

Active Learning

Making Charts. Have students work in pairs to make a chart of United States policies toward Latin America between 1900 and 1960. The chart should place the policies (with dates) along a continuum with Most Interference at one end and Least Interference at the other. Students can use the charts to discuss how United States policy toward Latin America changed during this time.

Writing About History

Newspaper Article. Remind students that newspaper writing concentrates on the five "Ws": Who, What, When, Where, and Why. Have students imagine they were journalists when the Organization of American States was formed. Using the five "Ws" as a guide, students should write newspaper articles about OAS.

Connections: Science and Technology
Sputnik (the name means "pilgrim" or "traveler") weighed about 185 pounds and was only about 23 inches in diameter. It circled the earth once every 96 minutes, with its radio transmitter beeping. A second, much larger *Sputnik* (1,100 pounds), with a dog (Laika) on board, was launched a month later.

Active Learning

Skits. Divide the class into teams. Each team can stage a skit portraying American reactions to Sputnik. (Skits could be of a family's dinner table conversation, reporters interviewing people on the street, or a meeting of government officials.) To get ideas for their skits students might research newspaper stories and editorials about Sputnik in October and November 1957.

Backyard History

Conducting an Interview. Have students try to find out what preparations for a possible Soviet missile attack (fallout shelters, Civil Defense drills, and so on) were made in their area during the late 1950s. Students can interview their parents or other adults about fears they may have had of such an attack (especially as children).

Reduced student page in the Teacher's Edition

in aid to Latin America. "We are not saints," he said. "We know we make mistakes but our heart is in the right place." Many Latin Americans, though, doubted whether the United States would truly pursue its "Good Neighbor Policy."

The Cold War Turns Frigid

While struggling to contain what they saw as Communist expansionism in Latin America, American policymakers faced a renewed Soviet threat in Europe. In November 1958 Khrushchev had abandoned talk of peaceful coexistence and threatened to force the Americans, British, and French to get out of West Berlin.

Khrushchev's boldness may have been spurred by a stunning technological success. In October 1957 the Soviets had launched into orbit the world's first satellite, *Sputnik I.* The feat delivered a blow to American self-confidence and intensified fears about American security. For if the Soviets could rocket satellites into outer space, they might also send intercontinental ballistic missiles (ICBMs) to shower nuclear warheads upon American cities. Scrambling to close the "missile gap," the United States launched a satellite four months later and accelerated ICBM research.

Having matched the American hydrogen bomb and feeling confident that he was leading in missile research, Khrushchev hoped to make the United States blink first in Berlin. Eisenhower and Dulles, however, held their ground. "We are most solemnly committed to hold West Berlin," announced Dulles, "if need be by military force." Neither side was willing to go to war, however, and the deadline passed without incident.

Hoping to "melt a little of the ice" of the Cold War and perhaps resolve the Berlin crisis, Eisenhower invited Khrushchev to the United States. Arriving in September 1959, the Soviet leader set off on a whirlwind tour of the nation. By the time he reached Camp David, the presidential retreat in Maryland, he was in a jovial mood.

As relations between the United States and the Soviet Union chilled, war seemed likely. To track planes and detect missiles, a chain of radar stations was raised facing the USSR across the Arctic Ocean. Private citizens took their own measures, optimistically placing their faith in backyard bomb shelters for protection from atomic blasts and radioactive particles.

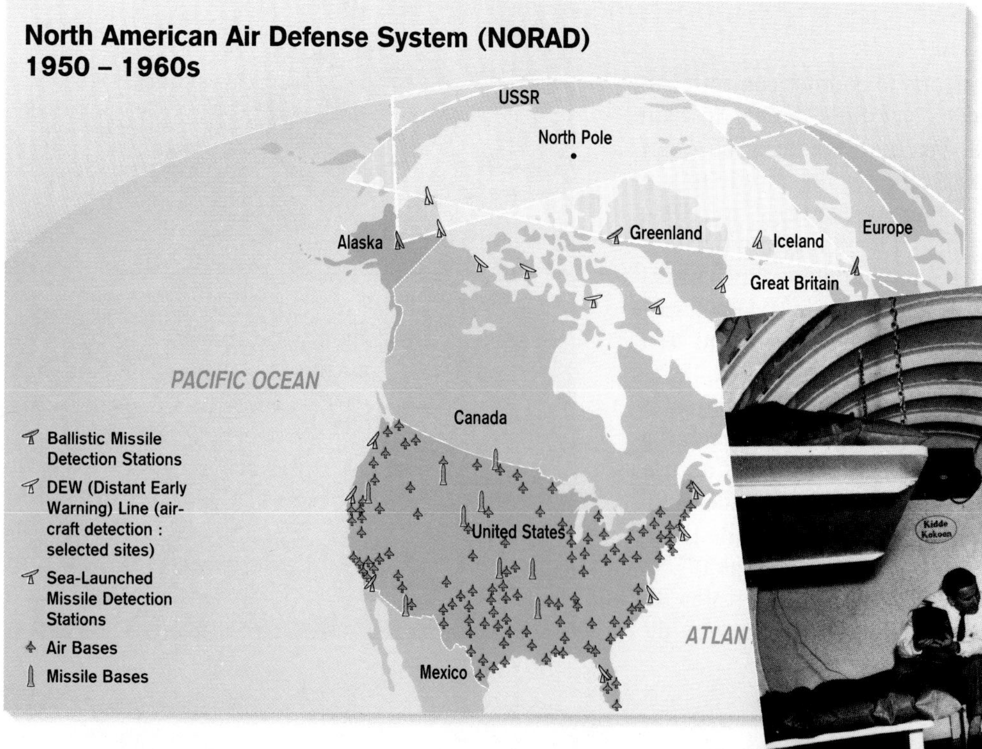

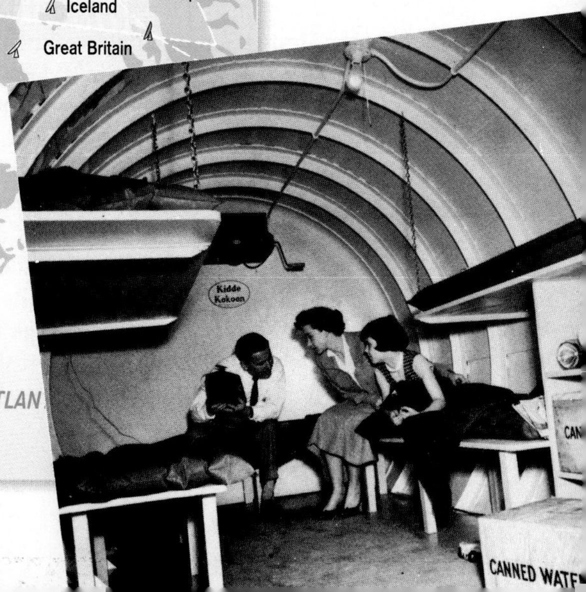

For three days the two leaders strolled the grounds and talked. As the meeting ended, they agreed that all future disputes "should be settled not by force but by peaceful means." Khrushchev extended indefinitely his Berlin ultimatum, and a summit conference with the leaders of Britain and France was planned for May 1960.

The U-2 incident. The warm spirit of Camp David abruptly ended on May 1, 1960, when an American U-2 spy plane was shot down in Soviet air space. At first the United States insisted that it was a weather plane that had strayed off course, but Khrushchev displayed the captured pilot and photographic equipment with pictures of military sites. Embarrassed American leaders then admitted that the U-2 was on a spy mission.

The summit took place as scheduled in Paris, but without handshakes or friendliness. Khrushchev harshly demanded an end to the U-2 flights, an apology from Eisenhower, and punishment for those responsible. Eisenhower announced that the flights had been suspended but offered no apology. The next day the Soviet leader went home, and the summit meeting collapsed.

With the Cold War blowing chilly gusts, some looked for comfort in remarks made later by the two leaders. Khrushchev still expressed his faith in negotiation, calling the clash "a passing phase," while Eisenhower said that "the path of reason and common sense is still open if the Soviets will but use it."

Section Review

1. Identification. Define *covert operations, massive retaliation,* and *domino theory.*

2. Evaluation. Contrasting their approach with Truman's, Eisenhower and Dulles said they had a "new look" policy toward communism. Do you think their description was accurate? Explain.

3. Comprehension. Why did tension between the Soviet Union and the United States increase during the late 1950s?

Linking Past and Present. How are the effects of the Cold War still evident in Latin America and the Middle East today?

Connections to Themes

Shaping Democracy

In announcing the containment policy in 1947, Truman said, "The free peoples of the world look to us for support in maintaining their freedoms." His words echoed those of Woodrow Wilson and Franklin Roosevelt in earlier crises. The belief that the United States has a responsibility to protect freedom and democracy became a moral rallying cry in the nation's Cold War against communism.

Containment, however, was not so much pro-democratic as it was anti-Communist. The United States found itself supporting dictators, such as those in Greece and Nationalist China, simply because they opposed communism. Furthermore, the use of military force against Communist rebels was viewed by some people, both in the United States and abroad, more as an effort to extend American power than as a struggle to protect freedom and democracy. In their eyes, both the United States and the Soviet Union were guilty of imperialism.

Has the quest to contain communism done more harm than good for the cause of democracy? That question, which continues to be asked to this day, emerged early in the Cold War. Not only was the Cold War pushing the United States into supporting dictatorships abroad but it was also threatening democracy at home. For on the "home front" during the 1950s, congressional committees were hunting for American Communists, as part of a new "Red Scare" similar to the one that had followed World War I.

Section Review

ANSWERS

1. Definitions for the following terms can be found on pages indicated in parentheses; *covert operations* (689), *massive retaliation* (689), *domino theory* (690).

2. Answers may include: Dulles believed Cold War a moral struggle against communism, encouraged propaganda broadcasts by Voice of America, had CIA covert actions play larger role, threatened massive retaliation, practiced brinkmanship. Under Eisenhower and Dulles, some aspects of Cold War more intensely pursued, but its nature not essentially different. Eisenhower ended Korean War.

3. Hostility toward Soviet Union increased after it put down Hungarian revolt. Rivalry between superpowers in oil-rich Middle East increased. U.S. troops sent to Lebanon to put down what was believed to be a Communist-inspired revolt. In Latin America, Communists and U.S. backed opposing forces. Cuban revolution increased American fear of Communist expansion. **Linking Past and Present:** Answers may include: American actions against Communist-inspired forces in Nicaragua, El Salvador and continued Cuban embargo; anti-American feelings in Iran, rooted in resentment of United States support of the Shah.

GTV Side 4

Chap. 7, Frame 29236

Immigration: 1911-1920; 1941-1950; 1971-1980 (Population Clocks, 3 Frames)

Search:

Step:

Chapter Survey

ANSWERS

Using New Vocabulary

1. *Domino theory* holds that one nation after another might fall to communism, much as had happened in the *Soviet bloc* nations.
2. To block the spread of communism during the *Cold War*, the United States adopted the policy of *containment.*

Reviewing the Chapter

1. Germany divided into four occupation zones, western Allies wanted to rebuild German economy, establish democratic government, while Soviets tightly controlled their zone, tried to cripple German economy. Japan was disarmed and occupied; it received aid in rebuilding economy, establishing democratic government.
2. Soviet Union dominated governments of Czechoslovakia, Poland, Bulgaria, Romania; tried to make inroads into Turkey, Iran.
3. Threat of communism in Europe and Middle East showed need for tougher stance against Soviets.
4. Western Allies merged occupation zones. Soviets retaliated by blockading Berlin. When airlift broke blockade, East and West were made into two separate nations.
5. Efforts concentrated on stopping any further Communist expansion in Europe through use of land forces now that Soviet Union had atom bomb.
6. At first, United States tried to avoid committing troops to Asia's mainland. Criticism of Truman as soft on communism and invasion of South Korea changed situation.
7. North Korean troops invaded South Korea in 1950. Truman sent U.S. troops, as UN forces, to push Communists back. At first they were driven southward but eventually pushed North Koreans out of South, drove as far as Chinese border. Chinese troops pushed Americans back to South Korea. Armistice at about 38th parallel, original dividing line. Dulles' policy changed focus from limited war to massive retaliation.
8. Dulles under Eisenhower wanted to wipe out communism, threatened massive retaliation. Acheson under Truman preferred to work through the Marshall plan and NATO to build up nations of western Europe so that they would not be tempted by communism.
9. Because Egypt began trading with Soviets, recognized Red China, Dulles withdrew offer of loan for Aswan Dam. Nasser then seized control of Suez Canal, which triggered invasion by Israelis, British, French.
10. United States supported anti-Communist dictatorship in Guatemala, embargoed

Chapter Survey

Using New Vocabulary

The vocabulary terms in each pair below are related to each other. For each pair, explain how the terms are related.

1. Soviet bloc, domino theory
2. Cold War, containment

Reviewing the Chapter

1. Compare and contrast the treatment of Germany and Japan after World War II.
2. Where and how was the Soviet Union expanding its influence?
3. Why did postwar American foreign policy shift its attention from the United Nations to the policy of containment?
4. Why did the Soviets blockade Berlin? How did the Allied response to the blockade lead to political changes?
5. Why did NATO become the focus of containment?
6. How and why did the containment strategy in Asia differ from the strategy in Europe?
7. Briefly trace the course of the Korean War from the roots of the conflict to the armistice. What effect did the Korean War have on American policy?
8. Compare Truman's policy with Eisenhower's.
9. How did the Cold War affect the Suez Crisis?
10. How did the Cold War affect Latin America and cause resentment of the United States?

Thinking Critically

1. Synthesis. Predict how the Security Council would function if the Big Five had no veto.
2. Analysis. Dean Acheson claimed that history taught the importance of alliances. Yet it could be argued that alliances entangled nations in World War I. Why do you think Acheson believed that NATO would work?
3. Evaluation. How successful was containment? Give examples to support your opinion.

Using Geography

Match each letter on the map with the correct nation or nations in the list below. Then explain why each country was a site of tension during the Cold War and what actions, if any, the United States took in that country.

1. North and South Vietnam
2. Iran
3. Hungary
4. Korea

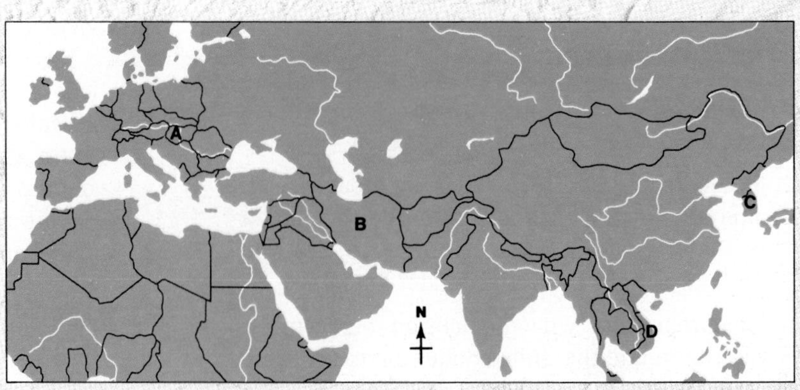

Cuban sugar imports. Latin Americans angry at U.S. interference in internal affairs of their countries.

Thinking Critically

1. UN might become embroiled, at behest of smaller nations, in a great many conflicts, and UN forces might be perpetually at war in one area of the world or another.
2. Acheson and others wanted NATO to be a bulwark against communism and probably thought the possibility of atomic warfare would deter the Soviets.
3. Answers will vary. Students who think containment successful can point to democracies of western Europe and to nations in Latin America and other areas (e.g., South Korea) that did not come under Communist control. Those disagreeing can point to Cuba and large parts of the world—e.g., China—that did become Communist.

Using Geography

1. (D) Communist North Vietnam invaded the south. The United States sent troops and became involved in a long costly war that many Americans opposed. Eventually South Vietnam fell.
2. (B) Suspecting Communist spies at work in Iran, CIA agents helped the shah overthrow the government. Control of its oil returned to the West.
3. (A) Hungarian rebels declared Hungary's independence from Soviet hegemony and the Warsaw Pact. When Soviets put down the revolt, U.S. did not intervene.
4. (C) After North Korea invaded South Korea, President Truman sent troops. The result was a long costly war.

History and You

Answers will vary.

Applying Social Studies Skills

1. Soviet Union 200, United States 2,600.
2. 16,100; heightened Cold War tensions, doctrine of massive retaliation.
3. The percentage increase was greater for the Soviets. Soviets attempting to catch up with the numerical difference in weapons that favored the United States.
4. The arsenals of both countries increased dramatically.

History and You

The launching of *Sputnik I* had a tremendous impact on American education. Interview several people who were students or teachers at that time to find out what changes they saw in schools. Have those changes continued to the present day?

Applying Social Studies Skills

Analyzing Bar Graphs

The graph below shows the results of enormous defense spending by the Soviet Union and the United States in the late 1950s and into the 1960s. Answer the following questions to help you analyze the graph.

The Nuclear Arms Race 1945 - 1965

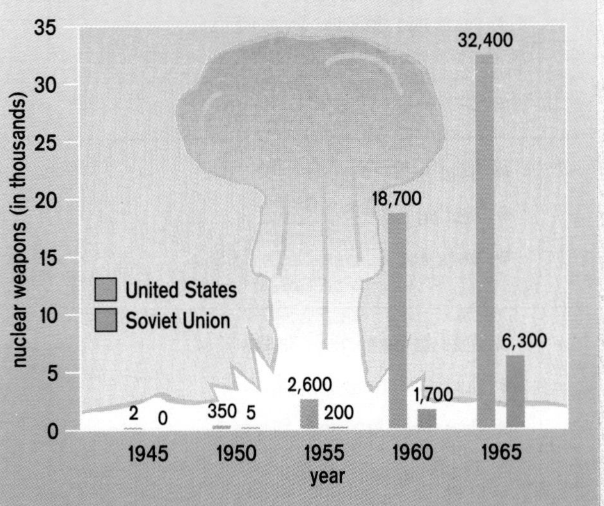

1. How many weapons did the Soviet Union and the United States each have in 1955?

2. How many more American nuclear weapons were there in 1960 than in 1955? What do you suppose accounts for the difference?

3. Compare the percentage increases of Soviet and American nuclear weapons between 1955 and 1965. What do you think accounts for the differing rates of increase?

4. How do you know that *both* sides participated in an "arms race" in the 1960s?

Writing About Issues

The Issue: *When should the United States go to war to protect weaker nations against stronger ones?*

When Truman sent troops to South Korea, he asserted that the United States had a responsibility to protect weaker nations from being overrun by stronger ones. Since the Korean War, other crises have raised the question of when and where the United States should go to war.

One such situation arose in 1991 when Iraqi troops under the command of Saddam Hussein invaded neighboring Kuwait. Alarmed at this aggression, the UN imposed an economic boycott against Iraq. When after several months the Iraqi troops did not withdraw, many people urged the United States and its allies to use military force. "If the world looks the other way," President George Bush stated, "other would-be Saddams will conclude, correctly, that aggression pays."

People opposed to fighting Iraq believed that the United States could not afford the economic cost of defending against aggression throughout the world. Others argued that protecting Kuwait was not worth American lives. "What happened to Kuwait was a tragedy," one veteran said, "but my heart is telling me that we don't need 50,000 of our young men to die over there. We have internal problems that are just as important as the problems in Kuwait."

What do you think? When should the United States go to war to protect weaker nations from the aggression of stronger ones? Imagine that you have a job as a speech writer for a candidate running for the Senate. Decide what stand to take. Then write a two-minute statement for a press conference, making your argument as persuasive as possible.

Chapter 26

Abundance and Uncertainty

Planning Guide

	Student Text	TWE Lesson Plans	Support Materials
SECTION 1	**Section 26–1 (1–2 Days)** **The Return to Peacetime,** pp 700–707 The American Spirit: Ernesto Galarza, p 702 Exploring Issues—Equal Opportunity: The Fair Employment Practices Committee, pp 706–707 Review/Evaluation Section Review, p 707	**Introducing the Chapter:** Themes of the Fifties—Class Activity, 30 minutes, p 697B **Teaching the Main Ideas:** Fair Deal Television Commercials—Cooperative Activity, one class period, p 697B **Teaching the Main Ideas:** Jukebox Hits—Cooperative Activity, one class period, p 697C **Reinforcement Activity:** The Dinner Party—Cooperative Activity, one class period, p 697C	★ **Read to Remember,** Section 1 ● **Section Activities,** Section 1 Δ **Enrichment Activities,** Section 1 Δ **Readings,** Jessie De La Cruz, Maxine Cheshire ● **Tests and Quizzes,** Section 1 Quiz
SECTION 2	**Section 26–2 (1–2 Days)** **Questions of Loyalty,** pp 708–710 Review/Evaluation Section Review, p 710	**Evaluating Progress:** Editorial on McCarthyism—Individual Activity, 30 minutes, p 697C **Enrichment Activity:** Survey on Communism—Cooperative Activity, homework, classwork, p 697C **Teaching the Main Ideas:** Jukebox Hits—Cooperative Activity, one class period, p 697C **Reinforcement Activity:** The Dinner Party—Cooperative Activity, one class period, p 697C	★ **Read to Remember,** Section 2 ● **Section Activities,** Section 2 Δ **Enrichment Activities,** Section 2 Δ **Readings,** Lillian Hellman ● **Tests and Quizzes,** Section 2 Quiz
SECTION 3	**Section 26–3 (1 Day)** **The Eisenhower Years,** pp 711–714 Review/Evaluation Section Review, p 714	**Teaching the Main Ideas:** Jukebox Hits—Cooperative Activity, one class period, p 697C **Reinforcement Activity:** The Dinner Party—Cooperative Activity, one class period, p 697C	★ **Read to Remember,** Section 3 ● **Section Activities,** Section 3 ● **Tests and Quizzes,** Section 3 Quiz
SECTION 4	**Section 26–4 (1–2 Days)** **Years of Abundance,** pp 715–721 Geography—Relationships Within Places: The Growth of Suburbs, p 719 Connections to Themes: The Search for Opportunity, p 721 Review/Evaluation Section Review, p 721 Chapter 26 Survey, pp 722–723 Skills, pp 722–723 Using New Vocabulary Thinking Critically Using a Time Line Applying Thinking Skills: Detecting Bias Writing About Issues	**Teaching the Main Ideas:** Jukebox Hits—Cooperative Activity, one class period, p 697C **Reinforcement Activity:** The Dinner Party—Cooperative Activity, one class period, p 697C	★ **Read to Remember,** Section 4 ● **Section Activities,** Section 4 ● **Geography Activities,** Section 4 Δ **Readings,** Ralph Martin ● **Tests and Quizzes,** Section 4 Quiz, Chapter 26 Test (Forms A and B) **Additional Resources** ● **Active Learning** Δ **GTV Videodiscs** Δ **Transparencies and Activity Book** ● **Testing Software** ★ **Chapter Summaries** **Key:** ★ For Extra Support ● For All Students Δ For Enrichment

Overview

In 1945 Americans wondered what the future would hold now that the war was over. Thousands of women had gone to work during the war; many wanted to continue. Members of ethnic groups had fought for democratic ideals overseas; now they pursued equal rights and opportunities at home.

Meanwhile, the nation faced the difficult shift from a wartime to a peacetime economy. Prices soared, and workers struck for wage increases. To curb labor's demands, Congress passed the Taft-Hartley Act, then overrode President Harry Truman's veto of the bill. Congress also voted down Truman proposals for civil rights legislation and a fair employment practices committee.

When conflict with the Soviet Union grew, a fear of communism took hold in the United States. Senator Joseph McCarthy gained national attention by charging that the government was infested with Communist infiltrators and traitors, but he provided little evidence to back his charges.

In 1952 Dwight Eisenhower was elected President. He moved to scale back the powers of the federal government in general and the executive branch in particular. During his term, the Supreme Court handed down the historic *Brown* v. *Board of Education of Topeka* ruling, ending segregation in public schools.

The Fifties were years of relative abundance, although not everyone shared in it. Freed from years of depression and war, people sought luxuries and comfort. Russia's launch of the first satellite focused attention on education. A baby boom, automation, television, nuclear power, suburbs, shopping centers, fast food drive-ins, and a tendency toward conforming behavior—all characterized life in the Fifties.

Activity Objectives

After completing the activities, students should be able to

- describe President Truman's solutions to postwar problems.
- describe the major social and political currents of the 1950s.
- analyze the experiences and attitudes of various groups of Americans in the 1950s.
- explain the events and attitudes that fostered McCarthyism.
- compare the attitudes toward communism and civil liberties prevalent in the 1950s with attitudes today.

Introducing the Chapter

Themes of the Fifties

This class activity requires a half a class period.

Before students read Chapter 26, engage their interest by discussing what they already know of the period. After the discussion, have students create a graphic web to show relationships among events, people, and ideas.

Explain to students that they probably already have some knowledge of the Fifties, perhaps from television shows and movies, such as *Happy Days, Leave It To Beaver*, and *American Graffiti*. Ask the class what words, phrases, and images this decade suggests to them. As students respond, make a list on the chalkboard. Encourage students to list a broad spectrum of occurrences, such as *Sputnik*, McCarthyism, Howdy Doody, and rock-and-roll.

Once a list has been generated, have students organize the information to show relationships between various occurrences. First, have students group the words and phrases into categories of their choosing, then name the categories. For example, the following words and phrases could be linked around the central theme Politics of Fear: McCarthy, spies, national television broadcasts, and House Committee on Un-American Activities. Some words and phrases may fit with more than one theme.

As the discussion continues, have two or three students display the relationships by creating a graphic web on the chalkboard. Following suggestions from the class, the students place each central theme or topic in a box or circle at the center of a web with the related words or phrases in circles or boxes arranged around the center. The subordinate boxes and circles can be linked to the central one with lines, producing a web pattern. An example of a graphic web appears on page 219C.

Conclude the activity by asking students to summarize the decade of the Fifties from the topics written on the board. Have students assess the areas of knowledge in which they are weak and encourage them to be alert for information on these areas as they read the chapter.

Teaching the Main Ideas

Section 26-1: Fair Deal Television Commercials

This cooperative activity requires a full class period, or part of the project may be assigned as homework.

In this activity students summarize the features of programs proposed by President Truman by creating television commercials to promote the programs.

After students have read Section 26-1, ask them to list the problems that Truman faced after World War II had ended. Answers should include skyrocketing prices, rising wages, and discrimination. Point out that Truman responded to these challenges with a series of proposals for legislation, but these proposals were rejected by Republicans and southern Democrats in Congress.

Remind students that in the late 1940s and the 1950s television became a popular medium. Ask students to imagine that President Truman has asked them to serve as consultants for a series of television commercials to build support for his proposals. Divide students into groups of three. Direct each group to prepare a two-minute advertisement on one of Truman's proposed programs. Tell students that they may focus on proposals that were not approved by Congress as well as those that were. Allow half a period for students to prepare their advertisements or assign the task as homework.

Have students present their advertisements to the class. After the presentations, discuss which programs were implemented and which were not and why.

Teaching the Main Ideas

Sections 26-1 26-2, 26-3, 26-4: Jukebox Hits

This cooperative activity requires one class period.

In this activity students are challenged to create song titles capturing aspects of life in the 1950s. Enlist an artistic student to draw a large representation of a jukebox on the chalkboard, a large sheet of paper, or posterboard. Have the artist provide a space in the drawing where students can write the titles of songs.

Ask students to name some of their favorite current songs and singing groups. Have students identify titles and names of groups that make a political or social statement. Discuss how songs reflect politics and social concerns today. Emphasize that songs of political and social comment have emerged in every era.

Divide the class into groups of three or four and direct each group to create five song titles that reflect some aspect of life in the 1950s. Along with their titles, students should name a singer or group, real or fictitious, to perform the songs. Provide examples such as "I See Red" by Joe McCarthy or "Opportunity Knocks" by the GIs. Encourage students to review the entire chapter for ideas.

Have students write the titles in the space on the jukebox. Allow time for the class to read the titles and discuss the social and political trends the titles suggest. Take a vote to award a Grammy in the "Best Title" category.

Reinforcement Activity

Sections 26-1, 26-2, 26-3, 26-4: The Dinner Party

This class activity requires one and a half class periods.

To more fully understand the uncertainty and abundance of the 1950s, students assume the roles of various people who lived during the decade. Inform the class that they will participate in role playing based on information throughout Chapter 25. In these roles students will simulate conversations that might have taken place at dinner parties in the 1950s.

Assign the following roles:

- *Dinner Party One:* returning GI, returning Japanese American, working woman, homemaker, member of a union, Ernesto Galarza, anti-labor senator, and a member of the NAACP.
- *Dinner Party Two:* J. Edgar Hoover, a government employee who resigned because of investigations, Joseph McCarthy, Margaret Chase Smith, a movie star accused of being a Communist, and a former Communist.
- *Dinner Party Three:* Charles Wilson, a Democratic member of Congress, John L. Lewis, A. Philip Randolph, Robert Taft, and Mary McLeod Bethune.
- *Dinner Party Four:* Raymond Chandler, Walter Reuther, a young couple, a farmer, a science teacher, a real estate agent, the owner of an appliance store, and an automobile dealer.

Direct students to develop their roles by listing the topics they would likely discuss and by thinking through their position on issues. Group the dinner party guests. Call on a student in each group to start the conversation and allow the conversations to continue for 10 to 15 minutes. If a guest is not participating, direct other group members to ask him or her a question.

Conclude by asking students to assess their conversations. What topics were discussed? Did conversations accurately reflect the issues of the 1950s? Which issues reflected the abundance of the 1950s? Which reflected the uncertainties?

Evaluating Progress

Section 26-2: Editorial on McCarthyism

This individual activity can be completed in half a class period or assigned as homework.

This activity is designed to evaluate the students' understanding of the threat to democracy posed by McCarthyism.

After students have read Section 26–2, discuss why so many people were afraid to criticize McCarthy. Tell students that their assignment is to put themselves in the role of a newspaper editor willing to risk writing an editorial against McCarthyism, the House Committee on Un-American Activities (HUAC), and the politics of fear.

Describe or write on the chalkboard the following characteristics of a good editorial: brief, to the point, defines the issues clearly, provides facts or examples, states the writer's personal viewpoints and the reasons for those views, recommends certain actions be taken, concludes with a punchy or thought-provoking sentence.

Direct students to exchange their completed editorials and evaluate each other's work. Criteria should include how well the editorials meet the characteristics stated above and how accurately they describe McCarthyism, HUAC, and the politics of fear.

Enrichment Activity

Section 26-2: Survey on Communism

This cooperative activity requires several days of out-of-class time as well as one class period for compiling information and discussing results.

In the following activity students will each ask three people five questions about communism. These same questions were originally asked in a public opinion survey in 1954.

Prepare a handout with the following questions or write them on the chalkboard for students to copy. Do not include the percentages shown in parenthesis; this information will be used for comparison after students have completed their surveys.

- Suppose an admitted Communist wants to make a speech in your community. Should he or she be allowed to speak or not? Yes (27%) No (68%) No opinion (5%)
- Suppose he or she is a high school teacher. Should he or she be fired or not? Yes (91%) No (5%) No opinion (4%)
- Should an admitted Communist have his or her American citizenship taken away or not? Yes (77%) No (13%) No opinion (10%)
- Which of the following statements is more important: To find out all the Communists, even if some innocent people should be hurt. To protect the rights of innocent people even if some Communists are not found out. Find out Communists (58%) Protect rights (32%) Don't Know (10%)
- How great a danger do you feel American Communists are to this country at the present time? A very great danger (19%) A great danger (24%) Some danger (38%) Hardly any danger (9%) No danger (2%) Don't know (8%).

Explain to students that in 1954 a cross section of Americans were surveyed about their views on communism and civil liberties. Review the questions. Tell students that their assignment is to repeat the poll to determine if views have changed.

When their surveys are completed, students are to compile the results and post their results on the chalkboard. When students have finished, write the 1954 responses beside the current findings. Ask the class to identify similarities and differences, then to offer explanations for any changes. Conclude by asking students to discuss what they would do if a new wave of hysteria and fear were to occur.

Bibliography and Audiovisual Material

Teacher Bibliography

Ambrose, Stephen E. *Eisenhower*. New York: Simon and Schuster, Inc., 1990.

García, Mario T. *Mexican Americans.* New Haven: Yale University Press, 1989.

Jackson, Kenneth. *The Crabgrass Frontier: The Suburbanization of America*. New York: Oxford University Press, 1987.

Kutler, Stanley I. *The American Inquisition: Justice and Injustice in the Cold War*. New York: Hill & Wang, 1983.

Manchester, William. *The Glory and the Dream.* New York: Bantam Books, 1984.

Miller, Merle. *Plain Speaking: An Oral Biography of Harry S. Truman*. New York: Berkley Publishing Group, 1986.

Rovere, Richard. *Senator Joe McCarthy*. New York: Harper-Collins Publishers, Inc., 1982.

Vaughn, Philip. *The Truman Administration's Legacy for Black America*. Reseda, Calif.: Mojave Books, 1976.

Student Bibliography

Bernstein, Leonard et al. *West Side Story*. New York: Random House, Inc., 1958.

Carlson, Rachel. *The Sea Around Us*. New York: NAL/Dutton Co., 1991.

Ellison, Ralph. *Invisible Man.* New York: Random House, Inc., 1989.

Kerouac, Jack. *On The Road*. New York: Viking Penguin, 1991.

Wilson, Sloan. *Man in the Gray Flannel Suit*. Cambridge, Mass.: Robert Bentley, Inc., Publishers, 1980.

Miller, Arthur. *Death of a Salesman*. New York: Viking Penguin, 1976.

Films, Videocassettes, and Videodiscs

1945–1989: The Cold War. 25 min. National Geographic. Videocassette.

The Eagle and the Bear—Dateline: 1961, Berlin. 23 min. Coronet/MTI. Videodisc.

Filmstrips

Decades of History: The 20th Century (The Middle Years): 1950's Prosperity and Cold War. 17 min. 1 filmstrip with cassette. National Geographic.

Chapter 26

Objectives

- Identify problems the nation faced after World War II.
- Describe how the fear of communism affected the nation.
- Relate events that challenged the Eisenhower administration.
- Describe what life was like in the 1950s.

Introducing THE CHAPTER

For suggestions on introducing Chapter 26, refer to page 697B in the Teacher's Edition.

Developing THE CHAPTER

For activities and teaching strategies to help you reinforce and enrich chapter content, see pages 697B–697D in the Teacher's Edition.

B · A · C · K · G · R · O · U · N · D

Chapter Opener Illustrations
The celebration of V-E Day was repeated on V-J Day. This time, however, happiness brought by peace was untroubled by warfare on another front.

In the 1950s a new kind of music, Rock-n'-Roll, emerged. Two of the most popular singers of the decade were Elvis Presley and Ray Charles.

The postwar housing boom resulted in an explosion in suburbia and the proliferation of tract houses like these.

Some teenagers under the age of sixteen had to rely on "wheels" such as this 1950 Schwinn Hornet. Without a bike, these teenagers were homebound in the suburbs.

Postwar prosperity extended to teenagers like these, whose parents often could afford to buy cars for their

Reduced student page in the Teacher's Edition

Chapter 26 1945-1960

Abundance and Uncertainty

children.

This photo taken at Union Station in Los Angeles shows the Second Marine Division returning home from the Pacific battlefront as a Japanese family returns from an internment camp in Rohwer, Arkansas.

American Voices

On V-J Day, August 15, 1945, writer Edna Ferber walked through the streets of New York City. All around her Americans were celebrating the end of World War II. With her "old reporter's instinct," she recorded the experience:

> "*I walked down Park Avenue from the Seventies, cut over to Fifth, and emerged at 59th Street and the Plaza. . . . The handsome square was almost peaceful. No din. . . .*
>
> *Out to a now crowded Fifth Avenue . . . and over to Broadway and 45th Street. Here, at last, was New York on the loose.*
>
> *They were marching in the middle of . . . Broadway. . . . They were strangers suddenly united by emotion. They simply marched in clumps, men and women, boys and girls, parents with their children. . . .*
>
> *As I stood at the curb on Broadway, . . . a young and handsome man in United States Army uniform made his erratic way, slowly and alone, in the street just at the curb's edge. He looked in our faces as we stood massed there, and we stared at him. His arms and hands were outstretched in a gesture of utter wonder and unbelief. . . . He repeated in a quiet and awestruck voice: 'I'm alive. I'm alive! The war's over—and I'm alive!'*"

Millions of Americans shared the feeling of the soldier. Eagerly, they turned away from the nightmare of war to face the challenge of peace.

Victory celebration; rock albums; San Francisco suburb; Schwinn Hornet; teens' weekend; homecoming at war's end.

Analyzing Primary Sources

American Voices

Edna Ferber, born in Kalamazoo, Michigan, in 1885, began her career as a journalist when she was seventeen. Later she became a successful novelist and playwright. By chance, she was in New York City on August 15, 1945. In her autobiography, *A Kind of Magic,* she later recalled the mood of Americans celebrating V-J Day.

Ask: How does Ferber describe the parading Americans? **(emotional; unorganized; marching in clumps)** What is the mood of the man in Army uniform? Why? **(incredulous; he can't believe that the war is over and he survived)** Based on this quotation, how would you describe the reaction of Americans to the end of the war? **(relieved, joyous, disbelieving)**

699

Section 26-1

Objectives

- ***Answer the Focus Question.***
- *Explain the situation of Japanese Americans after the war.*
- *Describe the rising expectations of women and ethnic groups.*
- *Describe the Taft-Hartley Act.*
- *Explain Truman's upset victory in 1948.*

Introducing THE CHAPTER

Review problems that faced the nation after World War I. **(economic downturn, racial conflict, rising labor unrest, resentment of immigrants)** **Ask:** Would the country face the same problems after World War II? Why? Remind students that during the war, Americans concentrated their efforts on defeating the enemy, subordinating their own goals. Review the ramifications of this all-out effort, stressing the military needs of the nation, industrial priorities, and wartime control of wages, and prices.

Lead students to speculate about the impact on the nation of the shift from war to peace. How would this affect the economy? The availability of consumer goods? The output of factories and farms? The relations between labor and management?

What policies did the government follow during the war to keep prices down? **(wage and price controls, rationing)** What would happen once these restrictions were lifted? **(Wages and prices would soar.)**

B · A · C · K · G · R · O · U · N · D

Time Line Illustrations

1. In 1956 John Bardeen, Walter H. Brattain, and William Shockley won the Nobel Prize in Physics for inventing the transistor. An early application was to small, highly portable radios like this one.

2. Artist Ben Shahn satirized the Truman-Dewey campaign of 1948, placing Truman at the keyboard—Truman's hobby was playing the piano—and Dewey on top of the piano singing "A Good Man Is Hard to Find."

3. Oveta Culp Hobby, first Secretary of Health, Education, and Welfare, was a highly accomplished administrator who served as Director of the WAACs during WW II.

4. Television was a means of entertainment from the moment it was widely available. The televised Army-McCarthy hearings solidified television's place as a main medium for news as millions of Americans watched the spectacle.

Reduced student page in the Teacher's Edition

CHAPTER TIME LINE

1945-1960

Ben Shahn, *A Good Man Is Hard to Find*, 1948

1945 — 1948 — 1951

1945 Last Japanese-American internment camp closed

1947 Transistor invented
Taft-Hartley Act

1948 Truman wins surprise victory

1950 Internal Security Act
Army seizes the railroads

1951 Rosenbergs convicted

26-1 *The Return to Peacetime*

Focus: What uncertainties did the nation face after the war?

In Times Square in August 1945, under an electric sign flashing news of the victory over Japan, nearly 2 million people gathered in celebration. Behind the elation, however, lay many uncertainties. For sixteen years the nation had faced one crisis after another—stock market crash, depression, and war. What would the future hold now that the war was over?

The Veterans Return Home

Congress ordered the military to disband the armed forces with haste, and enrollment shrank from over 12 million in 1945 to 1.5 million by the end of 1946. To help veterans return to civilian life—and to avoid a repeat of the disastrous unemployment that followed World War I—Congress had passed the Serviceman's Readjustment Act, or GI Bill of Rights, in 1944. The act offered veterans low-interest loans to start businesses or buy homes or farms, and grants to get an education. It also provided unemployment benefits for those veterans who were unable to find work.

The GI Bill of Rights had a far-reaching effect on American society. More than 2 million veterans attended college at government expense. This number included many veterans from ethnic groups and lower-income families, who would never have had such an opportunity before the war, when college was thought to be mostly for children of the middle and upper classes. A Veterans Administration official described the GI Bill's effect on the new students:

5. Soldiers protected African-American students integrating Central High School in Little Rock, Arkansas, after the Supreme Court ruled public school segregation unconstitutional.
6. After WWII, many Americans felt that Alaska and Hawaii were strategic stepping stones in any attack on the North American mainland. They became states in 1959.

1954 Army-McCarthy hearings
Brown v. *Board of Education of Topeka*

1957 School integration enforced at Little Rock

1954 — 1957 — 1960

1953 Oveta Culp Hobby, Secretary of HEW

1956 Federal-Aid Highway Act

1958 NASA formed
National Defense Education Act

1959 Alaska and Hawaii statehood

“I've talked to hundreds and hundreds of these kids, and you get the same story over and over again. They like the idea of making more money, but they like even more the idea—as they keep putting it—of 'getting to be somebody.'”

Returning Japanese Americans. Another group returning to "civilian" life was less fortunate than the GIs. The Japanese Americans who had been held in internment camps during the war were returning to communities where suspicions still lingered. In a few places local groups made an effort to help the returnees resume their pre-war lives.

In the rush following the internment order, many Japanese Americans had been forced to sell their businesses and homes at low prices, or simply to abandon them. Aiku Mifune described the dilemma of her parents, who had nothing left: "My parents did not know what to do or where to go after they had been let out of camp." One farmer who had sold his land and two houses for less than half their worth explained, "No use looking back. Go crazy thinking about all we lost. Have to start all over again like when we came from Japan, but faster this time."

At first, most Japanese Americans just concentrated on starting all over again. Only gradually did they speak out against the injustice of internment.

New Roles, Rising Hopes

Wartime experiences changed the expectations of many members of society. Millions of people had taken on new roles that gave them greater dignity or opportunity than they had had in the past.

First-class citizenship. Members of ethnic groups that had been discriminated against in the past had shouldered the same burdens as other Americans during the war. As members of the armed services, many had traveled to countries where people treated them simply as American GIs, not Mexican-American GIs or African-American GIs. They had fought for democracy around the world, and now they wanted equal rights and opportunities at home.

Developing
THE SECTION

Thinking Critically

Analysis. Discuss the effects of the GI Bill of Rights on American society. **Ask:** What effects would low-interest loans have on the economy? On society? Predict the long term effects government-financed college education would have upon American society. How did the government benefit by educating veterans? What aspects of the GI Bill are in operation today?

Analyzing Primary Sources

Roosevelt. At a press conference Roosevelt offered his vision of the future for Japanese Americans returning from internment camps.

“Probably half a dozen or a dozen families could be scattered around on the farms and worked into the community. After all, they are American citizens, and we all know that American citizens have certain privileges. And they wouldn't—[upset]—the existing population very much.”

Ask: Do you see an inconsistency in Roosevelt's statement and his previous actions? **(says Japanese Americans have rights as Americans, yet placed them in internment camps)** Assess FDR's sensitivity to the plight of returning Japanese Americans. **(wants them scattered; overlooks that citizens can choose where to live)**

Connections: Literature

Research and Report. Two African-American women wrote about the lives of black women with poignancy and dignity. Ann Petry published her first novel *The Street* in 1946 and *Country Place* in 1947. Gwendolyn Brooks won a Pulitzer Prize in 1950 for her poem *Annie Allen*.

Have interested students write reports on these women and read selections from their works aloud.

Analyzing Primary Sources

Women in the Fifties. Write the following quotations on the chalkboard:

“War jobs have uncovered unsuspected abilities in American women. Why lose all these abilities because of a belief that a ‘woman's place is in the home’? For some it is, for others it is not.”
—a female wartime worker

“[A woman must] accept herself fully as a woman [and] know . . . she is dependent on a man. There is not fantasy in her mind about being an independent woman, a contradiction in terms.”
—Farnham & Lundberg, *Modern Woman*

Ask: To what peacetime policy is the first speaker objecting? Why? Why were women encouraged to be homemakers? Which of the two quotations best reflects the spirit of the times? Which would have the most appeal to women today? Why?

Multicultural Perspectives

The GI Forum was born when a mortician in Three Rivers, Texas, refused to hold services in his chapel or to permit the burial of a Mexican-American GI in the local cemetery. The Forum was able to persuade then United States Senator Lyndon B. Johnson to arrange for Felix Longoria, killed in the battle for the Philippines, to be buried in Arlington National Cemetery. Although formed to assist Mexican-American veterans and their families, the GI Forum has broadened its activities to include raising money for scholarships and working for fair employment practices.

Reduced student page in the Teacher's Edition

THE AMERICAN SPIRIT

Ernesto Galarza

A Voice for Farm Workers

Born in a small village of thatch-roofed, adobe cottages high in the Sierra Madre of western Mexico, young Ernesto Galarza dreamed of becoming a driver of pack mules. Pack drivers traveled far over mountain trails, bringing news of the world outside the village.

One day in 1911, when Ernesto was five, a pack driver brought the news that rebels were planning to revolt against the dictator Porfirio Díaz. To escape the dangers of war, Ernesto's mother fled with her young son to the United States.

The family landed in Sacramento, California. Curious and bright, Galarza soon learned English. He remembered that his teacher also taught the class that “becoming a proud American, as she said we should, did not mean feeling ashamed of being a Mexican.”

Galarza's mother died while he was still in school, and he took odd jobs to help support himself. On the farm where he worked one summer, the workers' only source of water was a ditch. When a laborer's child died from drinking the polluted water, the young Galarza convinced a county inspector to help. The inspector advised him to get the workers to organize. This incident contributed to his lifelong concern for workers.

In all his many roles—as labor organizer, consultant to the United States Civil Rights Commission and the House of Representatives, university professor, and author—Galarza worked to bring about mutual understanding and respect between Mexican Americans and other Americans. Always a sympathetic voice for farm workers, Galarza wrote several books about their lives. He also wrote poetry. Shortly before his death in 1984, he wrote of his life's work:

“I only sang because the lonely road was long and now the road and I are gone but not the song. . . .”

Yet they met old prejudices. For instance, African, Hispanic, Filipino, and Japanese Americans could all tell about some GI who had won medals in wartime but who, on the basis of race, had been refused service in an American restaurant.

No longer willing to accept second-class citizenship, Hispanics began to organize. In Texas, Dr. Hector Garcia started the American GI Forum. In Los Angeles, Mexican Americans established the Community Service Organization. These groups registered Hispanic voters and sponsored Hispanic candidates for public office.

African-American veterans swelled the ranks of the NAACP. They led the way in black voter registration drives and in encouraging blacks to enter politics. Despite bitter opposition, they met with some success. In 1947 in Winston-Salem, North Carolina, for example, 3,000 newly registered black voters helped to elect the first black official in the town's history.

Women in the work force. The experience of war also contributed to changing expectations by women. During the war, women had been en-

Multicultural Perspectives

Ernesto Galarza was the first Mexican American to obtain a Ph. D. in social sciences in the United States, the first to lead a farm workers union, and the first to be nominated for a Nobel Prize in Literature.

Multicultural Perspectives

Puerto Ricans, who had fought during World War II for freedoms they themselves did not enjoy, pushed for greater self-government after the war. Although they elected their legislature, the U.S. President appointed the governor and other officials. In 1947 the U.S. Congress provided for the governor to be elected by popular vote, and in 1950 provided for a constitutional convention.

Connections: Economics

Discussion. People during the war had amassed savings of an estimated $140 billion. **Ask:** How did this contribute to rising prices? How did the government attempt to keep down prices? Why would farmers and business leaders urge government to end price controls? What is the meaning of the newspaper headline on this page "Prices Soar, Buyers Sore, Steers Jump Over the Moon"?

couraged to do their part. With millions of men away in the military, women in record numbers had taken jobs outside the home. After the war a woman steelworker expressed the feelings of many women who wanted to continue to work:

> *"If [women] are capable, I don't see why they should give up their position to men. . . . The old theory that a woman's place is in the home no longer exists."*

However, many people thought that women should return to more traditional roles. One senator proposed that Congress should make laws sending "wives and mothers back to the kitchen" to guarantee jobs to veterans.

Between September 1945 and November 1946, as industry converted to peacetime production, 3.25 million women were laid off or left their jobs. Later, when women began to return to the work force in growing numbers, they found they had to settle for lower paying jobs than they had had during the war.

Union workers. Like women workers, organized labor had benefited from the needs of wartime industry. Supported by the Wagner Act of 1935, union organizers had been enormously successful. Between 1941 and 1945, union membership grew by 50 percent to nearly 15 million workers.

When wartime restrictions were lifted, unions looked forward to winning increases in wages and benefits. However, their hopes would soon be carried away on a rising spiral of prices and wages.

The Wage-Price Spiral

During the war, the government had imposed widespread controls on prices and wages. Even so, by war's end consumer prices had risen 31 percent, and wages had more than doubled.

Although rationing ended after the war, there were still shortages of certain goods. As Congress began to lift controls in 1945 and 1946, the cost of scarce items, such as meat, skyrocketed. One newspaper headline lamented: "Prices Soar, Buyers Sore, Steers Jump Over the Moon."

Freed of the restraints of depression and war, consumers rushed to buy the new streamlined appliances and autos, like this Hudson. As travel increased, so did traffic.

Active Learning

Cooperative Activity. Discuss with students the various problems facing ethnic groups after the war and how they adjusted to these difficulties. Point out that through group efforts, they were able to improve conditions.

Divide the class into groups. Have each group select an ethnic group to research. The group should write a short paper on the problems they encountered after the war, organizations formed, progress made in eliminating obstacles, economic improvement, and social mobility. Each group can share its findings with the class.

Limited English Proficiency

Building Vocabulary. What is meant by a "closed shop"? **(work place where only union members were hired)** According to the Taft-Hartley Act, what was the purpose of a "cooling off" period? **(to allow time for negotiators to settle issues and prevent a strike)**

Connections: Politics

Discussion. During 1946 4.6 million workers were involved in strikes at a cost of 116 million person-hours. Have students discuss the pros and cons of striking as a negotiating tool. What were Truman's actions against the mine and railroad strikes? What political effect did these strikes, and Truman's subsequent actions, have? **(Truman lost support of unions; many blamed him for union activity)**

Writing About History

Editorial. Have students write editorials on the Taft-Hartley Act from the point of view of a Republican newspaper editor, a Democratic newspaper editor, or a Union newsletter editor in 1947.

Editorials should provide background to the act, explain the act's provisions and effect, and state why the act should or should not be made law. Have students read their editorials to the class and compare points of view.

Labor on strike. Industrial workers were especially hard hit by rising prices. Having worked 48-hour weeks, including eight hours of overtime at higher pay, they now returned to 40-hour work weeks—and shrunken paychecks.

In November 1945 auto workers went on strike against General Motors. That strike, and the resulting pay raise, set off a chain reaction. The steelworkers were next in line, and they, too, won increased pay.

Then in April 1946 John L. Lewis led 400,000 United Mine Workers out of the coal mines. The strike threatened the nation's supply of soft coal. If the supply ran out, steel mills and railroads would be paralyzed. After miners and mine owners negotiated without results, President Harry Truman ordered troops to seize the mines and end the strike.

Meanwhile, railroad workers threatened a walk-out. To prevent bringing the transportation system to a halt, Truman placed the railroads under federal control. However, railroad workers refused to work. On May 25, Truman asked Congress for authority "to draft into the armed forces of the United States all workers who are on strike against their government." The issue never came to a vote. Before Truman even left the platform, word came that the strike had been settled.

Political fallout from the strikes. Truman's hard line in the coal and rail strikes shocked union workers, who had been his staunchest supporters. "Labor," declared one union official, "is through with Truman." Yet people outside the labor movement blamed the Democratic President for letting the unions win higher wages, which in turn pushed prices higher. "Had enough?" asked the Republicans in the congressional elections of 1946. The answer was a resounding "Yes!" The Republicans won majorities in both houses of Congress for the first time since 1928.

American Voices

"I won both senatorial elections with all the press against me and a presidential election with ninety percent of them against me, all the pollsters, all the 'ivory tower' columnists, the gamblers and everybody but the people against me. And I'll do it again if it becomes necessary."

—Harry Truman, in a letter that was never mailed, 1949

The Taft-Hartley Act

On the first day of the Eightieth Congress, in 1947, Republicans introduced seventeen bills to curb organized labor. The most important bill was cosponsored by Ohio's Senator Robert A. Taft—son of former President William Howard Taft—and Representative Fred A. Hartley of New Jersey. The Taft-Hartley Act set up a "cooling off" period to allow federal mediators to negotiate a contract and avoid a strike. If a proposed strike threatened the national welfare, the cooling off period could be extended. The act ended the closed shop and allowed states to restrict the union shop.

Charging that the act would "discriminate against workers," Truman vetoed the bill in June 1947, but Congress overrode his veto. After the bill became law, Truman tried unsuccessfully to have it repealed. But by his strong opposition, Truman regained the support of many union leaders.

A "Common Man"

Harry Vaughn, an old friend of Truman's, described the feisty, outspoken President as the "common man." Comparing Truman to Roosevelt, he said, "After a diet of caviar, you like to get back to ham and eggs." Like Roosevelt, Truman paid particular attention to the needs of ordinary people. From 1946 to 1948, he struggled to get the Eightieth Congress to pass programs that carried on the spirit of the New Deal.

The conservative Congress defeated most of his proposals, however. Undaunted, he often found other ways to carry out his ideas. For example, when Congress turned down a new Fair Employment Practices Committee (FEPC) in 1946, Truman appointed a special President's Committee on Civil Rights. In 1947 this committee published its landmark report, "To Secure These Rights," recommending laws to end discrimination.

B · A · C · K · G · R · O · U · N · D

Connections: Politics

Henry Wallace challenged the United States with his strong civil rights platform. For example, he toured the South in 1948, appearing only before nonsegregated audiences. Wallace's challenge forced Truman and liberal Democrats to move on the civil rights issue, even at risk of Southern defection from the Democratic New Deal coalition.

The Chicago Daily Tribune *was not alone in expecting a Truman defeat in 1948. On election night, one broadcaster said, "He cannot win; his early lead will fold up." At midnight another said, "Mr. Truman is still ahead, but these are returns from [just] a few cities." Truman, however, remained confident.*

Discrimination and segregation in the armed forces had been a particularly sore point with African Americans during the war. In 1948, when A. Philip Randolph and other leaders threatened a massive civil disobedience campaign over the issue, Truman issued Executive Order 9981:

> *"It is hereby declared to be the policy of the President that there shall be equality of treatment and opportunity for all persons in the armed services without regard to race, color, religion, or national origin."*

This historic order was met with both acclaim and fierce opposition. Nevertheless, it marked the first step in the long, often painful process of desegregating the institutions of American society.

Truman Elected in 1948

In 1948 Republicans felt confident as they chose Governor Thomas E. Dewey of New York as their candidate. With Truman linked in many people's minds to inflation, shortages, and strikes, a Republican victory seemed assured. One newspaper suggested that "probably the best service that Truman could render to his party now is to step aside."

But Truman had no intention of quitting. At the Democratic convention in July, he had enough support to win the nomination on the first ballot. The convention was badly split, however, and two splinter parties broke off.

Southerners, angered by a strong civil-rights plank in the Democrat's platform, formed the States' Rights Democratic party, or Dixiecrats. They named Governor J. Strom Thurmond of South Carolina as their candidate. Liberals, who thought Truman's foreign policy was too anti-Soviet, formed the new Progressive party. Their candidate, Henry A. Wallace, had been Vice-President during Roosevelt's third term. With the party split three ways, few believed Truman would win.

Truman campaigned vigorously against the "do-nothing" Congress. He traveled 22,000 miles by train, averaging ten speeches a day. He told farmers that Congress's lack of action was the reason for lower grain prices. He reminded workers of the Taft-Hartley Act. When he attacked the Republicans, the crowds yelled, "Pour it on 'em, Harry!" Yet public opinion polls showed that "Mr. Dewey is just as good as elected."

A surprising victory. On election night in 1948, the *Chicago Daily Tribune* hit the stands with the headline: "Dewey Defeats Truman." But people who stayed up late listening to their radios were not so sure. The Dixiecrats were carrying only three or four states in the South, and Wallace was ahead only in California and New York. Truman was leading in the cities and splitting the farm areas with Dewey. By morning Truman had won—and the Democrats had recaptured Congress.

Backyard History

Activity. The Taft-Hartley Act made it possible for states to pass "right-to-work" laws (laws saying that union membership could not be a requirement for employment). Have students research "right-to-work" laws and determine whether such laws exist in their state.

Connections: Politics

Discussion. Goodman Ace, a humorist, said, *"Public opinion polls reach everyone in America from the farmer in his field right up to the President of the United States, Thomas E. Dewey."* Keep in mind that the polls predicted Dewey's victory: what joke is being made? Have students discuss how polls might influence elections.

Active Learning

Cooperative Activity. Ask students what issues dominated the election of 1948. (civil rights, policy toward Soviet Union, farming issues, union issues, and inflation) Divide the class into four groups to represent the four parties—Democratic, Republican, Progressive, and States' Rights Democratic (Dixiecrats). Have each group choose an issue to address and then write a campaign slogan, draw a campaign poster, and write a short speech for their candidate.

Thinking Critically

Application. Discuss fair employment practices today. **Ask:** What kind of groups seek protection from job discrimination today? (ethnic groups, women, gays and lesbians, people with certain diseases such as AIDS and cancer, for example) What government agency oversees laws assuring equal opportunity? (Equal Employment Opportunity Commission)

Relate the issue discussed here to the issue of affirmative action. How do you account for continuing job discrimination when the United States prides itself on giving everyone an equal opportunity?

Linking Past and Present

Researching Current Events. Have students examine newspapers for articles on job discrimination. Students can write short reports identifying the person or group involved, the nature of the complaint, and the decision or resolution reached.

Multicultural Perspectives

In April of 1947 Jackie Robinson broke the color barrier in major league baseball as a member of the Brooklyn Dodgers of the National League. Robinson, a football star at UCLA, was the son of a sharecropper and grandson of a slave. At the end of his first season, Robinson won the Rookie of the Year Award. Larry Doby, who played for the Cleveland Indians, was the first African-American player in the American League.

Reduced student page in the Teacher's Edition

Exploring Issues

EQUAL OPPORTUNITY

The Fair Employment Practices Committee

"In American democracy there is no room for racial discrimination," said Frank Paz, a Mexican-American leader from Chicago. "Our people do not want any special privileges," he went on. "All they want is the right to enjoy full citizenship."

Frank Paz was speaking in 1945 before a Senate committee considering a bill to establish a permanent Fair Employment Practices Committee (FEPC). It would investigate discrimination and enforce equal opportunity in employment.

Paz gave examples of discrimination in hiring. "Today in Chicago," he told the senators, "there are signs all over the city asking for workers to work on the streetcars. A boy . . . by the name of Vilar, decorated with the Purple Heart, . . . honorably discharged from the army, . . . applied for a position with this company." He was refused the job, Paz said, because he was a Mexican American.

Others echoed Paz's words. A. Philip Randolph of the Brotherhood of Sleeping Car Porters told of discrimination against African Americans. Donald Henderson said that in Pacific Coast canneries, Filipino and Mexican Americans were paid far less than other workers.

These speakers agreed that an FEPC could do much to end such unfairness. A man or woman who had been refused work or had been given lower pay could file a complaint. If the FEPC found evidence of discrimination, it could take legal action. Americans had just fought a war to preserve democracy, African-American leader Roy Wilkins told the committee. An FEPC, he said, would go far to prove "that the Negro, the Jew, the Catholic, the Spanish American, the new citizen, man or woman, who has served his country on the battlefronts, has not fought in vain."

One opponent, Senator Richard Russell of Georgia, argued that an FEPC "would destroy natural rights guaranteed every citizen by the Constitution." The Constitution, he said, "limits the powers of the federal government to those expressly conferred by that document." Those powers, he argued, did not include forcing one citizen to hire another. Yet under the FEPC, he warned, that is exactly what would happen.

Ben Shahn, *Welders,* 1943

Ben Shahn, *Welders.*

Russell predicted that the FEPC would become a vast bureaucracy. "People from all over the country would come to this agency to air their grievances . . . at the expense of the American Taxpayer." Business people would face "new regulations, investigations, hearings, and litigation, far beyond their time."

Russell also warned about reverse discrimination. Employers would hire members of ethnic groups, even if they were not as qualified, simply to avoid trouble with the FEPC. The government cannot "legislate tolerance," Russell concluded. By forcing different groups to work together against their will, the FEPC would only increase tension between them.

Educator Mary McLeod Bethune did not agree. Speaking at a congressional hearing, she said, "Laws against murder prohibit the taking of life. An FEPC would prohibit the taking away of one's livelihood because of race, creed, color, national origin, or ancestry."

For twenty years after World War II, bills to create an FEPC were proposed in Congress, but an FEPC was never established. In 1964, however, Congress passed a sweeping Civil Rights Act that outlawed job discrimination. The Equal Opportunity Commission was created to enforce the act. Today job discrimination on the basis of race, national origin, religion, or sex is clearly against the law.

1. What reasons did supporters give for wanting to create an FEPC? What did they hope it would accomplish?
2. Why did opponents think that the FEPC violated the Constitution? What other arguments did they give against it?
3. The Equal Opportunity Commission was created to stop discrimination in jobs. Do you think that such an agency is necessary today? Why or why not?

Truman's Fair Deal

Now that he had a more sympathetic Congress to work with, Truman pressed for many of the same programs that the Eightieth Congress had defeated. To emphasize their ties to the New Deal, Truman dubbed his programs the "Fair Deal."

Congress did enact some Fair Deal measures. It raised the minimum hourly wage from 40 cents to 75 cents and increased social security benefits as well as extending them to an additional 9.2 million people. It also approved housing for low-income families and passed new soil conservation, flood control, and rural electrification programs. However, a coalition of Republicans and southern Democrats defeated many of Truman's proposals, including the FEPC and national health insurance, and refused to repeal the Taft-Hartley Act.

With Harry Truman as President, none of the nation's worst fears had come to pass. Conversion from a wartime to a peacetime economy had not brought a new depression, and the Fair Deal had proved to be a moderate success. Yet a cautious Congress and nation were reluctant to make too many rapid changes.

The nation's conservative mood was also reflected in the passage of the Twenty-second Amendment to the Constitution. Proposed in 1947 in reaction to the unprecedented four terms of Franklin Roosevelt, it limited each future President to two terms in office.

Section Review

1. Comprehension. What uncertainties lay behind the celebrations at the end of the war?

2. Synthesis. Speculate about what challenges Japanese-Americans faced at the end of the war.

3. Comprehension. Select one group — either women or a racial or ethnic group — and explain how wartime experiences changed their expectations.

4. Synthesis. Write three different possible headlines for magazine articles about conditions for labor between 1945 and 1948.

5. Analysis. What groups of voters most likely approved of Truman's Fair Deal? Why?

Connections: Politics

Discussion. The issue of limiting the number of terms of elected officials in local, state, and national government is gaining widespread attention. **Ask:** What are some arguments for and against limiting the number of terms the President can serve?

Exploring Issues

ANSWERS

1. Minority workers suffered discrimination in hiring and in pay. A government agency would eliminate unfair practices and uphold American ideals.
2. The FEPC went beyond the powers expressly given to the federal government by the Constitution. It would create a vast, costly bureaucracy, and lead to litigation and reverse discrimination.
3. Opinions will vary.

Section Review

ANSWERS

1. Economic uncertainties stemming from conversion from a wartime economy, status of racial and ethnic groups and women.
2. Getting fair treatment and overcoming suspicions; starting all over again; getting compensation for losses.
3. Veterans from racial or ethnic groups expected equal rights and opportunities at home. Women wanted to continue to work outside the home.
4. Headlines might reflect rising prices and sinking wages, strikes, union solidarity, Taft-Hartley Act.
5. Groups included labor, small business people hurt by the wage-price spiral, farmers, low-income families, and African Americans.

Section 26-2

Objectives

- ***Answer the Focus Question.***
- *Explain why Truman created a loyalty review program.*
- *Describe the role of HUAC.*
- *Describe McCarthyism.*
- *Evaluate the validity of the charge that communists infested the federal government.*

Introducing

THE SECTION

Have students describe the American attitude toward the Soviet Union during the postwar years. **(Fears of Communist aggression lulled by wartime alliance were reawakened by Communist expansion in Eastern Europe and Asia.)**

Ask: What had motivated the red scare of 1919? **(fear of foreigners)** Were there more valid reasons for fearing communism in the 1940s? Explain. **(Postwar fears grew out of widely publicized cases of espionage; Soviet takeovers and attempted takeovers in Europe and elsewhere made Americans more susceptible to belief in a "communist conspiracy.")**

Social History

Many teachers refused to sign loyalty oaths because they believed the oaths violated academic freedom. Many argued that oaths in themselves would not stop communists from infiltrating schools. At the University of California, 157 faculty members were dismissed for refusal to sign loyalty oaths.

Reduced student page in the Teacher's Edition

26-2 *Questions of Loyalty*

Focus: How did fear of communism come to grip the nation?

Even as President Truman was struggling to push through his Fair Deal, the nation was undergoing a change that he could neither direct nor control: a growing fear of communism. In 1947 a public opinion poll showed that Americans favored a friendly policy toward the Soviet Union. By 1948, however, 76 percent believed the Soviet Union was out to rule the world. What accounted for this change in attitude?

For one thing, Cold War events made Americans suspicious. They watched the Soviets bring most of Eastern Europe under their influence, abolishing capitalism and suppressing religion wherever they gained control. As communist influence spread around the world, Americans wondered when they might have to defend against it at home.

Hunting for Communist Spies and Traitors

Many Americans became convinced that the Soviet Union would attack the United States. Even worse, they feared, the United States might fall to communism through **subversion**, being overthrown by traitors and spies lurking within the government. FBI Director J. Edgar Hoover encouraged fear. There was, he said, a "force of traitorous Communists, constantly gnawing away like termites at the very foundations of American society."

Rumors about traitors first circulated in 1945, when government agents found secret State Department documents in the office of *Amerasia*, a magazine sympathetic to Chinese and Russian communism. Then, in June 1946 the Canadian government uncovered a Soviet spy ring. The spies included more than twenty Canadians who had occupied "positions of trust" in government. According to Canadian sources, the Soviets had spy rings in other nations, too.

Although Truman thought the fear of spies in the government was exaggerated, he knew he would be a target for critics if he ignored the possibility. Thus, in March 1947 he created a loyalty review program. Between 1947 and 1951 the government investigated 3 million of its own employees, searching for anyone with ties to a group suspected of plotting harm to the country.

More than 2,000 government employees resigned in connection with the investigations, many because they objected to the investigations on principle. Only 212 were fired after the review found "reasonable grounds . . . that the person involved is disloyal." Those who were fired often were not told who had accused them or what they supposedly had done. No cases of spying were uncovered.

Secretary of State Dean Acheson later wrote that the reviews themselves had been the real threat because they violated the rules of fair trial.

> *"It was not realized how dangerous was the practice of secret evidence and secret informers, how alien to all our conceptions of justice and the rights of the citizen."*

In this atmosphere of suspicion, Congress gave the CIA authority to gather information about foreign threats. To protect the nation against internal subversion, Congress passed a series of laws, including the 1950 McCarran Act. This act required Communist organizations to register with the government. It also provided for the investigation of any group suspected of being un-American and permitted the arrest, without proof, of people suspected of disloyalty.

Truman vetoed the act, calling it "the greatest danger to freedom of press, speech, and assembly since the Sedition Act of 1798." Congress, however, passed the act over his veto.

Connections: Literature

In 1953 playwright Arthur Miller's drama, *The Crucible*, opened on Broadway. The subject was the Salem witch trials, but the play was a veiled attack on the activities of McCarthy and HUAC.

Committee on Un-American Activities. Meanwhile, in the House of Representatives, the House Committee on Un-American Activities (HUAC) had joined the battle. Established in 1938, the committee first investigated the activities of Nazis, Fascists, and Communists. Now HUAC's focus was mainly on "Communists and all who promote the Communist line."

In 1947 HUAC focused its spotlight on the motion picture industry, calling movie stars, directors, and screen writers to appear. Afraid of being branded as Communist sympathizers, film executives soon blacklisted, or refused to hire, ten of the witnesses, who had refused to answer questions on the grounds that HUAC had no right to examine a person's political or religious beliefs.

One of HUAC's most controversial investigations was of Alger Hiss. Hiss had been a State Department official from 1935 to 1947. According to testimony by Whittaker Chambers, a former spy for the Soviet Union, Hiss had given him copies of documents containing military secrets to turn over to Soviet agents.

Hiss denied the charge and sued Chambers for libel. Nevertheless, Hiss was brought to trial in 1949. He could not be charged with spying because too much time had passed. However, although he continued to protest his innocence, he was convicted of lying under oath.

With the guilty verdict, Truman's insistence that the Communist threat was largely imaginary came back to haunt him. HUAC member Richard M. Nixon, a Republican congressman who had been most vigorous in his pursuit of Hiss, charged that Truman and the Democrats were more interested in hiding "embarrassing facts than in finding out who stole the documents."

The Rosenberg Trial

While HUAC investigated Hiss, other unsettling events were unfolding. In October 1949 the Chinese Communists won that nation's long civil war and proclaimed the People's Republic of China. Then, in September 1949 Truman made an unexpected announcement: The Soviets had developed their own atomic bomb. The United States' monopoly on the weapon had vanished.

Americans wondered how the Soviet Union had managed to discover the secrets of the bomb so quickly. Many suspected that they had had help. These suspicions seemed confirmed when the British arrested Klaus Fuchs [FYOOKS], a German-born physicist who had worked on building the American atomic bomb, and charged him with giving atomic secrets to the Soviets.

Fuchs's arrest led to the arrest in the United States of Ethel and Julius Rosenberg on similar charges. Claiming they were being tried for their political beliefs and had committed no crime, the Rosenbergs were convicted, nonetheless. Later, in June 1953, they would be executed despite lingering doubts about their guilt.

Joe McCarthy and the Politics of Fear

The climate of fear was ripe for exploitation, which was not long in coming. On February 9, 1950, Senator Joseph McCarthy, a Wisconsin Republican, gave a speech in West Virginia. "I have here in my hand," he said, "a list of 205 . . . names that were known to the Secretary of State as being members of the Communist party and who nevertheless are still working and shaping the policy in the State Department."

Around the country and before the Senate committee investigating his charges, McCarthy repeated his theme. Traitors in the United States were responsible for the success of communism around the world, he said, especially in China.

McCarthy named names. As one person after another was brought before the committee, many observers thought it was clear that McCarthy's accusations were based on flimsy or even manufactured

Developing

THE SECTION

Active Learning

Cooperative Activity. Have students imagine that they have been called to testify before the House Committee on Un-American activities. In small groups have them discuss their options: (1) comply and risk informing on friends; (2) plead protection of First Amendment and incur charge of contempt of Congress; (3) invoke the Fifth Amendment against self-incrimination and risk assumed guilt. Have each group brainstorm other possible options.

After their discussions students can pair up with another in the group who shares the same opinions. In pairs, they are to write a position paper defending their actions before HUAC.

GTV Side 4

Chap. 6, Frame 27210

Echoes of War: The Fear of Communism (Movie Segment)

Search and Play:

B · A · C · K · G · R · O · U · N · D

Limited English Proficiency

Making a Time Line. Have students work in pairs to make a time line of events between 1946 and 1951 that heightened fears of communist subversion. **(Soviet nuclear tests, the Rosenberg case, for example)** Ask students what conclusions can be drawn about the growth of American fears of subversion. **(The events occurred in a relatively short period of time; there was evidence of espionage activities in Canada, Britain, and the United States; communism, with its victory in China, was expanding.)**

Connections: Politics

Opposition to McCarthy could have negative effects on a person's political career. The Tydings Committee stated that McCarthy's charges were a "fraud." Senator Tydings, a conservative Democrat, was defeated in his campaign for reelection. Commentators interpreted it as a victory for McCarthy. Margaret Chase Smith's criticism of McCarthy got her dropped from two Republican posts and isolated in her own party.

Section Review

ANSWERS

1. Definitions for the following terms are on text pages indicated in parentheses: *subversion* (708), *McCarthyism* (710).
2. He thought the fear exaggerated but took action to silence critics by creating a loyalty review program.
3. The State Department documents found at *Amerasia* and the Canadian spy ring indicated that there were some communist sympathizers in government positions. The assertion that the government was riddled with Communists was vastly exaggerated.
4. Democrats speaking out feared they would be branded Communists. Republicans feared being accused of weakening party unity.
Linking Past and Present: Claims made today might include: opponents are soft on crime, only in favor of certain ethnic or racial groups, or are in the pay of powerful business or labor interests.

Reduced student page in the Teacher's Edition

Investigations by Joseph McCarthy (left) were called "a fraud and a hoax" by Senator Millard Tydings of Maryland. Senator William Benton of Connecticut said that McCarthy lacked integrity and character.

"evidence." Yet unproven accusations were enough to ruin people's lives because friends and employers of the accused were afraid to associate with them any longer. Anyone who voiced criticisms or suggested changes in American society risked being called a Communist. Such use of unsupported accusations to intimidate people has come to be known as **McCarthyism.**

Maine's Margaret Chase Smith was a Representative from 1940 to 1948 and Senator from 1949 to 1973.

Few people had the courage to speak up against McCarthyism. One who dared was Senator Margaret Chase Smith of Maine. In June 1950 she declared:

> *"The American people are sick and tired of being afraid to speak their minds lest they be politically smeared as Communists or Fascists by their opponents. Freedom of speech is not what it used to be in America."*

Smith and six other Republican senators signed a Declaration of Conscience against such accusations. Their action did not stop McCarthy, however. His tirades against supposed Communists would continue to spread uncertainty for several years.

Section Review

1. Identification. Define *subversion* and *McCarthyism*.

2. Analysis. What was Truman's position on the hunt for Communists in government? What actions did the atmosphere of fear lead Truman to take?

3. Comprehension. In what respects was the fear of Communist subversion based on solid evidence? In what respects was it based on unfounded fear and suspicion?

4. Synthesis. Speculate about the difficulties Democrats faced in speaking out against McCarthyism. How did these differ from those faced by Republicans?

Linking Past and Present. During the McCarthy era, even a hint of sympathy for "commies" was enough to defeat many candidates. Do politicians today ever make unsubstantiated claims about their opponents? What kinds of accusations are made? Are they effective? Explain.

26-3 The Eisenhower Years

Focus: What events fractured the calm of the Eisenhower years?

In March 1952 Truman announced that he would not run for reelection. For the first time since 1932, the Democratic nomination was open to someone who was not already President. The Democratic convention approved Truman's own choice for the nomination, Governor Adlai E. Stevenson of Illinois.

Meanwhile, the Republicans were making quiet inquiries about General Dwight D. Eisenhower. When the county clerk in Eisenhower's hometown was asked "Ike's" party preference, he replied, "I don't think he has any politics." That was good enough. Eisenhower's easy-going style and enormous popularity made him the party's choice on the first ballot. Richard M. Nixon, the staunch McCarthyite, filled out the ticket.

The 1952 election campaign was the first to be widely televised. People watched eagerly as the Republicans blamed the Democrats for "Korea, Communism, and Corruption," and Eisenhower promised to bring about peace in Korea. The Democrats countered with, "You never had it so good." People were interested in Stevenson's ideas, but they "liked Ike," and Eisenhower won by more than 5 million votes. The Republican party also won narrow majorities in both houses of Congress.

The Middle-of-the-Road Presidency

As President, Eisenhower wanted to steer a moderate course. "The path to America's future," he declared, "lies down the middle of the road." However, he did want to make changes in the way government operated. First, believing that Roosevelt and Truman had had too much influence over Congress, he said he would restore the balance of power between the legislative and executive branches. He would work in "partnership" with Congress, proposing policies and letting members of Congress "vote their own consciences."

Eisenhower also thought the Democrats had concentrated too much power in Washington, D.C. He promised to run the federal government by "trying to make it smaller rather than bigger and finding things it can stop doing instead of seeking new things for it to do."

Like many Republican Presidents before him, Eisenhower placed his trust in business-minded advisors. Most members of his cabinet were industrialists. During Senate hearings on his appointment as Secretary of Defense, former General Motors Chairman Charles E. Wilson expressed his faith that what was "good for our country was good for General Motors, and vice versa."

Eisenhower not only vowed to streamline the government, he also promised to scale down its budget. His would be "an administration which knows how to practice the wiser spending of less of people's money." The President and his advisors focused on trimming public spending. They expected that by slowing the flow of government money into the economy, they would be able to keep prices down.

Eisenhower said that he planned to be "conservative when it comes to money and liberal when it comes to human beings." In 1953, he approved plans for consolidating social programs begun during the New Deal and Fair Deal into one agency, the Department of Health, Education, and Welfare (HEW). He named Oveta Culp Hobby, wartime director of the Women's Auxiliary Army Corps, as the first secretary of HEW.

Section 26-3

Objectives

- ***Answer the Focus Question.***
- *Explain how Eisenhower implemented his "middle of the road" approach.*
- *Describe the decline of McCarthyism.*
- *Explain the Supreme Court's school desegregation decision.*
- *Discuss why Eisenhower reluctantly implemented the decision.*

Introducing

THE SECTION

Review with students the leadership styles of the two Democratic Presidents: Roosevelt and Truman. **(active, dynamic, forceful, willing to use presidential power)** Tell students that Eisenhower, the first Republican President in twenty years, had a very different leadership style. He followed a middle-of-the-road policy, did not actively promote dramatic change, and was reluctant to use power. Have students note evidence of Eisenhower's leadership style as they read this section.

Developing THE SECTION

Limited English Proficiency

Discussion. Discuss how Eisenhower set *conservative* goals but followed *moderate* practices. **(He called for less executive power, more power for states, and a balanced budget. However, he did not cut New Deal programs, he formed HEW, and expanded social security.)**

Writing About History

News Stories. Write the following headlines on the chalkboard:

- *Eisenhower Wins Landslide Victory*
- *Eisenhower to Steer Middle of Road*
- *Millions Watch Army-McCarthy Hearings*
- *Eisenhower Sends Troops to Little Rock*
- *Another Landslide Victory for Eisenhower*

Have students assume they are journalists writing news stories for the front page for the headlines listed above. The opening paragraph of the story—the lead—should contain all the facts of the story. The remaining paragraphs should provide background information and deal with the significance of the event.

The End of McCarthyism

Meanwhile Senator McCarthy continued his attacks on supposed Communists in government. In 1953 he finally went too far.

As head of a Senate subcommittee, McCarthy began an investigation of the United States Army. One of McCarthy's aides, G. David Schine, had been drafted that fall, and McCarthy claimed the Army was holding Schine "hostage" to hinder the investigation. The Army countered that McCarthy had tried to get special treatment for Schine. These charges were aired in Senate hearings televised to the nation in the spring of 1954. An audience of more than 20 million watched in fascination.

The Army selected for its counsel Boston lawyer Joseph Nye Welch. As McCarthy rudely interrupted the proceedings and made one unsupported accusation after another, Welch quietly persevered. Then, when Welch was cross-examining a McCarthy aide, McCarthy attacked Welch, accusing him of harboring a Communist in his law firm, and naming the man.

Welch was outraged. He accused McCarthy of "reckless cruelty" in trying to ruin the career of a promising young lawyer. "Have you no sense of decency, sir? At long last, have you left no sense of decency?" There was a hush in the hearing room. Then Senators, lawyers, witnesses, spectators, and reporters broke into wild applause. Welch had finally said to McCarthy's face what many people had been thinking in private.

The hearings continued for thirty-six days. But the public had seen enough to get a true gauge of McCarthy's character. His reign of terror was over. In December 1954 the full Senate voted to "condemn" McCarthy for conduct that "tended to bring the Senate into dishonor and disrepute."

McCarthy lost most of his power in Washington, D.C., and soon dropped out of the headlines. He did not attend the Republican convention in 1956, and he died the following year.

Democratic Gains in 1954

Until the Army-McCarthy hearings, Democrats had been afraid to speak out against conservative candidates or condemn McCarthyism for fear of being accused of Communist leanings. Now they could go on the attack and expect public support.

In the congressional elections of 1954 the main issue was the economy. Eisenhower's budget trimming, including cuts in military spending after the Korean War, had triggered a mild recession in 1953 and 1954. As unemployment rose to more than 5 percent, Democratic candidates blamed the Republicans. Voters agreed, and in the 1954 elections, Democrats regained control of Congress.

"Separate But Equal" No More

In that same year the Supreme Court handed down a unanimous ruling in the case of *Brown* v. *Board of Education of Topeka*. The decision crackled through Washington like a bolt of lightning and sent shock waves thundering across the nation. It overturned the 1896 *Plessy* v. *Ferguson* ruling. In that case the Court had permitted segre-

CBS newsman Edward R. Murrow dared to risk McCarthy's wrath by televising a program that revealed to viewers the Senator's bullying tactics.

Multicultural Perspectives

Herman Sweatt was denied admission to the University of Texas Law School on racial grounds. With the assistance of NAACP lawyers, he carried his case to the Supreme Court. In 1950 the Court ruled that Sweatt, as well as other qualified black applicants, should be admitted. In another case, *McLaurin* v. *Oklahoma State Regents*, the Court again ruled against discriminatory practices at the University of Oklahoma. These victories encouraged the NAACP to begin building their case against segregation in public schools.

Thinking Critically

Evaluation. With regard to segregation, Eisenhower believed that hearts and minds could not be changed by laws. **Ask:** Do you agree or disagree? How important are lawmaking and courts in the fight against racism? Why?

Fifteen-year-old Elizabeth Eckford was threatened by an angry mob when she tried to enter Little Rock's Central High School. Eventually, Eisenhower sent federal troops to restore peace.

gation as long as facilities for blacks and whites were equal. Now, the Court ruled that "separate but equal" facilities were unconstitutional. Chief Justice Earl Warren read out the court's decision:

> *❝ We conclude that in the field of public education the doctrine of 'separate but equal' has no place. Separate educational facilities are inherently unequal. ❞*

The case had begun in 1950 when Oliver Brown tried to enroll his daughter Linda in a public school near their home in Topeka, Kansas, instead of in the school for African Americans on the other side of the city. The white school refused to accept her, citing a state law requiring separate schools for blacks. In all, seventeen states had such laws. Brown and other African Americans joined in a lawsuit that worked its way up to the Supreme Court.

Eisenhower was surprised by the Supreme Court's bold decision. He had appointed California's governor, Earl Warren, as Chief Justice of the Court because he thought Warren held safely conservative views. Furthermore, the President believed that improving race relations was a private matter. He told Booker T. Washington's daughter Portia, "We cannot do it by cold lawmaking, but must make these changes by . . . reason, by prayer."

Eisenhower's reluctance to use government power to end segregation was put to the test in Little Rock, Arkansas, three years after the Court's decision in the Brown case. Little Rock's Central High School had planned to desegregate gradually. But in the fall of 1957, a shrieking mob of whites prevented the first nine black students from registering. The situation went on for weeks. Finally, calling the incident a "disgraceful occurrence," Eisenhower dispatched federal troops to restore order and escort the black students into the school.

Under mounting pressure from African Americans, President Eisenhower also sent a civil rights bill to Congress. The resulting Civil Rights Act of 1957—the first civil rights law since Reconstruction—gave the federal government power to take action against states that blocked African Americans from voting.

Constitutional Heritage

Discussion. Tell students that the Supreme Court cited the equal protection clause of the Fourteenth Amendment as the basis for their decision in *Brown* v. *Board of Education.* Have students read the first section of the Fourteenth Amendment and explain how it relates to the Court's decision. **(The equal protection clause says that no state can deny any person the equal protection of the laws. It is state law that establishes public schools. The Court interpreted the equal protection clause to mean that state laws establishing schools should apply to everyone equally, and that the Court had determined that separate schools cannot be equal.)**

Global Connections

Research and Discussion. In 1959 Alaska and Hawaii became states. Have interested students research the process by which each achieved statehood. Students can also find newspaper articles relating to the events and share them with the class.

Students might also research Puerto Rico's status at this time. (In 1952 it became a commonwealth of the United States.) **Ask:** Why did Puerto Rico reject statehood at that time? What are the main opinions now about Puerto Rico's future status?

Global Connections

On June 26, 1959, Queen Elizabeth and President Eisenhower formally opened the St. Lawrence Seaway linking the Atlantic Ocean with the Great Lakes. People had dreamed of such a link since the 1500s, when Jacques Cartier sought a Northwest Passage through the continent. In modern times, the United States was at first reluctant to join Canada in the enterprise, rejecting treaties in 1932 and 1941, but Canada threatened to go it alone within its own territory. The discovery of vast iron ore deposits in Quebec and Labrador—ore much needed by U.S. steel mills—spurred Congressional approval in 1954. The 2,350 mile waterway allows bulk carriers to pass through the system of canals, locks, rivers, and lakes as far inland as Duluth, Minnesota.

Section Review

ANSWERS

1. Eisenhower thought Truman exercised too much influence over Congress. He planned to propose laws but not demand that Congress pass them.
2. The Army-McCarthy hearings and Joseph Welch's counterattack on McCarthy.
3. Eisenhower felt he had to uphold the Supreme Court decision in Brown. Possible reasons: to make sure the law was obeyed; restore order; other measures had failed.

Reduced student page in the Teacher's Edition

(Left to right) Soviet Premier Bulganin, President Eisenhower, French Premier Faure, and British Prime Minister Eden met in Geneva in 1955 to ease world tensions. Eisenhower's budget-trimming provoked a humorous response (below).

"I Don't Know Why Everything Has to Keep Changing. When I Was a Young Man—"
1959
U.S. SPENDING NEEDS
HERBLOCK

from STRAIGHT HERBLOCK (Simon & Schuster, 1964)

Eisenhower Reelected in 1956

In September 1955 Eisenhower suffered a heart attack, and people wondered if he would run for a second term. However, he soon resumed official duties, and in August 1956 he and Nixon easily won renomination at the Republican convention.

Adlai Stevenson was also renominated by his party and campaigned vigorously. But international conflicts affected the outcome of the election. Just days before the election, Soviet tanks crushed an uprising against Communist rule in Hungary, and Britain and France landed troops in Egypt to regain control of the Suez Canal. American voters chose the candidate whose military experience they trusted. Eisenhower swept to victory, although the Democrats kept control of Congress.

In 1958 the Democrats again made gains in the House and Senate, aided by a recession that began in 1957 and hit its lowest point in May 1958. As is usually the case, voters blamed the party in the White House. In all, Eisenhower had to work with a Democratic Congress for six of his eight years in office. Yet, on the whole, the nation prospered.

The nation also grew. In 1959 two more stars were added to the flag when Alaska and Hawaii joined the union as the forty-ninth and fiftieth states. Alaska became the nation's largest and least populous state. Hawaii, with its many people of Polynesian, Japanese, Chinese, Portuguese, and Filipino ancestry, became the most culturally diverse state in the union.

Section Review

1. Analysis. How did Eisenhower's leadership and his attitude toward Congress differ from Truman's?

2. Comprehension. What led to the decline of McCarthyism?

3. Synthesis. If Eisenhower personally believed that racial problems could not be solved by lawmaking, why did he send troops to Little Rock? Writing as the President, explain two reasons you might have given the public for your action.

Social History
Some popular children's TV shows of the 1950s include *The Lone Ranger, Hopalong Cassidy, Lassie, Howdy Doody,* and *The Mickey Mouse Club*. Television-inspired fads arose in the Fifties. Walt Disney's weekly show—*Davy Crockett*—caused millions of children to don coonskin caps in imitation of the show's hero.

26-4 Years of Abundance

Focus: What was life like in the United States in the middle of the twentieth century?

During the Eisenhower years, most Americans enjoyed a steadily rising standard of living. Wages rose faster than prices, unemployment averaged less than 6 percent, and veterans' benefits provided millions of young Americans with a purchasing power they had not known in this century. They used this purchasing power to buy cars, luxury items, labor-saving appliances, and television sets.

Television, developed before the war, was at first a toy for the rich. However, by 1950 more than 4 million families had TV sets. They were able to watch the first coast-to-coast broadcast in 1951, which covered President Truman at the Japanese Peace Treaty Conference. Three years later, the frozen "TV dinner" appeared on the scene. Mystery writer Raymond Chandler commented sarcastically on the effects of TV:

> *"It took a certain amount of effort to go to the movies. . . . Reading took less physical effort, but you had to concentrate a little. . . . Radio was a lot better, but there wasn't anything to look at. . . . But television's perfect. You turn a few knobs, a few of those mechanical adjustments at which the higher apes are so proficient, and lean back and drain your mind of all thought."*

The Second Industrial Revolution

One reason more Americans could afford television sets and other consumer goods was that new technologies had made these goods cheaper to produce. The tiny lightweight transistor, invented in 1947, revolutionized electronic equipment, making possible portable calculators, radios, and TV sets, and high-speed computers.

In the Fifties, the number of American homes with TV sets swelled from 5 million to 46 million.

Section 26-4

Objectives

- ***Answer the Focus Question.***
- *Analyze the factors that led to increased consumer spending and the move to the suburbs.*
- *Explain the problems that farmers faced in the 1950s.*
- *Relate what factors led to the passage of the National Defense Education Act.*

Introducing THE SECTION

Just as the Twenties, the Fifties have generally been looked upon with nostalgia. People tend to focus on the good rather than the bad. Have students list what words, objects, people, or events come to mind when they think of the Fifties. Write their responses on the chalkboard.

GTV Side 4

Chap. 5, Frame 22639

U.S. Population: 1920 and 1950 (Population Clocks, 2 Frames)

Search:

Step:

Developing

THE SECTION

Linking Past and Present

Discussion. The most popular early television programs were quiz shows, soap operas, and situation comedies. Have students cite some of the early TV shows they have seen in reruns, such as "I Love Lucy," "Leave it to Beaver," "The Adventures of Ozzie and Harriet." **Ask:** What values and attitudes were expressed in these shows? Do they accurately reflect American life in the 1950s? Do current shows accurately reflect today's values?

Active Learning

Debate. In the 1960s FCC Chairman Newton Minton declared television a "vast wasteland." Have students debate whether Minton's contention is true today. (Students might cite educational television and news programs that are beneficial; or cite programs that include violence or racial stereotypes.)

Connections: Politics
In 1955 the American Federation of Labor (AFL) and the Congress of Industrial Organizations (CIO) merged into a single organization, the AFL-CIO with 16 million members.

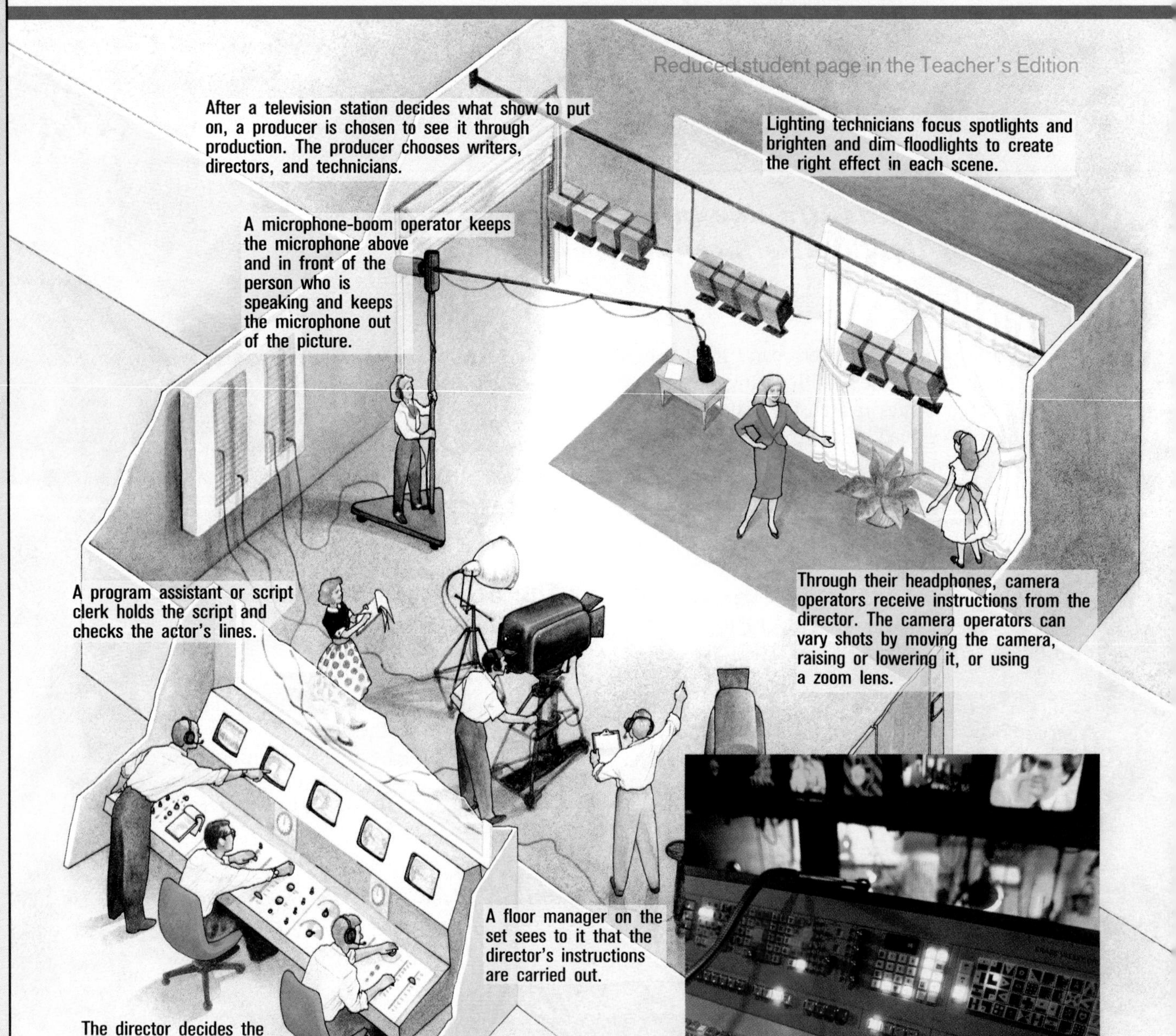
After a television station decides what show to put on, a producer is chosen to see it through production. The producer chooses writers, directors, and technicians.
Lighting technicians focus spotlights and brighten and dim floodlights to create the right effect in each scene.
A microphone-boom operator keeps the microphone above and in front of the person who is speaking and keeps the microphone out of the picture.
A program assistant or script clerk holds the script and checks the actor's lines.
Through their headphones, camera operators receive instructions from the director. The camera operators can vary shots by moving the camera, raising or lowering it, or using a zoom lens.
A floor manager on the set sees to it that the director's instructions are carried out.
The director decides the general behavior of the performers and what camera shots to use.
The directors and engineers work in the control room. Each monitor shows them scenes from a different camera or from some other source, such as a tape or another studio.
The technical director switches from camera to camera and from close-ups to more distant shots.
The audio engineer maintains the quality of the sound and determines what special sound effects to use.

Advances in technology give us clearer, more colorful images today than the fuzzy black-and-white images of early TV.

Learning From Art A TV Studio in the 1950s

In the mid-1950s some large companies began using computers to handle routine paper work. Other industrial firms installed computers to guide the production of steel, chemicals, and petroleum. On assembly lines, new electronic control-boards guided machines in performing each step of production automatically. Many people hailed this new process, called **automation,** as a "Second Industrial Revolution."

Walter Reuther, head of the United Auto Workers, saw the effects of automation in Detroit. Workers in the 1920s had taken a full day to machine—or finish—one engine block. Now, he said, a block moved along an automated line and "fourteen and six-tenths minutes later, it is fully machined, without a human hand touching it." Reuther and other union leaders did not fight automation as long as management protected workers' jobs and wages.

Fueling production. Thanks in part to automation, in the 1950s the United States was producing half of the world's goods. One effect of the boom in productivity was a rapid increase in energy requirements. More and more, this energy came from oil. Electric companies built power plants that burned oil. Cars, buses, trucks, and jet planes also increased the demand for petroleum products.

Until 1953 the United States had for the most part produced more oil than it consumed. But with the demand for oil rising at a rate of 6 percent per year, after 1953 the nation found it had to import oil to continue its industrial growth.

Hopes for a new, abundant source of energy were fueled in 1957 when the nation's first nuclear power plant opened at Shippingport, Pennsylvania. Similar plants would be built in the following decades. However, controversy about possible radiation hazards was to prevent nuclear power from becoming the answer to the nation's energy needs.

Settling in the Suburbs

Beginning in 1946, the nation experienced a **baby boom**—a dramatic rise in the birth rate. Between 1950 and 1956, the number of babies born per year increased from just over 3.6 million to more than 4.25 million. The birth rate hovered at that figure for several years before beginning to drop in the early 1960s. The baby boom had a major impact on the economy, as well as on patterns of American life.

With money in the bank and babies on the way, young couples went looking for housing. Rather than an apartment in the city, they wanted homes

TV became a primary source of entertainment. Families watched such favorites as The Honeymooners, Gunsmoke, *and* I Love Lucy. *Frozen foods were packaged as "TV dinners."*

Analyzing Primary Sources

John Kenneth Galbraith. In *The Affluent Society*, a book that became a best seller, economist John Kenneth Galbraith wrote:

"In their mauve and cerise air-conditioned, power-steered, and power-braked automobiles [people] pass through cities that are badly paved, made hideous by blighted buildings, billboards . . . decaying refuse. Is this, indeed, American genius?"

What was Galbraith's attitude toward the automobile? How did the automobile contribute to the deterioration of cities? What can be inferred about Galbraith's attitude toward American technology? **(Cars allowed people to move from cities to suburbs, isolating them from urban problems; technology can cause problems, not always a solution; cities took an economic downturn.)**

Connections: Literature

Discussion. During the baby boom Dr. Benjamin Spock's *The Common Sense Book of Baby and Child Care* became one of the most popular and influential books of the period. Have students ask their parents or grandparents if they read the book and if they were influenced by Dr. Spock in their child rearing.

Connections: Health

Discussion. A big change in American eating habits came in 1954 when Ray Kroc paid the McDonald brothers $2.7 million for the franchise rights to their hamburger diner in San Bernardino, California. A year later Kroc opened his own diner in Des Plaines, Illinois, complete with golden arches. Kroc's success begat dozens of imitators.

Ask: What effects did McDonald's have upon American eating habits? **(fast foods, fatty foods)** Upon social habits? **(less home cooking and family togetherness; employment for young people)** Upon the American landscape? **(fast-food outlets dot countryside)**

Thinking Critically

Evaluation. Discuss life in the suburbs. **Ask:** What were some of the advantages of living in the suburbs? Disadvantages? Why did living in the suburbs make owning one or more cars a necessity? How did the growth of suburbs contribute to the decline of cities? (Wealthier people moved to suburbs, reducing cities' tax base, making it hard for them to provide services. Many businesses moved out of cities too.)

Connections: Economics

Suburbanites forged a bond with the automobile. Between 1945 and 1960 the number of cars in the country increased by 133 percent as Americans rushed to buy the latest models with the largest fins. In 1955 a record 8 million cars were sold.

Reduced student page in the Teacher's Edition

America's landscape took on a new look as people rushed to the suburbs. The number of families owning their own homes rose dramatically—especially in the mainly all-white suburbs. To reach schools, hospitals, and businesses, suburban dwellers depended on their cars.

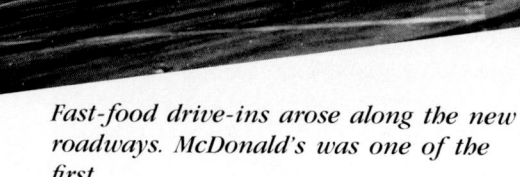

Fast-food drive-ins arose along the new roadways. McDonald's was one of the first.

of their own in the suburbs—communities that had begun to grow up at the edges of urban America. Inspired by the innovative ideas of William Levitt, builders cut costs by putting up hundreds of identical houses at a time. Thus, they could sell houses at prices young families could afford.

Suburban subdivisions sprang up across the nation. Between 1950 and 1955 suburbs grew seven times as fast as central cities. New housing developments sprawled across acres that had once been cropland or pasture. Shopping centers, schools, and businesses soon followed in their wake.

Some people fled the city for a place that was even beyond the suburbs. They commuted to the city to work each day and then commuted back home again. Writer Clifton Fadiman humorously described the lives of the commuters:

> *"The Communicators [white-collar commuters] are the frontiersmen of the 20th Century. They have made the dizzy . . . leap into the wilderness. . . . We . . . are blazing a trail and marking out new country. The 8:10 [train] is our Conestoga, the electric hedge-clipper our ax, the portable sprayer our rifle. And make no mistake: we may complain, . . . but we are not going back."*

Multicultural Perspectives

Those who left the city for the suburbs were mainly middle-class whites of various ethnic backgrounds. Sometimes ethnic and racial groups—Jews, African Americans, Hispanics, and Asian Americans—were excluded. The practices that assured this segregation included: segregation of such facilities as swimming pools, golf courses, theaters, and schools; discriminatory practices in lending, such as requiring mortgage applicants from certain ethnic groups to meet higher standards than other applicants; agreements among property owners and real estate people not to sell homes in certain areas to members of certain groups; and threats of violence against those who broke the rules.

Backyard History

Activity. If students live in a suburb or near one, have them find out when it was founded and how it has grown. What ties does it have to nearby cities? Students might research local resources to find maps and pictures of the area before it was developed and then trace its growth.

Geography

A KEY TO OUR PAST

Relationships Within Places: The Growth of Suburbs

To fulfill human needs, people often make changes in their physical environment. After World War II, human needs and new technology combined to bring about a great change in the American landscape.

After the war, the marriage rate doubled. Because there were not enough affordable homes, more than 2 million couples moved in with relatives, while others crowded into tiny apartments.

In 1946 readers of a New York newspaper spotted an advertisement for brand-new houses on already landscaped lots. Thousands flocked to Levittown on Long Island to see the rows of cozy homes. They found that a veteran could buy a two-bedroom house for $7,990 with $90 down and $58 a month for twenty-five years. In the first seven days, developer William Levitt sold 707 houses.

Levitt had kept costs down by applying mass-production techniques to home building. First, a fleet of earth-movers gouged out foundations. Then a squadron of cement trucks poured concrete slabs. Relay teams of workers laid brick foundations, raised walls, and added roofs, shingles, and paint. Construction was so rapid that eight new houses were ready each day.

If the earliest arrivals to Levittown spotted potatoes growing in their newly landscaped yards, it was because the land had once been a potato field. In just ten years, 17,000 houses sprang up on the one-time "potato patch."

Other builders adopted William Levitt's methods. They searched on the fringes of cities for level, well-drained land. That kind of land was usually agricultural land. Across the United States, farm land gave way to rows of box-like houses.

Between 1950 and 1960, whole communities seemed to spring up overnight. One-quarter of the nation's people moved to the new suburbs, while farmers retreated to land farther from the cities.

Americans viewed the rapid changes in their environment with mixed feelings. Millions of people now owned their own plot of land "in the country," but some of the nation's finest agricultural land was gone forever.

1. What needs led to great changes in the American landscape after World War II?
2. What role did technology play in these changes? What role did people's values play?
3. What were some consequences of the growth of suburbs? How did Americans view this rapid change in the relationship between humans and the environment in the 1950s?

Geography: A Key to Our Past

ANSWERS

1. The need for affordable housing; the baby boom.
2. Mass-production technology made it possible to build inexpensive houses. The high value placed on owning a home in a nice area led people to buy houses.
3. The disappearance of agricultural land; the addition of former farm people to the urban labor force. People viewed the suburbs with mixed feelings—satisfaction with better housing, concern with lost rural land.

Active Learning

Cooperative Activity. Divide the class into several "families." Have each "family" imagine that the farm they own has been in the family for four generations. A developer wants to buy it and build housing.

Ask: Will you sell the land or keep farming it? Before reaching a decision each group should compile a list of arguments for and against selling. Call upon each group for its decision and supporting arguments.

B · A · C · K · G · R · O · U · N · D

Connections: Literature

A literary and philosophical movement, the Beat Generation, emerged in the late Fifties; San Francisco was its center. The name "Beat" comes from the term *beatitude*—a state of inner grace that is idealized in the Eastern philosophy of Zen Buddhism. Two leading "beat" writers were novelist Jack Kerouac and poet Allen Ginsberg. Kerouac's novel *On the Road*, published in 1957, is an account of his three-week automobile journey across the country and his search for personal fulfillment. Beatniks shocked mainstream society by their rejection of authority and their attacks on middle-class standards of conduct and what they saw as smug conformity.

Reduced student page in the Teacher's Edition

Spotlight on the Suburbs

Songwriter Malvina Reynolds saw suburban living as one of the causes of the conformity of the Fifties. In 1963 she wrote a satirical song about the suburbs that had sprung up around her.

Little boxes on the hillside, little boxes
made of ticky tacky,
Little boxes on the hillside, little boxes
all the same.
There's a green one and a pink one and a blue one and a yellow one,
And they're all made out of ticky tacky and they all look just the same.
And the people in the houses all went to the university
Where they were put in boxes and they came out all the same;
And there's doctors and there's lawyers and there's business executives
And they're all made out of ticky tacky and they all look just the same.

The growth of suburbs intensified the demand for new roads. To link suburbs to cities—and to create a national road for rapidly moving armed forces in case of war—the federal government launched the nation's biggest public works project to date. Beginning in 1956 it built more than 41,000 miles of freeways at a cost of $76 billion.

Farmers Suffer Amid Plenty

The abundance of the Fifties was a mixed blessing for the nation's farmers. Even though the number of farms decreased, farm production actually rose by 10 percent. New types of equipment and improved seeds and fertilizers boosted the yield per acre. By 1960 one worker could produce as much wheat as two workers could produce a decade earlier. Gains in cotton and corn production were just as spectacular.

However, as in the 1880s and 1920s, crop surpluses caused prices, and therefore farm incomes, to drop. Government programs designed to eliminate surpluses were largely unsuccessful, so while 20 million Americans lived on farms in 1953, that number had dropped to 15 million by 1960.

People who were forced off the land moved into the cities looking for work. So, too, did new immigrants, particularly from Puerto Rico and Mexico. Poor themselves, these newcomers could not provide the cities with the tax revenues lost when wealthier people moved to the suburbs. As a result, in the midst of abundance, many central cities were troubled by poverty and declining public services.

from STRAIGHT HERBLOCK (Simon & Schuster, 1964)

Migrant farm workers did not share in the Fifties prosperity. Often they could not afford to buy the kind of food they provided for others.

Sputnik and Education

Despite problems on farms and in cities, more Americans lived in comfort than ever before. Their sense of security was shattered, however, when the Soviet Union launched *Sputnik I*. Americans now suspected that they were losing the race for scientific and military leadership of the world. Soviet Premier Nikita Khrushchev gloated, "People of the whole world . . . are saying that the U.S. has been beaten." Chief Soviet space scientist Leonid I. Sedov crowed:

Multicultural Perspectives

Included among the domestic migrant labor force were large numbers of Mexican Americans. Not covered by wage laws, not resident in one place long enough to qualify for aid programs, and not unionized, migrants were quartered in run-down housing and labored for low wages. Children fell behind in school because frequent moves and hard work (child labor laws were often overlooked on farms) kept them from attending regularly. Discrimination against Mexican Americans compounded their problems. In addition, in the 1940s, 1950s, and early 1960s Mexican-American workers found themselves in competition with temporary contract labor from Mexico, the *braceros*, who worked for very little.

Linking Past and Present

Discussion. In the Fifties Americans expressed as much concern over education as they do today. **Ask:** What prompted these concerns in the Fifties? **(fear of loss of military and scientific leadership)** In the Nineties? **(low student test scores, concern over the ability of the United States to compete economically)** Both movements for reform stress improvement in which areas? **(math and science)**

"You Americans have a better standard of living than we have. But the American loves his car, his refrigerator, his house. He does not, as we Russians do, love his country."

American critics argued that the nation's lagging performance was because the United States did not stress scientific education. To compete, Americans would have to strengthen science, math, and foreign language education. In 1958 Congress passed the National Defense Education Act, giving $280 million to the states to improve facilities for teaching science and modern languages.

Assessing the Fifties

The Fifties were marked by remarkable growth and prosperity. They were also a time of unusual conformity. Many people seemed to want to live their lives in the same way as everyone around them, due in part, perhaps, to the lingering effects of McCarthyism or the ideal lives they saw on TV. In dress and in thought, it was a conservative time.

The 1950s held more than their share of uncertainties, too. The threat of polio, a disease that killed thousands and crippled many more, hung over the nation until a vaccine to prevent it was put into use in 1954. The biggest fear of all came from the ever-present threat of a nuclear war. Against this backdrop, the poodle skirts, blue suede shoes, and rock n' roll that many young people favored seemed a splash of color in a sea of gray.

Section Review

1. Identification. Define *automation* and *baby boom.*

2. Analysis. What factors led to the increase in consumer spending in the 1950s?

3. Comprehension. What contributed to the problems farmers faced in the 1950s?

4. Comprehension. How did the launching of *Sputnik I* affect American education?

5. Analysis. Describe five features of American life today that first appeared on the scene in the 1950s.

Connections to Themes

The Search for Opportunity

From 1945 to 1960 Americans were "the people of plenty." The gross national product more than doubled from $208 billion to $506 billion. Automobile registrations also doubled. In supermarkets, shoppers chose from goods that had not even existed before the war.

Yet millions of Americans did not share in this prosperity. Lured to northern cities by the hope of jobs and education, "poor whites" and African Americans from the South and newcomers from Puerto Rico found instead unemployment, run-down housing, and overburdened schools. Conditions for those remaining behind were even worse, while in the West and Southwest, Asian and Mexican Americans met discrimination in school and on the job.

In the expanding economy, however, more opportunities opened up to members of ethnic groups than ever before—for example, as business owners, lawyers, ministers, and teachers. These men and women formed the core of a new political leadership, determined to turn the dream of economic opportunity for all into a reality.

At the same time, in colleges and universities students from different ethnic groups began to come together to seek equal educational opportunities and a political voice. In factories and on farms, workers began to press more aggressively for economic opportunities.

By the end of the Fifties, hundreds of grass-roots organizations had been formed to fight for a share of the country's abundance. They would soon introduce a new spirit of change.

Section Review

ANSWERS

1. Definitions for the following terms are on text pages indicated in parentheses: *automation* (717), *baby boom* (717).
2. Wages rose faster than prices; unemployment was down; veteran's benefits gave millions of young Americans purchasing power.
3. Technology led to overproduction, which lowered prices and hurt farmers.
4. Fear of Soviets "getting ahead" led to the National Defense Education Act, giving federal aid to improve teaching facilities for science and math.
5. Answers may include: automation, suburban housing developments, shopping centers, rock 'n roll, fast food, preoccupation with television, TV dinners.

Chapter Survey

ANSWERS

Using New Vocabulary

1. (c) Hoover believed United States endangered by federal employees bent on Communist *subversion* of government.
2. (a) William Levitt built subdivisions to house growing families of *baby boom.*
3. (b) Reuther, head of the auto workers' union, did not oppose *automation* as long as management protected workers' jobs and wages.

Reviewing the Chapter

1. For higher wages to keep up with rising prices. Truman's use of federal troops to end mining strike and his threats to draft striking railroad workers displeased union members.
2. Women who earned good money during war laid off or paid less after. African Americans and Mexican Americans fought as equals during the war but faced discrimination in civilian life. Japanese Americans interned during the war regained political rights but not property and had to start life anew with few if any resources.
3. Disagreed on curbing organized labor, instituting more New Deal-type programs. Congress more conservative than President, cool to federal spending.
4. Soviet Union took control of eastern and central Europe, Communists won civil war in China, Soviet spy ring uncovered in Canada, Soviets developed atomic bomb, Klaus Fuchs arrested in Britain for passing atomic secrets. Some basis for believing Communists were trying to expand influence in the United States, though exaggerated wildly.
5. Charged with giving secrets to Soviets when at State Department. Found guilty of lying under oath. His case heightened fears that communist threat did exist in the United States government.
6. Continued programs supporting human welfare started under FDR and Truman, but wanted to streamline the cost and role of federal government. Consolidated social programs under HEW, and increased social security.
7. Federal troops were used to enforce Supreme Court decision; led to passage of new civil rights act giving federal government power to act against states that kept blacks from voting.
8. United States began to import oil as demand multiplied to meet needs of more factories, power plants, automobiles.
9. Causes: great demand for goods, human and material resources to produce them, long period of peace. Effects:

Reduced student page in the Teacher's Edition

Chapter Survey

Using New Vocabulary

Match each numbered vocabulary term with the appropriate person. Then explain the connection between the person and the term.

1. subversion	(a) William Levitt
2. baby boom	(b) Walter Reuther
3. automation	(c) J. Edgar Hoover

Reviewing the Chapter

1. Why did industrial workers go on strike after the war? Why was Truman's response to the strikes unpopular?

2. How did the postwar experiences of women and members of minority groups differ from their wartime experiences?

3. On what issues did Truman and the Eightieth Congress disagree? What was the basis of their differences?

4. Why did a climate of suspicion of Communists develop in the United States in the postwar years? To what extent was it justified?

5. Explain the significance of the Alger Hiss case.

6. What did Eisenhower mean when he said that he intended to be conservative in money matters and liberal in human affairs? Give examples to support your answer.

7. How did *Brown* v. *Board of Education* lead to a change in the relationship between the federal government and the states?

8. In what way did the nation's demand for oil change in the 1950s? Why?

9. What were the main causes and effects of prosperity in the 1950s?

10. What Americans did not enjoy this prosperity? Why not?

Thinking Critically

1. Analysis. Compare actions taken by the government during the McCarthy era with those taken during the Red Scare of 1919-1920. What did they have in common? How did they differ?

2. Evaluation. Early in 1948 Truman asked Congress to pass civil rights legislation. An opponent said that Truman's request "has inflicted an apparently fatal blow, not only to the unity of the party, but to the unity of the country." When, if ever, do you think a President should overlook unity to achieve other goals? Do you think Truman was wise to ask for this legislation in an election year?

3. Synthesis. Soviet Premier Khrushchev said Americans were materialistic rather than patriotic. Write a response to Khrushchev from the point of view of an American of the 1950s.

History and You

Many people have compared the near-hysteria of the McCarthy era to a witch hunt, an investigation in which anyone who disagrees with official or established views is suspected of disloyalty. Do you think the same kind of intolerance could sweep America today? Why or why not? Give evidence to support your answer.

Using a Time Line

Match each date on the time line with the correct item in the list below. Write your answers in chronological order and explain the effect of each event on American society.

(A) Sputnik I
(B) McCarran Act
(C) Serviceman's Bill of Rights
(D) Executive Order 9981
(E) Start of interstate highway construction
(F) Taft-Hartley Act
(G) Army-McCarthy hearings
(H) First transcontinental television broadcast

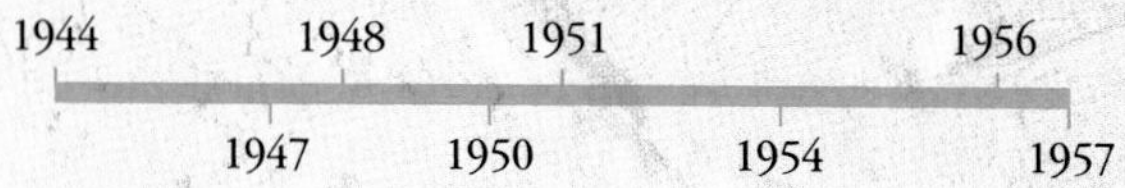

baby boom, move to suburbs, conformity.

10. Farmers did not prosper because overproduction led to low crop prices. Inner city residents suffered as cities lost tax revenue when middle class moved to suburbs; many racial and ethnic groups suffered from discrimination and racism.

Thinking Critically

1. In both periods: many feared suspected Communists; loyalty oaths were used; few of the people accused were actually guilty of the charges; some people recognized that the suppression of liberty was more dangerous than the supposed treachery; many claimed that Sacco and Vanzetti (during the Red Scare) and the Rosenbergs (during the McCarthy era) were executed more for political beliefs than for their actions. Suspicions focused more on aliens during the Red Scare, on influential citizens during McCarthy era. Red Scare was carried out by Attorney General's office, with suspects arrested, deported, or turned over to state authorities. McCarthy era accusations mainly made before congressional committees, broadcast on TV; suspects judged guilty by innuendo. McCarthy era lasted longer.
2. Some may argue that a President should ignore unity when a moral principle is at stake, such as basic human rights. Others may argue that a President can never ignore unity if he wants to achieve his objectives in a democratic society. Truman's timing did not help achieve goal in 1948.
3. Answers may include participation in World War II and Korean War as examples of patriotism.

History and You

Students arguing it could not happen again can point to tolerance of opposing opinions during the recent Persian Gulf War. Others may say it could happen again if those demanding "political correctness" gain control of media and shape public opinion, or if country has genuine cause to fear invasion.

Using a Time Line

(C) 1944, **(F)** 1947, **(D)** 1948, **(B)** 1950, **(H)** 1951, **(G)** 1954, **(E)** 1956, **(A)** 1957.

Detecting Bias

1. First is more biased, omits qualifications of second and all but calls the person a Communist.
2. Yes, since second statement makes up for omissions in the first, enables reader to detect its bias.
3. First statement, labeling person Communist, is the more damaging.
4. First statement.

Applying Thinking Skills

Detecting Bias

Often bias is easy to spot. But sometimes the slanting and twisting of information is not easy to detect unless one has some knowledge of the facts.

The statements below were made about the same State Department employee. One is from the official report of a 1947 Congressional investigation into the loyalty of State Department personnel. The other is from a speech by Senator Joseph McCarthy. Senator McCarthy used facts from the report as the basis of his remarks. Compare the two descriptions and answer the questions that follow.

"He was described in reports by various witnesses as interested in communism and by his roommate at the International House as a Communist."

"The subject was described in reports by various witnesses as interested in communism as an experiment, but his political philosophy is in keeping with liberal New Deal social reform under democratic processes of government. [One person said,] 'He is a very ardent New Dealer. He is a live liberal.' But an informant who also lived in the International House [with the subject] at one time said, 'He was one of those accused of being a Red here, but the people who do get up and talk communism are refuted.'"

1. Which description seems more biased or slanted? Why do you think so?

2. Did having the two different descriptions to compare make it easier for you to detect bias? Explain.

3. Which description was potentially more damaging to this employee and his career? Why?

4. From what you know about McCarthy and his anti-communist crusade, which of these statements do you think he made?

Writing About Issues

The Issue: *Should the United States use nuclear power to meet its energy needs?*

In the 1950s many Americans believed that nuclear power was the answer to the growing energy needs of the United States. Several electric power companies set about constructing nuclear plants, and by 1979 such plants provided 13.5 percent of all electricity consumed in the United States.

In that year, an accident occurred at the Three Mile Island Nuclear Power Plant near Harrisburg, Pennsylvania. Radioactive steam was released from the plant into the air. Believing that the accident endangered people living nearby, Pennsylvania Governor Richard Thornburgh closed public schools within five miles of the plant and warned that preschoolers and pregnant women should leave the area. The incident focused the nation's attention on the potential hazards of atomic energy.

People who had opposed nuclear power on grounds of safety argued that the accident at Three Mile Island proved them right. They urged government officials to shut down all nuclear power plants. One writer on environmental issues did not believe nuclear industry officials who tried to reassure the public. The writer stated, "We are being told that the levels of radiation [coming] from the Three Mile Island Nuclear Power Station are not alarming, even though it is an acknowledged fact that radiation, at any level, no matter how low, can cause genetic mutations [changes in the characteristics that children inherit]."

Supporters of nuclear power believed that it would be foolish to outlaw an entire industry because of a single accident. "The public has to be more realistic," a member of the Atomic Industrial Forum said. "There is a risk, but it's not particularly large compared to risks from other energy sources."

What do you think? Should our nation rely on nuclear power to meet its energy needs? Do research to make a list of reasons for and against. Use the list to help you form an opinion. Then write an editorial for your favorite radio station expressing your opinion.

Chapter 27

Camelot and the Great Society

Planning Guide

	Student Text	TWE Lesson Plans	Support Materials
SECTION 1	**Section 27-1 (1-2 Days)** **A Spirit of Change,** pp 726-732 Review/Evaluation Section Review, p 732	**Introducing the Chapter:** What Can You Do for Your Country?—Class Activity, 30 minutes, p 723B **Teaching the Main Ideas:** Peace Corps Recruitment Brochures—Cooperative Activity, one class period, p 723B	★ **Read to Remember,** Section 1 ● **Section Activities,** Section 1 Δ **Readings,** John Glenn, Anthony Lewis ● **Tests and Quizzes,** Section 1 Quiz
SECTION 2	**Section 27-2 (1-2 Days)** **Facing World Tensions,** pp 733-738 Review/Evaluation Section Review, p 738	**Teaching the Main Ideas:** Oral History of the Sixties—Individual Activity, homework, one class period, p 723B **Evaluating Progress:** Analyzing the JFK Presidency—Individual Activity, homework, p 723C	★ **Read to Remember,** Section 2 ● **Section Activities,** Section 2 Δ **Enrichment Activities,** Section 2 Δ **Readings,** Richard N. Goodwin ● **Tests and Quizzes,** Section 2 Quiz
SECTION 3	**Section 27-3 (1-2 Days)** **Johnson and the Great Society,** pp 739-747 Young in America: In the Sixties, pp 744-745 Connections to Themes: Shaping Democracy, p 747 Review/Evaluation Section Review, p 747 Chapter 27 Survey, pp 748-749 Skills, pp 748-749 Using New Vocabulary Thinking Critically Using a Time Line Applying Thinking Skills: Interpreting Political Cartoons Writing About Issues	**Reinforcement Activity:** Person of the Year! Event of the Year!—Cooperative Activity, one class period, p 723C **Enrichment Activity:** Campaign Speeches—Individual Activity, homework, p 723C	★ **Read to Remember,** Section 3 ● **Section Activities,** Section 3 ● **Geography Activities,** Section 3 Δ **Enrichment Activities,** Section 3 Δ **Readings,** Joan Didion ● **Tests and Quizzes,** Section 3 Quiz, Chapter 27 Test (Forms A and B) **Additional Resources** ● **Active Learning** Δ **Transparencies and Activity Book** ● **Testing Software** ★ **Chapter Summaries** **Key:** ★ **For Extra Support** ● **For All Students** Δ **For Enrichment**

Overview

In 1960 John Kennedy defeated Richard Nixon in a close election. Kennedy's "New Frontier" goals included building a volunteer Peace Corps, the Alliance for Progress with Latin American nations, government spending to increase economic growth, and stepping up the space program. During the Kennedy years the Supreme Court took an activist course in protecting individual rights.

Kennedy's foreign policy was dominated by crises and conflicts, including the Bay of Pigs, the Berlin Wall, Soviet arms buildup, communist pressures in South Vietnam, and the Cuban missile crisis.

Kennedy's assassination stunned the nation. Lyndon Johnson, who succeeded him as President, promised to continue to fight for reduced taxes, increased civil rights, and elimination of poverty. His "Great Society" programs sought to improve education and health care, expand voting rights and low-cost housing, and improve environmental quality and consumer safety. Profound social changes characterized Johnson's presidency, especially the rise of the counterculture with its emphasis on personal freedom, including experimentation with drugs, and rejection of middle-class values.

Activity Objectives

After completing the activities, students should be able to

- describe the goals of the Peace Corps and its appeal to American volunteers.
- identify different personal responses to major crises during the Kennedy years.
- recognize significant events and people of the Sixties.
- analyze successes, failures, and unfinished business of Kennedy's presidency.
- identify arguments for and against New Frontier and Great Society programs.

Introducing the Chapter

What Can You Do for Your Country?

This class activity requires half a class period.

This activity introduces students to the hope and optimism created by John F. Kennedy's election. Reflecting on Kennedy's inaugural address, students consider their expectations and responsibilities as American citizens.

Begin by asking a volunteer to read the quotation from Kennedy's address on page 725. Direct students' attention to the last line, " Ask not what your country can do for you—ask what you can do for your country." Explain that this statement inspired many young people in the 1960s to dedicate themselves to public service.

Have each student divide a piece of paper in half lengthwise and label one side *What I Expect from My Country* and the other side *What I Can Do for My Country*. Ask students to list their personal responses under each heading. Allow five to ten minutes of writing time.

Compile students' responses on the chalkboard under the two headings. Help the class identify the common themes under each heading. Encourage students, as they begin reading Chapter 27, to consider the mood of young people in the 1960s. (Common themes might include making a difference at home and abroad; activism—working for change; optimism; promoting international understanding; and so on.)

Teaching the Main Ideas

Section 27-1: Peace Corps Recruitment Brochures

This cooperative activity requires a full class period.

In this activity students create brochures to recruit Peace Corps volunteers. Provide blank paper and colored markers for students to use.

Introduce the activity by asking students to name other places in the world they would like to visit or work. List their answers on the chalkboard. When you have compiled a lengthy list, lead students in recognizing where most of the places are located and whether they are in developed or developing countries. Discuss some of the inconveniences Americans encounter in developing countries.

Explain to the class that President Kennedy founded the Peace Corps to help people in developing countries improve their standard of living, to foster understanding between Americans and peoples of other nations, and to promote world peace. The life of Peace Corps volunteers is generally hard and they often live in primitive conditions. Yet since 1961 tens of thousands of people have volunteered for service.

Divide the class into pairs of students. Each pair is to design a brochure to recruit young people to join the Peace Corps. The brochures should identify some of the countries to which volunteers might be assigned, the jobs they might do, and how their work might help promote peace. If possible, give students the opportunity to do additional research into the Peace Corps before they begin.

Display the completed brochures and discuss them with the class. Ask volunteers to tell what factors might motivate them to join the Peace Corps.

Teaching the Main Ideas

Section 27-2: Oral History of the Sixties

In this individual activity, students conduct interviews out of class and then participate in a discussion that requires a full class period.

This activity gives students insights into key events of the Kennedy era through oral history interviews. Each student conducts one interview and shares the results with the class.

Begin by explaining that the Kennedy years were exciting, and sometimes unsettling. Many people alive today vividly remember specific events of Kennedy's presidency but respond differently to them. Tell students that to capture the range of memories, they are each going to conduct an oral history interview with someone who was a teenager or adult in 1961.

Explain that to make their interviews effective, students are to write specific interview questions on the following topics:

- Bay of Pigs invasion
- Building of the Berlin Wall
- The Cuban Missile crisis
- The assassination of President Kennedy

Prepare students for their interviews by reviewing their questions and discussing interviewing etiquette.

On the day the assignment is due, rearrange the classroom seating so that all students can see each other as they share and discuss their interviews. Indicate that they will be evaluated on their participation, receiving points for sharing information and asking questions but losing points for interrupting or monopolizing the discussion. Direct students to discuss the responses of their interview subjects to each of the four topics.

Conclude the activity by summarizing the variety of responses to the four events covered in the interviews. Ask students to speculate on how people today might respond to similar crises.

Reinforcement Activity

Section 27-3: Person of the Year! Event of the Year!

This cooperative activity requires one class period.

This activity, in which students create magazine covers, reinforces knowledge of the events and people who made history in the 1960s. Students will need markers and sheets of 8½-by-11-inch paper.

Introduce the activity by asking students to name the single event and the one person they think were historically most important last year. Tell the class that some news magazines name a "person of the year" and feature the winner's picture on their cover for the first week of January. Ask if they think the people and events they named for the past year merit a magazine cover.

Group students in teams of three or four and assign them to create magazine covers that recognize important people and events in the 1960s. Each team is to select five events and five people from the decade and design a magazine cover for each. Covers should include a picture and a headline explaining the significance of the person or event. Specify that students may use both an event and a person for the same year but cannot name two people or two events for a single year.

Post the magazine covers and have students review them for common themes and trends.

Evaluating Progress

Section 27-2: Analyzing the JFK Presidency

This individual activity can be assigned as homework.

In this activity students demonstrate their understanding of the Kennedy presidency by creating a chart that identifies JFK's accomplishments, failures, and unfinished business.

Before making the activity assignment, remind students that John F. Kennedy's election was met with both excitement and concern. Similarly, his presidency inspired both admiration and criticism.

Tell students that the assignment has two parts. First, they are to prepare a chart entitled *Summarizing the Kennedy Presidency.* The chart is to have three headings: *Accomplishments, Failures*, and *Unfinished Business*. Direct students to review the first two sections of Chapter 27 for information to list under the three headings.

The second task is to write a paragraph supporting or disagreeing with the lines: *"Don't let it be forgot, that once there was a spot, for one brief shining moment that was known as Camelot."*

Students' charts will vary but should include:

- *Accomplishments*—Peace Corps, Alliance for Progress, space program, economic growth, test ban treaty, resolution of the Cuban missile crisis
- *Failures*—Bay of Pigs invasion, Berlin Wall, Vietnam, arms buildup
- *Unfinished Business*—arms limitation treaties, civil rights bill, New Frontier programs

Responses to the Camelot quote will vary.

Enrichment Activity

Section 27-3: Campaign Speeches

This activity is best assigned as homework, with a class period set aside for speeches and discussion.

In this activity students reflect on the social programs of Kennedy's New Frontier and Johnson's Great Society in the course of writing campaign speeches for congressional candidates.

Begin the activity by reviewing Section 27–3 with the class. Remind students that when Lyndon Johnson assumed the presidency, his stated goal was to continue and extend Kennedy's New Frontier programs to ensure civil rights and improve conditions for the nation's poorer citizens. Johnson's overwhelming victory in the election of 1964 encouraged him to proceed with even more ambitious programs to achieve what he called the Great Society.

Have students imagine that they are candidates for Congress in the election of 1966. Their task is to write campaign speeches either praising or condemning New Frontier and Great Society legislation and proposals and suggesting what action they will take if elected. Each student should decide which position to take, then gather information from the text—and from other sources if available—to use in the speech. Speeches in favor should describe and praise New Frontier and Great Society legislation. Speeches against should emphasize the high costs and uncertain benefits of such legislation. Encourage students to use their imaginations in playing the role of convincing political candidates. They may wish to review the propaganda techniques described on page 635 when writing their speeches.

On the day the assignment is due, ask two or three volunteers from each side to deliver their speeches to the class. Encourage class members to evaluate the speeches for accuracy and effectiveness and to add points from their own speeches that were left out of the presentations. Have students note examples of propaganda in the speeches, too, if appropriate.

Bibliography and Audiovisual Material

Teacher Bibliography

Caro, Robert A. *The Years of Lyndon Johnson*. 2 vols. New York: Alfred A. Knopf & Co., 1982 and 1990.

Gelb, Norman. *The Berlin Wall: Kennedy, Krushchev and a Showdown in the Heart of Europe*. New York: Simon & Schuster, Inc., 1988.

Kennedy, Robert F. *Thirteen Days: A Memoir of the Cuban Missile Crisis*. New York: NAL/Dutton Co., 1969.

Manchester, William. *The Death of a President, November, 1963*. New York: HarperCollins Publishers, Inc., 1988.

White, Theodore H. *The Making of the President, 1960*. New York: Macmillan, 1989.

Wyden, Peter. *Bay of Pigs*. New York: Simon & Schuster, Inc., 1980.

Student Bibliography

Drury, Allen. *Advise and Consent*. New York: Doubleday Co., 1959.

Kopit, Arthur. *Indians*. New York: Hill & Wang, Inc., 1965.

Van Itallie, Jean Claude. *American Hurrah*. New York: Grove/Weidenfeld, 1978.

Wolfe, Tom. *The Right Stuff*. New York: Bantam Books, 1984.

Films, Videocassettes, and Videodiscs

The Cuban Missile Crisis. 15 min. Guidance Associates. Videocassette.

The Eagle and the Bear—Dateline: 1962, Cuba. 23 min. Coronet/MTI. Videodisc.

The Fabulous 60s: Volumes 1 & 2 (1960 & 1961). 60 min. each. Social Studies School Services. 2 Videocassettes.

Footprints on the Moon: Achievements in Space Exploration. Guidance Associates. Videocassette.

John F. Kennedy: Great Figures in History. 104 min. CBS. Videocassette.

Kennedy: Years of Charisma. 24 min. LCA. Movie.

Filmstrips

The 1960's: American Decades Series. 6 color filmstrips, 3 cassettes, guide. United Learning.

The Sixties: The Best of Times, the Worst of Times. 2 color filmstrips, 2 cassettes, guide. New York Times.

Computer Software

American Foreign Policy. 1 Apple diskette, backup, guide. Focus Media.

Chapter 27

Objectives

- Contrast John F. Kennedy's approach to the presidency with Eisenhower's.
- Relate how Kennedy faced Cold War tensions.
- Explain how Lyndon Johnson launched the Great Society.
- Describe changes in American society during Johnson's administration.

Introducing THE CHAPTER

For suggestions on introducing Chapter 27, refer to page 723B in the Teacher's Edition.

Developing THE CHAPTER

For activities and teaching strategies to help you reinforce and enrich chapter content, see pages 723B–723D in the Teacher's Edition.

B · A · C · K · G · R · O · U · N · D

Chapter Opener Illustrations

John F. Kennedy and Jacqueline Kennedy at the main inaugural ball on January 20, 1961. There were five balls in all and each was so crowded there was almost no room for dancing.

Lyndon Baines Johnson, then Kennedy's Vice-President, visiting a poor family in Appalachia. When Johnson became President, he launched programs to combat poverty.

Fidel Castro on the cover of a 1961 *Life* magazine. At first many Americans supported Castro's revolt in Cuba, thinking him a liberator. After he revealed himself to be a Communist, many agreed with *Life* that he posed a threat to the United States.

John F. Kennedy, Jr., then known to his family and the public as "John-John" mourns the death of his father.

Reduced student page in the Teacher's Edition

Chapter 27 1960-1968

Camelot and the Great Society

For many, Bob Dylan's songs and Milton Glaser's posters and album covers recall the sixties. Dylan's songs—including "Blowin' in the Wind" and "The Times They Are A Changin'" are sometimes referred to as anthems of the youth counterculture.

American Voices

Washington, D.C., was brilliant with new-fallen snow on the morning of January 20, 1961, when a crowd gathered for the inauguration of the thirty-fifth President. After a rabbi, a Protestant minister, a Catholic cardinal, and a Greek Orthodox archbishop offered prayers, a young man stepped to the rostrum to take the oath of office. That man was John Fitzgerald Kennedy, the youngest man ever to be elected President.

"Let the word go forth from this time and place, to friend and foe alike, that the torch has been passed to a new generation of Americans. . . . Together let us explore the stars, conquer the deserts, eradicate disease, tap the ocean depths, and encourage the arts and commerce. . . .

In your hands, my fellow citizens, more than mine, will rest the final success or failure of our course. . . . The trumpet summons us . . . to bear the burden of a long twilight struggle . . . against the common enemies of man: tyranny, poverty, disease, and war itself.

Can we forge against these enemies a grand and global alliance, North and South, East and West that can assure a more fruitful life for all mankind? Will you join in that historic effort?

The energy, the faith, the devotion which we bring to this endeavor will light our country and all who serve it—and the glow from that fire can truly light the world.

And so, my fellow Americans—ask not what your country can do for you—ask what you can do for your country."

The young President rode into office on a wave of energetic idealism, a member of a generation committed to shaping the future of the world. Yet while the decade of the 1960s began on a note of high optimism, its idealism would be challenged by upheaval both at home and abroad.

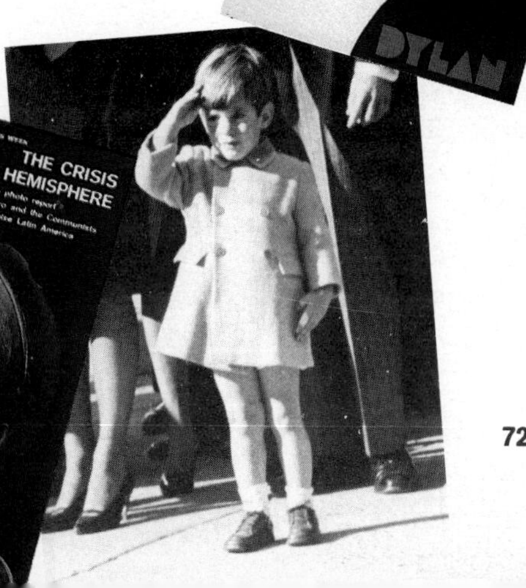

John and Jacqueline Kennedy at inaugural ball; Lyndon B. Johnson "pressing the flesh" in Appalachia; Fidel Castro; John Kennedy, Jr., at his father's funeral procession; Bob Dylan poster by Milton Glazer, 1966.

Analyzing Primary Sources

American Voices

John Kennedy's inaugural address is considered one of the most memorable and inspiring ever delivered. It spurred many Americans to think and hope that a new era in American history was beginning—an era of high goals and aspirations. Have the class discuss the excerpts from Kennedy's address.

1. What goals for the United States did Kennedy set forth? **(Students can mention the paragraph beginning "together let us . . ." Another goal to "forge a grand and global alliance" not only to contain communism but to "assure a more fruitful life for all mankind.")**

2. What sentences and phrases did you find most inspiring? Why? **(Answers will vary.)**

3. What might have been your reaction to his address? **(Answers will vary; some students might have been inspired to join the crusade Kennedy set forth.)**

725

Section 27-1

Objectives

- ***Answer the Focus Question.***
- *Identify the Peace Corps, and the Alliance for Progress.*
- *Evaluate the effectiveness of Kennedy's policies.*
- *List important rulings by the Warren Supreme Court.*

Introducing THE SECTION

Refer students to the journalist's comment on this page. Review Eisenhower's presidency in the context of this statement. Then tell students that after a narrow victory in 1960, President Kennedy spoke of the challenges of the "New Frontier"—the opportunities and perils of the coming decade. His goals included stopping the spread of Commmunist influence abroad, expanding domestic progress, and stepping up the space program to "land a man on the moon" by 1970.

.To reach his goals Kennedy designed programs to encourage economic growth and democratic government in Latin America and increased government spending, with resultant higher budget deficits.

Time Line Illustrations

1. The election poster conveyed JFK's message. Here was a young vigorous candidate—just the sort of President to get the country moving again.
2. In 1962 Americans were shocked to learn that Soviet missiles such as this were poised just 90 miles from the continent, able to reach any city in the eastern United States.
3. John F. Kennedy's assassination shocked the nation and the world. This banner newspaper headline scarcely conveys the sorrow and sense of loss most Americans felt.
4. Johnson's 1964 campaign button displays a Stetson hat and his campaign slogan. It conveys the message that a westerner with a westerner's vitality was the man for the White House.
5. In Florida, with its large population of elderly people,

Reduced student page in the Teacher's Edition

CHAPTER TIME LINE

1960-1968

1960 Kennedy elected President

1962 First American astronaut orbits the earth
Oct Cuban Missile Crisis

Aberdeen American-News
KENNEDY SLAIN
New College Lineup Proposed For S.D.
Sniper's Bullet Kills President

1960 | 1961 | 1963

1961 Peace Corps founded
Mar Alliance for Progress
Apr Bay of Pigs
Aug Berlin Wall

1963 Oct Test Ban Treaty
Nov President Kennedy assassinated

27-1 A Spirit of Change

Focus: How did the Kennedy administration's policies reflect a spirit of change?

As President Eisenhower prepared to leave office in 1960, he declared, "America is today the strongest, the most influential, and most productive nation in the world." Many Americans were satisfied that the nation was prosperous and at peace. A journalist expressed the nation's mood:

> *"For the time being our people do not have great purposes which they are united in wanting to achieve. The public mood of the country is defensive, to hold onto and to conserve, not to push forward and to create. We talk about ourselves these days as if we were a completed society, one which has achieved its purposes and has no further business to transact."*

Yet this conservative mood gradually gave way to a feeling of disquiet and a yearning for change. The concern with "national purpose" became a key issue in the presidential election of 1960.

Kennedy vs. Nixon, 1960

Of the two candidates in the 1960 election—Vice-President Richard M. Nixon of California and Senator John F. Kennedy of Massachusetts—Kennedy captured the spirit of change. In his acceptance speech for the Democratic nomination, he declared that "too many Americans have lost their way, their will, and their sense of historic purpose." He called for "a new generation of leadership."

Johnson gained strong backing for his support of federal medical aid for senior citizens. One Floridian and his Congressman delivered this four-foot trophy to the President to show their appreciation for Medicare.
6. This United States Postal Service stamp was made from a painting by the noted artist Robert Indiana. Many of his works came to be viewed as icons of the 1960s popular culture.

1965 **Apr** Johnson sends marines to the Dominican Republic
Apr-Oct Congress passes Great Society legislation

1967 "Summer of Love" in San Francisco

1964 — 1966 — 1968

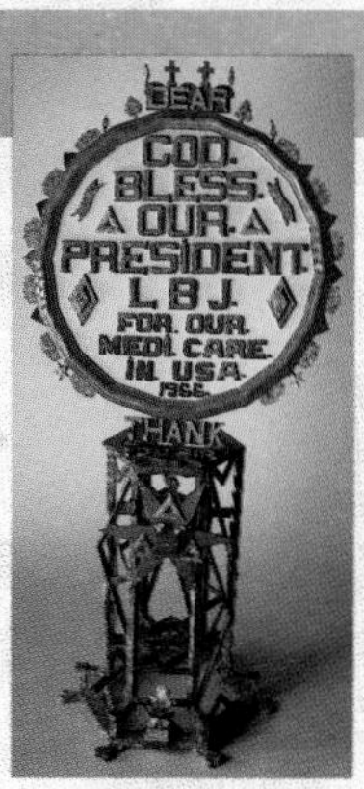

1964 Johnson elected President
Civil Rights Act of 1964
Economic Opportunity Act

1966 *Miranda* v. *Arizona*

Kennedy's youthful manner seemed a promise that he could offer just such new and energetic leadership. Nixon, though only a few years older, associated himself with the past, running on the record of the Eisenhower administration.

Yet in many instances, the candidates took similar positions. Both supported a military buildup to close the "missile gap" of Soviet rocket superiority. Both promised to extend freedom throughout the world. While Kennedy's style and wit were assets, his Catholicism was a political liability. Although he assured the public that his decisions would never be influenced by the Church, anti-Catholic prejudice was strong among some voters.

In the weeks before voting day, Nixon and Kennedy took part in the first televised debates in an American election. At the first debate Nixon, exhausted from the long campaign trail, appeared haggard and tense. Kennedy arrived tan and relaxed from a trip to Florida. His poise helped defuse criticism that he lacked the maturity needed to be President. While the radio audience ranked Nixon higher on the strength of his arguments, Kennedy benefited from his charismatic appeal.

A series of events that gained votes for Kennedy began when civil rights leader Martin Luther King, Jr., was given an especially severe jail sentence for joining a peaceful demonstration in Atlanta, Georgia, in October 1960. While Robert Kennedy worked for King's release, John Kennedy called King's wife, Coretta Scott King, to offer his support and sympathy. African-American churchgoers learned of these events the Sunday before the election. According to Coretta Scott King, "the difference in that election . . . had to do with Kennedy's intercession in Martin's case."

The election results were very close. Kennedy took 303 electoral votes to Nixon's 219. In the popular vote Kennedy's margin of 118,000 votes was the smallest in a presidential election since 1884.

As Kennedy took office he faced the spread of communism abroad and the threat of nuclear war. At home, racial tensions were increasing, the economy was sluggish, and the gap between rich and poor was widening. Yet Kennedy's inaugural address expressed the hope of the nation: that through hard work and commitment, Americans could make a difference both at home and abroad.

Developing
THE SECTION

Linking Past and Present

Discussion. The 1960 election was the first in which television played an important, and perhaps crucial, role. Have students discuss the effects TV has had on national politics. **Ask:** What physical and personal characteristics are likely to make a candidate appealing on TV? Are these characteristics important for carrying out the work of the presidency? What characteristics useful in a President might not be apparent in such appearances? Does television make it easier for people to judge candidates or does it make judgment harder or more inaccurate?

Connections: Politics

Discussion. The 1960 election was close enough that it could have been contested. There were questions about voting irregularities in Texas and Illinois. Nixon did not challenge the results, he said, because he felt that doing so would damage the image of the presidency and the United States. **Ask:** What might have happened if Nixon had challenged the election results? **(Answers may include: Kennedy might have still become President, but the country would have been divided, making it more difficult for Kennedy to carry out his plan for a better nation.)**

Analyzing Primary Sources

News Correspondence. Have students read the observation by a Washington correspondent on this page. **Ask:** Which groups might Kennedy and his followers appeal to? **(city people, well-educated people, middle and upper classes)**

Backyard History

Interview. Students can interview relatives or friends and neighbors to learn what their opinion of Kennedy was at the beginning of his administration. Have them report their findings to the class.

Connections: Language

Discussion. Have students discuss the "New Frontier" metaphor. What characteristics do they think were typical of "frontier" people in the mid-nineteenth century? Which of those characteristics might be desirable for people of the 1960's "new frontier"? Which might not be desirable? What new characteristics might be needed to meet the challenges of the 1960s?

Multicultural Perspectives

Watching the parade at his inauguration, Kennedy noted that there were no African Americans in the contingent of Coast Guard Cadets. Demanding an explanation, he was told that the Coast Guard Academy had no African-American students. He ordered that this be investigated immediately.

Connections: Politics

In his first days as President, Kennedy exhibited seemingly boundless energy. A New York *Times* correspondent wrote about one of these days that Kennedy *"did everything except shinny up the Washington Monument."* A senator reported, *"When you see the President, you have to get in your car and drive like blazes to the Capitol to beat his memo commenting on what you told him."*

The New Frontier

The public warmed to the youthful first family, and the White House became known as a center for the arts. (Left) The Kennedys on Cape Cod. (Below) Cellist Pablo Casals at the White House.

When John Kennedy, his wife Jacqueline, and their two small children moved into the White House, they were the youngest family to live there since Teddy Roosevelt's days. The Kennedys brought style and wit to the office, as well as youth, and soon the White House became a center for culture and the arts. Poets, musicians, writers, and movie stars were invited to gather there for parties and performances.

The leader of "the new generation of Americans" filled his cabinet with young, talented, vigorous achievers. A Washington correspondent wrote:

> *"He surrounded himself with bright, handsome . . . people, all activists, who worked and played hard . . . and perhaps removed the presidency for all time from the log-cabin tradition. Kennedy presented a picture of total urbanity, the first true reflection in the presidency of America at the mid-century, a country of city dwellers long gone from Main Street."*

Kennedy challenged his cabinet and the nation to work together to solve the problems of poverty, poor housing, and inadequate health care. He called his vision for domestic progress the "New Frontier." And, as one observer wrote, "Optimism was almost a requirement on the New Frontier."

Unlike the New Deal, the New Frontier never took the form of a well-defined set of plans. Nor was Kennedy as successful as Roosevelt had been in getting his programs enacted. His proposals for federal aid to public schools and for health insurance for the elderly were rejected by Congress. His efforts to enforce and expand civil rights for African Americans—the major domestic issue of his time in office—also fell short. (See Chapter 28.)

Kennedy's critics argued that he was more image than action, more words than deeds. Yet he stirred many Americans to a commitment to make change happen.

The Peace Corps

> *"To those peoples in the huts and villages across the globe struggling to break the bonds of mass misery, we pledge our best efforts to help them help themselves, for whatever period is required—not because the Communists may be doing it, but because it is right. If a free society cannot help the many who are poor, it cannot save the few who are rich."*

Multicultural Perspectives

Kennedy actively pursued a policy of appointing capable African Americans to important positions in his administration. He appointed Andrew Hatcher as Associate Press Secretary and Robert Weaver as Housing and Home Finance Administrator. African Americans were appointed as ambassadors to European as well as African nations. The number of African-American attorneys in the Justice Department rose from ten to over seventy. Supreme Court Justice Emeritus Thurgood Marshall was first appointed to the Court of Appeals by Kennedy.

Thinking Critically

Evaluation. Joseph Wiley, who served with the Peace Corps in Peru along with his wife, wrote: *"By Peace Corps standards we accomplished a lot, we were a success. But I gradually realized that these successes didn't last . . . . Seeing something progress and appear to be working, and then just slide back to where it was, with no harm done, was a very sobering experience."*

Ask: Why might "progress" have been temporary in many cases? (A society's problems might be too embedded for Peace Corps efforts to succeed in making important changes. Peace Corps approach might not have been appropriate to the culture.) What lesson do you think the Wileys learned from their experience? (Answers may vary.)

Within two months of making this promise in his inaugural address, Kennedy took steps to make it a reality. People who asked what they could do for their country now had an answer. They could promote peace by volunteering in a brand-new government organization, the Peace Corps.

The mission of Peace Corps volunteers was to offer their skills as teachers, engineers, farmers, carpenters, and so forth, to people in the cities and villages of developing nations in Asia, Africa, and Latin America. Eager to play a practical role in promoting international understanding, thousands of Americans, young and old, volunteered.

The Alliance for Progress

In his inaugural address Kennedy had also promised to foster international understanding in Latin America through partnership in economic development and the promotion of democratic governments. "To our sister republics south of our border" he had pledged

> *"to convert our good words into good deeds in a new alliance for progress—to assist free men and free governments in casting off the chains of poverty."*

Kennedy followed up this pledge in March 1961 by outlining a new program for the development of Latin America. He invited the nations of the Organization of American States (OAS) to form an alliance to promote economic growth and democracy in the region.

Nineteen Latin American nations and the United States joined the new Alliance for Progress. The Latin American governments agreed to spend $80 billion over ten years to improve economic and social conditions for their people. The United States pledged to contribute an additional $20 billion.

The Alliance for Progress had uneven results. Almost all of the Latin American countries met or exceeded the goal of a 2.5 percent annual economic growth rate and improved their educational and social welfare systems. In spite of the growth, however, goals for reducing unemployment went unmet. The alliance also did not consistently lead to the growth of democracy. In fact, in several nations military rule brought an end to democracy in the 1960s. By the end of the decade, Congress began to cut funds for the alliance.

The Peace Corps remains a lasting legacy of the Kennedy administration. Here, a Liberian teacher gives a warm embrace to a Peace Corps teacher.

Economic Growth

The early 1960s were a time of solid economic growth. Except for a brief dip in early 1961, the economy moved steadily up like a well-tuned car on a smooth grade. The gross national product (GNP) increased at an average annual rate of more than 5 percent during the Kennedy years. Inflation also grew year by year, but at a rate close to 1 percent. Unemployment declined from 8 percent in 1961 to less than 6 percent in the following years.

During the Great Depression, President Roosevelt had not shrunk from government inter-

Global Connections

Discussion. Point out that Cuba was not a member of the Alliance for Progress. **Ask:** Why might this have been so? Recall the state of relations between Cuba and the United States at this time. **(Cuba had a Communist government under Fidel Castro; the U.S. had refused to allow Americans to buy Cuban sugar, which is Cuba's major crop.)**

Connections: Economics

Discussion. Ask students whether they agree or disagree with Kennedy's ideas about deficit spending and why. **Ask:** Is running a deficit in the federal (or state) budget worthwhile if the government spending helps people (creates jobs, meets social needs, etc.)? Overall, does government spending help people?

Limited English Proficiency

Analyzing Cartoons. Refer students to the cartoon on this page. **Ask:** Who is the character represented by Kennedy? **(Superman)** How do you know? **(outfit; bending steel)** Do you think this is an appropriate caricature of Kennedy? Why or why not?

Analying Primary Sources

Kennedy Directive. On April 20, 1961 President Kennedy sent Vice-President Johnson a directive that read in part:

“Do we have a chance of beating the Soviets by putting a laboratory in space, or by a trip round the Moon, or by a rocket to go to the Moon and back with a man? Is there any other space program which promises dramatic results in which we could win?”

Ask: What does this directive suggest about Kennedy's reasons for promoting the space program? How might Kennedy's attitude have been influenced by the Bay of Pigs disaster?

Linking Past and Present

After Colonel John Glenn left the NASA Space Program he entered politics and in 1964 and 1970 ran in the Ohio primaries as a Democratic candidate for senator. Although neither run was successful, he did run and win in 1974, 1980, 1986 and 1992.

Reduced student page in the Teacher's Edition

vention to stimulate the economy. Following the ideas of British economist John Maynard Keynes, he and subsequent Presidents had used two methods—cutting taxes and increasing government spending—to encourage business investment, increase employment, and put more money in the hands of consumers. Both methods, however, resulted in the government running a **deficit**—the amount by which spending exceeds income.

While Eisenhower had tried to avoid deficit spending, Kennedy thought that deficits were sometimes proper, even in times of prosperity. He was convinced, for example, that the government needed to spend more for defense, space programs, and domestic measures. During his term federal spending rose, and so did the deficit, from about $3.5 billion to more than $7 billion a year.

New programs that Kennedy encouraged included the Area Redevelopment Act of 1961, which provided $300 million to create new businesses and retrain unemployed workers in depressed areas. In the same year Congress passed the Housing Act, authorizing $4.9 billion in federal loans for construction of low-cost housing and mass transportation systems. Kennedy also supported an increase in the minimum wage from $1 to $1.25.

One danger of deficit spending is that by pumping money into the economy it may cause inflation. To avoid this risk, Kennedy proposed “wage-price guideposts” to industry and labor. The idea was for industry and labor to cooperate to prevent inflationary price increases. Thus, when the steelworkers negotiated a new contract in March 1962, they kept their demands within the President's guidelines. However, in April the United States Steel Corporation announced a big price increase, which other steel companies soon matched.

Kennedy was furious. He denounced the increase as “wholly unjustified” and demanded that the companies cancel the price increases. Shocked by his strong reaction, the steel companies gave in and rolled back their prices.

Astronauts in Orbit

One area in which the President was eager to spend money was on the United States space program. The Soviet Union had shocked Americans by launching *Sputnik I*, the world's first artificial satellite, in 1957. Then, in April 1961, the Soviets placed the first human in orbit around the earth.

The sting of being in second place made the United States resolve to put an American on the moon before the end of the 1960s. Since 1958 the National Aeronautics and Space Administration (NASA) had been working toward putting an astronaut in space. In 1961 astronauts made brief flights as a part of the Mercury program. Then, in early 1962 John H. Glenn, Jr., became the first American to orbit the earth. On his return, he received a hero's welcome from Americans, who had watched the launch on television.

Meanwhile, in 1961 Kennedy had announced Project Apollo and asked Congress to appropriate $20 billion over the next ten years to reach the goal of “landing a man on the moon and returning him safely to earth.” The New Frontier in space, though costly, seemed within reach.

The Warren Court

When President Eisenhower named Earl Warren to be Chief Justice of the Supreme Court in 1953, he assumed that the Republican former governor of California would be a champion of the conservative viewpoint. In fact, however, under Warren the Court took an increasingly active role in bringing about reform in the United States in the 1950s and 1960s. In addition to important civil rights decisions, the Warren Court's rulings on a wide range of issues made it the subject of heated controversy.

Connections: Politics

After his fairly conservative record as governor, Earl Warren's actions as Chief Justice shocked and offended many Americans who had regarded him as sharing their views. Now conservatives saw Warren as a traitor to their cause. One *New Yorker* magazine cartoon depicted an old lady in a rocking chair making a sampler reading *Impeach Earl Warren.*

In 1962 the Court ruled that the public schools of New York State could not legally ask students to say an official school prayer. The prayer, the Court declared, violated the First Amendment, which prohibited government from establishing religion in the United States. Many Americans were shocked by the decision to ban school prayer. Some legislators even attempted to pass a constitutional amendment allowing prayer in schools. Nevertheless, the decision stood, and the separation of church and state was reinforced by later court decisions.

Two Court rulings on **reapportionment,** or the restructuring of voting districts, also caused controversy because they changed the balance of power in state legislatures. In many states, as populations shifted from rural to urban areas, voting districts were not changed. Thus rural districts, with relatively few voters, had a disproportionate number of representatives in state legislatures.

In 1962 the Court ruled that states could be required to redraw voting district lines to reflect population changes. Then, in a 1964 decision, the

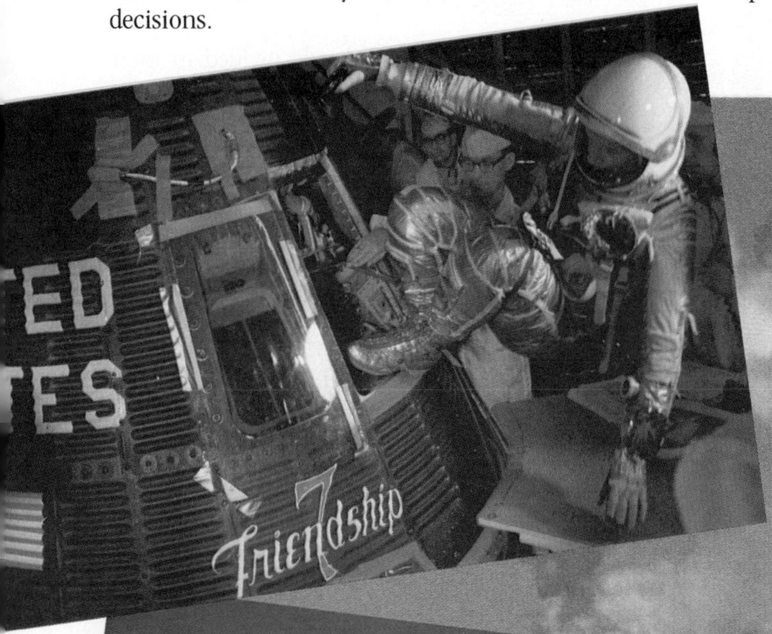

John Glenn (above left), one of the Mercury astronauts, boards the Friendship 7 capsule for launch on the United States' first orbital flight.

Limited English Proficiency

Making a Chart. Have students make a chart showing the court decisions mentioned in this section and the right or principle that each established. Additionally, or alternatively, they might list the court decisions and surround each with a cluster of words describing their feelings about it.

Thinking Critically

Evaluation. Even greater than the controversy stirred up by the Warren Court's individual decisions was the controversy over whether it should have been making those decisions at all. As Justice John M. Harlan wrote in a dissenting opinion in the 1964 reapportionment case: *"This Court ... does not serve its high purpose when it exceeds its authority, even to satisfy justified impatience with the slow workings of the political process. For when, in the name of constitutional interpretation, the Court adds something to the Constitution that was deliberately excluded from it, the Court in reality substitutes its view of what should be so for the amending process."*

Ask: What do you think the role of the Supreme Court should be? How should this role be limited, if at all? Do you agree or disagree with Justice Harlan? Explain.

Active Learning

Skit. Divide the class into groups and have each group choose one of the Supreme Court cases or issues discussed in this section. Have each group do research to find out more about the issues. The group can then perform a skit presenting the pro and con arguments about the issues or suggesting the consequences of the Supreme Court ruling.

Section Review

ANSWERS

1. Definitions for the following terms are on text pages indicated in parentheses: *deficit* (730), *reapportionment* (731).
2. To help people in developing nations help themselves; to offer skills to peoples in Asia, Africa, and Latin America.
3. Answers may include: Area Redevelopment Act, Project Apollo, Alliance for Progress.
4. Answers may include that Kennedy led in a different direction, citing programs he initiated. Those disagreeing may point to uneven results; for example, partial failure of Alliance for Progress.
5. Kennedy thought deficit spending was sometimes proper to initiate needed programs or stimulate the economy.
6. Critics accused the Court of making laws instead of interpreting them. Supporters approved of the Court's decisions strengthening equal rights.
Linking Past and Present: Students can point to the importance of television in campaigns today, or to the importance of debates in earlier elections (e.g. Lincoln-Douglas).

Clarence Earl Gideon wrote to the Supreme Court from prison, claiming that he had been denied a fair trial because he could not afford a lawyer.

Court held that state voting districts must be approximately equal in population. Writing for the Court, Chief Justice Earl Warren declared that "legislators represent people, not acres or trees." This "one man, one vote" ruling shifted power away from rural legislators.

In another series of controversial decisions, the Warren Court established new rules for the handling of criminal cases. In 1963, in *Gideon* v. *Wainwright*, the Court ruled that a person charged with a crime has a right to a lawyer even if the state must pay the lawyer's fee. In the 1964 case of *Escobedo* v. *Illinois* the Court held that police who question suspects in crimes must tell the suspects that they have the right to consult a lawyer. If police fail to inform them, the suspects' statements to police may not be used as evidence.

Finally, in the 1966 *Miranda* v. *Arizona* decision, the Court set strict guidelines for police when they are questioning suspects. Police must inform suspects of their rights, including the right to remain silent, the right to consult a lawyer before being questioned, and the right to have a lawyer, even if they are too poor to hire one. Admirers of the Court praised it for taking an active role in protecting individual rights. But many Americans believed the decisions would hinder the efforts of state and local police at a time when the crime rate was increasing.

In fact, Americans were deeply divided in their opinion of the activism of the Warren Court, which dated from the school desegregation case, *Brown* v. *Board of Education,* in 1954. Critics accused the Court of *making* laws instead of interpreting them, and roadside billboards urged, "Save our Republic! Impeach Earl Warren." Yet Americans who supported the spirit of change stirring the nation saw the Court's decisions as milestones in strengthening the rights of individuals and extending the promise of equality and justice to all.

Section Review

1. Identification. Define *deficit* and *reapportionment*.

2. Comprehension. Why was the Peace Corps founded and what was the mission of Peace Corps volunteers?

3. Application. Give three examples of Kennedy administration policies that reflect a concern with "national purpose."

4. Evaluation. In your opinion, did the Kennedy administration succeed in leading the nation in a direction different from the direction of the Eisenhower years? Explain your answer.

5. Analysis. How did Kennedy's view of deficit spending differ from Eisenhower's view?

6. Analysis. Why were the rulings of the Warren Court the subject of heated controversy?

Linking Past and Present. Agree or disagree with the following statement: The televised debates in the 1960 presidential election launched a new era in political campaigning. Explain your reasoning.

Connections: Economics
Between the Spanish-American War and Castro's takeover in 1958, the economy of Cuba had been almost totally dependent on the U.S. The U.S. bought such Cuban natural resources as sugar, minerals, and cattle. When Castro broke with the U.S., he had to find another economic ally to support the country's economy. He thus had economic as well as ideological reasons for turning to the USSR.

Connections: Politics
Several weeks after the Bay of Pigs fiasco, Kennedy commented glumly that if he had been prime minister of England, his government would have fallen. His secretary showed him a copy of a Gallup poll indicating that 83 percent of the American public was behind him. He commented, *"The worse I do, the more popular I get."*

Section 27-2

Objectives

- ***Answer the Focus Question.***
- *Compare the policy of flexible response with the policy of massive retaliation.*
- *Analyze factors leading to United States involvement in Vietnam.*
- *Evaluate Kennedy's role in the Cuban missile crisis and the Test Ban Treaty.*

Introducing

THE SECTION

Ask students to cite world tensions in 1961 based on their reading in previous chapters. Have them recount the policies toward communism and the Soviet Union pursued by Presidents from Franklin Roosevelt to Eisenhower. Ask them what policy they think Kennedy will follow.

27-2 Facing World Tensions

Focus: How did President Kennedy respond to tensions throughout the world?

"Let every nation know, whether it wishes us well or ill, that we shall pay any price, bear any burden, meet any hardship, support any friend, oppose any foe to assure the survival and the success of liberty."

When President Kennedy made this optimistic promise in his inaugural address, the nation cheered his generous and determined spirit. Once in office, however, Kennedy faced a world in turmoil, torn between communism and democracy and haunted by the specter of nuclear war. It seemed that wherever Kennedy and his advisors looked in the world, peace and freedom were being tested.

The Bay of Pigs

Soon after his election, Kennedy learned that the Central Intelligence Agency (CIA) was involved in a plot to overthrow the pro-Soviet government of Fidel Castro in Cuba. Eisenhower had approved the plan, and the CIA had been secretly training anti-Castro exiles for an invasion by sea. CIA experts were convinced that the Cuban people would welcome the invaders and join the fight against Castro.

Kennedy could disband the groups of exiles being trained in Florida and Guatemala, or he could allow the invasion to go ahead. Partly because plans were already set and partly to encourage anti-Castro Cubans, he chose to permit the invasion, but he refused to let United States forces take part in the fighting.

On April 17, 1961, a fleet of small boats landed some 1,500 invaders at the *Bahía de Cochinos*, the Bay of Pigs, on Cuba's southern coast. The result was a disaster. Castro's soldiers crushed the invasion and took 1,200 prisoners. The popular uprising predicted by CIA experts failed to take place.

Anti-Castro Cuban exiles planned the invasion of Cuba from a base in the Caribbean.

Global Connections
Two years after the Berlin Wall was built, President Kennedy gave a speech in West Berlin in which he said in part, "All free men, wherever they may live, are citizens of Berlin. And therefore, as a free man I take pride in the words, *'Ich bin ein Berliner'* (I am a Berliner)." These words showed that the United States supported West Germany in principle.

Linking Past and Present
Long after the Berlin Wall was built, East Germans continued to escape to the West both in Berlin and along the border between East and West Germany. Remind students that the Berlin Wall was torn down in 1989 and the two Germanies were reunited shortly thereafter. (See Chapter 31, page 849.)

Developing
THE SECTION

Thinking Critically

Evaluation. Refer students to Kennedy's remarks about the Bay of Pigs invasion on this page. Have the class discuss what Kennedy should have done about the planned invasion. What might have happened if he had disbanded the invasion? What might have happened if he had given it the full support of United States forces?

In 1964 President Richard Nixon stated that if he had been President then, he would have found "a proper legal cover" and gone in with air cover, ships, and infantry. **Ask:** Why do you think Kennedy did not follow this course? (He foresaw consequences: a long occupation, opposition from Cubans, a long, drawn-out military action.)

Limited English Proficiency

Analyzing Photographs. Refer students to the photographs of the Berlin Wall on this page. Have them contrast the two scenes. **Ask:** How do you think the person feels in the top photograph? Why? In the one on the right? Why?

Reduced student page in the Teacher's Edition

When the American role in the invasion became known, Communist nations condemned the United States. So did friendly nations in Latin America and Europe. Kennedy took full responsibility for the Bay of Pigs fiasco, but it was a hard lesson in the difficulties of trying to manage world events. Kennedy later said:

> *"How could everybody involved have thought such a plan would work? I don't know the answer, and I don't know anybody else who does."*

The Berlin Wall

The uproar over the Bay of Pigs invasion did not stop plans for a meeting between Kennedy and Soviet Premier Khrushchev. The two leaders met in Vienna, Austria, in June 1961 for talks. Khrushchev focused on the status of Berlin, located within Soviet-controlled East Germany. The city was still divided into East Berlin, which was the Soviet sector, and West Berlin, the combined American, British, and French sectors. Germans could travel freely between the two Berlins. Yet as the West German economy boomed, thousands of East Germans used West Berlin as an escape route to West Germany and economic opportunity.

At Vienna, Khrushchev demanded that the Americans, British, and French withdraw their troops from West Berlin and declare it an independent city. To gain access to the city, the United States and its allies would have to deal with the East German government, which they did not recognize. Khrushchev gave them until December to agree to his terms, threatening to seal off West Berlin.

The talks between Kennedy and Khrushchev ended in tense suspicion. Kennedy told Khrushchev, "It will be a cold winter," and he vowed not to abandon West Berlin. "All Europe is at stake in West Berlin," he said. In July, to give force to his position, Kennedy asked Congress for an extra $3.5 billion in defense spending and called up reserves. Fears of nuclear war ran high.

The next month, after the number of East German refugees reached a high of 2,662 in one day, Khrushchev ordered a barrier of barbed wire set up between East

The Berlin Wall was a stark reminder of the tense division between Communist and non-Communist countries. In 1989, the ugly symbol of the Cold War was torn down almost overnight.

Global Connections

In a special presidential message to Congress in March, 1961, Kennedy stated: *"The primary purpose of our arms is peace, not war. . . . The strength and deployment of our forces . . . should be sufficiently powerful and mobile to prevent the steady erosion of the free world through limited wars . . . Our defense posture must be both flexible and determined."*

Global Connections

People in South Vietnam had a number of reasons for opposing Ngo Dinh Diem, whether or not they were communists. Diem kept all power in his hands and the hands of his family. He did not allow self-government in the villages, and land was distributed very unevenly. His regime also practiced discrimination against the Buddhist majority.

Writing About History

Letter. Have students write a letter from a resident of East Berlin to a relative in West Berlin, describing his or her feelings at the sight of the Berlin Wall going up.

Thinking Critically

Evaluation. Have students discuss the advantages and disadvantages of Kennedy's policy of flexible response. Students should know that the policy of relying primarily on nuclear weapons depended partly on the fact that such weapons, expensive as they were, were cheaper than maintaining large numbers of conventional troops overseas.

Global Connections

Discussion. In a Paris conference Charles de Gaulle, France's leader, told Kennedy that France would no longer send troops to Vietnam or its neighboring countries. Southeast Asia, he said, was "a bad place to fight." **Ask:** What might de Gaulle have meant?

and West Berlin. Soon the wire was replaced with a concrete wall that stretched for miles, dividing neighbors and sometimes even families. Searchlights swept the wall at night, and East German armed guards patrolled around the clock.

Robert MacNeil, Berlin correspondent for an American network, wrote of "the dark mood of crisis" in Berlin:

"It [the wall] advertised in the crudest way to the impressionable Third World that a Communist state like East Germany could survive only if it became the jailer of its own people. . . . All I knew was that for a few weeks that summer I had lived where World War III could have started."

A Policy of "Flexible Response"

The Cold War tension so vividly represented by the Berlin Wall brought a horrifying truth into sharp focus: Any escalation of conflict between the United States and the Soviet Union was likely to lead to full-scale nuclear war. This realization led Kennedy to a change in policy.

Under Eisenhower, American policy had been to rely on nuclear weapons to stop Soviet aggression—the massive retaliation strategy. In pursuit of that policy, the government had built an arsenal of long-range bombers to carry nuclear weapons, and submarines that could launch Polaris missiles with nuclear warheads. The Soviets, meanwhile, had developed powerful rockets to propel intercontinental ballistic missiles (ICBMs).

Now Kennedy saw the grave danger of depending entirely on massive retaliation. He and his advisors developed a new policy of "flexible response," which stressed the use of troops and conventional weapons as well as nuclear arms, depending on the situation. Kennedy especially wanted forces to be trained in jungle warfare and guerrilla fighting, to be able to counter Communist-supported revolutions in developing nations. He foresaw that this preparation might be called upon in Southeast Asia, particularly in Vietnam.

American Voices

"[In 1962] it was a small, slow-motion war in a distant country."

—David Halberstam, *New York Times* reporter

Conflict in Southeast Asia

The division of Indochina into North and South Vietnam after the French were driven out in 1954 had not ended conflict there. In 1956 South Vietnam's leader, Ngo Dinh Diem, refused to allow UN-scheduled elections that were intended to reunite the nation. Under Diem's regime, land and power were concentrated in the hands of a few, and he feared that the dissatisfied South Vietnamese would vote for the Communists.

In 1957 both Communists and non-Communists in South Vietnam formed the National Liberation Front (NLF) to overthrow Diem and reunite the country. Diem called the NLF troops Viet Cong, meaning "Vietnamese Communists." The Viet Cong began a campaign of guerrilla warfare to topple Diem's regime.

When Kennedy took office, the United States was already sending money and military supplies to Diem, who was feeling pressure from the Viet Cong. It had also sent 700 military advisors to help train Diem's Army of the Republic of Vietnam (ARVN).

Aided by soldiers and supplies from the Communist government of North Vietnam, Viet Cong attacks against Diem increased in 1961. American advisors urged Diem to make reforms in order to strengthen his support. Instead, he responded to opposition with repression.

While Kennedy at first resisted the advice of Vice-President Johnson and others to send more military personnel, he did not want to let South Vietnam fall to Communists. By the end of 1961 the number of American "advisors" stationed in South Vietnam had grown to more than 3,000, and within a year there were more than 11,000 American troops there. Officially they were not combat units. Instead, they offered combat support, including helicopter transport, and advice and training.

Global Connections

On October 26–27 Kennedy received two communications from Khrushchev, one proposing removal of Soviet missiles in exchange for a United States guarantee against invasion of Cuba, and the second in exchange for dismantling of United States missiles in Turkey. Kennedy chose to respond to the first and ignore the second. Ironically, Kennedy had already ordered the removal of the outmoded missiles in Turkey, an action which was accomplished shortly after the crisis.

Connections: Literature

Book Report. Robert Kennedy, the President's brother and his Attorney General, wrote *Thirteen Days: A Memoir of the Cuban Missile Crisis*, a detailed, day-by-day account of the President's doubts, deliberations and decisions, as well as the advice he was given by others in government.

Interested students might read *Thirteen Days* and write a book report, perhaps focusing on one of the days, the problems confronting the President on that day, and what he did to resolve them.

Geography Skills

ANSWERS

Cuba located very close to the United States.

Reduced student page in the Teacher's Edition

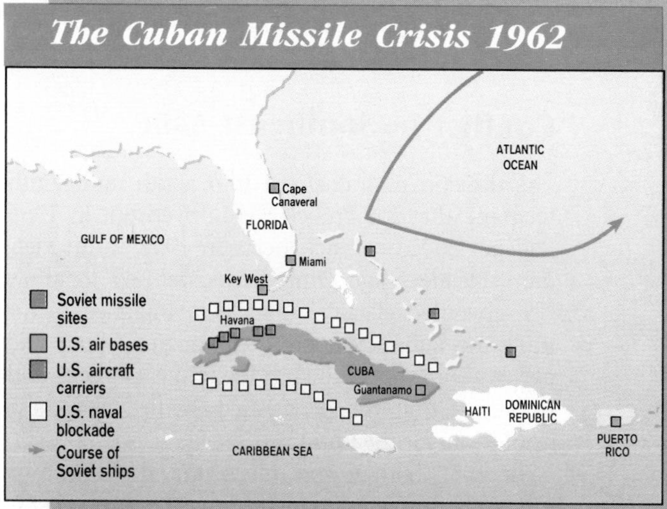

Geography Skills—Location. How did Cuba's location influence superpower decisions?

The President and his brother, Attorney General Robert Kennedy, confer.

The presence of American troops halted the advance of guerrilla forces in 1962. In February the President's brother Robert Kennedy traveled to Saigon (SĪ-GON), the capital of South Vietnam. "We are going to win in Vietnam," he told reporters. "We will remain here until we do win."

The Cuban Missile Crisis

Although the confrontation in West Berlin had heightened fears of nuclear war, tensions had eased after the Soviets avoided a showdown by building the wall. Meanwhile, the conflicts in Asia were not posing a direct threat to the United States.

To Castro and Khrushchev, however, American actions against the Cuban government, such as the Bay of Pigs, posed a direct threat to Cuban independence. They decided to install Soviet nuclear missiles in Cuba. That action led to a thirteen-day confrontation that brought the Soviet Union and the United States to the brink of nuclear war.

The crisis began on October 14, 1962, when photographs taken by a U-2 spy plane revealed construction of bases for Soviet missiles in Cuba—missiles that could reach targets more than 1,000 miles away. For the first time the United States faced Soviet missiles only 90 miles from its shores.

For five days, Kennedy and his advisors met secretly, pouring over possible options. The Joint Chiefs of Staff advised an air strike to knock out missile sites or an invasion to overthrow Castro and get rid of the missiles. Kennedy considered the risk. What if Soviet workers were killed? Would Khrushchev respond with a nuclear strike?

On October 22 Kennedy made the crisis public and announced his plan. The United States would impose a naval blockade to intercept "all offensive military equipment under shipment to Cuba." Kennedy also issued a demand for the "dismantling and withdrawal of all offensive weapons in Cuba." He directed the United States armed forces to be ready for action.

On October 24 a force of nineteen United States warships formed a line in the Atlantic, 500 miles from the shores of Cuba. They were preparing to block a fleet of Soviet ships bound for the island. Supporting the United States warships were aircraft carriers and B-52 bombers, plus troop ships ready for an invasion.

Connections: Science and Technology
In addition to worries about possible nuclear war, people were concerned about above-ground atomic testing because such tests released radioactive materials into the air and water. As "fallout," these materials were carried all over the world by wind and ocean currents. In time they could be consumed by humans and animals, increasing the risk of cancer and birth defects. Great concern was expressed when radioactive strontium-90 was found in samples of milk, for instance.

Active Learning

Drawing Cartoons. Have students work in teams to draw cartoons. The cartoons can express the dread people felt about the threat of nuclear war, or they can express opinions about the Test Ban Treaty. The cartoons should have a caption or dialogue, and clearly express a point of view.

As Soviet ships moved steadily toward Cuba, the two nations edged toward nuclear war. At last the leading Soviet ships reached the blockade. They then stopped and reversed course. Secretary of State Dean Rusk summed up the tensions of that moment when he remarked, "We're eyeball to eyeball, and I think the other fellow just blinked."

The crisis, however, was not over. Some missiles were already in place in Cuba. In spite of advice to invade, the President chose to negotiate with Khrushchev. On October 28, after two frantic days of bargaining, the Soviet Union agreed to withdraw or destroy its missiles, launching pads, and other offensive weapons in Cuba. In return, the United States agreed to end the blockade and pledged not to invade the island. In November 1962 the missiles were withdrawn, and the Cuban missile crisis came to an end.

The Test Ban Treaty

While the United States and the Soviet Union continued to build missiles, they also held talks about ways to limit the arms race. Such talks had been going on from time to time since the early 1950s. No formal agreements had been reached, but the United States, the Soviet Union, and Britain were observing a voluntary ban on atomic testing. They exploded no nuclear devices all through 1959, 1960, and most of 1961.

When the Soviet Union resumed atomic tests in September 1961, the United States quickly did the same. Following the Cuban missile crisis, however, Kennedy called for new talks, saying, "If we cannot end now all our differences, at least we can help make the world safe for diversity." American, Soviet, and British representatives discussed ways to ban tests of nuclear weapons underground, underwater, in the atmosphere, and in outer space.

The nations did not agree on a method of monitoring, or checking, underground tests. However, they did sign a limited test ban treaty to eliminate tests everywhere except underground. The treaty went into effect in October 1963. Many other nations agreed to the treaty, although France and the People's Republic of China refused to sign.

The treaty did not halt the arms race. In fact, soon after signing it, the Soviets began a massive arms buildup in an attempt to overtake the United States. President Kennedy expressed a concern, shared by many, that

> *"the deadly poisons produced by a nuclear exchange would be carried by wind and water and soil and seed to the far corners of the globe and to generations yet unborn."*

Thus, while the ban on testing was a significant safeguard against the ill effects of testing, the threat of war still hung heavy.

Kennedy's Assassination

Kennedy's handling of the Cuban missile crisis and the Test Ban Treaty had won the President acclaim, and he was now at the height of his career. The nation was prosperous, and at last his administration was making headway in facing the issue of civil rights. Kennedy looked forward with confidence to running for a second term.

To win the support he needed for reelection in 1964, Kennedy set about mending political fences. One target was Texas, where conservative Democrats were critical of his support of civil rights for African Americans.

On Friday, November 22, 1963, President Kennedy rode in a motorcade through the streets of Dallas, Texas. Governor John Connally later confessed that he had feared a hostile response from the crowds. Instead they greeted the President warmly, cheering as the motorcade passed.

Then, as Kennedy and his wife waved to the crowds, rifle shots rang out, and the President slumped forward. He was rushed to a hospital and pronounced dead within an hour. Aboard the presidential plane, Vice-President Johnson, visibly shaken, took the oath of office. Then the plane, bearing the new President and the body of his slain predecessor, took off on its flight to Washington.

Within hours, Dallas police had arrested Lee Harvey Oswald, a lonely, emotionally disturbed young man, and charged him with the President's assassination. Two days later, while being moved to another jail, Oswald himself was shot by a Dallas nightclub operator, Jack Ruby.

Backyard History

Interview. Students can interview relatives and others who were living in 1963 to learn what their reaction was when they learned of Kennedy's assassination. They can ask the interviewees what they were doing at the time they heard the news and what they felt and thought. The interviews can be presented to the class.

Writing About History

Poem. Have students imagine that they were alive at the time of Kennedy's assassination and write a poem describing their feelings about the event. They might focus on feelings of loss regarding Kennedy in particular or on feelings about violence attacking the presidency and society.

Thinking Critically

Evaluation. Review with the class the idea of Camelot and its "one brief shining moment." **Ask:** Do you think Kennedy lived up to this ideal? Would his presidency have been described in such idealistic terms if the assassination had not taken place? Speculate about how Kennedy's presidency would have been evaluated if he had lived and served two full terms.

Section Review

ANSWERS

1. CIA thought Cubans who were unhappy with Castro would welcome the invaders.
2. Flexible response depended as much on the use of troops and conventional weapons as on nuclear deterrent, less likely to lead to nuclear war, while the policy of massive retaliation left little choice but nuclear weapons.
3. National Liberation Front, aided by North Vietnam, tried to overthrow South Vietnam. Kennedy sent advisors to support friendly South Vietnam and oppose Communist North Vietnam.
4. Kennedy halted expanding Soviet influence with the blockade on Cuba and came very close to nuclear war.
5. Answers may include that Kennedy made progress with the Test Ban Treaty. However, there was an increase in conventional weapons.

B · A · C · K · G · R · O · U · N · D

Connections: Literature

According to Theodore Sorensen, Kennedy "had no fear or premonition of dying." One of his favorite poems, however, was Alan Seeger's "I Have a Rendezvous with Death." In this poem, Seeger predicts his own death on a World War I battlefield. What moved Kennedy about the poem was the fact that the brilliant young poet had died prematurely.

In this frame from a bystander's home movie (above), President Kennedy has just been hit in the throat by the first bullet. At left, Jackie Kennedy, still in her bloodstained suit, looks on as Lyndon Johnson is sworn in aboard Air Force One.

Oswald's death hindered murder investigations. A special commission headed by Chief Justice Warren concluded that Oswald had acted alone. Many Americans were unsatisfied with the Warren Commission's conclusions, though, and some maintained that Oswald had acted as a part of a conspiracy.

The news of the assassination stunned the nation. The hopes that the young President had offered seemed to have been dashed in one moment of violence. He had served little more than a thousand days. Jackie Kennedy was later to refer to those days as "Camelot," after a popular musical, and quoted a line from one of its songs: "Don't let it be forgot, that once there was a spot, for one brief shining moment that was known as Camelot."

With Kennedy's death, that "brief shining moment" of Camelot ended. A new President, with energy and ambition as big as his native state of Texas, moved into the White House, determined to make his own mark on the nation.

Section Review

1. Comprehension. Why did the CIA think that the invasion of Cuba would succeed?

2. Synthesis. How was the policy of flexible response an attempt to avert nuclear war? How did this policy differ from the earlier policy of massive retaliation?

3. Application. How was the American involvement in Vietnam during the Kennedy administration an example of his promise to "support any friend, oppose any foe" to defend liberty?

4. Analysis. The Cuban missile crisis has been called the pinnacle of the Cold War policy of containment. In what ways is this statement true?

5. Evaluation. Throughout his time in office, President Kennedy frequently called for greater efforts toward disarmament. Do you think that his administration made significant progress toward this goal? Give examples to support your opinion.

Connections: Politics
Like many Americans Johnson was almost paralyzed with grief following Kennedy's death. But, as he wrote in his memoirs: *"I knew I could not allow the tide of grief to overwhelm me. . . . It was imperative that I grasp the reins of power and do so without delay. Any hesitation or wavering . . . could have been disastrous."*

27-3 Johnson and the Great Society

Focus: How did Johnson pursue his vision of the Great Society and what changes were taking place in American society during his time in office?

The country was still reeling from the assassination when Vice-President Lyndon B. Johnson stepped into the role of President. Johnson later described the political climate at the time: "We were like a bunch of cattle caught in the swamp, unable to move in either direction, simply circling 'round and 'round." Johnson knew he needed to "take the lead, to assume command, to provide direction." The man from Texas took the reins with a firm hand.

Johnson brought with him to the office of President almost twenty-five years of congressional experience. Senator Hubert H. Humphrey of Minnesota described him as "a genius in the art of the legislative process." In addition to his understanding of the legislative process, Johnson also brought with him powers of persuasion which had won him the nickname, the "Great Persuader."

While Johnson was respected on Capitol Hill, he was not well known to the American people. Lacking a personal mandate, Johnson began his term in office by appealing to the memory of Kennedy and the Kennedy program, saying "Let us continue." Using his own legislative genius, Johnson helped push New Frontier proposals through Congress. But Johnson also had his own vision for change and a passion for social reform. Soon he would seek to launch his own program, which he called the "Great Society."

Extending the New Frontier

President Johnson stressed that his administration would honor commitments that the former President had made. Kennedy had planned a major tax cut to stimulate the economy. In February 1964 Johnson won congressional approval for a $10 billion tax cut. Kennedy had urged passage of a civil rights bill to outlaw discrimination in public accommodations and by employers, to strengthen federal powers in desegregating schools, and to protect the voting rights of African Americans. Johnson pushed the Civil Rights Act of 1964 through Congress by July, saying:

> *" No memorial oration or eulogy could more eloquently honor President Kennedy's memory than the earliest possible passage of the civil rights bill. . . . We have talked long enough in this country about equal rights. We have talked for one hundred years or more. It is time now to write the next chapter—and to write it in the books of law. "*

Spotlight on Presidents

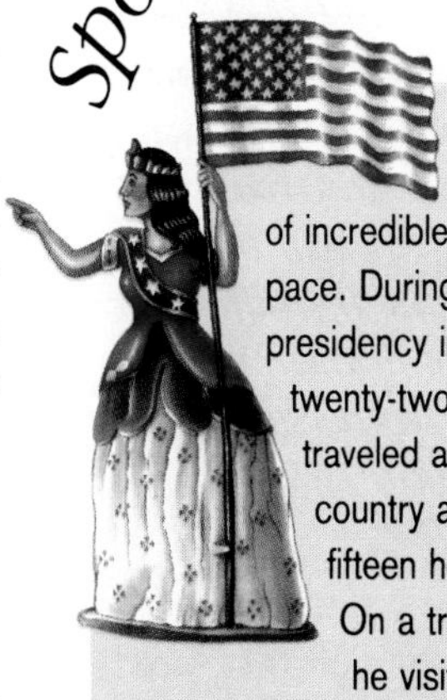

Lyndon B. Johnson was a man of incredible energy who kept up a frenetic pace. During his campaign for the presidency in 1964 he once gave twenty-two speeches in one day. Later he traveled around the world, visiting country after country, in only four days, fifteen hours, and fifty-eight minutes. On a trip to Central America in 1968, he visited five countries in one day. When one of his friends commented that on a public issue "Lyndon will go the way the wind blows," another friend quipped, "Maybe. But if he does, he'll probably beat the wind there."

Section 27-3

Objectives

- ***Answer the Focus Question.***
- *Compare the New Frontier and the Great Society.*
- *Explain Johnson's victory over Goldwater.*
- *Describe how the counterculture influenced American society.*
- *Explain Johnson's growing involvement in the cold war.*

Introducing

THE SECTION

On November 27, 1963, President Johnson made a speech to assembled Senators, Representatives, and Supreme Court Justices. He began *"Let us continue,"* and promised that *"the ideas and ideals which [Kennedy] so nobly represented must and will be translated into effective action."* He exhorted those assembled *"to do away with uncertainty and delay and doubt and to show that we are capable of decisive action. . . . John Kennedy's death commands what his life conveyed—that America must move forward."*

Ask: What do you think happened to Kennedy's New Frontier policies after Johnson took office? **(Johnson promised to carry on Kennedy's program.)** Kennedy had had difficulty in getting Congress to legislate his programs. Why might Johnson have been more successful? Refer students to the second paragraph on this page.

Developing

THE SECTION

Connections: Literature

Book Report. Refer students to the excerpt from Michael Harrington's book, *The Other America*, on this page. Interested students might read the book and make oral reports to the class. In their reports they might quote especially vivid and/or persuasive passages that account in part for the great impact the book made.

Thinking Critically

Synthesis. Have students note Harrington's definition of poverty. **Ask:** What "decisive factors" might Harrington have been referring to? Suggest some kinds of "help and resources" that you think Harrington would have society provide.

Multicultural Perspectives

African-American support for Democratic candidates had grown since 1932. In 1964 African-American voters gave Johnson 94 percent of their votes. Johnson called on several African Americans to hold important offices. He named Robert Weaver his Secretary of Housing and Urban Development, the first African American to serve in the cabinet. Attorney James M. Nabrit, Jr., became an ambassador to the UN, while biologist Samuel Nabrit served on the Atomic Energy Commission. Aileen C. Hernandez, an expert on labor education, sat on the Equal Employment Opportunity Commission, and Jeanne Noble, an educator, headed the Office of Economic Opportunities committee on the Girls' Job Corps.

Reduced student page in the Teacher's Edition

Poverty in the 1960s could be found amongst the urban, the rural, the young and the old. (Left) Children of an unemployed Appalachian coal miner who moved to Chicago in search of work.

The war on poverty. In 1962, Michael Harrington had published *The Other America*, a book that revealed the shocking extent of poverty in the United States. Like Jacob Riis in the late 1800s, Harrington focused public attention on the plight of the poor—a reality that many Americans, blinded by the affluence of the 1950s, failed to see.

> *"The poor are caught in a vicious circle. . . . In a sense, one might define the contemporary poor in the United States as those who, for reasons beyond their control, cannot help themselves. All the most decisive factors making for opportunity and advance are against them. . . . Only the larger society, with its help and resources, can really make it possible for [the poor] to help themselves. Yet those who could make the difference too often refuse to act because of their ignorant, smug moralisms. . . . Understanding the vicious circle is an important step in breaking down this prejudice."*

Harrington's book brought into view the "needless suffering in the most advanced society in the world." With the problem of domestic poverty now in the public eye, Kennedy had called for a "war on poverty."

Government studies in 1964 confirmed Harrington's claims and made Kennedy's call an urgent one. According to these studies, 18 percent of the population—some 34 million Americans—lived below the "poverty line," as defined by the federal government. Now Johnson, who himself had known hard times growing up in central Texas, used Kennedy's phrase as a rallying cry for new programs to combat poverty, the "domestic enemy."

One of the programs Congress approved in the War on Poverty was the Job Corps. It provided job training for unemployed young men and women in inner cities. Another program was Volunteers in Service to America (VISTA). Like the Peace Corps, VISTA recruited volunteers, but these volunteers worked in economically depressed areas of the United States rather than overseas. The goal of VISTA was to reduce unemployment and illiteracy.

Connections: Politics

In a speech to Congress on March 15, 1965, Johnson recalled his first teaching job in a small Mexican-American school in Texas: *"My students were poor. . . . They knew in their youth the pain of prejudice . . . It never occurred to me in my fondest dreams that I might have the chance to help the sons and daughters of those students. . . . But now I do have that chance. . . . I mean to use it."*

Another ambitious program, Head Start, set up preschools to prepare children from poor families to succeed in elementary school.

Congress approved these and similar programs in the Economic Opportunity Act, passed in August 1964. The act set up the Office of Economic Opportunity (OEO) and authorized it to spend almost $1 billion in the effort to wipe out poverty.

Launching the Great Society

Johnson's War on Poverty became the foundation for his own domestic vision. The Great Society, he said, would be based on "abundance and liberty for all" and would demand "an end to poverty and racial injustice." The election of 1964 would give Johnson the public mandate he needed to push ahead in building the Great Society.

The election of 1964. Johnson was the obvious choice for the Democratic nomination. He chose as his running mate Hubert H. Humphrey, a liberal senator from Minnesota. The Republicans, many of whom vehemently opposed President Johnson's attempts to solve domestic problems through increased federal action, chose Senator Barry Goldwater of Arizona.

Goldwater pleased his fellow conservatives by opposing a foreign policy of negotiation with the Communist bloc. Goldwater's conservatism contrasted sharply with the outlook of Johnson and Humphrey, and he claimed to offer "a choice, not an echo."

In the campaign the Democrats attacked Goldwater for his conservative views, pointing to his votes against the nuclear test ban treaty, against the tax cut, and against the Civil Rights Act of 1964. Above all, the Democrats tried to make Goldwater appear dangerous. They claimed that, if elected, he might recklessly start a nuclear war. Johnson won by a landslide, receiving more than 60 percent of the popular vote. His electoral vote margin was 486 to 52, the second biggest sweep of the century.

A flood of bills. Not only had Johnson won an overwhelming victory, but the Democrats had also strengthened their majority in Congress. Now, exuding confidence, Johnson set about pressing Congress to pass his Great Society program.

From April through October 1965, Congress passed more major bills than in any similar period since the New Deal. The Elementary and Secondary School Act granted more than $1 billion to school districts, based on the number of needy children enrolled. The Higher Education Act created federal scholarships for college students.

In health care, Congress established the Medicare program of federally funded health care for the aged. The Medicaid program, funded by state and federal governments, was created to assist the needy and the disabled who were too young for Medicare.

As a result of pressure from civil rights activists, Congress passed the Voting Rights Act of 1965. The act banned literacy tests, which had been used in some southern states to keep African and Mexican Americans from voting, and authorized federal officials to register eligible voters in states where they faced racial discrimination.

In the area of housing, Congress passed a housing act that provided federal aid for low-income families. The act was administered by the newly created Department of Housing and Urban Development (HUD),

"Did The Music Man Say When Our Instruments And Uniforms Are Coming?"

—from *The Herblock Gallery* (Simon & Schuster, 1968)

Writing About History

Letter. As American citizens in 1964, have students write letters to President Johnson, telling him what they think should be the role of the federal government in improving the lives of the poor in the United States. They can offer reasons to support programs that Johnson actually proposed, or they can suggest other programs that they think should be initiated.

Limited English Proficiency

Cooperative Activity. Have students work in pairs to prepare charts on the bills mentioned in the subsection "A Flood of Bills." For each bill passed, students can identify the problem it was intended to solve, and how successful it was.

Using the Visuals

Analyzing a Cartoon. Refer students to the cartoon on this page. **Ask:** What does the cartoon depict? **(a parade)** Who is the leader? **(Johnson)** To what does the label on the cartoon refer? **(Johnson's promise about achieving the Great Society)** What do the young people behind him symbolize? **(proposed governmental programs)** How does the cartoon contrast the leader of the parade and the followers? **(Johnson struts proudly, and the young people hobble behind him, confused.)** What does the caption—especially the word "instruments" suggest? **("Instruments" can mean musical instruments or means to achieve an end; the caption suggests that Johnson has yet to provide the means to achieve his promises.)**

Analyzing Primary Sources

Lyndon Johnson. In his April 1964 "Great Society" speech, President Johnson said:

"The Great Society is a place where every child can find knowledge to enrich his mind and to enlarge his talents. . . . It is a place where the city of man serves not only the needs of the body and the demands of commerce, but the desire for beauty and the hunger for community. It is a place where man can renew contact with nature. . . . It is a place where men are more concerned with the quality of their goals than the quantity of their goods."

Ask students to explain Johnson's goals for the Great Society in their own words. Have them discuss the degree to which these goals have (or have not) been achieved today.

Backyard History

Making a Chart. Have students find out what state and/or local laws protect the environment and consumers and when each was passed. They might prepare a chart for a class bulletin board, showing the name, date, and purpose of each law.

Multicultural Perspectives

Robert Clifton Weaver was born in Washington, D.C., in 1907. He received a Ph.D. in economics from Harvard University. As advisor to Harold Ickes, Secretary of the Interior in the 1930s, his specialty was public housing and slum clearance. He taught in several universities during the 1940s and 1950s. In 1961 President Kennedy made him head of the Federal Housing and Home Finance Agency, which became the nucleus of HUD. Weaver resigned in 1968 and returned to teaching.

Reduced student page in the Teacher's Edition

headed by economist Robert C. Weaver, the first African American to serve in a cabinet post.

The Immigration and Nationality Act of 1965 ended immigration quotas based on national origin, which had existed since the 1920s. The new law opened the way to newcomers from Asia and Latin America—a new tide of immigration that would have a profound impact on the culture of the United States.

Consumers and Environmentalists

During the Johnson administration, new forces began to play a part in shaping American democracy. Consumers and environmentalists organized to pressure Congress.

Lawyer Ralph Nader spearheaded the consumer movement with his attack on the auto industry. In a 1965 book, *Unsafe at Any Speed*, Nader argued that many people were being killed or injured needlessly because auto makers were more concerned with style than safety.

Despite objections by the powerful auto industry, Congress passed the National Traffic and Motor Vehicle Safety Act of 1966. The act set safety standards for cars and highways. Congress also created the Department of Transportation to oversee highway, air, and rail issues.

Rachel Carson awakened Americans to the dangers of pesticides.

Advocates for the environment. The environmental movement, which was in its infancy, was also gaining strength. Environmentalists pushed for laws to preserve wilderness areas, to beautify cities, and to reduce pollution.

Environmentalists were especially concerned about damage to the environment caused by chemical insect- and weed-killers. In her book *Silent Spring*, published in 1962, marine biologist Rachel Carson warned of the urgency of the threat:

"The central problem of our age has become the contamination of man's total environment with such substances of incredible potential for harm. . . . If the Bill of Rights contains no guarantee that a citizen shall be secure against lethal poisons distributed either by private individuals or by public officials, it is surely only because our forefathers, despite their considerable wisdom and foresight, could conceive of no such problem."

Silent Spring inspired many people to join the battle. Until the 1960s, the few laws that had been passed to control pollution were rarely enforced. Now, under pressure by environmentalists, Congress passed the Water Quality Act of 1965, requiring states to establish and enforce water-quality standards for interstate lakes and rivers. Air quality laws set federal emission standards for new cars produced by American manufacturers.

Finally, in the National Environmental Policy Act of 1969, Congress made protection of the environment a national policy. The act required federal agencies to consider the impact of their projects on the environment. In 1970 the Environmental Protection Agency (EPA) was created to enforce federal laws against pollution.

Connections: Literature
Rachel Carson was known for descriptive books about nature and warnings about environmental damage. *The Sea Around Us* and *At the Edge of the Sea* are noted for their evocative style. The title of *Silent Spring*, Carson's most famous book, refers to her contention that pesticides designed to kill insects were also killing the birds that ate the insects, and that someday there might be no birds left to sing.

Connections: Science and Technology
In addition to exposing unsafe cars, Nader carried out investigations of the meat and poultry industry, coal mines, and natural gas pipelines. These resulted in stricter health and safety laws. Nader has also pointed out damage to health from pesticides, food additives, and radiation from TV sets and X-rays.

Linking Past and Present

Research and Report. Today many ways to control insect pests without using pesticides are being explored. Encourage interested students to prepare reports on organic farming (farming without use of artificial chemicals) and biological pest control (use of other living things, such as parasitic insects and bacteria, to control insect pests).

Backyard History

Interview. Have students interview their parents or other adults to collect an oral history of memories about the 1960s. Are the adults' memories mostly positive, mostly negative, or a mixture of both?

The environmental movement has gained strength since the 1960s. (Above) New York City, 1966. (Left) "Redwood Summer," California, 1990.

The Counterculture

In the early 1960s Peter Max, a twenty-five year old commercial artist, had a vision of "a huge monumental wave of youth—the youth revolution coming." In anticipation of that revolution he created a wildly colorful new style of art.

Max's prediction was based on fact: the baby boom generation was growing up. Between 1960 and 1969, the number of Americans between the ages of fourteen and twenty-four swelled from 27 million to 40 million, or 20 percent of the population. The result was a youth culture unparalleled in American history. The interests of young people were to have a profound effect on society.

The "counterculture" that developed spread beyond any one age group. What members of the counterculture shared was a rejection of middle-class values and the ideas of those who stood for the status quo and for power. A popular bumper sticker said, "QUESTION AUTHORITY." Individuals and institutions that held the authority, such as government, police, schools, and corporations, were dubbed the "Establishment."

Author Tom Wolfe described the 1960s as the "decade when manners and morals, styles of living, attitudes towards the world changed the country." The spirit of change said that the time had come to start fresh, and new styles of living—mostly among the white, middle-class youth—emerged.

A reporter for the *San Francisco Chronicle* called members of the counterculture "hippies." Many flocked to urban centers, especially the East Village in New York and the Haight-Ashbury district in San Francisco. There they threw off the conformity and concern with material prosperity that had dominated the 1950s, opting instead to share what they owned and shun regular employment. They stressed love, individual freedom, and a sense of community. Street fairs, festivals, concerts, and events such as the "be-in" abounded.

Writing About History

"Eyewitness" Account. Have students do research to learn more about a famous event of the 1960s counterculture, for example, the "Summer of Love" in San Francisco, the Woodstock music festival, or the People's Park demonstrations in Berkeley. They can write an "eyewitness" account of the event from one of the following points of view: "hippie" participant, the parent of a participant, a reporter covering the event, or a police officer.

Connections: Music

One of the most memorable events of the counterculture was the Woodstock Festival—officially the Woodstock Music and Arts Fair. It took place on the weekend of August 15–17, 1969 on a small farm near Woodstock, New York. Among the performers were Jefferson Airplane; the Grateful Dead; Crosby, Stills, and Nash; Janis Joplin; and Jimi Hendrix. Almost 400,000 people attended.

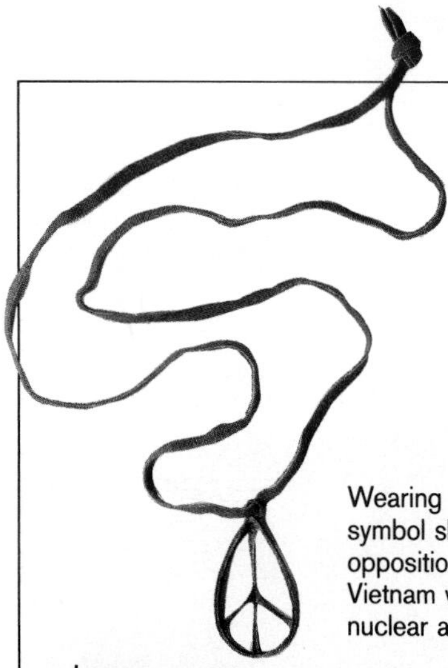

Wearing a peace symbol showed opposition to the Vietnam war and nuclear arms.

Bob Dylan

Jimi Hendrix

Janis Joplin

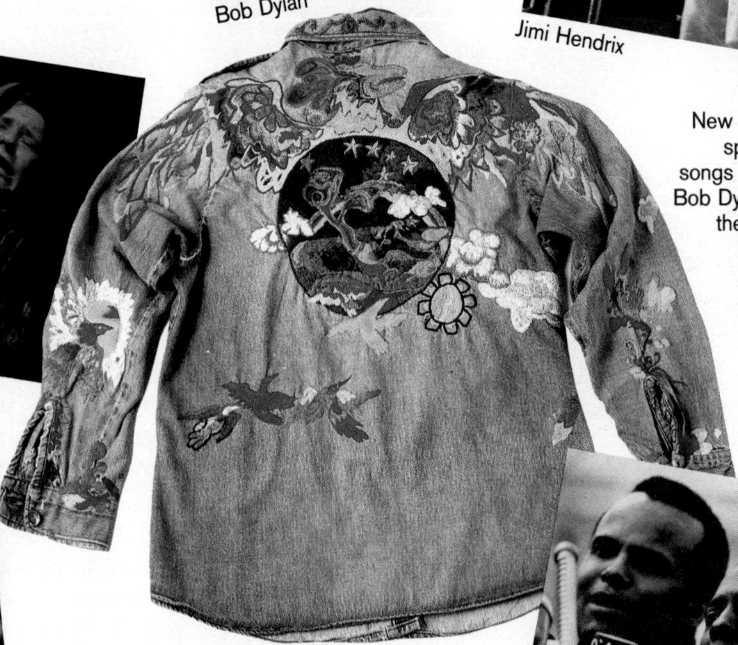

New music captured the spirit of the Sixties—songs of social protest by Bob Dylan and Joan Baez; the rock music of Jimi Hendrix and Carlos Santana, and Janis Joplin's raucous blues.

Retailers developed a booming business in "hippie" styles, such as decorated denim shirts and love beads.

Carlos Santana

Harry Belafonte, Leon Bibb, Joan Baez

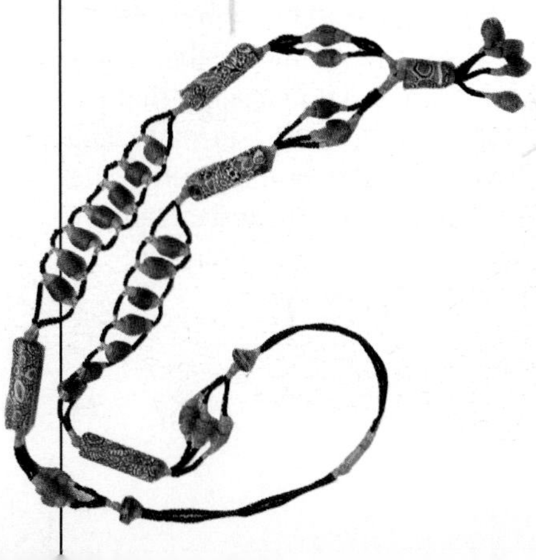

Connections: Music

The most popular musical group of the time—the Beatles—came from Liverpool, England. The band sold more records than any performer or group previously. Their concerts were mobbed with enthusiastic, screeching young people. After a performance one fan said, *"We don't come to hear them, really. We have their records. We came to scream at them."* Such songs as "All You Need Is Love" and "Lucy in the Sky with Diamonds"—spelling LSD—made the group especially popular with the counterculture.

Bright colors and wild designs decorated the bus of novelist Ken Kesey and his "Merry Pranksters."

young IN AMERICA

In the Sixties

"The times they are a-changin'" wrote folk singer and composer Bob Dylan in 1963. A large part of that change was the growing feeling among young people that something was wrong with a nation that permitted racism and discrimination to continue even as it plunged ever deeper into the war in Vietnam. Disturbing, too, was the value placed on conformity and material prosperity.

By the mid-1960s a "generation gap" had opened between rebellious young people and adults whose values they questioned. On high school and college campuses students protested restrictive rules and demanded courses that were "relevant" to the issues of the day. Hundreds of thousands of young people took part in the antiwar movement, and many joined the counterculture, hoping to "create a lifestyle which unites a generation in love and laughter."

Nearly 500,000 young people gathered at the Woodstock Festival in New York in 1969 for three days of music. Afterwards, Sixties youth were called the Woodstock Generation.

The powerful beat and youth-oriented lyrics of the Beatles and the Doors drew mobs of teenagers to their concerts.

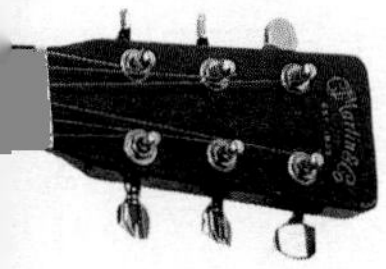

This guitar belonged to "Country Joe" McDonald.

Connections: Music

Listening to Music. If possible, play in class some of the popular music associated with the counterculture, such as the work of the Beatles, Jefferson Airplane, and Bob Dylan. Have students discuss the meaning of the lyrics as well as features that the music has in common.

Multicultural Perspectives

Point out the reference to Native-American culture suggested by the words *tribe* and *powwow* in the quotation on this page. Many people in the counterculture admired Native Americans for what they perceived as their superior spiritual and moral values and closeness to nature. Some Native Americans felt that these people idealized, and sometimes exploited, their beliefs without really understanding their culture, beliefs, and world view.

Connections: Science and Technology

LSD is produced by a fungus called ergot, which sometimes infects rye crops. LSD was used experimentally to treat and study mental illness. Some people who took LSD as part of the counterculture movement suffered permanent mental damage from it.

Thinking Critically

Analysis. Why did the counterculture movement appeal primarily to white, middle-class youth rather than to non-white or poor young people?

Connections: Art

Research. Have students look in books and magazines of the time (or at other sources, such as posters or record albums) for examples of "psychedelic" art. The term refers to art produced by people on mind-altering drugs such as LSD or meant to suggest the effect of such drugs (which often included vividly colored hallucinations). Have students note the features such art had in common, such as extremely bright colors and surrealistic designs. If possible, display some of the art in class.

Thinking Critically

Analysis. Have students point out similarities and differences between the idealism felt at the beginning of the Kennedy presidency and the idealism of the counterculture. Have them also consider similarities and differences in the attempts made to turn the ideals into reality.

The promise of the first "be-in," in San Francisco in 1967, was that

> *" Berkeley activists and the love generation of the Haight-Ashbury will join together with members of the new nation who will be coming from every state in the nation, every tribe of the young to powwow, celebrate, and prophesy the epoch of liberation, love, peace, compassion, and unity of mankind. "*

Part of the glorification of individual freedom expressed itself in the search for emotional and spiritual meaning through drugs and sex. After Harvard University fired Professor Timothy Leary for involving students in his experiments with lysergic acid diethylamide (LSD), he coined the phrase "turn on, tune in, drop out." Soon, a number of Americans were experimenting with LSD and other mind-altering drugs.

Meanwhile, the first birth control pill had gone on the market in 1960, and members of the counterculture celebrated sexual freedom, rejecting what they saw as conservative moralizing against premarital sex. Venereal disease rose dramatically, and in spite of the Pill, unplanned pregnancies, especially among teenagers, were widespread.

Religious experience also was on the rise. New sects attracted many converts, and traditional faiths experienced revivals. So-called "Jesus freaks" looked to the historical Jesus, not the established church, for guidance. They turned away from drug use and sought to reach out to those struggling to break free of addiction.

"Trouble in Hippieland." As the decade wore on, urban communities began to attract tourists and even dangerous hangers-on. *Newsweek* magazine, in a story titled "Trouble in Hippieland," reported the "murder, rape, racial clashes, and uncontrolled drug taking that have turned much of hippiedom into an urban nightmare."

Some members of the counterculture chose to move out of the urban jungle and form rural communities. These communities, like the utopian societies of an earlier age, sought to live out their values in a simple lifestyle, free from the materialism and societal restrictions that they rejected.

San Francisco's Haight-Ashbury district became known as a mecca of the 60s youth culture.

In the early years of the 1960s, *Life* magazine had described the times as marked by a "brisk feeling of hope, a generally optimistic and energetic shift from the calm of the late 50s." By the end of the decade, the magazine's editors reported,

> *" In a growing swell of demands for extreme and immediate change, the second part of the decade exploded—over race, youth, violence, life-styles, and above all, the Vietnam war. "*

In the end, the explosion would help bring about change. By focusing national attention on civil rights and on the futility of the Vietnam War, Americans—especially the young—who spoke out would make the "decade of tumult and change" one that would have a lasting effect on the fabric of American society.

Extending the Cold War

In 1965 former President Eisenhower reflected on a meeting he had had with Johnson the day after the assassination of President Kennedy:

> *" We also discussed foreign affairs. As far as I could see at that time, Lyndon Johnson's only intention was to find out what was going on and carry policy through. He suggested*

Global Connections
Cold War politics played a role in U.S. policy in the Middle East. As a result of the Six-Day War between Israel and the Arab nations (June 5–10, 1967), Israel gained Syria's Golan Heights, Egypt's Sinai Peninsula and Gaza Strip, and West Jordan, including Jerusalem. After a UN cease-fire, Israel's chief arms supplier, France, refused to send further arms to any of the combatants in the Middle East. Seeking political advantage, the Soviet Union immediately said that it would reequip the Arab air forces. The Johnson administration faced a dilemma: sell arms to Israel, possibly contributing to future wars and appearing to endorse Israel's occupation of the lands that had been part of Syria and Egypt, or refuse to sell arms, causing Israel to lose its military superiority over other nations in the area. The U.S. soon became Israel's main supplier of weapons.

nothing new or different. He wanted to talk about Laos, Cuba, and so forth. He did seem to be less informed about foreign policy than about domestic policy. ”

In the middle of 1965, President Johnson's wife, Lady Bird, had worried, "I just hope that foreign problems do not keep on mounting. They do not represent Lyndon's kind of Presidency." Ironically, however, it was foreign problems that would come to dominate Johnson's attention.

In April 1965, Johnson sent marines to the Dominican Republic, where he feared that unrest would lead to a Communist revolt. This action undermined the trust that Kennedy had gained through his Alliance for Progress. Critics said that Johnson lacked evidence of Communist involvement. They denounced him for bypassing the Organization of American States (OAS), which should have been consulted.

The foreign issue of greatest significance both at home and abroad was the Vietnam War. (See Chapter 29.) Johnson's role in launching the United States into a major war would not only cost him reelection; it would destroy his hopes of achieving his Great Society. As more and more of the nation's attention and resources were drained by the war, both the will and the funds to carry out Great Society legislation evaporated. As Martin Luther King, Jr., said, "The Great Society has been shot down on the battlefields of Vietnam."

Section Review

1. Comprehension. Name and describe two programs set up as part of Johnson's War on Poverty.

2. Analysis. In what sense did Goldwater offer voters "a choice, not an echo"?

3. Synthesis. Why do you think so many Americans were blind to the problem of poverty in the United States in the 1960s?

4. Synthesis. How could the alternative life styles of the 1960s be characterized as a "sequel to the 1950s"?

5. Analysis. How did the intervention in the Dominican Republic illustrate President Johnson's Cold War thinking?

Connections to Themes

Shaping Democracy

World War II and the Cold War convinced Americans that the nation had a mission as leader of the free world. A threat by anti-democratic forces anywhere was now seen as a threat to the United States.

While accepting this global commitment, many people assumed that all was well with democracy at home. Yet the nature of American democracy would come to be questioned and redefined as the decade wore on.

In a country where millions lacked civil rights, and millions lived in poverty while others enjoyed prosperity, the gap was widening between leaders and the people they sought to lead. The atmosphere that Eisenhower had described as one of "greater serenity and mutual confidence" could not continue as long as this gap existed.

John Kennedy suggested in 1962 that the economic and social changes that had taken place in the United States meant that there would be no further need for "the great sort of 'passionate movements' which have stirred this country so often in the past." The upheaval and change, the political awakening and reaffirming of American values that would occur in the late 1960s and early 1970s would show how wrong he was. As a growing number of Americans saw that the nation's democratic ideals were not reflected in reality, they would begin a massive push to reaffirm those ideals and make them a reality for a larger number of Americans.

Connections: Politics

Discussion. Would the Great Society, as President Johnson conceived it, have been successful even if the United States had not become involved in the Vietnam war? Why or why not?

Section Review

ANSWERS

1. Answers may include the Job Corps, Vista, and Head Start.
2. Goldwater disagreed with almost all Democratic policies and actions. He opposed the Test Ban Treaty and the Civil Rights Act and advocated a hard-line policy toward the Soviets.
3. Many prosperous people were too busy working, making money, and enjoying their success to notice the situation of the poor. Students might also suggest other likely explanations, such as that people with different income levels often live in different neighborhoods or communities and do not see how others live.
4. The alternative lifestyles of the hippies and others can be seen as a reaction to the conformity of the 1950s.
5. Johnson, like Kennedy, was determined to oppose the spread of communism. He sent marines to prevent a Communist revolution.

Chapter Survey

ANSWERS

Using New Vocabulary

Reapportionment involved redrawing (c) voting districts for (f) state legislatures to make them more equal in (a) population and give fair representation to (e) urban areas.

Reviewing the Chapter

1. Kennedy believed United States should help other nations overcome poverty; set up Peace Corps and Alliance for Progress.
2. Supreme Court outlawed school prayer, reinforcing separation of church and state. *Miranda v. Arizona* set guidelines for police questioning suspects; *Escobedo v. Illinois* required police to tell defendants of their right to a lawyer; latter decisions protected rights of accused.
3. Kennedy wanted to promote economic growth without dangerous inflation; cut taxes, increased government spending to stimulate consumer demand and drive economic growth. To control inflation, he urged steel companies to comply with voluntary wage-price guidelines.
4. Shift from massive retaliation with nuclear weapons to flexible response with some combination of nuclear weapons and conventional forces. Flexible response was way to prevent full-scale nuclear war.
5. Led to Test Ban Treaty, eliminated missiles in Turkey but did not eliminate arms race.
6. Job training through Job Corps, VISTA projects to reduce unemployment and illiteracy, other programs for job training and education, such as Head Start.
7. Goldwater opposed tax cut, Test Ban Treaty, Civil Rights Act, seemed "trigger happy" to start nuclear war.
8. Elderly helped by Medicare. Students helped by aid to schools from Elementary and Secondary Education Act and by scholarships from Higher Education Act. African Americans helped by Voting Rights Act of 1965, creation of Department of Housing and Urban Development.
9. Johnson sent marines to Dominican Republic to put down possible Communist revolt. Kennedy used Cuban exiles to invade Cuba; Johnson's operation overt, Kennedy's covert.
10. Counterculture arose from the baby boom as a reaction against 1950s materialism and conformity. Challenged morals and norms and impacted art, music, and forms of political protest.

Reduced student page in the Teacher's Edition

Chapter Survey

Using New Vocabulary

From the list below, select the four terms whose meanings relate to the underlined vocabulary word and explain the relationship.

reapportionment

(a) population	(d) caucus
(b) deficit	(e) urban
(c) voting district	(f) state legislature

Reviewing the Chapter

1. What vision did Kennedy have of America's responsibility to the world? How did he attempt to carry out that responsibility?

2. Give three examples of rulings of the Supreme Court under Chief Justice Earl Warren. Explain the significance of each.

3. State the goals of Kennedy's economic policies and explain how he sought to carry them out.

4. In what way did Kennedy shift the focus of American defense policy? Why did he develop a new policy?

5. What effect did the Cuban missile crisis have on the arms race?

6. By what methods did Johnson attempt to wage war on poverty?

7. In the election of 1964 on what grounds did the Democrats seek to discredit Goldwater?

8. List three groups of people affected by Great Society legislation and explain how these laws affected them. How did the Vietnam War affect Johnson's Great Society plans?

9. Compare and contrast Johnson's response to the threat of communism in Latin America in 1965 with Kennedy's response in the 1961 Bay of Pigs incident.

10. In what ways was the counterculture of the 1960s a result of events and ideas of the 1950s? What lasting changes in American society were influenced by the counterculture?

Thinking Critically

1. Analysis. What influences do you think the Bay of Pigs experience had on the decisions Kennedy made in the Cuban missile crisis? on the decisions Castro and Khrushchev made?

2. Evaluation. Describe Kennedy's response to the spread of communism in Cuba, Berlin, and South Vietnam. Which response do you think was most effective? Why?

3. Analysis. Compare the goals and methods of the consumer and environmental advocates of the 1960s to the Progressives of the early 1900s.

History and You

Since the Kennedy assassination, citizens' groups have worked for tighter gun control legislation. Investigate the movement for gun control in your state and at the national level. Which groups support greater control? These groups may not agree. What different kinds of control have they suggested, and what arguments have they offered? Which groups are against greater gun control? What reasons do they give? When you have concluded your investigation, give your opinion on gun control and support it with reasons.

Using a Time Line

Match each date on the time line with the correct event or events from the list below. Write your answers in chronological order and explain the significance of each event.

(A) Project Apollo
(B) Immigration and Naturalization Act
(C) Civil Rights Act
(D) Kennedy-Nixon debates
(E) Publication of *Silent Spring*
(F) Alliance for Progress
(G) Voting Rights Act
(H) *Gideon* v. *Wainwright*

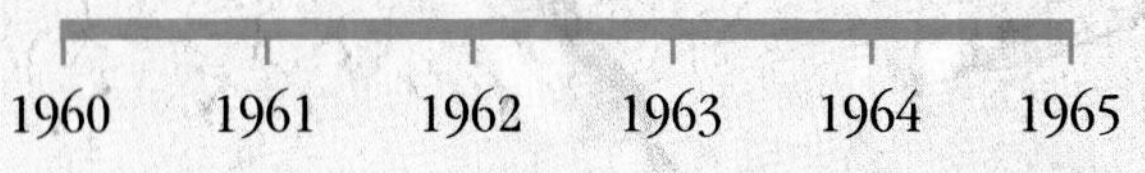

Applying Thinking Skills

Interpreting Political Cartoons

The cartoon below appeared in newspapers on October 30, 1962. At that time, "To tell the Truth" was a popular television program in which each of the three contestants claimed to be the same person. Panelists decided which of the three was telling the truth. Study the cartoon and answer the questions that follow.

"Will the real winner of the Cuba crisis please stand up?"

1. Which three nations were involved in the Cuban missile crisis?

2. Who are the three figures in the cartoon?

3. What is each of the figures claiming to be?

4. Consider each of the figures. What basis does each have for his claim?

5. Consider the people who saw this cartoon in 1962. Who was the real winner in their view?

Writing About Issues

The Issue: *Should there be a single six-year term for the President of the United States?*

In recent years, support has grown for a Constitutional amendment limiting the President of the United States to a single six-year term. The idea of this proposed change is to give the President a long enough term to develop and carry out his or her programs without the need to spend time and energy campaigning for reelection. Former President Lyndon Johnson supported the idea in his memoirs:

> *"The growing burdens of the office exact an enormous physical toll on the man himself and place incredible demands on his time. Under these circumstances the old belief that a President can carry out the responsibilities of the office and at the same time undergo the rigors of campaigning is, in my opinion, no longer valid."*

People who oppose such a change believe that eliminating the possibility of reelection would make the President less responsive to the people and therefore less likely to act in the public interest. In addition, they claim, voters would be deprived of the opportunity to express their views on the President's performance. Former presidential aide Thomas Cronin gives his opinion:

> *"The Presidency must be a highly political office, and the President an expert practitioner of the art of politics. Quite simply, there is no other way for Presidents to negotiate favorable [alliances] within the country, Congress, and the executive branch and to gather the authority needed to translate ideas into accomplishments. A President who remains aloof from politics, campaigns, and partisan alliances does so at the risk of becoming a prisoner of events, special interests, or his own wishes."*

What do you think? Should there be a single six-year term for the President, or two four-year terms? State your opinion and your reasons in a letter to one of your United States senators. Begin your letter "Dear Senator" and address it as follows:

The Honorable (name of Senator)
Senate Office Building
Washington, D.C. 20501

To obtain the names of your senators, ask your librarian.

Thinking Critically

1. Kennedy wanted to avoid possibility of another fiasco, wanted Soviets to appear the meddlers in Cuba, not U.S.
2. Ordered Bay of Pigs invasion in Cuba; used diplomacy and naval blockade to get Soviet missiles out of Cuba; called up reserves and asked for increase in defense spending in response to Soviet attempt to control all of Berlin. Sent more military advisors to South Vietnam.
3. Like Progressives, consumer and environmental advocates of 1960s worked to protect citizens from hazards caused by industry and big business. Also like them, they sought governmental regulation as the means to their ends.

History and You

Answers will vary by state: may include mention of NRA and the 1991 "Brady Bill."

Using a Time Line

(D) 1960; **(A)** 1961; **(F)** 1961; **(E)** 1962; **(H)** 1963; **(C)** 1964; **(G)** 1965, **(B)** 1965.

Interpreting Political Cartoons

1. The U.S., the Soviet Union, Cuba.
2. Kennedy, Khrushchev, Castro.
3. The winner of the confrontation.
4. Kennedy forced Khrushchev to withdraw missiles. Khrushchev got Kennedy to end blockade and promise not to invade Cuba. Castro remained in power.
5. Americans probably would have picked Kennedy because he forced Khrushchev to back down.

Chapter 28

"Let Justice Roll Down"

Planning Guide

	Student Text	TWE Lesson Plans	Support Materials
SECTION 1	**Section 28–1 (1–2 Days)** **Gaining Equality Under the Law,** pp 752–757 Review/Evaluation Section Review, p 757	**Introducing the Chapter:** The Dream of Equality—Class Activity, 30 minutes, p 749B **Evaluating Progress:** Challenging Segregation—Individual Activity, homework, p 749C	★ **Read to Remember,** Section 1 ● **Section Activities,** Section 1 ● **Geography Activities,** Section 1 Δ **Readings,** ● **Tests and Quizzes,** Section 1 Quiz
SECTION 2	**Section 28–2 (1–2 Days)** **Taking Direct Action,** pp 757–765 The American Spirit: Martin Luther King, Jr., p 760 Review/Evaluation Section Review, p 765	**Teaching the Main Ideas:** African-American Party Platform—Cooperative Activity, one class period, p 749B **Reinforcement Activity:** Charting the Struggle for Equality—Paired Activity, one class period, p 749C	★ **Read to Remember,** Section 2 ● **Section Activities,** Section 2 Δ **Enrichment Activities,** Section 2 Δ **Readings,** ● **Tests and Quizzes,** Section 2 Quiz
SECTION 3	**Section 28–3 (1–2 Days)** **From Civil Rights to Black Power,** pp 766–771 Connections to Themes: Shaping Democracy, p 771 Review/Evaluation Section Review, p 771 Chapter 28 Survey, pp 772–773 Skills, pp 772–773 Using New Vocabulary Thinking Critically Using Geography Applying Social Studies Skills: Analyzing Bar Graphs	**Teaching the Main Ideas:** The SCLC and the Black Panthers—Paired Activity, one class period, p 749C **Enrichment Activity:** Fighting Racism—Individual Activity, homework, p 749C	★ **Read to Remember,** Section 3 ● **Section Activities,** Section 3 Δ **Enrichment Activities,** Section 3 Δ **Readings,** ● **Tests and Quizzes,** Section 3 Quiz, Chapter 28 Test (Forms A and B) **Additional Resources** ● **Active Learning** Δ **Transparencies and Activity Book** ● **Testing Software** ★ **Chapter Summaries** **Key:** ★ **For Extra Support** ● **For All Students** Δ **For Enrichment**

Overview

In the 1950s and 1960s African Americans created a mass movement to gain the civil rights the Constitution guarantees to all Americans. The NAACP led the way by fighting discrimination and segregation in the courts. The Supreme Court's historic decision in *Brown* v. *Board of Education* in 1954 destroyed the legal basis for segregation, but federal efforts to desegregate schools in Virginia and the Deep South led to massive resistance and violence by white southerners. In 1957 President Eisenhower was forced to use federal troops in Little Rock, Arkansas, to enforce the Court's ruling.

African Americans also set out to achieve equality for themselves through direct action. In 1955 African Americans in Montgomery, Alabama, desegregated the bus system by a determined boycott. The example of Rosa Parks and the nonviolent boycotters, led by Martin Luther King, Jr., spurred direct action throughout the South, including student sit-ins, Freedom Rides, registration of black voters, and protest marches.

Violence against the protestors, which was shown on television, made the issue of racism impossible for the federal government to ignore. President Kennedy called for civil rights legislation, which was supported by a massive march on Washington, D.C. The Civil Rights Act of 1964, pushed through Congress by Kennedy's successor, Lyndon Johnson, was the nation's greatest step toward equality in a century. A year later, Johnson successfully urged Congress to pass the Voting Rights Act of 1965 after campaigns for voting rights in Mississippi and Alabama had led to bloodshed.

The new civil rights legislation did not end the deep-seated problems of racism and poverty. Frustration over injustice resulted in riots in northern cities in the mid-1960s and in increased demands for black power, which often rejected white society. The assassination of Martin Luther King in 1968 set off new riots, but it did not end the drive for equality.

Activity Objectives

After completing the activities, students should be able to

- describe the goals and actions of the civil rights movement in the 1950s and 1960s.
- compare the goals and methods of the Southern Christian Leadership Conference and the Black Panther party.
- summarize significant events in the civil rights movement.
- explain the reasoning behind the Supreme Court's historic Brown decision.
- analyze the relationship between racism and poverty.

Introducing the Chapter

The Dream of Equality

This class activity requires half a class period.

In this activity students, in the course of analyzing part of the "I have a dream" speech of Martin Luther King, Jr., consider whether the dream of civil rights activists in the 1950s and 1960s is now reality.

Begin the activity by having students turn to the excerpt from Dr. King's famous speech on pages 764–765 in the text. Call on a volunteer to read the excerpt.

Point out that Dr. King's speech became a rallying cry for many civil rights activists in the 1960s. Ask students whether the hopes described in the speech have been fulfilled. Encourage students to give examples of progress toward equality as well as examples of continuing racism and discrimination.

Give students several minutes to create their own "I have a dream" lists of conditions they want to see changed in the United States. Then have students select one or two of their dreams to post on the chalkboard or on large poster sheets.

Encourage the class to read the dreams. Leave the dreams posted and refer to them as the class studies Chapter 28.

Teaching the Main Ideas

Section 28-2: African-American Party Platform

This cooperative activity requires a full class period.

In Section 28-2 students learn that the African-American struggle for equality became a mass movement based on direct action. The following activity will enable students to identify different concerns and activities in the movement.

Begin the activity by asking students to name individuals and groups that took part in the civil rights movement in the 1950s and 1960s. Write their responses on the chalkboard. Then have students identify the specific concerns and forms of direct action used by the individuals and groups.

Tell students that they will use this information to write a platform for an African-American political party. Remind them that a platform is a statement of a political party's official stand on major public issues. The platform is made up of planks, position statements on each specific issue in a party's platform. These planks are often turned into government programs by party members who are elected to office.

Divide the class into groups of three and direct each group to develop a platform for a new political party that will represent African Americans. The platforms should include a party name, state the party's stand on major issues, and provide at least three planks, which outline beliefs about the issues and goals for government.

Direct groups to read their finished platforms to the class. Have the class compare platforms. Conclude the acitivity by challenging the class to choose one name and one platform for the new party and to give reasons for their choices.

Teaching the Main Ideas

Section 28-3: The SCLC and the Black Panthers

This paired activity requires one class period.

This activity gives students an opportunity to analyze the different approaches used by Martin Luther King, Jr., and the Southern Christian Leadership Conference (SCLC) and the Black Panther party to effect change for African Americans.

Begin the activity by asking students to review African–American reactions in the 1950s and 1960s to racism and discrimination in the United States. Point out that some groups, such as the SCLC led by Dr. King, believed in integration and nonviolent resistence, while others, such as the Black Panther party, advocated separatism and accepted the possibility of violence in the interest of self-defense.

Have students choose partners. In each pair assign one student to represent the views of Dr. King and the SCLC, and the other the views of the Black Panthers. Direct the pairs to review individually Sections 28–2 and 28–3 for arguments and supporting evidence.

On the chalkboard write the following questions:

- What methods should be used to bring about change for African Americans?
- What role should white Americans play in African-American efforts to bring about change?
- What is a reasonable amount of time to allow for change to occur?

Direct pairs to discuss each of these questions, with each partner representing his or her assigned point of view. Conclude the activity by asking students to identify areas in which different viewpoints were reconcilable and areas in which there was no common ground.

Reinforcement Activity

Sections 28-2: Charting the Struggle for Equality

This paired activity requires a full class period.

The following activity, in which students complete a summary chart, reinforces understanding of significant events in the civil rights movement.

Begin the activity by asking students to identify events described in the first two sections of Chapter 28 that required great courage and persistence. Have students speculate about the motivations of the people involved.

Divide the class into pairs. Have each pair create a chart that summarizes three significant events in the civil rights movement. Students are to select the events from Sections 28–1 and 28–2 and then set up a chart as follows:

	Event 1	*Event 2*	*Event 3*
Goals			
Individuals and Groups			
Forms of Protest			
Reactions			
Results			

Warn students to leave sufficient space to describe each topic listed in the left-hand column.

When students have finished their charts, ask volunteers to report on specific events. Have students make generalizations about forms of protest, reactions, and results. What forms of protest would students consider using? Why?

Evaluating Progress

Section 28-1: Challenging Segregation

This individual activity can be completed in class or assigned as homework.

This activity is designed to assess students' understanding of the Supreme Court decision in *Brown* v. *Board of Education* by having them imagine themselves as African-American parents who are trying to ensure an equal education for their children.

Begin by reading aloud the following description.

> *Your son or daughter is now attending Washington High School. The 1960 school year has just begun, and you are upset with the quality of education your child is receiving. At Washington, which is a school for African Americans, teachers are apathetic, courses are limited, textbooks are outdated, and test scores are low. Other schools in the district, which are for white students, are better. You tried but failed to get your child admitted to one of those schools. You decide to appeal to the local school board.*

Tell students to write a statement to the local school board. The letter is to include a brief introduction; arguments, including court decisions and laws regarding segregated schools as described in Section 28-1; and a summary.

Criteria for evaluating students' work should include accuracy of arguments and clearly expressed links between law, such as the 1954 Brown decision, desegregation efforts throughout the country, and this particular situation.

Enrichment Activity

Section 28-3: Fighting Racism

This individual activity may be assigned as homework and shared in class the following day.

In this activity students analyze the relationship between racism and poverty by preparing and presenting public service announcements.

Begin the activity by reviewing with students the report of the Commission on Civil Disorders, also known as the Kerner Commission, in Section 28-3. On the chalkboard or an overhead transparency, summarize the commission's conclusions as follows:

> *White racism is essentially responsible for widespread discrimination and segregation in employment, education, and housing. As a result, many urban African Americans live in areas that have higher unemployment and crime rates and that lack equal educational opportunities and adequate housing, health facilities, and city services.*

Begin the activity by discussing with students the use of public service announcements to make the public aware of problems and to encourage action to solve them. (Students were introduced to public service announcements in the Evaluating Progress activity in Chapter 17.)

Challenge students to write a 30-second public service announcement for television to address the problem of racism and discrimination as identified by the Kerner Commission and described under the subhead "Outbreak of Violence" in Section 28-3. The public service announcements are to identify a specific problem and suggest a solution. Encourage students to create public service announcements that have striking visual and strong verbal messages.

On the assignment's due date, have students present their public service announcements. After each presentation, have students discuss how the proposed solution may help to reduce not only the speicific problem addressed but racism in general.

Bibliography and Audiovisual Material

Teacher Bibliography

Anthony, Earl. *Spitting in the Wind*. Malibu, Calif.: Roundtable Publishing Co., 1990.

Banks, James A. and Cherry A. *March Toward Freedom: A History of Black Americans.* Carthage, Ill.: Fearon Teacher Aids, 1978.

Brown, Claude. *Manchild in the Promised Land*. New York: Macmillan Publishing Co., 1990.

Hampton, Henry and Steve Fayer. *Voices of Freedom.* New York: Bantam Books, 1991.

Oates, Stephen B. *Let the Trumpet Sound: The Life of Martin Luther King, Jr*. New York: NAL/Dutton Co., 1983.

Sitkoff, Harvard. *The Struggle for Black Equality, 1945–1980*. New York: Hill and Wang, Inc., 1981.

Viorst, Milton. *Fire in the Streets: America in the Nineteen Sixties*. New York: Simon & Schuster, Inc., 1981.

Williams, Juan. *Eyes on the Prize.* New York: Viking Penguin, 1987.

Student Bibliography

Baldwin, James. *Blues for Mr. Charlie*. New York: Dell Publishing Co., 1985.

Brooks, Gwendolyn. *Selected Poems*. New York: HarperCollins Publishers, Inc., 1982.

Gaines, Ernest. *Autobiography of Miss Jane Pitman*. New York: Bantam Books, 1982.

Haley, Alex. *Roots*. New York: Dell Publishing Co., 1980.

Hansberry, Lorraine. *Raisin in the Sun*. New York: NAL/Dutton Co., 1989.

Malcolm X. *The Autobiography of Malcolm X.* New York: Ballantine Books, Inc., 1987.

Styron, William. *Confessions of Nat Turner*. New York: Random House, Inc., 1967.

Taulbert, Clifton L. *Once Upon A Time When We Were Colored.* Tulsa, Okla.: Council Oaks Books, 1989.

Films, Videocassettes, and Videodiscs

American Documents: Martin Luther King, Jr.: Letter From Birmingham Jail. 25 min. Coronet/MTI. Videodisc.

Civil Rights Movement: The Personal View. 22 min. NBC; FI. Movie.

The Civil Rights Movement: Witness to History. 15 min. Guidance Associates. Videocassette.

"I Have a Dream": Martin Luther King. 28 min. Social Studies School Services. Videocassette.

King: Montgomery to Memphis. 103 min. FI. Movie.

Visions for American History: Struggles for Justice, Volumes 1 and 2. Scholastic. Videodisc.

Filmstrips

Civil Rights: Yesterday, Today, Tomorrow. 31 min. 4 color filmstrips, 4 cassettes, guide. VMA.

Dr. Martin Luther King, Jr. 21 min. 1 filmstrip with cassette. SVE.

Chapter 28

Objectives

- Explain how the NAACP sought to use the courts to end legal segregation.
- Describe how African-American resistance to segregation became a mass movement.
- Analyze factors that led advocates of black power to adopt more aggressive methods in the struggle for equality.

Introducing THE CHAPTER

For suggestions on introducing Chapter 28, refer to page 749B in the Teacher's Edition.

Developing THE CHAPTER

For activities and teaching strategies to help you reinforce and enrich chapter content, see pages 749B–749D in the Teacher's Edition.

BACKGROUND

Chapter Opener Illustrations

Those who attended the August 28, 1963, March on Washington, were present at a great moment in American history when Martin Luther King, Jr., delivered his "I Have a Dream" speech.

In May 1963 King's nonviolence faced a severe test. Birmingham, Alabama, police used fire hoses and police dogs to disperse civil rights marchers.

The effort to achieve desegregation of American schools contributed to dramatic changes in educational achievements of African Americans. In 1950 approximately 22.5 percent of black adults had had twelve or more years of schooling. In 1980 that figure had risen to nearly 75 percent.

A sharecropper grandmother taking care of a child reads the pamphlet "Civil Rights Under Federal Programs" to learn her rights as a citizen.

Chapter 28 1954-1968

"Let Justice Roll Down"

In 1982 the number of black-owned businesses totalled 339,239, up from 187,600 in 1972—a more than 80 percent increase. African Americans own about 3 percent of the total businesses in the United States. Two of the largest black-owned businesses are Johnson Publishing Company, which publishes *Jet* and *Ebony* magazines, and Motown Industries, a recording company that introduced such artists as Smokey Robinson and the Miracles and the Supremes to the public.

American Voices

For many Americans, the American Dream is of a life of opportunity and abundance. For African Americans, however, racism has too often turned that dream into a nightmare of discrimination and poverty. In a family memoir, Pauli Murray, a civil rights activist and lawyer, describes the racial barriers that, in part, sparked in her "a passion for equality."

> *"Every morning I passed white children as poor as I was going in the opposite direction on their way to school. We never had fights. I don't recall their ever having called me a single insulting name. It was worse than that. They passed me as if I weren't there! They looked through me and beyond me with unseeing eyes. Their [school] playground, a wonderland of iron swings, slides, see-saws, crossbars, and a basketball court, was barred from us by a strong eight-foot-high fence. . . .*
>
> *Our seedy run-down school told us that if we had any place at all in the scheme of things it was a separate place, marked off, and unwanted by the white people. We were bottled up and labeled and set aside—sent to the Jim Crow car, the back of the bus. . . .*
>
> *It seemed as if there were only two kinds of people in the world* —They *and* We—White *and* Colored. *The world revolved on color and variations in color. It pervaded the air I breathed."*

Caught in a system that kept her segregated in all areas of life, in the 1940s Pauli Murray joined other African Americans struggling to gain the civil rights the Constitution guaranteed to all Americans. That struggle had gone on for more than 300 years. In the 1950s and 1960s it became a mass movement. Created and led by African Americans, the civil rights movement tested the nation's willingness to expand the American dream to include all Americans.

Martin Luther King, Jr.; participants in the March on Washington, 1963; use of police dogs against civil rights marchers, Birmingham, 1963; college graduation, 1990; sharecroppers in South Carolina; a black businessman.

Analyzing Primary Sources

American Voices

Born in 1910, Pauli Murray grew up in Durham, North Carolina, with a thirst for learning. She graduated from Hunter College in New York but as an African American, was denied admission for graduate studies at the University of North Carolina. In 1940 her refusal to sit on a broken seat led to her arrest for resisting segregation on an interstate bus.

Those events, in part, prompted her to become a civil rights lawyer. While a student at Howard University's law school, she continued to protest segregation by organizing sit-ins at restaurants.

Murray earned law degrees at Howard University, the University of California at Berkeley, and Yale University and practiced law in New York and California. Her book *Proud Shoes: The Story of an American Family* was published in 1956. In 1973 Pauli Murray gave up the law to become a priest, and in 1977 she was ordained in the Protestant Episcopal Church.

1. What racial barriers does Murray describe? **(segregated schools, trains, and buses)**
2. What hurt Murray more than being called an insulting name? Why? **(being passed by as if she wasn't there; not being recognized as a person)**
3. How does Murray's description belie the idea of "separate but equal" schools for black students? **(Her school was seedy, rundown; black children were barred from the white children's toy-filled playground.)**

751

Section 28-1

Objectives

- ***Answer the Focus Question.***
- *Describe the nature of segregation in the United States prior to 1954.*
- *Explain the significance of* Brown *v.* Board of Education of Topeka.
- *Describe resistance to school desegregation.*

Introducing

THE SECTION

Explain to students the differences between "indirect" and "direct" action. Indirect action includes legal steps and personal negotiations that might lead to change in the law. An example of such steps would be discussions between African-American leaders and the President of the United States about ways of ending segregation. Direct action consists of legal or illegal confrontations. Examples include labor strikes, picketing, boycotting, demonstrations and marches, and the like.

B · A · C · K · G · R · O · U · N · D

Time Line Illustrations

1. An African-American child in a segregated school. NAACP lawyer Thurgood Marshall argued that because such schools were separate they could not be equal.

2. An empty bus during the Montgomery, Alabama, bus boycott. "EASE THAT SQUEEZE," the message on the side of the bus, does not refer to the boycott, but to traffic problems that can be solved if more people ride the bus. Ironically, the boycott increased the squeeze.

3. After more than a year of legal battles, on September 10, 1962, the United States Supreme Court upheld the right of James Meredith to enroll in the University of Mississippi.

4. In 1965 Martin Luther King, Jr., led a five-day march from Selma to Montgomery, the capital of Alabama, to pro-

Reduced student page in the Teacher's Edition

CHAPTER TIME LINE

1954-1968

1955 Montgomery bus boycott

1960 Greensboro sit-in
Student Nonviolent Coordinating Committee formed

1954 — 1957 — 1960

1954 School segregation ruled unconstitutional

1957 Southern Christian Leadership Conference formed
"Little Rock Nine" integrate Central High

1961 Freedom Rides begin

28-1 *Gaining Equality Under the Law*

Focus: How did the NAACP use the Constitution and the courts to break down legal barriers to equality?

" If there is no struggle there is no progress. Those who . . . favor freedom and yet [belittle] agitation, are men who want crops without plowing up the ground, they want rain without thunder and lightning. They want the ocean without the awful roar of its many waters. "

This warning, issued by Frederick Douglass in 1857, had rung in the ears of African Americans for a century. For a century, African Americans had been "plowing" with varying success, trying to force the nation to live up to its ideal of equal rights for all. But a mighty storm was brewing, and out of the thunder and lightning and the roar of the waters would come a movement that would change the place of black people in American society and point the way for other groups seeking to escape second-class citizenship.

Segregation from Cradle to Grave

In a park in Maryland stands a memorial on which are engraved the names of local soldiers who were killed during World War I. On the front of the monument is a list labeled "white," and on the back, a list labeled "colored." In the early 1950s, segregation affected all areas of life— and even of death— in the South.

test discrimination. This photograph catches the determination of the more than 25,000 marchers.

5. The emblem of the Black Panther party was the raised, clenched black fist. It came to signify "Black Power."

1962 James Meredith enters University of Mississippi

1963 Crisis in Birmingham
March on Washington

1964 24th Amendment: ban on poll tax
"Freedom Summer"
Civil Rights Act of 1964

1965 Selma-to-Montgomery march
The Autobiography of Malcolm X
Watts riot

1966 Black Panther party formed

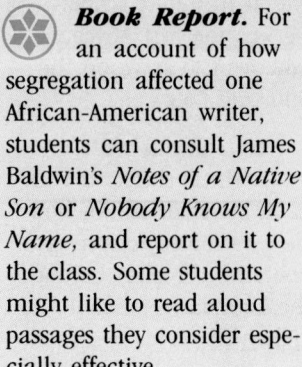

1968 Assassination of Martin Luther King, Jr.

1962 1965 1968

African Americans faced demeaning restrictions wherever they turned. Black children were born in separate hospitals, lived in "their own" neighborhoods, and went to segregated schools. On public transportation they sat in the black section. They were excluded from parks, beaches, and other recreation facilities. If they wanted to drink, eat, or go to the toilet, they had to find facilities reserved for them, or go without. They were restricted to the lowest paying jobs, and most were barred from voting. In court they were tried in front of all-white juries and sentenced by white judges to segregated jails. When they died, they were buried in black cemeteries.

Created in the late 1800s, racist policies of strict segregation and economic and political discrimination were designed to keep African Americans in their "place" and were enforced not only by laws but by terrorism. Most white southerners accepted the situation as normal, believing, as one Virginia newspaper editor said, that "the Negro race, as a race, is plainly not equal to the white race, as a race." These southerners resented criticism by outsiders and resisted interference by the federal government in what they considered to be state matters.

Working Through the Courts

The National Association for the Advancement of Colored People (NAACP) was in the forefront of resistance to segregation and discrimination. For decades, NAACP lawyers had been fighting such policies in court. Most had learned their skills from Charles H. Houston, the head of the law school at Howard University and a legendary NAACP lawyer. As a young man, Houston had vowed to "study law and use my time fighting for men who could not strike back." Houston inspired his students to follow in his footsteps. One who did was Thurgood Marshall, who became the chief NAACP lawyer and later the first African American to be appointed to the Supreme Court.

One of the goals of NAACP lawyers was to get the courts to overturn state laws that made it difficult for black people to vote. A large black vote could be a powerful weapon to force the government to act in the interest of African Americans. The *Chicago Defender* declared, "The ballot has become . . . the biggest gun in our battle for freedom."

NAACP lawyers won their first important victory in 1915 when the Supreme Court ruled that the

Developing

THE SECTION

Connections: Literature

Book Report. For an account of how segregation affected one African-American writer, students can consult James Baldwin's *Notes of a Native Son* or *Nobody Knows My Name,* and report on it to the class. Some students might like to read aloud passages they consider especially effective.

Writing About History

Interview. Aside from his work at Howard University Law School, Charles H. Houston (1895–1950) had a long, active legal career. Students might like to research two particular events in his life: his 1933 defense in Leesburg, Virginia, of George Crawford, an African American accused of murdering a white woman and his 1938 investigation of racial discrimination and violence at Chickamauga Dam, Tennessee.

Students can write what they have learned about these events in the form of an interview with Houston.

B · A · C · K · G · R · O · U · N · D

Writing About History

Biographical Sketch. Thurgood Marshall led the team of lawyers who won the case overturning legal segregation in public schools. He was the first African American to serve on the Supreme Court.

Have students write a biographical sketch of Thurgood Marshall telling how he contributed to American law and to society beyond the boundaries of civil rights law.

Limited English Proficiency

Building Vocabulary. Help students define *de facto* segregation and *de jure* segregation (see teacher background note in top margin). Discuss with students why de facto segregation is more difficult to eradicate than de jure segregation.

Thinking Critically

Analysis. Have students form hypotheses about why Houston and Marshall first decided to focus on graduate schools rather than on desegregating elementary and high schools. (Possible reason: Their actions would arouse less opposition but still serve as the thin end of the wedge to integration of all schools.)

Connections: Language

The terms *de jure* and *de facto* are Latin phrases. *De jure* means "by law"; *de facto* means "by deed," or "by customary behavior." Applied to racial policy, *de jure* segregation means separating the races by law. *De facto* segregation refers to separation of the races by custom. For example, in northern states many communities had no laws requiring separate schools for blacks and whites, but the economic realities and social customs forced blacks—and often Hispanics, Chinese and other groups—to go to school in their own neighborhoods.

grandfather clause violated the Fifteenth Amendment. A second victory came in 1944 when the Court ruled the all-white primary unconstitutional for the same reason. As a result of these decisions, the number of black registered voters increased in the South despite continuing illegal voter restrictions, such as poll taxes and literacy tests.

NAACP lawyers also sought equal opportunities for black Americans. As a result of African-American pressure, in 1941 President Roosevelt banned discrimination in defense and government work. Seven years later President Truman banned segregation in the armed forces, although it took years for his executive order to be fully implemented. Meanwhile, African Americans continued to face widespread discrimination in civilian employment not only in the South but elsewhere.

Discrimination was also widespread in housing. African Americans faced strong opposition when they tried to buy or rent in all-white neighborhoods. Home owners and new buyers often signed restrictive covenants, neighborhood agreements not to sell or rent to African, Hispanic, or Asian-American people. This type of separation, which developed by custom rather than by law, is called **de facto segregation**— segregation "in fact."

In 1948 the Supreme Court struck a blow against de facto segregation. It ruled that restrictive covenants denied prospective buyers the equal protection of the law and thus were unconstitutional. Informal agreements and social pressure, however, continued to keep black people and other groups from living in white neighborhoods.

Since the 1930s, NAACP lawyers had also been testing segregation established by law. Legal segregation had been strengthened by the *Plessy* v. *Ferguson* decision in 1896, which upheld the constitutionality of laws separating blacks from whites as long as the facilities available to both groups were equal. Many states used the separate but equal doctrine to segregate the races in public schools, transportation, and other facilities.

Houston and Marshall decided to attack segregation in public schools. They targeted graduate schools first. At that time most states did not provide separate law, medical, or other graduate schools. Between 1938 and 1950, the Court ruled in several cases that states had to provide an equal graduate education for black students. But could separate schools, no matter how good they were, ever be equal? NAACP lawyers decided to force the Court to review the constitutionality of the separate but equal doctrine.

Segregated schools were not "separate but equal." States that had segregated school systems spent far more on the education of white students than black students.

Multicultural Perspectives

Perhaps a key incident that sparked the civil rights movement was the death of Emmett Till, a 14-year-old boy killed for speaking to a white woman in Mississippi in 1955. Though the whites charged were acquitted, this marked the first trial in which black Mississippians were permitted to testify against whites. Till's death also brought wide support for the civil rights movement from outside the South.

Constitutional Heritage

The struggle for equal rights used every type of authority provided by the Constitution of the United States. Examples: The judicial branch ruled against segregation in the schools in 1954; the executive branch (President Eisenhower) protected the "Little Rock Nine" in 1957; the legislative branch passed civil and voting rights laws between 1957 and 1965 and the 24th Amendment, banning poll taxes.

NAACP lawyers (from left) George Hayes, Thurgood Marshall, and James Nabrit celebrate the Supreme Court's historic Brown decision.

Brown* v. *Board of Education

In 1952 four NAACP cases challenging segregation in elementary and secondary schools reached the Supreme Court. The cases were consolidated under the name of the first case the Court agreed to hear—*Brown* v. *Board of Education of Topeka, Kansas.*

In the Court hearings, Marshall and a team of NAACP lawyers argued that segregated schools were not equal and could never be made equal. Citing evidence by psychologists and sociologists, they claimed that the fact of being segregated made children feel inferior, no matter how good the facility might be. Thus, children forced to attend segregated schools were deprived of the equal protection of the laws guaranteed by the Fourteenth Amendment.

The defense argued that according to the Tenth Amendment, the states have all the powers that the Constitution neither gives to Congress nor denies to the states. One of the powers not mentioned in the Constitution, and thus reserved to the states, is the authority to establish schools.

Chief Justice Earl Warren delivered the Court's unanimous opinion on May 17, 1954. The Court, Warren said, "must consider public education in the light of . . . its present place in American life." In the Brown decision, which stands as one of the nation's landmarks, Warren wrote:

> *"It is doubtful that any child may be expected to succeed in life if he is denied the opportunity for an education. . . .*
>
> *Does segregation of children in public schools solely on the basis of race . . . deprive the children of the minority group of equal educational opportunities? We believe that it does. . . . [It] generates a feeling of inferiority as to their status in the community that may affect their hearts and minds in a way unlikely ever to be undone."*

The Court concluded that "separate educational facilities are inherently unequal." By destroying the legal basis for segregation, the Brown decision reopened the road to equality.

Massive resistance. The Supreme Court optimistically assumed that the Brown decision would lead to prompt desegregation of schools. In fact, states in the Upper South—Maryland, West Virginia, Kentucky, Missouri, Oklahoma—took steps

Backyard History

Research. Have students interview parents and grandparents to find out whether *de jure* or *de facto* segregation or other types of racial discrimination were practiced in their community during the 1950s and 1960s. They can then find out from relatives or old newspapers in the local library what measures were taken to end these injustices. Do some still exist? Students can report their findings to the rest of the class.

Constitutional Heritage

Activity. Tell students that Chief Justice Earl Warren wanted a unanimous decision in the Brown case. The court was widely split on the issue at the outset and the process by which it was able to reach a consensus is of great interest. Have students research Warren's role in securing unanimity, including the deal struck with Justice Stanley Reed. Students can present oral reports of their findings to the class.

Writing About History

Making Comparisons. Have students review the case of *Plessy* v. *Ferguson*, on page 345, and the case of *Brown* v. *Board of Education of Topeka* on this page. Then ask students to write an essay describing the two cases, comparing the rulings, and explaining why the Supreme Court decision in 1954 was momentous. Have students share their essays. Ask them to consider changes that took place in the nation during the half century between 1896 and 1954 that might account for the Brown decision.

Global Connections

Research. The United States was not the only nation to experience segregation. In the late 1940s South Africa set up a system of rigid racial segregation called *apartheid.* Have students gather information about apartheid, its supporters and opponents, and changes in the system since the early 1990s. Ask them to compare American segregation and apartheid.

Limited English Proficiency

Building Vocabulary. Have students look up the word *civil* in a dictionary and decide which of the several definitions pertains to the term *civil rights.* **(the definition having to do with rights of citizens)** Have them note the origin of *civil* **(from Latin *civis*, meaning of or pertaining to citizens)** and find other words that derive from the Latin word **(civic, civilian, civilization)**.

Section Review

ANSWERS

1. Definition for *de facto segregation* is on text page 754.
2. Easier to challenge explicitly stated law than vaguely defined social customs and informal racism.
3. Thurgood Marshall and team of lawyers able to prove that "separate" in practice means "unequal."
4. Greater strides made in enforcing the Supreme Court decision and in quashing actions of White Citizens Council, Ku Klux Klan, and other segregationists.

Multicultural Perspectives

The Civil Rights Act of 1957 was the result of many compromises in the Senate. Some civil rights leaders wanted to urge President Eisenhower to veto the bill as worthless. Finally, leaders including Martin Luther King, Jr., and Roy Wilkins of the NAACP decided to accept the bill. Wilkins defended his acceptance by saying, *"If you are digging a ditch with a teaspoon and a man comes along and offers you a spade, there is something wrong with your head if you don't take it because he didn't offer you a bulldozer."*

Reduced student page in the Teacher's Edition

to comply with the new "law of the land." So did western states that had permitted segregated schools. But Virginia and the Deep South held back.

To enforce the Brown ruling, in 1955 the Court now insisted that local school boards draw up desegregation plans "with all deliberate speed." Local courts were to enforce compliance.

Still the southern states resisted, arguing that public education was the responsibility of the states, not the federal government. President Eisenhower was reluctant to take sides in the desegregation battle. He believed that voluntary action by southern states, rather than federal force, would lead to the quickest progress with the fewest problems. Virginia and the Deep South showed few signs of undoing segregation, though.

As early as July 1954, the first White Citizens' Council was formed in Mississippi to preserve all-white schools. Other councils sprang up throughout the South. Virginia Senator Harry F. Byrd called for programs of "massive resistance," including the passage of state and local laws to prevent the Court decision from going into effect. Some districts closed schools to prevent integration.

American Voices

"I reached for the rock lying in the middle of the floor. A note was tied to it. I broke the string and unfolded a soiled piece of paper. Scrawled in bold print were the words: 'Stone this time. Dynamite next.'"

—Daisy Bates, Arkansas NAACP

Violence erupted. Membership in the Ku Klux Klan grew. Civil rights supporters were harassed. Lynching increased, with three incidents in Mississippi in 1955, including the murder of black teenager Emmett Till. In early 1956, when Autherine Lucy was admitted to the University of Alabama by a federal court order, rioting students drove her from the campus. Although she was later admitted by a new court order, the university expelled her permanently, claiming it was acting to avoid further violence. But Eisenhower took no action.

Later in 1956, 100 southern members of Congress signed the "Southern Manifesto." They denounced the Court's school desegregation decision as "a clear abuse of judicial power" and urged the states to use "all lawful means" to defy it. Citing the states' rights interpretation of the Constitution, Mississippi, Alabama, Florida, and Georgia declared the Brown decision null and void. Several states passed new measures to protect segregation. According to an Alabama judge, however, the appeal to states' rights was just a smoke screen for racial discrimination.

Civil Rights Act of 1957. Although Eisenhower was reluctant to press for school desegregation, he did propose legislation to support voting rights. The bill met massive resistance by southerners in Congress but was passed with the help of Senate Majority Leader Lyndon B. Johnson of Texas. The Civil Rights Act of 1957—the first since Reconstruction—set up the Civil Rights Commission to investigate voting abuses. The act also gave the federal government the power to seek court orders to stop states from denying black suffrage.

A second law, the Civil Rights Act of 1960, provided for federal court referees to register black voters where a court found a "pattern and practice" of discrimination. It also made interfering with any court order a federal crime.

Crisis at Little Rock. On September 2, 1957, the nation's attention was again drawn to the issue of school segregation. When a federal court order established a plan to integrate Central High School in Little Rock, Arkansas, Governor Orval Faubus of Arkansas called out the National Guard to prevent nine black students from enrolling. Faced with another court order, Faubus later withdrew the troops. But when the students tried to enter the school, a mob attacked them.

Before Little Rock, Eisenhower had said that he could not imagine sending federal troops because "the common sense of Americans will never require it." Now, faced with defiance of federal authority, he ordered paratroopers into Little Rock to protect the students. The soldiers stayed through the school year. For Melba Pattillo Beals, one of the "Little Rock Nine," it was a year of mixed feelings:

Social History

In August 1959 white demonstrators protested the reopening of integrated Central High School in Little Rock and had to be held back by police officers and firefighters. Twenty-nine were arrested for violence or refusing to obey police orders. Governor Faubus urged the demonstrators to "continue the struggle."

"There was a feeling of pride and hope that yes, this is the United States; yes, there is a reason I salute the flag; and it's going to be okay. . . . The troops did not, however, mean the end of harassment. It meant the declaration of war. . . . I worried about . . . which part of the hall to walk in that's the safest. Who's going to hit me with what? Is it going to be hot soup today? . . . How's this day going to go?"

In 1958 Governor Faubus closed all public high schools in Little Rock. They did not reopen as integrated schools until August 1959, after the Supreme Court ruled the closing unconstitutional. That year resistance also ended in Virginia after the courts struck down state laws that had cut off funds to integrated schools. Massive resistance continued, however, in the Deep South.

Despite the resistance to school integration, NAACP lawyers helped with dozens of law suits attacking other aspects of legal segregation. In case after case, the Court struck down segregation in facilities such as public parks, beaches, public housing, golf courses, and local and state transportation systems.

Section Review

1. **Identification.** Define *de facto segregation*.
2. **Analysis.** Why might legal segregation be easier to challenge in court than de facto segregation?
3. **Comprehension.** Why did the Supreme Court overturn the separate but equal doctrine in *Brown v. Board of Education*?
4. **Synthesis.** How might the struggle for school desegregation between 1954 and 1957 have been different if the federal government had acted more forcefully?

28-2 Taking Direct Action

Focus: How did the struggle for equality become a mass movement based on direct action?

"Having to take a certain section [on a bus] because of your race was humiliating, but having to stand up because a particular driver wanted to keep a white person from having to stand was, to my mind, most inhumane. . . .

When the driver saw me still sitting, he asked if I was going to stand up and I said, 'No, I'm not.' And he said, 'Well, if you don't stand up, I'm going to call the police.'

I said, 'You may do that.' . . .

He did get off the bus, and I still stayed where I was. Two policemen came on the bus. One asked me, 'Why don't you stand up?'

And I asked him, 'Why do you push us around?'

He said, 'I do not know, but the law is the law and you're under arrest.'"

In 1955 the drive for civil rights took a new turn in Montgomery, Alabama. There, on December 1, Rosa Parks was arrested for refusing to give up her seat on a city bus to a white man. This was not the first time that Rosa Parks had said no. She had been evicted from a bus in 1943 by the same driver. This time, however, her action set in motion a movement to break down segregation in the Montgomery bus system.

Section 28-2

Objectives

- ***Answer the Focus Question.***
- *Describe King's emergence as a leader in the Montgomery bus boycott.*
- *Identify SNCC and the Freedom Riders.*
- *Relate the confrontation over segregation in Birmingham.*
- *Evaluate government actions to bring equal rights to all citizens between 1955 and 1964.*

Introducing THE SECTION

Ask students to recall examples of citizen protests in American history that they have read about in previous chapters: boycotts of British goods, Boston Tea Party, Stamp Act protests, John Brown's raid, women's suffrage marches, labor strikes.

In this section students will learn how African Americans in the 1950s and 1960s participated in nonviolent protests against discrimination and segregation.

Multicultural Perspectives

Rosa Parks and many African-American leaders attended workshops on social change at the Highlander Folk School in Tennessee. The school was founded in 1932 by Myles Horton, a teacher and community activist who believed that people are not powerless. He initially offered workshops on labor unions, workers' rights, and race relations. In the 1950s and 1960s the center trained civil rights activists. Rosa Parks recalled her experience at Highlander: *"This was the first time in my life I had lived in an atmosphere of complete equality with the members of the other race. I gained there strength to persevere in my work for freedom, not just for blacks but for all oppressed people."* The school continues today, with a variety of agendas.

Developing
THE SECTION

Connections: Literature

Report. Martin Luther King, Jr., drew some of his ideas about nonviolent protest from the writings of Henry David Thoreau. Thoreau protested against the Mexican-American War of the 1840s by refusing to pay the Massachusetts poll tax, denying that obedience to the law was an American's highest responsibility. He wrote "Civil Disobedience" to explain his views.

Have interested students read "Civil Disobedience" and report on Thoreau's ideas to the class. Students can debate Thoreau's famous statement, *"Under a government which imprisons any unjustly, the true place for a just man is also a prison."*

You may wish to tell students that Mohandas Gandhi also read *Civil Disobedience* and was influenced by it. King used Gandhi's tactics (see page 760).

Reduced student page in the Teacher's Edition

Boycotting Buses in Montgomery

Rosa Parks was part of an organized civil rights movement that had been growing for years. She had been the secretary of the Montgomery branch of the NAACP for several years and had organized an NAACP Youth Council. In 1955 she agreed to be a test case in the local fight against segregation. E. D. Nixon, former head of the Montgomery NAACP, recalled: "We knew she was a determined, quiet woman. Once she said yes, we knew that we could go to work."

The day after Parks's arrest, black leaders met at Nixon's request to organize a bus boycott. Many were ministers who, Nixon believed, could help mobilize the people. The Reverend Ralph D. Abernathy was there. So was a newcomer to the community, Dr. Martin Luther King, Jr. Abernathy would take charge of negotiating with the city. At Nixon's suggestion, King was chosen to head the boycott. Nixon recalled,

> *❝ We wanted Dr. King because we knew he had not been here long enough for the city fathers to get hold of him and change his mind. He impressed us as a highly educated man and very honest and he hadn't been here long enough to create jealousy . . . among other ministers. King also believed in collective decision-making. He was not a one-man type of leader. ❞*

The boycott was set for Monday, December 5, 1955—the day of Parks' trial. Initial planning was done by the Women's Political Council, an organization of black professional women founded in the 1940s. By Monday, the council's president, teacher Jo Ann Gibson Robinson, and her students had distributed 35,000 leaflets calling for blacks to boycott public buses. Ministers had delivered the call from their pulpits, too.

On Monday morning, signs appeared at bus stops: "People, don't ride the bus today. Don't ride it for freedom." King and his wife, Coretta, watched bus after bus go by empty. The boycott was a success. But should it—could it—continue? At a meeting that night, the answer from the black community was a resounding yes.

Solidarity. The one-day bus boycott turned into a 382-day struggle to force the city to negotiate with the boycott committee, the Montgomery Improvement Association (MIA). MIA had not called for integration, only for an end to the most degrading practices on buses. Still, the city refused to negotiate, and MIA brought a case in federal court against bus segregation.

As the case made its way through the courts, King set the tone for the boycott—nonviolent re-

The arrest of Rosa Parks led to a long, organized protest against segregation, as the city held out against the boycott and against the pleas of a bus company tired of losing money.

Ain't gonna ride them
buses no more,
Ain't gonna ride no more.
Why don't all the white
folk know
That I ain't gonna
ride no more.

—Montgomery boycotters

Connections: Music

Those who protested, boycotted, sat-in, and marched for racial equality often used songs to bolster their courage and to show their unity. The most popular song was a spiritual sung by striking black tobacco workers in the 1940s. Its title was "I'll Be All Right." Folk singer Pete Seeger transformed it into "We Shall Overcome," which became the anthem of the civil rights movement.

Today, it is a universal song of protest. It was sung by South Korean protestors in 1987 and 1988, when they forced dictator Chun Doo Hwan to call free elections. It was sung by Lebanese during their civil war. At Vietnam War protests, the song became a call for international peace and nuclear disarmament. The non-violent movement of Northern Ireland adopted the song. It has also been part of the black struggle for equality in South Africa.

Thinking Critically

Have students debate the question: In a democracy, should people who oppose injustice resort to breaking the law to improve conditions?

Multicultural Perspectives

Discussion. In the 1890s, two approaches to gaining equality were debated in the African-American community. One approach was advocated by Booker T. Washington, the other by W.E.B. Du Bois. Have students reread pages 346–347 about the two approaches. Then have the class discuss whether these two men would have supported direct action for civil rights.

sistance to racial segregation. He rejected hatred and violence and called for self-respect and love. He told boycotters:

> *"If we are arrested every day, if we are exploited every day, if we are trampled over every day, don't ever let anyone pull you so low as to hate them. We must use the weapon of love. We must have compassion and understanding for those who hate us."*

King's stress on love and nonviolence drew sympathy and support for the boycott from Americans of all races.

The boycott proved almost 100 percent effective. Boycotters formed car pools, hitchhiked, or walked. They raised funds to buy vehicles to transport people to and from work. Funds also flowed in from black churches and organizations, especially the NAACP, as well as from sympathetic whites in Montgomery and elsewhere.

The boycott went on despite tension and violence. Police harassed drivers in the MIA car pool. King's house and then Nixon's house were bombed. Finally, in December 1956 the Supreme Court let stand an opinion of a lower court that bus segregation was unconstitutional. Segregated seating was abolished, and MIA ended its boycott.

Violence ended slowly, though. Bombs went off at four churches and at the homes of two anti-segregation ministers, one black and one white. Nonetheless, the Montgomery boycott had shown what could be accomplished by organized protests.

The boycott also thrust King to the forefront of the struggle. His philosophy of nonviolent protest inspired thousands to challenge discrimination with direct action.

American Voices

> *"The first thing that happened to whites like us who were sympathetic to the boycott was that we lost our businesses. People didn't come to us. We got a reputation."*
>
> —Virginia Foster Durr

Southern Christian Leadership Conference. In January 1957 leaders of the civil rights movement, almost all of them black Baptist preachers, formed the Southern Christian Leadership Conference (SCLC) to continue the struggle for civil rights. King became its president. Two years later he left his church in Montgomery to devote all of his time to the SCLC. "The time has come," he told his congregation, "for a broad, bold advance of the southern campaign for equality."

That campaign would not be as easy as many SCLC members expected. During the Montgomery bus boycott, Fred Shuttlesworth, a Birmingham minister, recalled, "All of us had the idea that all you had to do was just shame the conscience of the country." Before long, though, they learned that shame was not enough. Only through direct action could they focus the nation's attention on the evils of segregation and bring pressure on those who supported the system. As Shuttlesworth later said,

> *"A rattlesnake don't commit suicide, and ball teams don't strike themselves out. You got to* put *them out."*

Student Sit-Ins: Sparking Mass Protest

While King and the SCLC mobilized people, student sit-ins set off the largest direct-action protests of the civil rights movement. Sit-ins were not new. They had been used by the Congress of Racial Equality (CORE) and by college students since the 1940s to desegregate facilities. But the demonstrations had been small and had never caught fire. By the late 1950s, the Brown decision and the Montgomery boycott had occurred. Everywhere, the issue of civil rights was in the air.

On February 1, 1960, four black college students sat down and requested service at Woolworth's lunch counter in Greensboro, North Carolina. When the waitress refused to serve them, they sat there until the store closed. They returned daily, along with other students, until the store ended segregation.

Limited English Proficiency

Building Vocabulary. In the passage on this page beginning "If you want to say . . ." Dr. Martin Luther King, Jr., is using a metaphor, an implied comparison, to describe himself. **Ask:** What does King mean by comparing himself to a drum major? What does a drum major do? **(leads a parade)** What special gift of King's might be compared to what a drum major does? **(his eloquence, which directed and encouraged the "band" of civil rights workers)** What other metaphors can you think of to describe King's role as a leader in the civil rights movement?

Thinking Critically

Analysis. Harvey Gantt spoke for a generation of southern African Americans when he said, "Unlike our elders, we knew no fear." Have students discuss possible reasons why that generation seemed fearless in seeking equal rights.

Social History

Various publications and workshops prepared participants for nonviolent action against segregation. A group called the Fellowship of Reconciliation (FOR) printed several thousand pamphlets, in comic-book format, entitled *Martin Luther King and the Montgomery Story.* These offered instruction in passive resistance and in direct action against segregation, and were distributed throughout the South. James Lawson, an African-American divinity student, and Glenn Smiley, a white FOR minister, offered workshops on nonviolence across the South. They taught students and other activists, such as Diane Nash, the tactics of passive resistance.

Reduced student page in the Teacher's Edition

THE AMERICAN SPIRIT

Martin Luther King, Jr.

Striding Toward Freedom

In 1955, when Dr. Martin Luther King, Jr., became a leader of the Montgomery bus boycott, he was twenty-six years old and fresh out of Boston University's School of Theology. The boycott gave King the chance to test his commitment to using Christian love and nonviolent action to achieve social reform.

King's philosophy of nonviolence was rooted in the teachings of Christianity. Then, in college, he heard a lecture on Mohandas K. Gandhi, the leader of India's fight for independence from British rule. Gandhi had used passive resistance in which protesters engaged in sit-ins and other nonviolent actions. He had met hate and violence with love.

The lecture electrified King, and he read Gandhi's writings. Nonviolent resistance, King came to feel, "was the only morally and practically sound method open to oppressed people in their struggle for freedom." After the Montgomery boycott, that method was widely adopted by civil rights workers.

As one of the leading figures in the civil rights movement, King traveled thousands of miles annually, addressing two or three audiences a day. He spoke eloquently. Hearing him, one observer wrote, "was astonishing, the man spoke with such force." In 1964 he was awarded the Nobel Peace Prize for his nonviolent efforts to end racial injustice.

Despite his stress on nonviolence, King became the target of violence. Two months before his assassination in 1968, he spoke about what he would want said at his funeral:

"If you want to say that I was a drum major, say that I was a drum major for justice; say that I was a drum major for peace; I was a drum major for righteousness."

As news of the Greensboro sit-in spread, the tactic took hold elsewhere. Eventually it would become a nationwide campaign. Sit-ins at restaurants became "read-ins" at libraries, "wade-ins" at pools, and "kneel-ins" at churches. Everywhere, the protestors practiced nonviolence. They were polite and refused to retaliate, even when spattered with food or burned with cigarettes.

Violence and the threat of jail did not stop the movement. In fact, jail time became a "badge of honor." Harvey Gantt of Charleston, South Carolina, who had heard about the sit-ins elsewhere and then led his own, recalled the responsibility he and others felt "to do something to change the system." Unlike our elders, he said, "We knew no fear." For Diane Nash, who led the campaign to desegregate lunch counters in Nashville, Tennessee, the sit-ins changed her as well as society:

"The movement had a way of reaching inside me and bringing out things that I never knew were there. Like courage, and love for people. It was a real experience to be

Connections: Politics

John Kennedy's successful efforts to gain the release of Martin Luther King, Jr., jailed in Georgia in October 1960, and his call to King's wife, Coretta Scott King, to express his support and sympathy, had an enormous impact on black voters. At the start of the election campaign, Kennedy had been the least popular candidate among registered black voters. On election day seven out of ten African Americans who went to the polls voted for him.

seeing a group of people who would put their bodies between you and danger. And to love people that you work with enough that you would put your body between them and danger. . . . When the time came to go to jail, I was far too busy to be afraid.”

The sit-ins showed that there was a vital role for young people in the civil rights movement. And as they got involved, they changed the movement. Determined to confront discrimination wherever it occurred, the students focused on direct action rather than working through the courts. Instead of the gradual solutions to segregation sought by groups like the NAACP, they called for “freedom *now!*”

SNCC. By mid-April 1960 thousands of black students as well as sympathetic white students had taken part in sit-ins in the South. On April 16 student leaders of the movement formed the Student Nonviolent Coordinating Committee (SNCC) to coordinate the sit-in effort.

Ella J. Baker assisted in the formation of SNCC (pronounced “snick”). A former organizer for the NAACP and now executive secretary of the SCLC, she set up the April meeting and stressed the importance of working together to set goals and tactics. “In the long run,” she said, “people themselves are the only protection they have against violence or injustice.”

Members of SNCC became “the shock troops of the revolution” by going directly to the people. SNCC representatives moved into communities all over the Deep South. Joined by local African Americans, they organized community networks to protest against racism and to register people to vote. Despite terror and violence directed against them, they helped the civil rights movement take root and grow throughout the South.

Freedom Riders

CORE, headed by James Farmer, helped keep up the pressure against segregation with a “sit-in on wheels.” In May 1961 CORE sent a group of black and white “Freedom Riders” to travel by bus through the South.

One of CORE's purposes in the Freedom Ride was to test the new President, John F. Kennedy. They wanted to see whether he would enforce rulings by the Supreme Court and the Interstate Commerce Commission (ICC) that segregation in interstate travel was illegal. In his election campaign, Kennedy had promised to support civil rights, and the votes of African Americans had been a major factor in his victory. Now, however, he was moving very slowly on civil rights, perhaps hoping to win southern support in Congress for his New Frontier bills.

At workshops on nonviolence across the South, black student activists learned how to use the tactic of passive resistance at sit-ins. Nonviolence required discipline, courage, and faith.

Connections: Literature

Book Report. In 1919 Mary Church Terrell wrote in her diary about her plan to tell her life story. *“Be sure to be courageous and tell everything,”* she said. Her book, published in 1940, was the first full-length autobiography by an African-American woman. In 1952, ninety-year-old Terrell, carrying a picket sign in one hand and a cane in the other, led a group picketing restaurants in Washington, D.C., that discriminated against African Americans.

Interested students may read *A Colored Woman in a White World* and other sources about Terrell's life and write a report describing inequalities that blacks faced between 1863 and 1954 and Terrell's efforts to fight discrimination.

Active Learning

Skits. Divide the class into small groups. Each group is to imagine that it is a team of SNCC “shock troops.” Groups can prepare and perform skits showing the SNCC team preparing for its trip, framing its purposes and devising its plans; its encounter with African Americans and whites in a southern community; or its report to other teams after the trip about what it has experienced and achieved.

Writing About History

Editorial. Have students write editorials about Attorney General Robert Kennedy sending federal marshalls to Alabama. The editorials can either praise Kennedy for taking action to try to cool off a dangerous situation or condemn him for interfering in state matters.

Thinking Critically

Evaluation. Refer students to James Farmer's words on this page. Have the class discuss the issue: Should the Freedom Riders have agreed to a cooling-off period? Why or why not?

Social History

The Fellowship of Reconciliation (FOR) was founded in 1914 at England's Cambridge University by Quaker Henry Hodgkin. The FOR was established to promote pacifism and international understanding. The first American chapter was established in 1915. The group sponsored the first Freedom Ride in 1947. The FOR also worked closely with Dr. Martin Luther King, Jr., to plan the Montgomery bus boycott in 1955. The FOR has helped create other groups to work for social change, including the American Civil Liberties Union (ACLU), the National Conference of Christians and Jews, the Workers Defense League, and the Congress of Racial Equality.

Reduced student page in the Teacher's Edition

Civil Rights and Black Power Organizations

Organization	Founded	Major goals
National Association for the Advancement of Colored People (NAACP)	1909	End lynching, work through the courts to protect civil rights of African Americans
National Urban League	1911	Solve economic and social problems of urban African Americans
Nation of Islam (Black Muslims)	1931	Advocate racial separation, black pride, black self-sufficiency
Congress of Racial Equality (CORE)	1942	End segregation and discrimination through direct nonviolent action
Southern Christian Leadership Conference (SCLC)	1957	End segregation and discrimination through direct nonviolent action
Student Nonviolent Coordinating Committee (SNCC)	1960	Coordinate direct nonviolent action, organize communities, protest segregation and discrimination
Black Panthers	1966	Create programs for the black poor, defend them against the police, demand a separate black nation

The Freedom Riders left Washington, D.C., on May 4, headed for New Orleans. They never got there. In Alabama mobs beat the riders, paralyzing one of them for life, and burned one of the buses. Neither the police nor the federal government, which knew in advance about plans to attack the riders, did anything to stop the violence.

The Freedom Ride was far from over, though. A group of black and white SNCC members went to Alabama to continue the ride. In late May they were arrested and forced to leave the state. They returned and resumed their trip, only to be attacked in Montgomery by whites with baseball bats and pipes. By now, however, their story was making headlines around the world. From his hospital bed, white Freedom Rider Jim Zwerg told a television reporter:

> *"We are going on to New Orleans no matter what happens. We are dedicated to this. We will take hitting. We'll take beatings. We're willing to accept death. But we are going to keep coming until we can ride anywhere in the South . . . as Americans."*

Anxious to prevent further violence, Attorney General Robert Kennedy sent federal marshals to Montgomery. He also tried to get Farmer to stop the Freedom Ride and agree to have a cooling-off period to ease tension. After talking with the Freedom Riders, Farmer refused. "We'd been cooling off for 350 years, . . . and if we cooled off any more, we'd be in a deep freeze," he observed.

The Freedom Ride continued. Whenever the riders were arrested, new riders arrived and were also arrested. Throughout the summer, more than 300 Freedom Riders traveled through the Deep South, trying to desegregate travel facilities. In November, at the Attorney General's request, the ICC again banned segregation in interstate buses, trains, and terminals. Most quietly complied, but some continued to resist.

Growing Pressure for Change

The federal government had done little to support the civil rights movement until prodded into action by the Freedom Riders in the summer of 1961. A year later, the government was again forced into

Connections: Literature

Martin Luther King, Jr.'s *Letter From a Birmingham Jail* is considered one of the most eloquent statements by a public figure in American history.

Thinking Critically

Evaluation. Have the class discuss the effect that television had on the struggle for civil rights. **Ask:** What difference would it have made if there had been no coverage of violence and brutality?

action, this time by James Meredith, an African-American student who was determined to attend the all-white University of Mississippi. An air force veteran, Meredith set as his goal "total victory . . . over discrimination."

When the University of Mississippi refused to accept Meredith, the NAACP filed a suit that worked its way up to the Supreme Court. In September 1962 the Court ordered the university to desegregate. Governor Ross Barnett defied the order, vowing he would never allow Meredith to enroll. Federal marshals sent to enforce the law were attacked by more than 2,000 rioters. Federal troops finally broke up the mob, but only after two deaths and many injuries.

Meredith became the first black student to enroll at the university. Federal marshals stayed on campus to guard him. When he graduated in 1963, he wore a Ross Barnett campaign button that said "Never, never"— but he turned it upside down.

Confrontation in Birmingham. An even more dramatic confrontation began in Birmingham, Alabama, in April 1963. King had come to that city to lead nonviolent demonstrations against segregation and job discrimination. Birmingham, King later said, was "probably the most thoroughly segregated city in the United States." Desegregation there could influence the actions of other southern cities.

Thousands of African Americans, many of them young children, took part in the protest marches. At first, the police, led by Commissioner Eugene "Bull" Connor, arrested and jailed protesters, including children. Then police used fire hoses and police dogs. Millions of people were shocked by the daily newspaper and television pictures of police brutality. No longer could southern racism be easily ignored.

"WHAT DO YOU MEAN, 'NOT SO FAST'?"

King was arrested during the demonstrations. While he was in jail, several white Birmingham ministers issued a statement calling the demonstrations "unwise and untimely." In his reply, King wrote eloquently of the need for such action and the goals of the civil rights movement:

> *" I have never yet engaged in a direct action movement that was 'well-timed,' according to the timetable of those who have not suffered unduly from the disease of segregation. For years now I have heard the word 'Wait!' It rings in the ear of every Negro with piercing familiarity. This 'wait' has almost always meant 'never.' "*

In May, King and the city's business leaders negotiated a settlement. They agreed to desegregate some public facilities, hire blacks on an equal basis, and create a biracial committee in order to work out a timetable for further desegregation in Birmingham.

The issue was not fully resolved, however. City officials tried to scrap the agreement the business community had made. Bombs exploded at King's hotel and at his brother's home. When angry blacks rioted in protest, local and state police charged in with clubs swinging. Kennedy moved troops close to the city and threatened to intervene to preserve order. Finally, state and local officials restored peace, and a newly elected city government honored the agreement.

After the Birmingham crisis, nonviolent protests against segregation spread throughout the South. By the end of 1963, there had been more than 900 protests in the southern states. There were also more than 20,000 arrests, 35 bombings and 10 related deaths. Demonstrations had also occurred in the

Analyzing Primary Sources

Martin Luther King, Jr. Refer students to the last three sentences in the primary source on this page—part of Martin Luther King, Jr.'s "Letter from a Birmingham Jail."

Ask students to use the case of James Meredith to discuss how "wait" threatened to mean "never." Have them use the sit-ins to illustrate a kind of waiting that King accepted. **Ask:** What is the difference between the two kinds of waiting? **(In the case of Meredith, consider initial efforts to prevent his registration, student rioting, and need for federal troops for protection. In the case of sit-ins, consider the movement's tactics in terms of passive resistance. The sit-in movement relied on patience. If Meredith had waited for university acceptance without federal prodding, he might never have been admitted.)**

Connections: Literature

Activity. At the March on Washington, Martin Luther King, Jr., made a speech that transcended politics and became fine literature. From the library, get a copy of King's "I Have a Dream" speech. Select a few students to make a dramatic reading of the speech before the class. Have the entire class discuss key passages.

Writing About History

Obituary or Editorial. Have students research the murder of Medgar Evers and write about it in one of two forms: (a) an obituary summing up Evers's life and accomplishments and discussing the probable reasons behind his death; (b) an editorial describing and commentary on the murder and the circumstances that caused it.

Active Learning

Making Posters. Have students create posters urging people to join the March on Washington. The posters should relate to the struggle for equal rights and the opportunity for people to make their voices heard.

Connections: Music

At 10:00 A.M. on the day of the March on Washington, folksingers warmed up the crowd. Joan Baez sang "Oh Freedom." Odetta sang "I'm on My Way," and in his excitement, Josh White joined in with her. The folk trio Peter, Paul, and Mary sang a Bob Dylan song, "Blowin' in the Wind." Dylan himself followed with a song he had just written about the death of Medgar Evers. These performers were followed by the SNCC Freedom Singers from Albany, New York.

Pictures of these efforts to end segregation and discrimination flashed across the nation's newspapers and television news shows: Freedom Riders in Montgomery, 1961; fire hoses being turned on civil rights marchers, Birmingham, 1963; marcher for voting rights on Selma-to-Montgomery march, 1965.

North to protest unequal job opportunities and segregated schools.

Kennedy Takes Action

On June 11, 1963, President Kennedy finally took a strong public stand in the struggle for civil rights. "Are we to say . . . that this is a land of the free except for Negroes; that we have no second class citizens except Negroes?" he asked Americans in a television address. "Now the time has come for this nation to fulfill its promise."

Kennedy announced that he was sending a civil rights bill to Congress to provide "the kind of equality of treatment which we would want ourselves." Perhaps in reaction to the speech, the next day Medgar Evers, a prominent NAACP official in Mississippi, was murdered.

March on Washington. Civil rights groups called for a massive march on Washington to urge Congress to enact the President's bill and to protest against continuing job discrimination. Religious groups and labor organizations joined in. So did many people won to the cause of human rights by the courageous example of the civil rights workers.

More than 200,000 people—of all races and from all parts of the country—took part in the March on Washington for Jobs and Freedom on August 28. It was the greatest civil rights demonstration to date. Emily Rock, a black high school student, basked in a glow of optimism. She wrote:

> *“All around, in the face of everyone, there was this sense of hope for the future—that this march was the* big *step in the right direction. It could be heard in the voices of the people singing. It poured out in smiles.”*

Dr. King captured the mood of the day in his famous "I have a Dream" speech:

> *“In spite of the difficulties and frustrations of the moment I still have a dream. . . .*
>
> *I have a dream that one day this nation will rise up and live out the true meaning of its creed: 'We hold these truths to be self-evident: that all men are created equal.' . . .*
>
> *I have a dream that my four little children will one day live in a nation where they*

Connections: Politics

Edwin O. Guthman, Attorney General Kennedy's special assistant for public information, recalled that the Civil Rights Bill of 1964 had its roots in the 1963 confrontations in Birmingham. Justice Department officials told Kennedy, *"You've got to have a civil rights bill."* And he said, *"Why not, let's do it."* President Kennedy felt that because of public response to the graphic television pictures from Birmingham, there was a chance of getting the bill through. *"One thing about both Kennedys was they didn't like to tilt at windmills. They wanted to do something and have a chance of getting it done."*

In addition to the thousands of participants in the March on Washington, millions of television viewers watched the day's events on CBS. Both NBC and ABC broke programming to broadcast King's speech.

will not be judged by the color of their skin but by the content of their character. ❞

Much of white America, however, continued to reject King's vision. In September, eighteen days after the march, dynamite blew apart a Baptist Church in Birmingham. Four young girls were killed and twenty others were injured. The bombing shocked Coretta Scott King into realizing "how intense the opposition was."

The nation would never know whether President Kennedy could have succeeded in getting his civil rights bill passed. His assassination in November shifted the responsibility to his successor, Lyndon Johnson.

A second Emancipation Proclamation. When he was Senate majority leader, Lyndon Johnson had maneuvered two civil rights bills through the Senate: the Civil Rights Acts of 1957 and 1960. Now, using all his powers of persuasion, he pushed the Kennedy bill through Congress.

The Civil Rights Act of 1964 banned discrimination in restaurants, hotels, and other public accommodations. It required private employers and federally-assisted programs to end discrimination. An Equal Employment Opportunity Commission would oversee the ban on job discrimination by race, religion, or sex. Finally, the act gave the Attorney General the power to bring suits to require school desegregation.

Hailed as a second Emancipation Proclamation, the new law marked the nation's greatest step toward equality since Lincoln freed the slaves in 1863. It put the federal government squarely on the side of the fight for equality.

Section Review

1. Comprehension. Describe at least two steps African Americans took in response to the arrest of Rosa Parks. How successful was each step?

2. Analysis. Ella Baker said, "People themselves are the only protection they have against violence or injustice." What do you think she meant? Give at least two examples from this section to support your conclusion.

3. Synthesis. How might the struggle for civil rights have been different if Dr. King had not adopted a strategy of nonviolent resistance?

Backyard History

Interview. Have students interview parents, other relatives, and friends who lived at the time of the March on Washington and the "I Have a Dream" speech. Students can ask about emotional reactions to this event. Perhaps some students have relatives who attended the march and heard the speech. If so, these students may want to invite their relatives to school to share their experiences with the entire class.

Section Review

ANSWERS

1. Answers may include one-day bus boycott, continuing boycott, and suit in federal courts, all successful. In 1956 segregation on buses was declared unconstitutional.
2. Probably meant that only a vigilant people could protect themselves in cases where government was reluctant and/or slow to act. Cite bus boycotts; sit-ins; SNCC's activities; Freedom Riders; protest marches in Birmingham.
3. Some may answer that struggle would have led to far more violence, would have enlisted fewer white supporters. Also, Kennedy might not have taken action in 1963. Others may think greater change would have happened faster.

Section 28-3

Objectives

- ***Answer the Focus Question.***
- *Describe the effect of television in the effort to gain voting rights.*
- *Analyze the relationship between racism and poverty.*
- *Describe the "Black Power" movement and Martin Luther King's reaction to it.*

Introducing THE SECTION

Point out to students that, in spite of the exhilaration of African Americans when they heard King's "I Have a Dream" speech, the United States had a long way to go to make King's dream reality. Some African-American leaders doubted the possibility of an American society free from racial discrimination.

Malcolm X, supporter of a separate nation for black Americans, admired the speech, but had a sense of foreboding. He said, *"You know, this dream of King's is going to be a nightmare before it's over."* Tell students that they will now learn the extent to which Malcolm X's prophecy was fulfilled.

B · A · C · K · G · R · O · U · N · D

Connections: Politics

The Freedom Summer project received help from a number of lawyers' groups—the NAACP Legal Defense Fund, the American Jewish Committee, and the Lawyers' Constitutional Defense Committee (LCDC). One young lawyer the LCDC recruited was Edward Koch, who later served several terms as the mayor of New York City. When Koch first ran for mayor, he pointed with pride to his Mississippi summer, and it played a significant role in his being elected.

Reduced student page in the Teacher's Edition

28-3 From Civil Rights to Black Power

Focus: How and why did the struggle for equality change in the mid-1960s?

In 1960 Bob Moses, a young black teacher in New York, saw a newspaper photo of the Greensboro sit-in.

> *"The students in that picture had a certain look on their faces, sort of sullen, angry, determined. Before, the Negro in the South had always looked on the defensive. . . . This time they were taking the initiative. They were kids my age, and I knew this had something to do with my own life."*

Soon Bob Moses was working with SNCC in a campaign to help blacks in Mississippi register to vote. Hundreds of young people, mostly black but some white, went to the Deep South during the mid-1960s to work on the campaign. The work and the example of courage and conviction set by young and old, black and white, was to change southern race relations forever.

Working for Voting Rights

For years the NAACP had been working to help southern blacks exercise the right to vote. In the 1960 presidential election, less than 25 percent of the southern blacks eligible to vote were able to register. The worst situation existed in Mississippi. Some 45 percent of Mississippians were black, but only 5 percent were registered to vote. Unfair use of literacy tests and fear of reprisals were to blame.

Bob Moses set up SNCC's first project of voter registration in Mississippi in 1961. White resistance was fierce. SNCC workers were beaten, arrested, and jailed. One was killed. The following year, SNCC joined forces with CORE and the NAACP in a renewed campaign.

It took courage to register. Fannie Lou Hamer, a timekeeper and sharecropper on a cotton plantation, recalled her experience:

> *"I traveled 26 miles to the county courthouse to try to register to become a first-class citizen. . . . [After I returned home,] my husband came and said this plantation owner said I would have to leave if I didn't go down and withdraw. About that time the man walked up. . . . He said, 'Fannie Lou, you have been to the courthouse to try to register. . . . We are not ready for this in Mississippi.' I said, 'I didn't register for you, I tried to register for myself.'"*

Fannie Lou Hamer lost her job. She left the plantation and began registering other black voters.

Freedom Summer. In the summer of 1964, SNCC and other civil rights groups in Mississippi launched a massive campaign called "Freedom Summer" to register voters for the election of 1964. To focus national attention on the situation in Mississippi, hundreds of young white volunteers, especially from the North, were invited to help. Time and time again, they met with violence.

On June 21, 1964, three civil rights workers—James Chaney, a black CORE worker, and Michael Schwerner and Andrew Goodman, two white volunteers from New York—were arrested in Philadelphia, Mississippi. They were released from jail late at night, seized by the county deputy sheriff and members of the Ku Klux Klan, beaten, shot to death, and buried in an earthen dam.

The disappearance of Chaney, Schwerner, and Goodman horrified the nation. President Johnson immediately ordered the FBI to find the three men.

Citizenship

Volunteers for the Freedom Summer project attended a week-long training session. Each volunteer was told to bring $500 for bail and enough cash to cover living expenses, medical expenses that might occur, and transportation home at the end of the summer. The volunteers were warned by SNCC Executive Director James Forman, *"I may be killed. You may be killed. The whole staff may go."* Because of the danger, all civil rights workers, including the summer volunteers, were required to call Freedom Summer headquarters at regular intervals. If workers did not call within fifteen minutes of the appointed time, the local police, the FBI, and the Justice Department were notified.

A woman trying to register to vote for the first time in 1964 was rejected by officials. With enforcement of the Voting Rights Act of 1965, the number of African Americans who were able to register and vote soared.

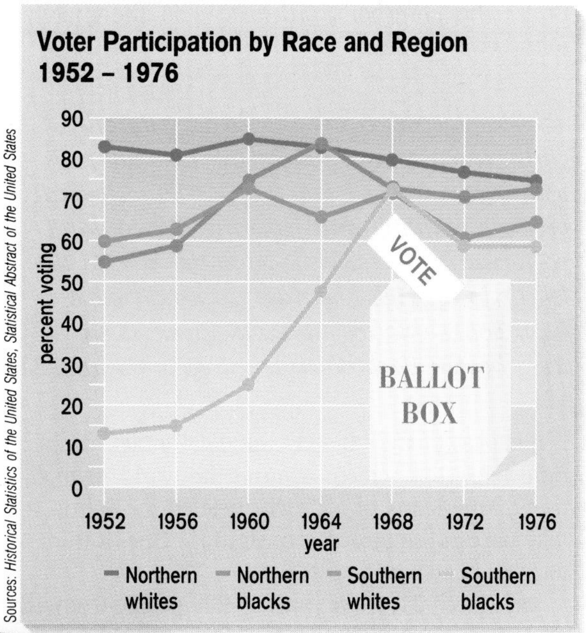

Aware that five black men, including Medgar Evers, had already lost their lives in voting campaigns, John Lewis of SNCC commented angrily, "It is a shame that national concern is aroused only after two white boys are missing." Ultimately the bodies were found, and seven people, including the deputy sheriff, went to jail.

The murders spread fear among Freedom Summer workers, but few quit. The incident, one volunteer said, made most of them "more determined to stay . . . and fight the evil system that people have to live under here." Their determination changed the attitudes of many African Americans who met them. Unita Blackwell, who became the mayor of the town where she had been denied the right to vote for much of her life, recalled:

> *"Students came and we wasn't a closed society anymore. They came to talk . . . that we had a right to register to vote, we had a right to stand up for our rights. That's a whole new era for us. . . . Hadn't anybody said that to us, in that open way, like what happened in 1964."*

Bloody Sunday. In early 1965 the SCLC joined the campaign for voting rights. It planned demonstrations in Selma, Alabama, where SNCC and local groups had been working since the early 1960s.

Day after day, Martin Luther King, Jr., led marchers to the Selma courthouse to register to vote. The sheriff barred their way and had them arrested when they refused to disperse. When King was arrested, children marched to protest. On television, Americans watched massive arrests and children being dragged off to jail. "There are more Negroes in jail with me than there are on the voting rolls," King wrote.

On March 7, some 600 protesters began a march to Montgomery to state their case to Governor George Wallace. On a bridge east of Selma, they were confronted by the Alabama highway patrol,

Developing

THE SECTION

Thinking Critically

Analysis. Have students discuss the following question: Why did Freedom Summer workers and other civil rights activists refuse to meet violence with violence? (Answers may include that they had learned how to use the tactic of passive resistance at workshops on nonviolence. They were well-disciplined and had faith in the use of nonviolent protest to challenge discrimination. They knew they would lose the sympathy of the country if they resorted to violence.)

Limited English Proficiency

Analyzing a Graph. Refer students to the graph on this page. **Ask:**

1. What does the graph show?
2. What do the colored lines on the graph represent? **(race and region)**
3. What percent of southern blacks voted in 1956? **(about 15 percent)** Northern blacks? **(about 62 percent)** What accounts for the difference? **(Terrorism and literacy tests in the South prevented many blacks from voting.)**
4. What percent of southern blacks voted in 1968? **(about 70 percent)** Northern blacks? **(about the same)** What accounts for the increase in black voter participation in the South? **(enforcement of Voting Rights Act of 1965 and 24th Amendment, and efforts to register black voters)**

Writing About History

News Articles. Have students write brief newspaper articles reporting civil rights news from Mississippi and Alabama. Students can write articles about events in 1964–1965, including Freedom Summer and the march from Selma to Montgomery. Encourage students to do research to report about various incidents that occurred. Have students read each other's articles and comment on them.

Limited English Proficiency

Making Time Charts. Have students work in pairs to prepare time charts of events in the movement for civil rights from the 1940s to 1964. The charts should have two headings: Date and Event. The charts should begin with Roosevelt banning discrimination in defense and government work in 1941, and end with the Civil Rights Act of 1964. Students can complete the charts after they read Section 3.

Discuss the charts by asking students what trends they see regarding African-American organization for civil rights and government support for civil rights.

Multicultural Perspectives

John Lewis, a Baptist minister, served as head of SNCC from 1963 to 1966. After leaving SNCC he administered the Voter Education Project, which coordinated voter education drives and provided assistance to elected black officials in the South. He served as an official with ACTION, the government agency that was responsible for volunteer activities such as VISTA, during Jimmy Carter's presidency, and from 1981 to 1986 was a city councilman in Atlanta, Georgia. In 1986 he was elected to Congress and reelected in 1988.

Reduced student page in the Teacher's Edition

under the governor's orders to stop the march. John Lewis recalled:

> “*The troopers came toward us with billy clubs, tear gas, and bullwhips, trampling us with horses. . . . I saw people rolling, heard people screaming and hollering. We couldn't go forward. We couldn't go to the side, to the left or to the right, because we would have been going into the Alabama River, so we were beaten back down the streets of Selma.*”

Pictures of the "Bloody Sunday" attack flashed onto television screens around the world. Sympathetic Americans of all races headed for Selma to take part in the next demonstration. One, a minister, was beaten and killed.

On March 21, more than 25,000 people from all over the nation took part in a march from Selma to Montgomery. Television crews came along to record it. President Johnson ordered the Alabama National Guard and military police to protect the marchers. Even so, a civil rights worker was killed.

Voting Rights Act of 1965. Several days before the Selma march, President Johnson had asked a special joint session of Congress to pass a law guaranteeing every American the right to vote. "All of us," he declared, "must overcome bigotry and injustice." He ended his plea with words from the anthem of the civil rights movement: "And we shall overcome." Congress passed the bill in August.

In the Voting Rights Act of 1965, the federal government acted to ensure the constitutional rights of African Americans. The law banned literacy tests and other measures that disenfranchised voters. It also gave the Attorney General the power to send federal examiners to register voters, and poll watchers to observe the fairness of elections.

The new law, combined with the Twenty-fourth Amendment, which banned poll taxes, opened voting booths to black voters in the South. Within two years, 430,000 blacks had registered to vote. As a result, African Americans began to be elected to office. One of the first was Julian Bond, a member of SNCC, who was elected to the Georgia House of Representatives in 1965.

Outbreak of Violence

The Civil Rights Acts of 1964 and 1965 had removed the most blatant forms of racial discrimination. But laws barring segregation and protecting voting rights did not end racism and poverty. Blacks in Harlem had voted for years, but they still lived in slums. The struggle for equality and economic opportunity, it was clear, was far from over.

Racism and poverty. A tragic fact of American society has been that racism breeds discrimination, and discrimination closes the doors to education and employment opportunities for its victims, thus reinforcing racist stereotypes. This vicious circle, popularly thought to be largely limited to the South, affected the whole country. Beginning in the 1940s, more than 5 million African Americans moved from farms and small towns in the South to northern cities, seeking better jobs and a freer racial climate.

Fifty percent of African Americans now lived outside the South, mostly in cities. But most migrants had merely traded rural poverty for urban poverty. The United States was changing from an industrial economy to a service economy. As a result, unskilled workers in manufacturing were less and less in demand, and jobs were hard to find.

The migrants also faced de facto segregation in housing and schools, the result of residential discrimination. African Americans were confined to black "ghettos" because whites refused to rent or sell them housing in white sections. Ghetto housing and schools were crowded, inferior, and often unsafe. Health care services were inadequate.

These deep-seated problems remained unsolved, waiting for a spark to ignite action. Roger Wilkins, who worked in the Justice Department, later wrote:

> “*Poor black people in the North had watched their TV sets just like everybody else and had seen progress made in the South. . . . Then they saw the Congress pass these laws in '64, '65. When they looked around, they saw that nothing, absolutely nothing, was changing in their lives. They were still poor, they were still jobless, they still*

Multicultural Perspectives

Like the Los Angeles riot, the Detroit riot was sparked by longstanding black grievances and increasing tension between the mostly white police force and the black community. More than 4,000 paratroopers were called in. When the five-day riot ended, 43 people were dead, and between 300 and 600 were wounded. As a result of fires, more than 5,000 people were left homeless. Property losses reached $45 million.

Ed Vaughn, a member of a revolutionary black group in Detroit, declared: *"It wasn't Black Power that caused the rebellion, it was the lack of power that caused the rebellions around the country. People did not see any hope for themselves. . . . We had no access to government."*

Thinking Critically

Analysis. Ask students where the civil rights movement of the 1950s and early 1960s was largely centered, in the North or the South? (South) In the mid- and late 1960s where did much of the rioting take place? (North) Ask students to explain this trend. (Legal segregation in the South was easier to change through nonviolent tactics and laws than de facto segregation in the North, which resulted from residential patterns. Also, northern blacks were frustrated because new laws did not end racism and poverty.)

lived in miserable housing, their kids still went to lousy schools. ”

Urban violence. Less than a week after the Civil Rights Act of 1965 went into effect, violence erupted in Watts, a largely African-American section of Los Angeles. Rumors of police brutality in the arrest of a black driver set off rioting. Stores were looted and burned. Police and the National Guard were called in. When the six-day riot ended, thirty-four were dead and hundreds injured, most of them black. Property damage exceeded $35 million.

The Watts riot was a reaction not just to one incident but to years of such incidents. Julius Lester, a young black writer, expressed the rage:

“ *America has had chance after chance to show that it really meant 'that all men are endowed with certain inalienable rights.'. . . Now it is over—the days of singing freedom songs and combating bullets with love.* ”

In the summer of 1966, Chicago, Cleveland, and forty other cities suffered race riots. The following summer, at least as many serious riots broke out. Eighty-three people died of gunfire, mostly in Newark and Detroit.

In 1967 President Johnson appointed the Commission on Civil Disorders, headed by Illinois Governor Otto Kerner, to study the riots and make recommendations for the future. The commission blamed white racism for the widespread discrimination and segregation that led to the riots and warned: "Our nation is moving toward two societies, one black, one white—separate and unequal." Faced with budget problems from the Vietnam war, however, Johnson did not act on proposals for new jobs and housing in ghettos.

Spotlight on People

For years Gordon Parks, a photographer, composer, and writer, believed that Hollywood would never accept a black director. But after his novel *The Learning Tree* was published, Parks had the following conversation with Kenneth Hyman of Warner Brothers.

"I'm serious," [Hyman] said. "I love your book and I'm convinced that it will make a good film, and that you should direct it. . . . Who would you like to write the screenplay?"

I was still cautious. "I don't know any screenwriters out here."

"Why not write it yourself? . . ."

"But I've never written a screenplay."

"You've never directed a picture either."

. . . "Okay—I'll give it a try."

"[I hear] you're a composer as well."

"That's right." . . . "Okay—why not. I'll take that on as well."

"Fine. Now you're going to be Hollywood's very first black director. There may be problems and you're going to need some clout. I suggest you act as executive producer as well."

Smiling, I shook my head. "Well why not."

Black Power, Black Pride

The riots, and the issues of economic injustice and segregation that sparked them, posed a challenge for Americans in the civil rights movement. For many, the dream of achieving integration through peaceful means had been shattered. Some of them turned to an approach called "black power."

This approach, proposed in the early 1900s, called on African Americans to strive for equality on their own and to stress their African, not American, heritage. Marcus Garvey carried this approach further in the 1920s. He urged blacks to create a separate society rather than working for an integrated one in a racist nation.

Malcolm X. As a young boy, Malcolm Little often went to meetings with his father, who was a Garvey organizer. Malcolm remembered the crowds chanting, "Up, you mighty race, you can accomplish what you will." The boy grew up to be one of the most eloquent advocates of black power in the United States. He renamed himself Malcolm X.

Connections: Literature

Analyzing Poetry. The black power movement found expression in the work of African-American writers. Poet-playwright Leroi Jones, who changed his name to Imamu Amiri Baraka, wrote:

We are beautiful people
with African imaginations
full of masks and dances
and swelling chants

We have been captured,
brothers. And we labor to
make our getaway, into
the ancient image, into a
new
correspondence with
ourselves
and our black family. We
need magic
now we need the spells, to
raise up
return, destroy, and
create. What will be
the sacred words?

Discuss what Baraka means by "been captured," and "we need the spells, to raise up/return, destroy and create." What might the "sacred words" be?

Multicultural Perspectives

According to Bobby Seale, the Black Panther party got its name from a conversation he had with Huey Newton about why a civil rights pamphlet had a black panther as its logo. Newton thought that *"if you drive a panther into a corner . . . then he will tend to come out of that corner to wipe out or stop its aggressor."* Seale replied, *"That's just like the black people. All civil rights people are getting brutalized . . . for exercising the First Amendment. . . . They can't go left . . . can't go right. So we just like the black panthers."*

Malcolm X first came to public notice as a spokesman for the Black Muslim religious sect in the 1950s and 1960s. Founded in 1931, the Black Muslims rejected "the white man's Christian world" and urged racial separation. Malcolm X stressed self-help, self-defense, solidarity, and pride for blacks in a nation where, he believed, they would never be accepted as equals:

> *"If you and I were Americans, there'd be no problem. . . . Everything that came out of Europe . . . is already an American. And as long as you and I have been here, we aren't Americans yet."*

For Malcolm X (left), black power meant, in part, creating black businesses. For Carl Stokes, it meant running for political office. In 1967 he was elected mayor of Cleveland, Ohio.

In 1964 Malcolm X broke with the Black Muslims and formed the Organization for Afro-American Unity. Just after his autobiography was published in 1965, he was assassinated. Thousands read his book, however, and were influenced by his view of the unity of black peoples everywhere and his call for political action.

Black power in action. In 1966, Stokely Carmichael, the new head of SNCC, yelled to a crowd, "We want black power." The crowd responded, "Black power!" Later, using labor unions as an example, he described what he meant:

> *"We must come together around the issue that oppressed us—which is our blackness. Unions needed power to stop their oppression. And black power just means black people coming together and getting people to represent their needs and stop that oppression."*

Across the nation, African Americans began to put black power into action to attack problems. They elected black city officials and created black schools, businesses, and community centers. By the end of the decade, almost 1,500 blacks held political office, including several mayors, state legislators, and members of Congress.

For some, black power meant a complete rejection of white society. In 1966 Huey Newton and Bobby Seale founded the Black Panther party in Oakland, California, and began to organize ghetto youth and create new programs to help the poor.

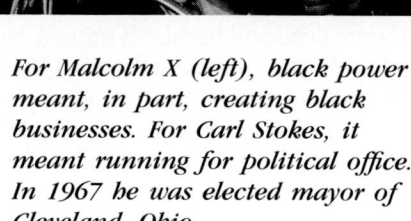

The Panthers inspired fear and hostility in many whites, however. They demanded land for a separate black nation, financial restitution for slavery, full employment, and decent housing. Their insistence on carrying guns for self-defense brought them into direct confrontation with police.

King's Assassination

Martin Luther King, Jr., applauded black self-help, unity, and pride. However, he opposed separatism, believing African Americans could achieve equality by working with whites to create change.

King became increasingly involved in efforts to solve the related problems of racism and poverty.

He tried to unite the poor of all races and in 1968 organized the Poor People's Campaign for a march on Washington. He also spoke out against the war in Vietnam, believing that it drained money and attention away from the struggle against poverty.

King was shot to death on April 4, 1968, in Memphis, Tennessee, where he had gone to support striking sanitation workers. His death set off an outpouring of grief among Americans of all races as well as riots in more than sixty cities.

Four weeks after the murder, the SCLC's new leader, the Reverend Ralph Abernathy, led marchers from Memphis to Washington, D.C., to open the Poor People's Campaign. As the marchers set out, Abernathy said:

> *"For any of you who would linger in the cemetery, I have news for you. We have business on the road to freedom. . . . We must prove to white America that you can kill the leader but you cannot kill the dream."*

Business *was* far from finished. But the civil rights movement had accomplished a great deal. It removed the legal basis for segregation. It gave the vote to African Americans, offering them entry into politics and to political office. Perhaps even more important, it raised the conscience of the nation, opening the door to greater understanding and moving the nation closer to the American ideal that all people deserve equal respect.

Section Review

1. Comprehension. What effect did television have on the success of voting rights demonstrations?

2. Analysis. President Kennedy said, "Those who make peaceful revolution impossible will make violent revolution inevitable." What do you think he meant? Do you agree? Why or why not?

3. Evaluation. Do you think that political equality, protected in civil rights laws, can be separated from economic equality? Give reasons for your answer.

4. Analysis. Martin Luther King said that "black supremacy is as evil as white supremacy." What do you think he meant?

Connections to Themes

Shaping Democracy

The general principles that form the framework of the United States Constitution — liberty, equality, and justice — have been reshaped time and again to meet the needs of a changing society. In the 1950s and 1960s, the impetus for change came largely from the African-American civil rights movement. Its success can be measured by landmark court decisions and new laws banning discrimination.

Discrimination was not just an African-American issue, however. Inspired by the activism of the black civil rights movement, Hispanic Americans, Native Americans, and women became more militant. In their struggles for political and social equality and economic opportunity, they adopted the tactics of black activists as well as the NAACP. In the Westminster case in 1945, Hispanics successfully challenged segregated schools in California. In the 1970s Native Americans would go to court to claim rights guaranteed in old treaties.

The activism that fired these movements continued to ripple outward, spreading to other groups that felt shut out of American society — the poor, homosexuals, the disabled, and the elderly. The struggle is far from over, though. "Where do we go from here?" Martin Luther King, Jr., asked in 1968. He called on all Americans to "move on with determination . . . to break down the unjust systems we find in our society."

Linking Past and Present

Discussion. Have students discuss the status of civil rights today. **Ask:** What inequalities in American society exist today? What is being done to remove them? What part can you play in this struggle?

Section Review

ANSWERS

1. TV showed violence with which demonstrations were put down, enlisted support of northern whites and blacks, led to passage of Voting Rights Act of 1965.

2. Meant that suppression, especially through violence, leads to violent reaction by suppressed, who lack other means to right wrongs. Students who agree can point to violent revolutions in countries (for example, Russia, Cuba) where dissent has been suppressed. Those who disagree can argue that, in modern times with modern technology, it is possible to suppress dissent indefinitely.

3. Answers will vary. Those who think political and economic equality separate can argue poor have played an important part in determining political results in past and that coupling the two leads to too much government control. Those disagreeing can argue that in many cases rich have greater influence than poor on legislation and exercise greater political power.

4. Meant that no group should tyrannize another.

Chapter Survey
ANSWERS

Using New Vocabulary

Restrictive covenants (a) and job discrimination (b) are part of de facto segregation, which CORE (d) and NAACP (e) fought.

Reviewing the Chapter

1. Separate schools inherently unequal and thus deprive African-American children of equal educational opportunities.
2. Massive resistance (including laws to block integration), closed schools, cut off funds to integrated schools, violently intimidated blacks attending.
3. Eisenhower believed voluntary action, rather than federal force, would lead to quickest progress with fewer problems. When governor of Arkansas defied federal law, Eisenhower sent troops.
4. Boycott succeeded in ending segregation on buses; also showed what could be accomplished by organized protests and inspired others.
5. Black students sat at white lunch counters, and black and white students became "freedom riders" to integrate interstate buses. Both groups met with violent resistance but also inspired others to act and spread message of civil rights movement.
6. Desegregated public accommodations, outlawed job discrimination, set up Equal Employment Opportunity Commission, gave Attorney General power to require school desegregation. Did not deal with voting rights or economic disadvantages.
7. Voter registration drives in Deep South, protest demonstrations. Activists threatened, harassed, beaten, arrested, some murdered, but Voting Rights Act passed in 1965.
8. Racism, poverty, frustration caused by continued *de facto* segregation.
9. Answers may include end of legal segregation, Voting Rights Acts of 1965, Civil Rights Act of 1964, greater pride and power for blacks, raised consciousness of whites, step toward ideal of equality.

Thinking Critically

1. Answers may include that philosophy of nonviolence won much support among whites removed from heat of controversy, did not necessarily bring reconciliation between southern whites and blacks.
2. Answers may include: black participation in World War II, desegregation of defense work and armed services, strong black leadership in churches and civil rights organizations and publicity in news media.

Reduced student page in the Teacher's Edition

Chapter Survey

Using New Vocabulary

From the list below, select the four words or phrases whose meanings relate to the underlined vocabulary term and explain the relationships.

<u>de facto segregation</u>

(a) restrictive covenants	(d) CORE
(b) job discrimination	(e) NAACP
(c) *Plessy* v. *Ferguson*	(f) massive resistance

Reviewing the Chapter

1. Explain the reasoning behind the Supreme Court decision in the Brown case.

2. Describe three methods southerners used to resist school integration.

3. Why was the Eisenhower administration slow to enforce the Brown decision? What finally caused it to take action?

4. Explain the immediate and long-range consequences of the Montgomery bus boycott.

5. Describe two methods used by students to promote integration in the South. How effective were these methods?

6. What did the Civil Rights Act of 1964 accomplish? What still needed to be done?

7. How did civil rights activists work for voting rights in the early 1960s? What were the results?

8. What caused urban violence in the mid-1960s?

9. List three accomplishments of the civil rights movement.

Thinking Critically

1. Evaluation. Martin Luther King, Jr., wrote that "nonviolence . . . does not seek to defeat or humiliate the opponent, but to win his friendship and understanding. . . . The end is . . . reconciliation." How effective do you think nonviolent protests were in the civil rights movement? How well did they achieve reconciliation between white and black Americans?

2. Analysis. African Americans had been working to achieve full citizenship since Reconstruction. What factors do you think enabled the civil rights movement to accomplish so much in the 1950s and 1960s?

History and You

Television coverage of the brutal treatment of black demonstrators had a tremendous impact on viewers and became a powerful tool for the civil rights movement. Interview people in your community to find out how watching these events on television influenced their thinking. Report your findings to the class.

Using Geography

Study the map below, then use it to answer the following questions.

1. Why do you think these years were chosen for a survey of school integration?

2. What geographic pattern can you see in the process of school integration?

3. How can you explain the absence of any integration in five states of the Deep South?

Desegregating Schools 1953-1960

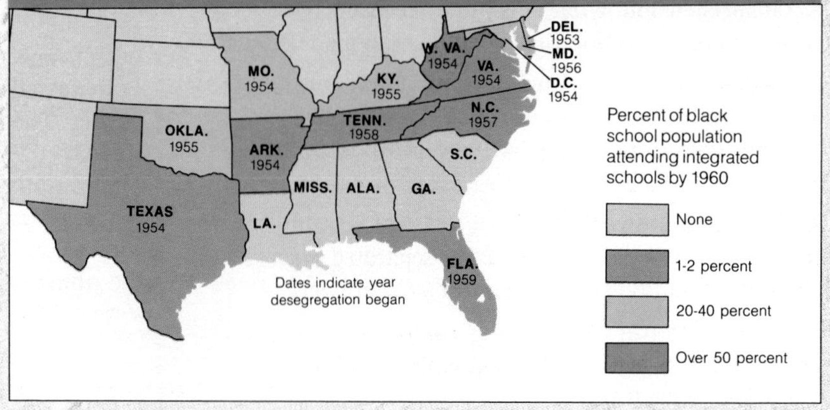

History and You

Answers will vary.

Using Geography

1. Delaware began desegregating its schools in 1953; school segregation declared unconstitutional in 1954; federal intervention already in use by 1960, a census year.
2. Border states and those in Upper South began desegregation before states in Deep South.
3. Massive resistance continued in the Deep South.

Analyzing Graphs

1. African-American man: $280,000. White man: $600,000.
2. African-American man: $6,364. White man: $13,636. (Lifetime income ÷ 44)
3. Increased for both blacks and whites; whites remained far ahead.
4. For African-American women the average increased more than 300 percent. Average for white women increased about 150 percent.
5. For women gap nearly disappeared; for men gap remained large.
6. Answers may include: from 1949 to 1969 expected earnings for all women and for black men remained lower than for white men.
7. African-American men: 22 percent, women: 26 percent. White men: 53 percent, women: 58 percent.
8. The percentage for all groups increased.
9. The rates are lower for African-American men and women than for white men and women.
10. Answers may include: family situation, economic condition, and interests of peer groups.
11. Answers may include: Civil rights movement may have given hope for the future where there was none before.

Applying Social Studies Skills

Analyzing Bar Graphs

Part of the legacy of racism and discrimination has been unequal opportunities for education and employment. The following graphs give data on schooling and income for black and white men and women during the 1950s and 1960s. Study the graphs and then answer the questions.

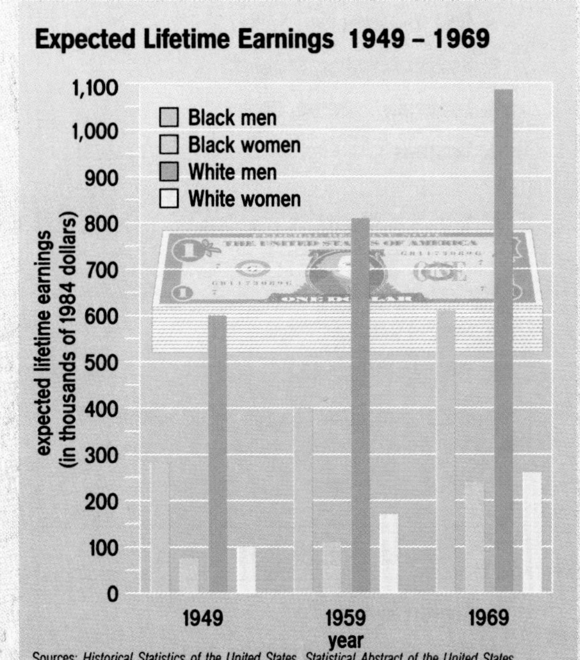

Sources: *Historical Statistics of the United States, Statistical Abstract of the United States*

1. Lifetime earnings are computed by adding average yearly income for each age from twenty to sixty-four. In 1949 what were the average expected lifetime earnings for an African American man? A white man?

2. Using the estimates for lifetime earnings in 1949, determine the average yearly income for black men and for white men in that year.

3. How did expected lifetime earnings for black and white men change between 1949 and 1969?

4. About how much did lifetime earnings for black and white women change between 1949 and 1969?

5. What happened to the gap between lifetime earnings of black women and white women between 1949 and 1969? What happened to the gap between black men and white men?

6. In a sentence or two, make a generalization about the differences between lifetime earnings of men and women, black and white.

7. In 1950 approximately what percentages of black women and men had completed twelve or more years of schooling? What percentages of white women and men?

8. Between 1950 and 1970, what happened to the percentages of each group that completed high school?

9. Compare the percentages of high-school completion for black men and women and for white men and women. What can you conclude?

10. What factors outside of school do you think might influence whether or not students completed high school?

11. Speculate about the effect that events described in the chapter may have had on the changes in percentages of high-school completion shown on the graph.

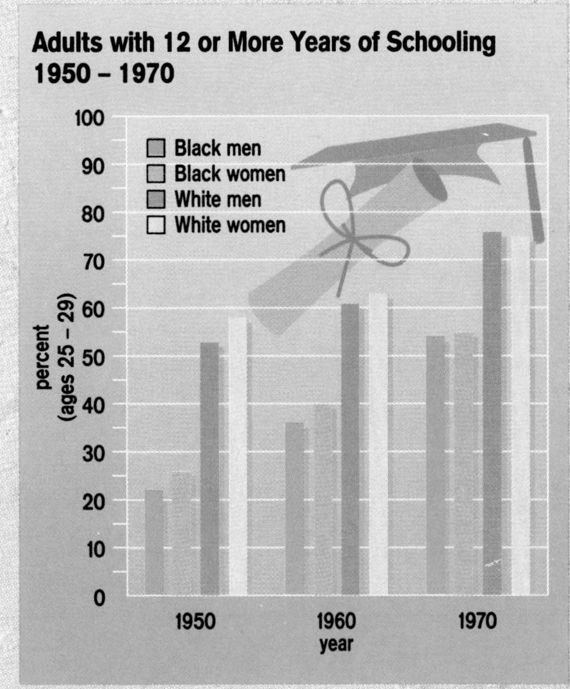

Sources: *Bureau of Labor Statistics, Historical Statistics of the United States, Statistical Abstract of the United States*

Chapter 29

The Ordeal of Vietnam

Planning Guide

	Student Text	TWE Lesson Plans	Support Materials
SECTION 1	**Section 29–1 (1–3 Days)** **Step by Step into the Quagmire,** pp 776–781 Review/Evaluation Section Review, p 781	**Introducing the Chapter:** Issues of War—Class Activity, 30 minutes, p 773B **Reinforcement Activity:** Rewriting History—Individual Project, 30 minutes, p 773C **Enrichment Activity:** A Gulf of Tonkin Exposé—Individual Project, homework, p 773D	★ **Read to Remember,** Section 1 ● **Section Activities,** Section 1 Δ **Enrichment Activities,** Section 1 Δ **Readings** ● **Tests and Quizzes,** Section 1 Quiz
SECTION 2	**Section 29–2 (1–3 Days)** **"In-Country" and at Home,** pp 782–789 Review/Evaluation Section Review, p 789	**Teaching the Main Ideas:** Tet Offensive Role Play—Class Activity, one class period, p 773B **Evaluating Progress:** Letters from "Nam"—Individual activity, homework, p 773C	★ **Read to Remember,** Section 2 ● **Section Activities,** Section 2 ● **Geography Activities,** Section 2 Δ **Readings** ● **Tests and Quizzes,** Section 2 Quiz
SECTION 3	**Section 29–3 (1–3 Days)** **A Peace Yet to Come,** pp 790–795 The American Spirit: Maya Lin, p 793 Point of View: Legacies of Vietnam, pp 796–797 Connections to Themes: Shaping Democracy, p 795 Review/Evaluation Section Review, p 795 Chapter 29 Survey, pp 798–799 Unit 9 Survey, pp 800–801 Skills, pp 798–799 Using New Vocabulary Thinking Critically Using Geography Applying Thinking Skills: Determining the Strength of an Argument Writing About Issues	**Teaching the Main Ideas:** American Intervention in Vietnam—Paired Activity, one class period, p 773C	★ **Read to Remember,** Section 3 ● **Section Activities,** Section 3 Δ **Enrichment Activities,** Section 3 ● **Tests and Quizzes,** Section 3 Quiz, Chapter 29 Test (Forms A and B), Unit 9 Test (Forms A and B) **Additional Resources** ● **Active Learning** Δ **Transparencies and Activity Book** ● **Testing Software** ★ **Chapter Summaries** **Key:** ★ **For Extra Support** ● **For All Students** Δ **For Enrichment**

Overview

The cold-war policy of containing communism led the United States to intervene in the longstanding conflict in Vietnam. Like Presidents Truman and Eisenhower, President Kennedy sent aid to South Vietnam in increasing amounts. Soon he was sending advisors and facing the possibility of American participation in combat. President Johnson, honoring Kennedy's commitments, used the Gulf of Tonkin Resolution to commit American military forces to action in Vietnam.

Massive bombing campaigns escalated the need for additional troops and by mid-1965 there were more than 500,000 American soldiers in Vietnam. American numbers and technical superiority, however, could not ensure victory against the Viet Cong's guerrilla tactics and Vietnam's geography. As a result of the Viet Cong's Tet Offensive in 1968 and growing divisiveness over the war, Johnson did not run for reelection.

Richard Nixon, the new President, faced the task of winning the war and withdrawing American troops. As criticism mounted against his policies, he ordered intensive bombing to force the North Vietnamese to negotiate a peace settlement. In 1973 an agreement to end the war was finally signed. Two years later, however, Communist forces took control of South Vietnam and Cambodia.

American veterans returning from Vietnam tried to adjust to physical disabilities and psychological damage resulting from the war. Meanwhile, thousands of war refugees settled in the United States.

Activity Objectives

After completing the activities, students should be able to

- describe the impact of the Tet Offensive.
- trace the efforts of American leaders to contain communism in Vietnam and the results.
- describe turning points in the history of Vietnam and the Vietnam War.
- recognize the unique experiences of American soldiers in the war in Vietnam.
- explain how President Johnson manipulated information to influence Congress and the public.

Introducing the Chapter

Issues of War

This class activity requires half a class period.

This activity gives students an opportunity to examine their opinions on some of the issues facing Americans during the Vietnam War.

Conduct a quick assessment of students' knowledge of the Vietnam War. Tell them they will have the opportunity to express their views on major issues debated by Americans at this time.

Designate an imaginary line down the middle of the classroom. Define one end of the line as the "agree" position and the other as the "disagree" position. Define the midpoint as the "no opinion" position. Explain that you will read a statement about which students may agree, disagree, or have no opinion. They are to indicate their opinion by standing in the appropriate location along the imaginary line.

Read the statement: *A democratic government is justified in withholding information from the public in wartime.* Direct students to move to the position along the line that expresses their opinion on the statement. When all are in line, call on students in both the agree and disagree positions to explain their reasons for holding these opinions. Allow students in the "no opinion" position to move if they are persuaded by the explanations. Continue the procedure by reading the following statements:

- A democratic government is justified in censoring the news media in wartime.
- Only Congress should have the power to send American troops into combat.
- Citizens have the obligation *not* to obey laws that they believe are wrong.
- Citizens should support their government's policies in wartime without question.
- Soldiers should obey orders without question.

Conclude the activity by asking students to identify issues from the Vietnam War era that are still issues today.

Teaching the Main Ideas

Section 29-2: Tet Offensive Role Play

This class activity requires at least one full class period.

In Section 29-2 students learn that Tet had a profound effect on the course of the Vietnam War. In this role-playing activity students analyze reactions to the offensive.

Ask students to describe the Tet Offensive. Emphasize that the offensive caught Americans by surprise and proved to be the major turning point in the war. Tell students that they will role play reactions to Tet in order to understand its significance.

Write the following roles on the chalkboard: American military leader, antiwar protestor, American news reporter, American soldier in Vietnam, Viet Cong soldier, North Vietnamese soldier, South Vietnamese civilian.

Divide the class into groups of seven, and direct each student to select one of the roles listed on the chalkboard. All seven roles should be represented in each group. Tell students to prepare for their roles by developing responses to the following questions:

- How would you describe the Tet Offensive?
- What effect do you think Tet will have on your future?
- What concerns or hopes do you have as a result of Tet?
- What would you do differently in the event of another offensive like Tet?

After preparation, have students begin their role play conversations using the questions above. Encourage them to go beyond the questions to discuss other issues related to Tet and the war in general.

Conclude the activity by asking students how the course of the war might have been different if the Tet Offensive had not occurred. Why?

Teaching the Main Ideas

Section 29-3: American Intervention in Vietnam

This paired activity requires one full class period.

Students learn in Chapter 29 that Presidents Truman, Eisenhower, Kennedy, and Johnson sought to prevent a Communist victory in South Vietnam. In this activity students will prepare time lines showing links between the Presidents' strategies, events in Vietnam, and events in the United States.

Divide the class into pairs and ask each pair to prepare a time line of American intervention in Vietnam from 1950 to 1968. Students should include the actions of Presidents Truman, Eisenhower, Kennedy, and Johnson; major events in Vietnam; and major events related to the war at home. Students may want to use the time line on pages 776–777 as an example. Encourage them to illustrate their time lines with copies of pictures or drawings.

When students have finished their time lines, review their work by having them work together to draw a class time line on the chalkboard. Discuss the time line by asking the following questions:

- Worried about American intervention in Vietnam, Undersecretary of State George Ball said, "Once on the tiger's back we cannot be sure of picking the place to dismount." What do you think he meant? Do you agree? Why or why not?
- How did the antiwar movement affect presidential action? How do you think it might have affected the actions of the Viet Cong?
- Historian George Brown Tindall said, "American military intervention was a logical culmination of the assumptions widely shared by the foreign policy establishment and leaders of both political parties since the early days of the Cold War." Do you agree? Why or why not?
- Was military victory in any traditional sense ever possible? Why or why not? (Have students consider U.S. fears of Soviet or Chinese intervention in the war.)

Reinforcement Activity

Section 29-1: Rewriting History

This individual activity requires half a class period.

In this activity students suggest actions that might have been taken to prevent or change the outcome of the Vietnam War.

Review Section 29-1 with students to reinforce their understanding of the history of Vietnam, including its efforts to gain independence from China and then from France. Point out that some historians believe that there were a number of points at which, if events had been handled differently, the United States would not have become involved in the Vietnam War. For example, if President Wilson had provided aid to Ho Chi Minh in 1919, right after World War I (see page 777), Vietnam might not have moved toward communism.

Direct students to select five events or actions in Section 29-1 that they would change if they could rewrite history. They are to list the five events and actions and explain how they would change them either to avoid United States involvement in fighting in Vietnam or to assure an American victory in the war. Explain that they may propose changing the actions of any country or person.

When the lists are complete, divide the class into small groups. Have group members share their responses and identify the most commonly proposed changes. Then have each group report to the class on the change most of its members proposed. Discuss together what the long-term implications of some of the changes might have been.

Evaluating Progress

Section 29-2: Letters from "Nam"

This individual activity may be assigned as homework.

This writing activity is designed to assess students' understanding of the dilemma that American soldiers faced in the Vietnam War.

Begin the activity by asking students to describe ways in which the war in Vietnam was different from other American wars. Students should consider not only the nature of the fighting but also the unity of the American fighting force.

Have students imagine that they are American combat soldiers in Vietnam and write a letter home to parents or friends. The letters should describe the land and climate of Vietnam, the nature of the fighting, and conditions in the fighting force. Have students conclude the letters with their personal views of the war, evidence to support opinions, and suggestions about how to win or end the war. Encourage students to use detail and creativity in their letters in order to give a sense of what serving "in-country" was like.

Criteria for evaluating students' letters should include accuracy of descriptions, clearly expressed links between views and suggestions, convincing evidence to support opinions, and creativity.

Enrichment Activity

Section 29-1: A Gulf of Tonkin Exposé

This individual activity may be assigned as homework.

In this activity, in which the class writes exposés of events surrounding the Gulf of Tonkin incident, students consider the ways government can manipulate information in order to influence Congress and the public.

Begin the activity by having students review information in Section 29-1 on the Gulf of Tonkin. Ask them to identify the information that was withheld from Congress and the American public.

Tell students that their assignment is to write a newspaper exposé (an article exposing something discreditable) in the form of an editorial on the Gulf of Tonkin incident. Emphasize that their editorials should call attention to misinformation or discrepancies in reports about the incident, and the effect of that misinformation on Congress. Writing from the point of view of a reporter in August 1964, they should also predict how the Gulf of Tonkin Resolution is likely to affect future American involvement in Vietnam. Finally, they should conclude their articles by recommending actions the President and/or Congress should take as a result of the exposé.

Have students exchange their completed articles and review each other's work for accuracy and completeness. Conclude the activity by having the class discuss the most common recommendation(s).

Bibliography and Audiovisual Material

Teacher Bibliography

Doyle, Edward and Stephen Weiss. *The Vietnam Experience.* 13 vols. Boston: Addison-Wesley, 1984.

Greene, Bob. *Homecoming: When the Soldiers Returned from Vietnam*. New York: Putnam, 1989.

Hayslip, Le Ly. *When Heaven and Earth Changed Places: A Vietnam Woman's Journey from War to Peace.* New York: Plume/Penguin, 1990.

Halberstam, David. *The Best and the Brightest*. New York: Viking Penguin, 1983.

Karnow, Stanley. *Vietnam: A History*. New York: Viking Penguin, 1984.

Palmer, Laura. *Shrapnel in the Heart: Letters and Remembrances from the Vietnam Memorial*. New York: Random House, Inc., 1987.

Salisbury, Harrison. *Vietnam Reconsidered: Lessons from a War*. New York: HarperCollins, 1985.

Santoli, Al. *Everything We Had: An Oral History of the Vietnam War*. New York: Ballantine, 1985.

Sheehan, Neil. *A Bright Shining Lie.* New York: Random House, 1989.

Wallace, Terry. *Bloods: An Oral History of the Vietnam War by Black Veterans.* New York: Random House, 1984.

Westmoreland, William C. *A Soldier Reports*. New York: Da Capo Press, 1989.

Student Bibliography

Alvarez, Everett, Jr. *Chained Eagle.* New York: D.I. Fine, 1989.

Caputo, Philip. *A Rumor of War*. New York: Ballantine Books, 1987.

Kovic, Ron. *Born on the Fourth of July*. New York: Pocket Books, 1990.

Marshall, Kathryn. *In the Combat Zone: An Oral History of American Women in Vietnam.* Boston: Little, Brown, 1987.

Mason, Bobbie A. *In Country*. New York: HarperCollins, 1989.

O'Brien, Tim. *Going After Cacciato*. New York: Doubleday, 1989.

Walker, Keith. *A Piece of My Heart: The Stories of 26 Women Who Served in Vietnam.* Novato, Calif.: Presidio Press, 1986.

Wright, Stephen. *Meditations in Green: A Novel of Vietnam*. New York: Macmillan, 1988.

Films, Videocassettes, and Videodiscs

After 'Nam. 30 min. CNN. Videocassette.

All The Unsung Heros: The Story of the Vietnam Veterans Memorial. 30 min. Heritage America. Videocassette.

America Takes Charge (1965–1967). 60 min. FI. Movie.

LBJ Goes To War (1964–1965). 60 min. FI. Movie.

Why Vietnam?. 32 min. U.S. Department of Defense. Videocassette.

Filmstrips

Vietnam: The War That Divided America. 48 min. 4 color filmstrips, 4 cassettes, guide. Guidance Associates.

The Vietnam War. 16 min each. 3 filmstrips with cassettes. National Geographic.

Chapter 29

Objectives

- Explain how the United States became involved in the Vietnam War.
- Describe how the Vietnam War differed from other American wars.
- Cite effects of the Vietnam War.

Introducing THE CHAPTER

For suggestions on introducing Chapter 29, refer to page 773B in the Teacher's Edition.

Developing THE CHAPTER

For activities and teaching strategies to help you reinforce and enrich chapter content, see pages 773B–773D in the Teacher's Edition.

B · A · C · K · G · R · O · U · N · D

Chapter Opener Illustrations

In the face of troops deployed to maintain order, a young American anti-war protestor places a flower in the barrel of a soldier's rifle.

On the Vietnam Veterans Memorial in Washington, D.C., appear the names of Americans killed or missing in action in the Vietnam War.

High-tech aircraft allowed American troops to arrive at the front quickly and redeploy with lightning speed.

Flowers played a symbolic part in this antiwar poster, this time combined with another traditional peace symbol, the dove.

President Johnson's presidency which began with progress in civil rights and a "War on Poverty," ended tragically as it sank into the quagmire of the Vietnam War.

Through print and television images, Americans witnessed

Reduced student page in the Teacher's Edition

Chapter 29 1954-1975

The Ordeal of Vietnam

the destruction of Vietnamese towns and came to sympathize with the anguish of the Vietnamese people.

The button on the right was worn by people who felt a need to speak out on behalf of American involvement. In past wars, support on the homefront was taken for granted; during the Vietnam conflict, it was not.

American Voices

Vietnam. For many, the name calls forth memories of the longest war the United States ever fought—and the first it ever "lost." From 1965 to 1973, thousands of American soldiers, most of them barely out of high school, fought against Communist forces in that Southeast Asian land. Lieutenant Robert Santos of the 101st Airborne Division described what happened as he led his platoon against North Vietnamese troops in 1968:

> " *I remember walking through the rice paddies that opened up and the small stream and the green on both sides. We were walking down the right side, near the trail, and there was another company on my left flank. All of a sudden . . . they opened up fire. . . .*
>
> *I moved, and as I ran forward I heard these noises. Kind of like* ping, ping—*no idea what that noise was . . . I finally got back after running around and sat down next to the RTO [radiotelephone operator]. . . . He said, 'Don't you know what that noise is?' I said no. He said, 'That's bullets going over your head!'* "

Vietnam was a country torn in half by war. Americans fought on the side of South Vietnam, a country not much larger than Santos's home state of New York. Santos tried to imagine "what it would be like if this took place in my hometown." At home the war did take place on millions of American television screens, and it bitterly divided the nation.

Protestor facing National Guardsmen in front of the Pentagon; the black granite surface of the Vietnam Veterans Memorial; helicopter dropoff; antiwar poster; President Johnson; Vietnamese civilians fleeing bomb attack; pro-war button.

Analyzing Primary Sources

American Voices

Robert Santos's description of a clash between American and North Vietnamese troops offers a frank look at the feelings of a soldier experiencing combat for the first time. Although Santos was twenty-one years of age then, he felt "young in terms of commanding men in combat." However, he grew quickly in experience and became one of the most decorated Vietnam veterans in New York State.

1. How would you describe what is happening to Santos and his platoon? **(They have been ambushed by North Vietnamese.)**
2. Why does the situation seem unreal to him? **(It is something he has never experienced before.)**
3. How does the extract reflect Santos's inexperience? **(He did not recognize the sounds of gunfire.)**

Section 29-1

Objectives

- ***Answer the Focus Question.***
- *Explain the reasons for the split between North and South Vietnam.*
- *Describe the Geneva Accords and the SEATO treaty.*
- *Cite steps taken by Johnson and Kennedy that increased United States involvement in South Vietnam.*

Introducing

THE SECTION

Review the policies the United States government developed in the 1950s in an attempt to contain the spread of communism. Recall the "domino theory" with students and discuss its implications.

Ask: What assumptions does the domino theory make about communism? **(that it is irresistible and spreads almost automatically)** Does it oversimplify social conflicts in Third World nations? What actions does it call for on the part of the United States? **(to police and contain any growth of communism)** What major event had made many Americans concerned about communism sweeping through all of Asia? **(Mao's successful establishment of communism in China and his alliance with the Soviet Union)**

B · A · C · K · G · R · O · U · N · D

Time Line Illustrations

1. The Geneva Accords of 1954 divided Vietnam along the 17th parallel.

2. WWII cartoonist Bill Maudlin continued his commentary during the Vietnam struggle. This cartoon, entitled *Backbone*, reflected a common American perception that the South Vietnamese lacked the will to fight on their own.

3. The peace symbol of the 1960s was created from the semaphore code for the letters *N* and *D*. The letters stood for nuclear disarmament.

4. In 1970 *Newsweek* magazine called Nixon's order to invade Cambodia a gamble. Nixon hoped that an attack across the Cambodian border would pressure the Viet Cong and North Vietnamese negotiators in Paris to take serious

Reduced student page in the Teacher's Edition

CHAPTER TIME LINE

1954-1975

Copyright 1964, Bill Mauldin, reprinted with permission

1963 Kennedy increases aid to Vietnam

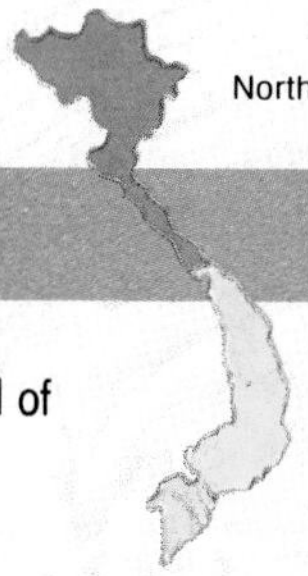

1954 | 1963 | 1966

1954 French lose control of Vietnam

Vietnam divided

1964 Gulf of Tonkin Resolution

1965 **Mar** Johnson sends first U. S. troops to Vietnam

Apr First large antiwar demonstrations

29-1 *Step by Step into the Quagmire*

Focus: What led to American intervention in Vietnam?

From the southern rim of the landmass of Asia juts the Indochina Peninsula. The interior is shared by the countries of Laos and Cambodia. Flexed like a backbone along its eastern edge is Vietnam, a small land that gradually loomed larger and larger in the effort of the United States to contain communism wherever it arose. Presidents Truman, Eisenhower, Kennedy, and Johnson each saw Vietnam as a cold-war battleground.

The cold-war view, however, gives an incomplete picture. The step-by-step process by which the United States became involved more and more deeply in the Vietnam War cannot be understood without exploring the Vietnamese people's ties to their land, and their history of struggle against foreign domination.

Vietnam: The Land and Its People

Vietnam naturally divides into northern and southern regions, both blessed with fertile delta farm lands. Between the Red River Delta in the north and the Mekong Delta in the south, a long narrow coastal plain rises to the west through thick forests to a chain of craggy mountains. For centuries the Red River Delta has nourished a culture centered on wet-rice farming, a process requiring a spirit of shared labor that is the basis of village life.

In 111 B.C. the Chinese conquered what is now North Vietnam, imposing a grim rule. As the Vietnamese struggled to retain their own culture, their sense of national identity grew. Finally, in the tenth century, they overthrew their Chinese rulers.

steps toward ending the war. A cease fire agreement was not reached for three more years.

5. When the two sides reached an agreement, Nixon's foreign policy advisor in Paris, Henry Kissinger, shook hands with Le Duc Tho, chief Vietnamese negotiator. Kissinger announced the decision with the words, "Peace is at hand."

6. The last United States combat troops left South Vietnam in 1973, but the war dragged on for two more years. In 1975, with North Vietnamese troops on the outskirts of the city, personnel of the American embassy in Saigon made a hasty departure.

1968 **Jan** Tet Offensive
Paris peace talks begin

1969 Nixon calls for Vietnamization

1973 **Jan** Cease-fire agreement
Mar Last U.S. combat troops leave South Vietnam

1969 — 1972 — 1975

1970 Nixon orders invasion of Cambodia

1975 South Vietnam surrenders

The following centuries were chaotic. As population soared and rival groups clashed over power, land-hungry Vietnamese pushed south to conquer new territory. Eventually, they spread through the Mekong Delta to the tip of the peninsula.

The French Conquest

French merchants and missionaries probed Vietnam in the 1600s. The merchants failed to set up ongoing trade, but the missionaries made inroads by converting about a tenth of the population to Catholicism. Meanwhile, France continued eyeing Vietnam as a source of raw materials. Eventually, in 1858, it sent soldiers to turn Vietnam into a French colony. The Vietnamese warrior spirit was unleashed against the invaders, and it was not until 1893 that the French finally subdued Indochina.

The French imposed heavy taxes and exported rice and raw materials for profit. French settlers and Vietnamese with close ties to the colonial government took control of most farm land. Before French rule, most Vietnamese had owned land. By the 1930s about half were landless.

The heavy-handed French rule sparked fierce opposition. Bands of guerrillas harassed the French. One French soldier complained, "They appear from nowhere in large numbers and then disappear." The French response was brutal, further inflaming resistance.

Nationalism on the Rise

The guerrillas found a powerful leader in Ho Chi Minh. Known to his followers as "Uncle Ho," he was a charismatic patriot dedicated to freeing his people from the French. Looking to the United States as a natural ally against colonialism, Ho asked President Wilson for support in 1919.

The United States did not come to Ho's aid, however. Loyalty to France, its World War I ally, was one reason. Another was growing fear of communism. Ho saw himself as a nationalist, but his supporters included Communists, which aroused American suspicions.

Denied American aid, Ho himself moved toward communism and founded a Communist party to attract Soviet support. A Communist state seemed

Developing

THE SECTION

Connections: Geography

Discussion. Have students locate the countries of Vietnam, Laos, and Cambodia on a contemporary world map such as the one on pages 904–905 of the text. **Ask:** How would the map have been different before 1954? **(The three countries were parts of the colony of French Indochina and some had different names.)** How would the map have been different between 1955 and 1975? **(Vietnam divided into two parts.)**

Chapter Connections

Discussion. Review with students reasons for colonization in North America in the 1600s and British policies toward the 13 colonies before the Revolution. Have them cite similarities in France's colonization of Southeast Asia. **(France colonized Indochina for mercantilistic reasons; imposed heavy taxes; exported goods for profit. Like Native Americans in North America, many Vietnamese were deprived of their lands. In Vietnam, however, it was the native population, not the colonists, who eventually rebelled.)**

Writing About History

Point of View. Ask students to imagine they are Vietnamese in 1858 or 1940. Have them write how they might have felt as French troops arrived and turned their homeland into a French colony, or as Japanese troops arrived in 1940.

Global Connections

Discussion. Why did the United States side with France in Indochina, despite American concern about corrupt colonial rule? **(Refer students to a map of post-World-War-II Europe, including divided Germany. Point out that the U.S. considered France to be an essential bulwark against the spread of communism in Europe.)**

Thinking Critically

Evaluation. Why did Ho Chi Minh believe he could win? (Ho's forces outnumbered the French. Refer students to Ho's words in the second column on this page.) Do you think Ho was correct in his prediction? Why, or why not?

Connections: Politics

People favoring American intervention in Vietnam tended to see Ho Chi Minh as a Communist, pure and simple. Opponents of the war, on the other hand, described him in strictly nationalistic terms. It is clear that Ho's involvement in communism, beginning in the 1920s, was deep and pervasive. He was a founder of the French Communist party and established the Intercolonial Union, an international communist and anti-imperialist group. He also studied in Moscow and established contacts there. Ho saw communism and nationalism as being two aspects of the same struggle, with nationalism providing emotional support and cultural identity, and communism offering a systematic ideology.

Reduced student page in the Teacher's Edition

Ho Chi Minh became a revolutionary hero for many Vietnamese by leading their struggle against the French, whose rule finally collapsed in 1954.

an appropriate ally since capitalism, French-style, had been a disaster for the Vietnamese. Ho later explained, "It was patriotism and not communism that originally inspired me."

When Japan invaded Indochina in 1940, Ho and his followers formed a nationalist organization known as the Vietminh to fight both the Japanese and the French. By the war's end the Vietminh controlled the north, and on September 2, 1945, Ho proclaimed Vietnam independent. Borrowing from the American Declaration of Independence, he declared, "We hold the truth that all men are created equal." A renewed appeal for American support, however, fell on deaf ears. At the Potsdam conference in July, no decision was made on the postwar status of Vietnam.

The Defeat of the French

The French moved quickly in their quest to reconquer Vietnam. By early 1946 they held the southern cities and roads. The Vietminh still controlled the north, though, and were supporting guerrilla resistance throughout the south. Defying the French, Ho Chi Minh declared,

"You can kill ten of my men for every one I kill of yours, but even at those odds, you will lose and I will win."

Seeking American aid, the French made a show of giving the Vietnamese a voice in government. In 1949 they appointed a former Vietnamese ruler, Bao Dai, as chief of state. The United States was unimpressed by the corrupt regime but continued to back it as a bulwark against the spread of communism. After Mao Zedong's victory in China, President Truman got Congress to approve sending $10 million in aid and fifty military advisors to Vietnam in 1950.

By 1954 American dollars were covering 80 percent of France's war costs, but the French were still losing. Soviet and Chinese military aid and training had helped transform guerrilla bands into a large, skilled military organization, and the Vietminh controlled much of Vietnam and neighboring Laos. In the spring of 1954 they launched a major strike at a large French force near the northern village of Dien Bien Phu.

As the Vietminh battered the French, France pleaded for American intervention, including nuclear strikes. Eisenhower refused, though, because he knew that America's allies would not join in and that Congress, with the memory of the Korean War still fresh, would not risk entanglement in another war. Dien Bien Phu fell in May. It was a final defeat for the French.

A Divided Country

In July 1954 representatives of France, Vietnam, Laos, Cambodia, China, Britain, and the Soviet Union met in Geneva, Switzerland, to work out a settlement for Indochina. American observers also attended.

Out of the meeting came the Geneva Accords. The agreement, which the United States did not sign, established a cease-fire and temporarily divided the country at the 17th parallel, leaving the Vietminh ruling the north from the city of Hanoi, and a pro-Western government in the south, with its capital at Saigon. Elections were to be held in 1956 to unify the country, and the Vietminh were expected to win.

Connections: Language

Viet is an ethnic term of unknown linguistic origin. It could be Chinese for "beyond" (the people beyond the boundary—outsiders), or "hatchet," referring to a common tool used in the region. *Nam* is a Chinese word meaning "South." Early Chinese history refers to a kingdom called Nam Viet. After the Chinese conquest of the Viets in 111 B.C., the Chinese word *Annam*, meaning "pacified South" was most often used. The term *Vietnam* dates from the early 19th century when the Vietnamese government was on good terms with the Chinese. The name was perhaps a compound of *Viet* and *Annam*.

The War in Vietnam 1954-1975

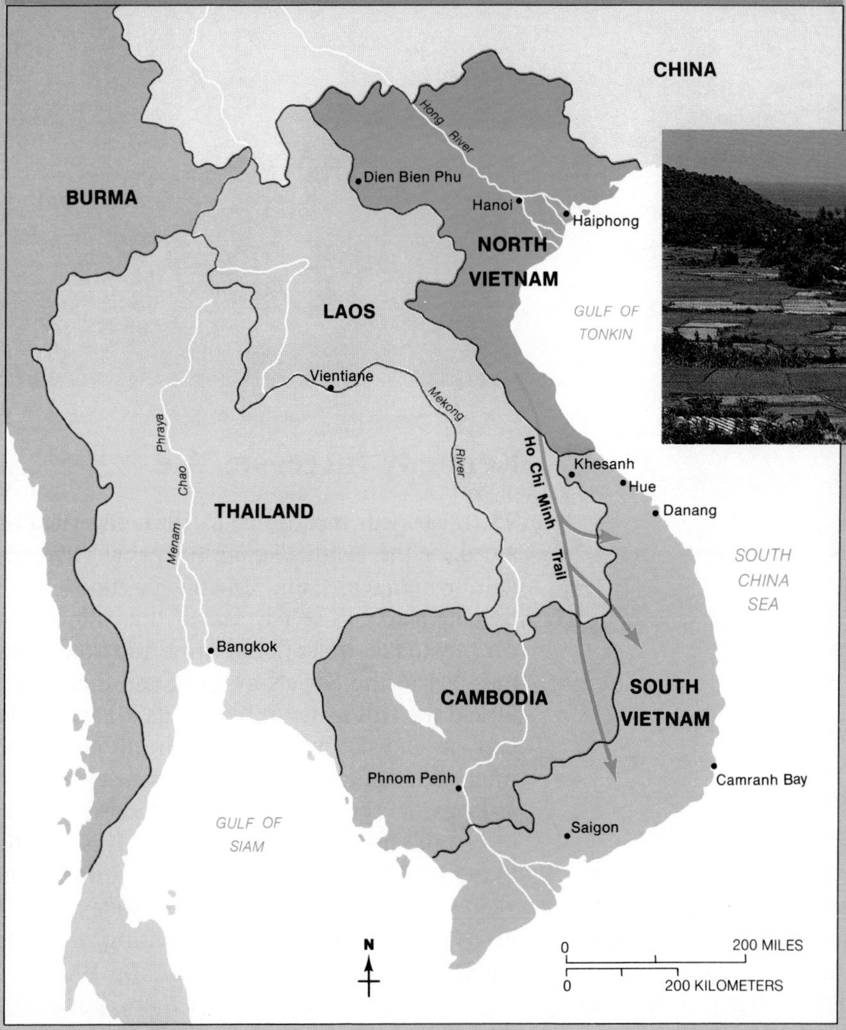

Rice fields in South Vietnam

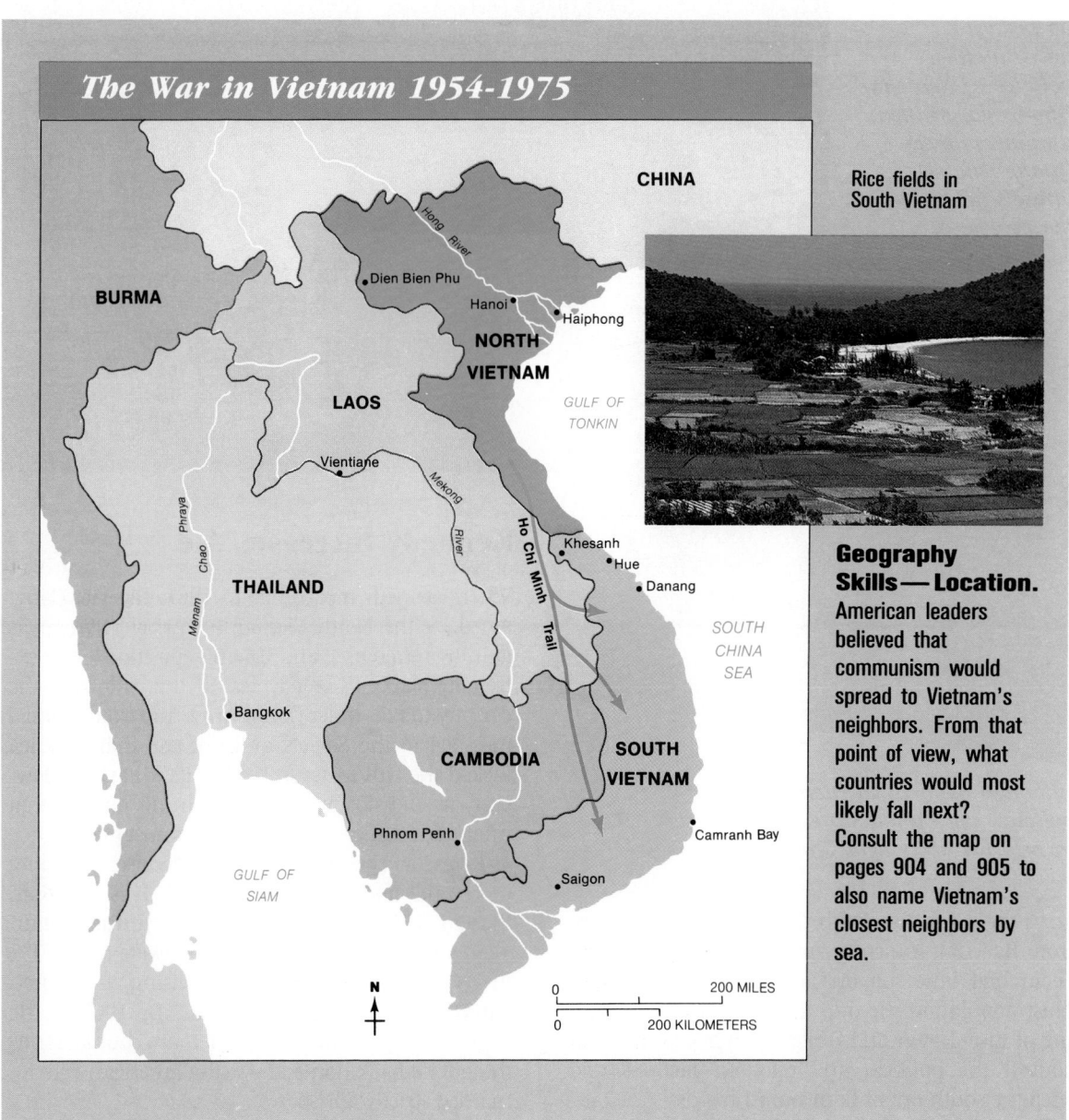

Geography Skills — Location. American leaders believed that communism would spread to Vietnam's neighbors. From that point of view, what countries would most likely fall next? Consult the map on pages 904 and 905 to also name Vietnam's closest neighbors by sea.

Fearing that a Communist victory would topple neighboring countries in Southeast Asia — the so-called domino effect — Secretary of State John Foster Dulles hastily engineered a regional alliance. In September 1954 New Zealand, Australia, Pakistan, the Philippines, and Thailand joined the United States, Britain, and France in the Southeast Asia Treaty Organization (SEATO). The Geneva Accords barred South Vietnam from joining, but American policymakers considered it protected by the treaty. The SEATO treaty would be used later to justify American intervention in Vietnam.

By 1955 the division between North and South Vietnam had hardened. In the north the Vietminh took firm control, redistributing land to landless farmers and executing or imprisoning former landlords. Thousands of government opponents fled south.

Active Learning

Making Charts. Have students begin making charts comparing the Korean and Vietnamese conflicts in terms of: status as civil wars, reasons for division of country, reasons for United States intervention, American attitudes toward the war, military strategies, and outcomes. As students work through the chapter they can add information to their charts.

Connections: Geography

Using a Map. Have students locate Vietnam on the world map on pages 904–905 of the text. Discuss its relative location and the geographical reasons it was important to France, Japan, and the United States.

Geography Skills

ANSWERS

1. Laos, Cambodia; possibly Thailand.
2. Singapore, Malaysia, Philippines, Indonesia.

Analyzing Primary Sources

John F. Kennedy. Read to students the following quotation from John F. Kennedy:

> “*[America would] pay any price, bear any burden, meet any hardship, support any friend, oppose any foe, to ensure the survival and the success of liberty.*”

Ask: What does this statement imply about American involvement in global conflicts? **(The United States would support its allies anywhere in the world to oppose communism.)** What “price” might the United States have to pay for this support? **(economic aid, American lives, for example)** Would “supporting any friend” and “opposing any foe” necessarily further liberty in all circumstances? Have students support their arguments by discussing events in recent history or current news.

Thinking Critically

Analysis. French President Charles de Gaulle warned President Kennedy about Vietnam in May 1961, saying, *“I predict you will sink step by step into a bottomless military and political quagmire.”* **Ask:** What did de Gaulle know that Kennedy did not? What experiences may account for de Gaulle's opinion?

Connections: Politics

Kennedy began to turn his attention to South Vietnam just two weeks after the United States' humiliation in the Bay of Pigs fiasco (see Chapter 27). One of Kennedy's advisors urged the Vietnam effort by saying, *“It is very important that the government have a major anti-Communist victory to its credit. . . . [In Vietnam] the odds are still in our favor.”* A little later Kennedy told a journalist: “Now we have a problem in making our power credible and Vietnam looks like the place.”

To protest anti-Buddhist policies of Ngo Dinh Diem's government, a monk named Quang Duc set himself on fire in the middle of a Saigon street.

Although opposed to Diem's harsh policies, the United States sent advisors to help his army fight Communist rebels.

In the south Ngo Dinh Diem had seized control from Bao Dai. A member of the Catholic minority, Diem had little support among the largely Buddhist population. He did, however, have the backing of Eisenhower and Dulles, who hoped he could control the political and religious factions and keep the south out of Communist hands.

Diem refused to schedule the election called for by the Geneva Accords because he feared a Vietminh victory. When Communist and non-Communist guerrillas joined together as the National Liberation Front to oppose him, he called them all Vietnamese Communists, or “Viet Cong.” To support him, the United States sent almost $2 billion in money and supplies between 1954 and 1959. American advisors trained Diem's army, the Army of the Republic of Vietnam (ARVN). By 1960 there were 685 advisors, the maximum allowed by the Geneva Accords.

Kennedy Increases Aid

When Kennedy took office in 1961, the Viet Cong, aided by the North Vietnamese Army (NVA), was gaining strength, and Diem's position was extremely shaky. Kennedy feared that allowing the country to fall under Communist rule would send a message to the Soviets and Chinese that America lacked the will to stand behind its alliances. However, he did not want to risk an all-out war that might draw in one or both Communist giants.

Kennedy chose a “flexible response,” sending more aid and military advisors. This solution, though, left the door wide open to further entanglement. The number of advisors swelled to 16,732 in 1963, and the line between advising and participating in combat began to blur. By 1963 nearly sixty Americans had died in Vietnam, but as far as the public back home knew, the American role remained strictly advisory.

Meanwhile, Diem would not bow to American urgings that he change repressive policies. He rejected land reform, and his “strategic hamlet” program forced villagers into detention compounds to keep them from aiding the Viet Cong. He replaced village councils with his own officials, appointed family members to powerful positions, and threw suspected opponents into detention camps. His only solid support was the privileged Catholic minority.

Diem's policies aroused protests from Buddhists. When his troops fired at demonstrators in May 1963, killing nine people, anger flared into more demonstrations. In an ultimate protest, a monk named Quang Duc set himself on fire, but the suicide failed to move Diem. Finally, encouraged by American diplomats, ARVN officers seized power in November 1963 and executed Diem.

Johnson Takes Further Steps

Twenty days after Diem's death, Kennedy was assassinated. His successor, Lyndon Johnson, now had to decide what to do about Vietnam. When Johnson was thrust into office, South Vietnam was in deeper trouble than anyone realized. For years, officials fearful of Diem's anger had concealed the extent of Viet Cong control. After his death they began sending in more accurate reports. One official's response when questioned about earlier reports was typical:

"How many villages are in your province?"
"Twenty-four."
"And how many do you control?"
"Eight."
"And how many did you tell Saigon you controlled?"
"Twenty-four."

Diem's overthrow plunged the south into chaos. The new rulers fought among themselves and could not direct the war effort. Within a year and a half the government changed hands nine times. This gloomy picture made a grim welcome for Johnson. Like Kennedy, he was bombarded by advice. Though knowing that increased involvement was risky, he shared Kennedy's fear of appearing weak-willed to the Soviets and Chinese. Having seen Truman condemned for being "soft" on communism, he decided that inaction would be political suicide in the upcoming 1964 election.

"Tell those generals in Saigon that Lyndon Johnson intends to stand by our word," Johnson declared. Publicly he steered a moderate course of continuing aid, but privately he authorized American-directed raids against Communist bases in Laos. Plans were also drawn up for bombing raids on North Vietnam, but officials balked at launching those without Congress's backing. The only event likely to gain the support of Congress would be a Viet Cong or NVA attack on Americans.

The Gulf of Tonkin Resolution. In August 1964 a report came out of the Gulf of Tonkin, off the coast of North Vietnam. Unknown to Congress and the public, two American destroyers were there supporting South Vietnamese gunboat raids. The captain of one radioed that he was being attacked by a North Vietnamese gunboat. Later, an attack on the other destroyer was reported.

Johnson did not wait for proof, but seized the opportunity to ask Congress for a resolution giving him power "to take all necessary measures to repel any armed attack against forces of the United States and to prevent further aggression." On August 7 the Gulf of Tonkin Resolution passed unanimously in the House. In the Senate only Wayne Morse of Oregon and Ernest Gruening of Alaska voted against it. Morse warned of giving the President "war-making powers in the absence of a declaration of war." Gruening said, "All Vietnam is not worth the life of a single American boy."

Johnson had misled Congress by not revealing that the destroyers were on a secret mission or that the attacks were unconfirmed. What actually happened in those waters remains a mystery. If Congress had known the truth it might not have been so quick to approve the resolution, which permitted a massive stepping-up of intervention in Vietnam. On the other hand, in the cold-war climate of the early 1960s, both Congress and the public still firmly supported the containment policy. Indeed, the two senators who voted against the resolution were defeated when they ran for reelection.

Section Review

1. Comprehension. Why did the United States oppose Ho Chi Minh's movement?

2. Analysis. How did South Vietnamese and American actions undercut the Geneva Accords?

3. Analysis. Why did Johnson seek stronger intervention, and how did he gain support for it?

Linking Past and Present. Compare American involvement in Vietnam with American efforts to contain communism in Central America.

Writing About History

Speech. Have students imagine they are Senators debating the Gulf of Tonkin Resolution. They are to prepare brief speeches giving a reason either for or against the resolution.

Active Learning

Cooperative Activity. Remind students that while Johnson was making decisions regarding the Vietnam conflict, he was also concerned with the "war" at home. What war was that? (War on Poverty, Chapter 27) Have students meet in small groups and carry on a cabinet meeting in which Johnson and his advisors debate options in government financing—military and economic, foreign and domestic.

Section Review

ANSWERS

1. Ho allied himself with Communists; the U.S. feared Communist victory in Vietnam would lead to rapid spread of communism in region.
2. Diem did not schedule the election called for by the Accords; U.S. sent advisors and aid to support Diem's government.
3. Johnson, after reports about chaos in South Vietnam, feared being called "soft" on communism. He used report of two American destroyers being attacked to get Congress to pass Gulf of Tonkin Resolution.
Linking Past and Present. Similarity: use of American funds to prevent spread of communism; difference: little reliance on American troops in Central America.

Section 29-2

Objectives

- ***Answer the Focus Question.***
- *Cite examples of racism during the Vietnam War.*
- *Explain the growing opposition to the war in the United States.*
- *Describe Nixon's policies in Vietnam, Cambodia, and Laos.*

Introducing THE SECTION

As students read this section, have them compare the experience of young Americans fighting in Vietnam with that of their relatives who might have fought in World War II.

Have them note how the composition of the fighting forces was different. **(in age, ethnicity, and other respects)** How might soldiers in World War II and in Vietnam have answered the question "What are you fighting for?" How was the atmosphere at home different during the two wars?

Developing THE SECTION

Backyard History

Research. Have students research the stories of local people who served in Vietnam or participated in antiwar activities in the community. **Ask:** In what ways did the war divide your community? Has there been evidence of reconciliation?

B · A · C · K · G · R · O · U · N · D

Social History

Because Vietnam was the first "television war," and images on the screen were the main experience most Americans had of the conflict, you may want to discuss movies such as *The Green Berets, Platoon, Born on the Fourth of July, In Country,* and *Apocalypse Now.* The PBS documentary *Vietnam: A Television History* is a factual complement to the fictional treatments.

Reduced student page in the Teacher's Edition

29-2 "In-Country" and at Home

Focus: How was the Vietnam War different from other American wars?

Though not a declaration of war, the Gulf of Tonkin Resolution freed the President to commit American military forces to action in Vietnam. Eventually hundreds of thousands of troops would be rotating in and out of Vietnam. After soldiers arrived "in-country," as they called Vietnam, the goal of containing communism became ever murkier in their minds. In a conflict that seemed to rewrite the "rules" of war, the primary goal was survival.

Expanding the War

Throughout 1964 North Vietnam channeled advisors and modern Chinese and Soviet weapons to the Viet Cong along a lifeline called the Ho Chi Minh Trail. This supply route, hacked out of thick jungles, snaked through Laos and Cambodia into the south. To strike at the source, Johnson launched Operation Rolling Thunder, a massive bombing campaign against North Vietnam.

Rolling Thunder continued for three years, hitting military sites, roads, and bridges, and laying waste to the countryside. However, no strikes were allowed on Hanoi's airfield, where Soviet and Chinese planes landed, or on the Ho Chi Minh Trail in Cambodia and Laos. As Secretary of State Dean Rusk later explained, "We took the situation very seriously in order to prevent the war from expanding into a war with the Soviet Union or China."

The operation failed to break the will of the NVA and the Viet Cong. In fact, NVA troops had begun heading down the Ho Chi Minh Trail to join the fighting in the south.

In early 1965 General William Westmoreland, the American commander, asked for two marine battalions to defend the air base at Da Nang. Marines waded ashore there on March 8, becoming the first American combat troops to arrive in Vietnam. Westmoreland soon asked for more troops and wider authority, and Johnson quickly agreed to **escalate,** or expand, the war. By the end of 1965 the troop level had risen to 180,000, and two years later it had soared to over 500,000.

Most Americans who fought in Vietnam were young, age nineteen on average, and had been drafted rather than volunteering. Most came from working-class backgrounds because many middle and upper-class youth got deferments, or postponements, of military service by enrolling in college.

On March 8, 1965, marines landed to defend the Da Nang airbase against guerrilla attacks. They were the first American ground troops to arrive in Vietnam.

African and Hispanic Americans bore far more than their fair share of the war's burden. For example, only 10 percent of the general population was African American, yet 18 percent of the troops were black, and they suffered 23 percent of the casualties. Likewise, California Hispanics, only 12 percent of the state's population, had 33 percent of its casualties. Many black and Hispanic soldiers were torn between their sense of patriotic duty and the pain of discrimination. As one said later, "We had been over in Vietnam fighting for our country, which at that point wasn't serving us properly."

One wounded marine reaches out to another during a lull in a battle against NVA troops in 1966. In such conflicts American firepower prevailed, but victory was never final. After sustaining heavy losses, NVA forces would regroup for future attacks on the South.

The unity of the fighting force was threatened not only by racial tensions but also by the constant rotation of soldiers. A new soldier was thrust into a platoon of strangers, and when his year-long tour of duty ended, or if he got a "million-dollar wound," he was sent home alone. Each platoon was in a state of flux, with officers and enlisted men changing every month. Many casualties resulted from soldiers being unaccustomed to each other as well as to the terrain and enemy strategies.

A Different Kind of War

From the moment soldiers arrived "in-country" until they returned to "the World," they were engulfed in a conflict unlike any other their country had fought. This was not a conventional war where the enemy and enemy territory could be clearly identified. This was "Nam," where the enemy was as likely to be a civilian as a soldier and could be lurking anywhere. One marine noted,

> *"You never knew who was the enemy and who was the friend. A woman watches your men walk down a trail and get killed or wounded by a booby trap. She knows the trap is there, but she doesn't warn them."*

The Americans were armed with modern weapons, with soldiers using infrared cameras to detect the heat of an unseen enemy. A highly flammable jellied gasoline called napalm and the chemical "Agent Orange" destroyed vegetation, depriving the enemy of food and cover. In the air, on the land, and on the sea, the American arsenal was superior.

Technical superiority did not ensure victory, though. The Viet Cong fought by guerrilla tactics: withdraw when the enemy advances, harass when he digs in, ambush when he least expects it. It was the infantry, the "grunts" trudging under sixty pounds of equipment, that took the heaviest casualties. Slogging through forests, they might set off grenades tied to vines or fall into brush-covered pits spiked with bamboo stakes.

Climate and terrain, too, were enemies. Monsoon rains grounded aircraft and created mud fields that sucked in artillery. Tropical heat roasted men carrying heavy equipment, and dense forests provided cover for guerrillas. "You begin to wonder if the VC are even out there," wrote a marine. "And all the time you know they are."

Search and destroy. To root out the hidden foe, patrols set out on "search and destroy" missions, sometimes burning villages suspected of

Connections: Music

Activity. Have students research attitudes toward the Vietnam War era reflected in music. Ask them to find recordings of several songs of the period and bring them to class. Play the recordings, asking students to note the lyrics and the songwriters' reactions to the war. "The Ballad of the Green Berets" by Barry Sadler tells of the valor of Vietnam soldiers. Song artists Bob Dylan, Phil Ochs, and Joan Baez sang songs of protest.

Linking Past and Present

Discussion. Ask students to compare the physical conditions in Vietnam with those faced by American soldiers in the desert in Kuwait and Iraq in 1991. **Ask:** How would equipment be affected differently in the two environments? Which conditions made it easier to locate and engage the enemy?

Analyzing Primary Sources

Vietnam Soldiers. Refer students to the soldier's description of "Killer" on this page. **Ask:** What reason does "Killer" give for killing the wounded prisoner? **(He'll recover from his wounds and kill more GIs.)** Why was the newcomer not trusted after that incident? **(He had spoken out in defense of a member of the Viet Cong.)**

Limited English Proficiency

Discussion. Ask students to describe some of the feelings and experiences that made the Vietnam War a fearful and frustrating experience for many American soldiers **(guerrilla tactics of Viet Cong, climate and terrain, contradictory American policies, cultural misunderstandings, racism)**.

Thinking Critically

Evaluation. Some people have said that the My Lai massacre was just one instance of a widespread pattern of atrocities. Others argue that the fact that Lt. Calley was court-martialed and convicted shows that the military tried to discourage such actions. **Ask:** Do you think atrocities are inevitable in war? Can they be minimized by proper training and supervision? Explain. (Students might feel that soldiers are less culpable than those who issue orders, others may believe that every soldier is responsible for his actions; still other may feel that the concept of "war crimes" is meaningless.)

Connections: Art

Artist William Linzee Prescott jumped into Normandy in World War II with the 82nd airborne division. He sketched and painted the invasion and his later experiences as a prisoner of war. In 1967 Prescott became the first civilian painter with the Army Combat Artist Program. His vibrant paintings show the frantic night life in Saigon as well as soldiers' daily lives and the devastation of bombed villages. His paintings appear in a portfolio *Vietnam Rhapsody*.

Reduced student page in the Teacher's Edition

hiding Viet Cong. Victory was measured by "structures" destroyed and the "body count." One newcomer described what happened after his unit, including a hardened veteran he called "The Killer," attacked a hideout and pulled out three bodies:

> *"I certainly wasn't expressing the confusion and doubt that was going on inside of me. The S2 [staff officer] is saying, 'Wow, body count three. You guys are really dynamite.' Then someone notices the third guy, the young one, that his chest is moving. He is breathing.*
>
> *The Killer kneels down, takes out his .38 snubnose, sticks it right into the kid's temple, and looks up. I guess he wanted to get some kind of permission. He says something like, 'We take no prisoners, right?'*
>
> *Something happened. I came back to earth. I became immediately decisive without a moment's hesitation. I said, 'You can't just kill that man.' The Killer went into a tantrum, 'We'll take this guy to the police and some relative will come and bribe whoever gets bribed and this guy will be back again planting mines in the road. If we don't kill this guy, he's going to be killing more GIs. . . .'*
>
> *Those guys never trusted me after that."*

Just as fear and frustration led some soldiers to "take no prisoners," the suspicion that anyone could be the enemy sometimes led to atrocities against civilians. One came to national attention a year after it occurred in March 1968. Soldiers had killed some 400 civilians in the village of My Lai, a suspected Viet Cong hideout. The officer in charge, Lieutenant William L. Calley, Jr., was court-martialed, but many Americans wondered if there were other "My Lai massacres" left unreported.

Spotlight on Vietnam Vocabulary

capping: shooting at
fire fight: a battle with the enemy
hooch: a hut or simple dwelling
KIA: killed in action
LZ: helicopter landing zone
medevac: medical evacuation by helicopter
million-dollar wound: a noncrippling wound serious enough to warrant return to the United States
point man: the first man in a combat patrol
rack: a bed or cot
slick: a helicopter
spider hole: a camouflaged enemy foxhole
two-digit midget: a soldier with less than 100 days left on his tour of duty

A Clash of Cultures

As Johnson "Americanized" the war, a transformation took place. The 600,000-man ARVN, which had been the front-line force fighting for South Vietnam, increasingly depended on the Americans. Noted one observer:

> *"I watched the South Vietnamese fighting spirit evaporate in direct proportion to increases in the level of U.S. aid, combat assistance, and advice that was poured in."*

The influx of American dollars and goods also contributed to government corruption in Saigon. Thus, while Americans spoke of protecting democracy, South Vietnamese leaders merely sought to tighten their grip on power.

American policies contradicted each other, too. The military campaign blotted out efforts to "win the hearts and minds" of villagers. Volunteers set up programs to help villagers, only to see their work undone by bombing raids. Many soldiers became frustrated with the confused policies, which one pilot summarized as "feed 'em and bomb 'em." Others failed to recognize the contradictions. After shelling a village, an officer bluntly declared, "It became necessary to destroy the town in order to save it."

Social History
In some cases, officers who placed their troops in high risk situations, exhibited racist behavior toward their men, or otherwise angered them, were targets of "fragging"—that is, fragmentation grenades were thrown into their tents. Some 730 incidents of fragging were reported between 1969 and 1971.

Deep cultural misunderstandings stood between the Vietnamese and the Americans. Seeing the strong value that Vietnamese place on family and village, many Americans falsely concluded that they did not value individual life.

Racism, too, played a role in hardening soldiers' attitudes toward Vietnamese allies as well as enemies. Calling them "gooks," as many soldiers did, somehow made them seem less than human. When asked about the killing of innocent civilians, one soldier replied, "What does it matter? They are all Vietnamese." Scoffing at the goal of winning hearts and minds, another stated flatly, "We're here to kill gooks, period."

The actions of Americans were influenced by the terrors and uncertainties of fighting an often-unseen enemy, resentment of lukewarm support from their ARVN allies, and prejudice against the very people they had been sent to defend. Many turned a blind eye to civilian casualties. Targets were designated "free fire zones," giving the green light for unrestricted bombing, artillery fire, and helicopter strafing.

American Voices

"You never knew who was the enemy and who was the friend."

—An American Marine

Lacking an understanding of the people's closeness to the land, soldiers insisted that farmers move to "pacified" areas. One old man replied,

> *"I have to stay behind to look after this piece of garden. Of all the property handed down to me by my ancestors, only this garden now remains. How can I have the heart to leave?"*

For most villagers, political differences between "democracy" and "communism" meant little. The Viet Cong also destroyed villages after suspecting residents of siding with the enemy. Thousands of civilians were killed each year by both sides, and some 4 million became refugees.

A contrast in technology: bicycles carrying supplies on the Ho Chi Minh Trail and an American fighter-bomber. Will-power proved to be a greater factor than firepower.

Connections: Literature

Reading Primary Sources. To help give students more perspective on the GI experience in Vietnam, have them read letters sent home by GIs. A good source is *Dear America: Letters Home from Vietnam,* edited by Bernard Edelman (see also Bibliography on page 773D).

Active Learning

Cooperative Activity. Divide the class into three groups. Have students imagine that they are Vietnamese village leaders forced to choose between the South Vietnamese (and Americans) and the Viet Cong. Have one group argue for each side and a third group argue a survival-oriented strategy.

Analyzing Primary Sources

An American Marine. Refer students to the "American Voices" quote on this page. **Ask:** Why was there confusion? What behavior resulted from such uncertainty?

Multicultural Perspectives

Analyzing Primary Sources. A group of African-American students in Mississippi, having heard that one of their classmates had been killed in Vietnam, distributed a leaflet that read as follows:

"No Mississippi Negroes should be fighting in Viet Nam for the White man's freedom, until all the Negro People are free in Mississippi. Negro boys should not honor the draft in Mississippi. Mothers should encourage their sons not to go.

No one has a right to ask us to risk our lives and kill other Colored People in . . . Viet Nam, so that the White American can get richer."

Ask: What were the two major objections these students had to the war? **(African Americans should not be fighting for freedom for others while inequality exists for them at home; people of color should not be fighting each other.)** How does this statement differ from statements at the start of World War II? **(Refer students to Chapter 24, pages 640–641.)** How does it compare with Col. Fred Cherry's statement on page 787?

Linking Past and Present

Research. Have students research newspaper and magazine accounts of the Tet Offensive in 1968. Was it reported as a victory for the Viet Cong or a defeat? How is it regarded today?

Connections: Science and Technology

Many Americans wondered how the Viet Cong could have mounted such an effective attack against supposedly secure territory. One reason was the vast network of underground tunnels and bunkers that the Viet Cong had constructed, reaching sometimes into the outskirts of major cities. The tunnel network included meeting rooms, storerooms, fuel storage tanks, even hospitals. South Vietnamese soldiers and short, wiry Americans on SWAT teams—"tunnel rats"—had the deadly job of going down into the tunnels, facing ambushes and booby traps and fighting desperate hand-to-hand combat in the dark.

Reduced student page in the Teacher's Edition

Tet: The Turning Point

By 1968 American and ARVN forces had gained much territory, but when they withdrew from "pacified" areas, the Viet Cong usually moved back in. American troops seemed to be merely buying time for a government that refused to earn the people's loyalty. If anything, the bombing increased opposition to the Saigon government.

Meanwhile, at home Johnson was losing support on two fronts. Some people felt that getting involved had been a mistake, while others called for a tougher policy. The frustration was reflected by a popular bumper sticker: "WIN OR GET OUT."

Eager to convince the doubters, Johnson put pressure on military leaders to show that the United States was winning. Unwilling to admit their problems, they sent falsely optimistic reports, and Johnson kept assuring the public that victory was in sight. In January 1968 the embassy in Saigon planned a party to celebrate Tet, the Vietnamese lunar New Year. "Come see the light at the end of the tunnel," said the invitations.

Such optimism was shattered on January 30, the first day of Tet, when 84,000 Communist soldiers launched a major offensive throughout the South. American and ARVN troops drove the invaders out of the cities and military bases they had overrun.

Learning From Art Viet Cong Tunnel System

For defense, the Viet Cong relied heavily on over 200 miles of tunnels. Dug by hand a few yards per day, they snaked underneath villages, some within a few miles of Saigon. Many tunnels were destroyed, but one American officer noted, "There isn't enough dynamite in Vietnam to blow up all of them." They helped the Viet Cong survive bombing attacks and disappear at will.

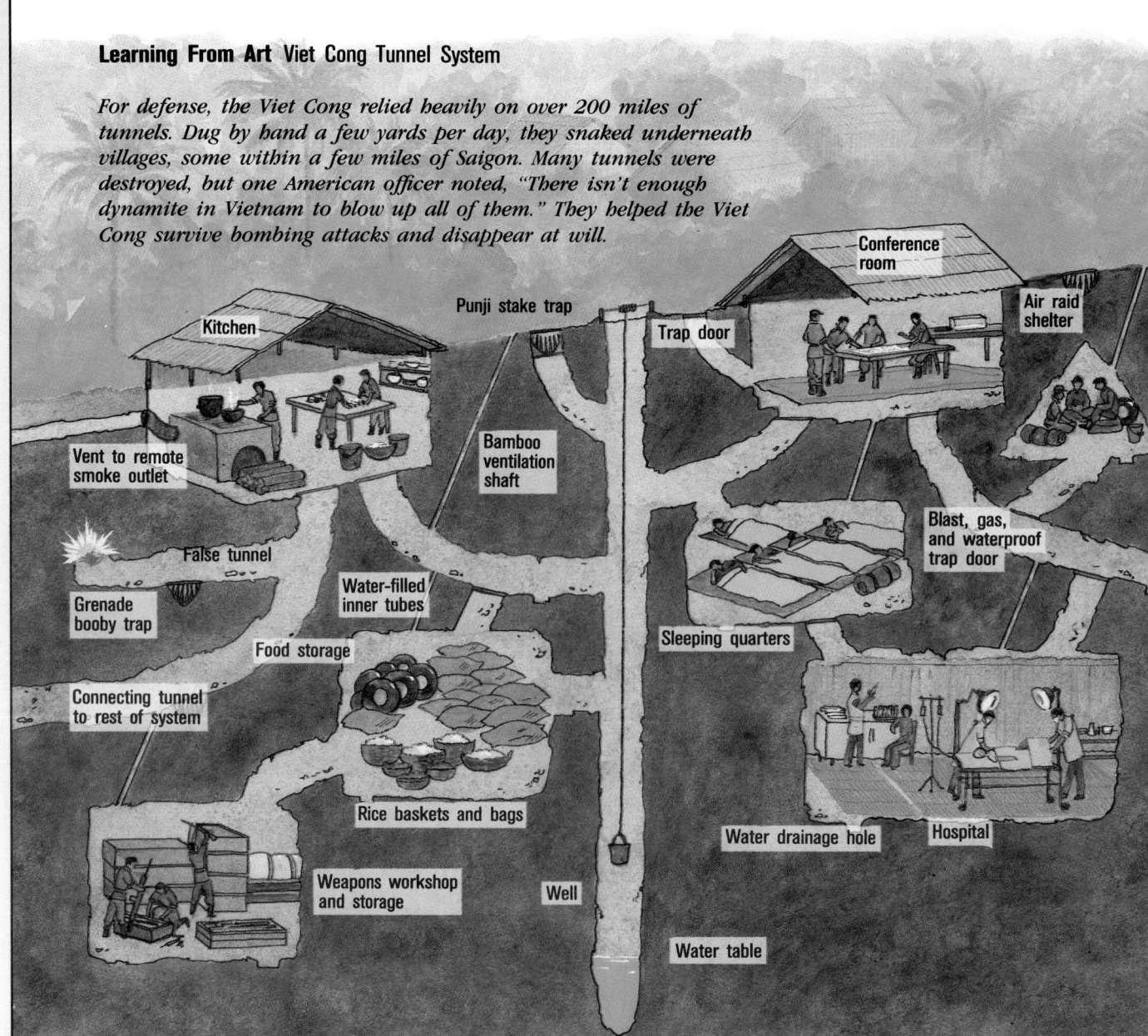

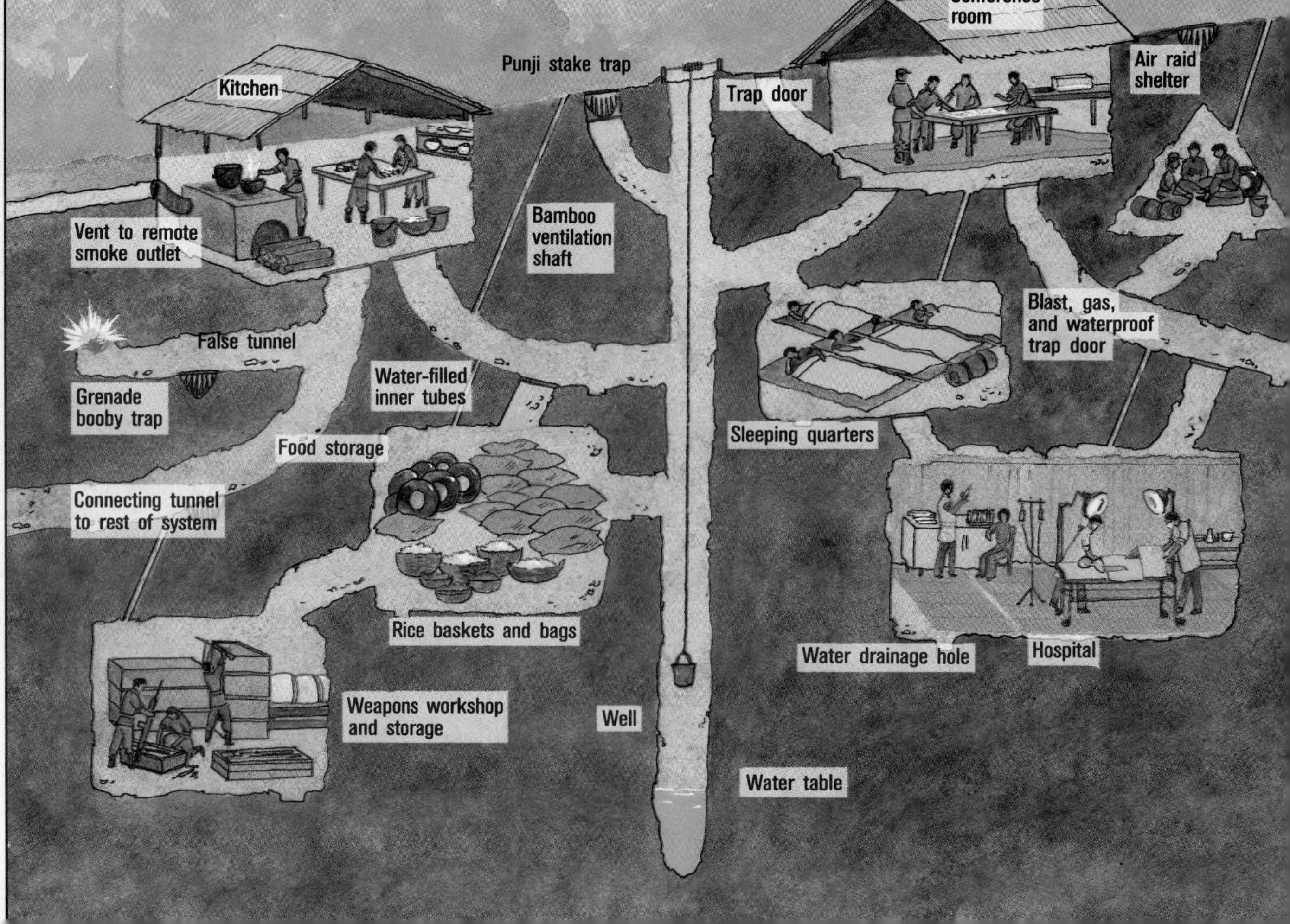

Social History
People opposed the war for a variety of reasons. Pacifists, often belonging to religious groups such as Quakers, opposed all war and killing. Some sought conscientious-objector status and served as noncombatants or in civilian jobs, while others refused to cooperate in any way with the government. An increasing number of moderate liberals viewed the war as a case of misplaced priorities and/or thought the U.S. was mistaken propping up an unpopular dictatorship in South Vietnam. A smaller but very vocal minority opposed the war on radical political grounds; Marxists and other members of the "New Left" sided with the North Vietnamese "struggle against imperialism" and urged that protestors take violent action against the authorities.

Still, the Communists had scored a stunning psychological victory by sweeping into cities thought safe and catching the south off guard.

The Tet Offensive proved to be the major turning point of the war. The *Wall Street Journal* warned, "The American people should be getting ready to accept, if they haven't already, that the whole Vietnam effort may be doomed."

The Antiwar Movement

The shock of Tet gave strength to the antiwar movement back home. By 1968 American casualties had risen to over 35,000, and the war was costing $25 billion a year. Many people thought that lives and dollars were being squandered to support a corrupt regime while anti-poverty programs at home were crying for funds.

Some critics agreed with the aim of containing communism but considered the war unwinnable, while others saw it as a civil war in which the United States had no business intervening.

As the war escalated, many young men had refused to be drafted. Some were **conscientious objectors,** people who refuse to take part in war because killing other persons is against their moral or religious principles. Others were opposed only to fighting in Vietnam. They burned their draft cards, went to jail, or starved or injured themselves to gain medical exemptions. About 100,000 took refuge in other countries, and in the armed forces an estimated 50,000 deserted.

American Voices

"Hey, hey, LBJ, how many kids did you kill today?"

—War Protestors' Chant

The war divided the nation as no issue had since the American Civil War, splitting it into opposing camps of prowar **hawks** and antiwar **doves.** Government policies bred distrust among many youth, adding fuel to the counterculture movement. Protestors on college campuses chanted "Hey, hey, LBJ, how many kids did you kill today?" Conversations in thousands of homes were poisoned by bitter arguments.

Meanwhile, support for the war was also weakening in Washington. Senator William Fulbright, chairman of the Senate Foreign Relations Committee, became a leading critic of Johnson's policy. At televised hearings of the committee in 1966 and 1967, government and business leaders, ministers, and educators spoke out against the war. Several of Johnson's advisors, including Secretary of Defense Robert McNamara, could no longer support his war policy, and resigned.

The turmoil tore at those serving in Vietnam. Some became protestors themselves when they came home. Many others, though, felt betrayed by the antiwar movement. One nurse, Lieutenant Lynda Van Devanter, wrote home,

"It hurts so much sometimes to see the paper full of demonstrators, especially people burning the flag. . . . Display the flag, Mom and Dad, please, every day. And tell your friends to do the same. It means so much to us to know we're supported, to know not everyone feels we're making a mistake being here."

Conflict over the war had erupted side by side with the civil rights struggle and particularly tore at African- and Hispanic-American soldiers. Many black soldiers wanted to quit the war after Martin Luther King, Jr., spoke out against it, and especially after he was murdered in 1968. The Communists tried to take advantage of the racial tensions. Fighter pilot Colonel Fred Cherry recalled that when he was captured, North Vietnamese guards pressured him to side with them as people of color:

"I told them, 'We have problems in the U.S., but you can't solve them. Like you, I am a uniformed soldier. . . . I can't do what you ask.' They never got to home plate. Just like when they beat me, I always kept in mind I was representing 24 million black Americans. If they are going to kill me, they are going to have to kill me. I'm not going to denounce my government."

Limited English Proficiency

Building Vocabulary. Refer students to the terms *hawks* and *doves* on this page. Discuss the use of these terms and their appropriateness. Then have students draw political cartoons using visual images of hawks or doves to indicate support or opposition to the war.

Constitutional Heritage

Discussion. Refer students to the Bill of Rights. Have volunteers read aloud the clauses related to the rights of citizens to disagree with elected officials and how those rights can be exercised. Have students consider whether the antiwar movement was constitutional.

Analyzing Primary Sources

Martin Luther King, Jr. In a speech in 1967 Martin Luther King, Jr., said:

"I am as deeply concerned about our own troops there as anything else. For it occurs to me that what we are submitting them to in Vietnam is not simply the brutalizing power that goes on in any war where armies face each other and seek to destroy. We are adding cynicism to the process of death, for they must know after a short period there that none of the things we claim to be fighting for are really involved."

Ask: According to Dr. King, why was this war different from other wars? What does he mean by "adding cynicism . . . to death"? How accurate do you think he was?

Citizenship

Discussion. The antiwar movement resulted in about 100,000 Americans of draft age fleeing the country and another 50,000 in the armed forces deserting. Were these actions legal? **(Fleeing the country to evade the draft is illegal, and deserting the military in wartime is a crime punishable by death.)** Many took these actions on moral grounds. Others chose to go to jail rather than be drafted. **Ask:** What should you do if a law goes against your beliefs? Do you have the right to disobey? What is a citizen's responsibility?

Global Connections

Discussion. In small groups, have students discuss Nixon's Vietnamization policy. What was its impact on the United States? What was the impact on North Vietnam? On South Vietnam? Given the condition of South Vietnam's government and society, did Vietnamization seem likely to succeed at the time? Explain.

Active Learning

Debate. Have students debate this proposition: The Nixon administration acted properly by withholding information from the public about the bombings in Cambodia and Laos.

Social History

Dickey Chapelle, a war correspondent, started her career covering the vicious fighting in Iwo Jima and Okinawa in World War II, and brought her camera to the line of fire in three wars and four revolutions. During the early fighting in Vietnam in 1962, she parachuted into Viet Cong territory, winning an award for "the best reporting, any medium, requiring exceptional courage and enterprise abroad." She was killed by a mine in 1965.

Reduced student page in the Teacher's Edition

The impact of the media. Military leaders blamed the media for the decline in public support. The war was the first to be widely televised as well as covered by newspaper and magazine reporters in the field. Articles, photographs, and especially video footage of death and destruction shocked Americans.

Prior to Tet, news coverage had generally supported American involvement. But Tet changed the mood of the media, which increasingly questioned optimistic government reports. Meanwhile, the sight of dead marines outside the American embassy had more impact on television viewers than did official statements about victory. And when CBS anchorman Walter Cronkite, the country's most trusted journalist, announced he had lost faith in the war policy, Johnson fretted, "If I've lost Walter, I've lost the support of Mr. Average Citizen."

Nixon Elected in 1968

1968 was a presidential election year. The Tet Offensive and growing opposition to the war crushed Johnson's hopes for reelection, and he decided not to run. His withdrawal intensified the Democratic race. Senator Eugene McCarthy had already attracted support among antiwar voters, especially young ones. Senator Robert Kennedy, now a dove himself, also entered the race. However, moments after he won the key California primary, Kennedy was killed by a lone assassin.

In the aftermath of Kennedy's death, Vice-President Hubert Humphrey emerged as the leading candidate. The Democratic Convention in Chicago nominated him, even though his defense of Johnson's Vietnam policy angered delegates who wanted a complete withdrawal.

While the Democrats conducted business inside the convention hall, the war issue was being thrashed out in the streets. Thousands of antiwar protestors who had gathered in Chicago clashed with National Guard troops and police. Battles between club-wielding police and taunting, bloodied demonstrators flashed across television screens. In stark contrast the Republicans, meeting in Miami, peacefully nominated Richard Nixon.

Capitalizing on public dismay at violent war protests, Nixon pledged to restore "law and order" and "bring us together." Competing for the conservative vote was Governor George Wallace of Alabama, candidate of the American Independent Party, whose campaign struck a more hawkish note. In a very close race, Nixon and Humphrey each received 43 percent of the popular vote. The final tally of electoral votes gave Nixon the victory, 301 to 191, with 46 for Wallace.

Vietnamization

Having promised "peace with honor," Nixon took office determined not to be the first President to lose a war. Yet he recognized that antiwar feeling was too strong to permit an all-out effort to achieve victory. In November 1969 he announced a gradual withdrawal of all American forces. Continued withdrawals, he explained, would depend on the enemy's actions and the progress of peace talks that had begun in 1968 in Paris.

Withdrawals would also depend on "Vietnamization," the key to Nixon's plan. The United States would equip the ARVN to fight the war. "As the South Vietnamese become strong enough to defend their own freedom," Nixon promised, Americans would come home. Meanwhile, Nixon supporters, whom he hailed as the "great silent majority," attended "pro-America" rallies. The antiwar movement responded with its own rallies, which also drew hundreds of thousands.

Into Cambodia and Laos. Along with his public policy, Nixon pursued a secret course in Cambodia. The NVA had set up bases in Cambodia, striking at South Vietnam and then retreating across the border to safety. In March 1969 Nixon launched a secret bombing campaign against these bases, hoping to prod North Vietnam to make concessions. But the peace talks remained stalled, and the Communists continued their cross-border raids.

By March 1970 Cambodian Communists were threatening the country's non-Communist government. Responding to the government's plea for help, Nixon ordered troops into Cambodia. Although the invasion slowed Communist activity in South Vietnam, it increased conflict in Cambodia.

At home, news of the invasion set off a furious wave of protests. On May 4, during a tense confron-

Social History

The Pentagon Papers contained the results of a study by the Department of Defense in 1967–1968 to determine how the United States had become so deeply committed to South Vietnam. The study began with the earliest policy decisions by Truman's administration and continued through the Johnson years. The Papers revealed that Johnson's escalation of the war had been planned, even as he was telling the American people there would be "no wider war." The Nixon administration took the *New York Times* to court requesting an injunction against further publication of the classified documents. The Supreme Court ruled that the government could file criminal charges against anyone stealing classified documents, but it could not impose prior restraint on a newspaper.

Reporters like CBS anchorman Walter Cronkite were free to tour the war zone and gather information. In contrast, during the Persian Gulf War of 1991, the military restricted the press's movement. Reporters mainly depended on whatever information officers provided at press conferences.

tation at Kent State University in Ohio, National Guard troops fired into a crowd, killing four students. Two more died during protests at Jackson State College in Mississippi. Meanwhile, the "silent majority" staged their own demonstrations in support of Nixon.

Members of Congress complained that Nixon had exceeded his powers by ordering troops into a neutral country without consulting Congress. In December 1970 Congress repealed the Gulf of Tonkin Resolution and prohibited the use of American troops in Cambodia or Laos.

Nixon, though, was intent on blocking the Ho Chi Minh Trail in Laos. Barred by Congress from sending troops, he had to settle for ARVN ground forces with American air support. It would be a test of Vietnamization. In February 1971 ARVN troops invaded Laos, but their blundering operation failed to dent the Communist supply line.

Gathering gloom. The Laotian campaign spread gloom among the South Vietnamese, many of whom believed that the Americans were abandoning them. Meanwhile, American troops, frustrated by a seemingly unwinnable war, grew more restless. Drug use soared, racial tensions flared, and some GIs even attacked their officers. "Everybody seemed to be at everybody else's throat," reported one soldier.

In Washington, D.C., 200,000 marchers protested the invasion. When a disapproving woman scolded a protestor, "Son, I don't think what you're doing is good for the troops," he replied, "Lady, we *are* the troops!" He was one of 2,000 Vietnam veterans at the demonstration.

Criticism continued to mount. In the summer of 1971 a former Defense Department aide named Daniel Ellsberg gave copies of secret government documents to the *New York Times.* They revealed that Johnson and Nixon administration officials had lied to the nation about Vietnam. When the *Times* published the "Pentagon Papers," opposition to the war reached a new high.

Section Review

1. Identification. Define *escalate, conscientious objectors, hawks,* and *doves.*

2. Comprehension. How did Vietnam differ from conventional wars like World War II?

3. Analysis. What were some examples of racism during the war?

4. Analysis. What led to the increase in public opposition to the war?

Thinking Critically

Synthesis. Recall with students that in 1964 Congress gave President Johnson the power to use whatever means necessary to aid South Vietnam. In 1970 Congress repealed the Gulf of Tonkin Resolution. What do you think happened to change the attitude of Congress? (Congress might have felt political pressure from constituents, for example.)

Section Review

ANSWERS

1. Definitions for the following terms are on text pages indicated in parentheses: *escalate* (782), *conscientious objectors* (787), *hawks* (787), *doves* (787).
2. Enemy could be soldiers or civilians, and spotting them was difficult; modern American weapons were pitted against guerrilla tactics; goals unclear, no "rules"; troops very young, constant rotation of soldiers.
3. Calling Vietnamese "gooks"; callousness about taking Vietnamese (including civilian) lives and destroying entire villages; racist attitudes of some white soldiers toward black and Hispanic soldiers.
4. The Tet Offensive showed the strength of the opposition and convinced many Americans that the attempt to shore up the South Vietnam government was doomed to failure.

Section 29-3

Objectives

- ***Answer the Focus Question.***
- *Describe how the Vietnam War ended.*
- *Explain why many veterans of the war felt bitter.*
- *Summarize the lessons of the Vietnam War.*

Introducing

THE SECTION

Direct American involvement in Vietnam ended in 1973, but the effects of the war on Americans continued. Returning veterans often faced hostility, limited opportunity, and severe psychological problems. After the fall of South Vietnam in 1975, "boat people" risked their lives to flee Vietnam, and those who made it to America faced racism as they struggled to build new lives. In Southeast Asia, political persecution and civil war resulted in death or poverty for millions of Vietnamese and Cambodians.

In discussing this section, consider the extent to which these problems continue today, long after the last American troops left Vietnam. Ask students to consider the various "lessons" that people with different perspectives say should be learned from the Vietnam experience.

B · A · C · K · G · R · O · U · N · D

Multicultural Perspectives

While Everett Alvarez was a prisoner of war, his sister, Delia Alvarez, came to believe that supporting the antiwar movement was the best way to speed the day her brother would come home. She spoke at rallies and went to the Paris peace talks to persuade the Viet Cong representatives to end the war. As Everett recalls in his book, *Chained Eagle*, the North Vietnamese taunted him with her actions: *"See, your own family disapproves of your criminal actions! Now you must change your attitude!"*

Delia faced harsh criticism, both for her views and for stepping beyond "a woman's place." Today, years after being reunited, the brother and sister still disagree about both Vietnam and the 1991 Gulf War. Yet, Everett says, *"We talk a lot and are probably the closest members of our family."*

29-3 A Peace Yet to Come

Focus: What were some effects of the Vietnam War?

By the beginning of 1972, Nixon had reduced the number of troops by over one half. But he continued air raids on the Viet Cong and the NVA in Vietnam, Cambodia, and Laos. In March the NVA launched a major offensive against South Vietnam. The Americans countered with intensive bombing of Hanoi and the port of Haiphong but failed to halt the advance.

Nixon tried to stop the flow of Soviet and Chinese supplies by ordering bombing strikes on supply routes and railroads and a naval blockade of North Vietnam. These would end, he said, when the North accepted a cease-fire.

Lieutenant Everett Alvarez, captured when his plane was shot down in 1964, was greeted by President Nixon after North Vietnam released him in 1973. He was the war's longest-held American POW.

The Paris Peace Talks

At last, peace negotiations began to show promise. But the real decisions were made not at the official talks but in secret meetings between Nixon's foreign policy advisor Henry Kissinger and North Vietnamese negotiator Le Duc Tho. Meeting outside Paris, the two could talk directly without interference from the Saigon regime or the Viet Cong. The meetings, which began in early 1970, had sputtered on and off for over two years as the two men matched diplomatic skills.

Finally, in October 1972, Kissinger announced a breakthrough and Nixon halted the bombing. But South Vietnamese President Nguyen Van Thieu objected, and then the North Vietnamese began to stall. An angry Nixon ordered round-the-clock bombing raids on Hanoi and Haiphong in December. After eleven days and 40,000 tons of bombs, the north agreed to talk again, and Nixon once more stopped the bombing.

In January 1973 all parties signed an "Agreement on Ending the War and Restoring Peace in Vietnam." The pact called for an immediate cease-fire, the withdrawal of all American forces, and the release of American prisoners of war (POWs). Thieu was instructed to work with the Viet Cong to organize elections in the south, and North Vietnam was permitted to keep 150,000 troops there.

By the end of March, over 500 POWs had been released, and the last American forces had departed. Some 7,000 American civilians and a few military personnel remained to staff government offices. Still, the situation was not settled.

The Fall of South Vietnam

When Thieu refused to cooperate with the Viet Cong, South Vietnam again plunged into warfare. In March 1975 the NVA launched their final assault. One city after another fell as they rolled south. Millions of refugees fled, some to the coast to escape by sea, others to Saigon with the retreating ARVN. On April 21 Thieu resigned, blaming the United States for his government's fall. By then, evacuation flights were leaving Saigon day and night.

On April 29 Saigon's American-owned radio station played "White Christmas," followed by a

Social History

Mary Stout, the first woman to become president of the Vietnam Veterans of America, served her tour of duty in 1966 as an intensive care nurse. Working twelve hours a day, seven days a week, she treated the war's worst casualties. But it was not until 1980 that the delayed effects of her ordeal hit her. She became hyperactive, unable to concentrate, and afraid to go to bed. Mary became involved in veteran's issues to help her own healing. When she learned that no special recognition had been given to nurses in the Vietnam Veterans Memorial in Washington, D.C., she lobbied to have a small statue of a nurse placed nearby.

weather report: "The temperature in Saigon is 105 degrees and rising." This was a signal for Americans to flee. Communist bombing had closed the airport, so the only way out was by helicopter. About 140,000 South Vietnamese were also airlifted to waiting ships, but in the panicky evacuation many more had to be left behind.

By the next morning only one rescue point remained: the rooftop of the American embassy. At 7:53 a.m. Marines lowered the American flag and boarded the last helicopter. That same day the government of South Vietnam surrendered.

Problems Facing Veterans

Some 2.7 million veterans came home alive. Their homecoming, like their war, was different. They did not return with their buddies on troop ships, with time to begin to adjust to civilian life. Far from being welcomed home with parades, they were often angrily blamed for the only war the nation had "lost." Americans who wanted to forget Vietnam simply ignored its veterans. Veteran John Kerry described his return:

> *"There I was, a week out of the jungle, flying from San Francisco to New York. I fell asleep and woke up yelling, probably a nightmare. The other passengers moved away from me—a reaction I noticed more and more in the months ahead."*

Many had to adapt to life with physical disabilities. Thanks to speedy medical evacuation, a higher proportion of injured soldiers survived in Vietnam than in previous wars. But they often needed painful, expensive, ongoing medical and surgical care. Some found that the benefits paid by

Fearing a bloodbath as Communist forces closed in on Saigon, South Vietnamese civilians surrounded the American embassy, hoping to be evacuated by helicopter.

Developing

THE SECTION

Writing About History

Descriptive Paragraphs. Have students look at the pictures on this page and write paragraphs describing how they think the following people felt about the fall of South Vietnam: a South Vietnamese civilian who had worked for the Americans, an American helicopter pilot, a North Vietnamese soldier entering the city with the victorious army.

Analyzing Primary Sources

WWII Veterans Welcomed Home. Read to students the following *New York Times* description of a returning ship after World War II:

> *"Blowing trumpets and banging brasses met the returning soldiers streaming back in 1945 and 1946. In New York Harbor, for example, as the first troopships to leave Europe after V-E Day entered into the narrows, the army's Welcome Home Boat Q200 chugged out into the rain to meet the four big vessels. The band, led by Marybelle Nissly, serenaded the troops with tunes of 'One Meatball' and 'The Pennsylvania Polka.'"*

Have students compare the homecoming of World War II veterans to that of returning Vietnam War veterans. Why was there a difference?

Connections: Science and Technology

Research. Have interested students research napalm and defoliants, such as Agent Orange. What were their effects on their targets? On American troops? What has been the outcome of recent suits by Vietnam veterans claiming ill effects from the chemicals?

Limited English Proficiency

Building Vocabulary. What is the purpose of a memorial? How was the erection of the Vietnam Veterans Memorial an important step in healing the nation after the war? What benefit is there in remembering?

Connections: Art

After Lin's design for the Vietnam Veterans Memorial was chosen, there was much political energy devoted to preventing it from being used. Jan Scruggs, the veteran who had steered the Vietnam memorial project into being nine years earlier, said, *"There were some very powerful people in Washington who were trying to stop this memorial from being built, saying, 'Why are all the others white and this is black?' They called it 'a scar, a black gash of shame and sorrow.'"* Retired Brigadier General George Price, a high-ranking African-American Army officer, loudly protested the reference to black as a "color of shame." The memorial's critics stopped using this analogy.

Reduced student page in the Teacher's Edition

the Veterans Administration (VA) did not adequately cover their expenses.

For years veterans pressed the VA to admit that many of their sicknesses stemmed from exposure to the chemical Agent Orange. Thousands charged that the chemical had caused cancer and liver disease, as well as birth defects in their children. Finally, in 1984 seven manufacturers of Agent Orange set up a fund to compensate victims.

The war also did psychological damage. An estimated half million veterans suffered from "post-traumatic stress disorder," involving anxiety, panic attacks, depression, and vivid flashbacks of war experiences. "Sometimes the terror is so deep-set you simply cannot remember. It comes back in nightmares," explained one veteran. It was not uncommon for a veteran, unable to recover, to commit suicide.

For many veterans bitter feelings eased with time. Very slowly they began to share their experiences with family, friends, and counselors. Some came to terms with the war through art. After years of painful silence, they poured out poems, novels, plays, films, paintings, and sculptures about Vietnam. This documenting of experiences helped bring a measure of understanding about the war to all Americans.

One veteran, Jan Skruggs, was convinced that the scars of the war would never truly heal until the United States erected a memorial to the American men and women who died in Vietnam. For years he worked to raise funds and gain support. At last, in November 1982, the Vietnam Veterans Memorial was dedicated in Washington, D.C. Carved on its V-shaped wall of polished black granite are the names of the war's dead and missing.

Thousands of veterans and their families poured into the capital for the dedication. Some wore business suits, while others wore combat fatigues. Some came in wheelchairs or on crutches. They held reunions and searched the wall for names of long-dead comrades. And the Vietnam veterans finally had their parade. Said one veteran,

> *"In this place there is no rancor, no debate. There is only reconciliation on basic human terms, strangers spontaneously hugging each other in tears."*

For some families, however, the names on the black wall provoked painful uncertainty. Over 2,000 Americans were listed as MIA, missing in action. Their deaths were never witnessed, and their bodies were never recovered.

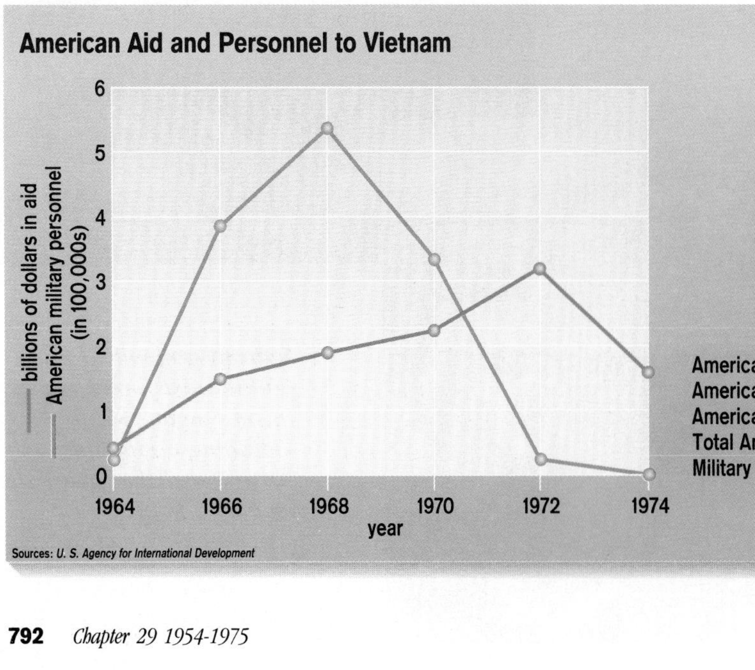

THE AMERICAN SPIRIT

Maya Lin

Monument Maker

Contest entries filled the huge airplane hangar. More than 1,400 people had submitted models of their designs for a memorial to the Americans who had died or were missing in the Vietnam War. Although the entrants included many well-known artists and architects, the winner was a twenty-one-year-old student named Maya Lin.

Many were shocked at the choice of a young, inexperienced artist who was still in high school when the war ended. Her unusual design also stirred controversy. She proposed a 500-foot-long, V-shaped wall rising out of the ground, angling up to a height of 10 feet, and sloping back into the earth. On its black granite surface would be carved the names of the dead and missing, beginning with the first casualties.

Maya Lin explained, "I just knew I wanted something horizontal that took you in, that made you feel safe within the park, yet at the same time reminding you of the dead. So I just imagined opening up the earth."

When the memorial was dedicated on Veterans' Day in 1982, any remaining doubt about its appropriateness vanished. Over 20 million people visited the memorial in the next few years, and millions more continue to visit, many reaching out to touch the name of a fallen relative or friend. All agree that the memorial has helped heal the wounds of a nation bitterly divided by the war.

In 1988 Maya Lin watched the unveiling of another of her designs, the Civil Rights Memorial in Montgomery, Alabama. It honors defenders of human rights and is inscribed with words from the Bible quoted by Dr. Martin Luther King, Jr.: "Until justice rolls down like waters and righteousness like a mighty stream." Maya Lin noted, "I've been incredibly fortunate to have been given the opportunity to work on not just one but both memorials. They are special. They mark the beginning and closing of a decade."

War Refugees

In Vietnam, an estimated 1.9 million people had been killed, 4.5 million wounded, and 9 million made refugees during the war. And the people's suffering continued. Under the Communists, thousands of city dwellers were forcibly relocated in the countryside as part of a plan to expand agriculture in the south. Opponents of the new regime were herded into harsh "reeducation camps." Meanwhile, a series of droughts and floods devastated the rice economy.

Seeking economic aid, Vietnam strengthened ties with the Soviet Union. At the same time, its relations with China and Cambodia worsened. In 1978 the Vietnamese invaded Cambodia and overthrew its Chinese-backed Communist government. China retaliated with raids into northern Vietnam.

By 1985 some 1.5 million Vietnamese, Cambodians, and Laotians had fled the turmoil in their

Active Learning

Designing a Memorial. Refer students to the illustration of the Vietnam Veterans Memorial on page 774. Gather pictures of other war memorials and have students compare them to the one for the Vietnam conflict. Have them discuss how their feelings differ when viewing pictures of different styles of memorials.

Divide the class into small groups to design a war memorial. Students can first design it on paper and then construct a model from clay, wood, cardboard, or other material. Have students display the finished memorials and explain their significance.

Thinking Critically

Synthesis. Have students research the massacre of Cambodians under Pol Pot. **Ask:** Why has this tragedy been compared to the murder of political opponents in the Soviet Union and China in earlier years? To what extent might American involvement in Southeast Asia have contributed to this situation?

Linking Past and Present

Discussion. Have students explain how the "Vietnam Syndrome"—the fear of becoming involved in another Vietnam-type war—affects American foreign policy today. Have students refer to recent policies concerning conflicts in Latin America and the Middle East.

Writing About History

Essays. Have students write essays comparing the Vietnam War and the 1991 Gulf War, illustrating the different "lessons" Americans took from Vietnam. Students should point out factors affecting public support and troop morale. **(In the Gulf War there was a clear-cut sense of "right and wrong"; a definite goal of driving Iraq from Kuwait; a total commitment of military force to achieve goal; conventional, rather than guerrilla warfare; a volunteer, professional army, rather than short-term draftees; a clear desire for quick results.)**

Connections: Economics

Free-market economic reforms began in Vietnam in 1986, sparking a revival in the cities—though 80 percent of the Vietnamese people live in the countryside. All land is owned by the state, but a contract system gives individual farmers control of the land for 15 to 30 years. Farmers grow what they want and sell it at market price. Vietnam has become the third largest exporter of rice in the world, after Thailand and the United States. An indication of better economic conditions is the sharp reduction in the number of boat people arriving in Hong Kong, down from about 1,800 in March 1989 to 730 in March 1990. The inflation rate dropped from 700 percent in 1989 to 50 percent in 1990. The annual per capita income of most Vietnamese, however, is less than $200, far below that in South Vietnam when the fighting ended in 1975.

Reduced student page in the Teacher's Edition

countries. Many crowded aboard flimsy boats, trying to reach safety in Thailand and other Asian countries. If they survived storms at sea and attacks by pirates, these "boat people" faced months or years in refugee camps waiting for permanent settlement in the West.

Over half settled in the United States. Like most new immigrants, they faced the difficulties of learning a new language and new customs. They also faced racial discrimination by Americans who saw them as an economic threat. Despite these obstacles, America's newest Asian immigrants set to work to build new lives.

A special group of refugees was made up of Amerasians, the children of Vietnamese mothers and American fathers. When the Americans left Vietnam, between 8,000 and 15,000 of these children remained with their mothers. But these mixed-race children were treated as outcasts in Vietnam. Some were sent alone to the United States, sometimes clutching photographs of fathers they hoped to find. Others, with their families, endured years of bureaucratic red tape before being reunited with American fathers and husbands.

Over 1.5 million refugees from Indochina fled by sea. Relief agencies estimated that up to one third of the "boat people" perished in storms or pirate attacks.

For Amerasians adjustment could be difficult. Still, many came to feel at home in their new country. One boy broke into tears upon his arrival at an American airport. He had never seen so many people who looked like him.

Lessons of the War

In the years since the war, some Americans have pointed to what they call a harmful "Vietnam syndrome," referring to the nation's reluctance in the wake of Vietnam to take decisive action overseas. Others, though, believe that the memory of Vietnam should keep the country cautious about entering another war.

In looking for military lessons, some have argued that the military's hands were tied by politicians and that the United States could have won with more firepower early in the war. Others, though, have noted that the Americans won every major battle, yet did not win the war. The United States, they argue, lacked a clear overall strategy, and in any case could not crush the will of the North Vietnamese and Viet Cong, who were prepared to take whatever losses were necessary to win.

Others focused on political and moral lessons. For Dean Rusk the main message was to look carefully at implications of alliances. For Senator Fulbright another lesson was more important:

> *"The biggest lesson I learned from Vietnam is not to trust government statements. I had no idea until then that you could not rely on government statements."*

Supporters said that the war's bloody aftermath proved that it was right to have tried to stop the Communists. Critics argued that the United States sided with an undemocratic regime. They also said the domino theory was disproved because Thailand, Malaysia, Singapore, and Indonesia did not fall to communism.

Former POW James Stockdale noted one lesson that most Americans could probably agree on:

> *“Only the Congress, only the people, can declare war. If the people don't understand a war, if they don't support it, our armed conflicts will degenerate into halfhearted deceptive measures.”*

Congress learned that lesson well. In 1973, it passed the War Powers Act, forbidding the President to send troops into combat for more than ninety days without congressional approval. Over the following years Congress placed added restrictions on the President's power to make war.

Some condemned the restrictions, claiming that they hampered diplomacy. George Shultz, who served as Secretary of State under President Reagan, insisted that a President should be able to use military force to back up diplomatic efforts. Shultz's colleague, Defense Secretary Caspar Weinberger, was more cautious. He argued that the military should be used only as a last resort, and only when American interests could be clearly defined.

In a 1985 *New York Times* poll, 73 percent said that war had been a mistake, and a *Newsweek* poll found that 75 percent thought the United States should be more cautious in using military force in the future. There was one final, and disturbing, lesson in the *Times* poll. Of those asked, 40 percent did not know that the United States had sided with South Vietnam. Americans were already forgetting what happened in the Vietnam War.

Section Review

1. Analysis. In what sense is the statement "The United States lost the war" true? In what sense is it misleading?

2. Comprehension. What angered many veterans after the war?

3. Analysis. In what ways can it be said that the Communists won the war but "lost the peace"?

Data Search. How is the declining American support for the war after the Tet Offensive in 1968 reflected in the graph on page 792?

Connections to Themes

Shaping Democracy

The use of military force in Vietnam had at first seemed to be a logical extension of the cold war policy of containment. In the early years of the Vietnam War, most Americans agreed that the survival of democracy depended on stopping the spread of communism everywhere in the world. When American planes began bombing North Vietnam, the *Washington Post* declared that "President Johnson has earned the gratitude of the free world."

By the end of the war, however, Americans were questioning the policy of containment. The belief that the United States has a mission to "police" the world took a severe beating in Vietnam, and in the future the public would be much more wary of the government's attempts to commit American troops overseas.

The war not only jolted people's confidence in the nation's global "mission" but also raised disturbing questions about democracy at home. Throughout the century, and especially since the New Deal era, the power of the presidency had grown enormously. The Vietnam War was a glaring example of how presidential power could be abused. Johnson and Nixon, most notably, used it to deceive both Congress and the American people. During this same period another misuse of presidential power, in connection with Nixon's reelection campaign in 1972, was to threaten American democracy with one of its gravest crises.

Linking Past and Present

Discussion. One of the few Vietnam lessons that all sides seem to agree on is that the United States should not go to war again without the informed consent of the American people.

Ask: How can the political system be used to make feelings about possible wars in the future known? Do people have access to enough information to make informed decisions about foreign policy issues? How might the government be prevented from starting "secret wars" such as the Iran-Contra affair, while still allowing timely response to genuine threats?

Section Review

ANSWERS

1. True: the United States withdrew from Vietnam and the Communists took over the country. Misleading: the United States won every "major battle." Also, the defeat of South Vietnam came only after American forces voluntarily left.
2. They felt ignored and/or blamed for "losing"; benefits did not cover all medical costs; Agent Orange victims had to fight for compensation.
3. Many people fled the country; droughts devastated the Vietnamese economy. Vietnam fought with other Communist nations: China and Cambodia.
Data Search: Number of personnel declined after 1968.

Thinking Critically

Evaluation. A good source of a variety of points of view on the war's legacy is an article in the May/June 1988 edition of *American Heritage* magazine titled "What Should We Tell Our Children About Vietnam?" The article was written by Bill McCloud, an Oklahoma teacher and Vietnam veteran who wrote to many prominent people—including politicians, veterans, journalists, and educators—asking them that very question.

Students might analyze the responses in the article and speculate about how people's varying occupations and political views influence what aspects of the war they choose to focus on or to ignore.

Reduced student page in the Teacher's Edition

POINT OF VIEW

Legacies of Vietnam

The war left behind lost lives, ravaged lands, and nightmare memories. Since it was the first American defeat in international conflict, it also raised questions about the nation's role in the world. What should Americans learn from the Vietnam War? Here are several views on the effects of the conflict.

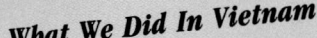

What We Did In Vietnam

"We destroyed their economy. . . . We separated families, we made orphans of so many children. We destroyed their beautiful cities. We destroyed the countryside—reduced triple-canopied jungle to bare red clay, left bomb craters everywhere. When you flew, you saw these enormous holes, like craters of the moon. . . . And yet the Vietnamese kept on. The farmers kept plowing. The women kept working. They're incredibly resourceful, incredibly industrious people. And so much courage. So much courage."

—Journalist Anne Allen

"A Vietnam Had to Happen"

"A Vietnam had to happen to us sometime. . . . When we came out of World War II we were artificially strong. We had a monopoly on nuclear weapons, the strongest conventional military forces, the most resilient economy, a vibrant political system. . . .

A lot of yahoos [superpatriots] in this country never accepted that things had inevitably changed. And eventually, just by sheer force of decibels [loudness], they got us around to the point that we were prepared to behave like John Wayne and sort of knock their teeth out, knock 'em back, put 'em back in their box, blow 'em back to the Stone Age, whatever phrase you want to use. Sooner or later we were going to run into a place where we tried to do that and it didn't work. . . .

We were damned lucky it happened in a place that didn't really matter all that much, like Indochina. Had we taken a stand in a place like Hungary, it could have blown up the world, including the United States. Fifty-eight thousand lives is too many to pay for a lesson, but it's probably smaller than we might have paid had we gone into Czechoslovakia in '68, or done something else that would have led to direct confrontation with the Soviets or with the Chinese. So Vietnam was a tragedy but it may have been the tragic price that American hubris [excessive pride] needed somewhere along the line to get back to reality."

—William Sullivan, who served as a State Department official throughout the Vietnam War

Mother's Heritage

A thousand years dominated by the Chinese
A hundred years enslaved by the French.
Then twenty years of destructive fratricidal war, day after day.
Mother! What heritage have you left to your children?
Mother! Your heritage is Vietnam in sorrow.

A thousand years dominated by the Chinese
A hundred years enslaved by the French.
Then twenty years of destructive fratricidal war, day after day.
Mother! Your heritage is a forest of dry bones.
Mother! Your heritage is an immense graveyard.

—From "Mother's Heritage," by Vietnamese songwriter Trinh Cong Son

Still in Saigon

Every summer when it rains
I smell the jungle
I hear the planes
I can't tell no one
I feel ashamed
Afraid some day
I'll go insane

That's been ten long years ago
And time has gone on by
But now and then I catch myself
Eyes searching through the sky

All the sounds of long ago
Will be forever in my head
Mingled with the wounded's cries
And the silence of the dead

Still in Saigon
Still in Saigon
Still in Saigon
In my mind

—From the song "Still in Saigon," by Vietnam veteran Dan Daley

"No More Vietnams"

"Our first reaction after Vietnam was to withdraw and in a sense be the way we had been for the first hundred and fifty years of our existence. There was a difference, though. We used to withdraw because we thought we were too good for the world: After Vietnam we said 'No, we're not good enough. We've failed. We supported a corrupt regime.'

We've come partly out of that, but the overhang still invests [affects] discussions about issues that have very little relevance to Vietnam. When we talk about Nicaragua or El Salvador we often say 'No more Vietnams.'. . . And I think that is unhealthy."

—Retired General Brent Scowcroft

1. How do Scowcroft and Sullivan differ in their views of the war's legacy?

2. Compare the views of Anne Allen and Trinh Cong Son on the legacy of this war for Vietnam.

3. In what sense was Dan Daley's Vietnam veteran "still in Saigon"?

Point of View

ANSWERS

1. Sullivan argues that a Vietnam had to happen sooner or later to force the United States to become more realistic and cautious in its use of military power throughout the world. He argues that we were lucky to learn this lesson in Indochina because a conflict there did not lead us into a direct nuclear confrontation with the Soviet Union or China. Scowcroft differs from Sullivan in that he sees the legacy of the war as less healthy. He argues that the war led Americans to withdraw from world affairs and to try to return to a more isolationist foreign policy, rather than making Americans more realistic.

2. Both Anne Allen and Trinh Cong Son see the legacy of the war for Vietnam as one of destruction and sorrow. Allen softens her picture with a tribute to Vietnamese courage. Trinh takes a longer view of this war, seeing it as part of a tragic thousand-year history of conflict pitting the Vietnamese first against the Chinese, then against the French, and finally against each other.

3. He is "still in Saigon" in the sense that the sounds, smells, and memories of that war still live in his mind and haunt his memory.

Chapter Survey

ANSWERS

Using New Vocabulary

1. *Hawks* supported the war and wanted military victory. One way to achieve this was to *escalate*, or step up, the fighting. The first term describes an attitude toward war, while the second describes a strategy.
2. Both *conscientious objectors* and *doves* opposed the war. Doves were any people specifically opposed to the Vietnam War. Conscientious objectors were only those men subject to the draft who refused to fight because they opposed all war for religious or moral reasons.

Reviewing the Chapter

1. North Vietnamese fought Chinese conquerors for 1,000 years, resisted French colonialism, fought French and Japanese during World War II, battled and defeated French attempts to recolonize country after World War II. Hatred of foreign domination forged spirit of nationalism which motivated VC and North Vietnamese during Vietnam War.
2. Ho wanted an independent country, Diem's goal was to keep the south out of Communist hands. Both leaders sought outside help. Ho created an effective army to drive out the French. Diem used brute force, political repression, and forced relocation.
3. Gave Johnson blank check to wage war without congressional declaration of war.
4. There are usually a clearly identifiable enemy and clearly drawn battle lines. Enemy—aided by civilians—was hard to identify and fought with guerrilla tactics.
5. Showed Americans that United States might lose war, strengthened anti-war movement.
6. Secret talks with North Vietnamese—ultimately successful. Attack Communist bases in Cambodia and Laos to stop flow of men and supplies from North—unsuccessful and very unpopular. Withdraw U.S. troops and turn fighting over to Vietnamese—placated some Americans. Increase bombing of North—December bombings finally led to cease-fire.
7. Cease-fire in 1973 called for removal of United States forces, but left Communist troops in South Vietnam. Viet Cong were supposed to become part of government. When they were excluded, fighting resumed, Communists took Saigon.
8. Ignored, blamed for "losing," not honored, inadequate medical benefits.
9. Economy of Vietnam ruined, anti-Communists forced into reeducation camps. War created millions of refugees, many of whom settled in United States.

Reduced student page in the Teacher's Edition

Chapter Survey

Using New Vocabulary

The vocabulary terms in each pair listed below are related to each other. For each pair, explain what the two terms have in common. Also explain how they are different.

1. escalate, hawks
2. conscientious objectors, doves

Reviewing the Chapter

1. Describe Vietnamese response to foreigners through 1954. What part did this attitude play in the Vietnam War?
2. Compare the goals of Ho Chi Minh and Ngo Dinh Diem. What steps did each leader take toward reaching his goals?
3. What was the significance of the Gulf of Tonkin Resolution?
4. Contrast conventional warfare with the fighting in Vietnam.
5. Why was the Tet Offensive a turning point in the war?
6. Describe the main elements of Nixon's strategy to end the war. How effective was each one?
7. How did the war finally come to an end?
8. What problems did Vietnam veterans face that soldiers in earlier wars did not?
9. What happened to the Vietnamese people after the war?
10. Explain two important lessons of the Vietnam War.

Thinking Critically

1. Analysis. Why was the war's outcome seen by some as a triumph of nationalism and by others as a victory for communism?
2. Evaluation. When, if ever, is a democratic government justified in withholding information from the public? Support your answer with examples.
3. Evaluation. What do you think is the major lesson to be learned from the Vietnam War? Explain.

History and You

Interview five people who were adults during the Vietnam War. Ask how the war affected their lives. Compare their responses with those gathered by your classmates. What generalizations can you make about the war's impact?

Using Geography

Match each location or event listed below with the correct letter on the map. Then explain the importance of each location or event in the history of the Vietnam War.

1. Start of the Ho Chi Minh Trail
2. Invasion by American troops in March 1970
3. Reported attack on destroyers in 1964
4. Target of December 1972 bombings
5. Invasion by ARVN troops in February 1971
6. Helicopter evacuation in April 1975

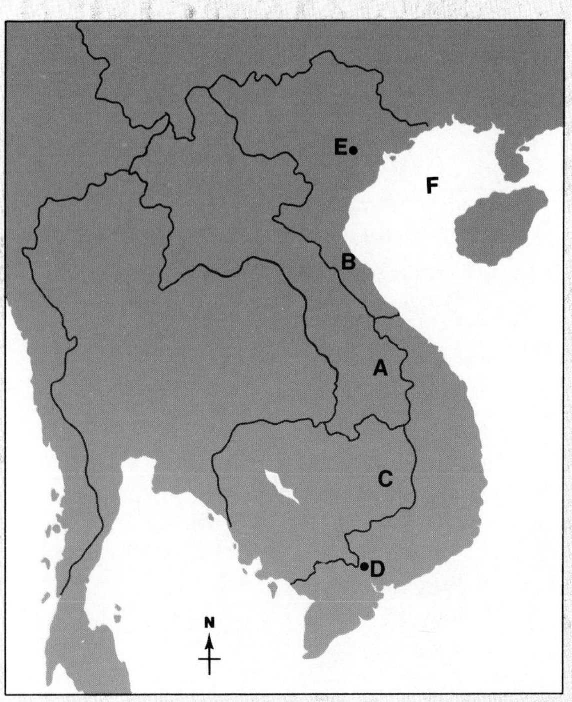

Some still live in refugee camps.
10. Popular support necessary for fighting a war; need to question government statements; do not give President power to wage war without formal declaration; military needs adequate firepower.

Thinking Critically

1. Many American policymakers saw it as part of the Cold War. Many Vietnamese saw it as a victory in their centuries-old struggle against foreign influence.

2. Some students may say there is never justification for withholding information in a democracy, and cite negative public reaction when truth was revealed. Others may argue that the government is justified in withholding vital strategic and tactical information to protect forces in time of war.
3. Answers may include: Do not back a corrupt regime. Do not go into a war unless determined to do everything possible to win it. Make sure the American people support and understand the war.

History and You

Answers will vary. Some trends which may emerge: young men who had to change career plans to go to war or avoid the draft, families split between hawks and doves, people who became politically active for the first time in their lives.

Using Geography

1. (B) **2.** (C) **3.** (F) **4.** (E) **5.** (A) **6.** (D)

Applying Thinking Skills

1. Answers will vary. Some may choose "It has played havoc with our domestic destinies" and the dramatic contrast between the money spent on Vietnam and that spent at home to combat poverty.
2. One possible answer: "We have alienated ourselves . . . . While many abroad opposed American involvement, the United States was by no means "politically isolated."
3. Answers will vary.

Applying Thinking Skills

Determining the Strength of an Argument

Shortly before his death in 1968, Martin Luther King, Jr., denounced the Vietnam War:

> *"Our involvement in the war in Vietnam has . . . put us against the self-determination of a vast majority of the Vietnamese people and put us in the position of protecting a corrupt regime. . . .*
>
> *It has played havoc with our domestic destinies. This day we are spending $500,000 to kill every Viet Cong soldier . . . while we spend only $53 a year for every person characterized as poverty-stricken in the so-called poverty program. . . .*
>
> *And here we are 10,000 miles away from home fighting for the so-called freedom of the Vietnamese people when we have not even put our own house in order. And we force young black men and young white men to fight and kill in brutal solidarity. Yet when they come back home they can't live on the same block together. . . .*
>
> *We have alienated ourselves from other nations so we end up morally and politically isolated in the world. There is not a single major ally of the United States of America that would dare send a troop to Vietnam. . . .*
>
> *Mankind must put an end to war or war will put an end to mankind, and the best way to start is to put an end to war in Vietnam because if it continues, we will inevitably come to the point of confronting China, which could lead the whole world to nuclear annihilation."*
>
> —From *A Testament of Hope: The Essential Writings of Martin Luther King, Jr.*, 1986.

1. Which of King's reasons for opposing the war do you find most convincing? Why?

2. What do you think is the weakest part of his argument? Explain.

3. Did King's argument convince you? Explain.

Writing About Issues

The Issue: *Should the armed forces be composed entirely of volunteers?*

Opposition to the military draft during the Vietnam War spurred a shift to an all-volunteer military force. However, some people argue for a return to the draft.

Those who believe in having a draft argue that it would ensure a large military force. They also say that it would lead to a "smarter," better-qualified fighting force. An all-volunteer force, they say, attracts relatively few people who go to college, while the draft would bring them into the military. They also argue that a draft is democratic and fair because it treats all young people, rich and poor, alike. Furthermore, they say, everyone who benefits from living in a democracy is responsible for defending it.

Supporters of the draft also see it as being more consistent with the democratic tradition of a citizen militia, in which defending the country is a duty above and beyond a person's regular job. Volunteer armed forces, they argue, are more likely to be made up of people who see the military mainly as a lifetime career to support themselves rather than primarily as a way to serve their country.

Supporters of all-volunteer armed forces argue that volunteers are more dedicated than draftees and therefore produce a more effective fighting force. They also declare that a draft has no place in a democracy because it takes away freedom of choice. There are many ways for people to serve their country besides military service, draft opponents say. They think people should be allowed to make their own decisions on that matter.

What do you think? Should the armed forces be composed entirely of volunteers? Write an editorial for your school newspaper expressing your opinion.

Unit 9 Survey

ANSWERS

Making Connections

1. Protect democracy by checking the spread of communism. Means: containment, economic aid, Marshall Plan, alliances such as NATO, confrontation in Korea and Vietnam, threat of massive retaliation, covert operations, flexible response, arms control, deténte.
2. Answers may include Randolph's 1941 march on Washington, CORE, postwar growth of NAACP, pressure for a FEPC, *Brown* v. *Board,* Montgomery bus boycott, SCLC, Greensboro sit-in, SNCC, Freedom Riders, March on Washington, Black Panthers. Successes include Supreme Court ruling against restrictive covenants, voter registration, Civil Rights acts, Voting Rights Act, desegregation of hotels, restaurants, transportation, schools, inroads against job discrimination. De facto segregation, inequalities in jobs, housing, education still exist.
3. Support for Israel while maintaining good will of Arab states; blocking Soviet influence. U.S. helped Shah gain power in Iran; pressured Britain and France to withdraw from Suez; sent marines to protect pro-western Lebanon.
4. During the McCarthy era, fear and intimidation were used to curtail freedom of speech and association. Outspoken disagreement with the government was a hallmark of the Vietnam era.
Using the Time Line. Students may consider the environment, space race, racial issues, communism.

Projects and Activities

1. Research topics include the first nationalist movement—United Gold Coast Convention in Ghana—and its leader, Kwame Nkrumah; Sékou Touré in Guinea; Jomo Kenyatta in Kenya; the independence of Nyasaland as Malawi, Northern Rhodesia as Zambia, Southern Rhodesia as Zimbabwe.
2. Conversations will vary.
3. On TV millions of people saw Freedom Riders, fire hoses turned on crowds in Birmingham, Selma-to-Montgomery March, March on Washington. Body counts and scenes of death and destruction in Vietnam were televised nightly. Television also fueled materialism with its bombardment of enticing ads.

Using the Time Line. Answers may include GI Bill, American G I Forum, Peace Corps, *Silent Spring,* Earth Day, and the EPA, as well as events related to the civil rights movement.

Unit Survey

Making Connections

1. What was the main goal of American foreign policy during the Cold War? By what means did the United States work toward this goal from the beginning of the Cold War to the mid-1970s?

2. Trace the development of the civil rights movement between the 1940s and the 1970s. List its accomplishments. What remains to be done?

3. What policy did the United States follow in Middle Eastern affairs after World War II? List actions the nation took to carry out this policy.

4. One characteristic of American democracy is the protection of individual rights granted by the First Amendment. Yet the limits of these rights have been interpreted differently over the years. Compare American attitudes toward individual rights during the McCarthy and Vietnam eras.

Using the Time Line. Between the end of World War II and the mid-1970s Americans were deeply concerned—and sometimes divided—about many issues. List three such issues of concern. For each find three events on the time line that reflect people's concern. Explain.

Projects and Activities

1. Do research on the emergence of independent nations in Africa in the 1950s and 1960s. What were the United States and the Soviet Union doing to gain influence in these countries? Write your findings as a magazine news article.

2. Each student writes the name of a famous person from the period 1945 to 1975 on a slip of paper and puts it into a bag. Each student then draws a name and assumes the role of that person. Meet in groups of five. In your role, carry out conversations about the communist threat, civil rights, and the Vietnam War.

3. With the class, discuss the role that television played in shaping events in the 1960s. How did television affect the civil rights movement? The Vietnam War? In what other ways did television influence the lives of Americans?

Using the Time Line. Speaking not only for African Americans, but for all Americans, Langston Hughes wrote of a continuing struggle for democracy and opportunity. (See text pages 669–671.) From the point of view of someone living in the mid-1970s write a letter to Hughes describing how people are continuing that struggle. Mention at least five events shown on the time line that represent a striving for the dream that Hughes wrote about. Explain.

Milestones	1945 (Truman)	1953
Political and Economic	• U.S. joins United Nations • People's Republic of China • Marshall Plan • Korean War begins • Taft-Hartley Act • American G I Forum, Hector Garcia	• *Brown* v. *Board of Education* • Army-McCarthy hearings
Social and Cultural	• Jitterbug is popular dance • Jackie Robinson integrates major leagues • *Black, Brown, and Beige*, Duke Ellington • First credit cards, Diner's Club • GI Bill signed into law • Disc jockey Alan Freed coins term *rock 'n' roll* • First issue of *Ebony*	
Technological and Scientific	• Streptomycin discovered • UNIVAC, first commercial computer • ENIAC, first electronic computer • Hydrogen bomb • Atomic Energy Commission established • Transistor invented	• DNA theory published, J. Watson, F. Crick

Assessment

Have partners plan their interviews. Both partners should be involved in writing questions—at least twenty. One partner might conduct the interview while the other tapes it or takes notes, or they might share interviewing and recording. To foster interview skills, you might want to model an interview or have students rehearse.

Scoring

To create a scoring system, or rubric, assign an achievement scale to each of the evaluation criteria. For example, you might evaluate "Thinking critically" on a scale of 0 to 4 as follows:

4—Exemplary response: questions are perceptive, structured around significant themes. Student draws conclusions and backs them with examples; provides reasonable interpretation; speculates about the relationship between information gained in the interview and in the classroom; elaborates on concepts gained, affirmed, or contradicted.

3—Good response: questions are clear, organized around important topics. Student's conclusions are backed by some interesting detail, personal observations, and interpretation. Student distinguishes newly gained information from information gained in class and explains concepts gained, affirmed, or contradicted as a result of the interview.

2—Adequate response: questions are clear, appropriate. Write-up summarizes the interview, incorporates personal observation. Student differentiates between information gained in the interview and in the class; identifies concepts gained from the interview.

1—Poor response: some questions not appropriate. Write-up doesn't provide sufficient information about the interview. Few personal observations or descriptive details. Student may not recognize and respond to new information and viewpoints.

0—No response/inappropriate response.

Follow-up Activity

Class discussion. Have students share the results of their interviews, focusing on how the interviews have affected ideas about the years 1945–1975.

Assessment: Demonstrating What You Know

Oral History Project

Poet Stephen Vincent Benét said, "Our history is not just a list of names and dates, declarations and proclamations. It is made up of the lives of millions upon millions of ordinary men and women who lived through war and peace, strove, struggled, succeeded, failed, built something together." Oral history—people telling their own stories in their own words—is one way to learn about the past.

Work in pairs for this oral history project. Contact someone who remembers events between 1945 and 1975. Introduce yourself, explain your project, and arrange an interview.

1. *Agree on a specific time for the interview.* Let the person know how much time you need.
2. *Tell the person what to expect.* Stress that you want to hear personal recollections rather than formal history. If you plan to tape the interview, get permission first.
3. *Make a list of questions.* Write questions about significant events, issues, and people in the unit. Focus on what the interviewee and his or her associates did, thought, and felt.
4. *Be flexible.* If the person says something that you want to hear more about, ask follow-up questions even if they are not on your list. If the person seems reluctant to pursue a topic, drop it. Ask permission to use the person's name in your write-up.
5. *Write up the interview.* Write an account of the interview, including your observations. Analyze how what you heard relates to the text. How does it add to your understanding?

Evaluation Criteria

Your work will be evaluated according to how well you meet the following criteria.

- **Completing the task**. You write questions for an interview, carry it out, and tape it or take notes. You write an account and an analysis.
- **Knowing history**. Your questions, write-up, and observations are based on accurate information about historic events.
- **Thinking critically**. Your write-up expresses both the interviewee's opinions and your observations. You compare information from the interview with textbook information and evaluate the effect of the interview on your views.
- **Communicating ideas**. You conduct the interview with respect and are a good listener. Your write-up and your analysis are well written, thoughtful, and creative.

1960		1968		1975
Eisenhower	Kennedy	L.B. Johnson	Nixon	

- Hiram Fong, first Senator from Hawaii
- Bay of Pigs
- Berlin Wall built
- Peace Corps formed
- March on Washington
- Gulf of Tonkin Resolution
- Voting Rights Act
- Black Panther party formed
- Tet Offensive
- Watergate break-in
- U.S. leaves Vietnam

- *West Side Story*, Leonard Bernstein
- Folk music becomes popular
- *A Raisin in the Sun*, Lorraine Hansberry
- Roger Maris hits 61 home runs
- Martin Luther King wins Nobel Prize
- *Autobiography of Malcolm X*
- *Star Trek* debuts
- Gateway Arch dedicated, St. Louis
- The Beatles disband
- U.S. outlaws cigarette ads on TV

- *Sputnik*
- NASA created
- First American satellite, *Explorer I*
- Laser developed, Schawlow and Townes
- First communications satellite
- *Silent Spring*, Rachel Carson
- DNA synthesized
- First heart transplant
- First moon landing
- First Earth Day
- Environmental Protection Agency
- *Skylab I*

801

B · A · C · K · G · R · O · U · N · D

Multicultural Perspectives: Art

After the Mexican Revolution of 1910–1917, mural painting—an artistic vehicle for educating a largely illiterate population about the ideals of a new society—gained great prominence in Mexico. The Mexican realist murals set a precedent for American social realists, especially during the New Deal (see pages 526, 574, 588). Starting in the 1960s, as a part of the Chicano movement for civil rights, Mexican Americans used murals widely as an organizing tool, a means for reclaiming cultural heritage, and a way of involving the local community in a collective statement of cultural pride. In Los Angeles, for example, it is estimated that between one thousand and fifteen hundred murals were painted between 1969 and 1990.

- Identify social change and reform since 1970.
- Describe successes and failures of Presidents Nixon, Ford, Carter, Reagan, and Bush.
- Identify key world events and trace United States foreign policy since 1970.
- Describe key problems facing the United States today and discuss and evaluate potential solutions.

Introducing

THE UNIT

Old as well as new challenges confronted the United States from the 1970s to the 1990s. Inspired by the African-American civil rights movement, other groups (including women, Hispanics, and Native Americans) spoke out for equality and justice. Conflict in the Middle East dominated foreign policy concerns in the 1970s. At home, the issue of presidential power took center stage as the nation faced the abuses of the Nixon administration, and as Ford and Carter sought to restore confidence. The 1980s dawned with an optimism that affluence and world leadership were the right of Americans. The late 1980s and early 1990s saw staggering global change, as many nations surged toward democracy. Persistent domestic problems of poverty, disease, and threats to the environment continued to present challenges to Americans.

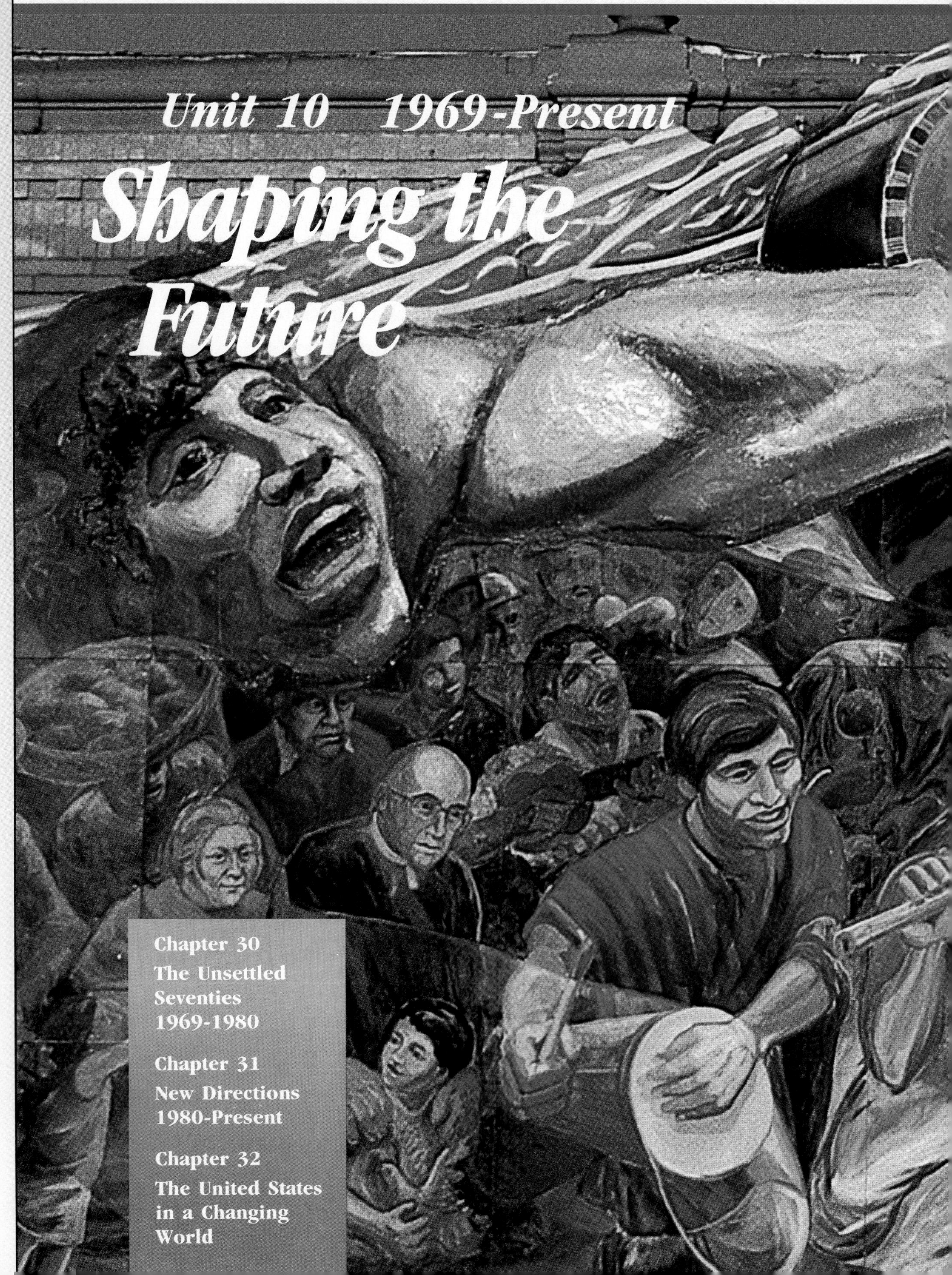

Unit 10 1969-Present

Shaping the Future

About the Authors

Lorna Dee Cervantes, Pat Mora, Rosario Morales, and Aurora Levins Morales say they write poetry, in part, to explore their own identities and experiences as Hispanic Americans. Of Mexican descent, Cervantes comes from an old *Californio* family which had settled originally in Santa Barbara. Pat Mora, also of Mexican descent, was born in El Paso, Texas. Puerto Rican Rosario Morales was raised in New York City and then returned to Puerto Rico to live with her Jewish-American husband. Their daughter Aurora Levins Morales was born and spent her early years in Puerto Rico. The family eventually returned to the United States.

Guided Reading

Discussion. As students read the poems, have them look for evidence of the ever-shifting balance between diversity and unity in the United States. Which poems reflect a clash of cultures, and why? Which poems reflect pride in a diverse heritage? Why?

Vocabulary Building

Discussion. Knowing the following words will help students understand "Ending Poem" on pages 804–805: *mestiza* (the offspring of Spanish or Portuguese and Native American marriages), *diaspora* (scattering of people with common origin, background, beliefs, etc.), *shtetl* (any of the former Jewish villages of Eastern Europe, especially in Russia), *Taína* (member of an extinct Indian people of the West Indies).

History Through Literature

The diversity of American life," wrote African-American author Ralph Ellison, "is often painful . . . and always a source of conflict, but in it lies our faith and our hope." The irony that underlies Ellison's observation is reflected in the works of many Hispanic-American poets. Among them are Mexican Americans Lorna Dee Cervantes and Pat Mora, and Puerto Rican Americans Rosario Morales and Aurora Levins Morales, mother and daughter.

"Freeway 280"

by Lorna Dee Cervantes

Las casitas[1] near the gray cannery,
nestled amid wild abrazos[2] of climbing roses
and man-high red geraniums
are gone now. The freeway conceals it
all beneath a raised scar.

But under the fake windsounds of the open lanes,
in the abandoned lots below, new grasses sprout,
wild mustard remembers, old gardens
come back stronger than they were,
trees have been left standing in their yards.
Albaricoqueros, cerezos, nogales . . .[3]

Viejitas[4] come here with paper bags to gather greens.
Espinaca, verdolagas, yerbabuena . . .[5]

I scramble over the wire fence
that would have kept me out.
Once, I wanted out, wanted the rigid lanes
to take me to a place without sun,
without the smell of tomatoes burning
on swing shift in the greasy summer air.

Maybe it's here
en los campos extraños de esta ciudad[6]
where I'll find it, that part of me
mown under
like a corpse
or a loose seed.

---

[1]little houses
[2]bear hugs
[3]apricot trees, cherry trees, walnut trees
[4]old women
[5]spinach, purslane, mint
[6]in the strange fields of this city

(Background) "Song of Unity," La Peña Cultural Center, Berkeley, California; (above) cover of* Saludos Hispanos *magazine.

Backyard History

Designing a Mural. While the subjects of Mexican-American murals vary widely, some common themes, motifs, and symbols recur. The following are some examples: religious symbols, both Catholic and pre-Columbian (Olmec, Toltec, Aztec, and Mayan); historical events and figures; Mexican symbols (flag, Mexican eagle); political and social issues on the local (education, drug abuse, gang pride, health care), national (strikes, marches, boycotts, United Farm Workers, laborers), and international (U.S. military, guerrillas) levels.

Have students discuss what themes and/or symbols a community mural in their neighborhood might include. Encourage them to consider local history, notable figures, problems and strengths, cultural heritage, distinctive characteristics, and/or ideals and aspirations. Then have students work individually or in groups to design murals expressive of their communities. Students may share their mural designs with the class.

"Sonrisas"[1]

by Pat Mora

I live in a doorway
between two rooms, I hear
quiet clicks, cups of black
coffee, *click, click* like facts
        budgets, tenure, curriculum,
from careful women in crisp beige
suits, quick beige smiles
that seldom sneak into their eyes.

I peek
in the other room señoras
in faded dresses stir sweet
milk coffee, laughter whirls
with steam from fresh *tamales*
        sh, sh, mucho ruido,[2]
they scold one another,
press their lips, trap smiles
in their dark, Mexican eyes.

Poster for the Hispanic Women's Network of Texas.

"Ending Poem"

by Rosario Morales and Aurora Levins Morales

I am what I am.
A child of the Americas.
A light-skinned mestiza of the Caribbean.
A child of many diaspora, born into this continent at a crossroads.
I am Puerto Rican. I am U.S. American.
I am New York Manhattan and the Bronx.
A mountain-born, country-bred, homegrown jíbara child,
up from the shtetl, a California Puerto Rican Jew
A product of the New York ghettos I have never known.
I am an immigrant
and the daughter and granddaughter of immigrants.
We didn't know our forbears' names with a certainty.
They aren't written anywhere.
First names only or mija, negra, ne, honey, sugar, dear

---

[1] smiles
[2] a lot of noise

804

I come from the dirt where the cane was grown.
My people didn't go to dinner parties. They weren't invited.
I am caribeña, island grown.
Spanish is in my flesh, ripples from my tongue, lodges in my hips,
the language of garlic and mangoes.
Boricua. As Boricuas come from the isle of Manhattan.
I am of latinoamerica, rooted in the history of my continent.
I speak from that body. Just brown and pink and full of drums inside.

I am not African.
Africa waters the roots of my tree, but I cannot return.

I am not Taína.
I am a late leaf of that ancient tree,
and my roots reach into the soil of two Americas.
Taíno is in me, but there is no way back.

I am not European, though I have dreamt of those cities.
Each plate is different.
wood, clay, papier mâché, metals basketry, a leaf, a coconut shell.
Europe lives in me but I have no home there.

The table has a cloth woven by one, dyed by another,
embroidered by another still.
I am a child of many mothers.
They have kept it all going

All the civilizations erected on their backs.
All the dinner parties given with their labor.

We are new.
They gave us life, kept us going,
brought us to where we are.
Born at a crossroads.
Come, lay that dishcloth down. Eat, dear, eat.
History made us.
We will not eat ourselves up inside anymore.

And we are whole.

Taking a Closer Look

1. *In what sense is the speaker in "Sonrisas" living between two "rooms"? In what ways do the rooms differ? Which one do you think she prefers and why?*

2. *What type of place is the speaker in "Freeway 280" describing? Why does she visit it?*

3. *How does "Ending Poem" express pride in a diverse heritage? In what ways does it point to effects of discrimination?*

Taking a Closer Look

ANSWERS

1. The speaker takes part in two different cultures, or "rooms." The first room has professional, academic women—it is probably where she spends her working days. The other room is the home/kitchen—it may represent her Mexican roots. The speaker seems to prefer the second room because it represents the warmth of her childhood.
2. The speaker is describing houses in a Mexican-American neighborhood torn down to make room for a freeway. She visits the neighborhood to try to rediscover her Mexican heritage.
3. The poem refers to being a "child of many mothers," with a variety of cultural roots—Puerto Rican and Jewish, urban and rural. References such as "Spanish is in my flesh, ripples from my tongue" express pride in the Latino heritage.

An economic effect of discrimination is noted in the references to "civilizations erected on their backs" and "dinner parties given with their labor," both of which refer to Puerto Ricans being forced into low-wage jobs, such as house servants. A social effect is noted in the reference to not being invited to dinner parties. The statement that "we will not eat ourselves up inside anymore" refers to a psychological effect of discrimination, which is to make people feel inferior.

Chapter 30

The Unsettled Seventies

Planning Guide

	Student Text	TWE Lesson Plans	Support Materials
SECTION 1	**Section 30–1 (1–2 Days)** **New Movements for Social Justice,** pp 808–814 Review/Evaluation Section Review, p 814	**Introducing the Chapter:** Presidential Leadership in the Seventies—Cooperative Activity, one class period, p 805B **Reinforcement Activity:** The Afternoon Show Discusses Social Justice—Cooperative Activity, one class period, p 805C	★ **Read to Remember,** Section 1 ● **Section Activities,** Section 1 Δ **Enrichment Activities,** Section 1 Δ **Readings** ● **Tests and Quizzes,** Section 1 Quiz
SECTION 2	**Section 30–2 (1–2 Days)** **Nixon: Triumph and Fall,** pp 814–821 The American Spirit: Barbara Jordan, p 820 Review/Evaluation Section Review, p 821	**Teaching the Main Ideas:** Writing a Presidential Resumé—Individual Activity, homework, p 805B **Evaluating Progress:** A Watergate Docudrama—Individual Project, homework, p 805C	★ **Read to Remember,** Section 2 ● **Section Activities,** Section 2 Δ **Readings** ● **Tests and Quizzes,** Section 2 Quiz
SECTION 3	**Section 30–3 (1–3 Days)** **A Crisis of Confidence,** pp 822–829 Connections to Themes: Balancing Unity and Diversity, p 829 Point of View: Affirmative Action, pp 830–831 Review/Evaluation Section Review, p 829 Chapter 30 Survey, pp 832–833 Skills, pp 832–833 Using New Vocabulary Thinking Critically Using a Time Line Applying Thinking Skills: Recognizing Stereotypes Writing About Issues	**Teaching the Main Ideas:** World Update—Cooperative Activity, one class period, p 805C **Enrichment Activity:** Planning and Energy Policy—Cooperative Activity, one class period, p 805D	★ **Read to Remember,** Section 3 ● **Section Activities,** Section 3 Δ **Enrichment Activities,** Section 3 ● **Geography Activities,** Section 3 Δ **Readings** ● **Tests and Quizzes,** Section 3 Quiz, Chapter 30 Test (Forms A and B) **Additional Resources** Δ **Twentieth Century Issues: Links to the Past** ● **Active Learning** Δ **GTV Videodiscs** Δ **Transparencies and Activity Book** ● **Testing Software** ★ **Chapter Summaries** **Key:** ★ **For Extra Support** ● **For All Students** Δ **For Enrichment**

Overview

In the 1970s women, Hispanics, and Native Americans struggled with increasing vigor for equality in education, the workplace, and politics. At the same time Hispanics and Native Americans found a new pride in their cultural heritage.

Richard Nixon took office as President in 1969. He improved relations with the People's Republic of China and established a policy of détente toward the Soviet Union. However, progress in arms control was overshadowed by the Watergate break-in and Nixon's participation in its coverup. The resignation of Nixon created a crisis of confidence across the nation.

President Gerald Ford tried to restore confidence, but his pardon of Nixon, as well as soaring inflation, led to his defeat in the 1976 election. President Jimmy Carter hoped to rebuild public trust. Carter, however, was soon occupied with a severe energy crisis; Congress reluctantly adopted some of Carter's energy conservation measures. His greatest foreign policy success was in arranging talks that led to the Camp David Accords, agreements between Israel and Egypt. The political effect of this success was undermined by Iran's taking of American hostages. In 1980 Carter was defeated in his bid for reelection by Ronald Reagan.

Activity Objectives

After completing the activities, students should be able to

- discuss the crisis of confidence in leadership posed by Watergate.
- compare relations with China, the Soviet Union, the Middle East, and Central America in the 1970s with current relations.
- explain movements for social justice in the 1970s.
- describe the sequence of events that led to President Nixon's resignation.
- display an awareness of the nation's continuing energy problems.

Introducing the Chapter

Presidential Leadership in the Seventies

This cooperative activity will requires one class period.

In this activity students will generate questions that help them compare the presidencies of Nixon, Ford, and Carter. After they have studied the chapter, students answer the questions as a review.

Introduce the chapter by telling students that when Leonid Breshnev died in 1982, former Presidents Carter, Ford, and Nixon together attended the funeral in Moscow. Ask them to imagine themselves as attendants on the flight carrying the three ex-Presidents. Explain that the flight offers the opportunity to talk to the three men about their presidencies and the Seventies.

Divide students into groups of three and direct each group to write three questions they would ask each former President about their presidencies and three questions to ask the men as a group. Read the questions to the class and encourage volunteers to answer any they can. Save the questions until students have finished reading the chapter, then have students answer them as a review.

Teaching the Main Ideas

Section 30-2: Writing a Presidential Resumé

This individual activity may be assigned as homework.

This activity will help students understand the crisis of confidence created by the Watergate scandal and the Vietnam War. Students suggest characteristics for the "perfect President," one who could have alleviated the disillusionment felt by Americans after Nixon's resignation.

Have students review Section 30-2 to identify events that raised doubts about the presidency and presidential power. These events may include obstructions of the Watergate investigation, withholding of evidence, any misuse of presidential power, the President's refusal to spend money as allocated by Congress, and the President acting "above the law."

Discuss with students the nature of a resumé. Ask students to invent the right person to apply for Richard Nixon's position after his resignation, a person who would restore the nation's faith in its leaders. (For purposes of this activity, students are to ignore vice-presidential succession.) Students then compose a resumé describing the characteristics of their applicant.

Students should first review the age and residency requirements set forth in Article 2 of the Constitution. The resumé should show that the applicant meets these requirements. Resumés should also include personal information about the applicant and his or her educational background and work experience. Encourage students to go beyond this basic data to include information that would convince voters that their candidate will avoid abuses of power and will restore confidence in the nation's leadership.

Circulate the resumés among student. When students have read them, have the class select the three top candidates. Hold an election to choose a President from these three.

Teaching the Main Ideas

Section 30-3: World Update

This cooperative activity requires one class period.

In this activity students compare foreign affairs of the 1970s with foreign affairs today. Before class write the following list on the chalkboard: *nonaligned nations, China, Soviet Union, Middle East, Vietnam, Nicaragua, Panama, nuclear disarmament, arms reduction, Iran, terrorism, hostages.*

Divide the class into pairs and direct each pair to choose two topics from the list. The pairs of students will investigate issues related to the topics they have chosen. Provide each pair with poster paper. Have them divide the paper in half, providing for two columns of information. They will label one column *1970s* and the other column *1990s*. In the column labeled *1970s* have students write sub-headings of the two topics they have chosen. Under each sub-heading they are to summarize the information they find in Chapter 30.

To complete the 1990s column, students are to skim magazines and newspapers for current information on their topics and summarize it as they have done with information from the 1970s. Students may use drawings, time lines, and other devices to show relationships between the affairs of the 1970s and the 1990s.

Post students' completed charts and allow time for class members to review each other's work. Discuss changes that have taken place over the past twenty to thirty years with regard to each of the topics on the list. Discuss in what areas foreign affairs have changed the most and in what areas they have changed the least in that time. Challenge students to identify issues they think will remain unresolved in their adult lives.

Reinforcement Activity

Section 30-1: The Afternoon Show Discusses Social Justice

This class activity requires one and a half class periods.

In the following activity students explore movements for social justice in the 1970s through a mock television talk show. Students play roles as the show's host, guests, and audience members.

Explain to students that they will participate in a mock talk show. Appoint three students to serve as hosts for the three segments of the show and one to serve as announcer. Allow volunteers to choose roles as guests from the list below. Explain that the remainder of the students will be members of the audience. They will be asked for their views during the show. Allow students one day to develop their roles—members of the audience included—by reviewing Section 30-1 of the text.

On one segment of the talk show the following guests will discuss the principle that women should have the same political, economic, and social rights as men: working woman who states that a male colleague is paid more than she is for the same work; female college student who has been refused admission to the geology department because "exploring for oil is not a suitable occupation for a woman"; campaigner for the ERA; someone who believes that it is important for women to remain at home to raise a family; someone who feels strongly that women should be able to choose to take time out from work to care for small children without losing a chance for advancement in their careers.

Segment two participants will discuss the importance of the participation of members of ethnic groups in the American political process: two Puerto Ricans, one who favors statehood for Puerto Rico and one who does not; Cuban who owns a business in Florida; member of the League of Latin American Citizens; Chicano member of a school board; Mexican American who belongs to a group that works to encourage Hispanics to vote.

Segment three guests will discuss the importance for Americans of pride in their ethnic backgrounds: Native-American artist; Native-American journalist; Hispanic college professor; Hispanic poet; Japanese-American politician; Scottish-American dancer; Jewish-American short story writer; Hawaiian chef.

On show day allow about 10 minutes for each segment. The host of each should ask the guests to state the issues that concern them, explain why they are concerned, and offer solutions to any problems they perceive. Make certain the host allows all guests to speak and then calls on audience members for their views.

At the end of the show, review the issues. Have the class summarize any calls for action. Then have each student select an issue and write a short essay voicing an opinion on the actions that were proposed during the show.

Evaluating Progress

Section 30-2: A Watergate Docudrama

This individual activity may be assigned as homework.

In this activity students demonstrate their knowledge of the Watergate burglary and the events that followed by creating a storyboard for a television docudrama on the subject.

Explain to students that television writers often create storyboards to plan their programs. A storyboard is a series of panels or frames, each with a drawing that illustrates a major event in the story. It looks somewhat like a comic strip. Storyboards also include an outline of the plot and the dialogue.

Ask students to imagine that they have been hired by a television studio to create a script for a docudrama on Watergate. Their contract calls for them to present the studio with a storyboard and a script outline. The storyboard should cover the Watergate story, from the break-in to Nixon's resignation. However, the plot does not have to be chronological. Encourage students to be creative in their storytelling but warn that their dramas must be historically accurate. Emphasize that they will be graded on thinking and creativity, not artistic ability.

Evaluate students' work on the content and originality of their presentations. An acceptable presentation should include: the burglary, McCord's letter to Judge Sirica, presidential firings, appointment of a special prosecutor, formation of Senate Select Committee, Senate hearings, tape battles, "Saturday Night Massacre," Agnew resignation, appointment of Ford, impeachment bills, Supreme Court ruling, release of the tapes, and Nixon's resignation.

Enrichment Activity

Section 30-3: Planning an Energy Policy

This cooperative activity requires one class period.

This activity is designed to encourage students to become aware of the nation's energy problems, conservation programs started in the Seventies, and challenges we face today in the use of energy. Students work in groups to suggest solutions to energy problems.

Tell students that petroleum is used in industry, in transportation, and in the home. Petroleum fuels motor vehicles, factories, and power plants that make electricity, and it is a major ingredient in lubricants, waxes, solvents, plastics, and textiles such as nylon, polyester, and acrylic.

Ask students to list 10 items they commonly use, such as automobiles, microwave ovens, and nylon stockings, that depend on petroleum. Then direct students to draw a line through the 3 items on their list they could most easily live without. Ask them to circle the 3 items they would least like to do without. Discuss why it is difficult to get people to give up such items.

Tell students that their task is to write an energy program for today. Divide the class into groups of three to write energy plans that include: an analysis of the sources of the energy crises of the 1970s, a list of measures taken during the Nixon and Carter administrations to combat the crises, an estimate of which sources of the energy crises are still a threat today, and a list of immediate as well as long-term proposals for improving the situation. Students may suggest actions that both government and individuals might take.

Ask volunteers to share their plans. After each presentation, poll the class to determine how many students would be willing to support the program. If not, is there a part of it they would be willing to support? Why or why not?

Bibliography and Audiovisual Materials

Teacher Bibliography

Ambrose, Stephen. *Nixon: The Triumph of a Politician, 1962–1972*. New York: Simon & Schuster, Inc., 1990.

Bernstein, Carl and Bob Woodward. *All the President's Men*. New York: Simon & Schuster, Inc., 1987.

Carroll, Peter N. *It Seemed Like Nothing Happened.* New York: Holt, Rinehart and Winston, 1982.

Friedan, Betty. *The Feminine Mystique*. New York: Dell Publishing Co., 1984.

Woodward, Bob, and Carl Bernstein. *The Final Days*. New York: Simon & Schuster, Inc., 1989.

Student Bibliography

Borland, Hal. *When the Legends Die*. New York: Bantam Books, 1984.

Crow Dog, Mary. *Lakota Woman*. New York: HarperCollins Publishers, Inc., 1991.

Dean, John. *Blind Ambition.* New York: Pocket Books, 1977.

Hoobler, Dorothy, and Thomas Hoobler. *An Album of the Seventies.* New York: Watts, 1981.

Taulbert, Clifton L. *The Last Train North.* Tulsa, Okla.: Council Oaks Books, 1992.

Films, Videocassettes, and Videodiscs

Dark Days at the White House: The Watergate Scandal and the Resignation of Richard Nixon. 60 min. ABC. Videocassette.

Nixon: Checkers To Watergate. 19 min. Pyramid Films and Video. Movie.

The Modern Presidency: Challenge of the Presidency, Richard Nixon, Gerald Ford, Jimmy Carter, Ronald Reagan. Social Studies School Services. 5 videocassettes.

Filmstrips

The 1970's: American Decades Series. 6 color filmstrips, 3 cassettes, guide. United Learning.

Computer Software

On the Campaign Trail: Decisions, Decisions. 1 Apple diskette, backup, booklets, guide. Tom Snyder Productions.

Watergate: Computer Version. 1 Apple diskette. Social Studies School Services.

Chapter 30

Objectives

- Cite changes brought about by women, Hispanics, and Native Americans in the 1970s.
- Explain why Nixon's presidency ended in disgrace.
- Relate what Ford and Carter did to restore confidence in the government and its leaders.

Introducing THE CHAPTER

For suggestions on introducing Chapter 30, refer to page 805B in the Teacher's Edition.

Developing THE CHAPTER

For activities and teaching strategies to help you reinforce and enrich chapter content, see pages 805B–805D in the Teacher's Edition.

B · A · C · K · G · R · O · U · N · D

Chapter Opener Illustrations

The widely displayed "Ecology Now" poster emphasizes the urgency of protecting the environment.

This campaign button is for Shirley Chisholm, the first African-American woman elected to Congress, where she served from 1969 to 1983. A New York Democrat, she ran unsuccessfully for the presidential nomination in 1972.

At the 1977 National Women's Conference in Houston, feminists proclaim their solidarity. Among those in the front line are Billie Jean King, Susan B. Anthony, II, Bella Abzug, Sylvia Ortiz, Peggy Kokernot, Michele Cearcy, and Betty Friedan.

Dolores Fernandez Huerta began working with César Chávez to organize farm workers in the 1950s. She played an important role in negotiating the terms that settled several strikes, including the Delano grape strike.

Reduced student page in the Teacher's Edition

Chapter 30 1969-1980

The Unsettled Seventies

CATALYST FOR CHANGE
SHIRLEY
CHISHOLM
FOR
PRESIDENT

WOMEN ON THE MOVE

Richard Nixon, the first President to visit Moscow, beams as Soviet Premier Leonid Brezhnev confirms a more positive relationship between the two countries.

After Watergate, Nixon's resignation, and Ford's installation as President, in a federal office a Marine replaces Nixon's picture with Ford's.

American Voices

As a San Antonio city councilman, Henry González fought for desegregation of public facilities. As Texas state senator, he championed equal rights for all peoples. In 1961 González became the first Texan of Mexican descent to win a seat in the House of Representatives. Speaking before the House in 1969, González gave voice to the hopes of Mexican Americans:

> *"I happen to be an American of Spanish surname and of Mexican descent. As it happens, my parents were born in Mexico and came to this country seeking safety from a violent revolution. . . .*
>
> *The question facing the Mexican American people today is, What do we want and how do we get it?*
>
> *What I want is justice. By justice I mean decent work at decent wages for all who want work; decent support for those who cannot support themselves; full and equal opportunity in employment, in education, in schools; I mean by justice the full, fair, and impartial protection of the law for every man; I mean by justice decent homes, adequate streets and public services; and I mean by justice no man being asked to do more than his fair share, but none being expected to do less. In short, I seek a justice that amounts to full, free, and equal opportunity for all; . . . and I believe in a justice that is for all the people all the time."*

González's words echoed the thoughts of millions whose demands for equal justice and opportunity would be heard, even as the nation grappled with challenges to the economy, to foreign policy, and to the institution of the presidency itself.

Ecology symbol; 1972 campaign button; March during the National Women's Conference, Houston, 1977; United Farm Workers organizer Dolores Huerta; Soviet leader Leonid Brezhnev with Richard Nixon; replacing Nixon's portrait.

Analyzing Primary Sources

American Voices

Henry González has served in the House of Representatives since 1961. He has fought for bills for better housing, benefits for farm workers, a youth conservation corps, and adult education.

Before students read the excerpt from Henry González's address to Congress, allow them a few minutes to think about their definitions of justice and to write them down. Then ask the following questions:

1. By justice, does González simply mean equality before the law, or more? If more, what else?
2. Do you think González's detailed definition of justice is acceptable to almost all Americans? If so, why? If not, what part of the definition might some object to and why?
3. Is it the government's job to secure this kind of justice? Why or why not? If yes, is it *only* the government's responsibility? Explain.

Section 30-1

Objectives

- ***Answer the Focus Question.***
- *Identify issues of concern to women in the Seventies.*
- *Compare the kinds of changes called for by Hispanics and Native Americans in the Seventies.*
- *Describe the goals of affirmative action and challenges to it.*

Introducing

THE SECTION

Have students make three lists of ways they believe women, Hispanics, and Native Americans have been discriminated against in the past century. The lists should include items relating to political, social, and economic discrimination. Have volunteers read their lists aloud and compile the items on the chalkboard under the headings: *Political, Social, Economic.* Ask students how these groups worked in the past to end such discrimination. Tell the class that in this section they will read about what these groups did in the 1970s.

B · A · C · K · G · R · O · U · N · D

Time Line Illustrations

1. The 1969 *Apollo 11* moon landing fulfilled a 1961 commitment made by Congress.
2. After the Senate passed the Equal Rights Amendment in 1972, many states ratified it. However, enough opposition later developed—generated in large part by Phyllis Schlafly and her followers—to prevent the amendment from being ratified by the required two-thirds of the states.
3. Dennis Banks, a leader of the American Indian Movement, was indicted by the federal government for his part in the occupation of Wounded Knee. However, the case was dismissed.
4. President Nixon in a rueful mood. His participation in Watergate shook the confidence of many Americans in their government and elected officials.
5. The 1976 Bicentennial of the signing of the Declaration

Reduced student page in the Teacher's Edition

CHAPTER TIME LINE

1969-1980

1970 Grape growers recognize United Farm Workers

1972 Senate passes ERA

1969 1971 1973

1969 First moon landing

1973 American Indian Movement seizes Wounded Knee

30-1 New Movements for Social Justice

Focus: What changes did women, Hispanics, and Native Americans bring about in the 1970s?

At his inauguration in 1969, President Richard Nixon echoed the "bring us together" theme he had sounded throughout his campaign. He called on all Americans to "surmount what divides us and cement what unites us."

American society, however, remained "torn by division." The Vietnam War dragged on into 1973, setting children against parents and hawks against doves. And while an uneasy peace settled over the inner cities, most black and white Americans still lived in different worlds.

Meanwhile, the voices of women, Hispanics, and Native Americans grew louder. Inspired by the successes of the black civil rights movement, these other groups brought a new militancy to their struggles for full equality and fair opportunities.

The Women's Movement

On August 26, 1970—exactly fifty years after their grandmothers had won the right to vote—tens of thousands of women went on strike across America. The strikers held parades and demonstrations in support of issues that ranged from equality of opportunity for women in the workplace to abortion rights and government-sponsored child care. Marchers carried signs saying, "REPENT MALE CHAUVINISTS—YOUR WORLD IS COMING TO AN END" and "DON'T IRON WHILE THE STRIKE IS HOT."

In New York, strikers protested corporations whose advertisements showed women as "servants and sex objects." In other cities, women invaded

of Independence reminded Americans of an event they could be proud of and of the ideals upon which the nation was founded.
6. Iranian revolutionaries seized the American embassy and took fifty-two Americans as hostages. Americans felt frustrated by their helplessness to free the hostages, who were led blindfolded to appear on international TV.

1974 Nixon resigns

1977 Panama Canal Treaties

1979 Iran hostage crisis begins

1975 1977 1979

1976 United States Bicentennial

1978 Camp David Accords

1980 U.S. boycotts summer Olympic games

males-only bars and restaurants as a demonstration of **feminism,** the principle that women should have the same political, economic, and social rights as men.

The new feminist movement grew out of the frustrations felt by two groups of women—housewives and women who worked outside the home. The housewives were protesting the idea that marriage and motherhood were all that a woman needed to be happy. In her 1963 book *The Feminine Mystique,* Betty Friedan chronicled the despair of wives and mothers who felt "empty" and "useless" in these traditional roles. One woman told her:

> *"All I wanted was to get married and have four children. I love the kids and Bob and my home. There's no problem you can put a name to. But I'm desperate. I begin to feel I have no personality. I'm a server of food and a putter-on of pants and a bed-maker, somebody who can be called on when you want something. But who am I?"*

Joining housewives in the new women's movement were thousands of frustrated working women. In 1940, only 25 percent of American women had held jobs. By 1970 that proportion had doubled. Although some women who entered the workforce were seeking new challenges outside the home, the great majority were women who had to work to support themselves and their families.

Regardless of education or training, most working women were limited to dead-end "female-only" jobs with lower pay and less power than their male counterparts. Women were often paid less than men doing the same job. Overall, women earned an average of 60 cents for every dollar earned by men.

Women's liberation. In the early 1970s, women began forming groups to talk about such problems and to "liberate" themselves from old ideas about "a woman's place." The largest of the new feminist groups was the National Organization for Women, or NOW. Founded in 1966, NOW's goal was "to bring women into full participation in the mainstream of American society *now* . . . in truly equal partnership with men."

Developing
THE SECTION

Writing About History

Biographical Sketch. The women's movement of recent years has historical roots in the nineteenth century. Ask students to prepare biographical sketches of feminists of the nineteenth century who were forerunners of twentieth century feminists. Possibilities include: Lucretia Mott, Elizabeth Cady Stanton, and Susan B. Anthony.

Students should indicate advances made by these women and how they prepared the way for the women's movement of the late twentieth century. Have students share their findings with the entire class.

Linking Past and Present

Research. Have interested students investigate the following: Under what circumstances was abortion legal from 1973 to the present? What groups supported and opposed abortion? On what grounds? What did Presidents Reagan and Bush say about the issue? How did they act to support their beliefs? What role has the Supreme Court played in the abortion controversy? Students may report their findings to the class.

Connections: Economics

Research. Have students consult almanacs or the *Historical Abstract of the United States* to find year-by-year statistics about women in the labor force from 1950 to the present. Ask them to look for data on the number of women in the labor force, the kinds of jobs they held, the pay they received, and so on.

Based on the data students find, discuss why women have played such roles in the work force and whether changes in these roles have taken place.

Social History

Not all women identified with the sentiments expressed in *The Feminine Mystique*. Phyllis Schlafly became a spokesperson for women who wanted to protect "traditional" roles for women as homemakers. She and her supporters were largely responsible for the failure of the Equal Rights Amendment.

Multicultural Perspectives

The Puerto-Rican organization ASPIRA, Spanish for "to strive," encourages young Puerto Ricans to get a better education and provides college scholarships. In Puerto Rico over 40 percent of all Puerto Ricans between the ages of 18 and 24 are in college. The Institute of Puerto Rican Culture gives scholarships to Puerto Rican artists to study in Europe.

Reduced student page in the Teacher's Edition

In 1972 Congress responded to women's demands for equality by passing legislation guaranteeing equal pay to women doing the same jobs as men. Congress also approved the Equal Rights Amendment (ERA) that year. The ERA consisted of twenty-four words: "Equality of rights under the law shall not be denied or abridged by the United States or any state on account of sex."

To become part of the Constitution, the ERA would have to be ratified by thirty-eight states. Approval came quickly from thirty-five. Then opposition began to mount. Some opponents argued that women already had equal rights under the Constitution. Others feared that the amendment would make women subject to the military draft and would force changes in the traditional role of women. Despite strong pressure from women's groups, the ERA failed to win approval.

NOW and other groups also campaigned for "the right of women to control their own reproductive lives." They worked to overturn state laws limiting access to birth control information and to legal abortions. While many feminists saw abortion as unfortunate, they believed that a woman should not be forced to bear an unwanted child. They also argued that legal abortions performed by doctors would save the lives of 10,000 women a year, the victims of botched illegal operations.

The abortion issue came before the Supreme Court in the 1973 case of *Roe* v. *Wade*. The Court ruled that a woman had the right to an abortion in the first three months of pregnancy. While the Roe ruling was cheered by feminists, it was denounced by the National Right to Life Committee and other groups that saw abortion as a form of murder. The dispute between the two groups centered on disagreement over when life begins, a question that would remain unresolved for some time to come.

Tennis star Billie Jean King fought for recognition of women's sports and equality for women athletes.

During the Seventies, women made some visible gains in their struggle for equality. In growing numbers, women moved into jobs once limited to men. Americans were no longer surprised to find female soldiers, miners, doctors, astronauts, rabbis, fire fighters, engineers, and airline pilots. Increasingly, women ran for and won political offices ranging from school board members to state legislators. In Connecticut, Ella Grasso became the first woman to be elected governor of a state.

As women moved into the Eighties and Nineties, they would find expanding opportunities in education, in the workplace, and in politics. Questions would continue to be raised, however, by critics—including many women—who feared the effects of the women's movement on the traditional American family.

Hispanic Americans

By the 1970s, Hispanics formed one of the largest ethnic groups in the United States. Many of the nation's 14 million Hispanics were relative newcomers from Mexico, Cuba, and Central America. Others were Mexican Americans whose families had lived in this country for generations.

Puerto Ricans have been American citizens since Puerto Rico became an American colony after the Spanish-American War. In the 1950s and 1960s, widespread unemployment in Puerto Rico drove thousands of Puerto Ricans to mainland cities in search of work. Because many knew little English and had few of the job skills required in a city, they often had to settle for the lowest paying jobs. Discrimination against Puerto Ricans also limited their opportunities. In the late 1960s Puerto Ricans formed several organizations to fight against discrimination and to open up new opportunities.

Thousands of Cubans sought refuge in the United States after Fidel Castro overturned the government of Cuba in 1959 and set up a new regime, which soon turned Cuba into a Communist state. So many Cubans settled in Miami, Florida, that the

Citizenship

Today, Armando Valladares, a former Cuban office worker, lives in the United States. He was imprisoned in Cuba for 22 years for questioning the Communist government of Fidel Castro. Amnesty International spoke out for Vallardares's release, and in 1982 he was freed. Vallardares is now a U.S. delegate to the UN Human Rights Commission and continues to speak out against Castro's regime.

Connections: Politics

The Mexican American Political Association (MAPA) was founded in Fresno, California, by Bert Corona and Eduardo Quevado in 1959. In 1962, with MAPA support, Californian Edward Roybal was elected to the United States Congress. Gloria Moreno-Wycoff is the founding president of Femenil de Rio Hondo, a women's organization that works to improve the image of Mexican-American women.

Multicultural Perspectives

Bulletin Board Display. Have students create a bulletin board display illustrating contributions to American culture by various Hispanic-American groups. The contributions may include achievements in food, music, literature, religion, architecture, politics, and the like.

Students may use school and public libraries as resources. If students show an inclination, hold an Hispanic/American achievement fair in which they demonstrate some of the contributions of Hispanic peoples to contemporary American life.

Union organizer César Chávez is shown speaking with California farm workers. Luis Valdez created a bilingual theater, El Teatro Campesino—The Farmworkers Theater—to bring attention to their cause. Its productions have gained international acclaim.

city became known as "Little Havana." Three thousand Spanish-speaking children entered local schools each month in the 1960s. As a result, Florida schools started widespread bilingual programs, teaching in two languages, a practice that had begun in German-American communities in the 1840s.

Many of the early Cuban refugees were business and professional people. Once they had become established, they helped other Cubans with jobs and aid. Cubans have become the most economically successful group of Hispanic Americans.

Mexican Americans. By far the largest group of Hispanics in the United States is Mexican American. In the 1950s and 1960s Mexican-American organizations such as the League of United Latin American Citizens and the American G.I. Forum achieved some success in expanding civil rights. A new generation challenged even more aggressively the conditions that kept Mexican Americans relatively poor and powerless.

Some of the new activists called themselves *Chicanos,* originally a slang word for Mexican-Americans. Now it became a symbol of unity and pride. The Chicano, or "brown power," movement took many forms. In Colorado, Rodolfo "Corky" Gonzáles formed the Crusade for Justice. The Crusade provided medical and legal aid to Mexican Americans, worked for better housing and jobs, and protested police brutality. In Texas José Angel Gutiérrez established a political organization, La Raza Unida, which was successful in getting Chicano candidates elected to city offices and school boards.

Many Chicano activists saw political power as the key to equal rights. During the Seventies they pressed for and won greater political representation in city and state governments through **redistricting**—the redrawing of voting district boundaries—to more fairly reflect the Hispanic population.

Not all Mexican Americans accepted all forms of the Chicano movement. Representative Henry González expressed his views in the House of Representatives in 1969:

“All over the Southwest new organizations are springing up; some promote pride in heritage, which is good, but others promote chauvinism [fanatical devotion], which is not; some promote community organization, which is good, but some promote race tension and hatred, which are not good.”

Another part of the Chicano movement focused on education. González, Gutiérrez, and others organized student groups to instill ethnic pride and bring about social change. In Los Angeles, 15,000 Chicano high school students staged a series of strikes, which they called "blow outs," to highlight

Connections: Language

Discussion. Hold a class discussion on the following issue: Should students who regularly use a language other than English be taught in school only in English, only in their native tongue, or in both? Why or why not?

Analyzing Primary Sources

Native-American Voices. Refer students to the four Native-American quotations on pages 812–813 and the Spotlight on Values. Have each quotation read aloud. **Ask:** How are these quotes evidence of the diversity within our nation? **(Students may refer to Michael Bush's words on page 812.)** What evidence is there of the Native-American belief that the land belongs to everyone? **(Hines' quote on page 812)** Cite evidence of pride in the Native-American heritage. **("We'll retain our beauty and still be Indian," and Lame Deer's quote, page 813)**

Multicultural Perspectives

Wounded Knee has a special significance for Native Americans. It is the place where a group of Miniconjou, a branch of the Teton Sioux, lost their last struggle with the United States Cavalry. Later, one Native American said: *"I can still see the butchered men, women, and children as clear as I saw them with my eyes still young. . . . A people's dream died there. It was a beautiful dream. Now the nation's hoop is broken and scattered. There is no center any longer."*

Reduced student page in the Teacher's Edition

their demand for a better education. The students stressed the need for "bilingual and bicultural education":

> *Teachers, administrators, and staff should be educated: they should know our language [Spanish], and understand the history, traditions, and contributions of Mexican culture. HOW CAN THEY EXPECT TO TEACH IF THEY DO NOT KNOW US?*

In 1968 Congress passed the Bilingual Education Act, establishing federal funding for certain bilingual programs. Other bilingual acts followed throughout the Seventies, and bilingual education spread, especially in states with large Spanish-speaking populations.

Some Chicano leaders concentrated on economic problems. In California, César Chávez organized Mexican-American farm workers into a labor union. The United Farm Workers staged strikes and boycotts to press demands for better pay and working conditions. In 1970, after years of bitter struggle, the union finally won the right to represent workers in contract talks with California's grape growers. By then, Chávez wrote, the union had also won something "even more important than money . . . a thing called dignity or self-respect or honor."

At the same time, Mexican American artists and writers began to express a new pride in their rich cultural heritage. "Chicanos are singing," wrote poet Sergio Elizondo, "singing and revealing the reality of our lives and our artistic presence."

Native Americans

Like Hispanics, Native Americans are not a single ethnic group with one history and culture. Mohawk leader Michael Bush wrote:

> *There are Mohawk people, there are Cheyenne people, there are Navajo people, Tlingit people, we are all different. . . . We have different histories. . . . We don't all think alike and we don't all act alike.*

In 1970 there were about 800,000 Native Americans in the United States. More than half lived on reservations. So limited were economic opportunities on most reservations that about one in four Indians resettled in urban areas during the 1970s.

Whether they lived on reservations or in cities, Native Americans felt a strong connection to their Indian heritage. After moving to New York from Oklahoma, Mifaunwy Shunatona Hines wrote:

> *To me, New York City is . . . Indian country for all of us whose roots are elsewhere. The ties are not cut, we have simply enlarged the endless Indian circle. And for a while, New York City is our reservation.*

A new militancy. In the 1970s, Native Americans, too, worked to gain fair treatment. In 1972 leaders of the American Indian Movement took over the Washington, D.C., offices of the Bureau of Indian Affairs and in 1973 occupied Wounded

Kiowa artist T. C. Cannon portrays an Indian in a setting with both Native-American and European traditions.

Connections: Religion

After the tragedy at Wounded Knee in 1890, the Sioux abandoned the Ghost Dance, which had been part of the Native-American religious revival of the late nineteenth century (see Chapter 14, page 363). During the occupation of Wounded Knee in 1973, Sioux Medicine Man Leonard Crow Dog revived the Ghost Dance. Later he explained his reasons, *"Eighty-five years ago the Ghost Dancers thought that by dancing they could change the earth. We dance to change ourselves. Only when we have done this can we try to change the earth."* Crow Dog's wife added the idea that the Sioux people's dreams of revival died during the 1890 tragedy, but in 1973 the renewal of the Ghost Dance mended the Sioux nation and gave them the pride they needed to work and fight for their rights.

Spotlight on Values

Lame Deer, a Lakota Sioux, made this satiric comment, with its humor based on differences in values between Native Americans and European Americans.

> "Before our white brother came to civilize us we . . . had no locks or keys, and so we had no thieves. If a man had no horse, tipi, or blanket, someone gave him these things. . . . We had no money, and therefore a man's worth couldn't be measured by it. We had no written law . . . therefore we couldn't cheat. We were really in a bad way before the white man came, and I don't know how we managed to get along without the basic things which, we are told, are absolutely necessary to make a civilized society."

Knee, South Dakota, to dramatize the need for sweeping changes in policies toward Native Americans. In 1978 another group of Indian activists organized a five-month march across the country. Part of their purpose was "to let America know that . . . we are still a way of life that survives."

During the 1970s, Native Americans also became more aggressive about defending their treaty rights in court. In Rhode Island, the Narragansetts forced the state to return some 1,800 acres of disputed land to tribal control. In Maine, the Penobscot, Maliseet, and Passamaquoddy laid claim to 12.5 million acres of land taken from them illegally a century before. They finally settled for $37 million and the right to expand their reservations. In 1980 the Supreme Court awarded the South Dakota Sioux more than $100 million as payment for land taken from them in "dishonorable dealings."

Native Americans fought to gain control of coal, oil, and uranium deposits discovered beneath their lands. The Northern Cheyenne and Crow of Montana won the right to halt destructive strip-mining operations on their reservations. "The coal can stay just where it is until they find a way to get it out without wrecking everything else," said Cheyenne president Allen Rowland.

The 1970s saw a rebirth of Native American pride. "Forty years ago," said a Crow college professor, "Indians would deny their religions because they didn't want to be persecuted. But now, Crow grandparents are teaching their children the old ways." For most, learning the "old ways" did not mean rejecting the benefits of modern life. A Northern Cheyenne newspaper editor wrote:

> *"We shall learn all these devices the white man has. We shall master his machinery, his inventions, his skills, his medicine, his planning. But we'll retain our beauty and still be Indian!"*

Affirmative Action

For women and for ethnic groups, one weapon in the fight for equal treatment was **affirmative action**— plans to counteract past discrimination in employment and in admission to colleges and universities. Affirmative action had begun in the Sixties as part of the civil rights movement. By executive order, large firms that did business with the federal government were required to establish affirmative action plans.

Some programs set up goals for hiring employees. The aim of the goals was for the ethnic and racial makeup of the firm's workforce to match that of the general labor force. Universities followed a similar plan in admitting students.

Affirmative action programs provoked an angry **backlash,** a strong reaction based on fear or resentment. Opponents charged that the goals resulted in **reverse discrimination**— unfair treatment of the majority— because, they claimed, qualified white males were often turned away in favor of less qualified people.

The ferment over affirmative action came before the Supreme Court in 1978 in the case of *Regents of the University of California* v. *Allan Bakke*. Bakke, a white, had been denied admission to the university's medical school although his entrance test scores were higher than those of students ad-

Writing About History

Report. Have students research the American Indian Movement (AIM). They should write a report on the founding of AIM, its leaders (Dennis Banks, Russel Means, Leonard Crow Dog, and others), and the steps it has taken to focus the efforts of all Native Americans on overcoming social, economic, and political problems.

Limited English Proficiency

Cooperative Activity. Divide the class into teams. Each team should represent one group of Americans fighting for equal rights. The group may be women, Native Americans, Hispanic Americans, or some other group the team thinks does not have a full measure of political, economic, and/or social rights. Have each team develop an equal-rights campaign, which might include posters, slogans, political cartoons, and TV commercials. The campaigns can be bilingual. Have each team share its campaign with the class.

GTV Side 4

Chap. 9, Frame 33307

Native American Population: 1920, 1950, and 1980 (Population Clocks, 3 Frames)

Search:

Step:

Section Review

ANSWERS

1. Definitions for the following terms are on text pages indicated in parentheses: *feminism* (809), *redistricting* (811), *affirmative action* (813), *backlash* (813), *reverse discrimination* (813).
2. Students may cite: (a) ERA; supporting: it was necessary to guarantee women equal rights; opposing: women already had equal rights; ERA would subject them to draft, change traditional roles. (b) Choice; supporting: a woman should not be forced to bear an unwanted child; opposing: abortion is a form of murder and a sin.
3. Others tend to think of Hispanics as a single ethnic group. However, Mexicans, Puerto Ricans, and Cubans come from different cultures with different traditions.
4. Both Hispanics and Native Americans worked to have their cultures respected. Both worked for affirmative action. Hispanics worked for bilingual education, while Native Americans worked to gain control of valuable mineral deposits on their lands and to regain or be compensated for land taken from them.

B · A · C · K · G · R · O · U · N · D

Chapter Connections
The Point of View feature on text pages 830–831 addresses the issue of affirmative action.

Connections: Science and Technology
As Neil Armstrong set foot on the moon at 10:56 P.M. Eastern Daylight Time, he said the memorable words—heard by the millions watching him on TV—"That's one small step for a man, one giant leap for mankind."

Reduced student page in the Teacher's Edition

mitted under the school's affirmative action program. He argued that he had been discriminated against because he was white. The Supreme Court agreed. The Court ruled that schools could take race or ethnic background into consideration to achieve variety, but a quota system was not legal.

Opponents of affirmative action cheered the Bakke decision, while supporters saw it as a painful set-back in their efforts. However, both opponents and supporters recognized that new winds were blowing in American society. Groups that throughout the nation's history had known discrimination and injustice had learned to organize and speak out, demanding equality, justice, and opportunity. In the coming decades, their voices would continue to be heard in the national debate over how to give everyone a chance to succeed.

Section Review

1. Identification. Define *feminism, redistricting, affirmative action, backlash,* and *reverse discrimination.*

2. Comprehension. Identify two issues of concern to women in the Seventies and explain opposing viewpoints on those issues.

3. Application. Explain Luisa Ezquerro's statement that to others Hispanics "may all look alike, but it doesn't work that way."

4. Analysis. What kinds of changes did Hispanics and Native Americans work to bring about? How were they similar and how were they different?

30-2 Nixon: Triumph and Fall

Focus: How did Richard Nixon's triumphs as President end in scandal and disgrace?

On July 20, 1969, astronauts Neil A. Armstrong and Edwin E. Aldrin, Jr. landed a spacecraft on the moon. The United States had fulfilled President Kennedy's dream of putting a man on the moon by the end of the decade.

Around the world people clustered in front of television sets to witness this astonishing event. President Nixon told the astronauts, "For one priceless moment in the whole history of man all the people on this earth are truly one."

Three days later, on the deck of a ship in the Pacific, Nixon welcomed the astronauts back to earth. From there he set out on a tour of Guam, the Philippines, Indonesia, Thailand, South Vietnam, India, Pakistan, Romania, and Britain. Nixon thrived on foreign policy. As President, he hoped to earn what he believed was "the greatest honor history can bestow: . . . the title of peacemaker."

Space Age marvels included Viking 2 *photos of Mars, astronauts on the moon, and movie robots R2D2 and C3PO.*

Global Connections
Nixon's trip to China was foreshadowed by two years of tension-easing events: In 1969 the United States eased travel and trade restrictions to and from China, in 1970 it resumed official diplomatic talks in a third country and ended a twenty-year-old trade embargo. But the event that caught the American public's imagination was a 1971 visit by the United States table tennis team to China. Chinese Premier Chou En-lai (Zhou Enlai) made a special point to greet the players personally, signalling that the Chinese government was eager to expand U.S.-China relationships. Newspaper reporters hastened to label the friendly contacts between the two countries "ping pong diplomacy."

In 1972 Nixon and Henry Kissinger (center) met China's Premier Chou En-lai (left) in Beijing. The U.S. had not had formal relations with China since 1949.

Nixon's Foreign Policy

Nixon was a staunch anti-Communist. Yet he and his foreign policy advisor Henry Kissinger agreed that it was time for the United States to move away from Cold War confrontation toward "a new era of negotiation." They recognized that the world had changed since the 1950s. The two blocs—Communist and non-Communist—had begun to splinter. Looking ahead, Nixon saw a world dominated by "five great economic superpowers: the United States, Western Europe, the Soviet Union, mainland China, and, of course, Japan."

Nixon also recognized the growing importance of the developing nations of Asia, Africa, and Latin America—the third world. While third-world nations were happy to receive aid from the superpowers, they had remained **nonaligned,** or not allied, with either side in the cold war.

In this changed world, Nixon and Kissinger based their foreign policy on *détente,* a French word meaning "relaxation of tension." Kissinger explained that under this policy "[we] have no permanent enemies." Instead, "we will judge other countries, including Communist countries, . . . on the basis of their actions and not . . . their ideology."

Opening doors to China. In line with this new approach, Nixon and Kissinger worked to improve relations with the People's Republic of China. For more than twenty years, the United States had refused to recognize the Communist government of China. Such a policy, Nixon believed, was no longer wise. He declared:

> *"We simply cannot afford to leave China forever outside the family of nations. There is no place on this small planet for a billion of its potentially most able people to live in angry isolation."*

Section 30-2

Objectives

- ***Answer the Focus Question.***
- *Evaluate Nixon's foreign policy achievements.*
- *Cite causes of the energy crisis.*
- *Discuss how the Watergate scandal affected Americans' attitudes toward government.*

Introducing

THE SECTION

Tell the class that Richard Nixon, in his 1969 inaugural address, pledged that the United States would seek "the title of peacemaker." Ask students to read this section to find out how Nixon sought this title for the nation and how political scandal at home destroyed his presidency.

Developing THE SECTION

Linking Past and Present

Discussion. Have the class discuss the relationship between the U.S. and China and the former Soviet Union today. What recent events have influenced these relationships? **(the breakup of the Soviet Union; the crackdown on democratic reforms in China; questioning of China's most favored nation trade status with the United States; and so on)**

Limited English Proficiency

Building Vocabulary. Ask students to define the term *détente.* Then have them cite at least two examples of how President Nixon used the policy of détente in dealing with Communist powers. **(Nixon reopened relations with China; he visited the Soviet Union; he and Brezhnev signed the SALT and ABM agreements and agreed to cooperate in space, science, and health research; and so on.)**

Multicultural Perspectives

Book Report. Interested students might like to write a book report on Shirley Chisholm's autobiography, *Unbought and Unbossed.* The report should touch on her early life, her years in the New York Assembly and the United States Congress, and her views on the seniority system. It also might include mention of her run for the presidency and an assessment of the book's title.

Global Connections
The United States and the People's Republic of China established formal diplomatic relations on January 1, 1979 (see pages 826–827).

Connections: Politics
Among those arrested for the Watergate break-in was James McCord (see page 818). McCord had worked for the Committee to Re-elect the President (CREEP) and answered to the committee's head, John Mitchell. Mitchell, Nixon's Attorney General, was later convicted for his part in Watergate.

Reduced student page in the Teacher's Edition

The Chinese had their own reason for seeking better relations. By 1970 fierce disagreements with the Soviet Union had led to armed clashes along the border separating the two nations. In dealing with this threat, the Chinese hoped, in their words, "to fight the near barbarian [the Soviet Union] with the far barbarian [the United States]."

In 1971 the United States dropped its opposition to UN membership for Communist China. Then Nixon stunned the world by announcing that he would visit the People's Republic of China. During this historic visit in 1972, Nixon and Chinese Premier Chou En-lai (JO en-LI) agreed to improve relations. "What we have done is simply opened the door," the President said, "opened the door for travel, opened the door for trade."

Détente with the Soviet Union. President Nixon expanded his policy of détente in 1972 when he became the first American President to visit Moscow. There, Nixon and Soviet leader Leonid I. Brezhnev (BREZH-nev) agreed to cooperative ventures in science, health, and space exploration.

The superpower leaders also signed two agreements designed to control the arms race. Over the last decade both nations had spent immense sums of money to build powerful weapons. American and Soviet representatives had been holding Strategic Arms Limitation Talks (SALT) in hopes of slowing this rush to destruction.

The 1972 SALT agreement limited each nation's offensive weapons to those already made or under construction. Critics pointed out that it failed to freeze or reduce nuclear arsenals. But it did establish the idea that the powers could set limits on their destructive weaponry.

The second agreement, the Anti-Ballistic Missile (ABM) Treaty, limited each nation to only two defense systems designed to shoot attacking missiles out of the sky. Nixon explained the reasoning behind the treaty.

> *"By giving up missile defenses, each side was leaving its population and territory hostage to a strategic missile attack. Each side therefore had an ultimate interest in preventing a war that could only be mutually destructive."*

Progress in arms control was not the only sign of détente. In May 1972 Nixon announced that the United States would sell a quarter of its grain supply to the Soviet Union, the largest grain-export deal in American history. Détente would even reach into space. In 1975 American and Soviet astronauts linked their two spacecraft while orbiting the earth.

Nixon Reelected in 1972

As the 1972 election approached, the Republican party enthusiastically renominated Nixon for President and Spiro Agnew for Vice-President. Victory seemed certain. Nixon's dramatic trips to China and the Soviet Union had sent his popularity soaring. Support rose even higher when Kissinger announced a breakthrough in the peace talks between the United States and North Vietnam.

Shirley Chisholm of New York, the first African-American woman to serve in Congress, ran for the Democratic nomination. However, the Democrats chose Senator George McGovern of South Dakota. Both Chisholm and McGovern opposed the Vietnam War. McGovern promised that if elected he would end the war and bring the troops home within ninety days.

A curious event occurred early in the election campaign. At 2:30 a.m. on June 17, five burglars were arrested in a Washington, D.C., building complex called Watergate. They had broken into the offices of the Democratic National Committee. The intruders carried electronic eavesdropping devices, which suggested they were political spies. The question was: Who was behind the burglary?

White House press secretary Ronald L. Ziegler dismissed the break-in as "a third-rate burglary attempt." Nixon assured the nation that "no one in this administration was involved in this very bizarre incident." By election day, it seemed to have been forgotten. Nixon was easily reelected with 47 million votes to McGovern's 29 million.

Global Connections

In his *Memoirs* Nixon writes that in the Yom Kippur War *"the Israelis had been overconfident about their ability to win a quick victory. They had already lost a thousand men . . . and were on their way to losing a third of their tank force. By . . . the fourth day of the war, we could see that if the Israelis were to continue fighting, we would have to provide them with planes and ammunition to replace their earlier losses. I had absolutely no doubt or hesitation about what we must do. I met with Kissinger and told him to let the Israelis know that we would replace all their losses . . . ."*

The Energy Crisis

A few months into Nixon's second term, the Middle East exploded into war. On October 6, 1973—the Jewish holy day of Yom Kippur—Egyptian and Syrian troops launched a surprise attack on Israel. Their goal was to recover land they had lost to Israel during the Six-Day War in 1967. Within days, however, Israeli troops had repelled the invasion and were pushing into Egypt and Syria. The fighting ended in late October, when both sides accepted a UN-sponsored cease-fire.

During the Yom Kippur War, the United States sent military supplies to Israel. In response, Arab nations friendly to Egypt and Syria halted oil shipments to the United States and its allies in Western Europe and Japan.

When the oil embargo began, the United States was importing a million barrels of oil per day from the Middle East. With these supplies cut off, heating oil and gasoline suddenly became scarce. To conserve precious fuel, Americans turned down thermostats, switched off unneeded lights, and carpooled to work. Congress reduced the national speed limit and passed other fuel-saving measures.

Despite these efforts, gasoline supplies were so limited that motorists had to wait in long lines just to buy a few gallons. Fuel oil was in short supply, too. As the weather grew colder, one newspaper warned: "THINGS WILL GET WORSE BEFORE THEY GET WORSE."

Meeting America's energy needs. The Arab nations ended the oil embargo in March of 1974, but the nation's energy woes were far from over. Analysts pointed out that the recent crisis was part of a larger problem: America's growing dependence on imported oil to meet its energy needs.

In 1960 Americans had imported 19 percent of their oil. However, the oil industry worldwide was controlled by a few American and European oil companies. They held the price of oil close to $1.80 a barrel.

The price of oil began to rise in 1970, the result of a shift in power from the western oil companies to members of the Organization of Petroleum Exporting Countries (OPEC). OPEC represented oil-producing nations in the Middle East, Africa, Asia, and Latin America. By the end of 1973, OPEC had boosted oil prices to $11.65 a barrel. "We are in a position to dictate oil prices," gloated Saudi Arabia's oil minister Sheikh Yamani, "and we are going to be very rich."

By 1973 Americans were importing 36 percent of the oil they used. In an effort to reduce the nation's dependence on imported oil, Congress approved construction of the Alaska pipeline. When completed in 1977, this 800-mile pipeline could transport up to 2 million barrels of crude oil per day from oil fields on the Arctic Coastal Plain to the ice-free port of Valdez. From there the oil was shipped by tanker to West Coast refineries.

"Have you noticed there's never any CAR shortage..."

Many people hoped that the pipeline from Prudhoe Bay, North America's largest oil field, would end U.S. energy problems.

Linking Past and Present

Oral Report. The energy crisis brought on by the Arab Oil Embargo of 1973 was not the first international crisis related to oil, nor was it the last. Ask students to investigate two other crises: the 1940 American oil embargo against Japan and the Iraqi invasion of Kuwait in 1990 and the subsequent Persian Gulf War of 1991. Students should report their findings to the class, stressing the reason why oil resources are so crucial to developed countries such as the United States.

Connections: Science and Technology

Discussion. Have students suggest ways in which consumption of fuel can be reduced. These can include ways to produce more fuel-efficient machines and ways students and their families can reduce fuel use.

Linking Past and Present

Discussion. Have students give examples of automobiles, buildings, and appliances that are designed to save energy. Have them explain how they save energy, and if possible, how they differ from similar products from the early 1900s. **(Students may consider washing machines, fluorescent lights, refrigerators, microwave ovens, automobiles, water heaters, and solar homes.)**

Thinking Critically

Analysis. Have students discuss the dilemma faced by Americans who on the one hand enjoy a lifestyle made possible by high energy consumption, and on the other hand are some of the world's most vocal environmentalists—urging oil producers to protect nature, for example. Have students attempt to reconcile these apparently conflicting values.

Connections: Politics

Research. Interested Students might research the careers of Sam Ervin, Daniel Inouye, and Howard Baker and report their finding to the class. Points to consider: what was the political reputation of these senators? Why were these two Democrats and one Republican chosen to investigate a scandal involving the President and important members of his staff.

Connections: Politics

During the Watergate scandal, the press played an indispensable role exposing crimes and cover-ups. The Washington *Post*, in particular, led the way in this regard. Editor-in-chief Benjamin Bradlee gave immense editorial freedom and support to two young reporters—Bob Woodward and Carl Bernstein—to ferret out the scandal. Their reporting, combined with judicial pressures and legislative investigations, eventually forced Nixon's resignation.

Chapter Connections

For a case study of Nixon and Watergate, refer back to Chapter 6, page 151.

Environmental concerns. People who believed energy independence should be a major national goal welcomed the Alaska pipeline. Environmentalists, however, protested that it threatened the region's ecological balance.

Responding to scientists' warnings, people had become more concerned with the environment during the Sixties and early Seventies. On April 22, 1970, the same year that Congress established the Environmental Protection Agency, Americans celebrated the first Earth Day. Across the country millions of people marched and rallied to focus attention on pollution and other environmental problems.

American Voices

"As certain of victory as any presidential candidate in recent history, President Nixon and/or his campaign workers seemed afraid to go with an honest campaign and an open one."

—Eugene McCarthy, *Up 'Til Now*

The Watergate Scandal

Nixon had begun his second term with ambitious domestic plans. At the top of his list was an assault on Johnson's Great Society programs. In Nixon's view, these programs gave "too much to those who were supposed to help the needy and too little to the needy themselves." But before he could put his plans in motion, he was overwhelmed by scandal.

Early in 1973, the men involved in the Watergate break-in were tried and convicted. One defendant, James W. McCord, wrote a letter to trial judge John J. Sirica, charging that high administration officials had pressured the defendants to plead guilty to hide the officials' part in the break-in.

McCord's charges transformed the "third rate burglary" into a major scandal. To restore confidence in his administration, Nixon announced that a White House investigation was underway. He fired four advisors for concealing facts about the break-in. He asked Attorney General Elliot L. Richardson to appoint a special prosecutor to investigate. Richardson chose Archibald Cox, a Harvard law professor. The Senate formed the Select Committee on Presidential Campaign Activities to carry on its own investigation.

Among the Senate Watergate committee's members were (left to right) Chairman Sam Ervin, Daniel Inouye, and Howard Baker.

Constitutional Heritage

The idea that a President or members of his administration may withhold information from the Congress and the courts is known as "executive privilege." Many Presidents have claimed this right although it is not recognized in the Constitution. Nixon argued, *"Under the doctrine of the separation of powers, the manner in which the President personally exercises his power is not subject to questioning by another branch of government."*

Senator Sam Ervin, Chairman of the Select Committee, labeled Nixon's arguments "executive poppycock." Ervin warned that White House officials were not "nobility and royalty" and would, like any other citizen, be subject to arrest if they refused to appear before a congressional committee.

Connections: Literature

Read and Report. Have students read parts of Woodward and Bernstein's book *All the President's Men*. Ask them to report on the methods and discoveries of these two reporters. You may also wish to show the class the film adaptation.

Constitutional Heritage

Discussion. Ask students to explain how the Watergate investigations were a struggle between the legislative and the executive branches of government. **(The Senate formed a committee to investigate the illegal activities of the executive.)** There were also struggles within the executive branch. Ask students to give examples. **(Members of the Nixon cabinet resigned rather than follow Nixon's orders: Elliot Richardson and William P. Ruckelshaus resigned rather than fire special prosecutor Cox.)** How does the Constitution provide for the Congress to protect against abuse of power in the federal government? **(Through system of checks and balances)**

The Watergate Hearings

On May 17, 1973, Senator Sam Ervin opened what he considered "the most important investigation ever entrusted to the Congress." For the next three months, Americans watched the televised hearings with fascination and dismay. Witnesses told a tangled tale of dirty campaign tricks, political spying, illegal break-ins and wiretaps, and White House efforts to cover up these illegal activities. The hearings revealed the existence of a White House "enemies list." This list included the names of politicians, journalists, and others who opposed the Nixon administration and were therefore targeted for government harassment.

Throughout the hearings Republican Senator Howard Baker repeatedly asked witnesses, "What did the President know and when did he know it?" This was, he knew, the "central question" of the Watergate scandal. But as the hearings ended, his question had not yet been answered.

The battle for the tapes. During the hearings, one witness revealed that Nixon had taped all of the conversations that took place in his office. The Ervin Committee asked the President for his tapes, as did Special Prosecutor Cox. Nixon refused.

Cox then obtained a subpoena, a written legal order, from Judge Sirica directing the President to turn over any tapes that related to the burglary and cover-up. Instead, Nixon ordered Attorney General Richardson to fire Cox. Richardson resigned rather than carry out the President's order, and so did Deputy Attorney General William D. Ruckelshaus. Finally, the third-ranking official in the Justice Department fired Cox. The resignations and firing became known as the "Saturday Night Massacre."

Vice-President Agnew resigns. Meanwhile, a fresh scandal broke. Federal investigators charged that Vice-President Agnew had accepted bribes while governor of Maryland and had cheated on his income tax. On October 10, 1973, Agnew re-

Former White House legal advisor John Dean testified about President Nixon's role in the Watergate affair. Watergate figures (below) point accusing fingers in a modern version of a nineteenth-century cartoon entitled "He did it!"

Backyard History

Interview. Have students interview parents, grandparents, or other relatives or friends who remember the Watergate scandal. Have them ask these people what their reactions were to the newspaper articles, congressional hearings, impeachment proceedings, the resignation of the President, and Ford's pardon of Nixon. Also, have students ask their subjects what they learned from Watergate.

Active Learning

Skits. Divide the class into groups. Each group is to create a skit about the Watergate scandal and perform it before the class. Possible subjects include: A reporter interviewing a citizen about Watergate; Nixon conferring with his associates about whether or not to resign; Democrats and Republicans in Congress debating the issue; a family at the dinner table discussing Nixon's possible guilt.

Global Connections

Discussion. Foreign policy experts worried about the Watergate scandal. **Ask:** How could Watergate threaten American foreign policy? Have students consider national unity and the President's ability to act. **(Consider the effect of the loss of confidence in the presidency, trust in government officials and their policies, congressional efforts to curb presidential power, damage to American prestige and credibility abroad.)**

Constitutional Heritage

See pages 934–935 for the text of the Twenty-Fifth Amendment. It lists procedures for choosing a President or Vice-President in case of resignation, disability, or death.

Reduced student page in the Teacher's Edition

signed as Vice-President and pleaded "no contest" to income-tax evasion. According to Agnew's judge, this was "the full equivalent to a plea of guilty."

The Twenty-fifth Amendment, ratified in 1967, set up procedures for choosing a new President or Vice-President in case of resignation, disability, or death. Acting under this amendment, Nixon named Representative Gerald R. Ford of Michigan as the new Vice-President, and Congress approved.

Impeachment and Resignation

The Saturday Night Massacre triggered a storm of protest. Huge crowds milled around the White House. More than a quarter million telegrams denouncing Nixon's actions poured into Washington the following week. And twenty-two bills were introduced in the House of Representatives calling for Nixon's impeachment.

THE AMERICAN SPIRIT

Barbara Jordan

The Congresswoman from Texas

During the long, tense impeachment hearings, television viewers were struck by the tough, penetrating questions posed by a young member of the House Judiciary Committee, Barbara Jordan. "She cuts right to the heart of every issue," a fellow member of Congress observed.

A brilliant student, Jordan had graduated with honors from Texas Southern University, then earned a law degree from Boston University. In 1966 she was elected to the Texas Senate—the first African American elected to that body since 1883. Six years later Jordan won a seat in the House of Representatives.

As a member of the Judiciary Committee, Jordan recalled, she "lived the impeachment matter—it was a 24-hour-a-day engagement." For her, it was vital that Congress act to restore "public confidence in the moral leadership of the presidency." It was also essential to Jordan that Congress preserve the Constitution, which had finally come to include all Americans. At the hearings, Jordan said:

"'We the people.' It is a very eloquent beginning. But when that document was completed, . . . I was not included in that 'We the people.' I felt somehow for many years that George Washington and Alexander Hamilton just left me out by mistake. But through the process of amendment, interpretation, and court decision, I have finally been included in 'We the People.'"

At the end of her third term, Barbara Jordan retired from politics to become a professor in the Lyndon B. Johnson School of Public Affairs at the University of Texas. Jordan soon became absorbed in her new career. "It takes a long time to be a good professor," she told an interviewer, "and I intend to be a very good one."

Jordan placed her hopes for moral leadership of the nation in her students. "I want them to be premier public servants who have a core of principles to guide them," she said. "They are my future and the future of this country."

Connections: Politics

What was in the White House tapes shocked both Republicans and Democrats. Republican Hugh Scott, the Senate minority leader, called them "deplorable," "disgusting," and "immoral." One Democratic Congressman said, "If this is what he thought he could release, I'd like to hear what else is on those tapes." Republican Congressman John Ashbrook of Ohio said "I read the March 21 transcript and it was incredible, unbelievable."

Nixon fought hard to save his presidency. He went on television to assure Americans that "I am not a crook!" He appointed a new special prosecutor, Texas lawyer Leon Jaworski.

The crisis surrounding the White House deepened, though. In April 1974 Special Prosecutor Jaworski requested the tapes from Nixon. The President again refused. In July, ruling unanimously that the President could not withhold evidence in a criminal case, the Supreme Court ordered Nixon to give Jaworski the tapes.

That same month the House Judiciary Committee adopted three articles of impeachment against Nixon. The first article charged that the President had obstructed the investigation of the break-in. The other articles charged that he had misused presidential powers and had illegally withheld evidence from the Senate committee.

Finally, Nixon released the tapes that he had guarded for so long. They revealed that less than a week after the Watergate break-in, Nixon had ordered the FBI to halt an investigation of the crime. The President had been part of the cover-up from the beginning. Impeachment by the House and conviction by the Senate seemed certain.

On August 8, 1974, President Nixon announced his resignation, effective the next day. He was the first President of the United States to resign.

The Honolulu Advertiser
Hawaii's Prizewinning Newspaper
home edition 20¢
Ford's in...
Nixon's out
Aloha!
New President sworn in today
'The interest of America first'
A presidency ends, a presidency begins

Reflections on Watergate. Nixon was gone. But the concerns he had raised about the use and abuse of presidential power lingered.

Even before the Watergate scandal broke, critics had worried that Nixon was creating an all-powerful "imperial presidency." As an example, they pointed to the size of his White House staff, more than twice as large as President Roosevelt's staff during World War II.

These same critics noted that when Congress voted money for programs that he opposed, Nixon refused to spend it as Congress had intended. Such action, they charged, jeopardized the balance between the legislative and executive branches. Even more troublesome to most Americans, Nixon had misused his powers to punish people he viewed as threats to his administration. In doing so, his critics said, he had tried to set himself above the law.

Watergate taught Americans a painful lesson about the dangers of presidential power. It also taught them something else—that the Constitution's system of checks and balances is still our best protection against abuses of power. "Our Constitution works," Gerald Ford reassured the nation in his first speech as President. "Our great republic is a government of laws and not of men. Here, the people rule."

Section Review

1. **Identification.** Define *nonaligned.*

2. **Evaluation.** What do you think was President Nixon's most valuable achievement? Why?

3. **Analysis.** What long-term problem was emphasized by the energy crisis? Explain.

4. **Evaluation.** What effects do you think the Watergate scandal might have had on Americans' attitudes toward their government? Why?

Past and Present. In general, do Americans today have confidence in their political leaders? Why or why not?

Constitutional Heritage

Discussion. Refer students to the Constitution at the back of the text. Have them read sections that deal with impeachment—Article 1, Section 2, Clause 5 (page 915); Article 1, Section 3, Clauses 6 and 7 (page 915); and Article 2, Section 4 (page 922). **Ask:** What does the term *impeach* mean? **(to accuse)** Which house of Congress impeaches the President? **(House of Representatives)** Which house of Congress serves as jury? **(Senate)** What crimes are causes for impeachment? **(treason, bribery, other high crimes and misdemeanors)** How many votes are required to be convicted? **(two-thirds majority vote of members present)** Of what crimes was Nixon accused? **(blocking Watergate investigation, misusing presidential power, withholding evidence from Congress)** Are these crimes grounds for impeachment and trial? **(could be considered high crimes or misdemeanors)**

Section Review

ANSWERS

1. Definition for *nonaligned* is on page 815.
2. Answers may include: lessening of tension with Soviet Union (and SALT agreement) or opening door to China. Both made nuclear war less likely.
3. Problem was dwindling supply of oil, dependence on politically troubled countries of Middle East.
4. Answers may include: loss of respect for public officials; worry about excessive presidential power; renewed faith in system of checks and balances.
Past and Present: Opinions will vary.

Section 30-3

Objectives

- ***Answers the Focus Question.***
- *Evaluate Ford's accomplishments as President.*
- *Explain how Carter applied his commitment to human rights to foreign policy.*
- *Describe how the Middle East affected events in the United States during the Carter administration.*

Introducing

THE SECTION

Have students discuss: What was most needed by the people and government of the United States in the wake of the Agnew resignation? The Watergate scandal? **(The nation needed a period of calm and of healing before tackling the challenges facing the nation.)** Ask students to be alert to steps taken during the Ford administration that were designed to recapture calm and help heal the nation.

B · A · C · K · G · R · O · U · N · D

Connections: Politics

In the aftermath of the Watergate scandal, Congress acted to limit presidential power. In July 1973 Congress passed the Congressional Budget and Impoundment Act. The act gave Congress greater control over government spending. It also set up ways to block a President from impounding funds appropriated by Congress. In October 1974 Congress passed the Campaign Reform Act. It was designed to prevent misuse of campaign funds. The act set limits on individual contributions to a single election campaign. The act also called for a thorough disclosure of sources and uses of campaign money.

30-3 A Crisis of Confidence

Focus: How did Presidents Ford and Carter try to restore public confidence in the government and its leaders?

The Watergate scandal left Americans deeply disillusioned with their leaders. Opinion polls showed a growing pessimism about the future and the ability of the government to deal with such problems as the energy crisis. News commentators spoke of a "crisis of confidence."

Having lost faith in their political system, many Americans turned inward. A new concern for personal fulfillment swept the country, fed by a stream of books, magazines, and television shows on how to achieve better health, greater peace of mind, and more satisfaction in love and work. Many people turned to religion for comfort and salvation. Others sought personal growth through meditation, self-help groups, or concentration on their careers. This shift of interest away from public concerns to personal ones led writer Tom Wolfe to describe the Seventies as the "Me Decade."

The Pardon of Nixon

The task of restoring faith in government fell to Gerald Ford, the first chief executive who had not been elected either President or Vice-President. Compared to Nixon, who often seemed remote and secretive, Ford was open and friendly. A modest man from the automobile-producing state of Michigan, he once told an audience "I am a Ford, not a Lincoln."

"Our long national nightmare is over," declared Ford. One of his first acts was to choose Nelson A. Rockefeller, a four-term governor of New York, to be Vice-President. Public confidence was shaken, however, when President Ford announced that he was granting Nixon "a full, free and absolute pardon for all offenses he committed or may have committed while in office." Ford said he was taking this action to help "heal the wounds" left by Watergate. Nixon, he added, had "suffered enough and will continue to suffer no matter what I do."

Instead of healing Watergate's wounds, the pardon reopened them. Many Americans suspected that it was part of a secret deal arranged by Nixon before he resigned. The Chicago *Tribune* complained of "a sour smell" in the White House.

Americans also questioned the justice of pardoning Nixon when his aides were facing trial for conspiracy, obstruction of justice, and perjury, or telling lies under oath. Eventually, more than forty people would serve time in jail for crimes related to the Watergate scandal. Why, many Americans asked, should the former president not share their fate?

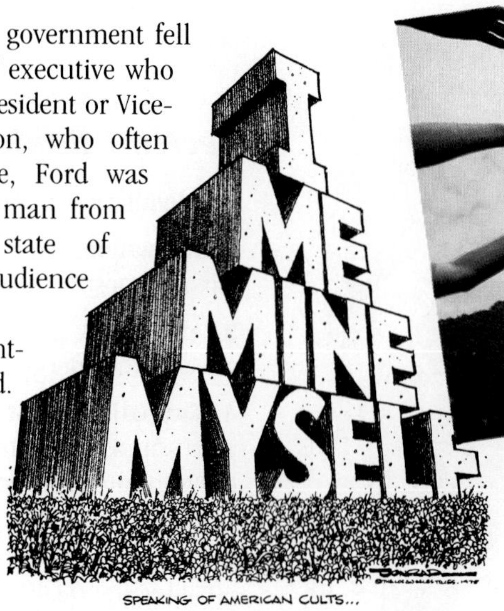
I
ME
MINE
MYSELF
SPEAKING OF AMERICAN CULTS...

During the 1970s people turned inward, following a variety of paths in search of spiritual and personal meaning.

Social History
Several television programs of the 1960s and 1970s reflected—and may have helped create—an atmosphere of cynicism about government. For some this cynicism revealed itself in the form of outrageous humor. "Laugh-In" savagely satirized Johnson's determination to pursue the war in Vietnam and Nixon's failure to quickly end it. "Saturday Night Live" parodied Nixon, Ford, and Carter. The programs exemplified a mood of disrespect for the presidency. A March 1975 poll surveying American attitudes included the statement, "the people running the country . . . don't tell us the truth." More than 83 percent of those polled agreed.

A Weak Economy

Meanwhile, the country faced grim economic news. Spurred by soaring oil prices, the cost of everything was shooting up. Inflation, Ford said, was "public enemy number one." Normally, high inflation meant a booming economy with low unemployment. But the economy was stagnant, not booming, and the number of people without jobs was growing. Economists coined a new word to describe this unhappy combination of rising prices and rising unemployment—**stagflation.**

In October 1974 Ford announced a broad anti-inflation crusade called "Whip Inflation Now," or WIN. As part of his WIN campaign, Ford called on Congress to reduce federal spending and urged every American to fight rising prices by spending less, saving more, and reducing waste. He explained:

> *"We waste food, gasoline, paper, electricity, natural resources. As a matter of fact, we waste almost everything. One friend told me we could probably whip—just understand this—whip inflation with the contents of our trash cans."*

Ford's WIN program did little, however, to reduce inflation. By encouraging consumers to stop spending, it may even have helped push the economy into recession. The jobless rate rose to over 7 percent, and by the end of 1974, the nation was in its worst economic downturn since the Great Depression.

The *Mayaguez* Incident

While fighting stagflation at home, President Ford faced other problems abroad. In the spring of 1975, the Communist forces of North Vietnam overwhelmed the government of South Vietnam. Communist regimes also seized power in nearby Laos and Cambodia. Around the world, newspaper headlines trumpeted a decline in American power.

Henry Kissinger, who had stayed on as Secretary of State, looked for some way to show that the United States was still "a world power." That opportunity came in May 1975 when the United States merchant ship *Mayaguez* was seized by Cambodian forces in the Gulf of Thailand. Kissinger advised Ford to "act . . . now, and act firmly."

President Ford ordered the marines to storm the island where the *Mayaguez* was held and free its crew. By the time marines attacked, the thirty-nine sailors had been released unharmed. News of their release, however, did not arrive in time to halt the rescue attempt. During this operation, forty-one Americans were killed.

Even so, haunted by the defeat in Vietnam, many Americans were pleased by this demonstration of American military might. It would not be the last time that Americans sought a victory to lay the ghosts of Vietnam to rest.

For advice on foreign policy, President Ford, shown here with Japanese emperor Hirohito, relied heavily on Secretary of State Henry Kissinger.

Developing

THE SECTION

Writing About History

Letter. Have students write letters to the Chicago *Tribune* responding to its complaint of a "sour smell" in the White House after Ford pardoned Nixon (see page 822, right column). Ask students to take a position either agreeing or disagreeing with the *Tribune* and give reasons to support their position.

Connections: Economics

Discussion. Democrats in Congress disagreed with Ford's methods of ending stagflation. Senator Hubert Humphrey warned, *"Any policy that brings high unemployment and lower real income . . . in the name of controlling inflation is simply unacceptable."* Speaker of the House Carl Albert recommended that one hundred thousand public service jobs be created and price increases be banned in monopoly industries.

Ask: Do you think Congressman Albert's plan would have been more effective than Ford's? Why or why not?

Connections: Literature

Read and Report. In 1975 Richard Reeves, a writer on politics, published a book called *A Ford, Not a Lincoln: The Decline of American Political Leadership.* Interested students might read the book and report back to the class. Points to consider: How does Reeves turn Ford's own description of himself ("I am a Ford, not a Lincoln") against him? Why does he think Ford represents a decline in leadership? Compared with whom? Do students agree or disagree?

Multicultural Perspectives

Although born and raised in the Deep South, James Earl Carter opposed segregation. In Plains he refused an invitation to join a local chapter of the White Citizens Council—a group opposing desegregation. He also opposed a proposal that his church ban blacks from membership.

In his 1971 governor's inaugural address, Carter stated, *"I say to you frankly that the time for racial segregation is over. No poor, rural, weak, or black person should endure the . . . burden of being deprived of an education, a job, or simple justice."* During his governorship the number of African-American state employees rose 40 percent. In 1974 a portrait of Martin Luther King, Jr., was hung in the Georgia state capitol.

Active Learning

Panel Discussion. Have students role-play Ford and Carter supporters in a panel discussion. Each participant can give reasons for supporting a candidate and answer questions and objections from the other side.

Thinking Critically

Evaluation. As Ford left office, many American leaders praised him for his efforts to rebuild confidence in government after Watergate. Have students debate whether Ford's pardon of Nixon hurt or helped these efforts.

Reduced student page in the Teacher's Edition

Carter Elected in 1976

Not long after the *Mayaguez* incident, Ford said that he would seek election as President in 1976—the year the nation celebrated its bicentennial. He faced opposition within his party from former California governor Ronald Reagan, but won the Republican nomination in a close fight.

The Democrats nominated a newcomer to national politics, James Earl Carter, Jr. When people first heard that Jimmy Carter was running for President, a common response was "Jimmy *who?*"

Carter campaigned tirelessly. People learned that he was a peanut farmer from Plains, Georgia. A graduate of the United States Naval Academy, he had served as an officer on one of the world's first nuclear-powered submarines. He had also served one term as governor of Georgia. Carter described himself as a "born again Christian." When asked to sum up his campaign in a word, Carter answered, "That word would be faith."

Carter appealed to Watergate-weary voters. "It's time for someone like myself to make a drastic change in Washington," he argued. Carter promised to bring honesty back into the White House, assuring voters, "I will never lie to you."

Neither Ford nor Carter inspired much enthusiasm. On election day, only 53 percent of eligible voters bothered to go to the polls. Carter won by a narrow margin.

Building Public Trust

On January 20, 1977, Carter took the oath of office, the first President from the Deep South since the Civil War. Walter F. Mondale, former senator from Minnesota, was sworn in as Vice-President.

President Carter hoped to rebuild Americans' trust in their government. His first act as President was to keep a promise made during the campaign to pardon those who had evaded the draft during the Vietnam War. Carter hoped that the pardon would help to heal the wounds left from Vietnam.

The President tried "to stay close to the people." When he traveled, he arranged to stay in the homes of ordinary citizens. He also worked to dismantle "the imperial presidency." Carter promised to eliminate "luxuries, such as door-to-door limousine service" for officials. "Government officials can't be sensitive to your problems," he explained, "if we are living like royalty here in Washington."

Ocean-going sailing ships from thirty-five nations were a stirring sight during bicentennial celebrations in New York and Boston harbors.

Connections: Politics

Democratic Congressman Morris Udall criticized Congress's slowness to enact Carter's energy programs as the triumph of special interests over the national interest: *"It's like it was the day after Pearl Harbor, and you interviewed the Congressman from Detroit, and he said 'The Japanese attack was outrageous, but before we rush into war, let's see how it would affect the [car] industry.' and then somebody else said, 'It was dastardly, but consider the effect on oil . . . .'"*

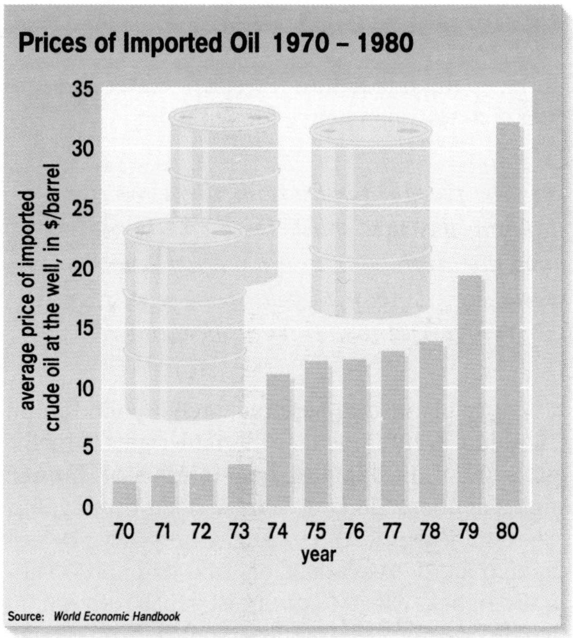

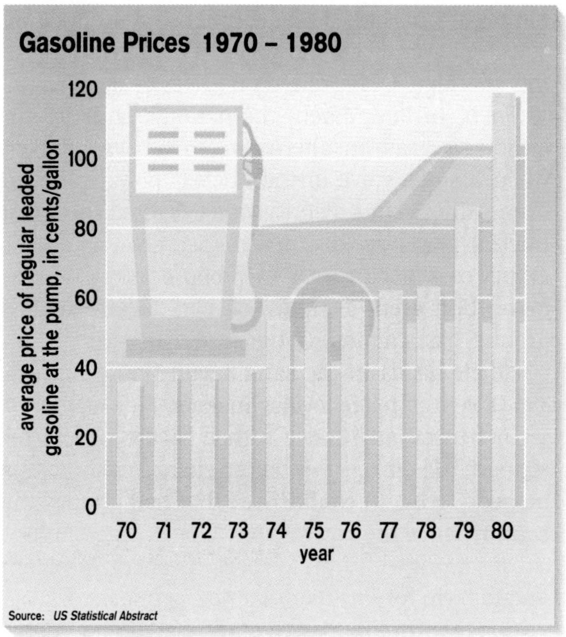

Skyrocketing Inflation

The new President inherited an economy plagued by high inflation and high unemployment. To stimulate the economy and create jobs, in early 1977 Carter asked Congress to fund public works projects and job-training programs. He also requested tax cuts for businesses in order to encourage them to expand.

Carter soon discovered that fighting one part of stagflation often only makes the other part worse. His programs did reduce the jobless rate by 1979, but in the next year inflation skyrocketed to an alarming 18 percent. Economists warned that the cost of living could double in less than four years.

Carter's energy program. One of the main causes of inflation was the soaring cost of imported oil. By 1977 the United States was importing more than half of its oil. Whenever the price of foreign oil went up, the effect rippled through the economy. Manufacturing, transportation, heating, and lighting costs escalated. Materials made from oil, such as plastics, rose in price as well.

To wean the nation from its dependence on imported oil, in April 1977 Carter unveiled an ambitious program. "This difficult effort," Carter warned, "will be the the moral equivalent of war." The President proposed to encourage energy conservation and promote the development of new energy sources. This could only be done, he argued, by **deregulation,** or ending government control of the price of domestic oil and natural gas.

For years, federal regulations had kept the price of oil and gas produced in this country very low. As Carter saw it, this policy had three bad effects. First, it encouraged waste. Second, the low oil and gas prices discouraged companies from looking for new supplies within the United States. Third, new sources of energy such as solar power could not compete with cheap oil and gas.

After two years of bitter debate, Congress passed most of Carter's energy program. The President was given power to deregulate domestic energy prices. Americans were offered tax breaks for conserving energy by insulating their homes and using alternative energy sources. Automobile makers were ordered to produce more fuel-efficient cars.

A new energy crisis. Before these measures could take effect, the nation was hit by a new crisis. In January 1979 a revolution in the Middle Eastern

Using the Visuals

Analyzing Graphs. Refer students to the two graphs on this page. **Ask:** What do the two graphs show? **(prices of oil and gasoline 1970–1980)** Cite three years in which the price of oil rose the most. **(1974, 1979, 1980)** By how much? **($8, $5, $14 respectively)** How did the rise in oil prices affect the price of gasoline in these years? **(Gas prices also rose.)**

Connections: Science and Technology

Research and Report. Divide the class into several groups to research alternative energy technology: solar, wind, geo-thermal, and nuclear energy, electric automobiles, and the like. Each group should investigate the potential for the technology to provide energy, to cause safety problems, and to raise environmental concerns. Have each group present its findings to the class.

Thinking Critically

Evaluation. Many Americans objected to small, light, fuel-efficient, cars, claiming they were less safe than big, heavy, gas-guzzling ones. Have the class discuss the pros and cons of the small, light, efficient auto and the large, heavy, high-gas-consumption car.

Thinking Critically

Evaluation. Have students discuss whether they think American foreign policy should be based, as Carter proposed, on an "absolute commitment to human rights" or on another assessment of the best interests of the nation.

Linking Past and Present

President Carter made an exception to his rule of using a good record on human rights as a criterion for foreign policy decisions. He established diplomatic relations with Communist China, a nation well known for flouting the human rights of its citizens. For 15 years China's economy and society seemed to be changing for the better. But in 1989, protesters began pressuring for more and greater reforms. The Communist leadership used soldiers and tanks to ruthlessly put down the protests in Beijing's Tiananmen Square. After that, many Americans demanded that the United States judge China on its human rights record, arguing that the brutality of the Tiananmen Square massacre was proof that China's rulers did not deserve American good will.

Connections: Economics

Book Report. In the 1970s many Americans espoused small-scale technology. They thought local communities and small groups should develop energy-saving and ecologically responsible technology. This movement got much of its impetus from a book, *Small is Beautiful*, by the economist E.F. Schumacher, who decried the "forward stampede" of society. Interested students might read Schumacher's book and report on it to the class.

Chapter Connections

Looking Back. Remind students of the history of the Panama Canal. Refer them to Chapter 18, pages 483–484.

Reduced student page in the Teacher's Edition

nation of Iran halted that country's oil production, causing a worldwide shortage. Taking advantage of this shortage, OPEC raised oil prices by 60 percent.

Then, in late March, the nation's faith in nuclear power as an alternative to oil was shaken when a stuck valve in the nuclear power plant at Three Mile Island, Pennsylvania, caused the worst nuclear-power accident in American history. These events convinced Carter to propose a new energy plan. But even as lines of cars again snaked around gas stations, Congress did not act. "They put their heads in the sand," said House Speaker Tip O'Neill of his fellow lawmakers.

In frustration, Carter turned to the people for support. He linked this latest energy crisis to the broader "crisis in confidence" that had gripped the country since the early 1970s. Carter urged Americans to work with him to solve the energy problem and to "win for our nation a new confidence."

Congress finally passed most of Carter's energy proposals in 1980. By then, the energy crisis had begun to ease. As deregulation took effect and domestic energy prices rose, shortages vanished. At the same time, Americans began to change their wasteful energy ways. By 1984 the United States was using less energy than it had in 1973.

Carter's energy policy encouraged use of alternative sources, such as solar heat captured by roof panels.

Carter's Foreign Policy

In his inaugural address, President Carter had spoken of a new approach to foreign policy:

> *"The passion for freedom is on the rise. Tapping this new spirit, there can be no nobler nor ambitious task for Americans to undertake . . . than to help shape a just and peaceful world that is truly humane."*

Carter planned to base his foreign policy on an "absolute commitment to human rights." In the past, the United States had overlooked human rights abuses as long as a ruler stood firm against Communism. Carter changed this policy. He cut foreign aid to many dictators who had abused human rights. When Communist rebels, known as Sandinistas, ousted Anastasio Somoza, the corrupt dictator of Nicaragua, Carter refused to intervene.

The Panama Canal treaties. Carter's concern for fairness in dealing with other nations led to two new Panama Canal treaties. Panamanians had long resented the Hay-Bunau-Varilla Treaty of 1903 because it gave the United States control of the canal "in perpetuity," or forever.

The new Panama Canal treaties called on the United States to shift control of the canal to Panama by the year 2000. Turning the canal over to Panama, Carter argued, was simply a matter of justice. Many Americans opposed this transfer, though. Ronald Reagan protested, "We're turning one of the world's most important waterways over to a country no one can believe." In the spring of 1978 the Senate barely ratified both treaties.

Recognition of China. In 1978, Carter told the nation that the United States would establish diplomatic relations with the People's Republic of China on January 1, 1979. He also announced an end to diplomatic relations with Taiwan.

Carter's announcement set off a storm of controversy. For three decades the United States had recognized the Nationalist Chinese on Taiwan as the rightful government of China. Senator Barry M. Goldwater of Arizona charged that the change in policy "stabs in the back the nation of Taiwan."

Connections: Politics

Much of the Senate opposition to Salt II arose from doubts about the United States' ability to monitor Soviet weapons. Some opposition arose because senators thought Carter had not adequately consulted military and diplomatic advisors. Marvin Stone, editor of *U.S. News and World Report*, raised the question: *"Do we or don't we have confidence in the President's judgment in dealing with questions of national security and the growing Soviet military threat?"*

Writing About History

Letter. Have students imagine themselves as members of the Olympic team of 1980. Ask them to write a letter home from their Olympic training camp, expressing their emotions upon learning that President Carter has ordered a boycott of the 1980 Olympic Games because of the Soviet invasion of Afghanistan.

Connections: Religion

Oral Report. Anwar el-Sadat risked his standing in the Arab world to make peace with Israel. At first it seemed that Sadat would not suffer from his gamble. But at the same time, a new and powerful movement was gathering strength among Arabs: Muslim fundamentalism.

Have students research Muslim fundamentalism: its roots and the role it played in shaping international relations in the Middle East. Students can report their findings to the class.

Carter defended his China policy, saying it would "contribute to the well-being of our own nation" and "enhance the stability of Asia." In March 1979 the United States and the People's Republic formally exchanged ambassadors. The United States gave the People's Republic special trade privileges.

President Carter shakes hands with Anwar Sadat of Egypt (left) and Menachem Begin of Israel after they signed the Camp David Accords.

Relations with the Soviet Union. President Carter continued Nixon's policy of détente with the Soviet Union. In June 1979 he and Soviet leader Leonid Brezhnev signed a new strategic arms limitation treaty at a summit meeting—SALT II—in Vienna, Austria. This agreement limited the number of missiles and long-range bombers each superpower could build, while allowing nuclear warheads to be doubled in number. "SALT II will not end the arms race," Carter said, "but it does make the arms race safer and more predictable."

The SALT II agreement faced stiff opposition in the Senate. Liberals charged that it was not "real arms control." Conservatives worried that it might weaken American military strength.

Late in 1979 the Soviet Union invaded its southern neighbor Afghanistan, claiming that Afghan leaders had asked for help in putting down a rebellion. Calling the invasion the "most serious threat to world peace since World War II," the President placed an embargo on the sale of grain, machinery, and technology to the Soviet Union. He also announced an American boycott of the 1980 Summer Olympic games in Moscow. Détente was dead. And with it died all hopes for Senate ratification of the SALT II agreement.

The Middle East

Carter's greatest foreign policy success came in the Middle East. In April 1977 he met with Egyptian president Anwar el-Sadat to discuss aid to Egypt and peace in the Middle East. The following November President Sadat stunned the world by announcing that he was ready to visit Israel in the cause of peace. Israeli prime minister Menachem Begin quickly extended an invitation. Millions of people throughout the world watched the historic meeting on television. The two nations, at war for thirty years, now agreed to settle their differences.

Soon after Sadat's visit, the Egyptians and the Israelis began peace talks, with the United States as mediator. But by mid-1978 the talks were faltering, with each side hurling charges at the other. "Unless there is some major breakthrough," Carter warned, "the whole thing will break down."

The Camp David Accords. In September Carter invited Sadat and Begin to meet with him at Camp David, the presidential retreat in Maryland. For thirteen days the three leaders worked out their differences. Writer Helen Bevington described their struggle:

> *"Carter's face was drawn with fatigue after close to total breakdown of negotiations, after daily prayers for enlightenment. . . . A Christian, a Jew, and a Muslim . . . sought together for peace."*

Limited English Proficiency

Cooperative Activity. Have students identify the various problems that President Carter faced during his term in office—energy crisis, inflation, human rights violations abroad, Middle East tensions, the arms race, the Soviet invasion of Afghanistan, revolution in Iran, and the hostage crisis.

Divide the class into eight groups and assign a problem to each. Have students skim the section to review the issues involved and how Carter dealt with them.

When finished, each group can appoint a spokesperson to present the issue and solutions to the class. Discuss the effectiveness of each one.

Thinking Critically

Analysis. Have students discuss how Carter's failure to effect release of the hostages might have affected his image as a President. What might it have contributed to his defeat in 1980?

B · A · C · K · G · R · O · U · N · D

Global Connections

On November 26, 1979, Ayatollah Khomeini made a speech condemning Carter and repeating the threat that the hostages would be killed if the United States attacked the embassy to try to save them. He declared, *"This is not a struggle between the United States and Iran. It is a struggle between Iran and blasphemy."* He urged the students holding the hostages to remain firm. *"Why should we be afraid? We consider martyrdom a great honor."*

Shouting "Death to America," Iranian students burn the American flag after seizing the embassy in Teheran and taking 52 hostages.

They finally hammered out two agreements known as the Camp David Accords. The first accord ended the state of war between Egypt and Israel. Israel agreed to return to Egypt the Sinai Peninsula, which it had occupied since 1967. The second agreement called for negotiations to settle the status of Palestinians living in two Israeli-controlled territories, the West Bank and the Gaza Strip.

Revolution in Iran. The Middle East, however, remained a region of conflict. Shah Mohammed Reza Pahlavi had ruled Iran since World War II. Under the Shah's rule, Carter declared, Iran was "an island of stability in one of the more troubled areas of the world."

The Shah encouraged modern industrial development. Conservative religious leaders, however, thought that the Shah was too worldly and that his plans for modernization threatened Islamic beliefs. Many Iranians also opposed the Shah because he had banned political parties and used secret police to silence dissent. They were also angered by his links with the CIA.

Opposition turned into bloody rioting in January 1979, forcing the Shah to flee the country. Soon after, the Ayatollah Ruhollah Khomeini (koh-MAY-nee), a religious leader, declared Iran an Islamic republic, governed by the laws of Islam.

The hostage crisis. In October 1979, the Shah entered the United States for medical treatment. Many Iranians demanded that the United States return him to Iran to stand trial for the brutality of his regime. Carter refused to surrender the Shah. Angered by Carter's support of the Shah, Iranian revolutionaries stormed the United States embassy, taking fifty-two Americans hostage. They vowed not to release the hostages until the Shah was returned to Iran.

The hostage crisis stretched into weeks, then months. Nightly television news broadcasts showed angry crowds marching through Teheran shouting "Death to America" and "Death to Carter."

Reagan Elected in 1980

The inability of the government to protect its citizens weighed heavily on Americans, and the hostage crisis hung like a dark cloud over the presidential campaign of 1980. Another cloud was the economy, with inflation, high taxes, and unemployment. Many felt that traditional Democratic policies and social programs were not working.

Former actor and governor Ronald Reagan appealed to voters with his philosophy of thrift, hard work, free enterprise, and patriotism. In July 1980

Reagan easily won the Republican nomination. He chose former CIA director George Bush as his running mate. The Democrats renominated Jimmy Carter and Walter Mondale.

Carter and Reagan met in Cleveland for a televised debate. Carter stressed peace, human rights, energy independence, and arms control. Reagan's main theme was the economy. He said that he would build up the military, cut taxes, and balance the budget. He promised "a new beginning."

In November Reagan defeated Carter by a wide margin. "This isn't an election," reported journalist Elizabeth Drew, "it's an earthquake."

The hostages return. Two days before the November election, Iranians agreed to negotiate the release of the hostages. But Iran waited to free captives until January 20, 1981, Reagan's Inauguration Day. On that date, after 444 days in captivity, the hostages left Iran. News of their release flashed across the world just after President Reagan had delivered his inaugural address. For the hostages, and for the nation as well, this happy moment did seem to promise "a new beginning."

Section Review

1. Identification. Define *stagflation* and *deregulation.*

2. Comprehension. What measures did Presidents Ford and Carter try to take to restore people's confidence in their leaders?

3. Application. Explain Carter's human rights policies. Should the United States continue to apply them?

4. Analysis. Describe two ways that events in the Middle East affected events in the United States during the Carter administration.

Data Search. Study the graphs on page 825. When did the price of imported oil nearly double? What happened to the price of gasoline that year? In what year did oil prices take their greatest leap? What event prompted this price rise? How were gasoline prices affected? Summarize in one sentence the relationship between events in the Middle East during the Seventies and the price of gasoline in the United States.

Connections to Themes

Balancing Unity and Diversity

One event after another during the 1970s tore at the fabric of national unity. As the decade opened, Americans were deeply divided over Vietnam and civil rights. Questions about abuses of power by President Nixon and Vice-President Agnew left many people feeling betrayed. Rapidly rising prices added to the national frustration.

Yet there was cause for optimism. The women's movement expanded opportunities for women. The number of people of diverse ethnic backgrounds who obtained an education and entered professions, managerial positions, and elective offices rose rapidly.

Even as members of ethnic groups were finding more opportunities in education and employment, they were also taking new interest in their heritage. In 1977 millions of Americans watched a television drama based on Alex Haley's book *Roots: The Saga of an American Family*. Haley had spent twelve years tracing his family's history from Africa to America and from slavery to freedom. The program—which remains one of the most watched in television history—led people of many different backgrounds to seek out their own roots.

Some observers saw the upswing of ethnic pride as a healthy sign. As people in large numbers gain a greater appreciation of their own cultural heritage, these observers said, they will also gain a greater appreciation of the one characteristic that all Americans share: the diversity of their backgrounds.

Active Learning

Get-Out-the Vote Campaign. Many young people did not vote for Carter or Reagan in 1980—they did not vote at all. One 18-year-old said, "I didn't want to be responsible for electing either one." A 20-year-old declared that politics has "nothing to do with me."

Divide the class into teams. Each team is to devise a get-out-the-vote campaign for 1980. The point of the campaign is to encourage people to go to the polls, no matter which candidate they vote for. Students can create posters, slogans, and TV commercials (with skits) that emphasize the importance of voting.

Section Review

ANSWERS

1. Definitions are on pages indicated in parentheses: *stagflation* (823); *deregulation* (825).
2. Ford: WIN program and handling of *Mayaguez* affair; Carter: "I will never lie to you," eliminating luxuries for government officials, keeping promise to pardon Vietnam draft dodgers.
3. Carter cut aid to countries that abused human rights.
4. Camp David Accords probably made Carter more popular; hostage crisis, partially responsible for his defeat in 1980; revolution in Iran set off U.S. energy crisis.
Data Search: (a) 1974 (b) rose sharply (c) 1980 (d) Political instability in the Middle East (e) Price of gas rose sharply (f) War, revolution, and instability in Middle East made gas prices rise.

Chapter Connections

Affirmative action is discussed in this chapter on text pages 813–814. The 1978 Supreme Court case of *Regents of the University of California* v. *Allan Bakke* is profiled.

Reduced student page in the Teacher's Edition

POINT OF VIEW

Affirmative Action

In the 1970s the policy of affirmative action became part of American life. Its purpose is to help women, African Americans, and members of other groups that have faced job discrimination to achieve full equality in the workplace. It calls on employers to hire people from these groups, even if that means favoring some job-seekers over others because of their sex or race.

Is affirmative action a reasonable policy for righting old wrongs? Or does it contradict the ideal of equality of opportunity? Here are two very different views.

Affirmative Racism

"A few years ago, I got into an argument with a lawyer friend who is a partner in a New York firm. I was being the conservative, arguing that preferential treatment of blacks was immoral; he was being the liberal, urging that it was the only way to bring blacks to full equality. In the middle of all this he abruptly said, 'But you know, let's face it. We must have hired at least ten blacks in the last few years, and none of them has really worked out.' . . .

My friend's comment was an outcropping of a new racism that is emerging to take its place alongside the old. . . . The new racists do not think blacks are inferior. They are typically longtime supporters of civil rights. But they exhibit the classic behavioral symptom of racism: they treat blacks differently from whites, because of their race. The results can be as concretely bad and unjust as any that the old racism produces: . . . blacks are denied the right to compete as equals. . . .

The most obvious consequence of preferential treatment is that every black professional, no matter how able, is tainted. Every black who is hired by a white-run organization that hires blacks preferentially has to put up with the knowledge that many of his co-workers believe he was hired because of his race; and he has to put up with the suspicion in his own mind that they might be right.

. . . Preferential treatment by race has sat as uneasily with America's equal opportunity ideal during the post-1965 period as it did during the days of legalized segregation. We had to construct tortuous rationalizations when we permitted blacks to be kept on the back of the bus—and the rationalizations to justify sending blacks to the head of the line have been just as tortuous. Both kinds of rationalization say that sometimes it is all right to treat people in different ways. For years, we have instinctively sensed this was wrong in principle. . . . I submit that our instincts were right. There is no such thing as good racial discrimination."

—Charles Murray, social policy researcher, in *The New Republic*, December 31, 1984

Yes to Affirmative Action

"I'm for affirmative action. I can make the argument on economic grounds—the disproportionate number of blacks out of work in this country should be enough evidence that the policy isn't taking jobs away from whites.

But there's a second reason for my bias. Except for a sweaty warehousing job that I was forced to take when laid off in 1984, all the jobs I've had since graduating from college in 1960 were because of affirmative action. In most cases, I was one of only a handful of black managers or professionals in an organization, and a few times I found myself to be the only one in a department. I never got around to feeling lonely, because I was too busy being grateful for being on the payroll.

Nor did I have gnawing doubts about my qualifications for the jobs I held. . . . I realized that somewhere there was someone who could do my job better than I could, but I also knew that every person . . . would have to say the same thing if he or she were strictly honest. Every single one of us—black and white, male and female—had been hired for reasons beyond our being able to do the job. . . . Some had connections who were able to get them interviewed and hired; others had attended the 'right' schools; still others had been hired because they were . . . members of a particular class, religion, nationality or fraternity. . . .

Affirmative action is needed in education as well as in the workplace. . . . Without the policy there would be a sharp drop in the already-small number of black professionals that colleges produce. . . . The affirmative action programs that raised the share of minorities in medical schools . . . produced tremendous benefits to society.

As for me, each morning I go to work with pride and confidence. I know I can do the job. I also know that I'm a beneficiary of a law . . . that does not require an organization to hire a person who clearly doesn't have the education, credentials or skills that a job demands. Any organization that has done this is guilty of ignoring qualified minority people."

—Hosea Martin, vice president of the United Way, *Wall Street Journal*, April 25, 1991

1. From Murray's point of view, what are troubling effects of affirmative action?

2. What positive effects does Martin see?

3. How might affirmative action affect you?

Point of View

ANSWERS

1. Murray argues that among white Americans affirmative action has spawned a new racism which perpetuates the belief that blacks are inferior to whites. He also believes that this policy hurts African-American employees, causing them to wonder whether they are qualified for their jobs or were hired because of their race.
2. Martin believes that the most positive affect of affirmative action has been to open the hiring process to qualified people who otherwise might have been discriminated against because of their race or sex. Noting that almost everyone in the workplace is hired because of some special connection, he argues that affirmative action hiring policies create such a connection for African Americans and others who have faced discrimination.
3. Answers will vary according to whether students perceive themselves as part of a group that could be helped or hurt by preferential hiring policies.

Chapter Survey

ANSWERS

Using New Vocabulary

1. (a) Opponents of *feminism* charged that it could lead to *reverse discrimination.*
2. (c) *Affirmative action* programs often caused a *backlash* of resentment.
3. (b) *Deregulation* aimed at combatting *stagflation.*

Reviewing the Chapter

1. Factors: dissatisfaction with "traditional" female role; discrimination in employment, lower pay and fewer chances for advancement; laws restricting women's reproductive freedom. Achievements: improvements in employment, education, participation in politics, liberalization of abortion and birth control laws.
2. Goals: expanding civil rights, political power, medical and legal aid; better housing, jobs, and education; economic protection. Methods: labor union, working through political parties, demonstrations, strikes, redistricting.
3. Like other groups, Native Americans wanted to be treated as equals in American society and to build up pride in their own heritage. Like Hispanics, Native Americans did not see themselves as a single group. Native Americans regained claims to land and mineral rights on their land.
4. Eisenhower followed policy of containment. Nixon followed a policy of détente by opening relations with China and signing arms limitation agreements with Soviet Union.
5. Americans conserved fuel used in transportation, electricity, production, and heating. Congress approved Alaska pipeline. These measures only slightly and temporarily reduced dependence on foreign oil.
6. President had abused his power, acted above the law in ordering cover-up, withholding evidence in criminal case. The power struggle between President and Congress resolved by Supreme Court ordering Nixon to release tapes.
7. Ford tried to heal the wounds of Watergate but made people even more disgusted with government because it looked as if deal had been made.
8. Promised to be truthful and honest. He did not significantly restore public confidence. Evidence includes persistent stagflation, energy crisis, Iran hostage crisis.
9. High inflation, high unemployment; Ford urged Americans to whip inflation by not being wasteful; this did not solve problems. Carter tried to reduce unemployment with public works projects, job training, tax cuts to spur business expansion, but only drove up

Reduced student page in the Teacher's Edition

Chapter Survey

Using New Vocabulary

Think about the meaning of each vocabulary term below. Then pair off terms with related meanings and explain how they are related.

1. feminism	(a) reverse discrimination
2. affirmative action	(b) stagflation
3. deregulation	(c) backlash

Reviewing the Chapter

1. What factors led to the growth of the women's movement in the 1970s? What were some of its achievements?

2. Explain the goals and methods of Hispanic organizations in the 1970s.

3. Compare the Native American movement of the 1970s with the women's and Hispanic movements.

4. How did Nixon's approach to foreign policy differ from Eisenhower's? Give examples to support your answer.

5. Evaluate the American response to the 1973-1974 energy crisis.

6. Why was the Watergate scandal a serious constitutional crisis?

7. Why did Ford pardon Nixon? What effect did the pardon have on the nation?

8. How did Jimmy Carter appeal to voters in 1976? Did his presidency restore confidence in the federal government? Give supporting evidence.

9. Describe the economic problems of the 1970s and evaluate Ford's and Carter's measures to deal with them.

10. Identify Carter's foreign policy successes and failures in the Middle East. What was the reason for each?

Thinking Critically

1. Evaluation. Do you think the nation was growing more democratic or less democratic during the 1970s? Give examples to support your answer.

2. Synthesis. Imagine that you are helping to prepare for a television debate between Nixon and Carter. Make "cue cards" for each President, listing arguments in favor of the basic principle underlying his foreign policy.

3. Analysis. In 1979 Jimmy Carter said to the nation, "I want to talk to you right now about a fundamental threat to American democracy. . . . It is a crisis of confidence. . . . The erosion of our confidence in the future is threatening to destroy the social and political fabric of America." Explain the causes of this crisis and how it endangered American society.

History and You

Consult an almanac to find out how much oil the United States imported in 1980, in 1985, and in a recent year. What percentage of the total amount of oil used in the United States was imported? This figure might be calculated by dividing the amount of oil imported in one year by the amount of oil consumed, as long as the units are the same. Next, compare gasoline prices today with prices in 1980 (see graph, page 825). From this information and your knowledge of current events, what influence would you say imported oil has on the American economy today?

Using a Time Line

Match dates on the time line with the events below. Write your answers in chronological order and explain the importance of each event. (Not all dates have events.)

(A) Panama Canal treaties
(B) seizure of *Mayaguez*
(C) Watergate burglary
(D) recognition of United Farm Workers
(E) Camp David Accords
(F) Nixon resignation
(G) recognition of People's Republic of China
(H) *Roe* v. *Wade*

1970 1972 1973 1974 1975 1977 1978 1979

inflation.
10. Successes: Camp David Accords worked because Carter able to bring Egyptian and Israeli leaders together and personally hammer out compromises. Failure: hostage crisis—no negotiation possible with Ayatollah and anti-American Muslim fundamentalists in power in Iran.

Thinking Critically

1. Answers may point to gains made by women, Hispanics, and Native Americans; or to Watergate and people's loss of confidence in government.
2. Cue cards for Nixon can touch on his diplomatic strategies and realpolitik maneuvers leading to SALT and a more open relationship with China. Those for Carter can touch on his more idealistic approach supporting human rights and achievement of Camp David Accords.
3. Crisis was result of Watergate. People suspicious that all public officials might be crooks. A democratic government lacking confidence and support of people cannot function well.

Applying Thinking Skills

Recognizing Stereotypes

Throughout the period of cold war and détente, American and Soviet citizens often held negative stereotypes, or unfavorable fixed notions, of each other. In 1980 Malcolm Toon, former ambassador to Moscow, stated that relations between the superpowers would not improve "without a basic change in Soviet philosophy and outlook." As you read Soviet scholar Georgi Arbatov's response, look for stereotypes of the United States.

"Suggesting that a significant improvement of relations is possible only if there is a basic change in Soviet philosophy and outlook is a sure prescription for greater tensions. . . . The gist of peaceful coexistence is that we can live side by side, have normal relations, even good relations, while remaining different from each other. . . .

Let us imagine a hypothetical situation where, instead of the Soviet Union, there is another superpower facing the United States, absolutely similar to it . . . with a similar Congress inhabited by quite a few trigger-happy politicians, . . . the same energy-wasting way of life, and very similar interests in . . . oil and other mineral resources around the world. Imagine that this United States II is just as egocentric [self-centered], self-righteous, and full of messianic [crusading] aspirations as [United States I], just as itching to reform the entire world to its liking. . . . Would our planet be better off and a safer place to live [in] than at present with the United States and the Soviet Union being as different from each other as they are?"

1. How does Arbatov stereotype the United States?
2. What stereotypes do you think most Americans would use to describe the Soviet Union today?

Writing About Issues

The Issue: *When should the United States use economic sanctions to influence the actions of other nations?*

Presidents use tools besides war to influence the actions of other nations. Diplomacy is one such tool. Economic sanctions, penalties such as the grain embargo Carter imposed on the Soviet Union in 1979, are another.

Many Americans agreed that the United States should oppose the Soviet invasion of Afghanistan. They said that if the Soviet Union got away with sending 85,000 troops into that country, other nations would be in danger of such aggression. Some Americans were especially concerned with keeping the Soviets out of the nearby oil-rich nations of the Middle East. But Americans did not agree that economic sanctions were the best way to oppose the invasion.

American farmers were strongly against the grain embargo. They had counted on the Soviet Union to purchase tons of grain and soybeans. If they could not find other customers to buy that grain, many farmers would be bankrupted. "Mr. Carter took aim at the Russians with a double-barreled shotgun, pulled the trigger, and hit the U.S. farmer," the president of the American Farm Bureau Federation said.

The Carter Administration tried to find alternative markets for the grain but insisted that economic sanctions were the best way to force the Soviets out of Afghanistan. The United States had used sanctions in the past, for example, the embargo on Cuban sugar that began in the 1960s. Now, Vice President Walter Mondale described the grain embargo as essential to counter "an absolutely outrageous, indefensible, and dangerous aggression."

What do you think? Under what circumstances should the United States use economic sanctions to oppose the actions of other countries? Imagine that you are a member of the President's cabinet. The President has asked you to submit written guidelines for deciding when economic sanctions should be used. Write a one-page paper stating your recommendations and the reasons for them.

History and You

Oil imports dropped in the early 1980s, then rose sharply at the end of the decade to exceed pre-energy crisis levels. Proportion of total consumption also fell, then reached 45 percent by early 1990. With demand for oil fairly constant, price on world market went up and down with supply, which was affected by political events.

Using a Time Line

(D) 1970, (C) 1972, (H) 1973, (F) 1974, (B) 1975, (A) 1978, (E) 1978, (G) 1979.

Applying Thinking Skills

1. Phrases such as: "trigger-happy politicians," "energy-wasting way of life," "egocentric, self-righteous," "messianic," and "itching to reform the world to its liking"; i.e., profligate and aggressively nationalistic and imperialist.
2. Answers may vary. Considering changes within the Soviet Union since the Cold War, students are less likely to see it as repressively and cruelly totalitarian and imperialist. One possible stereotype students can adduce is of a nation uncertainly groping for a freer way of life, with some Russians clinging to old ways and others thirsting for freedom and looking to the West for guidance.

Chapter 31

New Directions

Planning Guide

	Student Text	TWE Lesson Plans	Support Materials
SECTION 1	**Section 31-1 (1-2 Days)** **A Conservative Revolution,** pp 836-841 Review/Evaluation Section Review, p 841	**Introducing the Chapter:** Charting Government's Role—Class Activity, 30 minutes, p 833B **Teaching the Main Ideas:** Reagan Time Machine—Cooperative Activity, one class period, p 833B **Evaluating Progress:** Reagan's Supporters and Critics—Individual Activity, 30 minutes, p 833C	★ **Read to Remember,** Section 1 ● **Section Activities,** Section 1 Δ **Readings** ● **Tests and Quizzes and Quizzes,** Section 1 Quiz
SECTION 2	**Section 31-2 (1-2 Days)** **Foreign Policy in the Reagan Years,** pp 842-848 Review/Evaluation Section Review, p 848	**Teaching the Main Ideas:** Ethics in Government—Class Activity, 30 minutes, p 833C **Reinforcement Activity:** Reagan's Foreign Policy—Individual Activity, 30 minutes, p 833C	★ **Read to Remember,** Section 2 ● **Section Activities,** Section 2 Δ **Enrichment Activities,** Section 2 Δ **Readings** ● **Tests and Quizzes and Quizzes,** Section 2 Quiz
SECTION 3	**Section 31-3 (1-2 Days)** **From Cold War to New Challenges,** pp 848-857 Connections to Themes: Shaping Democracy, p 857 Review/Evaluation Section Review, p 857 Chapter 31 Survey, pp 858-859 Skills, pp 858-859 Using New Vocabulary Thinking Critically Using a Time Line Applying Social Studies Skills: Interpreting Diagrams	**Enrichment Activity:** Facing the 1990s—Cooperative Activity, one class period, p 833C	★ **Read to Remember,** Section 3 ● **Section Activities,** Section 3 Δ **Enrichment Activities,** Section 3 ● **Geography Activities,** Section 3 Δ **Readings** ● **Tests and Quizzes and Quizzes,** Section 3 Quiz, Chapter 31 Test (Forms A and B) **Additional Resources** ● **Active Learning** Δ **GTV Videodiscs** Δ **Transparencies and Activity Book** ● **Testing Software** ★ **Chapter Summaries** **Key:** ★ For Extra Support ● For All Students Δ For Enrichment

Overview

As President, Ronald Reagan's goals were to rekindle American pride and to diminish the role of government in American economic life. To stimulate investment and production he cut taxes, deregulated industry, and cut domestic programs. Although he advocated a balanced federal budget, he increased defense spending. His "new federalism" shifted many responsibilities to the states that had long belonged to the federal government. Among his legacies are his appointments of three conservative justices to the Supreme Court.

In foreign affairs, Reagan provided financial and military aid to help put down rebellions in Grenada and El Salvador, and he gave massive assistance to forces trying to topple the Marxist government of Nicaragua. The illegal activities of the Iran-contra affair shocked the American public. Changes in the Soviet Union under Mikhail Gorbachev eased East-West tensions in the final years of Reagan's presidency and led to an arms reduction treaty.

During the term of Reagan's successor, George Bush, dramatic developments occurred abroad, notably the end of the Cold War as communism collapsed in Eastern Europe and the Soviet Union dissolved. Bush took decisive action in gathering international support in the Persian Gulf War of 1991. At home, though, his lack of a clear domestic plan for dealing with the faltering economy led to his loss to Bill Clinton in the 1992 election. Though seeking to focus on the economy, Clinton soon found pressing foreign policy problems competing for his attention, such as ethnic conflicts that posed persistent threats to peace and stability.

Activity Objectives

After completing the activities, students should be able to

- compare Reagan's political philosophy with those of other periods in the nation's history.
- relate personal ethics to issues of governmental ethics.
- identify the chief goals and actions of Reagan's foreign policy.
- describe the major benefits or failures of Reagan's domestic policies.
- evaluate the most pressing domestic issues of the 1990s.

Introducing the Chapter

Charting Government's Role

This class activity requires about half a class period.

This activity is designed to help students formulate their views on the responsibility of state and federal government in dealing with the economy and providing social services.

Create a chart on the chalkboard or an overhead transparency. Down the left side of the chart write: *Small Businesses, Large Businesses, Working Conditions, Product Safety, Economic Security, Monetary Policy, Environmental Protection, Housing, Medical Research, Welfare, Crop Subsidies, Air and Water Quality,* and *Schools*. Across the top of the chart write: *State Government, Federal Government, Both*, and *Neither*.

Begin the activity by explaining that President Reagan sought to reduce the federal government's role in the economy and social services by giving more decision-making authority and fiscal responsibility to state governments and by deregulating business and industry.

Tell students that the topics on the left side of the chart are examples of areas of responsibility which came under discussion as Reagan advocated downsizing the federal government and removing government regulations.

For each topic, ask students to express (through a show of hands) their opinion as to whether the major responsibility for the matter should be assumed by state governments, the federal government, both, or neither. Use the chart to tally student responses.

Conclude by asking students to share reasons for their opinions on specific topics. Encourage them to be prepared to evaluate their opinions as they read about the goals and policies of the Reagan administration.

Teaching the Main Ideas

Section 31-1: Reagan Time Machine

This cooperative activity requires one class period.

In this writing activity students compare Ronald Reagan's political philosophy to conservative and liberal philosophies from other eras. They make their comparisons in the form of hypothetical diary entries.

Before giving the assignment, ask students to review the major points of Reagan's political philosophy. Emphasize that, like Reagan, past leaders have held strong views about the proper role of government in our society. Ask students to imagine former President Reagan traveling back through time and encountering some of these people and ideas: *National Recovery Act (NRA), President Hoover, Alexander Hamilton, States' Rights Doctrine, The Progressives, John Muir.*

Write the topics on the board and organize the class into groups of four. Direct each group to work cooperatively to prepare a series of diary entries that Ronald Reagan might have made as he traveled through time and encountered each of the people, actions, or movements listed. Direct groups to refer to their texts. The entries should first describe, as Reagan would, the philosophy represented by the person, act, or idea and record Regan's responses.

When the diaries are finished, ask a representative from one group to read an entry. Continue with other groups until entries for all the topics have been read. Conclude by asking students to speculate about what philosophy of the role of government will prevail in the 1990s.

Teaching the Main Ideas

Section 31-2: Ethics in Government

This class activity requires about 30 minutes.

In this activity students will explore questions of personal ethics. Then they will relate them to governmental ethics.

Introduce the activity by explaining that although public scandals tend to shock Americans, our nation's history has many such incidents. Ask students to name some government scandals they have studied during this course.

Tell students that you are going to read a series of statements and that they are to indicate with a show of hands whether they agree, disagree, or have no opinion. Encourage class discussion of each statement.

- When a cashier makes a mistake in your favor, it is all right to keep the money.
- It is all right to drive faster than the speed limit if you are late for an important appointment.
- Imagine that you had to spend the evening planning an important school meeting and did not have time to do your homework. If a friend offers to let you copy her homework, it is all right to do so.
- When it comes to catching dangerous criminals, it is all right for police to overlook some constitutional rights.

After the class has discussed all the statements, encourage students to relate them to historical events, such as Oliver North lying to Congress in the belief that he was helping to fight communism.

Reinforcement Activity

Section 31-2: Reagan's Foreign Policy

This individual activity requires about 30 minutes, or it may be assigned as homework.

In this activity students make a chart to help reinforce their understanding of Reagan's foreign policy.

Before class create a chart on the chalkboard or an overhead transparency. Down the left side of the chart write: *Grenada, El Salvador, Nicaragua, Lebanon, Soviet Union (1st Term)*, and *Soviet Union (2nd Term)*. Across the top of the chart write: *Country, Foreign Policy Goals*, and *Foreign Policy Actions.*

Ask students to reflect on strategies American Presidents have used to deal with international crises. Ask them to brainstorm to create a list of policy options a President has in dealing with foreign problems (giving or cutting off aid, imposing embargoes, arms build ups, threats or use of force, offering or withholding trade agreements, diplomatic discussions, treaties and alliances, declarations of neutrality).

Display the chart and explain that students can use it to summarize Reagan's foreign policy goals and actions.

When students have finished their charts, have them exchange papers and check for accuracy and completeness.

Evaluating Progress

Section 31-1: Reagan's Supporters and Critics

This individual activity requires half a class period, or it may be assigned as homework.

In this activity students show their understanding of Reagan administration policies by writing editorials supporting or criticizing them.

Remind students that Reagan was an extremely popular President, whose policies struck a responsive chord with millions of Americans. On the other hand, many critics fear that the long-range effects of his policies will be harmful to the nation. Ask students to imagine that they are newspaper editors. The assignment is to write an editorial assessing Reagan's domestic policies from today's perspective.

Emphasize that the editorials must refer to at least three of the following: *economic policy, deregulation, "new federalism,"* and *Supreme Court appointments*. Review the characteristics of a good editorial mentioned in the Evaluating Progress activity for Chapter 26.

In addition to meeting the criteria for a good editorial, students' work (depending on the viewpoint) should include the following ideas:

Economic policy: Pro–Tax and interest rate cuts and deregulation created unprecedented prosperity. *Con*–Prosperity did not reach the poor, and the income gap widened; deficit continued to soar.

Deregulation: Pro–Removing restrictions from businesses allowed them to function more efficiently and to use the money they saved to invest and expand. *Con*–Led to price wars that put small companies out of business. Fewer controls meant less environmental protection.

New Federalism: Pro–Transferred control back to state and local governments, which are closer and more responsible to the people. *Con*–Placed added burdens without providing adequate funds.

Supreme Court: Pro–Conservative justices practicing judicial restraint are more likely to reflect the opinions of the majority of the public. *Con*–Conservative justices are less likely to protect minority rights.

Enrichment Activity

Section 31-3: Facing the 1990s

This cooperative activity requires a full class period.

In this activity groups of students work together to propose solutions to domestic problems.

Introduce the activity by writing on the chalkboard the following list of domestic problems facing Americans in the 1990s: *AIDS, Homelessness, Crime, Drugs, Environmental Pollution*. Ask students to decide individually which problem they think is most serious.

Next, read the first problem and ask the students who considered it most serious to form a group. Using the same process, form other groups for the remaining problems. If any group exceeds five members, divide it into smaller groups.

Ask the class to imagine that Congress has appropriated one billion dollars to be spent on one of the problems. Each group is to prepare a proposal for using the money to help solve its problem. The proposals are to be in four parts:

- a description of the problem
- an explanation of how the money will be used to help solve the problem
- a description of the benefits to society that will result
- reasons for using the money to fight this problem rather than the others.

Ask representatives of each group to present the proposals to the class. Have the class vote for the one they think is most worthy of receiving the money.

Bibliography and Audiovisual Materials

Teacher Bibliography

Day, David. *The Environmental Wars: Reports from the Front Lines*. New York: Ballantine Books, Inc., 1991.

Hyland, William G. *The Cold War is Over*. New York: Random House, Inc., 1990.

Polk, William R. *The Elusive Peace: The Middle East in the Twentieth Century*. New York: St. Martin Press, 1979.

Ridley, Matthew. *Warts and All: The Men Who Would Be Bush*. New York: Viking Penguin, 1990.

Smith, Hedrick, et al. *Reagan: The Man, The President*. Riverside, N.J.: Pergamon Press, Inc., 1981.

Smith, Perry M. *The Gulf War Day by Day.* Garden City Park, N.Y.: Avery Publishing Group, 1991.

Student Bibliography

Gardner, John. *October Light*. New York: Random House, Inc., 1989.

Kingston, Maxine Hong. *Woman Warrior*. New York: Random House, Inc., 1989.

Piercy, Marge. *Small Changes*. New York: Fawcett, 1985.

Terkel, Studs, ed. *The Great Divide: Second Thoughts on the American Dream*. New York: Avon, 1989.

Films, Videocassettes, and Videodiscs

AIDS: Questions With Answers. 28 min. Meridian. Videocassette.

Drugs: A Plague Upon The Land. 60 min. ABC News. Videocassette.

Images of the 80s. 52 min. ABC News/Time. Videocassette.

A Line in the Sand. 50 min. Zenger Video. Videocassette.

Filmstrips

The Bush Administration-Challenges and Changes: Current Affairs. 19 min. 1 color filmstrip, cassette, guide. New York Times.

The Iran-Contra Affair: Current Affairs. 1 color filmstrip, cassette, guide. New York Times.

Our Nation's Homeless: Who, Where, and Why? 22 min. 1 color filmstrip with cassette. New York Times.

Computer Software

American Foreign Policy. 1 Apple diskette, backup, guide. Focus Media.

Chapter 31

Objectives

- Explain how President Ronald Reagan applied his conservatism to domestic policy.
- Cite Reagan's foreign policy goals.
- Describe domestic and foreign problems confronting President George Bush.

Introducing THE CHAPTER

For suggestions on introducing Chapter 31, refer to page 833B in the Teacher's Edition.

Developing THE CHAPTER

For activities and teaching strategies to help you reinforce and enrich chapter content, see pages 833B–833D in the Teacher's Edition.

B · A · C · K · G · R · O · U · N · D

Chapter Opener Illustrations
Reagan and Bush greeted the 1984 Republican Convention, confident of winning a second term.

At the 1988 Republican Convention, the party nominated George Bush for President and Dan Quayle, a senator from Indiana, as his running mate.

Tipper and Al Gore and Bill and Hillary Clinton wave to supporters in front of the Lincoln Memorial. Clinton and Gore represented a generational change, the first President and Vice-President born after World War II.

During the 1980s and 1990s, the AIDS epidemic was a major issue of public concern. Groups formed to serve and support those suffering with AIDS, to educate the public about AIDS, to help slow the spread of the virus, and to lobby for more money to be devoted to AIDS research.

During the Persian Gulf War, the United States Army in-

Chapter 31 1980-Present

New Directions

cluded thousands of women.

The last two photos here show stark contrasts in economic conditions in the 1980s and 1990s. Young, upwardly mobile business and professional people, called yuppies, enjoyed affluence, while increasing numbers of less fortunate Americans became homeless.

American Voices

Marian Wright Edelman, founder and president of the Children's Defense Fund, stood before a group of graduates in June of 1990. She reflected on the 1980s and looked ahead to the challenges of the 1990s, soberly but with hope.

> *"The 1990s' struggle is for America's conscience and future. The battles will not be as dramatic as Gettysburg or Vietnam, but they will shape our place in the twenty-first century no less. The bombs poised to blow up the American dream emanate from no enemies without. They are ticking away within ourselves, our families, our communities and our lack of community, and our moral drift.*
>
> *I believe we have lost our sense of what is important as a people. Too many young people of all races and classes are growing up unable to handle life, in hard places, without hope, and without steady compasses to navigate a world that is reinventing itself at an unpredictable pace both technologically and politically. . . .*
>
> *The political rhetoric of the 1980s that we can have our cake and eat it too was a national disaster. . . . Many Americans decry the growing gap between the rich and poor and middle class, as long as somebody else's taxes are raised and somebody else's program is cut. We all want to lower the deficit, while still trying to get everything we can. . . ."*

The 1980s dawned with an optimism that affluence and world leadership were the right of Americans. In his inaugural address, President Ronald Reagan spoke of a "new beginning," of a healthy economy and a "strong and prosperous America at peace with itself and the world." Yet while some Americans pursued prosperity, others faced the growing threats of poverty, crime, drugs, and disease. And the changing world scene forced Americans to face a new meaning for world leadership.

Ronald Reagan and George Bush; 1988 Republican National Convention; Tipper and Al Gore with Bill and Hillary Clinton; AIDS action; Persian Gulf War; the fast life; homelessness.

Analyzing Primary Sources

American Voices

Marion Wright Edelman is a member of the generation that fought for civil rights under the leadership of Martin Luther King, Jr., and others.

1. Is Edelman concerned with foreign or domestic issues? Explain. **(domestic; we should concentrate on problems within our society, not threats from foreign powers)**

2. What criticisms does Edelman make about the 1980s? **(American people lost their sense of community, morals, hope; growing gap between rich and poor, for example.)**

3. According to Edelman, what challenges face the American people in the 1990s? **(establishing moral priorities, such as helping others, not just ourselves)**

Section 31-1

Objectives

- ***Answer the Focus Question.***
- *Describe Reagan's economic policies.*
- *Explain Reagan's priorities in drawing up a federal budget.*
- *Evaluate arguments supporting and opposing Reagan's domestic policies.*

Introducing

THE SECTION

Refer students to Reagan's words on this page. Have them compare his vision with President Kennedy's "New Frontier" goals of the early 1960s (see Chapter 27). **Ask:** In what ways did the two Presidents have a similar vision of the role of the United States? **(Both spoke of the nation as a beacon of freedom and hope, and of a need to renew the country.)**

B · A · C · K · G · R · O · U · N · D

Time Line Illustrations

1. President Reagan appointed Sandra Day O'Connor to the Supreme Court. Here O'Connor poses with then Chief Justice Warren Burger.
2. This photo shows a member of the Nicaraguan contras. The Reagan White House's continued support for the contras, even after Congress cut off funds, caused the Iran-contra scandal of 1986.
3. This cartoon criticizes Reagan's support of the Nicaraguan contra rebels as meddling in the affairs of a foreign government. It implies that involvement there could produce tragic results similar to what occurred in Lebanon.
4. Bush, who shed his "nice guy" image and conducted a bruising campaign, easily defeated Michael Dukakis in 1988.
5. Liberal Chinese called for political reforms similar to the revolutionary changes in the rest of the Communist world.

Reduced student page in the Teacher's Edition

CHAPTER TIME LINE

1980-1993

1980 Ronald Reagan elected President

1981 Hostages released in Iran
Sandra Day O'Connor appointed to Supreme Court

1982 **Aug** Reagan sends troops to Lebanon

1983 Congress funds Nicaraguan contras
Oct United States intervenes in Grenada

"IT'S LIKE THE STRATEGY THAT WORKED SO WELL IN LEBANON"
CONGRESS
NICARAGUA
from HERBLOCK AT LARGE (Pantheon Books, 1987)

1984 Contra support cut off after CIA covert action revealed

1986 **Nov** Iran-contra scandal revealed

1980 | 1982 | 1984 | 1986

31-1 A Conservative Revolution

Focus: How did Ronald Reagan translate his conservative philosophy into domestic policy?

Millions of Americans watching Ronald Reagan's inauguration on television felt uplifted by his warm, optimistic style. "Let us renew our faith and hope," he encouraged Americans. "We have every right to dream heroic dreams." His upbeat tone gave a boost to Americans whose confidence was shaken by Vietnam, Watergate, the hostage crisis, and the stagnation of the economy. Reagan appealed to Americans' desire to feel good about themselves and to seem powerful in the eyes of the world:

> *"As we renew ourselves in our own land, we will be seen as having greater strength throughout the world. We will again be the exemplar of freedom and a beacon of hope for those who do not now have freedom."*

A former movie actor, Reagan brought great persuasive skills to his new job. He presented himself as an informal man, a man of the people. His own story had unfolded from his childhood in a small town in Illinois to a career in Hollywood, and on to become governor of California. Many Americans saw him as living proof that the United States is the land of opportunity.

During his campaign, Reagan appealed to voters yearning for material prosperity. "Are you better off now than you were four years ago?" he asked. He knew the answer would be "No." Americans had

Unlike the governments in Eastern Europe and the Soviet Union, Chinese leaders cracked down hard on demonstrators who had gathered in Tiananmen Square in Beijing.
6. As the Soviet Union dissolved, newly independent states cleared away icons of the old order. This giant statue of Lenin was removed from its place in Vilnius, Lithuania.
7. Bill and Hillary Rodham Clinton are shown at the 1993 inauguration ceremony.

1988 George Bush elected President

1991 **Jan-Feb** Persian Gulf War
Dec Soviet Union dissolves

1993 Bill Clinton inaugurated President

1988 — 1990 — 1993

1987 Iran-contra hearings
INF Treaty

1989 United States intervenes in Panama
Student demonstrations in China put down by force
Communist governments in Eastern Europe topple

1990 German reunification

been watching with dismay as their food and heating bills rose, factories closed, and interest rates soared.

Reagan's answer to these problems was a conservative one. He stressed patriotism and self-reliance and advocated a return to the traditional and wholesome values of an earlier time—values that the youth culture of the sixties and seventies had challenged. He strongly criticized the effects of big government. On an individual level, he thought that social welfare programs robbed people of their self-respect by making them dependent on the government. On a national level, he believed that high taxes and government regulation were damaging the economy.

Like the Republican Presidents of the 1920s, whom he greatly admired, Reagan promoted the benefits of laissez-faire capitalism. He believed that what was good for business was good for the nation as a whole. In his inaugural address he said:

> *“In this present crisis, government is not the solution to our problem; government is the problem. . . . It is time to reawaken this industrial giant, to get government back within its means, and to lighten our punitive tax burden.”*

Reaganomics

Reagan presented his ideas for economic recovery—later dubbed "Reaganomics"—to Congress soon after he took office. He said that his long-range goal was a balanced budget. His immediate goal was to attack the twin causes of stagflation—inflation and unemployment.

Reagan based his proposal on the theories of supply-side economists. Instead of increasing the *demand* for goods and services as the New Deal had tried to do, Reagan proposed to increase the *supply*. He believed that relaxing regulations on industry and lowering taxes, especially for wealthy individuals and corporations, would make more money available for business investments and thus for production. The benefit to the wealthy was expected to "trickle down" to the middle and lower economic classes as the economy revived.

Developing

THE SECTION

Connections: Language

Building Vocabulary. In small groups, have students do word studies of the terms *conservative* and *liberal*. They are to write definitions and a short etymology for each term. **Ask:** How has the meaning of these terms changed with time? **(Conservatism has emphasized traditional values, but the meaning of conservatism changes with the meaning of the values supported. For example, a "conservative" in the Soviet Union can be someone who opposes Gorbachev's reforms and supports traditional communism. The meaning of *liberalism* has also changed: in the 1700s and 1800s liberal political doctrine espoused freedom of the individual from interference by the state and supported laissez-faire capitalism. Today liberals tend to support an increase in the size and power of government in response to social problems.)**

GTV Side 4
Chap. 13, Frame 45534
U.S. Population: 1950 and 1980
(Population Clocks, 2 Frames)
Search:
Step:

Connections: Politics

Ronald Reagan was not always a conservative. During the 1940s he belonged to the Democratic party and campaigned for President Harry Truman in the 1948 presidential election. Reagan began his shift to conservative views in the 1950s.

Thinking Critically

Evaluation. Were Reagan's new policies likely to have an immediate effect on economic conditions? (Announcement of new policies can change peoples' perceptions, for example by making investors more or less hopeful and eager to invest. On the other hand, a massive economy such as that of the United States takes time to respond in areas such as employment.)

Limited English Proficiency

Building Vocabulary. **Ask:** What is *teflon*? **(a coating that prevents anything from sticking to a surface)** Why did Democrats use this term to describe Reagan? **(Criticism of Reagan seemed not to affect his popularity.)**

Using the Visuals

Analyzing a Graph. Refer students to the graph on this page. **Ask:** In 1980 what percent of the federal budget was spent on national defense? **(about 22.5 percent)** Human services? **(about 27.5 percent)** In what year were the budgets about the same? **(1982)** Describe the trend of defense and human services spending after 1982. **(Defense spending increased, human services spending decreased.)** Why? **(By increasing defense spending, Reagan had to decrease human services spending to try to balance the budget.)**

In addition to cutting taxes, Reagan also asked for a $1.3 trillion increase in defense spending. How would he live up to the promise of a balanced budget? Reagan's plan was to greatly reduce domestic spending, especially on social welfare programs. Despite criticism that a balanced budget would still be impossible and that the burden of the national debt would ultimately take its toll, Reagan gathered strong support for his program.

Reagan's first budget set federal priorities for the rest of the decade. Congress slashed billions of dollars from domestic spending, cutting back more than 200 federal aid programs, such as food stamps, Medicaid, and unemployment compensation. Congress also reduced taxes by $280 billion in Reagan's first year. Thus, while tax cuts benefited the rich the most, budget cuts reduced services to the poor. At the same time, military spending reached $508 million a day.

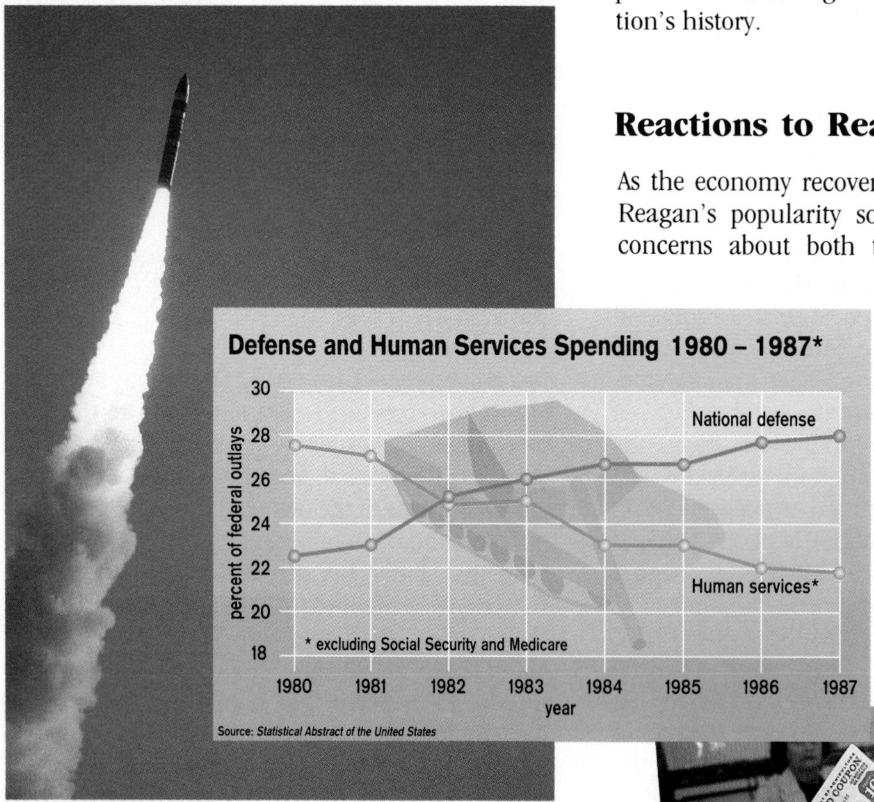

Defense spending reached $1.5 trillion over five years. Welfare and food stamps were cut dramatically.

Recession and Recovery

The economy had been in bad shape when Reagan took office. By fall 1981 it was slipping further. Unemployment topped 10 percent, thousands of businesses went bankrupt, and the stock market dropped. The budget deficit continued to grow. Once again the economy plunged into recession, this time the worst since the Great Depression.

Not until December 1982 did the economy begin to improve, due in part to a drop in oil prices. As the rate of inflation slowed, the Federal Reserve lowered interest rates, and investors began to buy stocks. New taxes and more deficit spending, which Reagan opposed, also helped to end the recession.

The recovery continued to gain ground in 1983. Hard-hit industries began to bounce back, and unemployment dropped below 10 percent. After years of penny pinching, consumers went on a spending spree. By 1984, prosperity had returned. It would prove to be the longest economic boom in the nation's history.

Reactions to Reagan

As the economy recovered, patriotism swelled and Reagan's popularity soared. While critics voiced concerns about both the immediate and long-range effects of his policies, the majority of Americans thought Reagan could do no wrong. Many Democrats called him the "Teflon" President because no criticism seemed to stick.

Connections: Religion
For a decade, fundamentalist Christian leaders had a profound effect on American politics and society. Then in the late 1980s, a series of sex scandals and charges of financial wrongdoing rocked religious right groups. These events seemed to discredit the morality of the entire movement. The Moral Majority disbanded in 1989. Some people's cars sported bumper stickers that read, "The Moral Majority is Neither."

Linking Past and Present

Discussion. While Geraldine Ferraro was the first woman to be nominated for the vice presidency by a major political party, outspoken suffragist Victoria Woodhull ran for President on the ticket of her own political party in 1872. **Ask:** Would a woman candidate for high office have been taken seriously in 1872? Did it cause much controversy in 1984?

Connections: Economics

Linking Past and Present. Ask students to locate current articles and research data about the state of the nation's economy today. News magazines and the business section of the newspaper often present economic data. Discuss economic trends and government policy. **Ask:** In what phase of the business cycle is the economy today? How do you know?

Active Learning

Drawing Political Cartoons. Have students draw political cartoons based on Reaganomics. The cartoons might support or oppose a particular action, such as slashing food stamps benefits, or his broad economic policy of supply-side economics. Have students share their cartoons and reactions to them.

Supporters. Not since the 1920s had the United States seen such a groundswell of conservative opinion. Reagan's supporters came from many segments of society. Some of the new conservatives were dissatisfied Democrats who thought that their party no longer spoke for their interests, or who saw the party's views as growing too liberal. Blue collar workers, for example, felt that the Democratic party had stopped fighting for issues such as decent jobs and fair pay.

A strong, well organized following came from a group newly vocal in American politics, the "religious right," or conservative evangelical Christians. In 1979 television evangelist Jerry Falwell helped form a group called the Moral Majority to apply conservative values to political issues and campaigns. The religious right adamantly opposed abortion and supported school prayer, and Reagan echoed their concerns.

In fact, Reagan took no action on these social issues. Yet his public statements strengthened his support among a wide range of conservatives in America. In turn, conservatives supported the President with extremely successful letter-writing campaigns and computerized fund raising.

Reagan's supporters also included people who benefited directly from his economic policies—"corporate America" and the upper middle class. The return to prosperity became the focus of Reagan's campaign for reelection in 1984. His best known slogan claimed it was "morning in America again." Now when he asked his 1980 question, "Are you better off now than you were four years ago?" he was assured of a resounding "Yes!" from many Americans.

Critics. Not everyone was better off. At the Democratic nominating convention in 1984, Governor Mario Cuomo of New York challenged Reagan's vision of America as "a shining city on a hill."

“But . . . there's another part to the shining city, the part where some people can't pay their mortgages and most young people can't afford one, where students can't afford the education they need and middle-class parents watch the dreams they hold for their children evaporate.

"In this part of the city there are more poor than ever, more families in trouble. More and more people who need help but can't find it. . . .

"There is despair, Mr. President, in the faces that you don't see, in the places that you don't visit in your shining city.”

The Democrats attacked Reagan's economic success story with the issue of fairness. Reagan's policies, they charged, hurt the elderly, the homeless, inner city youth, and many others. For President the Democrats nominated Walter Mondale, who had been Vice-President under Carter. Mondale named Geraldine Ferraro as his running mate, the first woman ever nominated for Vice-President.

This popular move did not make up for Mondale's unpopular message. Pointing to the budget deficit, which had doubled in 1982 alone, he warned that prosperity based on debt would not last, and urged higher taxes. "Let's tell the truth," Mondale told voters. "Mr. Reagan will raise taxes, and so will I. He won't tell you. I just did." But voters gave Reagan and Bush a landslide victory at the polls in November.

Lasting Legacies

During Reagan's eight years in office, his administration took a conservative path that will have a lasting effect on the nation. Among the areas in which Reagan policies may have their most enduring influence are government regulations, the balance between federal and state government responsibilities, and the makeup of the Supreme Court.

Government regulation. One of the ways Reagan sought to "take government off the backs" of the people was to remove or relax regulations he saw as interfering with business and industry. Giving companies more leeway would increase productivity, Reagan argued. He filled key posts in federal agencies with officials who shared his hands-off approach.

During the 1980s, for example, the price of oil was deregulated, the watchdog role of the Securities and Exchange Commission over Wall Street

Thinking Critically

Synthesis. Discuss Reagan's three major domestic legacies: deregulation, new federalism, and Supreme Court appointments. Then have students write a persuasive paragraph stating which of Reagan's legacies will have the most far-reaching effects on American society, and why.

Active Learning

Debate. One side should oppose the position taken by Reagan's Secretary of the Interior, James Watt, who said that Americans "*will mine more, drill more, cut more timber to use our resources rather than simply keep them locked up.*" The other side should support Watt's position. Have students support their arguments by citing data gathered from books and news-magazines.

Multicultural Perspectives

President Bush's nomination of Clarence Thomas to the Supreme Court in 1991, following the retirement of Thurgood Marshall, led to an intense controversy in the African-American community. Justice Marshall had been a civil rights pioneer and a strong advocate of affirmative action. Thomas, on the other hand, is a conservative who made statements opposing affirmative action and stressing self-help rather than government action as the road to success for blacks. The NAACP voted to oppose the nomination of Thomas, but a poll of blacks showed that 57 percent supported the nomination. Some who disagreed with Thomas nevertheless wanted to support a fellow African American.

Environmentalists criticized deregulation policy, which favored industry over the environment.

was eased, and limits on lending institutions were relaxed. The National Highway Traffic Safety Administration let up on its demands that auto manufacturers produce cars with air bags and greater fuel efficiency. Deregulation by the Federal Communications Commission allowed growth in the cable television industry. In some industries deregulation led to intense competition. Price wars put smaller companies out of business, leaving a few corporate giants.

Regulations aimed at protecting the environment were also eased. Reagan believed that the dangers of pollution by industry had been exaggerated in the 1970s. He also thought that some damage to the environment was the price the nation must pay for its industrial strength. His first Secretary of the Interior, James Watt, promised that Americans "will mine more, drill more, cut more timber to use our resources rather than simply keep them locked up." The EPA relaxed pollution standards and, with its budget slashed by one third, could no longer enforce remaining regulations effectively or conduct research.

"New federalism." Another way Reagan shrank the federal government was by shifting responsibility to the states, a plan he called "new federalism." Citizens had lost control over basic decisions about "schools, welfare, roads, and even garbage collection," he argued. Transferring responsibility to state and local governments would put control back in the people's hands.

Yet while the states were given more control, they were given *less* federal money. During the Reagan years federal grants for housing, education, mass transit, and public works were cut or eliminated. The federal government had been providing 25 percent of state and local budgets at the end of the 1970s. By the end of 1990 that amount had dropped to 17 percent.

The Supreme Court. Another lasting legacy of the Reagan years was his appointment of three conservative Supreme Court justices—Sandra Day O'Connor, the first woman justice, and Antonin Scalia and Anthony Kennedy. Furthermore, when Chief Justice Warren Burger retired, Reagan replaced him with the most conservative justice on the Court, William Rehnquist.

Unlike the Warren Court, which favored judicial activism, Reagan's appointees favored judicial restraint. The Court handed down decisions that curtailed affirmative action and limited the rights of criminal suspects. Although Reagan favored reversing earlier Court decisions prohibiting school prayer and upholding a woman's right to an abortion, those decisions stood during his presidency. However, in 1989 a decision of the Rehnquist Court gave states more power to restrict abortion.

The conservative majority on the Court was increased by Reagan's Republican successor, George Bush. Upon the retirement of William Brennan and Thurgood Marshall, the Court's staunchest supporters of individual rights, Bush appointed David Souter and Clarence Thomas, both thought to be conservative.

Connections: Economics
With the boom times of the 1980s, millions of Americans spent beyond their means. By the end of 1988, American consumers owed $728.9 billion in unpaid credit. This personal debt was more than twice what it had been at the end of 1980.

Credit Card Prosperity

Reagan maintained an immense popularity. Admirers referred to him as "the great communicator." He proposed simple answers to complex problems, and announced that they were working. But how well did they work, and for whom?

During the 1980s the pursuit of wealth was glorified. Designer clothes and luxury cars came into style, and millionaires, real and fictional, were the new national heroes. Yet this "conspicuous consumption" was part of a boom based on debt, a "credit card prosperity."

Upon taking office, Reagan had struck a note of caution:

"You and I, as individuals, can, by borrowing, live beyond our means, but only for a limited period of time. Why then, should we think that collectively, as a nation, we're not bound by that same limitation?"

Yet the government consistently spent more than it took in. In 1986 the deficit peaked at more than $221 billion. Paying interest on loans to cover the deficit kept adding to the national debt, which soon exceeded $3 trillion.

Ivan Boesky, a much-admired financier, was imprisoned for stock market manipulation. (Right) The media glorified "yuppie" lifestyle.

American Voices

"Greed is all right. . . . Everybody should be a little bit greedy. . . . You shouldn't feel guilty . "

—Ivan Boesky

The growing income gap. Although conspicuous consumption seemed the way of life of the 1980s, poverty was growing at an alarming rate. In March 1989 the House Ways and Means Committee reported that between 1979 and 1987 the standard of living for the poorest fifth of the nation fell 9 percent, while for the top fifth it rose 19 percent. During the 1980s the number of people living below the designated poverty line grew to 14 percent of the population and included more and more women and children. By the decade's end, one out of five American children lived in poverty.

The problems of poverty, along with the burden of the deficit and the debt, became a part of the legacy of the 1980s. The effects of the conservative revolution are still unfolding. While historians will credit Reagan with reviving the economy and reducing the role of the federal government, they will also examine whether his economic policies provided long-term growth and stability. The ultimate impact of the shift of responsibility back to state and local governments is another unknown.

Section Review

1. **Comprehension.** What does "trickle down theory" mean when applied to Reagan?

2. **Synthesis.** Some have called the federal budget a statement of priorities. Explain how the budget in the Reagan years reflected the priorities of the "conservative revolution."

3. **Evaluation.** In your opinion, why was President Reagan so popular with the American people?

4. **Synthesis.** Choose one of President Reagan's legacies and explain how it might affect the future.

Data Search. How could the graph on page 838 be used in a response to question two above?

Section Review

ANSWERS

1. Relaxing industry regulation and lowering taxes would increase business investment and revive the economy, thus benefitting the less affluent.
2. Cuts in welfare programs and unemployment compensation and increases in military spending reflected Reagan's priority on defense and the belief that welfare programs made people too dependent on government.
3. Possible answers: He gave Americans reason to hope; the country was prosperous; tax cuts appealed to many, as did the call for self-reliance; as an actor, he used TV well.
4. Answers will vary.
Data Search: Graph shows the growth of defense spending and decrease in human services spending during Reagan years.

Section 31-2

Objectives

- ***Answer the Focus Question.***
- *Discuss United States involvement in Grenada, El Salvador, and Nicaragua.*
- *Describe the Iran-contra scandal and the constitutional issues raised by it.*
- *Explain how Reagan and Gorbachev worked to end the Cold War.*

Introducing

THE SECTION

The Cold War between the superpowers began almost immediately after World War II and for more than 40 years dominated international relationships. But by the end of the 1980s, the Cold War had ended and new relationships were emerging.

Have students mention trouble spots and sources of conflict that arose as the Cold War ended. Ask students to make a list of these trouble spots and compare their lists with the topics discussed in this section.

Connections: Politics

In 1981 the release of 52 American hostages from Iranian hands delighted the people of the United States. Even as the hostages were arriving home, however, some Americans expressed suspicion about the timing of the release—within minutes of Reagan's assumption of office. Speculation about the apparent coincidence continued through the 1980s, and in 1991 high-ranking former State Department officials made public their own suspicions that influential Republicans had made a secret deal with Iran.

Reduced student page in the Teacher's Edition

31-2 Foreign Policy in the Reagan Years

Focus: What were the goals of Reagan's foreign policy?

Minutes after President Reagan took the oath of office in 1981, fifty-two American hostages were released from Iran following 444 days of captivity. Americans saw it as a positive step toward restoring the nation's image abroad and Americans' self-confidence at home.

A few months later Reagan told West Point cadets what the country wanted to hear: "The era of self-doubt is over." Reversing Carter's policies, he vowed to take a tough stance against communism and restore American military might and prestige. His foreign policy efforts began in two regions—in Central America and the Caribbean, and in the Middle East.

Fighting Communism in the Western Hemisphere

To Reagan, communism was the greatest threat facing the western hemisphere. He warned that violent revolutions, backed by the Soviet Union and organized by Cuba, would spread throughout Latin America and the Caribbean. Under Reagan, American aid to "defenders of freedom" in the region would take both open and secret forms.

Guerrillas fought the United States-backed government in El Salvador.

Invasion of Grenada. Before October 1983 most Americans could not locate the Caribbean nation of Grenada on a map. Then a Marxist-led coup overthrew the government of the tiny island nation, and Reagan sent in troops. The troops ousted the Marxist government after a few days of fighting, but stayed in Grenada for a year, until elections there provided a pro-American government.

Critics at home and abroad denounced the United States for using force to overthrow a foreign government. Still, many Americans were elated by the quick defeat of what they saw as a possible communist foe. Reagan proudly pointed to Grenada as a victory. He would have a harder time claiming victory in his actions in Central America.

Aid to El Salvador. Like other Central American nations, El Salvador suffered from extremes of wealth and poverty. For years this small country had been ruled by a military dictatorship. Then, in 1979 Salvadoran army leaders ousted the dictator and began needed land reforms.

The government of José Napoleon Duarte, however, met with opposition from both the left and the right, and by 1980 civil war raged. Leftist rebels wanting more land reform battled government forces, while right-wing "death squads" terrorized civilians and killed anyone suspected of sympathizing with the rebels.

Reagan responded with massive military aid to the anti-communist Duarte government. He also sought to stop the flow of arms to the rebels from Nicaragua. Despite his efforts, the war continued. Reagan's critics pointed to repressive and inhumane measures taken by the Salvadoran government and questioned his policies. Meanwhile, the situation in Nicaragua presented more problems.

Global Connections

As the 1980s progressed, supporters of Reagan's Nicaragua policy pointed to increasing repression by the Sandinistas, such as the closing of opposition newspapers and the use of gangs to attack dissenters in the streets. They also accused the Sandinistas of devastating Nicaragua's economy through poor management.

Opponents of Reagan's policies pointed to atrocities committed by the contras, such as the killing of teachers and social workers. They blamed Nicaragua's economic troubles on the devastation caused by the contras, the cost of a war forced on Nicaragua, and the American trade ban.

Central America and the Caribbean 1980s

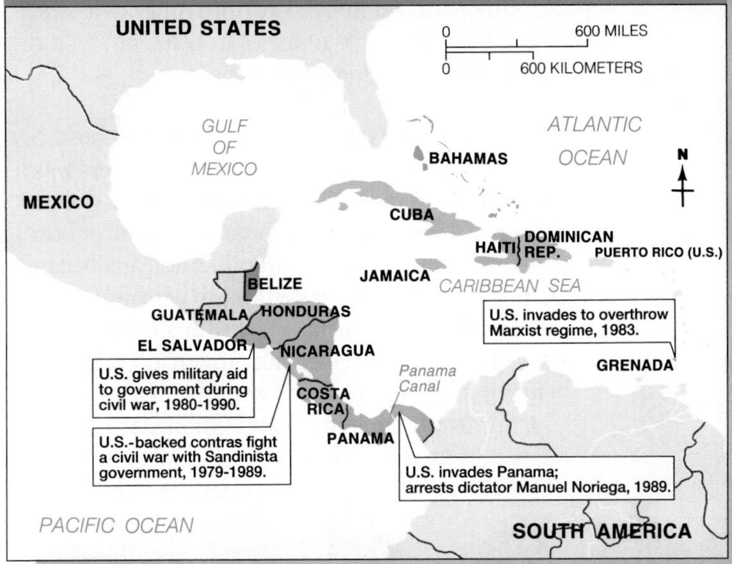

Geography Skills—Place. List the trouble spots of Central America and the Caribbean in the 1980s.

Violence in Nicaragua. Since the 1930s, the Somoza family had governed Nicaragua through a corrupt and repressive dictatorship. A rebel group, the Sandinistas, overthrew Anastasio Somoza in 1979 and set up their own government. They established an economic system mixing socialism and capitalism. Many Western European nations, as well as the Soviet Union and Cuba, gave aid to the new government.

Reagan saw the Sandinistas' success as proof that communism was spreading close to home. He cut off aid to Nicaragua and warned the Sandinistas to stop helping the Salvadoran rebels. Covertly, the Reagan administration backed the **contras** — Nicaraguan guerrillas who opposed the government. Reagan called the contras, many of whom were formerly in Somoza's army, "freedom fighters." They were trained at bases set up by the CIA over the border in Honduras.

When word of the CIA activity leaked out, the administration assured Congress that its purpose was to stop arms shipments to El Salvador. Congress agreed to fund the contras for this purpose in 1983, but said the money could not be used against the government. Yet in 1984 the public learned that CIA agents had planted mines in Nicaraguan harbors to disrupt the economy, thus weakening the government. Outraged, Congress cut off all funds to the contras.

The administration's actions against the Nicaraguan government appeared to end. In fact, they went underground and developed a strange link to another part of the world, the Middle East.

Aid to the contras became highly controversial. Demonstrators in Washington, D.C., and elsewhere protested United States involvement.

Developing THE SECTION

Multicultural Perspectives

Research and Report. The troubles in El Salvador and Nicaragua helped stimulate increased immigration from Central America to the United States. Have students do research to find out where most immigrants from Latin America settled.

Ask: From which countries did the largest number of refugees come? How might a Cuban refugee fleeing that country's Communist government differ from a refugee who had been threatened by right-wing death squads? What obstacles did refugees face in securing legal immigrant status? What extra dangers did illegal immigrants face?

Geography Skills ANSWERS

El Salvador, Nicaragua, Panama, Grenada.

Thinking Critically

Evaluation. Throughout the ordeal of the hostages held in Lebanon and Iran, American Presidents and other officials took the position that the United States would never make deals or negotiate for the release of its citizens held by terrorists. Their reason: Terrorists would only be encouraged to take more hostages if they experienced any gains from their behavior.

Have the class discuss the United States position on hostages. Some students may argue for the position, others that the United States should pay any price to free the hostages.

Global Connections

Terrorism affected not only victims, but all air travelers. Sometimes terrorists posed as passengers but, once in the air, revealed their weapons and forced pilots to take them to the airports of sympathetic nations. There they made demands, such as release of imprisoned comrades.

Sometimes terrorists secretly placed time bombs on board airplanes. Once aloft, the bombs detonated, killing hundreds of innocent passengers. These practices forced airports and airlines to institute rigorous policies of physical and electronic search of individuals and baggage. The freedom of movement of passengers and others at airports was thus limited.

Reduced student page in the Teacher's Edition

Conflict in Lebanon

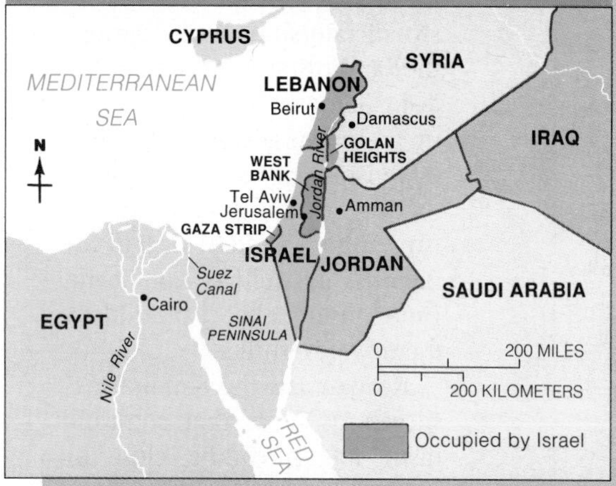

Geography Skills—Location. What countries could most easily move troops into Lebanon?

Geography Skills

ANSWERS

Countries surrounding Lebanon: Syria, Israel.

The attack on marines in Beirut called into question American military presence in Lebanon.

Terrorism in the Middle East

In 1982 Lebanon became the focus of Mideast tensions. In addition to a civil war between Muslim and Christian factions, Lebanon was also torn by fighting along its border with Israel. In June 1982 Israel invaded Lebanon to destroy military bases from which the Palestine Liberation Organization (PLO) was launching attacks on Israel. After the fighting ceased, a peacekeeping force of Americans, French, and Italians supervised the removal of PLO troops from Beirut.

Peace did not return to Lebanon, however. The civil war continued to rage, and some Muslims resented the presence of peacekeeping forces, which they saw as pro-Christian and pro-Israel. On October 23, 1983, an Arab suicide squad drove a truck full of explosives into marine headquarters, killing 241 Americans. At home, horrified Americans questioned the purpose of marines in Lebanon. As a result, Reagan withdrew the troops.

Acts of terrorism. Like the taking of hostages in Iran, the bombing of marine headquarters was a case of **terrorism**— the use or threat of violence to spread fear, usually in order to reach political goals. During the 1980s several Americans became victims of terrorism. Palestinians who wanted Israel to release prisoners hijacked a ship and a jetliner. In both incidents, an American was killed before the other passengers were rescued.

A number of Americans and Europeans were kidnapped in Lebanon by pro-Iranian Muslim fundamentalists who hated United States support of Israel. For these hostages, rescue seemed impossible. The Reagan administration's effort to win the release of these hostages would end up producing the most twisted tale of covert operations in United States history, and the greatest crisis of the presidency since Watergate.

The Iran-Contra Affair

"The U.S. gives terrorists no rewards, no guarantees. We make no concessions. We make no deals," Reagan told the nation after a 1985 hijacking. He had been talking tough against terrorists in general and Iran in particular since his 1980 campaign. In that year, the United States had broken off diplomatic relations with Iran. Thus, when Americans learned on November 4, 1986, that the United States had secretly sold arms to Iran, shock waves rocked the country.

The news of the arms sale appeared the same day that an American hostage was released by his captors in Lebanon. Since this was the third recent hostage release, there appeared to be an "arms for hostages" deal—exactly what the President had promised he would never approve. At first the White House denied the report. "We did not—repeat—did not trade weapons or anything else for hostages, nor will we," Reagan declared.

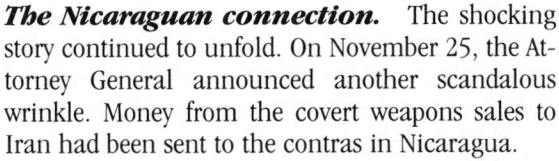

Oliver North took center stage in the televised Iran-contra hearings.

The Nicaraguan connection. The shocking story continued to unfold. On November 25, the Attorney General announced another scandalous wrinkle. Money from the covert weapons sales to Iran had been sent to the contras in Nicaragua.

These secret deals were clearly illegal. Stunned Americans wanted to know what part the President had played. Whatever the President's role, pointed out one senator, Reagan had acted improperly.

> *"If he knew about it, then he has willfully broken the law; if he didn't know about it, then he is failing to do his job. After all, we expect the President to know about the foreign policy activities being run directly out of the White House."*

As the story unraveled, it became known that a group called the "Enterprise" had carried out the intrigue. The Enterprise had arranged the arms sales through a third country, Israel. It deposited its profits—some $16 million—in secret Swiss bank accounts. It then funnelled a portion of the money back into the project for which it had originally been formed: support of the contras.

The mastermind of the Enterprise operation was Marine Lieutenant Colonel Oliver North, assistant to the President's national security advisor. When Congress cut off aid to the contras in 1984, Reagan had asked his aides to find some way to continue to help. North and others developed private funding for the contras from wealthy Americans and sympathetic countries like Saudi Arabia. Through the Enterprise, this money went to the contras in the form of guns, ammunition, and supplies.

Did Reagan know about the arms sales and the diversion of funds to the contras? The President claimed he did not. He appointed a commission, headed by former Senator John Tower, to investigate the case. The Tower Commission report, published in February 1987, faulted Reagan for delegating too much authority to others, but said that the President had not deliberately misled the American public.

Congressional investigation. During the spring and summer of 1987, a congressional committee held televised hearings to investigate the Iran-contra scandal. Taking the stand in his marine uniform was star witness Oliver North. North testified about the operations of the Enterprise and the "neat idea" of diverting funds from Iran to Nicaragua. He admitted to lying to Congress and to destroying and altering key documents in the case.

Thinking Critically

Evaluation. Two members of the congressional investigation committee declared that *"precisely because the sale of weapons to Iran and the diversion of money to the contras were perceived as misguided abuses of process rather than arrogant abuses of power, the central parallel to Watergate failed to take hold."*

Have students compare the Watergate and Iran-contra scandals. **Ask:** Which was the greater threat to the system of separation of powers and checks and balances in our government: Watergate or Iran-contra?

GTV Side 4

Chap. 14, Frame 45538

You've Grown Accustomed to My Face: The Information Age (Movie)

Search:

Play:

Limited English Proficiency

Building Vocabulary. In discussing the Spotlight on page 846, ask students to compare the words in the right column with those on the left. Why would people engaged in a secret and controversial enterprise prefer to use the words on the right? Tell students that a mild or vague word substituted for an offensive one is called a *euphemism.* Have them give examples of other euphemisms they have heard or read about.

Connections: Science and Technology

Oral Report. Have interested students do research on proposed ways of destroying incoming missiles. Have students investigate the Patriot Anti-Missile System used in the 1991 Gulf War and report their findings to the class.

Reduced student page in the Teacher's Edition

Spotlight on The Iran-contra hearings

During the Iran-contra hearings, *The Wall Street Journal* printed the "Dialogue of the Deaf," a guide to the jargon used by those involved in the scandal. The following is a selection.

Scandal — Flawed initiative
Terrorists — Iranian moderates
Cover-up — Executive privilege
Arms — Spare parts
Screw-up — Over-zealousness
Crimes — Technical violations
Lied — Misspoke

Why had North engaged in these clearly illegal activities? He claimed to be a patriot doing his duty to promote democracy in Nicaragua. To him the contras were "freedom fighters." To many others, however, they were more dedicated to military control than to democratic reform.

Although North had clearly broken the law, much of the public applauded him as a new American hero. Demonstrators carried banners proclaiming "Real Americans love Ollie!" Members of Congress were swamped with letters of support for this new standard-bearer of patriotism.

The congressional committee gave its report in November 1987. It found that while Reagan had approved the arms sale, it could not prove he knew the funds were diverted to the contras. So, while it could not find him guilty of a crime, it also said he should have known what his advisors were doing.

Furthermore, the covert operations of North and the Enterprise amounted to private diplomacy without public accountability. By arranging secret funding, the executive branch of the government had been making an end-run around Congress. Because it did not get its funds from Congress, the executive branch also evaded congressional limits on foreign policy. This "shadow government" violated the constitutional separation of powers and system of checks and balances.

Some people considered the Iran-contra affair a greater misuse of presidential power than the Watergate cover-up. Yet while Nixon resigned in the face of impeachment, Reagan seemed to get off with only a modest drop in popularity. Why? Some members of the Senate investigating committee explained that the Reagan administration had managed to convince people that its intentions were good, even if its methods were not.

Defrosting the Cold War

Long before he entered the White House, Reagan had preached against the dangers of communism. He called the Soviet Union an "evil empire" intent on taking over the world and overthrowing the traditional western values of individualism, free enterprise, religion, and democracy.

President Reagan chose to confront this menace from a position of military strength. During his first term of office, he initiated a huge military build-up, including work on the MX missile, the B-1 bomber, and the neutron bomb. He also proceeded with plans to place new missiles in Western Europe, despite protests from Europeans and Americans.

Meanwhile, hundreds of thousands of Americans spoke out in support of a nuclear freeze, or halt in production and placement of nuclear weapons. Freeze resolutions were passed by the House in 1982 and 1983 but failed in the Senate. Reagan argued that a freeze would leave the Soviets in the lead in the nuclear arms race.

In 1983 Reagan proposed the Strategic Defense Initiative (SDI), intended to protect the nation from nuclear attack. Nicknamed "Star Wars" after a film by that name, SDI would use lasers in space to shoot down incoming missiles. Its technology would cost billions of dollars to develop, and many scientists doubted that it could work. Soviet leaders warned that SDI might accelerate the arms race, as the superpowers rushed to build both offensive and defensive weapons. Nevertheless, Congress voted to approve SDI.

Summits with the Soviets. In his first term, Reagan had taken a hard-line stance against the Soviets. His military buildup signalled to the world

Global Connections

In 1991 the United States and Soviet Union signed a new arms reduction treaty called START. While hailed as an important sign of the new era of cooperation between the two powers, the new treaty actually only reduced the numbers of nuclear weapons to the level that existed when negotiations for the treaty began in 1982.

his dissatisfaction with détente. Yet in his second term, Reagan did an about-face.

Changes in United States-Soviet relations were in part the result of changes within the Soviet Union itself. The long war in Afghanistan was proving expensive and ineffective. Some called it the "Soviet Vietnam." Within the Soviet Union, the state-run economy was breaking down, unable to meet its citizens' basic needs.

In 1985 reformer Mikhail Gorbachev gained the leadership of the Communist party and the Soviet state. Gorbachev began a new policy of freedom in Soviet society, calling it *glasnost,* a Russian word meaning "openness." Under *glasnost,* the media had more freedom to report events and problems.

Meanwhile, Gorbachev's economic program of *perestroika,* or restructuring, encouraged limited free enterprise to make Soviet businesses efficient and consumer goods more available. Gorbachev also recognized that reviving the Soviet economy would require reducing military spending.

Gorbachev's ideas startled the world, and his policies led to a thaw in relations with the United States. Gorbachev and Reagan began talks toward slowing down the arms race. Their first two summit meetings, in November 1985 and October 1986, produced little in the way of concrete agreement, and SDI proved a major sticking point. But the ice was broken, and, in 1987 Gorbachev and Reagan signed an agreement to dismantle all of their intermediate-range missiles. This Intermediate–Range Nuclear Forces (INF) Treaty, while it made only a small dent in the superpowers' nuclear arsenals, was the first arms-reduction agreement since the start of the Cold War. It also gave Reagan's popularity, sagging since the Iran-contra affair, a much-needed boost.

Evaluating Reagan

Reagan's record on foreign policy is full of contrasts. The return of hostages opened his presidency in a burst of glory. Near the end, the shady deals of the Iran-contra scandal tarnished his reputation. The same President who entered the White House determined not to yield an inch to communism scored his greatest foreign policy triumph by improving relations with the Soviet Union and agreeing to reductions in arms.

Yet when Ronald Reagan left office, he was one of the most popular Presidents in United States history. Many Americans credited him with restoring their sense of national pride. They felt renewed confidence that their country held global power and leadership. That leadership would be tested in the next administration.

Section Review

1. **Identification.** Define *contras* and *terrorism*.

2. **Comprehension.** Give three examples of United States involvement in foreign countries during the Reagan administration. What was the purpose of the involvement?

3. **Analysis.** What constitutional issues did the Iran-contra scandal raise?

4. **Analysis.** How did Mikhail Gorbachev's leadership help thaw the Cold War?

At their 1987 summit in Washington, D.C., Gorbachev and Reagan signed the INF treaty, the first nuclear arms reduction agreement.

Backyard History

Research. Have students research and report on the involvement of their community in issues involving nuclear weapons. Have students identify and locate some of the following: potential targets for enemy nuclear attack; public fallout shelters or Civil Defense offices; resolutions passed by local authorities concerning nuclear weapons, such as "nuclear free zone" ordinances; organizations and activities pro and con nuclear disarmament.

Thinking Critically

Evaluation. Why has it usually been easier for a conservative President to get support for major changes in American foreign policy toward Communist states? Have students use Nixon's opening of China and Reagan's softening toward the Soviet Union as examples.

Section Review

ANSWERS

1. Definitions for the following term are on text pages indicated in parenthesis: *contras* (843), *terrorism* (844).
2. The invasion of Grenada, aid to El Salvador, and support of the contras in Nicaragua all meant to keep communism from spreading. In Lebanon, attempts to keep peace, rescue hostages.
3. Avoiding Congress by using secret funds violated the system of checks and balances set up by the Constitution.
4. His policies of *glasnost* and *perestroika,* reduction of military spending, and arms-reduction talks with Reagan all helped thaw the Cold War.

B · A · C · K · G · R · O · U · N · D

Multicultural Perspectives

Political observer P. J. O'Rourke claims that Jesse Jackson is *"the only living American politician with a mastery of classical rhetoric. . . . To listen to Jesse Jackson is to hear everything mankind has learned about public speaking since Demosthenes."* Jackson's oratorical skill also has its roots in the black religious tradition, as did the style of Martin Luther King, Jr., Jackson's mentor.

Section 31-3

Objectives

- ***Answer the Focus Question.***
- *Describe the effects of popular demands for democratic and economic reforms abroad.*
- *Explain the causes of economic and social crises in Bush's administration.*
- *Describe the major challenges facing the Clinton administration.*

Introducing

THE SECTION

Have small groups of students list ten challenges for the American people in the 1990s, without looking ahead in the text. Have each group explain its choices to the class. After students read this section, have them compare their lists with the text.

Reduced student page in the Teacher's Edition

31-3 From Cold War to New Challenges

Focus: What challenges faced George Bush, and why did he lose his bid for reelection?

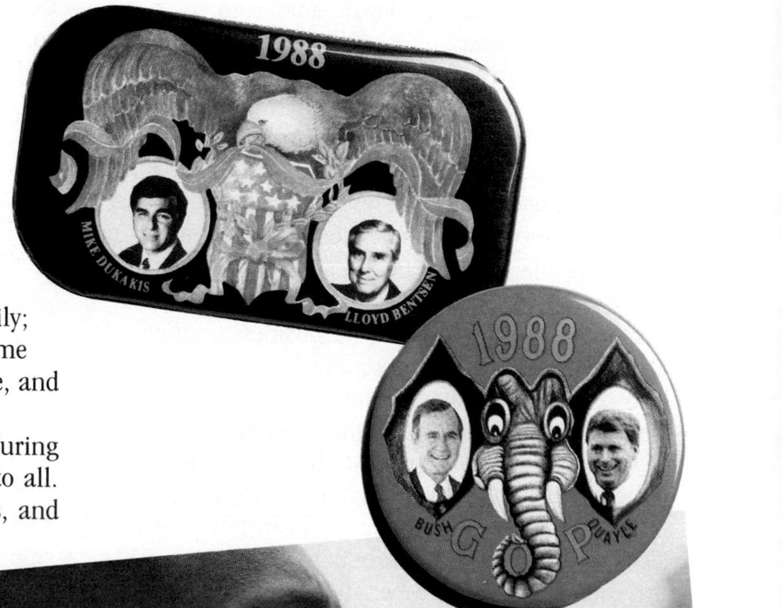

Read my lips— no new taxes," George Bush told the American people during his presidential campaign in 1988. With that slogan, the Republican candidate captured the attention of millions of middle-class Americans.

Despite the economic boom of the 1980s, the cost of living skyrocketed. Once, it had been possible for one parent to support a family; now it often took both parents working full time to pay the rising costs of housing, health care, and education.

Furthermore, the revival of the economy during the 1980s had not brought equal prosperity to all. It left out many farmers, blue-collar workers, and women. The Reverend Jesse Jackson, who had worked with Martin Luther King, Jr., and who already had a strong following among African Americans, worked to build a "rainbow coalition" to promote political action among members of all racial and ethnic groups. This following would support him for the Democratic nomination for President.

Jackson came to the 1988 Democratic convention with several primary victories. Yet many delegates saw his liberal views, his lack of experience in public office, and his race as obstacles to a presidential victory. They chose Governor Michael Dukakis of Massachusetts, who claimed credit for economic revival in his state.

The campaign of 1988 suffered woefully from negativity. Neither Bush nor his running mate, Senator Dan Quayle of Indiana, spelled out a plan. Instead, they focused on attacking their opponents with charges of being ultra-liberal, unpatriotic high spenders who were soft on crime. Dukakis and his running mate, Senator Lloyd Bentsen of Texas, scrambled to counter these charges but failed to come up with a specific program of their own.

Jesse Jackson made a strong showing in the 1988 Democratic primaries, but the party chose Michael Dukakis.

On election day, only 50 percent of voters went to the polls. Though lacking Reagan's overwhelming public support, Bush defeated Dukakis. The vagueness of his campaign, however, left Americans unsure about what his presidency would hold.

Connections: Economics
Boris Yeltsin's approach to converting Russia to a free-market economy included such policies as liberalizing prices of goods, reducing government subsidies and defense spending, raising taxes to cut the budget deficit, and reducing the artificially high value of the Russian ruble. This economic "shock therapy" created hardships for the Russian people. A Moscow research center reported in 1992 that the average Russian's purchasing power was only 42% of what it had been in 1990 and that the average family spent about 75% of its income on food.

Developing
THE SECTION

Thinking Critically

Evaluation. President Bush said the end of the Cold War made possible a "new world order" of international cooperation against threats to peace and stability. Have students explain their views on whether and to what extent a "new world order" has emerged.

Connections: Economics

Discussion. Have students discuss what problems former Communist countries are likely to face in establishing democracy and a free market economy. **Ask:** Why is it unlikely that these countries will receive a massive infusion of American aid similar to the Marshall Plan? What kinds of aid might be most helpful and from whom?

After the collapse of the Soviet Union, Russians looked to Boris Yeltsin for leadership in promoting democracy and moving toward a free-market economy.

The End of the Cold War

Reacting to criticism that the new President lacked a clear plan for the nation, a Bush aide declared, "Much of how a President is going to be evaluated is how he handles surprises, not necessarily how he handles his own agenda." Surprises were not long in coming. Most astonishing was the collapse of the communist states of the Soviet bloc, followed by the breakup of the Soviet Union itself.

Gorbachev's policies of *glasnost* and *perestroika* had not only brought more freedom to the Soviet Union, but had also spurred movements for freedom in Soviet bloc nations. In August 1989 Poland became the first Eastern European nation since World War II to form a non-communist government. Other nations followed, as their citizens demanded democracy and economic opportunity.

In November 1989 the world watched in awe as the Berlin Wall, symbol of the Cold War "iron curtain," was torn down. Eleven months later, in October 1990, East and West Germany were reunified in a single, democratic nation.

The collapse of the Soviet Union. In the Soviet Union, Gorbachev's policies had given people a taste of freedom—and they wanted more. Citizens grew impatient, and nationalist feelings long suppressed by communist rule erupted among the diverse peoples of the fifteen Soviet republics. Liberals blamed Gorbachev for not making reforms fast enough, while conservatives feared that change would destroy the Soviet Union.

In August 1991 conservative government leaders arrested Gorbachev. Their attempt to seize power, though, was met by mass protests in Moscow and Leningrad. Thousands of demonstrators rallied under the leadership of Boris Yeltsin, the liberal president of the Russian Republic. Lacking both popular support and military backing, the coup collapsed. The failure of the conservative coup sped the breakup of the Soviet Union.

While both Bush and Gorbachev had welcomed the end of the Cold War, neither had expected the collapse of the Soviet Union. The door to political and economic freedom had turned out to be a floodgate, and the rush of events reduced Gorbachev and Bush to bystanders. By the end of 1991, every Soviet republic had declared independence, the communist central government was dissolved, and the Soviet Union had ceased to exist.

Ten former Soviet republics formed a loose Commonwealth of Independent States, but major issues such as control over military forces and nuclear weapons remained unsettled. Meanwhile, the new states were plagued with problems as they tried to convert to market economies. Of greatest concern to the United States was maintaining the stability of Russia, the largest republic. With Gorbachev removed from power, focus shifted to Russian President Boris Yeltsin as the key figure trying to shape political and economic reform.

Connections: Science and Technology

Discussion. As Chinese authorities cracked down on student protesters, dissidents used fax machines and computer networks to spread news. **Ask:** How might modern communications and video technology aid in the spread of ideas of freedom?

Thinking Critically

Evaluation. In opposing trade sanctions against China, President Bush said "It is wrong to isolate China if we hope to influence it." Ask students to explain why they agree or disagree.

Connections: Music

Listening to Music. Recent decades have seen a dramatic increase in the popularity in the U.S. of music originating in other countries. Both the interest in and the influence of these new musical forms and styles have become widespread.

Additionally, recording artists such as Tracy Chapman, U2, Sting, and Jackson Browne emphasize social issues in their music. You may want to play music by these or other groups and discuss the lyrics with the class.

Multicultural Perspectives

The first steps toward dismantling apartheid in the early 1990s led to calls for removing American trade sanctions against South Africa. Those favoring removal argued that sanctions hurt economic opportunities for South African blacks, and that removing them would reward reformers. Others argued that sanctions should remain until blacks have true political power—one person, one vote.

Reduced student page in the Teacher's Edition

In a visit to the United States in June 1992, Yeltsin pleaded for economic aid to ensure the survival of democracy in Russia. He also agreed to an arms control pact between the United States and Russia that would reduce each country's stockpile of long-range nuclear weapons to less than half the number allowed under the 1991 START treaty.

For American leaders, the collapse of the Soviet Union aroused mixed feelings. The hope for democracy was tempered by fear of instability as ethnic conflicts and ailing economies continued to stir unrest in the former republics. Within Russia, for instance, Yeltsin's "shock therapy" approach of moving quickly to a market economy was causing painful price increases. Whether the Russian people were willing to continue to support his efforts remained to be seen. Meanwhile, the United States and other nations faced the issue of how much—and what kind of—help to provide.

Weighing Foreign Policy Goals

For over forty years the Cold War had framed American foreign policy. Policy makers had labeled communism the major threat to the goals of national security, political and economic stability, human rights, democracy, and sovereignty—the right of any government to control its own affairs. The end of the Cold War did not change these goals. Nor did it change the main tools for achieving them: negotiations, military force, and the use of **sanctions**—measures such as trade bans and blockades designed to put economic pressure on an offending nation. Even without communism as "the enemy," other world problems demanded the attention of American policy makers.

Toward a democratic South Africa. An example of applying economic sanctions in defense of human rights and democracy could be seen in policy toward South Africa. In the South African system of **apartheid**, the white minority maintained its dominance by denying the black majority basic civil and economic rights. Growing public outcry in the United States pressed Congress to pass a sanctions law in 1986. The law forbade American firms to invest in South Africa until that nation took concrete steps to dismantle apartheid.

Since his release from prison, Nelson Mandela has continued to rally support for democratic reform in South Africa.

The new government that took office in 1989 under President F. W. de Klerk at last moved toward change. De Klerk lifted the ban on the African National Congress (ANC), the main anti-apartheid group, and released Nelson Mandela, the ANC's most prominent leader, from prison.

In 1992, after the repeal of remaining apartheid laws, President Bush lifted the sanctions. Yet South Africa still had a long way to go in ensuring black South Africans civil rights. For example, the government still balked at giving blacks the right to vote. In 1993 negotiations on a new constitution centered on finding ways for blacks and whites to share power.

Dashed hopes in China. During the 1980s China had developed trade with the West and encouraged limited free enterprise. However, when students and workers demanded democratic reforms, the government reacted with harsh repression. In June 1989 the world watched in horror as troops crushed the protests of some 100,000 demonstrators in Beijing's Tiananmen Square. Thousands were injured or killed.

Believing that national security required stable relations with China, Bush responded cautiously. He argued against sanctions, saying they would only anger China's leaders rather than encourage reform. Congress agreed to renew China's "most favored nation" trade status but called on China to improve its human rights record.

Connections: Politics
Iraqi spokesmen had for months been blaming Kuwait for stealing Iraq's oil reserves and ignoring boundaries between the two nations. Shortly before the war, the American Ambassador to Kuwait, April Glaspie, delivered messages to Saddam Hussein, explaining the American position on events in the Gulf.

Their conversation, however, became a subject of controversy because there was no American transcript of the meeting. Testifying before congressional committees in March 1991, Glaspie said she had indicated that the United States would not tolerate an Iraqi invasion of Kuwait. Some commentators, though, doubted whether she had sent such a firm message to Hussein.

Central America. Though following a hands-off foreign policy toward China, Bush took a different stand with a country close to home—Panama. When Panama held elections in May 1989, the winner appeared to be Guillermo Endara. However, military dictator Manuel Noriega annulled the vote and continued to rule. Fearing that Noriega might block American access to the Panama Canal, Bush decided to act.

A United States court had indicted Noriega for drug dealing, and in late 1989 Bush sent troops to Panama to overthrow him and bring him to the United States for trial. Endara was sworn in as Panama's president. Other Latin American nations criticized the intervention, however, for violating Panama's sovereignty.

Meanwhile, in Nicaragua the Sandinistas—long labeled by President Reagan as a communist threat—fell from power when democratic elections were held in February 1990. The newly elected leader, Violeta Chamorro, formed a coalition to rebuild Nicaragua, but she faced the challenge of a devastated economy.

Conflict in the Persian Gulf. By invading Panama, Bush had shown willingness to use force against a perceived threat. Less than a year later he acted again, this time in the troubled Middle East.

On August 2, 1990, Iraq invaded Kuwait in a dispute over control of oil prices and oil fields. To force Iraqi president Saddam Hussein to withdraw his forces, Bush gathered international support for a series of economic sanctions. Fearing the possible effects of increased Iraqi control over the region's

American tanks played a key role in the Operation Desert Storm ground attack that forced Iraq to withdraw from Kuwait.

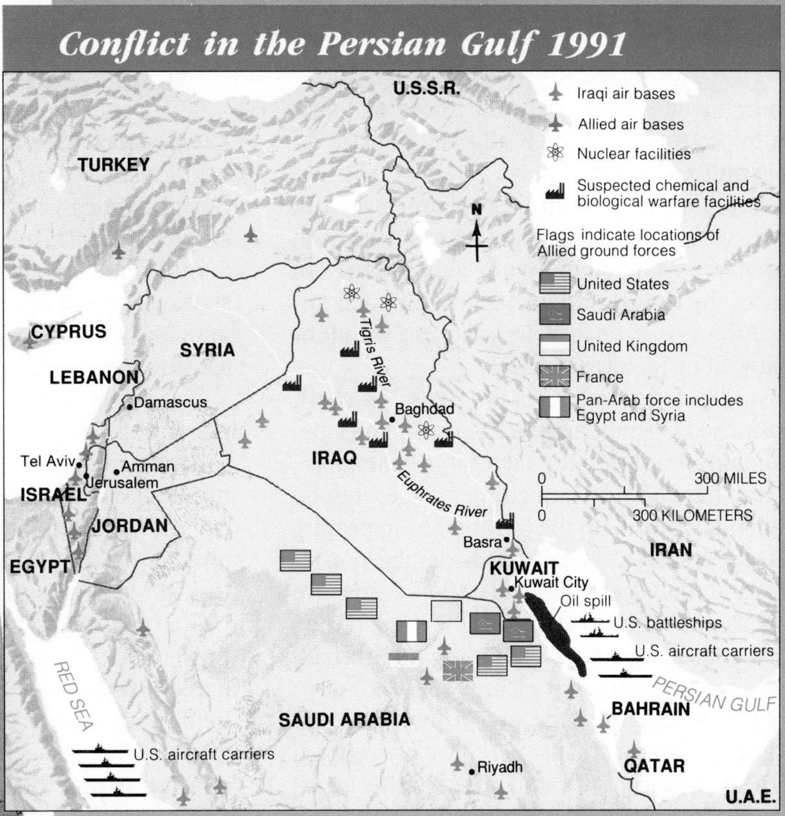

Geography Skills—Location. Why were Saudi Arabia, Egypt, Syria, the U.S., and USSR each worried by Iraqi power?

Writing About History

Position Paper. Have students write a position paper answering the following question: Which is the best rule to follow in establishing foreign policy: protecting national security, encouraging democracy and protecting human rights, or respecting national sovereignty? Have them use facts and historical examples to support their positions.

Geography Skills

ANSWERS

Saudi Arabia, Egypt, and Syria worried by Iraqi proximity and military might; United States concerned over Iraq's ability to control oil out of the Gulf; USSR concerned about Iraq destabilizing the region.

Thinking Critically

Evaluation. In 1993 President Clinton ordered a missile attack on the Iraqi Intelligence Ministry in Baghdad, acting on evidence that Iraq had planned an assassination attempt on President Bush during his visit to Kuwait. The attack heavily damaged its target but also caused civilian casualties. Have students discuss whether military retaliation is justified in response to terrorist threats or attacks and whether it is an effective deterrent.

Connections: Geography

Geography was a factor in the debate over military intervention to stop the ethnic civil war in the former Yugoslavia. Military leaders raised the issue of how effectively land forces could operate in the rugged terrain ("Balkan" means "mountain" in Turkish). Have students discuss the effect of geography on warfare in such a region, as compared with the desert terrain in the Persian Gulf War.

Thinking Critically

Evaluation. Situations like those in Bosnia and Somalia raise an issue: Under what circumstances do the United Nations in general and the United States in particular have the moral authority to intervene? Have students discuss what circumstances justify intervention in the affairs of a sovereign state.

Multicultural Perspectives

Conflicts among peoples of the former Yugoslavia are rooted in a long history of foreign conquest, religious differences, and power struggles. Serbs and Croats, the major groups in the region, are both Slavic peoples whose ancestors had formed independent kingdoms by the beginning of the twelfth century. The Ottoman Turks conquered the region in the late 1300s and ruled for over 400 years. Some Slavs, mostly in Bosnia, became Muslims, but most Serbs fiercely resisted Islam's influence, retaining their Eastern Orthodox faith. Most Croats remained Roman Catholic. Anti-Muslim feelings among Serbs and Croats largely reflect the legacy of struggle against Ottoman rule. Meanwhile, Serbs accuse Croats of collaborating with the Nazis during World War II, and Croats have long suspected Serbs of seeking to dominate other Slavic groups in the region.

Reduced student page in the Teacher's Edition

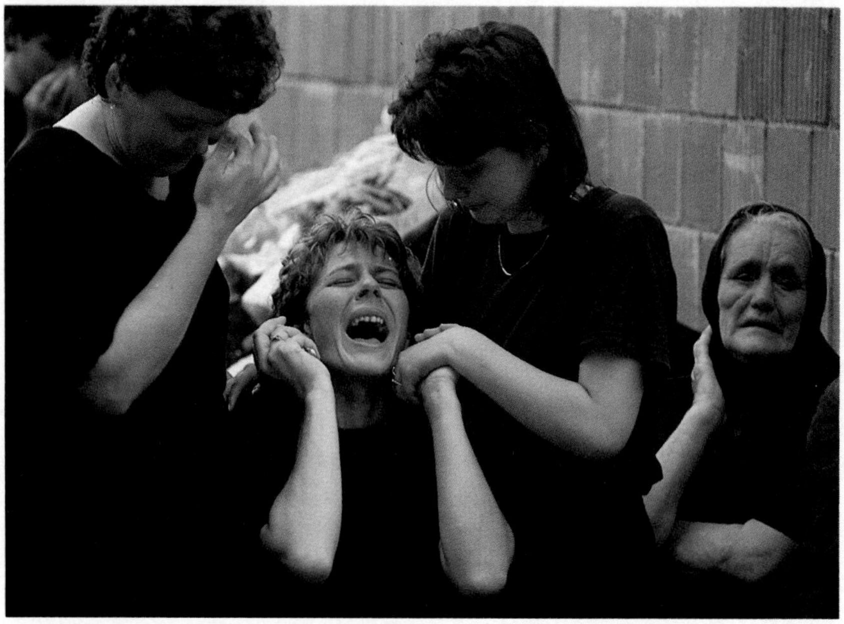

Women mourning at a funeral reflect the human tragedy of civil war in Bosnia, which moved many Americans to call for action.

vital oil supplies, Bush also sent troops to Saudi Arabia to protect that oil-rich ally and prepare for possible military action.

International support for use of force against Iraq was not as strong as for sanctions, but Bush put together a coalition of twenty-eight nations. In November the United Nations Security Council authorized the use of force if Iraq did not withdraw from Kuwait by January 15, 1991.

When talks failed to resolve the crisis, the coalition launched Operation Desert Storm. Planes began bombing Iraqi military targets on January 16, 1991. Iraq responded by launching missiles into Israel, hoping to break up the coalition by appealing to Arab opposition to Israel. But Israel did not retaliate, and the coalition held. After a massive ground assault quickly smashed the Iraqi army, Saddam Hussein agreed to a cease-fire on February 27, and Iraqi forces began to leave Kuwait.

In the United States, the use of force brought both celebration and criticism. The victory restored American military prestige and raised Bush's popularity to an all-time high. On the other hand, before and during the war an anti-war movement had mobilized to oppose the use of force.

The victory of the coalition forces did not solve the region's problems. Saddam Hussein remained in power, brutally suppressing attempts by Shiite Muslim and Kurdish groups to overthrow him. During and after the war, hundreds of thousands of Iraqis sought refuge in Iran and Turkey, many dying along the way from disease, exposure, and starvation. The United States and other coalition governments were criticized for not doing more to relieve their suffering.

Civil wars: Somalia and Bosnia. Though acting decisively in Panama and the Persian Gulf, Bush hesitated when faced with two civil wars that erupted in 1992, one in the East African nation of Somalia and the other in the newly dissolved Yugoslavia. The impact of these conflicts on civilians and, in the case of Bosnia, the threat of the conflict spreading eventually prompted American aid.

In Somalia, war between rival clan leaders was preventing UN relief supplies from reaching people suffering from famine. Over 1,000 people were dying each day of starvation. Amid a growing public call for action, Bush sent troops to guard UN supply convoys in December 1992. In May 1993 the United States turned military command over to a UN force. The famine crisis subsided, but the ongoing conflict between clans raised difficult questions. How long would UN forces need to remain? Could they be effective in helping resolve clan rivalries? What role should the United States play—either as part of the UN effort or on its own?

Meanwhile, the breakup of Yugoslavia into several independent states had brought to the surface ancient ethnic conflicts among Serbs, Croats, and Muslims in the state of Bosnia-Herzegovina. The heavily armed Serbs were taking control of Muslim areas, following a brutal policy of "ethnic cleans-

Connections: Economics

Some flagrant abuses in the savings and loan scandal included: (a) "Quid Pro Quo": Major borrowers were given bigger loans than they asked for in return for investing the extra money in the institution; (b) junk bonds: Some small depositors were persuaded to buy unsecured high-yield bonds, then lost their investments when the thrift collapsed; (c) "Daisy Chain": Real estate owned by one S&L would be sold to another, and then to another for an ever-increasing price, even if the value had not changed; (d) "Texas Premium": To get cash to keep afloat, a failing thrift would offer higher interest for deposits than it earned on loans.

ing"— killing Muslims or forcing them to flee. In spite of reports that drew parallels with the Holocaust in Nazi Germany, Bush hesitated to intervene out of fear of a Vietnam-like quagmire. Meanwhile, the UN and United States sanctions appeared to have little effect.

Facing Crises at Home

Although they supported foreign aid, Americans were increasingly preoccupied with problems at home— especially the struggling economy. Here President Bush faced thornier problems than Reagan's feel-good rhetoric had led people to expect.

Budget blues. A major problem was the huge **national debt**— the total the government owes on money it borrows to make up the difference between what it spends and what it receives in taxes. When Bush entered office, the national debt was rapidly reaching $3 trillion. So huge a debt endangered the economy by limiting the amount of money available for business investment. Also, paying interest on it used up an increasing amount of the federal budget.

In addition to the national debt, a crisis in the nation's savings and loan institutions (S&L's) heaped greater burdens on the federal government. Deregulation under Reagan had allowed S&L's to make more risky loans. Poor investments, dishonest bankers, or both, plunged a number of S&L's into bankruptcy, producing the nation's worst financial scandal. The problem was worse than a scandal, though, because the federal government has to pay depositors when an S&L fails. The bill for this "bailout" was estimated at $500 billion.

How would the government even begin to meet its obligations? Realizing that he could not keep his "no new taxes" promise, Bush joined Congress in approving a $500 billion deficit-reduction plan in 1990, which included large tax increases and domestic spending cuts.

Impact of "new federalism." Meanwhile, under "new federalism," the states faced their own budget crises. With less money from Washington, they had to cope with more problems— many related to the growing poverty of the 1980s— with fewer resources. People were no more willing to pay higher state taxes than higher federal taxes. One man summarized the voters' dilemma:

> *"We don't want to raise taxes. We don't want to spend money. Everybody wants his mother to have the very best health care and to have somebody else pay for it."*

Health care was the fastest growing state expense as the population aged and poverty increased. The federal government and the states share the cost of Medicaid— health care for the poor and disabled and nursing home care for the elderly. Yet while the federal government passed laws to expand coverage, it did not provide more money. Meanwhile, state tax revenues decreased as the economy dipped into recession in 1990.

The war on drugs. Increased drug use posed another serious problem for the nation. In 1990 Americans purchased an estimated $100 billion worth of illegal drugs— most notably the highly-addictive cocaine. Users ranged from the very rich to the very poor. Drug-related crime was rampant as addicts stole to support their habits, and dealers killed to protect their trade. Lacking hope of finding jobs, many youth turned to dealing drugs, believing they could get rich quick. Often they ended up addicted, imprisoned, or dead.

Like Reagan, Bush declared a "war" on drugs, but his efforts had minimal success. Bush attacked the source by sending military aid to Latin American countries to battle drug lords. His efforts, which focused on firmer law enforcement, were criticized for neglecting education and drug treatment programs.

The AIDS crisis. Another crisis faced Americans in the 1980s and 1990s— AIDS, or acquired immune deficiency syndrome. First identified in the United States in 1981, AIDS had caused the deaths of over 133,000 Americans as of January 1992. AIDS is caused by the human immune deficiency virus, or HIV, which destroys the body's immune system. A person with AIDS has no protection against illnesses such as pneumonia and cancer, the leading causes of death among AIDS patients.

Connections: Economics

Discussion. The high cost of the S&L bailout has raised questions about whether federal deposit insurance, instituted after the bank failures of the Great Depression, is fair. **Ask:** Who should pay for deposit insurance? Should it be the depositors themselves (as with life, car, and medical insurance)? Should it be the banks and savings institutions? Or should the risk continue to be spread among all taxpayers?

Connections: Politics

Analysis. Most states are not allowed to run a deficit. The only way they can pay for the services that the "new federalism" thrusts on them is to raise taxes. **Ask:** What happens when the public resists such taxes? **(Strong resistance to taxes usually results in cuts in government services.)**

Connections: Health

Discussion. Some people have argued that legalizing drugs would sharply reduce drug-related crime. Why might this be true? What are some objections to legalizing drugs?

Using the Visuals

Discussion. Have students discuss the message in the poster on page 854. **Ask:** Why might people who suspect they have AIDS be unwilling to be tested? **(Reasons might include fear of finding out one has a fatal disease and fear of discrimination or ostracism if one's condition is known.)**

Active Learning

Cooperative Activity. Divide the class into small groups and assign them an issue that is discussed in this section. Each group represents a task force commissioned by the President to combat the assigned social problem.

Groups are to brainstorm possible solutions to the problem, as well as strategies on how to educate the American people about the problem. Have each group present its plan to the class.

Backyard History

Interviewing. Have students interview people in their community to determine the number of homeless people. Have them interview local government officials to find out what economic, social, and legal problems cause and are caused by homelessness. Students should also investigate what help exists in their communities for the homeless. Have students report their findings to the class.

Connections: Science and Technology

By 1993 a cure for AIDS had not yet been discovered. One drug, AZT, was thought to slow the progress of AIDS and to make people with the AIDS virus less infectious to their sex partners. Other experimental drugs had been tried, but little progress had been made toward a cure. The Centers for Disease Control estimated that in 1990 between 800,000 and 1.3 million people were infected with AIDS, but most of them had not yet shown obvious symptoms. Scientists estimated that there were 60,000 AIDS cases with symptoms in the United States in 1990 and 68,000 in 1991, and that the number would rise to 90,000 in 1993.

Reduced student page in the Teacher's Edition

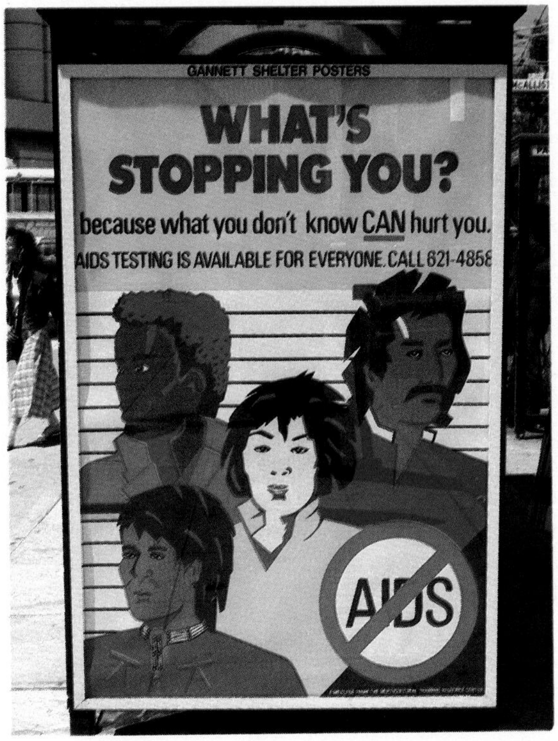

A number of organizations exist to reach the public with information and services related to the HIV virus.

The AIDS virus cannot be spread by casual contact. The most common ways AIDS spreads are through sexual intercourse, sharing of needles by intravenous (IV) drug users, and transmission from mother to child during pregnancy, birth, or breast-feeding. As AIDS touches a widening range of Americans, the costs of caring for the sick, finding a cure, and preventing the spread of the disease pose a challenge to the government.

Homelessness. Soaring housing prices and cutbacks in federal funds for low-cost housing contributed to another crisis—the dramatic increase in the number of homeless Americans, estimated at between 1 and 3 million. Homelessness exists in suburban and rural areas as well as in cities.

Some homeless people are mentally ill men and women released from institutions beginning in the 1960s. The intention was for them to be treated in outpatient clinics and to lead independent lives, but in many cases the services were inadequate.

Since the 1960s, a growing number of homeless people have been women, children, and families. One scenario is a single-income family whose breadwinner becomes ill, leaving the family without rent money. Another might be a woman, battered by her husband, choosing to live in her car rather than endure abuse. Teenagers who run away from home have also ended up on the street.

While thousands of Americans have pitched in to help homeless people by running shelters and soup kitchens, the challenge of finding more permanent solutions remains. One homeless man expressed his sense of defeat:

> *“[Homelessness] is a vicious cycle. You cannot get a job because you do not have an address, you do not have an address because you do not have any money, you do not have any money because you do not have a job.”*

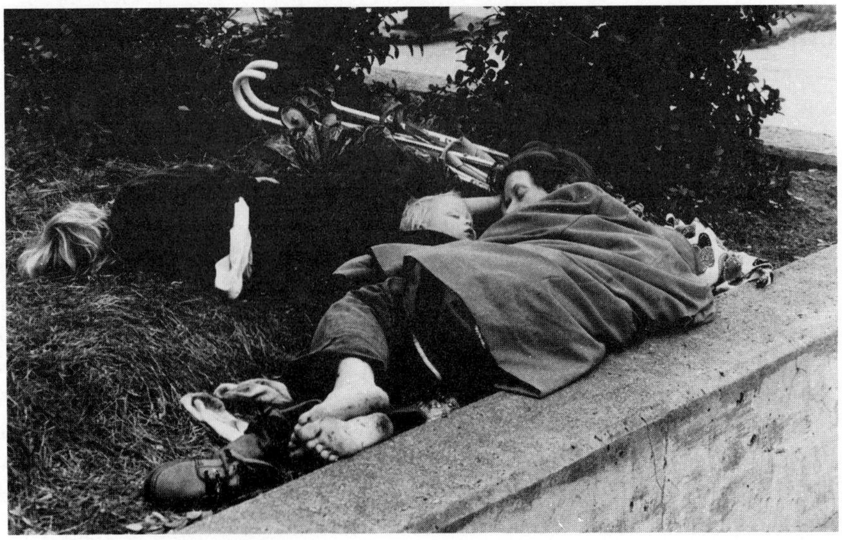

An increasing percentage of poor and homeless Americans are women and children.

Connections: Politics

The Electoral College vote in the 1992 election was 357 for Clinton, 168 for Bush, and 0 for Perot. Though Clinton's total far exceeded the 270 needed to win, the victory margin was not considered a landslide, and his 43% of the popular vote left in question how strong a mandate he could claim to have. The combined vote for Clinton and Perot, however, was a strong rejection of Bush, whose 38% of the popular vote was the lowest figure for an incumbent President since William Howard Taft lost a three-way race against Woodrow Wilson—the winner—and Theodore Roosevelt in 1912.

Connections: Economics

Research. Have students research the major issues in the presidential elections of the twentieth century. What conclusions can they draw regarding how the status of the economy affects the outcome of presidential elections?

Thinking Critically

Evaluation. During the 1992 campaign some people wondered whether a vote for Perot would be "wasted" if he did not have a realistic chance to win. Have students explain why they would or would not consider voting for a third-party candidate.

Debates between Bush, Perot, and Clinton drew large television audiences, reflecting high public interest in the 1992 election.

The Presidential Election of 1992

As President Bush entered the last year of his term, the ailing economy was clearly the key issue of the presidential election. Effects of a serious recession that had begun in 1990 could not be denied—thousands of workers were being laid off. In 1991 Bush had believed that the economy would cure itself; in 1992 he made economic proposals in his State of the Union speech, but many people thought his plans were too little, too late. As voter anger over his lack of action grew, his chances of reelection shrank.

The Democrats nominated Arkansas Governor Bill Clinton for President and Tennessee Senator Al Gore, Jr., for Vice-President. Clinton criticized the "trickle-down," laissez-faire economic policies of the Reagan-Bush era, saying that they had caused the increased gap between rich and poor. He promised more government involvement to "grow the economy" by investing in job training and reducing soaring health care costs.

Not all voters seeking change looked to Clinton, however. Frustrated by what they saw as the ineffectiveness of both parties, many voters turned to an independent candidate. Ross Perot, a Texas billionaire businessman, promised to focus on the national debt, a problem he said neither Republicans nor Democrats were truly willing to tackle.

Unable to run on his own economic record, Bush focused instead on attacking his opponents. He labeled Clinton a "tax and spend" liberal who could not be trusted. Clinton's campaign manager, meanwhile, posted the motto "The Economy, Stupid!" as a reminder not to get distracted by the negative attacks.

On election day Clinton's promise of economic change got a greater response than either Perot's focus on the national debt or Bush's warnings about higher taxes. Clinton won with 43 percent of the vote to Bush's 38 percent. Meanwhile, Perot's 19 percent was the strongest showing for a third-force candidate in eighty years, and a reminder that the national debt remained a critical concern of many voters.

Thinking Critically

Evaluation. William Bennett, who served in the Reagan and Bush administrations, gave this assessment of President Bush's performance:

"Clare Booth Luce once said that a President is accorded a single sentence in the history books. For George Bush it will read: 'He defeated a tyrant in the desert and presided over the end of the Cold War.' Not a bad sentence, that."

Have students compare Bennett's view with that of Arthur Schlesinger, Jr., in the quotation on page 856. Then ask them to make their own overall assessments of Bush, supporting their views with reasons and examples.

Using the Visuals

Discussion. Point out that the "Group of Seven" consists of the leaders of the United States, Japan, Canada, Great Britain, France, Germany, and Italy. **Ask:** Why would these particular countries have their own economic summit to address global issues? **(As leading economies, they can play major roles in addressing issues; agreements might be reached more easily with fewer parties.)**

Connections: Politics

In 1991 the nation's leading historians responded to a survey in which they rated Presidents according to categories ranging from "great" (Jefferson, Lincoln, Franklin D. Roosevelt, Washington) to "failure" (Buchanan, Grant, Harding, Andrew Johnson, Nixon). Six Presidents were rated "below average" (Fillmore, Pierce, Reagan, Taylor, Tyler). Among those rated "average" were Carter and Ford. Bush was not rated because he was still in office. As is evident in the rating of Reagan, the opinions of historians may not agree with the views of the majority of voters.

Looking Back on the Bush Years

In his 1988 campaign George Bush had promised to "stay the course"—to continue the Reagan policies of reducing domestic spending and government regulation of business. He also suggested, though, that government could play a role in softening the harsh effects of laissez-faire capitalism. He spoke of being an "Environmental President" and an "Education President," while also offering the goal of a "kinder, gentler nation."

Toward that end, Bush signed into law two major bills in 1990: the Clean Air Act and the Americans With Disabilities Act. The major focus of the Clean Air Act was to set stricter pollution-control goals for cars and factories. The Americans With Disabilities Act made it illegal to discriminate against physically or mentally disabled persons in jobs, public services, and public accommodations such as hotels. The law also required buses, trains, and large retail stores to be accessible to disabled persons. Both laws called for extensive regulation of businesses.

Although he signed some important laws, Bush had few legislative goals of his own. He allowed Congress to take the lead in domestic policy. A common observation about Bush is that he lacked "vision"—clear goals for the nation and strategies to reach those goals. Historian Arthur Schlesinger, Jr., believes that Bush mainly reacted to events rather than trying to shape them:

> *"Bush will be remembered as the ultimate 'in-box' president. If something is called to his attention, he reacts to it. But he will not be remembered as having the kind of capacity that creative Presidents have to see problems before they get into his box and try to do something about them."*

In the end, most voters did not judge Bush on his response to surprises—his careful monitoring of communism's collapse in Eastern Europe or his decisive reversal of Iraq's occupation of Kuwait. Instead, they held him accountable for lacking a clear domestic agenda—a plan for the nation's economy.

Challenges for Clinton

Clinton took office amid high public expectations. In the rise of a younger generation to leadership, many Americans saw hope for a more energetic, creative approach to public issues. Also, the combination of a Democratic President and a Democratic majority in Congress seemed to promise relief from gridlock, enabling government to make rapid progress on solving problems. The mood at the inauguration reflected these high hopes, and the nation looked to the new President for a fast-paced "first hundred days."

Clinton's major challenges were to create jobs, reduce the national debt, and reform the costly health-care system. In his State of the Union speech in February 1993, he announced a plan to stimulate the economy by funding job training and transportation projects, while reducing the national debt through spending cuts and tax increases. Meanwhile, first lady Hillary Rodham Clinton headed a task force assigned the project of proposing legislation to reform the health-care system. The goals of such reform were to reduce the costs of health care and make adequate care available to all Americans.

In July 1993 President Clinton met with world leaders at the Group of Seven Economic Summit in Tokyo.

Connections: Economics

Several major factors made health-care reform a major issue in the 1992 election: 37 million Americans had no medical insurance, health/Medicare spending was a large percentage of the federal budget—about 15% in 1992, and the cost of medical care was rapidly rising, adding to the budget deficit.

Thinking Critically

Evaluation. Hillary Rodham Clinton's leadership of a health-care reform task force raised the question of the proper role for the spouse of a President. Have students explain why they agree or disagree that a President's spouse should be able to play a prominent role in shaping national policy.

As chief advisor on health-care reform, Hillary Rodham Clinton listened to hours of testimony. Here she meets with Native Americans in March 1993.

Clinton soon learned that getting legislation approved would be even harder than winning the election. New to Washington, he and much of his staff were inexperienced at dealing with Congress. The well-organized opposition of congressional Republicans, bolstered by intense lobbying by interest groups, tested his skills and determination.

Meanwhile, foreign-policy issues pressed in on Clinton, competing for his attention with domestic concerns. He could not ignore the civil war in Bosnia, economic and political unrest in the former Soviet Union, continuing strains in the Middle East and Africa, and the spread of advanced weapons technology. Looking beyond Clinton's first hundred days in office, Americans could see that the instability of the post-Cold-War world might divert the "laser-like intensity" the President hoped to focus on the economy.

Section Review

1. Identification. Define *sanctions, apartheid,* and *national debt.*

2. Evaluation. Do you think the end of the Cold War made the world a safer or a more dangerous place? Explain.

3. Comprehension. Explain how the savings and loan crisis contributed to Bush's budget troubles.

4. Analysis. Contrast Clinton's and Bush's views of their roles and the role of government in general.

Connections to Themes

Shaping Democracy

For forty years after World War II, the global focus of the United States was on stopping the spread of communism. The long Cold-War struggle was costly for both sides as they competed to build up nuclear and conventional forces.

Then, in a series of dramatic events, the Soviet Union and its empire began to break apart under the demands of subject peoples for democracy, freedom, and economic opportunity. Americans could no longer view global politics as a military standoff between communism and democracy.

Neither the end of the Cold War nor the quick, startling victory over Iraq produced in Americans a confident vision for the future. Uncertainty about how the United States should use its power and influence in other parts of the world remained.

Even more troubling were questions about how well American democracy was functioning at home. Would the government remain paralyzed by such complex problems as poverty, crime, drugs, health care, and threats to the environment? Huge tax-supported programs had not solved similar problems in the past, and government cutbacks had only made today's problems more glaring.

Could the American people and their policy makers find effective solutions to domestic problems? Could they shape a new role for a democratic United States in the post-Cold-War world? These were the questions Americans would face.

Section Review

ANSWERS

1. Definitions for the following terms are on text pages indicated in parentheses: *sanctions* (850), *apartheid* (850), *national debt* (853).

2. Opinions will vary. Those seeing the world as safer may note the end of the threat of large-scale nuclear war and of indirect superpower conflict through support for warring factions in other countries. Russian-American cooperation may also help UN fulfill its role as peacekeeper. Others may argue that the superpower standoff created a certain stability, without which there is more potential for conflict between smaller countries and ethnic groups. They may also note increased danger of nuclear arms proliferation.

3. The federal government had to pay depositors of failed savings and loans. The cost was about $70 billion.

4. Bush believed that domestic policy should be essentially laissez faire and that Congress should take the lead if the government must take action on domestic problems. Clinton believed that government should play a major role in addressing domestic problems and that legislative leadership should come from the President.

Chapter Survey

ANSWERS

Using New Vocabulary

1. The Reagan administration overtly and covertly supported the *contras*—Nicaraguan guerrillas who opposed the government.
2. Acts of *terrorism* in the 1980s included Muslim fundamentalists taking hostages in the Middle East and blowing up marines headquarters in Lebanon.
3. In 1986 a law forbade American firms to invest in South Africa until political prisoners were released and steps were taken to dismantle *apartheid,* the system of legalized segregation and discrimination.

Reviewing the Chapter

1. Goals: end stagflation, restore prosperity. Means: reduced government spending on domestic programs, lower taxes.
2. He thought that deregulation would promote productivity. In business, it stimulated growth, but also price wars that put smaller companies out of business. In government, it limited the effectiveness of the Environmental Protection Agency.
3. "New federalism" turned responsibility for many programs over to states, reflected conservative belief in limiting size of federal government and strengthened local control.
4. Ousted Marxist leader of coup in Grenada; sent military aid to anti-communist government in El Salvador; through CIA, supported contra rebels against Sandinista government in Nicaragua.
5. Private group headed by ex-general arranged for sale of American weapons to Iran to get hostages released. Part of profits from sale used to support contras in Nicaragua, despite congressional ban on aid to them. Foreign policy out of White House avoided Congress.
6. Soviet failure in Afghanistan, crumbling Soviet economy, Gorbachev's *glasnost* and *perestroika* policies.
7. Foreign policy goals and methods remained the same, but focus shifted from seeing communism as the dominant threat. Interventions in Panama and the Persian Gulf, for instance, were largely in response to perceived national security threats unrelated to communism.
8. War removed Iraqis from Kuwait, prevented invasion of Saudi Arabia, raised U.S. self-confidence. Saddam Hussein still in power, no democratic reform in Kuwait, no solution of Palestine issue. New problems: devastation in Iraq, suffering refugees, environmental damage.
9. Federal: huge budget deficit resulting from increased spending, lower tax revenues, interest

Reduced student page in the Teacher's Edition

Chapter Survey

Using New Vocabulary

For each of the following vocabulary terms, write a short paragraph explaining its significance in American foreign policy in the 1980s and 1990s: *contras, terrorism,* and *apartheid.*

Reviewing the Chapter

1. What were the goals of Reaganomics? By what means were they to be achieved?

2. Why did Reagan support deregulation? What were its effects on business and government?

3. How did the "new federalism" apply to Reagan's conservative philosophy?

4. What methods did Reagan use to oppose communism in the western hemisphere?

5. Describe the Iran-contra affair and explain why it was a major crisis of the presidency.

6. What factors contributed to the improvement of relations between the United States and the Soviet Union at the end of Reagan's second term?

7. Did the end of the Cold War completely change American foreign policy? Give examples when explaining your answer.

8. What did the war in the Persian Gulf accomplish? What old problems were left unresolved?

9. Explain why both the federal and state governments were facing budget crises when President Bush took office.

10. Describe three social problems facing the United States in the 1990s and explain the difficulties in dealing with these problems.

11. What major domestic problems faced President Clinton, and what were the main obstacles to addressing them?

Thinking Critically

1. Synthesis. One of the oldest unwritten rules of politics is to avoid any mention of raising taxes in an election year. Why do you think Walter Mondale risked defying this tradition? What do you think he misjudged?

2. Evaluation. "Although he restored prestige to the presidency, Ronald Reagan crippled the federal government's ability to solve the nation's problems in the future." Do you agree or disagree with this statement? Give reasons to support your answer.

3. Application. What principles seemed to be guiding foreign policy under George Bush?

History and You

Statistics cited in this chapter point to a widening gap between rich and poor in the United States. Ask five people of your parents' age or older if they see specific examples of this trend in their daily lives. List their replies and compare them with those of your classmates. What are the most frequently mentioned differences between income distribution in the 1990s and earlier decades?

Using a Time Line

Match each date on the time line with the correct event or events in the list below. Explain what effect each event had on the United States.

(A) Student demonstrations in China put down
(B) Gorbachev comes to power in USSR
(C) Civil war breaks out in Bosnia
(D) Israel invades Lebanon
(E) Iraq invades Kuwait
(F) Sandinistas oust Somoza
(G) The Soviet Union collapses
(H) Civil war breaks out in El Salvador

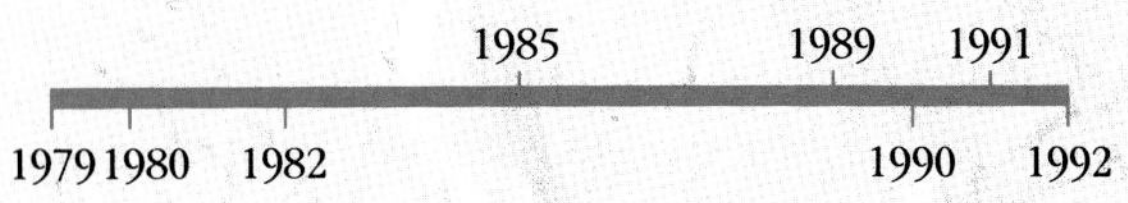

due on federal debt, S&L crisis. States: less funding from federal government, mounting social problems such as poverty.
10. Drugs—led to addiction, high crime rates; hard to stop drugs from entering country, hard to keep youth away from promise of profits from drug trade. AIDS—disease attacking body's immune system, no known cure, costs of research, prevention, and caring for sick very high. Homelessness—high cost of housing, lack of federal support for low-income housing and of local support programs, charities not adequate to handle problem.
11. Creating jobs, reducing the national debt, and reforming the health care system. Major obstacles were the new administration's inexperience with getting federal legislation approved and the potential diversion of attention and resources to foreign problems.

Thinking Critically

1. Mondale may have thought the problems were so serious that voters would put aside self-interest and vote for the well-being of the nation. He was not realistic about the degree to which people were focusing solely on their own needs at the expense of the common good.
2. Agree: Increases in budget deficit and federal debt leave nation with little money to solve problems. Disagree: Tax cuts force government to spend more efficiently.
3. Protect American business interests, such as oil in the Middle East and trade with China. Make the nation look strong militarily, as in Gulf War and Panama.

History and You

Possible responses include cost of housing, food, college education, medical care; level of savings; availability of stores selling goods in middle price range.

Using a Time Line

(F) 1979, **(H)** 1980, **(D)** 1982, **(B)** 1985, **(A)** 1989, **(E)** 1990, **(G)** 1991, **(C)** 1992.

Applying Social Studies Skills

1. Trying to stimulate the economy.
2. Cut taxes and deregulate to increase business production; create more jobs, thus expanding the economy.
3. Cut taxes and/or increase government spending to stimulate demand, which will cause businesses to increase output and hire more workers.
4. Reagan relaxed business regulations and decreased taxes for businesses and the wealthy.
5. FDR's New Deal offered work relief and direct relief programs to increase demand (made possible by government spending); he also taxed high personal incomes and company profits.

Applying Social Studies Skills

Interpreting Diagrams

Organizing information in a diagram can be a useful way to present complex ideas or processes clearly and in a way that can be quickly understood. Some diagrams show steps in a process or cause-and-effect relationships. Others provide a way to compare two or more processes or sets of data.

The diagram below outlines, side by side, two economic theories: supply-side economics and demand-side economics. Supply-side economists maintain that the government should seek to stimulate the production (supply) of goods and services. The result will be a revival of the economy. Demand-side economists claim that reviving the economy is best accomplished by stimulating consumption of goods and services (demand).

Study the diagram and answer the questions that follow.

1. What goal do both supply-side and demand-side economic theories share?
2. Explain how supply-side economists propose to reach the goal.
3. Explain how demand-side economists propose to reach the goal.
4. How did President Reagan's economic policies correspond to supply-side economics?
5. How did President Franklin Roosevelt's economic policies correspond to demand-side economics?

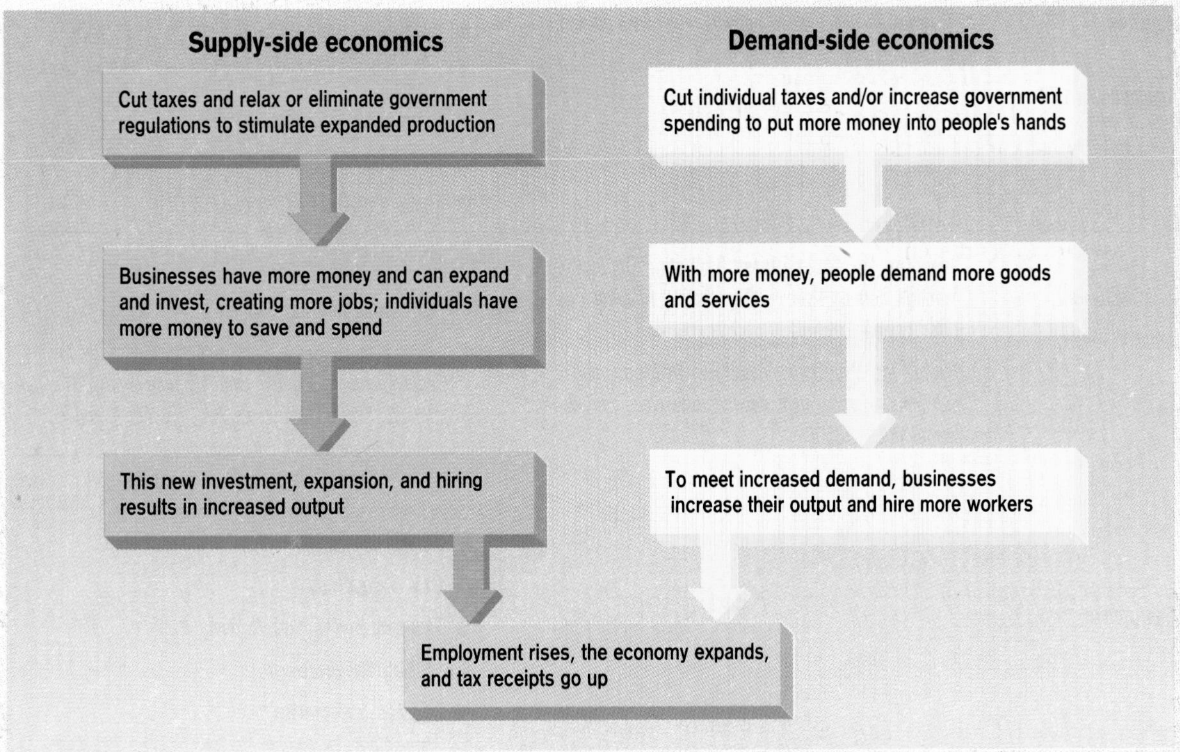

Supply-side economics
Cut taxes and relax or eliminate government regulations to stimulate expanded production
Businesses have more money and can expand and invest, creating more jobs; individuals have more money to save and spend
This new investment, expansion, and hiring results in increased output
Demand-side economics
Cut individual taxes and/or increase government spending to put more money into people's hands
With more money, people demand more goods and services
To meet increased demand, businesses increase their output and hire more workers
Employment rises, the economy expands, and tax receipts go up

859

Chapter 32

The United States in a Changing World

Planning Guide

	Student Text	TWE Lesson Plans	Support Materials
SECTION 1	**Section 32–1 (1–2 Days)** **A Portrait of a Diverse Nation,** pp 862–869 The American Spirit: Maxine Hong Kingston, p 863 The Creative Spirit: Artists, pp 864–865 Review/Evaluation Section Review, p 869	**Introducing the Chapter:** Finding Evidence of the Global Economy—Class Activity, 30 minutes, homework, p 859B **Teaching the Main Ideas:** "Microcosm of the World" Posters—Individual Activity, one class period, p 859B	★ **Read to Remember,** Section 1 ● **Section Activities,** Section 1 Δ **Enrichment Activities,** Section 1 Δ **Readings,** William L.H. Moon ● **Tests and Quizzes,** Section 1 Quiz
SECTION 2	**Section 32–2 (1–3 Days)** **Looking Toward Democracy's Future,** pp 869–873 Review/Evaluation Section Review, p 873	**Enrichment Activity:** Strategies to Get Out the Vote—Cooperative Activity, one-and-one-half class periods, p 859D	★ **Read to Remember,** Section 2 ● **Section Activities,** Section 2 Δ **Readings,** Maggie Kuhn ● **Tests and Quizzes,** Section 2 Quiz
SECTION 3	**Section 32–3 (1–3 Days)** **Economic Obstacles and Opportunities,** pp 874–880 Geography—Movement: Shifting Population, p 877 Review/Evaluation Section Review, p 880	**Reinforcement Activity:** Developing Television Programs—Cooperative Activity, one class period, p 859C	★ **Read to Remember,** Section 3 ● **Section Activities,** Section 3 Δ **Enrichment Activities,** Section 3 ● **Geography Activities,** Section 3 Δ **Readings,** Catherine Caufield ● **Tests and Quizzes,** Section 3 Quiz
SECTION 4	**Section 32–4 (1–3 Days)** **Global Links and Foreign Policy,** pp 880–887 Exploring Issues—Environment: Global Warming, pp 884–885 Chapter 32 Survey, pp 888–889 Unit 10 Survey, pp 890–891 Skills, pp 888–889 Using New Vocabulary Thinking Critically Using Geography Applying Social Studies Skills: Interpreting Diagrams Writing About Issues	**Teaching the Main Ideas:** Promoting Democracy Through Foreign Policy—Cooperative Activity, one class period, p 859C **Evaluating Progress:** Identifying Problems and Solutions—Cooperative Activity, one class period, homework, p 859C	★ **Read to Remember,** Section 4 ● **Section Activities,** Section 4 ● **Tests and Quizzes,** Section 4 Quiz, Chapter 32 Test (Forms A and B), Unit 10 Test (Forms A and B), Second Semester Test (Forms A and B) **Additional Resources** ● **Active Learning** Δ **GTV Videodiscs** Δ **Transparencies and Activity Book** ● **Testing Software** ★ **Chapter Summaries** **Key:** ★ **For Extra Support** ● **For All Students** Δ **For Enrichment**

Overview

Woven throughout the chapters of *The United States and Its People* are three recurrent themes in American history: the challenge of balancing unity and diversity, the continuing effort to make democracy work, and the struggle to fulfill the promise of economic opportunity for all Americans.

In the immediate future, balancing unity and diversity will remain a challenge, as the nation's population becomes increasingly diverse and as demands grow for the validation of diverse cultural traditions. The shaping of democracy will be manifested in efforts to increase voter participation, deal with political gridlock, and create a more broadly representative democracy. Familiar questions about equal economic opportunity will have to be tackled in the context of changes in technology, the workplace, and the global economy.

Foreign policy issues reflect all three recurrent themes, as the United States faces the problems of ethnic conflicts abroad, the challenge of promoting human rights and democracy abroad, and the trade issues inherent in a global economy.

Activity Objectives

After completing the activities, students should be able to

- analyze the nature and challenges of cultural diversity in the United States today.
- evaluate policy options for defending and encouraging democracy abroad.
- identify historical and contemporary examples of the text's three themes of American history.
- summarize major challenges facing the United States and the world.
- identify reasons and propose solutions for low voter turnout.

Introducing the Chapter

Finding Evidence of the Global Economy

This class activity requires half a class period and homework.

This activity is designed to help students appreciate the impact of the global economy. In the activity students make inventories to identify global connections in their daily lives.

Begin the activity by having students consider the amount of influence foreign countries have on their daily lives. Ask volunteers to give examples of such influence. Tell students that in today's activity they will collect evidence to show some of the economic impact of foreign influence on their lives.

Group students into pairs and ask each pair to predict how many of the clothing items they are wearing were made outside the United States. Then have the pairs examine the labels on their clothes to determine in what countries they were made. Direct students to write the names of the countries on the chalkboard, indicating with tally marks the number of items from each country. Save the list.

Challenge students to predict how many household items in their homes were foreign produced. As homework, assign them to conduct inventories of 20 household items to determine their countries of origin.

When the inventories are completed, compile a master list of the countries in which students' clothing and household items were produced. Have students compare their predictions with the results of the inventory and speculate why they were correct or incorrect. Tell students that they will have an opportunity to think further about the United States role in the global economy as they read Chapter 32.

Teaching the Main Ideas

Section 32-1: "Microcosm of the World" Posters

This individual activity requires a full class period.

In this activity students create posters to illustrate the quotation from Molefi Asante on page 860 of the text: "Once America was a microcosm of European nationalities. Today America is a microcosm of the world."

Write the term *melting pot* on the chalkboard and ask students to explain the term's meaning in relation to the nation's cultural diversity. As students contribute ideas, point out that many people today contend that the term does not reflect an accurate description of our nation's history because not all peoples "melted" into American society and because it is not necessarily desirable for newcomers to give up their cultural identity in order to be Americans. Ask students to suggest other analogies that more accurately reflect the balance between unity and diversity. (Possible analogies include mosaic, stew, salad bowl, each of which suggests that the individual "ingredients" keep their identity while combining to create a new whole.)

Distribute poster paper and colored markers and explain to students that their task is to design a poster illustrating the ideas underlying the Molefi Asante quotation. Encourage students to think about the text theme of balancing unity and diversity as they work. In addition, they may wish to review the Connections to Themes mini-essays throughout the text for poster ideas. Direct them to title their posters "The United States—Microcosm of the World."

Display students' completed posters. Use them as a springboard for a discussion of ideas about American identity and the challenges and opportunities posed by increasing diversity.

Teaching the Main Ideas

Section 32-4: Promoting Democracy Through Foreign Policy

This cooperative activity requires a full class period.

In this activity students consider and evaluate policies by which the United States can foster and protect democracy in foreign nations.

Begin the activity by asking students to discuss whether they think the United States, as the world's most powerful democratic nation, has an obligation to try to foster and protect democracy in other countries. As the discussion progresses, challenge students to identify specific ways in which our country can help defend democracy abroad.

Write on the chalkboard the following list: *Military Alliances, Covert Action, Weapons Sales, Military Force, Cultural and Educational Exchange Programs, Foreign Aid–Military, Foreign Aid–Development, Trade Agreements.* Explain that this is a list of some policy options available to the President and advisors when they decide how to encourage and defend democratic interests in other countries. Direct students individually to rank the options, from 1 for the option they think is most desirable to 8 for least desirable.

When students have completed their individual rankings, organize the class into groups of four. Instruct the groups to discuss their individual rankings and arrive at a group ranking. Encourage them to reach consensus, but permit minority reports.

When the groups have finished, bring the class back together and have representatives from the groups present their rankings. Encourage a class discussion in which each group explains the thinking behind its rankings.

Reinforcement Activity

Section 32-3: Developing Television Programs

This cooperative activity requires a full class period.

In the activity students reflect on the text's three themes by planning television programs based on those themes.

Begin the activity by asking students to identify the three themes that have been woven through the chapters of the text. As students identify them, write the themes on the chalkboard: *Balancing Unity and Diversity, Shaping Democracy,* and *The Search for Opportunity*.

Organize students into groups of three and ask them to imagine themselves as producers for "Channel TTT—Three Themes Television." They have been charged with the responsibility of developing ideas for a minimum of five programs to be broadcast in one evening. The programs are to address the three themes listed on the chalkboard. When the groups have created program ideas, they are to write descriptions of them in television guide form. They should give each program a name, identify its length, and write a short, enticing summary of it.

Encourage students to review the Connections to Themes sections of their text chapters for program ideas. Suggest that the programs may be historical or treat contemporary issues, and that they may focus on one theme or on combinations of themes.

When the program descriptions are complete, have the groups display them. Then ask a volunteer from each group to read the entry for one of its programs. Have students consider which of the programs they think might have potential for being developed into an actual television production.

Evaluating Progress

Section 32-4: Identifying Problems and Solutions

This cooperative and individual activity requires most of a class period plus homework.

In this activity students reflect on current global problems, then pose possible solutions. Students engage in cooperative brainstorming and then write personal essays based on the results of the brainstorming.

Before class, prepare five poster sheets. Write at the top of each sheet one of the following headings:

- Worldwide Environmental Problems
- Ways Individuals Can Help Solve Global Problems
- Approaches to Improving Understanding Between Groups of People
- Policies for Encouraging Democracy in Other Countries
- Reasons for Optimism about the Future.

Post the sheets at stations around the classroom and provide additional blank sheets.

Begin the activity by dividing the class into five groups. Assign a group to each poster-sheet station. Explain that each group is to brainstorm for three minutes about the topic indicated on the sheet at their station. Below the heading on the sheet they are to list all their knowledge and opinions about the topic.

After three minutes, direct the groups to move to a different station. Have them read what the preceding group has written and add their own thoughts. Allow three minutes for the task. Continue this process until each group has been to all five stations.

Reconvene the class and give students time to read the poster sheets. Tell students that they are to use the information from the sheets to stimulate their thinking for an essay entitled "What the World Needs Now." Explain that the essays are to summarize some of the major challenges facing the United States and the world and suggest specific solutions to those challenges. If the essay is to be completed as homework, students may want to take notes on the information on the poster sheets.

Evaluate students' essays on the clarity with which they identify problems and the specificity and reasonableness of the solutions they propose.

Enrichment Activity

Section 32-2: Strategies to Get Out the Vote

This cooperative activity requires one and a half class periods.

In this activity students consider ways to increase voter turnout and express their ideas in the form of a legislative bill.

Remind students that one of the problems addressed in Section 32-2 is low voter turnout. Ask the class to identify evidence of this problem and suggest possible reasons for it. Write their reasons on the chalkboard. Be sure that the following reasons are included:

- People think politicians avoid "real" issues.
- People think politicians do not address the average American's problems.
- Interest groups have too much influence because of their ability to make heavy financial contributions.
- Women and African, Hispanic, and Asian Americans think they are not fairly represented in elected offices.
- The actual process of registering and voting discourages voters.

Organize students into groups of three or four. Have each group choose one reason for low voter turnout from the chalkboard and brainstorm ways to address the problem. Direct groups to select the best suggestions from their brainstorming to develop into a legislative bill. Then they are to write a description of their bill, identifying the problem, specifying the provisions of the bill, and explaining how their proposed legislation would remedy the problem.

On the following day, allow time for each group to read its description to the class and have class members discuss the strengths and weaknesses of its bill. When all bills have been critiqued, conduct a class vote to identify the bill students think would be most effective in increasing voter turnout. Also have students consider which causes of voter apathy cannot be remedied by legislation.

Bibliography and Audiovisual Materials

Teacher Bibliography

Erickson, John. *Greenhouse Earth: Tomorrow's Disaster Today*. Blue Ridge Summit, Pa.: TAB Books, 1990.

Fehr, Ferenc and Andrew Arato, eds. *Crisis and Reform in Eastern Europe*. New Brunswick, N.J.: Transaction Publications, 1990.

Gorbachev, Mikhail, translated by David Floyd. *The August Coup: The Truth and the Lessons*. New York: HarperCollins, 1991.

Gordon, Bernard K. *New Directions for American Policy in East Asia*. New York: Routledge, 1990.

Hertzberg, Hazel W. *Search for an American Indian Identity: Modern Pan-Indian Movements*. Syracuse: Syracuse University Press, 1971.

Takaki, Ron. *Strangers from a Distant Shore: A History of Asian Americans.* Boston: Little, Brown & Co., 1989.

Student Bibliography

Bradbury, Ray. *Fahrenheit 451*. New York: Ballantine Books, Inc., 1987.

Bode, Janet. *New Kids on the Block: Oral Histories of Immigrant Teens.* New York: Watts, 1989.

Pringle, Laurence P. *Rain of Troubles: The Science and Politics of Acid Rain*. New York: Macmillan Children's Group, 1988.

Tan, Amy. *The Joy Luck Club.* New York: The Putnam Publishing Group, 1989.

Films, Videocassettes, and Videodiscs

The American Document Series: Hostages to Oil. 55 min. Coronet/MTI. Videocassette.

The Environment—New Global Concerns: Current Affairs. 20 min. New York Times. Videocassette.

Toward The Year 2000: Can We Survive the Future? 35 min. Center for Humanities. Videocassette.

Filmstrips

Why Cultures Are Different. 6 color filmstrips, 3 cassettes, guide. United Learning.

Computer Software

The Environment: Decisions, Decisions. Apple. Tom Snyder Productions.

Revolutions: Past, Present, and Future. 5 Apple diskettes, backups, guide. Focus Media.

Chapter 32

Objectives

- Explain effects of tension between unity and diversity in the United States today.
- Cite challenges the nation faces in implementing democracy at home.
- Describe economic obstacles and opportunities facing the nation.
- Describe foreign policy issues facing the nation.

Introducing THE CHAPTER

For suggestions on introducing Chapter 32, refer to page 859B in the Teacher's Edition.

Developing THE CHAPTER

For activities and teaching strategies to help you reinforce and enrich chapter content, see pages 859B-859D in the Teacher's Edition.

B · A · C · K · G · R · O · U · N · D

Chapter Opener Illustrations

Citizens of Ukraine rally for independence as the forces of communism collapse in Eastern Europe.

These Harvard Medical School graduates face a workplace radically different from their grandparents' time. A college education and advanced degrees are no longer a luxury but a requirement for many jobs.

As nations grow more interdependent, the role of the United Nations appears more crucial in helping to solve serious global issues. Troop transport vehicles in Bosnia represent the UN's effort to fulfill its main goal of peacekeeping.

Computer-aided design, as in this image of a helicopter turbine part, reflects the rapid technological change that is transforming the roles of workers and the way products are made.

Reduced student page in the Teacher's Edition

Chapter 32

The United States in a Changing World

"Save the Planet" is more than just a slogan for the Nineties, as environmental crises threaten public safety around the world.

American Voices

Three days before he was assassinated, the Reverend Dr. Martin Luther King, Jr., delivered a sermon at the National Cathedral in Washington, D.C. He spoke of the importance of taking a global perspective in our increasingly interdependent world.

"A new age is dawning in history in which we face new challenges and new opportunities. First, we are challenged to develop a new world perspective. No individual can live alone, no nation can live alone, and anyone who feels that he can live alone is sleeping through a revolution. The world in which we live is geographically one. The challenge we face today is to make it one in terms of brotherhood. . . . We must all learn to live together as brothers . . . or we will all perish as fools.

. . . And whatever affects one directly affects all indirectly. For some strange reason I can never be what I ought to be until you are what you ought to be. And you can never be what you ought to be until I am what I ought to be."

The futures of the United States and of other nations are becoming more intertwined. Efforts to balance unity and diversity, to shape a more representative democracy, and to expand economic opportunity are affecting not only the lives of Americans but also the lives of people around the globe.

Independence rally in Ukraine; Harvard Medical School graduation; UN peacekeeping forces in Bosnia; computer-aided design of helicopter turbine; ecology button.

Analyzing Primary Sources

American Voices

Martin Luther King, Jr.'s career took a dramatic turn between 1963 and 1968, the year of his death. His message, while remaining rooted in the movement for equal rights in the United States, became broader in nature. The quotation on this page is evidence of King's world-wide concerns.

Ask: Do you agree that "whatever affects one affects all"? Why or why not?

Section 32-1

Objectives

- ***Answer the Focus Question.***
- *Explain why the population of the United States is becoming more ethnically and racially diverse.*
- *Describe differing reactions to the nation's growing diversity.*
- *Describe some major changes in American family life.*

Introducing THE SECTION

As the twentieth century draws to a close, political, economic, and social relationships between racial and ethnic groups in the United States will be characterized by emphasis on cultural diversity rather than uniformity.

Ask: What are the implications of the changing racial and ethnic make-up of the nation's population?

B · A · C · K · G · R · O · U · N · D

Multicultural Perspectives

By the year 2056, if recent immigration trends continue, non-Hispanic white people may be a minority in the United States. From 1920 to 1955, they made up 90 percent of the total population. By 1985 they made up only about 80 percent. In 2020 they will be about 65 percent of the American population, and by 2056 they will be 50 percent or less.

Reduced student page in the Teacher's Edition

32-1 Portrait of a Diverse Nation

Focus: How do both unity and diversity continue to shape the United States?

"Once America was a microcosm [a little world] of European nationalities. Today America is a microcosm of the world."

This observation by African-American Studies Professor Molefi Asante refers to the growing diversity of the nation's population. If recent trends in immigration and birth rates continue, the United States might become a "nation of minorities" by the middle of the twenty-first century. In other words, no single ethnic group will make up more than half of the population. As the racial and ethnic mix of the nation continues to change, Americans face the challenge of embracing the strengths of diversity as well as the common bonds that tie Americans together.

Immigration by Region of Birth 1951 — 1990

	1951—1960	1961—1970	1971—1980	1981—1990*
Europe	1,492,200	1,238,600	801,300	705,600
Asia	157,100	445,300	1,633,800	2,817,400
Latin America	566,400	1,292,700	1,814,600	3,461,700
Africa/ Other	299,800	345,100	243,600	353,400

* Includes undocumented immigrants granted amnesty under the Immigration Reform and Control Act of 1986.

Source: *United States Immigration and Naturalization Service*

Diversity and Immigration Reform

In view of the 1990 census, calling the United States a microcosm of the world might seem like an exaggeration. After all, European Americans continue to form a large majority of the population—almost 80 percent. Yet that percent has been dropping as the proportions of other groups, especially Asian Americans and Hispanic Americans, have risen. This rise has largely resulted from changes in immigration.

In the last two decades, political and economic turmoil across the globe has forced millions of people to leave their homes in search of safety and a better life. At the same time, changes in United States immigration law and policy toward refugees have allowed large numbers of these displaced persons to settle in the United States. These factors have greatly enhanced American diversity.

The first landmark change was the Immigration and Nationality Act of 1965, which ended an ethnic quota system in place since 1924. The old system favored immigrants from northern and western Europe over those from southern and eastern Europe, while excluding Asians. In place of limits by country, the 1965 act set yearly quotas by hemisphere: 120,000 for the Western Hemisphere and 170,000 for the Eastern. It nearly doubled the number of immigrants allowed to enter the United States each year. Later, the Immigration Act of 1990 permitted more than twice the immigration allowed under the 1965 law.

Meanwhile, wars and political crises in Southeast Asia and Latin America created scores of refugees—persons escaping the threat of persecution. They were not subject to hemispheric limits, but were accepted on an emergency basis. Cuban, Vietnamese, Cambodian, and Laotian refugees swelled the numbers of newcomers. Once settled, many of these new Americans sponsored family members to immigrate under the 1965 act, which gave preference to immigrants reuniting with family.

Connections: Economics

According to the Census Bureau, by 2070 the Hispanic population in the United States will have multiplied to 57 million. In response to these significant numbers, advertisers are courting the Hispanic dollar. Procter and Gamble spent $30 million in 1990 advertising to Hispanics. Anheuser-Bush, Campbell's and other companies spent a combined total of $628 million in 1990, targeting Hispanic markets on the two Hispanic television networks, in the 145 Spanish-language magazines, and on the 450 Spanish-speaking radio stations.

In some cases, people seeking opportunity in the United States have entered the country without the proper visas. The Immigration and Naturalization Service has had great difficulty stopping this flow of immigration. In the early 1980s it estimated that several million undocumented immigrants were living in the United States. In 1986 Congress passed the Immigration Reform and Control Act. The act gave amnesty, or pardon, to undocumented immigrants who arrived before 1982, thus granting them legal status. At the same time, the act also increased the border patrol and fined employers who hired undocumented workers.

One People With Many Cultures

Recent immigrants from Latin America and Asia represent a wide variety of countries, cultures, and races. While we use the term *Latin America* to describe a region, there is no single "Hispanic" or "Latino" culture or race, because each Latin American country has its own traditions and racial mix. Likewise, as Chinese-American filmmaker Amy Lam notes,

> *"There is no such thing as an Asian American. We come from China, Japan, India, Vietnam, Korea, and the Philippines. We are as different as Russians are from English, as Brazilians are from Mexicans."*

The debate over assimilation. Greater diversity among new Americans has sparked renewed debate over whether American society can embrace a wide variety of cultures and yet still retain its unity. Immigration has always raised the question of whether newcomers will "fit in." Fitting in has traditionally meant assimilation—

THE AMERICAN SPIRIT

Maxine Hong Kingston

©Howard Schatz

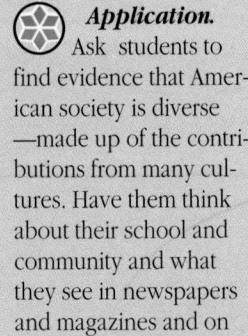

Growing Up as a Chinese American

Maxine Hong Kingston is a descendant of Chinese immigrants. Her father first came to the "Golden Mountain," as the Chinese called the United States, to earn money for his family. Later her mother, a doctor in China, joined him. Maxine, their first child, was born in Stockton in California's Central Valley, where her parents had opened a laundry.

Because she was born in the United States yet had roots in China, her childhood was rich but confusing. When she first went to school, she did not know English and remained silent, even on the playground, for more than a year. As she learned English, though, she soon showed a great gift for writing it.

After attending college, Kingston taught school and wrote about her childhood and Chinese heritage. In her first book, *The Woman Warrior,* she told what it was like to grow up Chinese American. She wove into it favorite Chinese stories that her mother had told her.

In her second book, *China Men,* she described Chinese-American men. She told of her great-grandfathers, who worked in the sugar cane fields of Hawaii. She told of her grandfather, paid a dollar a day in the 1860s to help build the transcontinental railroad. She also described her generation, through her brother who served in Vietnam. Like him, she calls the United States home, though she knows her Chinese roots will nourish her all her life.

Developing

THE SECTION

Thinking Critically

Application. Ask students to find evidence that American society is diverse—made up of the contributions from many cultures. Have them think about their school and community and what they see in newspapers and magazines and on television.

Active Learning

Making a Collage. Have students work in pairs to make a collage that shows the diversity of Americans. Finished projects can be part of a bulletin board display.

Connections: Music

Born in Paris of Chinese parents, cellist Yo Yo Ma is now an American citizen. He has played with all major American orchestras and throughout Europe.

By the age of 29, Wynton Marsalis had collected eight Grammy awards, both classical and jazz. His first public concert was at age 14 with the New Orleans Philharmonic.

(Above) In *Viva La Raza*—"Long Live Humanity"—Salvador Torres celebrates Chicano roots and the Chicano human rights movement.

The vivid colors and geometric patterns found in Indian art are reflected in this print by Crow-Blackfoot artist Susan Stewart.

Courtesy American Indian Contemporary Arts

Principal Dance Artists Hugue Magen and Virginia Brown are members of the Dance Theater of Harlem.

© 1988 by Jonathan Atkin

"One of the prime talents of our time," Chinese-American cellist Yo Yo Ma had his first recital at age six.

Painting on shaped canvases, New York artist Elizabeth Murray created *Mouse Cup*.

Chapter Connections

For information about the Chicano civil rights movement of the mid-1960s and 1970s, see Chapter 30, pages 811–812.

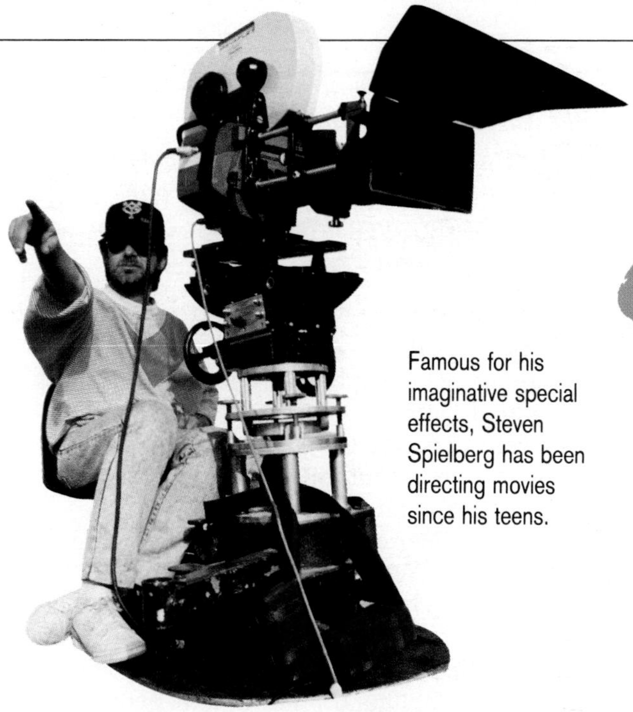

Famous for his imaginative special effects, Steven Spielberg has been directing movies since his teens.

THE CREATIVE *Spirit*

Artists

In the summer of 1991 a museum in San Francisco, California, electrified art lovers by presenting an exhibit of Chicano art. Celebrating Mexican-American cultural heritage and the struggle for civil rights that began in the 1960s, the exhibit reflected the fact that American art is as diverse as the American people themselves.

Over the years, American art has been enriched by the contributions of artists from many different cultures, many of whom have found inspiration and identity in their cultural heritage. Playwright August Wilson, who has written five plays describing African-American life in modern times, said, "What do you do with your legacy? How do you best put it to use? The one thing you cannot do is deny it, forget it—you cannot acquire a sense of self-worth by denying your past."

In this painting, Yolanda López proposes a new image of Mexican-American women as active and independent.

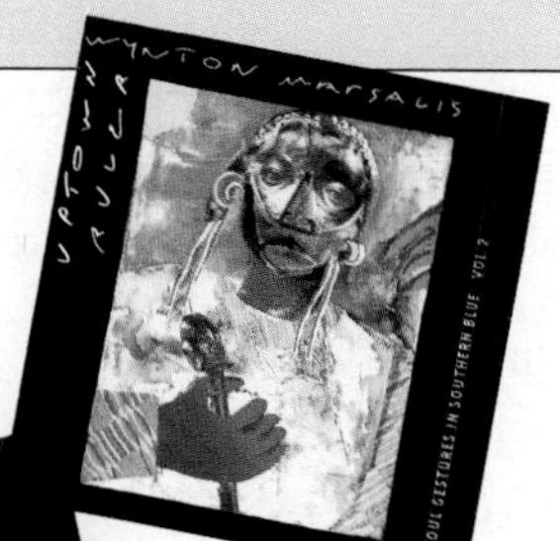

The art on this Wynton Marsalis album cover is *Ritual Dancer, Purple Lady* by the late artist Romare Bearden.

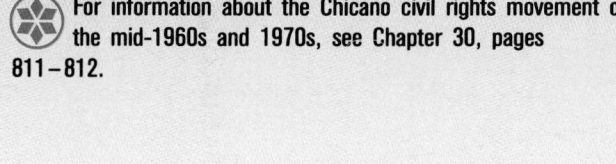

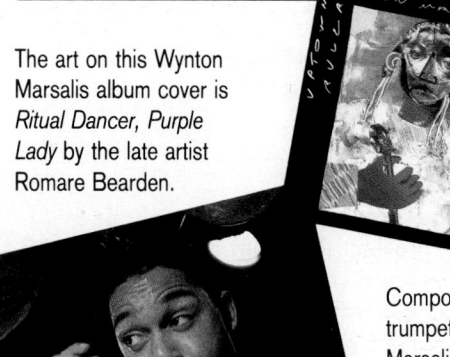

Composer and trumpeter Wynton Marsalis took the lead in sparking a jazz revival.

865

Connections: Religion

Religious beliefs are an important aspect of Native-American traditions. Although many American Indians are Christian, many more maintain beliefs and practices of their traditional religions. In 1978 Congress passed the American Indian Religious Freedom Act that affirmed the First Amendment right of Native Americans to practice their traditional religions.

Thinking Critically

Evaluation. Ask students the following question: What do you think are some advantages of being a diverse people? What are some of the problems that arise from diversity? (Answers may include the idea that a diverse nation is stronger or more interesting, but that diversity can lead to conflict between different groups.)

Active Learning

Role Play. Many "second generation" teenage children of immigrants who arrived after 1965 feel trapped between two worlds—between the mainstream American culture and the cultures of their parents. Have students role-play teenager-parent dialogues regarding these cultural differences. Afterwards, the class can note similarities and differences among the various "cultural collisions."

Reduced student page in the Teacher's Edition

A Native-American woman videotapes dancing at a powwow, a gathering to celebrate tribal traditions.

giving up one's culture to blend into the dominant English-American culture. Today, as in the past, there are Americans who believe that becoming an "American" means blending in and not maintaining one's distinct culture of origin.

Yet newcomers of many backgrounds are proving that they can adapt to new ways of life and embrace American values without giving up their culture and language of origin. For many Americans, what unites people in the United States is not a sharing of a common culture but instead a loyalty to democratic ideals and traditions. Maria Chavez, program director for a Spanish-language television station explains:

> *"I am not any less an American because I prefer to speak Spanish at home or because I would rather watch Latin American soccer than 'American' football. I still participate in our democracy and I believe in what our nation stands for, including the idea that we are all created equal."*

Signs of cultural pride. First-generation Americans are not the only ones who take pride in their cultural heritage. Americans of all backgrounds and generations add to the richness of American culture by affirming and maintaining their cultures of origin. Examples range from celebrations such as Mexican-American Cinco de Mayo and Chinese New Year to political action, for instance to establish bilingual education and African studies programs in schools.

The 1990 census yielded an example that points to an increase in cultural pride: a 38 percent increase in the number of people identifying themselves as American Indians since the 1980 census. As the increase was too big to be explained by births alone, a census official reasoned that people who did not call themselves Indians before were now doing so. One respondent explained:

> *"It was time to reclaim my heritage. For a long time, Native Americans have been told, 'If you can pass [as white], then do it.' We need to be telling our people, 'It's O.K. that you're Indian. Make your presence known.'"*

American Voices

"We need to be telling our people, 'It's O.K. that you're Indian. Make your presence known.'"

—John Homer

As Americans everywhere reclaim and celebrate their heritage, they increase the climate of diversity in the United States. To the extent that all Americans recognize the right to maintain one's heritage, and to the extent that they embrace diversity and recognize it as a source of national strength, cultural differences can flourish without undermining national unity.

Multicultural Perspectives

Some Americans endure multiple injustices. For example, Congresswoman Shirley Chisholm, an African-American woman, expressed the opinion that she had experienced more discrimination because she was a woman than because she was an African American. Women of other racial and ethnic groups have expressed similar opinions.

Global Connections

Backlashes against diversity are also evident in Britain, France, Germany, and Italy. In a recent French poll, 71% of respondents said the nation had too many Arabs, 45% said too many blacks, and 94% said racism was "widespread." A British poll found that 79% of blacks, 67% of whites, and 56% of Asians considered the country to be "very racist" or "fairly racist."

Backlash Against Diversity

However, misunderstandings and resistance frequently arise over the issue of cultural diversity. For instance, when Americans of African, Asian, Hispanic, or Native-American ancestry argue for inclusion—for respecting and embracing diverse beliefs and practices—they often are rejected. They see the white majority placing a higher value on the European heritage and the accomplishments of European Americans.

A controversy at a Chicago high school illustrates the kind of misunderstandings that can arise over the issue of inclusion. Thirty black students at the predominantly white school held a separate senior prom after none of their song requests were selected by the dance committee. To white seniors the selections were simply a matter of majority rule. "It's too bad," said one, "because it's our senior year and we should be together." Yet black seniors questioned how "together" blacks and whites had ever been. "We've been experiencing their culture for four years," said one. "But they don't seem ready to experience ours."

For Dr. Aldon Morris, a professor of sociology, the Chicago prom situation reflects not only misunderstanding between a majority and minority culture but also the debate over the meaning of integration itself:

> *"What integration has meant for many whites is that blacks had to interact with them on their terms. It is a kind of cultural arrogance. Not only do many [whites] not want to participate in other cultures, but they feel theirs is* the *culture, that theirs is very much American and what America is."*

This attitude helps explain why black students and white students at the Chicago school often ate lunch separately and went their separate ways after school.

Dr. Morris suggests that calls for inclusion can arouse more than misunderstanding. When members of the dominant culture hold an exclusive definition of what it means to be an American, calls for inclusion can prompt a backlash. Today, as in the past, Americans face the challenge of widening the national identity to reflect all Americans.

Racism: individual and institutional. While intolerance of other cultures remains an obstacle to unity, another serious obstacle is racial intolerance—especially the racism of the white majority. If people are discriminated against because of skin color, not even cultural assimilation can gain them full membership in society. Notes one Chinese American, "We're still vulnerable because of what we look like"—a comment that could be echoed by any person of color.

Bruce Yamashita, a third-generation Japanese American, encountered racism while training to be a Marine Corps officer. Some trainers discriminated against him and made remarks such as, "We don't want your kind around here. Go back to your own country." After being rejected for "unsatisfactory leadership," Yamashita protested. His case led to an investigation into why people of color were greatly underrepresented at officer levels despite a 1948 executive order desegregating the military.

Yamashita's experience reflected the fact that there can be two types of racism: individual and institutional. Individual racism is intentional acts by persons, such as insults, unequal treatment, and even violence. Institutional racism occurs when an organization's policies have the effect, even if unintentional, of denying equal treatment to persons of all races.

When riots erupted in Los Angeles in April 1992, the issues of individual and institutional racism gripped the nation's attention. The riots were triggered by a state court verdict finding four white policemen not guilty of excessively beating a black suspect, Rodney King. Americans debated whether racism played a role in the beating and in the verdict delivered by the jury of ten whites, one Asian, and one Hispanic. Some questioned whether the jury would have reached the same verdict if it had been a white suspect the police had beaten.

In a separate 1993 federal trial, a more racially diverse jury found two of the officers guilty of violating King's civil rights. Debate continued, though, over whether racism taints the legal system. Some said the first verdict was reasonably based on trial evidence, while others saw the jury as prejudiced and the beating as part of a pattern of police brutality. As for the riots, were they mainly unjustified lawlessness or rage over racial discrimination?

Thinking Critically

Analysis. Antonia Hernandez, as president of the Mexican American Legal Defense Fund, commented on the relationship between diversity and unity:

> *"Unity is the complete puzzle, diversity the pieces of the puzzle. And until we recognize every piece, we cannot have true unity."*

Ask: How do we go about "recognizing every piece"? What would true unity look like?

Writing About History

Essay. Ask students to write essays comparing the principle of majority rule as applied to the Chicago high school students and to the experiences of Native Americans between 1860 and 1890. What did the two situations have in common?

Section Review

ANSWERS

1. The Immigration and Nationality Act of 1965 ended the ethnic quota system and nearly doubled the amount of immigration allowed each year. The Immigration Reform and Control Act of 1986 was an effort to curb illegal immigration and also granted amnesty to undocumented immigrants who arrived before 1982. The Immigration and Nationality Act of 1990 opened the door to immigration even wider, more than doubling the amount allowed under the 1965 law.
2. Opinions will vary. Students may point to shared beliefs in democracy, free enterprise, and individual rights.
3. Answers will vary, but may include such examples of intolerance as slurs or jokes aimed at particular groups, lack of respect for other cultural traditions, and types of hate crimes. Suggestions for changing attitudes might include more instruction on cultural and religious differences and more opportunities for positive communication between people of differing backgrounds.
4. As a result of factors such as economic necessity and increases in the number of divorces and unwed mothers, there are more two-career and single-parent families. The two-parent family with one parent as homemaker is no longer typical.

Constitutional Heritage

In 1993 the Supreme Court ruled in a unanimous decision that people who commit hate crimes may be sentenced to more severe punishment without violating their right to freedom of speech. Explaining the Court's ruling, Chief Justice William Rehnquist wrote, "A physical assault is not by any stretch of the imagination expressive conduct protected by the First Amendment."

The ruling did not define new types of crimes. Rather, it allowed longer sentences for people convicted of violating existing laws if they chose their victims on the basis of race, culture, religion, disability, or sexual orientation. Crimes motivated by bias, declared Rehnquist, "inflict greater individual and societal harm."

Reduced student page in the Teacher's Edition

The first verdict on the Rodney King beating sparked the 1992 Los Angeles riots, which claimed fifty-eight lives and caused about $1 billion in property damage.

Hate crimes. The swirl of debate over the first Rodney King verdict reflected the fact that accusing people of any type of discrimination involves judging their motives. Often there is uncertainty because motives are difficult to prove. However, recent years have seen an increase in "hate crimes," violent acts clearly motivated by prejudice against a person's race, culture, religion, or sexual orientation.

Hate crimes range from property damage to murder. Some, such as painting swastikas on Jewish-American homes or Ku Klux Klan-style cross-burnings on lawns, aim to frighten people into leaving a community. Some people are targeted simply for being "different," as in beatings of homosexuals. Economic pressures or hard times often bring to the surface racist and nativist fears and an increase in hate crimes that scapegoat individuals or groups. In one extreme example, a white auto worker, in a rage over the effect of Japanese imports on the American economy, beat to death a Chinese-American man who he thought was Japanese.

American Voices

"We can all get along. We've just got to. I mean, we're all stuck here for a while. Let's try to work it out."

—Rodney King

The question remains how to foster true inclusion and the confidence that diversity is not a threat. The government punishes actions arising from intolerance, whether the violence of hate crimes or nonviolent discrimination in housing, education, and employment. Intolerant attitudes, though, can perhaps only be changed through education and through active efforts to make connections between people of diverse backgrounds.

The Changing American Family

Just as society's ethnic and racial mix is changing, so also is its nucleus—the family. A portrait of the typical family at mid-century showed the father as "breadwinner" and the mother as "housewife." However, increases in the number of divorces, remarriages, two-career couples, and single parents have greatly changed that picture. These factors have led to much greater variety in family life.

The number of single parents has increased dramatically over the past decades. Divorce has become commonplace, with about 50 percent of marriages breaking up. Unless a parent with custody of the children remarries, he or she often shoulders alone the tasks of breadwinner and homemaker. In addition to these single parents, there has also been a rise in the percentage of children born to unmarried women—from 11 percent in 1970 to 27 percent in 1989. About a third of these births in 1989 were to mothers age nineteen or under. The typical teenage mother receives no help from the child's father and must look to welfare aid or assistance from relatives.

The increase in the number of two-career couples has also changed the portrait of American family life. Economic and social factors have led many couples to decide that both will work outside the home. This change has raised public policy issues for many Americans. Finding

Global Connections

Many democracies, including Britain, Germany, Israel, and Japan, have a parliamentary system. Unlike American democracy, the parliamentary system has no clear separation between the legislative and executive branches. Executive leaders, including the prime minister, are members of Parliament and stay in power only as long as their party has a majority in the legislature.

high-quality, affordable day care for their children has become a high priority for working couples. While some businesses provide such care for children of their employees, in most cases couples must find their own solutions. One effort by Congress to encourage companies to provide such care was vetoed by President Bush as too costly for American business.

Another factor in the emerging portrait of family life is the steep increase in Americans over the age of sixty-five. Longer life spans have led to the current increase, and in the next twenty to thirty years today's baby boomers will swell these numbers. This trend raises the issue of whether the Social Security and health care systems will be overburdened in the coming decades.

Amid changes in family structure and responsibilities, some question whether Americans can preserve a strong sense of morality and stability in family relationships. Out of the variety of types of families, though, may emerge different forms of stability than ones Americans have known in the past. Notes Professor Maris Vinovskis, "The family is the most flexible, adaptive institution. It is constantly evolving." The same might be said of the nation as it continues along its path of diversity.

Section Review

1. Comprehension. Describe some changes in immigration policy in the second half of the 1900s.

2. Evaluation. What beliefs, values, or characteristics do you think unify Americans?

3. Application. Give your own examples of intolerance in American society. How would you suggest changing these attitudes?

4. Analysis. Explain why there is no longer a "typical American family."

32-2 Looking Toward Democracy's Future

Focus: What challenges does the nation face in shaping democracy?

Speaking to Congress in 1990, Vaclav Havel, leader of the newly democratic Czechoslovakia, expressed the challenge of democracy:

> *"As long as people are people, democracy, in the full sense of the word, will always be no more than an ideal. One may approach it as one would the horizon in ways that may be better or worse, but it can never be fully attained. In this sense, you [Americans], too, are merely approaching democracy."*

While the United States has served as a beacon of democracy to other parts of the world, Americans may never be able to boast that they have "gotten democracy right." As Havel points out, democracy can always be improved on, and the United States is no exception. For example, the number of Americans who vote is low, and many citizens consider *politics* a dirty word. Political writer E. J. Dionne warns, "A nation that hates politics will not long survive as a democracy." In short, making democracy work remains a pressing challenge.

The Problem of Voter Apathy

Some observers think that the greatest threat to American democracy is voter apathy. Congressional elections attract only a third of eligible voters, and local election turnouts can dip far lower.

Section 32-2

Objectives

- ***Answer the Focus Question.***
- *Identify reasons for voter apathy.*
- *Explain why many Americans are frustrated with the two-party system.*
- *Cite evidence that the federal government may be becoming more representative.*

Introducing

THE SECTION

Ask students to define the term *democracy.* Point out that democracy may take a variety of forms: direct democracy in a small state, representative democracy, parliamentary democracy, two-party democracy, one-party democracy, and multiple-party democracy.

Discuss why Americans must continually assess the characteristics of their own democracy and the challenges it faces. Remind students that other peoples may choose a different form of democracy to fit their own needs.

Developing THE SECTION

Active Learning

Debate. Have students conduct a debate. One side should defend the premise: "Democracy is dependent on the full participation of all citizens." The other side should defend the premise: "True democracy allows citizens to choose to be politically uninvolved."

Citizenship

Discussion. Some people believe that voter turnout would improve if local, state, and national elections were consolidated into one or two elections per year. Another plan suggests fining qualified nonvoters. Have students discuss the implications of such plans.

Thinking Critically

Evaluation. Have students meet in small groups to discuss this statement: "Bad officials are elected by good citizens who do not vote." Have them explain their answers and suggest ways to increase voter participation. Groups can share their ideas with the rest of the class.

Connections: Politics

Incumbents have a definite advantage in election campaigns. It is easier for politicians already in office to raise money to pay for their political campaigns. An incumbent can satisfy the legislative needs of special interests who in return may contribute to the incumbent's campaign fund. An incumbent can claim credit for public works profitable to the local community. An incumbent can also gain valuable media attention by virtue of his or her office.

Reduced student page in the Teacher's Edition

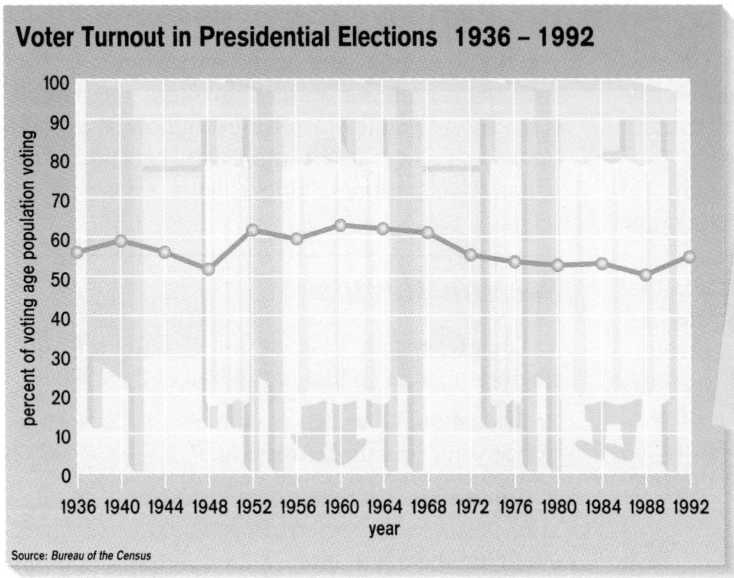

Cartoon by Richard Crowson. Copyright © 1991. Reprinted by permission of The Wichita Eagle.

Even in presidential election years, which generate the most interest, turnout hovers around a mere 50 percent. By comparison, major European democracies have turnout rates of over 75 percent.

Voter apathy can be traced to a variety of causes. Some Americans simply do not feel that government has anything to offer them. Others doubt that government can solve their problems. Some think that politicians do not address the concerns of average Americans. One elderly citizen complained, "Look, I voted for Roosevelt, I voted for Truman, I voted for Lyndon Johnson, I even voted for John F. Kennedy, the saint, and my street still isn't paved."

Indeed, many Americans think that political campaigns avoid the real issues. Instead of developing effective approaches to problems, candidates often engage in name-calling. Rather than discussing issues in detail, they pepper voters with brief television and radio appeals designed for short attention spans.

Of course, voters themselves bear some blame, because candidates are simply doing what works. Many voters respond to emotional appeals, simplistic slogans, and the most recognizable names, usually those of **incumbents**— politicians already in office. Too often, voters fail to insist that politicians take strong stands on controversial issues.

1992: A new trend? To the surprise of many observers, voter interest and participation showed an increase in the 1992 elections. Fears over the economy spurred voters to demand that the politicians directly address problems facing average Americans— unemployment, health care, and the national debt. In fact, when candidate Ross Perot paid for half an hour of television time to air his views on the national debt, he drew a larger television audience than a baseball playoff game.

Noting increased interest in issues, demand for more "straight talk" from candidates, and a jump in voter turnout to 55 percent, some observers called 1992 "The Year of the Voter." It remained to be seen, though, whether this change was simply a reaction to serious economic troubles or a new trend toward greater voter participation.

Two-Party Politics as Usual?

The strength of Ross Perot's third-party challenge for President in 1992 was fueled by voter frustration with both major parties. Accepting the view that there is not "a dime's worth of difference" between the Democrats and Republicans, many Americans blamed both parties for failing to solve the nation's economic problems. Their anger raised anew the question of how well the nation's two-party system serves the public interest.

In fact, only 20 percent of registered voters call themselves "strong Democrats" and only 10 percent say they are "strong Republicans." Needing to win the votes of the large number of voters who

Connections: Language

Catchy words or phrases can be powerful political tools. In the jargon of politics, many time-worn terms such as "pork barrel" and "pie in the sky" remain popular. Others have become obsolete, such as referring to bad legislation as a "bogus baby." Meanwhile, politicians continue to turn new phrases to rally support or deride opponents.

Safire's Political Dictionary traces the history of well-known political jargon. In introducing the first edition, author William Safire writes, *"This is a dictionary of the words and phrases that have misled millions, blackened reputations, held out false hopes, oversimplified ideas, . . . shouted down inquiry, and replaced searching debate with stereotypes that trigger approval or hatred."*

consider themselves to be "middle of the road," candidates avoid taking stands that might be seen as far "left"— too liberal — or far "right"— too conservative.

Party images. To appeal to the widest range of voters, candidates usually try to label their opponents while avoiding labels themselves. Democrats often label Republicans as heartless conservatives and Republicans typically portray their opponents as irresponsible, "tax and spend" liberals. Each party claims to represent "the American people" while painting the other as extreme.

The 1992 elections reflected the ongoing process within both parties of deciding how best to appeal to mainstream voters. Frustrated at being locked out of the White House for twelve years, many Democratic leaders concluded that voters thought their party was too liberal. Fresh in their minds was the memory of the 1988 campaign, when George Bush effectively tagged Michael Dukakis with the "L word"— liberal. Bill Clinton therefore delivered a moderate message with wider appeal, distancing himself from the old "tax and spend" image and running successfully as "a new Democrat."

© 1980 Mike Peters. Reprinted by permission: Tribune Media Services

After their defeat in 1992, Republican leaders debated whether their party needed a change in image to bring greater support. Some hoped for a "big tent" philosophy that would widen party appeal beyond its conservative base. They argued that moving too far to the right was a path to disaster. Others, however, insisted that "the future belongs to conservatism."

One focal point of the debate among Republicans was the abortion issue. Some leaders insisted that the party's best hope was to stick with its conservative position of making abortion illegal. Others, though, felt that the party should drop its strong anti-abortion stance which, they said, had led to many election losses. Republicans, they argued, could disagree on the abortion issue.

As both parties look for ways to attract as many — and offend as few — voters as possible, critics of the current system complain that candidates either avoid or only vaguely address specific issues. Thus they give voters little indication of where they stand or what actions they would take once in office. This vagueness can leave voters without clear alternatives.

Government gridlock. Two-party competition affects not only how politicians campaign for election but also how they govern once in office. For instance, legislation in Congress is often stalled by gridlock — standoffs between Republicans and Democrats who want to prevent each other from getting credit for solving problems. When the President and the majority in Congress are of different parties, as they were between 1980 and 1992, gridlock can be an especially serious obstacle to getting legislation passed.

When the Democrats emerged from the 1992 elections with both the presidency and a majority in Congress, many Americans hoped for an end to "divided government." However, the President would quickly learn that he could not expect the support of all the Democrats in Congress on every issue. Members of Congress also had to pay attention to the unique needs of their constituents, who did not always agree with Clinton's policies.

An example of how conflict between local and national needs can stall legislation was the reluctance of lawmakers in oil-producing states to support a Clinton energy tax proposal. Noted one, "It's a very dangerous thing for a Texas Democrat to vote for an unpopular tax and then have Republican senators going back to the state saying, 'Charlie voted for the tax and I saved you.' " Members of Congress must weigh their party loyalty against the needs of their constituents — and their desire to ensure their own reelection.

Backyard History

Interview. Have students interview relatives, neighbors, and friends on their views of the differences between the Democratic and Republican parties. Then have them write summaries of the responses for comparison in class. What generalizations can they make about public perceptions of the two parties?

Writing About History

Report. Have students refer to sources on political jargon such as *Safire's Political Dictionary* in order to write short reports on the origins, meanings, and uses of the following terms: *bleeding heart liberal, hidebound conservative, party of privilege, prophets of gloom and doom, redneck, pork barrel.* Discuss the findings in class, asking students how they think such labeling affects the political process.

B · A · C · K · G · R · O · U · N · D

Multicultural Perspectives

The four African Americans appointed to President Clinton's cabinet in 1993 were Commerce Secretary Ron Brown, Veterans Affairs Secretary Jesse Brown, Agriculture Secretary Mike Espy, and Energy Secretary Hazel O'Leary. The two Hispanic Americans were Housing and Urban Development Secretary Henry Cisneros and Transportation Secretary Frederico Pena.

Connections: Law

The retirement of Justice Byron White provided President Clinton with an opportunity to nominate a moderate Justice to help counterbalance the conservative appointees of Reagan and Bush. Ruth Bader Ginsburg became the first Supreme Court Justice appointed by a Democratic President since Thurgood Marshall was named to the Court in 1967.

Thinking Critically

Evaluation. Some civil rights advocates have proposed that, given the effects of racism, votes of African Americans and other people of color should count more than those of white voters on issues directly affecting the interests of minority groups. They point to a precedent in the disproportionate representation of large and small states in the Senate. Opponents counter that the "one person, one vote" principle is fundamental to democracy and that it is wrong to assume that racism is engrained in American society. Have students discuss whether minority interests can be adequately protected under the current system.

Backyard History

Research. Have interested students research their community to identify elected officials who are members of various ethnic and racial groups, as well as women and young people. Have them find out how these people gained office and what their achievements were. They can prepare reports to share with the class.

Reduced student page in the Teacher's Edition

Changing the Face of Government

While questions remain about the health of the two-party system, there are positive signs that American democracy is becoming more representative of the public at large. Americans of African, Hispanic, and Asian ancestry—and women of every background—are making their voices heard in government. The greater diversity of the American public was first reflected in both appointed and elected offices at the state and local levels. Recent years have seen an increase in diversity at the national level as well.

Greater diversity in national government has been measured in small but steady steps. The number of women and people of color appointed to cabinet positions has increased slowly since the mid-1970s, except for a decline during the Reagan years. The cabinet named by President Clinton in 1993 was the most diverse ever. Promising a cabinet that "looks like America," Clinton named four blacks and two Hispanics. The three women he appointed to cabinet positions included Janet Reno, a district attorney from Florida, whom he named attorney general—one of the most powerful cabinet posts. Clinton also named a woman, Ruth Bader Ginsburg, to the Supreme Court.

Diversity in Congress has been increasing, too. Between 1979 and 1993 the number of African-American senators and representatives in Congress rose from 16 to 39, and the number of Hispanics from 5 to 17. Meanwhile, the number of women increased from 17 to 54. Although Congress is still mostly white and male—90 percent in the Senate and 73 percent in the House in 1993—the views of women and people of color are having an impact. After the debate over a family medical leave bill, Senator Carol Moseley-Braun observed,

> *"We all had something to add. And I think it added a lot to the debate that would not have otherwise been heard or spoken to as forcefully or eloquently had women not been in that chamber."*

In 1992 more women ran for Congress and won than ever before. Here some candidates gather at the Democratic Convention.

Citizenship

The 1993 "Summer of Service" program was a pilot for one of President Clinton's main goals: a system of national service—a domestic version of the Peace Corps established during the Kennedy administration. Clinton proposed a voluntary system in which young Americans aged 17 to 25 would do community service in return for government loans for college. He recognized that there was little political support for mandatory service, largely because of fears of the following effects: high management costs, displacement of regular employees in the labor force by lower-wage national service workers, and increased competition with the military for young talent.

Vice-President Al Gore spoke to young Americans participating in a national program of service to local communities. Projects ranged from painting schools to restoring park trails.

The growing diversity among elected officials can be traced largely to efforts by fundraising and "get out the vote" organizations. Willy Velasquez of the Southwest Voter Registration Project notes potential Hispanic voting strength: "We're starting to register, we're starting to vote . . . That translates into political power." Ellen Malcolm, founder of a fundraising group that helped twenty-five women win election to Congress in 1992, says, "I want women to be powerful players in the middle, not just a fringe element."

Taking Action Locally

Although a greater variety of Americans are playing active roles in all levels of government, many citizens still think of state and national politics as far removed from them and "out of their hands." Seeing local politics as their best chance to be effective, they focus their efforts on school boards and city councils, urging elected officials to take action on local issues.

In the American tradition of self-help, citizens also continue to tackle problems themselves, banding together to rid neighborhoods of drug dealers, help the homeless, create health-care programs, and protect the environment. Action on a local problem such as a polluted stream or a community landfill can lead to pressure on corporations and governments for broader action.

Local action is a healthy sign, but few believe that the nation's ills can be corrected without ambitious effort by the national government as well. That effort must be spurred by voters. As historian David McCulloch points out,

> *"History shows that Congress acts when the country wants action. Leadership takes charge in Washington when it is clear the country will accept nothing less. . . . If the politicians of our time fail to meet the challenges of our time we have only ourselves to blame."*

Section Review

1. **Identification.** Define *incumbents.*

2. **Comprehension.** Describe some hopeful and some discouraging signs for the growth of democracy in the United States.

3. **Analysis.** Explain the meaning of the following statement: A nation that hates politics will not long survive as a democracy.

Active Learning

Conducting a City Council Meeting. Have students role-play a city council meeting, with some presenting opinions on a local issue (such as zoning, recreation, or education), and others acting as council members. After "citizens" present arguments, have "council members" vote and give reasons for their decisions.

Thinking Critically

Evaluation. Have students discuss which of the following national service proposals they would support: (1) making national service mandatory for all young people after graduation from high school, (2) offering financial aid for college in return for national service, or (3) encouraging volunteer service for its own sake.

Section Review

ANSWERS

1. Definition for the term ***incumbents*** is on text page 870.

2. Hopeful: local action groups; more women and people of color elected and appointed to office. Discouraging: apathy, low voter turnout, elected officials avoiding controversy.

3. Politics enables people to express their wants and needs. If people avoid politics, they avoid participating in democracy.

Section 32-3

Objectives

- ***Answer the Focus Question.***
- *Describe how the global economy and technological change affect the United States.*
- *Explain why the national debt and management of natural resources are important economic issues.*
- *Describe major changes and issues for the American work force.*

Introducing

THE SECTION

Have students read the following statement made by President Kennedy in Amherst, Massachusetts, in October 1963:

"I look forward to a great future for America, a future in which our country will match its military strength with our moral restraint, its wealth with our wisdom, its power with our purpose. I look forward to an America which will not be afraid of grace and beauty, which will protect the beauty of our natural environment."

Ask: What are some challenges and opportunities for Americans today that are implicit in this short quotation? What national challenges and opportunities would you add?

B • A • C • K • G • R • O • U • N • D

Connections: Economics
Two main factors in the dramatic growth of the trade deficit in the 1980s were the rising cost of imported oil and the dollar's rising value against foreign currencies, which made imports less expensive and more attractive to consumers. In the graph, the grain sacks and television illustrate that grains are a major export, while manufactured goods such as electronics and cars are major imports.

The balance of trade is the major factor in the balance of payments, the record of the value of transactions with foreign nations. Other factors are the flow of investment into and out of the country, borrowing from and lending to other nations, and net increase or decrease in holdings of foreign currency.

Reduced student page in the Teacher's Edition

32-3 Economic Obstacles and Opportunities

Focus: What economic challenges does the nation face?

In his inaugural address in January 1993, President Bill Clinton described some major economic challenges facing the United States in a rapidly changing world:

"Communications and commerce are global; investment is mobile; technology is almost magical; and ambition for a better life is now universal. We earn our livelihood in America today in peaceful competition with people all across the Earth. Profound and powerful forces are shaking and remaking our world, and the urgent question of our time is whether we can make change our friend and not our enemy."

As the nation nears a new century, two economic questions continue to face Americans: What roles should government, businesses, and individuals play in creating economic opportunity? How can the nation's resources best be used to the benefit of all Americans? Answering these questions means finding ways to compete more efficiently in a global economy, take advantage of technology, reduce the national debt, and manage limited natural resources.

Global Competition

For much of the 1900s, the United States had a surplus in its balance of trade, exporting a greater value of goods than it imported. The balance

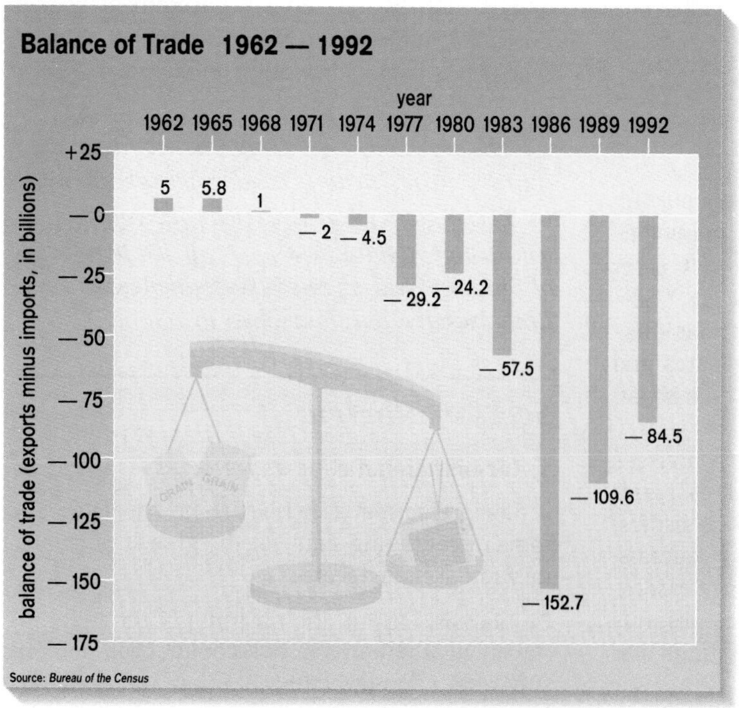

A Swiss watch and a Japanese video camera: two of the many factors in the trade deficit.

Connections: Economics

In 1991 the government began using gross domestic product (GDP) as the main measure of yearly economic activity. GDP is the market value of all goods and services produced in the country during one year, by both foreign-owned and American-owned companies. The previously used measure, gross national product (GNP), includes only production by American-owned businesses.

An abandoned steel factory and a new computerized production line are signs of the technological change that is transforming the work place.

shifted in the 1960s, as consumers increasingly purchased goods from other countries. An ever greater percentage of the economy has been exposed to foreign competition—from 7 percent in the 1960s to over 70 percent in the 1980s. The nation entered the 1990s with a huge trade deficit.

As trade increases the world over, Americans debate the effects of global competition on the nation's economy—particularly the impact on American jobs. Some see global competition as a trade war between countries, with the United States losing to Japan and Europe. They blame the trade deficit largely on unfair practices by other governments, such as high tariffs and aid to home industries. They argue that to protect American jobs the government must impose high tariffs on foreign products and urge consumers to "buy American."

Others argue that global competition is beneficial. It gives consumers more to choose from and forces greater efficiency and higher quality in production. Competition between products made in various countries, they say, is simply a matter of "survival of the fittest." They also note that increased global connections have produced many **multinationals**—companies operating in more than one nation. By opening up offices and factories in the United States, a foreign-owned multinational can create jobs for Americans.

American-owned companies, in short, are not the only source of American jobs. A case in point is one city council's decision to buy earthmovers from the John Deere Company instead of the Komatsu Company. The council had angrily rejected Komatsu after an official in Japan called American workers lazy. It did not realize that Komatsu made almost all its earthmovers in the United States. Most of the "American" John Deere earthmovers, meanwhile, were made in Japan.

People who welcome increased international trade argue that global competition is between companies, not countries. They say that better jobs for Americans—and therefore a higher standard of living—depend on playing a greater role in producing high-value, high-quality products, whether for American-owned or foreign-owned companies. Speaking at a high school graduation, economist William Felder pointed out,

> *"Don't think that a company has to fly the stars and stripes in order to be American. If a firm invests here, engages in research and development here, and creates new jobs, it is boosting the American economy. That's what counts. Your challenge is to maintain and improve this nation's standard of living."*

Technological Change

As companies and workers face increasing global competition, they must also adjust to changes in technology. New technology has always affected job

Developing

THE SECTION

Thinking Critically

Synthesis. Have students write a brief essay in which they pick a foreign language they would learn if their only consideration were making a living ten years from now. In their essay, ask students to justify their choice with information learned from reading this section.

Connections: Economics

To underscore the impact of multinationals, give students the following true/false quiz, asking whether each car is correctly matched with the country in which it is made:

1. Honda Accord Coupe, Japan (F, U.S.)
2. Chevrolet Lumina, U.S. (F, Canada)
3. Mercury Capri, Australia (T)
4. Mercury Tracer, Mexico (T)
5. Plymouth Voyager, Canada (T)

Have students consider the implications of these facts for "Buy American" campaigns. As a follow-up activity, they can research and write their own quizzes on cars and other products, further educating each other on the role of multinationals in the economy.

Active Learning

Cooperative Activity. In small groups, have students assemble photos, art, and articles pertaining to technological advances that occurred between 1970 and the present. Make sure to emphasize advances that affected the work place that students will enter in a few years. Include technologies such as electronics, computers, lasers, medical equipment, space science, and the like. Have students construct a bulletin board display showing these advances.

Connections: Economics

The U.S. Office of Management and Budget estimated the following federal outlays for the fiscal year ending 1992: 21% for national defense, 19% for Social Security, 13% for welfare, 13% for interest on the national debt, 8% for Medicare. These major areas of spending comprise approximately three quarters of federal expenditures.

opportunities—decreasing the number of some traditional jobs while paving the way for new ones. The industrial revolution moved the hub of the economy from farm to factory. Now the computer age is producing another dramatic change—a shift from "blue-collar" factory work to "white collar" office work.

Overall, the need for blue-collar labor is declining as computers and robots replace assembly-line workers. Foreign competition has also eliminated American jobs, most notably in the auto industry. Meanwhile, many American firms manufacture products overseas to take advantage of the lower wages there. A cordless phone that is a product of high-technology research in the United States may be stamped "Made in Indonesia."

Noting the effects of technological change and global competition, many economists believe that Americans seeking high-wage jobs will need higher levels of education and technical skill. "Today's high school and college graduates," observes economist Robert Miller, "will be entering a job market their grandparents would have trouble recognizing." Most high-wage opportunities will be in such areas as computer software, medical research, investment and banking services, and telecommunications. Writers Alvin and Heidi Toffler describe some characteristics of this changing job market:

> *"It is an economy whose primary resources are educated brainpower, innovative creativity, rapidly learned and unlearned skills. . . . It is an economy dependent on instantaneous communication through phone and fax; on computerization; . . . and, above all, on new attitudes and even newer (and ever-changing) skills. . . . The smokestacks and assembly lines of the past are not going to reappear. They, and the jobs they supplied, are gone forever."*

Changes in job requirements raise the issue of what roles government and businesses should play in fostering economic opportunity. How can each help improve schools so that graduates emerge with skills that companies need? What role can each play in retraining laid-off workers for new careers? How can they both promote research and development of new products for a global market? Questions like these must be addressed if Americans are to make a changing job market their ally rather than their enemy.

The National Debt

Another economic challenge is the national debt. The 1992 elections made the national debt a major public issue for the first time—tying it together in the minds of many with the health of the economy.

The debt is not new. After decades of gradual increase, it topped $1 trillion by the end of 1982. By 1992 it was more than $4 trillion. Still, Americans were reluctant to face the problem because to reduce the debt would require painful spending cuts and tax increases. Most spending goes for programs with strong public support: defense, social security, health, and welfare. Lawmakers also know that tax increases are unpopular. The cures have seemed more painful than the sickness.

A growing number of Americans, though, say they are prepared to swallow some bitter medicine. They find it unfair to dump a large debt on their children—the taxpayers of the future. They also worry that high interest payments, which soaked up over 13 percent of the 1992 budget, leave less money to spend on public needs. Another concern is that heavy government borrowing harms the economy by reducing the amount of money available to loan to businesses to help them grow.

Public opinion polls and heated debate in Congress reflect ongoing conflict over who should pay higher taxes and which government programs or services should be cut. The question remains whether Americans will make a long-term commitment to reduce the national debt—and be prepared to make sacrifices. Failure to reduce the debt may severely hamper economic growth, leaving future generations to pay the price.

Managing Natural Resources

Future generations may also pay the price if the nation fails to manage its natural resources wisely. For most of the nation's history, Americans took for

Multicultural Perspectives

Immigration—mainly from Latin America and Asia—has played a large role in the population growth of "Sunbelt" states, especially California, Texas, and Florida. In the census year of 1990 about 866,000 immigrants, 56 percent of the 1,536,483 admitted that year, chose to live in those three states. Of these immigrants, about 70 percent came from Mexico, El Salvador, and Guatemala.

Geography

A KEY TO OUR PAST

Movement: Shifting Population

Every year between 30 million and 40 million Americans pack up and move. Why do Americans "pull up stakes" so often? Climate is one reason. Most prefer mild, sunny climates, with temperatures hovering close to 65 degrees year-round. During the 1970s and 80s many moved from the "Frostbelt" of the Northeast and upper Midwest to the "Sunbelt" of the South and West. By 1980 more than half the population lived in the Sunbelt.

The changing economy is also a factor. In 1920 about one in three Americans lived on a farm. But new technology over the years led to large farming businesses that drove out family-owned farms, forcing small farmers to look elsewhere for jobs. Similarly, steel and automobile manufacturing gave way to high-technology industries such as aerospace, defense, and electronics. People tended to move where jobs in these fields were located—the Sunbelt.

Population shifts have brought more political power to states in the South and West, particularly Florida, Texas, and California, three states that accounted for 52 percent of the nation's population growth during the 1980s. As the map below shows, large population jumps can translate into significant gains in House of Representatives seats. Also, since state population affects electoral votes, the Sunbelt is prominent on the campaign trails of candidates for President.

Whether Americans will continue to flock to the Sunbelt remains to be seen. What does seem certain, though, is that they will continue the longstanding tradition of being a nation on the move.

1. What is the Sunbelt? What accounts for the large movement of people to the region?
2. Describe the political impact of movement to the Sunbelt.

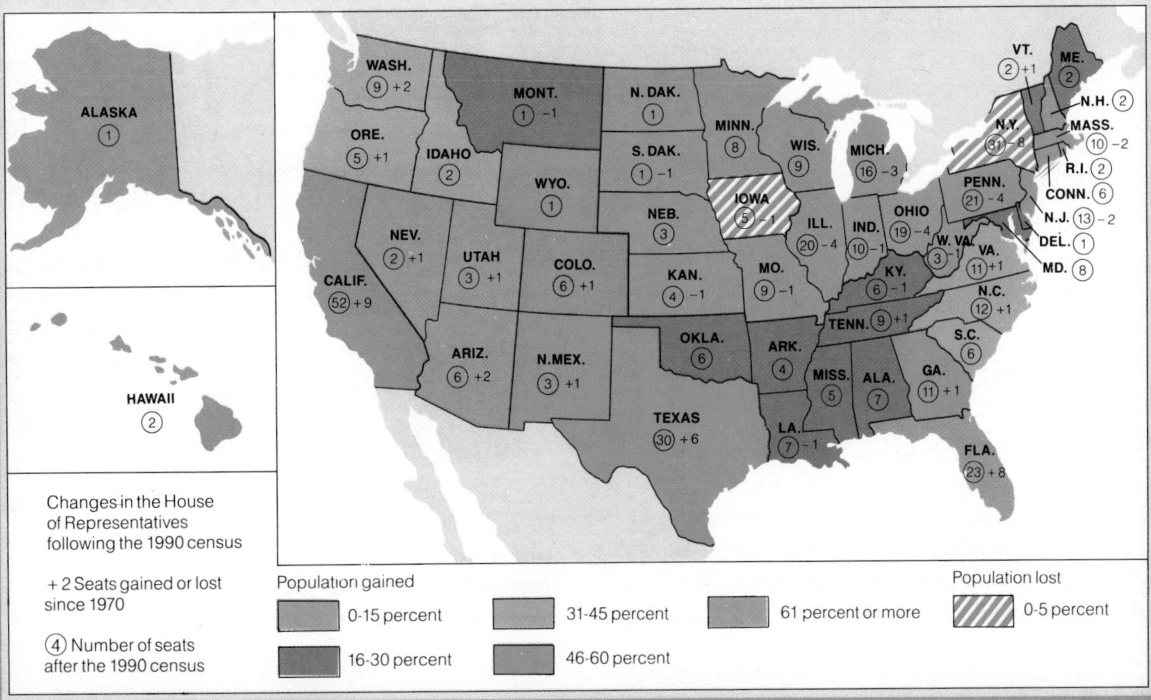

Geography: A Key to Our Past

ANSWERS

1. An area of mild sunny climates in the South and West. People find it more pleasant to live in this climate, and newer industries have located there.
2. States in the Sunbelt are gaining political power as they gain seats in the House of Representatives and electoral votes.

GTV Side 4

Chap. 8, Frame 29241

Shifting Winds: Migration Patterns Since the 1940s (Movie)

Search:

Play:

GTV Side 4

Chap. 10, Frame 33312

Where the Action Is: Changing American Cities (Movie)

Search:

Play:

GTV Side 4

Chap. 11, Frame 39466

U.S. Population, Urban/Rural: 1920, 1950, and 1980 (Population Clocks, 3 Frames)

Search:

Step:

Analyzing Primary Sources

Analysis. One of the first books advocating a national approach to solving the environmental crisis was Stewart Udall's *The Quiet Crisis* (1963). Udall wrote:

"What does material abundance avail if we create an environment in which man's highest and most specifically human attributes cannot be fulfilled? . . . We are all brief tenants on this planet. By choice, or by default, we will carve out a land legacy for our heirs. We can misuse the land and diminish the usefulness of resources, or we can create a world in which physical affluence and affluence of the spirit go hand in hand. . . . This, in brief, is the quiet conservation crisis."

Ask: How has our material abundance been detrimental to the environment? With regard to the environment, have Americans of the last decade acted out of choice or by default?

Backyard History

Discussion. Have students explain the difference between renewable and nonrenewable resources. Then ask them to name three things they have thrown away recently. **Ask:** Which were made from renewable and which from nonrenewable resources? Could any parts be recycled?

Social History

The increasing number of families in which both parents work outside the home raised significant problems for Americans in the 1980s and 1990s. Parents felt confused about how to handle their dual roles as workers and parents. In a newspaper poll taken in the San Francisco area in 1991, 84 percent of all parents polled believed raising children in the 1990s was more difficult than when they were children.

Half of the parents felt uneasy about the amount of time they could devote to their children. Half rated the jobs most parents were doing in raising their children as only average. More than three-quarters of the parents claimed they would turn down a new job with higher pay or a promotion to spend more time with their children.

Reduced student page in the Teacher's Edition

granted a seemingly unlimited supply of natural resources such as minerals, farm land, timber, and clean water. Only in recent years has awareness grown that American resources—and indeed those of the world—are limited. In large part, the health of the economy will depend upon using those resources efficiently.

Understanding the problem involves distinguishing between renewable and nonrenewable resources. **Renewable resources** are those that can be replaced naturally, such as trees and solar energy. When trees are cut, new ones can be planted. **Nonrenewable resources** cannot be replaced. Once fossil fuels like oil and coal are burned up, they are gone forever. Other mineral supplies, such as metals, are also nonrenewable. The world's known supplies of oil, tin, copper, and aluminum may be used up by the middle of the next century.

Shrinking supplies make it critically important to conserve existing resources and to look for alternatives. At the same time, many Americans have urged their leaders to develop policies that reduce dependence on foreign oil imports. Proposals for resource management have coupled conservation with greater reliance on alternative sources, such as nuclear, solar, and wind energy.

Another issue related to natural resources is the connection between environmental protection and economic growth. Some argue that protecting the environment can lead to the loss of jobs, while others stress that it keeps the economy healthier in the long run. Meeting stricter fuel efficiency standards, for example, can be costly to auto makers, perhaps leading to worker layoffs. However, greater fuel efficiency helps conserve oil, a long-run advantage, while also reducing emissions that pollute the air. Natural resource issues will continue to involve weighing short-term concerns against long-term ones.

The Work Force: Promoting Opportunity and Productivity

The nation's most important economic resource is, of course, its work force. Making the best use of that resource involves providing equal employment opportunity and encouraging worker productivity.

As the pool of available workers becomes more racially and ethnically diverse—and more female—ensuring equal employment opportunity becomes increasingly critical to the health of the economy. Affirmative action has been one measure government has used to ensure the hiring of more

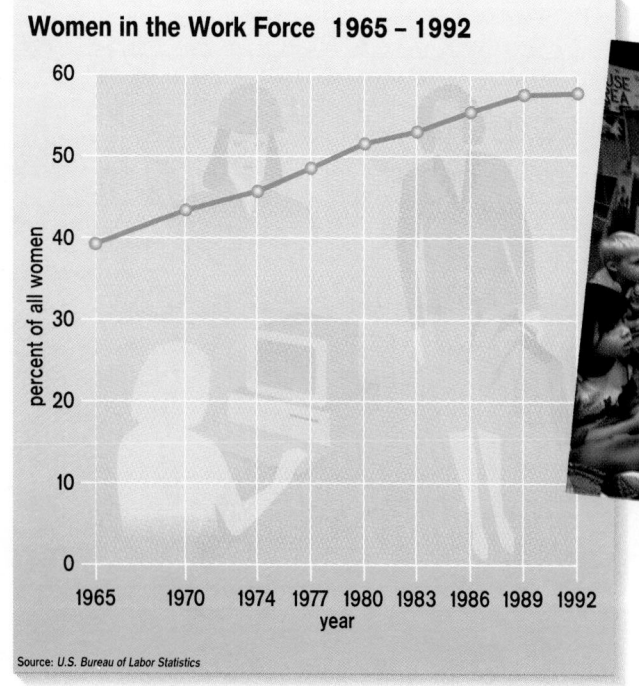

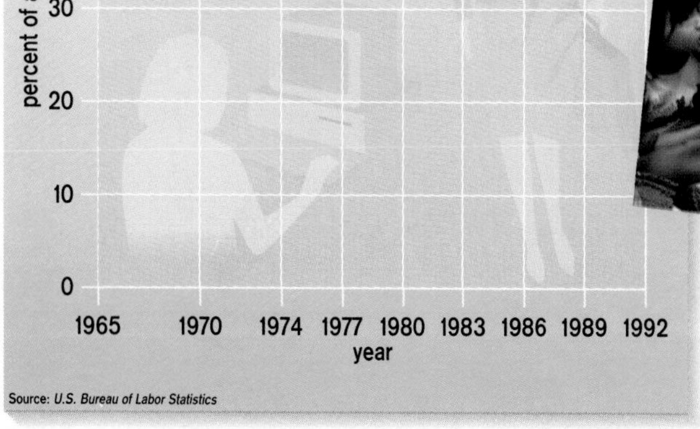

With more women in the work force and more two-career couples, the availability of quality, affordable day care has become a major issue.

Social History
Carole Leland, co-author of the book *Women of Influence, Women of Vision: A Cross-Generational Study of Leaders and Social Change,* claims that some leadership traits, such as being "inclusive and non-hierarchical," are more common among women than men. Leland's concern about the "glass ceiling" of discrimination that blocks women and people of color from top executive positions has intensified her interest in how women lead. Leland also claims that women at the top *"work harder than men because they have to."* Leland adds, *"Women should be valued and respected for what they bring to the workplace rather than constantly being criticized for what they do not."*

Social History

Oral Report. The increasing number of women in the work place has brought attention to several significant issues that have been ignored in the past. Have students prepare oral reports on one of the following topics and present them to the class: sexual harassment in the work place, equal pay for women, company-provided child-care, or parental leave.

women and people of color. Yet debate continues to swirl about affirmative action. Some see it as a fair and necessary step to "level the playing field," but others claim it leads to "racial quotas" and to reverse discrimination against white males.

Meanwhile, Americans are becoming increasingly aware that equal opportunity does not stop with hiring practices. As yet, few women and people of color have advanced beyond the level of middle management in American companies. In 1992, for example, women held only three of every one hundred top management positions at the nation's largest companies. The seemingly invisible barrier of discrimination that keeps women and people of color from advancing has been called the "glass ceiling." Furthermore, women and people of color have not yet achieved pay equity with white males.

As the work force becomes more diverse, pressure for change—at both corporate and government levels—will grow more intense. Already the increasing presence of women in the work force has led to changes in benefits policies. One notable example is the Family and Medical Leave Act of 1992, which gives employees the right to take several months off to care for children or other family members without losing their jobs. Another example is the growing number of companies providing on-site child-care programs. Furthermore, with more women and people of color in the workplace, many institutions are undergoing training for managing a diverse work force. Such efforts are aimed at creating a positive environment that will improve productivity.

An issue closely related to providing equal opportunity in the workplace is the issue of how to maximize worker productivity. While some companies recognize the link between their investment in their employees and the amount those employees produce, a current trend threatens to have a negative impact on productivity. The trend is for many businesses to hire fewer full-time permanent employees.

By 1993 about one third of American workers were hired on either a temporary or part-time basis—with predictions that they would outnumber full-time permanent workers by the turn of the century. Many businesses see this "disposable" work force as an effective way of saving costs in employee salaries and medical and retirement benefits. They say this policy provides flexibility to meet changing economic conditions. Short-term employees, however, may be less motivated and thus less productive. Robert Reich, Clinton's Secretary of Labor, describes the situation:

High unemployment is one sign of a troubled economy. When a hotel opened in Chicago, over 3,000 people waited in the snow to apply for 500 jobs.

> *"Unless people feel that they will be valued over the long term, they may be more reluctant to go the extra mile, to think a little harder, to contribute. In the same way, if the employer feels this is not a long-term relationship, the employer may be more reluctant to invest in on-the-job training of that worker."*

A continuation of this trend, coupled with the shortage of highly skilled, well-educated workers, might seriously impact the productivity of Ameri-

Section Review

ANSWERS

1. Definitions for the following terms are on text pages indicated in parentheses: *multinationals* (875), *renewable resources* (878), *nonrenewable resources* (878).

2. Global competition has been seen as harmful when jobs are lost to lower-wage workers overseas or when other nations place unfair tariffs on American exports. On the other hand, multinationals and other investment by foreigners can create American jobs. Also, global competition can lead to greater efficiency, higher-quality products, and lower prices, thus helping the nation's overall economic health.

3. With increasing global competition and rapid technological change, most high-wage job opportunities are in "white collar" work requiring higher education and technical skill. In order to compete in the global economy and maintain a high standard of living, the nation needs a better-educated work force.

Data Search: The graph shows the dramatic increase in the percentage of women in the work force, which has increased the need for child-care services. The statistic could be used to support the argument that it is in employers' best interest to help these workers balance their home and work life.

Multicultural Perspectives

In 1990, the year of the census, the United States government set the poverty level at $13,359 for a family of four. According to this definition, 33.6 million Americans, 13 percent of the population, lived below the poverty level. 31.9% of African Americans and 28.1% of Hispanic Americans lived below the poverty level, far more than the 10.7% figure for European Americans.

Reduced student page in the Teacher's Edition

can workers. Some companies have recognized the threat of the skills gap, and have even formed partnerships with schools to try to improve training at an early stage. The competition for skilled workers may ultimately lead companies to invest more in their employees and provide greater training.

Poverty and the work force. The goals of providing economic opportunity and improving worker productivity cannot be met without addressing the problem of poverty. The 1990 census revealed that more than 33 million Americans—13.5 percent of the population—live below the poverty level. The number of poor had increased in the 1980s, as the gap between rich and poor widened. Their ranks include not only the jobless but also the "working poor," people with low income from minimum-wage or part-time jobs.

Proposals for reducing poverty have included a variety of ideas for improving job opportunities for the poor. Job training programs for the unemployed and underemployed exist at all levels of government. Additionally, the federal government is experimenting with creating local "enterprise zones" in communities where at least 20 percent of the people live below the poverty line. The government provides tax incentives to businesses that create jobs by locating within these communities. It remains to be seen how well such efforts will work. Meanwhile, discussion will continue over how best to help people out of poverty as part of the overall effort to promote economic growth and ensure a decent standard of living for all Americans.

Section Review

1. Identification. Define *multinationals, renewable resources,* and *nonrenewable resources.*

2. Comprehension. Why has global competition been seen as both an obstacle and an opportunity for American workers?

3. Analysis. How does education play a key role in the health of the economy?

Data Search. How might the graph on page 878 on women in the work force support an argument for company-sponsored child-care centers?

32-4 Global Links and Foreign Policy

Focus: What are major foreign policy issues facing the nation?

Americans typically see a separation, even a competition, between foreign policy concerns and domestic issues. George Bush's defeat in 1992 can be largely traced to the widespread belief that he paid too much attention to foreign affairs and not enough to the economic crisis at home. His successor hoped that problems abroad, such as a civil war in Bosnia, would not interfere with efforts to fix the economy. "I don't want to have to spend any more time on [Bosnia] than is absolutely necessary," said President Clinton, "because what I got elected to do was to let America look at our own problems."

Clinton knew, though, that most Americans were not calling for a return to isolationism. In an interdependent world, issues at home and abroad are becoming increasingly linked. Global problems—such as military aggression, unfair trade practices, environmental threats, and disease—all affect life at home. Since these problems are not confined within borders, they cannot be solved unless nations work together.

What are the factors that motivate cooperation among nations—and what factors interfere? Confronted by military or economic threats to national security, nations are likely to band together, as in

Global Connections

In shifting the focus of foreign policy, the end of the Cold War also affected the world of espionage. While the bulk of the CIA's budget previously went for gathering intelligence on Soviet military strength, in 1993 less than 15% was spent on investigating the former Soviet republics. Some of the emphasis has moved to monitoring global threats such as arms proliferation, terrorism, and drug trafficking—problems involving international cooperation, even between the CIA and the Russian Intelligence Service, the successor to the KGB.

Meanwhile, the work of spies also focuses on the new major realm of international competition—trade. Notes one French intelligence agent, "Today's espionage is essentially economic, scientific, technological, and financial."

Section 32-4

Objectives

- ***Answer the Focus Question.***
- *Describe some major threats to global peace and stability.*
- *Identify differing views on international trade policy.*
- *Explain why it is difficult to get nations to cooperate on global environmental problems.*
- *Describe some international health issues.*

Introducing

THE SECTION

Have students explain the message of the political cartoon on this page. Ask why the end of the Cold War has presented a challenge for American foreign-policy makers.

the Gulf War when Iraq threatened the world's oil supply. Famines and disasters also bring nations together to protect human welfare.

Major barriers to cooperation among nations still exist, however, despite the end of the Cold War. One barrier is nationalism. Nations naturally tend to resist giving up—or sharing—sovereignty and independence. Another barrier to cooperation is competition for political and economic power and influence. A third barrier arises from the differences among nations in wealth, resources, and standard of living. Less developed nations are often unable or unwilling to shoulder equal responsibility for solving global problems—especially threats to the environment.

Confronted by problems around the world, the United States—like other nations—must make decisions about how to act. First, policy makers must determine whether taking action is in the national interest. Then they must assess what price, in terms of money and lives (in the case of military action), Americans are able and willing to pay—either alone, in cooperation with other nations, or in a global effort as part of the United Nations.

Promoting Peace and Stability

"We used to see a world divided into Free and Communist," remarked news analyst Daniel Schorr in 1992. "Now it threatens to be divided into Settled World and Chaotic World." Instead of the standoff between two superpowers that marked the Cold War, the early 1990s saw eruptions of conflict between ethnic groups within the former Soviet Union, in the former Yugoslavia, and elsewhere. Writer Hedrick Smith observed:

> *"With nuclear holocaust no longer a deterrent and without nuclear 'policemen' on both sides ready to intervene at once against any real or perceived threat to their interests, smaller nations and peoples were suddenly freer to fight petty wars. Not surprisingly, perhaps, what first emerged from the collapse of the Soviet empire was not a new order but old disorder—old passions, old feuds, old hatreds, old conflicts, in the same old places."*

"I DON'T KNOW—I'M A STRANGER HERE MYSELF"

© 1992 By Herblock in The Washington Post.

During the Cold War, American foreign policy decisions were dominated by the goal of containing communism. Today, in facing post-Cold-War threats, policy makers must weigh a variety of goals, such as defending human rights or protecting resources. As Secretary of State Warren Christopher noted, each problem is likely to be handled on a case-by-case basis rather than being fit into "the straightjacket of some neatly tailored doctrine."

Conflict in Bosnia. In the early 1990s, the conflict in Bosnia-Herzegovina confronted American policy makers with the difficulty of weighing goals. All sides in that ethnic conflict—Serbs, Muslims, and Croats—were killing and injuring thousands of civilians, and the vivid reports of cruelty, violence, and "ethnic cleansing" alarmed the world.

Some Americans, horrified by the human rights abuses and afraid that the conflict would spread, appealed for more vigorous action than the UN and

Developing

THE SECTION

Thinking Critically

Evaluation. Nobel Prize-winning scientist Linus Pauling has said, *"Extreme nationalism is a thing of the past. The idea that it is just as important to do harm to other nations as to do good for your own nation must be given up."* Have students discuss whether Pauling's view is realistic or unrealistic.

Active Learning

Role Play. Ask students to consider the following arms proliferation scenario: North Korea has developed nuclear missiles. American negotiators, fearful of further nuclear proliferation in the region, are meeting with representatives of South Korea, Japan, and Taiwan to try to convince these nations not to develop nuclear weapons in response to the North Korean threat. Have students role-play the negotiations.

Connections: Science and Technology

Chemical and biological weapons are a major problem in global arms proliferation because they are relatively easy to produce. The most common chemical weapons are tear gas, mustard gas, chlorine gas, and napalm. Biological weapons are designed to spread disease-causing viruses and bacteria.

The ability of modern technology to produce a great variety of chemical and biological weapons can make defense difficult, or even impossible. There may be no vaccines for new viruses produced through genetic engineering, and chemical weapons may be created to penetrate protective clothing.

Reduced student page in the Teacher's Edition

Arms Proliferation 1993

Country	Nuclear Warheads (Yes / Trying to obtain)	Chemical/Biological Warheads (Yes / Probably)	Ballistic Missiles (longest known range in miles)
Britain	Yes		2,900
China	Yes	Probably	9,300
France	Yes	Probably	3,100
India	Yes	Probably	1,550
Israel	Yes	Probably	930
Pakistan	Yes	Probably	190
Russia	Yes	Yes	8,100
*Belarus	Yes		6,500
*Kazakhstan	Yes		6,800
*Ukraine	Yes		6,200
United States	Yes	Yes	9,200
Algeria	Trying to obtain		40
Iran	Trying to obtain	Probably	300
Iraq	Trying to obtain	Yes	190
Libya	Trying to obtain	Probably	190
North Korea	Trying to obtain	Probably	300
Syria	Trying to obtain	Probably	300

*possessing nuclear warheads under Russian control

Sources: *Armed Forces Journal*, Arms Control Association

The spread of nuclear, chemical, and biological weapons is a major obstacle to world peace. Here, Russian soldiers prepare for a chemical-warfare drill.

United States sanctions in place. Stephen W. Walker, a State Department expert on Croatia, even resigned to protest United States policy. "A dangerous precedent is being set," he wrote. "Genocide is taking place again in Europe, yet we, the European Community, and the rest of the international community stand by and watch."

Unlike the Persian Gulf conflict in 1991, however, the conflict in Bosnia was a civil war, not a case of outside aggression. Thus it was hard to justify military intervention to protect national sovereignty. In addition, the chances of success in stopping a fierce civil war in mountainous terrain appeared slim, and European powers were reluctant to take steps beyond sanctions, humanitarian aid, and diplomatic negotiations. As a European negotiator noted, "There are all sorts of people out there who want to continue the war, on all three sides." Furthermore, the lack of a clear threat to American national security caused many Americans to view military intervention as too great a price to pay.

Arms proliferation. Another challenge that faces American foreign policy makers is controlling the worrisome proliferation, or spread, of powerful weapons. The United States and the former Soviet Union are not the only nations with large supplies of nuclear and conventional, or non-nuclear, weapons. In recent decades a growing number of other nations have stockpiled arms, including chemical and biological weapons. Years ago, instability in a particular region mostly threatened the security of that region alone. With the proliferation of powerful weapons, even small and less developed nations—or groups within a nation—might pose a threat to world security.

Although there are international controls on sales of nuclear technology and arms, not all nations abide by them. The largest seller is China. Although buyers of nuclear technology, notably North Korea and Iran, stress putting it to peaceful use, the United States suspects them of conducting

Linking Past and Present
Historian John Steele Gordon notes the changing impact of foreign trade: *"In the early days foreign trade was essential to the very survival of the tiny colonies. . . . After the Revolution, however, building the vast internal market more and more absorbed the economic energies of the country. By the early twentieth century, the American merchant marine had nearly ceased to exist and foreign trade was only about 6% of the American economy. . . . Today the situation has reversed again, and foreign trade is a larger component of the economy, in both scale and importance, than at any time since the early days of the Republic, about 15% and growing. At the end of the twentieth century our self-sufficiency is long gone."*

Thinking Critically

Evaluation. Accompanied by top auto company executives, President Bush traveled to Japan in January 1992 seeking trade concessions in auto sales. Following the trip, a January 10 *Wall Street Journal* editorial declared,

"If Mr. Bush's purpose was to demonstrate U.S. leadership in the post-Cold War world, he didn't succeed by turning his visit into a Commerce Department trade fair. The President who organized a global coalition against Saddam Hussein was reduced to the appearance of begging Japan to buy more American auto parts."

Ask students to explain why they agree or disagree that seeking economic concessions was a proper role for a President.

weapons research. Meanwhile, there is concern about who may gain control of the vast nuclear arsenal of the former Soviet Union.

While seeking to stop the spread of nuclear weapons, the United States does itself export conventional arms, as do other major suppliers like Russia, China, and Germany. Struggling to rebuild its economy, Russia has few controls on arms trade. Yet Americans fear the results of uncontrolled sales of arms. Until the nations that sell arms can agree on whether—and when—it is acceptable to sell weapons, arms sales will remain a threat to peace and political stability.

Trade Policy

International trade is likely to become an ever greater focus of American foreign policy. The central question is how to ensure a fair chance for American products and jobs in the global market. Opinions on the subject of trade policy reflect three major viewpoints.

One view, which supports free trade, wants all tariffs and other protections removed from products in international trade. Free traders argue that open competition forces businesses to operate more efficiently. The United States, they argue, should produce only what Americans can make most efficiently. Other goods should be imported. The result, they say, would be consumers paying less and Americans working at jobs they do best.

A second viewpoint holds that free trade is an unrealistic ideal because some countries will continue to protect certain industries, as Japan does with computer research. Those who hold this view favor managed trade, a government policy of supporting the most competitive American industries, such as high-technology. Managed trade could also include imposing high tariffs on foreign products and pressuring other countries to import American products.

A third view of trade policy favors negotiating individual trade agreements on a country-by-country basis. The United States could pursue free trade with any nation that would freely open its markets to American goods, while any country imposing high tariffs might face retaliation. Supporters of this approach point to its flexibility, but opponents see a problem with enforcing so many different agreements.

Trade agreements. The hope for freer trade is often clouded by distrust among governments that suspect each other of seeking unfair advantage. Nowhere is this distrust more apparent than in the rounds of world trade talks officially known as the General Agreement on Tariffs and Trade (GATT). In the talks held in the late 1980s and early 1990s, the different priorities of the 108 participating nations led to stormy debate. Still, many countries prefer continued negotiations to a complete breakdown into protectionist "trade wars."

Chrysler Chairman Lee Iacocca and Toyota Chairman Eiji Toyota did not see eye to eye at a 1992 meeting to discuss Japan's huge trade surplus with the United States.

Connections: Science and Technology

Research and Report. Have students prepare reports on acid rain and the depletion of the earth's ozone layer. Make sure they include the causes, effects, and potential remedies for both these environmental problems, as well as conflicting assessments of the severity of the problems. Direct students to school and local libraries to research these topics in newspapers, books, and magazines. Have students share their findings with the entire class.

Connection: Geography

One environmental crisis that has largely eluded the attention of Americans is the depletion of water in underground sources. Beneath the land exist natural aquifers, consisting of thousands of miles of underground rivers and even larger areas of porous rock containing vast quantities of fresh water. These natural aquifers are a precious resource, providing billions of gallons of well water for agricultural communities not served by surface rivers. In the northern Great Plains the Ogallala Aquifer has been tapped for centuries. So much water has been taken from it that this underground source of fresh water is running out. Only recently has this environmental problem been recognized.

Reduced student page in the Teacher's Edition

Many Americans see regional agreements, which promote freer trade with neighboring nations, as most realistic and useful. Yet regional agreements can be difficult to negotiate as well. In the debate over the North American Free Trade Agreement (NAFTA) between Canada, the United States, and Mexico, some believed all three nations would benefit from increased exports and more jobs. Others argued that the United States would, in fact, lose more jobs than it gained, as companies moved to Mexico to take advantage of lower wages and fewer pollution-control regulations.

Disputes over NAFTA's potential impact reflected the fact that Americans were uncertain about the "trade offs" of international trade. Therefore, proposed agreements—whether with a single nation, within a region, or among world nations—will continue to arouse debate. Meanwhile, the government will keep working to make global competition fair.

Environmental Issues: The Earth Summit

In 1992, leaders of more than 100 nations gathered in Rio de Janeiro, Brazil, for the United Nations Conference on Environment and Development, widely known as the Earth Summit. Climaxing many months of negotiations, this conference was not only the largest meeting of heads of state ever held, but was also the first to focus on the environment. The Earth Summit was a sign that nations saw the need to work together on such problems as endangered species, acid rain, ocean pollution, and global warming. However, it made only modest progress toward agreeing how to share the responsibility for solving such problems.

The major stumbling block was the difference in perspective between developed and developing nations. Awareness of environmental issues has come at a time when rich nations of the industrialized "North"—Europe, North America, and Japan—already enjoy high standards of living. Poor, developing nations of the "South"—most of Asia, Africa, and Latin America—are still trying to catch up. They point out that the "North" gained its wealth before people recognized the environmental damages industrial growth can cause.

Exploring Issues

ENVIRONMENT

Global Warming

In 1988, during one of the hottest summers ever recorded, Dr. James E. Hanson, a scientist from Goddard Institute for Space Studies, testified before Congress about the greenhouse effect—a threat to the environment that could alter climates throughout the world and change life on this planet forever. The "greenhouse effect" is the name scientists use to describe the global warming that many believe is currently affecting the environment.

Normally, the heat of the earth rises slowly through the atmosphere and passes harmlessly out into space. However, when wood and fossil fuels like gasoline, oil, and coal are burned, they release carbon dioxide (CO_2) into the air. This gas, along with methane and other "greenhouse gasses," traps the earth's heat and prevents it from escaping. The accumulation of heat in the atmosphere may be causing a general rise in temperature all over the earth.

Theorists warn that over the next 100 years the average global temperature (57 degrees Fahrenheit) could rise anywhere from 3 to 10 degrees. They point out that five of the warmest years in the twentieth century occurred during the 1980s, while the earth's average temperature had increased only 9 degrees since the end of the last ice age nearly 10,000 years ago. Some scientists also argue that deforestation accelerates the greenhouse effect. With each passing day more and more trees and other plants that naturally consume carbon

Global Connections

Never have international politics and worldwide environmental concerns come together as vividly as during the Gulf War of 1991. Iraqi soldiers, defeated and fleeing Kuwait, set off explosives on a reported 700 of the more than 1,000 producing oil wells. The Kuwaiti desert was awash with burning crude oil, which sent huge clouds of oily smoke into the air. Because of the smoke, mid-day in Kuwait seemed like midnight. Downwind from Kuwait, the people of Iran experienced an oily fallout from the smoke; thousands of acres of productive farmland were ruined.

dioxide are disappearing from the planet. The result is an ever greater build-up of CO_2 in the atmosphere.

Computer-generated mathematical models make it possible to predict the outcome of global warming. Scientists believe that glaciers and the polar ice caps will melt, causing the levels of seas and rivers to rise and leading to flooding in coastal regions all over the world.

Fundamental changes in the balance of nature may also occur. Relatively small increases in temperature could alter the climate in major cities. Cleveland could become a tropical paradise, for example, and Atlanta a swamp. Meanwhile, radical shifts in agricultural and forestry regions could change our ability to grow and distribute food at home and abroad.

Not surprisingly, scientists disagree about whether or not global warming is actually taking place and, if it is, just how severe the effects might be. Hugh W. Ellsaesser, a retired meteorologist, believes that the computer models "are seriously exaggerating the warming by at least two to threefold."

Ellsaesser and others also point to studies finding little change in temperature. In 1989 three Massachusetts Institute of Technology scientists examined ocean temperatures recorded by merchant ships since the middle 1800s. The computer models suggested that there should have been a rise of almost 2 degrees. On the contrary, the study concluded that "there appears to have been little or no global warming over the past century."

"It's not that we have a bad theory," says Reid A. Bryson of the University of Wisconsin. "We have an incomplete theory with a lot of bad science." One sign is a 1990 National Weather Service report that 250 of its temperature gauges may have been faulty.

Despite disagreement among scientists, many people believe that now is the time to reduce the release of greenhouse gases. "The problem," warns Beryl Magilavy, Executive Director of San Francisco Community Recyclers, "is that the effects of what we do today will not be seen for about twenty years. We cannot wait to act."

At the 1992 Earth Summit, leaders agreed in principle to reduce greenhouse gas emissions, but President Bush refused to accept a deadline for doing so. Though leaders in Europe and Japan criticized Bush, they did not follow through with firm steps of their own. In 1993 President Clinton reversed Bush's policy, announcing a commitment to reduce emissions to 1990 levels by the year 2000. As with other countries, though, the question remained whether that promise would be backed up by strong action.

1. What is the greenhouse effect?
2. What is some evidence for and against global warming?
3. Should the United States begin a program to reduce carbon dioxide emissions, or wait for more evidence?
4. What methods might the United States use to reduce carbon dioxide emissions?

Exploring Issues

ANSWERS

1. It is a global warming that may result when carbon dioxide released into the air combines with methane and other gases, prevents the earth's heat from escaping.
2. For: five of the warmest years in the twentieth century occurred in the 1980s; the burning of fossil fuels and deforestation are leading to carbon-dioxide build-up in the atmosphere. Against: flaws in mathematical models, recent studies finding no noticeable change in temperature, faulty temperature gauges.
3. Some may point to the harmful effects of carbon dioxide and claim it is better to act now before it is too late. Others can point to the cost of reducing carbon dioxide emissions and to Ellsaesser's statement that the models are exaggerating the warming.
4. Answers may include: Require more fuel-efficient cars; greater use of non-carbon energy sources; devices that prevent the release of carbon dioxide into the air.

GTV Side 4

Chap. 12, Frame 39471

What Goes Around Comes Around (Movie)

Search:

Play:

Active Learning

Role Play. Have half the students in the class imagine themselves residents of the region in Alaska where the *Exxon Valdez* went aground in 1989 and spilled millions of gallons of crude oil, which destroyed much plant and animal life on both land and water.

Have them write letters expressing their concerns and comments to the management of the Exxon Oil Company. Ask the other half of the students to play the role of an Exxon Oil Company manager charged with responding in a letter to the concerned citizens of Alaska.

Limited English Proficiency

Cooperative Activity. Have students work in small groups to collect newspaper and magazine clippings on a global problem. Have students report on progress made by groups and individuals to solve the problem and discuss challenges to be faced in dealing with the problem.

Global Connections

Americans usually focus on loss of rain forest in the Amazon Basin, where the largest forests lie. Yet in much of the Pacific Northwest, temperate rain forests are being cleared even faster. When calculated at an annual rate—the amount logged vs. the amount left standing—British Columbia is losing its rain forest twice as fast as Brazil.

Global Connections

The per-person impact on the environment differs greatly between developed and developing nations. According to the United Nations, developed nations represent only 25% of the world's population but consume 75% of all energy, 85% of all wood products, and 72% of all steel.

Clear-cutting in the Pacific Northwest shows that tropical rain forests are not the only endangered forests.

Therefore, they consider it unfair for the "North" now to expect them to pay the price—in slower development—of protecting the environment.

Debate over the fate of tropical rain forests perhaps best reflects the North-South conflict. Developed nations argue for preserving them as a home to diverse animal and plant life and as critical to controlling global warming. However, the developing nations where most of these forests still exist see them mainly as sources of income—the trees as timber and fuel, and the land as potential farms and pasture land. They also criticize industrialized nations, such as the United States, for causing more pollution and using more resources per person than any developing country.

Another problem in the Earth Summit negotiations was that most governments were unwilling to commit to agreements that might cause economic hardship in their countries. The Bush administration, for instance, rejected a deadline for reducing carbon dioxide emissions, fearing that it would hamper industry and cause job losses. Reacting to criticisms from developing nations, one American representative said, "They are trying to lay a collective guilt trip on us. The American life-style is not up for negotiation."

The limited ability and willingness of nations to take strong steps resulted in watered-down agreements on global warming, protection of species, and environmental cleanup. "The current level of commitment is not comparable to the size and gravity of the problems," summarized UN Secretary-General Boutros Boutros-Ghali. The need remains for decisive action to help solve both long-and short-range environmental problems.

Promoting International Health

Worldwide about 13 million people die every year from malnutrition and starvation. Lack of adequate health care leads to the deaths of tens of thousands of children every day in developing countries. By the turn of the century an estimated 30 to 40 million people will have AIDS. The World Health Organization reports an upsurge in the worldwide trafficking and use of illegal drugs. These and other mind-boggling statistics make it clear that all nations must cooperate to protect and promote health throughout the world.

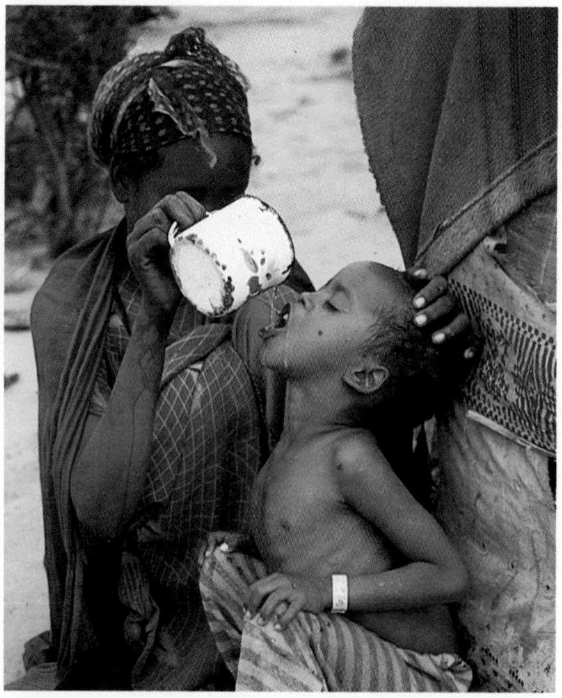

Efforts to fight famine include emergency relief and programs to increase farm output in developing nations.

Global Connections

Since 1988 the UN has undertaken more military operations than it did in the previous forty years. UN Secretary General Boutros Boutros-Ghali envisioned the UN extending beyond its traditional role of peacekeeping to more active peace-*making.* The intervention in Bosnia marked the first time UN military forces had ever launched a humanitarian mission into a war-torn nation where a cease fire had not already been declared.

The question remains, though, whether the UN has the power to bring peace when warring factions refuse to stop fighting. The UN remains hindered not only by lack of funds and troops but also by member nations' hesitation about commitment to peacemaking goals.

on Global Views

The view of earth from space can help bridge gaps between nations and cultures. Here are some comments from astronauts:

"The things that we share in our world are far more valuable than those which divide us."

—Donald Williams, USA

"It does not matter what country you look at. We are all Earth's children."

—Aleksandr Aleksandrov, Russia

"The first day or so we all pointed to our countries. The third or fourth day we were pointing to our continents. By the fifth day we were aware of only one Earth."

—Sultan Bin Salman al-Saud, Saudi Arabia

Three main issues emerge in the debate over the role of the United States in fighting hunger and disease. One is how to distribute aid fairly among many countries. Another is how to ensure that food and medicine get to those who need them, rather than falling into the hands of corrupt officials. A third is how to allot money most effectively for medical research on epidemic diseases.

With such complex and urgent problems, the need for coordinated efforts among nations is clear. One call for cooperation came from the Ninth International Conference on AIDS, held in Berlin in 1993 and attended by over 15,000 doctors and scientists. Stressing the urgency of the epidemic, one speaker showed a picture of Bangkok schoolgirls and said, "The first AIDS generation is here, for these adolescents are now at the leading edge of the global AIDS epidemic—not just in Thailand, but all over the world, including America."

The war on drug abuse, like the war on disease, cannot be confined within national borders. For instance, about four fifths of the heroin, cocaine, and other illegal drugs used by Americans comes from foreign countries, often smuggled in by worldwide networks of drug traffickers. In a declaration on drugs as a global problem, the United Nations committed itself to the goals of reducing drug demand in developed nations and helping developing nations destroy narcotic crops.

The United States and the UN

Most global problems are too complex for one nation, even a superpower, to face alone. Thus, in the 1990s nations increasingly sought to take action within the framework of the United Nations.

The working relationship between individual nations and the UN raises questions of sovereignty, however. For example, when, if ever, should the United States take orders from the UN? The sovereignty issue is likely to arise mainly over participation in peacekeeping missions, an area in which the UN has played an increasingly active role since the end of the Cold War. Should the United States be required to send troops to help a UN effort, even when there is no direct threat to American security?

Concern about sovereignty can also result in reluctance to be bound by international trade and environmental agreements, UN-sponsored or not. Other countries, of course, share this fear of giving up control. However, achieving global goals may require people to think of themselves as both citizens of a nation and citizens of the world.

Section Review

1. Analysis. Why can the post-Cold War world be described as "more free but less stable"?

2. Evaluation. Which view on trade policy do you think is most reasonable and why?

3. Comprehension. Explain what is meant by the conflict between "North" and "South" on environmental issues.

4. Synthesis. There is a saying: "Think globally, act locally." Pick a global problem and explain how that saying might apply to it.

Data Search. Study the table on page 882 and the map on pages 904–905. Why does arms proliferation pose a threat in the Middle East? Why is the United States particularly concerned about the control of missiles in the former Soviet Union?

Section Review

ANSWERS

1. The post-Cold War world is more free because former communist states in Eastern Europe are undergoing democratic reforms. It is less stable because of the resurgence of ethnic conflicts and the threat of accelerated arms proliferation.
2. Opinions on trade policy will vary but should be supported by analysis of the realities of the global economy.
3. Developed nations of the "North" and developing nations of the "South" view each other as having primary responsibility for global environmental problems. Developing nations believe they are unfairly asked to slow economic growth to curb problems rooted in earlier industrialization among developed nations.
4. Examples will vary, such as local recycling to reduce waste, carpooling to reduce pollution, and contributing to famine relief organizations.
Data Search. Five of the the six countries listed as trying to obtain nuclear weapons are in the Middle East. Missiles in the former Soviet republics of Belarus, Kazakhstan, and Ukraine are capable of reaching the United States.

Chapter Survey

ANSWERS

Using New Vocabulary

1. Multinationals are a result of (b) global economy.
2. One example of renewable resources is new trees planted by a program of (c) reforestation.
3. (a) Fossil fuels are non-renewable resources.

Reviewing the Chapter

1. Signs of intolerance range from narrowly defining what it means to be "American" to "hate crimes."
2. Some signs of progress are the increasing political participation by, and election of, women and people of color. Needs for improvement are evident in low voter turnout, gridlock, and failure of leaders to address issues.
3. Global competition has been seen as helpful in expanding markets, promoting efficiency and lower prices, and creating jobs through foreign-owned businesses. Critics argue that it exposes the economy to unfair trade and that lower wages in other countries lead multinationals to move jobs overseas.
4. Technological change has shifted opportunities to "white collar" work, resulting in greater demand for higher education. Nation faces shortage of highly skilled, well educated workers. Pool of available workers is more diverse—and more female—than ever. Increase of temporary or part-time workers.
5. Communism no longer seen as the major threat to peace and security—replaced by political instability, as in civil wars.
6. One main view favors free trade, removal of all tariffs. Another favors managed trade, government support of key industries. A third argues for country-by-country agreements, based on how open each market is.
7. Some examples: acid rain, depletion of ozone layer, possibility of global warming. Hampered by inability of scientists to agree, differing views on who bears most responsibility, and high costs of environmental protection.
8. Effectiveness of UN depends on member nations supporting goals and directives. U.S. may be reluctant to give over control, especially in peacekeeping where lives are at risk. Basic question remains: when should U.S. obey UN on matters such as security, trade, and the environment?

Thinking Critically

1. Possible recommendations to immigrants: learn language, culture, and traditions of new land; bring usable skills; value and nurture their cultural heritage as well. To people already

Chapter Survey

Using New Vocabulary

Match each numbered term with the lettered word or phrase most closely related to it. Then explain how the items in each pair are related.

1. multinationals	(a) fossil fuels
2. renewable resources	(b) global economy
3. nonrenewable resources	(c) reforestation

Reviewing the Chapter

1. In what ways is racial and cultural intolerance evident in American society?
2. In what ways is the United States today closer to becoming a true democracy? What evidence is there that more progress is needed?
3. Why has global competition been seen as both helpful and harmful to the economy?
4. Describe the major changes in the work force and explain why they have occurred.
5. Explain this statement: We used to see a world divided into Free and Communist. Now it threatens to be divided into Settled World and Chaotic World. Give examples.
6. Describe the differing views on trade policy.
7. Describe three threats to the environment. Why has it been hard for countries to cooperate in facing environmental problems?
8. Explain how the issue of sovereignty affects relations between the United States and the United Nations

Thinking Critically

1. **Synthesis**. Based on the American experience, what recommendations would you make to immigrants trying to make their home in a new land? What advice would you give to the people already living in that land?
2. **Analysis**. What might be some causes of the widening gap between the rich and the poor?
3. **Evaluation**. Does the United States have the right to interfere in another country's politics? Explain.
4. **Evaluation**. Should the United States lead efforts to deal with global environmental issues? Explain.

History and You

You have been examining three major themes in our nation's history: the balancing of unity and diversity, the shaping of democracy, and the search for opportunity. In what ways do these three themes touch your life? List at least seven items you would put into a time capsule to show future historians how these themes are reflected in our nation today. Compare your list with those of classmates.

Using Geography

Most world maps have the South Pole at the bottom. The maps below, showing Australia and Antarctica, give a different view.

1. Briefly summarize the change shown on the maps, telling what happened, where, and when.
2. Why do you think some scientists see the change as a global problem?
3. If you were a scientist being asked to recommend a way to stop this trend, what kinds of information would you need to gather?

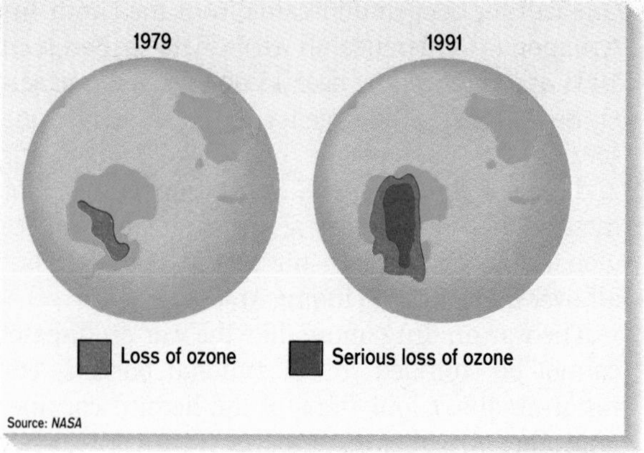

living in country: be prepared to accept cultural differences; provide training for new skills if skills are lacking; make sure job discrimination does not exist.
2. Possible causes: tax policies favoring the rich; racial prejudice; differences in education; fewer jobs for unskilled workers; apathy of homeless and other poor who see no future for themselves.
3. Those thinking U.S. has the right can argue it has a duty to foster democracy wherever it can and is ensuring its own security by doing so. Those disagreeing can argue the U.S. has as little right to interfere with self-determination of other countries as Britain had with American colonies.
4. Those thinking the U.S. should lead can argue it behooves the major world power to take the lead and that such action is in our own self-interest since such problems have a major effect on us. Those disagreeing can argue that U.S. should not have to bear the burden when some other nations have stronger economies and worse environmental policies.

Applying Social Studies Skills

Interpreting Diagrams

In the global economy, nations rely on one another for raw materials and manufactured goods. The diagram below shows how two nations and two regions are connected to one another through trade. The numbers indicate the value of goods traded in billions of dollars in a recent year.

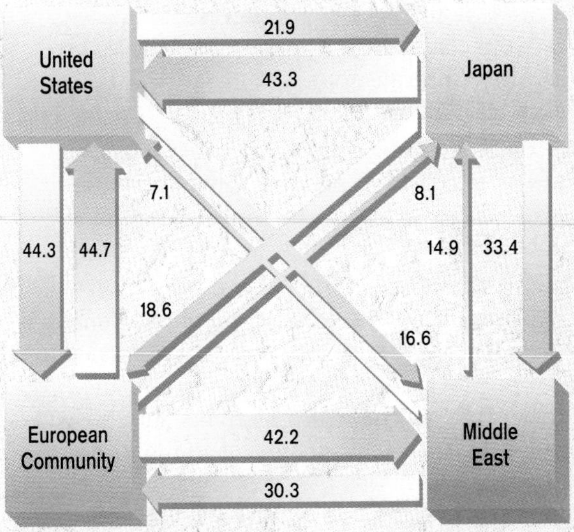

Numbers indicate value of goods traded in billions of dollars in a recent year.

1. Explain what the width of the lines between nations or regions indicates.

2. Of those shown on the diagram, which trades the most with the United States? Explain.

3. What do you notice about trade between the United States and Japan?

4. Between which two nations or regions on the diagram is trade most balanced?

Writing About Issues

The Issue: *Should companies provide day care for children of working parents?*

The women's movement of the 1970s and 1980s prompted many Americans to reconsider the roles of women and men in our society. Some mothers took more responsibility for the financial support of their families, while some fathers took more responsibility for at-home care of children.

In the years when women workers were only a small minority in most companies, day care remained a private problem. Mothers who suggested that day care should be a company concern were often regarded as troublemakers. They could be easily replaced from a vast pool of new workers. But experts predicted that the labor force would soon begin to shrink dramatically, making it hard to replace women who demanded company child care. In addition, some fathers who had taken more responsibility for raising their children began to raise the issue of day care on the job.

The day-care dilemma heated up throughout the 1980s and became a major issue in the 1988 presidential campaign. Both candidates proposed ways to solve the growing day-care problem. Newspapers, magazines, and television talk shows chronicled the national debate on the issue.

Those who opposed company-provided day care argued that parents, not employers, were responsible for taking care of children. Many small companies took this position because the cost of providing day care was higher than they could afford. A spokesperson for the national Chamber of Commerce pointed out that "not every employer is like IBM or General Motors."

Supporters of company-provided day care argue that being sensitive to the family needs of working parents could actually be good business. One study suggested that employers could improve employee morale, increase productivity, and decrease absenteeism by providing family benefits such as day care. "Provision of proper care for youngsters is a matter of supreme bottom-line [money-making] importance," a vice-president of American Express said.

What do you think? Do companies have a responsibility to provide day care for the children of their employees? Imagine that you are the director of personnel at a company that is considering this question. Then write a memorandum to the president of the company with your recommendations on the issue.

History and You

Answers will vary. Lists might include restaurant menus showing dishes from different cultures, music that reveals cultural diversity, a bilingual voter's pamphlet or handbook article about a local government issue, help wanted ads, ads and clothing labels reflecting global economy.

Using Geography

1. 1991 shows a much more serious loss of ozone over the South Pole.
2. Loss of ozone might prove to be a serious hazard to life on earth.
3. Answers may include: finding out what causes ozone depletion, and information on alternatives to processes and chemicals which lead to ozone depletion.

Applying Social Studies Skills

1. The value of goods traded in billions of dollars in a year.
2. The European Community trades the most, importing 44.3 billion dollars worth of goods from the U.S. and exporting 44.7 billion.
3. We import much more (21.4 billion) than we export to them.
4. The United States and Europe.

Unit 10 Survey

ANSWERS

Making Connections

1. Watergate scandal, energy crisis, stagflation, Iranian hostage crisis. Answers will vary.
2. Watergate: President ordered cover-up of illegal activities, withheld evidence from Congress. Iran-contra: Administration misused executive power to evade Congress. Unlike Watergate, it was believed that Reagan's intentions were good, even if his methods were not.
3. 1940s: Many women worked during the war. 1950s: Women left work world to raise families. 1960s and 1970s: Educational opportunities, divorce, cost of living, women's movement sent women back to work. 1980s and 1990s: Women met greater opportunity in education, workplace, politics.
4. U.S. aided Israel in Yom Kippur War, led to Arab oil embargo. Carter helped negotiate Camp David Accords. U.S. support for Shah of Iran brought on a wave of anti-Americanism. Carter's humanitarian gesture of medical care for the Shah led to seizure of American hostages. U.S. helped negotiate settlement between Israelis and PLO, but anti-American Arabs killed marines in peacekeeping force. Attempts to win release of American hostages led to Iran-contra scandal.
5. 1970s: Oil shortages drove up energy prices; inflation. Spending slowed; high unemployment, recession; stagflation. National deficit grew. 1980s: Oil prices dropped, inflation slowed, investors began to buy stocks, unemployment dropped, economy seemed to recover. Cost of living increased, poverty increased, gap between rich and poor widened. National deficit grew. 1990s: Deficit is part of staggering national debt, limiting money for investment. Savings and Loan crisis is costly. Severe recession.
Using the Time Line. Answers will vary.

Projects and Activities

1. Students may contact local and national organzations, community service and volunteer agencies, federal agencies, and church groups, and do research in newspapers and magazines.
2. Answers will vary.
3. Electricity may be generated from solar energy, nuclear energy, and water power. Fuels may include coal, natural gas, oil, uranium. Problems may be dwindling fuel supplies, old equipment, growing population.
Using the Time Line. Answers will vary.

Unit Survey

Making Connections

1. Why did the nation undergo a "crisis of confidence" in the 1970s? Do you think that crisis has been fully resolved? Explain.

2. Compare the Watergate and Iran-contra scandals. What was the issue in each case? Why do you think that Nixon was forced to resign but Reagan was not?

3. How have opportunities for women in American society changed between World War II and the present? What caused these changes?

4. List the major events in United States relations with the Middle East since the 1970s. What are our continuing interests in that region? What are our continuing problems?

5. Describe trends in the United States economy between 1970 and 1990. What situations were long-term problems? What factors contributed to the nation's economic problems?

Using the Time Line. Find five events on the time line that have touched your life in some way. Explain how they have affected you.

Projects and Activities

1. Work in groups of four. Choose one of the following topics: race relations, homelessness, drugs, education, health care, and crime. Do research into the nature and extent of problems related to the topic, their causes, and solutions people have offered. Each group will report its findings to the class and include its own recommendations to ease the problem.

2. Obtain census data for your community for 1970, 1980, and 1990. Consider the following topics: population, income levels, housing, business and industry, religion, schools. How has your community changed over those three decades? Illustrate your findings with a bulletin board display, including graphs.

3. Make an energy survey of your community. How is electricity generated? What fuels are used? Where do they come from? What energy problems might your area face in the future?

Using the Time Line. Working in groups of five, prepare a TV discussion program. Four students act as journalists one as the moderator, who provides a summary at the end of the show. The "journalists" use events shown on the time line in their discussion of the following questions: What was the most important news story of the past twenty years? Why? How will it affect the future?

Milestones 1969 — 1975

Milestones	1969	1975
Presidents	Nixon	Ford
Political and Economic	• American Indian Movement founded • Inflation increases worldwide • César Chávez and UFW to represent farm workers • Department of Defense ends draft • Energy crisis • House Watergate hearings open	• War Powers Act
Social and Cultural	• Navajo Community College founded • *Sesame Street* debuts • *Fiddler on the Roof* opens • Dance Theater of Harlem founded	• VCR's gain popularity • Mass-produced video games, Atari • Women enter military academies • Alex Haley's *Roots* televised
Technological and Scientific	• ARPANET, forerunner of Internet global electronic network • Microprocessor introduced • Endangered Species Act	• *Apollo and Soyuz* dock in space • *Vikings I and II* probe Mars • Personal computers introduced • TransAlaska pipeline

Assessment

Discuss the partial concept map on this page, noting that the central idea is in a diamond. The theme students choose will be the central idea of their map. To narrow the search for information, students might try the following. Focus on finding five or more developments—issues, events, situations, trends, people—related to the central idea. Review Chapter 1, which offers specific examples. Scan chapter titles, subtitles and illustrations, and read "Connections to Themes," beginning with Chapter 17.

Search for key terms. Terms related to democracy—*equal rights, civil rights, freedom, justice, citizenship, discrimination, voting, voter registration, reapportionment, redistricting*; to opportunity—*jobs, work force, labor, wages, employment, income, poverty*; diversity—*culture, ethnic groups, immigration, immigrants, racism, segregation, religion, pride, race relations, nativism.*

Scoring

To create a scoring system, or rubric, assign an achievement scale to each of the evaluation criteria. For example, you might evaluate "Thinking critically" on a scale of 0 to 4 as follows:

4—Exemplary response: many subordinate ideas; extensive web of lesser elements—issues, events, situations, trends, and people; clear understanding of relationships, e.g., main ideas and subordinate ideas, cause and effect, hypothesis and evidence.

3—Good response: several subordinate ideas; moderate web of lesser elements; good understanding of relationships.

2—Adequate response: some subordinate ideas; limited web of lesser elements; some understanding of relationships.

1—Poor response: a few subordinate ideas; minimal web of relevant lesser elements; little understanding of relationships.

0—No response/inappropriate response.

Follow-up Activity

Display. Have students create a display of news items and magazine stories related to the three themes, then discuss diversity, democracy, and opportunity in the U.S. today.

Assessment: Demonstrating What You Know

Concept Mapping

A concept map is a web of ideas. It shows relationships between key and subordinate ideas. The main idea is shown in a geometric shape in the center of the page with subordinate ideas clustered around it. Each subordinate idea also appears in a shape and is linked to the main idea by a line. A phrase written along the line explains the link. Other ideas may be attached to a subordinate idea, and subordinate ideas may be linked to each other.

Here is a partial concept map of the Cold War. Another Cold War concept map would probably look different because each person has different ways of demonstrating relationships.

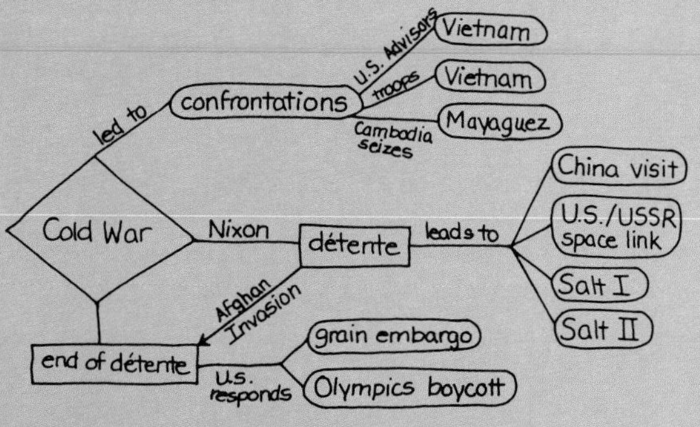

Choose one theme—balancing unity and diversity, shaping democracy, or the search for opportunity—and make a concept map illustrating major twentieth-century developments related to the theme. Note important issues and events and show relationships between them. Do some rough drafts first, to test out your ideas.

Evaluation Criteria

Your work will be evaluated according to how well you meet the following criteria.

- **Completing the task**. You complete a concept map based on twentieth-century developments related to one of the three themes.
- **Knowing history**. You identify several historically important trends, issues, and events related to your theme, based on information in your text or other sources.
- **Thinking critically**. You identify key concepts and subordinate ideas and determine relationships between them. You organize your concept map to show the relationships.
- **Communicating ideas**. You make at least one rough draft. Your final map is legible. The relationship of main ideas and subordinate ideas is clear, and connections are clearly drawn.

1981 | **1987** | **Present**

Carter | Reagan | Bush | Clinton

- American hostages taken in Iran
- U.S. recognizes China
- Bomb blast kills marines in Lebanon
- Congress declares World War II internment of Japanese Americans a grave injustice
- Iran-Contra Affair
- Berlin Wall falls
- Persian Gulf War
- U.S. troops into Somalia
- National Health Reform Task Force

- Equal Opportunity Commission makes sexual harassment in the workplace illegal.
- MTV begins broadcasting
- Martin Luther King Day becomes a national holiday
- U.S. rural population falls to 2 percent
- Census Bureau tries to count homeless people
- *Jurassic Park opens*
- Americans with Disabilities Act

- Mt. St. Helens erupts
- Chicken pox vaccine
- Supreme Court rules that genetically engineered organisms can be patented
- AIDS identified
- Plane, *Voyager*, circles the world without refueling
- Million-transistor microchip, Intel
- First gene therapy

Introducing

THE EPILOGUE

The Epilogue helps wrap up the year's study of United States history. It focuses on the Chicago World's Columbian Exposition of 1893 and the predictions made then about what life would be like in a hundred years—in the 1990s.

Tell students that the questions and activities will help them review, synthesize, and reflect on what they have learned about twentieth-century United States history. These activities will also reinforce for students the influence of history on present-day events and their own lives.

Have students write answers to questions individually, or form groups of three or four to discuss and collaborate on answers. Tell students to answer the questions as they would have been answered by people living in the 1890s.

B · A · C · K · G · R · O · U · N · D

Connections: Science and Technology
At the Chicago World's Columbian Exposition many fairgoers saw for the first time the dramatic power of electricity. High-speed electric trains, running on elevated tracks, circled the fairgrounds, and electric launches cruised along the fair's canals and lagoons. At night floodlights swept buildings and fountains outlined in electric lights. Within the Electricity Building itself, electricity was generated to operate lamps and machinery. Applications of the new technology included an all-electric kitchen, calculating machines, electric chairs for "humane" executions, and a telautograph for transmitting facsimile writing and drawings by telegraph—a nineteenth-century fax machine.

Reduced student page in the Teacher's Edition

Looking at the Past: The 1893 Fair

> *"Long before 1993, the journey from New York City to San Francisco, across the continent, and from New York City to London, across the sea, will be made between the sunrise and sunset of a summer day. The railway and the steamship will be as obsolete as the stagecoach. And it will be as common for the citizen to call for his dirigible balloon as it now is for his buggy or his boots."*

So said former Senator John J. Ingalls in 1893. Like 73 other noted Americans called on by the American Press Association (APA), Ingalls was looking 100 years into the future on the occasion of the World's Columbian Exposition in Chicago, the most dazzling world's fair of the nineteenth century.

Connections: Science and Technology

The Chicago World's Columbian Exposition introduced the world's first Ferris Wheel—and a new industry of mass entertainment. George Washington Gale Ferris, a bridge builder from Pennsylvania, designed and built the wheel in order to outdo the Eiffel Tower built for the Paris world's fair of 1889.

Built of 140-foot-high towers, a 250-foot-diameter wheel, and a 45-ton axle—the largest piece of steel forged up to that time—the top of the wheel's revolution was higher than the crown of the Statue of Liberty. Skeptical fairgoers were persuaded of the safety of the wheel only after Ferris, his wife, and a reporter, rode out hurricane winds in one of the cars.

The 1893 exposition celebrated—a year late—the landing of Columbus in the Americas. More importantly, it also celebrated the scientific and technological achievements of the United States, which was rapidly expanding its economy and commercial power and moving toward the industrial leadership of the world.

More than 27 million Americans—almost half the American population—visited the landmark fair. They saw a glimpse of the future in the inventions, machinery, and mass-produced products exhibited there. After viewing such sights, novelist Hamlin Garland hurriedly wrote to his parents on their Dakota farm. "Sell the cook stove if necessary and come," he urged. "You *must* see this fair!"

Considering the tremendous progress reflected by the fair's exhibits, the APA asked a group of experts from many fields to predict what life would be like in a hundred years. The experts were to answer a series of questions, some of which are shown in the box on the right.

Questions Asked in 1893

"**1.** What will be the state of great corporations and vast business aggregations in the 1990s?

2. What will be the condition and relationship of capital and labor in the 1990s?

3. What is the future in temperance legislation [banning the use of alcoholic beverages] in the United States?

4. What will be the state of transportation in the 1990s?

5. Is it likely that the railroads and telegraphs will be owned or managed by the state by the 1990s?

6. What changes in the structure and operation of the federal government will occur by the 1990s?

7. Will our soil and methods of agriculture improve so as to provide food without difficulty for all of our population in the 1990s?

8. What will be the status of women—particularly regarding suffrage—in the 1990s?

9. What improvements, inventions, and discoveries in mechanics [knowledge of machinery] and industrial arts do you foresee by the 1990s?"

Why do you think the APA asked these questions? What questions would you have asked? Why?

(Opposite) An overview of the fairgrounds; an incandescent light bulb from the fair; (this page) a hand-held "folding" Kodak camera used by some fairgoers; the world's first Ferris Wheel, with seats for 2,160 passengers in 36 cars.

Epilogue

ANSWERS

1. The late 1800s saw the consolidation of businesses into corporations, monopolies, and trusts to eliminate competititon. Public outcry against abuses led to the first federal attempts to regulate business (Ch 15).
2. The late 1800s saw the rise of organized labor to fight for improved wages and working conditions. Business-labor conflict had recently erupted in the Homestead Strike (Ch 16).
3. Reformers in the late 1800s urged a ban on the use of alcoholic beverages (Ch 17).
4. By 1890 the United States had an extensive railroad network, including four transcontinental lines (Ch 14). In addition, cities were installing electric streetcars (Ch 15).
5. In 1892 the Populist party called for government ownership of railroads and telegraphs (Chs 15, 16).
6. With the Interstate Commerce and Sherman Antitrust acts, the federal government established the precedent of setting rules to ensure fairness in business (Ch 15).
7. Agriculture was an unpredictable business in the late 1800s. Prairie farming was much more difficult than eastern farming (Ch 14), with bountiful crops often offset by natural disasters. Meanwhile technology and science were changing agriculture (Ch 16).
8. In the late 1800s the woman suffrage movement gained momentum, and advocates were using new strategies to build support (Ch 17).
9. The development of new processes in steelmaking and the explosion of inventions based on electricity made the late 1800s a time of great industrial expansion (Ch 15).
Questions students ask may refer to U.S. relations with other countries, education, religion, economic and social conditions of African Americans and/or Indians, immigration, and environmental issues.

Linking Past and Present

Research. Have students work in small groups. Each group will research and answer the questions about one or two of the predictions on pages 894 and 895 and then report to the class.

You may also want students to find out more about the people who made the predictions. The best source of brief biographical sketches is *Today Then: America's Best Minds Look 100 Years into the Future on the Occasion of the 1893 World's Columbian Exposition*, compiled and introduced by Dave Walter, American & World Geographic Publishing, 1992.

Analyzing Primary Sources

Predictions. Have students compare Walter Wellman's prediction about air travel on page 895 with that of John J. Ingalls on page 892. How do the predictions differ? **(Ingalls predicts air travel by balloon; Wellman, by airplane.)** Whose prediction do students think was most believable in 1893? Why?

Social History

In the late 1800s news-hungry Americans relied primarily on magazines and newspapers. One of the most widespread newspaper forms was syndicated copy—preset columns of news, humor, and special features provided by national syndicates such as the American Press Association. By using so-called "ready-print," newspaper publishers were able to offer a wider variety of materials to readers at a lower cost than if they had to set the type themselves. One effect was that Americans in all parts of the country were exposed to the same information and features.

THE HISTORY OF THE FUTURE

From the Past to the Present

From across the nation came answers to the questions asked by the American Press Association. Politicians, poets, business people, scientists, ministers, journalists—all looked boldly into the future and predicted what life would be like 100 years hence. For eleven weeks, the APA ran the predictions in its "America in the 1990s" series in newspapers across the country.

Reading these predictions now is like stepping back in time. In them we see not only the predictors' hopes and dreams, but also their assessment of the time in which they were living and their concerns about the future.

Answer the following questions about each prediction. Information in your textbook will help you. Give specific examples to support your answers.

1. What event, idea, or invention might have prompted the prediction?

2. What hope or concern seems to underlie the prediction?

3. Did the prediction come true? Fully? Partly? Not at all?

4. If the prediction did not come true, why not?

Based on your study of the 1893 predictions, write a short paragraph describing the difficulties of making realistic forecasts about the future.

> *Each reasonably well-to-do man (and there will be lots of them in 1993) will have a telephote in his residence. By means of this device, the entertainment at any place of amusement in that city may be seen as well as heard.*
>
> —Octavus Cohen, founder of *Charleston Daily World*

> *'Thought waves' go over this country with astonishing rapidity How much truer will it be 100 years hence, when to the mail, and the telegraph, and the railway, and the stagecoach are added postal telegraphy, electric railways, long-distance and short-distance telephoning . . . and heaven knows what other inventions?*
>
> —John W. Noble, Secretary of the Interior

> *Undoubtedly, in the twentieth century, the United States will take its place of destiny as pre-eminent among the governments of the world.*
>
> —Chauncey M. Depew, lawyer

> *Before the middle of the twentieth century, the increasing frequency of summer droughts will confront the farms of our middle states with . . . ruin.*
>
> —Felix L. Oswald, naturalist

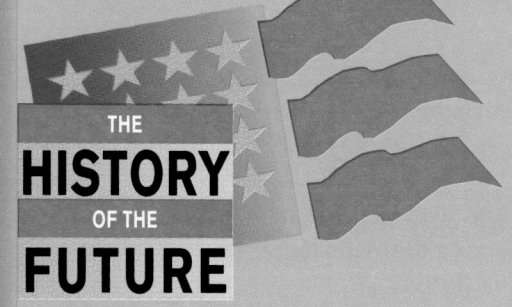

Epilogue Answers

1. Cohen prediction: Answers may include invention of telephone, phonograph, and/or motion picture camera (Ch 15). He is concerned with spread of theater, music. Prediction came true in part with TV (Ch 26).
2. Noble prediction: Answers may include production of electricity and/or invention of telephone (Ch 15). He is concerned with improving communication. Prediction came true with air travel, radio and TV, fax transmission, etc. (Chs 20, 26).
3. Depew prediction: Answers may include industrial expansion (Ch 15), commercial and naval expansion (Ch 18), and government intervention in economy (Ch 15). Answers may include concern with expansion and spread of democracy (Ch 18). Prediction came true (Chs 23, 24).
4. Oswald prediction: Answers may include population growth in prairie states and nature of prairie farming (Ch 14), and focus on cash crops (Ch 16). He is concerned with effects of large-scale farming. Prediction came true in 1930s (Ch 22).
5. Carty prediction is based on production of electricity (Ch 15). He is concerned with use of electricity to improve living and working conditions. Prediction came true in cities and in rural areas (Ch 22).
6. Wilcox prediction: Answers may include growth of women's rights movement (Ch 17). She thinks actions of women affect behavior of their children. Prediction came true only in part; some women have gained financial independence (Chs 20, 24, 26, 30), but theft and burglary are still serious social problems.
7. Lease prediction: Answers may include production of electricity and improvements in transportation (Ch 15). She hopes to use electricity for travel and space exploration. Although "Sunday trips to moon" are still in the future, prediction came true in part with trains, streetcars, motor vehicles, and ships, and electronic devices used on airplanes and space vehicles.
8. Wellman prediction: Answers may include production of electricity and engines (Ch 15). He is concerned with transportation. The prediction came true in that airplanes supplanted balloons; he was wrong in thinking they would not be in universal, commercial use, which they are (Chs 15, 20).
9. Brock prediction: Answers may include movement in late 1800s to ban alcoholic beverages. Answers may include that use of liquor causes crime and poverty. The prediction did not come true. Education did not end drinking, nor did prohibition (Ch 20).

Difficulties of making realistic forecasts may include: basing predictions on hopes rather than on how things really are, lack of adequate knowledge, and extrapolating beyond bounds of current information.

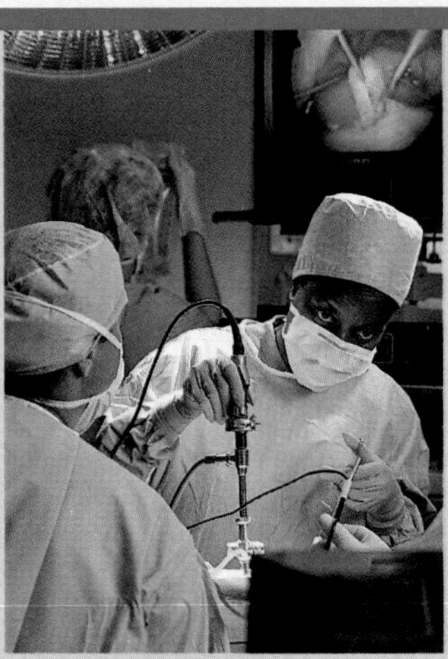

"We may reasonably expect to see, at least in the cities, electricity used generally for heating purposes . . . . It will also be used for lighting, I think, very generally."

—John L. Carty, engineer

"Woman will be financially independent of man, and this will materially lessen crime. No longer obliged to rifle her husband's pockets for money, she will not give birth to kleptomaniacs or thieves."

—Ella Wheeler Wilcox, poet

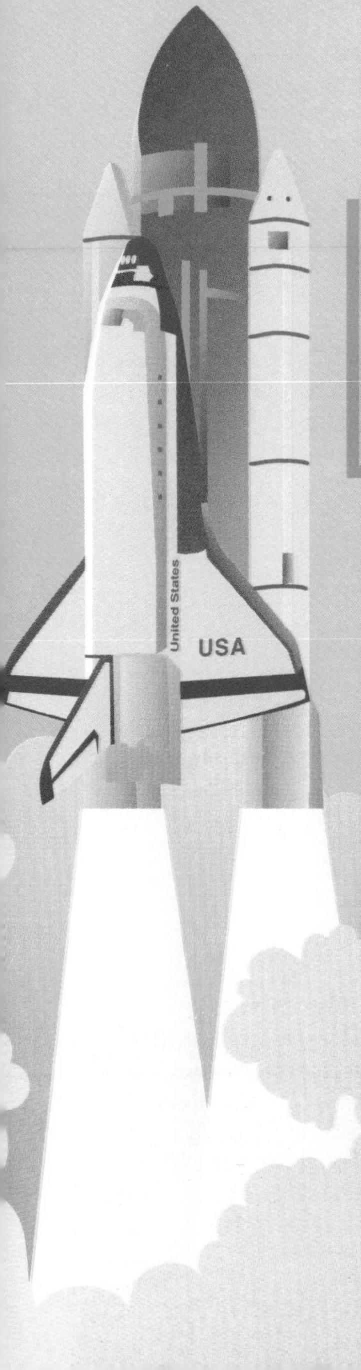

"We will travel over land and water and through the air by means of electricity. We will hold communication with the inhabitants of other planets, and Sunday excursions to the moon will not excite comment."

—Mary E. Lease, Populist leader

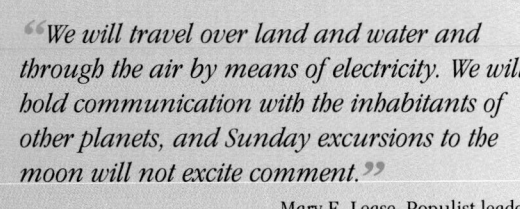

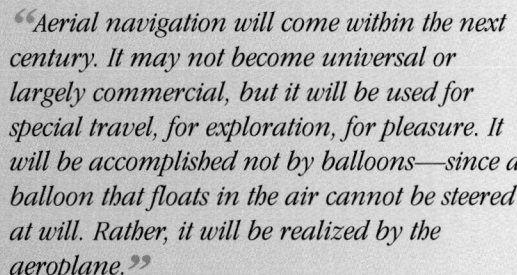

"Aerial navigation will come within the next century. It may not become universal or largely commercial, but it will be used for special travel, for exploration, for pleasure. It will be accomplished not by balloons—since a balloon that floats in the air cannot be steered at will. Rather, it will be realized by the aeroplane."

—Walter Wellman, journalist

"The people . . . will have become educated to such an extent that the vice of intemperance will largely cease. Saloons or public drinking places will probably no longer exist."

—Sidney G. Brock, Treasury Department

Predicting the Future

In this last section of the Epilogue, questions and alternative assessment activities direct students to synthesize what they have learned in their study of United States history in order to make predictions for the next century.

Have students work in groups of three or four to research, answer the questions, and complete the activities for one prediction project and then report to the class. For the final activity, "Plan a Fair for the New Century," you may want each group to work independently, or you may assign tasks under 1, 2, and 3 to different groups and have students complete 4, the final task, individually.

Advise students that their work will be evaluated according to how well they meet specific criteria (see below). For examples of how to create a scoring system for the evaluation criteria, see the teaching notes for "Assessment: Demonstrating What You Know" in the Unit Surveys.

Evaluation Criteria: Population

- **Completing the task.** Your group makes a line graph projecting the nation's population up to 2999.
- **Knowing history.** You accurately identify factors that cause population increases and decreases based on information in the text.
- **Thinking critically.** You make reasonable predictions about future population change based on information in the text and other information you may gather. You make reasoned judgments about the effect of population increases on the quality of life.
- **Communicating ideas.** You make at least one rough draft. Your final graph is legible. You make use of such devices as design, lettering, and color to help viewers understand the information.

Evaluation Criteria: Communication

- **Completing the task.** Your group writes questions for a class survey, carries it out, and records the results.
- **Knowing history.** You accurately identify significant technological developments in communication based on information in the text.

THE HISTORY OF THE FUTURE

Predicting the Future

Henry Adams, a leading historian, visited the World's Columbian Exposition twice. Later he wrote, "Chicago asked in 1893 for the first time the question whether the American people knew where they were driving." Today, as the twentieth century draws to a close, where do you think the American people are heading? What do you think life will be like in the next century?

The following activities will help you to reflect on current national as well as global developments and then to make predictions about the future. Use the graphs here together with information in your textbook to answer the questions.

Population

In 1893 labor leader Terence V. Powderly predicted that 300 million Americans "will in 1993 celebrate the landing of Columbus." In fact, Powderly overestimated the nation's future population growth. • What factors in the United States and in other countries cause our population to increase or decrease? Which factors seem to be dominant now? • Create a line graph projecting the nation's population up to 2999. • Predict how population change will affect the quality of our lives.

Communication

In the 1890s telephone systems created instant communication; within a century, interconnected computer networks were providing instant information as well. • Describe the growth of Internet, the largest network, which interconnects university, business, military, and science networks all over the world. • Conduct a survey in class to determine who uses computers. Do classmates think the impact of computers has been mainly positive or mainly negative. Why? • What do you think will be the next wave of technology? Describe its effects.

COMPUTERS REGISTERED ON INTERNET

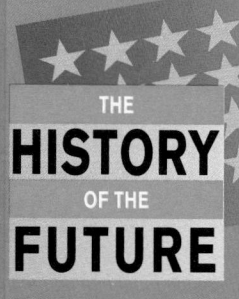

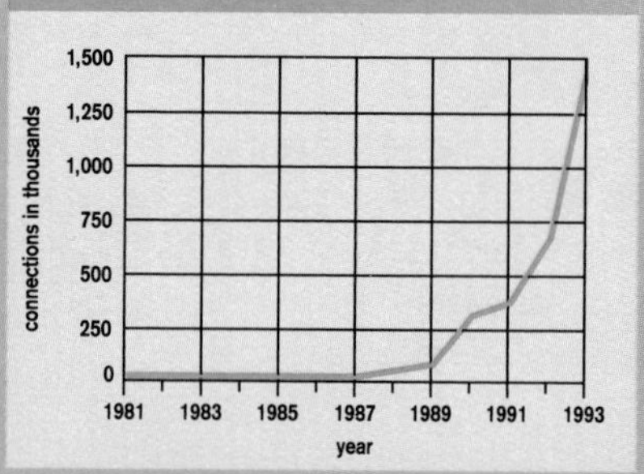

Source: SRI International

World Power

In 1893 Treasury official Asa C. Matthews predicted, "Isolated to some degree from the remainder of the world, we shall have little danger of entangling alliances or of troublesome contact." Matthews was far off the mark, for the United States went on to become a world power. • The graph on the right shows economic power. What other factors make a nation powerful? • Draw a map of the world and use colors to highlight the countries you think will be powerful in the future. Use different colors to show the kind or kinds of power you predict that each of those nations will have, and explain the colors in a legend.

- **Thinking critically.** You draw reasonable conclusions about the growth of Internet based on analysis of the graph. You make reasonable predictions about future developments in communication based on analysis of the graph and information in the text.
- **Communicating ideas.** Your written or oral report on the class survey is well organized. Your written or oral prediction is well organized, and connections between historical information and predictions are clearly drawn.

Evaluation Criteria: World Power

- **Completing the task.** Your group makes a world map, using different colors to highlight future powerful nations and explaining the kinds of power represented by the colors in a legend. (The geography supplement in the Teacher's Resource Package has outline world maps on pages 75 and 76).
- **Knowing history.** You accurately identify powerful nations today and create reasonable criteria for future world power (examples: economic power, military forces, state-of-the-art weapons, power of national ideals, power of cultural influences) based on information in the text.
- **Thinking critically.** You make reasonable predictions about the future power of countries based on your criteria and on information in the text.
- **Communicating ideas.** You make at least one rough draft. Your final map is legible. You make use of such devices as design, lettering, and color to help viewers understand the information.

Evaluation Criteria: Human Rights

- **Completing the task.** Your group makes a time line of major steps toward ending discrimination and segregation from 1893 to 1993 and projecting it into the future.
- **Knowing history.** You accurately identify goals in the struggle for equal rights and the significant events related to them based on information in the text.
- **Thinking critically.** You make plausible predictions based on analysis of historical information. You support your predictions with reasons based on evidence.
- **Communicating ideas.** Predictions of events and issues are clear and are

(continued on page 898)

UNITED STATES POPULATION 1890–1990

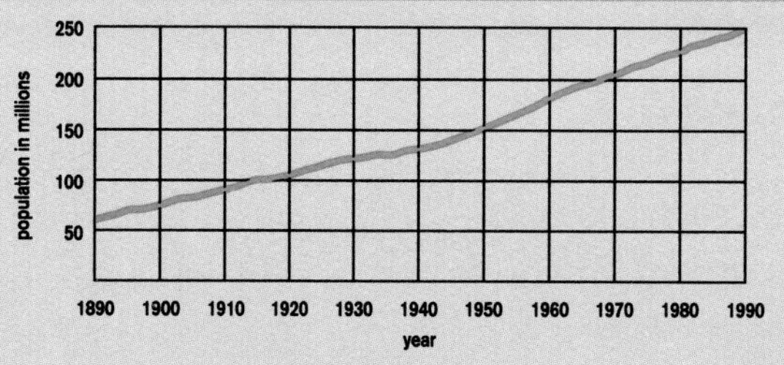

Sources: *Historical Statistics of the United States, U.S. Statistical Abstract*

BIRTHS AND IMMIGRATION 1890–1990

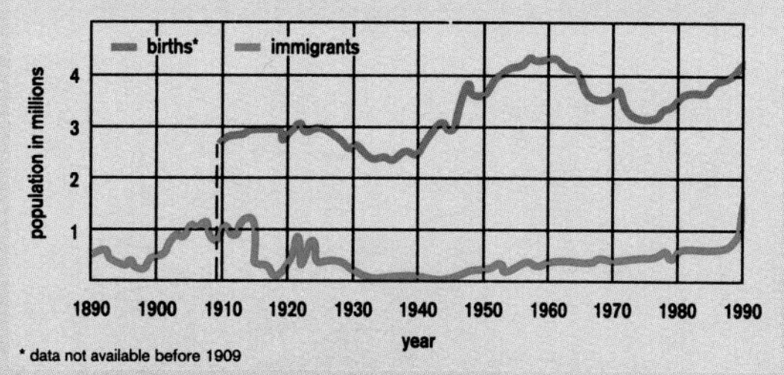

* data not available before 1909

Sources: *Historical Statistics of the United States, U.S. Statistical Abstract*

Human Rights

"We will take our stand on the solidarity of humanity, the oneness of life, and the . . . injustice of all special favoritisms, whether of sex, race, country, or condition. If one link of the chain is broken, the chain is broken."

—Anna Julia Cooper, Colored Women's League

Anna Julia Cooper made this stirring declaration at the World's Columbian Exposition, protesting the racial discrimination and segregation practiced there, as in much of the nation in the late 1890s. • Make a time line of events between 1893 and 1993 that marked major steps toward ending discrimination and segregation. • Project the time line into the future, predicting what will happen in the struggle for human rights. Consider actions by individuals, groups, and government.

Plan a Fair for the New Century

In 1893 President Grover Cleveland called fairs "the timekeepers of progress." Plan a fair that will encourage people to think about the next century.

1. Make plans for three displays to show scientific, technological, and cultural achievements. What can you show in each display to get people thinking about the future?
2. Make a poster that will create widespread interest in the fair and make people want to see it.
3. Write questions to use for making predictions about the future. Include economic, political, and social aspects of life in the United States. List six to ten Americans you would ask to make predictions and explain the reasons for your choices.
4. Write your own predictions for the future based on the questions.

IMPORTS AND EXPORTS OF MAJOR TRADING NATIONS 1970, 1980, 1990

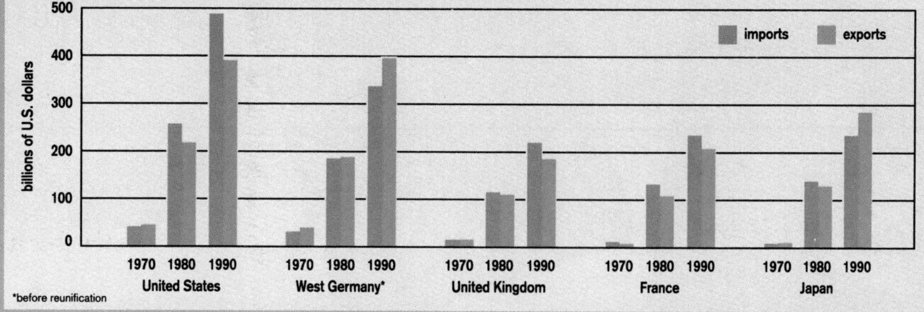

*before reunification

Sources: *United Nations Statistical Yearbook, U.S. Statistical Abstract*

Information and assistance provided by Professor Donald L. Miller, Department of History, Lafayette College, Easton, Pennsylvania.

(continued from page 897)

based on historical information in the text.

Evaluation Criteria: Plan a Fair for the New Century

- **Completing the task.** Your group plans scientific, technological, and/or cultural displays; makes a poster to create widespread interest in the fair; writes questions to guide prediction-making; chooses predictors; and writes predictions for the future.
- **Knowing history.** The items your group selected for the displays are related to the topics and are appropriate to the time period and the purpose. The poster is historically accurate, based on pictures and information in the text. The questions you write and the Americans you choose to make predictions are appropriate to the topics and the time period. You make reasonable predictions about the future, based on information in the text.
- **Thinking critically.** You explain clearly how each item in the displays relates to one of the topics. Your poster shows insight about how to appeal to the general public. You convincingly justify your choice of people to make predictions. You make reasonable predictions based on analysis of historical information.
- **Communicating ideas.** You plan displays that capture the interest of viewers. You take into consideration the purpose of the poster, and you produce clear, bold images. You write your predictions clearly and support them with convincing evidence.

Reference Center

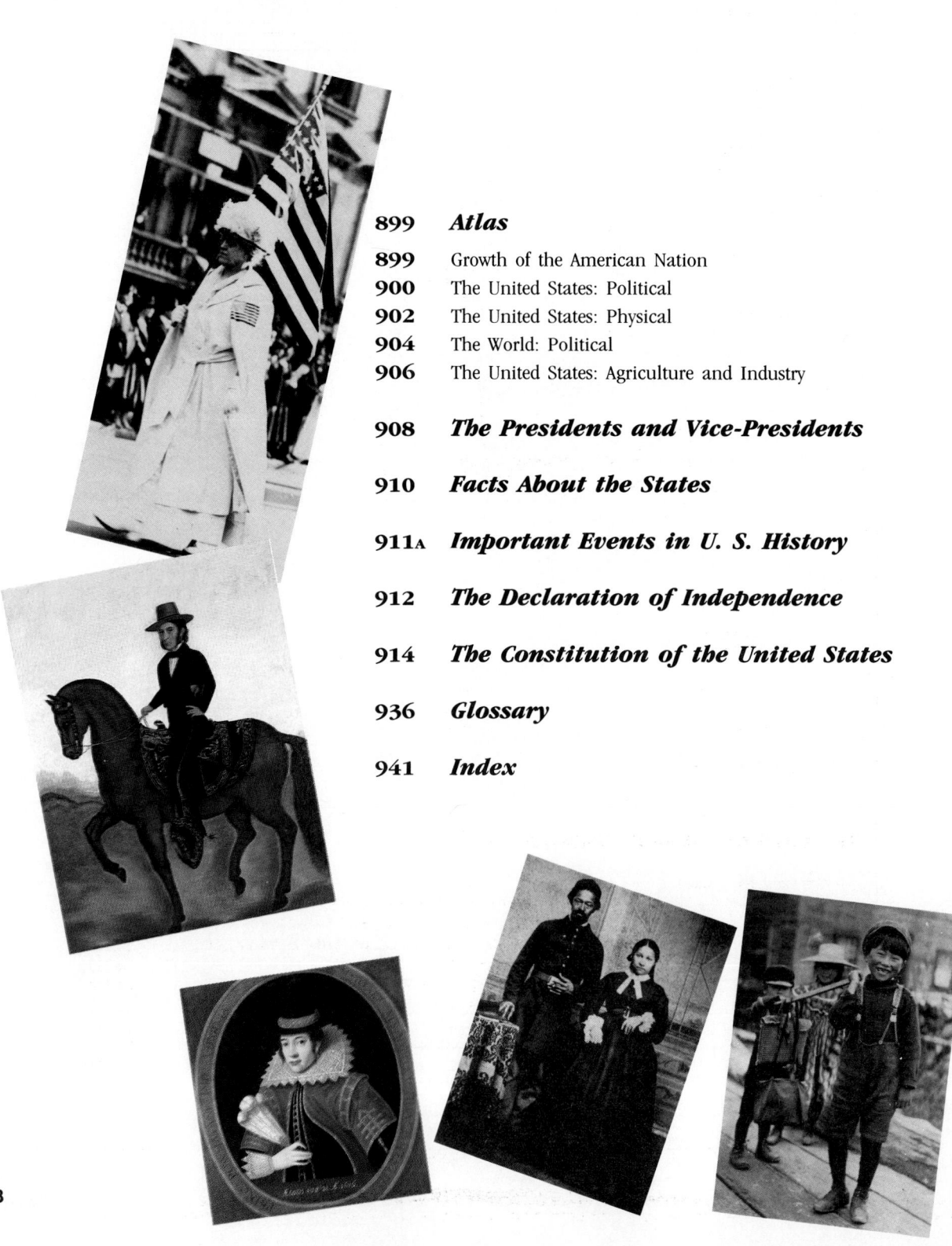

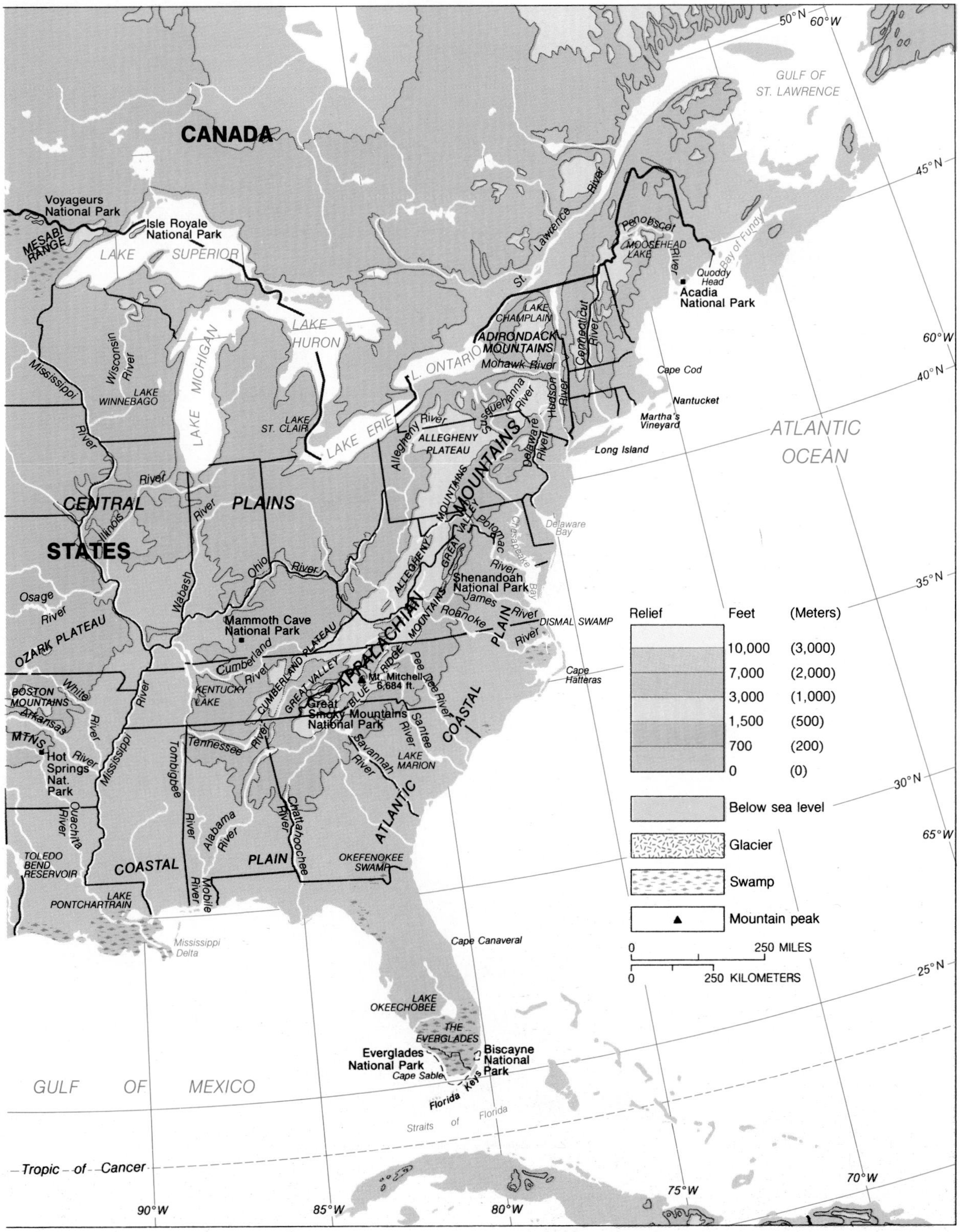
CANADA
UNITED STATES
GULF OF ST. LAWRENCE
ATLANTIC OCEAN
GULF OF MEXICO
Voyageurs National Park
Isle Royale National Park
MESABI RANGE
LAKE SUPERIOR
LAKE HURON
LAKE MICHIGAN
LAKE WINNEBAGO
LAKE ST. CLAIR
LAKE ERIE
L. ONTARIO
LAKE CHAMPLAIN
MOOSEHEAD LAKE
ADIRONDACK MOUNTAINS
Mohawk River
Hudson River
Connecticut River
Penobscot River
St. Lawrence River
Bay of Fundy
Quoddy Head
Acadia National Park
Cape Cod
Nantucket
Martha's Vineyard
Long Island
Delaware River
Delaware Bay
Susquehanna River
Allegheny River
ALLEGHENY PLATEAU
APPALACHIAN MOUNTAINS
ALLEGHENY MOUNTAINS
GREAT VALLEY
BLUE RIDGE MOUNTAINS
Chesapeake Bay
Potomac River
Shenandoah National Park
James River
Roanoke River
DISMAL SWAMP
Cape Hatteras
Mt. Mitchell 6,684 ft.
Great Smoky Mountains National Park
CUMBERLAND PLATEAU
Cumberland River
KENTUCKY LAKE
Mammoth Cave National Park
Wisconsin River
Mississippi River
Illinois River
Wabash River
Ohio River
CENTRAL PLAINS
Osage River
OZARK PLATEAU
BOSTON MOUNTAINS
White River
Arkansas River
OUACHITA MTNS.
Hot Springs Nat. Park
Ouachita River
TOLEDO BEND RESERVOIR
LAKE PONTCHARTRAIN
Mississippi Delta
Tennessee River
Tombigbee River
Alabama River
Mobile River
Chattahoochee River
Savannah River
Santee River
Pee Dee River
LAKE MARION
OKEFENOKEE SWAMP
ATLANTIC COASTAL PLAIN
COASTAL PLAIN
Cape Canaveral
LAKE OKEECHOBEE
THE EVERGLADES
Everglades National Park
Biscayne National Park
Cape Sable
Florida Keys
Straits of Florida
Tropic of Cancer
50° N
45° N
40° N
35° N
30° N
25° N
60° W
65° W
70° W
75° W
80° W
85° W
90° W
Relief
Feet
(Meters)
10,000 (3,000)
7,000 (2,000)
3,000 (1,000)
1,500 (500)
700 (200)
0 (0)
Below sea level
Glacier
Swamp
Mountain peak
0 250 MILES
0 250 KILOMETERS

The World: Political

Central America

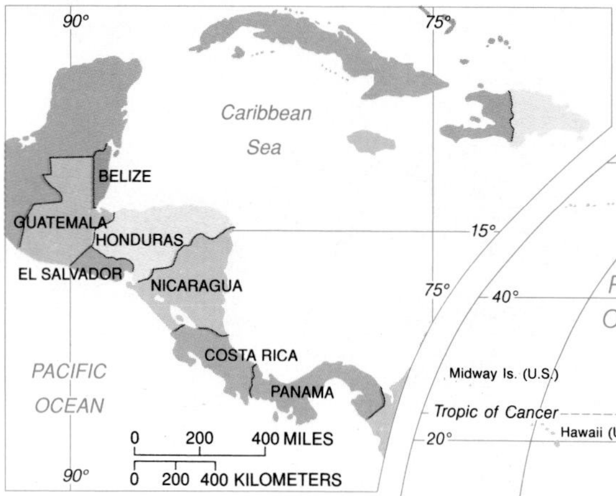

ALB.—ALBANIA
AUS.—AUSTRIA
CZ. REP.—CZECH REPUBLIC
GER.—GERMANY
HUN.—HUNGARY
LUX.—LUXEMBOURG
SLOV.—SLOVAKIA
SWITZ.—SWITZERLAND

Den.—Denmark
Fr.—France
G.B.—Great Britain
S. Afr.—South Africa
U.S.—United States

Europe

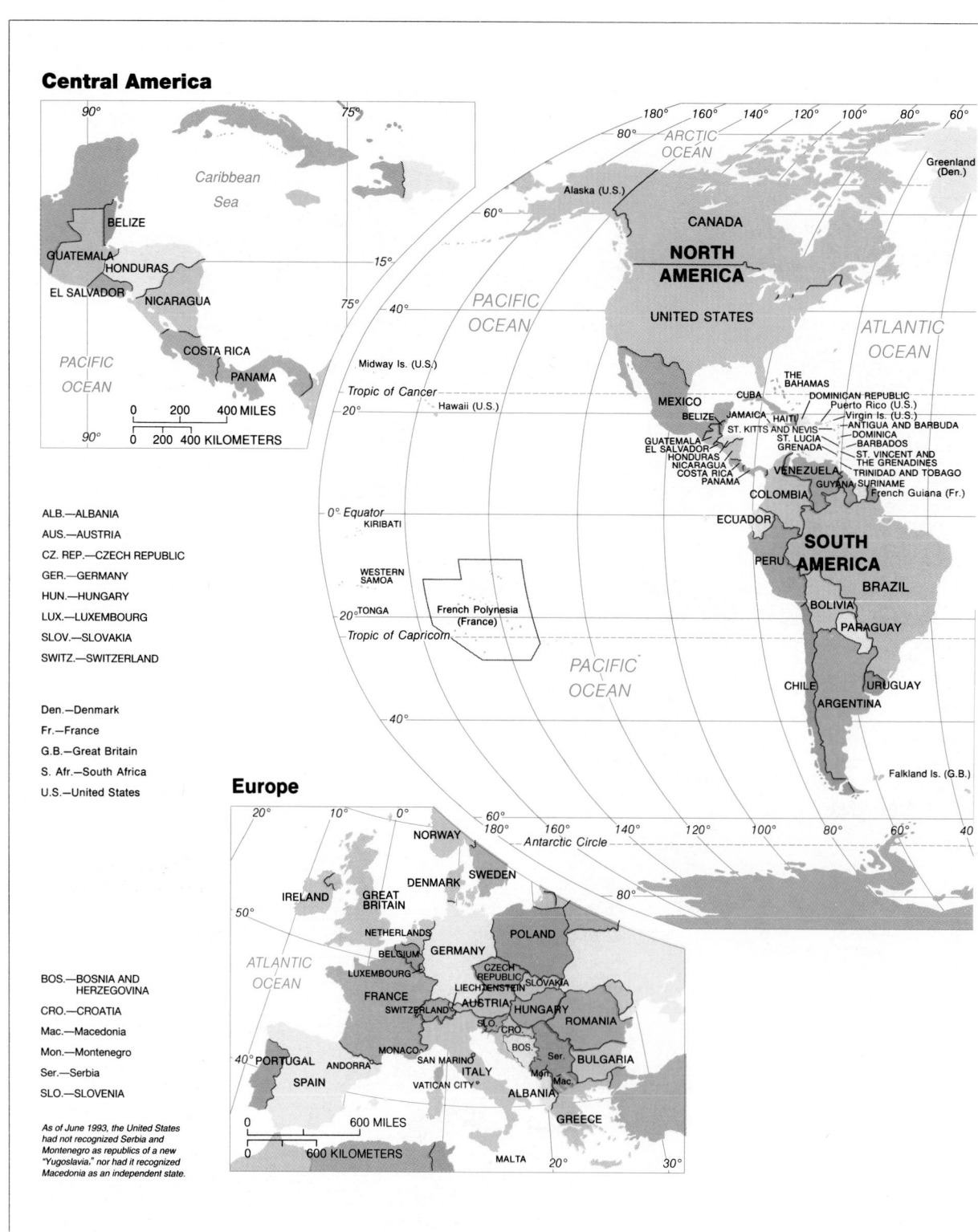

BOS.—BOSNIA AND HERZEGOVINA
CRO.—CROATIA
Mac.—Macedonia
Mon.—Montenegro
Ser.—Serbia
SLO.—SLOVENIA

As of June 1993, the United States had not recognized Serbia and Montenegro as republics of a new "Yugoslavia," nor had it recognized Macedonia as an independent state.

904

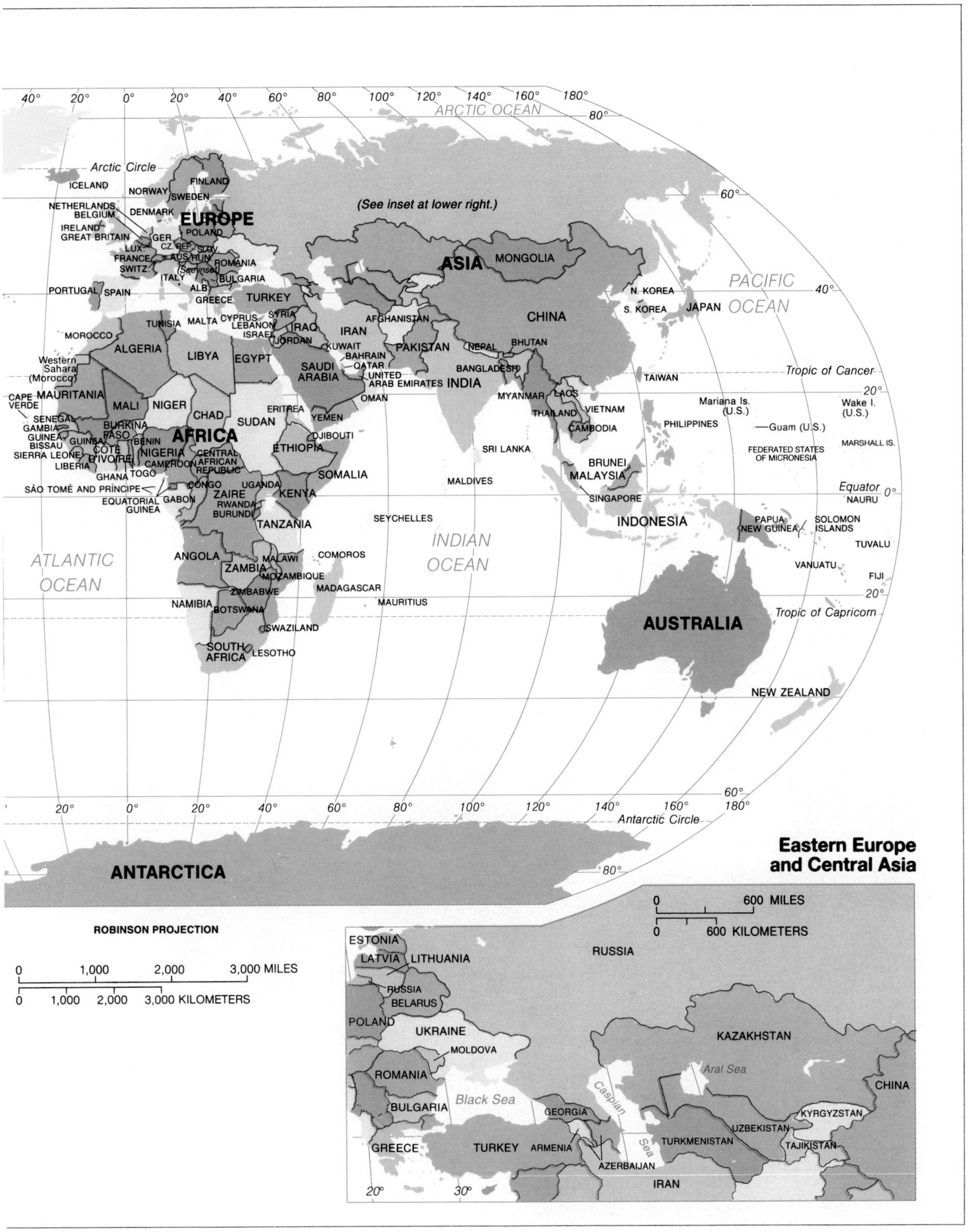
ARCTIC OCEAN
Arctic Circle
ICELAND
NORWAY
FINLAND
SWEDEN
NETHERLANDS
BELGIUM
DENMARK
EUROPE
IRELAND
GREAT BRITAIN
POLAND
GER.
CZ. REP.
LUX.
FRANCE
SWITZ.
AUS.
HUN.
SLOV.
ROMANIA
ITALY
(See inset)
BULGARIA
ALB.
PORTUGAL
SPAIN
GREECE
TURKEY
(See inset at lower right.)
ASIA
MONGOLIA
CHINA
N. KOREA
S. KOREA
JAPAN
PACIFIC OCEAN
TUNISIA
MALTA
CYPRUS
SYRIA
LEBANON
ISRAEL
IRAQ
JORDAN
IRAN
AFGHANISTAN
MOROCCO
ALGERIA
LIBYA
EGYPT
KUWAIT
BAHRAIN
QATAR
UNITED ARAB EMIRATES
PAKISTAN
NEPAL
BHUTAN
Western Sahara (Morocco)
SAUDI ARABIA
BANGLADESH
INDIA
TAIWAN
Tropic of Cancer
CAPE VERDE
MAURITANIA
MALI
NIGER
CHAD
SUDAN
ERITREA
YEMEN
OMAN
MYANMAR
LAOS
THAILAND
VIETNAM
CAMBODIA
PHILIPPINES
Mariana Is. (U.S.)
Wake I. (U.S.)
Guam (U.S.)
SENEGAL
GAMBIA
GUINEA-BISSAU
GUINEA
SIERRA LEONE
LIBERIA
BURKINA FASO
CÔTE D'IVOIRE
GHANA
TOGO
BENIN
NIGERIA
AFRICA
CAMEROON
CENTRAL AFRICAN REPUBLIC
DJIBOUTI
ETHIOPIA
SOMALIA
SRI LANKA
MALDIVES
BRUNEI
MALAYSIA
FEDERATED STATES OF MICRONESIA
MARSHALL IS.
SÃO TOMÉ AND PRÍNCIPE
EQUATORIAL GUINEA
GABON
CONGO
ZAIRE
UGANDA
KENYA
RWANDA
BURUNDI
TANZANIA
SEYCHELLES
SINGAPORE
INDONESIA
Equator
NAURU
PAPUA NEW GUINEA
SOLOMON ISLANDS
TUVALU
ATLANTIC OCEAN
INDIAN OCEAN
ANGOLA
ZAMBIA
MALAWI
COMOROS
MOZAMBIQUE
ZIMBABWE
MADAGASCAR
MAURITIUS
VANUATU
FIJI
NAMIBIA
BOTSWANA
SWAZILAND
Tropic of Capricorn
AUSTRALIA
SOUTH AFRICA
LESOTHO
NEW ZEALAND
Antarctic Circle
ANTARCTICA
ROBINSON PROJECTION
0 1,000 2,000 3,000 MILES
0 1,000 2,000 3,000 KILOMETERS
Eastern Europe and Central Asia
0 600 MILES
0 600 KILOMETERS
ESTONIA
LATVIA
LITHUANIA
RUSSIA
BELARUS
POLAND
UKRAINE
MOLDOVA
KAZAKHSTAN
Aral Sea
ROMANIA
Black Sea
Caspian Sea
BULGARIA
GEORGIA
UZBEKISTAN
KYRGYZSTAN
CHINA
GREECE
TURKEY
ARMENIA
AZERBAIJAN
TURKMENISTAN
TAJIKISTAN
IRAN

The United States: Agriculture and Industry

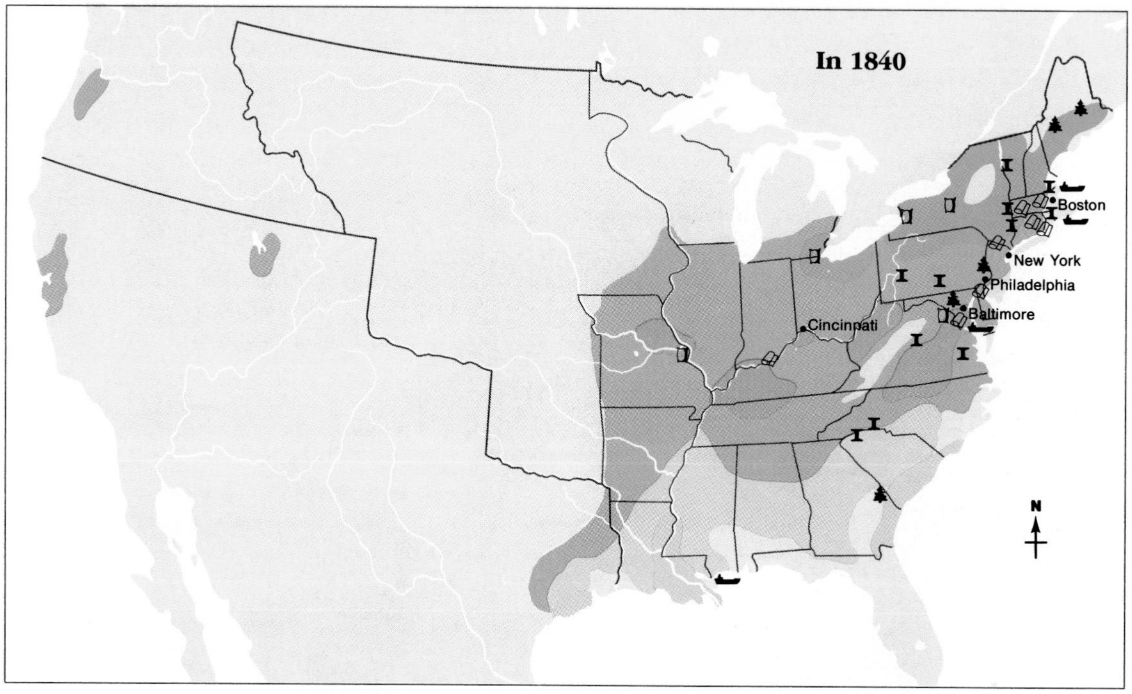

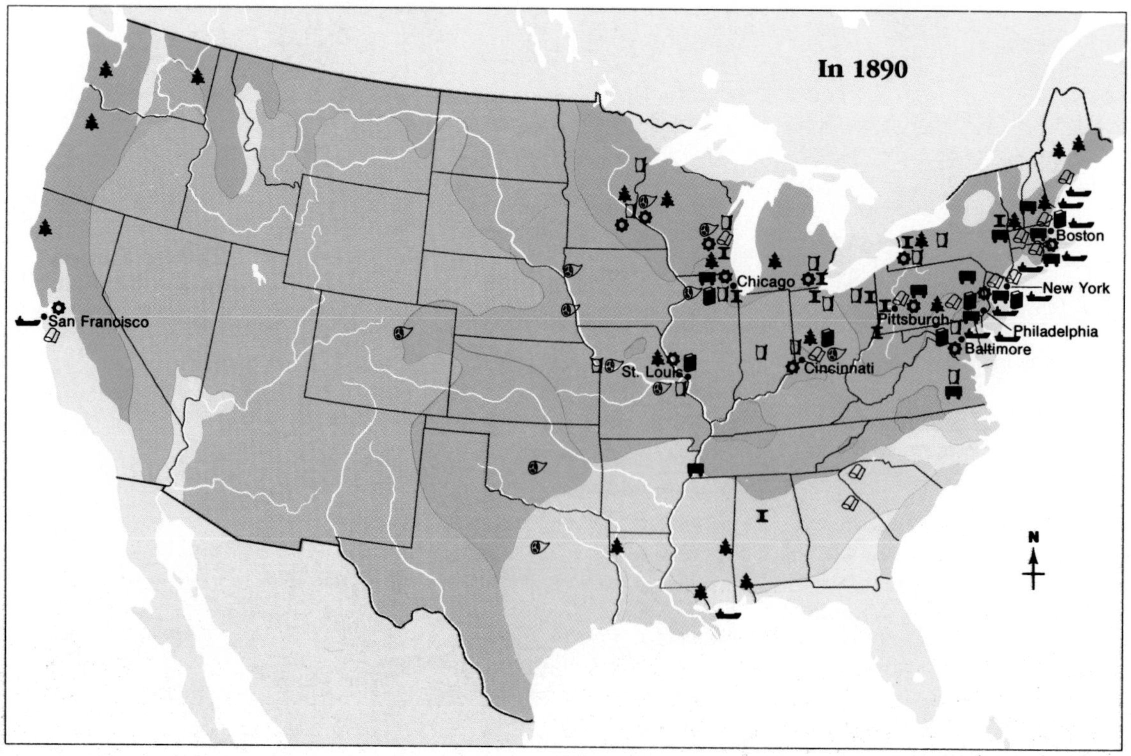

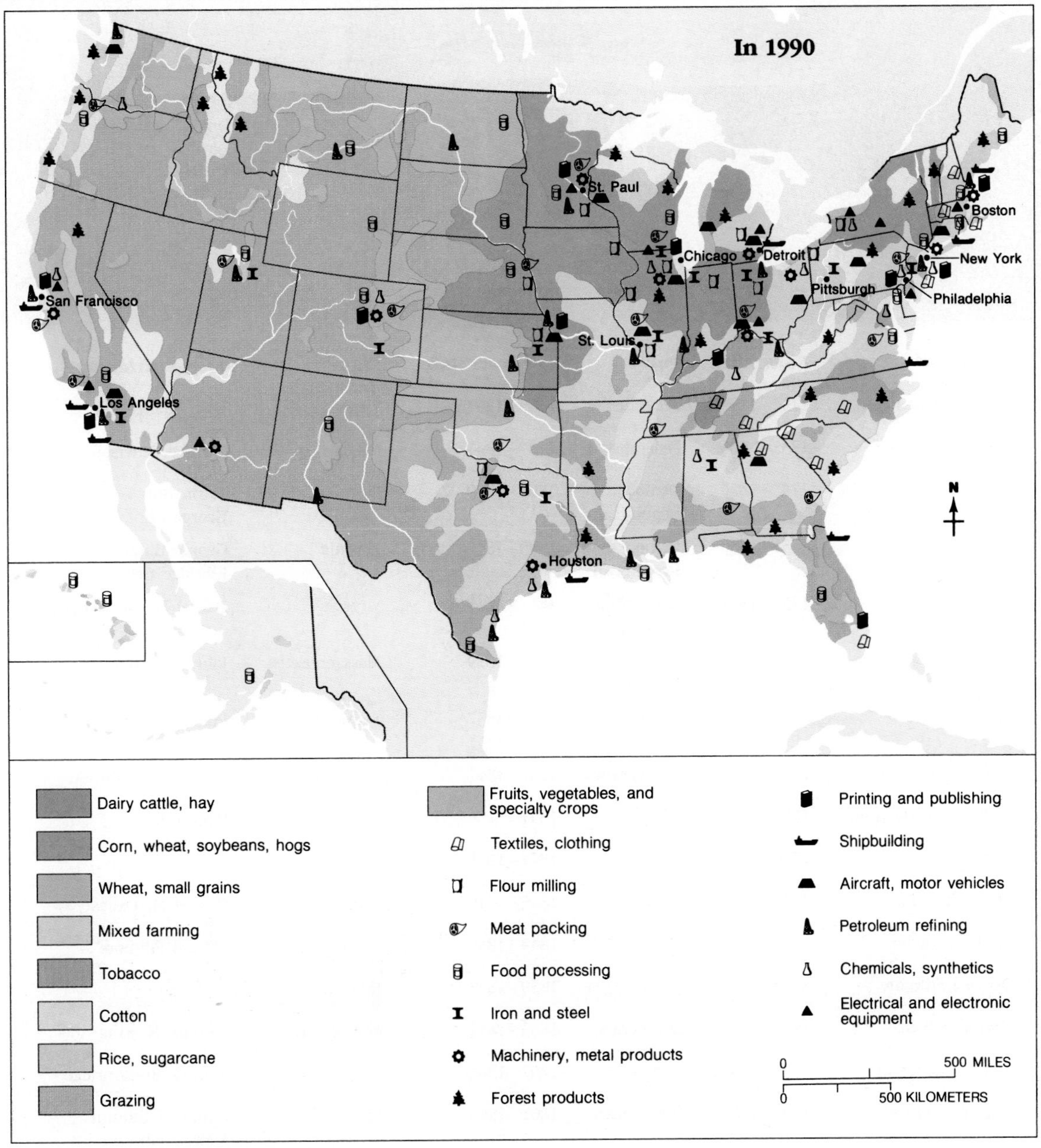

In 1840 the United States was mainly an agricultural nation, with nearly 70 percent of its labor force working on farms. With rapid growth in industry, though, many products were no longer made by artisans at home but by workers in factories. Between the Civil War and the early 1900s, the United States became the world's greatest industrial nation. Agriculture's importance did not end, however. In fact, farmland acreage more than doubled, and scientific technology in both agriculture and industry made production more efficient. Although farm acreage has been declining since 1959, productivity keeps rising. Meanwhile, as the nation moves toward the next century, industry continues to create new products.

Presidents and Vice-Presidents

	President	Born-Died	Party	Years in Office	State*	Vice-Presidents
1	George Washington	1732–1799	Federalist	1789–1797	Virginia	John Adams
2	John Adams	1735–1826	Federalist	1797–1801	Massachusetts	Thomas Jefferson
3	Thomas Jefferson	1743–1826	Democratic-Republican	1801–1809	Virginia	Aaron Burr George Clinton
4	James Madison	1751–1836	Democratic-Republican	1809–1817	Virginia	George Clinton Elbridge Gerry
5	James Monroe	1758–1831	Democratic-Republican	1817–1825	Virginia	Daniel D. Tompkins
6	John Quincy Adams	1767–1848	National-Republican	1825–1829	Massachusetts	John C. Calhoun
7	Andrew Jackson	1767–1845	Democratic	1829–1837	Tennessee	John C. Calhoun Martin Van Buren
8	Martin Van Buren	1782–1862	Democratic	1837–1841	New York	Richard M. Johnson
9	William H. Harrison	1773–1841	Whig	1841	Ohio	John Tyler
10	John Tyler	1790–1862	Whig	1841–1845	Virginia	
11	James K. Polk	1795–1849	Democratic	1845–1849	Tennessee	George M. Dallas
12	Zachary Taylor	1784–1850	Whig	1849–1850	Louisiana	Millard Fillmore
13	Millard Fillmore	1800–1874	Whig	1850–1853	New York	
14	Franklin Pierce	1804–1869	Democratic	1853–1857	New Hampshire	William R. King
15	James Buchanan	1791–1868	Democratic	1857–1861	Pennsylvania	John C. Breckinridge
16	Abraham Lincoln	1809–1865	Republican	1861–1865	Illinois	Hannibal Hamlin Andrew Johnson
17	Andrew Johnson	1808–1875	Democratic	1865–1869	Tennessee	
18	Ulysses S. Grant	1822–1885	Republican	1869–1877	Illinois	Schuyler Colfax Henry Wilson
19	Rutherford B. Hayes	1822–1893	Republican	1877–1881	Ohio	William A. Wheeler
20	James Garfield	1831–1881	Republican	1881	Ohio	Chester A. Arthur
21	Chester A. Arthur	1830–1886	Republican	1881–1885	New York	
22	Grover Cleveland	1837–1908	Democratic	1885–1889	New York	Thomas Hendricks

	President	Born-Died	Party	Years in Office	State*	Vice-Presidents
23	Benjamin Harrison	1833–1901	Republican	1889–1893	Indiana	Levi P. Morton
24	Grover Cleveland	1837–1908	Democratic	1893–1897	New York	Adlai E. Stevenson
25	William McKinley	1843–1901	Republican	1897–1901	Ohio	Garret A. Hobart Theodore Roosevelt
26	Theodore Roosevelt	1858–1919	Republican	1901–1909	New York	Charles Fairbanks
27	William H. Taft	1857–1930	Republican	1909–1913	Ohio	James S. Sherman
28	Woodrow Wilson	1856–1924	Democratic	1913–1921	New Jersey	Thomas R. Marshall
29	Warren G. Harding	1865–1923	Republican	1921–1923	Ohio	Calvin Coolidge
30	Calvin Coolidge	1872–1933	Republican	1923–1929	Massachusetts	Charles G. Dawes
31	Herbert Hoover	1874–1964	Republican	1929–1933	California	Charles Curtis
32	Franklin D. Roosevelt	1882–1945	Democratic	1933–1945	New York	John Garner Henry Wallace Harry S Truman
33	Harry S Truman	1884–1972	Democratic	1945–1953	Missouri	Alben Barkley
34	Dwight Eisenhower	1890–1969	Republican	1953–1961	New York	Richard Nixon
35	John F. Kennedy	1917–1963	Democratic	1961–1963	Massachusetts	Lyndon Johnson
36	Lyndon Johnson	1908–1973	Democratic	1963–1969	Texas	Hubert Humphrey
37	Richard Nixon	1913–	Republican	1969–1974	New York	Spiro Agnew Gerald Ford
38	Gerald Ford	1913–	Republican	1974–1977	Michigan	Nelson Rockefeller
39	Jimmy Carter	1924–	Democratic	1977–1981	Georgia	Walter Mondale
40	Ronald Reagan	1911–	Republican	1981–1989	California	George Bush
41	George Bush	1924–	Republican	1989–1993	Texas	J. Danforth Quayle
42	Bill Clinton	1946–	Democratic	1993–	Arkansas	Albert Gore, Jr.

*State of residence when elected

Facts About the States

State	Year of Admission	Capital	Estimated 1995 Population (Rank)		Area in Square Miles (Rank)		Nickname
Alabama	1819	Montgomery	4,307,000	(22)	51,609	(29)	Yellowhammer State
Alaska	1959	Juneau	636,000	(48)	586,412	(1)	The Last Frontier
Arizona	1912	Phoenix	4,218,000	(23)	113,909	(6)	Grand Canyon State
Arkansas	1836	Little Rock	2,482,000	(33)	53,104	(27)	Land of Opportunity
California	1850	Sacramento	31,463,000	(1)	158,693	(3)	Golden State
Colorado	1876	Denver	3,637,000	(26)	104,247	(8)	Centennial State
Connecticut	1788	Hartford	3,376,000	(27)	5,009	(48)	Constitution State
Delaware	1787	Dover	702,000	(46)	2,057	(49)	First State
Florida	1845	Tallahassee	14,189,000	(4)	58,560	(22)	Sunshine State
Georgia	1788	Atlanta	7,338,000	(10)	58,876	(21)	Peach State
Hawaii	1959	Honolulu	1,243,000	(40)	6,450	(47)	Aloha State
Idaho	1890	Boise	1,034,000	(42)	83,557	(13)	Gem State
Illinois	1818	Springfield	11,625,000	(6)	56,400	(24)	Prairie State
Indiana	1816	Indianapolis	5,545,000	(14)	36,291	(38)	Hoosier State
Iowa	1846	Des Moines	2,652,000	(31)	56,290	(25)	Hawkeye State
Kansas	1861	Topeka	2,515,000	(32)	82,264	(14)	Sunflower State
Kentucky	1792	Frankfort	3,745,000	(24)	40,395	(37)	Bluegrass State
Louisiana	1812	Baton Rouge	4,517,000	(20)	48,523	(31)	Pelican State
Maine	1820	Augusta	1,247,000	(39)	33,215	(39)	Pine Tree State
Maryland	1788	Annapolis	5,025,000	(17)	10,577	(42)	Old Line State
Massachusetts	1788	Boston	5,985,000	(13)	8,257	(45)	Bay State
Michigan	1837	Lansing	9,318,000	(8)	58,216	(23)	Wolverine State
Minnesota	1858	St. Paul	4,426,000	(21)	84,068	(12)	North Star State
Mississippi	1817	Jackson	2,792,000	(30)	47,716	(32)	Magnolia State
Missouri	1821	Jefferson City	5,304,000	(15)	69,686	(19)	Show Me State
Montana	1889	Helena	798,000	(44)	147,138	(4)	Treasure State

910

State	Year of Admission	Capital	Estimated 1995 Population (Rank)		Area in Square Miles (Rank)		Nickname
Nebraska	1867	Lincoln	1,574,000	(37)	77,227	(15)	Cornhusker State
Nevada	1864	Carson City	1,198,000	(41)	110,540	(7)	Sagebrush State
New Hampshire	1788	Concord	1,251,000	(38)	9,304	(44)	Granite State
New Jersey	1787	Trenton	8,252,000	(9)	7,836	(46)	Garden State
New Mexico	1912	Santa Fe	1,809,000	(35)	121,666	(5)	Land of Enchantment
New York	1788	Albany	17,886,000	(3)	49,576	(30)	Empire State
North Carolina	1789	Raleigh	7,106,000	(11)	52,586	(28)	Tar Heel State
North Dakota	1889	Bismarck	643,000	(47)	70,665	(17)	Flickertail State
Ohio	1803	Columbus	10,742,000	(7)	41,222	(35)	Buckeye State
Oklahoma	1907	Oklahoma City	3,318,000	(28)	69,919	(18)	Sooner State
Oregon	1859	Salem	2,828,000	(29)	96,981	(10)	Beaver State
Pennsylvania	1787	Harrisburg	11,689,000	(5)	45,333	(33)	Keystone State
Rhode Island	1790	Providence	1,029,000	(43)	1,214	(50)	Ocean State
South Carolina	1788	Columbia	3,740,000	(25)	31,055	(40)	Palmetto State
South Dakota	1889	Pierre	711,000	(45)	77,047	(16)	Coyote State
Tennessee	1796	Nashville	5,135,000	(16)	42,244	(34)	Volunteer State
Texas	1845	Austin	19,012,000	(2)	267,339	(2)	Lone Star State
Utah	1896	Salt Lake City	1,893,000	(34)	84,916	(11)	Beehive State
Vermont	1791	Montpelier	579,000	(49)	9,609	(43)	Green Mountain State
Virginia	1788	Richmond	6,551,000	(12)	40,817	(36)	Old Dominion
Washington	1889	Olympia	4,841,000	(18)	68,192	(20)	Evergreen State
West Virginia	1863	Charleston	1,786,000	(36)	24,181	(41)	Mountain State
Wisconsin	1848	Madison	4,811,000	(19)	56,153	(26)	Badger State
Wyoming	1890	Cheyenne	495,000	(50)	97,914	(9)	Equality State
District of Columbia			620,000		67		

Important Events in United States History

2000 B.C. Agriculture spreads north from Mexico
A.D. 1200 Aztecs build empire in Mexico
1492 Columbus sails to the Americas
1521 Spanish conquer Aztec Empire
1565 Spanish establish St. Augustine, Florida
1570 League of the Iroquois formed
1607 English establish Jamestown, Virginia
1608 French establish Quebec, Canada
1610 Spanish establish Santa Fe, New Mexico
1619 First Africans brought to Jamestown
Virginia House of Burgesses first meets
1620 Pilgrims land at Plymouth
1664 English seize New Netherland
1682 French claim Mississippi Valley
1718 Spanish establish San Antonio, Texas
1754 French and Indian War begins
1763 Treaty of Paris
1765 Parliament passes Stamp Act
1769 Spanish build first mission in California
1770 Boston Massacre
1773 Boston Tea Party
1774 Parliament passes Intolerable Acts
First Continental Congress meets
1775 Battles of Lexington and Concord
Second Continental Congress meets
1776 Declaration of Independence
1778 Treaty of alliance signed with France
1781 Articles of Confederation go into effect
1783 Treaty of Paris
1787 Constitution drafted
Northwest Ordinance
1788 Constitution ratified
1789 George Washington becomes President
1790 Conflict over Hamilton's financial program
1791 Bill of Rights becomes part of Constitution
1797 John Adams becomes President
1798 Alien and Sedition Acts
1801 Thomas Jefferson becomes President
1803 *Marbury* v. *Madison* decision
Louisiana Purchase
1809 James Madison becomes President
1812 United States declares war on Great Britain
1815 Treaty of Ghent
1817 James Monroe becomes President
1819 United States acquires Florida
McCulloch v. *Maryland* decision
1820 Missouri Compromise
1823 Monroe Doctrine
1825 John Quincy Adams becomes President
1829 Andrew Jackson becomes President
1830 Indian Removal Act
1832 Nullification crisis
1833 American Anti-Slavery Society founded
1836 Texans declare independence from Mexico
1837 Martin Van Buren becomes President
Panic of 1837

1841 William Henry Harrison becomes President
John Tyler becomes President on death of Harrison
1845 James K. Polk becomes President
United States annexes Texas
1846 United States declares war on Mexico
Oregon boundary settled
1848 Treaty of Guadalupe Hidalgo
Seneca Falls convention on women's rights
1849 Zachary Taylor becomes President
1850 Millard Fillmore becomes President on death of Taylor
Compromise of 1850
1851 Fort Laramie Treaty
1853 Franklin Pierce becomes President
Gadsden Purchase
1854 Perry opens Japanese ports to U.S. trade
Kansas-Nebraska Act
Republican party formed as antislavery party
1856 "Bleeding Kansas"
1857 James Buchanan becomes President
Dred Scott decision
1859 John Brown raids Harpers Ferry
1860 South Carolina secedes from Union
1861 Abraham Lincoln becomes President
Confederate States of America formed
Civil War breaks out
1862 Homestead Act
Indian-white conflict in North and West
Battle of Antietam
1863 Emancipation Proclamation goes into effect
Battles of Gettysburg and Vicksburg
1864 Union siege of Petersburg begins
Union forces seize Atlanta
1865 Lee surrenders at Appomattox
Andrew Johnson becomes President on assassination of Lincoln
Thirteenth Amendment abolishes slavery
1866 National Labor Union organized
1867 Congress passes Reconstruction Act
United States buys Alaska
1868 Andrew Johnson impeached
Fourteenth Amendment defines citizenship
1869 Ulysses S. Grant becomes President
1870 Fifteenth Amendment states rights of voters
1873 Panic of 1873
1877 Rutherford B. Hayes becomes President
Reconstruction ends
Great Railroad Strike
1881 James Garfield becomes President
Chester A. Arthur becomes President on assassination of Garfield
1882 Standard Oil trust formed
Chinese Exclusion Act
1883 Pendleton Civil Service Act
1885 Grover Cleveland becomes President

1886 Haymarket bombing
American Federation of Labor organized
1887 Interstate Commerce Act
Dawes Act
1889 **Benjamin Harrison becomes President**
1890 Sherman Antitrust Act
1891 Populist party organized
1892 Homestead Strike
1893 **Grover Cleveland becomes President**
Depression of 1893
1894 Pullman Strike
1896 *Plessy* v. *Ferguson* decision
1897 **William McKinley becomes President**
1898 Spanish-American War
United States annexes Hawaii
United States acquires Philippines, Puerto Rico, and Guam
1899 Open Door policy in China
1901 **Theodore Roosevelt becomes President on assassination of McKinley**
Progressive movement
1904 Construction of Panama Canal begins
Roosevelt Corollary to Monroe Doctrine
1909 **William H. Taft becomes President**
NAACP founded
1913 **Woodrow Wilson becomes President**
Federal Reserve Act
1914 World War I begins
1915 *Lusitania* sunk by German submarine
1916 U.S. troops sent to Mexico
1917 United States enters World War I
1919 United States rejects Treaty of Versailles
"Red Summer" and "Red Scare"
1920 Prohibition begins
Nineteenth Amendment gives women vote
1921 **Warren G. Harding becomes President**
First immigration quota law passed
1923 **Calvin Coolidge becomes President on death of Harding**
1929 **Herbert Hoover becomes President**
Stock market crash
1933 Lowest point of Great Depression
Franklin D. Roosevelt becomes President
Good Neighbor policy
New Deal begins
1934 Indian Reorganization Act
1935 Wagner Act and Social Security Act
1938 Congress of Industrial Organizations formed
1939 World War II begins
1941 United States enters World War II
1942 Japanese-American internment
Battle of Midway
1943 Battle of Stalingrad
Allies win in North Africa, invade Italy
1944 Allies invade France
1945 Yalta Conference
Harry S Truman becomes President on death of Roosevelt
Germany surrenders
Atomic bombs dropped on Japan
Japan surrenders
UN charter goes into effect
1946 Philippines become independent
1948 Marshall Plan goes into effect
Berlin airlift begins
1949 NATO formed
1950 Korean War begins
1953 **Dwight D. Eisenhower becomes President**
Armistice in Korea signed
1954 *Brown* v. *Board of Education* decision
Army-McCarthy hearings
1955 Montgomery bus boycott
1956 Suez crisis
1957 Soviet Union launches *Sputnik I*
1961 **John F. Kennedy becomes President**
Peace Corps established
Berlin crisis
1962 Cuban missile crisis
1963 March on Washington for civil rights
Nuclear Test Ban Treaty
Lyndon B. Johnson becomes President on assassination of Kennedy
1964 Twenty-fourth Amendment bans poll taxes
Civil Rights Act of 1964
1965 U.S. troop buildup begins in Vietnam
First large protests against Vietnam War
Voting Rights Act of 1965
Immigration quotas based on national origins ended
1966 National Organization for Women founded
1968 Martin Luther King, Jr., and Robert Kennedy assassinated
1969 **Richard M. Nixon becomes President**
American astronauts land on moon
1970 U.S. troops invade Cambodia
1971 Twenty-sixth Amendment lowers voting age to eighteen
1972 President Nixon visits mainland China
Watergate break-in
1973 Cease-fire agreement with North Vietnam
1974 **Gerald R. Ford becomes President on resignation of Nixon**
1975 South Vietnam falls to North Vietnam
1977 **Jimmy Carter becomes President**
1978 Camp David Accords
1979 Iranian hostage crisis
1981 **Ronald Reagan becomes President**
1983 U.S. troops invade Grenada
1986 Iran-contra scandal
1989 **George Bush becomes President**
U.S. troops invade Panama
Communist governments in Eastern Europe fall
1991 Persian Gulf War
Soviet Union collapses
1992 Los Angeles riots
Earth Summit
1993 **Bill Clinton becomes President**

The Declaration of Independence

When, in the course of human events, it becomes necessary for one people to dissolve the political bands which have connected them with another, and to assume, among the powers of the earth, the separate and equal station to which the laws of nature and of nature's God entitle them, a decent respect to the opinions of mankind requires that they should declare the causes which impel them to the separation.

We hold these truths to be self-evident, that all men are created equal, that they are endowed by their Creator with certain unalienable rights, that among these are life, liberty, and the pursuit of happiness. That, to secure these rights, governments are instituted among men, deriving their just powers from the consent of the governed. That, whenever any form of government becomes destructive of these ends, it is the right of the people to alter or to abolish it, and to institute new government, laying its foundation on such principles, and organizing its powers in such form, as to them shall seem most likely to effect their safety and happiness.

Prudence, indeed, will dictate that governments long established should not be changed for light and transient causes; and, accordingly, all experience has shown that mankind are more disposed to suffer, while evils are sufferable, than to right themselves by abolishing the forms to which they are accustomed.

But when a long train of abuses and usurpations, pursuing invariably the same object, evinces a design to reduce them under absolute despotism, it is their right, it is their duty, to throw off such government, and to provide new guards for their future security. Such has been the patient sufferance of these colonies; and such is now the necessity which constrains them to alter their former systems of government. The history of the present King of Great Britain is a history of repeated injuries and usurpations, all having in direct object the establishment of an absolute tyranny over these states. To prove this, let facts be submitted to a candid world.

He has refused his assent to laws the most wholesome and necessary for the public good.

He has forbidden his governors to pass laws of immediate and pressing importance, unless suspended in their operation till his assent should be obtained; and when so suspended, he has utterly neglected to attend to them.

He has refused to pass other laws for the accommodation of large districts of people, unless those people would relinquish the right of representation in the legislature; a right inestimable to them and formidable to tyrants only.

He has called together legislative bodies at places unusual, uncomfortable, and distant from the depository of their public records, for the sole purpose of fatiguing them into compliance with his measures.

He has dissolved representative houses repeatedly, for opposing with manly firmness his invasions on the rights of the people.

He has refused for a long time, after such dissolutions, to cause others to be elected; whereby the legislative powers, incapable of annihilation, have returned to the people at large for their exercise; the state remaining in the meantime exposed to all the dangers of invasion from without, and convulsions within.

He has endeavored to prevent the population of these states; for that purpose obstructing the laws for naturalization of foreigners; refusing to pass others to encourage their migrations hither, and raising the conditions of new appropriations of lands.

He has obstructed the administration of justice, by refusing his assent to laws for establishing judiciary powers.

He has made judges dependent on his will alone, for the tenure of their offices, and the amount and payment of their salaries.

He has erected a multitude of new offices, and sent hither swarms of officers to harass our people, and eat out their substance.

He has kept among us, in times of peace, standing armies, without the consent of our legislatures.

He has affected to render the military independent of and superior to the civil power.

He has combined with others to subject us to a jurisdiction foreign to our constitution, and unacknowledged by our laws; giving his assent to their acts of pretended legislation:

For quartering large bodies of armed troops among us;

For protecting them, by a mock trial, from punishment for any murders which they should commit on the inhabitants of these states;

For cutting off our trade with all parts of the world;

For imposing taxes on us without our consent;

For depriving us, in many cases, of the benefits of trial by jury;

For transporting us beyond seas to be tried for pretended offenses;

For abolishing the free system of English laws in a neighboring province, establishing therein an arbitrary government, and enlarging its boundaries, so as to render it at once an example and fit instrument for introducing the same absolute rule into these colonies;

For taking away our charters, abolishing our most valuable laws, and altering fundamentally the forms of our governments;

For suspending our own legislatures, and declaring themselves invested with power to legislate for us in all cases whatsoever.

He has abdicated government here, by declaring us out of his protection, and waging war against us.

He has plundered our seas, ravaged our coasts, burnt our towns, and destroyed the lives of our people.

He is at this time transporting large armies of foreign mercenaries to complete the works of death, desolation, and tyranny already begun with circumstances of cruelty and perfidy scarcely paralleled in the most barbarous ages, and totally unworthy the head of a civilized nation.

He has constrained our fellow citizens, taken captive on the high seas, to bear arms against their country, to become the executioners of their friends and brethren, or to fall themselves by their hands.

He has excited domestic insurrections among us, and has endeavored to bring on the inhabitants of our frontiers, the merciless Indian savages, whose known rule of warfare is an undistinguished destruction of all ages, sexes, and conditions.

In every stage of these oppressions, we have petitioned for redress in the most humble terms. Our repeated petitions have been answered only by repeated injury. A prince, whose character is thus marked by every act which may define a tyrant, is unfit to be the ruler of a free people.

Nor have we been wanting in attentions to our British brethren. We have warned them from time to time of attempts by their legislature to extend an unwarrantable jurisdiction over us. We have reminded them of the circumstances of our emigration and settlement here. We have appealed to their native justice and magnanimity, and we have conjured them by the ties of our common kindred to disavow these usurpations, which would inevitably interrupt our connections and correspondence. They too have been deaf to the voice of justice and of consanguinity. We must, therefore, acquiesce in the necessity, which denounces our separation, and hold them, as we hold the rest of mankind, enemies in war, in peace, friends.

We, therefore, the representatives of the United States of America, in General Congress assembled, appealing to the Supreme Judge of the world for the rectitude of our intentions, do, in the name and by authority of the good people of these colonies, solemnly publish and declare, that these United Colonies are and of right ought to be free and independent states; that they are absolved from all allegiance to the British Crown, and that all political connection between them and the state of Great Britain is and ought to be totally dissolved; and that, as free and independent states, they have full power to levy war, conclude peace, contract alliances, establish commerce, and to do all other acts and things which independent states may of right do. And for the support of this declaration, with a firm reliance on the protection of Divine Providence, we mutually pledge to each other our lives, our fortunes, and our sacred honor.

The Constitution of the United States

The text of the Constitution appears to the left below. In this version, spelling, capitalization, and punctuation have been modernized. Black lines through the text mark passages that have been changed or voided by amendments. The words to the right below are comments on the meaning and history of the Constitution.

Preamble

We the people of the United States, in order to form a more perfect Union, establish justice, insure domestic tranquility, provide for the common defense, promote the general welfare, and secure the blessings of liberty to ourselves and our posterity, do ordain and establish this Constitution for the United States of America

Preamble

The Preamble lists the purposes of the new government, based on the will of the people. Following the Preamble are the first three articles of the Constitution. They divide the powers of government among three distinct branches. They create a system of checks and balances.

Article 1

Section 1

All legislative powers herein granted shall be vested in a Congress of the United States, which shall consist of a Senate and House of Representatives.

Article 1. The Legislative Branch

Section 1. A Two-Part Congress

The legislative branch is empowered to make laws. Its powers are given to both the Senate and the House of Representatives.

Section 2

Clause 1. The House of Representatives shall be composed of members chosen every second year by the people of the several states, and the electors in each state shall have the qualifications requisite for electors of the most numerous branch of the state legislature.

Clause 2. No person shall be a representative who shall not have attained to the age of twenty-five years, and been seven years a citizen of the United States, and who shall not, when elected, be an inhabitant of that state in which he shall be chosen.

Clause 3. Representatives and direct taxes shall be apportioned among the several states which may be included within this Union, according to their respective numbers, ~~which shall be determined by adding to the whole number of free persons, including those bound to service for a term of years, and excluding Indians not taxed, three fifths of all other persons.~~ The actual enumeration shall be made within three years after the first meeting of the Congress of the United States, and within every subsequent term of ten years, in such manner as they shall by law direct. The number of representatives shall not exceed one for every thirty thousand, but each state shall have at least one representative; ~~and until such enumeration shall be made, the state of New Hampshire shall be entitled to choose three, Massachusetts eight, Rhode Island and Providence Plantations one, Connecticut five, New York six, New Jersey four, Pennsylvania eight, Delaware one, Maryland six, Virginia ten, North Carolina five, South Carolina five, and Georgia three.~~

Section 2. The House of Representatives

Clause 1. Elections and Voters. **All the members of the House are elected every two years. Voters for House members must be qualified to vote in certain state elections.**

Clause 2. Qualifications of Representatives.

Clause 3. Apportionment of Representatives. **The number of Representatives from each state is based on the state's population. Originally, indentured servants ("those bound to service") were counted as if they were free. But slaves ("all other persons") were counted as three fifths of a person. Thus it took 500 slaves to equal 300 free persons in deciding numbers of Representatives. When slavery was ended by the Thirteenth Amendment in 1865, the three-fifths rule became meaningless.**

The "actual enumeration," or census, was first made in 1790. It has been repeated every ten years since. Today there is no worry that the number of Representatives might exceed one for every thirty thousand persons. A typical House member now represents about five hundred thousand persons.

914

Clause 4. When vacancies happen in the representation from any state, the executive authority thereof shall issue writs of election to fill such vacancies.

Clause 4. Filling Vacancies. **The "executive authority" refers to a state governor. If a House seat becomes vacant between regular elections, the governor is empowered to call a special election to fill the seat.**

Clause 5. The House of Representatives shall choose their speaker and other officers, and shall have the sole power of impeachment.

Clause 5. Officers; Power of Impeachment. **The Speaker of the House is the leading officer of the House. Only the House can bring impeachment charges. (See Section 3, Clauses 6 and 7, below.)**

Section 3

Section 3. The Senate

Clause 1. The Senate of the United States shall be composed of two senators from each state, ~~chosen by the legislature thereof,~~ for six years; and each senator shall have one vote.

Clause 1. Elections. **Senators were elected by state legislatures until the Seventeenth Amendment, ratified in 1913. Since then, Senators have been chosen directly by the voters of each state.**

Clause 2. Immediately after they shall be assembled in consequence of the first election, they shall be divided as equally as may be into three classes. The seats of the senators of the first class shall be vacated at the expiration of the second year, of the second class at the expiration of the fourth year, and of the third class at the expiration of the sixth year, so that one third may be chosen every second year; ~~and if vacancies happen by resignation, or otherwise, during the recess of the legislature of any state, the executive thereof may make temporary appointments until the next meeting of the legislature, which shall then fill such vacancies.~~

Clause 2. Overlapping Terms of Office; Filling Vacancies. **By dividing Senators into three classes, or groups, the Constitution set up a system of overlapping terms in office. Every two years, one third of the Senators must leave office or stand for reelection. Thus the Senate changes somewhat every two years, even though Senators are elected to six-year terms.**

The method of filling vacancies in the Senate was changed by the Seventeenth Amendment. It gave the power of choosing replacements to the voters of each state.

Clause 3. No person shall be a senator who shall not have attained to the age of thirty years, and been nine years a citizen of the United States, and who shall not, when elected, be an inhabitant of that state for which he shall be chosen.

Clause 3. Qualifications of Senators.

Clause 4. The Vice-President of the United States shall be president of the Senate, but shall have no vote, unless they be equally divided.

Clause 4. President of the Senate **The Vice President serves as president of the Senate, but votes only in case of a tie.**

Clause 5. The Senate shall choose their other officers and also a president pro tempore, in the absence of the Vice-President, or when he shall exercise the office of President of the United States.

Clause 5. Election of Senate Officers. **The Senate elects officers, including a temporary president of the Senate. The president pro tempore, or pro tem, leads meetings when the Vice-President is absent.**

Clause 6. The Senate shall have the sole power to try all impeachments. When sitting for that purpose, they shall be on oath or affirmation. When the President of the United States is tried, the Chief Justice shall preside. And no person shall be convicted without the concurrence of two thirds of the members present.

Clause 6. Impeachment Trials. **The Senate serves as a jury in impeachment cases. A conviction requires a two-thirds vote of the members present. In 1868 the House impeached President Andrew Johnson, but the Senate acquitted him. In 1974 the House considered impeaching President Richard M. Nixon. Nixon resigned before the House made a final decision about impeachment.**

Clause 7. Judgment in cases of impeachment shall not extend further than to removal from office, and disqualification to hold and enjoy any office of honor, trust, or profit under the United States; but the party convicted shall nevertheless be liable and subject to indictment, trial, judgment, and punishment, according to law.

Clause 7. Penalty for Conviction. **If an impeached person is convicted, the person will be removed from office (see Article 2, Section 4) and barred from other federal office. The Senate cannot impose further punishment, but the convicted person can then be tried in a regular court. The Senate has convicted only four persons, all judges. They were removed from office but not tried in regular courts.**

Section 4

Clause 1. The times, places, and manner of holding elections for senators and representatives shall be prescribed in each state by the legislature thereof; but the Congress may at any time by law make or alter such regulations, ~~except as to the places of choosing senators.~~

Clause 2. The Congress shall assemble at least once in every year, ~~and such meeting shall be on the first Monday in December,~~ unless they shall by law appoint a different day.

Section 4. Times of Elections and Meetings

Clause 1. Elections. Each state regulates its own congressional elections, but Congress can change the regulations. In 1872 Congress required that every state hold congressional elections on the same day.

Clause 2. Meetings. Congress must meet once a year. The Twentieth Amendment, ratified in 1933, changed the first day of the meeting to January 3, unless Congress specifies a different day.

Section 5

Clause 1. Each house shall be the judge of the elections, returns, and qualifications of its own members, and a majority of each shall constitute a quorum to do business; but a smaller number may adjourn from day to day, and may be authorized to compel the attendance of absent members, in such manner and under such penalties as each house may provide.

Clause 2. Each house may determine the rules of its proceedings, punish its members for disorderly behavior, and, with the concurrence of two thirds, expel a member.

Clause 3. Each house shall keep a journal of its proceedings and from time to time publish the same, excepting such parts as may in their judgment require secrecy; and the yeas and nays of the members of either house on any question, shall, at the desire of one fifth of those present, be entered on the journal.

Clause 4. Neither house, during the session of Congress, shall, without the consent of the other, adjourn for more than three days, nor to any other place than that in which the two houses shall be sitting.

Section 5. Basics of Organization

Clause 1. Members; Attendance. Each house can judge whether new members have been elected fairly and are qualified to serve. A quorum is the minimum number of members who can act for all. Discussion and debate can go on without a quorum. A quorum is required for voting by either house, however.

Clause 2. Determining Procedures. Each house can set up its own rules of conducting business.

Clause 3. Written Records. Since 1873 the journals of the House and Senate have been published together in the *Congressional Record.* It is published daily when Congress is meeting. A member of either house may insert a speech in the published *Record* even though the speech was not actually delivered on the floor of the House or Senate.

Clause 4. Adjournment. Both houses must agree to any adjournment longer than three days.

Section 6

Clause 1. The senators and representatives shall receive a compensation for their services, to be ascertained by law, and paid out of the Treasury of the United States. They shall in all cases, except treason, felony, and breach of the peace, be privileged from arrest during their attendance at the session of their respective houses, and in going to and returning from the same; and for any speech or debate in either house, they shall not be questioned in any other place.

Clause 2. No senator or representative shall, during the time for which he was elected, be appointed to any civil office under the authority of the United States which shall have been created, or the emoluments whereof shall have been increased, during such time; and no person holding any office under the United States shall be a member of either house during his continuance in office.

Section 6. Special Rights and Restrictions

Clause 1. Salaries and Privileges. The members of Congress can by law set their own salaries. When Congress is in session, members cannot be arrested except on certain criminal charges. Thus the work of Congress cannot be disrupted by lawsuits against Senators and Representatives. In particular, the members of Congress cannot be sued for "any speech or debate in either house." While taking part in the work of Congress, members can write or say anything about anyone without fear of being sued for libel or slander.

Clause 2. Employment Restrictions. Members of Congress cannot create new federal jobs or increase the "emoluments," or payments, for old ones and then leave Congress to take those jobs. Nor can anyone holding a federal job outside Congress serve at the same time as a member of Congress. This restriction prevents the members of Congress from simultaneously working for other branches of the federal government.

Section 7

Clause 1. All bills for raising revenue shall originate in the House of Representatives; but the Senate may propose or concur with amendments as on other bills.

Clause 2. Every bill which shall have passed the House of Representatives and the Senate shall, before it becomes a law, be presented to the President of the United States. If he approve he shall sign it, but if not, he shall return it, with his objections, to that house in which it shall have originated, who shall enter the objections at large on their journal and proceed to reconsider it. If, after such reconsideration, two thirds of that house shall agree to pass the bill, it shall be sent, together with the objections, to the other house, by which it shall likewise be reconsidered, and, if approved by two thirds of that house, it shall become a law. But in all such cases the votes of both houses shall be determined by yeas and nays, and the names of the persons voting for and against the bill shall be entered on the journal of each house respectively. If any bill shall not be returned by the President within ten days (Sundays excepted) after it shall have been presented to him, the same shall be a law, in like manner as if he had signed it, unless the Congress by their adjournment prevent its return, in which case it shall not be a law.

Clause 3. Every order, resolution, or vote to which the concurrence of the Senate and House of Representatives may be necessary (except on a question of adjournment) shall be presented to the President of the United States; and before the same shall take effect, shall be approved by him, or being disapproved by him, shall be repassed by two thirds of the Senate and House of Representatives, according to the rules and limitations prescribed in the case of a bill.

Section 7 How a Bill Becomes a Law

Clause 1. Tax Bills. All tax bills must begin in the House. The Senate, however, can thoroughly revise such bills.

Clause 2. Submitting Bills to the President. After Congress passes a bill, it goes to the President. The bill can then become a law in one of three ways. First the President may approve the bill and sign it. Second, the President may veto the bill and return it to Congress with objections. If Congress is able to override the President's veto by a two-thirds vote of both houses, the bill becomes law. Third, the President may do nothing. In that case the bill becomes law after 10 days (not counting Sundays), provided Congress is in session at that time.

The bill can fail to become a law in two ways. First, the President may veto it. If Congress is unable to override the veto, the bill dies. Second, the President may do nothing. If Congress adjourns within 10 days, the bill dies. This method is called a pocket veto. A President may use it to avoid an open veto of a controversial bill.

Clause 3. Submitting Other Measures to the President. If other measures require agreement by both houses and are in effect bills, they must go to the President. Thus Congress cannot avoid submitting bills to the President by calling them orders or resolutions. When such measures reach the President, they are treated as bills.

Section 8

The Congress shall have power:

Clause 1. To lay and collect taxes, duties, imposts, and excises, to pay the debts and provide for the common defense and general welfare of the United States; but all duties, imposts, and excises shall be uniform throughout the United States;

Clause 2. To borrow money on the credit of the United States;

Clause 3. To regulate commerce with foreign nations, and among the several states, and with the Indian tribes;

Clause 4. To establish a uniform rule of naturalization and uniform laws on the subject of bankruptcies throughout the United States;

Clause 5. To coin money, regulate the value thereof, and of foreign coin, and fix the standard of weights and measures;

Clause 6. To provide for the punishment of counterfeiting the securities and current coin of the United States;

Clause 7. To establish post offices and post roads;

Section 8. Powers Granted to Congress

Clause 1. Taxation. Congress can impose "duties," taxes on imported goods. But Congress cannot tax exports. (See Section 9, Clause 5, below.) "Excises" are taxes on the manufacture, sale, or use of products, such as cigarettes, within the nation. "Imposts" are taxes of any sort.

Clause 2. Borrowing.

Clause 3. Regulating Interstate Trade. This is the "interstate commerce clause," the basis of many federal regulations.

Clause 4. Naturalization; Bankruptcy.

Clause 5. Coining Money. The federal government's power to print paper money derives from this clause.

Clause 6. Punishment of Counterfeiting. The "securities" referred to are government bonds.

Clause 7. Providing Postal Service.

Clause 8. To promote the progress of science and useful arts, by securing for limited times to authors and inventors the exclusive right to their respective writings and discoveries;

Clause 8. Encouraging Authors and Inventors. Through this clause authors receive copyrights and inventors receive patents.

Clause 9. To constitute tribunals inferior to the Supreme Court;

Clause 9. Establishing Lower Courts. Federal courts "inferior to the Supreme Court" include district courts and the United States Court of Appeals.

Clause 10. To define and punish piracies and felonies committed on the high seas and offenses against the law of nations;

Clause 10. Punishment of Crimes at Sea.

Clause 11. To declare war, grant letters of marque and reprisal, and make rules concerning captures on land and water;

Clause 11. Declaring War. "Letters of marque and reprisal" authorize private ships to attack and seize enemy ships.

Clause 12. To raise and support armies, but no appropriation of money to that use shall be for a longer term than two years;

Clause 12. Raising Armies.

Clause 13. To provide and maintain a navy;

Clause 13. Maintaining a Navy.

Clause 14. To make rules for the government and regulation of the land and naval forces;

Clause 14. Regulating the Armed Forces.

Clause 15. To provide for calling forth the militia to execute the laws of the Union, suppress insurrections, and repel invasions;

Clause 15. Calling Out the Militia. Congress can empower the President to call out state militia units, now known as the National Guard.

Clause 16. To provide for organizing, arming, and disciplining the militia, and for governing such part of them as may be employed in the service of the United States, reserving to the states respectively the appointment of the officers and the authority of training the militia according to the discipline prescribed by Congress;

Clause 16. Maintaining the Militia. The federal government and each state government share in providing funds for the National Guard.

Clause 17. To exercise exclusive legislation in all cases whatsoever over such district (not exceeding ten miles square) as may, by cession of particular states and the acceptance of Congress, become the seat of the government of the United States, and to exercise like authority over all places purchased by the consent of the legislature of the state in which the same shall be for the erection of forts, magazines, arsenals, dockyards, and other needful buildings; and

Clause 17. Control of Federal Property. Congress makes laws for the District of Columbia and for federal land on which forts, naval bases, and other federal structures stand.

Clause 18. To make all laws which shall be necessary and proper for carrying into execution the foregoing powers and all other powers vested by this Constitution in the government of the United States, or in any department or officer thereof.

Clause 18. Carrying Out Granted Powers. This clause, known as the "necessary and proper" clause, gives Congress a basis for dealing with matters not specifically named in the Constitution. The clause is also known as the "elastic clause."

Section 9

Clause 1. The migration or importation of such persons as any of the states now existing shall think proper to admit shall not be prohibited by Congress prior to the year 1808, but a tax or duty may be imposed on such importation, not exceeding ten dollars for each person.

Section 9. Powers Denied to Congress

Clause 1. Ending the Slave Trade. Congress was forbidden to end the importing of slaves before 1808. In that year, Congress declared that further importing of slaves was illegal.

Clause 2. The privilege of the writ of habeas corpus shall not be suspended, unless, when in cases of rebellion or invasion, the public safety may require it.

Clause 2. Suspending the Writ of Habeas Corpus. A writ of habeas corpus is a legal order saying that a person who is held in custody must be brought into court so that a judge can decide whether the person is being held illegally. During the Civil War (a case of "rebellion or invasion"), President Abraham Lincoln suspended the right to habeas corpus in some areas.

Clause 3. No bill of attainder or ex post facto law shall be passed.

Clause 3. Imposing Certain Penalties. A "bill of attainder" allows a person to be punished without a jury trial. An "ex post facto law" allows a person to be punished for an act that was not illegal when it was committed.

Clause 4. No capitation ~~or other direct~~ tax shall be laid, unless in proportion to the census or enumeration herein before directed to be taken.

Clause 4. Taxing Individuals Unfairly. A "capitation tax," also known as a "head tax," is paid by individuals directly to the government. This clause requires that any such tax be divided fairly among the states according to their population. The Sixteenth Amendment, ratified in 1913, prevents this clause from being applied to income taxes.

Clause 5. No tax or duty shall be laid on articles exported from any state.

Clause 5. Taxing Exports. Here "exported" means sent out of a state, whether to another state or to another country.

Clause 6. No preference shall be given by any regulation of commerce or revenue to the ports of one state over those of another; nor shall vessels bound to or from one state be obliged to enter, clear, or pay duties in another.

Clause 6. Taxing Trade Unfairly; Allowing Ships to Be Taxed in Trade Between States.

Clause 7. No money shall be drawn from the Treasury but in consequence of appropriations made by law; and a regular statement and account of the receipts and expenditures of all public money shall be published from time to time.

Clause 7. Unlawful Spending. The federal government can spend money only when Congress authorizes the spending. Federal spending and receipts must be recorded and published.

Clause 8. No title of nobility shall be granted by the United States. And no person holding any office of profit or trust under them shall, without the consent of the Congress, accept of any present, emolument, office, or title of any kind whatever from any king, prince, or foreign state.

Clause 8. Creating Titles of Nobility; Allowing Gifts from Foreign Countries Without Permission. Congress cannot give anyone a title such as duchess or count. Congress has passed laws letting federal officials accept small gifts from foreign countries. Larger gifts become the property of the United States government.

Section 10

Section 10. Powers Denied to the States

Clause 1. No state shall enter into any treaty, alliance, or confederation; grant letters of marque and reprisal; coin money; emit bills of credit; make anything but gold and silver coin a tender in payment of debts; pass any bill of attainder, ex post facto law, or law impairing the obligation of contracts, or grant any title of nobility.

Clause 1. Certain Foreign, Financial, and Legal Dealings. Some of these powers are given exclusively to the federal government. Others are denied to any government, state or federal.

Clause 2. No state shall, without the consent of the Congress, lay any imposts or duties on imports or exports, except what may be absolutely necessary for executing its inspection laws; and the net produce of all duties and imposts laid by any state on imports or exports shall be for the use of the Treasury of the United States; and all such laws shall be subject to the revision and control of the Congress.

Clause 2. Taxing Imports or Exports Without Permission. Except with the consent of Congress, a state cannot tax any goods entering or leaving the state. The state can charge a small fee, however, to pay for inspection of the goods.

Clause 3. No state shall, without the consent of Congress, lay any duty of tonnage; keep troops or ships of war in time of peace; enter into any agreement or compact with another state or with a foreign power; or engage in war, unless actually invaded, or in such imminent danger as will not admit of delay.

Clause 3. Taxing Ships or Making Military or Diplomatic Arrangements Without Permission. "Tonnage" is the number of tons of cargo a ship can carry. States cannot tax ships that use their ports without the agreement of Congress.

Except with the consent of Congress, a state cannot prepare for war or wage war unless there is a military emergency.

Article 2
Section 1

Clause 1. The executive power shall be vested in a President of the United States of America. He shall hold his office during the term of four years, and, together with the Vice-President, chosen for the same term, be elected as follows:

Clause 2. Each state shall appoint, in such manner as the legislature thereof may direct, a number of electors, equal to the whole number of senators and representatives to which the state may be entitled in the Congress; but no senator or representative, or person holding an office of trust or profit under the United States, shall be appointed an elector.

~~***Clause 3.*** The electors shall meet in their respective states and vote by ballot for two persons, of whom one at least shall not be an inhabitant of the same state with themselves. And they shall make a list of all the persons voted for and of the number of votes for each; which list they shall sign and certify, and transmit sealed to the seat of the government of the United States, directed to the president of the Senate. The president of the Senate shall, in the presence of the Senate and House of Representatives, open all the certificates, and the votes shall then be counted. The person having the greatest number of votes shall be the President, if such number be a majority of the whole number of electors appointed; and if there be more than one who have such majority, and have an equal number of votes, then the House of Representatives shall immediately choose by ballot one of them for President; and if no person have a majority, then from the five highest on the list the said house shall in like manner choose the President. But in choosing the President, the votes shall be taken by states, the representation from each state having one vote; a quorum for this purpose shall consist of a member or members from two thirds of the states, and a majority of all the states shall be necessary to a choice. In every case, after the choice of the President, the person having the greatest number of votes of the electors shall be the Vice-President. But if there should remain two or more who have equal votes, the Senate shall choose from them by ballot the Vice-President.~~

Clause 4. The Congress may determine the time of choosing the electors and the day on which they shall give their votes, which day shall be the same throughout the United States.

Clause 5. No person except a natural-born citizen, or a citizen of the United States at the time of the adoption of this Constitution, shall be eligible to the office of President; neither shall any person be eligible to that office who shall not have attained to the age of thirty-five years and been fourteen years a resident within the United States.

Clause 6. In case of the removal of the President from office, or of his death, resignation, or inability to discharge the powers and duties of the said office, the same shall de-

Article 2. **The Executive Branch**
Section 1. The Offices of President and Vice-President

Clause 1. The President as Executive; Term of Office. As chief executive, the President is responsible for executing, or carrying out, the laws passed by Congress.

Clause 2. Choosing Electors. This clause set up the electoral college, the group of people who elect the President and Vice-President. At first the electors were chosen mainly by state legislatures. After 1800 the electors were chosen increasingly by popular vote. Today all electors are chosen in this way.

Clause 3. Voting by Electors. Originally each elector voted for two candidates. Either might become President. As a result, the Republican candidate for President in 1800, Thomas Jefferson, received the same number of electoral votes as the Republican candidate for Vice-President, Aaron Burr. The choice was then left to the House of Representatives, which finally chose Jefferson.

To prevent similar ties between candidates for President and Vice-President, Congress passed the Twelfth Amendment in 1803. The amendment was ratified in June 1804, before the next presidential election. It required electors to cast one ballot for President and a separate ballot for Vice-President.

Clause 4. Time of Elections. Congress has decided that presidential elections are to be held every four years. The people vote on the Tuesday following the first Monday of November. Electoral votes are cast on the Monday after the second Wednesday in December.

Clause 5. Qualifications of the President.

Clause 6. Presidential Succession. In 1886 Congress specified that the line of succession would go from the Vice-President to members of the cabinet. In 1947 Congress changed the line of volve on the Vice-President, and the Congress may by law provide for the case of removal, death, resignation, or inability, both of the President and Vice-President, declaring what officer shall then act as President, and such officer shall act accordingly until the disability be removed or a President shall be elected.

succession to go from the Vice-President to the Speaker of the House, then to the president pro tempore of the Senate, and then to the cabinet. The Twenty-fifth Amendment, ratified in 1967, prevents a long vacancy in the office of Vice-President. The amendment also establishes procedures in case the President is disabled.

Clause 7. The President shall, at stated times, receive for his services a compensation, which shall neither be increased nor diminished during the period for which he shall have been elected, and he shall not receive within that period any other emolument from the United States or any of them.

Clause 7. Presidential Salary.

Clause 8. Before he enter on the execution of his office, he shall take the following oath or affirmation: "I do solemnly swear (or affirm) that I will faithfully execute the office of President of the United States, and will, to the best of my ability, preserve, protect, and defend the Constitution of the United States."

Clause 8. The Oath of Office. The Constitution does not say who will administer the oath. Ordinarily it is the Chief Justice of the Supreme Court. Federal Judge Sarah Hughes administered the oath of office to Lyndon Johnson after President John F. Kennedy's assassination in 1963.

Section 2

Section 2. Powers Granted to the President

Clause 1. The President shall be commander in chief of the army and navy of the United States, and of the militia of the several states when called into actual service of the United States. He may require the opinion, in writing, of the principal officer in each of the executive departments upon any subject relating to the duties of their respective offices. And he shall have power to grant reprieves and pardons for offenses against the United States, except in cases of impeachment.

Clause 1. Military Powers; Executive Powers; Reprieves and Pardons. Together, the military powers of the President and of Congress assure civilian control of the armed forces.

The President may grant a reprieve to stop punishment after a trial or grant a pardon to prevent a trial. In 1974 President Gerald R. Ford issued a pardon to Richard M. Nixon before the House could begin impeachment proceedings. Nixon then could not be tried on federal charges related to the Watergate scandal.

Clause 2. He shall have power, by and with the advice and consent of the Senate, to make treaties, provided two thirds of the senators present concur; and he shall nominate, and by and with the advice and consent of the Senate, shall appoint ambassadors, other public ministers and consuls, judges of the Supreme Court, and all other officers of the United States whose appointments were not herein otherwise provided for, and which shall be established by law; but the Congress may by law vest the appointment of such inferior officers as they think proper in the President alone, in the courts of law, or in the heads of departments.

Clause 2. Treaties and Appointments. The President may make treaties and appointments, but the Senate must approve them by a two-thirds vote. The president's power can be checked by the power of the Senate to reject the treaties and appointments.

Clause 3. The President shall have power to fill up all vacancies that may happen during the recess of the Senate, by granting commissions which shall expire at the end of their next session.

Clause 3. Temporary Appointments. When the Senate is not in session and cannot confirm appointments, the President may fill vacancies on a temporary basis.

Section 3

He shall from time to time give to the Congress information of the state of the Union, and recommend to their consideration such measures as he shall judge necessary and expedient; he may, on extraordinary occasions, convene both houses, or either of them, and in case of disagreement between them with respect to the time of adjournment, he may adjourn them to such time as he shall think proper; he shall receive ambassadors and other public ministers; he shall take care that the laws be faithfully executed, and shall commission all the officers of the United States.

Section 3. Duties of the President

The President delivers a State of the Union message to Congress each January. On many occasions, especially in the 1800s, the President has called Congress into special session. No President has needed to adjourn Congress.

The duty of receiving ambassadors fits the President's power to make treaties. The duty to "take care that the laws be faithfully executed" places the President in charge of enforcing federal law.

Section 4

The President, Vice-President, and all civil officers of the United States shall be removed from office on impeachment for, and conviction of, treason, bribery, or other high crimes and misdemeanors.

Section 4. Impeachment

Among the "civil officers" who can be impeached are cabinet members and federal judges.

Article 3

Section 1

The judicial power of the United States shall be vested in one Supreme Court, and in such inferior courts as the Congress may from time to time ordain and establish. The judges, both of the Supreme and inferior courts, shall hold their offices during good behavior, and shall, at stated times, receive for their services a compensation which shall not be diminished during their continuance in office.

Article 3. The Judicial Branch

Section 1. Federal Courts

Congress has established district courts and appeals courts under the Supreme Court.

Congress also has decided from time to time how many justices serve on the Supreme Court. But Congress can neither abolish the Supreme Court nor remove any federal judges unless they are impeached and convicted. Nor can Congress put pressure on judges by lowering their "compensation," or salaries.

Section 2

Clause 1. The judicial power shall extend to all cases, in law and equity, arising under this Constitution, the laws of the United States, and treaties made, or which shall be made, under their authority; to all cases affecting ambassadors, other public ministers and consuls; to all cases of admiralty and maritime jurisdiction; to controversies to which the United States shall be a party; to controversies between two or more states; ~~between a state and citizens of another state;~~ between citizens of different states; between citizens of the same state claiming lands under grants of different states; and between a state, or the citizens thereof, and foreign states, ~~citizens, or subjects.~~

Clause 2. In all cases affecting ambassadors, other public ministers and consuls, and those in which a state shall be party, the Supreme Court shall have original jurisdiction. In all the other cases before-mentioned, the Supreme Court shall have appellate jurisdiction, both as to law and fact, with such exceptions and under such regulations as the Congress shall make.

Clause 3. The trial of all crimes, except in cases of impeachment, shall be by jury; and such trial shall be held in the state where the said crimes shall have been committed; but when not committed within any state, the trial shall be at such place or places as the Congress may by law have directed.

Section 2. Jurisdiction of Federal Courts

Clause 1. Types of Cases. This clause names the types of cases that federal courts can rule on. These include "all cases . . . arising under this Constitution." Therefore the Supreme Court can exercise the right of judicial review, as asserted by Chief Justice John Marshall in the case of *Marbury* v. *Madison.* Thus the Court can declare a law unconstitutional. First, though, a case that involves the law must be brought before the Court. The Court cannot review a law unless it is presented to the Court as part of a case.

Clause 2. Original Cases and Appeals Cases. Cases of "original jurisdiction" go directly to the Supreme Court. Cases of "appellate jurisdiction" go first to lower courts. Then, if the lower court proceedings are appealed, the cases go to the Supreme Court. Congress sets the rules for appeal. Nearly all cases heard by the Supreme Court begin in the lower courts.

Clause 3. Cases Requiring Trials by Jury. This clause covers trials involving federal crimes. The clause does not require juries in civil cases, which involve individual rights, or in criminal cases under state laws.

Section 3

Clause 1. Treason against the United States shall consist only in levying war against them or in adhering to their enemies, giving them aid and comfort. No person shall be convicted of treason unless on the testimony of two witnesses to the same overt act, or on confession in open court.

Section 3. Treason

Clause 1. Limits of the Crime. To be convicted of treason against the United States, a person must commit an overt act, one that can be seen. Merely talking or thinking about treason is not a crime.

Clause 2. The Congress shall have power to declare the punishment of treason, but no attainder of treason shall work corruption of blood or forfeiture except during the life of the person attainted.

Article 4

Section 1

Full faith and credit shall be given in each state to the public acts, records, and judicial proceedings of every other state. And the Congress may by general laws prescribe the manner in which such acts, records, and proceedings shall be proved, and the effect thereof.

Section 2

Clause 1. The citizens of each state shall be entitled to all privileges and immunities of citizens in the several states.

Clause 2. A person charged in any state with treason, felony or other crime, who shall flee from justice and be found in another state, shall, on demand of the executive authority of the state from which he fled, be delivered up to be removed to the state having jurisdiction of the crime.

~~***Clause 3.*** No person held to service or labor in one state under the laws thereof, escaping into another, shall, in consequence of any law or regulation therein, be discharged from such service or labor, but shall be delivered up on claim of the party to whom such service or labor may be due.~~

Section 3

Clause 1. New states may be admitted by the Congress into this Union; but no new state shall be formed or erected within the jurisdiction of any other state; nor any state be formed by the junction of two or more states, or parts of states, without the consent of the legislatures of the states concerned as well as of the Congress.

Clause 2. The Congress shall have power to dispose of and make all needful rules and regulations respecting the territory or other property belonging to the United States; and nothing in this Constitution shall be so construed as to prejudice any claims of the United States, or of any particular state.

Section 4

The United States shall guarantee to every state in this Union a republican form of government, and shall protect each of them against invasion, and, on application of the legislature or of the executive (when the legislature cannot be convened), against domestic violence.

Clause 2. Limits of the Punishment. "Attainder of treason" and "corruption of blood" refer to punishing the family of a traitor. Such punishment is banned by this clause.

Article 4. **Relations Among the States, the Territories, and the United States**

Section 1. Official Acts of the States

Every state must recognize and honor the official acts of other states. Congress can decide what official proofs (for example, marriage certificates) must be accepted from state to state.

Section 2. Privileges and Liabilities of Citizens

Clause 1. Privileges. No state can discriminate against a citizen of another state except in special cases, such as residence requirements for voting or entrance requirements for state colleges.

Clause 2. Liabilities of Fugitive Criminals. If a person commits a crime in one state and then flees to another state and is caught, the governor of the state where the crime took place can demand the person's return.

Clause 3. Liabilities of Fugitive Slaves or Servants. The phrase "held to service or labor" refers to slavery or to service as an indentured servant. The Thirteenth Amendment nullified this clause.

Section 3. Admitting New States and Regulating Territories

Clause 1. New States. Congress can add new states to the Union. New states cannot be formed by dividing existing states (as when Maine separated from Massachusetts in 1820) or by combining parts of existing states unless both Congress and the states involved consent to the changes.

Clause 2. Territories. Besides having power over federal property of various kinds, Congress has the power to govern federal land. This land includes territory not organized into states and also federal land within states.

Section 4. Protection of the States

The federal government promises that each state will have some form of representative government. The federal government also promises to protect each state from invasion. It will send help, when requested, to stop rioting within a state.

Article 5

The Congress, whenever two thirds of both houses shall deem it necessary, shall propose amendments to this Constitution or, on the application of the legislatures of two thirds of the several states, shall call a convention for proposing amendments, which, in either case, shall be valid, to all intents and purposes, as part of this Constitution when ratified by the legislatures of three fourths of the several states, or by conventions in three fourths thereof, as the one or the other mode of ratification may be proposed by the Congress; provided ~~that no amendment which may be made prior to the year 1808 shall in any manner affect the first and fourth clauses in the ninth section of the first article; and~~ that no state, without its consent, shall be deprived of its equal suffrage in the Senate.

Article 5. **Methods of Amending the Constitution**

There are two ways to propose amendments to the Constitution. One is by a two-thirds vote of both the House and the Senate. The other way—which has not yet been used—is by a special convention demanded by two thirds of the states.

Once an amendment is proposed, there are two ways to ratify it. First, three fourths of the state legislatures may vote to approve it. Second, special conventions in three fourths of the states may approve the amendment. This way has been used only once, to ratify the Twenty-first Amendment. Congress decides which method of ratification to use.

The three-fourths requirement for ratification means that 38 states must now approve a proposed amendment before it becomes law.

Article 6

Clause 1. All debts contracted and engagements entered into before the adoption of this Constitution shall be as valid against the United States under this Constitution as under the Confederation.

Clause 2. This Constitution and the laws of the United States which shall be made in pursuance thereof, and all treaties made, or which shall be made, under the authority of the United States, shall be the supreme law of the land; and the judges in every state shall be bound thereby, anything in the Constitution or laws of any state to the contrary notwithstanding.

Clause 3. The senators and representatives before-mentioned, and the members of the several state legislatures, and all executive and judicial officers, both of the United States and of the several states, shall be bound by oath or affirmation to support this Constitution; but no religious test shall ever be required as a qualification to any office or public trust under the United States.

Article 6. **Federal Debts and the Supremacy of Federal Laws**

Clause 1. Federal Debts. **This clause promises that all debts incurred by Congress under the Articles of Confederation will be honored by the United States under the Constitution.**

Clause 2. Supremacy of the Constitution and of Federal Laws. **The Constitution and federal laws or treaties made under it are the highest laws of the nation. When federal laws are in conflict with state laws or constitutions, state judges must follow the federal laws.**

Clause 3. Oaths to Support the Constitution. **All federal and all state officials must promise to support the Constitution. But federal officials must not be required to meet any religious standards in order to hold office.**

State officials may be required to meet religious standards, but since the 1840s no state has set such requirements for its officials.

Article 7

The ratification of the conventions of nine states shall be sufficient for the establishment of this Constitution between the states so ratifying the same.

Done in convention by the unanimous consent of the states present the seventeenth day of September in the year of our Lord one thousand seven hundred and eighty-seven, and of the independence of the United States of America the twelfth. In witness whereof we have hereunto subscribed our names,

George Washington,
President and deputy from Virginia

Article 7. **Ratification of the Constitution**

"Conventions" refers to special conventions held in the states to approve or disapprove the Constitution. Nine state conventions voted their approval by June 21, 1788. The Constitution was signed on September 17, 1787, in the 12th year of the country's independence. George Washington signed first as the president of the Philadelphia convention. He was not elected President of the United States until 1789. Of the 55 delegates to the Philadelphia convention, 39 signed the Constitution and 16 did not.

New Hampshire
John Langdon
Nicholas Gilman

Massachusetts
Nathaniel Gorham
Rufus King

Connecticut
William Samuel Johnson
Roger Sherman

New York
Alexander Hamilton

New Jersey
William Livingston
David Brearley
William Paterson
Jonathan Dayton

Pennsylvania
Benjamin Franklin
Thomas Mifflin
Robert Morris
George Clymer
Thomas FitzSimons
Jared Ingersoll
James Wilson
Gouverneur Morris

Delaware
George Read
Gunning Bedford, Jr.
John Dickinson
Richard Bassett
Jacob Broom

Maryland
James McHenry
Dan of St. Thomas Jenifer
Daniel Carroll

Virginia
John Blair
James Madison, Jr.

North Carolina
William Blount
Richard Dobbs Spaight
Hugh Williamson

South Carolina
John Rutledge
Charles Cotesworth Pinckney
Charles Pinckney
Pierce Butler

Georgia
William Few
Abraham Baldwin

Amendments to the Constitution

The first ten amendments, called the Bill of Rights, were proposed as a group in 1789 and ratified in 1791. Other amendments were proposed and ratified one at a time. The dates in parentheses are the years of ratification.

Amendment 1

Congress shall make no law respecting an establishment of religion or prohibiting the free exercise thereof, or abridging the freedom of speech or of the press, or the right of the people peaceably to assemble and to petition the government for a redress of grievances.

Amendment 1 (1791). **Religious and Political Freedoms**

Congress cannot establish an official religion or interfere with freedom of worship. It cannot prohibit free speech or other political freedoms.

These freedoms are not absolute, though. They are limited by the rights of others. For example, the right of free speech does not include slander—the spreading of false stories to damage another person's reputation. Nor does the right of free speech include words that present what the Supreme Court has termed a "clear and present danger," such as screaming "fire" in a crowded theater.

Amendment 2

A well-regulated militia being necessary to the security of a free state, the right of the people to keep and bear arms shall not be infringed.

Amendment 2 (1791). **The Right to Bear Arms**

For the purposes of maintaining a state militia, citizens may keep and bear arms. Congress has prohibited the possession of certain firearms, however, such as sawed-off shotguns and machine guns.

Amendment 3

No soldier shall, in time of peace, be quartered in any house without the consent of the owner, nor in time of war but in a manner to be prescribed by law.

Amendment 3 (1791). **The Quartering of Soldiers**

In peacetime, soldiers cannot be quartered, or given lodging, in any private home unless the owner consents. In wartime, soldiers can be quartered in private homes, but only as directed by law.

Amendment 4

The right of the people to be secure in their persons, houses, papers, and effects against unreasonable searches and seizures shall not be violated, and no warrants shall issue, but upon probable cause, supported by oath or affirmation, and particularly describing the place to be searched and the persons or things to be seized.

Amendment 4 (1791). **Freedom from Unreasonable Searches and Seizures**

People and their homes and belongings are protected against unreasonable searches and seizures. As a rule, authorities must go before a court and obtain a search warrant before seizing evidence. They must get an arrest warrant before arresting someone. To obtain a legal warrant, the authorities must explain why it is needed, where the search will take place, and who or what will be seized.

Amendment 5

No person shall be held to answer for a capital or otherwise infamous crime unless on a presentment or indictment of a grand jury, except in cases arising in the land or naval forces, or in the militia, when in actual service in time of war or public danger; nor shall any person be subject for the same offense to be twice put in jeopardy of life or limb; nor shall be compelled in any criminal case to be a witness against himself, nor be deprived of life, liberty, or property without due process of law; nor shall private property be taken for public use without just compensation.

Amendment 5 (1791). **Rights Regarding Life, Liberty, and Property**

A person cannot be placed on trial in a federal court for a crime punishable by death or for any other major crime without a formal written accusation by a grand jury. This rule does not apply if the person is a member of the armed services during war or a time of public danger.

A grand jury can decide that there is not enough evidence to accuse a person of a crime. Or the jury can make a formal accusation. The charge can be based on evidence the jury gains on its own (a presentment) or on evidence presented by a prosecutor (an indictment). The accused person can then be held for trial before a trial jury.

If a person is found not guilty of a certain crime, the person cannot be tried again for the same offense (double jeopardy) in a federal court. This rule does not prevent the person from being tried for the same offense in a state court, however.

A person accused of a federal crime cannot be forced to give evidence against himself or herself. Nor can a person lose his or her life, liberty, or property in federal proceedings except as specified by law. When the government takes private property for public use (through the right of eminent domain), the government must pay a fair price.

Amendment 6

In all criminal prosecutions, the accused shall enjoy the right to a speedy and public trial by an impartial jury of the state and district wherein the crime shall have been committed, which district shall have been previously ascertained by law, and to be informed of the nature and cause of the accusation; to be confronted with the witnesses against him; to have compulsory process for obtaining witnesses in his favor, and to have the assistance of counsel for his defense.

Amendment 6 (1791). **The Right to a Trial by Jury in Criminal Cases**

A person accused of a crime has the right to a prompt, public trial. The case will be heard by a jury selected from the district in which the crime was committed. That district must be one that already has been described by law, such as an established city or county.

Accused persons must be informed of the exact charges against them. They must be allowed to face and question witnesses. Any accused person has the power to force witnesses to appear in court and has the right to a defense lawyer.

Amendment 7

In suits at common law, where the value in controversy shall exceed twenty dollars, the right of trial by jury shall be preserved, and no fact tried by a jury shall be otherwise re-examined in any court of the United States than according to the rules of the common law.

Amendment 7 (1791). **The Right to a Trial by Jury in Civil Cases**

Common law is based on customs and on decisions made by judges in previous cases. (Statute law, in contrast, is established by legislatures.)

Suits at common law usually involve disputes between private parties or corporations. They usually are tried in state courts. When such suits involve more than $20 and are tried in federal courts, either side can insist on a jury trial. If both sides agree, they can choose not to have a jury.

Once a jury reaches a decision, that decision cannot be overturned merely because a judge disagrees with the jury's findings.

Amendment 8

Excessive bail shall not be required, nor excessive fines imposed, nor cruel and unusual punishments inflicted.

Amendment 8 (1791). **Bail, Fines, and Punishments**

Bail is money or property that an accused person gives temporarily to a court as a guarantee that he or she will appear for trial. The amount of bail varies. The more serious the crime, usually the higher the bail. The amount also depends on the reputation and circumstances of the accused person. Unreasonably high bail is forbidden. So are unreasonably high fines and cruel and unusual punishments.

Amendment 9

The enumeration in the Constitution of certain rights shall not be construed to deny or disparage others retained by the people.

Amendment 9 (1791). **Further Rights of the People**

The naming of certain rights in the Constitution does not mean that people are limited to those rights only. People may claim other rights as well.

Amendment 10

The powers not delegated to the United States by the Constitution, nor prohibited by it to the states, are reserved to the states respectively, or to the people.

Amendment 10 (1791). **Powers Reserved to the States and to the People**

The federal government is granted certain powers under the Constitution. All other powers, except those denied to the states, belong to the states or to the people.

Amendment 11

The judicial power of the United States shall not be construed to extend to any suit in law or equity commenced or prosecuted against one of the United States by citizens of another state, or by citizens or subjects of any foreign state.

Amendment 11 (1795). **Lawsuits Against the States**

This amendment came about because the states feared a loss of authority if they could be sued in federal courts by foreigners or by citizens of other states. The amendment prevents such lawsuits from taking place in federal courts.

Amendment 12

The electors shall meet in their respective states and vote by ballot for President and Vice-President, one of whom at least shall not be an inhabitant of the same state with themselves; they shall name in their ballots the person voted for as President, and in distinct ballots the person voted for as Vice-President, and they shall make distinct lists of all persons voted for as President and of all persons voted for as Vice-President and of the number of votes for each, which lists they shall sign and certify and transmit sealed to the seat of government of the United States, directed to the president of the Senate. The president of the Senate shall, in the presence of the Senate and House of Representatives, open all the certificates and the votes shall then be counted. The person having the greatest number of votes for President shall be the President, if such number be a majority of the whole number of electors appointed; and if no person have such majority, then from the persons having the highest numbers not exceeding three on the list of those voted for as President, the House of Representatives shall choose immediately, by ballot, the President. But in choosing the President the votes shall be taken by states, the representation from each state having one vote; a quorum for this purpose shall consist of a member or members from two thirds of the states, and a majority of all the states shall be necessary to a choice. And if the House of Representatives shall not choose a President whenever the right of choice shall devolve upon them, ~~before the fourth day of March next following,~~ then the Vice-President shall act as President, as in the case of the death or other constitutional disability of the President. The person having the greatest number of votes as Vice-President shall be the Vice-President, if such number be a majority of the whole number of electors appointed, and if no person have a majority, then from the two highest numbers on the list the Senate shall choose the Vice-President; a quorum for the purpose shall consist of two thirds of the whole number of senators, and a majority of the whole number shall be necessary to a choice. But no person constitutionally ineligible to the office of President shall be eligible to that of Vice-President of the United States.

Amendment 12 (1804). **Separate Voting for President and Vice-President**

In each presidential election before 1800, the two leading candidates received differing numbers of electoral votes. The candidate with the higher number became President. The second-place candidate became Vice-President.

In 1800, electors voted along party lines. The Republican candidates for President and Vice-President received equal numbers of electoral votes. To prevent similar ties in later elections, this amendment requires separate electoral voting for President and Vice-President.

If no single candidate for President has a majority of the electoral votes for President, the House of Representatives must choose, by ballot, from the three leading candidates. In the balloting, each state may cast only one vote, no matter how many Representatives it has. If no single candidate for Vice-President has a majority of the electoral votes for Vice-President, the Senate must choose between the two leading candidates.

Amendment 13

Section 1

Neither slavery nor involuntary servitude, except as a punishment for crime whereof the party shall have been duly convicted, shall exist within the United States or any place subject to their jurisdiction.

Section 2

Congress shall have power to enforce this article by appropriate legislation.

Amendment 13 (1865). **Abolition of Slavery**

Section 1. Abolition

The Emancipation Proclamation, which took effect in 1863, applied only to the area then controlled by the Confederacy. This amendment bans slavery throughout the United States. The amendment also bans forced labor—"involuntary servitude"—except as legal punishment for crimes.

Section 2. Power of Enforcement

Congress has the power to pass laws to enforce this amendment.

Amendment 14

Section 1

All persons born or naturalized in the United States and subject to the jurisdiction thereof are citizens of the United States and of the state wherein they reside. No state shall make or enforce any law which shall abridge the privileges or immunities of citizens of the United States; nor shall any state deprive any person of life, liberty, or property without due process of law; nor deny to any person within its jurisdiction the equal protection of the laws.

Section 2

Representatives shall be apportioned among the several states according to their respective numbers, counting the whole number of persons in each state, ~~excluding Indians not taxed.~~ But when the right to vote at any election for the choice of electors for President and Vice-President of the United States, representatives in Congress, the executive and judicial officers of a state, or the members of the legislature thereof is denied to any of the ~~male~~ inhabitants of such state, being ~~twenty-one years of age and~~ citizens of the United States, or in any way abridged, except for participation in rebellion or other crime, the basis of representation therein shall be reduced in the proportion which the number of such ~~male~~ citizens shall bear to the whole number of ~~male~~ citizens ~~twenty-one years of age~~ in such state.

Section 3

No person shall be a senator or representative in Congress, or elector of President and Vice-President, or hold any office, civil or military, under the United States, or under any state, who, having previously taken an oath as a member of Congress or as an officer of the United States or as a member of any state legislature or as an executive or judicial officer of any state to support the Constitution of the United States, shall have engaged in insurrection or rebellion against the same, or given aid or comfort to the enemies thereof. But Congress may by a vote of two thirds of each house remove such disability.

Section 4

The validity of the public debt of the United States, authorized by law, including debts incurred for payment of pensions and bounties for services in suppressing insurrection or rebellion, shall not be questioned. But neither the United States nor any state shall assume or pay any debt or obligation incurred in aid of insurrection or rebellion against the United States or any claim for the loss or emancipation of any slave; but all such debts, obligations, and claims shall be held illegal and void.

Amendment 14 (1868). **Citizenship and Civil Rights**

Section 1. Citizenship

This section defines state citizenship. It prevents states from setting up their own definitions of citizenship in order to exclude African Americans or other groups.

The section also applies the due-process clause of the Fifth Amendment to actions by state governments. Since all citizens have "equal protection of the laws," states may not pass laws to discriminate unreasonably against any group.

Section 2. Representation and Voting Rights

Before 1865 each slave was counted as three fifths of a free person in determining the number of Representatives a state could send to Congress. This section does away with the three-fifths rule and sets up a different rule. If a state denies the right to vote ~~in federal elections~~ to male citizens age 21 or over—excepting those who have taken part in a rebellion or other crimes—that state would lose a proportional number of Representatives in Congress.

The rule was meant to force former slave states to allow black men to vote. It has never been enforced. Instead, the Fifteenth Amendment, ratified in 1870, has been used in lawsuits concerning voting rights for blacks.

Section 3. Disqualification of Former Confederate Leaders

Former state and federal officials who had served in the Confederacy were disqualified from holding state or federal office again, unless Congress voted otherwise. Congress did not completely remove this disqualification until 1898.

Section 4. Legal and Illegal Debts

The payment of the federal debt cannot be questioned, according to this section. This referred to debts that the Union incurred during the Civil War. Payment of the Confederate debt by any state or by the United States is illegal. Former slave owners have no legal claim to payment of any kind for their loss of slaves.

Former Confederate states were not allowed back into the Union until their legislatures ratified the Thirteenth and Fourteenth Amendments.

Section 5

The Congress shall have power to enforce, by appropriate legislation, the provisions of this article.

Section 5. Power of Enforcement

Congress has the power to pass laws to enforce this amendment.

Amendment 15

Section 1

The right of citizens of the United States to vote shall not be denied or abridged by the United States or by any state on account of race, color, or previous condition of servitude.

Section 2

The Congress shall have power to enforce this article by appropriate legislation.

Amendment 15 (1870). **Suffrage for African Americans**

Section 1. The Right to Vote

Race, color, or "previous condition of servitude"—status as an ex-slave—cannot be used by any state or by the United States to deny a person's right to vote. For a long time, states were able to use literacy tests and other devices to prevent many African-Americans from voting, despite this amendment.

Section 2. Power of Enforcement

Congress has the power to pass laws to enforce this amendment.

Amendment 16

The Congress shall have power to lay and collect taxes on incomes, from whatever source derived, without apportionment among the several states, and without regard to any census or enumeration.

Amendment 16 (1913). **Income Taxes**

Before this amendment, Congress could not levy an income tax. Article 1 of the Constitution (Section 2, Clause 3, and Section 9, Clause 4) says that federal taxes collected, state by state, must be in proportion to the states' population. This amendment allows an income tax to be levied on individuals and corporations without regard to the populations of the states.

Amendment 17

Section 1

The Senate of the United States shall be composed of two senators from each state, elected by the people thereof for six years; and each senator shall have one vote. The electors in each state shall have the qualifications requisite for electors of the most numerous branch of the state legislatures.

Section 2

When vacancies happen in the representation of any state in the Senate, the executive authority of such state shall issue writs of election to fill such vacancies, provided that the legislature of any state may empower the executive thereof to make temporary appointments until the people fill the vacancies by election as the legislature may direct.

Section 3

This amendment shall not be so construed as to affect the election or term of any senator chosen before it becomes valid as part of the Constitution.

Amendment 17 (1913). **Direct Election of Senators**

Section 1. Regular Elections

Article 1 of the Constitution (Section 3, Clause 1) says that Senators are to be elected by state legislatures. This amendment gives the power to elect Senators to the voters of each state.

Section 2. Special Elections

Any vacancy in the Senate must be filled through a special election called by the state governor. The state legislature may let the governor appoint someone to fill the vacancy temporarily, until an election can be held.

Section 3. Time of Effect

This amendment takes effect only when it is ratified as part of the Constitution, and not before.

Amendment 18

Section 1

After one year from the ratification of this article the manufacture, sale, or transportation of intoxicating liquors within, the importation thereof into, or the exportation thereof from the United States and all territory subject to the jurisdiction thereof for beverage purposes is hereby prohibited.

Section 2

The Congress and the several states shall have concurrent power to enforce this article by appropriate legislation.

Section 3

This article shall be inoperative unless it shall have been ratified as an amendment to the Constitution by the legislatures of the several states, as provided in the Constitution, within seven years from the date of the submission hereof to the states by the Congress.

Amendment 18 (1919). **National Prohibition**

Section 1. The Ban on Alcoholic Beverages

Manufacturing, selling, and transporting alcoholic beverages are to be illegal in the United States and its territories. The ban takes effect one year after the ratification of this amendment. Exporting and importing alcoholic beverages are to be illegal at the same time. This amendment was repealed in 1933 by the Twenty-first Amendment.

Section 2. Power of Enforcement

Both Congress and the states have the power to pass laws to enforce this amendment.

Section 3. Time Limit for Ratification

This amendment is not to take effect unless it is ratified by state legislatures within seven years.

Amendment 19

Section 1

The right of citizens of the United States to vote shall not be denied or abridged by the United States or by any state on account of sex.

Section 2

Congress shall have power to enforce this article by appropriate legislation.

Amendment 19 (1920). **Suffrage for Women**

Section 1. The Right to Vote

Women and men have an equal right to vote in the elections of the United States and of all the states.

Section 2. Power of Enforcement

Congress has the power to pass laws to enforce this amendment.

Amendment 20

Section 1

The terms of the President and Vice-President shall end at noon on the 20th day of January, and the terms of senators and representatives at noon on the 3rd day of January, of the years in which such terms would have ended if this article had not been ratified; and the terms of their successors shall then begin.

Amendment 20 (1933). **Terms of the President, Vice-President, and Congress**

Section 1. Ending Dates of Terms

The terms of the President and Vice-President end on January 20 in their final year. The terms of Senators and Representatives end on January 3.

Before this amendment, the terms of the President, Vice-President, and Congress ended on March 3. Defeated officeholders had to serve until March as "lame ducks," with little political power. This amendment, known as the "lame duck amendment," greatly reduces the time during which defeated officeholders remain in office.

Section 2

The Congress shall assemble at least once in every year, and such meeting shall begin at noon on the 3rd day of January, unless they shall by law appoint a different day.

Section 2. Meetings of Congress

Congress must meet at least once a year, beginning on January 3. Congress, however, can choose a different day.

Section 3

If, at the time fixed for the beginning of the term of the President, the President-elect shall have died, the Vice-President-elect shall become President. If a President shall not have been chosen before the time fixed for the beginning of his term, or if the President-elect shall have failed to qualify, then the Vice-President-elect shall act as President until a President shall have qualified; and the Congress may by law provide for the case wherein neither a President-elect nor a Vice-President-elect shall have qualified, declaring who shall then act as President, or the manner in which one who is to act shall be selected, and such person shall act accordingly until a President or Vice-President shall have qualified.

Section 3. Death or Lack of Qualification of a President-elect

If a President-elect dies before taking office, the Vice-President-elect will become President. If there is a deadlocked election and no President-elect has been qualified to take office, the Vice-President-elect will become President temporarily. If neither a President-elect nor a Vice-President-elect has been qualified to take office by the start of the term, Congress will decide on a temporary President.

Section 4

The Congress may by law provide for the case of the death of any of the persons from whom the House of Representatives may choose a President whenever the right of choice shall have devolved upon them, and for the case of the death of any of the persons from whom the Senate may choose a Vice-President whenever the right of choice shall have devolved upon them.

Section 4. Death of a Likely President-elect or a Likely Vice-President-elect

If no candidate for President receives a majority of the electoral votes, then, under the Twelfth Amendment, the House of Representatives must choose a President from among the three leading candidates. If one of those three dies before the House makes a choice, Congress can decide how to proceed, under this section.

Similarly, Congress can decide how to proceed in case a vice-presidential election goes to the Senate and one of the two leading candidates dies before the Senate makes its choice between them.

Section 5

Sections 1 and 2 shall take effect on the 15th day of October following the ratification of this article.

Section 5. Time of Effect

The first two sections of this amendment take effect on October 15 after the amendment is ratified.

Section 6

This article shall be inoperative unless it shall have been ratified as an amendment to the Constitution by the legislatures of three fourths of the several states within seven years from the date of its submission.

Section 6. Time Limit for Ratification

This amendment is not to take effect unless it is ratified by state legislatures within seven years.

Amendment 21

Section 1

The eighteenth article of amendment to the Constitution of the United States is hereby repealed.

Section 2

The transportation or importation into any state, territory, or possession of the United States for delivery or use therein of intoxicating liquors, in violation of the laws thereof, is hereby prohibited.

Amendment 21 (1933). **Repeal of Prohibition**

Section 1. Repeal

National prohibition is no longer required by law.

Section 2. Carrying Alcohol into "Dry" States

If a state is "dry"—that is, if it prohibits alcoholic beverages—then carrying alcoholic beverages into that state is a federal crime.

Section 3

This article shall be inoperative unless it shall have been ratified as an amendment to the Constitution by conventions in the several states, as provided in the Constitution, within seven years from the date of submission hereof to the states by the Congress.

Section 3. Method and Time Limit for Ratification

This amendment must be ratified by special state conventions. The amendment is not to take effect unless it is ratified by the state conventions within seven years.

Amendment 22

Section 1

No person shall be elected to the office of the President more than twice, and no person who has held the office of President or acted as President for more than two years of a term to which some other person was elected President shall be elected to the office of the President more than once. But this article shall not apply to any person holding the office of President when this article was proposed by the Congress, and shall not prevent any person who may be holding the office of President or acting as President during the term within which this article becomes operative from holding the office of President or acting as President during the remainder of such term.

Section 2

This article shall be inoperative unless it shall have been ratified as an amendment to the Constitution by the legislatures of three fourths of the several states within seven years from the day of its submission to the states by the Congress.

Amendment 22 (1951). **Presidents Limited to Two Terms**

Section 1. Limit on Presidential Terms

No person can be elected President more than twice. If a Vice-President or someone else succeeds to the presidency and serves for more than two years, that person cannot then be elected President more than once. This ban does not apply to the person who is President at the time of proposal of this amendment.

Harry S. Truman was President in 1947, when this amendment was proposed.

Section 2. Time Limit for Ratification

This amendment is not to take effect unless it is ratified by state legislatures within seven years.

Amendment 23

Section 1

The district constituting the seat of government of the United States shall appoint in such manner as the Congress may direct: A number of electors of President and Vice-President equal to the whole number of senators and representatives in Congress to which the district would be entitled if it were a state, but in no event more than the least populous state; they shall be in addition to those appointed by the states, but they shall be considered, for the purposes of the election of President and Vice-President, to be electors appointed by a state; and they shall meet in the district and perform such duties as provided by the twelfth article of amendment.

Section 2

The Congress shall have power to enforce this article by appropriate legislation.

Amendment 23 (1961). **Electoral Votes for the District of Columbia**

Section 1. The Number of Electors

The District of Columbia can have the same number of electors it would be entitled to if it were a state. But that number cannot be greater than the number of electors from the state with the smallest population. Since each state has at least one Representative and two Senators, the smallest number of electors possible is three. The District of Columbia may therefore have three electors.

The effect of this amendment is to let residents of Washington, D.C., vote in presidential elections.

Section 2. Power of Enforcement

Congress has the power to pass laws to enforce this amendment.

Amendment 24

Section 1

The right of citizens of the United States to vote in any primary or other election for President or Vice-President, for electors for President or Vice-President, or for senator or representative in Congress, shall not be denied or abridged by the United States or any state by reason of failure to pay any poll tax or other law.

Section 2

The Congress shall have power to enforce this article by appropriate legislation.

Amendment 24 (1964). **Abolition of Poll Taxes**

Section 1. Abolition

Neither the United States nor any state can require a citizen to pay a poll tax — a tax per head, or individual — in order to vote in a presidential or congressional election. The effect of this amendment is to prevent states from using poll taxes to keep poor people, especially thost who are African-American, from voting.

Section 2. Power of Enforcement

Congress has the power to pass laws to enforce this amendment.

Amendment 25

Section 1

In case of the removal of the President from office or of his death or resignation, the Vice-President shall become President.

Section 2

Whenever there is a vacancy in the office of the Vice-President, the President shall nominate a Vice-President who shall take office upon confirmation by a majority vote of both houses of Congress.

Section 3

Whenever the President transmits to the president pro tempore of the Senate and the speaker of the House of Representatives his written declaration that he is unable to discharge the powers and duties of his office, and until he transmits to them a written declaration to the contrary, such powers and duties shall be discharged by the Vice-President as Acting President.

Section 4

Whenever the Vice-President and a majority of either the principal officers of the executive departments or of such other body as Congress may by law provide, transmit to the president pro tempore of the Senate and the speaker of the House of Representatives their written declaration that the President is unable to discharge the powers and duties of his office, the Vice-President shall immediately assume the powers and duties of the office as Acting President.

Thereafter, when the President transmits to the president pro tempore of the Senate and the speaker of the House of Representatives his written declaration that no inability exists, he shall resume the powers and duties of his office unless the Vice-President and a majority of either the principal

Amendment 25 (1967). **Presidential Disability and Succession**

Section 1. Replacement of the President

If the President is removed from office or dies or resigns, the Vice-President becomes President.

Section 2. Replacement of the Vice-President

When the vice-presidency becomes vacant, the President will choose a Vice-President. The choice must be confirmed by both houses of Congress.

Section 3. Temporary Replacement of the President with the President's Consent

If the President sends Congress notice in writing that he or she is disabled from performing official duties, the Vice-President becomes Acting President. The President may resume office when he or she sends Congress written notice of renewed ability to serve.

Section 4. Temporary Replacement of the President Without the President's Consent

If a President is disabled and cannot or will not send written notice to Congress, the Vice-President and a majority of the cabinet (or some other group named by Congress) can send such notice. The Vice-President will then become Acting President.

The Vice-President will step down when the President sends Congress written notice of renewed ability to serve, unless the Vice-President and others disagree. If they disagree, they must send written notice to Congress within four days.

Congress then must meet within 48 hours to decide whether the President is still disabled. Within 21 days they must vote. If two thirds or more of both houses vote that the President is disabled, the Vice-President remains in office as Acting President. If they do not, the President resumes official duties.

officers of the executive department or of such other body as Congress may by law provide, transmit within four days to the president pro tempore of the Senate and the speaker of the House of Representatives their written declaration that the President is unable to discharge the powers and duties of his office. Thereupon Congress shall decide the issue, assembling within forty-eight hours for that purpose if not in session. If the Congress, within twenty-one days after receipt of the latter written declaration, or, if Congress is not in session, within twenty-one days after Congress is required to assemble, determines by two-thirds vote of both houses that the President is unable to discharge the powers and duties of his office, the Vice-President shall continue to discharge the same as Acting President; otherwise, the President shall resume the powers and duties of his office.

Amendment 26

Section 1

The right of citizens of the United States, who are eighteen years of age or older, to vote shall not be denied or abridged by the United States or by any state on account of age.

Section 2

The Congress shall have power to enforce this article by appropriate legislation.

Amendment 26 (1971). **Suffrage at Age Eighteen**

Section 1. The Right to Vote

Neither the United States nor any state can deny the vote to citizens of age 18 or older because of their age. The effect of this amendment is to lower the voting age from 21, the former minimum in federal and most state elections, to 18.

Section 2. Power of Enforcement

Congress has the power to pass laws to enforce this amendment.

Amendment 27

No law varying the compensation for the services of the senators and representatives shall take effect until an election of representatives shall have intervened.

Amendment 27 (1992). **Delay of Changes in Congressional Salaries**

If members of Congress vote to change their own salaries, the change cannot go into effect until after the next election for the House of Representatives. The intent is to make members of Congress accountable to the voters if they approve a pay raise for themselves.

Glossary

Terms important in the discussion of United States history are defined in the Glossary to clarify their meaning in the text. Page numbers refer to the places in the text where the terms first appear.

In the text some terms and names have been respelled as an aid to pronunciation. A key to pronouncing the respelled words appears at the right.

Pronunciation Key

Like certain other words in this book, the term *laissez faire* has been respelled to indicate its pronunciation: lehs-ay FEHR. A hyphen is used between syllables. Small capital letters mean that a syllable should be spoken with weak stress. Large capital letters mean that a syllable should be spoken with a strong stress. In *laissez faire,* the vowel sounds shown by the letters *eh* and *ay* in the respelling correspond to the vowel sounds in the key at the right.

Pronounce a as in hat

ah	father	ng	ring
ar	tar	o	frog
ay	say	ō	no
ayr	air	oo	soon
e, eh	hen	or	for
ee	bee	ow	plow
eer	deer	oy	boy
er	her	sh	she
ew	new	th	think
g	go	u, uh	sun
i, ih	him	z	zebra
ī	kite	zh	measure
j	jet		

absolute location: in geography, exact position on the globe as measured by a surveyor according to a system of latitude and longitude (page xxix)

affirmative action: plans to counteract past discrimination in employment and in admission to colleges and universities (page 813)

anarchism: the theory that all systems of government should be eliminated (page 393)

annexation: addition of new land to an existing country, state, city, etc. (page 260)

anti-Semitism: prejudice or discrimination against Jews (page 618)

apartheid: South Africa's racist policy of legalized segregation and discrimination (page 850)

appeasement: the policy of giving in to the demands of a hostile power to keep peace (page 624)

armistice: an agreement to stop warfare until a peace treaty is signed (page 511)

arms race: a peacetime competition to build more and better weapons (page 611)

assembly line: system in which a worker repeatedly performs one task in assembling a product, and a moving belt carries the product from worker to worker (page 536)

assimilated: absorbed into the dominant cultural group (page 125)

automation: manufacturing process in which production is guided electronically (page 717)

baby boom: a dramatic rise in the birth rate (page 717)

backlash: a strong reaction based on fear or resentment (page 813)

balance of power: situation where the power of rival nations or alliances is about equal (page 495)

balance of trade: the difference between the value of goods exported and the value of goods imported (page 51)

bicameral: describing a legislature made up of two houses (page 57)

big stick diplomacy: Theodore Roosevelt's policy of using the threat of military force to influence political events in other countries, particularly in Latin America (page 486)

bill of rights: a list of rights and freedoms guaranteed to the people (page 119)

blacklist: to put a person on a list of people to be censored or refused employment (page 281)

boycott: refusal to buy or use a product or service (page 91)

business cycle: a repeated series of "ups" of economic growth and "downs" of decline in business activity (page 564)

936

cabinet: a group of advisors to the President, including the secretaries of the federal executive departments and other presidential appointees (page 161)

carpetbaggers: northerners who moved to the South during Reconstruction (page 339)

cash crop: a crop raised for profit (page 62)

caucus: a private meeting of a few key political party members to select delegates or candidates or to decide on a course of action (page 223)

checks and balances: the system set up by the Constitution in which the branches of government can limit each other's power (page 151)

city manager: a manager hired by a city council to look after day-to-day city business (page 446)

civil rights: citizens' rights to equal opportunity and equal treatment under the law (page 335)

civil service: the body of employees who work in the administration of government and who are appointed rather than elected to their jobs (page 409)

coalition: a political alliance (page 592)

Cold War: from the 1950s through the 1980s, the state of tension between the Soviet Union and other Communist countries on one side and the United States and other non-Communist countries on the other (page 681)

collective bargaining: a process by which labor and management representatives can reach agreement about wages and conditions (page 420)

commission system: a system of city government in which different functions are each handled by a different elected commissioner (page 446)

communism: in theory, a system in which society as a whole owns all property and individuals share goods equally (page 393)

confederation: an alliance of independent groups or states (page 27)

conquistadores: the Spanish adventurers who conquered large parts of the Americas in the 1500s (page 38)

conscientious objectors: people who refuse to take part in war because killing other persons is against their principles (page 787)

conservation: protecting natural resources and managing them wisely for such uses as lumbering and irrigation (page 456)

constitutions: plans of government (page 118)

containment: the foreign policy of keeping communism within its current borders (page 680)

contraband: goods forbidden by law to be traded, such as war materials (page 169)

contras: Nicaraguan guerrillas who opposed the Sandinista government (page 843)

corporation: a type of business in which shares of stock are sold to investors, who then each own part of the business and share in the profits (page 385)

covert operations: secret activities by one government to undermine another government (page 689)

credit: allowing a buyer to make a purchase with a cash down payment followed by later payments that usually include interest (page 555)

critical thinking: the habit of making informed, thoughtful judgments about the meaning, accuracy, and worth of information (page xxvii)

de facto segregation: segregation "in fact" developed through custom rather than law (page 754)

deficit: the amount by which spending exceeds income (page 730)

deficit spending: a policy in which a government spends more than it receives in taxes (page 598)

depression: a long, sharp decline in economic activity (page 131)

deregulation: an end to government control (page 825)

direct primary: an election by the people to choose candidates for public office (page 447)

dividends: shares of a company's profits, paid to stockholders (page 385)

dollar diplomacy: William Howard Taft's policy of "substituting dollars for bullets" to influence political events in foreign countries, particularly in Latin America (page 486)

domino theory: the view that the fall of one country to communism would lead to the fall of neighboring countries to communism (page 690)

doves: people who oppose war as a means of settling conflicts (page 787)

durable goods: products made to last a long time (page 561)

embargo: a ban on trade (page 169)

encomienda: in Spanish colonies, system in which settlers were granted groups of Indians as labor, supposedly in return for care (page 42)

escalate: to expand rapidly, as in a war (page 782)

excise tax: a tax on goods produced, sold, and consumed within the country (page 165)

expansionist: someone with a policy of expanding a nation's territory or influence (page 260)

fascism: government system under total control of a dictator and a single political party (page 616)

federalism: the division of power between the states and the federal, or national, government (page 148)
feminism: idea that women have the same political, economic, and social rights as men (page 809)
freedmen: former slaves (page 333)
free enterprise: an economic system in which private companies freely compete with one another with little or no government regulation (page 385)

general strike: a work stoppage by all the workers in a community (page 417)
genocide: the systematic destruction of a national or ethnic group (page 514)
graduated income tax: taxation at rates proportional to incomes (page 428)
gross national product (GNP): the total dollar value of all final goods and services produced in a country in a year (page 536)

habeas corpus: the right of a person to appear in court so a judge can decide whether that person is being imprisoned lawfully (page 306)
hawks: people who favor an aggressive military solution to conflicts (page 787)
holding company: company organized to hold stock in other companies to control them (page 390)
Holocaust: the extermination of more than 6 million European Jews by the Nazis (page 654)

impeached: officially accused of wrongdoing in public office by the House of Representatives (page 151)
imperialism: the effort to dominate the trade and government of other lands (page 469)
incumbents: politicians already in office (page 870)
indentured servants: settlers who contracted to work for a colonist who paid their passage (page 52)
Industrial Revolution: shift of manufacturing from homes to factories and from hand tools to power tools and machines (page 203)
inflation: a rise in prices which causes a decline in the value of money (page 131)
initiative: bill placed on the ballot in a general election as a result of a voter petition (page 448)
interchangeable parts: parts that are so alike that one could be used in place of another (page 204)
isolationism: a foreign policy dedicated to withdrawing from international affairs (page 610)

joint-stock company: a business organization in which money is raised by selling shares in the company to investors (page 51)
judicial review: the power of the Supreme Court and other courts to declare a law or action unconstitutional (page 146)

kiva: an underground room used in Pueblo Indian religious ceremonies (page 25)

laissez faire: the idea that business should be free of government regulation (page 390)
legislature: a group of people chosen to make laws (page 53)
lobbyists: people acting on behalf of special interests in order to influence legislation (page 460)
location: in geography, where a place is and why it is there (page xxix)
loose construction: the view that the national government has powers implied in the Constitution as well as those directly stated (page 146)
Loyalists: colonists who were loyal to the Crown during the American War for Independence (page 103)

mandates: authority to govern; under the League of Nations, authority granted to nations temporarily to handle the affairs of other regions (page 516)
manifest destiny: the idea that the United States would and should extend across the whole continent (page 260)
martial law: rule by military rather than civil authorities (page 306)
massive retaliation: the policy of discouraging communist expansion by using the threat of nuclear attack on the Soviet Union or China (page 689)
mass production: manufacture of goods in large quantities (page 204)
McCarthyism: political use of unsupported accusations to intimidate people (page 710)
mercantilism: a policy of careful government regulation of the economy in an effort to fill a nation's treasury with gold and silver (page 50)
minutemen: in the English colonies in America, special militia units formed to "come in a moment's warning" to defend a colony (page 96)
mission: a community established by a religious organization to teach and spread its faith, especially in a foreign land (page 42)
mobilization: organization and preparation of people and resources for war (page 501)
moderates: people who prefer gradual change (page 96)
monopoly: a single business with the power to control prices in its market (page 387)

moral diplomacy: Woodrow Wilson's policy of using "the force of moral principle" to influence political events in foreign countries, particularly in Latin America (page 487)
movement: in geography, how people, things, and ideas move from place to place (page xxxi)
multinational company operating in more than one nation (page 875)

nation: a group of people with a feeling of unity based on sharing a common land and a common past (page 124)
nationalism: an intense feeling of national pride and unity (page 202)
national debt: the total outstanding debt of the federal government (page 853)
nativism: hostility toward immigrants based on the belief that they threaten traditional culture, institutions, and social order (page 283)
neutrality: a policy of not taking sides in a conflict (page 168)
nonaligned: not allied with either side in a clash of powers (page 815)
nonrenewable resources: minerals, coal, and iron; resources which cannot be replaced naturally (page 878)
nullify: to declare void; to refuse (on the part of a state) to enforce an act of Congress (page 176)

Open Door policy: the policy proposed by the United States in 1899 for keeping Chinese ports open to the trade of all nations (page 480)

pacifists: those who oppose the use of force under any circumstances (page 504)
parity: price levels that in bad years give farmers the same buying power as in good years (page 594)
Patriots: in the Revolutionary War, colonists who worked to rally public opinion against the British; colonists who fought for independence (page 91)
place: the concept that each locality is distinguished by physical and human characteristics (page xxx)
platform: statement of a political party's beliefs (page 223)
pluralistic: made up of different groups (page 129)
point of view: the position from which a person observes or considers something (page xxviii)
political machines: political organizations that control city or state governments, gaining their power, often, by bribery, delivery of phony votes, and exchange of political favors (page 401)
poll tax: a fixed tax levied on each adult, sometimes used as a requirement to vote (page 344)
popular sovereignty: concept that final political authority lies with the people; pre-Civil War, right of each new state to decide slavery issue (page 290)
potlatches: Northwest Coast Indian ceremonies, often involving generous gift giving (page 28)
preservation: keeping some wilderness areas in their natural state (page 456)
presidio: Spanish military garrison (page 42)
privateers: privately owned ships authorized by the government to attack enemy ships (page 105)
profiteering: making an unfair profit by charging high prices for scarce goods (page 105)
prohibition: ban on the manufacture, sale, and transport of alcoholic drinks (page 543)
protective tariff: tax imposed on imports to discourage the purchase of foreign goods (page 164)
protectorate: a weak country that is controlled and protected by a strong one (page 483)
public domain: unclaimed public lands (page 368)
pueblo: the Spanish word for "town;" the name Spanish explorers used for Native Americans living near the upper Rio Grande (page 25)

racism: believing that one's own race is superior to other races (page 66)
radicals: people who take an extreme position or favor extreme change (page 96)
ratify: approve officially, as in a vote by the people to approve a plan of government (page 120)
rationing: limiting the amount of scarce goods that each person can buy (page 640)
reapportionment: the restructuring of voting districts (page 731)
rebate: a refund of part of an amount paid (page 385)
recall: removing an elected official before his or her term expires, by a special election held as a result of a voter petition (page 448)
recession: a short economic decline (page 564)
Reconstruction: the restoration of the Confederate states to the Union (page 334)
redistricting: redrawing the boundaries of districts, for example, voting districts (page 811)
referendum: submission of a law to a vote of the people as result of a voter petition (page 448)
regions: in geography, areas defined by people according to one or more unifying characteristics (page xxxi)

relationships within places: how people both adapt to and modify their environments (page xxx)
relative location: in geography, the relationship of one place to all other places (page xxix)
renewable resources: resources that can be replaced naturally such as solar energy (page 878)
reparations: payment for war damages (page 514)
republic: a government run by representatives elected by the people (page 118)
reservations: public lands set aside for special use, such as for Native Americans (page 360)
reverse discrimination: unfair treatment of the majority (page 813)
revivals: public meetings intended to renew commitment to the Christian faith (page 234)
Roosevelt Corollary: Theodore Roosevelt's expansion of the Monroe Doctrine to include the assertion that the United States has the right to intervene in Latin America (page 486)

sanctions: measures such as trade bans and blockades designed to put economic pressure on an offending nation (page 850)
scalawags: white southerners who joined the Republican party during Reconstruction (page 339)
secession: official withdrawal; withdrawal of the southern states from the Union at the beginning of the Civil War (page 197)
secret ballot: voting in a private booth (page 448)
sectionalism: devotion to the interests of one section of a country over those of other sections (page 213)
segregation: the policy of keeping racial groups separate in public places (page 345)
separation of powers: the division of government power into executive, legislative, and judicial branches (page 149)
sharecroppers: tenant farmers who pay their rent with a share of their crops (page 344)
sit-down strike: a strike in which workers refuse to leave the workplace (page 594)
socialism: system where means of economic production and distribution are owned by the government or community, not by individuals (page 393)
sovereignty: the power of a government to control its own affairs (page 118)
Soviet bloc: Eastern European nations under the control of Communist parties backed by Soviet troops (page 679)
speculators: people seeking big profits from risky investments (page 74)
spheres of influence: areas in one nation in which other nations have strong political and economic influence or control (page 480)
spoils system: the practice by a public official of removing opposing appointed public officials and replacing them with supporters (page 223)
stagflation: economic condition with both rising prices and rising unemployment (page 823)
states' rights: the doctrine that the states have the right to judge whether Congress is going beyond its constitutional powers, based on the view that rights and powers not given to the federal government by the Constitution, and not forbidden to the states, belong to the states (page 176)
strict construction: the view that the national government has only those powers specifically spelled out in the Constitution (page 146)
strike: a refusal by employees to continue work, intended to pressure an employer to meet workers' demands (page 281)
subversion: being overthrown by traitors and spies lurking within the government (page 708)
suffrage: the right to vote (page 222)

tariffs: taxes on imports or exports (page 120)
temperance: moderation in or total abstinence from the use of alcoholic beverages (page 236)
tenant farmers: farmers who rent the land they live on and farm (page 344)
terrorism: the use or threat of violence to spread fear, usually for the purpose of achieving political goals (page 844)
third world: developing nations not aligned with either side in the Cold War (page 681)
totalitarian state: a state in which the government absolutely controls both the economic and political systems (page 617)
trust: a form of business combination in which a single board of trustees controls a group of member corporations (page 387)

utopias: attempts to create perfect societies based on economic and social ideals (page 234)

veto: to reject, especially the power to reject a proposed rule or law (page 54)
vigilantes: unofficial groups formed to control lawlessness (page 370)

writs of assistance: legal documents permitting customs collectors to search any building in which illegal goods might be hidden (page 90)

Index

Italicized page numbers preceded by an *i, f,* or *m* indicate an illustration, feature, or map. Page numbers set in **boldface** indicate pages on which glossary terms are introduced.

941

B

G

K

Q

Photo Acknowledgments

Cover: George B. Fry III*

Title Page: iiC National Portrait Gallery/Smithsonian Institution; **viiCL** Sophia Smith Collection; **iiCR** The Bettmann Archive; **iiL** *Paul Revere* by John Singleton Copley. Gift of Joseph W., William B. and Edward H.R. Revere, courtesy Museum of Fine Arts, Boston; **iiR** Staten Island Historical Society; **iiiCL** National Archives; **iiiCR** Dan Budnick/Woodfin Camp & Associates; **iiiL** Wyoming State Museum; **iiiR** Victor Aleman.

Table of Contents: vB SCALA/Art Resource, New York; **vBL** Rich Buzzelli/Tom Stack & Associates; **vR** Brown Brothers; **vTL** J.L. Atlan/Sygma; **viBL** Courtesy, the John Carter Brown Library at Brown University; **viBR** Courtesy, the John Carter Brown Library at Brown University; **viTR** *The New Life of Virginea,* London 1612; **viiB** The Granger Collection; **viiBR** Brown Brothers; **viiTR** Library of Congress; **viiiBL** The Bettmann Archive; **viiiR** California Section, California State Library Sacramento; **viiiTL** *Meriwether Lewis* by C.W. Peale. Independence National Historical Park Collection; **ixBR** Cook Collection/Valentine Museum; **ixL** U.S. Post Office; **ixTR** Nawrocki Stock Photo; **xBL** Library of Congress; **xR** Brown Brothers; **xTL** Denver Public Library; **xiBR** John Scheiber/The Image Bank; **xiL** National Archives; **xiTR** Brown Brothers; **xiiR** Culver Pictures; **xiiTL** The Bettmann Archive/Hulton Picture Library; **xiiBL** Culver Pictures; **xiiiBR** Brown Brothers; **xiiiL** Franklin D. Roosevelt Library; **xiiiTR** David Smart/Stock South; **xivBL** J.A.F. -Paris/Magnum Photos; **xivR** Leroy Woodson/Woodfin Camp & Associates; **xivTL** The Bettmann Archive; **xvBL** UPI/Bettmann Newsphotos; **xvBR** The Bettmann Archive; **xvTL** The Bettmann Archive; **xvTR** Photo by Alfred Eisenstaedt, LIFE Magazine (c) 1962 Time Warner Inc.; **xviL** Barbara R. Rascher/The Clarion-Ledger; **xviTR** D.B. Owen/Black Star; **xviBR** Wally McNamee/Sygma; **xviiL** *Soldier in World War I* by Sir William Orpen. Imperial War Museum, London; **xviiR** Francois Gohier/Photo Researchers; **xviiiBR** Kenneth Jarecke/Contact-Woodfin Camp & Associates; **xviiiBL** Culver Pictures; **xviiiTL** Sara Winnemucca Hopkins, c. 1874. Nevada Historical Society; **xviiiTR** FPG International; **xixB** Wade Spees; **xixT** National Baseball Hall of Fame and Museum, Inc.; **xxBL** The Bettmann Archive; **xxR** Culver Pictures; **xxTL** The Bettmann Archive; **xxi** The Metropolitan Museum of Art, Gift of I.N. Phelps Stokes, Edward S. Hawes, Alice Mary Hawes, Marion Augusta Hawes, 1937; **xxii**The National Portrait Gallery/Smithsonian Institution; **xxiiiB** Monty Roessell/Black Star; **xxivB** *General Schumacker* by Jacob Maentel, 1812. National Gallery of Art, Washington, gift of Edgar William and Bernice Chrysler Garbish; **xxivT** Southern Pacific Transportation Company; **xxvL** The Bettmann Archive; **xxvR** The New-York Historical Society;

Introducing the Book: xxvii (c) San Francisco Chronicle, 1962. Reprinted by permission; **xxviiiB** The Granger Collection; **xxviiiT** The Bettmann Archive; **xxix** Manuscripts Department, the Huntington Library, San Marino, California; **xxxB** Fred Ward/Black Star; **xxxi** *The Migration of the Negro, Panel 1: During the World War there was a great migration North by Southern Negros* by Jacob Lawrence, 1940-41. The Phillips Collection, Washington, D.C.; **xxxT** Print Collection, Miriam and Ira D. Wallach Division of Art, Prints and Photographs; The New York Public Library; Astor, Lenox and Tilden Foundations.

Unit 1: xxxii-1 Tom Bean/AllStock; **2-3** Tom Bean/AllStock; **2** Objects courtesy of Indian Gallery, Palo Alto, photo by Tim Davis*; **3** Lee Boltin.

Chapter 1: 4B Andy Levin/Photo Researchers; **4T** Library of Congress; **5BR** The Bettmann Archive; **5C** Bob Daemmrich/Stock, Boston; **5L** Frank Johnston/Black Star; **5TR** Curt Fischer*; **6C** Fred M. Dole/f-stop Pictures; **6L** The University of Texas, Institute of Texan Cultures; **6R** Bonnie Kamin/Comstock; **7** National Archives; **8B** Elliott Smith; **8T** Brown Brothers; **9B** The Bettmann Archive; **9T** J.L. Atlan/Sygma; **10B** The Bettmann Archive; **10T** Arthur Grace/Sygma; **11** Library of Congress; **12** *Hancock Shaker Village* by Kjakobsen, 1981. Jay Johnsons America's Folk Heritage Gallery, New York City; **13** "Smash the Hun" by Edward Hopper. Charles Rand Penney Collection. Photo by Charles A. Stainback; **14** Charles Gupton/TSW—Click/Chicago Ltd.; **15B** Lewis Hine photograph/Library of Congress; **15T** Thomas Ives/The Stock Market; **16** Office of Registrar of Voters; **17** John Epperson/The Denver Post.

Chapter 2: 20B Manuscripts Department, the Huntington Library, San Marino, California; **20T** Lee Boltin; **21C** The British Museum; **21L** Bibliotheque Nationale, Paris; **21R** Lee Boltin; **22BR** University Museum of National Antiquities, Oslo, Norway; **22L** Los Angeles County Museum of Natural History; **22TR** National Museum of the American Indian/Smithsonian Institution; **23BR** *Queen Elizabeth I ("The Armada Portrait")* by George Gower, ca. 1588. Woburn Abbey Collection/Newsweek Books/Laurie Platt Winfrey, Inc.; **23L** Rare Book Division, The New York Public Library, Astor, Lenox and Tilden Foundations; **23TR** Archiv de Indias, Seville/Laurie Platt Winfrey, Inc.; **24L** Courtesy, the Metropolitan Museum of Art; **24R** Library of Congress, courtesy National Geographic Society; **26BL** The Detroit Institute of Arts, Dirk Bakker (National Parks Service, Mound City National Monument, Chillicothe); **26BR** The Detroit Institute of Arts, Dirk Bakker; **26TL** Comstock; **26TR** The Detroit Institute of Arts, Dirk Bakker (Ohio Historical Society, Columbus); **27** *Buffalo Hunt Under White Wolf Skins* by George Catlin. The Thomas Gilcrease Institute of American History and Art, Tulsa, Oklahoma; **28L** National Museum of the American Indian/Smithsonian Institution; **28R** National Museum of the American Indian/Smithsonian Institution; **29BR** National Museum of the American Indian, Smithsonian Institution; **29L** Female ritual figure, wood and black, blue, yellow, red, and white earth pigments, c. 1150-1400, 35.6 × 17.1 cm, North American, New Mexico, Mimbres Culture. The Art Institute of Chicago, Major Acquisitions Centennial Fund Income; **29TR** Photo by A. Singer, Courtesy Department of Library Services, American Museum of Natural History; **30L** Lee Boltin; **30R** Christiana Dittman/Rainbow; **31** Bibliotheque Nationale, Paris; **32** SCALA/Art Resource, New York; **36-37B** Peabody Museum of Salem, photo by Mark Sexton; **36-37C** Rare Books and Manuscripts Division, The New York Public Library; Astor, Lenox and Tilden Foundations; **36C** Peabody Museum, Harvard University, photo by Hillel Burger; **36CL** Peabody Museum of Salem, photo by Mark Sexton; **36TL** *Village of Secotan* by Thomas De Bry. The Thomas Gilcrease Institute of American History and Art, Tulsa, Oklahoma; **36TR** National Museum of the American Indian/Smithsonian Institution; **37C**Peabody Museum, Harvard University, photo by Hillel Burger; **37T** Canadian Museum of Civilization, Negative #CMC 575-399; **39BR** Lee Boltin; **39CR** Lee Boltin; **39TL** Reproduced by courtesy of the trustees of the British Museum; **39TR** Lee Boltin; **40** Rich Buzzelli/Tom Stack & Associates; **43** John Elk III; **44** Lee Boltin.

Chapter 3: 48B Rare Book Division, The New York Public Library, Astor, Lenox & Tilden Foundations; **48T** Lee Boltin; **49C** *Mrs. Elizabeth Freake and Baby Mary* by an unknown artist, 1671-74. Worcester Art Museum, Worcester, Massachusetts; **49L** *The New Life of Virginea,* London 1612; **49R** Library of Congress; **50CL** Ashmolean Museum, Oxford; **50CR** *Burdens and Blessings;* **50T** American Antiquarian Society; **51CL** Philadelphia Museum of Art, given by John T. Morris; **51CR** Library of Congress; **51T** The Bettmann Archive; **53C** The Bettmann Archive; **53CL** The Bettmann Archive; **53CR** Universitats Bibliothek Erlangen, Manuscript Department; **53T** The Bettmann Archive; **55CR** Art Resource, New York; **55CL** The Granger Collection; **55T** The New York Public Library; **58** The New York Public

967

Library; **59CR** Manfred Gottschalk/Tom Stack & Associates; **59T** The New-York Historical Society, New York City; **60** Culver Pictures; **65BC** Jewish Museum/Art Resource, New York; **65BL** *Quaker Meeting* by unknown artist. Bequest of Maxim Karolik; courtesy, Museum of Fine Arts, Boston; **66** Burr Shafer, "Through More History with J. Wesley Smith", New York: The Vanguard Press, 1958; **67B** Thomas Gilcrease Institute; **67TL** Thomas Gilcrease Institute; **68TR** The New York Public Library; **69CL** Library of Congress; **69B** Library of Congress; **69CR** National Maritime Museum; **69T** The British Library; **70** The New-York Historical Society, New York City; **71CB** British Museum/Art Resource; **71CL** British Museum, photo by Ianthe Ruthven*; **71CT** The Nelson-Atkins Museum of Art, Kansas City, Missouri (Nelson Fund) 65-5; **72** Library of Congress; **73BL** *Puck the prentis boy* by Lewis Miller, I8I3. The Historical Society of York County, Pennsylvania; **73BR** Covered Pewter pitcher by Daniel Curtiss, c. 1822-1840. Yale University Art Gallery. The Mabel Brady Garvan Collection; **73CL** Linda Stinchfield collection, photo by Tim Davis*; **73CR** The New-York Historical Society, NYC; **73TL** Kenneth Martin; **75** Washington/Custis/Lee Collection, Washington and Lee University, Lexington, VA; **79** The Historical Society of Pennsylvania.

Unit 2: 82-83 M. Brodskaya/Bruce Coleman Inc.; **84-85** M. Brodskaya/Bruce Coleman Inc.; **84T** *Patrick Henry* by Lawrence Sully, 1795, watercolor on ivory, #1945.115. Mead Art Museum, Amherst College, bequest of Herbert L. Pratt, Class of 1895; **85** American Antiquarian Society.

Chapter 4: 86B The Granger Collection; **86T** Detail from *The Declaration of Independence* by John Trumbull. Yale University Art Gallery; **87BC** The Granger Collection; **87BL** Anne S.K. Brown Military Collection, Brown University Library; **87BR** Detail of *Deborah Sampson* by Joseph Stone. The Rhode Island Historical Society; **87TR** Concord Museum, Concord, MA; **88BL** Pontiac, Chief of the Ottawas, from *The American Book of Indians,* I854. American Heritage Archive; **88BR** American Antiquarian Society; **88T** Library of Congress; **89B** National Archives; **89TL** AP/Wide World Photos; **89TR** National Portrait Gallery, Smithsonian Institution/Art Resource, NY; **90C** The New York Public Library. Astor, Lenox & Tilden Foundations; **90L** The Granger Collection; **90R** The Historical Society of Pennsylvania; **91** Courtesy Essex Institute, Salem, Mass. Photo by Mark Sexton; **92L** Historical Pictures Service; **92R** Massachusetts Historical Society; **94** Courtesy, the John Carter Brown Library at Brown University; **96-97** Photri; **97** *The Engagement at the North Bridge in Concord* by Amos Doolittle, 1775. The Connecticut Historical Society, Hartford, Connecticut; **98** *Battle of Bunkers Hill* by John Trumbull, 1786. Yale University Art Gallery; **102** *Mrs. James Warren (Mercy Otis)* by John Singleton Copley, c. 1763. Courtesy, Museum of Fine Arts, Boston. Bequest of Winslow Warren; **106** Virginia Historical Society; **107** National Museum of American History/Smithsonian Institution. Photo by Charles H. Phillips; **109** West Point Museum; **111** American Philosophical Society.

Chapter 5: 116-117 *View of Mr. Joshua Winsors House* by Rufus Hathaway, 1795. Photo courtesy Stephen Score Antiques; **116** *Pennsylvania Farmstead with Many Fences,* by unknown artist. Courtesy, Museum of Fine Arts, Boston, Mr. and Mrs. Karolik Collection; **116BL** *Tontine Coffee House, New York City* by Francis Guy, c. 1797. The New-York Historical Society; **117C** Kentucky Historical Society, Military History Museum; **117R** Anne S.K. Brown Military Collection, Brown University Library; **118BL** National Archives; **118BR** National Archives; **119L** The Filson Club Historical Society; **119R** The National Portrait Gallery/Smithsonian Institution; **121** Detail from *Daniel Boone Escorting Settlers throughthe Cumberland Gap* by George Caleb Bingham, 1851-2. Washington University Gallery of Art, St. Louis; **122** *Fairview Inn or Three Mile House on Old Frederick Road* by Thomas Coke Ruckle. From the collection of The Maryland Historical Society; **124** Library of Congress; **125L** The Historical Society of York County, Pennsylvania; **125R** Library of Congress; **126L** Alon Rininger/Contact-Woodfin Camp & Associates; **126R** The Historical Society of Pennsylvania; **127** *Portrait traditionally said to be that of Abigail Adams* by unidentified artist. New York State Historical Association, Cooperstown; **128** The New York Public Library, Schomburg Collection; **129** *Miss Fillis and Child and Bill Sold at Public Sale* by Lewis Miller. Abby Aldrich Rockefeller Folk Art Center; **130L** The American Numismatic Society; **130R** The American Numismatic Society; **131C** The American Numismatic Society; **131L** Courtesy, the John Carter Brown Library at Brown University; **131R** The American Numismatic Society; **132L** Sam Abell; **132R** Culver Pictures.

Chapter 6: 136 Detail from *Constitutional Convention.* Independence National Historical Park Collection; **136-137** National Archives; **136T** *Benjamin Franklin* by Charles Wilson Peale. Courtesy of the Pennsylvania Academy of the Fine Arts, Philadelphia. Bequest of Mrs. Sarah Harrison (The Joseph Harrison, Jr. Collection); **137L** Kunio Owaki/The Stock Market; **137R** Independence National Historical Park Collection; **138L** Independence National Historical Park Collection; **138R** Independence National Historical Park Collection; **138T** *Portrait of William Paterson* by Mrs. B.S. Church. Oil on canvas, 36$\frac{1}{8}$ × 26$\frac{1}{8}$". Princeton University; **139L** American Antiquarian Society; **139R** American Antiquarian Society; **139T** *Banner of the Society of Pewterers, carried in The Federal Procession,* The New-York Historical Society, New York City; **140** *James Madison* by Charles Wilson Peale. The Thomas Gilcrease Institute of American History and Art, Tulsa, Oklahoma; **142-143** Robert Llewellyn; **143BR** Library of Congress; **143TR** The Print and Picture Department, Free Library of Philadelphia; **145** The Historical Society of Pennsylvania; **147** UPI/Bettmann Newsphotos; **149** Diana Walker/Time Magazine; **150** UPI/Bettmann Newsphotos; **151** Jacques Chenet/Woodfin Camp & Associates; **152** Brown Brothers; **154** The Granger Collection; **155** The Granger Collection.

Chapter 7: 158-159 Library of Congress; **158** Library of Congress, Geography and Map Division; **159C** Photri; **159L** Maryland Historical Society, Baltimore; **159TR** Library of Congress; **160C** Courtesy, the John Carter Brown Library at Brown University; **160L** *George Washington (Vaughan portrait)* by Gilbert Stuart, 1795. National Gallery of Art, Washington, Andrew W. Mellon Collection; **161C** National Archives; **160R** Chicago Historical Society; Portrait of Thomas Jefferson by Caleb Boyle, c. 1800. Lafayette College, Alan P. Kirby Collection; **161TL** The Bettmann Archive; **162BL** *The Residence of David Twining 1787,* by Edward Hicks, c. 1845-48. Abby Aldrich Rockefeller Folk Art Center; **162R** Detail from *The Republican Court* by Daniel Huntington, 1861. The Brooklyn Museum, gift of the Cresant-Hamilton Athletic Club; **162TL** Monticello, Thomas Jefferson Memorial Foundation, Inc.; **165** Atwater Kent Museum, Philadelphia; **166L** Library of Congress; **166R** The Granger Collection; **167** Bibliotheque Nationale, Paris; **170L** Chicago Historical Society; **170R** National Archives; **173** Franklin D. Roosevelt Library; **174** AP/Wide World; **176L** The New-York Historical Society, New York City; **176R** The New-York Historical Society, New York City; **178-179B** Detail from *Scenes from a Seminary for Young Ladies,* ca. 1810-1820. The Saint Louis Art Museum. Purchase and Decorative Arts Society Fund; **178BL** National Museum of American History/Smithsonian Institution; **178CR** Shelburne Museum, Shelburne, Vermont, photo by Ken Burris; **178TL** The Pierpont Morgan Library, New York. PML 85496; **178TR** Shelburne Museum, Shelburne, Vermont, photo by Ken Burris; **179BR** The Free Library of Philadelphia, photo by Joan Broderick; **179C** *The School Room* by Jonathan Jennings, I850s. Private Collection; **179T** Detail from *Children Playing,* attributed to Eunice Pinney, c. 1813. Abby Aldrich Rockefeller Folk Art Center, Williamsburg, Virginia; **181** The Bettmann Archive.

Unit 3: 184-185 Chad Ehlers/AllStock; **186-187** Chad Ehlers/AllStock; **186** Lee Boltin; **187B** Francois Gohier/Photo Researchers; **187T** Lee Boltin.

Chapter 8: 188B *Fourth of July at Center Square* by John Lewis Krimmel. The Historical Society of Pennsylvania; **188T** Library of ongress; **189C** Princeton University Library; **189L** I.N. Phelps Stoke ollection, Miriam and Ira D. Wallach Division of Arts, Prints and hotographs; The New York Public Library; Astor, Lenox and Tilden oundations; **189R** National Museum of American History/Smithsonian nstitution; **190T** Courtesy, American Antiquarian Society; **190BR** The lew-York Historical Society; **190BL** The Granger Collection; **191** The ranger Collection; **192** Naval Historical Foundation; **193B** John letcher, NGP/National Geographic Society; **193C** *Thomas Jefferson* y Rembrandt Peale, 1805. The New-York Historical Society, New ork City; **193T** Robert Llewellyn; **194** *Mahchsi-Karehde, Mandan Man* by Karl Bodmer. Joslyn Art Museum, Omaha, Nebraska; **195L** *Villiam Clark* by C.W. Peale. Independence National Historical Park ollection; **195R** *Meriwether Lewis* by C.W. Peale. Independence National Historical Park Collection; **196** Missouri Historical Society; **97** The New-York Historical Society; **199** Field Museum of Natural listory (Neg #A-93851.1c), Chicago; **200B** *General Schumacker* by acob Maentel, 1812. National Gallery of Art, Washington, gift of dgar William and Bernice Chrysler Garbish; **200T** Lee Boltin; **201** *he Constitution vs. the Guierrere.* New Haven Colony Historical ociety; **202** *Andrew Jackson* by C.W. Peale. Collections of the rand Lodge of Pennsylvania, on deposit with the Masonic Library nd Museum of Pennsylvania; **203** Linda Stinchfield Collection, photo y Tim Davis*; **205** P. Jones Griffiths/Magnum Photos; **207** *Junction of the Erie and Northern Canals, c. 1830-32* by John Hill. The lew-York Historical Society, New York City; **209** Smithsonian nstitution; **210L** The Granger Collection; **210R** The Bettmann Archive; **13** *Hauling the Whole Weeks Picking* by William Henry Brown. The listoric New Orleans Collection; **216** The Granger Collection.

Chapter 9: 220B *Trail of Tears* by Robert Lindneux. Woolaroc Auseum, Bartlesville, Oklahoma; **220C** The Granger Collection; **221BC** The Bettmann Archive; **221BR** Hancock Shaker Village, ittsfield, Massachusetts; **221CR** Rare Book Department, Free Library of Philadelphia; **222CL** Museum of the City of New York; **222CR** *Black Hawk and His Son Whirling Thunder* by John Wesley Jarvis. homas Gilcrease Institute; **222T** The Mattatuck Museum; **223** The ettmann Archive; **225** Monty Roessell/Black Star; **228C** Hood Auseum of Art, Dartmouth College, Hanover, N.H., Gift of Artists; **228T** Historical Pictures Service; **230-231** The New-York Historical ociety, New York City; **232BC** Stanley King Collection; **232BL** The lew-York Historical Society, New York City; **232BR** Boston Athenaeum; **233** The Granger Collection; **234** The Granger Collection; **235B** The Historical Society of Pennsylvania; **235T** Library of ongress; **236** The Bettmann Archive; **237TC** The Bettmann Archive; **237TL** The Bettmann Archive; **237TR** Oberlin College Archives; **238** he Metropolitan Museum of Art, Gift of I.N. Phelps Stokes, Edward S. lawes, Alice Mary Hawes, Marion Augusta Hawes, 1937; **239** Sophia mith Collection; **242** The Granger Collection; **245** The Granger ollection.

Chapter 10: 246B Colorado Historical Society; **246T** *A View from the Summit of Independence Rock* by Bruff. The Huntington Library, San Aarino, California; **247C** Denver Public Library, Western History epartment; **247L** *East Side Main Plaza, San Antonio, Texas* by William M.G. Samuel, 1849. Courtesy of the San Antonio Museum Association, San Antonio, Texas; on loan from Bexar County; **247R** eaver Center for Western History Research, Natural History Museum of Los Angeles County; **248B** Julius Fekete/The Stock Market; **248T** lerbert K. Barnett, courtesy of the Star of the Republic Museum, Washington, Texas; **249B** Abby Aldrich Rockefeller Folk Art Center, Williamsburg, Virginia; **249T** State Street Bank and Trust Company, oston, Massachusetts, photo by George M. Cushing; **250** *Trappers and Indians ferrying across a river* by Alfred Jacob Miller. The Walters Art Gallery, Baltimore; **252** Seaver Center for Western History esearch, Natural History Museum of Los Angeles County; **253** J.R. yerman, LIFE Magazine, courtesy Carl Schaefer Dentzel Collection, c) Time Warner Inc.; **255** Museum of Church History and Art, Salt ake City; **257B** Eric Beggs; **257C** Kunio Owaki/The Stock Market; **257T** Courtesy the R.W. Norton Gallery, Shreveport, Louisiana; **258** Library of Congress; **263** Oregon Historical Society; **264BR** The Oakland Museum History Department; **264C** California Section, California State Library, Sacramento; **264L** California Section, California State Library, Sacramento; **264TR** Lee Boltin; **266B** Detail from *Westside Main Plaza, San Antonio, Texas* by William G.M. Samuel, 1849. San Antonio Museum Association, San Antonio, Texas. On loan from Bexar County; **266CL** Seaver Center for Western History Research, Natural History Museum of Los Angeles County; **266TL** Portrait of Don Jose Sepulveda by Henri J. Penelon, c. 1856. Bowers Museum Collection, Santa Ana, CA; **266TR** The Oakland Museum History Department; **267BR** Collections of the Spanish Colonial Arts Society, Inc., in the Museum of International Folk Art, Museum of New Mexico, Santa Fe. Photo by Blair Clark; **267C** Gift of the Historical Society of New Mexico to the Museum of New Mexico, Museum of International Folk Art, Santa Fe. Photo by Blair Clark; **267T** Gail Russell.

Unit 4: 272-273 The Granger Collection; **274-275** The Granger Collection; **274B** John Running/Stock, Boston; **274T** Department of Special Collections and University Archives, Stanford University Library; **275** The Granger Collection.

Chapter 11: 276B The New-York Historical Society, New York City; **276T** National Portrait Gallery, Smithsonian Institution/Art Resource, NY; **277BC** Culver Pictures; **277BL** Brown Brothers; **277BR** Culver Pictures; **277CR** Kansas State Historical Society, Topeka, Kansas; **279TC** *John Brown was Found "Guilty of Treason and Murder in the First Degree" and was Hanged in Charles Town, Virginia on December 2, 1859,* by Jacob Lawrence, 1917. Screen print printed in color on wove paper, $13^{31}/32 \times 20$," F1983.18.22. The Detroit Institute of Arts, Founders Society Purchase, Commissioned by Founders Society, Detroit Institute of Arts; **279TL** The Granger Collection; **279TR** The Museum of the Confederacy; **280** Library of Congress; **281BC** Lynn Sanchez Collection, photo by Stephen Frisch*; **281BR** Janet Kodish Collection, photo by Stephen Frisch*; **282C** Print Collection, Miriam and Ira D. Wallach Division of Art, Prints and Photographs, The New York Public Library, Astor, Lenox and Tilden Foundations; **284** Library of Congress; **285BL** Brown Brothers; **285BR** Library of Congress; **285C** David Perdew/Stock South; **286** Brown Brothers; **288-289B** Carved cane with Figural Reliefs by Henry Gudgell ca. 1863. Yale University Art Gallery; **288BL** National Museum of American History/Smithsonian; Institution; **288CR** Wade Spees; **288T** National Museum of American History/Smithsonian Institution; **289BL** *The Banjo Lesson* by Henry Ossawa Turner, 1893. Hampton University Museum, Hampton, Virginia. Photo by Mike Fischer; **289BR** New York State Historical Association, Cooperstown; **289T** The Maryland Historical Society; **290** The New-York Historical Society, New York City; **292B** Smithsonian Institution; **292T** Schlesinger Library, Radcliffe College; **295** The Bettmann Archive; **296L** Missouri Historical Society; **296R** The National Portrait Gallery/Smithsonian Institution; **297** The Pennsylvania Academy of the Fine Arts, John Lambert Fund; **298** The Granger Collection.

Chapter 12: 302B David Muench; **302C** National Gallery of Art, Smithsonian Institution/Art Resource, NY; **302T** National Archives; **303BL** National Archives; **303BR** Old State House of Arkansas; **303CR** Barbara Robinson Collection, photo by Stephen Frisch*; **304** Chicago Historical Society; **304CL** The Museum of the Confederacy; **305CL** The Museum of the Confederacy; **305CR** The Granger Collection; **305TC** Nawrocki Stock Photo; **306C** The Granger Collection; **306T** Nawrocki Stock Photo; **308** Nawrocki Stock Photo; **309** National Archives; **312** Library of Congress; **314** Library of Congress; **315** Library of Congress; **316** National Archives; **317TC** U.S. Post Office; **318** National Archives; **319** The Bettmann Archive; **319TL** Library of Congress; **319TR** Massachusetts Commandery Military Order of the Loyal Legion and the US Army Military History Institute; **322** David Muench; **323** Library of Congress; **324BL** Library of Congress; **324C** Library of Congress; **324CR** Cook Collection/Valentine Museum; **326** Leslie Pinkney Hill Library, Cheyney University; **327** Library of Congress.

Chapter 13: 330L National Archives; **330R** Library of Congress; **331C** The Bettmann Archive; **331L** Library of Congress; **331R** The Oakland Museum History Department; **332BL** Library of Congress; **332BR** Culver Pictures; **332C** Stanley King Collection; **332T** Library of Congress; **333** Library of Congress; **334** Cook Collection, Valentine Museum, Richmond, Virginia; **337** Library of Congress; **338** Library of Congress; **339L** Courtesy the Newberry Library, Chicago; **339R** Library of Congress; **340** Library of Congress; **342** White House Historical Association; **343B** Photo Researchers; **343T** National Archives; **346** Fisk University Library's Special Collections; **347** Fisk University, photo by Vando L. Rogers.

Unit 5: 352-353 John Livzey/AllStock; **354** Kansas State Historical Society, Topeka, Kansas; **354-355** John Livzey/AllStock; **355** Kansas State Historical Society, Topeka, Kansas.

Chapter 14: 356B *Fort Laramie* by A.J. Miller Beinecke Rare Book and Manuscript Library, Western American Collection, Yale University; **356T** *Thighs, A Wichita Woman* by George Catlin, 1834, National Museum of American Art/Smithsonian Institution, Gift of Mrs. Joseph Harrison, Jr./Art Resource, N.Y.; **356TC** Deere & Company; **357L** *Cornfield* from Howling Wolfs "Drawing Book" ca. 1875. Joslyn Art Museum, Omaha, Nebraska; **357RB** Coffrins Old West Gallery, Bozeman, Montana; **357TR** The Denver Art Museum; **358L** The Oakland Museum; **358R** Formerly collection of Sy Seidman; **359L** Sara Winnemucca Hopkins, c. 1874. Nevada Historical Society; **359R** Library of Congress; **360** West Point Museum, photo by Joshua Nefsky*; **361** *Commanche Village* by George Catlin, 1834-35. National Museum of American Art, Smithsonian Institution/Art Resource, N.Y.; **362L** National Museum of the American Indian/Smithsonian Institution; **362T** Beinecke Rare Book and Manuscript Library, Western Americana Collection, Yale University; **363** National Portrait Gallery/Smithsonian Institution; **364B** Idaho State Historical Society; **364TL** National Museum of the American Indian/Smithsonian Institution; **364TR** Denver Public Library; **366** Southern Pacific Transportation Company; **367** Union Pacific Railroad Company; **368B** Stephen Frisch*; **368T** The Bancroft Library, University of California, Berkeley; **369** Courtesy, Colorado Historical Society. Photo by Benschneider; **371** Courtesy, Colorado Historical Society; **372-373B** National Archives; **373T** Missouri Historical Society; **375** Nebraska State Historical Society, Solomon D. Butcher Collection; **376** Library of Congress.

Chapter 15: 380BR Staten Island Historical Society; **380C** National Archives; **380TL** *The Unveiling of the Statue of Liberty—Enlightening the World* by Edward Moran, 1886. Museum of The City of New York, 37.100.260. The J. Clarence Davies Collection; **381C** The Edison Institute, Henry Ford Museum and Greenfield Village, Dearborn, Michigan; **381L** Culver Pictures; **381R** National Museum of American History/Smithsonian Institution; **382BR** The Granger Collection; **382C** National Museum of American History/Smithsonian Institution; **382L** Courtesy Bethlehem Steel Corporation; **383L** Culver Pictures; **383R** The Granger Collection; **384L** National Museum of American History/Smithsonian Institution; **384R** National Museum of American History/Smithsonian Institution; **385** Culver Pictures; **386B** Drake Museum, Titusville, PA; **386TL** Larry Lee/West Light; **388** The Granger Collection; **389BR** Walker Collection; Indiana Historical Society Library (neg. no. C3816); **389TL** Walker Collection; Indiana Historical Society Library (neg. no. C2140); **391** Library of Congress **393B** Museum of The City of New York, The Jacob A. Riis Collection, #167; **393T** Museum of the City of New York, The Jacob A. Riis Collecion, #170; **395** Prints Collection, Miriam and Ira D. Wallach Division of Arts, Prints and Photographs: The New York Public Library, Astor, Lenox and Tilden Foundations; **396** Chris Huie; **397** *The Bowery at Night* by Louis Sonntag, Jr., 1895. Museum of The City of New York,32.275.2. Gift of Mrs. William B. Miles; **398-399T** National Air & Space Museum/Smithsonian Institution. Photo by Charles H. Phillips; **398BC** Courtesy of the Museum of African American History of Detroit, Michigan. Photo by William Sanders; **398BL** Courtesy, the U.S. Postal Service; **398BR** Culver Pictures; **398CR** U.S. Department of Agriculture; **398TL** International Museum of Photography at George Eastman House; **399BL** National Museum of American History/Smithsonian Institution. Photo by Michael Freeman; **399BR** Herkimer County Historical Society, N.Y. Photo by Frank J. Forte; **399C** Courtesy, Vassar College Library; **401L** Museum of The City of New York, The Jacob A. Riis Collection; **401R** International Museum of Photography at George Eastman House; **402C** Culver Pictures; **402TL** Chicago Historical Society.

Chapter 16: 406B Library of Congress; **406C** Culver Pictures; **407CR** Culver Pictures; **407CL** National Archives; **407L** Library of Congress; **407R** Stanley King Collection; **408CL** Stanley King Collection; **408CR** Stanley King Collection; **408T** Tamiment Institute Library/Robert F. Wagner Labor Archives/New York University; **409** Museum of American Political Life/University of Hartford; **409CL** Historical Pictures Service, Chicago; **409TR** Culver Pictures; **411** Library of Congress; **413** Courtesy of the Ford Archives, Dearborn, Michigan; **414** Library of Congress; **415** Library of Congress; **417** The Bettmann Archive; **418** The Bettmann Archive; **419C** The Bettmann Archive; **419TL** The Filson Club, Louisville, Kentucky; **419TR** Kentucky Historical Society; **420TL** Brown Brothers; **421T** Hoda Bakhshandagi/Black Star; **422** Courtesy, Gordon Campbell; **425B** International Harvester Company; **425T** The Bettmann Archive; **427B** Wyoming State Museum; **427C** Runk-Schoenberger/Grant Heilman Photography; **428** The Granger Collection; **430** From Stefan Lorants *The Glorious Burden,* (Authors Edition); **431** The Granger Collection.

Unit 6: 436-437 John Scheiber/The Stock Market; **438-439** John Scheiber/The Stock Market; **438B** Renee Lynn*; **438T** Culver Pictures; **439** *Soldier in World War I* by Sir William Orpen. Imperial War Museum, London.

Chapter 17: 440B Maurice Prendergast: *The East River* (1901) Watercolor and pencil on paper, 13¾″ × 19¾″. Collection, The Museum of Modern Art, New York. Gift of Abby Aldrich Rockefeller; **440T** Tim Davis*; **441BR** *WCTU Parade* by Ben Shahn. Museum of the City of New York; **441C** Brown Brothers; **441L** The Bettmann Archive; **441TR** Stanley King Collection; **442BR** T. Kitchen/Tom Stack & Associates; **442L** The Granger Collection; **442TR** Indiana University, Lilly Library; **443C** Culver Pictures; **445B** Courtesy NCR Corporation; **445T** Culver Pictures; **446C** Brown Brothers; **446L** State Historical Society of Wisconsin; **446R** Library of Congress; **447L** UPI/Bettmann; **447R** The Bettmann Archive; **449B** Library of Congress; **449T** Schomburg Center for Research in Black Culture/New York Public Library; **450-45l** The Strong Museum, Rochester, New York (marbles); **450BC** The Strong Museum, Rochester, New York; **450BL** The Strong Museum, Rochester, New York; **450BR** The Oakland Museum History Department. Photo by Stephen Frisch*; **450T** The Strong Museum, Rochester, New York; **450TC** Culver Pictures; **451BC** National Museum of American History/Smithsonian Institution; **451BR** National Baseball Hall of Fame and Museum, Inc.; **451C** The Bancroft Library, University of California, Berkeley; **451T** Courtesy Margo Brown; **451TC** Stephen Frisch*; **452L** Museum of American Political Life/University of Hartford; **452R** Brown Brothers; **453** The New-York Historical Society; **455L** UPI/Bettmann; **455R** Brown Brothers; **456** Brown Brothers; **457L** Culver Pictures; **457R** Spencer Swanger/Tom Stack & Associates; **458** from the *Philadelphia Record,* January 10, 1910; **459** *Brown Brothers;* **460** Culver; **462L** Library of Congress; **462R** Brown Brothers; **463** Collection of Advertising History, Archives Center/Smithsonian Institution; **465** Library of Congress.

Chapter 18: 466 Courtesy, United States Naval Academy Museum; **466L** *New York Journal,* May 2, 1893; **467BR** Theodore Roosevelt Collection, Harvard College Library; **467C** from Joseph Pennell's *Pictures of the Panama Canal*; **467L** A cartoon by Charles R.

970

Macauley originally appeared in the *Democratic World;* **467TR** Laurie Platt Winfrey, Inc.; **468C** Cowlitz County Historical Museum; **468L** Library of Congress; **468R** *Colliers,* September 22, 1900; **469C** Brown Brothers; **469L** Theodore Roosevelt Collection, Harvard College Library; **469R** The American Numismatics Society; **470** Culver Pictures; **471** Hawaii State Archives; **471R** Bernice P. Bishop Museum, Honolulu; **473L** The New-York Historical Society; **473R** Chicago Historical Society; **474** The Bettmann Archive; **475BL** Library of Congress; **475RB** Stanley King Collection; **475TL** Chicago Historical Society; **475TR** Theodore Roosevelt Collection, Harvard College Library; **477** Franklin D. Roosevelt Library; **478** Library of Congress; **479L** National Archives; **479R** Andy Hernandez/Picture Group; **480** Culver Pictures; **481** The Bettmann Archive; **482** Culver Pictures; **484** National Archives; **484R** Library of Congress; **487** Library of Congress; **488L** Culver Pictures; **488R** Christopher Morris/Black Star.

Chapter 19: 492B Library of Congress; **492T** National Archives (Army); **493BR** *Armistice Night* by George Luks, oil on canvas, 37 × 68¾ inches, 1918. Collection of the Whitney Museum of American Art, New York; gift of an anonymous donor; **493C** Imperial War Museum, London; **493L** UPI/Bettmann Newsphotos; **493TR** West Point Museum, photography by Joshua Nefsky*; **494C** The Bettmann Archive; **494L** West Point Museum, photography by Joshua Nefsky*; **494R** Brown Brothers; **495C** National Archives; **495L** Library of Congress; **495R** Detail from *Signing of the Peace Treaty in the Hall of Mirrors, Versailles 28th June, 1919* by Sir William Orpen, R.A. By courtesy of The Trustees of the Imperial War Museum, London. Photographed by Larry Burrows; **496** The Bettmann Archive; **498B** Brown Brothers; **498T** Imperial War Museum, London; **499** Culver Pictures; **500** *New York Evening World,* 1917; **501** The Bettmann Archive; **502** National Archives; **503** National Archives; **505** The Bettmann Archive; **506** Imperial War Museum, London; **507** Culver Pictures; **509B** Imperial War Museum, London; **509T** The Bettmann Archive/Hulton Picture Library; **511** Collection, The Museum of Modern Art, New York. Gift of Edward Steichen; **513** UPI/Bettmann; **516** The Granger Collection; **519** Imperial War Museum, London.

Unit 7: 522-523 David Smart/Stock South; **524** Courtesy of the Dorothea Lange Collection. The City of Oakland, the Oakland Museum; **524-525** David Smart/Stock South; **525** Jerry Howard/Stock, Boston.

Chapter 20: 526 *City Activities with Dance Hall* by Thomas Hart Benton, 1930. (c) The Equitable Life Assurance Society of the United States; **526T** Courtesy Donna Mussenden-Van Der Zee; **527BR** UPI/Bettmann; **527L** *Men Parading for the Repeal of the 18th Amendment (Mural project for Central Park Casino)* by Ben Shahn. Museum of the City of New York, by permanent deposit of the Whitney Museum of American Art; **527TR** National Museum of American History/Smithsonian Institution; **528R** UPI/Bettmann Newsphotos; **528TL** Courtesy American Heritage Archives; **529C** Culver Pictures; **529L** From the Collection of Henry Ford Museum and Greenfield Village, Dearborn, Michigan; **529R** Culver Pictures; **530L** AP/Wide World Photos; **530R** *Bartolomeo Vanzetti and Nicola Sacco* from the Sacco-Vanzetti series of twenty-three paintings by Ben Shahn, 1931-32. Tempera on paper over composition board, 10½ × 14½". Collection, The Museum of Modern Art, New York. Gift of Abby Aldrich Rockefeller; **531L** L.S. Alexander Gumby Collection, Rare Book and Manuscript Library, Columbia University; **531R** AP/Wide World Photos; **533** Library of Congress; **534** Culver Pictures; **535** Culver Pictures; **536B** Chrysler Historical Collection; **536R** From the Collection of Henry Ford Museum and Greenfield Village, Dearborn, Michigan; **537** The Bettmann Archive; **537L** Erich Hartmann/Magnum Photos; **539** Fitzpatrick, "St. Louis Post Dispatch"/Culver Pictures; **540BC** The Granger Collection; **540BL** The Granger Collection; **540BR** Culver Pictures; **540C** National Museum of American History/Smithsonian Institution; **540CR** Courtesy of NBC, from the American Heritage Archive; **540TC** Culver Pictures; **540TL** Brown Brothers; **540TR** Courtesy Philip Hudner, photo by Stephen Frisch*; **541B** Brown Brothers; **541CL** National Museum of American History/Smithsonian Instutiton; **541CR** Sherwin Dunner Collection, photo by Stephen Frisch*; **541T** Culver Pictures; **542-543B** Courtesy Rachael Goodman Edelson; **542L** Culver Pictures; **542R** Courtesy of William Ransom Hogan Jazz Archive, Tulane University; **543T** Culver Pictures; **544R** *Bootleggers* (mural project for Central Park casino) by Ben Shahn. Museum of the City of New York, by permanent deposit of the Whitney Museum of American Art; **544T** Culver Pictures; **545C** Bob and Bobbi Watkinson Collection, photo by Stephen Frisch; **545L** Library of Congress; **545R** Brown Brothers; **546** Princeton University Library Collections; **547** *The Migration of the Negro, Panel 1: During the World Warthere was a great migration North by Southern Negroes* by Jacob Lawrence, 1940-41. The Phillips Collection, Washington, D.C.; **548** Library of Congress; **549** Courtesy, Estate of Carl Van Vechten, photo from the Schomburg Center for Research in Black Culture; The New York Public Library; Astor, Lenox and Tilden Foundations.

Chapter 21: 552B *Rainy Night* by Charles E. Burchfield, 1929-1930, Watercolor over pencil on paper, 30" H x 42" W, San Diego Museum of Art, Gift of Anne R. and Amy Putnam; **552C** University Microfilms; **552T** Courtesy Vanity Fair, (c) 1933 (renewed 1961) by the Conde Nast Publications Inc.; **553C** The Bettmann Archive; **553L** Courtesy Franklin D. Roosevelt Library, Hyde Park, N.Y.; **553R** The Granger Collection; **554BR** Courtesy of the Dorothea Lange Collection. The City of Oakland, the Oakland Museum; **554L** Stanley King Collection; **554T** The Boston Athenaeum; **555L** Strong Museum, Rochester, NY; **555R** (c) 1933, 1961 Peter Arno; **556L** Brown Brothers; **556R** Thelma Shumsky/The Image Works; **557L** Culver Pictures; **557R** The Bettmann Archive; **558** Brown Brothers; **559B** Culver Pictures; **559T** The Bettmann Archive; **560-561** D. Goldberg/Sygma; **560B** Wide World Photos; **560T** Icon Communications/FPG International; **563** UPI/Bettmann; **565** Margaret Bourke-White, LIFE Magazine (c) Time Warner Inc.; **566** Dorothea Lange, Library of Congress; **567** Courtesy of the Dorothea Lange Collection. The City of Oakland, the Oakland Museum; **568B** The Bettmann Archive; **568T** Sygma; **570** Culver Pictures.

Chapter 22: 574BL *Construction of a Dam* by William Gropper (from Croton, New York), 1939. Section of Fine Arts, Federal Works Agency, Public Building Adminstration Program. Photography courtesy of the U.S. Dept. of Interior; **574BR** Wide World Photos; **574T** Franklin D. Roosevelt Library; **575B** Library of Congress; **575C** The Fogg Art Museum, Harvard University, Cambridge, Massachusetts. Gift of Bernarda B. Shahn; **575CR** Library of Congress; **576CL** Culver Pictures; **576CR** Library of Congress; **576T** Library of Congress/George Mason University; **577CL** Culver Pictures; **577TC** Stanley King Collection; **577TR** Pictorial Parade; **578** Franklin D. Roosevelt Library; **579** Culver Pictures; **579C** Grant Heilman Photography; **580-581** Franklin D. Roosevelt Library; **583** Brown Brothers; **585** Library of Congress; **586** John D. Ecklund Collection, photo by Stephen Frisch*; **587T** Cleveland Public Library; **588B** *Detroit Industry* by Diego Rivera. Founders Society Purchase, Edsel B. Ford Fund and Gift of Edsel B. Ford; **588L** *Testimonial* by Dan Rico. Founders Society, Detroit Institute of Arts; **588R** Woodcut by Aimee Gorham. National Archives; **588TC** Library of Congress; **588TL** *La Citadelle-Freedom* by Augusta Savage. Howard University Gallery of Art; **590** Brown Brothers; **593** *Mary McLeod Bethune* by Betsy G. Reyneau. National Portrait Gallery/Smithsonian Institution; Gift of the Harmon Foundation; **594** Grant Heilman Photography; **595** Library of Congress; **595CR** Culver Pictures; **596** Library of Congress.

Unit 8: 604-605 Gordon Wiltsie*; **606-607** Gordon Wiltsie*; **606B** National Japanese-American Historical Society, photo by Renee Lynn*; **606T** National Japanese-American Historical Society, photo by Renee Lynn*; **607** Culver Pictures.

Chapter 23: 608B The Bettmann Archive; **608T** Brown Brothers; **609C** The Granger Collection; **609L** Culver Pictures; **609R** National Archives; **610L** Associated Press; **610R** Library of Congress; **611** National Archives; **613B** Cindy Karp/Black Star; **613T** National Archives; **614** Culver Pictures; **617** LIllustration/Sygma; **617R** Archiv fur Kunst und Geschichte, Berlin; **618** UPI/Bettmann Newsphotos; **618L** Courtesy Judah L. Magnes Museum, Berkeley, California; **618R** Associated Press; **620** Hugh Hutton, The Philadelphia Inquirer, courtesy Random House; **621** Michael S. Yamashita/West Light; **623B** The Granger Collection; **623T** UPI/Bettmann; **624** Bettmann/Hulton; **625** A Copyright 1940 Herblock cartoon; **626L** Bettmann/Hulton; **626R** Culver Pictures; **628** LIllustration/Sygma; **630** Wide World Photos; **632** National Archives.

Chapter 24: 636B Bill Weems/Woodfin Camp & Associates; **636TR** The Bettmann Archive; **637BCL** Peter Stackpole/LIFE Magazine c 1943 Time Inc.; **637BCR** Library of Congress; **637BL** National Archives; **637BR** National Archives; **637TR** W.S. Nawrocki/Nawrocki Stock Photo; **638C** Library of Congress; **638CL** Courtesy, A. Phillip Randolph Institute; **638TR** Ann Wilkinson Collection; **639CR** U.S. Air Force; **639TL** National Archives; **640BC** Library of Congress; **640BL** National Archives; **640CR** Library of Congress; **641BC** National Archives; **641BL** National Archives; **641CR** UPI/Bettmann; **642** *Zoot Suit Riots* by Judith F. Baca, 1981. Tujunga Wash Drainage Canal, San Fernando Valley, Los Angeles, total mural 1/2 mile long, this detail approximately 13′ × 8′; **643** Library of Congress; **645L** Presidio Army Museum, photo by Stephen Frisch*; **645R** National Archives; **646BL** National Archives; **646BR** Library of Congress; **646CL** Courtesy Mary Jo Portch, photo by Stephen Frisch*; **646CR** National Archives; **646TL** Library of Congress; **646TR** Chicago Historical Society (extinguisher), Presidio Army Museum, San Francisco, photo by Renee Lynn* (helmet), Stephen Frisch* (binoculars); **647B** UPI/Bettmann; **647C** Photo by Johnny Florea, LIFE Magazine (c) 1943 Time Warner Inc.; **647TC** The Research Libraries, The New York Public Library; **647TL** Library of Congress; **650** Copyright 1944, Bill Mauldin, reprinted with permission; **651** Library of Congress; **652C** Robert H. Watkinson Collection, photo by Stephen Frisch*; **653** Imperial War Museum, London; **654-655** Robert Harding Picture Library; **655C** UPI/Bettmann; **655CR** UPI/Bettmann; **655T** UPI/Bettmann; **656** National Archives; **657** Presidio Army Museum, photo by Stephen Frisch*; **658** National Archives; **659** Presidio Army Museum, photo by Stephen Frisch*; **660-661** Popperfoto; **662** John Launois/Black Star; **665BL** Brown Brothers; **665TR** Library of Congress.

Unit 9: 668-669 Leroy Woodson/Woodfin Camp & Associates; **670** Matt Herron/Black Star; **670-671** Leroy Woodson/Woodfin Camp & Associates; **671** Charles Moore/Black Star.

Chapter 25: 672B Hal Tretbar; **672T** Copyright 1957 Time Warner Inc. Reprinted by permission; **673C** UPI/Bettmann; **673L** UPI/Bettmann Newsphotos; **673R** AP/Wide World Photos; **674L** The United Nations; **674R** J.A.F.-Paris/Magnum Photos; **675BL** Sovfoto/Eastfoto; **675R** UPI/Bettmann Newsphotos; **675TL** AP/Wide World Photos; **677** Dennis Brack/Black Star; **678L** UPI/Bettmann; **678R** Lee Lockwood/Black Star; **679** Los Alamos National Laboratory; **680** Karsh, Ottawa/Woodfin Camp & Associates; **681L** UPI/Bettmann; **681R** Fred O. Seibel Collection (3/14/47), Manuscripts Division, Special Collections Department, University of Virginia Library; **682L** Bundesarchiv, Koblenz; **682R** AP/Wide World Photos; **683** Walter Sanders/LIFE Magazine (c) Time Warner Inc.; **685** Henri Cartier-Bresson/Magnum Photos; **686** National Archives; **688** The Bettmann Archives; **691L** Picture Post/Black Star; **691R** Patrick Forestier/Sygma; **693** Andrew St. George/Magnum Photos; **694** UPI/Bettmann.

Chapter 26: 698-699 Ed Pieratt/Black Star; **698C** FPG International; **698TR** Lynn Sanchez Collection, photo by Stephen Frisch*; **699BC** Wayne Miller/Magnum Photos; **699BR** Brown Brothers; **699CR** The Oakland Museum; **700CL** CTS-Turner Museum, photography by Joe Carlton; **700TR** *A Good Man Is Hard to Find* by Ben Shahn, 1948. Gouache on paper, 8 × 62″. Collection, The Museum of Modern Art, New York. Gift of the Artist; **701CL** FPG International; **701TL** Bob Wolf-Leeds T.V. Collection, photo by Stephen Frisch*; **701TR** Burt Glinn/Magnum Photos; **702** Special Collections, Occidental College; **703B** c 1987 Mark Gottleib; **703CR** Sickles Photo-Reporting; **703L** Loomis Dean/LIFE Magazine c Time Inc.; **705L** FPG International; **705R** W. Eugene Smith Estate/Black Star; **706** *Welders* by Ben Shahn, 1943. Tempera on cardboard mounted on composition board, 22 × 39 3/4″. Collection, The Museum of Modern Art, New York. Purchase.; **709** Elliott Erwitt/Magnum Photos; **710B** Calvin D. Campbell/Black Star; **710T** Brown Brothers; **711** Stanley King Collection; **712** Joe Covella/Black Star; **713L** Burt Glinn/Magnum Photos; **713R** UPI/Bettmann Newsphotos; **714L** Brown Brothers; **714R** *Straight Herblock* (Simon & Schuster, 1964); **715** FPG International; **716** Doug Handel/The Stock Market; **717L** Brown Brothers; **717R** Campbell Soup Company; **718CR** Sickles Photo-Reporting; **718L** J.R. Eyerman/LIFE Magazine c 1953 Time Inc.; **718TR** FPG International; **719** Fred Ward/Black Star; **720** *Straight Herblock* (Simon & Schuster, 1964).

Chapter 27: 724 Paul Schutzer, LIFE Magazine (c) 1961 Time Warner, Inc.; **724-725** Lyndon Baines Johnson Library, photo by Cecil Stoughton; **725** *Dylan* by Milton Glaser, 1966; **725C** UPI/Bettmann; **725L** LIFE Magazine, photo by Philippe Letellier; **726L** John Fitzgerald Kennedy Library; **726R** Library of Congress; **727C** Henry Groskinsky; **727L** Stanley King Collection; **727R** U.S. Postal Service; **728B** John F. Kennedy Library, photo by Robert Knudson. Photo no. KN-C 19428; **728T** John F. Kennedy Library (Photo No. ST-C267-5-63), photo by Cecil W. Stoughton; **729** Pierre Boulat/Cosmos; **730** Copyright 1962, Bill Mauldin, reprinted with permission; **731BL** NASA/Lyndon B. Johnson Space Center; **731R** Photo by Lynn Pelham, LIFE Magazine (c) Time Warner Inc.; **731TL** NASA/Lyndon B. Johnson Space Center; **732** Flip Schulke/Black Star; **733** El Panamericano photo from UPI/Bettmann; **734L** Roger Malloch/Magnum Photos; **734R** Anthony Suau/Black Star; **736** UPI/Bettmann; **738B** Cecil Stoughton/John F. Kennedy Library. Photo No. ST-1A-4-63; **738T** Photo by Abraham Zapruder, courtesy National Archives. Copyright 1967 by LMH Company. ALL RIGHTS RESERVED; **740** Owen Franken/Stock, Boston; **740L** Danny Lyon/Magnum Photos; **741** from The Herblock Gallery (Simon & Schuster, 1968); **742B** Photo by Alfred Eisenstaedt, LIFE Magazine (c) 1962 Time Warner Inc.; **742T** Copyright 1966 Time Warner Inc.; **743B** B. Nation/Sygma; **743T** Neal Buenzi/NYT Pictures; **744-745B** The Oakland Museum History Department; **744BCL** Catherine Leroy/Black Star; **744BL** Barbara Robinson Collection, photo by Stephen Frisch*; **744C** The Oakland Museum History Department; **744CR** Charles Moore/Black Star; **744TC** Photo by Bill Ray, LIFE Magazine (c) 1971 Time; **744TCL** Dan McCoy/Rainbow; **744TL** Gail Kefauver Collection, photo by Stephen Frisch*; **744TR** Ken Regan/Camera 5; **745BC** Lynn Sanchez Collection; **745BR** Jonathan Rubin Collections, photo by Stephen Frisch*; **745C** Photo by Bill Eppridge, LIFE Magazine (c) 1969 Time Warner Inc.; **745T** Ted Streshinsky/Photo 20/20; **746** Kent Reno/Jeroboam, Inc.; **749** (c) San Francisco Chronicle, 1962. Reprinted by permission.

Chapter 28: 750C Flip Schulke/Black Star; **750CR** Constantine Manos/Magnum Photos; **750TR** Dan Budnick/Woodfin Camp & Associates; **751BL** Charles Moore/Black Star; **751BR** Eve Arnold/Magnum Photos; **751CL** M. Dwyer/Stock Boston; **752CL** Bohdan Hrynewych/Stock, Boston; **752T** Wide World Photos; **753C** Dan Budnick/Woodfin Camp & Associates; **753TL** University of Mississippi; **753TR** Owen Franken/Stock, Boston; **754BL** Bruce Davidson/Magnum Photos; **754BR** Bruce Davidson/Magnum Photos; **755TL** Wide World Photos; **755TR** *Integration, Supreme Court* by Ben Shahn. Des Moines Art Center, Purchased with funds from the Edmundson Art Foundation, Inc., 1987-8; **758B** Dan Weiner/Magnum Photos; **758C** Wide World Photos; **760** Fred Ward/Black Star; **761B** Wide World Photos; **761C** Don Uhrbrock/LIFE Magazine c Time Inc.; **763** Copyright 1963 Bill Mauldin. Reprinted With Permission; **764C** Matt Herron/Black Star; **764TL** Bruce Davidson/Magnum Photos; **764TR** Charles Moore/Black Star; **765CR** Flip Schulke/Black Star; **765TL** Bob Henriques/Magnum; **767C** Bob Daemmrich/Stock, Boston; **769L** Bob Adelman/Magnum Photos; **770B** Charles Gatewood/The Image Works; **770C** John Launois/Black Star; **770T** Wide World Photos.

Chapter 29: 774B James Pickerall/Black Star; **774C** Wally McNamee/Woodfin Camp & Associates; **774T** Bernard Boston; **775BR** Dick Swanson/Black Star; **775C** The Bettmann Archive; **775L** *What if they gave a war and nobody came. . .* by Gino Beghe, photo by Howard Goodman. **775TR** Stephen Frisch*; **776B** Stephen Frisch*; **776T** Copyright 1964, Bill Mauldin, reprinted with permission; **777C** Presseagentur/Sven Simon; **777L** Photo by Wally McNamee. (c) 1970 Newsweek, Inc. All rights reserved. Reprinted by permission; **777R** Buffon-Darquenne/Sygma; **778** TASS from Sovfoto; **779** De Mulder/Sipa Press; **780** Wide World Photos; **782** Larry Burrows/LIFE Magazine (c) Time Warner Inc.; **783** Larry Burrows/LIFE Magazine (c) Time Warner Inc.; **785B** Larry Burrows/LIFE Magazine (c) Time Warner Inc.; **785T** Marc Riboud/Magnum Photos; **789B** Wally McNamee/Woodfin Camp & Associates; **789T** National Archives; **790** Dennis Brack/Black Star; **791B** Francolon/Gamma-Liaison; **791T** Nik Wheeler/Black Star; **792** Robin Hood; **793** UPI/Bettmann; **794** J.P. Laffont/Sygma; **796** Wally McNamee/Woodfin Camp & Associates.

Unit 10: 802-803 Mural in front of La Pena Cultural Center, Berkeley, California. Photo by Elliott Smith*; **803** Rod Rodriguez for *Saludos Hispanos* magazine; **804** Guadalupe Cultural Arts Center; **804-805** Mural in front of La Pena Cultural Center, Berkeley, California. Photo by Elliott Smith*.

Chapter 30: 806C Renee Lynn*; **806T** Curt Fischer*; **806B** Diana Mara Henry; **807C** Fred Ward/Black Star; **807L** Victor Aleman; **807R** Peter Mitchel/Sven Simon; **808BR** Wide World Photos; **808L** NASA; **808TR** Stephen Frisch*; **809BL** Fredrik D. Bodin/Stock, Boston; **809R** Alain Mingam/Gamma-Liaison; **809TL** J.P. Laffont/Sygma; **810** Nancy Moran; **811L** El Teatro Campesino, San Juan Bautista, California, photo by Renee Lynn*; **811R** Bob Fitch/Black Star; **812** *Collector #5 or Osage with Van Gogh* by T.C. Cannon. Walter Cannon and the University of Tulsa, Special Collections, McFarlin Library; **814** NASA; **814L** Courtesy Lucasfilm Ltd.; **814R** NASA; **815** Wally McNamee/Woodfin Camp & Associates; **816** Stephen Frisch*; **817L** Graysmith, (c) Chronicle Publishing Co.; **817R** B. Christensen/Stock, Boston; **818** Dennis Brack/Black Star; **819B** Stanley Tretick; **819T** Drawing by David Levine. Reprinted with permission from *The New York Review of Books;* **820** Nancy Schiff; **821** University Microfilms; **822L** Paul Conrad/(c) 1978 The Los Angeles Times. Reprinted by permission; **822R** Paul Fusco/Magnum Photos; **823B** Curt Fischer* **823T** Charles Habib/Gamma-Liaison; **824** Frank Wing/Stock, Boston; **26** Arthur Tress/Magnum Photos; **827** D.B. Owen/Black Star; **828** etboun/Sipa Press; **830-831** Robert Rathe/Stock, Boston.

hapter 31: 834T Wally McNamee/Woodfin Camp & Associates; **4B** John Ficara/Sygma; **834C** Matthew McVay/Stock, Boston; **5BC** David Turnley/Black Star; **835BL** J.R. Holland/Stock, Boston; **5BR** Gabe Palmer/The Stock Market; **835CR** Thomas Ives/The ock Market; **836CL** Fred Ward/Black Star; **836CR** *Herblock at rge* (Pantheon Books,1987); **836TC** Susan Meiselas/Magnum otos; **837BL** Stuart Franklin/Magnum Photos; **837BR** Ira man/Sygma; **837TL** Larry Downing/Woodfin Camp & Associates; **7TR** Sipa Press; **838BR** Maggie Stebe/Stock, Boston; **838L** Rick owne/Stock, Boston; **840** Auth c 1980 Philadelphia Inquirer. eprinted with permission of Universal Press Syndicate. All rights served; **841BL** David Burnett/Contact Press-Woodfin Camp & ssociates; **841BR** Paul Barton/The Stock Market; **842** Cindy arp/Black Star; **843L** Stacy Pick/Stock, Boston; **843R** James achtway/Magnum Photos; **844** Eli Reed/Magnum Photos; **845** Wally cNamee/Woodfin Camp & Associates; **847** Peter Turnley/Black Star; **48B** Roswell Angier/Stock, Boston; **848T** Stephen Frisch*; **849** Klaus eisinger/Black Star; **850** Louise Gubb/JB Pictures; **851** P. urand/Sygma; **852** Haviv/SABA; **854B** (c) William Viggiano from the ook *Homeless in America*; **854T** Herb Snitzer/Stock, Boston; **855** ally McNamee/Sygma; **856** Wally McNamee/Sygma; **857** Dennis rack/Black Star.

hapter 32: 860 A.F.P. Photo; **861BR** Hewlett-Packard Company; **61C** Luc Delahaye/Sipa-Press; **861L** Paula Lerner/Woodfin Camp & Associates; **861TR** Stephen Frisch*; **863** Maxine Hong Kingston from the "Gifted Woman" series (c) Howard Schatz 1990; **864BL** Courtesy Sony Classical; **864BR** *Mouse Cup* by Elizabeth Murray, 1981-82. Courtesy Mr. & Mrs. Harry W. Anderson; **864C** (c) 1988 Jonathan Atkin; **864TR** *Viva La Raza* by Salvador Roberto Torres, 1969; **864TL** *Awe Series* by Susan Stewart (Crow/Blackfeet), 1990. Courtesy, American Indian Contemporary Arts; **865BC** Reinhard Krumm; **865C** *The Guadalupe Triptych: Portrait of the Artist as the Virgin of Guadalupe* (detail) by Yolanda M. Lopez, 1978. Photo by the Wight Gallery, UCLA; **865R** Courtesy Romare Bearden Foundation, Inc. and Columbia Records; **865T** Michael Ochs Archives, Ltd; **866** Paul Kitagaki/San Jose Mercury News; **868** Catherine Leroy/Sipa-Press; **870** Cartoon by Richard Crowson. Copyright 1991. Reprinted by permission of The Wichita Eagle; **871** (c) 1980 Mike Peters. Reprinted by permission: Tribune Media Services; **872** Larry Downing/Woodfin Camp & Associates; **873L** Lloyd Francis/San Jose Mercury News; **873R** Brant Ward/San Francisco Chronicle; **874** Stephen Frisch*; **875L** Patrick Tehan; **875R** Michael L. Abramson; **878L** UPI/Bettmann Newsphotos; **878R** Drake Sorey; **879** Ralf-Finn Hestoft/SABA; **881** (c) 1992 by Herblock in The Washington Post; **882** Viktor Korotayev/Time Inc.; **883** A.F.P. Photo; **885** R. Watts/Westlight; **886B** Les Stone/Sygma; **886T** Deanne Fitzmaurice/San Francisco Chronicle; **892B** Chicago Historical Society (DIA 1956.359); **892T** Avery Architectural & Fine Arts Library, Columbia University; **893B** Chicago Historical Society; **893T** International Museum of Photography at George Eastman House; **894** Joseph Brignolo/The Image Bank; **895** Ted Horowitz/The Stock Market; **897** Dan Budnik/Woodfin Camp & Associates;

Reference Center: 898BL The National Portrait Gallery/Smithsonian Institution; **898C** The Granger Collection; **898CL** Portrait of Don Jose Sepulveda by Henri J. Penelon, c. 1856. Bowers Museum Collection, Santa Ana, CA; **898R** Brown Brothers; **898TL** The Bettmann Archive; **908** Jon Feingersh/Tom Stack & Associates; **909** Luis Villota/The Stock Market; **910–911** Sonya Jacobs/The Stock Market; **910BL** Alan G. Nelson/Animals, Animals; **910BR** Bill Ross/Woodfin Camp & Associates; **910TC** Michael J. Howell/Stock, Boston; **910TL** Larry Lipsky/Tom Stack & Associates; **910TR** Tim Thompson/The Stock Market; **911B** John Shaw/Tom Stack & Associates; **911TC** Jeff Gnass/The Stock Market; **911TL** Alan G. Nelson/Animals, Animals; **911TR** Barbara Alper/Stock, Boston.

Geography feature background images: Courtesy the Newberry Library. Edward E. Ayer Collection

*Photographed expressly for Addison-Wesley Publishing Company, Inc.

Literature Acknowledgments

1 From *Ceremony* by Leslie Marmon Silko. Copyright © 1977 by Leslie Silko. Used by permission of Viking Penguin, a division of Penguin Books USA Inc. **154** From "The Moral Legacy of the Founding Fathers" by John Hope Franklin. © 1975 University of Chicago Magazine. **353** From *Cimarron* by Edna Ferber. © 1929, 1930 by Edna Ferber. Renewed 1957, 1958. **376** From "The Trail of Ninety-Eight" by Robert Service. Reprinted by permission of the Putnam Publishing Group, Inc. Copyright © 1961 by Robert Service. **396** From Marion Hom, "Detained on Angel Island," from *Songs of Gold Mountain: Cantonese Rhymes from San Francisco Chinatown.* University of California Press. © 1987 The Regents of the University of California. **438** "Over There" by George M. Cohan. Copyright © 1917, renewed 1945. Leo Feist, Inc. All rights of Leo Feist, Inc. assigned to EMI Catalogue Partnership. All rights controlled and administered by EMI Feist Catalog Inc. All rights reserved. Used with permission. **438** From *Johnny Got His Gun* by Dalton Trumbo.

Lippincott © 1939 Dalton Trumbo. **523** From *The Grapes of Wrath* by John Steinbeck. Copyright 1939, renewed © 1967 by John Steinbeck. Used by permission of Viking Penguin, a division of Penguin Books USA Inc. **541** from "Jazz Fantasia" in *Smoke and Steel* by Carl Sandburg, © 1920 by Harcourt Brace Jovanovich, Inc., renewed 1948 by Carl Sandburg, reprinted by permission of the publisher. **547** From *Selected Poems* by Langston Hughes. Copyright © 1948 by Alfred A Knopf, Inc. Reprinted by permission of the publisher. **559, 562, 570, 571, 580, 595** From *Hard Times: An Oral History of the Great Depression* by Studs Terkel. Copyright © 1970 by Studs Terkel. Reprinted by permission of Pantheon Books, a division of Random House, Inc. **605** From *Farewell to Manzanar* by Jeanne Wakatsuki and James D. Houston. Copyright © 1973 by James D. Houston. Reprinted by permission of Houghton Mifflin Co. **669** "Let America Be America Again by Langston Hughes. Reprinted by permission of Harold Ober Associates Incorporated. Copyright 1938 by Langston Hughes. Copyright renewed 1965 by Langston Hughes. **720** From the song "Little Boxes" by Malvina Reynolds © 1962 Schroder Music Co. (ASCAP). Renewed 1990. Used by permission. All rights reserved. **803** Lorna Dee Cervantes, "Freeway 280," *Latin American Literary Review*, Vol. 5, No. 10, 1977, Pittsburgh, PA. Reprinted by permission of the publisher. **804** Pat Mora, "Sonrisas," from *Borders*, Arte Publico Press, University of Houston, 1986. Reprinted by permission of the publisher. **804** Aurora Levins Morales and Rosario Morales, "Ending Poem," from *Getting Home Alive,* copyright © 1986 Aurora Levins Morales and Rosario Morales. Ithaca, New York: Firebrand Books.

Illustration Acknowledgments

Ellen Emerson: Feature backgrounds and bars
Christa Kieffer: pages 42-43, 56-57, 62-63, 104-105, 168-169, 205, 312-313, 374, 375, 756
Susan Jaekel: *Spotlight* logo, pages 191, 249, 254
Jane McCreary: pages 119, 278, 333, 359
Alan Okamoto: pages 509, 510, 511, 536-537, 611, 674, 726
Sharron O'Neil: pages 260-261
D.J. Simison: page 716
John Weber Calligraphy: *Creative Spirit* features, page 258

Charts and Graphs
Precision Graphics

Maps
R.R. Donnelley Cartographic Services
John M. Isard Cartography